HANDBOOK OF RESEARCH ON MULTICULTURAL EDUCATION

SECOND EDITION

HANDBOOK OF RESEARCH ON MULTICULTURAL EDUCATION

SECOND EDITION

James A. Banks

Editor

Cherry A. McGee Banks

Associate Editor

JOSSEY-BASS
A Wiley Imprint
www.josseybass.com

Jossey-Bass books and products are available through most bookstores. To contact Jossey-Bass directly, call our Customer Care Department within the U.S. at (800) 274-4434, outside the U.S. at (317) 572-3985, or fax (317) 572-4002.

Jossey-Bass also publishes its books in a variety of electronic formats. Some content that appears in print may not be available in electronic books.

Library of Congress Cataloging-in-Publication Data

Handbook of research on multicultural education / James A. Banks, editor; Cherry A. McGee Banks, associate editor.—2nd ed.
    p. cm.
Includes bibliographical references and indexes.
  ISBN 0-7879-5915-4 (alk. paper)
1. Multicultural education—United States—Handbooks, manuals, etc.
2. Multicultural education—Research-United States—Handbooks,
manuals, etc. 3. Minorities—Education-United States—Handbooks,
manuals, etc. I. Banks, James A. II. Banks, Cherry A. McGee.
  LC1099.3.H35 2002
  370.117—dc21

                                        2002156022

Printed in the United States of America
SECOND EDITION
HB Printing   10 9 8 7 6 5 4 3 2

CONTENTS

PART VII   THE EDUCATION OF ETHNIC GROUPS

PART VIII   LANGUAGE ISSUES

PART IX   ACADEMIC ACHIEVEMENT: APPROACHES, THEORIES, AND RESEARCH

INTRODUCTION

The publication of the first edition of this *Handbook* in 1995 was a watershed event in the field of multicultural education and in the education profession. We conceived and initiated the *Handbook* project because we believed that multicultural education had come of age. Consequently, the field needed a *Handbook* to help educate future scholars and to provide scholars and practicing educators a one-volume overview and summary of the theory and research in the field.

The reception of the first edition of this *Handbook* by scholars and practitioners in both multicultural and general education was warm and enthusiastic. It was widely and positively reviewed in such journals as the *Journal of Teacher Education, Teachers College Record, Educational Leadership, Multicultural Education* (now *Multicultural Perspectives*), and *The Journal of Negro Education.* The *Handbook* was also the recipient of the 1997 Multicultural Education Book Award from the National Association for Multicultural Education (NAME). It contributed significantly to the institutionalization of multicultural education in the United States and abroad.

We were deeply gratified by the reception of the *Handbook* in both multicultural and general education in the United States and abroad. We undertook this second edition of the *Handbook* because the pace of change in the field has been substantial since the publication of the first edition in 1995. A new edition was needed to describe and analyze changes such as increased immigration to the United States as well as new developments in theory and research related to race, culture, ethnicity, and language. This new edition, which consists of 20 new chapters and 29 chapters revised from the first edition, describes new issues—such as assessment and standards—as well as such new research and trends as findings on the growth in interracial children and the characteristics of children in immigrant families. The educational implications of new research and trends are also described in the new and revised chapters in this edition.

MULTICULTURAL EDUCATION: HISTORY AND CHARACTERISTICS

Multicultural education is a field of study and an emerging discipline whose major aim is to create equal educational opportunities for students from diverse racial, ethnic, social-class, and cultural groups. One of its important goals is to help all students acquire the knowledge, attitudes, and skills needed to function effectively in a pluralistic democratic society and to interact, negotiate, and communicate with people from diverse groups to create a civic and moral community that works for the common good.

Because of its focus on equity, justice, and cultural democracy, multicultural education is consistent with the democratic ideals of the basic documents of the United States: the Declaration of Independence, the Constitution, and the Bill of Rights. One of its major aims is to actualize for all the ideals that the founding fathers intended for an elite few at the nation's birth.

Multicultural education has deep historical roots. It is linked directly to African American scholarship that emerged in the late 19th and early 20th centuries and indirectly to intercultural education, a research and curriculum reform movement formulated in the 1930s that had largely vanished by the time the civil rights movement emerged in the 1960s.

In its contemporary manifestation, multicultural education emerged out of the civil rights movement of the 1960s and 1970s. The civil rights movement developed when African Americans, frustrated by deferred and shattered dreams, took to the streets and used the ballot box to demand changes—symbolic and structural—throughout U.S. society. Many of their demands focused on change in the nation's schools, colleges, and universities. Individuals from many other ethnic and racial groups participated in and strongly supported the civil rights movement initiated by African Americans.

The first wave of responses by educational institutions resulted in the establishment of Black studies—and later other *ethnic studies*—courses and programs in the nation's schools, colleges, and universities. As the ethnic studies movement grew and became institutionalized, the realization arose among scholars and practitioners that although ethnic studies was a necessary component of educational reform, it was not sufficient to bring about the structural changes in schools, colleges, and universities that were needed to create educational equality for low-income students and students of color.

Consequently, *multiethnic education* was developed. It was designed to reform each of the variables in the educational environment to create equal educational opportunities for all students. Multiethnic education involves systemic and structural reform of these variables in educational institutions: (a) policy and politics; (b) the attitudes, perceptions, beliefs, and actions of teachers and professors; (c) formalized curriculum and course of study; (d) assessment and testing procedures; (e) the languages and dialects sanctioned within educational institutions; (e) teaching styles and strategies; and (f) instructional materials.

The ethnic studies and multiethnic education movements inspired other groups on the margins of society to push for change in the nation's educational institutions that would reflect their cultures, experiences, hopes, and dreams. One of the most successful political interest groups was made up of people with disabilities and their supporters. Using arguments borrowed from the 1954 *Brown* v. *Board of Education of Topeka* desegregation decision and from the civil rights movement, advocates for the rights of people with disabilities were able to win a number of important legal victories that resulted in substantial educational reforms. One of their most significant victories was passage of Public Law 94–142, enacted by Congress in 1975. Known as the Education for All Handicapped Children Act, it requires free public education for all students with disabilities, nondiscriminatory evaluation, and an individualized education program (IEP) for each student with a disability. It also stipulates that each student with a disability should be educated in the least restricted environment.

Feminists were also inspired by the civil rights movement to renew their historical quest for more rights for women in U.S. society, including equity in educational institutions. One of the most significant victories of the women's rights movement was Title IX of the 1972 Educational Amendments. Title IX prohibits sex discrimination in all educational programs receiving federal support. At the university level, women's studies programs emerged. They have since become institutionalized in colleges and universities throughout the United States, although they face important challenges.

A significant development in the last four decades has been the emergence of feminist scholarship. It seriously challenges the established knowledge in disciplines such as philosophy, the social and behavioral sciences, and the natural and physical sciences. New paradigms, concepts, and epistemological assumptions have emerged that are forcing scholars in the traditional disciplines to rethink and reconceptualize some of their major paradigms, concepts, and assumptions. Ethnic studies scholarship is also challenging the established disciplines and mainstream scholarship in similar ways.

As a new field of study and interdisciplinary discipline, multicultural education draws upon, reflects, and echoes concerns in ethnic studies, multiethnic education, women's studies, and to a lesser extent research and scholarship on exceptionality. Multicultural education incorporates concepts, paradigms, theories, assumptions, and pedagogy rooted in each of these interdisciplinary fields and applies them to practical educational settings in schools, colleges, and universities. The interrelationship of variables such as race, class, and gender—and how they interact to influence education—is an important concern in multicultural education theory and research.

Multicultural education not only draws content, concepts, paradigms, and theories from specialized interdisciplinary fields such as ethnic studies and women's studies (and from history and the social and behavioral sciences), it also interrogates, challenges, and reinterprets content, concepts, and paradigms from the established disciplines. Multicultural education applies content from these fields and disciplines to pedagogy and curriculum development in educational settings. *Consequently, we may define multicultural education as a field of study designed to increase educational equity for all students that incorporates for this purpose content, concepts, principles, theories, and paradigms from history, the social and behavioral sciences, and ethnic studies and women's studies.* It is because of these characteristics that Edmund W. Gordon calls multicultural education a *metadiscipline*.

An important aim of this *Handbook* is to clarify the meaning and boundaries of multicultural education and to stem the tide of the multiple misconceptions of the concept that are widespread and pernicious. Multicultural education focuses on ethnic, racial, cultural, language, and gender groups within the boundaries of a nation-state, such as the United States, the United Kingdom, and Japan. Yet there is widespread confusion among scholars, practitioners, publishers, and the public that multicultural education is the same as global education and international education.

Global and international education focus on the interrelationships among nations and the study of foreign nation-states, respectively. Even though multicultural education and global education both try to help students develop cross-cultural competencies and skills, each field makes unique contributions to educating students. Consequently, the two fields should not be confused. The integrity of each field should be recognized and respected.

THE NATURE OF THE HANDBOOK

The main purpose of this *Handbook* is to assemble in one volume the major research and scholarship related to multicultural education that has developed since the field emerged in the 1960s and 1970s. *Research* is defined broadly in this *Handbook* and includes studies using experimental and quasi-experimental designs, historical and philosophical inquiry, ethnographic studies, case studies, survey research, scholarship broadly defined, and insights gained from practice.

The chapters in the *Handbook* reflect the diverse disciplinary roots that constitute the foundations of the field. Consequently, among the contributors are researchers and scholars from a range of disciplines, including anthropology, history, psychology, social psychology, sociology, English and literature, and various fields within education.

DEVELOPMENT OF THE SECOND EDITION OF THE HANDBOOK

After seeking the advice and wisdom of the members of the Editorial Advisory Board and surveying the new research, trends, and developments in the field, the editors invited 29 of the authors of the first edition of the *Handbook* to update and revise their chapters, and 20 other scholars to write new chapters. Adding the new chapters to this edition necessitated dropping 18 chapters that appeared in the first edition of the *Handbook*.

The contributors were asked to critically review the research and scholarship within their topic areas in as comprehensive and balanced a way as possible, to conceptualize research broadly; to describe the implications of the research reviewed for further research, policy, and practice; and to use their own judgment to determine the scope and depth of their chapters. Most of the individuals invited to write chapters are established scholars with a national or international reputation. However, the editors invited and encouraged contributors to work with colleagues early in their careers. A number of authors invited a colleague or several to coauthor their chapters. In some cases, the coauthors are advanced graduate students or young scholars. The editors view the *Handbook* as a project not only to present the work of established scholars but also to mentor future scholars in the field.

The reviewers played a significant role in shaping the contents of the chapters, each of which had at least two reviewers. They gave each author of a new chapter comments on the chapter outline and on the first draft of the chapter. Reviewers gave the revising authors comments on their chapters. The chapter authors then incorporated comments from the reviewers and the editors into their final chapter drafts.

ORGANIZATION OF THE HANDBOOK

The *Handbook* is divided into 12 parts. Part I describes the nature, history, goals, and status of the field. The major purpose of the chapters in this section is to describe how the field has developed historically and its various components and dimensions. Several salient issues, trends, and developments that have significant implications for teaching and learning in a multicultural society are described in Part II: access and achievement in math and science; assessment, standards, and equity; and multiracial families and children.

Part III focuses on research and research issues in multicultural education. Its chapters offer examples of research in multicultural communities and classrooms as well as guidelines for conducting sound research in the field. How knowledge is constructed is a major research topic in both feminist and ethnic studies scholarship. Consequently, Part IV focuses on knowledge construction and critical studies. Critical multicultural education, which is discussed in Chapter 13, has emerged as a notable trend in the field. The chapters in Part V examine how researchers have described various ethnic groups in past and contemporary research and publications.

Throughout U.S. history, immigration and issues related to educating immigrants have been an enduring and significant problem. A persistent tension has existed between ensuring cultural freedom for immigrants and shaping a national civic culture with shared values and democratic ideals. The tension between *pluribus* and *unum* that has existed since the United States was established persists today. The three chapters that constitute Part VI describe the historical factors related to immigration and education in the United States, and the demographic, social, and psychological factors that influence the education of immigrant students.

The challenges and opportunities of educating specific ethnic groups is the focus of Part VII. These chapters describe the research, issues, and guidelines involved in educating ethnic groups of color in the past, present, and future. Effective ways to educate language minority groups and to help all students acquire second language competencies is becoming increasingly important as the percentage of students who speak a first language other than English increases in U.S. schools, colleges, and universities. The chapters in Part VIII examine the research on second language teaching and learning and describe its policy implications.

The mean academic achievement of Mexican American, Puerto Rican, American Indian, and African American students is significantly below that of Whites. The chapters in Part IX examine, summarize, and derive policy implications from the research regarding how to increase the academic achievement of students from diverse racial, ethnic, language, and social-class groups.

An important aim of multicultural education is to help all students—including White mainstream students—acquire the knowledge, attitudes, and values needed to function effectively in a pluralistic democratic society. The chapters in Part X focus on intergroup education and intercultural relations. Part X opens with a chapter on the history of intergroup education in the United States. The chapters in this part summarize research and describe guidelines for improving interracial and interethnic relations in the nation's educational institutions.

In part because of the increasing number of women and students of color entering their doors since the 1970s, institutions of higher education are facing a tremendous challenge and opportunity in their effort to respond effectively to these population groups and to deal with intergroup relations on campus. The chapters in Part XI summarize research in higher education that deals with students, ethnic studies, women's studies, curriculum reform, and multicultural teacher education.

Many individuals in the United States think of multicultural education and interracial problems as unique to the United States. Yet multicultural education is an international discipline and field of study. It takes unique forms in each nation, but it shares a number of overarching issues, concepts, and paradigms cross-nationally. The chapters in Part XII describe the historical development and current status of multicultural education research and developments in Australia, the United Kingdom, and South Africa.

ACKNOWLEDGMENTS

In preparing this second edition of the *Handbook*, the editors have incurred an enormous debt of gratitude. It is with pride that we acknowledge publicly the professionals who made this project possible. First, we would like to thank the members of the Editorial Advisory Board, who are identified in the front of this volume. Without their support, advice, wisdom, and encouragement, the *Handbook* and this second edition would not have been possible.

We are grateful to the contributing authors who wrote new chapters and to the authors who revised their first-edition chapters. We are deeply grateful to the reviewers for preparing excellent comments on chapter outlines and drafts. The *Handbook* is a much stronger publication because of their hard work and strong commitment to the profession. We hope this second edition is a source of continuing pride for the Advisory Board, the contributors, the reviewers, and the profession.

Since its inception, this *Handbook* has been a major project of the faculty affiliated with the Center for Multicultural Education at the University of Washington, Seattle. Most members of the Center have been heavily involved in the conception and development of this second edition. The Center has an ongoing project to facilitate its dissemination.

The Center staff involved in the conception and development of the *Handbook* includes the editor, who is the Center's director, and the associate editor, who is a faculty associate of the Center. Other faculty associates of the Center served as either contributors or reviewers; Geneva Gay and Michael Knapp are contributing authors. Gay, James Soto Anthony, and Rick Bonus reviewed manuscripts for the *Handbook*.

The Center's research assistants, past and present, took care of many of the daily details and research tasks for the *Handbook* revision project during its two-year duration. We extend warm thanks to Caroline Tamayo, Jennifer Outhouse, Caryn Park, Amrita Zahir, and John J. Juelis. Cristine Hinman, who assisted the senior editor in managing the Center, took major responsibility for coordinating and completing many essential tasks for the *Handbook* revision project. We are grateful for her contribution.

We wish to thank Stephen T. Kerr, former chair of the Area of Curriculum and Instruction in the College of Education—where the Center for Multicultural Education is housed—for his encouragement and support of the *Handbook* revision project. We wish to acknowledge the encouragement given to us by Patricia A. Wasley, dean of the College of Education. We are grateful for her visionary leadership and strong support of the Center.

We wish to thank Lesley Iura, our Jossey-Bass editor, who supported the first edition of the *Handbook* when it was moved from Macmillan—the first publisher of the *Handbook*—to Jossey-Bass, and who encouraged us to prepare this second edition. We wish to acknowledge the help of Elisa Rassen, editorial assistant at Jossey-Bass, who was responsive and helpful during the production phase of the *Handbook*. Kimberly McKaig helped the editors with proofreading. Finally, we wish to acknowledge our daughters, Angela Marie and Patricia Ann, whose presence and commitment to equity is a source of continuing inspiration for our work.

James A. Banks
Editor

Cherry A. McGee Banks
Associate Editor

CONTRIBUTORS

Rod Allan is senior lecturer emeritus in the School of Teacher Education at Charles Sturt University, Bathurst, New South Wales, Australia. He has been editor of *Mitchell Studies,* a handbook of teaching ideas in social studies for primary (elementary) schools. His research interests include multicultural education and analysis of political processes and their impact on tertiary students, details of which have been published in national and international journals.

Alfredo J. Artiles is associate professor of education at Vanderbilt University. His research interests focus on cultural diversity issues in special education and teacher learning for student diversity. He received the 2001 Early Career Award from the American Educational Research Association (AERA) Committee on the Role and Status of Minorities, and he was a National Academy of Education/Spencer Foundation Postdoctoral Fellow. His publications include *English Language Learners with Special Needs: Identification, Placement, and Instruction* and *Factors Associated with English Learner Representation in Special Education: Emerging Evidence from Urban School Districts in California.*

Cherry A. McGee Banks is professor of education at the University of Washington, Bothell, and faculty associate of the Center for Multicultural Education at the University of Washington, Seattle. In 1997, she received the Distinguished Teaching Award from the University of Washington, Bothell, and in 2000 she was named a Worthington Distinguished Professor. Her current research focuses on the intergroup education movement of the 1930s and 1940s. Professor Banks has contributed to numerous journals and is the author of *The Intergroup Education Movement: Insights from the Past, Lessons for the Present and Future* (in press), as well as coeditor of *Multicultural Education: Issues and Perspectives* and coauthor of *Teaching Strategies for the Social Studies.*

James A. Banks is Russell F. Stark University Professor and director of the Center for Multicultural Education at the University of Washington, Seattle. He is a past president of the American Educational Research Association (AERA) and of the National Council for the Social Studies (NCSS). He is a specialist in social studies education and multicultural education. His books include *Teaching Strategies for Ethnic Studies; Cultural Diversity and Education: Foundations, Curriculum, and Teaching; Teaching Strategies for the Social Studies;* and *Educating Citizens in a Multicultural Society.* He is the editor of the Multicultural Education Series of books published by Teachers College Press, Columbia University. Banks is a member of the Board of Children, Youth, and Families of the National Research Council and the Institute of Medicine of the National Academy of Sciences; and the National Academy of Education. In 2001, he received the Jean Dresden Grambs Distinguished Career Research in Social Studies Award from the National Council for the Social Studies.

Christine I. Bennett is professor of social studies and multicultural education at Indiana University in Bloomington. She also directs Project TEAM, a program to recruit and support talented students from underrepresented minorities in education into the teaching profession. Her funded research and publications have focused on the impact of a multicultural social studies curriculum on African American, Anglo, and Latino youth; the classroom climate in desegregated middle schools; causes of racial inequity in school suspension and expulsion in desegregated high schools; explanation of minority student attrition in predominantly White universities; the impact of multicultural teacher education; and preparation of preservice teachers of color at a predominantly White institution.

Dolores Delgado Bernal is assistant professor at the University of Utah with a joint appointment in the Department of Education, Culture, and Society and the Ethnic Studies Program. Her research and teaching draw from critical race theory, Latina/Latino critical theory, and Chicana and Black feminist theories to examine and improve the educational experiences of Chicanas/Chicanos and other students of color. She is the author of *Using a Chicana Feminist Epistemology in Educational Research* and *An Apartheid of Knowledge in Academia: The Struggle over the "Legitimate" Knowledge of Faculty of Color.*

Kelly Bikle is a doctoral candidate in educational linguistics at the Stanford University School of Education. Her career in professional education, which has included teaching in bilingual and ESL classrooms, exceeds 10 years. Her research interests focus on literacy development for English language learners and preparation of teachers to teach in linguistically diverse classrooms.

Elsa S. Billings is a doctoral candidate at Stanford University in the Language, Learning, and Culture Program in the School of Education. Prior to coming to Stanford, she was a bilingual elementary level teacher. Her research interests include academic equity issues, especially concerning language minority children; preparation of teachers to effectively teach in diverse classroom settings; and use of technology in teacher education and professional development.

Jomills Henry Braddock II is professor of sociology and director of the Center for Research on Sports in Society at the University of Miami. He was recently reappointed for a second term by the U.S. secretary of education to the National Educational Research Policy and Priorities Board. His broad research interests in issues of inequality and social justice have been supported by public and private grants and contracts addressing equality of opportunity in education, employment, and sports.

Johnnella E. Butler is associate dean and associate vice provost in the Graduate School at the University of Washington, Seattle, and professor of American ethnic studies with adjunct appointments in English and women's studies. She formerly taught at Smith College, where she served as chair of the Afro-American Studies Department and developed the Smith program in African American Studies. A specialist in African American literature and women's studies, Butler is particularly interested in how ethnic studies and women's studies can be interrelated. She has authored and edited numerous books and articles and is one of three editors of the *Encyclopedia of American Studies.*

Carlos E. Cortés is professor emeritus of history at the University of California, Riverside. He has lectured widely on topics such as multicultural education and media literacy. Since 1990, he has served on the summer faculty of the Harvard Institutes for Higher Education and on the faculty of the Summer Institute for Intercultural Communication. Cortés is the author of *The Children Are Watching* (2000) and *The Making and Remaking of a Multiculturalist* (2002). Cortés is currently working on a three-volume history of the U.S. motion picture industry's treatment of race, ethnicity, foreign nations, and world cultures.

Marilyn Cochran-Smith is professor of education and director of the doctoral program in curriculum and instruction at the Lynch School of Education at Boston College. She is also president-elect of AERA, editor of *The Journal of Teacher Education,* and coeditor of the Practitioner Inquiry Series published by Teachers College Press. She is cochair of AERA's Consensus Panel on Teacher Education and a member of the National Academy of Education's Committee on Teacher Education and the Advisory Board for the Carnegie Foundation's Academy for the Scholarship of Teaching and Learning. Among her award-winning publications is *Inside/Outside: Teacher Research and Knowledge.*

Elizabeth G. Cohen is professor emerita of the Stanford University School of Education and Department of Sociology. She was the founder and director of the Program for Complex Instruction, which develops research and strategies for teaching in heterogeneous classrooms with a focus on equity and conceptual learning. She conducted extensive research on interventions designed to produce equal-status behavior in cooperative classroom groups and received a Presidential Citation from AERA for this work. Her publications include *Designing Groupwork: Strategies for Heterogeneous Classrooms,* and *Working for Equity in Heterogeneous Classrooms: Sociological Theory in Practice* (edited with Rachel Lotan).

Linda Darling-Hammond is Charles E. Ducommun Professor of Education at Stanford University and faculty sponsor for the Stanford Teacher Education Program (STEP). Her research focuses on policy issues related to teaching quality and educational equity. She is a member of the National Academy of Education and the National Board for Professional Teaching Standards. She has edited the *Review of Research in Education* and coedited *The New Handbook of Teacher Evaluation.* Her books include *Learning to Teach for Social Justice* (with Jennifer French and Silvía Paloma García-Lopez); *The Right to Learn: A Blueprint for Creating Schools That Work; Teaching as the Learning Profession: Handbook of Policy and Practice* (edited with Gary Sykes); and *Authentic Assessment in Action: Case Studies of Schools and Students at Work.*

Danné Davis, who has more than 10 years' experience teaching in K–12 urban schools, is a doctoral student in curriculum and instruction at Boston College. She is a coeditor of the *AERA Graduate Student Council Newsletter* and active as a Holmes Scholar with the Holmes Partnership. Her research interests include teaching for diversity, particularly in the area of teacher preparation, which is the focus of her dissertation, *Learning to Teach Among School Children of Color.* She has published articles in *Multicultural Perspectives* and *The Public Manager: The Quarterly for Practitioners.*

Fabienne Doucet is on the staff of the Harvard Immigration Projects' Longitudinal Immigrant Student Adaptation Study and has initiated a parallel, comparative study of U.S.-born Haitian youth. She received her doctorate in human development and family studies from the University of North Carolina at Greensboro and completed a two-year term as a National Science Foundation Postdoctoral Fellow at the Harvard University Graduate School of Education. Her research focuses on parent-child relationships, with an interest in how race, class, gender, and structural factors influence parenting values, beliefs, and practices. She was awarded a National Academy of Education/Spencer Postdoctoral Fellowship for 2002–03.

Tamela McNulty Eitle is assistant professor at the University of Miami, where she teaches methods, statistics, and sociology of education courses. Her research focuses on the links between local racial and political-economic structures and racial inequalities in educational opportunities and outcomes. She is a member of a multiuniversity consortium studying educational reform in Florida (CERF) and is working on several projects exploring the relationship between racial segregation and school disorder, school crime, and delinquency. Her publications include articles in *Equity and Excellence in Education* and *Demography.*

Anne René Elsbree is assistant professor of education in curriculum and instruction at California State University, Chico. Her research examines how teacher educators make meaning of their efforts to disrupt homophobia with preservice teachers. Elsbree's research interests include multicultural education, queer pedagogy, feminist poststructural theory, and video documentation as a research methodology.

Joyce L. Epstein is director of the Center on School, Family, and Community Partnerships and the National Network of Partnership Schools; principal research scientist in the Center for Research on the Education of Students Placed at Risk (CRESPAR); and professor of sociology at Johns Hopkins University. Her recent books include *School, Family, and Community Partnerships: Preparing Educators and Improving Schools* and *School, Family, and Community Partnerships: Your Handbook for Action, Second Edition.* Epstein serves on numerous editorial boards and advisory panels on family involvement and school reform.

Peter Figueroa is professor emeritus of education at the University of Southampton. He has also been a lecturer and research officer at Oxford University; Australia National University; and the University of the West Indies, Jamaica. His main research interests are multicultural antiracist education, citizenship education in diverse societies, and the phenomenological philosophy of Maurice Merleau-Ponty. His books include *Education and the Social Construction of "Race"*; *Sociology of Education: A Caribbean Reader*; and *Education for Cultural Diversity.*

Ann K. Fitzgerald is senior researcher in the Department of Anthropology at the American Museum of Natural History. She conducted extensive fieldwork on contemporary tattoos and piercing for the expedition titled *Body Art: Marks of Identity* (1999) and as Jesup Centenary Coordinator for the Museum's exhibition titled *Drawing Shadows to Stone* (1998). She organized an international conference to reconceptualize the expedition Franz Boas led to Siberia and the Pacific Rim. Her most recent book, *Class, Culture, and Literature* (2001), was edited with Paul Lauter.

Suzanne Fondrie is a doctoral candidate at the University of Wisconsin, Madison. Her dissertation examines notions of Whiteness in Newbery Award books. She is the author of "Gentle Doses of Racism: Whiteness and Children's Literature," which was published in the *Journal of Children's Literature.* Prior to her doctoral studies, Fondrie was a high school English and German teacher. Her current research interests include critical literacy, multicultural education, and children's literature.

Kim Fries is assistant professor of education at the University of New Hampshire, where she teaches courses in educational change, classroom management, and instructional strategies and pedagogy. She is the project director for AERA's Consensus Panel on Teacher Education and former associate editor of AERA's Division K newsletter. With research interests in reflective practice, instructional strategies, and classroom management, she has presented regularly at AERA and coauthored an article in *Educational Researcher.* Prior to her doctoral studies, she taught in public and private schools.

Eugene E. García is professor of education and dean of the School of Education at Arizona State University. He has served as director of the Office of Bilingual Education and Minority Language Affairs of the U.S. Department of Education and dean of the Graduate School of Education at the University of California, Berkeley. He has published extensively in the area of language teaching and bilingual development and is currently conducting research on effective schooling for linguistically and culturally diverse student populations. His most recent books include *Hispanic Education in the United States: Raíces y Alas* and *Student Cultural Diversity: Understanding and Meeting the Challenge.*

Geneva Gay is professor of education and faculty associate of the Center for Multicultural Education at the University of Washington, Seattle. She is the recipient of the 1990 Distinguished Scholar Award presented by AERA's Committee on the Role and Status of Minorities in Educational Research and Development and the 1994 Multicultural Educator Award presented by the National Association of Multicultural Education. She is the author of *Culturally Responsive Teaching: Theory, Research and Practice*; *At the Essence of Learning: Multicultural Education*; and coeditor of *Expressively Black: The Cultural Basis of Ethnic Identity.*

Norma González is a research anthropologist at the Bureau of Applied Research in Anthropology, University of Arizona. Her research has appeared in several journals, including *Anthropology and Education Quarterly, Education and Urban Society,* and *Journal of Applied Behavioral Sciences.*

Carl A. Grant is the Hoefs-Bascom Professor of Teacher Education in the Department of Curriculum and Instruction and professor in the Department of Afro-American Studies at the University of Wisconsin, Madison. His awards include the Angela Davis Race, Gender, and Class Award from the Race, Gender, and Class Project (2001); the Multicultural Education Award from the National Association for Multicultural Education (NAME, 2001); and the School of Educator Distinguished Achievement Award (1997). His publications include *Global Constructions of Multicultural Education: Theories and Realities* and *Multicultural Research: A Reflective Engagement with Race, Class, Gender, and Sexual Orientation.* Grant served as president of NAME (1993–1999), editor of *Review of Educational Research* (1996–1999), and a member of the National Research Council's Committee on Assessment and Teacher Quality.

Ramón A. Gutiérrez is professor of ethnic studies and history, the founding chair of the Ethnic Studies Department, and the director of the Center for the Study of Race and Ethnicity at the University of California, San Diego. His publications include *When Jesus Came the Corn Mothers Went Away: Marriage, Sexuality and Power in New Mexico, 1500–1846; Recovering the U.S. Hispanic Literary Heritage; The Encyclopedia of the North American Colonies; Festivals and Celebrations in American Ethnic Communities; Contested Eden: California Before the Gold Rush;* and *Mexican Home Altars.* He is the recipient of several fellowships and awards, including the MacArthur Foundation Prize Fellowship.

Beverly Guy-Sheftall is Anna Julia Cooper Professor of Women's Studies at Spelman College and founding director of the Women's Research and Resource Center. She has written and edited a number of books, including *Sturdy Black Bridges: Visions of Black Women in Literature; Daughters of Sorrow: Attitudes Toward Black Women, 1880–1920; Words of Fire: An Anthology of African American Feminist Thought;* and *Traps: African American Men on Gender and Sexuality.* She has participated in the national women's studies movement since its inception and provided leadership for the establishment of the first women's studies major at a historically Black college.

Kenji Hakuta is the Vida Jacks Professor of Education at Stanford University. An experimental psychologist by training, his major areas of specialization are bilingual education and second language acquisition. His major publications include *Mirror of Language: The Debate on Bilingualism* and *In Other Words: The Science and Psychology of Second Language Acquisition.* He has served on a number of committees in education and the behavioral sciences at the national level, including the National Educational Research Policy and Priorities Board of the U.S. Department of Education.

Shirley Brice Heath is professor of English and linguistics (and, by courtesy, of anthropology and of education) at Stanford University and Senior Scholar for the Carnegie Foundation. She has held fellowships from the National Endowment for the Humanities, the Guggenheim Foundation, and the MacArthur Foundation. Known internationally for her work in literacy studies and language socialization, she has won awards from professional organizations across several fields, including English, anthropology, and education. In 2000, she received the Distinguished Scholarship and Service Award from the American Association for Applied Linguistics. Her books include *Telling Tongues: Language Policy in Mexico; Colony to Nation;* and *Ways with Words: Language, Life, and Work in Communities and Classrooms.*

Donald J. Hernandez is professor of sociology and affiliate with the Center for Social and Demographic Analysis at the University at Albany, State University of New York. He is the author of many articles and books on children, youth, and public policy, including *America's Children: Resources from Family, Government, and the Economy.* This was the first national research, since the Great Depression, to use children as the unit of analysis to document the timing, magnitude, and reasons for revolutionary changes in family composition, parents' education, fathers' and mothers' work, and family income and poverty.

Nitza M. Hidalgo is professor of education at Westfield State College and director of the Westfield Professional Development School Network. She teaches in the areas of multicultural education, philosophy of education, and ethnic studies. She is the coeditor of *Latino Communities: Resources for Educational Change* and *Facing Racism in Education*. Her research focuses on development of qualitative research methodologies in the study of Puerto Rican families. She is writing a literary memoir.

Bob Hill teaches social education at Charles Sturt University, Bathurst, New South Wales, Australia. He has published in the area of Aboriginal education, intercultural education, overseas teaching practicums, and political education. He is the author of *Overcoming Inequality* and coauthor of *The First of Its Kind, Perspectives on Childhood: An Approach to Citizenship Education*.

Evelyn Hu-DeHart is professor of history and director of the Center for the Study of Race and Ethnicity in America at Brown University. Her current research focuses on the Asian diaspora in Latin America and the Caribbean and on diaspora studies as a direction for ethnic studies. Her research—which is written in English, Spanish, and Chinese—has been published in numerous scholarly journals. Her books include *Missionaries, Miners, and Indians: History of Spanish Contact with the Yaqui Indians of Northwestern New Spain, 1533–1830* and *Yaqui Resistance and Survival: Struggle for Land and Autonomy, 1821–1910*.

Rebecca Joseph, a former middle school teacher, is a doctoral candidate at UCLA and a recipient of a Spencer RTG fellowship. She is currently researching how teachers respond to mandated use of scripted curricula. Her other research interest is in ways to train highly effective and resilient social justice urban educators.

Peter N. Kiang is professor of education and director of the Asian American Studies Program at the University of Massachusetts, Boston. His research, teaching, and advocacy related to Asian American immigrant/refugee students and communities in both K–12 and higher education have been honored or supported by the National Academy of Education, the National Endowment for the Humanities, the Spencer Foundation, the Massachusetts Teachers Association, the Massachusetts Association for Bilingual Education, the National Association for the Advancement of Colored People (NAACP), and the Anti-Defamation League.

Joyce Elaine King is professor of education at Spelman College. Her research and publications address teaching and learning, Black studies theory, epistemology and curriculum change, the role of cultural knowledge in the professional development of teachers, and community-mediated research and praxis at all levels. She has a special interest in global education, parent advocacy, service learning, innovative uses of new media technology, and other transformative educational approaches. Two of her books are *Preparing Teachers for Cultural Diversity* and *Black Mothers to Sons: Juxtaposing African American Literature with Social Practice*.

Michael S. Knapp is professor of educational leadership and policy studies at the University of Washington, Seattle, where he directs the Center for the Study of Teaching and Policy. His scholarship concentrates on the dynamics of policy and leadership, in relation to school improvement, teacher development, and the quality of teaching, especially in disenfranchised communities. He has written extensively about his research in *Teaching for Meaning in High-Poverty Classrooms* (1995); *Paths to Partnership* (1998); and a recent edited volume, *The School District and Instructional Renewal*.

Mindy L. Kornhaber is assistant professor in the Department of Education Policy Studies and a member of the faculty in the Children, Youth, and Families Consortium at the Pennsylvania State University. Her research interests are in how institutions, and the policies surrounding them, enhance or impede human potential, and how human potential is developed highly and equitably. She has published articles on intelligence, school change, and the use of standardized tests to select students for elite programs. She is the coauthor, with Howard Gardner, of *Intelligence: Multiple Perspectives* and coeditor, with Gary Orfield, of *Raising Standards or Raising Barriers? Inequality and High-Stakes Testing in Public Education*.

Gloria Ladson-Billings is professor of education in the Department of Curriculum and Instruction at the University of Wisconsin, Madison, and a former Senior Fellow in Urban Education at the Annenberg Institute for School Reform at Brown University. Her research interests concern the relationship between culture and schooling, particularly successful teaching and learning for African American students. Among her publications are *The Dreamkeepers: Successful Teachers of African American Children*, the *Dictionary of Multicultural Education* (with Carl A. Grant), and *Crossing Over to Canaan: The Journey of New Teachers in Diverse Classrooms*. She was formerly the editor of the Teaching, Learning and Human Development section of the *American Educational Research Journal* and a member of several editorial boards.

Paul Lauter is Allan K. and Gwendolyn Miles Smith Professor of Literature at Trinity College in Hartford, Connecticut. He has served as president of the American

Studies Association (of the United States) and general editor of the *Heath Anthology of American Literature* and was one of the founders of The Feminist Press. His recent books include *From Walden Pond to Jurassic Park: Literature, Class, and Culture* (edited with Ann Fitzgerald); *Thoreau's Walden;* and *Civil Disobedience* (general editor).

Carol D. Lee is associate professor of education in the School of Education and Social Policy at Northwestern University in Evanston, Illinois. She received her Ph.D. in curriculum and instruction from the University of Chicago. She has had many years of experience as a classroom teacher at the elementary, high school, and community college levels. Lee is a founder and former director of a 20-year-old independent school in Chicago that integrates African American culture throughout its curriculum. Her research interests and publications focus on cultural contexts for literacy instruction. She is the author of *Signifying as a Scaffold for Literary Interpretation.*

Angela Lintz is on the staff of High Tech High and directs the High Tech High Network Learning project. Her goal is to develop a national network of 10 charter schools based on the High Tech High design principles. Teachers and staff work to successfully integrate technical and academic education with the goal of preparing students for postsecondary education and professional employment in science and technology fields. Lintz came to High Tech High from the University of California, San Diego, Early Academic Outreach Program, where she directed a whole-school reform effort for an urban school in San Diego.

K. Tsianina Lomawaima is professor of American Indian Studies at the University of Arizona. Her research interests include American Indian history and education, and federal policy in the 20th and 21st centuries. Creek and Cherokee, she is a member of the editorial board for the *American Indian Lives Series.* Her books include *They Called It Prairie Light: The Story of Chilocco Indian School; Away From Home: American Indian Boarding School Experiences;* and *Uneven Ground: American Indian Sovereignty and Federal Law.*

Rachel A. Lotan is director of the Teacher Education Program at Stanford University and associate professor of education. Her teaching and research focus on aspects of teaching and learning in academically and linguistically diverse classrooms, teacher education, sociology of the classroom, and the social organization of schools. In addition to writing numerous articles and book chapters, she coedited *Working for Equity in Heterogeneous Classrooms: Sociological Theory in Action* and *Groupwork in Diverse Classrooms: A Casebook for Educators.*

Hugh Mehan is professor of sociology and director of the Center for Research on Educational Equity, Access, and Teaching Excellence (CREATE) at the University of California, San Diego. He has authored, coauthored, or edited nine books, among them *The Reality of Ethnomethodology; Learning Lessons; Handicapping the Handicapped;* and *Constructing School Success.* His most recent book, *Extending School Reform: From One School to Many,* discusses the processes, challenges, and consequences of "scaling up" educational reforms.

Pyong Gap Min is professor of sociology at Queens College and the Graduate Center of the City University of New York. His research focuses on Asian Americans and explores ethnic identity, immigrant entrepreneurship, immigrant women's gender role, and immigrant congregations. Min's publications include *Caught in the Middle: Korean Communities in New York and Los Angeles,* which won two book awards; *Changes and Conflicts: Korean Immigrant Families in New York; Asian Americans: Contemporary Trends and Issues; The Second Generation: Ethnic Identity Among Asian Americans;* and *Mass Migration in the United States: Classical and Contemporary Periods.*

Masahiko Minami is associate professor of Japanese and director of the Center for the Advancement of the Teaching of Japanese Language and Culture at San Francisco State University. He has written extensively on psycholinguistics and sociolinguistics. Since 1995, he has been teaching and conducting research on first and second language acquisition, development of literacy skills, and bilingualism. Minami has published works covering cultural constructions of meaning, child care quality in Japan, and East Asian students' experiences in U.S. classrooms. His books include *Culture-Specific Language Styles, Culture and Psychology: People Around the World,* and *New Directions in Applied Linguistics of Japanese.*

Luis C. Moll is professor in the Department of Language, Reading, and Culture at the University of Arizona. His research focuses on sociocultural approaches to child development and education, literacy and bilingual learning. His recent research combines ethnographic observations on the uses of knowledge in Latino and other households with teaching experiments designed to apply this knowledge in bilingual classrooms. In 1998, Moll was elected to membership in the National Academy of Education. His publications include *Vygotsky and Education; Funds of Knowledge: A New Approach to Culture in Education;* and *Ethnographic Experiments: A Socio-cultural Approach to Educational Research and Practice.*

Kogila A. Moodley is professor of sociology and anthropology in the Department of Educational Studies at the University of British Columbia, Canada. Born in South Africa, she moved to Canada during the apartheid era and currently lives there. She was the first holder of the David Lam Chair in Multicultural Education at the University of British Columbia. She is currently president of the International Sociological Association's Research Committee on Ethnic, Minority, and Race Relations. She has published several books and more than 60 articles on South African race relations, multiculturalism, and race and ethnic relations from a comparative and international perspective.

Kate Muir is professor of science and mathematics education at the University of Wyoming. Her research interests include how teachers make "science for all" a reality in classrooms and how these teachers' social justice ideals play a role in making science more critical and multicultural. She also has interest in the role environmental education plays in making students aware of their world. She has taught science in classrooms and in nonformal educational arenas such as the Monterey Bay Aquarium and the UCLA Ocean Discovery Center.

Sonia Nieto is professor of language, literacy, and culture at the University of Massachusetts, Amherst. She has written widely on multicultural education, Latino education, and education of students of linguistically and culturally diverse backgrounds. She is the author of *Affirming Diversity: The Sociopolitical Context of Multicultural Education* and *The Light in Their Eyes: Creating Multicultural Learning Communities*; she coedited *Puerto Rican Students in U.S. Schools*. Her most recent book is *What Keeps Teachers Going?* She serves on various national advisory boards that focus on educational equity and social justice and has received many awards for her community service, advocacy, and scholarly activities.

Jeannie Oakes is Presidential Professor in Educational Equity at the University of California, Los Angeles (UCLA), and director of UCLA's Institute for Democracy, Education, & Access (IDEA) and UC's All Campus Consortium on Research for Diversity. Her research examines schooling inequalities and follows the progress of educators and activists seeking socially just schools. She is the author of numerous journal articles in research publications and of *Keeping Track: How Schools Structure Inequality*; coauthor (with Martin Lipton) of *Teaching to Change the World*; and coauthor of *Becoming Good American Schools: The Struggle for Virtue in Education Reform* (2001), which received AERA's Outstanding Book Award.

Irma M. Olmedo is associate professor of education at the University of Illinois–Chicago. Her research interests focus on preparation of teachers for urban schools—especially for culturally and linguistically diverse classrooms—and on bilingualism and Latino cultures. She also has an interest in the international dimensions of multilingual/multicultural education. Her articles have been published in *Anthropology and Education Quarterly, Teaching and Teacher Education, Qualitative Inquiry,* and *Urban Education.* Olmedo is active in the AERA and the National Association for Bilingual Education.

Michael R. Olneck is professor of educational policy studies and sociology at the University of Wisconsin, Madison. His research interests include the study of historical and contemporary racial, ethnic, and linguistic diversity in American education. His analyses of the early-20th-century Americanization movement, the interwar intercultural education movement, and the contemporary bilingual education and multicultural education movements appear in a series of articles in the *American Journal of Education,* the *American Educational Research Journal,* and other venues. He is a contributor to the *Harvard Encyclopedia of American Ethnic Groups.*

Carlos J. Ovando is associate dean for teacher education, division director for curriculum and instruction, and professor of education at Arizona State University. He edited (with Peter McLaren) *The Politics of Multiculturalism and Bilingual Education: Students and Teachers Caught in the Cross Fire* and coauthored *The Color of Bureaucracy: The Politics of Equity in Multicultural School Communities* (with Colleen Larson). He is the coauthor of *Bilingual and ESL Classrooms: Teaching in Multicultural Contexts.*

Amado M. Padilla is professor of education at Stanford University. He received his Ph.D. in experimental psychology from the University of New Mexico. The American Psychological Association, AERA, and the Modern Language Association have recognized him for his research. Padilla is a Fellow of the American Association for the Advancement of Science and the APA. He has published extensively on a variety of topics; among his books are *Latino Mental Health, Introduction to Psychology,* and *Hispanic Psychology.* He is the founding editor of the *Hispanic Journal of Behavioral Sciences.*

Yoon K. Pak is assistant professor of educational policy studies at the University of Illinois at Urbana-Champaign and is a core faculty member of the Asian American Studies Program. Her research and teaching interests are in the history of American education from a multiracial perspective. She is a 2002–03 National Academy of Education/

Spencer Postdoctoral Fellow. She is the author of *Wherever I Go I'll Always Be a Loyal American: Schooling Seattle's Japanese Americans During World War II.*

John D. Palmer is a visiting assistant professor at Colgate University. His research concentrates on the sociocultural aspects of education, with specific interests in ethnic identity, cross-cultural competency, social justice educators, and Asian American immigrants. He is an AERA Spencer Predissertation Fellow and an Alumni Holmes Scholar. Currently, Palmer is secretary for the AERA Special Interest Group on Research on the Education of Asian Pacific Americans. He has a chapter titled "Korean Adopted Young Women: Gender Bias, Racial Issues, and Educational Implications" in *Research on the Education of Asian Pacific Americans.*

Valerie Ooka Pang is professor of teacher education at San Diego State University. She was a Senior Fellow with the Annenberg Institute for School Reform at Brown University and has been honored by AERA's Committee on the Role and Status of Minorities in Education, the National Association for Multicultural Education, San Diego State's Liberal Studies Program, and the University of Washington's College of Education. Pang authored *Multicultural Education: A Caring-Centered, Reflective Approach* and *Struggling to Be Heard: The Unmet Needs of Asian Pacific American Children.* Pang has published a number of journal articles and served as a member of several professional committees.

Thomas F. Pettigrew is research professor of social psychology at the University of California, Santa Cruz. He received his Ph.D. from Harvard University and has taught at the University of North Carolina and Harvard University. His books include *A Profile of the Negro American, Racially Separate or Together, Racial Discrimination in the U.S., The Sociology of Race Relations,* and *How to Think Like a Social Scientist.* He has received numerous honors, including sociology's Sydney Spivack Award for Race Relations Research, and social psychology's Kurt Lewin Award and the Distinguished Scientist Award.

Mariolga Reyes-Cruz is a predoctoral Ford Fellow in clinical/community psychology at the University of Illinois, Urbana-Champaign. Her research focuses on ethnic minority psychology, interracial relations, and qualitative research. Currently she is studying school racial climate from Latino/Latina immigrant perspectives. She is a member of the Society for the Psychological Study of Ethnic Minority Issues, the Society for Community Research and Action, and the Society for the Psychological Study of Social Issues. Her articles include "Thinking and Writing Skills in High-Ability Ethnic Minority High School Students" and "Deconstructing Whiteness and Liberation Psychology."

Clara E. Rodríguez is professor of sociology at Fordham University's College at Lincoln Center. She is the recipient of the American Sociological Association's Award for Distinguished Contributions to Research in Latina/Latino Sociology (2001). Her books include *Changing Race: Latinos, the Census, and the History of Ethnicity in the United States; "Adiós, Borinquen querida": La diáspora puertorriqueña, su historia y sus aportaciones; Latin Looks: Images of Latinas and Latinos in U.S. Media; Hispanics in the Labor Force: Issues and Policies; Historical Perspectives on Puerto Rican Survival in the United States;* and *Puerto Ricans: Born in the USA.*

Deborah Rosenfelt is professor of women's studies and director of the Curriculum Transformation Project at the University of Maryland, College Park. She writes about women, literature, and culture in the left and feminist movements in the United States, women's and diversity issues in higher education, and women's studies. Her recent publications include an anthology, *Tillie Olsen's Tell Me a Riddle;* the fall/winter 1998 *Women's Studies Quarterly* on internationalizing women's studies; a special issue of *American Studies* on international women's scholarship; a coauthored monograph, *Internationalizing Women's Studies;* and a coedited volume, *Encompassing Gender: Crossing Disciplinary and Geographic Borders.*

Maria P. P. Root, a clinical psychologist in private practice in Seattle, Washington, is president of the Washington State Psychological Association. She received her Ph.D. from the University of Washington where, in 1995, she served as an associate professor of American ethnic studies. Her publications, which include *Racially Mixed People in America* and *Love's Revolution: Interracial Marriage,* focus on the subject of diversity and identity. She is a fellow of the APA and recipient of the Washington State Psychological Association's Distinguished Psychologist Award.

Betty Schmitz is director of the Curriculum Transformation Project at the University of Washington, Seattle. A nationally known leader in curriculum, she has directed long-term faculty development projects and institutes at several major universities. She has lectured, written, and consulted extensively on curriculum and institutional change. Her books include *Core Curriculum and Cultural Pluralism: A Guide for Campus Planners* and *Integrating Women's Studies into the Curriculum.* She is currently working on new conceptual frameworks and models for faculty development for both university and K–12 teachers that take into account new scholarship on the intersectionality of race, ethnicity, gender, class, and sexuality.

Janet Ward Schofield is professor of psychology and a senior scientist at the Learning Research and Development Center at the University of Pittsburgh. She previously taught at Spelman College. Her research focuses on school desegregation and educational technology. She is a member of the Board on International Comparative Studies in Education at the National Academy of Sciences, a fellow of the APA, and a fellow of the American Psychological Society (APS). She has also served on APA's governing body, the Council of Representatives. Her books include *Black and White in School, Computers and Classroom Culture,* and *Bringing the Internet to School.*

Sau-Fong Siu is professor of social work and director of the Bachelor of Social Work Program at Wheelock College, Boston. Her research interests focus on Asian American educational issues and Chinese American families. The work she did as a researcher with the Center on Families, Communities, Schools, and Children's Learning has appeared as journal articles, research monographs, and book chapters. She is also principal author of an annotated bibliography on social work practice with Asian and Pacific Islander Americans, to be published by the Council on Social Work Education.

Diana T. Slaughter-Defoe is Constance E. Clayton Professor in Urban Education in the Graduate School of Education at the University of Pennsylvania. Her research and writing have emphasized the study of the relationship between parental socialization and children's school-related behavior and achievement, including parental involvement in Head Start programs. Among her publications are *Visible Now: Blacks in Private Schools* and *Black Children and Poverty: A Developmental Perspective.* She was the 1993 recipient of the Public Interest Directorate's Award for Distinguished Contribution to Research in Public Policy, given by the APA.

Christine E. Sleeter is professor in the College of Professional Studies at California State University, Monterey Bay. Her research focuses on antiracist multicultural education and multicultural teacher education. She was awarded the National Association for Multicultural Education Research Award, the AERA Committee on the Role and Status of Minorities in Education Distinguished Scholar Award, and the University of Wisconsin, Parkside, Research Award. Her books include *Culture, Difference and Power, Multicultural Education as Social Activism,* and *Turning on Learning* (with Carl Grant). She also edits the book series Social Context of Education for SUNY Press.

C. Matthew Snipp is professor of sociology at Stanford University. He has been a Research Fellow at the U.S. Census Bureau and a Fellow at the Center for Advanced Study in the Behavioral Sciences. Snipp has published three books and more than 60 articles and book chapters on demography, economic development, poverty, and unemployment. His current research and writing deals with the methodology of racial measurement, changes in the social and economic well-being of American ethnic minorities, and poverty and unemployment on American Indian reservations.

Claude M. Steele is the Lucie Sterns Professor in the Social Sciences at Stanford University. His research involves the processes of self-evaluation, especially in how people cope with self-image threat. This work has led to a general theory of the self-affirmation processes. Steele is president of the Society for Personality and Social Psychology and serves on the board of directors of the American Psychological Society. He is also a member of the National Academy of Sciences and the National Academy of Education.

Cookie White Stephan is professor of sociology at New Mexico State University. Stephan's major research focus is on racism. Currently, much of her research tests a model of the causes of prejudice, including prejudice directed toward the major minority groups in the United States, Whites, immigrants to the United States, and citizens of other cultures. Her publications include *Improving Intergroup Relations* (with Walter Stephan) and *Cognition and Affect in Cross-Cultural Relations.*

Walter G. Stephan is professor of social psychology at New Mexico State University. His areas of interest include intergroup relations, intercultural relations, attribution processes, and the relationship between cognition and affect. He is the recipient of the Klineberg Award for intercultural relations (1996) and the Allport Award (2002), given by Division 9 of the APA. He is the author or coauthor of *Desegregation: Past, Present and Future; Intergroup Relations: Reducing Prejudice and Stereotyping in Schools; Improving Intergroup Relations;* and *Learning Together: Intergroup Relations Programs* (in press).

Carola Suárez-Orozco is the executive director of the David Rockefeller Center for Latin American Studies at Harvard. She is also the coprincipal investigator of a five-year longitudinal study of immigrant adolescents. Her research focus in recent years has been on the intersection of cultural and psychological factors in the adaptation of immigrant and ethnic minority children. She is the coauthor, with Marcelo Suárez-Orozco, of *Children of*

Immigration and *Transformations: Migration, Family Life, and Achievement Motivation Among Latino Adolescents.* They are also the coeditors (with Desirée Qin-Hillard) of the six-volume series, *The New Immigration.*

Marcelo M. Suárez-Orozco is the Victor S. Thomas Professor of Education at Harvard University. He is the author of many scholarly essays, books, and edited volumes, the most recent of which are *Latinos: Remaking America; Children of Immigration; Interdisciplinary Perspectives on the New Immigration; Cultures Under Siege: Collective Violence and Trauma;* and co-author with Carola Suárez-Orozco of *Transformations: Immigration, Family Life and Achievement Motivation Among Latino Adolescents.* In 1995 and again in 1997, he was appointed Directeur d'Etudes Associé at the Ecole des Hautes Etudes en Sciences Sociales, Paris. He has been visiting professor at the University of Barcelona (Spain) and the Catholic University of Leuven (Belgium).

Derald Wing Sue is professor of psychology and education in the Department of Counseling and Clinical Psychology at Teachers College, Columbia University. He was the cofounder and first president of the Asian American Psychological Association and past president of the Society for the Psychological Study of Ethnic Minorities. Sue's coauthored books, *Counseling the Culturally Different: Theory and Practice* and *Counseling American Minorities: A Cross Cultural Perspective,* have been identified as the most frequently cited works in the field of multicultural counseling. He is also author of *A Theory of Multicultural Counseling and Therapy* and *Multicultural Counseling Competencies: Individual and Organizational Development.*

Stanley C. Trent is associate professor of special education in the Curry School of Education at the University of Virginia. His research interests focus on inclusive education for culturally and linguistically diverse students with disabilities and the impact of multicultural education courses on preservice and inservice teachers. His work on these topics has appeared in a number of journals. He is also an associate editor for the journal *Multiple Voices for Ethnically Diverse Exceptional Learners.*

John S. Wills is assistant professor of education in the Graduate School of Education at the University of California, Riverside. His research interests focus on the politics of historical representations in social studies classrooms, and efforts to construct inclusive narratives of U.S. history in K–12 classrooms. Wills is a recipient of a Spencer Foundation Postdoctoral Fellowship. In 2002, he served as Program Chair for Division B, Curriculum Studies, for the annual meeting of the AERA. His publications have appeared in various journals, including *Anthropology and Education Quarterly, Multicultural Education, Journal of Narrative and Life History,* and *Theory and Research in Social Education.*

Sara Woolverton holds an M.Ed. in special education and a Ph.D. in educational leadership and policy studies. Her teaching and research have focused on the dynamics of disenfranchisement and the roles of race, class, and gender in public K–12 education. She is currently an administrator for the Seattle School District.

REVIEWERS

Frances Aboud
McGill University, Montreal

James Soto Antony
University of Washington, Seattle

Eleanor Armour-Thomas
Queens College, City University of New York

Molefi Kete Asante
Temple University, Philadelphia

Kathryn Au
University of Hawaii, Honolulu

Ceola Ross Baber
University of North Carolina, Greensboro

Arnetha F. Ball
Stanford University

Rick Bonus
University of Washington, Seattle

A. Wade Boykin
Howard University, Washington, D.C.

Frank Brown
University of North Carolina, Chapel Hill

Deborah Faye Carter
Indiana University, Bloomington

Lillian Castaneda
California State University, Channel Islands

Courtney B. Cazden
Harvard University

Mitchell J. Chang
University of California, Los Angeles

Virgie O. Chattergy
University of Hawaii, Manoa

Nancy Chavkin
Southwest Texas State University

Donna Christian
Center for Applied Linguistics, Washington, D.C.

Robert L. Crain
Teachers College, Columbia University

Warren Crichlow
York University, Toronto

Jim Cummins
Ontario Institute for Studies in Education, Toronto

Carlos F. Diaz
Florida Atlantic University, Boca Raton

Mary E. Dilworth
American Association of Colleges for Teacher Education, Washington, D.C.

John F. Dovidio
Colgate University, Hamilton, New York

Margaret Eisenhart
University of Colorado, Boulder

Frederick D. Erickson
University of California, Los Angeles

Liza Fiol-Matta
New Jersey City University, Jersey City

Timothy P. Fong
California State University, Sacramento

Samuel L. Gaertner
University of Delaware, Newark

Patricia C. Gandara
University of California, Davis

Howard Gardner
Harvard University

Geneva Gay
University of Washington, Seattle

Russell Gersten
University of Oregon, Eugene

David Gillborn
Institute of Education, University of London

Claude Goldenberg
University of California, Los Angeles

Angela A. Gonzales
Cornell University, Ithaca, New York

David Gutiérrez
University of California, San Diego

Beth Harry
University of Miami

Willis D. Hawley
University of Maryland, College Park

HANDBOOK OF RESEARCH ON MULTICULTURAL EDUCATION

SECOND EDITION

PART

I

HISTORY, CHARACTERISTICS, AND GOALS

1

MULTICULTURAL EDUCATION

Historical Development, Dimensions, and Practice

James A. Banks

University of Washington, Seattle

Within the last two decades, scholars and researchers in multicultural education have developed a high level of consensus about the nature, aims, and scope of the field. Gay (1992) and J. A. Banks (2003a) have noted the high level of consensus about aims and scope in the literature written by multicultural education theorists. Gay, however, points out that there is a tremendous gap between theory and practice in the field. In her view, theory development has outpaced development in practice, and a wide gap exists between the two.

Gibson (1976) reviewed the multicultural education literature and identified five approaches, noting how they differ, overlap, and interrelate. In their review of the literature, published 11 years later, Sleeter and Grant (1987) also identified five approaches to multicultural education, four of which differ from Gibson's categories. Sleeter and Grant noted the lack of consensus in the field and concluded that a focus on the education of people of color is the only common element among the many definitions of multicultural education. Although there are numerous approaches, statements of aims, and definitions of multicultural education, an examination of the literature written by specialists in the field indicates that there is a high level of consensus about its aims and goals (J. A. Banks, 2003b; Banks et al., 2001; Bennett, 2001; Nieto, 1999; Parekh, 1986; Sleeter & Grant, 1999; Suzuki, 1984).

A major goal of multicultural education, as stated by specialists in the field, is to reform the schools and other educational institutions so that students from diverse racial, ethnic, and social-class groups will experience educational equality. Another important goal of multicultural education—revealed in this literature—is to give male and female students an equal chance to experience educational success and mobility (Klein, 1985; Sadker & Sadker, 1994). Multicultural education theorists are increasingly interested in how the interaction of race, class, and gender influences education (J. A. Banks, 2003b; Grant & Sleeter, 1986; Sleeter, 1991). However, the emphasis that theorists give to each factor varies considerably.

Although there is an emerging consensus about the aims and scope of multicultural education (J. A. Banks, 1992), the variety of typologies, conceptual schemes, and perspectives within the field reflects its emergent status and the fact that complete agreement about its aims and boundaries has not been attained (J. A. Banks, 2001; Bennett, 2001; Garcia, 1998; Gollnick & Chinn, 2001). The debate over the extent to which the histories and cultures of women and people of color should be incorporated into the study of Western civilization in the nation's schools, colleges, and universities has complicated the quest for sound definitions and clear disciplinary boundaries within the field (Asante, 1998; Asante & Ravitch, 1991; Ravitch, 1990; Schlesinger, 1991).

An earlier version of this chapter was published in *Review of Research in Education*, Vol. 19 (pp. 3–49), edited by Linda Darling-Hammond, 1993, Washington, DC: American Educational Research Association (AERA). It is used with the permission of AERA.

GOALS AND SCOPE

There is general agreement among most scholars and researchers that, for multicultural education to be implemented successfully, institutional changes must be made in the curriculum; the teaching materials; teaching and learning styles; the attitudes, perceptions, and behaviors of teachers and administrators; and the goals, norms, and culture of the school (J. A. Banks, 1992; Bennett, 2001; Sleeter & Grant, 1999). However, many school and university practitioners have a limited conception of multicultural education, viewing it primarily as curriculum reform that involves only changing or restructuring the curriculum to include content about ethnic groups, women, and other cultural groups. This conception of multicultural education is widespread because curriculum reform was the main focus when the movement first emerged in the 1960s and 1970s (Blassingame, 1972; Ford, 1973), and because the multiculturalism discourse in the popular media has focused on curriculum reform and largely ignored other dimensions and components of multicultural education (Gray, 1991; Schlesinger, 1991).

If multicultural education is to become better understood and implemented in ways more consistent with theory, its various dimensions must be more clearly described, conceptualized, and researched. Multicultural education is conceptualized in this review as a field that consists of the five dimensions formulated by J. A. Banks (1991a, 1992). The dimensions are based on his research, observations, and work in the field extending from the present back to the late 1960s (J. A. Banks, 1970, 1998). Because of the limited scope of this review, no attempt is made to review the research comprehensively in each of the five dimensions. Rather, a selected group of studies in each dimension are reviewed. Race, ethnicity, class, gender, and exceptionality—and their interaction—are each important factors in multicultural education. Since it is not possible within one review to examine each variable in sufficient depth, this review focuses on racial and ethnic groups.

THE DIMENSIONS OF MULTICULTURAL EDUCATION

The dimensions of multicultural education used to conceptualize, organize, and select the literature for review in this chapter are (a) content integration, (b) the knowledge construction process, (c) prejudice reduction, (d) an equity pedagogy, and (e) an empowering school culture and social structure (see Figure 1.1). Each dimension is

defined and illustrated, and a brief overview of each major section of the chapter is presented. The interrelationship of the five dimensions is discussed later.

Content Integration

Content integration deals with the extent to which teachers use examples, data, and information from a variety of cultures and groups to illustrate key concepts, principles, generalizations, and theories in their subject area or discipline. In many school districts, as well as in popular writings, multicultural education is viewed only, or primarily, as content integration. This widespread belief that content integration constitutes the whole of multicultural education might be the factor that causes many teachers of subjects such as mathematics and science to view multicultural education as an endeavor primarily for social studies and language arts teachers.

The historical development of content integration movements is discussed, beginning with the historical work of George Washington Williams (1882–83), who is usually considered the first African American historian in the United States (Franklin, 1985). The early ethnic studies movement, which began with Williams, continued quietly until the ethnic studies movements of the 1960s and 1970s. The rise and fall of the intergroup education movement is also described in this section.

Knowledge Construction

The knowledge construction process describes the procedures by which social, behavioral, and natural scientists create knowledge, and the manner in which the implicit cultural assumptions, frames of reference, perspectives, and biases within a discipline influence how knowledge is constructed within it (Berger & Luckman, 1966; Gould, 1996; Harding, 1991; Hartsock, 1998; Kuhn, 1970; Myrdal, 1969). When the knowledge construction process is implemented in the classroom, teachers help students to understand how knowledge is created and how it is influenced by the racial, ethnic, and social-class positions of individuals and groups.

This section describes how the dominant paradigms about ethnic groups established by mainstream social scientists were challenged by revisionist social scientists in the 1960s and 1970s; many of these revisionists were scholars of color (Acuña, 1972; Blassingame, 1972; Ladner, 1973), whereas others were not (Daniels, 1988; Genovese, 1972; Levine, 1977). Literature that illustrates how paradigm shifts are taking place and that identifies models useful in teaching students to understand the knowledge construction process is also described in this section.

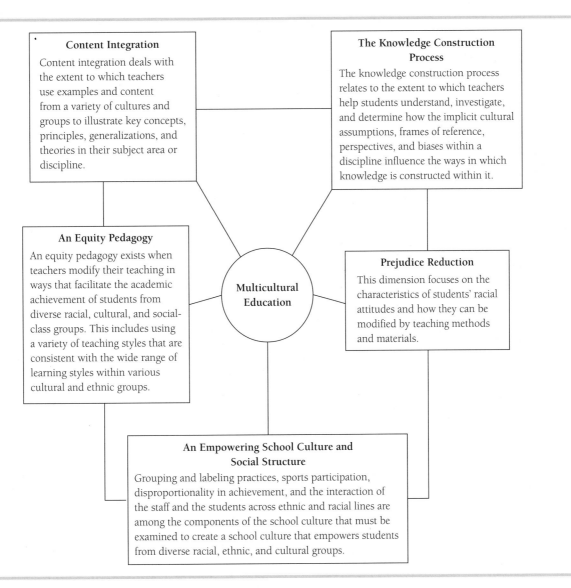

Content Integration

Content integration deals with the extent to which teachers use examples and content from a variety of cultures and groups to illustrate key concepts, principles, generalizations, and theories in their subject area or discipline.

The Knowledge Construction Process

The knowledge construction process relates to the extent to which teachers help students understand, investigate, and determine how the implicit cultural assumptions, frames of reference, perspectives, and biases within a discipline influence the ways in which knowledge is constructed within it.

An Equity Pedagogy

An equity pedagogy exists when teachers modify their teaching in ways that facilitate the academic achievement of students from diverse racial, cultural, and social-class groups. This includes using a variety of teaching styles that are consistent with the wide range of learning styles within various cultural and ethnic groups.

Multicultural Education

Prejudice Reduction

This dimension focuses on the characteristics of students' racial attitudes and how they can be modified by teaching methods and materials.

An Empowering School Culture and Social Structure

Grouping and labeling practices, sports participation, disproportionality in achievement, and the interaction of the staff and the students across ethnic and racial lines are among the components of the school culture that must be examined to create a school culture that empowers students from diverse racial, ethnic, and cultural groups.

FIGURE 1.1. The Dimensions of Multicultural Education.

Note: Copyright ©2002 by James A. Banks. Used with the permission of the author.

Prejudice Reduction

The prejudice reduction dimension of multicultural education describes the characteristics of children's racial attitudes and suggests strategies that can be used to help students develop more democratic attitudes and values. Researchers have been investigating the characteristics of children's racial attitudes since the 1920s (Lasker, 1929). Since the intergroup education movement of the 1940s and 1950s (Miel, with Kiester, 1967; Trager & Yarrow, 1952), a number of investigators have designed interventions to help students develop positive racial attitudes and values. This section briefly reviews selected studies on the characteristics of children's racial attitudes, and studies that describe the results of interventions designed to help students acquire more democratic racial attitudes (J. A. Banks, 1991b).

Equity Pedagogy

An equity pedagogy exists when teachers use techniques and methods that facilitate the academic achievement of students from diverse racial, ethnic, and social-class groups. This section consists of a review of selected studies of approaches, theories, and interventions that are designed to help students who are members of low-status population groups to increase their academic achievement (Delpit, 1988; Ogbu, 1990; Shade, 1989).

The literature reviewed in this section is discussed within a historical context. The kinds of theories constructed to help teachers develop effective strategies for use with students of color and low-income students have varied throughout time. In the early 1960s, the cultural deprivation paradigm was developed (Bloom, Davis, & Hess, 1965; Davis, 1948/1962; Riessman, 1962). The cultural difference theory emerged in the 1970s and challenged the cultural deprivationists (Baratz & Baratz, 1970; Ginsburg, 1972; Ramírez & Castañeda, 1974). The "at-risk" conception, which is akin to the cultural deprivation paradigm, emerged in the 1980s (Cuban, 1989; Richardson, Casanova, Placier, & Guilfoyle, 1989).

Empowering School Culture

The concept of an empowering school culture and social structure is used in this chapter to describe the process of restructuring the culture and organization of the school so that students from diverse racial, ethnic, language, and social-class groups will experience educational equality and cultural empowerment (Mehan, Villanueva, Hubbard, & Lintz, 1996; Valenzuela, 1999). Creating an empowering school culture for students of color and low-income students involves restructuring the culture and organization of the school.

Among the variables that must be examined to create a school culture that empowers students from diverse ethnic and cultural groups are grouping practices (Oakes, 1985; Yonezawa, Wells, & Serna, 2002), labeling practices (Mercer, 1989), the social climate of the school, and staff expectations for student achievement (Brookover, Beady, Flood, Schweitzer, & Wisenbaker, 1979; Levine & Lezotte, 2001). This section reviews literature that focuses on institutionalized factors of the school culture and environment that need to be reformed to increase the academic achievement and emotional growth of students from diverse ethnic, racial, and social-class groups.

Limitations and Interrelationships of the Dimensions

The dimensions typology is an ideal-type conception in the Weberian sense. It approximates but does not describe reality in its total complexity. Like all classification schemas, it has both strengths and limitations. Typologies are helpful conceptual tools because they provide ways to organize and make sense of complex and disparate data and observations. However, typological categories are interrelated and overlapping, not mutually exclusive. A typology is rarely able to encompass the total universe of existing or future cases. Consequently, some cases can be described only by using several of the categories.

The dimensions typology is a useful framework for categorizing and interpreting the extensive and disparate literature on diversity and education. The five dimensions are conceptually distinct but highly interrelated. Content integration, for example, describes any approach that is used to integrate content about racial and cultural groups into the curriculum. The knowledge construction process describes a method by which a teacher helps students understand how knowledge is created and how it reflects the experience of various ethnic and cultural groups.

Content integration is a necessary but not sufficient condition for the knowledge construction process (that is, content integration can take place without the knowledge construction process). Teachers can, for example, insert into the curriculum content about Mexican Americans without helping students view the content from Mexican American perspectives. However, the knowledge construction process cannot be included in the curriculum without content integration first taking place.

Some of the publications examined for this review crossed several categories of the dimensions. Cooperative learning techniques, for example, can help students increase their academic achievement, as well as develop positive racial attitudes. Consequently, some cooperative learning studies can be categorized as both equity pedagogy and prejudice reduction strategies (Aronson & Bridgeman, 1979; Slavin, 1985).

Criteria for selecting studies in each of the five dimensions included the extent to which the study or publication (a) is a prototype of the particular dimension being discussed; (b) has been influential in the field, as determined by how often it is cited and has contributed to the theoretical and empirical growth of the field; and (c) has promise, in the author's judgment, of contributing to the future development of theory, research, and practice in multicultural education.

CONTENT INTEGRATION

The literature on content integration focuses on what information should be included, how it should be integrated, and where it should be located within the curriculum (that is, whether it should be taught within a separate course or as part of the core curriculum). Another important issue discussed in this literature concerns who should be the audience for ethnic content (whether it should be for all students or primarily for students of color).

An exhaustive body of literature describes the various debates, discussions, and curricula that have focused on integrating content about ethnic groups and women into school, college, and university curricula (J. A. Banks, 2003c; Butler & Walter, 1991; Lauter, 1991). The scope of this section is limited primarily to a description of the literature that focuses on the integration of content about racial and ethnic groups into the curriculum. The literature that describes the effects of curricular materials on students' racial and ethnic attitudes is reviewed in the section that discusses the prejudice reduction dimension.

The Need for a Historical Perspective

It is important to view the movements by ethnic groups to integrate school, college, and university curricula with ethnic content from a historical perspective (see Table 1.1). A historical perspective is necessary to provide a context for understanding the contemporary developments and discourse in multicultural education and to restructure schools, colleges, and universities to reflect multicultural issues and concerns. Contemporary reformers need to understand, for example, why the intergroup education movement of the 1940s and 1950s ultimately failed (Cook, 1947; Taba & Wilson, 1946) and why early ethnic studies leaders such as Woodson (1919/1968), W.E.B. DuBois (1935), Wesley (1935), and Franklin (1947) and their successors were able to continue the early ethnic studies movement quietly with publications, research, and teaching from the turn of the century to the 1960s, when the new ethnic studies movement began.

At least a partial explanation is that the early ethnic studies movement was sustained by ethnic self-help organizations such as the Association for the Study of Negro Life and History (ASNLH, now the Association for the Study of Afro-American Life and History) and The Associated Publishers, two organizations cofounded and headed by Woodson. The Associated Publishers published many important and seminal works by such African American scholars as Woodson (1919/1968), Wesley (1935), and Bond (1939). African American schools and colleges were the major consumers of Black scholarship during the first decades of the 20th century. Ethnic community support might be essential for sustaining interest in ethnic studies and multicultural concerns over the long haul. Further investigations are needed to determine the fate of various early ethnic studies and intergroup education movements.

African Americans led the movement that pushed for the integration of ethnic content into the curriculum during the 1960s and 1970s. Consequently, it is appropriate to present a brief historical discussion of the movement to integrate the curriculum with ethnic content, using African Americans as a case study.

TABLE 1.1. Landmark Events and Publications in the Historical Development of Ethnic Studies and Multicultural Education.

Year(s)	Event/Publication
1882–83	*History of the Negro Race in America,* by George Washington Williams
1896	*The Suppression of the African Slave Trade to the United States of America, 1638–1870,* by W.E.B. DuBois
1899	*The Philadelphia Negro,* by DuBois
1915	The Association for the Study of Negro Life and History is founded in Chicago
1916	*The Journal of Negro History* begins publication
1921	The Associated Publishers is established
1922	*The Negro in Our History,* by Carter G. Woodson and Charles C. Wesley
1929	*Race Attitudes in Children,* by Bruno Lasker
1930	*Mexican Immigration to the United States,* by Manuel Gamio
1933	*The Mis-Education of the Negro,* by Carter G. Woodson
1936	Eugene Horowitz's study of young children's attitudes toward the Negro
1937	*The Negro History Bulletin,* designed for schools, begins publication
1939	*Negro Education in Alabama: A Study in Cotton and Steel,* by Horace Mann Bond; first reported study by Kenneth B. and Mamie P. Clark on young children's racial attitudes
1941	*Deep South: A Social Anthropological Study of Caste and Class,* by Allison Davis, Burleigh B. Gardner, and Mary R. Gardner
1944	*An American Dilemma: The Negro Problem and Modern Democracy,* by Gunnar Myrdal with Richard Sterner and Arnold Rose
1945	*Democratic Human Relations: Promising Practices in Intergroup and Intercultural Education in the Social Studies,* 16th yearbook of the National Council for the Social Studies, edited by Hilda Taba and William Van Til; *Black Metropolis: A Study of Negro Life in a Northern City,* by St. Clair Drake and Horace R. Cayton
1947	A review of research on intergroup education is published in the *Review of Educational Research,* by Lloyd A. Cook; first edition of *From Slavery to Freedom: A History of Negro Americans,* by John Hope Franklin
1950	*College Programs in Intergroup Relations,* by Lloyd A. Cook; *The Authoritarian Personality,* by T. W. Adorno et al.
1951	*Intergroup Relations in Teacher Education,* by Lloyd A. Cook

TABLE 1.1. Landmark Events and Publications in the Historical Development of Ethnic Studies and Multicultural Education. *(continued)*

Year(s)	Event/Publication
1952	*Intergroup Education in Public Schools*, by Hilda Taba, Elizabeth H. Brady, and John T. Robinson; *They Learn What They Live: Prejudice in Young Children*, by Helen G. Trager and Marian R. Yarrow; *Race Awareness in Young Children*, by Mary Ellen Goodman
1954	*The Nature of Prejudice*, by Gordon W. Allport
1962	*Social-Class Influences Upon Learning*, by Allison Davis
1965	*Compensatory Education for Cultural Deprivation*, by Benjamin S. Bloom, Allison Davis, and Robert Hess
1966	*Equality of Educational Opportunity*, by James Coleman et al.
1972	*Inequality: A Reassessment of the Effect of Family and Schooling in America*, by Christopher Jencks et al.
1973	*No One Model American* (American Association of Colleges for Teacher Education); *Teaching Ethnic Studies: Concepts and Strategies*, National Council for the Social Studies, 43rd yearbook, edited by James A. Banks
1974	*Cultural Democracy, Bicognitive Development, and Education*, by Manuel Ramírez and Alfredo Castañeda; *The Next Generation: An Ethnography of Education in an Urban Neighborhood*, by John U. Ogbu; *Students' Right to Their Own Language*, a position statement by the National Council of Teachers of English
1975	*Adolescent Prejudice*, by Charles Y. Glock, Robert Wuthnow, Jane A. Piliavin, and Metta Spencer, sponsored by the Anti-Defamation League of B'nai B'rith
1976	*Curriculum Guidelines for Multiethnic Education*, position statement issued by the National Council for the Social Studies; *Race, Color, and the Young Child*, by John E. Williams and J. Kenneth Morland, a synthesis of research conducted in the late 1960s and 1970s on young children's racial attitudes
1977	*Multicultural Education: Commitments, Issues, and Applications*, edited by Carl A. Grant, published by the Association for Supervision and Curriculum Development; *Pluralism and the American Teacher: Issues and Case Studies*, edited by Frank H. Klassen and Donna M. Gollnick, published by the American Association of Colleges for Teacher Education; *Pluralism in a Democratic Society*, edited by Melvin M. Tumin and Walter Plotch, sponsored by the Anti-Defamation League of B'nai B'rith; *Standards for the Accreditation of Teacher Education*, issued by the National Council for the Accreditation of Teacher Education, included a requirement for multicultural education in teacher education programs
1983	*Ways With Words: Language, Life, and Work in Communities and Classrooms*, by Shirley Brice Heath
1985	*Beginnings: The Social and Affective Development of Black Children*, edited by Margaret B. Spencer, Geraldine K. Brookins, and Walter R. Allen
1988	*The Education of Blacks in the South, 1860–1935*, by James D. Anderson
1989	*A Common Destiny: Blacks and American Society*, edited by Gerald D. Jaynes and Robin M. Williams, Jr., National Research Council report
1991	*Shades of Black: Diversity in African-American Identity*, by William E. Cross, Jr.
1995	*Handbook of Research on Multicultural Education*, edited by James A. Banks and Cherry A. McGee Banks

The Early Ethnic Studies Movement

The Black studies movement that emerged in the 1960s and 1970s has historical roots in the early national period (J. A. Banks, 1996; Brooks, 1990; White, 1973; Woodson, 1919/1968). It is directly linked to the work in ethnic studies research and the development of teaching materials by African American scholars such as G. W. Williams (1882–83), Woodson and Wesley (1922), and DuBois (1935, 1973). Those scholars created knowledge about African Americans that could be integrated into the school and college curriculum. Educators such as Woodson and Wesley (1922) worked during the early decades of the 20th century to integrate the school and college curriculum with content about African Americans.

Brooks (1990) discusses the early history of schools for African American children. He points out that from slavery to today, Black education has been characterized by desegregation in the colonial and early national periods,

a push for segregation in the early 1800s, a movement toward desegregation during the 1950s and 1960s, and another swing toward segregation today.

The first public schools that were organized in Massachusetts and Virginia were desegregated (Brooks, 1990; White, 1973; Woodson, 1919/1968). However, because of the discrimination they experienced in these schools, African Americans took the leadership in establishing separate schools for their children. When the city of Boston refused to fund separate schools for African American children in 1800, the Black community set up its own schools and hired the teachers. In 1818, the city of Boston started funding separate schools for African American children. The first schools established for African Americans in the South after the Civil War were segregated by laws formulated by White legislators.

Separate schools for African Americans proved to be a mixed blessing, especially in the southern states and later in northern cities. In the South, African American schools paper was titled "Freedom, Power, and Values in Our Present Crisis"; Allport's was called "Resolving Intergroup Tension: An Appraisal of Methods."

Alain Locke, an African American philosopher at Howard University, coedited a background book on intergroup education for the Progressive Education Association (Locke & Stern, 1942). This comprehensive book on race and culture consists of reprinted articles by some of the leading social scientists of the day, including Ruth Benedict, Franz Boas, John Dollard, E. Franklin Frazier, Melville J. Herskovits, Otto Klineberg, Ralph Linton, and Margaret Mead.

Allison Davis, the noted African American anthropologist at the University of Chicago and coauthor of *Deep South: A Social Anthropological Study of Caste and Class*, a classic study of an old southern city (Davis, Gardner, & Gardner, 1941), wrote a chapter for NCSS's 16th yearbook, titled "Some Basic Concepts in the Education of Ethnic and Lower-Class Groups." Davis urged social studies teachers to teach students "a devotion to democratic values, and group disapproval of injustice, oppression, and exploitation" (Taba & Van Til, 1945, p. 278). He also believed that teachers should teach social action: "Teach the underprivileged child to learn to help organize and improve his community" (p. 279). The fact that scholars of the stature of Davis and Locke contributed to books on intergroup education sponsored by educational organizations indicated that some of the leading social science scholars of the 1940s believed they should become involved in a major social problem facing the nation and the schools.

Several landmark studies in race relations were published during the intergroup education era. Jewish organizations, such as the American Jewish Committee and the Anti-Defamation League of B'nai B'rith, sponsored several of these studies. One important factor that contributed to the rise of the intergroup education movement was anti-Semitism in Western nations, which reached its peak in Germany during World War II. Jewish organizations were especially interested in taking action and sponsoring research that would ease racial tension and conflict. They were poignantly aware of the destructive power of ethnic hate (Wyman, 1984).

In 1950, *The Authoritarian Personality* (Adorno, Frenkel-Brunswik, Levinson, & Sanford, 1950) was published. In this landmark study, the authors identify the personality factors that contribute to the formation of prejudice. Although they overemphasize personality-factor explanations of prejudice and give insufficient attention to structural factors, their study remains an important one.

Allport's seminal study, *The Nature of Prejudice*, was published in 1954. In it he formulates his influential principles about how to create effective intergroup interactions. He states that positive interracial contact must be characterized by four conditions: (a) equal status, (b) common goals, (c) intergroup cooperation, and (d) the support of authorities (Pettigrew, Chapter 37, this volume). Allport's principles are highly influential in social science research today and are an important theoretical base for the work of Cohen (1972), Aronson and Bridgeman (1979), Slavin (1985), and other researchers.

Important theoretical and research work related to children's racial attitudes was also completed during the intergroup education period. The Anti-Defamation League of B'nai B'rith sponsored a major study by Goodman that was published in 1952. This study provided evidence that supported earlier findings by researchers such as E. L. Horowitz (1936), R. E. Horowitz (1939), and a series of studies by Kenneth B. Clark and Mamie P. Clark (1939a, 1939b, 1940, 1947). These studies established the postulate that preschool children have racial awareness and attitudes that mirror those of adults.

Intergroup educators wanted to help students develop democratic racial attitudes and values (Cook, 1947; Taba & Wilson, 1946). Investigations designed to determine the effects of curricular interventions on students' racial attitudes were an important part of the intergroup education movement. Significant intervention studies conducted during this period include those by Trager and Yarrow (1952) and by Hayes and Conklin (1953). Most of these studies support the postulate that multicultural lessons, activities, and teaching materials, when used within a democratic classroom atmosphere and implemented for a sufficiently long period, help students to develop democratic racial attitudes and values. Studies both prior to and during this period established that children internalize the adult attitudes that are institutionalized within the structures and institutions of society (Clark & Clark, 1947; Goodman, 1952; E. L. Horowitz, 1936).

Important textbooks and reports published during the intergroup education era include those by Locke and Stern (1942), Cook (1950), Taba et al. (1952), and Cook and Cook (1954), which reveal that intergroup educators emphasized democratic living and interracial cooperation within mainstream American society. The ethnic studies movements that preceded and followed the intergroup education movement emphasized ethnic attachment, pride, empowerment, and action to change society. The focus in intergroup education was on intercultural interactions within a shared, common culture (Cook, 1947; Taba & Wilson, 1946).

The Early Ethnic Studies and Intergroup Education Movements Compared

Woodson (1933) and W.E.B. DuBois (1973) were concerned that African Americans develop knowledge of

Black history and culture, and a commitment to empowering and enhancing the African American community. This was in contrast to the emphasis in intergroup education, which promoted a weak form of diversity and the notion that "we are different but the same."

The Sleeter and Grant (1987) typology consists of five categories: (a) teaching the culturally different, (b) human relations, (c) single-group studies, (d) multicultural education, and (e) education that is multicultural and social reconstructionist. Most of the literature and guides that were produced during the intergroup education era can be categorized as human relations. In this approach, according to Sleeter and Grant, multicultural education is "a way to help students of different backgrounds communicate, get along better with each other, and feel good about themselves" (p. 426).

Like the human relations books and materials examined by Sleeter and Grant that were published in the 1970s and 1980s, intergroup education materials devote little attention to issues and problems such as institutionalized racism, power, and structural inequality. However, unlike most of the human relations materials examined by Sleeter and Grant, some of the materials published during the intergroup education period are based on theories developed by psychologists and social psychologists (Taba, 1950, 1951; Taba & Wilson, 1946).

The intergroup education publications and projects emphasized interracial harmony and human relations. The early ethnic studies advocates endorsed ethnic empowerment and what Sleeter and Grant call "single group studies." Thus, the aims and goals of the intergroup education and ethnic studies movements were quite different. The ethnic studies movement emphasized the histories and cultures of specific ethnic groups (single-group studies). Taba and Wilson (1946) identified these focuses in intergroup education: concepts and understandings about groups and relations, sensitivity and goodwill, objective thinking, and experiences in democratic procedures.

The racial backgrounds and cultural experiences of the leaders of the two ethnic studies movements and those of the leaders of the intergroup education movement were factors that influenced the goals, aims, and nature of these movements. Most of the influential leaders of the early ethnic studies movement in the United States and the one that emerged in the 1960s and 1970s were people of color. Most of the leaders of the intergroup education movement were White liberal educators and social scientists who functioned and worked within mainstream colleges, universities, and other institutions and organizations. Hilda Taba (who taught at the University of Chicago and directed the Intergroup Education in Cooperating Schools Project for the American Council on Education) and Lloyd A. Cook (who taught at Wayne State University and directed the College Programs in Intergroup Relations project) were the most prolific and noted intergroup education leaders.

The different cultural experiences, perceptions, and values of the leaders of the ethnic studies and intergroup education movements significantly influenced their perceptions of the goals of citizenship education and the role of ethnic content in instruction. Ethnic studies scholars and educators probably endorsed a more pluralistic view of citizenship education than did intergroup educators because they worked and functioned primarily outside mainstream institutions and believed that parallel ethnic institutions were essential for the survival and development of ethnic groups in the United States. The experience of most intergroup educators in mainstream institutions influenced their view that assimilation into mainstream culture and its institutions was the most appropriate way to resolve ethnic tension.

The history of the early ethnic studies and intergroup education movements and analysis of current curriculum reform efforts reveal that movements related to integrating ethnic content into the curriculum move cyclically from a single-group to an intergroup focus. The fact that single-group studies movements continue to emerge within a society with a democratic ethos suggests that the United States has not dealt successfully with the American dilemma related to race that Myrdal (with Sterner & Rose, 1944) identified nearly 60 years ago.

The Ethnic Studies Movement of the 1960s and 1970s

A prominent vision within the intergroup education ideology was interracial harmony and desegregation; another name for the movement was *intercultural education*. Intergroup education emerged when the nation was sharply segregated along racial lines and was beginning its efforts to create a desegregated society. The early goal of the civil rights movement of the 1960s was racial desegregation. However, by the late 1960s many African Americans had grown impatient with the pace of desegregation. Imbued with racial pride, they called for Black power, separatism, and Black studies in the schools and colleges that would contribute to the empowerment and advancement of African Americans (Carmichael & Hamilton, 1967).

When the civil rights movement began, the intergroup education movement had quietly died without a requiem. The separatist ideology that emerged during the 1970s was antithetical to the intergroup education vision. The America envisioned by most intergroup educators was a nation in which ethnic and racial differences were minimized and all people were treated fairly and lived in harmony.

During the late 1960s and early 1970s, sometimes in strident voices, African Americans frustrated with deferred and shattered dreams demanded community control of their schools, African American teachers and administrators, and the infusion of Black history into the curriculum. At the university level, frequent demands included Black studies programs and courses, heritage rooms or houses, and Black professors and administrators. During this period there was little demand for the infusion of ethnic content into the core or mainstream curriculum; that demand would not emerge until the 1980s and 1990s. Rather, the demand was primarily for separate courses and programs (Blassingame, 1971; Ford, 1973; Robinson, Foster, & Ogilvie, 1969).

As schools, colleges, and universities began to respond to the demand by African Americans for curriculum changes, other ethnic groups of color that felt victimized by institutionalized discrimination in the United States began to demand similar programs (see Hu-DeHart, Chapter 43, this volume). These groups included Mexican Americans, Puerto Ricans, American Indians, and Asian Americans. A rich array of books, programs, curricula, and other materials that focused on the histories and cultures of ethnic groups of color were edited, written, or reprinted between the late 1960s and the early 1970s.

One major development during this period was the reprinting of books and research studies written during the early and more silent period of ethnic studies. A few of these publications had remained in print for many years and been best-sellers at all-Black colleges; noteworthy among them were John Hope Franklin's popular history, *From Slavery to Freedom,* first published in 1947, and *The Souls of Black Folk* by W.E.B. DuBois, first published in 1953.

However, more frequent was the reprinting of long-neglected works produced during the earlier period of ethnic studies. George Washington Williams's *History of the Negro Race in America* (1882–83) was reissued by Arno Press in 1968. Important earlier works on Hispanics reprinted during this period included Carey McWilliams's *North from Mexico: The Spanish-Speaking People of the United States* (1949), an informative overview of Hispanic groups in the United States; and Manuel Gamio's *Mexican Immigration to the United States* (1930), a well-researched description of the first wave of Mexican immigrants to the United States. Three important earlier works on Filipino Americans reissued during this period were *Filipino Immigration to the Continental United States and Hawaii,* by Bruno Lasker (1931); *Brothers Under the Skin,* also by McWilliams (1943); and *America Is in the Heart,* the powerful autobiography by the writer Carlos Bulosan (1943).

More significant than the older books that were kept in print or reissued was the new crop of publications focused primarily on the struggles and experiences of particular ethnic groups. The emphasis in many of these publications was on how ethnic groups of color had been victimized by institutionalized racism and discrimination in the United States. The quality and meticulousness of research of this rash of books varied widely. However, they all provided perspectives that gave Americans new ways to view the history and culture of the United States. Many of them became required reading in ethnic studies courses and degree programs. Among the significant books of this genre are *Japanese Americans,* by Harry H. L. Kitano (1969); *The Story of the Chinese in America,* by Betty Lee Sung (1967); *Occupied America: The Chicano's Struggle Toward Liberation,* by Rudy Acuña (1972); *Custer Died for Your Sins: An Indian Manifesto,* by Vine Deloria, Jr. (1969); and *The Rise of the Unmeltable Ethnics,* by Michael Novak (1971), a highly rhetorical and ringing plea for justice for such White ethnic groups as Poles, Italians, Greeks, and Slavs.

The Evolution of Multicultural Education

The intergroup education movement is an important antecedent of the current multicultural education movement but is not an actual root of it (J. A. Banks, 1996). The current movement is directly linked to the early ethnic studies movement initiated by scholars such as G. W. Williams (1882–83) and continued by individuals such as W.E.B. DuBois (1935), Woodson (1919/1968), Bond (1939), and Wesley (1935). The major architects of the multicultural education movement were cogently influenced by African American scholarship and ethnic studies related to other ethnic minority groups in the United States.

Baker (1977), J. A. Banks (1973), Gay (1971), and Grant (1973, 1978) have each played a significant role in formulating and developing multicultural education in the United States. Each of these scholars was heavily influenced by the early work of African American scholars and the African American ethnic studies movement. They were working in ethnic studies prior to participating in the formation of multicultural education. Other scholars who have helped to fashion multicultural education since its inception, and who were also influenced by the African American ethnic studies movement, are James B. Boyer (1974), Asa Hilliard III (1974), and Barbara A. Sizemore (1972).

Scholars who are specialists in other ethnic groups—such as Carlos E. Cortés (1973, 2002, Mexican Americans), Jack D. Forbes (1973, American Indians), Sonia Nieto (1986, Puerto Ricans), and Derald W. Sue (1981, Asian Americans)—also played early and significant roles in the evolution of multicultural education.

The first phase of multicultural education emerged when educators who had interests and specializations in the history and culture of ethnic minority groups initiated individual and institutional actions to incorporate the concepts, information, and theories from ethnic studies into the school and teacher-education curricula. Consequently, the first phase of multicultural education was ethnic studies.

A second phase of multicultural education emerged when educators interested in ethnic studies began to realize that inserting ethnic studies content into the school and teacher-education curricula was necessary but not sufficient to bring about school reform that would respond to the unique needs of students of color and help all students develop more democratic racial and ethnic attitudes. Multiethnic education was the second phase of multicultural education. Its aim was to bring about structural and systemic changes in the total school that were designed to increase educational equality.

A third phase of multicultural education emerged when other groups who viewed themselves as victims of the society and the schools, such as women and people with disabilities, demanded the incorporation of their histories, cultures, and voices into the curricula and structure of schools, colleges, and universities.

The fourth and current phase of multicultural education is developing theory, research, and practice that interrelate variables connected to race, class, and gender (J. A. Banks & C.A.M. Banks, 2003; Grant & Sleeter, 1986). It is important to note that each phase of multicultural education continues today. However, the later phases tend to be more prominent than the earlier ones, at least in the theoretical literature if not in practice.

During the 1970s, a number of professional organizations, such as the American Association of Colleges for Teacher Education (AACTE), the National Council of Teachers of English (NCTE), and NCSS, issued position statements and publications that encouraged schools to integrate the curriculum with content and understandings about ethnic groups. In 1973, AACTE published its brief and widely quoted statement, "No One Model American." That same year, the NCSS 43rd yearbook was titled *Teaching Ethnic Studies: Concepts and Strategies* (J. A. Banks, 1973). The following year, NCTE (1974) issued *Students' Right to Their Own Language.* An early landmark conference on multicultural education through competency-based teacher education was sponsored by AACTE in 1974 (Hunter, 1974). In 1976, NCSS published *Curriculum Guidelines for Multiethnic Education* (J. A. Banks, Cortés, Gay, Garcia, & Ochoa, 1976). This publication was revised and reissued in 1992 with a title change to *Curriculum Guidelines for Multicultural Education* (NCSS Task Force, 1992).

Several landmark developments in the emergence of multicultural education occurred in 1977. The Association for Supervision and Curriculum Development (ASCD) published a book on multicultural education

(Grant, 1977). That same year, AACTE published *Pluralism and the American Teacher: Issues and Case Studies* (Klassen & Gollnick, 1977). This book resulted from its conference series on the topic, supported by a grant from the U.S. Office of Education. Using the grant funds, AACTE established the Ethnic Heritage Center for Teacher Education, the unit that sponsored the conferences and the book. One of the most influential developments during the early emergence of multicultural education was the issuance of *Standards for the Accreditation of Teacher Education,* by the National Council for Accreditation of Teacher Education (NCATE) in 1977. These standards required all member teacher education institutions, which made up about 80 percent of the teacher education programs in the United States, to implement components, courses, and programs in multicultural education. The standards were issued in a revised form in 1987 (NCATE, 1987) and in 2000. They were revised and updated again in 2002 (www.ncate.org/standard/m_tds.htm).

Many professional associations, school districts, and state departments of education published guidelines and teacher's guides to help school districts integrate content about ethnic groups into the elementary and high school curriculum. The United Federation of Teachers published *Puerto Rican History and Culture: A Study Guide and Curriculum Outline* (Aran, Arthur, Colon, & Goldenberg, 1973). Like most materials produced by professional organizations, school districts, and commercial publishers during this period, this curriculum guide focused on a single ethnic group. Publications and materials about more than one ethnic group were developed later. One of the first publications to recommend a multiethnic approach to the study of ethnic groups was the NCSS 1973 yearbook (J. A. Banks, 1973). The guides and books published during this period varied in quality. Many were produced quickly, but others contained sound and thoughtful guidelines for integrating the curriculum with ethnic content.

Research Developments Since the 1960s

A rich array of research in the social sciences, humanities, and education focusing on people of color has been published since 1960. Much of this research challenges existing interpretations, paradigms, assumptions, and methodologies and contains pertinent data on long-neglected topics (Gates, 1988; Slaughter, 1988). The three decades between 1960 and 1990 were probably the most productive research period in ethnic studies in U.S. history. St. Claire Drake (1987, 1990), shortly before his death, completed a massive two-volume anthropological study, *Black Folk Here and There.* Bernal's (1987, 1991) comprehensive two-volume work, *Black Athena: The*

Afroasiatic Roots of Classical Civilization, challenges existing historical interpretations about the debt that ancient Greece owes to Africa and supports earlier works by African and African American scholars such as Diop (1974) and Van Sertima (1988). Many of the insights from this new scholarship are being incorporated into the school, college, and university curriculum.

The rich scholarship in ethnic studies continued throughout the late 1980s and 1990s, with notable publications such as *Strangers from a Different Shore: A History of Asian Americans* and *A Different Mirror: A History of Multicultural America,* both by Ronald Takaki (1989, 1993); *Black Women in America: An Historical Encyclopedia* (two volumes), edited by Darlene Clark Hine, Elsa Brakely Brown, and Roslyn Terborg-Penn (1993); and the *Encyclopedia of African-American Culture and History* (five volumes), edited by Jack Salzman, David L. Smith, and Cornel West (1996).

THE KNOWLEDGE CONSTRUCTION PROCESS

The ethnic studies research and literature published during the 1960s and 1970s (Acuña, 1972), like the ethnic studies scholarship in the early decades of the century (W.E.B. DuBois, 1935; Woodson, 1919/1968), challenged some of the major paradigms, canons, and perspectives established within mainstream scholarship (Blea, 1988; Gordon, 1985; Gordon, Miller, & Rollock, 1990; Ladner, 1973). Ethnic studies scholarship also challenges some of the key assumptions of mainstream Western empiricism (J. A. Banks, 1993a; Gordon & Meroe, 1991).

The construction of descriptions and interpretations of the settlement of the West (Turner, 1894/1989) and of slavery (Phillips, 1918) presents two examples of how people of color have been described and conceptualized in mainstream U.S. history and social science. Frederick Jackson Turner (1894/1989) constructed a view of the settlement of European Americans in the West that has cogently influenced the treatment and interpretation of the West in school, college, and university textbooks (Sleeter & Grant, 1991). Turner described the land occupied by the Indians as an empty wilderness to which the Europeans brought civilization. He also argued that the wilderness in the West, which required individualism for survival, was the main source of American democracy. Although revisionist historians have described the limitations of Turner's theory, its influence on the curricula of the nation's elementary and high schools and on textbooks is still powerful.

The interpretation of slavery within mainstream U.S. scholarship is another revealing example of how ethnic groups of color have been depicted in such scholarship. Ulrich B. Phillips's interpretation of slavery remained dominant from the time his book was published in 1918 to the 1950s, 1960s, and 1970s, when the established slavery paradigm was revised by a new generation of historians (Blassingame, 1972; Genovese, 1972; Stampp, 1956). Phillips's interpretation of slavery, which is essentially an apology for southern slaveholders, was one of the major sources for the conception of slaves as happy, contented, and loyal to their masters, a perspective that dominated textbooks in the 1950s and 1960s (J. A. Banks, 1969).

The descriptions of the settlement of Europeans in the western United States and the treatment of slavery in U.S. scholarship from the turn of the century to the 1950s indicate the extent to which knowledge reflects ideology, human interests, values, and perspectives (Collins, 2000; Habermas, 1971; Myrdal, 1969). Yet a basic assumption of Western empiricism is that knowledge is objective and neutral and that its principles are universal (Kaplan, 1964). Multicultural scholars (Acuña, 1972; Collins, 2000; Hilliard, Payton-Stewart, & Williams, 1990)—like critical theorists such as Habermas (1971) and Giroux (1983) and feminist postmodernists such as Farganis (1986), Code (1991), and Harding (1991)—reject these assumptions about the nature of knowledge.

Multicultural scholars maintain that knowledge reflects the social, cultural, and power positions of people within society, and that it is valid only when it "comes from an acknowledgment of the knower's specific position in any context, one always defined by gender, class, and other variables" (Tetreault, 2003, p. 160). Multicultural and feminist theorists maintain that knowledge is both subjective and objective and that its subjective components need to be clearly identified (Code, 1991; Collins, 2000; hooks, 1990). Multicultural theorists also contend that by claiming that their knowledge is objective and neutral, mainstream scholars are able to present their particularistic interests and ideologies as the universal concerns of the nation-state (Asante, 1998; Hilliard et al., 1990). According to Gordon and Meroe (1991):

> We often wonder if the socially adapted human being, who happens to be a scholar, is truly capable of discarding her or his individual frame of reference when it comes to the study of a subject to which she or he has chosen to commit her or his life's work. This is a precarious and dangerous situation because too many times "objectivity" has served as a mask for the political agenda of the status quo, thus marginalizing and labeling the concerns of less empowered groups as "special interests." (p. 28)

A number of conceptualizations have been developed by multicultural and feminist theorists that are designed to help teachers acquire the information and skills needed to teach students how knowledge is constructed, how to identify the writer's purposes and point of view, and how to formulate their own interpretations of reality.

Four approaches used to integrate ethnic content into the elementary and high school curriculum and to teach students about ethnic groups were conceptualized by J. A. Banks (2003a): contributions, additive, transformation, and social action (see Figure 1.2). The *contributions* approach focuses on heroes and heroines, holidays, and discrete cultural elements. When using the *additive* approach, teachers append ethnic content, themes, and perspectives to the curriculum without changing its basic structure. In the *transformation* approach, which is designed to help students learn how knowledge is constructed, the structure of the curriculum is changed to enable students to view concepts, issues, events, and themes from the perspectives of various ethnic and cultural groups. In the *social action* approach, which is an extension of the transformation approach, students make decisions on important social issues and take action to help solve them.

Tetreault (2003) describes a model for teaching content about women that is also designed to help students understand the nature of knowledge and how it is constructed. In this curriculum model, the teacher moves from a male-defined curriculum model to one that is gender-balanced. The phases are contributions curriculum, bifocal curriculum, women's curriculum, and gender-balanced curriculum. In the *contributions* curriculum, a male framework is used to insert women into the curriculum; the world is viewed through the eyes of women and men in the *bifocal* curriculum; subjects of primary importance to women are investigated in the *women's* curriculum, and the *gender-balanced* curriculum investigates topics and concepts that are important to women but also considers how women and men relate to each other.

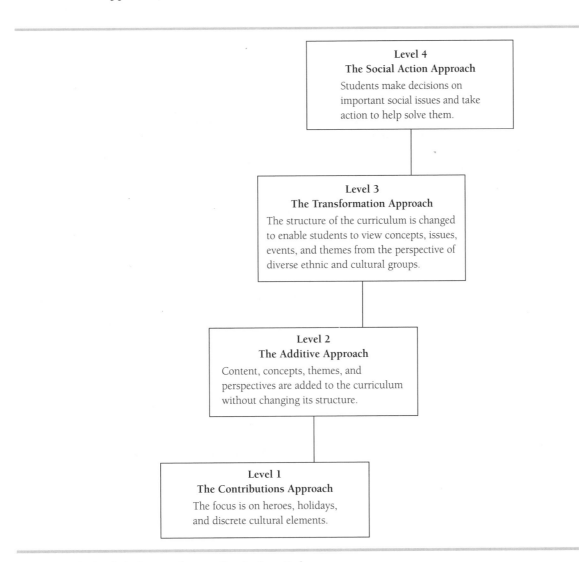

FIGURE 1.2. Banks's Approaches to Curriculum Reform.

Note: Copyright © 2002 by James A. Banks. Used with the permission of the author.

PREJUDICE REDUCTION

The prejudice reduction dimension of multicultural education is designed to help students develop democratic attitudes, values, and behaviors (Board on Children, Youth, and Families, 2000; Oskamp, 2000; Stephan, 1999; Van Ausdale & Feagin, 2001). Researchers and educators who are concerned about helping students develop democratic attitudes and behaviors have devoted much of their attention to investigating how children develop racial awareness, preferences, and identification (Aboud, 1988; Clark, 1963; Katz, 1976; Milner, 1983; Phinney & Rotheram, 1987). This discussion is divided into two sections: (a) the nature of children's racial attitudes and identities and (b) the modification of students' racial attitudes.

The Nature of Children's Racial Attitudes

A common belief among elementary school teachers is that young children have little awareness of racial differences and hold positive attitudes toward both African Americans and Whites. Many teachers with whom I have worked have told me that because young children are unaware of racial differences, talking about race to them merely creates racial problems that do not exist. This common observation by teachers is inconsistent with reality and research.

During a period of nearly 70 years, researchers have established that young children are aware of racial differences by the age of three (Aboud, 1988; Lasker, 1929; Phinney & Rotheram, 1987; Ramsey, 1998) and have internalized attitudes toward African Americans and Whites that are established in the wider society. They tend to prefer white (pinkish-colored) stimulus objects, such as dolls and pictures, to brown dolls and pictures, and to describe white (pinkish) objects and people more positively than brown ones.

Early studies by Lasker (1929) and Minard (1931) indicate that young children are aware of racial differences and that children's racial attitudes are formed early in life. Studies by E. L. Horowitz (1936) and R. E. Horowitz (1939) indicate that both African American and White nursery school children are aware of racial differences and show a statistically significant preference for Whites. The Horowitzes interpreted their findings to mean that the African American children in their studies evidenced self-rejection when they showed a White bias in their responses to stimulus objects and pictures.

In a series of pioneering studies conducted between 1939 and 1950, Kenneth B. and Mamie P. Clark confirmed the findings of the Horowitzes and gave considerable support to the self-rejection paradigm the Horowitzes formulated (Cross, 1991). The Clarks are usually credited with originating the paradigm; however, Cross states that the Horowitzes, and not the Clarks, created it. Nevertheless, the famous Clark studies gave the self-rejection paradigm wide visibility and credibility.

In the series of studies conducted by the Clarks, African American nursery school children were the subjects; the stimuli were brown and white (pinkish) dolls. The Clarks studied racial awareness, preference, and identification (Clark & Clark, 1939a, 1939b, 1940, 1947, 1950). They concluded that the children in their studies had accurate knowledge of racial differences, sometimes made incorrect racial self-identifications, and often expressed a preference for white. The Clarks concluded that many of the African American children in their studies evidenced self-rejection.

The self-rejection paradigm associated with the Clarks has had a cogent influence on research and the interpretation of research on children's racial attitudes and self-esteem for more than a half century. A series of significant and influential studies during the 1950s, 1960s, and 1970s confirmed the early findings by the Horowitzes and the Clarks (Morland, 1966; Porter, 1971; Radke & Trager, 1950; J. E. Williams & Morland, 1976): that young children are aware of racial differences and that both African American and White children tend to evidence a white bias.

The self-rejection paradigm was strongly challenged during the 1980s and 1990s on both methodological and interpretive grounds (W. C. Banks, 1976; Cross, 1991; Spencer, 1987). During the 1980s and 1990s, Spencer (1982, 1985, 1987) and Cross (1985, 1991) developed concepts and theories, and conducted research, that challenge the interpretation that the Horowitzes and the Clarks used to explain their findings. They have made a useful distinction between *personal* identity and *group* identity and have reinterpreted the early findings, as well as their own research findings, within this new paradigm.

An important group of studies by Spencer (1982, 1985, 1987) indicates that young African American children can distinguish their personal and group identities. They can express high self-esteem and a white bias at the same time. She formulates a cognitive theory to explain these findings: African American children often make white bias choices because they have learned from the wider society (a cognitive process) to make these choices, not because they reject themselves or have low self-concepts. In other words, the children are choosing the "right" answer when asked to select the white or colored stimulus. Research by J. A. Banks (1984) supports the postulate that African American children make choices related to race that indicate that personal and group identity are distinguished. Cross (1991) also provides strong theoretical and empirical evidence to support this conceptual distinction.

The Modification of Children's Racial Attitudes

Studies designed to modify children's racial attitudes have been conducted at least since the 1940s (Agnes, 1947; Jackson, 1944). However, the literature that describes the characteristics of children's racial attitudes is much richer than the modification literature. In two comprehensive reviews of the modification literature, J. A. Banks (1991b, 1993b) identifies four types of modification studies: (a) curricular intervention, (b) reinforcement, (c) perceptual differentiation, and (d) cooperative learning.

Curricular studies are the earliest type of intervention studies; they date back to the intergroup education period of the 1940s. In their studies, Agnes (1947) and Jackson (1944) concluded that reading materials about African Americans helped students develop positive racial attitudes. However, most of the early studies had serious methodological problems. One of the most well-designed and significant studies of the intergroup education period was conducted by Trager and Yarrow (1952). They found that a democratic curriculum had a positive effect on the racial attitudes of students and teachers. Hayes and Conklin (1953), with an experimental treatment that took place over a two-year period, also found that an intercultural curriculum had a positive effect on the racial attitudes of students. The description of the intervention, however, is imprecise.

Studies of the effects of units, courses, and curriculum materials have also been conducted by Fisher (1965); Leslie and Leslie (1972); Yawkey (1973); Lessing and Clarke (1976); Litcher and Johnson (1969); Litcher, Johnson, and Ryan (1973); and Shirley (1988). Most of these studies provide evidence for the postulate that curricular materials and interventions can have a positive effect on the racial attitudes of students. However, the studies by Lessing and Clarke and Litcher et al. had no measurable effect on student racial attitudes.

In an important study, Litcher and Johnson (1969) found that multiethnic readers had a positive effect on the racial attitudes of second-grade White students. However, when they replicated this study using photographs rather than readers (Litcher et al., 1973), no significant effects were attained. The investigators believe that the shorter duration of the latter study (one month compared with four) and the different ethnic compositions of the cities in which the studies were conducted may explain the conflicting findings in the two studies.

Ciullo and Troiani (1988) found that children who were excluded from a group exercise became more sensitive to the feelings of children from other ethnic groups. McGregor (1993) used meta-analysis to integrate findings and examine the effects of role playing and antiracist teaching on reducing prejudice in students. Twenty-six studies were located and examined. McGregor concluded that role playing and antiracist teaching "significantly reduce racial prejudice, and do not differ from each other in their effectiveness" (p. 215).

Aboud and Doyle (1996) designed a study to determine how children's racial evaluations were affected by talking about racial issues with a friend who had a different level of prejudice from their own. The researchers found that "high-prejudice children became significantly less prejudiced in their evaluations after the discussion. Changes were greater in children whose low-prejudice partner made more statements about cross-racial similarity, along with more positive Black and White evaluations" (p. 161).

In summarizing the effects of curriculum intervention studies, J. A. Banks (1991b) concludes:

The studies . . . indicate that curriculum intervention can help students to develop more positive racial attitudes but . . . the effects of such interventions are likely not to be consistent. . . . The inconsistencies may be due in part to the use of different measures to assess attitude change and because the duration of the interventions has varied widely. The duration of the intervention has rarely been varied to determine the effects. (p. 464)

J. E. Williams and his colleagues conducted a series of reinforcement studies with young children during the 1960s and 1970s (J. E. Williams & Edwards, 1969; J. E. Williams & Morland, 1976). The experiments were designed to reduce white bias in young children. In the typical design, the children are given pictures of black and white animals or objects and are reinforced for choosing the black objects or animals and for describing them positively. When they choose the white objects or animals, they receive negative reinforcement or no reinforcement. Williams and his colleagues (J. E. Williams, Best, Wood, & Filler, 1973; J. E. Williams & Edwards, 1969) have found that interventions of this type reduce white bias in children and that the children's responses are generalized from objects and animals to people. Laboratory reinforcement studies by other researchers have generally confirmed the findings by Williams and his colleagues (Hohn, 1973; Parish & Fleetwood, 1975; Parish, Shirazi, & Lambert, 1976).

Katz and her colleagues have conducted a series of studies that examine the perceptual components of the racial attitudes of young children. In one study, she confirmed her predictions that young children can more easily differentiate the faces of in-group members than the faces of out-group members, and that if young children are taught to differentiate the faces of out-groups, prejudice is reduced (Katz, 1973). She and Zalk (Katz & Zalk, 1978) examined the effect of four interventions on the racial attitudes of second- and fifth-grade White students: (a) perceptual differentiation of minority group faces, (b) increased positive racial contact, (c) vicarious interracial contact, and (d) reinforcement of the color black. Each intervention reduced prejudice. However, the most powerful were vicarious contact and perceptual differentiation.

Most of the research on cooperative learning has been conducted since the 1970s. Cooperative learning studies tend to support the postulate that cooperative learning situations, if based on the principles formulated by Allport (1954), can increase the academic achievement of students of color and help all students develop positive racial attitudes and cross-racial friendships (Aronson & Bridgeman, 1979; Cohen, 1972; Slavin, 1979, 1985). Cohen emphasizes the importance of giving students experiences that prepare them for equal-status interactions prior to assigning group tasks to students from different races. Her research indicates that if this is not done, both minority and White students will expect the White students to dominate the group situation. She calls this phenomenon *interracial interaction disability* and has demonstrated that pregroup treatment activities can enable African American students to experience equal status in group situations with Whites (Cohen, 1972; Cohen & Roper, 1972).

EQUITY PEDAGOGY

When the civil rights movement began in the 1960s, much attention was focused on poverty in the United States. In *The Other America*, Michael Harrington (1962) stirred the nation's conscience about the plight of poor people. Educational concepts and theories developed that reflected the national concern for low-income citizens and were designed to help teachers and other educators develop teaching techniques and strategies that would improve the academic achievement of low-income students.

The Cultural Deprivation Paradigm

The educational theories, concepts, and research developed during the early 1960s reflected the dominant ideologies of the time, as well as the concepts and theories used in the social sciences to explain the behavior and values of low-income populations. Social scientists developed the *culture of poverty* concept to describe the experiences of low-income populations (Lewis, 1965). In education, this concept became known as *cultural deprivation* or *the disadvantaged*. Cultural deprivation became the dominant paradigm that guided the formulation of programs and pedagogies for low-income populations during the 1960s (Bereiter & Engelmann, 1966; Bloom et al., 1965; Crow, Murray, & Smythe, 1966; Riessman, 1962).

A paradigm can be defined as a system of explanations that guides policy and action (Kuhn, 1970). When a paradigm becomes established and dominates public discourse, it is difficult for other systems of explanation to emerge or become institutionalized. When one paradigm replaces another, Kuhn states, a scientific revolution takes place. In education and the social sciences, rarely does one paradigm replace another. More typically, new paradigms compete with established ones and they coexist. Particular paradigms have been dominant at various times in the history of the education of low-income populations since the 1960s, but the educational landscape is usually characterized by competing paradigms and explanations.

A paradigm is not only a system of explanations, it is also a perspective on reality that reflects the experiences, perceptions, and values of its creators (Code, 1991; Harding, 1991). Cultural deprivation theorists, unlike geneticists (Herrnstein, 1971; Jensen, 1969), believe that low-income students can attain high levels of academic achievement, but socialization experiences in their homes and communities do not enable them to attain the knowledge, skills, and attitudes that middle-class children acquire and that are essential for academic success.

Cultural deprivation theorists consequently believe that the major focus of educational reform must be to change the students by enhancing their early socialization experiences. Cultural deprivation and disadvantaged theorists believe that the school must help low-income students to overcome the deficits that result from their early family and community experience. The focus on the deficits of low-income children often prevents cultural deprivation theorists from seeing their strengths. The emphasis on student deficits also does not allow the deprivationists to seriously consider structural changes that are needed in schools and in society.

When it emerged, the cultural deprivation paradigm was the most enlightened and liberal theory of the day that dealt with educating low-income populations. Some of the nation's most eminent and committed social scientists contributed to its formulation. Allison Davis did pioneering work on educating low-income students (Davis, 1948/1962). Davis was one of the organizers of the landmark Research Conference on Education and Cultural Deprivation, held at the University of Chicago in June 1964. Some of the nation's most eminent educators and social scientists participated in this conference: Anne Anastasi, Basil Bernstein, Benjamin Bloom, Martin Deutsch, Erik Erikson, Edmund W. Gordon, Robert J. Havighurst, and Thomas Pettigrew. In a book based on the conference, Bloom et al. (1965) defined *culturally deprived* children: "We refer to this group as culturally disadvantaged or deprived because we believe the roots of their problem may in large part be traced to their experiences in homes which do not transmit the cultural patterns necessary for the types of learning characteristic of the schools and the larger society" (p. 4). The book was highly influential among educational leaders.

Another influential book resulted from a conference held two years earlier at Teachers College, Columbia University, led by A. Harry Passow (1963), who edited *Education in Depressed Areas*. Like the Chicago conference, the Teachers College conference included papers by some of the nation's leading social scientists and educators, among them David P. Ausubel, Kenneth B. Clark, and Robert J. Havighurst.

Probably the most influential book published for teachers was *The Culturally Deprived Child*, by Frank Riessman (1962), which was used widely in teacher-preparation and in-service programs. He told teachers to respect low-income students and pointed out that he thought *culturally deprived* was an inappropriate term but he was using it because it was popular. He wrote: "The term 'culturally deprived' refers to those aspects of middle-class culture—such as education, books, formal language—from which these groups have not benefited" (p. 3). Implicit in this statement is the assumption that a student must be middle-class to have a culture.

The Cultural Difference Theorists

When the 1970s began, a new group of scholars strongly challenged the explanations and values that underlie the cultural deprivation paradigm. Some of the critics of the cultural deprivationists used powerful language in their critiques (Baratz & Baratz, 1970; Ryan, 1971). Head Start preschool programs were funded generously during the war on poverty of the 1960s. The most popular educational models used in these programs were based on the cultural deprivation paradigm. One of the most commercially successful of these programs was marketed as Distar; it was popularized by Bereiter and Engelmann (1966). In a highly influential article published in the *Harvard Educational Review*, Baratz and Baratz argued that many of these programs and models were an expression of institutional racism. Ryan stated that middle-class professionals were blaming the poor, who were victims.

The critics of the cultural deprivationists constructed another explanation for the school failure of low-income students. They contend that these students are not having academic success because they experience serious cultural conflicts in school. The students have rich cultures and values, but the schools have a culture that conflicts seriously with those of students from low-income and ethnic minority groups (Hale-Benson, 1987; Shade, 1982).

In developing their concepts and theories about the rich cultures of low-income students and students of color, the cultural difference theorists make far more use of ethnic culture than do cultural deprivationists (Ramírez & Castañeda, 1974). The cultural deprivationists focus on social class and the culture of poverty and tend to ignore ethnic culture as a variable. The cultural difference theorists emphasize ethnic culture and devote little attention to class (Boykin, 2000; Gay, 2000). Ignoring the ethnic cultures of students has evoked much of the criticism of the cultural deprivationists. The lack of attention to social class is problematic in the cultural difference literature (J. A. Banks, 1988). Cultural difference theorists have developed lists of cultural characteristics designed to help teachers build on the cultural strengths of ethnic students (Hale, 2001; Ramírez & Castañeda, 1974). However, the lists become problematic when teachers interpret them as static characteristics that apply to all members of the ethnic group (Cox & Ramírez, 1981).

The most influential work related to the cultural difference paradigm deals with learning styles, teaching styles, and language (Boykin, 2000; Gay, 2000; Hale, 2001; Heath, 1983). In their seminal book, Ramírez and Castañeda (1974) delineate two major types of learning style, *field-independent* and *field-sensitive*. They describe theoretical and empirical evidence to support the postulate that traditional Mexican American students tend to be more field-sensitive in their learning style than Anglo students. The school, however, most often uses a field-independent teaching style. Consequently, Mexican American students tend not to achieve as well as Anglo students. Ramírez and Castañeda state that the school should help all students, including Mexican American and Anglo students, become *bicognitive* in their learning style.

Theories similar to the one described by Ramírez and Castañeda have also been formulated by Hale-Benson (1987) and Shade (1982, 1989). Hale-Benson, for example, states that the African American child, more than the Anglo child, tends to be "highly affective, expresses herself or himself through considerable body language . . . [and] seeks to be people oriented" (p. 123). In a comprehensive review article, Shade (1982) summarizes an extensive body of research that supports the cultural learning style concept. In a study by Damico (1985), African American children took more photographs of people and Anglo children took more photographs of objects, thus confirming her hypothesis that African American students are more people-oriented than object-oriented and that Anglo children are more object-oriented.

Kleinfeld (1975, 1979) has spent much of her career researching the characteristics of effective teachers of Native American students. She has become skeptical of the learning-style concept and its usefulness in instruction. After they reviewed the few studies of the educational effects of adapting instruction to Native American learning styles, Kleinfeld and Nelson (1991) concluded that "virtually no research has succeeded in demonstrating that instruction adapted to Native Americans' visual learning style results in greater learning" (p. 273). The few weak studies reviewed by Kleinfeld and Nelson do not constitute a sufficient reason to abandon the learning-style paradigm. However, the paradigm is a contentious one. Both advocates and critics are strongly committed to their positions.

The controversy about learning-style theory and research is difficult to resolve. J. A. Banks (1988) examined the research literature to determine the extent to which learning style is a variable related to class and ethnicity. He concluded that the issue is a complex one, and that class mobility mediates (but does not eliminate) the effects of ethnic culture on the learning characteristics of Mexican American and African American students.

Some researchers believe that the best way to understand the learning characteristics of students of color is to observe and describe them in ethnographic studies, rather than classifying them into several brief categories. These researchers believe that thick descriptions of the learning and cultural characteristics of students of color are needed to guide educational practice. Influential ethnographic studies of the cultural characteristics of students of color have been conducted by researchers such as Heath (1983), Philips (1983), and Ladson-Billings (1994).

Since the 1960s, cultural difference theorists have done rich and pioneering theoretical and empirical work on the language characteristics of ethnic minority students. Prior to the 1960s, many teachers considered the version of English spoken by most low-income African Americans as an abnormal form of standard English. Within the last four decades, linguists have produced a rich body of literature that documents that Black English (Ebonics) is a legitimate communication system that has its own rules and logic (Delpit & Dowdy, 2002; Heath, 1983; Labov, 1969; Smitherman, 1977; F. Williams, 1970). Spanish-speaking children in schools of the Southwest were prohibited from speaking their first language for many decades. However, research in recent decades has revealed that it is important for the school to recognize and make use of a child's first language (August & Hakuta, 1997; Beykont, 2000).

The Rebirth of the Cultural Deprivation Paradigm

The history of the ethnic studies and intergroup education movements indicates that ideas related to these movements reemerge cyclically. We can observe a similar phenomenon in cultural deprivation. The cultural difference paradigm dominated discourse about the education of ethnic groups throughout much of the late 1970s and the early 1980s. However, during late 1980s the cultural deprivation/disadvantaged conception was exhumed and given new life in the form of the novel concept of at-risk (Richardson et al., 1989; Slavin, Karweit, & Madden,

1989). Like cultural deprivation, the definition of *at-risk* is imprecise. The term is used to refer to students who are different in many ways (Cuban, 1989).

The at-risk paradigm became popular, in part, because it was a funding category for state and federal educational agencies. When a term becomes a funding category, it does not need to be defined precisely to attain wide usage and popularity. Another reason the concept became politically popular was because it was used to refer to any population of youths experiencing problems in school. Consequently, every interest group could see itself in the term. Although the phrase is problematic, as Cuban (1989) points out in a thoughtful article, it was often used by both researchers and practitioners (Richardson et al., 1989; Slavin et al., 1989). The term *disadvantaged* also reemerged during the 1980s. Disadvantaged children are the subject of an informative book by Natriello, McDill, and Pallas (1990).

AN EMPOWERING SCHOOL CULTURE AND SOCIAL STRUCTURE

The four dimensions of multicultural education discussed earlier—content integration, the knowledge construction process, prejudice reduction, and an equity pedagogy—each deal with an aspect of a cultural or social system: the school. However, the school can also be conceptualized as one social system that is larger than its interrelated parts (e.g., for example, its formal and informal curriculum, teaching materials, counseling programs, and teaching strategies). When conceptualized as a social system, the school is viewed as an institution that "includes a social structure of interrelated statuses and roles and the functioning of that structure in terms of patterns of actions and interactions" (Theodorson & Theodorson, 1969, p. 395). The school can also be conceptualized as a cultural system (Erickson, 2003) with a specific set of values and norms, an ethos, and shared meanings.

A number of school reformers have used a systems approach to reform the school in order to increase the academic achievement of low-income students and students of color. There are a number of advantages to approaching school reform from a holistic perspective. To implement any reform successfully in a school (such as effective prejudice reduction teaching), changes are required in a number of other school variables. Teachers, for example, need more knowledge and have to examine their racial and ethnic attitudes; consequently, they require more time as well as a variety of instructional materials. Many school reform efforts fail because the roles, norms, and ethos of the school do not change in ways that make institutionalization of reform possible.

The effective-school reformers constitute one group of change agents who have approached school reform from a systems perspective. This movement emerged as a reaction to the work of Coleman et al. (1966) and Jencks et al. (1972); their studies indicate that the major factor influencing student academic achievement is the social-class composition of the students and the school. Many educators interpreted the research by Coleman et al. and Jencks et al. to mean that the school can do little to increase the academic achievement of low-income students.

Brookover (Brookover & Erickson, 1975) developed a social psychological theory of learning that states that students internalize the conceptions of themselves that are institutionalized within the ethos and structures of the school. Related to Merton's (1968) self-fulfilling prophecy, Brookover's theory states that student academic achievement increases if the adults within the school have high expectations for students, clearly identify the skills they wish them to learn, and teach those skills to them.

Research by Brookover and his colleagues (Brookover et al., 1979; Brookover & Lezotte, 1979) indicates that schools populated by low-income students within the same school district vary greatly in student achievement level. Consequently, Brookover attributes the difference to variations in a school's social structure. He calls the schools in low-income areas that have high academic achievement *improving* schools. Other researchers, among them Edmonds (1986), Lezotte (1993), and Levine and Lezotte (2001), call them *effective* schools.

Brookover and his colleagues (Brookover et al., 1979; Brookover & Lezotte, 1979) have identified the characteristics that differentiate effective from ineffective schools. Staff in an effective or improving school emphasize the importance of basic skills and believe that all students can master them. The principal is an assertive instructional leader and disciplinarian and assumes responsibility for evaluating the achievement of basic skills objectives. Staff members accept the concept of accountability, and parents initiate more contact than in a nonimproving school.

Edmonds (1986), who was a leading advocate of effective schools as an antidote to the doom that often haunts inner-city schools, identified characteristics of an effective school similar to those formulated by Brookover and his colleagues. Rutter, Maughan, Mortimore, Ouston, and Smith (1979) studied 12 secondary schools in an urban section of London. They concluded that some schools were much better than others in promoting the academic and social success of their students. Effective-schools researchers have conducted a large number of studies that support their major postulates (see Levine & Lezotte, 2001, for a review of this research). However, some educators have concerns about effective-school interventions, including the use of standardized tests as the major device

to ascertain academic achievement (Bliss, Firestone, & Richards, 1991; Cuban, 1983; Purkey & Smith, 1982).

Comer (1988) has developed a structural intervention model that involves changes in the social psychological climate of the school. Teachers, principals, and other school professionals make collaborative decisions about the school; parents also participate in the decision-making process. Comer's data indicate that this approach has been successful in increasing the academic achievement of low-income, inner-city students. He started a program in New Haven, Connecticut, that is now being implemented in a number of other U.S. cities using private foundation support (Comer, Haynes, Joyner, & Ben-Avie, 1996).

IMPLICATIONS FOR RESEARCH AND PRACTICE

Research

The historical development of multicultural education needs to be more fully described. Careful historical descriptions and analyses will help the field identify its links to the past, gain deeper insight into the problems and promises of multicultural education today, and plan more effectively for the future. Studies are needed to determine the details of the teaching of African American history in schools and colleges from the turn of the century to the 1960s. Studies are also needed to determine the extent to which the intergroup education movement intersected with the ethnic studies tradition initiated by George Washington Williams in 1882 and continued by his successors until the new ethnic studies movement began in the 1960s. The role of African American institutions (churches, schools, sororities, fraternities, women's clubs; see Hine, Brown, & Terborg-Penn, 1993; and Siddle Walker, 1996) in promoting the study and teaching of African American history should also be researched (Dabney, 1934).

A broad outline of the early ethnic studies movement related to African Americans has been described here. Additional studies are needed that can reveal the degree to which scholarship and teaching sources about other ethnic groups, such as American Indians and Mexican Americans, were developed from the turn of the century to the 1960s and 1970s.

A comprehensive history of the intergroup education movement, which is lacking, is being written by Cherry A. McGee Banks (in progress). We also need to determine the extent to which intergroup education practices became institutionalized within the typical school. The publications reviewed for this chapter indicate that intergroup education was often implemented as special projects within schools that were leaders in their cities or districts. Many of the nation's schools were tightly segregated when the movement arose and died, especially in the South. The geographical regions in which intergroup education project schools were located, as well as the types of schools, are important variables that should be investigated.

Other major issues that warrant investigation are (a) the reasons the movement had failed by the time the new ethnic studies movement emerged in the 1960s; and (b) why its leaders, such as Hilda Taba, Lloyd A. Cook, and William Van Til, did little work in intergroup education after the mid-1950s. Seemingly, intergroup education was not a lifetime commitment for its eminent leaders. In the 1960s, Taba became a leading expert and researcher in social studies education. Even though intergroup education was no longer a primary focus in the last part of her career, Taba incorporated many aspects of intergroup education into her subsequent work.

In her posthumously published book, coauthored with Deborah Elkins (Taba & Elkins, 1966), *Teaching Strategies for the Culturally Disadvantaged,* Taba incorporated concepts and strategies from the intergroup education project that she directed in the 1940s, funded by the National Conference of Christians and Jews and sponsored by the American Council on Education. Intergroup education concepts and aims also had a significant influence on her famous social studies curriculum (Taba, 1967). It focuses on thinking, knowledge, attitudes, feelings, and values, as well as on academic and social skills. These components are similar to the aims that Taba stated for intergroup education in an article she coauthored with Harold W. Wilson (Taba & Wilson, 1946).

Empirical studies need to be undertaken of each of the five dimensions of multicultural education described in this chapter. Content integration studies, using interview and ethnographic techniques, should describe the approaches that teachers use to integrate their curricula with ethnic content, the problems they face, and how they resolve them. The major barriers that teachers face when trying to make their curricula multicultural should also be identified.

The knowledge construction process is a fruitful topic for empirical research. Most of the work related to this concept is theoretical and philosophical (J. A. Banks, 1993a; Collins, 2000; Code, 1991; Gordon, 1985; Harding, 1991). This concept can be investigated by interventions that present students with documents describing different perspectives on the same historical event, such as the Japanese American internment, the westward movement, and Indian removal. Studies could be made of teacher questions and student responses when discussing conflicting accounts.

Studies that describe students' racial attitudes and intervention studies designed to modify them should be conducted. A literature search using ERIC, PsychLit, and Sociofile revealed that few intervention studies related to children's racial attitudes have been conducted since 1980. Most of the studies related to children's racial attitudes reviewed here were done before 1980. Since then, there has been little support for research in race relations; consequently, there are few studies. Perhaps multicultural researchers could implement small-scale observational studies funded by civil rights organizations. Jewish civil rights organizations funded a number of important studies during the intergroup education era.

Research related to effective teaching strategies for low-income students and students of color (equity pedagogy) should examine the complex interaction of race, class, and gender, as well as other variables such as region and generation (Grant & Sleeter, 1986; Ready, Edley, & Snow, 2002). The rising number of outspoken African American conservatives, such as Carter (1991), Sowell (1984), Steele (1990), and Wortham (1981), should help both the research and the wider community understand the enormous diversity within the African American community. Conservative Mexican American writers, such as Rodriguez (1982) and Chavez (1991), reveal the ideological and cultural diversity within the Mexican American community.

Since the 1960s, diversity within U.S. ethnic minority groups has increased greatly, as a significant number of African Americans, Mexican Americans, and Puerto Ricans joined the middle class and the exodus to the suburbs (Wilson, 1987). White flight has become middle-class flight. A sharp class schism has developed within ethnic minority communities (Wilson, 1987). Consequently, research on people of color—especially studies on learning styles and their cultural characteristics—that does not examine class as an important variable is not likely to result in findings that are helpful and generalizable.

Practice

The most important implication of this research review is that multicultural education must be conceptualized and implemented broadly if it is to bring about meaningful change in schools, colleges, and universities (Moreno, 1999; Moses & Cobb, 2001). Several serious problems result when multicultural education is conceptualized only, or primarily, as content integration. Teachers in subjects such as mathematics and science perceive multicultural education, when it is conceptualized only as content integration, as appropriate for social studies and language arts teachers but not for them.

When multicultural education is narrowly conceptualized, it is often confined to activities for special days and occasions, such as Martin Luther King's birthday or Cinco de Mayo. It may also be viewed as a special unit, an additional book by an African American or a Mexican American writer, or a few additional lessons. The knowledge were separate and unequal in terms of expenditures per pupil, teacher and administrator salaries, and the quality and newness of textbooks and other teaching materials (Anderson, 1988; Bond, 1939).

Although separate Black public schools in the South had African American teachers and administrators, their school boards, curricula, and textbooks were White controlled and dominated. Consequently, integration of the curriculum with content about African Americans was problematic. In his influential book *The Mis-Education of the Negro,* Woodson (1933) stated that schools and colleges were miseducating African Americans because they were being taught about European civilization but not about the great African civilizations and cultures of their own people. He described what he felt were the harmful effects that neglecting Black history and civilization had on the thinking and self-esteem of African American youth.

From 1920 until his death in 1950, Woodson probably did more than any other individual to promote the study and teaching of African American history in the nation's schools and colleges (Roche, 1996). He spent most of his career writing histories, editing journals, and building ASNLH. Woodson taught high school in Washington, D.C., from 1909 to 1918 and received his doctorate in history from Harvard in 1912. He was one of the founders of ASNLH and established the *Journal of Negro History* in 1916. In 1921, he established The Associated Publishers, a subsidiary of ASNLH, which published a score of histories about African Americans, many of them written by Woodson and his historian colleagues.

Woodson's books were widely used in African American high schools and colleges. He started Negro History Week (now National Afro-American History Month) in 1926 to promote the study and teaching of African American history in the elementary and secondary schools. In 1937, he started publishing the *Negro History Bulletin* to provide historical materials for use by elementary and secondary school teachers. Other early African American scholars, such as G. W. Williams (1882–83), DuBois (1935), Wesley (1935), Quarles (1953), and Logan (1954), played key roles in constructing the knowledge needed to develop teaching materials for the schools and colleges. However, none of these scholars were as directly involved as Woodson in promoting the inclusion of content about African Americans into the curriculum of the nation's schools and colleges.

The Intergroup Education Movement

The intergroup education movement, although not a direct link to the work of early African American scholars such as Woodson, Wesley, DuBois, and Logan, is an important precedent to the ethnic studies movement that emerged in the 1960s and 1970s. The intergroup educa-

tion movement is linked to the work of these scholars because content about religious, national, and racial groups was one of the variables it used to reduce prejudice and discrimination (C.A.M. Banks, 1996; Cook & Cook, 1954; Trager & Yarrow, 1952). It is linked to the contemporary multicultural education movement because it shared many of the goals of today's multicultural education movement and experienced many of the same problems (Taba & Wilson, 1946; J. A. Banks, 2001).

The social forces that gave rise to the intergroup education movement grew out of the consequences of World War II. The demands of the war created job opportunities in the North and the West that were not available in the South. Consequently, many African Americans, Mexican Americans, and Whites living in rural areas migrated to northern and western cities to find jobs in war-related industries. Ethnic and racial tension developed as Anglos and Mexican Americans in western cities and African Americans and Whites in northern cities competed for jobs and housing. These tensions resulted in a series of racial incidents and riots that stunned the nation.

Intergroup education emerged as an educational response to the racial and ethnic tension in the nation (C.A.M. Banks, Chapter 36, this volume; R. D. DuBois, 1984; Taba, Brady, & Robinson, 1952). One of its major goals was to help reduce prejudice and create interracial understanding among students from diverse national, religious, and racial groups (Cook & Cook, 1954; Taba & Wilson, 1946). Several national organizations, such as the Progressive Education Association (Locke & Stern, 1942), the National Council for the Social Studies (NCSS) (Taba & Van Til, 1945), and the American Council on Education (Cook, 1950), sponsored projects, activities, and publications in intergroup education. Projects and activities were developed for both elementary and secondary schools (Taba et al., 1952), as well as for teachers colleges (Cook, 1951).

Many of the intergroup education publications, like multicultural education publications today, were practical sources that described ways to set up an intergroup relations center (Clinchy, 1949; R. D. DuBois, 1984), identified objectives and methods for schools (Vickery & Cole, 1943), described curricula and units for schools (Taba, 1950, 1951, 1952), and described intergroup education programs and projects in colleges and universities (Cook, 1951). Some of these publications were based on intergroup theories developed by Louis Wirth (1928), Gordon W. Allport (1954), and other social scientists.

Some of the nation's leading social scientists and philosophers participated in the development of theoretical ideas about the reduction of interracial tension during the intergroup education era. Wirth, the University of Chicago sociologist, and Allport, the Harvard social psychologist, contributed chapters to a book edited by Lloyd A. Cook (1952), a leading intergroup educator. Wirth's construction dimension of multicultural education is an essential one. Using this concept, content about ethnic groups is not merely added to the curriculum. Rather, the curriculum is reconceptualized to help students understand how knowledge is constructed and how it reflects human interests, ideology, and the experiences of the people who create it. Students themselves also create interpretations. They begin to understand why it is essential to look at the nation's experience from diverse ethnic and cultural perspectives to comprehend fully its past and present.

The research reviewed in this chapter indicates that children come to school with misconceptions about outside ethnic groups and with a white bias. However, it also indicates that students' racial attitudes can be modified and made more democratic, and that the racial attitudes of young children are much more easily modified than the attitudes of older students and adults (Katz, 1976; Aboud & Doyle, 1996). Consequently, it suggests that if we are to help students acquire the attitudes needed to survive in a multicultural and diverse world, we must start early. Beginning in kindergarten, educators need to implement a well-conceptualized and sequential curriculum that is multicultural (Ramsey, 1998).

A school experience that is multicultural includes content, examples, and realistic images of diverse racial and ethnic groups. Cooperative learning activities in which students from diverse groups work to attain shared goals is also a feature of the school, as well as simulated images of ethnic groups that present them positively and realistically. Also essential within such a school are adults who model the attitudes and behaviors they are trying to teach. Actions speak much louder than words.

Jane Elliott (as described in Peters, 1987) has attained fame for a simulated lesson she taught on discrimination that is described in the award-winning documentary *The Eye of the Storm*. One day Elliott discriminated against blue-eyed children; the next day brown-eyed children experienced the sting of bigotry. In 1984, 11 of her former third graders returned to Riceville, Iowa, for a reunion with their teacher. This event is described in another documentary, *A Class Divided*, in which the students describe the power of a classroom experience that took place 14 years earlier. Elliott, who taught third grade in an all-White Iowa town, was moved to act because of the racial hate she observed in the nation. Racial discrimination is still prevalent throughout the United States (Feagin & Sikes, 1994). The research reviewed in this chapter, and in two previous reviews (J. A. Banks, 1991b, 1993b), can help empower educators to act to help create a more democratic and caring society. Jane Elliott acted and made a difference. She is a cogent example for us all.

References

Aboud, F. (1988). *Children and prejudice.* Cambridge, MA: Blackwell.

Aboud, F. E., & Doyle, A. B. (1996). Does talk foster prejudice or tolerance in children? *Canadian Journal of Behavioural Sciences, 28*(3), 161–171.

Acuña, R. (1972). *Occupied America: The Chicano's struggle toward liberation.* San Francisco: Canfield Press.

Adorno, T. W., Frenkel-Brunswik, E., Levinson, D. J., & Sanford, R. N. (1950). *The authoritarian personality.* New York: Norton.

Agnes, M. (1947). Influences of reading on the racial attitudes of adolescent girls. *Catholic Educational Review, 45,* 415–420.

Allport, G. W. (1954). *The nature of prejudice.* Cambridge, MA: Addison-Wesley.

American Association of Colleges for Teacher Education. (1973). *No one model American.* Washington, DC: Author.

Anderson, J. D. (1988). *The education of Blacks in the South, 1860–1935.* Chapel Hill: University of North Carolina Press.

Aran, K., Arthur, H., Colon, R., & Goldenberg, H. (1973). *Puerto Rican history and culture: A study guide and curriculum outline.* New York: United Federation of Teachers.

Aronson, E., & Bridgeman, D. (1979). Jigsaw groups and the desegregated classroom: In pursuit of common goals. *Personality and Social Psychology Bulletin, 5,* 438–446.

Asante, M. K. (1998). *The Afrocentric idea* (rev. expanded ed.). Philadelphia: Temple University Press.

Asante, M. K., & Ravitch, D. (1991). Multiculturalism: An exchange. *American Scholar, 60,* 267–276.

August, D., & Hakuta, K. (Eds.). (1997). *Improving schooling for language-minority children.* Washington, DC: National Academy Press.

Baker, G. (1977). Multicultural education: Two preservice approaches. *Journal of Teacher Education, 28,* 31–33.

Banks, C.A.M. (1996). The intergroup education movement. In J. A. Banks (Ed.), *Multicultural education, transformative knowledge, and action: Historical and contemporary perspectives* (pp. 251–277). New York: Teachers College Press.

Banks, C.A.M. (in progress). *The intergroup education movement: Insights from the past, lessons for the present and future.* New York: Teachers College Press.

Banks, J. A. (1969). A content analysis of the Black American in textbooks. *Social Education, 33,* 954–957, 963.

Banks, J. A. (1970). *Teaching the Black experience: Methods and materials.* Belmont, CA: Fearon.

Banks, J. A. (Ed.). (1973). *Teaching ethnic studies: Concepts and strategies* (43rd yearbook). Washington, DC: National Council for the Social Studies.

Banks, J. A. (1984). Black youths in predominantly White suburbs: An exploratory study of their attitudes and self-concepts. *Journal of Negro Education, 53,* 3–17.

Banks, J. A. (1988). Ethnicity, class, cognitive, and motivational styles: Research and teaching implications. *Journal of Negro Education, 57,* 452–466.

Banks, J. A. (1991a). The dimensions of multicultural education. *Multicultural Leader, 4,* 5–6.

Banks, J. A. (1991b). Multicultural education: Its effects on students' ethnic and gender role attitudes. In J. P. Shaver (Ed.), *Handbook of research on social studies teaching and learning* (pp. 459–469). New York: Macmillan.

Banks, J. A. (1992). Multicultural education: Approaches, developments, and dimensions. In J. Lynch, C. Modgil, & S. Modgil (Eds.), *Cultural diversity and the schools*, Vol. 1, *Education for cultural diversity: Convergence and divergence* (pp. 83–94). London: The Falmer Press.

Banks, J. A. (1993a). The canon debate, knowledge construction, and multicultural education. *Educational Researcher, 22*(5), 4–14.

Banks, J. A. (1993b). Multicultural education for young children: Racial and ethnic attitudes and their modification. In B. Spodek (Ed.), *Handbook of research on the education of young children* (pp. 236–250). New York: Macmillan.

Banks, J. A. (Ed.). (1996). *Multicultural education, transformative knowledge, and action: Historical and contemporary perspectives.* New York: Teachers College Press.

Banks, J. A. (1998). The lives and values of researchers: Implications for educating citizens in a multicultural society. *Educational Researcher, 27*(7), 4–17.

Banks, J. A. (2001). *Cultural diversity and education: Foundations, curriculum and teaching* (4th ed.). Boston: Allyn & Bacon.

Banks, J. A. (2003a). Approaches to multicultural curriculum reform. In J. A. Banks & C.A.M. Banks (Eds.), *Multicultural education: Issues and perspectives* (4th ed., rev., pp. 225–246). New York: Wiley.

Banks, J. A. (2003b). Multicultural education: Characteristics and goals. In J. A. Banks & C.A.M. Banks (Eds.), *Multicultural education: Issues and perspectives* (4th ed., rev., pp. 3–30). New York: Wiley.

Banks, J. A. (2003c). *Teaching strategies for ethnic studies* (7th ed.). Boston: Allyn & Bacon.

Banks, J. A., & Banks, C.A.M. (Eds.). (2003). *Multicultural education: Issues and perspectives* (4th ed., rev.). New York: Wiley.

Banks, J. A., Cookson, P., Gay, G., Hawley, W. D., Irvine, J. J., Nieto, S., Schofield, J. W., & Stephan, W. G. (2001). *Diversity within unity: Essential principles for teaching and learning in a multicultural society.* Seattle: University of Washington, Center for Multicultural Education.

Banks, J. A., Cortés, C. E., Gay, G., Garcia, R. L., & Ochoa, A. S. (1976). *Curriculum guidelines for multiethnic education.* Washington, DC: National Council for the Social Studies.

Banks, W. C. (1976). White preference in Blacks: A paradigm in search of a phenomenon. *Psychological Bulletin, 83*, 1170–1186.

Baratz, S. S., & Baratz, J. C. (1970). Early childhood intervention: The social science base of institutional racism. *Harvard Educational Review, 40*, 29–50.

Bennett, C. I. (2001). Genres of research in multicultural education. *Review of Educational Research, 71*(2), 171–217.

Bereiter, C., & Engelmann, S. (1966). *Teaching disadvantaged children in the preschool.* Englewood Cliffs, NJ: Prentice Hall.

Berger, P. L., & Luckman, T. (1966). *The social construction of knowledge: A treatise in the sociology of knowledge.* Garden City, NY: Doubleday.

Bernal, M. (1987, 1991). *Black Athena: The Afroasiatic roots of classical civilization* (Vols. 1 & 2). New Brunswick, NJ: Rutgers University Press.

Beykont, Z. F. (Ed.). (2000). *Lifting every voice: Pedagogy and the politics of bilingualism.* Cambridge, MA: Harvard Education Publishing Group.

Blassingame, J. W. (Ed.). (1971). *New perspectives in Black studies.* Urbana: University of Illinois Press.

Blassingame, J. W. (1972). *The slave community: Plantation life in the antebellum South.* New York: Oxford University Press.

Blea, I. I. (1988). *Toward a Chicano social science.* New York: Praeger.

Bliss, J. R., Firestone, W. A., & Richards, C. E. (Eds.). (1991). *Rethinking effective schools: Research and practice.* Englewood Cliffs, NJ: Prentice Hall.

Bloom, B. S., Davis, A., & Hess, R. (1965). *Compensatory education for cultural deprivation.* New York: Holt.

Board on Children, Youth, and Families (2000). *Improving intergroup relations among youth: Summary of a workshop.* Washington, DC: National Academy Press.

Bond, H. M. (1939). *Negro education in Alabama: A study in cotton and steel.* Washington, DC: The Associated Publishers.

Boyer, J. B. (1974). Needed: Curriculum diversity for the urban economically disadvantaged. *Educational Leadership, 31*, 624–626.

Boykin, A. W. (2000). The talent development model of schooling: Placing students at promise for academic success. *Journal of Education for Students Placed at Risk, 5*(1&2), 3–25.

Brookover, W. B., Beady, C., Flood, P., Schweitzer, J., & Wisenbaker, J. (1979). *School social systems and student achievement: Schools can make a difference.* New York: Praeger.

Brookover, W. B., & Erickson, E. (1975). *Sociology of education.* Homewood, IL: Dorsey.

Brookover, W. B., & Lezotte, L. W. (1979). *Changes in school characteristics coincident with changes in student achievement.* East Lansing: Michigan State University, College of Education, Institute for Research on Teaching.

Brooks, R. L. (1990). *Rethinking the American race problem.* Berkeley: University of California Press.

Bulosan, C. (1943). *America is in the heart.* New York: Harcourt.

Butler, J. E., & Walter, J. C. (Eds.). (1991). *Transforming the curriculum: Ethnic studies and women's studies.* Albany: State University of New York Press.

Carmichael, S., & Hamilton, C. V. (1967). *Black power: The politics of liberation in America.* New York: Vintage Books.

Carter, S. L. (1991). *Reflections of an affirmative action baby.* New York: Basic Books.

Chavez, L. (1991). *Out of the barrio: Toward a new politics of Hispanic assimilation.* New York: Basic Books.

Ciullo, R., & Troiani, M. Y. (1988). Resolution of prejudice: Small group interaction and behavior of latency-age children. *Small Group Behavior, 19*(3), 386–394.

Clark, K. B. (1963). *Prejudice and your child.* Boston: Beacon Press.

Clark, K. B., & Clark, M. P. (1939a). The development of consciousness of self and the emergence of racial identification in Negro preschool children. *Journal of Social Psychology, 10*, 591–599.

Clark, K. B., & Clark, M. P. (1939b). Segregation as a factor in the racial identification of Negro preschool children. *Journal of Experimental Education, 8*, 161–163.

Clark, K. B., & Clark, M. P. (1940). Skin color as a factor in racial identification and preference in Negro children. *Journal of Negro Education, 19*, 341–358.

Clark, K. B., & Clark, M. P. (1947). Racial identification and preference in Negro children. In T. M. Newcomb & E. L. Hartley (Eds.), *Readings in social psychology* (pp. 169–178). New York: Holt, Rinehart & Winston.

Clark, K. B., & Clark, M. P. (1950). Emotional factors in racial identification and preference of Negro children. *Journal of Negro Education, 19*, 341–350.

Clinchy, E. R. (1949). *Intergroup relations centers.* New York: Farrar, Straus & Giroux.

Code, L. (1991). *What can she know? Feminist theory and the construction of knowledge.* Ithaca, NY: Cornell University Press.

Cohen, E. G. (1972). Interracial interaction disability. *Human Relations, 25,* 9–24.

Cohen, E. G., & Roper, S. S. (1972). Modification of interracial interaction disability: An application of status characteristics theory. *American Sociological Review, 37,* 643–657.

Coleman, J. S., Campbell, E. G., Hobson, C. J., McPartland, J., Mood, A. M., Weinfeld, F. D., & York, R. L. (1966). *Equality of educational opportunity.* Washington, DC: U.S. Government Printing Office.

Collins, P. H. (2000). *Black feminist thought: Knowledge, consciousness, and the politics of empowerment* (2nd ed.). New York: Routledge.

Comer, J. P. (1988). Educating poor minority children. *Scientific American, 259,* 42–48.

Comer, J. P., Haynes, N. M., Joyner, E. T., & Ben-Avie, M. (Eds.). (1996). *Rallying the whole village: The Comer process for reforming education.* New York: Teachers College Press.

Cook, L. A. (1947). Intergroup education. *Review of Educational Research, 17,* 267–278.

Cook, L. A. (1950). *College programs in intergroup relations.* Washington, DC: American Council on Education.

Cook, L. A. (1951). *Intergroup relations in teacher education: An analytical study of intergroup education in colleges and schools in the United States—functions, current expressions, and improvements.* Washington, DC: American Council on Education.

Cook, L. A. (Ed.). (1952). *Toward better human relations.* Detroit: Wayne State University Press.

Cook, L., & Cook, E. (1954). *Intergroup education.* New York: McGraw-Hill.

Cortés, C. E. (1973). Teaching the Chicano experience. In J. A. Banks (Ed.), *Teaching ethnic studies: Concepts and strategies* (pp. 181–199). Washington, DC: National Council for the Social Studies.

Cortés, C. E. (2002). *The making and remaking of a multiculturalist.* New York: Teachers College Press.

Cox, B. G., & Ramírez, M., III (1981). Cognitive styles: Implications for teaching ethnic studies. In J. A. Banks (Ed.), *Education for the 80s: Multiethnic education* (pp. 61–71). Washington, DC: National Education Association.

Cross, W. E., Jr. (1985). Black identity: Rediscovering the distinction between personal identity and reference group orientation. In M. B. Spencer, G. K. Brookins, & W. R. Allen (Eds.), *Beginnings: The social and affective development of Black children* (pp. 155–171). Hillsdale, NJ: Erlbaum.

Cross, W. E., Jr. (1991). *Shades of Black: Diversity in African American identity.* Philadelphia: Temple University Press.

Crow, L. D., Murray, W. I., & Smythe, H. H. (1966). *Educating the culturally disadvantaged child: Principles and programs.* New York: David McKay.

Cuban, L. (1983). Effective schools: A friendly but cautionary note. *Phi Delta Kappan, 64,* 695–696.

Cuban, L. (1989). The "at risk" label and the problem of urban school reform. *Phi Delta Kappan, 70,* 780–801.

Dabney, T. L. (1934). The study of the Negro. *Journal of Negro History, 19,* 266–307.

Damico, S. B. (1985). The two worlds of school: Differences in the photographs of Black and White adolescents. *The Urban Review, 17,* 210–222.

Daniels, R. (1988). *Asian America: Chinese and Japanese in the United States since 1850.* Seattle: University of Washington Press.

Davis, A. (1962). *Social-class influences upon learning.* Cambridge, MA: Harvard University Press. (Original work published 1948)

Davis, A., Gardner, B. B., & Gardner, M. R. (1941). *Deep South: A social anthropological study of caste and class.* Chicago: University of Chicago Press.

Deloria, V., Jr. (1969). *Custer died for your sins: An Indian manifesto.* New York: Avon Books.

Delpit, L. D. (1988). The silenced dialogue: Power and pedagogy in educating other people's children. *Harvard Educational Review, 58,* 280–298.

Delpit, L. D., & Dowdy, J. D. K. (Eds.). (2002). *The skin that we speak: Thoughts on language and culture in the classroom.* New York: Free Press.

Diop, C. A. (1974). *The African origin of civilization: Myth or reality.* New York: Lawrence Hill.

Drake, St. C. (1987, 1990). *Black folk here and there* (Vols. 1 & 2). Los Angeles: University of California, Center for Afro-American Studies.

DuBois, R. D., with Okorodudu, C. (1984). *All this and something more: Pioneering in intercultural education.* Bryn Mawr, PA: Dorrance.

DuBois, W.E.B. (1935). *Black reconstruction.* New York: Harcourt Brace.

DuBois, W.E.B. (1953). *The souls of Black folk.* New York: Blue Heron Press.

DuBois, W.E.B. (1973). *The education of Black people: Ten critiques, 1906–1960.* New York: Monthly Review Press.

Edmonds, R. (1986). Characteristics of effective schools. In U. Neisser (Ed.), *The school achievement of minority children* (pp. 93–104). Hillsdale, NJ: Erlbaum.

Erickson, F. (2003). Culture in society and in educational practice. In J. A. Banks & C.A.M. Banks (Eds.), *Multicultural education: Issues and perspectives* (4th ed., rev., pp. 31–58). New York: Wiley.

Farganis, S. (1986). *The social construction of the feminine character.* Totowa, NJ: Rowman & Littlefield.

Feagin, J. R., & Sikes, M. P. (1994). *Living with racism: The Black middle-class experience.* Boston: Beacon Press.

Fisher, F. (1965). *The influence of reading and discussion on the attitudes of fifth graders toward American Indians.* Unpublished doctoral dissertation, University of California, Berkeley.

Forbes, J. D. (1973). Teaching Native American values and cultures. In J. A. Banks (Ed.), *Teaching ethnic studies: Concepts and strategies* (pp. 201–225). Washington, DC: National Council for the Social Studies.

Ford, N. A. (1973). *Black studies: Threat-or-challenge.* Port Washington, NY: Kennikat Press.

Franklin, J. H. (1947). *From slavery to freedom: A history of Negro Americans.* New York: Knopf.

Franklin, J. H. (1985). *George Washington Williams: A biography.* Chicago: University of Chicago Press.

Gamio, M. (1930). *Mexican immigration to the United States: A study of human migration and adjustment.* Chicago: University of Chicago Press.

Garcia, R. L. (1998). *Teaching for diversity.* Bloomington, IN: Phi Delta Kappa Educational Foundation.

Gates, H. L., Jr. (1988). *The signifying monkey: A theory of African-American literary criticism.* New York: Oxford University Press.

Gay, G. (1971). Ethnic minority studies: How widespread? How successful? *Educational Leadership, 29,* 108–112.

Gay, G. (1992). The state of multicultural education in the United States. In K. Adam Moodley (Ed.), *Education in plural societies: International perspectives* (pp. 47–66). Calgary, Alberta, Canada: Detselig Enterprises.

Gay, G. (2000). *Culturally responsive teaching: Theory, research and practice.* New York: Teachers College Press.

Genovese, E. D. (1972). *Roll, Jordan, roll: The world the slaves made.* New York: Pantheon Books.

Gibson, M. A. (1976). Approaches to multicultural education in the United States: Some concepts and assumptions. *Anthropology and Education Quarterly, 7,* 7–18.

Ginsburg, H. (1972). *The myth of the deprived child: Poor children's intellect and education.* Englewood Cliffs, NJ: Prentice Hall.

Giroux, H. A. (1983). *Theory and resistance in education.* South Hadley, MA: Bergin & Garvey.

Gollnick, D. M., & Chinn, P. C. (2001). *Multicultural education in a pluralistic society* (6th ed.). Upper Saddle River, NJ: Prentice Hall.

Goodman, M. A. (1952). *Race awareness in young children.* New York: Collier.

Gordon, E. W. (1985). Social science knowledge production and the Afro-American experience. *Journal of Negro Education, 54,* 117–133.

Gordon, E. W., & Meroe, A. S. (1991). Common destinies—Continuing dilemmas. *Psychological Science, 2,* 23–30.

Gordon, E. W., Miller, M., & Rollock, D. (1990). Coping with communicentric bias in knowledge production in the social sciences. *Educational Researcher, 19,* 14–19.

Gould, S. J. (1996). *The mismeasure of man* (rev. & updated ed.). New York: Norton.

Grant, C. A. (1973). Black studies materials do make a difference. *Journal of Educational Research, 66,* 400–404.

Grant, C. A. (Ed.). (1977). *Multicultural education: Commitments, issues, and applications.* Washington, DC: Association for Supervision and Curriculum Development.

Grant, C. A. (1978). Education that is multicultural: Isn't that what we mean? *Journal of Teacher Education, 29,* 45–48.

Grant, C. A., & Sleeter, C. E. (1986). Race, class, and gender in education research: An argument for integrative analysis. *Review of Educational Research, 56,* 195–211.

Gray, P. (1991, July 8). Whose America? *Time,* pp. 12–17.

Habermas, J. (1971). *Knowledge and human interests.* Boston: Beacon Press.

Hale, J. (2001). *Learning while Black: Creating educational excellence for African American children.* Baltimore: Johns Hopkins University Press.

Hale-Benson, J. (1987). Black children: Their roots, culture, and learning styles. In J. B. McCracken (Ed.), *Reducing stress in young children's lives* (pp. 122–129). Washington, DC: National Association for the Education of Young Children.

Harding, S. (1991). *Whose science? Whose knowledge? Thinking from women's lives.* Ithaca, NY: Cornell University Press.

Harrington, M. (1962). *The other America.* New York: Macmillan.

Hartsock, N.C.M. (1998). *The feminist standpoint revisited and other essays.* Boulder, CO: Westview Press.

Hayes, M. L., & Conklin, M. E. (1953). Intergroup attitudes and experimental change. *Journal of Experimental Education, 22,* 19–36.

Heath, S. B. (1983). *Ways with words: Language, life, and work in communities and classrooms.* New York: Cambridge University Press.

Herrnstein, R. J. (1971). *I.Q. in the meritocracy.* New York: Little, Brown.

Hilliard, A. G., III (1974). Restructuring teacher education for multicultural imperatives. In W. A. Hunter (Ed.), *Multicultural education through competency-based teacher education* (pp. 40–55). Washington, DC: American Association of Colleges for Teacher Education.

Hilliard, A. G., III, Payton-Stewart, L., & Williams, L. O. (Eds.). (1990). *Infusion of African and African American content in the school curriculum.* Morristown, NJ: Aaron Press.

Hine, D. C., Brown, E. B., & Terborg-Penn, R. (Eds.). (1993). *Black women in America: An historical encyclopedia* (2 vols.). Brooklyn: Carlson.

Hohn, R. L. (1973). Perceptual training and its effect on racial preference of kindergarten children. *Psychological Reports, 32,* 435–441.

hooks, b. (1990). *Yearning: Race, gender, and cultural politics.* Boston: South End Press.

Horowitz, E. L. (1936). The development of attitude toward the Negro. In *Archives of Psychology* (No. 104). New York: Columbia University.

Horowitz, R. E. (1939). Racial aspects of self-identification in nursery school children. *Journal of Psychology, 7,* 91–99.

Hunter, W. A. (Ed.). (1974). *Multicultural education through competency-based teacher education.* Washington, DC: American Association of Colleges for Teacher Education.

Jackson, E. P. (1944). Effects of reading upon the attitudes toward the Negro race. *Library Quarterly, 14,* 47–54.

Jencks, C., Smith, M., Acland, H., Bane, M. J., Cohen, D., Gintis, H., Heyns, B., & Michelson, S. (1972). *Inequality: A reassessment of the effect of family and schooling in America.* New York: Basic Books.

Jensen, A. R. (1969). How much can we boost IQ and scholastic achievement? *Harvard Educational Review, 39,* 1–123.

Kaplan, A. (1964). *The conduct of inquiry: Methodology for behavioral science.* San Francisco: Chandler.

Katz, P. A. (1973). Perception of racial cues in preschool children: A new look. *Developmental Psychology, 8,* 295–299.

Katz, P. A. (Ed.). (1976). *Towards the elimination of racism.* New York: Pergamon Press.

Katz, P. A., & Zalk, S. R. (1978). Modification of children's racial attitudes. *Developmental Psychology, 14,* 447–461.

Kitano, H.H.L. (1969). *Japanese Americans: The evolution of a subculture.* Englewood Cliffs, NJ: Prentice Hall.

Klassen, F. H., & Gollnick, D. M. (Eds.). (1977). *Pluralism and the American teacher: Issues and case studies.* Washington, DC: American Association of Colleges for Teacher Education, Ethnic Heritage Center for Teacher Education.

Klein, S. S. (Ed.). (1985). *Handbook for achieving sex equity through education.* Baltimore: Johns Hopkins University Press.

Kleinfeld, J. (1975). Effective teachers of Eskimo and Indian students. *School Review, 83,* 301–344.

Kleinfeld, J. (1979). *Eskimo children on the Andrearsky.* New York: Praeger.

Kleinfeld, J., & Nelson, P. (1991). Adapting instruction to Native Americans' learning styles: An iconoclastic view. *Journal of Cross-Cultural Psychology, 22,* 273–282.

Kuhn, T. S. (1970). *The structure of scientific revolutions* (2nd ed., enlarged). Chicago: University of Chicago Press.

Labov, W. (1969). *The study of nonstandard English.* Urbana, IL: National Council of Teachers of English.

Ladner, J. A. (Ed.). (1973). *The death of White sociology.* New York: Vintage Books.

Ladson-Billings, G. (1994). *The dreamkeepers: Successful teachers of African American children.* San Francisco: Jossey-Bass.

Lasker, B. (1929). *Race attitudes in children.* New York: Holt, Rinehart & Winston.

Lasker, B. (1931). *Filipino immigration to the continental United States and Hawaii.* Chicago: University of Chicago Press.

Lauter, P. (1991). *Canons and contexts.* New York: Oxford University Press.

Leslie, L. L., & Leslie, J. W. (1972). The effects of a student centered special curriculum upon the racial attitudes of sixth graders. *Journal of Experimental Education, 41,* 63–67.

Lessing, E. E., & Clarke, C. (1976). An attempt to reduce ethnic prejudice and assess its correlates. *Educational Research Quarterly, 1,* 3–16.

Levine, D. U., & Lezotte, L. W. (2001). Effective schools research. In J. A. Banks & C.A.M. Banks (Eds.), *Handbook of research on multicultural education* (pp. 525–547). San Francisco: Jossey-Bass.

Levine, L. W. (1977). *Black culture and Black consciousness: Afro-American folk thought from slavery to freedom.* New York: Oxford University Press.

Lewis, O. (1965). *La vida: A Puerto Rican family in the culture of poverty—San Juan and New York.* New York: Random House.

Lezotte, L. W. (1993). Effective schools: A framework for increasing student achievement. In J. A. Banks & C.A.M. Banks (Eds.), *Multicultural education: Issues and perspectives* (2nd ed., pp. 303–316). Boston: Allyn & Bacon.

Litcher, J. H., & Johnson, D. W. (1969). Changes in attitudes toward Negroes of White elementary school students after use of multiethnic readers. *Journal of Educational Psychology, 60,* 148–152.

Litcher, J. H., Johnson, D. W., & Ryan, F. L. (1973). Use of pictures of multiethnic interaction to change attitudes of White elementary school students toward Blacks. *Psychological Reports, 33,* 367–372.

Locke, A., & Stern, B. J. (Eds.). (1942). *When people meet: A study in race and culture contacts.* New York: Progressive Education Association.

Logan, R. W. (1954). *The betrayal of the Negro.* New York: Collier.

McGregor, J. (1993). Effectiveness of role playing and antiracist teaching in reducing student prejudice. *Journal of Educational Research, 86*(4), 215–226.

McWilliams, C. (1943). *Brothers under the skin.* Boston: Little, Brown.

McWilliams, C. (1949). *North from Mexico: The Spanish-speaking people of the United States.* Philadelphia: Lippincott.

Mehan, H., Villanueva, I., Hubbard, L., & Lintz, A. (1996). *Constructing school success: The consequences of untracking low-achieving students.* New York: Cambridge University Press.

Mercer, J. R. (1989). Alternative paradigms for assessment in a pluralistic society. In J. A. Banks & C.A.M. Banks (Eds.), *Multicultural education: Issues and perspectives* (pp. 289–304). Boston: Allyn & Bacon.

Merton, R. K. (1968). *Social theory and social structure.* New York: Free Press.

Miel, A., with Kiester, E., Jr. (1967). *The shortchanged children of suburbia: What schools don't teach about human differences and what can be done about it.* New York: American Jewish Committee.

Milner, D. (1983). *Children and race.* Beverly Hills, CA: Sage.

Minard, R. D. (1931). *Race attitudes of Iowa children.* Iowa City: University of Iowa.

Moreno, J. F. (Ed.). (1999). *The elusive quest for equality: 150 years of Chicano/Chicana education.* (Monograph.) Cambridge, MA: Harvard Educational Review.

Morland, J. K. (1966). A comparison of race awareness in northern and southern children. *American Journal of Orthopsychiatry, 36,* 22–31.

Moses, R., & Cobb, C. E., Jr. (2001). *Radical equations: Math literacy and civil rights.* Boston: Beacon Press.

Myrdal, G., with the assistance of Sterner, R., & Rose, A. (1944). *An American dilemma: The Negro problem and modern democracy.* New York: Harper & Row.

Myrdal, G. (1969). *Objectivity and social research.* Middletown, CT: Wesleyan University Press.

National Council for the Accreditation of Teacher Education. (1977). *Standards for the accreditation of teacher education.* Washington, DC: Author.

National Council for the Accreditation of Teacher Education. (1987). *NCATE standards, procedures, and policies for the accreditation of professional education units.* Washington, DC: Author.

National Council for the Social Studies Task Force on Ethnic Studies. (1992). Curriculum guidelines for multicultural education. *Social Education, 56,* 274–294.

National Council of Teachers of English. (1974). *Students' right to their own language.* Urbana, IL: Author.

Natriello, G., McDill, E. L., & Pallas, A. M. (1990). *Schooling disadvantaged children: Racing against catastrophe.* New York: Teachers College Press.

Nieto, S. (1986). Excellence and equity: The case for bilingual education. *Bulletin of the Council on Interracial Books for Children, 17,* 3–4.

Nieto, S. (1999). *The light in their eyes: Creating multicultural learning communities.* New York: Teachers College Press.

Novak, M. (1971). *The rise of the unmeltable ethnics.* New York: Macmillan.

Oakes, J. (1985). *Keeping track: How schools structure inequality.* New Haven: Yale University Press.

Ogbu, J. U. (1990). Overcoming racial barriers to equal access. In J. I. Goodlad & P. Keating (Eds.), *Access to knowledge: An agenda for our nation's schools* (pp. 59–89). New York: College Board.

Oskamp, S. (Ed.). (2000). *Reducing prejudice and discrimination.* Mahwah, NJ: Erlbaum.

Parekh, B. (1986). The concept of multicultural education. In S. Modgil, G. Verma, K. Mallick, & C. Modgil (Eds.), *Multicultural education: The interminable debate* (pp. 19–31). Philadelphia: The Falmer Press.

Parish, T. S., & Fleetwood, R. S. (1975). Amount of conditioning and subsequent change in racial attitudes of children. *Perceptual and Motor Skills, 43,* 907–912.

Parish, T. S., Shirazi, A., & Lambert, F. (1976). Conditioning away prejudicial attitudes in children. *Perceptual and Motor Skills, 43,* 907–912.

Passow, A. H. (Ed.). (1963). *Education in depressed areas.* New York: Teachers College Press.

Peters, W. (1987). *A class divided: Then and now* (Expanded ed.). New Haven: Yale University Press.

Philips, S. U. (1983). *The invisible culture: Communication in classroom and community on the Warm Springs Indian reservation.* New York: Longman.

Phillips, U. B. (1918). *American Negro slavery.* New York: Appleton.

Phinney, J. S., & Rotheram, M. J. (Eds.). (1987). *Children's ethnic socialization: Pluralism and development.* Thousand Oaks, CA: Sage.

Porter, J.D.R. (1971). *Black child, White child: The development of racial attitudes.* Cambridge, MA: Harvard University Press.

Purkey, S. C., & Smith, M. S. (1982). Too soon to cheer? Synthesis of research on effective schools. *Educational Leadership, 40,* 64–69.

Quarles, B. (1953). *The Negro in the Civil War.* New York: Da Capo Press.

Radke, M. J., & Trager, H. G. (1950). Children's perceptions of the social roles of Negroes and Whites. *Journal of Psychology, 29,* 3–33.

Ramírez, M., & Castañeda, A. (1974). *Cultural democracy, bicognitive development, and education.* New York: Academic Press.

Ramsey, P. G. (1998). *Teaching and learning in a diverse world: Multicultural education for young children* (2nd ed.). New York: Teachers College Press.

Ravitch, D. (1990). Diversity and democracy: Multicultural education in America. *American Educator, 14,* 16–48.

Ready, T., Edley, C., Jr., & Snow, C. E. (Eds.). (2002). *Achieving high educational standards for all: Conference summary.* Washington, DC: National Academy Press.

Richardson, V., Casanova, U., Placier, P., & Guilfoyle, K. (1989). *School children at risk.* New York: The Falmer Press.

Riessman, F. (1962). *The culturally deprived child.* New York: Harper & Row.

Robinson, A. L., Foster, C. C., & Ogilvie, D. H. (Eds.). (1969). *Black studies in the university.* New York: Bantam Books.

Roche, A. M. (1996). Carter G. Woodson and the development of transformative scholarship. In J. A. Banks (Ed.), *Multicultural education, transformative knowledge, and action: Historical and contemporary perspectives* (pp. 91–114). New York: Teachers College Press.

Rodriguez, R. (1982). *Hunger of memory: The education of Richard Rodriguez: An autobiography.* Boston: Godine.

Rutter, M., Maughan, B., Mortimore, P., Ouston, I., & Smith, A. (1979). *Fifteen thousand hours: Secondary schools and their effects on children.* Cambridge, MA: Harvard University Press.

Ryan, W. (1971). *Blaming the victim.* New York: Vintage Books.

Sadker, M. P., & Sadker, D. M. (1994). *Failing at fairness: How America's schools treat girls.* New York: Macmillan.

Salzman, J., Smith, D. L., & West, C. (Eds.). (1996). *Encyclopedia of African-American culture and history* (5 vols.). New York: Macmillan.

Schlesinger, A., Jr. (1991). *The disuniting of America: Reflections on a multicultural society.* Knoxville, TN: Whittle Direct Books.

Shade, B. J. (1982). Afro-American cognitive style: A variable in school success? *Review of Educational Research, 52,* 219–244.

Shade, B. J. (Ed.). (1989). *Culture, style and the educative process.* Springfield, IL: Charles C. Thomas.

Shirley, O.L.B. (1988). *The impact of multicultural education on self-concept, racial attitude and student achievement of Black and White fifth and sixth graders.* Unpublished doctoral dissertation, University of Mississippi.

Siddle Walker, V. (1996). *Their highest potential: An African American community school in the segregated south.* Chapel Hill: University of North Carolina Press.

Sizemore, B. A. (1972). Social science and education for a Black identity. In J. A. Banks & J. D. Grambs (Eds.), *Black self-concept: Implications for education and social science* (pp. 141–170). New York: McGraw-Hill.

Slaughter, D. T. (Ed.). (1988). *Black children and poverty: A developmental perspective.* San Francisco: Jossey-Bass.

Slavin, R. E. (1979). Effects of biracial learning teams on cross-racial friendships. *Journal of Educational Psychology, 71,* 381–387.

Slavin, R. E. (1985). Cooperative learning: Applying contact theory in desegregated schools. *Journal of Social Issues, 41,* 45–62.

Slavin, R. E., Karweit, N. L., & Madden, N. A. (1989). *Effective programs for students at risk.* Boston: Allyn & Bacon.

Sleeter, C. E. (Ed.). (1991). *Empowerment through multicultural education.* Albany: State University of New York Press.

Sleeter, C. E., & Grant, C. A. (1987). An analysis of multicultural education in the United States. *Harvard Educational Review, 7,* 421–444.

Sleeter, C. E., & Grant, C. A. (1991). Race, class, gender, and disability in current textbooks. In M. W. Apple & L. K. Christian-Smith (Eds.), *The politics of the textbook* (pp. 78–110). New York: Routledge.

Sleeter, C. E., & Grant, C. A. (1999). *Making choices for multicultural education: Five approaches to race, class, and gender* (3rd ed.). New York: Wiley.

Smitherman, G. (1977). *Talking and testifying: The language of Black America.* Boston: Houghton Mifflin.

Sowell, T. (1984). *Civil rights: Rhetoric or reality?* New York: Morrow.

Spencer, M. B. (1982). Personal and group identity of Black children: An alternative synthesis. *Genetic Psychology Monographs, 106,* 59–84.

Spencer, M. B. (1985). Cultural cognition and social cognition as identity correlates of Black children's personal-social development. In M. B. Spencer, G. K. Brookins, & W. R. Allen (Eds.), *Beginnings: The social and affective development of Black children* (pp. 215–234). Hillsdale, NJ: Erlbaum.

Spencer, M. B. (1987). Black children's ethnic identity formation: Risk and resilience of caste-like minorities. In J. S. Phinney & M. J. Rotheram (Eds.), *Children's ethnic socialization: Pluralism and development* (pp. 103–116). Beverly Hills, CA: Sage.

Stampp, K. M. (1956). *The peculiar institution: Slavery in the antebellum South.* New York: Vintage Books.

Steele, S. (1990). *The content of our character: A new vision of race in America.* New York: St. Martin's Press.

Stephan, W. (1999). *Reducing prejudice and stereotyping in schools.* New York: Teachers College Press.

Sue, D. W. (Ed.). (1981). *Counseling the culturally different: Theory and practice.* New York: Wiley.

Sung, B. L. (1967). *The story of the Chinese in America.* New York: Macmillan.

Suzuki, B. H. (1984). Curriculum transformation for multicultural education. *Education and Urban Society, 16,* 294–322.

Taba, H. (1950). *With a focus on human relations: A story of the eighth grade.* Washington, DC: American Council on Education.

Taba, H. (1951). *Diagnosing human relations needs.* Washington, DC: American Council on Education.

Taba, H. (1952). *Curriculum in intergroup relations: Case studies in instruction.* Washington, DC: American Council on Education.

Taba, H. (1967). *Teacher's handbook for elementary social studies.* Palo Alto, CA: Addison-Wesley.

Taba, H., Brady, E. H., & Robinson, J. T. (1952). *Intergroup education in public schools.* Washington, DC: American Council on Education.

Taba, H., & Elkins, D. (1966). *Teaching strategies for the culturally disadvantaged.* Chicago: Rand McNally.

Taba, H., & Van Til, W. (Eds.). (1945). *Democratic human relations* (16th yearbook). Washington, DC: National Council for the Social Studies.

Taba, H., & Wilson, H. (1946). Intergroup education through the school curriculum. *Annals of the American Academy of Political and Social Science, 244,* 19–25.

Takaki, R. (1989). *Strangers from a different shore: A history of Asian Americans.* New York: Little, Brown.

Takaki, R. (1993). *A different mirror: A history of multicultural America.* New York: Little, Brown.

Tetreault, M. K. (2003). Classrooms for diversity: Rethinking curriculum and pedagogy. In J. A. Banks & C.A.M. Banks (Eds.), *Multicultural education: Issues and perspectives* (4th ed. rev., pp. 152–173). New York: Wiley.

Theodorson, G. A., & Theodorson, A. G. (1969). *A modern dictionary of sociology.* New York: Barnes & Noble Books.

Trager, H. G., & Yarrow, M. R. (1952). *They learn what they live: Prejudice in young children.* New York: Harper & Brothers.

Turner, F. J. (1989). The significance of the frontier in American history. In C. A. Milner II (Ed.), *Major problems in the history of the American West* (pp. 2–34). Lexington, MA: Heath. (Original work published 1894)

Valenzuela, A. (1999). *Subtractive schooling: U.S.–Mexican youth and the politics of caring.* Albany: State University of New York Press.

Van Ausdale, D. V., & Feagin, J. R. (2001). *The first R: How children learn racism.* Lanham, MD: Rowman & Littlefield.

Van Sertima, I. (Ed.). (1988). *Great Black leaders: Ancient and modern.* New Brunswick, NJ: Rutgers University, Africana Studies Department.

Vickery, W. E., & Cole, S. G. (1943). *Intercultural education in American schools: Proposed objectives and methods.* New York: Harper & Brothers.

Wesley, C. H. (1935). *Richard Allen: Apostle of freedom.* Washington, DC: The Associated Publishers.

White, A. O. (1973). The Black leadership class and education in antebellum Boston. *Journal of Negro Education, 42,* 505–515.

Williams, F. (Ed.). (1970). *Language and poverty: Perspectives on a theme.* Chicago: Markham.

Williams, G. W. (1882–83). *History of the Negro race in America from 1619 to 1880: Negroes as slaves, as soldiers, and as citizens* (2 vols.). New York: Putnam.

Williams, J. E., Best, D. L., Wood, F. B., & Filler, I. W. (1973). Changes in the connotations of racial concepts and color names: 1963–1970. *Psychological Reports, 33,* 983–996.

Williams, J. E., & Edwards, C. D. (1969). An exploratory study of the modification of color and racial concept attitudes in preschool children. *Child Development, 40,* 737–750.

Williams, J. E., & Morland, J. K. (1976). *Race, color, and the young child.* Chapel Hill: University of North Carolina Press.

Wilson, W. J. (1987). *The truly disadvantaged: The inner city, the underclass, and public policy.* Chicago: University of Chicago Press.

Wirth, L. (1928). *The ghetto.* Chicago: University of Chicago Press.

Woodson, C. G. (1933). *The mis-education of the Negro.* Washington, DC: The Associated Publishers.

Woodson, C. G. (1968). *The education of the Negro prior to 1861.* New York: Arno Press. (Original work published 1919)

Woodson, C. G., & Wesley, C. H. (1922). *The Negro in our history.* Washington, DC: Associated Publishers.

Wortham, A. (1981). *The other side of racism: A philosophical study of Black race consciousness.* Columbus: Ohio State University Press.

Wyman, D. S. (1984). *The abandonment of the Jews: America and the Holocaust, 1941–1945.* New York: Pantheon.

Yawkey, T. D. (1973). Attitudes toward Black Americans held by rural and urban White early childhood subjects based upon multi-ethnic social studies materials. *Journal of Negro Education, 42,* 164–169.

Yonezawa, S., Wells, A. S., & Serna, I. (2002). Choosing tracks: "Freedom of choice" in detracking schools. *American Educational Research Journal, 39*(1), 37–67.

2

CURRICULUM THEORY AND MULTICULTURAL EDUCATION

Geneva Gay

University of Washington, Seattle

General curriculum theorists and multiculturalists typically have not all used the same conceptual paradigms, methodologies, and variables of analysis in developing their research and scholarship. However, they are not as discordant in principles, concepts, and intentions as initial impressions might suggest. Many logical and ideological similarities and potential connections exist between multicultural education and general curriculum theory, as well as among several specific curriculum theories that emerged in the United States during the 20th century. This is particularly true of policies, programs, and practices designed to make the educational enterprises more inclusive of, responsive to, and effective for ethnically diverse student populations. These connections and intersections are often more implicit than explicit. They are becoming increasingly apparent as multicultural education theorists contextualize their arguments in broader educational ideas, issues, and movements, and as general curriculum theorists respond more and more to the sociocultural realities of contemporary local, regional, national, and global schools and societies.

Some of the conceptual connections between general curriculum theory and multicultural education are explicated in this discussion. The conceptual model of curriculum theory developed by George Beauchamp (1968) guides this analysis. The major premises that anchor the discussion are that multicultural education (a) is consistent with and a continuation of some long-standing principles, values, and precedents in U.S. education; (b) is compatible with the basic egalitarian principles of democracy; and (c) has both intrinsic and instrumental value for translating some of the most fundamental ideals of Amer-

ican education into practice for select constituent groups of students.

GENERAL THEORETICAL PARAMETERS AND MULTICULTURAL EDUCATION

In a seminal document first published in the late 1960s, Beauchamp (1968) defines the conceptual parameters of curriculum theory. He argues that, like many other aspects of the education enterprise, curriculum theory and practice are driven more by external sociocultural pressures and political expediencies than by systematic and thoughtful internal analysis. Furthermore, curriculum theory operates at both a macro and a micro level. It encompasses several subtheories, as well as being a subtheory within educational theory. Some of its subtheories are curriculum design, development, implementation, history, inquiry, and evaluation. Curriculum theory is best understood when its functions and effects are explained in relation to other subtheories such as administration, instruction, educational psychology, policy studies, supervision, and evaluation. These interactive relationships evoke an ecological perspective in which theories about curriculum are shaped by knowledge and practice within the field, as well as by developments in other educational and societal domains (Beauchamp, 1968; Glatthorn, 1987; Ornstein & Hunkins, 1998; Schubert, 1986).

Beauchamp (1968) defines curriculum theory as "a set of related statements that give meaning to a school's curriculum by pointing up the relationships among its elements and by directing its development, its use, and its evaluation" (p. 66). Subsequent definitions of curriculum theory include essentially the same elements as those stated by Beauchamp. For example, Zais (1976) describes it as "a generalized set of logically interrelated definitions, concepts, propositions, and other constructs that represent a systematic view of curriculum phenomena" (p. 87), serving as a policy to guide curriculum practices. A decade later, Glatthorn (1987) noted that "a curriculum theory is a set of related educational concepts that afford a systematic and illuminating perspective on curricula phenomena" (p. 96). Ornstein and Hunkins (1998) suggest theory is "an expression of belief" that "challenges us to analyze why we think a curriculum should be developed in a certain way for particular students and focus on certain content" (p. 173). These and other theorists agree that the primary functions of curriculum theory are to define, describe, explain, critique, and evaluate phenomena endemic to the field, and to guide curriculum practice.

According to Schubert (1986), there are three generic types of curriculum theory: descriptive, prescriptive, and critical. Macdonald (1977) agrees with this conclusion but uses different labels (controls and hermeneutic) for two of the three types of theorizing. *Descriptive, or control, curriculum theory* focuses on practice and uses an empirical database to analyze existing realities. It is based on the linear-expert model of curriculum design that was first introduced by Franklin Bobbitt (1918) and then popularized by Ralph Tyler (1949). *Prescriptive or hermeneutic theory* "provides new viewpoints, perspectives, and interpretations of the human condition" (Molnar & Zahorik, 1977, p. 6). It assumes that curriculum is a set of recommendations, seeks to establish norms for action, and attempts to clarify and defend those principles upon which these advocacies are founded. *Critical theory* deals with practice and perspective, understanding and control, and the dialectical relationship between theory and practice. Its ultimate value commitment is human emancipation. Its goals are to expose contradictions in culture, explain how conventional curriculum and instruction perpetuate the socioeconomic exploitation and subjugation present in society at large, and create more egalitarianism in schools and societies. These goals are explicated through a combination of analytical, descriptive, and prescriptive analyses of schooling in particular historical and sociopolitical contexts (Aronowitz & Giroux, 1990; Giroux, 1983; Giroux & McLaren, 1989; Kreisberg, 1992; McLaren, 1989; Molnar & Zaharik, 1977; Schubert, 1986).

Another schema for understanding various theoretical conceptions of the nature and functions of curriculum was developed by Miller and Seller (1985). They identify three belief systems from which the educational enterprise is viewed. The *transmission position* emphasizes passing on to students the fund of knowledge, skills, and values that have accumulated over time. The *transaction position* views education as an interactive dialogue between students and the formal program of schooling in which they are given opportunities for inquiring, problem solving, critical thinking, questioning status quo norms, and reconstructing knowledge. The *transformation position* advocates individual responsibility and action, leading to the reconstruction of personal and social life. These positions parallel the descriptive, prescriptive, and critical theories, respectively, discussed earlier.

Generally, five key operations are involved in theory building in any area of scholarly inquiry:

1. Defining the key terms and constructs of the discipline
2. Classifying its known and assumed knowledge
3. Making and testing inferences and predictions
4. Creating physical, visual, and/or verbal models to represent key ideas, events, and interactions
5. Formulating subtheories to broaden the overall scope and conceptual clarity of the theory, and to improve the explanation of the events or issues involved in the design, implementation, and evaluation of the discipline (Beauchamp, 1968; Glatthorn, 1987; Oliva, 1997; Ornstein & Hunkins, 1998; Zais, 1976)

In the late 1960s, Beauchamp (1968) argued that uneven growth was taking place across these components of curriculum theory. While developments in definitions, models, and subtheories were flourishing, little progress was being made in the classifying and inferring/predicting dimensions of curriculum theorizing. Many changes have occurred in the field since then. Several kinds of curriculum inquiry and research are now taking place, and a variety of classification schemata have emerged. Illustrative of the available classification schemes are those proposed for categorizing curriculum theories and theorists (Gay, 1980; Giroux, Penna, & Pinar, 1981; Glatthorn, 1987; Orlosky & Smith, 1978; Pinar, 1974, 1975), types of curriculum designs (Ornstein & Hunkins, 1998; Smith, Stanley, & Shores, 1957; Taba, 1962; Zais, 1976), and kinds and sources of knowledge and ways of knowing (Eisner, 1985; Foshay, 1975; Phenix, 1964). This also means that curriculum theory is not nearly as prescriptive as it once was; more descriptive and critical theories now exist.

Multicultural education encompasses elements of all three types of theorizing. *Descriptive* analyses of educational systems and conditions that ignore or deny the importance of cultural diversity are frequently used to establish a baseline point of reference for changes. *Critical* explanations are then used to determine why these systems should be changed to be more representative of and responsive to ethnic and cultural diversity. *Prescriptive* recommendations suggest what the changes should embody in order for education to be maximally beneficial to an ever-increasing variety of culturally, ethnically, racially, socially, and linguistically pluralistic individuals, institutions, and communities. Multicultural education is also simultaneously transmissive, transactive, and transformative. It teaches content about culturally pluralistic contributions to humankind and U.S. society; engages students actively and interactively with their own and others' cultural identity; and develops the kind of social consciousness, civic responsibility, and political activism needed to reconstruct society for greater pluralistic equality, truth, inclusion, and justice.

When Beauchamp's conceptual model of curriculum theorizing is applied to multicultural education, several intersections are readily apparent. First, like general curricularists, multiculturalists use research findings, paradigms, principles, concepts, and perspectives from a variety of social science disciplines to construct their ideas about why culturally pluralistic education is imperative, how it can and should be implemented, and the benefits to be derived from it. These statements borrow heavily from sociology, cultural anthropology, political science, social psychology, cross-cultural communications, and sociolinguistics. Second, multicultural education theory dealing with curriculum and instruction is more fully developed than that concerned with administration, counseling, and evaluation. Third, multicultural education inferences and predictions based on empirical research are fewer in number and lesser in quality than theoretical definition of terms, classifications of knowledge, and conceptual models for designing curricula. Fourth, like general curriculum, most of the theoretical developments during the formative years of multicultural education were devoted to defining the field and clarifying its fundamental goals and purposes. As a result, its theoretical scholarship tends to be more prescriptive and critical than descriptive.

DEFINITIONS IN GENERAL CURRICULUM THEORY

Within curriculum theory, the key technical concept demanding definition is *curriculum* itself, and the primary challenge is to explain the relationships among the variables embedded within it. Beauchamp (1968) suggests that there are three major ways in which curriculum is theoretically conceived. First, it is viewed as a *substantive phenomenon,* or a document of some sort. Thus it is common for theorists to talk about "a curriculum." The major relationships that must be explained are those existing among the internal components of the document. Tyler (1949) describes these as four fundamental questions:

1. What educational purposes should the school seek to attain?
2. What educational experiences can be provided to achieve these purposes?

3. How can these educational experiences be effectively organized?
4. How can we determine whether these purposes are being accomplished?

Additionally, the sociocultural influences that impinge upon the curriculum need to be explained to make clear the reasons for primary decisions made about its components.

Another common conception of curriculum is as a *system,* or an organized framework in which all curricular decisions are made. It implies a cluster of relationships having to do with the "human engineering required in the process of curriculum development and curriculum usage" (Beauchamp, 1968, p. 69). The major tasks inherent in a curriculum system determine the parameters for establishing these relationships. They deal with developing, implementing, and evaluating the curriculum.

The third theoretical definition of curriculum is as *an area of professional scholarship and research.* Its purpose is to advance knowledge about various curricula and curriculum development systems. To explain the relationships among curriculum variables, individuals involved in these pursuits typically evoke psychological and philosophical foundations; historical precedents and experiences; social, political, and cultural influences; and research designs and procedures.

DEFINITIONS OF MULTICULTURAL EDUCATION

The various ways in which multicultural education is defined illustrate Beauchamp's notion (1968) that multiple approaches to defining a discipline are natural and need not impede its theoretical development. They vary with respect to content selection, methodological focus, and referent group orientations. However, these definitions can be grouped into several recurrent categories. Banks and Banks (2001, p. 1) identify the major ones when they explain that

multicultural education is an idea, an educational reform movement, and a process whose major goal is to change the structure of educational institutions so that male and female students, exceptional students, and students who are members of diverse racial, ethnic, language, and cultural groups will have an equal chance to achieve academically in school.

Garcia (1982), Grant (1977a, 1978), and L. Frazier (1977) agree and add that multicultural education is a concept, a framework, a way of thinking, a philosophical viewpoint, a value orientation, and a set of criteria for making decisions that better serve the educational needs of culturally diverse student populations.

As a *concept, idea, or philosophy,* multicultural education is a set of beliefs and explanations that recognize and value the importance of ethnic and cultural diversity in shaping lifestyles; social experiences; personal identities; and educational opportunities of individuals, groups, and nations. Consequently, it has both descriptive and prescriptive dimensions. Descriptively, it recognizes the ethnically and culturally diverse social structures of the United States and their relationship to national institutions, value beliefs, and power systems. Multicultural education also prescribes what should be done to ensure the equitable treatment for diverse groups (Baptiste, 1986). Parekh (1986) equates multicultural education with a refined version of liberalism, education for freedom, and celebration of the inherent plurality of the world. Bennett (1999), Banks (1990, 1991–92), Gay (1988, 1994), Garcia (1982), and Barber (1992) proclaim that it is a crucial part of the democratic imperative for U.S. schools and society.

Two influential professional organizations—the American Association of Colleges for Teacher Education (AACTE) and the Association for Supervision and Curriculum Development (ASCD)—published policy statements in the 1970s on multicultural education. They endorsed the idea that multicultural education is a set of value beliefs or a philosophy on the importance of students' learning about cultural diversity. The essence of the AACTE statement (1973) is that since there is "no one model American," schools should design and implement instructional programs that value and preserve cultural pluralism. ASCD (Grant, 1977b) connects multicultural education to its own value traditions by defining it as a humanistic concept; a conduit of quality education for ethnically diverse student populations; and an embodiment of principles of equality, human rights, social justice, and multiple realities. The conception of multicultural education as an alternative way of thinking about how to provide quality education for diverse groups within the context of democratic ideas is further refined by Baptiste (1979), Bennett (1999), Banks (1990, 1997), Sleeter (1991), Garcia (1982), Gay (1988, 1990, 1994), and Nieto (2000).

Gay (1988, 2000) proposes that educational equality and excellence for children of color, those from economically impoverished backgrounds, recent immigrants, and English language learners are inextricably interwoven. Pedagogical equality that reflects culturally sensitive instructional strategies is a precondition for and a means of achieving maximal academic outcomes for culturally diverse students. Banks (1990) argues that multicultural and citizenship education are reciprocal, interdependent processes. He explains that citizenship education in and for a culturally diverse society must help students "develop the knowledge, attitudes, and skills needed not only to participate in, but also to transform and reconstruct society . . . to become literate and reflective citizens who can participate productively in the work force . . . [who] care about other people in their communities and . . . take personal, social, and civic action to create a humane and just society" (p. 211). These conceptions of multicultural education satisfy Beauchamp's claim that curriculum theory building involves explaining relationships among the components of a phenomenon and its subtheories.

Multicultural education as a *reform movement* emphasizes revising the structural, procedural, substantive, and valuative components of the educational enterprise to reflect the social, cultural, ethnic, racial, and linguistic diversity of the United States. These elements are implied in Baptiste's explanation (1979) of multicultural education as a "process of institutionalizing the philosophy of cultural pluralism within the educational system" (p. 172). The operative word here is "institutionalizing," which requires systematic changes (Banks, 1992; Gollnick & Chinn, 1998; Nieto, 2000; Sleeter, 1991). Bennett (1999) extends the notion of systematic change by identifying some of the specific elements of a multicultural reform movement. According to her, it must encompass (a) curricula that develop understanding of ethnic groups' cultures, histories, and contributions; (b) processes for students' becoming multicultural in their attitudes, values, beliefs, and behaviors; and (c) action strategies for combating racism and other forms of oppression. Similar prescriptions are offered by Banks (1977, 1992), who contends that multicultural education involves modifications in the total school environment, including policies and politics; classroom instructional interactions, materials, and resources; extracurricular activities; formal and informal curricula; performance appraisal techniques; guidance and counseling; and institutional norms.

Frazier (1977), Gollnick and Chinn (1998), and Banks and Banks (2001) broaden the notion of multicultural education as comprehensive reform by extending the referent groups to include social class, gender, and disability, along with race and ethnicity. Sleeter and Grant (1999) and Sleeter (1996) do likewise, as well as include strong arguments for social reconstruction as the ultimate outcome in their definition of multicultural education. This goal is achieved by teaching social and political action skills and collaboration to bring about a more equitable distribution of resources and opportunities for all oppressed groups. Social transformation and personal empowerment are therefore fundamental themes within and characteristic traits of the conceptions of multicultural education as an emancipatory pedagogical and social reform movement.

Increasingly, multicultural education is seen as a *process* instead of a product. As a process, it is ways of thinking and behaving in educational settings that are pervasive and persistent (Banks, 2001b). It requires long-term investments of time and resources, and carefully planned and monitored actions. It evokes images similar to Beauchamp's conception of curriculum as a decision-making or "engineering" system for the creation, implementation, and evaluation of instructional plans. Grant (1978) captures the essence of this conception when he explains why he prefers to use *education that is multicultural* to identify the enterprise instead of *multicultural education*. Rather than a specific, discrete education program (such as social studies, bilingual, or science education), he sees multicultural education as a different approach to the entire educational enterprise in all its forms and functions.

The idea of a decision-making system is also embedded in Hunter's view of multicultural education as "the structuring of educational priorities, commitments, and processes to reflect the reality of cultural pluralism as a fact of life in the United States" (1974, p. 36). The California State Department of Education's policy on multicultural education (1979) says explicitly (as do other state policies, such as those of Iowa, Michigan, Minnesota, and Connecticut) that it is "an interdisciplinary process rather than a single program or a series of activities" (p. 1), or a "mode of experience and learning to be infused and integrated throughout the curriculum and throughout the school program" (p. 9).

Suzuki (1979, 1984) and Sizemore (1981) add the element of a "program" or an "artifact" to the definitional parameters of multicultural education. These are analogous to Beauchamp's conception of curriculum as a substantive phenomenon. Suzuki (1984) describes multicultural education as an interdisciplinary instructional program that "provides multiple learning environments matching the academic, social, and linguistic needs of students" (p. 305). This program also has multiple purposes, among them to (a) develop basic academic skills for students from different race, sex, ethnic, and social-class backgrounds; (b) teach students to respect and appreciate their own cultural groups and others; (c) overcome ethnocentric and prejudicial attitudes; (d) understand the sociohistorical, economic, and psychological factors that have produced contemporary ethnic alienation and inequality; (e) foster ability to analyze critically and make intelligent decisions about real-life ethnic, racial, and cultural problems; and (f) help students conceptualize and aspire toward a vision of a more humane, just, free, and equal society, and acquire the knowledge and skills necessary to achieve it (Suzuki, 1979). Sizemore uses "process" somewhat analogously to "program" in her conception of multicultural education as "the process of acquiring knowledge and information about the efforts of different

groups against adverse agencies and conditions for control of their destinies through the study of the artifacts and substances which emanated therefrom" (pp. 4–5).

A policy statement enacted by the Rochester, New York, School District in 1987 is representative of the way many local education agencies conceptualize multicultural education. This document mandates that "multicultural perspectives" and relevant facts, issues, values, and viewpoints of all cultural groups, especially those who have been historically omitted or misrepresented, be included in the development and dissemination of instructional materials (Swartz, 1989).

Probably the most inclusive and eclectic definition of multicultural education is the one crafted by Nieto (2000). Although many other scholars use multiple elements such as content, process, ideology, and reform in their conceptions of multicultural education, Nieto's is by far the most comprehensive. She places multicultural education in a sociopolitical context and incorporates substantive and procedural components, outcome expectations, and some interpretive comments. The result is a synergistic composite that includes some features of most of the various types of definition discussed here. Nieto states that multicultural education is a pervasive pedagogical process that is antiracist, egalitarian, and inclusive. Furthermore, it permeates the curriculum and instructional strategies used in schools, as well as the interactions among teachers, students and parents, and the very way that schools conceptualize the nature of teaching and learning. Because it uses critical pedagogy as its underlying philosophy and focuses on knowledge, reflection, and action (praxis) as the basis for social change, multicultural education furthers the democratic principles of social justice (Nieto, 2000, p. 305).

Multicultural education also meets the criterion of Beauchamp's third definitional category of theory building. It is a "field of study" because (a) there is a stable community of scholars who devote their professional time primarily, if not exclusively, to it; (b) a growing body of scholarship exists on philosophies and methodologies for incorporating ethnic diversity and cultural pluralism into the educational enterprise; (c) undergraduate and graduate programs at colleges and universities are preparing schoolteachers, administrators, and counselors to implement multicultural education; and (d) there is a considerable degree of continuity and longevity among the cadre of scholars who are leading voices in the field. Textbooks, monographs, journal articles, and book chapters about various multicultural education issues and dimensions are published regularly. Among the most prolific multicultural education authors in the United States are James A. Banks, Carl A. Grant, Geneva Gay, Christine I. Bennett, Christine E. Sleeter, Carlos E. Cortés, Joyce E. King, James

Boyer, Gloria Ladson-Billings, Sonia Nieto, Etta R. Hollins, Cherry McGee Banks, Joel Spring, Valerie Ooka Pang, and William Tate. The work of these scholars (and many others) is well known and well respected in the national and international professional communities of educators. Their visibility and significance extend beyond multicultural education into other disciplines as well, such as social studies, reading and language arts, mathematics, science, literature, sociolinguistics, history, and psychology. Many of these individuals are contributors to this *Handbook.*

These publications are not limited to the United States. A rich body of multicultural and antiracist pedagogical scholarship also is being produced in England, Canada, Australia, various nations in Western Europe, and Asian countries such as Taiwan and Japan (Banks & Lynch, 1986; Crittenden, 1982; Lynch, 1986, 1989; Modgil, Verma, Mallick, & Modgil, 1986; Moodley, 1992; Samuda, Berry, & Laferriere, 1984; Verma, 1989). These developments give an international dimension to the field (see Part Twelve of this *Handbook*).

Major colleges of education and universities throughout the United States are actively engaged in educating students to become multicultural education K–12 teachers, college professors, researchers, and scholars. Some of the leading ones are the University of Wisconsin at Madison, the University of Washington in Seattle, the University of Massachusetts, Indiana University at Bloomington, the University of California at Santa Cruz, the University of Houston, Teachers College at Columbia University, and San Diego State University.

Another strong indicator of multicultural education as a field of study is its presence in the agendas of professional associations. Over time it has become a central theme and determining influence in the programmatic activities of many national educational organizations. For example, the National Education Association (NEA) and the National Council of Teachers of English (NCTE) were among the first to declare their commitments to multicultural education in overt and highly significant ways through the creation of commissions, issuing policy statements, in publications, and at annual conference programs. In 1981, NEA published *Education in the 80s: Multiethnic Education* (edited by James A. Banks). Another publication with a similar theme, purpose, and focus was released in 1992, entitled *Multicultural Education for the 21st Century* and edited by Carlos Diaz. The Association for Supervision and Curriculum Development (ASCD) passed resolutions, developed media materials, published articles in *Educational Leadership,* created ethnically specific interest groups, and sponsored conferences on multicultural education and ethnic and cultural pluralism. Phi Delta Kappa used its journal, *Phi Delta Kappan,* and

topical monographs to disseminate to its members and subscribers the thinking of leading multiculturalists on key issues in the field. Later, the American Educational Research Association (AERA) joined this influential group of organizations by giving increasing attention to issues of ethnic, racial, cultural, and linguistic diversity in its policy statements, governance, and programmatic activities. These productions became what Beauchamp (1968) calls "milestones" in the formative years of multicultural education as a field of study.

In 1973, the National Council for the Social Studies (NCSS) published *Teaching Ethnic Studies* (edited by Banks), which became a best-seller. Three years later, it issued *Curriculum Guidelines for Multiethnic Education* (Banks, Cortés, Garcia, Gay, & Ochoa, 1976). This document—which was revised and reissued in 1992 with a change of title to *Curriculum Guidelines for Multicultural Education*—is the most comprehensive of its kind. It has served as a prototype for numerous groups and individuals interested in developing similar criteria. A 2001 document reminiscent of the NCSS multicultural education guidelines was published by the Center for Multicultural Education at the University of Washington, Seattle; it is entitled *Diversity Within Unity: Essential Principles for Teaching and Learning in a Multicultural Society.* These 12 principles were developed by a consensus panel of scholars who are specialists in race relations and multicultural education. They build upon the belief that schools should "forge a common nation and destiny from the tremendous ethnic, cultural, and language diversity" (p. 5) of the United States. To do this, "educators must respect and build upon the strengths and characteristics that students from diverse backgrounds bring to school . . . [and] help all students acquire the knowledge, skills, and values needed to becoming participating citizens of the commonwealth" (p. 5). The principles are organized into the categories of teacher learning, intergroup relations, student learning, school governance, and assessment.

The premier contribution of the National Council for the Accreditation of Teacher Education (NCATE) to establishing multicultural education as a field of study was to specify the need for its member colleges of education to include ethnically and culturally pluralistic content and experiences in their curricula as a condition of receiving unqualified accreditation. The initial standards were adopted in 1987. They have been revised and reissued several times since then. The latest version was released in 2002 as "Standard 4: Diversity." It requires NCATE member institutions to design, implement, and evaluate "curriculum and experiences for [teacher] candidates to acquire and apply the knowledge, skills, and dispositions necessary to help all students learn" (NCATE, 2002, p. 29). These experiences include working with teacher education and P–K school faculties and students from diverse ethnic, racial, gender, and socioeconomic groups, and demonstrating clearly articulated diversity proficiencies. Some of these proficiencies are understanding the influences of culture, diversity, and inequity on teaching and learning; designing school climates and teaching lessons that incorporate diversity; acquiring knowledge about the learning styles of ethnically diverse groups, and how to be culturally responsive to them in classroom instruction; and demonstrating dispositions that value equity and fairness for diverse students. Teacher education programs also have to include provisions for students to receive systematic evaluative feedback on their diversity development (NCATE, 2002).

Two other significant events mark the emergence of multicultural education as a field of study. The first is two journals dedicated to developing better understanding of ethnic, racial, and cultural diversity. *The Journal of Multicultural Counseling and Development* was started in 1985 by the Association of Multicultural Counseling and Development. Scholars concerned with issues related to the school counseling and guidance of ethnically diverse populations also published a *Handbook of Multicultural Counseling,* first released in 1995 and revised six years later (Ponterotto, 2001). *Multicultural Review* was initiated in 1992 by Greenwood Publishers; it is intended to provide reviews of multicultural materials and information on multiculturalism for a readership primarily of librarians.

The second event was the creation of a new professional organization to serve as a forum for educators committed to and actively engaged in the pursuit of multicultural education. During the 1990 annual conference of the Association for Teacher Education (ATE), 15 members of the Special Interest Group on Multicultural Education met and founded the National Association for Multicultural Education (NAME). Among the participants were nationally known multiculturalists Carl A. Grant of the University of Wisconsin at Madison, H. Prentice Baptiste and James E. Anderson of the University of Houston, Pritchy Smith of the University of North Florida, and James B. Boyer of Kansas State University. Rose M. Duhon-Sells of Southern University was designated the first chair; she organized the first national convention, which took place in New Orleans in February 1991. NAME released the first issue of its journal, *Multicultural Education,* in summer 1993. In 1999, the name changed to *Multicultural Perspectives.*

CLASSIFYING CURRICULUM THEORIZING

In addition to defining their domain of inquiry and its component parts, theorists arrange information about curriculum phenomena into coherent, integrated schemata to enhance the clarity of its meaning (Beauchamp, 1968; Ornstein & Hunkins, 1998). These efforts have generated a variety of classification systems in both general curriculum and multicultural education. Illustrative of the schemas available for organizing general curriculum knowledge are those devised by Eisner and Vallance (1974), Pinar (1974, 1975), Orlosky and Smith (1978), Gay (1980), and Glatthorn (1987). Frequently referenced classification systems in multicultural education are those developed by Banks (2001a, 2001b), Gibson (1976), Gay (1983, 1990), and Sleeter and Grant (1999).

Some curriculum theories are classified according to developmental maturity and increasing complexity. For Glatthorn (1987), the existence of an empirical database to support speculative hypotheses is what distinguishes between basic and more complex curriculum theories. According to him, *basic theory* sets up logically deduced but empirically untested hypotheses to explain curriculum phenomena and employs concepts that are not systematically refined in great detail. By comparison, *complex theory* is "an exclusive conceptual scheme for explaining an entire universe of inquiry" (p. 97).

The collective body of multicultural education theorizing is transitional and falls somewhere between these two polar positions. Much of it continues to be derived from logical deductions instead of an empirical database; it is therefore basic theory. However, the concepts and principles used to explain its major tenets are increasingly interdisciplinary and integrative, and include greater depth of conceptual analysis. Empirical databases verifying some of the subtheories are emerging (Gay, 1983, 1990, 2000). For example, explanations and justifications of what should be taught about ethnic and cultural diversity include reasoning that examines the intrinsic and instrumental value of multicultural knowledge and ways of knowing; the sociological and political needs of culturally pluralistic local, national, and global communities; the psychoemotional dispositions of culturally different students; the social construction of knowledge; skills needed for maximum personal development of individual students; and the reconstruction of society to achieve democratic equality within the context of racial, ethnic, cultural, and linguistic diversity.

Another set of criteria employed to classify curriculum knowledge addresses the degree of innovation and unorthodoxy evident in the primary conceptual orientations that theorists use in framing their arguments. Pinar (1975) and Giroux et al. (1981) use these criteria to classify general curriculum theorists as traditionalists, conceptual empiricists, or reconceptualists. *Traditionalists* are concerned primarily with the expeditious transmission of the cultural heritage of dominant society through a fixed body of knowledge and the perpetuation of the existing social order. Individuals such as Franklin Bobbitt, Ralph Tyler, and advocates of "back to basics" fall into this category. *Conceptual empiricists* such as Robert Gagné, Hilda Taba, James Popham, Joseph Schwab, and Jerome Bruner base their theorizing on data derived from research methodologies patterned after the physical and natural sciences. From these results, they attempt to compile general principles that will enable educators to predict and control what happens in schools. *Reconceptualists* such as William Pinar, Henry Giroux, James Macdonald, Maxine Greene, and Dwayne Huebner interpret and explain social, political, and economic factors impinging upon the structures, processes, and effects of schooling. They also explain how class conflict and unequal distribution of power correlate with access to high-quality, high-status educational opportunities and with academic achievement (Giroux et al., 1981; Pinar, 1974, 1975; McLaren, 1989).

In Glatthorn's assessment (1987), all of these schemas are lacking in one way or another. This discontent prompted him to create another system for classifying curriculum theory. He relies upon the work of Huenecke (1982) and Schwab (1970) to construct the conceptual parameters of his categories, which group theorists on the basis of their primary domain of inquiry within the curriculum field. The resulting classifications are structure-oriented, value-oriented, content-oriented, and process-oriented styles of curriculum theorizing.

Structure-oriented theorists analyze substantive components of the curriculum, their interrelationship, who makes decisions about them, and how these decisions are made. These theories are primarily descriptive in style and intent and evoke Beauchamp's notation (1968) of curriculum as a decision-making or engineering system.

Curriculum theories that are *value-oriented* are generally critical and transformative in nature. They analyze the value beliefs and assumptions that undergird curriculum actions and artifacts, envision educational possibilities that are less hegemonic and not skewed toward perpetuating the power and privilege of middle-class European American males, and promote more humane, just, and egalitarian learning and living across class, race, and gender categories. Glatthorn describes the work of these theorists as "educational consciousness-raising" (1987, p. 101) and identifies them as reconceptualists and critical theorists. Leading advocates include Pinar (1974, 1975), Giroux (1983, 1988, 1992), Peter McLaren (1989), Macdonald (1974, 1975, 1977), Michael Apple (1979), George Counts (1932), Huebner (Hillis, 1999), Greene (1978), and Nel Noddings (1992, 2002). Some, such as Macdonald, focus their discussion on the human condition, the search for personal transcendence, and the struggle of individuals to actualize the whole self. Others, like Noddings, emphasize building learning communities that are based on ethics of caring, collaboration, and reciprocity among students.

These person-oriented curriculum theorists gain support for their ideas from humanistic and perceptual psychologists such as the contributing authors to *Perceiving, Behaving, Becoming* (Combs, 1962) and Carl Rogers (1983). They contend that education is essentially a humanistic and moral endeavor; the learning process should engage students actively in constructing personal meaning; the journey toward self-actualization is a dialectic and dialogic interaction between self and society, explicit and implicit knowledge, change and stability; and the ultimate goal of education is to develop autonomous, self-actualizing individuals.

Other value-oriented theorists such as Apple (1979), Counts (1932), Giroux (1983, 1988, 1992), and McLaren (1989) ground their explanations of curriculum purposes and functions in analyses of the social milieu, the interrelationship between schools and society, cultural hegemony, uneven distribution of economic resources and political power, knowledge as cultural capital and a social construction, and the transformation of society and schools. More specific dimensions of these emphases are summarized by Giroux (1992) in his descriptions of border pedagogy, one of the operational tools of critical theory. Among its most salient features are linking education to critical social analysis and the imperative of representative democracy; advocating struggle against inequality; encouraging sociopolitical actions to ensure the human rights of oppressed and marginalized groups; and envisioning a new educational and social order that is more inclusive of a wider variety of students from various gender, class, racial, and ethnic groups. Although Dewey typically is not identified as a critical theorist or reconceptualist, he advocated a moderate version of these same themes, particularly the dialectic relationship among individuals, schools, and societies. They are apparent in his writing, in *My Pedagogic Creed* (1897), *Democracy and Education* (1916), and *The Child and the Curriculum* (1902).

The third type of curriculum theorizing in Glatthorn's classification is *content-oriented*. It attributes primary significance to students, formalized bodies of knowledge, or the social order in determining the selection and organization of curriculum content. Theorists who espouse child-centered curricula (Combs, 1962; Dewey, 1897, 1902; Entwistle, 1970; Jervis & Montag, 1991) argue that the child is the beginning point, the determiner, the center, and the end of the educational process. Therefore every phase of the child's development—the whole child—must be studied and provided for in the educational process. This is a pedagogical and a moral imperative (Entwistle, 1970; Frazier, 1976). Since children are psychological and social beings, and the welfare of individuals and society are inextricably interrelated, education must have both personal and societal development functions. Neither of these dimensions should be compromised by or subordinated to the other, because "if we eliminate the social factor from the child we are left only with an abstraction; if we eliminate the individual factor from society, we are left with only an inert and lifeless mass" (Dewey, 1897, p. 6). To achieve these goals, classroom teachers and curriculum designers need to understand the conditions in which children live, and how they are continuously shaping their intellectual powers, ideas, emotions, values, and behaviors.

Principles of child-centered education and the basic tenets of multicultural education are very similar. Proponents consistently explain that multicultural education has both personal and social content, goals, and consequences. The personal includes self-knowledge, self-affirmation, and self-empowerment of ethnically and culturally different individuals and groups. The social consequences have to do with changing other people's knowledge and attitudes about ethnic, racial, and cultural groups, and making society more reflective of and responsive to cultural diversity. These goals are dialectic. Ethnic and cultural perceptions of self and others are influenced by societal forces, and social conditions can be changed most effectively by individuals who know, value, and promote cultural diversity as a personal and societal strength. Furthermore, since cultural socialization influences every dimension of human values, beliefs, perceptions, and behavior, to demean, reject, or ignore the cultural heritage of diverse groups in curriculum and instruction constitutes an act of psychological and moral violence toward their human dignity (Novak, 1975; Pai, 1984, 1990).

Educators who theorize on what knowledge is most valid and valuable have tended to support either the structure-of-the-disciplines or different-ways-of-knowing viewpoints. The former was argued eloquently and persuasively by Bruner (1960) in *The Process of Education* and by Schwab (1969) in "Education and the Structure of the Disciplines." Bruner recommended that students study school subjects the same way disciplinary specialists (mathematicians, historians, economists, anthropologists, and so on) do. Phenix (1964) proposed that valid school knowledge should be derived from analyzing six distinctive modes of human understanding, or cluster domains of knowledge. These "realms of meaning" are symbolics, empirics, esthetics, synnoetics, ethics, and synoptics.

Ways-of-knowing theorists include the contributing authors to the 1985 Yearbook of the National Society for the Study of Education (NSSE), edited by Eisner, Gardner (1983), and Barbe and Swassing (1979). The NSSE Yearbook identifies eight modes of knowing: aesthetic, scientific, interpersonal, narrative, formal, practical, intuitive, and spiritual. Gardner makes basically the same observations but calls the ways of knowing *multiple intelligences*. His list includes linguistic, logical-mathematical, spatial, musical, bodily-kinesthetic, interpersonal, and intrapersonal

intelligences. Barbe and Swassing maintain that the preferred sensory channels through which individuals receive, process, and retain information are major determinants of learning. The three primary channels of information processing, or "modalities of learning," they identified are visual, auditory, and kinetic.

Process-oriented theories constitute the fourth category in Glatthorn's classification system (1987). They attempt to explain alternative approaches used to create curricula, or to activate what Beauchamp (1968) calls a curriculum engineering system. They analyze the organizational levels at which curriculum development takes place; who participates in the process, and their qualifications, roles, and functions; factors that influence decisions made about various curriculum phenomena; components of the substantive deliberations; how deliberative conflicts and problems are solved; how the scope and sequence of curriculum content are organized; plans for implementing and evaluating curriculum products; and criteria for assessing the quality and effectiveness of the curriculum processes and products.

Gay (1980) identifies four common ways in which curriculum theorists have conceptualized the curriculum development process. The *academic model* assumes that "curriculum development is a systematic process governed by academic rationality and theoretical logic" (p. 122). It also suggests that most curriculum decisions should be made by specialists, and that these decisions be guided by objective criteria, such as the Tyler rationale (Tyler, 1949), that can be applied universally. The *experiential model* is the reverse of the academic model. It concedes that the curriculum-creation process is a subjective, particularistic, and transactional endeavor in which the active involvement of students and teachers as well as environmental contexts are primary factors. The *technical model* of curriculum development is essentially a "scientific production" approach to instructional planning that emphasizes "systems" and "management" principles. It was first articulated by Bobbitt (1918) in his references to instructional planning as "educational engineering" and "scientific curriculum-making." The academic model appeals to academic rationality and theoretical logic to guide its decision making, and the experiential model emphasizes sociocultural and personal contexts; the technical model of curriculum development employs the logic of systems analysis, empiricism, scientific objectivity, and managerial efficiency.

A *pragmatic approach* to curriculum development is essentially an eclectic, political, reactive, and often fragmentary process. Decker Walker (1971) calls it a "naturalistic model" of curriculum development. Thus a pragmatic approach to curriculum planning is "a particularistic, localized process that is specific to the sociopolitical milieu of the school context in which it occurs. It concentrates on what individuals do in the daily operations of school bureaucracies to answer questions about what should be taught and how curriculum should be determined, organized, and evaluated. Of particular interest are the informal political negotiations, power allocations, and consensus building that take place among different interest groups" (Gay, 1980, p. 137).

GENERAL CHARACTERISTICS OF MULTICULTURAL EDUCATION THEORIZING

Most multicultural education theorizing tends to be eclectic in nature, cutting across many of the categories just identified. This is due to several factors. Multiculturalists bring a variety of disciplinary training and perspectives to bear upon their understanding and interpretations of multicultural education purposes, goals, content, methodologies, and benefits. Yet there is a high degree of substantive consensus that undergirds this perspective and methodological diversity. All the individuals and groups involved are seeking basically the same goals: a more equitable and effective educational system for ethnically and culturally diverse students, and a more democratic society in which there is much greater equality, freedom, and justice in all spheres of life. They also agree that the achievement of these goals is dependent upon changes in knowledge, attitudes, values, and human relationships among diverse groups, as well as fundamental structural changes in social, political, economic, and educational institutions (Banks, 1990; Darder, 1991; Nieto, 2000; Suzuki, 1979, 1984).

Multicultural education is essentially an affective, humanistic, and transformative enterprise situated within the sociocultural, political, and historical contexts of the United States. Endeavors of this kind are less amenable than emphases on cognition and conformity in traditional educational programs and practices to single perspectives and interpretations because they are so strongly influenced by values and beliefs. It is therefore not surprising that multicultural education generates eclectic theoretical explanations influenced by multiple disciplinary perspectives and the experiential viewpoints of many groups and individuals.

Another factor that helps account for the diversity and eclecticism within multicultural education theory is the various referent-group orientations that exist in the field. Some multiculturalists use ethnicity as their primary point of reference, while others emphasize gender, social class, and language diversity. These perspectives on common themes are analogous, in principle, to the diversity evident among general curriculum theorists. Some of them concentrate on the design process

but view it from a variety of vantage points; others do likewise with curriculum implementation, content, or evaluation.

Delpit (1988, 1995) provides some additional insights into why multiculturalists routinely incorporate multiple perspectives in their theorizing. She explains that students of color and poverty need to be taught the power codes and skills needed to participate fully in mainstream U.S. life, and strategies for personal fulfillment and social reform. This bicentric agenda accepts as legitimate the expert knowledge of educators and the experiential knowledge of students in creating valid, culturally pluralistic educational programs. Thus, multicultural education attends simultaneously to the personal and the social; content and process; microcultures and the macroculture; facts and experience; cognition and affect; rationality and intuition; self and others; and the past, present, and future. This eclectic orientation permeates and shapes almost all multicultural education theory and scholarship.

The concentration of multicultural education theory on personal development, social reform, and critical analysis is a logical consequence of the fact that it is fundamentally a reconstructive and transformative endeavor. Specifically, child-centeredness, social consciousness and civic responsibility, revisionist scholarship, educational equity, and social reconstruction are the benchmark principles of multicultural education theory. They are seen as operating dialectically to explain why multicultural education, in its substantive components and outcomes, is imperative for all students. Thus multiculturalists point out that their domain has many intrinsic and instrumental values. It can improve the academic achievement of culturally diverse students, as well as facilitate skill development in critical thinking, problem solving, decision making, and social activism needed for the creation of a more humane, egalitarian, democratic, and just society. It has potential for improving the personal competencies and empowerment of all students.

Another common theme in multicultural education theory that makes it consistent with process-, society-, child-, and reformist-centered general curriculum theories is the evocation of the social milieu and how it affects educational decision making. Changing school demographics, disparities in educational opportunities, and inequities in economic resources and political power along ethnic, racial, class, and gender lines are cited as reasons multicultural education is necessary.

Several scholars provide theoretical explanations that are illustrative of these trends. For example, Banks (1990, 1997), Bennett (1999), Nieto (2000), and Sleeter and Grant (1999) suggest that the goal of education is not merely to teach students to fit into the existing workforce, social order, and political structure but also to transform them. Conceding to the status quo "would be inimical to students from different cultural groups because it would force them to experience self alienation [since it fails] to incorporate their voices, experiences, and perspectives" (Banks, 1990, p. 211). Gay (1990, 2000) explains why changing school demographic trends are creating a significant "social distance" between students and teachers, and how this may further complicate making schooling relevant to the personal lives of ethnically, culturally, racially, and linguistically diverse students. She predicts that these social, cultural, and experiential gaps will make "achieving educational quality even more unlikely in the existing structure of schooling" (1990, p. 61).

MULTICULTURAL EDUCATION THEORIES OF KNOWLEDGE AND KNOWING

Furthermore, multicultural education is considered a means of acquiring a more accurate knowledge base and way of knowing about ethnic and cultural diversity in the United States (Asante, 1991–92; Banks, 1990, 1991; Bennett, 1999; Garcia, 1982; Gay, 2001; Hilliard, 1991–92; Nieto, 2000; Sleeter, 1991, 1996; Sleeter & McLaren, 1995; La Belle & Ward, 1994; Hollins, 1996). Banks (2001b) has developed a five-part knowledge typology for use in designing multicultural curriculum and instruction. *Personal/cultural knowledge* is "the concepts, explanations, and interpretations that students derive from . . . experiences in their homes, families, and community cultures" (p. 6). They act as reality screens through which school knowledge is made personally meaningful. *Popular knowledge* is facts, images, values, beliefs, and interpretations that are transmitted through and institutionalized in mass media. Within the context of schools, it is analogous to the *symbolic* (Gay, 1995) and *lived curricula* (Glatthorn, 1987) in form and effect.

The third part of the Banks typology, *mainstream academic knowledge,* is the presumed objective truths—the disciplinary canons—generated by Western-centric research and scholarship. It constitutes the dominant fund of knowledge in the various disciplines, from which the content taught in schools is extracted. *School knowledge* is the information that appears in textbooks, curriculum guides, and other instructional materials routinely used by classroom teachers, as well as the teacher's mediation and interpretation of this information. The fifth type of knowledge in Banks's typology is the bedrock of multicultural education. *Transformative academic knowledge* is concepts, paradigms, perspectives, and explanations that challenge mainstream assumptions about knowledge being neutral and devoid of particularistic human interests. Knowledge

is seen as a social construction, over which no one group has exclusive dominion. This type of knowledge provides alternative interpretations of history, life, and culture of ethnic, gender, and social groups, and it expands disciplinary canons to encompass the cultural diversity that characterizes U.S. society and the human story.

The essence of multicultural education as a pursuit of scholarly truth is summarized cogently by Hilliard (1991–92), Banks (1993), and Mitchell-Powell (1992). Hilliard makes an appeal for eliminating the Eurocentric dominance in the disciplinary knowledge taught in schools by including the contributions of ethnically diverse groups:

The primary goal of a pluralistic curriculum process is to present a truthful and meaningful rendition of the whole human experience. . . . Ultimately, if the curriculum is centered in truth, it will be pluralistic, for the simple fact is that human culture is the product of the struggle of all humanity, not the possession of a single racial or ethnic group. . . . We must awaken to the fact that no academic content is neutral nor is the specific cultural content of any ethnic group universal in and by itself . . . nothing less than the full truth of the human experience is worthy of our schools and our students. (pp. 13–14)

Nieto (2000) agrees with Hilliard that no one "canon of knowledge" stemming from a single monocultural base can ever be effective for the ethnically diverse U.S. student population. Crichlow, Goodwin, Shakes, and Schwartz (1990) offer additional support and clarification of this philosophical position. They credit multicultural education for making explicit a "politics of representation," which historically has been implicit in U.S. schools. This politics of representation "has to do with how a specific kind of knowledge, conception, or symbolic image of and about a thing, event, place or people is constructed" (p. 101). It also involves the "struggle over accuracy versus misrepresentation, emancipatory versus hegemonic scholarship, and the constructed supremacy of Western cultural knowledge transmitted in schools versus the inherent primacy of the multiple and collective origins of knowledge" (p. 102). As a result, no school programs can ever be considered excellent and equitable if they do not help students develop multicultural competence (Nieto, 2000; Gay 1988, 2000). Or, as O'Connor (1989, p. 69) suggests, "teaching must always be engaged in multivoiced dialogues." One of these critical "voices" should be ethnicity (Garcia, 1982). To provide less is to ensure that some cultural experiences, contributions, and perspectives will be ignored, and that ethnically diverse students will be left confused, alienated, and undereducated. These observations are consistent with the 1973 policy statement of the AACTE that there is "no one model American"—meaning, no one ethnic group's tradition, culture, experience, and canon are universally valid.

Banks makes a similar argument in his interpretation of the knowledge reconstruction and social transformation themes embedded in multicultural education. He encourages educators to recognize that the knowledge taught in schools is a form of cultural capital and is a social construction that reflects the values, perspectives, and experiences of the dominant ethnic group. It systematically ignores or diminishes the validity and significance of the life experiences and contributions of ethnic and cultural groups that historically have been vanquished, marginalized, and silenced (Banks, 1990, 1991, 1991–92, 1993, 1997). Delpit (1995), McElroy-Johnson (1993), Darder (1991), and Crichlow et al. (1990) suggest that this kind of intellectual discrimination and oppression can be corrected by "giving voice" to those groups and cultural traditions long silenced in U.S. society and schools. Voice is the power of affirmation, derived from seeing one's cultural heritage accurately represented in school programs, as well as the ability of individual students to express ideas and direct their lives toward the productive fulfillment of psychological and social needs. It is a sense of identity, self, relationships with others, purpose, and ethics (McElroy-Johnson, 1993).

Hegemonic research, teaching, and scholarship can be corrected by revising the traditional canons of knowledge and shifting the paradigms that govern mainstream educational values, structures, procedures, and programs. This shift should be toward the inclusion of more ethnically and culturally diverse contributions, perspectives, and experiences in school curriculum and instruction. Asante (1991–92), Bernal (1987), Drake (1987), and Van Sertima (1985) offer examples of how this works for African Americans. They provide new information and alternative interpretations about culture in ancient Africa and its influences in shaping contemporary African American cultural values and points of view. Different groups and cultures should be portrayed as producers, not just consumers, of knowledge; students should be exposed to multiple ways of knowing, thinking, and being (Crichlow et al., 1990). These transformations are imperative because all youths in the United States must understand that "the future of America is in their hands and that they can shape a new society when the torch is passed to their generation" (Banks, 1990, p. 213). As a result, these students will be more inspired and capable of pursuing freedom, equality, and justice in school and society.

Speaking in a tone and text reminiscent of Hilliard, Nieto, Banks, O'Connor, and Crichlow and colleagues, Mitchell-Powell (1992) highlights the themes of personal empowerment, knowledge reconstruction, and social reform ingrained in multicultural education. In her editor's notes for the April 1992 issue of *Multicultural Review*, she advises the readership (primarily librarians) to understand that appreciation of the U.S. common culture and values is enhanced by a recognition of the multiplicity of contributions that ethnically diverse groups have made. Moreover, for children to survive and prosper in a society and world destined for dramatic demographic, economic, social, and political changes, multicultural education is a necessity. Henry (1990) makes basically the same claims in his assessment of the broad-based effects of "the browning of America" on schools and society. Barber (1992) adds compelling explanations about why anticanonical curricular innovations and multicultural education are fundamentally products of Western cultural ideals. Their underlying principles include:

a conviction that individuals and groups have a right to self-determination; a belief in human equality coupled with a belief in human autonomy; the tenet which holds that domination in social relations, however grounded, is always illegitimate; and the principle that reason and the knowledge issuing from reason are themselves socially embedded in personal biography and social history, and thus in power relations. (p. 147)

Virtually all multicultural educators endorse these ideas and agree with the conclusion that when we educate our children for and about cultural diversity we enrich and empower ourselves as well as come closer to achieving a truly democratic civic society.

SPECIFIC CLASSIFICATIONS OF MULTICULTURAL EDUCATION THEORIES

This sample of a few prominent individuals, ideas, and explanations represents directional trends in multicultural education theory; it illustrates how they are compatible with some of the emphases and analyses in general curriculum theory. However, this is not the only kind of development taking place in multicultural education theory. Some classification schemas are unique to the field and illuminate theoretical developments specific to multicultural education. Many of them focus on distinguishing among the content emphasis, conceptual complexity, and outcome intentions of various program designs. Those developed by Gibson (1976) and Sleeter and Grant (1999) are of major and formative significance. They are prototypical because other multicultural educators have either built upon them or developed independent classification schemata that approximate their conceptual patterns, developmental directions, and descriptive features. For those reasons, the Gibson and the Sleeter and Grant models are discussed in greater detail. Elements of other classifications are juxtaposed to show parallels that exist in how educators conceptualize approaches to multicultural curriculum and instruction.

The classifications tend to exemplify Gay's contention (1983, 1992) that since its inception multicultural education theory has been continuously evolving and becoming more comprehensive, integrative, transformative, and scholarly. This growth is evident in the greater depth of analysis, clarity of meaning, and power of persuasion with which proponents talk about issues central to multicultural education, and the linkages they are making between their particular concerns and more general educational priorities such as academic excellence, school reform, knowledge construction, equality, and social justice.

Gibson's (1976) classifications are especially noteworthy because she was one of the first to provide a conceptual, developmental framework for multicultural education. Five approaches emerged from her review of advocacy literature on teaching for and about cultural pluralism on the basis of ethnicity. The first is *education of the culturally different, or benevolent multiculturalism.* Its focus is to help students develop skills for assimilation into mainstream culture and society. The second approach, *education about cultural pluralism,* emphasizes teaching all students culturally diverse knowledge as a basis for promoting better cross-cultural and interethnic group understanding. *Education for cultural pluralism,* the third approach, concentrates on preserving the culture and increasing the political power of groups of color. *Bicultural education* is the fourth approach, which prioritizes teaching ethnically diverse students skills needed to function effectively in their own microcultures and in the macroculture of the United States. This was as far as the field had advanced at the time of her analysis of the related scholarship, but Gibson saw the need for yet another approach to multicultural education. She suggested a fifth possibility, *multicultural education as the normal human experience,* wherein students are taught to operate in many cultural contexts as a routine part of their educational experiences. Her proposal was prophetic in that multiculturalists came to embrace and advocate this idea and to define teaching strategies associated with it. They support this stance with arguments to the effect that multicultural education is inherent to good quality education for all students, and cultural diversity is a personal, social, and national reality of the United States (Gay, 2000; Nieto, 2000; Parekh, 1986; Suzuki, 1979, 1984).

The most ambitious effort to date to organize scholarship systematically in the field of multicultural education was undertaken by Sleeter and Grant (1987, 1999; Grant & Sleeter, 1985, 2001; Sleeter, 1991). They compiled a list of approximately 200 articles on multicultural education, reviewed them, and classified them on the basis of their major themes, emphases, goals, content areas, and referent group orientations. The research technique is similar to that used by Schubert (1980) to catalogue

publications in the field of general curriculum. It builds upon the conceptual framework introduced by Gibson but broadens the units of analysis to include gender, class, and exceptionality, as well as ethnicity.

The Sleeter and Grant analyses (1987, 1999) generated five prevalent techniques in multicultural education theory and practice. The relationship among the various approaches is historical, developmental, progressional, and cumulative with respect to conformity to existing educational and societal structures, as opposed to their reform and transformation. The first approach, *teaching the exceptional and the culturally different,* is the most traditional and assimilationist; it is analogous to Gibson's stage of "education of the culturally different." It emphasizes teaching students who are different from the mainstream the cognitive skills, language, and values required to function in existing educational and societal structures. It is guided by a "deficit philosophy" and often takes the form of compensatory programs such as Upward Bound, Head Start, Outreach, and English-language immersion. Pratte (1983) refers to a similar category in his typology of education for cultural diversity as "restricted multicultural education."

The second category in Sleeter and Grant's classification of multicultural education approaches is *human relations.* It is similar to Gibson's "education *about* cultural differences" and Pratte's "modified restricted multicultural education" approaches, and it is reminiscent of the 1950s intergroup education movement. All of these give priority to promoting intergroup harmony and using a variety of instructional strategies to teach cultural awareness, prejudice and stereotype reduction, and ethnic group identity and pride. The expected outcomes are respect, tolerance, appreciation, and acceptance among diverse ethnic, racial, cultural, and ability groups; self-respect; and an understanding of the interdependence of groups and individuals.

Because the third approach to multicultural education focuses on acquiring knowledge, awareness, respect, and acceptance of one group at a time, Sleeter and Grant identify it as *single-group studies.* The target group of analysis can be chosen on the basis of ethnicity, social class, gender, or exceptionality. Students learn about the targeted group's culture, contributions, and forms of oppression, as well as its perspectives, experiences, and current and historical struggles. The single-group approach to multicultural education also "views school knowledge as political rather than neutral and presents alternatives to the existing Eurocentric, male-dominant curriculum . . . [is] oriented toward political action and liberation . . . [and] . . . develop[s] what Freire calls a 'critical consciousness'" (Grant & Sleeter, 2001, pp. 65–66).

Several other educators include parallel categories in their classification schema, but with some modification.

For example, Gay (1977) refers to her analogous category as "mono-minority studies" and restricts the referent groups to ethnicity. Comparable levels in the categories described by Banks (2001a) are the "contributions" and "additive" approaches. Level I in the Baptiste typology (1986, 1994), which is product-focused, encompasses all of Sleeter and Grant's first three approaches. Single-focus groups and events—such as ethnic celebrations, cultural contributions, and artifacts—and specific topics or courses are added to the regular school curricula to teach cultural diversity, human relations, and single-group studies.

The fourth approach that emerged from the analysis by Grant and Sleeter of the literature on cultural diversity in schools was *multicultural education*. Like the three preceding categories, it too emphasizes prejudice reduction, equal educational opportunities, social justice, and affirmation of cultural diversity. Its distinguishing procedures include dealing with multiple groups at the same time, reforming the total schooling process, and making all students benefactors of culturally sensitive education. The organizing center or core of curriculum reform shifts from separate groups to common concepts, themes, issues, and concerns across groups. Various school practices are revised to model equality and diversity or, as Asante (1991–92) suggests, to achieve pluralism without hierarchy.

Proponents of multicultural education also include conceptual schemes, experiential backgrounds, ways of thinking, and learning styles along with cultural contributions in educational policy, planning, and practice. Thus curriculum and instruction, content and climate, cognition and affect, and text and context are all essential elements for making education more reflective of and responsive to ethnic, cultural, social, language, and ability diversity. For these reasons, Baptiste (1986, 1994) refers to this analogous approach in his typology as Level II and describes it as emphasizing a process for incorporating multicultural products within the conceptual infrastructure or matrix of curriculum and instruction. It integrates culturally pluralistic concepts, content, perspectives, and experiences into all educational components. This category encompasses Gibson's viewpoint (1976) that diversity is a common feature of the human experience; Gay's ideas about "multiple-minority" and "ethnic studies" (1977); Banks's category of "transformation" (2001a); the idea of "knowledge redefinition" proposed by Cushner, McClelland, and Safford (1999); and Kendall's suggestions (1996) for multiculturizing instructional materials and school/classroom climates. Its philosophical orientations, content emphases, and intended outcomes also parallel those of the "four M curriculum" (multilingual, multicultural, multimodal, and multidimensional) envisioned by Sizemore (1979).

Education that is multicultural and social reconstructionist is the fifth category in Sleeter and Grant's classifications. It is committed to developing the critical thinking of students to improve the stratification in U.S. life by race, class, gender, and ability groups; engage in social action to reconstruct society; and empower themselves to control their own destinies. The "comprehensive approach to human relations education" proposed by Colangelo, Dustin, and Foxley (1985) advocates a similar agenda, with multicultural education being grounded in efforts to transform human relations and rethink morality in human conduct. It also approximates Level III in the Baptiste (1986, 1994) typology, in which educational leaders internalize multicultural values and processes. According to Colangelo et al. (1985), a transformative human relations approach to multicultural, nonsexist education "envisions both a present learning environment free of indignity and harassment and the foundations of a future society in which civil and personal equality are the norm, not merely the ideal. Such a goal is 'radical' . . . and awesome" (p. ix). These ideas, along with a related philosophical orientation, permeate the entire educational environment. The expected outcome is the elimination of discrimination, oppression, and inequities of all kinds among racial, ethnic, and cultural groups. This transformation involves accepting the tremendous variation within and among groups of people as an inherent trait of all members of the human family.

The emphases on critical analysis, knowledge reconstruction, social transformation, and personal empowerment among these authors are common themes in virtually all forms of and approaches to multicultural education beyond the most initial and formative ones. They are elaborated in greater detail in the writings of Bennett (1999); Banks (1991–92, 1992, 1993, 2001a, 2001b); Sleeter (1991); Nieto (2000); Banks and Banks (2001); Adams, Pardo, and Schniedewind (1991–92); Gay (1993, 2000); Kendall (1996); and Sleeter and Grant (1999; Grant & Sleeter, 2001). Banks (1992) describes the functions of these curricula as being transformative in helping students develop the knowledge, skills, and values they need to become critical and reflective decision makers; engage in effective political, social, personal, and economic actions; reexamine human conditions in the United States and the world; and understand the perspectives of cultural, ethnic, and social class groups in examining major issues, events, problems, and achievements. In other words, multiple multicultural voices and realities need to be incorporated into all aspects of teaching and learning. Such curricula are consistent with the mission of the multicultural education movement "to use schooling . . . to help shape a future America that is more equal, democratic, and just, and that does not demand conformity to one cultural norm" (Sleeter, 1989, p. 63).

Gay (1992, 1994) analyzes the growth patterns of multicultural education theory that can be extrapolated from the various ways it is conceptualized, and how related implementation techniques are described. Evolution of the theory from its inception in the late 1960s to the present has been developmental and progressional, and grounded in some of the ideological framework of many common values, ideals, and principles of U.S. education in general. Gay concludes that multicultural discourse is characterized by increasing ideological depth, logical coherency, and pedagogical prowess. Out of these analyses and conclusions emerges a portrayal of multicultural education as an interdisciplinary, integrative, inclusive, comprehensive, transformative, liberative, and celebratory enterprise. Consequently, a "central theme of most theoretical perceptions of multicultural education is its potential for revolutionizing education and, ultimately, revitalizing society" (Gay, 1992, p. 53).

MODELS OF MULTICULTURAL CURRICULUM DEVELOPMENT

Another theory-building activity closely related to developing classification systems for organizing knowledge about curriculum is the creation of models. They clarify, illustrate, and visualize key principles, concepts, components, and relationships in the area of inquiry. Beauchamp suggests that "it makes little difference whether models are 'borrowed' from other areas of knowledge or whether they are developed indigenously within the framework of curriculum constructs" (1968, p. 74). Thus, their functional utility is more important than their originality.

Since multicultural education is an eclectic field, it is not surprising that its theorists use elements from a number of conceptual models in other disciplines to construct their own. For example, Banks (1991) and Bennett (1999) often refer to Gordon Allport's work (1958) on the nature of prejudice and his social contact theory to develop antiracist and prejudice-reduction themes in multicultural education. Gay (1985) borrows from social and developmental psychologists such as William Cross (1991) and Erik Erikson (1968) in constructing models of ethnic identity development within the context of multiculturalism. Increasingly, educators such as Sleeter (1989, 1991), Sleeter and Grant (1999), Sleeter and McLaren (1995), Ladson-Billings and Henry (1990), King and Wilson (1990), Crichlow et al. (1990), and Darder (1991) are contextualizing multicultural education within critical theory traditions. Still others are using elements from representative democracy, interpersonal communications, ecological psychology, market-driven economics, cultural anthropology, the social construction of knowledge, the sociology of organizational change, and critical race theory to crystallize what multicultural education means, conceptually and operationally. Many of these efforts are still rather formative and are often restricted to segments of multicultural education rather than encompassing the entire field. Consequently, it is more appropriate to think of multicultural education models as minimodels, partial or skeletal in outline.

Three types of models are included here as representative samples of the trends evident in this dimension of multicultural education theory building. Bennett (1999) borrows from the 1948 United Nations Declaration of Human Rights, and from Native American traditional philosophy on respect for nature, to construct the core values of a "model for global and multicultural perspectives." Its four key democratic values are (a) acceptance of cultural diversity, (b) respect for human dignity, (c) responsibility for global community, and (d) respect for planet earth. These values serve as anchor points for grounding six main goals for multicultural and global perspectives in education: (a) multiple historical perspectives, (b) cultural consciousness, (c) intercultural competence, (d) skills to combat racism and other forms of oppression, (e) awareness of the state of the planet, and (f) social action skills. The dynamic interaction between the goals and values illustrates the mutual concerns of multicultural and global education for human rights, understanding, justice, and equality.

In 1979, Gay created an "integrative multicultural basic skills" (IMBS) model to demonstrate the interactive relationship between general education and multicultural curriculum planning. Of particular importance are principles of developmental growth, routine curriculum planning, and systemic change, and their implications for infusing multiculturalism into core learning skills and educational operations.

The IMBS model is composed of three concentric circles that are reciprocally related. The first circle represents the *core* curriculum—that is, universal basic skills routinely taught in schools, such as literacy, critical thinking, problem solving, and subject-specific content and techniques. The next circle contains the activities that educators view as essential to curriculum creation. These include determining student needs, selecting instructional content and materials, identifying student activities and teaching behaviors, and choosing performance appraisal tools and techniques. The third circle is multicultural resources; it surrounds and encases the other two. This configuration suggests that multicultural resources (culturally pluralistic contributions, perspectives, experiences, histories, cultures) should provide the ecological settings and points of reference for all operational decisions made about curriculum designs. If the IMBS model is used to design and implement an instructional program, students cannot avoid multicultural education if they succeed in learning basic academic skills, because the former serves as the context and text for mastery of the latter.

Banks (1991) has developed three important multicultural education models. One visualizes the organizing center or core of the multicultural curriculum as concepts, topics, themes, events, and experiences common to all ethnic groups but understood from the perspectives of multiple groups. He adds an international dimension to this basic construct by demonstrating how "ethnonational analyses" can be incorporated into the study of major issues affecting all ethnic groups. For example, a multiethnic model of the study of oppression would have students analyzing this issue from the perspectives of various ethnic groups in the United States, such as African Americans, Chinese Americans, and Jewish Americans. An ethno-national model would focus on how the oppression of similar groups has operated in other countries (such as Germany, England, Canada, and Australia). These models demonstrate the differences among mainstream-centered, ethnic-additive, multiethnic, and ethnonational approaches to multicultural education, relative to their central focus or organizing core.

Banks (1991) also has designed visual models to illustrate the study of comparative ethnic and cultural perspectives on key social issues, and use of interdisciplinary conceptual approaches to multicultural education. Both build upon three other ideas commonly advanced in multicultural education theory: (a) the interdependence of ethnic and cultural groups in the United States; (b) the contributions and influence of diverse ethnic, cultural, and social groups in shaping the life and culture of the United States and humankind; and (c) the need to use interdisciplinary conceptual content and techniques to achieve maximum effectiveness in teaching multicultural education.

The third multicultural education model created by Banks (1991) demonstrates the relationships between the various microcultures and the macroculture of the United States. These relationships are depicted as being simultaneously distinct, overlapping, interactive, and reciprocal. The models indicate that members of an ethnic group have some cultural characteristics that are not shared with other groups; some traits that are shared with some ethnic groups but not with others; and some traits that are shared by all ethnic groups by virtue of their being citizens of the United States and members of humankind. These models also illustrate the idea proposed by most multicultural theorists that students need to become multicultural and develop cross-cultural social competencies

so they can function comfortably in their own and others' cultures as well as the national culture.

CONCLUSIONS AND IMPLICATIONS FOR FUTURE DIRECTIONS

The major premise underlying the discussion presented in this chapter is that developments in multicultural education scholarship meet the general criteria of curriculum theorizing. The conceptual model of curriculum theorizing created by George Beauchamp (1968) was used to examine this premise. The analysis reveals that almost all of the elements Beauchamp identified as essential to curriculum theory building are present in multicultural education scholarship. These are defining the key concepts and parameters of the field; classifying knowledge in multicultural education; building models to clarify and explain the imperative of educating about and for cultural diversity; and constructing subtheories to clarify issues related to the design, implementation, and evaluation of multicultural education. This examination has also indicated that the field exhibits many of the same growth trends that are characteristic of other types of curriculum theorizing at comparable stages of development. It suggests further that multicultural education is well on the way to becoming a mature curriculum theory in its own right.

Another noteworthy observation emerges from the analysis. A high degree of consensus exists among multicultural educators on the major principles, concepts, concerns, and directions for changing curriculum and instruction to make them more reflective of and responsive to the racial, ethnic, cultural, social, and linguistic diversity that exists in the United States. Differences are located more in semantics, points of emphasis, and constituent orientations than in the substantive content of what constitutes the essence of multicultural education. This observation defies the claims of many critics that multicultural education is chaotic, confused, lacking in conceptual clarity, and devoid of a consensual voice. A more comprehensive examination of this consensus needs to be conducted. The results will be helpful in minimizing some of the confusion about the purposes and meanings of multicultural education. They also will crystallize the fundamental elements of the field, which in turn can become quality-control criteria for designing multicultural education programs and determining their adequacy and effectiveness.

The analytical technique used in this chapter is a form of metacognition that allows productive and enriching reflective dialogue on multicultural education to take place. It provides a precedent and a methodology for future analysis on how multicultural education is related to other dimensions, trends, and priorities in U.S. educational theory and practice. The field has reached a level of conceptual maturity that warrants more analyses of this kind to explore how multicultural education illustrates universal pedagogical principles, and how it can be appropriately centered within U.S. educational and democratic ideals.

Two other lines of analytical inquiry worthy of pursuit are similar in kind and purpose to the one undertaken in this chapter. First is the premise that multicultural education is not ahistorical; nor does it exist in a theoretical void. Many ideological analogues exist for the major principles and concerns of multicultural education in the United States. They are located in programs that attempt to extend the democratic principles of human dignity, equality, justice, and freedom to the educational arena. Similarities among these and other basic tenets of multicultural education need to be explicated. Some possibilities are progressive, affective, humanistic, open, alternative, developmental, and critical-theory education. The analyses should demonstrate how each initiative is a variation on the common consensus of (a) reforming education for the benefit of students who are underserved by schools, (b) being more inclusive and comprehensive by teaching the whole child, and (c) aligning schooling with the promises of democratic ideals.

The second set of analytical inquiries should explicate the commonly proclaimed contention that multicultural education is a methodological conduit, tool, or bridge for making the schooling process more relevant, representational, and effective for ethnically and culturally different students. These claims are often made without sufficient explanation relative to their practical operations. The absence of these details limits the reformative potential of multicultural education, as well as making it susceptible to misinterpretations and distortions. Carefully executed analyses that explain the *operational* elements of multicultural education—which can be used to improve teaching and learning at the *functional level*—will be a significant contribution to its theory and practice. They also will generate a rich body of variables and hypotheses capable of being tested empirically as to which operational features are most effective, and under what kinds of conditions.

Further analysis of the prominent bridging potentials of multiculturalism to make general education more successful for culturally different students is needed in matching teaching and learning styles; extending the democratic principles of equality, freedom, and justice to the education of ethnically diverse students; improving the empowerment of diverse students through self-knowledge and self-affirmation; developing personal competence and sociopolitical efficacy; increasing mastery of basic literary and subject-matter skills; and using culturally specific materials and methods to teach common learning outcomes to ethnically diverse students. Educational practitioners and researchers need help in specifying the action or behavioral dimension of these principles before they can act responsibly upon them. In fact, decisions to act on or not to act on implementing multicultural education may be direct reflections of the extent to which educators understand it operationally. Therefore, more analytical research and scholarship in multicultural education are imperative to its future survival, integrity, and progress.

Future reflective analysis undoubtedly will reveal that multicultural education is very Western and American in spirit and intent. It grew out of a libertarian philosophy and embodies its major principles. It falls well within the "critical and alternative voice traditions" of U.S. education. It shares with critics of this persuasion the belief that democratic and human rights imperatives demand that existing educational programs and practices be reformed to make them more accessible and responsive to ethnic, racial, and social groups that historically have been disenfranchised educationally, economically, and politically.

Educational equity and excellence for all children in the United States are unattainable without the incorporation of cultural diversity in all aspects of the educational enterprise. Curriculum plays a key role in this process; it is a powerful avenue through which multiculturalism can penetrate the core of educational systems. Consequently, more exploration of the interconnections among specific types of curricular innovations and ideologies and particular elements of multicultural education is fundamental to maximizing school success for students from diverse racial, ethnic, cultural, linguistic, and social-class backgrounds.

References

Adams, B. S., Pardo, W. E., & Schniedewind, N. (1991–92). Changing "the way we do things around here." *Educational Leadership, 49,* 37–42.

Allport, G. (1958). *The nature of prejudice.* Garden City, NY: Doubleday.

American Association of Colleges for Teacher Education. (1973). *No one model American.* Washington, DC: Author.

Apple, M. W. (1979). *Ideology and curriculum.* London: Routledge & Kegan Paul.

Aronowitz, S., & Giroux, H. A. (1990). *Education under siege: The conservative, liberal, and radical debate over schooling.* South Hadley, MA: Bergin & Garvey.

Asante, M. (1991–92). Afrocentric curriculum. *Educational Leadership, 49,* 28–31.

Banks, J. A. (Ed.). (1973). *Teaching ethnic studies: Concepts and strategies* (43rd yearbook). Washington, DC: National Council for the Social Studies.

Banks, J. A. (1977). Pluralism and educational concepts: A clarification. *Peabody Journal of Education, 54*, 73–78.

Banks, J. A. (Ed.). (1981). *Education in the 80s: Multiethnic education*. Washington, DC: National Education Association.

Banks, j. A. (1990). Citizenship education for a pluralistic democratic society. *Social Studies, 81*, 210–214.

Banks, J. A. (1991). *Teaching strategies for ethnic studies* (5th ed.). Boston: Allyn & Bacon.

Banks, J. A. (1991–92). Multicultural education: For freedom's sake. *Educational Leadership, 49*, 32–36.

Banks, J. A. (1992). A curriculum for empowerment, action and change. In K. A. Moodley (Ed.), *Beyond multicultural education: International perspectives* (pp. 154–170). Calgary, Alberta: Detselig Enterprises.

Banks, J. A. (1993). The canon debate, knowledge construction, and multicultural education. *Educational Researcher, 22*(5), 4–14.

Banks, J. A. (1997). *Educating citizens in a multicultural society*. New York: Teachers College Press.

Banks, J. A. (2001a). Approaches to multicultural curriculum reform. In J. A. Banks & C.A.M. Banks (Eds.), *Multicultural education: Issues and perspectives* (4th ed., pp. 225–246). Boston: Allyn & Bacon.

Banks, J. A. (2001b). Multicultural education: Characteristics and goals. In J. A. Banks & C.A.M. Banks (Eds.), *Multicultural education: Issues and perspectives* (4th ed., pp. 3–30). Boston: Allyn & Bacon.

Banks, J. A., & Banks, C.A.M. (Eds.). (2001). *Multicultural education: Issues and perspectives* (4th ed.). Boston: Allyn & Bacon.

Banks, J., Cookson, P., & Gay, G. (2001). *Diversity within unity: Essential principles for teaching and learning in a multicultural society*. Seattle: University of Washington, Center for Multicultural Education.

Banks, J. A., Cortés, C. E., Garcia, R. L., Gay, G., & Ochoa, A. S. (1976). *Curriculum guidelines for multiethnic education*. Washington, DC: National Council for the Social Studies.

Banks, J. A., Cortés, C. E., Garcia, R. L., Gay, G., & Ochoa, A. S. (1992). *Curriculum guidelines for multicultural education* (rev. ed.). Washington, DC: National Council for the Social Studies.

Banks, J. A., & Lynch, J. (Eds.). (1986). *Multicultural education in Western societies*. New York: Holt, Rinehart and Winston.

Baptiste, H. P. (1979). *Multicultural education: A synopsis*. Washington, DC: University Press of America.

Baptiste, H. P. (1986). Multicultural education and urban schools from a sociohistorical perspective: Internalizing multiculturalism. *Journal of Educational Equity and Leadership, 6*, 295–312.

Baptiste, H. P. (1994). The multicultural environment of schools: Implications to leaders. In L. W. Hughes (Ed.), *The principal as leader* (pp. 89–109). New York: Merrill/Macmillan.

Barbe, W. B., & Swassing, R. H. (1979). *Teaching through modality strengths: Concepts and practices*. Columbus, OH: Zaner-Bloser.

Barber, B. R. (1992). *An aristocracy of everyone: The politics of education and the future of America*. New York: Ballantine.

Beauchamp, G. A. (1968). *Curriculum theory* (2nd ed.). Wilmette, IL: Kagg Press.

Bennett, C. I. (1999). *Comprehensive multicultural education: Theory and practice* (4th ed.). Boston: Allyn & Bacon.

Bernal, M. (1987). *Black Athena: The Afroasiatic roots of classical civilization* (Vol. 1). London: Free Association Books.

Bobbitt, F. (1918). *The curriculum*. Boston: Houghton Mifflin.

Bruner, J. S. (1960). *The process of education*. Cambridge, MA: Harvard University Press.

California State Department of Education. (1979). *Planning for multicultural education as a part of school improvement*. Sacramento: Office of Intergroup Relations.

Colangelo, N., Dustin, D., & Foxley, C. H. (Eds.). (1985). *Multicultural nonsexist education: A human relations approach*. Dubuque, IA: Kendall/Hunt.

Combs, A. W. (Ed.). (1962). *Perceiving, behaving, becoming: A new focus for education*. Washington, DC: Association for Supervision and Curriculum Development.

Counts, G. (1932). *Dare the schools build a new social order?* Carbondale: Southern Illinois University Press.

Crichlow, W., Goodwin, S., Shakes, G., & Swartz, E. (1990). Multicultural ways of knowing: Implications for practice. *Journal of Education, 172*, 101–117.

Crittenden, B. (1982). *Cultural pluralism and common curriculum*. Melbourne, Australia: Melbourne University Press.

Cross, W. E., Jr. (1991). *Shades of black: Diversity in African-American identity*. Philadelphia: Temple University Press.

Cushner, K., McClelland, A., & Safford, P. (1999). *Human diversity in education: An integrative approach* (2nd ed.). New York: McGraw-Hill.

Darder, A. (1991). *Culture and power in the classroom: A critical foundation for bicultural education*. New York: Bergin & Garvey.

Delpit, L. D. (1988). The silenced dialogue: Power and pedagogy in educating other people's children. *Harvard Educational Review, 58*, 280–298.

Delpit, L. D. (1995). *Other people's children: Cultural conflict in the classroom*. New York: New Press.

Dewey, J. (1897). *My pedagogic creed*. New York: E. L. Kellogg.

Dewey, J. (1902). *The child and the curriculum*. Chicago: University of Chicago Press.

Dewey, J. (1916). *Democracy and education*. New York: Macmillan.

Diaz, C. (Ed.). (1992). *Multicultural education for the 21st century*. Washington, DC: National Education Association.

Drake, St. C. (1987). *Black folk here and now* (Vol. 1). Los Angeles: University of California, Center for Afro-American Studies.

Eisner, E. W. (Ed.). (1985). *Learning and teaching: The ways of knowing* (84th Yearbook of the National Society for the Study of Education, Part II). Chicago: University of Chicago Press.

Eisner, E. W., & Vallance, E. (Eds.). (1974). *Conflicting conceptions of curriculum*. Berkeley: McCutchan.

Entwistle, H. (1970). *Child-centered education*. London: Methuen.

Erikson, E. H. (1968). *Identity, youth, and crisis*. New York: Norton.

Foshay, A. W. (1975). *Essays on curriculum*. New York: Columbia University, A. W. Foshay Fund.

Frazier, A. (1976). *Adventuring, mastering, associating: New strategies for teaching children*. Washington, DC: Association for Supervision and Curriculum Development.

Frazier, L. (1977). Multicultural facet of education. *Journal of Research and Development in Education, 11*, 10–16.

Garcia, R. L. (1982). *Teaching in a pluralistic society: Concepts, models, strategies*. New York: Harper & Row.

Gardner, H. (1983). *Frames of mind: The theory of multiple intelligences*. New York: Basic Books.

Gay, G. (1977). Changing conceptions of multicultural education. *Educational Perspectives, 16*, 4–9.

Gay, G. (1979). On behalf of children: A curriculum design for multicultural education in the elementary school. *Journal of Negro Education, 48*, 324–340.

Gay, G. (1980). Conceptual models of the curriculum-planning process. In A. W. Foshay (Ed.), *Considered action for curriculum improvement* (pp. 120–143). Alexandria, VA: Association for Supervision and Curriculum Development.

Gay, G. (1983). Multicultural education: Historical developments and future prospects. *Phi Delta Kappan, 64,* 560–563.

Gay, G. (1985). Implications of selected models of ethnic identity development for educators. *Journal of Negro Education, 54,* 43–55.

Gay, G. (1988). Designing relevant curricula for diverse learners. *Education and Urban Society, 20,* 327–340.

Gay, G. (1990). Achieving educational equality through curriculum desegregation. *Phi Delta Kappan, 70,* 56–62.

Gay, G. (1992). The state of multicultural education in the United States. In K. A. Moodley (Ed.), *Beyond multicultural education: International perspectives* (pp. 41–65). Calgary, Alberta: Detselig Enterprises.

Gay, G. (1993). Building cultural bridges: A bold proposal for teacher education. *Education and Urban Society, 25,* 287–301.

Gay, G. (1994). *At the essence of learning: Multicultural education.* Lafayette, IN: Kappa Delta Pi.

Gay, G. (1995). A multicultural school curriculum. In C. A. Grant & M. L. Gomez (Eds.), *Making school multicultural: Campus and classroom* (pp. 37–54). Englewood Cliffs, NJ: Prentice Hall/Merrill.

Gay, G. (2000). *Culturally responsive teaching: Theory, research, & practice.* New York: Teachers College Press.

Gay, G. (2001). Educational equality for students of color. In J. A. Banks & C.A.M. Banks (Eds.), *Multicultural education: Issues and perspectives* (4th ed., pp. 197–224). New York: Wiley.

Gibson, M. A. (1976). Approaches to multicultural education in the United States: Some concepts and assumptions. *Anthropology and Education, 7,* 7–18.

Giroux, H. A. (1983). *Theory and resistance in education: A pedagogy for the opposition.* South Hadley, MA: Bergin & Garvey.

Giroux, H. A. (1988). *Teachers as intellectuals: Toward a critical pedagogy of learning.* South Hadley, MA: Bergin & Garvey.

Giroux, H. A. (1992). *Border crossings: Cultural workers and the politics of education.* New York: Routledge.

Giroux, H. A., & McLaren, P. (Eds.). (1989). *Critical pedagogy, the state, and cultural struggle.* Albany: State University of New York Press.

Giroux, H. A., Penna, A. N., & Pinar, W. F. (Eds.). (1981). *Curriculum and instruction: Alternatives in education.* Berkeley: McCutchan.

Glatthorn, A. A. (1987). *Curriculum leadership.* Glenview, IL: Scott, Foresman.

Gollnick, D. M., & Chinn, P. C. (Eds.). (1998). *Multicultural education in a pluralistic society* (5th ed.). Columbus, OH: Merrill.

Grant, C. A. (1977a). Education that is multicultural and P/CBTE: Discussion and recommendations for teacher education. In F. H. Klasen & D. M. Gollnick (Eds.), *Pluralism and the American teacher: Issues and case studies* (pp. 63–80). Washington, DC: American Association of Colleges for Teacher Education, Ethnic Heritage Center for Teacher Education.

Grant, C. A. (1977b). *Multicultural education: Commitments, issues, and applications.* Washington, DC: Association for Supervision and Curriculum Development.

Grant, C. A. (1978). Education that is multicultural—Isn't that what we mean? *Journal of Teacher Education, 29,* 45–49.

Grant, C. A., & Sleeter, C. E. (1985). The literature on multicultural education: Review and analysis. *Educational Review, 37,* 97–118.

Grant, C. A., & Sleeter, C. E. (2001). Race, class, gender and disability in the classroom. In J. A. Banks & C.A.M. Banks (Eds.), *Multicultural education: Issues and perspectives* (4th ed., pp. 59–81). New York: Wiley.

Greene, M. (1978). *Landscapes of learning.* New York: Teachers College Press.

Henry, W. A., III (1990, April 9). Beyond the melting pot. *Time, 135,* 28–31.

Hilliard, A. G., III (1991–92). Why we must pluralize the curriculum. *Educational Leadership, 29,* 12–14.

Hillis, V. (Ed.). (1999). *The lure of the transcendent: Collected essays by Dwayne E. Huebner.* Mahwah, NJ: Erlbaum.

Hollins, E. R. (Ed.). (1996). *Transforming curriculum for a culturally diverse society.* Mahwah, NJ: Erlbaum.

Huenecke, D. (1982). What is curriculum theorizing? What are its implications for practice? *Educational Leadership, 39,* 290–294.

Hunter, W. A. (Ed.). (1974). *Multicultural education through competency-based teacher education.* Washington, DC: American Association of Colleges for Teacher Education.

Jervis, K., & Montag, C. (Eds.). (1991). *Progressive education for the 1990s: Transforming practice.* New York: Teachers College Press.

Kendall, F. E. (1996). *Diversity in the classroom: A multicultural approach to the education of young children* (2nd ed.). New York: Teachers College Press.

King, J. E., & Wilson, T. L. (1990). Being the soul-freeing substance: A legacy of hope in Afro humanity. *Journal of Education, 172,* 9–27.

Kreisberg, S. (1992). *Transforming power: Domination, empowerments, and education.* Albany: State University of New York Press.

La Belle, T. J., & Ward, C. R. (1994). *Multiculuralism and education: Diversity and its impact on schools and society.* Albany: State University of New York Press.

Ladson-Billings, G., & Henry, A. (1990). Blurring the borders: Voices of African liberatory pedagogy in the United States and Canada. *Journal of Education, 172,* 72–88.

Lynch, J. (1986). *Multicultural education: Principles and practice.* Boston: Routledge and Kegan Paul.

Lynch, J. (1989). *Multicultural education in a global society.* New York: Falmer Press.

Macdonald, J. B. (1974). A transcendental developmental ideology in education. In W. F. Pinar (Ed.), *Heightened conscience, cultural revolution, and curriculum theory* (pp. 85–116). Berkeley: McCutchan.

Macdonald, J. B. (1975). Curriculum and human interest. In W. F. Pinar (Ed.), *Curriculum theorizing: The reconceptualists* (pp. 283–298). Berkeley: McCutchan.

Macdonald, J. B. (1977). Value bases and issues in curriculum. In A. Molnar & J. A. Zahorik (Eds.), *Curriculum theory* (pp. 10–21). Washington, DC: Association for Supervision and Curriculum Development.

McElroy-Johnson, B. (1993). Giving voice to the voiceless. *Harvard Educational Review, 63,* 85–104.

McLaren, P. (1989). *Life in schools: An introduction to critical pedagogy in the foundations of education.* New York: Longman.

Miller, J., & Seller, W. (1985). *Curriculum perspectives and practice.* New York: Longman.

Mitchell-Powell, B. (1992). From the editor. *Multicultural Review, 1,* 3.

Modgil, S., Verma, G. K., Mallick, K., & Modgil, C. (Eds.). (1986). *Multicultural education: The interminable debate.* London: Falmer Press.

Molnar, A., & Zahorik, J. A. (Eds.). (1977). *Curriculum theory.* Washington, DC: Association for Supervision and Curriculum Development.

Moodley, K. A. (Ed.). (1992). *Beyond multicultural education: International perspectives.* Calgary, Alberta: Detselig Enterprises.

National Council for the Accreditation of Teacher Education. (1987). *NCATE standards, procedures, and policies for the accreditation of professional education units.* Washington, DC: Author.

National Council for the Accreditation of Teacher Education (2002). *Professional standards for the accreditation of schools, colleges, and departments of education.* Washington, DC: Author.

Nieto, S. (2000). *Affirming diversity: The sociopolitical context of multicultural education* (3rd ed.). New York: Longman.

Noddings, N. (1992). *Educating moral people: A caring alternative to character education.* New York: Teachers College Press.

Noddings, N. (2002). *The challenge to care in schools: An alternative approach to education.* New York: Teachers College Press.

Novak, M. (1975). Variety is more than a slice of life. *Momentum, 6,* 24–27.

O'Connor, T. (1989). Cultural voice and strategies for multicultural education. *Journal of Education, 171,* 57–73.

Oliva, P. F. (1997). *Developing the curriculum* (4th ed.). New York: Longman.

Orlosky, D. E., & Smith, B. O. (Eds.). (1978). *Curriculum development: Issues and insights.* Chicago: Rand McNally.

Ornstein, A. C., & Hunkins, F. P. (1998). *Curriculum: Foundations, principles, and issues* (3rd ed.). Boston: Allyn & Bacon.

Pai, Y. (1984). Cultural diversity and multicultural education. *Lifelong Learning, 7,* 7–9, 27.

Pai, Y. (1990). *Cultural foundations of education.* New York: Merrill/Macmillan.

Parekh, B. (1986). The concept of multicultural education. In S. Modgil, G. K. Verma, K. Mallick, & C. Modgil (Eds.), *Multicultural education: The interminable debate* (pp. 19–31). London: Falmer Press.

Phenix, P. H. (1964). *Realms of meaning: A philosophy of the curriculum for general education.* New York: McGraw-Hill.

Pinar, W. F. (Ed.). (1974). *Heightened consciousness, cultural revolution, and curriculum theory.* Berkeley: McCutchan.

Pinar, W. F. (Ed.). (1975). *Curriculum theorizing: The reconceptualists.* Berkeley: McCutchan.

Ponterotto, J. G. (Ed.). (2001). *Handbook of multicultural counseling* (2nd ed.). Thousand Oaks, CA: Sage.

Pratte, R. (1983). Multicultural education: Four normative arguments. *Educational Theory, 33,* 21–32.

Rogers, C. (1983). *Freedom to learn for the 80s.* Columbus, OH: Merrill.

Samuda, R. J., Berry, J. W., & Laferriere, M. (Eds.). (1984). *Multiculturalism in Canada: Some social and educational perspectives.* Boston: Allyn & Bacon.

Schubert, W. H. (1980). *Curriculum books: The first eighty years.* Lanham, MD: University Press of America.

Schubert, W. H. (1986). *Curriculum: Perspective, paradigm, and possibility.* New York: Macmillan.

Schwab, J. J. (1969). Education and the structure of the disciplines. In I. Westbury and N. J. Wilkof (Eds.), *Science, curriculum and liberal education* (pp. 229–270). Chicago: University of Chicago Press.

Schwab, J. J. (1970). *The practical: A language for curriculum.* Washington, DC: National Education Association.

Sizemore, B. (1979). The four M curriculum: A way to shape the future. *Journal of Negro Education, 47,* 341–356.

Sizemore, B. A. (1981). The politics of multicultural education. *Urban Education, 5,* 4–11.

Sleeter, C. E. (1989). Multicultural education as a form of resistance to oppression. *Journal of Education, 171,* 510–571.

Sleeter, C. E. (Ed.). (1991). *Empowerment through multicultural education.* Albany: State University of New York Press.

Sleeter, C. E. (1996). *Multicultural education as social activism.* Albany: State University of New York Press.

Sleeter, C. E., & Grant, C. A. (1987). An analysis of multicultural education in the U.S.A. *Harvard Educational Review, 57,* 421–444.

Sleeter, C. E., & Grant, C. A. (1999). *Making choices for multicultural education: Five approaches to race, class, and gender* (3rd ed.). Upper Saddle River, NJ: Merrill.

Sleeter, C. E., & McLaren, P. L. (Eds.). (1995). *Multicultural education, critical pedagogy, and the politics of difference.* Albany: State University of New York Press.

Smith, B. O., Stanley, W. O., and Shores, J. H. (1957). *Fundamentals of curriculum development.* Yonkers-on-Hudson, NY: World Book.

Suzuki, B. H. (1979). Multicultural education: What's it all about? *Integrateducation, 17,* 43–50.

Suzuki, B. H. (1984). Curriculum transformation for multicultural education. *Education and Urban Society, 16,* 294–322.

Swartz, E. (1989). *Multicultural curriculum development: A practical approach to curriculum development at the school level.* Rochester, NY: Rochester City School District.

Taba, H. (1962). *Curriculum development: Theory and practice.* New York: Harcourt, Brace & World.

Tyler, R. W. (1949). *Basic principles of curriculum and instruction.* Chicago: University of Chicago Press.

Van Sertima, I. (1985). *African presence in early Europe.* New Brunswick, NJ: Transactions Books.

Verma, G. K. (Ed.). (1989). *Education for all: A landmark in pluralism.* London: Falmer Press.

Walker, D. F. (1971). A naturalistic model for curriculum development. *School Review, 80,* 51–65.

Zais, R. S. (1976). *Curriculum: Principles and foundations.* New York: Crowell.

3

NEW DIRECTIONS IN MULTICULTURAL EDUCATION

Complexities, Boundaries, and Critical Race Theory

Gloria Ladson-Billings

University of Wisconsin, Madison

The Sunday, May 20, 2001, headline on the *Chicago Tribune* read, "A Multicultural State for Sears." The subheading pointed out that Sears, one of the largest retailers in the United States, was targeting Black and Latino consumers. (In this chapter, the term *Black* designates all individuals of African descent. In cases where the reference is solely to Blacks who also have a U.S. heritage, the term is *African American*.) The ease with which a major newspaper used the term *multicultural* tells us something about how power and domination appropriate even the most marginal voices. Multicultural has made it to Main Street.

This chapter examines the ways current ideas about the term *multicultural* must give way to new expressions of human and social diversity. It argues for reconceptualized views of difference that often are forced to operate in old social schemes. Placed in a linear chronology, this chapter would necessarily cover a large volume, not a chapter. Thus the liberty taken with this discussion is to appropriate a metaphor—jazz—to scaffold the changing, often conflicting, developments and iterations of this field we call multicultural education.

Carl Engel's discussion of jazz in 1922 pointed out that "good jazz is a composite, the happy union of seemingly incompatible elements. . . . It is the upshot of a transformation . . . and culminates in something unique, unmatched in any other part of the world" (p. 6). Engel further asserts that "jazz is rag-time, plus 'Blues,' plus orchestral polyphony; it is the combination . . . of melody, rhythm, harmony, and counterpoint" (p. 8). Finally,

Jazz is abandon, is whimsicality in music. A good jazz band should never play, and actually never does play, the same piece twice in the same manner. Each player must be a clever musician, an originator as well as an interpreter, a wheel that turns hither and thither on its own axis without disturbing the clockwork." (p. 9) (A number of these jazz references come from the *Atlantic Monthly*'s jazz archives, which can be found on the Internet at www.theatlantic.com/unbound/jazz.)

Indeed, what we now call multicultural education also is a composite. It is no longer solely race, or class, or gender. Rather, it is the infinite permutations that come about as a result of the dazzling array of combinations human beings recruit to organize and fulfill themselves. Like jazz, no human being is ever the same in every context. The variety of "selves" we perform have made multicultural education a richer, more complex, and more difficult enterprise to organize and implement than previously envisioned. In 1955, Arnold Sundgaard pointed out:

A song of itself is not jazz, no matter what its origin. Jazz is what the jazzmen [sic] searching together bring to it, take from it, find within it. . . . Much is left free for improvisation, and no precise method of notation has been developed to indicate its rhythmic and emotional complexities. . . . The song and its arrangement become

The author is indebted to Thomas Popkewitz of the University of Wisconsin, Madison, for his helpful comments on an earlier draft of this chapter.

. . . a means to an end. The music used . . . is somewhat incidental to the inspired uses to which it is put. For this reason jazz . . . thrives on endless exploration and ceaseless discovery. (pp. 1–2)

Again, like jazz, multicultural education is less a thing than a process. It is organic and dynamic, and although it has a history rooted in our traditional notions of curriculum and schooling its aims and purposes transcend all conventional perceptions of education. Early attempts at multicultural education were rooted in what Hollinger (1995) called the ethnoracial pentagon, that is, African Americans, Asian Americans, Latinas/os, Native Americans, and European Americans. These static categories held some political sway but began to lose their social and symbolic meanings because of the changes in the everyday lives of most people. Racial and ethnic inequity and discrimination had played significant roles in contouring the U.S. landscape. But demographic shifts, a growing understanding of the multiple identities that people inhabit and embrace, and an awareness of other forms of oppression made the ethnoracial distinctions a limited way to talk about multiculturalism and multicultural education.

Perhaps the limitation in this thinking about multiculturalism stems from limited thinking about the term *culture*. Most common definitions of culture describe it either as "an aesthetic phenomenon" (Coffey, 2000, p. 38) or a particular way of life that includes knowledge, values, artifacts, beliefs, and other aspects of human endeavor peculiar to any group or groups of people (Williams, 1976). It is this latter definition that has come to be associated with multiculturalism. However, Coffey (2000) cites Tony Bennett in describing new thinking about culture:

[It] is more cogently conceived . . . when thought of as a historically specific set of institutionally embedded relations of government in which the forms of thought and conduct of extended populations are targeted for transformation—in part via the extension through the social body of the forms, techniques, and regimens of aesthetic and intellectual culture. (Bennett, 1992, p. 26)

Bennett's (1992) work is informed by Foucault's (1991) writing on governmentality and argues that culture is created through the processes of social management, and that it is both the object and the instrument of government. This definition does not negate the materiality of culture (that is, the objects and practices of culture) but expands conventional notions of culture to include the way both specialized and everyday practices are marked as culture. The very human endeavors that may be seen as normal or commonsensical are culturally bounded. Multiculturalism cannot be seen merely as a study of the other, but rather as multiple studies of culture and cultural practices in the lives of all humans.

Another theme of this chapter is that the notion of America, like jazz, does not lend itself easily to definition and prescription. Ward and Burns (2000) link jazz to America:

It is America's music—born out of a million American negotiations: between having and not having; between happy and sad, country and city; between black and white and men and women; between the Old Africa and the Old Europe—which could only have happened in an entirely New World.

It is an improvisational art, making itself up as it goes along—just like the country that gave it birth.

It rewards individual expression but demands selfless collaboration.

It is forever changing but nearly always rooted in the blues.

It has a rich tradition and its own rules, but it is brand-new every night.

It is about just making a living and taking terrible risks, losing everything and finding love, making things simple and dressing to the nines.

It has enjoyed huge popularity and survived hard times, but it has always reflected Americans—all Americans—at their best (p. xxi)

I argue that this multilayered, eclectic description of America is similarly evident in new notions of multicultural education. The early beginnings of multicultural education (see J. A. Banks, Chapter 1, this volume) are reminiscent of the early beginnings of jazz. Scholars as far back as George Washington Williams in the 1880s and W.E.B. DuBois in the first decades of the 20th century began to articulate a new vision of history that positioned African Americans as fully human cultural agents. The dissonance caused by this "new" vision of history parallels the dissonance from early jazz stirrings. The editor of *Etude* magazine (cited in Ward & Burns, 2000) asserted that the music was "syncopation gone mad. . . . Whether it is simply a passing phase of our decadent art culture or an infectious disease which has come to stay . . . time alone can tell" (pp. 14–15).

However, by the 1960s and 1970s social movements concerning the rights of African Americans, Latinas/os, Native Americans, Asian Americans, women, and the poor were sweeping across America. By appropriating the language of civil rights and the strategy of legal remedies, various groups were able to make use of existing laws and push for new ones that recognized their basic humanity. The parallel moment in jazz was roughly between 1917 and 1924, or the emergence of the jazz age. It was during this era of World War I and the Roaring Twenties that jazz became clearly established in the United States. In 1926, R.W. S. Mendl stated that "jazz is the product of a restless age: an age in which the fever of war is only now beginning to abate its fury: when men and women, after their efforts in the great struggle, are still too much disturbed to be content with a tranquil existence" (quoted in Ward & Burns, 2000, p. 102).

In the Ward and Burns volume (2000), a quotation from Duke Ellington captures another central point of this discussion, that of freedom and liberation:

Jazz is a good barometer of freedom. . . . In its beginnings, the United States of America spawned certain ideals of freedom and independence through which eventually jazz was evolved, and the music is so free that many people say it is the only unhampered, unhindered expression of complete freedom yet produced in this country. (p. vii)

Multicultural education, like America itself, is about the expression of freedom, but notions of freedom and liberation almost always involve contestation. The work of the social movements was taken up by theorists and practitioners to create new curriculum and instructional practices to reflect changes in the sociopolitical landscape. Work by James A. Banks, Gwendolyn Baker, Carl Grant, and Geneva Gay built on the ethnic studies work of scholars such as Carlos Cortés, Jack Forbes, Asa Hilliard, Barbara Sizemore, and others to create rubrics for curriculum designers and teachers who took on the task of aligning school curricula with emerging scholarly evidence about the histories, cultures, lives, and experiences of various peoples. More important, this work challenged old perceptions of America as a "White" country.

Today it is almost impossible to walk into an elementary school in the United States and not find representation of "multicultural America." These representations take the form of characters in reading books, bulletin board displays, assembly programs, and even school supplies (Crayola crayons offers what it calls a "multicultural" crayon set purportedly with hues that represent various skin colors). But it is just this commonality (as expressed earlier in the Sears store example) that has forced scholars and activists to begin pushing the boundaries of multicultural education and argue against the ways dominant ideologies are able to appropriate the multicultural discourse (McCarthy, 1988; Wynter, 1992). At the secondary school level, there are an array of courses (typically electives) and clubs that acknowledge the cultural contributions of various groups formerly ignored by the school curriculum. However, these efforts typically represent what King (2001) calls "marginalizing knowledge," which "is a form of curriculum transformation that can include selected 'multicultural' curriculum content that simultaneously distorts both the historical and social reality that people actually experienced. . . . This form of marginalizing inclusion is justified in the (indivisible) interest of 'our common culture'" (p. 274).

McLaren (1994, 2000) introduces the notions of "critical multiculturalism" and/or "revolutionary multiculturalism" to interrupt the diversity discourse that emerged to supplant and subvert the original intentions of theorists who set out to create a pedagogy of liberation and social justice. King (2001) calls for "deciphering culture-centered knowledge" that leads to "changed consciousness and cognitive autonomy [that] can be a foundation for curriculum transformation" (p. 276). This "new multiculturalism," like the new jazz ushered in by alto saxophonist Ornette Coleman, represents a "permanent revolution" (Davis, 1985, p. 1). In his discussion of Coleman's work, Davis said:

What must have bothered musicians . . . more than the unmistakable southern dialect of Coleman's music was its apparent formlessness, its flouting of rules that most jazz modernists had invested a great deal of time and effort in mastering. In the wake of bebop, jazz had become a music of enormous harmonic complexity. By the late 1950s it seemed to be in danger of becoming a playground for virtuosos, as the liberating practice of running the chords became routine. If some great players sounded at times as though they lacked commitment and were simply going through the motions, it was because the motions were what they had become most committed to. (p. 4)

Critical multiculturalism that relies on a deciphering knowledge seeks to push past going through the motions of multiculturalism. The remainder of this chapter discusses a rubric for thinking about multicultural education, the extant tensions within the field, a rearticulation of race, and a look at current trends in multicultural education.

A RUBRIC FOR THINKING ABOUT MULTICULTURAL EDUCATION

The discomfort is also there, of course, in the music's structure. Rather than following standard chord progressions and traditional solo structures, large portions of the ensemble's repertoire are devoted to impromptu explorations of a semiotic freedom (Heble, 2000).

Banks (Chapter 1, this volume) puts forth five dimensions of multicultural education that help us understand its comprehensive and multifaceted nature: content integration, knowledge construction, prejudice reduction, equity pedagogy, and an empowering school culture (see Banks for a full explanation of these elements). This chapter focuses more directly on the knowledge construction aspect of his dimensions because new notions of knowledge, what is knowable—or the epistemological basis of a discipline or area of study—determines its theoretical, conceptual, methodological, and pedagogical trajectory. Gordon (1997) reminds us that "mainstream social science knowledge is grounded in the standards for knowledge production that have developed in the physical sciences (Keto, 1989), in which the main purpose of research is seen as seeking universal 'truths,' generalizations one can apply to all—'totalizing schemas'" (p. 47).

Gordon further asserts that epistemological paradigms emerging from the experiences of people of color and women offer a challenge to these mainstream perspectives.

Culturally centered research (here the term *cultural* refers to a variety of human groupings: race, ethnicity, gender, social class, ability, sexuality, and religion) argues against the claims of universality and objectivity of knowledge that mainstream research presumes. It recognizes that both the knower and the known have particular standpoints grounded in historical, political, social, and economic contexts. Thus it is important to make clear the frame of reference from which the researcher works and understands the world. Gordon (1997) argues that this challenge to mainstream research has caused an "epistemological crisis" (p. 49). However, mainstream scholars have found ways to construe multicultural education as a part of the dominant paradigm. Both McLaren (1994) and King (2001) provide clear examples of this.

McLaren (1994) argues that multiculturalism has taken on a variety of forms that move it away from ideals of liberation and social justice. He terms these forms conservative (or corporate) multiculturalism, liberal multiculturalism, and left-liberal multiculturalism. McLaren is careful to identify these forms as heuristic devices, not meant to serve as essentialized and fixed categories but rather as useful categories to describe an array of thought and practice evident in schools and society today. One reason these categories become important is, as McLaren states, that "multiculturalism without a transformative political agenda can be just another form of accommodation to the larger social order" (p. 53).

Conservative or corporate multiculturalism is a strategy for disavowing racism and prejudice without conceding any of the power or privilege the dominant class enjoys. For example, the approach of the Sears store mentioned in the beginning of this chapter represents the way corporate interests have attempted to mobilize the multicultural rhetoric to promote consumption (and perhaps exploitation of workers). Their message, like that of Glazer (1997), is that we are all multiculturalists now. Corporate or conservative multiculturalism has a veneer of diversity without any commitment to social justice or structural change. Like King's (2001) description of marginalizing knowledge, conservative multiculturalism is a "form of curriculum transformation that can include selected 'multicultural' curriculum content that simultaneously distorts both the historical and social reality that people actually experienced" (p. 274). So even though students might see representations of various groups in their texts and school curriculum, how those people are represented may be conservative or marginalizing. A typical textbook strategy for accomplishing this is to place

information about racially and ethnically subordinated peoples in a special features section while the main text, which carries the dominant discourse, remains uninterrupted and undisturbed by "multicultural information."

The second type of multiculturalism McLaren (1994) identifies is liberal multiculturalism. This rests on a perspective of "intellectual sameness among the races . . . or the rationality imminent in all races that permits them to compete equally in a capitalist society" (p. 51). In King's (2001) analysis, this might be thought of as "expanding knowledge." This represents a kind of curriculum transformation, but the "rotation in the perspective of the subject can multiculturalize knowledge without changing fundamentally the norm of middle-classness in the social framework's cultural model of being" (p. 275). This type of multiculturalism finds a ready home in the academy because it tries to address the concerns of all groups equally without disturbing the existing power structure. Thus most campuses offer programs and activities directed at African Americans, Latinas/os, Asian Americans, Native Americans, women, gays, lesbians, the disabled, and other identified groups. However, these programs and groups operate in isolation from each other, and the campus community rarely calls into question the way White middle-class norms prevail.

The perspectives of liberal multiculturalism are similar to what Sleeter and Grant (1987) identified as a human relations approach to multicultural education. Here emphasis on human sameness fails to reveal the huge power differentials that exist between the White middle class and other groups in U.S. society. By acknowledging the existence of various groups while simultaneously ignoring the issues of power and structural inequity, liberal multiculturalism functions as a form of appeasement. As previously stated, liberal multiculturalism argues for intellectual sameness among distinctive cultural groups. This form of multiculturalism also holds on to notions of meritocracy and argues for equal opportunities to compete in a capitalist market economy. This thinking fails to recognize the structural and symbolic practices that militate against the ability of the poor, women, and non-White ethnic and cultural groups to access (and succeed in) the society.

For example, Conley (2000) describes his growing up poor in a New York housing project that was almost all Black and Latino. Even here, his White skin privilege prevailed. All of his Black classmates were regularly struck by teachers for misbehavior, but "everyone involved, teacher and students, took it for granted that a Black teacher would never cross the racial line to strike a White student" (Conley, p. 45). Later, as a sociology professor, Conley began to ask his students a simple question: how they got their first job. Almost all of his African American and Latina/o students reported that they searched the newspaper classified advertisements or responded to help wanted signs in store and business windows to search for work. Almost none of the White students found their first jobs that way. Instead, family, friends, and other familiar connections meant that employment came to them.

It is important to point out that the advantage of White skin privilege is not totally invisible to Whites. Hacker (1992) asked his White students at Queens College how much they would want in the way of "compensation" if they were to become Black for the next 20 years. Hacker reminded the students that they would suffer no loss of resources, intellect, or social status in this hypothetical skin change experiment. Still, students reported that they would want $1 million in compensation. Thus White college students believe their White skin is worth at least $50,000 a year.

Sims (1982) gave curriculum examples of liberal multiculturalism in her description of children's fiction. She categorized those books that merely colored in the faces of children while maintaining a story line that gave no indication of the characters' racial and cultural experiences as "culturally neutral." Classics such as Ezra Jack Keats's *A Snowy Day* or *Whistle for Willie* are prototypical examples of such books. The story purports to be a universal one, where the characters' racial identity adds nothing to the story line. Rather, such books attempt to underscore the human commonality rather than differences.

A third approach to multiculturalism is what McLaren (1994) calls "left-liberal multiculturalism." This form of multiculturalism emphasizes cultural differences to the point of exoticism. According to McLaren, "the left liberal position tends to exoticize 'otherness' in a nativistic retreat that locates difference in a primeval past of cultural authenticity" (p. 51). The reliance on separate and distinct campus programs of identity politics fosters this essentialized notion of culture. Few, if any, programs in ethnic studies, gender, sexuality, or disability integrate across identities; rarely are there Black women's studies programs or Latino gay programs.

Current academy relations treat identity politics as monolithic and essentialized. Even within programs, there is often little room for perspectives that stretch the epistemological and ideological boundaries. Dyson (1994) argues that "contemporary African American culture is radically complex and diverse, marked by an intriguing variety of intellectual reflections, artistic creations, and social practices" (p. 218). Surely the same can be said of every other cultural group. Scholars such as Lowe (1996), Anzaldua (1987), and Warrior (1995) examine the complexities of ethnic identities within Asian American, Latina/o, and American Indian groups, respectively.

In speaking of the cultural complexities of Black identities and cultures, Gilroy (1993) urges people of African descent (particularly those in the Diaspora) to avoid the "lure of ethnic particularism and nationalism" (p. 4) in favor of "global, coalitional politics in which anti-imperialism and anti-racism might be seen to interact" (p. 4). Further, Gilroy encourages people of various racial and cultural identities to break out of linear, absolutist renderings of their cultural selves that often characterize ethnic studies agendas. Instead, Gilroy points back to DuBois's (1953/1989) powerful notion of double consciousness as an appropriate rubric for understanding the identity challenge of all peoples who suffer the oppression of dominant culture norms and constraints. McKay and Wong (1996) provide another compelling example of the way people eschew the ethnic, racial, and/or cultural boundaries established by totalizing discourses, to act in ways that more accurately reflect current identities. In their study of adolescent Chinese immigrants, they found that the students had different motivations for learning (or not learning) English, tied to their identities and influenced by economic status, peer groups, neighborhoods, and academic ability.

Finally, McLaren (1994) offers a notion of critical multiculturalism. Here he calls for a restructuring of the social order through a radical approach to schooling. McCarthy (1988) suggests that because multiculturalism originates in the liberal pluralist paradigm it is limited in its ability to create long-lasting substantive social change. Instead, from McCarthy's perspective multicultural education represents a "curricular truce" (p. 267) that was designed to pacify the insurgent demands of African Americans, Latinas/os, Asian Americans, and Native Americans during the 1960s and 1970s.

King (2001) offers what she terms "deciphering knowledge" as an emancipatory form of cultural knowledge. Drawing heavily on the work of Sylvia Wynter (1989, 1992) and novelist Toni Morrison (1989, 1991), King asserts that deciphering knowledge is "aimed at changed consciousness and cognitive autonomy" as the "foundation for curriculum transformation" (p. 276). Though not specifically postmodern, this work engages Foucault's notion (1972) of the archaeology of knowledge to reveal the discursive practices that support the racial and power ideologies that contour the social order. Such work examines both the explicit and implicit texts to articulate meaning and intentions. For example, Morrison's (1991) examination of classics from the American literary canon exposes how race was configured throughout the texts without ever having to use the familiar terms and codes. A much less sophisticated example of "text" can be seen in everyday advertising and media representations. For example, when George Herbert Bush ran for president in 1988 his campaign aired what came to be known as the "Willie Horton ad." The literal representation of the ad was one of a particular criminal, Willie Horton, who was released from jail by Mr. Bush's opponent, only to kill again. Applying deciphering knowledge to the ad/text allows us to see the way Horton was a proxy for the supposed danger and criminality of African American men. On the opposite end of the spectrum is the way that various ethnic and cultural groups members are recruited to represent a form of "contained diversity." For example, high-level government officials and appointees can be used to reflect a commitment to diversity regardless of their lack of interest or personal commitment to social justice and transformative social change. Deciphering knowledge helps people see through the veneer of inclusion to the ways in which diversity or multiculturalism is being manipulated to maintain and justify the status quo.

Another example of critical multiculturalism and deciphering knowledge is the postcolonial project. Smith (1999) points out that from the perspective of the colonized, the very term *research* is linked to European imperialism and colonialism. This notion was established earlier by Fanon (1963, 1967), who explained the ways European education creates a sense of alienation and self-negation in the colonized. Writing from a place of "alterity" (Wynter, 1992), those who are positioned as "others" see the social framework from another perspective, not unlike DuBois's (1953/1989) double-consciousness:

the Negro is a sort of seventh son, born with a veil, and gifted with second sight in this American world—a world which yields him no true self consciousness, but only lets him see himself through the revelation of the other world. It is a peculiar sensation, this double consciousness, this sense of always looking at one's self through the eyes of others, of measuring one's soul by the tape of a world that looks on in amused contempt and pity. (p. 3).

TENSIONS WITHIN THE FIELD

[John] Coltrane seemingly forsook lyricism for an unfettered quest for ecstasy. The results remain virtually indescribable, and they forestall criticism with the furious directness of their energy. Yet, their effect depends more on the abandonment of rationality, which most listeners achieve only intermittently if at all.

—Strickland (1987)

For the sake of argument, let us presume that we agree that McLaren's (1994) critical multiculturalism and King's (2001) deciphering knowledge are indeed what we mean when we refer to multiculturalism. Such agreement does not necessarily resolve tensions within the field of multiculturalism. Although multicultural education began as a challenge to the inequities that students of color experienced in school and society, it soon became an umbrella movement for a variety of forms of difference—

particularly race, class, and gender. Within each category of difference, other issues emerged: linguistic, ethnic and cultural, sexual orientation, and ability.

The work of feminists gave rise to demands for social equity for women and supported an epistemological challenge to the academy. Work by Gilligan (1977), Noddings (1984), Lather (1991), Code (1991), and others challenged the notion that conventional positivist paradigms represent the full spectrum of social and educational experiences. Feminist scholars demanded that new forms of scholarship be represented in the academy. Thus gender work became another task of the multicultural project. Schmitz, Butler, Rosenfelt, and Guy-Sheftall (2001) point out that there exists a "continuing tension in feminist scholarship, the tension between an emphasis on equality . . . and an emphasis on difference" (p. 710). I would argue that this tension runs deeper because of the complex and multiple identities women assume. Jaimes and Halsey (1992) suggest that the work of Native American women is one of sovereignty over Western feminism. Similarly, African American women such as Audrey Lourde, bell hooks, Alice Walker, and Patricia Hill Collins have asked about the place of Black women and their particular issues in the feminist discourse. Although Frankenberg (1993) has clearly acknowledged that race shapes White women's lives, many others have ignored race and class in their discussions of feminist work. Trinh T. Minh-ha (1989) argues that we cannot think of race and gender as separate and distinct identities because this creates dichotomous thinking that serves the interests of the dominant order:

Many women of color feel obliged [to choose] between ethnicity and womanhood: how can they? You never have/are one without the other. The idea of two illusorily separated identities, one ethnic, the other woman (or most precisely female), partakes in the Euro-American system of dualistic reasoning and its age–old divide-and-conquer tactics. . . . The pitting of anti-racist and anti-sexist struggles against one another allows some vocal fighters to dismiss blatantly the existence of either racism or sexism within their lines of action, as if oppression only comes in separate, monolithic forms. (p. 105)

Perhaps the emblem of the fissure between race and gender in the United States was the O. J. Simpson trial (see Morrison & Lacour, 1997). Feminists (many of the more vocal ones were White) advocated constructing the trial around the worrisome women's issue of domestic violence. However, both Simpson's defense team and segments of the African American community saw the trial as an opportunity to underscore the way the justice system (and the society) uses a racial measurement to determine the kind of available justice defendants receive.

Another point of tension for feminists is around class issues. The seemingly stunning efforts of the women's movement to help women gain access to middle-class positions in the corporate sector, the academy, and social services pale in comparison to the continued problems of women in poverty, women's health, and child support and care. Women of color often find themselves in poverty alongside men of color (James & Busia, 1993). Thus their social and political allegiances are complex and multiple. Recognizing the masculinist discourse of the 1960s civil rights movement (both the nonviolence of Martin Luther King and the self-determination of the Black Panther Party), African American women still understand the need to work with African American men who are locked out of economic opportunities right along with them.

Still another source of tension regarding multiculturalism and feminism is in the global realm. In an edited volume entitled *Is Multiculturalism Bad for Women?* (Okin, Cohen, Howard, & Nussbaum, 1999), Okin raises important questions about ways that group rights may trump women's rights on issues of polygamy, genital mutilation, forced marriage, differential access for men and women to health care and education, disparate rights of ownership, and unequal vulnerability to violence. Her main argument is that some group rights can endanger women. However, there are non-Western feminists who challenge the essentialized and stereotypical representations of women within their cultures (Afsaruddin, 1999). These feminists offer a variety of perspectives, some of which challenge notions of moral universalism and the imposition of Western standards on all women in all circumstances. Afsaruddin points out that the lives of women in Muslim societies are not uniform, unchanging, or monolithic. Rather than accept the idea that feminism is incompatible with Islam, Afsaruddin asserts that Western readings of Muslim traditions such as veiling by educated women in urban centers may be "the farthest thing from tradition" (p. 23). The meaning of the veil in these contexts may reflect Muslim women's decision to claim both private and public identities on their own terms.

It is not just feminism and its warrants on equity and social justice that have caused a sort of "family feud" in multiculturalism, but also the new studies that emerged around linguistic diversity, immigrant status, social class, ability, and sexuality. Although these varied and multiple identity categories do not compete as they are embodied in single individuals (for example, a Mandarin-speaking disabled lesbian Asian American woman), politically the categories are pitted against each other and compete for primacy on academic and policy agendas. Reed (1997) and Palumbo-Liu (1995) grapple with the intercultural and intracultural struggles that emerge from our increasing diversity. Tensions between older and newer immigrant communities (for instance, Chinese American, Vietnamese, Laotian, and Hmong immigrants), tensions between immigrant communities and constitutive communities of color (such as Korean Americans and African Americans), and tensions resulting from biracial and multiracial identities all are examples of the changing cultural landscape. Political issues like those that emerged in California around undocumented workers (Proposition 187), affirmative action (Proposition 209), and bilingual education (the Unz Amendment) often reveal fissures and fractures in loosely aligned coalitions of oppressed peoples.

Of course, the tensions of class and economic asymmetry continue to plague discussions of multiculturalism. Because so much of the debate has centered on equal access and improved achievement in schools (Banks & Banks, 2001; Grant & Sleeter, 1997), a major interpretation of the project has been one of gaining access to the extant economic order. Sleeter & Grant (1987) analyzed the various forms multicultural education takes and concluded that only those that included a social reconstructionist perspective could be legitimately seen as multicultural. However, few expressions of multicultural education in school take on the critique of capitalism as systemically inequitable (McCarthy, 1993; Olneck, 1990). Increasing disparities between the rich and poor, the concentration of wealth in the hands of a few, and a burgeoning underclass (Collins & Yeskel, 2000) make very real Justice Brandeis's comment that "you can have great wealth concentrated in the hands of a few, or democracy. But you cannot have both" (Goldman, 1953, p. xi). These economic disparities occur both internationally and intranationally. Thus the concerns of a middle-class White woman or a middle-class African American man seem to take on less urgency in the face of the exploitation of Latin American and Southeast Asian workers who toil for pennies a day to make high-priced basketball shoes or baseballs. The cries of environmentalists to save the rain forests meet with hostilities from starving indigenous peoples. As Nobel Prize–winning economist Amatrya Sen (1995) argues, everyone is for equality; it's just that what constitutes equality for one is not the same as for another. For instance, amid the affirmative action debate, both sides lay claim to the rhetoric of equality. Those on the left insist that the need to redress past wrongs is the only way to ensure the disruption of the cycle of inequity (Bell, 1987; Crenshaw, 1988). Those on the right insist that granting special preferences only furthers inequity (see, for example, arguments advanced by McWhorter, 2001; Sowell, 1984; and Steele, 1990).

In the face of the events that occurred in the United States on September 11, 2001 (reference is to the attack on the World Trade Center in New York City; the Pentagon in Washington, D.C.; and the downed airplane in Pennsylvania), new fault lines have been drawn concerning diversity, inclusion, and democracy. Despite the long-standing presence of Muslims in the United States, the national gaze on Islam cast the religion in quite a different light. Now, those who practice Islam are configured in a narrow outline: Arab, Middle Eastern, religious fundamentalist, terrorist, fanatic. They have become the new "other" in the same way that American Indians, African Americans, Latinos, and Asian Americans were at various points in our history. Of course, this current depiction of Muslims narrows and limits the full spectrum of people who practice the religion. For instance, there are 1,209 mosques in the United States, the typical mosque is ethnically diverse, and 30 percent of Muslims in this country are African Americans (U.S. Department of State, 2001). So although Muslims of Middle Eastern origin have been made the proxy for all who practice Islam, the empirical evidence reveals that adherents to the faith are as diverse and complex as any other human group (Eck, 2001).

What does a critical resistant multiculturalism look like in a community where African American Christians, Yemeni immigrant Muslims, Orthodox Jews, Korean Buddhists, and Spanish-speaking Chicana/o Catholics all must vie for rights and opportunities? What happens when among this group there are feminists and gays, lesbians, and bisexuals at odds with some of the religious tenets of one or more of these groups? It is this "big tent" multiculturalism that has rendered much of what happens in the name of multiculturalism ineffective. The Democratic Party in the United States refers to itself as a big tent party because it purports to include everyone; unfortunately, this inclusion has not considered what happens when some groups under the tent are at odds with others.

What one group perceives as the multicultural agenda is something else for another. Victims of racism and ethnic discrimination and violence worry that attention to other forms of human diversity dilutes multicultural education's ability to address their concerns. Feminists and other proponents of gender equity may feel marginalized within the multicultural education discourse. The complexity of identities that individuals experience makes it difficult to craft a multicultural mission that speaks to the specificity of identity. However, attempts to be all things to all people seem to minimize the effective impact of multicultural education as a vehicle for school and social change.

The identity politics of multicultural education is cast as a struggle for rights. The discussion of various groups within the rhetoric of rights provides a new way to think about these conflicts. The next section discusses Critical Race Theory as a way to formulate a rights-based discourse. It is important to note that by taking up Critical Race Theory as a theoretical framework, one is not necessarily privileging race over class, gender, or other identity category. Critical Race Theory is a complex legal and intellectual tool for making sense of all forms of human inequity. The strategies it deploys can be used by scholars working on issues of gender, class, ability, and other forms of human difference. Its use in this chapter is as an exemplar of new scholarship. The references made here are specifically to race because of the body of scholarship that has emerged in this area.

CRITICAL RACE THEORY AS A MULTICULTURAL HEURISTIC

I did not come to America to interpret Wagner for the public. I came to discover what young Americans had in them and to help them express it. I am now satisfied that the future of music in this country must be founded upon what are called the Negro melodies. In the Negro melodies of America I discovered all that is needed for a great noble school of music. They are pathetic, tender, passionate, melancholy, solemn, religious, bold, merry, gay, or what you will.

—Antonín Dvořák, 1892 (cited in Ward & Burns, 2000, p. 10)

It may seem strange to return to a discussion of race after going to great lengths to explain the human complexity with which we are now faced. However, this argument is not about race as positivist social science defines it or how notions of liberalism embrace it. Rather, Critical Race Theory (CRT) is about deploying race and racial theory as a challenge to traditional notions of diversity and social hierarchy.

Although we are just beginning to see CRT in education (Ladson-Billings, 1998; Ladson-Billings & Tate, 1995; Tate, 1997), it has its beginnings in the 1970s with the early work of legal scholars Derrick Bell and Alan Freeman and their growing dissatisfaction with the slow pace of racial reform in the United States (Delgado, 1995). Soon they were joined by others; by the mid-1990s legal scholars had written more than 300 leading law review articles and a dozen books on the topic.

CRT incorporates scholarship from feminism, continental social and political philosophy, postmodernism, cultural nationalism, and a variety of social movements. Cornel West (1995) identifies CRT as

an intellectual movement that is both particular to our postmodern (and conservative) times and part of a long tradition of human resistance and liberation. On the one hand, the movement highlights a creative—and tension ridden—fusion of theoretical self-reflection, formal innovation, radical politics, existential evaluation, reconstructive experimentation and vocational anguish. But, like all bold attempts to reinterpret and remake the world to reveal silenced suffering and to relieve social misery, Critical Race Theorists put forward novel readings of a hidden past that disclose the flagrant shortcomings of the treacherous present in the light of unrealized—though not unrealizable—possibilities for human freedom and equality. (pp. xi–xii)

CRT begins with a number of premises. First and foremost is the proposition that "racism is normal, not aberrant, in American society" (Delgado, 1995, p. xiv). Because racism is such an integral part of our society, "it looks ordinary and natural to persons in the culture" (p. xiv). For instance, from time to time instances of racist behavior are exposed in "surprising" places such as corporate boardrooms (see, for example, White, 1996). These incidents are followed by public outrage and demands for redress. However, these instances keep happening over and over because they are normal, ordinary features of the society. Similarly, sexism, patriarchy, heterosexism, able-ism, classism, linguisticism, and other forms of hierarchy that come from dominance and oppression are also normal. Thus the theory's identification of racism as normal provides an important tool for identifying other such "normal, ordinary" thinking in the society.

A second aspect of CRT is the use of storytelling to challenge racial (and other) oppression. The significance of this storytelling is not merely to exhibit another form of scholarship but rather to use stories to "analyze the myths, presuppositions, and received wisdoms that make up the common culture about race" (Delgado, 1995, p. xiv). CRT storytelling begins with the premise that a society "constructs social reality in ways that promote its own self-interest (or that of elite groups)" (p. xiv). Thus, it is the responsibility of CRT theorists to construct alternative portraits of reality—portraits from subaltern perspectives.

A third aspect of CRT is Derrick Bell's (1980) concept of interest convergence. Here Bell argues that a society's elites allow or encourage advances by a subordinated group only when such advances also promote the self-interest of the elites. Two examples of interest convergence are the way affirmative action policies are enacted and the specific instance of the state of Arizona and the Martin Luther King, Jr., holiday. Despite all of the conservative arguments against affirmative action, an analysis of affirmative action policies indicates that White women, because of their large number, are the major beneficiaries of affirmative action (U.S. Census Bureau, 2000). However, most White women have some relationship to White men, whether as spouses, partners, siblings, parents, or children. This means that White men and White children can share the financial and social benefits that White women enjoy as a result of affirmative action. Thus the interests of women and people of color converge with that of White men who receive the ancillary benefit of White women's improved labor conditions.

In the specific case of the state of Arizona and Martin Luther King, Jr., Day, then-governor Evan Mecham argued that the state could not afford to observe the holiday. However, after threatened boycotts from tourists, various African American civil rights groups, and the National Basketball Association, the state reversed its decision. It did not have a change of heart about the significance of honoring Martin Luther King, Jr.; rather, the potential loss of revenue meant that the state had to have its interests converge with that of African Americans.

CRT theorists have also tried out new forms of writing. Since some are postmodernists, they believe that form and substance are intimately linked. They use biography, autobiography, narratives, and counternarratives to expose the way traditional legal scholarship uses circular and self-serving doctrines and rules to bolster its arguments. Most mainstream legal scholarship embraces universalism over particularism, but CRT responds to a "call to context" (Delgado, 1995, p. xv) and a critique of liberalism, which is a system of civil rights litigation and activism that depends on incremental change, faith in the legal system, and hope for progress.

Although a number of the more prominent names in CRT are African Americans (Derrick Bell, Robin Barnes, Kimberle Crenshaw, Lani Guinier, Cheryl Harris, Charles Lawrence, Patricia Williams), Latina/o scholars (and other scholars of color) also have served as important architects of this movement. Richard Delgado, Ian Haney Lopez, Michael Olivas, Gerald Torres, Margaret Montoya, Mari Matsuda, Robert Chang, Leslie Espinoza, Jayne Chong-Soon Lee, and Lisa Ikemoto all have written important law review articles that sculpt the body of knowledge we have come to know as Critical Race Theory. This work is not just about the Black-White binary. The group known as the LatCrits (see Delgado, 1992, 2000; and Olivas, 1995) are developing a stream of CRT focused on language and immigration issues. Other CRT scholars work primarily on issues facing women of color; there are still other scholars (Grillo & Wildman, 1995; Haney Lopez, 1995) who focus on making systems of privilege more apparent. Through their work they examine the social construction of Whiteness and how Whiteness becomes the default racial identity—never occupying a space of otherness or difference.

For those who think that CRT is only about race, in the narrowest sense of the term, Delgado (2000) has an important response:

Minority groups in the United States should consider abandoning all binaries, narrow nationalisms, and strategies that focus on cutting the most favorable possible deal with whites, and instead set up a secondary market in which they negotiate selectively with each other. . . . The idea would be for minority groups to assess their own preferences and make tradeoffs that will, optimistically, bring gains for all concerned. Some controversies may turn out to be polycentric, presenting win-win possibilities so that negotiation can advance goals important to both sides without compromising anything either group deems vital. . . .

Ignoring the siren song of binaries opens up new possibilities for coalitions based on level-headed assessment of the chances for mutual gains. It liberates one from dependence on a system that has advanced minority interests at best sporadically and unpredictably. It takes interest convergence to a new dimension. (p. 306)

Although CRT's relationship to law is evident, its use in education represents a new dimension and challenge to liberal orthodoxy in the field. However, several scholars have attempted to address the way CRT creates a new way to analyze and critique current practices in schooling and education (Ladson-Billings, 1998; Ladson-Billings & Tate, 1995; Parker, Deyhle, & Villenas, 1999; Tate, 1997; Taylor, 1998). CRT connections to issues like school funding (Kozol, 1991) and school desegregation (Shujaa, 1996) are fairly evident. But other aspects of schooling are amenable to a CRT analysis, for example, curriculum, instruction, and assessment.

Curriculum

CRT sees the official knowledge (Apple, 1993) of the school curriculum as a culturally specific artifact designed to maintain the current social order. As Swartz (1992) suggests:

Master scripting silences multiple voices and perspectives, primarily legitimizing dominant, White, upper-class, male voicings as the 'standard' knowledge students need to know. All other accounts and perspectives are omitted from the master script unless they can be disempowered through misrepresentation. Thus, content that does not reflect the dominant voice must be brought under control, *mastered,* and then reshaped before it can become a part of the master script. (p. 341)

This kind of master scripting means stories of people of color, women, and anyone who challenges this script are muted and erased. The muting or erasing of these voices is done subtly, yet effectively. Instead of omitting them altogether, they can be included in ways that distort their real meaning and significance (King, 1992). Examples of this muting and erasure are evident in the way cultural heroes are transformed in textbooks to make them more palatable to dominant constituencies. Rosa Parks becomes the tired seamstress rather than a lifelong community activist. Martin Luther King, Jr., becomes a sanitized folk hero who enjoyed the support of all "good" Americans rather than the FBI's public enemy number one who challenged an unjust war and economic injustice (Dyson, 2000). Che Guevara, the Black Panthers, Japanese American resistance to the internment camps, and countless other counternarratives rarely exist in the curriculum.

In addition to the content of the curriculum, CRT also raises questions about its quality. Many children of the dominant group have an opportunity for "enriched" and "rigorous" curriculum. Poor, immigrant, bilingual, and children of color usually are confined to the "basics." As Kozol (1991) observes:

The curriculum [that the White school] follows "emphasizes critical thinking, reasoning and logic." The planetarium, for instance, is employed not simply for the study of the universe as it exists. "Children also are designing their own galaxies," the teacher says. . . .
"Six girls, four boys. Nine white, one Chinese. I am glad they have this class. But what about the others? Aren't there ten Black children in the school who could enjoy this also?" (p. 96)

Recent emphasis on testing in the nation's schools has meant that many schools serving subordinated students spend most of the day with no curriculum outside of test preparation. McNeil (2000) states that students experience "phony curricula, reluctantly presented by teachers in class to conform to the forms of knowledge their students would encounter on centralized tests" (p. 5).

Students who are not in the social, political, economic, and cultural mainstream find their access to high-quality curriculum restricted. Such restriction is a good example of CRT theorist Cheryl Harris's (1993) notion of use and enjoyment of property. Harris argues that Whiteness is a form of property that entitles Whites to rights of disposition, use and enjoyment, reputation and status—and the absolute right to exclude. The failure of many groups to participate in advanced classes and other school-sponsored enrichment activities is not by happenstance. The infrastructure and networks of Whiteness provide differential access to the school curriculum.

Instruction

Haberman (1991) describes what he terms the "pedagogy of poverty," reflecting the basic mode of teaching in schools serving poor urban students (who are likely to be students of color, immigrants, and children whose first language is not English). This pedagogy consists of "giving information, asking questions, giving directions, making assignments, monitoring seatwork, reviewing assignments, giving tests, reviewing tests, assigning homework, reviewing homework, settling disputes, punishing noncompliance, marking papers, and giving grades" (p. 291). According to Haberman, none of these functions is inherently bad, and in fact some might be beneficial in certain circumstances. But "taken together and performed to the systematic exclusion of other acts they have become the pedagogical coin of the realm in urban schools" (p. 291). Haberman contrasts this pedagogy of poverty with "good" teaching, which he says involves student engagement with issues important to their lives; explanations of human differences; major concepts and ideas; planning what they will be doing; applying ideals to their world; heterogeneous groups; questioning common sense; redoing, polishing, or perfecting their work; reflecting on their own lives; and accessing technology in meaningful ways. It is no surprise that the kinds of instruction students have access to breaks along racial fault lines.

McLaren (2000) calls for a critical pedagogy that is a "way of thinking about, negotiating, and transforming the relationship among classroom teaching, the production of knowledge, the institutional structure of the school, and the social and material relations of the wider community, society, and nation-state" (p. 35). Of course, critical pedagogy must be performed by critical pedagogues, and few, if any, teacher preparation programs systematically prepare such teachers.

CRT's project is to uncover the way pedagogy is racialized and selectively offered to students according to the setting, rather than to produce critical pedagogy. Ladson-Billings's (1994) writing on culturally relevant pedagogy describes the work of teachers whose sociopolitical consciousness infused their teaching in a community primarily serving African American students. These teachers understood the decidedly racial and political perspective of their work and unashamedly took on oppressive structures from the school administration and state mandates.

Assessment

Current cries for accountability almost always mean some form of testing, preferably standardized testing. The George W. Bush administration claims that it will "leave no child behind" through the use of "state-of-the-art tests" and argues that "teaching to the test is really teaching those things we have already decided every child should know and be able to do" (U.S. Department of Education, 2001, pp. 7–8). For the CRT theorists, most of the tests children of color, poor children, immigrant children, and limited-English-speaking children experience inevitably legitimize their deficiencies.

In the classroom, a poor-quality curriculum, coupled with poor-quality instruction, a poorly prepared teacher, and limited resources add up to poor performance on the so-called objective tests. CRT theorists point out that the assessment game is merely a validation of the dominant culture's superiority. In his "Chronicle of the Black Crime Cure," Bell (1987) tells a story of a Black street gang member who finds a magical stone that he ingests. Instantly, the gang member is converted. He stops all wrongdoing and begins fighting crime wherever he finds it. Then he distributes the magical stones to the rest of his band. They too become converts and fight crime everywhere. By some mechanism, the group is able to distribute the magic stones to every Black community in the country. Crime plummets. There are no more muggings,

burglaries, rapes, or murders in the communities. However, all of the social barriers that supposedly were closed because of Black "criminal tendencies" remain intact. Jobs do not become available to Blacks. White neighborhoods do not welcome Blacks. Schools, which are now filled with well-behaved and eager Black children, continue to offer poor-quality teaching.

More important, the "Black Crime Cure," which to this point in the chronicle has been a perennial excuse for inequitable treatment and policies, begins to undermine the crime industry. Police officers, judges, court workers, prison guards, and weapons manufacturers experience serious job cutbacks. Hundreds of millions of dollars are lost, and many begin to see how the lack of Black crime undermines the social order. The cave that holds the magical stones is mysteriously blown up.

The "Black Crime Cure" is a good example of a CRT narrative. Bell has taken a fanciful story as a canvas on which to reveal the ways that race and other social inequity are important tools for maintaining the privilege of the dominant group. An analogous education story might be called the "Achievement Gap Cure," where Black, Latino, and American Indian families find a magical potion that allows their children to equal and exceed the academic performance of White middle-class students. Were this to happen, the dominant group would be deeply affected. All the education positions in remediation and special education would be lost. Every researcher who has made a career describing low performance and prescribing remedies would have to develop a new research agenda. More important, White middle-class parents would lobby for a new way to identify their children as superior. Such was the case in an upper-middle-class California school community that tried to detrack mathematics courses (Kohn, 1998). White middle-class parents vehemently opposed detracking because there would be no way to determine how much better their children were than other children—and to keep their children from forming social networks with the "others."

From a CRT perspective, current assessment schemes continue to instantiate inequity and validate the privilege of those who have access to cultural capital (Bourdieu, 1977). Indeed, the entire history of standardized testing has been one of exclusion and social ranking rather than diagnosis and school improvement. Intelligence testing, for example, has been a way to legitimate the ongoing racism aimed at non-White peoples (Aleinikoff, 1991; Gould, 1981). The history of the United States is replete with examples of how people of color have been subordinated by "scientific" theories, each of which depends on racial stereotypes that make the socioeconomic condition of these groups seem appropriate. Crenshaw (1988) contends that the point of controversy is no longer that these stereotypes were developed to rationalize the oppression of people of color but rather that they "serve a hegemonic function by perpetuating a mythology about both [people of color] and Whites even today, reinforcing an illusion of a White community that cuts across ethnic, gender, and class lines" (p. 1371).

The promise of CRT is that it can be deployed as a theoretical tool for uncovering many types of inequity and social injustice—not just racial inequity and injustice. Some aspects of this new scholarship are beginning to appear in the current scholarly efforts in multiculturalism and multicultural education. Examples of this work are presented in the next section.

CURRENT TRENDS IN MULTICULTURALISM

My music is the spiritual expression of what I am—my faith, my knowledge, my being. . . . When you begin to see possibilities of music, you desire to do something really good for people, to help humanity free itself from its hang-ups.

—John Coltrane (quoted in Ward & Burns, 2000, p. 436)

The possibilities that this current era offers for multiculturalism and multicultural education seem endless. In addition to adding new areas such as disability studies (Linton, 1998; Shakespeare, 1998) and queer studies (Fuss, 1991; Sedgwick, 1990), cultural studies, postcolonial, postmodern, and poststructuralist studies all attempt to push past conventional and essentialized thinking about race, class, and gender. But these "new studies" are not unproblematic. Multicultural education's seeming allegiance to the triumvirate of race, class, and gender may have rendered it less useful to scholars and practitioners who have to work with the complexities of identities that do not fit into fixed categories. Thus cultural studies, with its multiple lenses and multilayered perspectives, began to fill this space. Unfortunately, the complexity of identity may also mean that some explanations offered by cultural studies are too diffuse and rhetorical to be meaningful in everyday lives, especially in pre-K–12 classrooms. Sometimes what is pushing up against an individual is racism or sexism, or class discrimination plain and simple. An argument about one's complex identity does not alleviate that oppression.

Similarly, although postcolonial theory serves as a useful rubric for scholarship, the people who live under these regimes ask, as Aboriginal activist Bobbi Sykes did most memorably,

"What? Post-colonialism? Have they left?" (cited in Smith, 1999, p. 24). Smith further asserts that "there is also, amongst indigenous academics, the sneaking suspicion that the fashion of post-colonialism has become a strategy for reinscribing or reauthorizing the privilege of non-indigenous academics because the field of 'post-colonial' discourse has been defined in ways which can still leave out indigenous peoples, our ways of knowing and our current concerns." (p. 24)

On the question of the postmodern, multiculturalism again offers an important challenge. Clearly oppressed peoples have argued about the contested nature of history and other social phenomena (Smith, 1999). West (1993) argues that postmodernism is attractive, for example, to Black intellectuals because it "speaks to the black postmodern predicament, defined by rampant xenophobia of bourgeois humanism predominant in the whole academy, the waning attraction to orthodox reductionist and scientific versions of Marxism, and the need for reconceptualization regarding the specificity and complexity of African American oppression" (p. 80). But as Smith points out, "there can be no 'postmodern' for us until we have settled some business of the modern" (p. 34).

Perhaps the place where these new trends can most help multiculturalism and multicultural education is methodology. Early scholarship in multiculturalism seemed to mimic mainstream scholarship, with its use of surveys, interviews, content analysis, and other apparently positivist approaches to research. Multiculturalism and multicultural education have access to more expanded methodologies such as narrative inquiry (Tierney, 1995), counterstories (Bell, 1998), historical ethnographies (Siddle Walker, 1996), autobiography, portraiture (Lawrence-Lightfoot & Davis, 1997), and a full range of indigenous projects: claiming, testimonies, celebrating survival, remembering, indigenizing, intervening, revitalizing, gendering, connecting, envisioning, reframing, restoring, returning, democratizing, naming, protecting, creating, and sharing (Smith, 1999). Fewer academic writers have taken up the challenge to "talk back" (hooks, 1989) in their own languages. Notable exceptions are the work of Ngugi Wa Thiong'o (1986) and Anzaldua (1987), which use native languages to work against oppression. Wa Thiong'o asserted that "language carries culture and the language of the colonizer became the means by which the 'mental universe of the colonized' was dominated" (quoted in Smith, 1999, p. 36).

The other more present trend in multiculturalism and multicultural education is globalization. Even though multicultural education has always included some acknowledgment of international iterations (Moodley, 1983; Troyna & Williams, 1986; Verma & Bagley, 1982), like their U.S. counterparts they were local expressions of multiculturalism that deal primarily with the cultural landscape of particular nation states. Now with the increasing blurring of national geopolitical borders, notions of difference and otherness take on new meaning. Technological advances mean that the West can (and does) assert its hegemony over what people see and hear, how they speak, and ultimately what they think. Communication satellites, fiber optic cables, the Internet, and e-mail bring every corner of the world into our homes. Almost everywhere in the world, people have access to CNN, ESPN, and other U.S.-generated images and perspectives. Thus a worldwide vision of civilization, progress, aesthetics, standard of living, and advance reflects what the world of Western television and other media project.

In this more global environment, the question of group rights versus individual rights takes on new meaning (Kymlicka, 1995). Group and individual rights in South Africa shape up differently from such rights in Germany. Pan-ethnic rights signal new alignments and configurations. Despite the controversy over Huntington's (1997) assessment of realignment in world allegiances, he clearly raised some important questions about how culture may be positioned to trump nationality. Huntington argues that instead of national allegiances, the world is divided along what he terms civilizational allegiances. Thus Spanish speakers, regardless of their national residence, may demonstrate a strong affinity to each other in relation to other groups, or Muslims worldwide may cohere in opposition to Jews or Christians. However, it is equally important to avoid the single-explanation trap that substitutes culture for economy. Indeed, the melding of culture, economy, and politics makes for a new calculus where disruption in one part of the world causes tremors throughout the world. The breakup of the Soviet Union, war in the Balkans, the Palestinian-Israeli conflict, and famine in East Africa all work to configure nation-states in different ways. Previously "White" nations find their streets and communities home to immigrants from Black, Brown, and Yellow nations. Those nations that formerly talked about diversity and multiculturalism in the abstract now come face to face with multicultural, multilingual everyday lives.

The enduring question facing multicultural education is what to do as a school reform effort in the face of this rapid social and cultural change. Multicultural education faces pressure from forces of school reform and standardization on one end of the spectrum and the complexities and changes occasioned by globalization on the other. Gay (2001) points out the current lag between multicultural education theory and practice. Such a gap is likely to be exacerbated by the call for standardized tests as the primary measure of achievement as well as the sheer volume of new knowledge about the world and increasing global interactions. College and university programs seem to be moving in two directions related to these pressures. To conform to the demands of state and national external reviews, some programs of teacher preparation are developing standards-based programs (National Council for Accreditation of Teacher Education, 2002)

that at least nominally address diversity. At the same time, more graduate programs include opportunities for advanced work in multicultural education, multiculturalism, and cultural studies.

Where multiculturalism and multicultural education go from here is difficult to predict. Will it follow the 1970s jazz lead, succumb to the pressures of conformity, and produce a fusion that is palatable but without substance? Or will it be the jazz that Wynton Marsalis (cited in Ward & Burns, 2000) recognizes?

That's the thing in jazz that got Bix Beiderbecke up out of his bed at two o'clock in the morning to pick that cornet up and practice with it into the pillow for another two or three hours. Or that would make Louis Armstrong travel around the world for fifty years non-stop, just get up out of his sickbed, crawl up on the bandstand, and play. The thing that would make Duke Ellington, Thelonius Monk, Miles Davis, Charlie Parker—any of these people that we've heard about—all these wonderful people—give their lives. And they did give their lives for it, because it gives us a glimpse into what America is going to be when it becomes itself. And this music tells you that it *will* become itself. (p. 460)

SUMMARY COMMENTS AND FUTURE QUESTIONS

This chapter began by highlighting the growing presence of multicultural forms in the society. It points out that the current popularity of multiculturalism and multicultural education does not necessarily speak to the complexity and dissonance that is occurring within the field. The chapter uses work by McLaren (1994) and King (2001) as rubrics for rethinking and rearticulating what we mean by multiculturalism and multicultural education. Rather than one multiculturalism, both theorists offer multiple representations of multiculturalism that are aimed at decidedly different agendas. The chapter endorses McLaren's critical resistant multiculturalism and King's deciphering knowledge as a form of emancipatory practice.

Next, the chapter discusses some of the tensions that exist within the field. It points out that some traditional issues of multiculturalism began to bump up against each other around race, class, gender, language, immigrant status, ability, and sexuality. Uneasy alliances seem to find multiculturalism an uncomfortable space, and several movements for social justice and equity actually worked against each other. Out of this discussion flows an explanation and analysis of Critical Race Theory (CRT) as a heuristic for multiculturalism and multicultural education. The chapter explains CRT as a strategy for reinventing legal scholarship in civil rights and then explores ways it might apply to education. Finally, the chapter points out the ongoing challenges multiculturalism and multicultural education face with increasing demands by diverse groups, the growing complexities of the human condition, and expanding methodologies. The chapter concludes by recognizing globalization as an ever-present force in our thinking about multiculturalism and multicultural education.

In the midst of the complexity and seeming confusion, what, then, are the research and scholarship agendas for multiculturalism and multicultural education? How will academics take on the challenge of writing and researching in a rapidly changing sociocultural reality? Where do the concerns of schoolchildren (no matter where they are in the world) who are left behind in the information age surface as we attempt to unravel and unpack our projects? What, if anything, is to be done about the fissures and fractures? What will constitute the next generation of new scholarship for even newer directions in multicultural education?

These are important questions as we move into a world where globalization defines the economy, culture, and politics of people everywhere (Suárez-Orozco, 2001). The fact of a worldwide media that transports not only news and information but also cultural images of how to be and act in the world means that our conceptions of culture can no longer be simplistic, one-dimensional, and essentialized. The hegemony of world English reinscribes the power of the West—particularly the United States and its allies—at the same moment the West itself is being contested. The United States and the Western European nations are undergoing demographic changes that challenge perceptions of them as White, Christian nations.

Scholars will need to respond to the postcolonial and multiple discourses that worldwide change demands. Their work will have to incorporate heterogeneity, hybridity, and multiplicity and be more tentative in its assertions. Scholarship will be more like everyday life: less certain, less definitive, and less prescriptive. In K-12 classrooms, teachers will have to work back and forth between individual and group identities, while at the same moment taking principled stands on behalf of students who, because of some perceived difference or sense of otherness, are left behind. The new work of multicultural education must be more generative. Both scholars and classroom teachers must look for opportunities, new ways to think and learn about human diversity and social justice. They must be willing to push innovation in multicultural education. Multicultural education must be open to conflict and change, as is true of any culture and cultural form if it is to survive. Multicultural education, like jazz, must remain "gloriously inclusive" (Ward & Burns, 2000, p. 460). Each epoch must offer us a new direction in multicultural education.

References

Afsaruddin, A. (Ed.). (1999). *Hermeneutics and honor: Negotiating female public space in Islamic/ate societies*. Boston: Harvard University Press.

Aleinikoff, T. A. (1991). A case for race-consciousness. *Columbia Law Review, 91*, 1060–1125.

Anzaldua, G. (1987). *Borderlands/la frontera: The new mestiza*. San Francisco: Ante Lute Press.

Apple, M. W. (1993). *Official knowledge: Democratic education in a conservative age*. New York: Routledge.

Banks, J. A., & Banks, C.A.M. (Eds.). (2001). *Multicultural education: Issues and perspectives* (4th ed.). New York: Wiley.

Bell, D. (1980). *Brown v. Board of Education* and the interest convergence dilemma. *Harvard Law Review, 93*, 518–533.

Bell, D. (1987). *And we are not saved: The elusive quest for racial justice*. New York: Basic Books.

Bell, D. (1998). *Afrolantic legacies*. Chicago: Third World Press.

Bennett, T. (1992). Putting policy into cultural studies. In L. Grossbert, C. Nelson, & P. Treichler (Eds.), *Cultural Studies* (pp. 23–27). London: Routledge.

Bourdieu, P. (1977). Cultural reproduction and social reproduction. In J. Karabel & F. Halsey (Eds.), *Power and ideology in education* (pp. 487–511). New York: Oxford University Press.

Code, L. (1991). *What can she know? Feminist theory and the construction of knowledge*. Ithaca, NY: Cornell University Press.

Coffey, M. (2000). What puts the "culture" in "multiculturalism"? An analysis of culture, government, and the politics of Mexican identity. In R. Mahalingam & C. McCarthy (Eds.), *Multicultural curriculum: New directions for social theory, practice, and policy* (pp. 37–55). New York: Routledge.

Collins, C., & Yeskel, F. (2000). *Economic apartheid: A primer on economic inequality and security*. New York: New Press.

Conley, D. (2000). *Honky*. New York: Vintage Books.

Crenshaw, K. (1988). Race, reform, and retrenchment: Transformation and legitimation in antidiscrimination law. *Harvard Law Review, 101*, 1331–1387.

Davis, F. (1985). Ornette's permanent revolution. [On-line]. Available: www.theatlantic.com/unbound/jazz/dornette.htm

Delgado, R. (1992). Rodrigo's chronicle. *Yale Law Journal, 101*, 1357–1383.

Delgado, R. (Ed.). (1995). *Critical race theory: The cutting edge*. Philadelphia: Temple University Press.

Delgado, R. (2000). Derrick Bell's toolkit—Fit to dismantle that famous house? *New York University Law Review, 75*, 283–307.

DuBois, W.E.B. (1953/1989). *The souls of Black folk*. New York: Bantam Books. (Originally published in 1953)

Dyson, M. E. (1994). Essentialism and the complexities of racial identity. In D. T. Goldberg (Ed.), *Multiculturalism: A critical reader* (pp. 218–229). Cambridge, MA: Blackwell Press.

Dyson, M. E. (2000). *I may not get there with you: The true Martin Luther King, Jr.* New York: Free Press.

Eck, D. (2001). *A new religious America: How a "Christian country" has become the world's most religiously diverse nation*. San Francisco: Harper.

Engel, C. (1922). Jazz: A musical discussion. [On-line]. Available: www.theatlantic.com/unbound/jazz/cengel.htm

Fanon, F. (1963). *The wretched of the earth*. New York: Grove Press.

Fanon, F. (1967). *Black skins, White masks*. New York: Grove Press.

Foucault, M. (1972). *The archaeology of knowledge* (A. M. Sheridan-Smith, Trans.). London: Tavistock.

Foucault, M. (1991). Governmentality. In G. Burchell, C. Gordon, & P. Miller (Eds.), *The Foucault effect: Studies in governmentality* (pp. 87–104). Chicago: University of Chicago Press.

Frankenberg, R. (1993). *White women, race matters: The social construction of whiteness.* Minneapolis: University of Minnesota Press.

Fuss, D. (Ed.). (1991). *Inside/out: Lesbian theories, gay theories.* New York: Routledge.

Gay, G. (2001). Curriculum theory and multicultural education. In J. A. Banks & C.A.M. Banks (Eds.), *Handbook of research on multicultural education* (pp. 25–43). San Francisco: Jossey-Bass.

Gilligan, C. (1977). In a different voice: Women's conceptions of self and of morality. *Harvard Educational Review, 47,* 481–517.

Gilroy, P. (1993). *The Black Atlantic: Modernity and double consciousness.* Cambridge, MA: Harvard University Press.

Glazer, N. (1997). *We are all multiculturalists now.* Cambridge, MA: Harvard University Press.

Goldman, S. (Ed.). (1953). *The words of Justice Brandeis.* New York: Schuman.

Gordon, E. W. (1997). Task force on the role and future of minorities: American Educational Research Association. *Educational Researcher, 26*(3), 44–52.

Gould, S. J. (1981). *The mismeasure of man.* New York: Norton.

Grant, C. A., & Sleeter, C. E. (1997). *Turning on learning: Five approaches for multicultural teaching plans for race, class, gender, and disability* (2nd ed.). Upper Saddle River, NJ: Merrill/Prentice Hall.

Grillo, T., & Wildman, S. M. (1995). Obscuring the importance of race: The implication of making comparisons between racism and sexism (or other-isms). In R. Delgado (Ed.), *Critical Race Theory: The cutting edge* (pp. 564–572). Philadelphia: Temple University Press.

Haberman, M. (1991). The pedagogy of poverty versus good teaching. *Phi Delta Kappan, 73,* 290–294.

Hacker, A. (1992). *Two nations: Black and White, separate, hostile, unequal.* New York: Basic Books.

Haney Lopez, I. (1995). White by law. In R. Delgado (Ed.), *Critical Race Theory: The cutting edge* (pp. 542–550). Philadelphia: Temple University Press.

Harris, C. (1993). Whiteness as property. *Harvard Law Review, 106,* 1707–1791.

Heble, A. (2000). *Landing on the wrong note: Jazz, dissonance and critical practice.* New York: Routledge.

Hollinger, D. (1995). *Postethnic America: Beyond multiculturalism.* New York: Basic Books.

hooks, b. (1989). *Talking back: Thinking feminist, thinking Black.* Boston: South End Press.

Huntington, S. (1997). *The clash of civilization and the remaking of world order.* New York: Touchstone.

Jaimes, M. A., & Halsey, T. (1992). American Indian women at the center of indigenous resistance in contemporary North America. In M. A. Jaimes (Ed.), *The state of Native America: Genocide, colonization, and resistance* (pp. 311–344). Boston: South End Press.

James, S., & Busia, A. (Eds.). (1993). *Theorizing Black feminisms: The visionary pragmatism of Black women.* New York: Routledge.

King, J. E. (1992). Diaspora literacy and consciousness in the struggle against miseducation in the Black community. *Journal of Negro Education, 61,* 317–340.

King, J. E. (2001). Culture-centered knowledge: Black studies, curriculum transformation, and social action. In J. A. Banks & C.A.M. Banks (Eds.), *Handbook of research on multicultural education* (pp. 265–290). San Francisco: Jossey-Bass.

Kohn, A. (1998). Only for *my* kid: How privileged parents undermine school reform. *Phi Delta Kappan, 79,* 568–577.

Kozol, J. (1991). *Savage inequalities: Children in America's schools.* New York: HarperCollins.

Kymlicka, W. (Ed.).(1995). *The rights of minority cultures.* New York: Oxford University Press.

Ladson-Billings, G. (1994). *The dreamkeepers: Successful teachers of African American children.* San Francisco: Jossey-Bass.

Ladson-Billings, G. (1998). Just what is critical race theory and what's it doing in a nice field like education? *International Journal of Qualitative Studies in Education, 11*(1), 7–24.

Ladson-Billings, G., & Tate, W. F. (1995). Toward a critical race theory of education. *Teachers College Record, 97*(1), 47–68.

Lather, P. (1991). *Getting smart: Feminist research and pedagogy with/in the postmodern.* New York: Routledge.

Lawrence-Lightfoot, S., & Davis, J. H. (1997). *The art and science of portraiture.* San Francisco: Jossey-Bass.

Linton, S. (1998). *Claiming disability: Knowledge and identity.* New York: New York University Press.

Lowe, L. (1996). *Immigrant acts.* Durham, NC: Duke University Press.

McCarthy, C. (1988). Reconsidering liberal and radical perspectives on racial inequality in schooling: Making the case for nonsynchrony. *Harvard Educational Review, 58,* 265–279.

McCarthy, C. (1993). After the canon: knowledge and ideological representation in the multicultural discourse on curriculum reform. In C. McCarthy & W. Crichlow (Eds.), *Race, identity and representation in education* (pp. 289–305). New York: Routledge.

McKay, S., & Wong, S. (1996). Multiple discourses, multiple identities: Investment and agency in second-language learning among Chinese adolescent immigrant students. *Harvard Educational Review, 66,* 577–608.

McLaren, P. (1994). White terror and oppositional agency: Towards a critical multiculturalism. In D. T. Goldberg (Ed.), *Multiculturalism: A critical reader* (pp. 45–74). Cambridge, MA: Blackwell.

McLaren, P. (2000). *Che Guevara, Paulo Freire, and the pedagogy of revolution.* Lanham, MD: Rowman & Littlefield.

McNeil, L. (2000). *Contradictions of school reform: Educational costs of standardized testing.* New York: Routledge.

McWhorter, J. (2001). *Losing the race: Self-sabotage in Black America.* New York: HarperPerennial Library.

Minh-ha, T. T. (1989). *Woman, native, other: Writing postcolonially and feminism.* Bloomington: Indiana University Press.

Moodley, K. A. (1983). Canadian multiculturalism as ideology. *Ethnic and racial studies, 6,* 320–331.

Morrison, T. (1989). Unspeakable things unspoken: The Afro-American presence in American literature. *Michigan Quarterly Review, 28*(1), 1–34.

Morrison, T. (1991). *Playing in the dark: Whiteness in the literary imagination.* Cambridge, MA: Harvard University Press.

Morrison, T., & Lacour, C. B. (Eds.). (1997). *Birth of a nation'hood: Gaze, script, and spectacle in the O. J. Simpson case.* New York: Pantheon Books.

National Council for Accreditation of Teacher Education. (2002). *Professional standards for the accreditation of schools, colleges, and departments of education.* Washington, DC: Author.

Noddings, N. (1984). *Caring: A feminine approach to ethics and moral education.* Berkeley: University of California Press.

Okin, S., Cohen, J., Howard, M., & Nussbaum, M. (Eds.). (1999). *Is multiculturalism bad for women?* Princeton, NJ: Princeton University Press.

Olivas, M. (1995). The chronicles, my grandfather's stories, and immigration law: The slave traders chronicle as racial history. In R. Delgado (Ed.), *Critical Race Theory: The cutting edge* (pp. 9–20). Philadelphia: Temple University Press.

Olneck, M. (1990). The recurring dream: Symbolism and ideology in intercultural and multicultural education. *American Journal of Education, 98*(2), 147–174.

Palumbo-Liu, D. (Ed.). (1995). *The ethnic canon: Histories, institutions and interventions.* Minneapolis: University of Minnesota Press.

Parker, L., Deyhle, D., & Villenas, S. (Eds.). (1999). *Race is . . . race isn't: Critical race theory and qualitative studies in education.* Boulder, CO: Westview Press.

Ravitch, D. (1990). Multiculturalism: E pluribus plures. *American Scholar, 59*(3), 337–354.

Reed, I. (Ed.). (1997). *Multi-America: Essays on cultural wars and cultural peace.* New York: Viking Press.

Schlesinger, A. (1991). *The disuniting of America: Reflections of a multicultural society.* Knoxville, TN: Whittle Direct Books.

Schmitz, B., Butler, J., Rosenfelt, D., & Guy-Sheftall, B. (2001). Women's studies and curriculum transformation. In J. A. Banks & C.A.M. Banks (Eds.), *Handbook of research on multicultural education* (pp. 708–728). San Francisco: Jossey-Bass.

Sedgwick, E. (1990). *Epistemology of the closet.* Berkeley: University of California Press.

Sen, A. (1995). *Inequality reexamined.* Cambridge, MA: Harvard University Press.

Shakespeare, T. (Ed.). (1998). *Disability reader: Social sciences perspectives.* London: Cassell.

Shujaa, M. (Ed.). (1996). *Beyond desegregation.* Thousand Oaks, CA: Corwin Press.

Siddle Walker, E. V. (1996). *Their highest potential: An African American school community in the segregated south.* Chapel Hill: University of North Carolina Press.

Sims, R. (1982). *Shadow and substance: Afro-American experience in contemporary children's fiction.* Urban, IL: National Council of Teachers of English.

Sleeter, C. E., & Grant, C. A. (1987). An analysis of multicultural education in the United States. *Harvard Educational Review, 7,* 421–444.

Smith, L. T. (1999). *Decolonizing methodologies: Research and indigenous peoples.* London: Zed Books.

Sowell, T. (1984). *Civil rights: Rhetoric or reality?* New York: Morrow.

Steele, S. (1990). *The content of our character: A new vision of race in America.* New York: St. Martin's Press.

Strickland, E. (1987). What Coltrane wanted. [On-line]. Available: www.theatlantic.com/unbound/jazz/strickla.htm

Suárez-Orozco, M. (2001). Globalization, immigration, and education: The research agenda. *Harvard Educational Review, 71,* 345–365.

Sundgaard, A. (1955). Jazz, hot and cold. [On-line]. Available: www.theatlantic.com/unbound/jazz/sungaar.htm

Swartz, E. (1992). Emancipatory narratives: Rewriting the master script in the school curriculum. *Journal of Negro Education, 61,* 341–355.

Tate, W. F. (1997). Critical race theory and education: History, theory, and implications. In M. Apple (Ed.), *Review of Research in Education* (vol. 22, pp. 195–247). Washington, DC: American Educational Research Association.

Taylor, E. (1998, Spring). A primer on CRT. *Journal of Blacks in Higher Education, 19,* 122–124.

Tierney, W. (1995). (Re)presentation and voice. *Qualitative Inquiry, 1,* 379–390.

Troyna, B., & Williams, J. (1986). *Racism, education, and the state: The racialisation of education policy.* London: Croom Helm.

U.S. Census Bureau. (2000). *Report of the Population.* [On-line]. Available: www.census.gov

U.S. Department of Education. (2001, August). *Back to school, moving forward.* Washington, DC: Educational Publications Center.

U.S. Department of State. (2001). [On-line]. Available: http://usinfo/state/gov/products/pubs/muslimlife

Verma, G., & Bagley, C. (Eds.). (1982). *Self-concept, achievement and multicultural education.* London: Macmillan.

Wa Thiong'o, N. (1986). *Decolonizing the mind: The politics of language in African literature.* London: Currey.

Ward, G. C., & Burns, K. (2000). *Jazz: A history of America's music.* New York: Knopf.

Warrior, R. A. (1995). *Tribal secrets: Recovering American Indian intellectual traditions.* Minneapolis: University of Minnesota Press.

West, C. (1993). *Keeping faith: Philosophy and race in America.* New York: Routledge.

West, C. (1995). Foreword. In K. Crenshaw, N. Gotanda, G. Peller, & K. Thomas (Eds.), *Critical race theory: The key writings that formed the movement* (pp. xi–xii). New York: New Press.

White, J. E. (1996, November 25). Texaco's high-octane racism problems. *Time, 148,* pp. 33–34.

Williams, R. (1976). *Keywords.* London: Fontana.

Wynter, S. (1989). Beyond the word of man: Glissant and the new discourse of the Antilles. *World Literature Today, 63,* 637–648.

Wynter, S. (1992). *Do not call us "Negroes": How "multicultural" textbooks perpetuate racism.* San Francisco: Aspire Books.

PART

II

ISSUES, TRENDS, AND DEVELOPMENTS

4

ACCESS AND ACHIEVEMENT IN MATHEMATICS AND SCIENCE

Inequalities That Endure and Change

Jeannie Oakes
University of California, Los Angeles

Rebecca Joseph
University of California, Los Angeles

Kate Muir
University of Wyoming, Laramie

In July 1999, Rasheda Daniel and three of her fellow students at Inglewood High School in Southern California launched a legal challenge to achieve equitable access to advanced placement (AP) courses. Represented by the American Civil Liberties Union (ACLU) of Southern California, the Inglewood High School students filed a statewide class-action lawsuit against their school district and the State of California (*Daniel* v. *California*, no. BC 214156). Their complaint stated that this differential access to AP classes denied Rasheda Daniel and a class of primarily low-income students of color equal educational opportunity. Like students at many other comprehensive urban high schools serving primarily poor African American and Latino students, Rasheda Daniel and her schoolmates could not enroll in AP classes in math and science, because Inglewood High School did not offer AP courses in these core academic subjects. Indeed, at the time of the filing, Inglewood High School offered only three AP courses, none in math or science. By contrast, other California public high schools such as Beverly Hills High School and Arcadia High School, which serve large numbers of White and affluent students, offered more than 14 AP courses, among them calculus, computer programming, and physics. Without such access, Rasheda and her lawsuit peers claimed, they would be severely disadvantaged when seeking admission to competitive universities.

The *Daniel* case demonstrates that unequal access to mathematics and science course taking and achievement remains a serious, self-evident problem in K-12 schools. Moreover, the case also illuminates that the face of the problem has changed significantly over the past decade and that possible solutions are less than straightforward. The case and its proposed remedy reveal both what we know and what we do not about the enduring, yet changing, relationship among diversity, mathematics and science course taking, achievement, and equity.

In what follows, we review research from the past decade that has examined various dimensions of this persistent and troubling problem. Our review reveals that, even though both achievement and course taking have increased for all groups, serious gaps remain. They relate at least in part to persistent inequality in opportunity to learn, linked to race and social class, between schools and within them. This finding suggests that, although continuing to add and/or require additional mathematics and science coursework may have some ameliorative effects in the future, these solutions will not touch the core of the inequality problem.

At the same time, considerable work studying curricular reforms and equity-minded interventions suggests a number of strategies for bridging the gaps in course taking and achievement. We have also learned that translating effective strategies into wide-scale school change is enormously challenging. In addition to new curricula, teaching strategies, and supplemental supports for low-income students and students of color, reducing inequality will require significant shifts in the current low educational expectations our culture holds for low-income students and students of color, and in our political unwillingness to provide them high-quality schooling.

We conclude from this review that we need to better understand the practices that will lead to more equitable patterns of course taking and achievement. However, we also need far more knowledge of these cultural and political dimensions of the problem. Because all of these areas would profit from further investigation, we offer a list of promising questions for future work.

We begin, however, by sketching the larger social and political context that helps us see how and why inequality exists even in the face of the increases in course taking and achievement.

EDUCATIONAL EQUITY IN THE 1990S: BROAD THEMES

Three themes emerged repeatedly in our examination of the past decade's research on the relationship between equity, math and science course taking, and achievement: (a) the press for standards and accountability, (b) the still separate and unequal K-12 education system, and (c) the redefinition of college eligibility. We describe these themes to provide a context for our discussions of what we have learned from research and what we still need to know.

Press for Standards and Accountability

Despite the Reagan administration's attempt to minimize the federal role in education, the late 1980s and 1990s witnessed an increased emphasis on national goals and federal standards for education, and, under the rubric of "systemic reform," the alignment of these national policies with state accountability systems. Anxiety about potentially powerful competitors in the new global economy triggered a national conversation about what American students should know and be able to do to ensure our prosperity; it pressed diverse groups of subject matter experts and policy makers to develop, implement, and adopt a standards-based approach to education reform.

The National Council of Teachers of Mathematics (NCTM) was the first group to release national goals and guidelines (NCTM, 1989, 2000). In the field of science, two organizations released documents that guide reform, the American Association for the Advancement of Science (AAAS) Project 2061's *Benchmarks for Science Literacy* (AAAS, 1993) and the National Research Council's (NRC) *National Science Education Standards* (NRC, 1996). Equity

issues were salient, albeit contentious, in the framing of these documents, and the emerging foundation of these standards declares that all students can learn high-level math and science. For example, the underlying principle of the *National Science Education Standards* reads:

Science is for all students. This principle is one of equity and excellence.

> Science in our schools must be for all students: All students regardless of age, sex, cultural or ethnic background, disabilities, aspirations, or interest and motivation in science, should have the opportunity to attain high levels of scientific literacy. (NRC, 1996, p. 20)

We do not yet know the full impact the movement for high standards will have on equity in course taking and achievement, but we have already seen a significant reduction in the number of low-level mathematics and science classes and increasing pressure for all students to complete algebra 1 in high school.

However, the same climate that produced an emphasis on higher educational standards also produced a rapid expansion of statewide accountability programs. These programs feature high-stakes assessments to hold students, teachers, and schools accountable for meeting academic standards set by the states (Hanushek, 1994; Ladd, 1996; Millman, 1997). To give these standards teeth, the accountability systems often include dire consequences for failure to meet the academic standards, including grade retention or failure to earn a high school diploma and whole school reconstitution or state take-over. Increasingly, however, analysts worry that these programs will have a disproportionately negative effect on low-income minority students. Recent studies suggest that standards-based accountability reforms can serve to widen the gap between these students and their more advantaged peers in their access to significant mathematics and science opportunities and achievement, even as the gap on basic skills tests may narrow. For example, high-stakes assessments, like those used in Texas, lead to students in low-income schools receiving significantly less science instruction and low-level math instruction at all levels in the K-12 educational system (McNeil & Valenzuela, 2000).

We return to the impact of reform on achievement and course taking later in this chapter. Here, we simply note that the past decade's standards and accountability reforms affect nearly every effort to achieve equity in opportunities and outcomes.

Still Separate and Still Unequal

In the last 10 years, as our nation has become more diverse and multicultural, different responses have emerged to address these societal changes. Growing segregation has been one. Urban schools, for example, are more likely than ever to serve a population of low-income, minority students, given increased residential segregation and recent court decisions releasing schools across the country from desegregation orders (Orfield & Yun, 1999).

Segregated minority schools remain less likely to offer access to upper courses, despite considerable recent evidence of the benefit of rigorous curricula for all students, regardless of their educational backgrounds (Adelman, 1999). Research in the past decade also demonstrates that, although a school's ability to enable students to succeed in a rigorous curriculum depends on its teacher corps, schools serving minority and low-income students are least likely to have highly qualified faculties (Darling-Hammond, 2000; Ferguson, 1991, 1998; Greenwald, Hedges, & Laine, 1996; Murnane, 1996; Wright, Horn, & Sanders, 1997). The very real teacher shortage in many parts of the nation, coupled with policies that discourage teachers from working in racially segregated minority schools, means that fewer well-qualified teachers are available to teach students of color in segregated schools. Moreover, schools serving low-income students of color have yet to counter the growing "digital divide" that brings race and social class inequity in access to technology (Educational Testing Service Policy Information Report, 1997).

Additionally, counseling shortages in urban schools affect both the quality and quantity of advisement for low-income students. This lack, combined with the pervasiveness of tracking, restricts these students' access to challenging mathematics and science classes. Despite numerous efforts to detrack K-12 education institutions since the mid-1980s, tracking still exists and thrives in schools across the country (U.S. Commission on Civil Rights, 1999). Within racially mixed schools, minorities are still disproportionately overrepresented in low-level courses and underrepresented in critical courses. An ironic impact of the detracking movement may be the dramatic increase and emphasis on advanced placement courses and testing in the past decade (Oakes, Welner, Yonezawa, & Allen, 1998). As schools began to eliminate some of their low-level courses, many middle-class parents sought ways to maintain their children's perceived competitiveness for college. As a result, the math and science pipelines began earlier and became more extensive, with college-bound students taking algebra I in eighth grade and ending their high school career in advanced placement courses, including calculus.

College Eligibility: An Ever-Rising Bar

Changes in college admissions make it far more difficult for students lacking access to rigorous K-12 mathematics and science education to qualify. Most salient, the national movement to discredit and dismantle affirmative action in college admissions has increased the importance of K-12 academic achievement, particularly for low-income students of color. Minority admissions to public universities in California and Texas have declined significantly since those states banned the use of racial preferences in their admissions processes (Orfield & Miller, 2000). As a result, minority enrollment in college preparatory courses is even more important than ever.

Relevant here, too, is that AP classes have become an ever more important factor in college admissions. For example, in the past decade alone, the number of AP exams taken in California has almost tripled, from 78,379 in 1989 to 203,523 in 1999. The increase in California can be traced to the decision of the University of California in 1984 to boost student grades in AP classes when calculating student grade point average (GPA) for university admission. California's rate of AP participation exceeds that of most other states, but it is not alone in this trend. Moreover, as the demand for college rises, policy makers, educators, and members of the public now expect a highly competitive admissions process to elite universities. Further, most people recognize that college preparatory curricula must now include AP courses. Because these new expectations emerged without planning or publicity, only certain high schools—primarily those serving advantaged populations—have been in the position to embrace them. Without a plan for supporting schools to realize these new expectations, the state transformed the rules of the game in a way that negatively affects its poorest and most vulnerable communities (Oakes et al., 2000).

WHAT WE KNOW FROM RESEARCH ABOUT COURSE TAKING AND ACHIEVEMENT

Whether you view the glass as half empty or half full, positive trends exist in mathematics and science course taking and achievement. First, we will note these positive trends and then describe other patterns that have developed over the past 10 to 15 years. Then we analyze course taking patterns. Within these positive trends, patterns of differential access (both between schools and within schools) to math and science course taking continue to disadvantage poor children.

Trends in Achievement

As Rodriguez (1997) states, "There is cause for cautious celebration regarding student achievement in science" (p. 13). Positive patterns occurred in mathematics achievement as well. Over the last 20 years, scores on the science and math portions of the National Assessment of Educational Progress (NAEP) have increased for all student populations. From 1973 to 1996, all ethnic groups improved their NAEP math and science scores with the greatest increases for all tested age groups in both subject areas occurring in the 1970s and 1980s (Snyder & Hoffman,

	1978	1986	1990	1996
White	272	274	276	281
Black	230	249	249	252
Hispanic	238	254	255	256

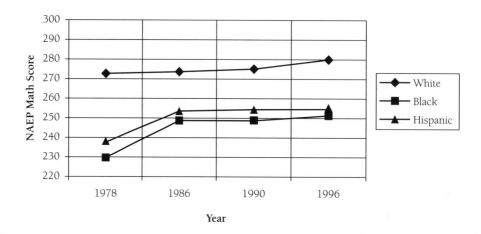

FIGURE 4.1. NAEP Math Scores, 13-Year-Olds.

2000). Figures 4.1 and 4.2 display NAEP scores for 13-year-olds in math and science, respectively.

Other positive trends in NAEP assessments are the steady disappearance of a gender gap in science achievement and the almost nonexistent gender gap in math achievement. For example, 1996 male and female students' science scores in grades 4 and 8 "did not differ to a statistically significant degree" (O'Sullivan, Reese, & Mazzeo, 1997, p. 28). Even though in 1996, among students in grade 12, on average males scored higher on the NAEP science assessment than their female peers (National Science Foundation [NSF], 1999), the gender gap is one of the smallest internationally, as reported by the Third International Mathematics and Science study (U.S. Department of Education, 1998).

Despite these science and math gains in NAEP, performance gaps persist between White students and Hispanic students (National Science Board, 2000; NSF, 1999; Rodriguez, 1997; Snyder & Hoffman, 2000). In fact, Hispanic 13-year-olds score slightly lower in science than White 9-year-olds (Snyder & Hoffman). A gap also exists in achieving advanced scores on NAEP tests. Table 4.1 displays the 1996 math and science NAEP test scores for 12th graders. Black and Hispanic students do not score at the advanced level in math, and only 1 percent of Hispanic students score at the advanced level in science. Socioeconomic gaps occur as well: Title I students and those receiving free or reduced lunch score lower than students ineligible for these benefits.

Moreover, minority groups exhibit gender gaps that raise troubling questions about the overall patterns of decreasing gaps that we noted earlier. Underrepresented minority males fall far behind their female counterparts in achievement and attainment. That males earned only 36 percent of the bachelor's degrees accorded to African Americans in the mid-1990s attests to a pattern of differential achievement among males and females from the earliest grades (College Board, 1999).

Trends in Course Taking

Who has access to mathematics and science courses, and who is taking them? These are the questions to which we

TABLE 4.1. Percentage of 12th-Grade Students Within the Proficient and Advanced Achievement Ranges on the NAEP 1996 Math and Science Tests.

	Proficient		Advanced	
	Math	Science	Math	Science
White	18	24	2	3
African American	4	4	0	0
Hispanic	6	6	0	1
Asian	26	19	7	3
Native American	3	10	0	0

Source: College Board, 1999.

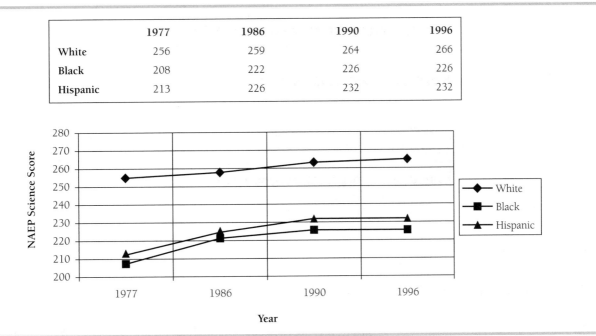

	1977	1986	1990	1996
White	256	259	264	266
Black	208	222	226	226
Hispanic	213	226	232	232

FIGURE 4.2. NAEP Science Scores, 13-Year-Olds.

now turn. Minority enrollment and completion of advanced-level math and science courses rose dramatically during the past twenty years. The percentages of Black and Hispanic high school graduates taking algebra II more than doubled from 1982 to 1994. As Figure 4.3 demonstrates, calculus course taking doubled as well. In science, almost all high school graduates take biology (93 percent in 1994), as compared to only 77 percent in 1982 (NSF, 1999). Changes in chemistry enrollment are shown in Figure 4.4.

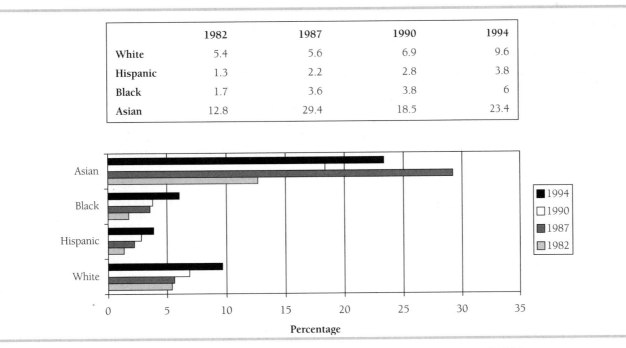

	1982	1987	1990	1994
White	5.4	5.6	6.9	9.6
Hispanic	1.3	2.2	2.8	3.8
Black	1.7	3.6	3.8	6
Asian	12.8	29.4	18.5	23.4

FIGURE 4.3. Percentage of High School Graduates Taking Calculus, 1982, 1987, 1990, and 1994.

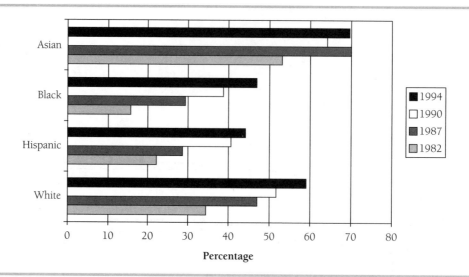

FIGURE 4.4. Percentage of High School Graduates Taking Chemistry, 1982, 1987, 1990, and 1994.

Despite these tremendous gains, there is still a great difference among racial and ethnic groups. Aggregated data from 1998 show similar patterns in advanced mathematics (an aggregate of trigonometry and calculus) and advanced science (chemistry II and physics II) course taking. Asian students take advanced mathematics (56 percent of high school graduates who took these courses) and advanced science (17 percent) more often than their high school peers (see Table 4.2).

On the remedial end, "Black and Hispanic high school graduates in 1994 were far more likely than White and Asian students to have taken remedial mathematics courses: 31 percent of Blacks, 24 percent of Hispanics compared to 15 percent of Whites and Asians" (NSF, 1999, p. 16). On the honors or advanced end, Asians far outpaced other racial and ethnic groups in advanced mathematics course taking (NSF, p. 16).

Similar patterns occur in science course taking. Moreover, an apparent gender gap occurs in the type of science enrollment: "Females were slightly more likely than males to have taken Biology and Chemistry and males were

slightly more likely than females to have taken Physics" (NSF, 1999, p. 12). Madigan (1997) also notes that males were more likely to have taken physics than their female peers.

These gaps among groups in Table 4.2 are actually far larger than the numbers show. Low-income students of color, and particularly Latino youth, experience far higher dropout rates than their White and Asian peers. The Latino dropout rate, for example, hovers around 50 percent. Consequently, figures showing the participation of students of high school age in the population at large would show significantly greater gaps in participation.

These achievement and course-taking gaps are unnecessary and dangerous (Education Trust, 1998). They are unnecessary because low-income and minority students will achieve at the highest levels given appropriate learning opportunities and support, and dangerous because we cannot afford the loss of these students' talents and future efforts. Although the gaps narrowed in the late 1970s and 1980s, they stagnated in the 1990s. We turn now to explanations of why these tenacious gaps remain.

TABLE 4.2. Percentage of High School Graduates Who Took Advanced Mathematics or Science Courses, 1998.

Race or Ethnicity	Advanced Mathematics	Advanced Science
White	45	7
African American	30	5
Hispanic	26	6
Asian or Pacific Islander	56	17
American Indian or Alaskan Native	27	2

Source: NSF (1999).

WHY DO INEQUALITIES PERSIST? BETWEEN-SCHOOL DIFFERENCES

A student can take a high-level class in science and mathematics only if his or her school offers such classes or if his or her school opens up access to these courses to all students. In other words, how far a student can go down either the mathematics or science pipeline depends on his or her access to particular courses. We will focus on high-level gatekeeping courses such as algebra II and calculus in math and physics and chemistry in science to elucidate patterns of access and nonaccess to such courses. We find that, despite the standards movement, segregated minority schools remain less likely to offer access to upper-level math and science courses. Many schools do not offer math beyond algebra II. Many do not offer three basic lab science classes. Poor and minority students form a disproportionate number of those affected by these differences in course taking opportunities (Oakes, 1990a).

For example, participation in advanced courses differs with a school's socioeconomic status (SES) level (Ma & Willms, 1999). Ma and Willms write, "With all factors being equal, students were more likely to pursue advanced mathematics if they attended a high SES school than if they attended a low SES school" (p. 379). Similarly, using data from two sources—the National Education Longitudinal Study of 1988 (NELS 88) (NCES, n.d.) and the High School Effectiveness Study (HSES)—Lee, Burkham, Chow-Hoy, Smerdon, and Geverdt (1998) define school types on the basis of average pipeline completion. Two types relate to our discussion: "low-progress schools" (15.8 percent of the sample) and "high-progress schools" (17.4 percent). Low-progress schools, all of which are public schools, include schools in which the average progress through the mathematics pipeline ends at algebra. Most of these schools feature high minority enrollments (40 percent or more minority students) and on average have lower-achieving students. High-progress schools, of which 14 percent are public, are defined as schools where all students reach calculus. All high-progress schools offered calculus, "but less than half of the low-progress schools offer this course" (Lee et al., 1998, p. 21). Low-progress schools offered "nearly twice as many math courses below Algebra as high-progress schools" (p. 21).

Similar patterns occur in science course offerings. Differentiating schools by community type, Matti and Weiss (1994) found that students in disadvantaged urban schools along with many of their rural peers "were less likely to have the opportunity to take advanced science courses" (p. 37). Students from low SES backgrounds in NELS 88 "were clearly less likely than those from high SES backgrounds to take eight or more semesters of science or to take Physics" (Madigan, 1997, p. 11).

These gaps extend to advanced placement courses. Oakes and her colleagues (2000) found that high schools across the state of California vary greatly in their AP offerings. Some high schools offer multiple sections of more than 14 AP courses. Many other California high schools offer only a single section of two or three AP courses, with 177 California high schools not offering any AP classes. These differences in AP offerings correlate to several factors, including school size and location, but they clearly correspond to a high school's racial composition. Comprehensive urban high schools that serve predominantly

poor Latino and African American students typically offer far fewer AP courses than suburban high schools of comparable size serving mainly White and middle-class students. Regardless of high school size, the availability of AP courses decreases as the percentage of African Americans and Latinos in the school population increases (Oakes et al., 2000). Moreover, differential access to AP classes is starkest and most consequential in mathematics and science. Table 4.3 shows that schools that enroll a primarily African American and Latino student population have far fewer offerings than schools that serve predominantly White and/or Asian students.

Same Courses Differ Between Schools

As early as 1980, researchers commented on the curricular differences in schools with varying levels of socioeconomic status. Ironically, these differences continue and may be made worse by standards-based accountability systems.

Content Differences. High-poverty elementary school curricula often focus on basic facts and skills, while affluent school curricula provide access to challenging, problem-based learning and "enrichment" activities. For example, Anyon noted differences in elementary school curricula between what she termed a "working class school" and an "executive elite school" (Anyon, 1980). In particular, science and math instruction differed at these two types of schools. Teachers at the working-class school used procedure-driven techniques in their classes and often failed to gauge whether their students understood what they were making or doing. In science, "children were never called upon to set up experiments or to give explanations for facts or concepts" (p. 75). In contrast, at the executive elite school teachers expected students to develop "analytical intellectual powers" (p. 83). In math, teachers encouraged students to evaluate each other's decision-making strategies; in science, as an executive elite school teacher explains, students "generate hypotheses and devise experiments to solve the problem" (p. 86).

Later studies confirm Anyon's findings of teachers in low-SES elementary schools emphasizing problem solving and inquiry skills less than their higher-SES peers

TABLE 4.3. Disparities in Math and Science Offerings.

African American and Latino	Number of AP Math or Science Offerings
Greater than 70%	3.8
Less than 30%	5.3

Source: Tomas Rivera Center (1999).

(Matti & Weiss, 1994; Oakes, 1990a). Higher emphases on standardized testing in many states exacerbate these differences, with teachers teaching toward basic skills necessary to achieve well on statewide assessments (McNeil & Valenzuela, 2000). Elementary teachers in low-SES schools often eliminate most science instruction to focus on basic reading and math skills (McNeil and Valenzuela). In states that mandate performance-based assessments, such as portfolios, some improvements in access to higher level math and science instruction and curriculum do occur in low-income elementary schools (Darling-Hammond, 1997; Koretz, Mitchell, Barron, & Keith, 1996; Stecher & Mitchell, 1995).

In high-poverty and high-minority secondary schools, courses offer less content coverage, depth, and laboratory time. For example, Lee and her colleagues determined that "disadvantaged students . . . are often found in classrooms that emphasize lower-order skills, basic knowledge, drill and practice, recitation, and desk work" (Lee, Smith, & Croninger, 1997, p. 130). Similarly, Weiss (1994), replicating Oakes's 1990a and 1990b findings, found that math and science teachers in classes with high proportions of minority students are more likely than others to emphasize standardized test preparation (these tests often focus on low-level skills) and less likely to attempt to prepare students for further study in these fields. For example, examining data from High School and Beyond, a national database, Adelman (1999) concluded that algebra II classes in high-poverty schools often resemble algebra I classes found in more affluent schools. In their analysis of TIMMS data, Cogan, Schmidt, and Wiley (2002) note a disturbing difference in content between eighth-grade math classes both within and between schools. In fact, they identify four levels of eighth-grade math curricula: remedial, typical, enriched, and algebra. Three years' worth of learning content differentiates the remedial and algebra classes. Forty percent of schools serving urban and rural students do not offer eighth-grade algebra, while 80 percent of suburban schools do. Moreover, with increasing numbers of schools requiring algebra in the eighth grade, more minority students are failing because of a failure of schools to offer necessary supports to help students succeed in these classes.

Teacher Quality Differences. Teacher quality affects differences in course offerings. Generally, students in high-poverty schools more often have less-qualified teachers than their suburban peers do, and these trends are most extreme in math and science. Forty percent of math teachers and 20 percent of science in high-poverty schools teach out of field, as compared to 28 percent and 14 percent, respectively, in low-poverty schools (Ingersoll, Han, & Bobbitt, 1995). Out-of-field teachers and uncertified teachers are more likely to have onerous teaching loads. Their

lack of experience and expertise makes it probable that they rely heavily on textbooks and short-answer questions. Consequently, they spend less time developing students' critical-thinking skills and attending to students' interests.

Importantly, districts with low-income students often pay less and offer poorer working conditions (larger class sizes, more bureaucratic regulations, and less teacher autonomy) that make them less able to attract and retain qualified urban teachers (Darling-Hammond, 1997; Gilford & Tenebaum, 1995; Ingersoll, 1999). Ineffective and uncoordinated hiring practices also contribute to qualified math and science teacher shortages in urban districts. Applicants to urban schools often encounter unwieldy personnel offices, which routinely lose files, answer questions incorrectly or not at all, and ignore qualifications in favor of compliance. Late budget decisions and seniority transfer policies often make it impossible for urban recruiters to specify the school to which the prospective teachers will be assigned (Darling-Hammond, 1997; Gilford & Tenebaum, 1995). Rather than conducting full job searches, urban schools often fill midyear vacancies with out-of-field teachers or substitutes (Ingersoll, 1999). All these policies mean that urban districts hire less-qualified teachers, who are assigned to their neediest schools.

Making matters worse, math and science teachers often do not feel prepared to teach students from diverse cultural backgrounds. Results of the 1993 National Survey of Science and Math demonstrate that only 29 percent of these teachers feel comfortable teaching English language learners (Weiss, 1994). The 1993 National Survey of Science and Math Education included a national probability sample of 1,250 schools and 6,000 K-12 teachers (Weiss, 1994).

WITHIN-SCHOOL DIFFERENCES: TRACKING

We've known for years that tracking has allocated quite different instruction to students in different tracks, socialized them to accept their position in the school's status hierarchy, and signaled their appropriate futures to the outside world. American schools have quite consistently assigned children from privileged families (usually White) to academic tracks, and those who are poor and non-White to the others. Despite numerous efforts to detrack K-12 education institutions since the mid-1980s, tracking still exists and thrives in schools across the country. Recent efforts at raising student achievement paradoxically may exacerbate tracking. Also, the content coverage and teaching objectives vary within the different levels and ability-grouped courses. Through tracking policies, then, students have differential access to high-level courses, and in turn to science and math achievement (Hoffer, 1992; Lee, Smith, & Croninger, 1997; Mason &

Good, 1993; Oakes, 1990b, 1995; Oakes, Gamoran, & Page, 1992).

Prevailing norms about the desirability of tracking underlie its persistence. Interestingly, although more than 75 percent of science and math teachers believe that almost all children can develop mathematical and scientific thinking skills, most teachers do not believe they can bring about such learning in heterogeneous classes. Approximately 30 percent of elementary school teachers and 70 percent of high school teachers favor ability grouping for effective math and science instruction (Weiss, 1994). Ironically, the movement away from tracking and toward high standards for all students may have increased emphasis on advanced placement courses. As schools eliminate their lower-level courses, middle-class parents often look to advanced placement as a way to maintain their children's perceived competitiveness for college (Oakes, Welner, Yonezawa, & Allen, 1998). As a consequence, more students are taking algebra I in eighth grade and hoping to complete advanced placement courses, including calculus, during high school.

Track-Level Differences in Content

Although national standards call for high expectations for all students, teachers set objectives for students that depend on the perceived academic composition of the class. High-ability classes focus on skill building, while low-ability courses focus on the importance of science and math in daily life. Teachers of low-level classes are more

likely to emphasize awareness of the importance of math and science in daily life, while they focus more on developing reasoning and inquiry skills in their high-level classes. Weiss (1994) writes, "Instructional activities follow similar patterns; low ability science classes spend more time reading from textbooks and completing worksheets than high ability classes, and they spend less time than high ability classes participating in hands-on activities or being asked to write about their reasoning about solving a math problem" (p. 20; see also, Oakes, 1990a). Figure 4.5 demonstrates the significant differential between math and science objectives in low- and high-ability classes (Weiss).

Raudenbush, Rowan, and Cheong's (1993) multilevel analyses of data about secondary teachers' instructional goals found that the variation in emphasis on teaching higher-order thinking across subjects (and most strongly in mathematics and science) was a function of hierarchical conceptions of teaching and learning related to perceived ability group (track). That is, teachers who taught classes at more than one level varied their instructional goals among those classes. Teachers placed much greater emphasis on higher-order thinking and problem solving in their high-track classes than in others. These goals included generic thinking and problem-solving skills, as well as advanced academics topics and skills.

Track-Level Differences in Teacher Quality

In tracked schools, students in lower tracks are more likely to have out-of-field math or science teachers than

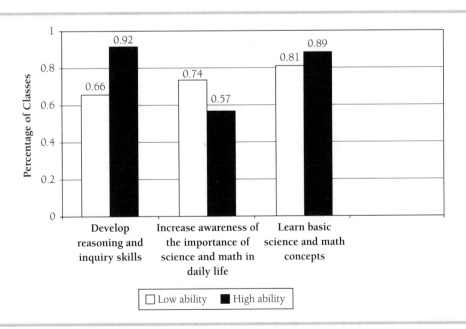

FIGURE 4.5. Percentage of Low- and High-Ability High School Science and Mathematics Classes Where Selected Objectives Are Heavily Emphasized.

students in higher tracks (Ingersoll, 1999). Using data from the High School and Beyond study's 1984 Teacher and Administrator Survey, Talbert and Ennis (1990) also found track-related teacher differences. Their analyses suggest that although teachers of high-track students also teach other ability groups, teachers of low-track students are more often tracked themselves. Twenty-four percent of the teachers in the national sample indicated that they teach predominantly low-ability students in tracked classes, compared with only 14 percent reporting that they are comparably tracked into classes with high-ability students.

The extent of teacher tracking (inequalities in the distribution of teachers among high and low tracks) is partly a function of social inequalities among students and teachers—that is, social-class background, race, and ethnicity (Talbert & Ennis, 1990). Teacher tracking is far less extensive in schools with relatively high-SES student populations and more extensive in schools with comparatively high proportions of minority students, minority teachers, and women teachers. Women teachers are more likely than men to be tracked into low-ability classes. Talbert and Ennis also found that teachers with low-track assignments had less influence over school policies and less administrative and collegial support. Finally, teachers' track assignments were related to their instructional efficacy, with high-track teachers feeling more efficacious than others. Talbert and Ennis concluded:

Regardless of whether relatively ineffective teachers are assigned to teach low-track classes or teachers assigned to teach low-tracked classes come to feel inefficacious, teacher tracking practices exacerbate student inequalities. Students in low-track classes are more likely than their academic- or general-track peers to have teachers with low status in the school, with fewer resources for personal growth, and who feel relatively ineffective in promoting student learning. (p. 30)

Racial Consequences of Tracking

Within racially mixed schools, minorities remain disproportionately overrepresented in low-level math and science courses and underrepresented in critical gatekeeping math and science courses. For example, Braddock and Dawkins's (1993) analyses of the base-year and first follow-up data from the National Educational Longitudinal Study of 1988 (NCES, n.d.) found African American, Latino, and American Indian 8th and 10th graders to be significantly underrepresented in high-ability classes and significantly overrepresented in low-ability classes. This disproportionate placement is a product of two somewhat distinct dynamics. First, schools with predominantly low-income and minority student populations offer relatively smaller numbers of high-track classes and larger numbers of low-track, remedial, and vocational programs than do schools serving Whiter, more affluent student bodies (Oakes, 1990a). Second, in racially mixed schools that offer upper-level math and science courses, low-SES students and students of color are much less likely to enroll in them (Atanda, 1999; Horn, Nunez, & Bobbitt, 2000; Ma & Willms, 1999).

Low-SES students and non-Asian minorities are less likely than others to take math and science courses beyond mandated graduation requirements (Ma & Willms, 1999; Weiss, 1994). Nationwide, although 20 percent of high school biology takers are African American and Latino, only 10 percent of high school physics students are from these groups (Weiss, 1994). Similarly, 34 percent of students in remedial or review math classes are non-Asian minorities, but they constitute only 8 percent of algebra II and more advanced math classes (Weiss, 1994).

A relaxing of the rigid three-track structure (academic, general, and vocational) of high schools over the past 20 years may have actually disadvantaged students from lower-class families (Lucas, 1999). Currently, course titles usually suggest that classes at different ability levels are simply modified versions of the same course, and few make clear their consequences for college eligibility. Lower-income families lack the experience of middle-class and upper-class families in recognizing and negotiating placements that provide better opportunities (Yonezawa, 1997). Moreover, Oakes and Guiton (1995) found that educators did not compensate for parental lack of access to knowledge, but rather justified the disproportionate enrollment of Whites and Asians in high-track classes as the result of meritocratic selection or from student choice. Some faculty members brushed aside the disproportionate representation of Hispanics—even those whose test scores were comparable to high-track White and Asian students—attributing these disparities to differences in students' motivation and choices, or to racial differences in educational values or family support. Oakes's (1995, 2000) studies of Rockford, Illinois, and San Jose, California, found that course placement practices consistently skewed enrollments in favor of Whites over and above what can be explained by measured achievement. African American and Latino students were much less likely than comparably scoring White or Asian students to be placed in accelerated courses. Table 4.4 illustrates the placement disparities in mathematics and English.

The table shows discrimination *at both high and low levels of achievement*. Even minority students in the highest-scoring groups fared worse than majority students did, and the combined impact across the ranges is considerable.

Other studies suggest how this discriminatory effect occurs. Increasingly, school systems do not use fixed

TABLE 4.4. Placement of Majority and Minority High School Students with Comparable Math and Reading Achievement in Regular and Advanced Classes 1998–99, Rockford, Illinois.

Math and Reading Achievement—NCEs*	Majority Students		Minority Students	
	Number	Percentage Advanced	Number	Percentage Advanced
Decile 1	775	3	962	2
Decile 2	973	6	1056	4
Decile 3	1,199	10	959	6
Decile 4	1,371	16	895	13
Decile 5	1,482	21	689	19
Decile 6	1,787	34	583	23
Decile 7	1,810	46	444	43
Decile 8	1,925	58	305	45
Decile 9	2,350	72	207	59
Decile 10	1,853	85	92	63

* NCE = normal curve equivalent

criteria to assign students to particular course levels. Teacher and counselor track-placement recommendations include, in addition to test scores and grades, highly subjective judgments about students' personalities, behavior, and motivation, especially at critical transitions between elementary, middle, and high schools (Paul, 1995). Some schools allow considerable student choice, and many routinely honor parent requests. Not surprisingly, parent involvement often increases students' chances of taking higher-level math and science courses (Ekstrom, Goertz, & Rock, 1988; Horn, Nunez, & Bobbitt, 2000; Useem, 1992b).

These aspects of course placement interweave with race and social class. Dornbush (1994) analyzed track assignment practices and tracking consequences in a stratified random sample of students in six diverse northern California senior high schools. Using a combination of survey and longitudinal record data (beginning in grade 5), Dornbush compared the impact of course taking, grades, attendance, and disciplinary patterns and test scores on college preparatory course taking of comparable students in different racial groups. Dornbush found marked variation in science and math, with Asians and non-Hispanic White student groups enrolling in college prep courses at more than twice the rates of African American and Latino peers with comparable high school grades. Parent education differences explained some of these group differences, but having highly educated parents did not have nearly as strong a positive impact on disadvantaged minority students' course taking as it did on Whites' course taking.

According to Dornbush, this disproportionality resulted partially from overt discrimination against African American and Latino students in high school class placement. To a much larger extent, this resulted from a combination of racial and ethnic differences in eighth-grade math test scores, grades, attendance records in elementary school, and negative comments about their behavior. In contrast, Asian enrollment patterns were greatly affected by positive discrimination during the high school enrollment process, in that Asians enrolled in college-track classes at rates greater than expected, given the predictor variables.

Other studies also find that counselors play a role in the lower participation rates of low-income and African American and Latino students in higher-level math and science courses. For example, Paul (1995) noted that although counselors used test scores or current math placements to bar these students from high-level courses, they permitted middle-class students with similar qualifications to enroll if their parents intervened on their behalf (Paul, 1995; Romo & Falbo, 1996). Similarly, controlling for student achievement levels, McDonough (1997) found that students in middle-class schools get significantly more supportive guidance counseling than do their peers in lower-income schools. Additionally, counselors in the latter schools more often steered students toward postsecondary programs for which they were overqualified.

Finally, in a study using the NELS 88 and subsequent follow-up survey data (NCES, n.d.), Horn, Nunez, and Bobbitt (2000) compared the high school academic performance of students who would be first-generation college goers (a group in which minorities and low-income students are disproportionately represented) with peers from college-educated families. Twenty-seven percent of the 1992 high school graduates included in the Horn, Nunez, and Bobbitt study were first-generation students. Half of these students came from a low-income family, compared to less than one-third whose parents had some postsecondary education and one-tenth whose parents were college graduates. First-generation students were more likely to be Hispanic (16%) than were students from other ethnic groups (6%). They were also more likely to be female (53%) compared to others (48%), because of the higher likelihood of male first-generation students dropping out of high school. Controlling for academic achievement, family income, and family structure, the researchers found the first-generation students less likely to participate in college preparatory programs and much less likely to enroll in college within two years of high school graduation. However, for both groups parent participation in college preparation activities and high school assistance in the application process increased a student's chance of going to college.

The influence of middle-class parent interventions appear as early as middle school (Horn, Nunez, & Bobbitt, 2000; Useem, 1992b), as students vie for eighth-grade algebra placements. Useem (1992a), for example, found a strong relationship between parents' education levels and placement in middle school mathematics, with college-educated parents involved in school programs and parent information networks, intervening in placement decisions, and influencing their children's course choices. The Horn, Nunez, and Bobbitt (2000) findings mirror these patterns, even after controlling for students' math ability. Thirty-one percent of parents of first-generation students encouraged their students to take algebra, compared to 53 percent of college graduate parents.

To better understand the relative contributions of between-school differences, tracking, and individual student characteristics on high school math and science course taking, Hoffer and Nelson (1993) used Hierarchical Linear Modeling (HLM) to examine the Longitudinal Study of American Youth 1987–1989 (LSAY) data. They found that about 80 percent of course taking differences occurred within schools. Although students' prior achievement and aspirations accounted for much of the differences in participation, lower socioeconomic status and minority status had independent negative effects. The influence of between-school differences on course taking was much smaller; students attending high schools with large concentrations of low-income, minority students took fewer demanding math and science courses than did comparable students at schools with more advantaged students. Additionally, higher rates of course taking took place at schools where greater proportions of the students with comparable ability levels were placed in high-level math and science classes.

DIFFERENCES BETWEEN AND WITHIN SCHOOLS MATTER

In this section, we examine the impact of differences in access to and participation in math and science courses on students' achievement and postsecondary opportunities. The relevant body of research yields five conclusions:

1. Advanced course taking enhances achievement.
2. Advanced course taking determines eligibility for competitive colleges.
3. Completion of a rigorous high school program is the strongest predictor of college success, and it has a particularly strong impact on underrepresented students of color.
4. Taking courses from qualified teachers increases achievement.

5. A school's tracking policies play an important role in all of these outcomes.

Advanced Course Taking Enhances Achievement

A straightforward relationship exists between course taking and achievement: the more academic courses high school students take, the more positive their schooling outcomes. Advanced courses, in particular, positively affect student achievement, particularly in science and mathematics, in students' preparedness for college and in their success in college-level work.

In a study that examines the access patterns and outcomes of 4,000 students in six public high schools and one Catholic school, Hallinan (2000) found that assigning a student to an advanced, high-level class affects student achievement dramatically for all students, regardless of their previous academic performance. These students in higher-track classes, particularly math, benefit from the intellectual challenge of the material covered and become more successful in future classes. Unfortunately, students of color were much more likely in this study to be assigned to lower-level classes.

NAEP data, for example, show that eighth graders who take algebra perform considerably better in mathematics, and that the more math they take the better they do (U.S. Department of Education, 1997). Similarly, evaluations of the 1993 decision requiring all New York City public high schools students to take tougher Regents-level math and science courses (courses traditionally reserved for college-bound students) showed the number of Hispanic students passing Regents science tripled in a single year and the number of African American students passing doubled (Education Trust, 1998).

In data drawn from the 1995–96 Beginning Postsecondary Students Survey, Horn and Carroll (2001) found a strong association between the rigor of a high school curriculum and a student's likelihood of enrolling in college. They found that 71 percent of students completing a rigorous high school curriculum enroll in a selective four-year college, while 40 percent of their peers taking midlevel curricula and only 32 percent of those completing core curricula do. Rigorous curricula include four years of math, with precalculus or higher, and three years of science (two from among biology, chemistry, or physics), and at least one AP test taken. Midway curricula include the same science requirements as the rigorous category but no AP component; students take at least geometry. In core curricula, students take three years of math and three years of science with no specific levels required.

The rigor of the curricula that high school students take also has an impact on their likelihood of persisting within college. More than two-thirds of students completing a rigorous high school curricula were still enrolled in their four-year college program, according to the Horn and Carroll study, as compared to 62 percent and 55 percent, respectively, of those students taking midlevel or core curricula.

A clear link also exists between 12th grade NAEP math achievement and the highest mathematics course taken (Snyder & Hoffman, 2000). Students who take precalculus or calculus score higher than students in lower-level classes. This trend is consistent across gender and race.

Similar patterns occur in science. Using NELS 88 data (NCES, n.d.) to investigate the link between science course taking and achievement, Madigan (1997) found "that students who take higher level science courses are more likely to gain in science proficiency" (p. 12), as measured on the NELS scientific achievement measure. Madigan compared scores from the same set of students twice—when they were in 8th grade and then again in 12th grade.

Table 4.5 summarizes Madigan's findings. More students at all three levels of eighth grade science proficiency increased their scores if they took physics.

Recent tracking studies find similar effects on student achievement. Oakes's studies (1995, 2000) of San Jose and Rockford schools, for example, found that high-track placement led to greater achievement gains than low-track participation for students at all ability levels. In San Jose, for example, "average" students (those with prior math achievement between 50 and 59 normal curve equivalents, or NCEs) placed in low-track courses lost an average of 2.2 NCEs after one year and lost a total of 1.9 NCEs after three years. By contrast, students in the same group who were placed in a regular track gained 0.1 NCEs after one year and gained 3.5 NCEs after three years. Most striking, the students in this average group who took an accelerated course experienced the greatest gain: 6.5 NCEs after one year, and a total of 9.6 NCEs after three years. Oakes found similar results across prior achievement levels. That is, whether students began with relatively high or relatively low achievement, those who were placed in lower-level courses showed lesser gains over time than similarly situated students who were placed in higher-level courses.

Dornbush (1994) demonstrates an overall low correlation between eighth-grade test scores and subsequent math and science grades—a relationship that is especially low for students in the low track. However, students who scored above the 50th percentile as eighth graders and who were placed in low-track classes did poorly in those classes and did worse in terms of grades than comparably scoring peers who were placed in high-track classes. Such findings contradict the belief that low-track classes permit students to earn higher grades than they would earn if they were placed in more challenging classes.

Advanced Course Taking Determines Eligibility for College

Enrollment in upper-level courses also correlates with long-term benefits. Paul (1995) found, for example, that placement in general math or algebra I in junior high highly corresponds to counselors' recommendations for high school placement. Those students taking eighth- or ninth-grade algebra were much more likely to be placed in college prep programs. Similarly, a U.S. Department of Education analysis showed that 83 percent of students taking algebra I and geometry went to college within two years of their high school graduation, compared to 36 percent of students who did not take these two courses (U.S. Department of Education, 1997). Almost 89 percent of students taking chemistry in high school attend college, compared to 43 percent of those not taking it (U.S. Department of Education).

These results are explained, in part, because college prep students receive more information and help in developing four-year high school plans and long-term educational and career plans than general education students do (McDonough, 1997; Paul, 1995). Counselors use academic program placement to determine how much potential students have for college and how strongly to recommend students for postsecondary and career opportunities.

Differences in access to AP courses in math and science are particularly important in access to highly competitive colleges. For example, discrepancies in AP participation have a major impact on student competitiveness for admission to California's universities. The University of California counts the total number of AP courses students take as indicators of a rigorous curriculum and student potential when evaluating applications. Student performance on AP tests is used as an important marker of student achievement. Moreover, it allows students to boost their grades in AP classes (by 1 point on a 4-point scale) for the purpose of calculating their GPA. Since students can receive a 5 on the 4-point scale for an A in an AP class, the median GPA of students admitted to UCLA and UC Berkeley is now well over 4.0. Consequently, students

TABLE 4.5. Percentage of Students Gaining Science Proficiency Between Grades 8 and 12.

Course	Low in Eighth Grade	Medium in Eighth Grade	High in Eighth Grade
No chemistry or physics	58	37	18
Chemistry, no physics	65	59	41
Physics	86	75	63

Source: NELS 88 data, Madigan (1997).

who lack meaningful access to AP classes find themselves at a competitive disadvantage in the UC admissions process (Oakes et al., 2000).

The disadvantage to students without AP is particularly pronounced in a post–affirmative action era. Prior to passage of Proposition 209 (which prohibits the University of California from taking race into account in college admissions) in 1994, African American and Latino students who did not take AP classes could gain admission to UCLA or UC Berkeley through affirmative action policies. In the wake of Proposition 209, students at a high school with low AP availability are expected to compete for admission with students from more advantaged schools that offer extensive AP programs.

In addition to shaping college competitiveness in general, AP courses in biology, calculus, and physics also serve as a gate through which prospective science, mathematics, and engineering majors must pass.

Rigor Is the Strongest Predictor of Minority Student Success in College

In his analysis of the new and restricted 1998 edition of the High School and Beyond sophomore cohort files, Adelman (1999) found that finishing a course beyond algebra II more than doubles the chances that students who go to college will complete it. In fact, the highest level of math studied in high school has an effect on bachelor's completion more than any other precollege variable. As with algebra II, advanced placement course taking strongly correlates with completion of a bachelor's degree, even more so than to college access (Adelman, 1999).

Taking calculus in high school has tremendous consequences. Students who persist through calculus are much more likely to pass college calculus courses, which serve as the gateway to more than half of college majors (Burton, 1989).

The cumulative effects of rigorous middle and high school math and science courses are particularly strong for low-income students. Low-income students who take algebra and geometry are almost three times as likely to attend college as those who do not (Atanda, 1999). When low-income students take rigorous courses, income effects on college entrance decrease significantly (Horn, Nunez, & Bobbitt, 2000; U.S. Department of Education, 1997).

Taking Courses from Qualified Teachers Promotes Achievement

Students learn more in courses taught by teachers who have majored in the academic subjects they teach and who are certified (Darling-Hammond, 2000; Ferguson, 1991;

1998; Greenwald, Hedges, & Laine, 1996; Murnane, 1996; Wright, Horn, & Sanders, 1997). These benefits have been documented in math and science specifically. Analyzing eighth-grade scores from the 1996 NAEP, for example, Hawkins, Stancavage, and Dossey (1998) found that students who are taught by teachers with either an undergraduate or a graduate mathematics major scored higher than their peers taught by other teachers. Teachers with teaching certificates in mathematics, moreover, affected student achievement more than teachers certified in other areas (Hawkins, Stancavage, & Dossey, 1998). In a study of Stanford 9 test scores in California, Fetler (1999) replicated Hawkins's findings. According to Fetler's analysis, well-prepared math teachers, as measured by certification and education levels, outperformed all other teachers on student achievement scores.

The powerful impact of well-qualified teachers can be explained, in part, by the fact that such teachers possess a range of teaching strategies, including the ability to ask high-order questions and respond to students' needs and curriculum goals (Darling-Hammond, 2000; Ingersoll, 1999).

Tracking Matters

Tracking practices also influence students' access to various courses and thereby their exposure to curriculum knowledge, their classroom learning experiences, and their learning outcomes. To the extent that tracking reduces students' access to rigorous courses and well-qualified teachers, it diminishes students' achievement and postsecondary opportunities. However, tracking also has an independent effect. For example, using data from the Longitudinal Study of American Youth 1987–89 (LSAY), Hoffer (1992) investigated middle school ability grouping and student achievement in science and mathematics. In mathematics, he found that "high-group students learn more than non-grouped students and low-group students learn much less" (p. 218), and "ability grouping in seventh and eighth grade mathematics and science is clearly not an optimal arrangement compared with the non-grouped alternative, for low-group students are significant losers" (p. 221).

Gamoran's work also shows that the type of tracking structure affects students' learning. Gamoran (1992) used HLM analyses with High School and Beyond data on more than 20,000 students in nearly 900 public and Catholic senior high schools to simultaneously assess the impact of tracking on achievement within schools and the impact of between-school differences in tracking structures on those track-related outcomes. He found that the structural differences among schools' tracking systems affect the magnitude of track-related effects on math achievement and schools' average levels of achievement in both math and verbal skills. Schools where students have greater mobility among tracks produced higher math achievement overall; they also had smaller gaps among tracks in both math and verbal achievement. Schools permitting more students to take high-track courses tended to have higher math achievement than did those with less inclusive systems, and both math and verbal scores increased with the inclusiveness of schools' track structures.

A REMEDY FOR RASHEDA DANIEL

With all the evidence of the many benefits of the access to high-level math and science classes, solutions come in many shapes and sizes. In this section, we first describe the proposed remedies for Rasheda Daniel's quest for increased access to AP courses. We then describe some solutions that do not work, as well as some that do. Even so, none comes close to eliminating systemic school resource or segregation issues.

After filing the complaint with the court, the ACLU convened a meeting with the attorneys and high-level staff from the governor's office, the state Board of Education, and the California Department of Education—the defendants in the case. Few disputed the validity of Rasheda's complaint or that other students like her across the state faced similar barriers; all seemed eager for a political solution. So, rather than pressing ahead with court action, the parties agreed to work together and enlist the assistance of the state legislature. The timing was right, they believed, to place the issue before the public as part of the governor's agenda for 2000–01 and to include support in the budget for a plan to address the inequities that Rasheda Daniel and other students like her face.

As might be expected, however, the early agreement has not brought an easy (or, for many, even satisfactory) resolution. The governor did develop a plan for ensuring that all California high school students have access to at least three AP courses. According to this plan, the legislature program would provide a small amount of funding for schools that needed to add courses and to provide teachers at these schools with some training in how to teach advanced placement courses.

This executive and legislative remedy has not entirely satisfied Rasheda Daniel and the ACLU, whose proposed remedy went much further to ensure that the state provide students with what they called "meaningful access" to AP programs (Oakes et al., 2000). They defined the term as a process that enables a broad cross section of students at a high school to take advantage of AP offerings in a way that makes these students competitive for selective public universities in California. Simply requiring a minimum

number of AP courses at each school, they argued, is not sufficient if other conditions for success in these courses are not met. They specified certain necessary conditions: (a) experienced and qualified teachers teaching AP courses; (b) rigorous academic curricula provided to all students in the pipeline courses leading up to the AP classes; (c) intensive academic supports (tutoring, counseling, and so forth) that enable students to negotiate challenging academic courses in light of their own backgrounds, understandings, and experiences; (d) information and supports to enhance the ability of students and family to understand the importance of AP as part of a broader strategy for becoming competitive for college admission; and (e) creation of alternative approaches to advanced study that would provide greater access and success for students of color.

Without guarantees of these necessary conditions, efforts to address the defendants' past failures to provide equal access to college via competitive high school programs would be insufficient. The governor—whose signature was required to enact any AP reform—disagreed. The resulting legislation provided only a small amount of funding for a broad array of schools to establish AP courses over the next four years. By 2002, 556 of the state's 800 comprehensive high schools had received a share of this funding.

Simply Adding Course Offerings Will Not Be Enough

To what degree does the proposed remedy in the *Daniel* case reflect what research tells us? Raising high school graduation requirements, as Ma and Willms (1999) claim, may serve as one way to ensure that all schools offer access to high-level math and science courses. Doing so "will likely improve students' preparation in high school mathematics, without creating an insurmountable barrier for the majority of students" (p. 380). Confirming this finding, Williams, Atash, and Chaney (1995) and Chaney, Burgdor, and Atash (1997) determined that minorities take more math and science courses in schools with higher math and science graduation requirements. Ma and Willms (1999) recommend that all high schools offer a core math curriculum in grades 9 and 10 of at least algebra I and geometry and provide instruction, if necessary, for low achievers.

However, we also have evidence that simply adding courses to a high school's offerings is insufficient to narrow the gaps in course taking and achievement. For example, the Los Angeles Unified School District recently pressed all of its high schools to offer more advanced placement classes. Yet comprehensive high schools in low-income L.A. neighborhoods have proven to be far less able than schools in more advantaged neighborhoods to offer

TABLE 4.6. Success in Advanced Placement Courses in Selected LAUSD High Schools, 1999.

School	Science and Math AP Courses	Science, Math AP Tests	Science, Math Scores of 3+	Science and Math Scores of 5
Low income				
Washington Prep	5 (+1 CS)*	63	14	0
Crenshaw	4	74	0	0
Dorsey	1	3	0	0
Fremont	6	71	5	0
Jefferson	1	17	2	1
Jordan	3	11	0	0
Locke	4	31	9	4
Manual Arts	6	44	2	0
Garfield	5	92	26	6
Roosevelt	3	87	25	2
San Fernando	5	123	18	3
South Gate	3	121	18	2
High income				
Palisades	6	220	153	59
University	5	143	73	28
Chatsworth	6	114	84	28
El Camino Real	7	196	165	75
Taft	5	217	154	39

* Computer science courses

Source: Oakes et al. (2000).

students opportunities that lead to AP success. Only 693 students across 12 very large high schools in low-income neighborhoods sat for AP exams in math and science in 1999, an average of 53 per school. Of these, only a total of 119, or an average of less than 10 exams at each school, received a passing score. In contrast, at five of the comprehensive high schools in the district's wealthiest neighborhoods, students took 890 math and science exams, an average of 178 per school; of these, 629, or an average of 126 per school, earned a passing score. Even more striking, a total of only 18 students at the low-income schools earned a score of 5, an average of only 1.5 per school. In contrast, 229, an average of 46 students per school, earned a score of 5 at schools in the wealthier neighborhoods (Table 4.6).

Increased Participation and Achievement Through Integrated Math and Science

Instead of just tacking on classes, some schools are making systemic changes to the classes they currently offer. Responding to calls for integration that come from national standards in math (NCTM, 1989, 2000) and science (NRC, 1996), more and more high schools offer integrated courses. A nationwide survey, conducted by the Biological Sciences Curriculum Study (BSCS) for the NSF, found that more than thirty states offer integrated science courses. Such courses "integrate content knowledge across discipline boundaries . . . providing

substantive opportunities for learning for a broad range of students" (BSCS, 2000). Integrated math courses benefit students as well. Mendieta (1999) cites a 1998 Kentucky Department of Education integrated mathematics study entitled *Results Based Practices Showcase,* which states, "The results gathered from schools around the country show that the Integrated Mathematics Program increases student understanding and improves student performance" (p. 11).

Houghton Mifflin's Integrated Mathematics Program (IMP), an intensely studied integrated curriculum, is aligned with the National Council of Teachers of Mathematics standards (Mendieta, 1999; Wisconsin Center for Education Research [WCER], 1996). WCER researcher Norman Webb found that IMP students took more math courses, maintained higher grade point averages, and achieved Scholastic Aptitude Test (SAT) scores similar to those of their peers in traditional mathematics courses. All of these results were statistically significant at the .01 level for all students, whether male or female, White or Hispanic (WCER). Of note is that 87 percent of IMP students took the SAT, while only 58 percent of the non-IMP students took the test. Mendieta notes that the "IMP group maintained a comparable level of achievement, while expanding the pool of students interested in meeting college entrance requirements" (p. 13).

These students may also be more prepared for college because the IMP curriculum integrates traditional material with additional topics recommended by the NCTM standards, such as statistics, probability, curve fitting, and matrix algebra (Mendieta, 1999). Webb designed assessments to evaluate 9th through 11th grade student achievement in three additional areas: statistics, problem solving, and quantitative reasoning. On all three assessments, IMP students demonstrated substantial knowledge and proficiency compared to their peers enrolled in traditional math courses (Mendieta).

Equity-Minded Interventions to Increase Participation and Achievement

Successful interventions aimed at boosting minority course taking and achievement in math and science take several forms. Some work within schools to increase minority enrollment in college prep classes, such as the College Board's College 2000 (U.S. Department of Education, 1997). This program requires participating school districts to eliminate lower-level math in favor of college prep math. Focusing on grades 6–9, teachers received assistance in working with mixed-ability classes, creating back-up classes, and increasing parental support. The program also includes Saturday and summer academies on college campuses for entire families. All six pilot sites dramatically increased student enrollment in algebra I by the ninth grade; in three pilot districts, all ninth graders took algebra I. The percentage of students passing algebra did not decline significantly and in some cases rose, as more students from discontinued lower tracks enrolled in an algebra class.

QUASAR (Quantitative Understanding Amplifying Student Achievement and Reasoning) aims to raise low levels of student participation and performance in mathematics. Based in urban middle schools, this demonstration project of the Learning Research and Development Center at the University of Pittsburgh helps all students acquire a deeper and more meaningful understanding of math ideas and demonstrate their proficiency in mathematical reasoning and complex problem solving. Schools in the project eliminated most forms of academic tracking and implemented programs to develop deeper student understanding and high-level thinking and reasoning skills. All project sites received extensive attention to professional development and teacher support. Students in the program performed as well as others did on basic and traditional items from the 1992 NAEP math assessment and outperformed others on less-traditional middle school math content (U.S. Department of Education, 1997).

In the Living Up to Their Potential program, 20 school districts from Chicago's North Shore began collaborating in 1995 to provide their students with "a world class education" in math and science. Using the Third International Math and Science Study (TIMSS) as a guide, this program tries to include all members of the community in helping students meet international learning standards. Fourth- and eighth-grade program participants who took the TIMSS assessment in 1996 ranked along with other top performers around the world, outperforming the average U.S. student. Other results include 50% of eighth-grade students taking algebra or geometry compared to 25% nationwide (U.S. Department of Education, 1997).

The College Board (1999) cites the absence of an "extensive supplementary educational system designed to support the high academic performance of minority students as a major challenge and opportunity" (p. 25). The College Board notes that Project SEED, an elementary school program, does help low-SES students acquire and master abstract mathematical concepts to help them succeed in more advanced math later in their school career. Project SEED employs scientists, mathematicians, and engineers to teach its curriculum in the school, typically using Socratic discussion techniques. While Project SEED typically works within existing school structures, the College Board believes that it has potential as an external program.

Advancement Via Individual Determination (AVID) supports the notion that top-track curriculum can be made available to all students, even in school systems where students have been tracked at earlier grades. AVID places "high potential/low-performance," low-income, and ethnic and linguistic minority students in college-prep senior high school classes alongside their high-achieving peers and provides them an additional AVID course in which they learn study skills and receive academic tutoring. Mehan and his colleagues (1994b) found that AVID graduates' rate of four-year college attendance outpaced those of San Diego and the national average (50, 37, and 39 percent, respectively). It is particularly impressive that the AVID minority graduates' rates far exceed those of their African American and Hispanic peers (44 percent of the AVID Hispanic group, compared with 25 percent across San Diego and 29 percent nationally; 50 percent of the AVID African American group, compared with 35 percent in San Diego and 33 percent nationally).

Additionally, using interview and observation data, Mehan and his colleagues documented other social benefits accruing to AVID participants. Hispanic and African American participants developed what Mehan terms a "reflective system of beliefs, a critical consciousness . . . about the limits and possibilities of the actions they take and the limitations and constraints they face in life" (Mehan, Hubbard, & Villanueva, 1994a, p. 100). That is, AVID taught students that they could achieve if they were motivated and studied hard. Even so, AVID students did not adopt a belief that their hard work would automatically bring success; nor did they abandon their cultural identities. Rather, they maintained "dual identities" and adopted the view that, even though they would continue to face considerable discrimination and inequality, they could succeed if they developed "certain cultural practices, notably achieving academically, that are acceptable to the mainstream" (Mehan et al., p. 105). Mehan terms this response "accommodation without assimilation."

Mehan attributes these positive outcomes to three characteristics of the AVID program. First, the special AVID class isolates its students for a period of time each day, during which they are simultaneously shielded from counterinfluences and provided with necessary social and academic supports, including direct instruction in the "hidden curriculum of the school" (Mehan, Hubbard, & Villanueva, 1994a, p. 109). Second, special AVID notebooks and other paraphernalia "emblazoned with the AVID logo" provide public markers of group identity that earn students recognition as "special." Third, because the AVID students are a group, participants form academically oriented friendships with their AVID peers. If Mehan and his colleagues are correct about how AVID works, detracking may work best as a combination of integrating low-achieving students into rigorous academic classes and at the same time giving them separate high-status experiences that provide both social and academic support.

Together these studies support the claims made by the remedy for Rasheda Daniel that we propose. Reducing the gaps in course taking and achievement will not be accomplished by simply offering and requiring more courses, although such measures may further boost these outcomes overall. However, reducing the inequalities among groups will require what the College Board's National Task Force on Minority High Achievement termed "affirmative development." By affirmative development, the Task Force meant "the notion that our nation has both strong moral and practical interests in taking an extensive array of public and private actions designed to ensure that underrepresented minority groups significantly increase their rates of educational progress" (College Board, 1999, p. 3). Reflecting the findings of the research we have cited here, the Task Force called for preschool and parent education programs and formal and informal supplementary interventions targeted specifically at students of color from all economic groups, as necessary complements to much-needed reforms that upgrade the quality of the curriculum and teaching in K-12 schools.

WHAT DO WE NEED TO KNOW? RESEARCH FOR THE FUTURE

Our review of research on equity in mathematics and science course taking and achievement reveals that, in a decade of policies pressing for high standards in schools that remain separate and unequal, we've made

some progress in raising the levels of course taking and achievement of all racial groups. At the same time, however, we've done little to reduce the gaps among them. The increases are encouraging, but they have served to raise standards for admission to competitive colleges in ways that prevent most low-income and minority students from translating their improved accomplishments into enhanced educational and life chances. However, our review also supports the claim made last year by the Task Force on Minority High Achievement that we have learned a great deal "about how minority educational outcomes can be improved, despite having made only modest investments in educational R&D" (College Board, 1999, p. 14). Along with the Task Force, we conclude that we must "redouble our efforts and our investments" to promote minority opportunities and high achievement (p. 14). To forward this agenda, we offer a set of research questions about the general educational system as well as questions specific to math and science education. We believe that questions of both sorts are necessary as researchers and policy makers implement what we already know and mount new, vigorous initiatives to learn more and do more to achieve equitable course taking and achievement.

Questions About Diversity and Learning

Currently we are unable to draw on the full range of talents in our diverse population because we lack specific understanding of the value of diversity in learning and social advancement. We must dismiss the idea that we value diversity for diversity's sake and start believing in the idea that diversity is needed to better us all. We must take the challenge posed by Rita Colwell (cited in NSF, 1999) in her foreword to *Women, Minorities, and Persons with Disabilities in Science and Engineering*, "A challenge for our country is to attract the best talent from all sources to science and engineering to stimulate creativity, innovation, and change; contribute to the advancement of science and engineering; and foster a scientifically literate population. Different perspectives, talents and experiences produce better ideas" (p. ii).

Answers to these questions will help us better engage a broader section of our population in learning and contributing in science and mathematics:

- What can educators learn from science about the advantages of diversity in the natural world?
- What contributions do diversity and heterogeneity make to learning and change in social institutions?
- Why is it that certain constructs from sociocultural perspectives on learning ("communities of practice," learning through "apprenticeship," "changing participation over time" as "identity development," etc.), contribute

to our general understanding of learning in diverse settings?

- How can math and science courses capitalize on diversity and heterogeneity to maximize learning? How, for example, might a greater emphasis on diversity contribute to all students' multiple ways of knowing math and science?

Questions About Creating Equitable Structures and Cultures

We have specific evidence, from research and equity interventions, about school conditions likely to promote more equitable course taking and achievement. A college-going culture at school, high-quality curriculum, well-prepared and knowledgeable teachers, special academic assistance when needed, supportive relationships with caring school adults, and connections with families focused on high achievement and college going all seem to foster the outcomes we seek for low-income students and students of color. But to translate these features of exemplary schools and effective special programs into the routine, everyday practices experienced by low-income students of color presents enormous challenges. Research focused on these questions should help:

- How can states, districts, and schools undo the structural impediments to equitable course participation—for instance, uneven resources for high-level math and science among schools, tracking practices within schools, and uneven assignment of teachers to schools and to tracks within schools?
- How do schools create academic, college-going cultures where adults and peers see college going as expected and attainable, and where they see the effort and persistence that preparation for college requires as normal?
- How can we piece together what we know from effective "equity programs"—including their provision of intensive academic and college-going support and close relationships between students and adults—to create an equitable science and mathematics educational *system*?
- How can schools, working with community organizations, develop connections with parents and neighborhoods that enhance their knowledge and access to mathematics and science courses, high achievement, and college preparation?

Questions About the Form and Substance of Equitable Courses

How can we create courses that make mathematics and science content more accessible to all American students? In contrast to commonly held views that low-income and minority students devalue education, studies suggest that they more likely turn away because of a real or perceived lack of opportunities (Steinberg, 1996). A RAND study of low-income high school graduates who were eligible to attend the University of California but chose not to found that the students were most deterred by their beliefs that the university is "not for people like me" (Krop et al., 1998). These perceptions arise, in part, as students internalize negative labels assigned to their racial and cultural groups—what Claude Steele (1997) terms "the stereotype threat" (see Chapter 21, this volume). Creating courses where minority students can see the connections between themselves and the content of science and mathematics and where teachers use pedagogy that builds on students' culture and languages is one way to counter this threat. However, we need to know far more about what such courses might be like. Research into these math and science education questions should help us develop a system in which students hold identities that are simultaneously multicultural and academic:

- How can science and mathematics be treated as everyone's "everyday practices"?
- What are multicultural curricula and culturally relevant pedagogies in mathematics and science?
- Does the absence of multicultural and diversity issues in the National Science Education Standards prohibit equitable implementation of the standards?
- What assessments capture and respect multiple ways of knowing mathematics and science?
- Is advanced placement and the pipeline of courses that lead to it an equitable (or even the best) approach to advanced study in math and science?

Questions About Social and Political Support for Equitable Schooling

The National Task Force on Minority High Achievement put it simply: "America is a diverse society in which educational differences have the potential to become a progressively larger source of inequality and social conflict" (College Board, 1999, p. 1). Efforts to construct the math and science education system in ways that the literature suggest are necessary to make participation and high achievement possible for low-income students of color will inevitably bring political resistance from powerful forces bent on preserving the status quo. California's rejection of affirmative action provides a sobering example. This response is understandable in a stratified educational system where opportunities are based on ideologies of intelligence and merit that disadvantage some groups and favor others. Are we to just sit by and let conflicts build? Or might research on certain issues reveal ways for Americans to move more harmoniously toward a diverse, high-achieving, and equitable society?

- What is the impact of our culture's framing of mathematics and science achievement as "culture-free" and ideologically neutral? How do we dismantle the elite and esoteric status of science and mathematics as fields of study?
- How can we change prevailing attitudes about who can learn mathematics and science? What alternative measures of competence and potential help reduce race and social-class sorting?
- How do we develop norms whereby Americans see deep engagement, high achievement, and hard work in math and science as *normal* and expected of all?

- How can we counter the often-unspoken race and social-class fears that complicate efforts to create equitable course taking and achievement?
- How can we unseat ideologies of competition and merit in schools that perpetuate social and racial stratification in school and beyond?
- How can more equitable schools hold on to children from families used to having a competitive advantage?
- How can we make it salient that our goal is not simply to accommodate "minorities" but also to educate well everyone in an increasingly diverse society?

References

Adelman, C. (1999). *Answers in the tool box: Academics, intensity, attendance patterns, and bachelor's degree attainment.* Washington, DC: U.S. Department of Education, Office of Educational Research and Improvement.

American Association for the Advancement of Science. (1993). *Benchmarks for science literacy.* New York: Oxford University Press.

Anyon, J. (1980). Social class and the hidden curriculum of work. *Journal of Education, 162*(1), 67–92.

Atanda, R. (1999). *Do gatekeeper courses expand education options?* Washington, DC: National Center for Education Statistics.

Biological Sciences Curriculum Study. (2000). Making sense of integrated science: A guide for high schools. Colorado Springs, CO: Author.

Braddock, J. H., & Dawkins, M. P. (1993). Ability grouping, aspirations, and attainments: Evidence from the National Educational Longitudinal Study of 1988. *Journal of Negro Education, 62*(3), 1–13.

Burton, M. B. (1989). The effect of prior calculus experience on "introductory calculus." *American Mathematical Monthly, 96,* 350–354.

Chaney, B., Burgdor, K., & Atash, N. (1997). Influencing achievement through high school graduation requirements. *Educational Evaluation and Policy Analysis, 12,* 229–244.

Cogan, L. S., Schmidt, W. H., & Wiley, D. E. (2002). Who takes what math and in which tracks? Using TIMSS to characterize U.S. students' eighth grade mathematics learning opportunities. Unpublished paper.

College Board. (1999). *Reaching the top: A report of the national task force on minority high achievement.* New York: Author.

Darling-Hammond, L. (1997). *The right to learn: A blueprint for creating schools that work.* San Francisco: Jossey-Bass.

Darling-Hammond, L. (2000). Teacher quality and student achievement: A review of state policy evidence. *Education Policy Analysis Archives.* Retrieved May 2000 from http://epaa.asu.edu/epaa/v8n1

Dornbush, S. (1994). *Off the track.* Paper presented as the Presidential Address to the Society for Research on Adolescence, San Diego, CA.

Educational Testing Service Policy Information Report. (1997). *Computers and classrooms: The status of technology in the U.S.* Princeton, NJ: Author.

Education Trust. (1998). *Education watch 1998: State and national data book* (Vol. 11). Washington, DC: Author.

Ekstrom, R. B., Goertz, M., & Rock, D. A. (1988). *Education and American youth.* Philadelphia: Falmer Press.

Ferguson, R. F. (1991). Paying for public education: New evidence on how and why money matters. *Harvard Journal on Legislation, 28,* 465–498.

Ferguson, R. F. (1998). Can schools narrow the Black-White test score gap? In C. Jencks and M. Phillips (Eds.), *The Black-White Test Score Gap* (pp. 318–374). Washington, DC: Brookings Institution.

Fetler, M. (1999). High school characteristics and mathematics test results. *Educational Policy Analysis Archives, 7*(9). Retrieved May 2002 from http://epaa.asu.edu/epaa/v7n9html

Gamoran, A. (1992). The variable effects of high school tracking. *American Sociological Review, 57*(6), 812–828.

Gilford, D. M., & Tenebaum, E. (Eds.). (1995). *Precollege science and mathematics teachers: Monitoring supply, demand, and quality.* Washington, DC: National Academy Press.

Greenwald, R., Hedges, L. V., & Laine, R. D. (1996). The effects of school resources on student achievement. *Review of Educational Research, 66*(3), 361–396.

Hallinan, M. T. (2000). Ability group effects on high school learning outcomes. Paper presented at the annual meeting of the American Sociological Association, Washington, DC.

Hanushek, E. (1994). *Making schools work: Improving performance and controlling costs.* Washington, DC: Brookings Institution.

Hawkins, E., Stancavage, F., & Dossey, J. (1998). *School policies and practices affecting instruction in mathematics: Findings from the National Assessment of Educational Progress.* Washington, DC: U.S. Department of Education, Office of Educational Research and Improvement. (NCES 98–495)

Hoffer, T., & Nelson, C. (1993). High school effects on coursework in science and mathematics. Paper presented at the annual meeting of the American Educational Research Association.

Hoffer, T. B. (1992). Middle school ability grouping and student achievement in science and mathematics. *Educational Evaluation and Policy Analysis, 14*(3), 205–227.

Horn, L., & Carroll, C. D. (2001). High school academic curriculum and the persistence path through college: Persistence and transfer behavior of undergraduates after entering 4-year institutions. Washington, DC: U.S. Department of Education, Office of Educational Research and Improvement. (NCES 2001–163)

Horn, L., Nunez, A., & Bobbitt, L. (2000). *Mapping the road to college: First generation students' math track, planning strategies, and context of support.* Washington, DC: U.S. Department of Education, National Center for Education Statistics. (NCES 2000–153)

Ingersoll, R. M. (1999). The problem of underqualified teachers in American secondary schools. *Educational Researcher, 28*(20), 26–37.

Ingersoll, R. M., Han, M., & Bobbitt, S. (1995). *School staffing survey: Teacher supply, teacher qualifications, and teacher turnovers: 1990–1991.* Washington, DC: U.S. Department of Education, National Center for Education Statistics. (NCES 95–744)

Koretz, D., Mitchell, K. M., Barron, S., & Keith, S. (1996). *Final report: Perceived effects of the Maryland school performance assessment.* (CSE technical report 409.) Los Angeles: CRESST/RAND Institute on Education and Testing.

Krop, C., Brewer, D., Gates, S., Gill, B., Reichardt, R., Sundt, M., & Throgmorton, D. (1998). *Potentially eligible students: A growing opportunity for the University of California.* Santa Monica: RAND.

Ladd, H. (Ed.). (1996). *Holding schools accountable: Performance-based reform.* Washington, DC: The Brookings Institute.

Lee, V. E., Burkham, D. T., Chow-Hoy, T., Smerdon, B. A., & Geverdt, D. (1998). *High school curriculum structure: Effects on coursetaking and achievement in mathematics for high school graduates—An examination of data from the National Education Longitudinal Study of 1988.* (Working Paper No. 98). Washington, DC: U.S. Department of Education, National Center for Education Statistics.

Lee, V. E., Smith, J. B., & Croninger, R. G. (1997). How high school organization influences the equitable distribution of learning in mathematics and science. *Sociology of Education, 70*(2), 128–150.

Lucas, S. R. (1999). *Tracking inequalities: Stratification and mobility in American schools.* New York: Teachers College Press.

Ma, X., & Willms, J. D. (1999). Dropping out of advanced mathematics: How much do students and schools contribute to the problem? *Educational Evaluation and Policy Analysis, 21*(4), 365–383.

Madigan, T. (1997). *Science proficiency and course taking in high school.* Washington, DC: U.S. Department of Education, National Center for Education Statistics. (NCES 97–838)

Mason, D. A., & Good, T. L. (1993, Summer). Effects of two-group and whole-class teaching on regrouped elementary students' mathematics achievement. *American Educational Research Journal, 30*(2), 328–360.

Matti, M. C., & Weiss, I. R. (with Boyd, S. L., Boyd, S. E., Kroll, J. L., Montgomery, D. L., et al.). (1994). *Science and mathematics education: Briefing book volume IV.* Chapel Hill, NC: Horizon Research.

McDonough, P. (1997). *Choosing colleges: How social class and schools structure opportunity.* Albany: State University of New York Press.

McNeil, L., & Valenzuela, A. (2000). *The harmful impact of the TAAS system of testing in Texas: Beneath the accountability rhetoric.* Cambridge, MA: Harvard Civil Rights Project.

Mehan, H. B., Hubbard, L., & Villanueva, I. (1994a). Forming academic identities: Accommodation without assimilation among involuntary minorities. *Anthropology and Education Quarterly, 25*(2), 91–117.

Mehan, H. B., Hubbard, L., Lintz, A., & Villanueva, I. (1994b). Tracking untracking: The consequences of placing low track students in high track classes. (Research Report No. 10.) San Diego, CA: San Diego County Department of Education.

Mendieta, G. (1999). Should the Los Angeles Unified School District support phase-out of progressive mathematics curricula? (Unpublished report by the Achievement Council.) Los Angeles: Achievement Council.

Millman, J. (Ed.). (1997). *Grading teachers, grading students: Is student achievement a valid evaluation measure?* Thousand Oaks, CA: Corwin Press.

Murnane, R. J. (1996). Staffing the nation's schools with skilled teachers. In E. A. Hanushek & D. W. Jorgenson (Eds.), *Improving America's schools: The role of incentives* (pp. 241–258). Washington, DC: National Academy Press.

National Center for Educational Statistics. *National Education Longitudinal Study of 1988.* (n.d.). Retrieved July 17, 2002, from http://www.nces.ed.gov/surveys/nels88

National Council of Teachers of Mathematics. (1989). *Curriculum and evaluation standards for school mathematics.* Reston, VA: Author.

National Council of Teachers of Mathematics. (2000). *Principles and standards for school mathematics.* Reston, VA: Author.

National Research Council. (1996). *National science education standards.* Washington, DC: National Academy Press.

National Science Board. (2000). Science and engineering indicators— 2000. Arlington, VA: National Science Foundation. (NSB-00–1)

National Science Foundation. (1999). *Women, minorities, and persons with disabilities in science and engineering: 1998.* Arlington, VA: Author. (NSF 99–338)

Oakes, J. (1990a). *Multiplying inequalities: Race, social class, and tracking on students' opportunities to learn mathematics and science.* Santa Monica: RAND.

Oakes, J. (1990b). Opportunities, achievement, and choice: Women and minority students in science and mathematics. In C. Cazden (Ed.), *Review of Research in Education* (No. 16, pp. 153–222). Washington DC: American Educational Research Association.

Oakes, J. (1995). Two cities: Tracking and within-school segregation. In L. Miller (Ed.), *Brown plus forty: The promise.* New York: Teachers College Press.

Oakes, J. (2000). *Within-school integration, grouping practices, and educational quality in Rockford schools.* (Report prepared in conjunction with *People Who Care, et al.* v. *Rockford Board of Education, et al.*)

Oakes, J., Gamoran, A., & Page, R. N. (1992). Curriculum differentiation: Opportunities, outcomes, and meanings. In P. Jackson (Ed.), *Handbook of research on curriculum.* New York: Macmillan.

Oakes, J., & Guiton, G. (1995). Matchmaking: The dynamics of high school tracking decisions. *American Educational Research Journal, 32*(1), 3–33.

Oakes, J., Rogers, J., McDonough, P., Solorzano, D., Mehan, H., & Noguera, P. (2000). *Remedying unequal opportunities for successful participation in Advanced Placement courses in California high schools.* Unpublished report of the ACLU of Southern California.

Oakes, J., Welner, K., Yonezawa, S., & Allen, R. I. (1998). Norms and politics of equity-minded change: Researching the "zone of mediation." In A. Hargreaves, A. Lieberman, M. Fullan, and D. Hopkins (Eds.), *International handbook of educational change, Part 2.* London: Kluwer.

Orfield, G., & Miller, E. (Eds.). (2000). *Chilling admissions: The affirmative action crisis and the search for alternatives.* Cambridge, MA: Harvard Civil Rights Project.

Orfield, G., & Yun, J. T. (1999). *Resegregation in American schools.* Cambridge, MA: Harvard Civil Rights Project.

O'Sullivan, C. Y., Reese, C. M., & Mazzeo, J. (1997). *NAEP 1996 science report card for the nation and the states.* Washington, DC: U.S. Department of Education, National Center for Education Statistics.

Paul, F. (1995). Academic program in a democratic society: Structured choices and their consequences. *Advances in Educational Policy* (No. 2). Philadelphia: Falmer Press.

Raudenbush, S. W., Rowan, B., & Cheong, Y. F. (1993). Higher order instructional goals in secondary schools: Class, teacher, and school influences. *American Educational Research Journal, 30*(3), 523–553.

Rodriguez, A. (1997). *Counting the runners who don't have shoes: Trends in student achievement in science by socioeconomic status and gender within ethnic groups* (Research Monograph No. 3). Madison: University of Wisconsin, National Institute for Science Education.

Romo, H., & Falbo, T. (1996). Latino high school graduation: Defying the odds. Austin, TX: University of Texas Press.

Stecher, B. M., & Mitchell, K. J. (1995). *Portfolio-driven reform: Vermont teachers' understanding of mathematical problem-solving and related classroom practices.* (CSE technical report 400.) Los Angeles: CRESST/RAND.

Steele, C. M. (1997). A threat in the air: How stereotypes shape intellectual identity and performance. *American Psychologist, 52,* 613–629.

Steinberg, L. (1996). *Beyond the Classroom.* New York: Simon & Schuster.

Snyder, T. D., & Hoffman, C. M. (2000). *Digest of education statistics, 1999.* Washington, DC: U.S. Department of Education, National Center for Education Statistics. (NCES 2000–031)

Talbert, J., & Ennis, M. (1990). Teacher tracking: Exacerbating inequalities in the high school. Paper presented at the annual meeting of the American Educational Research Association, April, Boston, MA.

Tomas Rivera Center. (1999). Unpublished analysis for the ACLU and personal communication. Los Angeles: Author.

U.S. Commission on Civil Rights. (1999). *Equal educational opportunity and nondiscrimination for minority students: Federal enforcement of Title VI in ability group practices.* Washington, DC: Author.

U.S. Department of Education. (1997). Mathematics equals opportunity. (White Paper presented for U.S. Secretary of Education Richard W. Riley.) Washington, DC: Author.

U.S. Department of Education, National Center for Educational Statistics. (1998). *Pursuing excellence: A study of U.S. twelfth-grade mathematics and science achievement in international context.* Washington, DC: U.S. Government Printing Office. (NCES 98–049)

Useem, E. (1992a). Getting on the fast track in mathematics: School organizational influence on math track assignment. *American Journal of Education, 100,* 325–353.

Useem, E. (1992b). Middle school and math groups: Parents' involvement in children's placement. *Sociology of Education, 65*(4), 263–279.

Weiss, I. (1994). *A profile of science and mathematics education in the United States: 1993.* Chapel Hill, NC: Horizon Research.

Williams, T., Atash, N., & Chaney, B. (1995). *Legislating achievement: Graduation requirements, course taking, and achievement in mathematics and science.* Paper presented at the meeting of the American Educational Research Association, April, San Francisco, CA.

Wisconsin Center for Education Research. (1996–97, Winter). Mathematics curriculum boosts performance. *WCER Highlights, 8*(4). Retrieved May 2000 from www.wcer.wisc.edu/Publications/WCER_Highlights/

Wright, S. P., Horn, S. P., & Sanders, W. L. (1997). Teacher and classroom content effects on student achievement: Implications for teacher evaluation. *Journal of Personnel Evaluation, 11,* 57–67.

Yonezawa, S. S. (1997). Making decisions about students' lives: An interactive study of secondary school students' academic program selection. Unpublished dissertation, University of California, Los Angeles.

5

ASSESSMENT, STANDARDS, AND EQUITY

Mindy L. Kornhaber

Pennsylvania State University, University Park

Educational assessment—the evaluation of what students know and can do—has many purposes and takes many forms. It includes ascertaining whether topics have been learned; diagnosing learning difficulties; shaping classroom instruction; placing students in remedial, gifted, or other special classes; certifying student accomplishment; and evaluating the effectiveness of educational programs (American Educational Research Association [AERA], American Psychological Association [APA], National Council on Measurement in Education [NCME], 1999; Heubert & Hauser, 1999; Pellegrino, Chudowsky & Glaser, 2001). Among the forms that assessment can take are informal observation, teacher-made tests, individually administered test batteries, systematically reviewed portfolios, performances of writing or other discipline-based work, and standardized tests.

There are many purposes and forms of assessment. However, there should be just *one* motivation: assessment should serve as a tool to enhance all students' knowledge, skills, and understanding so that they can function at the highest possible level in the wider world. In theory, then, educational assessment could be well aligned with the broad aims of multicultural education: to enable students from all circumstances to use their minds to the fullest, to explore social and cultural phenomena from diverse perspectives, to participate thoughtfully in a democratic society, and to apply their knowledge and skills in ways that can improve the human condition (for examples, see Banks & Banks, 1993; Banks, 1994a, 2001; Sleeter, 1991; Sleeter & Grant, 1994).

However, from its inception, educational assessment has been intertwined with conflicting assumptions about the educability of people from different social groups (Terman, 1916). Alongside constructive motivations, educational assessment has been widely used in ways that have

steered students toward differentiated levels of functioning, levels closely associated with differences of race and class (Fierros & Conroy, 2002; Frasier, Garcia, & Passow, 1995; Grossman, 1995; Oakes, 1985; Oakes, Gamoran, & Page, 1992).

This chapter examines the relationship among educational assessment, standards, and equity. It does so in five sections. The first traces the history of contradictory assumptions underlying the development and broad deployment of educational assessment. The second focuses on explanations for the persistent disparities in average test scores attained by different cultural and ethnic groups. This paves the way for a third section, which examines recent policies of state-developed standards and high-stakes tests as a solution to these disparities. Section four explores whether those policies are likely to foster equity in enabling young people to function at a high level in the wider society. The fifth section describes how the appropriate use of assessments can help to promote equity.

HISTORY OF CONFLICTING ASSUMPTIONS UNDERLYING EDUCATIONAL ASSESSMENT

The first large-scale program of mental testing was developed by the British scientist Francis Galton in 1884. Over the next six years, he compiled data from 9,300 individuals who participated in brief tests of their reaction times and sensory discrimination abilities. Galton's testing program was inspired by his years of prior research into the distribution of "genius" and "imbecility" in the British population. His statistical research indicated that "grades of natural ability" followed a bell curve, thus emphasizing that these grades could be measured by their distance from the mean. In addition, a line of historical inquiry led Galton to assert that the highest reaches of ability were largely found among those from the most eminent families (Galton, 1869). These investigations, along with the influence of his cousin, Charles Darwin, led Galton to conclude that intelligence was an inherited characteristic. Galton further asserted that education or environment had little influence on mental ability. Given this, Galton believed that governments should ascertain, through testing programs such as his, who was mentally capable and implement eugenic policies to encourage them to procreate—and to discourage others from doing so.

Across the English Channel, very different motivations spurred a new form of testing from which markedly different inferences were drawn. In 1904, the French Ministry of Public Instruction was struggling to educate a newly diverse student population arising from the advent of mass education. The Ministry charged psychologist Alfred Binet to develop an assessment that could distinguish between students capable of learning, despite differences in school behavior that challenged their teachers, and those who were genuinely "unable to profit . . . from the instruction given in the ordinary schools" (Binet & Simon, 1916/1973, p. 9). Binet and his colleague, Théophile Simon, developed mental assessments consisting of short questions that primarily tested memory, math, factual knowledge, and vocabulary. The assessment was to be used as a diagnostic tool for detecting whether youngsters were solving problems at a level appropriate for their age. Students who succeeded on most of the questions for 10-year-olds were said to have a mental age of 10, which may have been equal to, higher than, or below their chronological age. Essentially, a child whose chronological age was markedly above his or her mental age was deemed to need additional support in a special classroom.

In addition to his testing program, Binet instituted a program of educational interventions that he claimed successfully stimulated these students' cognitive development. Thus, unlike Galton, Binet claimed that intelligence was very much influenced by the environment and that it could be enhanced with education. He also argued that intelligent thought varied from person to person and rested on many types of problem-solving abilities. Therefore it was "altogether different" (Binet & Simon, 1916/1973, p. 243) from height or other characteristics that might be measured against a single standard or dimension.

The only point upon which both Binet and Galton might have agreed was that individuals differ in their performance on assessments of thinking and learning, and that differences also exist across social groups. Both men died in 1911, leaving generations of test developers, educators, policy makers, and ordinary citizens to wrestle

with, and act on, a host of otherwise divergent assumptions. These span such fundamental issues as the origins of intellectual differences (to what extent genetic or environmental), the nature of intelligence (how malleable or fixed), the standards against which it should be measured (one yardstick or many), and the purposes of assessment (for the student's improvement or for broader social engineering).

Three influential developments in assessment followed within a decade after the deaths of Binet and Galton. The first was the invention of the intelligence quotient, or IQ. This statistic was introduced by the German psychologist William Stern (1912/1965) and was initially derived by dividing a child's mental age by his or her chronological age. Although contrary to Binet's idea, the IQ enabled ready comparisons of everyone's mental test performance against a single scale. This statistic was said to measure "general intelligence": one underlying, general mental ability that was thought to be involved in any type of problem solving (Spearman, 1904).

The second development was the move to mass administrations of mental tests. This was the work of a small group of psychologists, among them Harvard's Robert Yerkes and Stanford's Lewis Terman, who stepped forward to design a test for efficiently classifying and assigning jobs to U.S. Army recruits during World War I. The Army tests were devised and administered to nearly 1.75 million soldiers in just a few months' time. By today's standards, the tests were seriously flawed by numerous culture- and class-specific items and by nonstandardized practices of administration (Gould, 1981; Gardner, Kornhaber, & Wake, 1996; see Yerkes, 1921). Nevertheless, Army psychologists highlighted two results whose themes have been echoed by more recent authors (e.g., Herrnstein & Murray, 1994). First, they claimed that there were so few "A" men—those at the highest level of ability— that the nation was threatened by low intelligence and a potential lack of able leaders. Second, they noted that average scores differed across racial and ethnic groups, with native Anglo-Saxons scoring higher than immigrants, and immigrants outscoring Black Americans (Yerkes, 1921).

Despite heated debates in the press over these two claims (see Block & Dworkin, 1976, in which relevant texts are reprinted) a third key development occurred. Lewis Terman and several other Army psychologists produced and popularized mass-administered intelligence tests for students. As with the Army tests, the new student examinations were intended to provide an efficient and scientific means for determining how different individuals should be trained or educated.

Terman's test, the Stanford-Binet, explicitly acknowledged Binet's work (Terman, 1916). Nevertheless, for most of his long career Terman's explanations for test score disparities were consistent with Galton's ideas. Terman believed that intelligence was innate, inherited, and immutable. Unlike Binet, he was dismissive of the idea that students' knowledge and skills could be enlarged to enable them to function at a higher-than-tested level. His beliefs were evident in his widely read volumes on intelligence testing in schools (Terman, 1916, 1919, 1922), and they set the tone for institutionalizing educational opportunity along race and class lines.

To illustrate, in the first published version of his Stanford-Binet test, Terman (1916) asserted that the better scores attained by "children of the superior social classes . . . is probably due, for the most part, to a superiority in original endowment" (p. 72). Later in the same volume, he described two lower-scoring children as representative of

the level of intelligence which is very, very common among Spanish, Indian and Mexican families of the Southwest and also among negroes. [sic] Their dullness seems to be racial, or at least inherent in the family stocks from which they come. The fact that one meets this type with such extraordinary frequency among Indians, Mexicans, and negroes [sic] suggests quite forcibly that the whole question of racial differences in mental traits will have to be taken up anew and by experimental methods. The writer predicts that when this is done there will be discovered enormously significant racial differences in general intelligence, differences which cannot be wiped out by any scheme of mental culture.

Children of this group should be segregated in special classes and be given instruction which is concrete and practical. They cannot master abstractions, but they can often be made efficient workers, able to look out for themselves. There is no possibility at present of convincing society that they should not be allowed to reproduce, although from a eugenic point of view they constitute a grave problem because of their unusually prolific breeding. (pp. 91–92)

Terman's books and testing programs were widely adopted by public school administrators, who had an immediate need to organize student populations that were burgeoning from an influx of immigrants, the spread of compulsory education, and restrictions on child labor (Cremin, 1988). The new tests were advertised to these administrators as a quick and scientific approach for student placement. In addition, testing was compelling because schools were under increasing scrutiny to use their resources efficiently, and testing was promoted as a cost-saving measure.

Their promise of objectivity and efficiency, alongside popular belief in general intelligence, enabled IQ tests to occupy a prominent position in the educational landscape into the 1970s. However, in recent decades, the popularity of mass-administered intelligence tests has waned. Part of this decline may be due to powerful arguments that such tests are not different from those that purport to measure what a student has learned (Mercer, 1989; *Larry P. v. Wilson Riles*, 1984). Both kinds of tests require an individual to draw on the pool of information, strategies, and skills to which he or she has been exposed. Neither test can isolate any kind of raw intellectual capacity from what an individual has learned.

Another reason for the decline of standardized intelligence tests is a desire to avoid the notion that human potential is innate and fixed (Cizek, 1998). There have also been legal challenges to the use of IQ testing for school placement of African American children (*Larry P. v. Wilson Riles*, 1984). Part of the decline in intelligence testing may also stem from the rise in popularity of theories of intelligence that assert that intelligence consists of a variety of abilities that are not tapped by tests but are harnessed in the workplace and in other culturally valued endeavors (Gardner, 1983; Sternberg, 1985).

Even as intelligence testing has waned, greater emphasis has been placed on standardized achievement testing. These are tests meant to assess what has actually been learned, rather than some innate capacity to learn. This conceptual distinction is important, to the extent that it underscores the ideas that human ability can be enhanced and is entwined with the wider culture. Yet many achievement tests are not markedly different from standardized tests of intelligence. Both kinds of tests tend to rely heavily on multiple-choice questions, language skills, problem solving undertaken by individuals in isolation, and time limits and content coverage designed to maximize the spread of scores (Gardner, 1995; Popham, 2001). Not surprisingly, therefore, on a range of assessments clear differences remain in average scores across economic, racial, and ethnic groups. These score differences continue to affect access to higher-level learning opportunities for students in the primary grades through graduate school (for example, Ford, 1995; Frasier, Garcia, & Passow, 1995; Gewertz, 2002; Orfield & Kornhaber, 2001, passim; Orfield & Miller, 1998).

With some notable exceptions (Jensen, 1980; Herrnstein & Murray, 1994), relatively few scholars now attribute score differences to a fundamental disparity in innate mental abilities across races or ethnic groups. It has become increasingly plain that there is no parsimonious explanation for linking these score differences to some unknown genetic source (Gardner, 1995; Nisbett, 1995, 1998). In contrast, across social groups there are a multitude of well-documented differences above the level of the genome that are clearly associated with test results (e.g., Coleman et al., 1966; Ferguson, 1998; Fordham & Ogbu, 1986; Gaudet, 2000; Kamin, 1995; Natriello & Pallas, 2001; Steele, 1997; Steele & Aronson, 1995, 1998; Young & Smith, 1997). As the next section highlights, it is obvious that people situated differently in society encounter and respond to different experiences. Nevertheless, there is still no clear-cut explanation for the disparities in average test scores (Jencks & Phillips, 1998).

EXPLANATIONS FOR DISPARITIES IN SCORES

Social scientists have made sustained efforts to link score disparities to many phenomena, ranging from problems with the tests themselves to differences in the sociological, psychological, educational, and economic situations of different social and ethnic groups. Reviewing these explanations here facilitates a later analysis of the adequacy of high standards and high-stakes testing policies to foster equity in young people's ability to function at high levels in the world beyond school.

Test Bias

Critics of standardized testing have often attributed group differences to problems of test bias (Gould, 1981; Helms, 1992; Kamin, 1995). In lay or popular definitions, *test bias* refers to several issues: the fact that there are test score differences across groups, the different impact such scores might have for different social groups, and the inclusion of questions that appear to tap knowledge and experiences more readily available to White and middle-class people (Schwartz, 1999; Sturm & Guinier, 1996). Thus, in the lay view, college admissions exams may be considered biased solely because there are score disparities. They may also be considered biased because affluent and White students' access to good schooling and expensive test preparation courses make it more likely they will obtain higher average scores, which in turn may yield advantages for them in college admissions or merit-based scholarships.

However, within the field of testing and measurement, bias refers to something narrower: problems in the test, its administration, or its scoring that yield discrepancies in the meaning of test scores for different groups of people (AERA et al., 1999). In other words, experts hold that when test bias is present, a given score may not enable equally accurate inferences for members of different groups. In this view, differences in average scores across groups are not biased unless the scores themselves say something inaccurate about one group or the other. For example, if a given test yields a score that accurately predicts males' college grades but underpredicts females' college grades, then experts consider that test to be biased.

There are many sources for such test bias. Even so, over the years test developers have devised a host of statistical and subjective methods to scrutinize whole tests and individual test items to greatly reduce test bias. For example, they seek to eliminate elements of the test that are irrelevant to the content or skill in question. They strive to make instructions clear. They often employ panels of diverse individuals to weed out language and content that might hold different meanings to members of different groups or that might be offensive to some

groups. Panels also scrutinize the test to ensure that its content is adequately engaging to diverse test takers and that scoring methods credit different yet correct solutions (AERA et al., 1999). In addition, test developers avoid items whose terms are unfamiliar to particular groups in the society. Such procedures have minimized the kinds of more obvious problems that led earlier critics to condemn standardized tests and their results.

Although debates on item selection and other technical points continue (see Bernal, 2000; Hambleton et al., 2000; Mercer, 1989; Pellegrino, 2000) and these may spur further refinements, test developers can now make a compelling case that similar test scores tend to represent similar levels of skill and knowledge for different groups. Given this, some test experts argue that group scores differ according to the groups' average acquisition of the knowledge and skills the test is sampling (Phelps, 1998, 1999; Phillips, 2000). A less aggressive interpretation is also possible, namely, that differences in scores across Whites and Asians on the one hand, and Latinos and African Americans on the other, are not likely to be largely attributable to problems with test items, instructions, or scoring. Score differences may or may not reflect similar acquisitions of knowledge and skill, partly because students' capacity or willingness to demonstrate that knowledge or skill may vary systematically across groups (more on social-psychological explanations later in this chapter).

Cultural Disadvantage and Differences

Especially during the 1960s and 1970s, score differences on standardized tests across racial, ethnic, linguistic, and socioeconomic groups were often attributed to "cultural disadvantages" among lower-scoring groups. Those who took this position located the source of score disparities primarily *within* the group of low scorers, rather than with the tests themselves or with school practices. These problems were often considered to be educational in nature. For example, language usage or early learning opportunities were regarded as limited relative to groups with higher achievement (Bernstein, 1971). Sometimes the values and behaviors of the lower-scoring groups were regarded as contrary to those needed for success in school groups (Lewis, 1968; Moynihan, 1967). Such explanations have been roundly critiqued for blaming the victims, and for ignoring the strengths of different social and ethnic groups (Baratz & Baratz, 1970; Leacock, 1971). Critics have argued that there are systemic causes for poverty and that the government should respond with programs and policies to ameliorate inadequate income and provide educational opportunities.

Those who have advanced theories of cultural difference argue that the score gaps are due to a collision between students' home cultures and the culture of schools (Delpit, 1995; Heath, 1983). The source of achievement disparities then resides neither in the test nor in the students' culture, but in good measure with the approaches that schools use when educating students from diverse backgrounds. Those who maintain this position find that educators do not understand, appreciate, or know how to work with students whose language, communication methods, or behaviors differ from their own (Delpit, 1995; Heath, 1983; Knapp & Woolverton, 2001; Ladson-Billings, 2001a, 2001b). In the absence of such knowledge, educators view lower achievement as a problem involving student deficiencies. This perception often leads educators to label such students with learning or behavioral problems and to refer them to programs for behavioral or learning remediation. In these programs, students' opportunities to tap more challenging curricula are limited and their learning languishes (Artiles & Trent, 1994; Couhtino & Oswald, 2000; Fierros & Conroy, 2002).

Given this explanation for achievement disparities, solutions take other forms. Among them are reducing the divide between school and home culture by working with parents and tapping community resources (Epstein, 1997; Heath, 1983). In addition, solutions focus on professional development to help build teachers' knowledge and repertoire of practices and inclusive, empowering curricula so that they can better serve students from diverse socioeconomic, racial, and linguistic backgrounds (Banks, 1994b, 2001; Delpit, 1995; Heath, 1983; Sleeter & Grant, 1994).

Social-Psychological Explanations

Another set of explanations ascribes group differences in measured achievement to social and psychological forces that affect students' performance. One prominent strand of research in this area concerns students' motivation in school. Another strand concerns their psychological responses to testing situations.

Some researchers have argued that students from different minority groups show differences in their motivation to perform well in school. Ogbu (1978, 1991) has asserted that students from voluntary minority groups—those who have emigrated in search of better conditions relative to their home country—do not suffer depressed academic achievement. They tend to believe that high educational achievement will enable them to surmount social barriers. In contrast, those from involuntary minority groups—groups that have been colonialized or enslaved, or whose status is ascriptively fixed at the bottom of the social hierarchy—do not necessarily maintain strong beliefs in social mobility through education. Students from involuntary minority groups routinely manifest markedly depressed academic outcomes. This held

true even when, as in Japan, the groups were racially identical (Ogbu, 1978), a finding that helped to cast doubt on racial inferiority theories. Fordham and Ogbu (1986) argued that in response to White oppression, African Americans have evolved a collective identity that is distinct from White mainstream culture. This collective identify tends to reject activities, behaviors, and symbols that are typical of the White majority (Fordham & Ogbu). To the extent that mass education reflects White values and cultures and effaces their own, African American students (and other involuntary minority youth) regard school as a subtractive process (Fordham & Ogbu; see also Valenzuela, 1999). Pursuing academic activities in line with the majority threatens students' ties to this collective culture. Therefore, according to these researchers, students' motivation and effort are depressed. Their standardized test scores reflect their lower level of motivation.

Although work among several other researchers aligns with Fordham and Ogbu's (1986) basic ideas (e.g., Garrison, 1989; Mickelson, 1990), other investigators have critiqued their thesis. Cross (1995) has drawn finer distinctions in the notion of oppositional culture, saying that the phenomenon described by Fordham and Ogbu is primarily a response to the recent, extreme segregation from opportunity experienced by young African Americans in the inner city (see Wilson, 1987, 1996). As a result, Ogbu's work (1978, 1991) doesn't reflect the fact that, historically, African Americans have prized education and emphasized the importance of schooling. Empirical work by Spencer, Noel, Stoltzfus, and Harpalani (2001), involving surveys of African American students, refutes the notion that African American youth show any less effort in school. An analysis by Cook and Ludwig (1998) of data from the National Education Longitudinal Study (NELS) finds that if family income, mother's education, and family structure are held constant, many differences across Black and White students disappear. These researchers assert that given similar backgrounds, academically successful African American students actually feel slightly more popular than White students who are academically successful and also more popular than Black students with lower achievement. Cook and Ludwig also find no significant differences in educational aspiration or effort between African American and White high school students. They conclude that "Black high school students are not particularly alienated from school" (p. 391).

If effort, motivation, and engagement are similar among Black and White students from similar family situations, how might continuing achievement disparities be understood? Research conducted by Steele (Steele, 1997; Steele & Aronson, 1995, 1998) offers an explanation from the psychological perspective, namely, stereotype threat. In essence, African American students know that weaker performance can lead others to view them in a stereotyped, negative way. Steele finds this awareness to be especially true of stronger students whose self-identity is tied to school achievement. The threat of being stereotyped disrupts these students' performance. In experimental work, Steele manipulated conditions to prime very able Black college students to think that the negative stereotype was or was not a salient feature of a testing situation. When the stereotype threat was present, these students overworked problems and were less willing to guess. They therefore solved fewer problems and attained lower scores than Whites with equally high SAT scores. If the stereotype threat was removed, the scores of White and Black students were equivalent. Steele finds similar effects on test scores when stereotype threat is primed for White males in a situation that compares them with Asian males. Steele (1997) has also induced depressed results when stereotype threat is primed for women in testing situations with men. Thus stereotype threat appears to be a human, rather than a race- or gender-specific, response among achievement-oriented students. Nevertheless, it is prominent among those who are frequently subjected to negative stereotypes of their abilities.

Given social and psychological explanations of this sort, there are a whole host of possible policy responses. For example, Fordham and Ogbu's (1986) first suggestion is to reduce the economic disparities that may make educational achievement seem irrelevant to some Black students. Indeed, it was during the period when civil rights enforcement was greatest that the gap in test scores most narrowed (Levin, 2001). In addition, Fordham and Ogbu have suggested the development of community programs that highlight and publicly value achievement among minority students. Steele (1997) has described several "situational changes" (p. 624) in the learning environment that can reduce stereotype threat. For example, he highlights the importance of "optimistic teacher-student relationships" (p. 624), which can diminish students' concerns that others doubt their academic abilities. He calls upon educators to emphasize that intelligence is not fixed but develops with experience, instruction, and effort. In addition, he advocates a focus on challenging curriculum, rather than remediation. These changes each have implications for policies governing preprofessional education, professional development programs, and remedial education.

Educational Disparities

As many scholars have pointed out, there are myriad important differences in the schooling of students from lower- and higher-scoring groups. Within the same school, students from groups with lower average scores are treated differently from those in groups with higher

average scores. For example, teacher expectations for African American students are often lower (Baron, Tom, & Cooper, 1985; Ferguson, 1998; Howard & Hammond, 1985). An extensive review of educators' perceptions and expectations concludes that low expectations not only exist for Black students but "probably do help to sustain, and perhaps even to expand, the black-white test score gap" (Ferguson, 1998, p. 313). Different expectations also play out in different learning opportunities. Disproportionately few African Americans and Latinos participate in programs for the gifted or in advanced high school courses (Ford, 1995; Frasier, Garcia, & Passow, 1995). They are disproportionately overrepresented, however, in lower tracks, remedial classes, and special education (Artiles & Trent, 1994; Fierros & Conroy, 2002; Mickelson, 2001; Oakes, 1985; Oakes, Gamoran, & Page, 1992).

Furthermore, African American and Latino students tend to go to schools that differ importantly from schools that are largely attended by White, middle-class (or wealthier) students. Throughout the 1990s, public schools actually became more segregated by race and ethnicity (G. Orfield, 2001; Orfield & Yun, 1999). Segregated schools are separated both by color and class. Thus students of color are also far more likely to attend schools where there are high levels of poverty (G. Orfield, 2001; Young & Smith, 1997).

Practices, beliefs, and climate within schools do matter (Cole, 1995; Darling-Hammond, 1997; DeLuca & Rosenbaum, 2001; Edmonds, 1982; Ferguson, 1998; Lee & Burkam, 2001; Legters & Kerr, 2001; Levine & Lezotte, 2001; Valenzuela, 1999), but the fact remains that a great deal of the variance in educational performance is associated with the demographics of the school population (Coleman et al., 1966; Gaudet, 2000; Natriello & Pallas, 2001; Schellenberg, 1999; Young & Smith, 1997). Among other differences, schools whose students are predominantly of color and from low-income families are more likely to have students with special needs (Lanckford & Wyckoff, 1996). At the same time, such schools are also less likely to have teachers certified in their area of instruction, offer challenging curriculum, maintain high standards for performance, or provide adequate supplies of up-to-date equipment and books (Darling-Hammond, 2001; Ferguson & Ladd, 1996; Firestone, Camilli, Yurecko, Monfils, & Mayrowetz, 2000; Kozol, 1991; McNeil, 2000). In essence, segregated schools offer vastly unequal educational opportunities (G. Orfield, 2001). Assessment outcomes clearly reflect these differences. In turn, these school environments mirror policy decisions in areas such as income support, housing, and metropolitan development that are beyond the scope of this chapter and that have been off the radar screen of most policy makers since the early 1980s (G. Orfield, 1993; M. Orfield,

1997; Powell, Kearney, & Vina, 2001; Wilson, 1987, 1996).

In sum, there is no one single explanation for the disparities in achievement across socioeconomic, racial, and ethnic groups in the United States. Nevertheless, the range of explanations suggests that a variety of interventions might be helpful. As has been noted, these interventions range from emphasizing the malleability of intelligence to reducing barriers among schools, parents, and communities, to improving professional development and curriculum, and providing more equitable educational resources. Nevertheless, since the mid-1980s there has been one overwhelming policy response to disparities in test scores: raising standards and testing students to see whether the standards are being met.

STANDARDS AND HIGH-STAKES TESTS AS A SOLUTION FOR INEQUITY

The origins of the movement to raise standards and increase testing reach back to the 1983 federal report, *A Nation at Risk* (National Commission on Excellence in Education, 1983). This report asserted that there was a crisis of low demand and low performance in U.S. schools, which represented a threat no less dangerous than that of a hostile enemy. To combat this, the authors of the report argued that schools should require students to take more courses and pursue more demanding courses.

The report's message was widely and favorably received. Although 37 states already required minimum competency tests, *A Nation at Risk* faulted these for setting too low a standard (National Commission on Excellence in Education, 1983). Within three years of the report, 35 states pushed through education reforms, many requiring increased course taking and testing (Pipho, 1986). At the 1989 Summit on Education, President George Bush, together with the nation's governors, argued for even higher standards and additional assessments aimed at yielding great achievement gains by the year 2000 (Hoffman, 1989). Support for such reforms remains strong among state governors through the present (National Governors Association, 2001).

In 1989, the federal government helped to launch the so-called standards movement by urging the development of national standards for all major school subjects (Stotsky, 2000). National discipline-based groups, such as the National Council of Teachers of English, the National Council of Teachers of Mathematics, and the National Council for Social Studies, soon began writing their own standards, which states began drawing on (National Council of Teachers of English, 1996; National Council

of Teachers of Mathematics, 1995; Raimi, 2000; Stotsky, 2000).

Shortly thereafter, federal and state officials formed the National Education Goals Panel, which promoted "Goals 2000." Included among the panel's six goals was that "all students leaving grades 4, 8 and 12" will have "demonstrated competency over challenging subject matter including English, mathematics, science, history, and geography" (National Education Goals Panel, 1991, p. ix). The Educate America Act, passed by Congress in 1994, was intended to provide a framework for achieving the aims of Goals 2000. In the act, Congress called for more equal achievement and stated that "the distribution of minority students in each quartile will more closely reflect the student population as a whole" (U.S. Congress, 1994). In 2002, the reauthorization of Title I went further by embracing President George W. Bush's campaign promise to "leave no child behind." For this promise to be fulfilled, Bush successfully argued that states should test all students who are enrolled in grades three through eight (Robelen, 2002; U.S. Department of Education, 2001).

Alongside governmental actors, business groups have consistently endorsed the move to higher standards and increased testing. Business leaders, often noting the changing demographics of the workforce, regard standards and testing as an essential tool for developing workers suitable for the new, knowledge-based economy. In addition, many leaders assert that standards and tests can be used to hold schools accountable for performance and tax dollars. Indeed, a number of business organizations have been formed or reconfigured specifically to promote higher standards and higher achievement as measured on standardized tests (see Business-Higher Education Forum, 2002; National Alliance of Business, 2002; Platzer, Novak, & Kazmierczak, 2002).

A number of researchers and education reformers have also supported higher standards and increased testing as a means to improve educational equity (Ravitch, 1996; Resnick & Nolan, 1995; Stotsky, 2000). Stotsky (2000), for example, has claimed that standards provide educators and parents with "clear expectations of what all students should learn. . . . Standards that reflect high expectations for all students in a state contribute strongly to the goal of equity" (p. xiii). Similarly, Ravitch (1996) has argued that an "essential purpose of standards is to ensure that students in all schools have access to equally challenging programs and courses of study" (p. 26). In addition, some researchers and advocates assert that understanding where all students stand against a given test yardstick is an important step in improving educational equity (Bishop & Mane, 2001; Murnane, 2000). Therefore, testing is regarded as an essential component of standards-based reform.

Various organizations that are explicitly concerned with civil rights—among them the Citizens Commission for Civil Rights, the Campaign for Fiscal Equity, and the Education Trust—have also advocated standards-based reform. Leaders of these groups argue that clear and high standards, and accountability for the performance of *all* students, can help improve achievement for African American and Latino students (see Lindsay, 1995; Sack, 1999; Taylor, 2000). Some of these leaders view higher standards and more testing as a wedge for other reforms that can improve educational equity—for example, better funding and staff development.

In sum, beginning with *A Nation at Risk* and through 2002, there has been strong support across key sectors of society for higher standards for all students. Testing students to see if they have been taught and have learned the standards is also broadly supported across these groups. Opinion polls from the mid-1990s through the time of this writing have also found that the general public supports standards and tests (Phelps, 1998; Public Agenda, 2002; Public Education Network & Education Week, 2002).

THE LOGIC BEHIND STANDARDS-BASED REFORM

The broad appeal of high standards and increased testing may reflect the straightforward logic on which it rests: for too long, American students have been held to low and poorly articulated educational standards. Clear and high standards for academic performance must therefore be developed and disseminated to improve student achievement. Schools must focus on these standards so that students can reach them. To check whether teachers and students are working toward the standards, students will be tested. To ensure that the tests and standards are taken seriously, test results will carry consequences, or stakes. The stakes can be either carrots (e.g., teacher or school bonuses, good school publicity) or sticks (e.g., dismissal of school staff, school takeovers, student retention, denial of high school diplomas, bad school publicity), or often both. The data from the test should also inform decisions about where additional professional development or other educational resources should be directed. This line of thinking has produced variations of standards-and-test-based reforms across the great majority of states.

Even so, it is worth noting that there is another straightforward and logical approach to introducing higher standards in schools. It is usually termed "authentic assessment" or "performance assessment," because it emphasizes performances and products that incorporate qualities valued beyond, and not only in, schools or formal testing situations (Darling-Hammond, Ancess, &

Falk, 2001; Wiggins, 1998; Zessoules & Gardner, 1991). Under the logic of performance assessment, teachers and students learn the characteristics of high-quality work in a number of disciplines by studying examples and practices that embody it. They clearly articulated these characteristics. (For example, characteristics for a strong paper in history might include the use of multiple sources, well-reasoned use of evidence, a clear sense of chronology and of the relationship among events, and well-organized writing.) Students then seek to produce work that incorporates the characteristics of high-quality work. Using ongoing, formative feedback from teachers and classmates, students revise their work until it embodies the identified qualities. Their grades reflect the extent to which the specified characteristics are incorporated. In some places, graduation from high school depends on showing high-quality work on performance assessments in a variety of disciplines. Many schools in different states have used this approach, but no state is currently relying exclusively on a performance assessment system to promote and raise statewide standards.

Each approach to fostering high standards has complementary strengths and weaknesses. Among the strengths of the authentic assessment approach is that the standards are rich and accessible, because they are generated and discussed using concrete examples at the classroom or school level (Darling-Hammond, Ancess, & Falk, 2001; Wiggins, 1998; Zessoules & Gardner, 1991). These examples can be quite adaptable to individual and local issues and interests, and they can draw upon what is most compelling and meaningful in a given community. Thus standards that are employed in authentic assessments are more readily owned and understood by teachers and students. Another strength is that, compared to a test score, a relatively low level of inference is needed to know whether students have or have not mastered a particular area (Fredericksen & Collins, 1989): a student's paper incorporates the articulated qualities to a visible extent. Therefore, authentic assessment lends itself to clear feedback on the specific qualities that have yet to be met and the processes for meeting them. In addition, feedback can be immediate and ongoing. This tight feedback loop makes it more likely that a given student will have the information needed to improve performance in a timely way. These features make authentic assessments powerful tools to help students learn (Black & Wiliam, 1998; Eisner, 1999; Pellegrino, Chudowsky, & Glaser, 2001; Wiggins, 1998).

However, performance assessments have several drawbacks. One weakness is that locally developed standards for quality may be extremely variable and even idiosyncratic. Thus what constitutes high-quality work in School A can look much better or worse than high-quality work in School Z. In addition, it is unwieldy for the state to use performance assessment in evaluating every student and every school's actual work. It is also costly to look at large samples of actual student work, and more difficult and costly to achieve reliability in judging such work (Haertel, 1999; Koretz, Klein, McCaffrey, & Stecher, 1994). Furthermore, the results from performance assessment do not readily yield a single summary statistic that permits clear comparison across students, classrooms, schools, and districts. Therefore, this kind of assessment is better at guiding teaching and learning than it is at monitoring or auditing educational systems for teaching and learning.

The weaknesses and strengths of the standards-and-testing approach are largely reversed, with the audit function being powerful and the instructional function being much weaker (Wiggins, 1998). Consequently, among the weaknesses of the current high-standards and high-stakes reforms is the fact that the standards are set far outside of the school and classroom level. Recent research indicates that the standards often do not make it into the classroom level in the systemic fashion that state policy makers are seeking (Blank, Porter, & Smithson, 2001). Not surprisingly, then, these standards are less likely to be owned or well understood by teachers and students. Furthermore, because they are set far outside local communities, when the standards ultimately arrive in the classrooms they are less likely to engage students and teachers through powerful local questions and issues. It is partly this inability that gives rise to claims that such assessments are undemocratic (see Meier, 2000). Another weakness is that a much higher degree of inference is required to determine whether a score truly reflects whether a student knows the qualities of good work in a given discipline and can actually produce high-quality work (Fredericksen & Collins, 1989; Gardner, 1999). In addition, there is a longer and more summative feedback loop to students, teachers, and schools. In fact, feedback sometimes reaches the teacher only as, or even after, the student is moving on to another grade or classroom (Snow & Jones, 2001). Relatedly, feedback on the standards tends to be thin ("proficient," "70th percentile," "fail"). This makes the emphasis on testing less useful in informing classroom practice for particular students (Black & Wiliam, 1998; Wiggins, 1998). Finally, although the summary statistic readily permits comparisons, the statistic can also be easily "gamed." That is, the statistic can be made to look better by manipulating conditions unrelated to teaching and learning the qualities of good work in a discipline. Gaming techniques include altering the pool of test takers, teaching test-taking skills, comparing students against old norms, or changing students' answer sheets; all of these improve scores without improving learning (Amrein &

Berliner, 2002). Prominent leaders in educational assessment have pointed out that the higher the stakes, the higher the temptations to game the system (Cizek, 1998; Haney, 2000, 2001; Linn, 2000; Madaus & Clarke, 2001). Researchers in the area of school reform have seen these temptations enacted in practice (Amrein & Berliner, 2002; McNeil, 2000; McNeil & Valenzuela, 2001).

However, the strengths of the standards-and-testing approach complement the weaknesses of authentic assessment. Test-based measures of standards have much higher reliability and more easily allow all schools and students to be assessed. Their statistics can give information useful in comparing performances across students, schools, and districts. The cost per student is much lower than for broad efforts at authentic assessment. (Indeed, the popularity of testing may be related to its cost, which is much lower than for programs to reduce class size, put a certified teacher in every classroom, or ensure every student has a set of up-to-date textbooks.) Because of statewide efforts to develop standards and tests, this approach provides a uniform direction across diverse districts and schools far more readily than authentic assessments. As Natriello and Pallas (2001) point out, test-focused reforms "are among the most important methods of exercising state influence. . . . Formal testing of students has the potential to influence the behavior of all major actors in the educational system" (p. 20). These strengths, together with the support of government, business and civic leaders, as well as researchers and the public, have clearly won out in practice. Nevertheless, a National Research Council report has recently stated that a balanced use of school-based performance assessments and standardized testing is likely to be more beneficial in advancing learning and informing policy decisions (Pellegrino et al., 2001).

EQUITY IN THE ERA OF HIGH-STAKES TESTING

Historically, as described in the first part of this chapter, overreliance on testing for making decisions about students has not produced sustained efforts to improve educational equity in the United States. That is, overreliance on testing has not facilitated equity in enabling students from diverse social groups to function at the highest possible level in the wider world. This characterization holds true even when testing is designed for that purpose (Madaus, 1994). For example, although Binet's tests were intended to improve the chances that students from different social classes were educated, his technology applied in a U.S. context fostered classroom and curriculum assignments that largely reinforced, rather than altered, social inequalities. The same might be said for the SAT, which was designed to provide a common instrument for many elite colleges to use in admitting students from different high schools (College Entrance Examination Board, 1926), and it was also thought to enable the identification of applicants from humble circumstances (Lemann, 1999). But when the SAT serves as a key determinant of admissions, the chances for African Americans, Latinos, Native Americans, or students from poverty to attend the best universities plummet (Crouse & Trusheim, 1988; Kornhaber, 1998; Orfield & Miller, 1998). Similarly, legal challenges to affirmative action in admissions to the best public high schools have driven up the salience of test scores and driven down the number of Latino and African American students who gain access to these elite institutions (Gewertz, 2002).

Proponents of the newest generation of high standards and high-stakes testing have argued that their approach will not follow this trajectory. Instead, proponents assert, equally high standards and equally demanding testing will bring greater equity across diverse schools (Bishop & Mane, 2001; Howard, 1995; Ravitch, 1996; Robelen, 2002; Stotsky, 2000). The debate between supporters and skeptics of high standards and high-stakes tests focuses on whether the reforms improve curriculum, improve effort and motivation, produce genuine learning gains or merely higher scores, and foster more similar educational attainment across groups, or instead yield greater disparities. Each of these debates is considered in the next sections.

Curricular Access Versus Curricular Narrowing

Because testing drives instruction (Elmore & Rothman, 2000; Fredericksen & Collins, 1989; Linn, 2000), proponents of higher standards and high-stakes testing have argued that the new reforms will improve access by focusing instruction on substantive curriculum. It is this sort of curriculum that underserved students were often not provided with, avoided, or were steered away from (Bishop & Mane, 2001; Stotsky, 2000).

Proponents of the new reforms acknowledge that in the past testing did not adequately spur a focus on substance. They often attribute this to the use of norm-referenced tests (Howard, 1995). Such tests indicate how students and schools perform relative to each other, but they do not reveal what it is that students, and groups of students, actually know and can do. Proponents of high standards and high stakes argue that these new reforms should rely on tests that are criterion-referenced and aligned with the states' new challenging content standards. Because of their relationship to the curriculum, and because they have the potential to focus teachers' and students' effort on things that matter, they will be "tests worth teaching to" (Simmons & Resnick, 1993; Spalding, 2000; Viadero, 1994).

These ideas, however, are not necessarily playing out in reality. First, several states (most notably California) and big districts (most notably Chicago) have continued to rely on norm-referenced tests such as the Stanford 9 and Iowa Test of Basic Skills. Consequently, students' test scores are not providing much substantive information about what they can do relative to particular criteria. Nevertheless, because stakes are still associated with scores on these tests, instruction in at least some cases has strenuously focused on test preparation. For example, a report on Chicago's strategies for school improvements notes that "the current school system leadership has strongly emphasized drill in preparation for the test. . . . Furthermore, the curriculum options that they propose to mandate for low achieving schools place an overriding emphasis on teacher-directed drill" (Moore & Hanson, 2001, p. 6).

Instruction focused on test preparation has happened even in states that have developed tests that are aligned with their standards. Because teachers and students are held accountable on the basis of test performance, those schools and students where performance is likely to be problematic will more likely gear instruction toward test preparation (Firestone et al., 2000; Hillocks, 2002; McNeil, 2000; McNeil & Valenzuela, 2001). For such schools and students, the curriculum can shrink to the tested subjects. For instance, McNeil and Valenzuela's (2001) investigation into several predominantly poor and minority schools in Texas indicates that writing had been refocused simply to teaching and learning the format of the persuasive essay required on the state test. In addition, reading was reduced from actual literature to short passages of the sort found on the test. Furthermore, time was siphoned away from teaching and learning those subjects that were not tested, including history and science, to make additional room for test preparation.

Tests that are more demanding or more "authentic" might seem to offer a solution. Unfortunately, when the stakes are high, these exams can also channel students more toward drill and memorization and away from thinking in the discipline. One well-known example is based on research on a high-stakes test in Ireland. This investigation uncovered virtually identical "essays" prepared by a number of students over several years. Students had been taught to memorize a response rather than to craft writing (Madaus & Clarke, 2001).

Proponents of high stakes and standards note that there may be some overzealous preparation, but that good school leaders avoid such practices (Barthe, 2001). The problem, however, is that some school leaders will be better able to avoid these practices than others. Because stakes fall on school leaders and not just students, leaders' ability to avoid such pressures will logically tend to divide along the lines of lower- and higher-scoring schools. Because higher-scoring schools tend to have more affluent and predominantly White populations, more qualified teachers, and better educational resources, educators in those schools need not worry much about showing score gains. They can spend marginal time acquainting students with the test format and then continue to teach mostly the content of the disciplines: writing in various genres, reading a range of literature, exploring patterns of relationships in mathematics. Lower-scoring schools tend to have weaker educational resources alongside higher proportions of students of color and students from poverty. In these schools, improving test scores will be a salient concern among educators, and narrow drill and test preparation will be much more common (Firestone et al., 2000; McNeil, 2000). Therefore, even if students are being prepared for the same test, the curriculum is pushed in different directions depending on the relative advantages present at the start of the reform. Consequently, it is unlikely that high-stakes testing systems can drive curricular equality into schools with widely disparate economic and demographic characteristics.

Actual Learning Versus Test Score Gains

Even if high-stakes testing does not yield equivalent curriculum, and even if it drives instruction of minority and poor youth toward test preparation, proponents of such reforms make the commonsense argument that students still need to learn the knowledge and skills the tests sample. These proponents argue that unless the reforms focus on these essentials, they will continue to remain beyond the reach of the students who have been historically underserved by public schools (Bishop & Mane, 2001; Phelps, 1998). This argument is nevertheless problematic because test-driven reforms do not necessarily boost actual English or math skills even when they boost test scores (Amrein & Berliner, 2002; Elmore & Rothman, 1998; Klein, Hamilton, McCaffrey, & Stecher, 2000; Koretz & Barron, 1998; Linn, 2000; Neill, 2001; Pellegrino et al., 2001). Nor do such reforms necessarily close the gap in learning between those who are well served and those who have been poorly served by the education system.

It is typical for test scores to rise for a few years after a new testing program has been implemented (Linn, 2000). However, to understand whether such increases reflect growth in learning and not mostly growth in test scores, it is important to see if the gains on the new test generalize to gains on other kinds of tests or assessments. Several studies that explore whether students' gains on state tests generalize to other tests are decidedly mixed. For example, an analysis conducted by Neill (2001)

found no clear patterns of gains on the National Assessment of Educational Progress among states that had or did not have a high-stakes graduation test. In other words, states with test-driven reforms, whose scores typically rise for a period of time, did not necessarily show NAEP gains. Another study by Koretz and Barron (1998) found that score gains on Kentucky's own state test during the early 1990s were three and a half to four times larger than NAEP gains, even though Kentucky's test was supposed to tap NAEP content and skills. At the high school level, gains on the Kentucky test were also substantially larger than gains on the ACT. Koretz and Barron (1998) asserted that state and local education agencies need to assess whether recorded score gains are valid. Amrein and Berliner (2002) investigated the 18 states with the highest-stakes testing programs and found only scant indications of generalized gains in learning on the NAEP, college entrance examinations, or advanced placement tests. They concluded that "we have little evidence at the present time that such programs work" (p. 52).

Even in Texas—the state that has gotten the most notice for its education reforms and test score gains—the relationship between score increases and learning increases is not clear. According to one RAND Corporation study, Texas and North Carolina showed the largest average gains among all states on the NAEP between 1990 and 1996 (Grissmer, Flanagan, Kawata, & Williamson, 2000). This study also found that gains among African American and Latino students in Texas were larger than gains among Whites (Grissmer et al., 2000). However, another team of RAND researchers that looked at fourth- and eighth-grade NAEP reading and math scores found that Texas outpaced the nation only on the fourth-grade math exam. In fourth- and eighth-grade reading and in eighth-grade math, "the gains in Texas were comparable to those experienced nationwide" (Klein et al., 2000, p. 12). In addition, these researchers discovered that between 1994 and 1998 the Black-White gap in NAEP scores in the state actually increased in fourth-grade reading and in fourth- and eighth-grade math. The NAEP score gap between Latinos and Whites also grew slightly wider. These gaps grew even as Texas declared gaps to be narrowing on its own state assessment (Klein et al., 2000).

A serious concern, then, with these standards and test-driven reforms is that their focus on making test scores rise—and even their success in raising scores—does not necessarily generalize or transfer to performances elsewhere. It should be noted that transfer is hard to achieve throughout the educational enterprise. Students who learn information for use in one context (a test, or only in school) typically experience difficulty transferring or applying that knowledge to other tests or situations (diSessa, 1982; Lave, 1990; Perkins & Salomon, 1989; Salomon & Perkins, 1989; Singley & Anderson, 1989). To foster transfer, students need opportunities to work in varied contexts and with varied representations of concepts and information (Pellegrino et al., 2001; Gardner, 1992; Perkins & Salomon, 1989). However, because of their tendency to overemphasize the kind of performance valued on a single test, the current high-stakes test policies will exacerbate, rather than mitigate, this central educational problem. Given the greater focus on raising test scores in schools with higher concentrations of students of color and students from poverty, transfer of knowledge and generalized gains will be even less likely for these young people (Amrein & Berliner, 2002).

Catching Up Versus Falling Behind in Educational Attainment

It is often argued that higher standards and high-stakes testing will help students catch up, because the consequences associated with the tests will push students and their teachers to make more effort. One possible consequence is retaining students in grade until they meet the standard. For example, President Bill Clinton wrote that he

repeatedly challenged States [sic] and school district to end social promotions—to require students to meet rigorous academic standards. . . . Students should not be promoted past the fourth grade if they cannot read independently and well, and should not enter high school without a solid foundation in math. They should get the help they need to meet the standards before moving on. (quoted in Hauser, 2001, p. 152)

Policy makers in at least seven states have accepted this message and now require state assessments to be used in making promotion decisions in certain grades (Hauser, 2001). Some test-based accountability systems, such as those in Georgia, Louisiana, and North Carolina, explicitly call for retention if a student fails the state test.

Despite such arguments, there are at least four problems with calls to increase retention. First, presidential rhetoric aside, retention is actually widespread. A cautious estimate using federal data to infer the number of children who are overage for their grade *after* ages six to eight (during which retention is common) indicates that about 20 percent of students are retained at least once (Hauser, 2001). Texas is one of the few states that collect good data on retention, and its numbers are revealing: in the late 1990s approximately 17 percent of students were retained at least once between first and eighth grade (Hauser, 2001). However, in the ninth grade—the year before the state's mandatory high school graduation test—nearly 18 percent of students were retained (McCollum, Cortez, Maroney, & Montes, 1999).

Even when there is not an explicit policy to use test scores to promote or retain students, test-based accountability systems foster perverse incentives to increase retention in order to game the scores. Although retention commonly yields negative consequences for students (Hauser, 2001; Holmes, 1989; Moore, 2000; Shepard & Smith, 1989), retention can give the impression that school performances are improving. This is because retention removes from the test-taking cohort those students who are likely to score poorly or fail. Once these students are removed, the net score for the cohort is likely to rise. It is common to see retention increase markedly among students in the year prior to a high-stakes test, and it is common to see school retention rates go up alongside rising scores on high-stakes tests (Haney, 2001).

A third problem with retention policies is that they are disproportionately applied to students of color as well as to males. The good data from Texas help to illustrate this point. Of the nearly 18 percent of ninth graders who were retained, 60 percent were male. Disparities grew wider with race and class: the retention rate among Latinos and African American students in Texas was two and a half times higher than for Whites. Retention was also much more prevalent in urban districts and in other areas serving high proportions of minority students and students from poverty (McCollum et al., 1999). Although some states and districts have a process by which retention can be appealed, the process may not work equally for all students. For example, an investigation of Chicago's retention policy, which included an appeal system, noted that the appeal process was "highly capricious and inequitable and was strongly influenced by . . . principals' individual attitudes towards retention and towards particular families and students" (Moore, 2000, p. 10).

Fourth, although it may be argued that the students who are retained need time to catch up, retention does not foster gains in student learning. Researchers consistently find that students who have been retained ultimately learn less than those with similar test scores who are promoted (Hauser, 2001; Holmes, 1989; Moore, 2000; National Research Council, 1999). Retained students may learn less because they are often given limited curriculum with teachers who are less well prepared, and they are far more likely to drop out (Hauser, 2001; Holmes, 1989). Though retention may motivate some students to work harder, it is also clear that a substantial percentage of retained students ultimately walk away from school without obtaining important skills or a high school diploma.

In essence, despite rhetoric that says "leave no child behind," widespread policies focusing on standards and testing are unlikely to yield broad improvements in genuine educational attainment. That is, they are not likely to foster equity in enabling students to use their minds well in the real world. Under these policies, curriculum tends to veer toward test drill in schools that primarily serve children of color and students from poverty, while enriched curriculum is left largely intact in schools serving the affluent. These reforms seek to advance learning, but there is evidence that measured gains on high-stakes tests do not generalize to other tests or contexts. To the extent that education for many poor students and students of color becomes more focused on testing, there will be even less likelihood of generalized and equitable gains. Finally, testing policies are associated with increases in retention, a practice that reduces achievement and graduation rates and that disproportionately affects males and African American and Latino students. Even if such reforms are intended to reduce inequitable education and achievement, equity is not likely to flow from them.

USING ASSESSMENTS TO PROMOTE EQUITY

Building an equitable educational system in the context of U.S. society is an exceedingly complex task: the school system is highly decentralized; students bring to school different cultures, languages, early childhood experiences, and economic circumstances; and they are provided with very disparate educational resources. As with any complex task, many tools are necessary, rather than a single one. Not surprisingly therefore, assessment is insufficient to instill school quality or educational equity across the entire society. Overreliance on any one type of assessment—be it authentic or a high-stakes standardized test—warps the educational system in ways that can undermine educational equity. However, when used appropriately, good tests balanced with good classroom-level assessment can contribute helpful information about students and educational systems (National Research Council, 1999; Pellegrino et al., 2001).

Several prominent organizations, including the National Research Council, the American Educational Research Association, the American Psychological Association, and the National Council on Measurement in Education, have published revised guidelines and recommendations for appropriate test use (AERA et al., 1999; National Research Council, 1999; McDonnell, McLaughlin, & Morison, 1997). These publications underscore several important points. One is that results from a single test should never be used to make an important decision about an individual student. Because of random error, even test scores that are obtained under optimal conditions are never wholly accurate. Therefore, test scores should not be used exclusively in decisions about promotion, graduation, tracking, or school quality (AERA et

al., 1999; National Research Council, 1999).

Nevertheless, heavy reliance on data from one test is a common practice in graduation and promotion decisions across many states and districts. One reason for this is that a gray area exists in the Standards for Educational and Psychological Testing (AERA et al., 1999), the key document used by psychometricians and test developers to guide test design and use: repeated testing of a student using one exam, such as a state's graduation test, is regarded by some as equal to obtaining results from many tests, rather than one. Retesting is considered a route to reducing measurement error and getting closer to the student's "true" score (Gong & Hill, 2001). It has also been viewed in court as a way to provide students with multiple chances to show whether they have learned the skills the state requires (GI Forum v. Texas Education Agency, 2000).

Although the notion of repeated testing may pass muster from the legal and measurement perspectives, it does not work from an educational one. In essence, overemphasizing a single assessment narrows the educational landscape rather than opens it up. Test preparation classes may ultimately equip many students to pass their high-stakes test, but as noted earlier it will not equip them to apply whatever knowledge they have gleaned to situations beyond the test, where the vast majority of problem solving lies.

A second and related key point is that a single test should not be used to judge an entire school or educational system (AERA et al., 1999). Scores in a school can vary for many reasons wholly unrelated to teaching and learning. For example, a great deal of the variance in yearly school scores is due to small student cohorts in a given grade. Thus very strong or weak scores from just a few students can make a major difference in the score of the cohort, even though there may actually be little real change (Haney, 2002; Kane & Staiger, 2001). In addition, random circumstances, such as noise beyond the school walls or a disruptive student in the test site, can readily affect scores (Kane & Staiger, 2001). Yearly fluctuations in the composition of the student population, especially in schools with high mobility rates, may make for sizeable changes in scores without comparable gains or losses in actual learning by students. Given this, it is important to use multiple measures, disaggregated by race and class, and to interpret school performance using trends over several years' duration rather than year-to-year.

A critical indicator to consider in judging schools at the secondary level is disaggregated information about student dropout rates. Because high school completion is vital to students' real-world success, a crucial measure is the ability of schools to keep students until graduation (Balfanz & Letgers, 2001). In some states and districts, the pressure to raise scores on high-stakes tests has come into conflict with educating students who score poorly. The upshot has been increased dropout rates among already vulnerable Latino, African American, and low-income youth (Haney, 2001; Hauser, 2001).

A third key point, underscored by the National Research Council, is that assessment results cannot be used to justify placing students in typical low-track or remedial classes (Heubert & Hauser, 1999). Because they emphasize drill and are often staffed by less experienced teachers, such placements commonly do not enable students to improve their knowledge and skills. They erode, rather than build, students' educational and life chances. Placements should be made only into programs that benefit students. Furthermore, these placements should be based on a range of information, including grades and input from teachers and parents (AERA et al., 1999).

Fourth, to use tests appropriately, it is also necessary to understand whether the score is attributable to, or accurately reflects, students' knowledge. This requires that tests themselves be as free as possible from technical bias and that they be administered in a way that is respectful of the test takers (AERA et al., 1999). In interpreting test results, it is important to consider a range of explanations for a given score. It is inappropriate for those using test results to infer that a score simply reflects students' current knowledge. For instance, a low score can result from events during testing, weak opportunities to learn the curriculum, or language differences. These and other possible explanations need to be ruled out before a score is used in making a decision of consequence (Heubert & Hauser, 1999).

Fifth, to obtain results that accurately reflect the knowledge and skills of students with special needs or learning differences, it is important to make test accommodations, especially when those accommodations do not conflict with the content area being assessed. For example, to know whether an English language learner has mastered algebra, the test questions and instructions should be comprehensible in the student's native language. A report by the National Research Council (Heubert & Hauser, 1999) has asserted that the increasing inclusion of English language learners in large-scale assessments creates demands on testing that "are greater than the current knowledge and technology can support" (p. 296). Unless accommodations are provided for such students, "their scores will not accurately reflect their knowledge" (p. 296). In turn, judgments about these students and the systems that educate them will be faulty. Such possibilities grow as bilingual programs come under siege and testing demands increase.

Under the Individuals with Disabilities Education Act of 1997, students with disabilities are also increasingly participating in large-scale testing programs. This is seen by many educators and policy makers as a way to bring greater accountability for the education of these students and for bringing greater comparability across schools, districts, and states (McDonnell et al., 1997). To facilitate these students' participation, it is reasonable to provide testing accommodations. For example, these students may need to have the test administered in a small-group or individual setting. They may need additional time. They may need modifications in the way the test materials are presented (such as Braille or audiotaped versions of the test). It may be necessary to provide modifications in the way they are allowed to respond, as with dictated answers instead of written responses (McDonnell et al.).

Finally, if the results from tests or any other form of assessment are to be properly interpreted and used, it is essential to determine whether students have had an adequate opportunity to learn the material on the test. Low scores from those who have not had the opportunity to learn are not equivalent to low scores from those who have had reasonable learning opportunities but who have not acquired the expected knowledge and skills. A major difficulty, however, is defining what constitutes an adequate opportunity to learn (AERA et al., 1999).

In some influential legal cases, judges and policy makers have narrowly interpreted opportunity to learn in terms of alignment between the test content and the classroom curriculum (*Debra P.* v. *Turlington,* 1979; *GI Forum* v. *Texas Education Agency,* 2000). Nevertheless, research indicates that opportunity to learn depends as well on a host of other variables: teacher quality, bilingual status, class size, prevalence of school poverty, and racial segregation (Finn, Gerber, Achilles, & Boyd-Zaharias, 2001; Natriello & Pallas, 2001; G. Orfield, 2001; Orfield & Yun, 1999; Young & Smith, 1997). Alignment between test and curriculum may provide some schools with needed standards and direction, even as it narrows instruction in others. However, alignment cannot compensate for the full range of other differences across students and schools.

To the extent that standardized testing helps to illuminate systemic disparities in youngsters' opportunity to learn, the appropriate use of test information should entail systemic redress and resources. An effective policy response to group differences in test scores must reach well beyond proclamations that emphasize additional tests with higher stakes. It must engage other tools to tackle disparities in the host of factors known to affect students' opportunity to learn. Using the auditing power of standardized tests in this fashion, alongside specific and timely information from well-designed performance assessments, would enhance students' knowledge, skills, and understanding within classrooms and across disparate schools. In turn, this would more equitably enable diverse learners to function at the highest possible level in the wider world.

References

American Educational Research Association, American Psychological Association, National Council on Measurement in Education (1999). *Standards for educational and psychological testing.* Washington, DC: American Educational Research Association.

Amrein, A. L., & Berliner, D. C. (2002). High-stakes testing, uncertainty, and student learning. *Education Policy Analysis Archives, 10*(18) [On-line]. Available: http://epaa.asu.edu/epaa/v10n18/

Artiles, A., & Trent, S. (1994). Overrepresentation of minority students in special education: A continuing debate. *Journal of Special Education, 27*(4), 410–437.

Balfanz, R., & Letgers, N. (2001, January). How many central city high schools have a severe dropout problem, where are they located, and who attends them? Initial estimates using the common core of data. Paper presented at the Conference on Dropouts in America, Harvard Graduate School of Education, Cambridge, MA.

Banks, J. A. (1994a). *Multicultural education: An introduction.* Boston: Allyn & Bacon.

Banks, J. A. (1994b). *Multiethnic education: Theory and practice* (3rd ed.). Boston: Allyn & Bacon.

Banks, J. A. (2001). Multicultural education: Historical development, dimensions, and practice. In J. A. Banks & C.A.M. Banks (Eds.), *Handbook of research on multicultural education* (pp. 3–24). San Francisco: Jossey-Bass.

Banks, J. A., & Banks, C.A.M. (1993). *Multicultural education: Issues and perspectives* (2nd ed.). Boston: Allyn & Bacon.

Baratz, S. S., & Baratz, J. C. (1970). Early childhood intervention: The social science base of institutional racism. *Harvard Educational Review, 40,* 29–50.

Baron, R., Tom, D., & Cooper, M. (1985). Social class, race, and teacher expectations. In J. B. Dusek (Ed.), *Teacher expectancies* (pp. 251–269). Hillsdale, NJ: Erlbaum.

Barthe, P. (2001, November). Standards-based reforms and their impact on families. Paper presented at the University of Maryland Journalism Fellowships in Child & Family Policy Conference, Washington, DC.

Bernal, E. M. (2000). Psychometric inadequacies of the TAAS. *Hispanic Journal of Behavioral Sciences, 22*(4), 481–507.

Bernstein, B. (1971). *Class, codes and control.* London: Routledge and K. Paul.

Binet, A., & Simon, T. (1973). *The development of intelligence in children (the Binet-Simon Scale)* (E. S. Kite, Trans.). New York: Arno Press. (Original work published 1916)

Bishop, J., & Mane, F. (2001). The impacts of minimum competency exam graduation requirements on college attendance and early labor market success of disadvantaged students. In G. Orfield & M. L. Kornhaber (Eds.), *Raising standards or raising barriers? Inequality and high-stakes testing in public education* (pp. 51–84). New York: Century Foundation Press.

Black, P., & Wiliam, D. (1998). Inside the black box: Raising standards through classroom assessment. *Phi Delta Kappan, 80*(2), 139–148.

Blank, R. K., Porter, A., & Smithson, J. (2001). New tools for analyzing teaching, curriculum and standards in mathematics & science: Results from the survey of enacted curriculum project. Washington, DC: Council of Chief State School Officers.

Block, N., & Dworkin, G. (1976). *The IQ controversy.* New York: Pantheon Books.

Business-Higher Education Forum. (2002). Investing in people: Developing all of America's talent on campus and in the workplace. [On-line]. Available: http://www.acenet.edu/bookstore/pdf/investing_in_people.pdf

Cizek, G. (1998). Putting standardized tests to the test. *Fordham Report, 2*(11), 1–51.

Cole, R. (Ed.). (1995). *Educating everybody's children: Diverse teaching strategies for diverse learners.* Alexandria, VA: Association for Supervision and Curriculum Development.

Coleman, J. S., Campbell, E. Q., Hobson, C. J., McPartland, J., Mood, A. M., Weinfeld, F. D., & York, R. L. (1966). *Equality of educational opportunity.* Washington, DC: U.S. Government Printing Office.

College Entrance Examination Board. (Ed.). (1926). *The work of the College Entrance Examination Board, 1901–1926.* Boston: Ginn.

Cook, P. J., & Ludwig, J. (1998). The burden of "acting white": Do black adolescents disparage academic achievement? In C. Jencks & M. Phillips (Eds.), *The Black-White test score gap* (pp. 375–400). Washington, DC: Brookings Institution Press.

Couhtino, M., & Oswald, D. (2000). Disproportionate representation in special education: A synthesis and recommendations. *Journal of Child and Family Studies, 9*(2), 135–156.

Cremin, L. A. (1988). *American education: The metropolitan experience, 1876–1980.* New York: Harper & Row.

Cross, W. E. (1995). Oppositional identity and African-American youth: Issues and prospects. In W. D. Hawley & A. W. Jackson (Eds.), *Toward a common destiny: Improving race and ethnic relations in America* (pp. 185–204). San Francisco: Jossey-Bass.

Crouse, J., & Trusheim, D. (1988). *The case against the SAT.* Chicago: University of Chicago Press.

Darling-Hammond, L. (1997). The right to learn: A blueprint for creating schools that work. San Francisco: Jossey-Bass.

Darling-Hammond, L. (2001). Inequality and access to knowledge. In J. A. Banks & C.A.M. Banks (Eds.), *Handbook of research on multicultural education* (pp. 465–483). San Francisco: Jossey-Bass.

Darling-Hammond, L., Ancess, J., & Falk, B. (2001). *Authentic assessment in action: Studies of schools and students at work.* New York: Teachers College Press.

Debra P. v. Turlington, 474 F. Supp. 244 (M. D. FL 1979).

Degler, C. (1991). *In search of human nature.* New York: Oxford University Press.

Delpit, L. (1995). *Other people's children.* New York: New Press.

DeLuca, S., & Rosenbaum, J. (2001, January). Are dropout decisions related to safety concerns, social isolation, and teacher disparagement? Paper presented at the Conference on Dropouts in America, Harvard Graduate School of Education, Cambridge, MA.

diSessa, A. (1982). Unlearning Aristotelian physics: A study of knowledge-based learning. *Cognitive Science, 6*(1), 37–75.

Edmonds, R. (1982). Programs of school improvement: An overview. *Educational Leadership, 40*(3), 4–12.

Eisner, E. W. (1999). The uses and limits of performance assessment. *Phi Delta Kappan, 80*(9), 658–660.

Elmore, R., & Rothman, R. (1998). (Eds.), *Testing, teaching, and learning: A guide for states and school districts.* National Research Council Committee on Title I Testing and Assessment. Washington, DC: National Academy Press.

Epstein, J. L. (1997). *School, family, and community partnerships: Your handbook for action.* Thousand Oaks, CA: Corwin Press.

Ferguson, R. (1998). Teachers' perceptions and expectations and the black-white test score gap. In C. Jencks & M. Phillips (Eds.), *The black-white test score gap* (pp. 318–374). Washington, DC: Brookings Institution Press.

Ferguson, R., & Ladd, H. (1996). How and why money matters: An analysis of Alabama schools. In H. Ladd (Ed.), *Holding schools accountable* (pp. 265–298). Washington, DC: Brookings Institution Press.

Fierros, E. G., & Conroy, J. W. (2002). Double jeopardy: An examination of restrictiveness in special education. In G. Orfield & D. Losen (Eds.), *Racial inequity in special education* (pp. 39–70). Cambridge, MA: Harvard Education Publishing Group.

Finn, J., Gerber, S., Achilles, C. M., & Boyd-Zaharias, J. (2001). The enduring effects of small classes. *Teachers College Record, 103*(2), 145–183.

Firestone, W. A., Camilli, D., Yurecko, M., Monfils, L., & Mayrowetz, D. (2000). State standards, socio-fiscal context and opportunity to learn in New Jersey. *Education Policy Analysis Archives, 8*(35) [On-line]. Available: http://epaa.asu.edu/epaav8n35/

Ford, D. Y. (1995). Desegregating gifted education: A need unmet. *Journal of Negro Education, 64*(1), 52–62.

Fordham, S., & Ogbu, J. (1986). Black students' school success: Coping with the "burden of 'acting white.'" *Urban Review, 18*(3), 176–206.

Frasier, M., Garcia, H. H., & Passow, A. H. (1995). *A review of assessment issues in gifted education and their implications for identifying gifted minority students.* Storrs, CT: National Research Center on the Gifted and Talented.

Fredericksen, J. R., & Collins, A. (1989, December). A systems approach to educational testing. *Educational Researcher, 18*(9), 27–32.

Galton, F. (1869). Hereditary genius: An inquiry into its laws and consequences. London: Macmillan.

Galton, F. (1892). Hereditary genius: An inquiry into its laws and consequences (2nd ed.). London: Watts. (Original work published in 1869)

Gardner, H. (1983). *Frames of mind: The theory of multiple intelligences.* New York: Basic Books.

Gardner, H. (1995). Cracking open the IQ box. In S. Fraser (Ed.), *The bell curve wars: Race, intelligence, and the future of America* (pp. 23–35). New York: Basic Books.

Gardner, H. (1999). *The unschooled mind: How children think and how schools should teach.* New York: Basic Books.

Gardner, H., Kornhaber, M., & Wake, W. (1996). *Intelligence: Multiple perspectives.* Forth Worth, TX: Harcourt Brace.

Garrison, L. (1989). Programming for the gifted American Indian student. In C. J. Maker & S. Schiever (Eds.), *Critical issues in gifted education: Defensible programs for cultural and ethnic minorities.* Austin, TX: Pro-Ed.

Gaudet, R. (2000). Effective school districts in Massachusetts [Online]. Available: http://www.donahue.umassp.edu/publications/donapub.htm

Gewertz, C. (2002). Affirmative reaction. *Education Week, 21*(21), 26–32.

GI Forum, Image de Tejas v. *Texas Education Agency,* 87 F. Supp. 667 (W.D. Tex. 2000).

Gong, B., & Hill, R. (2001, March). Some consideration of multiple measures in assessment and school accountability. Paper presented at the Seminar on Using Multiple Measures and Indicators to Judge Schools' Adequate Yearly Progress under Title I, Washington, DC.

Gould, S. (1981). *The mismeasure of man.* New York: Norton.

Grissmer, D. W., Flanagan, A., Kawata, J., & Williamson, S. (2000). Improving student achievement: What state NAEP scores tell us. Santa Monica, CA: RAND.

Grossman, H. (1995). *Special education in a diverse society.* Boston: Allyn & Bacon.

Haertel, E. (1999). Performance assessment and education reform. *Phi Delta Kappan, 80*(9), 662–666.

Hambleton, R. K., Brennan, R. L., Brown, W., Dodd, B., Forsyth, R. A., Mehrens, W. A., Nellhaus, J., Reckase, M., Rindone, M., van der Linden, W. J., & Zwick, R. (2000). A response to "setting reasonable and useful performance standards" in the National Academy of Sciences' *Grading the nation's report card. Educational Measurement: Issues and Practice, 19*(2), 5–14.

Haney, W. (2000). The myth of the Texas miracle in education. *Education Analysis and Policy Archives, 8*(41) [On-line]. Available: http://epaa.asu.edu/epaa/v8n41/

Haney, W. (2001, January). Revisiting the myth of the Texas miracle in education: Lessons about dropout research and dropout prevention. Initial estimates using the common core of data. Paper presented at the Conference on Dropouts in America, Harvard Graduate School of Education, Cambridge, MA.

Haney, W. (2002). Lake Woebeguaranteed: Misuse of test scores in Massachusetts, Part I. *Education Policy Analysis Archives, 10*(24) [On-line]. Available: http://epaa.asu.edu/epaa/v10n24/

Hauser, R. (2001). Should we end social promotion? Truth and consequences. In G. Orfield & M. L. Kornhaber (Eds.), *Raising standards or raising barriers? Inequality and high-stakes testing in public education* (pp. 151–178). New York: Century Foundation Press.

Heath, S. B. (1983). *Ways with words: language, life, and work in communities and classrooms.* Cambridge and New York: Cambridge University Press.

Helms, J. E. (1992). Why is there no study of cultural equivalence in standardized cognitive ability testing? *American Psychologist, 47*(9), 1083–1101.

Herrnstein, R., & Murray, C. (1994). *The bell curve: Intelligence and class structure in American life.* New York: Free Press.

Heubert, J. P., & Hauser, R. M. (Eds.). (1999). *High stakes: Testing for tracking, promotion, and graduation.* Washington, DC: National Academy Press.

Hillocks, G. (2002). *The testing trap: How state writing assessments control learning.* New York: Teachers College Press.

Hoffman, D. (1989, January 20). George Bush promises to keep. *The Washington Post,* p. A25.

Holmes, C. T. (1989). Grade level retention effects: A meta-analysis of research studies. In L. Shepard & M. L. Smith (Eds.), *Flunking grades: Research and policies on retention* (pp. 16–33). London: Falmer Press.

Howard, J. (1995). You can't get there from here: The need for a new logic in education reform. *Daedalus, 124*(4), 85–92.

Howard, J., & Hammond, R. (1985, September 9). Rumors of inferiority: The hidden obstacles to black success. *New Republic, 3686,* 17–21.

Jencks, C., & Phillips, M. (1998). The black-white test score gap: An introduction. In C. Jencks & M. Phillips (Eds.), *The black-white test score gap* (pp. 1–51). Washington, DC: Brookings Institution Press.

Jensen, A. (1980). *Bias in mental testing.* New York: Free Press.

Kamin, L. (1995). Bad science under the bell curve: What it doesn't tell us about IQ. *Scientific American, 272*(2), 99–103.

Kane, T., & Staiger, D. O. (2001). Volatility in school test scores: Implications for test-based accountability systems [On-line]. Available: http://www.dartmouth.edu/~dstaiger/Papers/kanes-taigerbrookings.pdf

Klein, S. P., Hamilton, L. S., McCaffrey, D. F., & Stecher, B. M. (2000). *What do test scores in Texas tell us?* Santa Monica, CA: RAND.

Knapp, M., & Woolverton, S. (2001). Social class and schooling. In J. A. Banks & C.A.M. Banks (Eds.), *Handbook of research on multicultural education* (pp. 548–569). San Francisco: Jossey-Bass.

Koretz, D., & Barron, S. (1998). The validity of gains in scores on the Kentucky Instructional Results Information System (KIRIS). Santa Monica, CA: RAND.

Koretz, D., Klein, S., McCaffrey, D., & Stecher, D. (1994). *Can portfolios assess student performance and influence instruction?* Santa Monica, CA: RAND.

Kozol, J. (1991). *Savage inequalities: Children in America's schools.* New York: Crown.

Ladson-Billings, G. (2001a). Multicultural teacher education: Research, practice, and policy. In J. A. Banks & C.A.M. Banks (Eds.), *Handbook of research on multicultural education* (pp. 747–759). San Francisco: Jossey-Bass.

Ladson-Billings, G. (2001b). *Crossing over to Canaan: The journey of new teachers in diverse classrooms.* San Francisco: Jossey-Bass.

Lanckford, H., & Wyckoff, J. (1996). The allocation of resources to special education and regular instruction. In H. Ladd (Ed.), *Holding schools accountable* (pp. 221–257). Washington, DC: The Brookings Institution Press.

Larry P. v. Wilson Riles, 793 F. 2d 969 (9th Cir. 1984).

Lave, J. (1990). The culture of acquisition and the practice of understanding. In J. W. Stigler, R. A. Shweder, & G. Herdt (Eds.), *Cultural psychology: Essays on comparative human development* (pp. 309–327). New York: Cambridge University Press.

Leacock, E. B. (Ed.). (1971). *The culture of poverty: A critique.* New York: Simon & Schuster.

Lee, V. E., & Burkam, D. T. (2001, January). Dropping out of high school: The role of school organization and structure. Paper presented at the Conference on Dropouts in America, Harvard Graduate School of Education, Cambridge, MA.

Lemann, N. (1999). *The big test: The secret history of the American meritocracy.* New York: Farrar, Straus & Giroux.

Letgers, N., & Kerr, K. (2001, January). Easing the transition to high school: An investigation of reform practices to promote ninth grade success. Paper presented at the Conference on Dropouts in America, Harvard Graduate School of Education, Cambridge, MA.

Levin, H. M. (2001). High-stakes testing and economic productivity. In G. Orfield & M. L. Kornhaber (Eds.), *Raising standards or raising barriers? Inequality and high-stakes testing in public education* (pp. 39–49). New York: Century Foundation Press.

Levine, D., & Lezotte, L. (2001). Effective schools research. In J. A. Banks & C.A.M. Banks (Eds.), *Handbook of research on multicultural education* (pp. 525–547). San Francisco: Jossey-Bass.

Lewis, O. (1968). The culture of poverty. In D. P. Moynihan (Ed.), *On understanding poverty: Perspectives from the social sciences* (pp. 187–200). New York: Basic Books.

Lindsay, D. (1995, March 29). Two finance cases spur N.Y. Court to consider how to measure equity. *Education Week,* p. 13.

Linn, R. (2000). Assessments and accountability. *Educational Researcher, 29*(2), 4–16.

Madaus, G. F. (1994). A technological and historical consideration of equity issues associated with proposals to change the nation's testing policy. *Harvard Educational Review, 64*(1), 76–95.

Madaus, G., & Clarke, M. (2001). The adverse impact of high-stakes testing on minority students: Evidence from one hundred years of test data. In G. Orfield & M. Kornhaber (Eds.), *Raising standards or raising barriers? Inequality and high-stakes testing in public education* (pp. 85–106). New York: Century Foundation Press.

McCollum, P., Cortez, A., Maroney, O. H., & Montes, F. (1999). Failing our children: Finding alternatives to in-grade retention. San Antonio, TX: Intercultural Development Research Association [On-line]. Available: www.idra.org/Research/ingrade.pdf

McDonnell, L. M., McLaughlin, M. J., & Morison, P. (Eds.). (1997). *Educating one and all: Students with disabilities and standards-based reform.* National Research Council, Committee on Goals 2000 and the Inclusion of Students with Disabilities. Washington, DC: National Academy Press.

McNeil, L. (2000). *Contradictions of school reform: Educational costs of standardized testing.* New York: Routledge.

McNeil, L., & Valenzuela, A. (2001). The harmful impact of the TAAS system of testing in Texas: Beneath the accountability rhetoric. In G. Orfield & M. L. Kornhaber (Eds.), *Raising standards or raising barriers? Inequality and high-stakes testing in public education* (pp. 127–150). New York: Century Foundation Press.

Meier, D. (2000). Educating a democracy. In J. Cohen & J. Rogers (Eds.), *Will standards save public education?* (pp. 3–31). Boston: Beacon Press.

Mercer, J. R. (1989). Alternative paradigms for assessment in a pluralistic society. In J. A. Banks & C.A.M. Banks (Eds.), *Multicultural education: Issues and perspectives* (2nd ed., pp. 289–304). New York: Macmillan.

Mickelson, R. A. (1990). The attitude-achievement paradox among black adolescents. *Sociology of Education, 63*(1), 44–61.

Mickelson, R. A. (2001). Subverting Swann: Tracking as second generation segregation in Charlotte, North Carolina. *American Educational Research Journal, 38,* 215–252.

Moore, D. (2000). *Chicago's grade retention program fails to help retained students.* Chicago: Designs for Change.

Moore, D., & Hanson, M. (2001). School system leaders propose ineffective strategies contradicted by results and research. Chicago: Designs for Change.

Moynihan, D. P. (1967). The Negro family: The case for national action. In L. Rainwater and W. L. Yancy (Eds.), *The Moynihan Report and the politics of controversy* (pp. 39–124). Cambridge, MA: MIT Press.

Murnane, R. (2000). The case for standards. In J. Cohen & J. Rogers (Eds.), *Will standards save public education?* (pp. 57–63). Boston: Beacon Press.

National Alliance of Business. (2002). About the organization [On-line]. Available: http://www.nab.com/about.htm

National Commission on Excellence in Education. (1983). *A nation at risk: The imperative for education reform.* Washington, DC: U.S. Government Printing Office.

National Council of Teachers of English. (1996). *Standards for the English language arts.* Urbana, IL: Author.

National Council of Teachers of Mathematics. (1995). *Assessment standards for school mathematics.* Reston, VA: Author.

National Education Goals Panel. (1991). *The national education goals report: Building a nation of learners.* Washington, DC: U.S. Government Printing Office.

National Governors Association (2001). *Standards, assessments and accountability* [On-line]. Available: www.nga.org/center/topics/1,1188,D_413,00.html

Natriello, G., & Pallas, A. (2001). The development and impact of high-stakes testing. In G. Orfield & M. L. Kornhaber (Eds.), *Raising standards or raising barriers? Inequality and high-stakes testing in public education* (pp. 19-38). New York: Century Foundation Press.

Neill, M., with Gayler, K. (2001). Do high-stakes graduation tests improve learning outcomes? Using state-level NAEP data to evaluate the effects of mandatory graduation tests. In G. Orfield & M. L. Kornhaber (Eds.), *Raising standards or raising barriers? Inequality and high-stakes testing in public education* (pp. 105-205). New York: Century Foundation Press.

Nisbett, R. (1995). Race, IQ, and scientism. In S. Fraser (Ed.), *The bell curve wars: Race, intelligence, and the future of America* (pp. 36–57). New York: Basic Books.

Nisbett, R. (1998). Race, genetics, and IQ. In C. Jencks & M. Phillips (Eds.), *The black-white test score gap.* Washington, DC: Brookings Institution Press.

Oakes, J. (1985). *Keeping track: How schools structure inequality.* New Haven, CT: Yale University Press.

Oakes, J., Gamoran, A., & Page, R. (1992). Curriculum differentiation: Opportunities, outcomes, and meanings. In P. W. Jackson (Ed.), *Handbook of research on curriculum* (pp. 570–608). New York: Macmillan.

Ogbu, J. U. (1978). *Minority education and caste: The American system in cross-cultural comparison.* New York: Academic Press.

Ogbu, J. U. (1991). Immigrant and involuntary minorities in comparative perspective. In M. A. Gibson & J. U. Ogbu (Eds.), *Minority status and schooling: A comparative study of immigrant and involuntary minorities* (pp. 3–33). New York: Garland.

Orfield, G. (Ed.). (1993). *Separate and unequal in the metropolis: The changing shape of the school desegregation battle.* Washington, DC: Brookings Institution Press.

Orfield, G. (2001). Schools more separate: Consequences of a decade of resegregation [On-line]. Available: http://www.law.harvard.edu/groups/civilrights/publications/resegregation01/presssegexs.html

Orfield, G., & Kornhaber, M. L. (2001). *Raising standards or raising barriers? Inequality and high-stakes testing in public education.* New York: Century Foundation Press.

Orfield, G., & Miller, E. (Eds.). (1998). *Chilling admissions: The affirmative action crisis and the search for alternatives.* Cambridge, MA: Harvard Education Publishing Group.

Orfield, G., & Yun, J. T. (1999). *Resegregation in American schools.* Cambridge, MA.: Harvard Civil Rights Project [On-line]. Available: http://www.law.harvard.edu/groups/civilrights/publications/resegregation99/resegregation99.html

Orfield, M. (1997). *Metropolitics: A regional agenda for community and stability.* Washington, DC: Brookings Institution Press.

Pellegrino, J. W. (2000). A response to ACT's technical advisors on NAEP standard setting. *Educational Measurement, 19*(2), 14–15.

Pellegrino, J. W., Chudowsky, N., & Glaser, R. (Eds.). (2001). *Knowing what students know: The science and design of educational assessment.* Washington, DC: National Academy Press.

Perkins, D. N., & Salomon, G. (l989). Are cognitive skills context-bound? *Educational Researcher, 18*(1), 16–25.

Phelps, R. P. (1998). The demand for standardized student testing. *Educational Measurement: Issues and Practice, 17*(3), 17–22.

Phelps, R. P. (1999). Why testing experts hate tests. *Fordham Report, 3*(1), vii-33 [On-line]. Available: www.edexcellence.net/library/phelps.htm

Phillips, S. E. (2000). *GI forum v. Texas education agency:* Psychometric evidence. *Applied Measurement, 13*(4), 343–385.

Pipho, C. (1986, May 12). Tracking the reforms, part 12. *Education Week,* p. 20.

Platzer, M., Novak, C., & Kazmierczak, M. (2002). *Cybereducation 2002.* Washington, DC: American Electronics Association.

Popham, W. J. (2001). *The truth about testing: An educator's call to action.* Alexandria, VA: Association for Supervision and Curriculum Development.

Powell, J., Kearney, G., & Vina, K. (2001). *In pursuit of a dream deferred: Linking housing and education policy.* New York: Peter Lang.

Public Agenda. (2002). *Reality Check 2002* [On-line]. Available: http://www.publicagenda.org/specials/rcheck2002/reality.htm

Public Education Network and Education Week. (2002). *Accountability for all: What voters want from education candidates* [On-line]. Available: http://www.publiceducation.org/download/2002PollReport.pdf

Raimi, R. A. (2000). The state of state standards in mathematics. In C. E. Finn & M. J. Petrilli (Eds.), *The state of state standards.* Washington, DC: Thomas B. Fordham Foundation [On-line]. Available: http://www.edexcellence.net/library/soss2000/2000soss.html#Mathematics

Ravitch, D. (1996). *National standards in American education: A citizen's guide.* Washington, DC: Brookings Institution Press.

Resnick, L., & Nolan, K. (1995, March). Where in the world are world-class standards? *Educational Leadership, 52*(6) [On-line]. Available: http://www.ascd.org/readingroom/edlead/9503/resnick.html

Robelen, E. W. (2002, January 9). ESEA to boost federal role in education. *Education Week, 21*(6), 1, 28, 29, 31.

Sack, J. (1999, December 15). Group seeks help for minority achievement. *Education Week, 19*(6), 23, 26.

Salomon, G., & Perkins, D. N. (1989). Rocky roads to transfer: Rethinking mechanisms of a neglected phenomenon. *Educational Psychologist, 24*(2), 113–142.

Schellenberg, S. J. (1999). Concentration of poverty and the ongoing need for Title I. In G. Orfield & L. Debray (Eds.), *Hard work for good schools: Facts not fads in Title I reform* (pp. 130–146). Cambridge, MA: Civil Rights Project, Harvard University.

Schwartz, T. (1999, January 10). The test under stress. *The New York Times,* p. 30.

Shepard, L. A., & Smith, M. L. (Eds.). (1989). Flunking grades: Research and policies on retention. New York: Falmer Press.

Simmons, W., & Resnick, L. (1993, February). Assessment as the catalyst of school reform. *Educational Leadership,* pp. 11–15.

Singley, M. K., & Anderson, J. R. (1989). *The transfer of cognitive skill.* Cambridge, MA: Harvard University Press.

Sleeter, C. E. (1991). Multicultural education and empowerment. In C. Sleeter (Ed.), *Empowerment through multicultural education* (pp. 1–23). Albany: State University of New York Press.

Sleeter, C. E., & Grant, C. A. (1994). *Making choices for multicultural education: Five approaches to race, class, and gender* (2nd ed.). New York: Macmillan.

Snow, C. E., & Jones, J. (2001). Making a silk purse. . . . *Education Week, 20*(32), 60.

Spalding, E. (2000). Performance assessment and the new standards project: A story of serendipitous success. *Phi Delta Kappan, 81*(10), 758–764.

Spearman, C. (1904). General intelligence, objectively determined and measured. *American Journal of Psychology, 15,* 201–293.

Spencer, M. B., Noll, E., Stoltzfus, J., & Harpalani, V. (2001). Identity and school adjustment: Revisiting the "acting white" assumption. *Educational Psychologist, 36*(1), 21–30.

Steele, C. (1997, June). A threat in the air: How stereotypes shape the intellectual identities and performance of women and African Americans. *American Psychologist, 52*(6), 613–629.

Steele, C., & Aronson, J. (1995). Stereotype threat and the intellectual performance of African Americans. *Journal of Personality and Social Psychology, 69*(5), 797–811.

Steele, C., & Aronson, J. (1998). Stereotype threat and the test performance of academically successful African Americans. In C. Jencks & M. Phillips (Eds.), *The black-white test score gap* (pp. 401–427). Washington, DC: Brookings Institution Press.

Stern, W. (1965). The psychological methods for testing intelligence. In R. J. Herrnstein & E. G. Boring (Eds.), *A source book in the history of psychology* (pp. 450–453). Cambridge, MA: Harvard University Press. (Original work published 1912)

Sternberg, R. J. (1985). *Beyond IQ: A triarchic theory of human intelligence.* Cambridge: Cambridge University Press.

Stotsky, S. (2000). What's at stake in the K-12 standards war. New York: Peter Lang.

Sturm, S., & Guinier, L. (1996). The future of affirmative action: Reclaiming the innovative ideal. *California Law Review, 84*(4), 953–1036.

Taylor, W. (2000). Standards, tests, and civil rights. *Education Week, 20*(11), 40-41, 56.

Terman, L. (1916). *The measurement of intelligence: An explanation of and a complete guide for the use of the Stanford revision and extension of the Binet-Simon intelligence scale.* Boston: Houghton Mifflin.

Terman, L. (1919). *The intelligence of school children.* Boston: Houghton Mifflin.

Terman, L. (1922). *Intelligence tests and school reorganization.* Yonkers-on-Hudson, NY: World Book.

U.S. Congress. (1994). *Goals 2000: Educate America act* [Online]. Available: http://www.ed.gov/legislation/GOALS2000/TheAct/

U.S. Department of Education (2001). *No Child Left Behind Act of 2001* [On-line]. Available: www.ed.gov/legislation/ESEA02

Valenzuela, A. (1999). Subtractive schooling: U.S.-Mexican youth and the politics of caring. Albany: State University of New York Press.

Viadero, D. (1994, July 13). Teaching to the test. *Education Week,* pp. 21–25.

Wiggins, G. (1998). Educative assessment: Designing assessments to inform and improve student performance. San Francisco: Jossey-Bass.

Wilson, W. J. (1987). The truly disadvantaged: The inner city, the underclass, and public policy. Chicago: University of Chicago Press.

Wilson, W. J. (1996). When work disappears: The world of the new urban poor. New York: Knopf.

Yerkes, R. M. (1921). Psychological examining in the United States Army. Memoirs of the National Academy of Sciences (Vol. XV). Washington, DC: Government Printing Office.

Young, B. A., & Smith, T. M. (1997). The social context of education. In National Center for Education Statistics (Ed.), *The condition of education, 1997.* Washington, DC: Office of Educational Research and Improvement [On-line]. Available: http://nces.ed.gov/pubs/ce/c97004.html

Zessoules, R., & Gardner, H. (1991). Authentic assessment: Beyond the buzzword and into the classroom. In V. Perrone (Ed.), *Assessment in schools* (pp. 47–71). Washington, DC: Association for Supervision and Curriculum Development.

6

MULTIRACIAL FAMILIES AND CHILDREN

Implications for Educational Research and Practice

Maria P. P. Root

Seattle, Washington

The 2000 census reflected an evolving twist to a centuries-old drama around notions of race. People could identify themselves by more than one race, and 2.4 percent did (U.S. Census Bureau, 2001). Furthermore, 6.8 percent of youths under 18 years of age were identified by more than one race. This change in the racial classification scheme fundamentally challenges a race system wedded to notions of racial purity and one-drop rules to enforce a monoracial reality (meaning, you can be only one race). Omi and Winant (1994), like others before and after them, note that race is a construction driven by legal, political, and historical interests and injury.

All U.S. racial groups represent multiracial populations. Despite the lack of evidence for a notion of pure race, the assignment of single race categories in the United States confines the reality and fate of individuals and the nation (Nash, 1999). The result is a society that has been very race-discriminating and illogical. Although not erasing the make-believe tale of race, the paradigm of multirace in the public domain challenges the monoracial orientation of U.S. society. The change in the 2000 census acknowledged the increased mixing of the U.S. population across racial lines and a trend toward younger persons identifying themselves as mixed, biracial, multiracial, and the specific variants these labels imply: Black/White, Asian/White, Asian/African American, American Indian and White.

This chapter presents some historical and demographic trends by which to understand why the educational system is challenged to consider how this change in numbers and identification of the young population has implications for training and curriculum. This chapter provides a framework for understanding mixed race identity and the familial and social variables that influence it. In this way, scholars, researchers, and practitioners may remain effective and facilitate new ways of thinking about race. In the words of American writer Peter DeVries, "The value of children is that they grow to become adults who in turn have children" (in Andrews, 1987, p. 167). Educators have the opportunity to equip students, from young child to university adult, with a knowledge base that can affect the critical thinking of hundreds if not thousands of students during their careers.

DEMOGRAPHIC TRENDS AND CIVIL RIGHTS INFLUENCES

He explained to me his theory—that the mulatto in America functions as a canary in the coal mine. The canaries, he said, were used by coal miners to gauge how poisonous the air underground was. They would bring a canary in with them, and if it grew sick and died, they knew the air was bad and that eventually everyone else would be poisoned by the fumes. My father said that likewise, mulattos had historically been the gauge of how poisonous American race relations were. The fate of the mulatto in history and in literature, he said, will manifest the symptoms that will eventually infect the rest of the nation. He pointed to the chart. "See, my guess is that you're the first generation of canaries to survive, a little injured perhaps, but alive. . . ."

—Senna (1998, pp. 335–336)

110

For the first time in history, the multiracially identified population was documented with a multiple race checkoff at 2.4 percent of the U.S. population (U.S. Census Bureau, 2001). This was quite a different option from tracking the fractions of African American heritage in the U.S. census at the end of the nineteenth and the beginning of the twentieth century (Lee, 1993). On the 2000 census form, individuals were allowed to identify themselves by checking more than one race in answer to the race question. Those who did so were located primarily in the western United States. These states have representation greater than the average: Alaska, 5.4 percent; California, 4.7 percent; Hawaii, 21.4 percent; Nevada, 3.8 percent; New Mexico, 3.6 percent; and Washington, 3.6 percent. Oklahoma had 4.5 percent of its population identify as multiracial, primarily of American Indian and White European descent. Among those who checked more than one race, 93 percent identified themselves as being of two races, while the remaining seven percent checked three or more races. Seventy-two percent of the biracial people identified as being mixed with European heritage; for example, American Indian/White or Black/White. Approximately 20 percent of the remaining biracial respondents checked boxes indicating that they were of two minority racial groups such as Asian/African American.

The increase in the contemporary mixed heritage population is real, as evidenced by the steadily increasing number of people who have been recorded as interracially married since 1970, shortly after the Supreme Court repeal of the last antimiscegenation laws in 1967. Fourteen states still had laws declaring these marriages illegal in 1967 (Spickard, 1989).

In 1960, the census counted only 148,000 interracially married couples. The majority of these marriages were between White men and Black women. A decade later, the number had doubled. By 1980, the number was triple the count in the 1970 census and six times the number in the 1960 census. By 1990, Black-White intermarriage almost doubled again within a decade, and other intermarriages grew by approximately 50 percent (Root, 2001). With the last population accounting in 2000, the number of interracial marriages increased significantly (U.S. Census Bureau, 2001). The public seems to be more attentive to Black and White interracial union. However, intermarriage is proportionally most frequent among other racial groups such as Asian Americans (Kitano, Fujino, & Sato, 1998), American Indians, and Latinos in some parts of the country (Root, 2001).

Two facts related to the growth of the U.S. multiracial population are relevant to educational practice. First, by 2003 federal law requires that government forms be in compliance with this "check all that apply" format for race. Although individual school districts and universities may not be required to be in compliance, states often follow federal law.

Second, 6.8 percent of the population younger than 18 years of age was identified as mixed race (U.S. Census Bureau, 2001). This change will spur more dialogue and nomenclature about mixed heritage that challenges some aspects of curriculum and classroom discussion. For example, racial construction may become a necessary part of Black History month as students learn that many of the early Black leaders were mixed, but the political and economic system was constructed to enforce hypodescent (assignment to the racial group of lower social ranking). History may need to teach that Homer Plessy of *Plessy* v. *Ferguson* was Black by virtue of a great-grandparent and the rule of hypodescent. Japanese Americans of fractional percentage were interned, again because of hypodescent and racial phobia (Spickard, 1989).

The experience and the declaration of a mixed race identity have changed over the last 50 years. Prior to that period of time, the only discussion about mixed race was cast in Black and White. Themes and images of the tragic mulatta or mulatto abounded (Sollors, 1997). Although the Harlem Renaissance clearly included many multiracial persons of African and European descent, there was no room in U.S. society to resolve the disparity in status and worlds between Black and White. For example, Langston Hughes questioned his liminal position in the poem "Cross": "My old man died in a fine big house. My ma died in a shack. I wonder where I'm gonna die, Being neither white nor black?" (Hughes, 1926).

Three contemporary generations of mixed race persons currently exist (Root, in press). Each successive generation occurs over a compressed time period and has its own options for identity. The first generation (see Table 6.1) was born between the late 1940s and the late 1960s and grew up or experienced its young adult years during the civil rights movement. The second generation was born between the repeal of the antimiscegenation laws and approximately 1980. The third generation was born after 1980 and is now going through the school system, from kindergarten through college. There is reason to believe that another generation recently born, from the mid-1990s to the present, will experience being multiracial even differently than did the generation just coming of age.

Each generation's identity options differ. The first generation could not publicly declare a mixed race identity without being thought to be confused, disturbed, or self-hating. The civil rights movement further required solidarity, and a mixed race identity was not perceived as being in solidarity with any of the racial pride movements. The middle generation grew up during the last phase of major civil rights reform, with the enactment of the 1978 Office of Management and Budget's racial categories being used to protect civil rights in housing,

TABLE 6.1. Public Racial Identity Possible by Cohort of Racially Mixed People.

| | Possible Identities | | | | |
Cohort	Accept Identity Society Assigns	Monoracial Identity	Multiple Races	New Race	Symbolic Race
Exotic (born before the late 1960s)	Yes	Yes	No	No	No
Vanguard (born between the late 1960s and late 1970s)	Yes	Yes	Yes	No	No
Biracial boomer (born after 1980, post–civil rights)	Yes	Yes	Yes	Yes	Yes

employment, lending, and other practices that had been racially discriminating. However, with the increasing number of mixed race persons, public declaration of mixed race identity was discouraged but situationally declared nevertheless in the 1980s and early 1990s.

The youngest generation grows up with distance from the civil rights movement while being beneficiaries of it. The reforms that characterized the third quarter of the twentieth century are history for them. This generation, whether monoracial or multiracial, is exposed less to the virulent forms of racism experienced by previous generations. Until they leave home, many are often not familiar with racism, though this does not necessarily mean they have not been subjected to it. This generation grows up amid many youths with similar multiracial backgrounds and media figures acknowledging their background: golfer Tiger Woods, actress Halle Berry, and speed skater Apollo Ono. Public declaration of mixed race identity is not unusual. Claiming a White identity, though uncommon, is not necessarily associated with maladjustment (Root, 1998).

Despite evidence that the United States is being forced to shift its racial paradigm, and younger people seem more capable of doing so, injurious policing or gatekeeping occurs, particularly in the middle school to college years when students of color are establishing their racial and ethnic identity. This often requires rejection of people and values that are not conventionally Black, Asian, Indian, or Latino (Azoulay, 1997; Funderburg, 1994; Rockquemore & Brunsma, 2002; Root, 1992, 1996; Wijeyesinghe & Jackson, 2001; Zack, 1995). For example, persons of mixed heritage, particularly of European heritage, are often seen as less authentic African Americans, Asian Americans, Latinos or Chicanos, or American Indians. Authenticity tests are a form of racial hazing and illogically enforce a limited, superficial solidarity. These membership tests, posed by peers and learned from elders, authenticate the gatekeeper by their oppressive action and attitudes to those who are not conventionally conforming or who are vulnerable to rejection. Authenticity tests hurt, reject, and marginalize mixed race youth (Gaskins, 1999; No Collective, 1992; Wardle, 1999).

Negative experiences of gatekeeping, rejection, and hazing expel or push multiracial people out of communities with which they might otherwise identify (Funderburg, 1994; Hall, 1992; Rocquemore & Brunsma, 2002; Root, 1990; Williams-Leon & Nakashima, 2001). Thus some children and adolescents avoid situations where they are tested, taunted, and rejected and fulfill the fear of some ethnic communities that they will be lost to that community (Gaskins, 1999; No Collective, 1992; Rocquemore & Brunsma, 2002; Root, 1998, 1999). To pass these tests, one must exhibit stereotypic behavior, possibly shun or hide family members, and become a two-dimensional caricature of what racial groups have internalized as White definitions of racially identified behaviors for people of color. The rules for passing the test are determined by the gatekeeper. Simultaneously, these youths are subject to the same discrimination as other people of color.

Lastly, because of the unresolved history of racial injuries and trauma sustained in this nation, a racial hierarchy exists (Montagu, 1997). Within this hierarchy, a clear demarcation existed for centuries between Whites and everyone else. Non-White status was a caste marker until recently. This caste status seems to be eroding, but more slowly for African Americans than for other groups of color (Root, 2001).

RACIAL IDENTITY DEVELOPMENT

There are advantages to not being this or that. You have a million stories, one for every occasion, and in a way they're all lies and in another way they're all true. When Indians say to me, "What are you?" I know exactly what they're asking, and answer Coeur d'Alene. I don't add, "Between a quarter and a half," because that's information they don't require, first off—though it may come later if I screw up and they're looking for reasons why. If one of my Dartmouth colleagues wonders, "Where did you study?" I pick the best place, the hardest one to get into, in order to establish that I belong. . . . There are times when I control who I'll be, and times when I let other people decide. I'm not all anything, but I'm a little bit of a lot. My roots spread in every direction, and if I water one set of them more often than others, it's because they need it more.

—Erdrich and Dorris (1991, pp. 166–167)

Normative Behavior and Experience

The contemporary literature on the adjustment and well-being of youths of mixed race who identify multiracially generally demonstrates good adjustment (Field, 1996; Cauce, Hiraga, Mason, Aguilar, Ordonez, & Gonzales, 1992; Gibbs & Hines, 1992; R. C. Johnson, 1992; Johnson & Nagoshi, 1986; Stephan, 1992). Field's study in 1991 of 31 biracial Black and White adolescents found that they had similarly positive self-concepts as their Black peers. Cauce and colleagues (1992) compared 22 biracial adolescents with 22 monoracial peers of color. They found no difference in self-reports or maternal reports on life stress, general distress, behavior problems, or self-worth. Gibbs and Hines (1992) suggest that from their study of 12 adolescents from 1987 to 1989, identity conflicts about belonging, sexuality, control, and future directions are associated with confusion. Though present to some degree in all, they found 9 (75 percent) of their participants were well adjusted. Those who were not well adjusted were more likely than the well-adjusted adolescents to live in a single-parent family, lack contact with the noncustodial parent and relatives, and avoid talking about racial issues.

In an earlier study, R. C. Johnson (1992) summarized the findings of reports from the Hawai'i Family Study of Cognitions. They tested 180 children of intermarriage for aspects of personality and found no difference on aspects of personality that are correlated with poor adjustment. The offspring of these marriages were compared with children of within-group marriages. R. C. Johnson summarizes (1992): "The only empirical data available support the position that whether one is the offspring of within- or across-racial mating does not significantly influence one's personal adjustment" (p. 247).

Many typical behaviors of persons of mixed heritage are nevertheless misunderstood and interpreted as signs of poor adjustment. Some of these behaviors stem from ways of sorting out the meaning of race and ethnicity from a mixed perspective, exposure to multiple types of discriminating comments, and ways of coping with the dynamics of situations. Historically, it was thought that mixed race people of European descent would aspire to be White and therefore try to pass (Daniel, 1992). Although this was true for some individuals of generations before the first generation outlined earlier, times are changing. Many young people from the middle or youngest generation who may phenotypically appear to be White, and are passed as White, make it clear that they do not wish to identify as White, but as a person of color. That passing remains a point of contention is evidence of the salience of race and how it is used to demarcate social status.

Situational ethnicity or race is an often-misunderstood expression of identity. Stephan (1992) reported a summary of findings for her studies on mixed heritage youth of Asian descent in Hawai'i and of mixed heritage Hispanic descent in New Mexico. She asked them about the identity they would use in five situations. The overwhelming majority of respondents gave answers differing with the situation. No respondent used the same identity across all five. Several findings emerged. Stephan found that cultural exposure was not a necessary condition for ethnic identity to occur, since a quarter of her respondents identified with a group to which they had little exposure. Furthermore, cultural exposure did not guarantee identification since 15 percent of participants did not identify with groups from which they were descended or to which they were consistently exposed. In combining results of her studies, she found that the status of the particular minority group in its region, acceptance, surnames, and physical appearance contributed to identity decisions.

Variability in identity and situational declarations that Stephan (1992) found has often been misunderstood to be confusion, rather than flexibility and adaptability. At some ages, it reflects experimentation. Code switching, usually a manifestation of situational identity, further adds to an observer's confusion and speculation as to the motives of mixed race people. It refers to changed expressions of behavior and speech (Root, 1998; Williams, 1992). Exaggerated code switches are often a response to thwart racial hazing or authenticity tests to be accepted by a particular ethnic group.

When contemporary studies have offered evidence of negative adjustment (Dimas, 1995; Field, 1996; Gibbs & Hines, 1992; Root, 1998; Tomishima, 1999), the researchers suggest that it is not being of mixed race per se but rather conflict arising in the family and environment or the lack of guidance in resolving developmental crisis that is responsible. For example, Dimas suggests that with Latino-identified adolescents of mixed parentage, the more stereotypically identified the adolescent was, the more psychological problems he or she reported. Dimas attributed this to the possibility that they were more frequently the recipient of negative attitudes and stigmatization that was internalized. Gibbs and Hines found that 3 of their 12 biracial Black White adolescents had some adjustment difficulties, correlated with living in a single-parent family and having less contact with the noncustodial parent and relatives and lack of conversation about race in the family. Field found that those adolescents whose reference group was White and who held negative feelings about Black persons had poorer adjustment. She notes that Helms (1990) has suggested that a White reference group would not predict poor adjustment. Rather, it might be this identity combined with negative feelings about being Black that would be associated with dissonance within oneself. Tomishima (1999) found that the family strife her 15 research participants had experienced (divorce, an addicted parent or sibling, an absent parent, abuse, adoption) confused identity or derailed it. These findings are born out by Root (1998), who studied a small cohort that identified as White as well as biracial. However, they did not feel negative toward the racial minority aspect of their heritage. Root's findings also support the conclusions of the four studies that identified evidence for poor adjustment. She suggested that when racial identity is associated with poor adjustment, it is often because family dysfunction and traumas were color-coded at a young age. This color coding of the dysfunction attaches to external negative stereotypes associated with being a person of color. These findings would suggest that mixed race youths who are in the foster care system and experience repeated loss or abuse may have poorer adjustment than same race peers if they attach their lack of permanent placement or mistreatment to being mixed race or being a child of color. This research begs to be conducted.

Racial Identity Models

It is important that the racial identity models reviewed in this chapter be identified within specific eras. The first group of models reviewed was developed in the 1970s and early 1980s, corresponding with the civil rights and racial pride movements. They are stage models and place specific values on accomplishment of particular identity, whether it is Black, Asian, or biracial.

Stage Models. The most widely acknowledged and used racial identity models are those developed by Cross (1978), Helms (1990), and Parham (1989). They emerged from the Black Pride movement and are stage models. In more recent years, in response to observed variety in accomplishing identity and testing of theories, these models are less rigidly stage models (for instance, Cross, 1981) but have difficulty accommodating persons who declare mixed race. In general, the models suggest that there is an initial stage of internalization of a White reference group that necessarily is accompanied by internalization of devalued messages about Black people, values, and culture.

A signifying and often traumatic event awakens the individual to the lack of equity and fairness in this society. There is a retreat and immersion into the racial group of origin to gain support and affirmation as part of a process of undoing the harm of internalized racism. Subsequently, one emerges with an understanding of how racism works, and an appreciation for oneself and for Black people. An ability to embrace all people to work toward social justice while maintaining awareness of one's racial self in an affirmative sense characterizes the last stage of Cross's model.

Phinney (1989) has developed the most commonly cited model of panethnic and panracial identity. She combines Nigrescence models, the evolution of a positive Black identity, with stages of ego identity development based on Marcia's work (1966). Phinney suggests that racial identity development occurs in tandem with other aspects of identity development.

Overlapping with the development of these models, the contemporary body of work on mixed race identity began to emerge. The first models paralleled the work of monoracial theorists and developmental theorists in their form as stage models. In a study of people of Asian and European ancestry, Kich (1982, 1992) proposed a stage model for an evolved mixed race identity. His model is unique for clearly articulating a process of developing a mixed race identity, suggesting that this is a desirable one and starting the model from childhood. He suggests that from ages 3 to 10 children contend with their difference and the disparity between their experiences and the projections and perceptions of others. In his second stage, from age 8 to adolescence or young adulthood, he suggests that there is a developmental struggle for acceptance from others, parallel to many developmental models of child development. In the third stage, the resolution of the combined work of these previous two stages results in adoption of a biracial and bicultural identity.

Jacobs (1977, 1992) likewise offered a stage model based upon tasks posed to Black/White children three to eight years of age, corresponding to the ages encompassed by Kich's first stage. Jacobs suggests that issues of size, color, and gender have different dimensions and degrees of constancy that must be resolved during this period of time. In stage I, he notes that children have no valence attached to color, because racial color constancy has not been attained. In stage II, children achieve some notion of race and acquire a sense of constancy or stability to their sense of people's racial color by about four and a half years of age.

However, with the dawning awareness of racial prejudice, children experience ambivalence about their racial status. Ambivalence may be experienced sequentially, with rejection or ambivalence toward Blackness and then toward Whiteness. He notes that these preferences, rejections, and ambivalences were also projected onto Asians.

Simultaneously, children are attempting to cognitively make sense out of the biracial label. They observe a perceptual distortion of color as a way of trying to make sense of racial labels and of reconciling color assignments in the family. Half of the children in this stage assigned themselves a color one or two shades darker than they were in order to make their color more clearly brown or blended.

The stages were extended by including 8-to-12-year-old children in a second phase of the study. In stage III, children have resolved the correlation between skin color and racial grouping and understand that racial group is determined by parentage. Implicit in this accomplishment is that children have acquired some sense of racial hierarchicalization and hypodescent. For example, in the era in which this study was conducted (second generation) a biracial Black/White child could be Black or biracial, but not White.

Poston (1990) presented a direct translation of the Nigrescence models for his stages, offering a five-stage model. In the first stage, the awareness of race and ethnicity was not necessarily attached to ethnic background (similar to Jacobs's stage II). In his second stage, people had to choose a racial identity; their cognitive capacity usually allowed a single identity. The third stage is driven by dissonance between the chosen identity and the incomplete match with ethnic and racial identity. Through the third and fourth stages, a person still tended to choose a single, monoracial identity, though moving to an appreciation of both parent cultures. In the fifth stage, the parent cultures were personalized and individuals integrated this knowledge and experience into their identity. They might choose a mixed race identity.

Ecological Models. Cross (1981) noted that his work and that of others were influenced by the naturalistic event of Black identity change during the civil rights and racial pride movements. Further, he notes that Bronfenbrenner, a sociologist, had stated that it was important "to make detailed observations when a system is undergoing change in its 'real world' environment" (Cross, 1981, p. x). Thus, the Nigrescence models both evolved and were a response to needed real-world change. Similarly, the emergence of a visible and growing cohort of people of mixed heritage, identifying as such, marks the emergence of a different type of racial identity model. These models do not offer stages; they typically focus on social process and variables, and they suggest that different identities may be viable and reflect certain needs. The models emerge within a similar time frame (D. J. Johnson, 1992; Miller, 1992; Ramirez, 1983, 1998; Root, 1990; Stephan, 1992; Tomishima, 1999; Trimble, 2000; Wijeyesinghe, 2001).

Tomishima (1999) used a grounded theory methodology to examine application of Cross's (1978) model of Nigrescence and Root's (1998; 1999) "ecological framework for understanding racial identity development." She used 15 participants from ages 20 to 32, of different mixes but of whom two-thirds had White mothers. She found evidence for stage movement in line with Cross's model but noted that the biracial experience did not afford racial shelter because of intraethnic prejudice. The immersion in the racial group of origins associated with monoracial stage models does not extend the same protection to multiracial individuals as to monoracial individuals. As Root (1998) and others suggest, racial hazing may be experienced with this attempt at shelter or immersion. Tomishima further suggested that combining two heritages is a task that is neither accommodated nor explained by the stage models. Thus she concluded that these additional experiences add to the tasks included in racial identity making some of the process distinctly different in some important ways. Consequently she found support for Root's model.

Acknowledging that this model was just being outlined, Tomishima (1999) noted that it was important for the role of oppression, clearly outlined in Cross's (1978) model and implied in Root's (1998) model, to be explicitly stated in the ecological framework model if it is to be genuinely useful. Tomishima further found that it was useful to have a model that detailed more specific aspects of the family environment such as family strife, the dominant caretaker, the extended family's reaction to the interracial marriage, and siblings, all of which were detailed in Root's study of biracial siblings as critical and explanatory factors for identity (Root, 1998).

Tomishima's (1999) findings also significantly overlapped with Wijeyesinghe's (2001) "factor model of multiracial identity." In this model, eight life factor experiences have an impact on one's racial identity choice: racial ancestry, cultural attachment, early experiences and socialization, political awareness and orientation, spirituality, physical appearance, social and historical context, and other social identities. This model also overlaps significantly with Root's (1998, 1999) model. It is unique in that it explicitly lists spirituality as a significant factor in combating racism and subsequently influencing racial identity. It explains through narrative how early-life experiences shape identity, and it combines different aspects and locations of variables in Root's model under this category.

Root's (1998; 1999) ecological framework for understanding racial identity is outlined later in this chapter (see Figure 6.1). The theoretical basis for this model is symbolic interactionism, from sociology. The research on monoracial and biracial identity finds that there is much variation in identity, whether it be influenced by the situation, the generation, or some other mediating variable. Furthermore, a particular identity is not necessarily correlated with self-esteem. Whereas certain experiences and processes influence identity, the presence and meaning of these experiences vary across generations.

Table 6.1 lists five identity options for the three generational cohorts, as a way of understanding generational shifts in identity options. Interviewing adults in the mid-1980s and combing through the research on multiraciality conducted by multiracial people, Root (1990) outlined four types of identity resolution for multiracial people. These identities were subject to change in a person's lifetime. None was better than the other, but all were governed by circumstances, personality, generation, geographical location, and other external influences. The identities are (a) accept the monoracial identity society assigns, (b) actively choose a monoracial identity (congruent with the identity society would assign), (c) define self as biracial or multiracial, or (d) develop a "new race" identity. Her research a decade later included interviews with biracial baby boomers, the youngest cohort studied; a fifth identity

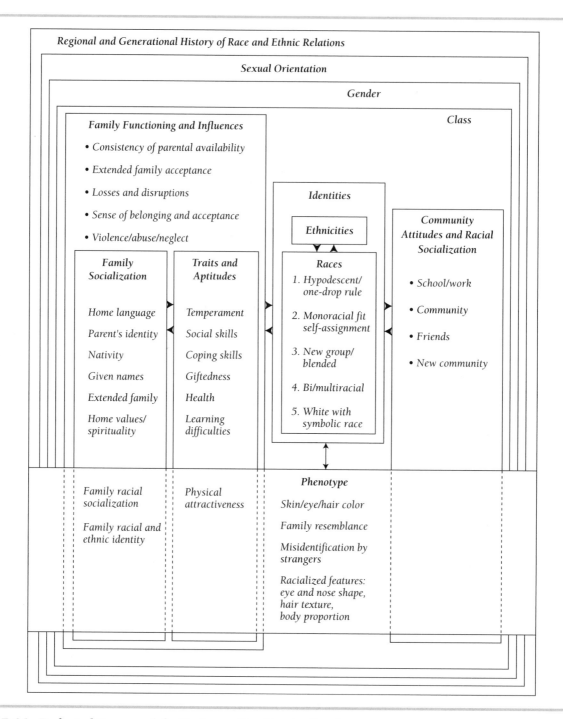

FIGURE 6.1. Ecological Framework for Understanding Identity Development.

emerged: (e) symbolic race, the declaration of a White identity with simultaneous attachment to and detachment from one's heritage of color (Root, 1998).

The macro lenses of the model are gender, regional history of race relations, class, and generation. *Regional history* is influenced by and subsequently influences racial history, racial proportions, and economics (Miller, 1992).

Gender affects identity significantly because it is a master status (Collins, 1991; Comas-Diaz, 1996; Hurtado, 1996; Root, 1994; Zack, 1997). *Class* is conflated with race. *Generational history* has been explained previously in this chapter as subsuming a set of historical experiences that interact with the region of the country within which one is raised and the identity choices possible.

Theoretically, certain experiences and influences can change salience during one's lifetime and situation. The salience of the screening lenses varies with the individual. For example, though the model can have sexual orientation as a sublens under "family socialization," there is a period of time in sorting out sexual identity in which this salient experience of identity is a macro lens through which other experiences are screened (Allman, 1996; Kich, 1996).

The middle lenses cluster certain experiences as inherited influences, traits, social interactions with the community, phenotype, and eventually identity. The *family socialization influences* primarily do not reflect biology but rather influences originating in the home that are often external markers of identity such as language, nativity, given names, values, customs, parent's identity, family identity, presence of extended family, and sexual orientation. The *traits* are a combination of tendencies combined with environmental influences such as temperament, social skills, talents (other social identities), and coping skills. Temperament is important to how hazing influences an individual. Individuals who are particularly sensitive, despite their constructive coping skills and social skills, are likely to be affected more by the rejection hazing poses than are individuals who are rather thick-skinned.

Community attitudes and racial socialization are a combination of personal and group relationships within each category of home, school or work, community (for instance, religious community), friends and peers, and foreign communities. Within each category, the level of acceptance, belonging, and oppressive experience influences the salience of the category. For example, if the home is dysfunctional, the child may seek a home away from home among friends at school, at church, or in athletic involvement. This method of seeking a source of attachment may be positive or negative. If it is negatively tainted by prevailing negative racial messages at home, school, or the community, the individual may seek refuge in places that further derail a positive construction of racial identity. This is briefly discussed later. When someone leaves a community in which she or he has been raised or attended school for a significant period of time, moving to a new community with or without family often requires renegotiation of racial identity. The possibilities and the obstacles interact with the history of the new community and the regional history of the country. Micro lenses under inherited influences as well as traits may also affect this process of negotiation.

The revision of Root's ecological framework mapped here magnifies the lens of *phenotype* listed originally under inherited influences. It is clearly shown cutting across all three middle lenses (inherited influences, traits, and community). Phenotype is clearly a major experiential piece of multiracial identity (Hall, 1992; Rocquemore & Brunsma, 2002; Wijeyesinghe, 2001; Williams, 1996).

Certain phenotypes look more ambiguous in racial group belonging than others. Persons of Asian and European ancestry may be mistakenly identified as Latino (Williams, 1996). Hall (1980) found that individuals of Black and Japanese ancestry have a multitude of phenotypes. Root (1990) determined that one's racial appearance may also vary by age, which further complicates the type of feedback and interaction one may experience in a lifetime.

Thus racial and ethnic identity predictably vary from individual to individual and even for siblings within a family. It is a dynamic process that may change over a lifetime and be expressed situationally. However, Root (1994) suggests that despite this flexibility, the multiracial individual's ultimate task is to establish a core identity of values.

PROCESSES AFFECTING IDENTITY DEVELOPMENT

Whether offering monoracial stage models or ecological models of identity development, researchers agree that lived experience as it interacts with the paradigm of race in this country drives racial identity. Virtually all researchers of biracial identity find it important to discuss the influences of phenotype, environment, family environment, and racial awareness. Those researchers cited earlier who attend to family dynamics observe that the biracial experience is unique in that neither parent knows what it is like to be biracial, and neither is likely to have experience with the type of hazing to which a biracial individual may be subjected. These are significant issues for educators as the classroom, school, and university are home away from home for many students and a source of significant information, process, and interaction—and ultimately a significant influence in perception of self. Glass and Wallace (1996) emphasize that "educators can help to dismantle racism and to reconstruct common-sense meanings of race . . . recent multicultural educational approaches are inadequate because they often reinscribe essentialist notions of race and fail to challenge the structures of racism" (p. 343). Reexamining diversity and multicultural approaches to education through the experience of a multiracial experience offers instruction as to where we need to seek to improve our discussions and deconstruction of race in order to challenge racism.

Despite suggestions that phenotype is a significant determinant of identity, Hall (1980) did not find a strong correlation. Root (1998) found that an individual's perception of self was not always correlated with how the person was perceived. Jacobs's (1977) early work suggested that because of the racial paradigm in the United States, at an early age some cognitive distortions around color must be made to understand the categories. Featurism abounds across racial groups. This is the process of devaluing, critiquing, and tormenting physical aspects of self that are usually measured against a white European standard or the reference group of color. Whereas it is usually discussed in terms of skin color, it may include characteristics such as hair, eyes, body proportions, assumptions about male genital size, and nose shape. Dimas (1995) noted how appearance did serve as an external signifier of identity whether or not it was consistent with one's identity. The issue seems to be more salient if one's physical appearance does not match what people expect (Williams, 1996).

Several researchers have pointed out the significance of the family environment (Gibbs & Hines, 1992; Kich, 1992; Root, 1990, 1998; Tomishima, 1999; Wijeyesinghe, 2001). They cite the potential impact of family cutoff, rejection, oppressive behavior and attitudes, and parental abandonment. Root (1998) explains that on the basis of cognitive problem solving and the degree of egocentricity of young children, negative behaviors between parents can be race coded by children. This coding is primed by a society that codes and stereotypes racial behaviors. The result is that an individual may internalize negative aspects of a parent as racial and thus try to disavow herself of this connection with her parent, with people who belong to the same group as the parent, and ultimately with some aspect of herself.

Root (2001) describes three types of cutoff from extended family, which may shape the balance and outcome of racial identity. If the family views race as a commodity (something to be reproduced in its "purity"), dysfunction plays out in distancing, to varying degrees. Using three business models, *merger, franchise,* and *acquisition,* she outlines the outcomes of marriages when race is not a commodity as opposed to when it is. If race is a commodity, the results vary. With the *merger* model, based upon a notion that clans merge with marriage, the family recognizes the marriage, expels the family member, and rejects the couple; the clans do not merge. The *franchise* model promotes separateness of a new couple even when race is not an issue. If race is an issue, the family further distances itself from the couple but may maintain contact. At the most extreme is the *acquisition* model, which ordinarily incorporates only the marital partner into the fold of the family. If this goes awry, the family member is disowned and the marriage is never acknowledged.

All three models deprive the couple of support useful for negotiating the stresses of married life and of having children. When such models are in effect, couples may move away from their families of origin to cope with the emotional distance more effectively, merge or franchise themselves to the other partner's family, or find community support. This type of distancing sometimes becomes problematic in the marriage since much is expected of the partner and pressure may be put on children to be exceptional (Root, 2001).

Family cutoff sometimes makes conversation about race difficult (Root, 2001). Four problematic family approaches to race can be mirrored in the classroom. The first one is a color-blind approach, held in the sentiment that "we're all members of the human race." The second is that "race is everything." Youths often rebel against this view and adopt the first or third approach, the third being "don't make race an issue." Children usually are not sure whether this means it is or is not. The last approach is most frequent among immigrant parents who are not a racial minority in their country of origin but become a racial minority and members of an oppressed group once they immigrate. As their children grow up they may express, "We don't understand Americans and race."

Any of these perspectives is problematic because it deprives children of the opportunity to learn a vocabulary with which to talk about race. It also deprives them of the opportunity to think critically about racial paradigms. Children and adolescents may be discouraged from going to their parents with hurtful and oppressive experiences. This lack of discussion, unless it takes place elsewhere, limits their exploration of their racial identity. Lastly, an absence of overt discussion of race, racial classification, and racism limits the way in which children and adolescents can learn from their parents how to recognize and defend themselves against racial insults toward them or their family.

In multiracial family support groups, enlightened parents of color often tell White parents that whereas they know what it is like to grow up as a person of color in this country, they do not know what it is like to grow up biracial. Thus there are aspects of guiding their children through this experience of race and negotiating social space that are new and experimental for them, just as for White parents (Wehrly, Kenney, & Kenney, 1999). The difference for the younger generation of multiracial individuals is that they are growing up amid a significant cohort of other mixed people, either immediately in their extended family or school or in imagined role models. This was hardly available to previous generations. As a result, although parents may know that there are things they might learn, they are also aware that there are other parents with whom they can consult, family support groups they can join, and newsletters to which they can subscribe that can facilitate their child's experience and their parenting (Brown & Douglass, 1996; Wardle, 1999).

Some children and youths have strong individual and family identities that are skills-based. For example, a youth might identify primarily as an athlete, musician, dancer, or chess player. Thus racial identity plays a background to these identities occurring in an environment in which a certain culture is created. The young person is bonded to a community through shared commonality. Often, in moving to a new community, these individuals seek out a similar replacement community. Their skill base is their entry and ticket to acceptance into the community. This is not to say that race does not matter in the equation. But in the same way as religion does for some people, this community and sense of belonging brings resilience for some of the racial insults and assaults.

Lastly, peer acceptance and rejection are critical racial identity influences. These experiences, which can constitute hazing and amount to authenticity tests, interact with individual personalities, the availability of parents, family, and teachers to facilitate coping and dissecting these experiences, and the nature of the school and community. The experience associated with hazing may bring physical appearance, behavior, accent, bilingual capabilities, dialectical proficiencies, choice of friends, choice of romantic partner, class, parent's occupation, clothing preference, body type, and neighborhood into the equation.

FIVE TYPES OF IDENTITY

I don't drink alcohol, never have, mostly because I don't want to maintain and confirm any of my ethnic stereotypes, let alone the most prevalent one, but also because my long-lost father, a half-breed, is still missing somewhere in the bottom of a tequila bottle. I had always wondered if he was a drunk because he was Indian or because he was white or because he was both.

—Alexie (2000, p. 47)

Continuing away from stage models as a way of embracing the diversity that exists and the functions it serves, Root (1990) outlined four types of identity that could be found among multiracial people. The first two identities are monoracial and may be expressed in the same way but are driven by different processes. Hypodescent and one-drop rules drive the first identity; one takes on the racial status the community assigns, and it is always the racial identity of lower status. Until recent times, this was the only option publicly available to mixed race people.

The second identity is also monoracial and may result in the same resolution. However, the individual does examine how this identity fits, works for the person, and is consistent with experience. This may be a difficult resolution if one arrives at an identity different from how people perceive one and based upon one's physical appearance, parentage, and defiance of hypodescent rules (as with a White identity in previous generations).

The third identity is one that was not available or easily workable in early generations of mixed heritage people. Identifying with both groups of parentage is part of this resolution. Sometimes one aspect of one's heritage may be more salient than the other, depending on the demands of the situation and the aspects of identity that resonate. This is a frequent normative identity for mixed race young adults and youths in this period of history.

The fourth identity was the most radical of the original four. It was to identify as a new racial group and refuse to do racial addition, as in Black and White. Rather, one might identify as multiracial with no separate racial signifiers or fractions attached as a descriptor or qualifier.

These four identities were derived from the first contemporary generation of biracial people and the oldest cohort of people in the middle generation (see Table 6.1). It was also reinforced by some parents, particularly White parents, who approached such a label as a way of de-essentializing racial construction (Graham, 1996).

In a study conducted ten years later (Root, 1998), these identities were still confirmed, but a fifth identity emerged: symbolic race. In some ways, it is the most radical and challenging identity. It demonstrates how history and generation change the meaning of identity choices. Of 30 biracial sibling pairs, a few people of European heritage who appeared well adjusted and were phenotypically mixed looking identified as White. They did not ignore the fact that they had Asian, American Indian, or African heritage; they did not denigrate it. In fact, they even felt pride in having this heritage, but they did not feel the affinity they did to the markers of Whiteness. At the same time, they were detached from this aspect of their heritage for either having been raised away from family and community of ethnic origins or having experienced significant and repeated rejection from communities of color such that they stopped trying to join in group activities. Their approach to race was similar to what Waters (1990) described as symbolic ethnicity, where people of European ancestry took pride in their ethnic roots of Irish, German, or Polish descent but no longer had much meaning or attachment to it through cultural practice or engagement. As Helms noted in 1990, the orientation to Whiteness may not be problematic if there is not a simultaneous denigration of Blackness.

DEVELOPMENTAL TASKS ASSOCIATED WITH IDENTITY DEVELOPMENT

From the time I started elementary school to the time I started junior high, strangers, teachers, and friends' parents often let me know I was different by asking, "Where are you from?" I would name my street, my city, or a geographic marker near my house. But I knew these answers, although they sometimes stopped the inquiry, were not replying to the question they intended. Sometimes if the inquiry continued, I would give my birth country, the Philippines, a place I could no longer remember. For some strange reason, this of all answers seemed to satisfy them. Some would go further and knowingly ask, "Your dad in the military?" a question I dreaded and disliked. Then sometime in my teens, in the era of ethnic and racial pride movements, the question about my difference more frequently became "What are you?" By then I understood that the question was mostly about my physical ambiguity, asked by someone wondering "whose side I was on." I gave various fractions and explanations, trying to hurry my explanation away from this difference.

—Root (1996, p. xiii)

Various developmental theorists have outlined essential tasks of identity development. It should be noted that the importance of individual identity is a thoroughly Western notion. Thus the theories that guide child development are rooted in some assumptions that are not universal. The major developmental theories that have guided child development are behavioral, humanistic, and psychodynamically based. One of the most influential theorists was Erikson (1968). He was the only influential classic child developmentalist to address racial identity as a task to be resolved. Although progressive at the time, his theoretical thinking was limited by the era in which it was produced and the paradigm of race. The "mature" stage of human development overlaps among theorists, whether it is clarification (Erikson), self-actualization (Maslow, 1962), or being (Rogers, 1962).

Researchers of racial identity suggest that resolution of racial identity has several tasks, beginning in childhood (Phinney & Rotheram, 1987), and is dependent upon one's cognitive capacity. Because race is a social construction, an individual's understanding of race and resolution of racial identity requires a certain level of cognitive complexity. Whereas categorization seems to be a natural human propensity, we are socialized and oriented toward what differences matter. Sex and eventually gender are master statuses in all societies, though their expression and what constitutes desirable behavior are culturally shaped. Before kindergarten, virtually all children can classify most individuals correctly on the basis of whether they are boys or girls, women or men.

Phinney and Rotheram correlate children's ethnic identity socialization with their cognitive capabilities, which become increasingly complex with age. First they are inconsistent and idiosyncratic, then overly general, then entirely concrete. Adolescence is a time in which they gain the capacity for complex abstraction, which allows fuller understanding of ethnicity, race, and racism. All the researchers cited in this chapter fundamentally believe, as Phinney and Rotheram do, that "children's ethnic socialization is a function of both the immediate environment and the sociocultural context" (p. 276). However, not all researchers are grounded in Eriksonian theory, as Phinney and Rotheram are.

Piagetian theory suggests that certain cognitive tasks are ordered, although this has been culturally challenged in more recent years. What is relevant is that physical objects develop constancy (size, volume, shape). Jacobs's (1977) work on biracial identity with young children four to eight years of age suggested that in a society in which race matters, skin color is transformed into an object that must achieve a sense of constancy in spite of the variability among people even within the same group (Russell, Wilson, & Hall, 1992; Spickard, 1992). He notes that this constancy is developed at the cusp of beginning formal schooling and is later associated with the social dynamics of racism and oppression. To achieve this constancy, the child must learn to distort color in people, assigning them to the correct racial categories with some confidence on the basis of a monoracial paradigm. Children must be taught a racially loaded schema; it is not natural. Extrapolating from his work, we can assume that such color constancy would not be a necessary task in a society that did not have race as a master status and that acknowledged continuity and blendedness among individuals along many dimensions of physical features.

Gibbs (1987) focuses on the relational tasks that a person may cycle through at various stages of life, in ever more complex ways with age. The five identity conflicts she poses derive from Eriksonian theory. The conflicts that Gibbs poses in her framework, although derived from ego psychology, explicitly address the racial aspects of each challenge to identity (Gibbs & Hines, 1992):

1. "Who am I?" Conflicts about integrating racial identities that might be socially disparate must be resolved.
2. "Where do I fit in?" Conflicts about social marginality must be resolved.
3. "What is my social role?" Conflicts about sexuality, gender identity, and general impulsivity must be resolved. Feelings about these roles are tied to feelings toward parents.
4. "Who is in charge of my life?" Conflicts over separation and individuation from parents must be resolved. Parental views and feelings about their own race and the degree to which they can appropriately equip and guide their children to understanding independence may well interact with unresolved parental issues around their own interracial union, rejection, or fears for their children.
5. "Where am I going?" The conflict to be resolved touches on achievement and career. Gibbs's discussion suggests that internalization of negative stereotypes by race may limit achievement and ambitions.

Another focus on child development revolves around the transition from dependence upon parents and family as the reference group and source of reflection of the self to transferring more of this dependence to peers. It should be noted that this is culture-specific. Thus Hartup (1978) suggests that the establishment and quality of friendships is the goal and measure of social competence. Several researchers' findings suggest that peer relationships are not merely a replacement or extension of familial relations; rather, they operate independently. These observations are consistent with those of many researchers on biracial identity, who describe the importance of peer interaction, the choice of friends, parents' choice of neighborhood and school in which to raise their children, and the impact of hazing. Little specific empirical research has focused on this aspect of biracial children's development. Some theorists suggest that mixed race children have multiple groups from which to draw friends (Hall, 1980). Cauce et al. (1992) found no difference between mixed race early adolescents and the comparison cohort of monoracial children of color in terms of peer relationships. Gibbs and Hines (1992) found that all of the adolescents in their study reported good peer relationships.

IMPLICATIONS FOR THEORY AND RESEARCH

This chapter has presented a summary and critique of long-standing racial identity models and their limitations for understanding the process of identity resolution for a growing population of individuals who identify as multiracial. Although population mixing is not new, and neither is racial mixing in the United States, theoretical revaluation and acceptance suggest that a critical shift is taking place in racial construction. Researchers are necessarily attempting to reconsider how monoracial models of identity might accommodate multiracial identity. The emphasis on process and multiple outcomes as well as heavy reliance on historical factors to explain this shift move us into an era in which ecological models seem to accommodate the identity resolutions of multiracial individuals in a way that other models cannot.

Research must study both the subjects of multiracial identity and their families, but also the environments in which their identities are shaped. Now that several qualitative studies have independently shown that family dysfunction as well as peer rejection may derail identity development, quantitative studies might be useful to further test these conclusions. Not all family dysfunctions may influence identity equally.

Although the research on multiracial people has focused on those of multiracial heritage, it is important to conduct research on persons who have no investment in such an identity, or who are indeed against such public identity. This research needs to include both people with parents of different races and persons who are monoracial in origin. It would allow us to further understand what are the contemporary external obstacles to accepting mixed race people and the concept of multirace. Researchers also have to be specific about their sample of mixed race people on the basis of the research questions. It may not be appropriate to mix persons of Black/White and Asian/White and Native American/White and Latino/White in the same samples, particularly if the sample numbers are small. Historical issues specific to the ethnic groups may predictably confound the results.

Root (2002) discusses methodological approaches to multiracial identity in the context of the number of dissertations and theses that have proliferated on this topic. She notes that proportionally few offer new information. Some of these difficulties are because of sampling considerations. Here are common flaws that must be corrected in subsequent research:

- Mixed race people are not randomly distributed geographically in the United States (U.S. Census Bureau, 2001). This leads to other methodological challenges, particularly self-selection into studies.
- Self-selection limits the breadth of findings. Studies of multiracial people typically include persons who identify as such. Root (1998) introduced leveraged sampling, in which a sibling had to engage another sibling to participate in the same study. Siblings often identify differently within the same family.
- Generational changes in the meaning of mixed race and the support for mixed race identities imply that research findings from 15 to 20 years ago may not be replicable or as relevant to persons who are of mixed race in their early twenties.
- Heterogeneity versus homogeneity is often the rule in small qualitative studies. However, from a theoretical standpoint, it is time to be careful about the research questions and whether or not a heterogeneous mixed race sample can answer the question. It is important to study individuals who identify with specific combinations of mixed race to make sure the findings and their implications are understood.
- Restricted sampling limits the generalizability of results. Many studies use college-age students, who represent a restricted age cohort and are in a specific development stage in their lives. Community samples are harder to obtain but yield a broader scope of influences on people's identities.
- Secondary analysis versus primary analysis may obtain larger samples. However, the data collection is not usually constructed to answer many questions about an issue and multiracial identity. For example, one does not know how an individual identifies even if the person is asked questions about parental ancestry.
- Determining the appropriate control group is more complex and must have conceptual validity. Should the control for a group of Black/White adolescents be Black, White, or another mixed race group? Should the control group be based upon something other than race, such as socioeconomic status?

- Nativity of parents and participants in studies of multiraciality must be considered. For example, the early contemporary studies of mixed race individuals of Asian ancestry typically had mothers who were Asian, not Asian American. The issues of identity were not solely around race but included nationality and cultural brokering for mothers. These issues are not present for persons with a U.S.-born Asian American parent.

Educators are challenged to examine their own thinking about race and ethnicity. Their impact is profound, because they are role models for critical thinking about race. Without specific training or life experience to examine their assumptions about race, they are likely to replicate conventional meanings of race and reinforce standard racial identities that alienate an increasing number of students. Hollins (1999) outlines three types of educators' racial and ethnic identity development as it influences classroom practice, discussion, and interaction with students. Many multiracial students, particularly by high school and college, have grappled with the meaning of race, have had to be critical about racial stereotypes, and may be assertive about creating spaces and places in which to live an integrated life. They are a challenge to teachers who have not examined racial construction in a way that allows students to develop their critical thinking around race.

SUMMARY

This chapter attempts to present background for rethinking the constricted paradigm of monorace and its potential impact on the growing number of mixed race students who identify with multiple heritages. To facilitate a shift in how race is taught and analyzed in the classroom, especially precollege, a brief background history of concepts around race has been provided to understand the generational change in thinking about and expressing mixed race identities. Concepts that are central to the mixed race experience are laid out, such as hypodescent, one-drop rules, passing, code switching, authenticity tests, situational ethnicity, and multiracial identity. The chapter has proposed a framework for thinking about racial identity, as well as explanation of some normative expressions of

being mixed race and where developmental issues around race arise. Lastly, recognition of mixed race people requires us to reconsider the implications for theory and research on racial identity, multicultural education, and the educator's need for critical thinking and personal development.

Educators have a surrogate-parent role in terms of guiding critical thinking; protecting students from harmful practices, interactions, and attitudes in the classroom and curriculum; and engaging them in learning when students are away from home. Most racial socialization takes place outside of the home. The educator who is sensitive to the reform that is needed to accommodate the growing number of multiracial students, many more of whom will assert mixed race identity, may embrace a forthcoming challenge. The paradigm of mixed race, although not eliminating race, challenges some of the fallacies and limitations of the cognitive complexity and flexibility constricted by the current system.

Sheets (1999) states that educators lack awareness of how suppression, denial, and coercion of racial and ethnic identities cause emotional and cognitive stress for students. This invisibility of multiracial realities in the classroom and multicultural curricula sends an unhealthy message (Wardle, 1996). Glass and Wallace (1996) note that to reform multicultural education and challenge racism, educators must be equipped to disrupt racial formation in the way that McCarthy (1993) has outlined. These authors suggest that critical thinking is necessary to expose contradictions and structuring principles currently inherent in the various approaches to multicultural education so that the educational system does not perpetuate and legitimize an oppressive racial ideology. Ideally, such a progressive transgression would challenge the notion of race itself (Glass & Wallace).

The creators of multicultural curricula will, it is hoped, reexamine how conventional multicultural education presents race in a way that discourages flexible thinking and critical questions. Multiracial individuals in history are a vehicle by which to examine race relations in this country and our assumptions about race. Will multicultural education take on the challenge of being a twist in a centuries-old make-believe tale of race that is firmly entrenched into the fabric of everyday life in the United States?

References

Alexie, S. (2000). *The toughest Indian in the world*. New York: Grove Press.

Allman, K. M. (1996). (Un)natural boundaries: Mixed race, gender, and sexuality. In M.P.P. Root (Ed.), *The multiracial experience: Racial borders as the new frontier* (pp. 277–291). Thousand Oaks, CA: Sage.

Azoulay, K. G. (1997). *Black, Jewish, and interracial: It's not the color of your skin, but the race of your kin, and other myths of identity*. Durham, NC: Duke University Press.

Brown, N. G., & Douglass, R. E. (1996). Making the invisible visible: The growth of community network organizations. In M.P.P. Root (Ed.), *The multiracial experience: Racial* borders as the new frontier (pp. 323–340). Thousand Oaks, CA: Sage.

Cauce, A. M., Hiraga, Y., Mason, C., Aguilar, T., Ordonez, N., & Gonzales, N. (1992). Between a rock and a hard place: Social adjustment of biracial youth. In M.P.P. Root (Ed.), *Racially mixed people in America* (pp. 207–222). Thousand Oaks, CA: Sage.

Collins, P. H. (1991). *Black feminist thought: Knowledge, consciousness, and the politics of empowerment.* New York: Routledge.

Comas-Diaz, L. (1996). LatiNegra: Mental health issues of African Latinas. In M.P.P. Root (Ed.), *The multiracial experience: Racial borders as the new frontier* (pp. 167–190). Thousand Oaks, CA: Sage.

Cross, W. E., Jr. (1978). The Thomas and Cross models of psychological Nigrescence: A review. *Journal of Black Psychology, 5,* 12–31.

Cross, W. E., Jr. (1981). *Shades of Black: Diversity in African-American identity.* Philadelphia: Temple University Press.

Daniel, G. R. (1992). Passers and pluralists: Subverting the racial divide. In M.P.P. Root (Ed.), *Racially mixed people in America* (pp. 91–107). Thousand Oaks, CA: Sage.

Dimas, J. M. (1995). *Psycho-social adjustment in children of inter-ethnic families: The relationship to cultural behavior and ethnic identity.* (Doctoral dissertation, University of California, Berkeley.)

Erdrich, L., & Dorris, M. (1991). *The crown of Columbus.* New York: HarperPaperbacks.

Erikson, E. H. (1968). *Identity: Youth and crisis.* New York: Norton.

Field, L. D. (1996). Piecing together the puzzle: Self-concept and group identity in biracial Black/White youth. In M.P.P. Root (ed.), *The multiracial experience: Racial borders as the new frontier* (pp. 211–226). Thousand Oaks, CA: Sage.

Funderburg, L. (1994). *Black, White, other: Biracial Americans talk about race and identity.* New York: Morrow.

Gaskins, P. F. (1999). *What are you? Voices of mixed-race young people.* New York: Henry Holt.

Gibbs, J. T. (1987). Identity and marginality: Issues in the treatment of biracial adolescents. *American Journal of Orthopsychiatry, 57,* 265–278.

Gibbs, J. T., & Hines, A. M. (1992). Negotiating ethnic identity: Issues for Black-White biracial adolescents. In M.P.P. Root (Ed.), *Racially mixed people in America* (pp. 223–238). Thousand Oaks, CA: Sage.

Glass, R. D., & Wallace, K. R. (1996). Challenging race and racism: A framework for educators. In M.P.P. Root (Ed.), *The multiracial experience: Racial borders as the new frontier* (pp. 341–358). Thousand Oaks, CA: Sage.

Graham, S. (1996). The real world. In M.P.P. Root (Ed.), *The multiracial experience: Racial borders as the new frontier* (pp. 37–48). Thousand Oaks, CA: Sage.

Hall, C.C.I. (1980). *The ethnic identity of racially mixed people: A study of Black-Japanese.* (Doctoral dissertation, University of California, Los Angeles, 1980). *Dissertation Abstracts International, 41,* 1565.

Hall, C.C.I. (1992). Please choose one: Ethnic identity choices for biracial individuals. In M.P.P. Root (Ed.), *Racially mixed people in America* (pp. 250–264). Thousand Oaks, CA: Sage.

Hartup, W. W. (1978). Children and their friends. In H. McGurk (ed.), *Childhood social development.* London: Methuen.

Helms, J. E. (1990). *Black and white racial identity: Theory, research and practice.* New York: Greenwood Press.

Hollins, E. R. (1999). Relating ethnic and racial identity development to teaching. In R. H. Sheets and E. R. Hollins (Eds.), *Racial and ethnic identity in school practices: Aspects of human development* (pp. 183–194). Mahwah, NJ: Erlbaum.

Hughes, L. (1926). *Selected poems by Langston Hughes.* New York: Knopf.

Hurtado, A. (1996). *The color of privilege: Three blasphemies on race and feminism.* Ann Arbor: University of Michigan Press.

Jacobs, J. H. (1977). *Black/White interracial families: Marital process and identity development in young children* (Doctoral dissertation, Wright Institute Graduate School of Psychology, 1977). *Dissertation Abstracts International, 38,* 5023.

Jacobs, J. H. (1992). Identity development in biracial children. In M.P.P. Root (Ed.), *Racially mixed people in America* (pp. 190–206). Thousand Oaks, CA: Sage.

Johnson, D. J. (1992). Developmental pathways: Toward an ecological theoretical formulation of race identity in Black-White children. In M.P.P. Root (Ed.), *Racially mixed people in America* (pp. 37–49). Thousand Oaks, CA: Sage.

Johnson, R. C. (1992). Offspring of cross-race and cross-ethnic marriages in Hawaii. In M.P.P. Root (Ed.), *Racially mixed people in America* (pp. 239–249). Thousand Oaks, CA: Sage.

Johnson, R. C., & Nagoshi, C. T. (1986). The adjustment of offspring of within-group and interracial/intercultural marriages: A comparison of personality factor scores. *Journal of Marriage and the Family, 48,* 279–284.

Kich, G. K. (1982). *Eurasians: Ethnic/racial identity development of biracial Japanese/White adults.* (Doctoral dissertation, Wright Institute Graduate School of Psychology, Berkeley, CA.)

Kich, G. K. (1992). The developmental process of asserting a biracial, bicultural identity. In M.P.P. Root (Ed.), *Racially mixed people in America* (pp. 304–317). Thousand Oaks, CA: Sage.

Kich, G. K. (1996). In the margins of sex and race: Difference, marginality, and flexibility. In M.P.P. Root (Ed.), *The multiracial experience: Racial borders as the new frontier* (pp. 263–276). Thousand Oaks, CA: Sage.

Kitano, H. L., Fujino, D. C., & Sato, J. T. (1998). Interracial marriages: Where are the Asian Americans and where are they going? In L. C. Lee and N. W. Zane (Eds.), *Handbook of Asian American Psychology* (pp. 233–260). Thousand Oaks, CA: Sage.

Lee, S. (1993). Racial classifications in the U.S. census: 1890–1990. *Ethnic and Racial Studies, 16*(1), 75–94.

Marcia, J. (1966). Development and validation of ego identity status. *Journal of Personality and Social Psychology, 3,* 551–558.

Maslow, A. H. (1962). Some basic propositions of a growth and self-actualization psychology. In A. W. Combs (Ed.), *Perceiving, behaving, becoming: A new focus for education* (pp. 34–49). Washington, DC: Association for Supervision and Curriculum Development.

McCarthy, C. (1993). After the canon: Knowledge and ideological representation in the multicultural discourse on curriculum reform. In C. McCarthy and W. Crichlow (Eds.), *Race, identity, and representation in education* (pp. 289–305). New York: Routledge.

Miller, R. L. (1992). The human ecology of multiracial identity. In M.P.P. Root (Ed.), *Racially mixed people in America* (pp. 24–36). Thousand Oaks, CA: Sage.

Montagu, A. (1997). *Man's most dangerous myth: The fallacy of race* (6th ed.). Walnut Creek, CA: AltaMira Press.

Nash, G. B. (1999). *Forbidden love: The secret history of mixed-race America.* New York: Henry Holt.

No Collective (Eds.). (1992). *Voices of identity, rage and deliverance: An anthology of writings by people of mixed descent.* Berkeley, CA: No Press.

Omi, M., & Winant, H. (1994). *Racial formation in the United States: From the 1960s to the 1990s.* New York: Routledge.

Parham, T. A. (1989). Cycles of psychological Nigrescence. *Counseling Psychologist, 17(2),* 187–226.

Phinney, J. S. (1989). Stages of ethnic identity development in minority group adolescents. *Journal of Early Adolescence, 9,* 34–49.

Phinney, J. S., & Rotheram, M. J. (1987). Children's ethnic socialization: Themes and implications. In J. S. Phinney and M. J. Rotheram (Eds.), *Children's ethnic socialization: Pluralism and development* (pp. 274–292). Thousand Oaks, CA: Sage.

Poston, C. W. (1990). The biracial identity development model: A needed addition. *Journal of Counseling and Development, 69,* 152–155.

Ramirez, M., III (1983). *Psychology of the Americas: Mestizo perspectives on personality and mental health.* Elmsford, NY: Pergamon Press.

Ramirez, M., III (1998). *Multicultural/multiracial psychology: Mestizo perspectives in personality and mental health.* Northvale, NJ: Aronson.

Rocquemore, K. A., & Brunsma, D. L. (2002). *Beyond Black: Biracial identity in America.* Thousand Oaks, CA: Sage.

Rogers, C. R. (1962). Toward becoming a fully functioning person. In A. W. Combs (Ed.), *Perceiving, behaving, becoming: A new focus for education* (pp. 21–33). Washington, DC: Association for Supervision and Curriculum Development.

Root, M.P.P. (1990). Resolving "other" status: Identity development of biracial individuals. In L. Brown and M.P.P. Root (Eds.), *Complexity and diversity in feminist theory and therapy* (pp. 185–205). New York: Haworth Press.

Root, M.P.P. (Ed.). (1992). *Racially mixed people in America.* Thousand Oaks, CA: Sage.

Root, M.P.P. (1994). Mixed race women. In L. Comas-Diaz and B. Greene (Eds.), *Women of color and mental health: Integrating ethnic and gender identities in psychotherapy* (pp. 455–478). New York: Guilford Press.

Root, M.P.P. (Ed.). (1996). *The multiracial experience: Racial borders as the new frontier.* Thousand Oaks, CA: Sage.

Root, M.P.P. (1998). Preliminary findings from the biracial sibling project. *Cultural Diversity and Mental Health, 4(3),* 237–247.

Root, M.P.P. (1999). The biracial baby boom: Understanding ecological constructions of racial identity in the twenty-first century. In R. H. Sheets and E. R. Hollins (Eds.), *Aspects of human development: Racial and ethnic identity in school practices* (pp. 67–90). Mahwah, NJ: Erlbaum.

Root, M.P.P. (2001). *Love's revolution: Interracial marriage.* Philadelphia: Temple University Press.

Root, M.P.P. (2002). Methodological issues in multiracial research. In G. N. Hall and S. Okazaki (eds.), *Asian American psychology: The science of lives in context.* Thousand Oaks, CA: Sage.

Root, M.P.P. (in press). From exotic to a dime a dozen. In A. Gillem and C. Thompson (Eds.), *Biracial women in therapy: Between the rock of gender and the hard place of race.* (Available Spring 2003). New York: Haworth Press.

Russell, K., Wilson, M., & Hall, R. (1992). *The color complex: The politics of skin color among African Americans.* Orlando: Harcourt Brace.

Senna, D. (1998). *Caucasia.* New York: Riverhead Books.

Sheets, R. H. (1999). Human development and ethnic identity. In R. H. Sheets and E. R. Hollins (Eds.), *Racial and ethnic identity in school practices: Aspects of human development* (pp. 91–101). Mahwah, NJ: Erlbaum.

Sollors, W. (1997). *Neither Black nor White yet both: Thematic explorations of interracial literature.* New York: Oxford University Press.

Spickard, P. R. (1989). *Mixed blood: Intermarriage and ethnic identity in twentieth-century America.* Madison: University of Wisconsin Press.

Spickard, P. R. (1992). The illogic of American racial categories. In M.P.P. Root (Ed.), *Racially mixed people in America* (pp. 12–23). Thousand Oaks, CA: Sage.

Stephan, C. W. (1992). Mixed heritage individuals: Ethnic identity and trait characteristics. In M.P.P. Root (ed.), *Racially mixed people in America* (pp. 50–63). Thousand Oaks, CA: Sage.

Tomishima, S. A. (1999). *Factors and experiences in biracial and biethnic identity development.* Unpublished doctoral dissertation, University of Utah, Salt Lake City.

Trimble, J. E. (2000). Social psychological perspectives on changing self-identification among American Indians and Alaska Natives. In R. H. Dana (Ed.), *Handbook of cross-cultural/multicultural personality assessment.* Mahwah, NJ: Erlbaum.

U.S. Census Bureau. (2001). [On-line]. Available: http://www.census.gov/population/cen2000

Wardle, F. (1996). Multicultural education. In M.P.P. Root (Ed.), *The multiracial experience: Racial borders as the new frontier* (pp. 380–391). Thousand Oaks, CA: Sage.

Wardle, F. (1999). *Tomorrow's children: Meeting the needs of multiracial and multiethnic children at home, in early childhood programs, and at school.* Denver, CO: Center for the Study of Biracial Children.

Waters, M. C. (1990). *Ethnic options: Choosing identities in America.* Berkeley: University of California Press.

Wehrly, B., Kenney, K. R., & Kenney, M. E. (1999). *Counseling multiracial families.* Thousand Oaks, CA: Sage.

Wijeyesinghe, C. L. (2001). Racial identity in multiracial people: An alternative paradigm. In C. L. Wijeyesinghe and B. W. Jackson III (Eds.), *New perspectives on racial identity development: A theoretical and practical anthology* (pp. 153–181). New York: New York University Press.

Wijeyesinghe, C. L., & Jackson, B. W., III (Eds.). (2001). *New perspectives on racial identity development: A theoretical and practical anthology.* New York: New York University Press.

Williams, T. K. (1992). Prism lives: Identity of binational Amerasians. In M.P.P. Root (Eds.), *Racially mixed people in America* (pp. 280–303). Thousand Oaks, CA: Sage.

Williams, T. K. (1996). Race as process: Reassessing the "What are you?" encounters of biracial individuals. In M.P.P. Root (Ed.), *The multiracial experience: Racial borders as the new frontier* (pp. 191–210). Thousand Oaks, CA: Sage.

Williams-Leon, T., & Nakashima, C. (2001). *The sum of our parts: Mixed heritage Asian Americans.* Philadelphia: Temple University Press.

Zack, N. (1995). *American mixed race: The culture of microdiversity.* Lanham, MD: Rowman & Littlefield.

Zack, N. (1997). *Race/sex: Their sameness, difference, and interplay.* New York: Routledge.

PART
III

RESEARCH AND RESEARCH ISSUES

7

QUANTITATIVE METHODS IN MULTICULTURAL EDUCATION RESEARCH

Amado M. Padilla

Stanford University

Quantitative educational research with ethnic minorities has a long history. The earliest studies with educational implications focused on the intellectual assessment and school achievement of African American, immigrant, and other ethnic minority students (Kamin, 1974; Valencia & Suzuki, 2001). This research legacy is now well known for its failure to consider many variables that are critical for assessing student ability (Valencia & Suzuki, 2001; Padilla, 1988). For example, in assessing intelligence, IQ tests were given special status, and it was assumed that instruments such as the Stanford Binet Test could be used to uncover differences in intellectual ability between individuals or racial groups. With the special status ascribed to IQ tests, little attention was given to the fact that in the development of IQ tests minority children were not included in standardizing the instrument (Kamin, 1974). Further, in actually carrying out research on differences between groups on IQ tests, little if any attention was given to social class or language background of the subject, or cultural differences between the groups being compared. Researchers today recognize the many problems inherent with the older body of IQ-related research, but great reliance is still placed on standardized tests of achievement; many of the same problems still exist in properly using and interpreting findings from these tests.

More important is the recognition of a set of assumptions inherent in the older IQ studies that are still operative today in educational research involving ethnic minorities. Complex, interrelated, and conforming to commonsense qualities that make them appealing, these identifiable assumptions are that (a) the White middle-class American is the standard against which other groups should be compared; (b) the instruments used for assessing differences are universally applicable across groups, with perhaps only minimal adjustment for culturally diverse populations; and (c) although we need to recognize such sources of potential variance as social class, educational attainment, gender, cultural orientation, and proficiency in English, these are nuisances that can later be discarded.

This chapter challenges these assumptions and offers numerous suggestions for improving quantitative research with ethnic minority respondents. There are many forms of quantitative research: controlled experiment, quasi-experiment, survey, observational study, case study, statistical simulation, meta-analysis (a study of studies), and others. Some of these are hypothesis-generating, meaning that they explore data to form or sharpen a hypothesis about a population so as to assess future hypotheses. Some are hypothesis-testing, which means they seek to assess specific a priori hypotheses or estimate parameters by random sampling from a population.

In this chapter, the primary focus is on nonexperimental quantitative research since this is the primary mode of research in education (Johnson, 2001). However, the methodological difficulties to be identified in conducting research with ethnic populations are also applicable to experimental studies involving a treatment and control group. In addition, problems of instrumentation and measurement of constructs are discussed in a way that is applicable to research in general, regardless of the specific methods used.

THE SOCIAL CONSTRUCTION OF KNOWLEDGE

Before these issues can be investigated meaningfully, it is important to examine how the construction of knowledge has proceeded in the social sciences and what impact this has had on the study of minority populations generally, as well as in education specifically. Within this discussion, questions and challenges are directed at Eurocentric paradigms that have dominated our approach to accumulating scientific facts. Critique of Eurocentric approaches to the study of ethnic minority populations in social science research, and in educational research particularly, is based on the fact that such approaches have resulted in erroneous interpretations because of specific biases inherent in the paradigms themselves.

In a discussion of quantitative research with minority populations, it is important to address the topic of scientific paradigms used by researchers to define their approach. A starting point for our discussion is the distinction between universalistic and relativistic methods. Allport (1937) framed the central tenets of these two methods with respect to their use in psychology, but the distinction is equally appropriate to educational research since educational researchers employ the same paradigms.

Universalistic Versus Relativistic Approaches to Educational Research

The universalistic approach seeks confirmation of general truths that extend across cultural groups. In contrast, the relativistic approach seeks to uncover a particular truth that is confined to a single culture or social group. Since its initial formulation, the debate has been recast in terms of etic and emic principles (Matsumoto, 1994). Proponents of the universalistic or etic view believe that concepts and methodologies are basically valid across different cultures. Conversely, the relativistic or emic view maintains that concepts and methodologies do not have universal validity; they may be appropriate only within a narrow range of cultural groups.

Educational researchers have generally followed the social sciences in their adoption of acceptable paradigms that rest on a universal framework (Banks, 1993; Kerlinger, 1979). According to the universalistic framework, theory and hypothesis testing should guide research. Thus, quantitative methods are employed and statistical inferences are used to draw conclusions that support the universal principles. In addition, advocates of a universalistic framework also adopted a research strategy that calls for the logic of the laboratory, where experimentation, control, and random assignment of subjects to experimental and control groups is possible (Dehue, 2001). It wasn't long before it was apparent to social scientists and educational researchers alike that a strictly experimental research approach was not possible in the real world of people, schools, and large-scale societal problems such as class size reduction or curriculum reform. However, Campbell and Stanley (1966) showed that quasi-experiments could be designed in a natural context, with varying degrees of experimental or statistical control and where the necessary statistical assumption of random assignment of respondents to groups could be maintained. Dehue presents an invaluable historical critique of the idea of randomized controlled studies.

The important concern here is that this approach eschews the importance of such variables as culture; rather, emphasis is on a comparative approach that uses similar measures to compare males and females, children of different age or ethnic groups, etc. Investigators who use this approach argue that universal principles can be uncovered only by means of a comparative approach to research.

The universal approach has come under sharp criticism from numerous sources, notably feminist and minority researchers, because of its Eurocentric perspective (for a summary of this critique, see Banks, 1993). The most salient feature of the Eurocentric paradigm is its focus on a monocultural, male-oriented, and comparative approach to research (Yoder & Kahn, 1993). White male researchers from a monocultural perspective using White and generally middle-class students as the normative population have developed the majority of instruments and research procedures used in educational research. These instruments and procedures are then used primarily to assess some psychological or educationally relevant construct with a White (male and female) middle-class student population. This approach lends itself to a narrow database, resulting in biased conclusions of substantive educational outcomes that are problematic even for White samples that differ from the normative population. The problem is worse if use of the instruments and procedures is extended to ethnic minority populations who do not share all the demographic characteristics of the normative group (e.g., immigrant students who are not proficient in English). A related point has been made by Sears (1986), who showed how research based on college students tested in academic laboratories on academic-like tasks has culminated in social psychological theories that are incompatible with the everyday life experiences of most non–college-age majority-group adults.

There is nothing wrong with this approach to research so long as whatever groups are being compared are equivalent in all demographic characteristics including social class, cultural background, and proficiency in English. However, there is still room for caution when, for example, men and women from the same social class and cultural background are compared on a task requiring interpersonal competition and men are found to score higher on competition (Griffen-Pierson, 1990). Is this difference due to the use of an inappropriate male-oriented task, or a real difference between the sexes resulting from a genetic disposition found in males but not females? It should be obvious that an informed person would agree with the former and not the latter conclusion. Yet in comparisons of cultural or ethnic groups, conclusions similar to the latter "genetic" interpretation can be found, with no consideration for the fact that the instruments may have been biased to begin with because of a conceptual framework and set of tasks that favored one group over the other (Griffen-Pierson).

The problem arises when "biased" instruments that favor non-Hispanic whites are used in a comparative research framework to examine differences between racial or ethnic groups (Azibo, 1996; Rogler, 1999; Sue, 1999). The comparative research framework requires a statistical test between at least two groups that have been equated on all variables known to have an influence on the behavior in question (Plutchik, 1974). However, if both the construct being assessed and the method for assessing the construct originate in the same cultural context, then a comparative approach may seriously increase the potential for research bias. Thus it would be inappropriate to use the instrument developed for one cultural group to assess group differences, as necessitated by the comparative research framework (Sue, 1999). Proof that such comparisons are the mainstay of much of the empirical research in education is evident from a cursory examination of our major professional journals in education.

The situation is even more problematic because the comparative research framework assumes that there is some standard by which comparisons are made. Although not always stated explicitly, the standard is usually the non-Hispanic White middle class, and any deviations are interpreted negatively as deficits or differences that possibly require intervention. In sum, no fewer than three potentially harmful consequences can be identified when a White, privileged male norm is adopted: (a) overgeneralization of findings that benefit members of the "norm" group, (b) exaggeration of differences that extend beyond the true nature of the between-group difference, and (c) evaluation of deficiency levied at a low-status contrast group.

In sum, studies driven by a universalistic approach have the potential to blind the researcher to important between-group differences that go uncontrolled, the result of which is erroneous conclusions if mean score differences are found to be statistically significant. Many minority students are subjected to institutionalized practices of racism (English-only instruction, academic tracking, and so on) that may have the effect of devaluing self-esteem and academic achievement. Consequently, between-group differences in academic performance as measured by

grade point average or standardized test scores (SAT and others) might be a reflection of unmeasured variance (such as unequal educational opportunity) that is due to extraneous factors not taken into account by researchers (Lee, 2002).

A Paradigm Shift in Ethnic Research

African American researchers (Azibo, 1996; Parham, White, & Ajamu, 1999; and others) have challenged the Eurocentric approach because it typically assumes a White standard reference group. This has led to an emic or Afrocentric approach employing conceptual categories and worldviews adopted from traditional African cultures that serve as the standard for understanding African Americans. According to Azibo (1996), the Afrocentric approach challenges comparative studies that employ theory or methods designed to maintain African American inferiority.

In a less philosophical and more methodological challenge to the universalistic or etic approach, Marín and Marín (1991) and Rogler (1999) argue that researchers must be knowledgeable of Hispanic culture and demographic information to carry out useful research with this population. Yee (1992) makes a similar case in discussing the stereotypes and misperceptions that persist when Asian Americans are studied by educational researchers.

Rogler (1989), for example, argues in favor of a culturally sensitive research approach that places culture at the center of the research enterprise. According to Rogler:

Research is made culturally sensitive through a continuing and open-ended series of substantive and methodological insertions and adaptations designed to mesh the process of inquiry with the cultural characteristics of the group being studied. . . . The insertions and adaptations span the entire research process, from the pretesting and planning of the study, to the collection of data and translation of instruments, to the instrumentation of measures, and to the analysis and interpretation of the data. Research, therefore, is made culturally sensitive through an incessant, basic, and active preoccupation with the culture of the group being studied throughout the process of research. (p. 296)

It is important to understand that the merits of the scientific method are not being challenged here. What is being called into question is the claim to objectivity by some researchers who believe that their scientific paradigms are neutral as far as minority groups (including women) are concerned. The scientific method consists of a series of paradigms, each governed by distinct assumptions, rules, and methods of conducting research (Kuhn, 1970). However, a culturally sensitive approach to research holds that empirically derived facts are not valid for all time but need to be examined from the perspective of the assumptions, language, and activities of the community of scientists. If the "community" has not included minority researchers, then it is small wonder that culture and other salient characteristics of ethnic groups are not considered important in mainstream research. A more emic-oriented approach thus has the responsibility to examine these "established facts" through a new lens.

In sum, if we begin with Rogler's (1989) definition of culturally sensitive research and couple this with the criticisms of the Eurocentric paradigm discussed above, a new paradigm is called for, in which the study of a specific ethnic group is valued for its own sake and that group need not be compared to another. Proponents of this view of research argue that it is valuable first to research and understand within-ethnic-group differences; and only when intragroup heterogeneity is well understood is comparative ethnic-group research meaningful. An alternative way of stating this is that if majority group researchers are not admonished for including *only* a White sample in their study, why should ethnic researchers be cautioned against not including a White comparison group in their research?

We shall now turn to discussion of major challenges in conducting research with ethnic minority groups. Important considerations that are required of the researcher intending to conduct quantitative research with ethnic groups are identified and assessed in the next sections of this chapter.

CHALLENGES IN CONDUCTING RESEARCH WITH ETHNIC GROUPS

There are numerous problems in conducting research with ethnic minority populations, many of which are frequently overlooked by investigators unfamiliar with research topics that may be particularly sensitive for these populations. A useful guide for conducting research in ethnic minority communities is available from the American Psychological Association (2000). Some of these issues are related to identifying and selecting a sample. Because of the diversity of the U.S. population, the researcher has to be careful not to confound culture, ethnicity, and social class in selecting a sample. A related concern is the failure to recognize heterogeneity (for instance, differences in level of acculturation) existing within an ethnic group, which can lead to variation in outcome measures and result in misinterpretation of the findings. Finally, we consider language and culture barriers confronting researchers in ethnic minority communities.

Properly Identifying, Describing, and Selecting a Sample

When minority students are included in quantitative research, it usually results—intentionally or not—in

documenting the low academic achievement of Hispanic, African American, and Native American students in comparison to non-Hispanic white students (Lee, 2002) and the higher mathematics attainment of Chinese, Korean, and Japanese students compared to Caucasian students (Flynn, 1991; Sue & Okazaki, 1990). Many educational studies involving Hispanic and African American students examine them from the perspective of their failure in the educational system, or how to improve our understanding of factors associated with (under)achievement, such as achievement motivation (Marchant, 1991) and parenting styles (Dornbusch, Ritter, Leiderman, Roberts, & Fraleigh, 1987; Lamborn, Mounts, Steinberg, & Dornbusch, 1991). There are, however, a few excellent quantitative studies of the educational achievement of language-minority, usually Spanish-speaking, students in bilingual education programs (August & Hakuta, 1997).

Few studies have examined ethnic minority students with respect to their success in education. It is rare to find research such as Kraft's (1991) study of what makes a Black student successful on a predominantly White campus; Alatorre Alva's (1991) examination of the academic invulnerability of Mexican American high school students; Arrelano and Padilla's (1996) study of highly successful undergraduates at Stanford University and the role played by personal, family, and school resources in understanding high academic attainment of Mexican American students; Duran and Weffer's (1992) study of the influential family and school factors associated with the achievement of successful Mexican American immigrant high school students; or Strom, Johnson, Strom, and Strom's (1992) investigation of programs for gifted Hispanic children and their parents. Specialized topics such as desegregation and bilingual education also include ethnic minority students, but empirical research in these areas is scant.

Understanding the characteristics of the population is critical if we are to generalize the results properly and replicate the findings. However, many studies do not describe the subject population sufficiently to enable replication. Two examples of subject description from research journals are presented here to illustrate the lack of information that would enable true replication:

1. "Subjects were 32 children from the Berkeley area. Subjects included 15 boys and 17 girls. Children came from a variety of socioeconomic and ethnic backgrounds, though most were Caucasian and middle class" (Gopnik & Meltzoff, 1992, p. 1094).

2. "In all, 423 sixth- and seventh-grade students . . . participated in the study. The school was in a predominantly working-class [geographic location here in original] community. The average student age was 11.87 and 13.08 for sixth and seventh graders,

respectively. The sample was equally representative of males (52%) and females (48%), with 68% of the sample being Caucasian, 23% Black, 5% Hispanic, and 7% other minority status (Wentzel, 1991, p. 1068).

Each description offers the basic information about number of students, gender, age, social status, and ethnicity. However, the information is much too general, and each variable is described for the sample as a whole. To be specific, it is not known whether the social class of the non-Hispanic white students was similar to that of the other ethnic groups. What does predominantly, mostly White or Caucasian, and middle-class mean? Does it mean 51% of the sample, or something closer to 100%? Do the categories of White and Caucasian include Hispanic, as they should? Does a sample of 60% White and 40% Black from diverse social backgrounds mean 50% White middle-class, 35% Black working-class, and the remaining White and Black subjects representing other social classes? Are the Hispanic students from English- or Spanish-speaking homes? Are the Hispanic students of Mexican, Cuban, Puerto Rican, or Guatemalan heritage? Do they belong to some other Latino national group? Are they biracial? Does diverse social background include children from homeless families or poverty conditions? What about single-parent versus two-parent families?

In the latest edition of the *APA Publication Manual* (American Psychological Association, 2001), authors are given quite explicit guidelines about the detail required when describing subjects in a study:

Report major demographic characteristics such as sex, age, and race/ethnicity, and, where possible and appropriate, characteristics such as socioeconomic status, disability status, and sexual orientation. When a particular demographic characteristic is an experimental variable or is important for the interpretation of results, describe the group specifically—for example, in terms of national origin, level of education, health status, and language preference and use. . . . Even when a characteristic is not an analytic variable, reporting it may give readers a more complete understanding of the sample (pp. 18–19).

Clearly, this level of detail cannot always be attained. However, if researchers know beforehand that they are going to employ a diverse subject pool in their research, they can make provision to collect demographic information that can be used to enhance their description of the population studied. This has two benefits. First, by gathering important demographic information the researcher is in a better position to interpret the findings in terms of the context of culture, social class, acculturation level, and length of residence in the United States. Second, by adequately describing the subject population, other interested researchers can replicate the study using a comparable subject population. The advantage of replication is that it allows researchers to test the robustness of findings and thereby adds an element of truthfulness to them if replication results in similar outcomes. However, it is commonplace to find little information regarding culturally diverse respondents in the methods section of an article. Apparently many authors, peer reviewers, and journal editors do not question the absence of critical information when it comes to a culturally diverse population.

In identifying and selecting a sample, keep in mind that several major methodological issues are essential:

• What important demographic characteristics of the population does the researcher need to know in order to properly interpret findings and make generalizations?
• Are the procedures for sample selection adequately described so that replication can be carried out?
• If the sample was not randomly selected and is therefore not representative of the population, what limitations does this pose for generalizing?

One critical issue in identifying a population is to understand its demographic characteristics. What diversity is represented? Understanding the heterogeneity that exists in various communities is essential if the researcher is to understand how best to move forward in gaining information about culturally different respondents. Further, if we are to lessen the potential for bias found in research with ethnic minority individuals (and found in what passes as truth in the field), we need to rethink our designation of respondents. Bond (1988) discusses the bias of labels and perspectives in research with culturally diverse populations. Designations such as "deprived background," "disadvantaged," "lack of stimulation," "poverty," and the more current "limited English proficient" and "at-risk learners" have been widely associated with culturally diverse individuals. As Bond states:

Discussions of the effects of poverty on development frequently equate minority membership with the poor. Although it is important to acknowledge the disproportionate representation of certain ethnic and racial groups at the lower socioeconomic levels and the significance of such environments to these groups' development, this oversimplified equation of minority status with poverty perpetuates stereotypes and obscures the factors that contribute to this relationship. (p. 46)

The frequent failure of researchers to understand that poverty imposes constraints on the choices a person or family has available also causes problems. Poverty limits the educational, social, and recreational choices a family can make for their children, so it is no small wonder that poorer children do less well academically than middle-class children. The fact that low SES results in limited educational choices is frequently overlooked when between-ethnic-group comparisons are made.

When studies do incorporate culturally diverse individuals, it is generally within a cross-racial/ethnic comparison. In many such comparisons, ethnicity is confounded with social class, whereby the comparison is made between a middle-class White population and a working-class African American or Hispanic (perhaps immigrant) population. Such glaring differences between groups would not be acceptable in any other area of education-related research. Imagine a study of differences on the SAT equating girls from upper-class backgrounds attending a private school with boys from working-class families enrolled in a public school vocational track. A reviewer of such a study would immediately recognize the problem of trying to infer gender differences from a sample that ignores differences in socioeconomic status between the two groups of students and would likely recommend that a peer-refereed journal reject the paper. Yet as Sue (1999) points out, this level of critique on the part of a journal reviewer may not occur in a research study involving ethnic groups.

In addition, as mentioned previously, the subject section of an article might not describe the background of the research subjects sufficiently so that one knows what "Hispanic" or "Asian" means. Is the subject a third-generation American of Chinese ancestry from a middle-class home, or an immigrant from a working-class mainland Chinese family who arrived illegally in the United States? These two individuals differ in fundamentally important ways, and to gloss over these differences by merely indicating that the sample consisted of Asian Americans is to miss the important point being made here.

In order that culture, ethnicity, and social class not be confounded, it is important to understand the unique cultural features of the group. For example, length of residence in the United States is important for immigrants; language usage and preference is also significant if for no other reason than to determine what language to use in data collection. Another variable is the ethnic or racial self-identification of the person. If a respondent prefers *Pilipino* to Filipino or Pacific Islander, then this conveys important information about political orientation and level of acculturation to U.S. culture and customs. When studying children, parents' level of education (or human capital) is often critical in understanding how and why children perform as they do on standardized tests. Children from homes with more human capital perform at a higher level than children whose parents possess less education.

Few researchers have actually taken these factors into account when conducting research. Laosa (1982) demonstrated, in a study of Anglo and Chicana mothers' teaching strategies, that any differences in teaching strategies between the two ethnic groups disappeared when the mother's level of formal education was a controlling factor. Similarly, Gutierrez and her colleagues (Gutierrez &

Sameroff, 1990; Gutierrez, Sameroff, & Karrer, 1988) examined the heterogeneity of acculturation and social class in a study of Mexican American and Anglo mothers' concepts of development. They included Anglo upper-class and lower-class groups and six Mexican American groups representing various socioeconomic status and low, medium, and high acculturation. Results showed significant SES effects for both Anglo and Mexican American mothers, and considerable within-group variability for the Mexican American group. In addition, comparisons between the Mexican American highly acculturated and Anglo American, both higher SES, indicated that Mexican American mothers gave more cognitively complex responses.

In another study of low-income Mexican mothers, Richman, Miller, and LeVine (1993) also demonstrated that "maternal schooling emerges from this study as an important influence on maternal responsiveness during infancy in and of itself, rather than as reflecting the social variables with which it is often associated" (p. 62). The significance of these research studies is in demonstrating the varying effects of both educational background and acculturation level in responses of Mexican American subjects, and even between similar Mexican American subgroups (grouped by acculturation level).

Several researchers have included ethnic minority individuals in their studies so that the subject sample would be representative of a particular geographic area. This representative sampling approach can be useful in understanding some component of behavior or development as reflected by the diversity of individuals in the community. An example of a representative sample is Stevenson, Chen, and Uttal's (1990) study of the achievement of 3,000 first-, third-, and fifth-grade Black, White, and Hispanic children, and a subsample of the parents' beliefs about academic achievement. They selected "20 elementary schools covering the range of socioeconomic and ethnic groups within the area. Two classrooms each at first, third, and fifth grades within each school were randomly selected for study" (p. 509). Subsamples of students were selected for individually administered tests. Stevenson et al. provided information about the age of students by ethnic group and the percentage of students in each group born in the United States. In addition, they presented information on family structure, language spoken at home, educational level, and family income. Black, Hispanic, and White families differed significantly in both education and occupation level, though multiple comparison analyses were not employed to examine specific differences among the groups. The researchers analyzed student achievement according to both ethnicity and SES (mother's level of education). Results indicated that ethnic differences in children's mathematics performance, but not reading performance, were no longer significant when mother's education level was controlled. There were many ethnic differences in parental attitudes, but unfortunately, effects resulting from educational differences were not analyzed. Thus the confounding effects of education were examined in children's academic performance, but not in parental beliefs, despite the previously identified significant differences in education level among the ethnic groups.

This example illustrates one of the problems in conducting research with ethnic populations. The issue of confounding is substantial even in a carefully conducted study. Even when results include statistical controls, findings are not always discussed with respect to the confounding. Thus the results may be representative of the population, but the comparisons made among groups may be inappropriate because of the serious problem of confounding.

We have just seen some of the problems that may arise in representative samples. What about random samples? Culver, Wolfle, and Cross (1990) wanted to obtain a random sample from a population of 9,753 teachers who were identified as early in their career (those with six years of full-time teaching or less) and who were currently teaching. However, a simple random sample would not be likely to yield enough African American teachers for the researchers' purposes because teachers from this racial group made up only 13.5% of the population. Thus they decided to "sample at random approximately equal numbers of Blacks and Whites (actually 350 Whites and 375 Blacks)" (p. 329). Since it was not possible, in this case, simply to select a random sample from the population, another sampling procedure was used that included a random sample of White teachers and an oversample of African American teachers. In many research projects, especially of the survey type, investigators should seriously consider the advantages of oversampling of an ethnic group to have a large enough sample size to carry out statistical tests of significance.

In another work, Finn and Achilles (1990) conducted an experimental study of class size and used random sampling effectively in composing their classrooms:

All school systems in the State of Tennessee were invited to participate. . . . About one third of the districts, representing 180 schools, expressed an interest in participating. After negotiation, the final sample consisted of 76 elementary schools that were large enough to have at least three kindergarten classes. . . . Within each school, children entering kindergarten were assigned at random, by the project staff, to one of three class types: small, with an enrollment range of 13–17 pupils; regular, with an enrollment of 22–25 pupils; or regular with aide, with 22–25 pupils but with a teacher aide formally assigned to work with the class. Teachers were assigned at random to classes as a separate step. (pp. 559–560)

Classes were categorized by composition, as containing all White students, all minority students, or a mixture of White and minority. They were also classified by location, as inner-city, urban, suburban, or rural. However, within this well-controlled experimental study was a serious confound concerning race and ethnicity, location, and social class (participation in the free lunch program was considered as designating low income). There were no inner-city classes with all White students and no suburban or rural classrooms with only minority students. Only five classrooms were inner-city and mixed. There was also a "strong association between minority status and participation in the free lunch program. About 70% of the student sample is either minorities receiving free lunches, or Whites not receiving free lunches; Yule's Q association measure is .78" (Finn & Achilles, 1990, p. 561). Consequently, in this "randomized experiment" there is certainly helpful information about class-size effects, but the effects for ethnic minority status are seriously confounded with location and social class. Fortunately, the researchers recognized this problem and conducted their analyses to take this confound into consideration.

In sum, researchers need to take seriously the problem of confounding variables when they do research with ethnic minority populations. How a sample is selected for study can greatly influence the results and hence the generalizations that can be made on the basis of the findings. Moreover, if sufficient attention is given beforehand to possible confounding variables while selecting a subject population, misinterpretation of findings is reduced (Wilkinson, 1999). When an ethnic population is studied, there is often a confound between social class and cultural group membership. To state the obvious, a difference in reading achievement between African American students and non-Hispanic White students does not mean that African American students come from a culture that does not value learning to read, but it could mean that because of poverty the home conditions are not optimal for early reading development.

Understanding the Heterogeneity Within an Ethnic Group

Similar to the problem of confounding is the lack of understanding by most researchers of the heterogeneity within an ethnic minority population. Some researchers state that they include Asians without going into further detail about who these Asians are (Yee, 1992). Are they middle-class, or working-class? Are they Chinese, Japanese, Hmong, Korean, Vietnamese, or Cambodian? Were they born in the United States? If not, how long have they lived in this country? Similarly, for Hispanics, there are considerable differences among Mexican American, Cuban, Puerto Rican, Argentinean, Chilean, Colombian, Guatemalan, and Central American Mayans (for whom Spanish is a second language). Within each ethnic subgroup are social-class (e.g., educational background), acculturation, and language differences (particularly dialect and language variations among Central American Indians).

To illustrate the point made in the preceding paragraph, consider how Keefe and Padilla (1987) showed that newly arrived Mexican immigrants differed in many ways from second- and third-generation Mexican Americans. Puerto Ricans who live on the mainland differ from those who commute between the island and the mainland, as well as from those who have always lived on the mainland (Rodriguez, 1989). The Cubans who fled Castro in the 1960s differ in social class and color (White) from the poor and largely Black Cuban exiles who came in the 1970s (Suarez, 1993). There are Black Hispanics who are frequently identified by the majority group as African American, without any understanding of their Latino roots. Berndt, Cheung, Lau, Hau, and Lew (1993) showed that perceptions of parenting differed among Chinese parents living in mainland China, Taiwan, and Hong Kong. In the United States, where Chinese (and Asians in general) are frequently treated as though they are homogeneous, this study demonstrates important socialization differences among Chinese families on the basis of country of origin. Also of importance is the growing number of interracial children. Increasingly in our schools, there are children who are of mixed ethnic or racial heritage. It is important for researchers to be aware of mixed-heritage individuals in conducting research because these individuals often have loyalty to both of their heritage backgrounds and cultures (Yee, 1992). These examples all illustrate complex intragroup differences that must be understood to facilitate replicability and generalizability.

Difficulties from Cultural and Language Barriers

Another difficulty in conducting research with ethnic minority populations concerns language and cultural barriers. Superficial speculation on this point suggests that one can always get someone to translate instruments and broker with community members, but issues are more intricate than the simple term *language and cultural barriers* suggests. As asserted in the previous section, there are a number of subject-selection and subject-description issues that can introduce serious methodological flaws into research, though these serious flaws do not often draw the attention of journal peer reviewers. How can an outsider interpret the results of a study involving ethnic respondents if individuals who understand the ethnic community are not included in a significant capacity on the research team (Rogler, 1999)?

De la Luz Reyes and Halcón (1988) make this assertion regarding research on Hispanics:

As Hispanic academics, our research interests often stem from . . . a compelling need to lend a dimension of authenticity to the prevailing theories about our communities. Said another way, we want to provide our own perspectives regarding prevailing negative assumptions about our values, culture, and language. . . . Our interest in these research areas is also motivated by a concern for assisting our community in improving its second-rate status in the education, economic, and political arenas. Tired of reading about ourselves in the social science literature written by non-minorities, we want to speak for ourselves, to define, label, describe, and interpret our own condition from the "inside out." We feel strongly about providing a balance to the existing literature and research on Chicanos. (p. 306)

Marín and Marín (1991) make a similar point in their book *Research with Hispanic Populations,* noting that "some [Hispanic] community members perceive social science research as a form of exploitation in which nonminority individuals reap the benefits of the data collection effort" (p. 42).

In addition, Marín and Marín (1991) delineate several other cultural barriers that make it difficult for minority and nonminority researchers alike to work within an ethnic minority community. Although their comments are aimed at Hispanics, many of these points are relevant for other ethnic communities as well:

Suspicion of government involvement in a research project is more likely when individuals or their family members and friends have lived in political climates where oppressive governments make use of informers and home visits to gather compromising information to be used in surveillance, social control, or other abuses of a person's rights. In addition, many Hispanics, regardless of their immigration status (documented, undocumented, refugee, parolee), live in fear of being stopped by agents of the Immigration and Naturalization Service and of being asked to document their citizenship or immigration status. . . . Also of relevance in determining the rate of cooperation with an investigation is the type of personal or community benefit that is to be accrued by participating in the study. (pp. 43–44)

In recent years, with the backlash against newcomers observed through nativist movements such as "English only"; with state restrictions designed to limit social services to immigrants; and with new federal laws calling for greater restrictions in immigration policies, especially after the September 11, 2001, attacks on the World Trade Center and the Pentagon, immigrants are more cautious than ever about volunteering to participate in any type of research project.

Language barriers can also be problematic for researchers. For example, Spanish is not the same in all Hispanic communities. Hispanics from numerous countries may be able to communicate with one another, but there are significant dialect differences that should be reflected in letters of introduction, human subject consent forms, questionnaires, and other written and oral forms of communication with the group of interest. Issues of instrument translation are discussed in the next section of this chapter.

Some cultural and language barriers can be surmounted by including members of the community on the research team. However, including a Mexican American graduate student raised in a middle-class suburban neighborhood who learned Spanish in high school in a project of Latino immigrant parents and children may not constitute inclusion of an informed community member in the research enterprise. Similarly, including a Cuban or Puerto Rican educated on the East Coast as an interviewer may not be so helpful with a Mexican American population in South Texas, particularly with respect to language issues, even if the interviewer is perfectly fluent in Spanish; the reverse would be equally inappropriate. As another example, a highly acculturated Filipino American may have difficulty collecting data from recently arrived Filipinos on attitudes toward schooling. Unless investigators are culturally aware of traditional customs, they could ask questions in such a way as to promote inaccurate responses or to offend the respondent. Thus to minimize culture and language barriers it is necessary to have thorough cultural knowledge of the target population.

It is equally important to know something about the language background and proficiency level of individuals who serve as translators of materials or interviewers for non–English speaking respondents. I am reminded of a case where an investigator working with Chinese immigrants in the San Francisco area assumed that all Chinese spoke the same dialect. Consequently, when he showed up with a Mandarin-speaking interviewer to meet with parents who spoke Cantonese, he was both embarrassed by his lack of familiarity with the very community he wished to study and disappointed that his effort to identify and train an interviewer had been wasted.

In sum, the challenges in researching ethnic minority communities are considerable. I do not want to leave the impression that only minority researchers should study minority communities. The take-home message is that unless the researcher knows the community well, it is critical to include members of the community in the research study as true partners and not just as translators, interviewers, or data coders.

Community leaders are often more vested in the research conducted in their neighborhood or school than is the actual researcher. But they want to see the research findings used in ways that benefit the community, not just in ways that benefit the researcher's career or the interests of the sponsoring agency. For this reason, it makes good sense to identify community advocates and to find ways to make them legitimate partners in the research process.

INSTRUMENTATION AND MEASUREMENT

Critical to any quantitative study are the issues of instrumentation and measurement. Regardless of whether one uses a rating scale, an inventory, a standardized achievement test, or any other type of performance-based outcome measure, the issues are the same. That is, the instrument must be appropriate for measuring change resulting from an educational program or intervention. If the research involves a survey questionnaire, then the items must reliably assess how the sample population evaluates the items. Accordingly, this section includes a general discussion of these instrumentation concerns because of their relevance in identifying suitable measures when conducting research with an ethnic population.

One issue in research with ethnic groups concerns identifying *appropriate* outcome measures. Many instruments may be suitable for White middle-class subjects but not for a culturally diverse sample. In identifying and selecting outcome measures, one has to consider the psychometric qualities of the instrument. There are several questions that should provoke serious consideration whenever we use an instrument with ethnic respondents:

- Are the selected instruments reliable and valid with the ethnic group in question? Is there equivalence of meaning of key concepts across cultures (e.g., self-esteem, independence-dependence, etc.) used in educational research?
- Do we have to translate the instrument into another language? If so, what is the best way to do this?
- Is it necessary to use specially designed instruments to assess such characteristics as acculturation, ethnic identity, English-language proficiency, or culture-specific learning strategies? How are such instruments identified for use with an ethnic population?
- Do ethnic respondents answer paper-and-pencil instruments such as a questionnaire or personal inventory in the same manner as majority-group respondents? Are there response biases that researchers need to be knowledgeable of?

Are the Instruments Appropriate?

Many studies have examined instruments to assess their suitability for a particular ethnic minority population. For example, Knight, Tein, Shell, and Roosa (1992) evaluated the cross-ethnic equivalence of parenting and family interaction measures between Hispanic and non-Hispanic White families. In the study they assessed four instruments: the Children's Report of Parental Behavior Inventory, the Parent-Adolescent Communication Scale, the Family Adaptability and Cohesion Evaluation Scale II, and the Family Routines Inventory. These instruments were selected because the authors believed them to be most useful in large-scale field assessments that would include ethnic minorities. They examined the interaction measures by using small panels of Hispanic individuals with some training in measurement. The examination involved having panel members evaluate each item for cultural relevance, that is, "the degree to which the behaviors and attitudes reflected in the items were applicable in the Hispanic culture" (p. 1394). Panel members also evaluated the items according to their underlying construct using two formats. Then the panel members "identified three rejection items, three cohesion items, three adaptability items, and seven family routine items as potentially irrelevant or as questionably relevant for the Mexican American culture" (p. 1394). As Knight et al. (1992) point out, "The explanations provided by the panel members of the lack of relevance for each item fell into one of two categories: (1) the item itself, or some wording or phrasing in the item, either has an ethnically specific meaning or has unclear meaning to members of the Mexican American culture; and (2) the item was worded poorly or vague terms were used, such that it is unlikely that subjects would understand the meaning of the item regardless of their ethnicity" (p. 1394).

The conclusion from this panel approach was that "there appears to be a small subset of items . . . that are likely of limited item equivalence because the behaviors or attitudes represented in these items are of limited applicability or generalizability to the Hispanic family" (Knight et al., 1992, p. 1395). The study then went on to assess the item equivalence and functional equivalence of the latent structure and subscale intercorrelations between Hispanic and non-Hispanic samples. From the findings, it was clear that some scales, minus certain subscales, had sufficient cross-ethnic equivalence for English-speaking Hispanic samples, while other scales required further scale development.

Many other scales have been assessed for their appropriateness for various cultural groups. Two scale categories are used to illustrate the psychometric work that has been conducted to address the issues of instrument appropriateness: (a) achievement scales, and (b) self-esteem scales. Numerous other types of scale could have been selected for discussion here, but achievement and self-esteem scales have a long history of use with ethnically diverse populations and serve to exemplify some points that we wish to emphasize regarding proper use of instruments with ethnic respondents.

Achievement Scales. Considerable research has examined achievement differences between ethnic minority and nonethnic minority students (Valencia & Suzuki, 2001). However, it is often not clear whether the various

achievement measures in use are comparable in what they measure and in how they should be used in the research. Frisby (2001) has produced a readable account of the many types of achievement test currently available to researchers interested in culturally diverse students. For example, there are individual standardized achievement tests used to evaluate individual students who are believed to be in need of some form of special treatment in school because of a suspected learning disorder, or for determining giftedness. There are group standardized achievement tests such as the National Assessment of Educational Progress (NAEP) test, the California Test of Basic Skills, the Stanford Achievement Test, etc. These are standardized tests used broadly across the country to monitor trends in achievement by grade level, content area (reading, math), gender, ethnic differences, and social class of the learner.

Achievement measures have been translated into other languages, but rarely are the instruments carefully assessed for their comparability. For example, the Metropolitan Achievement Test (MAT) was translated into Chinese and is used by Chinese bilingual programs because there are no alternative measures. Similarly, the Comprehensive Tests of Basic Skills (CTBS) have a Spanish version, the Spanish Assessment of Basic Education (SABE). The SABE was developed by Spanish-speaking experts and normed with a native Spanish-speaking U.S. student population. However, the SABE is not equivalent to the CTBS. The SABE was not developed as a translation of the CTBS, but as a separate measure that was to be comparable to the CTBS; careful studies have not been conducted as to how comparable the two versions are. There are also other Spanish-language achievement tests: *La Prueba Riverside de Realización en Español (La Prueba)* and *Aprenda: La Prueba de Logros en Español*. Both are norm-referenced with Spanish-speaking populations in the United States.

Aside from the comparability across languages, there is the issue of content comparability for middle-class English-speaking non-Hispanic white students and for culturally and linguistically diverse students. In an important conceptual article, Helms (1992) has argued that cognitive ability test items are not all culturally equivalent for African Americans and Whites. As she points out, there is an "absence of clearly articulated, theoretically based models for examining the influence of race-related cultural factors on cognitive ability" (p. 1089). Helms maintains that cultural equivalence of standardized cognitive ability testing remains to be studied. The problem is partially because no commonly accepted alternatives to statistical approaches for instigating such an investigation are available. More problematic still is the inability of psychologists and psychometricians to articulate the relevant issues as they affect test takers from various racial and ethnic groups within the United States. Therefore, the conclusion that whatever construct is measured by standardized CATs (Cognitive Ability Tests) constitutes universal intelligence or general cognitive ability for all racial and ethnic groups in this country is dubious at best.

Achievement tests suffer from the same validity and cultural bias problems discussed earlier. Even criterion-referenced achievement tests based on students' classroom curriculum fall short. In Stevenson et al.'s (1990) study of the achievement of African American, White, and Hispanic children, the researchers carefully constructed criterion-based achievement measures of mathematics and reading. The results showed significant ethnic differences in reading, but not mathematics, even after carefully controlling for mother's education background. Stevenson et al.'s conclusion clearly identifies the problem associated with achievement tests and even criterion-referenced tests:

> Our interpretation of this finding [of significant ethnic differences in reading achievement after controlling for mother's level of education] is that the content of the material the children were asked to read was based on experiences and knowledge that were less likely to be part of the daily lives of the Black and Hispanic than of the White children. Comprehending the meaning of text is difficult when the topics lie outside the child's everyday experience. Hispanic children bore the additional burden of being asked to read a language that typically was not the native language of their parents. The content of reading classes, more than that of mathematics classes, reflects situations that exist in the dominant culture. Minority children may be penalized in reading because the materials require information to which they have had less exposure outside of school than the White children have had. However, our use of tests based on the textbooks to which the children had been exposed may have been responsible for reducing the magnitude of ethnic differences in this study compared to studies that have relied on standardized tests of achievement. Typically, standardized achievement tests are based on what children are expected to know, rather than on what they necessarily have encountered. (p. 520)

In sum, the point made by Stevenson et al.(1990) is that important contextual, experiential, and cultural factors need to be considered when assessing achievement across ethnic and cultural groups. Much progress along these lines has already taken place from the time when little to no effort was made to ensure that the content of a test was equivalent for all groups who took it. The practical significance of this has taken on greater importance today, with increased implementation of high-stakes testing in schools for purposes of teacher and student accountability such as teacher merit pay and high school exiting.

Self-Esteem Scales. Another category of instrument that has been used extensively in educational research with ethnic minority students encompasses the many self-esteem scales that are available. There are some important issues exemplified by self-esteem measurement that also affect psychosocial development in children and adolescents. One concerns the definition of self-esteem. Theorists have long debated how to conceptualize and measure self-esteem (Rosenberg, 1979). Two major conceptual camps are distinguished, in terms of whether we view self-esteem as a unidimensional construct of self-worth (global view) or whether we evaluate an individual along several domains in addition to an overall global self-worth, or differentiated, view (for a review, see Harter, 1999).

These theoretical perspectives have not incorporated considerations relevant to culturally diverse students. Early literature suggested that ethnic minority children showed a lower level of self-esteem than White majority group children (for reviews, see Rosenberg, 1979; Wylie, 1979), a finding contested on several methodological and conceptual grounds (Wylie, 1979). However, despite the frequency with which self-esteem measures are used, there is still little theory that is relevant to ethnic minority students. As Clark (1965) suggested four decades ago, living in a racist and oppressive society that keeps people of color in poverty impinges on how they appraise their self-worth. For example, to continue with Harter's (1999) formulation of self-esteem, adolescents describe themselves in terms of characteristics from many domains: academic competence, athletic competence, job competence, physical appearance, social acceptance, close friendships, romantic appeal, and so on. Self-appraisal on many of these domains is made in the context of social comparison (I am smart because I am taking honors U.S. history and calculus, but I am not an athlete because I couldn't make the varsity basketball team!). As a result, depending on an adolescent's academic, social, and athletic standing in school, self-appraisal of worth may vary widely among all these domains (Harter, 1999). Further, minority adolescents in a school where there are few students from their same ethnic community may appraise themselves even more negatively on a larger number of domains because of their "outsider status" and possibly because of perceived prejudice and discrimination directed at them by peers.

Martinez and Dukes (1987) have conceptualized self-esteem according to the differentiated viewpoint, which suggests that ethnic minority students may evaluate themselves differentially among two major domains. They hypothesized that ethnic minority students would evaluate themselves lower than majority group members on *public* aspects of self-esteem (such as intelligence) but rate themselves high in *private* domains (satisfaction with self, for one). The rationale for this hypothesis was that in the public domain of self-esteem the majority group is the standard, whereas in the private domain the individual or the ethnic group is the standard. In their study, Martinez and Dukes found support for their thesis. The private-domain self-esteem ratings of African American and Hispanic students were higher than those of non-Hispanic

White students, while in the public domain of intelligence, which is measured in terms of the majority school-based culture, Hispanic and African American students rate themselves lower than non-Hispanic White students.

Scales for measuring self-esteem among ethnic minority students also fall short. In addition to the typical psychometric problems, they do not assess any cultural items that may affect self-esteem, and they are oriented toward middle-class norms. For example, in Harter's (1982) Perceived Competence and Social Acceptance Scale for Young Children (Grades 1–2), there is an item that asks children whether they have spent the night at a friend's house. In determining a child's social competence (which Harter views as a part of self-esteem), those first- and second-grade children who have stayed overnight at their friends' homes get higher scores than those who have not and thus attain a higher social competence score. Clearly, this item may be biased against some children whose culture is less permissive about sleepovers. Many ethnic children, especially girls, are not allowed to spend the night away from home unless it is the home of a trusted family member, and certainly not the home of a schoolmate whom the family does not know intimately. Children from traditional homes (Chinese, Muslim, Mexican, Vietnamese) may have stayed at their grandparents' or other family members' homes overnight, but this would not be credited on the Harter scale.

A study of Chinese children in Taiwan using the Perceived Competence Scale for Children (a translated version) reported the factorial validity of the scale for the Chinese sample (Stigler, Smith, & Mao, 1985). As with White American samples, there was a high correlation between the perceived cognitive competence and actual achievement. However, in keeping with Chinese culture and concerns of modesty, children tended to underrate their competence compared to White American children. In addition, unlike White American children, Chinese children differentiated satisfaction with self from the desire to change for the better. Stigler et al. conclude, "Whereas idealized perceptions of the self might reflect social desirability bias among American children, this same bias might produce self-effacement among Chinese children" (p. 1269). A similar finding would not be unlikely with Chinese American and other Asian background children living in the United States.

In a related study, Rotenberg and Cranwell (1989) assessed the self-concept of Native American and White American children using the "20 statements" test, an open self-description measure. They found that Native American children referred more frequently in their open description to kinship roles, traditional customs and beliefs, and moral worth than did White American children.

Thus, the findings differ with the instrument in comparison of ethnic minority and White children. As a whole, these results clearly point out that theories of self-esteem need to take into account how culture influences the manner in which a person defines his or her role in the social group (Dana, 1997). Also important is how the level of acculturation interacts with the social context to influence the self-esteem of culturally diverse individuals. Only when scales have been developed that incorporate culture into the items will we really understand how children evaluate themselves. Similar findings would result from an examination of other categories of scales.

Ethnic-Specific Instruments

The second set of issues concerns the question of whether it is necessary to use a specially designed instrument to assess characteristics such as acculturation, ethnic identity, or stress. As we have seen in the preceding discussion, mainstream scales that assess cognitive ability, achievement, and psychosocial development have not been generated with ethnic minority populations in mind. They have largely been produced by and for a majority-group middle-class population. The problem becomes even more complex when we focus on culturally specific behaviors or areas of development (such as ethnic identity, acculturation, or acculturative stress) that have not been viewed as significant issues for most White middle-class individuals.

As we have discussed, it is important for purposes of research to recognize the heterogeneity within certain ethnic groups. One important source of heterogeneity that has received considerable attention in recent years is acculturation (Moyerman & Forman, 1992; Rogler, Cortes, & Malgady, 1991; Shen & Takeuchi, 2001). It is well known that with contact between majority-group members and immigrants, the newcomers and their offspring eventually acquire the language, values, beliefs, and behaviors of the majority group. Theorists such as Berry (1990); Bourhis, Moise, Perreault, and Senecal (1997); Olmedo (1979); and Padilla (1980) have discussed the conceptual and methodological issues involved in the study of acculturation. Many questions have arisen regarding the process of acculturation and such considerations as gender, age of immigration, educational level, length of residence, and extent of intergroup contact with members of the majority group. More recently, Landrine and Klonoff (1996) have shown that African Americans also demonstrate differences in level of acculturation that are unrelated to social class and educational attainment.

There is no agreed-upon universal scale for measuring acculturation; neither is there, for that matter, any agreed-upon best scale for use with a particular ethnic group. However, most scales can be characterized by two general item categories: (a) self-rated proficiency and use of the home language, and (b) preference for ethnic-related activities and friends. By way of illustration, numerous scales can be found in the literature for use with diverse ethnic groups: African Americans (Landrine & Klonoff, 1996), Koreans (Kim, 1988), Mexican Americans (Cuellar, Harris, & Jasso, 1980), Asian Americans (Suinn, Richard-Figueroa, Lew, & Vigil, 1987), and American Indians (Oetting & Beauvais, 1990, 1991).

The important consideration regarding acculturation, for our purposes, is that the relationship among culture change, psychosocial adjustment, and educational attainment is in need of more attention. Most of the research on acculturation involves various indexes of mental health such as depression (Moyerman & Forman, 1992) and, more recently, the relationship between acculturation and ethnic identity (Buriel & Cardoza, 1993; Marín, 1993).

There is evidence in the literature suggesting that immigrant and second-generation students who are more traditionally oriented perform better academically than their later-generation and more acculturated counterparts (Buriel & Cardoza, 1988; Caplan, Whitmore, & Choy, 1989; Padilla & Gonzalez, 2001; Portes & Rumbaut, 2001; Suárez-Orozco, 1989). Thus immigrant youths who identify with their ethnic group and who are more traditional in beliefs and values have better grades and are more likely to go on to college than their acculturated peers. For example, Portes and Rumbaut (2001) found that for Southeast Asian students high grade point average was related to how their parents answered four questions on an acculturation measure. The questions pertained to preservation of culture and identity; "sticking together" for social support and mutual assistance; living where there are people of their own ethnic group; and no interest in returning to their country of origin. Using a 6-point scale from "strongly disagree" (0) to "strongly agree" (6), Rumbaut found that high parental scores were positively related to student high school GPA.

A similar finding appears to hold true for Mexican immigrants (Buriel, 1984; Buriel & Cardoza, 1988; Padilla & Gonzalez, 2001), Punjabi Sikh students (Gibson, 1988), and Central American children (Suárez-Orozco, 1989). A complicating factor also has to do with whether we are describing a situation of accommodation without assimilation, or a form of biculturalism in which students acquire English-language proficiency, know the culture of their parents *and* of the school, and have friends from different ethnic groups. As a consequence, they feel more comfortable in school *and* at home and do better overall in their academic work (Alatorre Alva, 1991).

In sum, the finding that immigrant students are more motivated to study and have more positive school attitudes than later-generation ethnic students is important. Further, how school achievement is influenced by ethnic and cultural maintenance via a strategy of accommodation without assimilation or biculturalism is still an open question. Much more research is required before we fully understand the relationship for immigrant students between school performance and acculturation.

Another consideration in ethnic-related research has to do with the attitude that minority-group members have toward their own ethnicity. Phinney (1990) and Bernal and Knight (1993) have given us useful reviews of the relevant literature on ethnic identification. As Phinney states, there is much research on how majority group members stereotype minorities, but much less on how minority-group members perceive themselves. The issues here have to do with the evaluation of self-worth in a social context that frequently discriminates against or disparages ethnic groups.

The difficulty with ethnic identification research to date is that there are widely differing approaches to the study of ethnic identity, since groups vary in their experiences as members of a minority group. This has resulted in diverse measurement instruments designed to assess ethnic identity. For example, Phinney and Rotheram (1987) and Bernal and Knight (1993) offer a useful starting point for understanding the various avenues that have been pursued in ethnic identification research.

Assessing the Response Patterns of Ethnic Respondents

The third set of questions in this section has to do with how ethnic respondents answer questions on objective instruments that do not coincide with the intent or content of the instrument. This is a serious matter that merits extensive discussion. One aspect of this question in the research literature concerns what is described as *response set preferences* in answering questions on various types of objective instrument. For example, some respondents choose the extremes on Likert-type scales, while others prefer the middle choice. Other informants respond to questions even if they have no opinion on the topic addressed in the survey instrument. Still other subjects offer *socially desirable or acquiescent* answers (yea-sayers) on an instrument or during an interview. These respondents use strategies in answering that make them look good in the eyes of the examiner or that reduce the possibility of more questions. Whatever the reason for response bias in answering, the crucial matter is that such bias results in error that can be consequential because it raises questions about the validity of the data obtained from respondents.

Response Set. Bachman and O'Malley (1984) have shown that African Americans have a preference for selecting the extreme responses on instruments that use a Likert-type scale. According to Bachman and O'Malley, this is why African Americans have sometimes been found to be higher in self-esteem than Whites. This extreme response set means that African Americans use the extreme scores (both positive and negative) more than Whites. The result, then, is a distribution of scores on a measure of self-esteem that may be a reflection of the response set rather than of actual between group differences on self-esteem.

Hui and Triandis (1989) have found that Hispanics are also more likely to use an extreme response set on a 5-point Likert scale than are non-Hispanic Whites. Similar findings are discussed by Marín and Marín (1991), who state that such extreme responding is particularly evident with low-acculturated Hispanic respondents. It is unknown whether other ethnic groups follow a pattern similar to African Americans and Hispanics in answering Likert-type questions.

The reason for being concerned about whether extreme response set has occurred is that such responding can seriously affect the results and interpretation of a study by giving a misleading impression of group variances. According to Bachman and O'Malley (1984), one solution to the problem of extreme set responding is to collapse the extreme category on each end of the scale (collapse "disagree" with "strongly disagree" on one end of the scale, and "agree" with "strongly agree" on the other). Scores between ethnic and majority group subjects then become more similar. However, before collapsing the extreme categories of a 5-point scale the investigator needs to be aware that compressing a scale from five to three categories results in what is no longer an interval scale, even though we may use it as such. A more satisfactory way to address the question of biased response pattern is to ensure that any scale includes a healthy dose of reverse-keyed items.

Another question that arises in this context that has remained largely unexplored is whether the race of the examiner influences response bias on the part of ethnic minority respondents. In other words, do minority respondents offer more or less face-saving positive responding when the examiner is of a race other than the respondent's? Thus, in the absence of a theory to explain why ethnic respondents prefer the extreme response categories, it may simply be sufficient to examine the pattern of responses on a Likert scale to determine whether extreme responding has occurred and to note this in reporting the results.

Social Desirability and Acquiescence. Another concern in conducting research with ethnic respondents has to do with the possible problem of social desirability or acquiescence in responding. Social desirability refers to the tendency to "deny socially undesirable traits and to claim socially desirable ones" (Nederhof, 1985, p. 264); responding in a socially desirable manner may occur consciously or unconsciously (Paulhus, 1984). Acquiescence

refers to a type of responding wherein respondents agree (yea-saying) with statements presented to them regardless of their content. Whether or not social desirability or acquiescence responding is deliberate matters little, since either way it creates a major concern in assessing the validity of self-reported measures (Rogler, Mroczek, Fellows, & Loftus, 2001).

The question of social desirability is raised here because ethnic differences in the tendency to offer socially desirable responses have been reported in the literature. For instance, Ross and Mirowsky (1984) administered a questionnaire with a battery of measures—including social desirability, locus of control, and psychological distress—to a sample of non-Hispanic Whites and Mexican Americans in El Paso, Texas. An additional sample of Mexicans from Juarez, Mexico, was administered the same battery of instruments, but in Spanish. It was found that the greatest level of social desirability was reported by the Mexican sample, followed in turn by the Mexican Americans, and finally the non-Hispanic Whites. Ross and Mirowsky also found an inverse relationship between social class and social desirability; individuals lower in socioeconomic status were most likely to present a pattern of socially desired responses.

Ross and Mirowsky (1984) interpreted their findings by suggesting that as we move down the socioeconomic ladder, acquiescence appears as a self-presentation strategy of those who are relatively powerless in society. According to these authors, people of greater powerlessness attempt to present a good face to those members of society whom they perceive to be higher in social standing in an effort to be more accepted in society.

In a reanalysis of four data sets that included responses by nearly 2,000 Hispanics and more than 14,000 non-Hispanic Whites, Marín, Gamba, and Marín (1992) reported that Hispanics showed a greater tendency to agree with items than did Whites. Two variables were found by Marín et al. to correlate with acquiescence responding. The first was educational level; those respondents, regardless of ethnicity, who possessed fewer than 12 years of formal schooling showed more response acquiescence than did the more highly educated respondents. The other variable was acculturation; it was found that Hispanics who were more acculturated evidenced less response acquiescence. An important cultural interpretation is offered by Marín and Marín (1991) to explain the findings. According to them, Hispanic culture promotes social acquiescence through the social script of *simpatia*, which "mandates politeness and respect and discourages criticism, confrontation, and assertiveness. Providing socially desirable answers could be a way to promote positive, smooth relationships between researcher and participant" (p. 106).

These few studies demonstrate the importance of understanding how the cultural background that the ethnic respondent brings to the task of completing an interview, survey, or questionnaire of various types determines the response patterns that emerge. Equipped with this understanding, the investigator might anticipate responses quite different from those obtained from the White respondents on whom most instruments are standardized. Clearly, more research is required on the question of ethnic differences in response patterns on objective measurement instruments.

Another consideration in this discussion pertains to approaching use of an instrument with members of an ethnic group for which the scale was not normed. It is always a good practice to determine the adequacy of such a scale with the ethnic group in question. We recommend at least two methods for doing this: Cronbach alpha (internal-consistency reliability) and exploratory factor analysis. In the earlier discussion of a study by Knight et al. (1992), we showed how Knight and his colleagues tested their instruments for their appropriateness with ethnic samples. The discussion that follows elaborates on the approach taken by Knight et al. and offers suggestions for using instruments appropriately.

Internal-Consistency Reliability. It is good practice for researchers to question the reliability of their instruments whenever they conduct a study involving ethnic samples. At a minimum, Cronbach alpha for internal-consistency reliability should be computed on the scales used in a study. This should be done for each of the ethnic groups *separately* if two or more groups are being compared. On the basis of the resulting alpha coefficients, the researcher must decide whether to proceed with the study or search for a more appropriate instrument.

A frequently asked question is, What is the minimum acceptable level of reliability to gauge the suitability of a scale for use with a sample? Pedhazur and Pedhazur-Schmelkin (1991) maintain that the acceptability of a reliability estimate depends on the "decisions made on the basis of the scores and the possible consequences of the decisions" (p. 109). Thus, the reliability of an instrument should be as high as possible (minimum of $r = .70$) for more consequential (high-stakes) program or policy decisions, but it can be lower ($r = .50$) for research purposes involving low-stakes outcomes to be made about assessing differences between groups on a psychological or educational measure where no intervention is planned.

If the reliability estimates are low for an ethnic group, then it is always the responsibility of the investigator to point out that the estimates were low and offer caution regarding any interpretations to be drawn from the study. An item-by-item analysis may also enable the researcher to understand why a particular scale is more tenuous for one population than for another.

In conducting quantitative research with ethnic populations, it is also essential to determine, whenever possible, whether the constructs being measured by the instruments have the same meaning for each ethnic group being studied. Depending on the instrument in question and the sample size, it may be possible to examine the construct validity of instruments across groups by means of exploratory factor analysis.

Exploratory Factor Analysis. It is commonplace today for many of our educational and psychological scales to be developed using methods of factor analysis. For example, a researcher may have a theory about the underlying construct of learning anxiety, or about which attitudinal predispositions are important in learning a foreign language (Gardner, 1985). Armed with a theory, the researcher develops a set of items that appear to measure the constructs of learning anxiety and attitude toward learning a second language. The items are then formatted into an objective questionnaire and (usually) arranged using a Likert scoring continuum; respondents are instructed to check whether they agree with each item on the continuum, which is arranged from "strongly agree" to "strongly disagree." The instrument is administered to a large number of respondents and the data analyzed by means of a factor analysis. Factor analysis is a data-analytic procedure for arriving "at a relatively small number of components that will extract most of the variance of a relatively large set of indicators (variables, items)" (Pedhazur & Pedhazur-Schmelkin, 1991, p. 598).

There are several types of factor analysis, but the one most commonly used in the literature is called principal components factor analysis with Varimax rotation. The important thing about this statistical procedure is that it produces clusters of items that are statistically independent of each other. The researcher is then able to examine the items within a cluster and determine whether they fit the construct the researcher has in mind. For example, if the researcher believes that two separate constructs (say, anxiety and predisposition toward second-language learning) underlie the learning of English by nonnative speakers, she can then examine the clusters of items to determine whether the two key constructs are reflected in the items. Technically speaking, those items that contribute to (or load on) a component (or factor) using some criterion level such as 0.30 are then retained and those that do not are discarded. In this way, scales are developed that can be refined further to determine whether they measure the construct in question.

To continue our example, suppose we have developed an instrument using factor analysis that has two subscales: one measures learning anxiety and the other attitudinal disposition toward second-language acquisition. We then hypothesize that a good second-language learner would be characterized as showing little learning anxiety and a positive attitude toward learning a new language.

We can test this hypothesis by administering our new instrument to a large group of Latino immigrant students enrolled in high school ESL classes. As dependent measures, we could use class grades and a measure of English language oral proficiency. If we find that students who score low on anxiety and high on disposition to learn English also have higher grades and higher oral proficiency assessments in English than students who show a pattern of high anxiety and low disposition to learn English, then we may have confidence in our instruments and in their utility to measure our key constructs of anxiety and attitude toward learning of a second language.

The proof of how good our instrument is, however, depends on whether the constructs hold up in the same way with other groups of English language learners. Thus we might then administer our questionnaire to a group of newcomer Pakistani students. However, bear in mind that the original items were most likely developed with Spanish speakers in mind and written and administered in Spanish. Now, to use the instrument with a new group of English language learners, the items must be translated into Urdu (following the guidelines for translation discussed earlier in this chapter). After the translated questionnaire has been administered to the students, a new factor analysis should be carried out to ensure that our underlying constructs of anxiety and predisposition to learning a second language are applicable to this new population of English language learners. Accordingly, if factor analysis indicates a similar factor structure as that found with Spanish speakers, then we can be confident that our measuring instrument is suitable for cross-cultural generalization. Bear in mind that the factor loadings (the items) may not be identical in our two respondent groups. However, if there is sufficient similarity in how the items load on the two subscales, then we can have confidence in our constructs, in how we have measured them, and in the translation equivalence across two quite distinct languages (Pedhazur & Pedhazur-Schmelkin, 1991).

On the other hand, if a factor structure emerges that is different from that found with the Latino students, we need to rethink our constructs and how we define them operationally so that they are measurable. Perhaps there is an issue in the way we have attempted to arrive at equivalence of meaning in our translation of the instrument. This is a common problem in cross-cultural research. Or perhaps the worldviews and attitudes toward learning generally of the other sample populations are so distinct that our constructs do not make sense to one of the groups of students for whom we are attempting to find the best pedagogical strategies for teaching English.

In sum, quantitative research with culturally and linguistically diverse populations is not always easy. Issues of instruments and their external validity and reliability with diverse populations must be a core concern to the educational researcher intent on studying ethnic groups (Sue, 1999). The issues are by no means insurmountable, and various strategies have been offered for thinking constructively about the appropriateness of instruments and ways of collecting data that will prove to be meaningful to the investigator and the community of respondents involved in the research (Messick, 1995).

CONCLUSION

This chapter has covered a number of critical issues that must be considered in doing quantitative research with ethnic minority populations. The chapter opened with discussion of the social construction of knowledge and how two research approaches have shaped, in different ways, how quantitative research is conducted. Central to this discussion is the Eurocentric paradigm. In recent years, it has been called into question because of potential bias in favor of White middle-class (male) college students, who are used as the standard by which to evaluate research findings and to draw inferences to a broader population. Critics of this approach (Sears, 1986; Sue, 1999) have pointed to the dangers for both social sciences generally and cross-cultural research specifically. In opposition to this approach, ethnic minority researchers and educational scholars have called for a shift away from the Eurocentric paradigm and moved toward more ethnic-sensitive paradigms (Afrocentric, for one). Advocates of these new paradigms maintain that standards should lie with the specific ethnic group in question and that they should be based on the values and worldviews of that ethnic group alone. In addition, researchers (Azibo, 1996; Marín and Marín, 1991; Rogler, 1989) have called for more culturally sensitive approaches to quantitative research with ethnic communities.

In line with the culturally sensitive approaches to quantitative research, the critical challenges to conducting quantitative research with ethnic groups were identified and discussed in the chapter. These challenges involve (a) the importance of identifying, describing, and selecting a sample; (b) understanding of the heterogeneity within an ethnic group; and (c) the difficulties posed by language differences. The importance of each challenge was discussed, pointing out that they are not insurmountable and in fact pose no serious threat to the integrity of a research study so long as there is understanding of the ethnic group being studied.

A recommendation was made that, whenever possible, members of the ethnic community under study be incorporated into the planning and implementation of the research project. This increases the potential for more relevant research questions and approaches. Further, a more appropriate or bias-free sample may be a likely outcome if the ethnic community is involved in the research enterprise. Also, interpretation of certain findings can be enhanced if "community insiders" are part of the research team.

The final section of this chapter was devoted to issues of instrumentation and measurement. Quantitative research is only as good as the data on which it is based, and this means special attention must be given to the instruments used in research with ethnic populations. The importance of measurement was illustrated by a review of research involving achievement and self-esteem scales. This was followed by a discussion of acculturation and ethnic identification, which have emerged as two central constructs in ethnic-related research. It was shown that there are conceptual reasons for giving significant attention to acculturation and ethnic identification in

our research. This section closed with a discussion of response bias and patterns of socially desirable (acquiescence) responding that have been found in some research with African American and Hispanic informants. This could be a serious concern both in interpreting findings and in deciding what strategies should be followed in future development of instruments for use with ethnic populations.

The chapter closed with two analytic strategies to determine whether the ethnic informants show similar patterns of reliability and interpretation of specific items on a scale. These strategies involved internal-consistency reliability and exploratory factor analysis. This discussion was intended to suggest that the research base with ethnic minority populations can be improved by giving serious attention to the psychometric properties of all of the instruments used in educational research.

References

Alatorre Alva, S. (1991). Academic invulnerability among Mexican-American students: The importance of protective resources and appraisals. *Hispanic Journal of Behavioral Sciences, 13,* 18–34.

Allport, G. (1937). *Personality: A psychological interpretation.* New York: Henry Holt.

American Psychological Association. (2000). *Guidelines for research in ethnic minority communities.* Washington, DC: Author.

American Psychological Association. (2001). *Publication Manual of the American Psychological Association* (5th ed.). Washington, DC: Author.

Arellano, A. R., & Padilla, A. M. (1996). Academic invulnerability among a select group of Latino university students. *Hispanic Journal of Behavioral Sciences, 18,* 485–507.

August, D., & Hakuta, K. (1997). *Improving schooling for language-minority children: A research agenda.* Washington, DC: National Academy Press.

Azibo, D. (1996). *African psychology in historical perspective and related commentary.* Trenton, NJ: African World Press.

Bachman, J. G., & O'Malley, P. M. (1984). Black-White differences in self-esteem: Are they affected by response styles? *American Journal of Sociology, 90,* 624–639.

Banks, J. A. (1993). The canon debate, knowledge construction, and multicultural education. *Educational Researcher, 22*(6), 4–14.

Bernal, M. E., & Knight, G. P. (Eds.). (1993). *Ethnic identity: Formation and transmission among Hispanics and other minorities.* Albany, NY: State University of New York Press.

Berndt, T. J., Cheung, P. C., Lau, S., Hau, K., & Lew, W.-J.F. (1993). Perceptions of parenting in mainland China, Taiwan, and Hong Kong: Sex differences and societal differences. *Developmental Psychology, 29,* 156–164.

Berry, J. (1990). Psychology of acculturation: Understanding individuals moving between cultures. In R. Brislin (Ed.), *Applied cross-cultural psychology* (pp. 232–253). Thousand Oaks, CA: Sage.

Bond, L. A. (1988). Teaching developmental psychology. In P. A. Bronstein & K. Quina (Eds.), *Teaching a psychology of people:*

Resources for gender and sociocultural awareness (pp. 45–52). Washington, DC: American Psychological Association.

Bourhis, R. Y., Moise, L. C., Perreault, S., & Senecal, S. (1997). Towards an interactive acculturation model: A social psychological approach. *International Journal of Psychology, 32,* 369–386.

Buriel, R. (1984). Integration with traditional Mexican American culture and sociocultural adjustment. In J. L. Martinez, Jr., & R. H. Mendoza (Eds.), *Chicano psychology* (2nd ed., pp. 95–130). Orlando, FL: Academic Press.

Buriel, R., & Cardoza, D. (1988). Sociocultural correlates of achievement among three generations of Mexican American high school seniors. *American Educational Research Journal, 25,* 177–192.

Buriel, R., & Cardoza, D. (1993). Mexican American ethnic labeling: An intrafamilial and intergenerational analysis. In M. E. Bernal & G. P. Knight (Eds.), *Ethnic identity: Formation and transmission among Hispanics and other minorities* (pp. 197–210). Albany, NY: State University of New York Press.

Campbell, D. T., & Stanley, J. C. (1966). *Experimental and quasi-experimental designs for research.* Skokie, IL: Rand McNally.

Caplan, N., Whitmore, J. K., & Choy, M. H. (1989). *The boat people and achievement in America.* Ann Arbor, MI: University of Michigan Press.

Clark, K. B. (1965). *Dark ghetto: Dilemmas of social power.* New York: HarperCollins.

Cuellar, I., Harris, L. C., & Jasso, R. (1980). An acculturation scale for Mexican American normal and clinical populations. *Hispanic Journal of Behavioral Sciences, 2,* 199–217.

Culver, S. M., Wolfle, L. M., & Cross, L. H. (1990). Testing a model of teaching satisfaction for Blacks and Whites. *American Educational Research Journal, 27,* 323–349.

Dana, R. H. (1997). *Understanding cultural identity in intervention and assessment.* Thousand Oaks, CA: Sage.

Dehue, T. (2001). Establishing the experimental society: The historical origin of social experimentation according to the randomized controlled design. *American Journal of Psychology, 114,* 283–302.

Dornbusch, S. M., Ritter, P. L., Leiderman, H., Roberts, D. F., & Fraleigh, M. J. (1987). The relation of parenting style to adolescent school performance. *Child Development, 58,* 1244–1257.

Duran, B. J., & Weffer, R. E. (1992). Immigrants' aspirations, high school process, and academic outcomes. *American Educational Research Journal, 29,* 163–181.

Finn, J. D., & Achilles, C. M. (1990). Answers and questions about class size: A statewide experiment. *American Educational Research Journal, 27,* 557–577.

Flynn, J. R. (1991). *Asian Americans: Achievement beyond IQ.* Mahwah, NJ: Erlbaum.

Frisby, C. L. (2001). Academic achievement. In L. Suzuki, J. G. Ponterotto, & P. J. Meller (Eds.), *Handbook of multicultural assessment* (2nd ed., pp. 541–568). San Francisco: Jossey-Bass.

Gardner, R. C. (1985). *Social psychology and second language learning: The role of attitudes and motivation.* London: Arnold.

Gibson, M. A. (1988). *Accommodation without assimilation: Sikh immigrants in an American high school.* Ithaca, NY: Cornell University Press.

Gopnik, A., & Meltzoff, A. N. (1992). Categorization and naming: Basic-level sorting in 18-month-olds and its relation to language. *Child Development, 63,* 1091–1103.

Griffen-Pierson, S. (1990). The competitiveness questionnaire: A measure of two components of competitiveness. *Measurement and Evaluation in Counseling and Development, 23,* 108–115.

Gutierrez, J., & Sameroff, A. (1990). Determinants of complexity in Mexican-American and Anglo-American mothers' conceptions of child development. *Child Development, 61,* 384–394.

Gutierrez, J., Sameroff, A., & Karrer, B. M. (1988). Acculturation and SES effects on Mexican-American parents' concepts of development. *Child Development, 59,* 250–255.

Harter, S. (1982). The perceived competence scale for children. *Child Development, 53,* 87–97.

Harter, S. (1999). *The construction of the self: A developmental perspective.* New York: Guilford Press.

Helms, J. E. (1992). Why is there no study of cultural equivalence in standardized cognitive ability testing? *American Psychologist, 47,* 1083–1101.

Hui, C. H., & Triandis, H. (1989). Effects of culture and response format on extreme response style. *Journal of Cross-Cultural Psychology, 20,* 296–309.

Johnson, B. (2001). Toward a new classification of nonexperimental quantitative research. *Educational Researcher, 30,* 3–13.

Kamin, L. J. (1974). *The science and politics of I.Q.* Mahwah, NJ: Erlbaum.

Keefe, S. E., & Padilla, A. M. (1987). *Chicano ethnicity.* Albuquerque, NM: University of New Mexico Press.

Kerlinger, F. N. (1979). *Behavioral research.* Austin, TX: Holt, Rinehart and Winston.

Kim, U. (1988). *Acculturation of Korean immigrants to Canada: Psychological, demographic and behavioural profiles of emigrating Koreans, non-emigrating Koreans and Korean-Canadians.* Unpublished doctoral dissertation, Queen's University, Kingston, Ontario, Canada.

Knight, G. P., Tein, J. Y., Shell, R., & Roosa, M. (1992). The cross-ethnic equivalence of parenting and family interaction measures among Hispanic and Anglo American families. *Child Development, 63,* 1392–1403.

Kraft, C. L. (1991). What makes a successful Black student on a predominantly White campus? *American Educational Research Journal, 28,* 423–444.

Kuhn, T. S. (1970). *The structure of scientific revolutions* (2nd ed.). Chicago: University of Chicago Press.

Lamborn, S. D., Mounts, N. S., Steinberg, L., & Dornbusch, S. M. (1991). Patterns of competence and adjustment among adolescents from authoritative, authoritarian, indulgent, and neglectful families. *Child Development, 62,* 1049–1065.

Landrine, H., & Klonoff, E. A. (1996). *African American acculturation.* Thousand Oaks, CA: Sage.

Laosa, L. (1982). School, occupation, culture and the family: The impact of parental schooling on the parent-child relationship. *Journal of Educational Psychology, 74,* 791–827.

Lee, J. (2002). Racial and ethnic achievement gap trends: Reversing the progress toward equity. *Educational Researcher, 31,* 3–12.

de la Luz Reyes, M., & Halcón, J. J. (1988). Racism in academia: The old wolf revisited. *Harvard Educational Review, 58,* 299–314.

Marchant, G. J. (1991). A profile of motivation, self-perceptions and achievement in black urban elementary children. *Urban Review, 23,* 83–99.

Marín, G. (1993). Influence of acculturation on familialism and self-identification among Hispanics. In M. E. Bernal & G. P. Knight (Eds.), *Ethnic identity: Formation and transmission among Hispanics and other minorities* (pp. 181–196). Albany, NY: State University of New York Press.

Marín, G., Gamba, R. J., & Marín, B. V. (1992). Extreme response style and acquiescence among Hispanics: The role of acculturation and education. *Journal of Cross-Cultural Psychology, 23,* 498–509.

Marín, G., & Marín, B. V. (1991). *Research with Hispanic populations.* Thousand Oaks, CA: Sage.

Martinez, R., & Dukes, R. L. (1987). Race, gender, and self-esteem among youth. *Hispanic Journal of Behavioral Sciences, 9,* 427–443.

Matsumoto, D. (1994). *Cultural influences on research methods and statistics.* Pacific Grove, CA: Brooks/Cole.

Messick, S. (1995). Validity of psychological assessment: Validation of inferences from persons' responses and performances as scientific inquiry into score meaning. *American Psychologist, 50,* 741–749.

Moyerman, D. R., & Forman, B. D. (1992). Acculturation and adjustment: A meta-analytic study. *Hispanic Journal of Behavioral Sciences, 14,* 163–200.

Nederhof, A. J. (1985). Methods of coping with social desirability: A review. *Journal of European Social Psychology, 15,* 263–280.

Oetting, E. R., & Beauvais, F. (1990/1991). Orthogonal cultural identification theory: The cultural identification of minority adolescents. *International Journal of the Addictions, 25,* 655–685.

Olmedo, E. (1979). Acculturation: A psychometric perspective. *American Psychologist, 34,* 1061–1070.

Padilla, A. M. (Ed.). (1980). *Acculturation: Theory, models, and some new findings.* Boulder, CO: Westview Press.

Padilla, A. M. (1988). Early psychological assessment of Mexican-American children. *Journal of the History of the Behavioral Sciences, 24,* 111–117.

Padilla, A. M., & Gonzalez, R. (2001). Academic performance of immigrant and U.S. born Mexican heritage students: Effects of schooling in Mexico and bilingual/English language instruction. *American Educational Research Journal, 38,* 727–742.

Parham, T. A., White, J. L., & Ajamu, A. (1999). *The psychology of Blacks: An African-centered perspective.* Upper Saddle River, NJ: Prentice Hall.

Paulhus, D. L. (1984). Two-component models of socially desirable responding. *Journal of Personality and Social Psychology, 46*, 598–609.

Pedhazur, E. J., & Pedhazur-Schmelkin, L. (1991). *Measurement, design, and analysis: An integrated approach* (2nd ed.). Mahwah, NJ: Erlbaum.

Phinney, J. S. (1990). Ethnic identity in adolescents and adults: Review of research. *Psychological Bulletin, 108*, 499–514.

Phinney, J. S., & Rotheram, M. J. (Eds.). (1987). *Children's ethnic socialization*. Thousand Oaks, CA: Sage.

Plutchik, R. (1974). *Foundations of experimental research*. New York: HarperCollins.

Portes, A., & Rumbaut, R. G. (2001). *Legacies: The story of the immigrant second generation*. Berkeley, CA: University of California Press.

Richman, A. L., Miller, P. M., & LeVine, R. A. (1993). Cultural and educational variations in maternal responsiveness. *Developmental Psychology, 28*, 614–621.

Rodriguez, C. E. (1989). *Puerto Ricans born in the U.S.A*. Boston: Unwin Hyman.

Rogler, L. H. (1989). The meaning of culturally sensitive research in mental health. *American Journal of Psychiatry, 146*, 296–303.

Rogler, L. H. (1999). Methodological sources of cultural insensitivity in mental health research. *American Psychologist, 54*, 424–433.

Rogler, L. H., Cortes, D. E., & Malgady, R. G. (1991). Acculturation and mental health status among Hispanics: Convergence and new directions for research. *American Psychologist, 46*, 585–597.

Rogler, L. H., Mroczek, D. K., Fellows, M., & Loftus, S. T. (2001). The neglect of response bias in mental health research. *Journal of Nervous and Mental Disease, 189*, 182–187.

Rosenberg, M. (1979). *Conceiving the self*. New York: Basic Books.

Ross, C. E., & Mirowsky, J. (1984). Socially desirable response and acquiescence in a cross-cultural survey of mental health. *Journal of Health and Social Behavior, 25*, 189–197.

Rotenberg, K. J., & Cranwell, F. R. (1989). Self-concept in American Indian and White children. *Journal of Cross-Cultural Psychology, 20*, 39–53.

Sears, D. O. (1986). College sophomores in the laboratory: Influence of a narrow data based on social psychology's view of human nature. *Journal of Personality & Social Psychology, 51*, 515–530.

Shen, B., & Takeuchi, D. T. (2001). A structured model of acculturation and mental health status among Chinese Americans. *American Journal of Community Psychology, 29*, 387–418.

Stevenson, H. W., Chen, C., & Uttal, D. H. (1990). Beliefs and achievement: A study of Black, White, and Hispanic children. *Child Development, 61*, 508–523.

Stigler, J. W., Smith, S., & Mao, L. (1985). The self-perception of competence by Chinese children. *Child Development, 56*, 1259–1270.

Strom, R., Johnson, A., Strom, S., & Strom, P. (1992). Educating gifted Hispanic children and their parents. *Hispanic Journal of Behavioral Sciences, 14*, 383–393.

Suarez, Z. E. (1993). Cuban Americans: From golden exiles to social undesirables. In H. P. McAdoo (Ed.), *Family ethnicity: Strength in diversity* (pp. 164–176). Thousand Oaks, CA: Sage.

Suarez-Orozco, M. M. (1989). *Central American refugees and U.S. high schools: A psychosocial study of motivation and achievement*. Stanford, CA: Stanford University Press.

Sue, S. (1999). Science, ethnicity, and bias: Where have we gone wrong? *American Psychologist, 54*, 1070–1077.

Sue, S., & Okazaki, S. (1990). Asian American educational achievements: A phenomenon in search of an explanation. *American Psychologist, 45*, 913–920.

Suinn, R. M., Richard-Figueroa, K., Lew, S., & Vigil, P. (1987). The Suinn-Lew Asian self-identity acculturation scale: An initial report. *Educational and Psychological Measurement, 47*, 401–407.

Valencia, R. R., & Suzuki, L. A. (2001). *Intelligence testing and minority students: Foundations, performance factors, and assessment issues*. Thousand Oaks, CA: Sage.

Wentzel, K. R. (1991). Relations between social competence and academic achievement in early adolescence. *Child Development, 62*, 1066–1078.

Wilkinson, L. (1999). Statistical methods in psychology journals: Guidelines and explanations. *American Psychologist, 54*, 594–604.

Wylie, R. (1979). *The self-concept: Vol. 2. Theory and research on selected topics*. Lincoln, NB: University of Nebraska Press.

Yee, A. H. (1992). Asians as stereotypes and students: Misperceptions that persist. *Educational Psychology Review, 4*, 95–132.

Yoder, J. D., & Kahn, A. S. (1993). Working toward an inclusive psychology of women. *American Psychologist, 48*, 846–850.

8

ETHNOGRAPHY IN COMMUNITIES

Learning the Everyday Life of America's Subordinated Youth

Shirley Brice Heath

Stanford University

The concept of *community* has been central to the American ethos since the settlement of the colonies, both as a fundamental idea and as an actual physical construct grounded in the interconnectedness of place, people, history, and purpose. In the widely read book of the mid-1980s, *Habits of the Heart* (Bellah, Madsen, Sullivan, Swidler, & Tipton, 1985), the authors observe that "the community of civic-minded, interlocking families rooted in two hundred fifty years of tradition does not really exist" (p. 11) for most Americans. Instead, a wide array of organizations and regroupings serve to bond people together and include their individual voices in the "currents of communal conversation" (p. 135). Some of these communities are intentionally identified around their founders' central purpose (e.g., Mothers Against Drunk Driving). Others bear more general labels and are classified together on the basis of general perceptions about their members' shared beliefs and values (e.g., the Christian community, the gay community, the Hispanic community, or the nation as community). Still others seem shaped around a bond that unites some people and differentiates them from others at particular stages of their life (e.g., support groups, computer networks). In spite of the proliferation of what are often either temporarily or loosely aggregated communities, the quest continues for the utopia of the ideal community as a place of roots and connection, linking people to cycles of nature and grounding them in attachments to their neighbors.

Since the beginnings of social science, scholars, as well as the public at large, have quarreled over what makes and sustains *community*. (Arensberg, 1961, remains perhaps the most comprehensive discussion of this concern,

particularly with respect to the community as a unit of analysis.) Of particular debate has been the question of whether or not modernity and urban industrial life within nation-states force a fundamental shift away from the agricultural bases of community: shared territory, kinship, close links to nature's cycles, and consensual group solidarity. Ferdinand Toennies (1887/1963) distinguished *Gemeinschaft* (community)—with emphasis on clearly defined social structure and loyalties to close personal relationships—from *Gesellschaft* (society), or impersonally, even artificially, contracted associations. Emile Durkheim's (1933) analysis of organic and mechanical solidarity stressed that within modern urban society both psychological consensus and interdependence resulting from the division of labor coexisted as two aspects of the same reality. Yet some social scientists have continued to contend that the larger society and mass communication have replaced communal associations of primary affiliations, while others argue that new "intentional communities," by their interactive nature, achieve the goals of face-to-face, homegrown, territorially based nature communities (Gusfield, 1975; Warren, 1978; Wilkinson, 1986). Pointing to the power of all-inclusive public interests and the ideology of community, B. Anderson (1983) has maintained that nations are communities because their citizens have faith in the "steady, anonymous, simultaneous activity" of fellow members moving through "homogeneous, empty time" (p. 31).

What, then, does *community* mean? This question is more difficult to answer as the 21st century opens than is the reshaped question of *who* does community mean? Rare is the contemporary individual who will claim membership in a community based on physical proximity, residence, or even face-to-face contact. Few people live close by groups with which they feel the strongest communal association. Hence, large societal institutions of all sorts—athletic, ethnic, recreational, occupational, religious, and professional—allow individuals to branch off to create their own subgroups called "communities" that provide emotional and common-interest ties as well as a sense of subjective wholeness.

This chapter considers first a brief chronology of community within American life and the influence of ideals remaining from this history. Next is a quick look through ethnographic portrayals of different kinds of contemporary communities and their ways of socializing individuals into their membership. Without the benefit of early shared learning experiences gained by playing in the same block, walking to the same school, and sharing backyards—as is the case in communities of close spatial connection—members come to association as individuals who must often undergo a self-conscious socialization to new affiliations and self-identities. All of the portrayals in this section include subtexts of members' collective views of learning through formal and nonformal education. Finally, implications of current community life for the future of research, policy, and practice in multiculturalism or pluralism in American education close the chapter.

A STEP BACK TO COMMUNITY ROOTS

In rural parts of the nation during its first 100 years, separate households at distant spots over plains and in isolated mountain hollows held their sense of connectedness by bringing residents together during particular seasons and for rites of intensification—weddings, family reunions, barn raisings, and celebrations of harvests. During the early Industrial Revolution, American villages grew up around mills, and millworker and mill owner lived in sight of each other. Laborers, inventors, entrepreneurs, managers, investors, and those who hung on around the town's edges shared common spaces and came together less and less often as a group, except during those occasions of sponsorship by the town's industrialists or mill owners (Hall et al., 1987; Hareven & Langenbach, 1978; Wallace, 1978).

In ensuing decades, as more and more towns began to dot the countryside, weekend events, such as baseball games, parades, carnivals, and celebrations of school or church affairs, divided along gender, class, and racial lines. Competitions of male teams in local athletic events were sustained in large part by the "benevolent work" of women in local institutions, such as churches, schools, and community centers, which facilitated occasions of public congregation, celebration, and recreation. Wealthier families

formed clubs, set on great expanses of land near their residential areas, to provide exclusive recreational facilities for themselves. Blacks and Whites worked, worshiped, lived, and played separately throughout not only the South but also most parts of the United States. In recently admitted states or areas preparing for statehood in the Southwest, Mexican and Anglo families often lived in separate towns despite the symbiotic nature of their economic contributions to the region's development (Camarillo, 1979; Steiner, 1969).

Despite the untenable conditions of slavery and racial division, strong coalitions of community evolved across regions and in the face of hostile opposition. These came first through the Underground Railroad and later through religious and political affiliations—often covertly and always from a sense of critical human need. In the South slavery created communities spatially based on plantations and, for freed Blacks, in the back alleys such as Savannah and Richmond. As early as the 1830s more than 300,000 free Blacks lived in the United States, many forming strong middle- and upper-class communities that sustained churches, social clubs, libraries, and literary groups, primarily in northern cities. Almost entirely neglected in accounts of American history, these groups shaped key institutions, such as antislavery societies, the Black press, professional groups, and literary journals, that played significant roles in creating the cultural and social landscape during Reconstruction and into the 20th century (DuBois, 1899; Edwards, 1959; Frazier, 1947, 1957; Gatewood, 1990).

Following the Civil War and again during the period between World Wars I and II, migration to northern cities resulted in urban zones occupied exclusively by Blacks (Drake & Cayton, 1945/1962). Poverty and employment in the lowest-paying economic niches helped create ghettos of Blacks who came to compete with immigrants and refugees from Europe in the first half of the 20th century for jobs, local business development, and decent housing. Entertainment, newspapers, radio stations, occupational niches, and union memberships divided along racial, ethnic, and linguistic lines—Black, Italian, Irish, Polish, Scandinavian (Myrdal, 1944; Fishman, 1966).

Immigrant newcomers marked their identities in the architecture of homes and churches, choices of neighborhood stores and wares, and preferences for music, food, and recreational pastimes. In the late 19th century, cities such as New York, Cleveland, and San Francisco developed community schools that taught in the languages of the students until the xenophobia of World War I forced the reduction of publicly supported efforts to retain the linguistic identities of immigrant communities (Fishman, 1966). The explosion of suburbs after World War II further scattered the face-to-face commonalities of old urban neighborhoods, as the second generation of immigrants moved out to shape their lives around their chosen new American identity and to shed much of the language, traditional lore, and values of the "old country."

Social Science in the Study of Community and Society

Dynamic changes in the factors that brought people together in American life captured the attention of social scientists from the second decade of the 20th century through the 1950s. At the University of Chicago, Robert Park and his colleagues in urban sociology opened up some of the complexities of the urban community and began the tradition of the detailed case study and ecological approach to communities that influenced social scientists such as David Riesman (1950), Oscar Lewis (1951), and Robert Redfield (1941). Sociologists described Midwestern towns, documenting the increasing social stratification that created separate communities of distinct values and institutional affiliations even for those of the same ethnic and national backgrounds (Lynd & Lynd, 1929; West, 1945).

From the University of North Carolina in Chapel Hill, a team of researchers scattered across the South to document the varieties of types of communities there (Gilman, 1956; H. Lewis, 1955; Morland, 1958). Other social scientists began to study communities-in-the-making and subgroups such as gangs in urban society, purposefully formed by young and old for mutual protection of urban territory and maintenance of separate identities from other groups in poverty (Thrasher, 1927; Whyte, 1943). By the end of the 1950s the variation in what counted as *community* for social scientists ranged from occupational groupings (such as hospitals; see Becker, 1961/1976) to media-constructed entities (such as "Hollywood"; see Powdermaker, 1950).

Absence of a consensual operational definition of *community* continued to hinder social scientists from reaching any agreement on unit of analysis. Certain obvious, older, traditional requisites of community—such as territoriality, contact with the cycles of nature, and inclusion of more than one generation—were weakened considerably in favor of interactionist perspectives that focused on attachments and common processes of formation and sustenance grounded in communication. The old issue of whether or not community disappears as society expands its influence appeared repeatedly. Throughout the 20th century in the United States, as government bureaucracies seemed to take over more and more matters previously handled informally in face-to-face encounters, social scientists periodically questioned how, and indeed if, little communities could persist with so many forces of government and mass communication at work in the society at large. Some social commentators and scholars saw this intrusion of external "problem solvers" as killing off just

what communities needed for their survival: the seeking of collective solutions to their own problems. As controls of the local group over the behavior of its members weakened, communities died and larger frames of reference and temporary memberships took over former loyalties (Gallaher & Padfield, 1980).

Little Communities at the End of the 20th Century

The work of anthropologist Robert Redfield in Mexico, perhaps more than that of any other social scientist, brought together conceptual bases for distinguishing among the many types of "little communities" and the conditions of their development and persistence. In the scattered small groups of the Yucatan peninsula (1941) Redfield found what members called "*communidades*," and characterized these in ways that foreshadowed what would by the end of the 20th century characterize communities in North America—spatially scattered individuals brought together through communication networks and as face-to-face groups primarily in seasonal rites of intensification. He noted that habits of travel, different occupational patterns, and the mix of separate groups through intermarriage and resettlement would increasingly make of community a *sense* of bondedness rather than a *place* of mutual dwelling (Redfield, 1956/1960).

His views were echoed in work of the 1970s and 1980s that documented the diversity of Americans' responses to the need to build new shapes and formulations of group bondings from the ashes of the traditional community. Groups, seeing themselves primarily in terms of their occupations and wishing to set apart their specific abilities and interests, included in their reasons for existence not only socialization opportunities for their increased professionalization, but also advocacy and recreational goals (Salaman, 1974). Having much in common with the Underground Railroad community of the 19th century, numerous late 20th-century communities formed themselves around crises, feelings of common suffering and struggle, and the need to regroup outside "ordinary" communities to compete and survive. (Wallace's 1970 study of the rise and rebirth of the Seneca Iroquois through religion is an example of such work, as is Kreiger, 1983, a study of a lesbian community.) "Dying" communities, those attempting rebirth, and those struggling to be born all work to sustain membership and loyalties, and to overcome insecurities that spring from a lack of economic, natural, and human resources (Gallaher & Padfield, 1980, provide 10 studies of such communities beset with such problems as lack of economic and technological resources, ethnic and social class conflicts, and demographic isolation).

As the 21st century begins, membership in a community with no territorial basis or shared early socialization experience occurs at least as frequently as groupings that do bear these traditional features. Shared bonds of national origin, ethnicity, and religion are diminishing for many who find that their primary glue of community is instead a self-conscious sense of purpose and self-interest, as well as socioeconomic class ties and degree of assimilation of or resistance to mainstream values and behaviors. In earlier decades individuals were drawn together through a sense of common history; now a sense of disparate present and diverging future leads to purposeful choices of language, norms, and goals that separate many Americans from the primary-group connections of former generations.

During the civil rights era and through the 1970s, inner cities depended on the power of their subdivisions into zones of similarity in ethnicity, race, language, and religion to make self-affirming declarations (e.g., Black Is Beautiful) and to display pride in their differences. Increase in Black pride soon brought numerous efforts to revive ethnic heritages and to celebrate diversities of history, dress, music, costume, food, and art. Federal efforts, such as the Ethnic Heritage Act, encouraged artists and art institutions to take seriously the promotion of diverse art forms and traditions to widespread public attention (Kilbride, Goodale, & Ameisen, 1990). Professional and college athletics expanded efforts to recruit players from Black and Hispanic communities and to provide new opportunities for financial and educational advancement. Public consciousness about overt discrimination in public spheres, especially employment, real estate, and education, opened new possibilities of social and geographic movement to members of populations formerly subordinated in and excluded from these areas.

Within a decade these societal changes—often effected in the interest of desegregation, civil rights, and affirmative action—brought drastic shifts in allegiances to spatial communities that had previously been *all*-Black, *all*-Hispanic, *all*-Polish, *all*-Chinese (Alba, 1990; Blackwell, 1984). New economic possibilities meant chances for different patterns of residence and recreation; families began to move into new neighborhoods, many of which had only recently been the urban sites to which earlier European immigrants had come from their urban ghettos. Middle-class neighborhoods on the outskirts of cities or in towns across America were no longer predictable from household to household as to culture, race, religion, or language. Friendships came more and more to be formed through work and less through common place of residence. Telephones increasingly provided the interstices of the networks held together by communication. Soon computer networks greatly supplemented the telephone as a communication net that bound together individuals who never saw each other but coalesced around common information needs and goals. As corporations

and factories steadily sought regions that would offer cheaper labor and better tax incentives, employees at executive and managerial levels were relocated frequently about the country and found safety in community formations that centered around common interests—recreational, religious, aesthetic, civic, and professional. In addition, "intentional" communities sprouted up, linking themselves together through what they termed "the technologies of cooperation and electronic communications" (see *Communities*, 1992).

In the 1960s and 1970s, communities of poverty—especially those of Blacks—had been portrayed as full of pride and a centeredness in their cultural past (e.g., Stack, 1974; Hannerz, 1969). However, the late 1980s brought drastic economic changes that cut in several directions, often contradictory to one another. Numerous factors resulted in a radical decrease in the need for unskilled labor in manufacturing and construction, leaving those without formal education and specialized skills unable to find work except in the low-paying service sector (Wilson, 1987). Communities of recent migrants from Mexico struggled to establish themselves as viable economic neighborhoods with churches and businesses. Yet most were without priests from among their own group or economic entrepreneurs who could establish local businesses of sufficient strength to sustain themselves through hard times. The young turned away from their parents' older ways and tried to find themselves within a youth subculture dictated to by commercial music and entertainment (Moore & Pinderhughes, 1993). Economic migrants and political refugees entering the United States willingly stepped into low-paying jobs providing service within establishments owned by others. A few found small-business niches in the increasingly ethnically mixed and poorest inner-city areas. Many industries found that global competition meant they had to upgrade the workplace to require new technological, computational, and literacy skills of workers; displaced unskilled workers and young workers without education often could find no employment.

These changes brought rapid shifts in inner-city neighborhoods and high-rise projects that had formerly been the province of one ethnic group. By the mid-1980s urban projects often housed as many as 20 different language groups. Drug trafficking and gang violence gave "*neighborhood*" new meanings fraught with fear and desperation. Groups of youth claimed their own "hoods" (neighborhoods or claimed territories in various parts of the city) with automatic weapons, "beepers" as local communication resources, and fax machines and airline travel as means to stay in touch with counterparts in other urban areas. Gang life substituted for families that had either disintegrated through alcohol and drug abuse or incarceration, or had been incomplete to start with because of single parenthood, or devolved as powerless to influence the younger generation to hope for a brighter future resulting from hard work and continued education (Hagedorn, 1988; Padilla, 1987). Young men and women found few models in their parents' lives or media representations of their ethnic heritage; instead they sought to form collective identities through gang membership (Vigil, 1993). Sexual codes centered in street norms of gender-based groups, and the value of bearing children tied more to status within these groups than to perceived role in a new generational family unit (E. Anderson, 1990). In place of the local jobs former generations of young people had held as street vendors, newspaper deliverers, and helpers in the kitchens and stockrooms of small family-owned businesses, gang members now found the entrepreneurial opportunities of gangs their only "hood" source of financial support (Padilla, 1992; Rodriguez, 1993). Male gangs shifted somewhat their earlier structures and functions of the 1940s, and they and newly organized female gangs cooperated with social scientists to document continuities and variations across as many as three generations in some neighborhoods (Moore, 1991).

WITH AN ETHNOGRAPHER'S EYE

But what is happening within these diverse groups that all go under the name of *community*? What holds these groups together, and how do they differ in the education of their members? To act responsibly, social planners have to ask both what is happening and who is calling for responses (Bellah, Madsen, Sullivan, Swidler, & Tipton, 1991, p. 283). Answers to these questions can best come from getting inside these groups and taking a comparative perspective on their historical, structural, and behavioral features. Ethnographers learn about beliefs and behaviors of groups by becoming, to the extent possible, participants and observers of these groups. But as sites of ethnographers' studies, communities and families have been the most difficult social arenas for intense study. By their very definition and rationale of existence, communities do not include outsiders such as researchers; they are not open institutions inviting general membership, and their everyday interactions are guided by unspoken (often out-of-awareness) rules of behavior and language. Writing an ethnography requires long-term immersion, continuing involvement with community members, and some degree of comparative perspective that attempts to distinguish between what is common and what is unique across such groups.

Portrayed here will be five contemporary communities of very different types, each of which has been studied by an ethnographer as insider/outsider over a long period of time. The five are: (a) a Puerto Rican *barrio* in New York City; (b) a pre–World War II Japanese fishing community in California and its current nonspatial community; (c) a rural-oriented African American community of the 1970s and its current nonspatially based connections; (d) a community-based youth organization in a high-crime inner-city area; (e) and a community of street youth in a university neighborhood. Taken together, these five do not give a representative picture of all possible types of communities in the final decade of the 20th century. Instead, they focus on groupings shaped in arenas that serve as the source of an increasing proportion of America's public school students. These portrayals offer insider perspectives of subordinated populations— individuals often either ignored or maligned by the public media and public policies and badly served by the tendency toward aggregate clustering of cultural patterns in current approaches to multicultural education.

El Bloque: Then and Now

In the late 1970s in Manhattan, *el bloque,* home to 20 Puerto Rican families with school-age children in three five-story tenements abandoned by their landlords, buzzed on warm days with the sounds of children playing happily around open water hydrants, young men alternately washing and lounging on their cars, and women and young children sitting on the steps leading into the mailbox vestibule (see Zentella, 1981, 1997). The general pattern of language was Spanish among parents and elders and often to children, and both Spanish and English among the children. Return trips to Puerto Rico, along with frequent visits from relatives, kept both the language and the sense of link to the island alive for young and old through the end of the 1970s.

Eleven of the families were related in some way to one another, but all of *el bloque* acted like a large family, with members alternately quarreling and caring for each other, lamenting losses together, and celebrating small victories with vigor. Stops at the local *bodega,* visits to nearby relatives, and occasional church celebrations punctuated the routine of daily life, which was by no means easy. Sickness, disrupted relations between husband and wife, money shortages, alcoholism, and job disappointments seemed to mark every day for someone there. Few teenagers made it through high school; the local high school had been closed down because of disrepair, violence, and failed programs. Adults worried over the educational futures of their children and the loss of blue-collar jobs for themselves; between 1950 and 1980 New York City lost 59% of its apparel and textile industry jobs. In 1985 Puerto Ricans suffered the highest unemployment rate in the city (17.5%). Of all persons below the poverty line in the city, 47.5% were Puerto Ricans, a poverty rate exceeding that of Puerto Rico, which itself fared worse than any state in the United States (Torres, 1989).

Most adults knew more Spanish than English. Those who used English most were those whose employment brought them into contact with English speakers on a daily basis, but the high unemployment rate of Puerto Ricans in the city meant that very few had this opportunity. Children became English dominant within a year of entering school, even in bilingual programs, but most were able to manage both languages, switching back and forth as needed for particular speakers, situations, or discourse strategies.

By the 1990s the close-knit community Zentella had studied a decade earlier showed the bitter effects of unemployment, drug dealing, violence, and social-service failures (Zentella, 1997). Much of the sense of guardianship that families once had for each other seemed supplanted by the needs of individuals to protect themselves from the ravages of dislocation, unpredictability, and danger that ripped into their lives with regularity.

The immediate signs of loss of community for *el bloque* came in the displacement of its people. Most of the girls who had played sidewalk games in the 1970s under the watchful eyes of their mothers and often of fathers, relatives, and a network of older fictive kin, now were raising their own children in their parents' apartments away from the block. Their old tenements had been partially destroyed by fires in the 1980s and were slowly and haphazardly being rebuilt by city and federal authorities. The slow pace of the rebuilding, plus the appearance of unoccupied zones given the neighborhood by construction scaffolding as it cut off entrances to buildings and provided hiding places for drug activities and squatters, helped push old-time residents to accept relocation elsewhere, usually to large city projects. As the apartments were finished, newcomers—formerly homeless—were moved in from shelters by city officials.

By the early 1990s *el bloque* was more African American in population than Puerto Rican, and few of the residents had been in their neighbors' apartments. The easy availability in the neighborhood of drugs and alcohol fed domestic violence and what often seemed to be open warfare on buildings and cars. Only 6 of the 20 families that had been there in the 1970s remained; 8 others lived within 12 blocks of the old block and sometimes returned to visit. The others had scattered farther afield or were no longer heard from. Several of their children now had surrogate parents or relatives or lived in foster homes. Some of *el bloque's* young men were headed for jail, sentenced for armed robbery, drug dealing, or domestic violence. All of the young women continued to live with their parents when they had children, because the children's fathers had unsteady jobs—if they had jobs at all—public housing

had a six-year waiting list, private apartments were too expensive, and no one would rent to families on welfare.

Those left on the block or those who remembered it from their childhood lamented its passing and perhaps romanticized its former embracing role:

Una cosa que yo llamo bloque, se sentaba—era como una familia, no como gente separada. Ahora la gente no se conocen. No se quieren ayudar. La mayoria està en drogas. Los niños de todo el mundo era una familia. Los niños eran de todo el mundo. ["Something that I call block, it sat—it was like a family, not like separate people. Now people don't know each other. They don't want to help each other. The majority is into drugs. Everybody's children was a family. The children belonged in [to] everybody."] (Zentella, 1997)

Scattered as they now are—in domestic units that few would acknowledge to be the same as their ideal of a family and in geographic locations they do not yet acknowledge as their own communities in the ways *el bloque* was—the former second-generation residents of *el bloque* see themselves adopting and adapting aspects of other identities, both African American and Anglo.

Socialization patterns—including changes in primary agents and directions of learning—shifted in accordance with the different family living arrangements and patterns of peer friendships now available. Many of the young women dress, dance, and sing to the African American styles that surround them, as well as speak with African American vernacular English dialect features. For both lighter- and darker-skinned Puerto Ricans, speaking and acting Black are the natural result of intense contact with African Americans in schools and public housing. (See Brady, 1988, and Flores, 1988, for discussions of the doubleness of African American and Puerto Rican cultural traditions merged in Afro-Latin arts; see *Centro de Estudio Puertorriquenos*, 1992–93, for discussion of the special problems of Puerto Rican youth and their ambivalence with regard to place and culture.) The darker-complexioned often are mistaken for African Americans, and they may identify more closely with that community, especially if they know little Spanish. But when their Spanish surname suggests to newcomers from the Caribbean that they should speak Spanish, local non-Spanish speakers feel they are missing out on something.

Shifts of self-identification among the young follow the lines of both skin color and place of residence. *El bloque* residents—both light and dark—who have moved or aspire to move to suburban areas populated by Anglos find that speaking English in ways that label them as "acting White" is a kind of self-protection and insurance for slipping into school networks. A few feel that speaking Spanish might hold them and their children back, because they have adopted the idea that only English is a ticket to a better life. They choose to think of their current interests and occupational goals for their children as providing the communal connections they need to help them in the future. This small minority tend to see themselves as Americans or Hispanic Americans.

Most individuals, even those whose behavior and speech sometimes proclaim their affinity to things African American or Anglo, speak Puerto Rican English, a dialect that identifies them as second-generation native bilinguals. They also profess allegiance to being Puerto Rican and see such an identity as distinct from just being "American." In contrast to their elders, however, speaking Spanish is not an indispensable part of "being Puerto Rican" for them; Puerto Rican heritage is enough. The power of English, generational change, and participation in non–Puerto Rican networks have made the pattern of retention of Spanish spotty, and the young are unwilling to exclude from the Puerto Rican family those of their sisters and brothers who do not speak Spanish.

Thirty years later, *el bloque's* children of the 1970s have transferred their allegiance from one block to *el barrio* (East Harlem) in general, and to a redefined New York Rican or "Nuyorican" identity in particular. Just as their parents had originally defined themselves in relation to a particular *barrio* in their island hometown and then became more pan–Puerto Rican in *el barrio,* the second generation is embracing a larger community than the one in which they were raised, but one less island-linked and more pan-Latino in the greater New York context. Both old and young share a uniform collective memory of their earlier life on *el bloque* "like a family," but now that it is not safe to send children to play in the syringe-filled playgrounds of the projects they find themselves confined to apartments that often house three generations. This makes the young women more dependent on their mothers than their mothers had been, because in the 1970s their grandmothers were either in Puerto Rico or deceased. Now they rely on their mothers to care for their children while they look for jobs and schools.

In these efforts they meet other young women whose situations are similar to their own. For example, job-training programs become their extended network for a period of time, while they share common goals and common learning situations. Once out of the program, some of these ties remain, but they tend to be more individual than communal. Ties are often bound to technology. Friends keep their networks alive by telephone, preferring to hold to the safety of their own households rather than risk taking the elevators or walking the streets. DVDs bring groups of people together to watch a film at home—more cheaply and safely than at movie houses. Young men were the first to keep in touch through beepers and cellular telephones; theirs is a network that circulates information related to economic entrepreneurship, both legal and underground. Now young mothers carry cell phones so

they can be reached anywhere in case of a child-care emergency. Information about the latest technology is shared in the extended networks, as is the equipment itself, along with cars, furniture, and job applications. Families respond to the similarities they see in other families struggling to survive and to make sense of the mismatch between opportunities and their hopes for the future.

Puerto Ricans in New York and other major metropolitan areas, such as Philadelphia and Chicago, have experienced many of the same expanding and contracting aspects of community life as those described by Zentella (1981, 1997). Latino politics, as well as community development efforts and school reform movements, have reinforced a sense of community cutting across spatial boundaries and residing in common bonds of poverty and family struggles (see, for example, Gonzalez, 1989; Pantoja, 1989). For some, temporary communal memberships come increasingly through shared hardships and opportunities to protest these to an authority, and through newly gained opportunities to try for new housing, employment, or educational opportunities. For example, neighbors in a city who formerly did not recognize each other as living in the same area create a community around a special purpose—increased safety in an elementary school where an intruder has killed several youngsters with an automatic weapon. School councils and community safety committees work to organize collections of individuals into a communal voice to pressure school boards, precinct leaders, or the mayor's office (Caballero, 1989). These efforts, often led by the more upwardly mobile of the neighborhood, provide socialization into literacy, mathematical skills, video production, and a professional manner on the telephone for women and men who never found formal schooling or self-teaching sufficient motivation for picking up these new skills. In another instance, the violent death of very young children in a neighborhood ballpark or nearby alley can lead to reform efforts of community cleanup that draw formerly reticent women into increasing public advocacy roles. In the 1990s, union groups made up almost exclusively of immigrant women—whom outsiders formerly believed neither could nor would protest their conditions of work or lack of health benefits—learned in literacy and English as a second language classes that they could speak out about their needs and begin to reshape their unions' thinking.

Terminal Island(ers): Community Constituted, Reconstituted, and Mythologized

Located in San Pedro Bay in Southern California, at the beginning of World War II Terminal Island was the residence of Japanese families who made their living primarily by fishing (see Yamashita, 1985). In the 1990s, no physical traces exist of the former community, yet the Terminal

Islanders Club members come together annually for celebrations and renewals of their connections to a common past. The *issei* (first generation) who immigrated from Japan at the turn of the century have disappeared, and their children, the *nisei* (second generation), are in their 70s, watching the *sansei* (third generation) gradually lose any awareness of the early life of their grandparents and parents on Terminal Island.

Between the turn of the century and World War II, Terminal Island was a microcosm of the Japanese villages left behind by the *issei* immigrants. Age and gender status relations held as they had in Japan. The social structure of families as well as that of the commercial fishing industry divided and distinguished man from woman, young from old, one type of fisherman from another. Though many of the trappings of their community seemed like that of other American communities—an elementary school, church, and several social organizations, including a Boy Scout troop—they remained very much outside or set apart, through their physical isolation on the island and through their strong retention of the habits and beliefs of the prefecture from which most of them had come. On Terminal Island, the mixture of old and new came in inexplicable social alignments: the Boy Scouts, sponsored by the Buddhists, met at the Buddhist Hall. Annual Christmas festivities were held in both English and Japanese at the Baptist Mission, where the Japanese Language School also met. Judo training went on at the Shinto Shrine, and the annual Buddhist Festival of the Dead took place on the street in front of the Shrine. Beyond the elementary school level, students had to leave the island by the passenger ferry to San Pedro for middle or high school, but almost no friendships formed between the Island *nisei* and their mainland counterparts.

By the 1940s language patterns showed some of the same kinds of mixtures. Almost all of the *issei* on Terminal Island knew standard Japanese (*kokugo*), and it was taught in the Japanese Language School. But daily contacts were carried on in *Kii-shu ben,* a dialect marked by informality and English loan words, without the honorifics of standard Japanese. Those who returned to Japan for their education (*Kibei*) and then came back to Terminal Island and used the honorific forms drew derision. Before World War II it was common for *nisei* parents to use Japanese while their children responded to them in English. The children grew up with strong receptive knowledge of Japanese, but were less than fully competent speakers of their parents' mother tongue. The mixture of Japanese and English, with the development of particular vocabulary items, came to have a distinctive form accentuated by the specialized technical vocabulary related to the fishing industry. Those who returned to Japan as adults found that their form of Japanese learned on Terminal Island was not wholly comprehensible. These features remain in the speech of the Terminal Islanders as part of their sense of group identity. Use of any of these terms or markers of syntax and pronunciation immediately makes a Terminal Islander identifiable as such.

With the outbreak of war in December 1941, it became clear that commercial fishing for the Japanese would end. By February of 1942 all the *issei* fishermen were arrested and evicted, their homes and businesses destroyed and replaced by commercial canning facilities. Most of the Terminal Islanders lived in adjoining blocks in the internment camp at Manzanar. There was little integration with other Japanese for them, and many retained features that marked them as having *shimaguni konjo* ("an island country mentality"). They kept to themselves, excluded as a small enclave within this sea of exclusion and labeled as aggressive, rough, and uncouth.

After the war, some scattered to the East Coast but still remained in touch with those who returned to California. In a curious twist of fate for the *kibei* who had returned to Japan for education before the war, a peculiar vocational contact enabled them to obtain employment with a company in New Jersey and allowed a large number of Terminal Islander families to resettle there together. These individuals had been trained in Japan to be "chick sexers"—to differentiate between roosters and hens just shortly before birth, an important talent in the chicken-raising business. Their skills were in demand and gave them the basis for establishing a subcommunity of their former island. Others who went to New Jersey set up businesses that served those who worked in the chicken business, and still others soon became owners of food markets and other local enterprises to serve their neighbors.

Most, however, returned to California, especially the Long Beach area, where many found work in fish canneries. There they lived in either a trailer camp established as Federal Emergency Housing, in low-cost housing, or in rental units within the area of Long Beach occupied by shipyard and defense-facility workers. The mixture in the poorest sections of town of the Terminal Islanders with others in poverty—Yugoslavian-, Portuguese-, Philippine-, and Mexican-origin families—led to considerable economic competition. The few efforts of the Islanders to take up commercial fishing again were sabotaged by other immigrants who had moved into this occupation during the war. Thus returning Japanese turned to establishing small businesses that contributed goods and services desired by their Japanese neighbors. Others took up gardening and nursery services for the burgeoning Los Angeles residential areas. Many of these businesses have passed from the hands of the original owners to the next generation of Terminal Islanders.

But creating units of organization to sustain the families in their sense of togetherness, now that their physical isolation and common livelihood were gone, came with difficulty. No longer was a Fishermen's Association possible, because no central location for gathering existed; their children were minorities among minorities in the city schools, making celebrations there of New Year's *mochi-tsuki* or Girls Day or Boys Day impossible. Gradually some new units of organization were established: the Japanese church, a Buddhist temple, and the Long Beach Japanese Community Hall, all of which provided gathering places for cultural activities.

By the early 1950s the idea of a Terminal Islander reunion came about through the efforts of some *nisei* who often came together to share their memories of "the good old days." Women and men were enlisted to help locate former Terminal Islanders, and the first reunion was finally held in 1970—at a large Chinese restaurant in Los Angeles. The enthusiasm of this occasion led to the formation of the Terminal Club, which in ensuing years has sponsored the annual New Year's party (*shinnen kai*), summer picnics, and annual events such as golfing tournaments for the males. The activity building at the local California Retirement Home, constructed through funds donated from Terminal Islanders, is dedicated to the club.

Trackton: A Community Connected No More

The residents of Trackton, a working-class community of Black Americans in a rapidly growing town of the Piedmont Carolinas, were ready for the civil rights era and its accompanying proclamations of Black pride (see Heath, 1983, 1990). Textile mills had been the major employer in this region since World War I, competing with agriculture as a primary regional employer. With the lifting of legal restrictions against the employment of Blacks in the mills, and White workers moving out of the mills to what they regarded as more upwardly mobile jobs, Blacks readily took up mill jobs. In the first flush of social services and desegregated education in the 1970s, Black families looked positively on their opportunities for moving up and out of the patterns of poverty and stagnation that had encased their parents and grandparents.

In spite of the availability of public housing, many communities of working-class Blacks preferred to rent the small former mill houses scattered around small communities and in sections of larger towns that often contained several textile mills. Families shared the two-family wooden structures, whose primary identifying features were the wide open front porch and steps that led to the central dirt plaza on which residents parked their cars and children played. While some residents of these communities worked one of the shifts at the mills, others held part-time jobs as domestic laborers, and others stayed at home, "minding" the children of those who worked. Informal hierarchical social structures developed in each of these communities, often with an older male serving as

unofficial "mayor," and others falling in line to help maintain social control in the community—over children as well as the adults who occasionally fell into family or neighbor disputes fueled by alcohol. Cars, tools, and household goods were shared with care and caution, each family wary of acquiring too many evident belongings and thereby becoming thought of as chief supplier for the community. Food was the exception, and young and old gave food willingly. And so long as requests did not come too often, return requests or favors were not refused and always seemed to be in balance.

Boys in the community grew up as kings of the plaza, exchanging verbal challenges with adults and older children who taunted and teased them with questions and mock attacks on their toys or games. Preschool girls rarely figured in central roles in the public roughhousing of the boys on the plaza, instead staying close to the women of the household, who spent as much time as possible on the porches. These girls played with dolls or younger siblings, talking with them and engaging in conversation with the porch sitters by the time they themselves were toddlers.

School-age children of both sexes played together often during the primary years, but as adolescence approached each group separated into specialized activities and private opportunities to talk about members of the opposite sex. Opportunities for reading and writing centered around practical matters: going to the store, reading directions for a new item to adorn a bicycle, helping parents decipher messages from school, and joining in the communal reading of letters from relatives who had moved up north. Church life, especially "meeting time" or revivals in August or homecoming weekends, drew community members together, sometimes for all-day occasions of celebration with friends from surrounding rural areas as well as different parts of town. Here men and women, young and old, separated from one another for various parts of the day. The men told stories and discussed local social and political changes in the wake of new local bureaucracies deriving from the legislation of the "Great Society." The women often worked with the choir director to create new musical performances for choir exchange with regional churches during rotating weeks of "meeting time." Between such tasks and cleaning up the church kitchen after the midday meal, the women talked of changes in schools under desegregation, new public housing regulations and possibilities, and deaths of older community members since the last time they had held such a large church affair.

The physical groupings of houses of Trackton's community no longer exist, bulldozed in the late 1980s to make room for a highway expansion. But the houses had been abandoned for several years by most of the original families, whose older members had given up their 1960s goal of independent living and gone into public housing. Many of their older children had left the area and others lived in various parts of town, subsisting on welfare and occasional part-time jobs.

By the early 1980s it was clear that the bottom was falling out of the textile industry in the Piedmont Carolinas. Closure of the mills had been forced by a combination of factors, primary among them foreign competition and the failure of local owners to update equipment to keep pace with regional divisions of textile companies now part of national and multinational conglomerates. Blacks had stayed on in many of the mills until the bitter end, unable in the recession of the time to find jobs elsewhere. When the mills finally closed, most found themselves on welfare rolls for the first time, able to secure only occasional work in the new motels and fast-food restaurants springing up along the recently constructed interstate highways. Families that had managed to survive together in the 1970s broke apart, and public-housing units increasingly filled with mothers trying to keep their adolescents in school and out of harm's way, while taking on the additional responsibility of caring for infants born to their teenagers. Fathers had often either drifted away from the area or into heavy alcohol use. Almost all of the Trackton youth who had entered school in the early 1970s dropped out of high school in the mid-1980s. They thereby added to their mothers' financial burdens, as they remained at home, unable to find work or to enter the armed services or regional vocational programs because they lacked high school diplomas.

The young who moved away to major metropolitan areas generally resided in high-rise apartment units of public housing, among strangers who had also set out from rural areas and small towns of the Southeast without high school diplomas and often with infants (Heath, 1990). The communal base of church life both in the region around Trackton and in inner cities began to erode. Many country churches that had been served by circuit preachers closed for lack of support; inner-city churches were cleared for urban redevelopment or relocated to new areas of town where a rising middle class of African Americans increasingly developed and chose primarily to serve their own needs and not those of inner-city populations.

Suspicion, fear, and despair marked social relations in public-housing units, in place of the shared communal guardianship and social control hierarchy of earlier days. Dealing drugs, buying and selling handguns, stealing cars and car parts, and promoting prostitution came to be occupational choices for the young. Growing numbers of young men ended up in juvenile detention centers or jail, while the mothers of their children were left on welfare in public housing, without either the personal network or the motivational resources and modeling of older family members to inspire them to start again with their education or job seeking. As immigrants with different languages, dress, and backgrounds came to be the norm rather than the exception on the floors or in the buildings of inner-city public housing in the Southeast, ethnic differences periodically flared and subsided, as each group worked out survival strategies. For the young, membership in gangs, often ethnically based, promised affiliations and economic opportunities offered by neither families nor community-building institutions such as churches.

Community became a concept only minimally associated with affective response, and only as an appendage to the names of major public-housing units, such as "Boyd Hill Community" or "Rayland Project Community." Bonding for young people beyond the age of 8 to 10 was increasingly not to historical traditions and a collective memory of their parents' past but to the survival strategies and flourishes of dress, symbols, and language that marked gangs. Most of the adolescents who formed male-female bondings and tried to establish households of their own found that their educational and employment failures forced the girl to stay with her mother's household, while the male remained with his mother or stayed on a casual basis with friends. Young mothers alternated between feeling abandoned and bitter and hoping still for the ideal romance of a man who would stay with them and help take care of the children. The primary group bonding became that of "us women"—the young single mothers in high-rise projects who tried to care for their children apart from the family, church, and neighborhood supports of their own childhood.

BEST: A Safe Place in a Danger Zone

BEST is not a community that uses space in expected ways; it is not a region or a group of residences. It is only a couple of buildings located several blocks apart along the streets of an inner-city area infamous for gang-related deaths and local drug-war casualties. The same activities take place in both buildings, and a single administration looks over both. BEST is a community youth center, opened in 1963 as an outreach program of a nearby White church (see Heath & McLaughlin, 1993; McLaughlin, Irby, & Langman, 1994). Throughout the year, in after-school and summer day programs, BEST serves as community for the youth of the nearby high-risk projects.

The neighborhood of BEST, located in a large midwestern city, provides a counterpart to the more recently built public-housing projects of the Southeast to which some of Trackton's children had gone. The housing projects of BEST's neighborhood were established back in the 1940s and renovated in the 1960s after massive urban unrest had turned their streets into battlegrounds. Here gangs of youth have been power brokers of city neighborhoods since the 1920s, though today's gangs differ considerably because of their links to drug dealing and the intense isolation of youth from older residents of the immediate neighborhood. Unlike the "tough old man" of past gang eras who lived just two apartments down the street, the bosses of "hood" gangs in the 1990s were more likely to be inmates whose communication networks spread across the state and even the nation.

Nearby schools are bullet scarred and have metal detectors at every entry; school personnel try to ban all possible signs of gang membership exhibited by students. Young people learn to walk quickly along the street, careful not to walk too close to a building held by a gang that may not regard them as "homies." Once they reach their own high-rise project buildings, they pass by the local gang members who guard the doors and sometimes use their positions of power to arrange drug deals.

For some children of this neighborhood, leaving school at the end of the day does not mean going home or heading to the streets to gangbang. It means heading for BEST, their home away from home, their surrogate family that provides help with homework, after-school activities, and friends in a safe place shut off from the streets and the projects.

Daily over 100 youngsters between the ages of 8 and 18 go to BEST. For several groups of high schoolers, BEST is their "scholarship" home, a sponsoring agency for cohorts of 20 or so member students who move as a single group through high school as BEST scholars. This special "family within a family" membership avails these young people of a sustaining primary group between ninth grade and high school graduation. The young people go to BEST daily to do homework and projects with their group leaders, adults who have committed to staying with them through their entire "scholar" cycle. Afternoon activities vary. Homework comes first, as older students team up with one or two younger peers, set out their school books, and hear about the week of work and projects ahead. On some days homework takes several hours. On other afternoons the older youngsters can join together in "club" activities in which they work on supplementary projects on African American–, Caribbean-, Puerto Rican–, and Mexican-origin heroes and heroines, with the goal of preparing a hall exhibit. On other days they plan puppet shows, story-telling, and art programs for presentation in the auditorium to their younger peers.

As the dark shadows of evening begin to fall along the streets down from the high-rise projects, the youngsters collect at the door of BEST to walk home in groups. By 6 o'clock the grade school children have left the buildings, but the junior high and high school students head down the street to a restaurant to get a quick dinner, so they can return to BEST by 7 P.M. each evening with a group of local law students and other adults who are their tutors. These sessions involve not only homework of the day or week from their schools, but also preparations for taking standardized tests, and researching scholarships, employment,

and career choices. Values clarification, discussion about appropriate times for standard English, and debate over recent police crackdowns in the neighborhood also come up during these evening sessions. On weekends, tutors and BEST teens join in tennis lessons, art classes, mural projects, and an occasional movie.

BEST socializes its young along the lines of traditional family life. Manners, goals, values, speech, work, play, friendships, and current events circulate through the lives of the adults and young people within BEST's halls. BEST also provides the services often expected of communities in affluent suburbs: a safe place to congregate; library resources; reliable adults to offer advice, help, and discipline; recreational equipment, spaces, and programs; and opportunities for occasional aesthetic and athletic events. In addition, BEST constantly creates and sustains a collective memory. Its "graduates"—those who have moved out of the community to jobs and higher education—return often to talk with current BEST young people. Photographs, trophies, and newspaper clippings throughout the buildings announce the achievements of those who have preceded the current generation. Many of the staff have been with BEST since its beginning in the fall of 1963, and their stories of the past bring laughter and tears on many of the informal occasions that take place in the halls of BEST.

Young people of BEST talk of their community there in romanticized terms, crediting it with "saving my life," "making me what I am now," "giving me a chance," "protecting me and being there for me," and "being there for me to trust." The institution is thus a combination of personified agent and glorified place. Friendships, sponsorships, disciplined occasions, interdependent living and learning, and motivation to grow and learn in peace mark BEST, just as they mark community in the traditional sense of something more than a building and a set of associations. The common endeavors and shared outlook, firmly but not obtrusively grounded in the Christian fellowship and ethos of the sponsoring church, ensure that daily needs (ranging from shoes to praise) can be met for youngsters. Like many communities, BEST serves as a transition or border zone between the families and households of the young and the outside world of strangers, new opportunities, and different expectations.

Homeless City: A "Kid Community" of the Streets

"Spare change?" "Excuse me, sir, can you spare a quarter for a starving kid?" "Ma'am, how about a few cents, so I don't have to sell my body?" "Could you spare some money, so I can buy milk for my kitten?"

Along the streets of University Avenue, a 10-block zone near the state university located in a large Pacific Northwest city, young men and women address passersby with these greetings. Scattered strategically at different corners, in supermarket parking lots, and in doorways of video stores and "counterculture" shops, about two dozen teens are at work panhandling by noon on any given day. For six to eight hours they will shuttle back and forth between their chosen posts, collecting their change to a point where they can enter the muffin shop for a cup of coffee, a stop in the bathroom, and a quick face wash. By 8 P.M. several days of the week they are nowhere to be seen, for all of them have gathered at Teen Feed, occasions for a free hot meal at one of the local churches (see Heath, 1992a, 1992b).

Shortly before the doors of the church educational building open, the young people gather outside on the steps to have a final smoke, for the rules of Teen Feed prohibit smoking, drinking, or dealing or taking drugs while in the building. Once the doors open, they shuffle into a semblance of a line and move to the trays and along the cafeteria line, where they can pick up their plates of steaming hot spaghetti, garlic bread, salad, jello, and cake. Behind the cafeteria line and scattered among the tables of the auditorium are adults from the church and a few students from the university. "Hey, Melissa, great color on those fingernails! How'd you get those sequins to stick? Did you get over to the office to see about getting your GED?" Such combinations of compliments, teasing, and nudging flow back and forth, as the young people take their seats at bare wooden tables and begin to eat. They run over their plans with each other, bringing friends up-to-date on recent trials with relationships, their latest contact with their parents, brushes with the law, and music they've heard or movies they've seen. Often they discuss plans for trips to San Francisco or perhaps the Oregon coast. They dream of these trips for months. A few save enough money to catch a bus one day and disappear for a few months. But almost always they return, striding in the door of the church sporting a new haircut or hair color and eager to share their adventures with their old friends.

By 10 P.M. on any evening of Teen Feed, they are out the door of the church building and scattering their separate ways. Some head back to their homes, trying once again for a short while to see whether they can live with their parents. Others know where they will sleep—in a now-familiar doorway of a store along Main Street or with a couple of friends who recently got enough money together to rent a room at the transient hotel. A close look at their knots of friendship illustrates the interests and circumstances that both connect and sometimes scatter them.

For a period of more than four weeks, Susie, Mel, and Jennifer were always together (Heath, 1992a). The three of them shared a "squat," the name the young people have given the abandoned buildings two streets back of Main Street. They had plans to panhandle, save their money, and rent a room together. Once they had a room, they hoped to find jobs.

Susie and Jen had arrived in town together after meeting on the streets of a midwestern city. Jen had left home because she "could not stand" what she regarded as "overbearing parents who only want to control my life." They had given her a horse when she was 8 years old, and by the age of 16 she had ridden her way to numerous ribbons and trophies. But at 16 she was tired of the endless competition and was no longer sure she even wanted to go to college. Her parents responded with higher demands and tighter controls. She decided to run away with Susie, whom she had met at school.

Susie's life fascinated Jen, for Susie seemed to have had everything Jen lacked in the way of freedom, choice, and experiences. Susie had left home at 13 because "nobody cared." Her older sister had been in a treatment center for cocaine abuse and then in jail, and Susie's single parent, her mother, always seemed either mentally occupied or physically absent, because she was trying "to do something with your sister." Susie took off, frustrated at "always trying to be the good kid." She sometimes returned to her mother's apartment for short stays, but she always left soon: "My sister was going through a lot of shit, and I was the scapegoat. I tried so hard to take care of everyone. Mom used to say stuff like, 'I'll be back in a couple of weeks. Call me every day, and see if I'm back. I've got to take care of your sister.'"

When Jen joined Susie on the street, the two decided to travel. They settled for a while in University City, a place Susie had visited a year or so earlier and where she had thought life on the streets was better than in other cities. The university atmosphere made people "more giving, smarter, and not so mean."

Soon after the two arrived in University City, they met Mel, who had grown up there. Mel had left home at 14 and had been on the streets two years when she welcomed Jen and Susie in and agreed to teach them how to become "a part of our community here." She taught them the best places to panhandle, the days when unfriendly policemen took their beats, the clerks at the muffin shop who would sneak day-old muffins to the street kids, and the restaurants whose waitresses would not yell when you went in to use the bathroom and just have a cup of coffee. These learning sessions came in informal talks, primarily around the dinner table at Teen Feed and on strolls along Main Street, where strangers would not have distinguished the girls from their age peers who were sophomores and juniors at the local high school. Mel introduced them to others of the "street kid" community, giving them brief biographies of those she knew best and dropping brief warnings about those she did not know or had learned not to trust. The girls shared their very different background stories. Jen and Susie listened to Mel's stories of physical and mental abuse from her stepfather, remembering the forms abuse took in their own families—highly restrictive outings, unpredictable support, and verbal harangues. Susie's sister had told her bloodcurdling tales of events that took place when she was just an infant: Her natural father had chased her mother around the house with a knife to "drive the demons from her." They asked Mel about her real father and learned that she had lived with him for three months when she was 15, but "he kicked me out, 'cause we had differences, and he was an addict." Before she met Susie and Jen, Mel's best friend had been a big "mutt," Jupiter, that she had inherited from another street friend who had left the area three months earlier. Mel coached the newcomers on the guys to stay away from, the ones who were homosexual or bisexual, those who had a reputation for liking "kinky sex," and how to get condoms. For the most part, the girls had little private contact with boys of the community, who tended to hang in small groups, as did the girls.

For several months the girls were never apart except when they panhandled, finding it more profitable to operate on different sides of Main Street, about a block apart. They always entered Teen Feed as a threesome, taking their places in line with friends and sitting together to discuss their present plans, recent incidents, and "grapevine" news about friends who had "moved on" out of the University area. After three months the threesome gave up their plans to rent a room together, because "we figure we'll never find a place that would take a dog."

Mel decided to head for San Francisco as soon as she earned "some extra money to take enough food for Jupiter." Susie found a job through a local counseling and employment agency recommended by one of the Teen Feed adults and moved to a suburb of town, where she was going to live in a youth center and work with a youth coordinator. Jen decided to go back home after her father found her and pleaded with her to come back and try again. Susie commented: "You know, it's funny about parents. They can't stand us while we're with them, but as soon as we do something to prove that we might be able to make something out of life by ourselves, they just want us back."

For the short time they formed part of the transient community of the University District, the three girls shared everything from their spare change to the ramshackle abandoned building where they slept. They made definite plans to provide for each other and to build a future together. The realities of disparate needs led them to outgrow each other and to separate. Mel knew she did not want a job, because she would find it too confining. Susie wanted a job to prove to her mother and the world that she could survive on her own. Jen chose to return to her family and to put in place some lessons she had learned from slowing her life down.

In spite of media presentations about the violence of the streets, the "street kids" in the University District have created a "community" life. In place before the arrival and after the departure of individual community members were structures of organization, rules of territory and exchange of goods, and patterns of socialization. Teen Feed and the adults and students there provided information, encouragement, conversation, and family-like meal times when young and old came together around "a lot of talk about nothing" (S. B. Heath, 1983). School, church, police, physicians, and other "typical" ministering agents of community were largely absent from the lives of these young. Most had left school around age 14 and depended on their mature looks and experiences to allay suspicions by a stranger that they were "school-age." They regarded the church as "a place to eat," and, in fact, many were unaware of any relationship between church teachings and the service that members provided them a few nights a week at Teen Feed. When any of them became sick enough to need a doctor, they went to the emergency room at the hospital; those who had families in the area went home and hoped that parents would get them help. They read papers they collected from trashcans, knew which clinics had open days for certain kinds of screenings or tests, and frequently checked the bulletin board of the local youth-counseling and employment center to see if possibilities might convince them to move on.

Each one had learned to be a "street kid," adopting and adapting as best he or she could certain aspects of idealized features of "family"—promises of mutual caring, some regularity of group meals, and generally regular hours of working and sleeping. They had also chosen to leave behind in their current existence features of home life they had detested: control, demands, abuse, and drugs. They had built bonds of shared exclusion and common dilemmas; they had learned how to find places of acceptance. They had spent lots of time telling stories, planning the next step in their lives, and sharing oral and written sources of information. They took advantage of the abilities of the group to get what they needed; for example, Jen could read better than Mel and Susie, so she helped Susie interpret the forms she had to fill out for her job. Among themselves, and occasionally branching out to ask for advice and help from other young people of the street, they managed access to medical services, travel information, and housing and clothing networks. Though for many their time on the street away from their damaged and damaging families was relatively short—often less than two years—they forged a sense of deep horizontal comradeship with each other and, to some extent, with "street kids" in general (as do children of the streets in cities all over the world; see Boyden, 1991; Webber, 1991). The absence of sustained time with caring adults and lack of models for their own rapid transition from child to adult throw them very much on their own resources and often into the temptation of relieving their pain through drugs. But both for those who manage to leave the streets for good and those who keep returning, there is the bond created by inclusion in being ignored by others. For years beyond their own time on the streets, they connect primarily to peers and to those who have also experienced streets as places to call home.

THE FUTURE OF COMMUNITY

As the 21st century begins, the demographic profile of the United States suggests that communities such as those portrayed here may persist and even proliferate for some decades to come. Their values and realignments of dependencies and interdependencies suggest strongly that the "habits of the heart" of America have moved its citizens away from the realities of traditional spatial community and into new organizational alignments that create bondings more directly and pragmatically than did the loosely aggregated amorphous communities of the past (Bellah et al., 1985). Groups, ranging from professional affiliations to local youth recreational associations, offer protection of one sort or another and socialize their members into patterns of behavior, language use, and value systems that work for the benefit of individual members and, more vaguely, for the benefit of the group as a whole or for a particular cause or enterprise espoused by the group. Locating community in people's lives requires understanding of the nature and levels of the network of social relations that provides several different normative frameworks simultaneously (Bender, 1978; Milroy, 1992). This network approach examines sets of social relations at work at the same time and sequentially over the life course of an individual, and considers how the coincidence of normative frameworks within an individual's map of social relations amounts to one's ongoing socialization.

The togetherness of the multiple and somewhat unpredictable forms of communities in the next century will be far less spontaneous and, no doubt, considerably less enduring—in both reality and collective memory—than that of communities that dominated through most of the 20th century. Neighborhoods such as el bloque, University City, and the projects that surround BEST and take in former residents of Trackton incorporate dysfunctional elements of society such as drugs, alcohol, and spousal and child abuse. Individuals in these situations, struggling to meet everyday subsistence needs, have few resources of reform that can bring back into place older bonds based on "little communities" occupying common spatial territory. Therefore, they will no doubt continue to turn to groupings based on needs, communication networks, and selective appeals to common histories and languages.

Communities have historically served five central functions (Dynes, 1970, p. 84): mutual support, social control, social participation, socialization, and production. Within their provisions of mutual support and social participation, they have met key individual and group needs through interaction, generally assumed to take place on a face-to-face and regular basis. Their socialization and social control functions have ensured not only conformity to certain norms and practices, but also a process of continuation of the information, values, and behaviors of their members through enculturation processes at various points after childhood (Brim & Wheeler, 1966). Their production and distribution functions, though generally linked in the past to food and service, have also increasingly included information and technical services (often linked to further expansion of information and increased communication networks; see Gottschalk, 1975; Scherer, 1972).

The array of communities noted here, with the exception of the disrupted community and current collection of individuals of Trackton, all include these key functions. Moreover, the communities described here arose out of crises or critical environmental and socioeconomic changes that thrust on their members and leaders a sense of mutual need, a feeling of loss, and a sense of connection as a way station along the path to improved conditions. In all cases, these communities have only in the past decade come to include individuals of different ethnic groups and language backgrounds. For example, whereas Trackton and el bloque were all Black and all Puerto Rican, respectively, the current neighborhoods of those who used in live in Trackton and el bloque are ethnically mixed. When BEST began, all the young people there were Black; in the 1990s some Puerto Rican children, as well as immigrant youth, became part of the community. University City's street youth include young people from several different ethnic groups; their elder counterparts, who have their special posts along the street for panhandling, also represent several different ethnic backgrounds.

What do these nontraditional and ethnically mixed communities mean for education and for the movement in the name of "multiculturalism"? The usual answer might be that multicultural education will bring the separate cultures that have always made up the United States population into consideration in the content of classrooms, allowing students to learn about groups other than their own and thereby grow to appreciate them. But such an answer does not adequately take into account the conditions of variety among communities today.

The ethnographic cases here reflect structural and behavioral features of communities from which an increasing percentage of American students will come in the next century. Their diversity is not that usually associated with portrayals in education of "multicultural diversity," but rather comes in diversity of access to mainstream institutions, stable predictable home lives, daily language uses and calls for particular identities, and resources on which to fall back in times of family crisis incited by poverty, illness, and random violence. Many of today's young do not see their community or their identity as that of a single ethnic group, place, or family; instead they pick and choose, change and reshape their affiliations of primary socialization.

Multicultural education will be hopelessly caught in cultural lag if it tries to plead for the dignity of cultural differences and respect merely through repeated portrayals of individuals of color who have conquered their oppressive backgrounds to contribute to mainstream society, or in capsule histories of the immigration patterns of certain nationalities. Discussions of African American, Hispanic, Latino, Asian American, or Pacific cultures that present all members of each of these groups as homogeneous and securely locked within the membranes of their ethnic membership and identity as "a community" also reflect an inability to stay in touch with the out-of-school socialization networks of today's youth. Multicultural education must go considerably further than the introduction of new content into literature, social studies, and art and music classes. The history of groups taught under the rubric of "multicultural education" must not present all the struggles as those of the past, with no concurrent attention to recent and contemporary regional, economic, and social stresses and strains carrying strong influence on institutions such as families, communities, community organizations (such as gangs and other youth groups), and occupations.

The term *multicultural* is, more often than not, a collective category for "others"—those outside the perceived mainstream of ethnic background (northern European and British Isles) and Caucasian racial membership. Implicit within such a category is the notion that all those that are multicultural are non-White, defined for what they are *not* rather than for what they are. That which is White and mainstream remains very much the norm against which such projections are made. To speak of "ethnic communities" or even of "multicultural" communities is to perpetuate myths that such communities are, on the one hand, homogeneous across classes, regions, and histories of immigration, or, on the other hand, to suggest that there is homogeneity of culture, language, and socialization within local communities. Yamashita's work (1985) and that of Zentella (1981, 1997) make it abundantly clear that such is not the case, even among individuals who identify themselves as Japanese or Puerto Rican. Numerous other studies of individuals in transition and of communities responding—as those included here did—to social and economic crises and drastic shifts in conditions (Barton, 1969; Dynes,

1970; Erickson, 1976) echo the need to ensure that "multicultural education" [does] not become a consolidating mechanism.

In such a view of education, "others" are categorized together, stripped of their variations and individual differences, and uniformly pictured as victimized and dependent on the White "majority" to come to their aid or provide their models for the future. Preferential endogamy—or choosing to marry within one's own group—as a trend toward continuity (Schermerhorn, 1978, p. xiv) cannot be assumed of all individuals or groups. More and more individuals will be of "mixed" cultures, ethnicities, and identities, and will learn to declare themselves of one or another ethnic group according to current rewards for such declarations. For example, during the 1980s the San Francisco Unified School District learned that parents and high schoolers were shifting their self-assignments of ethnic labels in order to help their argument for entry into magnet schools. The district ruled that an individual could change his or her identity only once every three years. The U.S. Bureau of the Census, national survey organizations, and local school districts present choices of ethnic identity as though they were clear-cut and permanently set along racial and group affiliations; for example, students in state colleges often have to tag themselves as "non-Hispanic White" or "non-Hispanic Black" (Brady, 1988). The offspring of families that include several ethnicities increasingly find themselves negotiating their language, dress, manners, and announcements of affiliation on a regular situational basis in job interviews, arrangements with social service agencies, and dealings with school personnel. For example, the offspring of a Jewish father from eastern Europe and a mother from Mexico may find that she can "prove" her Hispanic identity on school forms only by using her mother's maiden name as her own rather than her legal name—that of her father. Increased intermarriage and geographic mobility mean that the biological bases, cultural values, and communication patterns of ethnic groups (Barth, 1969) can no longer be counted on to create and sustain community. (For discussion of the transformation of identity among White Americans, see Alba, 1990.)

Future research must continue to integrate paradigms, bringing together census data (Farmer, Luloff, Ilvento, & Dixon, 1992), literary and historical representations, and participation observation (Bender, 1978). These must be long-term accounts that draw in every way possible from the knowledge gained by the long-term insider-outsider perspectives of anthropologists, descendants of earlier communities, and individuals who claim several communities of origin through intermarriage, acculturation, and biculturalism (E. Anderson, 1990; Driben, 1985; Yamashita, 1985). Moreover, community studies must increasingly explore the socialization powers of short-term communities, such as refugee camps (Long, 1993), drug-dealing affiliations (Adler, 1985; Agar, 1973), and communities of purposeful intent and endeavor (such as science-fiction readers and writers) linked by distance technologies (Laffler, in press). Community studies can no longer take historical identities as given; researchers must attend much more to ways that groups and institutions create alternative historical identities for themselves (Dorst, 1989).

As the 21st century begins, more than one quarter of the nation's youngsters are at "serious risk" of never reaching maturity; another one quarter are at moderate risk of leading unproductive lives to the detriment of themselves and others (Dryfoos, 1990; Schorr, 1988). Many of the reasons for this state of affairs among the young of America lie within policies dominated by idealized images of community, family, school, and ethnic homogeneity. Policies and promises have tended to focus on those things the public would like to believe have gone unchanged, and to ignore those that have changed (Wilkinson, 1986). In addition, this reductionism can continue to hide the power of institutions and downplay their possibilities for both benefit and harm (Bellah et al., 1991).

The young of the projected majority of "minorities" entering the workforce at the opening of the 21st century can meet their own potential and the needs of society only if education, health, employment, and housing policies take into account contemporary diversities of communities. Myths, ideals, and dependencies on old social structures and their roles have to shift so that policy makers and contemporary institutions can provide contexts and conditions of learning that will be relevant to the present realities of American communities and facilitate their productive, positive futures.

References

Adler, P. A. (1985). *Wheeling and dealing: An ethnography of an upper-level drug dealing and smuggling community*. New York: Columbia University Press.

Agar, M. (1973). *Ripping and running: A formal ethnography of urban heroin addicts*. New York: Seminar Press.

Alba, R. D. (1990). *Ethnic identity: The transformation of White America*. New Haven: Yale University Press.

Anderson, B. (1983). *Imagined communities: Reflections on the origin and spread of nationalism*. London: Verso.

Anderson, E. (1990). *Street wise: Race, class, and change in an urban community*. Chicago: University of Chicago Press.

Arensberg, C. (1961). The community as object and as sample. *American Anthropologist, 63*, 241–264.

Barth, F. (Ed.). (1969). *Ethnic groups and boundaries*. Boston: Little, Brown.

Barton, A. H. (1969). *Communities in disaster: A sociological analysis of collective stress behavior*. Garden City, NY: Doubleday.

Becker, H. (1976). *Boys in white: Student culture in medical school*. New York: Transaction Books. (Originally published 1961)

Bellah, R. N., Madsen, R., Sullivan, W. M., Swidler, A., & Tipton, S. M. (1985). *Habits of the heart: Individualism and commitment in American life*. Berkeley: University of California Press.

Bellah, R. N., Madsen, R., Sullivan, W. M., Swidler, A., & Tipton, S. M. (1991). *The good society*. New York: Knopf.

Bender, T. (1978). *Community and social change in America*. New Brunswick, NJ: Rutgers University Press.

Blackwell, J. (1984). *The Black community: Diversity and unity*. New York: Harper & Row.

Boyden, J. (1991). *Children of the cities*. London: Zed Books.

Brady, V. (1988). Black Hispanics: The ties that bind. *Centro, 2*(3), 44–47.

Brim, O. G., & Wheeler, S. (1966). *Socialization after childhood: Two essays*. New York: Wiley.

Caballero, D. (1989). School board elections: Parents against the odds. *Centro, 2*(5), 86–94.

Camarillo, A. (1979). *Chicanos in a changing society: From Mexican pueblos to American barrios in Santa Barbara and Southern California, 1848–1930*. Cambridge, MA: Harvard University Press.

Centro de Estudio Puertorriquenos. (1999–93, Winter) [entire volume].

Communities, Journal of Cooperation. (1992, Fall), 79 [entire issue].

Dorst, J. D. (1989). *The written suburb: An American site, an ethnographic dilemma*. Philadelphia: University of Pennsylvania Press.

Drake, S. C., & Cayton, H. R. (1962). *Black metropolis: A study of Negro life in a northern city*. New York: Harper Torchbooks. (Originally published 1945)

Driben, P. (1985). *We are Metis: The ethnography of a halfbreed community in Northern Alberta*. New York: AMS Press.

Dryfoos, J. G. (1990). *Adolescents at risk*. New York: Oxford University Press.

DuBois, W.E.B. (1899). *The Philadelphia Negro: A social study*. Philadelphia: University of Pennsylvania Press.

Durkheim, E. (1933). *The division of labor in society*. Glencoe, IL: Free Press.

Dynes, R. R. (1970). *Organized behavior in disaster*. Lexington, MA: Heath Lexington Books.

Edwards, G. F. (1959). *The Negro professional class*. New York: Free Press.

Erickson, K. T. (1976). *Everything in its path*. New York: Simon & Schuster.

Farmer, F. L., Luloff, A. E., Ilvento, T. W., & Dixon, B. L. (1992). Rural community studies and secondary data: Aggregation revisited. *Journal of the Community Development Society, 23*(1), 57–70.

Fishman, J. A. (1966). *Language loyalty in the United States*. The Hague: Mouton.

Flores, J. (1988). Rappin', writin', & breakin'. *Centro, 2*(3), 34–41.

Frazier, E. F. (1947). *The Negro in the United States*. New York: Macmillan.

Frazier, E. F. (1957). *Black bourgeoisie*. Glencoe, IL: Free Press.

Gallaher, A., & Padfield, H. (1980). *The dying community*. Albuquerque: University of New Mexico Press.

Gatewood, W. B. (1990). *Aristocrats of color: The Black elite, 1880–1920.* Bloomington: Indiana University Press.

Gilman, G. (1956). *Human relations in the industrial Southeast.* Chapel Hill: University of North Carolina Press.

Gonzalez, N. (1989). Latino politics in Chicago. *Centro, 2*(5), 46–57.

Gottschalk, S. S. (1975). *Communities and alternatives: An exploration of the limits of planning.* New York: Wiley.

Gusfield, J. R. (1975). *Community: A critical response.* Oxford, England: Blackwell.

Hagedorn, J. M. (1988). *People and folks: Gangs, crime and the underclass in a rustbelt city.* Chicago: Lake View Press.

Hall, J. D., Leloudis, J., Korstad, R., Murphy, M., Jones, L. A., & Daly, C. B. (1987). *Like a family: The making of a southern cotton mill world.* Chapel Hill: University of North Carolina Press.

Hannerz, U. (1969). *Soulside: Inquiries into ghetto culture and community.* New York: Columbia University Press.

Hareven, T. K., & Langenbach, R. (1978). *Amoskeag: Life and work in an American factory-city.* New York: Pantheon Books.

Heath, S. B. (1983). *Ways with words: Language, life, and work in communities and classrooms.* Cambridge: Cambridge University Press.

Heath, S. B. (1990). The children of Trackton's children: Spoken and written language in social change. In J. E. Stigler, R. A. Shweder, & G. Herdt (Eds.), *Cultural psychology: Essays on comparative human development* (pp. 496–519). Cambridge: Cambridge University Press.

Heath, S. B. (1992a, November 13). How can we help homeless teens in U district? *Daily of the University of Washington,* p. 9.

Heath, S. B. (1992b). *Street youth of Seattle.* Seattle, WA: University Street Ministry.

Heath, S. B., & McLaughlin, M. W. (Eds.). (1993). *Identity and inner-city youth: Beyond ethnicity and gender.* New York: Teachers College Press.

Kilbride, P. L., Goodale, J. C., & Ameisen, E. R. (1990). *Encounters with American ethnic cultures.* Tuscaloosa: University of Alabama Press.

Kreiger, S. (1983). *The mirror dance: Identity in a women's community.* Philadelphia: Temple University Press.

Laffler, J. (in press). *The science fiction community of readers and writers.* Doctoral dissertation, Stanford University, Stanford, CA.

Lewis, H. (1955). *Blackways of Kent.* Chapel Hill: University of North Carolina Press.

Lewis, O. (1951). *Life in a Mexican village: Tepoztlan restudied.* Urbana: University of Illinois Press.

Long, L. D. (1993). *Ban Vinai: The refugee camp.* New York: Columbia University Press.

Lynd, R. S., & Lynd, H. M. (1929). *Middletown.* New York: Columbia University Press.

McLaughlin, M. W., Irby, M. A., & Langman, J. (1994). *Urban sanctuaries: Neighborhood organizations in the lives and futures of inner-city youth.* San Francisco: Jossey-Bass.

Milroy, J. (1992). *Linguistic variation and change.* Oxford, England: Blackwell.

Moore, J. W. (1991). *Going down to the barrio: Homeboys and homegirls in change.* Philadelphia: Temple University Press.

Moore, J. W., & Pinderhughes, R. (1993). *Latinos and the underclass debate: Latino communities in the United States.* New York: Russell Sage Foundation.

Morland, J. K. (1958). *Millways of Kent.* Chapel Hill: University of North Carolina Press.

Myrdal, G. (1944). *An American dilemma: The Negro problem and modern democracy.* New York: Harper.

Padilla, F. M. (1987). *Puerto Rican Chicago.* Notre Dame, IN: University of Notre Dame Press.

Padilla, F. M. (1992). *The gang as an American enterprise.* New Brunswick, NJ: Rutgers University Press.

Pantoja, A. (1989). Puerto Ricans in New York: A historical and community development perspective. *Centro, 2*(5), 20–31.

Powdermaker, H. (1950). *Hollywood: The dream factory.* New York: Columbia University Press.

Redfield, R. (1941). *The folk culture of Yucatan.* Chicago: University of Chicago Press.

Redfield, R. (1960). *The little community.* Stanford, CA: Stanford University Press. (Originally published 1956)

Riesman, D. (1950). *The lonely crowd.* New Haven, CT: Yale University Press.

Rodriguez, L. J. (1993). *Always running: La vida loca—Gang days in LA.* Willimantic, CT: Curbstone Press.

Salaman, G. (1974). *Community and occupation.* Cambridge, England: Cambridge University Press.

Scherer, J. (1972). *Contemporary community: Sociological illusion or reality?* London: Tavistock.

Schermerhorn, R. A. (1978). *Comparative ethnic relations.* Chicago: University of Chicago Press.

Schorr, L. B. (1988). *Within our reach.* Garden City, NY: Anchor Press/Doubleday.

Stack, C. B. (1974). *All our kin: Strategies for survival in a Black community.* New York: Harper & Row.

Steiner, S. (1969). *La raza: The Mexican Americans.* New York: Harper & Row.

Thrasher, F. (1927). *The gang.* Chicago: University of Chicago Press.

Toennies, F. (1963). *Community and society.* New York: Praeger. (Originally published 1887)

Torres, A. (1989). New York in the year 2000: A sober assessment. *Centro, 2*(6), 48–54.

Vigil, J. D. (1993). Gangs, social control, and ethnicity: Ways to redirect. In S. B. Heath & M. W. McLaughlin (Eds.), *Identity and inner-city youth: Beyond ethnicity and gender* (pp. 94–120). New York: Teachers College Press.

Wallace, A.F.C. (1970). *The death and rebirth of the Seneca.* New York: Knopf.

Wallace, A.F.C. (1978). *Rockdale: The growth of an American village in the early industrial revolution.* New York: Knopf.

Warren, R. (1978). *The community in America.* Chicago: Rand McNally.

Webber, M. (1991). *Street kids: The tragedy of Canada's runaways.* Toronto: University of Toronto Press.

West, J. (1945). *Plainfield.* New York: Columbia University Press.

Whyte, W. F. (1943). *Street corner society.* Chicago: University of Chicago Press.

Wilkinson, K. P. (1986). In search of the community in the changing countryside. *Rural Sociology, 51*(1), 1–18.

Wilson, W. J. (1987). *The truly disadvantaged.* Chicago: University of Chicago Press.

Yamashita, K. S. (1985). *Terminal Island: Ethnography of an ethnic community—Its dissolution and reorganization to a non-spatial community.* Dissertation, University of California, Irvine.

Zentella, A. C. (1981). *Hablamos los dos: Bilingualism in el bloque.* Unpublished doctoral dissertation, University of Pennsylvania, University Park.

Zentella, A. C. (1997). *Growing up bilingual: Puerto Rican children in New York.* New York: Blackwell.

9

ETHNOGRAPHIC STUDIES OF MULTICULTURAL EDUCATION IN U.S. CLASSROOMS AND SCHOOLS

John S. Wills
University of California, Riverside

Angela Lintz
High Tech High, San Diego

Hugh Mehan
University of California, San Diego

This chapter reviews ethnographic studies of multicultural education in U.S. classrooms and schools. We emphasize those studies that have made intentional—that is, self-conscious—attempts to be culturally inclusive by modifying classroom organization, discourse patterns, or the curriculum. Space limitations and the focus of this chap-. ter mean, unfortunately, that other research cannot be included. Of necessity, we have omitted studies of desegregation (such as Hanna, 1982; Metz, 1980, 1986; Peshkin, 1991; Rist, 1979; Schofield, 1982; and Wagner, 1969) and ethnographies of urban schools (Anyon, 1997; Devine, 1996; Fine, 1991; Ogbu, 1974; Olsen, 1997; Solomon, 1992; Weis, 1985, 1990; Yon, 2000; and others).

The chapter is organized into three parts. In the first part, we examine the educational and social consequences of attempts to achieve multicultural education by modifying classroom discourse patterns and participation structures. In the second part, we examine what happens when the manifest content of the history–social studies instructional curriculum is modified in order to (a) teach a multicultural history so that students will gain an under-

standing of the experiences of different groups, and (b) foster ethnoracial identity. In the third part, we draw the implications of these studies for classrooms composed of students from many linguistic and cultural backgrounds.

THE CONSEQUENCES OF MODIFYING CLASSROOM DISCOURSE

The language that teachers use with students is constitutive. The way in which teachers ask questions and engage in discourse with students both constrains and enables the ways in which they can display what they know. Because of the co-occurrence relationships that operate in conversation, what students can say in lessons depends on the frames established by what teachers say, the questions they ask.

The "recitation script" (Tharp & Gallimore, 1988) is the prevailing way in which lessons are organized in U.S. classrooms. Although everyday conversations are organized in two-part sequences (Sacks, Schegloff, & Jefferson,

The authors wish to thank James A. Banks, Frederick Erickson, and Peter McLaren for their helpful suggestions on the version of this chapter published in the first edition of this book and Bradley Levinson and Margaret Eisenhart on this revised version of this chapter. The contribution of Hugh Mehan to the original version of this chapter was supported by the Linguistic Minority Research Institute of the University of California and the office of Educational Research and Improvement (OERI); the contribution of Angela Lintz was supported by the Girard Foundation; the contribution of John Wills was supported by the Spencer Foundation.

1974), classroom lessons are organized in three-part sequences: a teacher's initiation act induces a student's reply, which in turn invokes a teacher's evaluation (Mehan, 1979). This three-part I-R-E structure exists because teachers often ask "known information questions" (Mehan, 1979; Shuy & Griffin, 1978; Sinclair & Coulthard, 1975) in which students' knowledge is tested rather than new information sought from them. Recitation lessons are therefore teacher-centered and require students to respond, often individually, with student behavior evaluated quite publicly. Such lessons create a highly competitive classroom interaction situation.

Discontinuity Between the Language of the Home and the School

Students of language use in homes and schools (Cazden, 1988; Heath, 1982, 1986; Laosa, 1973; Mehan, 1979; Philips, 1982; Schultz, Florio, & Erickson, 1982; Lee, 1995; Gutierrez, in press; Gutierrez, Baquedano-Lopez, & Tejada, 1997; Gutierrez, Rymes, & Larson, 1995) have suggested that recitation-type lessons in school may be compatible with the discourse patterns in Anglo families but may be incompatible with the discourse patterns of certain minority group families. This discontinuity, in turn, may contribute to the lower achievement and higher dropout rate among minority students.

In the hallmark study in this tradition, Philips (1982) found that Native American children performed very poorly in classroom contexts that demanded individualized performance and emphasized competition among peers, but they performed more effectively in classroom contexts that minimized the obligation of individual students to perform in public contexts. The classroom contexts in which Native American students operated best were similar in organization to local Native American community contexts, where *cooperation* and not *competition* was valued, and *sociality* and not *individuality* was emphasized. Philips attributes the generally poor performance of Native American children to differences in the "structures of participation" normatively demanded in the home and in the school. It seems that the patterns of participation normally expected in conventional classrooms create conditions that are unfamiliar and threatening to most Native American children.

Erickson and Mohatt (1982) showed that an Athabaskan Indian teacher taught Athabaskan Indian children differently than did a Canadian teacher in the same school. The Indian teacher's manner of exercising control over the classroom focused on groups; she dispensed praise in public, made criticism in private, and allocated turns so that students were not obligated to participate as individuals but could choose to join in group answers to questions. More interesting than the congruence between the cultural style of this Native teacher and her Native students is the fact that the Canadian teacher began to modify his teaching practices in the direction of his students' culture. His Indian students informally socialized him to use more group-based instruction, facilitate more voluntary contributions, and keep evaluations private as they worked together through time (see Barnhardt, 1982).

McCullum (1989) makes a similar point about the cultural congruity of a Puerto Rican teacher's turn-allocation practices with her Puerto Rican students. An English-speaking teacher of Puerto Rican students in Chicago allocated turns competitively and individually—in ways that conform precisely to the recitation script. However, a Spanish-speaking teacher of Puerto Rican students in Puerto Rico deployed turn-allocation strategies that were group-oriented and permitted students to volunteer answers. McCullum suggests that the language patterns used in the Puerto Rican classroom signaled a social relationship between teacher and students that was closer to an "instructional conversation" (Tharp & Gallimore, 1988) than a recitation lesson. This instructional conversation was more consistent with the conversational patterns in everyday Puerto Rican life.

Heath (1982) reports that the children of middle-income teachers in "Trackton" (see Chapter 8, this volume) were taught to label and name objects and to talk about things out of context, which were the skills demanded of students in school. These same teachers talked to the students in their classrooms in ways that were very similar to the ways in which they talked to their own children at home. They instructed students primarily through an interrogative format using known-information questions and taught students to label objects and identify the features of things.

However, this mode of language use and language socialization was not prevalent in the homes of low-income students. Low-income adults seldom addressed questions to their school-age children at home, and even less often to preverbal children. Where Trackton teachers would use questions, Trackton parents would use statements or imperatives. When questions were asked of Trackton children by their parents, they were much different from the types of questions asked by teachers. Questions at home called for nonspecific comparisons or analogies as answers. They were not the known-information or information-seeking questions associated with the classroom. Heath (1982) concludes that the language used in Trackton homes did not prepare children to cope with the major characteristics of the language used in classrooms: utterances that were interrogative in form but directive in pragmatic function, known-information questions, and questions that asked for information from books.

Modifying Classroom Discourse for Cultural Compatibility

Although it is a powerful antidote to cultural-deprivation explanations of educational inequality, the cultural-discontinuity account is not without its detractors. Critics (Foley, 1990; Levinson, Foley, & Holland, 1996; MacLaren, 1997; Ogbu, 1987, 1991) fear that its liberal assimilationist assumptions are inadequate to the real challenges of creating equity in a racialized capitalist order because this perspective can mistakenly reduce inequality to a problem of miscommunication. Even if parents read more stories to their children at bedtime, or teachers learned to respect language minority students' codes or learned to communicate effectively with them, critics argue that structural inequities (glass ceilings, downsized corporations, and institutional discrimination in the workplace, for example) would remain. Despite these disclaimers, a vigorous set of recommendations for improving classroom pedagogy has emerged from research on cultural discontinuity.

Piestrup (1973) documented the positive benefits of compatible relationships between home and school language in 14 predominantly African American first-grade classrooms in the Oakland, California, public school system. When teachers employed a style that reflected the taken-for-granted speech patterns of the African American community, instruction was the most effective. Students in classrooms where teachers implicitly incorporated the taken-for-granted features of culturally familiar speech events in classrooms, including rhythmic language, rapid intonation, repetition, alliteration, call and response, variation in pace, and creative language play, scored significantly higher on standardized reading tests than students in classrooms where teachers used other styles.

According to M. Foster (1989), Marva Collins, the well-known teacher from Chicago's Westside Prep School, employed strategies similar to those of the successful teachers in Piestrup's (1973) study. Collins attributes her own success to a phonics curriculum; Foster gives more credit to the congruence between her interactional style and the children's cultural experience. Familiar language and participation structures, including rhythmic language, call and response, repetition, and deliberate body motions, make up the interactional pattern.

M. Foster (1989) complemented her informal discussion of Collins's teaching with a more formal analysis of teachers in a predominantly African American community college. She found (M. Foster 1989, 1995) that classroom discussion increased in degree and intensity when teacher-student interaction was symmetrical (teachers and students had equivalent numbers of turns) and cooperative learning groups were formed. This finding parallels a more general one about the value of cooperative learning for linguistic minority youth (Duran & Szymanski, 1992; Kagan, 1986; Slavin, 2001). Successful community college teachers also called for active vocal audience responses and descriptions of personal experiences, strategies that act in ways that model performance patterns in the local African American community.

To increase Trackton students' verbal skills in naming objects, identifying their characteristics, providing descriptions out of context, and responding to known-information questions, Heath (1982) worked with the Trackton teachers on ways to adapt to the community's ways of asking questions. After reviewing tapes with researchers, teachers began social studies lessons with questions that ask for personal experiences and analogic responses, such as "What's happening there?" "Have you ever been there?" "What's this like?" These questions were similar to the questions that parents asked their children at home. Their use in early stages of instruction was productive in generating active responses from previously passive and nonverbal Trackton students. Once the teachers increased the students' participation in lessons using home questioning styles, they were able to move them through a zone of learning toward school-based questioning styles (cf. Taylor & Dorsey-Grimes, 1988).

In an analogous fashion, teachers working with the Kamehameha (Hawaii) Early Education Program (KEEP) spontaneously introduced narratives jointly produced by the children into the beginning of reading lessons—a detail later observed by researchers associated with the project (Au, 1980; Tharp & Gallimore, 1988). In addition, they shifted the focus of instruction from decoding to comprehension, implemented small-group instruction to encourage cooperation, and included children's experiences as part of the discussion of reading materials. All of these modifications were consistent with Hawaiian cultural norms and had significant consequences. Student participation in lessons increased, and their scores on standardized tests improved. Both of these effects were notable because they contravened the notoriously low school performance of Native Hawaiians.

Moll and his colleagues (Moll, Vélez-Ibáñez, & Greenberg, 1988, 1989; Moll & Gonzalez, this volume; Gonzalez, Moll, & Amanti, in press; see also Moll & Diaz, 1987; Díaz, Moll, & Mehan, 1986) have systematized the use of ethnographic techniques to exploit the social and cultural practices of the community for instructional purposes in the classroom. Employing a collaborative approach to research, teachers and researchers first work together to learn about the demographic and economic patterns, the social networks, and the social knowledge of existing households and neighborhoods within the local community. Then teachers mobilize the information they acquire for instructional purposes.

Moll et al. (1989) relate a provocative example in which a sixth-grade teacher incorporated information about construction gleaned from the local *barrio* to enliven literacy instruction. After students were sent to the library in the usual fashion to gather and read books on constructing houses and other buildings, the teacher invited members of the local community (some of whom were the parents of the students) to share their knowledge about building. A mason told the students how to mix mortar, measure straight lines, and stack bricks neatly and strongly. A carpenter told about the relative strength of brick and wood, and about sawing and nailing techniques. Students applied this knowledge to a model they built in their classroom. Analysis of the students' writing during and after the model building showed that the students incidentally acquired new vocabulary (joists, ridge hangers, waffle boards), wrote eloquently about the skills involved in the building trades, and perhaps most important developed an appreciation for their parents' "funds of knowledge." The students were surprised and pleased that the school would validate their parents' skills and experience, even though they did not have formal education.

This study has wider implications. It helps redefine the Latino family for educators, researchers, and the public. Educational activities such as these demonstrate that the households and neighborhoods of even the poorest families are not devoid of knowledge and are not disorganized. Economically poor conditions do not create culturally poor conditions. Rural and urban poor Latino families are connected to extensive social networks that provide different forms of economic assistance and labor cooperation that help families avoid the cost of plumbers, car mechanics, even physicians. These social networks also provide emotional and service support in the form of child care, job information, and "connections." Although educators are correct when they say they are strapped for material resources in the classroom, they can learn from Moll and his colleagues that even the poorest neighborhood is rich in cultural resources that can connect the classroom to the world.

By modifying classroom discourse to emphasize inquiry and information-seeking questions, McCarty, Wallace, Lynch, and Benally (1991) help dispel the myth of the nonverbal Indian student, and in the process challenge the concept of learning styles. For decades, Native American students have been portrayed in the literature as quiet, passive, and nonresponsive (John, 1972). They have been said to learn by observing and doing, not through listening and saying (More, 1989; Tharp, 1989). Often in the name of cultural compatibility, educators have emphasized nonverbal means of instruction and cue-response scripted drills as a way to reach passive Indian students. McCarty and colleagues say that these erstwhile attempts had an unfortunate side effect: Indian students

are not taught with higher-order questioning and inquiry methods.

Working with the Navajo-staffed Native American Materials Development Center, staff members of the Rough Rock Indian reservation school implemented an inquiry-based bilingual social studies program. In the first lesson, the teacher-demonstrator showed students local scenes and asked them to identify things needed in their community. After accumulating a long list, students were asked to group like items and justify their choices. Eventually they reached a consensus, identifying things needed and things they'd like to have. That consensus led to the lesson generalization "Rough Rock is a community because people work together to meet their needs and solve mutual problems" (McCarty et al., 1991, p. 57).

The lessons in "Navajo Humanities" suggest that Navajo students will indeed respond enthusiastically to inquiry-based questioning. What made these lessons work? McCarty and her coauthors (1991) suggest that this curriculum was effective because it encouraged students to draw upon their prior knowledge to solve new problems. The materials presented familiar scenes, and the teachers' questions tapped students' knowledge and experience. When the classroom environment was changed, Navajo children became verbal, assertive, and able to make innovative generalizations.

In addition to illustrating that Native American children will respond to inquiry-based instruction when it is grounded in the experiences of their everyday life, this study shows us the limitations of the cognitive styles concept. Native American and other minority children may in fact appear to be nonverbal when classroom discourse patterns limit their expression, but if the expression of students' ideas is sought, if aspects of students' life are meaningfully incorporated into curricular content, and if students are encouraged to use their cultural and linguistic knowledge to solve new problems, then Native American students will respond eagerly and verbally to questioning. This validates the observation by Cole and Scribner (1974) that cognitive differences reside more in the situations in which particular cognitive processes are applied than in the existence of a process in a cultural group and its absence in another.

Organizing classroom discourse around inquiry and students' everyday knowledge has produced similar results with Haitian students. Current research in the sociology of science (e.g., Knorr-Cetina & Mulkay, 1983; Latour & Woolgar, 1986) suggests that scientists do their work within a community of practice. They transform their observations into findings through interpretation and argumentation, not simply through measurement and discovery. Scientists may claim that they discover facts passively, but close observation of their practice reveals they construct findings actively. Although textbooks depict the scientific *method* as orderly, logical, and rational, sociological studies show that scientific *practice* entails making sense out of contradictory observations, choosing among competing hypotheses, and convincing others about the importance of findings.

Roseberry, Warren, and Conant (1992) explored this idea that scientific understanding is shaped by a community through scientific argument, rather than received from authority, with a class of seventh- and eighth-grade Haitian students in Cambridge, Massachusetts. The "Water Taste Test" was designed to investigate the "truth" of a belief held by most of the junior high school students that the water from the fountain on the third floor was superior to the water from the other fountains in the school (in part because "all the little kids slobber" in the first-floor fountain). After discussing methodological issues of sampling, masking the identity of the water, and ways to overcome bias in voting, the students conducted a blind taste test of water from several fountains. Test results showed a vast majority of the junior high school students thought they preferred water from the third-floor fountain, but they chose the first-floor fountain. In order to interpret their findings, the students analyzed the school's water. Analysis showed that the water from the first-floor fountain was 20 degrees colder than that from the other fountains (and theorized that the water was cooled by underground pipes and warmed as it flowed to the third floor). Therefore, they concluded that temperature was probably a deciding factor in students' preferences.

This sense-making approach to science with language minority students is a radical departure from the textbook memorizing, or even experimental demonstrations, found in most classrooms. Here we see students constructing scientific understandings through an iterative process of theory building, hypothesis testing, and data collection. These students posed their own questions, generated their own hypotheses, and analyzed their own data. This activity facilitated students' appreciation of responses that were different from their own, which Vygotskians and Piagetians alike agree is essential in learning to take the perspective of the other. Like scientists in real-life laboratories, these students challenged one another's thoughts, negotiated conflicts about evidence and conclusions, and shared their knowledge in order to achieve an understanding that looks just like scientific understanding. Like scientists in real-life laboratories, these students were working in a community of practice in which the exploration of individual participants was guided and supported by the whole group (cf. Brown & Palinscar, 1989; Brown, Ash, Rutherford, Nakagawa, Gordon, & Campione, 1993).

Labov's (1972) path-breaking work showed that youngsters who seemed linguistically deprived in formal testing situations provided linguistically elaborate and logical statements in less formal conversations. Organizing classroom participation structures so that these discourse strategies could be transferred to the classroom has proven to be a vexing task. Lee (1995) has described how one teacher accomplished this important goal by introducing and building upon material drawn from popular cultural routines and rituals. Convinced that African American youth who are skilled at signifying use certain strategies to process dialogue that are comparable to those that expert readers use to construct inferences from narratives, the teacher designed instruction to make students' tacit knowledge explicit and useable when analyzing short stories and passages from novels.

In a similar model of cognitive apprenticeship, Gutierrez (in press) and her colleagues (Gutierrez et al., 1995; Gutierrez et al., 1999) have documented teachers' use of the "third space" (between the formal, official classroom discourse space and unofficial, out-of-school conversational space) as a tool to build upon students' cultural knowledge. In her Spanish immersion classroom, "Ms. Rivera" capitalized on students' informal name calling ("homos") to construct a lesson on homosexuality and human reproduction. Analysis of classroom transcripts shows that the teacher combined students' local knowledge, generated in unofficial discourse space, with formal scientific terms (such as *esperma*) to expand Latino students' learning horizons.

The research discussed in this section reinforces a more general point made by Erickson and Schultz (1992): The engagement of students in learning activities results from a connection between social participation structure (form) and academic curriculum (content). If the social participation structure is familiar to students, then performing with new academic content is not very alienating (as in the KEEP reading lessons described in Au, 1980; Tharp & Gallimore, 1988). On the other hand, if the academic content is familiar or engaging, then students may be willing to try out new ways of interacting and using language (as in the Rough Rock lessons in McCarty et al., 1991). The issue underlying both cases is safety: not having to risk looking clumsy or stupid in front of others. Lesson content and form, taken together or separately, can reduce the risk of embarrassment, which in turn triggers resistance—the withholding of assent to learn and to participate in learning activities.

THE CONSEQUENCES OF MODIFYING THE CURRICULUM

A second approach to multicultural education modifies the curriculum, especially in history and social studies, to achieve one of two goals: (a) to include the experiences, perspectives, and contributions of women and people of color in historical narratives, or (b) to build an ethnoracial identity. Since the publication of the first edition of this *Handbook,* there has still been virtually no ethnographic research on multicultural curriculum practice in actual classrooms. As a consequence, we will, once again, highlight our own case studies here, after first reporting on related research that engages issues of multiculturalism and diversity in history and social studies education and then arguing for the need for ethnographic investigations of multicultural curriculum practice in schools and classrooms.

Analyzing Textbooks and Investigating Adolescents' Historical Understanding

We begin this section by noting two main approaches to researching issues of multiculturalism and diversity in history and social studies education. We do not raise this research in order to present an exhaustive review of these studies. Rather, we use our discussion to indicate the significant gap in our knowledge regarding the consequences of efforts to modify K-12 history and social studies curriculum to embody diversity in actual classrooms. The lack of ethnographic research on multicultural curriculum practice empowers us to continue proposing and theorizing what multicultural education should be, without being able to state with any confidence, supported by a body of ethnographic case studies, what multicultural education actually is in K-12 history and social studies classrooms.

One body of research addressing the issue of diversity and multiculturalism in K-12 history and social studies education consists of analyses of curriculum content, especially textbooks. Content analyses of textbooks have been a favored means for critiquing what students learn, or do not learn, from their schooling (cf. Apple & Christian-Smith, 1991; Fitzgerald, 1980; Sleeter & Grant, 1991). Recent analyses have investigated issues of multicultural reform and the treatment (or rather, lack of treatment) of discrimination, racism, and injustice in history and social studies textbooks. Loewen (1995) analyzed 12 high school U.S. history textbooks and concluded, among other things, that omissions, distortions, and misrepresentations often rendered Native Americans and African Americans invisible in U.S. history, and that the structure of textbook discussions promoted a "white supremacist viewpoint" (p. 157) of U.S. history. Willinsky (1998) analyzed textbooks and other curricular materials to demonstrate how the legacy of imperialism continues to educate students with a "colonial imagery" that divides the world according to race and ethnicity. Similarly, Kaomea (2000) finds that the Hawaiian studies curriculum, a well-intended multicultural curriculum reform effort, embodies colonial dynamics that educate Native Hawaiian students with a "tourist-catering mentality"

(p. 332) that prepares them for future roles as tour guides, hotel workers, and other low-paid laborers in the tourist industry.

In addition to analyses of curriculum content, researchers in history and social studies education have investigated the historical-reasoning and interpretive practices of adolescents. Scholars working in this tradition have been concerned with the effectiveness of instruction and the divide between the historical reasoning exhibited by historians and the historical thinking exhibited by students and found in history textbooks (Brophy, VanSledright, & Bredin, 1993; Gabella, 1994; McKeown & Beck, 1990, 1994; Wineburg, 1991; see also Paxton, 1999, for a recent review of this literature, as well as helpful discussions in Levstik & Barton, 1996; and Wineburg, 2001). More recently, a number of scholars have shifted the focus from issues of historical reasoning to studying adolescents' interpretations of historical actors, events, and themes (Barton & Levstik, 1996; Epstein, 1998; Levstik & Barton, 1996, 1997; Seixas, 1993; Wineburg, 2001). Informed by debates over multicultural reform in history and social studies education (Gitlin, 1995; Nash, Crabtree, & Dunn, 1997) and battles over public commemorations and museum exhibits (Linenthal & Engelhardt, 1996; Wineburg, 2001), these studies have attempted to understand the factors that mediate adolescents' representation and narration of history. Drawing on cognitive psychology and employing a "sociocultural approach" (Epstein, 2000, p. 191), these studies have used questionnaires, individual and group interviews, and the manipulation of historical images to understand the interpretive practices of adolescents as they offer their explanations of important people, events, and themes in U.S. history.

Fournier and Wineburg (1997) found gender differences in girls' and boys' illustrations of history, with boys depicting a past in which women were virtually invisible and girls depicting a past dominated mainly by solitary male figures. Barton and Levstik (1998) found that both African American and European American eighth graders constructed narratives of U.S. history that reflected a progressive view of national development, even though they could cite examples from history that challenged this narrative. Levstik (2000) reports on differences between teachers' and students' investment in a progressive narrative of expanding rights and opportunities in U.S. history. Teachers were firmly wedded to a progressive story of nation building; students were interested in pursuing more coercive and negative aspects of U.S. history. The group interviews with students in this research also demonstrated diverse perspectives on history among African American and European American students. Epstein (1998, 2000) examined the effects of adolescents' racial identities on their interpretations of U.S. history.

She found racial differences reflected in students' selections of historically significant people and events, their understandings of racism, inequality, and oppression in U.S. history, and their perspectives on racial diversity in U.S. history. Epstein concluded that differences in adolescents' historical understandings were due to race-related differences in the lived experiences of students and their family members.

We mention these studies of textbook content and of students' interpretation and narration of history because it would be wrong to conclude that there is no research (including qualitative research) investigating important issues regarding diversity and multicultural education in history and social studies education. Textbook analyses demonstrate the continuing Eurocentic, colonialist, and imperialist perspectives in history and social studies textbooks. Investigations of students' interpretations and narration of U.S. history indicate a privileging of narratives that reflect a White perspective but also indicate contradictions and discordant representations of people and events that could provide avenues for deconstructing and revising school-based histories of the United States. But even with the important insights of these studies, they are no substitute for ethnographic studies of multicultural curriculum practice in actual classrooms.

Ethnographic studies of the curriculum have demonstrated how the use of curriculum in constructing school knowledge is mediated by the organizational forms of schooling (McNeil, 1986), school culture (Page, 1991), teacher expectations (Keddie, 1971), and popular cultural knowledge (Wills, 1994). Readers are not passive consumers of fixed meanings that are located in textbooks and other curricular texts. Instead, curricular content takes on meaning as teachers and students actively draw upon these materials as resources in representing historical figures and events in lessons and activities. Textbook content does not determine the representation and narration of history by teachers and students. In fact, the role of textbook content in determining classroom representations of the past is complicated by the fact that textbooks often contain multiple, even contradictory, representations of historical figures and events (Wills, 1994, 2001b). Textbooks are also often used in conjunction with other media, such as documentary and popular film, literature, popular articles, library research, and various other multimedia, situating the textbook as one of many resources that teachers and students draw upon to construct meaningful accounts of historical figures and events. Understanding student knowledge of the past as a product of curriculum practice therefore becomes a complex enterprise for which an ethnographic approach is well suited.

That students' interpretation and narration of the past is mediated by gender, racial, and ethnic differences argues for the need for teachers to take students' historical

perspectives into account when developing curriculum and making instructional decisions to support a multicultural history and social studies education. But the interpretation and narration of history in classrooms is not only an individual cognitive phenomenon; it is a complex social and cultural process involving the interaction of teachers, students, and a variety of cultural texts. Although these studies rightly note the influence of nonschool factors (family, the media, popular culture) on students' historical perspectives, understanding the remembering and forgetting of the past as a product of curriculum practice has been ignored in these studies. Even Epstein (1998), who observed classroom lessons and activities as part of her research, does not engage curriculum practice beyond mentioning themes, ideas, and explanations evident in students' explanations of important historical actors and events that were also mentioned by the teacher.

Our point here is not to criticize these two areas of research, which are valuable and important in advancing our understanding of multicultural curriculum and efforts to construct more inclusive narratives of the past. Rather, we mention this research to illuminate and illustrate a perspective on and method of studying issues of curriculum, diversity, and multiculturalism that has been missing from the research literature. What are the social, cultural, and institutional practices that transform official curriculum into classroom knowledge of U.S. history and society? How does multicultural curriculum, as constructed in classroom lessons and activities, transform teachers' and students' representation of historical figures and events and their narration of U.S. history? What counts as multicultural curriculum practice in actual classrooms, and what are the consequences of these practices for students and society?

For example, Wills (Mehan & Wills, 1988; Wills & Mehan, 2001) also asked eighth-grade students to construct narratives of U.S. history but did so to discover what aspects of the curriculum in use would affect students' narration of the past. By analyzing these narratives, Wills was able to connect the absence of Native Americans in students' representations of U.S. history to curriculum practice. Native Americans were present in the curriculum in use—in exercises and activities exploring their traditional culture, contrasting Native American culture to White culture, and establishing their perspective on historical events. However, they were absent as historical actors and agents in accounts of historical events. They were, in effect, present in the curriculum but absent in history. Student narratives in this instance were clearly products of curricular practice and illuminated the trap of focusing on culture as an approach to including diverse groups in a supposedly multicultural history of the United States. This is the kind of insight concerning the consequences of modifying curriculum to achieve a multicultural history of the United States that an ethnographic approach to studying curriculum can achieve, and that is difficult to discern solely through textbook studies or investigations of adolescents' interpretations of history.

Modifying Classroom Curriculum to Embody Diversity

In this section, we describe the struggles of three teachers to construct a multicultural history of the United States using a new textbook, *A More Perfect Union* (Armento, Nash, Slater, & Wixson, 1991), part of a textbook series adopted by the state of California to meet the requirements of a new *History/Social Science Framework* (California State Department of Education, 1988) approved in 1987. This series, published by Houghton Mifflin, was intended to provide students with a multicultural history of the United States and the world. Wills (1994, 1996, 2001b; see also Mehan & Wills, 1996; and Wills & Mehan, 2001) examined the influence of the official curriculum on the representation of racial and ethnic groups and the creation of inclusive narratives of U.S. history in three eighth-grade classrooms in one predominantly White, suburban middle school in San Diego. The approach taken by the textbook series and by the teachers Wills observed consisted mainly of injecting the contributions, experiences, and perspectives of African Americans and Native Americans into a traditional, Eurocentric narrative of U.S. history.

The three teachers whose classrooms were observed—"Judy," "Ruth," and "Tom"—were chosen for their different teaching styles, interests, and conceptions of a multicultural U.S. history curriculum. Wills observed their use of different instructional materials throughout the 1991–92 school year and compared and contrasted their use of the same eighth-grade U.S. history textbook, *A More Perfect Union* (Armento et al., 1991). In addition to nonparticipant observation, Wills videotaped lessons and activities, thus providing a record of classroom discourse and the interpretive practices of teachers and students as they used a variety of texts to construct a history of the United States. Analysis of this data was supplemented by formal and informal interviews with teachers and students and collection and analysis of student work, including brief narratives of U.S. history written by students specifically for the researcher.

One long-standing hope of multicultural curriculum reform is that it will help teach students some degree of understanding of different racial, ethnic, and religious groups, and that this understanding will translate into improved relations in our increasingly diverse society (Banks & Banks, 1989; Sleeter & Grant, 1987). By focusing on the experiences of men and women of diverse racial, ethnic, and religious groups in U.S. history, a

multicultural history curriculum will provide students with a historical context in which to situate and understand the experiences and perspectives of these groups in U.S. society today. Over the past decade, critical multiculturalists have called for curriculum and pedagogy that moves beyond liberal goals of improving cultural understanding between diverse groups to engage the unequal distribution of power and resources in U.S. society and recognizes the normative status of Whiteness in American culture. By making visible the economic, political, and cultural power of Whiteness in U.S. history and society, White students are provided a critical space in which they can move beyond White guilt to engage issues of structured inequality in U.S. society (Giroux, 1997; Jackson & Solis, 1995; Ladson-Billings & Tate, 1995; McCarthy, 1998; McCarthy & Crichlow, 1993; McCarthy & Willis, 1995; McLaren, 1997).

Whether critical or liberal, advocates of multicultural education recognize the necessity to educate all students with knowledge that may ultimately improve race and ethnic relations in our increasingly diverse society. This was also the goal of both proponents and opponents of the Houghton Mifflin textbook series adopted in California, who shared the belief that education could be a positive force for social change by influencing students' attitudes and beliefs about different racial and ethnic groups. For White students and teachers, multicultural education (what it could and should be, not necessarily what it is in practice) means challenging the assumptions and biases of mainstream White American culture (Grant & Sleeter, 1986; McLaren & Estrada, 1993), assumptions and biases that often remain invisible in curriculum practice. The purpose of Wills's ethnography was to understand the "how" of multicultural curriculum practice in these teachers' classrooms: what counted as multicultural histories of the United States in these classrooms, and how the construction of historical knowledge was mediated by the textbook and other curricular and popular texts. Here we report the main findings of his research, a story of the sincere efforts of three teachers to modify the curriculum to present a multicultural history of the United States and the unintended, even paradoxical effects of these modifications.

Multicultural Curriculum Practice in Three U.S. History Classrooms

The adoption of the Houghton Mifflin textbook series in California was met with intense criticism from a multitude of racial, ethnic, and religious groups who charged that the textbooks misrepresented the experiences of their people, presented stereotypical portrayals of their people, and contained an unacknowledged Eurocentric perspective on history (Gitlin, 1995; Nash et al., 1997). These groups feared that these textbooks would perpetuate stereotypes and promote prejudice among the students who used them. Wills (1994) found that the curriculum in use in three eighth-grade U.S. history classrooms did perpetuate a stereotypical representation of Native Americans, but attributing this only to use of a biased textbook is too simple an explanation. What Wills found in these classrooms was a remembering, and then a forgetting, of Native American diversity as the representation of Native Americans as nomadic, buffalo hunting Plains Indians was privileged over alternative representations.

Although *A More Perfect Union* (Armento et al., 1991) presents diverse representations of Native Americans, Wills argued that the textbook does exhibit a bias toward privileging the culture and presence of Plains Indians over other American Indian groups. For example, while noting that most Native Americans were successful farmers on one page, the text on the facing page celebrates the buffalo hunting of the Plains Indians, and the dominant visual image is of an American Indian on horseback about to shoot an arrow into a fleeing buffalo (pp. 26–27). Although it expands upon the traditional Eurocentric narrative by including a lesson on the Shawnee, the Cherokee, and the Trail of Tears (pp. 201–207), more time is spent providing information on the culture, literature, and history of the Plains Indians (pp. 415–426). *A More Perfect Union* does attempt to expand the narrative of U.S. history by recognizing the diversity of Native Americans and their experiences in U.S. history, but at heart the narrative is still organized around a Eurocentric perspective on U.S. history.

But the content of *A More Perfect Union* (Armento et al., 1991), or the other curricular and popular materials used by these teachers, does not determine the representation of Native Americans or the narration of U.S. history. Ruth and Tom noted the racist views of Whites toward Native Americans and the diversity of Native American groups in U.S. history, and they used the textbook as a resource in these classroom lessons and discussions. But they also ultimately constructed a history of the United States that privileged a romanticized and stereotypical representation of Native Americans as nomadic, buffalo hunting Plains Indians over all others. Wills (1994) argued that this was due not only to the influence of popular images of American Indians found in mainstream American culture but also to the use of a Eurocentric narrative of U.S. history that necessarily constricted the diversity of Native Americans that was sustainable throughout U.S. history. In this narrative, the history of Native American–White relations was almost exclusively understood through the experience of the Plains Indians during the westward movement, which was the only developed story of American Indians in U.S. history. As a consequence, the remembering of Plains Indians resulted

in the forgetting of other Native American groups, thereby perpetuating the stereotype that all American Indians were nomadic buffalo hunters.

Judy's approach to including the experiences and perspectives of Native Americans in U.S. history is different from Ruth's and Tom's and illustrates the problems of studying the cultures of diverse groups as an approach to multicultural curriculum in history and social studies. Finding less information than she thought was appropriate on Native Americans during the Colonial period in *A More Perfect Union* (Armento et. al., 1991), Judy decided to spend three weeks supplementing the textbook with additional reading, research, and cooperative group activities. The curriculum in use was focused on studying the traditional cultures of Native American tribes, exploring the cultural differences between Native Americans and Whites, and understanding the diverse perspectives of cultural groups on events in U.S. history. As Mehan & Wills (1988; see also Wills & Mehan, 2001; and Wills, 2001) argue, this approach to including Native Americans in U.S. history not only promotes an essentialist understanding of culture but more importantly fails to include Native Americans as actors and agents in U.S. history.

Judy had her students read Conrad Richter's *The Light in the Forest* (1953) to provide information on Native American groups during the Colonial period in U.S. history. This novel, coupled with library research on Native American tribes who lived in the eastern woodlands during the Colonial period, provided the curricular content for discussing stereotypes of Native Americans, Native American culture, and cultural differences between Native Americans and Whites. In addition to this work, Judy also used a variety of role-playing activities to include the perspectives of diverse groups in discussions of important events in U.S. history. These activities can provide students with an understanding of history that is multiperspectival, allowing students to see how specific historical events were interpreted differently by people on the basis of gender, race, and ethnicity.

Judy's efforts were a sincere attempt to create a more inclusive narrative of U.S. history, but they fell victim to the trap of "cultural tourism" (Mehan & Wills, 1988, p. 6). This approach can lead teachers and students away from the study of history and leave diverse groups "missing in interaction" in narratives of U.S. history (Wills, 2001a). The problem of focusing on culture in creating a multicultural history and social studies curriculum, as evidenced in Judy's classroom, is that the focus on culture often leads teachers to focus their attention on the cultural attributes of diverse groups and not on social action in history. To the extent that Native Americans were present in the curriculum, they were present as cultural representatives, exotic "others" who view, experience, and live in the world differently than Whites do; or as cultural commentators, addressing the actions of others (White males) in significant historical events in U.S. history. As a consequence, diverse groups remain outside the narratives of U.S. history constructed in classrooms, as teachers and students construct deterministic and essentialist understandings of the diverse cultures of racial and ethnic groups while failing to represent them as actors and agents in specific historical events. Paradoxically, the presence of Native Americans in the curriculum in use told students little to nothing about their role in U.S. history, their actions in specific historical events, and their interactions with Whites and other groups present during the Colonial period.

Judy's attempt to create a more inclusive narrative of U.S. history also applied to African Americans. She hoped her students' study of African Americans in U.S. history would enable them to address contemporary race relations in the United States and engage issues of inequality, economic opportunity, and African Americans' struggle for civil rights. To support this goal, Judy spent eight weeks studying the Civil War period, with a specific emphasis on examining the experiences of enslaved African Americans in the South. Paradoxically, this focus on exploring the brutalities and injustices that characterized the lives of enslaved African Americans in the South during the Civil War period did little to enable Judy's students to critically examine contemporary race relations in U.S. society (Wills, 1996).

As with her students' work on Native Americans during the Colonial period, Judy drew upon many sources beyond the textbook to inform her students' understanding of slavery during their study of the Civil War period. For example, she used the documentary film *Roots of Resistance: The Underground Railroad* (Thomas, 1990), which discusses slave resistance, the Underground Railroad, the Fugitive Slave Act, and the Dred Scott decision, as a starting point for discussing southern slavery. Her students also read Julius Lester's *To Be a Slave* (1968), a collection of interviews with African Americans who were former slaves, gathered by the Federal Writers Project in the 1930s. Students kept a dialectical journal in which they responded to passages from each chapter of Lester's book. In addition to class discussion that drew upon these materials, her students also completed Civil War projects that were then presented in class, as well as writing a final essay dealing with slavery. *A More Perfect Union* (Armento et al., 1991) supported this examination of the experiences of enslaved African Americans with, for example, Solomon Northup's description of the whippings slaves received while picking cotton (p. 285) and Frederick Douglass's discussion of Mr. Covey, a master who succeeded in breaking Douglass "in body, soul, and spirit" (pp. 296–297).

By the end of their unit on the Civil War, Judy's students had become "virtual witnesses" to the experiences of African Americans under slavery. All the work the students did and the materials they read were focused on imparting some sense, however imperfect, of the indignities, brutalities, and injustices of slave life. The students seemed sincere, both in their writing and comments in class, in their expressions of shock and outrage at the treatment of enslaved African Americans. Slavery was clearly immoral, and they had difficulty understanding how White slaveholders could have been so mean and cruel. African Americans had experienced unimaginable cruelty at the hands of slaveholders, who considered them inferior and less than human, and this was a lesson Judy's students learned well. But, surprisingly, this lesson was little help to her students in using this past to understand the racism, inequities, and injustices experienced by African Americans in contemporary U.S. society.

Wills (1996) argued that for Judy's students, African Americans' experiences of racism and injustice in U.S. history and society were "anchored" in slavery, a product of the enslavement of African Americans, and this historically specific "problem" had been solved by the freeing of slaves and the conclusion of the Civil War. For Judy's students to be able to connect their knowledge of slavery to the experiences of African Americans in contemporary society, they would need to be able to conceptualize slavery as part of a larger, continuous history of race relations in the United States. But this is exactly what was missing from her students' study of African Americans in U.S. history. As with Ruth's discussions of Native Americans in U.S. history, Judy's failure to seriously challenge the Eurocentric narrative of U.S. history contributes significantly to her students' inability to connect the history of slavery to contemporary race relations. Outside the context of slavery, her students had little historical knowledge to draw upon for thinking about African Americans' experiences of racism, discrimination, and injustice in the United States.

In all three teachers' classrooms, African Americans are "fully present" only as slaves during the Civil War period. African Americans are mentioned in other times and places, as in discussions of the Middle Passage and their presence during the Colonial period, especially in the person of Crispus Attucks, but never studied in any depth. Tom attempts to expand this Eurocentric perspective by having his students study African American Revolutionary War heroes, but his students find little information in the library to support this research project. *A More Perfect Union* also expands the presence of African Americans somewhat by, for example, briefly discussing the existence of communities of free African Americans in the North and South (Armento et al., 1991, pp. 193–195, 304–305). But these revisions do little to challenge the construction of a Eurocentric narrative of U.S. history, or to construct a continuous history of race relations that would enable Judy's students to see beyond slavery when conceptualizing the experiences of African Americans in the United States.

Wills's research (1996) suggests that many efforts that appear to be multicultural steps forward can in fact be counterproductive in unintended, even paradoxical ways. A detailed study of the experiences of enslaved African Americans during the Civil War period, and their virtual absence in the remainder of U.S. history, anchored Judy's students' understandings of racism and injustice in slavery. This provided them with few tools for understanding or critically engaging the historical present of contemporary race relations in U.S. society. Studying the cultures of diverse groups is a widespread approach to multicultural education, not only in K–12 classrooms but also in teacher education programs. But the consequences of this approach in studying Native Americans in Judy's classroom suggests that focusing on cultural diversity can undermine efforts to create narratives of history that embody social and cultural diversity.

Finally, the study of Native Americans in Ruth and Tom's classes illustrate how sincere efforts to challenge stereotypes can be undermined by the continuing use of a Eurocentric narrative. By determining where different groups belong in U.S. history and, consequently, necessitating how they must be represented and remembered in U.S. history, continuous reliance on a Eurocentic history of the United States presents a major obstacle to realizing a multicultural history and social studies curriculum in K–12 classrooms.

Modifying Classroom Curriculum to Build Racial-Ethnic Identity

Widespread dissatisfaction with the public schools has led some parents to seek alternative forms of education for their children, most notably private schools. Approximately 5.3 million students attend at least 22 types of private schools (*Key Statistics . . .*, 1989). *Religious* private schools have been created because parents and educational leaders are dissatisfied with the moral climate of the public school. Religious schools attempt to create environments where students are self-consciously exposed to deep religious values (Parsons, 1987). *African American* private schools have been created because Black children have had such limited success in public schools in the face of long-standing patterns of racism and discrimination that have not been broken down by desegregation and busing. Often affiliated with African American churches, African American independent schools offer an environment that emphasizes ethnoracial identity formation, high academic expectations, and a firm disciplinary code based on religious principles (G. E. Foster, 1991).

The life and organization of White Christian fundamentalist schools has received some attention (Parsons, 1987; Peshkin, 1986; Rose, 1988). Other than the research by Ratteray and Shujaa (1987), the rise of independent schools attempting to build ethnoracial as well as religious identities is largely undocumented. The interaction of ethnoracial and religious identity politics demands academic attention, especially since more than 70 percent of the ethnoracial secular and religious schools Ratteray and Shujaa surveyed have been founded *since* the landmark 1954 U.S. Supreme Court desegregation decision of *Brown* v. *Board of Education of Topeka*.

The Social Organization of the Church and the School. Disciple's Academic Christian Academy (DACA) is an African American independent school in California with an ethnoracial identity project (Lintz, 2000). Operating autonomously, this African American Christian fundamentalist school functions largely as a result of the political efforts of the local African American community. Most teachers, administrators, parents, and students are African American and make the decisions that define the school's character and set the agenda. As in most other Christian fundamentalist schools, DACA's parent organization owns the physical facilities in which its school is housed. Disciple's church is part of an African American charismatic denomination, Church of God in Christ, an association of churches (Lincoln & Mamiya, 1990). In this denomination, a preacher is ordained, approved for church leadership by a local church, and then founds his own church, rather than being sent to the pulpit by a central office. A number of churches in this organization have schools, but they operate independently of any national or central church authority.

According to Bishop Ralph Jackson, founder of DACA, the school has a strong religious agenda because many of the students require direction and spiritual guidance owing to their extreme backgrounds. It is not uncommon for DACA students to be faced with one or more drug abusers in their immediate family, a family tragedy caused by gang activity, a member of the immediate family in jail, or having no parents at all. Given the desperate conditions of her students' lives, the principal of the school, Sister Sheila Robinson, declared that the students' most important concern is to build self-esteem and confidence. Acknowledging that college is not for everyone, she wants to ensure that her students will mature as productive adults and obtain jobs in the mainstream of society.

Disciple's is located in an inner city. The surrounding community is predominantly African American and Latino, and gang activity is prevalent. The school and church facilities are located in a 13,000-square-foot building. There are 114 students (K–12), nine teachers, and two teacher's aides who are supervised by the principal.

Bishop Jackson said that the teachers need not be members of his church, but they must hold spiritual values derived from Christianity. The school has five classrooms, each with 23 students, which produces a teacher-student ratio much more favorable than that of public schools. Grades are combined (K–1, 2–3, 4–6, 7–8, 9–12) because there are not enough students at each grade to fill separate classrooms.

The complexion of Disciple's is striking in contrast to most U.S. public schools. Virtually all of the teachers, students, and administrators are African American, but the school is separatist in neither ideology nor practice; a small number of non-Black students and non-Black teachers participate. The very presence of so many African American staff and administrators provides a culture-affirming atmosphere. Such schools are often the only places where African American children can observe members of their own cultural group as autonomous operators and managers, as individuals in control of an important institution (G. E. Foster, 1991).

Both students and teachers wear navy and white clothing—white blouses and navy skirts for females, white shirts and navy slacks for males. This religiously motivated attention to gender, dress, and etiquette is not unique to Disciple's. It permeates Catholic and White Christian fundamentalist schools (Parsons, 1987; Peshkin, 1986; Rose, 1988).

Only one teacher holds a California teaching credential. Two have credentials (one foreign and the other out-of-state) that are not accepted by the state of California. Five teachers have a B.A. degree, and of those five two have an M.A. One teacher is working toward her B.A. in secondary education at a local private university.

The physical organization of the classrooms at Disciple's—a legacy from the Accelerated Christian Education curriculum that the school once used—is different from traditional public schools. Each classroom has two large desks for instructors, while student desks line the perimeter, with wooden slats separating them. Without compartments in the desks, books and other materials must be stacked underneath.

Disciple's classrooms are similar to public school classrooms in that teachers are constantly negotiating with the students for order. The seventh- and eighth-grade teacher frequently raises his voice to the students in a calm manner, telling them that control and discipline are the necessary determinants of success. The second- and third-grade teacher constantly gives commands and imperatives to which the students quickly respond without question. The teacher is quick to correct anyone who is out of order: "What are you doing standing up? Why were you talking? Turn around and keep working." The teachers' disciplinary style demands that students conform to externally imposed rules, a type of authority system that can produce passive, conforming students (Wilcox, 1982).

Teachers at Disciple's routinely employ the recitation script described in the first part of this chapter. Teachers structure participation by calling on individual students to perform in front of the group. The student's knowledge of almost any subject is informally tested through known-information questions. Ability grouping prevails in reading and math. Because grade levels are combined, teachers often work with one grade while the other students work silently at their desks. The K–5 students are taught traditionally with textbooks and workbooks. The children learn to work quietly and must raise their hands when questions arise. As in many public school classrooms, the transmission of knowledge moves in only one direction, from teacher to student. Cooperative or collaborative groups and inquiry or discovery methods are virtually nonexistent.

Different participation structures are imposed in the upper grades. Students must raise their hands when a formal lesson is being taught, but otherwise they may talk among themselves. The senior high class has a self-directed curriculum because so many grade levels are combined. Since lectures are not a regular part of the curriculum, students complete assignments at their desks for most of the day but do not seem to be doing intensive work because they constantly talk to one another. There are no science labs or advanced math and literature courses. Thus the upper grades at Disciple's provide less academic content than at comparable public schools, concentrating instead on building self-esteem and confidence.

The Overt Curriculum: Building Ethnoracial Identity Through Religion. The academic day at DACA begins with prayer, followed by religious studies. These studies are biblical text readings with teacher-directed exegesis. Religious instruction in the primary grades comes largely from collections of biblical stories. Starting with the second- and third-grade classes, however, religious pedagogy includes reading aloud from biblical text. Tutelage in faith not being limited to morning prayer or biblical studies, students also attend chapel two days per week. It may be spiritually focused (a salvation message by a visiting missionary) or instructional, but even when instructional—a health presentation about the dangers of smoking, for example—explicit religious guidance accompanies the material. Children are not to smoke because it can cause health problems, but also because their bodies are "a temple of the Holy Spirit" (I Corinthians 6:19); a habit causing physical decay of the corporal person also causes spiritual malaise.

All of the educational materials used at Disciple's are published by A Beka, a company affiliated with the ministry of Pensacola Christian College. These books present a complete Christian education program, including day-to-day lesson plans, in materials heavily infused with a religious message. For example, Bible verses are displayed at the bottom of each math workbook page; sentences that need to be written in grammatically correct form include references and persons from the Bible; and more than half of the fiction and poetry included in the literature books is religious-oriented. The science book for the upper grades rejects evolution and espouses creationism: "It is very important to understand that the theory of evolution is not science; it is simply an idea that certain men thought up after they rejected God's Word. To call evolution scientific is to insult science itself" (Howe, 1984, p. xx).

In the highly structured, teacher-centered classrooms, students are not encouraged to be critical thinkers or to have meaningful discourse about theories of origination. Students are taught to accept only one perspective, not only when studying the origins of the universe but in other subjects as well. Even though the A Beka curriculum does give accurate representations of most acts, it ultimately limits students' understanding of the world. A paternalistic approach to gender relations and the economy is apparent throughout the curriculum and does not actively promote a sense of gender difference. The traditional family unit and traditional lifestyles are portrayed frequently. For example, sketches from the high school literature anthology reinforce traditional sex roles. Women are depicted as either wife or mother, while men are shown in many roles (worker, thinker, scientist, father, judge, mountain climber). Only 10 representations of women, compared with 60 of men, appeared in a 500-page textbook.

Disciple's chapel, daily prayer, and Christian curriculum constitute a spiritual exercise that is absent from the public school environment, but the religious orientation is not the only difference in its academic life. The substantial focus on African American culture and history throughout the academic year is an example of a curriculum priority that occurs uniquely in African American independent schools. The educators at Disciple's see African American culture and history as an important component of their curriculum, though somewhat less so than the spiritual. The religious and ethnoracial identity agendas are at odds with one another, however, because the fundamentalist Christian orientation of the A Beka books is so highly Eurocentric. A Beka texts portray Western societies as the most technologically advanced and attribute this developmental superiority to the belief that Christianity is the one true religion. In the fourth-grade history book, for example, the section on Native Americans discusses their heathen status and celebrates the

missionaries who brought them the Christian religion. Howe's (1986) introduction alerts the reader:

The very first Americans did not know anything about the Bible until the Europeans brought it to them. Because they did not have the Bible, which tells us about the one true God, they worshipped false gods. Their worship of false gods kept them from advancing the way the Europeans had. (p. 38)

After establishing the heathen status of the Native Americans, the text tells of how the White men "improved their way of life" with the Bible. The text states that the missionary Roger Williams was "willing to treat the Indians fairly. He offered to buy the land from them" (Howe, 1986, p. 44). This narrative of Western progressivism, which dominates public school texts described earlier in this chapter, attributes no value to any cultural perspective other than the European Christian. Other religions are simply heathen. Contact with Whites and the culture that evolved from Christianity presents the only possibility for non-White Christian cultures. The implication for African Americans is clear: Any African cultures are heathen and consequently primitive.

The commitment to ethnoracial identity at Disciple's forces teachers to use materials to supplement the Eurocentric Christian fundamentalist curriculum. To instruct students about their ethnoracial identity, teachers infuse the curriculum with drama, Black history texts, and movies. They often rely on homemade learning materials and research from college-level publications. Ratteray and Shujaa (1987) found "teacher-designed materials" to be prevalent in black independent schools, because teachers insisted that "commercially produced materials inadequately represented their cultural group" (p. 6). One of the DACA teachers who said she "didn't make much of race" in fact displayed just the opposite propensity. For Black History Month she composed an elaborate drama for the children to perform in front of their parents. Included were the views of a variety of African American historical figures about the plight of and solution for African Americans, including Sojourner Truth: "America owes to my people some of the dividends. . . . She can afford to pay, and she must pay. I shall make them understand that there is a debt to the Negro people which they can never repay. At least, then, they must make amends."

Most of the quotations in the play, like this one, affirm the common experience of African Americans, thereby fostering a group destiny. To enhance understanding of and pride for the students' African American heritage, teachers also include lessons from films and Black history texts. Franklin's (1969) *From Slavery to Freedom: A History of Negro Americans* and Blum's (1971) *Key Issues in the African American Experience* are examples of texts used by teachers to integrate African American history into their curriculum. The teacher who introduced these texts acquired them in a Black studies course in college. The movie *Roots* was shown to the fourth through sixth grades. The teachers supplemented the film with commentary, explaining the historical racial-cultural context of scenes. Black identity is also expressed in prideful slogans and pictures of famous African American scientists, athletes, and educators displayed on the classroom walls.

The Covert Curriculum: A Critique of Black Linguistic and Cultural Expression. The overt instruction in ethnoracial identity during formal lessons at DACA does not proceed without tension. Often the overt curriculum of ethnic pride is contradicted by a covert curriculum that critiques Black linguistic expression and popular culture. In addition, the collective sense of pride taught in Black history and social studies runs up against informal entreaties to the individual pursuit of success.

Much important writing has been dedicated to the subject of interaction between Anglo teachers and linguistic and cultural-minority students. As the research we reviewed in the first part of this chapter shows, the communication challenges that result from differing linguistic patterns, beliefs, values, and experiences can interfere with the learning process. Implicit in the cultural-discontinuity position is that closing the gap between the linguistic and cultural styles of teachers and students will facilitate the educational process. The work of Piestrup (1973), Erickson and Mohatt (1982), M. Foster (1989, 1995), and Berlack and Moyenda (2001) can be interpreted to suggest that employing teachers from the same ethnolinguistic background as the students can help close this gap.

African American independent schools present an opportunity for a common linguistic-cultural code between teacher and student to fortify cultural identity in classroom interaction. Our work at DACA shows that cultural-linguistic continuity between teacher and students does not necessarily result in cultural tolerance, however. Similar experiences do not essentially constitute relational fluency or support. Some communication barriers attributed to the cultural differences between Anglo teachers and their African American pupils also arise between African American teachers and their African American pupils, an observation made by Rist (1970) more than 30 years ago about interactions between Black teachers and Black students in public schools.

Most notably, some DACA teachers denigrate the use of Black English vernacular (BEV) by their students. They find it necessary to correct BEV, whether the lesson is a discussion of a PBS educational program or a grammar exercise. One teacher referred to BEV as "ghettoese," combining a poverty term with a language suffix and thereby making this a language of destitution. This high school teacher studied African American history and Swahili as an undergraduate and feels strongly that many aspects of African American culture should be abandoned, particularly BEV. Gilmore (1983) found African American teachers engaged in a similar linguistic critique of African American rhyming games because teachers thought the games were coarse (cf. Perry, 1998).

These critiques are not limited to the students' linguistic expression; they also attack other aspects of Black popular culture. A member of the church leadership, Elder Ford, spoke to the students during a school chapel about the need to abandon such physical expressions of ethnoracial identity as hairstyle in order to achieve mobility. He advised the boys not to get "ridiculous" haircuts; otherwise, when they go to job interviews "the man" will tell them to follow one of the arrows shaved into their hair out to the next exit.

DACA students are also told that Black identity should be tempered with a positive Black heritage. The high school teacher said that there is no benefit in trying to "Africanize" because Blacks have been Americans for seven generations. Aspirations for success involve cultural change and sacrifice. Students need to aspire to "nerd" as opposed to "cool" status, finding new friends who have the same success-oriented goals and leaving old companions behind.

Another message communicated implicitly to students concerns strategies for achieving success in U.S. society. Students are encouraged to seek individual rather than collective strategies for mobility. The high school teacher also told his students: "You can't bring the whole tribe with you. You have to get there first and *then* help people." In so doing, this teacher critiques a popular effort to form an African American group identity. He discourages collective strategy as a solution for poverty in the African American community, advocating instead an individual solution. If there is to be mobility for African Americans, it will be achieved by individuals striving personally without coalescing with others.

These critiques are not expressed out of malice. These African American teachers who unintentionally employ a culture-of-poverty perspective when encountering African American popular culture all *care* for their students, wanting them to be academically successful. In fact, critiques of students' language and culture are rendered with a motivation to encourage students to speak and behave in ways that will clear barriers on their paths to success. In their historical research, Higginbotham (1993), Lasch-Quinn (1993), and Gaines (1996) found middle-class or elite African Americans critiquing working-class culture to encourage upward mobility for working-class African Americans. These critiques generated negative consequences, however, that were manifested in classroom interaction. When encountering criticism of their speech and behavior, students often acted flustered (blowing air through pursed lips, stammering) and withdrew from the lesson. That is, these *African American* students withdrew from learning situations with their *African American* teachers; but this resistance is passive, not active. Truancy, drug use, and verbal conflict with teachers are not part of the milieu at DACA. MacLeod's (1987) "hallway hangers," Willis's (1979) "lads," and Foley's (1990) "*cholos*" are noticeably absent from this independent school. Rather than playing the role of class clown or disrupter, which Ogbu (1974) and Hanna (1982) found in their studies of African American students in public schools, the DACA students are more likely to resist passively, conduct that has been more commonly attributed to Native Hawaiian and Native American students (Au & Jordan, 1981; Erickson & Mohatt, 1982; Philips, 1982).

Even though the overt curriculum for the entire school is religiously based, teachers do not invoke the Bible in the covert curriculum—that is, in providing explanation or guiding students' conduct. According to Peshkin (1986), teachers and administrators at Bethany Baptist Academy put Christ at the center of all subjects and concentrated on teaching proper Christian behavior. In the Academy classrooms he studied, teachers used references from the Bible as often as possible in their lessons, and students were expected to regard the Bible as the absolute truth and guide for life. By contrast, teachers and aides at Disciple's teach all subjects (except devotion) without reference to the tenets of Christianity or the Bible. The difference between such schools as DACA and Bethany Baptist Academy and typical public schools is found in the explicit curriculum, then, not the implicit curriculum of teacher-student discourse.

This observation does not imply that the teachers at Disciple's are not deeply religious. Brother Grant Brown, senior high school co-teacher, asserts that the most important component of Disciple's is the spiritual atmosphere. He says that students can learn to recognize their problems and use their spiritual values, knowing that God will give them strength to overcome. Brother Brown claims that if students do not learn any spiritual values, then they cannot use their knowledge correctly. Other teachers feel just as strongly about the spiritual aspect of the school, but they realize that students also need discipline, mastery of basic subjects, and confidence to succeed in the real world.

Dilemmas and Contradictions of Multicultural Education in Separate Schools. The teaching practices at DACA are not too much different from those found in public schools. A major rationale for opening private schools is that they are freed from bureaucratic constraints and governmental regulations (Chubb & Moe, 1990). Even though independent schools are able to organize in any manner they choose and use any teaching techniques they wish, Disciple's has not deviated radically from the traditional approach to teaching. Supplements are used when teaching African American history, and peer tutoring is employed in one of the lower-grade classes. But these are the exceptions, not the rule. Ability grouping, rigid daily schedules, customary participant structures, and conventional teaching techniques are practiced every day. Thus there is little evidence that Disciple's exercises its freedom from bureaucratic constraints by implementing innovative instructional strategies or using time and space creatively in the classroom.

African American culture is bountifully displayed in the distinctive presence of African American educators, curriculum materials, and striking classroom wall designs. At the same time, popular Black culture is exorcised. The African American teachers at Disciple's critique their students' linguistic and cultural expression. When communication difficulties occur with Anglo teachers, African American pupils are likely to explain the disrespect of their terminology in terms of racism. When their linguistic and cultural patterns are censored by their African American teachers, however, the students attribute the censorship to cultural treason. There are even long-lived labels for those who compromise Black cultural tradition to please Whites: "Tom," "Uncle Tom," or "oreo." Though separate independent schools are a potential solution to the cultural communication gap between teachers and students, minority teachers may make choices, for the same reasons as do their White counterparts, that frustrate minority students and thus limit classroom interaction and the learning process. Multicultural education requires more than teachers who are from the same ethnic background as their students.

The overt agenda at DACA to build a collective sense of pride, taught in the formal Black history and social studies portions of the curriculum, ran up against entreaties in the informal curriculum to pursue success individually. Students were encouraged to achieve success on their own first, and to worry about the African American community second. This attitude fuels Wilson's (1987) argument that the African American urban community is truly disadvantaged in part because the African American middle class has abandoned the inner city.

Because of the desperate circumstances of their students' lives, the school officials of Disciple's believe that firm discipline is required. Seeking their answer to the discipline problem in a fundamentalist Christian curriculum raises a host of other problems. This same curriculum is Eurocentric and antiscience, relies on externally imposed authority (which fosters passive students), and contradicts the thrust of the ethnic pride curriculum.

Consistent with the religious base of its supporting church, the teachers see teaching as a calling or vocation, not a job. But these teachers have relatively little formal education and teacher training, which limits the quality of academic instruction in the upper grades, especially in math and laboratory science courses. As a result, the school's goal of building self-esteem is met better than the school's goal of developing academic sophistication.

CONCLUSIONS AND IMPLICATIONS FOR MULTICULTURAL EDUCATION

As American society continues to grapple with difficult issues involving race and ethnic relations, and as many continue to look to education as a vehicle for improving relations among diverse groups, it is important to understand the various strategies that educators have employed to incorporate diversity into the curriculum and the schools. To this end, we have reviewed ethnographic studies of multicultural education in three areas: (a) those that describe attempts to achieve equality in classroom interaction by modifying discourse patterns and participation structures; (b) those that describe attempts to implement a curriculum that includes the contributions, experiences, and perspectives of women and racial and ethnic groups; and (c) those that describe attempts to build an ethnoracial identity.

If one goal of multicultural education is to construct an inclusive multiracial and multiethnic definition of American identity, then our review of the design and implementation of the multicultural textbooks being used in California public and private schools demonstrates the limitations of curricular reforms that attempt to achieve a multicultural history through the *addition* or *injection* of racially and ethnically diverse individuals and groups into an already existing narrative of U.S. history. It seems more productive to employ totally restructured narratives of U.S. history that are both honest and respectful. Such narratives would provide students with an image of "Americans" that captures and celebrates the diversity of the United States, both today and in the past, and would acknowledge that conflict, oppression, and prejudice have been enduring features of U.S. history, not isolated incidents confined to unusual periods of time.

To be sure, we want a "critical multiculturalism" (Sleeter & Bernal, this volume; Banks & Banks, 1989; Giroux, 1988, 1997; Grant & Sleeter, 1986; Jackson & Solis, 1995; Ladson-Billings & Tate, 1995; McCarthy, 1998; McCarthy & Crichlow, 1993; McCarthy & Willis, 1995; McLaren, 1997; McLaren & Estrada, 1993) that encourages students to challenge racism and inequality and to respect social and cultural diversity. But we feel we need to go beyond critique, to the systematic inclusion of

new narratives in the curriculum. African American, Native American, and Latino narratives all have different stories, with different plots, major events, and characters. These narratives need to be juxtaposed with the mainstream "narrative of progress" so that students can recognize experiences different from their own, and learn to take the perspectives of others. Exposing students to the multiplicity of narratives that make up U.S. society and teaching them about the contested nature of our history encourages them to challenge inequality and to rethink American identity.

This is an important first step, but difficult to achieve in practice. Supplementing the prevailing narrative of U.S. history with separate histories of different racial and ethnic groups does not guarantee a decentering or reinterpretation of this narrative. The experiences and perspectives of African Americans, Native Americans, and other groups would be included in the curriculum. However, their inclusion might still be on terms dictated by assumptions of historical relevance and significance as defined by mainstream White American culture. Ultimately, what is needed is a new narrative of U.S. history, one focused on historical moments in which diverse groups interacted over, even fought over, issues of justice, equality, and civil and political rights. Such a narrative would provide students with new and different resources for remembering our common, and continuing, struggle to imagine an inclusive American identity and a just society.

Although the studies we have reviewed are provocative, there is a problem with this line of research. The investigators have examined primarily monocultural or bicultural classrooms. Although not easy by any means, it is a relatively uncomplicated task to modify practices and reorganize classrooms when they are composed of no more than two culturally different groups. The job grows enormously in complexity when the classrooms are composed of students from many ethnic and linguistic groups. Are there lessons to be learned from these monocultural and bicultural studies for *multi*cultural classrooms? We glean several generalizations from these studies about ways to organize classroom practices for the benefit of many cultural groups.

- *Academic rigor with social supports.* Especially in a time of emphasizing "standards" and "accountability," maintaining high expectations and focusing on comprehension rather than decoding and on sense making rather than decontextualized skills drills may very well be better ways of teaching all children. When academically rigorous instruction is conducted within a community of scholarship accompanied by a system of social supports, then all students seem to benefit. But if culturally sensitive features are added to the curriculum without adding academically demanding curriculum, then minority students may not benefit and achieve.

- *Variety.* It makes sense for all students to express their knowledge in a variety of modalities, to experience multiple grouping arrangements, to be challenged at the upper ends of their zones of development with accompanying systems of social support, to be criticized in private and not embarrassed in public, to have their cultural knowledge treated with respect and used as a resource in classroom instruction.

Note carefully: this is a general recommendation. It is not the same as telling teachers to use a particular pedagogic practice (for example, small groups, cooperative groups, or voluntary turn-allocation strategies) exclusively and repeatedly. If cultural compatibility is interpreted narrowly as asking teachers to match school to home, then members of language and ethnic-minority groups may not be encouraged to expand their repertoire to include new possibilities (McCarty, Wallace, Lynch, & Benally, 1991).

- *Flexibility.* Flexibility is the key to our conclusion. As we are reminded by Vogt's experiences when she attempted to duplicate the key elements of the KEEP program from Hawaii in the Rough Rock Navajo reservation, teachers are mistaken if they try to match a particular pedagogic practice with a particular cultural group. Doing so limits educational opportunities and reduces cultural groups to hollow, one-dimensional stereotypes.

The classroom management technique of quickly confronting trouble ("quick nice") that worked so well with native Hawaiians antagonized young Navajo boys; Vogt learned to control misbehavior by ignoring or lowering her eyes and giving a short but stern lecture to the whole group, not singling out the offending student. The boy-girl cooperative learning groups that worked so well with native Hawaiians did not work with Native Americans. Vogt had to segregate the sexes in order to keep interaction moving (Vogt, Jordan, & Tharp, 1987).

- *Adaptation to local circumstances.* Teachers always need to be sensitive to nuances in teacher-student relations and must be able to change their behavior year to year, day to day, even moment to moment. As Jacob and Jordan (1993) caution us:

Good educational practice does not exist outside of a particular educational context and . . . "*just* good teaching" is not just good teaching at all, but a complex process of combining information from a number of different sources to produce practice well adapted to the population and setting at hand. (p. 256)

That is, no matter how impressive, no matter how provocative, pedagogic practices must be artfully fitted

to local circumstances (Cazden & Mehan, 1989; Goldenberg & Gallimore, 1989; Mehan, Hubbard, Villanueva, & Lintz, 1996).

- *Particularity.* Researcher/educators (we are included) are fond of saying to teachers, "Go explore the community; learn about your kids' culture." That may be a difficult if not impossible task, especially given the rich diversity in today's urban classrooms, which have as many as 20 language groups present. If we're not careful, teachers will draw stereotypic conclusions in their exuberance to be ethnographers of their classrooms. Instead of trying to learn the generalities of ethnic groups in the abstract, the studies reviewed here recommend that teachers learn about the details of their students' lives in particular. This means teachers will have to explore their students' funds of knowledge (Moll & González, this volume) and experiences by observing their students in the classroom, on the playground, and in the community, talking with their students, their families, and members of the community. The context-specific nature of cultural knowledge means that what the teacher learns about students one year may not apply to students the next year. Therefore, teachers will have to engage in this ethnographic process regularly.

These studies signal a new relationship between teacher, researcher, and pedagogical knowledge. Many of the insights into culturally compatible instruction emerged when teachers and researchers collaborated. In this new configuration, the teacher moves from being a passive recipient of packaged research knowledge to a collaborative constructor of pedagogical knowledge useful in local circumstances. Indeed, the teacher-as-researcher model has become the hallmark of many teacher education efforts (Florio-Ruane, 2001).

- *Adapt general principles to local circumstances.* This is itself a general principle. No matter how impressive, no matter how provocative, general recommendations must be modified to fit local circumstances (Cazden & Mehan, 1989). Or to paraphrase Goldenberg and Gallimore (1989, p. 45): To be successful, universally valid principles must be artfully fitted to the local niches of schools and classrooms. It is true that small-group instruction, voluntary turn-allocation procedures, and funds of knowledge seem to be universally productive forms of instruction, but each school experience, each classroom, is different. Therefore, each school will have to adopt a local version of these universal principles. As Vogt, Jordan, and Tharp's attempt (1987) to implement the Hawaiian version of the KEEP curriculum with Navajos shows, each artful implementation will have to be sensitive to the features of the children's experience in local circumstances.

References

Anyon, J. (1997). *Ghetto schooling*. New York: Teachers College Press.

Apple, M. W., & Christian-Smith, L. K. (1991). *The politics of the textbook*. New York: Routledge.

Armento, B. J., Nash, G. B., Slater, C. L., & Wixson, K. K. (1991). *A more perfect union*. Boston: Houghton Mifflin.

Au, K. (1980). Participation structures in a reading lesson with Hawaiian children. *Anthropology and Education Quarterly, 11*(2), 91–115.

Au, K., & Jordan, C. (1981). Teaching reading to Hawaiian children: Finding a culturally appropriate solution. In H. Trueba, G. P. Guthrie, & K. H. Au (Eds.), *Culture and the bilingual classroom* (pp. 139–152). Rowley, MA: Newbury House.

Banks, J. A., & Banks, C.A.M. (Eds.). (1989). *Multicultural education: Issues and perspectives*. Boston: Allyn & Bacon.

Barnhardt, C. (1982). "Tuning in": Athabaskan teachers and students. In R. Barnhardt (Ed.), *Cross-cultural issues in Alaskan education* (pp. 87–98). Fairbanks, AK: University of Alaska, Center for Cross-Cultural Studies.

Barton, K. C., & Levstik, L. S. (1996). "Back when God was round and everything": Elementary students' understanding of historical time. *American Educational Research Journal, 33*, 419–454.

Barton, K. C., & Levstik, L. S. (1998). "It wasn't a good part of history": National identity and students' explanations of historical significance. *Teachers College Record, 99*, 478–513.

Berlack, A., & Moyenda, S. (2001). *Taking it personally: Racism in the classroom from kindergarten to college*. Philadelphia: Temple University Press.

Blum, A. (1971). *Key issues in the African American experience*. New York: Harcourt Brace Jovanovich.

Brophy, J., VanSledright, B., & Bredin, N. (1993). "What do entering fifth graders know about U.S. history?" *Journal of Social Studies Research, 16/17*(1), 2–19.

Brown, A. L., Ash, D., Rutherford, M., Nakagawa, K., Gordon, A., & Campione, J. C. (1993). Distributed expertise in the classroom. In G. Salomon (Ed.), *Distributed cognitions: Psychological and educational considerations* (pp. 188-228). New York: Cambridge University Press.

Brown, A. L., & Palinscar, A. M. (1989). Guided cooperative learning and individual knowledge acquisition. In L. B. Resnick (Ed.), *Cognition and instruction: Issues and agendas* (pp. 393–451). Hillsdale, NJ: Erlbaum.

California State Department of Education. (1988). *History-social science framework for California public schools kindergarten through grade 12*. Sacramento: Author.

Cazden, C. B. (1988). *Classroom discourse*. Portsmouth, NH: Heinemann.

Cazden, C. B., & Mehan, H. (1989). Principles from sociology and anthropology: Context, code, classroom and culture. In M. C. Reynolds (Ed.), *Knowledge base for the beginning teacher* (pp. 42–57). Oxford: Pergamon Press.

Chubb, J. E., & Moe, T. M. (1990). *Politics, markets and America's schools*. Washington, DC: Brookings Institution.

Cole, M., & Scribner, S. (1974). *Culture and thought*. New York: Wiley.

Devine, J. (1996). Maximum security: The culture of violence in inner-city schools. Chicago: University of Chicago Press.

Diaz, S., Moll, L. C., & Mehan, H. (1986). Sociocultural resources in instruction: A context specific approach. In *Beyond Language* (pp. 187–230). Los Angeles: California State University, Evaluation, Dissemination and Assessment Center.

Duran, R. P., & Szymanski, M. (1992, December). *Activity and learning in cooperative learning*. Paper presented at the annual meeting of the American Anthropological Association, San Francisco.

Epstein, T. L. (1998). Deconstructing differences in African-American and European-American adolescents' perspectives on U.S. history. *Curriculum Inquiry, 28*(4), 397–423.

Epstein, T. L. (2000). Adolescents' perspectives on racial diversity in U.S. history: Case studies from an urban classroom. *American Educational Research Journal, 37*(1), 185–214.

Erickson, F., & Mohatt, G. (1982). Participant structures in two communities. In G. D. Spindler (Ed.), *Doing the ethnography of schooling* (pp. 132–175). New York: Holt, Rinehart, & Winston.

Erikson, F., & Schultz, J. (1992). Student experience and the curriculum. In P. W. Jackson (Ed.), *Handbook of research on curriculum* (pp. 465–485). New York: Macmillan.

Fine, M. (1991). *Framing dropouts: Notes on the politics of an urban public high school*. Albany: State University of New York Press.

Fitzgerald, F. (1980). *America revised: History textbooks in the 20th century*. New York: Vintage Books.

Florio-Ruane, S. (2001). Teacher education and the cultural imagination. Mahwah, NJ: Erlbaum.

Foley, D. (1990). *Learning capitalist culture: Deep in the heart of Tejas*. Philadelphia: University of Pennsylvania Press.

Foster, G. E. (1991). *Independent schools owned by African Americans*. New York: Toussaint Institute.

Foster, M. (1989). "It's cookin' now": A performance analysis of the speech events in an urban community college. *Language in Society, 18*, 1–29.

Foster M. (1995). Talkin' that talk: The language of control, curriculum, and critique. *Linguistics and Education, 7*, 129–150.

Fournier, J. E., & Wineburg, S. S. (1997). Picturing the past: Gender differences in the depiction of historical figures. *American Journal of Education, 105*(2), 160–185.

Franklin, J. H. (1969). *From slavery to freedom: A history of Negro Americans* (3rd ed.). New York: Vintage Books.

Gabella, M. S. (1994). Beyond the looking glass: Bringing students into the conversation of historical inquiry. *Theory and Research in Social Education, 22*(3), 340–363.

Gaines, K. K. (1996). *Uplifting the race: Black leadership, politics, and culture in the 20th century*. Chapel Hill: University of North Carolina Press.

Gilmore, P. (1983). "Spelling Mississippi": Recontextualizing a literacy-related speech event. *Anthropology and Education Quarterly, 14*, 235–256.

Giroux, H. (1988). *Schooling and the struggle for public life: Critical pedagogy in the modern age*. Minneapolis: University of Minnesota Press.

Giroux, H. A. (1997). Rewriting the discourse of racial identity: Towards a pedagogy and politics of Whiteness. *Harvard Educational Review, 67*(2), 285–320.

Gitlin, T. (1995). *The twilight of common dreams: Why America is wracked by culture wars*. New York: Metropolitan.

Goldenberg, C. N., & Gallimore, R. (1989). Teaching California's diverse student populations: The common ground between educational and cultural research. *California Public Schools Forum, 3*, 41–65.

González, N., Moll, L. C., & Amanti, C. (Eds.) (in press). Theorizing practices: Funds of knowledge in households and classrooms. Cresskill, NJ: Hampton.

Grant, C. A., & Sleeter, C. E. (1986). Educational equity: Education that is multicultural and reconstructionist. *Journal of Educational Equity and Leadership, 6*(2), 105–118.

Gutiérrez, K. D. (in press). Studying cultural practices in urban learning communities. *Human Development.*

Gutiérrez, K. D., Baquedano-López, P. O., & Tejada, C. (1999). Rethinking diversity: hybridity and hybrid language practices in the third space. *Mind, Culture and Activity, 6*(4), 286–303.

Gutiérrez, K. D., Rymes, B., & Larson, J. (1995). Script, counter-script and underlife in the classroom: James Brown vs *Brown v. Board of Education. Harvard Educational Review, 65*(3), 445–471.

Hanna, J. L. (1982). Public policy and the children's world: Implications of ethnographic work for desegregated schooling. In G. D. Spindler (Ed.), *Doing the ethnography of schooling* (pp. 316–335). New York: Holt, Rinehart & Winston.

Heath, S. B. (1982). Questioning at home and at school: A comparative study. In G. D. Spindler (Ed.), *Doing the ethnography of schooling* (pp. 96–101). New York: Holt, Rinehart & Winston.

Heath, S. B. (1986). Sociocultural contexts of language development. In *Beyond Language* (pp. 143–186). Los Angeles: California State University, Evaluation, Dissemination, and Assessment Center.

Higginbotham, E. B. (1993). *Righteous discontent: The women's movement in the Black Baptist church, 1820–1920.* Cambridge, MA: Harvard University Press.

Howe, J. E. (Ed.). (1984). *Matter and motion.* Pensacola, FL: A Beka Books.

Howe, J. E. (Ed.). (1986). *The history of our United States.* Pensacola, FL: A Beka Books.

Jackson, S., & Solis, J. (1995). *Beyond comfort zones in multiculturalism: Confronting the politics of privilege.* Westport, CT: Bergin & Garvey.

Jacob, E., & Jordan, C. (Eds.). (1993). Minority education. Norwood, NJ: Ablex.

John, V. K. (1972). Styles of learning—styles of teaching: Reflections on the education of Navajo children. In C. B. Cazden, D. Hymes, & V. K. John (Eds.), *Functions of language in the classroom* (pp. 331–343). New York: Teachers College Press.

Kagan, S. (1986). Cooperative learning and sociocultural factors in school. In *Beyond Language* (pp. 231–298). Los Angeles: California State University, Evaluation, Dissemination and Assessment Center.

Kaomea, J. (2000). A curriculum of aloha? Colonialism and tourism in Hawai'i's elementary textbooks. *Curriculum Inquiry, 30*(3), 319–344.

Keddie, N. (1971). Classroom knowledge. In M.F.D. Young (Ed.), *Knowledge and control.* London: Collier Macmillan.

Key statistics for private elementary and secondary education: School year 1989–90. (1989, December). (Early Estimates, Survey Report No. NCES 90–206). Washington, DC: U.S. Department of Education, National Center for Educational Statistics.

Knorr-Cetina, K. D., & Mulkay, M. (Eds.). (1983). *Science observed: Perspectives on the social study of science.* London: Sage.

Labov, W. (1972). *Language in the inner city: Studies in the Black English vernacular.* Philadelphia: University of Pennsylvania Press.

Ladson-Billings, G., & Tate, W. R. (1995). Toward a critical race theory of education. *Teachers College Record, 97*(1), 47–68.

Laosa, L. M. (1973). Reform in educational and psychological assessment: Cultural and linguistic issues. *Journal of the Association of Mexican-American Educators, 1,* 19–24.

Lasch-Quinn, E. (1993). Black neighbors: Race and the limits of reform in the American settlement house movement, 1890–1945. Chapel Hill: University of North Carolina Press.

Latour, B., & Woolgar, S. (1986). *Laboratory life: The social construction of scientific facts.* Princeton, NJ: Princeton University Press.

Lee, C. D. (1995). A culturally based cognitive apprenticeship: Teaching African American high school students skills in literary interpretation. *Reading Research Quarterly, 50*(4), 608–630.

Lester, J. L. (1968). *To be a slave.* New York: Scholastic.

Levinson, B., Foley, D., & Holland, D. (Eds.) (1996). The cultural production of the educated person. Albany: State University of New York Press.

Levstik, L. S. (2000). Articulating the silences: Teachers' and adolescents' conceptions of historical significance. In P. N. Stearns, P. Seixas, & S. Wineburg (Eds.), *Knowing, teaching, and learning history: National and international perspectives* (pp. 284–305). New York: New York University Press.

Levstik, L. S., & Barton, K. C. (1996). "They still use some of their past": Historical salience in elementary children's chronological thinking. *Journal of Curriculum Studies, 28*(5), 531–576.

Levstik, L. S., & Barton, K. C. (1997). *Doing history: Investigating with children in elementary and middle schools.* Mahwah, NJ: Erlbaum.

Lincoln, C. E., & Mamiya, L. H. (1990). *The Black church in the African American experience.* Durham, NC: Duke University Press.

Linenthal, E. T., & Engelhardt, T. (1996). *History wars: The Enola Gay and other battles for the American past.* New York: Henry Holt.

Lintz, A. (2000). The tectonics of class culture and resources in education: A case study of two African American private schools. Unpublished dissertation, University of California, San Diego.

Loewen, J. W. (1995). *Lies my teacher told me: Everything your American history textbook got wrong.* New York: Touchstone.

MacLeod, J. (1987). *Ain't no makin' it.* Boulder, CO: Westview Press.

McCarthy, C. (1998). *The uses of culture: Education and the limits of ethnic affiliation.* New York: Routledge.

McCarthy, C., & Crichlow, W. (1993). *Race, identity, and representation in education.* New York: Routledge.

McCarthy, C., & Willis, A. I. (1995). The politics of culture: Multicultural education after the canon debate. In S. Jackson and J. Solis (Eds.), *Beyond comfort zones in multiculturalism: Confronting the politics of privilege.* New York: Bergin & Garvey.

McCarty, T. L., Wallace, S., Lynch, R. H., & Benally, A. (1991). Classroom inquiry and Navajo learning styles: A call for reassessment. *Anthropology and Education Quarterly, 22,* 42–59.

McCullum, P. (1989). Turn-allocation in lessons with North American and Puerto Rican students. *Anthropology and Education Quarterly, 20,* 133–156.

McKeown, M. G., & Beck, I. L. (1990). The assessment and characterization of young learners' knowledge of a topic in history. *American Educational Research Journal, 27*(4), 688–726.

McKeown, M. G., & Beck, I. L. (1994). Making sense of accounts of history: Why young students don't and how they might. In G. Leinhardt, Beck, I. L., & Stainton, C. (Eds.), *Teaching and learning in history* (pp. 1–26). Hillsdale, NJ: Erlbaum.

McLaren, P. (1997). *Revolutionary multiculturalism: Pedagogies of dissent for the new millennium*. Boulder, CO: Westview Press.

McLaren, P., & Estrada, K. (1993). A dialog on multiculturalism and democratic culture. *Educational Researcher, 22*(3), 27–33.

McNeil, L. (1986). *Contradictions of control: School structure and school knowledge*. New York: Routledge.

Mehan, H. (1979). *Learning lessons*. Cambridge, MA: Harvard University Press.

Mehan, H., Hubbard, L., Villanueva, I., and Lintz, A. (1996). *Constructing school success: The consequences of untracking low achieving students*. Cambridge: Cambridge University Press.

Mehan, H., & Wills, J. S. (1988). MEND: A nurturing voice in the nuclear arms debate. *Social Problems, 35*(4), 363–383.

Metz, M. H. (1980). *Classrooms and corridors: The crisis of authority in desegregated secondary schools*. Berkeley: University of California Press.

Metz, M. H. (1986). *Different by design*. London: Kegan Paul.

Moll, L. C., & Diaz, S. (1987). Change as the goal of educational research. *Anthropology and Education Quarterly, 18*, 300–311.

Moll, L. C., Vélez-Ibáñez, C., & Greenberg, J. (1988). *Project implementation plan: Community knowledge and classroom practice—Combining resources for literacy instruction*. Tucson: University of Arizona Press.

Moll, L. C., Vélez-Ibáñez, C., & Greenberg, J. (1989). *Fieldwork summary: Community knowledge and classroom practice—Combining resources for literacy instruction*. Tucson: University of Arizona Press.

More, A. J. (1989). Native Indian learning styles: A review for researchers and teachers. *Journal of American Indian Education, 3*, 15–28.

Nash, G. B., Crabtree, C., and Dunn, R. E. (1997). *History on trial: Culture wars and the teaching of the past*. New York: Knopf.

Ogbu, J. U. (1974). *The next generation: An ethnography of education in an urban neighborhood*. New York: Academic Press.

Ogbu, J. U. (1987). Variability in minority school performance: A problem in search of an explanation. *Anthropology and Education Quarterly, 18*, 312–334.

Ogbu, J. U. (1991). Immigrant and involuntary minorities in comparative perspective. In M. Gibson & J. Ogbu (Eds.)., *Minority status and schooling*. New York: Garland.

Olsen, L. (1997). Made in America: Immigrant students in U.S. schools. New York: New Press.

Page, R. N. (1991). Lower-track classrooms: A curricular and cultural perspective. New York: Teachers College Press.

Parsons, P. F. (1987). *Inside America's Christian schools*. Macon, GA: Mercer University Press.

Paxton, R. J. (1999). A deafening silence: History textbooks and the students who read them. *Review of Educational Research, 69*(3), 315–339.

Perry, T. (1998). "I'on know why they be trippin'": Reflections on the Ebonics debate. In T. Perry and L. Delpit (Eds.), *The real Ebonics debate: Power, language, and the education of African-American children*. Boston: Beacon Press.

Peshkin, A. (1986). *God's choice: The total world of a fundamentalist Christian school*. Chicago: University of Chicago Press.

Peshkin, A. (1991). *The color of strangers, the color of friends*. Chicago: University of Chicago Press.

Philips, S. U. (1982). *The invisible culture: Communication in classroom and community on the Warm Springs reservation*. New York: Longman.

Piestrup, A. (1973). *Black dialect interference and accommodation of reading instruction in the first grade*. (Monographs of the Language Behavior Research Lab). Berkeley: University of California Press.

Ratteray, J. D., & Shujaa, M. (1987). *Dare to choose: Parental choice at independent neighborhood schools*. Washington, DC: Institute for Independent Education.

Richter, C. (1953). *The light in the forest*. New York: Knopf.

Rist, R. C. (1970). Student social class and teacher expectations: The self-fulfilling prophecy in ghetto education. *Harvard Educational Review, 40*(3), 411–451.

Rist, R. C. (1979). *Desegregated schools: Appraisals of an American experience*. New York: Academic Press.

Rose, S. (1988). *Keeping them out of the hands of Satan: Evangelical schooling in America*. London: Routledge & Kegan Paul.

Roseberry, A. S., Warren, B., & Conant, F. R. (1992). *Appropriating scientific discourse: Findings from language minority classrooms*. (Working Paper No. 1). Cambridge, MA: Technical Educational Research Center.

Sacks, H., Schegloff, E., & Jefferson, G. (1974). A simplist systematics for the organization of turn-taking in conversation. *Language, 50*, 696–735.

Schofield, J. W. (1982). *Black and White in school: Trust, tension or tolerance?* New York: Praeger.

Schultz, J., Florio, S., & Erickson, F. (1982). Where's the floor? *Quarterly Newsletter of the Laboratory of Comparative Human Cognition, 4*, 2–9.

Seixas, P. (1993). Historical understanding among adolescents in a multicultural setting. *Curriculum Inquiry, 23*(3), 301–327.

Shapin, S. (1984). Pump and circumstance: Robert Boyle's literary technology. *Social Studies of Science, 14*, 481–520.

Shapiro, M. J. (1988). *The politics of representation: Writing practices in biography, photography, and policy analysis*. Madison: University of Wisconsin Press.

Shuy, R., & Griffin, P. (1978). *The study of children's functional language and education in the early years*. Arlington, VA: Center for Applied Linguistics.

Sinclair, J. M., & Coulthard, R. M. (1975). *Toward an analysis of discourse*. New York: Oxford University Press.

Slavin, R. E. (2001). Cooperative Learning and Intergroup Relations. In J. A. Banks & C.A.M. Banks (Eds.), *Handbook of research on multicultural education* (pp. 628–634). San Francisco: Jossey-Bass.

Sleeter, C. E., & Grant, C. A. (1987). An analysis of multicultural education in the United States. *Harvard Educational Review, 57*(4), 421–444.

Sleeter, C. E., & Grant, C. A. (1991). Race, class, gender, and disability in current textbooks. In M. W. Apple & L. K. Christian-Smith (Eds.), *The politics of the textbook* (pp. 78–110). London: Routledge & Kegan Paul.

Solomon, R. P. (1992). *Black resistance in high school: Forging a separatist culture*. Albany: State University of New York Press.

Taylor, D., & Dorsey-Grimes, C. (1988). *Growing up literate: Learning from inner city families*. Portsmouth, NH: Heinemann.

Tharp, R. G. (1989). Culturally compatible education: A formula for designing effective classrooms. In H. T. Trueba, G. Spindler, & L. Spindler (Eds.), *What do anthropologists have to say about dropouts?* (pp. 51–66). New York: Falmer Press.

Tharp, R., & Gallimore, R. (1988). *Rousing minds to life: Teaching, learning, and schooling in social context.* Cambridge: Cambridge University Press.

Thomas, T. (Writer) & Bagwell, O. (Director). (1990). Roots of resistance [video recording]. Boston: PBS Video.

Vogt, L. A., Jordan, C., & Tharp, R. (1987). Explaining school failure, producing school success: Two cases. *Anthropology and Education Quarterly, 18*(4), 276–288.

Wagner, J. (1969). *Misfits and missionaries.* Beverly Hills, CA: Sage.

Weis, L. (1985). *Between two worlds.* London: Routledge & Kegan Paul.

Weis, L. (1990). *Working class without work.* London: Routledge & Kegan Paul.

Wilcox, E. (1982). Differential socialization in classrooms: Implications for equal opportunity. In G. D. Spindler (Ed.), *Doing the ethnography of schooling* (pp. 268–309). New York: Holt, Rinehart & Winston.

Willinsky, J. (1998). *Learning to divide the world: Education at empire's end.* Minneapolis: University of Minnesota Press.

Willis, P. (1979). *Learning to labor.* New York: Teachers College Press.

Wills, J. S. (1994). Popular culture, curriculum, and historical representation: The situation of Native Americans in American history and the perpetuation of stereotypes. *Journal of Narrative and Life History, 4*(4), 277–294.

Wills, J. S. (1996). Who needs multicultural education? White students, U.S. history, and the construction of a usable past. *Anthropology and Education Quarterly, 27*(3), 365–389.

Wills, J. S. (2001a). Missing in interaction: Diversity, narrative, and critical multicultural social studies. *Theory and Research in Social Education, 29*(1), 43–64.

Wills, J. S. (2001b). Schooling and the production of collective memory: Curriculum, popular culture, and the politics of historical representation. Paper presented at the annual meeting of the American Educational Research Association, April, Seattle.

Wills, J. S., & Mehan, H. (2001). Recognizing diversity within a common historical narrative: Culture, history, and the study of social life. In J. Liu and P. Kahaney (Eds.), *Contested terrain: Exploring cultural diversity through writing.* Ann Arbor: University of Michigan Press.

Wilson, W. J. (1987). *The truly disadvantaged.* Chicago: University of Chicago Press.

Wineburg, S. (1991). On the reading of historical texts: Notes on the breach between school and academy. *American Educational Research Journal, 28*(3), 495–519.

Wineburg, S. (2001). *Historical thinking and other unnatural acts.* Philadelphia: Temple University Press.

Yon, D. A. (2000). Elusive Culture: Schooling, Race, and Identity in Global Times. Albany: State University of New York Press.

10

A DECADE OF RESEARCH ON THE CHANGING TERRAIN OF MULTICULTURAL EDUCATION RESEARCH

Carl A. Grant
University of Wisconsin, Madison

Anne René Elsbree
California State University, Chico

Suzanne Fondrie
University of Wisconsin, Madison

This chapter is a review of multicultural education research from 1990 to 2001. Our intention was to build on the earlier review in the first edition of the *Handbook of Research on Multicultural Education* by Grant and Tate (1995). At times, this review is compared to the earlier one. In this chapter, we cover (a) a definition of our use of the term *multicultural education*, (b) the troubled state of multicultural education research, (c) theoretical framework, (d) methodological framework, (e) studies in multicultural education literature from 1990 to 2001, (f) discussion, (g) research concerns and suggestions, and (h) concluding remarks. In the theoretical section, we present two research paradigms, assimilation and pluralism, which serve as the lens for our analysis. We also present Grant and Sleeter's (1985) five approaches to multicultural education (1985), which serve as a typology for categorizing the studies: teaching the exceptional and culturally different, human relations, single-group studies, multicultural education, and education that is multicultural and social-reconstructionist. In the studies of multicultural education literature, we report on research that

focuses on specific populations: K–12 students, preservice teachers, K–12 teachers, teacher educators, and others. In the discussion section, we offer general observations, selected observations, gaps in the research, and barriers to multicultural education research. We continue with a question: How has the terrain of multicultural education changed in the last decade?

OUR DEFINITION OF MULTICULTURAL EDUCATION

From our perspective, the term *multicultural* itself has become widely accepted in both academia and public discourse. In addition, over the last decade we have noticed more stability and organization around multiculturalism, reflected by, for example, the development of the University of Washington's Center for Multicultural Education, the founding of the National Association of Multicultural Education, and the publication of the first edition of the *Handbook of Research on Multicultural Education* and the

This chapter builds on work by Carl A. Grant and William F. Tate from the first edition of the *Handbook*. We acknowledge and appreciate their efforts and scholarship.

Dictionary of Multicultural Education. This stability is also reflected in the steady increase in the number of journal articles involving issues of multiculturalism, as well as the variety of journals that serve to inform multicultural education.

However, a contradictory parallel exists between the academy and prekindergarten–12th-grade classrooms (PK–12), with the former beginning to explore the hierarchical power relationships between and among socially constructed categories such as race, class, gender, ethnicity, ability, sexuality, language, and religion, although we acknowledge that not all multiculturalists include all social constructs or give equal significance across the categories. In contrast, PK–12 classrooms are primarily concerned with how to work with specific groups in the realm of classroom instruction.

In this review of research in multicultural education, we use Grant's (1994) definition of multicultural education:

Multicultural education is a philosophical concept and an educational process. It is a concept built upon the philosophical ideals of freedom, justice, equality, equity, and human dignity. . . . Multicultural education is a process that takes place in schools and other educational institutions and informs all subject areas and other aspects of the curriculum. It prepares all students to work actively toward structural equality in the organizations and institutions of the United States. . . . Multicultural education does this by providing knowledge about the history, culture, and contributions of the diverse groups that have shaped history, politics, and culture of the United States. Multicultural education acknowledges that the strength and riches of the United States are a result of its human diversity. . . . It confronts social issues involving race, ethnicity, socioeconomic class, gender, homophobia, and disability. It accomplishes this by providing instruction in familiar contexts and building on students' diverse ways of thinking. It encourages student investigations of world and national events and how these events affect their lives. It teaches critical thinking skills, as well as democratic decision making, social action, and empowerment skills. (Grant, 1994, p. 31)

THE (STILL-)TROUBLED STATE OF MULTICULTURAL EDUCATION RESEARCH

In the first edition of this *Handbook,* Grant and Tate (1995) describe the nature of multicultural education research as troubled. The research from 1990 to 2001 suggests that this description holds true today. The troubled state of current multicultural education research can be explained by exploring how researchers include or exclude problematic aspects of race, class, gender, ethnicity, ability, sexuality, language, and religion. To begin, we locate the roots of multicultural education research in the antiracist and desegregation literature, and we then describe how identity factors have developed in education research in recent years.

After the 1954 *Brown* v. *Board of Education of Topeka* decision, a substantial increase occurred in research on race, particularly relating to desegregation and other antiracist practices. This research, as Taeuber (1977) notes, had methodological, theoretical, and conceptual problems. Weinberg (1977) suggests that we place research on minority students in a broader framework than has been customary:

Factors treated at some length [should] include historical and legal background, the ideology of racism, a continuing reexamination and questioning of prevailing views of the role of social class and race in learning, and the impact of minority communities upon the schools. . . . Too often theoretical studies proceed in virtual ignorance of this reality. Curiously, this failing is rarely commented on in the research literature. (p. v)

Lightfoot's (1980) critique that research on minority students has many shortcomings holds true today. Her argument that much of this research lacks insight into the context in which students live, cope, and survive is still problematic in current multicultural education research.

Race, ethnicity, and class variables vital to antiracist and desegregation research are also vital to multicultural education research. However, during the 1960s through the 1980s, an important distinction between these two areas of research is that much of the earlier antiracist and desegregation research was "decision oriented" (see Tate, Ladson-Billings, & Grant, 1993). Green, Bakan, McMillan, and Lezotte (1973) made this point when they observed that most of the research funded by the federal government and foundations was designed to provide information to decision makers. Taeuber (1977) concluded:

Despite repeated pleas for a coordinated and systematic research effort, despite establishment of sundry desegregation assistance and research centers, and despite sporadic governmental and private conferences, symposia, and reports, the flood of publications roars on, largely unharnessed by those most in need of its power. Educational administrators in search of advice on how to desegregate effectively, attorneys in search of empirical information on complex issues of feasibility and effectiveness, social scientists in search of new knowledge from a vast national experiment in social change, all find themselves inundated. (p. iii)

Besides being decision-oriented, much of the desegregation research conducted during the 1970s and 1980s—and research in general that used race, class, and gender as variables—was narrowly conceived. Much of the desegregation research dealt with Black achievement (for instance, Crain, 1971; Scott, 1969; Vane, Weitzman, & Applebaum, 1966) and Black aspirations (Ausubel & Ausubel, 1963; Coleman, 1967) and did not situate race and gender in a historical context where Whiteness and maleness were privileged (Weinberg, 1977).

In the 1990s, desegregation research moved gradually away from a decision-oriented focus and toward an understanding of the impact of desegregation on the classroom. There exists today a distinction between research that looks at the effects of desegregation and multicultural education research, which grew out of the former area. Studies in multicultural education now attempt to include a richer description of social or psychological factors, particularly relating to schoolchildren and their attitudes and identity. Peshkin and White (1990) exemplify this shift in focus in their study of four African American students coming of age in a multiethnic high school. In the same vein, Goto (1997) examines how peer interactions among Chinese American high school students influence them to accommodate or resist societal norms. At the same time, however, some research still explores ethnicity in a superficial way. For example, researchers often employ the term *Hispanic* instead of identifying which specific ethnic name members of that group prefer, such as Latino or Latina, Puerto Rican, Cuban. Similarly, *American Indian* continues to be a popular umbrella label used by researchers, rather than revealing the specific tribal affiliations represented in the studies. Even when studies identify participants, the researchers often do not analyze how the participants' identities and contexts are reflected in the research findings.

In past decades, social class and socioeconomic status were often reduced in educational research to variables used to categorize student achievement data. This research tended to ignore the cultural reproduction and the transmission of knowledge related to race, class, and gender. For example, Apple (1979) suggests there is a relationship between the curriculum, pedagogy (teacher and instructional approach), and forms of evaluation in schools on the one hand and the structural inequality in the larger society on the other. He contends that researchers must get inside both the school and the workplace in order to develop a more complete analysis of the relationship between education and the state and between culture and economy in education (see also Bourdieu, 1973; Popkewitz, 1998).

Currently, researchers persist in conflating lower socioeconomic class with ethnicity, so that poverty is more likely associated with students of color and being economically advantaged is associated with Whiteness. Even in research that identifies the context of the study in terms of socioeconomic factors, there is a lack of follow-up and analysis. For example, some research in this review identifies the percentage of students receiving free or reduced-price lunch but fails to analyze it in the discussion. Also, research continues to focus primarily on urban settings, ignoring the economic disparities present in rural education. In addition, most present research avoids addressing how issues of social privilege and cultural capital play out in the area of education. Since Jonathan Kozol's (1991) documentation of social and economic inequalities in educational settings, we find little evidence that others are exploring similar themes in their research.

Gender also continues to be problematic in educational research. Spender (1982) characterizes the troubled state of gender research in education at the time of Grant and Tate's review this way: "Our problems had not been perceived as problems" (quoted in Grant & Tate, 1995, p. 141). Spender and other feminists pointed out that the perspectives of women had not appeared across the disciplines of the academy and in research conducted by the academy. The absence of women's voices in academic discourse kept "their problems" on the margins of educational research and preserved them as the others in the academic community. Gender research in education was also complicated by the failure of researchers to address different ethnic and racial group experiences within the feminist analysis (e.g., hooks, 1990). However, these problems regarding gender in education persist, as researchers in the 1990s focused primarily on girls and their relationship to and achievement in the areas of math and science (Menis, 1997; Streitmatter, 1997). Although a few studies take into consideration the intersection of gender and ethnicity and/or social class, the majority examine gender in isolation from other factors or tend to focus predominantly on African American students (O'Halloran, 1995; Price, 1998).

More troubling is the evidence that little research exists in the areas of sexuality, multiethnicity, and religion. One must wonder why this is true. Despite the increase—albeit minimal—in acceptance of diverse sexualities, these researchers' voices are still silent. Also, multiethnicity, though always visible in society, has only recently achieved legitimacy in educational discourse. Some studies exist in the sociological literature, but educational research has been slow in coming. Similarly, religion remains underexamined, although increasingly it is an active agent in educational discourse and policy, particularly in the areas of curriculum standards and school choice. Perhaps the area most lacking in the research is attention to the intersections between and among the myriad factors included under the multicultural umbrella.

In two areas, ability and language, we found abundant research. Studies on ability focus on the participants' ability labels and how they experience schooling, though few studies analyze intersections of social constructs such as race, gender, and ability. Studies on ability frequently lack recognition of culture and ethnicity, with researchers omitting attention to race and ethnicity. Similarly, research on language is highly visible in the literature, but the focus remains on second-language acquisition. Little research addresses how first or second languages affect learning, attitude, and identity, or how language relates to issues of knowledge and power.

In sum, for many scholars educational research becomes problematic when it does not include race, class, gender, ethnicity, ability, sexuality, language, and religion, and/or when these constructs are not rigorously examined. For others, educational research becomes problematic when it *does* include these multiple factors. For still others, the impact and influence of these constructs are somewhat muted when their intersections are left unexamined. However, not including these social constructs, not providing a rigorous interrogation, and not examining their intersections means, for example, that the day-to-day life of students in their social milieu and the interaction of the school within that milieu are not studied vigorously and extensively. Furthermore, there is not sufficient consideration given to the idea that school itself reproduces social inequities.

THEORETICAL FRAMEWORK

As we read through the multicultural education research literature, we place the research within two paradigms and five approaches to multicultural education. Our research paradigms are *assimilation* and *pluralism*. Although the assimilation and pluralism paradigms are not perfect tools of analysis, they do in most cases lend themselves well to reporting the diversity we find in the research literature. As a typology for reporting the conceptualization of multicultural education authors employed, we use Grant and Sleeter's (1985) approaches to multicultural education, which consist of teaching the exceptional and culturally different, human relations, single-group studies, multicultural education, and education that is multicultural and social-reconstructionist.

Two Paradigms

The assimilation and pluralism paradigms (see Table 10.1) can be used to guide decision making for educational policy and practice. Both can employ different types of methodological procedures. Assimilation and pluralism paradigms use as primary themes race, class, gender, ethnicity, ability, sexuality, language, and religion, but there are also distinct practical differences between them.

The assimilation paradigm espouses tolerance and acceptance of difference in an effort to uphold the existing social structure and power relations. Discussions of power relationships are absent, as the focus or purpose of the research supports business as usual. Assimilationistic research tends to focus on single social constructs for data collection and analysis. For example, this research might examine race or class or gender in a classroom context

Table 10.1. Two Multicultural Education Research Paradigms.

Research Characteristics	Assimilation	Pluralism
Focus on population	Single social construct (e.g., race, or class, or gender)	Multiple or intersectionality of social constructs (e.g., races, classes, genders; or intersection of race, class, and gender)
Use of relational power	Power status quo; seeks tolerance and acceptance of differences	Transformation of power; seeks freedom, justice, equality, equity, and human dignity

without considering the intersection of multiple social constructs or the social constructs of other individuals in that classroom.

The pluralism paradigm is built upon the philosophical ideas of freedom, justice, equality, equity, and human dignity. The intention and purpose of pluralistic research is to facilitate an understanding of students, the instructional context, and the influence of educational policy in order to improve students' learning experience and the schooling process. Much of pluralistic research recognizes multiple social constructs within educational contexts and includes multiple perspectives and voices of the school community in its research. Some pluralistic research takes this a step farther and recognizes that intersections of the social constructs of race, class, gender, ethnicity, ability, sexuality, language, and religion are essential variables in analyzing data. The relationships between knowledge and power are at the forefront of the analysis and discussion of pluralistic research with the intention to seek equity by transforming power relations.

Approaches to Multicultural Education

Since the inception of multicultural education and throughout its continuous growth, several approaches (among them Grant & Sleeter, 1985; Grant, Sleeter, & Anderson, 1986; Sleeter & Grant, 1987) or dimensions (Banks, 1992) have been used to define or characterize research; scholarship; and educational policy, practices, and procedures. These approaches or dimensions have illuminated the direction taken in, and the epistemological boundaries of, multicultural education. We use the approaches as benchmark criteria to classify and judge the various studies that are reported in the subsequent sections of this chapter. We describe these approaches in reference to Grant and Sleeter (1985) and Sleeter and Grant (1987).

Research literature we identify as using the teaching the exceptional and culturally different (TECD) approach has as its main purposes:

> to challenge the cultural deficiency orientation, to establish the importance of maintaining one's own cultural identity, and to describe aspects of culture a teacher can build on. . . . Authors advocating this approach emphasize building bridges between cultures to facilitate individual achievement and social mobility, rather than combating unequal distribution of goods and power among [marginalized groups]. (Sleeter & Grant, 1987, p. 423)

Research literature we identify as conceptualizing multicultural education from the human relations (HR) approach seeks to "help students from different backgrounds get along better with each other and feel good about themselves" and to increase school and social harmony (Sleeter & Grant, 1987, p. 424).

Research literature we identify as conceptualizing multicultural education from the single-group studies (SGS) approach promotes social structural equality for, and immediate recognition of, an identified group. Commonly implemented in the form of ethnic studies or women's studies, this literature argues that knowledge about particular oppressed groups should be studied separately. Authors of research literature from a single-studies approach seek to raise consciousness concerning an identified group (for example, the Hmong) (Grant & Sleeter, 1985).

The research literature we identify as conceptualizing from a multicultural education (ME) approach promotes social structural equality and cultural pluralism. The authors examine how race, class, gender, ethnicity, ability, sexuality, language, and religious inequities play out in the various areas of society. Authors using this approach keep power relationships at the forefront of their research analysis in an effort to seek social justice goals.

In research literature we identify as using an approach of education that is multicultural and social-reconstructionist (EMSR), the authors analyze inequality and oppression in society critically and are concerned with structural equality, cultural pluralism, and the potential for social action.

These approaches provide a theoretical framework for analyzing the studies included in this chapter. The approaches can be applied to different research foci (PK-12 students, preservice education, in-service education, teacher education) to determine their attention to the philosophy and ideology of multicultural education (Grant, 1992). The purpose of the methodological section is to discuss the education research on various areas of schooling in relationship to the paradigms and approaches just delineated.

METHODOLOGICAL PROCEDURES

This section presents the research criteria, selections of research studies, testing of research procedures, data recording chart, and analysis of data.

Research Criteria

We examined research studies to determine if they met the definition of multicultural education as discussed earlier and if the research was conducted within a classroom context. Our last criterion was to determine if qualitative or quantitative methods were used.

Selection of Research Studies

To start, we reviewed more than 200 education journals in order to identify those that published multicultural education research studies and eliminate those that did not. From this pool, we identified 107 journals that published multicultural education research during the 1990s. From this pool of journals, we identified 1,207 articles on multicultural education research (for comparison purposes, Sleeter and Grant's (1985) analysis of multicultural education literature found a mere 200 articles in this area). Our next step was to eliminate any studies that would possibly be reviewed in another chapter of this edition of the *Handbook*. For example, we excluded all studies on language, ability, and studies from countries other than the United States. Additionally, we eliminated nonclassroom-based research. In other words, a study conducted at the Boys and Girls Club would not be included. In the interests of space limitations, we excluded prekindergarten populations and postsecondary studies other than those in teacher education. Finally, because other chapters in this *Handbook* address multicultural education from a single-group perspective, we excluded articles that explored only one social construct (such as ethnicity) in isolation from other factors such as class, gender, or sexuality. Our final number of articles included in this review is 184, representing 37 education journals.

Testing Research Procedures

Each of the three authors was given copies of the same ten journal articles to review and place within the assimilation or pluralism paradigms and the multicultural education approaches. We selected articles from various journals and years to make certain that our plan of review would remain consistent regardless of the journal and the nature of the study. Next, we met to compare our analyses and discuss differences in placement according to the paradigms and approaches. We resolved disagreements through discussion, finding no cases where we were unable to reach agreement.

Data Recording Chart

We developed a chart for the purpose of recording information from each of the studies that we reviewed. The chart includes author, date, title, journal, purpose of research, methodology, subjects of study, duration of study, research paradigm, approach to multicultural education, chain of inquiry, funding, and nature and place of study.

Analysis of Data

Each author was given one-third of the articles to analyze and record on the chart. We provided the others with a copy of the chart and met to discuss our findings. As each author discussed an article, the other two were able to agree or disagree on the placement in the paradigms or multicultural approaches and ask for clarification. When there was a disagreement on the placement, all the authors reread the article in order to come to a consensus. We tabulated the results according to paradigms, multicultural approaches, and populations in research studies. From this discussion and analysis, we looked for themes and patterns in the research literature.

STUDIES IN THE MULTICULTURAL EDUCATION LITERATURE

In this section, we present a discussion and analysis of the areas represented in the research: K–12 students, preservice teachers, K–12 teachers, teacher educators, and other outlying studies. These areas were selected because they represent the educational areas that have most received "multicultural" research attention; in addition, there is less possibility that they would duplicate other research reported in this volume. In the first edition of the *Handbook,* Grant and Tate (1995) found a dominant focus on two areas: student-teacher relationships and curriculum and text materials. This new review suggests a focus on attitudes and curriculum/instruction, with some attention to achievement and overall programs. For each study, we indicate both their research paradigm (either assimilation [A] or pluralism [P]) and their multicultural education approach: again, teaching the exceptional and culturally different (TECD), human relations (HR), single-group study (SGS), multicultural education (ME), and education that is multicultural and social-reconstructionist (EMSR). After each section, we provide examples of one

or two studies from that group that represent research operating within a pluralistic research paradigm. Table 10.2 presents the breakdown of the studies by paradigm and approach.

Students

By far, the majority of research on K–12 student populations deals with attitudes (44 studies). Achievement (29) and curriculum/instruction (23) follow, with a few that investigate school programs (6).

Student attitude studies relate either to their perceptions of self and others or perceptions of schooling. The majority of student attitude studies (18) involved attitudes toward school (Abi-Nader, 1990, P/ME; Atwater, Wiggins, & Gardner, 1995, P/TECD; Brickhouse, Lowery, & Schultz, 2000, P/SGS; Dehyle, 1992, P/SGS; Epstein, 1998, P/HR; Graham, Taylor, & Hudley, 1998, P/HR; Kaplan, 1999, A/TECD; Katz, 1999, P/SGS; MacMillan, Widaman, Balow, Hemsley, & Little, 1992, P/TECD; Martinez & Cranston-Gingras, 1996, P/SGS; Mather, 1997, P/SGS; Mickelson, 1990, P/SGS; Price, 1998, P/SGS; Rizzo-Tolk & Varenne, 1992, P/ME; Slaughter-Defoe & Carlson, 1996, P/TECD; Stanton-Salazar & Dornbusch, 1995, P/SGS; Voelkl, Welte, & Wieczorek, 1999, A/SGS; Willson-Quayle & Pasnak, 1997, P/TECD).

Sample studies include Abi-Nader's ethnographic inquiry (1990), which examines motivation for success among inner-city Latina/o students in a college preparatory program. She found that specific teacher strategies motivated students to "create a vision of the future, redefine their image of self, and build a supportive community" (p. 41). Slaughter-Defoe and Carlson (1996) presented their findings of a self-report survey of third-grade Comer School students' perceptions of school

Table 10.2. Paradigms and Approaches in the Multicultural Education Research Literature.

	Research Paradigm	
Grant and Sleeter Multicultural Education Approach	Assimilation	Pluralism
Teaching the exceptional and culturally different	10	17
Human relations	16	19
Single-group studies	4	49
Multicultural education	0	50
Education that is multicultural and social-reconstructionist	0	19
Total	30	154

climate. The survey, given to 1,000 African American and 260 Latino/a children in high-poverty urban schools, reveals that there are both similarities and differences between the two populations regarding school climate. Each emphasizes the importance of following school rules and doing well in school, but they differ in their perceptions of teacher-child interactions.

We located seven studies that examine students' attitudes toward others (Dickinson, Holifield, Holifield, & Creer, 2000, A/HR; DiPardo, 2000, P/ME; Dyson, 1994, P/ME; Parsons, 1997, P/SGS; J. A. Schneider, 1997, P/ME; Yamauchi, Nakagawa, & Murdoch, 1992, P/ME; Zisman & Wilson, 1992, P/HR). For example, Yamauchi et al. (1992) conducted a two-study examination of age-related ethnic attitudes of K–6 students toward peers in multiethnic Hawaiian classrooms. The authors found that when asked to nominate peers for a particular role (friend, helpful classmate, not a good leader, trip companion), students tend to nominate more on the basis of gender preference than ethnic preferences.

There were also seven studies on students' attitudes toward themselves (Hemmings, 2000, P/ME; McCarthey, 1998, P/ME; O'Brien, Martinez-Pons, & Kopala, 1999, A/HR; O'Connor, 1999, P/EMSR; Okwumabua, 2000, P/SGS; Oliver, 1999, P/EMSR; Townsend & Fu, 1998, P/HR). Representative of these is Oliver's (1999) critical narrative study, which examines how four inner-city middle school adolescent girls construct the meanings of their bodies through fashion. Interviews, interactions, and discussion reveal the girls' perceptions of "fashion in" and "fashion out." The author notes that her ethics demanded that she give back to the participants, the intent being "to help the girls begin to think critically about some of the issues they were writing about and discussing" (p. 228). Hemmings's (2000) two-year ethnographic study (2000) focuses on how urban high school students construct postoppositional identities. Specifically, the author is interested in "how historically marginalized youths managed to work out identities that carried them to the brink of graduation" (p. 152).

Twelve student studies deal with multiple attitudes: toward self and other, self and school, and so on (Cousins, 1999, P/SGS; Goto, 1997, P/HR; Hall, 2000, P/SGS; Horvat & Antonio, 1999, P/SGS; Kistner, Metzler, Gatlin, & Risi, 1993, P/HR; Machamer & Gruber, 1998, P/SGS; Miron & Lauria, 1998, P/HR; Patthey-Chavez, 1993, P/SGS; Peshkin & White, 1990, P/SGS; Pewewardy & Willower, 1993, P/SGS; Proweller, 1999, P/ME; Watson, Bell, & Chavez, 1994, A/TECD). For example, Miron and Lauria's (1998) comparative case study interviews academically successful and unsuccessful students at two inner-city high schools in the southeastern United States. The results describe "how students' racial/ethnic identity . . . becomes both a means of *resistance* and

accommodation to white hegemony" (p. 189). Proweller's (1999) ethnographic approach directs attention to the social construction of Whiteness among girls at a predominantly White private high school for girls. The study also provides narratives of students of color in order to complete the discussion of relationally constituted identities.

These studies on student attitudes represent a recent change in multicultural research, as researchers from 1990 to 2001 move away from quantitative surveys of attitudes regarding different ethnic groups and toward qualitative discoveries of attitudes about educational opportunities or self-identity. Researchers also tend to focus their efforts on high school students, accounting for more than two-thirds of the total number. This is troubling, as it concentrates attention on already existing attitudes, rather than devoting efforts to discover how and why such attitudes are formed in elementary and middle schools.

Studies assessing student achievement are situated predominantly in elementary and secondary settings, with only 4 of the 29 taking place in middle school. The majority of the achievement studies focus on African American students (11), followed by Latino/a (7), Asian Pacific American (4), and American Indian (3), while 4 studies explore achievement of multiple ethnic populations (Bankston & Zhou, 1995, P/SGS; Bergin & Cooks, 2000, P/ME; Bowker, 1992, P/SGS; Brady, Tucker, Harris, & Tribble, 1992, P/ME; Caldas & Bankston, 1998, P/TECD; Carver, 1994, A/TECD; Flores-Gonzalez, 1999, P/SGS; Fordham, 1993, P/SGS; Gauvain, Savage, & McCollum, 2000, A/TECD; Hebert & Reis, 1999, P/SGS; Hemmings, 1996, P/ME; Hubbard, 1999, P/SGS; Jimenez, 1997, P/EMSR; Kennedy, 1992, P/ME; Langer, Bartolome, Vasquez, & Lucas, 1990, P/SGS; Lee, Fradd, & Sutman, 1995, P/TECD; Lee, Fradd, & Sutman, 1996, A/TECD; McInerney & Swisher, 1995, P/SGS; Nasir, 2000, P/SGS; Noll, 1998, P/SGS; Nozaki, 2000, P/SGS; Portes & Hao, 1998, P/ME; Rodney, Crafter, Rodney, & Mupier, 1999, A/SGS; Rumberger & Larson, 1998, A/TECD; B. Schneider & Lee, 1990, P/SGS; Signer, Beasley, & Bauer, 1997, P/ME; Singh, Vaught, & Mitchell, 1998, P/SGS; Timm, Chiang, & Finn, 1998, A/TECD).

One example of these studies is Jimenez (1997), who examines the reading abilities and potential of low-literacy Latino/a middle schoolers. His qualitative research involves a formative experiment framework, which engages the researcher with the participants. The students' responses to cognitive strategy lessons are used to "shape and modify the experiment . . . so as to best promote students' comprehension of text" (p. 229). In addition to a fine portrait of low-literacy Latino/a students, the study offers their metacognitive comments and reactions to this instructional approach. Signer et al. (1997) use open-ended interviews with 100 White and African American urban high schoolers to discover their educational aspirations, academic aspirations in math, and math self-concepts. The authors found that "mathematics achievement level interacted with ethnicity, SES, and gender to influence students' mathematics self-concept and academic aspirations" (p. 386).

Curriculum and instruction studies relating to students are divided into three categories: best-practice approaches (10 studies), culturally relevant curriculum and pedagogy (9), and student learning (5). Unlike the student attitude studies, this group includes studies situated fairly evenly at all three levels: elementary, middle, and secondary.

Best-practice research examines the effectiveness of various approaches to instruction (Fitzgerald & Noblit, 2000, P/TECD; Hollingsworth, Teel, & Minarik, 1992, P/TECD; Kahle, Meece, & Scantlebury, 2000, P/SGS; McCarty, Wallace, Lynch, & Benally, 1991, P/SGS; O'Halloran, 1995, P/SGS; Polinard & Wrinkle, 1995, A/TECD; Schlosser, 1992, P/SGS; Sperling & Woodlief, 1997, P/ME; Sweeney, 1993, P/EMSR; Yeh, 1998, P/TECD).

Examples of best-practice approaches include a fourth-grade teacher's self-study (Sweeney) on attempting to change her students' perceptions of Columbus in particular and history in general (Sweeney, 1993). At the end of the unit, the students take on roles as social activists by preparing a documentary, which they shared with other students, parents, and teachers. Because of the students' efforts, Sweeney notes, the fifth-grade teachers revised their exploration unit, making it much more critical. Fitzgerald and Noblit (2000) investigate using a balanced literacy method with emergent readers in a diverse first-grade classroom. Using multiple data sources and a participant observer, the authors suggest that balanced instruction can result in students constructing a balanced view of reading and that students develop the kinds of knowledge the teacher presents. In other words, "If the terrain is ideologically diverse, then children are more likely to construct an ideologically diverse sense of reading" (p. 16).

The culturally relevant curriculum and pedagogy studies investigate materials, learning styles, and pedagogical strategies (Barba, 1993, P/TECD; Brenner, 1998, P/TECD; Grignon, 1993, P/SGS; Lee, 1995, P/HR; Matthews & Smith, 1994, P/TECD; Murrell, 1994, P/SGS; Park, 1997, P/TECD; Park, 2000, A/HR; Teel, Debruin-Parecki, & Covington, 1998, P/EMSR). A representative study is Matthews and Smith (1994), who employ quantitative methods to examine the use of culturally relevant science materials with fourth- through eighth-grade American Indians across multiple tribal affiliations. Teel, Debruin-Parecki, and Covington's two-year study describes a school-university collaboration "resulting in the development of alternative teaching strategies which honored and motivated inner-city African-American middle-school

students" (1998, p. 479). Following two cohorts (one each year), the authors use teacher research to provide a rich examination of pedagogical practices and student responses.

Student learning research analyzes the ways and contexts in which students take in curriculum and instruction (Britzman, Santiago-Valles, Jiménez-Muñoz, & Lamash, 1991, P/ME; Fine, Weis, Centrie, & Roberts, 2000, P/ME; Fordham, 1999, P/SGS; Hemphill, 1999, P/TECD; Schultz, 1996, P/HR).

The fact that the last review (Grant & Tate, 1995) included no student curriculum/instruction studies reflects a current emphasis on how students interact with curriculum and respond to different pedagogies. For example, Fordham's (1999) discourse analysis of African American high school students' use of either Ebonics or "standard English" demonstrates the ways in which these students both "lease" and "disrespect" the hegemonic school discourse. The author documents the effects of this practice on academic achievement and notes several implications for policy, one of which is that attempting to alter students' use of Ebonics is "largely counterproductive" (p. 288). Britzman et al. (1991) explore how "the politics of identity are played out in a high school English class" and use poststructural text analysis to demonstrate the ways racism and sexism manifest in this setting.

Six studies look at school programs and their effect on students (Nichols, Ludwin, & Iadicola, 1999, A/HR; Phillips, 1992, A/TECD; Tucker et al., 1995, P/SGS; Ulichny, 1996, P/ME; Volk, 1997, P/TECD; Willie, Alves, & Hagerty, 1996, A/HR).

Tucker et al. (1997), for example, report on an after-school tutoring and skill-training partnership program in a county school district in Florida involving parents, community members, and school and university teachers. The study suggests that the efforts of those involved in the partnership hold promise for raising the academic performance of the low-achieving African American students in the program.

Preservice Teachers

In contrast to the studies involving students, research involving preservice teachers (39 total studies) is primarily focused on attitudes (17 studies) and curriculum/instruction (16). A few articles focused on programs (5) and achievement (1).

Preservice teachers' attitudes covered perceptions of self (5 studies) and others (10) and perceptions of school (2). Five studies focus on preservice teachers' attitudes toward self (Duesterberg, 1998, P/ME; Guyton, Saxton, & Wesche, 1996, P/ME; McIntyre, 1997, P/EMSR; Meacham, 2000, P/SGS; Zulich, Bean, & Herrick, 1992, P/ME).

For example, in Duesterberg's (1998) study of 46 elementary student teachers, she discovers how they used culture in their classrooms and engaged in efforts to learn about their students' communities. The author uses action research to examine how her preservice teachers theorize their identities and the schooling procedures they engage in as they learn to teach. Duesterberg (1998) claims that preservice students need "more work in identifying the power relations set up by [school] configurations" in their teaching practice, such as parent conferences (p. 771). The author claims that teacher education programs can aid preservice teachers in identifying how some bureaucratic structures may put limitations on home school relationships and exclude some groups. Duesterberg suggests that benefit can be achieved from renegotiation of "rules and requirements which make exclusions possible" (p. 510).

There are 10 articles focusing on the attitudes preservice teachers have toward others, specifically students who are different from them (Avery & Walker, 1993, A/HR; Barry & Lechner, 1995, P/HR; Bowie & Bond, 1994, P/HR; Duesterberg, 1999, P/EMSR; Groulx, 2001, P/HR; Pattnaik, 1997, P/HR; Ross & Smith, 1992, P/ME; Terrill & Mark, 2000, P/ME; Tettegraph, 1996, P/ME; Tran, Young, & Di Lella, 1994, P/HR).

One example is Terrill and Mark's (2000) examination of preservice teachers' expectations for schools with children of color and English language learners by analyzing 97 preservice teachers with a questionnaire. The authors articulate three main findings: "(a) conducting this type of study helps identify and document the profile of candidates accepted into [teacher education] programs and their specific expectations, strengths, and limitations" (p. 154); (b) "service learning opportunities in diverse settings must be offered"; and (c) "teacher educators and their students require strategies to explore their cultural, linguistic, and racial identities before they can explore their particular biases toward others and appreciate different worldviews" (2000, p. 154).

Attitudes toward school appear in two studies (Burant, 1999, P/SGS; Su, 1996, P/ME). Burant (1999) explores how one working-class female Mexican American preservice teacher, Monica, found, used, or lost her political voice during her practicum experience. Burant uses a case study approach to collect data on how Monica's attitude toward schooling changes over a six-month period. The author found that the preservice teacher's participation in the community was a tool in her experience. It influenced how she used multiple literacies to make sense of experiences and how she transformed or shifted her practices, understandings, and voice in relationship to her attitudes toward school.

Curriculum and instruction studies involving preservice teachers fall into the same three categories as for students: best practice (12 studies), learning (2), and culturally relevant pedagogy (2). There are 13 studies of best practices for preservice teachers (Barton, 1999, P/EMSR; Bondy, Schmitz, & Johnson, 1993, A/HR; Causey, Thomas, & Armento, 2000, P/ME; Garmon, 1998, P/ME; Houser & Chevalier, 1995, P/EMSR; King, 1991, P/EMSR; Lawrence & Bunche, 1996, P/ME; Lawrence, 1997, P/ME; McCall, 1995, P/ME; Montecinos, 1994, P/ME; Obidah, 2000, P/EMSR; Sernak & Wolfe, 1998, P/EMSR).

As an example, Lawrence and Bunche (1996) use a white racial identity model to examine how an education course operates as a catalyst for the development of a positive White antiracist identity. Course writings and interview data are used in analyzing "to what extent a one semester course in multicultural education could help white teacher education students develop a white antiracist identity" (1996, p. 531). Analysis indicates that the course "served as a catalyst for development of students' racial identities," but the authors claim that more than one course is needed (p. 531). Sernak and Wolfe (1998) author one of the few studies in the last decade involving technology, exploring e-mail as an instructional tool to bridge multicultural theory and practice for preservice teachers at two midwestern colleges. The authors analyze e-mail communications between the students at the two colleges as well as the students' journals over three semesters with three student groups. The authors claim that the e-mail communications deepened the students' conceptual understandings through the act of writing and enhanced the community building within the courses.

The student learning studies include an examination of the impact of preservice teachers' involvement in a multicultural education course from the human relations approach to multicultural education (Bennett, Niggle, & Stage, 1990, A/HR; Reed, 1993, P/HR). One example is Reed (1993), who studies the implementation of a multicultural education unit in a preservice teacher course. The author's findings suggest that the preservice teachers perceived themselves to be better prepared to work in an urban school setting after the course unit, but the findings also indicated that preservice teachers' attitudes about students of color did not change after the unit.

Culturally relevant pedagogy studies (Tellez, 1999, P/SGS; Nel, 1992, P/ME) include research that focuses on how preservice teachers are integrating culturally relevant knowledge and strategies into their emerging pedagogies. For example, Tellez (1999) investigates how Mexican American preservice teachers use their ethnicity in their curriculum and instruction during their student teacher experience. Analysis of interview data indicates that there was little room for injecting the student teachers' cultural knowledge into the preestablished curriculum, but the Mexican American student teachers did take advantage of some opportunities that did not affect the formal curriculum. Tellez suggests that student teachers need more "opportunities to infuse the curriculum with their cultural knowledge in a development setting" (p. 568).

Studies on programs (Bullock, 1997, P/EMSR; Davis, 1995, P/ME; Hood & Parker, 1994, P/SGS; Loving & Marshall, 1997, A/HR; McDiarmid, 1992, P/ME) and achievement (Pailliotet, 1997, P/EMSR) are rarer. In a four-year study, McDiarmid (1992) assesses the multicultural component of the teacher trainee program for the Los Angeles Unified School District for preservice intern teachers. The author indicates that the periodic presentations on multicultural education appeared to have little effect on how teachers think about multiculturalism and education. Pailliotet's two-year achievement study examines the student teaching struggles of a language-minority preservice teacher, Vivian, who identifies herself as culturally Chinese, although she was born in Vietnam. Pailliotet used observation, interview, and documentational analysis for methodology. "Analysis revealed that Vivian faced many difficulties: conflicts among past and present experiences, language and communication problems, home/school tensions, financial concerns, social isolation, stereotyping and prejudice" (1997, p. 675).

In comparison to the first edition of the *Handbook's* report of 47 studies involving preservice students, our current review found slightly fewer (40), with the majority focusing on university courses for preservice teachers and only a few on preservice programs. As in the last review, current scholars pay little attention to student teaching experiences or the impact of cooperating teachers, although both components are critical to the new teachers' emerging pedagogy. Similarly, practicum and student teaching supervisor studies are nonexistent in the last decade.

K–12 Teachers

Our search for work dealing with practicing K–12 teachers revealed 28 studies, while the previous *Handbook* reported a total of only 5. As with students and preservice teachers, attitude once again is the focus of the majority of research on K–12 teachers (18 studies); curriculum/instruction (6) and programs (4) follow.

Eleven of the teacher attitude studies involve teacher perceptions of and attitudes toward others (Baker, 1999, P/SGS; Becket, 1998, P/ME; Birrell, 1995; Byrnes, Kiger, & Manning, 1997, P/TECD; Davidson, Howell, & Hoekema, 2000, P/ME; Freeman, Brookhart, & Loadman, 1999, P/HR; Fuller, 1994, P/ME; Kailin, 1999, P/ME; Lawrence & Tatum, 1997, P/EMSR; Plata & Masten, 1998, A/HR; Powell, 1996, P/ME). We discovered, surprisingly, only three studies examining teachers' attitudes toward themselves (Datnow, 1997, P/HR; Gordon, 1994, P/SGS; Paccione, 2000, P/ME). Similar to attitudes among

preservice teachers, few of the teacher attitude studies ask for teacher self-analysis or introspection, preferring instead to discover how they perceive others. Attitudes toward school are also underexamined, with only four studies encountered (Brown & Butty, 1999, A/SGS; Culver, Wolfle, & Cross, 1990, A/HR; Gordon, 2000, P/SGS; Rong & Preissle, 1997, P/SGS).

Studies on attitude toward others include Kailin (1999), whose questionnaire examines 222 White teachers' attitudes toward racism in their schools, which are situated in a "highly rated middle-class Midwestern school district" (p. 724). The author's findings indicate that a majority of the teachers blame the victim for the racism. Also, most teachers who witness racist acts or behavior from peers do not intervene, choosing instead to remain silent. Assessing teachers' perceptions of unknown writers, Davidson et al. (2000) provide 144 teachers from both urban and rural schools with nearly identical writing samples, which differ in either ethnocultural markers or violent content. Results suggest that rubric scores may be influenced by "teachers' attitudes regarding both students' ethnicity and the content they write" (p. 370).

One example of an attitude-toward-self study is Paccione (2000), who surveyed 330 members of the National Association for Multicultural Education (NAME) to reveal factors that led to their "commitment to multicultural education and/or educational equity" (p. 985). Follow-up interviews with 45 volunteers provide deeper understanding of the factors, two of the most important of which are cultural immersion and multicultural education course work that provides a critical social analysis.

Gordon (2000) explores teacher attitudes toward school, searching for the reasons Asian Pacific Americans do not choose teaching as a career. The author first interviews preservice Asian Pacific American teachers about their values regarding teaching. Then those interviewees conduct similar interviews with Asian Pacific American nonteachers in several California communities. Although she does not break "Asian American" into distinct Asian Pacific groups, Gordon does focus on the influence traditional Chinese teaching roles have on the choice of an education career. She also notes that most participants do not regard race-matched teaching as either necessary or valuable.

The surprisingly few pieces (five) of research on teachers and their curriculum and instruction approaches are mostly classified as culturally relevant pedagogy (Ennis, 1998, P/ME; Howard, 2001, P/HR; Lipka, 1991, P/SGS; Stodolsky & Grossman, 2000, P/ME), with one involving curriculum (Saldana & Waxman, 1997, A/HR). Comparing the difference between the number of attitude and curriculum/instruction studies leads us to wonder why scholarship chooses to focus on the former rather than the latter. One would expect that teachers' choice and/or delivery of material (for example, working with standards) would be a major educational concern, but this expectation is not reflected in actual research.

A case study of a single Yup'ik teacher, part of a larger collaborative research project with Yup'ik teachers in southwest Alaska, attempts to discover what culturally relevant pedagogical practices are in use in his classroom (Lipka, 1991). The article focuses on a single fifth-grade art lesson incorporating ideas about art and survival. The author notes the social relations and cultural values present in the class and lesson that convey the culturally relevant approaches. Stodolsky and Grossman's (2000) case study focuses on four teachers who work with a changing student population. The authors' intent is to discover how the teachers—two who adapt and two who do not—change or do not change their goals, curriculum, and beliefs. A larger survey of teachers confirms what the case study suggests about how teachers relate to a changing population.

The single teacher curriculum study, by Saldana and Waxman (1997), uses the Multicultural Teaching Observation Instrument to assess the types of multicultural teaching that occur in 76 fourth- and fifth-grade teachers' classrooms from 12 desegregated elementary schools. The authors found that although incidents of "teacher support of student" were frequent, there was relatively little "integration of students' culture." Five of the 28 studies involving teachers look at programs (Anyon, 1994, A/HR, and 1995, P/ME; Cook & Van Cleaf, 2000, A/HR; Sleeter, 1992b, P/ME; Smith, 1989–90, P/HR). Sleeter's (1992b) article draws on data from an ethnographic study of 30 teachers participating in a two-year multicultural education staff development project. The teachers volunteered to participate in the program, and Sleeter's focus is to determine the extent to which they made use of what they were learning at the staff development sessions. The author notes that the program's impact on classroom teaching was limited by multiple factors: lack of time, class size, required curriculum, existing program structures, the disjuncture between school and community, and the teachers' position in the administrative/bureaucratic context.

Teacher Educators

Of the entire sample, only four studies involve university teacher educators—a small change from the last *Handbook,* which included no studies on this population. All four employ a pluralistic research approach, in that they consider intersections of social constructs and power. Using an approach that is multicultural and social-reconstructionist, Ellsworth (1992, P/EMSR) simultaneously examines her own practice and describes her experience teaching a graduate course on using media in education,

where diverse participants reacted in different ways to a presentation by the American Indian Dance Theatre. In her analysis, Ellsworth describes how the class discussion became an act of assimilation as students spoke, speculated, and judged the American Indian Dance Theatre as if there were no American Indians present in the room. Ellsworth indicates that the Dance Theatre was measured against the dominant cultural norms. In terms of the American Indian culture, she states, "an 'unfamiliar,' historically subordinated culture's self-representation is discussed by those from outside that culture, in terms that position their own cultural expectations and norms at the center, as given and self-evident" (1992, p. 6). Ellsworth suggests teachers need to focus on assumptions, goals, and ground rules of classroom discussion formats in an effort to reverse power relations.

Kumashiro (2000, P/EMSR) similarly describes both his practice as a queer teacher educator working with preservice teachers and his involvement with high school students of color during a summer program. He analyzes his efforts to create antioppressive education and describes how desire, crisis, and difference play a key role in teaching and learning. Kumashiro claims teachers and students must enter a state of crisis if they are to teach and learn. He also claims that we must stop affirming the self and remaining the same and begin to desire crisis in order to teach and learn about difference.

Abt-Perkins, Hauschildt, and Dale (2000, P/ME), three preservice teacher supervisors, examine their practice regarding questions of racial and gender equity. The authors' findings indicate that preservice teaching supervisors can become multicultural supervisors by framing management and planning issues by organizing such problems along cultural dimensions, taking sufficient advantage of cooperating teachers' expertise, using storytelling when engaging supervisory dialogue, and collaborating with other supervisors in critically reflective conversations in an attempt to become aware of their own cultural positions and biases.

Although the first three of the four teacher educator studies are self-reports, the remaining one looks at large populations. Kitano, Lewis, Lynch, and Graves (1996, P/ME) ask 56 teacher educators to give written responses to a teaching vignette, to gather information about their perceptions of appropriate practice in teaching students from diverse groups. The authors then evaluate these responses to determine the teacher educators' familiarity with multicultural education practices and ability to respond to the needs of diverse populations in the classroom. In this study, the researchers identify the teacher educators as either expert or novice. The teacher educators were identified as experts if they had one or more publications in the area of multicultural education or taught one or more multicultural education courses. The findings indicate that expert and novice teacher educators in multicultural education differ in terms of the specificity, depth, and linkage to classroom practices that the teacher educators offer regarding how the teacher in the vignette can approach the situation with a multicultural perspective.

Perhaps more in-depth case studies on teacher educators might reveal how their identities (social constructs) and motivations influence their work with preservice teachers. Once again, the scarcity of research into this population demonstrates a shortcoming in the educational knowledge base about teacher educators and their pedagogy, despite the fact that teacher educators are the ones who work most closely with future teachers and who may have a great deal of influence on future teachers' emerging pedagogies.

Other Studies

Several topics appear in such small numbers that we designate them outlying studies (11 studies total). They include a combination of two studies on preservice/inservice teachers (Greenleaf, Hull, & Reilly, 1994, P/EMSR; Greenman & Kimmel, 1995, P/ME), two studies on parents (Lareau & Horvat, 1999, P/TECD; Taylor & Alves, 1999, A/HR), two studies on curriculum/texts (Chisholm & Wetzel, 1997, A/HR; Kaomea, 2000, P/SGS), one study on a bilingual liaison staff member (Hones, 1999, A/SGS), one study on environmental influence on student achievement (Bruno, 2000, P/ME), one study on school funding inequities within a district (Necochea & Cline, 1996, P/SGS), one study on a program (Freeman, 2000, P/EMSR), and one study on teacher recruitment (Young, Place, Rinehart, Jury, & Baits, 1997, A/TECD).

Both studies on preservice and in-service teachers focus on teacher training activities that address multicultural education (Greenleaf, Hull, & Reilly, 1994; Greenman & Kimmel, 1995). Greenleaf, Hull, and Reilly (1994) analyzed 36 participants (including teachers, tutors, and preservice teachers) for their responses to three case studies. The participants worked in small groups to discuss the cases. The participants were given a set of data about an individual student's academic and social behaviors and were asked to collaboratively decide on what pedagogical actions they would take to meet the students' needs. The authors analyze the responses for the accounts given for the problematic interactions articulated in the cases and the pedagogical design chosen on the basis of the case accounts. Their findings indicate that data in the form of open-ended cases create opportunities for teachers to engage in critically reflective problem solving with an emphasis on rethinking their expectations of diverse students.

The articles that report on research on parents include examination of parental preferences for their children's school enrollment and parental involvement. Taylor and Alves (1999) survey parents of a Rockford, Illinois, controlled choice program to determine their attitude toward the program and their priorities in making their school choice. The findings indicate that the teaching staff is the most significant asset a school has for attracting parent choice. They also find that parents of color put higher priority on curriculum, teachers, and facilities.

Lareau and Horvat (1999) perform a case study of parents' involvement with third-grade children using interview and classroom observations. Their research reveals how some African American parents approach schooling with open criticism, indicating that race and class mediate the ways parents express their concerns for the children's education. Their study highlights the difference between possession and activation of capital and how that capital plays out in particular settings.

It is important to note that the presence of only two studies on either curriculum or texts represents a continuing decline of research in these areas. Grant and Tate (1995) found 10 articles addressing these topics in the 1970s and 6 during the 1980s, the majority of which involved sexism or gender bias in textbooks. In 1997, Chisholm and Wetzel used a multicultural criterion to examine 32 technology-based instructional units for elementary schools (A/HR). They found that the curriculum focused on higher-level thinking and integration of technology but lacked adaptations for languages other than English, second-language acquisition, parental involvement, and collaborative student work at the computer. Three Hawaiian elementary textbooks come under scrutiny from Kaomea (2000, P/SGS), who assesses the postcolonial perspectives of the texts. The findings indicate that the images and representations in the textbooks are similar to those first projected upon Hawaiians by early colonial voyagers and since perpetuated through the travel industry. Kaomea juxtaposes the school texts with documents used for the training of tourist industry workers. Her findings warn indigenous and disadvantaged groups to think cautiously before lobbying for inclusion that may ultimately do more damage than good.

Hones's narrative inquiry studies the "role of a [Hmong] bilingual liaison in helping to resolve conflicts and build bridges of understanding between the school and diverse community" (1999, p. 106, A/SGS). Hones's analysis indicates that the relationship among the bilingual liaison, the community, and the school is dependent on three themes rooted in the Hmong and American culture: resourcefulness, relationship, and respect. Hones suggests that schools could improve their relationships with diverse communities by renegotiating their role in the community with an emphasis on these three themes.

Bruno's (2000) research focuses on school environment as he examines the correlation between Los Angeles International Airport (LAX) flight paths and math attainment in the K–12 schools near those corridors. Bruno examines the complex equity and excellence issues at inner-city school sites that are located in the geographical space under the flight paths. The findings indicate that the LAX flight paths magnify the effects of traditional at-risk factors such as poverty, make extreme demands on teachers, attenuate the impact of school district resources and school reform efforts, and make the home and community support for schooling very difficult.

Necochea and Cline (1996) analyze 10 school budgets within a single district to discover how funding is allocated on the basis of school diversity. The study compares the per student general fund expenditures at each of the ten schools. They found a $600 discrepancy, indicating that the diversity of the school population, the large size of the school, and the need for project fund allocations decreases the funding expenditures per student. The findings indicate that the higher the concentration of language-minority students in a school, the lower the allocation of general district funds to the school. The three largest schools received the least amount of per student expenditures. There is a negative correlation between the allocation of per school categorical funds and the overall level of per student expenditures from the general fund.

Freeman (2000) examines how a team of urban middle school educators in Philadelphia developed a dual language program to address the needs of their low-income, predominantly Puerto Rican students. Freeman uses action-oriented ethnographic methodology to study the dual-language program over a two-year period. Her findings indicate a discrepancy between the team's ideal plan and the actual implementation of the dual-language program. She claims that the program must be understood as a work in progress, and the team's recognition of the discrepancies was helpful to inform practice and work toward the ideal goals for the program.

Young et al. (1997) study teacher recruitment. Their participants include 60 African American females, 60 African American males, 60 White females, and 60 White males who were students in a college of education, across four states. The participants were shown a number of videotaped teacher recruitment messages and asked what they believed was the likelihood of being offered, and of accepting, the teaching position. The findings indicate that "racially similar pairings produced more positive results than racially dissimilar pairings" (p. 86). African American applicants preferred female representatives presenting recruitment messages, while Whites preferred male representatives.

In summary, there is a lack of research into equity issues involving school funding, the physical environment of the school, school choice, class size, technology, or standards, although currently these themes are important topics of discussion in education.

DISCUSSION

What follows in this discussion are (a) general observations regarding changes in the research over the last decade, (b) selected observations that we believe will contribute to further understanding of multicultural education research, and (c) suggestions to scholars who engage in multicultural education research.

General Observations

In terms of research paradigms and approaches (see Table 10.1), the studies from the last decade are concentrated in the pluralism research paradigm (154 out of 184 total), with the majority of those using a single-group (49 studies) or multicultural education (50) approach. Studies employing the assimilation research paradigm (31 out of 184) primarily use either the teaching the exceptional and culturally different (10) or human relations (17) approach.

Beyond the paradigms and approaches evident in the studies, there are several interesting points to note about the results from the review of multicultural education research. For one, the vast majority of studies deal with K-12 students and teachers: of the 184 total, 130 involve students and classroom teachers. This is a noticeable contrast to the Grant and Tate (1995) results, where much of the research reported on the field of teacher preparation. The previous edition of the *Handbook* also noted a concern in the literature with teacher-student relationships, whereas our sample finds only a few studies with this focus.

Another point of interest in the current review of research is the attention to particular groups, specifically African American, Asian Pacific Americans, Latino/as, and American Indians. The trend remains a focus on African Americans, similar to what the last review revealed. In addition, even though it is encouraging to note that many studies include diverse populations, it is discouraging to see that only a few examine or differentiate in the results among the multiple ethnicities. There is also a tendency in the research to consider some of these groups (Asian Pacific Americans, American Indians) as monolithic entities, rather than pointing out within-group differences.

We should also call attention to the fact that when researchers conduct studies on particular groups, the focus varies according to the group involved. For example, African American and Latino/a students are most often studied to reveal their attitudes or achievement, with little mention of how the information garnered from the study might inform educational policy or classroom practice. In these studies, the students are often situated as the main (or only) focus, rather than revealing how the intersection of curriculum and/or pedagogy affects them in the classroom.

A final note involves the use of "newer" frameworks in research, namely postmodern, postcolonial, poststructural, postfeminist, and ethnic feminist approaches. Only two of the articles (Ellsworth, 1992; Lareau & Horvat, 1999) employ any one of these approaches in their research, a fact that we find intriguing in light of the recent attention paid to this scholarship in academia.

Selected Observations

This section addresses the gaps we find evident in the research literature and the problem of the lack of consideration of intersectionality. We identify barriers to conducting quality multicultural education research, namely conceptual confusion, epistemological bias, funding, and acceptance of research interests.

Gaps in the Research. Certain lacks or gaps exist in the sample of research from the last decade. For one, sexuality receives very little mention in these studies, demonstrating perhaps that queerness is not yet accepted under the umbrella of multiculturalism or that research on it carries risks for both researcher and participants. Although there are organizations that publish education resources relating to queer curriculum and pedagogy (for example, the Gay, Lesbian, & Straight Education Network), much of the material is not oriented toward classroom research. In comparison to other groups, queer research in education is minimal, appearing primarily in the form of books or in journals not associated with education (see *Hatred in the Hallways*, 2001; and Letts & Sears, 1999). Given that research on queer teachers, queer students, and students from queer families is problematic because of the safety issues associated with identifying them, one would expect that this population would be underrepresented. However, this does not rule out the possibility of exploring how schools deal with harassment, how their policies support (or do not support) queer students, how teachers introduce (or avoid) topics of sexuality, or the ways in which queerness is integrated into curriculum and texts.

Another unexamined issue is religion and its place within the multicultural education paradigm. Despite the fact that religion is tied closely with culture and ethnicity, there is little to show how it affects pedagogy, learning, school/classroom environment, or curriculum selection. Several questions come to mind: Are advocates of religion as a social construct unwilling to align themselves with multicultural education efforts? Does the separation of church and state become an obstacle to research in this area, despite the fact that religion does in fact have an impact on education? How do religious convictions affect student or parent interactions with the school? Which religions are included or excluded in the classroom, particularly in light of the fact that classrooms are increasingly diverse (see, for instance, Eck, 2001)?

Intersectionality. Multicultural education research seeks to analyze the contextual aspects of educational resources, classrooms, and student experiences. However, in the past, multicultural education research tended to limit itself (see Grant, Sleeter, & Anderson, 1986b; hooks, 1990; Sleeter, 1992a) to an examination of the impact of single variables such as race, class, and/or gender instead of examining the intersections and interactions of these social constructs. Although recent educational discourse points out the importance of intersectionality in research and theorists in multicultural education embrace and promote the idea of intersectionality, there has been little impact on actual research. For example, Sleeter's comments hold true today:

It is quite possible for an individual to profess one theoretical perspective regarding one axis of inequality, such as gender, and another regarding other axes of inequality. For example, bell hooks (1990) criticizes avant-garde Whites who take a radical position on gender and/or social class, but accept implicitly more conservative beliefs about race; or African American men who view racism from a radical perspective but regard women, including African American women, as their inferiors. In analyzing a person's beliefs about the social structure and inequality, it is important not to assume *consistency*. (1992a, pp. 13–14; emphasis added)

Our survey of research finds only a few exemplary studies that model what we feel is a productive approach to including intersections of social constructs. Hemmings (2000) discovers how postoppositional identities within an urban teen clique include multiple factors such as ability, sexuality, poverty, and race. The author emphasizes the need to understand the multifaceted nature of the students and how their complex identities inform their individual adaptations: "This is especially critical in studies of historically marginalized youths who are often fighting ongoing struggles to assert a viable sense of self on multiple fronts in multiple worlds" (p. 170). She proposes that "documenting individual variations provides more accurate representations of students' identity work" (p. 170).

Similarly, Henry's (1995) analysis gives special attention to the intersectionalities of an African American, working-class, female teacher. The study explores how this teacher's consciousness, developed through her experiences of marginality, informs her current teaching. The author, citing Kathryn Riley, first points out the limitations of narrowly focused research that does not take into account multiple constructs: "It is easy to assume that to find out about young black women all we have to do is to add up what we already know about young people, black people and women" (p. 296). She implies that merely combining the evidence of these three groups does not result in an understanding of this particular young Black woman. Henry next articulates the possibilities inherent in research that considers contextualized social constructs:

We need critical, qualitative investigations of black girls and schooling which not only are distinctly gender-specific but also make participants' lives, voices, and meanings the starting points and foci of the research. We need to be asking not only new feminist questions but new *black feminist* questions about how race, class, gender, and patriarchy are inscribed into the social, academic, emotional experiences of young black girls and women. (pp. 296–297)

Intersectional studies such as these examples include in-depth examinations of interactions among multiple social constructs, providing the reader with a rich, panoramic understanding of how the politics of power and privilege affect the studies' participants.

Barriers to Multicultural Education Research

Next we examine possible explanations for why the gaps in research we have noted exist in current research. There are many roadblocks to conducting the kind of quality research necessary to advancing the understanding of multicultural issues in education, but here we focus on the main barriers evident in our examination of the last decade's research: conceptual confusion, epistemological bias, funding, and acceptance of research interests by the academy.

Conceptual Confusion Over Multicultural Education. Although the field of multicultural education is in its third decade, the lack of an agreed-upon definition continues to be a barrier (see discussion by Banks, 1977; Gay, 1983; Grant & Sleeter, 1985). Scholars have pointed out this problematic area, but little has resulted to respond to the call. In the 1970s, some advocates of multicultural education proposed that it should concern itself with matters of race and ethnicity, while others opined that it should include class and gender. More recently, what has occurred is a broadening of the multicultural umbrella, which over the years has for many come to include ability, sexuality, language, and religion. However, both sexuality and religion continue to be controversial elements in the multicultural debate, which is reflected in the lack of studies in educational journals of the last decade that give attention to these two areas.

The lack of a definition for multicultural education leads to competing interpretations and notions, thus allowing critics to dismiss multicultural education or view it as an idea without theoretical underpinnings. The impact of this confusion can be found in research, curriculum frameworks, textbooks, teacher education, and other school artifacts that claim to be multicultural yet lack any coherent guiding philosophy. Moreover, definition confusion extends into the very difference between what we identify as the two paradigmatic frameworks in multicultural education research. Failure to differentiate between the quite different agendas present in pluralism research and assimilation research paradigms may result in research that espouses a multicultural focus yet actually promotes policy antithetical to the tenets of multicultural education. In examining such research, it is crucial to look at the researchers' goals and consider whether they are working to perpetuate the status quo or seeking to promote social justice and/or social reconstruction. Without engaging in such an examination, we allow research to wander directionless, a ship without a rudder.

Researchers' Epistemological Bias. One barrier to multicultural education research relates to how researchers conjecture about certain features of their areas of interest and how these features are related. Delgado (1990) argues that feminists and scholars of color are able to tell stories different from those heard in traditional academic discourse. Albert Einstein makes a similar argument on this point:

To the discoverer . . . the constructions of his imagination appear so necessary and so natural that he is apt to treat them not as the creations of his thoughts, but as given realities. . . . The stereotypical categories that we use are rarely without some point of tangency with reality (biological, social, medical), but their interpretation is colored by the ideology that motivates us. (cited in Minow, 1987, pp. 173–174)

Like Einstein, Delgado (1990) recognizes that scholars' previous experience and personal convictions affect their research (see also Gould, 1981). Rather than hide behind the tenets of scientific empiricism, Delgado (1990, 1991) argues that the researcher's previous experiences are important components of disciplined inquiry (see also Banks, 1992; Grant, 1992). Delgado (1990) contends that marginalized populations in our society speak with experiential knowledge framed by that marginality. This framework gives their stories a common structure warranting the term *voice*. Incorporating the voice of diverse scholars challenges the manner in which political, moral, and scientific analysis is conducted in educational research.

For many multicultural education scholars, social reality is constructed by the creation and the exchange of stories about individual situations (Brickhouse, Lowery, & Schultz, 2000; Ladson-Billings, 2001; Luttrell, 1997). Delgado (1989) reminds us that outgroups throughout U.S. history have used stories to heal wounds caused by racism, sexism, and other forms of oppression. These stories also provide a mechanism to challenge dominant groups of society who use stock stories (stereotypes) to legitimize privilege (Bell, 1992; Crenshaw, 1988;

Lawrence, 1987; Takaki, 1993). Our review of the last decade's educational research reveals a wealth of such stories in the form of ethnographic studies that seek to understand and give voice to marginalized people (see Dehyle, 1992; Hemmings, 1996; Katz, 1999; Schneider, 1997). Yet these stories are in jeopardy if multicultural education researchers do not fend off arguments against research that incorporates marginalized voices.

Another aspect of epistemological bias is researchers' tendency to address only one or two social constructs in the overall body of their research. Often the rationales for this narrow focus include lack of sufficient interest in exploring multiple constructs, lack of time, and lack of financial resources. In addition, the absence of mentoring or modeling of an approach to research involving multiple constructs and their intersectionality might lead to new scholars' perpetuating the methodologies and paradigms modeled for them in the past.

One of the past paradigms we find revealed in current research is the use of a deficit model in studying students and classrooms. Much research still looks at ways to assimilate students and align their behavior and attitudes more closely to traditional schooling and classroom life, rather than attempting to discover ways in which policy, pedagogy, and curriculum might better serve students. This deficit approach may be a reflection of the issue mentioned before: the lack of attention to the multiple facets present in education. Seeing a student or teacher only in terms of race or gender or class limits the research.

Research Funding. Funding continues to be a key factor in the slow development of long-term and sustained multicultural education research. Lack of funding is a barrier to multicultural education research for two reasons. First, formal and informal socialization of future multicultural education scholars should take place in graduate programs with the resources required for thorough scholarly preparation. Popkewitz (1984) states:

As people are trained to participate in a research community, the learning involves more than the content or the field. Learning the exemplars of a field of inquiry is also to learn how to see, think about and act towards the world. An individual is taught the appropriate expectations, demands, and consistent attitudes and emotions that are involved in doing science. (p. 3)

In the academy, a key ingredient for providing graduate students the type of experience described here is research funding. A lack of funding can result in a void in the future leadership of multicultural education research. Additionally, scholars in the field often lack the resources and opportunities to engage in staff development that might help them analyze and enhance their research approach.

A second reason lack of funding for multicultural education research is problematic is its impact on the type, depth, and length of studies that are possible. It is difficult to study multiple educational systems, schools, classrooms, and/or teachers without financial backing. Grant and Secada's review (1990) of research studies reveals that only a few were supported with institutional, state, or federal funds. Similarly, 20% of the 184 studies surveyed for this review received some sort of funding, but of those, 30% were Spencer Foundation awards for graduate research. Of greater interest is the fact that government funding accounts for only 8% of the studies included in this chapter. Because diversity and ever-changing demographics are important facets of policies and practices in U.S. institutions, we find the lack of government support for research into this area a profound barrier to meeting the needs of all students.

Acceptance of Varied Research Interests. A nonmonetary barrier to multicultural education research—but one that still haunts multicultural education researchers—is hesitancy on the part of scholars in pursuing their research interests for fear that they will not be taken seriously or advanced up the academic career ladder. For example, the lack of research involving sexuality might indicate that scholars either do not perceive it as important or are concerned with how including sexuality in their research would be received or accepted by their academic community.

In sum, conceptual confusion, research bias, inadequate funding, and lack of acceptance of varied research interests continue to plague multicultural education research. As long as this is the case, we miss valuable opportunities to increase understanding about students and teachers and address issues of educational equity. The barriers we have noted frame our next section: suggestions for and concerns about multicultural education research.

RESEARCH CONCERNS AND SUGGESTIONS

On the basis of our review and analysis of 184 research articles dealing with multicultural issues in education, we find encouraging signs of progress, but we also offer several continuing concerns and suggestions for future direction. At the most basic level, our initial number of education studies with a multicultural perspective (more than 1,200) represents a considerable increase in research. Furthermore, it is positive to note that about four-fifths of the articles operate in a pluralism research paradigm instead of an assimilation research paradigm. This is significant, as the former paradigm espouses ideas of freedom, justice, and equity as it moves toward an understanding of students and their total education and attempts to understand the influence of social constructs and the relationship between knowledge and power, using multiple perspectives.

Another noteworthy aspect of the studies in general is that an increasing number of them (more than one-third) use an approach that is either multicultural education or education that is multicultural and social-reconstructionist in nature. This indicates a shift in multicultural education research since the last review, as scholars move away from a single-group or human relations approach. We hope that this trend continues and future research examines the many social constructs, including equity and social justice concerns. Finally, although a number of the studies use attitudinal surveys or a quantitative approach to the research, the majority employ a qualitative or ethnographic methodology that often involves rich detail and description of the setting and participants.

Although these positive aspects are promising, problems exist in the research. We have examined several barriers to multicultural education research: conceptual confusion, researcher epistemological bias, funding, research acceptance in the academy. Our first suggestion addresses possible ways researchers can mitigate the effects of these barriers. Like any other field, multicultural education has varying conceptions of its own definition. Researchers should clarify how they define multicultural education in the context of the study, instead of assuming knowledge on the part of the reader. In the absence of this guiding definition, the research confuses and misleads the reader and opens the field to criticism from the outside. Similarly, epistemological bias leads to a less thorough approach to research. Researchers need to understand and examine marginalized voices, explore intersectionalities, and avoid employing a deficit approach to research. Bringing together a collaborative team that is more broadly based, with multiple backgrounds and experiences, could result in research that contains multiple dimensions and a fuller understanding of the issues under scrutiny.

However, without adequate funding, such collaboration remains only a possibility. The lack of research funds often determines who conducts the research and the issues on which they choose to focus. Researchers need to be more proactive in seeking out funds for multicultural education research, recognizing that studies in this area are critical to matters of national and international interest. Nevertheless, even with adequate funding, there is still the chance that researchers' efforts will be ignored or not accepted by the research community. The research community must be open to multiple approaches on diverse topics of interest, considering the quality of the research over the nature of the study itself.

A second area of concern is the focus of the study. Research questions need to focus less on a single attribute and be more attentive to how multiple social constructs are affected by issues of equity, power, and social justice. Although the majority of the studies in our pool of articles do consider more than one population within a classroom, the analysis is often superficial and does not discuss the implications of these differences for improving the educational process. Future research should both introduce and analyze the presence of multiple, intersecting social constructs, indicating how these intersections illuminate the issues at hand and better help the researcher understand that the problems under investigation are complex and multilayered.

A third area of concern is the lack of a chain of inquiry evident in the research. Of the authors involved with the 184 studies, only six authored a multicultural education research article more than once in the last decade. In addition, very few authors appear both in this review and in the last, and replication studies are almost totally absent. Multicultural education scholars need to conduct research on multiple sites to confirm and disconfirm findings over time and situations (Erickson, 1986). A related point is a need for multicultural education researchers to establish chains of inquiry to formulate conceptions of knowledge. We wonder where the authors who were reviewed in the first edition of the *Handbook* have gone and why they are no longer doing research in this area, although we recognize that many of these scholars engage in theoretical and philosophical writing, such as producing textbooks and responding to journal editors' invitations to appear in upcoming issues. The absence of long-term and consistent research agendas makes it difficult for the field to have the chains of inquiry necessary in order to understand the multiple dimensions of how power and equity play out in educational policy and practices.

A fourth concern exists in the foci chosen for these studies. The majority of the research looks at attitudes and behavior, employing a human relations or teaching the exceptional and culturally different approach. Such studies involve a deficit perspective as they seek ways to better fit the participants into the existing education system, rather than displaying how power and privilege operate on the participants and limit their educational potential.

A fifth concern relates to the underserved issues and populations in research. Issues such as multicultural perspectives on technology, sexuality, religion, and rural and multiethnic populations are almost nonexistent in studies in the last decade. In addition, research that includes umbrella terms for groups such as American Indians, Latino/as, or Asian Pacific Americans should instead identify the specific cultural group dealt with in the research, rather than generalizing the results across what is a very diverse aggregate.

The final issue of concern involves methodological practices. Many of the studies do not describe in detail the procedures and methods used to collect data. Most often lacking are an explicit statement of the research question(s), a full description of the methodological approach, a description of the researcher as an insider or outsider to the issue, rich detail about the participants and their multiple social constructs, and comprehensive discussion and analysis that follow up on the participants identified at the outset. Research that does not fully articulate these methods and procedures displays a lack of research sophistication and calls into question the quality of multicultural education research.

CONCLUDING REMARKS

We conclude with four remarks that inform future multicultural education research. First, in our effort to narrow our field by excluding prekindergarten populations, language, international studies, and ability studies, we recognize that we have missed opportunities within the initial 1,200 articles to examine multicultural education research in the last decade as a whole. Because of this, we are unable to determine how our sample connects across the field of multicultural education research. On the other hand, the large initial sample is encouraging. The sheer number of articles—and the explosion of the number of journals publishing those articles—signals to future researchers that there are numerous outlets for their research interests and efforts. This is a distinct change from the last review, continuing the trend over the past 30 years.

Second, it is encouraging to note that several articles offer a potential model for future research that uses a multicultural and social-reconstructionist approach. In a field that is plagued with conceptual confusion, scholars and practitioners are often searching for new ways to conceptualize and analyze research, and this review finds that there are examples available to researchers in the fields to help them do just that.

Third, the trend toward conducting research in the classroom is very promising. Yet at the same time, it is important not to swing away from (for example) teacher education in favor of another focus, as important as that focus might be. A balanced research agenda is crucial to advancing multicultural education, and focusing attention on one area over another does a disservice to the field in general.

As we conclude this two-year-long study, our final observation is that multicultural education research is alive and well and involves active scholarly commitment, scholarship that works with a language that provides understanding and enlightenment and leads to the construction and/or reconstruction of hope and agency for all people.

References

Abi-Nader, J. (1990). A house for my mother: Motivating Hispanic high school students. *Anthropology & Education Quarterly, 21,* 41–58.

Abt-Perkins, D., Hauschildt, P., & Dale, H. (2000). Becoming multicultural supervisors: Lessons from a collaborative field study. *Journal of Curriculum & Supervision, 16*(1), 28–47.

Anyon, J. (1994). Teacher development and reform in an inner-city school. *Teachers College Record, 96*(1), 14–31.

Anyon, J. (1995). Race, social class, and educational reform in an inner-city school. *Teachers College Record, 97*(1), 69–94.

Apple, M. W. (1979). *Ideology and curriculum.* Boston: Routledge & Kegan Paul.

Atwater, M. M., Wiggins, J., & Gardner, C. M. (1995). A study of urban middle school students with high and low attitudes toward science. *Journal of Research in Science Teaching, 32*(6), 605–677.

Ausubel, D. P., & Ausubel, P. (1963). Ego development among segregated Negro children. In H. A. Passow (Ed.), *Education in depressed areas* (pp. 109–141). New York: Teachers College Press.

Avery, P. G., & Walker, C. (1993). Prospective teachers' perceptions of ethnic and gender differences in academic achievements. *Journal of Teacher Education, 44*(1), 27–37.

Baker, J. A. (1999). Teacher-student interaction in urban at-risk classrooms: Differential behavior, relationship quality, and student satisfaction with school. *Elementary School Journal, 100*(1), 57–70.

Banks, J. A. (1977). The implications of multicultural education for teacher education. In F. H. Klassen & D. M. Gollnick (Eds.), *Pluralism and the American teacher* (pp. 1–34). Washington, DC: American Association of Colleges for Teacher Education.

Banks, J. A. (1992). Multicultural education: Historical development, dimensions, and practice. In L. Darling-Hammond (Ed.), *Review of research in education* (pp. 3–49). Washington, DC: American Educational Research Association.

Bankston, C. L., III, & Zhou, M. (1995). Effects of minority-language literacy on the academic achievement of Vietnamese youths in New Orleans. *Sociology of Education, 68,* 1–17.

Barba, R. H. (1993). A study of culturally syntonic variables in the bilingual/bicultural science classroom. *Journal of Research in Science Teaching, 30*(9), 1053–1071.

Barry, N. H., & Lechner, J. V. (1995). Preservice teachers' attitudes about and awareness of multicultural teaching and learning. *Teaching and Teacher Education, 11*(2), 149–161.

Barton, A. C. (1999). Crafting a multicultural science teacher education: A case study. *Journal of Teacher Education, 50*(4), 303–314.

Becket, D. R. (1998). Increasing the number of Latino and Navajo teachers in hard-to-staff schools. *Journal of Teacher Education, 49*(3), 196–205.

Bell, D. (1992). *Faces at the bottom of the well: The permanence of racism*. New York: Basic Books.

Bennett, C., Niggle, T., & Stage, F. (1990). Preservice multicultural teacher education: Predictors of student readiness. *Teaching and Teacher Education, 6*(3), 243–254.

Bergin, D. D., & Cooks, H. C. (2000). Academic competition among students of color: An interview study. *Urban Education, 35*(4), 442–472.

Birrell, J. E. (1995). "Learning how the game is played": An ethnically encapsulated beginning teacher's struggle to prepare Black youth for a White world. *Teaching & Teacher Education, 11*(2), 137–147.

Bondy, E., Schmitz, S., & Johnson, M. (1993). The impact of coursework and fieldwork on student teachers' reported beliefs about teaching poor and minority students. *Action in Teacher Education, 15*(2), 55–62.

Bourdieu, P. (1973). Cultural reproduction and social reproduction. In J. Karabel & A. H. Halsey (Eds.), *Power and ideology in education* (pp. 487–510). New York: Oxford University Press.

Bowie, R. L., & Bond, C. L. (1994). Influencing future teachers' attitudes toward Black English: Are we making a difference? *Journal of Teacher Education, 45*(2), 112–118.

Bowker, A. (1992). The American Indian female dropout. *Journal of American Indian Education, 31*(3), 3–20.

Brady, B. A., Tucker, C. M., Harris, Y. R., & Tribble, I. (1992). Association of academic achievement with behavior among Black students and White students. *Journal of Educational Research, 86*(1), 43–51.

Brenner, M. E. (1998). Adding cognition to the formula for culturally relevant instruction in mathematics. *Anthropology & Education Quarterly, 29*(2), 214–244.

Brickhouse, N. W., Lowery, P., & Schultz, K. (2000). What kind of a girl does science? The construction of school science identities. *Journal of Research in Science Teaching, 37*(5), 441–458.

Britzman, D. P., Santiago-Valles, K. A., Jiménez-Muñoz, G. M., & Lamash, L. (1991). Dusting off the erasures: Race, gender, and pedagogy. *Education and Society, 9*(2), 88–99.

Brown, J. W., & Butty, J. M. (1999). Factors that influence African American male teachers' educational and career aspirations: Implications for school district recruitment and retention efforts. *Journal of Negro Education, 68*(3), 280–292.

Bruno, J. E. (2000). Geographical space surrounding school settings as an issue of social justice. *Equity & Excellence in Education, 33*(2), 50–60.

Bullock, L. D. (1997). Efficacy of a gender and ethnic equity in science education curriculum for preservice teachers. *Journal of Research in Science Teaching, 34*(10), 1019–1038.

Burant, T. J. (1999). Finding, using, and losing(?) voice: A preservice teacher's experiences in an urban educative practicum. *Journal of Teacher Education, 50*(3), 209–219.

Caldas, S. J., & Bankston, C., III. (1998). The inequality of separation: Racial composition of schools and academic achievement. *Educational Administration Quarterly, 34*(4), 533–557.

Carver, B. A. (1994). Defining the context of early computer learning for African American males in urban elementary schools. *Journal of Negro Education, 63*(4), 532–544.

Causey, V. E., Thomas, C. D., & Armento, B. J. (2000). Cultural diversity is basically a foreign term to me: The challenges of diversity for preservice teacher education. *Teaching and Teacher Education, 16*, 33–45.

Chisholm, I. M., & Wetzel, K. (1997). Lessons learned from a technology-integrated curriculum for multicultural classrooms. *Journal of Technology & Teacher Education, 5*(4), 293–317.

Coleman, J. S. (1967). *Race relations and social change*. Baltimore, MD: Johns Hopkins University, Center for the Study of Social Organization of Schools.

Cook, D. W., & Van Cleaf, D. W. (2000). Multicultural perceptions of 1st-year elementary teachers' urban, suburban, and rural student teaching placements. *Urban Education, 35*(2), 165–174.

Cousins, L. H. (1999). Playing between classes: America's troubles with class, race, and gender in a Black high school and community. *Anthropology & Education Quarterly, 30*(3), 294–316.

Crain, R. L. (1971). School integration and the academic achievement of Negroes. *Sociology of Education, 44*(1), 1–26.

Crenshaw, K. W. (1988). Race, reform, and retrenchment: Transformation and legitimation in anti-discrimination law. *Harvard Law Review, 101*, 1331–1387.

Culver, S. M., Wolfle, L. M., & Cross, L. H. (1990). Testing a model of teacher satisfaction for Blacks and Whites. *American Educational Research Journal, 27*(2), 323–349.

Datnow, A. (1997). Using gender to preserve tracking's status hierarchy: The defensive strategy of entrenched teachers. *Anthropology & Education Quarterly, 28*(2), 204–228.

Davidson, M., Howell, K. W., & Hoekema, P. (2000). Effects of ethnicity and violent content on rubric scores in writing samples. *Journal of Educational Research, 9*(6), 367–372.

Davis, K. A. (1995). Multicultural classrooms and cultural communities of teachers. *Teaching & Teacher Education, 11*(6), 553–563.

Dehyle, D. (1992). Constructing failure and maintaining cultural identity: Navajo and Ute school leavers. *Journal of American Indian Education, 31*(2), 24–47.

Delgado, R. (1989). Storytelling for oppositionists and others: A plea for narrative. *Michigan Law Review, 87*, 2411–2441.

Delgado, R. (1990). When a story is just a story: Does voice really matter? *Virginia Law Review, 76*, 95–111.

Delgado, R. (1991). Brewer's plea: Critical thoughts on common cause. *Vanderbilt Law Review, 44*, 2–14.

Dickinson, G., Holifield, M., Holifield, G., & Creer, D. (2000). Elementary magnet school students' interracial interaction choices. *Journal of Educational Research, 93*(6), 391–394.

DiPardo, A. (2000). What a little hate literature will do: "Cultural issues" and the emotional aspect of school change. *Anthropology & Education Quarterly, 31*(3), 306–332.

Duesterberg, L. M. (1998). Rethinking culture in the pedagogy and practices of preservice teachers. *Teaching and Teacher Education, 14*(5), 497–512.

Duesterberg, L. M. (1999). Theorizing race in the context of learning to teach. *Teachers College Record, 100*(4), 751–775.

Dyson, A. H. (1994). The Ninjas, the X-Men, and the ladies: Playing with power and identity in an urban primary school. *Teachers College Record, 96*(2), 219–239.

Eck, D. L. (2001). *A new religious America: How a "Christian country" has become the world's most religiously diverse nation*. San Franciso: HarperSanFrancisco.

Ellsworth, E. (1992). Teaching to support unassimilated difference. *Radical Teacher, 42*, 4–9.

Ennis, C. D. (1998). The context of a culturally unresponsive curriculum: Constructing ethnicity and gender within a contested terrain. *Teaching and Teacher Education, 14*(7), 749–760.

Epstein, T. (1998). Deconstructing differences in African-American and European-American adolescents' perspectives on U.S. history. *Curriculum Inquiry, 28*(4), 397–425.

Erickson, F. (1986). Qualitative methods in research on teaching. In M. C. Wittrock (Ed.), *Handbook of research on teaching* (3rd ed., pp. 119–161). New York: Macmillan.

Fine, M., Weis, L., Centrie, C., & Roberts, R. (2000). Educating beyond the borders of schooling. *Anthropology & Education Quarterly, 31*(2), 131–151.

Fitzgerald, J., & Noblit, G. (2000). Balance in the making: Learning to read in an ethnically diverse first-grade classroom. *Journal of Educational Psychology, 92*(1), 3–22.

Flores-Gonzalez, N. (1999). Puerto Rican high achievers: An example of ethnic and academic identity compatibility. *Anthropology & Education Quarterly, 30*(3), 343–362.

Fordham, S. (1993). "Those loud Black girls": (Black) women, silence, and gender "passing" in the academy. *Anthropology & Education Quarterly, 24*(1), 3–32.

Fordham, S. (1999). Dissin' "the standard": Ebonics as guerrilla warfare at Capital High. *Anthropology & Education Quarterly, 30*(3), 272–293.

Freeman, D. J., Brookhart, S. M., & Loadman, W. E. (1999). Realities of teaching in racially/ethnically diverse schools: Feedback from entry-level teachers. *Urban Education, 34*(1), 89–114.

Freeman, R. (2000). Contextual challenges to dual-language education: A case study of a developing middle school program. *Anthropology & Education Quarterly, 31*(2), 202–229.

Fuller, M. L. (1994). The monocultural graduate in the multicultural environment: A challenge for teacher educators. *Journal of Teacher Education, 45*(4), 269–277.

Garmon, M. A. (1998). Using dialogue journals to promote student learning in a multicultural teacher education course. *Remedial & Special Education, 19*(1), 32–45.

Gauvain, M., Savage, S., & McCollum, D. (2000). Reading at home and at school in the primary grades: Cultural and social influences. *Early Education & Development, 2*(4), 447–463.

Gay, G. (1983). Multiethnic education: Historical developments and future prospects. *Phi Delta Kappan, 64*(8), 560–563.

Gordon, J. A. (1994). Why students of color are not entering teaching: Reflections from minority teachers. *Journal of Teacher Education, 45*(5), 346–353.

Gordon, J. A. (2000). Asian American resistance to selecting teaching as a career: The power of community and tradition. *Teachers College Record, 102*(1), 173–196.

Goto, S. T. (1997). Nerds, normal people, and homeboys: Accommodation and resistance among Chinese American students. *Anthropology & Education Quarterly, 28*(1), 70–84.

Gould, S. J. (1981). *The mismeasure of man.* New York: Norton.

Graham, S., Taylor, A. Z., & Hudley, C. (1998). Exploring achievement values among ethnic minority early adolescents. *Journal of Educational Psychology, 90*(4), 606–620.

Grant, C. A. (1992). *Research and multicultural education: From the margins to the mainstream.* London: Falmer Press.

Grant, C. A. (1994). Toward a common definition of multicultural education. *Insights on diversity.* West Lafayette, IN: Kappa Delta Pi.

Grant, C. A., & Secada, W. G. (1990). Preparing teachers for diversity. In W. R. Houston (Ed.), *Handbook of research on teacher education* (pp. 403–422). New York: Macmillan.

Grant, C. A., & Sleeter, C. E. (1985). The literature on multicultural education: Review and analysis. *Educational Review, 37*(2), 97–118.

Grant, C. A., Sleeter, C. E., & Anderson, J. (1986). The literature on multicultural education: Review and analysis. *Educational Studies, 12,* 47–71.

Grant, C. A., & Tate, W. F. (1995). Multicultural education through the lens of the multicultural education research literature. In J. A. Banks & C.A.M. Banks (Eds.), *Handbook of research on multicultural education* (pp. 145–166). New York: Macmillan.

Green, R. L., Bakan, R. F., McMillan, J. H., & Lezotte, L. W. (1973). Research and the urban school: Implications for educational improvement. In R. M. W. Travers (Ed.), *Second handbook of research on teaching* (pp. 601–631). Skokie, IL: Rand McNally.

Greenleaf, C., Hull, G., & Reilly, B. (1994). Learning from our diverse students: Helping teachers rethink problematic teaching and learning situations. *Teaching & Teacher Education, 10*(5), 521–541.

Greenman, N. P., & Kimmel, E. B. (1995). The road to multicultural education: Potholes of resistance. *Journal of Teacher Education, 46*(5), 360–368.

Grignon, J. R. (1993). Computer experience of Menominee Indian students: Gender differences in coursework and use of software. *Journal of American Indian Education, 32*(3), 1–15.

Groulx, J. G. (2001). Changing preservice teacher perceptions of minority schools. *Urban Education, 36*(1), 60–92.

Guyton, E., Saxton, R., & Wesche, M. (1996). Experiences of diverse students in teacher education. *Teaching & Teacher Education, 12*(6), 643–652.

Hall, J. (2000). Canal Town boys: Poor white males and domestic violence. *Anthropology & Education Quarterly, 31*(4), 471–485.

Hatred in the hallways: Violence and discrimination against lesbian, gay, bisexual, and transgender students in U.S. schools. (2001). New York: Human Rights Watch.

Hebert, T. P., & Reis, S. M. (1999). Culturally diverse high-achieving students in an urban high school. *Urban Education, 34*(4), 428–457.

Hemmings, A. (1996). Conflicting images? Being Black and a model high school student. *Anthropology & Education Quarterly, 27*(1), 20–50.

Hemmings, A. (2000). Lona's links: Postoppositional identity work of urban youths. *Anthropology & Education Quarterly, 31*(2), 152–172.

Hemphill, L. (1999). Narrative style, social class, and response to poetry. *Research in the Teaching of English, 33,* 275–303.

Henry, A. (1995). Growing up Black, female, and working class: A teacher's narrative. *Anthropology & Education Quarterly, 26*(3), 279–305.

Hollingsworth, S., Teel, K., & Minarik, L. (1992). Learning to teach Aaron: A beginning teacher's story of literacy instruction in an urban classroom. *Journal of Teacher Education, 43*(2), 116–127.

Hones, D. F. (1999). Making peace: A narrative study of a bilingual liaison, a school and a community. *Teachers College Record, 101*(1), 106–134.

Hood, S., & Parker, L. (1994). Minority students informing the faculty: Implications for racial diversity and the future of teacher education. *Journal of Teacher Education, 48*(3), 164–171.

hooks, b. (1990). *Yearning: Race, gender and cultural politics.* Boston: South End Press.

Horvat, E. M., & Antonio, A. L. (1999). "Hey, those shoes are out of uniform": African American girls in an elite high school and the importance of habitus. *Anthropology & Education Quarterly, 30*(3), 317–342.

Houser, N. O., & Chevalier, M. (1995). Multicultural self-development in the preservice classroom: Equity education for the dominant culture. *Equity & Excellence in Education, 28*(3), 5–13.

Howard, T. C. (2001). Powerful pedagogy for African American students: A case of four teachers. *Urban Education, 36*(2), 179–202.

Hubbard, L. (1999). College aspirations among low-income African American high school students: Gendered strategies for success. *Anthropology & Education Quarterly, 30*(3), 363–383.

Jimenez, R. T. (1997). The strategic reading abilities and potential of five low-literacy Latina/o readers in middle school. *Reading Research Quarterly, 32*(3), 224–243.

Kahle, J. B., Meece, J., & Scantlebury, K. (2000). Urban African-American middle school science students: Does standards-based teaching make a difference? *Journal of Research in Science Teaching, 37*(9), 1019–1041.

Kailin, J. (1999). How White teachers perceive the problem of racism in their schools: A case study in "liberal" Lakeview. *Teachers College Record, 100*(4), 724–750.

Kaomea, J. (2000). A curriculum of Aloha? Colonialism and tourism in Hawai'i's elementary textbooks. *Curriculum Inquiry, 30*(3), 319–344.

Kaplan, E. B. (1999). "It's going good": Inner-city Black and Latino adolescents' perceptions about achieving an education. *Urban Education, 34*(2), 181–213.

Katz, S. R. (1999). Teaching in tensions: Latino immigrant youth, their teachers, and the structures of schooling. *Teachers College Record, 100*(4), 809–840.

Kennedy, E. (1992). A multilevel study of elementary male Black students and White students. *Journal of Educational Research, 86*(2), 105–110.

King, J. E. (1991). Dysconscious racism: Ideology, identity, and the miseducation of teachers. *Journal of Negro Education, 60*(2), 133–146.

Kistner, J., Metzler, A., Gatlin, D., & Risi, S. (1993). Classroom racial proportions and children's peer relations: Race and gender effects. *Journal of Education Psychology, 85*(3), 446–452.

Kitano, M. K., Lewis, R. B., Lynch, E. W., & Graves, A. W. (1996). Teaching in a multicultural classroom: Teacher educators' perspectives. *Equity & Excellence in Education, 29*(3), 70–77.

Kozol, J. (1991). *Savage inequalities.* New York: Crown.

Kumashiro, K. K. (2000). Teaching and learning through desire, crisis, and difference: Perverted reflections on anti-oppressive education. *Radical Teacher, 58,* 6–11.

Ladson-Billings, G. (2001). *Crossing over to Canaan: The journey of new teachers in diverse classrooms.* San Francisco: Jossey-Bass.

Langer, J. A., Bartolome, L., Vasquez, O., & Lucas, T. (1990). Meaning construction in school literacy tasks: A study of bilingual students. *American Educational Research Journal, 27*(3), 427–471.

Lareau, A., & Horvat, E. M. (1999). Moments of social inclusion and exclusion: Race, class, and cultural capital in family-school relationships. *Sociology of Education, 72,* 37–53.

Lawrence, C. R. (1987). The id, the ego, and equal protection: Reckoning with unconscious racism. *Stanford Law Review, 39,* 317–388.

Lawrence, S. (1997). Beyond race awareness: White racial identity and multicultural teaching. *Journal of Teacher Education, 48*(2), 108–117.

Lawrence, S. M., & Bunche, T. (1996). Feeling and dealing: Teaching White students about racial privilege. *Teaching & Teacher Education, 12*(5), 531–542.

Lawrence, S. M., & Tatum, B. D. (1997). Teachers in transition: The impact of antiracist professional development on classroom practice. *Teachers College Record, 99*(1), 162–178.

Lee, C. D. (1995). A culturally based cognitive apprenticeship: Teaching African American high school students skills in literacy interpretation. *Reading Research Quarterly, 30*(4), 608–630.

Lee, O., & Fradd, S. H. (1996). Literacy skills in science learning among linguistically diverse students. *Science Education, 80*(6), 651–671.

Lee, O., Fradd, S. H., & Sutman, F. X. (1995). Science knowledge and cognitive strategy use among culturally and linguistically diverse students. *Journal of Research in Science Teaching, 32*(8), 797–816.

Letts, W. J., & Sears, J. T. (1999). *Queering elementary education: Advancing the dialogue about sexualities and schooling.* Lanham, MD: Rowman & Littlefield.

Lightfoot, S. L. (1980). Families as educators: The forgotten people of *Brown.* In D. Bell (Ed.), *Shades of Brown: New perspectives on school desegregation* (pp. 2–19). New York: Teachers College Press.

Lipka, J. (1991). Toward a culturally based pedagogy: A case study of one Yup'ik Eskimo teacher. *Anthropology & Education Quarterly, 22,* 203–223.

Loving, C. C., & Marshall, J. E. (1997). Increasing the pool of ethnically diverse science teachers: A mid-project evaluation. *Journal of Science Teacher Education, 8*(3), 205–217.

Luttrell, W. (1997). *School-smart and mother-wise: Working-class women's identity and schooling.* New York: Routledge.

Machamer, A. M., & Gruber, E. (1998). Secondary school, family, and educational risk: Comparing American Indian adolescents and their peers. *Journal of Educational Research, 91*(6), 357–369.

MacMillan, D. L., Widaman, K. F., Balow, I. H., Hemsley, R. E., & Little, T. D. (1992). Differences in adolescent school attitudes as a function of academic level, ethnicity, and gender. *Learning Disability Quarterly, 15*(1), 39–50.

Martinez, Y. G., & Cranston-Gingras, A. (1996). Migrant farmworker students and the educational process: Barriers to high school completion. *High School Journal, 80*(1), 28–38.

Mather, J.R.C. (1997). How do American Indian fifth and sixth graders perceive mathematics and the mathematics classroom? *Journal of American Indian Education,* 9–18.

Matthews, C. E., & Smith, W. S. (1994). Native American related materials in elementary science instruction. *Journal of Research in Science Teaching, 31*(4), 363–380.

McCall, A. L. (1995). Constructing conceptions of multicultural teaching: Preservice teachers' life experiences and teacher education. *Journal of Teacher Education, 46*(5), 340–350.

McCarthey, S. J. (1998). Constructing multiple subjectivities in classroom literacy contexts. *Research in the Teaching of English, 32*(2), 126–160.

McCarty, T. L., Wallace, S., Lynch, R. H., & Benally, A. (1991). Classroom inquiry and Navajo learning styles: A call for reassessment. *Anthropology & Educational Quarterly, 22,* 42–59.

McDiarmid, G. W. (1992). What to do about differences? A study of multicultural education for teacher trainees in the Los Angeles Unified School District. *Journal of Teacher Education, 43*(2), 83–93.

McInerney, D. M., & Swisher, K. G. (1995). Exploring Navajo motivation in school settings. *Journal of American Indian Education,* 28–51.

McIntyre, A. (1997). Constructing an image of a White teacher. *Teachers College Board, 98*(4), 653–681.

Meacham, S. J. (2000). Black self-love, language, and the teacher education dilemma: The cultural limbo of African American preservice teachers. *Urban Education, 34*(5), 571–596.

Menis, J. (1997). Factors affecting female students' choice of science studies at university. *Curriculum and Teaching, 12*(10), 45–54.

Mickelson, R. A. (1990). The attitude-achievement paradox among Black adolescents. *Sociology of Education, 63,* 44–61.

Minow, M. (1987). When difference has its home: Group homes for the mentally retarded, equal protection and legal treatment of difference. *Harvard Civil Rights-Civil Liberties Law Review, 22*(1), 111–189.

Miron, L. F., & Lauria, M. (1998). Student voice as agency: Resistance and accommodation in inner-city schools. *Anthropology & Education Quarterly, 29*(2), 189–213.

Montecinos, C. (1994). Teachers of color and multiculturalism. *Equity & Excellence in Education, 27*(3), 34–42.

Murrell, P. C., Jr. (1994). In search of responsive teaching for African American males: An investigation of students' experiences of middle school mathematics curriculum. *Journal of Negro Education, 63*(4), 556–569.

Nel, J. (1992). The empowerment of minority students: Implications of Cummins' model for teacher education. *Journal of the Association of Teacher Educators, 14*(3), 38–45.

Nasir, N. S. (2000). Points ain't everything: Emergent goals and average and percent understandings in the play of basketball among African American students. *Anthropology & Education Quarterly, 31*(3), 283–305.

Necochea, J., & Cline, Z. (1996). A case study analysis of within district school funding inequities. *Equity & Excellence in Education, 29*(2), 69–77.

Nichols, J. D., Ludwin, W. G., & Iadicola, P. (1999). A darker shade of gray: A year-end analysis of discipline and suspension data. *Equity & Excellence in Education, 32*(1), 43–55.

Noll, E. (1998). Experiencing literacy in and out of school: Case studies of two American Indian youths. *Journal of Literacy Research, 30*(2), 205–232.

Nozaki, Y. (2000). Essentializing dilemma and multiculturalist pedagogy: An ethnographic study of Japanese children in a U.S. school. *Anthropology & Educational Quarterly, 31*(3), 355–380.

Obidah, J. (2000). Mediating boundaries of race, class, and professorial authority as a critical multiculturalist. *Teachers College Record, 102*(6), 1035–1060.

O'Brien, V., Martinez-Pons, M., & Kopala, M. (1999). Mathematics self-efficacy, ethnic identity, gender, and career interests related to mathematics and science. *Journal of Educational Research, 92*(4), 231–235.

O'Connor, C. (1999). Race, class, and gender in America: Narratives of opportunity among low-income African American youths. *Sociology of Education, 72,* 137–157.

O'Halloran, C. S. (1995). Mexican American female students who were successful in high school science courses. *Equity & Excellence in Education, 28*(2), 57–64.

Okwumabua, J. O. (1999). An investigation of the decision-making skills of at-risk African American male youth. *Journal of Negro Education, 68*(2), 154–163.

Oliver, K. L. (1999). Adolescent girls' body-narratives: Learning to desire and create a fashionable image. *Teachers College Board, 101*(2), 220–246.

Paccione, A. V. (2000). Developing a commitment to multicultural education. *Teachers College Record, 102*(6), 980–1005.

Pailliotet, A. W. (1997). "I'm really quiet": A case study of an Asian, language minority preservice teacher's experiences. *Teaching and Teacher Education, 13*(7), 675–690.

Park, C. C. (1997). Learning style preferences of Asian American (Chinese, Filipino, Korean, and Vietnamese) students in secondary schools. *Equity & Excellence in Education, 30*(2), 68–77.

Park, C. C. (2000). Learning style preferences of Southeast Asian students. *Urban Education, 35*(3), 245–268.

Parsons, E. C. (1997). Black high school females' images of the scientist: Expression of culture. *Journal of Research in Science Teaching, 34*(7), 745–768.

Patthey-Chavez, G. G. (1993). High school as an arena for cultural conflict and acculturation for Latino Angelinos. *Anthropology & Education Quarterly, 24*(1), 33–60.

Pattnaik, J. (1997). Cultural stereotypes and preservice education: Moving beyond our biases. *Equity & Excellence in Education, 30*(3), 40–50.

Peshkin, A., & White, C. J. (1990). Four Black American students: Coming of age in a multiethnic high school. *Teachers College Record, 92*(1), 21–38.

Pewewardy, C. D., & Willower, D. J. (1993). Perceptions of American Indian high school students in public schools. *Equity & Excellence in Education, 26*(1), 52–55.

Phillips, N. H. (1992). Two-tiered kindergartens: Effective for at-risk 5-year-olds? *Early Childhood Research Quarterly, 7,* 205–224.

Plata, M., & Masten, W. G. (1998). Teacher ratings of Hispanic and Anglo Students on a behavior rating scale. *Roeper Review, 21*(2), 139–144.

Polinard, J. L., & Wrinkle, R. D. (1995). The influence of educational and political resources on minority students' success. *Journal of Negro Education, 64*(4), 463–474.

Popkewitz, T. (1984). *Paradigm and ideology in educational research.* London: Falmer Press.

Popkewitz, T. (1998). *Struggling for the soul: The politics of schooling and the construction of the teacher.* New York: Teachers College Press.

Portes, A., & Hao, L. (1998). E pluribus unum: Bilingualism and loss of language in the second generation. *Sociology of Education, 71,* 269–294.

Powell, R. R. (1996). Epistemological antecedents to culturally relevant and constructivist classroom curricula: A longitudinal study of teachers' contrasting world views. *Teaching & Teacher Education, 12*(4), 365–384.

Price, J. N. (1998). Accommodation and critique in the school lives of six young African-American men. *Curriculum Inquiry, 28*(4), 443–471.

Proweller, A. (1999). Shifting identities in private education: Reconstructing race at/in the cultural center. *Teachers College Record, 100*(4), 809–840.

Reed, D. F. (1993). Multicultural education for preservice students. *Action in Teaching Education, 15*(3), 27–34.

Rizzo-Tolk, R., & Varenne, H. (1992). Joint action on the wild side of Manhattan: The power of the cultural center on an educational alternative. *Anthropology & Education Quarterly, 23,* 221–249.

Rodney, L. W., Crafter, B., Rodney, H. E., & Mupier, R. M. (1999). Variables contributing to grade retention among African American adolescent males. *Journal of Educational Research, 92*(3), 185–190.

Rong, X. L., & Preissle, J. (1997). The continuing decline in Asian American teachers. *American Educational Research Journal, 34*(2), 267–293.

Ross, D. D., & Smith, W. (1992). Understanding preservice teachers' perspectives on diversity. *Journal of Teacher Education, 43*(2), 94–103.

Rumberger, R. W., & Larson, K. A. (1998). Toward explaining differences in educational achievement among Mexican American language-minority students. *Sociology of Education, 71,* 69–93.

Saldana, D. C., & Waxman, H. C. (1997). An observational study of multicultural education in urban elementary schools. *Equity & Excellence in Education, 30*(1), 40–46.

Schlosser, L. K. (1992). Teacher distance and student disengagement: School lives on the margin. *Journal of Teacher Education, 43*(2), 128–140.

Schneider, B., & Lee, Y. (1990). A model for academic success: The school and home environment of East Asian students. *Anthropology & Education Quarterly, 21,* 358–377.

Schneider, J. A. (1997). Dialectics of race and nationality: Contradictions and Philadelphia working-class youth. *Anthropology & Education Quarterly, 28*(4), 493–523.

Schultz, K. (1996). Between school and work: The literacies of urban adolescent females. *Anthropology & Education Quarterly, 27*(4), 517–544.

Scott, R. (1969). Social class, race, seriating and reading readiness: A study of their relationship at the kindergarten level. *Journal of Genetic Psychology, 115,* 87–96.

Sernak, K. S., & Wolfe, C. S. (1998). Creating multicultural understanding and community in preservice education classes via email. *Journal of Technology & Teacher Education, 6*(4), 303–329.

Signer, B., Beasley, T. M., & Bauer, E. (1997). Interaction of ethnicity, mathematics achievement level, socioeconomic status, and gender among high school students' mathematics self-concepts. *Journal of Education for Students Placed at Risk, 2*(4), 377–393.

Singh, K., Vaught, C., & Mitchell, E. W. (1998). Single-sex classes and academic achievement in two inner-city schools. *Journal of Negro Education, 67*(2), 157–167.

Slaughter-Defoe, D. T., & Carlson, K. G. (1996). Young African American and Latino children in high-poverty urban schools: How they perceive school climate. *Journal of Negro Education, 65*(1), 60–70.

Sleeter, C. E. (1992a). *Keepers of the American dream.* London: Falmer Press.

Sleeter, C. E. (1992b). Restructuring schools for multicultural education. *Journal of Teacher Education, 43*(2), 141–148.

Sleeter, C. E., & Grant, C. A. (1987). An analysis of multicultural education in the United States. *Harvard Educational Review, 57,* 421–444.

Smith, A. L. (1989–90). Collaborative induction model to support first-year minority teachers. *Action in Teacher Education, 11*(4), 42–53.

Spender, D. (1982). *Invisible women.* New York: Writers and Readers Publishing Cooperative.

Sperling, M., & Woodlief, L. (1997). Two classrooms, two writing communities: Urban and suburban tenth-graders learning to write. *Research in the Teaching of English, 31,* 205–239.

Stanton-Salazar, R. D., & Dornbusch, S. M. (1995). Social capital and the reproduction of inequality: Information networks among Mexican-origin high school students. *Sociology of Education, 68,* 116–135.

Stodolsky, S. S., & Grossman, P. L. (2000). Changing students, changing teaching. *Teachers College Record, 102*(1), 125–172.

Streitmatter, J. (1997). An exploratory study of risk-taking and attitudes in a girls-only middle school math class. *Elementary School Journal, 98*(1), 15–26.

Su, Z. (1996). Why teach: Profiles and entry perspectives of minority students as becoming teachers. *Journal of Research and Development in Education, 29*(3), 117–133.

Sweeney, M. (1993). Columbus, a hero? Rethinking Columbus in an elementary classroom. *Radical Teacher, 43,* 25–29.

Taeuber, K. E. (1977). Foreword. In M. Weinberg (Ed.), *Minority students: A research appraisal* (p. iii). Washington, DC: Government Printing Office.

Takaki, R. (1993). *A different mirror: A history of multicultural America.* Boston: Little, Brown.

Tate, W. F., Ladson-Billings, G., & Grant, C. A. (1993). The *Brown* decision revisited: Mathematizing social problems. *Educational Policy, 7*(3), 255–275.

Taylor, D. G., & Alves, M. J. (1999). Controlled choice: Rockford, Illinois, desegregation. *Equity & Excellence in Education, 32*(1), 18–30.

Teel, K. M., Debruin-Parecki, A., & Covington, M. V. (1998). Teaching strategies that honor and motivate inner-city African-American students: A school/university collaboration. *Teaching & Teacher Education, 14*(5), 479–495.

Tellez, K. (1999). Mexican-American preservice teachers and the intransigency of the elementary school curriculum. *Teaching and Teacher Education, 15,* 555–570.

Terrill, M., & Mark, D.L.H. (2000). Preservice teachers' expectations for schools with children of color and second-language learners. *Journal of Teacher Education, 51*(2), 149–155.

Tettegraph, S. (1996). The racial consciousness attitudes of White prospective teachers and their perceptions of the teachability of students from different racial/ethnic backgrounds: Findings from a California study. *Journal of Negro Education, 65*(2), 151–163.

Timm, J. T., Chiang, B., & Finn, B. D. (1998). Acculturation in the cognitive style of Laotian Hmong students in the United States. *Equity & Excellence in Education, 31*(1), 29–35.

Townsend, J. S., & Fu, D. (1998). Quiet students across cultures and contexts. *English Education, 31*(1), 4–19.

Tran, M. T., Young, R. L., & Di Lella, J. D. (1994). Multicultural education courses and the student teacher: Eliminating stereotypical attitudes in our ethnically diverse classroom. *Journal of Teacher Education, 45*(3), 183–189.

Tucker, C. M., Chennault, S. A., Brady, B. A., Fraser, K. P., Gaskin, V. T., Dunn, D., & Frisby, C. (1995). A parent, community, public schools, and university involved partnership education program to examine and boost academic achievement and adaptive functioning skills of African-American students. *Journal of Research and Development in Education, 28*(3), 174–185.

Ulichny, P. (1996). Cultures in conflict. *Anthropology & Education Quarterly, 27*(3), 331-364.

Vane, J. R., Weitzman, J., & Applebaum, A. P. (1966). Performance of Negro and White children and problem and nonproblem children on the Stanford Binet Scale. *Journal of Clinical Psychology, 22*, 431–435.

Voelkl, K. E., Welte, J. W., & Wieczorek, W. F. (1999). Schooling and delinquency among White and African American adolescents. *Urban Education, 34*(1), 69–88.

Volk, D. (1997). Questions in lessons: Activity settings in the homes and school of two Puerto Rican kindergartners. *Anthropology & Education Quarterly, 28*(1), 22–49.

Watson, D. N., Bell, P. A., & Chavez, E. L. (1994). Conflict handling skills used by Mexican-American and white Non-Hispanic students in the educational system. *High School Journal, 78*(1), 35–39.

Weinberg, M. (1977). *Minority students: A research appraisal.* Washington, DC: Government Printing Office.

Willie, C. V., Alves, M., & Hagerty, G. (1996). Multiracial, attractive city schools: Controlled choice in Boston. *Equity & Excellence in Education, 29*(2), 5–19.

Willson-Quayle, A., & Pasnak, R. (1997). The training of class inclusion and English language skills in young Latino children. *Journal of Research in Childhood Education, 11*(2), 152–162.

Yamauchi, L. A., Nakagawa, T., & Murdoch, K. (1998). Ethnic attitudes among elementary school students in a multiethnic school community. *Journal of Research in Childhood Education, 12*(2), 155–165.

Yeh, S. S. (1998). Empowering education: Teaching argumentative writing to cultural minority middle-school students. *Research in the Teaching of English, 33,* 49–83.

Young, I. P., Place, A. W., Rinehart, J. S., Jury, J. C., & Baits, D. F. (1997). Teacher recruitment: A test of the similarity-attraction hypothesis for race and sex. *Educational Administration Quarterly, 33*(1), 86–106.

Zisman, P., & Wilson, V. (1992). Table hopping in the cafeteria: An exploration of racial integration in early adolescent social groups. *Anthropology & Education Quarterly, 23,* 199–220.

Zulich, J., Bean, T. W., & Herrick, J. (1992). Charting stages of preservice teacher development and reflection in a multicultural community through dialogue journal analysis. *Teaching & Teacher Education, 8*(4), 345–360.

PART
IV

KNOWLEDGE CONSTRUCTION
AND CRITICAL STUDIES

11

KNOWLEDGE CONSTRUCTION AND POPULAR CULTURE

The Media as Multicultural Educator

Carlos E. Cortés

University of California, Riverside

Discussions of education often, and erroneously, use "schools" and "education" as synonymous. Certainly schools are a powerful component of the educational process. However, they do not monopolize education, nor could they even if they wished.

Students learn not only in schools, but also *outside* of schools through the "societal curriculum"—that massive, ongoing, informal curriculum of families, peer groups, neighborhoods, churches, organizations, institutions, mass media, and other socializing forces that educate all of us throughout our lives (Berry, 1980; Cortés, 1981; Leifer, Gordon, & Graves, 1974; Leiss, Kline, & Jhally, 1986; Spring, 1992). Much of that societal curriculum provides multicultural education.

Through both the school and the societal curriculum, students learn language, acquire culture, obtain knowledge, develop beliefs, internalize attitudes, and establish patterns of behavior. They learn about themselves and others. They learn about the groups to which they and others belong. They learn about their nation and other nations and cultures. In short, as part of this combined process of school and societal multicultural education, students learn about diversity in various forms, including racial, ethnic, cultural, gender, religious, regional, and national.

The mass media serve as a major element of societal multicultural education. Through such avenues as newspapers, magazines, motion pictures, television, and radio, they disseminate information, images, and ideas concerning diversity . . . for better *and* for worse. This media multicultural curriculum functions regardless of whether individual mediamakers perceive themselves as educators, realize that they are spreading ideas about diversity, or operate in the realm of fact or fiction. Moreover, media-based multicultural learning may occur whether or not learners approach the media as a source of knowledge and information, are aware that they are learning from the media, or recognize how their previous experiences—including their media experiences—may be influencing the meanings that they consciously or unconsciously construct from their interactions with the media.

Media play a powerful role in the social construction of knowledge about diversity (Hall, 1977). Through the repetition of themes, messages, and images, they foster group pride and erode self-esteem (Allen & Hatchett, 1986). Sometimes contributing to intergroup understanding through sensitive examinations of ethnic experiences, cultures, and problems, at other times media exacerbate intergroup misunderstanding through repeated presentation of derogatory stereotypes and overemphasis on negative themes about selected groups or nations. At times striving for truth, accuracy, nuance, and balance, at other times media consciously distort for purposes of sensationalism, commercialism, and transmission of ideological messages. By participating in the social construction of knowledge about race, ethnicity, and other aspects of diversity, media multicultural education interacts with and affects personal identity; challenges and reinforces intergroup prejudice; contributes to intergroup understanding and misunderstanding; and influences public norms, expectations, hopes, and fears about diversity.

Media multicultural education incorporates news and entertainment media, including the evolving media dimensions of the Internet (Ebo, 1998; Gorski, 2001). Audiences learn not only from programs and publications intended to inform but also from media presumably designed merely to entertain (and make money). Moreover, audiences sometimes have difficulty distinguishing nonfictional from fictional media presentations.

Although some mediamakers state that they merely offer entertainment, in fact they simultaneously teach, whether intentionally or incidentally. Reverse the equation. Whatever the stated or unstated goals of the image-makers, audiences learn from and construct knowledge that is based on both fictional and nonfictional media, without necessarily realizing that such media-based learning is occurring. In *The Republic*, Plato recognized the power of fictional narrative, particularly for young people, when he asserted, "Then shall we so easily let the children hear just any tales fashioned by just anyone and take into their souls opinions for the most part opposite to those we'll suppose they must have when they are grown up?" (Basic Books 2nd ed., Bloom trans., 1968, pp. 54–55). In *The Empire's Old Clothes: What the Lone Ranger, Babar, and Other Innocent Heroes Do to Our Minds*, Ariel Dorfman (1983) argued:

Industrially produced fiction has become one of the primary shapers of our emotions and our intellect in the twentieth century. Although these stories are supposed to merely entertain us, they constantly give us a secret education. We are not only taught certain styles of violence, the latest fashions, and sex roles by TV, movies, magazines, and comic strips; we are also taught how to succeed, how to love, how to buy, how to conquer, how to forget the past and suppress the future. We are taught, more than anything else, how not to rebel. (p. ix)

In a comparable manner, sociologist Herbert Gans (1967) likened television to schools and television programs to school courses:

Almost all TV programs and magazine fiction teach something about American society. For example, *Batman* is, from this vantage point, a course in criminology that describes how a superhuman aristocrat does a better job eradicating crime than do public officials. Similarly, *The Beverly Hillbillies* offers a course in social stratification and applied economics, teaching that with money, uneducated and uncultured people can do pretty well in American society, and can easily outwit more sophisticated and more powerful middle-class types. . . . And even the innocuous family situation comedies such as *Ozzie and Harriet* deal occasionally with ethical problems encountered on a neighborhood level. . . . Although the schools argue that they are the major transmitter of society's moral values, the mass media offer a great deal more content on this topic. (pp. 21–22)

Among this "great deal more content," the mass media transmit an enormous body of material on diversity, thereby contributing to the social construction of multicultural knowledge. The *degree* to which media actually *construct* multicultural knowledge, perceptions, and stereotypes can be debated. Beyond debate, however, is the fact that they *contribute* to the construction of intergroup knowledge, beliefs, perceptions, and attitudes. Specifying precisely what the media have taught and identifying what different individuals, groups, or nations have learned from the media, however, poses a considerable challenge. In addressing the media's role in the social construction of multicultural knowledge, scholars have explored at least four basic analytical areas:

1. *Content analysis:* What the mass media have *taught* about race, ethnicity, culture, foreignness, and other aspects of diversity
2. *Control analysis:* The process by which mediamakers have created, repeated, modified, and disseminated this multicultural content
3. *Impact analysis:* The short-term and long-term influences of the media on individual and societal learning about diversity, including the roles that readers, viewers, and listeners have played in that process
4. *Pedagogical analysis:* The relationship between mass media and school education in the construction of multicultural knowledge, including ways in which schools can address, contend with, build from, and draw upon the media as a multicultural educational tool.

CONTENT ANALYSIS: THE MEDIA CURRICULUM ON DIVERSITY

Using race and ethnicity as principal examples, what have the mass media taught about diversity? Three generalizations can be formulated about such research.

First, most published content analyses deal with a single ethnic group (such as Chinese Americans), a constellation of related ethnic groups (such as Asian Americans), or a single foreign area (such as Asia). Studies sometimes link the related ethnic and foreign cultures, such as Asian Americans and Asians.

Second, most studies focus tightly on the subject group or area, with sporadic efforts at placing them in the comparative context of the media treatment of other ethnic groups or foreign areas. This sometimes leads to false conclusions about the asserted or implied uniqueness of the media's treatment of the subject group. In contrast, a comparative multicultural approach may reveal that such treatment was not group-specific and that, during a particular era, the media were giving similar treatment to other ethnic groups or cultures, or for that matter to Americans in general.

Third, some of these studies involve attempts to examine systematically and comprehensively the long-term chronological development of the treatment of the target ethnic group or culture by the media (or by one element of the media, such as television or motion pictures). However, most studies merely provide snapshots of media treatment within limited periods of time rather than extended longitudinal analyses. Such limited studies often provide valuable insights, but they sometimes also fall into the trap of asserting broad long-term generalizations about media images, messages, and stereotyping on the basis of fragmentary, overly selective, or temporally restricted pieces of media evidence. Occasionally this even leads to the stereotyping of assumed and asserted, but unproven, media stereotyping.

Motion pictures have drawn the greatest amount of book-length scholarly content analysis concerning the media treatment of race and ethnicity. In assessing the historical development of the treatment of specific racial and ethnic groups in U.S. motion pictures, some scholars have also engaged the control analysis issue of the *process* by which mediamakers have created, repeated, and modified movie multicultural content, including some of the reasons and forces behind this content creation.

African Americans in film have received the most extensive examination, ranging from Donald Bogle's (2001b) engagingly iconoclastic and idiosyncratic *Toms, Coons, Mulattoes, Mammies & Bucks: An Interpretive History of Blacks in American Films*, to impressionistically provocative essays on individual films such as James Snead's (1992) *White Screens/Black Images: Hollywood from the Dark Side* and more archive-based studies such as Thomas Cripps's (1977, 1993) *Slow Fade to Black: The Negro in American Film, 1900–1942* and *Making Movies Black: The Hollywood Message Movie from World War II to the Civil Rights Era.* Books on Jewish Americans have earned the statistical runner-up spot, with such studies as Lester Friedman's (1982) *Hollywood's Image of the Jew* and Patricia Erens's (1984) *The Jew in American Cinema*, as well as books on Yiddish cinema (discussed later).

The mainstream film treatment of U.S. Latinos has been studied in Allen Woll's (1980) *The Latin Image in American Film* and Arthur Pettit's (1980) *Images of the Mexican American in Fiction and Film*, while Gary Keller's (1985) *Chicano Cinema: Research, Reviews, and Resources* and Chon Noriega's (1992) *Chicanos and Film: Essays on Chicano Representation and Resistance* address the role of both mainstream and Chicano media in the creation of the Chicano film image. The depiction of American Indians has been discussed in Ralph Friar and Natasha Friar's (1972) *The Only Good Indian . . . The Hollywood Gospel*, John O'Connor's (1980) *The Hollywood Indian: Stereotypes*

of Native Americans in Films, and Gretchen Bataille and Charles Silet's (1980) *The Pretend Indian: Images of Native Americans in the Movies.* Other books on the film treatment of specific groups are Eugene Franklin Wong's (1978) *On Visual Media Racism: Asians in the American Motion Pictures*, Joseph Curran's (1989) *Hibernian Green on the Silver Screen*, and Jack Shaheen's (2001) *Reel Bad Arabs: How Hollywood Vilifies a People.*

The treatment of ethnic groups in other media has generated far fewer comprehensive book-length content analysis efforts. The television depiction of African Americans has been addressed in Bogle's (2001a) *Prime Time Blues: African Americans on Network Television*, while Darrell Hamamoto (1994) examined Asian Americans in *Monitored Peril: Asian Americans and the Politics of TV Representation* and Jack Shaheen (1984) discussed Arab Americans as well as Arabs in *The TV Arab.* Bradley Greenberg, Michael Burgoon, Judee K. Burgoon, and Felipe Korzenny's (1983) *Mexican Americans and the Mass Media* and Robert Entman and Andrew Rojecki's (2000) *The Black Image in the White Mind: Media and Race in America* address treatment in a variety of media.

Beyond books, there has been a cottage industry of content analysis articles on individual ethnic groups and intergroup relations (Woll & Miller, 1987). These include multiple articles on certain significant television programs, such as *Roots, All in the Family, Star Trek*, and *The Cosby Show*, and motion pictures, such as *The Birth of a Nation, Dances with Wolves, Guess Who's Coming to Dinner, Pocahontas*, and *The Jazz Singer* (in its several versions). Nevertheless, some ethnic groups have not yet earned even a single scholarly article concerning their media treatment.

Other scholarly gaps still exist. No book to date deals systematically with the larger issue of the history of the treatment of race and ethnicity by the media in general. For that matter, there have been no book-length scholarly studies of the historical comparative treatment of race and ethnicity in any one segment of the media.

The most comprehensive books to date are collections of essays on motion pictures. These include Randall Miller's (1978) edited volume of original essays, *The Kaleidoscopic Lens: How Hollywood Views Ethnic Groups*, Allen Woll and Randall Miller's (1987) *Ethnic and Racial Images in American Film and Television: Historical Essays and Bibliography*, Friedman's (1991) edited collection, *Unspeakable Images: Ethnicity and the American Cinema*, and Robert Brent Toplin's (1993) *Hollywood as Mirror: Changing Views of "Outsiders" and "Enemies" in American Movies.*

In addition to race and ethnicity, the last three decades have produced myriad books on the relationship of the media to various other groups (Holtzman, 2000). These include the media treatment of gender (Haskell, 1987;

Kitch, 2001; Tasker, 1998), religion (Hoover, 1998; Keyser & Keyser, 1984), disability (Norden, 1994; Wahl, 1995), and sexual orientation (Alwood, 1996; Gross, 2002; Russo, 1987).

Although the themes of individual and, to a far lesser extent, comparative group treatment have dominated multicultural media content analysis, there is also the larger question of the general *categories* of multicultural knowledge that the media have disseminated. In his book *The Children Are Watching: How the Media Teach about Diversity,* Carlos Cortés (2000) posits the following five different but interrelated *types* of content that media contribute to multicultural knowledge construction.

Media Provide Information About Diversity

Because people cannot be in all places at all times, they have to rely on mediating forms of communication—particularly the mass media—for much of their learning about today's world as well as the past. Therefore they necessarily acquire much of what they know about diversity through what historian Daniel Boorstin (1961) has termed the "pseudoenvironment," principally the mass media.

Moreover, the issue of media as multicultural information source goes well beyond the question of accuracy. In news, the constant reiteration of certain themes, even when each story is accurate in and of itself, may unjustifiably emphasize limited information about a group (Keever, Martindale, & Weston, 1997). This process becomes even more powerful if news and entertainment treatments of a group coincide and mutually reinforce each other in theme, approach, content, perspective, and frequency.

Media Help Organize Multicultural Information and Ideas

More than simply providing information, media also influence viewer and reader structures for perceiving, receiving, thinking, and remembering—the way people process and organize information and ideas as they construct their personal multicultural knowledge (Adoni & Mane, 1984; Lester, 1996; Naficy & Gabriel, 1993; O'Barr, 1994). Fictional and nonfictional narratives, for example, perform roles comparable to those of folk stories and fairy tales (Bettelheim, 1976; Giroux, 1997; Hunt, 1997). They provide a type of "ritualized glue" that helps recipients make sense out of the pseudoenvironment's increasing information overload, which has been hypertrophied by the Internet.

Reporting in 1977 that there had been more than 2,300 research papers on television and human behavior, social psychologist George Comstock addressed the relationship of the entertainment media to the reification of social structures:

Several writers have argued that television is a powerful reinforcer of the status quo. The ostensible mechanisms are the effects of its portrayals on public expectations and perceptions. Television portrayals and particularly violent drama are said to assign roles of authority, power, success, failure, dependence, and vulnerability in a manner that matches the real-life social hierarchy, thereby strengthening that hierarchy by increasing its acknowledgement among the public and by failing to provide positive images for members of social categories occupying a subservient position. Content analyses of television drama support the contention that portrayals reflect normative status. (pp. 20–21)

To the degree that the media assert the normality of racial, ethnic, and other social hierarchies or reiterate intergroup taboos, they serve to reinforce the legitimacy and even the naturalness of these relationships and attitudes (Bernardi, 1998; Williams, 2001). When news media continually disseminate selected patterns of treatment about diversity, they help to shape cognitive and attitudinal frameworks for interpreting future information and ideas about certain groups and issues (Chavez, 2001; Campbell, 1995; King & Wood, 2001; Wykes, 2001). When the entertainment media repeatedly depict intergroup dominance or subservience or consistently portray members of specific groups in limited spheres of action, they contribute to the formation of viewer organizational schema for perceiving those groups and absorbing future images into a meaningful and consistent, if distorted, conceptual framework (Wiegman, 1989).

For example, a Children Now study (2001) determined that prime time television became increasingly segregated as it moved from the 10:00 P.M. to the 8:00 P.M. time slot. Two-thirds of the 10:00 P.M. shows had mixed opening credit casts compared to only 13 percent at 8:00 P.M., when young viewers are more likely to be watching.

In a study of the comparative treatment of Blacks and Whites by Chicago local television news, communications scholar Robert Entman (1990) concluded:

In the stories analyzed, crime reporting made blacks look particularly threatening, while coverage of politics exaggerated the degree to which black politicians (as compared to white ones) practice special interest politics. These images would feed the first two components of modern racism, anti-black affect and resistance to blacks' political demands. On the other hand, the positive dimension of the news, the presence of black anchors and other authority figures, may simultaneously engender an impression that racial discrimination is no longer a problem. (p. 342)

Media Disseminate Diversity-Related Values

For decades, critics of the media have been asserting the value-influencing power of movies. The Payne Fund studies of motion picture impact during the 1930s, for example, included Henry James Forman's (1933) provocatively titled *Our Movie Made Children.*

The 1930 Motion Picture Production Code (the Hays Code) provides a primer on Hollywood's response to public concerns over the motion picture industry's role in teaching values. For example, one values position of the code, its opposition to interracial love (Smith, 2001), appeared in Section II, Rule 6: "Miscegenation (sex relationship between the white and black races) is forbidden" (Stanley & Steinberg, 1976, p. 82). Until that rule was deleted in 1956, Hollywood drummed home the repeated values message of the importance of avoiding miscegenation, not only between "the white and black races" but also between Whites and other people categorized as "colored." In those rare screen instances where interracial love or sex occurred or seemed about to occur, failure, punishment, and retribution predictably resulted (Cortés, 1991).

To an extent, this values curriculum reflected widespread American social mores. When surveys conducted for Gunnar Myrdal's (1944) classic *An American Dilemma: The Negro Problem and Modern Democracy* asked southern Whites what discriminatory lines must be maintained, their most common answer was "the bar against intermarriage and sexual intercourse involving white women" (p. 60). Similar Anglo opposition to intermarriage with Mexican Americans was documented through interviews for economist Paul Taylor's (1930) study of Mexican labor in the United States.

Although interracial marriage had long existed in the United States, Hollywood elevated antimiscegenation values lessons over the presentation of multiethnic reality. In adopting this pattern of portrayals, moviemakers functioned simultaneously as learners (reacting to the public presence of certain social mores), as values teachers (creating antimiscegenation "curriculum guidelines" and transmitting this "thou-shall-and-shall-not" lesson to the viewing public), and as profit-at-all-cost commercialists (fearing that movies with interracial love might not sell to White audiences, particularly in the South) (Cripps, 1970).

Media Help Shape Multicultural Expectations

In *Hollywood vs. America*, film critic Michael Medved (1992) argued, "If nothing else, repeated exposure to media images serves to alter our perceptions of the society in which we live and to gradually shape what we accept—and expect—from our fellow citizens" (p. xxiii). I agree. Mass media do help shape expectations.

To examine the phenomenon of media-created intercultural expectations, media scholar Chon Noriega (1988–1990) examined film reviews in thirty publications to assess how Hispanic and non-Hispanic movie critics responded to Latino-made films about the U.S. Latino experience (*La Bamba, Stand and Deliver, Born in East L.A.*). Through this process, he discovered the operation of the "selective perception" phenomenon, in which ethnicity

served as one determinant in predicting critic expectations and reactions. Nor did the ideology of non-Hispanic publications seem to be a factor. According to Noriega:

Liberal non-Hispanic publications often relied on the same outsider's assumption about the *barrio* that characterized the conservative publications. The *barrio* was a problem space, denied a history, culture and separate point of view, not to mention internal complexity. That assumption manifested itself first and foremost in the mistranslation of *barrio* as "slum," rather than as the more appropriate "neighborhood." As a result, the films were often discussed in the context of social problems, rather than in the context of cultural identity or even film history. (p. 23)

At the transnational level, concerns were raised about the possible impact of the movie *Pearl Harbor* (2001) on intergroup expectations. *Pearl Harbor* was shot almost entirely from the perspective of the United States (as contrasted with the 1970 U.S.-Japanese coproduction *Tora! Tora! Tora!*, which consciously alternated perspectives on this seminal historical event). Moreover, *Pearl Harbor* made little effort to suggest Japanese American loyalty to the United States. Further buttressing Japanese American fears was the April 2001 release of a Yankelovich national poll, reporting that 32 percent of Americans believed that Chinese *Americans* were more loyal to China than to the United States!

Media Present Models of Diversity-Related Behavior

Anecdotal evidence offers myriad examples of media popularization of clothing styles, verbal expressions ("Make my day" and "Show me the money"), and other forms of behavior. Aware of the possibility of imitation, protesters railed against the release of such youth gang films as *A Clockwork Orange* (1971), *The Warriors* (1979), *Colors* (1988), *Boyz N the Hood* (1991), and *American Me* (1992) for fear that young people would imitate screen violence. Although a few fights did break out near theaters, massive waves of imitative gang violence did not occur, which came as a shock to those who proclaimed such deterministic positions about media impact.

However, there is also the issue of "disinhibiting effects." Instead of asking just whether media provoke people into action, we also need to consider their potential for removing inhibitions to previously repressed actions. For example, does cable dissemination of African American comedians who repeatedly use the word *nigger* in their routines unwittingly lower public inhibitions against employing this brutalizing word, thereby unintentionally legitimizing its use by non-Blacks? The behavioral ramifications of racial labeling were addressed in the March 18, 2001, episode of Lifetime Channel's *Any Day Now* and in the February 25, 2002, episode of Fox's *Boston Public*. The latter, in fact, dealt specifically with the disinhibiting effect, when a White student casually refers to a Black friend as "nigger," setting off a classroom confrontation that ultimately involves the entire school.

Media participation in the social construction of multicultural knowledge, then, involves more than the creation and dissemination of images. The media also transmit information (correct or incorrect, balanced or distorted, contextualized or stereotypical), organize information and ideas, disseminate values, create expectations, and model behavior.

CONTROL ANALYSIS: MEDIAMAKERS AS MULTICULTURAL CURRICULUM DEVELOPERS

Content analysis of media multicultural education raises the collateral issue of control analysis: Why have the media disseminated these multicultural images and messages? When it comes to giving reasons for such dissemination, mediamakers differ (Carr, 2001; Wilson & Gutiérrez, 1995). Some intentionally try to teach about diversity, while others do so only incidentally, such as by publishing news stories with multicultural dimensions or by including certain characters in movie or television narratives without any particular goal of multicultural image making or message sending. Yet whatever the mediamakers' intentions, they may teach by contributing to multicultural knowledge construction (Diawara, 1992). In examining the media creation of multicultural content, control analysts have generally focused on three levels: the media at large, an entire media industry, or individual components of the media.

Some scholars have argued that the creation of media content must be addressed in structural terms of the media at large, including the societal context in which the media operate (Gandy, 1998). For example, in analyzing the British media, Stuart Hall (1981) contended:

If the media function in a systematically racist manner, it is not because they are run and organized exclusively by active racists; this is a category mistake. This would be equivalent to saying that you could change the character of the capitalist state by replacing its personnel. The media, like the state, have a *structure*, a set of *practices* which are *not* reducible to the individuals who staff them. What defines how the media function is the result of a set of complex, often contradictory, social relations; not the personal inclinations of its members. (p. 46)

Other analysts have looked at specific media industries (Chaisson, 2000; Heider, 2000). Some critics of the media, including politicians and special-interest pressure groups, have proclaimed various types of media conspiracies to influence diversity-related popular thinking. Although they have discovered a few spent shells, neither critics nor scholars have effectively demonstrated many mediawide (or even single-industry) smoking guns of multicultural educational intentions.

Possibly the closest they have come is through their analysis of the 1930 Motion Picture Production Code, which laid out movie content rules that Hollywood filmmakers had to follow in order to earn the official industry seal of approval for commercial exhibition. Some of its provisions applied directly to, or had serious implications for, the treatment of race and ethnicity. Yet with the admittedly important exception of miscegenation, even this critical document does not provide evidence of any major industry concern about the treatment of this theme.

For example, Section V stated that

the Production Code Administration may take cognizance of the fact that the following words and phrases are obviously offensive to the patrons of motion pictures in the United States and *more particularly* [emphasis added] to the patrons of motion pictures in foreign countries: Chink, Dago, Frog, Greaser, Hunkie, Kike, Nigger, Spic, Wop, Yid. (Stanley & Steinberg, 1976, p. 83)

The code's emphasis on the concerns of foreign patrons suggests that the commercial issue of overseas ticket sales provided a stronger imperative than did the moral issues of ethnic sensitivities or interethnic bigotry. (When the 2001 film *Pearl Harbor* was released in Japan, the word *enemies* was reportedly used in the Japanese subtitle whenever an American character said *Japs*.)

At times, however, certain media industries and even the media at large have appeared to follow a relatively regimented approach to the treatment of specific multicultural topics. Under federal government pressure to support World War II mobilization, for example, Hollywood consciously created a pro-war multicultural curriculum by cranking out movies featuring multiethnic military units, each containing at least one Grabowski, one Ginsberg, one González, one Graziano, and one O'Grady. Hollywood thereby issued a clarion call to arms by spreading the message that Americans of all backgrounds have fought for their country in the past and should be happy to do so now (Koppes & Black, 1987).

Finally, when scholars drop down from mediawide and industrywide analyses, they have identified more limited collaborations around specific diversity-related themes, concerns, issues, or media products. Some individual newspapers, magazines, stations, and even movie studios have had their own multicultural ideologies.

For example, in its early years Warner Brothers took a special interest in making social-problem films that often dealt with issues of racial inequality, antiethnic bigotry, and discrimination; Fox became the first national noncable TV network to emphasize Black-oriented programming (Zook, 1999). At one time, assimilation-oriented Jewish movie studio heads took steps to reduce the screen visibility of Jewish Americans, particularly during the rise of European anti-Semitism in the 1930s (Gabler, 1988).

In contrast, during the past two decades such ethnic filmmakers as Spike Lee, Gregory Nava, Wayne Wang, Francis Ford Coppola, and Martin Scorsese have each emphasized the making of movies that explore their own ethnic group.

Alternative independent film movements, not just individual filmmakers, have occasionally arisen around selected multicultural themes and issues, such as Black "race movies" (Cripps, 1978), Native American films (Singer, 2001), and Yiddish films of the 1920s and 1930s. Jewish American moviemakers in the Yiddish film movement provided a sharp contrast with mainstream Jewish studio heads by consciously emphasizing the celebration and maintenance of Jewish culture, as opposed to the assimilationist screen ideology of the Hollywood moguls (Goldberg, 1983; Goldman, 1983; Hoberman, 1991).

Individual mediamakers have sometimes tried to influence societal attitudes toward specific ethnic groups (Crowdus & Georgakas, 2001). Over the years, selected films have consciously tried to reduce bigotry by challenging ethnic prejudice. This was a common stance in such post–World War II movie textbooks as *Home of the Brave* (African Americans), *A Medal for Benny* (Mexican Americans), *Broken Arrow* (American Indians), *Saturday's Hero* (Polish Americans), *Crossfire* (Jewish Americans), and *Knock on Any Door* (Italian Americans) (Holt, 2001). Some filmmakers have tried to deliver broader multicultural messages, such as celebrating ethnic diversity as integral to American national character, culture, and values. In contrast, other films have just as consciously traded on antiethnic bigotry, a process begun during the early silent era in the anti-Mexican "greaser" movies (as an example, *The Greaser's Revenge*); a parade of Indian savage movies; and even classics such as D. W. Griffith's *The Birth of a Nation*, which featured some of the most despicable portrayals of African Americans ever to reach the screen.

Mediamakers often take advantage of the audience's presumed previous multicultural knowledge construction and resulting predispositions in order to provoke media-conditioned emotional responses. Sometimes filmmakers play upon personal fears by providing an ethnic menace, iconographically generated—examples being a band of Indians (or merely a smoke signal accompanied by the beating of tom-toms) in westerns, or a large group—presumably a gang—of young Latinos or African Americans in contemporary urban films. Or they may go for cheap intercultural laughs by using "odd" surnames; inserting a crowd of Japanese tourists loaded with cameras; or, in the 1978 film *The End*, presenting an asylum inmate who admits that he strangled his father because he was "too Polish."

Trading on and manipulating presumed audience predispositions, moviemakers also reinforce the audience's constructed knowledge and thereby make it more convenient for other mediamakers to draw upon. However, like school textbook writers, mediamakers ultimately lose control of their multicultural creations. Once media products appear, they take on lives of their own. Media authors often find that their original conceptions become severely modified, seriously undermined, or even drastically distorted in the editing and production process. Therefore, media images and messages may diverge, to some degree, from the intent of the mediamakers.

The process by which makers of broadcast and print media have created diversity content has received less attention than has the work of filmmakers. Sally Miller's (1987) seminal work, *The Ethnic Press in the United States: A Historical Analysis and Handbook,* assesses how ethnic newspapers and magazines have contributed to their own group's popular knowledge construction. Other examinations of print press knowledge dissemination are Ronald Jacobs's (2000) *Race, Media and the Crisis of Civil Society: From Watts to Rodney King* (a comparison of African American newspapers and mainstream media); Catherine Lutz and Jane Collins's (1993) *Reading National Geographic;* Abby Arthur Johnson and Ronald Maberry Johnson's (1979) *Propaganda and Aesthetics: The Literary Politics of Afro-American Magazines of the Twentieth Century;* Carolyn Martindale's *The White Press and Black America;* and Katherine Sender's (2001) "Gay Readers, Consumers, and a Dominant Gay Habitus: 25 Years of the *Advocate* Magazine."

Television's role in the construction of knowledge about two ethnic groups is explored in J. Fred MacDonald's (1992) *Blacks and White TV: African Americans in Television since 1948* and Chon Noriega's (2000) *Shot in America: Television, the State, and the Rise of Chicano Cinema.* Melvin Patrick Ely's (1991) *The Adventures of Amos 'n' Andy: A Social History of an American Phenomenon* examines the rise and fall of that popular and controversial radio and later television show. The diversity-teaching role of advertising has also received scholarly attention (Leiss et al., 1986). Finally, in recent years we have witnessed the rapid growth of foreign-language television and radio in the United States, but scholars have barely begun to address the knowledge-construction aspects of this phenomenon (Subervi-Vélez, 1986).

Ely's (1991) study, which includes an examination of the role of African American protests in affecting *Amos 'n' Andy*'s fate, also illustrates an additional aspect of control analysis: that the forces influencing the creation of media content do not come entirely from within the media. External pressure groups—watchdog groups, ratings producers, protesters, ethnic organizations, and multiethnic coalitions—have often tried, sometimes with success, to influence media content (Lewels, 1974). These groups have ranged from the Catholic Legion of Decency, formed in the 1930s to assign content ratings, to such ethnic protest groups as the Italian-American Anti-Defamation Committee and the Polish-American Guardian Society (Black, 1998).

Most important, both the media industry and mediamakers individually have embodied reigning (or at least competing) national ideologies, which are often transitory or in conflict. From commitment to the idea of the melting pot to the championing of contemporary multiculturalism, from support for the U.S. government during World War II to support for (and sometimes opposition to) the civil rights movements, from celebration of diversity to opposition to immigration, ideology has penetrated and provided a subtext for American media making. Even though the media have never been the curricular monolith sometimes claimed by critics, and though specific newspapers, magazines, networks, stations, and studios as well as individual mediamakers have provided varying treatments of diversity, the deeper patterns of media multicultural curricular messages often outweigh the surface variations (Cortés, 2000).

IMPACT ANALYSIS: ASSESSING MEDIA CONSTRUCTION OF MULTICULTURAL KNOWLEDGE

As any teacher knows, teaching and learning are not synonymous. We teach and then, through examinations—often to our chagrin—we discover great variations in the extent, content, and quality of student learning, multicultural education included (Banks, 1991, 1993). The same teaching-learning gap applies to media teaching and reader/viewer/listener learning.

Mediamakers intentionally or unintentionally develop multicultural curriculum, and media products themselves become intended or unintended multicultural textbooks; audiences also become coparticipants in multicultural knowledge construction. They may react as conscious, analytical learners, pondering the media's treatment of diversity and thoughtfully integrating this pseudoenvironmental experience into their knowledge bases, ideational frameworks, attitudinal structures, and value systems. Or they may react and learn unconsciously, unaware of the process by which they are connecting these new ideas to their previously existent knowledge, perceptions, attitudes, values, and mental schemata. Given the conscious and unconscious filtering power of media receivers, their varying sets of experiences, cognitive frameworks, and expectations, the presence of often deeply imbedded values and beliefs (including prejudices), and their differing information bases, it is clear that caution must temper assertions about the elusive topic of the *precise* content of audience learning (Gilman, 1985).

Scholarly and popular analyses of the media's societal impact have tended to become polarized. Many analysts have treated the media as virtually all-powerful forces that inculcate audiences with their beliefs (Fox, 1996; Winn, 1977). Some have taken a nearly deterministic position, drawing direct causal (sometimes unicausal) links between media and the development of individual, group, and national beliefs, attitudes, and behavior. So popular and fallacious in many early media studies, this common trap of media determinism—the assumed "hypodermic needle" media effect—remains popular in protest-group proclamations and political pontifications. Although most present only sporadic concrete evidence of media impact on knowledge construction, some content analysis scholars suggest or even categorically assert what viewers learn from the media, inappropriately using media content (teaching) to proclaim audience impact (learning). In the area of schooling, this would be analogous to substituting an analysis of textbooks and lectures for final examinations and achievement tests in assessing student learning.

In contrast to these deterministic assertions, other analysts have viewed the media as having limited power to influence audiences, treating the media as a reflector of social consensus or fulfiller of audience desires, or emphasizing the audience's activist role in constructing meaning from the media (Jenkins, 1992). Those who take these limited-influence positions fall into two groups. First are many mediamakers, particularly those involved in entertainment, who reject responsibility for what their movies, TV programs, or musical releases might incidentally or unintentionally teach. At times they even deny their teaching potential. Second are scholars, particularly proponents of certain varieties of "reception theory," who assert that the reader/viewer/listener is the primary force in the media-based construction of knowledge.

In the middle stand those scholars who agree that media, including movies and fictional television, do teach, but they argue that audiences, especially young viewers, are not passive receptacles and play a vital role in the media knowledge construction process (Comstock & Paik, 1991; DeAngelis, 2001). Despite the major scholarly challenges inherent in assessing media impact, research has provided some insights (Cantor, 1998; Davies, 1997; Huston et al., 1992). Such multicultural scholarship has generally fallen into three categories: empirical, projective, and theoretical.

Empirical Scholarship

Empirical scholarship has been sporadic and temporally limited, focusing almost entirely on such topics as the short-range effects of specific films or television shows, often in experimental settings. Even though results vary, they do coalesce convincingly around two essential conclusions. The first is that media, including feature films and fictional television, do influence intragroup and interethnic perceptions. Second, the nature of that influence—the extent, content, and tenacity of conscious and unconscious learning—varies with the individual reader, listener, or viewer. In short, scholarship confirms the old social science axiom that *some* people are influenced by *some* media, at *some* time.

For example, one pioneering study of the 1930s involved the classic 1915 silent film *The Birth of a Nation,* which included a degrading portrayal of African Americans during the Reconstruction era of U.S. history. The study concluded that when White students viewed *Birth* as part of their courses on U.S. history, an increase in student prejudice toward African Americans resulted (Peterson & Thurstone, 1933).

But media (in particular entertainment media) can also help reduce prejudice, even if audiences do not realize it. Some scholars found that the 1947 anti-anti-Semitism film *Gentleman's Agreement* had such an effect. In one study, students who saw the film reported improved attitudes toward Jews, even though most of the surveyed students also stated that the film *had not* influenced their attitudes (Rosen, 1948).

One of the most extensive examinations of the entertainment media's impact on popular knowledge construction was the Payne Fund motion picture project, carried out during the early 1930s by leading sociologists, psychologists, and educators located principally at the University of Chicago. The project began in response to public expressions of concern about movie effects; the public, particularly powerful politicians, literally demanded absolute conclusions and agendas for action, rather than traditional academic calls for more research. Fearful of being considered too cautiously academic, some of the scholars went beyond the bounds of their evidence, making claims and recommendations that ultimately brought much of their research into scholarly ill repute. In retrospect some of their methodologies seem empirically crude, but their research results—as contrasted with their often poorly grounded cries of alarm and calls for action—did provide evidence of viewer learning about race, ethnic groups, and foreign nations among other things (Jowett, Jarvie, & Fuller, 1996).

Unfortunately for those interested in the effect of films on the social construction of multicultural knowledge, such film-impact studies virtually ended in the late 1940s with the advent of television, as communications researchers turned their impact-study attention to the new kid on the media block. Moreover, by the 1960s such behaviorist pretest-posttest direct-impact studies had lost stature among communications scholars, who had become frustrated by the failure of this approach to determine more than limited and short-range media effects on attitude and overt behavior (Chaffee & Hochheimer, 1985; Hall, 1982; Rogers, Dearing, & Bregman, 1993). Instead, scholars developed a variety of other models to examine the knowledge construction relationship between media and media recipients.

For example, use-and-gratification research emphasizes the role of viewers and readers as active seekers of specific media that serve useful functions for them or that provide certain personal gratifications (Tan & Tan, 1979). Some studies have concluded that Black children, more than White children, consider entertainment television to be an important source of learning about the world, especially regarding behavior with the opposite sex and other types of social adaptation (Atkin, Greenberg, & McDermott, 1978).

Agenda-setting research began with the principle that the media may not be able to tell audiences what to think, but they can tell them what to think about. (The spiral-of-silence model provides the flip side to agenda setting, by focusing on the power of the media to limit public discussion by avoiding certain issues.) Later agenda-setting research expanded its domain, demonstrating the ability of the media to "frame" public issues and to "prime" the public on *how* to think about those issues (Goffman, 1974; Iyengar & Kinder, 1987). As argued by the agenda-setting scholars Maxwell McCombs and Donald Shaw (1993):

Agenda setting is considerably more than the classical assertion that the news tells us *what to think about.* The news also tells us *how to think about it.* Both the selection of objects for attention and the selection of frames for thinking about these objects are powerful agenda-setting roles. (p. 62; emphasis in original)

Most agenda-setting scholars have restricted their attention to the news, ignoring the comparable role of the entertainment media. They have found evidence that racial and ethnic differences influence audience reactions to media agenda-setting efforts. For example, Oscar Gandy and Larry Coleman (1986) concluded that Black college students rejected mainstream press criticism of the Reverend Jesse Jackson during his 1984 campaign for the Democratic presidential nomination.

Other empirical research has reconfirmed the variability of learner responses to the media, particularly when audiences reflect different cultural positions (Children Now, 1998; Korzenny & Ting-Toomey, 1992; Tobin, 2000) or when the subject is as emotion-laden as bigotry and prejudice (Cooper & Jahoda, 1947). Scholars have taken a variety of approaches to such reception analysis in an effort to determine or posit how different audiences have, or may have, interpreted and drawn meaning from various media (Bryant & Zillmann, 1991). One approach to such reception research has been the intensive study of audience reactions to important media products. For example, media scholar Janne Seppanen (2001) determined enormous interpretive variations by Finnish university students when observing Benetton's controversial racial and gender-bending advertisement "Family of the Future." Two major television phenomena, *All in the Family* and *Roots,* illustrate those learning variations.

Norman Lear's weekly television series *All in the Family,* which burst onto the American TV scene in 1971, generated a series of empirical studies that revealed varying audience responses. This popular series portrayed antihero Archie Bunker as a classic bigot—racist, sexist, and just about every other kind of anti-"ist" imaginable. The show sought to critique racial and ethnic prejudice by making Bunker's expressions of bigotry appear to be comically absurd. By provoking viewers to laugh at Archie and by portraying bigotry as imbecilic, Lear consciously sought to reduce prejudice. The ploy succeeded, but only for *some* viewers. Unfortunately, others identified with the cuddly, ingratiating, laugh-provoking Archie, the lovable racist, and found his expression of bigoted beliefs to be a confirmation of the validity of their own prejudices (Leckenby & Surlin, 1976). Studies of *All in the Family* with American and Canadian audiences confirmed the operation of the selective perception hypothesis—that is, already highly prejudiced or dogmatic viewers tended to admire Bunker and condone his racial and ethnic slurs (Surlin & Tate, 1976; Vidmar & Rokeach, 1974). In contrast, a comparable study concluded that the hypothesis did not seem to operate with Dutch viewers (Wilhoit & de Bock, 1976).

Roots, the January 1977 eight-night television miniseries tracing the history of the family of author Alex Haley from African origins to the post–Civil War United States, also drew a swarm of researchers. Stuart Surlin (1978) analyzed and compared the results of five studies conducted concurrently with or immediately after the showing of *Roots.* All focused on the topic of the viewer's "incidental learning," but results varied. The studies generally concluded that a higher percentage of Blacks than Whites viewed *Roots,* with 60–80% of the viewers believing in the accuracy of the show's treatment of history. However, even though three of the studies concluded that the series seemed to have a positive impact on viewers, two tended to support the selective perception hypothesis.

Still another approach to the study of the role of media in the social construction of multicultural knowledge has involved analyses of the interaction of the media with specific ethnic audiences (Comstock & Cobbey, 1979). These include studies of the relationship of the media to the acculturation of Asian American immigrants (Yum, 1982); American Indian communication practices (Worth & Adair, 1972); the maintenance and decline of ethnic pluralism among U.S. Latinos (Subervi-Vélez, 1986);

intercultural interpretations by Inuit children (Caron, 1979); self-esteem and group identification on the part of various sectors of the African American community (Allen & Hatchett, 1986); White college-student perceptions of Black socioeconomic progress and decline (Armstrong, Neuendorf, & Brentar, 1992); and the influence of race on the interpretation of news stories (Lind, 1996). For example, a retrospective study of Black viewers of *Roots* (Fairchild, Stockard, & Bowman, 1986) found that differences of region, urbanicity, age, education, and income (but not gender) influenced viewers' reactions to the program in terms of their evaluation of its significance and role as evidence of Black social progress.

In contrast to the *obtrusive* empiricism of pretest-posttest and survey research, in which audiences respond to specific scholarly queries, other scholars have drawn upon already existent evidence as the basis for *unobtrusive* empiricism. For example, in his *War Without Mercy: Race and Power in the Pacific War,* historian John Dower (1986) assessed the development of racial pride and cross-cultural stereotypes of the enemy in both Japan and the Allied nations prior to and during World War II. Casting a wide investigatory net that included media along with other forms of evidence, Dower explored multiple Japanese and Allied sources, from scholarly studies to propaganda tracts, from government reports to military training materials, and from popular periodicals to motion pictures. But Dower took an additional step, pointing to examples of both sides' political and military decisions that revealed how these stereotypes had become internalized and operationalized, even when acting on them led to military and diplomatic excesses and blunders.

Projective Scholarship

Alongside empirical scholarship stands the second category of media impact scholarship, projective studies in which scholars have attempted to suggest how different audiences *may* or *are likely to* construct personal knowledge from specific media. Sam Keen's (1986) *Faces of the Enemy: Reflections of the Hostile Imagination* and Vamik Volkan's (1988) *The Need to Have Enemies and Allies: From Clinical Practice to International Relationships* argued that people *need* to hate, and that "the other"—the racial, ethnic, cultural, or foreign other—serves as a convenient outlet for that hate. Some media scholars have focused on specific examples of "otherness." For example, Blaine Lamb (1975) asserted that Mexican characters served that "other" role for early U.S. movie audiences, who needed an easily identifiable, easily despised foil.

Some projective studies have attempted to reconstruct historical learning. For example, scholars have drawn upon autobiographies to suggest the impact of media learning on ethnic identity (Erben & Erben, 1991–92). Others have ventured into the challenging area of projective assessment of historical audiences' likely reactions to the media treatment of diversity (Douglas, 1994; Farmer, 2000; Staiger, 2000). For example, Jane Gaines (1987) used social and cultural characteristics of African American moviegoers during the 1920s to posit how such viewers probably "read" the film *The Scar of Shame,* as contrasted to latter-day reinterpretations of the movie that tend to be burdened with distorting presentist assumptions.

Some scholars have based their projections about the media-based social construction of knowledge on their own "readings" of specific media "texts." For example, *The Cosby Show* television series has elicited nearly polaric conclusions concerning potential impact (Real, 1991). Is *Cosby* the ideal positive-role-model minority show, featuring a well-educated, sophisticated, financially successful African American family? Or, by commission and omission, whether intentionally or unintentionally, does the series provide less salutary lessons to some viewing audiences?

Although observing that racism was never mentioned in 15 episodes that he analyzed, media scholar John D. H. Downing (1988) lauded the series for its dignified emphasis on Black culture; its championing of Black familial unity; its direct, continuous critique of sexism; and its portrayal of Black-White relations in a manner that challenged racist thinking by transcending racism. Yet *The Cosby Show* has also drawn concerned reactions from analysts who feared that the series' concentration on well-heeled African Americans and its failure to deal with the Black underclass might unintentionally encourage viewers to ignore the fact that the majority of American Blacks still face tremendous social and economic problems (Dyson, 1989; Jhally & Lewis, 1992). As media scholar Paula Matabane (1988) wrote:

The Cosby Show, for example, epitomizes the Afro-American dream of full acceptance and assimilation into U.S. society. Both the series and Bill Cosby as an individual represent successful competitors in network television and in attaining a high status. Although this achievement is certainly not inherently negative, we should consider the role television plays in the cultivation of an overall picture of growing racial equality that conceals unequal social relationships and overestimates of how well blacks are integrating into white society (if at all). The illusion of well-being among the oppressed may lead to reduced political activity and less demand for social justice and equality. (p. 30)

Finally, the media themselves sometimes provide grudging projective recognition of their power to contribute to the social construction of multicultural knowledge. For example, when in 2001 the Cartoon Network presented a two-day marathon of "all" Bugs Bunny cartoons, it actually pulled 12 of the cartoons because they contained what the network considered to be racially offensive content.

Prior to the 1977 U.S. national network television showing of Francis Ford Coppola's *The Godfather Saga* (a revised and expanded version of the two theatrical motion pictures, *The Godfather* and *The Godfather: Part II*), these words appeared on screen, simultaneously intoned by a solemn voice: "*The Godfather* is a fictional account of the activities of a small group of ruthless criminals. It would be erroneous and unfair to suggest that they are representative of any ethnic group." Forewarned that the characters were not "representative of any ethnic group," a nationwide audience then watched the violent, multigenerational saga of the Corleone family. The film began in Sicily; large segments were spoken in Italian with English subtitles; and most of the characters bore such names as Clemenza, Barzini, Tattaglia, and Fanucci (Lebo, 1997).

Moreover, this became the model for future media disclaimers. Subsequent controversial films that exploited criminal violence in presenting other ethnic groups, such as the 1983 *Scarface* (Cuban Americans) and the 1985 *Year of the Dragon* (Chinese Americans), copied and only slightly modified the "*Godfather* disclaimer." Such pro forma words could do little to mitigate the teaching impact of these movie textbooks (in fact, howls of laughter during the disclaimers suggested that the warnings may have done more harm than good), but the disclaimers did serve as a media admission that feature films do in fact teach, influencing audience learning about diversity.

Theoretical Scholarship

Finally, alongside scholars who conduct empirical and projective analysis are those who have addressed the process of media-based construction of knowledge by proposing and applying *theories* of audience reception (Bryant & Zillmann, 1991; Jensen, 1987; Schwartz, 1973). Some use schema theory, according to which each learner (viewer/reader/listener) develops an operational internal mental and emotional schema—referred to by such names as "ideational scaffolding," "cognitive maps," or "anticipatory schemes"—that is based on his or her own personal experiences, including school and societal learning. This personal schema then becomes the reception framework by which learners process, interpret, and organize new information, ideas, and images, including those disseminated by the media (Gentner & Stevens, 1983; Graber, 1984).

Related to schema theorists are media analysts who draw upon Gestalt psychology. According to this approach, viewers and readers encounter a piece of communication and alter it by omitting some of its content from their reception or memory, while supplementing or contextualizing its content on the basis of their own beliefs and biases, thereby changing its meaning for them. This Gestalt approach would suggest that if the media challenge preexistent beliefs, particularly those with strong and deep emotional roots, these challenges will tend to be blunted by omission, supplementation, and contextualization (Cooper & Jahoda, 1947). In light of this theory, it can be hypothesized that media would be more likely to influence viewer beliefs about specific groups or intergroup relations if they dealt with topics about which viewers knew little or did not have firmly held preconceptions.

Psychologist Leon Festinger (1957) went one step further with his "theory of cognitive dissonance," according to which once an individual's cognitive structure takes firm shape, it tends to repel those ideas that seem too dissonant. Application of this theory suggests that when media or school frontal assaults on firmly rooted prejudices lack subtlety, they may well be rejected by some because they create too much dissonance.

As part of his social learning theory, psychologist Albert Bandura (1977) described the "sleeper effect," which provides insights for better understanding of how media teaching/learning works. In relation to the media, the sleeper effect suggests that ideas, often clothed as entertainment, can subconsciously enter and become part of a viewer's cognitive or affective storehouse and then lie dormant until provoked by some external stimulus, perhaps a personal or mediated experience (Comstock, 1978). People may not realize that they have prejudices, which might be media-fostered prejudices, about a certain group until they encounter individuals from that group or are exposed to a media barrage about that group, at which point these sleeping beliefs and attitudes awaken and become activated.

Overall, then, scholarship has demonstrated that the media curriculum does contribute to the social construction of multicultural knowledge. Content analysis has provided insights into the media multicultural curriculum of information, messages, ideas, values, and images. Control analysis has provided insights into the process by which mediamakers have made decisions about whether, when, and how to treat multicultural themes. Impact analysis has provided insights into the ways in which media and audiences interact in the social construction of multicultural knowledge.

Yet the *precise* assessment of the media's *long-range* historical influences on multicultural knowledge construction remains a complex scholarly challenge. Research has not dealt with the long-range impact of continuous media experience on learning about diversity. For example, as Garth Jowett and James Linton (1980) noted:

Most of the research on movie influence deals with individual movies, but it is the cumulative effect of years of viewing movies which so far defies adequate measurement and which is of real interest in any assessment of the movies' impact on society and culture. (p. 10)

RELATIONSHIP OF MEDIA AND SCHOOLS IN THE SOCIAL CONSTRUCTION OF MULTICULTURAL KNOWLEDGE

One final scholarly problem has been the difficulty of controlling variables and separating media influence from the impact of other teaching forces, such as schools, families, and other societal institutions (McLeod & Reeves, 1981). Two questions are particularly critical. First, how have the media interacted with schools in the construction of multicultural knowledge? Second, how can educational institutions build most effectively upon growing media-based scholarship?

To date, media and educational scholars have tended to operate in separate worlds regarding the social construction of multicultural knowledge. As this chapter has demonstrated, media scholars have employed a variety of approaches for looking at the media and diversity. Conversely, as reflected in this *Handbook*, scholars involved in multicultural education have explored myriad facets of multicultural teaching and learning. These parallel efforts suggest similarities and differences between educational and media scholarship.

Media scholars analyze media content; educational scholars analyze textbooks and curricula. Media scholars examine media decision making and actions; educational scholars dissect decision making and actions within the textbook industry, within school systems, and by teachers and administrators. Media scholars attempt to assess reader, viewer, and listener learning; educational scholars assess student learning. Seldom have these scholarly efforts intersected (Spring, 1992; Zornado, 2001).

Some communications scholars have focused on the role of the media in fostering interracial, interethnic, and intercultural learning among those of school age (Berry & Asamen, 1993; Cortés, 2000; Dates, 1980; Tobin, 2000) and in socializing children of different racial and ethnic backgrounds (Berry & Mitchell-Kernan, 1982; Stroman, 1991). For example, Bradley Greenberg (1972) discovered that White children often considered television depictions of Blacks to be more representative than Blacks whom they knew in real life. In order to develop more effective multicultural education in the school, teachers and curriculum developers must become more aware of such research and draw upon it in their pedagogical approaches. Moreover, scholars need to explicitly investigate the relationship between media and school multicultural knowledge construction.

The potential for media/school multicultural educational research is raised by the article "Harmony and Conflict of Intercultural Images: The Treatment of Mexico in U.S. Feature Films and K–12 Textbooks," by Gerald Michael Greenfield and Carlos Cortés (1991). The authors compared and contrasted the ways in which U.S. social studies textbooks and feature films have treated both Mexico in general and a series of critical themes in Mexican history, such as the immigration of undocumented Mexican workers into the United States. On the basis of their content analysis, the authors indicated the places where textbooks and feature films reinforced each other's intercultural messages, where they challenged each other, and where by omission they conceded pedagogical dominance to the other educational force.

Even more critical than mere understanding is the need for educators to develop more effective pedagogical strategies for using the mass media as a multicultural teaching source (Carson & Friedman, 1995; Martindale, 1993). During the past two decades, interest in the areas of media literacy and critical pedagogy has grown, especially scholarship and curriculum materials aimed at helping teachers draw upon media at various grade levels (Alvarado & Boyd-Barrett, 1992; Buckingham, 1993; Semali & Pailliotet, 1999). Although most media literacy materials deal only tangentially with diversity, a few scholars have dealt directly with the question of integrating media critically into multicultural education (Cortés, 2000; Summerfield & Lee, 2001). In addition, others have dealt with the development of media intended to reduce prejudice, confront stereotyping, and improve intergroup understanding (McLaughlin & Brilliant, 1997; Stephan, 1999; Summerfield, 1993). Yet much more needs to be done to increase the effective use of media to strengthen multicultural education.

CONCLUSION

The mass media, it can be seen, play a critical role in the social construction of diversity-related knowledge. Teachers, administrators, students, parents, and others involved in school education live in an environment of intended and unintended media multicultural education. Yet most published scholarship on and proposals for implementing multicultural education have failed to effectively engage the existence, persistence, and power of the media as a multicultural educator, including its implications for multicultural schooling.

Scholars need to expand their exploration of the process of media-based multicultural knowledge construction, with regard to the media-derived multicultural beliefs, perceptions, and attitudes that students bring to school. Moreover, school educators need to develop far more effective ways of incorporating media scholarship in order to strengthen multicultural educational pedagogy and curriculum development.

References

Adoni, H., & Mane, S. (1984). Media and the social construction of reality: Toward an integration of theory and research. *Communication Theory, 11,* 323–340.

Allen, R. L., & Hatchett, S. (1986). The media and social effects: Self and system orientations of Blacks. *Communication Research, 13*(1), 97–123.

Alvarado, M., & Boyd-Barrett, O. (Eds.). (1992). *Media education: An introduction.* London: British Film Institute.

Alwood, E. (1996). *Straight news: Gays, lesbians, and the news media.* New York: Columbia University Press.

Armstrong, G. B., Neuendorf, K. A., & Brentar, J. E. (1992). TV entertainment, news, and racial perceptions of college students. *Journal of Communication, 42*(3), 153–176.

Atkin, C., Greenberg, B., & McDermott, S. (1978). Race and social role learning from television. In H. S. Dordick (Ed.), *Proceedings of the sixth annual telecommunications policy research conference* (pp. 7–20). Lexington, MA: Heath.

Bandura, A. (1977). *Social learning theory.* Englewood Cliffs, NJ: Prentice Hall.

Banks, J. A. (1991). Multicultural education: Its effects on students' racial and gender role attitudes. In J. P. Shaver (Ed.), *Handbook of research on social studies teaching and learning* (pp. 459–469). New York: Macmillan.

Banks, J. A. (1993). Multicultural education for young children: Racial and ethnic attitudes and their modification. In B. Spodek (Ed.), *Handbook of research on the education of young children* (pp. 236–250). New York: Macmillan.

Bataille, G. M., & Silet, C.L.P. (Eds.). (1980). *The pretend Indian: Images of Native Americans in the movies.* Ames: Iowa State University Press.

Bernardi, D. L. (1998). *Star Trek and history: Race-ing toward a White future.* New Brunswick, NJ: Rutgers University Press.

Berry, G. L. (1980). Children, television and social class roles: The medium as an unplanned educational curriculum. In E. L. Palmer & A. Dorr (Eds.), *Children and the faces of television* (pp. 71–81). New York: Academic Press.

Berry, G. L., & Asamen, J. K. (Eds.). (1993). *Children and television: Images in a changing socio-cultural world.* Beverly Hills, CA: Sage.

Berry, G. L., & Mitchell-Kernan, C. (Eds.). (1982). *Television and the socialization of the minority child.* New York: Academic Press.

Bettelheim, B. (1976). *The uses of enchantment: The meaning and importance of fairy tales.* New York: Knopf.

Black, G. D. (1998). *The Catholic crusade against the movies, 1940–1975.* New York: Cambridge University Press.

Bloom, A. (1968). (Trans.). *The republic of Plato* (2nd ed.). New York: Basic Books.

Bogle, D. (2001a). *Prime time blues: African Americans on network television.* New York: Farrar, Straus & Giroux.

Bogle, D. (2001b). *Toms, coons, mulattoes, mammies & bucks: An interpretive history of Blacks in American films* (4th ed.). New York: Continuum.

Boorstin, D. J. (1961). *The image or whatever happened to the American dream?* New York: Atheneum.

Bryant, J., & Zillmann, D. (Eds.). (1991). *Responding to the screen: Reception and reaction processes.* Hillsdale, NJ: Erlbaum.

Buckingham, D. (Ed.) (1993). *Reading audiences: Young people and the media.* Manchester, UK: Manchester University Press.

Campbell, C. R. (1995). *Race, myth and the news.* Thousand Oaks, CA: Sage.

Cantor, J. (1998). *"Mommy, I'm scared": How TV and movies frighten children and what we can do to protect them.* San Diego: Harcourt Brace.

Caron, A. H. (1979). First-time exposure to television: Effects on Inuit children's cultural images. *Communication Research, 6,* 135–154.

Carr, S. (2001). *Hollywood & anti-Semitism: A cultural history up to World War II.* Cambridge: Cambridge University Press.

Carson, D., & Friedman, L. D. (Eds.). (1995). *Shared differences: Multicultural media and practical pedagogy.* Urbana: University of Illinois Press.

Chaffee, S. H., & Hochheimer, J. L. (1985). The beginnings of political communication research in the United States: Origins of the "limited effects" model. In E. M. Rogers & F. Balle (Eds.), *The media revolution in America and in Western Europe* (pp. 267–296). Norwood, NJ: Ablex.

Chaisson, R. L. (2000). *For entertainment purposes only? An analysis of the struggle to control filmic representations.* New York: Lexington Books.

Chavez, L. R. (2001). *Covering immigration: Popular images and the politics of the nation.* Berkeley: University of California Press.

Children Now (1998). *A different world: Children's perceptions of race and class in the media.* Oakland, CA: Author.

Children Now (2001). *Fall colors 2000–2001 prime time diversity report.* Oakland, CA: Author.

Comstock, G. (1977). *The impact of television on American institutions and the American public.* Honolulu: East-West Center, East-West Communications Institute.

Comstock, G., & Cobbey, R. (1979). Television and the children of ethnic minorities. *Journal of Communication, 29*(1), 104–115.

Comstock, G., & Paik, H. (1991). *Television and the American children.* San Diego, CA: Academic Press.

Comstock, G. A. (1978). *Trends in the study of incidental learning from television viewing.* Syracuse, NY: ERIC Clearinghouse on Information Resources.

Cooper, E., & Jahoda, M. (1947). The evasion of propaganda: How prejudiced people respond to anti-prejudice propaganda. *Journal of Psychology, 23,* 15–25.

Cortés, C. E. (1981). The societal curriculum: Implications for multiethnic education. In J. A. Banks (Ed.), *Education in the '80s: Multiethnic education* (pp. 24–32). Washington, DC: National Education Association.

Cortés, C. E. (1991). Hollywood interracial love: Social taboo as screen titillation. In P. Loukides & L. K. Fuller (Eds.), *Plot conventions in American popular film* (pp. 21–35). Bowling Green, OH: Bowling Green State University Popular Press.

Cortés, C. E. (2000). *The children are watching: How the media teach about diversity.* New York: Teachers College Press.

Cripps, T. (1970). The myth of the southern box office: A factor in racial stereotyping in American movies, 1920–1940. In J. C. Curtis & L. L. Gould (Eds.), *The Black experience in America: Selected essays* (pp. 116–144). Austin: University of Texas Press.

Cripps, T. (1977). *Slow fade to Black: The Negro in American film, 1900–1942.* New York: Oxford University Press.

Cripps, T. (1978). *Black film as genre.* Bloomington: Indiana University Press.

Cripps, T. (1993). *Making movies Black: The Hollywood message movie from World War II to the civil rights era.* New York: Oxford University Press.

Crowdus, G., & Georgakas, D. (2001). Thinking about the power of images: An interview with Spike Lee. *Cineaste, 26*(2), 4–9.

Curran, J. M. (1989). *Hibernian green on the silver screen.* New York: Greenwood Press.

Dates, J. L. (1980). Race, racial attitudes and adolescent perceptions of Black television characters. *Journal of Broadcasting, 24*(4), 549–560.

Davies, M. M. (1997). *Fake, fact, and fantasy: Children's interpretations of television reality.* Mahwah, NJ: Erlbaum.

DeAngelis, M. (2001). *Gay fandom and crossover stardom: James Dean, Mel Gibson, and Keanu Reeves.* Durham, NC: Duke University Press.

Diawara, M. (Ed.). (1992). *Black American cinema: Aesthetics and spectatorship.* New York: Routledge, Chapman, and Hall.

Dorfman, A. (1983). *The empire's old clothes: What the Lone Ranger, Babar, and other innocent heroes do to our minds.* New York: Pantheon.

Douglas, S. J. (1994). *Where the girls are: Growing up female with the mass media.* New York: Times Books.

Dower, J. (1986). *War without mercy: Race and power in the Pacific war.* New York: Pantheon.

Downing, J.D.H. (1988). "The Cosby Show" and American racial discourse. In G. Smitherman-Donaldson & T. A. van Dijk (Eds.), *Discourse and discrimination* (pp. 46–73). Detroit: Wayne State University Press.

Dyson, M. (1989). Bill Cosby and the politics of race. *Z Magazine, 2*(9), 26–30.

Ebo, B. (Ed.). (1998). *Cyberghetto or cybertopia? Race, class, and gender on the Internet.* Westport, CT: Praeger.

Ely, M. P. (1991). *The adventures of Amos 'n' Andy: A social history of an American phenomenon.* New York: Free Press.

Entman, R. M. (1990). Modern racism and the images of Blacks in local television news. *Critical Studies in Mass Communication, 7,* 332–345.

Entman, R. M., & Rojecki, A. (2000). *The Black image in the White mind: Media and race in America.* Chicago: University of Chicago Press.

Erben, R., & Erben, U. (1991–92). Popular culture, mass media, and Chicano identity in Gary Soto's "Living up the Street" and "Small Faces." *MELUS, 17*(3), 43–52.

Erens, P. (Ed.). (1984). *The Jew in American cinema.* Bloomington: Indiana University Press.

Fairchild, H. H., Stockard, R., & Bowman, P. (1986). Impact of "Roots": Evidence from the national survey of Black Americans. *Journal of Black Studies, 16*(3), 307–318.

Farmer, B. (2000). *Spectacular passions: Cinema, fantasy, gay male spectatorship.* Durham, NC: Duke University Press.

Festinger, L. (1957). *A theory of cognitive dissonance.* Evanston, IL: Row, Peterson.

Forman, H. J. (1933). *Our movie made children.* New York: Macmillan.

Fox, R. F. (1996). *Harvesting minds: How TV commercials control kids.* Westport, CT: Praeger.

Friar, R. E., & Friar, N. A. (1972). *The only good Indian . . . the Hollywood gospel.* New York: Drama Book Specialists.

Friedman, L. D. (1982). *Hollywood's image of the Jew.* New York: Frederick Ungar.

Friedman, L. D. (Ed.). (1991). *Unspeakable images: Ethnicity and the American cinema.* Urbana: University of Illinois Press.

Gabler, N. (1988). *An empire of their own: How the Jews invented Hollywood*. New York: Crown.

Gaines, J. (1987). *The Scar of Shame*: Skin color and caste in Black silent melodrama. *Cinema Journal, 26*(4), 3–21.

Gandy, O., Jr. (1998). *Communication and race: A structural perspective*. New York: Oxford University Press.

Gandy, O., Jr., & Coleman, L. G. (1986). The Jackson campaign: Mass media and Black student perceptions. *Journalism Quarterly, 63*(1), 138ff.

Gans, H. J. (1967). The mass media as an educational institution. *Television Quarterly, 6*(2), 20–37.

Gentner, D., & Stevens, A. L. (Eds.). (1983). *Mental models*. Hillsdale, NJ: Erlbaum.

Gilman, S. L. (1985). *Difference and pathology: Stereotypes of sexuality, race, and madness*. Ithaca, NY: Cornell University Press.

Giroux, H. A. (1997). *Channel surfing: Racetalk and the destruction of today's youth*. New York: Routledge.

Goffman, E. (1974). *Frame analysis*. Boston: Northeastern University Press.

Goldberg, J. N. (1983). *Laughter through tears: The Yiddish cinema*. Rutherford, NJ: Fairleigh Dickinson University Press.

Goldman, E. A. (1983). *Visions, images, and dreams: Yiddish film—past and present*. Ann Arbor, MI: UMI Research Press.

Gorski, P. C. (2001). *Multicultural education and the Internet: Intersections and integrations*. New York: McGraw-Hill.

Graber, D. A. (1984). *Processing the news: How people tame the information tide*. New York: Longman.

Greenberg, B. S. (1972). Children's reactions to TV Blacks. *Journalism Quarterly, 49*(1), 5–14.

Greenberg, B. S., Burgoon, M., Burgoon, J. K., & Korzenny, F. (1983). *Mexican Americans and the mass media*. Norwood, NJ: Ablex.

Greenfield, G. M., & Cortés, C. E. (1991). Harmony and conflict of intercultural images: The treatment of Mexico in U.S. feature films and K–12 textbooks. *Mexican Studies/Estudios Mexicanos, 7*(2), 283–301.

Gross, L. (2002). *Up from invisibility: Lesbians, gay men, and the media in America*. New York: Columbia University Press.

Hall, S. (1977). Culture, the media and the "ideological effect." In J. Curran, M. Gurevitch, & J. Wollacott (Eds.), *Mass communication and society* (pp. 315–348). London: Arnold.

Hall, S. (1981). The whites of their eyes: Racist ideologies and the media. In G. Bridges & R. Brunt (Eds.), *Silver linings: Some strategies for the eighties* (pp. 28–52). London: Lawrence & Wishart.

Hall, S. (1982). The rediscovery of "ideology": Return of the repressed in media studies. In M. Gurevich, T. Bennet, J. Curran, & J. Woollacott (Eds.), *Culture, Society, and the Media* (pp. 56–90). New York: Methuen.

Hamamoto, D. Y. (1994). *Monitored peril: Asian Americans and the politics of TV representation*. Minneapolis: University of Minnesota Press.

Haskell, M. (1987). *From reverence to rape: The treatment of women in movies* (2nd ed.). Chicago: University of Chicago Press.

Heider, D. (2000). *White news: Why local news programs don't cover people of color*. Hillsdale, NJ: Erlbaum.

Hoberman, J. (1991). *Bridge of light: Yiddish film between two worlds*. New York: Museum of Modern Art and Schocken Books.

Holt, J. (2001). Hollywood and politics caught in the Cold War crossfire. *Film & History, 31*(1), 6–12.

Holtzman, L. (2000). *Media messages: What film, television, and popular music teach us about race, class, gender, and sexual orientation*. Armonk, NY: Sharpe.

Hoover, S. M. (1998). *Religion in the news: Faith and journalism in American public discourse*. Thousand Oaks, CA: Sage.

Hunt, D. M. (1997). *Screening the Los Angeles "riots": Race, seeing, and resistance*. New York: Cambridge University Press.

Huston, A. C., Donnerstein, E., Fairchild, H., Feshbach, N. D., Katz, P. A., Murray, J. P., Rubinstein, E. A., Wilcox, B., & Zuckerman, D. (1992). *Big world, small screen: The role of television in American society*. Lincoln: University of Nebraska Press.

Iyengar, S., & Kinder, D. R. (1987). *News that matters: Agenda-setting and priming in a television age*. Chicago: University of Chicago Press.

Jacobs, R. N. (2000). *Race, media and the crisis of civil society: From Watts to Rodney King*. New York: Cambridge University Press.

Jenkins, H. (1992). *Textual poachers: Television fans and participatory culture*. New York: Routledge, Chapman, and Hall.

Jensen, K. B. (1987). Qualitative audience research: Toward an integrative approach to reception. *Critical Studies in Mass Communication, 4*, 21–36.

Jhally, S., & Lewis, J. (1992). *Enlightened racism: "The Cosby Show," audiences, and the myth of the American dream*. Boulder, CO: Westview Press.

Johnson, A. A., & Johnson, R. M. (1979). *Propaganda and aesthetics: The literary politics of Afro-American magazines of the twentieth century*. Amherst: University of Massachusetts Press.

Jowett, G. S., Jarvie, I. C., & Fuller, K. H. (1996). *Children and the movies: Media influence and the Payne Fund controversy*. Cambridge: Cambridge University Press.

Jowett, G., & Linton, J. M. (1980). *Movies as mass communication*. Beverly Hills, CA: Sage.

Keen, S. (1986). *Faces of the enemy: Reflections of the hostile imagination*. New York: Harper & Row.

Keever, B.A.D., Martindale, C., & Weston, M. A. (Eds.). (1997). *U.S. news coverage of racial minorities: A sourcebook, 1934–1996*. Westport, CT: Greenwood Press.

Keller, G. D. (Ed.). (1985). *Chicano cinema: Research, reviews, and resources*. Binghamton, NY: Bilingual Review/Press.

Keyser, L., & Keyser, B. (1984). *Hollywood and the Catholic church: The image of Roman Catholicism in American movies*. Chicago: Loyola University Press.

King, R., & Wood, N. (Eds.). (2001). *Media and migration: Constructions of mobility and difference*. New York: Routledge.

Kitch, C. L. (2001). *The girl on the magazine cover: The origins of visual stereotypes in American mass media*. Chapel Hill: University of North Carolina Press.

Koppes, C. R., & Black, G. D. (1987). *Hollywood goes to war: How politics, profits and propaganda shaped World War II movies*. New York: Free Press.

Korzenny, F., & Ting-Toomey, S., with Schiff, E. (Eds.). (1992). Mass media effects across cultures. *International and Intercultural Communication Annual, No. 16*. Newbury Park, CA: Sage.

Lamb, B. S. (1975). The convenient villain: The early cinema views the Mexican-American. *Journal of the West, 14*(4), 75–81.

Lebo, H. (1997). *The Godfather legacy*. New York: Fireside.

Leckenby, J. D., & Surlin, S. H. (1976). Incidental social learning and viewer race: "All in the Family" and "Sanford and Son." *Journal of Broadcasting, 20*(4), 481–494.

Leifer, A. D., Gordon, N. J., & Graves, S. B. (1974). Children's television more than mere entertainment. *Harvard Educational Review, 44*(2), 213–245.

Leiss, W., Kline, S., & Jhally, S. (1986). *Social communication in advertising*. Toronto: Methuen.

Lester, P. M. (Ed.). (1996). *Images that injure: Pictorial stereotypes in the media*. Westport, CT: Praeger.

Lewels, F. J., Jr. (1974). *The uses of the media by the Chicano movement: A study in minority access*. New York: Praeger.

Lind, R. A. (1996). Diverse interpretations: The "relevance" of race in the construction of meaning in, and the evaluation of, a television news story. *Harvard Journal of Communications, 7,* 53–74.

Lutz, C. A., & Collins, J. A. (1993). *Reading National Geographic*. Chicago: University of Chicago Press.

MacDonald, J. F. (1992). *Blacks and White TV: African Americans in television since 1948* (2nd ed.). Chicago: Nelson-Hall.

Martindale, C. (1986). *The White press and Black America*. New York: Greenwood Press.

Martindale, C. (Ed.). (1993). *Pluralizing journalism education: A multicultural handbook*. Westport, CT: Greenwood Press.

Matabane, P. W. (1988). Television and the Black audience: Cultivating moderate perspectives on racial integration. *Journal of Communication, 38*(4), 21–31.

McCombs, M. W., & Shaw, D. L. (1993). The evolution of agenda-setting research: Twenty-five years in the marketplace of ideas. *Journal of Communication, 43*(2), 58–67.

McLaughlin, K. A., & Brilliant, K. J. (1997). *Healing the hate: A national bias crime prevention curriculum for middle schools*. Newton, MA: Education Development Center.

McLeod, J. M., & Reeves, B. (1981). On the nature of mass media effects. In S. B. Withey & R. P. Abeles (Eds.), *Television and social behavior: Beyond violence and children* (pp. 17–54). Hillsdale, NJ: Erlbaum.

Medved, M. (1992). *Hollywood vs. America: Popular culture and the war on traditional values*. New York: HarperCollins.

Miller, R. M. (Ed.). (1978). *The kaleidoscopic lens: How Hollywood views ethnic groups*. Englewood, NJ: Ozer.

Miller, S. M. (Ed.). (1987). *The ethnic press in the United States: A historical analysis and handbook*. Westport, CT: Greenwood Press.

Myrdal, G. (1944). *An American dilemma: The Negro problem and modern democracy*. New York: Harper & Brothers.

Naficy, H., & Gabriel, T. (Eds.). (1993). *Otherness and the media: The ethnography of the imagined and the imaged*. Langhorne, PA: Harwood Academic.

Norden, M. F. (1994). *The cinema of loneliness: A history of physical disability in the movies*. New Brunswick, NJ: Rutgers University Press.

Noriega, C. (1988–1990). Chicano cinema and the horizon of expectations: A discursive analysis of recent film reviews in the mainstream, alternative and Hispanic press, 1987–1988. *Aztlan, a Journal of Chicano Studies, 19*(2), 1–31.

Noriega, C. (Ed.). (1992). *Chicanos and film: Essays on Chicano representation and resistance*. New York: Garland.

Noriega, C. (2000). *Shot in America: Television, the state, and the rise of Chicano cinema*. Minneapolis: University of Minnesota Press.

O'Barr, W. M. (1994). *Culture and the ad: Exploring otherness in the world of advertising*. Boulder, CO: Westview Press.

O'Connor, J. E. (1980). *The Hollywood Indian: Stereotypes of Native Americans in films*. Trenton: New Jersey State Museum.

Peterson, R. C., & Thurstone, L. L. (1933). *Motion pictures and the social attitudes of children*. New York: Macmillan.

Pettit, A. G. (1980). *Images of the Mexican American in fiction and film*. College Station: Texas A&M University Press.

Real, M. R. (1991). Bill Cosby and recoding ethnicity. In L. R. Vande Berg & L. A. Wenner (Eds.), *Television criticism: Approaches and applications* (pp. 58–84). New York: Longman.

Rogers, E. M., Dearing, J. W., & Bregman, D. (1993). The anatomy of agenda-setting research. *Journal of Communication, 43*(2), 68–84.

Rosen, I. C. (1948). The effect of the motion picture *Gentleman's Agreement* on attitudes toward Jews. *Journal of Psychology, 26,* 525–536.

Russo, V. (1987). *The celluloid closet: Homosexuality in the movies* (rev. ed.). New York: Harper & Row.

Schwartz, T. (1973). *The responsive chord*. Garden City, NY: Doubleday.

Semali, L., & Pailliotet, A. (Eds.). (1999). *Intermediality: The teachers' handbook of critical media literacy*. Boulder, CO: Westview Press.

Sender, K. (2001). Gay readers, consumers, and a dominant gay habitus: 25 years of the *Advocate* magazine. *Journal of Communication, 51*(1), 73–99.

Seppanen, J. (2001). Young people, researchers and Benetton: Contest interpretations of a Benetton advertisement picture. *Nordicom: Nordic Research on Media & Communication Review, 22*(1), 85–96.

Shaheen, J. G. (1984). *The TV Arab*. Bowling Green, OH: Bowling Green State University Popular Press.

Shaheen, J. G. (2001). *Reel bad Arabs: How Hollywood vilifies a people*. Brooklyn, NY: Olive Branch Press.

Singer, B. R. (2001). *Wiping the war paint off the lens: Native American film and video*. Minneapolis: University of Minnesota Press.

Smith, J. D. (2001). Patrolling the boundaries of race: Motion picture censorship and Jim Crow in Virginia, 1922–1932. *Historical Journal of Film, Radio and Television, 21*(3), 273–291.

Snead, J. (1992). *White screens/Black images: Hollywood from the dark side*. New York: Routledge, Chapman, and Hall.

Spring, J. (1992). *Images of American life: A history of ideological management in schools, movies, radio, and television*. Albany: State University of New York Press.

Staiger, J. (2000). *Perverse spectators: The practices of film reception*. New York: New York University Press.

Stanley, R. H., & Steinberg, C. S. (1976). *The media environment: Mass communications in American society*. New York: Hastings House.

Stephan, W. (1999). *Reducing prejudice and stereotyping in schools*. New York: Teachers College Press.

Stroman, C. A. (1991). Television's role in the socialization of African American children and adolescents. *Journal of Negro Education, 60*(3), 314–327.

Subervi-Vélez, F. A. (1986). The mass media and ethnic assimilation and pluralism: A review and research proposal with special focus on Hispanics. *Communication Research, 13*(1), 71–96.

Summerfield, E. (1993). *Crossing cultures through film*. Yarmouth, ME: Intercultural Press.

Summerfield, E., & Lee, S. (2001). *Seeing the big picture: Exploring American cultures*. Yarmouth, ME: Intercultural Press.

Surlin, S. H. (1978). "Roots" research: A summary of findings. *Journal of Broadcasting, 22*(3), 309–319.

Surlin, S. H., & Tate, E. D. (1976). "All in the Family": Is Archie funny? *Journal of Communication, 26*(4), 61–68.

Tan, A., & Tan, G. (1979). Television use and self-esteem of Blacks. *Journal of Communication, 29*(1), 123–135.

Tasker, Y. (1998). *Working girls: Gender and sexuality in popular cinema.* New York: Routledge.

Taylor, P. S. (1930). *Mexican labor in the United States* (Vol. 1). Berkeley: University of California Press.

Tobin, J. (2000). *"Good guys don't wear hats": Children's talk about the media.* New York: Teachers College Press.

Toplin, R. B. (1993). *Hollywood as mirror: Changing views of "outsiders" and "enemies" in American movies.* Westport, CT: Greenwood Press.

Vidmar, N., & Rokeach, M. (1974). Archie Bunker's bigotry: A study in selective perception and exposure. *Journal of Communication, 24*(1), 36–47.

Volkan, V. (1988). *The need to have enemies and allies: From clinical practice to international relationships.* Northvale, NJ: Aronson.

Wahl, O. F. (1995). *Media madness: Public images of mental illness.* New Brunswick, NJ: Rutgers University Press.

Wiegman, R. (1989). Negotiating AMERICA: Gender, race, and the ideology of the interracial male bond. *Cultural Critique, 13,* 89–117.

Wilhoit, G. C., & de Bock, H. (1976). "All in the Family" in Holland. *Journal of Communication, 26*(4), 75–84.

Williams, L. (2001). *Playing the race card: Melodramas of Black and White from Uncle Tom to O. J. Simpson.* Princeton, NJ: Princeton University Press.

Wilson, C. C., II, & Gutiérrez, F. (1995). *Race, multiculturalism, and the media: From mass media to class communication.* Thousand Oaks, CA: Sage.

Winn, M. (1977). *The plug-in drug.* New York: Viking Press.

Woll, A. L. (1980). *The Latin image in American film* (rev. ed.). Los Angeles: University of California, Latin American Center.

Woll, A. L., & Miller, R. M. (Eds.). (1987). *Ethnic and racial images in American film and television: Historical essays and bibliography.* New York: Garland.

Wong, E. F. (1978). *On visual media racism: Asians in the American motion pictures.* New York: Arno Press.

Worth, S., & Adair, J. (1972). *Through Navajo eyes: An exploration in film communication and anthropology.* Bloomington: Indiana University Press.

Wykes, M. (2001). *News, crime, and culture.* London: Pluto Press.

Yum, J. O. (1982). Communication diversity and information acquisition among Korean immigrants in Hawaii. *Human Communication Research, 8*(2), 154–169.

Zook, K. B. (1999). *Color by Fox: The Fox network and the revolution in Black television.* New York: Oxford University Press.

Zornado, J. L. (2001). *Inventing the child: Culture, ideology, and the story of childhood.* New York: Garland.

12

RACE, KNOWLEDGE CONSTRUCTION, AND EDUCATION IN THE UNITED STATES

Lessons from History

James A. Banks

University of Washington, Seattle

The *Studies in the Historical Foundations of Multicultural Education Series* (hereafter, Series) was initiated by the Center for Multicultural Education at the University of Washington in 1992. The purpose of this research project is to uncover the roots of multicultural education, to identify the ways in which it is connected to its historical antecedents, and to gain insights from the past that can inform school reform efforts today related to race and ethnic diversity (J. A. Banks, 1996b).

Another aim of the Series is to identify the ways in which the knowledge constructed within a society reflects the social, political, and economic contexts in which it is created as well as the subsocieties and personal biographies of historians and social scientists (J. A. Banks, 1998). Studies in the Series identify important ways in which theory, research, and ideology in multicultural education are both linked to and divergent from past educational reform movements related to race and ethnic diversity (J. A. Banks, 1995, 1996a, 1996b, 1998; C.A.M. Banks, 1996, in progress; Hillis, 1996; Roche, 1996).

This chapter extends the ongoing work of the Series by examining the historical and social contexts from 1911 to 2000 to identify ways in which the research and knowledge constructed about race and ethnic groups mirrored and perpetuated these contexts. This historical survey will of necessity be highly abbreviated and condensed. Race relations research on both adults and children will be discussed and related to the social, historical, and political contexts in which it was conducted. In this chapter, I describe research that supports the claims I made in an earlier publication in the Series project (J. A. Banks, 1998):

- The cultural communities in which individuals are socialized are also epistemological communities that have shared beliefs, perspectives, and knowledge.
- Social science and historical research are influenced in complex ways by the life experiences, values, personal biographies, and epistemological communities of researchers.
- Knowledge created by social scientists, historians, and public intellectuals reflects and perpetuates their epistemological communities, experiences, goals, and interests.
- How individual social scientists interpret their cultural experiences is mediated by the interaction of a complex set of status variables, such as gender, social class, age, political affiliation, religion, and region. (p. 5)

An earlier version of this chapter was published in *Race, Ethnicity and Education*, 2002, 5(1), 7–27. Copyright © 2002 Taylor & Francis Ltd. Used with the permission of the author. It was presented as a paper when the author received the Jean Dresden Grambs Distinguished Career Research in Social Studies Award at the 81st Annual Conference of the National Council for the Social Studies, Washington, DC, Nov. 16–18, 2001.

I am grateful to Cherry A. McGee Banks for her insightful and encouraging comments on an earlier draft of this chapter. I especially appreciate her keen observations about my discussion of the intercultural and intergroup education movements.

THE RISE OF NATIVISM IN THE EARLY 1900S

In the early decades of the last century—1900 to 1924—the United States experienced massive immigration from southern, central, and eastern Europe. Europeans were leaving their homelands in massive numbers because of economic dislocations in Europe and the power and promise of the American dream. The American dream and its promises were conveyed across the Atlantic to potential newcomers by letters from European immigrants already in America and by steamship companies. The companies were anxious to profit from the "huddled masses" from Europe, described in Emma Lazarus's poem inscribed on the base of the Statue of Liberty (1886/1968).

The "old" European immigrants—who had come largely from northern and western Europe—considered themselves "native Americans" by the turn of the century. They became alarmed by the large number of immigrants from southern, eastern, and central Europe who were settling in the United States because, they believed, these immigrants differed from themselves in several important ways (Higham, 1972). A large percentage of the new immigrants were Catholics, and most spoke languages different from those spoken by the so-called native Americans. Also, the old immigrants believed that the new immigrants were easy pawns for city politicians because they exchanged their votes for patronage. Consequently, argued individuals who spoke for the old immigrants, the new immigrants threatened democracy in America. They were also a threat to U.S. democracy because of the possibility of a papal takeover in the United States (Higham). This belief developed because of the large percentage of the new immigrants who were Catholic. A significant percentage were also Jews; some also came from China and, after 1882, Japan.

The nativists were also alarmed about the new immigrants because they considered the immigrants—such as Jews, Italians, and Poles—to be members of races that were separate from and inferior to the descendants of northern and western Europeans (Jacobson, 1998). Madison Grant (1923) argued that the mixing of these inferior races with the northern and western European groups would result in the emergence of a lower type of civilization in the United States. His book had the evocative title, *The Passing of the Great Race.*

THE CONSTRUCTION OF KNOWLEDGE ABOUT RACE IN THE EARLY 1900S

As is usually the case during a particular historical period, conflicting and oppositional paradigms were constructed about the southern, central, and eastern European immigrants during the early decades of the twentieth century.

One was a *nativist paradigm,* which was given voice and legitimacy by a number of influential books and other publications. Researchers and writers who embraced this paradigm documented ways in which the new immigrants differed from the northern and western Europeans and how they were a threat to American democracy and to the survival of the Anglo-Saxon "race."

Researchers and writers such as Grant (1923) and T. Lothrop Stoddard (1920) documented the ways in which southern, central, and eastern Europeans were genetically inferior to northern and western Europeans by using findings from craniometry, the method and science of measuring skull sizes (Gould, 1996). This research indicated that southern, central, and eastern Europeans had smaller skulls than those of northern and western Europeans and consequently were genetically inferior. Jews and Blacks, both regarded as inferior to northern and western Europeans, were also targets of the nativists. Jews were targets because they were considered a distinct race from Whites in the early 1900s and made up a significant percentage of the new immigrants (Brodkin, 1998; Jacobson, 1998). African Americans had been in America since 1619 and made up a substantial percentage of the nation's population, especially in the Southern states. In 1790, for example, African Americans made up approximately 19.2 percent of the U.S. population (Bailey, 1961).

An Oppositional Paradigm Emerges

A group of social scientists and philosophers within marginalized ethnic communities—primarily Jewish and African American scholars—created a *transformative paradigm* that challenged nativist theories (J. A. Banks, 1993a). They included the anthropologist Franz Boas (1910) and the philosophers Horace Kallen (1924) and Randolph Bourne (1916). Boas (1938/1963) rejected genetic explanations of racial differences and argued that human behavior could best be explained by the interaction of genetic characteristics with the environment. In response to calls by educators and policy makers for the forced and rapid assimilation of the new immigrants, Kallen and Bourne argued that the new immigrants were entitled to "cultural democracy" in America, which was an extension of the political democracy guaranteed by the Constitution. Kallen and Bourne argued that the new immigrants had the right to maintain important aspects of their ethnic cultures and identities as they became Americans. Gordon (1964), summarizing Kallen's work, writes:

> A second theme that highlights Kallen's development of the cultural pluralism position is that his position is entirely in harmony with the traditional ideals of American political and social life, and that, indeed, any attempt to impose Anglo-Saxon conformity constitutes a violation of those ideals. (p. 145)

NATIVISM TRIUMPHS

The nativistic sentiments directed against the southern, central, and eastern European immigrants gave rise to the influential and inflammatory nativistic Know-Nothing movement (Bennett, 1988), whose aim was to rid the United States of foreign influences. In 1911, the Dillingham Commission—a congressional committee created in 1907 to investigate immigration—issued a report that validated and reinforced the views of the nativists. The Commission concluded that the new and the old immigrants were different in significant ways. Historical research today indicates that the two groups of immigrants were more alike than different (Higham, 1972; Bennett, 1988).

The Dillingham Commission, which was appointed by members of Congress who represented and identified with powerful groups in America, created knowledge and findings that reinforced the dominant prejudices, sentiments, and perceptions of mainstream groups in the United States. The Commission, in the words of Manning Marable (1996), did not "speak truth to power." Rather, it reinforced and legitimized mainstream popular knowledge and the groups that exercised the most power in society rather than challenged prevailing conceptions and the people who benefited from them.

The nativists won several major congressional victories that eventually curtailed the flow of southern, eastern, and central European immigrants to the United States and completely stopped immigration from China. These victories included the Chinese Exclusion Act of 1882, the first immigration act directed toward a specific nationality group. The Immigration Act of 1917 required immigrants to pass a literacy test in their native language. The era of massive immigration to the United States was ended by the Immigration Act of 1924, which discriminated blatantly against the southern, central, and eastern European immigrants.

The nativists and the assimilationists were victorious in part because most of the immigrants themselves surrendered their ethnic cultures and languages to gain full inclusion into American society. This was a possibility for White European immigrants, but not for people of color such as Native Americans, Mexican Americans, and African Americans. Even when people of color became highly culturally assimilated, they were still denied structural inclusion into American society. This is to a large extent still true today, although it is mediated and made more complex by social-class factors (Wilson, 1978). In the United States today, in large part because of opportunities that resulted from the civil rights movement of the 1960s and 1970s, there is a significant group of middle-class African Americans. Although middle-class Blacks are able to enjoy most of the material benefits that middle-class Whites experience, they encounter racism in their personal and professional lives (Feagin & Sikes, 1994).

KNOWLEDGE, POWER, AND TRANSFORMATIVE KNOWLEDGE

A significant finding of the Series is that individuals and groups on the margins often challenge mainstream and established paradigms that violate human rights and American democratic ideals (J. A. Banks, 1996b). Boas, Kallen, and Bourne were immigrant Jews. African American social scientists such as W.E.B. DuBois (Aptheker, 1983; Lewis, 1995), Carter G. Woodson (1933), and Kelly Miller (1908) also challenged the prevailing theories about race and intelligence during the early decades of the twentieth century. As Okihiro (1994) has perceptively argued, it is "outsiders" and groups and individuals in the margins who frequently keep democratic ideals and practices alive in democratic nation-states because they are among the first people to take actions to defend these ideals when they are most seriously challenged.

Social scientists and philosophers such as Boas, Bourne, Kallen, DuBois, Woodson, and Miller created oppositional knowledge—which I call *transformative knowledge*—because of their socialization and experiences within marginalized communities (J. A. Banks, 1993a). These communities enable individuals to acquire unique ways to conceptualize the world and an epistemology that differs in significant ways from mainstream assumptions, conceptions, values, and epistemology. Knowledge is in important ways related to power. Groups with the most power within society often construct—perhaps unconsciously—knowledge that maintains their power and protects their interests. Scholars and public intellectuals who are outside the mainstream often construct transformative knowledge that challenges the existing and institutionalized metanarrative (C.A.M. Banks, 1996).

The Series' hypotheses about the relationship between knowledge and power are influenced by the work of transformative scholars such as Mannheim (1936), Clark (1965), Myrdal (1969), Ladner (1973), Code (1991), Harding (1991), and Collins (2000). These scholars have described the ways in which knowledge is not neutral but is highly related to the social, economic, and political contexts in which it is created. Code, the feminist epistemologist, writes, "Knowledge does not transcend, but is rooted in and shaped by, specific interests and social arrangements" (p. 68).

Scholars and researchers less centered in the mainstream tend to have different epistemologies, in part because change and reform, rather than maintenance of the status quo, more frequently serve their social, cultural, political, and economic interests. The epistemological communities in which researchers on the margins are socialized provide them with a unique standpoint or cultural eye, which Patricia Hill Collins, the African American sociologist, calls the "outsider/within" perspective.

Despite the oppositional knowledge created by scholars such as Boas, Bourne, and Kallen, the nativists were destined to win the battle to stop the massive influx of immigrants from southern, eastern, and central Europe; culturally assimilate the immigrants; and maintain Anglo-Saxon cultural and political hegemony. The nativists won the battle for several reasons. Although the knowledge and arguments created by Boas, Bourne, Kallen, and other scholars were incisive and cogent, they largely fell on deaf ears. The political and economic power was on the side of the nativists. Knowledge, no matter how thoughtful and logical, usually fades when it goes against powerful political and economic forces. *Knowledge is viewed as most influential when it reinforces the beliefs, ideologies, and assumptions of the people who exercise the most political and economic power within a society.* Neither the knowledge created by nativist scholars nor that created by transformative scholars such as Boas, Kallen, and Bourne was the decisive factor that resulted in the victory of the nativists. Political and economic factors, rather than knowledge, were the most significant factors in their triumph.

THE INTERCULTURAL AND INTER-GROUP EDUCATION MOVEMENTS

The Intercultural Education Movement

The assimilationist and pluralist paradigms that emerged within the larger society were mirrored in the nation's schools, colleges, and universities. In the 1930s, an educational movement emerged in the United States to help immigrant students adapt to American life, maintain aspects of their ethnic heritages and identity, and become effective citizens of the commonwealth. This movement was called the *intercultural education movement* (Montalto, 1982). New York City, where most of the European immigrants arrived when they came to the United States, became one of the most important sites for the intercultural education movement.

Rachel Davis DuBois, one of the leaders of the intercultural education movement, initiated ethnic assemblies in schools that celebrated the cultures of the immigrants (C.A.M. Banks, 1996). An important aim of the assemblies was to teach immigrant youths ethnic pride and to help mainstream students appreciate the cultures of immigrant youths.

The Intergroup Education Movement

When World War II began, most African Americans lived in Southern states, such as Arkansas, Mississippi, and South Carolina. Blacks were heavily concentrated in the South because as captive workers they most frequently worked in cotton and tobacco fields. African Americans began the Great Migration to northern, midwestern, and western cities when the war began (Lemann, 1991). They rushed to cities such as St. Louis, Chicago, New York, and Los Angeles. Like the southern, central, and eastern European immigrants, African American migrants were searching for better economic opportunities and for the elusive American dream. They also left the South in large numbers to escape the institutionalized racism and discrimination that became pernicious and rampant in the decades after the Civil War (Logan, 1954/1997).

When they arrived in northern and western cities, African Americans discovered that these regions were not promised lands. They experienced discrimination in housing, employment, and public accommodation. Racial tensions developed and erupted in a series of race riots that destroyed many lives and millions of dollars' worth of property. In 1943, riots occurred in Los Angeles, Detroit, and New York City. The Detroit riot lasted more than 30 hours. When it was over, 25 African Americans and nine Whites had been killed and millions of dollars in property had been destroyed.

The racial riots and incidents in the nation's cities, as well as Nazi anti-Semitism in Europe, provided a new emphasis for intercultural educators. By this time, they frequently referred to themselves as intergroup educators (C.A.M. Banks, in progress). During the 1940s, the intergroup education movement in the nation's schools, colleges, and universities gave birth to a new era of research in race relations and intergroup relations. Like intercultural education, the aims of intergroup education were to minimize ethnic cultures and affiliations, help students become mainstream Americans and effective citizens, and teach racial and ethnic tolerance (Taba, Brady, & Robinson, 1952).

Research During the Intergroup Education Era, 1940–1954

The intergroup education period in the United States, from about 1940 to 1954, was one of the nation's most prodigious periods for interracial and intergroup research, theory development, and activities. Although the nation's schools, as well as most of its other institutions—especially in the South—were tightly segregated along racial lines, a group of the nation's social scientists, educators, civil rights organizations, and foundations focused on what Myrdal (1944) called the "American Dilemma." Most of this research, theory development, and activities originated within ethnic communities that were rather separate and apart from mainstream institutions. Jewish American and African American scholars and civil rights organizations provided much of the leadership in the intergroup and ethnic studies developments during the years that preceded and followed World War II.

Three seminal studies marked this period: *An American Dilemma* (Myrdal, 1944), *The Authoritarian Personality* (Adorno, Frenkel-Brunswik, Levinson, & Sanford, 1950), and *The Nature of Prejudice* (Allport, 1954). Each of these studies was designed to provide knowledge and insights that would improve race relations and contribute to the development of theory and research in the social sciences.

An American Dilemma, funded by the Carnegie Corporation of New York, is the most comprehensive single study of race relations in the United States (Myrdal, 1944). Gunnar Myrdal, a Swedish economist, led the research team that gathered the data for this ambitious study and authored the book that resulted from it. One of Myrdal's key findings was that the discrepancy between American democratic ideals and institutionalized racism and discrimination created an "American dilemma" that had the potential to lead to the reform of race relations in the United States. He believed that most Americans had internalized American creed values such as equality and justice, and that a dilemma was created for Americans because of the gap between their ideals and realities. Effective leaders, he argued, could bring about reform in race relations by making this dilemma visible to Americans and appealing to their basic democratic beliefs.

The leaders at the Carnegie Foundation who funded the study, and who identified with America's power elite, were surprised and embarrassed by Myrdal's candid criticism of racism and discrimination in the American South. They responded to the study with benign neglect. The major findings of the study challenged the status quo in the South. Although *An American Dilemma* was destined to attain the status of a classic within the American academic community, it received a chilly response in the foundation and corporate worlds (Southern, 1987). One consequence of its publication and reception was a drying up of foundation support for race relations research. Substantial funds for race relations research in the United States would not become available again until the civil rights era of the 1960s and 1970s.

The Authoritarian Personality (Adorno et al., 1950) was another path-breaking research study during the intergroup education period in the United States. Supported and sponsored by the American Jewish Committee as a volume in its *Studies in Prejudice Series*, it was created in the aftermath of Nazi anti-Semitism. It was designed to reveal the personality and social conditions that caused individuals to become anti-Semitic. The lead author of the study, Theodor W. Adorno, was a founder of the Frankfurt School in Germany. He was considered Jewish by the Nazi authorities; his father was an assimilated Jew and his mother was a Catholic (Jarvis, 1998; O'Connor, 2000). Adorno immigrated to the United States to escape anti-Semitism in Germany and to find work.

Adorno and his colleagues (1950) concluded that family socialization practices were a major factor that caused individuals to develop authoritarian personalities and consequently to become anti-Semitic. Their research indicated that certain individuals, because of their early childhood experiences, have insecure personalities and need to dominate and feel superior to other individuals. These individuals, concluded the authors, have an authoritarian personality, which is manifested not only in their anti-Semitism but also in their religious and political views. Although Adorno and his colleagues overemphasized personality variables as a cause of prejudice and underestimated structural factors, their theory is an important one. It made substantial contributions to methodology and to theory development in race relations research.

Gordon Allport's 1954 book, *The Nature of Prejudice*, has had a major influence on intergroup education theory and research since its publication. Allport presented his now-famous contact hypothesis in this book. He stated that contact between groups will improve intergroup relations if the contact is characterized by these conditions: (a) equal status, (b) intergroup cooperation, (c) common goals, and (d) support by authorities (see Pettigrew, Chapter 37, this volume).

Most of the research on cooperative learning and interracial contact that has been conducted within the last three decades is based on Allport's (1954) contact hypothesis. This research lends considerable support to the postulate that cooperative interracial contact situations in schools, if the conditions stated by Allport are present in the contact situations, have positive effects on both student interracial behavior and student academic achievement (Aronson & Gonzalez, 1988; Slavin, 1979, 2001).

African American Scholarship During the Intergroup Education Period

The books by Myrdal (1944), Adorno et al. (1950), and Allport (1954) received notable attention, discussion, and reviews in mainstream academic publications and discourse. However, the mainstream intellectual and popular communities largely ignored most of the research, work, and publications written by African American scholars during this period. An exception was *The Souls of Black Folk,* by W.E.B. DuBois (1953/1973), which was widely reviewed and sold briskly. DuBois was the most prolific African American scholar during this period (Lewis, 1995). Although he was a historian and sociologist of the first rank, DuBois found it difficult to secure funds to support his research and was unable to obtain a teaching position at a predominantly White university.

Carter G. Woodson, an African American historian who obtained his doctorate from Harvard, produced a long list of distinguished scholarly works. He also wrote textbooks for students in the elementary and high schools. Woodson's publications, like those of other African American historians such as John Hope Franklin and Rayford Logan, were widely used in predominantly Black schools, colleges, and universities. Woodson probably had more influence on the teaching of African American history in the nation's schools and colleges from the turn of the century until his death in 1950 than any other scholar (J. A. Banks, 1996a). With others, he founded the Association for the Study of Negro Life and History in 1912. He established the *Journal of Negro History* in 1916.

A number of other publications and research studies by African American scholars during this period also became very influential in predominantly Black colleges and universities, among them John Hope Franklin's *From Slavery to Freedom: A History of Black Americans,* first published in 1947; and Rayford Logan's (1954/ 1997) *The Betrayal of the Negro,* a study of the post-Reconstruction period. Oliver C. Cox's (1948) important study, *Caste, Class and Race: A Study in Social Dynamics,* never became influential in the mainstream academic community. Cox, an African American sociologist who taught at Lincoln University, a historically Black college, gave a Marxist interpretation of race and class.

Research on Children's Racial Attitudes During the Intergroup Education Period

The pace of research on children's racial attitudes quickened during the intergroup education period, and attempts to modify their racial attitudes with experimental interventions began. Scholars within the Jewish and African American communities did most of this research. Research on children's racial attitudes had begun as early as 1929, with the publication of *Race Attitudes in Children* by Bruno Lasker. Eugene and Ruth Horowitz (1938) and Kenneth and Mamie Clark (1939) conducted other early studies of children's racial attitudes in the 1930s. This early research was designed to describe, not modify, children's racial attitudes.

The early research on children's racial attitudes by researchers such as Horowitz and Horowitz, Clark and Clark, and Goodman (1946) indicates that very young children are aware of racial differences, that their racial attitudes mirror those of adults that are institutionalized within mainstream society, and that both African Americans and White children express a white bias. This early research established a paradigm in race relations research that is still highly influential. It states that the preference African American children express for white indicates self-rejection or self-hate. More recent research by Spencer (1982) and Cross (1991) confirms the early findings that both White and Black young children express a white bias. However, they interpret the findings quite differently.

Spencer distinguishes *personal identity* and *group identity.* Her research indicates that children can have a high personal self-concept and yet express a bias against their ethnic group. She concludes that the White bias often expressed by young African American children indicates an accurate understanding of the status of Blacks and Whites in American society rather than a rejection of self.

Intervention Studies During the Intergroup Education Years

During the intergroup education period of the 1940s and 1950s, a number of curriculum interventions were conducted by researchers to determine the effects of teaching units, lessons, multicultural materials, role-playing activities, and other kinds of simulated experiences on the racial attitudes of students. Jackson (1944) and Agnes (1947) found that curriculum materials about African Americans had a positive effect on the racial attitudes of students. Trager and Yarrow (1952) found that a democratic curriculum helped students develop more positive racial attitudes. They titled their study *They Learn What They Live.* A variety of curriculum interventions helped students acquire more positive racial attitudes in a study conducted by Haynes and Conklin (1953). Collectively, these studies indicate that curriculum interventions can help students develop more positive racial attitudes if certain conditions exist in the interventions.

THE AMERICAN CIVIL RIGHTS MOVEMENT

When a group of African American college students sat down at a lunch counter reserved for Whites in a Woolworth's store in Greensboro, North Carolina, on February 1, 1960, and refused to leave until they were served, the civil rights movement had begun (Halberstam, 1998). Race relations in the United States were destined to be transformed. A series of events had given rise to the civil rights movement, including the desegregation of the public universities in the Southern and border states, and the desegregation of the armed forces by President Harry Truman with Executive Order 9981 in 1948. The *Brown v. Board of Education* Supreme Court decision, which declared *de jure* school segregation unconstitutional in 1954, was also an important precedent of the civil rights movement of the 1960s and 1970s. The movement had a profound influence on most of the nation's institutions, including schools, colleges, and universities, as well as on research and theory in the social sciences and education.

The National Advisory Commission on Civil Disorders (1968) was established by President Lyndon B. Johnson to identify the causes of the urban race riots that had raged in many American cities in the late 1960s.

Many people had died and millions of dollars' worth of property had been destroyed in this series of riots. The Commission's report set the tone for much of the research, publications, and public declarations of this period. The Commission, which issued its report in 1968, concluded that institutionalized racism was the root cause of the riots and that America was moving toward two societies, one Black and one White. The Commission called upon the nation to act decisively to heal its racial wounds:

This is our basic conclusion: our Nation is moving toward two societies, one black, one white—separate and unequal. . . . What white Americans have never fully understood—but what the Negro can never forget—is that white society is deeply implicated in the ghetto. White institutions created it, white institutions maintain it, and white society condones it. (vol. 1, p. 1)

This was also the period in which Michael Harrington published *The Other America* (1962), President Johnson initiated affirmative action with Executive Order 11246 (in 1971), and the nation began its war on poverty. There was a widespread belief within the nation, which was often voiced by its leaders, that by harnessing its tremendous human resources the United States could eliminate racism and poverty. These ideals were publicly expressed by such influential leaders as John F. Kennedy, Martin Luther King, Jr., and Johnson. In a message to Congress in 1964 in which he declared a war on poverty in America, President Johnson (1964) said:

The path forward has not been an easy one. But we have never lost sight of our goal—an America in which every citizen shares all the opportunities of his society, in which every man has a chance to advance his welfare to the limit of his capacities. We have come a long way toward this goal. We still have a long way to go.

The distance which remains is the measure of the great unfinished work of our society. To finish that work I have called for a national war on poverty. Our objective: total victory. (p. 212)

The American civil rights movement, initiated and led by African Americans, played a major role in the democratization and humanization of American society. As a direct result of action by African Americans and their supporters in the civil rights movement, Congress passed the Civil Rights Act of 1964. Franklin and Moss (1988) call it "the most far-reaching and comprehensive law in support of racial equality ever enacted by Congress" (p. 449). As a result of the legal, political, and human rights precedent set by the Civil Rights Act of 1964, equal rights were extended to many other groups in American society, including women, people with disabilities, and groups immigrating to the United States. Related legislation that Congress passed after it enacted the Civil Rights Act of 1964 included Title IX of the Elementary and Secondary

Education Act in 1972, which made sex bias in education illegal; and Public Law 94–142 in 1975, the Education for All Handicapped Children Act, which requires free public education and nondiscrimination for all students with disabilities.

The Immigration Reform Act of 1965 was also an extension of the ideas embodied by the civil rights movement and the Civil Rights Act of 1964. It abolished the highly discriminatory national origins quota system and made it possible for immigrants from nations in Asia and Latin America to enter the United States in significant numbers for the first time in U.S. history. The tremendous demographic changes now taking place in American society are a direct result of this act, and consequently of the civil rights movement. Because of its passage, massive numbers of immigrants from nations in Asia and Latin America are now entering the United States. The U.S. Census Bureau projects that people of color will make up 47 percent of the U.S. population by 2050. In that year, the population is projected to be 53 percent White, 25 percent Hispanic, 14 percent African American, 8 percent Asian Pacific American, and 1 percent American Indian and Alaska Native (Franklin, 1998).

Research During the Civil Rights Era

Much of the research and publications during the 1960s and 1970s reflected the social and political ethos of possibility, hope, and the quest for knowledge that would help to eliminate poverty, create equality, and eradicate racism in the United States. People of color (African Americans, Mexican Americans, Puerto Rican Americans, and others) entered predominantly White colleges and universities in significant numbers for the first time in U.S. history as both students and professors. They established ethnic studies programs, conducted research within their communities, and published a score of academic works that described their histories and cultures from "insider" perspectives (Gutiérrez, 2001; Rodríguez, 2001).

Scholars of color published critiques of much of the previous research that had been done on their histories and cultures by White scholars. They argued that much of this research presented inaccurate and distorted views of their experiences, histories, and cultures (Ladner, 1973; Acuña, 1981). They revealed ways in which many White scholars described their histories and cultures from deficit perspectives (Rodríguez, 2001). These scholars developed and published a group of studies that presented their histories and cultures from insider perspectives that were more accurate, complex, and compassionate (Acuña, 1981; Gates, 1988; Rodríguez, 1989; Takaki, 1993; Collins, 2000).

Research on Children's Racial Attitudes: 1960 Through the 1980s

The hope ushered in by the civil rights movement resulted in federal and foundation funds for research on children's racial attitudes and on ways to intervene to help students acquire democratic racial attitudes and values. I will discuss only the intervention research studies in this chapter, although much descriptive research was also published during the 1970s and 1980s (Aboud, 1988; Stephan, 1999). I will use a Weber-like typology to classify this research into four types: (a) reinforcement studies, (b) perceptual differentiation studies, (c) curriculum intervention studies, and (d) cooperative activities and contact studies (J. A. Banks, 1993b). Although these categories overlap, they highlight the important ways in which the four groups differ.

Reinforcement Studies. In the late 1960s, John E. Williams and his colleagues at Wake Forest University conducted a series of studies with preschool children that were designed to modify their attitudes toward the colors black and white and to determine whether a reduction of white bias toward animals and objects would generalize to people (Williams & Edwards, 1969). Using reinforcement techniques, the researchers were able to reduce—but not eliminate—white bias in preschool children. This reduction in bias was generalizable to people. Williams and Morland (1976) summarize this work in their book.

Perceptual Studies. In a series of trenchant and innovative studies, P. A. Katz (1973) and Katz and her colleagues (P. A. Katz, M. Sohn, & S. Zalk, 1975; P. A. Katz & S. Zalk, 1978) were able to help preschool White and African American children acquire more positive racial attitudes by teaching them to perceptually differentiate the faces of outgroup members. Katz and Zalk also investigated the effects of perceptual differentiation, vicarious interracial contact, direct interracial contact, and reinforcement of the color black on the racial attitudes of second- and fifth-grade children. They found that each of these interventions resulted in a short-term reduction of prejudice.

Curriculum Intervention Studies. A number of researchers working between 1969 and 1980 investigated the effects of curriculum interventions such as teaching units and lessons, multiethnic materials, role playing, and simulation on children's racial attitudes. These investigators included Litcher and Johnson (1969), Weiner and Wright (1973), and Yawkey and Blackwell (1974). In general, these studies indicate that curriculum interventions can modify student racial attitudes if certain conditions exist in the experimental situations. Highly focused interventions of sufficient duration are more likely to modify the racial attitudes of students than those that lack these characteristics. The younger students are, the more likely interventions will be successful. It becomes increasingly difficult to modify the racial attitudes of students as they grow older.

Cooperative Learning and Interracial Contact Studies. During the 1970s and 1980s, a group of investigators accumulated an impressive body of research on the effects of cooperative learning groups and activities on students' racial attitudes, friendship choices, and academic achievement. Most of this research is based on the contact hypothesis of intergroup relations formulated by Allport (1954; see Chapter 37, this volume). Investigators such as Aronson and his colleagues (Aronson & Bridgeman, 1979; Aronson & Gonzalez, 1988), Cohen (Cohen, 1972; Cohen & Roper, 1972), D. W. Johnson and R. T. Johnson (1981), and Slavin (1979) have conducted much of this research. It strongly supports the postulate that cooperative interracial contact situations in schools, if the conditions stated by Allport exist in the contact situations, have positive effects on both student interracial behavior and student academic achievement.

Very few studies on children's racial attitudes were published during the 1990s (Van Ausdale & Feagin, 2001). Several factors may explain the paucity of studies during this decade: the rise of conservatism in the United States during this time, the shifting of the nation's priorities to other research areas, and the view held by some leaders that the nation had focused enough energy and attention on the problems of minority groups and race. Many Americans also believed that the nation's racial problems had been solved during the civil rights period of the 1960s and 1970s (Schuman, Steeh, Bobo, & Krysan, 1997).

A ray of hope in race relations research on children developed when the Carnegie Corporation of New York funded 16 studies in the late 1990s that investigated ways to improve race relations among adolescents (National Research Council and Institute of Medicine, 2000). This group of studies produced important findings and provided essential support for scholars doing race relations research in schools. The National Research Council sponsored a workshop that focused on these studies. However, funding for this project was discontinued when the new leadership at the Carnegie Corporation formulated its priorities for the late 1990s and early 2000s.

THE LOSS OF HOPE AND
THE FADING OF THE DREAM

By the beginning of the 1980s, hope about the possibility of America eliminating poverty and racism had begun to fade, a culture of narcissism was on the rise, and conservative politicians were gaining increasing power in the states and in the federal government. The election of Ronald Reagan, the conservative Republican governor of California, to the presidency in November 1980 epitomized the political mood of the nation. Write Franklin and Moss (1988):

Ronald Reagan had said during his campaign—and he repeated it after his election—that government handouts made people "government dependent, rather than independent," and he wanted to put a stop to that. In office he pushed through Congress a number of programs in keeping with his views. His first budget as well as subsequent ones reduced the number of people eligible to participate in federal social programs such as food stamps, Medicaid, student loans, unemployment compensation, child nutrition assistance, and Aid to Families with Dependent Children. (p. 475)

A group of neoconservative scholars, notably Edward Banfield and Charles Murray, argued in books and articles that the federal government should reduce help to the poor because it made people dependent. Murray's book *Losing Ground: American Social Policy, 1950–1980,* published in 1984, marked the birth of a new paradigm that attacked the poor and argued for little government intervention. Just as Michael Harrington's 1962 book signaled the beginning of the war on poverty, Murray's book marked the beginning of "the war against the poor," the apt title of Herbert J. Gans's (1995) incisive book. The war against the poor experienced a major victory when the Welfare Reform Act of 1996 was enacted by both houses of Congress and signed by President Bill Clinton. This bill drastically reduced welfare benefits and institutionalized the idea that many low-income people were "the undeserving poor" (Katz, 1989).

THE COEXISTENCE OF CONSERVATIVE AND
PROGRESSIVE POLITICAL FORCES IN U.S. SOCIETY

The neoconservative movement in the United States that began in the post–civil rights years is characterized by attacks on the poor, affirmative action (Edley, 1996), ethnic studies programs (D'Souza, 1991), and bilingual education (Epstein, 1977). However, the period from 1980 to 2000 was marked by contradictions and competing forces in U.S. society. Both progressive and neoconservative forces competed to shape a new American identity and to influence research, policy, and educational practice.

Two political developments of the 1990s indicate the extent to which both progressive and conservative forces are influencing American society. Proposition 209, which prohibits affirmative action in state government and universities, was passed by the voters in California in November 1996. However, President Clinton, who opposed the initiative, received the electoral votes for the state, which helped him win reelection. Clinton's "mend it, but don't end it" position on affirmative action epitomizes the extent to which both progressive and conservative forces are competing to influence public policy in the United States.

The inability of conservative candidate George W. Bush to win a plurality of the popular votes in the 2000 presidential election and the remarkable showing of Green Party candidate Ralph Nader in several western states also indicate the extent to which conservative and progressive forces coexist in the United States. The strong negative reaction by many American citizens to the U.S. Supreme Court making a decision that resulted in Bush becoming the winner of the disputed election of 2000 is another indication of the political divisions and competing political forces in U.S. society.

Neoconservative and progressive forces and movements are both influencing research, curriculum, and teaching in U.S. society today. Books that attack diversity, such as Arthur M. Schlesinger, Jr.'s, (1991) *The Disuniting of America* and Dinesh D'Souza's (1991) *Illiberal Education,* became best-sellers and were widely discussed and influential within the academic and popular communities. *The Bell Curve,* by Herrnstein and Murray (1994), which argues that poor people and African Americans have less intellectual ability than middle-class Whites, was on the *New York Times* best-seller list for a number of weeks. It echoed and gave academic legitimacy to many of the institutionalized beliefs about poor people and African Americans within American society.

At the same time that books attacking ethnic studies and multicultural education and supporting inequality were enjoying a wide public reception, seminal research was being conducted and published in ethnic studies and in multicultural education. The years from 1980 to 2000 were one of the most prolific and productive periods in the development of ethnic studies scholarship and curriculum reform in the United States. Seminal and important works published in ethnic studies during this period include *The Signifying Monkey: A Theory of African-American Literary Criticism,* by Henry Louis Gates, Jr. (1988); *Black Feminist Thought,* by Patricia Hill Collins (2000); *A Different Mirror: A History of Multicultural America,* by Ronald Takaki (1993); *Black Women in America: An Historical Encyclopedia,* by Darlene Clark Hine (1993, two volumes); and the *Handbook of Research on Multicultural*

Education, edited by James A. Banks and Cherry A. McGee Banks (1995/2001). Each of these titles has enjoyed remarkable sales and warm receptions within the academic community.

The work by multicultural scholars has not been as successful at reaching the popular market as has the work of conservative scholars. There are a few notable exceptions, such as works by African American public intellectuals bell hooks, Henry Louis Gates, and Cornel West. West's (1993) *Race Matters* was on the *New York Times* best-seller list for many weeks. hooks has written a score of popular books that enjoy wide sales and high visibility among the public. Gates has published several popular books that have been widely disseminated. He also frequently contributes editorials to popular newspapers and magazines such as the *New York Times* and the *New York Times Book Review.* The reception of works by public intellectuals such as West, hooks, and Gates—and the success of the books by conservatives such as Schlesinger and D'Souza—indicate that the American public is as divided in its views as the academic community is.

LESSONS FROM HISTORY: TRANSFORMATIVE KNOWLEDGE AND HUMAN FREEDOM

The studies examined in this chapter indicate that the knowledge that scholars and public intellectuals create reflects the epistemological communities in which they are socialized; their social, political, economic, and cultural interests; and the times in which they live. This review also indicates that in every historical period, competing paradigms and forms of knowledge coexist; some reinforce the status quo and others challenge it. The groups exercising the most power within a society heavily influence what knowledge becomes legitimized and widely disseminated.

Scholars and public intellectuals in marginalized communities create knowledge that challenges the status quo and the dominant paradigms and explanations within a society. However, this knowledge is often marginalized within the mainstream academic community and remains largely invisible to the larger public. The knowledge that emanates from marginalized epistemological communities often contests existing political, economic, and educational practices and calls for fundamental change and reform. It often reveals the inconsistency between the democratic ideals within a society and its social arrangements and educational practices.

By revealing and articulating the inconsistency between the democratic ideals within a society and its practices, transformative knowledge becomes a potential source for substantial change. When combined with political and social action that reinforces its major claims, assumptions, and tenets, transformative knowledge can become an important factor in social, political, and educational change that promotes human rights and other democratic values.

The ethnic studies and multicultural education movements in the United States, which grew out of and reinforced the civil rights movement of the 1960s and 1970s, have created transformative knowledge that has brought many benefits to American intellectual and scholarly life. It has not only facilitated the process of democratization in the United States but has deeply influenced mainstream academic knowledge by helping to make it more truthful and more consistent with the realities of American life. It has also helped to liberate American students from many national myths and misconceptions and consequently given them more human freedom—which includes having the capacity to choose, the power to act to attain one's purposes, and the ability to help transform a world lived in common with others (Greene, 1988).

References

Aboud, F. (1988). *Children and prejudice.* Cambridge: Blackwell.

Acuña, R. (1981). *Occupied America: A history of Chicanos* (2nd ed.). New York: Harper & Row.

Adorno, T. W., Frenkel-Brunswik, E., Levinson, D. J., & Sanford, R. N. (1950). *The authoritarian personality.* New York: Norton.

Agnes, M. (1947). Influences of reading on the racial attitudes of adolescent girls. *Catholic Educational Review, 45,* 415–420.

Allport, G. W. (1954). *The nature of prejudice.* Reading, MA: Addison-Wesley.

Aptheker, H. (Ed.). (1983). *The complete published works of W.E.B. DuBois: Writings in periodicals edited by W.E.B. DuBois, selections from the crisis* (Vol. 1, 1911–1925). Millwood, NY: Kraus-Thomson.

Aronson, E., & Bridgeman, D. (1979). Jigsaw groups and the desegregated classroom: In pursuit of common goals. *Personality and Social Psychology Bulletin, 5,* 438–446.

Aronson, E., & Gonzalez, A. (1988). Desegregation, jigsaw, and the Mexican-American experience. In P. A. Katz & D. A. Taylor (Eds.), *Eliminating racism: Profiles in controversy* (pp. 301–314). New York: Plenum Press.

Bailey, T. A. (1961). *The American pageant: A history of the republic.* Boston: Heath.

Banks, C.A.M. (1996). The intergroup education movement. In J. A. Banks (Ed.), *Multicultural education, transformative knowledge, and action: Historical and contemporary perspectives* (pp. 251–277). New York: Teachers College Press.

Banks, C.A.M. (in progress). *The intergroup education movement: Insights from the past, lessons for the present and future.* New York: Teachers College Press.

Banks, J. A. (1993a). The canon debate, knowledge construction, and multicultural education. *Educational Researcher, 22*(5), 4–14.

Banks, J. A. (1993b). Multicultural education for young children: Racial and ethnic attitudes and their modification. In B. Spodek (Ed.), *Handbook of research on the education of young children* (pp. 236–250). New York: Macmillan.

Banks, J. A. (1995). The historical reconstruction of knowledge about race: Implications for transformative teaching. *Educational Researcher, 24*(2), 15–25.

Banks, J. A. (1996a). The African American roots of multicultural education. In J. A. Banks (Ed.), *Multicultural education, transformative knowledge, and action: Historical and contemporary perspectives* (pp. 30–45). New York: Teachers College Press.

Banks, J. A. (1996b). *Multicultural education, transformative knowledge, and action: Historical and contemporary perspectives.* New York: Teachers College Press.

Banks, J. A. (1998). The lives and values of researchers: Implications for educating citizens in a multicultural society. *Educational Researcher, 27*(7), 4–17.

Banks, J. A., & Banks, C.A.M. (Eds.). (2001). *Handbook of research on multicultural education.* San Francisco: Jossey-Bass.

Bennett, D. H. (1988). *The party of fear: From nativist movements to the new right in American history.* Chapel Hill: University of North Carolina Press.

Boas, F. (1910). The real racial problem. *Crisis, 1*(2), 2–15.

Boas, F. (1963). *The mind of primitive man* (Rev. ed.). New York: Free Press. (Original work published 1938)

Bourne, R. S. (1916, July). Trans-national America. *Atlantic Monthly, 18,* 95.

Brodkin, K. (1998). *How the Jews became White folks and what that says about race in America.* New Brunswick, NJ: Rutgers University Press.

Clark, K. B. (1965). *Dark ghetto: Dilemmas of social power.* New York: Harper & Row.

Clark, K. B., & Clark, M. P. (1939). The development of consciousness of self and the emergence of racial identification in Negro preschool children. *Journal of Social Psychology, 10,* 591–599.

Code, L. (1991). *What can she know? Feminist theory and the construction of knowledge.* Ithaca, NY: Cornell University Press.

Cohen, E. (1972). Interracial interaction disability. *Human Relations, 25,* 9–24.

Cohen, E. G., & Roper, S. S. (1972). Modification of interracial interaction disability: An application of status characteristic theory. *American Sociological Review, 37,* 643–657.

Collins, P. H. (2000). *Black feminist thought: Knowledge, consciousness, and the politics of empowerment* (Rev. ed.). New York: Routledge.

Cox, O. C. (1948). *Caste, class and race: A study in social dynamics.* New York: Monthly Review Press.

Cross, W. E., Jr. (1991). *Shades of Black: Diversity in African-American identity.* Philadelphia: Temple University Press.

D'Souza, D. (1991). *Illiberal education: The politics of race and sex on campus.* New York: Free Press.

DuBois, W.E.B. (1973). *The souls of Black folk: Essays and sketches.* Millwood, NY: Kraus-Thompson. (Original work published 1953)

Edley, C. (1996). *Not all Black and White: Affirmative action, race and American values.* New York: Hill & Wang.

Epstein, N. (1977). *Language, ethnicity, and the schools.* Washington, DC: George Washington University, Institute for Educational Leadership.

Feagin, J. R., & Sikes, M. P. (1994). *Living with racism: The Black middle-class experience.* Boston: Beacon Press.

Franklin, J. H. (1947). *From slavery to freedom: A history of Negro Americans* (1st ed.). New York: Knopf.

Franklin, J. H. (Chairman). (1998). *One America in the 21st century: Forging a new future.* President's Initiative on Race, Advisory Board's Report to the President. Washington, DC: U.S. Government Printing Office.

Franklin, J. H., & Moss, A. A., Jr. (1988). *From slavery to freedom: A history of Negro Americans* (6th ed.). New York: McGraw-Hill.

Gans, H. J. (1995). *The war against the poor: The underclass and antipoverty policy.* New York: Basic Books.

Gates, H. L., Jr. (1988). *The signifying monkey: A theory of African-American literary criticism.* New York: Oxford University Press.

Goodman, M. E. (1946). Evidence concerning the genesis of interracial attitudes. *American Anthropologist, 48,* 624–630.

Gordon, M. M. (1964). *Assimilation in American life.* New York: Oxford University Press.

Gould, S. J. (1996). *The mismeasure of man* (Rev. & expanded ed.). New York: Norton.

Grant, M. (1923). *The passing of the great race.* New York: Scribner.

Greene, M. (1988). *The dialectic of freedom.* New York: Teachers College Press.

Gutiérrez, R. A. (2001). Historical and social science research on Mexican Americans. In J. A. Banks & C.A.M. Banks (Eds.), *Handbook of research on multicultural education* (pp. 203–222). San Francisco: Jossey-Bass.

Halberstam, D. (1998). *The children.* New York: Random House.

Harding, S. (1991). *Whose knowledge? Whose science? Thinking from women's lives.* Ithaca, NY: Cornell University Press.

Harrington, M. (1962). *The other America.* New York: Macmillan.

Haynes, M. L., & Conklin, M. E. (1953). Intergroup attitudes and experimental change. *Journal of Experimental Education, 22,* 19–36.

Herrnstein, R. J., & Murray, C. (1994). *The bell curve: Intelligence and class structure in American life.* New York: Free Press.

Higham, J. (1972). *Strangers in the land: Patterns of American nativism 1860–1925.* New York: Atheneum.

Hillis, M. R. (1996). Research on racial attitudes: Historical perspectives. In J. A. Banks (Ed.), *Multicultural education, transformative knowledge, and action: Historical and contemporary perspectives* (pp. 278–293). New York: Teachers College Press.

Hine, D. C. (Ed.). (1993). *Black women in America: An historical encyclopedia* (2 vols.). Brooklyn, NY: Carlson.

Horowitz, E. L., & Horowitz, R. E. (1938). Development of social attitudes in children. *Sociometry, 1,* 301–338.

Jackson, E. P. (1944). Effects of reading upon attitudes toward the Negro race. *Library Quarterly, 14,* 47–54.

Jacobson, M. F. (1998). *Whiteness of a different color: European immigrants and the alchemy of race.* Cambridge, MA: Harvard University Press.

Jarvis, S. (1998). *Adorno: A critical introduction.* New York: Routledge.

Johnson, D. W., & Johnson, R. T. (1981). Effects of cooperative and individualistic learning experiences on interethnic interaction. *Journal of Educational Psychology, 73,* 444–449.

Johnson, L. B. (1964). The war on poverty. In *The annals of America* (Vol. 18, pp. 212–216). Chicago: Encyclopedia Britannica.

Kallen, H. (1924). *Culture and democracy in the United States.* New York: Boni & Liveright.

Katz, M. B. (1989). *The undeserving poor: From the war on poverty to the war on welfare.* New York: Pantheon.

Katz, P., Sohn, M., & Zalk, S. (1975). Perceptual concomitants of racial attitudes in urban grade school children. *Developmental Psychology, 11,* 135–144.

Katz, P. A. (1973). Perception of racial cues in preschool children: A new look. *Developmental Psychology, 8,* 295–299.

Katz, P. A., & Zalk, S. R. (1978). Modification of children's racial attitudes. *Developmental Psychology, 14,* 447–461.

Ladner, J. (1973). *The death of White sociology.* New York: Vintage Books.

Lasker, G. (1929). *Race attitudes in children.* New York: Henry Holt.

Lazarus, E. (1968). The new colossus. In *The Annals of America* (Vol. 11, p. 108). Chicago: Encyclopedia Britannica. (Original work published 1886)

Lemann, N. (1991). *The promised Land: The great Black migration and how it changed America.* New York: Knopf.

Lewis, D. L. (Ed.). (1995). *W.E.B. DuBois: A reader.* New York: Henry Holt.

Litcher, J. H., & Johnson, D. W. (1969). Changes in attitudes toward Negroes of White elementary school students after use of multiethnic readers. *Journal of Educational Psychology, 60,* 148–152.

Logan, R. W. (1997). *The betrayal of the Negro: From Rutherford B. Hayes to Woodrow Wilson.* New York: Da Capo Press. (Original work published 1954)

Mannheim, K. (1936). *Ideology and utopia: An introduction to the sociology of knowledge.* New York: Harper.

Marable, M. (1996). *Speaking truth to power: Essays on race, resistance, and radicalism.* Boulder, CO: Westview Press.

Miller, K. (1908). *Race adjustment: Essays on the Negro in America.* New York: Neale.

Montalto, N. V. (1982). *A history of the intercultural education movement 1924–1941.* New York: Garland.

Murray, C. (1984). *Losing ground: American social policy, 1950–1980.* New York: Basic Books.

Myrdal, G. (1944). *An American dilemma: The Negro problem and modern democracy.* New York: Harper & Row.

Myrdal, G. (1969). *Objectivity in social research.* Middletown, CT: Wesleyan University Press.

National Advisory Commission on Civil Disorders. (1968). *Report of the national advisory commission on civil disorders* (2 vols.). Washington, DC: U.S. Government Printing Office.

National Research Council and Institute of Medicine. (2000). *Improving intergroup relations among youth: Summary of a workshop.* Washington, DC: National Academy Press.

O'Connor, B. (Ed.). (2000). *The Adorno reader.* Malden, MA: Blackwell.

Okihiro, G. Y. (1994). *Margins and mainstreams: Asians in American history and culture.* Seattle: University of Washington Press.

Roche, A. M. (1996). Carter G. Woodson and the development of transformative scholarship. In J. A. Banks (Ed.), *Multicultural education, transformative knowledge, and action: Historical and contemporary perspectives* (pp. 91–114). New York: Teachers College Press.

Rodríguez, C. E. (1989). *Puerto Ricans born in the USA.* Boston: Unwin Hyman.

Rodríguez, C. E. (2001). Puerto Ricans in historical and social science research. In J. A. Banks & C.A.M. Banks (Eds.), *Handbook of research on multicultural education* (pp. 223–244). San Francisco: Jossey-Bass.

Schlesinger, A. M., Jr. (1991). *The disuniting of America: Reflections on a multicultural society.* Knoxville, TN: Whittle Direct Books.

Schuman, H., Steeh, C., Bobo, L., & Krysan, M. (1997). *Racial attitudes in America* (Rev. ed.). Cambridge, MA: Harvard University Press.

Slavin, R. E. (1979). Effects of biracial learning teams on cross-racial friendships. *Journal of Educational Psychology, 71,* 381–387.

Slavin, R. E. (2001). Cooperative learning and intergroup relations. In J. A. Banks & C.A.M. Banks (Eds.), *Handbook of research on multicultural education* (pp. 628–634). San Francisco: Jossey-Bass.

Southern, D. W. (1987). *Gunnar Myrdal and Black-White relations: The use and abuse of an American dilemma.* Baton Rouge: Louisiana State University Press.

Spencer, M. B. (1982). Personal and group identity of Black children: An alternative synthesis. *Genetic Psychology Monographs, 106,* 59–84.

Stephan, W. (1999). *Reducing prejudice and stereotyping in schools.* New York: Teachers College Press.

Stoddard, T. L. (1920). *The rising tide of color against White world supremacy.* New York: Scribner.

Taba, H., Brady, E., & Robinson, J. (1952). *Intergroup education in public schools.* Washington, DC: American Council on Education.

Takaki, R. (1993). *A different mirror: A history of multicultural America.* New York: Little, Brown.

Trager, H. G., & Yarrow, M. R. (1952). *They learn what they live: Prejudice in young children.* New York: Harper.

United States Census Bureau (2000). *Statistical abstract of the United States: 2000* (120th ed.). Washington, DC: U.S. Government Printing Office.

Van Ausdale, D. V., & Feagin, J. R. (2001). *The first R: How children learn race and racism.* New York: Rowman & Littlefield.

Weiner, M. J., & Wright, F. E. (1973). Effects of undergoing arbitrary discrimination upon subsequent attitudes toward a minority group. *Journal of Applied Social Psychology, 3,* 94–102.

West, C. (1993). *Race matters.* Boston: Beacon Press.

Williams, J. E., & Edwards, C. D. (1969). An exploratory study of the modification of color and racial concept attitudes in preschool children. *Child Development, 40,* 737–750.

Williams, J. E., & Morland, J. K. (1976). *Race, color, and the young child.* Chapel Hill: University of North Carolina Press.

Wilson, W. J. (1978). *The declining significance of race: Blacks and changing American institutions.* Chicago: University of Chicago Press.

Woodson, C. G. (1933). *The mis-education of the Negro.* Washington, DC: Associated Publishers.

Yawkey, T. D., & Blackwell, J. (1974). Attitudes of 4-year-old urban Black children toward themselves and Whites based upon multiethnic social studies materials and experiences. *Journal of Educational Research, 67,* 373–377.

13

CRITICAL PEDAGOGY, CRITICAL RACE THEORY, AND ANTIRACIST EDUCATION

Implications for Multicultural Education

Christine E. Sleeter
California State University, Monterey Bay

Dolores Delgado Bernal
University of Utah

Multicultural education grew out of social protest movements of the 1960s, particularly challenges to racism in education. Banks (Chapter 1, this volume) traces the roots of multicultural education to the ethnic studies movement of the 1960s, which is itself a legacy of earlier ethnic studies pioneers such as Carter G. Woodson and W.E.B. DuBois. During the 1960s, in the context of social activism addressing a range of manifestations of racism, community groups, students, and ethnic studies scholars pressed for the inclusion of ethnic content in the curriculum in order to bring intellectual counternarratives to the dominant Eurocentric narratives. Multicultural education thus began as a scholarly and activist movement to transform schools and their contexts. Over time, as more and more people have taken up and used multicultural education, it has come to have an ever wider array of meanings. In the process, ironically (given its historical roots), a good deal of what occurs within the arena of multicultural education today does not address power relations critically, particularly racism. This chapter will review some of today's critical discourses for their implications for multicultural education. Our intent is not to move multicultural education away from its core conceptual moorings, but rather to anchor the field more firmly in those moorings.

Many contemporary renderings of multicultural education examine difference without connecting it to power or a critical analysis of racism. This is probably because the great majority of classroom teachers and school administrators are White and bring a worldview that tacitly condones existing race and class relations. For example, Sleeter (1992) studied a group of teachers who had volunteered to participate in a staff development project in multicultural education. Of 26 who discussed what multicultural education meant to them by the second year of the project, 7 White teachers saw it as irrelevant to their work and 6 White teachers saw its main purpose as helping students learn to get along with each other. Eight teachers (1 African American and the rest White ESL or special education teachers) saw multicultural education as building students' self-esteem in response to exclusion of some students' experience in school and the wider society. Five (2 African American and 3 White) had more complex conceptions, but only one of these directly connected multicultural education with social activism. In short, almost all of these educators filtered their understanding of multicultural education through conceptual discourses of individualism and psychology and took for granted as neutral the existing structures and processes of school and its relationship to communities.

At the same time that multicultural education has been acquiring a range of meanings, many theorists and educators (inside and outside multicultural education) who are concerned about racism, oppression, and how to build democracy in historically racist and hierarchical multicultural societies have advanced perspectives that explicitly address social justice. To distinguish these perspectives from noncritical orientations toward multicultural education, some have begun using the term *critical multiculturalism* (e.g., Kanpol & McLaren, 1995; May, 1999a; Obidah, 2000).

Some conceptions of critical multiculturalism foreground racism. On the basis of an analysis of teacher education student responses to a discussion of race, Berlak and Moyenda (2001) argued that liberal conceptions of multiculturalism support "white privilege by rendering institutional racism invisible," leading to the belief that injustices will disappear if people simply learn to get along (p. 94). They stated that "central to critical multiculturalism is naming and actively challenging racism and other forms of injustice, not simply recognizing and celebrating differences and reducing prejudice" (p. 92). McCarthy (1995) argued that various models of multicultural education rest far too heavily on attitude change as a means of social transformation and take for granted essentialized racial identities, failing to situate racial inequality within global relations. Critical multiculturalism "links the microdynamics of the school curriculum to larger issues of social relations outside the school" (p. 43). Similarly, in an effort to join antiracism with multicultural education, May (1999a) stated that critical multiculturalism "incorporates postmodern conceptions and analyses of culture and identity, while holding onto the possibility of an emancipatory politics" (pp. 7–8).

Other conceptions link multiculturalism with critical pedagogy (Kanpol & McLaren, 1995; Kincheloe & Steinberg, 1997). Kanpol and McLaren used the term *critical multiculturalism* to emphasize that "justice is not evenly distributed and cannot be so without a radical and profound change in social structures and in terms of a development of historical agency and a praxis of possibility" (p. 13). Obidah (2000) described herself as a critical multiculturalist because the tools of both critical pedagogy and multicultural education have helped her link a dynamic conception of culture, identity, and lived experience with an analysis of power structures and pedagogy.

This chapter explores the implications of critical traditions for multicultural education in order to connect it more firmly to its transformative roots and to encourage dialogue across contemporary critical traditions. We realized that in order to keep the chapter manageable, we could focus on only three traditions. We selected critical pedagogy, critical race theory, and antiracist education. The chapter therefore omits groundbreaking work in multicultural feminism (e.g., Collins, 1990), critical cultural studies (e.g., Hall, 1993), and disability studies (e.g., Linton, 1998), which also have implications for multicultural education. Each section that follows provides a brief genealogy, implications, and limitations for each of the three bodies of literature as they relate to multicultural education. The final section of the chapter sketches out a

synthesis of this analysis; in the process it suggests the need to expand the dialogue among critical pedagogy, critical race theory, antiracist education, and multicultural education.

CRITICAL PEDAGOGY AND MULTICULTURAL EDUCATION

Critical pedagogy can be defined as "an entry point in the contradictory nature of schooling, a chance to force it toward creating conditions for a new public sphere" (Giroux, 1983, p. 116). According to Giroux (1992), critical pedagogy should "explore how pedagogy functions as a cultural practice to *produce* rather than merely *transmit* knowledge within the asymmetrical relations of power that structure teacher-student relations" (p. 98). Theorists of critical pedagogy view schools as "contradictory social sites" (Giroux, 1983, p. 115) in which class relations are not simply reproduced but also contested through the actions students and educators construct every day. As such, youth could learn collectively to construct a new democratic public sphere. Critical pedagogy, then, offers a language of both "analysis and hope" (McLaren, 1991, p. 30). Gay (1995) described many conceptual parallels between multicultural education and critical pedagogy and advocated an active coalition between the fields.

Critical pedagogy can be traced to at least two genealogical roots: (a) critical theory and the Frankfurt School and (b) the work of Paulo Freire and Latin American liberation movements. The Frankfurt School, which began in Germany prior to World War II, connected a Marxist analysis of class structure with psychological theories of the unconscious to understand how oppressive class relations are produced and reproduced. The culturalist paradigm of the Frankfurt School emphasized human agency, focusing on the lived experiences of people and how consciousness is formed within class struggles. The structuralist paradigm analyzed how oppressive political and economic structures are reproduced, but it tended to ignore or deny personal agency (Giroux, 1983). The rise of Nazism in Germany caused many members of the Frankfurt School to flee to the United States, where theorists in many disciplines took up critical theory. Critical theorists do not necessarily practice or write about critical pedagogy. In the 1980s, theorists such as Henry Giroux and Peter McLaren applied critical theory's analytical tools to pedagogy, creating a "pedagogy of critical theory" (Pruyn, 1994, p. 38). According to Giroux (1983), critical pedagogy seeks to "bridge the agency-structural dualism" of the Frankfurt School by viewing youth culture as a site of cultural production, social struggle, and social transformation (p. 139).

A second genealogical root of critical pedagogy is the work of Freire (1970, 1973, 1976) and Latin American liberation movements. Freire began writing while in exile in Chile. He had promoted popular literacy in Brazil, connecting the act of reading with the development of critical consciousness. Freire argued throughout his life that oppressed people need to develop a critical consciousness that will enable them to denounce dehumanizing social structures and announce social transformation. In the process of teaching literacy to adults, he created culture circles in which students took up topics of concern to them, discussed and debated in order to clarify and develop their thinking, and developed strategies for action. Freire did not call these culture circles "schools" because of the passivity traditionally associated with school learning. A fundamental task in culture circles was to distinguish between what humans have created and what nature created, in order to examine what role humans can play in bringing about change. Freire's connection between critical education and political work for liberation took up questions similar to those being asked by critical theorists.

Potential Implications of Critical Pedagogy for Multicultural Education

Critical pedagogy has four main implications for multicultural education: (a) conceptual tools for critical reflexivity; (b) an analysis of class, corporate power, and globalization; (c) an analysis of empowering pedagogical practices within the classroom; and (d) a deeper analysis of language and literacy than one finds generally in the multicultural education literature.

Critical pedagogy as a theoretical space develops several concepts that relate to multicultural education, among them voice, culture, power, culture, and ideology. In so doing, it offers tools for critical reflexivity on those concepts. *Voice* is grounded in Freire's notion of dialogical communication, which rejects both the authoritarian imposition of knowledge and also the idea that everyone's beliefs are equal. To Freire (1998), the development of democratic life requires critical engagement with ideas through dialogue. Dialogue demands engagement; it occurs neither when some parties opt out silently nor when those with the most power simply impose their views. Voice is rooted in experience that is examined for its interests, principles, values, and historical remembrances (Darder, 1995; Giroux, 1988; hooks, 1994). The concepts of voice and dialogue act as tools for uncovering whose ideas are represented and whose ideas have been submerged, marginalized, or left out entirely.

Critical pedagogy offers tools for examining the concept of *culture*. Simplistic conceptions of culture are common in multicultural education, although many multiculturalists

also critique them. McCarthy (1998) noted that too often "culture, identity, and community are narrowly read as the final property of particular groups based on ethnic origins" (p. 148); for example, teachers commonly conflate ethnicity and culture, seeing them as synonymous. Within this conception of culture, "multiculturalism is generally about Otherness" in a way that makes Whiteness and racial struggle invisible and takes for granted boundaries of race, ethnicity, and power (Giroux, 1992, p. 117). Whose conceptions of culture tend to predominate, and what gets left out of those conceptions? For example, hybrid cultural identities defy fixed and essentialized definitions of culture (e.g., see Darder, 1995; McCarthy, 1998). Dominant cultures can be examined with much greater depth when contextualized within relations of colonialism and power than when they are decontextualized (McLaren & Mayo, 1999). Popular culture as a form of collective meaning making also "counts" as culture (Giroux & Simon, 1989; Livingstone, 1987; Shor, 1980).

Power is yet another concept within multicultural education that critical pedagogy helps to examine (Kincheloe & Steinberg, 1997). Giroux (1985) pointed out that some progressive and multicultural education discourses "quietly ignore the complexity and sweat of social change" and reduce power and domination to misunderstandings that can be corrected by providing accurate information (p. 31). Challenging power relations is central to critical pedagogy (Freire, 1970), which is based on an analysis of structural as well as cultural power. It is the centrality of interrogating how power works and how power relations can be challenged that led McLaren (2000) to focus on revolution rather than reform. Multicultural education in its inception challenged power relations, particularly racism, and for some multicultural educators power remains a central concept. However, power is often displaced by more comfortable concepts such as tolerance. Critical pedagogy offers an important critique of that displacement and continues to ask the question, Comfortable for whom?

Ideology is a concept that is central to critical pedagogy but used surprisingly little in multicultural education. Ideology refers to "the formation of the consciousness of the individuals" in a society, particularly their consciousness about how the society works (Apple, 1979, p. 2). Within multicultural education, curriculum is often discussed in terms of bias, a concept that does not necessarily lead to an analysis of power and consciousness. Similarly, examining teachers in terms of attitudes focuses on individual psychology rather than collective power. Ideology offers a much more powerful conceptual tool, connecting meanings with structures of power on the one hand and with individuals on the other. Ideology as a tool of analysis "helps to locate the structuring principles and ideas that mediate between the dominant society and the everyday experiences of teachers and students" (Giroux, 1983, p. 161). It helps us examine who produces what kinds of ideologies, why some ideologies prevail, and whose interests they serve (see Apple, 2000). Ideology can also serve as a reflexive tool of critique when multicultural education itself is conceived as a field of discourse. Lei (2001), for example, examined the ideology of multicultural education as it was used in specific contexts in order to question whose interests those conceptions served, what issues they foreground, and whose interests and points of view were displaced.

A second potential implication of critical pedagogy is its analysis of social class, class power, corporate power, and global corporate control. Although multicultural education grew primarily out of racial and ethnic struggle, critical pedagogy grew primarily out of class struggle. In the United States, connections between race and class tend to be undertheorized partially because of the myth that the United States is a "classless" society, which leads to a general refusal to examine class relations critically. Yet the forms and persistence of racism can be understood more clearly when racism is connected historically with capitalism (Marable, 2000; Roediger, 1991; Sleeter, 2001). Freire (1973) specifically located his work in a history of colonialism and class struggle: "It was upon this vast lack of democratic experience, characterized by feudal mentality and sustained by a colonial economic and social structure, that we attempted to inaugurate a formal democracy" (p. 28).

Connections between racism and global capitalism lend urgency to the significance of class. Over the past two decades, a small corporate elite has extended global control markedly and consolidated means for wealth accumulation. At the same time, however, even critical pedagogues have retreated from concern with class and capitalism. McLaren (1998) argued that the "growing diasporic movements of immigrants in search of employment across national boundaries" has led to an increased discourse around ethnicity, but domesticated ways of thinking about it have displaced critiques of capitalist expansion. Given the rampant and unchecked expansion of global capitalism, critical pedagogy and multicultural education need to "address themselves to the adaptive persistence of capitalism and to issues of capitalist imperialism and its specific manifestations of accumulative capacities through conquest" (1998). Multicultural education could benefit from a trenchant analysis of capitalist expansion and global capitalism. Increased poverty, racial strife, incarceration of youth of color, movements of people around the globe, and corporate-driven school reforms can be understood more clearly when class is part of the analysis. That is not to imply that class should be given primacy over race or gender, but rather that these

concepts should be developed as connected structures of oppression, lenses of analysis, and sites of struggle.

A third potential implication of critical pedagogy for multicultural education is its examination of how power plays out in the classroom, and its connection of pedagogical processes with empowerment. In this regard, critical pedagogy and feminist pedagogy share similar concerns (hooks, 1994; Lather, 1991). Multicultural education as a field has extensively examined school knowledge and developed insights for transformative curricula, usually discussing pedagogy mainly in relationship to strategies that support high achievement for all students (e.g., Banks, 1999; Bennett, 1998). Critical pedagogy complements this work by conceptualizing students as creators of knowledge and by connecting student-generated knowledge with student empowerment. Freire (1970) explicitly rejected a "banking" form of pedagogy "in which students are the depositories and the teacher is the depositor" (p. 53), viewing it as an instrument of control over the masses. Instead, he viewed empowering pedagogy as a dialogical process in which the teacher acts as a partner with students, helping them examine the world critically, using a problem-posing process that begins with their own experience and historical location.

Several critical pedagogy theorists have written about the use of this form of pedagogy in their own classrooms. Most of these discussions focus on adult students (e.g., Ada, 1988; Curtis & Rasool, 1997; Mayo, 1999; Shor, 1980, 1992; R. I. Simon, 1992; Sleeter, 1995; Solorzano, 1989), although a few focus on the K-12 level (Bigelow, 1990; Goldstein, 1995; Peterson, 1991). In all of these discussions, pedagogy starts with students' lived experience and involves students in analysis of that experience. Students are treated as active agents of knowledge creation, and classrooms as democratic public spheres. Class materials are used as tools for expanding students' analyses, rather than as content that is simply deposited into the students. This view of pedagogy complements multicultural education well.

A fourth potential implication of critical pedagogy for multicultural education is its analysis of language and literacy, which connects to concerns of bilingual educators. Multicultural education and bilingual education have emerged as distinct fields, with some overlap. For example, an ERIC search in June 2001 yielded 5,117 journal articles with *multicultural education* as a keyword and 3,216 journal articles with *bilingual education* as a keyword, but only 431 articles with both *multicultural education* and *bilingual education*. Language and culture are part of each other; the fields need bridging, and critical pedagogy is one bridge.

Drawing from his experience teaching literacy to adults, Freire distinguished between technical and critical approaches to literacy. A technical approach focuses on language as a subject distinct from the world of students, or "words emptied of the reality they are meant to represent" (Freire, 1973, p. 37). Critical literacy begins with words within students' experience and then situates them historically, helping students learn to question their world, with language serving as a tool of critical analysis. Language, then, is a key tool in development of consciousness and voice. Macedo and Bartolome (1999) challenged the notion that multicultural education can take place in English only, noting that "one cannot celebrate different cultural values through the very dominant language that devalues, in many ways, the cultural experiences of different cultural groups," and that "language is the only means through which one comes to consciousness" (p. 34). Identity, values, experiences, interpretations, and ideologies are encoded linguistically; one knows the world and oneself through language. Because consciousness is shaped through language, language can serve as a means of control as well as a means of liberation (Giroux & McLaren, 1992; Macedo, 1994).

These ideas resonate with many second language teachers and bilingual educators who are conscious of oppression. For example, on the basis of his work as an ESL (English as a Second Language) teacher to adult farmworkers, Graman (1988) explained that when language was treated as a subject abstracted from everyday life, students lost interest. Drawing language from life and then examining students' problems and dreams politically in the context of second language instruction engaged them in learning and helped them use education to act on their own behalf. In short, critical pedagogy can enrich analysis of language within multicultural education.

Limitations of Critical Pedagogy and Its Implications for Multicultural Education

Critical pedagogy has two major limitations that need to be acknowledged. First, although it developed through practice in Latin America, within the United States it has been developed mainly at a theoretical level, often leaving practitioners unclear about what to do. Its theoretical writings tend to be conceptually dense, which many practitioners find difficult to understand, although one can find literature that shows what critical pedagogy "looks like" in practice (e.g., Bromley, 1989; Pruyn, 1994, 1999; Students for Cultural and Linguistic Democracy, 1996; Wink, 1997). In this, a strength and limitation of critical pedagogy are joined. Critical pedagogues argue that the ideology of the teacher is of central importance; critical pedagogy cannot be reduced to method or technique. At the same time, teachers need guidance when translating ideological clarity into practice; radical teachers can still teach in very traditional ways (Pruyn, 1999). This translation needs to go far beyond learning steps or seeing

lesson plans, since critical pedagogy directly opens up very difficult and painful issues in the classroom (Ellsworth, 1989; Obidah, 2000). We have worked with many teachers who, even when they are drawn to ideas of critical pedagogy, end up dismissing it because they do not know what to do with it in their classrooms. Particularly given the back-to-basics turn of the past several years, critical pedagogy suggests a very different paradigm from that institutionalized in most schools. There is a need for practical guidance that does not, in the process, sacrifice conceptual grounding.

Second, most of the literature in critical pedagogy does not directly address race, ethnicity, or gender, and as such it has a White bias. Since much of it grows from a class analysis, with some exceptions it foregrounds social class. Critical pedagogy may well appeal to radical White educators who see class as the main axis of oppression, but doing so can marginalize race and have the effect of elevating the power of largely White radical theorists over theorists of color, even if this is not intended. Further, White theorists taking on race and racism does not resolve the problem of Whites having the power to define how race and racism are theorized. In a discussion of Chicana/o border pedagogy, Elenes (1997) argued that people of color must articulate theory for themselves. However helpful writings of White critical pedagogues might be, White writers still produce silences and assumptions that arise from lived experiences. She writes:

Much of the problematic of this discussion over differences is that until recently only those who were marked as different were considered in the theorization of difference. If differences are going to be constituted in nonessentialist ways, it is necessary to mark, deconstruct, and decenter whiteness and privilege. (p. 371)

Elenes found much value in critical pedagogy writings, but at the same time she pointed out that the privilege of White theorists needs to be examined critically.

Grande (2000) took this argument further, pointing out ideas and assumptions that are central to critical pedagogy that clash with indigenous perspectives. Critical pedagogues question essentialized identities and value border crossing, while the history of border crossing and blending cultures has meant "Whitestream America . . . appropriating Native lands, culture, spiritual practices, history and literature" (p. 481). Further, the "seemingly liberatory constructs of fluidity, mobility, and transgression" are part of "the fundamental lexicon of Western imperialism" (p. 483). Thus, although the insights of critical pedagogy and their implications for multicultural education are valuable, one also needs to be concerned with how the power to name the issues affects both which issues get addressed and whose interests are served in the process.

CRITICAL RACE THEORY AND MULTICULTURAL EDUCATION

Critical race theory is an analytical framework developed primarily, though not exclusively, by legal scholars of color to address social justice and racial oppression in U.S. society. According to Delgado and Stefancic (2001), "The critical race theory (CRT) movement is a collection of activists and scholars interested in studying and transforming the relationship among race, racism, and power" (p. 2). Among CRT's basic theoretical themes is that of privileging contextual and historical descriptions over abstract or ahistorical ones. It is therefore important to understand the genealogy of CRT in education with respect to its contextual and historical relations to critical legal studies, the civil rights movement, radical/U.S. third-world feminisms, and the other theoretical traditions from which it borrows (Matsuda, Lawrence, Delgado, & Crenshaw, 1993). Its conception can be located in the mid-1970s with the work of legal scholars such as Derrick Bell and Alan Freeman, who were frustrated with the slow pace of racial reform within the liberal civil rights tradition in the United States. They were joined by other legal scholars, students, and activists who felt that the advances of the civil rights movement had been stalled and in fact were being rolled back (Delgado & Stefancic, 2000).

During the 1980s, CRT continued to emerge as a response to critical legal studies (CLS). CLS originated with a predominantly White male group of leftist law professors who challenged the traditional legal scholarship that creates, supports, and legitimates social power in U.S. society (Matsuda et al., 1993). As Wing (1997) pointed out, "People of color, white women, and others were attracted by CLS because it challenged orthodox ideas about the inviolability and objectivity of laws that oppressed minorities and white women for centuries" (p. 2). However, some of these scholars also felt that CLS excluded the perspectives of people of color and that the CLS movement was inattentive to racism's role in both the U.S. legal system and U.S. society. As a result, legal scholars of color began articulating a theory of race and racism that "allows us to better understand how racial power can be produced even from within a liberal discourse that is relatively autonomous from organized vectors of racial power" (Crenshaw, Gotanda, Peller, & Thomas, 1995, p. xxv).

Just as CRT builds on the insights and weaknesses of CLS, it also draws on the work of ethnic studies and U.S. third-world feminisms. Some would argue that the genealogy of CRT goes back as far as W.E.B. DuBois, Sojourner Truth, Frederick Douglass, Cesar Chavez, and the Black Power and Chicano movements of the 1960s and 1970s (Delgado & Stefancic, 2001). Most recently, critical race theory has borrowed much from the postmodern cultural revolution in the humanities and from postcolonialism and poststructuralism (Roithmayr, 1999). Indeed, CRT has expanded to include complementary branches such as Latina/o critical race theory (LatCrits), critical race feminists (FemCrits), and Tribal Crits (Brayboy, 2001). These branches continue to influence and reshape a growing CRT movement that includes more than 400 CRT law review articles and dozens of books (Solorzano & Yosso, 2001).

Although CRT began in legal studies, it has spread to other disciplines, including education. One might think of CRT in education as a developing theoretical, conceptual, methodological, and pedagogical strategy that accounts for the role of race and racism in U.S. education and works toward the elimination of racism as part of a larger goal of eliminating other forms of subordination (Solorzano, 1998). Since 1994, scholars of color in the field of education have been increasingly employing it in their research and practice. Tate's autobiographical article in *Urban Education* (1994) was the first explicit use of CRT in education. A year later, Ladson-Billings and Tate (1995) laid the conceptual background for much of the applied CRT work done shortly thereafter. Today a growing body of scholarship in education uses CRT as a framework to examine a variety of educational issues at both the K-12 and the postsecondary levels (e.g., Aguirre, 2000; Gonzalez, 1998; Ladson-Billings, 1998, 1999, 2000; Lynn, 1999; Parker, Deyhle, & Villenas 1999; Solorzano, 1997, 1998; Solorzano & Delgado Bernal, 2001; Solorzano & Villalpando, 1998; Solorzano & Yosso, 2000, 2001; Tate, 1997; Villenas & Deyhle, 1999). Special journal issues on CRT in education have also appeared (*International Journal of Qualitative Studies in Education*, 1998; *Qualitative Inquiry*, 2002; *Equity and Excellence in Education*, 2002).

Potential Implications of Critical Race Theory for Multicultural Education

Critical race theory has at least three important implications for multicultural education: (a) it theorizes about race while also addressing the intersectionality of racism, classism, sexism, and other forms of oppression; (b) it challenges Eurocentric epistemologies and dominant ideologies such as meritocracy, objectivity, and neutrality; and (c) it uses counterstorytelling as a methodological and pedagogical tool.

Although multicultural education emerged as a challenge to racism in schools, its writings tend to focus on classroom practices without necessarily contextualizing classrooms within an analysis of racism. Teacher training in multicultural education often takes the form of offering solutions to problems connected to race and ethnicity without digging very deeply into the nature of the problem. CRT in education is similar to antiracist education (discussed in the next section) because it is a social justice paradigm that seeks to combat racism as part of a larger goal of ending all forms of subordination. Education scholars using CRT theorize about "raced" education in ways found too infrequently in multicultural education. As Ladson-Billings and Tate (1995) pointed out, there is a need to do this because race remains untheorized as a topic of scholarly inquiry in education. Although scholars have examined race as a tool for understanding social inequities, "the intellectual salience of this theorizing has not been systematically employed in the analysis of educational inequality" (p. 50). CRT scholars believe that race as an analytical tool, rather than a biological or socially constructed category used to compare and contrast social conditions, can deepen the analysis of educational barriers for people of color, as well as illuminate how they resist and overcome these barriers.

One example of using race as an analytical tool is found within what Ladson-Billings and Tate (1995) called the "property issue." Critical race legal scholars introduced the property issue by examining the historical construction of Whiteness as the most valued type of property and how the concept of individual rights has been linked to property rights in the United States since the writing of the U.S. Constitution (Bell, 1987, Harris, 1993). Ladson-Billings and Tate demonstrated that property relates to education in explicit and implicit ways. One obvious example is how property owners largely reap the highest educational benefits: those with the best property are entitled to the best schools. They write, "Recurring discussions about property tax relief indicate that more affluent communities (which have higher property values, hence higher tax assessments) resent paying for a public school system whose clientele is largely non-white and poor" (p. 53). An implicit way in which property relates to education is the way in which curriculum represents a form of "intellectual property" that is interconnected to race. The quality and quantity of the curriculum varies with the "property values" of the school so that intellectual property is directly connected to "real" property in the form of course offerings, classroom resources, science labs, technology, and certified and prepared teachers (Ladson-Billings & Tate, 1995).

In addition to using race as an analytical tool, critical race theorists challenge the separate discourses on race, class, and gender and focus on the intersectionality of subordination (Solorzano & Yosso, 2002). Crenshaw (1993) saw intersectionality as a concept that links various forms of oppression (racism, classism, sexism) with their political consequences (e.g., global capitalism, growing poverty, large numbers of incarcerated youth of color). The property issue is an example of how the intersection of race and class interests offers a more complete understanding of the current inequities in schools and districts in which the majority of students are poor and of color.

Recently, the branch of CRT called Latina/o critical race theory (LatCrit) has added layers of complexity to the concept of intersectionality by analyzing Latina/o identities and positionalities in relation to race, class, and gender, as well as language (Romany, 1996), immigration (Garcia, 1995; Johnson, 1996–97), culture (Montoya, 1994, 1997), religion/spirituality (Iglesias & Valdes, 1998; Sanchez, 1998), and sexuality (Iglesias & Valdes, 1998). For example, Villalpando (2003) used a CRT and LatCrit framework to examine how Chicana/o college students draw from their language, religion/spirituality, and culture as tools in their struggle for success in higher education. He uses a counterstory methodology and an intersectional analysis to highlight cultural practices and beliefs of the peer group that function as empowering and nourishing cultural resources for Chicana/o students. One of the more important cultural practices is how the peer group adopts roles and characteristics of a student's family of origin. In other words, Chicana/o peers often offer support, understanding, or admonishment similar to what they receive at home. This cultural practice helped Chicana/o students cope with the marginalization they experienced via racist structures, practices, and discourses in higher education.

These types of analyses could contribute to multicultural education by interrogating the racialized context of teaching, and connecting race with multiple forms of oppression. Multicultural research conducted within a CRT framework might offer a way to understand and analyze the multiple identities and knowledges of people of color without essentializing their various experiences.

A second potential contribution of CRT is the way that it challenges Eurocentric epistemology and questions dominant discursive notions of meritocracy, objectivity, knowledge, and individualism. The concept of epistemology is more than just a "way of knowing" and can be defined as a "system of knowing" that is linked to worldviews that are based on the conditions under which people live and learn (Ladson-Billings, 2000). Ladson-Billings argues that "there are well-developed systems of knowledge, or epistemologies, that stand in contrast to the dominant Euro-American epistemology" (p. 258). Critical race theorists ground their research in these systems of knowledge and "integrate their experiential knowledge, drawn from a shared history as 'other' with their ongoing struggles to transform" (Barnes, 1990, pp. 1864–1865).

For example, in his study of socially active African American teachers, Lynn (1999) drew from African-centered epistemological paradigms and critical race theory to theorize about a critical race pedagogy that is in part based on a system of knowledge that counters the dominant Euro-American epistemology. He defined critical race pedagogy as "an analysis of racial, ethnic, and gender subordination in education that relies mostly on the perceptions, experiences, and counterhegemonic practices of educators of color" (p. 615). On the basis of the reflections of African American educators, he argued that critical race pedagogues are concerned with a number of issues: the endemic nature of racism in the United States; the importance of cultural identity; the necessary interaction of race, class, and gender; and the practice of liberatory pedagogy. Practicing a liberatory pedagogy was in some ways similar to the Freirean notion of critical pedagogy that encourages inquiry, dialogue, and participation in the classroom. However, Lynn demonstrated two key differences between a critical pedagogy and a critical race pedagogy: the daily struggle against racist discursive practices provided African American teachers with a unique position from which to build their curricula, and there was a strong emphasis on developing and maintaining a sense of cultural identity by teaching children about Africa and African American cultural experiences.

By grounding itself in systems of knowledge that counter a dominant Eurocentric epistemology, critical race theory in education offers a tool for dismantling prevailing notions of fairness, meritocracy, colorblindness, and neutrality (Parker, Deyhle, & Villenas, 1999). Raced and gendered epistemologies allow CRT scholars to deconstruct master narratives and illustrate the way in which discursive and cultural sites "may be a form of colonialism, a way of imparting white, Westernized conceptions of enlightened thinking" (Roithmayr, 1999, p. 5). For example, Gutiérrez (2000) examined Walt Disney's ideological shift from conservatism (1930s–1970s) to present-day liberal multiculturalism, particularly within its Spanish-speaking market. He argued that the discursive notions promoted by Disney continue to be based on dominant Eurocentric ideologies that maintain a form of cultural hegemony. He offered critical race theory as one of several ways to examine the master narratives (capitalist, racist, and heterosexist ideals) exposed specifically to Latina/o children and believed Disney movies provide "numerous opportunities for children and adults to engage in critical discussions regarding power, domination, and repression" (p. 31). These types of critical discussions that challenge the insidious nature of a Eurocentric epistemological perspective and dismantle master narratives can and should take place more frequently in multicultural classrooms. As this example shows, by engaging teachers and students in a critical analysis of epistemologies that underlie curriculum and other school processes, critical race theory offers tools that dig deeply into issues and problems that concern multicultural education.

A third (and potentially the greatest) contribution of CRT is its justification and use of storytelling in legal analysis and scholarship. CRT work in storytelling provides a rich way of conceptualizing multicultural curriculum. Because critical race scholars view experiential knowledge as a strength, they draw explicitly on the lived experiences of people of color by including such methods as storytelling, family history, biographies, parables, *testimonios, cuentos, consejos,* chronicles, and narratives. Storytelling has a rich legacy and continuing tradition in African American, Chicana/o, Asian American, and American Indian communities. Indeed, Delgado (1995) asserted that many of the "early tellers of tales used stories to test and challenge reality, to construct a counter-reality, to hearten and support each other and to probe, mock, displace, jar, or reconstruct the dominant tale or narrative" (p. xviii).

Counterstorytelling is a methodological tool that allows one to tell the story of those experiences that are not often told (i.e., by those on the margins of society) and to analyze and challenge the stories of those in power (Delgado, 1989). The stories people of color tell often counter the majoritarian or stock story that is a natural part of the dominant discourse. Building on the work of Delgado (1989), some education scholars argue that these counterstories serve multiple methodological and pedagogical functions such as building community among those at the margins of society, putting a human and familiar face on educational theory and practice, and challenging perceived wisdom about the schooling of students of color (Solorzano & Delgado Bernal, 2001; Solorzano & Yosso, 2001).

One way that education scholars are attempting to put a "human and familiar face to educational theory and practice" is through the development of composite characters that are based on interviews, focus groups, and biographical narratives in the humanities and social science literature. This work builds on the scholarship of Bell (1985, 1987), who tells stories of society's treatment of race through his protagonist and alter ego, Geneva Crenshaw; and Delgado (1995, 1999), who addresses race, class, and gender issues through Rodrigo Crenshaw, the half-brother of Geneva. The web of composite characters that have recently appeared in educational journals and chapters represent very real life experiences and are created to illuminate the educational system's role in racial, gender, and class oppression, as well as the myriad responses by people of color (Delgado Bernal, 1999; Solorzano & Delgado Bernal, 2001; Solorzano and Villalpando, 1998; Solorzano & Yosso, 2000, 2001; Villalpando, 2003). In addition, these composite characters allow students and educators of color to relate to or empathize with the experiences described in the counterstories, through which they can better understand that they are not alone in their position. Solorzano (1998) writes:

In that space or moment when one connects with these experiences, these stories can be the catalyst for one's own coming to voice, of not feeling alone, and knowing that someone has gone before them, had similar experiences, and succeeded. (p. 131)

Counterstorytelling can serve as a pedagogical tool by allowing multicultural educators to better understand and appreciate the unique experiences and responses of students of color through a deliberate, conscious, and open type of listening. In other words, an important component of using counterstories includes not simply telling nonmajoritarian stories but also learning how to listen and hear the messages in them (Delgado Bernal, 2002). Legal scholar Robert Williams (1997) believes that counterstorytelling and critical race practice are "mostly about learning to listen to other people's stories and then finding ways to make those stories matter in the legal system" (p. 765). Likewise, learning to listen to counterstories and then making those stories matter in the educational system is an important pedagogical practice for teachers and students.

Indeed, Gay (1995) asserted that the foundation of multicultural curriculum should be counterstories, but much of what ends up passing for multicultural curriculum is the dominant story with "Others" incorporated into it. Yosso (2002) proposed a critical race curriculum that is based on counterstories, thereby providing "students with an oppositional language to challenge the deficit societal discourses with which they are daily bombarded" (p. 15). Rather than adding on the experiences of Others or pushing students toward "discovering" a monolithic people of color, her understanding of a critical race curriculum "explores and utilizes shared and individual experiences of race, class, gender, immigration status, language, and sexuality in education" (p. 16). As such, a multicultural curriculum that grounds itself in the counterstorytelling of critical race theory has the potential to move a watered-down multicultural curriculum away from simply celebrating difference and reducing prejudice, to a "critical race curriculum" that actively names and challenges racism and other forms of injustice.

Limitations of Critical Race Theory and Its Implications for Multicultural Education

Critical race theory has received numerous critiques within legal studies, but few within education. We will address two of these critiques: the essentialist critique and the personal stories and narratives critique. We will also address the problems associated with being a relatively new area of study in education.

Within legal studies, some critics of CRT argue that it is an essentialist paradigm based on race. In general, essentialism is rooted in an identity politics that is based on a unidimensional characteristic, such as race, ethnicity, or gender. Critics argue that an essentialist notion of identity is simplistic and does not allow for the myriad experiences that shape who we are and what we know. Crenshaw and colleagues write, "To be sure, some of the foundational essays of CRT could be vulnerable to such a critique, particularly when read apart from the context and conditions of their production" (Crenshaw et al., 1995, p. xxv). However, what many critics do not understand is that despite the name critical *race* theory, most critical race scholars argue against an analysis based solely on race or some other unitary essentialized defining characteristic. For example, Harris (2000) points to the inherent problem of race and gender essentialism in fragmenting people's identities and experiences:

In this essay I use the term "gender essentialism" to describe the notion that there is a monolithic "women's experience" that can be described independently of other facets of experience like race, class, and sexual orientation. A corollary to gender essentialism is "racial essentialism"—the belief that there is a monolithic "black experience" or "Chicano experience." The effect of gender and racial essentialism (and all other essentialisms, for the list of categories could be infinite) is to reduce the lives of people who experience multiple forms of oppression to addition problems: "racism + sexism = straight black women's experience," or "racism + sexism + homophobia = black lesbian experience." (p. 263)

Certainly, "critical legal scholarship of race (and gender or sexual orientation) in recent times has interrogated and helped debunk various essentialisms and power hierarchies based on race . . . and other constructs" (Valdes, 1996, p. 3). With increased transnational labor and communication, many critical race scholars argue to move beyond essentialist notions of identity and of what counts as knowledge. Although race is forefronted in CRT, it is viewed as a fluid and dynamic concept and as one of the many components that are woven together to form one's positionality in a shifting set of social relationships.

There are numerous critiques of critical race scholars' use of stories and narratives in legal scholarship (e.g., see Farber & Sherry, 1993, 1997; Posner, 1997). Many critical race scholars have responded in more detail than we can offer within the scope of this chapter. The critiques are grounded in a debate over alternative ways of knowing and understanding, subjectivity versus objectivity, and different conceptions of truth. Briefly stated, critics believe that CRT theorists

relentlessly replace traditional scholarship with personal stories, which hardly represent common experiences. The proliferation of stories makes it impossible for others to debate. . . . An infatuation with narrative infects and distorts [their] attempts at analysis. Instead of scientifically investigating whether rewarding individuals according to merit has any objective basis, [they] insist on telling stories about their personal struggles. (T. W. Simon, 1999, p. 3)

Farber and Sherry (1993) argued against the pedagogical and methodological use of stories in legal scholarship, stating that "storytellers need to take greater steps to ensure that their stories are accurate and typical, to articulate the legal relevance of the stories, and to include an analytic dimension in their work" (p. 809). They also argued that just because counterstories draw explicitly on the lived experiences of people of color does not prove the existence of a new perspective based on "a voice of color." They, in fact, disagreed that people of color write in a different voice or offer a new perspective that differs from traditional scholarship.

Interestingly, most critics do not acknowledge that Eurocentrism has become the dominant mind-set that directly affects the mainstream stories told about race. Because Eurocentrism and White privilege appear to be the norm, many people continue to believe that education in the United States is a meritocratic, unbiased, and fair process. Delgado (1993) points out that "majoritarians tell stories too. But the ones they tell—about merit, causation, blame, responsibility, and social justice—do not seem to them like stories at all, but the truth" (p. 666). At the same time, critics argue that critical race scholars' stories, narratives, and autobiographies are unreliable sources of truth (Posner, 1997). At issue is the question of what counts as truth and who gets to decide. Also at issue is the matter of how to generalize. Counterstories derive generalization through their resonance with lived experiences of oppressed peoples, rather than through parametric statistics, but some empirical researchers do not see this as a valid way of making claims that generalize.

Finally, critical race theory is a relatively new area of study in education with a limited amount of literature using it as an analytical framework, and with few specific connections to multicultural education. Although education scholars are reshaping and extending critical race theory in ways very different from what legal scholars are doing, they need more time to study and understand the legal literature from which it emerges (Ladson-Billings, 1998; Roithmayr, 1999). Most education scholars who use CRT make a sharp distinction between CRT and multicultural education on the basis of the popular manifestations of multicultural education that pay little attention to racism and its intersections with other forms of subordination. With a few exceptions (Ladson-Billings & Tate, 1995; Ladson-Billings, 1999), education theorists have not offered direct implications of CRT for multicultural education. The future of critical race theory in education and in multicultural education depends on the efforts of educators to explore its possible connections to racism in schools and communities of color (Parker, 1998; Tate, 1997).

As a relatively new area of study, CRT may face a problem that multicultural education has experienced: transmutation into a depoliticized discourse in schools.

Ladson-Billings (1998) warns that CRT in education may continue to generate scholarly papers and debate, but she doubts that it will ever penetrate the classrooms and daily experiences of students of color. If it does, she worries that it may become a very different innovation, similar to the transmutation of multicultural education theory. She points out that many scholars such as James A. Banks, Carl Grant, and Geneva Gay began a "scholarly path designed to change schools as institutions so that students might be prepared to reconstruct the society" (p. 22). Yet in its current practice multicultural education is often superficial and based on holidays and food. In order to remain true to its principles of social justice and advocacy, critical race scholars will need to be attentive to the possibility of the transmutation of CRT into depoliticized discourses and practices in schools.

ANTIRACIST EDUCATION

Antiracist education emerged largely in opposition to multicultural education, particularly in Britain (Brandt, 1986), where it challenged "the apolitical and folksy orientation of multicultural education" (Bonnett & Carrington, 1996). Contexts in which multicultural and antiracist education emerged have differed across national borders, so national debates have differed (Bonnett & Carrington; May, 1999a); but debates have been vigorous, particularly in Canada and Britain (Modgil, Verma, Mallick, & Modgil, 1986). In both Britain and Canada during the late 1970s and 1980s, multicultural education was codified into national policy and school programs, drawing "its inspiration and rationale from white middle-class professional understandings of how the educational system might best respond to the perceived 'needs' and 'interests' of black students and their parents" (Troyna, 1987, p. 308). Its critics saw multicultural education as a way for White educators to "manage" the "problems" brought about by ethnic minority students (e.g., James, 2001; Troyna, 1987). Antiracist education grew, mainly in urban areas, out of community activism addressing racism in various dimensions of public life (Steiner-Khamsi, 1990). Antiracist education "can be defined as an action-oriented strategy for institutional, systemic change to address racism and the interlocking systems of social oppression" (Dei, 1996, p. 25).

In Britain, antiracist education was severely attacked by the New Right in the late 1980s. After 1988, national educational policy was "deracialized," in that references to race and ethnicity were replaced by references to authority and national identity. Antiracist education was also criticized by its allies, who argued that it had marginalized culture and overly essentialized racial categories (Gillborn, 1995). Antiracism as a movement declined in

Britain and subsequently reemerged by making connections with critical versions of multicultural education (Bonnett & Carrington, 1996; May, 1994; Gillborn, 1995). In Canada, Australia, and elsewhere, distinctions between antiracism and multicultural education were less sharply drawn (May, 1999a). Antiracist education in Canada, for example, made connections with critical pedagogy and African-centered pedagogy (Dei, 1993, 1996).

In the United States, multicultural education initially grew out of the Black struggle in the context of the civil rights movement, rather than out of national policy debates. Therefore it did not prompt an activist counter-discourse until, over time, it had taken on watered-down and apolitical meanings. For some, multicultural education and antiracism are or should be interchangeable (see Nieto, 1992; Perry & Fraser, 1993; Sleeter & Grant, 1998; Thompson, 1997). Others, however, do not ground multicultural education in an analysis of structural racism, but rather in interpersonal prejudice, cultural difference, and cross-cultural misunderstandings. For example, Tiedt and Tiedt (1999) emphasize individual uniqueness, unity with diversity, and community building; the word *racism* does not appear in their book.

There have been a number of efforts to bring antiracist education and multicultural education together (e.g., May, 1999a). However, because multicultural education often takes forms that avoid racism, and because, like critical race theory, antiracism foregrounds race as a site of struggle, it has significant implications for multicultural education.

Potential Implications of Antiracist Education for Multicultural Education

Antiracist education has five main implications for multicultural education. It (a) directs attention specifically to challenging racism in education; (b) addresses racist school structures such as tracking, which are often not addressed in multicultural education; (c) situates culture within power relations; (d) connects school with community; and (e) problematizes Whiteness. As noted earlier, some multicultural educators also address these issues.

Antiracist education challenges systemic racism. Despite the work of many of its leading theorists, multicultural education is often enacted in schools by adding in contributions, advocating "let's all get along," or promoting individual upward mobility within hierarchical structures rather than critiquing the structures themselves (Kailin, 1998–99). Too often it takes the form of telling "white children about the lifestyles and cultural achievements of ethnic minorities" (Short & Carrington, 1996). The term itself—multicultural—suggests starting with the idea of "many cultures." For Whites, this idea can fit within the taken-for-grantedness of White dominance, the

assumed normality and superiority of European and Euro-American cultures, and the assumption that society is already structured fairly.

Troyna's critique (1987) of four assumptions of multicultural education in Britain is relevant to the discussion here. First, "Britain is a multicultural society" (p. 313); the same can be said of Canada, the United States, and most other countries. Troyna argued that this assumption correctly describes what is, but not what should happen as a result. Beginning with the premise of diversity rather than justice and solidarity leads to addressing only diversity and not necessarily justice. Second, "the curriculum should reflect that substantive fact [of multiculturalism]," and third, "learning about other cultures will benefit all students" (p. 313). Troyna did not dispute the desirability of making the curriculum multicultural but questioned whether learning about "other cultures" is actually a corrective for racism. For members of oppressed groups, this proposition suggests that learning about diverse lifestyles enhances their life chances, which is fallacious. Assuming that White students will adopt antiracist behavior simply by learning about lifestyles of others is also questionable, and "increased knowledge of other groups might in fact enhance feelings of 'differentness'" (p. 313). Flecha (1999) agreed, pointing out that neo-Nazis also "use the concept of difference to support their programs of hate" (p. 152). Also, adding into the curriculum other cultures does not necessarily lead to a critical examination of the dominant culture. The problem here is not learning about others, but rather doing so within a conceptual framework that does not question relationships between dominant and subordinate groups. Fourth, "cultural relativism is a desirable and tenable position" (p. 313). This assumption leads to "anything goes" rather than dialogue across groups about how to work through differences. In addition, the entire formulation following this line of reasoning assumes the state and its institutions to be culturally neutral.

Antiracist education, in contrast, focuses on "the racist underpinnings and operation of white dominated institutions . . . rather than ethnic minority cultures and lifestyles" (Troyna, 1987, p. 310). In so doing, it directs attention to White supremacy, and to needs articulated by communities who are oppressed on the basis of race (Dei, 1996; Thompson, 1997). Antiracist education begins not with a description of changing demographics, which suggests a new problem stemming from immigration, but with an analysis of historic and contemporary imperialism and racism (Blumer & Tatum, 1999; Brandt, 1986; Derman-Sparks & Phillips, 1997; Walker, 1989). It examines how a racist system is maintained, roles of individuals in maintaining it, and how racism can be challenged both collectively and individually. Antiracist teaching entails helping students identify manifestations of racism, learn how racism works, and learn to interrupt it. Antiracism gives tools not only to talk about racism but also to do something about it (James, 2001; Lee, Menkart, & Okazawa-Rey, 1998).

A second implication of antiracist education is that it questions various ways in which schools structure unequal access to education (Brandt, 1986; James, 1995; Lee, 1985; Perry & Fraser, 1993). Racist structures and processes can include institutionalizing better instruction for White children than for children of color; using tracking, special education, and gifted programs to differentiate instruction along racial lines; using racially biased tests and other assessment processes; employing mainly White professionals; and so forth. In other words, antiracism critiques the supposed neutrality of institutions such as schools; this does not necessarily happen in some versions of multicultural education (May, 1999b).

For example, the anthology *Rethinking Schools: An Agenda for Change* (Levine, Lowe, Peterson, & Tenorio, 1995) included a section critiquing tracking. The section examined race and class biases in tracking systems, class and race biases in standardized testing, biases in access to algebra, and teaching in untracked secondary-level classrooms. Similarly, Lee (1985) examined racism in academic expectations, career counseling, assessment, and placement. Although numerous multicultural educators also address racism in the structure and operations of schools, many do not. For example, Davidman and Davidman (1994) directed their book toward prospective teachers, offering mainly suggestions for how to integrate ethnic content into lesson plans. The book simply did not address patterns of racism institutionalized in schools.

A third implication of antiracist education is that it situates culture within relations of power (Dei, 1996). As mentioned earlier, multicultural education enacted in schools often assumes culture to be fixed and bounded, groups to be relatively homogeneous, and culture to be separate from its material and relational contexts. Antiracist educators point out that the experience of subjugation itself acts on the cultures of both those who are subjugated and those who dominate (May, 1999b). People take up and adapt cultural forms in response to experiences; rap music, for example, is a form of popular Black youth culture that often speaks to racial subjugation (Rattansi, 1999). Further, global movements of peoples produce complex cultural identities that cannot be reduced to essentialist portrayals. Antiracist education is similar to critical pedagogy in conceptualizing culture within a nexus of power relations, overlapping histories, and complex identities (Dei, 1996).

A fourth implication of antiracist education is that it situates schooling in the broader community, viewing parents and community members as necessary parts of the education process (Perry & Fraser, 1993). Again,

although some multicultural educators also do this, many do not. Part of the issue involves how one views race, power sharing, and professionalism. If one views teaching as "a series of technical decisions made by experts who have a claim to authority" (Sleeter & Montecinos, 1999, p. 116), then professionally trained educators should not share authority with parents. However, "for oppressed groups, framing teaching as a series of technical decisions made by experts constitutes cultural invasion—the dominant society renders as illegitimate systems of meaning and reality originating in oppressed communities" (p. 117). Antiracism directs attention toward relationships between historically oppressed communities and professionals who are complicit in perpetuating racism. Antiracist educators argue that transformation initiatives need to come at least in part from communities that are usually excluded from decision making, particularly communities of color (Dei, 1996; Lee, 1985). One reason antiracist education makes sense to First Nations people in Canada is that it advocates stronger community control of education for their own children (Young, 1995).

A fifth implication of antiracist education is that it problematizes Whiteness and White dominance (Stanley, 1998). Whiteness tends to be normalized in traditional discourse, and very often in multicultural education as well (Dei, 1996; Lee, 1995). White ethnic identities might be named, but Whiteness is not. When teachers teach what they believe are universals, they draw from European and Euro-American culture and experience. Multicultural becomes, then, the Other, implicitly exoticized and still deficient. By shifting the gaze, antiracism names and critiques dominance (Stanley, 1998). Teaching about racism, however, can place White students in the position of being the named oppressor, thus alienating them from dialogue and engagement (Gillborn, 1995). This presents a pedagogical dilemma for antiracist educators who embrace a student-centered pedagogy (Thompson, 2002). A goal of antiracist education is to help students make significant political shifts in their thinking around racism and privilege, and this "sits uneasily with the aims of student-centered education, which is meant to be open-ended and emergent" (p. 443). To understand and address the pedagogical tension, Thompson highlighted antiracist pedagogies articulated to Whiteness theorizing. Her work and that of other critical White theorists is beginning to offer alternative conceptions of Whiteness that take account of White responsibility for maintaining or challenging racism (see, for example, Curry, 2000; Daniels, 1997; Roediger, 1994; Scheurich, 2002; Segrest, 1994). Although we do not have space to review that literature here, it is important to note that antiracism helps to locate White people within multicultural education, and to critique depoliticized White identities.

Limitations of Antiracist Education and Its Implications for Multicultural Education

Antiracist education has three limitations. First, the term itself, with its oppositional stance toward multicultural education, suggests a binary with two opposing agendas, each of which supposedly has an internally consistent body of ideas and practices. This assumed binary has been problematic on a number of fronts. Banks (1984) pointed out that "the critics [of multicultural education] have chosen some of the worst practices that are masquerading as multicultural education and defined these practices as multicultural education" (p. 60). In fact, a fair amount of literature in antiracist education and multicultural education is virtually interchangeable.

Binaries assume that people within each camp think alike and define one camp as "good" and the other as "bad," which closes off dialogue rather than encouraging it (Bonnett, 1990; Bonnett & Carrington, 1996; Green, 1982; Rattansi, 1999). Further, the terms themselves do not have the same meanings across national borders, which also confuses or greatly truncates discussion.

Second, antiracism has been criticized for giving too little attention to culture and too much attention to race, and in the process essentializing race as a construct. Gillborn (1995) and Mansfield and Kehoe (1994) synthesized criticisms of antiracism made by Paul Gilroy, Tariq Modood, and Kogila Moodley. Briefly, these critics argued that many groups see race as a construct that is used against non-Anglos and would rather give serious attention to culture, language, and religion instead. Antiracism is often too reductive, painting the world in black and white and leaving too little space for diverse ethnic minorities, which in Britain has alienated Asian Muslims. Further, antiracism has reduced even the experiences of Black people solely to race, giving too little credence to culture. Gillborn (1995) argued that rather than privileging either race or culture, we need to connect both, situating culture within a sociopolitical context. Similarly, Flecha (1999) pointed out that the older racial categories do not work well today, yet racist movements aimed toward exclusion are gathering momentum. Antiracism needs to develop a dialogic approach "emphasizing the need for equal rights among ethnicities" (p. 164). This means that an essential agenda for antiracist education is to work toward dialogue among diverse groups "that is oriented toward creating conditions for people from different cultures and ethnicities to live together" (p. 165).

A third limitation is that antiracist education can end up subsuming multiple forms of oppression (such as gender and class) under racism. Some educators who are trying to connect multiple forms of oppression, and who enter the dialogue through an interest in sexism or class oppression, do not see antiracist education as a venue for addressing anything except racism. For example, the focus on racism to the exclusion of other forms of oppression has alienated many White working-class youth who find it difficult to develop a sense of solidarity with oppressed people when the only identity they see for themselves is as the oppressor (Bonnett & Carrington, 1996). At the same time, in Canada antiracist educators have been making connections with multiple forms of oppression (e.g., Dei, 1999; James, 2001; Ng, Staton, & Scane, 1995) and offer ways of framing antiracism that address multiple oppressions without losing focus on racism, similar to the work of critical race theorists.

DISCUSSION

Like the other three fields discussed in this chapter, multicultural education emerged as an intellectual and activist movement to transform social institutions. In its inception, its primary focus was challenging racism, but it became transmuted as it filtered through schools and mainstream discourses. Although multicultural education today has taken on a wide range of meanings and practices, there are many within the field who have continued to develop it consistently with its original conceptual moorings. This chapter has attempted to act as a corrective to superficial and depoliticized versions of multicultural education by connecting the field to critical intellectual work. This chapter has also sought to develop the field by pointing out conceptual tools that can enrich and deepen its analyses.

What seems to distinguish critical traditions is their insistence on grounding practice in ideological clarity that explicitly critiques at least one form of collective oppression. Multicultural education that is critical, then, is not simply practice, but very explicitly politically guided practice. Multicultural education writings, however, with their focus on classroom practice, too often assume that educators bring ideological clarity and a sophisticated understanding of oppression, culture, and difference, and that they will change practice accordingly with guidance. But subsequent practice too often remains grounded in dominant discourses of individualism, implicit Eurocentrism, and naiveté about embedded power relations. In that context, multicultural education is enacted as strategies for sharing information about lifestyles, learning to get along, and examining the other. Critical race theory, antiracist education, and critical pedagogy writings generally spend more time examining the nature of oppression and culture in depth in order to develop ideological clarity, even though they may have less to say about teaching practice. This chapter suggests drawing from these fields, as well as additional fields such as multicultural feminism, to steer the course of transforming education more strongly.

At this point, one might reasonably ask to what extent it is possible and useful to attempt to synthesize multicultural education, critical pedagogy, critical race theory, and antiracist education. After considering this question, we concluded that it is more useful to expand the dialogue between these fields. All four fields emerged as oppositional discourses to dominant discourses about education. Each came about through specific histories to address social justice from specific vantage points. As such, each illuminates some issues and strategies while occluding others, and each speaks to realities of some communities more than others. Conceptually, theoretical differences among the fields can provide overlapping but still distinct lenses for viewing schooling, each revealing somewhat different issues and possibilities. Politically, the fields themselves represent overlapping but distinct groups of people, embedded within histories of power conflicts. It is helpful to think of the differences as creative tensions that are grounded in the theoretical, practical, and political realities of each field.

At a theoretical level, literature in multicultural education, critical pedagogy, antiracist education, and critical race theory provide somewhat different insights. Let us consider creative tensions around how each views the concept of culture and how each addresses structure and agency, since these concepts directly involve the nature of oppression, social change, and shared ways of making sense of the world. Critical pedagogy, antiracist education, and critical race theory situate culture within relations of power more explicitly than does much of the multicultural education literature. Yet even these three do not necessarily agree entirely on the relationship between culture and structures of power. Even though multicultural education attends actively to ethnic culture that is transmitted from generation to generation, critical pedagogy focuses mostly on the culture of everyday life, viewing culture as created within historic as well as contemporary power struggles. Antiracist education (particularly in its inception) and critical race theory give far more attention to race and racism than to culture per se. Similarly, at a theoretical level the fields place different emphases on structure versus agency. Multicultural education tends to emphasize, more than the other fields, individual agency and personal attitudes over power structures and institutional practices by highlighting what teachers can do. On the other hand, critical race theory and antiracist education focus primarily on oppressive structures and racist practices such as tracking, school funding, school (de)segregation, and the media. Critical pedagogy attempts to link the structure-agency dichotomy, but with a focus on class more than on the intersections of multiple oppressions.

Rather than suggesting a grand theory, we find it more useful to ask what insights each perspective can offer, and

how these insights might overlap and complement each other. For example, White Americans can be described as being preoccupied with measuring and organizing time, viewing time as linear, tangible, and scarce. Historically one might trace the roots of this practice, in part, to German culture (ethnic cultural transmission perspective with an emphasis on agency); one can also connect this practice to industrialization and the construction of factories (institutional perspective with an emphasis on structure; Alred, 1997). Current intensification of work due to economic shifts has intensified the scheduling of lives (culture within social class relations structured by capitalism). In addition, one can view the clock as a tool of racism that the monochronic dominant society uses to regulate subordinate groups (racism perspective with an emphasis on structure). Monochronic White Americans (who tend to see individual agency and not culture or structure) judge polychronic uses of time—in which time is conceptualized as circular, overlapping, and flexible—as disorganized. At an institutional level, this matters when organizations such as schools operate in a highly monochronic manner, penalizing communities that construct time more flexibly (racism and culture conflict perspective with an emphasis on structure). Which conception of culture is most helpful and how to address the relationship of structure to agency depends on one's question.

Thompson (1997) cautioned that attempting to create one grand narrative from the left would end up pushing aside too many very significant issues. Therefore, our discussion of the four bodies of literature attempts to illustrate creative tensions and clarify what each field brings to bear on schooling, so that depending on one's question and focus, educators can benefit from the unique insights of multiple frameworks. Learning to use multiple frameworks can help us avoid the dangers of one grand narrative while examining significant issues related to schools, students, and their community contexts.

At a practical and political level, tensions surround the historic and contemporary discourse communities represented by each of the four fields. Each was created by and speaks to a group of people, and these groups do not necessarily blend easily or readily. For example, since critical pedagogy has its conceptual basis in a social class analysis and its theorists speak to class issues, it appeals more than the other three fields to a White leftist constituency. Critical race theory, on the other hand, developed as an oppositional discourse to critical theory, as scholars of color sought to place race rather than class at the center of analysis. As such, its discourse community is largely scholars of color. Multicultural education speaks largely to practicing teachers, a community that is not at the center of critical race theory. Each field has historic roots; connecting fields means addressing tensions that are based on historic as well as contemporary power struggles among the people who have created them. If historically the White working class participated in the subjugation of African Americans, to what extent does the historical baggage of racism accompany critical theory? If K-12 teachers tend to be marginalized in the process of constructing academic theory, to what extent would attempts to merge the fields reproduce this marginalization?

At the same time, there is a need to continue trying to connect various forms of oppression and various communities struggling for justice. Over the past several years, significant attempts have been made to connect an analysis of racism with an analysis of sexism and class oppression; our chapter is only one additional effort. Struggles to define the nature of oppression are often couched in terms of binaries: White versus people of color, men versus women, gay/lesbian versus heterosexual, working-class and impoverished versus wealthy, and so forth. Binaries help to define power relations and demarcate conflict and struggle; but historically binaries have also been used as a means of control. Okihiro (2001) provides an excellent example of using the vantage point of Asian American history to challenge the binaries of East-West, Black-White, male-female, and heterosexual-homosexual. He showed how each of these was socially constructed within specific historic circumstances, and how each breaks apart when viewed from an angle within Asian American history. For example, 18th- and 19th-century White Americans constructed images of Chinese men as asexual but Chinese women as prostitutes, as a way of controlling the sexuality of White women and making both White women and women of color available to White men. Attempts to connect multiple forms of oppression and multiple diversities end up challenging binaries. Okihiro pointed out that "binaries resist change, perhaps, because they offer coherence" (p. 125). Binaries may work as conceptual tools, but they also impose simplistic solutions and serve as means of controlling some Other. Practice uninformed by a critical reanalysis of how one understands social relations may end up reproducing the status quo.

As critical traditions attempt to connect analyses of various forms of oppression, they work to dislodge existing binaries while retaining a critical analysis of power, struggle, oppression, and social change. This is complicated work, both theoretically and practically. Since practice is often uninformed by a complex understanding of oppression, culture, and power, one might ask if it is truly possible to use oppositional discourses in mainstream schools. Is it likely that critical theories, as they interact with practice, will be altered or diluted to meet the everyday practical needs of educators? It seems that although multicultural education, critical pedagogy, critical race theory, and antiracist education emerged as oppositional discourses, there remains a strong possibility for their transmutation in practice. This seems to be especially true if dialogue among the different discourse communities is limited or restrained.

References

Ada, A. F. (1988). The Pajaro Valley experience. In T. Skutnabb-Kangas & J. Cummins (Eds.), *Minority education: From shame to struggle* (pp. 223–238). Philadelphia: Multilingual Matters.

Aguirre, A. (2000). Academic storytelling: A critical race theory story of affirmative action. *Sociological Perspectives, 43,* 319–339.

Alred, G. J. (1997). Teaching in Germany and the rhetoric of culture. *Journal of Business & Technical Communication, 11*(3), 353–379.

Apple, M. W. (1979). *Ideology and curriculum.* Boston: Routledge and Kegan Paul.

Apple, M. W. (2000). *Official knowledge: Democratic education in a conservative age.* New York: Routledge.

Banks, J. A. (1984). Multicultural education and its critics: Britain and the United States. *New Era, 65*(3), 58–65.

Banks, J. A. (1999). *An introduction to multicultural education* (2nd ed.). Needham Heights, MA: Allyn & Bacon.

Barnes, R. (1990). Race consciousness: The thematic content of racial distinctiveness in critical race scholarship. *Harvard Law Review, 103,* 1864–1871.

Bell, D. (1985). The civil rights chronicles. *Harvard Law Review, 99,* 4–83.

Bell, D. (1987). *And we are not saved: The elusive quest for racial justice.* New York: Basic Books.

Bennett, C. I. (1998). *Comprehensive multicultural education* (4th ed.). Needham Heights, MA: Allyn & Bacon.

Berlak, A., & Moyenda, S. (2001). *Taking it personally.* Philadelphia: Temple University Press.

Bigelow, W. (1990). Inside the classroom: Social vision and critical pedagogy. *Teachers College Record, 91*(3), 437–448.

Blumer, I., & Tatum, B. D. (1999). Creating a community of allies: How one school system attempted to create an anti-racist environment. *International Journal of Leadership in Education, 2*(3), 255–267.

Bonnett, A. (1990). Anti-racism as a radical educational ideology in London and Tyneside. *Oxford Review of Education, 16*(2), 255–268.

Bonnett, A., & Carrington, B. (1996). Constructions of anti-racist education in Britain and Canada. *Comparative Education, 32*(3), 271–288.

Brandt, G. L. (1986). *The realization of anti-racist teaching.* Lewes, England: Falmer Press.

Brayboy, B. McK. (2001, November). Toward a tribal critical race theory. Paper presented at the annual meeting of the Association for the Study of Higher Education, Richmond, VA.

Bromley, H. (1989). Identity politics and critical pedagogy. *Educational Theory, 39*(3), 207–223.

Collins, P. H. (1990). *Black feminist thought*. New York: Routledge.

Crenshaw, K. (1993). Beyond racism and misogyny: Black feminism and 2 Live Crew. In M. J. Matsuda, C. R. Lawrence, R. Delgado, & K. W. Crenshaw (Eds.), *Words that wound: Critical race theory, assaultive speech, and the first amendment* (pp. 111–132). Boulder, CO: Westview Press.

Crenshaw, K., Gotanda, N., Peller, G., & Thomas, K., (Eds.). (1995). *Critical race theory: The key writings that formed the movement*. New York: New Press.

Curry, R. R. (2000). *White women writing white*. Westport, CT: Greenwood Press.

Curtis, A. C., & Rasool, J. A. (1997). Motivating future educators through empowerment: A special case. *Educational Forum, 61*(4), 307–313.

Daniels, J. (1997). *White lies: Race, class, gender, and sexuality in white supremacist discourse*. New York: Routledge.

Darder, A. (1995). Buscando America: The contributions of critical Latino educators to the academic development and empowerment of Latino students in the U.S. In C. E. Sleeter & P. McLaren (Eds.), *Multicultural education, critical pedagogy, and the politics of difference* (pp. 319–348). Albany: State University of New York Press.

Davidman, L., & Davidman, P. T. (1994). *Teaching with a multicultural perspective: A practical guide*. White Plains, NY: Longman.

Dei, G.J.S. (1993). The challenges of anti-racist education in Canada. *Canadian Ethnic Studies, 25*(2), 36–52.

Dei, G.J.S. (1996). *Anti-racism education*. Halifax, Nova Scotia: Fernwood.

Dei, G.J.S. (1999). Knowledge and politics of social change: the implication of anti-racism. *British Journal of Sociology of Education, 20*(3), 395–410.

Delgado, R. (1989). Storytelling for oppositionists and others: A plea for narrative. *Michigan Law Review, 87*, 2411–2441.

Delgado, R. (1993). On telling stories in school: A reply to Farber and Sherry. *Vanderbilt Law Review, 46*, 665–676.

Delgado, R. (1995). *The Rodrigo chronicles: Conversations about America and race*. New York: New York University Press.

Delgado, R. (1999). *When equality ends: Stories about race and resistance*. Boulder, CO: Westview Press.

Delgado, R., & Stefancic, J. (Eds.). (2000). *Critical race theory: The cutting edge* (2nd ed.). Philadelphia: Temple University Press.

Delgado, R., & Stefancic, J. (2001). *Critical race theory: An introduction*. New York: New York University Press.

Delgado Bernal, D. (1999). Chicana/o education from the civil rights era to the present. In J. F. Moreno (Ed.), *The elusive quest for equality: 150 years of Chicano/Chicana education* (pp. 77–108). Cambridge, MA: Harvard Educational Review.

Delgado Bernal, D. (2002). Critical race theory, Latino critical theory, and critical raced-gendered epistemologies: Recognizing students of color as holders and creators of knowledge. *Qualitative Inquiry, 8*(1), 105–126.

Derman-Sparks, L., & Phillips, C. B. (1997). *Teaching/learning antiracism*. New York: Teachers College Press.

Elenes, C. A. (1997). Reclaiming the borderlands: Chicana/o identity, difference, and critical pedagogy. *Educational Theory, 47*(3), 359–375.

Ellsworth, E. (1989). Why doesn't this feel empowering? Working through the repressive myths of critical pedagogy. *Harvard Educational Review, 59*(3), 297–324.

Farber, D., & Sherry, S. (1993). Telling stories out of school: An essay on legal narratives. *Stanford Law Review, 45*, 807–855.

Farber, D., & Sherry, S. (1997). *Beyond all reason: The radical assault on truth in American law*. New York: Oxford University Press.

Flecha, R. (1999). Modern and postmodern racism in Europe: Dialogic approach and anti-racist pedagogies. *Harvard Educational Review, 69*(2), 150–171.

Freire, P. (1970). *Pedagogy of the oppressed*. New York: Seabury Press.

Freire, P. (1973). *Education for critical consciousness*. New York: Seabury Press.

Freire, P. (1976). *Education and the practice of freedom*. London: Writers and Readers Publishing Cooperative.

Freire, P. (1998). *Pedagogy of freedom*. Boulder, CO: Rowman & Littlefield.

Garcia, R. (1995). Critical race theory and Proposition 187: The racial politics of immigration law. *Chicano-Latino Law Review, 17*, 118–148.

Gay, G. (1995). Mirror images on common issues: Parallels between multicultural education and critical pedagogy. In C. E. Sleeter & P. McLaren (Eds.), *Multicultural education, critical pedagogy, and the politics of difference* (pp. 155–190). Albany: State University of New York Press.

Gillborn, D. (1995). *Racism and anti-racism in real schools*. Buckingham, England: Open University Press.

Giroux, H. A. (1983). *Theory and resistance in education*. South Hadley, MA: Bergin & Garvey.

Giroux, H. A. (1985). Critical pedagogy, cultural politics, and the discourse of experience. *Journal of Education, 167*(2), 22–41.

Giroux, H. A. (1988). Literacy and the pedagogy of voice and political empowerment. *Educational Theory, 38*(1), 61–75.

Giroux, H. A. (1992). *Border crossings*. New York: Routledge.

Giroux, H. A., & McLaren, P. (1992). Writing from the margins: Geographies of identity, pedagogy and power. *Journal of Education, 174*(1), 7–30.

Giroux, H. A., & Simon, R. I. (Eds.). (1989). *Popular culture, schooling and everyday life*. Granby, MA: Bergin & Garvey.

Goldstein, B.S.C. (1995). Critical pedagogy in a bilingual special education classroom. *Journal of Learning Disabilities, 28*(8), pp. 463–476.

González, F. (1998). The formations of Mexicananess: Trenzas de identidades multiples. Growing Up Mexicana: Braids of multiple identities. *International Journal of Qualitative Studies in Education, 11*(1), 81–102.

Graman, T. (1988). Education for humanization: Applying Paulo Freire's pedagogy to learning a second language. *Harvard Educational Review, 58*(4), 433–448.

Grande, S.M.A. (2000). American Indian geographies of identity and power. *Harvard Educational Review, 70*(4), 467–498.

Green, A. (1982). In defense of anti-racist teaching: A reply to recent critiques of multicultural education. *Multicultural Education, 10*(2), 19–35.

Gutiérrez, G. (2000). Deconstructing Disney: Chicano/a children and critical race theory. *Aztlán, 25*(1), 7–46.

Hall, S. (1993). What is this "black" in black popular culture? *Social Justice, 20*(1–2), 104–115.

Harris, A. (1993). Whiteness as property. *Harvard Law Review, 106*, 1707–1791.

Harris, A. (2000). Race and essentialism in feminist legal theory. In R. Delgado & J. Stefancic (Eds.), *Critical race theory: The cutting edge* (2nd ed.). Philadelphia: Temple University Press.

hooks, b. (1994). *Teaching to transgress: Education as the practice of freedom*. New York: Routledge.

Iglesias, E. M., & Valdes, F. (1998). Religion, gender, sexuality, race, and class in coalitional theory: A critical & self critical analysis of LatCrit. *Chicano-Latino Law Review, 19*, 503–588.

James, C. (1995). Multicultural and anti-racism education in Canada. *Race, Gender and Class, 2*(3), 31–48.

James, C. (2001). Multiculturalism in the Canadian context. In C. A. Grant & J. L. Lei (Eds.), *Global constructions of multicultural education* (pp. 175–204). Mahwah, NJ: Erlbaum.

Johnson, K. R. (1996–97). The social and legal construction of nonpersons. *Inter-American Law Review, 28*(2), 263–292.

Kailin, J. (1998–99). Preparing urban teachers for schools and communities: An anti-racist perspective. *High School Journal, 82*(2), 80–88.

Kanpol, B., & McLaren, P. (Eds.). (1995). *Critical multiculturalism: Uncommon voices in a common struggle*. Westport, CT: Bergin & Garvey.

Kincheloe, J. L., & Steinberg, S. R. (1997). *Changing multiculturalism*. Buckingham, England: Open University Press.

Ladson-Billings, G. (1998). Just what is critical race theory and what's it doing in a nice field like education? *International Journal of Qualitative Studies in Education, 11*(1), 7–24.

Ladson-Billings, G. (1999). Preparing teachers for diverse student populations: A critical race theory perspective. *Review of Research in Education, 24*, 211–247.

Ladson-Billings, G. (2000). Racialized discourses and ethnic epistemologies. In N. K. Denzin & Y. S. Lincoln (Eds.), *Handbook of qualitative research* (2nd ed., pp. 257–277). Thousands Oaks, CA: Sage.

Ladson-Billings, G., & Tate, W. (1995). Toward a critical race theory of education. *Teachers College Record, 97*, 47–68.

Lather, P. (1991). *Getting smart*. New York: Routledge.

Lee, E. (1985). *Letters to Marcia: A teacher's guide to anti-racist education*. Toronto, Ontario: Cross Cultural Communication Centre.

Lee, E. (1995). Taking multicultural, antiracist education seriously. In D. P. Levine et al. (Eds.), *Rethinking schools: An agenda for change* (pp. 10–16). New York: New Press.

Lee, E., Menkart, D., & Okazawa-Rey, M. (Eds.). (1998). *Beyond heroes and holidays: a practical guide to K-12 anti-racist, multicultural education and staff development*. Washington, DC: Network of Educators on the Americas.

Lei, J. L. (2001, April). "Displacing" race in multicultural education. Paper presented at the American Educational Research Association, Seattle, WA.

Levine, D. P., Lowe, R., Peterson, B., & Tenorio, R. (Eds.). (1995). *Rethinking schools: An agenda for change*. New York: New Press.

Linton, S. (1998). *Claiming disability*. New York: New York University Press.

Livingstone, D. W. (Ed.). (1987). *Critical pedagogy and cultural power*. South Hadley, MA: Bergin & Garvey.

Lynn, M. (1999). Toward a critical race pedagogy: A research note. *Urban Education, 33*(5), 606–626.

Macedo, D. (1994). *Literacies of power*. Boulder, CO: Westview Press.

Macedo, D., & Bartolome, L. I. (1999). *Dancing with bigotry: Beyond the politics of tolerance*. New York: St. Martin's Press.

Mansfield, E., & Kehoe, J. W. (1994). A critical examination of antiracist education. *Canadian Journal of Education, 19*(4), 419–430.

Marable, M. (2000). *How capitalism underdeveloped Black America: Problems in race, political economy, and society*. Cambridge, MA: South End Press.

Matsuda, M., Lawrence, C., Delgado, R., & Crenshaw, K. (Eds.). (1993). *Words that wound: Critical race theory, assaultive speech, and the first amendment*. Boulder, CO: Westview Press.

May, S. (1994). *Making multicultural education work*. Philadelphia: Multilingual Matters.

May, S. (Ed.). (1999a). *Critical multiculturalism: Rethinking multicultural and antiracist education*. London: Falmer Press.

May, S. (1999b). Critical multiculturalism and cultural difference: Avoiding essentialism. In S. May (Ed.), *Critical multiculturalism: Rethinking multicultural and antiracist education* (pp. 11–41). London: Falmer Press.

Mayo, P. (1999). *Gramsci, Freire and adult education: Possibilities for transformative action*. London: Zed Books.

McCarthy, C. (1995). Multicultural policy discourses on racial inequality in American education. In R. Ng, P. Staton, & J. Scane (Eds.), *Anti-racism, feminism, and critical approaches to education* (pp. 21–44). Westport, CT: Bergin & Garvey.

McCarthy, C. (1998). *The uses of culture*. New York: Routledge.

McLaren, P. (1991). Critical pedagogy: Constructing an arch of social dreaming and a doorway to hope. *Journal of Education, 173*(1), 9–34.

McLaren, P. (1998). Revolutionary pedagogy in post-revolutionary times: Rethinking the political economy of critical education. (Online version.) *Educational Theory, 48*(4), 431–462.

McLaren, P. (2000). *Che Guevara, Paulo Freire, and the pedagogy of revolution*. Boulder, CO: Rowman & Littlefield.

McLaren, P., & Mayo, P. (1999). Value commitment, social change, and personal narrative. *International Journal of Educational Reform, 8*(4), 397–408.

Modgil, S., Verma, G., Mallick, D., & Modgil, C. (Eds.). (1986). *Multicultural education: The interminable debate*. London: Falmer Press.

Montoya, M. (1994). *Mascaras, trenzas, y grenas*: Un/masking the self while un/braiding Latina stories and legal discourse. *Chicano-Latino Law Review, 15*, 1–37.

Montoya, M. E. (1997). Academic *mestizaje*: Re/producing clinical teaching and re/framing wills as Latina praxis. *Harvard Latino Law Review, 2*, 349–373.

Ng, R., Staton, P., & Scane, J. (Eds.). (1995). *Anti-racism, feminism, and critical approaches to education*. Westport, CT: Bergin & Garvey.

Nieto, S. (1992). *Affirming diversity*. White Plains, NY: Longman.

Obidah, J. E. (2000). Mediating boundaries of race, class, and professional authority as a critical multiculturalist. *Teachers College Record, 102*(6), 1035–1060.

Okihiro, G. Y. (2001). *Common ground: Reimagining American history*. Princeton, NJ: Princeton University Press.

Parker, L. (1998). "Race is . . . race ain't": An exploration of the utility of critical race theory in qualitative research in education. *International Journal of Qualitative Studies in Education, 11*(1), 7–24.

Parker, L., Deyhle, D., and Villenas, S. (Eds.). (1999). *Race is . . . race isn't: Critical race theory and qualitative studies in education*. Boulder, CO: Westview Press.

Perry, T., & Fraser, J. W. (1993). *Freedom's plow: Teaching in the multicultural classroom*. New York: Routledge.

Peterson, R. E. (1991). Teaching how to read the world and change it: Critical pedagogy in the intermediate grades. In C. E. Walsh

(Ed.), *Literacy as praxis: Culture, language and pedagogy* (pp. 156–182). Norwood, NJ: Ablex.

Posner, R. A. (1997). Narrative and narratology in classroom and courtroom. *Philosophy and Literature, 21*(2), 292–305.

Pruyn, M. (1994). Becoming subjects through critical practice: How students in one elementary classroom critically read and wrote their world. *International Journal of Educational Reform, 3*(1), 37–50.

Pruyn, M. (1999). *Discourse wars in Gotham West.* Boulder, CO: Westview Press.

Rattansi, A. (1999). Racism, "postmodernism," and reflexive multiculturalism. In S. May (Ed.), *Critical multiculturalism: Rethinking multicultural and antiracist education* (pp. 77–112). London: Falmer Press.

Roediger, D. R. (1991). *The wages of whiteness.* New York: Verso.

Roediger, D. R. (1994). *Towards the abolition of whiteness.* New York: Verso.

Roithmayr, D. (1999). Introduction to critical race theory in educational research and praxis. In L. Parker, D. Deyhle, & S. Villenas (Eds.), *Race is . . . race isn't: Critical race theory and qualitative studies in education.* Boulder, CO: Westview Press.

Romany, C. (1996). Gender, race/ethnicity and language. *La Raza Law Journal, 9*(1), 49–53.

Sanchez, V. (1998). Looking upward and inward: Religion and critical theory. *Chicano-Latino Law Review, 19,* 431–435.

Scheurich, J. J. (Ed.). (2002). *Anti-racist scholarship: An advocacy.* Albany: State University of New York Press.

Segrest, M. (1994). *Memoir of a race traitor.* Boston: South End Press.

Shor, I. (1980). *Critical teaching and everyday life.* Boston: South End Press.

Shor, I. (1992). *Empowering education: Critical teaching for social change.* Chicago: University of Chicago Press.

Short, G., & Carrington, B. (1996). Anti-racist education, multiculturalism and the new racism. *Educational Review, 48*(1), 65–77.

Simon, R. I. (1992). *Teaching against the grain: Texts for a pedagogy of possibility.* New York: Bergin & Garvey.

Simon, T. W. (1999). Racists versus anti-Semites? Critical race theorists criticized. *Newsletter on Philosophy, Law, and the Black Experience, 98*(2), 1–11.

Sleeter, C. E. (1992). *Keepers of the American dream.* London: Falmer Press.

Sleeter, C. E. (1995). Reflections on my use of multicultural and critical pedagogy when students are white. In C. E. Sleeter & P. L. McLaren (Eds.), *Multicultural education, critical pedagogy and the politics of difference* (pp. 415–438). Albany: State University of New York Press.

Sleeter, C. E. (2001). *Culture, difference and power.* New York: Teachers College Press.

Sleeter, C. E., & Grant, C. A. (1998). *Making choices for multicultural education: Five approaches to race, class and gender* (3rd ed.). New York: Wiley.

Sleeter, C. E., & Montecinos, C. (1999). Forging partnerships for multicultural teacher education. In S. May (Ed.), *Critical multiculturalism: Rethinking multicultural and antiracist education* (pp. 113–137). London: Falmer Press.

Solorzano, D., & Yosso, T. (2000). Toward a critical race theory of Chicana and Chicano education. In C. Tejeda, C. Martinez, & Z. Leonardo (Eds.), *Charting new terrains of Chicana(o)/Latina(o) education* (pp. 35–65). Cresskill, NJ: Hampton Press.

Solorzano, D., & Yosso, T. (2001). Critical race and LatCrit theory and method: Counter-storytelling, Chicana and Chicano graduate school experiences. *International Journal of Qualitative Studies in Education, 14*(4), 471–495.

Solorzano, D., & Yosso, T. (2002). Critical race methodology: Counter-storytelling as an analytical framework for education research. *Qualitative Inquiry, 8*(1), 23–44.

Solorzano, D. G. (1989). Teaching and social change: Reflections on a Freirean approach in a college classroom. *Teaching Sociology, 17,* 218–225.

Solorzano, D. G. (1997). Images and words that wound: Critical race theory, racial stereotyping and teacher education. *Teacher Education Quarterly, 24,* 5–19.

Solorzano, D. G. (1998). Critical race theory, race and gender microaggressions, and the experience of Chicana and Chicano scholars. *International Journal of Qualitative Studies in Education, 11*(1), 121–136.

Solorzano, D. G., & Delgado Bernal, D. (2001). Examining transformational resistance through a critical race and LatCrit theory framework: Chicana and Chicano students in an urban context. *Urban Education, 36*(3), 308–342.

Solorzano, D. G., & Villalpando, O. (1998). Critical race theory, marginality, and the experiences of students of color in higher education. In C. A. Torres & T. R. Mitchell (Eds.), *Sociology of education: Emerging perspectives* (pp. 211–224). Albany: State University of New York Press.

Stanley, T. (1998). The struggle for history: Historical narratives and anti-racist pedagogy. *Discourse: Studies in the Cultural Politics of Education, 19*(1), 41–52.

Steiner-Khamsi, G. (1990). Community languages and anti-racist education: The open battlefield. *Educational Studies, 16*(1), 33–47.

Students for Cultural and Linguistic Democracy. (1996). Reclaiming our voices. In C. E. Walsh (Ed.), *Education reform and social change* (pp. 129–145). Mahwah, NJ: Erlbaum.

Tate, W. (1994). From inner city to ivory tower: Does my voice matter in the academy? *Urban Education, 29,* 245–269.

Tate, W. F. (1997). Critical race theory and education: History, theory, and implications. *Review of Research in Education, 22,* 195–247.

Thompson, A. (1997). For: Anti-racist education. *Curriculum Inquiry, 29*(1), 7–44.

Thompson, A. (2002). Entertaining doubts: Enjoyment and ambiguity in White, antiracist classrooms. In E. Mirochnik & D. C. Sherman (Eds.), *Passion and pedagogy: Relation, creation, and transformation in teaching* (pp. 431–452). New York: Peter Lang.

Tiedt, P. L., & Tiedt, I. M. (1999). *Multicultural teaching* (5th ed.). Boston: Allyn & Bacon.

Troyna, B. (1987). Beyond multiculturalism: towards the enactment of anti-racist education in policy, provision and pedagogy. *Oxford Review of Education, 13*(3), 307–320.

Valdes, F. (1996). Latina/o ethnicities, critical race theory, and post-identity politics in postmodern legal culture: From practices to possibilities. *La Raza Law Journal, 9*(1).

Villalpando, O. (2003). Self-segregation or self-preservation? A critical race theory and Latina/o critical theory analysis of a study of Chicana/o college students. *International Journal of Qualitative Studies in Education, 16*(5).

Villenas, S., & Deyhle, D. (1999). Critical race theory and ethnographies challenging the stereotypes: Latino families, schooling, resilience and resistance. *Curriculum Inquiry, 29*(4), 413–445.

Walker, H. (1989). Towards anti-racist, multicultural practice with under fives. *Early Child Development and Care, 41,* 103–112.

Williams, R. (1997). Vampires anonymous and critical race practice. *Michigan Law Review, 95,* 741–765.

Wing, A. K. (Ed.). (1997). *Critical race feminism: A reader.* New York: New York University Press.

Wink, J. (1997). *Critical pedagogy: Notes from the real world.* White Plains, NY: Longman.

Young, J. (1995). Multicultural and anti-racist teacher education. In R. Ng, P. Staton, & J. Scane (Eds.), *Anti-racism, feminism, and critical approaches to education* (pp. 43–63). Westport, CT: Bergin & Garvey.

Yosso, T. (2002). Toward a critical race curriculum. *Equity and Excellence in Education, 35*(2), 93–107.

PART
V

ETHNIC GROUPS IN HISTORICAL
AND SOCIAL SCIENCE RESEARCH

14

ETHNIC MEXICANS IN HISTORICAL AND SOCIAL SCIENCE SCHOLARSHIP

Ramón A. Gutiérrez
University of California, San Diego

Historical and social science writing on Mexican Americans has a long tradition that reaches back almost a century and a half in the United States. At various points in this history, Mexican Americans were characterized as a regionally conquered people, an immigrant group, a minority, a nationality, and an emerging majority population. In this historiographical survey, the extant scholarship under review has been divided thematically into five subsections: Mexicans as a regionally conquered people, 1821–1880; the Mexican as immigrant, 1880–1993; the Mexican American minority, 1920–1965; Chicanos as a nationality, 1965–1993; and recent research trends, 1985–2001. The dates for each of these subsections denote when a particular theme and specific representation of the Mexican was prominent in the scholarly literature. Sometimes the actual research was produced in the period under review, but often it was not; as any bibliophile will attest, revisionist research continues and is produced every day. Bear in mind, too, that the five themes and periods elaborated here are rough approximations for the primacy of specific discourses on the Mexican population in the United States. Obviously, population movements, paradigm shifts, and the diffusion of information do not always conform to such neat temporal and thematic divides. The same can be said of ethnic Mexicans in the United States. They have moved across the U.S.-Mexico border over the course of many years, producing population nodes in which conquered residents, immigrant workers, assimilated Mexican Americans, and nationalistic Chicanos all reside side by side.

MEXICANS AS A REGIONALLY CONQUERED PEOPLE, 1821–1880

Mexicans first attracted the attention of the American reading public in 1821, when the newly independent Republic of Mexico began welcoming the world's traders and settlers. Mexico's leaders were convinced that if they did not populate their vast expanses of seemingly "vacant" national territory, it would quickly become the envy of expansionistic neighbors. To accomplish this, in 1824 Mexico promulgated a colonization law that encouraged immigrants to petition for land and settlement grants. Scouts from the United States seeking natural resources, merchants in search of markets, trappers hunting pelts, settlers desperate for land, and adventurers seeking just that all responded rapidly to Mexico's newly opened borders. They arrived in *Nuevo México* (New Mexico), which had been colonized in 1598; in *Tejas* (Texas) and the *Pimería Alta* (southern Arizona), whose settlements dated from the 1720s; and in the towns of *Alta California,* colonized in the years following 1769. These were the only population centers that had been established in Mexico's far north under Spanish colonial rule. The Kingdom of New Mexico, which in the colonial period encompassed the northern half of Arizona, was by far the most densely populated in 1820, with some 28,500 nominally "Spanish" settlers and 10,000 Christianized Indians as residents. California boasted a populace of 3,400 "Spaniards" and 23,000 mission Indians; Arizona counted about 700 "Spanish" and 1,400 Indian mission residents; and Texas had roughly 4,000 "Spaniards" and 800 Christianized Indians congregated in missions (R. A. Gutiérrez, 1991, 1992).

The men and women who ventured from the United States into Mexican territory and who were literate enough to record their observations and experiences became important cultural map makers for their stay-at-home compatriots, as literary historian Martin Padget (1993) has explained. As the initial mappers of a complex cultural terrain, these early-19th-century American writers were largely responsible for creating the types and stereotypes of the Mexican that would be etched into the minds of militant jingoists, politicians, and patriots as they articulated the God-ordained providential mission of the United States: territorial expansion. "Manifest Destiny" became the war cry with which they impassioned their readers about the necessity to lay claim to Mexican terrain (Horsman, 1981; Merk, 1963). As the gospel of American state nationalism, Manifest Destiny was steeped in anti-Spanish and anti-Catholic attitudes, anchored to a republican ideology that disparaged feudal and monarchical forms of government, and wedded to an evolutionary science that deemed it the duty of superior races to eradicate inferior mongrels.

These sentiments are readily apparent in such best-selling narratives as James O. Pattie's *The Personal Narrative of James O. Pattie* (1831), Richard Henry Dana's *Two Years Before the Mast* (1840), and Josiah Gregg's *Commerce of the Prairies* (1844). The negative stereotypes of the Spaniard and Mexican, crafted by American travel writers, have been extensively studied over the last 40 years by Gardiner (1952), Lacy (1959), Noggle (1959), Robinson (1963, 1977), Gunn (1974), Paredes (1977a, 1977b), Langum (1978), Meyer (1978), Weber (1979), Pettit (1980), Monsiváis (1984), and R. A. Gutiérrez (1989a).

The accumulated scholarly evidence concludes that most of the American travel narratives were but panegyrics for the territorial expansion of the United States. American travelers attested to the greatness of the United States and, in comparison, the moral and physical decay of Mexico, as most demonstrably embodied in Mexican men. The women were another matter. In the eyes of American men who described them, they were beautiful "Spanish" *señoritas* who suffered none of the character deficits of the "Mexican" mixed-blood men who had inherited all the degenerate traits of the Spanish and Indian races (Lacy, 1959; Meyer, 1978). Mexican men were typically portrayed as a breed of cruel and cowardly mongrels who were indolent, ignorant, and superstitious, given to cheating, thieving, gambling, drinking, cursing, and dancing. Expansionists drew on such stereotypes to build the case for territorial aggrandizement by asking, Was it not the duty of the United States to rescue such "greasers" from themselves? Dana as much as said so,

speculating in his 1840 classic *Two Years Before the Mast*, "In the hands of an enterprising people, what a great country this could be" (Monsiváis, 1984, p. 55). So it was. First in Texas, Anglo American settlers united with a small group of elite Mexican *Tejanos* and declared their independence from Mexico as the Republic of Texas in 1835. In 1846, sparked by border conflicts between Texas and Mexico, the United States declared war—a war that ended by dispossessing Mexico of one third of its national territory.

The causes, the events, and the consequences of the U.S.-Mexican War have been the topic of numerous tomes from the vantage points both of the victors and the vanquished. Singletary's *The Mexican War* (1960) remains the most succinct history of the war itself, with all its various military campaigns. Mexican historian Ramón Eduardo Ruiz (1963) carefully dissected the political (the personal ambitions of President James K. Polk) and economic motives (the expansion of plantation slave economies and the desire to acquire more land) for the war in *The Mexican War: Was It Manifest Destiny?*, a theme Brack (1975) addressed largely through Mexican sources in *Mexico Views Manifest Destiny, 1821–1846*. Johannsen's *To the Halls of the Montezumas* (1985) studied the war in the American imagination. Horsman (1981) went one step further, teasing out the Anglo-Saxon racial ideology that justified war in Texas and Mexican territory. Finally, an interpretation best classified as "Manifest Destiny in reverse" was advanced by Weber in *The Mexican Frontier 1821–1846* (1982). He argued that American conquest was made possible, if not inevitable, by the inefficiency and decadence of Mexican civil and ecclesiastical institutions on the northern frontier. Dobyns (1991) aggressively rebutted the Weber thesis, arguing that, at least with respect to popular Catholicism in northern Mexico, no such decay was apparent.

The Texas Revolution and the Mexican War were the two events that legally transformed Mexicans into American citizens. Given the centrality of these historical events in forging the modern political identity of Chicanos, a large part of the scholarly research undertaken by Chicano scholars educated since the mid-1960s has focused on the periods right before and right after territorial annexation by the United States. The overarching themes in all of these works—themes largely of concern to the contemporary Mexican American experience—are the nature and meaning of community, the dynamics and politics of race, the sex and gender stratification of society, and the covert and overt dimensions of Mexican resistance to United States annexation and Anglo domination.

In rewriting and revisioning the history of the Southwest before U.S. rule, Chicano scholars have usually focused their studies on the various regions Spain initially colonized: *Nuevo México, Tejas, Alta California,* and the

Pimería Alta, or southern Arizona. New Mexico, the oldest and most densely populated of these territories, was the topic of R. A. Gutiérrez's *When Jesus Came, the Corn Mothers Went Away* (1991). As the title suggests, Gutiérrez investigated the nature of interactions between the Pueblo Indians and their Spanish conquerors, looking specifically at the conflictual politics that characterized marriage, religion, and patriarchal rule, as men and women, young and old, slave and free negotiated their behavior in a colonial context. Sketching the cultural concepts of *honor* (honor) and *vergüenza* (shame) that formed Spanish notions of the self, Gutiérrez shows how race and color were imagined as central components of the status hierarchy governed by honor, and how the legacy of this hierarchy persisted up to and after territorial conquest in 1848. Shorter articles on the status of Spanish women in Santa Fe (J. L. Aragón, 1976), on their property rights and wills (Veyna, 1986, 1993), and on life and labor in late-18th-century Albuquerque (Ríos-Bustamante, 1976) have also greatly enhanced our knowledge of New Mexico.

The history of Spanish, Mexican, and Republican Texas has been intensely scrutinized by several generations of scholars. Herbert E. Bolton (1915) laid the foundation for Texas studies in *Texas in the Middle Eighteenth Century: Studies in Spanish Colonial History and Administration.* Chipman's *Spanish Texas, 1519–1821* (1992) covered many of the same themes over a longer historical period. Simons and Hoyt (1992), in their encyclopedic *Hispanic Texas: A Historical Guide,* catalogued the wide array of Hispanic contributions to Texas culture, including such things as architecture and cuisine. Poyo and Hinojosa (1991) have sought the origins of *Tejano* identity in the area of San Antonio in the 18th century. The arrival of Anglo American settlers, and the changes that produced, was the topic of De León's *The Tejano Community, 1836–1900* (1982), which surveyed the experiences of daily life for *Tejanos* (Texans of Mexican origin) through their religious rituals, forms of entertainment, work, and politics. De León argued, sometimes without much evidence, that *Tejanos* accepted their circumstances of conquest and "developed a bicultural identity that equipped them to resist oppression" (1982, p. xii).

One such *Tejano* hero who resisted oppression was Juan Seguín, a wealthy landowner. In 1835, he allied himself with the Anglos during Texas independence, only to be removed in the 1840s as the mayor of San Antonio and driven out of Texas once the Anglos had consolidated their power. This tragic turn of events in Seguín's life has made him a resistance hero for many Mexican Americans. Seguín's story became the theme of Jesús Treviño's 1982 movie *Seguín.* De la Teja (1991) recently prepared a critical edition of Juan Seguín's diary and correspondence.

Montejano's *Anglos and Mexicans in the Making of Texas, 1836–1986* (1987) is the most comprehensive work on Anglo-Mexican race relations in Texas. Montejano examined the origin, growth, and demise of the racial order in Texas, specifically as tied to class development that evolved from a ranch to a farm and to an urban-industrial economy. According to Montejano, unique and peculiar "racial situations" were created under each of these modes of production, resulting in years of racial quiescence (1836–1900), a period of intense "Jim Crow" segregation (1920–1940), and a period of integration (1940–1986) when Mexican-origin residents of Texas demanded their civil rights, first peacefully and then more militantly.

Studies of Spanish colonial and Mexican California produced by Chicano scholars have been few. Like R. A. Gutiérrez's work on New Mexico (1991), which explores Indian-White relations through the intimate politics of the libido, Monroy in *Thrown Among Strangers: The Making of Culture in Frontier California* (1990) and Castañeda (1990, 1993) have studied the Spanish colonization of California and the hybridization that occurred when Spaniards, *mestizos,* and Indians mixed biologically through marriage, concubinage, and rape. Both Monroy and Castañeda tell much larger stories about how colonizers and colonized eked out a meager subsistence; how poverty and marginality precipitated sexual violence; and how constant conflicts erupted among settlers, missionaries, and Indians over labor, food, and love.

Although much of the historical research on Mexicans as a conquered population has focused on New Mexico, Texas, and California, undoubtedly because of the sheer number of Mexicans who ultimately settled in these states, a few monographs have been written on Arizona and Colorado in the pre- and post-1848 periods. For Arizona, Officer's *Hispanic Arizona, 1536–1856* (1987) and Sheridan's *Los Tucsonenses: The Mexican Community in Tucson, 1854–1941* (1986) are essential baseline reading. In *Songs My Mother Sang to Me: An Oral History of Mexican American Women,* Martin (1992) interviewed 10 women regarding the role of gender and cultural resistance as Arizona's Mexican ranches were transformed into *barrios.* Similar studies do not exist for Colorado. Deutsch's *No Separate Refuge: Culture, Class, and Gender on an Anglo-Hispanic Frontier in the American Southwest, 1880–1940* (1987) studied the transformation of women's work and culture in northern New Mexico and southern Colorado. An anthology edited by De Onis, *The Hispanic Contribution to the State of Colorado* (1976), has contributed some groundbreaking essays on the history of Colorado's ethnic Mexicans.

During the late 19th and first half of the 20th centuries, scores of works were written on the two institutions that still dominate the mythic imagination of the Southwest: the missions and the presidios. Rarely was much attention given to the third institution of colonial conquest, the independent town. Cruz (1998) filled this lacuna with *Let There Be Towns,* tracing the municipal origins of Santa Fe, New Mexico; El Paso, San Antonio, and Laredo, Texas; and Los Angeles and San José, California, focusing specifically on town plans, the institutions of town government (*cabildos*), and how they actually functioned. Though very institutional and legalistic in his approach, Cruz set down the foundation for more detailed town studies. Indeed, M. J. González (1993) used Cruz's work in his study of the municipal origins of Los Angeles, which explored the republican philosophy of the town founders, the ecclesio-political ideals manifested in town planning, and the role of Indians in the town's economy both before and after secularization.

What all of these studies indicate is that in New Mexico, Texas, and California, and by implication in Arizona and Colorado, the personal identities that European settlers developed were initially based on membership in a religious community as Old Christians or as New Christian converts. Residence on New Spain's northern frontier gradually transformed the Old World regional consciousness that the colonists initially proclaimed as Castilians, Catalans, Leoneses, and Galicians into a single national identity as Spaniards. But the Spaniards of Mexico's north, as a contingent largely of young and single men, by necessity took American Indian and African slave women as lovers, concubines, and occasionally as legal brides. Quickly a cultural *mestizaje* developed, resulting in a syncretic culture born of biological, linguistic, and social mixing. Thus when the colonists proclaimed that they were Spaniards they did so to differentiate themselves culturally from those they defined as "Indians."

Despite the realities of extensive physical amalgamation, the Spaniards maintained the fiction that they were biologically pure in order to create and perpetuate their social privileges in relationship to Indians, whom they stigmatized through conquest, subjugation, and toil. In the 18th century, as racial mixing rapidly rendered physical color categories meaningless as visual markers of status, new strictures were established in law to regulate relations that could no longer be assessed visually. The legal color categories of the *Regimen de Castas* (the Society of Castes) defined in excruciating detail the precise racial status of every particular mix of ancestry, thus buttressing the authority of local pigmentocracies at precisely the moment when they were most contested from below. Since racial codes were largely cultural fictions used to create social boundaries and hierarchies of prestige, they too ultimately gave way in the 1790s to a renewed consciousness of place, a *conciencia de sí,* and an identification with the *patria chica,* or the "small fatherland." By the early 1800s *Tejanos* proclaimed their uniqueness as settlers of this zone. The *Californios* celebrated their own pastoral ways. The *Tucsonenses* (residents of Tucson, then

Arizona's major settlement) explained that their character had been forged by the aridity of their desert terrain. The *Nuevo Mexicanos* boasted of the distinct regional culture they had preserved. The highly developed sense of regional and local community that developed in each of these areas was undergirded by a common religion, a common cycle of rites of passage and calendric events, a common language, and an identity as Spaniards forged in opposition to and conflict with Indians (R. A. Gutiérrez, 1989b). This sense of community was what gave Spaniards, transformed into Mexicans with independence in 1821, the will and strength to resist their domination by Anglos.

Sketching the parameters of Anglo American legal domination, though crucial to any history of Mexican Americans, has yet to gain much sustained attention. The legal incorporation of Mexicans into the United States transpired with the ratification of the Treaty of Guadalupe-Hidalgo in 1848, and with its extension through the 1853 Gadsden Purchase. The U.S. government assured Mexicans residing in the conquered territory that their lands would be protected, their religion honored, their language preserved, and their livelihoods left undisturbed. Mexican American and Chicano scholars since the mid-1960s have repeatedly shown how those legal protections were violated and rendered meaningless. The history of the Treaty of Guadalupe-Hidalgo, its debate, and its ultimate ratification by the United States was the topic of a monograph by Griswold del Castillo (1992). Martínez, in *Troublesome Border* (1988), also focused on the 1848 treaty within a broader history of border conflicts between Mexico and the United States, from 1795 to the present.

How Mexicans residing in the United States after 1848 lost their lands and power, despite promises by the U.S. government that these would be protected, has been the topic of extensive study. Most of the book-length monographs to date have examined this process as it unfolded in California. Pitt (1971) studied Mexican-Anglo relations in northern California from the gold rush until 1890. Griswold del Castillo (1979) focused on the morselization of land rights, the disappearance of livestock production, and the political disenfranchisement of *Californios* in the Los Angeles Basin, parallel themes splendidly explored by Hass (1994) in her book on the history of racial identities in Santa Ana, California.

But undoubtedly the best of the California studies on the disenfranchisement of Mexicans is Camarillo's *Chicanos in a Changing Society: From Mexican Pueblos to American Barrios in Santa Barbara and Southern California, 1848–1930* (1979). Other historians described a dichotomous ethnic structure that pitted Anglos against Mexicans or Chicanos, but Camarillo carefully documented a much more complex social structure with internal class cleavages in every ethnic group. Here was a complex story of how California's *Mexicano* population was deprived of its land, politically disempowered, and socially segregated into ethnic enclaves or barrios. These themes were illuminated through an examination of racial and ethnic conflicts, and an analysis of ethnic and class alliances forged either to seize power or to dominate in the struggle to keep it. That Camarillo got the story right can be seen in any contemporary newspaper story about electoral reapportionment in California. By showing Chicanos precisely how Mexicans lost their political power in the state, Camarillo outlined a political strategy for how best to regain it as ethnic Mexicans became an emerging majority population in California.

A full-length history of New Mexican land and water rights controversies has yet to be written. What does exist is a splendid anthology edited by Briggs and Van Ness, *Land, Water, and Culture: New Perspectives on Hispanic Land Grants* (1987). Herein Ebright (1987) surveyed the legal background of New Mexican land grants, while Hall (1987) explored the conflicts between Hispano and Pueblo Indians over these grants. Van Ness (1987) looked at the functions of Spanish land grants at the local level. The two best contributions in the volume are those by Briggs (1987) and Rodriguez (1987). Briggs explained how oral histories can be used in land grant litigation. Rodriguez focused on Taos, New Mexico, to show how the "Land of Enchantment" was metaphysically constructed for touristic consumption.

The history of overt and covert resistance to Anglo domination in the Southwest has been an important and recurrent theme in Chicano-inspired scholarship over the last 20 years. Writing from a lesbian feminist perspective, and interrogating her sources for their class and racial bias, D. J. González (1993) studied the facts and fiction surrounding Doña Gertrudis Barcelo, a Santa Fe woman who allegedly ran a brothel in the 1850s and 1860s. González argued that Doña Barcelo really was a businesswoman of considerable skill who adapted to changing social, political, and economic dislocations and adroitly profited from the American invaders. De León's *They Called Them Greasers: Anglo Attitudes Toward Mexicans in Texas, 1821–1900* (1983) analyzed the more general topic of American stereotypes of Mexicans as they were generated in Texas.

One of the persistent myths of American Western historiography has been that *Mexicanos* happily greeted American soldiers, offered little resistance to their domination, and allowed the conquest to occur without spilling a drop of blood. Rosenbaum (1981) shattered this myth in *Mexicano Resistance in the Southwest*. He chronicled how New Mexicans assassinated the occupational governor, Charles Bent, in 1847; how *Mexicanos* fought and died during numerous campaigns of the Mexican War; and how, when overpowered militarily by 1848, they maintained a resistance to domination and the dispossession of their lands. Rosenbaum showed how resistance to displacement took various forms: so-called bandit activity (Tiburcio Vásquez and Joaquín Murieta in California; Gregorio Cortez, José Mosqueda, and Mariano Reséndez in Texas), secret societies (New Mexico's *La Mano Negra* and *Las Gorras Blancas*), political parties (*El Partido del Pueblo Unido*), and anarchist and syndicalist groups. Castillo and Camarillo (1973) contributed immensely to this general theme by proposing that *Mexicano* resistance fighters had to be understood as primitive rebels and not as the unruly "bandits" of the Anglo American imagination.

One of the most exciting developments in historical scholarship on Mexican Americans has been the revival of Spanish and *Mexicano* literary voices from 1598 to the early 1900s. Two recent anthologies analyzing these writings have appeared: Herrera-Sobek's *Reconstructing a Chicano/a Literary Heritage* (1993) and R. A. Gutiérrez and Padilla's *Recovering the U.S. Hispanic Literary Heritage* (1993). The former primarily focused on Spanish colonial texts produced within what is now the United States; the latter delved into nontraditional sources such as periodical literature (Kanellos, 1993), the privately published works of 19th-century New Mexican novelists Vicente Bernal and Felipe Maximiliano Chacón (Gonzales-Berry, 1993), the *Californio* oral histories collected by Hubert H. Bancroft's assistants in the 1880s (R. Sánchez, 1993), Mexican American autobiographies (G. Padilla, 1993b), and the bibliographic sources for the study of Mexican American literary culture in the United States from 1821 to 1945 (R. A. Gutiérrez, 1993c).

At a more detailed and monographic level, G. Padilla expanded our knowledge of the 19th-century formation of Mexican American autobiographical identity in *History, Memory, and the Struggles of Self-Representation* (1993a). Herein he analyzed the ways in which war and social domination shaped the contours of the Mexican American autobiographical voice from 1836 on, arguing that Mexican Americans wrote autobiographies as a response to their fear, both real and imagined, of social erasure and literary oblivion. As a literary archaeologist, Padilla recovered the autobiographical utterances of his colonized compatriots, reminding moderns that to do this we must imagine a historical moment that did not exclusively privilege the individual. The men and women Padilla studied—Juan Seguín, Rafael Chacón, Mariano Vallejo, Manuel Otero, Cleofas Jaramillo—were representatives of the larger communitarian politics in which these subjects were engaged.

Much research remains to be done on the conquest period. The literary voices of Mexican women are still waiting to be heard. Little has been written about the politics of conquest. No one has yet written the history of

Mexicans in Colorado or any area outside the Southwest. Much more has yet to be said about the intimate politics of daily life in which men and women, Anglo and Mexican, young and old, rich and poor constantly interacted.

THE MEXICAN AS IMMIGRANT, 1880–1992

Once the U.S. victory over Mexico's ceded territory was complete and the economic, political, and cultural subordination of Mexicans residing in the Southwest had been accomplished, Mexico became a close and convenient source of cheap immigrant labor. The development of Arizona, California, New Mexico, and Texas as economically productive areas necessitated cheap, tractable, unskilled labor. One sector of the American economy after another called on Mexicans, first to mine the vast mineral deposits of the West; then to construct the railroads that moved these minerals to ports and eastern manufacturing centers; and finally, when rail lines made it possible to transport agricultural products to markets quickly and cheaply, as laborers to till, tend, and harvest the fields.

Mexicans became the immigrant laborers of choice in the 1880s, primarily because the Chinese workers who had provided the bulk of California's labor during the gold rush were excluded from entry into the United States in 1882 by the Chinese Exclusion Act. In 1882 as well, the Alien Contract Labor Law was repealed, prohibiting labor contractors from recruiting workers in distant lands. Experimentation with Japanese workers ended with the so-called Japanese Gentlemen's Agreement of 1907, which restricted the number of Japanese immigrant laborers allowed into the country. Mexico was thus the closest and most abundant source of workers available. By 1930, the census of the United States listed 16,668 Mexicans as legally employed in mining, 70,799 in transportation and communication (primarily as railroad field hands), and 189,000 in agricultural industries (initially sugar beets and cotton, and later citrus and table vegetables) (Cardoso, 1980; R. A. Gutiérrez, 1976; McWilliams, 1949; Reisler, 1976).

Mexican peasant laborers began entering the United States in the 1880s largely because of the rural poverty they faced at home, a situation that culminated in the 1910 Mexican Revolution. Landless and increasingly unable to produce or purchase the basic necessities of life, these men and women were forced to migrate to known work sites. In the 1880s, President Porfirio Díaz began a massive modernization program in Mexico, centered on the creation of an extensive infrastructure that ultimately connected the country's productive areas with markets. Railroad construction was the cornerstone of this plan, primarily through rail links between Mexico and the United States. Many landless peasants left their ancestral homes in search of work on railroad construction in Mexico's northern states. No physical barrier other than the easily forded Rio Grande separated Mexico from the United States before 1924. The availability of jobs at wages significantly higher than those found in Mexico made the move all the more irresistible. Caught in the midst of the revolutionary violence that rocked Mexico between 1910 and 1924, many migrants found the United States a peaceful and attractive haven.

The Mexican emigration/immigration literature published in Mexico and the United States is immense and often contradictory. Some of it is based on facts. Much of it is based on fallacious assumptions that have been widely accepted as facts and compounded through dissemination as national fictions. It is impossible to summarize all of this literature here, but what follows illustrates some of the major themes.

Two very different and often contradictory representations of the "Mexican Immigrant" exist in the public policy and scholarly literature. The Mexican immigrant has been viewed either as a "problem" that threatens the racial, hygienic, and economic basis of life in the United States (Bamford, 1923–24; Jenks & Lauck, 1917) or as a valuable asset that contributes to American prosperity by performing tasks at wages that citizen workers will not accept, and by contributing taxes from which the immigrant rarely benefits (Borjas, 1990). Advocates of the Mexicans-as-problem position have demanded severe immigration restrictions, particularly at times of economic hardship. The Mexicans-as-asset advocates have generally favored open doors or more tempered governmental regulation, particularly during times of prosperity. The average person on the street probably embodies attitudes about immigrants drawn from both viewpoints.

The tenor of these polemics and debates has been remarkably consistent, whether in 1903 or 1993. In 1908, for example, labor contractors in the Southwest explained to Victor S. Clark, a U.S. Bureau of Labor economist, that they preferred Mexican to Japanese laborers because "when you have occasion to dismiss one Japanese, all quit. If a Mexican proves poor or an undesirable workman, you can let him go without breaking up the gang" (Clark, 1908, p. 478). Clark characterized the Mexican immigrant laborer as

ambitious, listless, physically weak, irregular and indolent. On the other hand, he is docile, patient, usually orderly in camp, fairly intelligent under competent supervision, obedient, and cheap. If he were active and ambitious, he would be less tractable and would cost more. (p. 496)

From this point of view—that of California growers—the Mexican was characterized by many of the negative stereotypes that American writers had first created in the 1820s.

At the opposite end of the spectrum, in the 1920s, nativist and patriotic societies and eugenicist organizations demanded a solution to the "Mexican Problem" through immigration restriction because, explained sociologist Robert L. Garis (1930) of Vanderbilt University:

Their minds run to nothing higher than animal functions—eat, sleep, and sexual debauchery. In every huddle of Mexican shacks one meets the same idleness, hoards of hungry dogs, and filthy children with faces plastered with flies, disease, lice, human filth, stench, promiscuous fornication, bastardy, lounging, apathetic peons and lazy squaws, beans and dried chili, liquor, general squalor, and envy and hatred of the gringo. . . . Yet there are Americans clamoring for more of this human swine to be brought over from Mexico. (p. 436)

Princeton economist Robert Foerster (1925) voiced similar opposition to Mexican immigration on purely racial grounds. He asked rhetorically whether Mexican *mestizo* and African mulatto racial stocks should be welcomed in the United States. Foerster argued that they should not, because "these groups merely approach but do not attain the race value of the white stocks, and therefore . . . the immigrants from these countries—Latin America—tend to lower the average of the white population of the United States" (p. 55). He warned that it was foolhardy to succumb to momentary profits while the racial purity of the nation was under attack (p. 57).

As various interest groups in the United States have attempted to advance their agendas, the question of appropriate policy about Mexican immigrants has been a recurrent concern. Of primary interest to these debates has been the question, How many Mexicans emigrate to the United States? This has not been a simple question to answer. Statistics on Mexican entries into the United States along the southern border were not kept until 1924. Before that, the only Mexicans who entered U.S. immigration records were those that arrived at official ports of entry, such as New York and San Francisco. Since few Mexicans ever saw the Statue of Liberty, those numbers rarely reached the hundreds before 1924. Estimates gathered by the U.S. census in 1930 placed the number of Mexicans permanently residing in the United States at 1 million, a number Mexican scholars fiercely contested as too high. The census was taken in July, at the peak period in the use of Mexican labor, Gamio maintained (1930a, 1930b, 1931); if one estimated the number of immigrants on the basis of monetary remittances in December, after the temporary migrants had returned home, the number of permanent residents was closer to 500,000.

The first systematic statistical count of Mexicans living in the United States came shortly after the 1929 economic depression. Restrictionist pressures mounted and eventually led to the deportation of many Mexicans. From 1930 to 1937, massive repatriation campaigns were conducted throughout the U.S. Southwest and Midwest. According to state and federal reports, the deportees were all Mexicans, but the reality was that many Americans of Mexican descent were deported or emigrated back to Mexico under duress. From official Mexican records, Carreras (1974) concluded that 311,717 Mexicans had reentered Mexico between 1930 and 1933. Working with American welfare records, newspaper accounts, and state and federal statistics, Hoffman (1974) placed the number of Mexican deportees at 458,039, a number comparable to that advanced by Gamio in 1930. Further information on the repatriation movement can be found in Kiser & Silverman (1972), Betten & Mohl (1973), and Dinwoodie (1977).

Not until 1942, as the United States entered World War II, were Mexican immigrants allowed to reenter in large numbers. To stem labor shortages in industries that were deemed essential to the war effort, Congress authorized Public Law 45, which became widely known as the *bracero* program. Though this legislation was initially deemed a temporary emergency war measure, it was repeatedly extended in various forms and with slightly different names until 1964. To stem some of the most notorious abuses suffered by Mexican immigrant laborers—unsanitary living conditions, payment failures, peonagelike contracts, overt racism—Mexico and the United States agreed that firms requiring workers would petition the U.S. Department of Labor. The Labor Department would serve as the contracting agent, guaranteeing the wage, the length of work, and the living conditions of the contracted workers. The Labor Department also made provisions to hold a portion of the workers' wages in escrow until they returned to Mexico, thereby assuring that temporary guests would not become permanent residents (Calavita, 1992; Craig, 1971; Galarza, 1964, 1977; Gamboa, 1990; Samora, 1971). Approximately 4.6 million *braceros* entered the United States between 1942 and 1964, a statistic considered accurate by most American and Mexican authorities.

The initiation of the *bracero* program coincided with another major trend in Mexican emigration: the movement of undocumented immigrants into the United States. According to official statistics compiled by the Immigration and Naturalization Service, 22 million undocumented Mexican immigrants have been apprehended and deported back to Mexico since 1942. The precise meaning of this number has been the topic of heated debate. Statistics often do not account for repeat offenders; the same individual may have been apprehended by American authorities on as many as 50 occasions in a lifetime. Nevertheless, depending on the user, the number can be exaggerated to show how the nation's borders have been eroded, or conversely the necessity of better monitoring and more accurate statistics.

Some clarity was brought to the issue with the passage of the U.S. Immigration Reform and Control Act of 1986. Undocumented immigrants who had entered the country before January 1, 1982, were given the right to legalize their status; a special amnesty was extended to those persons that had spent at least 90 days working in agriculture in the year preceding May 1, 1986. A mere 2.3 million applicants came forward (Durand & Massey, 1992), thus greatly deflating the projections in the 1980s of 7 to 8 million undocumented Mexican immigrants in the United States. Of course, the critics of these numbers have argued that not all Mexicans eligible for legalization took advantage of the statute.

Who migrated? The standard historical truism worldwide has been that the poorest cannot afford to move and the rich have no reason to, so the stratum in between is the one that has the wherewithal and motives to move. But the answers one finds to this question in the emigration literature on Mexicans are as varied as the scholars who framed them. Some have asserted that it was the landless and poor who migrated (Reichert, 1979; Stuart & Kearney, 1981). Other scholars have confirmed the truism, noting that the migrants were poor but not at the bottom of the social hierarchy (Cornelius, 1976; Wiest, 1973). One scholar (E. J. Taylor, 1986) argued that no relationship between social class and migration could be established.

The most insightful analysis of who migrates has been offered by Douglas Massey and his coauthors (Massey, Alarcón, Durand, & González, 1987). Massey et al. argued that the class composition of the migrants was a historically varied, dynamic, and ever-shifting process dependent on the age of the migration stream from a particular Mexican locality to the United States and the social inequality present in the community of origin. In a typical scenario, when the migrant stream from a particular Mexican area initially developed, the individuals who migrated were from the middle sectors of the social hierarchy as reckoned by wealth and/or occupation. They left Mexico without kinship or social ties in the United States to draw on and thus were the only social group economically capable of risking a move to initiate a migrant stream from their home community. Once they were established in the United States, ties of kinship and friendship made it possible for the poorer members of their home community to enter and eventually dominate the migrant stream, because they could join an established support network when they arrived. Once the support networks became extensive, migration was less dependent on class or the resources a particular migrant could garner.

Which geographic regions did Mexican migrants come from, and where have they settled in the United States? Gamio (1930a, 1931) studied the geographic origin of Mexicans who migrated to the United States, as did his Mexican compatriot Loyo (1969) in the mid-1960s. Both concluded that the bulk of migrants left the central Mexican states of Guanajuato, Michoacán, México, and Jalisco; since 1965 many have also come from the state of Oaxaca. Although the revolutionary violence between 1910 and 1917 probably accounted for the majority of emigrants during those years, abundant work, higher wages, and the possibility of upward mobility have continued to attract them to the United States in the years that followed. Mexicans historically have settled overwhelmingly in the Southwest, with California and then Texas receiving the bulk. Recently, however, Washington (Gamboa, 1990), the Great Lakes region (Valdés, 1991; Vargas, 1993), and New York have developed sizeable Mexican communities. Both the geographic distribution and demographic profile of these immigrants have been studied by Alvarez (1966); Bean and Tienda (1987); Boswell (1979); Martínez (1975); and Teller, Estrada, Hernández, and Alvírez (1977).

Much of the writing produced by the Chicano scholars in the period after 1967 has focused on the work experiences of Mexican laborers in the United States. Undoubtedly part of the reason for this focus was the scholars' desires to trace their own immigrant roots. But one cannot dismiss the influence of one historian, Juan Gómez-Quiñones, the founder of the UCLA Chicano Studies Research Center. He mentored the first generation of Chicano scholars at UCLA. It was inevitable that the research themes of his students and disciples would bear the mark and concerns of the master. Much of the important work of Gómez-Quiñones has been on Mexican immigrants as workers (1972, 1982), focusing on their culture (1977), their relationships with state authorities (1975), and their political organizations on both sides of the border (1990).

His own students, and those influenced by his models, have studied the origins of labor union activism in the form of fraternal organizations and mutual aid societies (Briegel, 1974; Hernández, 1983; Vélez-Ibañez, 1983), the role of the Mexican consulates in protecting workers in the United States (Balderrama, 1982), Mexican workers in Texas (Zamora, 1993), and the roles of various labor unions and political parties, such as the Communist Party of the United States (Almaguer & Camarillo, 1983; Arroyo, 1975). The bulk of this literature focused on class and class formation in the United States and gave little attention to the dynamics of racism. For these authors, race was but an ideological ploy the ruling class used to divide workers; it was a form of false consciousness that had no role in the activity of militants. The only strategy for seizing power was a class strategy, or so claimed the Socialist and Communist organizers of Mexican workers from the 1920s to the 1960s. How Chicanos reacted to this formulation of their oppression will be examined in some detail in the section on the Chicano movement.

The published story of the Mexican immigrant has largely been a heroic male tale. Women have rarely entered the historical and sociological record. But whatever the mythology, the reality has been that women formed a major component of the migrant stream since the 1880s. Between 1930 and 1933, for example, Carreras (1974) discovered that of the 311,717 Mexicans repatriated, two thirds were women. More recent studies have estimated that since 1945, slightly more than one half of all Mexican immigrants have been women (Cardenas & Flores, 1986; V. L. Ruiz & Tiano, 1987).

Historically, Mexican women usually entered the migrant stream only after a particular community had a well-established immigrant support network in the United States. Men usually migrated first, familiarized themselves with labor markets and work demands, and, when they felt secure, sent for their wives and children (Durand & Massey, 1992). Thus those communities that have had long histories of sending emigrants to the United States usually also have had a large number of women among those migrants. If the community's history of sending workers to the United States is more recent, the number of women in that migrant stream is usually smaller.

The nature of gender relations in Mexican immigrant families has been of some concern to feminist scholars. Studying a sample of 26 families containing 44 adult women, and controlling for the length of separation between a husband and wife caused by the migration process, Hondagneu-Sotelo (1992) found that the longer a couple was separated the greater was the erosion of domestic patriarchy. During long periods of separation, women became independent and "were no longer accustomed or always willing to act subserviently before their husbands." When the separation was only a few years, "daily housework arrangements were not radically transformed once the families were reconstituted in the United States" (pp. 408–409).

The new research trends in the Mexican immigration literature can be found in the work of D. Gutiérrez (1994) and Foley (1990). In *Walls and Mirrors: Mexican Americans, Mexican Immigrants, and the Politics of Ethnicity in the American Southwest, 1910–1986*, Gutiérrez focused on the differences that were generated over 150 years within the Mexican and Mexican American communities as their populations were transformed into Americans. Over the course of these years, as Mexicans forged a situational ethnicity, responding to forces generated both within their communities and outside of them by the discriminatory practices of American society, they constantly grappled with the "crucial distinctions between 'native' and 'foreigner,' 'citizen' and 'alien,' 'American' and 'Mexican'" (p. 12). How these statuses were mobilized for political purposes, to promote or curtail the flow of Mexican immigrants, is the story that Gutiérrez tells with considerable finesse. It is a story full of nuance and complexity; a story devoid of black or white, but quite florid in its various hues of gray. There are Mexican Americans who hate Mexicans and ally themselves with Americans to curtail Mexican immigration, just are there are working-class Mexican Americans who favor continued immigration, while cursing their middle-class ethnic brothers who want to stem the flow.

Foley (1990) also explored social complexity, linking theoretical concerns in Chicano and African American history with issues central to labor history and post-emancipation studies. In *The New South in the Southwest: Anglos, Blacks, and Mexicans in Central Texas, 1880–1930* (1990), Foley examined the complex triangular relationship that developed among Anglo owners and tenants, Black and Mexican sharecroppers, and Mexican migrant workers in the fertile cotton-producing area of Central Texas from 1880 to 1930. Historically, Central Texas (roughly from Dallas in the north to San Antonio and Corpus Christi in the south) represented the border between the cotton-growing U.S. South, with its history of slavery and emancipation, and the semi-arid region of southwestern Texas, with its history of ranching and migrant Mexican labor. At the end of the 19th century, the populations from these two geographically distinct regions began to overlap. Mexicans began moving north, pushed by political and economic turmoil in Mexico and pulled by economic opportunities in the fertile fields to the north and east. By 1900, large numbers of Mexicans had settled in the cotton-producing counties north of San Antonio, where, along with African Americans, they began displacing Anglo share tenants on farms and came to form the labor supply in this predominantly Anglo region.

The trend in Chicano-inspired immigration studies increasingly has begun to look at conflicts within and between ethnic groups, incorporating information from diverse fields of study.

THE MEXICAN AMERICAN MINORITY, 1920–1965

The emergence of a Mexican American minority population in the United States between 1920 and 1965 is the theme that has received the least attention in the vast scholarly corpus examined here. The very appellation *Mexican American* signifies that something Mexican and something American have mixed, and from this mixture an entirely new hybrid has been produced. This hybridity historically has been studied by anthropologists and sociologists as *assimilation,* a process initiated by marriage, by acquiring a new language or religion, by obtaining a distinct job, and by entering a new culture.

The Mexicans' transition from the status of conquered group to assimilated Americans has been long and rather confining. From the time the first Anglo American settlers arrived in the Mexico that became the United States, extensive Anglo-Mexican intermarriage occurred. Racially mixed progeny were born. Protestants converted to Catholicism and vice versa, to make a good or advantageous match. Spanish-English bilingualism became a necessity for anyone who married exogamously or traded in the labor or products of the Southwest. Social scientists have long described this process of cultural mixing and blending, in which cultural partners both give and take from each other, as *transculturation.* Historically, transculturation has been the norm when cultures and peoples reside side by side, sharing foodways and folkways, love and life. But when a relationship of domination and subordination has developed that was coded as a racial, ethnic, or national divide, transculturation was no longer the operative process. Instead, power was exercised by the dominant group to make the subordinate become more like them. In social science writing, such cultural movement in one direction only, toward the ideals of the dominant culture, has been described as *acculturation,* which can occur at either the structural or the personal level. At the personal level, acquisition of the dominator's language, forms of comportment, dress, and demeanor, as well as aspirations, has been defined as *assimilation.*

By the 1880s, given some 60 years of cohabitation in the Southwest, there were sizeable numbers of the Mexicans who thought of themselves as Americans—as indeed they were by law—and who objectively had assimilated or were in the process of assimilating to the dominant Anglo American culture. They had accepted or passively acquiesced to the realities of the domination under which they lived. Some of them married Anglos, some learned the language, and a few even mastered it (Carver, 1982; Dysart, 1976; Miller, 1982; Myres, 1982).

Then, starting in the 1880s, large numbers of dirt-poor Mexican immigrants started to arrive in the old Spanish towns and villages of the Southwest, resuscitating latent Anglo perceptions of the social types that had inspired vicious stereotypes of Mexicans in the 1820s. In the Anglo-American imagination, once again the Mexican was poor, dirty, indolent, disease-ridden, superstitious, and dumb. Such caricatures fed the racist science and xenophobic ideologies of the day. Indeed, in the 1880s one did not call another a "Mexican," a "Meskin," or a "Mex" in polite company. It was considered an insult, particularly to women and men who had resided in the Southwest since the times of the Spanish *doñas* and *dons.*

As was noted in the first section of this chapter, in the 1820s a bifurcated image of Mexicans developed in American travel literature. The beautiful women were described as Spanish, and the indolent men as Mexican. In the 1880s this bifurcation was reanimated, with the long-time Mexican residents of the Southwest labeled Spanish and Spanish Americans, and the recent immigrants Mexicans. With this naming strategy, ethnic Mexicans resident in the United State were distanced and differentiated as a distinct nationality from Mexican immigrants. This differentiation also had racial implications, for by accepting and even proclaiming a Spanish identity ethnic Mexicans created a genealogy rooted in Europe that lacked the degenerate racial elements presented in Mexican *mestizos* or mixed-bloods (R. A. Gutiérrez, 1989b, 1993b).

One cannot make sense of the sociological and anthropological literature on Mexican Americans as a minority group published from roughly 1920 to 1965 without understanding this Mexicans-and-Spaniards distinction. In this period, the three major analytic paradigms of societal analysis—biological determinism, environmental/structural determinism, and cultural determinism—repeatedly invoked the Spanish and Mexican categories to explain why Mexican Americans, despite many years of residence in the United States, were not assimilating as quickly or as completely as northern Europeans had. The assimilation models of the day had been constructed on the basis of the experiences of the "old" northern European immigrants who had settled the Northeast between 1776 and 1880. However, with the United States seemingly flooded by the arrival of numerous "new" immigrants from southern and eastern Europe and Mexico between 1880 and 1930, new models were necessary to explain everything from the desirability of racial mixing with these immigrants to the biological determinants of the crimes they committed, their poor health, and unemployment rates.

Strongly influenced by the racial science of the late 19th and early 20th centuries, the biological determinists in psychology sought to confirm empirically what many already suspected: that Mexicans and southern and eastern European immigrants were innately less intelligent. The IQ test was the instrument used to prove this; when administered to nonnative English speakers, these tests invariably confirmed that these groups had lower IQs. The work of Young (1922) on mental difference in immigrant groups; of Garth (1923) on the intelligence of Mexican American, American Indian, and mixed-blood children; of Garretson (1928) on the causes of retardation among Mexican children in Arizona; and of Haught (1931) on the language difficulties of "Spanish American" children all conclusively pointed to the linguistic shortcomings of their research subjects as measured by intelligence tests—proof positive of their inferior mental abilities. These were studies and findings, coincidentally, that advocates of immigration restrictions were always quick to publicize in their testimony before congressional committees; such studies persisted as late as 1950 (Carlson & Henderson, 1950).

The riposte to these biological determinists came from anthropologists, sociologists, and educational psychologists, who rejected biological explanations and instead turned their attention to the structural environment in which Mexican Americans lived, learned, and worked to explain the characteristics of Mexican workers. The very organization of the American agricultural economy, rather than the mental capacities of individual Mexicans, had to be examined to understand the "Mexican problem." Why Mexican Americans as a group were "unstable, subject to irregular employment, low earning, and more importantly the social and political disabilities of non-residents," explained Paul S. Taylor (1938, p. 226), had more than anything else to do with the fact that the demand for their labor was largely seasonal, widely dispersed regionally, and poorly compensated.

Emory Bogardus (1940) and Norman D. Humphrey (1943) echoed similar sentiments when they explained that the structure of work and levels of discrimination were the environmental factors that most affected the life outcomes of Mexican workers. Migratory labor resulted in "deplorable housing accommodations, and the Mexican and his family have suffered," noted Bogardus (p. 170). Mexican American boys were attracted to gangs, not because they had low IQs or were culturally deprived but because they were "discriminated against occupationally. Some of the work opportunities open to other youth are closed to him because he is 'Mexican'" (Bogardus, 1943, p. 65). Writing about Mexican immigrants in Detroit, Humphrey concluded that "discrimination against Mexicans in the southern and western states is favorable neither to assimilation nor to the acquisition of United States citizenship" (p. 333).

In scathing critiques of IQ testing, native New Mexican George I. Sánchez (1932, 1934, 1940) demanded that test instruments become more carefully constructed and that investigators build in environmental variables (such as diet, home environment, social class, the physical nature of schools, rural versus urban setting) to explain school and test score performance. On the basis of his own studies, Sánchez argued that Mexican American children were no less intelligent than any other American group. The racist policies of school boards and teachers were the real problem, as demonstrated "in the nature and quality of the educational facilities available to these children. . . . In the counties with the largest proportions of Spanish-speaking people," Sanchez (1940) argued further,

school terms are shorter, teachers are less well prepared and their salaries are lower, and materials of instruction and school buildings are inferior to those found elsewhere in the state [of New Mexico]. . . . The unresponsiveness of the school to the environment of New Mexican children tends to force them out of school. (pp. 31–32)

In fact, Sanchez (1932) demonstrated that Spanish-speaking children who had initially been judged dull and feeble-minded on the basis of intelligence tests had, after only two years of English-language tutoring, shown perfectly normal IQs.

The powerful correctives offered by Sánchez (1934) in psychology were buttressed by others who were eager to understand the relationship between environment and educational success. West (1936) wanted to know whether teachers' racial prejudices influenced their assessment of a child's performance. Comparing a Southwestern sample of "Spanish-American" and "Anglo-American" teachers, he found that the Anglo teachers "were more strongly inclined than were the Spanish to claim superiority for pupils of their own race" (p. 337).

Thomas Garth and his colleagues (Garth, Elson, & Morton, 1936) used three achievement tests (one nonverbal, two verbal) to assess the role English-language competence played in the intelligence test results of Anglo and Mexican school-aged children. Controlling for age and grade, the IQ scores of the Mexican American children on the nonverbal test were "about equal to the American White I.Q." (p. 58), though they scored much lower than Anglo students on the verbal tests.

Keston and Jiménez (1954) extended this line of research on the relationship between language and intelligence by administering Spanish and English versions of the Stanford-Binet Intelligence Test to bilingual children in Albuquerque, New Mexico. The results were quite unexpected. The children had higher IQs when tested in English than in Spanish, explained largely by the fact that though the children were verbally competent in Spanish, they had no formal training in reading and writing the language—skills necessary to do well on the standardized tests. From this study, it became clear that simply translating a test into Spanish was no solution to the larger educational problems face by Mexican Americans.

The third major paradigm shift used extensively to analyze Mexican Americans—cultural determinism—grew out of 19th-century racial science and studies of national character precipitated by the rise of state nationalisms. In country after country, historians, philosophers, and pedants intensively scrutinized the behaviors of their compatriots to sketch the collective portrait of the nation.

The national character of Mexico was largely depicted by psychologist Samuel Ramos (1938), philosopher Leopoldo Zea (1952), and poet/critic Octavio Paz (1961).

These three men generally agreed that the Mexican psyche had been deeply affected by three centuries of Spanish colonial domination and repeated foreign penetration of their sovereign national space. The living legacy of this past was a profound sense of inferiority among Mexicans, compensated for and displayed by men as hypermasculinity, or *machismo*. Using observations from his own practice, psychiatrist Diaz-Guerrero (1955) delineated precisely how this inferiority/hypermasculinity manifested itself. For him, the dominant Mexican family pattern consisted of the absolute and unquestioned authority of the father and the necessary and absolute self-sacrifice of the mother. Boys were socialized to display *machismo*, while girls were taught that their femininity was tied to the home and maternity. In adolescence, men simultaneously sought both homey maternal wives and eroticized sexual playmates. Their strength, courage, and virility, symbolized by the size of their penis and testicles, were displayed by the convention of protecting one's own womenfolk, while trying to seduce those of other men. Although before marriage men placed women on pedestals as queens, after marriage they became slaves who had to submit to the unquestioned authority of their husbands. Diaz-Guerrero concluded that the inability of both sexes, particularly the females, to fulfill these expectations commonly led Mexicans to develop neuroses. Many Mexican personality disorders were due to the exaggerated *machismo* in the culture, a thesis that found validation in the works of Lewis (1951) and Gilbert (1959). Lewis's study was largely impressionistic, but Gilbert reached the conclusion by administering 106 Rorschach tests to residents of a *mestizo* village close to Mexico City. There was a pronounced tendency, he argued,

to either severely constricted affect or to morbid-depressed-hypochondriacal types of responses among the older males. . . . [T]his may be indicative of increasing impotence and "castration anxiety" as the males fail in the life-long struggle to live up to the demands of machismo. (p. 212)

The study of Mexicans living in the United States followed similar lines of inquiry. Mexicans were deemed initially identical on both sides of the border, with assimilation fundamentally transforming generational power relations within the home. "Mexican men in Detroit generally expect their wives to behave in much the same fashion that they did in Mexico," explained Humphrey (1944). "Most Mexican women in Detroit have remained subordinate, home-centered creatures" (p. 624). Assimilation produced a role reversal that effectively emasculated the father and elevated the eldest assimilated son to the role of "protector, orderer, and forbidder; in short a foster parent, schooled in American ways" through the mastery of English and monetary earnings. The mother retained her status as the guardian of "Mexican meanings and understandings" (p. 624). Jones (1948) reached the similar conclusion that the impact of emigration to the United States was to break up the "web of culture" (p. 452) that had previously kept the Mexican family intact.

Throughout the 1950s and early 1960s, little substantive research was added to these psychological profiles. Increasing, though, Mexican American culture came to be seen as based on "values" and "value orientations" that were diametrically different from those found in Anglo culture, values that bred underachievement and educational failure (Kluckhohn & Strodtbeck, 1961; Saunders, 1954). Mexican Americans would best enjoy the benefits of assimilation, explained educational psychologist H. T. Manuel (1965), only by embracing "Anglo-American values, both because of the weight of numbers in the dominant group and because of better adaptation" (p. 44). In the chapter "Failure of the Culture," Carter (1970) explained that Mexican American culture itself was responsible for orienting its children to devaluation of formal education; to placing interpersonal relationships over material goods; and to fatalism, stasis, apathy, presentism, superstition, and devaluation of time—"the Anglo concept of wasting time is not understood" (p. 42).

In general, Spanish Americans were portrayed as "a poor, proud, stable and cohesive group, with a value orientation strongly emphasizing interpersonal relations rather than ideas, abstractions or material possessions." They scorned upward mobility and equated it "with craft and dishonor," or so opined sociologist Robert G. Hayden (1966, p. 15). In domestic relations,

the family is under the firm authority of the father, while the mother assumes the traditional subservient and severely proscribed role of homemaker, the model of purity, bearer and trainer of children. This is a reflection of "hombría" or "machismo," i.e., supreme male dominance, and male individualism, assertiveness, and extreme pride. (p. 20)

Harking back to the work of Samuel Ramos (1938) and Paz (1961), Madsen (1964) proposed that *machismo* was a reactive response to the Mexican American male's subordination in the United States: "To a large extent the supremacy of the male within his own home compensates for subservice he may have to demonstrate on the job or in the presence of a social superior" (p. 48).

As obtuse and ethnocentric as these research results may now seem, their impact was far-reaching. Many of the conclusions of the biological determinists and value orientation theorists were diffused broadly through American culture via films. Woll (1977, 1980), Pettit (1980), Keller (1985), Greenfield and Cortés (1991), and Cortés (1992) have all shown that Hollywood films created such "scientific" caricatures of the Mexican and Mexican American to underscore the point that they lacked the values for upward mobility and full citizenship in the United States. Though some thematic variations were screened, Mexicans largely were portrayed in the movies as bandits and villains who rarely managed to romance the beautiful girls or to triumph in the conflicts in which they found themselves (Woll, 1977, 1980). That triumph was always reserved for Anglo men. American social science and image making persistently emasculated Mexican men and rendered the women passive and erotic trophies of conquest.

Much of this scholarship and popular myth making, which blamed the victims for their own marginalization and subordination in American life, was gradually eclipsed in the early 1960s as a result of social protest. Given the passivity, docility, and apathy social scientists said characterized the culture of African Americans, American Indians, and Mexican Americans, how was it possible that these groups had mobilized themselves to demand change?

CHICANOS AS A NATIONALITY, 1967–1993

Mexican Americans fought in World War II to make the world safe for democracy (Morin, 1966). Fighting beside other assimilated immigrants, they believed the national promise that when they returned home, the American Dream of social mobility and middle-class status would be theirs. The troops returned to what became a period of unprecedented economic growth in the United States. It was between 1945 and 1960 that America's global economic hegemony was truly consolidated. For white American men, the dream was indeed realized. The GI Bill of Rights helped educate many of them. The consumer goods, the cars, the stocked refrigerators, money to spare, and government loans to educate their children and buy homes soon followed. But by 1960, it was clear to Blacks, Mexican Americans, and Asian Americans that the benefits, the dreams, and the cash had not been distributed equitably. Indeed, the 1960 census graphically showed how far minorities lagged behind white America.

For Mexican Americans, these realizations were made potent in the mid-1960s as they saw their sons drafted and killed in the escalating war in Vietnam. In newspapers, they read about the worldwide crumbling of imperialism and the rise of new nationalisms, and at home they were moved by the peaceful activism of Cesar Chavez, who was trying to win better wages and work conditions for farmworkers and by Reies López Tijerina's attempts to regain lands fraudulently stolen from New Mexico's Hispanos. This complex conjuncture of structural forces was what sparked the Chicano movement. What differentiated the

Chicano movement from the civil rights activities of such groups as the League of United Latin American Citizens (LULAC), the American GI Forum, or the numerous mutual aid societies that Mexicanos had created to better their socioeconomic situation was the *Movimiento's* radical political stance. The civil rights movement of the 1940s and 1950s had sought slow, peaceful change through assimilation, through petitions for governmental beneficence, and through appeals to white liberal guilt. The Chicanos, largely a contingent of educated students, in a revolution sparked by rising expectations, insisted on equality with white America, demanded an end to racism, and asserted their right to cultural autonomy and national self-determination.

Chicanos saw themselves confronted by social emasculation and cultural negation and thus sought strength and inspiration in a heroic Aztec past that emphasized the virility of warriors and the exercise of brute force. Young Chicano men, a largely powerless group, invested themselves with images of power—a symbolic inversion commonly found in the fantasies of powerless men worldwide, a gendered vision that rarely extends to women. Aztlán, the legendary homeland of the Aztecs, was the nation Chicanos claimed, which they situated in a global community of oppressed nations and theorized through the emerging paradigm of internal colonialism.

Internal colonialism emerged as an interpretive social science model in the 1950s to explain racism, the segregation of racial groups, and socioeconomic inequality. Originally elaborated to explain the "development of underdevelopment" in Africa, Asia, and Latin America (Frank, 1967), the model was employed in Latin America as a theory of ethnic relations between indigenous groups and the larger *mestizo* (mixed-blood) class societies in Mexico, Guatemala, and Peru (Cotler, 1967–68; González-Casanova, 1969; Stavenhagen, 1965). By 1967, Stokeley Carmichael and Charles Harris employed the idea of internal colonialism in their book *Black Power,* an interpretation that was quickly adopted by other cultural nationalists in the United States.

Internal colonialism as a model appropriate for the description of American minorities received its fullest elaboration in the work of sociologist Robert Blauner (1972). Blauner maintained that although the United States was never a "colonizer" in the 19th-century European sense, it had nonetheless established its development through the conquest and seizure of Indian lands, the enslavement of Africans, and the usurpation of Mexican territory through war. Thus "western colonialism brought into existence the present-day patterns of racial stratification; in the United States, as elsewhere, it was a colonial experience that generated the lineup of ethnic and racial divisions" (p. 12).

Blauner (1972) admitted that internal colonialism by itself could not theorize race relations and social change in the United States because the country was a combination of colonial-racial and capitalist class realities. Internal colonialism was a modern capitalist practice of oppression and exploitation of racial and ethnic minorities within the borders of the state characterized by relationships of domination, oppression, and exploitation. Such relationships were apparent as (a) forced entry, (b) cultural impact, (c) external administration, and (d) racism.

White skin racial privilege was at the heart of the colonial relationship, manifested as an "unfair advantage, a preferential situation or systematic 'headstart' in the pursuit of social values, whether they be money, power, position, learning, or whatever" (Blauner, 1972, p. 22). White people had historically advanced at the expense of and because of the presence of Blacks, Chicanos, and other third world peoples, particularly in the structure of dual labor markets and occupational hierarchies. Given these realities, racism was not a form of false consciousness; it resulted in concrete benefits for Whites.

Chicanos quickly accepted the internal colonial model, and by the 1960s and 1970s they increasingly conceptualized themselves as a socially, culturally, and economically subordinated and regionally segregated people. These ideas received elaboration in Acuña (1972) and R. A. Gutiérrez (1976) in the discipline of history; Almaguer (1971, 1974, 1975) in the field of sociology; and Barrera (1979) and Barrera, Muñoz, and Ornelas (1972) in political science.

When internal colonialism was taken from the realm of the global and applied as a local concept, the *barrio,* or ghetto, became its focus, as evidenced in the titles of scholarly works by Camarillo, *Chicanos in a Changing Society: From Mexican Pueblos to American Barrios in Santa Barbara and Southern California, 1848–1930* (1979); Griswold del Castillo, *The Los Angeles Barrio, 1850–1890* (1979); and Romo, *East Los Angeles: A History of a Barrio* (1983).

If anything defined the ethics of the Chicano moral community, it was the belief in collectivism and an explicit rejection of individualism (Acuña, 1972). *Chicanismo* meant identifying with *la raza* (the race or people), and collectively promoting the interests of *carnales* (brothers) with whom they shared a common language, culture, and religion.

Examining any of the Chicano scholarly or artistic productions between 1965 and 1975 clearly indicates one point. The history of Chicanos was thought to have begun in 1848, at the end of the U.S.-Mexican War. This date emphasized the legacy of Anglo racism toward Chicanos. As Armando Navarro (1974) would write, "Chicano politics [and history have] always been imbued with a spirit of resistance toward Anglo-American oppression and

domination." The relationship between Anglos and Chicanos "was conceived out of a master-servant relationship between the Anglo conqueror and the Chicano conquered" (pp. 57–58).

The years 1965 to 1969 saw extensive Chicano activism in the Southwest. As Chicano students were recruited to college and university campuses, the protest from the streets was brought into the classroom. Chicanos demanded Chicano studies programs, cultural pride day, and diversification of the curriculum. Coming from working-class backgrounds and feeling privileged by their college draft exemptions, these Chicanos identified with workers and peasants, and indeed imagined themselves as speakers for these groups.

Few Chicano militants, however, were willing to consider women as an important component of their emancipatory project. By 1969, at the very moment Corky Gonzales was trying to weld a fractured Chicano student movement into a national force, the more radical Chicanas were beginning to see themselves as triply oppressed: by their race, their gender, and their class. "Women students were expected by their male peers to involve themselves actively but in subordination," recalled Adelaida Del Castillo (1980). It was not uncommon in those days for the movement's men "to request sexual cooperation as proof of commitment to the struggle, by gratifying the men who fought it" (p. 7). Although the movement persistently had advocated the self-actualization of all Chicanos, women soon discovered that *Chicanos* meant only men.

Within the Chicano student movement, women were denied leadership roles and were asked to perform only the most traditional stereotypic roles—cleaning up, making coffee, executing the orders given by men, and servicing their needs. Women who did manage to assume leadership positions were ridiculed as unfeminine, sexually perverse, and promiscuous; at the extreme, they were all too often taunted as lesbians.

Consequently, by the early 1970s articles began to appear in the movement press highlighting the contradiction between racial and sexual oppression in the Chicano movement. Irene Rodarte (1973) posed the question, "machismo or revolution?" which Guadalupe Valdes Fallis (1974) reformulated as, "tradition or liberation?" Chicano men initially regarded the feminist critique as an assault on their Mexican cultural past, their power, and by implication their virility; they responded with crass name calling, labeling Chicana feminists as *malinchistas,* traitors who were influenced by ideas foreign to their community, namely, bourgeois feminist ideology.

The men exhorted the women to be Chicanas first and foremost, to take pride in their cultural heritage, and to reject women's liberation (Longauex y Vásquez, 1970,

1972). Theresa Aragón (1980) was but one of the many women who responded by stating clearly and unequivocally that Chicanas, by incorporating feminist demands in their anticolonial revolution, were not dupes of White bourgeois feminists. "The white women's movement at present is not generally aware of or sensitive to the needs of the Chicana," Aragón wrote, and so, "Chicanas would have to define their own goals and objectives in relationship to their culture, and their own feminist ideology in relation to those goals" (p. 27).

Just as Chicanos interested in interpreting the history of the Southwest as a history of racial conflict between Anglos and Mexicans explicitly chose 1848 as the beginning of Chicano history, Chicana feminists began envisioning a history ordered by a different sense of time. For women, it was not the U.S.–Mexican War that was most important; instead, it was the first major act of conquest in the Americas, Spain's defeat of the Aztec empire (Mirandé & Enríquez, 1979; Sweeney, 1977). A Chicana history that began in 1519, not 1848, placed the issues of gender and power at the very center of the political debate about the future and the past. By choosing 1519, women focused attention on one of Mexico's most famous women, Doña Marina, a Maya woman of noble ancestry given as a gift to Hernán Cortés in 1517. Cortés availed himself of Doña Marina's considerable knowledge of the local political geography and of various indigenous languages. Acting as his mistress, translator, and confidante, Marina helped Cortés to forge local antipathies toward the Aztecs into a fighting force that Cortés successfully unleashed on Tenochtitlan.

In Mexican history, Doña Marina, or la Malinche, had always been seen as a villain, as the supreme betrayer of her race. Luis Valdez, in his 1971 play *The Conquest of Mexico*, depicted Malinche as a traitor because "not only did she turn her back on her own people, she joined the white men and became assimilated" (p. 131). For activist Chicanas, the historical representations of Malinche as a treacherous whore who betrayed her own people were but profound reflections of the deep-seated misogynist beliefs in Mexican and Mexican American culture. The only public models open to Mexican women were those of the virgin and the whore (Stevens, 1973). If women were going to go beyond them, then they had to begin by rehabilitating Malinche, seeing her as the primordial source of *mexicanidad* and *mestizaje*. Malinche, noted Del Castillo (1977),

is the beginning of the mestizo nation, she is the mother of its birth, she initiates it with the birth of her mestizo children. Even her baptism is significant. She is, in fact, the first Indian to be christianized (catechized and baptized to Catholicism) in her native land, that land which metamorphizes into our mundo mestizo—again she is the starting point! Thus any denigration made against her indirectly defames the character of the . . . chicana female. If there is shame for her, there is shame for us; we suffer the effects of those implications. (p. 126)

Whatever the facts—in the case of Malinche there are dreadfully few—the crafting of a *her*story and feminist chronology had shifted the debate away from racism to sexism, away from the male ethos of *carnalismo*, or brotherhood, and *chicanismo*, to *mexicanidad* and *mestizaje*, or pride in one's Mexican ancestry and a recognition of race mixture.

The aim of the male Chicano movement was to decolonize the mind. Chicanas wanted to decolonize the body. Male concerns over job discrimination, access to political power, entry into educational institutions, and community autonomy and self-determination gave way to female demands for birth control (T. Aragón, 1980; Delgado, 1978; Flores, 1976) and against forced sterilization (Velez-Ibañez, 1980), for welfare rights, for prison rights for *pintas*, for protection against male violence, and most important for sexual pleasure both in marriage and outside of it.

As should be apparent from these writings, the impact of Chicano-inspired scholarship and activism was to challenge the status quo and to displace the century-old stereotypes and caricatures of Mexicans and Mexican Americans in the dominant imagination. The alleged passivity of the Mexican American could no longer be reconciled with the images that appeared daily on network television news and in newspapers. "Docile" Mexican Americans had demanded their rights; had affirmed the vibrancy and importance of their culture, religion, and language; and, like other nationalist movements in the United States, were demanding a reinscription into the body politic.

RECENT RESEARCH TRENDS

Since 1985, there has been a great deal of research activity generated by scholars of Chicano ancestry, by individuals who were active in the movement, and by sympathetic fellow travelers. Foremost in the minds of many has been serious reexamination of the Chicano movement, focusing on the social origins of the leaders, the ideologies that inspired them, and impact on society. What this new scholarship shows is that the Chicano movement has largely been misunderstood. Scholars describe it in monolithic and unitary terms, lumping together and projecting onto a national stage what were, in fact, disparate activities of local import. The plight of Mexican Americans first gained national visibility through the activities of César Chávez and his attempts to win better wages and working conditions for agricultural laborers in the central valley of California through the United Farm Workers of America, the labor union he had formed. Rodolfo "Corky" Gonzales began the Crusade for Justice in Denver to militate against police brutality and the poverty Mexican Americans suffered, and from this base mobilized Chicano students in the Southwest. The long-time Hispano residents of northern New Mexico, seeking to regain the lands they had been defrauded of after U.S. territorial conquest, found a leader for their cause in Reies López Tijerina. In Crystal City, Texas, José Angel Gutiérrez organized ethnic Mexicans to seize political power through electoral campaigns, first winning representation on the school board and then creating La Raza Unida Party for larger regional goals. Although student protest over educational access and against the War in Vietnam are often factored into the mix, these men and their organizations are what is still deemed the Chicano movement.

Few scholarly attempts have yet been made to assess the accomplishments and larger historical significance of the Chicano movement. The National Latino Communications Center, in conjunction with Los Angeles-based KCET public television, undertook one of the best attempts, producing in 1996 a four-hour program called "Chicano! The History of the Mexican American Civil Rights Movement," which provides both a history of ethnic Mexican experiences in the United States from 1836 to 1980 and a description of various organizations, leaders, and their ideologies. Two companion books to the television series were published, the first a copiously illustrated program narrative, the second a collection of historical documents (Rosales, 1997, 2000).

A second and much more artistic attempt to analyze the Chicano movement was undertaken as part of a museum exhibition called "Chicano Art: Resistance and Affirmation, 1965–1985," or simply CARA, which toured the United States between 1990 and 1993. The exhibition catalogue placed Chicano art within a larger social and political context and by so doing offered an explanation of the movement's various components and concerns (Griswold del Castillo, McKenna, & Yarbro-Bejarano, 1991). A. Gaspar de Alba (1998) studies the politics of the CARA exhibition itself as a window into the larger history and significance of the Chicano movement. R. A. Gutiérrez (1993a) likewise places Chicano student activism on college and university campuses within larger movements of decolonization in the United States.

Only one essay critical of the Chicano movement's ideology has appeared, T. Almaguer's "Ideological Distortions in Recent Chicano Historiography" (1989). Almaguer argues that, motivated primarily by the desire to challenge the dominant assimilationist model of the 1950s, Chicano radicals embraced a very simplistic colonial analysis that depicted the history of Chicanos as that of an internally colonized minority. However strongly these sentiments were felt in the 1960s, the analysis was wrong because Mexican-Americans historically had occupied several classes, including the upper class, and racially stood in an intermediate position between Blacks and Whites. In short, much of what he and others had written about Chicano oppression was an ideological distortion of the past, fashioned to fit the political tenor of the day.

Over the last fifteen years, the major leaders of the Chicano movement have been the topic of more research. Despite his death in 1998, César Chávez remains the most extensively studied. In 2000, California declared his birthday a state holiday and mandated that all public schools create curricular materials on the issues Chávez devoted his life to. Mexican farm laborers in the United States have continued to garner scholarly attention with a number of works focusing on areas other than California. E. Gamboa (1990) studies the Pacific Northwest, W. K. Barger and E. M. Reza (1994) the Midwest, and D. Valdés (1991, 2000) the Great Lakes. R. Griswold del Castillo and R. García (1995) have written an important new biography of Chávez. Y. Broyles-González (1994) looks at how Chávez used popular theatre, the Teatro Campesino, to attract union members among a largely illiterate working class. Although most of the early scholarship on Chávez focused on his unionizing campaigns, two dissertations explore his religious rhetoric. F. Dalton (1998) studies the moral foundations of Chávez's national appeals, while A. Watt (1999) examines the multiple religious traditions Chávez drew on to provoke America's national conscience.

Corky Gonzales is now also deceased. A collection of his speeches, poems, and plays was recently published (R. Gonzales, 2001), allowing a closer look at the ideology of this leader. E. B. Vigil (1999), his comrade in the Crusade for Justice, recently penned an insider account of the organization's origin, leadership, ideals, and larger impact. What is particularly noteworthy about this study is its extensive use of FBI documents. Vigil shows the FBI constantly monitoring and disrupting the Crusade's activities.

Reies López Tijerina, the New Mexican land militant, drew considerable scholarly attention in the early 1970s, at the very moment of confrontation with state authorities, but very little since. R. Busto's (1991) dissertation on Tijerina's Baptist ministry and the messianic content of his public appeals is the notable exception. Tijerina's (1978) own massive autobiography, originally published in Mexico in Spanish some twenty-five years ago, finally has been translated into English in abbreviated form (2000).

During the late 1950s, many Mexican American civil rights organizations in the United States believed that they would improve their social and economic lot through peaceful appeals to government and through participation in organized political parties. This civil rights strategy, and the retreat from it, has been documented in a number of recent works. I. García (2000) chronicles Mexican American mobilization to elect John F. Kennedy president in 1960, the formation of Viva Kennedy Clubs, campaigns to get out the vote, and the high levels of disillusionment that resulted when Kennedy failed to deliver on his campaign promises. These same episodes are covered from the vantage point of Lyndon B. Johnson and his ascendancy to national politics in J. L. Pycior's (1997) study. The formulation of Johnson's Great Society programs and their specific impact on Mexican Americans are excellently analyzed herein, as well as in J. R. Chavez's (1998) history of Great Society programs in Los Angeles. Mexican American community leaders gained administrative experience and political connections to the Democratic Party through these organizations, which they later used to launch political careers.

For many Chicano activists, there was a clear realization by 1964 that participation in the Democratic Party had produced few tangible results. If true structural change was to occur, Chicanos needed to create their own political party. José Angel Gutiérrez chose this path, starting La Raza Unida Party in Crystal City, Texas, in 1970 to fight discrimination and political disenfranchisement. His reminiscences (J. A. Gutiérrez, 1998) about the party's formation and demise were recently published. Therein he describes how the idea for a Chicano party was born in 1960 when as a student he and his classmates struggled with the all-Anglo Crystal City school board to gain access to college preparatory courses and better educational resources. A. Navarro (1998) deepens our understanding of José Angel Gutiérrez's role in educational reform in Crystal City and offers a different narrative of the events that led to the formation of La Raza Unida Party (Navarro, 2000).

The scholarship on the Chicano movement has quite naturally focused on the leaders and organizations that came to the nation's attention. Some works are just beginning to appear on the largely nameless student activists who also militated for civil rights, for the end of the war in Vietnam, and whose egalitarian aspirations led them to demand gender and sexual equality for women, lesbians, and gays. The radicalization of Mexican American students in the 1960s and 1970s is studied extensively by C. Muñoz (1989) in California and by A. Navarro (1995) in Texas. Many of these student radicals, out of solidarity with Blacks, emulated black nationalist rhetoric and cultural politics to create a group of Brown Berets, which mimicked the Black Panther Party's Black Berets. D. Espinoza's (1996) dissertation studies these manifestations among Chicanos and Chicanas.

Chicano participation in the war in Vietnam and in the American peace movement against it has been the topic of a number of new works. R. Benavidez (1995),

F. Munguía (1986), J. Ramirez (1999), and C. Trujillo (1990) were all soldiers who served in Vietnam and wrote self-consciously as Chicanos about those experiences. Chicano opposition to the war in the United States is the topic of L. Oropeza's (1996) dissertation. G. Mariscal (1999) has compiled an anthology of original poems, short stories, newspaper editorials, and personal narratives about Chicano and Chicana reactions to the war, which is a welcome addition to the literature.

The impact of feminism on the Chicano student movement and on the development of Chicana studies has largely been told through anthologies rather than book-length monographic studies. A. García's (1997) foundational anthology gathers much of the early Chicana feminists' writings. C. Trujillo (1998) collected a number of autobiographical essays by Chicana activists in which they describe their experiences and lessons learned. A. de la Torre and B. Pesquera (1993) produced a similarly foundational anthology on Chicana studies, demonstrating how interpretations of work, family, and economy profoundly change when women's participation is seriously considered.

Homosexuality, a theme that was previously studied largely as taboo, perversion, and pathology, in the 1990s emerged as an important theme of personal identity. Inspired by Chicana feminist works, a number of important anthologies on lesbianism and sexuality have appeared, by C. Trujillo (1991); N. Alarcón, A. Castillo, and C. Moraga (1993); and J. Ramos (Ramos, 1994). These collections are largely autobiographical, describing personal experiences and explorations of sexuality. C. Moraga (1997) and G. Anzaldúa (1987; Keating, 2000), two of the first Chicana women to publicly discuss their lesbianism, each reflect on those experiences in recent books.

Writing by and about gay Mexican American men has not been quite as extensive, nor has it been as openly revealing as the work by women. Take for example public television essayist Richard Rodriguez. His autobiographical, largely anti-affirmative-action tract *Hunger of Memory: The Education of Richard Rodriguez* (1982) is full of homoerotic passages describing his fantasies about the sweaty muscled bodies of Mexican day laborers. Similar impulses are more explicitly described in *Days of Obligation* (1992), but nowhere does he reveal, much less reflect on, his well-known gay identity.

The most comprehensive analysis yet of Chicano homosexual behavior and identity remains A. Almaguer's (1991) comparison of Anglo American and Latin American sexual systems. Though the essay is flawed by its overly rigid dichotomies, it is nevertheless the only interpretive piece that tries to compare sexual scripts people use to eroticize bodies. This essay has been reprinted in many anthologies, precipitated controversies, and generated much exciting new research. Spurred primarily by the spread of AIDS and HIV infection, younger scholars are also now giving serious scholarly attention to ethnic Mexican men who have sex with other men but who do not identify as gay (Cantú, 1999; Díaz, 1998).

The impact of feminist scholarship can also be seen in a number of studies on the social and cultural construction of manhood and masculinity among Mexicans, Mexican Americans, and Chicanos. Undoubtedly the most substantial of these is M. Gutmann's (1996) study of the ideology, roles, and practices of working-class men in one of Mexico City's neighborhoods. He concludes that strict role division does not exist, that men actively participate in child rearing and domestic work, and that the hypermasculine ethos of machismo is more fiction than fact, at least in this specific locale. A. Mirandé (1997) relies on interviews to reinscribe the very stereotypic portrait Gutmann debunks. R. González's anthology (1996) of writing by Latino men reflecting on their manhood gives a great deal of variance, contingency, and complexity to how men are formed and reformed through social practice.

These new assessments of the components that made up the Chicano movement have deepened our understanding of the role Mexican Americans played in the larger civil rights movement in the United States. Such activities occurred at the very moment that new levels of immigration began. In 1965, Congress abolished the so-called national origins quotas, which since 1924 had limited the number of Mexicans allowed legal entry into the United States. Whereas in the twenty years between 1941 and 1960 a grand total of only 3,550,000 immigrants had gained entry into the United States, over the next 40 years more than 20 million legally did. Of these immigrants, Mexicans were the largest single national group to arrive, representing roughly 25% of this total (U.S. Department of Commerce, 1999). Aggregating as a whole the immigrants from Mexico, Central America, South America, and the Caribbean accounted for roughly half of all immigrants who entered between 1965 and 1980.

The rapid arrival of so many immigrants provoked a range of national responses, not unlike those that greeted new arrivals at the beginning of the twentieth century. Jubilant employers hailed the abundant supply of cheap Mexican labor while anxious xenophobes expressed their racial fears. L. R. Chavez (2001) excellently surveys the negative print media stories on this immigration in his recent book, *Covering Immigration.*

As was already noted earlier in this chapter, popular anxiety about the presence of immigrants has long been closely correlated with economic cycles. Prosperity brings abundant work that cannot be accomplished without immigrants, and in such moments they are praised as indispensable additions to the republic. In moments of economic depression, immigrants are scapegoats, blamed

for economic hardships and for taking jobs from American workers. P. Brimelow's *Alien Nation* (1995) is rather typical of anti-immigrant tracts produced during the economic recession of the early 1990s. "The American nation has always had a specific core . . . and that core has been white," wrote Brimelow. He insisted that Americans had a right to demand that government stop shifting the nation's racial balance; "indeed, it seems to me that they have a right to insist that it be shifted back" (p. 265). Sentiments similar to these from the extreme political right can be found in L. Auster's *The Path to National Suicide* (1990) and R. D. Lamm and G. Imhoff's *The Immigration Time Bomb* (1985), as well as from the liberal left, such as A. Schlesinger, Jr.'s, *The Disuniting of America* (1992). Racist ideas about the relationship between race and intelligence, dismissed a century ago, reemerged in the 1990s to buttress arguments against immigration. In their book *The Bell Curve* (1994), R. J. Herrnstein and C. Murray claimed that on the average Latinos scored 9% lower than Whites on IQ tests. Such disparity, they warned, would lower the overall intelligence of the United States and ultimately lead to crime, women on welfare, and single-parent households.

The U.S. economy experienced rapid growth between 1995 and 2001. The Mexican immigrant population, which only a few years earlier had been denigrated as parasitic and contributing to America's mongrelization, quickly became an essential source of vitality. The July 12, 1999, issue of *Newsweek* magazine, for example, had as its cover story "Latin U.S.A.," announcing that "Hispanics are hip, hot and making history" (Larmer, 1999). The story chronicled transformations in America's population wrought by high levels of Latin American immigration, which were producing a new national geometry of culture, politics, and money radiating from Miami, Los Angeles, Chicago, Houston, New York, and San Jose. "By 2005, Latinos will be the largest U.S. minority; they're already shaping pop culture and presidential politics. The Latin wave will change how the country looks—and how it looks at itself," *Newsweek* proclaimed, nevertheless worried that this population would be "ground zero for a demographic upheaval" (Larmer, 1999).

Given the importance of immigration to contemporary economic life in the United States, it quite naturally has remained an important scholarly theme. Although earlier work focused largely on immigrant men, a pronounced shift in the gender balance of the immigrant stream has led to heightened attention to women's issues. Recent studies estimate that since 1945 slightly more than one half of all Mexican immigrants have been women, and since 1990, particularly in Los Angeles County, women have constituted the bulk (Cardenas & Flores, 1986; Cornelius, 1999; Ruiz & Tiano, 1987). This sex-ratio shift has led to the study of women's work; rates of labor force participation; comparable worth; occupational preferences; their roles in secondary labor markets; the production and reproduction of material life; gender ideology; and family, kinship, and sexuality (Cardenas, 1982; Cooney, 1975; Cravey, 1998; Fernández-Kelly, 1983; Hondagneu-Sotelo, 2001; Kossoudji & Ranney, 1984; Romero, 1992; V. Ruiz, 1987; Zavella, 1987).

As was noted above, one of the consequences of the 1965 Immigration Reform Act was to increase the number of immigrants of Latin American origin in the United States, adding significant numbers from the Caribbean, Central America, and South America. To acknowledge this change, scholars have increasingly turned their attention to the panethnic political identity that these nationalities have invented as Latinos. The U.S. census of 2000 concludes that there are 35 million Latinos in the United States today, constituting roughly 14% of the total population, and projected to represent 18% in the year 2025 and 25% by 2050. Already in states like California, Texas, Florida, and New York, the Latino proportion of the total population is much higher. In 1998 they accounted for 40% of the population in New Mexico, 31% in California, 30% in Texas, 15% in Florida, and 14% in New York. The population in the first three of these five states is largely of Mexican origin, while for the last two it is Cuban and Puerto Rican. These proportions are even higher in specific metropolitan areas. El Paso in 1997 was 75% Latino, San Antonio 53%, Fresno 42%, Albuquerque 39%, Los Angeles 39%, and Miami–Fort Lauderdale 37% (U.S. Department of Commerce, 1999).

Latinos are extremely diverse. Most of the 1.2 million Cubans fled Cuba in the early 1960s and came from educated, middle-class, and professional families. They were joined in 1980 by a group of lower-class origin known as the Marielitos. Puerto Ricans are U.S. citizens. Of the 2.4 million currently living on the mainland, most emigrated from the island between 1945 and 1960 and arrived poor, and few have improved their lot. Class, race, ethnicity, and date of entry complexly stratify Mexicans. The original Spanish and Mexican settlers of the Southwest were joined by wave after wave of compatriots in every decade since the 1880s. Mexican emigration to the United States never stopped. To this mix, add emigrants from the Caribbean and Central and South America, and the complexity of Latino identity becomes apparent (Moore & Pachón, 1985; Oboler, 1995).

Latinos are largely concentrated at the bottom of the socioeconomic ladder. Very few have managed to ascend into the ranks of the rich. When *Hispanic Business* identified the richest "Hispanics" in the United States in 1995, it listed 75—out of a population of roughly 30 million. The majority of these, 27, were Cuban Americans; 25 were Mexican Americans, 8 were Spaniards, 7 were Puerto Rican (5 lived in the United States and 3 on the island), and one each were from Chile, Colombia, Costa Rica, the Dominican Republic, Ecuador, Uruguay, and Venezuela ("Emerging Wealth," 1996).

The number of Latinos in the corporate elite is just as small. Again, *Hispanic Business* reported that between 1990 and 1995 the number of Hispanics on the board of directors of a Fortune 1000 company did not exceed 1% of all corporate directors. In 1990, they numbered 40, and in 1995, 51, with roughly one out of every five of these a Latina. Analyzing the personal histories of these individuals, sociologists R. L. Zweigenhaft and G. W. Domhoff (1998) found that most had been born into well-connected middle-class families with access to elite education and included very few rags-to-riches stories.

Economist E. López, heading a California Research Bureau team in 1998, reported that Latinos had the state's lowest median wages (López, Ramirez, & Rochin, 1999). The median wage for California's 15.6 million workers was $21,000; for Whites it was $27,000, for Asians $24,000, for Blacks $23,000, and for Latinos $14,560. Holding all other factors constant, such as immigrant status and length of time in the United States, most of the wage disparity could be explained by level of educational achievement. Only 7% of White workers lacked a high school diploma. Seven percent of Black workers had failed to reach this basic benchmark, 12% of Asians, and 45% of Latinos. Only 8% of Latinos had a bachelor's degree or higher. Twenty-four percent of black workers had this level of education, as did 33% of Whites and 43% of Asians. Projecting the size and composition of California's population forward to the year 2025, López predicted dire fiscal consequences for the state if investments in Latino educational achievement were not radically increased. In 2025, Latinos would constitute 43% of the population. If roughly 50% of Latinos continued to drop out of high school, this would account for about a fourth of the state's population.

What other economists have also found particularly worrisome about this wage and employment pattern is that over the last decade Latino males have had the highest rates of labor force participation. In 1990, 85% of age-eligible Latinos worked, while only 77% of Anglos did. What these statistics show is a pattern of working poverty, not joblessness, due to low levels of educational achievement and limited social networks for acquiring better-paid work (Hayes-Bautista, 1993; Melendez, 1993; Pastor, 1995).

A number of factors explain Latino working poverty. In his study of Mexican emigration to the United States, sociologist D. Massey and a group of researchers found highly developed "bonding" networks that connected Mexicans in their country to work in the United States (Massey, Alarcón, Durand, & González, 1987). In San Diego and Los Angeles, 70% of Mexican immigrants found work through such ties. These networks provided steady access to work, but it was poorly paid, nonunionized work in the service and light manufacturing sectors that often provided no benefits and offered little possibilities for upward mobility. To expand their economic opportunities, Mexican immigrants needed "bridging" networks, ties that cut across geography, class, and ethnicity to offer access to higher-paid work. As economist M. Pastor has argued, when communities are boxed in by residential segregation, racial discrimination, and weak educational structures, broadened opportunities develop only through the construction of bridging networks in the form of community-based employment and training agencies (Pastor, 2000).

Sociologists D. López and Y. Espiritu (1990) have analyzed the structural and cultural forces that account for the development of panethnic identities such as Latino and argue that they emerge when members of different nationalities share a common structural relationship to race, class, generation, and geography. If subethnicities "look alike" to dominant outsiders and are the targets of racial discrimination, panethnic solidarity is likely to develop. A shared class position, a high level of residential proximity, and several generations of residence in the United States have often led marginalized ethnic/national groups to enhance their power through ethnic alliances. Cultural factors, such as common language and religion, are also important but not determinative.

Although they recognize that Latino identity has on occasion played an important political role, such as that described in Chicago by F. Padilla (1987), López and Espiritu (1990) do not believe that it will ever be a structurally significant identity because of the racial, class, and generational diversity it subsumes. Sixty percent of all Mexicans are geographically concentrated in California and the Southwest. The majority of Puerto Ricans on the mainland live in New York and New Jersey. Cubans reside primarily in South Florida. Each group has different political priorities, histories, memories, and objective class interests not easily abandoned in the name of Latino identity goals.

A common language (Spanish) and religion (Catholicism) certainly create strong affective ties at the cultural level among Latinos, argue López and Espiritu (1990). But these are not structurally significant, for if one looks at the popular manifestations of Latino identity in the United States today, they are primarily at the cultural level of consumption: shared language, religion, literature, and music. Cuban American Gloria Estefan sings in her popular 1993 song *Hablemos el mismo idioma* ("Let's Speak the Same Language"), that "Latinos" must put aside their differences, stand united, speak their shared Spanish language, and be proud of being Latinos, regardless of national origin. What the media increasingly celebrates as Latino is the music of Ricki Martin, Marc Anthony, Junot Diaz, and Shakira; the popularity of boxing champion Oscar de la Hoya and baseball player Alex Rodriguez; and the sexiness of Latino movie stars.

What all this recent research has poignantly established is that the Mexican-origin population of the United States is complexly stratified by class, color, gender, generation, and level of assimilation. Ethnic Mexicans, when considered along with other immigrants of Latin American origin, are no longer a minority but an emerging majority population in the United States. This reality has prompted new research on Latinos, whom outsiders perceive as a much more potentially powerful group than realities would suggest.

IMPLICATIONS FOR RESEARCH AND PRACTICE

Looking over the course of almost 200 years, this chapter has surveyed the historical and social science literature on Mexican, Mexican Americans, Chicanos, and Latinos. What becomes apparent is that in each of the periods reviewed here the ethnic Mexican population of the United States was negatively stigmatized by their culture and its occupations, and persistently and repeatedly viewed as a problem that had to be cured, if not eradicated. Scholarship written by Chicanos themselves, and by intellectuals sympathetic to their aspirations, did a great deal to change the topics and tenor of the research. Studies that once vilified Mexicans, that blamed victims for their own problems, or that celebrated victimization were supplanted by scholarship that explored historical agency, subjectivity, and differentiation of various sorts.

If one glances over the research corpus discussed here, it is readily apparent that there are still numerous themes in the history of Mexican Americans that are desperately in need of study. The issue of transculturation has been only slightly explored, and much remains to be written on the process of assimilation and acculturation as it has affected a highly mobile population that has consistently refused to cut its ties to Mexico. Most of the theoretical work on assimilation and acculturation was based on the experiences of European immigrants who were separated by an ocean from their country of origin, who rarely visited Europe once they emigrated, and who quickly cast their lot with their new home in the United States. Mexicans have never fit this pattern, and thus perhaps it is time to rethink assimilation as an explanatory model for Americanization.

Because so much of the scholarship on ethnic Mexicans focused on immigration, little has been written about the generational experiences of these immigrants in the United States. Some attention has been given to marital and linguistic assimilation, to educational attainment and occupational patterns, but very little to the experiences of the first or immigrant generation. We know for a fact that English-language proficiency is the major determinant of wage level for Mexican immigrants. The challenge is how to teach adult immigrants English. Second-generation pathologies (juvenile crime, poor health, poor school performance) are largely the result of the low and unstable incomes of first-generation parents. If we bear in mind the feminization of Mexican immigration over the last three decades, the monumentality of the challenge becomes even more pressing (Cornelius, 1999).

As the United States tries to imagine its future in a new world order devoid of the threat of communism, how the nation's borders are constructed both physically and metaphysically will be an issue of utmost importance. To respond to the challenges and opportunities posed by the rise of global corporations and major regional trading blocs, the hemispheric relationship among Mexico, Canada, and the United States is being renegotiated. Perhaps in the not-too-distant future physical borders will cease to exist in North America and workers will move about freely without constraint, pushed and pulled by market forces rather than the forces of state repression.

The racialization of Mexicans and Latinos as non-Whites continues to be a significant barrier to upward mobility. Latin American societies have long been extremely color-conscious, recognizing fine gradations of mixture between Africans, Europeans, and Indians. In the United States, these complex racial classifications have been reduced to three categories—Black, White, and non-White—primarily on the basis of visual assessments of a person's color. Mexicans and Latinos are daily racialized as non-White, suffering the disabilities such an assessment brings: lower wages, occupation segregation, fewer educational opportunities, racial profiling by the authorities, and residential segregation (Arce, Murguía, & Frisbie, 1987; Telles & Murguía, 1990).

These, then, are some of the challenges and opportunities that await scholars, researchers, students, and cultural workers—reimagining the Mexican past in order to challenge the future before us.

References

Acuña, R. (1972). *Occupied America: The Chicano struggle toward liberation*. New York: Canfield Press.

Alarcón, N., Castillo, A., & Moraga, C. (Ed.). (1993). *The sexuality of Latinas*. Berkeley, CA: Third Woman Press.

Almaguer, T. (1971). Toward the study of Chicano colonialism. *Aztlán, 2*(1), 7–21.

Almaguer, T. (1974). Historical notes on Chicano oppression: The dialectics of racial and class domination in North America. *Aztlán, 5*(1–2), 27–56.

Almaguer, T. (1975). Class, race, and Chicano oppression. *Socialist Revolution, 25*, 71–99.

Almaguer, T. (1989). Ideological distortions in recent Chicano historiography. *Aztlán, 18*, 7–27.

Almaguer, T. (1991). Chicano men: A cartography of homosexual identity and behavior. *Differences: A Journal of Feminist Cultural Studies, 3*(2), 75–100.

Almaguer, T., & Camarillo, A. (1983). Urban Chicano workers in historical perspective: A review of the literature. In A. Valdez, A. Camarillo, & T. Almaguer (Eds.), *The state of Chicano research on family, labor, and migration: Proceedings of the first Stanford symposium on Chicano research and public policy* (pp. 3–32). Stanford, CA: Stanford Center for Chicano Research.

Alvarez, H. (1966). A demographic profile of Mexican immigration to the United States, 1910–1950. *Journal of Inter-American Studies, 8*(1), 471–496.

Anzaldúa, G. (1987). *Borderlands, La frontera: The new mestiza*. San Francisco: Spinsters/Aunt Lute Book Company.

Aragón, J. L. (1976). The people of Santa Fe in the 1790s. *Aztlán, 7*(3), 391–417.

Aragón, T. (1980). Organizing as a political tool for the Chicana. *Frontiers: A Journal of Women's Studies, 5*(2), 9–34.

Arce, C. H., Murguía, E., & Frisbie, W. P. (1987). Phenotype and life chances among Chicanos. *Hispanic Journal of Behavioral Sciences, 9*(1), 19–32.

Arroyo, L. (1975). Notes on past, present and future directions of Chicano labor studies. *Aztlán, 6*(2), 137–150.

Auster, L. (1990). *The path to national suicide: An essay on immigration and multiculturalism*. Monterey, VA: American Immigration Control Foundation.

Balderrama, F. E. (1982). *In defense of La Raza: The Los Angeles Mexican consulate and the Mexican community, 1929–1936*. Tucson: University of New Mexico Press.

Bamford, E. F. (1923–24). The Mexican casual problem in the Southwest. *Journal of Applied Sociology, 8*, 364–371.

Barger, W. K., & Reza, E. M. (1994). *The farm labor movement in the Midwest: Social change and labor adaptation among migrant farmworkers*. Austin: University of Texas Press.

Barrera, M. (1979). *Race and class in the southwest: A theory of racial inequality*. Notre Dame, IN: Notre Dame University Press.

Barrera, M., Muñoz, C., & Ornelas, C. (1972). The barrio as internal colony. *Urban Affairs Annual Reviews, 6*, 465–498.

Bean, F. D., & Tienda, M. (1987). *The Hispanic population of the United States*. New York: Russell Sage Foundation.

Benavidez, R. (1995). *Medal of honor: A Vietnam warrior's story*. Washington, DC: Brasseys.

Betten, N., & Mohl, R. A. (1973). From discrimination to repatriation: Mexican life during the great depression. *Pacific Historical Review, 42*(3), 370–388.

Blauner, R. (1972). *Racial oppression in America*. New York: Harper & Row.

Bogardus, E. (1940). Current problems of Mexican immigrants. *Sociology and Social Research, 24*, 168–173.

Bogardus, E. (1943). Gangs of Mexican-American youth. *Sociology and Social Science Research, 27,* 60–72.

Bolton, H. E. (1915). *Texas in the middle eighteenth century: Studies in Spanish colonial history and administration.* Berkeley: University of California Press.

Borjas, G. J. (1990). *Friends or strangers: The impact of immigrants on the U.S. economy.* New York: Basic Books.

Boswell, T. D. (1979). The growth and proportional distribution of the Mexican-stock population of the United States: 1910–1970. *Mississippi Geographer, 7*(1), 57–76.

Brack, G. M. (1975). *Mexico views manifest destiny, 1821–1846: An essay on the origins of the Mexican War.* Albuquerque: University of New Mexico Press.

Briegel, K. L. (1974). *The Alianza Hispano Americana, 1894–1965: A Mexican fraternal insurance society.* Unpublished doctoral dissertation, University of Southern California.

Briggs, C. (1987). Getting both sides of the story: Oral history in land grant research and litigation. In C. L. Briggs & J. R. Van Ness (Eds.), *Land, water, and culture: New perspectives on Hispanic land grants* (pp. 217–268). Albuquerque: University of New Mexico Press.

Briggs, C. L., & Van Ness, J. R. (1987). *Land, water, and culture: New perspectives on Hispanic land grants.* Albuquerque: University of New Mexico Press.

Brimelow, P. (1995). *Alien nation: Common sense about America's immigration disaster.* New York: Random House.

Broyles-González, Y. (1994). *El teatro campesino: Theatre in the Chicano movement.* Austin: University of Texas Press.

Burroughs, F. (1988). Joining the future and the past. In L. Hernández & T. Bénitez (Eds.), *Palabras Chicanas* (pp. 55–57). Berkeley, CA: University of California Press.

Busto, R. V. (1991). *Like a mighty rushing wind: The religious impulse in the life and writing of Reies López Tijerina.* Unpublished doctoral dissertation, University of California, Berkeley.

Calavita, K. (1992). *Inside the state: The Bracero Program, immigration, and the I.N.S.* New York: Routledge.

Camarillo, A. (1979). *Chicanos in a changing society: From Mexican pueblos to American barrios in Santa Barbara and Southern California, 1848–1930.* Cambridge, MA: Harvard University Press.

Cantú, L. (1999). *Border crossing: Mexican men and the sexuality of migration.* Unpublished doctoral dissertation, University of California, Irvine.

Cardenas, G. (1982). Undocumented immigrant women in the Houston labor force. *California Sociologist, 5*(2), 98–118.

Cardenas, G., & Flores, E. (1986). *The migration and settlement of undocumented women.* Austin, TX: Mexican American Studies Center.

Cardoso, L. (1980). *Mexican emigration to the United States, 1897–1931.* Tucson: University of Arizona Press.

Carlson, H., & Henderson, N. (1950). The intelligence of American children of Mexican parentage. *Journal of Abnormal Psychology, 33,* 540–553.

Carmichael, S., & Hamilton, C. (1967). *Black power.* New York: Random House.

Carreras, M. (1974). *Los mexicanos que devolvió la crisis 1929–1932.* Mexico City: Secretaría de Relaciones Exteriores.

Carter, T. (1970). *Mexican Americans in school: A history of educational neglect.* New York: Russell Sage Foundation.

Carver, R. (1982). *The impact of intimacy: Mexican-Anglo intermarriage in New Mexico, 1821–1846.* El Paso: Texas Western Press.

Castañeda, A. (1990). *Presidarias y pobladoras: Spanish-Mexican women in frontier Monterey, California, 1770–1821.* Unpublished doctoral dissertation, Stanford University.

Castañeda, A. (1993). Sexual violence in the politics and policies of conquest: Amerindian Women and the Spanish conquest of Alta California. In A. de la Torre & B. M. Pesquera (Eds.), *Building with our hands: New directions in Chicana studies* (pp. 15–33). Berkeley: University of California Press.

Castillo, P., & Camarillo, A. (1973). *Furia y muerte: Los bandidos Chicanos.* Los Angeles: Aztlán.

Chávez, J. R. (1998). *Eastside landmark: A history of the East Los Angeles Community Union, 1968–1993.* Stanford: Stanford University Press.

Chavez, L. R. (2001). *Covering immigration: Popular images and the politics of the nation.* Berkeley: University of California Press.

Chipman, D. E. (1992). *Spanish Texas, 1519–1821.* Austin: University of Texas Press.

Clark, K. (1965). *Dark Ghetto.* New York: Harper and Row.

Clark, V. S. (1908). Mexican labor in the United States. *U.S. Bureau of Labor Bulletin, 78,* 450–503.

Cooney, R. S. (1975). Changing labor force participation of Mexican-American wives: A comparison with Anglos and Blacks. *Social Science Quarterly, 56,* 252–261.

Cornelius, W. A. (1976). *Mexican migration to the United States: The view from rural sending communities.* Cambridge, MA: Massachusetts Institute of Technology, Center for International Studies.

Cornelius, W. A. (1999). *Trends in Mexican migration to California: Implications for politics and research in the 21st century.* Unpublished paper.

Cortés, C. E. (1992). To view a neighbor: The Hollywood textbook on Mexico. In J. Coatsworth & C. Rico (Eds.), *Images of Mexico in the United States* (pp. 91–118). San Diego: University of California, Center for U.S.-Mexican Studies.

Cotler, J. (1967–68). The mechanics of internal domination and social change in Peru. *Studies in Comparative International Development, 3*(12), 229–246.

Craig, R. (1971). *The Bracero Program: Interest groups and foreign policy.* Austin: University of Texas Press.

Cravey, A. J. (1998). *Women and work in Mexico's maquiladoras.* Lanham, MD: Rowman & Littlefield.

Cruz, G. R. (1988). *Let there be towns: Spanish municipal origins in the American Southwest, 1610–1810.* College Station: Texas A&M University Press.

Dalton, F. J. (1998). *The moral vision of César E. Chávez: An examination of his public life from an ethical perspective.* Unpublished doctoral dissertation, Graduate Theological Union, Berkeley, CA.

Dana, R. H. (1840). *Two years before the mast.* New York: Harper-Collins.

De la Teja, J. F. (1991). *A revolution remembered: The memoirs and selected correspondence of Juan N. Seguín.* Austin: Texas Historical Society.

De la Torre, A., & Pesquera, B. M. (Ed.). (1993). *Building with our hands: New directions in Chicana studies.* Berkeley: University of California Press.

De León, A. (1982). *The Tejano community, 1836–1900.* Albuquerque: University of New Mexico Press.

De León, A. (1983). *They call them greasers: Anglo Attitudes toward Mexicans in Texas, 1821–1900.* Austin: University of Texas Press.

Del Castillo, A. R. (1977). Malintzin Tenépal: A preliminary look into a new perspective. In R. Sánchez (Ed.), *Essays on la mujer* (pp. 124–149). Los Angeles: UCLA, Chicano Studies Center.

Del Castillo, A. R. (1980). Mexican women in organization. In M. Mora & A. R. Del Castillo (Eds.), *Mexican women in the United States* (pp. 7–16). Los Angeles: UCLA, Chicano Studies Center.

Delgado, S. (1978). Young Chicana speaks up on problems faced by young girls. *Regeneración, 1*(1), 5–7.

De Onís, J. (1976). *The Hispanic contribution to the state of Colorado.* Boulder, CO: Westview Press.

Deutsch, S. (1987). *No separate refuge: Culture, class and gender on an Anglo-Hispanic frontier in the American Southwest, 1880–1940.* New York: Oxford University Press.

Díaz, R. M. (1998). *Latino gay men and HIV: Culture, sexuality, and risk behavior.* New York: Routledge.

Diaz-Guerrero, R. (1955). Neurosis and the Mexican family structure. *American Journal of Psychiatry, 112,* 411–417.

Dinwoodie, D. H. (1977). Deportation: The Immigration Service and the Chicano labor movement in the 1930s. *New Mexico Historical Review, 52*(3), 193–206.

Dobyns, H. F. (1991). Do-it-yourself religion: The diffusion of folk Catholicism on Mexico's northern frontier, 1821–1846. In N. R. Crumrine & A. Morinis (Eds.), *Pilgrimage in Latin America* (pp. 53–70). New York: Greenwood Press.

Durand, J., & Massey, D. S. (1992). Mexican migration to the United States: A critical review. *Latin American Research Review, 27*(2), 3–42.

Dysart, J. (1976). Mexican women in San Antonio, 1830–1860: The assimilation process. *Western Historical Quarterly, 7*(4), 365–377.

Ebright, M. (1987). New Mexican land grants: The legal background. In C. L. Briggs & J. R. Van Ness (Eds.), *Land, water, and culture: New perspectives on Hispanic land grants* (pp. 15–66). Albuquerque: University of New Mexico Press.

Emerging wealth: The Hispanic business rich list. (1996). *Hispanic Business,* p. 18.

Espinoza, D. (1996) *Pedagogies of nationalism and gender: Cultural resistance in selected representational practices of Chicana/o movement activists, 1967–1972.* Unpublished doctoral dissertation, Cornell University, Ithaca, NY.

Fernández-Kelly, M. P. (1983). *For we are sold, I and my people: Women and industry in Mexico's frontier.* Albany: State University of New York Press.

Flores, K. (1976). Chicano attitudes toward birth control. *Imagenes de la Chicana, 1*(1), 19–21.

Foerster, R. F. (1925). *The racial problems involved in immigration from Latin America and the West Indies to the United States: A report to the Secretary of Labor.* Washington, DC: Government Printing Office.

Foley, N. (1990). *The New South in the Southwest: Anglos, Blacks, and Mexicans in central Texas, 1880–1930.* Unpublished doctoral dissertation, University of Texas, Austin.

Frank, A. G. (1967). *Capitalism and underdevelopment in Latin America.* New York: Monthly Review Press.

Galarza, E. (1964). *Merchants of labor: The Mexican bracero story.* Santa Barbara, CA: McNally & Loflin.

Galarza, E. (1977). *Farm workers and agribusiness in California, 1947–1960.* Notre Dame, IN: Notre Dame University Press.

Gamboa, E. (1990). *Mexican labor and World War II: Braceros in the Pacific Northwest, 1942–1947.* Austin: University of Texas Press.

Gamio, M. (1930a). *The life story of the Mexican immigrants.* Chicago: University of Chicago Press.

Gamio, M. (1930b). *Número, procedencia y distribución geográfica de los inmigrantes mexicanos en los Estados Unidos.* Mexico City: Talleres Gráficos y Diario Official.

Gamio, M. (1931). *Mexican immigration to the United States.* Chicago: University of Chicago Press.

García, A. M. (Ed.). (1997). *Chicana feminist thought: The basic historical writings.* New York: Routledge.

García, I. M. (2000). *Viva Kennedy: Mexican Americans in search of Camelot.* College Station: Texas A&M University Press.

Gardiner, H. (1952). Foreign travelers' accounts of Mexico, 1810–1910. *Americas, 8*(3), 321–351.

Garis, R. L. (1930). *Mexican immigration: A report by Roy I. Garis for the information of the members of Congress.* In U.S. House of Representatives, *Western Hemisphere immigration* (pp. 420–455). Washington, DC: Government Printing Office.

Garretson, O. (1928). A study of causes of retardation among Mexican children in a small public school system in Arizona. *Journal of Educational Psychology, 19,* 31–40.

Garth, T. (1923). A comparison of the intelligence of Mexican and mixed and full blood Indian children. *Psychological Review, 30,* 388–401.

Garth, T., Elson, T. H, & Morton, M. M. (1936). The administration of non-language intelligence tests to Mexicans. *Journal of Abnormal Psychology, 23,* 101–145.

Gaspar de Alba, A. (1998). *Chicano art inside/outside the master's house.* Austin: University of Texas Press.

Gilbert, G. M. (1959). Sex differences in mental health in a Mexican village. *International Journal of Psychiatry, 5*(3), 208–213.

Gómez-Quiñones, J. (1972). The first steps: Chicano labor conflict and organizing, 1900–1920. *Aztlán, 3*(1), 13–50.

Gómez-Quiñones, J. (1975). Piedras contra la luna, México en Aztlán y Aztlán en México: Chicano-Mexican relations in the Mexican consulates, 1900–1920. In J. W. Wilkie, M. C. Meyer, & E. Monzón de Wilkie (Eds.), *Contemporary Mexico: Papers of the IV International Congress of Mexican History* (pp. 43–97). Mexico City: Colegio de México.

Gómez-Quiñones, J. (1977). On culture. *Revista Chicano-Riqueña, 5*(2), 35–53.

Gómez-Quiñones, J. (1982). *Development of the Mexican working class north of the Rio Bravo: Work and culture among laborers and artisans, 1600–1900.* Los Angeles: UCLA, Chicano Studies Research Center.

Gómez-Quiñones, J. (1990). *Chicano politics: Reality and promise, 1940–1990.* Albuquerque: University of New Mexico Press.

González, D. J. (1993). La Tules of image and reality: Euro-American attitudes and legend formation on a Spanish-Mexican frontier. In A. de la Torre & B. M. Pesquera (Eds.), *Building with our hands: New directions in Chicana studies* (pp. 75–90). Berkeley: University of California Press.

González, M. J. (1993). *In search of the plumed serpent: Mexican Los Angeles, 1781–1850.* Unpublished doctoral dissertation, University of California, Berkeley.

González, R. (Ed.). (1996). *Muy macho: Latino men confront their manhood.* New York: Anchor Books.

Gonzales, R. (2001). *Message to Aztlán: Selected writings.* Houston, TX: Arte Público Press.

Gonzales-Berry, E. (1993). Two texts for a new canon: Vicente Bernal's Las primicias and Felipe Maximiliano Chacón's Poesía y prosa. In R. A. Gutiérrez & G. Padilla (Eds.), *Recovering the U.S. Hispanic literary heritage* (pp. 129–152). Houston, TX: Arte Público Press.

González-Casanova, P. (1969). Internal colonialism and national development. In I. L. Horowitz (Ed.), *Latin American Radicalism* (pp. 118–137). New York: Random House.

Greenfield, G. M., & Cortés, C. E. (1991). Harmony and conflict of intercultural images: The treatment of Mexico in U.S. feature films and K-12 textbooks. *Mexican Studies/Estudios Mexicanos, 7*(2), 283–301.

Gregg, J. (1844). *Commerce of the prairies.* New York: H. G. Langley.

Griswold del Castillo, R. (1979). *The Los Angeles barrio, 1850–1890.* Berkeley: University of California Press.

Griswold del Castillo, R., & García, R. A. (1995). *César Chávez: A triumph of spirit.* Norman: University of Oklahoma Press.

Griswold del Castillo, R., McKenna, T., & Yarbro-Bejarano, Y. (Eds.). (1991). *Chicano art: Resistance and affirmation, 1965–1985.* Los Angeles: UCLA, Wright Art Gallery.

Gunn, D. W. (1974). *American and British writers in Mexico, 1556–1973.* Austin: University of Texas Press.

Gutiérrez, D. (1994). *Walls and mirrors: Mexican Americans, Mexican immigrants, and the politics of ethnicity in the American Southwest, 1910–1986.* Berkeley: University of California Press.

Gutiérrez, J. A. (1998). *The making of a Chicano militant: Lessons from Cristal.* Madison: University of Wisconsin Press.

Gutiérrez, R. A. (1976). *Mexican migration to the United States, 1880-1930: The Chicano and internal colonialism.* Unpublished master's thesis, University of Wisconsin, Madison.

Gutiérrez, R. A. (1989a). Aztlán, Montezuma, and New Mexico: The political uses of American Indian mythology. In R. A. Anaya & F. Lomelí (Eds.), *Aztlán: Essays on the Chicano homeland* (pp. 172–190). Albuquerque, NM: Academia/El Norte.

Gutiérrez, R. A. (1989b). Ethnic and class boundaries in America's Hispanic past. In S. Chan (Ed.), *Intersections: Studies of ethnicity, gender, and inequality* (pp. 47–63). Lewiston, NY: Edwin Mellin Press.

Gutiérrez, R. A. (1991). *When Jesus came, the corn mothers went away: Marriage, sexuality and power in New Mexico, 1500–1846.* Stanford, CA: Stanford University Press.

Gutiérrez, R. A. (1992). The colonial worlds: The southern part of the United States. In M. Ramírez (Ed.), *Ibero-American heritage: Latinos in the making of the United States of America* (Vol. 2, pp. 719–738). Albany: New York State Education Department.

Gutiérrez, R. A. (1993a). Community, patriarchy and individualism: The politics of Chicano history. *American Quarterly, 45*(1), 44–72.

Gutiérrez, R. A. (1993b). Nationalism and literary production: The Hispanic and Chicano experiences. In R. A. Gutiérrez & G. Padilla (Eds.), *Recovering the U.S. Hispanic literary heritage* (pp. 309–314). Houston: Arte Público Press.

Gutiérrez, R. A. (1993c). The UCLA bibliographic survey of Mexican American literary culture, 1821–1945: An overview. In R. A. Gutiérrez & G. Padilla (Eds.), *Recovering the U.S. Hispanic literary heritage* (pp. 309–314). Houston, TX: Arte Público Press.

Gutiérrez, R. A., & Padilla, G. (1993). *Recovering the U.S. Hispanic literary heritage.* Houston, TX: Arte Público Press.

Gutmann, M. C. (1996). *The meanings of macho: Being a man in Mexico City.* Berkeley: University of California Press.

Hall, G. E. (1987). The Pueblo grant labyrinth. In C. L. Briggs & J. R. Van Ness (Eds.), *Land, water, and culture: New perspectives on Hispanic land grants* (pp. 67–140). Albuquerque: University of New Mexico Press.

Hass, L. (1994). *Race identities and the politics of space: From Spanish colony to immigrant society.* Berkeley: University of California Press.

Haught, B. F. (1931). The language difficulty of Spanish-American children. *Journal of Applied Psychology, 15,* 92–95.

Hayden, R. G. (1966). Spanish-Americans of the Southwest: Life style patterns and their implications. *Welfare in Review, 4*(4), 14–25.

Hayes-Bautista, D. E. (1993). Mexicans in southern California: Societal enrichment or wasted opportunity? In A. F. Lowenthal & K. Burgess (Eds.), *The California-Mexico connection* (pp. 131–46). Stanford, CA: Stanford University Press.

Hernández, J. A. (1983). *Mutual aid for survival: The case of the Mexican Americans.* Malabar, FL: Krieger.

Herrera-Sobek, M. (1993). *Reconstructing a Chicano/a literary heritage: Hispanic colonial literature of the Southwest.* Tucson: University of Arizona Press.

Herrnstein, C. J., & Murray, C. (1994). *The bell curve: Intelligence and class structure in American life.* New York: Free Press.

Hoffman, A. (1974). *Unwanted Mexican Americans in the Great Depression: Repatriation pressures, 1929–1939.* Tucson: University of Arizona Press.

Hondagneu-Sotelo, P. (1992). Overcoming patriarchal constraints: The reconstruction of gender relations among Mexican immigrant women and men. *Gender & Society, 6*(1), 393–415.

Hondagneu-Sotelo, P. (2001). *Doméstica: Immigrant workers cleaning and caring in the shadows of affluence.* Berkeley: University of California Press.

Horsman, R. (1981). *Race and Manifest Destiny: The origins of American racial Anglo-Saxonism.* Cambridge, MA: Harvard University Press.

Humphrey, N. D. (1943). The Detroit Mexican immigrant and naturalization. *Social Forces, 22,* 332–335.

Humphrey, N. D. (1944). The changing structure of the Detroit Mexican family: An index of acculturation. *American Sociological Review, 9*(6), 622–626.

Jenks, J. W., & Lauck, W. J. (1917). *The immigrant problem: A study of American immigration conditions and needs.* New York: Funk and Wagnalls.

Johannsen, R. W. (1985). *To the halls of the Montezumas: The Mexican War in the American imagination.* New York: Oxford University Press.

Johnson, L. (1938). A comparison of the vocabularies of Anglo-American and Spanish-American high school pupils. *Journal of Educational Psychology, 15,* 222–240.

Jones, R. C. (1948). Ethnic family patterns: The Mexican family in the United States. *American Journal of Sociology, 53*(6), 450–452.

Kanellos, N. (1993). A socio-historic study of Hispanic newspapers in the United States. In R. A. Gutiérrez & G. Padilla (Eds.), *Recovering the U.S. Hispanic literary heritage* (pp. 107–126). Houston, TX: Arte Público Press.

Keating, A. L. (Ed.). (2000). *Interviews-entrevistas/Gloria E. Anzaldúa.* New York: Routledge.

Keller, G. D. (1985). *Chicano cinema: Research, reviews, and resources.* Binghamton, NY: Bilingual Review Press.

Keston, M., & Jiménez, C. (1954). A study of the performance on English and Spanish editions of the Stanford-Binet Intelligence Test by Spanish-American children. *Journal of Genetic Psychology, 30,* 250–267.

Kiser, G. C., & Silverman, D. (1972). Mexican repatriation during the Great Depression. *Journal of Mexican American History, 2*(2), 122–142.

Kluckhohn, F., & Strodtbeck, F. (1961). *Variations in value orientations.* Evanston, IL: Row, Peterson.

Kossoudji, S. A., & Ranney, S. I. (1984). The labor market experience of female immigrants: The case of temporary Mexican migration to the United States. *International Migration Review, 18*(3), 1120–1143.

Lacy, J. H. (1959). New Mexico women in early American writings. *New Mexico Historical Review, 34*(2), 41–59.

Lamm, R. D., & Imhoff, G. (1985). *The immigration time bomb.* New York: Truman Talley Books.

Langum, D. J. (1978). Californios and the image of indolence. *Western Historical Quarterly, 9*(2), 181–196.

Larmer, B. (1999, July 12). Latino America. *Newsweek,* pp. 48–51.

Lewis, O. (1951). *Life in a Mexican village.* Urbana: University of Illinois Press.

Longauex y Vásquez, E. (1970). The Mexican-American woman. In R. Morgan (Ed.), *Sisterhood is powerful* (pp. 426–432). New York: Random House.

Longauex y Vásquez, E. (1972). Soy Chicana primero. *El Cuaderno, 1,*17–22.

López, D., & Espiritu, Y. (1990). Panethnicity in the United States: A theoretical framework. *Ethnic and Racial Studies, 13*(2), 198–224.

López, E., Ramirez, E., & Rochin, R. I. (Eds.). (1999). *Latinos and economic development in California.* (No. CRB-99–008). Sacramento: California Research Bureau.

Loyo, G. (1969). Notas preliminares de Gilberto Loyo sobre la migración de Mexicanos a los Estados Unidos de 1900 a 1967. In M. Gamio (Ed.), *El inmigrante mexicano: la historia de su vida* (pp. 28–37). Mexico City: Universidad Nacional Autónoma de México.

Madsen, W. (1964). *The Mexican-Americans of south Texas.* New York: Holt, Rinehart, and Winston.

Manuel, H. T. (1965). *Spanish-speaking children of the Southwest.* Austin: University of Texas Press.

Mariscal, G. (Ed.). (1999). *Aztlán and Viet Nam: Chicano and Chicana experiences of the war.* Berkeley: University of California Press.

Martin, P. P. (1992). *Songs my mother sang to me: An oral history of Mexican American women.* Tucson: University of Arizona Press.

Martínez, O. J. (1975). On the size of the Chicano population: New estimates, 1850–1900. *Aztlán, 6*(1), 43–67.

Martínez, O. J. (1988). *Troublesome border.* Tucson: University of Arizona Press.

Massey, D., Alarcón, R., Durand, J., & González, H. (1987). *Return to Aztlán: The social process of international migration from Western Mexico.* Berkeley: University of California Press.

McWilliams, C. (1949). *North from Mexico: The Spanish-speaking people of the United States.* Philadelphia: Lippincott.

Melendez, E. (1993). Understanding Latino poverty. *Sage Race Relations Abstracts, 18*(2).

Merk, F. (1963). *Manifest destiny and mission in American history.* New York: Random House.

Meyer, D. L. (1978). Early Mexican-American responses to negative stereotyping. *New Mexico Historical Review, 53*(3), 75–91.

Miller, D. A. (1982). Cross-cultural marriages in the Southwest: The New Mexico experience, 1846–1900. *New Mexico Historical Review, 57*(4), 335–359.

Mirandé, A. (1997). *Hombres y machos: Masculinity and Latino culture.* Boulder, CO: Westview Press.

Mirandé, A., & Enríquez, E. (1979). *La Chicana: The Mexican-American woman.* Chicago: University of Chicago Press.

Monroy, D. (1990). *Thrown among strangers: The making of culture in frontier California.* Berkeley: University of California Press.

Monsiváis, C. (1984). Travelers in Mexico: A brief anthology of selected myths. *Diogenes, 125,* 48–74.

Montejano, D. (1987). *Anglos and Mexicans in the making of Texas, 1836–1986.* Austin: University of Texas Press.

Moore, J., & Pachón, H. (1985). *Hispanics in the United States.* Englewood Cliffs, NJ: Prentice Hall.

Moraga, C. (1997). *Waiting in the wings: Portrait of a queer motherhood.* Ithaca, NY: Firebrand Books.

Morin, R. (1966). *Among the valiant: Mexican-Americans in WWII and Korea.* Alhambra, CA: Borden.

Munguía M. F. J. (1986). *Un mexicano en Vietnam.* Mexico City: Harper & Row Latinoamericana.

Muñoz, C. (1989). *Youth, identity, power: The Chicano movement.* New York: Verso.

Myres, S. L. (1982). Mexican Americans and westering Anglos: A feminine perspective. *New Mexico Historical Review, 57*(4), 317–333.

Navarro, A. (1974). The evolution of Chicano politics. *Aztlán, 5,* 57–84.

Navarro, A. (1995). *Mexican American youth organization: Avantgarde of the Chicano movement in Texas.* Austin: University of Texas Press.

Navarro, A. (1998). *The Cristal experiment: A Chicano struggle for community control.* Madison: University of Wisconsin Press.

Navarro, A. (2000). *La Raza Unida Party: A challenge to the U.S. two-party dictatorship.* Philadelphia: Temple University Press.

Noggle, B. (1959). Anglo observers of the Southwest borderlands, 1825–1890: The rise of a concept. *Arizona and the West, 1*(2), 105–131.

Oboler, S. (1995). *Ethnic labels, Latino lives.* Minneapolis: University of Minnesota Press.

Officer, J. E. (1987). *Hispanic Arizona, 1536–1856.* Tucson: University of Arizona Press.

Oropeza, L. (1996). *La batalla esta aqui! Chicanos oppose war in Vietnam.* Unpublished doctoral dissertation, Cornell University, Ithaca, NY.

Padget, M. (1993). Cultural geographies: Travel writing in the Southwest, 1869–97. Unpublished doctoral dissertation, University of California, San Diego.

Padilla, F. (1987). *Latino ethnic consciousness.* Notre Dame, IN: Notre Dame University Press.

Padilla, G. (1993a). *History, memory and the struggles of self-representation: The formation of Mexican American autobiography.* Madison: University of Wisconsin Press.

Padilla, G. (1993b). Recovering Mexican American autobiography. In R. A. Gutiérrez & G. Padilla (Eds.), *Recovering the U.S. Hispanic literary heritage* (pp. 153–178). Houston, TX: Arte Público Press.

Paredes, R. A. (1977a). The Mexican image in American travel literature, 1831–1869. *New Mexico Historical Review, 52*(1), 5–29.

Paredes, R. A. (1977b). The origins of anti-Mexican sentiment in the United States. *New Scholar, 6,* 139–165.

Pastor, M., Jr. (1995). Economic inequality, Latino poverty and the civil unrest in Los Angeles. *Economic Development Quarterly, 9*(3).

Pastor, M., Jr. (2000). The California economy: Servant or master? In D. López (Eds.), *Latino inequality: California's challenge.* Berkeley, CA: California Policy Seminar.

Pattie, J. O. (1831). *The personal narrative of James O. Pattie*. Cincinnati, OH: John H. Wood.

Paz, O. (1961). *The labyrinth of solitude: Life and thought in Mexico*. New York: Random House.

Pettit, A. G. (1980). *Images of the Mexican American in fiction and film*. College Station: Texas A&M University Press.

Pitt, L. (1971). *The decline of the Californios: A social history of the Spanish-speaking Californians, 1846–1890*. Berkeley: University of California Press.

Poyo, G., & Hinojosa, G. (1991). *Tejano origins in eighteenth-century San Antonio*. Austin: University of Texas Press.

Pycior, J. L. (1997). *LBJ & Mexican Americans: The paradox of power*. Austin: University of Texas Press.

Ramirez, J. (1999). *A patriot after all: The story of a Chicano Vietnam vet*. Albuquerque: University of New Mexico Press.

Ramos, J. (Ed.). (1994). *Compañera: Latina lesbians*. New York: Routledge.

Ramos, S. (1938). *El perfil del hombre y la cultura en México*. México, D.F.: Pedro Robredo.

Reichert, J. A. (1979). *The migrant syndrome: An analysis of U.S. migration and its impact on a rural Mexican town*. Unpublished doctoral dissertation, Princeton University, Princeton, NJ.

Reisler, M. (1976). *By the sweat of their brows: Mexican immigrant labor in the United States, 1900–1940*. Westport, CT: Greenwood Press.

Ríos-Bustamante, A. (1976). New Mexico in the eighteenth century: Life, labor and trade in La Villa de San Felipe de Albuquerque, 1706–1790. *Aztlán, 7*(3), 357–389.

Robinson, C. (1963). *With the ears of strangers: The Mexican in American literature*. Tucson: University of Arizona Press.

Robinson, C. (1977). *Mexico and the Hispanic Southwest in American literature*. Tucson: University of Arizona Press.

Rodarte, I. (1973). Machismo vs. revolution. In D. Moreno (Ed.), *La mujer en pie de lucha* (pp. 4–34). Mexico City: Espina del Norte.

Rodriguez, R. (1982). *Hunger of memory: The education of Richard Rodriguez*. New York: Bantam Books.

Rodriguez, R. (1992). *Days of obligation: An argument with my Mexican father*. New York: Viking.

Rodríguez, S. (1987). Land, water and ethnic identity in Taos. In C. L. Briggs & J. R. Van Ness (Eds.), *Land, water, and culture: New perspectives on Hispanic land grants* (pp. 313–403). Albuquerque: University of New Mexico Press.

Romero, M. (1992). *Maid in the U.S.A.* New York: Routledge.

Romo, R. (1983). *East Los Angeles: A history of a barrio*. Austin: University of Texas Press.

Rosales, F. A. (1997). *Chicano! The history of the Mexican American civil rights movement*. Houston, TX: Arte Público Press.

Rosales, F. A. (2000). *Testimonio: A documentary history of the Mexican American struggle for civil rights*. Houston, TX: Arte Público Press.

Rosenbaum, R. J. (1981). *Mexicano resistance in the Southwest: The sacred right of self-preservation*. Austin: University of Texas Press.

Ruiz, R. E. (1963). *The Mexican war: Was it manifest destiny?* New York: Holt Rinehart.

Ruiz, V. L. (1987). *Cannery women, cannery lives: Mexican women, unionization, and the California food packing industry, 1930–1950*. Albuquerque: University of New Mexico Press.

Ruiz, V. L., & Tiano, S. (1987). *Women on the U.S.-Mexico border: Responses to change*. Boston: Allen and Unwin.

Samora, J. (1971). *Los mojados: The wetback story*. Notre Dame, IN: Notre Dame University Press.

Sánchez, G. (1932). Scores of Spanish-speaking children on repeated tests. *Pedagogical Seminary and Journal of Genetic Psychology, 23*, 223–231.

Sánchez, G. (1934). Bilingualism and mental measures: A word of caution. *Journal of Applied Psychology, 18*, 765–772.

Sánchez, G. (1940). *Forgotten people*. Albuquerque: University of New Mexico Press.

Sánchez, R. (1993). Nineteenth-century Californio narratives: The Hubert H. Bancroft collection. In R. A. Gutiérrez & G. Padilla (Eds.), *Recovering the U.S. Hispanic literary heritage* (pp. 279–292). Houston, TX: Arte Público Press.

Saunders, L. (1954). *Cultural difference and medical care: The case of the Spanish-speaking people of the southwest*. New York: Russell Sage Foundation.

Schlesinger, A. B. (1971). Las Gorras Blancas, 1889–1891. *Journal of Mexican American History, 1*, 87–143.

Schlesinger, A. M., Jr. (1992). *The disuniting of America: Reflections on a multicultural society*. New York: Norton.

Sheridan, T. (1986). *Los Tucsonenses: The Mexican community in Tucson, 1854–1941*. Tucson: University of Arizona Press.

Simons, H., & Hoyt, C. (1992). *Hispanic Texas: A historical guide*. Austin: University of Texas Press.

Singletary, O. (1960). *The Mexican War*. New York: Oxford University Press.

Stavenhagen, R. (1965). Classes, colonialism, and acculturation. *Studies in Comparative International Development, 1*(6), 53–77.

Stevens, E. (1973). Marianismo: The other face of machismo in Latin America. In A. Pascetello (Ed.), *Female and male in Latin America* (pp. 89–102). Pittsburgh, PA: University of Pittsburgh Press.

Stuart, J., & Kearney, M. (1981). *Causes and effects of agricultural labor migration from the Mixteca of Oaxaca to California*. La Jolla, CA: University of California at San Diego, Center for U.S.-Mexican Studies.

Sweeney, J. (1977). Chicana history: A review of the literature. In R. Sánchez (Ed.), *Essays on la mujer* (pp. 99–123). Los Angeles: UCLA, Chicano Studies Center.

Taylor, E. J. (1986). Differential migration, networks, information and risk. In O. Stark (Ed.), *Research in human capital and development: Migration, human capital, and development* (pp. 147–171). Greenwich, CT: JAI Press.

Taylor, P. S. (1938). Migratory agricultural workers on the Pacific Coast. *American Sociological Review, 35*, 220–239.

Teller, C., Estrada, L., Hernández, J., & Alvírez, D. (1977). *Cuantos somos: A demographic study of the Mexican American population*. Austin: University of Texas, Mexican American Studies Center.

Telles, E. A., & Murguía, E. (1990). Phenotypic discrimination and income differences among Mexican Americans. *Social Science Quarterly, 71*, 682–696.

Tijerina, R. L. (1978). *Mi lucha por la tierra*. Mexico City: Fondo de Cultura Económia.

Tijerina, R. L. (2000). *They called me "King Tiger": My struggle for the land and our rights* (José Angel Gutiérrez, Trans.). Houston, TX: Arte Público Press.

Trujillo, C. (1990). *Soldados: Chicanos in Viet Nam*. San Jose, CA: Chusma House.

Trujillo, C. (Ed.). (1991). *Chicana lesbians: The girls our mothers warned us about*. Berkeley, CA: Third Woman Press.

Trujillo, C. (Ed.). (1998). *Living Chicana theory*. Berkeley, CA: Third Woman Press.

U.S. Department of Commerce. (1999). *Statistical abstract of the United States, 1999*. Washington, DC: Government Printing Office.

Valdés, D. N. (1991). *Al norte: Agricultural workers in the Great Lakes region, 1917–1970*. Austin: University of Texas Press.

Valdés, D. N. (2000). *Barrios norteños: St. Paul and Midwestern Mexican communities in the twentieth century*. Austin: University of Texas Press.

Valdes Fallis, G. (1974). The liberated Chicana: A struggle against tradition. *Women: A Journal of Liberation, 3*(4), 20–21.

Valdez, L. (1971). La conquista de Méjico: Actos y el Teatro Campesino. San Juan Bautista, CA: Menvan.

Van Ness, J. R. (1987). Hispanic land grants: Ecology and subsistence in the uplands of northern New Mexico and southern Colorado. In C. L. Briggs & J. R. Van Ness (Eds.), *Land, water, and culture: New perspectives on Hispanic land grants* (pp. 141–216). Albuquerque: University of New Mexico Press.

Vargas, Z. (1993). *Proletarians of the north: Mexican industrial workers in Detroit and the Midwest, 1917–1933*. Berkeley: University of California Press.

Vélez-Ibañez, C. G. (1980). Se me acabó la canción: An ethnography of non-consenting sterilizations among Mexican women in Los Angeles. In M. Mora & A. Del Castillo (Eds.), *Mexican women in the United States* (pp. 71–94). Los Angeles: UCLA, Chicano Studies Center.

Vélez-Ibañez, C. G. (1983). *Bonds of mutual trust: The cultural systems of rotating credit associations among urban Mexicans and Chicanos*. New Brunswick, NJ: Rutgers University Press.

Veyna, A. F. (1986). Women in early New Mexico: A preliminary view. In T. Córdova (Ed.), *Chicana voices: Intersections of class, race, and gender* (pp. 120–135). Austin: University of Texas Press.

Veyna, A. F. (1993). "It is my last wish that . . .": A look at colonial Nuevo Mexicanas through their testaments. In A. de la Torre & B. M. Pesquera (Eds.), *Building with our hands: New directions in Chicana studies* (pp. 91–108). Berkeley: University of California Press.

Vigil, E. B. (1999). *The Crusade for Justice: Chicano militancy and the government war on dissent*. Madison: University of Wisconsin Press.

Waldman, E. (1980). Profile of the Chicana: A statistical fact sheet. In M. Mora & A. del Castillo (Eds.), *Mexican Women in the United States* (pp. 195–204). Los Angeles: UCLA, Chicano Studies Center.

Watt, A. J. (1999). *The religious dimensions of the farm worker movement*. Unpublished doctoral dissertation, Vanderbilt University, Nashville, TN.

Weber, D. J. (1979). "Scarce more than apes": Historical roots of Anglo American stereotypes of Mexicans in the border region. In D. J. Weber (Ed.), *New Spain's far northern frontier: Essays on Spain in the American West, 1540–1821* (pp. 295–307). Albuquerque: University of New Mexico Press.

Weber, D. J. (1982). *The Mexican frontier 1821–1846: The American Southwest under Mexico*. Albuquerque: University of New Mexico Press.

West, G. A. (1936). Race attitudes among teachers in the Southwest. *Journal of Abnormal Psychology, 23*, 146–159.

Wiest, R. (1973). Wage-labor migration and the household in a Mexican town. *Journal of Anthropological Research, 29*(1), 108–209.

Woll, A. L. (1977). *The Latin image in American film*. Los Angeles: University of California Press.

Woll, A. L. (1980). Bandits and lovers: Hispanic images in American film. In R. M. Miller (Ed.), *The kaleidoscopic lens: How Hollywood views ethnic groups*, (pp. 54–72). New York: Jerome S. Ozer.

Young, K. (1922). *Mental differences in certain immigrant groups*. Eugene: University of Oregon Press. (1993). *The world of the Mexican worker in Texas*. College Station: Texas A&M University Press.

Zavella, P. (1987). *Women's work and Chicano families: Cannery workers of the Santa Clara Valley*. Ithaca: Cornell University Press.

Zea, L. (1952). *Conciencia y posibilidad del Mexicano*. Mexico City: Porrua y Obregón.

Zweigenhaft, R. L., & Domhoff, G. W. (1998). *Diversity in the power elite: Have women and minorities reached the top?* New Haven, CT: Yale University Press.

15

DECONSTRUCTING AND CONTEXTUALIZING THE HISTORICAL AND SOCIAL SCIENCE LITERATURE ON PUERTO RICANS

Clara E. Rodríguez
Fordham University

Irma M. Olmedo
University of Illinois at Chicago

Mariolga Reyes-Cruz
University of Illinois at Urbana-Champaign

This review of the literature finds that colonialism has been a major, albeit sometimes unrecognized, issue influencing the writing on and by Puerto Ricans. Because of space limitations, this review includes mainly historical and social science books—not articles—that focus on Puerto Ricans. A couple of exceptional dissertations are included. This omits many otherwise significant articles, monographs, special journal issues, and reports. It also does not include writings in the sports area, bibliographic listings, or an extensive review of literary works. In order to reach a broader audience and in view of the fact that the audience for this *Handbook* is predominantly English speaking, our review emphasizes English language texts, though some relevant Spanish language texts are cited for bilingual readers. A review of the relevant Spanish language literature would require a separate chapter, given that this literature is wide ranging and of extraordinary depth. Bilingual readers are encouraged to consult some of the main research centers for a more in-depth exploration of those texts, for instance, the Centro de Investigaciones Sociales and the Instituto de Estudios del Caribe, both at the University of Puerto Rico, Río Piedras, P.R.; the Centro de Investigaciones Sobre el Caribe y Latinoamérica, at the Universidad Interamericana, San Germán, P.R.; the Centro de Investigaciones Académicas at the Universidad del Sagrado Corazón; as well as the Center for Puerto Rican Studies at Hunter College, City University of New York, in New York City, among others.

The literature reviewed here is divided into two periods: books published before and after 1970. In general, the majority of books published before 1970 were, implicitly or explicitly, reflective (and in some cases supportive) of Puerto Rico's colonial relationship to the United States. The bulk of works published after 1970 were critical of this relationship and attempted to deconstruct the earlier literature and contextualize Puerto Rico and Puerto Ricans. The year 1970 represents a somewhat arbitrary selection because there is not a sharp division in the literature—that is, works similar to the 1970 literature continued to be produced after 1970, and works akin to the

The authors would like to thank the following for important contributions to this chapter: S. Baver, H. Cordero-Guzmán, J. Duany, T. Feliciano, G. Haslip-Viera, J. Hernández, M. Hyacinth, S. Nieto, F. Ortiz, N. Pérez, V. Sánchez-Korrol, C. Schmidt-Nowara, A. Torres, and J. Vásquez.

Permission to quote from the following is gratefully acknowledged: Lewis, O. (1966). *La vida: A Puerto Rican family in the culture of poverty—San Juan and New York.* New York: Random House; and Rigdon, S. M. (1988). *The culture façade: Art, science, and politics in the work of Oscar Lewis.* Urbana and Chicago: University of Illinois Press.

post-1970 literature existed prior to this cutoff point. Nonetheless, the year does provide a convenient marker, for it is in the early to mid-seventies that there is the substantial development of a critical literature that responds to the earlier literature. It is in the late sixties that there is also the beginning of the establishment of Puerto Rican studies programs in the United States. To a large degree, the post-1970 literature mirrors many of the principles embodied in Puerto Rican studies.

The review of the pre-1970s literature reveals a number of subthemes: (a) an obfuscation of the colonial relationship and the neglect of political sovereignty issues; (b) an exclusive, noncomparative focus on Puerto Rico—as if Puerto Rico existed in isolation; (c) a preponderance of non–Puerto Ricans writing about Puerto Ricans; (d) the dominance of an assimilationist, immigrant paradigm; (e) a tendency to overgeneralize from small numbers or extreme cases to all Puerto Ricans; and (f) the application of paradigms, categories, and contexts developed in the United States but not necessarily relevant to Puerto Ricans. As a result, in this academic literature Puerto Ricans tended to be defined by others, and Puerto Rican history tended either to be excluded or presented from a Eurocentric perspective. Implicit deficit models highlighted negative as opposed to positive dimensions among Puerto Ricans, and revisionist or critical work tended to be marginalized.

In the late 1960s and early 1970s, there was a surge in English-language literature that challenged these earlier perspectives. This literature came about as a result of a number of factors. One was the development of English-language works by Puerto Ricans in Puerto Rico. Another factor was the growth of a new generation of English-dominant, activist Puerto Ricans in the United States who were influenced by (a) the political and social currents of the time, such as the Black power and the civil rights movements, the antiwar movement, and the general challenge to social and ethical mores of the time; and by (b) the long-standing Spanish-language tradition of political radicalism on the status issue in Puerto Rico. These contributed to the development of a historically based, clearly articulated anticolonial perspective. The early literary works and autobiographical works of second-generation Puerto Ricans also served to stimulate and support more critical work (e.g., Thomas, 1967). In addition, the establishment of Puerto Rican studies programs was a stimulus to, as well as the result of, the development of this literature.

This chapter begins by emphasizing the political and thematic similarities in the literatures of Puerto Ricans and Native American peoples. This comparison is meant to illuminate the unique political relationship both groups have had with the U.S. government, and to emphasize how this relationship has influenced the literature written.

It is not meant to suggest that Puerto Ricans and Native American Indians are the same in other regards (e.g., culturally). Works on the early 1898–1910 period; subsequent governors' memoirs; and the major political, economic, and anthropological-sociological books written in the 1950s and 1960s are then examined, and their relevant characteristics denoted. An analysis of Oscar Lewis's *La Vida* (1966) follows as a detailed case study of literature sculpted by colonialism. Next, the literature in the post-1970 period is reviewed, highlighting the proclivity in these works to deconstruct colonialism and contextualize the earlier works in a way that represents the Puerto Rican reality more validly. The chapter ends with a discussion of the implications of this literature for multicultural education.

PUERTO RICANS AND NATIVE AMERICAN PEOPLES

Although some early writers recognized the political similarities between Native American Indians and Puerto Ricans (see, for example, Miller Gould, 1900), this comparison is a departure from current and past academic practice. In the past, Puerto Ricans were often compared with previous European immigrant groups (e.g., Fitzpatrick, 1971; Glazer & Moynihan, 1970). Subsequently, analogies were found between Puerto Ricans and African Americans (F. Bean & Tienda, 1988; A. Torres, 1994). These comparisons are important because Puerto Ricans share many characteristics with both African Americans and previous immigrant groups. However, some of these comparisons have failed to adequately recognize the importance (and the history) of the political relationship between Puerto Rico and the United States. Because the relationship of Native American nations to the U.S. government is one of even longer duration, it provides a unique historical perspective within which to discuss the relationship between the United States and Puerto Rico. Consequently, an analysis of the similarities between Native American nations and Puerto Ricans facilitates greater insight into the subtle distinctiveness of, and difficulties with, particularly the early literature on Puerto Ricans.

Both Puerto Ricans and Native Americans share a historical and still unresolved issue: political sovereignty in relation to the United States (Tinker, 1992). Indeed, the Domestic Dependent Nation Policy, which was applied to Puerto Rico in 1898, was first articulated in Supreme Court decisions regarding the Cherokee nation (Hernández, 1992/1997). In contrast to Native American peoples, who originally participated in treaty making as nations, Puerto Ricans did not participate in the 1898 Treaty of Paris negotiations and have never entered into bilateral agreements with the United States. However, because of their common political histories as wards of the U.S. Congress, both groups have experienced difficulty in bringing forward their concerns. This is because in so doing they bring attention to policies of inequality (e.g., colonial, military, legal, economic, and imperialist) that the United States would prefer either not to discuss or to define in quite different ways. For example, it has taken a long time for the American majority to understand that the "expansion of the West" also meant "the vanishing of the West" from the perspective of Native Americans. Similarly, in the case of Puerto Ricans the U.S. victory in the war with Spain in 1898 also meant the invasion and conquest of Puerto Rico by a foreign power.

In essence, the study of the history of Puerto Rico requires us to examine the foray by the United States into colonial administration in the 20th century. This is neither pleasant nor easy to do in those academic contexts that have been created to gloss over or interpret these aspects of U.S. history in seemingly positive ways. For this reason, the political situation of Puerto Rico vis-à-vis the United States is often better understood outside of the United States than within it. As a consequence, both Native Americans and Puerto Ricans often look to international law and international arenas as courts of appeal and for definitions of their status and rights.

Both also share issues involving current and past political prisoners, a history of invasion, land takeovers, and installation of authoritarian regimes by the U.S. government. Both groups were administered, for a time, by the Department of War and then by the Department of the Interior. Moreover, both groups have had decades of persistent exposure to programs of forceful cultural assimilation, language dominance, and economic exploitation. Yet both groups have also resisted attempts to be completely assimilated or to be recreated as marginal laborers "in the White man's image" (1991). Finally, socioeconomic data on both groups has documented a similarly bleak picture of persisting disadvantage.

EDUCATION AND COLONIALISM: THE PUERTO RICO CASE

Although quite real in its consequences, the control and influence that the United States has exerted on Puerto Rico is seldom noted. The history of education and language is a good example of this somewhat concealed, but quite determining, control. The first American educators who came to the island after 1898 thought that "the Spanish spoken in Puerto Rico was not an appropriate vehicle to transmit the culture the people already had and much less the culture the educators wanted to introduce" (Rodríguez Bou, 1966, p. 159). Indeed, Dr. Victor S.

Clark, prior to his 1900 report on Puerto Rico, said: "There does not seem to be among the masses the same devotion to their native tongue or to any national ideal that animates the Frenchman" (quoted in Rodríguez Bou, p. 159). Subsequent events would prove this observation wrong, because—even after 100 years of U.S. rule and strenuous efforts to make them English-speaking, Puerto Ricans have persisted in their strong loyalty to the Spanish language in Puerto Rico and in the United States.

Nonetheless, Clark's idea was shared by many others who proceeded to alter the school system and institute English as the sole language of instruction. At the time this decision was made, the people of Puerto Rico had been Spanish-speaking for close to 400 years. This was 250 years longer than the majority of the people in the United States (who are not of British origin) had been speaking English. Until 1949, the presidents of the United States appointed the commissioners of education in Puerto Rico. Although they were responsible for educational policy, many of these commissioners had no previous experience in educational administration or practice; nor had they ever been to Puerto Rico prior to their appointment. They were political appointees sent to enforce the English-only policy. Few spoke Spanish.

Soon after the U.S. occupation began, a strong popular resistance developed against the English-only policy (Morales Carrión, 1983). Deprived of any political means of expressing their dissatisfaction with the new regime, Puerto Ricans demonstrated their discontent by continuing to speak their language. Spanish was spoken at home and in public when American officials were not present. The wisdom of the English-only policy was continuously questioned. It became apparent that the Spanish-speaking students did not have a clue as to what many of the English-only, U.S.-imported teachers were trying to say. This was also evident in the poor academic performance of students, who left school recalling the boredom, frustration, and humiliation of the experience (Negrón de Montilla, 1975). However, it took decades for an educational language policy to be established that took into account Puerto Ricans' native tongue and cognitive pattern of learning. It was not until 1949 that Spanish was used as the language of instruction in all grades, and English was taught as a second language.

Educational language policies fluctuated, depending in large part on who had been appointed commissioner. The consequences of these changing policies for Puerto Ricans have never been fully assessed; nonetheless, their impact was clearly felt. For example, one policy that was in effect for some time during the period 1916–1934 had Spanish as the language of instruction in grades one through four and English as the language of instruction in grades six through eight. The fifth grade was a grade of transition.

American women teachers were brought to Puerto Rico when English was made the school language and "imported with them were U.S. textbooks, materials and methods" (Walsh, 1991, p. 9). Puerto Rican teachers were expected to start teaching in English. The consequences of this policy become clearer when we consider the average fourth to fifth grade education of many Puerto Rican elderly. As one elderly Puerto Rican gentleman vividly related, he had been an enthusiastic, bright, and eager student in school until the fifth grade when, frustrated by his English-language books, he angrily cast them into a ditch on his way home from school, never to return. This anecdote and dimension of Puerto Rican history emphasize, in a personalistic way, how determinant colonialism has been in the everyday lives of Puerto Ricans and in most of the policies developed in Puerto Rico. Actual implementation of the policies varied widely, being perhaps stronger in large cities, where the strength of U.S. control was greater. Nonetheless, control over Puerto Rico's educational system served to advance the goal of the Americanization and militarization of Puerto Rico (see Canino, 1981; Collazo, 1998; Walsh, 1991). Although the control over educational policy is less stringent today, U.S. educational associations and educational training in the United States continue to influence education. This past history of language and education in Puerto Rico demonstrates the absolute necessity of viewing Puerto Rico and Puerto Ricans contextually.

PRE-1970 LITERATURE

Despite the significance and pervasiveness of the colonial structure in the history of Puerto Ricans, close attention to the U.S. role in this structure is generally absent from the English language literature written prior to 1970. The colonial relationship tends to be obfuscated or depicted as benign, as creating more opportunities than obstacles to progress, and/or as eminently "fixable." Consequently, and as in the case of Native American peoples and other groups, Puerto Ricans who read the literature on their people were confronted with unquestioned myths, sins of omission and commission, and distortions and suppression of evidence concerning their historical relationship with the United States. The limited distribution of critical works contributed to the problem. These distortions, assumptions, and perceptions are often quite subtle as regards Puerto Rico. They are also typically wrapped in verbal complexity. An example of this subtlety and complexity can be seen in a seemingly innocuous statement written by one of the more socially committed U.S. presidents, Franklin D. Roosevelt. In a letter appointing José M. Gallardo to be Puerto Rico's commissioner of educa-

tion, he stated: "What is necessary, however, is that the American citizens of Puerto Rico should profit from their unique geographical situation and the unique historical circumstance which has brought to them the blessings of American citizenship by becoming bilingual" (quoted in Rodríguez Bou, 1966, p. 163).

Implicit in this statement is the assumption that Puerto Ricans are fortunate to have been blessed with American citizenship. The letter contains no indication that this citizenship was thrust upon Puerto Ricans, without their consent. For some, the fact that citizenship was granted just prior to World War I seems to have been a justification for their recruitment into the armed forces and U.S. military use of Puerto Rico—but see also Cabranes (1979) on this issue. (A Puerto Rican request for an opportunity to vote on this issue was denied.) It is not clear that "the unique historical circumstance" alluded to in the letter was a war in which Puerto Rico was invaded by the United States—a war in which some Puerto Ricans supported the United States because they thought that the United States would assist them in their struggle for independence from Spain. At present, Puerto Rico enjoys less independence in its current relationship with the United States than it did in 1897 with Spain (Rodríguez, 1989/1991).

Glossed over in Roosevelt's statement was the fact (made clear in later histories) that those who profited from the "unique geographical situation" were actually the U.S. government and business (Dietz, 1986; Figueroa, 1974; Maldonado Denis, 1972). Indeed, soon after the 1898 war ended, Puerto Rico's military importance to the United States was made clear (Hernández, 1992/1997). Puerto Rico has continuously served this role up to the present. In 1991, Puerto Rico had half of the U.S. military personnel in the Caribbean, with military installations covering 72,634 acres of Puerto Rico's land (García Muñiz, 1993). The Puerto Rican island of Vieques has for six decades been used for military live-fire training exercises. In 1999, bombs launched by F-18 airplanes mistakenly killed one civilian and left four others wounded. ("Mortal Bombing . . . ," 1999, p. 1) Furthermore, decisions regarding the presence of the military in Puerto Rico are made unilaterally by the United States, responding to their economic and political interests in the region. Thus, the U.S. military presence in Puerto Rico is an obstacle for Puerto Ricans' self-determination (see Rodríguez Beruff, 1996; García Muñiz & Rodríguez Beruff, 1999). See Paralitici (1998) for a discussion of induction and military service in Puerto Rico.

What is also not stated in Roosevelt's letter is that historically, "becoming bilingual" has often meant assimilating monoculturally to the U.S. Anglo way of life—without regard for traditional Puerto Rican customs and language. Last, there is no indication in the letter that the citizenship referred to does not allow Puerto Rico to have political representation in the U.S. Congress, nor to participate in presidential elections. Discontent over lack of representation in the British Parliament was one of the reasons the American colonists fought a war with England and became the United States.

Earliest Literature

Immediately after the U.S. invasion in 1898, the earliest descriptions of Puerto Rico were stock-taking accounts. Although one American geographer's book about Puerto Rico prior to the conquest found the economic and social situation to be relatively stable and comfortable (J. Hernández, 1992/1997), North American reports after the conquest (Carroll, 1898; Davis, 1900) found a backward society with a great number of social problems, including high illiteracy, low health standards, and inadequate sanitation facilities. Another perspective on this period is offered by Morales Carrión (1952) and Berbusse (1966), who portray the initial period of occupation as one fraught with conflict. The "temporary" military government, which persisted for two years, proclaimed the supremacy of the military and published copies of the U.S. Constitution and its territorial laws. Other changes were put into effect: the name of the island was changed to "Porto Rico," which remained the official name until 1932, when Puerto Ricans succeeded in passing legislation to return it to its original spelling, Puerto Rico. In 1899, when rumors of revolt spread, all periodicals were placed under the direct control of the military. Berbusse (1966) concludes that the greatest failings of the military governors were their lack of understanding of a people with a different tradition and their rather blunt expression of chauvinism.

Puerto Rico's political situation changed to civilian rule after the military government ceased in 1900 as a result of the Foraker Act (see Cabranes, 1979; Hunter, 1966, for a description of this act). However, despite Puerto Rican expectations (of liberation and greater political and economic freedoms), and some intense legal and intellectual debate in the United States around how to reconcile territorial expansion and colonialism with the U.S. Constitution (Cabranes, 1979), the change did not result in improvement. A total of 13 Anglo American governors would be appointed between 1900 and 1946—without consulting Puerto Ricans. Most of the appointments were political payoffs for men who lacked any prior experience with Puerto Rico. Many could not speak the language, had little interest in the culture, felt the job carried little prestige, and "were interested in being elsewhere" (G. K. Lewis, 1963, p. 119). In 1947, Puerto Ricans managed to have legislation passed that would enable them to elect their own governor.

Governors' Memoirs

The memoirs of two appointed governors (Tugwell, 1946/1977; Roosevelt, 1937/1970) provide insight into official government perspectives at the time. Theodore Roosevelt, Jr., served as the governor of Puerto Rico between 1929 and 1932. He was the son of President Theodore Roosevelt, who had a decisive role in planning and carrying out the U.S. war with Spain and had become president in 1901, soon after the invasion of Puerto Rico. It is clear from Roosevelt's memoirs that he was imbued with an imperialist vision similar to the one his father had earlier articulated as president (p. 83). His memoirs also make clear the previous policy of the United States, which was in the main "to Americanize Puerto Rico and thereby confer on her the greatest blessing, in our opinion, within our gift" (p. 97). In accordance with this policy of Americanization, all the laws were changed to conform to U.S. laws. According to Roosevelt (1937/1970), the civil code in Puerto Rico, which had been derived from Roman law, was "superseded in general with our adaptation of the English common law" (p. 98). Roosevelt also was quite explicit about the perceived need to change the language of the people as part of the Americanization policy: "Perhaps more significant of the line we were following was our attitude on education. . . . We set out deliberately to change this [the fact that Puerto Ricans spoke Spanish] and to make Puerto Rico English speaking" (p. 99).

Roosevelt's views on the ability of Puerto Ricans to govern themselves are more subtle. But it is apparent that he implicitly minimized the level of political knowledge, participation, and especially resistance among the Puerto Rican people. He also dismissed as natural and inevitable the dissatisfaction of Puerto Ricans. He said: "The fact remains, however, that never in any part of the world have I known a country financed by foreign capital and administered by foreigners where there was not local dissatisfaction and irritations" (Roosevelt, 1970, p. 103).

Mintz (1990) describes the economic changes Puerto Rico experienced during this period. In contrast to the political "benefits" cited by Roosevelt earlier, Mintz underscores the economic gain that accrued to the "sugar bosses":

Almost overnight, the island's placid countryside was remade by the conquerors, so that Puerto Rico could supply her colossal northern neighbor with the ever vaster quantities of sugar, molasses, and rum her fertile lands would yield. The central highlands, with their coffee lands and small farmers, declined, while the sugar coasts rapidly grew in extent and importance. . . . Between the First World War and the crash, Puerto Rico was turned into an enormous agrosocial sweatshop; during the Great Depression, its workers suffered while the sugar corporations, both Puerto Rican and North American, prospered. (p. 2)

Apparently, there were unrecognized economic costs that accompanied the "blessings of citizenship."

Rexford Tugwell, a member of Franklin D. Roosevelt's brain trust, was the appointed governor of Puerto Rico between 1941 and 1946. In his memoirs, he painted a more sympathetic and detailed picture than his predecessors did of the economic and political control the United States exercised over Puerto Rico. He remarked that Puerto Rico was just as much a colony as Massachusetts and New York had been under George III. He also discussed the president's concern over "the frightening increase of the population" (Tugwell, 1946/1977, p. 35) and the need for this to be stopped. Last, he recognized the lack of sympathy of the U.S. Congress and the generally difficult odds Puerto Rico faced there. Tugwell drew a distinction between the policy of the government and the attitude of the American people. He said: "Americans intend well for Puerto Ricans, but the United States somehow does not intend well for Puerto Rico" (p. 93). With regard to actual government practice, Tugwell said there was "no policy" and he described the prevailing governmental attitude as one that was "neither selfish nor generous; it was indifferent" (p. 7).

As Mintz (1990) has said more recently, "The propensity to view Puerto Rico as not very significant has never vanished from either the official North American psyche or the popular view" (p. 2). According to Tugwell (1946/1977), time spent on Puerto Rico was seen as "a political waste" (p. 71). What was demanded of a Puerto Rican governor "was that Puerto Rico should never be heard of" (p. 84). There was also the predominant attitude that it was "better to keep issues foggy" (p. 71). These attitudes influenced the subsequent economic and political changes Puerto Rico would undertake, as well as its literature.

Tugwell's departure was immediately followed by the appointment of the first Puerto Rican governor, Jesús Piñero, and subsequently by the election of a Puerto Rican governor, Luis Muñoz Marín, in 1948, and the development of a constitution that was approved through popular vote in 1952. The economy of the island also went through a series of transitions. First, there was an attempt to reform Puerto Rico's economy. State-owned enterprises were developed and were shown to induce foreign investment on the island. These state-owned firms were quickly sold to the private sector. This was followed by a labor-intensive industrial economy called Operation Bootstrap, which gave way, after 1960, to the present "capital-intensive economy" (J. Hernández, 1992/1997). Both of the latter economic approaches relied heavily on the use of tax incentives, low wages, and lenient regulation to attract foreign capital and industry to the island. In this regard, Puerto Rico became the U.S. model for programs established in other developing parts of the world. It also served as a well-publicized and convenient counter to socialist models inspired by the Cuban Revolution. During this period (1950s–1970s), Puerto Rico made major advances in education, housing, electrification, water and sewage systems, roads, and transportation. There was a large increase in consumerism, as well as growth of the middle class. This was also the period during which Puerto Rico developed its tourism industry and experienced the greatest exodus of its residents to the United States.

Economic and Political Studies of Puerto Rico

In the period following World War II, a number of studies focused on the politics and economics of Puerto Rico. These works were limited exclusively to the island, with little critical attention paid to the colonial relationship between the United States and Puerto Rico. The economic analyses included an early study by Perloff (1950), which focused on the future of the economy, and later works that assessed the consequences of economic growth. For example, Reynolds and Gregory (1965) focused on the Puerto Rican economy, with particular attention to economic push-and-pull factors affecting migration, wages, productivity, and industrialization. Another major economic treatise was Friedlander's (1965) study of labor migration and economic growth. This study documented the relative decline of employment in the agricultural sector and the accompanying decrease in agricultural output in Puerto Rico. It noted that despite changes in the kinds of work done by the total employed, such as labor shifts into mining, manufacturing, construction, services, and government, the volume of unemployment and underemployment remained high. These studies also noted that unemployment would have been higher but for the high rate of out-migration. However, these works gave little attention to contextual or political factors affecting the economic planning, or the decisions previously made by the U.S. colonial administration.

Political analyses included works by Anderson (1965), Hanson (1960), Wells (1969), and Goodsell (1965). These works also tended to focus exclusively on Puerto Rico and on the dramatic economic and political changes occurring in Puerto Rico after World War II, while avoiding explicit discussion of the colonial relationship. Anderson, for example, says the intent of his book is to explain "the dynamics of Puerto Rican party politics in terms of the perceptions and expectations of the political actors involved, not in terms of the relations—real or desired—between Puerto Rico and the United States" (p. vii). Nonetheless, these books reflect (some more explicitly than others) the ability of Puerto Ricans to cope successfully with the limitations imposed by the colonial relationship. Hanson describes how Puerto Rico was able to challenge radically the political dominance of absentee sugar interests. Goodsell analyzes politics in Puerto Rico after 1917 and demonstrates how the political elite in Puerto Rico managed to defeat U.S. political control. He describes how appointed governors were blocked or circumvented by the Puerto Rican legislature, and how the governors' attempts to supervise their political administrations were often impeded by their own cultural unfamiliarity, the language barrier, their short tenure, and an informal system developed by Puerto Rican leaders to facilitate legislation useful to the island.

There was also in the literature a more celebratory tone. Anderson (1965) refers to this shift of perspective in his preface, declaring,

In the years since the Second World War there has been a marked change in the literature on Puerto Rico. . . . During the thirties and early forties the island territory was usually described in terms of despair and hopelessness. . . . After the war Puerto Rico became an island of hope. . . . Such words as "miracle," "showcase of democracy," "the answer to Communism in Latin America" have been used to describe the transformation of this island over the past twenty years. (p. vii)

Although this review is largely limited to books, two very significant articles produced during this period reflected a similar orientation: Baggs (1962) and Galbraith and Shaw Soto (1953). Both emphasized the success of Puerto Rico's economic development program. Galbraith and Shaw Soto also chronicle the success of the governor, Muñoz Marín, in eliciting popular support for the program and for political reforms.

Sociological, Anthropological, and Journalistic Works

Between 1938 and 1972, there were a total of 20 major social science works written on Puerto Ricans. These include, in order of publication, books that focused specifically on Puerto Rico by Vincenzo Petrullo (1947); Julian H. Steward, Robert A. Manners, Eric R. Wolf, Elena Padilla Seda, Sidney W. Mintz, and Raymond L. Scheele (1956); David Landy (1959); Sidney W. Mintz (1960); Melvin Tumin and Arnold Feldman (1961); Gordon K. Lewis (1963); and Anthony La Ruffa (1971). These authors focused specifically on Puerto Ricans in the United States: Lawrence Chenault (1938/1970); C. Wright Mills, Clarence Senior, and Rose Goldsen (1950); Elena Padilla (1958); Oscar Handlin (1959); Beatrice Berle (1958); Dan Wakefield (1959/1975); Clarence Senior (1961); Patricia Cayo Sexton (1965); Nathan Glazer and Daniel P. Moynihan (1970); Eva Sandis (1970); and Rev. Joseph Fitzpatrick (1971). Only two works, Handlin's and Glazer and Moynihan's, focus on other groups as well as Puerto Ricans, while Oscar

Lewis's *La Vida* (1966) examines three families in Puerto Rico and two in New York. Christopher Rand's (1958) work discusses both Puerto Rico and Puerto Ricans in the United States. With few exceptions, this literature was characterized by an approach that emphasized fieldwork, community studies, structured questionnaires, and personal accounts. The social scientists generally used a variety of descriptive, ethnographic, and survey research methods in their studies, while the journalists based their works on conversations and impressions.

Characteristics of the Literature

With a Blind Eye: Exclusive Focus and Obfuscation of the Colonial Relationship. In this literature there was often an exclusive focus on the group without (a) the standard contrast and comparison methodologies used to study and assess groups; and (b) with minimal analysis of U.S. motives, policies, and impact on the group. There was a concurrent obfuscation of the colonial relationship. Although some works made reference to the "status" issue (or to the all-consuming preoccupation with it) in Puerto Rico, few discussed the role of the United States in originating or sustaining the issue. When the colonial relationship was not overlooked, it was viewed as benign, commensurate with what Puerto Ricans wanted, or eminently fixable. Certain inequalities were acknowledged, but it was thought that, with certain reforms and more education in English, these could be improved. Thus, although the colonial relationship was a very significant influence in the everyday life of the people, it and its consequences tended to be ignored or obfuscated in many of the major English-language works.

These characteristics of the early literature reflect, to a degree, the nonreflexive view that most Americans had (and many still have) of Puerto Rico. Puerto Rico is often approached as if it didn't have a historical and current-day political and economic context. Visitors to Puerto Rico are often surprised at the all-pervasive nature of the status issue in Puerto Rico—the extent to which it permeates political and social life, as well as the extent to which it influences decisions in education, the environment, language policy, and economic planning.

The methodologies and approaches common in much of the early literature contributed to the exclusive focus on Puerto Rico and the tendency to obfuscate the colonial relationship. Reports on Puerto Rico and memoirs were, by definition, exclusive focuses on the island written by representatives of the U.S. government. Many of the subsequent political analyses (Anderson, 1965; Goodsell, 1965; Hanson, 1960; Wells, 1969) also represented insular, noncontextualized views of Puerto Rico. Economic studies of the island (e.g., Friedlander, 1965; Perloff, 1950; Reynolds & Gregory, 1965) gave scant attention to contextual or political factors affecting economic planning, or to comparative situations. In addition, the works written by sociologists, anthropologists, and journalists—which constituted the bulk of the pre-1970s literature on Puerto Ricans—also focused exclusively on Puerto Rico or on Puerto Ricans in the continental United States. In many cases, the ethnographic approaches used in these works also reinforced these tendencies and supported Eurocentric biases.

Despite this tendency toward obfuscation, it was the colonial relationship that allowed and facilitated works on Puerto Ricans by many noted North Americans. Ironically, it is also the presumed need for "fixing" that has facilitated the production of so many works by North Americans. With regard to research, Puerto Rico has been accessible, exploitable, enjoyable, and fundable. Last, and most unfortunate, it has been this colonialist relationship that has also predisposed some authors either to view Puerto Ricans negatively and/or to misunderstand them totally. As Gordon Lewis (1963) pointed out, Puerto Ricans have the dubious distinction of being one of the most researched but least understood people in the United States, if not in the world.

In this regard, Puerto Rico served as something of a social science laboratory for many academics. Clearly, the data, the material gathered, and the works written provided many of the Puerto Rican scholars who surfaced in the subsequent period with points of departure. Some were trained by, or had studied the works of, these pre-1970s writers. Yet little is known about the development side of this process, on either an institutional or an individual basis. Although there is growing interest in this area among researchers today, little has been written about the impact of this scholarly production on subsequent scholars and on academic succession in Puerto Rico and in the United States. Although not yet thoroughly researched, the pre-1970s literature, though biased and faulty in many respects, very likely had a significant impact on developments in quantitative and qualitative methodology in the social sciences both in Puerto Rico and in the United States.

The tendency to ignore the role of larger political-economic contexts in the lives and outcomes of both Puerto Ricans and Native American peoples was a common theme in the literatures of both. Hawaiians and the South Pacific peoples in the U.S. territories have also often seen their historical and contemporary situation as similar to that of Native Americans, and yet these groups are seldom compared or studied together. There has been a tendency to view these groups as "unique" and apparently without parallel. This tendency was particularly evident in the early literatures on these groups, but in the case of Puerto Ricans there are still, for example, few comparative analyses with U.S. territories such as Guam. This "one-case" focus has delimited analysis of more contextual and structural issues that may have been common to people similarly situated. For example, Puerto Rico's status issue was often analyzed without reference to the experiences of other nations such as Cuba, the Dominican Republic, and the Philippines, and without reference to the United States' own resolution of its status issue.

Preponderance of Non–Puerto Ricans. Just as there has been a preponderance of non–Native Americans who have written about Native Americans, the English-language literature on Puerto Ricans was also dominated by non–Puerto Ricans. Of the 20 major social science works noted earlier, only one author was Puerto Rican. Puerto Ricans were used, in some cases, as fieldworkers and assistants, but they were viewed merely as helpers and their contributions were seldom acknowledged. The University of Puerto Rico Social Science Research Center was administered for a considerable period of time by Anglo Americans who consistently identified young Anglo scholars who came to do their doctoral dissertations (Lauria-Perricelli, 1990). Many of these works were published by major presses and were conducted by persons who were either prominent at the time or were to become celebrated scholars.

Consequently, autonomous indigenous perspectives tended to lack representation. Much of the literature suffered because there was little cultural, linguistic, and/or historical familiarity with the group studied. Given that language, culture, and knowledge of a people's history are basic bridges to be crossed when studying groups different from one's own, it is surprising how little attention this issue received in the early literature. For example, few works bothered to indicate how many of their research personnel were familiar with these three areas, nor did they discuss how their own lack of familiarity might have influenced their work.

As a result, much of the literature suffered from an "otherness" approach, in which Puerto Ricans were examined as "others" without histories or "convincing" cultural rationales. Although there were works written by Puerto Ricans on Puerto Ricans in the early 1970s (e.g., Seda Bonilla, 1973; Fernández Méndez, 1972; Buitrago Ortiz, 1974), they were few in number and, with scant exceptions (e.g., Padilla, 1958), did not receive as much attention as the works by non–Puerto Ricans.

Dominance of the Assimilationist, Immigrant Paradigm. Another characteristic of this literature was the tendency to view Puerto Ricans within an assimilationist, immigrant paradigm. Yet there are significant differences between the Puerto Rican migration and that of previous immigrant groups to the United States. For example, their arrival as U.S. citizens and colonial subjects—that is, as colonial (im)migrants—their Caribbean as opposed to European point of origin, and their multiracial composition are key differentiating factors. Nonetheless, it was the immigrant paradigm that was predominantly used in the pre-1970 literature to analyze Puerto Ricans in the United States (see, e.g., Chenault, 1938/1970; Fitzpatrick, 1971; Glazer & Moynihan, 1970; Handlin, 1959; Mills et al., 1950). In keeping with this paradigm, it was expected that, despite initial difficulties, Puerto Ricans would assimilate in due time, as had previous European immigrants. To the degree that the multiracial nature of the group was recognized, it was predicted that those who could not pass for White would assimilate into communities of African ancestry.

A number of factors combined to make this the paradigm of choice. First, it was the reigning paradigm, within which many of those who studied Puerto Ricans were educated. It was also the paradigm that coincided with the "melting pot" ethos that evolved with the large migrations at the end of the 19th and the beginning of the 20th centuries. In addition, Puerto Ricans arrived in greatest numbers in the 1950s, which was a unique historical period. The immigration laws of 1921 and 1924 had closed U.S. doors to free, unrestricted immigration, so large numbers of immigrants had not arrived for a number of years. New York, in particular, had lost much of its earlier (and current) ethnic immigrant flavor.

This was also a period of extreme political conservatism—the McCarthy era. The degree to which this conservative political climate influenced the reception of Puerto Ricans has not yet been fully assessed. Baver (1984) has noted that Puerto Ricans' political resistance to U.S. domination had a negative effect on the position that established political parties took vis-à-vis Puerto Ricans. But within this politically conservative context, groups that were culturally and linguistically distinct—as were migrating Puerto Ricans—were seen to be "immigrants." Citizenship status, multiracial composition, or U.S. military experience did not matter. Puerto Ricans were seen as the last in the continuum of (European) immigrant groups to this country. That this was not the "best-fitting" paradigm within which to understand Puerto Ricans would become evident as the work of revisionist writers and protestors helped to usher in an era in which diversity and multiculturalism would combine with the arrival of greater numbers of immigrants from Asia and Latin America and begin the formation of a new paradigm.

Overgeneralizations: Assuming the Part to Be the Whole. Another important and cross-cutting theme that is still to be found in the literature on Puerto Ricans is the tendency to generalize from a small number of observations and extreme cases to the whole group. Such gener-

alization presents a homogeneous but very distorted picture of the group. The rich and heterogeneous reality that typifies not just Puerto Ricans but most groups is missed. There is a selectivity of observation, and the complexity of the structures affecting individuals is not understood—especially the social, economic, and political institutions within which behavior takes place. It is this tendency that has been the most problematic and, unfortunately, the most recurrent in the literature on Puerto Ricans. (For a discussion, see A. Torres & Rodríguez, 1991.)

Misapplication of Categories, Concepts, and Contexts. The use of categories and concepts developed in one context and applied uncritically to another context was another theme in the literature that continues in the present. For example, the socioeconomic categories used by U.S. researchers often placed federal government employees in Puerto Rico in lower status positions than they were seen to occupy by the population they served. This tendency to apply categories and concepts uncritically is often evident in studies relying on secondary data. In such studies, basic issues, such as contextual analysis, the definition and measurement of variables, and the validity and relevance of constructs, seldom surface as points of discussion. This approach is common and accepted in mainstream social science research, but its primary purpose is not to generate knowledge about Puerto Rico and Puerto Ricans. Hypotheses often flow from, and build upon, the results of preceding studies that have used methodological and theoretical orientations that are similarly abstract. Consequently, the correct application and execution of the preestablished methodology becomes the basis upon which the research is evaluated. The extent to which it reveals new, useful, and accurate information about Puerto Ricans is often secondary. This tendency has been particularly evident in some journal articles written about Puerto Ricans.

Neglect of Indigenous Voices and Histories. The precontact cultural traditions and heritages of both Puerto Ricans and Native Americans were severely neglected. Histories of both groups tended to begin with the official date of conquest and were thereby constructed within the official U.S. canon. Thus, in the case of Puerto Ricans, the literature "began" after 1898. Literature written prior to that time by Puerto Ricans, or by others, tended not to be incorporated into the new English-language literature on Puerto Ricans. It was as if there had not been at least a 3,500-year history in Puerto Rico prior to its conquest by the United States. An example of this continuing neglect is the work of Eugenio M. de Hostos, who was an eminent social writer, philosopher, and intellectual leader in the late 19th century. Although he was a prolific writer and quite well known in Latin American literature, very few of his works have been translated into English. In addition, references to de Hostos, in the English-language literature, tend to be limited to his political role as an advocate for the independence movement at the time of conquest.

Definitions. With time, a struggle over definitions and perspectives has become more evident in the literatures of both Native American peoples and Puerto Ricans (Churchill, 1992; Jaimes, 1992). "Indigenous" writers sought to find their own voice and often struggled against definitions of themselves by others as "others." This still ongoing conflict is most clearly seen in discussions over the ostensibly straightforward task of counting people. The criteria, issues, and consequences of defining what constitutes a "Native American person" or "Indian" have been well detailed by Snipp (1989). Different criteria have resulted in different counts. Historically, Native American peoples have preferred criteria identifying them as members of a nation instead of the genetically based criteria of the U.S. government. Genetically based criteria (such as the proportion of Indian "blood") have resulted in lower numbers of Native Americans counted, as well as in fewer persons being declared eligible for entitlement programs that grew out of treaty stipulations or tribal agreements with the U.S. government.

Similarly, for most intents and purposes, the data generally presented on Puerto Ricans is on the 3.4 million Puerto Ricans who reside in the continental United States. Yet in 1999, there were also 3.8 million Puerto Ricans living in Puerto Rico (U.S. Census Bureau, 2000). This practice of presenting just data on Puerto Ricans in the states is common despite the fact that Puerto Ricans in Puerto Rico and the United States are all citizens of the United States. Consequently, this practice underestimates (a) the absolute numbers of Puerto Ricans, (b) the number and proportion of Latinos in the United States, and (c) the proportion of Latinos who are Puerto Rican. Indeed, in 1990, the Puerto Rican share of the Latino population in the United States almost doubled when Puerto Ricans from Puerto Rico were included in the count—from 12.2% to 24.1% (U.S. Census Bureau, 1990a, 1990b). This practice also underestimates the needs of Puerto Ricans in Puerto Rico and, in some instances, pits the groups against one another as they compete for public and private funds, such as scholarships, student financial aid, and research grants. With the availability of census 2000 data on the Web (www.census.gov), a few reports include data on Puerto Ricans both in Puerto Rico and in the states.

In summary, many of the works produced in the pre-1970s period manifested the problems noted earlier. They ignored issues of political sovereignty; they obfuscated or viewed as benign the political relationship; they focused exclusively on Puerto Ricans without contrasting them with similar groups; they misrepresented, underrepresented, or totally ignored indigenous histories and voices; they used inappropriate contexts, categories, and concepts to examine Puerto Ricans; and they generalized from extreme cases to the whole population. Although some works were less problematic than others, as a whole the works conveyed a strong sense of otherness in their depictions of Puerto Ricans. Although these were the major patterns, there were also important exceptions. For example, Morales Carrión's (1952) book placed Puerto Rico in the context of the Antilles and examined the multiple sociocultural and economic encounters that took place under Spanish colonialism.

The literature that emerged after the 1970s would critique the earlier literature on a number of grounds: (a) overuse of the Malthusian view that Puerto Rico's problems are the result of overpopulation (see J. Hernández, 1992/1997; Hernández Cruz, 1988; and History Task Force, 1979, for criticisms of this view); (b) the tendency to apply an accusatory or deficit model that views Puerto Rico and Puerto Ricans as "a problem," the source of their own problems, or an expensive liability with few accomplishments or contributions; (c) the incorrect assumption that the history of the Puerto Rican community in the United States has been undistinguished and of fairly short duration; (d) a tendency to ignore issues and perspectives of concern to Puerto Ricans; and (e) disparagement of Puerto Rican language and culture. In Puerto Rico, the social literature by U.S. social scientists on Puerto Rico was also critically examined (see Rivera Medina & Ramírez, 1989).

Oscar Lewis and *La Vida* (1966). Oscar Lewis's *La Vida* (1966) is the book that most dramatically represents some of the difficulties noted here. It won the National Book Award for nonfiction in 1967 and received great attention in the popular press and in the scholarly community, being reviewed in a variety of major journals and newspapers by some of the foremost authors of the day (see, for example, Caplow, 1967; "The Culture of Poverty," 1966; Day, 1967; Fitzpatrick, 1966; Glazer, 1967; Harrington, 1966; Maloff, 1966; Renek, 1966). It also received much attention in Puerto Rico, being the subject of a special issue of the *Revista de Ciencias Sociales,* the social sciences journal of the University of Puerto Rico (Maldonado Denis, 1967). It appeared just five years after *West Side Story* (1961)—the now-classic musical that introduced Puerto Ricans in New York to America as ghettoized, gang-warring, "immigrants"—won a multitude of prestigious awards, Oscars, and top grossing receipts for the year.

Lewis claimed to write the book for "teachers, social workers, doctors, priests, and others—who bear the major responsibility for carrying out anti-poverty programs" (Rigdon, 1988, p. 151). Written in a narrative form and highly readable, it also appeared during the peak of the Johnson administration's War on Poverty and reflected to some degree the concerns of this period.

It was perhaps the most controversial book ever written on Puerto Ricans. Within Puerto Rico and Puerto Rican communities in the United States, the book generally elicited outrage. Reviewers were divided on whether Lewis misrepresented Puerto Ricans or whether readers "misinterpreted" the work (see, e.g., von Eckardt, 1967; Fitzpatrick, 1966; Glazer, 1967). Still others felt the problems with the work went beyond misrepresentation of Puerto Ricans to the misrepresentation of people in poverty. Opler (1967), for example, argued that the concept of the culture of poverty blurred, leveled, and stereotyped the indigent of various cultures of the world, and that this was "a middle-class or ethnocentric stereotype" (p. 488). Valentine (1968) argued that Lewis's work had more pragmatic, negative implications; he maintained that it was Lewis's works and his concept of the culture of poverty that deserved part of the blame for the failure of the War on Poverty program (see also Rigdon, 1988).

The Colonial Context Displayed. *La Vida* (O. Lewis, 1966) illustrates a good many of the themes just discussed. It was an ethnography written by an Anglo-American with a strong assimilationist and immigrant background. The book had an exclusive focus, obfuscated the colonial relationship, conveyed a strong sense of "otherness," used a deficit model, applied inappropriate contexts for analysis, generalized from extreme cases to the whole group, and depreciated the indigenous view of political events. For example, it focuses exclusively on one extended family, the Ríos family, living in a slum area of San Juan, Puerto Rico, and in New York City. There is an introduction followed by five chapters, each of which is devoted to one person in the family. The family consists of the mother plus her four children. Each chapter describes a day in their lives and then presents a narrative by an individual family member.

The colonial relationship is only obliquely referred to in the narrative, as when Lewis's respondents express their opinions about politics or about Americans. However, the effect of the colonial relationship weaves its way implicitly into the narrative. It is evident in the need of the Ríos family members to move to the United States to work. Family members indicate they came to New York to live and earn money away from Puerto Rico.

Lewis seemed to have selected Puerto Rico for his study for a variety of reasons. Crucial to this selection were important components of Puerto Rico's colonial context: political approval and timing, funding, and the availability of informants. He argued in his work that Puerto Rico had been under U.S. control and influence since 1898, it was an unincorporated territory, Puerto Ricans had citizenship status, and there had been a large migration of Puerto Ricans to the United States (O. Lewis, 1966). In essence, since Puerto Ricans were legally citizens, fears of repercussions or deportation, or potential problems of cooperation during the research, were not anticipated (Rigdon, 1988).

Lewis also viewed Puerto Ricans through outside contexts and applied concepts and categories developed in another context without taking the Puerto Rican experience into consideration. In his introduction, he faults Puerto Ricans for not developing "a great revolutionary tradition" (O. Lewis, 1966, p. xvi) like that of Mexico, and for not identifying as richly and as deeply with their traditions as do the Mexicans. Lewis also argued that the native culture in Puerto Rico was relatively simple and had never reached the high degree of civilization achieved by Mexico in pre-Hispanic times. These comparisons demonstrated an astounding lack of awareness of Puerto Rican history and the consequences of a colonial policy. Contrasting Puerto Ricans with Mexicans, he said:

In Mexico even the poorest slum dwellers have a much richer sense of the past and a deeper identification with the Mexican tradition than do Puerto Ricans with their tradition. . . . In San Juan the respondents showed an abysmal ignorance of Puerto Rican historical figures. Some knew more about George Washington and Abraham Lincoln than about their own heroes. (p. xvii)

In making this statement, Lewis was oblivious to the fact that, along with changes in language policy, colonialism had brought changes in the content of education. For several years after publication of Lewis's book, Puerto Ricans were still taught the history of the United States and not the history of Puerto Rico. This was not the case in Mexico. A number of Marxists in Puerto Rico defended Lewis's work, and it is important to understand why, for their position further highlights the colonial context of Puerto Rico. Maldonado Denis (1967), for example, argued that Lewis's respondents represented the double alienation that comes from the combination of class and colonialist oppression. In essence, the Ríos family was seen to represent the lumpen proletariat within a colonial structure. He contended that the politically conservative attitudes of the family indicated that Marx was right when he said the lumpen proletariat were a potential ally of the propertied classes. Fundamentally, Marxists argued that it was important to confront this reality so as to change the structure that gave rise to it; others argued that the image was not representative. The issue was not whether there was a problem, but how that problem was to be described and categorized—within pathological, deficit models, or within more structuralist frameworks.

Methodological Critiques. Oscar Lewis's *La Vida* (1966) received two major methodological criticisms: his use of a selective sample and of a selective site (Padilla, 1967). He selected all five of the members of his family from one barrio "from a group Lewis thought was most likely to manifest subculture traits" (Rigdon, 1988, p. 109). Consequently, by "relying on individuals who were the most accessible and willing to cooperate, Lewis selected out many people who were fully employed and hard working, as well as those with a strong sense of personal privacy" (p. 111).

The Ríos family was one of 120 multiproblem families that had been under study by the School of Social Work at the University of Puerto Rico. A serious flaw in the book is Lewis's inability to demonstrate the representativeness of his respondents. On the one hand, he announces: "I should like to emphasize that this study deals with only one segment of the Puerto Rican population and that the data should not be generalized to Puerto Rican society as a whole" (O. Lewis, 1966, pp. xii–xiii). But then he declares subsequently:

The intensive study of the life of even a single extended family by the methods used in this volume tells us something about individuals, about family life, about lower-class life as a whole, and about the history and culture of the larger society in which these people live. (p. xv)

The representativeness of the Ríos family was also questioned because they were engaged in prostitution, while only a minority of families in the area studied were so engaged (Glazer, 1967; Pérez de Jesús, 1967). Fitzpatrick (1966) also questioned the representativeness of the sexual patterns depicted and cited other studies in Puerto Rico (e.g., Landy, 1959; Mintz, 1960; Steward et al., 1956) that had found results quite at variance with Lewis's presentation.

Another question raised about the respondents' representativeness is the degree to which they may have been mentally ill. Rigdon (1988), who also worked on the Puerto Rico study, said that "among his Puerto Rican informants in particular were a number of people whose behavior was, in the context of their own communities, deviant and even bizarre" (p. 97).

The second methodological criticism concerns the typicality of the area chosen. As Padilla (1967) notes in her review, "La Esmeralda, as any San Juan resident would tell, is a center of prostitution, the unofficial red light district of the city" (p. 651).

At the conceptual level, there is also in Lewis's work little awareness of the role of class. This is curious, because his work is premised on the assumption that cultural differences exist because of class. In von Eckardt's (1967) own study of middle-class Puerto Rican youth, she showed that the values that predominate in this group are opposite to those in *La Vida*. She argues that Lewis should have placed the Ríos family more clearly within the Puerto Rican societal structure. Padilla (1967) agrees and adds that Lewis "has failed to use unbiased sampling procedures in the selection of his respondents and has neglected to use historical methods to place the Ríoses in their proper historical and social perspective" (p. 652). This "contextualizing" is especially important when the intended readership is non–Puerto Rican.

Lewis's work is also criticized because he never clarified the criteria he used to select or edit his original tapes. He says that, in the process of taping, he asked informants to repeat the histories that he already knew with the goal of having them "in their own words" (O. Lewis, 1966, p. xx). He also says that few notes were taken during the day, when observation took place, and that memory was relied on to reproduce the dialogue and the details. According to Rigdon (1988), Lewis never kept records, logs, or diaries in the field. It is unclear what was included and what was excluded from the tapes, and what criteria were used to select themes and conversations in *La Vida* (Beattie, 1967; Rodríguez Bou, 1967).

There are other questions that could be raised about Lewis's research in Puerto Rico. Contrary to earlier studies in which he was quite actively involved, in Puerto Rico he personally administered only a small number of questionnaires (Rigdon, 1988). There is also a question as to the "fit" between his theory and his data. Rigdon says: "The use of culture of poverty theory to force an integration was not only artificial but led Lewis to postulate relationships he did not demonstrate, let alone prove, with his own data" (p. 81).

La Vida was used to generalize to many groups, most importantly Puerto Ricans, yet the representativeness of this one family can be questioned on a variety of grounds. It is clear that they are not representative of all Puerto Ricans, it seems evident that they are not representative of Puerto Ricans in poverty or of most people in poverty, and it is questionable whether they are even representative of the barrio within which they lived. Although the book is subtitled *A Puerto Rican Family in the Culture of Poverty,* it is difficult to determine whether this is a study of the culture of poverty or a study of prostitution within the culture of poverty.

Puerto Rican communities dealt with the spillover effects generated by the book. Teachers read it in their faculty lounges; well-intentioned social workers and other service providers read it en route to work. They concluded that they now understood Puerto Ricans. As Rodríguez Bou (1967) argued, the study would have a negative impact on the poor, because many poor people would now be rejected by the nonpoor, who would assume they followed the practices depicted in *La Vida*.

In the end, the book served important, if dispiriting, political purposes. Writes Rigdon (1988), "In the 1960s, the eradication of poverty was a central political issue and the culture of poverty was a dramatic yet conveniently vague phrase that helped to call attention to the problems of the poor—or, from another perspective, to the problem of the poor" (p. 87).

Puerto Ricans became further identified with the problem of the poor. Subsequent funded research on Puerto Ricans would focus on poverty, and *La Vida* would provide a major point of departure. But what is perhaps most lamentable is that even if we were to accept Lewis's study as representative or legitimate, it would have taught us nothing new, nor could it prescribe policy that would alleviate the dramatic expression of hunger and deprivation (Rodríguez Bou, 1967).

DECONSTRUCTING AND CONTEXTUALIZING: THE POST-1970 LITERATURE

Many of the themes in the earlier literature still persist (see, e.g., Hauberg, 1974), some in slightly altered fashion; for example, the culture-of-poverty thesis was transformed into the underclass conception. There was also a shift from a focus on Puerto Rico and Puerto Ricans to the more generic Hispanic group, within which Puerto Ricans were subsumed. (Within this rubric, there was a tendency to lose sight of what was specific to one group and what was common to all Latino groups.) There was also a shift to a more quantitative approach. Private and public funding would assist these shifts. However, there was also the development of a literature that was deconstructionist in its intent and that sought to contextualize Puerto Rico and Puerto Ricans. As was to be expected, resistance to, and misinterpretation of, the new literature would also become manifest.

It was also during the late 1960s and early 1970s that many Puerto Rican studies programs were started in the United States. These programs rejected traditional approaches to learning about Puerto Ricans and defined new sources of learning that stemmed from within the Puerto Rican experience. Puerto Rican studies discarded apologist and colonizing ideologies and designed new theoretical constructs within which fresh analyses about the Puerto Rican condition were generated (Nieves, 1987). The Puerto Rican studies thrust emphasized the accountability of scholars to represent the community accurately. This thrust also spread to scholars in Puerto Rico. One example is Quintero Rivera, González, Campos, and Flores's essays (1981) on national identity and social classes, originally presented at a university-sponsored colloquium. The scholars explore the issue of Puerto Ricans' national identity from literary, historical, and ideological perspectives.

However, the early efforts (in English and in Spanish) to combat and correct the homogeneous and distorted views of Puerto Ricans were often ignored or summarily dismissed because they challenged the prevailing notions. These pioneering writers and researchers were often accused of reflecting bias and were perceived as lacking in competence or qualifications. At best they were seen as marginal, or not important in addressing the major research questions of the day. In addition, until very recently, publisher interest in these efforts was minimal. Unless the images coincided with stereotypical expectations, most publishers did not avail themselves of these transformative works, arguing that they would have no market. Consequently, many of these works were not published in mainstream outlets. This was the case both in the United States and in Puerto Rico, where the internalized colonialism and the divisions created by it restrained publishers from publishing on these issues. When critical or revisionist works were printed at all, it was often through less well-established and less prestigious avenues, with distribution networks that were typically not extensive. Thus they became in many respects phantom or fugitive works—seldom referenced, less well known, and less read.

Moreover, there was a subtle academic exclusion. U.S.-based scholars who might have been considered "deconstructionists" or "postmodernists" were instead often "derogatively labeled 'ghetto' scholars" (Vázquez, 1992, p. 1043). According to Vázquez, their work was often devalued because, in large measure, their subject matter was devalued. Despite the fact that

others could and did study Puerto Rico and Puerto Ricans in great profusion during the 1940s, 1950s, and 1960s, [when] Puerto Ricans started studying other Puerto Ricans it was seen as nothing more than the scholarly contemplation of one's own navel. If American scholars [studied] American culture and society through American studies, this was considered serious scholarship. However, when a Puerto Rican researcher [studied] the Puerto Rican culture—any aspect of it—it [was] not seen as quite scholarly enough. (p. 1043)

Nonetheless, despite the protestations of more traditional (and threatened) mainstream academics, the energetic efforts of the new writers succeeded in transforming the literature on Puerto Ricans. The number of Puerto Ricans contributing to the literature increased significantly after 1970 and even more so in the 1990s.

Focus on the Colonial Relationship and Its Negative Consequences

The literature that surfaced during this period reflected many of the new intentions. It also focused directly on the colonial relationship and its negative consequences.

Challenging the assimilationist, immigrant paradigm, it questioned the use of deficit models and gave attention to indigenous issues and histories that had been neglected. It compared Puerto Ricans with other, similar groups and examined Puerto Ricans within national and international contexts. As was the case with the literatures of other racial/ethnic groups, there was a search for a "buried past." The histories of Puerto Rico and of the Puerto Rican communities in the United States examined more closely colonial relationships and their negative consequences— see, for example, Bergad (1983), Scarano (1984), Baralt (1999), Ayala (1999), Findlay Suárez (1999), and Schmidt-Nowara (1999), who investigate Puerto Rico's buried past; Matos Rodríguez's (1999) gender and class analysis of urban change in 19th-century San Juan; Harris (1980), who examined the involvement of Puerto Ricans in military service; Colón (2001), whose formerly "buried" manuscript recounts the history of early Puerto Rican migrants to Brooklyn, New York; and the extensive writings of Fernando Picó on 19th-century Puerto Rico (e.g., Picó, 1979, 1981).

The late 1960s and early 1970s have been referred to as a period of "nationalist revitalization" within the Puerto Rican communities in the United States (Falcón, 1984). During this period a number of works appeared that were widely read and that stressed the heretofore-neglected perspectives of "independentistas." Significant among these were Figueroa (1974), Maldonado Denis (1972), Silén (1971), and López (1973). Many of these works offered an interpretation of Puerto Rico's history that emphasized the inequality of the colonial relationship and the consequences of domination. López and Petras (1974) and López (1980) echoed these views. They were also critical of earlier studies that focused on symptoms and did not point out that these symptoms were consequences of larger exploitative relationships that had been cultivated and institutionalized over time. In López and Petras (1974), a number of the chapters were devoted to "the Puerto Rican Diaspora" in the United States. In this new literature, the political relationship was central, not obscured or seen as benevolent.

Many works began to unearth the history of the independence movement and to clarify its current-day distortions. Ribes Tovar's (1971) volume on the independence leader Albizu Campos is an example of such a work oriented to a less academic audience. All of these works were instrumental in establishing in the United States a literary tradition that had already existed in Puerto Rico in Spanish. Other works that followed in this tradition are those by G. Lewis (1974), Zavala and Rodríguez (1980), Liden (1981), Blaut (1987), Fernández (1992), Meléndez and Meléndez (1993), and Bosque Pérez and Colón Morera (1997). Meléndez and Meléndez presented critical perspectives on contemporary Puerto Rico and focused on questions often neglected in earlier research, such as the extent of military control and ownership of land in Puerto Rico; the struggle for independence in contemporary times; and an assessment of Puerto Rico's current role in the Caribbean economy. Bosque Pérez and Colón Morera (1997) present a collection of essays and documents on the persecution of independentistas. What was evident in this ongoing tradition of scholarship was that "behind the complacency that sometimes seems to dominate U.S. colonial rule over Puerto Rico lurks a will of national affirmation that refuses to die" (Carrión, 1993, p. 75).

In keeping with more radical and revisionist perspectives were works examining the impact of the U.S.–Puerto Rico political relationship on Puerto Rico (Cabán, 1999; Heine, 1983; Maldonado Denis, 1980; Márquez, 1976; Meléndez, 1996; Navarro, 1995; Santiago-Valle, 1994; Trías Monjes, 1997) and upon Puerto Ricans in the United States (History Task Force, 1979). This relationship was no longer viewed as benign and malleable, but rather as highly determinant. For example, the earlier literature had viewed migration as a response to push-and-pull forces, but still very much the result of individual choice. The Centro de Estudios Puertorriqueños focused upon the influence of the political-economic relationship on migration (History Task Force). Scholars at the Centro argued that one cannot separate analysis of migration from analysis of economic structure and change; that the massive migration of Puerto Ricans to the United States in the post–World War II period was a labor migration that could only be understood by examining the colonial-capitalist framework of Puerto Rico; that it was, in effect, driven by U.S. capitalist forces functioning within a colonial context.

In subsequent works, the political-economic relationship and the post–World War II industrialization program in Puerto Rico received closer examination (see Baver, 1993; Bloomfield, 1985; Bonilla & Campos, 1986; Carr, 1984; Dietz, 1986; Lapp, 1991; López, 1987; Meléndez & Meléndez, 1993; Pantojas-García, 1990; Ross, 1976; Santiago, 1992; Weisskoff, 1985). Similarly, an emphasis on examining larger contextual and structural issues affecting Puerto Ricans in the United States was provided by Rodríguez (1974, 1989/1991), J. Morales (1986), and Padilla (1987). These works began with the assumption that Puerto Ricans in the United States and in Puerto Rico could not be accurately understood without understanding the context from which they came, the context they had entered, and the structural contexts within which they functioned.

Some authors questioned traditional views of economic development. Berman-Santana (1996), for example, used a case study approach in Salinas, Puerto Rico, to examine the problems created as a result of Puerto Rico's economic development program, such as the exploitation of natural resources and the policies of Operation Bootstrap, which eliminated jobs and did not create enough new ones to replace them. Others detailed the history, goals, and activities of the development program (Maldonado, 1997), and still others examined more independent or autonomous approaches to economic development on the community level (Meléndez Vélez & Medina Piña (1999).

Still others used larger quantitative databases and challenged generally accepted but often-untested theories. Rivera-Batiz and Santiago (1994/1997), using decennial census data, found evidence for increasing bipolarization in the socioeconomic status of Puerto Ricans in the United States. Rivera-Batiz and Santiago (1996) also used decennial census data to describe social and economic changes in Puerto Rico during its fifty years as a U.S. commonwealth. Sotomayor (1998) examined the structure, trends, and sources of poverty and income inequality in Puerto Rico from the 1970s to the 1990s. J. Hernández (1983) found that human capital theory could not be applied to Puerto Rican youth without considering their health, family, and residential situation; migration background; and veteran status. Meléndez, Rodríguez, and Barry Figueroa's (1991) collection examined structural economic factors affecting Puerto Ricans, as well as the effect of national and international intersections of race, color, class, and colonialism. Some authors developed innovative perspectives within traditional subject areas. Building on the earlier work of J. Hernández (1967) and Torruellas and Vásquez (1984), Torre, Rodríguez-Vecchini, and Burgos (1994) developed new perspectives on return migration. These works differed from the earlier literature in that they focused more on the structures affecting Puerto Ricans as opposed to the cultural attributes considered to be characteristic of the group.

Puerto Ricans and Other Groups

Closely allied to this approach was the growing research that examined Puerto Ricans in relation to similar groups. Examples include Padilla's (1985) accounts of the factors responsible for the development of Latino ethnic consciousness among Puerto Ricans and Mexicans in Chicago; Acosta-Belén and Sjostrom's (1988) collection of articles on Hispanics in the United States; Fox's (1996) analysis of Hispanic identity; Flores and Benmayor's (1997) study of the concept of citizenship among Latinos; de la Garza, Desipio, Garcia, Garcia, and Falcón's study (1992) of political attitudes; R. Morales and Bonilla's (1993) study of Latinos in a changing U.S. economy; and Gonzalez's (2000) analysis of the Latinization of the United States. Another instance is J. Hernández's (1992/1997) interdisciplinary work, which surveys the peoples and nations made part of the United States by war and occupation and focuses on Puerto Ricans, Filipinos, Hawaiians, Chicanos, and Native Americans. Gautier Mayoral and Alegría Ortega (1994) focus on the politics of decolonization for the Caribbean, specifically Puerto Rico, the U.S. Virgin Islands, Guyana, and Guadalupe. Finally, the work by A. Torres (1994) compares the effects of national and regional trends on Puerto Ricans and African Americans in New York City.

In addition to deconstructing and reconstructing earlier views, works began to focus on issues that had been ignored in the previous literature. For example, Pérez y Mena (1991) explored the historical roots of spiritualism, while Harwood (1977) and Morales-Dorta (1976) considered its mental health functions; Moreno Vega (2000) described the living traditions of Santería; Díaz-Stevens (1993) examined Puerto Rican Catholicism in New York; and Dolan and Vidal (1994) edited a volume examining the history of Puerto Rican and Cuban Catholics in the United States between 1900 and 1965.

At the same time as renewed interest in immigration studies in the United States (because of the large numbers of immigrants coming to the United States during the 1980s and 1990s), there was also attention paid to immigration to Puerto Rico. Although in the past the emphasis had been to study Puerto Ricans returning to or leaving Puerto Rico, now there was increased attention given to the migration of Cubans and Dominicans to Puerto Rico—see, for example, Cobas and Duany (1995, 1997) and Duany (1990). In journal articles and monographs, there were also comparisons made of communities established by these groups in both the United States and Puerto Rico.

Popular Culture

Popular culture also became an important area of study, with Aparicio (1998), Calvo Ospina (1995), Block (1973), Flores (2000), and Glasser (1995) all examining the history and role of music within the Puerto Rican community, and Perez and Mejias (1997) profiling the life of one popular singer. Some of this literature recognizes that popular culture can also be an excellent source for researching issues of race, culture, class, and gender. With the legitimization of cultural studies as a field among mainstream researchers, this literature opened up new venues for exploring Puerto Ricans on the island and in the Diaspora. This literature is especially important since one of the principal ways that non–Puerto Ricans confront the reality of Puerto Rican culture is through music and the arts. The Aparicio (1998) volume, for example, combines sociology with literary analysis to explore the various meanings of salsa and other Puerto Rican popular music forms in terms of issues such as race, gender, and class. It situates contemporary salsa music in the broader context of the historical development of other music forms in Puerto Rico. The Flores (2000) work contains a series of essays on various aspects of popular culture, including musical styles, literary traditions, and the use of urban space. The works of Dávila (1997, 2001) focus on the influence of marketing and the commercial media on the construction of contemporary Puerto Rican and Latina/o culture and identity. Finally, Quintero Rivera (1999) presents a sociological study of "tropical" music that centers on Puerto Rico and expands through the rest of the Spanish Caribbean and the Latino-Caribbean diasporas in the United States.

Crime was not a new area of research, but the foci within this area were new: Bourgois (1995) focused his ethnographic research on crack addicts in East Harlem, Schneider (1999) on gang activity in New York, Padilla (1992) on the gang as an American enterprise, and Padilla and Santiago (1993) on prisoners' families.

The collection of readings edited by Rodríguez, Sánchez Korrol, and Alers (1980/1984) is an early example of a work that focuses on previously ignored issues. Developed as a reader for Puerto Rican studies courses, this volume included articles that were vital to the Puerto Rican community at the time but were generally ignored within more mainstream contexts. This interdisciplinary volume included chapters on Puerto Rican women, the Young Lords, Latin music, the struggle for local political control, spiritualism, the struggles within the Catholic church, the Puerto Rican Day Parade, race within ethnicity, political activism, the economy, and a beginning critique of the conceptual models and methods used to "measure" the quality of life among Puerto Ricans. This attention to neglected issues was a first step in developing knowledge that would help to resolve community issues. The highly interdisciplinary nature of the chapters, ranging from literary selections by nonacademic writers to more traditional social science commentaries, would also typify other works published during this period and subsequently (see, for example, Santiago, 1995).

This reader also departed from traditional approaches in that it asserted that the experience of being Puerto Rican would enhance the work, if based on valid observations related to commonly accepted knowledge. It was not suggested that one had to be Puerto Rican to write accurately about the Puerto Rican community, or that being Puerto Rican was any guarantee of accuracy or insight, but that the experience of being Puerto Rican, if understood correctly, would be an asset in dealing with the issues. Thus it was no accident that nearly all of those involved with this collection were second-generation Puerto Ricans or had experienced life in U.S. Puerto Rican

communities. The editors stated that "the authors have been intimately involved in the issues they address and this sets their work apart from many traditional social scientists" (Rodríguez, Sánchez Korrol, & Alers, 1980/ 1984, p. 3). The collection also endeavored to speak to "the new reality of Puerto Ricans, their future, and a more accurate past than had been depicted in the traditional literature" (p. 3). This collection and the others described here attempted to put forth a more representative view by allowing those affected to speak for themselves within a framework of personal integrity and dignity. The second edition of this volume (Rodríguez & Sánchez Korrol, 1996) and other works that followed the first edition (e.g., Acosta-Belén, 1986; Hidalgo & McEniry, 1985) were similar in their orientations. (The latter was targeted to government officials and service providers interested in the Hispanic community.)

Search for a Buried Past

The post-1970 literature contained the same search for a buried past undertaken by Native Americans, and by other groups whose stories have often been excluded from official U.S. history. Examples are the continuing work of the Centro de Estudios Puertorriqueños in assembling historical documentation on the migration and on Puerto Rico (Flores, 1987; History Task Force, 1983; Oral History Task Force, 1986; Reynolds, Rodríguez-Fraticelli, & Vásquez Erazo, 1989) and the volumes by Wagenheim and Jiménez de Wagenheim (1973/1994). Acosta (1987), Picó (1990), Scarano (1993), and Jiménez de Wagenheim (1998) present Puerto Rican history textbooks in this tradition. In women's studies, the reconstruction of migrant women's lives using oral history methods is another example (Benmayor, Juarbe, Alvarez, & Vásquez, 1987). Moreover, there are a number of works that present "portraits of the early migration" (Hernández Cruz, 1988), such as those by Sánchez Korrol (1983/1994), which depicts the pre–World War II Puerto Rican community; and by Iglesias (1984), which compiles the memoirs of Bernardo Vega, an early migrant and socialist writer who gives us a glimpse of life in the late 19th- and early 20th-century Puerto Rican community. Works by Acosta-Belén and Sánchez Korrol (1993) and Colón (1982) describe the Puerto Rican community in the 1930s, 1940s, and 1950s. There is also the work of Stevens-Arroyo (1988), Rouse (1992), and Chanlatte Baik and Narganes Storde (1990) on the world of the Taínos, the pre-Columbian inhabitants of Puerto Rico.

The search for a buried past also focused on the history of slaves in Puerto Rico and Puerto Rico's African heritage. Many writers focused on the history of slavery and the experiences of African slaves in Puerto Rico (e.g., Mayo Santana, Negrón Portillo, & Mayo López, 1997; Morales Carrión, 1978; Negrón Portillo & Mayo Santana, 1999; Sued Badillo & López Cantos, 1986). Others explored the impact of slavery on Puerto Rican society and culture. For example, Kinsbruner (1996) examined racial prejudice in 19th-century Puerto Rican society, Scarano (1984) examined slavery and the plantation economy between 1800 and 1850, and Díaz Quiñones (1985) critically reviewed earlier analyses of racial prejudice in Puerto Rico. González's (1993) seminal essays presented an in-depth analysis of Puerto Rican cultural history and proposed that Puerto Rico's culture is primarily Afro-Caribbean.

Works focusing on the Puerto Rican communities in the United States also examined the early histories of these communities; in so doing they contested the notion, then generally accepted, that these communities had begun at about the time that *West Side Story* made its debut on Broadway in 1957. There were also numerous works documenting more recent history (e.g., Bonilla-Santiago, 1988; Cardona, 1974; Díaz-Stevens, 1993; Figueroa, 1989; Estades, 1978; Haslip-Viera & Baver, 1994; Martínez, 1974; Ribes Tovar, 1968, 1970, 1972; Rogler, 1972; Sanchez & Stevens-Arroyo, 1987) and pictorial treatments, such as those by Matos Rodríguez and Hernández (2001), Maldonado (1984), and Young Lords Party (1971). Many of the works also moved the Puerto Rican perspective to a more national level (see, for example, U.S. Commission on Civil Rights, 1976; and Wagenheim, 1975).

In addition, there were works that began to reassess long-standing issues, such as nationalism, language, religion, race, residential segregation, employment, and education. Negrón-Muntaner and Grosfoguel's (1997) collection of critical essays focused on colonialism and nationalism, incorporating the perspectives of underrepresented groups such as Puerto Rican youth, gays and lesbians, blacks, and women. However, many of these discussions are not to be found in published books but rather outside the realm of this review, in reports and monographs published by such community organizations as ASPIRA, the Puerto Rican Forum, the National Puerto Rican Coalition, the Institute for Puerto Rican Policy, and the Latino Institute; in theses; and in articles in journals developed by Puerto Ricans, such as *The Rican, Revista, Centro Boletín, Journal of Latino Studies, METAS,* and the *Latino(a) Research Review.* It is also to be found in the monographs produced by the Hispanic Research Center (1990), and in the work on culture and language by the Centro de Estudios Puertorriqueños (Alvarez, Bennett, Greenlee, Pedraza, & Pousada, 1988; Attinasi, Pedraza, Poplack, & Pousada, 1988; Benmayor, Torruellas, & Juarbe, 1992; Cultural Studies Task Force, 1987; Pedraza, 1987; Poplack & Pousada, 1981; Torruellas, Benmayor, Goris, & Juarbe, 1991).

Language Issues

Given the controversies over bilingual education in the United States, the issue of language has taken on an additional prominence in the literature. Language issues had received particular attention in the Working Papers of the Centro de Estudios Puertorriqueños (Language Policy Task Force, 1978, 1980, and 1982). Book-length treatments expanded on these concerns. For instance, Fishman, Cooper, and Ma (1971); L. Torres (1997); Urciuoli (1996); and Zentella (1997) all examined the development of language and identity in the United States. Urciuoli discussed how processes of racialization and ethnicization are conflated with language usage, often to the detriment of Spanish speakers. Zentella (1997) undertook a sociolinguistic analysis of the language usage of 20 families on a block in "El Barrio" (East Harlem) in New York, which took into consideration broader issues of community life, identity, and socioeconomic issues. Walsh (1991) reexamined language issues in Puerto Rico, contextualizing current controversies by describing the history of colonial language policies on the island.

This is an important historical record for those seeking a broader understanding of why language carries such weighty symbolic meanings not only in the educational arena but even in discussions of the political status of Puerto Rico. Language issues in Puerto Rico are inextricably connected to broader sociopolitical and economic issues, as well as issues of identity. Such connections are explored in three recent texts, one analyzing language policies passed by the Puerto Rican government in the 1990s (Barreto, 2001); a second focusing on the popular consciousness, creative expression, and national identity (Guerra, 1998); and a third comparing language controversies in Puerto Rico with those of Quebec, another site where language and politics frequently surface and where sentiments on these issues are also quite intense (Barreto, 1998).

Questioning Assumptions

In many works, questions were raised about earlier assimilationist assumptions, but the following authors gave particular attention to this area: Fishman et al. (1971), Flores (1993), J. Morales (1986), Padilla (1985, 1987), Rodríguez (1974, 1989/1991), and Rogler and Santana Cooney (1984). In keeping with the new thrust and research in the post-1970 literature, the updated edition of Fitzpatrick's *Puerto Rican Americans* (1987) moderated former claims about assimilation. Although a number of works would continue to reflect the perspectives of the past (for example, Aliotta, 1991), there was also evidence of a shift to a more sympathetic, albeit sometimes patronizing and stereotypic, view (e.g., Larsen, 1994; Sheehan, 1976; Steiner, 1974; Wojcicka Sharff, 1998). There were also a number of attempts to provide profiles of commonplace Puerto Ricans (e.g., C. Bean, 1974; Cooper, 1972) or of the perspectives of Puerto Rican leaders in the United States (Cordasco & Bucchioni, 1973; Mapp, 1974) and in Puerto Rico (Heine, 1993).

Other works addressed the generally neglected or stereotyped view of Puerto Rican politics in the United States by taking a broad view. Jennings and Rivera's *Puerto Rican Politics in Urban America* (1984), for example, included chapters on the history of Puerto Rican politics, from the mid-19th century to current times, both in and outside of New York. The book also focused on topics often neglected, such as labor activism and the Puerto Rican struggle for educational equality. In addition, it began to detail the growing literature on the Puerto Rican community in the United States, noting the still-assimilationist perspective of some writers, and presented a more analytical shift in perspective with regard to Puerto Rican politics. Finally, it drew attention to the repression of Puerto Rican political activists (Falcón, 1984).

The volume by Fernandez (1987) and that edited by A. Torres and Velázquez (1998) also addressed Puerto Rican political involvements in the United States. Fernandez (1987) examined one particular group of independentistas, while the A. Torres and Velázquez (1998) book focused on a variety of political activities. The latter contained 19 articles on topics ranging from a history of the Puerto Rican socialist party in the United States to political prisoners; the Young Lords; and gays, lesbians, and activists engaged in political movements in various communities, such as Hartford, Philadelphia, New York, and Boston. One article also discusses the solidarity movement in support of Vieques in the United States. The Vieques issue has aroused a great deal of general public and press interest and mobilized island residents across all political and religious persuasions.

Other works have also raised questions about earlier assumptions and taken a similarly broad look at the history of Puerto Ricans in the United States, for example, Cardona (1995), Pérez y González (2000), and Cruz (1998), all of whom focus on the political arena.

Puerto Rican Communities Throughout the United States

The growing literature on Puerto Rican communities in the United States was characterized by case studies in a number of cities. Though much of the early literature of Puerto Ricans living in the United States was based on New York City, a growing number of studies examined the reality of Puerto Ricans in other areas. Examples of these case studies are Whalen (2001), who presents a history of

Puerto Rican labor migration to Philadelphia—the third largest Puerto Rican community in the United States—and explores both structural factors and human agency in issues of migration; Bigler (1999), who examined efforts of a Puerto Rican community in upstate New York to institute multicultural education in its urban school system and the conflicts between Puerto Ricans and White ethnics over schooling; Cruz (1998), who considered the activities of Puerto Rican activists in Hartford, Connecticut, to demonstrate the power of ethnic mobilization and strategies in confronting the political power structure; Glasser's (1997) work on Puerto Ricans in Middletown, Connecticut; and Antonsen (1997), who chronicled the evolution of the Puerto Rican community in Bethlehem, Pennsylvania.

More recent works have continued to document the history of Puerto Ricans in the United States. An interesting development in this area is the bilingual publication of books. For example, the volume by Acosta-Belén et al. (2000) was simultaneously published in English and Spanish and was distributed in both Puerto Rico and the United States. The illustrated volume includes essays on the Puerto Rican Diaspora, its history and contributions in the areas of literature and the arts, politics, media, education, migration, social movements, the armed forces, sports, business, and the professions, as well as the forging of new spaces by Puerto Ricans in the social, behavioral, and health sciences. Another example is the bilingual edition by Matos Rodríguez and Hernández (2001), which is an illustrated history of the Puerto Rican *pioneros,* or pioneers, who migrated to New York City between 1896 and 1948. (An earlier bilingual, photographic essay book was that by Delano, 1990, which focused on social change over four decades in Puerto Rico.)

Literature on and by Puerto Rican Women

The literature on and by women also increased in the post-1970 period. We also saw in this period works examining gender more generally and a focus on the meaning of Puerto Rican masculinity (Ramírez, 1999). Although many Latinas were critical of Ribes Tovar's (1972) early book on Puerto Rican women because of what appeared to be unsubstantiated and subjective generalizations, it did provide a popular history of women and drew attention to famous women of the 19th and 20th centuries. Acosta-Belén's (1979, 1986) works served a number of important purposes. They provided a link between the work being done in Puerto Rico and in the United States, and they focused on areas that had generally been neglected, including images of women in literature, role expectations, discrimination, lesbianism, the Black Puerto Rican woman, and stories of success. The work of

Sánchez Korrol (1983/1994) emphasized the unacknowledged contributions of women to the household economy and to the functioning of the early Puerto Rican communities in the United States. The personal essays of Levins Morales and Morales (1986) and Padilla and Santiago's (1993) volume shed light on identity struggles of Puerto Rican women, while Hidalgo and McEniry (1985) gave particular emphasis to service delivery issues affecting women.

Works begun on women by Benmayor et al. (1987), Benmayor et al. (1992), and Torruellas et al. (1991) were interesting in that they used the same oral history method employed by Oscar Lewis but arrived at very different depictions. Cafferty San Juan and Rivera-Martínez (1981) examined the issues in bilingual education, while García Coll and Mattei's (1989) collection explored the psychological and social development of Puerto Rican women from a life span developmental perspective. Azize (1985) investigated the links between working-class organizing and women's rights in late 19th- and 20th-century Puerto Rico. These works have served to stimulate newer efforts. This new research on Puerto Rican women has grown considerably in the 1990s, with full-length books and edited volumes by researchers from a variety of disciplines. For example, Lamberty and García Coll (1994) examined the health status of Puerto Rican women and children, Matos Rodríguez and Delgado (1998) investigated new perspectives on the roles played by Puerto Rican women in 19th-century Puerto Rico, and Barceló Miller (1997) examined the sociopolitical history of women's struggle for the right to vote in Puerto Rico. Ortiz (1996) edited works on the nature of Puerto Rican women's work; Hardy-Fanta (1992) and Muñiz (1998) concentrated on the role of women in community and political organizing in the states. Also contributing to this literature were new works that focused on individual Puerto Rican women, such as the Valle Ferrer (2000) work on pioneer feminist and union organizer Luisa Capetillo; and Ramos (1992), who published in Spanish an edited collection of Capetillo's writings.

Many of the works on women have continued the established traditions of incorporating research from both Puerto Rico and the United States, and of focusing on important areas often neglected in the earlier literature. Work at the intersection of women's studies and Puerto Rican studies also expanded the boundaries of the field. According to Acosta-Belén (1992), there is emerging a literary discourse based upon cultural subjectivities that involve being a Latina and sharing experiences (at the individual and interethnic levels). This discourse transcends national origins and speaks to a spirit of solidarity and identification with the liberation movements of all women and other groups oppressed because of class position, race, ethnicity, or sexual preference.

The Literary Arena

In the broader literary arena, there were similar developments. Acosta-Belén (1992) argues that the literature produced by both male and female Puerto Ricans in the United States provided cultural validation and affirmation of a collective sense of identity. Analyzing this literature, she finds that these qualities served to counteract the detrimental effects of the marginalization experienced in the United States. She cites a number of other characteristics of this literature: its antiestablishment cast, its commitment to denouncing inequality and injustice, and its use as a consciousness-raising tool for promoting social change. Furthermore, she finds that the writings revealed the prevalence of a strong political activism, cultural effervescence, and communal spirit, which helped to counter the alleged cultural deficiency notions promulgated by earlier writers. Writers' experiences with cultural, linguistic, and racial prejudice as well as their sense of displacement and triumph are revealed in C. D. Hernández's (1997) collection of interviews with Puerto Rican writers living in the United States and, to some degree, in Turner's (1991) edited collection. The book by Rodríguez de Laguna (1987) on Puerto Rican literature reflected "the bridging tradition"; it examined images and identities in the creative literature of Puerto Ricans in two world contexts.

Acosta-Belén (1992) views the literature produced in the United States as part of the larger multicultural revitalization movement that was a component of ethnoracial minorities' response to their structural and cultural marginalization and to the assimilation pressures from the dominant Anglo-American society. This multicultural revitalization challenged cultural hegemony and engendered, within U.S. academic circles, an intellectual reevaluation and redefinition of "ethnocentric Western cultural theories and canons" (p. 983).

IMPLICATIONS

The implications of this literature review for educators and students in multicultural education are many. Given the previous literature on Puerto Ricans, special efforts need to be made to develop material that is more sensitive to Puerto Rican culture, writings, insights, and ideas. This would counter, to a degree, the earlier errors. It would also introduce students to knowledge and perspectives to which, in all likelihood, they have not been exposed. For teaching, there are a number of urgent needs:

• Make clear that Puerto Rico has (a) at least a 3,500-year history before 1898; (b) a Native American civilization prior to 1493 that many Puerto Ricans still consider to be an important component of their heritage; (c) a history of enslavement and forced migration of Africans from 1510 to 1876, the contributions of which continue as significant components of Puerto Rican culture; (d) a Puerto Rican community in the United States with a history dating back to the 19th century; and (e) a culture that is a blend of European (mainly Spanish), African, Native American, and Anglo American traditions.

- Clarify the role of the United States in Puerto Rico, both historically and currently. It is incumbent on educators to be very specific when discussing the current situation of Puerto Ricans in Puerto Rico—for example, to talk about how Puerto Ricans on the island are citizens and serve in the military but do not have the right to vote in U.S. presidential or congressional elections. Puerto Ricans on the island lack representation in the U.S. Congress and have limited control over immigration to Puerto Rico, commercial trade with other countries, Caribbean security issues, U.S. military bases, and environmental policy. This is all related to the political status of Puerto Rico. It is also important to explore how both the United States and Puerto Rico benefit from or lose as a result of the colonial relationship. It would also seem important to discuss the cultural impact of Anglo-American industry and tourism on Puerto Ricans. Lastly, it should be noted that, in contrast to the embassies and consulates of other countries, the Puerto Rican government lacks power to negotiate—whether for good or for bad—on behalf of Puerto Ricans living in the United States.

  Educators should examine with students how creatively and cleverly Puerto Ricans have coped with these limitations historically. Thus it is important to discuss how colonialism induces not just a colonized mentality but also an "oppositional mentality" (Rodríguez, 1989/1991).

- Stress the need to view Puerto Ricans as a heterogeneous people, having various racial and ethnic backgrounds, as well as divergent cultural and political views and migrant status. Given the confusion and general lack of information about Puerto Ricans, educators may have to be prepared to dispel students' previous homogeneous or stereotypic images.
- Given the tendency in the literature to overgeneralize (that is, to go from specific or extreme cases to the whole group), special efforts need to be made to avoid falling into this trap when using personal stories or singular cases for illustrative purposes.
- Given the earlier exclusive and limiting focus, it is important to highlight the similarities and differences between Puerto Ricans and such other groups as Native Americans, other Latinos, African Americans,

Asian Americans, and migrants to Europe from former European colonies. However, educators might well have to be prepared to discuss Puerto Ricans within more conventional frameworks, for example, why and how Puerto Ricans fit into this society as U.S. citizens, and how they also fit into Latin American history and culture.

- Given the controversies about bilingual education and the use of ethnic languages in American schools, it is important that educators be able to discuss the English educational policies that the colonial administration imposed on the Puerto Rican people during the earlier part of this century, and to examine what impact this may have had on Spanish literacy, language proficiency, and the attitudes of some Puerto Ricans toward English and Spanish.
- Given the extent to which Puerto Rican history has been omitted or obscured in the curriculum, it is important to stress the accomplishments of Puerto Ricans prior to 1898, including the work of ordinary people who contributed to the island's wealth but were kept as slaves, the long struggle for liberation, and the establishment of a unique self-determination in 1897.
- Similarly, it is important to stress the contributions of Puerto Ricans from 1898 to the present, both in Puerto Rico and in the United States.
- The recent growth in books by and about Puerto Ricans in English provides opportunities for educators to more effectively integrate themes about Puerto Rican life and culture into school curricula. This integration should not be limited to ethnic studies courses, nor to history-related topics, but should include literature and other works of fiction that are valuable for understanding Puerto Ricans, and American life in the latter half of the 20th century. Literary works in English and Spanish provide another vehicle for looking at Puerto Ricans and Puerto Rico from Puerto Ricans' perspectives. The reader is referred to these authors: Jack Agueros, Miguel Algarin, Marta Aponte Alsina, Pura Belpre, Pedro Cabilla, Judith Cofer, Abelardo Díaz Alfaro, Martín Espada, Sandra María Estevez, Rosario Ferré, José Angel Figueroa, Magali García Ramis, David Hernández, Victor Hernández-Cruz, Enrique Laguerre, Tato Laviera, Luis López Nieves, René Marquéz, Aurora Levins Morales, Carmen Lugo Filippi, Julio Marzán, Jesús Papoleto Meléndez, Nicolasa Mohr, Luis Palés Matos, Pedro Pietri, Miguel Piñero, Manuel Ramos Otero, Rosa Vanesa Otero, Ernesto Quiñones, José Ramos Meléndez, Juan Antonio Ramos, Carmen Rivera, Edward Rivera, Abraham Rodríguez, Edgardo Rodríguez Juliá, Carmelo Rodríguez Torres, Luis Rafael Sánchez, Edgardo Sanabria Santalíz, Esmeralda Santiago, Mayra Santos Febres, Pedro Juan Soto, Piri Thomas, Candido Tirado, Luz María Umpierre, Ana Lydia Vega, and Ed Vega.

- The unique political position of Puerto Rico also implies that it is important to discuss both the benefits and problems of Puerto Rico as a U.S. territory, such as the gains in standard of living after Puerto Ricans elected their own governor, along with the disruptions caused by industrialization and mass migration. A related and important theme would be to explore with students the various meanings of development, including issues such as the environmental impact that political and economic policies have on less powerful countries. Such a theme would provide students with new perspectives for examining development policies in different areas of the United States as well as related issues in other countries.
- Puerto Rico's political status lends itself to lively discussions among students regarding continued commonwealth, statehood, or independence. However, students should be reminded that the U.S. Congress and the American people will ultimately decide this issue as well, and that other territories may be affected, such as the District of Columbia, Guam, and the Virgin Islands. The comparison of Puerto Ricans and Native American peoples should help students reflect on the colonial politics of the United States and the consequences of these policies on groups affected by these policies.
- Last, given the difficulties noted with much of the early writing (and some contemporary works) on Puerto Ricans, educators must avoid repeating the mistakes of the past, such as using deficit models, conveying a strong sense of "otherness," using inappropriate contexts for analysis, generalizing from singular or extreme cases to the whole group, depreciating indigenous views, obscuring the colonial relationship, and overemphasizing an assimilationist perspective.

A broader, multicultural approach should result in a more valid presentation of Puerto Ricans. It should also assist in the integration of Puerto Rican studies into a broader perspective that is inclusive and representative of the commonalities and differences among all groups. Focusing on the case of Puerto Rico can help broaden understanding of other issues, for example, the relationship of the United States to other countries as well as the various ethnic groups that constitute this nation.

References

Acosta, U. (1987). *New voices of old: Five centuries of Puerto Rican cultural history.* Santurce, PR: Permanent Press.

Acosta-Belén, E. (Ed.). (1979). *The Puerto Rican woman.* New York: Praeger.

Acosta-Belén, E. (Ed.). (1986). *The Puerto Rican woman* (2nd ed.). New York: Praeger.

Acosta-Belén, E. (1992). Beyond island boundaries: Ethnicity, gender, and cultural revitalization in Nuyorican literature. *Callaloo, 15*(4), 979–998.

Acosta-Belén, E., & Sánchez Korrol, V. (1993). *The way it was and other writings.* Houston, TX: Arte Público Press.

Acosta-Belén, E., & Sjostrom, B. (Eds.). (1988). *The Hispanic experience in the U.S.* (2nd ed.). New York: Praeger.

Acosta-Belén, E., Benítez, M., Cruz, J. E., González-Rodríguez, Y., Rodríguez, C. E., Santiago, C. E., et al. (2000). *"Adiós, Borinquen querida": The Puerto Rican diaspora, its history, and contributions.* Albany: State University of New York-Albany, CELAC. (Also published in Spanish under the title *"Adiós, Borinquen querida": La diáspora puertorriqueña, su historia y sus aportaciones*)

Aliotta, J. J. (1991). *The Puerto Ricans.* New York: Chelsea House.

Alvarez, C., Bennett, A., Greenlee, M., Pedraza, P., & Pousada, A. (1988). *Speech and ways of speaking in a bilingual Puerto Rican community.* New York: City University of New York, Hunter College, Centro de Estudios Puertorriqueños.

Anderson, R. (1965). *Party politics in Puerto Rico.* Stanford, CA: Stanford University Press.

Antonsen, P. J. (1997). *A history of the Puerto Rican community in Bethlehem, PA, 1944–1993.* Bethlehem, PA: Council of Spanish Speaking Organizations of the Lehigh Valley.

Aparicio, F. (1998). *Listening to salsa: Gender, Latin popular music and Puerto Rican cultures.* Hanover, NH: Wesleyan University Press.

Attinasi, J., Pedraza, P., Poplack, S., & Pousada, A. (1988). *Intergenerational perspectives on bilingualism.* New York: City University of New York, Hunter College, Centro de Estudios Puertorriqueños.

Ayala, C. J. (1999). *American sugar kingdom: The plantation economy of the Spanish Caribbean, 1898–1934.* Chapel Hill: University of North Carolina Press.

Azize, Y. (1985). *La mujer en la lucha.* Río Piedras, PR: Editorial Cultural.

Baggs, W. C. (1962). *Puerto Rico: Showcase of development.* San Juan, PR: Commonwealth of Puerto Rico. (Reprinted from *1962 Britannica Book of the Year*)

Baralt, G. A. (1999). *Buena Vista: Life and work on a Puerto Rican hacienda, 1833–1904* (A. Hurley, Trans.). Chapel Hill: University of North Carolina Press. (Original work published in 1988)

Barceló Miller, M. de F. (1997). *La lucha por el sufragio femenino en Puerto Rico, 1896–1935.* San Juan, PR: Centro de Investigaciones Sociales, Ediciones Huracán.

Barreto, A. A. (1998). *Language, elites, and the state: Nationalism in Puerto Rico and Quebec.* Gainesville: University Press of Florida.

Barreto, A. A. (2001). *The politics of language in Puerto Rico.* Gainesville: University Press of Florida.

Baver, S. (1984). Puerto Rican politics in New York City: The post-World War II period. In J. Jennings & M. Rivera (Eds.), *Puerto Rican politics in urban America* (pp. 43–59). Westport, CT: Greenwood Press.

Baver, S. (1993). *The political economy of colonialism: The state and industrialization in Puerto Rico.* New York: Praeger.

Bean, C. (1974). *My name is José.* Chicago: Herald Press.

Bean, F., & Tienda, M. (1988). *The Hispanic population in the U.S.* New York: Russell Sage Foundation.

Beattie, J.H.M. (1967). Review of *The children of Sánchez, Pedro Martínez,* and *La Vida. Current Anthropology, 8*(5), 484.

Benmayor, R., Juarbe, A., Alvarez, C., & Vásquez, B. (1987). *Stories to live by: Continuity and change in three generations of Puerto Rican women* (working paper). New York: City University of New York, Hunter College, Centro de Estudios Puertorriqueños.

Benmayor, R., Torruellas, R. M., & Juarbe, A. L. (1992). *Responses to poverty among Puerto Rican women: Identity, community and cultural citizenship.* New York: City University of New York, Hunter College, Centro de Estudios Puertorriqueños.

Berbusse, E. J. (1966). *The United States in Puerto Rico, 1898–1900.* Chapel Hill: University of North Carolina Press.

Bergad, L. W. (1983). *Coffee and the growth of agrarian capitalism in nineteenth-century Puerto Rico.* Princeton, NJ: Princeton University Press.

Berle, B. (1958). *80 Puerto Rican families in New York City.* New York: Columbia University Press.

Berman-Santana, D. (1996). *Kicking off the bootstraps: Environment, development and community power in Puerto Rico.* Tucson: University of Arizona Press.

Bigler, E. (1999). *American conversations: Puerto Ricans, White ethnics and multicultural education.* Philadelphia: Temple University Press.

Blaut, J. (1987). *The national question: Decolonizing the theory of nationalism.* London: Zed Books.

Block, P. (1973). *La-le-lo-lai: Puerto Rican music and its performers.* New York: Plus Ultra.

Bloomfield, R. (1985). *Puerto Rico: The search for a national policy.* Boulder, CO: Westview Press.

Bonilla, F., & Campos, R. (1986). *Industry and idleness.* New York: City University of New York, Hunter College, Centro de Estudios Puertorriqueños.

Bonilla-Santiago, G. (1988). *Organizing Puerto Rican migrant farmworkers: The experience of Puerto Ricans in New Jersey.* New York: Lang.

Bosque Pérez, R., & Colón Morera, J. J. (1997). *Las carpetas: Persecución política y derechos civiles en Puerto Rico, ensayos y documentos.* Río Piedras, PR: Centro para la Investigación y Promoción de los Derechos Civiles.

Bourgois, P. (1995). *In search of respect: Selling crack in El Barrio.* New York: Cambridge University Press.

Buitrago Ortiz, C. (1974). *Esperanza: An ethnographic study of a peasant community in Puerto Rico.* Tucson: University of Arizona Press.

Cabán, P. A. (1999). *Constructing a colonial people: Puerto Rico and the United States, 1898–1932.* Boulder, CO: Westview Press.

Cabranes, J. A. (1979). *Citizenship and the American Empire: Notes on the legislative history of the United States citizenship of Puerto Ricans.* New Haven, CT: Yale University Press.

Cafferty San Juan, P., & Rivera-Martínez, C. (Eds.). (1981). *The politics of language: The dilemma of bilingual education for Puerto Ricans.* Boulder, CO: Westview Press.

Calvo Ospina, H. (1995). *Salsa! Havana heat, Bronx beat.* New York: Monthly Review Press.

Canino, M. (1981). *A historical overview of the English language policy in Puerto Rico's educational system: 1898–1949.* Unpublished doctoral dissertation, Harvard University.

Caplow, T. (1967). Review of *The children of Sánchez, Pedro Martínez,* and *La Vida. Current Anthropology, 8*(5), 485–486.

Cardona, L. A. (1974). *The coming of the Puerto Ricans.* Washington, DC: Unidos.

Cardona, L. A. (1995). *A history of the Puerto Ricans in the United States of America.* Bethesda, MD: Carreta Press.

Carr, R. (1984). *Puerto Rico: A colonial experiment.* New York: New York University Press.

Carrión, J. M. (1993). The national question in Puerto Rico. In E. Meléndez & E. Meléndez (Eds.), *Colonial dilemma: Critical perspectives on contemporary Puerto Rico* (pp. 67–75). Boston: South End Press.

Carroll, H. K. (1898). *Report on the island of Porto Rico.* Submitted by the Special Commissioner for the United States to Puerto Rico to President William McKinley, Washington, DC: U.S. Government Printing Office.

Cayo Sexton, P. (1965). *Spanish Harlem.* New York: HarperCollins.

Chanlatte Baik, L. A., & Narganes Storde, Y. M. (1990). *La nueva arqueología de Puerto Rico (su proyección en las Antillas).* Santo Domingo, DR: Taller.

Chenault, L. (1938/1970). *The Puerto Rican migrant in New York City.* New York: Columbia University Press. (Original work published in 1938)

Churchill, W. (1992). Naming our destiny: Towards a language of Indian liberation. *Global Justice, 3*(2 & 3), 22–33.

Cobas, J., & Duany, J. (1997). *Cubans in Puerto Rico: Ethnic economy and cultural identity.* Gainesville: University Press of Florida.

Cobas, J. A., & Duany, J. (1995). *Los cubanos en Puerto Rico: economía étnica e identidad cultural.* Río Piedras: Editorial de la Universidad de Puerto Rico.

Collazo, J. (1998). *Guerra y educación: La militarización y americanización del puertorriqueño durante la Segunda Guerra Mundial, 1939–1945.* Santo Domingo, DR: Editora Centenario.

Colón, J. (1982). *A Puerto Rican in New York and other sketches.* New York: International Publishers.

Colón, J. (2001). *Pioneros: Puertorriqueños en Nueva York, 1917–1947.* Houston, TX: Arte Público Press.

Cooper, P. (1972). *Growing up Puerto Rican.* New York: Arbor House.

Cordasco, F., & Bucchioni, E. (Eds.). (1973). *The Puerto Rican experience: A sociological sourcebook.* Totowa, NJ: Rowman & Littlefield.

Cruz, J. (1998). *Identity and power: Puerto Rican politics and the challenge of ethnicity.* Philadelphia: Temple University Press.

Cultural Studies Task Force. (1987). *Aprender a luchar, luchar es aprender.* New York: City University of New York Hunter College, Centro de Estudios Puertorriqueños.

The Culture of Poverty. (1966, November 25). *Time, 88,* pp. 133ff.

Dávila, A. (1997). *Sponsored identities: Cultural politics in Puerto Rico.* Philadelphia: Temple University Press.

Dávila, A. (2001). *Latinos Inc.: The marketing and making of a people.* Berkeley: University of California Press.

Davis, Gen. M. (1900). *Report on civil affairs in Porto Rico, 1899.* Washington, DC: Government Printing Office.

Day, D. (1967, April-May). How blessed the poor. *The Critic,* pp. 74–76.

de la Garza, R., Desipio, L., Garcia, C., Garcia, J., & Falcón, A. (1992). *Latino voices: Mexican, Puerto Rican, and Cuban perspectives on American politics.* Boulder, CO: Westview Press.

Delano, J. (1990). *Puerto Rico mío: Four decades of change.* Washington, DC: Smithsonian Institution Press.

Díaz Quiñones, A. (1985). Tomás Blanco: Racismo, historia, esclavitud. In T. Blanco & A. Díaz Quiñones (Eds.), *El prejuicio racial en Puerto Rico, con estudio preliminar de Arcadio Díaz Quiñones* (pp. 13–83). Río Piedras, PR: Ediciones Huracán.

Díaz-Stevens, A. M. (1993). *Oxcart Catholicism on Fifth Avenue.* Notre Dame, IN: University of Notre Dame Press.

Dietz, J. L. (1986). *Economic history of Puerto Rico*. Princeton, NJ: Princeton University Press.

Dolan, J. P., & Vidal, J. R. (Eds.). (1994). *Puerto Rican and Cuban Catholics in the U.S., 1900–1965* (Notre Dame History of Hispanic Catholics in the U.S., Vol. 2). Notre Dame, IN: University of Notre Dame Press.

Duany, J. (Ed.). (1990). *Los dominicanos en Puerto Rico: Migración en la semi-periferia*. Río Piedras, PR: Ediciones Huracán.

Estades, R. (1978). *Patterns of political participation of Puerto Ricans in New York City* (dissertation translated by author and printed in Spanish). Rio Piedras: Universidad de Puerto Rico, Editorial Universitaria.

Falcón, A. (1984). An introduction to the literature of Puerto Rican politics in urban America. In J. Jennings & M. Rivera (Eds.), *Puerto Rican politics in urban America* (pp. 145–154). Westport, CT: Greenwood Press.

Fernandez, R. (1987) *Los macheteros: The Wells Fargo robbery and the violent struggle for Puerto Rican independence*. New York: Prentice Hall.

Fernández, R. (1992). *The disenchanted island: Puerto Rico and the United States in the twentieth century*. New York: Praeger.

Fernández Méndez, E. (Ed.). (1972). *Portrait of a society: Readings in Puerto Rican sociology*. Rio Piedras, PR: University of Puerto Rico Press.

Figueroa, J. (1989). *Survival on the margin: A documentary study of the underground economy in a Puerto Rican ghetto*. New York: Vantage Press.

Figueroa, L. (1974). *History of Puerto Rico*. New York: Anaya.

Findlay Suárez, E. (1999). *Imposing decency: The politics of sexuality and race in Puerto Rico, 1870–1920*. Durham, NC: Duke University Press.

Fishman, J. A., Cooper, R. L., & Ma, R. (1971). *Bilingualism in the barrio*. Bloomington: University of Indiana Press.

Fitzpatrick, J. P. (1966). Oscar Lewis and the Puerto Rican family. *America, 115*, 778–779.

Fitzpatrick, J. P. (1971). *Puerto Rican Americans*. Englewood Cliffs, NJ: Prentice Hall.

Fitzpatrick, J. P. (1987). *Puerto Rican Americans* (2nd ed.) Englewood Cliffs, NJ: Prentice Hall.

Flores, J. (Ed.). (1987). *Divided arrival: Narratives of the Puerto Rican migration, 1920–50*. New York: City University of New York, Hunter College, Centro de Estudios Puertorriqueños.

Flores, J. (1993). *Divided borders: Essays on Puerto Rican identity*. Houston, TX: Arte Público Press.

Flores, J. (2000). *From bomba to hip-hop: Puerto Rican culture and Latino identity*. New York: Columbia University Press.

Flores, W. V., & Benmayor, R. (1997). *Cultural citizenship: Claiming identity, space and rights*. Boston: Beacon Press.

Fox, G. (1996). *Hispanic nation: Culture, politics and the construction of identity*. Tucson: University of Arizona Press.

Friedlander, S. L. (1965). *Labor migration and economic growth*. Boston: MIT Press.

Galbraith, J. K., & Shaw Soto, C. (1953). Puerto Rican lessons in economic development. *Annals of the American Academy of Political and Social Sciences, 1*(285), 55–59.

García Coll, C., & Mattei, M. (Eds.). (1989). *The psychosocial development of Puerto Rican women*. Westport, CT: Praeger.

García Muñiz, H. (1993). U.S. military installations in Puerto Rico controlling the Caribbean. In E. Meléndez & E. Meléndez (Eds.), *Colonial dilemma: Critical perspectives on contemporary Puerto Rico* (pp. 53–65). Boston: South End Press.

García Muñiz, H., & Rodríguez Beruff, J. (Eds.). (1999). *Cuadernos de paz y fronteras en conflicto: Guerra contra las drogas, militarización y democracia en el Caribe, Puerto Rico y Vieques*. San Juan, PR: Red Caribeña de Geopolítica, Seguridad Regional y Relaciones Internacionales afiliada al Proyecto ATLANTEA.

Gautier Mayoral, C., & Alegría Ortega, I. E. (Eds.). (1994). *Políticas de descolonización de las potencias en la región caribeña*. Río Piedras, PR: Centro de Investigaciones Sociales.

Glasser, R. (1995). *My music is my flag: Puerto Rican musicians and their New York communities 1917–1940*. Berkeley: University of California Press.

Glasser, R. (1997). *Aquí me quedo: Puerto Ricans in Connecticut*. Middletown: Connecticut Humanities Council.

Glazer, N. (1967, February). One kind of life. *Commentary*, pp. 83–85.

Glazer, N., & Moynihan, D. P. (1970). *Beyond the melting pot* (2nd ed.). Cambridge, MA: MIT Press.

Gonzalez, J. (2000). *Harvest of empire: A history of Latinos in America*. New York: Viking Press.

González, J. L. (1993). *Puerto Rico: The four-storeyed country and other essays*. Princeton, NJ: M. Wiener.

Goodsell, C. (1965). *Administration of a revolution*. Cambridge, MA: Harvard University Press.

Guerra, L. (1998). *Popular expression and national identity in Puerto Rico: The struggle for self, community and nation*. Gainesville: University Press of Florida.

Handlin, O. (1959). *The newcomers: Negroes and Puerto Ricans in a changing metropolis*. Cambridge, MA: Harvard University Press.

Hanson, E. P. (1960). *Puerto Rico: Land of wonders*. New York: Knopf.

Hardy-Fanta, C. (1992). *Latina politics, Latino politics: Gender, culture, and political participation in Boston*. Philadelphia: Temple University Press.

Harrington, M. (1966, November 20). Everyday hell. *New York Times Book Review*, pp. 1, 92.

Harris, W. W. (1980). *Puerto Rico's fighting 65th Infantry*. San Rafael, CA: Presidio Press.

Harwood, A. (1977). *Rx-spiritist as needed: A study of a Puerto Rican community mental health resource*. New York: Wiley.

Haslip-Viera, G., & Baver, S. (Eds.). (1994). *Latinos in New York: A community in transition*. Notre Dame, IN: University of Notre Dame Press.

Hauberg, C. A. (1974). *Puerto Rico and the Puerto Ricans*. New York: Twayne.

Heine, J. (1983). *Time for decision: The United States and Puerto Rico*. Lanham, MD: North-South.

Heine, J. (1993). *The last cacique: Leadership and politics in a Puerto Rican city*. (Pitt Latin American Series). Pittsburgh, PA: University of Pittsburgh Press.

Hernández, C. D. (1997). *Puerto Rican voices in English: Interviews with writers*. Westport, CT: Praeger.

Hernández, J. (1967). *Return migration to Puerto Rico*. Berkeley: University of California Press.

Hernández, J. (1983). *Puerto Rican youth employment*. Maplewood, NJ: Waterfront Press.

Hernández, J. (1992/1997). *Conquered peoples in America* (Fifth Centennial Ed.). Dubuque, IA: Kendall/Hunt.

Hernández Cruz, J. E. (1988). Puerto Rico in the Ibero-American heritage project. *Proceedings of the second annual meeting of the International Advisory Panel*, Santillana del Mar, Spain, October 6–9, 1988 (pp. 165–176). Albany: State Education Department, University of the State of New York.

Hidalgo, H., & McEniry, J. L. (Eds.). (1985). *Hispanic temas: A contribution to the knowledge bank of the Hispanic community.* Newark, NJ: Rutgers University, Puerto Rican Studies Program.

Hispanic Research Center. (1990). *Report of activities, 1977–1990.* New York: Fordham University, Hispanic Research Center.

History Task Force. (1979). *Labor migration under capitalism.* New York: Monthly Review Press.

History Task Force. (1983). *Sources for the study of Puerto Rican migration 1879–1930.* New York: City University of New York, Hunter College, Centro de Estudios Puertorriqueños.

Hunter, R. J. (1966). Historical survey of the Puerto Rico status question, 1898–1965. In United States-Puerto Rico Commission on the Status of Puerto Rico, *Status of Puerto Rico: Selected background studies of the Status Commission Report* (pp. 50–146). Washington, DC: Government Printing Office.

Iglesias, C. A. (Ed.). (1984). *Memoirs of Bernardo Vega.* New York: Monthly Review Press.

In the White man's image. (1991). (Videorecording, presented by WGBH/Boston, WNET/New York, and KCET/Los Angeles.). Alexandria, VA: PBS Video.

Jaimes, M. A. (1992). Federal Indian identification policy. In M. A. Jaimes (Ed.), *The state of Native America: Genocide, colonization and resistance* (pp. 123–138). Boston: South End Press.

Jennings, J., & Rivera, M. (Eds.). (1984). *Puerto Rican politics in urban America.* Westport, CT: Greenwood Press.

Jiménez de Wagenheim, O. (1998). *Puerto Rico: An interpretative history from pre-Columbian times to the 1900.* Princeton, NJ: Markus Wiener.

Kinsbruner, J. (1996). *Not of pure blood: The free people of color and racial prejudice in nineteenth-century Puerto Rico.* Durham, NC: Duke University Press.

Lamberty, G., & García Coll, C. (Eds.). (1994). *Puerto Rican women and children: Issues in health, growth, and development.* New York: Plenum.

Landy, D. (1959). *Tropical childhood.* Chapel Hill: University of North Carolina Press.

Language Policy Task Force. (1978). *Language policy and the Puerto Rican community.* New York: City University of New York, Hunter College, Centro de Estudios Puertorriqueños.

Language Policy Task Force. (1980). *Social dimensions of language use in East Harlem.* New York: City University of New York, Hunter College, Centro de Estudios Puertorriqueños.

Language Policy Task Force. (1982). *Intergenerational perspectives on bilingualism: From community to classroom.* New York: City University of New York, Hunter College, Centro de Estudios Puertorriqueños.

Lapp, M. (1991). *Managing migration: The migration division of Puerto Rico and Puerto Ricans in New York City, 1948–1968.* Ann Arbor, MI: University Microfilms International.

Larsen, R. J. (1994). *Puerto Ricans in America.* Minneapolis, MN: Lerner.

La Ruffa, A. (1971). *San Cipriano: Life in a Puerto Rican community.* New York: Gordon and Breach.

Lauria-Perricelli, A. (1990). *A study in historical and critical anthropology: The making of the people of Puerto Rico.* Ann Arbor, MI: University Microfilms.

Levins Morales, A., & Morales, R. (1986). *Getting home alive.* Ithaca, NY: Firebrand Books.

Lewis, G. (1974). *Notes on the Puerto Rican revolution: An essay on American dominance and Caribbean resistance.* New York: Monthly Review Press.

Lewis, G. K. (1963). *Puerto Rico: Freedom and power in the Caribbean.* New York: Monthly Review Press.

Lewis, O. (1961). *The children of Sánchez.* New York: Random House.

Lewis, O. (1966). *La vida: A Puerto Rican family in the culture of poverty—San Juan and New York.* New York: Random House.

Liden, H. (1981). *History of the Puerto Rican independence movement, 19th century* (Vol. 1). Maplewood, NJ: Waterfront Press.

López, A. (1973). *The Puerto Rican papers.* New York: Bobbs-Merrill.

López, A. (Ed.). (1980). *The Puerto Ricans: The history, culture and society.* Cambridge, MA: Schenkman.

López, A. (1987). *Doña Licha's island: Modern colonialism in Puerto Rico.* Boston: South End Press.

López, A., & Petras, J. (Eds.). (1974). *Puerto Rico and Puerto Ricans.* Cambridge, MA: Schenkman.

Maldonado, A. A. (1984). *Portraits of the Puerto Rican experience.* Bronx, NY: IPRUS.

Maldonado, A. W. (1997). *Teodoro Moscoso and Puerto Rico's Operation Bootstrap.* Gainesville: University Press of Florida.

Maldonado Denis, M. (1967). Oscar Lewis, *La Vida,* y la enajenación. *Revista de Ciencias Sociales, 11*(2), 253–259. Rio Piedras, P.R.: Universidad de Puerto Rico.

Maldonado Denis, M. (1972). *Puerto Rico: A socio-historic interpretation.* New York: Random House.

Maldonado Denis, M. (1980). *The emigration dialectic: Puerto Rico and the U.S.A.* New York: International Publishers.

Maloff, S. (1966, November 21). "Man's fate?" *Newsweek,* p. 131.

Mapp, E. (Ed.). (1974). *Puerto Rican perspectives.* Metuchen, NJ: Scarecrow Press.

Márquez, R. (1976). *The docile Puerto Rican.* Philadelphia: Temple University Press.

Martínez, A. (Ed.). (1974). *Rising voices.* New York: New American Library.

Matos Rodríguez, F. V. (1999). *Women and urban change in San Juan, Puerto Rico, 1820–1868.* Gainesville: University Press of Florida.

Matos Rodríguez, F. V., & Delgado, L. (Eds.). (1998). *Puerto Rican women's history: New perspectives.* Armonk, NY: M. E. Sharpe.

Matos Rodríguez, F. V., & Hernández, P. D. (2001). *Pioneros, Puerto Ricans in New York City, 1896–1948.* Charleston, SC: Arcadia.

Mayo Santana, R., Negrón Portillo, M., & Mayo López, M. (1997). *Cadenas de esclavitud . . . y de solidaridad: Esclavos y libertos en San Juan, siglo XIX.* San Juan, PR: Universidad de Puerto Rico, Centro de Investigaciones Sociales.

Meléndez, E. (1996). *Puerto Rico en "Patria."* Río Piedras: Editorial Edil.

Meléndez, E., & Meléndez, E. (Eds.). (1993). *Colonial dilemma: Critical perspectives on contemporary Puerto Rico.* Boston: South End Press.

Meléndez, E., Rodríguez, C. E., & Barry Figueroa, J. (Eds.). (1991). *Hispanics in the labor force: Issues and policies.* New York: Plenum Press.

Meléndez Vélez, E., & Medina Piña, N. (1999). *Desarrollo económico comunitario: Casos exitosos en Puerto Rico.* Rio Piedras, PR: Ediciones Nueva Aurora.

Miller Gould, H. (1900). The duty of our people to the people of Puerto Rico and the Hawaiian Islands. *Lake Mohonk Conference of Friends of the Indian, Proceedings.*

Mills, C. W., Senior, C., & Goldsen, R. (1950). *The Puerto Rican journey: New York's newest migrants.* New York: Harper & Bros.

Mintz, S. W. (1960). *Worker in the cane: A Puerto Rican life history.* New Haven, CT: Yale University Press.

Mintz, S. W. (1990). The island. In J. Delano (Ed.), *Puerto Rican mio: Four decades of change/photographs* (pp. 1–6). Washington, DC: Smithsonian Institution Press.

Morales, J. (1986). *Puerto Rican poverty and migration: We just had to try elsewhere.* New York: Praeger.

Morales, R., & Bonilla, F. (1993). *Latinos in a changing U.S. economy.* Thousand Oaks, CA: Sage.

Morales Carrión, A. (1952). *Puerto Rico and the non-Hispanic Caribbean: A study in the decline of Spanish exclusivism.* Río Piedras, PR: University of Puerto Rico Press.

Morales Carrión, A. (1978). *Auge y decadencia de la trata negrera en Puerto Rico (1820–1860).* San Juan, PR: Centro de Estudios Avanzados de Puerto Rico y el Caribe, Instituto de Cultura Puertorriqueña.

Morales Carrión, A. (Ed.). (1983). *Puerto Rico: A political and cultural history.* New York: Norton.

Morales-Dorta, J. (1976). *Puerto Rican espiritismo: Religion and psychotherapy.* New York: Vantage Press.

Moreno Vega, M. (2000). *The altar of my soul: The living traditions of Santería.* New York: Ballantine.

"Mortal Bombing in Vieques." (1999, April 20). *El Nuevo Dia,* p. 1.

Muñiz, V. (1998). *Resisting gentrification and displacement: Voices of Puerto Rican women of the Barrio.* New York: Garland.

Navarro, J. M. (1995). *Creating tropical Yankees: The "spiritual conquest" of Puerto Rico, 1898–1908.* Unpublished doctoral dissertation, University of Chicago.

Negrón de Montilla, A. (1975). *Americanization in Puerto Rico and the public school system, 1900–1930.* Rio Piedras, PR: University of Puerto Rico Press.

Negrón-Muntaner, F., & Grosfoguel, R. (Eds.). (1997). *Puerto Rican jam: Rethinking colonialism and nationalism.* Minneapolis: University of Minnesota Press.

Negrón Portillo, M., & Mayo Santana, R. (1999). *Urban slavery in San Juan* (M. Negrón, Trans.). Río Piedras, PR: Universidad de Puerto Rico, Centro de Investigaciones Sociales.

Nieves, J. (1987). Puerto Rican studies: Roots and challenges. In M. Sánchez & A. Stevens-Arroyo (Eds.), *Toward a renaissance of Puerto Rican studies: Ethnic and area studies in university education* (pp. 3–12). Boulder, CO: Social Science Monographs; Highland Lakes, NJ: Atlantic Research and Publications.

Opler, M. K. (1967). Review of *The children of Sánchez, Pedro Martínez,* and *La Vida. Current Anthropology,* 8(5), 488–489.

Oral History Task Force. (1986). *Extended roots: From Hawaii to New York.* New York: City University of New York, Hunter College, Centro de Estudios Puertorriqueños.

Ortiz, A. (Ed.). (1996). *Puerto Rican women and work: Bridges in transnational labor.* Philadelphia: Temple University Press.

Padilla, E. (1958). *Up from Puerto Rico.* New York: Columbia University Press.

Padilla, E. (1967, December). Book review of *La Vida. Political Science Quarterly,* 82, 651–652.

Padilla, F. (1985). *Latino ethnic consciousness: The case of Mexican-Americans and Puerto Ricans in Chicago.* Notre Dame, IN: University of Notre Dame Press.

Padilla, F. (1987). *Puerto Rican Chicago.* Notre Dame, IN: University of Notre Dame Press.

Padilla, F. (1992). *The gang as an American enterprise.* New Brunswick, NJ: Rutgers University Press.

Padilla, F., & Santiago, L. (1993). *Outside the wall: A Puerto Rican woman's struggle.* New Brunswick, NJ: Rutgers University Press.

Pantojas-García, E. (1990). *Development strategies as ideology: Puerto Rico's export-led industrialization experience.* Boulder, CO: Lynne Rienner.

Paralitici, C. (1998). *No quiero mi cuerpo pa' tambor: El servicio militar obligatorio en Puerto Rico.* San Juan, PR: Ediciones Puerto.

Pedraza, P. (1987). *An ethnographic analysis of language use in the Puerto Rican community of East Harlem.* New York: City University of New York, Hunter College, Centro de Estudios Puertorriqueños.

Perez, J. A., & Mejias, A. I. (1997). *The Hector Lavoe story, 1946–1993.* New York: Infante.

Pérez de Jesús, M. (1967). Comentarios en torno a *La Vida,* obra publicada por el Dr. Oscar Lewis. *Revista de Ciencias Sociales,* 11(2), 264–274.

Pérez y González, M. E. (2000). *Puerto Ricans in the United States.* Westport, CT: Greenwood Press.

Pérez y Mena, A. I. (1991). *Speaking with the dead: Development of Afro-Latin religion among Puerto Ricans in the United States.* New York: AMS Press.

Perloff, H. S. (1950). *Puerto Rico's economic future: A study in planned development.* Chicago: University of Chicago Press.

Petrullo, V. (1947). *Puerto Rican paradox.* Philadelphia: University of Pennsylvania Press.

Picó, F. (1979). *Libertad y servidumbre en Puerto Rico del siglo XIX: Los jornaleros utuadeños en vísperas del auge del café.* Río Piedras, PR: Ediciones Huracán.

Picó, F. (1981). *Amargo café: Los pequeños y medianos caficultores de Utuado en la segunda mitad del siglo XIX.* Río Piedras, PR: Ediciones Huracán.

Picó, F. (1990). *Historia general de Puerto Rico.* Río Piedras, PR: Ediciones Huracán.

Poplack, S., & Pousada, A. (1981). *A comparative study of gender assignment to borrowed nouns.* New York: City University of New York, Hunter College, Centro de Estudios Puertorriqueños.

Quintero Rivera, Á. G. (1999). *Salsa, sabor y control: Sociología de la música tropical.* México D.F.: Siglo Veintiuno Editores.

Quintero Rivera, Á. G., González, J. L., Campos, R., & Flores, J. (1981). *Puerto Rico: Identidad nacional y clases sociales (coloquio de Princeton).* Río Piedras, PR: Ediciones Huracán.

Ramírez, R. L. (1999). *What it means to be a man: Reflections on Puerto Rican masculinity* (R. Casper, Trans.). New Brunswick, NJ: Rutgers University Press. (Original work published in 1993)

Ramos, J. (Ed.). (1992). *Amor y anarquía: Los escritos de Luisa Capetillo.* Río Piedras, PR: Ediciones Huracán.

Rand, C. (1958). *The Puerto Ricans.* New York: Oxford University Press.

Renek, M. (1966, December 3). "New Windows on Poverty." *New Republic,* pp. 23–24.

Reynolds, L. G., & Gregory, P. (1965). *Wages, productivity and industrialization in Puerto Rico.* Homewood, IL: R. D. Irvin.

Reynolds, R. M., Rodríguez-Fraticelli, C., & Vásquez Erazo, B. (Eds.). (1989). *Campus in bondage: A 1948 microcosm of Puerto Rico in bondage.* New York: City University of New York, Hunter College, Centro de Estudios Puertorriqueños.

Ribes Tovar, F. (1968). *Handbook of the Puerto Rican community* (Vol. 1). New York: El Libro Puerto Rico.

Ribes Tovar, F. (1970). *Enciclopedia puertorriqueña ilustrada: The Puerto Rican heritage encyclopedia.* New York: Plus Ultra.

Ribes Tovar, F. (1971). *Albizu Campos: Puerto Rican revolutionary.* New York: Plus Ultra.

Ribes Tovar, F. (1972). *The Puerto Rican woman.* New York: Plus Ultra.

Rigdon, S. M. (1988). *The culture façade: Art, science, and politics in the work of Oscar Lewis.* Urbana: University of Illinois Press.

Rivera-Batiz, F. L., & Santiago, C. (1994/1997). *Puerto Ricans in the United States: A changing reality.* Washington, DC: National Puerto Rican Coalition.

Rivera-Batiz, F. L., & Santiago, C. E. (1996). *Island paradox: Puerto Rico in the 1990s.* New York: Russell Sage Foundation.

Rivera Medina, E., & Ramírez, R. L. (Eds.). (1989). *Del cañaveral a la fábrica: Cambio social en Puerto Rico.* Río Piedras, PR: Ediciones Huracán.

Rodríguez, C., Sánchez Korrol, V., & Alers, O. (Eds.). (1980/1984). *The Puerto Rican struggle: Essays on survival in the U.S.* Maplewood, NJ: Waterfront Press.

Rodríguez, C. E. (1974). *The ethnic queue: The case of Puerto Ricans.* San Francisco: R & E Research Associates.

Rodríguez, C. E. (1989/1991). *Puerto Ricans: Born in the USA.* Boston: Unwin & Hyman. (Reissued by Westview Press 1991)

Rodríguez, C. E., & Sánchez Korrol, V. (Eds.). (1996). *Historical perspectives on Puerto Rican survival in the United States.* Princeton, NJ: Markus Wiener.

Rodríguez Beruff, J. (1996). Strategic military interests and Puerto Rican self-determination. In J. Rodríguez Beruff & H. García Muñiz (Eds.), *Security problems and policies in the post-cold war Caribbean* (pp. 155–177). New York: St. Martin's Press.

Rodríguez Bou, I. (1966). Significant factors in the development of education in Puerto Rico. In United States-Puerto Rico Commission on the Status of Puerto Rico, *Status of Puerto Rico: Selected background studies of the Status Commission Report* (pp. 147–314). Washington, DC: Government Printing Office.

Rodríguez Bou, I. (1967). Comentarios en torno a *La Vida* de Oscar Lewis. *Revista de Ciencias Sociales, 11*(2), 205–225.

Rodríguez de Laguna, A. (Ed.). (1987). *Images and identities: The Puerto Rican in two world contexts.* New Brunswick, NJ: Transaction Books.

Rogler, L. H. (1972). *Migrant in the city: The life of a Puerto Rican action group.* New York: Basic Books.

Rogler, L. H., & Santana Cooney, R. (1984). *Puerto Rican families in New York City: Intergenerational processes.* Maplewood, NJ: Waterfront Press.

Roosevelt, T., Jr. (1937/1970). *Colonial policies of the United States: American imperialism.* New York: Arno Press & New York Times. (Original work published 1937)

Ross, D. (1976). *The long uphill path: A historical study of Puerto Rico's program of economic development.* San Juan, PR: Editorial Edil.

Rouse, I. (1992). *The Tainos: Rise and decline of the people who greeted Columbus.* New Haven, CT: Yale University Press.

Sánchez, M. E., & Stevens-Arroyo, A. (Eds.). (1987). *Toward a renaissance of Puerto Rican Studies: Ethnic and area studies in university education.* Boulder, CO: Social Science Monographs; Highland Lakes, NJ: Atlantic Research and Publications.

Sánchez Korrol, V. (1983/1994). *From colonia to community: The history of Puerto Ricans in New York City, 1917–1948.* Berkeley: University of California Press. (Original work published 1983)

Sandis, E. (Ed.). (1970). *The Puerto Rican experience.* New York: Selected Academic Readings.

Santiago, C. E. (1992). *Labor in the Puerto Rican economy: Postwar development and stagnation.* New York: Praeger.

Santiago, R. (1995). *Boricuas: Influential Puerto Rican writings—An anthology.* New York: Ballantine.

Santiago-Valle, K. A. (1994). *"Subject people" and colonial discourses: Economic transformation and social disorder in Puerto Rico, 1898–1947.* Albany: State University of New York Press.

Scarano, F. A. (1984). *Sugar and slavery in Puerto Rico: The plantation economy of Ponce, 1800–1850.* Madison: University of Wisconsin Press.

Scarano, F. A. (1993). *Puerto Rico: Cinco siglos de historia.* San Juan, PR: McGraw-Hill.

Schmidt-Nowara, C. (1999). *Empire and antislavery: Spain, Cuba, and Puerto Rico, 1833–1874.* Pittsburgh, PA: University of Pittsburgh Press.

Schneider, E. C. (1999). *Vampires, dragons, and Egyptian kings: Youth gangs in postwar New York.* Princeton, NJ: Princeton University Press.

Seda Bonilla, E. (1973). *Social change and personality in a Puerto Rican agrarian reform community.* Evanston, IL: Northwestern University Press.

Senior, C. (1961). *Strangers, then neighbors: From pilgrims to Puerto Ricans.* New York: Freedom Books.

Sheehan, S. (1976). *A welfare mother.* Boston: Houghton Mifflin.

Silén, J. A. (1971). *We, the Puerto Rican people: A story of oppression and resistance.* New York: Monthly Review Press.

Snipp, M. C. (1989). *Native Americans: The first of this land.* New York: Russell Sage Foundation.

Sotomayor, O. J. (1998). *Poverty and income inequality in Puerto Rico, 1970–1990.* San Juan, PR: Centro de Investigaciones Sociales.

Steiner, S. (1974). *The islands: The worlds of the Puerto Ricans.* New York: Harper & Row.

Stevens-Arroyo, A. M. (1988). *The cave of the Jagua: The mythological world of the Taínos.* Albuquerque: University of New Mexico Press.

Steward, J. H., Manners, R. A., Wolf, E. R., Padilla Seda, E., Mintz, S. W., & Scheele, R. L. (1956). *The people of Puerto Rico: A study in social anthropology.* Urbana: University of Illinois Press.

Sued Badillo, J., & López Cantos, A. (1986). *Puerto Rico negro.* Río Piedras, PR: Editorial Cultural.

Thomas, P. (1967). *Down these mean streets.* New York: Knopf.

Thompson, L. (1995). Nuestra isla y su gente: La construcción del "otro" puertorriqueño. *Our islands and their people.* Rio Piedras, PR: Centro de Investigaciones Sociales y Departamento de Historia de la Universidad de Puerto Rico.

Tinker, G. (1992). Indigenous autonomy and the next 500 years. *Global Justice, 3*(2 & 3), 1–3.

Torre, C., Rodríguez-Vecchini, H., and Burgos, W. (1994). (Eds.). *The commuter nation: Perspectives on Puerto Rican migration.* Río Piedras, PR: Editorial de la Universidad de Puerto Rico.

Torres, A. (1994). *Between melting pot and mosaic: African Americans and Puerto Ricans in the New York political economy.* Philadelphia: Temple University Press.

Torres, A., & Rodríguez, C. E. (1991). Latino research and policy: The Puerto Rican case. In E. Meléndez, C. E. Rodríguez, & J. Barry Figueroa (Eds.), *Hispanics in the labor force: Issues and policies* (pp. 247–263). New York: Plenum Press.

Torres, A., & Velázquez, J. E. (Eds.). (1998). *The Puerto Rican movement: Voices from the Diaspora.* Philadelphia: Temple University Press.

Torres, L. (1997). *Puerto Rican discourse: A sociolinguistic study of a New York suburb.* Mahwah, NJ: Erlbaum.

Torruellas, R. M., Benmayor, R., Goris, A., & Juarbe, A. L. (1991). *Affirming cultural citizenship in the Puerto Rican community.* New York: City University of New York, Hunter College, Centro de Estudios Puertorriqueños.

Torruellas, L. M., & Vásquez, J. L. (1984). *Puertorriqueños que regresaron: Un análisis de su participación laboral*. Río Piedras, PR: University of Puerto Rico.

Trías Monjes, J. (1997). *Puerto Rico: The trials of the oldest colony in the world*. New Haven, CT: Yale University Press.

Tugwell, R. G. (1946/1977). *Stricken land: The story of Puerto Rico*. New York: Greenwood Press. (Original work published 1946)

Tumin, M., & Feldman, A. (1961). *Social class and social change in Puerto Rico* (2nd ed.). Princeton, NJ: Princeton University Press.

Turner, F. (Ed.). (1991). *Puerto Rican writers at home in the USA: An anthology*. Seattle, WA: Open Hand.

Urciuoli, B. (1996). *Exposing prejudice: Puerto Rican experiences of language, race, and class*. Boulder, CO: Westview Press.

U.S. Census Bureau. (1990a). *1990 census of the population*, series #1990 CP-1–1, table 253, p. 323 (general population characteristics). Washington, DC: Government Printing Office.

U.S. Census Bureau. (1990b, August). *The summary: Population and housing characteristics*, series #CPH-1–53, table 1, pp. 1–17. Washington, DC: Government Printing Office.

U.S. Census Bureau. (2000). *The Hispanic population: 2000 brief*. Retrieved from www.census.gov.

U.S. Commission on Civil Rights. (1976). *Puerto Ricans in the continental United States: An uncertain future*. Washington, DC: Author.

Valentine, C. A. (1968). *Culture and poverty: Critique and counterproposals*. Chicago: University of Chicago Press.

Valle Ferrer, N. (2000). *The story of Luisa Capetillo: A pioneer Puerto Rican feminist*. New York: Peter Lang.

Vázquez, J. M. (1992). Embattled scholars in the academy. *Callaloo, 15*(4), 1039–1051.

von Eckardt, U. M. (1967). *La Vida* de Oscar Lewis: Reseña y comentario. *Revista de Ciencias Sociales, 11*(2), 240–252.

Wagenheim, K. (1975). *A survey of Puerto Ricans on the U.S. mainland in the 1970s*. New York: Praeger.

Wagenheim, K., & Jiménez de Wagenheim, O. (Eds.). (1973/1994). *The Puerto Ricans: A documentary history*. Princeton, NJ: Markus Weiner. (Original work published in 1973)

Wakefield, D. (1959/1975). *Island in the city: The world of Spanish Harlem*. New York: Arno Press. (Original work published 1959)

Walsh, K. (1991). *The struggle for voice: Issues of language, power, and schooling for Puerto Ricans*. New York: Bergin & Garvey.

Weisskoff, R. (1985). *Factories and food stamps*. Baltimore, MD: Johns Hopkins University Press.

Wells, H. (1969). *The modernization of Puerto Rico: A political study of changing values and institutions*. Cambridge, MA: Harvard University Press.

Whalen, C. T. (2001). *From Puerto Rico to Philadelphia: Puerto Rican workers and postwar economies*. Philadelphia: Temple University Press.

Wojcicka Sharff, J. (1998). *King Kong on 4th Street: Families and the violence of poverty on the Lower East Side*. Boulder, CO: Westview Press.

Young Lords Party. (1971). *Palante: Young Lords Party*. New York: McGraw-Hill.

Zavala, I. M., & Rodríguez, R. (1980). *The intellectual roots of independence: An anthology of Puerto Rican political essays*. New York: Monthly Review Press.

Zentella, A. C. (1997). *Growing up bilingual: Puerto Rican children in New York*. Malden, MA: Blackwell.

16

AMERICAN INDIAN STUDIES

C. Matthew Snipp

Stanford University

American Indian studies is an interdisciplinary blend of many fields in the social sciences and humanities; history and anthropology have been especially prominent, along with contributions from education, sociology, psychology, economics, and political science. In recent years, American Indian writers and artists have produced a substantial body of original writings, literary criticism, and other artistic works. A casual glance at the literature in American Indian studies will reveal that it is divided about equally between historical research and studies of contemporary American Indians, no doubt reflecting the strong influence of history and anthropology. Historical studies of American Indians tend to focus on culture and tradition, precontact social structure, or episodes in relations with Euro-Americans. Contemporary research focuses on a range of issues, from modern culture to socioeconomic conditions to law and public policy. In addition to this scholarly work, authors such as Joy Harjo, Leslie Silko, Sherman Alexie, and Louise Erdrich have written critically acclaimed novels that provide unique insights into the modern lives of American Indians.

American Indian studies overlaps many disciplines and is better characterized as an "area study," like Soviet studies or Latin American studies, than as a traditional academic discipline. American Indian studies also lacks a single coherent theoretical paradigm that structures intellectual inquiry (cf. Mihesuah, 1998; Thornton & Snipp, 1998). Instead, a plethora of intellectual perspectives from diverse disciplines have been used to explain the variety of subjects related to American Indians. In fact, the single unifying theme of American Indian studies is its link to the culture and experiences of American Indians, as a people separate from the mainstream of American society and Euro-American culture.

This literature can be roughly classified into several major subject areas encompassing both historical and contemporary interests: demographic behavior, socioeconomic conditions, political and legal institutions, and culture and religion. Of course, a great deal of overlap exists among these areas. Another notable point is that this literature deals almost exclusively with North American aboriginals and their descendants. As the field has evolved, relatively little attention has been devoted to the natives of South America or the Pacific Islands. Finally, this review focuses mainly on work done in the social sciences and history. Reviews are necessarily selective, and an in-depth discussion of work in the arts and literature is far afield from the issues addressed in this chapter.

AMERICAN INDIANS

Before turning to the topical areas of American Indian studies, some background information about American Indians may be helpful. No one knows with certainty when populations of Homo sapiens first appeared in North America. It is widely believed that the first immigrants to North America migrated from what is now Siberia, perhaps in pursuit of game, across the Beringia land bridge now submerged in the Bering Sea. This land bridge existed during several ice ages, leading to speculation that the first populations arrived as early as 40,000 years ago or as recently as 15,000 years ago; 24,000 years is considered a particularly credible estimate (Thornton, 1987). Traditionalists view this explanation with a great deal of skepticism, preferring instead their own accounts of Native origins (Deloria, 1995).

Nonetheless, these populations moved southward, settling throughout the Americas. In North America, dense populations developed along the East and West coasts, in the Southeast and Southwest regions, and in the Mississippi River valley. The size of the 15th-century aboriginal population is currently the subject of intense debate (Verano & Ubelaker, 1992). Once thought to number less than 1 million, the precontact native population is now believed to have been much larger. The most conservative estimates calculated that 3 to 5 million natives were living in North America in 1492, though other, more controversial estimates range upward to 18 million (Dobyns, 1983; Ramenofsky, 1987; Thornton, 1987).

The aboriginals of North America did not prosper after the arrival of Europeans. European-borne diseases were devastating and, along with warfare, genocidal practices, forced removals, and a changing ecology, very nearly annihilated American Indians. Census records indicate that by the end of the 19th century fewer than 250,000 American Indians survived in the United States. By 1900 the culture, lifestyle, social organization, and even the languages of these survivors were vastly different from their ancestors of 400 years earlier.

Since 1900, American Indians in the United States and Canada have staged a remarkable comeback (Shoemaker, 1999). Growing in number throughout this century, there were 1.9 million American Indians and Alaska Natives counted in the 1990 U.S. census. About half of this population live in rural areas, most often on specially designated tribal lands (reservations or trust properties). Though more numerous than in the past, American Indians are still not prosperous. The standard of living for most American Indians in the United States is about the same as for African Americans, and well below the standards of White Americans (see Sandefur, Rindfuss, & Cohen, 1996).

Although less variegated than in the past, American Indians today retain a diverse representation of tribal cultures. Broad generalizations about American Indians are often difficult to make, and exceptions are usually easy to find. The American Indian studies literature typically deals with this problem by focusing exclusively on a single tribe or a group of similar tribes, or by seeking reasonable generalizations that appear valid for many tribal cultures. The literature concerned with American Indian demography has most often been concerned with large-scale processes affecting American Indian people across the nation.

AMERICAN INDIAN DEMOGRAPHY

American Indian demography focuses on the size, distribution, and composition of the American Indian population. Improvements in the data for American Indians, especially that gathered by the U.S. census, have

facilitated studies of their contemporary demography, and this work has been especially important in planning and public policy applications. However, a great deal of attention has been given to pre-Columbian historical demography, and since the mid-1960s this literature has been filled with significant breakthroughs and controversies.

HISTORICAL DEMOGRAPHY

Understanding the prehistoric and historic demographic behavior of American Indians is a prerequisite for gaining knowledge about the indigenous societies of North America and for assessing the impact of European contacts. For example, large populations are usually associated with economic surpluses, and complex societies with highly developed systems of religion, culture, and governance. Archaeological evidence of such societies exists in the Southwest, the Pacific Northwest, and the Mississippi River valley (Thornton, 1987; Willey, 1966). Because American Indians almost disappeared in the late 19th century, large numbers of earlier generations of Indians would indicate that the arrival of Europeans had a substantial, if not devastating, impact on native mortality and, by implication, native social organization.

The first systematic estimates of the American Indian population were published in 1918 by a Smithsonian anthropologist, James Mooney (Thornton, 1987). He reckoned that 1.15 million American Indians were living around 1600. Alfred Kroeber reviewed Mooney's early estimates in 1938 and deemed them essentially correct, though he adjusted the total population estimate downward to 900,000 (Denaven, 1976). The Mooney-Kroeber estimates of around 1 million in 1600 have been the benchmark for scholars throughout this century, though other estimates were published. However, the Mooney-Kroeber estimates were flawed because they failed to take into account the effects of epidemic disease.

Noting the shortcomings in the Mooney-Kroeber figures, Dobyns (1966) published a revised estimate for the 1492 population. According to Dobyns, the 1492 North American population was perhaps as large as 12 million. This launched a debate that is still far from being resolved. Despite these disagreements, it is fairly certain that the Mooney-Kroeber figures were too low. Even very conservative estimates now number the indigenous 1492 population at approximately 3 to 5 million (Thornton, 1987; Ubelaker, 1976). At the other end of the spectrum, Dobyns's (1983) subsequent estimates suggest a population numbering 18 million.

Dobyns's work in particular has started lively debates about a variety of issues in American Indian historical demography. Some of these disputes are disagreements about methodology (Driver, 1969; Henige, 1998;

Thornton & Marsh-Thornton, 1981). For example, the projection methods used in this work depend heavily on estimates of the nadir population, that is, the approximate year and numeric size of the Indian population before it began to rebound in number. Some critics make a convincing case that Dobyns's 1966 estimates are flawed because he uses the wrong nadir (Driver, 1969; Thornton & Marsh-Thornton, 1981). However, there is little agreement about the nadir population, except that it happened around the turn of the 20th century and was much smaller than the precontact population. For example, Thornton (1987) suggests that the nadir was around 228,000 in 1890, but Ubelaker (1992) argues that it was later and larger than Thornton's figure—namely, 530,000 in 1900. The geographic areas about which Thornton and Ubelaker are writing are not strictly comparable, but this discrepancy exemplifies the current debate.

Despite the apparent ubiquity of disputes in this literature, there is little disagreement that the population estimates by Mooney and Kroeber are too low, and that Dobyns's revisions are probably too high. But some observers find this range, between 1 million and 18 million, troubling. Henige (1986, 1992, 1998), for instance, argues that the theory, methodology, and data for estimating precontact populations are irredeemably flawed, so defective that it is simply impossible to draw any conclusions whatsoever about the size of the populations in the Western hemisphere before 1492. Perhaps, but precontact population estimates are so heavily laden with implications about precontact societies that it seems unlikely scholars will heed Henige's advice to abandon this effort.

In fact, there is a growing body of archaeological research that deals with this issue. Substantially larger population estimates than the Mooney-Kroeber figures are certainly consistent with the archaeological record (Ramenofsky, 1987). This work clearly indicates that relatively complex societies occupied regions of North America before the arrival of Europeans (Milner, 1992). However, the archaeological work also makes it abundantly evident that the process of depopulation was considerably more complex than it has often been portrayed. In fact, there is a growing body of evidence that the American Indian population did not precipitously collapse. Instead, diseases reached some populations sooner than others and affected populations in some areas more than in others (Verano & Ubelaker, 1992). This body of literature shows that the impact of European contact was certainly greater than once believed, as the introduction of European diseases, slavery, genocidal practices, and the intensification of conflict nearly exterminated the native population (Stannard, 1992). Recent research has noted that population recoveries normally follow epidemic mortality; the European recovery following the spread of the bubonic plague is evidence for this observation (Thorn-

ton, Warren, & Miller, 1992). This poses the vexing question of why North American native populations did not recover in the same manner as Europeans. One possible explanation is that the expansion of mercantile capitalism and the attendant depredations by Europeans (slavery, genocide), as well as the loss of traditional subsistence sources, made population recovery impossible for American Indians, at least until the late 19th century (Thornton, 1992).

Massive population losses also undoubtedly caused a large-scale amalgamation and reorganization of groups struggling to survive, and profound changes in the cultures and social structures of these populations (Merrell, 1989; Nagel & Snipp, 1993). Beyond the archaeological record, not much is known about the distribution and composition of these populations before and after the arrival of Europeans (Milner, 1992). This remains a promising subject for future studies of American Indian historical demography.

CONTEMPORARY DEMOGRAPHY

As mentioned, the American Indian population stopped declining and began to increase sometime around 1890 to 1900. Since that time, the American Indian population has grown very quickly, especially since 1950. As Figure 16.1

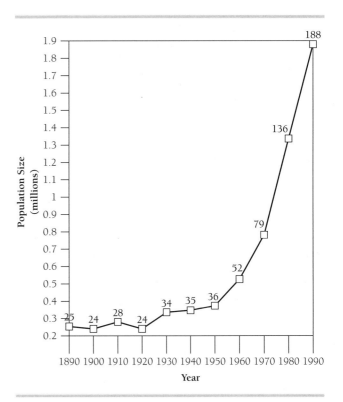

Figure 16.1. American Indian Population, 1890–1990.

shows, population growth was modest in the first half of this century, and the deadly influenza epidemic of 1918–19 (Prucha, 1984) resulted in a slight population decline in 1920. This low rate of growth is somewhat surprising considering that American Indian women had (and have) relatively high fertility rates (Thornton, Sandefur, & Snipp, 1991). However, high infant mortality rates and the propensity of mixed-ancestry offspring to shed their Indian identity may have kept American Indian population growth at low levels.

There was a sharp increase in the Indian population beginning in about 1950. Some (and possibly a great deal) of this increase was due to procedural changes in the 1960 census that resulted in a more accurate enumeration, but other factors, such as improved health care, also played a role. For instance, in 1955 health care delivery to reservations was improved when the Indian Health Service was moved from the Bureau of Indian Affairs (BIA) to the Public Health Service (Rhoades, 2000; Sorkin, 1988). Studies indicate that because American Indians often have better access to health care (from the Indian Health Service) than do other equally impoverished groups, infant mortality has diminished and longevity has increased (Snipp, 1996; Taffel, 1987).

Although other types of deaths, such as those related to alcoholism and violence, continue to be a problem (Howard, Walker, Walker, & Rhoades, 2000; Wissow, 2000), American Indian fertility is exceedingly high, even higher than that of Black women (Snipp, 1996; Thornton et al., 1991). The large excess of American Indian births over deaths has contributed significantly to the population growth of this century.

A peculiar characteristic of American Indian population growth, at least since 1970, is that a large share of this increase can be attributed to changing racial identification. That is, much of the expansion in the American Indian population since 1970 has been the result of persons switching their racial identification to American Indian from some other racial category (Harris, 1994; Passell, 1976; Passell & Berman, 1986). The U.S. census, virtually the only comprehensive source of data for American Indians, depends on the voluntary self-identification of respondents to identify and enumerate members of the American Indian population as well as all other racial groups. Declining social discrimination, growing ethnic pride, and a resurgence in tribal organization have been cited as possible reasons so many individuals have switched their racial identity to American Indian (Passell & Berman, 1986; Quinn, 1990).

The fluid boundaries of the American Indian population underscore a particularly problematic concern for demographers and anyone else desiring to study the American Indian population: defining who is a member of the American Indian population. Definitions are abundant,

and there is no single agreed-upon standard. Some federal agencies and a number of tribes use an arbitrary measure of descendancy, such as ¼ blood quantum. Blood quantum standards for tribal membership vary greatly from ½ to ⅟₆₄ Indian blood (Thornton, 1996).

For many other applications, the genealogical verification of blood quantum standards is too complex. This leads agencies such as the U.S. Census Bureau to rely simply on self-identification. By default, most studies of American Indians also rely on self-identification, especially if they use secondary data from federal government sources. To complicate this matter for comparative purposes, the Canadian government uses a somewhat different set of standards for defining the boundaries of its native Indian population.

Beyond the complexities of counting, studies show that American Indians, more than other minorities, are concentrated in rural areas; slightly fewer than half reside in metropolitan regions. Most American Indians live west of the Mississippi River, mainly because of 19th-century removal programs directed at eastern American Indians. A number of studies document that American Indians are one of the least educated, most unemployed, poorest, and least healthy groups in American society (see Sandefur et al., 1996). Nonetheless, American Indians are more likely than other groups, especially African Americans, to live in a large husband-wife household, and about a third of the population speaks a native language; this is provisional evidence of the continuing influence of traditional culture in family organization and language use (Sandefur & Sakamoto, 1988; Snipp, 1989).

The recent movement of American Indians to urban areas is a demographic event of major significance. As late as 1930, when about half of American society lived in cities, only about 10 percent of the American Indian population could be found in urban environs. However, World War II, federal policy, and prevailing migration streams in the postwar era were responsible for urbanizing the American Indian population. World War II was significant because American Indian participation in this conflict was widespread; approximately 25,000 American Indians served in the military (Bernstein, 1991). This experience provided many American Indians with their first glimpse of life away from the reservation. It also gave many in the service an opportunity to learn job skills and, perhaps even more important, skills in dealing with the cultural practices and expectations of Euro-American society.

The impact of the GI Bill following the war also should not be underestimated. This program gave many American Indians an opportunity for higher education, resulting in a generation of relatively well-educated Indian men for whom there were no job opportunities on the reservation (Fixico, 1986). Needless to say, job opportunities in expanding postwar urban America were a powerful incentive for migration away from rural reservations. Because of their limited participation in the uniformed services, Indian women benefited little from the GI Bill, and neither their education nor their labor-force participation increased noticeably after the war in the same way as for Indian men (Snipp, 1989).

Federal relocation policies have also had an impact on Indian urbanization. In the 1950s and 1960s, federal relocation programs were established to encourage reservation Indians to move to preselected relocation centers in cities such as Los Angeles, San Francisco, Chicago, and Denver (Sorkin, 1978). Participants in these programs typically were provided job training and/or counseling, moving expenses, and a stipend until they found work. Critics faulted these programs for being ineffective as well as being a reservation brain drain (Fixico, 1986; O'Brien, 1989). Nonetheless, they had a significant impact on Indian urbanization insofar as more than 100,000 American Indians participated in these programs until they were sharply curtailed in the early 1970s (Margon, 1976; Sorkin, 1978).

Despite the abolition of relocation programs in the early 1980s, American Indians continue to be a highly mobile population. However, evidence from the decennial census suggests that although American Indians have higher migration rates than either African Americans or Whites, they tend to follow the same migration streams as other Americans (Eschbach, 1995; Snipp, 1989). American Indians joined the streams moving out of the Northeast and upper Midwest in favor of destinations in the West and South.

These developments have tended to produce "generations" of urban Indians. For example, studies in Los Angeles have found distinct generations of urban Indians, divided between those who moved there in the 1930s or 1940s and those who came later in the relocation programs. These groups have distinctive characteristics with respect to their reservation ties, tribal allegiances, and the Indian organizations in which they are active (Price, 1968; Weibel-Orlando, 1991).

Urbanization has profound implications for the American Indian population that are manifest in several ways. This development is directly related to other social and economic characteristics, as well as to measures of well-being for the Indian population. Urbanization also has influenced American Indian political ideologies, in addition to cultural events and practices. These issues are addressed in the next section.

STUDIES OF SOCIAL AND ECONOMIC STATUS

The literature on the social and economic status of American Indians is relatively large. One area of research,

development studies, includes a variety of perspectives concerned with the structure of economic relations between Euro-Americans and Indians. This literature is often historical, but there is also a small but growing body of work that deals with contemporary economic processes that affect the well-being of American Indians. Another research perspective concerns the human resources of American Indians, especially in terms of education, unemployment, and the prevalence of poverty.

DEVELOPMENT STUDIES

From a historical perspective, studies of the early social and economic status of American Indians have often focused on the development of so-called dependency relations between Euro-Americans and American Indians (Hall, 1989; White, 1983). Dependency theory, a variant of neo-Marxist world system theory, has been widely criticized for a number of shortcomings, but it has gained a measure of acceptance among scholars of White-Indian relations (Dunaway, 1996; Hall, 1989; White, 1983; Wolf, 1982). In this perspective, economic dependency arises from trade relations in which Euro-Americans enjoy a disproportionate economic advantage over American Indians. The source of this advantage stems from a near monopoly over items such as manufactured goods and rum (White, 1983; Wolf, 1982). The introduction of such European business practices as the use of credit also played a role in fostering dependency.

Dependency relations between Euro-Americans and American Indians led to highly exploitive trading conditions that were often detrimental to American Indians. Trade relations were a frequent source of conflict that periodically erupted into serious violence. Unscrupulous traders and a growing commerce in Indian captives, for example, ignited the Yamassee War, which marked the end of Indian slavery in the Southeast (Merrell, 1989). Early colonial officials frequently complained about the conflicts created by the unethical practices of frontier traders and sought to curb their abuses, though with little success (Bateman, 1989). Beyond the conflicts between traders and their Indian clients, the introduction of European innovations such as guns, horses, and metal implements represents a subtler and more profound impact of economic dependency that is not fully appreciated; such items altered forever the culture and lifestyles of North American Indians (White, 1991).

Recent scholarship also has made clear that American Indians were not merely the passive victims of unchecked capitalism. On the contrary, American Indians were active participants in trade relations with Europeans, acting in their own self-interests to advance their own well-being. Large tribes in particular, such as the Iroquois in the

Northeast, the Cherokee in the Southeast, and the Ojibwa in the Great Lakes, often enjoyed substantial advantages in dealing with European traders (Dunaway, 1996; White, 1999).

The onset of the Industrial Revolution, growing urbanization, and an influx of immigrants from Europe and slaves from Africa changed dramatically the relations between Euro-Americans and American Indians. The role of American Indians as trading partners decreased in favor of policies and measures designed to remove them from lands desired for development by Euro-Americans. The emergence of industrial capitalism diminished the importance of American Indian productivity in the national economy, while the natural resources belonging to American Indians have become ever more valued (Jacobsen, 1984). Throughout the 19th century, American Indians were more or less forcibly induced to cede their lands for the development of agriculture, timber, and water. Efforts to develop petroleum, coal, and other minerals on tribal lands were first initiated in the late 19th century (Miner, 1976).

Tribes have responded by organizing to prevent the wholesale expropriation of reservation resources. For example, the Council of Energy Resource Tribes (CERT) is an intertribal consortium that provides technical assistance and information to reservations seeking to lease or develop oil, gas, or other energy resources (Ambler, 1990). This organization was formed in the mid-1970s to help tribes negotiate effectively with highly sophisticated multinational energy corporations. In this period, when energy prices were rising rapidly, there were numerous cases of gross incompetence and a few cases of fraud involving federal officials responsible for managing tribal energy resources (Ambler, 1990; Fixico, 1998). In the aftermath of these cases, the tribes became more heavily involved in the negotiations for exploration and development leases; CERT has often played a major role in those discussions as a technical adviser.

Many other reservations have struggled to achieve economic self-sufficiency. There are various explanations for the limited success that tribes have had in stimulating economic activity on reservations. Some studies of reservation economies blame the isolated locales for many of the economic woes that are experienced (Levitan & Johnston, 1975; Sorkin, 1971). These studies argue that lack of physical infrastructure, absence of raw materials, distance from markets, and a workforce with few skills severely limit development opportunities, especially in manufacturing. Lack of capital for investment also has been identified as a serious obstacle to development. However, a number of tribes have adopted innovative strategies such as microenterprises to stimulate economic activity (Mushinski & Pickering, 1996; Pickering, 2000).

Economic development in Indian country is also frequently complicated by the collision of traditional native values and the ethics of capitalism and business development (Vinje, 1982). In fact, Cornell and Kalt (1990, 1992a, 1992b) argue that for economic development to be successful, development projects must be structured in ways that are consonant with tribal culture and practices. Projects with authoritarian or highly centralized management practices will be neither welcome nor likely to succeed in reservation communities that are highly egalitarian and communalistic. They have also argued that institutions such as the tribal government are essential in this process.

Despite the many obstacles to economic development, in recent years a number of reservations have enjoyed limited (and in a few instances, spectacular) success in spurring economic growth, especially in tourism, gambling, and light manufacturing (Snipp & Summers, 1991). For example, White (1990) describes the development successes of the Passamaquoddy in Maine and of the Mississippi Choctaw. The Passamaquoddy are particularly interesting because they parlayed a substantial land claims settlement into an even larger estate through investments in agriculture, manufacturing, and investment portfolios. The Passamaquoddy are not alone in their use of a legal decision to obtain economic leverage. In Washington State, tribes have used a court decision affirming their fishing rights to build a successful aquaculture industry.

There are many paths on the legal road to economic development. Reservation tobacco outlets gain a competitive advantage because tribal sovereignty makes them immune from state taxes and hence able to sell their products for lower prices than their off-reservation competitors. States have been known to complain bitterly about this loss of tax revenue, and merchants about unfair competition. However, the sums of money and the controversies related to reservation tobacco sales pale in comparison to the disputes surrounding gambling. Reservation gambling is a relatively recent development that started with a 1980 court decision (*Seminole Tribe of Florida* v. *Butterworth*), which allowed high-stakes bingo on the Florida Seminole reservation (Kersey, 1992). Within a few years, reservation gambling has grown explosively. Some of these operations are small-scale, marginally profitable bingo operations, but others, such as the one owned by the Pequot tribe in western Connecticut, are large, full-service casinos that take in millions of dollars annually. Surprisingly, there are few studies of reservation gaming (Anders, 1999; Cornell & Kalt, 1992b; Midwest Hospitality Advisors [MHA], 1992), and most of what has been published is in trade publications such as the one from the Indian Gaming Association.

HUMAN RESOURCES

Contemporary studies of the social and economic status of modern American Indians consistently point to the widespread poverty and economic hardships facing them. The Meriam Report, published in 1928 (Institute for Government Research), furnished the first systematic empirical assessment of the economic status of American Indians. Since the publication of that report, numerous studies have documented the disadvantaged status of American Indians (see Brophy & Aberle, 1966; Levitan & Hetrick, 1971; Sandefur et al., 1996; Snipp, 1989).

Although a number of studies have described in detail the economic conditions among American Indians, fewer have attempted to isolate the causes of poverty and unemployment. However, it is clear that a number of factors can be blamed for these conditions. Primary among them is that American Indians have very low levels of education, and this, of course, limits access to job opportunities, especially well-paid jobs (Gregory, Abello, & Johnson, 1996; Trosper, 1996; Ward, 1998).

The persistent finding that American Indians lack the skills, and especially the education, to compete successfully in the job market underscores a pressing problem. In 1980, 56% of American Indian adults had completed high school, while 70% of White adults had done so (Snipp, 1989). Ten years later, 71% of American Indians reported 12 or more years of schooling (80% for White adults), but such gains are somewhat misleading because GEDs are widespread among American Indians. In particular, as holders of compensatory certificates, students with GEDs may be less likely to pursue postsecondary education. Indeed, this is reflected in the fact that the percentage of White adults with a baccalaureate or higher degree was in 1990 twice as high as the percentage of American Indians holding such a degree, 24% and 12%, respectively. Perhaps a more telling statistic is that in 1990, 19.3% of Indian youths aged 16 to 19 had withdrawn from school without a diploma (U.S. Census Bureau, 1993).

The lack of education among American Indians should not be construed as resulting from a lack of exposure to educational institutions. American Indians have a long history of experience with Western education under the auspices of missionaries and federal authorities (Fuchs & Havighurst, 1972; Szasz, 1977, 1988). Until recently, these schools were far more concerned with "civilizing" American Indians—detribalizing and acculturating them—than with educating them (Fuchs & Havighurst; Lomawaima, 1994; Szasz, 1977).

Changes in federal policy since the mid-1970s facilitated the participation of American Indians in educational systems (Gross, 1989). Indian school board members and tribally controlled school systems are considerably more common than in the past. Perhaps most significant is that 24 tribally controlled colleges have formed in the past 25 years (Carnegie Foundation for the Advancement of Teaching, 1989). Most of these fledgling institutions are two-year community colleges, though a few offer baccalaureate and master's degrees. These institutions are especially meaningful because of the dearth of American Indians with advanced education.

The sharp rise in the number of high school graduates has not translated into an equal rise in college attendance. In fact, there is some evidence to suggest that transitions to college have diminished for American Indians since the 1960s (Snipp, 1989; Ward, 1998). American Indians who attend college are enrolled overwhelmingly in public institutions, approximately 88% (Fries, 1987). Furthermore, from 1975 to 1981 the number of American Indian baccalaureate degree recipients stayed nearly constant—about 3,500—despite an increase in the "college-age" population (Fries, 1987). There was a small increase in American Indian doctorates, but the numbers are exceedingly low, rising from 93 in 1975–76 to 130 in 1980–81, and virtually unchanged in 1993, with 134 awarded (Fries, 1987; National Center for Educational Statistics, 1998).

American Indian students have marked preferences for certain areas of study. Over half of these degrees were in the social sciences, education, and the humanities. Barely 20% were in the physical or biological sciences. The relative underrepresentation of American Indians in the latter fields may reflect a preference for subjects that promise to ameliorate the problems or meet the needs of their communities. For example, an education major would allow one to become a teacher and serve a pressing need on many reservations. It is not surprising then, that about one half of American Indian students receiving a baccalaureate degree in 1994 obtained them in fields related to education and business management (National Center for Educational Statistics, 1998).

In the past, the role of economic discrimination in limiting opportunities for American Indians has been unclear. Some research has suggested that discrimination has not been a significant disadvantage for American Indians (Sandefur & Scott, 1983), while other studies have disagreed with this conclusion (Gwartney & Long, 1978). However, unlike the case with women and African Americans, there is little research showing that American Indians are systematically segregated into lower-status, lesser-paid occupations. That is, there is little evidence to suggest that there are "Indian jobs" in the same manner as there is "women's work" (for instance, lower-paid clerical employment). The absence of systematic labor market discrimination does not mean that American Indians are immune from other types of discrimination, such as in housing or education.

Of course, American Indian women are not exempt from gender discrimination. American Indian women are systematically paid less than their male counterparts in comparable circumstances (Snipp, 1989, 1990; Snipp & Aytac, 1990). American Indian women also appear to be constrained by many of the same concerns that affect other women. For example, family obligations such as child-rearing duties limit their ability to participate in the workforce, and the so-called feminization of poverty has been especially burdensome for Indian women. Unfortunately, very little has been written about the special circumstances of American Indian women; this is an area in which much more work needs to be done (see Shoemaker, 1995).

The economic conditions on reservations, where many Indians reside, are particularly harsh. Reservations are typically located in remote rural areas and are often bereft of economic activity and job opportunities. Reservation unemployment rates in excess of 50% are not unusual. The impact of spatial isolation or lack of economic opportunity is underscored by data that typically show that urban American Indians enjoy a higher standard of living than their counterparts living in rural areas, usually reservations.

There is disagreement about the benefits of rural-urban migration for American Indians; some studies have identified tangible benefits for urban immigrants (Clinton, Chadwick, & Bahr, 1975; Sorkin, 1978), while other research finds evidence to the contrary (Pickering, 2000; Snipp & Sandefur, 1988). One argument against programs that assist urban migration is that such efforts typically help most those who need the least help; that is, such efforts assist the brightest and most able-bodied. Conversely, these same programs take poorly educated and unemployed Indians from reservations and turn them into poorly educated and unemployed urban Indians. Federal policies that encouraged urban immigration for American Indians in the 1950s and 1960s were abandoned amid controversies over their effectiveness and overall impact (Fixico, 1986; O'Brien, 1989).

Persistently high poverty rates have led some researchers to suggest that some reservations are ripe for the development of an "underclass" (Sandefur, 1989). However, there is little or no research about reservation underclasses, and disagreements about the meaning of this concept are certain to limit work on this subject (Sandefur, 1989). Along similar lines, informal economies are known to thrive on reservations, but little has been written about them (Sherman, 1988).

The poverty and economic hardship facing rural and urban American Indians alike have been a major source of other serious distress. Alcoholism, suicide, and homicide are leading causes of death for American Indians (Howard et al., 2000; Wissow, 2000). One study found

that programs sponsored by the Indian Health Service have improved some measures of public health, such as infant mortality. However, other health problems associated with poverty and social malaise, such as mental disorders and alcoholism, are likely to remain unchanged in the absence of significant improvements in economic conditions (Rhoades, 2000; Sandefur et al., 1996).

POLITICAL ORGANIZATIONS AND LEGAL INSTITUTIONS

Historical Background

The political and legal status of American Indians in the United States is an extremely complicated subject, tangled in a conflicting multitude of treaties, formal laws, bureaucratic regulations, and court decisions (Pommersheim, 1995). Unlike any other racial or ethnic group in American society, American Indians have a distinctive niche in the legal system, acquired through a long history of conflicts and agreements with federal authorities. As a result of this history, a separate agency within the federal government (the Bureau of Indian Affairs), a volume of the Code of Federal Regulations (25), and a multiplicity of other rules exist for dealing with American Indians.

The current legal and political status of American tribes is the product of a long and circuitous history. The relevant literature overlaps modern studies in law and political science, as well as in history (Biolsi, 2001; Deloria & Lytle, 1983; O'Brien, 1989; Pommersheim, 1995). Initially, before the arrival of Europeans, the indigenous societies of the Western hemisphere were self-governing entities with political systems of varying degrees of complexity. The Mississippian culture (approximately A.D. 1200–1400) may have had a highly complex political structure akin to the systems of pre-Columbian Central and South America (Champagne, 1992; Milner, 1992).

The arrival of Europeans in the Western hemisphere certainly altered the political systems of these societies, but this did not mean that these populations were no longer self-governing. On the contrary, dwindling numbers in the aftermath of disease may have manifested simpler, devolved systems of governance. At the same time, there is some evidence that political consolidation occurred for the purpose of mobilizing military power and controlling access to European traders. For example, the Iroquois confederation may have become more tightly knit for monopolizing trade with Europeans. This allowed them to drive the Huron out of upstate New York and to gain exclusive trading rights with Europeans in this part of the country (Bradley, 1987).

The English Crown maintained a healthy respect for the sovereign rights of tribes. The Royal Proclamation of

1763 made it clear that the colonies were obligated to respect the rights of tribes (O'Brien, 1989; Prucha, 1984). Needless to say, this was an extremely unpopular position among the colonists, and this proclamation was eventually repealed. Nonetheless, it was an important document because it established doctrine for dealing with Indian tribes that was later to shape Indian policy in the new United States (O'Brien, 1989).

Early Federal-Indian Relations

Dealings with American Indian tribes by the new United States were at first highly circumscribed. The new U.S. government had neither the financial nor the military resources to wage a protracted war (Prucha, 1984). There was little choice for federal authorities except to negotiate with tribes on a "government-to-government basis." Prucha writes about a memorandum from Henry Knox, the secretary of war, to George Washington, in which

he [Knox] concluded that to crush the Indians would require men and money "far exceeding the United States' ability to advance, consistently with a due regard to other indispensible objects." To treat the Indians by a "conciliatory system" would not only cost far less but, more important, would absolve the nation from "blood and injustice which would stain the character of the nation . . . beyond all pecuniary calculation." (pp. 61–62)

The War of 1812 and conflicts with Indians after the war were a turning point in federal policy (Dippie, 1982). The War of 1812 decisively limited Britain's influence in North America, especially as an ally of the Indians against the expanding U.S. frontier. Perhaps more significant, Andrew Jackson successfully prosecuted the Creek Wars and established beyond doubt the federal government's ability to wage war successfully against a formidable Indian force. This made negotiation merely a convenient alternative to military action and considerably increased the options available to the rapidly expanding nation.

Although the federal government initially dealt with tribes as equals, this practice was short-lived, especially after 1812, when pressure to remove Indians from the eastern United States resulted in a series of measures that culminated in the infamous removal legislation of the 1830s. This legislation also prompted a succession of legal confrontations that have made the political status of American Indian tribes difficult to characterize. In 1831, Chief Justice John Marshall described Indian tribes as "domestic, dependent nations" (*Worcester* v. *Georgia*). In another decision (*Cherokee* v. *Georgia*, 1832), Marshall affirmed the idea that tribes were sovereigns with the same rights as "foreign powers," and that treaties with them had the same standing in law. With these opinions, he set forth the principle that tribes are autonomous political entities that enjoy quasi-sovereignty, subject only to the authority of the federal government (Barsh & Henderson, 1980; O'Brien, 1989; Pommersheim, 1995).

The limits on tribal political autonomy have fluctuated as a result of court decisions and federal legislation that curtail or extend tribal powers. The Congress forbade any further treaties to be made with Indian tribes in the Appropriations Act of 1871. This action reflected congressional impatience in dealing with Indian tribes as political entities with sovereign rights, especially when the wherewithal existed to conduct successful military campaigns. In fact, the prohibition against treaty making left military action as the only recourse for resettling tribes reluctant to give up their homes and move to their appointed reservations. Passage of this statute was followed by outbreaks of bloodshed and violence in which the tribes of the West were forcibly settled on reservation lands, distant from tribal lands rapidly being occupied by Euro-American settlers.

Sixteen years later, in an effort to break up the reservations and liquidate the remaining tribal lands, the disastrous General Allotment (Dawes) Act was passed. The Dawes Act, which became law in 1887, and related legislation were designed to parcel out small, privately owned tracts of land to individual Indian families. It was expected that this land, along with the gift of a mule and a plow, would be enough to turn Indians into yeoman farmers (Carlson, 1981; Hoxie, 1984). But Indians who were once nomadic hunters had little knowledge of agriculture and little desire to pursue small-scale farming as a livelihood, while among Indian farmers agricultural production actually fell because allotment disrupted traditional systems (Carlson, 1981).

Twentieth-Century Federal-Indian Relations

The allotment process continued until the early 1930s and very nearly succeeded in completely dispersing Indian lands. Ultimately, this policy caused nearly 90 million acres of Indian land to pass into non-Indian hands through sales, fraud, and tax seizures. By 1934, Indian tribes controlled only a third of the land they had possessed in 1887 (O'Brien, 1989). A number of tribes are trying to cope with this problem today by repurchasing property or reclaiming land illegally seized during allotment.

The allotment programs were curtailed as policy by the passage of legislation known as the "Indian New Deal." The most significant enactment in the Indian New Deal was the Wheeler-Howard Indian Reorganization Act (IRA), passed in 1934. This act rescinded earlier federal legislation outlawing tribal governments. The IRA permitted tribes to organize their own governments to handle a limited number of issues on their reservations. However, tribal governments wishing to organize under the IRA legislation were required to adopt a system of representative democracy similar in form to the federal government (O'Brien, 1989; Prucha, 1984); other forms of government, such as traditional theocracies, were not permitted. For many years, these tribal governments had little real power and very circumscribed jurisdictions, but this began to change in the early 1970s.

In the years following World War II, the federal government unilaterally decided to extricate itself from Indian affairs with a three-pronged public policy known as "termination and relocation." The first step in this process began shortly after World War II, when the federal government established the Indian Claims Commission (ICC). This commission was created to settle outstanding claims made by Indian tribes involving such disputes as treaty violations and illegally seized land. Although it was expected that the ICC would expedite these claims, many of them were still pending when the commission was dissolved in 1978 (Fixico, 1986). The second part of termination and relocation dissolved reservation boundaries and withdrew federal recognition from tribal governments. Ultimately, only two reservations were terminated, the Menominee in Wisconsin and the Klamath in Oregon, and the former was restored to reservation status in 1975. In theory, once the claims were settled and the reservations abolished, the third step would be to move American Indians from isolated rural areas to urban labor markets. To accomplish this objective, in the early 1950s the BIA established programs to encourage reservation Indians to move to preselected urban "relocation centers" in cities such as Seattle, Los Angeles, and San Francisco. By 1972, more than 100,000 American Indians had participated in these programs (Sorkin, 1978).

Termination and relocation came under increasing attack from numerous quarters. Supporters complained that it was not implemented quickly or effectively enough, while opponents argued that these policies did more harm than good (Castile, 1998). By the mid-1960s, the time was ripe for a dramatic change in federal policy toward American Indians. Until the 1960s, federal actions curtailed tribal rights more often than extending them. However, the past 25 years have marked a political resurgence among American Indians (Cornell, 1988). Active opposition to termination and relocation eventually led to the passage of a number of legislative acts affirming, among other things, Indian religious freedom and rights to self-government. The Indian Self-Determination and Educational Assistance Act of 1975 was an especially important bill. This legislation formally recognized the rights of tribes to administer their reservations with minimal interference from Congress, the courts, or the BIA. In particular, the BIA was directed to hand over control of many of its programs and activities.

Tribal sovereignty, as mentioned, is a complex legal doctrine affecting the political autonomy of tribal governments. It is distinct from a closely aligned political principle known as self-determination. The principle of self-determination, unlike tribal sovereignty, is relatively recent in origin and initially was meant as a claim for administrative control of reservation affairs. As a political ideology, self-determination developed in response to the unilateral actions of the federal government in implementing policies such as the termination legislation of the 1950s. In the 1960s, self-determination was a rallying theme for promoting greater tribal involvement in the development and implementation of federal policies affecting American Indians. This principle was formally enacted into public law with the passage of the Indian Self-Determination and Educational Assistance Act of 1975. Federal agencies have complied with the mandates of this legislation by gradually divesting control over programs and services, such as those once administered by the BIA. For example, many tribal governments now have contracts to provide social services, similar to the arrangements formerly made with state and local governments.

Arguments promoting self-determination have been enlarged in recent years to the point where self-determination is indistinguishable from tribal sovereignty (Gross, 1989). The most influential statement merging these principles is a report presented to the Senate by the American Indian Policy Review Commission (AIPRC) in 1976. The AIPRC report was a comprehensive though highly controversial evaluation of federal Indian policy. Every presidential administration since Richard Nixon has acknowledged the principle of self-determination, but most have not sought to expand tribal powers. The Clinton administration augmented the notion of self-determination by issuing a statement that it would adhere to a "government-to-government" relationship in dealing with federally recognized tribes. At this time, there is no indication that the Bush administration plans either to restrict or expand the principle of self-determination as it has been implemented during past administrations.

PAN-INDIAN POLITICAL IDEOLOGY

Pan-Indianism is a supratribal ideology that places the common interests and well-being of American Indians as a collectivity above the narrower interests of individual tribes. Not surprisingly, the goals of tribalism and pan-Indianism do not always coincide. The roots of modern pan-Indian organizations can be traced to the Omaha leader Pontiac, and later to the Shawnee leader Tecumseh, and to Joseph Brant, a Mohawk. These leaders organized pan-Indian movements opposing Euro-American frontier settlement in the late 18th and early 19th centuries (for example, Pontiac's Revolt in 1763).

In the late 19th century, pan-Indian messianic movements known as Ghost Dances swept across the West (Thornton, 1986). There were two major episodes of the Ghost Dance. The first began in the early 1870s and was confined mainly to California, Nevada, and Oregon. The second was more widespread, with adherents across the Southwest and the Plains, and started around 1890. The Ghost Dances began with the visionary dreams of Paviotso spiritual leaders. Wodziwob's visions sparked the first movement, and another Paviotso, Wovoka, was responsible for the second movement. The practice of the Ghost Dance varied, but adherents believed that the dance would resurrect dead warriors, bring back wildlife, and remove Euro-Americans from the land. Some believed that the special shirts worn for the Ghost Dance would protect them from soldiers' bullets (Thornton, 1986).

The federal government moved aggressively to repress the Ghost Dance and forbade its practice on reservations. This ultimately led one group of Sioux, led by Big Foot, to leave the reservation. The military was dispatched to force them back. The confrontation between the military and Big Foot's followers ended in the 1890 Wounded Knee (South Dakota) massacre, in which 146 men, women, and children were killed and buried in a mass grave, and another 7 died later from their wounds (Prucha, 1984). This was the last major conflict involving American Indians and the U.S. military.

Despite the Ghost Dance tragedy, pan-Indian organizations have persisted since the late 19th century. Federal boarding schools were established in the late 1800s for civilizing and detribalizing Indian children. Ironically, boarding schools became seedbeds for pan-Indianism as Indian youth realized that the experiences of their tribe were not unique, and that American Indians had many problems in common regardless of tribal affiliation (Dippie, 1982; Nagel, 1997). In the early decades of this century, especially before 1930, many of these students migrated to urban areas. They organized urban-based pan-Indian organizations to promote the well-being of American Indians across the nation (Hertzberg, 1971). These organizations were particularly active in the 1910s and 1920s, but most had disappeared before World War II.

Creation of the National Congress of American Indians in 1944 marked the renewal of pan-Indian interests, although the next major burst of pan-Indian activity did not occur until the late 1960s and early 1970s. The political resurgence of American Indians coincided with the gains of the civil rights movement. It is impossible to credit this development to civil rights activism alone, but certainly they are not unrelated. The political climate of the 1960s and early 1970s was clearly favorable to social change, especially for ensuring equal rights for ethnic minorities. American Indian leaders and their supporters moved quickly to capitalize on these sentiments.

Some observers have also suggested that Indian political activism in the 1960s was a response to the postwar termination policies that aimed to liquidate the special status accorded to Indian tribes. For example, restoration of the Menominee reservation in Wisconsin served as a focus for Indian activists in the Midwest. Relocation programs in the termination era accelerated the urbanization of American Indians and contributed eventually to building the critical mass necessary for the political mobilization of urban Indians (Fixico, 1986).

The highly diverse tribal composition of the urban Indian population has meant that it is virtually impossible to organize urban Indians around narrowly defined issues germane to only one or a few tribes. In the face of this constraint, the ideology of pan-Indianism is a theme peculiar to urban Indian groups (Hertzberg, 1971), a supratribal ideology committed to broad issues such as economic opportunity and social justice, and to the preservation of Indian culture through pan-Indian events such as intertribal powwows.

The urbanization of American Indians in the 1950s and 1960s accelerated the development of pan-Indian organizations and activities (Nagel, 1997). Some of these organizations, such as the National Congress of American Indians, have moderate political agendas focused on lobbying, while others, such as the American Indian Movement, are highly militant. The latter was involved in the occupation of the Washington, D.C., BIA office in 1972, and later participated in the armed conflict at Wounded Knee in 1973 (Churchill & Vanderwall, 1988). Today, most cities with large Indian populations have pan-Indian organizations involved in political activities, cultural events, and social service delivery (Weibel-Orlando, 1991).

It is important to note that pan-Indian ideology and issues have somewhat less appeal in reservation communities. It is not that pan-Indian sentiments are absent among reservation Indians, but rather that tribal homogeneity is much greater on and near reservations, and issues directly affecting the reservation and the structure and function of tribal government are typically more salient than more global kinds of intertribal concerns.

CULTURE AND RELIGION

The cultures of American Indians are extremely diverse and broad generalizations are difficult to make, although contemporary American Indians are probably less heterogeneous than their ancestors were before the arrival of

Europeans. The same can be said about the religions of American Indians. Not much is known about the spiritual life of American Indians before the 15th century; such information is available only from archaeological evidence, which, regrettably, seldom captures the rich complexity of religious symbol systems. Most knowledge about American Indian religions is based on the reports of explorers, missionaries, traders, and anthropologists (Brown, 1982).

SPIRITUALITY

The spiritual practices of contemporary American Indians reflect several types of religious observances: Christian, neotraditional, and traditional. Participation in one or another of these observances may or may not limit participation in another. For example, adherents to Christianity may feel that participation in other religious ceremonies is a violation of their beliefs. But these practices are not always mutually exclusive and are sometimes blended into new religious practices. Besides the variation in religious beliefs, it is also important to keep in mind that there is a great deal of tribal variation in these practices.

American Indians who are practicing Christians represent the legacy of European missionaries. The Christian affiliation of many, if not most, American Indians reflects their tribal membership and the denomination of the missionaries responsible for their tribe's conversion. Numerical estimates are not available, but there are many Catholic Indians in the Southwest, while American Indians in the Midwest are often Lutheran, to mention only two examples.

American Indians who participate in neotraditional religions often belong to a branch of the Native American Church (NAC). NAC is a pan-Indian religion that is practiced throughout the United States and Canada. The NAC combines elements of Christian religion with traditional religious beliefs and practices. A particularly controversial NAC practice is the use of peyote, a hallucinogenic drug and an otherwise illegal substance, as a sacrament paralleling the use of wine in the Christian Church.

In the early part of this century, prior to World War I, reformers seeking to civilize American Indians advocated the abolition of peyote. This effort, along with other endeavors such as the Prohibition movement, which led to the Harrison Act, prompted a small group of Indians in Oklahoma to organize the NAC. This was a deliberate strategy designed to preserve peyote ceremonies under the constitutional protections of religious freedom. After numerous legal challenges, the NAC won the right to use peyote within narrowly defined limits prescribed by the courts (Prucha, 1984). However, the Supreme Court has recently upheld a decision (*Employment Division, Department of Human Resources* v. *Smith,* 110 S. Ct. 1595, 1990) involving the use of peyote that raised serious questions about its legality. This has fostered concerns about how the conservative Court will interpret freedom-of-religion cases in the future (Deloria, 1992).

Traditional American Indian religious practices often take place in the context of informally organized groups, such as sweatlodge or feasting societies. Some of these groups are remnants of the older religious movements, such as the Ghost Dance discussed earlier. Not much is written about these groups because they are ordinarily not open to outsiders. An exception is the Sun Dance, and the ceremonies of this belief have attracted numerous chroniclers. The ceremony is held in a number of locations, mainly in the northern Plains, and involves the participation of numerous tribes. It is perhaps best known for the ritual scarification and trances of the Sun Dancers (Jorgensen, 1972).

The secrecy in which many traditional religions are practiced may be the result of the intense repression once directed at these observances by the federal government. In 1883, the BIA established Courts of Indian Offenses that prosecuted American Indians for practicing their traditional culture. Among other things, the courts forbade the use of traditional medicines, shaman healers, and all ceremonial observances, including religious ceremonies. Despite their dubious legal foundation, the Courts of Indian Offenses were active until their mandate was rewritten in 1935 (Prucha, 1984).

In 1935, the federal government ended its official opposition to the practice of tribal culture and religion. However, this did not end the conflicts between government authorities and American Indians trying to practice a non-Christian religion. Many American Indians regard freedom of religion as an elusive promise. Besides the controversies surrounding NAC ceremonies, the preservation of sacred areas and the repatriation of religious artifacts and skeletal remains from museum collections are highly contentious issues that concern many American Indians (Loftin, 1989).

Preservation of sacred areas is an issue that places Indian groups at odds with land developers, property owners, local governments, and others who would develop sites deemed sacred by American Indian spiritual leaders. In one such case, the Navajo and Hopi went to court in 1983 to petition against the development of a ski resort that was alleged to intrude on sacred ground. In this and in several similar cases, the courts ruled against the Indians (Loftin, 1989). A more recent case (*Lyng* v. *Northwest Indian Cemetery Protective Association,* 108 S. Ct. 1319, 1988) challenged the U.S. Forest Service's authority to construct a logging road that would desecrate an area in northern California deemed sacred by Yurok, Karok, and Tolowa tribes. The upshot of these rulings is that the courts have little tolerance for Indian claims when they threaten economic interests (Deloria, 1992).

Similar conflicts have arisen over the repatriation of religious artifacts and skeletal remains held in museums, pitting academics such as scientists and museum curators against Indian groups (Thornton, 1998). Scientists, especially archaeologists, claim that these remains are important "data" that may hold the keys to scientific discoveries in the future. Tribes and other Indian organizations counter that these are the remains of their ancestors, over whom no one has a proprietary right and who should be left to rest undisturbed. In some instances, remains and artifacts have been returned to tribes; Stanford University returned burial remains to the Ohlone tribe in California, for example. Other institutions have opposed repatriation or are studying the matter. The Smithsonian Institution has developed a complex policy for repatriation, and the University of California has appointed a committee to develop such a policy. For the foreseeable future, this controversy is likely to linger in the courts, Congress, and academic institutions.

CULTURAL SURVIVAL

Compared with repatriation, cultural studies are a less controversial though no less important domain of American Indian Studies. Whereas the doctrine of religious freedom and its impact on the practice of Indian religion defines one of the central forms of native culture, cultural studies emphasize the content of Indian lifestyles, values, and symbol systems. Some of these studies focus on the internal content of tribal culture, while other research deals with the impact of tribal culture on other forms of behavior.

Two other themes have been extremely important in the study of American Indian culture. One has been the study of traditional cultural knowledge for the purpose of renewing and extending it to others. For example, there has been a well-known renaissance in Pueblo pottery, but the resurrection of tribal arts and crafts has also included basketry, wood carving, and decorative arts such as beadwork and jewelry made from porcupine quills. A second theme has been manifest in the use of native materials or knowledge to express the contemporary experience of American Indians. For example, the use of native folklore in contemporary novels or poetry is a common practice among American Indian writers.

For decades, studies of American Indians were dominated by ethnologists recording for posterity details about Indian culture, especially material culture, or documenting the ways that European contact influenced the content of tribal culture. Much of this research was spurred by the belief that American Indians were destined for extinction, and thus it was necessary to chronicle

tribal culture before it disappeared; one scholar describes this tradition as "salvage ethnography" (Dippie, 1982). The popularity of this type of research has declined significantly, partially because there are few "pristine" cultures left anywhere in the world, much less in North America. It is also fairly clear to most observers that American Indians are not in imminent danger of extinction. Another, perhaps more damaging, reason for the decline in research is the growing realization among scholars that studies purporting to document precontact Indian culture were based on secondhand accounts of periods that were themselves not truly pristine. The influence of European diseases and trade goods often arrived far in advance of the physical presence of Europeans (Dobyns, 1983).

Although American Indian ethnologies have fallen out of favor, studies of American Indian culture have persisted. Such studies now resemble literary or artistic criticism, and a discussion of this work is somewhat far afield for this chapter. Nonetheless, it is noteworthy that writers such as Leslie Silko, Scott Momaday, Joy Harjo, Louise Erdrich, and Michael Dorris have received a great deal of public recognition, as well as artists such as R. C. Gorman and William Rabbitt. This work is especially notable insofar as it blends the themes, concepts, and experiences of American Indian tribal culture with non-Indian media such as literary styles of printmaking.

Other work has focused on how European innovations have been incorporated into tribal culture in ways that are unique among American Indians; silversmithing and rug weaving are two well-known examples. Still other studies have examined how the symbolic culture of American Indians has gradually adapted to changing environmental conditions (Fowler, 1987). For example, urban Indians from Oklahoma living in Los Angeles have constructed their churches and conduct their services in ways that closely mirror the practices of Indian churches in Oklahoma (Weibel-Orlando, 1991).

A related set of studies deals with the resurgence in American Indian culture. Cultural resurgence among American Indians is manifest in a number of ways. The spread of pan-Indianism described earlier is clearly one sign of cultural renewal. Another is that the use of American Indian languages and the number of native speakers have increased significantly in recent years (Leap, 1988). The resurgence of American Indian language use is particularly fascinating. The number of American Indians who do not speak English, especially among those under age 40, is very small (Snipp, 1989). Despite the widespread use of English, about a fourth of the American Indian population also regularly use a native language, and there is some evidence that this may be on the increase (Leap, 1988).

One reason for this resurgence is that many tribes are engaged in active efforts to encourage native-language use

(Valentine, 1998). In areas where there are large concentrations of native-language speakers, such as the Navajo reservation, it seems likely that these efforts to preserve the language will be successful. However, some tribes such as the Catawba in South Carolina have all but lost their language (the last two native speakers died in the 1950s), and it remains to be seen whether it will be possible to reintroduce a native language (Taukchiray & Kasakoff, 1992). It seems likely that for some tribes the native language will remain a vital part of the culture, while for others native-language instruction will not be unlike Latin training, something to be learned and used occasionally but not in everyday life.

The influence of American Indian culture on other types of behavior is perhaps most prominent in a large literature on American Indian mental health, education, and rehabilitation (Bennett & Ames, 1985; Foster, 1988; Rhoades, 2000). The bulk of these studies show that education and rehabilitation efforts can be made more effective if they are sensitive to cultural nuances. In fact, many specialists take this idea as a given point of departure and focus their research on the ways in which Euro-American educational and therapeutic practices can be adapted to the cultural predisposition of American Indian clients. For example, substance-abuse programs might incorporate elements of tribal culture such as sweat lodges, or talking circles as a part of their therapeutic regime, or traditional values such as respect for elders or for women may be advocated as a device for preventing domestic abuse.

CONCLUSION

It was once widely believed that the American Indian was destined for extinction—the "vanishing American." This led to a plethora of early studies of American Indians that sought to document and catalogue the culture and lifestyles of American Indians before they disappeared forever. Along with this effort, a great deal of work was done to classify disparate elements of tribal culture, such as family and kinship structures, language, property relations, housing design, and artwork. This work adopted a view of American Indians as the passive objects of scientific inquiry.

Modern American Indian studies are a sharp departure from this earlier tradition of scholarship in a number of important respects. One crucial difference is that American Indians are viewed as a dynamic and vital population that shows no sign of disappearing from the ethnic mosaic of American society. Another difference is that American Indian studies focus on tribal culture as an evolving phenomenon that is continuously changing as American Indians adapt to the world around them. In fact, it is the dynamic character of American Indian culture that has made possible the survival of American Indians into the 20th century and beyond. In many respects, the raison d'être of American Indian studies arises from a fundamental concern about American Indian culture, lifestyles, and traditions, and a basic commitment to the well-being of American Indian people.

Like the American Indian population, American Indian studies is a highly diverse and growing field of inquiry. It is interdisciplinary and extremely eclectic in the perspectives it employs. Once primarily the domain of historians and anthropologists, American Indian studies has rapidly expanded beyond the bounds of these disciplines, with contributions from scholars in a variety of fields. Given the scope and breadth of these endeavors, the field of American Indian studies will continue to expand and develop for the foreseeable future.

References

Ambler, M. (1990). *Breaking the iron bonds.* Lawrence: University Press of Kansas.

Anders, G. C. (1999). Indian gaming: Financial and regulatory issues. In T. R. Johnson (Ed.), *Contemporary Native American political issues* (pp. 163–173). Walnut Creek, CA: Altamira Press.

Barsh, R. L., & Henderson, J. Y. (1980). *The road: Indian tribes and political liberty.* Berkeley: University of California Press.

Bateman, R. (1989). The deerskin trade in the Southeast. Unpublished manuscript, Johns Hopkins University, Department of Anthropology, Baltimore.

Bennett, L. A., & Ames, G. M. (Eds.). (1985). *The American experience with alcohol: Contrasting cultural perspectives.* New York: Plenum.

Bernstein, A. R. (1991). *American Indians and World War II.* Norman: University of Oklahoma Press.

Biolsi, T. (2001). *Deadliest enemies: Law and the making of race relations on and off Rosebud Reservation.* Berkeley: University of California Press.

Bradley, J. W. (1987). *Evolution of the Onondaga Iroquois.* Syracuse, NY: Syracuse University Press.

Brophy, W. A., & Aberle, S. D. (1966). *The Indian: America's unfinished business.* Norman: University of Oklahoma Press.

Brown, J. E. (1982). *The spiritual legacy of the American Indian.* New York: Crossroad.

Carlson, L. A. (1981). *Indians, land, and bureaucrats.* Westport, CT: Greenwood Press.

Carnegie Foundation for the Advancement of Teaching. (1989). *Tribal college: Shaping the future of Native Americans.* Princeton, NJ: Princeton University Press.

Castile, G. P. (1998). *To show heart: Native American self-determination and federal Indian policy, 1960–1975.* Tucson: University of Arizona Press.

Champagne, D. (1992). *Social order and political change.* Stanford, CA: Stanford University Press.

Churchill, W. A., & Vanderwall, J. K. (1988). *Agents of repression: The FBI's secret wars against the Black Panther party and the American Indian movement.* Boston: South End Press.

Clinton, L., Chadwick, B. A., & Bahr, H. M. (1975). Urban relocation reconsidered: Antecedents of unemployment among Indian males. *Rural Sociology, 40,* 117–133.

Cordeiro, E. E. (1992). The economics of bingo: Factors influencing the success of bingo operations on American Indian reservations. In S. Cornell and J. P. Kalt (Eds.), *What can tribes do? Strategies and institutions in American Indian economic development* (pp. 205–238). Los Angeles: UCLA, American Indian Studies Center.

Cornell, S. (1988). *The return of the native.* New York: Oxford University Press.

Cornell, S., & Kalt, J. P. (1990). Pathways from poverty: Economic development and institution-building on American Indian reservations. *American Indian Culture and Research Journal, 14,* 89–125.

Cornell, S., & Kalt, J. P. (1992a). Reloading the dice: Improving the chances for economic development on American Indian reservations. In S. Cornell and J. P. Kalt (Eds.), *What can tribes do? Strategies and institutions in American Indian economic development* (pp. 1–59). Los Angeles: UCLA, American Indian Studies Center.

Cornell, S., & Kalt, J. P. (Eds.). (1992b). *What can tribes do? Strategies and institutions in American Indian economic development.* Los Angeles: UCLA, American Indian Studies Center.

Deloria, V., Jr. (1992). Trouble in high places: Erosion of American Indian rights to religious freedom in the United States. In M. A. Jaimes (Ed.), *The state of native America* (pp. 267–290). Boston: South End Press.

Deloria, V., Jr. (1995). *Red earth, white lies: Native Americans and the myth of scientific fact.* New York: Scribner.

Deloria, V., Jr., & Lytle, C. M. (1983). *American Indians, American justice.* Austin: University of Texas Press.

Denevan, W. M. (Ed.). (1976). *The native population of the Americas in 1492.* Madison: University of Wisconsin Press.

Dippie, B. W. (1982). *The vanishing American.* Lawrence: University Press of Kansas.

Dobyns, H. F. (1966). Estimating aboriginal American population: Estimating techniques with a new hemispheric estimate. *Current Anthropology, 7,* 395–416.

Dobyns, H. F. (1983). *Their number become thinned.* Knoxville: University of Tennessee Press.

Driver, H. E. (1969). *Indians of North America* (2nd ed., rev.). Chicago: University of Chicago Press.

Dunaway, W. A. (1996). *The first American frontier: Transition to capitalism in southern Appalachia, 1700–1860.* Chapel Hill: University of North Carolina Press.

Eschbach, K. (1995). The enduring and vanishing American Indian: American Indian population growth and intermarriage in 1990. *Ethnic and Racial Studies, 18,* 89–108.

Fixico, D. L. (1986). *Termination and relocation.* Albuquerque: University of New Mexico Press.

Fixico, D. L. (1998). *The invasion of Indian Country in the twentieth century: American capitalism and tribal natural resources.* Niwot: University Press of Colorado.

Foster, D. V. (1988). Consideration of treatment issues with American Indians detained in the Federal Bureau of Prisons. *Psychiatric Annals, 18,* 698–701.

Fowler, L. (1987). *Shared symbols, contested meanings.* Ithaca, NY: Cornell University Press.

Fries, J. E. (1987). *The American Indian in higher education, 1975–1976 to 1984–1985.* Washington, DC: U.S. Department of Education, Center for Education Statistics.

Fuchs, E., & Havighurst, R. J. (1972). *To live on this earth.* Albuquerque: University of New Mexico Press.

Gregory, R. G., Abello, A. C., and Johnson, J. (1996). The individual economic well-being of Native American men and women during the 1980s: A decade of moving backwards. In G. D. Sandefur, R. R. Rindfuss, & B. Cohen (Eds.), *Changing numbers, changing needs: American Indian demography and public health* (pp. 133–171). Washington, DC: National Academy Press.

Gross, E. R. (1989). *Contemporary federal policy toward American Indians.* Westport, CT: Greenwood Press.

Gwartney, J. D., & Long, J. E. (1978). The relative earnings of Blacks and other minorities. *Industrial Labor Relations Review, 31,* 336–346.

Hall, T. D. (1989). *Social change in the Southwest, 1350–1880.* Lawrence: University Press of Kansas.

Harris, D. (1994). The 1990 census count of American Indians: What do the numbers really mean? *Social Science Quarterly, 75,* 580–593.

Henige, D. (1986). Primary source by primary source? On the role of epidemics in New World depopulation. *Ethnohistory, 33,* 293–312.

Henige, D. (1992). Native American population at contact: Standards of proof and styles of discourse in the debate. *Latin American Population History Bulletin, 22,* 2–23.

Henige, D. P. (1998). *Numbers from nowhere: the American Indian contact population debate.* Norman: University of Oklahoma Press.

Hertzberg, H. W. (1971). *The search for an American Indian identity.* Syracuse, NY: Syracuse University Press.

Howard, M. O., Walker, R. D., Walker, P. S., & Rhoades, E. R. (2000). Alcoholism and substance abuse. In E. R. Rhoades (Ed.), *American Indian health: Innovations in health care, promotion, and policy* (pp. 281–298). Baltimore, MD: Johns Hopkins University Press.

Hoxie, F. E. (1984). *A final promise: The campaign to assimilate the Indians, 1880–1920.* Lincoln: University of Nebraska Press.

Institute for Government Research. (1928). *The problem of Indian administration* [Meriam Report]. Baltimore, MD: Johns Hopkins University Press.

Jacobsen, C. K. (1984). Internal colonialism and Native Americans: Indian labor in the United States from 1871 to World War II. *Social Science Quarterly, 65,* 158–171.

Jorgensen, J. C. (1972). *The sun dance religion.* Chicago: University of Chicago Press.

Kersey, H.A.J. (1992). Seminoles and Miccosukees: A century in perspective. In J. A. Paredes (Ed.), *Indians of the southeastern United States in the late 20th century* (pp. 102–119). Tuscaloosa: University of Alabama Press.

Leap, W. L. (1988). Indian language renewal. *Human Organization, 47,* 283–291.

Levitan, S. A., & Hetrick, B. (1971). *Big Brother's Indian programs: With reservations.* New York: McGraw-Hill.

Levitan, S. A., & Johnston, W. B. (1975). *Indian giving: Federal programs for Native Americans.* Baltimore, MD: Johns Hopkins University Press.

Loftin, J. D. (1989). Anglo-American jurisprudence and the Native American tribal quest for religious freedom. *American Indian Culture and Research Journal, 13,* 1–52.

Lomawaima, K. T. (1994). *They called it prairie light: The story of Chilocco Indian School.* Lincoln: University of Nebraska Press.

Margon, A. (1976). Indians and immigrants: A comparison of groups new to the city. *Journal of Ethnic Studies, 4,* 17–28.

Merrell, J. H. (1989). *The Indian's new world: Catawbas and their neighbors from European contact through the era of removal.* Chapel Hill: University of North Carolina Press.

Midwest Hospitality Advisors (MHA). (1992). *Impact: Indian gaming in Minnesota.* Minneapolis: Marquette Partners.

Mihesuah, D. A. (1998). *Natives and academics: Researching and writing about American Indians.* Lincoln: University of Nebraska Press.

Milner, G. R. (1992). Disease and sociopolitical systems in late prehistoric Illinois. In W. Verano & D. H. Ubelaker (Eds.), *Disease and demography in the Americas* (pp. 103–116). Washington, DC: Smithsonian Institution Press.

Miner, H. C. (1976). *The corporation and the Indian.* Columbia: University of Missouri Press.

Mushinski, D., and Pickering, K. A. (1996). Micro-enterprise credit in Indian country. *Research in Human Capital and Development, 10,* 147–169.

Nagel, J. (1997). *American Indian ethnic renewal: Red power and the resurgence of identity and culture.* New York: Oxford University Press.

Nagel, J., & Snipp, C. M. (1993). Ethnic reorganization: American Indian social, economic, political, and cultural strategies for survival. *Racial and Ethnic Studies, 16,* 203–235.

National Center for Educational Statistics. (1998). *American Indians and Alaska Natives in postsecondary education.* (Technical Report NCES 98–291.) Washington, DC: U.S. Department of Education.

O'Brien, S. (1989). *American Indian tribal governments.* Norman: University of Oklahoma Press.

Passell, J. S. (1976). Provisional evaluation of the census count of American Indians. *Demography, 13,* 397–409.

Passell, J. S., & Berman, P. A. (1986). Quality of 1980 census data for American Indians. *Social Biology, 33,* 163–182.

Pickering, K. A. (2000). *Lakota culture, world economy.* Lincoln: University of Nebraska Press.

Pommersheim, F. (1995). *Braid of feathers: American Indian law and contemporary tribal life.* Berkeley: University of California Press.

Price, J. A. (1968). The migration and adaptation of American Indians to Los Angeles. *Human Organization, 27,* 168–175.

Prucha, F. P. (1984). *The great father.* Lincoln: University of Nebraska Press.

Quinn, W. W., Jr. (1990). The Southeast syndrome: Notes on Indian descendant recruitment organizations and their perceptions of Native American culture. *American Indian Quarterly, 14,* 147–154.

Ramenofsky, A. F. (1987). *Vectors of death: The archaeology of European contact.* Albuquerque: University of New Mexico Press.

Rhoades, E. R. (2000). *American Indian health: Innovations in health care, promotion, and policy.* Baltimore, MD: Johns Hopkins University Press.

Sandefur, G. D. (1989). American Indian reservations: The first underclass areas? *Focus, 12,* 37–41.

Sandefur, G. D., Rindfuss, R. R., & Cohen, B. (Eds.). (1996). *Changing numbers, changing needs: American Indian demography and public health.* Washington, DC: National Academy Press.

Sandefur, G. D., & Sakamoto, A. (1988). American Indian household structure and income. *Demography, 25,* 44–68.

Sandefur, G. D., & Scott, W. J. (1983). Minority group status and the wages of Indian and Black males. *Social Science Research, 12,* 44–68.

Sherman, R. T. (1988). A study of traditional and informal sector micro-enterprise activity and its impact on the Pine Ridge Indian Reservation economy. Unpublished manuscript.

Shoemaker, N. (1995). *Negotiators of change: Historical perspectives on Native American women.* New York: Routledge.

Shoemaker, N. (1999). *American Indian population recovery in the twentieth century.* Albuquerque: University of New Mexico Press.

Snipp, C. M. (1989). *American Indians: The first of this land.* New York: Russell Sage Foundation.

Snipp, C. M. (1990). A portrait of American Indian women and their labor force experiences. In S. E. Rix (Ed.), *The American woman, 1990–1991: A status report* (pp. 265–272). New York: Norton.

Snipp, C. M. (1996). The size and distribution of the American Indian population: Fertility, mortality, migration, and residence. In G. D. Sandefur, R. R. Rindfuss, & B. Cohen (Eds.), *Changing numbers, changing needs: American Indian demography and public health* (pp. 17–52). Washington, DC: National Academy Press.

Snipp, C. M., & Aytac, I. (1990). The labor force participation of American Indian women. *Research in Human Capital and Development, 6,* 189–211.

Snipp, C. M., & Sandefur, G. D. (1988). Earnings of American Indians and Alaska natives: The effects of residence and migration. *Social Forces, 66,* 994–1008.

Snipp, C. M., & Summers, G. F. (1991). American Indians and economic poverty. In C. M. Duncan (Ed.), *Rural poverty in America* (pp. 155–176). Westport, CT: Auburn House.

Sorkin, A. L. (1971). *American Indians and federal aid.* Washington, DC: Brookings Institution.

Sorkin, A. L. (1978). *Urban American Indians.* Lexington, MA: Heath.

Sorkin, A. L. (1988). Health and economic development on American Indian reservations. In C. M. Snipp (Ed.), *Public policy impacts on American Indian economic development* (pp. 145–165). Albuquerque: University of New Mexico, Institute for Native American Development.

Stannard, D. E. (1992). *American holocaust.* New York: Oxford University Press.

Szasz, M. C. (1977). *Education and the American Indian.* Albuquerque: University of New Mexico Press.

Szasz, M. C. (1988). *Indian education in the American colonies, 1607–1783.* Albuquerque: University of New Mexico Press.

Taffel, S. M. (1987, June 19). *Characteristics of American Indian and Alaska native births: United States* (NCHS Monthly Vital Statistics Report, vol. 36, no. 3). Hyattsville, MD: U.S. National Center for Health Statistics.

Taukchiray, W. D., & Kasakoff, A. B. (1992). Contemporary Native Americans in South Carolina. In J. A. Paredes (Ed.), *Indians of the southeastern United States in the late 20th century* (pp. 72–101). Tuscaloosa: University of Alabama Press.

Thornton, R. (1986). *We shall live again* (Rose Monograph Series). New York: Cambridge University Press.

Thornton, R. (1987). *American Indian holocaust and survival.* Norman: University of Oklahoma Press.

Thornton, R. (1992, October). *North American Indians and the demography of colonialism: Population dynamics, the epidemic disease "myth," and adaptations following 1492.* Paper presented at the conference Discovery: Meaning, Legitimations, Critiques, University of Wisconsin, Madison.

Thornton, R. (1996). Tribal membership requirements and the demography of "old" and "new" Native Americans. In G. D. Sandefur, R. R. Rindfuss, & B. Cohen (Eds.), *Changing numbers, changing needs: American Indian demography and public health* (pp. 103–112). Washington, DC: National Academy Press.

Thornton, R. (1998). Who owns our past? The repatriation of Native American human remains and cultural objects. In R. Thornton (Ed.), *Studying Native America: Problems and prospects* (pp. 385–415). Madison: University of Wisconsin Press.

Thornton, R., Sandefur, G. D., & Snipp, C. M. (1991). American Indian fertility in 1910, and 1940 to 1980. *American Indian Quarterly, 15,* 359–367.

Thornton, R., & Snipp, C. M. (1998). A final note. In R. Thornton (Ed.), *Studying Native America: Problems and prospects* (pp. 416–421). Madison: University of Wisconsin Press.

Thornton, R., Warren, J., & Miller, T. (1992). Depopulation in the southeast after 1492. In J. W. Verano and D. H. Ubelaker (Eds.), *Disease and demography in the Americas* (pp. 187–195). Washington, DC: Smithsonian Institution Press.

Thornton, R. T., & Marsh-Thornton, J. (1981). Estimating prehistoric American Indian population size for the United States area: Implications of the nineteenth century population decline and nadir. *American Journal of Physical Anthropology, 55,* 47–53.

Trosper, R. L. (1996). American Indian poverty on reservations, 1969–1989. In G. D. Sandefur, R. R. Rindfuss, & B. Cohen (Eds.), *Changing numbers, changing needs: American Indian demography and public health* (pp. 172–195). Washington, DC: National Academy Press.

Ubelaker, D. H. (1976). The sources and methodology for Mooney's estimates of North American Indian populations. In W. M. Denevan (Ed.), *The native populations of the Americas in 1492* (pp. 243–288). Madison: University of Wisconsin Press.

Ubelaker, D. H. (1992). North American Indian population size: Changing perspectives. In J. W. Verano and D. H. Ubelaker (Eds.), *Disease and demography in the Americas* (pp. 169–176). Washington, DC: Smithsonian Institution Press.

U.S. Census Bureau. (1993). *1990 census of population, social and economic characteristics: United States, CP-2–1.* Washington, DC: Government Printing Office.

Valentine, J. R. (1998). Linguistics and languages in Native American studies. In R. Thornton (Ed.), *Studying Native America: Problems and prospects* (pp. 152–181). Madison: University of Wisconsin Press.

Verano, J. W., & Ubelaker, D. H. (Eds.). (1992). *Disease and demography in the Americas.* Washington, DC: Smithsonian Institution Press.

Vinje, D. C. (1982). Cultural values and economic development: U.S. Indian reservations. *Social Science Journal, 19,* 87–99.

Ward, C. (1998). The importance of context in explaining human capital formation and labor force participation of American Indians in Rosebud County, Montana. *Rural Sociology, 63,* 451–480.

Weibel-Orlando, J. (1991). *Indian country, LA.* Urbana: University of Illinois Press.

White, R. (1983). *The roots of dependency.* Lincoln: University of Nebraska Press.

White, R. (1991). *The middle ground: Indians, empires, and republics in the Great Lakes region, 1650–1815.* New York: Cambridge University Press.

White, R. H. (1990). *Tribal assets.* New York: Henry Holt.

Willey, G. R. (1966). *An introduction to American archaeology.* Englewood Cliffs, NJ: Prentice Hall.

Wissow, L. S. (2000). Suicide among American Indians and Alaska Natives. In E. R. Rhoades (Ed.) *American Indian health: Innovations in health care, promotion, and policy* (pp. 260–280). Baltimore, MD: Johns Hopkins University Press.

Wolf, E. R. (1982). *Europe and the people without history.* Berkeley: University of California Press.

17

SOCIAL SCIENCE RESEARCH ON ASIAN AMERICANS

Pyong Gap Min

Queens College, and the Graduate Center, the City University of New York

The abolition of the 40-year-old Asian Exclusion Act in 1965, along with the U.S. government's military, political, and economic linkages with several Asian countries, ignited a mass influx of Asian immigrants and refugees to the United States during the post-1965 period. Approximately 25% (7 million) of the 28 million post-1965 immigrants admitted between 1965 and 2000 originated from Asian countries (Min, 1999). The influx of Asian immigrants over the last three decades has expanded the Asian American population in the United States from less than 1.5 million in 1970 to about 11 million in 2000 (Min, 1995b; U.S. Census Bureau, 2002). It has also led to diversity among Asian Americans; in addition to the Chinese, Japanese, and Filipino groups with sizable populations in the early 20th century, Koreans, Indians, and Vietnamese have emerged as major Asian American groups. Although the earlier Asian immigrants were heavily concentrated in California, Hawaii, and other West Coast states, post-1965 immigrants are more widely dispersed throughout the United States. At the beginning of the 21st century, many children of post-1965 Asian immigrants have completed their formal education and entered the labor market.

The expansion of Asian American studies programs and the increase in the number of Asian American faculty members in social science disciplines have contributed to an expansion of the literature on contemporary Asian immigrants. Several publishers, including Temple University Press, University of Hawaii Press, Altamira Press, and Stanford University Press, have established special book series on Asian American experiences. All these factors have accelerated publication of many social-science books focusing on contemporary Asian immigrants. The

establishment of two journals specializing in Asian American studies, *Amerasia Journal* in 1971 and the *Journal of Asian American Studies* in 1998, has also facilitated publication of articles on Asian American experiences.

Asian Americans consist of national origin groups with differing population sizes and immigration histories. According to 1990 U.S. Census data, the U.S.-born population accounted for 68% of the Japanese Americans, compared to 36% of Filipino Americans, 31% of Chinese Americans, 27% of Korean Americans, 25% of Indian Americans, and 20% of Vietnamese Americans (Min, 1995b). Most studies of Asian Americans focus on particular Asian ethnic groups and are usually conducted by scholars who are members of the groups being investigated. Because Asian American groups have been studied separately, it is difficult to prepare an overview of the social science research on Asian Americans. This chapter analyzes major perspectives, new directions of inquiry, and popular research topics that exist in a number of social science studies dealing with post-1965 Asian immigrants and their children.

THE CRITIQUE OF THE "MODEL MINORITY" THESIS

Probably the most frequently cited concept in the Asian American social science literature over the past two decades is the "model minority" thesis. It is not a popular thesis Asian American scholars and activists have used to support their arguments, but probably the most unpopular thesis they have criticized. Beginning in the 1960s, the U.S. media described Asian Americans as having achieved high social mobility through cultural mechanisms such as hard work, frugality, family ties, and sacrifice for children's education (Kasindorf, 1982; Peterson, 1966; D. A. Williams, 1984). Several scholars offered similar cultural explanations for the achievements of Chinese and Japanese Americans, focusing on their cultural mechanisms for adaptations and neglecting to examine their problems (Kitano, 1969; Kitano & Sue, 1973; Marden & Meyer, 1973). Many Asian American community leaders might have felt appreciative of the success image, taking it as a positive acceptance of Asian Americans by U.S. society. Yet Asian American scholars, teachers, social workers, and activists have never appreciated the success image. Instead, they have provided harsh criticisms of the so-called model minority thesis, examining its inadequacies and its political basis and negative consequences (Chan, 1991; Cheng & Yang, 1996; Chun, 1980; Crystal, 1989; Divoky, 1988; Espiritu, 1996; Hamamoto, 1992, 1994; Hurh & Kim, 1982, 1989; Kim & Hurh, 1983; Kwong, 1987; Lee, 1996b; Okihiro, 1988; Osajima, 1988; Shim, 2000; Suzuki, 1977; Takagi, 1992). Indeed, the critique of the model minority thesis has had a powerful influence on the Asian American literature over the past 25 years. Not only major social scientists but also historians (Chan, 1991; Takaki, 1989) have attacked the model minority thesis.

The success image of Asian Americans is partly based on the fact that the median family income of Asian Americans is higher than that of White Americans. However, many Asian American social scientists have pointed out the problems of using the median family income as an indicator of the economic conditions of Asian Americans (Cabezas & Kawaguchi, 1988; Cabezas, Shinagawa, & Kawaguchi, 1987; Hurh & Kim, 1982, 1989; Kwong, 1987; Lee, 1989). They have argued that the median family income is not a good measure of the economic success of Asian Americans because they have more workers per family and residentially concentrate in large cities, such as San Francisco, Los Angeles, and New York, with a higher cost of living.

The critics of the model minority thesis have also indicated that basing it on the median or mean family income of Asian Americans distorts their economic condition because of their socioeconomic diversity. Many college-educated Asian immigrants have high earnings from professional and managerial occupations, but many others struggle for economic survival trapped in low-level, service-related jobs. A number of researchers have documented poverty among Asian immigrants to highlight their economic problems (Ching-Louie, 1992; Endo, 1980; Kwong, 1987; Ong, 1984; Toji & Johnson, 1992). They have shown that although many Asian immigrants become poor from joblessness many employed Asian immigrants encounter poverty that is due to their concentration in the secondary labor market or the ethnic market.

The critics of the success image do not consider Asian Americans successful mainly for the reason that Asian immigrants do not get rewards for their educational investments equal to White Americans (Cabezas et al., 1987; Cabezas & Kawaguchi, 1988; Cho, 1993; Hirschman & Wong, 1984; Hurh & Kim, 1989; Tienda & Lii, 1987; Tsukada, 1988; Wong, 1982; Zhou, 1993; Zhou & Kamo, 1994). For example, using 1980 census data Hurh and Kim (1989) compared the earnings of major Asian groups with the White U.S.-born population. Their data analyses revealed that all Asian groups, with the exception of Japanese Americans, earned less than White Americans under equivalent conditions of human capital investment, and that the White-Asian earnings disparity was much greater for Asian immigrants than for native-born Asian Americans. Asian immigrants' earnings were about 75% of native-born White Americans' earnings when education was controlled. On the basis of these results, they concluded that "as long as this inequity exists, the success image of Asian Americans remains largely a myth rather than a reality" (Hurh & Kim, 1989, p. 529).

The great disparity in earnings between White Americans and Asian immigrants with comparable educational levels suggests that many Asian immigrants cannot find occupations commensurate with their educational levels. A number of studies have documented underemployment among Asian immigrants (I. Kim, 1981; Min, 1984; Zhou, 1993). Korean immigrants with a college education often turn to labor-intensive small businesses to avoid low-paying service and blue-collar jobs (Min, 1984). Some studies have indicated that even Asian immigrants who hold professional and government jobs are concentrated in periphery specialty areas or less influential positions (Ishi, 1988; I. Kim, 1981; Shin & Chang, 1988; Taylor & Kim, 1980). Asian Americans are overrepresented in science and engineering in which professional skills are supposed to determine job performance. Yet Tang (1993) has documented that Asian American engineers are disadvantaged compared to White engineers in managerial representation and upward mobility. Several researchers have shown that Asian Americans encounter the glass-ceiling problem in attaining influential executive and managerial positions (Dunleep & Sanders, 1992; Liu-Wu, 1997; Tang, 1993, 1997; U.S. Commission on Civil Rights, 1992).

The mainstream media's stereotype of Asian Americans as successful is partly based on the high academic achievement of Asian American students. Challenging the stereotype, both Asian American educators and researchers have emphasized the diversity in educational achievements among Asian ethnic groups and diversity within each group (Endo, 1980; Hu, 1989; Kao, 1995; S. J. Lee, 1996a, 1996b). Asian Americans surpass White

Americans in the rate of college graduation but have a lower rate of high school graduation. Also, Asian American students include proportionally more overachievers and more underachievers. From this data, Hu suggested that Asian Americans should be referred to as a dual minority rather than a model minority. Some Asian American researchers (Endo, 1980; S. J. Lee, 1996a, 1996b) have admitted that Asian American parents put more emphasis on and invest more in their children's educational achievements than parents in other ethnic groups. But they have pointed out that Asian American parents' emphasis on their children's education reflects their recognition of social barriers rather than their cultural norms.

Asian American critics of the model minority thesis have argued that the success image of Asian Americans is not only invalid but also detrimental to the welfare of Asian Americans (Crystal, 1989; Gould, 1988; Hurh & Kim, 1989; Osajima, 1988; Takaki, 1989). They have pointed out that because of their image as successful and problem-free, Asian Americans have frequently been eliminated from affirmative action and other social service programs designed for disadvantaged minority groups. For example, the poverty rates of Chinese residents in New York Chinatown and Korean residents in Los Angeles Koreatown in 1990 were 25% and 26%, respectively (Ong & Umemoto, 2000). Yet those poor Chinese and Korean residents were not eligible for many welfare programs for which poor African Americans were eligible. The critics have also indicated that the success stories of Asian Americans stimulated anti-Asian sentiment and violence on college campuses and communities (Cho, 1993; Takaki, 1989; Wong-Hall & Hwang, 2001).

Asian American social work and mental health professionals in particular have been concerned about the negative implications of the success image for various social services to Asian Americans (Crystal, 1989; Gould, 1988; B. L. Kim, 1973, 1978; Snowden & Cheung, 1990; Sue & McKinney, 1980). Because of their success image and their low level of dependency on formal social services, policy makers and non-Asian social workers tend to assume that Asian Americans generally do not have serious juvenile, elderly, and other family problems. However, Asian American social workers have argued that Asian Americans' underuse of social services does not imply that they have fewer social and psychological problems than the general population. In their view, Asian Americans' underuse of social services reflects their help-seeking behavior patterns rather than the level of their social and psychological well-being. As Sue and Morishima (1980) indicated, moderately disturbed Asian Americans are reluctant to seek help from mental health services because of their cultural norms emphasizing shame and family integrity. Several studies reveal that Asian immigrants have a higher rate of stress and other mental health problems than White Americans (Guillermo, 1993; Hurh & Kim, 1990a; Kuo, 1984; Loo, Tong, & True, 1989; Ying, 1988).

Finally, Asian American scholars and activists have been critical of the model minority thesis partly because it negatively affects other minority groups as well (Chun, 1980; Crystal, 1989; Hurh & Kim, 1989; S. J. Lee, 1996a, 1996b; Osajima, 1988). By emphasizing the importance of cultural factors for the successful adjustment of Asian Americans, the success image in effect blames other less successful minority groups for their failure. It thus legitimates the supposed openness of American society and leads people to fail to recognize social barriers encountered by other minority groups. As Hurh and Kim (1989) comment:

The dominant group's stereotype of Asian Americans as a model minority also affects negatively other minorities. Since the Asian Americans' "success" may be considered by the dominant group as a proof of openness in the American opportunity structure, there is a constant danger that other less successful minorities could be regarded as "inferior" and/or "lazy." These less achieving minorities could be blamed for their own failure and become victims of scapegoating ("Japanese have made it. Why can't they?"). (p. 530)

ETHNIC SOLIDARITY VERSUS CLASS CONFLICT

Social scientists who did research on the Chinese and Japanese immigrants in the first half of the 20th century emphasized ethnic solidarity or ethnic ties as an important aspect of Chinese and Japanese communities (Light, 1972; Miyamoto, 1939; Montero, 1975). However, since the late 1970s researchers have increasingly focused on class division and conflict in Asian immigrant communities. Both a greater class diversity within each Asian immigrant population and the increasing adoption of the Marxian class analysis by Asian American scholars have led to this shift in research focus.

The Chinese immigrant community is more socioeconomically polarized than any other Asian immigrant community. Even though a higher proportion of Chinese immigrants than White Americans were engaged in professional occupations, a much higher proportion of them were also involved in low-level service occupations (Wong, 1995). As a result, a number of researchers have applied a class analysis to examining Chinese communities. In a 1975 study of class analysis, Light and Wong highlighted the class division and conflicts between Chinese business owners and co-ethnic employees in New York's Chinatown. In his study of the Chinese community in Toronto, Thompson (1979, 1980) also suggested that a modified Marxian class analysis best captures the structure of Chinese communities in North America. In his widely read book, Kwong (1987) highlighted the class division between "Downtown Chinese" and "Uptown Chinese" in the New York Chinese community. He also highlighted the exploitation of Chinese workers by Chinese business owners and of Chinese renters by Chinese landlords in Chinatown.

There are many other studies that have examined the class conflict between Chinese business owners and Chinese employees and the labor movement in Chinatown (Kwong, 1997; Mar, 1984; Ong, 1984; Sanders & Nee, 1987; Zhou & Nordquist, 2000). In their view, business owners in Chinatown—garment subcontractors and owners of Chinese restaurants in particular—survive or achieve economic mobility largely by exploiting Chinese employees. Chinese workers in Chinatown are vulnerable to exploitation partly because they have a severe language barrier and partly because many of them are illegal residents (Kwong, 1997). Sanders and Nee showed that although Chinese business owners in the San Francisco Chinese enclave achieved economic mobility, Chinese employees did not benefit from the enclave economy. This finding sharply conflicts with the enclave economy thesis that emphasizes the economic benefits of the enclave businesses to both owners and employees (Portes & Bach, 1985; Wilson & Portes, 1980; Zhou, 1992).

Since Light and Wong (1975) exposed picketing by Chinese workers against Chinese restaurants in New York's Chinatown, a number of researchers/labor activists have continued to analyze labor movements among Chinese workers in Chinatowns in New York and other cities (Ching-Louie, 1992; Kwong, 1987, 1997; J. Lin, 1998; Lowe, 1992). Chinese immigrants employed in Chinese-owned garment factories and Chinese restaurants have been involved in labor organizing. Not only Chinese but also other Asian immigrant employees are subjected to exploitation, often by co-ethnic garment subcontractors who in turn are subjected to exploitation by White manufacturers. Social scientists (such as Edna Bonacich and Paul Ong, along with Glenn Omatsu, a labor activist) have dedicated their professional energy to exposing the levels of labor exploitation involved in the garment industry (Bonacich & Appelbaum, 2000; Bonacich, Cheng, Chinchilla, Hamilton, & Ong, 1994; Bonacich and Modell, 1980; Ong, Bonacich, & Cheng, 1994). In her editorial forum published in a special issue of *Amerasia Journal* focusing on "Asian American labor," Bonacich (1992) recommended that Asian American studies should adopt more working-class than middle-class issues. The exploitation of Asian immigrant garment workers has a gender implication because the vast majority of them are women (Bonacich & Appelbaum, 2000; Ching-Louie, 1992; Loo & Ong, 1982; Woo, 1989).

THE STRUCTURAL APPROACH TO STUDYING ASIAN IMMIGRANT (AMERICAN) FAMILIES

Traditionally, both the mainstream media and academic researchers took the cultural approach to studying Asian immigrant families in that they interpreted Asian immigrants' family ties, transplanted from their home countries, as contributing to their economic adjustment (Kitano, 1969; Light, 1972). However, since the early 1980s researchers have taken the structural approach, focusing on how Asian immigrants' adaptation to the United States has affected their family system. In her 1983 article, Glenn tried to show how the structural constraints encountered by Chinese Americans in different historical periods strongly influenced the structure of Chinese American families in those periods. A number of researchers have recently used the structural approach to study Asian American families (Chow, 1995; Glenn & Parrenas, 1995; Kibria, 1993; Lim, 1997; Min, 1998, 2001; Wong, 1988).

The increased economic role of Asian immigrant women serves as the major structural factor for changes in Asian immigrant families in general and marital relations in particular. Few Asian immigrants in the United States at the turn of the 20th century were women, with even fewer of those immigrant women participating in the labor market. By contrast, slightly more Asian women immigrated to the United States in the post-1965 era than Asian men (Barringer, Gardner, & Levin, 1993). More significantly, post-1965 Asian immigrant women, like other Third World immigrant women, actively participate in the labor market (Agbayani-Siewert & Revilla, 1995; Barringer et al., 1993; Foner, 1999; Min, 1998). For example, according to 1990 census data, about 73% of Filipino immigrant women and 58% of all Asian immigrant women participated in the labor force, compared to 57% of native-born female adults (U.S. Bureau of the Census, 1993). Many Asian immigrant women immigrated through occupational preferences, often as nurses or as housemaids, and later invited their marital partners from their home countries (I. Kim, 1981; Ong & Azores, 1994; Tyner, 2000). Many other Asian women did not work in their home countries, but they need to work in the United States for economic survival.

The increased economic role of Asian immigrant wives and the concomitant decline in their husbands' economic power and social status have contributed to marital conflicts. In the 1970s, a few researchers described marital conflicts in Vietnamese refugee families created by the change in the traditional gender role orientation (Liu, Lamanna, & Mirata, 1975; Sluzki, 1979). In her book on ethnographic research, Kibria (1993) showed how

Vietnamese men's reduction in the economic role and patriarchal authority, and their wives' concomitant increase in economic role and marital power, contributed to marital and intergenerational conflicts in Vietnamese immigrant families. In the introduction to the book, she stated that "immigrant families must be studied in relation to the external structural conditions encountered by immigrants in the host society" (p. 22). Using a similar ethnographic research method, Min (1998, 2001) showed how the discrepancy between Korean immigrant women's increased economic role and persistency of their husbands' traditional patriarchal ideology caused marital conflicts and tensions.

THE ROLE OF IMMIGRANT CONGREGATIONS IN ASIAN IMMIGRANTS' ADJUSTMENT

Asian Buddhist and Hindu temples, Muslim mosques, and Catholic and Protestant churches have mushroomed over the past 30 years in many American cities, which reflects Asian immigrants' active participation in religious congregations. But the topic of Asian immigrants' religious experiences did not receive much scholarly attention in the 1970s and 1980s. Asian American scholars' bias against religion as the "opiate of the masses" and their postcolonial association of Asian Christianity with Western missionary activities was partly responsible for the paucity of research on the religious experiences of Asian Americans (Min, 2002a; Yoo, 1996). The dominant pattern of immigrant research in the United States focused on immigrants' economic adjustment, neglecting to examine their cultural adjustment. It also contributed to the dearth of research on the religious experiences of Asian immigrants (Ebaugh & Chafetz, 2000; Min, 2002a; S. Warner, 1998).

However, Asian American scholars specializing in Asian immigrants have paid increasing attention to the role of religious institutions in Asian immigrants' adjustment since the late 1980s. The interest in Asian Americans' religious experiences is reflected by publication of a special issue of *Amerasia Journal* in 1996 focusing on the topic. More than a dozen books (Fenton, 1988; Iwamura & Spickard, 2003; A. Kim, 1996; Kwon, Kim, & Warner, 2001; Min & Kim, 2002; Numrich, 1996; R. B. Williams, 1988, 1996; Yang, 1999; Yoo, 1999) and a number of articles and book chapters focusing on Asian American religious experiences have been published (Alumkal, 1999, 2001; Bankston, 1997; Bankston & Zhou, 1995, 1996; Busto, 1996; Chai, 1998, 2001; Chong, 1998; George, 1998; Hurh & Kim, 1990b; J. H. Kim, 1996; Kim & Kim, 2001; Kurien, 1998, 1999, 2001; Min, 1992, 2000; Shin & Park, 1988; Yang, 1998).

Asian immigrants' religious practices are interesting to researchers especially because Asian immigrants have brought with them several non-Christian religions—Buddhism, Hinduism, Islam—as well as Asianized Christian religions. Following the dominant theoretical perspective derived from studies of turn-of-the-century Judeo-Christian immigrant groups (Herberg, 1960; Ostergren, 1981; W. Warner & Srole, 1945), most studies of contemporary Asian immigrants' religions have examined cultural retention/ethnic identity functions of religious congregations (Bankston & Zhou, 1995, 1996; Fenton, 1988; Hurh & Kim, 1990b; Kurien, 1998, 2001; Min, 1992, 2000; R. B. Williams, 1988; Yang, 1999). Asian Buddhists, Hindus, and worshippers of other "Eastern religions" can use their religious practices effectively for preserving their ethnic culture and identity because the religious practices are embedded in their cultural traditions and can be used as ethnic markers in a Christian country. Thus, Kurien (1998) has shown how Asian Indian Hindus use their "religious organizations as means to forge ethnic communities and articulate their ethnic identities as Indian Americans" (p. 59). In his study of a Chinese temple in Los Angeles, I. Lin (1998) also says that the temple "provides the context for overseas Chinese to reinforce and reinvent Chinese identity through religion, ethnicity, nationality, culture, family, and education" (p. 145).

Asian Christian immigrants, too, use their participation in religious congregations as a mechanism for maintaining their cultural traditions and ethnic identity. For example, various studies reveal that Korean immigrants, heavily of Protestant background, try to maintain their Confucian cultural traditions, including more patriarchal customs, through active participation in Korean churches (A. R. Kim, 1996; Kim & Kim, 2001; Min, 1992, 2000). Yang (1999) also indicates that Chinese evangelical Christians find Confucian values compatible with Christian values although they reject Buddhism without reservation (pp. 151–158). From the results of a survey of Vietnamese high school students in New Orleans, Bankston and Zhou (1995) have concluded that "religious participation consistently makes a greater contribution to ethnic identification than any of the family or individual characteristics, except recency of arrival" (p. 530).

Another theme that has derived from studies of turn-of-the-century Judeo-Christian immigrant groups (Doran, 1985; Links, 1985) and has been popularly applied to studies of contemporary Asian immigrant groups (Hurh & Kim, 1990b; I. Lin, 1998; Min, 1992; Yu, 1988; Zhou, Bankston, & Kim, 2002) is the social service function of congregations. Christian churches are found to play the role of the most important social service agencies in Korean immigrant communities (Hurh & Kim, 1990b;

Kim & Kim, 2001; Min, 1992). For example, results of Min's (1992) survey of Korean immigrant churches in New York reveal that they offer multiple social services for their members, including immigration orientation, counseling, educational services, job referral, and monetary aid to unemployed families. Other Asian Protestant and Catholic churches have been found to offer similar services (Yang, 2000; Zhou et al., 2002).

Asian immigrant Buddhist temples are found to provide services, but not to the extent Asian immigrant Christian churches do (Lin, 1998; Yu, 1988; Zhou et al., 2002). But piecemeal information suggests that Hindu temples and mosques mostly remain a place of worship without offering services (Ebaugh & Chafetz, 2000; Min, 2000).

Many other studies have paid special attention to issues related to gender, intergenerational conflict and transmission, and transnational ties (Alumkal, 2001; Chai, 1998, 2001; George, 1998; A. R. Kim, 1996; J. H. Kim, 1996; Kim & Kim, 2001; Kurien, 1999, 2001; Min, 1998; Yang, 1999). In explaining patriarchal customs practiced in Korean immigrant churches, a few scholars have focused on the transplantation of Korean Confucian cultural traditions as the major cause (A. R. Kim, 1996; Min, 1992) while another group of scholars (Alumkal, 1999; J. H. Kim, 1996) has emphasized the nature of the Protestant religion itself. Race or racial formation is an important issue in the religious experiences of Asian Americans. Yet there is only one social science study that has used racial analysis in examining contemporary Asian Americans' religious experiences (Jeung, 2002).

KOREAN-BLACK CONFLICTS

A topic that has been subjected to both high media publicity and scholarly attention with regard to the economic adjustment and intergroup relations of Asian immigrants is Korean-Black conflicts. Korean immigrants' concentration in Black-oriented businesses has led to Korean-Black conflict in the form of boycotts of Korean stores, physical violence against Korean merchants, and destruction of Korean stores during the 1992 Los Angeles riots (C. J. Kim, 2000; K. C. Kim, 1999; Light & Bonacich, 1988; Min, 1996). Korean immigrants' business-related intergroup conflicts have been extensively studied. About 10 books and a number of articles focusing on the topic have been published (Abelmann & Lie, 1995; Asante & Min, 2000; Chang, 1996; Chang & Leong, 1994; Chang & Oh, 1995; Cheng & Espiritu, 1989; Cho, 1993; Jo, 1992; C. J. Kim, 2000; I. S. Kim, 1981; K. C. Kim, 1999; J. Lee, 2000; Light & Bonacich, 1988; Light, Har-Chi, & Kan, 1994; Min, 1990, 1996; Min & Kolodney, 1994; Park, 1995, 1996; Weitzer, 1997; Yoon, 1997; Yu, 1994). All authors

and/or editors of these works, with only a few exceptions, are Korean scholars. Although many Korean social scientists have examined Korean-Black conflicts, few African American scholars have paid attention to it (among the authors and editors or coeditors of the works just cited, Asante is the only African American scholar).

It is interesting to note the differences in explaining Korean-Black conflicts between Korean immigrant scholars on the one hand and "1.5-generation" (those who were born in Korea and who immigrated to the United States at an early age, usually 12 or younger) and second-generation scholars on the other. According to middleman minority theory (Blalock, 1967; Rinder, 1958–59; Turner & Bonacich, 1980), middleman merchants play an economically intermediate role in a racially stratified society, by distributing products made by members of the ruling group to minority customers. Korean immigrant scholars, often using middleman minority theory, explained Korean-Black conflicts as a result of Black residents' scapegoating of the nearest targets in reaction to their poverty and other economic problems (H. C. Kim, 1999; Kim & Kim, 1999; Min, 1990, 1996; Min & Kolodney, 1994). As the title of this author's book suggests, Min (1996) tried to explain the business-related intergroup conflicts of Korean immigrants and their reactive solidarity in New York and Los Angeles using middleman minority theory. In explaining the 1990 boycott of two Korean stores in Brooklyn, H. C. Kim (1999) even charged Sonny Carlson and other Black Nationalist boycott leaders with exploiting the boycott to increase their political power within the Black community.

By contrast, 1.5- and second-generation Korean researchers (Abelmann & Lie, 1995; Cho, 1993) considered Korean-Black conflicts merely as a by-product of the mainstream media's construction to make minority groups fight against each other. As Abelmann and Lie write, "Many Korean Americans dismissed the 'black-Korean conflict' not only as a media fabrication but also as an attempt to engender intra-minority conflict" (p. 153). Rejecting the racial scapegoating argument, C. J. Kim (2000), another second-generation Korean scholar, argued that the boycott leaders considered Korean merchants not as "pawns or proxy targets" but as "frontline representatives of the white power structure" and thus as "legitimate targets of protest" (p. 110).

ETHNIC IDENTITY AMONG SECOND-GENERATION ASIAN AMERICANS

Social scientists have conducted research on the children of post-1965 Asian immigrants since the late 1980s. Interestingly, most studies on second-generation Asian

Americans, largely conducted by 1.5- and second-generation Asian Americans, have focused on issues directly or indirectly related to ethnic identity. Several books (Gibson, 1988; S. J. Lee, 1996a; Min, 2002b; Min & Kim, 1999) and a number of journal articles and book chapters (Alsaybar, 1999; Bacon, 1999; Espiritu, 1994; Hong & Min, 1999; Katrak, 2001; Kibria, 1997, 1999; Min & Kim, 2000; Park, 1999; Rudrappa, 2002; Thai, 1999) that focus on ethnic identity among second-generation Asian Americans have been published. Several of these articles were published in a special issue (number one of 1999) of *Amerasia Journal,* focusing on ethnic identity among second-generation Asian Americans.

Many of the studies just cited are based on personal interviews with and personal narratives by young second-generation Asian Americans (Alsaybar, 1999; Bacon, 1999; Espiritu, 1994; Kibria, 1997, 1999; Min, 2002b; Min & Kim, 1999, 2000; Park, 1999; Thai, 1999). Results of these studies reveal that during their childhood and adolescence many second-generation Asian Americans felt ashamed of their ethnic culture and non-White physical characteristics and "acted White," pretending to be Whites and associating mainly with White students. As one of the Vietnamese American interviewees in Thai's study said: "I thought I was one of the white girls. I tried dying my hair blonde once and I put on makeup to look like one of them" (p. 65). But in young adulthood they grew increasingly conscious of their ethnic culture and non-White racial background and felt increasingly comfortable with both. Their recognition of the fact that as racial minority members they are not fully accepted as American citizens is the crux of ethnic and racial identities among second-generation Asian Americans.

Third- and fourth-generation White Americans have an option to choose their ethnic identity (or not) because they are accepted as full American citizens (Alba, 1990; Waters, 1990). However, an ethnographic study of third- and fourth-generation Japanese and Chinese Americans shows that these multigeneration Asian Americans do not have the same option (Tuan, 1999). The study reveals that although most Japanese and Chinese respondents are thoroughly acculturated to American society, they are forced to accept their ethnic and racial identities by societal expectations.

Many other studies focusing on ethnic identity have taken the postmodernist or postcolonial approach (Bonus, 2000; Katrak, 2001; Revilla, 1998; Root, 1998; Rudrappa, 2002; San Juan, 1994; Shankar & Srikanth, 1998; Strobel, 1998). The authors of these studies are mostly anthropologists and other cultural studies scholars of Filipino or Indian ancestry. Both the Philippines and the Indian subcontinent have a long history of Western colonization. Given the combination of cultural studies with the colonial history of the home countries, it is not surprising that

the scholars of both Filipino and South Asian Americans have often used postcolonial or postmodernist theory.

Although the postcolonial thesis has marked historical studies of Filipino Americans, it has also inevitably influenced the limited social science studies dealing with Filipino Americans (Bonus, 2000; Espiritu, 1994, 1995; Pido, 1986; Root, 1998). As far as the ethnic identity issue is concerned, Maria Root's (1998) edited book *Filipino Americans: Transformation and Identity* deserves special mention. It was a by-product of the centennial anniversary of the 1896 revolution that challenged the 350 years of Spanish rule of the Philippines. In the introduction to the book, the editor comments: "The pages of this book, filled with pride, sorrow, anger, and courage, analyze and interpret the far-reaching impact of the insidious traumas euphemistically called history on contemporary Filipino Americans . . ." (p. xii).

South Asian postmodernist analysts stress not only South Asians' collective memory of colonial India but also three other factors as major sources of Indian ethnic or South Asian pan-ethnic identities. They are the experiences of South Asians with racial discrimination, their transnational ties with homelands, and their perceptions of "authentic Indian culture" (Dave et al., 2000; Katrak, 2001; Radhakrishnan, 1994; Rudrappa, 2002; Shankar & Srikanth, 1998; Shukla, 1999–2000). The last point has significant gender implications. To resist a racial categorization in a racialized society, Indian community leaders, dominated by upper-class professional and religious male leaders, have presented "the figure of the chaste, nurturing, and self-sacrificing Indian woman" as the center of the Indian family values and work ethic (Kurien, 1999, p. 665). However, 1.5- and second-generation South Asian women activists and academicians have contested the presentation of women's subservience and other patriarchal values as the core of the "authentic Indian culture" (Abraham, 1995; Bhattacharjee, 1992, 1997; Katrak, 2001; Lynch, 1994; Maira, 1999–2000; Rudrappa, 2002). In reaction to a "one-sided emphasis" on patriarchal customs and values by South Asian immigrant community leaders, many younger generation South Asian women have turned into feminist activists (Dasgupta, 1998; Das DasGupta & DasGupta, 1996; S. Gupta, 2002; Kukke & Shah, 1999–2000; Shah, 1999–2000; J. Vaid, 1999–2000; U. Vaid, 1999–2000). Many of them have mobilized themselves against family violence in South Asian communities (Bhattacharjee, 1992, 1997; J. Vaid, 1999–2000).

PAN-ASIAN ETHNICITY AMONG YOUNGER-GENERATION ASIAN AMERICANS

A topic closely related to ethnic identity that has gained a great deal of popularity in Asian American studies over the past 10 years is pan-Asian ethnicity or solidarity. Espiritu (1992) defined pan-Asian American ethnicity as "the development of bridging institutions and solidarities among several ethnic and immigrant groups of Asian ancestry" (p. 14). The book that has influenced pan-Asian research probably most significantly is *Racial Formation in the United States: From the 1960s to the 1980s* by Omi and Winant (1986). In the book, they criticized culture-, class-, and nation-based theories of race relations and racial inequality and offered a racial formation theory that "emphasizes the social nature of race, the absence of any racial characteristics, [and] the historical flexibility of racial meanings and categories" (p. 4). Omi and Winant noted that the U.S. government's racial policies, including the Census Bureau's racial classification, in the post–civil rights era led members of various Asian ethnic groups to frame their common (pan-Asian) identity.

In a major work on pan-Asian ethnicity, Espiritu (1992) showed how different Asian groups in Los Angeles and other cities established coalitions to protect their common interests in politics, social services, Asian American studies, and physical security against anti-Asian violence. For example, in Chapter 4 she described how various Asian American groups in Chicago, Los Angeles, and other cities created pan-Asian social service agencies to effectively compete with other ethnoracial minority groups for influence with funding agencies. In *Race and Politics*, Saito (1998) showed how Chinese immigrants and U.S.-born Japanese Americans in the San Gabriel Valley of California made a political coalition to get Japanese or Chinese American candidates elected as city councilmen and councilwomen.

The development of Asian American studies programs, the emergence of many younger-generation Asian Americans in Asian American studies programs, and government policies encouraging identity politics have led to the expansion of the literature emphasizing pan-Asian identity or pan-Asian solidarity (Aguilar-San Juan, 1994; Dave et al., 2000; Espiritu, 1992; Kurashige, 2000; S. J. Lee, 1996a, 1996b; Lopez & Espiritu, 1990; Omi & Winant, 1986; Shinagawa & Pang, 1996; Takagi, 1992, 1994; Vo, 1996; Wei, 1993). The popularity of pan-Asianism in the field of Asian American studies is reflected by the fact that each of the two major journals in Asian American studies devoted a special issue to the topic in 1996 and 2000 (*Amerasia Journal* in 1996, issue two; and *Journal of Asian American Studies* in the June issue of 2000).

The pan-Asian studies cited earlier have focused on the pan-Asian coalitions built at the collective level for common interests. With a few exceptions (Kibria, 1997, 1999; Min & Kim, 2000), they have neglected to examine pan-Asian attachment among members of various Asian ethnic groups at the individual level. Although political identity is central to pan-Asian coalitions, private identity

figures prominently in pan-ethnic attachment at the individual level. Asian Americans with activist orientations usually participate in pan-Asian politics. Pan-Asian politics are most salient on college campuses (Kibria, 1999), but even most second-generation Asian American college students do not take an activist stance and thus are not affiliated with any pan-Asian club (Kibria, 1999).

Because Asian American communities are marked by a great deal of diversity in language, religion, immigration history, and physical characteristics, they have difficulty maintaining pan-ethnic attachment at the individual level in friendship, dating, and intermarriage. However, East Asians—Chinese, Japanese, and Korean Americans—and South Asians—Indians, Pakistani, and Bangladeshi—have significant similarities in culture, physical characteristics, and premigrant historical experiences within each cluster and significant differences between the two clusters. Thus a number of studies have indicated that second-generation East and South Asian Americans maintain a moderate level of pan-ethnic attachment within each cluster but rarely interact with each other in their private domain (Dave et al., 2000; A. Gupta, 1998; Kibria, 1996, 1997; Min & Kim, 1999, 2000; Prashad, 1998; Shankar & Srikanth, 1998).

For example, Kibria's (1997) study reveals that although Chinese and Korean informants adopted their ethnic identity as their primary identity they had a moderate level of pan-Asian identity based on their personal racial history. Significantly, the Chinese and Korean informants did not include all Asian-origin groups in the "Asian" category; they included largely East Asian Americans who they believed shared a common culture and race. Explaining why South Asian students at Brown University left the Asian club, A. Gupta (1998) made a comment on the differences in culture and physical characteristics between East and South Asians: "However, despite these inclusionary efforts, a segment of South Asian American community still feels that the substantial differences (of religion, appearance, and experiences), between South Asian Americans and other Asian Americans . . . are reasons to insist on the organization's speaking as its own advocates . . ." (p. 134). Several other second-generation South Asians have made similar comments to indicate the East and South Asian differences (Dave et. al., 2000; Prashad, 1998).

SOCIOECONOMIC ADJUSTMENTS AMONG YOUNGER-GENERATION ASIAN AMERICANS

As noted earlier, the ethnic and pan-ethnic identities of second-generation Asian Americans have been extensively studied, largely by second-generation Asian American scholars. By contrast, research on their socioeconomic adjustments has been conducted mainly by Asian immigrant and White scholars (Cheng & Yang, 1996; Gibson, 1988; Hurh & Kim, 1989; Jiobu, 1988; Zhou, 1999; Zhou & Bankston, 1998; Zhou & Kamo, 1994). Research on socioeconomic adjustment usually involves quantitative data analyses, often census data. In fact, the most widely used data set to examine the socioeconomic adjustments of minority groups is the 5% Public Use Microdata Sample (PUMS) of the U.S. Census, collected every 10 years. All of the studies cited here, with the exception of Gibson (1988) and Zhou and Bankston (1998), are quantitative studies based on 1980/1990 PUMS data and conducted by Asian immigrant or non-Asian scholars. The major reason for second-generation Asian American scholars' noninvolvement in research on Asian Americans' socioeconomic adjustment is that few of them are interested in or equipped with the quantitative research skills needed for research on social class.

Analyses of 1980 and 1990 PUMS data reveal that overall U.S.-born Asian Americans had a higher college completion rate than Asian immigrants, who were also far ahead of White Americans (the reference group) in the college completion rate (Agbayani-Siewert & Revilla, 1995; Barringer et al., 1993; Cheng & Yang, 1996). Major survey studies of high school students have consistently shown that Asian American students as a group outperform White students in grade point average and in achievement scores and on SAT tests in mathematics (Hacker, 1995; Kao, 1995; Rumbaut, 1995). But ethnic differences within the U.S.-born Asian American population are significant. U.S.-born Chinese and Vietnamese Americans achieved substantially higher levels of intergenerational educational mobility than other Asian groups. At the other extreme, U.S.-born Filipinos had a substantially lower college completion rate than Filipino immigrants. In school performance, too, Filipino students had lower levels of achievement than other Asian groups, although Filipino immigrants achieved the highest level of education second to Indian immigrants.

Most U.S.-born Asian American young adults, with the exception of the Japanese group, are children of Asian immigrants who came to the United States in the 1960s and the early 1970s. They do very well in education partly because their parents, the Asian immigrant cohorts in the 1960s and 1970s, have exceptionally high educational levels and professional backgrounds (Barringer et al., 1993). The Asian immigrants who came to the United States in the 1980s and the 1990s have lower educational levels, and thus their children are unlikely to achieve the high educational levels comparable to young second-generation Asian Americans today. However, research shows that the children of immigrants, regardless of their ethnic background and generation status, perform better in school and have higher educational aspirations than the

children of U.S.-born Americans (Kao, 1995; Kao & Tienda, 1995). This suggests that the children of post-1965 Asian immigrants, including the U.S.-born second generation, outperform White students because of their parents' higher social class backgrounds and higher educational aspirations than those of White parents.

It is instructive to note the conclusion from Kao's (1995) study, that the "immigrant status of youth and parents accounts for much more of the variation in educational outcomes among Asian students than other minority or white students" (p. 16). The immigrant status of parents has significant effects on school performance and educational aspiration, especially among Asian American students, because Asian parents instill in their children values emphasizing the importance of hard work, education, and respect for adults. Gibson's (1988) ethnographic study shows that Punjabi Sikh parents' pressure on children to stick to these traditional values and to avoid excessive Americanization helped their children succeed in school. A study of Vietnamese high school students in New Orleans (Zhou & Bankston, 1998) also demonstrates the positive effects of traditional values imbedded in immigrant families and the immigrant community on children's academic achievements. The critics of the model minority thesis would underestimate these findings, which show the importance of Asian immigrants' traditional values for their children's achievement. The significance of immigrant values for students' academic achievements implies that the children of contemporary second-generation Asian Americans may not do as well as their parents. Indeed, Kao's data show that third- or higher-generation Asian American students do not perform better than White students.

Only a few studies have examined second-generation Asian Americans' occupational and economic adjustments using independent survey data (D. Y. Kim, 2000; Kasinitz, Mollenkoph, & Waters, 2002). This can be explained by the fact that sampling second-generation households in any city is extremely difficult and costly for any Asian group because of their relatively small number. However, studies based on the PUMS data of the 1980 and 1990 U.S. Census have provided data on Asian Americans' socioeconomic adjustments by nativity status (Barringer et al., 1993; Hurh & Kim, 1989; Light & Roach, 1996; Min, 1995a; Zhou & Kamo, 1994). Since for all Asian groups, with the exception of Japanese Americans, the vast majority of U.S.-born adults belong to the second generation, these studies based on census data shed light on second-generation Asian Americans' occupational and economic adjustments.

Because of their language problems and other disadvantages for employment in the general labor market, many Asian immigrants have started their own businesses (Gold, 1994; Kim, Hurh, & Fernandez, 1989; Min, 1984).

Thus, several Asian immigrant groups, including Koreans, Taiwanese, and Indians, have high self-employment rates, much higher than the national average (Light & Roach, 1996; Yoon, 1996). Census and independent survey data, however, suggest that second-generation Asian Americans avoid the tendency of Asian immigrants to create their jobs through self-employment. For example, an analysis of the PUMS of the 1990 U.S. Census shows that U.S.-born Chinese and Koreans had lower self-employment rates than White Americans while the respective immigrant groups had much higher self-employment rates than Whites (Light & Roach, 1996; Min, 1996). This finding is not surprising considering that second-generation Asian American professionals do not face the language barrier that pushes many Asian professional immigrants to turn to small business.

Cheng and Yang (1996) analyzed the 1970, 1980, and 1990 PUMS data to examine both the levels of intergenerational mobility and improvement over time in occupational status among Asian Americans in Los Angeles. Their analyses reveal that for four of the six major Asian groups in Los Angeles the U.S.-born had a higher level of representation in three high-skill occupations (professional, managerial, and technical) than the foreign-born. Japanese and Chinese Americans in particular achieved impressively high levels of intergenerational mobility in terms of representation in high-skill occupations (26% and 11% increases, respectively). Other studies based on census aggregate data consistently indicate that for all Asian groups but Filipino Americans the U.S.-born outperform the foreign-born in representation in professional and managerial occupations (Barringer et al., 1993; Min, 1995a).

As already indicated with regard to the model minority thesis, because of their language barrier and other disadvantages Asian immigrants get much lower returns on their educational and other human capital investments than White Americans. An important question, then, is whether U.S.-born Asian Americans get earnings for their human capital investments comparable to White Americans. A number of studies based on census data have consistently shown that U.S.-born Asian Americans did much better than Asian immigrants in translating their human capital investments into earnings, but that they still had a slight disadvantage compared to White Americans (Cheng & Yang, 1996; Hirschman & Wong, 1981, 1984; Hurh & Kim, 1989; Wong, 1982; Zhou & Kamo, 1994). These studies have also revealed that U.S.-born Asian American women were much closer to their White counterparts than men in returns for their human capital investments. Even the 1990 5% PUMS data included too small a number of U.S.-born Korean, Indian, and Vietnamese adults. Thus, only Japanese, Chinese and Filipinos were examined in the census-based studies just

mentioned. The 2000 census data are likely to have enough U.S.-born samples for all major Asian groups to permit meaningful analyses. Accordingly, future studies based on the 2000 census data will shed light on the effects of ethnicity, as well as gender and nativity, on returns for human capital investments among Asian Americans.

CONCLUSION

Active research on post-1965 Asian immigrants and their children by sociologists and other social scientists over the past 30 years has produced a long list of monographs, edited books, journal articles, and book chapters. It is impossible to summarize the rich social science literature on Asian American experiences in one chapter. Thus, the chapter does not pretend to have provided a comprehensive summary of social science studies focusing on Asian Americans. Rather, it has tried to introduce the reader to dominant themes, major directions of inquiry, and popular topics in the social science literature on Asian Americans during the past 30 years.

A critique of the model minority thesis and pan-Asian solidarity as two dominant themes in Asian American studies since the early 1980s has been presented, along with analysis of the shifts in emphasis from ethnic solidarity to class conflicts and from the cultural to the structural approach to studying Asian American families as two new directions of inquiry that have become popular since the early 1980s. The two dominant themes and the two new directions of social science inquiry have been strongly influenced by two interrelated forces, both of which emerged in the early 1970s. The first is the general trend in U.S. social sciences to reject the assimilation paradigm and cultural arguments and to emphasize White racism and other structural barriers in explaining the adjustments of minority groups.

The other major force is "academic activism," which has strongly affected Asian American studies. Academic activism has touched all ethnic studies and women's studies fields. But it seems to have affected Asian American studies more strongly, at least in the past two decades, because many Asian American studies programs have been established during this period through the active struggles and claims making of Asian American students and faculty members. Asian American faculty members and students with activist orientations have played an important role in establishing Asian American studies programs. Once their activism has helped to establish Asian American studies programs, it further affects their teaching, curriculum, and research on Asian Americans. Not surprisingly, Asian American professors and researchers with activist orientations have emphasized social barriers and problems encountered by Asian Americans and the need for pan-Asian solidarity to protect a common interest for all Asian groups. Many social scientists of Asian ancestry not affiliated with Asian American studies programs may not feel comfortable with activist research. But these social scientists are careful not to focus on Asian Americans' achievement and not to provide cultural explanations for their achievement because the faculty members and students in Asian American studies programs compose the main readers of their academic productions.

It is also interesting to note interethnic differences in social science research on Asian immigrants. There are enough social science data and information about Chinese and Korean Americans mainly because many Chinese and Korean social scientists have studied their own groups. Vietnamese and other Southeast Asian refugees have received a great deal of scholarly attention, too, but not because there are many Southeast Asian social scientists who have conducted research on their own groups. White American and Latino scholars have largely studied the refugee groups because more research grants have been available for research on refugees.

By contrast, there is a paucity of social science literature on Filipino, Asian Indian, and Japanese Americans. But these three groups have been understudied for different reasons. There is not much social science information about Filipino Americans mainly because few Filipino American social scientists have studied their own group. There are few social science studies on Japanese Americans mainly because not many Japanese have immigrated to the United States in the post-1965 era. Since third and higher generations compose the majority of Japanese Americans, limited recent social science studies of Japanese Americans have focused on intergenerational changes, using more historical data than sociological (Bonacich & Modell, 1980; Fugita & O'Brien, 1991; Glenn, 1986; Kessler, 1993). There are no hard social science data on Indian and other South Asian immigrants either, mainly because there are few sociologists of South Asian ancestry. As has been noted, many South Asian anthropologists and literary scholars have studied the ethnic and pan-ethnic identities of South Asians. They have usually taken the postmodernist approach, often using discursive analysis.

References

Abelmann, N., & Lie, J. (1995). *Blue dream: Korean Americans and the Los Angeles riots.* Cambridge, MA: Harvard University Press.

Abraham, M. (1995). Marital violence: South Asian women's organizations in the United States. *Gender and Society, 9,* 450–468.

Agbayani-Siewert, P., & Revilla, L. (1995). Filipino Americans. In P. G. Min (Ed.), *Asian Americans: Contemporary trends and issues* (pp. 134–168). Thousand Oaks, CA: Sage.

Aguilar-San Juan, K. (Ed.). (1994). *The state of Asian America: Activism and resistance in the 1990s.* Boston: South End Press.

Alba, D. R. (1990). *Ethnic identity: Transformation of White America.* New Haven, CT: Yale University Press.

Alsaybar, B. D. (1999). Deconstructing deviance: Filipino American youth gangs, "party culture," and ethnic identity in Los Angeles. *Amerasia Journal, 25*(1), 117–138.

Alumkal, A. (1999). Preserving patriarchy: Assimilation, gender norms, and second-generation Korean American evangelicals. *Qualitative Sociology, 22,* 127–140.

Alumkal, A. (2001). Being Korean, being Christian: Particularism and universalism in a second-generation congregation. In H. Y. Kwon, K. C. Kim, & S. Warner (Eds.), *Korean Americans and their religion* (pp. 157–180). University Park: Pennsylvania State University Press.

Asante, M. K., & Min, E. J. (Eds.). (2000). *Socio-cultural conflict between African Americans and Korean Americans.* Lanham, MD: University Press of America.

Bacon, J. (1999). Constructing collective ethnic identities: The case of second-generation Asian Indians. *Qualitative Sociology, 22,* 141–159.

Bankston, C., III. (1997). Bayo Rotus: Theravada Buddhism in southwestern Louisiana. *Sociological Spectrum, 38,* 473–489.

Bankston, C., III, & Zhou, M. (1995). Religious participation, ethnic identification, and adaptation of Vietnamese adolescents in an immigrant community. *Sociological Quarterly, 36,* 523–534.

Bankston, C., III, & Zhou, M. (1996). The ethnic church, ethnic identification, and the social adjustment of Vietnamese adolescents. *Review of Religious Research, 38,* 18–37.

Barringer, H., Gardner, R. W., & Levin, M. J. (1993). *Asians and Pacific Islanders in the United States.* New York: Russell Sage Foundation.

Bhattacharjee, A. (1992). The Habit of ex-nomination: Nation, women, and the Indian women bourgeoisie. *Public Culture, 5*(1), 19–44.

Bhattacharjee, A. (1997). A slippery path: Organizing resistance to violence against women. In S. Shah (Ed.), *Dragon ladies: Asian American feminists breathe fire* (pp. 29–45). Boston: South End Press.

Blalock, H. (1967). *Toward a theory of minority group relations.* New York: Wiley.

Bonacich, E. (1992). Reflections on Asian American labor. *Amerasia Journal, 18*(1), xxi–xxvii.

Bonacich, E., & Appelbaum, R. P. (2000). *Behind the label: Inequality in the Los Angeles apparel industry.* Berkeley: University of California Press.

Bonacich, E., Cheng, L., Chinchilla, N., Hamilton, N., & Ong, P. (Eds.). (1994). *Global production: The apparel industry in the Pacific Rim.* Philadelphia: Temple University Press.

Bonacich, E., & Modell, J. (1980). *The economic basis of ethnic solidarity: Small business in the Japanese American community.* Berkeley: University of California Press.

Bonus, R. (2000). *Locating Filipino Americans: Ethnicity & the cultural politics of space.* Philadelphia: Temple University Press.

Busto, B. (1996). The Gospel according to model minority: Hazarding an interpretation of Asian American evangelical college students. *Amerasia Journal, 22*, 133–248.

Cabezas, A., & Kawaguchi, G. (1988). Empirical evidence for continuing Asian American income inequality: The human capital model and the labor market segmentation. In Y. G. Okihiro, S. Hune, A. A. Hansen, & J. M. Liu (Eds.), *Reflections on Shattered windows: Promises and prospects for Asian American studies* (pp. 144–164). Pullman: Washington State University Press.

Cabezas, A., Shinagawa, L., & Kawaguchi, G. (1987). New inquiries into the socio-economic status of Filipino Americans in California. *Amerasia Journal, 13*, 1–22.

Chai, K. (1998). Competing for the second generation: English-language ministry at a Korean Protestant church. In S. Warner & J. Wittner (Eds.), *Gatherings in diaspora* (pp. 295–332). Philadelphia: Temple University Press.

Chai, K. (2001). Intra-ethnic religious diversity: Korean Buddhists and Protestants in Greater Boston. In H. Y. Kwon, K. C. Kim, & S. Warner (Eds.), *Korean Americans and their religions* (pp. 273–294). University Park: Pennsylvania State University Press.

Chan, S. (1991). *Asian Americans: An interpretive history.* Boston: Twayne.

Chang, E. (1996). African American boycotts of Korean-owned stores in New York and Los Angeles. In P. R. Brass (Ed.), *Riots and pogroms* (pp. 235–252). New York: New York University Press.

Chang, E., & Leong, R. (Eds.). (1994). *Struggles toward multiethnic community: Asian, American, African American and Latino perspectives.* Seattle: University of Washington Press.

Chang, E., & Oh, A. E. (1995). Korean American dilemma: Violence, vengeance, vision. In D. A. Harris (Ed.), *Multiculturalism from the margins: Non-dominant voices on difference and diversity* (pp. 129–138). Westport, CT: Bergin & Garvey.

Cheng, L., & Espiritu, Y. L. (1989). Korean businesses in Black and Hispanic neighborhoods. *Sociological Perspectives, 32*, 521–534.

Cheng, L., & Yang, P. Q. (1996). Asians: The "model minority" deconstructed. In R. Waldinger and M. Bozorgmehr (Eds.), *Ethnic Los Angeles* (pp. 305–344). New York: Russell Sage Foundation.

Ching-Louie, M. (1992). Immigrant Asian women in Bay Area garment sweatshops. *Amerasia Journal, 18*(1), 1–26.

Cho, S. M. (1993). Korean Americans vs. African Americans: Conflict and construction. In R. Gooding-Williams (Ed.), *Reading Rodney King/Reading urban uprising* (pp. 196–211). New York: Routledge.

Chong, K. (1998). What it means to be Christians: The role of religion in the construction of ethnic identity and boundary among Korean Americans. *Sociology of Religion, 59*, 259–286.

Chow, E. N. (1995). Family, economy, and the state: A legacy of struggle for Chinese American women. In S. Pedraza and R. Rumbaut (Eds.), *Origins and destinies: Immigration, race, and ethnicity* (pp. 110–124). Belmont, CA: Wadsworth.

Chun, K. T. (1980). The myth of Asian American success and its educational ramifications. *ICRD Bulletin, 15*, 1–12.

Crystal, D. (1989). Asian Americans and the myth of the model minority. *Social Casework, 70*, 405–413.

DasGupta, S. (Ed.). (1998). *A patchwork shawl: Chronicles of South Asian women in America.* New Brunswick, NJ: Rutgers University Press.

DasGupta, S., & DasGupta, S. (1996). Women in exile: Gender relations in the Asian Indian community. In S. Maira & R. Srikanth (Eds.), *Contours of the heart: South Asians map North America* (pp. 381–400). New York: Asian American Writers Workshop.

Dave, S., Dhingra, P., Maira, S., Mazumdar, P., Shankar, L., Singh, J., & Srikanth, R. (2000). De-privileging positions: Indian Americans, South Asian Americans, and politics of Asian American Studies. *Journal of Asian American Studies, 3*(1), 67–100.

Divoky, D. (1988). The model minority goes to school. *Phi Delta Kappan, 70*, 219–222.

Doran, J. (1985). *The American Catholic experience: A history from colonial times to the present.* New York: Doubleday.

Dunleep, H. O., & Sanders, S. (1992). Discrimination at the top: American-born Asian and White men. *Industrial Relations, 31*, 416–432.

Ebaugh, H. R., & Chafetz, J. S. (2000). (Eds.). *Religion and the new immigrants: Continuities and adaptations in immigrant congregations.* Walnut Creek, CA: Altamira Press.

Endo, R. (1980). Asian Americans and higher education. *Phylon, 40*, 367–379.

Espiritu, Y. L. (1992). *Asian American panethnicity: Bridging institutions and identities.* Philadelphia: Temple University Press.

Espiritu, Y. L. (1994). The intersection of race, ethnicity, and class: The multiple identities of second-generation Filipinos. *Identities, 1*, 249–273.

Espiritu, Y. L. (1995). *Filipino American lives.* Philadelphia: Temple University Press.

Espiritu, Y. L. (1996). *Asian American women and men: Labor, law, and love.* Thousand Oaks, CA: Sage.

Fenton, J. (1988). *Transplanting religious traditions: Asian Indians in America.* New York: Praeger.

Foner, N. (1999). Immigrant women and work in New York City, then and now. *Journal of American Ethnic History, 18*, 95–113.

Fugita, S. S., & O'Brien, D. J. (1991). *Japanese American ethnicity: The persistence of community.* Seattle: University of Washington Press.

George, S. (1998). Caroling with the Keralites: The negotiation of gendered space in an Indian immigrant church. In S. Warner & J. Wittner (Eds.), *Gatherings in Diaspora* (pp. 265–294). Philadelphia: Temple University Press.

Gibson, M. A. (1988). *Accommodation without assimilation: Sikh immigrants in an American high school.* Ithaca, NY: Cornell University Press.

Glenn, E. N. (1983). Split household, small producer, dual wage earner: An analysis of Chinese-American family strategies. *Journal of Marriage and the Family, 45*, 35–45.

Glenn, E. N. (1986). *Issei, nissei, warbride: Three generations of Japanese American women in domestic service.* Philadelphia: Temple University Press.

Glenn, E. N., & Parreñas, R. S. (1995). The other issei: Japanese immigrant women in the pre–World War II period. In S. Pedraza and R. Rumbaut (Eds.), *Origins and Destinies: Immigration, Race, and Ethnicity* (pp. 125–140). Belmont, CA: Wadsworth.

Gold, S. (1994). Chinese-Vietnamese entrepreneurs in California. In P. Ong, E. Bonacich, & L. Cheng (Eds.), *The New Asian Immigration in Los Angeles and Global Restructuring* (pp. 196–226). Philadelphia: Temple University Press.

Gould, K. H. (1988). Asian and Pacific Islanders: Myth and reality. *National Association of Social Workers, 37*, 142–147.

Guillermo, T. (1993). Health care needs and service delivery for Asian and Pacific Islander Americans. In LEAP Asian Pacific American Public Policy Institute & UCLA Asian American Studies Center (Eds.), *The State of Asian Pacific America: Policy Issues to the Year 2020* (pp. 61–78). Los Angeles: Editors.

Gupta, A. (1998). College activism and its impact on Asian American identity formation. In L. D. Shankar & R. Srikanth (Eds.), *A Part, Yet Apart: South Asia in Asian America* (pp. 127–145). Philadelphia: Temple University Press.

Gupta, S. (Ed.). (2002). *South Asian women in the Diaspora.* Thousand Oaks, CA: Sage.

Hacker, A. (1995). *Two nations: Black and White, separate, hostile, unequal* (2nd ed.). New York: Ballantine Books.

Hamamoto, D. Y. (1992). Kindred spirits: The contemporary Asian American family on television. *Amerasia Journal, 18*(2), 35–53.

Hamamoto, D. Y. (1994). *Monitored peril: Asian Americans and the politics of representation.* Minneapolis: University of Minnesota Press.

Herberg, W. (1960). *Protestant, Catholic, and Jew: An essay in American religious sociology.* Garden City, NJ: Doubleday.

Hirschman, C., & Wong, M. G. (1981). Trends in socioeconomic achievement among immigrant and native-born Asian-Americans, 1960–1976. *Sociological Quarterly, 22,* 495–513.

Hirschman, C., & Wong, M. G. (1984). Socioeconomic gains of Asian Americans, Blacks and Hispanics: 1960–1976. *American Journal of Sociology, 90,* 584–607.

Hong, J., & Min, P. G. (1999). Ethnic attachment among second-generation Korean adolescents. *Amerasia Journal, 15*(1), 165–180.

Hu, A. (1989). Asian Americans: Model or double minority? *Amerasia Journal, 15*(1), 243–257.

Hurh, W. M., & Kim, K. C. (1982). Race relations paradigm and Korean-American research: A sociology of knowledge perspective. In E.-Y. Yu, E. Phillips, & E. S. Yang (Eds.), *Koreans in Los Angeles* (pp. 219–246). Los Angeles: California State University, Center for Korean-American and Korean Studies.

Hurh, W. M., & Kim, K. C. (1989). The "Success" image of Asian Americans: Its validity and its practical implications. *Ethnic and Racial Studies, 12,* 512–538.

Hurh, W. M., & Kim, K. C. (1990a). Correlates of Korean immigrants' mental health. *Journal of Nervous and Mental Disease, 178,* 703–711.

Hurh, W. M., & Kim, K. C. (1990b). Religious participation of Korean immigrants in the United States. *Journal of the Scientific Study of Religion, 29,* 19–34.

Ishi, T. (1988). International linkage and national class conflict: The migration of Korean nurses in the United States. *Amerasia Journal, 14*(1), 23–50.

Iwamura, J. N., & Spickard, P. (Eds.). (2003). *Revealing the sacred in Asian and Pacific America.* New York: Routledge.

Jeung, R. (2002). Asian American pan-ethnic formation and congregational culture. In P. G. Min & J. H. Kim (Eds.), *Religions in Asian America* (pp. 215–244). Walnut Creek, CA: Altamira Press.

Jiobu, R. M. (1988). *Ethnicity and assimilation: Blacks, Chinese, Filipinos, Japanese, Koreans, Mexicans, Vietnamese, and Whites.* Albany: State University of New York Press.

Jo, M. H. (1992). Korean merchants in the Black community: Prejudice among the victims of prejudice. *Ethnic and Racial Studies, 15,* 395–411.

Kao, G. (1995). Asian Americans as model minorities: A look at their academic performance. *American Journal of Education, 103*(2), 121–159.

Kao, G., & Tienda, M. (1995). Optimism and achievement: The educational performance of immigrant youth. *Social Science Quarterly, 76*(1), 1–19.

Kasindorf, M. (1982, December 6). Asian-Americans: A model minority. *Newsweek,* 40–51.

Kasinitz, P., Mollenkoph, J., & Waters, M. (2002). Becoming American/becoming New Yorkers: Immigrant incorporation in a majority/minority city. *International Migration Review, 36*(4), 1020–1036.

Katrak, K. H. (2001). Body boundarylands: Locating South Asian ethnicity in performance and daily life. *Amerasia Journal, 27*(1), 2–33.

Kessler, R. (1993). *Three generations in the life of a Japanese American family: Stubborn twig.* New York: Penguin Books.

Kibria, N. (1993). *Family tightrope: The changing lives of Vietnamese Americans.* Princeton: Princeton University Press.

Kibria, N. (1996). Not Asian, Black or White?: Reflections on South Asian racial identity. *Amerasia Journal, 22*(2), 77–86.

Kibria, N. (1997). The construction of "Asian American": Reflections on intermarriage and ethnic identity among second-generation Chinese and Korean Americans. *Ethnic and Racial Studies, 20,* 77–86.

Kibria, N. (1999). College and the notions of "Asian American": Second-generation Chinese and Korean Americans negotiate race and identity. *Amerasia Journal, 25*(1), 29–52.

Kim, A. R. (1996). *Women struggling for a new life: The role of religion in the cultural passage from Korea to America.* Albany: State University of New York Press.

Kim, B. L. (1973). Asian Americans: No model minority. *Social Work, 18*(1), 44–53.

Kim, B. L. (1978). *The Asian Americans, changing patterns, changing needs.* Montclair, NJ: Association of Korean Christian Scholars in North America.

Kim, C. J. (2000). *Bitter fruits: The politics of Black-Korean conflict in New York City.* New Haven, CT: Yale University Press.

Kim, D. Y. (2000). *Immigrant entrepreneurship and intergenerational mobility among second-generation Korean Americans in New York.* Unpublished doctoral dissertation, Graduate Center, City University of New York.

Kim, H. C. (1999). The dynamics of Black-Korean conflict: A Korean-American perspective. In K. C. Kim (Ed.), *Koreans in the hood: Conflict with African Americans* (pp. 91–112). Baltimore: Johns Hopkins University Press.

Kim, I. S. (1981). *New urban immigrants: The Korean community in New York.* Princeton, NJ: Princeton University Press.

Kim, J. H. (1996). The labor of compassion: Voices of "churched" Korean American women. *Amerasia Journal, 22,* 93–105.

Kim, K. C. (Ed.). (1999). *Koreans in the hood: Conflict with African Americans.* Baltimore, MD: Johns Hopkins University Press.

Kim, K. C., & Hurh, W. M. (1983). Korean Americans and the "success" image: A critique. *Amerasia Journal, 10*(2), 3–22.

Kim, K. C., Hurh, W. M., & Fernandez, M. (1989). Intra-group differences in business participation: A comparative analysis of three Asian immigrant groups. *International Migration Review, 23*(1), 73–95.

Kim, K. C., & Kim, S. (1999). The multiracial nature of Los Angeles unrest in 1992. In K. C. Kim (Ed.), *Koreans in the Hood: Conflict with African Americans* (pp. 17–38). Baltimore, MD: Johns Hopkins University Press.

Kim, K. C., & Kim, S. (2001). The ethnic role of Korean immigrant churches in the U.S. In H. Y. Kwon, K. C. Kim, & S. Warner (Eds.), *Korean Americans and their religions* (pp. 71–94). University Park: Pennsylvania State University Press.

Kitano, H.H.L. (1969). Japanese Americans: The evolution of a sub-culture. Englewood Cliffs, NJ: Prentice Hall.

Kitano, H.H.L., & Sue, S. (1973). The model minorities. *Journal of Social Issues, 29*(1), 1–9.

Kukke, S., & Shah, S. (1999–2000). Reflections on queer South Asian progressive activism in the U.S. *Amerasia Journal, 25*(3), 129–137.

Kuo, W. H. (1984). Prevalence of depression among Asian Americans. *Journal of Nervous and Mental Disease, 172,* 449–457.

Kurashige, S. (2000). Pan-ethnicity and community organizing: Asian American United Campaign Against Anti-Asian Violence. *Journal of Asian American Studies, 3,* 163–190.

Kurien, P. (1998). Becoming American by becoming Hindu: Indian Americans take their place at the multicultural table. In S. Warner & J. Wittner (Eds.), *Gatherings in diaspora* (pp. 37–70). Philadelphia: Temple University Press.

Kurien, P. (1999). Gendered ethnicity: Creating a Hindu Indian identity in the United States. *American Behavioral Scientist, 42,* 648–670.

Kurien, P. (2001). Religion, ethnicity and politics: Hindu and Muslim Indian immigrants in the United States. *Ethnic and Racial Studies, 24,* 263–293.

Kwon, H. Y., Kim, K. C., & Warner, S. (Eds.). (2001). *Korean Americans and their religions: Pilgrims and missionaries from a different shore.* University Park: Pennsylvania State University.

Kwong, P. (1987). *The new Chinatown.* New York: Noonsday.

Kwong, P. (1997). *Forbidden workers: Illegal Chinese immigrants and American labor.* New York: New Press.

Lee, J. (2000). Striving for the American dream: Struggle, success, and intergroup conflict among Korean immigrant entrepreneurs. In M. Zhou & J. V. Gatewood (Eds.), *Contemporary Asian America: A multidisciplinary reader* (pp. 278–294). New York: New York University Press.

Lee, S. (1989). Asian immigration and American race relations: From exclusion to acceptance. *Ethnic and Racial Studies, 12,* 368–390.

Lee, S. J. (1996a). Perceptions of panethnicity among Asian American high school students. *Amerasia Journal, 22*(2), 109–126.

Lee, S. J. (1996b). *Unraveling the "model minority" stereotype: Listening to Asian American youth.* New York: Teachers College Press.

Light, I. (1972). *Ethnic enterprise in North America: Business and welfare among Chinese, Japanese, and Blacks.* Berkeley: University of California Press.

Light, I., & Bonacich, E. (1988). *Immigrant entrepreneurs: Koreans in Los Angeles.* Berkeley: University of California Press.

Light, I., Har-Chi, H., & Kan, K. (1994). Black/Korean conflict in Los Angeles. In S. Duan (Ed.), *Managing divided cities.* Keele, UK: University of Keele Press.

Light, I., & Roach, E. (1996). Self-employment: Mobility ladder or economic lifeboat? In R. Waldinger & M. Bozorgmehr (Eds.), *Ethnic Los Angeles* (pp. 193–214). New York: Russell Sage Foundation.

Light, I., & Wong, C. C. (1975). Protest or work: Dilemmas of the tourist industry in American Chinatown. *American Journal of Sociology, 80,* 1342–1368.

Lim, I. S. (1997). Korean immigrant women's challenge to gender inequality at home: The interplay of economic resources, gender and family. *Gender and Society, 11,* 31–51.

Lin, I. (1998). Journey to the Far West: Chinese Buddhism in America. In D. Yoo (Ed.), *New Spiritual Homes: Religions and Asian Americans* (pp. 134–166). Honolulu: University of Hawaii Press.

Lin, J. (1998). *Reconstructing Chinatown: Ethnic enclave, global change.* Minneapolis: University of Minnesota Press.

Links, R. M. (1985). *American Catholicism and European immigrants.* Staten Island, NY: Center for Migration Studies.

Liu, W. T., Lamanna, M., & Mirata, A. (1975). *Transition nowhere: Vietnamese refugees in America.* Nashville, TN: Charter House.

Liu-Wu, D. T. (1997). *Asian Pacific Americans in the workplace.* Walnut Creek, CA: Altamira Press.

Loo, C., & Ong, P. (1982). Slaying demons with a sewing needle: Feminist issues for Chinatown's women. *Berkeley Journal of Sociology, 27,* 77–88.

Loo, C., Tong, B., & True, R. (1989). A bitter bean: Mental health status and attitudes in Chinatown. *Journal of Community Psychology, 17,* 183–226.

Lopez, D., & Espiritu, Y. (1990). Panethnicity in the United States: A theoretical framework. *Ethnic and Racial Studies, 13,* 198–224.

Lowe, L. (1992). Paving the way: Chinese immigrant workers and community-based labor organizing in Boston. *Amerasia Journal, 18*(1), 39–48.

Lynch, C. (1994). Nation, women, and the Indian bourgeoisie: An alternative formulation. *Public Culture, 6*(2), 425–437.

Maira, S. (1999–2000). Ideologies of authenticity: Youth, politics, and Diaspora. *Amerasia Journal, 25*(3), 139–149.

Mar, D. (1984). Chinese immigrant women and the ethnic labor market. *Critical Perspectives of Third World America, 2,* 62–74.

Marden, C. F., & Meyer, G. (1973). *Minorities in American society.* New York: Van Nostrand.

Min, P. G. (1984). From White-color occupations to small business: Korean immigrants' occupational adjustment. *Sociological Quarterly, 25,* 333–352.

Min, P. G. (1990). Problems of Korean immigrant entrepreneurs. *International Migration Review, 24,* 436–455.

Min, P. G. (1992). The structure and social functions of Korean immigrant churches in the United States. *International Migration Review, 26,* 1370–1394.

Min, P. G. (Ed.). (1995a). *Asian Americans: Contemporary trends and issues.* Thousand Oaks, CA: Sage.

Min, P. G. (1995b). An overview of Asian Americans. In P. G. Min (Ed.), *Asian Americans: Contemporary trends and issues* (pp. 38–57). Walnut Creek, CA: Sage.

Min, P. G. (1996). *Caught in the middle: Korean communities in New York and Los Angeles.* Berkeley: University of California Press.

Min, P. G. (1998). *Changes and conflicts: Korean immigrant families in New York.* Needham Heights, MA: Allyn & Bacon.

Min, P. G. (1999). A comparison of contemporary and turn-of-the-century immigrants in intergenerational mobility and cultural transmission. *Journal of American Ethnic History, 18,* 65–94.

Min, P. G. (2000). Immigrants' religion and ethnicity: A comparison of Indian Hindu and Korean Christian immigrants in the United States. *Bulletin of the Royal Institute of Inter-Faith Studies, 2,* 122–140.

Min, P. G. (2001). Changes in Korean immigrants' gender role and social status, and their marital conflicts. *Sociological Forum, 16,* 301–320.

Min, P. G. (2002a). Introduction. In P. G. Min & J. H. Kim (Ed.), *Religions in Asian America: Building faith communities* (pp. 1–14). Walnut Creek, CA: Altamira Press.

Min, P. G. (Ed.). (2002b). *The second generation: Ethnic identity among Asian Americans*. Walnut Creek, CA: Altamira Press.

Min, P. G., & Kim, J. H. (Eds.). (2002). *Religions in Asian America: Building faith communities*. Walnut Creek, CA: Altamira Press.

Min, P. G., & Kim, R. (Eds.). (1999). *Struggle for ethnic identity: Narratives by Asian American professionals*. Walnut Creek, CA: Altamira Press.

Min, P. G., & Kim, R. (2000). Formation of ethnic and racial identities: Narratives by young Asian-American professionals. *Ethnic and Racial Studies, 23,* 735–760.

Min, P. G., & Kolodny, A. (1994). The middleman minority characteristics of Korean merchants in the United States. *Korean Journal of Population and Development, 23,* 179–202.

Miyamoto, S. F. (1939). *Social solidarity among the Japanese in Seattle*. Seattle: University of Washington.

Montero, D. M. (1975). *The Japanese American community: A study of generational changes in ethnic affiliation* (Doctoral Dissertation, University of California at Los Angeles.) *Dissertation Abstracts International.* 36/07, 4802.

Numrich, P. D. (1996). *Old wisdom in the New World: Americanization in two immigrant Theravada Buddhist temples*. Knoxville: University of Tennessee Press.

Okihiro, G. Y. (1988). The idea of community and a "particular type of history." In G. Y. Okihiro, S. Hune, A. A. Hansen, & J. M. Liu (Eds.), *Reflections on shattered windows* (pp. 175–183). Pullman: Washington State University Press.

Omi, M., & Winant, H. (1986). *Racial formation in the United States: From the 1960s to the 1980s*. New York: Routledge.

Ong, P. (1984). The Chinatown unemployment and the ethnic labor market. *Amerasia Journal, 11,* 35–54.

Ong, P., & Azores, T. (1994). The migration and incorporation of Filipino nurses. In P. Ong, E. Bonacich, & L. Cheng (Eds.), *The new Asian immigration in Los Angeles and global restructuring* (pp. 164–195). Philadelphia: Temple University Press.

Ong, P., Bonacich, E., & Cheng, L. (1994). *The new Asian immigration in Los Angeles and global restructuring*. Philadelphia: Temple University Press.

Ong, P., & Umemoto, K. (2000). Life and work in the inner city. In M. Zhou & J. Gatewood (Eds.), *Contemporary Asian America: A multidisciplinary reader* (pp. 233–253). New York: New York University Press.

Osajima, K. (1988). Asian Americans as a model minority: An analysis of the popular press image in the 1960s and 1980s. In G. Y. Okihiro, S. Hune, A. Hansen, & J. Liu (Eds.), *Reflections on shattered windows* (pp. 165–174). Pullman: Washington University Press.

Ostergren, R. (1981). The immigrant church as a symbol of community and place in the Upper Midwest. *Great Plains Quarterly, 1,* 225–238.

Park, K. (1995). The re-invention of affirmative action: Korean immigrants' changing conceptions of African Americans and Latin Americans. *Urban Anthropology, 24*(1–2), 59–92.

Park, K. (1996). Use and abuse of race and culture: Black-Korean tension in America. *American Anthropologist, 98,* 492–499.

Park, K. (1999). "I really do feel I'm 1.5": The construction of self and community by young Korean Americans. *Amerasia Journal, 15*(1), 139–164.

Peterson, W. (1966, January 9). Success story, Japanese-American style. *New York Times Magazine,* 20–21.

Pido, A.J.A. (1986). *The Pilipinos in America: Macro/micro dimensions of immigration and integration*. Staten Island, NY: Center for Migration Studies.

Portes, A., & Bach, R. (1985). *Latin journey: Cuban and Mexican immigrants in the United States*. Berkeley: University of California Press.

Prashad, V. (1998). Crafting solidarity. In L. D. Shankar & R. Srikanth (Eds.), *A part, but apart: South Asians in Asian America* (pp. 105–126). Philadelphia: Temple University Press.

Radhakrishnan, R. (1994). Is the ethnic "authentic" in the diaspora? In K. Aguilar-San Juan (Ed.), *The state of Asian America: Activism and resistance in the 1990s* (pp. 219–234). Boston: South End Press.

Revilla, L. A. (1998). Filipino American identity: Transcending the crisis. In M.P.P. Root (Ed.), *Filipino Americans: Transformation and identity* (pp. 80–94). Thousand Oaks, CA: Sage.

Rinder, I. (1958–59). Stranger in the land: Social relations in the status gap. *Social Problems, 6,* 253–260.

Root, M.P.P. (Ed.). (1998). *Filipino Americans: Transformation and identity*. Thousand Oaks, CA: Sage.

Rudrappa, S. (2002). Disciplining desire in making home: Endangering ethnicity in Indian immigrant families. In P. G. Min (Ed.), *The second generation: Ethnic identity among Asian Americans* (pp. 85–111). Walnut Creek, CA: Altamira Press.

Rumbaut, R. G. (1995). The new Californians: Comparative research findings on the educational progress of immigrant children. In R. Rumbaut & W. Cornelius (Eds.), *California's immigrant children: Theory, research, and implications for educational policy* (pp. 17–69). San Diego: University of California, Center for U.S.-Mexican Studies.

Saito, L. T. (1998). *Race and politics: Asian Americans, Latinos, and Whites in a Los Angeles suburb*. Urbana: University of Illinois Press.

Sanders, J., & Nee, V. (1987). The limits of ethnic solidarity in the enclave economy. *American Sociological Review, 52,* 745–767.

San Juan, E., Jr. (1994). The predicament of Filipinos in the United States. In K. Aguilar-San Juan (Ed.), *The state of Asian America: Activism and resistance in the 1990s* (pp. 205–218). Boston: South End Press.

Shah, S. (1994). Presenting the Blue Goddess: Toward a national, Pan-Asian feminist agenda. In K. Aguilar-San Juan (Ed.), *The state of Asian America: Activism and resistance in the 1990s* (pp. 147–158). Boston: South Asian Press.

Shankar, L. D., & Srikanth, R. (Eds.). (1998). *A part, yet apart: South Asians in Asian America*. Philadelphia: Temple University Press.

Shim, D. B. (2000). From yellow peril through model minority to renewed yellow peril. In B. Mori (Ed.), *Stand! Contesting ideas and opinions: Race and ethnicity*. Madison: Coursewise.

Shin, E. H., & Chang, K. S. (1988). Peripherization of immigrant professionals: Korean physicians in the United States. *International Migration Review, 22,* 609–626.

Shin, E. H., & Park, H. (1988). An analysis of causes of schisms in ethnic churches: The case of Korean-American churches. *Sociological Analysis, 49,* 234–248.

Shinagawa, L. H., & Pang, G. Y. (1996). Asian American panethnicity and intermarriage. *Amerasia Journal, 22*(2), 127–152.

Shukla, S. (1999–2000). New immigrants, new forms of transnational community: Post-1965 Indian migrations. *Amerasia Journal, 25*(3), 19–36.

Sluzki, C. E. (1979). Migration and family conflict. *Family Process, 18*(4), 381–394.

Snowden, L. R., & Cheung, F. K. (1990). Use of inpatient mental health services by members of ethnic minority groups. *American Psychologist, 45*, 347–355.

Strobel, L. M. (1998). Coming full circle: Narratives of decolonization among post-1965 Filipino Americans. In M.P.P. Root (Ed.), *Filipino Americans: Transformation and identity* (pp. 62–79). Thousand Oaks, CA: Sage.

Sue, S., & McKinney, H. (1980). Asian Americans in the community mental health care system. In R. Endo, S. Sue, & N. Wagner (Eds.), *Asian Americans: Social and psychological perspectives*, vol. 2 (pp. 291–310). Palo Alto, CA: Science and Behavior Books.

Sue, S., & Morishima, J. (1980). *The mental health of Asian Americans*. San Francisco: Jossey-Bass.

Suzuki, B. H. (1977). Education and the socialization of Asian Americans: A revisionist analysis of the "model minority" thesis. *Amerasia Journal, 4*(1), 25–51.

Takagi, D. Y. (1992). *The retreat from race: Asian American admissions and racial politics*. New Brunswick, NJ: Rutgers University Press.

Takagi, D. Y. (1994). Post-civil rights politics and Asian-American identity: Admissions and higher education. In S. Gregory & R. Sanjek (Eds.), *Race* (pp. 229–242). New Brunswick, NJ: Rutgers University Press.

Takaki, R. (1989). *Strangers from a different shore: A history of Asian Americans*. Boston: Little, Brown.

Tang, J. (1993). The career attainment of Caucasian and Asian engineers. *Sociological Quarterly, 34*, 467–496.

Tang, J. (1997). The glass ceiling in science and engineering. *Journal of Socio-Economics, 26*, 383–406.

Taylor, P. A., & Kim, S. S. (1980). Asian Americans in the federal civil service. *California Sociologist, 3*, 1–16.

Thai, H. C. (1999). "Splitting things in half is so White": Conceptions of family life and friendship and the formation of ethnic identity among second-generation Vietnamese Americans. *Amerasia Journal, 25*(1), 53–88.

Thompson, R. H. (1979). Ethnicity vs. class: An analysis of conflict in a North American Chinese community. *Ethnicity, 6*, 306–326.

Thompson, R. H. (1980). From kinship to class: A new model of urban overseas Chinese social organization. *Urban Anthropology, 9*, 265–293.

Tienda, M., & Lii, D.-T. (1987). Minority concentration and earnings inequality: Blacks, Hispanics and Asians compared. *American Journal of Sociology, 2*, 141–165.

Toji, D. S., & Johnson, J. H. (1992). Asian and Pacific Islander American poverty: The working poor and the jobless poor. *Amerasia Journal, 18*(1), 83–91.

Tsukada, M. (1988). Income parity through different paths: Chinese Americans, Japanese Americans, and Caucasians in Hawaii. *Amerasia Journal, 14*(2), 47–60.

Tuan, M. (1999). *Forever foreigners or honorary White? The Asian ethnic experience today*. New Brunswick, NJ: Rutgers University Press.

Turner, J., & Bonacich, E. (1980). Toward a composite theory of middleman minorities. *Ethnicity, 7*, 144–158.

Tyner, J. A. (2000). The social construction of gendered migration from the Philippines. In M. Zhou & J. V. Gatewood (Eds.), *Contemporary Asian America: A multidisciplinary reader* (pp. 207–228). New York: New York University Press.

U.S. Census Bureau. (1993). *1990 census of population, Asians and Pacific Islanders in the United States* (C-P-3–5). Washington, DC: Government Printing Office.

U.S. Census Bureau. (2002). [On-line]. Available: www.census.gov/Press-Release/www/2002/Cb02cn59.html/.

U.S. Commission on Civil Rights. (1992). *Civil rights issues facing Asian Americans in the 1990s*. Washington, DC: Government Printing Office.

Vaid, J. (1999–2000). Beyond a space of our own: South Asian women's groups in the U.S. *Amerasia Journal, 25*(3), 111–126.

Vaid, U. (1999–2000). Inclusion, exclusion and occlusion: The queer idea of Asian Pacific American-ness. *Amerasia Journal, 25*(3), 1–16.

Vo, T. L. (1996). Asian immigrants, Asian Americans, and the politics of economic mobilization in San Diego. *Amerasia Journal, 22*(2), 89–108.

Warner, S. (1998). Immigration and religious communities in the United States. In S. Warner & J. Wittner (Eds.), *Gatherings in diaspora* (pp. 3–36). Philadelphia: Temple University Press.

Warner, W. L., & Srole, L. (1945). *The social system of American ethnic groups*. New Haven, CT: Yale University Press.

Waters, M. (1990). *Ethnic options: Choosing identities in America*. Berkeley: University of California Press.

Wei, W. (1993). *The Asian American movement*. Philadelphia: Temple University Press.

Weitzer, R. (1997). Racial prejudice among Korean merchants in African American neighborhoods. *Sociological Quarterly, 38*, 587–606.

Williams, D. A. (1984, April 23). A formula for success. *Newsweek*, pp. 77–78.

Williams, R. B. (1988). *Religions of immigrants from India and Pakistan: New threads in the American tapestry*. Cambridge: Cambridge University Press.

Williams, R. B. (1996). *Christian pluralism in the United States: The Indian immigrant experience*. New York: Cambridge University Press.

Wilson, K., & Portes, A. (1980). Immigrant enclaves: An analysis of the labor market experiences of Cubans in Miami. *American Journal of Sociology, 86*, 305–319.

Wong, M. (1982). The cost of being Chinese, Japanese, and Filipino in the United States 1960, 1970, 1976. *Pacific Sociological Review, 25*, 59–78.

Wong, M. (1988). The Chinese American family. In C. Mindel, R. Habenstein, & R. Wright, Jr. (Eds.), *Ethnic families in America: Patterns and variations* (pp. 230–256). New York: Elsevier.

Wong, M. (1995). Chinese Americans. In P. G. Min (Ed.), *Asian Americans: Contemporary trends and issues* (pp. 58–94). Thousand Oaks, CA: Sage.

Wong-Hall, P., & Hwang, V. M. (Eds.). (2001). *Anti-Asian violence in North America: Asian American and Asian Canadian reflections on hate, healing, and resistance*. Walnut Creek, CA: Altamira Press.

Woo, D. (1989). The gap between striving and achieving: The case of Asian American women. In Asian Women United of California (Ed.), *An anthology of writings by and about Asian American women* (pp. 185–194). Boston: Beacon Press.

Yang, P. (1998). Chinese conversion to evangelical Christianity: The importance of social and cultural contexts. *Sociology of Religion, 59*, 237–257.

Yang, P. (1999). *Chinese Christians in America: Conversion, assimilation, and adhesive identities*. University Park: Pennsylvania State University Press.

Yang, P. (2000). Chinese Gospel Church: The Sinicization of Christianity. In H. R. Ebaugh & J. S. Chafetz (Eds.), *Religion and the*

new immigrants: Continuities and adaptations in immigrant congregations (pp. 89–108). Walnut Creek, CA: Altamira Press.

Ying, Y. (1988). Depressive symptomatology among Chinese Americans as measured by CES-D. *Journal of Clinical Psychology, 44,*
739–746.

Yoo, D. (1996). For those who have eyes to see: Religious sightings
in Asian America. *Amerasia Journal, 22,* xiii–xxii.

Yoo, D. (Ed.). (1999). *New spiritual homes: Religion and Asian Americans.* Honolulu: University of Hawaii Press.

Yoon, I. J. (1996). Self-employment rates of U.S. ancestry groups,
1990. *Korea Journal of Population and Development, 25*(1),
123–154.

Yoon, I. J. (1997). *On my own: Korean businesses and race relations
in America.* Chicago: University of Chicago Press.

Yu, E. Y. (1988). The growth of Buddhism in the United States, with
special reference to Southern California. *Pacific World, 4,* 82–93.

Yu, E. Y.(Ed.). (1994). *Black-Korean encounter: Toward understanding and alliance.* Los Angeles: California State University, Institute for Asian American and Pacific Asian Studies.

Zhou, M. (1992). *Chinatown: The socioeconomic potential of an
urban enclave.* Philadelphia: Temple University Press.

Zhou, M. (1993). Underemployment and economic disparities
among minority groups. *Population Research and Policy Review,
12*(2), 139–157.

Zhou, M. (1999). Coming of age: The current situation of Asian
American children. *Amerasia Journal, 25*(1), 1–27.

Zhou, M., & Bankston, C., III. (1998). *Growing up American: How
Vietnamese children adapt to life in the United States.* New York:
Russell Sage Foundation.

Zhou, M., Bankston, C., III, & Kim, R. (2002). Rebuilding spiritual
lives in the new land: Religious practices among South East
Asian refugees in the United States. In P. G. Min & J. H. Kim
(Eds.), *Religions in Asian America: Building faith communities* (pp.
37–70). New York: Altamira Press.

Zhou, M., & Kamo, Y. (1994). An analysis of earnings patterns for
Chinese, Japanese, and non-Hispanic White males in the United
States. *Sociological Quarterly, 35,* 581–602.

Zhou, M., & Nordquist, R. (2000). Work and its place in the lives
of immigrant women: Garment workers in New York City's
Chinatown. In M. Zhou & J. V. Gatewood (Eds.), *Contemporary
Asian America: A multidisciplinary reader* (pp. 254–277). New
York: New York University Press.

18

CULTURE-CENTERED KNOWLEDGE

Black Studies, Curriculum Transformation, and Social Action

Joyce Elaine King

Spelman College

At this level of Otherness the "negro" was not even considered, since he was not imagined to have languages worth studying, nor to partake in culture, so total was his mode of Nigger Chaos.

—Sylvia Wynter, 1984

It has not occurred to the members of the neo-plantation school of social science that working-class Blacks have their own epistemology, their own theory of social change, and their own theories of class and ethnic depravity.

—Clyde Woods, 1998

The problem here is that few Americans know who and what they really are . . . most American whites are culturally part Negro American without even realizing it.

—Ralph Ellison, 1986

To be white in America is to be very black. If you don't know how black you are, you don't know how American you are.

—Robert Farris Thompson, 1992

This chapter is an interpretive review of selected sources in Black studies; historical, literary, and cultural studies scholarship; research in the social sciences, multicultural education, and the emergent field of research and writing

in Black education. One purpose of this review is to delineate the contours of this evolving field of theorizing and praxis. Another purpose is to clarify the nature and production of culture-centered knowledge in African American (and Diasporan/African) intellectual thought, educational research, and practice. The primary purpose is to summarize and draw conclusions from this literature regarding the uses of cultural knowledge and culture-centered knowledge in curriculum transformation and social action, particularly for the educational benefit of Black people.

All but the culturally conservative "Western traditionalists" (Banks, 1993) recognize the partiality of knowledge and the importance of understanding how culture, ideology, and hegemony affect knowledge, its production, and its social uses. In addition, criteria are needed to distinguish between dominating as compared to liberating culture-centered knowledge and curriculum transformation. For example, a central concern in Black studies and Black education (and in some variants of multicultural education) has been how education can be used as a social weapon for human freedom (Rodney, 1990; S. W. Williams, 1991). Relatedly, "How can research become one of the forms of struggle in Black education?" (J. E. King, 2002, p. 6). Although this chapter does not include a comprehensive review of the discipline of Black studies, it discusses relevant scholarship and research directions that address these critical issues. The literature has been selected in accordance with these aims.

THE BLACK STUDIES CRITIQUE:
EDUCATION FOR HUMAN FREEDOM

Education and knowledge and intellectual production are contested, nonneutral terrains. In the last decades of the 20th century, contestation about education frequently took the form of vituperous academic debate and media hyperbole about curriculum transformation at all levels. This debate over the curriculum and the literary canon was not "merely academic" and was so fierce precisely because it involved "the attempt to redefine American cultural identity under new historical circumstances" (Erickson, 1992, p. 97). At the dawn of the new millennium, the conservative forces that used the "language of liberalism and pluralism" (Giroux, 1992) in the 1990s to attack African-centered education and multicultural education are promoting "reforms" that effectively nullify these efforts. Government-mandated high-stakes testing, one outgrowth of the academic "standards movement," hostile take-overs, seizure and "sale" of public schools to private for-profit enterprises, as well as school vouchers—the so-called "choice movement" that is being touted for the benefit of poor students—dominate the educational landscape and policy agendas. A troubling silence about the content of school knowledge with respect to these "reforms" suggests that the fate of cultural democracy and public education hang in the balance.

New "accountability" requirements, operating in the guise of "equal opportunity" (but without equitable resource deployment), are reproducing unequal educational outcomes and life chances for those least well served by the education system. This predictable "achievement gap" reflects the society's failure to resolve the persistent problems of racial hierarchy and cultural hegemony that engendered debates and struggles in education in the last decade. These irruptions in the academy over the curriculum (Erickson, 1992; Graff, 1993) coincided with community struggles against racism in education—resistance, ostensibly multicultural textbooks (Cornbleth & Waugh, 1993; Epstein & Ellis, 1992; J. E. King, 1992; Sanford, 1990; Wynter, 1992a), and efforts to include African American home language in instruction in schools (Delpit & Dowdy, 2002). Although the battleground seemingly has shifted, disagreements in preceding decades about the literary canon; about what should be taught in school; and about curriculum transformation among liberals, progressives, and conservatives are instructive. Even as U.S. society appears to be more "diverse," the analytical task that remains for Black studies and Black education praxis is to undo the forms of knowledge that sustain unjust and inequitable racialized educational outcomes.

Historically, education has facilitated the absorption of recurrent waves of newly arriving immigrants. In contrast, with regard to the troublesome, inassimilable "Negro presence" in this country, Chafets (2001) offers this astute observation:

Traditionally America has turned its immigrants (except those who look African-American) into white people. . . . No matter how people identify themselves, what counts is how they are identified by society. . . . Eventually America treats all its ethnics as whites—except blacks. . . . [A] permanent fault line runs between the perennially disadvantaged descendents of African slaves and everybody else, in various stages of upward (i.e., whiteward) mobility. (p. 3)

Indeed, the United States has never been the "White" country of popular imagination and ideology, and "American cultural identity" continues to be formed not only along the boundaries of the "color line"—that enduring problem of the 20th century that W.E.B. DuBois predicted (DuBois, 1903/1953)—but also within the normative cultural demarcations that denote and connote degrees of assimilation to an idealized White Euro-American middle-class cultural norm (Cruse, 1987). These social divisions along racial and cultural lines require equally trenchant analysis because, as Cruse (1967) observes:

Racial democracy is, at the same time, cultural democracy; and the question of cultural democracy in America [continues to be] posed in a way never before seen or considered in other societies. This uniqueness results historically from the manner in which American cultural developments have been influenced by the Negro presence. (p. 96)

It is in the context of persisting systemic social injustice and inequity that this chapter asks, *What needs to be analyzed and understood about curriculum transformation and social action that is in the best interest of African Americans?* Close consideration of historical contestation over the curriculum as well as the contemporary absence of audible concern about such curriculum matters in national educational reforms reveal a recurring pendulumlike pattern of cultural affirmation/revitalization versus cultural negation/assimilation within a historical dialectic of ideological conflict, cultural hegemony, and White supremacy. Often oversimplified as a choice between integration or separatism, this dialectic has a long history in concrete struggles that African Americans have waged for liberating knowledge, intellectual autonomy, and education for human freedom. The epistemological critique of knowledge brought on by the modern Black studies movement is one legacy of this struggle.

THE BLACK STUDIES LEGACY

Debates about Black studies, African-centered education, and multicultural curriculum transformation in the 1990s have been argued in earlier historical periods, albeit in other vocabularies. For example, objections to Black studies arose as this movement converged with the Black arts movement to challenge Eurocentric intellectual and cultural hegemony in the academy and liberate African American and African culture, consciousness, and aesthetics from institutionalized White cultural supremacy. Both of these movements had historical antecedents that go back at least to David Walker's *Appeal to the Colored Citizens of the World but in Particular and Very Expressly to those of the United States of America* in 1829 (D. Walker, 1829/1971), to the Garvey Movement, and to the Harlem Renaissance in the 1920s. The base of contemporary African American, Caribbean, and African literary scholarship can also be located in the "New Negro, Indigenist and Negritude movements of the 1920s and 1930s" (V. Clark, 1991, p. 40). In the 1960s, both Black studies and the new letters movement were correctly linked to the political and cultural values in the concept of Black Power (Gayle, 1971).

In the next decade, calls for "education for liberation" (Banks, 1973) as well as "Black feminist criticism" and theorizing emerged in the 1970s from the convergence of the "new Black consciousness" and the women's movement—both of which can be traced to the political and social action that grew out of the civil rights movement. This convergence influenced subsequent developments in ethnic studies and Black/Third World/women's studies. Christian (1989) recounts, for instance, that this conjuncture of Black consciousness and the women's movement "provided a context to imagine questions" about Black women's writing that were "never imagined before" (p. 61). Presently, "minority" and postcolonial literary theory and criticism, multicultural education, critical race theory and antirace theorizing, cultural studies, and teacher education have benefited from the new forms of consciousness engendered by these earlier convergences of critical thought and social action (Apple, 1993; Banks, 1992; Berlak & Moyenda, 2001; Boyce Davies, 1994; Delgado, 1995; Feagin, 2001; E. W. Gordon, 1985; B. M. Gordon, 1992; Guy-Sheftall, 1992; Henry, 2000; Ladson-Billings, 1991a).

From its inception as an "interdisciplinary mode of critical investigation" (Marable, 1992, p. 31), Black studies distinguished itself from Negro history and ethnic studies (Aldridge, 1992; J. H. Clarke, 1992). Black studies evolved beyond Negro history and Black history to encompass a particular epistemological and axiological mission across the disciplines. Harding (1970) explains the crucial difference between Black history and Negro history: "Black History does not seek to highlight the outstanding contributions of special black people to the life and times of America. Rather our emphasis is on exposure, disclosure, on reinterpretation of the entire American past" (p. 279). In other words, Black history raises questions that were never asked by Negro history—questions about the European heritage of the United States, for example. That is, Black history is "forced to ask about the meaning of America itself" (p. 281). Such questions are not only about "exclusively black things" and Black people, for Black history "sees with Indian eyes as well" (p. 280). Black studies is an interdisciplinary fulfillment of the task and hope of Black history: to create a newly defined world "in which the best of blackness has prevailed" and Black manhood and womanhood "will be vindicated" (p. 291). Or as Margaret Walker envisioned in her poem, "For My People," this is a world that "will hold all the people" (Harding, 1970, p. 291).

The interdisciplinary body of knowledge that constitutes "Black, African American, or African studies" is, according to Semmes (1992), "tied to explicating social and historical processes that affect the status and development of people of African descent on a global scale . . . [and] this emerging discipline is able to provide universals for understanding the human experience in general" (p. ix). The point is that Black studies link the development of African-descent people with the *transmutation* of knowledge. Rather than merely "multiculturalizing" knowledge or "opening up" the traditional disciplines (Gates, 1992a, p. 6), this intellectual perspective asks, "Where is the social philosophy, the social, political and economic theory that could *change the condition* of African Americans?" (Semmes, p. 72, emphasis added). Black studies offers the possibility of an epistemological critique of social reality and the social organization of knowledge. The object of this critique includes the societal obstacles to Black people's development as well as the knowledge that sustains and legitimates societal inequity.

BLACK STUDIES, AFRICAN-CENTERED THOUGHT, AND CULTURAL DEMOCRACY

In an article published in 1993, Watkins describes the Black studies curriculum development movement of the previous 25 years as an evolution of the "Black nationalist orientation" that combined "Pan Africanist," "cultural nationalist," and "separatist" views on education (p. 329). According to Watkins, this nationalist outlook in curriculum development contrasts sharply with the optimism of earlier Black liberal education aims. Watkins concludes that "its focus on separateness indicates little optimism for integration" (p. 331), and that this nationalist outlook is "reflected in part in contemporary renditions of Afrocentrism" (p. 331). From the perspective of Black studies as a mode of critical investigation, however, it is the ideology *underlying* the social ethic of integration that should be analyzed (Semmes, 1992). Semmes stresses this aspect of Afrocentrism or "Afrocentric social science" that is the "act of examining phenomena in terms of their relationship to the survival and prosperity of African peoples." Such critical examination is "crucial to developing a social science approach within the context of African American studies," or Black studies (p. 18). Semmes's description of African-centered theorizing emphasizes "the importance of an epistemological center" (p. 18) in Black studies/Afrocentric social science that also affirms the importance of the humanities in analyzing the Black experience and Euro-American cultural hegemony.

Semmes (1992) compares the way E. Franklin Frazier (1957, 1973) and Harold Cruse (1967) systematically examined the liberal integrationist ethic. He concludes that their scholarship demonstrates that this ethic requires African American cultural or group negation, and this negation blocks the kind of group-based strategies that enabled other groups to develop. This suggests that achieving racial and cultural democracy is not a dualistic either-or choice between integration or separation but requires overcoming "blocked cultural pluralism." It is in this context that Semmes identifies group-affirming African-centered thought with the Black studies tradition of intellectual autonomy that extends legitimacy to the "study of plural impulses among African Americans" (p. 76). That is, studying group-based strategies for social action can be legitimately pluralist. Also, such study need not be equated with "separatism" or "self-segregation." Semmes shows that "over time dominant society elites have changed the meaning of segregation for African Americans to fit their political needs" and interests (p. 105):

The label "segregation" is incorrectly applied to any group-focused effort by African Americans and others to meet the social and cultural needs that are not automatically provided to African Americans, as they are to European Americans, or to rectify the past and current effects of White supremacist oppression and structured inequality. (p. 105)

Thus, equating the "variegated expressions" of African-centered theorizing and "group-directed strategies" (p. 105) with separatism/segregation uncritically accepts normative liberal assumptions concerning integration, democracy, and social change.

Moral and Epistemological Panics

In the 1960s, the Black studies critique of liberal assumptions, "mainstream" knowledge, and ideology across the disciplines precipitated a series of stunning breakaways from Western traditional forms of knowledge, thought, and influence (V. Clark, 1991; West, 1985). Both epistemological and "moral panics" ensued in reaction against

the alternative perspective and social action possibilities that the Black studies critique of knowledge and society represents. The term *moral panic* refers to "the emergence of a perceived threat to the values and interests of a society in its mass media" (Carby, 1987, p. 190, n. 15). (Cohen, 1972, originated the term; S. Hall, Critcher, Jefferson, Clarke, & Roberts, 1978, use it in the British context.) *Epistemological panic* is used here to suggest a corollary perceived threat to certain values and interests in the disciplines and curriculum knowledge (Schlesinger, 1991). These epistemological and moral panics can be seen in a book on teaching social studies published as Black history challenged Negro history 30 years ago (Banks & Joyce, 1971).

In the 1970s, Banks (1971a), McIntosh (1971), and other contributors to Banks and Joyce (1971) made explicit social justice claims upon the social studies to make the curriculum relevant to the lives and needs of "culturally different" children. Particularly revealing are articles by Cuban (1971), which first appeared in the *Saturday Review* in 1968, and an essay critique by Grambs (1971) of a 1965 children's biography of Crispus Attucks. (See Swartz, 1992, for a more recent discussion of the transformation of curriculum knowledge about Attucks.) Cuban stressed that Negro history belonged in the public schools because of its "restraint and balance," but not Black history, which, despite its merits, aimed at "instilling racial pride" through "propaganda" (pp. 317–318). Cuban preferred Negro history to both the presumed "mythology" of Black history and the "white mythology" of the existing school curriculum that Negro history could rectify. Grambs complained that the children's biography featuring Crispus Attucks as a hero distorted the historical facts by substituting "non-history" and "ethnic chauvinism" for "authentic history" (p. 327). Banks (1971b) wrote a lengthy response to these criticisms in a letter to the editors of the *Harvard Educational Review* (which had published the Grambs essay). He argued that their liberal assumptions about and interpretation of the "canons of scholarly objectivity and historical accuracy" (Cuban, 1971, p. 318), as well as their claim that these standards of historicity are lacking in Black history, not only were profoundly misguided but missed the point of teaching history in general.

Recent and particularly rancorous debate among White scholars and conservative politicians concerning the national history standards (Nash, Crabtree, & Dunn, 1997; National Center for History in the Schools, 1994) recalls these earlier allegations against Negro history. At the 1997 American Historical Association meeting, Wineburg (1999) offered an analysis of this debate that closely parallels the defense of Black history Banks was compelled to make 30 years ago. Addressing not "Whose history?"—the question that frames the history standards debate—but "Why study history at all?" Wineburg stresses the ultimate importance of teaching historical thinking.

The Restoration Agenda

The complaint that Black history lacked scholarly objectivity and appropriate "balance" and promoted propagandistic "ethnic chauvinism" persisted into the education "culture wars" in the late 1980s and 1990s. As Black studies (and ethnic studies) replaced Negro history and became institutionalized, however, the object of moral and epistemological panics concerning curriculum transformation shifted to African-centered theorizing and education practice. Critics, whose aim was not to promote cultural democracy but rather to preserve Eurocentric hegemony, regularly characterized African-centered education as academic "separatism" and excoriated it as "ethnic cheer leading" and self-esteem building "filiopietism" (i.e., excessive reverence for one's ancestors) (Ravitch, 1990a, p. 46). In fact, such efforts to constrain the transformation of the curriculum in schools and the academy in the last decade—efforts by both conservatives and liberals—can be best understood as a "restoration agenda" (Asante, 1991a, 1991b; Banks, 1993; Cornbleth & Waugh, 1993; J. E. King, 1992; Ladson-Billings, 1991b; Shor, 1986; Sizemore, 1990). The academic content standards and high-stakes testing "movements" are recent manifestations of this agenda. Moreover, certain ways of "talking about race," as well as multicultural education, its various perspectives notwithstanding, are also being appropriated and positioned within this agenda as more politically and academically acceptable alternatives to African-centered curriculum reform. Such appropriation is reminiscent of the way Negro history was positioned in relation to the perceived threat of Black history.

Liberals, progressives, and conservatives alike continue to condemn the political implications of African-centered scholarship and curriculum, but usually without adequately acknowledging the ideological distortion of knowledge and cultural hegemony this alternative epistemological approach seeks to rectify (Semmes, 1992). For example, Eugene Genovese; Nathan Glazer; Arthur Schlesinger, Jr.; Diane Ravitch; and C. Vann Woodward, to name a few, have criticized aspects of multicultural curriculum reform but unequivocally denounced the "Afrocentric idea" in education (Asante, 1987, 1991a). These scholars may not equally support the opinion media pundit George F. Will stated in the *Baton Rouge Morning Advocate* at the height of the "culture wars" (December 19, 1989, p. 3, cited in McCarthy, 1990, p. 118), but Will's position epitomizes the ideology of Euro-American superiority within the restoration agenda. Will states: "Our country is a branch of European civilization. . . .

'Eurocentricity' is right, in American curricula and consciousness, because it accords with the facts of our history." It is such ideological antithesis to cultural democracy to which African-centered theorizing responds.

Another exchange among historians 30 years ago further illuminates this ideological struggle. In a response to Woodward's criticism of DuBois, Stuckey (1971) addressed the "long history" of White historians and the media admonishing and "disrespecting" Black scholars and Black studies (pp. 280–281). (See Genovese, 1971, for another example of the tendency of White scholars in this regard.) Woodward had chided DuBois for publishing "uninhibited" expressions of "racial pride." This charge further illustrates that the anxiety (or panics) about Black intellectual autonomy and group consciousness—be it Black history or African-centered theorizing—is a recurring theme. Stuckey's rejoinder to Woodward includes this incisive closing comment:

Of this we may be certain: white historians, save perhaps the most radical of the future, will never acknowledge what blacks have done for the country or what Americans have done to blacks. To do so would be tantamount to blotting out the America they have known and written about and would bring to an end ways in which, as white men, they look out on the world and in at themselves. (p. 286)

The Cultural Recuperation Agenda

As scholarly debate about the epistemological legitimacy and theoretical adequacy—or truthfulness—of Black studies has become more complex (Asante, 1992), there is a deeper understanding of the intellectual paradigm-in-use as an epistemological (not biological) issue of fundamentally hermeneutic importance to cultural democracy (Foster, 1998; E. W. Gordon, 1999; Meacham, 1998). Hermeneutics concerns the philosophical problem of interpretation and understanding. Such understanding of intellectual paradigm or worldview perspective is discernible in new millennium studies of the Black experience globally, including transformative research and praxis in Black education, that challenge existing knowledge paradigms of history, identity, culture, and cultural resistance (S. Walker, 2001; Watkins, 2001). A complete review of this burgeoning literature across the disciplines is beyond the scope of this chapter, but several examples will suffice.

One example is an interdisciplinary, cross-national collection of scholarship entitled *African Roots/American Cultures* (S. Walker, 2001) in which contributors from the United States, Latin America, and the Caribbean illustrate "Afrogenic" perspectives and methods of explanation, interpretation, and cultural recuperation. As an alternative to Eurocentric "concepts, norms, and terminologies" that suppress, distort, and erase the truth about "Africa in the creation of the Americas," Afrogenic scholarship provides "new data, interpretations and theories." According to Walker, "Afrogenic simply means growing out of the histories, ways of being and knowing, and interpretations and interpretive styles of African and African Diaspora peoples" (p. 8). Although this interpretive method is mediated by "belonging," for African Diaspora scholar/activists, others of non-African ancestry can "manifest an Afrogenic perspective" by "acknowledging African and African Diaspora agency, assuming the 'blackness' as well as the 'whiteness' of the Pan-American experience, challenging Eurocentric (mis)interpretations of Afrogenic behaviors, and being committed to telling an inclusive and accurate story of the Americas" (p. 8).

Like earlier vindicationist scholarship (Drake, 1987) within the Black history/Black studies intellectual continuum that challenged Eurocentrism, truth-telling is a critical element of the cultural recuperation agenda.

Two recent publications concerning indigenous African American music, the blues and the spirituals, illustrate how cultural recuperation differs from knowledge production *about* the "Black experience" that is primarily a referent for analyzing the White experience of "blackness." In *Development Arrested*, Woods (1998) states his purpose is to "bridge the gap between the blues as a widely recognized aesthetic tradition and the blues as a theory of social action and economic development and change" (p. 20). As an expression of African American working-class thought, the blues function(ed) as a form of social explanation and critique of plantation culture and power. Woods uses the "blues epistemology" not only to analyze and critique the plantation-based economic system and historical power relations in the Mississippi Delta but also to recuperate "heroic movements" of Black cultural resistance that have been purged from "both historical texts and popular memory" (p. 4). He explains that

by reestablishing the original connection between regional political economy, culture, and consciousness, we now have the beginnings of a *method of investigation* capable of recovering forgotten conflicts between the plantation tradition of explanation and the blues tradition of explanation within the Delta. (Woods, 1998, p. 21, emphasis added)

The result is a brilliant explication of the autonomous social vision of African Americans and the role of music, as an expression of Black thought, in sustaining the struggle for justice.

By contrast, the emphasis in *Culture on the Margins* (Cruz, 1999) is not on illuminating or documenting Black agency in particular but the "discovery" of the spirituals by elite White northern abolitionists in the nineteenth century. Cruz's interest is to explore "the central role that black music played in the rise of American cultural interpretation" by tracing "modern modes of interpretation" through the "transformation of the hearing of black music" by White people (p. 18). The book jacket notes that "this interpretive shift—which the author calls—'ethnosympathy'—marks the beginning of a mainstream American interest in the country's cultural margins." Interestingly, neither the term *mainstream America* nor *abolitionist* is among the Library of Congress catalogue categories listed in the book. Rather, the category *Afro-Americans* appears in both these volumes. The point is that criteria are needed to clearly distinguish the social interests of scholarship that goes beyond labeling the object of inquiry.

In addition to differences of perspective, internal differences exist among scholars representing divergent postmodern, progressive, Marxist, conservative, liberal pluralist, and feminist epistemological perspectives and theoretical positions. Within this shifting intellectual terrain and complex political landscape, knowledge, culture, and cultural identity intersect and are used for different theoretical, ideological, and educational purposes. It is with respect to this intersection of culture, ideology, and knowledge that a heuristic construct of culture-centered knowledge is used in this chapter as a conceptual tool to analyze forms of knowledge and curriculum transformation that can be identified with hegemony and autonomy. Such an analysis is needed to distinguish between dominating versus liberating forms of knowledge of, by, for, and about African-descent people and their education. This examination of culture-centered knowledge and curriculum transformation builds on the epistemological critique and axiological foundations of the Black studies movement.

KNOWLEDGE PRODUCTION, SOCIAL INTERESTS, AND CONCEPTUAL PARADIGMS

It is a common understanding in the social sciences that knowledge is a social construction of reality (Holt, 2000) and that both reality and knowledge pertain to specific social contexts (Berger & Luckmann, 1967). Yet according to E. W. Gordon (1985) and others, "mainstream" social science has inadequately and insufficiently addressed the life experiences of African Americans and other cultural groups (p. 118). African American scholars are well-represented among those who have revealed links among methodological bias in social science knowledge production, culture, ideology, and hegemony (Alkalimat, 1969; Ani, 1994; Childs, 1989; Dixon, 1971;

Ladner, 1973; Semmes, 1992). Besides exposing ethnocentric perspective bias in social science knowledge production, African American scholars are exploring a liberatory role for African American cultural knowledge as an alternative to hegemony and ideology in education, the arts and humanities, and the social sciences (Childs; B. M. Gordon, 1985b, 1990; J. E. King & Mitchell, 1990/1995; S. Walker, 2001). This includes using "culture as a weapon for liberation" (B. M. Gordon, 1993, p. 458).

Alternatives to Ideology and Cultural Hegemony

Asa Hilliard (2000) emphasizes that people of African ancestry "must keep in our consciousness that domination involves structures and systematic practices *founded on ideology*" that is,

suppress the history of the victims; destroy the practice of their culture; prevent the victims from coming to understand themselves as part of a cultural family; teach systematically the ideology of white supremacy; control the socialization process; control the accumulation of wealth; and perform segregation or apartheid. (pp. 24–25, emphasis in original)

According to McLaren (1989), hegemony refers to processes of domination that are maintained "not by sheer force" but through "consensual social practices." It is a struggle by which the "powerful win the consent of those who are oppressed" (p. 173). Palestinian educator Fasheh (1990) describes one effect of hegemony in education: "Generally speaking, hegemonic education produces intellectuals who have lost their power base in their own culture and society and who have been provided with a foreign culture and ideology, but without a power base in the hegemonic society" (p. 25).

Semmes (1992) emphasizes this key element of hegemony with respect to African Americans: "progress for the subordinated group meant the uncritical assimilation and regurgitation of the conquering culture" (p. 3). In other words, as Semmes writes, "the perspective of the oppressed shifted to that of the imperial group. This rotation in perspective affirmed the legitimacy of the world view of the oppressors, which sought to present subordination as a normative order" (p. 3). This does not mean that dominated social groups are homogeneous and exist with no internally stratifying divisions or opposing interests. However, as Collins (1990) points out, such "contradictory elements" can "foster both compliance with and resistance to oppression" (p. 18, n. 4). Also, as Semmes explains, hegemonic domination of African Americans has been complicated because of the "self-generative character of the human spirit" that has produced "distinctive parameters for cultural reconstruction" and revitalization (pp. 2–3). Black studies, including African-centered

theorizing and Afrogenic interpretive methods, are indicative of such opposition to cultural hegemony and ideological constraints on thought.

E. W. Gordon, Miller, and Rollock (1990) also criticize the tendency among researchers to "make one's own community the center of the universe and the conceptual frame that constrains all thought." This applies to conceptual paradigms as well as to the methodological paradigms used to study social phenomena. "The problem," as they put it, "is cultural and methodological hegemony" (p. 15). Gordon et al. suggest an approach to this problem of "communicentric bias" that is consistent with a holistic and critical interdisciplinary Black studies approach to knowledge and education praxis. They suggest that a "marriage between the arts, humanities and the social sciences" is needed "in order to understand the lived experiences of Blacks, Latinos, and Native Americans" (p. 18). They write: "We may need to turn to the arts and humanities . . . because the meanings of our behavior are often better explicated in artistic and fiction work" (p. 18). Because literature can also function as a vehicle of hegemonic domination, however, its use in research, social theorizing, and curriculum transformation may require demystification.

Writers in the Black arts movement, theorists/critics of literature, including Black children's literature (Johnson, 1990; Sims, 1982), as well as intellectuals in formerly colonized societies in the Caribbean and Africa have written extensively on both the need to combat literature as a tool of cultural domination/colonization (Césaire, 1960; Touré, 1969; Wa Thiong'o, 1986) and its potential as a tool for liberation. The novelist John O. Killens stressed the role of "art as a weapon" that could be used to liberate all people. That is, art (literature) could also "liberate white people . . . of their prejudice, their preconceived notions of what the world is about" (Peeples, 1984, p. 12). In an examination of current literary scholarship, which is pertinent to this liberatory potential, Fishkin suggests that "African traditions may be essential to understanding" and re-writing modern American literature and the "Black presence in mainstream (American) culture" (Fishkin, 2001, p. 82; 1993). This reviewer found it both necessary and constructive to include examples of literary theory and criticism in this chapter in order to examine oppositional discursive practices in African American and African Diaspora thought that have implications for curriculum transformation.

Conceptual Intervention Is Needed

Though a problem of bias in knowledge production may be acknowledged, it can also be argued that the existing organization of knowledge sustains and legitimates the social framework through ideology and cultural hegemony in education. Rectifying the ideological and partial nature of knowledge production in the disciplines and school curricula has been one focus of the Black studies movement. Conceptual confusion continues to exist regarding what constitutes ideological bias and hegemony. This confusion, partly related to a tendency to conflate ideology, worldview or philosophical perspective, and identity, generates such questions as, "Who is qualified to teach Black studies?" (Aldridge, 1992, p. 63) "Can White teachers/professors teach Black literature?" and "Can't a White person write a multicultural textbook?" Elsewhere, this reviewer (J. E. King, 1992) explains the specious nature of such questions that conflate ideology with identity, responding, to the last of the three questions: "The answer, of course, is yes; the issue, however, is the social interests of the intellectual paradigm within which any scholar writes, regardless of ethnicity, gender, religion, etc." (p. 325; see also Wiggington, 1991/1992; S. Walker, 2001). Moreover, Carruthers (1994) argues that ideology ought not to be confused with worldview (or a philosophical perspective). He writes: "The concept of an African world-view must be distinguished from any connotation of ideology . . . [that] is largely associated with the rationalization of class interests" (p. 53). W. M. King (1990) makes a similar point with respect to the scholar's "mind-set." The issue is "not so much the color of the scholar's skin," he explains, "as the mind-set that is brought to the examination of the intergroup dynamic" (p. 170). These scholars are writing about ideology in education, but the literature in educational research is not presently organized in a way that permits one to locate references such as these that address the relationship among culture, identity, ideology, hegemony, and knowledge production in education.

Although computerized databases such as ERIC, EBSCOR, and RIES permit limited access to publications about "cultural knowledge," the vast majority of the citations generated using this term are not focused on African Americans and education. Other publications and book chapters discussed in this review also contain this term in their titles or content (Banks, 1993; B. M. Gordon, 1985b, 1993; Lee, 1991) but were not accessible electronically. Another finding of the literature review undertaken for this chapter is that the Black studies epistemological critique has not sufficiently influenced the conceptual paradigms-in-use in education research or those used to organize computerized databases, and much less those that reflect a global or African Diaspora perspective. Conceptual intervention in the organization of educational research literature is needed to facilitate a systematic examination of scholarship that addresses ideological influences on knowledge in curriculum and education practice, particularly with regard to the education of Black people in the United States and worldwide.

CULTURE-CENTERED KNOWLEDGE AND CURRICULUM TRANSFORMATION

Before examining the sources that were selected for this review, it will be useful to consider some basic definitions of the key concepts used to analyze culture-centered knowledge in this chapter (as compared to the cultural knowledge of a specific racial/ethnic group). These concepts are culture and cultural knowledge, culture-centered knowledge, and African American cultural knowledge.

Culture and Cultural Knowledge

The concept of *culture* can be used broadly to refer to humans in general, a nationality, or a particular group. Culture usually refers to group ways of thinking and living. At the most specific level, it is a group's "design for living" (Nobles, 1985); it includes the shared knowledge, consciousness, skills, values, expressive forms, social institutions, and behavior that enable their survival as a people. This usage is consistent with a definition Bullivant (1989) prefers: Culture is "a social group's design for surviving in and adapting to its environment" (p. 27). In other words, culture is the total product of a people's being and consciousness that "emerges from their grappling with nature and living with other humans in a collective group" (Ogundipe-Leslie, 1984, p. 81). As it adapts to changing societal needs and goals, culture is also "both enduring and changing" (Semmes, 1981, p. 4).

A people's particular ways of interpreting and perceiving reality—their social thought and folk wisdom—constitute one aspect of collectively generated autochthonous cultural knowledge. The term *cultural knowledge* refers to the learned behaviors, beliefs, and ways of relating to people and the environment that members of a cultural group acquire through normal processes of enculturation (Spradley, 1972). In a typology of knowledge that Banks (1993) constructs, this sociocultural dimension is the first of five categories of knowledge: (a) personal/cultural, (b) popular, (c) mainstream academic, (d) transformative academic, and (e) school knowledge. African American cultural knowledge will be discussed following an explanation of culture-centered knowledge.

Culture-Centered Knowledge

All knowledge is centered or grounded in some cultural context. Culture-centered knowledge (CCK) is used heuristically in this chapter as an organizing concept (not a descriptive category) to denote integrating factors that aid in holding a social framework together. This concept includes forms of knowledge, that is, thought, perception, and belief structures, that (by making certain ways of knowing oneself and the world possible) function in behalf of integrating the extant (or an envisioned) social framework. The centered nature of CCK denotes its role in generating the coherence a referent social framework requires in order to secure the loyalty, motivated participation, and relevant consciousness of its subjects (adherents). For example, individuals from different subgroups can be socially integrated (assimilated) within the referent (White, Anglo-Saxon, or European American) middle-class culture because CCK induces the perceptions and interpretations of social reality, behaviors, consciousness, and consensual (but not necessarily conscious) meanings that support the middle-class normative cultural model of the social framework. Culture-centered knowledge, as ideology, can make certain perceptions and interpretations of reality (of self and "different" others) possible or "dysconsciously" improbable. Dysconsciousness is defined as "an uncritical habit of mind (including perceptions, attitudes, assumptions, and beliefs)"; it is a form of thought that "justifies inequity and exploitation by accepting the existing order of things as given" (J. E. King, 1991a, p. 135; J. E. King, 1997, p. 129).

This formulation of the concept of culture-centered knowledge attempts to denote objectively the manner in which certain ways of knowing and perceiving social reality function within a given social framework. It is adapted from Wynter's (1991) discussion of ideology, not in the pejorative sense of false-consciousness but as a description of the "system function," as Ricoeur (1979) and others suggest, which "all ideologies serve" (p. 252). This formulation of CCK also draws on Asante's (1992) explanation of how Afrocentricity differs from the ideology of Eurocentricity as well as S. Walker's (2001) analysis of the "lack of Afrogenic intellectual balance in our academic training" (p. 15).

For example, Euro-American cultural knowledge that is represented and valorized in school curricula is culture-centered with respect to its referent, the existing U.S. social framework, not because it is Eurocentric but because it serves to *legitimate* the dominant White middle-class normative cultural model (Castenell & Pinar, 1993). This is so even if White American culture is actually hybrid or "culturally part Negro" (Ellison, 1986, p. 108). On the other hand, an Afrocentric or African-centered worldview refers to the culture-specific social thought or perspective of African-descent people (in terms not of biology but of social and historical experience and empirical reality). In contrast to Eurocentric thought, this worldview perspective does not rationalize or justify a universal or normative cultural model of being and way of knowing the world. That is, as Asante (1992) states, "Afrocentricity is not a black version of Eurocentricity" (p. 22). This would imply that White cultural authority in the curriculum or the disciplines would

simply be replaced by the hegemony of Black cultural authority. There has been a failure to distinguish among differing conceptions of Black studies and African-centered thought (Weider, 1992), and these differences involve more than "ongoing debate over nomenclature" in the field of Black studies (Hine, 1990, p. 15).

Hegemony and Autonomy. Analysis is required in order to determine whether the referent social framework of culture-centered knowledge (i.e., the framework that CCK holds together) is dominating or culturally democratic (liberating). Under conditions of domination, race and ethnic difference, for example, are negated and a single, normative "common culture" model based on individualism is emphasized. In this instance culture-centered knowledge can be identified with hegemony, if it induces the belief that the social interests of various groups are indivisible (i.e., isomorphic), whereas diverse communities of interests actually exist (Alinsky, 1971). A central element of critical race theory developed by Derrick Bell (and others) emphasizes that "racial advances" for Black people are possible only where a "convergence" of the divergent interests of Black people and White exists (Delgado, 1995, p. xiv). Such socially constructed consensus is in the particular interest of a dominant group that prevails over and against the various interests of less powerful groups. On the other hand, culture-centered knowledge that enables social cohesion through democratic or "shared pluralism" (A. Walker, 1991, p. 25)—recognizing and valuing group differences and freedom in choice and thought—can be identified with autonomy. In this instance, the larger interest of human freedom predominates. Under conditions of autonomy, differences are not suppressed or ranked. In addition, under conditions either of hegemony or autonomy, CCK produces (and/or privileges) forms of subjectivity and thought that dislocate or locate individual and collective identity, behavior, and consciousness.

To recapitulate, because it is a social product culture-centered knowledge (like knowledge more generally) is built up as a result of the social activity of men and women (Cornforth, 1971), but also in particular social and cultural contexts. An important point is that under conditions of hegemony, CCK conflicts with or disparages the cultural knowledge and interests of dominated groups, and the "sameness" of individuals (for instance, "e pluribus unum") serves as a rationalizing principle for domination that is represented as societal cohesion ("our" national identity, national security interest). Curiously, sameness can be represented ideologically as pluralism: "We are all multicultural."

The Belief Structure of Race. A final point is that the culture-centered knowledge that constitutes a given society's claims about itself does not necessarily correspond to the reality of how the social framework actually works. In the Caribbean, Brazil, and America's "southern cone" (S. Walker, 2001), a socially integrating belief structure of race powerfully contradicts the appearance of pluralism in these societies (Goveia, 1970; Moore, 1964; Wynter, 1992a). Because diverse groups people the Caribbean Islands, the islands are thought to constitute "plural societies" with no "common culture or common set of values, shared by the population as a whole" (Goveia, p. 9). However, Goveia points out that the integrating factor (or CCK) that unifies the Caribbean in a way that transcends "internal divisions" of class, language, and politics is the "acceptance of the inferiority of Negroes to whites" (p. 9). The social framework in Brazil is also sustained by such a system-integrating structure of belief in Black inferiority. This culture-centered knowledge legitimates "racial democracy," the central myth of societal cohesion in Brazil. That is, one becomes "White" with enough money. Despite the reality of racial hierarchy in Brazil, the idea of Brazil as a racial democracy was documented and promulgated for years in government-sponsored social science research (Fontaine, 1985).

In the United States, people also proclaim their society to be a democracy, yet the social framework is also based on a system of racial hierarchy and a belief structure of racial superiority and inferiority (Feagin, 2001; Hacker, 1992). Wynter (1984) maintains that one of the ways that social cohesion has been forged in U.S. society is through the collectively imagined threat of "Nigger Chaos" that inheres in the alter ego role of the conceptual "black" or "Negro" (p. 2). The conceptual Black embodies a totalizing belief in Black inferiority that rationalizes racial inequality in the social framework. Such beliefs, induced by culture-centered knowledge in the education system and as part of normal processes of enculturation, indicate some of the ways in which the social framework of these societies is sustained by a lack of cognitive autonomy. Such hegemonic CCK can either enable certain social illusions to be maintained or provoke the cognitive or intellectual autonomy needed to call the belief structure into question. Before analyzing and comparing different forms of culture-centered knowledge in educational discourse and curriculum transformation, this chapter discusses African American cultural knowledge and the tradition of autonomous Black social thought.

African American Cultural Knowledge and Thought

To acknowledge that individuals enculturated within a common group experience share a distinct mode of social thought and a shared body of cultural knowledge is not to imply an essentialized, romantic, biocentric ethnorationality. Although certain individuals will no doubt prove the exception, empirical evidence exists in various disciplines that African American culture differs from European American culture(s) in various ways, among them perceptual and value orientations, language patterns, ethos, aesthetics, and worldview (Collins, 1990; Dixon, 1971; Heath, 1989; Kochman, 1981; Nobles, 1985; A. Walker, 1991; S. W. Williams, 1991). This shared cultural knowledge includes the skills, awareness, consciousness, and competence that permit African American people and others of African descent in the Diaspora to participate meaningfully in a shared culture—in all of its changing socioeconomic and regional variations. The cultural competence involved is more than learning "a conglomeration of superficial aspects of life such as dance, dress, hairstyles" or other artifacts (Ogundipe-Leslie, 1984). An expanding body of literature also suggests that, despite the rupturing effects of enslavement and dislocating miseducation, the cultural knowledge that enables African people in various national contexts to maintain a collective group identity has been passed on, at least in part, through oral and literate expressive traditions, technology and material culture, spirituality and religion, and folkways (Asante, 1987; Gay & Baber, 1987; Harris, 1992; Holloway, 1990; Stuckey, 1987; S. Walker, 2001). Spirituality, a recognizable feature in African cultures worldwide, is a distinctive and profoundly important dimension of African American cultural knowledge and consciousness as well (Cone, 1972; Drake, 1977; Levine, 1977; Mitchell, 1991; Richards, 1980; Thompson, 1983). It is expressed in both religious music, such as spirituals, and the secularized blues (Woods, 1998). According to Cone, this spirituality (and particularly the blues) affirms the worth of Black humanity, embraces the value of universal humanism, and acknowledges but refuses to accept "the absurdity of White society" (Cone, p. 117). The literature also suggests that African American cultural knowledge includes a "distinctly African American mode of rationality" that evolved out of the shared history of "resistance against the various effects of capitalism and racism" (B. M. Gordon, 1985b, p. 7).

Competing Perspectives and Positions. The suggestion that African Americans share a distinct cultural perspective or worldview evokes skepticism about the cultural and "racial identity politics" that are implied. Scholars writing from within various theoretical positions—about African American social thought, Black studies, and multicultural education reforms, for example, including Black feminist scholars and literary critics and theorists—tend to stress the importance of recognizing gender and social-class differences or more fluid multiple or "hybrid" identities. Emphasis is also placed on the "duality" of African American identity (Gates, 1992b; Marable, 1993). What many perceive to be problematic and to which they take exception in "narrow notions of Afro-American identity" (Giroux, 1992, p. 127) that are equated with African-centered theorizing includes "scholarly" versus "vulgar" positivist claims to universality and cultural "authenticity" (Lemelle, 1993; Marable); "an untenable binary opposition" or (false) dichotomy between Europeans and Africans or Whites and Blacks (White, 1990, p. 84); "ethnic absolutisms" (Gilroy, 1993, p. 3); or unitary, fixed, biological conceptions of cultural identity that are reflected in conceptions of the "subject" as generically White/female or Black/male (Gates, 1992b; Giroux, 1992; S. Hall, 1991; Guy-Sheftall, 1992; hooks, 1990; hooks & West, 1991; Said, 1993; West, 1993).

Black feminist scholar D. K. King (1988) criticizes the "theoretical invisibility of black women" in "mainstream" scholarship and Black studies, while Collins (1990) locates her theoretical analysis of Black women's thought and experience in the nexus of race, class, and gender *within* an Afrocentric epistemological paradigm. She defines Black women's standpoint as Afrocentric feminist consciousness. White (1990), on the other hand, is critical of both Afrocentric theorizing and Collins's Afrocentric feminist standpoint. White asserts that "Black feminists do not have any essential, biologically-based claim on understanding black women's experience" because this group is "divided by class, region, and sexual orientations" (p. 82). White also argues that Afrocentric theorizing, like the Eurocentric perspective it criticizes, is essentially positivist and therefore also makes false claims to universal truth (p. 93). Other objections are raised on the basis of the perception that this theoretic is counterproductive to interracial collaboration, that it represents a form of racial "essentialism," "cultural separation," or an overdetermined modernist notion of the "fixed subject" (McCarthy & Crichlow, 1993). Giroux (1992) suggests that the writing of women of color avoids such problems. In a discussion of "some meanings of blackness," Gates (1992b) disparages what he calls "the paranoid dream of cultural autarky" (pp. 131–151). Gates indicates his preference for "blackness without blood," that is to say, "elective affinities, unburdened by an ideology of descent" over the "cultural ensolacements of nationalism" (p. 151).

S. A. Clarke (1991) acknowledges that "political practices and mobilizations that are based on cultural and social identities" such as race have "serious limitations," but he argues that racial identity politics "also embody possibilities for empowerment." This is because "the most powerful constructions of common sense about identity politics . . . are deeply influenced by racial symbols, racial meanings, and racial understandings" (p. 37). Yet this potential for empowerment must contend with "formidable hostility," because political

mobilizations around race appear (to liberals and conservatives) to constitute a "danger to the body politic" (p. 37). That is, "identity politics are positioned"—in a socially constructed and media-supported "common sense" way—"to starkly reflect the need for a reassertion of 'traditional' liberal values of individualism, privatism, and authoritarian nationalism" (p. 38). Progressives have argued that racial identity politics ignore divergent cultural differences within groups (immigrant Africans, Haitians, and so forth) and block class-based coalition building with other groups (Marable, 1993). One problem, of course, is who decides what is progressive (or valid), and by which criteria. Clearly, the race of the protagonists in such discussions is not a reliable indicator of their political perspective, worldview, or theoretical position.

Cultural Assimilation/Miseducation/Liberation. It is not necessary to conclude that African American social thought is homogeneous to recognize that one of its predominant concerns, well represented in the work of DuBois (Aptheker, 1973), Woodson (1933), and others, is the relationship between preserving African American cultural originality and liberating education. In his introduction to a collection of essays on the education of Black people, Aptheker (1973), DuBois's editor and biographer (and a radical White historian in his own right), explains that

DuBois saw education (to be truly education) as partisan and—given the realities of the social order—fundamentally subversive. Specifically, in this connection, he wrote as a Black man in the United States; in this sense he was concerned in the first place with the education of his people in the United States, and that education as part of the process of the liberation of his people. Thus, his writing on education—as on everything else—has a kind of national consciousness, a specific motivation which—while directed towards his people—at the same time and therefore was meant to serve all humanity. (p. xi)

That education ought to be for service to "all humanity" while preserving African American culture—and not just for class-based personal gain and profit making—constituted no contradiction for DuBois. This is indicative of the significant human interest in the social thought of African American intellectuals like DuBois who were at the same time committed to "saving the race" (Carruthers, 1994). One of DuBois's last commentaries on this matter was written in 1960, just three years before his death:

Any statement of our desire to develop American Negro culture, to keep up our ties with coloured people, to remember our past is being regarded as "racism." I, for instance, who have devoted my life to efforts to break down racial barriers, am being accused of desiring to emphasize differences of race. This has a certain truth about it. (quoted in H. Aptheker, 1973, p. 150)

It is interesting to note that scholars of various persuasions cite DuBois's *The Souls of Black Folk* (1903/1953) to support both pluralist and nationalist interpretations of the aims of Black studies, curriculum transformation, and social action (Gates, 1992a; Marable, 1993; Stuckey, 1987). However, DuBois explained that he was "not fighting to settle the question of racial equality" in America by "getting rid of black folk" (p. 150). Rather his commitment was to the "possibility of black folk and their cultural patterns existing in America without discrimination; and on terms of equality" (p. 150). This requires the "preservation of African history and culture as a valuable contribution to modern civilization as it was to medieval and ancient civilization" (pp. 150–151).

DuBois's commitment to these multiple goals was long-term and not one-dimensional. As early as 1897, he wrote that he did not believe Black folk were destined to "imitate Anglo-Saxon culture" but to maintain an "originality which shall unswervingly follow Negro ideals" (Stuckey, 1987, p. 398, n. 59). According to Stuckey, DuBois "considered originality the highest nationalist objective intellectually and spiritually," yet he also expressly admired aspects of Euro-American culture and emphasized the worth of all humanity (p. 398, n. 61). In order to take into consideration the importance of economic and psychological factors, Stuckey notes that DuBois later modified his early belief in "racial gifts as the motive force of history" (pp. 265, 298, n. 59).

This commitment to uplifting humanity by struggling to transform the United States into a "socially just society" (Semmes, 1992, p. 73), while valorizing African American culture and autonomy, is an important dimension of the tradition of Black studies and African American social thought. Other Black intellectuals who have demonstrated this commitment (the list could be longer) include Ida B. Wells-Barnett (Dray, 2002; Wells-Barnett, 1969; McMurry, 1998), John Henrik Clarke (Adams, 1992; J. H. Clarke, 1992), Anna Julia Cooper (Carby, 1987; Cooper, 1892/1988), Vincent Harding (1974, 1990), C.L.R. James (Hamilton, 1992; C.L.R. James, 1948, 1970), Arturo Schomburg (Childs, 1989), and Sylvia Wynter (Scott, 2000; Wynter, 1992b, 1992c). As Frazier (1973) also observed, this struggle requires "intellectual freedom" from "an implied or unconscious assimilationist philosophy, holding that Negroes should enter the mainstream of American life as rapidly as possible leaving behind their social heritage and becoming invisible as soon as possible" (p. 56). Earlier, Woodson (1933) had described how the "mis-education of the Negro" produced the abject conformity that contributed to this "failure of the Negro intellectual" that Frazier (1957, 1973) and Cruse (Cobb, 2002; Cruse, 1967) also criticize.

HEGEMONY/AUTONOMY: CULTURE-CENTERED KNOWLEDGE AND CURRICULUM TRANSFORMATION

The remainder of this chapter will use the formulation of CCK presented earlier to compare forms of culture-centered knowledge in educational discourse and curriculum transformation. Culture-centered knowledge that represents divergent conceptions of "difference" and social interest can be organized into four overlapping categories of curriculum transformation. The knowledge in these categories is identified as culture-centered because each category is associated with a type of curriculum transformation (or restoration) that can serve a socially integrating function on behalf of a particular social framework. The four categories are marginalizing knowledge, invisibilizing knowledge, expanding knowledge, and deciphering knowledge. Each category corresponds to divergent ways of perceiving and knowing social reality, particularly with regard to the social constructions of "sameness" or "difference." These social constructions have implications for the way social interests are represented—as "indivisible," for example, or as "communities of interest." Table 18.1 shows the four categories of culture-centered knowledge and curriculum transformation in relation to the conception of sameness and difference and the interest with which each is associated.

As Table 18.1 shows, these categories are also identified with hegemony or autonomy. As such, each also involves dominating or liberating forms of curriculum transformation and education practice as social action. The two categories identified with hegemony and indivisible social interests are marginalizing knowledge and invisibilizing knowledge. Both emphasize sameness; that is, the social construction of difference (as sameness) corresponds to a unitary conception of social interests, but to a greater extent (invisibilizing knowledge) or a lesser one (marginalizing knowledge).

Expanding knowledge and deciphering knowledge are forms of curriculum transformation that can be identified with autonomy; that is, knowledge and curriculum transformation in these categories are autonomous or

TABLE 18.1. Categories of Culture-Centered Knowledge and Curriculum Transformation.

Hegemony/Sameness Indivisible Interest	Autonomy/Difference Communities of Interest
Marginalizing knowledge	Expanding knowledge
Invisibilizing knowledge	Deciphering knowledge

free to a greater extent (deciphering knowledge) or a lesser extent (expanding knowledge) from socially constructed cognitive constraints (beliefs) that suppress difference. Under such conditions of autonomy, culture-centered curriculum knowledge values cultural difference and recognizes diverse communities of social interests. Democracy or "pluralism without hierarchy" (Asante, 1992, p. 22) and cultural affirmation is the "Ideological" interest (in the Wynterian sense) in the social framework this type of curriculum transformation seeks to bring about. These four categories, as presented here, are not intended to be mutually exclusive but are dynamically interrelated. Each one contains in itself the conditions of possibility of another category (C.L.R. James, 1948).

Marginalizing Knowledge

Marginalizing knowledge is a form of curriculum transformation that can include selected "multicultural" curriculum content that simultaneously distorts the historical and social reality that people actually experienced. Marginalization can take the form of bias and omission (McCarthy, 1990; Swartz, 1992), but it is most particularly a form of selective inclusion. The ideology of pluralism in California's *History/Social Science Framework* (California State Department of Education [CSDE], 1987), more recently developed academic content standards, and state-adopted textbooks illustrate this kind of marginalizing knowledge in the transformation of a curriculum. This form of marginalizing inclusion is justified in the (indivisible) interest of "our common culture." That diverse cultures make the United States a multicultural society, that the perspectives of diverse groups should be acknowledged, and that the right to "be different" should be "respected" are clearly stated principles in this document. The *Framework* also states that it "incorporates a multicultural perspective throughout" (CSDE, p. 5). However, the ideology of pluralism in this curriculum guide marginalizes the actual experiences of African Americans, Latinos, and American Indians in the development of U.S. society. This is done through the use of conceptual terms that privilege the historical experiences of White Euro-American immigrant groups. J. E. King (1992) and Wynter (1992a) analyze the conceptual flaws in the *Framework* and the state-adopted textbooks; they demonstrate how the conceptualizations of "immigrant" and "immigration" in these curriculum materials reify the historical experiences of dominant Whites and rationalize the social construction of racial hierarchy and societal inequity in textbooks. These representations of "our common culture" mask the enduring significance of racial and cultural social divisions.

An example from the *Framework's* course guide for the fifth-grade "story of the development of the nation" is illustrative. The focus is on "one of the most remarkable stories in history: the creation of a new nation peopled by *immigrants* from all parts of the globe" (CSDE, 1987, p. 50, emphasis added). In Chapter 1 of the state-approved fifth-grade textbook, *America Will Be* (Armento, Nash, Salter, & Wixson, 1991), ideological representations of this (mis)conceptualization are stated as incontrovertible fact (about which historians agree). This statement appears in the text: "Everyone who lives in the United States is either an immigrant or a descendant of immigrants." Alongside it, to provide reinforcement, a study question asks: "Why do you think historians call the United States 'a nation of immigrants?'" (p. 13). The contradictory interests that are suppressed by this representation of everyone in the United States in terms of the idealized Euro-American immigrant "model of being" becomes apparent when this construct is applied to the actual historical experiences of American Indians, Native Hawaiians and Alaskans, or the indigenous peoples of the Southwest and their ongoing struggles over the land, including disputed claims, resistance to the disposal of toxic wastes in their communities, their rights to natural resources, and their right not to be treated as "illegal aliens" in their ancestral homelands. This representation makes the African American experience of enslavement an anomaly of the normative cultural model (J. E. King, 1992).

Yet students are to be taught that all groups have the same indivisible social interest. Descriptions of U.S. society as a "common community" that mask the racially and economically divided social reality is another way that dominant-group interests are represented as the indivisible interest of all individuals and groups. Consider this statement:

> We are strong because we are united in a pluralistic society of many races, cultures, and ethnic groups; we have built a great nation because we have learned to live in peace with each other, respecting each other's right to be different and supporting each other as members of a common community. (CSDE, 1987, p. 56)

This passage from the *Framework* adroitly transforms difference into a form of homogenizing pluralism or sameness in the ostensible interest of "our common public culture." According to J. E. King (1992), interests of dominant power groups that might be at stake in the promulgation of this form of culture-centered knowledge include the official validation of "established" scholars and the reification of the White Euro-American immigrant experience as a model of success to be emulated by Latino and Asian immigrant "newcomers," who are often placed in an "intermediate status" on the black-to-white continuum

(Feagin, 2001). This representation of social reality does not provide students with culture-centered knowledge needed to critique the basis of social cohesion in the U.S. social framework (e.g., the belief structure of race) or the motivation to participate in continued struggle against racism and injustice (J. E. King, 1992). B. M. Gordon (1992) suggests that this may be because "pluralism is used and defended in the United States because pluralism can assist the dominant power in maintaining their structures" (p. 28).

Invisibilizing Knowledge

Curriculum transformation and knowledge in this category also serve the ideology of the sameness and indivisibility of social interests, but not in terms of pluralism. Rather, invisibilizing knowledge is monocultural; it simply obliterates the historical presence, unique experience, contributions, and perspectives of diverse people in the development of the United States and Western civilization. This category can include not only forms of erasure but also defamation or denial of group achievements (LaFrance, 1992). The interest involved is the restoration or preservation of Western cultural and intellectual dominance through the curriculum. This occurs in curriculum narratives such as the "we came to an empty land" White colonial settler identity story of the development of the United States, and the "our Western heritage of Ancient Rome, Greece, Egypt, and Sumer, but not Africa" White ethnic identity story (Bernal, 1987; Diop, 1981; Hilliard, 1992; Young, 1990).

The "we" and "our" induce the conceptually excluded to identify with these social constructions of the self-identity of the dominant group (Martinez, 1992/1993; Wynter, 1992a). Such narratives also constitute a discourse of cultural hegemony that transmutes the "real environment"(Fasheh, 1990) into an ideological one: cultural identity is positioned hegemonically within the dominant group's social interest. This erasure does not just marginalize difference; it obliterates the self-identities and communities of interest of the dominated as well. Paradoxically, this erasure may even be achieved by means of "structured absences" and silences on certain topics (Morrison, 1989) that writers use to construct an imagined "White self," a conception of "mainstream culture," or "our" national identity (Fishkin, 2001). Curriculum restoration of Western dominance through invisibilizing knowledge is articulated by Neusner (1989) in an example of CCK that is vigorously defended as universally valid objective scholarship in the popular media (Leo, 1989) and in academic writing such as this:

A critical question that demands our study of other cultures is why it is that the West has created what the rest of the world now wants. Why did capitalism not begin in India, for example? . . . Why is there no science in Africa? Why has democracy only been grafted onto the political structures in Asia? And conversely, why are all of them to be found indigenously in the West? To answer such questions, we must begin where science, economics, politics, and technology began and from whence they were diffused. They uniquely flourished in the West, and, to begin with, in Western Europe. (Neusner, 1989, p. B1)

Sizemore (1990, p. 78) cites this statement to make the point that such claims to the superiority, objectivity, and universality of the disciplines of Western knowledge are themselves based on "distinctly political ideologies" (p. 77). Consequently, the sociohistorical record becomes an unrelenting monocultural narrative of White superiority, while denial of any influence of culture and ideology on knowledge also invisibilizes the connection between the power to define reality and ideological distortions of knowledge and curriculum transformation (restoration). Both expanding knowledge and invisibilizing knowledge are responses to the moral and epistemological panics discussed earlier.

Expanding Knowledge

The other two categories of curriculum transformation recognize that various perspectives on knowledge, divergent social interests, and multiple social identities exist in consequence of the diversity of people's historical and lived experiences. In the expanding knowledge category, curriculum transformation incorporates multiple narratives and rotating standpoints from which to view and interpret social reality. This category can be likened to an "additive" model of multicultural curriculum change (Banks, 1989). Curriculum transformation that expands knowledge can replace "Whiteness" in the mode of the subject (the normative representation of the social framework's desired self) with a racially "hybrid" middle-classness (not homelessness or wagelessness). However, this rotation in the perspective of the subject can multiculturalize knowledge without changing fundamentally the norm of middle-classness in the social framework's cultural model of being (Wynter, 1992c). With the expansion and inclusion of the multiple perspectives of diverse "Others," traditional knowledge in the curriculum and the disciplines can be multiculturalized and thereby "saved" (Wynter, 1992c). Only "incremental additions to a body of knowledge" (Aldridge, 1992, p. 65) or to the disciplines are possible as curriculum expands in this way (Asante, 1992, pp. 22–23). These additions do not undo, uninvent, or uncover the social framework's prescriptive rules governing inclusion and exclusion (Wynter, 1992b,

1992c). Ishmael Reed's 1993 novel about multicultural change at a fictional college satirizes this limitation of expanding knowledge. As the number of oppositional (i.e., multicultural) studies programs increase and vie for centrality, Professor Puttbutt, the novel's Black protagonist, concludes sardonically that "Everybody was a nigger . . . Women, gays, always comparing their situations [subject positions] with blacks" (p. 9). In other words, knowledge within traditional disciplines can be expanded (e.g., "multiculturalized," "genderized," or "Africanized") by adding the perspectives of the formerly excluded, but fundamental assumptions of human existence in the social organization of knowledge can remain unquestioned and thereby leave in place faulty conceptions of being within those disciplines.

The inclusion of African American literature at all levels of education is a common form of curriculum transformation in the category of expanding knowledge (McElroy-Johnson, 1993; Spears-Bunton, 1990). Gates (1992a, 1992b) is widely recognized for his successful efforts to "open up" mainstream literature to include a Black literary canon. Both Gates (1988) and Baker (1984) have used "vernacular" forms of African American expressive culture like blues music and "signifyin'" (indirect, boastful, critical, or reproachful speech) to articulate complex, complementary theories of the distinctive character of African American literature and writing. Their stated aim is to "enlarge" the literary canon by institutionalizing this vernacular tradition (Gates, 1992a, 1992b). In Wynter's (1992c) estimation, the theory of literary criticism offered by Gates does not liberate people's knowledge and consciousness from dominating social constructs but is instead a culturally original way of *interpreting* Black texts. Wynter is also doubtful about the establishment of what she calls Gates's "ethno-literary" or "cultural-indigenous" school of thought in the arts (pp. 263–266).

In sum, individual scholars and practitioners engaged in expanding knowledge may exercise sufficient cognitive autonomy to increase the available perspectives, but perhaps not so "vastly" as is often asserted (Adell, 1990; Baker, 1984; Gates, 1992a; Giroux, 1992; West, 1993). Christian (1989) and R. W. Gilmore (1993) caution that the "system" can "reproduce itself" through the work of "individualistic" scholars who have become a "multiculturalized professional managerial class" by virtue of opportunistically studying whatever is "politically and oppositionally 'new'" (R. W. Gilmore, 1993, pp. 71–72). Other critical analyses of Black vernacular traditions (Childs, 1989; Cone, 1972; Stuckey, 1987), when compared to theorizing that is aimed primarily at institutionalizing a Black literary canon, reveal autonomous critiques

of the social framework in African American thought that are articulated in analyses that not only expand but transcend the "mainstream" canon. These limitations of curriculum transformation through expanding knowledge are also suggested in a critical comparison of "capitalistic" and "democratic" versus "liberationist" forms of Afrocentrism (Weider, 1992).

Other forms of curriculum transformation that involve expanding knowledge in schools and the academy include collaborative efforts among teachers, students, and researchers to recover and use in school learning students' cultural knowledge related to their home and community experiences (Moses & Cobb, 2001; Wiggington, 1989). Lee (1991, 1992) extends Gates's theory of African American vernacular oral traditions to create "culturally sensitive scaffolding," an innovative teaching strategy that uses "students' existing cultural knowledge" of traditional African American community language practices such as "signifyin'" to enable them to interpret figurative language in Black literary texts. Moll, Amanti, Neff, and Gonzalez (1992) prepare teachers to use the tools of anthropology to study the "funds of knowledge" in the households of Mexican American and African American families. A team of researchers and teachers then translates this cultural knowledge into meaningful classroom lessons. The object in both of these research projects is the improvement of student academic learning.

Deciphering Knowledge

Examination of the theoretical and literary analyses of Wynter (1984, 1989, 1991, 1992a, 1992c) and Morrison (1989, 1992) will show that deciphering knowledge that is aimed at changed consciousness and cognitive autonomy can be a foundation for curriculum transformation. This is not to imply that deciphering knowledge alone can change society; social action directed at fundamental social change requires the "emancipation of human cognition" (C.L.R. James, 1948; Semmes, 1992). Both Wynter and Morrison use a theoretical and methodological vocabulary like that of Foucault's "archaeology of knowledge" (1972) to expose the belief structure of race in literature, school texts (Wynter, 1992a), and other discursive practices. Foucault's method involves "deciphering," "excavating," and analyzing "discursive literary formations" in the social organization of knowledge "whose lineage can be traced and whose regularities are discoverable" (Baker, 1984, pp. 17–18). Wynter locates her theoretical project within Black studies and describes her method as a "deciphering practice." She uses Foucault's insights (1970) regarding knowledge and power to "decipher" the governing cultural rules of knowledge in the academic disciplines and in society. One such rule is the classifying duality of "conceptual" Whiteness and Blackness, which, Wynter (1984, 1989, 1992b) argues, sustains and legitimates human misery.

In two analytical essays, Morrison (1989, 1992) examines critically the socially constructed nature of Whiteness and Blackness in the "literary imagination." Morrison deciphers the presence and use of invented "ideological Africanism" in fiction (1992, p. 80) by "excavating" the "denotative and connotative blackness that African peoples have come to signify" in literature (p. 6). Together these analyses demonstrate the liberating possibilities of curriculum transformation that uses autonomous culture-centered knowledge to decipher the social framework and the social organization of knowledge that legitimates it.

The Perspective Advantage of "Alterity"

Wynter's examination (1992a) of the belief structure of race suggests that the social constructions of Blackness/Whiteness embedded in literature that Morrison has uncovered reveal the "cultural mode of rationality" of the social framework. Wynter demonstrates that the founding integrative conception of the U.S. social framework is a "prescriptive value-opposition between Black and White" (p. 7), to which the society's racially based classifying system—or episteme that values and ranks people, their knowledge, and culture unequally—is a *logical* response. Within this classifying system, the conceptual Black is the alter ego (of the conceptual White) that "embodies the alternative of (Nigger) chaos" (Wynter, 1984, p. 2) to the "orthodox behaviors" that express the "normative national [White] identity" (Wynter, 1992a, p. 17). This conceptual difference between Blackness and Whiteness is the CCK upon which racialized social cohesion and inequity are founded. Wynter analyzes the epistemology of this prescriptive conception of human difference and concludes that *alterity* gives Black studies a perspective advantage. Semmes also argues that the "normative Eurocentric propensity" of cultural hegemony gives an advantage to Black studies as a social and epistemological critique (Semmes, 1992, p. 44). S. Walker (2001) concludes that "only by adding the real Afrogenic pieces can the rich mosaic of the Americas be correctly portrayed" (p. 42).

This perspective advantage is not due to an inherent racial/cultural difference, Wynter (1992a) argues, but is the result of the dialectical nature of constructed otherness that prescribes the liminal status of Blacks (and, for instance, American Indians) as beyond the normative boundary of the conception of Self and Other. Davis (1983a) makes an analogous observation about the dialectical nature of the Black-White experience of oppression-liberation, or what Morrison describes as the "parasitical nature of white freedom" (1992, p. 57). This perspective advantage of alterity can be likened to the "second-sight" Negroes are "gifted with" in the "American world" (DuBois, 1903/1953, pp. 16–17). This is not a racial advantage but a function of the normative racial categories of value that are operative in the social framework.

The alternative suggested here is not a dualistic position that there are multiple (and equally partial) standpoints that are either equally valid (because equally partial) or inexorably ranked hierarchically. Recognizing the alterity perspective of Black studies (or "seeing with Indian eyes, as well") does not essentialize "Blackness" as a homogenizing reverse epistemic (West, 1990, p. 585). Nor does Wynter's analysis of the perspective of alterity reduce the social complexity to a single explanatory factor or the so-called "black-white" paradigm (Feagin, 2001). At times, other differences (for instance, gender) may assume centrality in an analysis of the social reality, but *within* the belief system of race, given the way the classifying system of race functions as a belief structure in the society. The alternative to the prescriptive hierarchy of Otherness, insofar as curriculum transformation is concerned, is neither imposing an inverted "Black over White" hegemony nor emphasizing "multiple identities." The solution Wynter and others propose is abolition of the race-based classifying belief structure itself (Feagin, 2001; Wynter, 1992b, 1992c).

The next section of this chapter, which further considers the social effects of deciphering knowledge and its explanatory power to penetrate social myths, suggests a specific role for Black studies in curriculum transformation that abolishes this belief structure. It is also important to emphasize that the referent social framework of the deciphering culture-centered knowledge in the work of Morrison and Wynter is not a world dominated by Blackness or a world that multiculturalizes the Other and leaves conceptual Blackness intact. Rather, the social "Imaginary" (Wynter, 1989, p. 639) is the "newly defined world" (Harding, 1970, p. 290) that will "hold all the people" (p. 292) and constitute an altogether different "order of knowledge" and "changed quality of consciousness" (Blumenberg, 1983, p. 205; cited in Wynter, 1989, p. 643). According to Wynter, cognitive autonomy from the social framework's existing "cultural specific model of reality" is a necessity of human freedom (pp. 640–641). This suggests that liberating education can make more visible "the mode of production of the symbolic" (Simon, 1992, pp. 109–110) as well as the "real environment and power relations" (Fasheh, 1990, p. 28).

This section has presented four types of culture-centered knowledge and curriculum transformation that can be identified with hegemony or autonomy. The next section presents a further explication of the belief structure of race in the work of Wynter and Morrison.

DECIPHERING THE SOCIAL ORGANIZATION OF KNOWLEDGE

Henry and Buhle (1992) note that Wynter's "critical works contain one of the most powerful and comprehensive recastings of the problems of colonial discourses in the light of poststructuralist theory" (p. 116). Their assessment is perhaps a reflection of the interdisciplinary breadth and scope of Wynter's theoretical project. Her analysis of the belief structure of race draws together recent theory in biology, environmental studies, the history of European thought and colonization of the "New World," and African/Diaspora theorizing and social analysis. It presents a comprehensive, interdisciplinary analysis of the epistemological and axiological foundations of a Black studies approach to curriculum transformation. Wynter's theoretical project is grounded in a commitment to scientific description and ethical concern for social justice that is shared by other Caribbean, African, and African American scholars, including Angela Davis (United States, 1983a, 1983b), Chiekh Anta Diop (Senegal, 1981), Frantz Fanon (Martinique and Algeria, 1963), Elsa Goveia (Jamaica, 1970), Vincent Harding (United States, 1970, 1974, 1990), C.L.R. James (Trinidad, 1948, 1963), Asmarom Legesse (Eritrea, 1973), Donna M. Richards and Mi-rimba Ani (United States, 1980; Ani, 1994), Walter Rodney (Guyana, 1975, 1990), Arturo Schomburg (United States, Childs, 1989), Sheila Walker (United States, 2001), Ida B. Wells-Barnett (United States, 1969), and Carter G. Woodson (United States, 1933), to name only a few. One of Wynter's major contributions is that her work brings together elements of a transnational tradition of intellectual autonomy in African/Diaspora social thought (Scott, 2000). Wynter (1989) points out, for instance, that Frantz Fanon (1963) and the Martinican writer Edouard Glissant (1981) had been "impelled" by their recognition of the "Abject Otherness" of African-descent people to raise the "question of the historical and, therefore, relative nature of our modes of subjectivity" *before* Foucault (1970, 1972) was awakened to this problem in the aftermath of the 1968 "cultural revolts" in France (Wynter, 1989, p. 640).

Wynter's work extends that of such African American scholars as George Washington Ellis, an ethnographer whose writing appears in the *Journal of Race and Development* as early as 1915; DuBois; and Woodson, who raised the issue of subjectivity in racist scholarly justifications of slavery (Childs, 1989, pp. 83–87). According to Childs, "Ellis argued that scholarly activity had to be moved from the ideological position of racism to the ideological position of democracy" (p. 87). Childs notes that Ellis's "sense of the partiality of knowledge" was "intimately linked" to his "belief in the multifariousness of social reality" (p. 94).

Wells-Barnett exposed economic motives for the lynching of African Americans that were masked in racial and sexual rationalizations (Carby, 1987; Davis, 1983b; Wells-Barnett, 1969).

Deciphering the Belief Structure of Race/Invented Africanism in the White Literary Imagination

Wynter uses an interdisciplinary approach across the humanities and science to decipher the belief structure of race as a founding element of the Western model of culture, knowledge, and the "mode of the subject." This "cultural model analysis" calls for a *rewriting* of the academic disciplines from a "Black Studies Intellectual Perspective" (of alterity). This belief structure is *in* the disciplines and needs to be abolished in order to "emancipate human knowledge" from the semiolinguistic (symbolic) rules of inclusion-exclusion—the sign systems that inhere in the very "Founding Narratives of Origin" that "we tell ourselves." These rules govern all human cultures (Wynter, 1991, 1992c). Wynter argues that as humans we are not consciously aware of them; nor do we knowingly choose these behavior-orienting rules because we are subjects within an episteme or our "order of knowledge" and, as such, we are "always already" socialized by these rules. (The term *always already,* as used by Derrida (1976), denotes the socially determining power of language practices and is frequently found in the work of scholars writing from within "poststructuralist" and "deconstructionist" theoretical positions.) These governing rules represent the order's "desired mode of the subject" to us—what it means, for example, to be a good man or woman—and govern our behaviors and attitudes toward ourselves and others.

Morrison (1992) deciphers the ways that race, in the form of invented "Africanism," functions dialectically in literature and in the social imagination of White authors and readers. "Through a close look at 'literary blackness,'" she writes, "it may be possible to discover 'literary whiteness'" (p. 9). Morrison examines the "impact of racial hierarchy, racial exclusion, and racial vulnerability and availability" in fiction on non-Black readers and writers. This examination of the "problem that race causes" in the nation's literature (p. 14) shows how writers position readers as "White" by using "serviceable" representations of "the Black." Thus Morrison's analysis also reveals how the "sycophancy of white identity" (p. 19) functions hegemonically in these relations of representation. Because hegemony legitimates the social framework's White normative cultural model of being and identity, the analyses by both Wynter and Morrison suggest that Black people's humanity can only be affirmed and valued—and everyone else freed from the conceptual incarceration of the belief structure of race—if society is reinvented and reorganized around a different cultural model of the human. As Morrison explains: "Statements to the contrary, insisting on the meaninglessness of race to the American identity are themselves full of meaning. The world does not become raceless or will not become unracialized by assertion" (p. 46).

Therefore, a condition of a radically changed social framework is autonomous knowledge, and according to Wynter, autonomous knowledge must include knowledge of the "cultural model" itself. Both Morrison and Wynter point out that the belief structure of race that sustains the existing social framework is built into the culture, in the epistemic or social organization of knowledge, including the education system, the academic disciplines, curriculum knowledge, and the national literature. The disciplines of the West's cultural heritage are deeply implicated. This is why Wynter traces the history of their development through the intellectual, economic, and political expansion that followed Europe's Middle Ages.

A Deciphering Role for Black Studies in Curriculum Transformation

Just as the European bourgeoisie had to disestablish (theocentric) scholasticism to find freedom for their own proper being, Wynter (1992c) argues that postcolonial subjects must "establish a new order" of knowledge to get beyond the present crisis of societal and self-negation. Wynter contends that the Black studies intellectual perspective can bring into being an epistemological break from the biological/racial/hierarchical narrative about humanity's origins that "we" still tell ourselves. Wynter finds support for her position in the work of Woodson (1933) and of Fanon, a psychiatrist and revolutionary theoretician who documented his empirical observations of the psychological consequences of "alienating material conditions" and "alienated consciousness" (Hansen, 1977) in his book *Black Skins, White Masks* (Fanon, 1967). As with Fanon, a primary concern of both Wynter and Morrison is to explicate the conditions of human freedom from all forms of alienation and oppression. Since people have the capacity to question and to act upon humanly instituted ideological and self-negating cultural structures, such as the belief in the "genetic defectivity of race," cognitive autonomy is a condition of freedom.

Wynter urges Black studies scholars to investigate the conditions under which autonomous thought and social action are possible. Citing Hartmann's observation (1980) that "literature is to the modern mind as the Bible was to medieval thought," Wynter (1992c, p. 263) points out that literary criticism must perform a deciphering "allegorical exegesis" to provide cognitive alternatives to the social framework's governing mode of knowledge and being.

Wynter's critical aesthetics project is for liberating knowledge not only in behalf of African-descent people, but also for the most inclusive interest of human freedom. Both Wynter and Morrison are contributing to an emergent body of deciphering knowledge that exemplifies the dynamically evolving Black studies epistemological critique.

THE PRACTICE OF FREEDOM: DECIPHERING CULTURE-CENTERED KNOWLEDGE

The remainder of this chapter presents selected examples of CCK in research and education practice that deciphers aspects of the social framework to prepare people for the practice of freedom, that is, to change society and themselves (Freire, 1980). It should be clear from the preceding discussion that culture-centered knowledge can serve different interests and purposes with different outcomes (e.g., invisibilization, marginalization, expanding the canon). The literature discussed in this section will demonstrate this point further and suggest criteria that can be used to distinguish between the two forms of autonomous culture-centered knowledge identified in this chapter. There are several important reasons to focus on identifying differences between curriculum transformation that expands the canon and deciphering knowledge in education practice and research. One is that scholars not only conceptualize Black studies, African-centered, and multicultural curriculum transformation differently but also conceptualize and use African American cultural knowledge in very different ways in curriculum transformation. A second reason to examine closely such applications of cultural knowledge is because scholars using the same conceptual paradigm and theoretical vocabulary (Fanon, Foucault, or DuBois) can, of course, reach very different conclusions (Robinson, 1993). For example, Wynter's (1992c) critical exegesis or "re-thinking" of aesthetics identifies "signifying practices" in both popular films and Black music, as do Gates (1988) and Baker (1984, 1993), but with different theoretical aims. In another example, Asante (1992) uses "dislocation, location, and relocation" as theoretical terms within the "Afrocentric position" to describe what he calls the "locational fallacy," or what occurs when a person is "de-centered, misoriented, or disoriented" from his or her own cultural reality (p. 20). When writing about theorists who "displace" dominating/colonial representations (master narratives) that relegate difference to marginalized "otherness," Giroux (1992) cites Young's notion of "dislocating" postcolonial discourse (1990, p. 20). Similar terms thus derive from very different theoretical positions.

The literature reviewed in this section of the chapter suggests two primary criteria that can be used to identify deciphering knowledge in education practice and research. The first criterion is the *social effects of knowledge*, particularly with respect to the uses of knowledge for social action in organic connection with "the larger struggle for social change" (R. W. Gilmore, 1993, p. 72). Deciphering knowledge gives priority to the most urgent needs of real-life citizens as a criterion of validity—as compared to whether new scholarship is institutionalized as a discipline or expands a traditional academic canon. An important example of this criterion is Wynter's insistent plea urging intellectuals to "marry their thought" to the jobless, "the global new poor," or "les damnés (de la terre)"—Fanon's "wretched of the earth" (1993)—the "captive populations of the U.S. inner cities and the Third World shantytown archipelagoes" (Wynter, 1992c, p. 241). Stated another way, deciphering knowledge is necessarily holistic, explicitly accountable to and linked to the needs of real communities (J. James, 1993b; Orr, 1992). Both expanding and deciphering knowledge can make useful contributions to curriculum transformation and social action, but by differing means. For instance, a growing body of African-centered curriculum materials, Web-based and multimedia learning resources, as well as service-learning approaches that are not reviewed in this chapter are expanding curriculum knowledge and the social action possibilities that are available to schools (M. Hall, 1991; Pinkard, 2001).

The ethos of deciphering knowledge is nonelitist and inclusive with regard to the fluid roles of the scholar/activist/knower (intellectual, teacher, student, researcher, or community person), who is committed to rigorous truth-seeking demystification (Harding, 1974; J. James, 1993a; J. James & Farmer, 1993). A second criterion follows from this: the *effects of knowledge on consciousness or cognitive autonomy*, that is, the extent to which culture-centered knowledge penetrates social myths linked to objective and subjective problems of human existence and gives people "power over their own lives" (Boggs, 1974, p. 80). Such knowledge is necessarily nonassimilationist and embraces democratic racial and cultural pluralism. These criteria assume the dialectical mutability of the social framework and people (Giddens, 1979). Liberating, autonomous knowledge can change consciousness, and a new social "Imaginary" (Wynter, 1989) can empower and motivate people to take action, that is, to take charge of their circumstances.

Deciphering Knowledge, Consciousness, and Social Change

This next section presents several examples of research and scholarship that demonstrate these criteria in different contexts, though not necessarily to the same extent. The researchers and practitioners involved aim to make the curriculum and other education practices more liberating and inclusive, while also meeting the real and urgent needs of people by using knowledge for action and change. (Personal biographical information that is included about several researchers, such as race, accords with an "ethic of personal accountability," or a value-based criterion, that Collins, 1990, suggests is useful for assessing knowledge claims in an alternative Afrocentric epistemology.)

Education to Govern. Grace Lee Boggs, a Chinese American woman formally trained in philosophy, is a grassroots scholar-activist in the Black community of Detroit. She and her late husband, James Boggs (noted for publications like *Pages from a Negro Worker's Notebook* and *Racism and the Class Struggle*), have been at the forefront of radical social changes for decades (Boggs, 1998). An essay Boggs first published in 1970 and that is still powerfully relevant critiques society and education from the perspective of the Black experience. As the title of a later version of this essay ("Education: The Great Obsession," Boggs, 1974) suggests, this work penetrates pervasive social myths like "making it"—namely, that education is for "achieving the *good life*" and for "fitting people into the framework of our present industrial society" (p. 72). Although Boggs explains how a new role for education would benefit all students, she demonstrates how the education system works to the particular disadvantage of the Black community. Because the education system supports the social framework, Boggs observes that "the overwhelming majority of black youth see no relationship" between education, "their daily lives in the community or the problems of today's world which affect them so intimately" (p. 69). That is, education promotes opportunist individualism over communal needs; unquestioning acceptance of textbook authority; and irrelevance in the face of changing economic conditions, locally and globally. Boggs proposes a new role for education to prepare students "to govern" in the best interests of their communities and the society. The key principles of this new system of education are:

1. *Education must be based on a philosophy of history* to enable students to realize their "highest potential as a human being" with the "unique capacity . . . to shape and create reality in accordance with conscious purposes and plans" (pp. 72–73).
2. *Education must include clearly defined goals* and social purposes "for changing society and changing ourselves simultaneously" (p. 72).
3. *Education must be responsive to the community*, that is, "the community itself with its needs and problems must become the curriculum of the schools. . . . [T]hrough a realistic curriculum, research becomes a means of building the community . . . rather than pacification programs against the community" (p. 74).

4–5. *Education must include a wide variety of resources and environments* (e.g., books and computers, the city and countryside) and *productive activity* as well, because "experiencing the consequences of their own activity" is the way students learn best (pp. 75–76).

6. *Education must include living struggles* to enable students "to develop the technical skills to rebuild their communities" and "transform themselves along with their communities" (p. 76).

7–8. *Education must include development in bodily self-knowledge and well-being; and education must include preparation to govern.* This is because "young people whose *self-concept* has undergone a fundamental change must be given concrete opportunities to change the *actual* conditions of their life" (p. 77, emphasis in original).

Since Boggs first articulated these principles, the U.S. education system has not enabled most young Black people to develop the "sense of black pride, black consciousness, and total rejection of the present social system" that Boggs envisioned (p. 77). Yet a body of scholarship has developed, here and in other parts of the world, that critiques curriculum knowledge and provides empirical and conceptual support for liberating education. This scholarship accords with many of the principles Boggs articulated and contributes in various ways to culture-centered knowledge, curriculum transformation, and pedagogy that can benefit African American students and is also in the interest of a more just and equitable world. Here are selected examples:

1. *Critiques of the curriculum/alternative knowledge:* Anyon (1981); Banks (1991, 1993); Carruthers and Harris (1997); B. M. Gordon (1985b); Hilliard (1991/1992, 1992); Holloway (1990); J. E. King (1992); J. E. King and Wilson (1990); Ladson-Billings (1991b); McCarthy (1990); Obenga (1990); Sleeter and Grant (1991)

2. *Teaching approaches that recuperate, valorize, and/or use African American/Diaspora/student cultural knowledge and social practice:* Asante (1991a); Ballenger (1992); Heath (1989); Hollins (1982); Hollins and Spencer (1990); Hudicourt-Barnes (2003); Jordan (1988); J. E. King (1994); Moses and Cobb (2001); Perry (1995); Tate (1995); S. W. Williams (1991)

3. *Critical teaching of African American literature:* Fishkin (2001); Johnson (1990); Jordan (1988); Lee (1991, 1992); McElroy-Johnson (1993); Sims (1982); Spears-Bunton (1990)

4. *Oppositional/emancipatory pedagogy:* Childs (1991); Crichlow, Goodwin, Shakes, and Swartz (1990); J. James and Farmer (1993); J. E. King (1990, 1991b);

Ladson-Billings and Henry (1990); MacLeod (1991); Shujaa (1994).

These examples and categories are only illustrative and not mutually exclusive. Other sources can be identified related to critical pedagogy, multicultural education, and African-centered curriculum strategies that aim to empower and influence student development positively (e.g., Bennett, 2001; Bigelow, 1990; Gay, 1988; Hale, 1994; Nieto, 1992; Pang, 2001; Simon, 1990, 1992; Swartz, 1992; Tatum, 1992a). An extensive body of research also exists on culturally responsive pedagogy for culturally different children, of which research with Native Hawaiian children is one of the best-known examples (Au & Kawakami, 1994).

Next is an important historical precedent for the kind of education that Boggs proposes. With few exceptions, the research just cited is disconnected from this historical legacy. Contemporary education theorizing and practice related to liberating knowledge, curriculum transformation, and social action for change rarely build on the philosophical foundations and living struggles that influenced scholar-activists like Boggs.

The Historical Legacy of the Mississippi Freedom Schools. Striking parallels exist between what Boggs proposes as "education to govern," the Citizenship Schools the Southern Christian Leadership Conference organized across the South to prepare disenfranchised Black people to assert their voting rights, and the Mississippi Freedom Schools organized by the Student Nonviolent Coordinating Committee (SNCC) in 1964. The purpose of the Freedom Schools was to "start young Mississippians thinking about how they could change the society in which they lived" (Perlstein, 1990, p. 319). Educators and community activists organized these schools to awaken students and adults to their highest human potential. The problems in southern Black communities dominated by virulent racism became the curriculum for these schools, and the "scars of the system" possessed by the people, as well their survival knowledge and "living struggles," provided creative learning resources. As Perlstein reports, in SNCC schools for Black Mississippi teenagers "teachers generally incorporated students' lives into lessons and worked to break down the authority of whiteness" (p. 317). Often this pedagogy was constructed with the students, whom the volunteer teachers believed had as much to teach them as the other way around. The "art, dance, song, drama" and "the emancipatory capacities of these free forms . . . helped to promote a synthesis of experience, learning and politics [that] depended on the opportunities for activism that other components" of the Freedom Schools provided (p. 318). Both the Citizenship Schools and

Freedom Schools embodied what Freire (1980) later called "education as the practice of freedom." The expectation in these schools was that people would become empowered to govern themselves and their communities (S. Clark, 1986; Perlstein, 1990; Stembridge, 1971).

Cultural Knowledge, Curriculum Transformation, and Black Education

The struggle for education that redirects learning toward community needs and control of Black communities and schools seems to have been taken up in some independent Black educational institutions (Lee, Lomotey, & Shujaa, 1990; Shujaa, 1994). In addition, the Algebra Project, the inspiration of former SNCC activist Bob Moses, is recognized as a legacy of the civil rights movement's popular education activities (Moses & Cobb, 2001). Teacher retraining and curriculum development in this project make algebra, traditionally a "gatekeeping" course, accessible to middle school students in inner-city and southern schools. Some Algebra Project lessons build on African American cultural knowledge, such as African drumming to teach math concepts.

Other approaches get students directly involved in studying their culture and emphasize the need for social action through collaborative research that also enhances their academic learning. MacLeod (1991) adapted the Foxfire method that had been developed by Wiggington (1985, 1991/1992) to engage Black Mississippi high school students in studying the history of their own community's involvement in the civil rights movement. The Bloodlines Project enabled these students to use "tools of social analysis" to understand and decipher "how inequities in wealth, power, and privilege affect them" (MacLeod, 1991, p. 274). According to MacLeod, "this critical awareness of selfhood in relation to society" becomes for some a motivating force to struggle for a better world (p. 274). MacLeod's students published their study in *Minds Stayed on Freedom* (Youth of the Rural Organizing and Cultural Center, 1991). The skills and knowledge these students gain through these projects also accord with many of Boggs's education principles.

Lessons from the Decolonized World

Other examples of liberating knowledge, curriculum transformation, and social action-oriented practice created out of urgent necessity in the African Diaspora and the decolonized world share elements in common with the new education system Boggs proposes (Gonçalves e Silva, 1992; Jansen, 1990). Two will be discussed briefly; the first example is from Palestine, the second is from Mali (West Africa). They exemplify ways that cultural knowledge and curriculum transformation can make education more responsive to community needs. They also point to new directions in research.

Munir's Mother's Math. Just as extreme social disruption in France in 1968 enabled Foucault to rethink the nature of knowledge, Munir Fasheh, a Palestinian teacher and professional mathematician, was compelled to regard his discipline in an entirely new way and rethink the relationship between knowledge and hegemony. The urgent reality of war in his society and the Palestinian youth rebellion—the Intifadeh—brought the real needs of the Palestinian people to his attention. Fasheh (1990) compares his math with his mother's math. Her math consists of turning rectangles of fabric into "perfectly fitted clothing for people" (p. 21) and her sewing, despite her "illiteracy," "demonstrated another way of conceptualizing and doing mathematics, another kind of knowledge, and the place of that knowledge in the world" (p. 24). Even with "few measurements and no patterns," his mother's sewing involved math nonetheless in the way that "it embodied order, pattern, relations, and measurement" (p. 21). Fasheh discovered, by looking at their math in their two contexts, that his math was "biased toward the manipulation of symbols and theories linked . . . to technological advancement . . . that usually lead(s) to military, political, and economic power and control" (p. 22), whereas his mother's math was "biased toward life, action, production, and personal experience, and it was linked to immediate and concrete needs in the community" (p. 22). Yet her math and her knowledge, though not "intrinsically disempowering," were "continually discredited by the world around her" (p. 24). Although Fasheh is an experienced teacher and math professional, he realized that his mother's math was "beyond" his comprehension; it was "so deeply embedded in the culture that it was invisible to eyes trained by formal education" (p. 22).

Fasheh also realized that "the power of Western hegemony rests on claims of superiority, universality, and ethical neutrality of Western math, positivistic science, technology, and education" (1990, p. 25). He concludes that continuing to accept these Western claims of superiority, universality, and authoritativeness in math, science, and education "is detrimental to creating a healthier and more humane world" (p. 25). For education to be responsive to this challenge, according to Fasheh, it must play a new role in community transformation by enabling people to critique the "basic premises and values that govern their conceptions, practices, and production" (p. 25). The kind of math people need involves organic praxis, a combination of the practical aspects of his mother's math that is linked to community needs and the articulated theoretical constructs of his discipline. This kind of education will allow people to "reclaim and develop what has been made invisible by hegemony" (p. 25).

The Gao (Mali) School Museum. Hassimi Maiga, another professional educator and senior researcher, developed an innovative educational approach in Mali, West Africa, that plays the kind of role in community transformation that both Fasheh and Boggs envision. From its philosophy to classroom practice and learning-by-doing service in the community, the Gao School Museum approach exemplifies the principles of the new system of education that Boggs outlines (Maiga, 1995). In each classroom, the students and teachers collaboratively develop a repository of materials, resources, and teaching aids that they use to balance the theoretical knowledge in the school curriculum with students' cultural knowledge, practical skills, and know-how. Maiga (1993) explains that the Gao School Museum permits "each child to learn the curriculum content and to put what he or she is learning into practice . . . by actively participating with the teacher in the search for, creation and production of knowledge" (p. 9). In the process, the teachers and students are able "to transcend the limitations of the present curriculum in so far as the future needs of the students, their community and society are concerned" (p. 11).

The Gao School Museum is also innovative in preparing and training teachers as researchers: it enables them to rethink their subject matter so as to meet real community needs. This innovation was partly designed to improve the implementation of Mali's national ruralization program, which created practical learning activities such as gardening, tending animals and poultry, carpentry, and sewing to enhance the academic learning of Malian students (Maiga, 1993). In the Malian context of severe environmental and economic constraints (e.g., recurring drought), education is constantly endangered. Behind this visible and urgent economic crisis lies a deeper one: students need to develop the kind of knowledge and skills that will enable them to be flexible, self-directed creators of solutions to their economic and social problems. The aim of the Gao School Museum is to develop students who are problem solvers for the positive transformation of their society. As Fasheh (1990) observed in the Palestinian context, this requires using the theoretical insights of the disciplines of the school curriculum, and recovering and reclaiming indigenous cultural knowledge and autonomous cognitive resources for education and social change. Consequently, the methodology of the Gao School Museum requires that teachers carefully study the curriculum first, and then select and integrate learning activities that reinforce this kind of experiential learning across the curriculum. Teachers and students form research teams to study, analyze, and produce selected aspects of the curriculum together; they engage in productive community problem solving to test their knowledge and apply what they learn in situations with real, immediate consequences. The underlying philosophy serves as a "concrete bridge between learners and their social, cultural and economic environment; as a laboratory for studying and improving the presentation of school subjects; and therefore as a permanent pedagogical support for both teachers and students" (Maiga, 1993, p. 21).

Indigenous Cultural Knowledge, Professional Education, and Grassroots Development

Recent developments in the professional education of lawyers, teachers, researchers, social workers, and international development specialists among others demonstrate the importance of recuperating indigenous cultural knowledge, as these lessons from the decolonized world also suggest. From preparation for professional advocacy in environmental poverty law (Cole, 1992) to the use of the clients' "subjugated knowledge" in social work (Hartman, 1992) to reexaminations of the value of indigenous knowledge systems by development specialists (D. L. Williams & Muchena, 1991), researchers (L. T. Smith, 1999), and environmentalist educators (Orr, 1992), there is an interest in identifying and using (indigenous) cultural knowledge for liberating purposes (G. H. Smith, 1990, 2002). Community educators and grassroots development specialists in Africa (National Education Crisis Committee, 1987), Latin America (Kleymeyer & Moreno, 1988), and the United States are using participatory research, "by the people for the people" strategies (Dubell, Erasmie, & de Vries, 1980), as well as critical pedagogies of organic social action research to recuperate subjugated cultural knowledge (J. E. King & Mitchell, 1990/1995; Borda, 1980). These strategies involve participants in the study of their own lives and community needs in ways that can enable people to recognize and value their cultural knowledge and promote cultural "revitalization" and group self-help.

The research discussed thus far in this chapter underscores the importance of considering the social effects of knowledge and the ways that curriculum transformation can contribute to demystification of the social framework and thereby prepare people to change themselves and society. Research that bridges "street and school" can be a form of organic praxis that links scholarly work with community needs and with the cultural knowledge of the people engaged in the research. Two examples of this type of research are summarized briefly in the next section, which will also point to directions in research that can support these effects.

Organic Praxis, Research, and Social Action

J. E. King and Mitchell (1990/1995) provide a model of participatory Afrocentric research that can engage participants in thinking critically about changing themselves and society. This research is a grounded (Rodney, 1975) model of organic praxis that involves professionals and community participants in analyzing, theorizing, and discussing African American literature, their own social practice as mothers of sons, and myths of the social framework and the education system. Together the researchers and participants collectively decipher and recuperate cultural knowledge they can use in family, school, and community contexts. This methodology, according to King and Mitchell, "recognizes that particular knowledge of the world contained in people's daily cultural practice and social experience is not just distorted by the dominant ideology . . . but can be liberating as well" (pp. 89–90). One criterion of validity the researchers use in this praxis-oriented research is the impact of collaborative inquiry on the "consciousness and practice" of the participants (p. 100). This study is an organic approach to the collective production of cultural knowledge "for the sake of the communal good and individual human liberation" (J. James, 1993b, p. 133, n. 17).

Ballenger (1992), a White professional preschool teacher of young Haitian children, describes another research approach that values and uses the cultural knowledge of a community and enables the researcher to reflect critically upon her own knowledge and assumptions. Ballenger's research method parallels the engaged scholarship of King and Mitchell. By comparing her own methods and language of classroom control with those of Haitian teachers and parents, and by engaging in reflective discussion with them, Ballenger learned that the "process of gaining multicultural understanding in education must . . . be a dual one" (p. 207). What she learned from the children and their Haitian teachers enabled her to reevaluate the emphasis on (and the presumed superiority of) individualism in North American teaching practice, compared with the shared values and responsibilities of membership in a moral community that Haitian children derive within their cultural group at a very young age. Ballenger describes her attempts to use the cultural knowledge of the community by emulating the language (reciprocal dialogue) and methods of classroom control that she learned from the Haitian teachers, parents, and children. She reports that she feels "especially connected to the children" when she gets "it right" (p. 205).

A Lack of Conceptual and Pedagogical Resources

As Black students move through the education system, they face "the school's undermining doubt about their ability" (P. Gilmore, 1985, p. 124). Their dignity and positive group identity may be further undermined by hegemonic school knowledge and curricula that traumatize and humiliate many Black students, especially when

dealing with topics concerning their ancestry, such as slavery (Hawkins, 1990; J. E. King, 1992; Tatum, 1992b). Although some educators admit that they lack conceptual tools to intervene in this dynamic (Hawkins, 1990), others are oblivious or able to perceive only ethnocentric bias and ideology in materials that depart from and attempt to rectify a normative Eurocentric perspective bias (J. E. King, 1991a). That the problem of dislocating cultural hegemony in education persists, even as textbooks have become more multicultural, reveals a conceptual, methodological, and pedagogical lack in curriculum knowledge and research (Wynter, 1992a). In fact, there has been generalized silence about these matters in research in the disciplines and fields of pedagogical inquiry that might otherwise be of help to teachers. This is partly because educational researchers fail to draw upon the insights of research and theorizing in Black studies (B. M. Gordon, 1992; J. James, 1993b).

Wineburg's research (1991, 1999) is an intriguing example of this lack in research on learning, teaching, and curriculum. Wineburg is an "educational psychologist interested in how people learn from texts," and he presents evidence that even "bright," "successful" high school students with in-depth factual knowledge of history and excellent academic and "generic" reading skills do not recognize distortion, polemic, or bias in history texts. Wineburg asks: "How could they know so much history, yet have so little sense of how to read it?" (1991, p. 511). The Black studies epistemological critique can aid in the search for answers to such important questions.

Woodson's observations more than 60 years ago—that African Americans are miseducated as a result of the social organization of knowledge; that this bias has "invaded the teaching profession" (1933, p. 20); and that "false education" contributes to social nefariousness—are still relevant. Woodson wrote: "There would be no lynching if it did not start in the classroom" (p. 3). Organic, praxis-oriented research is needed that enables students, teachers, and researchers to recognize ways that ideological bias and hegemony in the disciplines constrain their own thinking (Rodney, 1990). This applies not just to the humanities but to science (Bazin, 1993) and mathematics (Fasheh, 1990) as well. As the research and experiences of Ballenger (1992), Fasheh (1990), J. E. King (1994), J. E. King and Mitchell (1990/1995), MacLeod (1991), Maiga (1993), and S. Walker (2001) indicate, rethinking the disciplines can be linked fruitfully with community praxis and inquiry related to the use of cultural knowledge. Such organic, praxis-oriented research is a first step toward rethinking the social framework and the knowledge that legitimates it. Educators at all levels need to study the intellectual and historical antecedents of Black studies and African-centered approaches to education to clear away the mystification and confusion surrounding group-based perspectives and strategies for education, curriculum transformation, and social change.

In addition, community needs should become a subject and object of study and a resource for learning as well (J. James, 1993a, 1993b). Also, in contrast to "the pattern of thinking about racialism in terms of its consequences on the victim" (Morrison, 1992, p. 11), research is needed that examines how students, teachers, and academics (including textbook authors) are affected by and can overcome various societal myths—such as the belief system of race—that are embedded in the social organization of knowledge. Before they can decide whether to "challenge the status quo" (Farmer, 1993) in order to reinvent school knowledge and transform the curriculum (Bigelow, 1990), "teach the conflicts" (Graff, 1993), or teach "against the grain" (Simon, 1992), educators at all levels need to be able to recognize and overcome their own miseducation (J. E. King, 1991a). However, the general research community has not pursued these research directions. Finally, research that focuses on the education of Black students often emphasizes sociocultural deficits as an obstacle to assimilation or acculturation (Ogbu, 1992; Steele, 1992). This research paradigm misses the point of a fundamental insight of Black studies: cultural and racial democracy requires pluralism, not cultural negation or absorption.

CONCLUDING COMMENTS

The examination of culture-centered knowledge and curriculum transformation suggests that marginalizing and/or invisibilizing historical reality can alienate the identity and consciousness of subordinated groups or create the conditions of intellectual autonomy that are requisite for cultural and racial democracy and human freedom. That is, a dialectical theory of social change suggests that the experience of subordination and liminality can also give such groups a perspective advantage of alterity. Although expanding knowledge through the inclusion of multiple perspectives on reality is an alternative to dominating curriculum transformation and knowledge, from such a perspective of alterity Wynter (1984, 1989, 1992c) and Morrison (1989, 1992) decipher the belief structure that legitimates the social framework and contributes to alienated and self-negating consciousness. Both these analyses suggest that the knowledge in the academic disciplines themselves needs to be changed. Such changes could create further possibilities for cognitive autonomy and human freedom. The "canon wars" over curriculum transformation have been replaced by capitulation to high-stakes testing and the elusive quest for "equal opportunity" in privatized education. Deciphering knowledge, a category of the emergent field of Black education—like oppositional aspects of African American cultural knowledge in the intellectual autonomy of the Black studies tradition—is a resource that can link curriculum transformation with the "wider struggle" for social change in order to bring about the alternative social vision of Black studies: "a world that will hold all the people."

CODA

To have any practical relevancy to the actual conditions and problems experienced by African American people, Black Studies must conceive itself as a type of praxis, a unity of theory and practical action. It is insufficient for black scholars to scale the pristine walls of the academic tower, looking below with calculated indifference to the ongoing struggles of Black people. We must always remember that we are the product and beneficiaries of those struggles, and that our scholarship is without value unless it bears a message that nourishes the hope, dignity and resistance of our people (Marable, 1992, p. 32).

References

Adams, B. E. (1992). *John Henrik Clarke: The early years.* Hampton, VA: United Brothers and Sisters Communications.

Adell, S. (1990). A function at the junction. *Diacritics, 20*(4), 43–56.

Aldridge, D. P. (1992). The kitchen's filled—but who are the cooks? What it takes to teach Black studies. *Phylon, 49*(1/2), 61–70.

Alinsky, S. (1971). *Rules for radicals.* New York: Random House.

Alkalimat, A. H. [McWorter, G.]. (1969). The ideology of Black social science. *Black Scholar, 4*(2), 28–35.

Ani, M. [Richards, D. M.]. (1994). *Yurugu: An African-centered critique of European cultural thought and behavior.* Trenton, NJ: Africa World Press.

Anyon, J. (1981). Social class and school knowledge. *Curriculum Inquiry, 11,* 3–42.

Apple, M. (1993). *Official knowledge: Democratic education in a conservative age.* New York: Routledge.

Aptheker, H. (Ed.). (1973). *The education of Black people: Ten critiques by W.E.B. DuBois, 1906–1960.* New York: Monthly Review.

Armento, B., Nash, G., Salter, K., & Wixson, K. (1991). *America will be.* Boston: Houghton Mifflin.

Asante, M. K. (1987). *The Afrocentric idea.* Philadelphia: Temple University Press.

Asante, M. K. (1991a). The Afrocentric idea in education. *Journal of Negro Education, 60*(2), 170–180.

Asante, M. K. (1991b). Multiculturalism: An exchange. *American Scholar, 60*(2), 267–276.

Asante, M. K. (1992). African American studies: The future of the discipline. *Black Scholar, 22*(3), 20–29.

Au, K. H., & Kawakami, A. J. (1994). Cultural congruence in instruction. In E. R. Hollins, J. E. King, & W. C. Hayman (Eds.), *Teaching diverse populations: Formulating a knowledge base.* Albany: State University of New York Press.

Baker, H. A., Jr. (1984). *Blues, ideology and Afro-American literature: A vernacular theory.* Chicago: University of Chicago Press.

Baker, H. A., Jr. (1993). *Black Studies, rap and the academy.* Chicago: University of Chicago Press.

Ballenger, C. (1992). Because you like us: The language of control. *Harvard Educational Review, 62*(2), 199–208.

Banks, J. A. (1971a). Relevant social studies for Black pupils. In J. A. Banks & W. W. Joyce (Eds.), *Teaching social studies to culturally different children* (pp. 202–209). Menlo Park, CA: Addison-Wesley.

Banks, J. A. (1971b). Varieties of history: Negro, Black, White. In J. A. Banks & W. W. Joyce (Eds.), *Teaching social studies to culturally different children* (pp. 329–332). Menlo Park, CA: Addison-Wesley.

Banks, J. A. (1973). Curriculum strategies for liberation. *School Review, 81*(3), 405–414.

Banks, J. A. (1989). Integrating the curriculum with ethnic content: Approaches and guidelines. In J. A. Banks & C.A.M. Banks (Eds.), *Multicultural education: Issues and perspectives* (pp. 189–207). Boston: Allyn & Bacon.

Banks, J. A. (1991). Multicultural literacy and curriculum reform. *Educational Horizons, 69*(3), 135–140.

Banks, J. A. (1992). African American scholarship and the evolution of multicultural education. *Journal of Negro Education, 61*(3), 273–286.

Banks, J. A. (1993). The canon debate, knowledge construction, and multicultural education. *Educational Researcher, 22*(5), 4–13.

Banks, J. A., & Joyce, W. W. (Eds.). (1971). *Teaching social studies to culturally different children.* Menlo Park, CA: Addison-Wesley.

Bazin, M. (1993). Our sciences, their science. *Race & Class, 34*(4), 35–47.

Bennett, C. (2001). Genres of research in multicultural education. *Review of Educational Research, 71*(2), 171–217.

Berger, P. L., & Luckmann, T. (1967). *The social construction of reality.* Garden City, NY: Doubleday Anchor.

Berlak, A., & Moyenda, S. (2001). *Taking it personally: Racism in the classroom from kindergarten to college.* Philadelphia: Temple University Press.

Bernal, M. (1987). *Black Athena: The Afro-Asiatic roots of classical civilization* (Vol. 1). London: Free Association Books.

Bigelow, W. (1990). Inside the classroom: Social visions and critical pedagogy. *Teachers College Record, 91*(3), 437–448.

Blumenberg, H. (1983). *The legitimacy of the modern age* (R. M. Wallace, Trans.) Cambridge, MA: MIT Press.

Boggs, G. L. (1974). Education: The great obsession. In Institute of the Black World (Ed.), *Education and Black struggle: Notes from the colonized world* (pp. 61–81). (Monograph no. 2.) *Harvard Educational Review.*

Boggs, G. L. (1998). *Living for change.* Minneapolis: University of Minnesota Press.

Borda, O. F. (1980). Science and the common people. In F. Dubell, T. Erasmie, & J. de Vries (Eds.), *Research for the people—Research by the people* (pp. 13–40). Linkoping, Sweden: Linkoping University.

Boyce Davies, C. (1994). *Black women, writing and identity: Migrations of the subject.* London: Routledge.

Bullivant, B. M. (1989). Culture: Its nature and meaning for educators. In J. A. Banks & C. A. Banks (Eds.), *Multicultural education: Issues and perspectives* (pp. 27–45). Boston: Allyn & Bacon.

California State Department of Education (CSDE). (1987). *History/social science framework.* Sacramento: Author.

Carby, H. (1987). *Reconstructing womanhood: The emergence of the Afro-American woman novelist.* New York: Oxford University Press.

Carruthers, J. H. (1994). Black intellectualism and the crisis in Black education. In M. J. Shujaa (Ed.), *Too much schooling, too little education: A paradox of Black life in White societies* (pp. 37–55). Trenton, NJ: Africa World Press.

Carruthers, J. H., & Harris, L. C. (1997). *African world history project: The preliminary challenge.* Los Angeles: ASCAC.

Castenell, L. A., Jr., & Pinar, W. F. (Eds.). (1993). *Understanding curriculum as racial text: Representations of identity and difference in education.* Albany: State University of New York Press.

Césaire, A. (1960). *Return to my native land.* (2nd ed.; E. Snyders, Trans.). Paris: Présence Africaine.

Chafets, Z. (2001). Changing races. *New York Daily News,* March 25, pp. 3–4.

Childs, J. B. (1989). *Leadership, conflict and cooperation in Afro-American social thought.* Philadelphia: Temple University Press.

Childs, J. B. (1991). The pedagogy of peace and war. *Journal of Urban and Cultural Studies, 2*(1), 81–92.

Christian, B. (1989). But what do we think we're doing anyway: The state of Black feminist criticism(s) or my version of a little bit of history. In C. A. Wall (Ed.), *Changing our own words: Essays on criticism, theory, and writing by Black women* (pp. 58–74). New Brunswick, NJ: Rutgers University Press.

Clark, S., with C. S. Brown (Ed.). (1986). *Ready from within: Septima Clark and the civil rights movements.* Navarro, CA: Wild Trees Press.

Clark, V. (1991). Developing Diaspora literacy and *Marasa* consciousness. In H. Spillers (Ed.), *Comparative American identities* (pp. 40–61). New York: Routledge.

Clarke, J. H. (1992). The influence of Arthur A. Schomburg on my concept of Africana studies. *Phylon, 49*(1/2), 4–9.

Clarke, S. A. (1991). Fear of a Black planet: Race, identity politics and common sense. *Socialist Review, 21*(3/4), 37–56.

Cobb, W. J. (2002). *The essential Harold Cruse: A reader.* New York: Palgrave.

Cohen, S. (1972). *Folk devils and moral panics: The creation of the Mods and Rockers.* London: MacGibbon and Kee.

Cole, L. W. (1992). Empowerment as the key to environmental protection: The need for environmental poverty law. *Ecology Law Quarterly, 19,* 619ff.

Collins, P. H. (1990). *Black feminist thought: Knowledge, consciousness, and the politics of empowerment.* London: Unwin Hyman.

Cone, J. H. (1972). *The spirituals and the blues.* New York: Seabury Press.

Cooper, A. J. (1988). *A voice from the South.* New York: Oxford University Press. (Original work published 1892)

Cornbleth, C., & Waugh, D. (1993). The great speckled bird: Education policy-in-the-making. *Educational Researcher, 22*(7), 31–37.

Cornforth, M. (1971). *The theory of knowledge.* New York: International Publishers.

Crichlow, W., Goodwin, S., Shakes, S., & Swartz, E. (1990). Multi-cultural ways of knowing. *Journal of Education, 172*(2), 101–117.

Cruse, H. (1967). *The crisis of the Negro intellectual: From its origins to the present.* New York: Morrow.

Cruse, H. (1987). *Plural but equal: A critical study of Blacks and minorities and America's plural society.* New York: Morrow.

Cruz, J. (1999). *Culture on the margins: The Black spiritual and the rise of American cultural interpretation.* Princeton, NJ: Princeton University Press.

Cuban, L. (1971). Black history, Negro history, and White folk. In J. A. Banks & W. W. Joyce (Eds.), *Teaching social studies to culturally different children* (pp. 317–320). Menlo Park, CA: Addison-Wesley.

Davis, A. (1983a). Unfinished lecture on liberation—II. In L. Harris (Ed.), *Philosophy born of struggle: Anthology of Afro-American philosophy from 1917* (pp. 130–136). Dubuque, IA: Kendall/Hunt.

Davis, A. (1983b). *Women, race & class.* New York: Vintage Books.

Delgado, R. *Critical race theory: The cutting edge.* Philadelphia: Temple University Press, 1995.

Delpit, L., & Dowdy, J. K. (2002). *The skin that we speak: Thoughts on language and culture in the classroom.* New York: New Press.

Derrida, J. (1976). *Of grammatology.* Baltimore, MD: Johns Hopkins University Press.

Diop, C. A. (1981). *Civilization or barbarism? An authentic anthropology.* Chicago: Lawrence Hill Books.

Dixon, J. (1971). African-oriented and Euro-American–oriented worldviews: Research methodologies and economics. *Review of Black Political Economy, 7*(2), 119–156.

Drake, S. C. (1977). *The redemption of Africa and Black religion.* Chicago: Third World Press.

Drake, S. C. (1987). *Black folk here and there* (Vol. 1). Los Angeles: UCLA, Center for Afro-American Studies.

Dray, P. (2002). *At the hands of persons unknown: The lynching of Black America.* New York: The Modern Library.

Dubell, F., Erasmie, T., & de Vries, J. (Eds.). (1980). *Research for the people—Research by the people.* Linkoping, Sweden: Linkoping University.

DuBois, W.E.B. (1953). *The souls of Black folk.* New York: Fawcett. (Original work published 1903)

Ellison, R. (1986). What America would be like without Blacks. In R. Ellison, *Going to the territory* (pp. 104–112). New York: Random House.

Epstein, K. E., & Ellis, W. F. (1992). Oakland moves to create its own multicultural curriculum. *Phi Delta Kappan, 73*(3), 635–638.

Erickson, P. (1992). Multiculturalism and the problem of liberalism. *Reconstruction, 2*(1), 97–101.

Fanon, F. (1963). *The wretched of the earth.* New York: Grove Press.

Fanon, F. (1967). *Black skins, white masks.* New York: Grove Press.

Farmer, R. (1993). Place but not importance: The race for inclusion in academe. In J. James & R. Farmer (Eds.), *Spirit, space and survival: African American women in (White) academe* (pp. 196–217). New York: Routledge.

Fasheh, M. (1990). Community education: To reclaim and transform what has been made invisible. *Harvard Educational Review, 60*(1), 19–35.

Feagin, J. R. (2001). *Racist America: Roots, current realities, and future reparations.* New York: Routledge.

Fishkin, F. S. (1993). *Was Huck Black? Mark Twain and African-American Voices.* New York: Oxford University Press.

Fishkin, F. S. (2001). Reclaiming the Black presence in "Mainstream Culture." In S. Walker (Ed.), *African roots/American cultures: Africa in the creation of the Americas* (pp. 81–88). Lanham, MD: Rowman & Littlefield.

Fontaine, P. (Ed.). (1985). *Race, class and power in Brazil.* Los Angeles: UCLA, Center for Afro-American Studies.

Foster, M. (1998). Race, class, and gender in education research: Surveying the political terrain. *Educational Policy, 13*(1), 77–85.

Foucault, M. (1970). *The order of things: An archeology of the human sciences.* New York: Vintage Books.

Foucault, M. (1972). *The archeology of knowledge.* (A. M. Sheridan Smith, Trans.) New York: Harper & Row.

Frazier, E. F. (1957). *Black bourgeoisie: The rise of a new middle class.* New York: Free Press.

Frazier, E. F. (1973). The failure of the Negro intellectual. In J. A. Ladner (Ed.), *The death of White sociology* (pp. 52–66). New York: Vintage Books.

Freire, P. (1980). *Education for critical consciousness.* New York: Continuum.

Gates, H. L. (1988). *The signifying monkey: A theory of African-American literary criticism.* New York: Oxford University Press.

Gates, H. L. (1992a). African American studies in the 21st century. *Black Scholar, 22*(3), 3–11.

Gates, H. L. (1992b). *Loose canons: Notes on the culture wars.* New York: Oxford University Press.

Gay, G. (1988). Designing relevant curricula for diverse learners. *Education and Urban Society, 20*(4), 327–340.

Gay, G., & Baber, W. L. (Eds.). (1987). *Expressively Black: The cultural basis of ethnic identity.* New York: Praeger.

Gayle, A. (Ed.). (1971). *The Black aesthetic.* Garden City, NY: Doubleday.

Genovese, E. D. (1971). Black studies: Trouble ahead. In J. W. Blassingame (Ed.), *New perspectives on Black studies* (pp. 104–115). Urbana: University of Illinois Press.

Giddens, A. (1979). *Central problems in sociological theory.* Berkeley: University of California Press.

Gilmore, P. (1985). "Gimme room": School resistance, attitude, and access to literacy. *Journal of Education, 167*(1), 111–128.

Gilmore, R. W. (1993). Public enemies and private intellectuals: Apartheid USA. *Race and Class, 35*(1), 69–78.

Gilroy, P. (1993). *The Black Atlantic: Modernity and double consciousness.* Cambridge, MA: Harvard University Press.

Giroux, H. (1992). *Border crossings: Cultural workers and the politics of education.* New York: Routledge.

Glissant, E. (1981). *Le discours antillais.* Paris: Seuil.

Gonçalves e Silva, P. B. (1992, April). *Black-women-teachers' resistance to racism in São Carlos (São Paulo, Brazil).* Paper presented at the meeting of the American Educational Research Association, San Francisco.

Gordon, B. M. (1985). Toward emancipation in citizenship education: The case for African-American cultural knowledge. *Theory and Research in Social Education, 12*(4), 1–23.

Gordon, B. M. (1990). The necessity of African-American epistemology for educational theory and practice. *Journal of Education, 172*(3), 88–106.

Gordon, B. M. (1992). The marginalized discourse of minority intellectual thought in traditional writings on teaching. In C. A. Grant (Ed.), *Research and multicultural education: From the margins to the mainstream* (pp. 19–31). London: Falmer Press.

Gordon, B. M. (1993). African American cultural knowledge and liberatory education: Dilemmas, problems and potentials in a postmodern American society. *Urban Education, 27*(4), 448–470.

Gordon, E. W. (1985). Social science knowledge production and minority experiences. *Journal of Negro Education, 54*(2), 117–133.

Gordon, E. W. (1999). *Education and justice: A view from the back of the bus.* New York: Teachers College Press.

Gordon, E. W. (2000). *Education and justice: A view from the back of the bus.* New York: Teachers College.

Gordon, E. W., Miller, F., & Rollock, D. (1990). Coping with communicentric bias in knowledge production in the social sciences. *Educational Researcher, 19*(3), 14–19.

Goveia, E. (1970). The social framework. *Savacou* [University of the West Indies, Mona, Jamaica], *1,* 7–15.

Graff, G. (1993). *Beyond the culture wars: How teaching the conflicts can revitalize American education.* New York: Norton.

Grambs, J. (1971). Crispus Attucks. In J. A. Banks & W. W. Joyce (Eds.), *Teaching social studies to culturally different children* (pp. 320–328). Menlo Park, CA: Addison-Wesley.

Guy-Sheftall, B. (1992). Black women's studies: The interface of women's studies and Black studies. *Phylon, 49*(1/2), 33–41.

Hacker, A. (1992). *Two nations: Black, White, separate, hostile, unequal.* New York: Scribner.

Hale, J. E. (1994). *Unbank the fire: Visions for the education of African American children.* Baltimore: The Johns Hopkins University Press.

Hall, M. (1991). Gadugi: A model of service-learning for Native American communities. *Phi Delta Kappan, 72*(10), 754–757.

Hall, S. (1991). Brave new world. *Socialist Review, 21*(1), 57–64.

Hall, S., Critcher, C., Jefferson, T., Clarke, J., & Roberts, B. (1978). *Policing the crisis: Mugging, the state and law and order.* London: Macmillan.

Hamilton, C. (1992). A way of seeing: Culture as political expression in the works of C.L.R. James. *Journal of Black Studies, 22*(3), 429–443.

Hansen, E. (1977). Freedom and revolution in the thought of Frantz Fanon. *Pan-African Journal, 10*(1), 1–22.

Harding, V. (1970). Beyond chaos: Black history and the search for the new land. In J. A. Williams & C. F. Harris (Eds.). *Amistad 1* (pp. 267–292). New York: Vintage Books.

Harding, V. (1974). The vocation of the Black scholar and the struggles of the Black community. In Institute of the Black World (Ed.), *Education and Black struggle: Notes from the colonized world* (pp. 3–29). (Monograph no. 2.) *Harvard Educational Review.*

Harding, V. (1990). *Hope and history: Why we must share the story of the movement.* Mary Knoll, NY: Orbis Books.

Harris, V. (1992). African-American conceptions of literacy: A historical perspective. *Theory Into Practice, 31*(4), 276–286.

Hartman, A. (1992). In search of subjugated knowledge. *Social Work, 37*(6), 483–484.

Hartmann, G. (1980). *Criticism in the wilderness: A study of literature today.* New Haven, CT: Yale University Press.

Hawkins, J. A. (1990, June/July). The cries of my ancestors: The "uncomfortable" story of slavery must be told honestly. *Teacher,* pp. 8–9.

Heath, S. B. (1989). Oral and literate traditions among Black Americans living in poverty. *American Psychologist, 44*(2), 367–373.

Henry, P. (2000). *Caliban's Reason: Introducing Afro-Caribbean philosophy.* New York: Routledge.

Henry, P., & Buhle, P. (1992). Caliban as deconstructionist: C.L.R. James and postcolonial discourse. In P. Henry & P. Buhle (Eds.), *C.L.R. James's Caribbean* (pp. 111–142). Durham, NC: Duke University Press.

Hilliard, A. G. (1991/1992). Why we must pluralize the curriculum. *Educational Leadership, 49*(4), 12–14.

Hilliard, A. G. (1992). The meaning of KMT history. *Phylon, 49*(1/2), 10–22.

Hilliard, A. G. (2000). "Race," identity, hegemony, and education: What do we need to know now? In W. H. Watkins, J. H. Lewis, & V. Chou (Eds.), *Race and education: The roles of history and society in educating African American students* (pp. 7–33). Boston: Allyn & Bacon.

Hine, D. C. (1990). Black studies: An overview. In R. L. Harris, D. C. Hine, & N. McKay, *Three essays: Black studies in the United States* (pp. 15–25). New York: Ford Foundation.

Hollins, E. R. (1982). The Marva Collins Story revisited: Implications for regular classroom instruction. *Journal of Teacher Education, 33*(1), 37–40.

Hollins, E. R., & Spencer, K. (1990). Restructuring schools for cultural inclusion: Changing the schooling process for African American youngsters. *Journal of Education, 172*(2), 89–100.

Holloway, J. E. (Ed.). (1990). *Africanisms in American culture.* Bloomington: University of Indiana Press.

Holt, T. C. (2000). *The problem of race in the 21st century.* Cambridge: Harvard University Press.

hooks, b. (1990). *Yearning: Race, gender and cultural politics.* Boston: South End Press.

hooks, b., & West, C. (1991). *Breaking bread: Insurgent Black intellectual life.* Boston: South End Press.

Hudicourt-Barnes, J. (2003). The use of argumentation in Haitian Creole science classrooms. *Harvard Educational Review, 73*(1), 73–93.

James, C.L.R. (1948). *Notes on dialectics.* Westport, CT: Lawrence Hill.

James, C.L.R. (1963). *The Black Jacobins.* New York: Vintage Books.

James, C.L.R. (1970). The Atlantic slave trade and slavery: Some interpretations of their significance in the development of the United States and the Western world. In J. A. Williams & C. F. Harris (Eds.), *Amistad 1* (pp. 119–164). New York: Vintage Books.

James, J. (1993a). African philosophy, theory, and "living thinkers." In J. James & R. Farmer (Eds.), *Spirit, space and survival: African American women in (White) academe* (pp. 31–46). New York: Routledge.

James, J. (1993b). Teaching theory, talking community. In J. James & R. Farmer (Eds.), *Spirit, space and survival: African American women in (White) academe* (pp. 118–135). New York: Routledge.

James, J., & Farmer, R. (Eds.). (1993). *Spirit, space and survival: African American women in (White) academe.* New York: Routledge.

Jansen, J. (1990). In search of liberation pedagogy in South Africa. *Journal of Education, 172*(2), 62–71.

Johnson, D. (1990). *Telling tales: The pedagogy and power of African American literature for youth.* New York: Greenwood.

Jordan, J. (1988). Nobody means more to me than you and the future life of Willie Jordan. *Harvard Educational Review, 58*(3), 363–374.

King, D. K. (1988). Multiple jeopardy, multiple consciousness: The context of a Black feminist ideology. *Signs, 14*(1), 42–72.

King, J. E. (Ed.). (1990). In search of African liberation pedagogy: Multiple contexts of education and struggle (theme issue). *Journal of Education, 172*(2).

King, J. E. (1991a). Dysconscious racism: Ideology, identity, and the miseducation of teachers. *Journal of Negro Education, 60*(2), 133–146.

King, J. E. (1991b). Unfinished business: Black student alienation and Black teachers' emancipatory pedagogy. In M. Foster (Ed.), *Readings on equal education* (Vol. 11, pp. 245–271). New York: AMS Press.

King, J. E. (1992). Diaspora literacy and consciousness in the struggle against miseducation in the Black community. *Journal of Negro Education, 61*(3), 317–340.

King, J. E. (1994). The purpose of schooling for African American children: Including cultural knowledge. In E. R. Hollins, J. E. King, & W. C. Hayman (Eds.), *Teaching diverse populations: Formulating a knowledge base* (pp. 25–56). Albany: State University of New York Press.

King, J. E. (1997). Ideology, identity and miseducation. In R. Delgado & J. Stefancic (Eds.), *Critical White studies: Looking behind the mirror* (pp. 128–132). Philadelphia: Temple University Press.

King, J. E. (2002). *Facing the new millennium: A transformative research and action agenda in Black education*. Washington, D.C. American Educational Research Association, Commission on Research in Black Education.

King, J. E., & Mitchell, C. A. (1990/1995). *Black mothers to sons: Juxtaposing African American literature with social practice*. New York: Peter Lang.

King, J. E., & Wilson, T. L. (1990). Being the soul-freeing substance: A legacy of hope in Afro humanity. *Journal of Education, 172*(2), 9–27.

King, W. M. (1990). Challenges across the curriculum: Broadening the base of how knowledge is produced. *American Behavioral Scientist, 34*(2), 165–180.

Kleymeyer, C., & Moreno, C. (1988). La feria educativa: A wellspring of ideas and cultural pride. *Grassroots Development, 12*(2), 32–40.

Kochman, T. (1981). *Black and White styles in conflict*. Chicago: University of Chicago Press.

Ladner, J. A. (Ed.). (1973). *The death of White sociology*. New York: Vintage Books.

Ladson-Billings, G. (1991a). Beyond multicultural illiteracy. *Journal of Negro Education, 60*(2), 147–157.

Ladson-Billings, G. (1991b, November). Distorting democracy: Social studies curriculum development and textbook adoption in California. Paper presented at the meeting of the National Council for the Social Studies, Washington, DC.

Ladson-Billings, G., & Henry, A. (1990). Blurring the borders: Voices of African liberatory pedagogy in the United States and Canada. *Journal of Education, 172*(2), 72–88.

LaFrance, J. (1992). Lessons from Maine. *Harvard Educational Review, 62*(3), 384–395.

Lee, C. D. (1991). Big picture talkers/words walking without masters: The instructional implications of ethnic voices for an expanded literacy. *Journal of Negro Education, 60*(3), 291–304.

Lee, C. D. (1992). Literacy, cultural diversity, and instruction. *Education and Urban Society, 24*(2), 279–291.

Lee, C. D., Lomotey, K., & Shujaa, M. J. (1990). How shall we sing our song in a strange land? The dilemma of double consciousness and the complexities of an African-centered pedagogy. *Journal of Education, 172*(2), 45–61.

Legesse, A. (1973). *Gada: Three approaches to the study of an African society*. New York: Free Press.

Lemelle, S. J. (1993). The politics of cultural existence: Pan-Africanism, historical materialism and Afrocentricity. *Race & Class, 35*(1), 93–112.

Leo, J. (1989, November 27). Teaching history the way it happened. *U.S. News & World Report*, p. 73.

Levine, L. W. (1977). *Black culture and Black consciousness: African American folk thought from slavery to freedom*. New York: Oxford University Press.

MacLeod, J. (1991). Bridging street and school. *Journal of Negro Education, 60*(3), 260–275.

Maiga, H. O. (1993). *From whole to part: The Gao School Museum—Restoring a learning tradition*. San Francisco: Aspire Books.

Maiga, H. O. (1995). Bridging classroom, curriculum, and community: The Gao School Museum. *Theory Into Practice, 34*(3), 209–215.

Marable, M. (1992). Blueprint for Black studies and multiculturalism. *Black Scholar, 22*(3), 30–36.

Marable, M. (1993). Beyond racial identity politics: Towards a liberation theory for multicultural democracy. *Race & Class, 35*(1), 113–130.

Martinez, E. (1992/1993). How Calif. texts portray Latinos. *Rethinking Schools, 7*(2), 10–11.

McCarthy, C. (1990). Multicultural education, minority identities, textbooks, and the challenge of curriculum reform. *Journal of Education, 172*(2), 118–129.

McCarthy, C., & Crichlow, W. (Eds.). (1993). *Race, identity, and representation in education*. New York: Routledge.

McElroy-Johnson, B. (1993). Giving voice to the voiceless. *Harvard Educational Review, 63*(1), 85–104.

McIntosh, G. A. (1971). Black liberation and the social studies curriculum. In J. A. Banks & W. W. Joyce (Eds.), *Teaching social studies to culturally different children* (pp. 366–369). Menlo Park, CA: Addison-Wesley.

McLaren, P. (1989). *Life in schools: Introduction to critical pedagogy in the foundations of education*. New York: Longman.

McMurry, L. O. (1998). *To keep the waters troubled: The life of Ida B. Wells*. New York: Oxford University Press.

Meacham, S. J. (1998). Threads of a new language: A response to Eisenhart's "On the subject of interpretive review." *Review of Education Research, 68*(4), 401–407.

Mitchell, C. A. (1991, Autumn). "I love to tell the story": Biblical revisions in *Beloved. Religion & Literature, 23*(3), 27–42.

Moll, L., Amanti, C., Neff, D., & Gonzalez, N. (1992). Funds of knowledge for teaching: Using a qualitative approach to connect homes and classrooms. *Theory Into Practice, 31*(2), 132–141.

Moore, C. (1964). Cuba: The untold story. *Présence Africaine, 52*(24), 177–229.

Morrison, T. (1989). Unspeakable things unspoken: The Afro-American presence in American literature. *Michigan Quarterly Review, 28*(1), 1–34.

Morrison, T. (1992). *Playing in the dark: Whiteness in the literary imagination*. Cambridge, MA: Harvard University Press.

Moses, R. P., & Cobb, C. E., Jr. (2001). *Radical equations: Math literacy and civil rights*. Boston: Beacon Press.

Nash, G., Crabtree, C. & Dunn, R. E. (1997). *History on trial: Culture wars and the teaching of the past*. New York: Knopf.

National Center for History in the Schools. (1994). *National Standards for United States History: Exploring the American experience*. Los Angeles: University of California Press.

National Education Crisis Committee. (1987). *What is history? A new approach to history for students, workers and communities*. Johannesburg, South Africa: Skotaville.

Neusner, J. (1989). It is time to stop apologizing for Western civilization and start analyzing why it defines world culture. *Chronicle of Higher Education, 35*(23), B1–B2.

Nieto, S. (1992). *Affirming diversity: The sociopolitical context of multicultural education.* White Plains, NY: Longman.

Nobles, W. W. (1985). *Africanity and the Black family.* Oakland, CA: Black Family Institute.

Obenga, T. (1990). *The African origin of philosophy.* Paris: Présence Africaine.

Ogbu, J. (1992). Understanding cultural diversity and learning. *Educational Researcher, 21*(8), 5–14, 24.

Ogundipe-Leslie, M. (1984). African women, culture and another development. *Journal of African Marxists, 5,* 77–92.

Orr, D. W. (1992). *Ecological literacy: Education and the transition to a postmodern world.* Albany: State University of New York Press.

Pang, V. O. (2001). *Multicultural education: A caring-centered, reflective approach.* New York: McGraw-Hill.

Peeples, K. (1984). The artist as liberator: An interview with John Oliver Killens. *Community Review, 5*(2), 6–14.

Perlstein, D. (1990). Teaching freedom: SNCC and the creation of the Mississippi Freedom Schools. *History of Education Quarterly, 30*(3), 287–324.

Perry, T. (Ed.) (1995). *Teaching Malcolm X.* New York: Routledge.

Pinkard, N. (2001). Rappin' Reader and Say Say Oh Playmate: Culturally responsive beginning literacy computer-based learning environment. *Journal of Computing Research, 25*(1), 17–34.

Ravitch, D. (1990a). Diversity and democracy. *American Educator, 14*(1), 16–20ff.

Reed, I. (1993). *Japanese by spring.* New York: Atheneum.

Richards, D. M. (1980). *Let the circle be unbroken: The implications of African spirituality in the Diaspora.* Trenton, NJ: Red Sea Press.

Ricoeur, P. (1979). Ideology and utopia as cultural imagination. In D. M. Borchert & D. Stewart (Eds.), *Being human in a technological age* (pp. 107–126). Athens: Ohio University Press.

Robinson, C. (1993). The appropriation of Frantz Fanon. *Race & Class, 35*(1), 79–91.

Rodney, W. (1975). *The groundings with my brothers.* London: Bogle-L'Ouverture.

Rodney, W. (1990). *Walter Rodney speaks: The making of an African intellectual.* Trenton, NJ: Africa World Press.

Said, E. W. (1993). *Culture and imperialism.* New York: Knopf.

Sanford, A. (1990). An education agenda. *Essence, 21*(4), 126.

Schlesinger, A., Jr. (1991). *The disuniting of America: Reflections on a multicultural society.* Knoxville, TN: Whittle Direct Books.

Scott, D. (2000, September). The re-enchantment of humanism: An interview with Sylvia Wynter. *Small Axe, 8,* 119–207.

Semmes, C. E. (1981). Foundations of an Afrocentric social science. *Journal of Black Studies, 12*(1), 3–17.

Semmes, C. E. (1992). *Cultural hegemony and African American development.* Westport, CT: Praeger.

Shor, I. (1986). *Culture wars: School and society in the conservative restoration 1969–1984.* Boston: Routledge & Kegan Paul.

Shujaa, M. J. (Ed.). (1994). *Too much schooling, too little education: A paradox of Black life in White societies.* Trenton, NJ: Africa World Press.

Simon, R. I. (1990). Jewish applause for a Yiddish Shylock: Beyond the racist text. *Journal of Urban and Cultural Studies, 1*(1), 69–86.

Simon, R. I. (1992). *Teaching against the grain: Texts for a pedagogy of possibility.* New York: Bergin & Garvey.

Sims, R. (1982). *Shadow and substance: Afro—American experience in contemporary children's fiction.* Urbana, IL: National Council of Teachers of English.

Sizemore, B. A. (1990). The politics of curriculum, race, and class. *Journal of Negro Education 59*(1), 77–85.

Sleeter, C. E., & Grant, C. A. (1991). Mapping terrains of power: Student cultural knowledge versus classroom knowledge. In C. E. Sleeter (Ed.), *Empowerment through multicultural education* (pp. 49–68). Albany: State University of New York Press.

Smith, G. H. (1990). The politics of reforming Maori education. In H. Lauder & C. Wylie (Eds.) *Towards successful schooling* (pp. 73–88). London: Falmer Press.

Smith, G. H. (2002, Apr. 1–5). *Kaupapa Maori Theory: An indigenous theory of transformative praxis.* Paper presented at the annual meeting of the American Educational Research Association, New Orleans, LA.

Smith, L. T. (1999). *Decolonising methodologies: Research and indigenous peoples.* London: Zed Books.

Spears-Bunton, L. A. (1990). Welcome to my house: African American and European American students' responses to Virginia Hamilton's *House of Dies Drear. Journal of Negro Education, 59*(4), 566–576.

Spradley, J. P. (1972). Foundations of cultural knowledge. In J. P. Spradley (Ed.), *Culture and cognition: Rules, maps, and plans* (pp. 3–38). Prospect Heights, IL: Waveland Press.

Steele, C. M. (1992). Race and the schooling of Black Americans. *Atlantic Monthly, 269*(4), 68–78.

Stembridge, J. (1971). Notes on a class. In S. Carmichael, *Stokely speaks: Black power to Pan-Africanism* (pp. 3–4). New York: Vintage Books.

Stuckey, S. (1971). Twilight of our past: Reflections on the origins of black history. In J. A. Williams & C. F. Harrison (Eds.), *Amistad 2* (pp. 261–296). New York: Vintage Books.

Stuckey, S. (1987). *Slave culture: Nationalist theory and the foundations of Black America.* New York: Oxford University Press.

Swartz, E. (1992). Multicultural education: From a compensatory to a scholarly foundation. In C. A. Grant (Ed.), *Research and multicultural education: From the margins to the mainstream* (pp. 32–43). London: Falmer Press.

Tate, W. (1995). Returning to the root: A culturally relevant approach to mathematics pedagogy. *Theory Into Practice: Multicultural Education, 34*(3), 166–173.

Tatum, B. D. (1992a). African-American identity, academic achievement, and missing history. *Social Education, 56*(6), 331–334.

Tatum, B. D. (1992b). Talking about race, learning about racism: The application of racial identity development theory in the classroom. *Harvard Educational Review, 62*(1), 1–24.

Thompson, R. F. (1983). *Flash of the spirit: African and Afro-American art and philosophy.* New York: Random House.

Thompson, R. F. (1992, Feb.). *The Kongo Atlantic tradition.* Lecture at the University of Texas, Austin.

Touré, S. (1969). A dialectical approach to culture. *Black Scholar, 1*(1), 11–26.

Wa Thiong'o, N. (1986). *Decolonizing the mind: The politics of language in African literature.* London: James Currey.

Walker, A. (1991). *Reach wisely: The Black cultural approach to education.* San Francisco: Aspire Books.

Walker, D. (1971). Article 11. Our wretchedness in consequence of ignorance. In H. A. Baker, Jr. (Ed.), *Black literature in America* (pp. 55–65). New York: McGraw-Hill. (Original work published 1829)

Walker, S. (2001). *African roots/American cultures: Africa in the creation of the Americas.* Boston: Rowman and Littlefield.

Watkins, W. H. (1993). Black curriculum orientations: A preliminary inquiry. *Harvard Educational Review, 63*(3), 321–338.

Watkins, W. H. (2001). *The White architects of Black education: Ideology and power in America, 1865–1954.* New York: Teachers College Press.

Weider, A. (1992). Afrocentrism: Capitalist, democratic, and liberationist portraits. *Educational Foundations, 6*(2), 33–43.

Wells-Barnett, I. B. (1969). *On lynchings.* New York: Arno Press and New York Times.

West, C. (1985). The dilemma of the Black intellectual. *Cultural Critique, 3*(1), 109–124.

West, C. (1990). The new cultural politics of difference. In R. Ferguson, M. Gever, & T. Minh-ha (Eds.), *Out there: Marginalization and contemporary cultures* (pp. 577–589). Cambridge, MA: MIT Press.

West, C. (1993). *Race matters.* Boston: Beacon Press.

White, E. F. (1990). Africa on my mind: Gender, counter discourse and African-American nationalism. *Journal of Women's History, 2*(1), 73–97.

Wiggington, E. (1985). *Sometimes a shining moment: The Foxfire experience.* Garden City, NY: Doubleday.

Wiggington, E. (1989). Foxfire grows up. *Harvard Educational Review, 59*(1), 24–49.

Wiggington, E. (1991/1992). Culture begins at home. *Educational Leadership, 49*(4), 60–64.

Williams, D. L., & Muchena, O. N. (1991). Utilizing indigenous knowledge systems in agricultural education to promote sustainable agriculture. *Journal of Agricultural Education, 32*(4), 52–57.

Williams, S. W. (1991). Classroom use of African American language: Educational tool or social weapon? In C. E. Sleeter (Ed.), *Empowerment through multicultural education* (pp. 199–216). Albany: SUNY Press.

Wineburg, S. (1991). On the reading of historical texts: Notes on the breach between school and academy. *American Educational Research Journal, 28*(3), 495–519.

Wineburg, S. (1999, March). Historical thinking and other unnatural acts. *Phi Delta Kappan,* pp. 488–499.

Woods, C. (1998). *Development arrested: The blues and plantation power in the Mississippi Delta.* London: Verso.

Woodson, C. G. (1933). *The mis-education of the Negro.* Washington, DC: The Associated Publishers.

Wynter, S. (1984). The ceremony must be found. *Boundary/2, 12*(3)/*13*(1), 19–61.

Wynter, S. (1989). Beyond the word of man: Glissant and the new discourse of the Antilles. *World Literature Today, 63,* 637–648.

Wynter, S. (1991). Columbus and the poetics of the *Propter Nos.* In D. Kadir (Ed.), *Discovering Columbus: Annals of Scholarship, 8*(2), 251–286.

Wynter, S. (1992a). *Do not call us "Negroes": How multicultural textbooks perpetuate racism.* San Francisco: Aspire Books.

Wynter, S. (1992b). No humans involved: An open letter to my colleagues. *Voices of the African Diaspora, 8*(2), 13–16.

Wynter, S. (1992c). Rethinking "aesthetics": Notes towards a deciphering practice. In M. Cham (Ed.), *Exiles: Essays on Caribbean cinema* (pp. 237–279). Trenton, NJ: Africa World Press.

Young, R. (1990). *White mythologies: Writing history and the West.* London: Routledge.

Youth of the Rural Organizing and Cultural Center. (1991). *Minds stayed on freedom.* Boulder, CO: Westview Press.

PART

VI

THE EDUCATION OF IMMIGRANT CHILDREN AND YOUTH

19

IMMIGRANTS AND EDUCATION IN THE UNITED STATES

Michael R. Olneck

University of Wisconsin–Madison

The schooling of immigrants holds substantial symbolic power in American culture. Educators' responses to immigrants in the early part of the 20th century established an ideology of social reform and provided terms of debate that endure (Cohen, 1970; Fass, 1989). What Americans believe about the schooling of immigrants in the past has significant bearing on their expectations for both recent immigrants and nonimmigrant minorities (Montero-Sieburth & La Celle-Peterson, 1991). The responses of schools to the influx of immigrant students since 1965, and the responses of immigrant students and their families and communities to the schools, are of enormous significance to contemporary struggles over cultural diversity and racial hierarchy (Olsen, 1997). These struggles are conditioned and intensified by worldwide patterns of continuing large-scale immigration, technological change, and marketization associated with processes of globalization (M. Suárez-Orozco, 2000, 2001). For these reasons, research on immigrants and education illuminates important societal beliefs and aspirations, responses to social change, prevailing educational policies and practices, and contentious debates about multiculturalism.

Drawing on historical and social scientific research, this chapter examines how educators and schools have responded to the children of immigrants, the nature of the encounter between immigrants and the schools, and the patterns and causes of education outcomes among immigrants and their children.

SCHOOLS' RESPONSES TO THE PRESENCE OF IMMIGRANTS

The responses that schools make to immigrants are shaped by social changes concomitant with immigration, broader political currents, professional educational philosophies and paradigms, and the local school ethos. Across the variations shaped by these influences, there has been a continuity of purpose to acculturate immigrants and incorporate them into existing or emergent social structures, moral orders, and symbolic systems, using schooling to inculcate dominant modes of social participation and belonging, and to periodically reestablish the "once imagined neat fit between language, culture, and nation" (Suárez-Orozco, 2001, p. 346) that large-scale immigration unsettles. The discussion in this section of the chapter centers on the goals of and means to immigrant acculturation, immigrants' responses to them, the accommodations to immigrants' cultural differences that schools have made, and the degree of conflict attending each of these factors.

The Goals of and Means to Immigrant Acculturation

In the antebellum 19th century, there were close relationships between immigration and the development of common schooling. The growth of northern urban immigrant populations became associated in the minds of native Americans with class conflict, persistent poverty, crime, social disorganization and disorder, cultural deviance and foreign habits, and the threat of Catholicism (Kaestle, 1973, 1983; Schultz, 1973). Anxious social reformers promoted schools as "culture factories" (Schultz, 1973) in which to inoculate immigrant children against the moral depravity of their environment, to inculcate principles of republican virtue, and to cultivate American habits and identities through association with native-born children.

On the assumptions that the social morality of the nation depended crucially on the moral character of each individual, and that extant American institutions were both superior and fragile, antebellum schools stressed a pan-Protestant ideology of unity, assimilation, obedience, restraint, self-sacrifice, and industriousness that was directed at all but deemed especially necessary for lower-class immigrants (Kaestle, 1983; Troen, 1975). To these ends, educators placed reliance on moralizing textbooks (Elson, 1964; Schultz, 1973) and on the educative effects of "non-sectarian" King James Bible reading and Protestant prayers.

The responses of 19th-century immigrants to the common schools cannot be easily summarized (Kaestle, 1983). For many, the cultural and religious alienation and denigration with which the public schools confronted their children sparked political protest and provided reasons to attend parochial schools or to not attend school at all (Kaestle, 1973, 1983; Ravitch, 1974; Schultz, 1973). For others, the opportunities provided by the schools, or the local accommodations compelled by developing political power among immigrant communities—for example, permitting scriptural choice and purging textbooks of ethnic slurs, or making provisions for the use of non-English vernaculars—sufficed to make attendance attractive.

Toward the end of the 19th century, and persisting through the first quarter of the 20th century, massive population influxes from southern and eastern Europe to crowded and disorderly urban centers, as well as transformations in the nature of the workplace, intensified anxiety over American national identity and social cohesion. Educators both broadened the reach of the school in socializing all children and adopted distinctive curricular, extracurricular, and disciplinary innovations intended to "Americanize" the children of immigrants. These included, for example, kindergartens; instruction in hygiene, manners, and the conduct of daily life; home visitations; and special classes for teaching English (Berrol, 1978; Brumberg, 1986; R. Cohen & Mohl, 1979; Lazerson, 1971; Olneck, 1989; Raftery, 1992; Tyack, 1974).

Steven Brumberg (1986) provides an especially meticulous account of the schooling of European immigrants in the early part of the 20th century. Reconstructing the efforts of New York's schools to transform immigrant children from "aliens" into "Americans," Brumberg emphasizes the connections educators made between outward behavior and inner identity. In explicitly instructing youngsters in middle-class hygiene and manners, diet and food preparation, home management, dress, aesthetic and literary standards, recreation, the rights and duties of citizenship, accentless English, and the myths and legends of U.S. history, and in providing them with role models, educators sought not merely to induce behavioral conformity but more fundamentally to inculcate American values, logics, sensibilities, and identities. Similarly, regimentation of movement, patriotic assemblies, the flag salute, exhortative speeches, and other rituals were intended not merely to regulate behavior and extract professions of loyalty but to reorder students' dispositions, orientations, and the communities and symbols with which they identified.

Although Brumberg (1986) concedes that excluding immigrant cultures from recognition in the curriculum and prohibiting children from using their native languages was denigrating, he rejects the characterization by revisionist scholars (Carlson, 1987; Greer, 1972; Violas, 1973) that Americanization in the schools was coercive. Instead, on the basis of the facts that (a) many of the approaches used by the New York public schools were innovated by private philanthropic institutions that were heavily and voluntarily patronized by immigrants; (b) immigrants faced a real need for structure and direction in a difficult new environment; and (c) immigrant parents, at least the Eastern European Jews upon whom his study concentrates, appear to have endorsed the schools' efforts, Brumberg (1986) gives credence to the Progressives' desires to "share" American life with the newcomers, and to provide them with the knowledge required for successful participation in a modern, urban society.

Even some less sympathetic interpreters of Americanization than Brumberg (1986) question the extent to which Americanizers imposed their requirements upon unwilling families and students. R. Cohen and Mohl (1979) note that despite immigrant objections to the linkages between Americanization and Protestantism forged in such practices as the released time plan adopted by the Gary, Indiana, public schools and the city's Protestant churches, public school attendance remained high even though parochial schools were available. David Tyack (1974) may have best summarized the dual nature of Americanization by observing that it cultivated modern habits and Anglo-conformity, and that it promoted equal opportunity and social control.

Although immigrants may have for the most part accepted the efforts of the schools to acculturate their children, they were less accepting of the efforts to differentiate and vocationalize secondary education. Immigrant communities sometimes collectively and publicly resisted plans (like the Gary Plan) that intensified curricular differentiation and appeared to limit their children's opportunities for social mobility through schooling (Brumberg, 1986).

After enactment of immigration restriction in 1924 (King, 2000), and with abatement of anxieties over the threat to national cultural identity, the schools turned from their emphasis on Americanizing new immigrants to addressing the "second-generation problem." Hoping to overcome the alienation experienced by relatively acculturated children of immigrants who were cut off from their parents but not fully accepted into the American mainstream, and hoping to reduce the ongoing tensions between hyphenated Americans and Anglo-Saxons, between Jews and Gentiles, and even between White and Black Americans, educators began to develop "intercultural education" to recognize the contributions of diverse groups to American history and society, teach appreciation of cultural differences, and enhance the self-respect of minority children (Goodenow, 1975; Montalto, 1982; Olneck, 1990). Foreshadowing aspects of the debates over multicultural education in the post-1965 period, interculturalists debated the relative emphasis that should be placed on recognizing distinctive contributions and cultures of particular groups as compared with the emphasis that should be placed on commonalities among individuals of diverse origins. In the context of the Second World War, the latter position prevailed (Montalto, 1982).

As this account suggests, the historiography of immigrant education has been overwhelmingly devoted to the schooling of European immigrants. Historians investigating the schooling of Mexican and Asian immigrants in the Southwest and West detail Americanization, IQ testing, and vocationalizing measures paralleling those applied to European immigrants and find similar tensions between coercion and beneficence, between immigrant acquiescence and resistance, as were found by those studying the schooling of European immigrants (Gonzalez, 1990; Raftery, 1992; San Miguel, 1987). They detail, as well, the somewhat paradoxical ties, unique to non-White immigrants, between Americanization on the one hand and systematic racial segregation and economic, political, and social subordination on the other.

After passage of the Immigration Reform Act of 1965, revoking the 1924 national quota regulations, large-scale immigration into the United States resumed, particularly from Mexico, Latin America, and Asia, and once again the question of how to school immigrant children arose, persisting into the present. Despite contemporary rhetoric rejecting melting pot ideology, schools continue to seek to integrate immigrant children into an assumed American mainstream (Becker, 1985; Gibson, 1995; Goldstein, 1985; Grey, 1990; Katz, 1999; Olsen, 1997; Patthey-Chavez, 1993). Their approaches continue to reflect what Marcelo Suárez-Orozco (2000) has termed the "clean break" assumption: that immigration should and does involve ultimately a complete exchange of prior cultures and identities for new. Schools rarely recognize the transnational aspects of their immigrant students' identities and lives (Sarroub, 2001; M. Suárez-Orozco, 2000).

In some settings in which immigration is a volatile political issue, pressures on immigrant students to Americanize rapidly have intensified. California's Proposition 227, passed in 1998, attempts to ban most bilingual education in the state's schools (Crawford, 1999). Teachers often adopt a "color-blind, difference-blind" stance in the face of a culturally diverse student body and resist the idea that the school's "regular" practices and curriculum require change (Olsen, 1997). They also misperceive or refuse to acknowledge the extent to which superficial harmony among students may mask fissures and antagonisms between immigrant and native groups (Lee, 1996; Lei, 2001). Curriculum that does not recognize the perspectives of immigrants contributes to an overall context of "subtractive schooling" (Valenzuela, 1999). Teachers, like community members at large, often resent giving immigrant students "something special" (Olsen, 1997). Voicing concern that immigrant children be provided equal opportunity to acquire the skills necessary for participation in U.S. labor markets and social arenas, contemporary educators insist that newcomers be encouraged and prepared to enter so-called regular classrooms and participate in the elaborate social life of U.S. schools. Despite the evident difficulties of English monolinguals in their schools (Valenzuela, 1999), in large measure educators view the rapid acquisition of English as the necessary prerequisite for participation, and some informally try to enforce the "English-only" practices reminiscent of earlier official prohibitions on the use of languages other than English (Gibson, 1995, 1998; Olsen, 1997). Immigrant students are pressured as well by ridicule, demands, and shunning from other students, including co-ethnics of the second and third generations, to abandon use of their home languages while at school (Katz, 1999; Olsen, 1997). The response of contemporary immigrants to U.S. schools is discussed later in this chapter.

Accommodations to Cultural Diversity

The degree and manner in which schools have acknowledged and accommodated cultural differences varies over time and locale. Accommodations by the public schools have, however, been generally limited and conflictual.

Throughout much of the 19th century, the combination of decentralized control and concentrations of immigrant settlement in the agricultural upper Midwest permitted considerable use of vernacular mother tongues in rural schools, the hiring of native homeland language speakers as teachers, and modifications (or benign neglect) of Protestant-inspired observances such as Bible reading (Kaestle, 1983; Kuyper, 1980). School officials turned a blind eye to such practices, even when they were legally prohibited, because of the political power of immigrant communities and their desire to entice immigrant children into the "Anglicizing" environment of the common school.

Such accommodations, though widespread, were nevertheless subject to criticism and controversy. English-language parents objected when their own children were assigned to schools in which instruction in German predominated, necessitating the redrawing of district lines and time sharing of school buildings (Kuyper, 1980; Schlossman, 1983). At the state level, nativist-inspired legislation limiting language of instruction to English, even when it had little instrumental effect, took on symbolic importance (Jorgenson, 1987).

Mid- to late-19th-century urban school officials in such cities as St. Louis and Milwaukee were motivated for reasons similar to those of their rural counterparts to provide opportunities for the study of German as a subject in elementary schools—an opportunity that, for example, almost half of the students in St. Louis availed themselves of by 1874, and that, by 1880, had drawn 80 percent of the German students into the public schools (Troen, 1975). Nevertheless, even as they provided for the study of German in their schools, urban school officials insisted that the amount of time devoted to such study be strictly limited, and that such study be a bridge into a wholly English-language curriculum (Schlossman, 1983). Moreover, school authorities did not consider similar measures for linguistic groups whose numbers were fewer than the Germans, and whose children were already within the embrace of the public schools (Troen, 1975).

Even in relatively favorable contexts, linguistic accommodation engendered ongoing debate. Opponents of German language instruction in St. Louis invoked arguments over cost, interference with the regular curriculum, threat to the standing and universality of English, and special privilege; they succeeded in eliminating such instruction even before the onset of anti-German hysteria around 1914 (Schlossman, 1983; Troen, 1975). Outside of the Midwest, accommodations were fewer and less durable (see Kaestle, 1973; Shultz, 1973), though, in Buffalo, New York, the politics of language and schooling was a focal point for the pre–Civil War emergence of a German ethnic group out of diverse religious, regional, and linguistic elements. It remained an arena for the advancement and recognition of German Americans in the mid-1870s (Gerber, 1984).

Accommodation to the religious and cultural demands of 19th-century Catholic immigrants proved inherently more difficult than accommodation to the linguistic demands of Germans. Common school reformers sought an inclusive school system that would culturally and morally reform and homogenize the republic's children (Kaestle, 1973, 1983). To this end, they demanded and won a public school monopoly on tax monies for schooling and insisted upon such practices as nonsectarian moral education and Bible reading without commentary that were anathema to Catholic immigrants and their clerical leaders (Jorgenson, 1987; Kaestle, 1973; Ravitch, 1974; Sanders, 1977; Troen, 1975). They also confronted immigrant children with texts that denigrated Catholicism, Catholics, the nations from which Catholic immigrants originated, and the moral character of immigrant populations, most notably the Irish (Elson, 1964; Jorgenson, 1987; Kaestle, 1973; Sanders, 1977). The result was periodic eruption of intense conflict between Catholics and Protestants over school policy, periods of uneasy and tenuous local accommodations such as banning Bible reading, and the growth of parochial schooling (see Jorgenson, 1987; Kaestle, 1973; Ravitch, 1974; Sanders, 1977; Schultz, 1973; Troen, 1975; Vinyard, 1998).

The 19th-century growth of parochial schooling did not, however, depend solely on the nativism of the public schools or on overt conflict between Catholics and Protestants (Sanders, 1977; Troen, 1975). Those immigrants, like German-speaking Lutherans and Catholics in St. Louis, who looked to schooling to guarantee their children's membership in ongoing ethnic, linguistic, and religious communities, rather than to train them for wider civic participation, relied upon parochial schooling until their linguistic demands were met. In the early 20th century, Slavic groups, whose use of schooling was directed more toward ethnic solidarity than toward economic mobility, also attended parochial schools in large numbers (R. Cohen & Mohl, 1979; Bodnar, 1976, 1982).

Patterns and rates of growth of urban parochial schools were determined by ongoing immigration, economic conditions, concentrations of population, and the size and attitudes of particular groups (Sanders, 1977). In such cities as Chicago, parochial schools proliferated, in particular, as ethnically and linguistically specific parishes, called "national parishes," were established (Sanders, 1977; Troen, 1975; Vinyard, 1998). The question of national parishes created conflict among groups and between particular groups and the episcopate, thereby propelling the creation of new parochial schools into the 20th century.

Scholars have often contrasted the culturally conservative functions of parochial schools with the Americanizing functions of public schools (R. Cohen & Mohl, 1979), but under the impact of immigration restriction, diminished ethnic cohesion, residential dispersal and ethnic commingling, social mobility, language attrition, and the centralizing and standardizing policies of the church hierarchy, parochial schools from the 1920s onward played more the role of organizing an Americanized Catholic community than of preserving ethnically bounded immigrant communities (Sanders, 1977).

Public schools during the first quarter of this century made, for the most part, even fewer and more grudging accommodations to cultural diversity than had 19th-century schools. A few experts advocated and a few schools occasionally experimented with the employment of bilingual teachers and even some bilingual instruction, but educational orthodoxy held that any use of home languages in the classroom detracted from English acquisition and perpetuated the use of non-English languages in immigrant homes. Moreover, educators intent upon facilitating immigrant children's rapid assimilation were exceedingly reluctant to separate them from their English-speaking classmates (Olneck, 1989). Nevertheless, teachers and administrators recognized that sink-or-swim practices and the placement of older children into primary grades could cause difficulty and be counterproductive.

To facilitate the speedy acquisition of English by immigrant children, various localities experimented with "vestibule" or "steamer" classes and "special rooms" that were intended to equip non–English-speaking students with sufficient English comprehension to enable them to join regular classrooms (Berrol, 1978; Lazerson, 1971; Montero-Sieburth & La Celle-Peterson, 1991). Such experimental classes were regarded as expedients, were intended to be conducted solely in English, were limited to language instruction, and were to be attended only for so long as was absolutely necessary. Nor were they universal or necessarily prevalent. In Gary, Indiana, during the mid-1920s, only one school had even one special class in which to teach immigrant children English (R. Cohen & Mohl, 1979).

During the 1920s and 1930s, in the absence of continuing infusions of new, non–English-speaking immigrants into the schools, the issue of accommodating linguistic diversity receded. As second-generation immigrants constructed American-based ethnic identities, the question became the extent to which the public schools were permissible arenas in which to collectively organize and express these identities.

Introduction of foreign languages such as Hebrew and Italian as subjects of study in the high schools came to serve as ethnic insignias of Americanized middle-class groups even as the proportion of ethnic students enrolling in such courses was minimal (Dash Moore, 1981). Even though school boards looked askance at the formation of religio-ethnic clubs and associations within the schools, or at the use of school facilities for community-based religio-ethnic activities, school principals proved more accommodating (Dash Moore, 1981; Raftery, 1992). The social distance between the schools and immigrant children diminished as second-generation Euro-Americans

entered the teaching force in increasing numbers, and as school officials endeavored to place ethnic teachers with co-ethnic student populations (Berrol, 1978).

In the period since the 1965 Immigration Reform Act, the schooling of immigrants has been conditioned by post–civil rights movement education policies and practices that originated in relation to the schooling of students of color and nonimmigrant linguistic minorities. These policies and practices, at least nominally, propound the value of multiculturalism (Glazer, 1985, 1997; C. Suárez-Orozco & M. Suárez-Orozco, 2001; M. Suárez-Orozco, 2000, 2001). Official education policy assumes that the limited recognition and incorporation of minority cultural and linguistic repertoires is an appropriate, and perhaps necessary, means to assure students that they are respected and that they belong, and to facilitate levels of linguistic and subject matter comprehension adequate to participation in regular classrooms. This assumption is most commonly implemented through transitional bilingual education and English as a Second Language (ESL) programs, which schools provide with varying degrees of willingness and varying levels of support, and which are structured so as to leave undisturbed the normal school programs and prevailing local academic values (Goldstein, 1985; Katz, 1999; Olsen, 1997; Patthey-Chavez, 1993).

School ethnographers have found that by virtue of physical and social isolation from the regular academic program, the very programs intended to facilitate the incorporation of immigrant students can highlight and perpetuate those students' and their teachers' marginal and peripheral status within the school (Becker, 1985; Davidson, 1997; Gibson, 1988; Goldstein, 1985; Grey, 1990; Katz, 1999; Olsen, 1997; Patthey-Chavez, 1993). Immigrant parents and students, though often appreciative of the support and guidance these programs offer, are aware that the education they provide is not fully recognized, and they express concern that students not be assigned to them needlessly or unnecessarily retained in them (Gibson, 1988; Montero-Sieburth & La Celle-Peterson, 1991; M. Suárez-Orozco, 1991). Although assignment to special classes for "LEPs," or limited English speakers (now more likely to be termed "English language learners") can lower the self-esteem of students (Rumbaut, 1996), it is nevertheless usually only within such "special" programs or classrooms that teachers are willing to modify curriculum and pedagogy to accommodate the distinctive learning needs of immigrant children, and only there that immigrant children may comfortably express themselves (Goldstein, 1985; Lee, 2001b; Olsen, 1997; T. Trueba, Jacobs, & Kirton, 1990). In some rare circumstances, where non–English-speaking students outperform their American peers, special language classes can provide advantaged opportunities and higher status (Centrie, 2000b).

Despite the fact that local bilingual and ESL programs are highly circumscribed and often funded with federal and state funds, they are, as California's Proposition 227 illustrates, a source of protest by established Americans. Resistance arises because the programs do not mesh with perceptions of what the local school is and does, and how it is related to the existing community (Grey, 1990), because (a) local parents fear that special programs will interfere with their own children's educations, and they resent "their" tax dollars being used to fund instruction that uses "other people's" languages (Gibson, 1988), (b) some community members fear that bilingual education impedes assimilation (Gibson, 1988), and (c) some community members hold nativist sentiments of the sort exemplified by the English-only movement (Kiang, 1990; Montero-Sieburth & La Celle-Peterson, 1991). The unwillingness of communities to more fully respond to and accommodate the distinctive needs of immigrant communities has, in some cases, prompted those communities to organize on the model of (and sometimes in cooperation with) long-term American minority communities (Kiang, 1990; Montero-Sieburth & La Celle-Peterson, 1991).

THE ENCOUNTER BETWEEN THE IMMIGRANT AND THE SCHOOLS

The encounter between immigrant children, families, and communities and the schools is conditioned by local school cultures; by perceptions relevant actors hold of one another and of themselves; by the diverse meanings immigrants and educators assign to schooling; by tacit as well as explicit pedagogical, curricular, and administrative practices; by the degree of discontinuity that obtains between immigrant and school cultures; and by the structural characteristics and cultural practices of immigrant communities. The results of that encounter may be seen in status orders within schools, in the nature of mutual interactions, in the degree of acculturation immigrants experience, in the manner in which immigrants appropriate and use their educational experiences, and in how schooling becomes a site for the construction and experience of ethnic identity.

Local School Cultures

Immigrants do not enter undifferentiated "American" schools. Rather, they enter specific schools whose immediate contexts, histories, memories, and commitments shape their organization and practices. Mediated by day-to-day routines and by the interpretations assigned to events, differences among schools may be highly consequential for the ways in which boundaries between immigrant and native students are either transcended or solidified.

Goode, Schneider, and Blanc (1992), for example, found appreciable differences in the practices and outcomes of two nearby Philadelphia schools serving socioeconomically comparable populations. One, a public school, symbolically celebrated schooling as an avenue of individual mobility and deemphasized cultural differences. It provided short-term rather than long-term ESOL (English for Speakers of Other Languages) or ESL programs and established classroom and lunchroom assignment and seating rules that ensured intermingling. The school's policies and practices appeared to encourage easy interactions and strong attachments among students from diverse groups, as well as the muting of expressions of ethnic distinctiveness, including the informal use of languages other than English. By contrast, a nearby parochial school symbolically recognized distinctive community entities, addressed recruitment appeals explicitly to particular identity groups, and recognized and supported group-based activities and associations. This school's policies and practices appeared to accentuate the salience of group boundaries.

Goode et al.'s (1992) specific findings should not be generalized. In some contexts, it is institutional silence about immigrant cultural distinctiveness that seems to reinforce separation and lack of communication between immigrant and native students (Grey, 1990). What Goode and colleagues do demonstrate is the salience of the immediate school context for social relations between immigrants and natives.

The terms on which immigrants encounter native students may be affected by a school ethos that antedates their entrance into a particular school. In her ethnographic study of two contrasting high schools, Goldstein (1985) found that in one school institutional commitments to sustaining a public reputation for academic rigor and to upholding strict academic standards encouraged bilingual and bicultural programs markedly isolated from the remainder of the school. In the other school a prior commitment to strong discipline and racial integration encouraged the placement of immigrant students in classes among natives, though in pedagogical regimes not conducive to constructive interactions.

Intergroup Perceptions

The views in which students, parents, and teachers hold one another significantly shape the degree, quality, and consequences of interactions between immigrants and their fellow students and teachers, and the views immigrant youths come to hold of themselves. The result is often exacerbated social distance and marginality for immigrant students even in the absence of intentional exclusion.

In the eyes of many American students and teachers, immigrants have entered—even intruded into—"our" country and are therefore obligated to adopt our ways and evaluative standards (Gibson, 1988). Native students and teachers are especially frustrated by immigrants' lack of participation in the social and extracurricular lives of the schools; echoing complaints of previous generations of educators and students, they also complain about immigrants' "clannishness" (Lei, 2001; Patthey-Chavez, 1993). Students often do not comprehend the restrictions some immigrant parents place on their children; nor do they comprehend immigrants' apparent lack of concern with dating, or the degree to which immigrant students seem to take school seriously (Gibson, 1988; Goldstein, 1985). Generally, neither American teachers and students nor immigrant students recognize the extent to which their assessments of one another are complicated by misinterpretations of behavior and by mutual ignorance of differing subjective values and standards (Delgado-Gaitan & Trueba, 1991; Goldstein, 1985).

Both in earlier periods and in the contemporary period, teachers have categorized immigrant groups according to their conformity to prevailing definitions of the "good student" and have held mixed views of the educational values, capabilities, and futures of immigrant students. Early-20th-century educators praised the studiousness and academic talent displayed by Jewish students, while criticizing Italians as nonacademic (Brumberg, 1986; Cowan & Cowan, 1989; Olneck & Lazerson, 1974; Ravitch, 1974). Contemporary educators praise the academic prowess and hard work of Vietnamese and some other "Asian" students, appreciate the cooperation and effort of Hmong and recently arrived Mexican immigrant students despite their modest academic success, and regard U.S.-born Mexican Americans as unruly and untalented (Caplan, Choy, & Whitmore, 1991; Delgado-Gaitan & Trueba, 1991; Gibson, 1988; Goldstein, 1985; Grey, 1990; Matute-Bianchi, 1991; Patthey-Chavez, 1993; M. Suárez-Orozco, 1991; T. Trueba et al., 1990). In some contexts, Asian students are upheld by teachers and staff as "model minorities," to the detriment especially of African American students with whom they are contrasted (Lee, 1996; Centrie, 2000b).

Immigrant students are well aware of the negative judgments being passed upon them (Davidson, 1997; C. Suárez-Orozco, 2000; C. Suárez-Orozco & M. Suárez-Orozco, 2001), though the degree to which they are in return critical of teachers and fellow students seems to vary by their length of residence or by their membership in a group that has a collective memory of discrimination within the United States. In Garden City, Kansas, for example, Latino students explain their high dropout rate as a reaction in part to the low expectations their teachers express toward them (Grey, 1990). Recent Portuguese immigrants in New England, however, see their teachers as being helpful and interpret their teachers' more favorable views toward African Americans and Southeast Asians as an effect of the larger school environment, not as an effect of their teachers' volition (Becker, 1985). In contrast, those who have lived longer in the United States perceive their teachers as neglecting them, favoring other groups, and ignoring their language. Similarly, Mexican American immigrant students, solidly grounded in their Mexican *national* identity, as yet unfamiliar with Mexican American *minority* status, and focused on swift acculturation, do not respond to the school's Americanizing project as negatively as do longer-resident immigrant students and second- and third-generation immigrant students (Valenzuela, 1999). They perceive teachers as more caring and accessible, and school climate as more positive, than do their U.S. counterparts, even when there is no direct evidence of greater teacher proactive support for them than for their co-ethnic peers (Olsen, 1997; Stanton-Salazar, 2001; Valenzuela, 1999). In part, this view derives from immigrants' optimism rooted in their "dual frame of reference," in which the opportunities offered in the United States are contrasted with the absence of opportunity at "home" (Ogbu, 1987, 1991). Additionally, teachers in fact express more approval of immigrant students than of the U.S.-born peers, appreciating their more conservative dress and deference, and assuming that they "care more" about school (Valenzuela, 1999).

Second- and third-generation Mexican American students, however, often perceive their teachers as holding racist ideas about their intellectual competence (Patthey-Chavez, 1993)—favoring Asian students (Katz, 1999; Patthey-Chavez)—and they mistrust and resist schools' "de-Mexicanizing" efforts (Gibson, 1998; Valenzuela, 1999). Dynamics of antagonism and hostility between teachers and students arise in which teachers perceive expressions of powerlessness and alienation as indifference and opposition to schooling per se and act to simply confirm the students' views that the teachers do not care about them (Valenzuela, 1999).

The judgments that teachers render of immigrant students' academic competence are integrated into the students' views of themselves. When these views are negative, not only are students deterred from learning but their sense of marginality is accentuated (T. Trueba et al., 1990). Immigrant students perceive and are injured as well by the hostility, disapproval, condescension, and indifference they sense from American students, leading to even greater hesitance and withdrawal than produced merely by newcomer status and cultural uncertainty (Becker, 1985; Goldstein, 1985). Over time, in the face of denigration and neglect by teachers and fellow students, even initially resilient immigrant students may have their optimism eroded, their engagement diminished, and their marginalization magnified (Davidson, 1997).

Just as native students assess immigrant students, so too immigrants assess the natives with whom they come into contact. These assessments can impede mutual interaction. In particular, many immigrants judge African Americans unfavorably, which significantly affects relationships in the urban schools that both attend (Becker, 1985; Caplan et al., 1991).

Immigrant students are often disconcerted by American students' apparent disrespect toward teachers, and by the constant socializing that occurs in classes, making them likely to rebuff overtures made toward them in the classroom setting (Goldstein, 1985). By contrast, immigrant youths, recognizing the status enjoyed by native students, often do aspire to friendships and associations with their established fellows (Goldstein, 1985). In contexts where second- and third-generation Mexican Americans and other working- or lower-class students resent their beliefs in meritocratic opportunity, acceptance requires immigrants to change their relationship to the school from conformist to resistant (Olsen, 1997), very likely putting them at odds with their parents' exhortations in the value of schooling and hard work (Rumbaut, 1996).

Tacit and Explicit Pedagogical, Curricular, and Administrative Practices

Established pedagogical, curricular, and administrative practices can create the boundaries and strengthen the hierarchies that define the immigrant's marginal location within the school and limit relationships among immigrants and natives.

For example, laissez-faire practices ceding students appreciable choice in their patterns of association inhibit cooperation and interaction between immigrant and native students. Exempting immigrant girls from gym requirements, though responsive to particular cultural prohibitions, fails to provide inclusive accommodations to immigrant needs (Becker, 1985).

Reliance on whole-class instruction and on public student participation renders immigrants whose skills in English are limited, and who are reluctant participants, problematic to teachers. They are less problematic in the lower-ability-level classes that rely on individual worksheets, drills, and in-class exercises than in the upper-ability-level classrooms that rely on lectures and homework (Goldstein, 1985). Even in lower-ability-level classes, immigrants may be seated apart from others, encouraged to rely upon one another, and graded for effort alone, resulting in isolation from mainstream students and ongoing classroom activities.

The perceptions and interpretations that teachers hold of immigrant youth guide their practices with them. Expectations of poor performance, early school leaving, and resistance to assimilation, as held by New England teachers of Portuguese immigrants, result in neglect and indifference to poor academic performance, while high expectations, like those held with respect to Asian students, result in encouragement and individualized attention (Becker, 1985). Interpretation of immigrants' reticence as lack of interest, coupled with practices dependent upon student voluntarism and initiative, limit immigrant students' classroom participation.

Cultural Discontinuities

For immigrant groups, schools present challenges to valued ways and inherited meanings. For immigrant students, schools are one among the multiple, incongruent, and noncomplementary worlds they must negotiate each day (Phelan, Davidson, & Yu, 1993; Sarroub, 2001; M. Suárez-Orozco, 2001). Not merely behavioral patterns are at issue. Rather, concepts of God, personhood, family, community, and society; responsibilities and futures; models of success, right, and wrong; and gender identities and roles are at stake (C. Suárez-Orozco, 2000). These challenges have had profound consequences for the experiences of immigrant youth, for rending relationships between the generations, and for transforming immigrant culture and identities.

The most obvious challenge is to the place of community languages. Among turn-of-the-century Eastern European Jewish immigrant youth, Yiddish rapidly became a source of shame that was to be readily relinquished (Brumberg, 1986). At the same time, reliance on Yiddish deterred parental visits to the schools, no doubt to the relief of their children, who dreaded exposure of their parents' broken and accented English (Dash Moore, 1981). Whether because of schools' efforts to foster an English-only environment, or the need to communicate among fellows who come from different home language environments, or the necessities of the workplace, or the general cultural message (sometimes shrill) that *being* American *means* using exclusively English, contemporary immigrant youth in massively large numbers both acquire and prefer to use English (A. Portes & Hao, 1998; A. Portes & Rumbaut, 1996, 2001; A. Portes & Schauffler, 1996; C. Suárez-Orozco & M. Suárez-Orozco, 2001). Among immigrant youth, the transition to English is a largely uncontested aspect of "becoming American" and participating in the life of the school (Olsen, 1997). The process generally leads to the home language of second-generation adults being English, and to the loss of even residual proficiency in a foreign language by the third generation (A. Portes & Rumbaut, 2001). The shift to English monolingualism is slower among Spanish-speaking immigrants than among Asians, especially among those attending schools with large concentrations of Spanish-speaking peers (A. Portes & Hao, 1998), but it is nonetheless evident in survey and ethnographic data (Katz, 1999; D. Lopez & Stanton-Salazar, 2001). Predictions by some that, because of greater residential concentration compared with early-20th-century East European immigrants, transnational contacts, ethnic media, and multicultural policy, fluent bilingualism and strong biculturalism among contemporary immigrants is likely to be considerably higher than in the early 20th century (Min, 1999) appear to be off the mark. Conclusions to the contrary (Zhou & Bankston, 1998) most likely result from misinterpreting cross-sectional data that include young children, whose process of language shift is less complete.

American teachers and fellow-students present immigrant youths with models that put in doubt their own sense of what is normal, right, and proper, and that beckon them away from the worlds of their families and communities. Immigrant youths face the dilemma of how to fulfill the roles and responsibilities that family and community membership require—for example, assuming early employment or entering marriage at a young age—while at the same time conforming to the expectations of American culture and institutions (Goldstein, 1985; Sarroub, 2001).

Social scientists and historians have frequently commented upon the power of individualism in American culture and social structure. The practices and values of American schooling are premised on deeply ingrained perceptions of the individual as the fundamental sociological and moral unit of society. In contrast, for many immigrants, family and community are the fundamental sociological and moral constructs, and the practices and values of American schools that are rooted in individualism are a source of tension, discomfort, and conflict (Caplan et al., 1991; Gibson, 1988; Goldstein, 1985; T. Trueba et al., 1990).

The extracurricular and social lives of American schools, for example, not only compete with the obligations immigrant students may have to contribute to the family's economic and domestic well-being but may, in their premise that individuals must discover and develop their unique interests during a period of adolescence, present a foreign model of personhood (Goldstein, 1985; Sarroub, 2001). Expectations that students must develop their skills as "decision makers" who "make up their own minds" and select their own futures may conflict with models of family and community decision making that rely on collective wisdom and respect for elders (Gibson, 1988). Expectations that students will compete academically on an individualistic basis may conflict with immigrants' practices of cooperation, aversion to atomistic behavior, and reluctance to distinguish oneself publicly (Delgado-Gaitan & Trueba, 1991; Gibson, 1988; Goldstein, 1985).

Classrooms and schools are governed by linguistic, sociocultural, and social interaction codes that may well diverge from those governing the home, peer, and community lives of immigrant children (Delgado-Gaitan & Trueba, 1991). Language and literacy acquisition, in particular, may be impeded when the social organization of teaching and learning ignores these differences and fails to provide opportunities and activities that permit students to integrate and build upon the culture, cognitive patterns, and skills they bring to the classroom.

The Mexican children whom Guadalupe Valdes (1996) studied, for example, refused to engage in fantasy play and initially held back from peers, having been raised to play primarily with siblings and extended family members. Having been trained not to be disruptive or to interrupt adult speech, they did not readily speak out loud, ask for teachers' attention, volunteer, call out answers, or otherwise display information. They did not respond well to the competitive individualism governing U.S. classrooms. In response, teachers viewed the children as having communication or social developmental problems, or as simply coming from homes where parents did not care a great deal about education (Valdes, 1996), which predisposed them to place the children in lower-ability groups until the students were able to "snap out of it." Similarly, Delgado-Gaitan and Trueba (1991) found that pedagogical practices in the California elementary schools they studied contradicted culturally sanctioned patterns of sharing, leadership, and oral storytelling among Mexican American students. Mainstream teachers, rather than modify their pedagogies to accommodate their students, attributed students' difficulties to "deficiencies" and insisted upon adherence to Anglo norms. T. Trueba et al. (1990) report similar findings for the elementary school attended by the Hmong students they studied. In these cases, students did not necessarily or successfully adopt the American patterns insisted upon in the classrooms. Rather, they engaged in a variety of strategies to resist or disengage from classroom learning, further reinforcing their teachers' negative assessments of the students' academic capabilities.

It is, perhaps, in the matter of gender relations that schooling poses the greatest challenge to immigrant communities. Whereas the education of sons is regarded with some anxiety, the education of girls has proven especially problematic. Immigrant parents worry that schools undermine the close supervision and protection they seek to exercise over their daughters, and they fear that through Americanized social behavior their daughters will be spoiled as prospective wives for men within the ethnic group. They also worry that American ideas of individual fulfillment will lead their daughters away from their responsibilities as caretakers of the home and as future mothers, and possibly into marriages with Americans (Becker, 1985; Gibson, 1988; Goldstein, 1985; Matute-Bianchi, 1991; Olsen, 1997; Sarroub, 2001).

Nevertheless, immigrant parents appreciate the value of education for girls within the U.S. context. They recognize that lengthier schooling and high academic achievement strengthen young women's ability to contribute economically to the family and enhance the prospects of marriage to more successful young men (Lee, 1997; Olsen, 1997; Zhou & Bankston, 1998). Mothers, in particular, value the additional bargaining power within marriage that education will provide their daughters (Zhou & Bankston, 1998; Lee, 1997). Rather than adhering strictly to traditional limitations on girls' education, immigrant parents are adapting and transforming their values and practices in ways that take account of their new context. Many Hmong parents, for example, now permit their daughters to finish high school before marrying (Lee, 2001a), while some even support their daughters' aspirations for higher education (Lee, 1997). In some cases parents may compromise by supporting higher education for their daughters—so long as further schooling is limited to community college programs destining their graduates for office work (Gibson, 1988).

For the girls, schooling offers models and possibilities of less burdened and constrained lives, and greater empowerment and equality, but it has posed them with highly charged conflicts that are not easy to resolve (Goldstein, 1985; Lee, 2001b; Olsen, 1997; Rumbaut, 1996). The negotiation of gender roles has proven central to how immigrant girls negotiate the path into "becoming American" (Olsen, 1997). Buffeted by the judgments of American classmates, ethnic peers, school staff, and family members, as well as by conflicting desires and judgments of their own, immigrant girls struggle over such matters as clothing, dating, sexuality, independence, participation in the extracurricular and social life of the school, and plans for higher education (Olsen). Not surprisingly, girls report greater degrees of conflict with their parents than do boys (Rumbaut, 1996).

Despite the conflicts that schooling poses for immigrant girls, their academic success has in general proven higher than that of boys (A. Portes & Rumbaut, 2001; C. Suárez-Orozco & M. Suárez-Orozco, 2001), though some local ethnographies have reported the opposite (Gibson, 1998; but contrast Lee, 2001b). Girls have proven more adept than boys at establishing constructive and useful relationships with teachers (Stanton-Salazar, 2001). The (relatively unreciprocated) academic support and assistance girls give to boys may enhance their own learning and performance (Valenzuela, 1999). Their greater embeddedness in home life and the higher behavioral standards to which they are subject may also contribute to their greater academic success. Moreover, immigrant young women are not so much abandoning traditional

commitments or their ethnic identities through success in education as they are reinterpreting and redefining the conditions of those commitments and identities for themselves *and* for their communities as well (Lee, 1997; Centrie, 2000b).

Cross-Group Interactions

The interactions between immigrant students and natives range from virtually nonexistent to hostile. There is little evidence of sustained and mutually fruitful interaction across boundaries, either within the confines of the school or beyond (Becker, 1985; Gibson, 1988; Goldstein, 1985; Lee, 1996). Students often territorially self-segregate racially and ethnically in schools' public spaces, reinforcing immigrants' isolation from others and reproducing group boundaries (Olsen, 1997; Lei, 2001). In the Midwestern city studied by Goldstein (1985), for example, virtually no Hmong high school students met with American classmates outside of school. Within the high schools Goldstein studied, on those rare occasions when social conversations occurred between Americans and Hmong, they were filled with misunderstood responses and disparaging undertones on the part of the American students. On occasion, the Hmong encountered subtle forms of discrimination, such as American students deliberately speaking fast, making plays on words, and using sarcasm at their expense. Direct discrimination also occurred in the use of racial slurs. More recently, in the school studied by Lei (2001), Hmong and African American students came to blows, proximately because of Hmong frustration with racial taunting, but fundamentally because of competition for position in the school's racial hierarchy.

For immigrant parents, schools are often opaque, confusing, distant, and uninviting, leading to a "noninterventionist" stance toward the school (Gibson, 1995). Parents are, for example, uncertain about what programs their children are following, about graduation and college-entrance requirements, and about grading systems (Valdes, 1996). In part impeded by lack of facility in English, they are unlikely to initiate contact with teachers or other school staff about academic matters, often believe that it is inappropriate to bother teachers with requests about their children's progress, are reluctant to attend school events, and are uncomfortable approaching teachers even at structured parent-teacher events (Delgado-Gaitan & Trueba, 1991; Gibson, 1988; Goldstein, 1985; Valdes, 1996). Moreover, immigrant parents often believe that their direct involvement with their children's schooling would be inappropriate (C. Suárez-Orozco & M. Suárez-Orozco, 2001). Consequently, they do not display the kind of involvement with their children's schooling that teachers interpret as evidence of "caring about" and "supporting" education (Lareau, 1989). Nor do immigrant parents see themselves as "adjunct teachers," thereby violating norms the current emphasis on parent involvement imposes and further contributing to teachers' impressions that some parents "do not care" about their children's education (Valdes, 1996). Ironically, in some cases parents who are more acculturated and have lived longer in the United States are *less likely* to visit and be involved in school than are more recently arrived immigrant parents (Stanton-Salazar, 2001).

The Meaning of Schooling to Immigrants

Although myths and symbols exaggerate and idealize reality, the identification of education with opportunity in America, and of the school with American society itself, are facts of crucial significance conditioning the encounter between immigrant communities and American schools. Immigrants have tended, both in the past and the present, to regard schools, despite the cultural threats they pose, as welcome avenues to participation and mobility (Cowan & Cowan, 1989; Dash Moore, 1981; Gibson, 1991; Goldstein, 1985; C. Suárez-Orozco & M. Suárez-Orozco, 2001). Immigrant parents express confidence that in the United States educational credentials will be respected and rewarded irrespective of the origins of their holders, and they press strongly upon their children the connections between educational success and occupational attainment (Caplan et al., 1991; Delgado-Gaitan & Trueba, 1991).

The value that immigrants assign schooling arises in part from the recognition that only superior educational credentials will overcome discriminatory barriers to advancement (Gibson, 1988). Success in school is not, however, necessarily perceived by parents or children as an instrument of individual mobility or competitive success. Rather, in a number of immigrant or refugee communities, schooling is collectively supported and pursued as a strategy for enhancing family status and mobility, and for recompensing adults for their sacrifices on behalf of children (Caplan et al., 1991; Gibson, 1988; M. Suárez-Orozco, 1991; Louie, 2001).

Immigrant belief in and dependence on the efficacy of schooling is not an obdurate article of faith that is unresponsive to objective realities and to shifts in a group's perception of its status and opportunities. Sikh confidence in higher education is strong in Northern California, but in Britain it is on the wane as awareness of persistent discrimination becomes more acute (Gibson & Bhachu, 1991). In California, immigrant Mexicanos hold a far stronger faith in the efficacy of education than do non-immigrant Mexican Americans and Chicanos (Matute-Bianchi, 1991).

School as a Site for Constructing and Evolving Ethnic and Racial Identities

Ethnic identities are not inheritances or preservations; rather, they are ongoing active constructions that emerge out of interactions among groups within sociopolitical and institutional contexts. Within American schools, immigrant youths become ethnic as they develop images of themselves and of their place on the "map" of American society (Goldstein, 1985; Olsen, 1997), and as they cope with the confusions inherent in wanting to maintain their identities and to become Americans (T. Trueba et al., 1990). Processes of ethnic differentiation, stratification, and identification define, as much as do processes of cultural diffusion and incorporation, the manner of Americanization (Fass, 1989).

For example, from the social distance induced by school sorting mechanisms and classroom management practices, from the treatment they received from American teachers and students, from the competition of their own cultural and power orders with those of the dominant society, and from the necessity of self-consciously making cultural choices, the Hmong high school students whom Goldstein (1985) studied developed a distinctive sense of themselves as a separate category, and as a marginal and inferior group. So too did those studied by Lee (2001b) and the younger Hmong students studied by Trueba and his colleagues (T. Trueba et al., 1990). A social identity as Hmong immigrants was therefore not simply the projection forward of premigration identities; nor was it inconsistent with the adoption of American cultural symbols and behavioral norms (Goldstein, 1985).

Not only is ethnic identity among immigrants constructed; its expression may vary situationally and be systematically patterned by gender, suggesting that the school is itself salient in the refashioning of identity (Becker, 1985; Fass, 1989). For example, among long-term Portuguese immigrant students in New England, within the school context, boys far more than girls approximate culturally their Anglo counterparts, yet within the home and community no gender differences obtain in the expression of Portuguese identity.

The world of extracurricular activities, as much as the classroom, may be a stage upon which ethnicity is contingently and variably enacted; it is thus a sphere in which variable patterns of association and acculturation arise. Paula Fass (1989) found pronounced ethnic differences, particularly among young men, in patterns of extracurricular participation in New York City's high schools during the 1930s and 1940s. More importantly, the nature of those differences varied from school to school, depending upon patterns of social class and ethnic composition. This latter variation suggests strongly that the dynamics of ethnic participation were not simple extrapolations of traditional affinities but arose out of context-specific interaction between groups seeking a place within each school's prestige and status hierarchies. In the contemporary period, Stacey Lee (1996) has found ethnic clubs to be important sites both for promoting pan-ethnic perspectives, and for enacting and preserving particularistic identities.

As immigrant students negotiate the world of schooling, they acquire competencies, make choices, and take on roles that both transform their own identities and alter their relationships with their families and communities and, indeed, begin to reconfigure family and community. In very real ways, immigrant children take school home with them. But what they take is selected, filtered, reinterpreted, applied in novel contexts, and transformed through processes that cannot be readily comprehended as "assimilation" (Brumberg, 1986; Goldstein, 1985).

In part as a reaction to ostracism and discrimination, and in part as an expression of wanting to belong, immigrant children readily adopt the outward manifestations of American culture, including the use of English, American clothing styles, listening to American music, and eating American food; they develop a distance from and ambivalence about their native culture (Becker, 1985; Gibson, 1988; Goode, Schneider, & Blanc, 1992). Delgado-Gaitan and Trueba (1991) suggest that the deeper interactional, linguistic, and cultural codes that immigrant students appropriate at school are also transported into familiar family, peer, and community contexts.

In their adoption of American practices, immigrant children are ambivalently encouraged by parents eager for their offspring not to incur the objections of natives, and eager that they take advantage of opportunity (Gibson, 1988; T. Trueba et al., 1990). Such acculturation is not, however, intended or regarded as relinquishing inherited identities but is rather part of elaborating a dual identity (Gibson, 1988). Indeed, peer pressures to socialize solely within the group may intensify even as acculturation proceeds apace.

Immigrants' relationships to schooling may themselves become an integral component of students' collective and individual identities. This is seen clearly when diverse orientations toward school characterize distinctive identities within a single ethnic group. Maria Matute-Bianchi (1986, 1991) has, for example, detailed for one high school in a California coastal community the ways in which positive and negative orientations toward school are highly salient in defining the identities, respectively, of "Mexicanos" (recent Mexican immigrants and long-term immigrants retaining an orientation toward Mexico) and "homeboys" and "homegirls" or Chicanos (who are largely second-generation or longer U.S. residents from lower socioeconomic strata). Students whose

perceptions and understandings accorded with the modal immigrant model emphasizing opportunity (Ogbu, 1987, 1991; Gibson, 1991) incorporated favorable outlooks about schooling into their sense of what it means to be a Mexicano. Students who held to the modal involuntary minority model stressing opposition to the culture of historical and contemporary oppressors incorporated rejection of schooling into their sense of what being a homeboy or homegirl means. Lee (1996) observed similar phenomena in an academically elite high school, in which students who identified themselves as "Korean" and "Asian" incorporated school success as part of their identities, while Asian immigrant students identifying as "new wavers" incorporated resistance to school as part of their identities. Significantly, students in the study who identified as "Asian American" incorporated school success into their identities as part of their overt resistance to racism.

In some settings, the contemporary American school is less a site in which immigrants are transformed into "Americans" and more a site where immigrants must find and take their place as racialized "minorities." Whereas immigrants may initially see themselves and their schoolmates at school in terms of various national and linguistic identities, they come to acquire the "social maps" replete with racial categorizations with which longer-resident immigrants and others operate (Olsen, 1997; C. Suárez-Orozco & M. Suárez-Orozco, 2001). Most significantly, they learn that "American" *means* White (Lee, 1996), as well as English-speaking, and they learn that the national and linguistic distinctions they make among themselves are unknown and irrelevant to American students (Olsen, 1997). They are thus confronted with having to participate in the school from the position of a racialized group, or remaining marginalized within traditional identities.

West Indian and Haitian immigrants, in particular, who are susceptible to being identified by others as Black, "hold the image of the urban underclass as a pivotal referent to delineate their own place in society" (Fernández-Kelly & Schauffler, 1996, p. 31). Some members of these groups accentuate national identities and inherited cultural practices in order to differentiate the group from African Americans, and to sustain an immigrant identity and ethos in the face of the adversarial culture associated with urban underclass African Americans (Fernández-Kelly & Schauffler, 1996; Stepick, Stepick, Eugene, Teed, & Labissiere, 2001; Waters, 1996). On the other hand, some members of non-White immigrant groups attempt to blend in with African Americans in an effort to escape discrimination by Black schoolmates, and in heavily Black inner-city communities and schools, immigrants such as Haitians and West Indians are increasingly likely to identify racially as "Black" (Kasinitz, Battle, & Miyares, 2001; A. Portes & Rumbaut, 2001; Waters, 1996). Through these processes, the U.S. racial hierarchy placing African Americans on the bottom is reinforced.

Conflictual relations with African Americans that arise out of competition for status and opportunities in stratified schools, and negative views of African Americans' behaviors in school, also play a significant role in the identities some Asian students construct for themselves (Lee, 1996; Centrie, 2000b; Lei, 2001). In some cases, where African Americans predominate, becoming Americanized is equated by immigrants with emulating them and is viewed pejoratively (Centrie, 2000b).

Immigrant youths who have acquired racialized minority identities are, in many cases, characterized by identification with versions of national or pan-ethnic identity labels, and abandonment of American-referenced identity labels. The emergence of such "reactive" ethnic identities (Espiritu & Wolf, 2001) entails the politicization of ethnic culture and should not be mistaken for a return to traditional or immigrant identities. This was the case in the Children of Immigrants Longitudinal Study (CILS), which reported an appreciable shift between the beginning and the end of high school away from self-reported labels such as "American" or "Nicaraguan American" to pan-ethnic labels like Hispanic or to national identity labels like "Nicaraguan" (A. Portes & Rumbaut, 2001). Unlike their parents, who often answered "White," the youths offered these labels as answers to questions about their *racial* identity. From these results, Portes and Rumbaut (2001) concluded that, even as they rapidly shifted to the use of English, "second-generation youths seemed to become increasingly aware of and adopt ethnoracial markers in which they are persistently classified by the schools and other U.S. institutions" (p. 157). "Fully exposed to American culture and its racial definitions, children learn to see themselves more and more in these terms and even to racialize their national origin" (p. 177; see also Espiritu & Wolf; Fernández-Kelly & Curran, 2001). The propensity to conflate national with racial identity is strongest among U.S.-born second-generation youths, and among youths who report having experienced discrimination (A. Portes & Rumbaut, 2001). These findings suggest that Perlmann and Waldinger's (1997) argument that immigrants perceived as people of color in today's schema may well be able to escape being relegated to castelike status is probably overly sanguine. Whether or not they are relegated to caste status, they appear very likely to locate themselves and to be located by others as *racial minorities*, with possibly detrimental effects on education outcomes and the prospects for social mobility.

This outcome is made more probable when immigrants react to their circumstances by mobilizing their identities and cultural practices against White or Anglo cultural domination in ways that include resistance to schooling, as has been the case among numerous Mexican American students (Katz, 1999; D. Lopez & Stanton-Salazar, 2001; Matute-Bianchi, 1986, 1991; C. Suárez-Orozco & M. Suárez-Orozco, 2001; Valenzuela, 1999). In some schools, rejection of English in favor of use of Spanish has become a badge of loyalty and solidarity contributing to broader cultural resistance to coercive assimilation and cultural denigration, especially among *U.S.-born* Mexican American youths. In other schools, being Mexican might mean choosing Mexican friends; standing by other Latinos who have experienced discrimination; adopting aspects of urban street talk, particular clothing and hair styles; and cutting classes (Delgado-Gaitan & Trueba, 1991; Katz, 1999; Olsen, 1997; Patthey-Chavez, 1993; Valenzuela, 1999). In Ogbu's (1987, 1991) terminology, we witness the emergence of "secondary cultural traits" within what some (for instance, H. Trueba, 1988)—though not Ogbu himself—regard as a "voluntary" immigrant group. This finding, along with the finding that heretofore oppressed and subordinated "involuntary" minority groups can undertake cultural revitalization movements that redefine ethnic identities in ways conducive to educational achievement and attainment (Foley, 1991), is evidence that the distinctions Ogbu draws need not be permanent, and that they are imperfectly associated with original conditions of incorporation into society (Gibson, 1997).

THE CAUSES OF VARIABILITY IN EDUCATIONAL ACHIEVEMENT AND ATTAINMENT AMONG IMMIGRANTS

Fascination with education outcomes among immigrants is long-standing. During the last 30 years, social scientists and historians have attempted to assess and explain the dimensions and variability of immigrant school performance.

Patterns of Educational Performance Among Prerestriction Euro-American Immigrant Groups

In a pioneering study of Euro-American immigrant school performance based on studies in the first third of the 20th century, David Cohen (1970) identified a relatively consistent rank ordering of groups' performances that persisted over the first three decades of this century. Children of parents from northern European countries did about as well as children of native Whites. Eastern European Jews ranked at or above native Whites, while non-Jewish central and southern Europeans were at a serious disadvantage. The studies Cohen (1970) used were, however, inadequate for disentangling the effects of ethnicity per se from the effects of other relevant factors on which ethnic groups might differ.

Working with a wider array of published studies than Cohen (1970) had, Olneck and Lazerson (1974) attempted, albeit crudely and indirectly, to manipulate and combine cross-sectional results from a number of sources from the first third of the 20th century in ways that would more precisely distinguish direct "ethnic" effects from the effects of confounding and intervening influences. They found pronounced and fairly consistent differences among national origin groups in rates of grammar school overage enrollment, likelihood of entering high school, and rates of progress in high school. As did Cohen (1970), Olneck and Lazerson (1974) found that the children of Italian and Polish parents fared poorly, while the children of Eastern European Jews fared well. Failing to account for variation among immigrant groups by the effects of differences on socioeconomic and other measured factors known to influence education outcomes, Olneck and Lazerson (1974) advanced a cultural explanation that took note of the fact that ethnic cultures are not free-floating and static but are rooted in historical experiences that shape a collective outlook. They argued that group-specific cognitive and intellectual orientations, as well as attitudinal and behavioral dispositions toward schooling, contributed favorably to Russian Jewish immigrant school success, while militating against the success of southern Italian immigrant youths.

The most significant study of the determinants of Euro-American immigrant school achievement and attainment in the past is that by Joel Perlmann (1988). Using local and state school and census records, and the manuscript U.S. census, Perlmann assembled and analyzed longitudinal data for individuals from Providence, Rhode Island, covering the period 1880–1930. Perlmann's (1988) findings attest to the salience of both structural and cultural factors. Increasing political, social, and economic power and participation among the Irish appear, for example, to account for the convergence between 1880 and 1890 of Irish and Yankee high school entry and school enrollment rates. On the other hand, cultural factors appear implicated in persistent disadvantages for Italians that cannot be explained by differentials in socioeconomic background or nativity.

A number of scholars have questioned the extent to which independent cultural factors are implicated in education differentials among immigrant groups. Jacobs and Greene (1994), on the basis of analyses of individual-level data from the 1910 decennial census, argue that controls for parental occupation, self-employment, recency of immigration, region, urbanicity, parental literacy, parental English ability, and presence of the father in the household generally account for observed disparities in school enrollment among ethnic groups, and between the offspring of immigrants and those of native White parents. They claim that remaining differentials are best explained

by variations in economic opportunity. Nevertheless, even in Jacob and Greene's (1994) data, disparities in school enrollment favoring Jewish immigrant children over the children of Italians and Poles are quite striking.

Stephen Steinberg (1981) argues that only after they had secured an economic foothold through small-scale entrepreneurial success or savings from arduous labor were Jews able to act upon values conducive to lengthier schooling. However, if Steinberg (1981) was correct, differentials in educational attainment favoring the children of Jewish immigrants should occur only above certain socioeconomic thresholds, and the degree to which Jews enjoy educational advantages in comparison with others should rise, at least up to a point, with socioeconomic status. The average socioeconomic level of a group, creating a socioeconomic context or environment beyond that of the family, might be expected to influence individuals' educational attainments. No such patterns are evident in Perlmann's (1988) data or others' data.

Without gainsaying the powerful impact that socioeconomic status and social class location have on differentiating education outcomes among individuals and groups, both direct and inferential evidence suggest the salience of cultural factors that distinguish otherwise structurally comparable groups. But cultural factors do not operate in a vacuum; nor are they impervious to material and historical circumstances. Thus the durability of a distinctive education ethos and of its consequences is an important question.

Durability of Educational Differences Among Euro-American Ethnic Groups

S. Steinberg (1981) rightly observes that immigrant groups starting out with less favorable cultural dispositions with respect to education did experience educational mobility once they experienced economic mobility, and that ethnic differentials did not persist unchanged. Similarly, Miriam Cohen (1982) argues that increasing levels of persistence in schooling among Italian Americans in New York City, beginning in the 1930s, demonstrate that socioeconomic and demographic circumstances, as well as labor market incentives, contribute to what otherwise appears to be ethnically determined educational behavior.

David Hogan (1978), too, has provided evidence for the convergence of education attainment among immigrant groups. Hogan explains the lengthier schooling pursued by various Chicago immigrant groups in the 1920s as an outcome of the evolution among working-class immigrants of an instrumental attitude toward schooling aimed at ensuring their children's economic welfare. Ewa Morawska (1985) describes a similar evolution among East Central European immigrants in post–World War II Johnstown, Pennsylvania. With the proviso that Jewish education attainment remained distinctive, the convergence of education outcomes among diverse European immigrant groups evident in local data is evident as well in national survey data (Duncan & Duncan, 1968; Featherman & Hauser, 1978; Hirschman & Falcon, 1985; Lieberson, 1980; Lieberson & Waters, 1988).

The Education Performance of Recent Immigrants

The education performance of the children of recent immigrants receives both public and scholarly attention. News media routinely comment on Vietnamese valedictorians, Chinese science fair winners, and the other accomplishments of Asian "model minorities" (Lee, 1996). More generally, the success of Asian immigrants in the schools is contrasted with the persistently high dropout rates and low test scores of inner-city African Americans, Native Americans, and Mexican Americans. There is considerable variation among individuals within any ethnic group, and academic difficulties and failure may attend members of even unusually successful groups (Lee, 1996), but social science data largely accord with popular perceptions. We must, however, not overgeneralize the advantages or disadvantages of any broadly defined groups such as "Asians" or "Hispanics." Within broadly defined classifications, there is considerable variation among specific ethnic or national-origin groups (Driscoll, 1999; Goyette & Xie, 1999; Kao, 1995).

As in historical data, observed variations in school performance and attainment among contemporary immigrant groups to some extent reflect the consequences of differences among groups in socioeconomic status, parental education, parental literacy, parental proficiency in English, nativity, and the like. In some cases, observed advantages can be attributed almost entirely to background factors correlated with ethnic group membership. With this caveat in mind, then, I turn to patterns of ethnic variation in education achievement and attainment among recent immigrant groups.

Synthesizing across a range of studies, certain generalizations appear warranted. First, despite the burdens of poverty and difficulties with English, Vietnamese students in particular do unusually well in school (Caplan et al., 1991; A. Portes & Rumbaut, 2001; Zhou & Bankston, 1998). So too do the offspring of Chinese, Korean, and South Asian immigrants (A. Portes & Rumbaut, 1990, 2001; Zhou & Bankston, 1998), though much of their advantage stems from parental socioeconomic advantages (Kao, 1995; but see Zhou & Bankston, 1998). Hmong students apparently earn good grades despite not evidencing high test scores (Rumbaut, 1995). Haitian immigrant children do even less well than their socioeconomic background would lead one to expect (A. Portes & MacLeod, 1996). Cuban students whose parents arrived

in the United States before 1970 do noticeably well (Portes & MacLeod, 1996); however, on the whole Cuban students receive lower grades and drop out of high school to a greater degree than might be expected (Perez, 2001). A very substantial proportion, but by no means the entirety, of achievement disparities between students of Mexican origin and others is accounted for by socioeconomic and other background disparities (Kao, Tienda, & Schneider, 1996; A. Portes & Rumbaut, 2001). Low second-generation Mexican school achievement and attainment replicates historical patterns evident in earlier generations of immigrants (D. Lopez & Stanton-Salazar, 2001).

Some of the proximate causes for patterns of differential education advantage and disadvantage among immigrant groups are the higher-than-average amount of time many Asian-origin students spend on homework (Kao et al., 1996; A. Portes & Rumbaut, 2001; Wong, 1990), the fewer hours spent on homework by Mexican-origin students (Portes & Rumbaut, 2001), and the high expectations of education success for their children held by Cuban and Vietnamese parents compared with pessimistic assessments by Haitian and Mexican parents (A. Portes & MacLeod, 1996). No doubt, cultural discontinuities between home and community on the one hand and schooling on the other, of the sort discussed earlier and further on in this section, also play a role in explaining patterns of variation in immigrant school performance.

Although it is true that ethnic cultures are not static, and that groups selectively apply and adapt their cultural repertoires (P. Portes, 1999; Zhou & Bankston, 1998), the role of values, perspectives, dispositions, orientations, and practices originating in a group's preimmigration history and culture cannot be discounted in accounting to some extent for immigrant education behavior and outcomes in the United States. Valdes (1996), for example, in a close study of Mexican immigrant families in Texas, identified a number of ways in which the values, beliefs, and practices of families did not prepare their children or parents for the demands of U.S. schools. These included a skeptical attitude toward those who are merely "book smart"; concern that being well educated would go to their children's heads; reluctance to push children who were not evidently likely to excel at school; placing paramount importance on filial loyalty, reciprocity, and conformity to social convention even when these conflicted with children's school obligations; and not assigning value to children's academic success as a status symbol. In contrast, adherence to traditional values of obedience, industriousness, mutual assistance, and commitment to family well-being are credited by some researchers as contributing to the success of Vietnamese and other Asian immigrant pupils (Centrie, 2000a, 2000b; A. Portes & Rumbaut, 2001; Zhou & Bankston, 1996, 1998).

By the same token, simplistic and stereotypic cultural-ist explanations should be avoided. The role of "Confucian" values in the higher achievement of Asian students, for example, has certainly been exaggerated, especially when one recognizes that *Southeast* Asian students are *not* Confucian (A. Portes & Rumbaut, 2001). Suárez-Orozco and Suarez-Orozco (1995), in a study of Mexicans in Mexico and Mexican immigrants in the United States, found that Mexican culture *does* value self-initiated achievement and does recognize the necessity of hard work for success, albeit played out in a context of familial interdependence. They conclude that their findings "suggest that problems in the motivational dynamics and schooling experiences of Mexico-origin second-generation youths cannot be attributed to cultural background per se" (p. 177). Others, too, have found strong recognition and appreciation of the value of schooling among Mexican immigrant families (D. Lopez & Stanton-Salazar, 2001; G. Lopez, 2001; Stanton-Salazar, 2001; Valdes, 1996; Valenzuela, 1999), albeit unaccompanied by the resources to translate this commitment into effective institutional support of their children (D. Lopez & Stanton-Salazar).

It is noteworthy that numerous researchers have found that, within linguistic minority groups, students who are fluently bilingual—that is, who are adept in their native language and fully proficient in English—outperform students whose proficiency in both their home languages and English is limited and *also* outperform students who are monolingual in English. These findings occur in a number of samples even when socioeconomic background is controlled (Bankston & Zhou, 1995; Hao & Bonstead-Bruns, 1998; A. Portes & Rumbaut, 1990, 1996, 2001; A. Portes & Schauffler, 1996; A. Portes & Rumbaut, 1996, 2001; Zhou & Bankston, 1998). Mouw and Xie (1999), however, find that in the NELS: 88 data bilingual fluency in and of itself has *negative* effects on achievement outcomes, and that use of native language has positive effects on achievement only when parents are low in English proficiency. From this, Mouw and Xie (1999) argue that the only significance of bilingual fluency for education achievement is in ensuring communication between parents and children at points where the children's fluency in English exceeds that of their parents.

Although it is in dispute, the possibility of a positive effect of fluent bilingualism on education achievement is consistent with the more general finding that affirmative ethnic identities and commitment to ethnically rooted values among immigrants and their children are often associated with greater success in school. In Rumbaut's (1995) mid-1980s San Diego sample, for example, an index of ethnic resilience and cultural reaffirmation was positively associated with higher grades. Similarly, in their study of the Indochinese refugee children, Caplan et al. (1991)

found that the children having the strongest respect for the past and its relevance to the present, and those most committed to familial and communal loyalty and responsibilities, enjoyed the most success at school. Finally, Zhou and Bankston (1996, 1998) found that strong ethnic identification and affiliation were central to the success of Vietnamese children in New Orleans schools. Findings such as these fly in the face of teachers' beliefs that rapid Americanization and abandonment of home languages facilitate school success (Matute-Bianchi, 1991; Olsen, 1997), and they support A. Portes and Rumbaut's (1990) conclusion that "it is not parents most willing to assimilate—in the sense of 'subtracting' from their cultural background—who seem to motivate their children effectively, but those most inclined to reaffirm their cultural heritage within ethnic neighborhoods" (p. 214).

This is not to be confused with static cultural preservation or unwavering allegiance to tradition. It is better understood as "selective acculturation" (A. Portes & Rumbaut, 1996, 2001) or "accommodation without assimilation" (Gibson, 1988), in which immigrant parents and children acquire the elements from American cultural repertoires that are essential to success, while at the same time maintaining distinct identities, values, and practices that sustain parental and community authority and norms. Indeed, Stacey Lee (2001b) has found that Hmong parents' willingness and ability to adopt aspects of the dominant culture are directly related to their ability to maintain aspects of Hmong culture. Lee concludes: "In other words, my data suggest that academic success is the result of both cultural transformation and cultural preservation" (p. 525).

Ethnic identity can, however, as Matute-Bianchi's findings (1986, 1991) and others' (D. Lopez & Stanton-Salazar, 2001; Katz, 1999; Valenzuela, 1999) regarding students of Mexican descent show, be used to mobilize sentiments against educational engagement. Whether ethnic identity is a positive or a negative influence on educational performance depends, as Rumbaut (1995) observes, on "the specific nature, content, and style of the minority group's perceptions and adaptive responses to their specific social and historical contexts" (pp. 65–66).

The relationships that immigrant families have with one another and their ethnic communities—and the relationships that immigrant students have with their families; their communities; their peers; and their teachers, counselors, and school administrators—are important sources of variability in education success among immigrant groups. These relationships operate as forms of *social capital* (Coleman, 1988), facilitating the transmission of and adherence to shared norms, the cultivation of trust, reciprocal assistance and mutual support, and the provision of institutional resources and opportunities necessary for academic success and social mobility (A. Portes & Rumbaut, 2001; P. Portes, 1999).

Social capital works to make values efficacious, so it is differences in social capital, rather than in values, that may account for differing outcomes among groups and individuals (Zhou & Bankston, 1998). The Mexican immigrant families studied by Stanton-Salazar (2001), for example, attempted to maintain traditional norms of *confianza en confianza* (trusting mutual trust) and tried to instill and reinforce a core set of values and a sense of familial attachment and obligation in their children. But because the families were not well embedded in tightly knit kinship networks, and only a few of the families were integrated into church or other institutional and organizational domains, their efforts lacked the reinforcement they would have received had they been mirrored in extended family and community networks.

The unusual success of Vietnamese has been directly attributed to the ways in which Vietnamese immigrant youths remain embedded in dense family and community networks, which make ethnically sanctioned norms of academic success salient and effective (Bankston, 1997, 1998; Centrie, 2000a, 2000b; A. Portes & Rumbaut, 2001; Zhou & Bankston, 1998). In contrast, immigrant Mexican student communities are characterized by low bonds of solidarity and low levels of mutual support among co-ethnics (A. Portes & Rumbaut; D. Lopez & Stanton-Salazar, 2001; Stanton-Salazar, 2001). Also in striking contrast to Vietnamese families, the families of Haitian students, whose low education achievement has been noted, are notably weak in social capital. Within the Haitian families included in the CILS, there is strong cultural dissonance between children and parents, characterized by a disproportionate incidence of conflict between the generations, feelings of shame among Haitian youth associated with their home culture, and their rapid abandonment of their parents' language (Stepick et al., 2001). As will be seen, the capacity for an immigrant community to provide its members with social capital has a good deal to do with the manner in which the group has been received and incorporated into U.S. society.

The social capital provided by ethnic communities is expressed institutionally in such endeavors as afternoon schools, like those found among the Vietnamese and Chinese in New Orleans (Zhou & Bankston, 1998) or in New York City's Chinatown (Zhou, 1997), in community civic institutions that celebrate and support the education success of the community's children (Bankston, 1997; Zhou & Bankston, 1998), in periodic meetings of community leaders as well as organized holiday celebrations (Centrie, 2000a, 2000b), and in the system of private bilingual schools in Miami's Cuban enclave (Perez, 2001). It is expressed informally in the ways in which education

success of family members garners praise from others, while educational failure produces shame, and in the exercise of authority and moral guidance by adults other than members of the nuclear family (Centrie, 2000a, 2000b; Gibson, 1988, 1998; A. Portes & MacLeod, 1996; Zhou, 1997; Zhou & Bankston, 1996, 1998), as well as in the ways in which community members, like those in the Cuban enclave of Miami, provide one another with information, job opportunities, and recommendations (Fernández-Kelly & Schauffler, 1996), or the ways in which New York City Chinese immigrant coworkers exchange information about the relative desirability of specific public schools (Louie, 2001).

Student and peer networks provide social capital in a number of ways. Immigrant students who remain closely associated with co-ethnics tend to do better in school than those whose ties to co-ethnics have loosened (A. Portes & Rumbaut, 2001). In New Orleans, Vietnamese students, already likely to persist in their schooling, are even less likely to drop out of high school when they attend schools and live in neighborhoods in which there are heavy concentrations of other Vietnamese (Zhou & Bankston, 1998). Normatively required cooperation among siblings also enhances Vietnamese students' academic engagement and achievement (Bankston, 1998). Where they do exist, networks among Mexican immigrant students of achievement-oriented peers facilitate the sharing of school-related information, material resources, and school-based knowledge, as well as the adoption of collective achievement strategies (Davidson, 1997; Valenzuela, 1999); but all too often, Mexican students are left to "go it alone" (D. Lopez & Stanton-Salazar, 2001). This is true in part because schools' aggressively assimilationist stances, including denigration of Spanish, undermine sources of solidarity and cooperation among students, with particularly negative effects on second- and third-generation students, who are alienated from and repudiated by recent immigrant students (Valenzuela, 1999; Stanton-Salazar, 2001).

Close relationships with teachers, counselors, and other school personnel can be an important source of social capital, providing students with "funds of knowledge" (Chapter 33, this volume), including access to necessary institutional discourses, as well as information about school procedures and requirements and opportunities for college, with advice and guidance, with advocates and bridges to gatekeepers, with role models, and with emotional and moral support (Stanton-Salazar, 1997). All too often, however, ethnic minority students do not forge the kinds of relationships with school staff that can serve as social capital (Stanton-Salazar, 2001); nor do schools provide the kinds of "social scaffolding" that would promote such relationships (Conchas, 2001).

As Stanton-Salazar (2001) explains, activating social capital requires a willingness to ask for help and be receptive to help when it is proffered. Students who lack self-confidence, who are ashamed, fearful, angry, and distrustful—as many ethnic minority students are—are unlikely to engage in help seeking or readily accept help if it is offered outside an established trusting relationship. The relationships that provide social capital are often formed outside of the regular classroom, in extracurricular activities, sports, clubs, nonacademic classes, and even detention halls, yet ethnic minority students are less likely to participate in extracurricular activities (Stanton-Salazar, 2001). Moreover, ethnic minority students often lack command of the cultural codes on which access to and participation in resource-providing networks depends—command these students can obtain only from already having access to such networks. Further, several facets of urban school organization and practice impede the formation of such relationships. These include high student-to-teacher and student-to-counselor ratios, the periodic severing of bonds through promotion, the absence of native-language–speaking school staff, the predominance of academic classes that do not engage teachers and students with one another in cooperatively solving problems, curricular tracking, and the norms of competitive individualism through which access to resources and opportunities must be *earned*. Consequently, "[r]elationships between school agents and students seldom have the opportunity to develop beyond a superficial, ephemeral, transitory state; in the end, students' social webs remain perilously anemic" (Stanton-Salazar, 2001, p. 205).

The manner in which and the context into which an immigrant group is received influences, for better or ill, the formation of social capital within the group, and the impact of social capital on education outcomes. Post-Mariel Cuban immigrants, for example, already low in human capital, entered an unwelcoming and hostile climate, but a context in which preexisting co-ethnic entrepreneurs had use for their labor. The interaction of these factors contributed to their lower school achievement and earlier school leaving (A. Portes & Rumbaut, 2001; Perez, 2001). Mexican immigrants have been "*the* textbook example of theoretically anticipated effects of low human capital combined with negative context of reception" (A. Portes & Rumbaut, 2001, p. 277; emphasis in original).

It is important to distinguish apparent ethnic effects from the effects of immigrant status per se. There is substantial evidence that the children of immigrants do better in school and aspire to and acquire more schooling than co-ethnics of comparable socioeconomic status whose parents are born in the United States (Driscoll,

1999; Gibson, 1998; Goyette & Xie, 1999; Kao, 1995; Kao & Tienda, 1995, 1998; Kao, Tienda, & Schneider, 1996; Kasinitz et al., 2001; Rong & Brown, 2001; Rumbaut, 1995; Valenzuela, 1999). Consequently, advantages in education performance that members of "voluntary minorities" (Ogbu, 1987, 1991) enjoy tend to dissipate. Notably, the often-cited advantages of some groups of Asian students do not persist into the third generation (Kao, 1995), though it is premature to speculate whether this will prove to be the case as well among the Vietnamese.

Second-generation immigrants as parents, despite their *own* higher-than-expected achievement and attainment, apparently are unable to motivate their children in the same way that their parents motivated them. Indeed, a decline in education commitment and performance can be observed not only across generations but among second-generation high schoolers over time (A. Portes & Rumbaut, 2001). Both birth in the United States and lengthier residence in the United States appear to depress education performance within immigrant groups. What remains unclear is the extent to which "immigrant optimism" (Kao & Tienda, 1995) has eroded among second-generation parents, whose own experiences with American society and schooling may have recast them as minorities rather than immigrants (Rumbaut, 1996; M. Suárez-Orozco & C. Suárez-Orozco, 1995) or the extent to which their optimism endures but is counteracted by their children's negative encounters with American schools and their affinity for American culture. Ethnographic accounts of "toxic" school environments that children of immigrants encounter (Davidson, 1997; C. Suárez-Orozco & M. Suárez-Orozco, 2001) suggest the former; however, finding no differences among recent-immigrant, children-of-immigrant, and grandchildren-of-immigrant American high school students' beliefs about the long-term consequences of doing poorly in school, Lawrence Steinberg (1996) has rejected the "dashed hopes" hypothesis for intergenerationally declining academic engagement and achievement in favor of a "socialization of indifference" hypothesis that locates the explanation in a general, American cultural devaluation of academic excellence.

CONCLUSION

The results of scholarship about immigrants and schooling unsurprisingly reveal greater ambiguity and complexity than popular mythology represents. Immigrants have embraced American schools, but not as unreservedly as mythology holds. Schools have been places where immigrant children joined American society, but not necessarily on the terms educators preferred or with the ease that is sometimes imagined. American schools have, however reluctantly, always had to revise their practices and policies to accommodate immigrant languages, cultures, and identities, but their success in educating immigrant children has been uneven. Immigrants have availed themselves of schooling as an avenue of social mobility, but not equally successfully, and often as a hedge against discrimination, not as an affirmation of equal opportunity.

The results of the historical research that this chapter has reviewed suggest that contemporary opposition to multiculturalism is often premised on mistaken representations of the past. The charge of "Eurocentricity" that people of color raise against the contemporary curriculum is not a novel kind of charge. Nineteenth-century Catholics, especially the Irish, were acutely aware that public school textbooks, staffing patterns, and approaches to socialization were Anglo-Protestant. Conflict over the monocultural character of the public schools persisted into the 20th century.

The demand for African American immersion schools, whatever its merits, is not an entirely novel one. European immigrants in the 19th century on occasion sought similar accommodations. The demand that public school curricula incorporate culturally specific content has precedent in the incorporation of European immigrant languages into post–World War I course offerings. The contemporary use of schools for ethnic expression also has a precedent in the use of schools during the interwar period for Euro-American religio-ethnic organizations and activities. Most notably, although there may be no "American tradition" of bilingual education (Schlossman, 1983), there is ample precedent for the incorporation of non-English vernaculars into pedagogical repertoires.

Valid representation of the past would not dictate particular resolutions to our contemporary dilemmas. It could, however, challenge the claim that the authority of history lies with the critics of multiculturalism.

Valid representation of the past, as well as scrutiny of recent ethnographic and survey data, could also lend support to the claim that it is culturally responsive schools, not monocultural schools, that are most integrative and least divisive. Although insistence on Anglo-Protestant schools during the 19th century impelled many Catholic immigrants to forswear the public schools, accommodation to the linguistic demands of Germans drew German immigrant children into the public schools.

Insistence on culturally discontinuous pedagogical regimes can often provoke disengagement and resistance, while culturally responsive pedagogy seems more often to prompt engagement and assent to learning.

Maintenance of ethnic loyalty and participation in ethnic communities by immigrant parents and children, combined with their acculturation to American culture and language, rather than assimilation, appears associated with stronger school performance among immigrant children.

There remains a theoretical and practical need to more fully integrate historical research on the schooling of European immigrants with research on the schooling of Latino and Asian immigrants, and to more fully integrate social scientific research on the schooling of contemporary immigrants with research on the schooling of involuntary minorities. In particular, the possibility that variations in the social organization, and therefore in the social capital of East European immigrant communities in the early 20th century, may have contributed to education differentials that have otherwise been attributed to differences in values about education warrants attention.

Because, as Sylvia Wynter has pointed out, the European immigrant has been represented as the "generic" American (Olneck, 1993), it is important to a more inclusive symbolic representation of American identity that the connotation of the historical, pre-1965 "immigrant" be expanded to embrace Latinos and Asians. Theoretically, historical research that paid comparative attention to Latino, Asian, and European immigrants could better elucidate the dynamics of ethnicity, race, and class that are entailed in the political economy of the schooling of immigrants.

Finally, because immigrants and involuntary minorities are compared in the popular imagination; because recent theoretical work has turned on the distinction between the immigrant experience and that of involuntary minorities; and because interactions within schools among Whites, African Americans, nonimmigrant Latinos, and immigrants are critical to the social and individual outcomes of schooling, it is important that richer empirical work be undertaken to establish how the dynamics of schooling differ and overlap between immigrants and involuntary minorities. In particular, further ethnographic research, such as that by Lee (1996) and Lei (2001), is needed at sites in which immigrants and involuntary minorities attend school together. Such research could not only bring into sharper relief the perspectives of diverse students but also better address whether and how teachers' ideologies, pedagogies, and social relations with students distinguish between immigrant youths and involuntary minorities. Those distinctions might prove as relevant to achievement differentials as any distinctions in students' culturally shaped frames of reference.

References

Bankston, C., III. (1997). Education and ethnicity in an urban Vietnamese village: The role of ethnic community involvement in academic achievement. In M. Seller & L. Weis (Eds.), *Beyond Black and White: New faces and voices in U.S. schools* (pp. 207–230). Albany: State University of New York Press.

Bankston, C., III. (1998). Sibling cooperation and scholastic performance among Vietnamese-American secondary school students: An ethnic relations theory. *Sociological Perspectives, 41*(1), 167–184.

Bankston, C., III, & Zhou, M. (1995). Effects of minority-language literacy on the academic achievement of Vietnamese youths in New Orleans. *Sociology of Education, 68*(1), 1–17.

Becker, A. (1985). *The role of the public school in the maintenance and change of ethnic group affiliation.* Unpublished doctoral dissertation, Brown University, Providence, RI.

Berrol, S. (1978). *Immigrants at school, New York City, 1898–1914.* New York: Arno Press.

Bodnar, J. (1976). Materialism and morality: Slavic-American immigrants and education, 1890–1940. *Journal of Ethnic Studies, 3*(4), 1–19.

Bodnar, J. (1982). Schooling and the Slavic-American family. In B. Weiss (Ed.), *American education and the European immigrant: 1840–1940* (pp. 78–95). Urbana: University of Illinois Press.

Brumberg, S. E. (1986). *Going to America, going to school: The Jewish immigrant public school encounter in turn-of-the-century New York City.* New York: Praeger.

Caplan, N., Choy, M. H., & Whitmore, J. K. (1991). *Children of the boat people: A study of educational success.* Ann Arbor: University of Michigan Press.

Carlson, R. (1987). *The Americanization syndrome: A quest for conformity.* New York: St. Martin's Press.

Centrie, C. (2000a). Free spaces unbound: Families, community, and Vietnamese high school students' identities. In L. Weis & M. Fein (Eds.), *Construction sites: Excavating race, class, and gender among urban youth* (pp. 65–83). New York: Teachers College Press.

Centrie, C. (2000b). *New lives, new freedoms: The identity formation of Vietnamese youth in an American high school.* Unpublished doctoral dissertation, State University of New York, Buffalo.

Cohen, D. K. (1970). Immigrants and the schools. *Review of Educational Research, 40*(1), 13–27.

Cohen, M. (1982). Changing education strategies among immigrant generations: New York Italians in comparative perspective. *Journal of Social History, 15*(3), 443–466.

Cohen, R., & Mohl, R. (1979). *The paradox of progressive education: The Gary Plan and urban schooling.* Port Washington, NY: Kennileat.

Coleman, J. (1988). Social capital in the creation of human capital. *American Journal of Sociology, 94*, 95–120.

Conchas, G. (2001). Structuring failure and success: Understanding the variability in Latino school engagement. *Harvard Educational Review, 71*(3), 475–504.

Cowan, N. M., & Cowan, R. S. (1989). *Our parents' lives: The Americanization of Eastern European Jews.* New York: Basic Books.

Crawford, J. (1999). *Bilingual education: History, politics, theory, and practice.* Los Angeles: Bilingual Educational Services.

Dash Moore, D. (1981). *At home in America: Second-generation New York Jews.* New York: Columbia University Press.

Davidson, A. L. (1997). Marbella Sanchez: On marginalization and silencing. In M. Seller and L. Weis (Eds.), *Beyond Black and White: New faces and voices in U.S. schools* (pp. 15–44). Albany: State University of New York Press.

Delgado-Gaitan, C., & Trueba, H. (1991). *Crossing cultural borders: Education for immigrant families in America.* London: Falmer Press.

Driscoll, A. (1999). Risk of high school dropout among immigrant and native Hispanic youth. *International Migration Review, 33*(4), 857–875.

Duncan, B., & Duncan, O. D. (1968). Minorities and the process of stratification. *American Sociological Review, 33*(3), 356–364.

Elson, R. (1964). *Guardians of tradition: American schoolbooks of the nineteenth century.* Lincoln: University of Nebraska Press.

Espiritu, Y. L., & Wolf, D. L. (2001). The paradox of assimilation: Children of Filipino immigrants in San Diego. In R. Rumbaut & A. Portes (Eds.), *Ethnicities: Children of immigrants in America* (pp. 157–186). Berkeley: University of California Press.

Fass, P. (1989). *Outside in: Minorities and the transformation of American education.* New York: Oxford University Press.

Featherman, D. & Hauser, R. (1978). *Opportunity and change.* New York: Academic Press.

Fernández-Kelly, M. P., & Curran, S. (2001). Nicaraguans: Voices lost, voices found. In R. Rumbaut & A. Portes (Eds.), *Ethnicities: Children of immigrants in America* (pp. 127–156). Berkeley: University of California Press.

Fernández-Kelly, M. P., & Schauffler, R. (1996). Divided fates: Immigrant children and the new assimilation. In A. Portes (Ed.), *The new second generation* (pp. 30–53). New York: Russell Sage Foundation.

Foley, D. (1991). Reconsidering anthropological explanations of ethnic school failure. *Anthropology and Education Quarterly, 22*(1), 60–86.

Gerber, D. (1984). Language maintenance, ethnic group formation, and public schools: Changing patterns of German concern, Buffalo, 1837–1874. *Journal of American Ethnic History, 4*, 31–61.

Gibson, M. (1988). *Accommodation without assimilation: Sikh immigrants in an American high school.* Ithaca, NY: Cornell University Press.

Gibson, M. (1991). Minorities and schooling: Some implications. In M. A. Gibson & J. U. Ogbu (Eds.), *Minority status and schooling: A comparative study of immigrant and involuntary minorities* (pp. 357–381). New York: Garland.

Gibson, M. (1995). Additive acculturation as a strategy for school improvement. In R. Rumbaut & W. Cornelius (Eds.), *California's immigrant children: Theory, research and implications for educational policy* (pp. 77–105). San Diego: University of California, San Diego, Center for U.S.-Mexican Studies.

Gibson, M. (1997). Complicating the immigrant/involuntary minority typology. *Anthropology and Education Quarterly, 28*(3), 431–454.

Gibson, M. (1998). Promoting academic success among immigrant students: Is acculturation the issue? *Educational Policy, 12*, 615–633.

Gibson, M., & Bhachu, P. K. (1991). The dynamics of educational decision making: A comparative study of Sikhs in Britain and the United States. In M. A. Gibson & J. U. Ogbu (Eds.), *Minority status and schooling: A comparative study of immigrant and involuntary minorities* (pp. 63–95). New York: Garland.

Glazer, N. (1985). Immigrants and education. In N. Glazer (Ed.), *Clamor at the gates: The new American immigration* (pp. 213–239). San Francisco: Institute for Contemporary Studies Press.

Glazer, N. (1997). *We are all multiculturalists now.* Cambridge, MA: Harvard University Press.

Goldstein, B. L. (1985). *Schooling for cultural transitions: Hmong girls and boys in American high schools.* Unpublished doctoral dissertation, University of Wisconsin, Madison.

Gonzalez, G. (1990). *Chicano education in the era of segregation.* Philadelphia: Balch Institute Press.

Goode, J. G., Schneider, J. A., & Blanc, S. (1992). Transcending boundaries and closing ranks: How schools shape interrelations. In L. Lamphere (Ed.), *Structuring diversity: Ethnographic perspectives on the new immigration* (pp. 173–213). Chicago: University of Chicago Press.

Goodenow, R. (1975). The Progressive educator, race and ethnicity in the Depression years: An overview. *History of Education Quarterly, 15,* 365–394.

Goyette, K., & Xie, Y. (1999). Educational expectations of Asian American youths: Determinants and ethnic differences. *Sociology of Education, 72*(1), 22–36.

Greer, C. (1972). *The great school legend: A revisionist interpretation of American education.* New York: Basic Books.

Grey, M. A. (1990). Immigrant students in the heartland: Ethnic relations in Garden City, Kansas high school. *Urban Anthropology 19*(4), 409–427.

Hao, L., & Bonstead-Bruns, M. (1998). Parent-child differences in educational expectations and the academic achievement of immigrant and native students. *Sociology of Education, 71*(3), 175–198.

Hirschman, C., & Falcon, L. M. (1985). The educational attainment of religio-ethnic groups in the United States. In A. C. Kerckhoff (Ed.), *Research in sociology of education and socialization, Vol. 5* (pp. 83–120). Greenwich, CT: JAI Press.

Hogan, D. (1978). Education and the making of the Chicago working class, 1880–1930. *History of Education Quarterly, 18*(3), 227–270.

Jacobs, J., & Greene, M. (1994). Race and ethnicity, social class, and schooling. In S. Watkins (Ed.), *After Ellis Island: Newcomers and natives in the 1910 census* (pp. 209–255). New York: Russell Sage Foundation.

Jorgenson, L. (1987). *The state and the non-public school, 1825–1925.* Columbia: University of Missouri Press.

Kaestle, C. (1973). *The evolution of an urban school system: New York City, 1750–1850.* Cambridge, MA: Harvard University Press.

Kaestle, C. (1983). *Pillars of the republic: Common schools and American society, 1780–1860.* New York: Hill and Wang.

Kao, G. (1995). Asian Americans as model minorities: A look at their academic performance. *American Journal of Education 103*(2), 121–159.

Kao, G., & Tienda, M. (1995). Optimism and achievement: The educational performance of immigrant youth. *Social Science Quarterly, 76*(1), 1–19.

Kao, G., & Tienda, M. (1998). Educational aspirations of minority youth. *American Journal of Education, 106*(3), 349–384.

Kao, G., Tienda, M., & Schneider, B. (1996). Racial and ethnic variation in academic performance. In A. Pallas (Ed.), *Research in sociology of education and socialization, Vol. 11* (pp. 263–297). Greenwich, CT: JAI Press.

Kasinitz, P., Battle, J., & Miyares, I. M. (2001). Face to Black? The children of West Indian immigrants in South Florida. In R. Rumbaut & A. Portes (Eds.), *Ethnicities: Children of immigrants in America* (pp. 267–300). Berkeley: University of California Press.

Katz, S. (1999). Teaching in tensions: Latino immigrant youth, their teachers, and the structures of schooling. *Teachers College Record, 100*(4), 809–840.

Kiang, P. N. (1990). *Southeast Asian parent empowerment: The challenge of changing demographics in Lowell, Massachusetts.* Jamaica Plain, MA: MABE Monographs.

King, D. (2000). *Making Americans: Immigration, race, and the origins of diverse democracy.* Cambridge, MA: Harvard University Press.

Kuyper, S. J. (1980). *The Americanization of German immigrants: Language, religion and schools in nineteenth century rural Wisconsin.* Unpublished doctoral dissertation, University of Wisconsin, Madison.

Lareau, A. (1989). *Home advantage: Social class and parental intervention in elementary education.* London, England: Falmer Press.

Lazerson, M. (1971). *The origins of the urban school: Public education in Massachusetts, 1870–1915.* Cambridge, MA: Harvard University Press.

Lee, S. J. (1996). *Unraveling the "model minority" stereotype: Listening to Asian American youth.* New York: Teachers College Press.

Lee, S. J. (1997). The road to college: Hmong American women's pursuit of higher education. *Harvard Educational Review, 77*(4), 803–827.

Lee, S. J. (2001a). Exploring and transforming the landscape of gender and sexuality: Hmong American teenaged girls. *Race, Gender, & Class, 8*(1), 35–46.

Lee, S. J. (2001b). More than "model minorities" or "delinquents": A look at Hmong American high school students. *Harvard Educational Review, 71*(3), 505–528.

Lei, J. (2001). *Claims to belonging and difference: Cultural citizenship and identity construction in schools.* Unpublished doctoral dissertation, University of Wisconsin, Madison.

Lieberson, S. (1980). *A piece of the pie: Blacks and White immigrants since 1880.* Berkeley: University of California Press.

Lieberson, S., & Waters, M. (1988). *From many strands: Ethnic and racial groups in contemporary America.* New York: Russell Sage Foundation.

Lopez, G. (2001). The value of hard work: Lessons on parent involvement from an (im)migrant household. *Harvard Educational Review, 71*(3), 416–437.

Lopez, D., & Stanton-Salazar, R. (2001). Mexican Americans: A second generation at risk. In R. Rumbaut & A. Portes (Eds.), *Ethnicities: Children of immigrants in America* (pp. 57–90). Berkeley: University of California Press.

Louie, V. (2001). Parents' aspirations and investment: The role of social class in the educational experiences of 1.5- and second-generation Chinese Americans. *Harvard Educational Review, 71*(3), 438–474.

Matute-Bianchi, M. E. (1986). Ethnic identities and patterns of school success and failure among Mexican-descent and Japanese American students in a California high school: An ethnographic analysis. *American Journal of Education, 95*(1), 233–255.

Matute-Bianchi, M. E. (1991). Situational ethnicity and patterns of school performance among immigrant and nonimmigrant Mexican-descent students. In M. A. Gibson & J. U. Ogbu (Eds.), *Minority status and schooling: A comparative study of immigrant and involuntary minorities* (pp. 205–247). New York: Garland.

Min, P. G. (1999). A comparison of post-1965 and turn-of-the-century immigrants in intergenerational mobility and cultural transmission. *Journal of American Ethnic History, 18*(3), 65–94.

Montalto, N. (1982). *A history of the intercultural education movement.* New York: Garland.

Montero-Sieburth, M., & La Celle-Peterson, M. (1991). Immigration and schooling: An ethnohistorical account of policy and family perspectives in an urban community. *Anthropology and Education Quarterly, 22*(4), 300–325.

Morawska, E. (1985). *For bread with butter: The life-worlds of East Central Europeans in Johnstown, Pennsylvania, 1890–1940.* Cambridge, England: Cambridge University Press.

Mouw, T., & Xie, Y. (1999). Bilingualism and the academic achievement of first- and second-generation Asian Americans: Accommodation with or without assimilation? *American Sociological Review, 64*(2), 232–252.

Ogbu, J. U. (1987). Variability in minority school performance: A problem in search of an explanation. *Anthropology and Education Quarterly, 18*(4), 312–334.

Ogbu, J. U. (1991). Immigrant and involuntary minorities in comparative perspective. In M. A. Gibson & J. U. Ogbu (Eds.), *Minority status and schooling: A comparative study of immigrant and involuntary minorities* (pp. 3–33). New York: Garland.

Olneck, M. (1989). Americanization and the education of immigrants, 1900–1925: An analysis of symbolic action. *American Journal of Education, 97*(4), 398–423.

Olneck, M. (1990). The recurring dream: Symbolism and ideology in intercultural education and multicultural education. *American Journal of Education, 98*(2), 147–174.

Olneck, M. (1993). Terms of inclusion: Has multiculturalism redefined equality in American education? *American Journal of Education, 101*(3), 234–260.

Olneck, M. R., & Lazerson, M. F. (1974, Winter). The school achievement of immigrant children: 1900–1930. *History of Education Quarterly, 14*, 453–482.

Olsen, L. (1997). *Made in America: Immigrant students in our public schools.* New York: New Press.

Patthey-Chavez, G. (1993). High school as an arena for cultural conflict and acculturation for Latino Angelinos. *Anthropology and Education Quarterly, 24*(1), 33–60.

Perez, L. (2001). Growing up in Cuban Miami: Immigration, the enclave, and new generations. In R. Rumbaut & A. Portes (Eds.), *Ethnicities: Children of immigrants in America* (pp. 91–125). Berkeley: University of California Press.

Perlmann, J. (1988). *Ethnic differences: Schooling and social structure among the Irish, Italians, Jews and Blacks in an American city, 1880–1935.* New York: Cambridge University Press.

Perlmann, J., & Waldinger, R. (1997). Second generation decline? Children of immigrants, past and present—a reconsideration. *International Migration Review, 31*(4), 893–922.

Phelan, P., Davidson, A. L., & Yu, H. C. (1993). Students' multiple worlds: Navigating the borders of family, peer, and school cultures. In P. Phelan & A. L. Davidson (Eds.), *Renegotiating cultural diversity in American schools* (pp. 52–88). New York: Teachers College Press.

Portes, A., & Hao, L. (1998). E pluribus unum: Bilingualism and loss of language in the second generation. *Sociology of Education, 71*(4), 269–294.

Portes, A., & MacLeod, D. (1996). Educational progress of children of immigrants: The roles of class, ethnicity, and school context. *Sociology of Education, 69*(4), 255–275.

Portes, A., & Rumbaut, R. (1990). *Immigrant America: A portrait.* Berkeley: University of California Press.

Portes, A., & Rumbaut, R. (1996). *Immigrant America: A portrait* (2nd ed.). Berkeley: University of California Press.

Portes, A., and Rumbaut, R. (2001). *Legacies: The story of the immigrant second generation.* Berkeley: University of California Press.

Portes, A., & Schauffler, R. (1996). Language and the second generation: Bilingualism yesterday and today. In A. Portes (Ed.), *The new second generation* (pp. 8–29). New York: Russell Sage Foundation.

Portes, P. (1999). Social and psychological factors in the academic achievement of children of immigrants: A cultural history puzzle. *American Educational Research Journal, 36*(3), 489–507.

Raftery, J. R. (1992). *Land of fair promise: Politics and reform in Los Angeles schools, 1885–1941.* Stanford, CA: Stanford University Press.

Ravitch, D. (1974). *The great school wars: A history of the New York City public schools.* New York: Basic Books.

Rong, X., & Brown, F. (2001). The effects of immigrant generation and ethnicity on educational attainment among young African and Caribbean Blacks in the United States. *Harvard Educational Review, 71*(3), 536–565.

Rumbaut, R. (1995). The new Californians: Comparative research findings on the educational progress of immigrant children. In R. Rumbaut & W. Cornelius (Eds.), *California's immigrant children: Theory, research and implications for educational policy* (pp. 17–69). San Diego: University of California at San Diego, Center for U.S.-Mexican Studies.

Rumbaut, R. (1996). The crucible within: Ethnic identity, self-esteem and segmented assimilation among children of immigrants. In A. Portes (Ed.), *The new second generation* (pp. 119–170). New York: Russell Sage Foundation.

Sanders, J. W. (1977). *The education of an urban minority: Catholics in Chicago, 1833–1965.* New York: Oxford University Press.

San Miguel, G., Jr. (1987). *"Let all of them take heed": Mexican Americans and the campaign for educational equality in Texas, 1910–1981.* Austin: University of Texas Press.

Sarroub, L. K. (2001). The sojourner experience of Yemeni American high school students: An ethnographic portrait. *Harvard Educational Review, 71*(3), 390–415.

Schlossman, S. L. (1983). Is there an American tradition of bilingual education? German in the public elementary schools, 1840–1919. *American Journal of Education, 91*(2), 139–186.

Schultz, S. (1973). *The culture factory: Boston Public Schools, 1789–1860.* New York: Oxford University Press.

Stanton-Salazar, R. (1997). A social capital framework for understanding the socialization of racial minority children and youths. *Harvard Educational Review, 67*(1), 1–40.

Stanton-Salazar, R. (2001). *Manufacturing hope and despair: The school and kin support networks of U.S.-Mexican youth.* New York: Teachers College Press.

Steinberg, L., with Brown, B., & Dornbusch, S. (1996). *Beyond the classroom: Why school reform has failed and what parents need to do.* New York: Simon & Schuster.

Steinberg, S. (1981). *The ethnic myth: Race, ethnicity, and class in America.* New York: Atheneum.

Stepick, A., Stepick, C., Eugene, E., Teed, D., & Labissiere, Y. (2001). Shifting identities and intergenerational conflict: Growing up Haitian in Miami. In R. Rumbaut & A. Portes (Eds.), *Ethnicities: Children of immigrants in America* (pp. 229–266). Berkeley: University of California Press.

Suárez-Orozco, C. (2000). Identities under siege: Immigration stress and social mirroring among the children of immigrants. In A.C.G.M. Robben & M. Suárez-Orozco (Eds.), *Cultures under siege: Collective violence and trauma* (pp. 194–226). New York: Cambridge University Press.

Suárez-Orozco, C., & Suárez-Orozco, M. (2001). *Children of immigration.* Cambridge, MA: Harvard University Press.

Suárez-Orozco, M. (1991). Immigrant adaptation to schooling: A Hispanic case. In M. A. Gibson & J. U. Ogbu (Eds.), *Minority status and schooling: A comparative study of immigrant and involuntary minorities* (pp. 37–61). New York: Garland Publishing.

Suárez-Orozco, M. (2000). Everything you ever wanted to know about assimilation but were afraid to ask. *Daedalus, 129*(4), 233–262.

Suárez-Orozco, M. (2001). Globalization, immigration, and education: The research agenda. *Harvard Educational Review, 71*(3), 345–365.

Suárez-Orozco, M., & Suárez-Orozco, C. (1995). The cultural patterning of achievement motivation: A comparison of Mexican, Mexican immigrant, Mexican American, and non-Latino white American students. In R. Rumbaut & W. Cornelius (Eds.), *California's immigrant children: Theory, research and implications for educational policy* (pp. 160–190). San Diego: University of California, San Diego, Center for U.S.-Mexican Studies.

Troen, S. K. (1975). *The public and the schools: Shaping the St. Louis school system, 1838–1920.* Columbia: University of Missouri Press.

Trueba, H. (1988). Culturally based explanations of minority students' academic achievement. *Anthropology and Education Quarterly, 19*(3), 270–287.

Trueba, T., Jacobs, L., & Kirton, E. (1990). *Cultural conflict and adaptation: The case of Hmong children in American society.* New York: Falmer Press.

Tyack, D. (1974). *The one best system: A history of American urban education.* Cambridge, MA: Harvard University Press.

Valdes, G. (1996). *Con respeto: Bridging the distance between culturally diverse families and schools.* New York: Teachers College Press.

Valenzuela, A. (1999). *Subtractive schooling: U.S.-Mexican youth and the politics of caring.* Albany: State University of New York Press.

Vinyard, J. (1998). *For faith and fortune: The education of Catholic immigrants in Detroit, 1805–1925.* Urbana: University of Illinois Press.

Violas, P. (1973). Jane Addams and the new liberalism. In C. Karrier, P. Violas, & J. Spring, *Roots of crisis: American education in the twentieth century* (pp. 66–83). Chicago: Rand McNally.

Waters, M. (1996). Ethnic and racial identities of second-generation black immigrants in New York City. In A. Portes (Ed.), *The new second generation* (pp. 171–196). New York: Russell Sage Foundation.

Wong, M. (1990). The education of White, Chinese, Filipino, and Japanese students: A look at "High School and Beyond." *Sociological Perspectives, 33*(3), 355–374.

Zhou, M. (1997). Social capital in Chinatown: The role of community-based organizations and families in the adaptation of the younger generation. In M. Seller & L. Weis (Eds.), *Beyond Black and White: New faces and voices in U.S. schools* (pp. 181–205). Albany: State University of New York Press.

Zhou, M., & Bankston, C., III. (1996). Social capital and the adaptation of the second generation: The case of Vietnamese youth in New Orleans. In A. Portes (Ed.), *The new second generation* (pp. 197–220). New York: Russell Sage Foundation.

Zhou, M., & Bankston, C., III. (1998). *Growing up American: How Vietnamese children adapt to life in the United States.* New York: Russell Sage Foundation.

20

CHILDREN AND YOUTH IN IMMIGRANT FAMILIES

Demographic, Social, and Educational Issues

Donald J. Hernandez

University at Albany, State University of New York

Children and youths in immigrant families are the fastest-growing component of the child and youth population in the United States. Between 1990 to 1997, the number in immigrant families grew by 47%, compared to only 7% for those with native-born parents. By 2000, one of every five children and youths (20.1%, or 14.6 million) was the child of an immigrant (Hernandez & Charney, 1998). Most expansion in the child and youth population during the next three decades will occur through immigration and through births to current immigrants and their descendants.

As a result, because most immigrants are Hispanic or Asian, the proportion of children and youth who are non-Hispanic White is projected to drop from 69% in 1990 to less than 50% by 2040. Conversely, children and youth who are Hispanic, Black, Asian, or of some other racial minority will by 2040 constitute more than one-half of all children and youth in the United States (U.S. Census Bureau, 2002). But the timing and growth in the population of racial and ethnic minorities varies greatly by age. In 2030, when the baby boom generation born between 1946 and 1964 will be in the retirement ages of 66 to 84, the most recent U.S. Census Bureau (2002) projections indicate that 74% of the elderly will be non-Hispanic White, compared to only 59% for working-age adults and 52% for children and youth. Thus, as the predominantly White, non-Hispanic baby boom generation ages, it will depend increasingly for its economic support on the productivity, health, and civic participation of adults who grew up as children and youths in minority immigrant families.

The circumstances of and resources for these members of immigrant families merit special attention, because the children and youths of today are the parents, workers, and citizens of the future, and because those who grow up in immigrant families will play an increasingly important role during coming decades. This chapter begins by portraying major social and economic resources and circumstances of children and youth in immigrant families, compared to those in native-born families. It then discusses the demographic circumstances of children and youth in immigrant families that pertain specifically to their immigrant status, and access to public benefits and health insurance coverage. The chapter concludes by comparing the physical health, psychological well-being, and educational accomplishments of children and youth in immigrant and native-born families.

This chapter draws especially on the work of the Committee on the Health and Adjustment of Immigrant Children and Families, established by the National Academy of Sciences' National Research Council and Institute of Medicine, including eleven new studies commissioned by the Committee (Hernandez & Charney, 1998). These new studies involved extensive analyses of nationally or regionally representative surveys and censuses focusing, for the first time, on the circumstances of children and youth in immigrant families (Hernandez, 1999).

The indicators presented here distinguish, insofar as possible, among children and youths (ages 0–17) who are first generation (foreign-born), second generation (native-born in the United States with least one foreign-born parent), and third or later generation (native-born with native-born parents). To reflect the sometimes great differences among immigrants that are associated with the social, economic, and cultural conditions in their countries of origin, indicators presented here also distinguish, insofar as possible, between children and youth in immigrant families according to their country or region of origin. Because life chances differ greatly by race and ethnicity in the United States, and because the representation of Hispanics and non-Whites among immigrants has increased markedly during recent decades, this chapter often compares the situation of immigrants and natives who are White, Black, Hispanic, or Asian.

COUNTRY OF ORIGIN AND RACE/ETHNICITY

The number, country of origin, and race/ethnicity of children and youth in immigrant families have shifted greatly during the 20th century (Hernandez & Darke, 1999a). The number of children and youth in immigrant families dropped from 9.3 to 3.7 million between 1910 and 1960 and then jumped to 14.6 million in 2000, exceeding the level of 1910 by 57%. But the total population of children and youth was rising as well. Hence, as a proportion of all children and youth, those in immigrant families plummeted from 28% to only 6% between 1910 and 1960, and the subsequent rise to 20% in 2000 represented slightly less than three-fourths the level of 1910.

To focus on region and country of origin, most children and youth in immigrant families in 1910 had origins in the northern and western European countries of Germany, Scandinavia, Ireland, or the United Kingdom (50%); in the southern or eastern European countries of Russia, Hungary, Poland, Italy, or Austria (35%); or in Canada (10%; Hernandez & Darke, 1999a). Perceived differences in culture and race separating southern and eastern European immigrants from the native-born population were viewed as enormous at the turn of the century. A massive government study of the time by the Joint U.S. Immigration Commission (popularly known as the Dillingham Commission) drew sharp distinctions between the "old" northern and western European immigrants and "new" southern and eastern European immigrants (U.S. Immigration [Dillingham] Commission, 1911). Anthropologists, scientists, and policy makers shared the public sentiment that the new immigrants were likely to dilute the racial and cultural purity of Americans with a mainly northwestern European heritage (Ross, 1914; Stoddard, 1920/1971). Despite these concerns, however, a comprehensive assessment using 1980 census data found that, although White ethnic groups maintain some distinctive patterns, differences on many measures have disappeared, including fertility rates and socioeconomic measures such as educational attainment. The high degree of assimilation of White ethnic groups also is reflected in extensive intermarriage across ethnic lines (Lieberson & Waters, 1988).

The proportion of children and youth with European or Canadian origins declined substantially from 87% to 71% between 1910 and 1960 (Hernandez & Darke, 1999a), and then dramatically to only 19% in 2000 (derived by author from U.S. Census Bureau Current Population Survey). Corresponding increases occurred among sending countries in Latin America and Asia. The proportion of children and youth in immigrant families with origins in Latin America or the Caribbean jumped from only 2% in 1910 to 18% in 1960, and then to 61% in 2000. Meanwhile, the proportion from Asia jumped from 1% to 7% between 1910 and 1960, and then to 22% in 2000. Since the beginning of the 20th century, then, the countries of origin of children and youth in immigrant families have become increasingly diverse, with rising proportions from Latin America and Asia. In addition to the increasing diversity associated with a shift from primarily European origins to widely global origins, the very large increase in the proportion with origins in one country, Mexico, is quite striking, from 2% in 1910 to 13% in 1960, and then to 39% in 2000.

These changes in country of origin have brought corresponding changes in the race/ethnicity of children and youth in immigrant families and overall. As of 2000, 76% of children and youth in immigrant families were Hispanic (52%), Asian (18%), or Black (6%). As a consequence, children and youth in immigrant families in 2000 accounted for 65% of all Hispanic children and youth, and 87% of all Asian children and youth. Thus, by 2000 the proportion of all children and youth who were members of minority race/ethnic groups had climbed to 37% (derived by author from U.S. Census Bureau Current Population Survey).

Throughout the past century, most children and youth in immigrant families have, however, been second generation, born in the United States. In 1910, the second generation accounted for 89% of all children and youth in immigrant families; this declined to 83% in 1960 and still further to 77% in 1990. Yet only one-fourth of children and youth in immigrant families in 1990 were themselves foreign-born; three-fourths were United States citizens by virtue of birth in this country.

SOCIOECONOMIC AND DEMOGRAPHIC RISK FACTORS

The extent to which the risks and needs of children and youth in immigrant and native-born families differ depends, at least in part, on the extent to which they are similar or different in family circumstances that have been found to influence outcomes among children and youth generally. These circumstances include experience with poverty, parental educational attainments and paid work by various family members, living in a two-parent or one-parent family, living with a large or small number of siblings, and exposure to overcrowded housing conditions (Hernandez & Darke, 1999a).

One of the best-documented relationships in epidemiology and in child and youth development is that social and economic inequality has negative consequences for health and other important outcomes for persons of low socioeconomic status—that is, persons experiencing poverty, job insecurity and unemployment, and limited educational attainments (Duncan & Brooks-Gunn, 1997; Hill & Duncan, 1987; Montgomery & Carter-Pokras, 1993; Montgomery, Kiely, & Pappas, 1996; Newacheck, 1994; Newacheck, Jameson, & Halfon, 1994; Newacheck & Starfield, 1988; Starfield, 1982, 1991, 1992; U.S. Department of Health and Human Services, 1981; Wilkinson, 1996). Children and youths living in poverty have comparatively limited access to economic resources required to purchase necessary goods and services, such as housing, food, clothing, and health care.

Parental educational attainments are important, because they influence parental values in socializing children and youth, as well as parental occupation and income, but also because they influence education attainments and income that children and youth achieve when they, in turn, become adults (Alwin, 1984; Blau & Duncan, 1967; Featherman & Hauser, 1978; Kohn, 1969; Kohn & Schooler, 1983; Sewell & Hauser, 1975; Sewell, Hauser & Wolf, 1980). Thus, children and youths whose parents have completed relatively few years of school are disadvantaged, compared to those with more highly educated parents, because their parents are less likely to have paid jobs that provide access to health insurance and to income required to buy important goods and services, and because these children and youths are less likely to complete high school or college and hence to achieve economic success in adulthood.

Because parents' paid work is the primary source of income for most children and youth, the number of parents who work for pay and whether they work part-time or full-time are key determinants of whether children and youth live in poverty. Father's paid work has been the primary factor determining trends since the Great Depression in child poverty, but mother's paid employment has become increasingly important (Hernandez, 1993, 1997).

Children and youths with only one parent in the home are at risk of a variety of negative outcomes, because those living with two parents have greater access, potentially, to personal care and economic resources from parents than do children and youths living with one parent, and because those in one-parent families experience greater personal or parental stress (Alwin, 1984; Blau & Duncan, 1967; Cherlin, 1999; Cherlin et al., 1991; Featherman & Hauser, 1978; Furstenberg, Nord, Peterson, & Zill, 1983; Hernandez, 1986; Hetherington, Cox, & Cox, 1978; Kohn, 1969; Kohn & Schooler, 1983; Kominski, 1987; McLanahan & Sandefur, 1994; Sewell & Hauser, 1975; Sewell et al., 1980).

Many children and youths in one-parent families live in poverty, partly because fathers' incomes are not available in the home, and partly because low socioeconomic status strongly influences both family disruption and out-of-wedlock childbearing. Poverty has major effects on child and youth outcomes independent of family structure; but those living with one parent are also at risk of negative life outcomes beyond the effect of poverty (Cherlin, 1999; Conger & Elder, 1994; Conger et al., 1990; Elder, 1974; Elder, Conger, Foster, & Ardelt, 1992; Hernandez, 1993; McLanahan & Sandefur, 1994).

Most children and youths live not only with their parent(s) but also with one or more brothers or sisters who are potential sources of lifelong loving companionship, but they are also potential competitors for the scarce time and economic resources parents can devote to their children. Although research has found the number of siblings to have little effect on psychological well-being later during adulthood, children and youth in large families with five or more siblings do tend to complete fewer years of schooling than those from smaller families and are therefore less likely to enter high-income, high-status occupations when they reach adulthood (Blake, 1981, 1985, 1987, 1989; Featherman & Hauser, 1978; Glenn & Hoppe, 1982; Hernandez, 1986).

In addition, overcrowded housing conditions often associated with low family income can facilitate the transmission of communicable diseases such as tuberculosis, hepatitis A, and other enteric and respiratory infections (Hernandez & Charney, 1998).

POVERTY

Children and youth in immigrant families experienced a somewhat greater risk of living in poverty in the 1990 census (income during 1989) than those in native-born families, at 22% and 17%, respectively (Hernandez &

Darke, 1999b). Most of the difference was due to the high poverty rate for the first generation (33%); the second generation was only slightly more likely (19%) to be poor than children and youth in native-born families (17%).

Poverty rates in 1989 differed enormously among children and youth in immigrant and in native-born families and among those in immigrant families by race and ethnicity (Hernandez & Darke, 1999b). The poverty rate for White non-Hispanic children and youth in native-born families was only 11%, but three to four times greater for Black, Hispanic, and American Indian children and youth in native-born families (at 40%, 28%, and 35%, respectively).

Similarly, among children and youth in immigrant families with origins in about two dozen countries spread across Latin America and the Caribbean, Asia, Europe, the Middle East, and Africa, poverty rates were about equal to, or substantially less than, the rate of 11% for White non-Hispanic children and youth in native-born families. But among children and youth in immigrant families from 12 other countries, poverty rates were quite high, ranging from 26% to 51% depending on the country of origin.

In view of the negative risks associated with poverty generally, the situation of children and youths from these 12 countries is of particular concern. Five of these 12 countries are the source of many officially recognized refugees (former Soviet Union, Cambodia, Laos, Thailand, Vietnam); three are war-torn countries in Central America (El Salvador, Guatemala, and Nicaragua); and three are small and impoverished Central American or Caribbean countries (Honduras, Haiti, Dominican Republic) that are sources of unskilled labor migrants. The 12th country is Mexico, which currently sends the largest number of both legal and illegal unskilled labor immigrants, and which has been a ready source of unskilled labor for the U.S. economy throughout the 20th century (Romo, 1996; Rumbaut, 1996). Within the racial and ethnic stratification system of the United States, most children and youths from 11 of these 12 countries, with the former Soviet Union as the sole exception, are classified as Hispanic, Asian, or Black.

Children and youth with origins in these 12 countries accounted for 47% (3.9 million) of all children and youth in immigrant families in 1990 (8.3 million), but they accounted for 72% of the children and youth in immigrant families who lived in poverty. Moreover, Mexico alone accounted for 31% (2.6 million) of all children and youth in immigrant families, but 49% of those officially classified as poor in the 1990 census (Hernandez & Darke, 1999b).

Poverty rates were lower, sometimes much lower, for second-generation children and youth than for the first generation for nearly all countries of origin, including most of the 12 countries with the highest poverty rates. But for children and youth with origins in Mexico, which

accounts for about two-thirds of the children and youth in immigrant families from these 12 countries, the poverty rates for the second and later generations were quite similar, at 32% and 28% respectively, which is 2.5 to 3 times greater than for White non-Hispanic children and youth in native-born families (Hernandez & Darke, 1999b).

PARENTS' EDUCATION

First-, second-, and later-generation children and youths in families with a father or mother in the home were about equally likely in 1990 to have fathers who had graduated from college (23% to 26%) or mothers who had graduated from college (14% to 18%; Hernandez & Darke, 1999a). But in 1990, among children and youth in immigrant families from about two dozen countries, at least 35% with fathers in the home had fathers who were college graduates, and at least 25% with mothers in the home had mothers who were college graduates. These proportions are substantially higher than the corresponding figures for non-Hispanic Whites in native-born families (28% for fathers and 20% for mothers). All of these proportions with parents graduating from college were at least two to three times greater than the corresponding rates for children and youth in native-born families who were Black, Hispanic, or American Indian (Hernandez & Darke, 1999a).

Children and youth in immigrant families were, overall, also much more likely than those in native-born families to have parents with very low educational attainments. This was especially true for children and youth from the 12 countries of origin at greatest risk of living in poverty, with the sole exception of the former Soviet Union. For example, among children and youth living with fathers, the overall proportions with fathers not graduating from high school were two to three times greater for the first and second generations than for the later generations (at 49%, 36%, and 15%, respectively); this difference is accounted for almost completely by differences in the proportions with fathers completing no more than eight years of schooling, which for the three generations were 34%, 23%, and 3%, respectively. Patterns in mothers' education were quite similar (Hernandez & Darke, 1999a).

As with poverty, parental educational attainments vary enormously by country of origin, and among children and youth in native-born families by race and ethnicity (Hernandez & Darke, 1999a). In the 1990 census, children and youth in immigrant families from the 12 countries with the highest poverty rates were also, with the exception of the former Soviet Union, more likely (from somewhat to enormously) than non-Hispanic Whites in native-born families to have parents in the home who had not graduated from high school or elementary school. Among children and youths from these 11 countries, parental educational attainments generally increase substantially from the first to the second to the third generation. Although few third-generation children and youths from these countries for which estimates are available have parents who have completed eight or fewer years of schooling, few have parents who have completed college.

Especially noteworthy is the 30–34% of Mexican-origin children and youth in native-born families whose parents have not graduated from high school, a level similar to Blacks in native-born families and American Indians (26–29%), and two to three times higher than White, non-Hispanic children and youth in native-born families (12%; Hernandez & Darke, 1999a).

PARENTS' LABOR FORCE PARTICIPATION

Throughout the century, the overwhelming majority of children and youth in both immigrant and native-born families had fathers who worked in the labor force (Hernandez & Darke, 1999a). Among first-, second-, and later-generation children and youth the proportions as of 1990 were 88% for the first generation and 94–95% for the second and later generations. The combined proportion for the first and second generations in 1990 was 93%, only slightly less than the 95% for the third and later generation. Differences in labor force participation rates among fathers in the homes of children and youth in immigrant and native-born families cannot therefore account for most of the poverty differences between the two in the 1990 census (Hernandez & Darke, 1999a). Even among children and youth in immigrant families from the 12 countries of origin with very high poverty rates of more than 25% in the 1990 census, the proportions with fathers in the home who were in the labor force fell below 89% for only 5 countries (Cambodia, Laos, Thailand, Vietnam, and the former Soviet Union).

Despite high levels of employment among fathers in the homes of children and youth in immigrant families, overall and for most specific countries of origin many had fathers who worked less than full-time year-round. In 1990, the difference was 10 percentage points (69% versus 79%). In fact, it is the lack of full-time year-round work among fathers in the home, along with very low father's educational attainments and linguistic isolation from English-speaking culture, that is especially common among children and youths from the 12 countries of origin with very high poverty rates (Hernandez & Darke, 1999a).

Although children and youth in immigrant families from 16 additional countries in 1990 had very high proportions with fathers not working full-time year-round, children and youth from most of these 16 countries had two advantages compared to those from the 12 very-high-poverty countries of origin. Most did not have high proportions with very limited parental educational attainments, and most had at least one person in the household, no doubt often the parent, who spoke English exclusively or very well. Thus very high poverty rates for children and youth in immigrant families tend to occur among those from countries with very low parental educational attainments (eight years of schooling or less), fathers who cannot find full-time year-round work, and parents who do not speak English exclusively or very well. These results suggest that the combination of very limited father's educational attainments and linguistic isolation of the household are key factors making it difficult for fathers in immigrant families to obtain full-time year-round work that pays well enough to lift the family out of poverty.

Of course, many mothers also work for pay, contributing to family income. Among children and youths with mothers in the home, mother's labor force participation rates were broadly similar for immigrant and native-born families, at 58% and 66% respectively in 1990. Full-time year-round employment rates for mothers also were similar for children and youth in immigrant and native-born families, at 28% and 31%, respectively.

As of 1990, of the 12 countries of origin with high proportions (50% or more) of children and youth with mothers not in the labor force, seven had high proportions (68% to 80%) with fathers working full-time year-round. Children and youth in immigrant families from the 5 remaining countries were among the 12 with very high poverty rates, and they had comparatively high proportions with fathers not working full-time year-round (38% to 68%). But they also had high proportions with mothers not graduating from high school (55% to 76%), and four had high proportions with five or more siblings in the home (19% to 42%). This pattern suggests that among mothers with very low educational attainments, large family size may often be incompatible with mother's employment outside the home, perhaps because of the trade-off between mother's work and providing care for younger children in the home.

ONE-PARENT FAMILIES

The proportion of children living with only one parent was smaller for the second than for the first generation overall, and for most specific countries of origin. But overall and for most specific countries of origin for which estimates can be calculated in 1990, third- and later-generation children and youths were more likely to live with only one parent (Hernandez & Darke, 1999a). Third- and later-generation children and youths from most of these countries were at least twice as likely as the corresponding third and later generation to live in one-parent families.

To focus on children and youth in immigrant families from the 12 countries of origin with very high poverty rates, those from Cambodia and from 6 of 7 Central American and Caribbean countries (excepting only Mexico) were substantially more likely to live in one-parent families (26% to 48%) than were White non-Hispanic children and youth in native-born families (17%). Children and youth from these countries tended to have smaller proportions with 5 or more siblings in the home than from those high-poverty countries with higher proportions in two-parent families, and they tended to have higher proportions with mothers in the labor force. Thus, children and youth in immigrant families from the 12 countries of origin with very high poverty rates in 1990 tended to live in families with a large number of siblings and comparatively few working mothers, or to live in one-parent families, but not both.

FAMILIES WITH MANY SIBLINGS

Although the proportion of children and youth living in one-parent families increases, sometimes dramatically, from the second to the third generation, the proportion of children and youth living in families with a large number of siblings declines consistently across generations (Hernandez & Darke, 1999a). Specifically, the proportion of children and youth living in families with five or more siblings in 1990 dropped from 17% to 9% to 5%, respectively, across the first, second, and later generations. For most specific countries of origin, not only did the second generation in 1990 have smaller proportions in large families than first-generation children and youth from the same countries; the proportions usually were similar to native-born non-Hispanic White children and youth, at 10% or less for the second generation. The proportion in large families for third- and higher-generation minority children and youth also were similar overall, but not identical to the level for native-born non-Hispanic Whites. Among children and youth in native-born families, those of Mexican origin were somewhat less likely than Blacks to live in large families, at 8% versus 10%, respectively, and somewhat more likely than non-Hispanic Whites to live in such families (4%).

OVERCROWDED HOUSING

Only 12% of third-generation children and youth lived in overcrowded housing with more than one person per room in 1990, compared to 38% for the second generation, and 62% for the first generation (Hernandez &

Darke, 1999a). Children and youth in immigrant families from most specific countries of origin in 1990 also had high proportions living in overcrowded housing, although children and youth in immigrant families from the 12 countries with very high poverty were much more likely than most to live in such conditions. For children and youth from most of these 12 countries, declines in overcrowding are substantial across the first and second (and, where measurable, to the later) generations. But third and later generations continue to experience high levels of overcrowding, especially Mexican-origin children and youth at an extraordinary 31%, which is similar to the 26% and 29% experienced respectively by Blacks and American Indians, and five times greater than the 7% experienced by non-Hispanic White children and youth in native-born families.

ENGLISH LANGUAGE FLUENCY

Children and youth in immigrant families from countries where English is not the native language or is not widely taught may be at special risk, compared to children and youth in native-born families, because they may not themselves speak English well, or they may live with parents who do not speak English well. A lack of English fluency can limit effective communication and functioning in health facilities, schools, or other settings that provide essential resources to children and youths and their families.

At least 60% of children and youth in immigrant families from most countries of origin spoke a language other than English at home in 1990 (Hernandez & Darke, 1999a). The exceptions were English-speaking countries of origin, as well as Austria, Germany, The Netherlands, Nigeria, and South Africa. But for only 13 countries of origin did the proportion of children and youth in immigrant families not speaking English exclusively or very well reach a substantial level of 30% or more. Eleven of these countries are among the 12 with children and youth who experience especially high poverty rates (excluding only Haiti), and the remaining two were China and Hong Kong. Differences across generations are large, however, as the proportion who speak English exclusively or very well rises from only 55% for the first generation to 81% for the second generation. Thus, by the second generation the vast majority of children and youths speak English exclusively or very well. For children and youth in immigrant families from 11 of the 12 countries with very high poverty rates, the range is 35% to 53% for the first generation, but this rises for 10 of 12 countries (excluding Cambodia and Laos) to 65% to 91% for the second generation—substantial to overwhelming majorities.

Lack of English fluency may not pose enormous difficulties for immigrants in communities with a large number of residents from their home country. But it does isolate immigrants from the broader, mainstream society. The U.S. Census Bureau defines a linguistically isolated household as one in which no person age 14 or over speaks English either exclusively or very well (U.S. Census Bureau, 1992). Among children and youth in immigrant families in 1990, 26% lived in linguistically isolated households. But among children and youth from each of the 12 countries of origin with high poverty rates, the proportions in linguistically isolated households were 30–39% for 3 countries, 40–49% for 7 countries, and 60% for 2 (Laos and Cambodia). Children and youth from only 4 additional countries had 30% or more in linguistically isolated households (China, Hong Kong, Taiwan, and Colombia).

CITIZENSHIP AND WELFARE REFORM

Prior to welfare reform, legal immigrants and U.S.-born citizens were eligible for public benefits on essentially the same terms (Fix & Zimmerman, 1995; Hernandez & Charney, 1998). But changes in eligibility rules under the 1996 federal welfare reform restricted or barred many legal immigrants from eligibility for important public programs. Additional changes in rules and regulations may act further as a disincentive to enrollment; and the devolution of responsibility for immigrant policy implies that children and parents in immigrant families may be exposed to quite different eligibility criteria depending on their state or locality of residence. Thus, with the enactment of welfare reform, lack of U.S. citizenship became a potential risk factor for children and youths and their parents. Even among children and youths who are citizens by virtue of being born in the United States, a substantial proportion may be at risk of not receiving important public benefits, because their immigrant parent(s) may be unaware of their children's eligibility for essential services or may fear contact with authorities on behalf of their children.

Of the 8.4 million children and youth in immigrant families in 1990, 75% were citizens by birth, 4% were naturalized citizens, and 21% (1.7 million) were not citizens (Hernandez & Darke, 1999a). Of the citizen children and youth, 82% had at least one parent in the home who was not a citizen; thus, approximately two-thirds of children and youth in immigrant families in 1990 were either themselves not a citizen or lived with a noncitizen parent.

In the 1990 census, the official poverty rate for noncitizen children and youth was 34%, and the rate for children and youth who were not citizens or had at least one noncitizen parent was 27%. Children and youth in immigrant families from 9 of the 12 countries of origin with high levels of poverty were especially likely to be noncitizens,

at 29% or more. The proportion was 21% to 23% for the remaining high-poverty countries of origin (Dominican Republic, Mexico, Haiti). Three additional countries had 29% or more of children and youth who were noncitizens and poverty rates greater than among native-born non-Hispanic Whites (Venezuela, Romania, Guyana).

For children and youth in immigrant families with origins in 2 of the 12 countries with high poverty rates, 62% or 63% were not citizens or had at least one parent in the home who was not a citizen; this rose to 73–75% for 5 of these countries and 81% to 89% for the remaining 5 countries. The figure was 50% or more for 18 of the other 26 countries of origin with child poverty rates at least as high as native-born non-Hispanic Whites (11%). Thus children and youth in immigrant families from countries of origin with high poverty rates also are often not citizens or have at least one parent who is not a citizen.

Two studies provide a baseline for assessing the effect of welfare reform for children and youth in immigrant families on the levels of participation of their families in AFDC, SSI, other welfare, food stamps, Medicaid, housing, and heating assistance programs (Brandon, 1999; Hofferth, 1999). Compared to third- and later-generation children and youth, prior to welfare reform, those in immigrant families were about equally likely, or only slightly more likely, to live in families receiving public assistance. Existing differences reflected higher participation rates of families of first-generation children and youth, which are mainly accounted for by their more disadvantaged sociological and demographic circumstances. Comparison of children and youth in immigrant and native-born families at the same socioeconomic levels shows that the differences either disappear, or children and youth in immigrant families (including those of Mexican origin) are less likely than those in native-born families to rely on public assistance (Hernandez & Charney, 1998). Special refugee status for many immigrants from Southeast Asia and the former Soviet Union does, however, appear to involve comparatively high participation in public programs for the first generation.

HEALTH SERVICES ACCESS AND USE

Children and youths require access to health care to assure that they receive recommended preventive services, that acute and chronic conditions are diagnosed and treated in a timely fashion, and that health and development are monitored so that minor health problems do not become serious and costly medical emergencies (Hernandez & Charney, 1998). Health insurance coverage and having a usual source of care facilitate access to health services.

A baseline study prior to welfare reform of access to and use of health services indicates that first-generation children and youth are three times more likely than second-generation children and youth, and twice as likely as those in native-born families, to lack health insurance coverage (Brown, Wyn, Yu, Valenzuela, & Dong, 1999). Hispanic children and youth are especially likely to not be covered by health insurance. The lack of health insurance coverage for all groups is mainly due to the high cost and lack of coverage from parents' employers. Immigrant children and youth also are less likely than others to have been seen by a physician during the previous 12 months, and less likely to have a usual health care provider or source of care. Medicaid has acted to reduce the risk of uninsurance among children and youth in immigrant families; about one in four were covered by Medicaid prior to welfare reform. The automatic eligibility of refugees for Medicaid leads to the very low rate of uninsurance among Southeast Asian children and youth, despite their low socioeconomic status. The role of public policy in ensuring that children and youth in immigrant families have access to health insurance and health services merits special attention with the continuing evolution of welfare reform.

PHYSICAL HEALTH: OVERVIEW

The physical health of children and youth in immigrant families encompasses a range of issues. Because few surveys or health monitoring systems in the United States distinguish among first-, second-, and later-generation children and youth, scientific evidence is limited. Nevertheless, available evidence along several important dimensions suggests that children and youth in immigrant families experience better health than do those in native-born families, a finding that is counterintuitive in light of the racial and ethnic minority status, the overall lower socioeconomic status, the higher poverty rates, and the lower rates of health insurance coverage that characterize children and youth in immigrant families.

Evidence on this issue is patchy, focusing on some immigrant groups and some age groups and frequently relying on parental or adolescent reports rather than direct medical examinations, but the research that exists is quite consistent. However, the relative advantage of children and youth in immigrant families appears to decline with length of time in the United States and from one generation to the next. Moreover, immigrant children and youth may be at particular risk for selected health conditions, including parasitic infections, some of which may be unfamiliar to many U.S. physicians and most of which, if left untreated, can lead to serious conditions. Care must be taken not to overgeneralize, however,

because children and youth from various countries of origin differ greatly, and available evidence is often for children and youth from only a few countries of origin (Hernandez & Charney, 1998).

INFANT BIRTHWEIGHT AND MORTALITY

Two commonly used indicators of infant health are the rate of low birthweight (less than 2,500 grams) and infant mortality (death in the first year of life; Institute of Medicine, 1985; U.S. Department of Health and Human Services, 1986). Significantly lower rates for these two indicators have been found among the immigrant population than among the native-born mothers for the Mexican American population, despite the lower socioeconomic status of the immigrants (Guendelman & English, 1995; Guendelman, English, & Chavez, 1995; Markides & Coreil, 1986; Scribner & Dwyer, 1989; Ventura, 1983, 1984; Williams, Binkin, & Clingman, 1986). Research across immigrant groups based on single births in the 1989–1991 Linked Birth/Infant Death Data Sets (Landale, Oropesa, & Gorman, 1999) found similar patterns for other ethnic groups. The nativity differentials in birthweight and infant mortality in these groups are often smaller than they are for Mexican Americans, however, and are sometimes consistent with expectations based on socioeconomic differences between immigrant and native-born women. Differences in rates of cigarette smoking are one important determinant of the differences between immigrant and native-born women.

CHILD AND ADOLESCENT HEALTH

Analyses of parent reports from the 1994 National Health Interview Survey (NHIS) indicate that children and youth in immigrant families experience fewer acute and chronic health problems than those in native-born families, including infectious and parasitic diseases; acute ear infections; acute injuries; chronic respiratory conditions such as bronchitis, asthma, and hay fever; and chronic hearing, speech, and deformity impairments (Brown et al., 1999; Hernandez & Charney, 1998). Additional estimates for children and youth of Mexican origin using the 1996 National Health and Nutrition Examination Survey (NHANES III), which also rely on parent reports, similarly indicate that noncitizen children and youths, and citizen children and youths with an immigrant parent, have fewer acute injuries and poisonings and fewer major activity limitations than citizen children and youths with U.S.-born parents (Mendoza and Dixon, 1999; Hernandez & Charney, 1998).

Although these differences are not always statistically significant because of the limited sample sizes of available data sets, they are quite consistent. Analyses using the National Longitudinal Survey of Adolescent Health (Add Health) for adolescents in grades 7 through 12 in 1995 found the same generational pattern of deterioration of health over time, based on self-reports of neurological impairment, obesity, and asthma; health risk behaviors such as early sexual activity, use of cigarettes, alcohol, marijuana, or hard drugs; delinquency; and use of violence (Harris, 1999).

These estimates raise the intriguing possibility that immigrant children and youths are somewhat protected, albeit temporarily, from the deleterious health consequences that typically accompany poverty, minority status, and other indicators of disadvantage in the United States.

However, not all conclusions that can be drawn about the health of immigrant children and youths are favorable. Children and youth in immigrant families from Mexico, for example, are more likely to be reported by parents as having teeth in only fair to poor condition, and those over age 6 are reported much more likely to ever have had anemia and, especially for those age 12 to 16, to have vision problems (Mendoza & Dixon, 1998). In addition, epidemiological evidence as well as physician reports indicate that children and youth of recently arrived immigrants, and particularly those from selected high-risk countries of origin, are at elevated risk of harboring or acquiring tuberculosis, hepatitis B, and parasitic infections, and of having unsafe levels of lead in the blood (Hernandez & Charney, 1998).

Exposure to pesticides is an additional health risk of great concern for children and youth of migrant farm workers in light of its documented links to specific ailments and chronic health conditions (Hernandez & Charney, 1998). Mines (1999) reports analyses of the National Agricultural Workers Survey (NAWS), for example, indicating that 29% of U.S.-based children and youth with a migrant farm worker parent (250,000 out of 900,000) in any given year between 1993 and 1995 had a parent who mixed or applied pesticides, or they themselves mixed or applied pesticides. These children and youths may, as harvesters, encounter pesticide residues on crops; they may eat, drink, or smoke in the fields, and thereby ingest pesticides; or they may be exposed to direct spray or drift while working in the field or at home in adjacent migrant labor camps. These chemicals cause acute ailments such as skin rashes, eye irritation, flulike symptoms, and even death. They may also cause chronic harm such as birth defects, sterility, neurological damage, liver and kidney disease, and cancer (Wilk, 1993). Children and youths are more likely to be harmed by pesticide exposures than are adults because of their lower body weight, higher metabolism, and immature immune and neurological systems (National Research Council, 1993).

PSYCHOLOGICAL ADJUSTMENT

Measures of psychological adjustment are available from the National Educational Longitudinal Survey (NELS) of 1988 for 8th graders from China, the Philippines, Mexico, and other Hispanic countries (Kao, 1999); and from the National Longitudinal Study of Adolescent Health (Add Health) for adolescents in grades 7 through 12 in 1995 with origins in Mexico, Cuba, Central and South America, China, the Philippines, Japan, Vietnam, Africa and the Afro-Caribbean, and Europe and Canada (Harris, 1999). The Add Health measured psychological distress and psychological well-being; the NELS measured feelings of having control over the direction of one's life (self-efficacy), self-esteem, and feelings of being popular or unpopular among school peers (alienation).

The NELS analyses (Kao, 1999) found that first- and second-generation adolescents had significantly lower feelings of self-efficacy and higher feelings of alienation from their schoolmates than children and youth in native-born families. In contrast, adolescents in immigrant and native-born families did not differ in their self-esteem. The Add Health analyses (Harris, 1999) found no differences between youth in immigrant and native-born families in psychological well-being or psychological distress. Taken together, these results suggest that adolescents in immigrant families may be able to maintain positive feelings about themselves and their general well-being despite perceiving that they have relatively less control over their lives and are less well accepted by their school peers.

Important differences among adolescents in immigrant families emerge, however, in analyses distinguishing youth by country of origin and racial and ethnic group, and when controls for socioeconomic status are added. In the NELS data, lower levels of feeling control over their own life occurred among first- and second-generation Mexican-origin and other Hispanic-origin adolescents, and among first-generation Chinese, Filipino, and Black adolescents, but not among the second generation of the latter groups, nor among first- or second-generation White youth in immigrant families (Kao, 1999). The lack of popularity of adolescents in immigrant families, compared to youth in native-born families, was found specifically among first- and second-generation Mexican and Chinese youth, not but not among other groups. Although adolescents in immigrant families do not experience greater psychological distress in the Add Health data than those in native-born families, overall, the first- and second-generation Mexican and Filipino youth are more likely to feel such distress than White non-Hispanic adolescents (Harris, 1999).

After controls for socioeconomic status are added, the NELS data continue to show relatively lower self-efficacy and greater feelings of alienation among most of the Hispanic, Asian, and Black generational groups experiencing these disadvantages, compared to non-Hispanic Whites in native-born families. Socioeconomic controls have little effect on the magnitude of the disadvantage for Asian youth (both Chinese and Filipino), but 40–60% of the disadvantage for Hispanic and Black youth is accounted for by their lower parental education and income. Moreover, the lower self-esteem of first- and second-generation Mexican adolescents, compared to non-Hispanic Whites in native-born families, is accounted for entirely by the lower socioeconomic status of these Mexican-origin youths (Kao, 1999).

When controls for socioeconomic influences, such as family poverty and disadvantaged neighborhood circumstances, are introduced in the Add Health data, these factors were found to be very influential predictors of psychological distress for all adolescents, and especially for Mexican-origin youth. This pattern of results suggests (with the noteworthy partial exception of Mexican youths) a protective influence of immigrant status among adolescents who, for reasons of exposure to poverty and inner-city neighborhoods, would be expected to show poor psychological health (Harris, 1999).

The Children of Immigrants Longitudinal Study (CILS), conducted in Southern California (San Diego) and South Florida (Miami and Fort Lauderdale), is the first large-scale survey of changes in the family, community, and educational experiences of children and youth in immigrant families from nine countries of origin in the Western hemisphere and Asia (see Portes, 1995, 1996; Portes & MacLeod, 1996; Portes & Rumbaut, 1996, 2001; Rumbaut, 1994a, 1994b, 1995, 1997a, 1997b). Although it does not provide nationally representative estimates for children and youth from these countries of origin and does not include comparative data from native-born families, the survey is a rich source of psychological data and offers insights into the processes that might underlie patterns in the psychological well-being of immigrant youth.

Recent research focused on children and youth in immigrant families living in San Diego who were from Mexico, the Philippines, Vietnam, Cambodia, and Laos (Rumbaut, 1999). This research assessed possible risk and protective factors for low self-esteem and depressive symptoms, including gender, country of origin, intrafamily and extrafamily contexts and stressors, educational aspirations and achievement, language preference and skills, and physical looks and popularity with the opposite sex.

The study found lower self-esteem and higher depressive symptoms among immigrant youth for females and for children and youth experiencing high parent-child conflict, low family cohesion, recent serious illness or disability in the family, a high proportion of English-only spoken in the neighborhood, a school perceived as unsafe, dissatisfaction with physical looks, and lack of popularity with the opposite sex. Seven additional factors associated with higher depression were a later age at arrival in the United States, a nonintact family, a recent worsening of the family's economic situation, perceptions of poor teaching quality or unfairness, experience with stress in school, high proportion of friends not planning to attend college, and experience with racial or ethnic discrimination. Also associated with low self-esteem were being of Filipino or Vietnamese origin, a recent family move to another home, low grades and educational aspirations, limited English proficiency (LEP), and LEP status in 1991. The NELS data already discussed also revealed the importance of language factors and school experiences for feelings of self-efficacy among Hispanic and Black immigrant youths, but not for Asian immigrant youths (Kao, 1999).

Despite the potential importance of these factors for enhancing or reducing self-esteem and depression among children and youth in immigrant families, national estimates of the prevalence of experience with most of these factors are not available for children and youth in immigrant families.

EDUCATIONAL EXPERIENCES OF CHILDREN

The National Household Education Survey (NHES) has been used to assess important aspects of family and school support for educational success among children ages three to eight in immigrant families for Hispanics, Asians, and Whites and for the foreign-born and native-born (Nord & Griffin, 1999). Estimates for specific countries of origin are not possible because of the limited sample size and lack of information on countries of origin.

Family members can foster school success by engaging in various activities with their young child, including teaching them letters and numbers, reading to them, and working on projects with them. For seven activities of this type in 1996, among children in native-born families who were non-Hispanic White, the proportion of children with parents engaged in such activities during the past week ranged from 75% to 93%; the proportions for children in immigrant families were about the same to no more than 11 percentage points smaller. Among children in immigrant families, the proportions were usually higher for second-generation children than for the first generation, and the proportions tended to be 10 to 15 percentage points lower for Hispanic children than for Asians (Nord & Griffin, 1999).

Parents also can foster school achievement by taking their children on a variety of educational outings. Estimates of the proportion with parents taking them on six types of outings in 1996 ranged widely from 12% to 65% and did not vary systematically between immigrant and native-born children, between first- and second-generation immigrants, or between Hispanic and Asian children in immigrant families (Nord & Griffin, 1999).

Parental involvement in their children's schools is a third set of activities that foster school achievement. Among native-born children in 1996, 68% of non-Hispanic Whites had parents highly involved in school, somewhat more than the 59% for Hispanics and 56% for non-Hispanic Blacks. Among children in immigrant families, the proportion with parents highly involved in school was 57%, although most of the difference between these children and native-born non-Hispanic White children was accounted for by the higher proportion with a moderate level of parental involvement. Parental involvement was greater for the second generation than the first (58% versus 50% highly involved). Among children in immigrant families, Hispanics were less likely than Asians to have highly involved parents (49% versus 57%; Nord & Griffin, 1999).

Early childhood programs prior to kindergarten help children and youths prepare for school. The proportions attending early childhood programs among native-born children were 58%, 66%, and 47%, respectively, for non-Hispanic Whites, Blacks, and Hispanics, compared to 42% for children in immigrant families. The second generation was more likely than the first to attend such programs, and Hispanic children in immigrant families were slightly less likely than Asians to attend such programs (Nord & Griffin, 1999).

Children are able to learn better if the schools they attend are well disciplined, and parental participation may be encouraged by a variety of school practices that foster such involvement. In parental ratings of children's schools along 10 dimensions, the proportion with favorable or very favorable parental responses was 45% to 67% for non-Hispanic White children. The proportions with favorable ratings were 2 to 10 percentage points lower along most dimensions for non-Hispanic Blacks and Hispanics in native-born families. These proportions varied between about 15 percentage points less and 15 percentage points more for children in native-born families. They also varied substantially but in no specific direction for first- and second-generation children in immigrant families and for Hispanic and Asian children in immigrant families (Nord & Griffin, 1999).

ACADEMIC ACHIEVEMENT OF YOUTH

Children and youth from immigrant families face a variety of potential challenges to their educational success. Many of them come from homes in which English is not the main spoken language. Parents may be unfamiliar or uncomfortable with avenues for participation in the schooling of their children and youth, and many have received little formal education. Immigrant families tend to settle in large urban areas that have troubled school systems (Fuligni, 1998). It follows that these children and youth may experience difficulties at school. Yet recent studies suggest that adolescents from immigrant families perform in school just as well as, if not better than, their peers from native-born families (Fletcher & Steinberg, 1994; Fuligni, 1997; Kao & Tienda, 1995; Rosenthal & Feldman, 1991; Rumbaut, 1995).

First- and second-generation adolescents in immigrant families nationally have slightly higher grades and math test scores than adolescents in native-born families, but the reading test scores of the first generation are somewhat lower than those of adolescents in native-born families (Kao, 1999). The relationship is not uniform for adolescents in immigrant families; it varies with country of origin.

First-, second-, and later-generation Mexican adolescents are similar in grades and in math test scores, although there is a tendency, especially for reading test scores, toward improvement across the generations. Mexican adolescents of all generations have substantially lower educational achievements than White non-Hispanic adolescents in native-born families; most of the difference for each generation is explained by lower parent education and family income among Mexican adolescents (Kao, 1999).

Chinese adolescents in immigrant families, especially the second generation, exceed Chinese adolescents in native families in grades and math test scores. However, only the second generation exceeds the later generations in reading test scores. Chinese first- and second-generation adolescents also exceed White non-Hispanic adolescents in native-born families in grades and math test scores. The second generation has higher reading scores as well. The superior grades and math test scores of first-generation Chinese are not explained by socioeconomic status, psychological well-being, or other school experience. For the second generation, however, one-third to one-half of the superior performance is explained by these factors, particularly parent education and family income (Kao, 1999).

Among Filipino adolescents, the second generation also achieves better grades and math and reading test scores than the first or third and higher generations. Compared to White non-Hispanic adolescents in native-born families, first- and second-generation Filipino adolescents achieve higher grades. The second generation achieves higher grades and math and reading test scores (Kao, 1999). One-half to three-fourths of the Filipino advantage in math and reading test scores, compared to White non-Hispanic adolescents in native-born families, is accounted for by differences in parents' education and family income.

In the San Diego study, adolescents in immigrant families at every grade level had higher grades than the districtwide average, and the school dropout rate was lower among the adolescents in immigrant families, even among Mexican-origin adolescents, despite significant socioeconomic and linguistic handicaps (Rumbaut, 1999). Factors contributing to these outcomes are the amount of time spent doing homework, time spent watching television, and the educational aspirations of the adolescents and their parents (Rumbaut, 1999; Fuligni, 1997).

YOUTH NOT IN SCHOOL AND EDUCATIONAL ATTAINMENTS

The greater the number of years of schooling completed by youths, the more likely they are to obtain well-paid jobs during adulthood. In 1990, first-generation youth were substantially more likely than second- and later-generation youth to not be enrolled in school and to have limited educational attainments. But most of the difference is accounted for by youths from Mexico, from five war-torn countries (Laos, Vietnam, El Salvador, Guatemala, and Nicaragua), and from three impoverished countries (Honduras, Haiti, and Dominican Republic), all with very high child poverty rates.

At age 12, the proportions not enrolled in school were essentially identical at 3–4% for the second and later generations overall, and the third and later generations of Whites, Blacks, American Indians, and Hispanics, and for second- and third-generation youth of Mexican origin. The proportion was slightly higher for the first generation, but most of this small difference is accounted for by the high proportion (7%) of Mexican-origin youths not in school.

Important differences emerge at older ages, however. By age 17 in 1990, 7–9% of second- and later-generation youth were not enrolled in school; among the third and later generations, the proportion rises from 8% for non-Hispanic Whites to 11% for Blacks and 13–14% for Hispanics and American Indians (Hernandez & Darke, 1999b). Among Mexican-origin youths age 17, 10–11% of the second and later generations were not enrolled in school, a level similar to later-generation Blacks and somewhat higher than corresponding non-Hispanic Whites. But among the first generation age 17 overall, 20% were not enrolled in school; this increased to 38% for Mexican-origin youths. In fact, Mexico and the other eight impoverished and war-torn countries of origin just listed account for 92% of all the first-generation youth age 17 not enrolled in school; 29% of all the first-generation youth age 17 from these nine countries were not enrolled in school. Among other countries of origin, excluding these nine, 10% are not enrolled in school—only 1.5 percentage points more than among non-Hispanic Whites in native-born families. Not only were many of the youths from these nine countries not enrolled in school, many had extremely low educational attainments, having completed no more than nine years of school. Among second- and later-generation youth as a whole, 8–9% at age 17 had completed no more than nine years of school, the same as non-Hispanic Whites in native-born families. This increased to 14% to 16% for youth age 17 in native-born families who were Black, American Indian, or Hispanic. Among both second- and later-generation Mexican-origin youth age 17, 13–14% had completed no more than nine years of education; but 23% of all first-generation youth had completed so little school, and this jumped to 38% for first-generation Mexican-origin youth. In fact, Mexican-origin youth age 17 accounted for 59% of all first-generation youth at this age who had completed no more than nine years of schooling, and 79% of these youth were born in Mexico or one of the other eight countries with high proportions not enrolled in school.

Thus, among youth age 17 from these nine countries, 29% were not enrolled in school and a nearly identical 32% had completed no more than nine years of education. The very limited educational attainments of many of these youths no doubt reflect the limited educational opportunities available to them in their countries of birth, and the recency of their migration to the United States, since school enrollment rates among the first generation at age 12 are much more similar to those for second- and later-generation children and youth.

In fact, most of the enormous disadvantage of Mexican-origin youth as a whole (23% completing no more than nine years of schooling) is accounted for by the first generation, and no doubt by first-generation youth who are very recent immigrants. Thus, insofar as Mexican-origin youth, and more generally Hispanic youth, have comparatively high proportions not attending school and low educational attainments, much of the disadvantage occurs among recent immigrants from Mexico who enter the United States with very low educational attainments. These youths may have educational and related needs that are quite different from those of children and youths who immigrate at earlier ages, and from second- and later-generation youth.

YOUTH NOT IN SCHOOL AND NOT WORKING

Youth who are neither in school nor working for pay experience lower earnings and less stable employment over the long run than peers who stay in school or secure jobs (Federal Interagency Forum on Child and Family Statistics, 1997). Only 4–6% of all second- and later-generation adolescents age 17 were neither in school nor working in 1990, compared to 7–8% for second- and later-generation Mexican-origin youth, and 9–11% for Black, American Indian, and Hispanic youth in native-born families (Hernandez & Darke, 1999b).

Among first-generation youth age 17, 12% were neither in school nor working, but this high level is accounted for by the very high proportion (21%) among first-generation Mexican-origin youth. If adolescents of Mexican origin are excluded, only 7% of the first generation age 17 were neither working nor in school. Thus, among youth age 17 in native-born families, Blacks, American Indians, and Hispanics were about twice as likely as corresponding non-Hispanic Whites to be neither in school nor working, and second- and later-generation Mexican-origin adolescents lie between the two. But first-generation Mexican-origin adolescents are about twice as likely as racial and ethnic minorities in native-born families to not be engaged in school or work, mainly because many of these youths are not enrolled in school.

CONCLUSIONS

Research on children and youth in immigrant families suggests that, compared to children and youth in native-born families, they were (prior to welfare reform) on average exposed to greater socioeconomic risks, had less access to health insurance and health care, and among those at greatest socioeconomic risk were less likely to live in families receiving a range of welfare benefits and services. Surprisingly, then, children and youth in immigrant families were doing at least as well as, or better than, those in native-born families along a variety of indicators measuring physical health, psychological adjustment, and school achievement.

This conclusion must be tempered, however, for four reasons (Hernandez & Charney, 1998). First, available evidence regarding the health and well-being of children and youth in immigrant families is consistent across a variety of domains, but it is limited both in quality and number of domains for which research is available. Second, available evidence suggests there is enormous variability across children and youth with different countries of origin for many indicators. Third, the health and well-being of children and youth in immigrant families appears to deteriorate through time and across generations, suggesting that the protective benefits of immigrant culture become more diluted the longer they live in the United States. Fourth, the federal welfare reform of 1996 places many children and youth in immigrant families at risk of losing potentially important economic and health resources.

At the beginning of the 21st century, these results suggest the need to address several major issues (Hernandez & Charney, 1998; Zhou, 1997). First, attention needs to be paid to the role of racial and ethnic discrimination and intergroup relations as they affect children and youth in immigrant and native-born families, either similarly or differently. Second, particular attention should be paid to neighborhood and cross-national social networks, to family traditions and expectations, and to connections to ethnic communities and resources within the United States. Third, these issues must be addressed in the context of the great diversity of children and youth in immigrant and native-born families regarding their family structure, their socioeconomic status, their economic opportunities, their race and ethnicity, their family circumstances, the social contexts in which they live, and their language and culture. Key questions for the future include these:

- What are the nature and causes of different child and family trajectories?
- Will they involve access to middle-class opportunities? Or will they instead involve exposure to the challenges and stresses that result from experiencing a severely limited set of resources and opportunities?
- How will the United States adjust to and accommodate the increasing racial, ethnic, and cultural diversity that many cities and states are experiencing today, and that promises to increase during the coming decades?
- What will happen to children and youths who are members of racial and ethnic minorities as they become, together, a numerical majority of the children and youths in the United States?

As the growing elderly population of the predominantly White baby boom generation reaches retirement age, it will increasingly depend for its economic support during retirement on the health, productive activities, and civic participation—that is, voting—of working-age adults who are members of racial and ethnic minorities, many of whom lived in immigrant families as children and youths. Consequently, a focus on the future of children, youth, and families in the United States must increasingly attend to the circumstances of racial and ethnic minorities, including immigrants.

References

Alwin, D. F. (1984). Trends in parental socialization values: Detroit, 1958–1983. *American Journal of Sociology, 90,* 359–382.

Blake, J. (1981). Family size and the quality of children and youth. *Demography, 18,* 321–342.

Blake, J. (1985). Number of siblings and educational mobility. *American Sociological Review, 50,* 84–94.

Blake, J. (1987). Differential parental investment: Its effects on child quality and status attainment. In J. B. Lancaster, J. Altmann, A. S. Rossi, & L. R. Sherrod (Eds.), *Parenting across the life span: Biosocial dimensions* (pp. 351–375). New York: Aldine de Gruyter.

Blake, J. (1989). *Family size and achievement.* Berkeley: University of California Press.

Blau, P. M., & Duncan, O. D. (1967). *The American occupational structure.* New York: Wiley.

Brandon, P. D. (1999). Receipt of public assistance by immigrant children and their families: Evidence from the Survey of Income and Program Participation. In D. J. Hernandez (Ed.), *Children of immigrants: Health, adjustment, and public assistance* (pp. 584–619). Washington, DC: National Academy Press.

Brown, E. R., Wyn, R., Yu, H., Valenzuela, A., & Dong, L. (1999). Access to health insurance and health care for children in immigrant families. In D. J. Hernandez (Ed.), *Children of immigrants: Health, adjustment, and public assistance* (pp. 126–186). Washington, DC: National Academy Press.

Cherlin, A. J. (1999). Going to extremes: Family structure, children's well-being, and social science. *Demography, 36,* 421–428.

Cherlin, A. J., Furstenberg, F. F., Chase-Lansdale, P. L., Kiernan, K. E., Robins, P. K., Morrison, D. R., et al. (1991). Longitudinal studies of effects of divorce on children in Great Britain and the United States. *Science, 252,* 1386–1389.

Conger, R. D., Elder, G. H., Jr., Lorenz, F. O., Conger, K. J., Simons, R. L., Whitbeck, L. B., et al. (1990). Linking economic hardship and marital quality and instability. *Journal of Marriage and the Family, 52,* 643–656.

Conger, R. D., & Elder, G. H. (1994). *Families in troubled times: Adapting to change in rural America.* Hawthorne, NY: Aldine de Gruyter.

Duncan, G. J., & Brooks-Gunn, J. (Eds.). (1997). *Consequences of growing up poor.* New York: Russell Sage Foundation.

Elder, G. H., Jr. (1974). *Children of the Great Depression: Social change in life experience.* Chicago: University of Chicago Press.

Elder, G. H., Jr., Conger, R. D., Foster, E. M., & Ardelt, M. (1992). Families under economic pressure. *Journal of Family Issues, 13,* 5–37.

Featherman, D. L., & Hauser, R. M. (1978). *Opportunity and change.* New York: Academic Press.

Federal Interagency Forum on Child and Family Statistics. (1997). *America's children: Key national indicators of well-being, 1997.* Washington, DC: U.S. Government Printing Office.

Fix, M., & Zimmerman, W. (1995). When should immigrants receive public benefits? In I. V. Sawhill (Ed.), *Welfare reform: An analysis of the issues* (pp. 69–72). Washington, DC: Urban Institute.

Fletcher, A., & Steinberg, L. (1994, February). *Generational status and country of origin as influences on the psychological adjustment of Asian-American adolescents.* Paper presented as part of a symposium entitled Psychological Adjustment of Asian-American Adolescents at the meetings of the Society for Research on Adolescence, San Diego.

Fuligni, A. J. (1997). The academic achievement of adolescents from immigrant families: The roles of family background, attitudes, and behavior. *Child Development, 68,* 351–363.

Fuligni, A. J. (1998). Adolescents from immigrant families. In V. McLoyd and L. Steinberg (Eds.), *Research on minority adolescents: Conceptual, theoretical and methodological issues* (pp. 127–143). Hillsdale, NJ: Erlbaum.

Furstenberg, F. F., Nord, C. W., Peterson, J. L., & Zill, N. (1983). The life course of children of divorce: Marital disruption and parental contact. *American Sociological Review, 48,* 656–668.

Glenn, N. D., & Hoppe, S. K. (1982). Only children as adults: Psychological well-being. *Journal of Family Issues, 56,* 363–382.

Guendelman, S. (2000). Immigrants may hold clues to protecting health during pregnancy: Exploring a paradox. In M. S. Jamner & D. Stokols (Eds.), *Promoting human wellness: New frontiers for research, practice, and policy* (pp. 222–257). Berkeley: University of California Press.

Guendelman, S., & English, P. B. (1995). Effects of United States residence on birth outcomes among Mexican immigrants: An exploratory study. *American Journal of Epidemiology, 142,* S30-S38.

Guendelman, S., English, P. B., & Chavez, G. (1995). Infants of Mexican immigrants: Health status of an emerging population. *Medical Care, 33,* 41–52.

Harris, K. M. (1999). The health status and risk behavior of adolescents in immigrant families. In D. J. Hernandez (Ed.), *Children of immigrants: Health, adjustment, and public assistance.* Washington, DC: National Academy Press.

Hernandez, D. J. (1986). Childhood in sociodemographic perspective. In R. H. Turner & J. J. Short, Jr. (Eds.), *Annual Review of Sociology, 12,* 159–180.

Hernandez, D. J. (1993). *America's children: Resources from family, government, and the economy.* New York: Russell Sage Foundation.

Hernandez, D. J. (1997). Poverty trends. In G. J. Duncan & J. Brooks-Gunn (Eds.), *Consequences of growing up poor* (pp. 18–34). New York: Russell Sage Foundation.

Hernandez, D. J. (Ed.). (1999). *Children of immigrants: Health, adjustment, and public assistance.* Washington, DC: National Academy Press.

Hernandez, D. J., & Charney, E. (Eds.). (1998). *From generation to generation: The health and well-being of children in immigrant families.* Washington, DC: National Academy Press.

Hernandez, D. J., & Darke, K. (1999a). Socioeconomic and demographic risk factors and resources among children in immigrant and native-born families: 1910, 1960, and 1990. In D. J. Hernandez (Ed.), *Children of immigrants: Health, adjustment, and public assistance* (pp. 19–125). Washington, DC: National Academy Press.

Hernandez, D. J., & Darke, K. (1999b). The well-being of immigrant children, native-born children with immigrant parents, and native-born children with native-born parents. In *Trends in the well-being of America's children: 1998* (pp. 421–543). Washington, DC: U.S. Department of Health and Human Services.

Hetherington, E. M., Cox, M., & Cox, R. (1978). The aftermath of divorce. In J. J. Stevens, Jr., & M. Matthews (Eds.), *Mother-child, father-child relations.* Washington, DC: National Association for the Education of Young Children and Youth.

Hill, M. S., & Duncan, G. J. (1987). Parental family income and socioeconomic attainment. *Social Science Research, 16,* 39–73.

Hofferth, S. L. (1999). Receipt of public assistance by Mexican American and Cuban American children in native and immigrant families. In D. J. Hernandez (Ed.), *Children of immigrants: Health, adjustment, and public assistance* (pp. 546–583). Washington, DC: National Academy Press.

Institute of Medicine. (1985). *Preventing low birthweight.* Washington, DC: National Academy Press.

Kao, G. (1999). Psychological well-being and educational achievement among immigrant youth. In D. J. Hernandez (Ed.), *Children of immigrants: Health, adjustment, and public assistance* (pp. 410–477). Washington, DC: National Academy Press.

Kao, G., & Tienda, M. (1995). Optimism and achievement: The educational performance of immigrant youth. *Social Science Quarterly, 76*(1), 1–19.

Kohn, M. L. (1969). *Class and conformity.* Homewood, IL: Dorsey.

Kohn, M. L., & Schooler, C. (1983). *Work and personality.* Norwood, NJ: Ablex.

Kominski, R. (1987). *What's it worth? Educational background and economic status.* (Current Population Reports, series P-70, no. 21.) Washington, DC: Government Printing Office.

Landale, N. S., Oropesa, R. S., & Gorman, B. (1999). Immigrant and infant health: Birth outcomes of immigrant and native women. In D. J. Hernandez (Ed.), *Children of immigrants: Health, adjustment, and public assistance* (pp. 244–285). Washington, DC: National Academy Press.

Lieberson, S., & Waters, W. C. (1988). *From many strands: Ethnic and racial groups in contemporary America.* New York: Russell Sage Foundation.

Markides, K. S., & Coreil, J. T. (1986). The health of Hispanics in the southwestern United States: An epidemiologic paradox. *Public Health Reports, 101,* 253–265.

McLanahan, S., & Sandefur, G. (1994). *Growing up with a single parent: What hurts, what helps.* Cambridge, MA: Harvard University Press.

Mendoza, F. S., & Dixon, L. B. (1999). The health and nutritional status of immigrant Hispanic children: Analyses of the Hispanic Health and Nutrition Examination Survey. In D. J. Hernandez (Ed.), *Children of immigrants: Health, adjustment, and public assistance* (pp. 187–243). Washington, DC: National Academy Press.

Mines, R. (1999). Children of immigrant farm workers. In D. J. Hernandez (Ed.), *Children of immigrants: Health, adaptation, and public assistance* (pp. 620–658). Washington, DC: National Academy Press.

Montgomery, L., & Carter-Pokras, O. (1993). Health status by social class and/or minority status: Implications for environmental equity research. *Toxicology and Industrial Health, 9,* 729–773.

Montgomery, L. E., Kiely, J. L., & Pappas, G. (1996). The effects of poverty, race, and family structure on US children and youth's health: Data from the NHIS, 1978 through 1980 and 1989 through 1991. *American Journal of Public Health, 6,* 1401–1405.

National Research Council. (1993). *Pesticides in the diets of infants and children.* Washington, DC: National Academy Press.

Newacheck, P. W. (1994). Poverty and childhood chronic illness. *Archive of Pediatric Adolescent Medicine, 48,* 1143–1149.

Newacheck, P. W., Jameson, W. J., & Halfon, N. (1994). Health status and income: The impact of poverty on child health. *Journal of School Health, 65,* 229–233.

Newacheck, P. W., & Starfield, B. (1988). Morbidity and use of ambulatory care services among poor and nonpoor children. *American Journal of Public Health, 78,* 927–933.

Nord, C. W., & Griffin, J. A. (1999). Educational profile of 3-to-8-year-old children of immigrants. In D. J. Hernandez (Ed.), *Children of immigrants: Health, adjustment, and public assistance* (pp. 348–409). Washington, DC: National Academy Press.

Portes, A. (1995). Children of immigrants: Segmented assimilation and its determinants. In A. Portes (Ed.), *The economic sociology of immigration: Essays on networks, ethnicity, and entrepreneurship* (pp. 248–279). New York: Russell Sage Foundation.

Portes, A. (1996). *The new second generation.* New York: Russell Sage Foundation.

Portes, A., & MacLeod, D. (1996). Educational progress of children of immigrants: The roles of class, ethnicity, and school context. *Sociology of Education, 9,* 255–275.

Portes, A., & Rumbaut, R. G. (1996). *Immigrant America: A portrait* (2nd ed.). Berkeley: University of California Press.

Portes, A., & Rumbaut, R. G. (2001). *Legacies: The story of the immigrant second generation.* Berkeley: University of California Press.

Romo, H. (1996). 'The newest outsiders': Educating Mexican migrant and immigrant youth. In J. Flores (Ed.), *Children of La Frontera* (pp. 61–91). Charleston, WV: ERIC Clearinghouse on Rural Education and Small Schools.

Rosenthal, D. A., & Feldman, S. S. (1991). The influence of perceived family and personal factors on self-reported school performance of Chinese and Western high school students. *Journal of Research on Adolescence, 1,* 135–154.

Ross, E. A. (1914). *The old world in the new.* New York: Century.

Rumbaut, R. G. (1994a). The crucible within: Ethnic identity, self-esteem, and segmented assimilation among children of immigrants. *International Migration Review, 28,* 748–794.

Rumbaut, R. G. (1994b). Origins and destinies: Immigration to the United States since World War II. *Sociological Forum, 9,* 583–621.

Rumbaut, R. G. (1995). The new immigration. *Contemporary Sociology, 24,* 307–311.

Rumbaut, R. G. (1996). Origins and destinies: Immigration, race, and ethnicity in contemporary America. In S. Pedraza & R. G. Rumbaut (Eds.), *Origins and destinies: Immigration, race, and ethnicity in America* (pp. 21–42). Belmont, CA: Wadsworth.

Rumbaut, R. G. (1997a). Paradoxes (and orthodoxies) of assimilation. *Sociological Perspectives, 40,* 483–511.

Rumbaut, R. G. (1997b). Ties that bind: immigration and immigrant families in the United States. In A. Booth, A. C. Crouter, & N. Landale (Eds.), *Immigration and the family: Research and policy on U.S. immigrants* (pp. 3–46). Mahwah, NJ: Erlbaum.

Rumbaut, R. G. (1999). Passages to adulthood: The adaptation of children and youth of immigrants in Southern California. In D. J. Hernandez (Ed.), *Children of immigrants: Health, adjustment, and public assistance* (pp. 478–545). Washington, DC: National Academy Press.

Scribner, R., & Dwyer, J. H. (1989). Acculturation and low birthweight among Latinos in the Hispanic HANES. *American Journal of Public Health, 79,* 1263–1267.

Sewell, W. H., & Hauser, R. M. (1975). *Education, occupation, and earnings.* New York: Academic Press.

Sewell, W. H., Hauser, R. M., & Wolf, W. C. (1980). Sex, schooling, and occupational status. *American Journal of Sociology, 83,* 551–583.

Starfield, B. (1982). Family income, ill health, and medical care of U.S. children. *Journal of Public Health Policy, 3,* 244–259.

Starfield, B. (1991). Childhood morbidity: Comparisons, clusters, and trends. *Pediatrics, 88,* 519–526.

Starfield, B. (1992). Effects of poverty on health status. *Bulletin of the New York Academy of Medicine,* 17–24.

Stoddard, T. L. (1920/1971). *The rising tide of color again White-world supremacy.* Westport, CT: Negro Universities Press. (Original work published 1920)

U.S. Census Bureau. (1992). *Census of population and housing, 1990: Public use microdata sample.* (U.S. Technical Documentation.) Washington, DC: U.S. Census Bureau. (www.census.gov/population/www/projections/natdet-D1A.html)

U.S. Department of Health and Human Services. (1981). *Better health for our children: A national strategy.* (Report of the Select Panel for the Promotion of Child Health to the United States Congress and the Secretary of Health and Human Services, Executive Summary. DHHS publication PHS 79–55071.)

Washington, DC: Office of the Assistant Secretary for Health and Surgeon General.

U.S. Department of Health and Human Services. (1986). *Infant Mortality and Low Birthweight.* (Report of the Secretary's Task Force on Black and Minority Health, Vol. VI.) Bethesda, MD: National Institutes of Health.

U.S. Immigration [Dillingham] Commission. (1911). *Reports of the Immigration Commission: Vol. 4. Emigration conditions in Europe.* Washington, DC: U.S. Government Printing Office.

Ventura, S. J. (1983). Births of Hispanic parentage, 1980. *Monthly Vital Statistics Report, 32,* 1–18.

Ventura, S. J. (1984). Births of Hispanic parentage, 1981. *Monthly Vital Statistics Report, 33,* 1–17.

Wilk, V. A. (1993). Health hazards to children in agriculture. *American Journal of Indian Medicine, 24,* 283–290.

Wilkinson, R. G. (1996) *Unhealthy societies: The afflictions of inequality.* London: Routledge.

Williams, R. L., Binkin, N. J., & Clingman, E. J. (1986). Pregnancy outcomes among Spanish-surname women in California. *American Journal of Public Health, 76,* 387–391.

Zhou, M. (1997). Growing up American: The challenge confronting immigrant children and children of immigrants. *Annual Review of Sociology, 23,* 63–95.

21

THE ACADEMIC ENGAGEMENT AND ACHIEVEMENT OF LATINO YOUTH

Carola Suárez-Orozco

Harvard University

Marcelo M. Suárez-Orozco

Harvard University

Fabienne Doucet

Harvard University

The United States is undergoing a dramatic transformation of its youth population. According to figures from the 2000 census, Latino youths under age 18 make up 35% of the Latino population in the United States (currently estimated at 12.5%). By 2020, it is projected that 17% of the U.S. population will be of Latino origin, reaching 33.3% by 2100 (U.S. Census Bureau, 2000). Although some of this growth is due to birth rates, it is also related to Latino immigrants arriving in unprecedented numbers, reshaping urban, suburban, and rural settings throughout the nation. The Latino presence is now being felt not only in the traditional immigrant regions of the Eastern seaboard and the Southwest but also throughout the South and Midwest—areas of the country that in the past rarely have encountered Latinos in large numbers. Nevada, for example, has had a 123% increase in Latino population since 1990. Likewise, since that time, Arkansas has had a 148% increase, North Carolina a 110% increase, and Nebraska has experienced a growth of 96% (U.S. Census Bureau).

Latino youth are extraordinarily diverse, and their experiences resist facile generalizations. The ancestors of some were established on what is now U.S. territory long before the current borders were set through conquest and land purchases. Today, large numbers of Latinos are immigrants coming from dozens of countries, with a rich range of cultural traditions. Some are the children of highly educated professionals, while others have parents who are illiterate, low-skilled, and struggling in the lowest-paid sectors of the service economy (M. Suárez-Orozco, 2000).

Some Latino families are escaping political, religious, or ethnic persecution; others are lured by the promise of better jobs and the hope for better educational opportunities. Some are documented, and others are not. Some immigrant origin youth come to settle permanently, over time losing their ties to their homelands; others follow their parents from one migrant work camp to another. Some Latinos engage in transnational strategies, living both "here and there"—that is, shuttling between their country of birth and their country of choice (Levitt, 1996; Suárez-Orozco & Suárez-Orozco, 2001).

An estimated two-thirds of Latinos are either immigrants or the children of immigrants (M. Suárez-Orozco & Páez, 2002). When we refer to "immigrant children" we mean foreign-born children who have migrated—not the U.S.-born second generation. "Children of immigrants," however, refers to both U.S.-born and foreign-born children. Although the experience of U.S.-born and foreign-born youth differ in many respects (the U.S.-born are citizens, for example), they nonetheless share important common denominators, including immigrant parents.

Much of the recent scholarship on Latino youth well-being has focused on schooling adaptations, as schooling processes and outcomes are a powerful barometer of current as well as future psychosocial functioning (Mandel & Marcus, 1988; Steinberg, Brown, & Dornbusch, 1996). Findings from a number of recent studies suggest that although some are successfully navigating the American educational system, many others struggle academically, leaving school without acquiring the tools that will enable them to manage in the highly competitive knowledge-intensive economy. Nationwide, nearly a third of all Latino youths drop out of school (President's Advisory Commission on Educational Excellence for Hispanic American Education, 1996). Immigrant youth who are unschooled or unskilled will encounter dim odds in today's economy. Many will be facing a life below the poverty line, on the lower rungs of the service sector of the economy. Some will gravitate toward gangs and face the danger of incarceration in the new country—a country that today has the largest prison population in the postindustrial world (Kennedy, 2001; Zimbardo & Haney, 1998). Some of these gang-involved youths will be deported to their "home" countries, with potentially catastrophic outcomes (Vigil, 2002). Many of the youths who are deported no longer speak the language of their country of origin, and they lack the skills and ties to make viable contributions, whether economic or social.

ACADEMIC OUTCOMES AMONG LATINO YOUTH

There is much to be concerned about as we consider a variety of indicators of Latino academic outcomes. The National Center for Education Statistics (Kaufman, Alt, & Chapman, 2001) reports that among young people age 16 to 24, 44.2% of "Hispanics" born outside the United States are high school dropouts. Those born in the United States were less likely to drop out, but at 30.5% the proportion was still higher than that among young adults from other ethnic groups. (These figures include all young people in the 16-to-24 age range who had dropped out of school or did not have high school credentials as of October 2000.) The needs of Limited English Proficient (LEP) students are rarely met in schools, which also contributes to school dropout rates. In 1995, children of Hispanic origin (with U.S.-born parents) classified as LEP had a dropout rate of 66.4%, compared to 41.8% of their non-LEP counterparts (Ruiz-de-Velasco, Fix, & Clewell, 2000).

The high-stakes testing movement currently sweeping the United States also has implications for dropout patterns (Bracey, 2000). The introduction of statewide tests in Texas in the late 1980s was accompanied by a sharp increase in dropout rates for Black and Latino students, and these rates have not returned to previous levels since (Bracey, 2000). Close to 83% of Latino students graduating from Texas high schools in 1998 had passed the Texas Assessment of Academic Skills (TAAS) required for a high school diploma at some point between their 10th and 12th grade years, compared to 94% of White students (Natriello & Pallas, 1998). In 1997, the Mexican American Legal Defense and Educational Fund filed a suit against the Texas Education Agency in a federal district court, pointing out that "over half of Texas' minority students in the

sophomore year do not pass one or more parts of the TAAS test, and approximately 85% of the students who do not pass the TAAS in May before graduation are Mexican American or African American" (as cited in Natriello & Pallas, 1998).

Massachusetts recently joined Texas in the growing number of states requiring test scores for high school graduation. The class of 2003 is the first to be required to pass all components of the Massachusetts Comprehensive Assessment System (MCAS) at some point between 10th and 12th grade in order to be awarded a high school diploma. In 2001, as 10th graders, these students showed alarming disparities in failure rates. Although 12% of White students failed the English language arts component of the exam, 48% of Latino students did so. For the mathematics component, 18% of White students failed, compared to 58% of Latino students. For LEP students, the disparities are even more astounding—84% did not pass the English language arts test, and 74% did not pass the mathematics test. Overall, in 2001, 77% of White students earned a "competency determination," while only 29% of Latino students did so. According to a study by the Gastón Institute for Latino Community Development and Public Policy (2001) at the University of Massachusetts, Boston, Latino students are significantly underrepresented in higher-level math and science courses that will prepare them for the MCAS exam, thus barring them from the knowledge and skills necessary for high school graduation in Massachusetts.

These findings have implications not only for the short-term outcomes of Latino students in American schools but for long-term outcomes as well. As Natriello and Pallas (1998) pointed out, Claude Steele's work on stereotype threat suggests that the academic performance of racial and ethnic minorities is impaired by negative stereotypes about their competency in school settings (Steele, 1997; Steele & Aronson, 1995). Although we certainly do not argue that measures of competency for students and accountability for schools are unnecessary, we concur with Robert Linn (2000) that "the unintended negative effects of the high-stakes accountability uses often outweigh the intended positive effects" (p. 15).

RESEARCH ON IMMIGRANT YOUTH

In recent years, a counterintuitive trend has been emerging from a number of studies conducted in a variety of disciplines. We have identified a somewhat paradoxical pattern: compared to second-generation Latino youth, more recent immigrants have more optimistic and positive attitudes about school and school authorities (Suárez-Orozco & Suárez-Orozco, 1995). A number of recent studies have verified that, for many immigrants, length of residence in the United States seems to be disconcertingly associated with *declining* health, attitudinal, and schooling outcomes (Hernández & Charney, 1998; Kao & Tienda, 1995; Rumbaut, 1995; Steinberg, Brown, & Dornbusch, 1996; Suárez-Orozco & Suárez-Orozco, 1995, 2001). A large-scale National Research Council (NRC) study considered a variety of measures of physical health and risk behaviors among children and adolescents from immigrant families, including general health, learning disabilities, obesity, emotional difficulties, and risk behaviors. The NRC researchers found that immigrant youths were healthier than their counterparts from nonimmigrant families. These findings, as the authors reported, are counterintuitive in light of the racial and ethnic minority status, lower overall socioeconomic status, and higher poverty rates that characterize many immigrant children and families. The NRC meta-analysis revealed that the longer immigrant youths are in the United States, the poorer their overall physical and psychological health. Furthermore, the more "Americanized" they become, the more likely they are to engage in risky behaviors such as substance abuse, unprotected sex, and delinquency (Hernández & Charney, 1998). This directly refutes assimilation theories of adaptation that hypothesize that immigrant youth would do better over time and across generations (C. Suárez-Orozco, 2000).

In the area of schooling, an ambitious study of more than 5,000 immigrant and second-generation students in San Diego, California, and Dade County, Florida, by sociologists Alejandro Portes and Rubén Rumbaut (2001) found that "U.S. nativity and long term residence among the foreign-born increase English skills but significantly lower grades. . . . These findings strongly suggest that second-generation children gradually lose their achievement drive with increasing acculturation" (p. 239). A similar pattern was established in a large-scale study conducted of Canadian immigrant families: length of residence seemed to be associated with declining well-being and academic engagement (Beiser, Dion, Gotowiec, Hyman, & Vu, 1995). Research by Laurence Steinberg et al. (1996), based on a national study of more than 20,000 teenagers attending nine high schools, uncovered the same alarming trend, that "the longer a student's family has lived in this country, the worse the youngster's school performance and mental health" (pp. 97–98). This trend was evident not only among Latino youth but among Asian students as well. The data, coming from many sources, concentrating on a range of immigrant countries of origin, using various methodologies, and crossing disciplines, suggest "that becoming Americanized is detrimental to youngsters' achievement, and terrible for their overall mental health" (Steinberg et al., pp. 97–98).

A number of social scientists have explored the issues of variability and decline in schooling performance and

social adaptation of immigrant children. As we discuss in this chapter, several factors are implicated. Social scientists have argued that the "capital" immigrant families bring with them—including financial resources, social class and educational background, psychological and physical health, as well as social supports—all shape the immigrant experience. Legal status, race, color, and language also mediate how children adapt to the upheavals of immigration. Economic opportunities and neighborhood characteristics—including the quality of schools where families settle, racial and class segregation, neighborhood decay, and violence—all contribute significantly to the adaptation process. Discriminatory experiences also play a role. These factors combine in ways that lead to very different outcomes (Suárez-Orozco & Suárez-Orozco, 2001).

In this chapter, we offer a framework for understanding in broad psychosocial terms the diverse adaptations and outcomes of Latino youth. We structure this discussion around several conceptual domains. First, we examine the dynamics that shape opportunity: socioeconomic status, neighborhood characteristics such as poverty and segregation, and the schools Latino youth most often attend. These structural features shape the opportunities and mold the experiences of immigrant youth as they journey to their varied American destinies. Because the human experience is never solely the product of impersonal structural forces, we also examine how agency and changing identities are implicated in the making of today's immigrant story. We introduce the concept of "social mirroring" to explain the vicissitudes of identity formation among Latino youth. We consider carefully how networks of social relations function to mediate academic outcomes. We argue that, taken together, these psychosocial formations are at the heart of any understanding of the complexities of the academic engagement and academic outcomes among Latino youth.

STRUCTURING OPPORTUNITY

Educational Background

Latino immigrant youths arrive in American neighborhoods and schools from very different backgrounds. On one end of the spectrum, we find youths from middle-class, upper-status urban backgrounds. These young people are typically highly literate and have well-developed study skills. In sharp contrast are those youngsters arriving from strife-ridden or poverty-stricken countries with little or no schooling. Many of them have missed critical years of classroom experience and often cannot read and write in Spanish (Páez, 2001). Such varied experiences and backgrounds have profound implications for their transition to the U.S. setting. Others are born in the United States to Latino American–born parents and may either enter middle-class life or become entrenched in the urban underclass, depending in part upon the neighborhoods where they live and are schooled.

Not surprisingly, more-educated parents are better equipped to guide their children in various aspects of life in the new country: how to study; structure an essay; access information for school projects; and provide necessary resources, including additional books, a home computer, and even tutors. These parents are more likely to know to ask the right questions and insist that their children be placed in educational programs that will ensure viable options in the future. They will know that not all courses are the same and indeed that not all schools produce the same outcomes. Children who have parents with limited education are at a clear disadvantage.

Poverty

Poverty has long been recognized as a significant risk factor for youth (Luthar, 1999; Weissbourd, 1996). Children raised in circumstances of socioeconomic deprivation are vulnerable to an array of psychological distresses, among them difficulties concentrating and sleeping, anxiety, and depression as well as a heightened propensity for delinquency and violence. Those living in poverty often experience major life event stress as well as the stress of daily hassles (Luthar, 1999; Weissbourd, 1996). Poverty frequently coexists with a variety of other factors that augment risks, such as single parenthood, residence in neighborhoods plagued with violence, gang activity, and drug trade, as well as school environments that are segregated, overcrowded, and poorly funded (Luthar; Weissbourd).

Although some Latino youths come from privileged backgrounds, large numbers today suffer from the challenges associated with poverty. Poverty might be a preexisting condition prior to migration, or it may be accentuated as immigrants experience some downward mobility in the process of settlement. The 2000 U.S. Census Bureau report on the foreign-born population shows that 21.9% of persons originating in Latin America live below the poverty line—the highest percentage among the foreign-born, and more than twice as high as the portion of the native population living below the poverty line (11.2%). Nationwide, 34.4% of all Latino children live below poverty, and 37% of Latino immigrant families report difficulties affording food. Immigrant children are more than four times as likely as native-born children to live in crowded housing conditions (Capps, 2001). A study by Brown, Wyn, Yu, Valenzuela, and Dong (1998) of access to health insurance and health care among Mexican American families revealed that noncitizen Mexican American children are twice as likely as citizen children in immigrant families to lack insurance coverage, and three times as likely as native-born children to be uninsured.

Neighborhoods, Segregation, and Schools

Where immigrant families settle shapes the immigrant journey and the experiences and adaptations of children. Now, Latinos are settling in unprecedented numbers in highly segregated, deeply impoverished urban settings (Orfield & Yun, 1999). Orfield and Yun found that Latino-origin students attend the most highly segregated schools of any group in the United States today—in 1996, only 25% of Latino students attended majority White schools. The degree of segregation will have a series of consequences (Massey & Denton, 1993). New immigrants of color who settle in predominantly minority neighborhoods will have virtually no direct, systematic, and intimate contact with middle-class White Americans. This in turn will affect the kinds of languages and dialects encountered by the youths, the quality of schools they will attend, and the networks that are useful to access desirable colleges and jobs (Orfield, 1995; Portes, 1996).

Concentrated poverty is all too often associated with an absence of gratifying work opportunities with the promise of mobility to the more appealing sectors of the opportunity structure (Wilson, 1997). Youngsters in such neighborhoods are chronically underemployed or unemployed and must search for work elsewhere. In such neighborhoods with few opportunities in the formal economy, underground or informal activities tend to flourish. Exposure to violence in both neighborhoods and schools is an everyday reality for many immigrant youths today (Collier, 1998; Suárez-Orozco & Suárez-Orozco, 2001). Sociologists Portes and Rumbaut (2001) have argued that these structural features interact to generate a pattern they have termed "segmented assimilation," whereby over time large numbers of poor immigrant youths of color will tend to gravitate toward the American underclass rather than approaching middle-class norms.

The neighborhood characteristics outlined here are reflected in the schools attended by a large segment of Latino youth. They enroll in schools that cover the range from well-functioning institutions with a culture of high expectations and a focus on achievement to dysfunctional ones characterized by ever-present fear of violence, distrust, low expectation, and institutional anomie. Unfortunately, poor Latino youths who need the most academic help tend to enroll in inferior schools—many of them characterized by a culture of violence. An ethnographic study of a number of immigrant schools in Miami found that three factors were consistently present in such schools (Collier, 1998). First, administrators tended to deny that the school had problems with violence or drugs.

Second, many of the staff members exhibited "noncaring" behaviors toward the students. Lastly, the schools took lax security measures.

These schools typically have limited and outdated resources and offer an inferior education. Buildings are poorly maintained as a rule, and classrooms are overcrowded. Textbooks and curriculum are outdated; computers are few and obsolete. Many of the teachers may not have credentials in the subjects they teach. Clearly defined tracks limit immigrant students to noncollege destinations. Lacking English skills, Latino immigrant students are often enrolled in the least demanding and competitive classes that eventually exclude them from courses needed for college.

Meier and Stewart (1991) discussed the inherent problems in using already biased placement tests written in English to place Latino students with limited English proficiency in academic groups. These students are often wrongly assigned to classes intended to meet the needs of students with developmental delays (for example, special education classrooms), or they are tracked into academic groups where they receive little or no advanced instruction. Placement in such groups has serious implications for the future educational trajectories these students will follow. As Olsen (1997) poignantly put it, "With insufficient English language development and insufficient access to the curriculum in a language they can understand, most immigrant students are (through the forces of schooling) denied equal access to an education. Some manage to achieve, but many drop out of school or become stuck in the category of 'ESL lifers'" (p. 241). Latino students also often attend schools that generally offer few advanced placement courses critical for entry to many of the more competitive colleges. Because the settings are so undesirable, teachers and principals routinely transfer out in search of better assignments elsewhere (Orfield, 2002). As a result, in many such schools there is little continuity or sense of community to foster academic engagement.

Conchas (2001) conducted a study of Latino high school students in California, examining how the institutional mechanisms of a school mediate academic engagement. He argued that within a school, school structures and practices form opportunity tracks that can lead to optimism or pessimism among students, as the students become divided along structural lines. Conchas found that Latino students who were enrolled in the general school program were exposed to fewer examples of opportunities for academic success in comparison to their counterparts enrolled in the school's more prestigious academies (e.g., medical, graphics). There were also variations within the academies, with some offering more support for Latino youth than others. This study counters widely accepted assumptions that the onus is upon students themselves to achieve by demonstrating variations among Latinos in a single school setting. As Conchas stated, "while schools often replicate existing social and economic inequality present in the larger society and culture, they can also circumvent inequality if students and teachers work in consort towards academic success" (p. 502).

Undocumented Status

Lack of Immigration and Naturalization Service (INS) documentation presents an additional obstacle to academic success. There are an estimated 8–10 million undocumented immigrants within the foreign-born population of the United States (Deardorff & Blumerman, 2001), and children constitute a significant portion of the undocumented population. Although precise figures are impossible to acquire, since schools do not keep records of this sort, it is estimated, for example, that several hundred thousand undocumented children attend public schools in California. In 1982, the U.S. Supreme Court ruled, in *Plyler* v. *Doe,* that it was unconstitutional to deny public education to undocumented alien children. The Court stated that denying undocumented children access to public education was, *inter alia,* unfair punishment for their parents' actions. The ruling specifies that schools cannot deny admission to a student on the basis of undocumented status, treat a student fundamentally differently from others to determine residency, engage in practices to "chill" access to school ("chilling" refers to actions that create fear among undocumented children and their families, such as requirements to provide vaccination records), require students or parents to disclose or document immigration status, make inquiries of students or parents that may expose their undocumented status, or require social security numbers from all students (Morse & Ludovina, 1999).

These measures, meant to provide some protection for undocumented children in schools, do not prevent other threats. Undocumented children often arrive in the United States under traumatic circumstances, and once they are here they continue to experience fear and anxiety about being apprehended, separated from their parents, and deported (Suárez-Orozco & Suárez-Orozco, 2001). Such psychological and emotional duress can take its toll on the academic experiences of undocumented children. Another obstacle to academic success for these youths comes at the end of the high school years. Every year, thousands of bright and gifted undocumented young adults with dreams of getting a college education are gravely disappointed when they discover that their legal status stands in the way of their access to postsecondary education. Most colleges and universities require a social security number (or some other form of legal documentation) for financial aid. Thus even students who qualify for academic scholarships may not be able to accept them because of their undocumented status. Our work in various immigrant communities has shown that this issue is of great concern to students, parents, teachers, and community leaders.

Seasonal Migrants

Being a child in a migrant family presents particular challenges. The youngster faces multiple moves, frequent interruptions in schooling, and deep poverty, as well as harsh working and living conditions. Latinos constitute 94% of the migrant worker population, with 80% born in Mexico. (Information cited in this subsection was drawn from a series of papers in the ERIC Digests on migrant families: ERIC, 1991; Huang, 1993; Martin, 1994.) Most migrant workers are men (82%), and 52% are married with children. The primary industries for migrant workers are in agriculture and fishing, and the average migrant worker earns $5,000 per year. It is estimated that approximately 600,000 children travel with their migrant parents in the United States each year. Of those children, about 40% work with their families; among working children, 40% have worked in fields wet with pesticides, and 40% have been sprayed while they were working in fields. It is thus not surprising that migrant workers are in much poorer health than the rest of the population. Compared with the national life expectancy rate of 75 years, migrant workers live to an average of 49 years. The infant mortality rate among migrant workers is 125% higher than the general population, and 10.9% of migrant children suffer from chronic health problems, compared to the national rate of 3%.

Migrant children are the least likely among other population groups to be enrolled in school. The lack of continuity in their schooling trajectories (because of interruptions during the school year, the difficulty of transferring school records, health problems, and lack of English language skills) contributes both to their low attendance and to the high dropout rate among migrant children. The dropout rate after grade six among these children is twice the national average, and typically they only reach the eighth grade.

Late Entry into American Schools

Data suggest that Latino immigrant youths who arrive during adolescence are at a particular disadvantage in their schooling (Ruiz-de-Velasco et al., 2001). Although many immigrants arrive during their secondary school years, most school-based programs targeting immigrant youth are designed for the needs of primary school students. Many immigrants who arrive in adolescence must overcome several often-insurmountable obstacles.

Frequently, they are not awarded credits for previous course work completed in their countries of origin. They may enter settings with high-stakes testing that have not been designed with second language learners in mind. Older immigrant youth may have had longer gaps in their previous schooling and enter schools far behind their age levels. Therefore, dropout rates among older Latino immigrant youth have reached disturbingly high levels (C. Suárez-Orozco, 2001). As discussed earlier, even when older immigrant adolescents are able to graduate, if they lack documented status they are often unable to have access to higher education (Suárez-Orozco & Suárez-Orozco, 2001).

Clearly, Latino youth face myriad obstacles that all too often severely truncate their academic trajectories. There is no doubt, of course, that structural constraints play a critical role in academic outcomes. Parental education and income is highly predictive of such educational outcomes, as are performance on high-stakes graduation tests, as well as grades and college attendance rates. Focusing entirely on such structural issues, however, overlooks the critical role of agency in the schooling experience.

ACADEMIC ENGAGEMENT AND DISENGAGEMENT

Achievement motivation has been viewed by many psychologists to be closely related to academic outcomes and defined as the motive related to performance according to standards of excellence (Eccles, Wigfield, & Schiefele, 1998). Eccles, Wigfield, and Schiefele argue that three motivational questions are at the heart of achievement motivation theory. The first question—Does the individual feel capable of doing the task?—considers in particular issues of locus of control (Weiner, 1994) and self-efficacy (Bandura, 1994; Schunk, 1991). The next question—Is the task motivating, and why?—focuses on the issues of intrinsic motivation (Dewey, 1913), internalization (Ryan, 1992), and interest (Schiefele, 1991). The last question—Does the individual understand what he or she must do to succeed at the task?—is concerned with issues of volition (Corno, 1993; Schiefele, 1991), self-regulation (Borkowski & Thorpe, 1994; Zimmerman, 1989), and help-seeking behaviors (Nelson-Le Gall & Jones, 1990; Newman & Goldin, 1990). In general, the focus on achievement motivation is largely based on a Western model of individualism.

In our view, emphasis on achievement motivation as a lens for understanding academic outcomes for Latino youth has limited value. This model of understanding tends to ignore the harsh implications of structural barriers and blames the victim: if a poor Latino child does not perform well in school, it is because she is not motivated. Emphasizing achievement motivation also ignores the fact that although many poor high school students of color attending urban schools say they believe a college education is important and they intend to go to college, few will actually attend (Ogbu, 1995).

As part of the data collection for the Harvard Longitudinal Immigrant Student Adaptations study (a five-year interdisciplinary longitudinal study of 400 immigrant youths ranging in age from 9 to 14 at the beginning of the study, arriving from the Dominican Republic, Mexico, Central America, Haiti, and China) we found that 75% indicated a college education is "very important," and close to 75% intended to go on to college or obtain a professional degree in fields such as medicine and law. In the last year of the study, however, it is evident that far fewer are likely to have the grades and credits necessary to go on to college in the immediate future. Valuing education and achievement motivation, without actual academic engagement, may be only loosely linked to tangible academic outcomes.

In order to perform optimally on the educational journey, the student must be engaged in learning. When a student is engaged, she is both intellectually and behaviorally involved in her schooling. She ponders the materials presented, participates in discussions, completes assignments with attention and effort, and optimally applies newfound knowledge in new contexts. Conversely, when academically disengaged, students "simply go through the motions" (Steinberg, Lamborn, Dornbusch, & Darling, 1992, p. 15), putting forth minimum effort and, in extreme cases, none.

In recent years, a number of scholars have argued that academic achievement and adjustment are in large part a function of academic engagement (Jordan, 1999; Pierson & Connell, 1992; Steinberg et al., 1992; Wick, 1990, 1990). However, academic engagement is a term that has been defined and used in a variety of ways (Jordan, 1999; Pierson & Connell, 1992; Steinberg et al., 1992; Wick; Zeidner & Schleyer, 1999). Rather than viewing academic engagement as an end product, we conceptualize degrees of academic engagement and disengagement as occurring along a continuum. Highly engaged students are both interested and actively engaged in the process of learning. Their motivation may be intrinsic (a thirst for knowledge and understanding) or extrinsic (pursuit of good grades as an entrée to the academic and career opportunity structure) and may combine both features. Whatever the motivation, the student is meeting his academic potential by engaging in schooling. A moderately engaged student may complete a school's basic requirements (such as attending and completing most assignments) but not work to his full potential and find the content of learning to be only sporadically interesting. The more disengaged student learns significantly less than if he were cognitively or behaviorally engaged and receives lower grades than

that which he is capable of. In its most extreme form, academic disengagement leads to a pattern of multiple failures. In such cases, the student has stopped engaging in his schooling—he is habitually truant, rarely completes assignments, and shows little or no interest in the materials presented.

Conceptually, we separate academic engagement into three dimensions: cognitive, behavioral, and relational. A student's reported intellectual or *cognitive engagement* with schoolwork includes the elements of intellectual curiosity about new ideas and domains of learning as well as the pleasure that is derived in the process of mastering new materials. Do the students report that learning is inherently interesting to them? *Behavioral engagement* refers to the degree to which students actually engage in the behaviors necessary to do well in school: attending classes, participating in class, and completing assignments. We consider general academic behaviors as well as subject-specific behaviors from both student and teacher perspectives. *Relational engagement* is the degree to which students report meaningful and supportive relationships in school with adults as well as peers. These relationships can serve emotional as well as tangible functions (Figure 21.1).

Cognitive and behavioral engagements are viewed as manifestations of engagement, while relational engagement is viewed as a mediator of these engagements. Background characteristics, as well as family and contextual risks, have independent effects upon academic outcomes. Background characteristics such as socioeconomic status, a history of trauma, and whether or not the student is documented have a direct effect on academic outcomes not completely mediated by academic engagement. Contextual risks, including neighborhood and school segregation, also have a direct effect on academic outcomes. A student with highly educated parents attending a quality suburban school will be at a distinct advantage over a student with a less-privileged background on achievement test results as well as course grades, independent of effort or engagement. We maintain that family risks, including single-parent structures and lack of parental supervision, are likely to influence such individual student attributes as a sense of self-efficacy, future orientation, or attitude toward school authorities, which in turn affect academic engagement. Relational supports can serve to mediate the effects of family and contextual risks on individual attributes.

Varying levels of academic engagement have clear implications. We view academic engagement as a particularly important dimension of schooling because it would appear to be malleable and hence a promising level for intervention. Our conceptual model recognizes the role of characteristics each student has, such as parental education, poverty, INS documentation, family constellation,

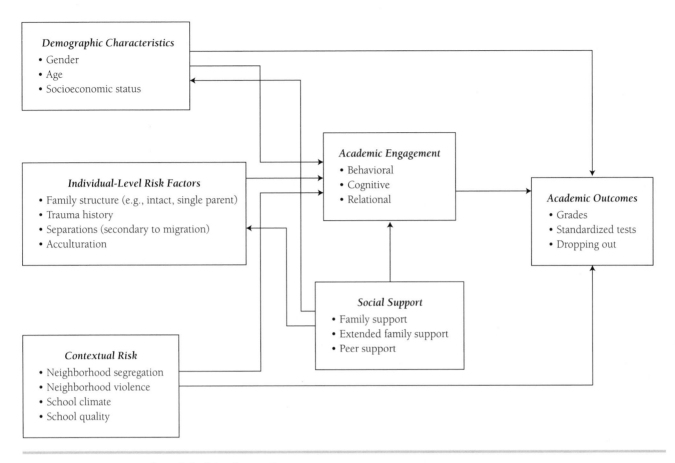

Figure 21.1. Conceptual Model of Academic Engagement.

neighborhood characteristics, and networks of social relations. It also takes into consideration the individual dimensions that can influence academic outcomes: behavioral and cognitive engagement, self-efficacy, motivation, attitude toward school authorities, and future goals, along with ethnic and academic identities. Taken together, a clearer understanding of academic outcomes begins to emerge.

IDENTITY FORMATION

Any understanding of Latino youth growing up in a diaspora must take into consideration identity. How they come to define themselves, as well as how others define them, has important implications for where they live, with whom they live, where they work, and how they envision their future and mobilize toward that realization. Erik Erikson (1968) argued that at no time in the lifespan is the urge to define oneself vis-à-vis the society at large as great as during adolescence. He claimed that for optimal development, the individual's sense of self and the varied social milieus should complement each other. If there is

too much cultural dissonance, cultural hostility, and role confusion, and if the cultural guides are inadequate, Latino adolescents may find it difficult to develop a flexible and adaptive sense of identity. They may be torn between an attachment to the parental culture of origin, the lure of the often more intriguing adolescent peer culture, and aspirations to join the "mainstream" American culture.

In a society structured by "the color line" (Du Bois, 1986), race and color are significant forces shaping the lives of immigrant youth. Research demonstrates that immigrant youth of color are quickly socialized into America's racial and class regime (Bailey, 2001; Stepick, 1997; Waters, 1999). Indeed, entry into American identities today is via the culture of multiculturalism (Suárez-Orozco & Suárez-Orozco, 2001). One experiments, names, and performs American identities by crafting a hyphenated self. Many important questions are relevant to an understanding of the realities new immigrants will face. How do phenotypically (but not culturally) Black new Latino immigrants come to terms, over time and across generations, with the ever-charged folk racial binary in the American urban setting (Bailey)? How does a Dominican child respond when she suddenly discovers she is Black in the American sense of the term? Will the new immigrants, by sheer force of numbers, finally break the binary logic of American racial regime? How do these transformations in racial and ethnic self-identities affect (if at all) the schooling of children? As Americanization now appears to lead to dystopic adaptations (e.g., obesity, diabetes, drug taking, lower grades), are there protective features in the crafting and performing of hyphenated identities (Hernández & Charney, 1998; Steinberg et al., 1996)? Is an immigrant youth who identifies herself as Mexican more likely to do better in school than one who self-identifies as Chicana? Although a number of scholars have looked at these important questions, more interdisciplinary work is needed in this area (Portes & Rumbaut, 2001; Suárez-Orozco & Suárez-Orozco, 2001; Waters 1999).

How others view her is one of the vectors by which the adolescent struggles to sort out a sense of identity and self. Immigrant youths must contend with the fact that they are culturally, ethnically, and racially "Other." Sociologists have documented how immigration generates ambivalence at best, and latent and manifest hostilities at worst (Espenshade, 1998). Hence, immigrant youths must face the usual challenges of adolescence while contending with the winds of xenophobia their presence generates (Suárez-Orozco & Suárez-Orozco, 2001).

Identity has been conceptualized and defined in many ways by diverse social science disciplines as well as by individual researchers (Phinney, 1990). We place ethnic and racial identities in an interdisciplinary framework and define identity as a feeling, intersubjectively shared by individuals in a given group, that is based on a sense of common origin, common beliefs and values, common goals, and a sense of shared destiny. We maintain that ethnic and racial identity development does not occur in a linear sequence of stages, from least to most aware as some psychological theorists have posited (Suárez-Orozco & Suárez-Orozco, 2001). Rather, we view identities as contextual and contingent upon a variety of circumstances throughout the lifespan (Suárez-Orozco & Suárez-Orozco, 2001). Implied in this definition is the idea of cultural pluralism, where dominant majorities and ethnic and racial minorities cohabit a national space (De Vos & Suárez-Orozco, 1990). These identities are powerfully shaped by the "social mirror" and by a variety of contextual factors.

Racial and ethnic identities are at once achieved and ascribed. Identities are achieved when there is a sense, in Appiah's words, that this "identity is mine. . . . I can choose how central my identification with it will be—choose, that is, how much I will organize my life around that identity" (Appiah & Gutmann, 1998, p. 80). Ascription of group membership has two main sources: those made by group members ("You are a member of *our* group") and those made by the majority group ("You are a member of *that* group"). In highly stratified plural societies, the process of ascription involves instrumental and expressive considerations. On the instrumental level, it delimits the spaces in the opportunity structure that the minority group is allowed to inhabit as well as their avenues for status mobility. On the expressive level, ascription involves collective perceptions of the minority group that almost always include stereotypic attitudes toward them. Negative distortions of the social mirror have profound implications for the development of identity among members of ethnically and racially marked groups (C. Suárez-Orozco, 2000).

SOCIAL MIRRORING

Are immigrant youth aware of stereotypic xenophobic attitudes and anti-immigrant hostilities? Data from the Harvard Longitudinal Immigrant Student Adaptation study reveal that discrimination and anti-immigrant sentiment were recurring concerns discussed by many youths. A 13-year-old Chinese girl reported, "Americans discriminate. They treat you badly because you are Chinese or Black. I hate this most." "They treat immigrants like animals. There are a lot of racist people," said a 13-year-old Mexican girl. All the participants were asked to complete the sentence "Most Americans think [people from my country] are _____" (for example, Haitian children were asked, "Most Americans think Haitians are _____"; Mexican children were asked, "Most Americans think Mexicans are _____"; and so forth). Fully 65% of our respondents had negative associations, such as:

Most Americans think that we are garbage. (14-year-old Dominican boy)

Most Americans think that we are members of gangs. (9-year-old Central American girl)

Most Americans think that we are lazy, gangsters, drug-addicts that only come to take their jobs away. (14-year-old Mexican boy)

Immigrant youth of color indeed perceive that many in the dominant culture do not like them or welcome them. Psychologically, what do adolescents do with this reception? Are these attitudes of the host culture internalized, denied, or resisted?

Winnicott (1958) suggests that the child's sense of self is profoundly shaped by the reflections mirrored back to her by significant others. Indeed, all human beings no matter their age are dependent upon the reflection of themselves mirrored by others. "Others" include not just the mother (Winnicott's focus) but also nonparental relatives, adult caretakers, siblings, teachers, peers, employers, people on the street, and even the media. If the reflected image is generally positive, the individual (adult or child) will be able to feel that she is worthwhile and competent. If the reflection is generally negative, it is extremely difficult to maintain an unblemished sense of self-worth.

At times, the reflection can be a positive distortion. In such a situation, the response to the individual may be out of proportion to his actual contribution or achievements. In the most benign case, positive expectations can be an asset. The classic "Pygmalion in the classroom" study, in which teachers were told that certain students were brighter than others (on the basis of the experimenter randomly assigning some children that designation, unsubstantiated in fact), the teachers treated the children more positively and assigned them higher grades (Rosenthal & Jacobson, 1968). It is possible that some immigrant students, such as Asians, benefit somewhat from positive expectations of their competence as a result of being members of a "model minority" (Takaki, 1989). There is no doubt, however, that this comes at the cost of constantly having to live up to a standard of perfection (Lee, 1990).

We are more concerned, however, with negative distortions. What happens to youths who receive mirroring on the societal level that is predominantly negative and hostile? Du Bois (1986) beautifully articulated this challenge of what he termed "double-consciousness": a "sense of always looking at one's self through the eyes of others, of measuring one's soul by the tape of a world that looks on in amused contempt and pity" (pp. 364–365). If the expectations are of sloth, irresponsibility, low intelligence, and even danger, the outcome can be toxic. If these reflections are received in a number of mirrors, including the media, the classroom, and the street, the outcome is devastating.

Even when parents provide positive mirroring, it is often insufficient to compensate for the distorted reflections that children encounter in their daily lives. In some cases, the immigrant parent is considered out of touch with the reality in the new culture. Although parents' opinions may be considered valid, they may not be enough to compensate for the intensity and frequency of the distortions of the "house of mirrors" immigrant children of color encounter in their everyday lives.

What meanings do young people construct, and how do they respond? One possible pathway is for youth to become resigned to the negative reflections, leading to hopelessness and self-depreciation that may in turn result in low aspirations and self-defeating behaviors. The general affect associated with this pathway is one of depression and passivity. In this scenario, the child is likely to respond with self-doubt and shame, setting low aspirations in a kind of self-fulfilling prophecy: "They're probably right. I'll never be able to do it." Other youths mobilize to resist the mirrors and injustices they encounter. Here we differentiate between two types of resistance. The first is a project infused with hope, a sense of justice, and a faith in a better tomorrow. The other form of resistance occurs when the child is eventually overcome by alienation leading to anomie, hopelessness, and a nihilistic view of the future. In this latter case, young people may actively resist the reflections they encounter but are unable to maintain hope for change or a better future. Without hope, the resulting anger and compensatory self-aggrandizement may lead to acting-out behaviors, including the kinds of dystopic cultural practices typically associated with gang membership. For these youths, the response is one of "If you think I'm bad, let me show you just how bad I can be."

The social trajectories of youth are more promising for those who are actively able to maintain and cultivate a sense of hope for the future. Whether they are resigned, oblivious, or resistant to the reflections in the social mirror, those who are able to maintain hope are in fundamental ways partially inoculated to the toxicity they encounter. These youths are better able to maintain a sense of pride and preserved self-esteem. In these circumstances, their energies are freed and mobilized in the service of day-to-day coping. Some not only become focused on their own advancement but also harness their energies in the service of their communities by volunteering to help others, acting as role models, or actively advocating and mobilizing for social change. In this scenario, youths respond to the negative social mirror by being goaded into "I'll show you I can make it in spite of what you think of me."

Theoretical and empirical research suggest that exposure to a negative social mirror can adversely affect academic engagement. Social psychologist Steele (1997) demonstrated that under the stress of "identity threats," performance goes down on a variety of academic tasks. He maintains that when negative stereotypes about one's group prevail, "members of these groups can fear being reduced to the stereotype" (p. 614). Under such circumstances, self-handicapping goes up. This "threat in the air" has both an immediate effect on the specific situation that evokes the stereotype threat and a cumulative erosive effect as events that evoke the threat continually occur. Steele argues that stereotype threat shapes both intellectual performance and intellectual identity.

Data from a variety of studies demonstrate that immigrant students enter U.S. schools with highly positive attitudes toward education (Fuligni, 1997; Kao & Tienda, 1995; S. Steinberg et al., 1996; Suárez-Orozco & Suárez-Orozco, 2001). But these attitudes cannot be maintained in a climate of insurmountable obstacles, cultural hostility, identity threats, and psychological disparagement; under such circumstances most youths will not continue to invest in school as an avenue for status mobility. Indeed, facing toxic levels of cultural violence, children will tend to invest significant amounts of their psychic energy to "defend" against these assaults on their sense of self.

A number of studies in recent years have demonstrated a link between racial and ethnic identity pathways and academic outcomes (Gibson, 1988; Matute-Bianchi, 1991; Ogbu & Herbert, 1998; Suárez-Orozco & Suárez-Orozco, 2001; Waters, 1997). These studies suggest a pattern that implies that those who forge bicultural identities are more successful academically. As our research unfolds, we have come to believe that ethnic identity has in some ways been confounded with academic identity. Methodologically, future research should strive to assess each of these dimensions separately before searching for patterns of covariance.

In our extensive fieldwork with the Harvard Longitudinal Immigrant Student Adaptation study, we have found a variety of ethnic identities. Some immigrant-origin youth develop ethnic flight identity whereby they embrace the dominant culture while rejecting their own culture and language. Others maintain a co-ethnic focus, remaining largely involved in their group of origin. Many who maintain a co-ethnic focus live in highly segregated neighborhoods and have limited exposure to the dominant culture. Others with a co-ethnic identity actively reject the dominant culture (after being rejected by it), developing an adversarial posture. Still others, who live in segregated neighborhoods in which they have little contact with the dominant culture coupled with sustained negative interactions with African Americans, develop a hyperethnic identity in reaction to African American youth culture. The most adaptive ethnic identity involves forging a transcultural sense of self. In such cases, the individual develops the instrumental competencies of the new culture while maintaining expressive contact with the culture of origin. Such individuals move fluidly between cultures, creatively code-switching according to circumstance. Individuals with transcultural identities may move between two cultures (e.g., Mexican and American) or among three or more (e.g., Dominican, American mainstream, African American) according to circumstances. Here exposure and imposed identities play critical roles.

Turning to academic identities, preliminary analyses of longitudinal data also indicate emerging patterns. At one end of the continuum, we find immigrant students who are highly engaged in the academic enterprise and who view schooling as central to their sense of self. At the other end of the continuum are students who are completely disengaged from their schooling; such students simply do not view schooling as playing a critical role in their lives and engage in very few of the tasks required in school. Some students fall somewhere on this spectrum across subjects, while others demonstrate subject-specific patterns in which they are highly engaged in some courses and not in others. For some students, engaged schooling identities are sustained across time, while with others there may be significant downward or upward trajectories.

We are systematically assessing these separate dimensions of ethnic identity and academic identity through a combination of responses to structured questionnaires, sentence completion tests, ethnographic observations, behavioral checklists completed by teachers, and evaluations of report cards. In the final stage of analysis, we will systematically search for patterns of covariance between these two dimensions of identity. Emerging findings reveal that a critical mediating variables for identity formation and academic engagement are the networks of relations available to the immigrant student.

SOCIAL CONTEXTS OF LEARNING

Role of Social Relations

The presence of a healthy social support network has long been regarded to be a key mediator to stress and a predictor of well-being for adults and children alike (Cobb, 1976; Cohen & Syme, 1985). Interpersonal relationships perform a number of functions. Social companionship, a basic human need, serves to maintain and enhance self-esteem as well as provide acceptance and approval (Wills, 1985). Instrumental social support gives individuals and their families tangible aid (such as running an errand or making a loan) as well as guidance and advice (including information, job, and housing leads). These instrumental supports are particularly critical for disoriented immigrant newcomers. Quite predictably, a well-functioning social support network is closely linked to better adjustment (Wills, 1985).

Affiliative Motivations

Particularly for Latino students, social relations also play a critical role in initiating and sustaining motivations. This form of motivation stands in sharp contrast with classic conceptualizations of achievement motivation developed on White mainstream populations. McClelland and his associates at Harvard conducted a series of pioneering studies of achievement motivation among White American students in the 1950s (McClelland, Atkinson, Clark, & Lowell, 1953). Their studies suggested that achievement motivation flourishes when youngsters are trained to become independent from their families. These studies suggested that for White American students, achievement-oriented individuals were motivated in the context of attempting to gain independence from the family. Hence, according to this model, achievement motivation and individualism are highly correlated. In contrast, we have found in the course of several studies that successful Latino students are typically highly motivated to achieve *for* their families (M. Suárez-Orozco, 1989; Suárez-Orozco & Suárez-Orozco, 1995, 2001). Using a variety of methodologies (interviews, ethnographies, projective narrative techniques, and others), we have found that a principal stated motivation for being successful academically is a desire to help family and community. Further, we have found that Latino students (more so than for Chinese or Haitian students) perceive that receiving the help of others is critical to their success (Suárez-Orozco, Suárez-Orozco, & Todorova, in press).

The Family

In all social systems, the family is a basic structural unit. Indeed, the family is the most significant gravitational field in the lives of young people. Family cohesion and the maintenance of a well-functioning system of supervision, authority, and mutuality are perhaps the most powerful factors in shaping the well-being and future outcomes of all children, Latino and non-Latino alike. Although parents play the central role in traditional two-parent nuclear mainstream American family systems, Latino families often involve a larger cast of characters. For Latino immigrant families, extended family members—godparents, aunts, uncles, older cousins, and the like—are often critical sources of tangible instrumental and emotional support.

Families can support children's schooling in a variety of ways. At a minimum, good parenting provides an emotional safe haven for children, fostering the development of a healthy sense of belonging, self-esteem, and emotional well-being. Wentzel (1999) deconstructs the key elements of parental support for academic adjustment. She notes that parents concretely support educational outcomes by maintaining a value of education and establishing a standard of expectations regarding the minimum acceptable standard for grades or for level of educational pursuit. Wentzel also argues that parents are crucial in their ability to make educational opportunities and resources available. Further, parents establish expectations about appropriate behaviors and attitudes vis-à-vis school authorities and peer interactions. Lastly, by actively scaffolding their children as they complete assignments, parents can offer role modeling in how to be successful in school.

Parents with higher educational levels are able to provide a variety of resources to their children that place them at a clear advantage. As noted earlier, there is a direct relationship between parental education and performance on achievement tests, grades, and dropping out (Bourdieu & Passeron, 1977; Jencks et al., 1972; Madaus & Clarke, 1998). Their children tend to enter school with more sophisticated vocabularies, higher literacy levels, and computer skills. Further, better educated parents know firsthand how to play the academic game, allowing them to actively scaffold homework assignments, advocate for their children with teachers, and provide private SAT instruction, as well as access college pathway information and the like (Suárez-Orozco & Suárez-Orozco, 2001).

Latino parents who work long hours and may have limited schooling are at a distinct disadvantage in this regard. Stanton-Salazar (2001) found that although low-income Mexican immigrant parents highly valued educational success for their children, few of them actually understood their children's school experiences or the role they as parents had in facilitating their children's access to postsecondary education. Although Latino parents generally have high educational aspirations for their children's education, they are often unable to tangibly support their children in ways that are congruent with American cultural models and expectations. Many come from traditions that revere school authorities and expect parents to keep a distance from the day-to-day workings of their child's education. This stands in sharp contrast to U.S. expectations of parental involvement, whereby "good" parents are expected to volunteer in the classroom or as fundraisers, actively help with parent-child homework projects, and advocate for their children. Most Latino immigrant parents consider it presumptuous to impose their expectations onto teachers. Unfortunately, teachers often interpret this distance and respect as lack of caring on the parent's part and may judge their children accordingly (Lopez, 2002).

Community Relationships

Because no family is an island, its cohesion and functioning are enhanced when the family is part of a larger community displaying effective forms of what Felton Earls (1997) has termed "community agency." Likewise, cultural psychologist George De Vos (1992) has argued that culturally constituted patterns of community cohesion and supervision can "immunize" immigrant youth from the more toxic elements in their new settings. This line of research suggests that when communities are cohesive and when adults within the community can monitor youngsters' activities, they will tend to do better. Earls found that children who live in such communities are less likely to be involved with gangs and delinquency and are more focused on their academic pursuits.

Our ethnographic data suggest the crucial role of networks of social relations extending beyond the family in the successful adjustment of immigrant youth. In nearly every story of immigrant success, there is a caring adult who took an interest in the child and became actively engaged in her life. Connections with nonparent adults—a community leader, a teacher, a member of the church, a coach—are important in the academic and social adaptation of Latino adolescents (Hamilton & Darling, 1996; Lynch & Cicchetti, 1997; Pianta, 1999; Roeser & Eccles, 1998; Rhodes, 2002; Stanton-Salazar, 2001). These youngsters are often undergoing profound shifts in their sense of self and are struggling to negotiate changing circumstances in relationships with their parents and peers (Rhodes, 2002). Protective relationships with nonparent adults can provide Latino youth with compensatory attachments, safe contexts for learning new cultural norms and practices, and information that is vital to success in school (Roffman, Suarez-Orozco, & Rhodes, 2003).

The support of nonparental adults, through either volunteer mentoring programs or community youth-serving agencies, can prove invaluable in minimizing the risks associated with the stresses of immigration and transculturation, as well as in facilitating the vicissitudes of identity formation and transformation. Mentors and supportive adults in community organizations and schools can complement the efforts of parents to guide Latino youth through adolescence. Rather than supplanting the role of parents, these nonparental adults can support parents' efforts as the entire family attempts the difficult task of adapting to life in a new and often hostile country (Roffman et al., 2003).

Community-based youth organizations provide structured activities and settings in which to interact with peers while under the supervision of adult staff. These organizations can represent an important form of social capital at work in immigrant communities (Furstenberg & Cherlin, 1991). The presence of social resources in a family, a school, agency, or neighborhood engenders positive interactions between individuals and contributes to positive outcomes (Furstenberg & Cherlin, 1991; Stevenson & Shin-Ying, 1990). Youth-serving organizations and individuals, much like ethnic-owned businesses and family networks, enrich immigrant communities and foster healthy development among its youth through the support they provide to parents and families (Nevarez-La Torre, 1997).

At the most basic level, participation in a community youth program translates into out-of-school time that is not spent in isolation, unsupervised, or on the streets with one's peers. These programs are often seen by participants as a safe haven from the pressures of the street or as a "second home"—a place where youths feel comfortable expressing themselves and letting down their guard (Hirsch et al., 2000; Villaruel & Lerner, 1994). The existence of a setting in which youngsters can congregate and participate in recreational activities during their out-of-school hours represents an important option as they react to the lack of supervision while parents are at work or are emotionally unavailable. Instead of having to stay home to care for younger siblings or seek an alternate family structure in peer groups or street gangs, families can choose for their adolescents to attend a community center or club. This option allows youths to feel supervised by caring adults, while at the same time preserving their freedom to choose activities and interact with peers, an autonomy that becomes more and more important as they grow older (Beck, 1999; Bryant, 1989). Parents can feel that their children are in a safe setting, without feeling threatened by the intensity of a one-on-one relationship with a volunteer mentor.

The adults who work in community programs are often equipped to provide tutoring, educational guidance, advice about the college application process, and job search assistance, information often inaccessible to immigrant youth whose parents have not navigated the academic system in the United States and who attend schools with few guidance counselors. Youth programs may be a welcome alternative to the environment in many schools serving disadvantaged communities where immigrant youth may not feel comfortable or welcome. This is often the case among low-income Latino immigrants, who report feeling discriminated against by their teachers, who are placed disproportionately into lower-track and special needs classes, and who cite a sense of rejection by the school as an important reason for dropping out (García, Wilkinson, & Ortiz, 1995; Katz, 1999). Valenzuela (1999) exposed the disrespect Mexican and Mexican American high school students experience in schools where their identities are devalued or are ignored, where they are alienated from teachers and one another, and where feelings of not being cared about are rampant. Staff members at community youth-serving agencies often report that they believe an important part of their role is the reversal of inner-city schools' and teachers' negative impact on the educational trajectories and academic achievement of minority youth (McLaughlin, Irby, & Langman, 1994).

In addition to the provision of safety and the opportunity for tutoring and other forms of direct academic enrichments, many community youth workers can serve as role models for immigrant students embroiled in the difficult process of identity development within a bicultural context. Staff members can create an atmosphere in an after-school context where Latino youth feel comfortable exploring the intersections between their multiple identities: immigrant, Latino, Latino American, and the like (Camino, 1994). With supportive staff to guide them, through role modeling, and through simply creating a norm of self-expression, joint ownership, and the communal responsibility and fictive kinship that are associated with their Latino background, youths can find ways to fuse various parts of their identities, expressing each at different times and for different purposes. Similarly, Cooper, Denner, and Lopez (1999) express the difficulties inherent in Mexican immigrant children's transitions from elementary to middle school, describing ways in which community program staff can serve as "culture brokers" for youth. These culture brokers act as intermediary figures "bridging" the disparate norms that are in place in children's homes and those in place at school (Heath, 1994). Support from figures such as these youth workers increases the chances of academic success among Latino youth entering middle school and encountering numerous challenges to their newly forming bicultural identities.

"Urban sanctuaries" focus on the potential of youth and operate in a respectful and informal manner (McLaughlin et al., 1994). The staff at these community-based youth programs fills many gaps that exist for low-income minority individuals and their children. The benefits of belonging to a caring organization that can perform such a bridging function are particularly salient for many immigrant youths, whose most challenging tasks involve the reconciliation of multiple cultures and value systems, against a backdrop that is often characterized by hostility. Through the provision of activities, instruction, or supervised time to interact with peers, these programs are an opportunity for young people who might not have access to mentoring programs, or for whom (for reasons discussed below) a one-on-one mentoring relationship might not be appropriate, to form supportive relationships with caring adults.

Mentoring Relationships

Mentoring relationships foster a one-on-one relationship between an older, more experienced adult and an unrelated, younger protégé. In these relationships, an adult provides guidance and encouragement aimed at developing the competence and character of the protégé. Over time, a special bond of mutual respect, affection, and loyalty may develop, which facilitates the protégé's transition into adulthood (Hamilton & Darling, 1989; Rhodes, 2002). Youth in successful mentoring relationships have been found to benefit in terms of improved academics, healthier family and peer relationships, and reduced incidence of substance abuse and aggressive behavior (Grossman & Tierney, 1998; Rhodes, 2002).

Formal or informal mentoring relationships may have special implications for Latino immigrant youth. During the course of migration, loved ones are often separated from one another and significant attachments are ruptured. Mentoring relationships can give immigrant youth an opportunity to be involved in reparative relationships engendering new significant attachments. Since immigrant adolescents' parents and other adult relatives may be unavailable due to long work hours or emotional distress, the guidance and affection of a mentor may help to fill the void created by parental absence. The mentor, as an adult who has been in the United States longer than the protégé, can also offer information about and exposure to American cultural and educational institutions, and help as the adolescent negotiates developmental transitions. If the mentor is of the same ethnic background as the protégé, he or she can interpret the rules of engagement of the new culture to parents and consequently help to attenuate cultural rigidities. Furthermore, bicultural mentors can serve as role models in the challenging process of developing a bicultural identity, exemplifying the ways in which elements of the ethnic identity can be preserved and celebrated even as features of the more mainstream culture of the United States are incorporated into youths' lives.

Although there are many benefits associated with mentoring for the development of Latino youth, there are also ways in which mentoring may not be ideally suited to the needs of some families. First, an intense one-on-one relationship with another adult may represent a source of discomfort for some immigrant parents in particular, who may feel threatened by the prospect of a nonrelative adult usurping parental authority, or who may be mistrustful of the intentions of an adult from outside the family who will be learning intimate family information through his or her relationship with a child (Roffman et al., 2003). Second, many of the volunteers who come into adolescents' lives are from different ethnic and socioeconomic backgrounds than the youth they are mentoring. Such differences can have implications for immigrant youths, who may face language barriers if matched with a mentor who only speaks English, and who may not receive the support they need related to the formation of a bicultural identity from a mentor who identifies too closely with the mainstream culture. Third, mentoring relationships are not suitable for all young people. Adolescents who are experiencing psychological, emotional, or behavioral distress may have difficulty engaging in a mentoring relationship. Further, older youths may be more peer-oriented than younger children and hence less amenable to becoming invested in a relationship that requires spending significant amounts of time alone with an adult (Rhodes, 2002).

Finally, not all mentoring relationships are successful; an estimated half of all matches dissolve after only a few months (Freedman, 1993; Roffman et al., 2003; Styles &

Morrow, 1992). These premature terminations may occur if a child's emotional needs are too great, if a mentor is not able to spend enough time with the protégé to build up the necessary trust and mutual respect, or if for some other reason the two individuals do not forge a strong connection. When this occurs, the resulting feelings of rejection and loss of another adult support figure can be devastating for the adolescent (Rhodes, 2002; Roffman et al., 2003), exacerbating feelings of loss and rejection engendered by previously ruptured attachments. This type of loss may be particularly destructive for an immigrant adolescent, who has likely already experienced the loss of family members and cherished adults during the difficult process of migration (Suárez-Orozco & Suárez-Orozco, 2001). For these reasons, immigrant youth are often better served when they form mentoring relationships with nonparental adults they encounter in programs oriented around activities, thereby eliminating some of the pressures involved in more intensive mentoring programs.

Peer Relationships

Peers can also provide important emotional sustenance to support the development of significant psychosocial competencies in young people (Selman, Levitt, & Schultz, 1997). In a variety of ways, peers can specifically serve to support *or* detract from academic engagement (Berndt, 1999). By valuing (or devaluing) certain academic outcomes and by modeling specific academic behaviors, peers establish the "norms" of academic engagement (Berndt, 1999; Ogbu & Herbert, 1998; Steinberg et al., 1996). Peers may further support academic engagements through conversations and discussions where ideas are exchanged (Berndt, 1999; Vygotsky, 1978). Peers can tangibly support academic engagement by clarifying readings or lectures, helping one another in completing homework assignments, and exchanging information (about SATs, helpful tutors, volunteer positions, and other college pathway knowledge). Because, however, immigrant youth often attend highly segregated schools in low-income communities (Orfield, 1998), they may have limited access to knowledgeable networks of peers.

Taken together, these networks of relationships can make a significant difference in Latino youths' lives. They can serve to help Latino youth develop healthy bicultural identities, engender motivation, and provide specific information about how to successfully navigate schooling pathways. When successful, these relationships help Latino youth and their families overcome some of the barriers associated with poverty and discrimination that prevent full participation in the new country's economic and cultural life (Stanton-Salazar, 2001; Valenzuela, 1999).

CONCLUDING THOUGHTS

Latinos are now the largest minority group in U.S. schools. The majority of them are immigrants or the children of immigrants. Like other immigrants, Latinos share an optimism and hope for the future that must be cultivated and treasured; they come to see schooling as the key to a better tomorrow. Tragically, over time Latino immigrant youngsters—especially those enrolling in highly impoverished and deeply segregated schools—face negative odds and uncertain prospects. Too many Latino youngsters are leaving our schools without developing and mastering the kinds of higher-order skills needed in today's global economy and society. The future of the United States will in no small measure be tied to the fortunes of all young Americans. Because Latinos, immigrant and U.S.-born, are an increasing part of the American future, harnessing their energy, optimism, and faith in the future is in everyone's interest. Doing so is arguably one of the most important challenges for our country's democratic promise.

References

Appiah, A., & Gutmann, A. (1998). *Color conscious: The political morality of race.* Princeton, NJ: Princeton University Press.

Bailey, B. H. (2001). Dominican-American ethnic/racial identities and United States social categories. *International Migration Review, 35*(3), 677–708.

Bandura, A. (1994). *Self-efficacy: The exercise of control.* New York: Freeman.

Beck, E. L. (1999). Prevention and intervention programming: Lessons from an after-school program. *Urban Review, 31*(1), 107–124.

Beiser, M., Dion, R., Gotowiec, A., Hyman, I., & Vu, N. (1995, March). Immigrant and refugee children in Canada. *Canadian Journal of Psychiatry, 40,* 67–72.

Berndt, T. J. (1999). Friends' influence on students' adjustment to school. *Educational Psychologist, 34*(1), 15–28.

Borkowski, J., & Thorpe, P. K. (1994). Self-regulation and motivation: A life-span perspective on underachievement. In D. H. Schunk & B. J. Zimmerman (Eds.), *Self-regulation of learning and performance.* Hillsdale, NJ: Erlbaum.

Bourdieu, P., & Passeron, J. (1977). *Reproduction in education, society and culture.* Beverly Hills, CA: Sage.

Bracey, G. (2000). *High stakes testing* (Education Policy Project, CERAI-00–32). Milwaukee: University of Wisconsin-Milwaukee, Center for Education Research, Analysis, and Innovation.

Brown, R., Wyn, R., Yu, H., Valenzuela, A., & Dong, L. (1998). Access to health insurance and health care for Mexican American children in immigrant families. In M. M. Suárez-Orozco (Ed.), *Crossings: Mexican immigration in interdisciplinary perspective*. Cambridge, MA: David Rockefeller Center for Latin American Studies/Harvard University Press.

Bryant, B. K. (1989). The need for support in relation to the need for autonomy. In D. Belle (Ed.), *Children's social networks and social supports* (pp. 332–351). New York: Wiley.

Camino, L. A. (1994). Refugee adolescents and their changing identities. In L. A. Camino & R. M. Krulfeld (Eds.), *Reconstructing lives, recapturing meaning: Refugee identity, gender, and culture change* (pp. 29–56). Amsterdam, Netherlands: Gordon & Breach.

Capps, R. (2001). *Hardship among children of immigrants: Findings from the 1999 National Survey of America's families*. Washington, DC: Urban Institute.

Cobb, S. (1976). Social support as a moderator of life stress. *Psychosomatic Medicine, 38*(5), 300–314.

Cohen, S., & Syme, S. L. (1985). Issues in the study and application of social support. In S. Cohen & S. L. Syme (Eds.), *Social support and health* (pp. 3–22). Orlando, FL: Academic Press.

Collier, M. (1998). *Cultures of violence in Miami-Dade public schools*. Miami: Florida International University.

Conchas, G. Q. (2001). Structuring failure and success: Understanding the variability in Latino school engagement. *Harvard Educational Review, 71*(3), 475–504.

Cooper, C. R., Denner, J., & Lopez, E. M. (1999). Cultural brokers: Helping Latino children on pathways toward success. *The Future of Children, 9*(2), 51–57.

Corno, L. (1993). The best laid plans: Modern conceptions of volition and educational research. *Educational Researcher, 22,* 14–22.

Deardorff, K. E., & Blumerman, L. M. (2001, December). *Evaluating components of international migration: Estimates of the foreign-born population by migrant status in 2000*. (Population Division Working Paper no. 58). Washington, DC: U.S. Census Bureau.

De Vos, G. (1992). The passing of passing. In G. De Vos (Ed.), *Social cohesion and alienation: Minorities in the United States and Japan*. Boulder, CO: Westview Press.

De Vos, G., & Suárez-Orozco, M. (1990). *Status inequality: The self in culture*. Newbury Park: CA: Sage.

Dewey, J. (1913). *Interest and effort in education*. Boston: Riverside Press.

DuBois, W.E.B. (1986). *The souls of Black folks*. In N. Huggins (Ed.), *W.E.B. DuBois: Writings* (pp. 357–547). New York: Library of America.

Earls, F. (1997, Nov.–Dec.). Tighter, safer, neighborhoods. *Harvard Magazine*, 14–15.

Eccles, J. S., Wigfield, A., & Schiefele, U. (1998). Motivation to succeed. In W. Damon & N. Eisenberg (Eds.), *Handbook of child psychology* (5th ed., Vol. 3, pp. 1017–1095). New York: Wiley.

ERIC. (1991, June). *Highly mobile students: Educational problems and possible solutions*. (ED338745, ERIC/CUE Digest, No. 73). (www.ed.gov/databases/ERIC_Digests/ed338745.html)

Erikson, E. (1968). *Identity: Youth and crisis*. New York: Norton.

Espenshade, T. M. B. (1998). Immigration and public opinion. In M. M. Suárez-Orozco (Ed.), *Crossings: Mexican immigration in interdisciplinary perspective*. Cambridge, MA: David Rockefeller Center for Latin American Studies.

Freedman, M. (1993). *The kindness of strangers: Adult mentors, urban youth, and the new volunteerism*. San Francisco: Jossey-Bass.

Fuligni, A. (1997). The academic achievement of adolescents from immigrant families: The roles of family background, attitudes, and behavior. *Child Development, 69*(2), 351–363.

Furstenberg, F. F. J., & Cherlin, A. J. (1991). *Divided families: What happens to children when parents part*. Cambridge, MA: Harvard University Press.

García, S. B., Wilkinson, C. Y., & Ortiz, A. A. (1995). Enhancing achievement for language minority students: Classroom, school and family contexts. *Education and Urban Society, 27*(4), 441–462.

Gastón Institute for Latino Community Development and Public Policy. (2001, Summer). New study finds few Latinos prepared for MCAS. *Newsletter of the Mauricio Gastón Institute for Latino Community Development and Public Policy*.

Gibson, M. A. (1988). *Accommodation without assimilation: Sikh immigrants in an American high school*. Ithaca, NY: Cornell University Press.

Grossman, J. B., & Tierney, J. P. (1998). Does mentoring work? An impact study of the Big Brothers/Big Sisters Program. *Evaluation Review, 22,* 403–426.

Hamilton, S. F., & Darling, N. (1989). Mentors in adolescents' lives. In K. Hurrelmann (Ed.), *The social world of adolescents: International perspectives*. Berlin: Walter de Gruyter.

Hamilton, S. F., & Darling, N. (1996). Mentors in adolescents' lives. In K. Hurrelmann & S. F. Hamilton (Eds.), *Social problems and social contexts in adolescence: Perspectives across boundaries* (pp. 199–215). New York: Aldine D. Gruyter.

Heath, S. B. (1994). The project of learning from the inner-city youth perspective. *New Directions for Child Development, 63,* 25–34.

Hernández, D., & Charney, E. (Eds.). (1998). *From generation to generation: The health and well-being of children of immigrant families*. Washington, D.C.: National Academy Press.

Hirsch, B. J., Roffman, J. G., Deutsch, N. L., Flynn, C., Loder, T. L., & Pagano, M. E. (2000). Inner-city youth development programs: Strengthening programs for adolescent girls. *Journal of Early Adolescence, 20*(2), 210–230.

Huang, G. (1993, January). *Health problems among migrant farmworkers' children in the U.S.* (ED357907, ERIC Digests. Available: www.ed.gov/databases/ERIC_Digests/ed357907.html.

Jencks, C., Smith, M., Acland, H., Bane, M. J., Cohen, D., & Ginits, H., et al. (1972). *Inequality: A reassessment of the effect of family and schooling in America*. New York: Basic Books.

Jordan, W. J. (1999). Black high school students' participation in school-sponsored sports activities: Effects on school engagement and achievement. *Journal of Negro Education, 68*(1), 54–71.

Kao, G., & Tienda, M. (1995). Optimism and achievement: The educational performance of immigrant youth. *Social Science Quarterly, 76*(1), 1–19.

Katz, S. R. (1999). Teaching in tensions: Latino immigrant youth, their teachers and the structures of schooling. *Teachers College Record, 100*(4), 809–840.

Kaufman, P., Alt, M. N., & Chapman, C. D. (2001, November). *Dropout rates in the United States: 2000* (NCES 2002–114). Washington DC: National Center for Education Statistics.

Kennedy, R. (2001). Racial trends in the administration of criminal justice. In N. J. Smelser, W. J. Wilson, & F. Mitchell (Eds.), *America becoming: Racial trends and their consequences* (Vol. 2, pp. 1–20). Washington, DC: National Academy Press.

Lee, F. R. (1990, Mar. 20). "Model minority" label taxes Asian youth. *New York Times,* p. B1.

Levitt, P. (1996). *Immigration and transnationalism* (paper presented). Cambridge, MA: Harvard Graduate School of Education.

Linn, R. (2000). Testing and accountability. *Educational Researcher, 29*(2), 4–17.

Lopez, N. (2002). *Hopeful girls, troubled boys: Race and gender disparity in urban education.* New York: Routledge.

Luthar, S. (1999). *Poverty and children's adjustment.* Thousand Oaks, CA: Sage.

Lynch, M., & Cicchetti, D. (1997). Children's relationships with adults and peers: An examination of elementary and junior high school students. *Journal of School Psychology, 35,* 81–99.

Madaus, G., & Clarke, M. (1998, Dec. 4). *The adverse impact of high stakes testing on minority students: Evidence from 100 years of test data.* Paper presented at the conference on the Civil Rights Implications of High Stakes K-12 Testing, New York.

Mandel, H. P., & Marcus, S. I. (1988). *The psychology of underachievement: Differential diagnosis and differential treatment.* New York: Wiley.

Martin, P. (1994, November). *Migrant farmworkers and their children* (ED376997, ERIC Digests). Available: www.ed.gov/databases/ERIC_Digests/ed376997.html.

Massey, D., & Denton, N. (1993). *American apartheid.* Cambridge, MA: Harvard University Press.

Matute-Bianchi, M. E. (1991). Situational ethnicity and patterns of school performance among immigrant and non-immigrant Mexican-descent students. In M. A. Gibson & J. Ogbu (Eds.), *Minority status and schooling: A comparative study of immigrant and involuntary minorities* (pp. 205–247). New York: Garland.

McClelland, D. J., Atkinson, J. W., Clark, R. H., & Lowell, E. L. (1953). *The achievement motive.* New York: Appleton-Century-Crofts.

McLaughlin, M., Irby, M., & Langman, J. (1994). *Urban sanctuaries: Neighborhood organizations in the lives and futures of inner-city youth.* San Francisco: Jossey-Bass.

Meier, K., & Stewart, J. (1991). *The politics of Hispanic education.* Albany: State University of New York Press.

Morse, S. C., & Ludovina, F. S. (1999, September). *Responding to undocumented children in the schools* (EDO-RC-99-1). ERIC Digests. Available: www.ed.gov/databases/ERIC_Digests/ed433172.html.

Natriello, G., & Pallas, A. M. (1998, December 4). *The development and impact of high stakes testing.* Paper presented at the Conference on the Civil Rights Implication of High Stakes K-12 Testing, New York.

Nelson-Le Gall, S., & Jones, E. (1990). Cognitive-motivational influences on task-related help-seeking behavior of Black children. *Child Development, 61,* 581–589.

Nevarez-La Torre, A. A. (1997). Influencing Latino education: Church-based community programs. *Education and Urban Society, 30*(1), 58–74.

Newman, R. S., & Goldin, L. (1990). Children's reluctance to seek help with schoolwork. *Journal of Educational Psychology, 82,* 92–100.

Ogbu, J. U. (1995). *Community forces and minority educational strategies—A comparative study: Final report.* Berkeley: University of California, Berkeley, Department of Anthropology.

Ogbu, J. U., & Herbert, S. (1998). Voluntary & involuntary minorities: A cultural-ecological theory of school performance with some implications for education. *Anthropology and Education Quarterly, 29,* 155–188.

Olsen, L. (1997, May). *Made in America: Immigrant students in our public schools.* New York: New Press.

Orfield, G. (1995). *Latinos in education: Recent trends* (Paper presented). Cambridge, MA: Harvard Graduate School of Education.

Orfield, G. (1998). The education of Mexican immigrant children: A commentary. In M. M. Suárez-Orozco (Ed.), *Crossings: Mexican immigration in interdisciplinary perspective.* Cambridge, MA: David Rockefeller Center for Latin American Studies/Harvard University Press.

Orfield, G. (2002). Commentary. In M. Suárez-Orozco & M. Páez (Eds.), *Latinos: Remaking America* (pp. 389–297). Berkeley: University of California Press.

Orfield, G., & Yun, J. T. (1999). *Resegregation in American schools.* Cambridge, MA: Harvard University, Civil Rights Project.

Páez, M. (2001). *Language and the immigrant child: Predicting English language proficiency for Chinese, Dominican, and Haitian students.* Cambridge, MA: Harvard Graduate School of Education.

Phinney, J. (1990). Ethnic identity in adolescents and adults: A review of the literature. *Psychological Bulletin, 108*(3), 499–514.

Pianta, R. C. (1999). *Enhancing relationships between children and teachers.* Washington, DC: American Psychological Association.

Pierson, L. H., & Connell, J. P. (1992). Effect of grade retention on self-system processes, school engagement, and academic performance. *Journal of Educational Psychology, 84*(3), 300–307.

Portes, A. (1996). Children of immigrants: Segmented assimilation and its determinants. In A. Portes (Ed.), *The economic sociology of immigration: Essays on networks, ethnicity, and entrepreneurship* (pp. 248–280). New York: Russell Sage Foundation.

Portes, A., & Rumbaut, R. G. (2001). *Legacies: The story of the second generation.* Berkeley: University of California Press.

President's Advisory Commission on Educational Excellence for Hispanic American Education. (1996). *Our nation on the fault line: Hispanic American education.* Washington, DC: Author.

Rhodes, J. E. (2002). *Stand by me: The risks and rewards of youth mentoring relationships.* Cambridge, MA: Harvard University Press.

Roeser, R. W., & Eccles, J. S. (1998). Adolescents' perception of middle school: Relation to longitudinal changes in academic and psychological adjustment. *Journal of Research on Adolescence, 8*(1), 123–158.

Roffman, J., Suárez-Orozco, C., & Rhodes, J. (2003). Facilitating positive development in immigrant youth: The role of mentors and community organizations. In F. Villaruel, D. Perkins, L. Borden, & J. Keith (Eds.), *Community youth development: Programs, policies, and practices* (pp. 90–117). Thousand Oaks, CA: Sage.

Rosenthal, R., & Jacobson, L. (1968). *Pygmalion in the classroom: Teacher expectations and pupil intellectual development.* New York: Holt, Rinehart and Winston.

Ruiz-de-Velasco, J., Fix, M., & Clewell, B. C. (2000). *Overlooked and underserved: Immigrant students in U.S. secondary schools.* Washington, DC: Urban Institute.

Rumbaut, R. (1995). The new Californians: Comparative research findings on the educational progress of immigrant children. In R. Rumbaut & W. Cornelius (Eds.), *California's immigrant children: Theory, research, and implications for educational policy* (pp. 17–70). San Diego, CA: Center for U.S.-Mexican Studies.

Ryan, R. M. (1992). Agency and organization: Intrinsic motivation, autonomy, and the self in psychological development. In J. Jacobs (Ed.), *Nebraska Symposium on Motivation* (Vol. 40, pp. 1–56). Lincoln: University of Nebraska Press.

Schiefele, U. (1991). Interest, learning, and motivation. *Educational Psychologist, 26,* 299–323.

Schunk, D. H. (1991). Self-efficacy and academic motivation. *Educational Psychologist, 26,* 207–231.

Selman, R. L., Levitt, M. Z., & Schultz, L. H. (1997). The friendship framework: Tools for the assessment of psychosocial development. In R. L. Selman, M. Z. Levitt, & L. H. Schultz (Eds.), *Fostering friendship: Pair therapy for treatment and prevention* (pp. 31–52). New York: Walter de Gruyter.

Stanton-Salazar, R. D. (2001). *Manufacturing hope and despair: The school and kin support networks of U.S.-Mexican youth.* New York: Teachers College Press.

Steele, C. M., & Aronson, J. (1995). Stereotype threat and the intellectual test performance of African Americans. *Journal of Personality and Social Psychology, 69*(5), 797–811.

Steele, C. (1997). A threat in the air: How stereotypes shape intellectual identity and performance. *American Psychologist, 52*(6), 613–629.

Steinberg, L., Lamborn, S. D., Dornbusch, S. M., & Darling, N. (1992). Impact of parenting practices on adolescent achievement: Authoritative parenting, school involvement, and encouragement to succeed. *Child Development, 63,* 1266–1281.

Steinberg, L., Brown, B. B., & Dornbusch, S. M. (1996). *Beyond the classroom: Why school reform has failed and what parents need to do.* New York: Simon & Schuster.

Stepick, A. (1997). *Pride against prejudice: Haitians in the United States.* Boston: Allyn & Bacon.

Stevenson, H., & Shin-Ying, L. (1990). *Contexts of achievement: A study of American, Chinese, and Japanese children.* Chicago: University of Chicago Press.

Styles, M. B., & Morrow, K. V. (1992). *Understanding how youth and elders form relationships: A study of four Linking Lifetimes programs.* (Research report). Philadelphia: Public/Private Ventures.

Suárez-Orozco, C. (2000). Identities under siege: Immigration stress and social mirroring among the children of immigrants. In A. Robben & M. Suárez-Orozco (Eds.), *Cultures under siege: Social violence & trauma.* Cambridge, England: Cambridge University Press.

Suárez-Orozco, C. (2001). Afterword: Understanding and serving the children of immigrants. *Harvard Educational Review, 71*(3), 579–589.

Suárez-Orozco, C., & Páez, M. (Eds.) (2002). *Latinos: Remaking America.* Berkeley: University of California Press.

Suárez-Orozco, C., & Suárez-Orozco, M. (1995). *Transformations: Immigration, family life, and achievement motivation among Latino adolescents.* Stanford, CA: Stanford University Press.

Suárez-Orozco, C., & Suárez-Orozco, M. (2001). *Children of immigration* (1st ed.). Cambridge, MA: Harvard University Press.

Suárez-Orozco, C., Suárez-Orozco, M., & Todorova, I. (in press). Wandering souls: Adolescent immigrant interpersonal concerns. In G. De Vos & E. De Vos (Eds.), *Narrative analysis cross culturally: The self as revealed in the Thematic Apperception Test.* Boulder, CO: Rowman & Littlefield.

Suárez-Orozco, M. (1989). *Central American refugees and U.S. high schools: A psychosocial study of motivation and achievement.* Stanford: Stanford University Press.

Suárez-Orozco, M. (2000). Everything you ever wanted to know about assimilation but were afraid to ask. *Daedalus—Journal of the American Academy of Arts and Sciences, 129*(4), 1–30.

Takaki, R. (1989). *Strangers from a different shore.* Boston: Little and Brown.

U.S. Census Bureau. (2000). *Current population reports.* Washington, DC: Author.

Valenzuela, A. (1999). *Subtractive schooling: U.S.-Mexican youth and the politics of caring.* Albany: State University of New York Press.

Vigil, J. D. (2002). *A rainbow of gangs: Street cultures in the megacity.* Austin: University of Texas Press.

Villaruel, F. A., & Lerner, R. M. (1994). *Promoting community-based programs for socialization and learning.* San Francisco: Jossey-Bass.

Vygotsky, L. S. (Ed.). (1978). *Mind in society: The development of higher psychological processes.* Cambridge, MA: Harvard University Press.

Waters, M. (1999). *Black identities: West Indian dreams and American realities.* Cambridge, MA: Harvard University Press.

Waters, M. C. (1997). Ethnic and racial identities of second-generation Black immigrants in New York City. *International Migration Review, 28*(4), 795–820.

Weiner, B. (1994). Integrating school and personal theories of achievement striving. *Review of Educational Research, 64*(4), 557–573.

Weissbourd, R. (1996). *The vulnerable child.* Reading, MA: Perseus Books.

Wentzel, K. R. (1999). Social influences and school adjustment: Commentary. *Educational Psychologist, 34*(1), 59–69.

Wick, J. W. (1990). *Technical manual and norms for School Attitudes Measure.* Chicago: American Testronics.

Wills, T. A. (1985). Supportive functions of interpersonal relationships. In S. Cohen & S. L. Syme (Eds.), *Social Support and Health* (pp. 61–82). Orlando, FL: Academic Press.

Wilson, W. (1997). *When work disappears: The world of the new urban poor.* New York: Vintage Books.

Winnicott, D. W. (1958). *Through pediatrics to psycho-analysis.* London: Hogarth Press.

Zeidner, M., & Schleyer, E. J. (1999). The effects of educational context on individual difference variables, self-perceptions of giftedness, and school attitudes in gifted adolescents. *Journal of Youth and Adolescence, 28*(6), 687–703.

Zimbardo, P., & Haney, C. (1998). The past and future of U.S. prison policy: Twenty-five years after the Stanford Prison Experiment. *American Psychologist, 53*(7), 709–727.

Zimmerman, B. J. (1989). A social cognitive view of self-regulated learning. *Journal of Educational Psychology, 81,* 329–339.

THE EDUCATION OF ETHNIC GROUPS

22

EDUCATING NATIVE AMERICANS

K. Tsianina Lomawaima

University of Arizona, Tucson

Educating Native Americans. These words still encapsulate a battle for power: the power to define what education is—the power to set its goals, define its policies, and enforce its practices—and the power to define who Native people are and who they are not. (In this chapter, I use the terms *Native American, Native,* and *Indian education* to refer to all Indian people in the lower 48 states and to Alaska Natives. The federal government maintains two separate listings of American Indian tribes and Alaska Native villages.) European and American colonial governments, operating through denominations of the Christian church, first defined Indian education as the cleansing, uplifting, thoroughly aggressive and penetrating force that would Christianize, civilize, and individualize a heathen, barbaric, and tribal world (Axtell, 1981; Hoxie, 1984; Prucha, 1979, 1984; Szasz, 1988; Szasz & Ryan, 1988).

Over two centuries, the U.S. colonial administration of Indian affairs has diligently built a bureaucracy dedicated to controlling every aspect of Native lives (Castile & Bee, 1992; Fixico, 1998). Rules and regulations have authorized mineral extraction, controlled individual bank accounts, directed land use, homogenized housing, and mandated schooling—in short, created an edifice of federal surveillance that might astonish the average U.S. citizen secure in the image of a democratic nation. The "Indian education" devised to transform and assimilate Native people has been at loggerheads with the education of Native children by their parents and communities within indigenous systems of knowledge and practice. The tensions between the two systems have not relaxed much in the years since the first edition of this volume, but the political relations among tribal sovereigns, the federal sovereign, and the states continue to shift and evolve, and developments in education have always been deeply implicated in that process.

A discussion of tribal sovereignty, federal policy, and the singular government-to-government relationship that exists between tribes and the United States must begin this story. Native nations are distinct from other ethnic or linguistic "minority groups." As indigenous nations with an inherent sovereignty that predates the constitutionally based sovereignty of the United States, American Indian tribes and Alaska Native villages retain a status recognized by the Constitution and the legal supremacy of treaty law. They have agreed to a protectorate relationship under federal authority, above the jurisdiction of the states, unless Congress explicitly and appropriately authorizes state jurisdiction.

Second, a brief overview of the demographic history and characteristics of the U.S. Native population includes statistics on educational participation, achievement, and degrees earned. The historical narrative of federal Indian education began with colonial efforts to Christianize and civilize indigenous people, and it continued through the establishment of mission and federal boarding schools. Boarding schools shaped thousands of Native American people; their attitudes and responses to those institutions are discussed briefly.

A review of contemporary issues includes research on dropouts, learning styles, and interactional styles in classrooms; theories of cultural congruence or discontinuity and their shortcomings; self-determination; the development of Native leadership and control in Indian education; and curriculum development, school reform, and

The author is indebted to Teresa L. McCarty, at the University of Arizona, and to the reviewers of this manuscript for their generous and thoughtful contributions.

language policy. After a discussion of current trends, the chapter concludes with an assessment of the past and implications for the future of Native American education.

TRIBAL SOVEREIGNTY AND FEDERAL INDIAN POLICY

Federal powers have devised an educational system wedding ideology and practice in order to reshape Native American people (Adams, 1995; V. Deloria & Wildcat, 2001; Lomawaima, 2002). Other arms of the federal bureaucracy have manufactured definitions of Indianness, tribal rolls, lists of recognized tribes, and certificates of degree of Indian blood—all to control who has American Indian or Alaska Native status and who does not (National Archives, 1988a, 1988b; Pascal, 1991). Native nations have creatively resisted federal powers even as they have had to adapt to them (Nabokov, 1991; Olson & Wilson, 1984). The assertion of tribal power is and has always been the assertion of inherent sovereignty: to retain or reclaim rights to self-government, self-definition, and self-education (Wilkins & Lomawaima, 2001). Indian education can only be understood against this historical, political, economic, legal, and social battleground.

In approximately the last half century, the balance of power has shifted as tribes struggle with changing definitions of self-government and work to strengthen and expand tribal sovereignty (V. Deloria & Lytle, 1984; V. Deloria & Wilkins, 1999; Pommersheim, 1995). The shift in power toward tribal self-determination in education has not been uniform, or rapid, or uncontested; it has grown slowly from deep roots. It has significantly changed educational practice and policy but has by no means reformed schools to satisfy all the needs of Native American children, parents, and communities (Swisher & Tippeconnic, 1999). It is the aim of this chapter to delineate the course of research on Native education without losing sight of the larger political context, where Native people patiently labor to check the erosion of their sovereign rights. We need the vantage point of sovereignty in order to imagine what Native education should be and might become (Lomawaima & McCarty, 2002).

Since the federal government turned its attention to the "problem" of civilizing Indians, its overt goal has been their complete transformation (Adams, 1995; Szasz & Ryan, 1988). Since the late 1800s, most federal policy has not equated the civilizing process with simple assimilation into U.S. society. Educational policies have been designed to prepare Indians as a subservient working class, amenable to federal control, to provide domestic and manual labor to the U.S. economy (Adams, 1988; Littlefield, 1993; Lomawaima, 1993; Trennert, 1988). Native

Americans have challenged that model of Indian education by seeking access to Euro-American schools, and to academic and professional training. In the twentieth century, tribes and the courts refined a theory of political rights that defines educational opportunity as a treaty right promised in partial exchange for the cession of huge tracts of land (V. Deloria & Lytle, 1984; V. Deloria & Wilkins, 1999; Wilkinson, 1987). As indigenous nations exercising internal sovereignty, tribes occupy a unique legal and political space within the United States. American Indian tribes and Alaska Native villages are federally acknowledged as political entities with a government-to-government relationship with the United States; that status distinguishes them from all other ethnic or racial minorities and places them above state jurisdiction (Wilkins & Lomawaima, 2001).

Most Native Americans believe their right to education should not necessitate eradication of heritage languages, cultures, religions, or identities (Cajete, 1994; V. Deloria & Wildcat, 2001; McCarty, 2002). As Native American parents and communities have challenged and changed the working definition of Indian education and created education for and by Native people, the questions and solutions proposed by Native and nonnative educational researchers have also evolved.

One of the great challenges to research on Native Americans is the exhilarating range of diversity among our cultures. The federal government currently recognizes more than 550 tribes, including 223 Alaska Native villages. Federal officials have estimated there are as many as 250 indigenous groups who are not recognized by the United States (Prucha, 1984). Each Native community is distinguished by its own language, customs, religion, economy, historical circumstances, and environment. Native people are not all the same. A fluent member of a Cherokee Baptist congregation living in Tahlequah, Oklahoma, is different from an English-speaking, powwow-dancing Lakota born and raised in Oakland, California, who is different from a Hopi fluent in Hopi, English, Navajo, and Spanish who lives on the reservation and supports her family by selling "traditional" pottery in New York, Santa Fe, and Scottsdale galleries. The idea of being generically "Indian" really was a figment of Columbus's imagination.

It is a cornerstone of tribal sovereignty today that tribal governments set the criteria for their tribal membership; the criteria vary widely across the nations. Some tribes specify a "blood quantum" of ancestry within that specific tribe, typically ranging between one-eighth and one-half, for membership; others do not. Some tribes specify Native language fluency as a condition for service in the tribal government; others do not. Despite tribal control of tribal membership, certain federal criteria for Native American identity still carry weight. The federal government, for instance, requires one-quarter blood quantum as recorded in a federal "certificate of degree of Indian blood," which is based on agency records, in order to qualify for Bureau of Indian Affairs (BIA) college scholarships. Other federal programs—such as the census, or educational opportunity entitlement funds—rely on self-identification, where an American Indian or Alaskan Native is someone who checks the right box on the right form.

DEMOGRAPHIC TRENDS

The scholarly effort to piece together a demographic history of indigenous American populations has proved a difficult and depressing chore. There is no consensus on how many people lived on the North American continent prior to 1492 (see Ramenofsky, 1987, and Ubelaker, 1992, for an overview of the debate). We do know indigenous Americans were devastated by European expansion and newly introduced epidemic diseases, smallpox foremost among them. Although scholars do not agree on absolute Native population numbers, they have slowly but surely revised numbers upward, to current estimates for precontact Native North America ranging from more than 5 million in the present United States (Thornton, 1987) to the highest estimate, 18 million north of Mexico (Dobyns, 1983).

Native populations plummeted as much as 90% to 95% to their nadir of less than 250,000 in the early 1900s. The U.S. Census Bureau first attempted a complete census of American Indians in 1890, when they counted 248,000. By 1900 that number had shrunk to 237,000. The numbers have been climbing ever since 1920, as populations recovered, health care improved, and census methods changed: 357,000 in 1950, 524,000 in 1960 (Shoemaker, 1999; U.S. Census Bureau, 1988).

The numbers shot upward as the census allowed more citizens to self-identify and in 1960 began to alter the questions on race and ethnicity: 793,000 Native Americans in 1970, 1.42 million in 1980, 2.06 million in 1990, 2.48 million in 2000 (U.S. Census Bureau, 1988, 1992, 2001). Self-identification has influenced the count, as "only about 40% of the difference between the 1970 and 1980 census counts of American Indians can be accounted for by natural increase" (Thornton, Sandefur, & Snipp, 1991, p. 365). Of the 1.37 million (excluding Alaska Natives) enumerated in the 1980 census, "fewer than 900,000 were enrolled as members in federally recognized" tribes (Thornton, Sandefur, & Snipp, p. 365).

By 1980, the total Native American population was split roughly evenly between those who lived on or near reservations and those who lived in or near urban areas. By 2000, the percentage living in or near urban areas had climbed to 63%. In 1980, the 1.42 million American Indians and Alaska Natives enumerated by the census constituted 0.6% of the total U.S. population; by 1990 the percentage rose slightly to 0.85%; and in 2000, 2.47 million Natives composed 0.86% of the national population (U.S. Census Bureau, 1984, 1992, 2001).

Since the early 1970s, Native American students have constituted 0.7% to 0.9% of the enrollment in public elementary and secondary schools; the Native population has consistently been statistically younger than the U.S. norm (Pavel, Curtin, & Whitener, 1998; U.S. Census Bureau, 1992). Roughly 76% of Native students in 1980 attended public or private schools, and the remaining 24% attended schools operated by the BIA or by tribes (U.S. Bureau of the Census, 1988). By 1993–94, 91% of American Indian students (K-12) were enrolled in public schools, a total of more than 447,600 students (Pavel, Curtin, & Whitener). As of 2000, approximately 500,000 Native students were in school, and the approximate percentages of their distribution across schools has held steady since the early 1990s: about 90% in public schools, about 10% in BIA or tribal schools. See Table 22.1 for numbers of schools operated and/or funded by BIA or other federal agencies or funds. As Pavel points out, a relatively small number of schools enroll "a relatively large number of Native students"; "BIA/tribal schools and HIE [high Indian enrollment: 25% or more] schools represent approximately 1.7% of the total number of publicly funded schools but enroll 47% of the total Native student population" (Pavel, 1999, p. 1).

TABLE 22.1. Types and Numbers of Schools Enrolling American Indian/Alaska Native Students.

	School Year 1990–91	School Year 2000–01
BIA-operated schools		
Day schools and on-reservation boarding schools	87	65
Off-reservation boarding schools	5	4
Dormitories attached to public schools	8	1
Tribally operated schools run with BIA contract funds		
Day schools and on-reservation boarding schools	73	120
Off-reservation boarding school	1	3
Dormitories attached to public schools	6	13

Note: In 1990–91, federal funds supported about 225,870 Indian students enrolled in public schools (U.S. Department of the Interior, 1991). In 2000, approximately 440,000 Native students were enrolled in public schools, and approximately 60,000 were enrolled in BIA/tribal schools (Faircloth & Tippeconnic, 2000).

Sources: Office of Indian Education Programs (2001); U.S. Department of the Interior (1991).

In the mid-1990s, at least one-third of students enrolled in BIA or tribal schools spoke a language other than English in the home (Pavel, Curtin, & Whitener, 1998); in public schools with 25% or more Indian enrollment, 16% of the Native students spoke a language other than English in their homes (Pavel, 1999b). There are striking disparities in the percentages of Native teachers in the public versus tribal/BIA schools: less than 1% of all public school teachers were identified as American Indian or Alaska Native in 1993–94, while 38% of the teachers in BIA/tribal schools were of Native descent (Pavel, Curtin, & Whitener). Compared to BIA schools, however, public high schools in the 1990s graduated a higher percentage of their Indian students (91% versus 86%), and a higher percentage of their Indian graduates applied to colleges—58% from the public schools versus 47% from the BIA schools (Pavel, Curtin, & Whitener).

Across all school types, overall high school graduation rates for Native students increased from 56% in 1980 to 66% in 1990, while national rates climbed from 67% to 75%. Similarly, completion of college preparatory curricula by Native high school graduates jumped from 6% in 1982 to 31% in 1992, while national averages also showed significant increases, 13% to 47% (U.S. Department of Education, 1998). Although Natives were making gains, they were not catching up to national numbers, which also increased during these years: "In 1992, most Native American college-bound high school graduates failed to meet all five criteria used to assess student competitiveness in the college admissions process" (U.S. Department of Education, p. 2–2). We can see the low numbers of Native Americans relative to the total national population earning higher degrees in Tables 22.2 and 22.3, but it is important to note that within the Native population the percentage of people earning higher degrees climbed significantly from 1977 to 1994, compared to national norms; see Table 22.4 (U.S. Department of Education).

TABLE 22.2. Bachelor's, Master's, and Doctoral Degrees Earned by American Indians/Alaska Natives, 1976–1995.

	1976–77	1984–85	1989–90	1994–95
Bachelor's degrees	3,326	4,246	4,392	6,606
Percentage of total, all races	0.4	0.4	0.4	0.5
Master's degrees	967	1,256	1,101	1,621
Percentage of total, all races	0.3	0.4	0.3	0.4
Doctoral degrees	95	119	99	130
Percentage of total, all races	0.3	0.4	0.3	0.3

Sources: Based on data from U.S. Department of Education, National Center for Education Statistics (1981, 1985–86, 1990a, 1992, 1997).

In 1980, Native American students made up 0.7% of the total enrollment in institutions of higher education, earning 0.4% of the bachelor's degrees, 0.3% to 0.4% of the master's degrees, and 0.3% to 0.4% of the doctoral degrees throughout the decade of the 1980s (National Center for Education Statistics [NCES], 1981, 1985–86, 1990a). In 1980, Indian children and young adults were not completing higher education at rates close to national norms: 8% of the Native population completed four years of college, half the national rate of 16% (U.S. Bureau of the Census, 1988). By 1996, the numbers improved for Native students but still did not match national norms: at NCAA Division I institutions, public and private, a six-year graduation rate of 36% for Native students compared to 56% for all students (U.S. Department of Education, 1998).

Closer examination of degrees awarded, especially graduate degrees, reveals that Native Americans have concentrated their studies in a few fields and disciplines, particularly education. In 1989–90, for example, 14% (598) of the bachelor's degrees, 37% (405) of the master's degrees, and 37% (38) of the doctoral degrees earned by Native people were in education. In that same academic year, Native Americans earned only 5 Ph.D.s in the physical sciences and 4 Ph.D.s in the life sciences (NCES, 1992). In 1996, the National Research Council (1998) reported 187 doctorates earned by American Indians; of those, 60 (32%) were earned in education. It should be noted that disturbing disparities in number of degrees reported as earned have existed over the years among various statistical sources (see Table 22.3).

The NCES and the National Research Council (NRC) cite significantly different numbers of doctorates earned by American Indians. The NRC (1976) reports 143 American Indian doctorates in 1975 (Vaughn, 1985), but other sources cite only 36 (Thurgood, 1991). The NRC (1982) cites 89 American Indian doctorates in 1981, but NCES (1990a) cites 130. More recent and reliable publications commissioned of Native authors by the U.S. Department of Education (1998) integrate statistics from a variety of sources and pay close attention to difficulties stemming from "limited data availability, high standard errors, weighting problems, and reliability issues" (U.S. Department of Education, 1998).

One of the most encouraging trends in higher education for American Indians/Alaska Natives is the continued development of tribally controlled community colleges and universities, a trend that began with the establishment in 1968 of Navajo Community College, now called Diné College (Carnegie Foundation for the Advancement of Teaching, 1989; Tippeconnic, 1999). Native participation in higher education promises to grow with the tribal college system; in the nontribal higher education institutions, however, it appears that "the academic

TABLE 22.3. Doctorates Earned by Native Americans (N.A.) 1975–1995: Disparate Statistics.

		NRC-SR Data[a]	NRC 1991 Data[b]	DES Data[c]	MSGE Data[d]	USDOE Data[e]
	U.S.	N.A.	N.A.	N.A.	N.A.	
1975	27,009[x]	143 (34% of N.A. doctorates earned in education)	36			
1976	27,195[x]	148 (35%)	40		148	
1977	26,007[x]; 33,126[y]	220 (31%)	65	95		95
1978	25,186[x]	174 (32%)	60			
1979	25,369[x]; 32,675[y]	165 (39%)	81	104 (41%)		104
1980	25,108[x]	106 (50%)	75			
1981	24,990[x]; 32,839[y]	89 (47%)	85	130	89	130
1982	24,309[x]	77 (38%)	77			
1983	24,292[x]	81 (54%)	81			
1984	23,951[x]	74 (43%)	74			
1985	23,241[x]; 32,307[y]	93 (42%)	96	119		119
1986	22,984[x]	100 (26%)	99			
1987	22,863[x]; 34,041[y]	116 (35%)	115	104		105
1988	23,172[x]	93 (38%)	94			
1989	23,172[x]; 38,113[y]; 35,659[z]	93 (26%)	94	99		85
1990			93	102 (37%)		
1991	24,721[x]	130 (41%)				
1993–94	43,149[z]			134	134	
1994–95	44,427[y]			130		

Notes: U.S. = total doctorates earned by citizens in United States, although these numbers also vary among sources; see notes on *x, y,* and *z.*

N.A. = Native American doctorates.

Where statistics were unavailable, the table was left blank.

Sources: [a] National Research Council summary reports (see References).

[b] Thurgood (1991). Despite its similarity to the NRC reports cited in this table, this summary report has a different Library of Congress catalogue number, and the figures Thurgood cites vary drastically from statistics reported in other NRC summary reports.

[c] National Center for Education Statistics (1981, 1985–86, 1990, 1992, 1997).

[d] Vaughn (1985).

[e] U.S. Department of Education (1998), pp. 4–34, Table S4–1.

[x] National Research Council summary reports (see References).

[y] National Center for Education Statistics (1997), Table 271.

[z] U.S. Department of Education, National Center for Education Statistics (1998), pp. 4–34, Table S4–1.

pipeline for the American Indian people is leaking badly" (Dingman, Mroczka, & Brady, 1995, p. 17).

Dedicated to community, cultural continuity, local control, and economic development, as well as the professional development of teachers and curriculum materials for elementary and secondary education, the colleges strengthened their position when Congress passed the Tribally Controlled College or University Assistance Act (P.L. 95–471) in 1978, even though federal support has never met the full level of authorized appropriations (Carnegie Foundation for the Advancement of Teaching, 1989; Stein, 1992). In 1994, Congress "designated Tribal Colleges as land-grant institutions, in recognition of the essential ties between the colleges, tribal lands, and local economic development" (American Indian Higher

TABLE 22.4. Increases from 1977 to 1994, by Percentage, in Number of Higher Education Degrees Earned by American Indians/Alaska Natives.

	Percentage Increase in Number of Degrees Earned from 1976–77 to 1993–94	
	American Indians/ Alaska Natives	Total population
Associate degrees	95	31
Bachelor's degrees	86	27
Master's degrees	75	22
First professional degrees	89	18
Doctoral degrees	41	30

Source: U.S. Department of Education (1998), pp. 4–34, Table S4–1.

Education Consortium, 1999, p. A-4). As of 2002, there are 32 tribal colleges serving more than 30,000 students (www.aihec.org; Office of Indian Education Programs, 2001).

HISTORICAL BACKGROUND: POLICIES AND PRACTICES IN INDIAN EDUCATION

If history is the bequest of meaning from the past to the present, then Indian education has had a remarkably constant inheritance until recent times. Unfortunately, school-based education has not often included the education of Indian children by their parents or by other tribal adults. Native American autobiographies (Brumble, 1981) are excellent sources of information on tribally specific education in the 1800s and 1900s, but the lessons of home and heritage language were under direct attack in those centuries and beyond.

Euro-American nations and churches have consistently sought to replace the profound lessons of indigenous instruction with a new language, Christianity, patriarchal family structure, subordinate political status, and capitalist economy—all part of a conscious agenda to disenfranchise Native Americans from their land (Adams, 1988). Four principal methods have been harnessed toward these goals: (1) the relocation of Native Americans into newly created, closely controlled communities separate from European settlements, such as Spanish missions and Puritan praying towns; (2) instruction in the language of civilized society, be it French, Spanish, English, or some other (training in literacy varied considerably); (3) conversion to Christianity; and (4) the restructuring of Native economies to fit European-style practices of sedentary agriculture, small-scale craft industry, and gendered labor (Lomawaima, 1999). The hopes of colonial educators were epitomized by Eleazar Wheelock, founder of Moor's Charity School for Indians as well as Dartmouth College, who sought "to save the Indians from themselves and to save the English from the Indians" (Axtell, 1981, p. 97).

American Indian parents and children have resisted colonial programs of total assimilation in many ways. From armed revolts in the Southwest to epidemic-induced conversions in the Northeast, the course of proselytization was never smooth (Bowden, 1981). Reprisals for resistance could be harsh. The Spanish flogged, amputated the hands and feet of, or set fire to Pueblo "heretics" in the 17th century (Simmons, 1979), and in 1895 the United States sent Hopi men who resisted federal agents to Alcatraz (James, 1974). More recent assimilatory practices, such as mandatory school enrollment, may seem humane compared to earlier horrors, yet they have also provoked resistance. Indian children, for example, have devised ingenious ways to subvert or escape the disciplines and expand the possibilities of boarding school life (Archuleta, Child, & Lomawaima, 2000).

Through the 18th and 19th centuries, the United States left Indian education largely in the hands of the clergy, subsidizing the work of mission boards in agricultural, domestic, manual labor, and academic instruction (Prucha, 1979). Diverse Native nations met diverse denominations—Quakers, Moravians, Catholics, Presbyterians, Mennonites—some of whom were dedicated to high academic standards, the development of writing systems, and literacy instruction in both English and Native languages (Neely, 1975). Bilingual/bicultural education developed in the early 1800s at mission stations serving the Choctaw and other Eastern tribes (Noley, 1979). Tribal governments continued this educational tradition as Eastern tribes were relocated to Indian Territory (eventually to become the state of Oklahoma) by the middle of the 19th century. The Creek, Choctaw, and Cherokee nations, among others, built their own academies and seminaries in Indian Territory, such as the Cherokee Female Seminary, established in 1851 (Mihesuah, 1993).

By the late 1800s, the federal government began to displace missions as the primary educator of Native Americans (Prucha, 1979). In 1875 Colonel Richard Henry Pratt began a federal experiment in education among Kiowa and Cheyenne prisoners of war incarcerated at Fort Marion, St. Augustine, Florida. After three years of imprisonment, a number of the young Kiowa and Cheyenne requested further schooling. Convinced that equal educational opportunity was all that separated Native people from the advantages of civilization, Pratt tried in vain to locate an agricultural college that would accept his students. Samuel Armstrong accepted them into Hampton Institute, a school for African Americans, but the Indian college at Hampton was short-lived. Armstrong, staunchly committed to a racially determined hierarchy of human achievement, and Pratt, with his progressive notions of racial equality, respected one another, but their views were too divergent to easily coexist (Adams, 1977; Utley, 1964).

Pratt successfully lobbied Secretary of the Interior Carl Schurz and the Congress to establish the first federal off-reservation boarding school for American Indian youth at unused military barracks in Carlisle, Pennsylvania, in 1879 (Ryan, 1962; Utley, 1964). Within five years, similar schools were established: Chilocco Indian School in Oklahoma; Genoa Indian School in Nebraska; and Haskell Institute at Lawrence, Kansas. By the turn of the century, the federal government ended its subsidies of mission schools and operated 25 off-reservation boarding schools and dozens of local day schools and on-reservation boarding schools.

Federal policy of total assimilation of Indian people and educational practices of military regimentation, strict discipline, and intensive manual labor clearly reveal the government's intent to train young Indians in subservience to federal authority (Adams, 1988; Littlefield, 1993; Lomawaima, 1993). Nonnative and Native reformers have objected to the principles and/or the practices of assimilatory education since its inception. Religious and political groups have, at various times, fought corruption and graft in the federal administration of Indian affairs and advocated more humane treatment of Indian students. Perhaps the best-known and most effective critique of federal Indian administration was the 1928 report *The Problem of Indian Administration* (Meriam et al., 1928). The Meriam Report's chapter on Indian education targeted boarding schools as inappropriate places to raise children; it recommended public and on-reservation day schools as alternatives.

Under the leadership of John Collier, President Franklin D. Roosevelt's commissioner of Indian affairs, the education division of the BIA began to shift support from boarding to day schools, from federal to public schools, from assimilatory to respectful attitudes toward Native cultures (Szasz, 1999). Critical legislation, the Johnson-O'Malley Act (49 Stat. 1458)—known as J-O'M—was passed on April 16, 1934, to fund the enrollment of Native students in public schools. Federal subsidies to public schools for Indian student enrollment are necessary because federal trust lands (such as Indian and military reservations) are exempt from the local property taxes that support public school education in most states (children of military personnel are subsidized through similar arrangements).

Johnson-O'Malley replaced a complex system of contracting between BIA and literally thousands of individual school districts (Szasz, 1999). J-O'M gave the bureau "the authority to centralize its contracting on a federal-state basis" (Szasz, p. 92). J-O'M injected significant levels of federal funds into public schools, but the relationship between the BIA and the states has often been strained, and concerns over public school unwillingness to meet the needs of Indian students have never been fully resolved (Szasz).

The decades after Collier's tenure witnessed a shift back toward repressive political and educational treatment of Native nations, as the American nation continued to struggle with the linked issues of its national self-identity, the appropriate place of American Indians in the nation, and the difficult distinction between cultural differences believed to be innocuous and those considered so different as to be dangerous (Lomawaima, 2002; Lomawaima & McCarty, 2002). The windows of opportunity for bilingual instruction, locally relevant schooling, and respect for Native values that Collier and his staff opened in the 1930s were firmly shut in the post–Word War II nationalism and intolerance of cultural pluralism characteristic

of the Cold War decades. Assimilation policies once more deemed Native cultural values, practices, and languages too dangerous to warrant federal encouragement. By the late 1950s, civil rights and social justice movements reasserted themselves, but the assimilatory view has certainly not disappeared from the scene, as recent movements advocating an "English only" language policy clearly reveal.

RESEARCH ON INDIAN EDUCATION

Professional discussion of Indian education began as early as 1884, when the Indian Service, later called the Bureau of Indian Affairs (BIA), began an annual tradition of teachers' summer institutes. By 1903, Superintendent of Indian Schools Estelle Reel had organized 10 such institutes (Reel, 1903). As part of her plan to professionalize her teacher corps, Reel applied to the National Education Association (NEA) for recognition. In 1899 the Indian education group met for the first time at the NEA annual meeting to present papers and exchange ideas.

In 1936, the Education Division of the Indian Service began to publish the field letter *Indian Education* to present "concise and clear-cut statements of the philosophy, policy and preferred procedures of Indian education" (Beatty, 1953, p. 10). During the administrations of Directors of Education Willard W. Beatty (1936–1952) and Hildegard Thompson (1952–1965), the newsletter provided a forum for communication among teachers and administrators within the federal system for Indian education. Beatty was not ultimately successful in developing "an education relevant to Indian life" (Szasz, 1999, p. 49), but community schooling, reservation day schools, and bilingual education programs did flourish for a short time. Thompson faced the more difficult Cold War era. Congressional legislation to terminate tribes' distinctive government-to-government relationship with the federal government and mandates to relocate Indians to urban areas (Lobo & Peters, 2001) threatened tribal sovereignty during her tenure (Szasz).

Research on the Boarding School Experience

Indian resistance to assimilation within boarding schools has proved rich ground for research. Early research on boarding schools tended to focus on the social, cultural, psychological, or intellectual pathologies of Indian students or the pathologies of the environment (Birchard, 1970; Krush, Bjork, Sindell, & Nelle, 1966). Alternatively, authors investigating the history of particular schools focused on federal policy and documentary evidence (Ryan, 1962; Trennert, 1988). In 1983, McBeth introduced the voices of Native alumni of boarding schools, paving the way for research and films about Native people in U.S. boarding schools (Archuleta, Child, & Lomawaima, 2000; Child, 1998; Ellis, 1996; Lomawaima, 1994) and Canadian residential schools (Haig-Brown, 1988; Johnston, 1988; Nuu-chah-nulth Tribal Council, 1996; Pittman, 1989; Sterling, 1998).

Basil Johnston's (1988) memoir of his education at "Spanish," a Jesuit boarding school in northern Ontario in the 1930s, is the 20th-century counterpoint to Francis LaFlesche's (1900/1978) moving account of Presbyterian mission education of young Omaha children in the 1880s. Boarding-school attendance has left a range of legacies, from family enrollment at an "alma mater" over generations (McBeth, 1983; Lomawaima, 1994) to very negative attitudes toward all schools (Butterfield & Pepper, 1991). Recent publications and a growing number of museum exhibits explore boarding school legacies nationally and locally, expanding the scope of inquiry into the transformation of Native homes and domestic spaces; the meaning of school sports and teams; and the exploration and creation of new forms of music, dance, and pageantry among alumni (Archuleta, Child, & Lomawaima, 2000).

Some ethnographic study of contemporary boarding schools was undertaken in the 1970s in Alaska (Kleinfeld, 1973b). In 1985, the governors of the 19 pueblos of New Mexico sponsored an oral history of the Santa Fe Indian School (Hyer, 1990), eloquently conveying Native voices, lives, and educational self-determination. Meanwhile, a few off-reservation boarding schools survive as an educational option for Native students: Chemawa Indian High School in Salem, Oregon; Flandreau Indian School north of Sioux Falls, South Dakota; Sherman Indian High School in Riverside, California; Santa Fe Indian School in northern New Mexico; and Haskell Institute, established in 1884 in Lawrence, Kansas, continuing today as Haskell Indian Nations University.

Self-Determination: Rhetoric or Reality?

The civil rights movement of the 1950s and 1960s radically shifted the status quo across America. More and more Indian children had been enrolling in public schools, and Indian parents and communities exercised newfound political power to reform existing schools or establish new schools of their own (Johnson, 1968). Congressional and federal investigations of Indian education uncovered scandals and advocated reforms (Aurbach & Fuchs, 1970; U.S. Senate, Committee on Labor and Public Welfare, 1969; Fuchs & Havighurst, 1972; NAACP Legal Defense and Educational Fund, 1971). Congress responded with a landslide of legislation promoting tribal self-determination in education: the 1965 Elementary and Secondary Education Act (P.L. 89–10, amended in 1966 to include BIA schools), the 1964 Economic Opportunity Act, the 1972 Indian Education Act (Title IV of Public Law 92–318), the 1975 Indian Self-Determination and Education Assistance Act (P.L. 93–638), and the Educational Amendments Act of 1978 (P.L. 95–561 and its technical amendments P.L. 98–511, 98–89, and 100–297).

The Indian Self-Determination and Education Assistance Act of 1975 (P.L. 93-638) exemplifies how rhetoric—what sounds good on paper—collided with administrative reality in American Indian education. P.L. 93–638 regulated the existing practice of contracting federal monies to Indian communities to run local programs (Senese, 1986). The practice of "638 contracting" has been praised by some as the greatest opportunity in history for Indian people to control their own destiny (Szasz, 1999), while others have condemned it as yet another link in the chain of BIA bureaucratic oppression (Grell, 1983; Senese).

Senese (1986) argued that 638 contracting offered Indian communities only an "illusion of control" (p. 154), while the law's language, implementation, and flawed disbursement of funds crippled community-based education. McCarty (1987, 1989) detailed similar obstacles—program instability, student transfers, staff turnover, and unpredictable funding—on the Navajo reservation. In a case study of the Kickapoo National School, Grell (1983) concluded that "control of the school is not a panacea" for Indian education because "the incompatibility of externally imposed restrictions and tribally-oriented values in education remains" (p. 9).

McCarty's (2002) more recent work on the history and development of Rough Rock, the first Indian community-controlled school, established in 1966 (with funding from the BIA and the Office of Economic Opportunity), details the frustrations and accomplishments of Navajo people who persevered to create a school environment where it is healthy, safe, and productive to simply "be Navajo." As Goddard and Shields (1997) remind us in their comparison of two school districts in the United States and Canada, there is "no automatic link between local control and more empowering educational practices" (p. 19). Effective local control of schools requires both effective structures of governance and effective educational strategies. Today, most Indian-controlled schools take advantage of the congressional option to receive grants rather than contracts: grants afford less federal micromanagement, more flexibility, and more local control. Despite the obstacles that remain, it is undeniably clear that Indian parents, communities, and professional educators have made tremendous gains in the last 30 years, largely as a result of determined Native leadership at all levels (Tippeconnic, 1999, 2000).

The Disadvantaged Child

Throughout the late 1960s and early 1970s, educational and social scientists began to study the school experiences of minority children (including at times American Indian students) and document their achievement levels on standardized tests. Some researchers focused on the validity of testing instruments, others on the inadequacies of minority children—asserting, for example, that Nez Percé kindergartners had "less developed" visual perception than White students (Lowry, 1970, p. 303) or that Native students possessed severely inadequate linguistic skills (Ramstad & Potter, 1974).

A "culture of poverty" model labeled children, their families, and communities as "disadvantaged"—culturally, socially, linguistically, and/or economically unprepared to melt into the American pot (Crow, Murray, & Smythe, 1966; Webster, 1966). Salisbury's research (1974) in Alaska blamed cultural disadvantage for the maladjustment of Native students to college life. Salisbury hoped to teach the students to "verbalize problems freely" in order to make the "transition toward a culture in which [they] must find a place" (p. 199). Disadvantage models continued the assimilationist thrust of two centuries of Indian education by assuming that Indian children *must* "find their place" by giving up their Indianness.

Other scholars removed the onus of disadvantage from Indian students and placed responsibility elsewhere for minority student "failure." Bryde's (1970) classic study of scholastic failure and personality conflict examined the "cross-over phenomenon" (Brown, 1979) among Sioux students. These students achieved at or above national norms in their first few school years but then crossed over and "reverse[d] their performance by underachieving for the rest of their scholastic lives" (Bryde, 1970, p. i). By the seventh or eighth grade, students sensed "themselves caught by forces beyond their command" and responded with rejection, depression, alienation, and anxiety (Bryde, p. 67). Bryde and others recognized that systematic social inequities were being played out in the schools as well as in the larger society (Ogbu, 1983, 1987, 1989; Parmee, 1968).

The Dropout Rate: Problems of Comparability

Disproportionately high Native dropout rates and low graduation and retention rates at all educational levels have motivated statistical inquiry and policy concern for decades. The NCES sponsored three longitudinal studies of dropout rates during the 1970s and 1980s (NCES, 1988, 1989, 1990b). The studies were hampered by very small sample sizes of American Indian/Alaska Native students, making statistical analysis impossible (but see descriptive reports for some of the data sets; Bureau of Indian Affairs,

1988). The 1980 survey of 30,000 sophomores and 28,000 seniors across the country found a 31.8% dropout rate for American Indian females, 27.2% for American Indian males, 18% for Hispanics, 14.1% for Blacks, 11.5% for Whites, and 2.7% for Asian Americans (Peng & Takai, 1983). The National Educational Longitudinal Study of 1988 tracked 24,599 eighth graders (including 307 students coded as Native) and reported dropout rates of American Indian/Alaska Native 9.2%; Black, non-Hispanic, 10.2%; Hispanic 9.6%; White, non-Hispanic, 5.2%; and Asian/Pacific Islander 4% (NCES, 1990b).

In 1992 the *Journal of American Indian Education* (Swisher, 1992a, 1992b) devoted two special issues to dropout research, as "the statistics regarding these rates among Indian/Native students have been highly speculative, inaccurate, and/or embedded in the innocuous category of 'other' when reported . . . there is not a clear picture of the reasons that Indian/Native students are leaving school" (Swisher, 1992c, p. 1).

Swisher and Hoisch (1992) reviewed dropout studies from the 1960s through the 1980s, revealing disparities from study to study among measurement techniques, sample sizes and compositions, and data sets that made it very difficult to obtain nationally comparable or meaningful figures.

In an effort to calculate Indian dropout rates more accurately, Swisher, Hoisch, and Pavel (1991) drew data from 26 state and national educational agencies, BIA offices, and tribal entities in the 20 states identified by the census with the largest Indian/Native populations. Although state data response was timely and complete, data were difficult to obtain and/or compare across BIA and tribal sources. A subsequent follow-up study focusing on BIA schools found a 25% dropout rate in grades 9 through 12, compounded by a transfer rate that ranged from 10% in BIA elementary schools to 30% in BIA high schools and 50% at Chemawa, a BIA boarding school in Oregon (Swisher & Hoisch, 1992). Student transfers at such high rates can confound dropout statistics.

Researchers have explored students' school experiences and reasons for dropping out, identifying a variety of social, cultural, economic, and academic factors. Studies tend to focus on "school-based" reasons for dropping out, such as uncaring teachers or inappropriate curriculum (Reyhner, 1992); on "home-based" reasons, such as lack of parental support or first language other than English (Platero, Brandt, Witherspoon, & Wong, 1986); or on "student-based" reasons, such as life goals unrelated to school instruction, pregnancy, or substance abuse (Bowker, 1992). In a two-year study of 991 Indian females of diverse backgrounds from seven northern Plains groups, Bowker found no strong correlates for school failure, "no formula for success or dropping out" (p. 17). The strongest indicator Bowker found for school success was "the support of . . . families," especially mothers and grandmothers (p. 16).

Brandt (1992) reported the findings of the Navajo Area Student Dropout Study, or NASDS (Platero et al., 1986). Prior to NASDS, reported dropout rates across the reservation ranged from 30% to 95% (Brandt). NASDS tracked students through their Navajo census numbers and interviewed 889 students—670 stayers and 219 leavers. The investigators found that "over 50% of the students that the schools identified as 'dropouts' had in fact either transferred to another school or had graduated" (p. 52). NASDS estimated a transfer rate for the study area of 30% and a dropout rate of 31%. Academic factors were minimally involved for school leavers, strong Navajo cultural ties were found among stayers and leavers, and bilingual proficiency in Navajo and English was *positively* linked to *persistence* in school. Brandt concluded that for both stayers and leavers, schools were not "challenging or engaging Navajo students socially or intellectually" (p. 61).

Deyhle's (1992) seven-year ethnographic study of Navajo and Ute "school leavers" provides a rich source of evidence. Deyhle found that Native students and nonnative teachers and administrators neither trusted nor cared for one another. Students were not blind to the institutional racism of the schools or to their limited opportunities outside schools. Deyhle calls their decision to leave school "a rational response" to racism (p. 25), and established an overall dropout rate of 21.3%. Deyhle used Ogbu's (1987) concept of castes to explain failure among the Native students attending a border town high school and attributed school success among the students attending the on-reservation school to the cultural integrity between school and community.

Learning and Interactional Styles

As educators have struggled to develop culturally relevant classroom materials and pedagogic methods (Lipka, 1991), researchers have addressed the issue of how children might learn and exhibit knowledge in culturally specific ways. In their review of this literature, Swisher and Deyhle (1987) defined learning style as "the way in which knowledge is acquired," and interactional style as "the way in which knowledge is demonstrated" (p. 345). The cultural discontinuity/congruence hypothesis predicts that cultural discontinuities between teachers and students (King, 1967; Sindell, 1974; Vogt, Jordan, & Tharp, 1987), between Indian and non-Indian learning styles (Cazden & John, 1971; John, 1972), or between teacher-imposed and community-sanctioned interactional styles (Philips, 1972, 1983) will hinder children's achievement as measured by standardized tests. Deyhle (1983) raises

provocative questions about standardized tests. She posits that a culture that values process over product, coupled with students' realization of the personal judgment entailed in passing or failing, conspire to create students who reject testing itself.

Researchers have focused on a range of critical parameters defining how children learn and how they display what they learn, including (a) linguistic performance (Cazden & Leggett, 1981; Philips, 1972, 1983; Scollon & Scollon, 1981) and linguistic nonperformance, or silence, in the classroom (Dumont, 1972; Wax, Wax, & Dumont, 1964/1989); (b) observational or "private" versus trial-by-error learning (John, 1972; Wolcott, 1967); (c) cooperative versus competitive learning strategies (Brown, 1980; Miller & Thomas, 1972); (d) field-dependent versus field-independent perceptual and personality organization (Dinges & Hollenbeck, 1978); (e) cultural congruence; and (f) brain hemispheric dominance (not discussed further here; see Chrisjohn & Peters, 1989; and Rhodes, 1990, for rebuttals to this theory).

Linguistic Performance/Silence. Philips's (1972, 1983) seminal study of Warm Springs, Oregon, reservation education outlined different standards of linguistic performance—called "communicative competencies"—in the community and in the school. Communicative competency means knowing the cultural standards for who speaks when, for how long, in what order, and in what context. Philips called the framework of rules that govern speech "participant structures." She concluded that Indian children at Warm Springs resisted school-defined, teacher-dominated participant structures that required students to recite publicly as a sign of mastering knowledge. One of the most cited studies of Indian education, her 1972 work laid the groundwork for subsequent decades of research on linguistic performance and classroom interaction.

The classroom interaction model has been productively applied to studies of reading instruction developed for Native Hawaiian children (Au & Jordan, 1981) and for Athabascan children in Alaska (Van Ness, 1981). Greenbaum and Greenbaum (1983) reviewed the literature on cultural differences in classroom interaction, and the possible negative effects when teachers and students nonverbally regulate conversation in conflicting ways. Although concluding that Indian and non-Indian classroom interactions differ in the frequency or duration of utterances, voice loudness, and degree of visual attention, they caution that "it has yet to be shown empirically that such differences obstruct the students' comprehension of what they are being taught" (Greenbaum & Greenbaum, p. 28).

Studies have attempted to demonstrate empirically what teachers report anecdotally: that Indian children are much quieter than other children in the classroom

(Guilmet, 1978, 1981). In their study of Oklahoma Cherokee children's behavior in classrooms, Dumont and Wax (1969) posit a "Cherokee school society" created by students to resist an imposed, alien institution. Students

surrounded themselves with a wall of silence impenetrable by the outsider, while sheltering a rich emotional communion among themselves. The silence is positive, not negative or withdrawing, and it shelters them so that . . . they can pursue their scholastic interests in their own style and pace. By their silence they exercise control over the teacher. (Dumont & Wax, p. 222)

Private Learners? Philips (1972, 1983) also discussed how Warm Springs adults taught children to pay attention, to observe, to practice on their own, and only then to undertake public performance or demonstration of a new skill or knowledge. This notion of "private learning" (Swisher & Deyhle, 1989, p. 4) has been attested as well for Navajo children (Longstreet, 1978), Oglala Sioux children (Brewer, 1977), and Yaqui children (Appleton, 1983).

Cooperation or Competition? It is commonly asserted that Indian children are raised to be more "cooperative" than White children, and that competition is expressed by Indian children only in group contexts such as team sports. Miller and Thomas (1972) compared 48 Blood children from a reserve school in Alberta, Canada, with 48 non-Indian children in an urban school. The children, between the ages of 7 and 10, were tested with the Madsen Cooperation Board under two experimental reward conditions. Both Indian and non-Indian groups cooperated effectively to achieve a group reward. Under an individual reward system, however, the "performance level of Indian children continued to increase while that of the non-Indian children deteriorated" (Miller & Thomas, p. 1109). Miller and Thomas note "it is tempting to relate these differences to differences in the cultural background of the groups . . . but the specific ways that these . . . cultural factors find expression in cooperative behaviors . . . are not known in detail at the present time" (p. 1110).

Field-Dependent or Field-Independent? Swisher and Deyhle (1989) note that the little research on Indian students' degree of field dependence or field independence contradicts the model Ramírez and Castañeda (1974) developed on the basis of their study of Mexican American children. This cognitive model proposes that formally organized families who promote strong individual identity (i.e., Anglos) produce field-independent children, and that shared-function families who promote group identity—especially groups isolated from the U.S. mainstream, such as Mexican Americans—produce field-dependent children (Ramírez & Castañeda). The

Ramírez and Castañeda model predicts that Navajo children would be more field dependent than White children. The 1978 study by Dinges and Hollenbeck demonstrates exactly the opposite. Dinges and Hollenbeck propose genetic, environmental, experiential, and linguistic factors to account for this unexpected result. Their recognition of cultural and grammatical imperatives that privilege "perceptual-cognitive abilities" is noteworthy, but their devaluation of Navajo creativity is not. Dinges and Hollenbeck claimed that Navajo women do not create rug patterns according to a cultural aesthetic, but that they merely "duplicate" them "from memory" (p. 218).

Cultural Congruence. The theory of cultural discontinuity/cultural congruence predicts that cultural/linguistic difference among teacher, school, and student can result in student underachievement or failure; and that cultural/linguistic congruence among teacher, school, and student leads to student success. The theory, however, has been taken for granted more often than it has been empirically tested. Mohatt and Erickson (1981) described the teaching styles of two "effective and experienced" teachers, one an Indian female, the other a non-Indian male, in a study that resulted only in a recommendation to conduct more research to "see whether more culturally congruent participant structures will increase achievement among native students" (p. 119). Kleinfeld (1974) examined whether altering nonverbal cues that communicate "warmth" in teaching styles would stimulate learning, question answering, and question asking among 20 White and 20 Eskimo students. The cues were ethnographically defined according to Eskimo values. She found that "warm" college guidance sessions did increase learning for both groups, but that "ethnic group differences were few and not altogether consistent" (p. 3).

Ledlow (1992) tackled the whole question of cultural discontinuity as an adequate explanation for dropping out. Her critical review of earlier research found "little or no explicit research to prove the hypothesis" (p. 21). Ledlow supported the cultural congruence hypothesis as a research question but objected to unquestioned assumption of its validity. She proposed that macrostructural explanations of minority schooling, rooted in a Marxist perspective, might more productively focus on "economic and social issues"—pregnancy, drugs, boredom, institutional racism, poverty—"which are not culturally specific to being Indian" (p. 29). Brady (1996) echoed her approach in a Canadian study that found wide diversity in dropping-out factors within and among Native communities, and a core constellation of similar economic and social influences operating among Native and non-Native dropouts. Some studies (Coggins, Williams &

Radin, 1997; Deyhle, 1992) indicate that "a strong sense of traditional cultural identity . . . provides a student with an advantage in school. The idea that traditional Indian students may have an academic advantage over more 'acculturated' students is an important issue" (Ledlow, 1992, p. 34).

Ogbu (1989), in his differentiation of voluntary and involuntary minorities, has pointed out that some minority groups who do well in school are more culturally different from mainstream school culture than groups who do poorly. A simple model of cultural congruence does not account for their school success. In Indian education, Osborne (1989) questioned the entire rationale of the cultural congruence hypothesis by pointing out that complete cultural congruence between Indian (specifically Zuni Pueblo, New Mexico) and U.S. values is not possible—or, perhaps, even desirable—in the classroom. Osborne proposed a conceptual framework of "fused biculturalism" to describe the juxtaposition of irreconcilable but coexisting cultural traditions.

Yet another critique of research in Indian education zeroes in on the lack of evidence supporting the abundant literature suggesting that Indian children have "special strengths" in spatial abilities and visual memory, so-called "visual learning styles" (Kleinfeld & Nelson, 1988, p. 1–2). Kleinfeld and Nelson searched the psychological, ethnographic, and educational research for studies that empirically tested the claim that "instruction adapted to Native American learning styles increases achievement" (p. 8). They found three: two studies did *not* show that Native American students learn more with visually based instruction; the third had conflicting results but found that visually based instruction was *more* effective for White than for Indian children. Kleinfeld and Nelson concluded that the lack of evidence notwithstanding, the "learning-style" construct remains popular because educators want to avoid "deficit" language and because the terminology is useful in grant proposals and to describe the many adjustments teachers make when dealing with specific Native American groups. Similarly, Irvine and York (1995) propose that "widespread conclusions in the [learning style] literature . . . are premature and conjectural" (p. 484). Their critical review of the literature leads them to the conclusion that "research on learning styles using culturally diverse students fails to support the premise that members of a given cultural group exhibit a distinctive style" (p. 494).

Indigenous Languages and Epistemologies, Educational Theories, and Reforms

The debates over learning and teaching styles and cultural congruence raise profound questions for American Indian

education. How we teach children, and how they learn, are critically important issues, but they should not obscure the critical nature of *what* is being taught. Anyone who has suffered through a television miniseries on "How the West Was Won," or a high school history lecture lauding Columbus's bold, adventurous spirit of "discovery," or an elementary classroom reenactment of the first Thanksgiving knows this lesson. What if teachers scrupulously develop culturally/linguistically sensitive pedagogical methods but never alter the content of what they teach?

Can we expect Indian children to "succeed" in school when Indian history, cultures, and peoples are systematically excluded from, marginalized within, or brutalized by curricular content? Perhaps classrooms that value Native cultures and use local knowledge as bridges to "mainstream" curricular content in an atmosphere of mutual trust and respect—Osborne's (1989) notion of fused biculturalism—might foster Native academic achievement (Demmert, 2001). Research findings from the Rough Rock Demonstration School on the Navajo reservation describe the introduction of an experimental social studies curriculum based on local values, which began locally but expanded to global content. Children blossomed from silent "concrete" learners into talkative, analytical students who responded to questions with as much enthusiasm as any interlocutor of Socrates (McCarty, Wallace, Lynch, & Benally, 1991).

Projects in curriculum development have achieved positive results in some Indian-controlled schools. The Kickapoo Nation School introduced new curriculum in 1985 and reversed declining performance on test scores (Dupuis & Walker, 1989); Okakok (1989) stressed the benefits of integrating Inupiat and Western Alaskan cultural values into the administration and curriculum of the North Slope Borough School District. What goes on within schools is only part, of course, of the influences to which children are exposed. DeMarrais, Nelson, and Baker's (1992) delightful description of the cognitive skills reinforced by "storyknifing," the storytelling activity of young Alaska Native girls along the muddy banks of the Kuskokwim River, concluded with the discouraging observation that this childhood pastime has been supplanted by hours in front of the TV. The overwhelming onslaught of contemporary American culture, ruled by music, media, and the mall, threatens to overwhelm more than indigenous childhood games. Native languages, the very fabric of cultural expression and cultural production, are critically endangered.

Language Policy and Language Renewal. Native American language use, maintenance, and renewal are tremendously important influences on educational experiences and policies, but it would require another chapter to review them adequately. At one end of the continuum, groups such as the Navajo nation try to maintain a language still spoken by a majority of members (Rosier & Holm, 1980). Along the middle, the Tachi-Yokuts in central California struggle to revive interest in a language spoken only by an elderly few (Britsch-Devany, 1988). At the other end of the continuum, heritage languages have virtually disappeared, leaving their traces in a locally specific version of "Indian English" (Leap, 1977).

Long-standing federal policy to eradicate Native languages has only recently been revised to provide grudging support for bilingual education (McCarty, 1992; Zepeda, 1990). Since the passage of the Bilingual Education Act in 1968 (other federal titles also supply monies to support bilingual/bicultural education), at least 70 Native communities have developed language education projects (McCarty; St. Clair & Leap, 1982). Federal bilingual policies have supported "transitional" bilingual programs, to move children from fluency in a Native language to English (Grant & Goldsmith, 1979; Spolsky, 1972, 1978). Most Native people, however, are committed to maintaining Native languages, in programs ranging from Makah on the northwest tip of Washington state (Renker & Arnold, 1988) to Passamoquoddy in Maine (Spolsky, 1978).

Tribes have turned to professionally and academically trained linguists to help develop educational programs in spoken and written language (Hale, 1973; Leap, 1988; Watahomigie & Yamamoto, 1987; Young, 1972). Fluent Native speakers of Hopi, Navajo, Tohono O'odham, and other languages have earned graduate degrees in linguistics and applied their training to educational development. Native Americans may not willingly surrender their languages, but many communities are deeply troubled that fluent speakers grow fewer and older, and younger generations grow up inundated by the constant English chatter transmitted via cable, satellite dish, and digital media.

Bilingual/Bicultural Education and Language Development. According to recent estimates, only 16% of the remaining 210 indigenous languages spoken in the United States and Canada have new speakers to ensure their survival into the next generations (Krauss, 1998). Native communities across the continent teeter on the brink of language extinction, while dedicated speakers of these precious, irreplaceable heritage languages fight to preserve their future (McCarty, Watahomigie, & Yamamoto, 1999; McCarty & Zepeda, 1995). The challenge in reversing "language shift"—that is, the shift from indigenous heritage languages to English—is not only "to bring the language 'back,' but . . . [to move] it *forward* into new social contexts" (McCarty & Watahomigie, 1999, p. 6).

Immersion programs based on models developed by Maori speakers in New Zealand, Native Hawaiians, and First Nations in Canada have proven attractive (Yamauchi & Ceppi, 1998), although they may prove more difficult to implement in mixed urban settings where Native families are scattered and are from diverse tribal homelands. The goal of creating "new habitats where the language can be reconstructed and used" has been successfully accomplished, notably by the master-apprentice program in Native California communities (Apodaca, 2000), and in yearly gatherings such as the American Indian Language Development Institute at the University of Arizona and the Oklahoma Native American Language Development Institute (McCarty & Watahomigie, 1999). Congress has articulated its support through the 1990/1992 Native American Languages Act, "the only federal legislation which explicitly vows to protect and provides some financial support for indigenous languages" (McCarty & Watahomigie, 1999, p. 11).

Indigenous Literacies. Some Native communities have used orthographic systems developed by Christian missionaries from colonial languages for a century or more, while in other communities literacy practices are new. Across the spectrum, communities are producing published and online materials such as dictionaries, grammars, and school curricula (Hopi Dictionary Project, 1998; Lipka & Ilustik, 1997). The comprehensive, thought-provoking anthology edited by Nancy Hornberger (1997) presents a diversity of indigenous literacy projects across North, Central, and South America, illustrating the modern tensions within multilingual nations, and the potential of literacy to act simultaneously as "liberator and a weapon of oppression" (p. 4). "For literacy developers in multilingual contexts, then, the question is not so much: how to develop literacy? But, which literacies to develop for what purposes?" (Hornberger, p. 4).

Native Epistemologies. Acknowledging Native ways of knowing requires more than language reclamation. Teacher training, school reform, curricular renovation, secure and predictable funding bases, community participation, the integration of Native and Western educational goals and practices—all must go hand in hand to achieve progress (Demmert, 2001; Lipka, 2002). The transformation of school culture in a Yup'ik (Eskimo) community in Alaska (Lipka et al., 1998) is a model for the committed, courageous intercultural dialogue and willingness to change that is also being developed through the Alaska Native Knowledge Network (www.ankn.uaf.edu) and the Creating Sacred Places for Children initiative of the National Indian School Board Association (Fox, 2000). School reform of this kind depends on a kind of scholarship that has not been widely available to most educators, an indigenous scholarship that plumbs the depths of Native epistemologies.

Like Basil Johnston (1976), the noted scholar of education and Anishinabe language and philosophy, Yup'ik scholar A. O. Kawagley (1995, 1999) presents an intellectually engaged, analytic view of his own culture: a specific indigenous system of thought that is profoundly complex and demanding, deeply imaginative, and respectful of "the mysteries of the world" (Kawagley, 1999, p. 31). Scholars such as these, who recognize the multiple levels of understanding within each Native system of "ancient knowledge" (Lang, 1989), offer a welcome counterpoint to the genericized, pan-Indian, never-well-defined notions of "holistic" or "spiritual" or "ecological" education proposed by some (Cajete, 1994; van Hamme, 1996).

Kawagley eloquently distills the real-world sovereign demands of indigenous education: "If the Yupiaq people are to really exercise the option of educational control it will require that the schools become Yupiaq controlled, Yupiaq administered, and Yupiaq in practice" (1999, p. 45). Dalton and Youpa (1998) describe a similar program of reform at Zuni, New Mexico, that integrates Zuni values of fortitude, stoicism, responsibility, and initiative into a system of standards that extends an invitation to students to join a community of learners. As laudable and difficult as these goals are for small, self-contained communities, what are the options in highly diverse urban and semiurban environments, where more than half of all Native Americans now live?

Surely it does not well serve any students to isolate Native curricular content in some unit focused on Thanksgiving (Huff, 1997; Rains & Swisher, 1999). Multicultural education needs to achieve more than that, but meaningful integration of profoundly different cultural philosophies, pedagogies, and curricula is a daunting task. Realistically, most teachers of Native children are not Native themselves: in 1993–94, even in HIE [high Indian enrollment, 25% or more] public schools "only 15% of the teachers . . . were American Indian or Alaska Native" (Pavel, 1999, p. 2). Non-Native teachers are often as sincerely interested in serving Native students better as they are sincerely frustrated by the lack of materials, training, and institutional support available to them. Cleary and Peacock's (1998) collection of teachers' testimonials is eloquent and compelling reading, even as it demonstrates how difficult it is to remember the diversity of indigenous lives and guard against the tendency to stereotype and overgeneralize.

Trends

Research on Indian education has tended to move away from models that propose deficiencies—in the students' language abilities (Philion & Galloway, 1969; Salisbury, 1974) or neural organization (Ross, 1989) or cultural background—to theories of social and economic discrimination (Ogbu, 1983, 1987, 1989) that contextualize schools within the larger society. Current research trends define Native cognitive skills as strengths, not weaknesses (Macias, 1989), and try to discover the characteristics of successful students, successful programs, successful teachers, and successful schools (Benjamin, Chambers, & Reiterman, 1993; Demmert, 2001; Shutiva, 1991; Swisher & Tippeconnic, 1999).

As researchers turn their attention toward student success, gifted programs become a topic of interest, especially since it seems clear that "the patterning tests for giftedness and other standardized tests do not, as presently constructed, allow for cultural differences" (Gamati & Weiland, 1997, p. 47). DeMarrais et al. (1992) focus on storytelling skills of Alaska Native girls; Kleinfeld (1973a) studies Eskimos' visual skills; Nelson and Lalami (1991) discuss Tohono O'odham children's "visual-spatial, pattern-symbol and kinesthetic" skills for the creative process. Romero (1994) reports on a two-year survey designed to develop a culturally coherent definition of "giftedness"—specifically among New Mexico communities who speak the Keres language—another example of Native educators articulating indigenous philosophy and leading schools to value and incorporate community values. Native educational leaders also played key roles in formulating a recent federal policy statement on Indian education.

On August 6, 1998, President Clinton issued Executive Order 13096, calling for the development and implementation of a comprehensive, federally funded research agenda in American Indian education. Federal officials convened meetings of academics, educators, and tribal representatives to draft research initiatives, and in November 2001 the *American Indian and Alaska Native Education Research Agenda* (which includes the text of Executive Order 13096) was published on the Web (Research Agenda Working Group, 2001). In the fall of 2001, the first grants were funded under the Office of Educational Research and Innovation (OERI).

The *Research Agenda* details its assumptions about *how* research in Indian education should be approached—it should focus on success as well as deficits, respect tribal sovereignty, and recognize tribal difference—and *what* research methods should be used, including the need for detailed national data, generalizable research findings, and an independent clearinghouse focused on Native education. The *Agenda* repeatedly emphasizes the critical need for Native participation in, if not control of, research efforts. The call for Native researchers, tribal oversight of research protocols, and strict adherence to the ethical and methodological demands of tribal sovereigns permeates recent literature on Indian education (Lomawaima, 2000;

Nason, 1996; Swisher, 1996; Swisher & Tippeconnic, 1999).

Meanwhile, at Sinte Gleske College in Sioux country, Native scholars map the constellations and their earthly correlates among the geographic features of the Black Hills (P. Deloria, 1984); Native scholars gather at the Institute for Native Knowledge at Humboldt State University in Northern California to exchange ideas. Finally, Native scholarship is being shaped by Native people. Scholars continue to identify and battle against the legacies of institutional racism in the American public school system (Huff, 1997), but they also nurture a spirit of optimism: "As we close out another decade and another century, the state of Indigenous education is in better shape than ever before in history" (Swisher & Tippeconnic, 1999, p. vii).

ASSESSMENTS AND IMPLICATIONS FOR FUTURE RESEARCH

Native Americans face multiple challenges in the coming century as they work to maintain sovereignty, build economies, preserve or regain language, and ensure educational access and achievement for their young people. Significant obstacles to all these goals exist within U.S. society, as the same struggles over sovereignty, reserved rights, and self-determination that began the 20th century also usher in the 21st century.

It is perhaps ironic that a pan-tribal identity has become more real over time, but that pan-tribal linkage today complicates educational policy making and educational research. Too much policy has been predicated on creating viable solutions to "Indian" problems, generically defined. Too often, provocative but slender evidence from a tribally specific research site has been generalized to all "Indian" children. Educators need to understand the diversity of Native cultures and experiences and work locally to develop relevant content and methods. It may be that their achievements will never be generalizable. We need a wider range of research in the increasingly multicultural, increasingly poor urban schools where more and more children are being educated, far from traditional tribal homes.

Diversity in the classroom means we must attend to the skills, strengths, and needs of each child as an individual, building on Native values (Fiordo, 1988) without romanticizing them or stereotyping an "Indian learning style." Well-meaning educators and policy makers may long for a simple answer, be it whole-language instruction (Kasten, 1992) or generic spirituality (Locust, 1988), but the search for a single best way to educate any human population is like the search for the Holy Grail. It risks becoming a sacred calling that consumes resources in the search for an illusory panacea for complex social and educational ills.

History, politics, and education have always been and will forever be inextricably bound up with one another in Indian America. Activism for educational change and empowerment has served as a political proving ground for Native American leadership. In the wake of the 1960s civil rights movement, the birth of the National Indian Education Association offered a forum for nationwide communication and organization. The Indian Historian Press, *Wassaja, Akwesasne Notes, Indian Country Today,* and other Native presses have linked tribal communities and provided unprecedented opportunity to disseminate information and exchange ideas. The Chicago Indian Conference in 1961, the formation of the National Indian Youth Council in the early 1960s, and the first Convocation of American Indian scholars at Princeton in 1970 brought people together and developed new levels of political consciousness and cooperation (Indian Historian Press, 1970; Lynch & Charleston, 1990).

Their legacy has been inherited and enriched by the National Indian Education Association, the National Indian School Board Association, the scholars and community members who contributed to the 2001 *Research Agenda,* and the many dedicated individuals working tirelessly across Indian country to improve educational methods and opportunities. Schools have frequently been the flash point for political organization in Indian communities. When Native Americans occupied Alcatraz Island in San Francisco Bay on November 20, 1969, they resolved to "plan our own futures and educate our own children" (blue cloud, 1972, p. 21). Their plan for Alcatraz included a Center for Native American Studies with "traveling colleges" to visit reservations, a training school, and a museum. Education was foremost in their minds; their vision was realized in part when D-Q University was established at Davis, California (blue cloud, 1972; Lutz, 1980). The vision flourishes today on the 32 campuses of the tribal community college system. Education, politics, and history still walk hand in hand across Indian country.

Native American communities know their own history well, and that highly developed historical consciousness tends to make them skeptical of federal promises of change or educators' promises of improvement. The special legal and political status of tribes and the implications of sovereignty may mitigate against a wholehearted acceptance of multicultural education if "multicultural concepts seem to promote the assimilative trend by standardization at the expense of self-determination in Indian education" (Jaimes, 1983, p. 17). If self-determination means a tribal community college, or an all-Indian urban school (Butterfield & Pepper, 1991), it runs the risk of alienating those who believe in U.S.

ideals of desegregation and cultural sharing. Self-determination must be understood as expressing a possibility of cultural pluralism, and the rights of Native communities to claim certain places, practices, and beliefs as their own (Tippeconnic, 2000).

Native America has insisted for 500 years on the right to exist; Native America has hoped for 500 years for the right to prosper and thrive. If Native people make educational decisions according to their own ideals of cultural survival and sovereign status, they must be respected.

Their rights to self-determination are rooted in the mature inherent sovereignty that predates the U.S. Constitution; in the constitutional recognition of Native peoples as distinctive peoples with distinctive political identities; in the constitutionally based recognition of the relationship between tribal governments and the federal government accomplished through the negotiation of treaties and the articulation of a trust relationship; and the principle of constrained, just government that lies at the heart of the American democratic ideal.

References

Adams, D. W. (1977). Education in hues: Red and Black at Hampton Institute, 1878–1893. *South Atlantic Quarterly, 76,* 159–176.

Adams, D. W. (1988). Fundamental considerations: The deep meaning of Native American schooling, 1880–1900. *Harvard Educational Review, 58*(1), 1–28.

Adams, D. W. (1995). *Education for extinction: American Indians and the boarding school experience, 1875–1928.* Lawrence: University Press of Kansas.

American Indian Higher Education Consortium. (1999). *Tribal colleges: An introduction.* Arlington, VA: Author. (www.aihec.org)

Apodaca, P. (2000). California tongues. *Native Americas, 17*(4), 50–55.

Appleton, N. (1983). *Cultural pluralism in education.* New York: Longman.

Archuleta, M. L., Child, B. J., & Lomawaima, K. T. (2000). *Away from home: American Indian boarding school experiences, 1879–2000.* Phoenix, AZ: Heard Museum.

Au, K., & Jordan, C. (1981). Teaching reading to Hawaiian children. In H. Trueba, G. Guthrie, & K. Au (Eds.), *Culture and the bilingual classroom* (pp. 139–152). Rowley, MA: Newbury House.

Aurbach, H., & Fuchs, E. (1970). *The status of American Indian education.* University Park: Pennsylvania State University Press.

Axtell, J. (1981). Dr. Wheelock's little red school. In J. Axtell (Ed.), *The European and the Indian: Essays in the ethnohistory of colonial North America* (pp. 87–109). Oxford, England: Oxford University Press.

Beatty, W. (1953). *Education for culture change.* Chilocco, OK: Bureau of Indian Affairs.

Benjamin, D. P., Chambers, S., & Reiterman, G. (1993). A focus on American Indian college persistence. *Journal of American Indian Education, 32*(2), 24–40.

Birchard, B. (1970). *Boarding schools for American Indian youth.* National Study of American Indian Education, Ser. 2, no. 2. Minneapolis: University of Minnesota Center for Urban and Regional Affairs.

blue cloud, p. (1972). *Alcatraz is not an island.* Berkeley: Wingbow Press.

Bowden, H. (1981). *American Indians and Christian missions.* Chicago: University of Chicago Press.

Bowker, A. (1992). The American Indian female dropout. *Journal of American Indian Education, 31*(3), 3–20.

Brady, P. (1996). Native dropouts and non-Native dropouts in Canada: Two solitudes or a solitude shared? *Journal of American Indian Education, 35*(2), 10–20.

Brandt, E. (1992). The Navajo area student dropout study: Findings and implications. *Journal of American Indian Education, 31*(2), 48–63.

Brewer, A. (1977). An Indian education. *Integrateducation, 15,* 21–23.

Britsch-Devany, S. (1988). The collaborative development of a language renewal program for preschoolers. *Human Organization, 47,* 297–302.

Brown, A. D. (1979). The cross-over effect: A legitimate issue in Indian education? In *Multicultural education and the American Indian* (pp. 93–113). Los Angeles: UCLA, American Indian Studies Center.

Brown, A. D. (1980). Cherokee culture and school achievement. *American Indian Culture and Research Journal, 4,* 55–74.

Brumble, H. D., III. (1981). *An annotated bibliography of American Indian and Eskimo autobiographies.* Lincoln: University of Nebraska Press.

Bryde, J. (1970). *The Indian student: A study of scholastic failure and personality conflict* (2nd ed.). Vermillion, SD: Dakota Press.

Bureau of Indian Affairs. (1988). *Report on BIA education: Excellence in Indian education through effective school process.* Washington, DC: U.S. Department of the Interior.

Butterfield, R., & Pepper, F. (1991). Improving parental participation in elementary and secondary education for American Indian and Alaska Native students. In *Indian Nations at Risk Task Force commissioned papers.* Washington, DC: Department of Education. (ERIC Document Reproduction Service no. ED 343 763)

Cajete, G. (1994). *Look to the mountain: An ecology of indigenous education.* Skyland, NC: Kivakí Press.

Carnegie Foundation for the Advancement of Teaching. (1989). *Tribal colleges: Shaping the future of Native America.* Princeton, NJ: Author.

Castile, G., & Bee, R. (1992). *State and reservation: New perspectives on federal Indian policy.* Tucson: University of Arizona Press.

Cazden, C., & John, V. (1971). Learning in American Indian children. In M. L. Wax, S. Diamond, & F. Gearing (Eds.), *Anthropological perspectives on education* (pp. 253–272). New York: Basic Books.

Cazden, C., & Leggett, E. L. (1981). Culturally responsive education: Recommendations for achieving Lau remedies II. In H. Trueba, G. Guthrie, & K. Au (Eds.), *Culture and the bilingual classroom* (pp. 69–86). Rowley, MA: Newbury House.

Child, B. J. (1998). *Boarding school seasons: American Indian families, 1900–1940.* Lincoln: University of Nebraska Press.

Chrisjohn, R. D., & Peters, M. (1989, August). The right-brained Indian: Fact or fiction? *Journal of American Indian Education* [Special issue], 77–83.

Cleary, L. M., & Peacock, T. D. (1998). *Collected wisdom: American Indian education.* Boston: Allyn and Bacon.

Coggins, K., Williams, E., & Radin, N. (1997). The traditional tribal values of Ojibwa parents and the school performance of their children: An exploratory study. *Journal of American Indian Education, 36*(3), 1–15.

Crow, L., Murray, W., & Smythe, H. (1966). *Educating the culturally disadvantaged child.* New York: David McKay.

Dalton, S. S., & Youpa, D. G. (1998). Standards-based teaching reform in Zuni Pueblo middle and high schools. *Equity and Excellence in Education, 31*(1), 55–68.

Deloria, P. (Director). (1984). *Eyanopopi: Heart of the Sioux* [Film]. Boulder, CO: Centre Productions.

Deloria, V., Jr., & Lytle, C. (1984). *The nation within: The past and future of American Indian sovereignty.* New York: Pantheon Books.

Deloria, V., Jr., & Wildcat, D. R. (2001). *Power and place: Indian education in America.* Golden, CO: American Indian Graduate Center and Fulcrum Resources.

Deloria, V., Jr., & Wilkins, D. E. (1999). *Tribes, treaties, and constitutional tribulations.* Austin: University of Texas Press.

DeMarrais, K., Nelson, P., & Baker, J. (1992). Meaning in mud: Yup'ik Eskimo girls at play. *Anthropology and Education Quarterly, 23,* 120–144.

Demmert, W. G., Jr. (2001). *Improving academic performance among Native American students: A review of the research literature.* Charleston, WV: ERIC Clearinghouse on Rural Education and Small Schools.

Deyhle, D. (1983). Measuring success and failure in the classroom: Teacher communication about tests and the understandings of young Navajo students. *Peabody Journal of Education, 61*(1), 67–85.

Deyhle, D. (1992). Constructing failure and maintaining cultural identity: Navajo and Ute school leavers. *Journal of American Indian Education, 31*(2), 24–47.

Dinges, N. G., & Hollenbeck, A. R. (1978). Field dependence-independence in Navajo children. *International Journal of Psychology, 13,* 215–220.

Dingman, S. M., Mroczka, M. A., & Brady, J. V. (1995). Predicting academic success for American Indian students. *Journal of American Indian Education, 34*(2), 10–17.

Dobyns, H. F. (1983). *Their number become thinned.* Knoxville: University of Tennessee Press.

Dumont, R. (1972). Learning English and how to be silent: Studies in Sioux and Cherokee classrooms. In C. Cazden, V. John, & D. Hymes (Eds.), *Functions of language in the classroom* (pp. 344–369). New York: Teachers College Press.

Dumont, R., & Wax, M. (1969). Cherokee school society and the intercultural classroom. *Human Organization, 28,* 217–226.

Dupuis, V. L., & Walker, M. (1989). The circle of learning at Kickapoo. *Journal of American Indian Education, 28*(1), 27–33.

Ellis, C. (1996). *To change them forever: Indian education at the Rainy Mountain Boarding School, 1893–1920.* Norman: University of Oklahoma Press.

Faircloth, S., & Tippeconnic, J. W., III. (2000). *Issues in the education of American Indian and Alaska Native students with disabilities.* (ERIC Digest.) Charleston, WV: ERIC Clearinghouse on Rural Education and Small Schools. (ERIC Document Reproduction Service no. EDO-RC-00-3)

Fiordo, R. (1988). The great learning enterprise of the Four Winds Development Project. *Journal of American Indian Education, 27*(3), 24–34.

Fixico, D. (1998). *The invasion of Indian country in the 20th century: American capitalism and tribal natural resources.* Boulder: University Press of Colorado.

Fox, S. (2000). *Creating a sacred place to support young American Indian and other learners* (Vols. 1 & 2). Polson, MT: National Indian School Board Association.

Fuchs, E., & Havighurst, R. (1972). *To live on this earth.* New York: Doubleday.

Gamati, C., & Weiland, M. (1997). An exploration of American Indian students' perceptions of patterning, symmetry and geometry. *Journal of American Indian Education, 36*(3), 27–47.

Goddard, J. T., & Shields, C. M. (1997). An ethnocultural comparison of empowerment in two districts: Learning from an American Indian and a Canadian First Nations school district. *Journal of American Indian Education, 36*(2), 19–45.

Grant, J. H., & Goldsmith, R. (1979). *Bilingual education and federal law: An overview.* (Project report). Austin, TX: Dissemination and Assessment Center for Bilingual Education.

Greenbaum, P. E., & Greenbaum, S. D. (1983). Cultural differences, nonverbal regulation, and classroom interaction: Sociolinguistic interference in American Indian education. *Peabody Journal of Education, 61*(1), 16–33.

Grell, L. (1983, October). *Indian self-determination and education: Kickapoo Nation School.* Paper presented at the meeting of the American Anthropological Association, Chicago. (ERIC Document Reproduction Service no. ED 247 056)

Guilmet, G. M. (1978). Navajo and Caucasian children's verbal and nonverbal visual behavior in the urban classroom. *Anthropology and Education Quarterly, 9,* 196–215.

Guilmet, G. M. (1981). Oral-linguistic and nonoral-visual styles of attending: Navajo and Caucasian children compared in an urban classroom and on an urban playground. *Human Organization, 40,* 145–150.

Haig-Brown, C. (1988). *Resistance and renewal: Surviving the Indian residential school.* Vancouver, BC: Tillacum Library.

Hale, K. (1973). The role of American Indian linguistics in bilingual education. In R. Turner (Ed.), *Bilingualism in the Southwest* (pp. 203–225). Tucson: University of Arizona Press.

Hopi Dictionary Project. (1998). *Hopi dictionary: Hopìikwa lavàytutuveni.* Tucson: University of Arizona Press.

Hornberger, N. H. (Ed.). (1997). *Indigenous literacies in the Americas: Language planning from the bottom up.* Berlin: Mouton de Gruyter.

Hoxie, F. (1984). *A final promise: The campaign to assimilate the Indians, 1880–1920.* Lincoln: University of Nebraska Press.

Huff, D. J. (1997). *To live heroically: Institutional racism and American Indian education.* Albany: State University of New York Press.

Hyer, S. (1990). *One house, one voice, one heart: Native American education at Santa Fe Indian School.* Santa Fe: Museum of New Mexico Press.

Indian Historian Press. (1970). *Indian voices: The first convocation of American Indian scholars.* San Francisco: Author.

Irvine, J. J., & York, D. E. (1995). Learning styles and culturally diverse students: A literature review. In J. A. Banks & C.A.M. Banks (Eds.), *Handbook of research on multicultural education* (pp. 487–497). New York: Macmillan.

Jaimes, M. A. (1983). The myth of Indian education in the American education system. *Action in Teacher Education, 5*(3), 15–19.

James, H. (1974). *Pages from Hopi history.* Tucson: University of Arizona Press.

John, V. (1972). Styles of learning—styles of teaching: Reflections on the education of Navajo children. In C. Cazden, D. Hymes, & V. John (Eds.), *Functions of language in the classroom* (pp. 331–343). New York: Teachers College Press.

Johnson, B. (1968). *Navaho education at Rough Rock.* Rough Rock, AZ: Rough Rock Demonstration School, D.I.N.E..

Johnston, B. H. (1976). *Ojibway heritage.* New York: Columbia University Press.

Johnston, B. H. (1988). *Indian school days.* Norman: University of Oklahoma Press.

Kasten, W. (1992). Bridging the horizon: American Indian beliefs and whole language learning. *Anthropology and Education Quarterly, 23,* 108–119.

Kawagley, A. O. (1995). *A Yupiaq worldview: A pathway to an ecology and spirit.* Prospect Heights, IL: Waveland Press.

Kawagley, A. O. (1999). Alaska native education: History and adaptation in the new millennium. *Journal of American Indian Education, 39*(1), 31–51.

King, A. R. (1967). *The school at Mopass: A problem of identity.* New York: Holt, Rinehart, & Winston.

Kleinfeld, J. S. (1973a). Intellectual strengths in culturally different groups: An Eskimo illustration. *Review of Educational Research, 43,* 341–359.

Kleinfeld, J. S. (1973b). *A long way from home: Effects of public high schools on village children away from home.* Fairbanks, AK: Center for Northern Educational Research.

Kleinfeld, J. S. (1974). Effects of nonverbal warmth on the learning of Eskimo and white students. *Journal of Social Psychology, 92,* 3–9.

Kleinfeld, J., & Nelson, P. (1988). *Adapting instruction to Native Americans' "learning styles": An iconoclastic view.* (ERIC Document Reproduction Service no. ED 321 952)

Krauss, M. (1998). The condition of Native North American languages: The need for realistic assessment and action. *International Journal of the Sociology of Language, 132,* 9–21.

Krush, T., Bjork, J., Sindell, P., & Nelle, J. (1966). Some thoughts on the formation of personality disorder: Study of an Indian boarding school population. *American Journal of Psychiatry, 122,* 868–876.

LaFlesche, F. (1978). *The middle five.* Lincoln: University of Nebraska Press. (Original work published 1900)

Lang, J. (1989). It's hard to be an Indian. *News From Native California, 3*(1), 3.

Leap, W. (1977). *Studies in southwestern Indian English.* San Antonio, TX: Trinity University Press.

Leap, W. (1988). Applied linguistics and American Indian language renewal: Introductory comments. *Human Organization, 47,* 283–291.

Ledlow, S. (1992). Is cultural discontinuity an adequate explanation for dropping out? *Journal of American Indian Education, 31*(3), 21–36.

Lipka, J. (1991). Toward a culturally based pedagogy: A case study of one Yup'ik Eskimo teacher. *Anthropology and Education Quarterly, 22,* 203–223.

Lipka, J. (2002). *Schooling for self-determination: Research on the effects of including Native language and culture in the schools* (ERIC Digest). Charleston, WV: ERIC Clearinghouse on Rural Education and Small Schools. (ERIC Document Reproduction Service no. EDO-RC-01-12)

Lipka, J., & Ilustik, E. (1997). Ciulistet and the curriculum of the possible. In N. H. Hornberger (Ed.), *Indigenous literacies in the Americas* (pp. 45–67). Berlin: Mouton de Gruyter.

Lipka, J., with Mohatt, G. V., & Ciulistet Group. (1998). *Transforming the culture of schools: Yup'ik Eskimo examples.* Mahwah, NJ: Erlbaum.

Littlefield, A. (1993). Learning to labor: Native American education in the United States, 1880–1930. In J. Moore (Ed.), *The political economy of North American Indians* (pp. 43–59). Norman: University of Oklahoma Press.

Lobo, S., & Peters, K. (Eds.). (2001). *American Indians and the urban experience.* Walnut Creek, CA: Altamira Press.

Locust, C. (1988). Wounding the spirit: Discrimination and traditional American Indian belief systems. *Harvard Educational Review, 58,* 315–330.

Lomawaima, K. T. (1993). Domesticity in the federal Indian schools: The power of authority over mind and body. *American Ethnologist, 20*(2), 1–14.

Lomawaima, K. T. (1994). *They called it Prairie Light: The story of Chilocco Indian School.* Lincoln: University of Nebraska Press.

Lomawaima, K. T. (1999). The un-natural history of American Indian education. In K. G. Swisher & J. W. Tippeconnic, III (Eds.), *Next steps: Research and practice to advance American Indian education* (pp. 3–31). Charleston, WV: ERIC Clearinghouse on Rural Education and Small Schools.

Lomawaima, K. T. (2000). Tribal sovereigns: Reframing research in American Indian education. *Harvard Educational Review, 70*(1), 1–21.

Lomawaima, K. T. (2002). American Indian education: By Indians versus for Indians. In P. J. Deloria & N. Salisbury (Eds.), *A companion to American Indian history* (pp. 422–440). Malden, MA: Blackwell.

Lomawaima, K. T., & McCarty, T. L. (2002). When tribal sovereignty challenges democracy: American Indian education and the democratic ideal. *American Educational Research Journal, 39*(2), 279–305.

Longstreet, W. S. (1978). *Aspects of ethnicity.* New York: Teachers College Press.

Lowry, L. (1970). Differences in visual perception and auditory discrimination between American Indian and White kindergarten children. *Journal of Learning Disabilities, 3,* 359–363.

Lutz, H. (1980). *D-Q University: Native American self-determination in higher education.* Davis: University of California, Native American Studies/Applied Behavioral Sciences, Tecumseh Center. (ERIC Document Reproduction Service no. ED 209 049)

Lynch, P. D., & Charleston, M. (1990). The emergence of American Indian leadership in education. *Journal of American Indian Education, 29*(2), 1–10.

Macias, C. J. (1989, August). American Indian academic success: The role of indigenous learning strategies. *Journal of American Indian Education,* 43–52.

McBeth, S. (1983). *Ethnic identity and the boarding school experience of west-central Oklahoma American Indians.* Washington, DC: University Press of America.

McCarty, T. L. (1987). The Rough Rock demonstration school: A case history with implications for educational evaluation. *Human Organization, 46,* 1103–1112.

McCarty, T. L. (1989). School as community: The Rough Rock demonstration. *Harvard Educational Review, 59,* 484–503.

McCarty, T. L. (1992). *Federal language policy and American Indian education.* (Rev. ed.). (ERIC Document Reproduction Service no. ED 355 060)

McCarty, T. L. (2002). *A place to be Navajo: Rough Rock and the struggle for self-determination in indigenous schooling.* Mahwah, NJ: Erlbaum.

McCarty, T., Wallace, S., Lynch, R., & Benally, A. (1991). Classroom inquiry and Navajo learning styles: A call for reassessment. *Anthropology and Education Quarterly, 22,* 42–59.

McCarty, T. L., & Watahomigie, L. J. (1999). Indigenous education and grassroots language planning in the USA. *Practicing Anthropology, 20*(2), 5–11.

McCarty, T. L., Watahomigie, L. J., & Yamamoto, A. Y. (1999). Reversing language shift in indigenous America: Collaborations and views from the field. *Practicing Anthropology, 20*(2).

McCarty, T. L., & Zepeda, O. (Eds.). (1995). Indigenous language education and literacy [Theme issue]. *Bilingual Research Journal. 19*(1).

Meriam, L., with Brown, R. A., Cloud, H. R., Dale, E. E., Duke, E., Edwards, H. R., et al. (1928). *The problem of Indian administration.* Baltimore, MD: Johns Hopkins Press for the Institute for Government Research.

Mihesuah, D. A. (1993). *Cultivating the rosebuds: The education of women at the Cherokee Female Seminary, 1851–1909.* Urbana: University of Illinois Press.

Miller, A. G., & Thomas, R. (1972). Cooperation and competition among Blackfoot Indian and urban Canadian children. *Child Development, 43,* 1104–1110.

Mohatt, G., & Erickson, F. (1981). Cultural differences in teaching styles in an Odawa school. In H. Trueba, G. Guthrie, & K. Au (Eds.), *Culture and the bilingual classroom* (pp. 105–119). Rowley, MA: Newbury House.

NAACP Legal Defense and Educational Fund. (1971). *An even chance: A report on federal funds for Indian children in public school districts.* Annandale, VA: Graphics 4.

Nabokov, P. (Ed.). (1991). *Native American testimony.* New York: Penguin Books.

Nason, J. D. (1996). Tribal models for controlling research. *Tribal College, 8*(2), 17–20.

National Archives. (1988a). Indian tribal entities within the contiguous 48 states recognized and eligible to receive services from the U.S. B.I.A. *Federal Register, 53,* 52829–52831.

National Archives. (1988b). Native entities within the state of Alaska recognized and eligible to receive services from the U.S. B.I.A. *Federal Register, 53,* 52832–52835.

National Center for Education Statistics. (1981). *Digest of education statistics.* Washington, DC: Government Printing Office.

National Center for Education Statistics. (1985–86). *Digest of education statistics.* Washington, DC: Government Printing Office.

National Center for Education Statistics. (1988). *High school and beyond—A descriptive summary of 1980 high school sophomores: Six years later* (DOE Report no. CS88–404). Washington, DC: Government Printing Office.

National Center for Education Statistics. (1989). *Analysis report: Dropout rates in the United States 1988* (NCES 89–609). Washington, DC: U.S. Department of Education, Office of Educational Research and Improvement.

National Center for Education Statistics. (1990a). *Digest of education statistics.* Washington, DC: Government Printing Office.

National Center for Education Statistics. (1990b). *National education longitudinal study of 1988: A profile of the American eighth grade* (NCES 90–458). Washington, DC: U.S. Department of Education, Office of Educational Research and Improvement.

National Center for Education Statistics. (1992). *Digest of education statistics.* Washington, DC: Government Printing Office.

National Center for Education Statistics. (1997). *Digest of education statistics.* Washington, DC: Government Printing Office.

National Research Council. (1976, 1977, 1978, 1979, 1980, 1981, 1982, 1983, 1986, 1987, 1989, 1990, 1991, 1993, 1998). *Doctorate recipients from United States universities.* (Summary reports.) Washington, DC: National Academy Press.

Neely, S. (1975). The Quaker era of Cherokee Indian education, 1880–1892. *Appalachian Journal, 2,* 314–322.

Nelson, A., & Lalami, B. (1991). The role of imagery training on Tohono O'odham children's creativity scores. *Journal of American Indian Education, 30*(3), 24–32.

Noley, G. (1979). Choctaw bilingual and bicultural education in the nineteenth century. In *Multicultural education and the American Indian* (pp. 25–39). Los Angeles: UCLA, American Indian Studies Center.

Nuu-chah-nulth Tribal Council. (1996). *Indian residential schools: The Nuu-chah-nulth experience.* Port Albert, BC: Author.

Office of Indian Education Programs. (2001). *Fingertip facts.* (www.oiep.bia.edu/news.htm)

Ogbu, J. U. (1983). Cultural discontinuities and schooling. *Anthropology and Education Quarterly, 13,* 290–307.

Ogbu, J. U. (1987). *Minority education and caste: The American system in cross-cultural perspective.* New York: Academic Press.

Ogbu, J. U. (1989). The individual in collective adaptation: A framework for focusing on academic underperformance and dropping out among involuntary minorities. In L. Weis, E. Farrar, & H. Petrie (Eds.), *Dropouts from school: Issues, dilemmas, and solutions* (pp. 181–204). Albany: State University of New York Press.

Okakok, L. (1989). Serving the purpose of education. *Harvard Educational Review, 59,* 405–422.

Olson, J., & Wilson, R. (1984). *Native Americans in the twentieth century.* Urbana: University of Illinois Press.

Osborne, B. (1989). Cultural congruence, ethnicity, and fused biculturalism: Zuni and Torres Strait. *Journal of American Indian Education, 28*(2), 7–20.

Parmee, E. (1968). *Formal education and culture change: A modern Apache Indian community and government education programs.* Tucson: University of Arizona Press.

Pascal, R. (1991). The imprimatur of recognition: American Indian tribes and the federal acknowledgment process. *Washington Law Review, 66,* 209–226.

Pavel, D. M. (1999). Schools, principals, and teachers serving American Indian and Alaska Native students. (ERIC Digest.) Charleston, WV: ERIC Clearinghouse on Rural Education and Small Schools. (ERIC Document Reproduction Service no. EDO-RC-98–9)

Pavel, D. M., Curtin, T. R., & Whitener, S. D. (1998). Characteristics of American Indian and Alaska Native education: Results from the 1990–91 and 1993–94 Schools and staffing surveys. *Equity and Excellence in Education, 31*(1) 48–54.

Peng, S. S., & Takai, R. T. (1983). *High school dropouts: Descriptive information from high school and beyond* (Bulletin, pp. 1–9). Washington, DC: National Center for Educational Statistics.

Philion, W. L., & Galloway, C. G. (1969). Indian children and the reading program. *Journal of Reading, 12,* 553–560, 598–602.

Philips, S. U. (1972). Participant structures and communicative competence: Warm Springs children in community and classroom. In C. Cazden, V. John, & D. Hymes (Eds.), *Functions of language in the classroom* (pp. 370–394). Prospect Heights, IL: Waveland.

Philips, S. U. (1983). *The invisible culture: Communication in classroom and community on the Warm Springs Indian reservation.* New York: Longman.

Pittman, B. (Director). (1989). *Where the spirit lives* [Film]. Canada: Amazing Spirit Productions.

Platero, P. R., Brandt, E., Witherspoon, G., & Wong, P. (1986). *Navajo students at risk. Final report for the Navajo area student dropout study.* Window Rock, AZ: Platero Paperwork.

Pommersheim, F. (1995). *Braid of feathers: American Indian law and contemporary tribal life.* Berkeley: University of California Press.

Prucha, F. P. (1979). *The churches and the Indian schools.* Lincoln: University of Nebraska Press.

Prucha, F. P. (1984). *The Great Father* (Vols. 1–2). Lincoln: University of Nebraska Press.

Rains, F. V., & Swisher, K. G. (1999). Authentic voices. *Social Education, 63*(1), 46–53.

Ramenofsky, A. (1987). *Vectors of death: The archaeology of European contact.* Albuquerque: University of New Mexico Press.

Ramírez, M., & Castañeda, A. (1974). *Cultural democracy, bicognitive development, and education.* New York: Academic Press.

Ramstad, V., & Potter, R. (1974). Differences in vocabulary and syntax usage between Nez Percé Indian and White kindergarten children. *Journal of Learning Disabilities, 7,* 491–497.

Reel, E. (1903). *Report of the superintendent of Indian schools.* Estelle Reel papers, Arden Sallquist collection, Cheney-Cowles Museum, Eastern Washington State Historical Society, Spokane, WA.

Renker, A., & Arnold, G. (1988). Exploring the role of education in cultural resource management: The Makah cultural and research center example. *Human Organization, 47,* 302–307.

Research Agenda Working Group, with Strang, W., & von Glatz, A. (2001). *American Indian and Alaska Native Education Research Agenda.* Washington, DC: U.S. Department of Education.

Reyhner, J. (1992). American Indians out of school: A review of school-based causes and solutions. *Journal of American Indian Education, 31*(3), 37–56.

Rhodes, R. W. (1990). Measurements of Navajo and Hopi brain dominance and learning styles. *Journal of American Indian Education, 29*(3), 29–40.

Romero, M. E. (1994). Identifying giftedness among Keresan Pueblo Indians: The Keres study. *Journal of American Indian Education, 34*(1), 35–58.

Rosier, P., & Holm, W. (1980). *The Rock Point experience: A longitudinal study of a Navajo school program (Saad naaki bee Na'nitin).* Bilingual Education Series, no. 8. Arlington, VA: Center for Applied Linguistics.

Ross, A. C. (1989, August). Brain hemispheric functions and the Native American. *Journal of American Indian Education,* pp. 72–76.

Ryan, C. (1962). *The Carlisle Indian industrial school.* Unpublished doctoral dissertation, Georgetown University, Washington, DC.

Salisbury, L. H. (1974). Teaching English to Alaska Natives. In R. Deever, W. Abraham, G. Gill, H. Sundwall, & P. Gianopulos (Eds.), *American Indian education* (pp. 193–203). Tempe: Arizona State University.

Scollon, R., & Scollon, S. (1981). *Narrative, literacy, and face in interethnic communication.* Norwood, NJ: Ablex.

Senese, G. (1986). Self-determination and American Indian education: An illusion of control. *Educational Theory, 36,* 153–164.

Shoemaker, N. (1999). *American Indian population recovery in the twentieth century.* Albuquerque: University of New Mexico Press.

Shutiva, C. (1991). Creativity differences between reservation and urban American Indians. *Journal of American Indian Education, 31*(1), 33–52.

Simmons, M. (1979). History of Pueblo-Spanish relations to 1821. In A. Ortiz (Ed.), *Handbook of North American Indians* (Vol. 9, pp. 178–193). Washington, DC: Smithsonian Institution Press.

Sindell, P. (1974). Some discontinuities in the enculturation of Mistassini Cree children. In G. Spindler (Ed.), *Education and cultural process* (pp. 333–341). New York: Holt, Rinehart, & Winston.

Spolsky, B. (Ed.). (1972). *The language education of minority children: Selected readings.* Rowley, MA: Newbury House.

Spolsky, B. (1978). American Indian bilingual education. In B. Spolsky & R. Cooper (Eds.), *Case studies in bilingual education* (pp. 332–361). Rowley, MA: Newbury House.

St. Clair, R., & Leap, W. (1982). *Language renewal among American Indian tribes: Issues, problems, and prospects.* Rosslyn, VA: National Clearinghouse for Bilingual Education.

Stein, W. J. (1992). *Tribally controlled colleges: Making good medicine.* New York: Peter Lang.

Sterling, S. (1998). *My name is Seepeetza.* Toronto: Groundwood Books.

Swisher, K. G. (Ed.). (1992a). *Journal of American Indian Education* [Special issue], *31* (2).

Swisher, K. G. (Ed.). (1992b). *Journal of American Indian Education* [Special issue], *31* (3).

Swisher, K. G. (1992c). Preface. In K. Swisher (Ed.), *Journal of American Indian Education* [Special issue], *31*(2), 1.

Swisher, K. G. (1996). Why Indian people should be the ones to write about Indian education. *American Indian Quarterly, 20*(1), 83–90.

Swisher, K. G., & Deyhle, D. (1987). Styles of learning and learning of styles: Educational conflicts for American Indian/Alaskan Native youth. *Journal of Multilingual and Multicultural Development, 8*(4), 345–360.

Swisher, K. G., & Deyhle, D. (1989, August). The styles of learning are different, but the teaching is just the same: Suggestions for teachers of American Indian youth. *Journal of American Indian Education,* pp. 1–14.

Swisher, K. G., & Hoisch, M. (1992). Dropping out among American Indians and Alaska Natives: A review of studies. *Journal of American Indian Education, 31*(2), 3–23.

Swisher, K. G., Hoisch, M., & Pavel, D. (1991). *American Indian/Alaska Native dropout study, 1991.* Washington, DC: National Education Association.

Swisher, K. G., & Tippeconnic, J. W., III. (Eds.). (1999). *Next steps: Research and practice to advance Indian education.* Charleston, WV: ERIC Clearinghouse on Rural Education and Small Schools.

Szasz, M. C. (1988). *Indian education in the American colonies, 1607–1783.* Albuquerque: University of New Mexico Press.

Szasz, M. C. (1999). *Education and the American Indian: The road to self-determination, 1928–1973* (3rd ed.). Albuquerque: University of New Mexico Press.

Szasz, M. C., & Ryan, C. S. (1988). American Indian education. In W. Washburn (Ed.), *Handbook of North American Indians* (Vol. 4, pp. 284–300). Washington, DC: Smithsonian Institution Press.

Thornton, R. (1987). *American Indian holocaust and survival.* Norman: University of Oklahoma Press.

Thornton, R., Sandefur, G., & Snipp, C. M. (1991). American Indian fertility patterns: 1910 and 1940 to 1980. A research note. *American Indian Quarterly, 15,* 359–367.

Thurgood, D. (1991). *Summary report 1990: Doctorate recipients from United States universities.* Washington, DC: National Academy Press.

Tippeconnic, J. W., III. (1999). Tribal control of American Indian education. In K. G. Swisher & J. W. Tippeconnic, III (Eds.), *Next steps: Research and practice to advance Indian education* (pp. 33–52). Charleston, WV: ERIC Clearinghouse on Rural Education and Small Schools.

Tippeconnic, J. (2000). Towards educational self-determination. *Native Americas, 17*(4), 42–49.

Trennert, R. (1988). *The Phoenix Indian School: Forced assimilation in Arizona.* Norman: University of Oklahoma Press.

Ubelaker, D. (1992). North American Indian population size: Changing perspectives. In J. Verano & D. Ubelaker (Eds.), *Disease and demography in the Americas* (pp. 169–176). Washington, DC: Smithsonian Institution Press.

U.S. Bureau of the Census. (1984). *American Indian areas and Alaska Native villages: 1980.* (Supplementary report PC80-S1–13.) Washington, DC: Government Printing Office.

U.S. Bureau of the Census. (1988). *We, the first Americans.* Washington, DC: Government Printing Office.

U.S. Census Bureau. (1992). *Statistical abstract of the United States* (112th ed.). Washington, DC: Government Printing Office.

U.S. Census Bureau. (2001). *General demographic characteristics by race for the United States: 2000.* (Census report PHC-T-15.) (www.census.gov/population/cen2000/phc-t15)

U.S. Department of Education. National Center for Education Statistics. (1998). *American Indians and Alaska Natives in postsecondary education.* (NCES 98–291, by D. M. Pavel, R. R. Singer, E. Farris, M. Cahalen, & J. Tippeconnic.) Washington, DC: Government Printing Office.

U.S. Department of the Interior. (1991). *American Indians today* (3rd ed.). Washington, DC: Author.

U.S. Senate, Committee on Labor and Public Welfare. (1969). *Indian education: A national tragedy—A national challenge.* Washington, DC: Government Printing Office.

Utley, R. (Ed.). (1964). *Battlefield and classroom: Four decades with the American Indian.* New Haven, CT: Yale University Press.

Van Hamme, L. (1996). American Indian cultures and the classroom. *Journal of American Indian Education, 35*(2), 21–36.

Van Ness, H. (1981). Social control and social organization in an Alaskan Athabaskan classroom: A microethnography of "getting ready" for reading. In H. Trueba, G. Guthrie, & K. Au (Eds.), *Culture and the bilingual classroom* (pp. 120–138). Rowley, MA: Newbury House.

Vaughn, J. C. (1985). Minority students in graduate education. In B.L.R. Smith (Ed.), *The state of graduate education* (pp. 151–168). Washington, DC: Brookings Institution.

Vogt, L., Jordan, C., & Tharp, R. (1987). Explaining school failure, producing school success: Two cases. *Anthropology and Education Quarterly, 18,* 276–286.

Watahomigie, L., & Yamamoto, A. Y. (1987). Linguistics in action: The Hualapai bilingual/bicultural education program. In D. D. Stull & J. J. Schensul (Eds.), *Collaborative research and social change: Applied anthropology in action* (pp. 77–98). Boulder, CO: Westview Press.

Wax, M. L., Wax, R. H., & Dumont, R. V. (1964/1989). *Formal education in an American Indian community: Peer society and the failure of minority education.* Prospect Heights, IL: Waveland Press.

Webster, S. (Ed.). (1966). *Understanding the educational problems of the disadvantaged learner.* San Francisco: Chandler.

Wilkins, D. E., & Lomawaima, K. T. (2001). *Uneven ground: American Indian sovereignty and federal law.* Norman: University of Oklahoma Press.

Wilkinson, C. (1987). *American Indians, time, and the law.* New Haven, CT: Yale University Press.

Wolcott, H. (1967). *A Kwakiutl village and school.* New York: Holt, Rinehart, & Winston.

Yamauchi, L. A., & Ceppi, A. K. (1998). A review of indigenous language immersion programs and a focus on Hawai'i. In D. A. Almeida (Ed.), *Equity and Excellence in Education, 31*(1) [Special issue on the education of indigenous people], 11–20.

Young, R. (1972). *Written Navajo: A brief history.* (Navajo Reading Study Progress Report 19.) Albuquerque: University of New Mexico. (ERIC Document Reproduction Service no. ED 068 229)

Zepeda, O. (1990). American Indian language policy. In K. Adams & D. Brink (Eds.), *Perspectives on official English* (pp. 247–256); J. Fishman (Gen. Ed.), *Contributions to the sociology of language 57.* Berlin: Mouton de Gruyter.

23

HISTORICAL AND SOCIOCULTURAL INFLUENCES ON AFRICAN AMERICAN EDUCATION

Carol D. Lee

Northwestern University

Diana T. Slaughter-Defoe

University of Pennsylvania

In this chapter on African American education, we explore the influences of culture and political status on the schooling experiences and educational achievement of African Americans. We also discuss the influences of culture and political status on educational research regarding African Americans. In scope, this chapter focuses primarily on elementary through secondary school education. Using culture and political status as filters, we trace the educational status of African Americans historically. We analyze the historical foundations of critical contemporary issues in the education of African Americans and document major educational problems that can be traced to issues of culture and political status. We describe both theoretical and programmatic responses, based on culturally responsive foundations, to the educational needs of African American children and adolescents. The studies reported include theoretical research and historical studies, as well as qualitative and quantitative research. Because of space limitations, the chapter does not include issues of school administration, higher education, and early childhood education. Where possible, however, continuities between early and later schooling experiences are noted.

MAJOR EDUCATIONAL PROBLEMS IN SCHOOLS

Several studies published during the Reagan-Bush years (1980–1992) indicate that African Americans, particularly

males from lower socioeconomic backgrounds, are disproportionately represented in the grade-retention, school-suspension, and dropout rates of public schools (Bennett & Harris, 1981; Campbell, 1982; Hess & Greer, 1987; Hess & Lauber, 1985; Kaufman, 1991). Prior to leaving school during the adolescent years, the same students are frequently poor academic achievers in the elementary grades and experience academic suspensions for related disciplinary problems.

Further, since the beginning of public schooling in the United States, African American children have been labeled, and even misclassified and tracked, relative to educational standing, as a combined result of inequitable resource allocations; the application of inadequately developed and normed intelligence and achievement tests; disproportionately inappropriate placements in special educational classrooms and settings; and insufficient attention to the learning styles evidenced by many of the children (e.g., Designs for Change, 1982; Epps, 1992; Hale-Benson, 1986; Hilliard, 1976; Miller-Jones, 1988, 1989; Myrdal, 1944; Shade, 1982).

The studies of the Chicago Panel on Public School Policy and Finance, and others of similar persuasion, suggest that prevention and/or intervention begin early in the elementary schools the students attend, focusing particularly on raising the level of teacher academic expectations for African American students and improving teacher quality, in addition to revitalizing the overall school climate of

The authors are indebted to Craig Brookins, North Carolina State University, for his assistance with the sections of this chapter that discuss the rites of passage.

the public schools attended by these youths (e.g., Anson, Cook, & Habib, 1991; Baron, Tom, & Cooper, 1985; Clark, 1965; Comer, 1988a; Haynes & Comer, 1993; Hess & Greer, 1987). Other intervenors have emphasized the importance of preschool intervention for school readiness, including the contribution of such national programs as Project Head Start, to the early development of social and academic competence among African American children (e.g., Schorr, 1988; V. Washington & Oyemade, 1987). Today, many who stress intervention to improve the educational prospects of African American children offer strategies for effectively involving parents and family within the social context of the school (Comer, 1980, 1988b; Slaughter & Epps, 1987; Slaughter-Defoe, 1991; K. R. Wilson & Allen, 1987). It is encouraged that evaluations of the longer-term effects of Head Start, for example, apply a two-generational model in which outcomes for parents and families, as well as children, are stressed (Grimmett & Garrett, 1989; Head Start Research and Evaluation, 1990; Slaughter, Lindsey, Nakagawa, & Kuehne, 1989; Slaughter, Washington, Oyemade, & Lindsey, 1988).

Perhaps the most radical effort at reform of public schools in the past 15 years was introduced by Chicago's School Reform Act, effective July 1, 1989. The Chicago School Reform Act followed the assertion of then-Secretary of Education William Bennett in November 1987 that Chicago's public schools were the worst in the United States, whether measured by dropout rates, disciplinary incidents, or achievement scores. This act established local school councils at each of the 539 Chicago public schools that had the authority and power to establish a school improvement plan, allocate appropriate resources for implementation, and evaluate the performance of the principal in relation to realization of the goals of that plan at four-year intervals ("Chicago Schools," 1991). The Chicago plan essentially sought to take power from school administrators and give it to the parents of attending schoolchildren.

The overall strategy is consistent with efforts to involve parents meaningfully, particularly lower-income, minority-status, and culturally different parents, in their children's education (Epps, 1992; Slaughter & Epps, 1987). However, despite best intentions, monitors of this effort suggest that African American and other parents have not yet achieved the measure of authority in their children's education and schooling toward which restructuring and decentralization efforts have aimed (Ayers, 1991; Boo, 1992). The observers note that teacher involvement and commitment to the reform effort have been minimal, and that restructuring has not directly affected the classroom (teacher behavior and teacher-pupil interaction). Thus the mere presence of parents may be necessary, but not sufficient, to have an impact on school administrative policies

and practices. This was particularly true because school resources continued to be limited, the councils had limited powers to raise revenues or set curricula, and teachers and administrators were better positioned to "wait out 'reform' until public interest wanes" (Boo, p. 23).

The data on disproportionate rates indicative of educational failure on the part of African American children, as well as contemporary approaches to the educational problems presented by African American students, are familiar. However, we appreciate less often the considerable historical continuity between the failures of schools in relation to African American children and families today and such failures throughout the history of the African American presence in the United States. At the least, these historic and continuing experiences have influenced attitudes held by African Americans toward the educational system of the United States. Valuing education highly, African Americans typically have less positive responses toward the educational system itself. Indeed, we posit that a major aspect of the relationship between U.S. educational institutions and African Americans has been the struggle between educational ideology and related policies and practices, including access and equity of resources advanced. Traditional learning environments, notably public schools, in which African Americans have participated in the greatest numbers have emphasized cultural assimilation, rather than cultural difference or competence, the latter two of which would affirm the African American cultural heritage.

HISTORICAL FOUNDATIONS OF CRITICAL CONTEMPORARY ISSUES

J. D. Anderson (1988) states that "there have been essential relationships between popular education and the politics of oppression. Both schooling for democratic citizenship and schooling for second-class citizenship have been basic traditions in American education" (p. 1). In the history of African American education, tensions surrounding the content and focus of schooling and the question of who should control the schools can be traced from Reconstruction through the present (Bullock, 1967; Butchart, 1980; Woodson, 1919/1991). There is significant evidence that the African American community has historically recognized the political ramifications of education and how education could be used as a tool either of liberation or for maintaining second-class citizenship (Woodson, 1933/1969). Woodson (1919/1991) documents efforts of African Americans to gain education prior to the Civil War. The intensity of the interest in education on the part of the newly freed African Americans after the Civil War ended has been well documented by many researchers (J. D. Anderson, 1988; Franklin, 1984;

Stowe, 1879; B. T. Washington, 1902). Anderson (1988) quotes one ex-slave who said: "There is one sin that slavery committed against me which I will never forgive. It robbed me of my education" (p. 5). Harding (1981) notes the observations of the White northern journalist Sidney Andrews in 1866:

Yesterday's "ignorant slaves" . . . now seemed fiercely determined to educate themselves and their people . . . the epitome of this quest could be seen in Macon, Georgia: "a young negro woman with her spelling book fastened to the fence, that she might study while at work over the wash tub." Such testimony of black determination to master the printed word came from every corner of the South. (p. 308)

In response to this tremendous desire for education and the new legal rights of citizenship, the government established the Freedman's Bureau in 1865. Among the responsibilities assigned to the bureau was to establish and provide oversight for schooling for the newly freed African Americans. From 1867 to 1872, the Freedman's Bureau established day schools, night schools, and industrial schools. However, from the end of the Civil War and before the inroads of the bureau, an entire movement of independent schools had been established by African Americans themselves. According to J. D. Anderson (1988), both the Freedman's Bureau and northern missionaries discovered "that many ex-slaves had established their own educational collectives and associations, staffed schools entirely with black teachers, and were unwilling to allow their educational movement to be controlled by 'civilized' Yankees" (p. 6). John W. Alvord, the national superintendent of schools for the Freedman's Bureau, in astonishment conducted many investigations of what he called, in part because of his own incredulity, "native schools." His investigations provide one body of evidence on the quantity, distribution, and administration of these schools established by African Americans. In 1866, one year after the end of the Civil War, Alvord estimated that there were "at least 500 schools of this description . . . already in operation in the South" (p. 7). These schools were supported by the monetary and labor contributions of formerly enslaved African Americans, who were responsible as well for the supervision and administration of the schools (J. D. Anderson, 1988; Gutman, 1979). Gutman notes that this educational movement had its foundations in African American communal values. Butchart (1980) has documented not only that the formerly enslaved African Americans developed and supported their own schools in large numbers, but also that they resisted efforts to control these schools from outside their own communities. Anderson writes, "A white observer noted that 'in all respects apart from his or her competency to teach—they will keep their children out of school, and go to work, organize and [sic] independent school and send their children to it'" (p. 12).

An additional significant component of African American efforts in education after the Civil War was through church-operated "Sabbath schools." They were conducted in the evenings and on weekends, providing basic instruction in literacy for those who could not attend regular schools during weekdays. According to reports in 1869 by Alvord's field agents, conservative estimates indicated there were "1,512 Sabbath schools with 6,146 teachers and 107,109 pupils" (J. D. Anderson, 1988, p. 13).

Out of both the missionary interests and the emerging interests of northern capitalist philanthropists issued a vision of an appropriate education for African Americans based on an industrial model of education. These interests were intricately linked to the interests of the class of traditional planters in the South. The combined efforts of African American communities, the Freedman's Bureau, and northern missionaries had laid the foundations in practical terms for universal public schooling in the South for both Blacks and Whites (Du Bois, 1935/1962). According to J. D. Anderson (1988), "Proponents of southern industrialization increasingly viewed mass schooling as a means to produce efficient and contented labor and as a socialization process to instill in black and white children an acceptance of the southern racial hierarchy" (p. 27). The model was exemplified in the curriculum and administration of both Hampton Normal and Agricultural Institute of Virginia, founded by White Brigadier General Samuel Chapman Armstrong, and the Tuskegee Institute, developed in Alabama by Booker T. Washington (J. D. Anderson, 1978). This model of education reflected both market interests and the interests of maintaining the existing racial hierarchy (J. D. Anderson, 1975). However, the schools developed and operated by African Americans (with the notable exception of Washington and the Tuskegee Institute) did not accept this model as appropriate for the interests of the African American community. According to J. D. Anderson (1988), Black educators of the postwar common school movement believed that education could help raise the freed people to an appreciation of their historic responsibility to develop a better society, and that any significant reorganization of the southern political economy was indissolubly linked to their education in the principles, duties, and obligations appropriate to a democratic social order.

Ironically, the curriculum model adopted by Black schools did not differ significantly from courses taught in northern White schools (Woodson, 1933/1969). J. D. Anderson (1988) suggests that although this curriculum did not focus on "the historical and cultural forces that enabled Afro-Americans to survive the most dehumanized aspects of enslavement" (p. 29), it did counter the prevailing attitudes that Blacks were intellectually inferior and incapable of learning. An interesting example of how educated African Americans related their studies of European classics to the liberatory aims of education as they envisioned them is captured in the 1883 testimony of Richard Wright to the U.S. Senate Committee on Education and Labor about the education and work conditions of Georgia Blacks. Wright was the principal of the only public high school for Blacks in the state of Georgia. He stated:

I believe too, that our methods of alphabetic writing all came from the colored race, and I think the majority of the sciences in their origin have come from the colored races. . . . Now I take the testimony of those people who know, and who, I feel are capable of instructing me on this point, and I find them saying that the Egyptians were actually woolly-haired negroes. (J D. Anderson, 1988, p. 29)

According to Anderson, although the short-range goals of schooling envisioned by Blacks were for basic literacy and citizenship training, the long-range goals were to develop "a responsible leadership class that would organize the masses and lead them to freedom and equality" (1988, p. 31).

The tensions inherent in this brief history of the beginnings of formal education for African Americans in the United States capture conflicting themes and interests that have been maintained into the present. Four educational philosophers who wrote from the turn of the century through the 1920s capture the essence of the conflicting positions regarding what an appropriate education for African Americans should be and who should control educational institutions providing services to Black students: W.E.B. DuBois, Booker T. Washington, Horace Mann Bond, and Carter G. Woodson. The core of these tensions revolved around how a responsible leadership class would best be educated.

Between 1860 and 1935, three models for educating a responsible leadership class developed. The first model was based on a combination of curricula from the New England *liberal classical curriculum,* implemented in schools established both by northern missionary societies and by the Black education movement organized by former enslaved African Americans. The second model was based on the notion of *industrial education* developed at Hampton Institute of Virginia, founded by Armstrong in 1868 and later propagated by Armstrong's tutee, Washington. The third model *critiqued* the limitations of the liberal classical and industrial curricula.

The industrial model, whose foundation was laid through that of Hampton Institute, was aimed at influencing generations of leaders in the Black community who would become teachers. Armstrong himself said, "Let us make the teachers and we will make the people" (J. D. Anderson, 1988, p. 45). Armstrong argued against Black political participation. Washington reactivated that same position when he said, "In their present condition it is a mistake for them to enter actively into general political agitation and activity" (Anderson, p. 52). At the famous

Atlanta Exposition in 1895, Washington announced that Tuskegee Institute would produce Black workers who would be "the most patient, faithful, law abiding and unresentful people that the world has seen" (Anderson, p. 73). This model of Black education received widespread support from such political and philanthropic leaders as Ulysses S. Grant, Rutherford B. Hayes, James A. Garfield, Theodore Roosevelt, William Howard Taft, Woodrow Wilson, Andrew Carnegie, John D. Rockefeller, and Julius Rosenwald. In contrast, there was highly vocal opposition to the industrial model, proclaimed by leaders of northern missionary societies but more importantly by the leadership of the Black intelligentsia.

This debate did not begin with DuBois, as is commonly thought; in fact, the Hampton industrial model was initiated the year DuBois was born, 1868. However, the debate reached its pinnacle within the first two decades of the 20th century. The vocal Black leadership who opposed this industrial model of Black education included such figures as William Monroe Trotter (editor of the *Boston Guardian*), Charles Chestnutt, John S. Durham, John Hope, Bishop Henry McNeil Turner, Ida Wells-Barnett, and DuBois. The critical difference was that these Black leaders believed that education should provide training for direct political empowerment along with an intellectual curriculum. This was believed to be especially important for education at the secondary and college levels, from which professional leadership for the Black community developed. DuBois (1903/1968, 1908/1969) labeled these incipient leaders the "talented tenth." By 1905, he and other members of the opposition organized the Niagara Movement, which advocated direct action to achieve civil rights for African Americans. By 1910, the Niagara Movement had organized the National Association for the Advancement of Colored People (NAACP).

This ideological battle continued long after the death of Booker T. Washington in 1915, primarily because of the heavy investment of capital and political pressure from northern capitalists and politicians. Much of this investment was intended to develop alternative industrial normal schools to train teachers and county training schools in rural districts to provide secondary education where public high schools did not exist. In fact, by 1933, 66% of Black high school students in the south were being educated in county training schools that were based on the industrial model (J. D. Anderson, 1988). However, by 1935 many of these schools were phased out because of more stringent licensing requirements for those preparing to teach, and the evolution of a public, though segregated, school system in the South. DuBois and Dill (1911) accurately noted that the existence of a public education system in the South is due in large part to the efforts of African Americans to be adequately educated in order to compete both economically and politically.

DuBois's critique of Black education spanned a period from 1903 through 1960. In an address at Howard University in 1930 (DuBois, 1973a), DuBois succinctly and elegantly summarized the tensions between the New England model of education, aimed at Euro-classic intellectual traditions, and the industrial model, aimed at training a docile workforce. Whether based on a Euro-classical model (Howard, Fisk, and Atlanta Universities) or an industrial education model (the land-grant colleges and former industrial schools such as Hampton Institute and Tuskegee), by 1930 the Black college still mimicked curriculum and social organization patterns found in predominantly White colleges. DuBois acknowledged the tremendous increase in Black school enrollment (1973a, p. 65) and the Black leadership produced from the Black colleges, "trained in modern education, able to cope with the white world on its own ground and in its own thought, method, and language" (p. 66). However, DuBois criticized the Black colleges for focusing inadequately on the problems of economic development within the Black community, and training graduates to cluster in white-collar jobs without building a solid foundation for businesses and independent institutions within the African American community. He also criticized a social milieu in which Black college men focused more on superficial social life (athletics and Greek-letter societies) than on rigorous intellectual study. He argued that these colleges were producing a generation of leaders who were committed to personal wealth rather than to the service and leadership of the masses of their communities. DuBois reasoned that changes in technology required a different kind of education that neither the intellectual focus of the Black colleges nor the antiquated vocational focus of the industrial schools addressed. He wrote:

The industrial school secured usually as teacher a man of affairs and technical knowledge, without culture or general knowledge. The college took too often as teacher a man of books and brains with no contact with or first-hand knowledge of real everyday life and ordinary human beings. . . . Both types of teacher failed. (p. 76)

As had been the case throughout his many years of critique, this challenge laid by DuBois in 1930 is no less relevant today. DuBois said in 1930 before his Howard University audience:

We are not going to share modern civilization just by deserving recognition. We are going to force ourselves in by organized far-seeing effort—by outthinking and outflanking the owners of the world today who are too drunk with their own arrogance and power successfully to oppose us, if we think and learn and do. (DuBois, 1973a, p. 77)

DuBois recognized throughout his illustrious intellectual career that the problem of education for African Americans was no simple matter. He articulated in 1946, and again in 1960, the delicate tensions between political and economic integration of African Americans into the fabric of American life and the maintenance of African American cultural integrity. Any analysis of the movement to integrate public education in the United States and current trends in multicultural education must acknowledge his insights. DuBois wrote that although in 1960 some resolution to the problems of Blacks' right to vote and equal protection under the law was in sight, "it brings not as many assume an end to the so-called Negro problems, but a beginning of even more difficult problems of race and culture" (DuBois, 1973c, p. 149). He continued:

I am not fighting to settle the question of racial equality in America by the process of getting rid of the Negro race; getting rid of black folk, not producing black children, forgetting the slave trade and slavery, and the struggle for emancipation; of forgetting abolition and especially ignoring the whole cultural history of Africans in the world. What we must . . . do is to lay down a line of thought and action which will accomplish two things: The utter disappearance of color discrimination in American life and the preservation of African history and culture as a valuable contribution to modern civilization as it was to medieval and ancient civilization. (pp. 150–151)

DuBois's Harvard-educated contemporary, Carter G. Woodson, founder of the Association for the Study of Negro Life and History (later African American Life and History) and of the concept of Black History Week (later African American History Month), made similar criticisms of education offered in Black colleges based on a Euro-classical model:

No systematic effort toward change has been possible, for, taught the same economics, history, philosophy, literature and religion which have established the present code of morals, the Negro's mind has been brought under the control of his oppressor. The problem of holding the Negro down, therefore, is easily solved. When you control a man's thinking you do not have to worry about his actions. . . . You do not need to send him to the back door. He will go without being told. In fact, if there is no back door, he will cut one for his special benefit. His education makes it necessary. (Woodson, 1933/1969, p. xxxiii)

We have articulated this history of the major conceptions of what education for African Americans should entail because they form the basis on which current trends and issues must be understood. In fact, many of the critical contemporary issues around the education of African Americans parallel in fundamental ways these same historical tensions (Franklin & Anderson, 1978). Table 23.1 summarizes these three foundational models and their contemporary manifestations. For a full review of these historical tensions and how they have been treated by historians of African American education, see Butchart (1988).

TABLE 23.1. Historical Models of Education Appropriate for Blacks, 1860–1935 and Contemporary Parallels.

	Euro-Classical Liberal Curriculum	*Industrial Education Hampton/Tuskegee Model*	*Education for Black Self-Reliance*
Supporters	Northern missionary societies; White liberals; Blacks who supported liberal education	Booker T. Washington; northern capitalists; national, state, and local White political leaders	W.E.B. DuBois, William Monroe Trotter, Ida B. Wells, Martin Delaney, Carter G. Woodson, Mary McLeod Bethune
Historical sites of operation	Black land-grant colleges, normal schools, missionary colleges	Black land-grant colleges, Southern county school system, Hampton Institute, Tuskegee Institute	Schools set up by formerly enslaved Africans, Sabbath schools, Black literary societies (Porter, 1936)
Key characteristics	1. Curriculum content drawn from Euro-classical traditions 2. Belief that understanding foundations of Western civilization is a necessary prelude to participation in democratic citizenship	1. Train workers who are dutiful, hard working, and capable of contributing to the growing labor needs of the postwar South 2. Do not focus on politics and oppression 3. Train teachers for public schools	1. Administration controlled by Blacks 2. Curriculum reflecting African and African American cultural and historical traditions 3. Explicit goals related to political empowerment 4. Education to challenge existing political and cultural norms
Contemporary parallels	Movement to integrate public schools without an explicit focus on the content and delivery of instruction that is culturally diverse and sensitive	Tracking in vocational programs and inequitable tracking in less challenging academic courses and special education	Freedom schools of civil rights movement, Black Independent school movement, Black studies in higher education, Afro-centric curriculum movement, rites-of-passage movement

AFRICAN AMERICAN ACHIEVEMENT IN EDUCATION

J. D. Anderson (1984) offers an extensive review of data documenting the evolution of African American achievement in education from Reconstruction through the 1980s. Anderson proposes that an appropriate framework for analyzing data regarding the educational achievement of African Americans should "chart the ingroup achievement patterns of black school children through the twentieth century, to study those patterns on their own terms, and to see how recent developments compare with those of earlier decades" (p. 103). He also proposes that these developments can be properly understood only in the context of the political and economic conditions under which they were achieved. It is also important to note that the standards and instruments by which educational achievement have been measured since the late 1800s have changed in response to the expansion of mandatory public education, the educational requirements of the labor market, and the development of formalized instruments for measuring proficiency in basic school subject matters. Thus the data for achievement reflect the historical era during which they were collected, and any broad conclusions to be drawn from such data must be considered tentative.

Definitions of minimal literacy as measured by school attendance between Reconstruction and the first decade of the 20th century are substantively different from definitions of minimal literacy as measured by high school completion rates after 1960. From the Reconstruction era through the dawn of the 20th century, literacy rates were measured using census data on school enrollment. By 1930, high school enrollment became the benchmark. Any discrepancies between Whites and Blacks concerning high school enrollment are certainly influenced by the fact that at this period there were only a small number of high schools available for Blacks in the South, and the vast majority of African Americans lived in the South. According to the Bureau of Education in 1917, in 1915 90% of African American schoolchildren lived in the

South, with only 64 public secondary schools available for Blacks (J. D. Anderson, 1984). After the introduction of standardized IQ testing in the U.S. Army during World War I, the formal study of standardized measures of mental ability sharply increased. From the late 1920s on, these standardized measures were used to assess the (presumed) native abilities of American students, including African Americans, and thus were initiated as a gauge of educational achievement. Following the landmark U.S. Supreme Court decision in *Brown* v. *Board of Education of Topeka,* from 1954 on college enrollment (and later, graduation rates) was added as a measure of educational achievement. Achievement according to each of these measures must be weighed in light of the extreme political, social, and economic hardships that Blacks had to overcome in order to attend school and achieve. In addition, the motivation for schooling within the African American community should also be evaluated in relationship to the economic and political benefits achievable from schooling during different historical periods. For example, it was not unusual in the 1940s and 1950s to see Black college graduates working as mail carriers, waiters, railroad porters, and redcaps (Lincoln, 1969). In 1982, the jobless rate among African American teenagers was reported at 50%, in contrast with 16.5% in 1954 (cited in J. D. Anderson, 1984, p. 120).

In the decades immediately following Reconstruction, literacy rates were measured by percentages of school-age children enrolled in school. It should be noted that the ranges specifying school age substantively changed over time as well. The period from 1860 to 1880 reveals the greatest increase in the rates of literacy within the African American community, from a 2% literacy rate in 1860 to a 34% literacy rate in 1880 (J. D. Anderson, 1984). Following Reconstruction there was a harsh political backlash that resulted in terrorism and Jim Crowism. Thus between 1880 and 1900, although there was a 25% increase in the number of school-age children within the African American community (in itself a devastating commentary on the mortality rates under the African holocaust of enslavement), there was a decrease in the percentage of Black school-age children enrolled in school (Anderson). Under the direst of political, economic, and social conditions, however, illiteracy rates in the Black community decreased drastically, from 70% in 1880 to 44% in 1900 and 19% by 1910, as defined by rates of school enrollment. By 1910, school enrollment for Blacks and Whites in the North and West were nearly the same. The biggest discrepancies in school-enrollment figures were in the South, where no mandatory school attendance laws were in effect. As noted earlier, DuBois and Dill (1911) credit the evolution of a public school system in the South to the educational demands of the African American community and to federal efforts to support

those demands. Despite differences in high school enrollment figures in the South due to lack of adequate availability of facilities for Blacks, analysis of growth figures within the African American community indicates that the period between 1917 and 1931 records the greatest increase in high school enrollment (J. D. Anderson, 1984).

In the period following *Brown* v. *Board of Education,* the benchmarks that served as measures of educational achievement began to shift. The *Brown* decision made possible greater opportunity for college enrollment among African Americans. The greatest increases in high school completion, college enrollment, and college graduation rates within the African American community occurred between 1960 and 1980. Between 1966 and 1976, there was a 275% increase in Black student college enrollment (J. D. Anderson, 1984). During the same period, the data reveal that Blacks were more likely to enroll in two-year colleges than four-year institutions (p. 118). College enrollment and graduation rates decreased between 1980 and 1986 and thereafter increased to slightly more than the 1980 level (Carter & Wilson, 1993).

Around the 1920s, standardized test data began to be used as a measure of educational achievement in the United Sates. Most of the data involved the use of standardized measures of native intelligence in the form of IQ tests. There is ample evidence to support the claim that IQ testing was used from its inception in the United States to justify claims of native mental inferiority among African Americans (Gould, 1981; Hilliard, 1991b). From the beginning there were challenges to the assumptions that these measures were unbiased instruments. Foreman (1932), a White Georgian who became an advisor on racial matters to President Franklin Delano Roosevelt, had as his assistant African American educator and researcher Horace Mann Bond (J. D. Anderson, 1984; Urban, 1993). Foreman and Bond studied test scores of African American children enrolled in Black schools in Jefferson County, Alabama, operated by the Tennessee Coal, Iron and Railroad Company. The company had dedicated itself to providing the best possible resources to its schools. Foreman and Bond found that average scores for these Black children at the third grade were consistent with national norms. They concluded that better educational and social environments had a positive effect on the educational achievement of African American children, thus challenging the assumptions of Black intellectual inferiority fostered by mainstream research on standardized testing and Blacks (J. D. Anderson, 1984).

Similar arguments can be made today about the effects of the quality of educational environments and resources on African American student achievement on standardized measures. Dreeben and Gamoran (1986) found "that when black and nonblack first graders are exposed to similar instruction, they do comparably well" (p. 667). Mullis, Dossey, Foertsch, Jones, and Gentile (1991) have analyzed data on the trends in academic progress among American students between 1969 and 1990 on the National Assessment of Educational Progress (NAEP). This analysis focuses on trends according to subject matter, age, race, ethnicity, and gender. Although there were significant gains in achievement by African Americans as measured by the NAEP tests between 1969 and 1990, Black and Latino students continue to score significantly below Whites on every measure. The improvements in Black achievement on these measures are evident in each subject. In science, gains between 1969 and 1990 have been for 9-year-olds (statistically significant) and 11-year-olds; 17-year-old African Americans maintained their level of achievement, while that for 17-year-old Whites decreased. In mathematics and reading, there were significant improvements for all three ages (9, 11, and 17). Despite these improvements, the gaps between African Americans and Whites remain great. For 17-year-olds, even though there has been some decline in NAEP reading scores from 1990 for both African American and White students, the differences in achievement between the two groups remain relatively the same. On the other hand, in mathematics the average scale scores of 17-year-old White students have shown small gains, while that of African American students have declined (Campbell, Hombo, & Mazzeo, 2000). It can be argued that these continuing gaps in Black and White achievement may be attributable in part to the continuing distinctions in quality of educational practice and resources—as they relate to tracking, course content, classroom pedagogy, and technological facilities—between schools serving predominantly White student populations and schools serving predominantly African American and Latino students (Darling-Hammond, 1985; Darling-Hammond & Green, 1990; Marshall, 1990; Means & Knapp, 1991; Mullis et al., 1991; Oakes, 1985, 1990; Page, 1991; Scott, Cole, & Engel, 1992). These distinctions in resources and quality of instruction have been consistently documented in NAEP surveys (Campbell, Hombo, & Mazzeo, 2000).

Standardized testing measures have been used to categorize and limit educational access for African American students. Such measures include both achievement tests and IQ tests. A special issue of the *Negro Educational Review* (Hilliard, 1987), republished as *Testing African Students* (Hilliard, 1991b), provides critiques of the historical and psychological foundations of standardized psychological assessment as they relate to the educational opportunities of African American youth.

Irvine and Irvine (1983) assert that any discussion of discrepancies in educational achievement between Black and White students must address the consequences of the 1954 Supreme Court decision that called for the desegregation of public schooling. These consequences may be viewed as being at the interpersonal, institutional, and community levels. Epps (1992) offers a comprehensive overview of key events and issues in the evolution of the battle over segregated public schools. The *Brown* decision did not address issues of school achievement, but there was an underlying assumption that the desegregation of public schools would have a positive impact on the life chances of African American students. Irvine and Irvine challenge the research community to provide "analyses which assess the effect of desegregation on black pupil achievement and on life outcome chances for black children" (p. 410). Offering an in-depth analysis of the broader social ramifications of school desegregation, they cite Charles Johnson (1954) of Fisk University, who predicted that the *Brown* decision would result in the "demise of racially separate schools" and in "dramatic . . . changes in the institutional structures of the black community" (Irvine & Irvine, p. 142).

Irvine and Irvine (1983) argue that, at the interpersonal level, teacher-pupil interactions and relationships that they say characterized traditionally all-Black schools were changed as a result of the significant loss in number of Black teachers and principals in those historically all-Black schools, particularly in the South (M. Foster, 1993; Gadsden, 1993). Picott (1976) collected data that indicated "a 90% reduction in the number of black principals in the South between the years 1964 and 1973" (Irvine & Irvine, p. 417). It should be noted, however, that the number and percentage of African American teachers in some northern districts, such as Chicago, increased significantly after 1954 (E. G. Epps, personal communication, October 1993). Irvine and Irvine cite Beady and Hansell (1981), who found that the race of the teacher "was strongly associated with expectation for students' future success in college" (Irvine & Irvine, p. 414). They conclude that the factors influencing student achievement prior to the *Brown* decision were reflective of an interaction between pupil ability and social class. After the *Brown* decision, the influencing interaction included race. Although differences in the placement of Black teachers in the immediate post-Brown era were problematic, today a major problem is the decreasing absolute number of Black teachers. In 1998, 17% of K–12 students were African American but only 4% of teachers were African American (Freeman, Alfeld, & Vo, 2001). There is evidence that the proportion of African American teachers in schools serving predominantly African American students has a positive impact on the quality of students' school experiences (Irvine, 2001; Meier, Stewart, & England, 1989).

At the institutional level, Irvine and Irvine (1983) claim that the school in the African American community prior to the *Brown* decision served, along with the Black church, as a central pillar of the community. Schools under desegregation were relatively autonomous. Sowell (1976) states:

Under the dual school system in the era of racial segregation the lack of interest in black schools by all-white boards of education allowed wide latitude to black subordinates to run the black part of the system so long as no problems became visible. (pp. 36–37)

The Black school in this context provided inspirational role models for upward mobility (the professionals associated with the school lived in the community), emphasized social values that promoted positive self-concept and identity, and was a site for communitywide events and support services. Similar observations about the centrality of the Black school prior to the widespread desegregation of public schools, particularly the Black high school in the African American community, have been made by F. C. Jones (1981) and Rodgers (1975). Whereas a case has been made for the positive role of the model Black school, others have noted class biases and tracking in such schools as the famous Dunbar High School of Little Rock, Arkansas (E. G. Epps, personal communication, October 1993).

The third level on which desegregation has influenced educational achievement in the Black community, according to Irvine and Irvine (1983), is that of the community. They state that "understanding the black community involves understanding its basis for solidarity, its implied sense of control, its values and its collective aspirations for its young" (p. 419). In what they call the "historic black community," members of the community functioning through the community's primary institutions—the church and the school—served as a source of achievement and socialization for youngsters. They cite Billingsley's (1968) historic study on the African American family:

In every aspect of the child's life a trusted elder, neighbor, Sunday school teacher, school teacher, or other community member might instruct, discipline, assist, or otherwise guide the young of a given family. Second, as role models, community members show an example to and interest in the young people. Third, as advocates they actively intercede with major segments of society (a responsibility assumed by professional educators) to help young members of particular families find opportunities which might otherwise be closed to them. Fourth, as supportive figures, they simply inquire about the progress of the young, take a special interest in them. Fifth, in the formal roles of teacher, leader, elder, they serve youth generally as part of the general role or occupation. (1968, p. 99)

Irvine and Irvine conclude that desegregation has changed the concept of "the collective whole, the collective struggle, and the collective will" to a focus on individual achievement through individual effort for individual development (p. 420). They cite Kroll (1980), who found no "statistically significant research from 1955–77 which showed that desegregation influenced black student achievement positively" (Irvine & Irvine, 1983, p. 421).

Orfield and Ashkinaze (1991) take just the opposite view on the effects of school desegregation on Black student achievement. Although a primary focus of their study of the Atlanta metropolitan area is on the effects of national and local political and economic policies on opportunities for Blacks (particularly low-income Blacks) to achieve upward mobility, they offer extensive data on the achievement of Black and White students on standardized achievement tests over time in segregated and desegregated schools. They conclude that the overwhelming evidence for the Atlanta region between 1975 and 1987 is that the schools with the highest achievement on the standardized measures were those schools that were integrated, regardless of economic background of students, and regardless of whether the schools were within metropolitan Atlanta or the surrounding suburbs. Crain and Mahard (1981) also found that desegregation had a positive effect on education, especially when initiated in the early grades. They also found "that desegregation enhances IQ test scores as much or more than it does achievement test scores" (p. 76). Thus, 40 years after *Brown*, race continues to be a salient issue in African American education. Lewis and Nakagawa (1994), for example, report that race played a significant role during the late 1980s and early 1990s in the restructuring efforts of Chicago and other big city school systems throughout the nation.

BLACK STUDIES, AFROCENTRICITY, AND MULTICULTURAL EDUCATION: FOUNDATIONS

Banks (1992) and Karenga (1992) acknowledge the interrelationships among Black studies within the university, the conceptual frameworks of Afrocentricity, and multicultural education. Banks illustrates that key leaders in the current movement for multicultural education were initially grounded in the intellectual foundations of African American studies.

The links among the evolution of Black studies as a discipline within the university, Afrocentricity, and multicultural education are evident in the history of Black studies. The struggle for Black studies began in the 1960s and was influenced by the radicalism of the civil rights movement, the antiwar movement, and the student movement (Karenga, 1982). Leadership of the Student Non-Violent Coordinating Committee (SNCC) trained thousands of Black students as well as White students in social and political activism. Radical White students who initiated the free speech movement at the University of

California at Berkeley in 1964, as well as students leading the antiwar movement—including leadership of the Students for a Democratic Society (SDS)—were initially trained as SNCC workers in the South (Carson, 1981; Karenga, 1982). In its opposition to the Vietnam War, the student movement challenged the political links of the university to the structures of power that sustained the war. SNCC opposed the war because it was seen as another example of U.S. intervention in Third World liberation struggles; SNCC felt that the war deflected resources and energy needed to correct injustices against African Americans (Carson, 1981; Karenga, 1982).

Out of this political environment, fueled in 1966 by the Watts revolt and a more broadly defined Black power movement, Black students in 1966 at San Francisco State College demanded the establishment of the first Department of Black Studies. At that time, the Black Student Union at San Francisco State initiated the Experimental College, which carried out service activities with the surrounding community. After an extensive student strike in 1968 that included formal organizational support from other Third World student groups, the first Black Studies program and department was founded, under the leadership of Nathan Hare (Hare, 1972). The Third World Liberation Front that supported the Black Student Union in the strike included the Mexican American Student Confederation, the Asian-American Political Alliance, the Intercollegiate Chinese for Social Action, the Philippine American Collegiate Endeavor, and the Latin American Student Organization (Karenga, 1982). The model for Black studies established by Hare (1972, p. 33) included the call to "bring both the college to the community and the community to the college," increasing the enrollment of Black students as well as their representation in decision-making bodies, and improving their overall treatment on campus. This early model for Black studies also strove to develop a leadership of Black intellectuals who would view service to the Black community as fundamental, reflecting earlier positions stated by scholars and activists such as DuBois (1973b), Woodson (1933/1969), and Bethune (1939). By 1969, most of the major universities and colleges had agreed to the establishment of some form of Black studies (Karenga, 1982). Initially there was resistance on the part of many historically Black colleges to organize Black studies programs and departments, but after universities such as Harvard, Yale, and Columbia established such programs many of the Black colleges began to follow suit (Brisbane, 1974; Karenga, 1982). R. Allen (1974) reports that by 1971 at least 500 colleges and universities had established Black studies programs; however, by 1974 that number had dropped to 200.

Black studies has faced and continues to face challenges to its rigor as an intellectual discipline, as well as a diminution of power by relegation of the discipline to program and institute status, rather than full departmental status within the university (Karenga, 1982). These challenges mirror in many ways the challenges to implementation of multicultural education at both the precollegiate and collegiate levels. The Black studies movement introduced the concept of relevance in educational curriculum, expanding the curriculum to include ethnic studies and infusing it with a concern for social consciousness, commitment, and action. The movement for multicultural education at both K–12 and collegiate levels, as well as current movements toward African-centered pedagogy, clearly rests on the legacy of the history of the Black studies movement (Banks, 1992; see also Banks, Chapter 1, this volume).

The intellectual construct of Afrocentricity provides the philosophical foundation of the Black studies movement as well as the historical movement we have labeled in Table 23.1 as "Education for Black Self-Reliance." The early educational philosophy of Du Bois (1973b), Bond (1935), Woodson (1933/1969), and Bethune (1939) can be generally grouped under the umbrella of Afrocentric thought. Karenga (1992) states:

When one speaks of the Afrocentric project, one should always keep in mind that one is not talking about a monolithic position, but rather a general conceptual orientation among Africana Studies scholars whose fundamental point of departure and intellectual concerns and views are centered in the African experience. (p. 7)

The African experience is broadly defined as a shared orientation among peoples of African descent both on the continent of Africa and throughout the Diaspora, based on similar cultural, historical, and political experiences (Asante, 1987; Bastide, 1979; Herskovits, 1958; J. R. King, 1976; Mbiti, 1970; Nobles, 1974, 1985; Pasteur & Toldson, 1982; Skinner & Nwokah, 1987; Stuckey, 1987). Karenga (1992) states that this shared orientation or African worldview minimally includes these principles: "1) the centrality of community; 2) respect for tradition; 3) a high level spirituality and ethical concern; 4) harmony with nature; 5) the sociality of selfhood; 6) veneration of ancestors; and 7) the unity of being" (p. 12). Adaptations of these themes are also reflected in the literature on Black learning styles that will be discussed later in this chapter. As was the case with the arguments at the turn of the century among African American leaders against the industrial model of education for Blacks, contemporary articulations of Afrocentric theories have engendered an ideological battle.

Karenga (1992) emphasizes the difference between the terms *Afrocentrism* and *Afrocentricity*. He advocates use of the latter term to delineate an intellectual category, a quality of thought and practice, rather than simply an ideological tool. Although the term *Afrocentricity* was introduced by Asante (1980) in the late 1970s, what Banks (1992) calls the African American ethnic studies movement has a long tradition of scholarship linking the culture, experiences, and worldview of African Americans, Africans in other parts of the Diaspora, and Africans on the continent. That tradition of scholarship does not represent a monolithic view, but rather an ongoing discussion among African scholars, bounded by a broad sense of shared cultural and historical experience (Carruthers & Karenga, 1986; Diop, 1974). Afrocentric thought has been made institutionally operational in the freedom school of the civil rights movement (Howe, 1965), the independent school movement from the 1970s until the present (Lee, 1992b; Shujaa, 1994), the current rites-of-passage movement in African American communities across the nation (Warfield-Coppock, 1992), and the production of history texts and readers reflecting African and African American experiences (Harris, 1990, 1992; D. Johnson, 1991). All of these manifestations of Afrocentric orientations in education highlight the importance of linking intellectual study to service in the Black community and of grounding intellectual thought in the cultural experiences and the historical traditions of Black people (Bethune, 1939; Bond, 1935; DuBois, 1973b; Hare, 1972; Woodson, 1933/1969). Karenga (1992) argues that Afrocentricity has both particular and universal dimensions. He writes: "For even as there are lessons for humanity in African particularity, there are lessons for Africans in human commonality" (p. 9). These lessons in human commonality include "respect and concern for truth, justice, freedom [and] the dignity of the human person" (p. 10).

CULTURAL CONTEXTS INFLUENCING AFRICAN AMERICAN EDUCATION

In this section we look at research that explores how African American culture has been used to improve teaching and learning for Black students. Spradley (1980) defines "culture as *the acquired knowledge people use to interpret experience and generate behavior*" (p. 6, emphasis in original). This acquired knowledge is often transmitted through language and includes knowledge about social roles and relationships, structures for communicating, norms about what is appropriate to be communicated to whom and under what circumstances, and conceptions about the natural world and the individual's role in it (Hymes, 1974; Gee, 1989). Farr (1991) writes, "Culture can be viewed as a (cognitive) system of knowledge that both gives rise to behavior and is used to interpret experience" (p. 365). Thus any discussion of African American education within a multicultural context must use as

a primary filter the implications of African American cultural knowledge, values, and language for the learning process.

Language and Literacy

Language is an essential tool through which we not only communicate but also construct knowledge or think through new problems. Thus any discussion of factors influencing the learning of African American children, adolescents, and adults must take into account the variable of language use. This variable becomes particularly problematic in a society, such as the United States, in which language varieties are valued hierarchically. The conditions under which there are low- and high-prestige language varieties in a society have been labeled *diglossia* by Saville-Troike (1989). Sociolinguists have pointed out that developing communicative competence in a language variety entails learning not only the structure, phonology, and lexicon of the language or dialect but also a set of cultural values that determine what is appropriate to be said, how the communication should be articulated, and under what circumstances (Hymes, 1974; Gee, 1989; Robinson, 1988). Such communicative competence entails what Saville-Troike terms *biculturalism*. Because of the low prestige that Black English carries, especially in its vernacular variety (in contrast to standard Black English), the influences of language on learning for African Americans are both complex and problematic.

The discussion here, regarding the impact of competency in Black English (standard or vernacular) on the acquisition of literacy competencies, is influenced by two major trends in the reconceptualization of what it means to be literate in contemporary terms. Langer (1984) proposes that literacy be conceptualized as a way of thinking, as opposed to being limited to the ability to decode and comprehend printed matter, especially extended texts, at basic levels. She suggests that the ability to analyze critically a television newscast, for example, not only displays literate thinking but is also a prerequisite to democratic citizenship. Pursuing the same concept, Cole and Keyssar (1985) discuss the idea of film literacy. This reconceptualization of literacy as a way of thinking critically may focus on knowledge communicated through both print and oral media. In the same vein, Denny Taylor (1989) proposes thinking about teaching reading and writing as problem-solving activities, methods through which readers think through problems and construct new knowledge.

The variety of English spoken by the majority of African Americans is referred to as Black English or African American English. Although much attention has been paid by researchers to its vernacular variety, Orlando Taylor (1992) argues that there are both standard and vernacular forms of Black English (see also Dillard, 1972; Kochman, 1981; Labov, 1969; Smitherman, 1977). The syntax of the standard variety may more closely approximate the syntax of the standard variety of English. However, standard Black English shares with its vernacular counterpart essential defining features related to phonology, intonation, and other tonal characteristics, and formal modes of discourse. Smitherman classifies Black modes of discourse into general categories: call and response, signification, tonal semantics, and narrative sequencing. These genres of discourse have been studied extensively (Abrahams, 1970; Kochman, 1972; Mitchell-Kernan, 1981; Smith, 1972a, 1972b). Smitherman and others (Gates, 1988; Turner, 1949; Vass, 1979) document the influence of West African languages on the structure, phonology, lexicon, and modes of discourse of Black English. In fact, Smitherman specifically refers to Black English vernacular as "Africanized English" (1977, p. 103). Although this body of linguistic research documents the logic of the grammar (Labov, 1969, 1972), as well as its creative and imaginative qualities (Delain, Pearson, & Anderson, 1985; Gates, 1988; Mitchell-Kernan, 1981; Smitherman), research on practical implications for teaching and learning has been limited. Research that has investigated the practical implications for educational settings has fallen into three broad categories: educational programming based on deficit assumptions; analyses of the effects of mismatches between the language of the school and that of the community, based on the assumption that competence in Black English is not a deficit but a difference; and proactive research that builds upon the identified strengths of Black English.

In the late 1960s and early 1970s, there were many funded educational programs to implement curricula aimed at compensating for what was termed "cultural deprivation," largely reflected in the language uses displayed by many African American children (see Hall & Guthrie, 1980, for a full review). Attempts were made to organize what were called "dialect" readers on the basis of the assumption that the phonology and syntax of Black English interfered with the abilities of Black children to learn to read. A review of the research shows mixed results, with no clear advantage to the use of dialect readers and no substantive support for the claim that use of Black English interfered with learning to read (Hall & Guthrie, 1980).

In contrast to these educational interventions and research based on models of cultural and linguistic deprivation, and in response to the research just cited regarding the distinctive and positive qualities of Black English, other researchers have investigated the effects of the home-school language differences on learning, without attributing fault to the child or the home. O. Taylor and Lee (1987), Michaels (1981, 1986), and Cazden, Michaels,

and Tabors (1985) conducted ethnographic observations of sharing time in primary grade classrooms. They found that the African American children told stories in what Michaels called a topic-associative style, whereas the White children used a more linear narrative style that more closely approximated the linear expository style of writing and speaking into which the school was attempting to apprentice the students. In the topic-associative style, African American children told stories in which the segments of the story appeared on the surface as anecdotal, with no explicit relationship to one another. Instead, the relationships between segments of the story must be inferred and often relate to some unarticulated internal point of view of the narrator. This stands in contrast to the sequential series of events and explicit thematic cohesion of the topic-centered storytelling style used by the White children in the studies. The teachers saw no logic to the Black children's narratives and were thus unable to coach them to make connections between episodes and to make details more explicit. Cazden (1988) reports differences in the judgments of White and Black adults about topic-centered and topic-associative children's narratives:

White adults were much more likely to find the episodic stories hard to follow and they were much more likely to infer that the narrator was a low-achieving student. Black adults were more likely to evaluate positively both topic-centered and episodic stories, noticing differences, but appreciating both. (p. 17)

Gee (1989) extended this analysis of the topic-associative narrative style by arguing that it was more aligned with a high literary style and was, in fact, more complex and subtle than the topic-centered style that the school advocated. Champion (1998) as well as Hyon and Sulzby (1994) found a wider array of narrative repertoires among African American children, including topic-associative, topic-centered, and other culturally rooted styles.

This issue of narrative style is significant because children's sense of genres influences how they approach writing tasks and what story grammars they use as templates for comprehending stories (Stein & Palicastro, 1984). Ball (1992) investigated the expository structures used by a group of African American high school students in their school and personal expository writing. She found a preference for the use of structures grounded in African American linguistic traditions among these students, although they were not necessarily conscious of why they used them. Lee (Lee, Mendenhall, & Tynes, 2000; Lee & Rosenfeld, 2001) demonstrated the positive effects of drawing on oral narrative competencies of African American elementary-aged students to produce higher-quality written narratives. Lee (1991, 1992a, 1993, 1997) and Delain et al. (1985) investigated how competencies in

Black English related to procedural knowledge or heuristics in interpreting figurative language. Delain et al. showed that competency in Black English was the most significant variable influencing comprehension of figurative language for the middle school Black children in their study, whereas general language ability was the determining factor for the White children.

Lee (1993, 1995a, 1995b) demonstrated how signifying, a genre of Black discourse, could be successfully used to teach skills in interpreting fiction. Lee argued that the language experiences of African American students at the middle school and high school levels offered rich cognitive models from which to extrapolate strategies for interpreting fiction. In addition, she claimed that the prior knowledge such students brought, particularly to texts of African American fiction, when coupled with the teaching of culturally scaffolded reading strategies, offered a rich learning environment for complex thinking about literary texts. Lee proposed that such learning environments helped apprentice students into a community of readers that would then address a diverse array of literary texts. Lee (2001, 2000a, 2000b) has expanded this conceptualization into a framework for the design of culturally responsive curriculum, called "cultural modeling," that involves productive uses of Black English to enhance instructional discourse, as well as uses of artifacts of rap culture to support complex literary reasoning. Mahiri (1991) investigated how a group of adolescent African American boys in a youth basketball organization used specific aspects of Black English to develop skills in argumentation and as a jumping-off point for extensive reading about sports. Moss (1994) investigated how specific forms of argumentation are structured within the African American sermon and the many uses of literacy in the Black churches she studied. These studies are important because they take a proactive stance on specific ways in which education for African American children can be improved by drawing on particular language strengths evident in Black English.

In addition to the research on using specific characteristics of Black English to teach and learn academic skills related to literacy, there is also a body of research that considers the socializing effects of competency in Black English and the implications of that socializing for schooling. Delpit (1986, 1988) warned that misunderstandings often occurred in classrooms when teachers used an indirect communicative and teaching style with African American children. She argued that teachers should be direct and explicit about the power relationships embedded in the use of different language varieties. DiPardo (1993) investigated the effects of interventions on a college campus to help basic writers, often from ethnically and linguistically diverse backgrounds, make successful transitions to college-level composition classes. Case studies including

African American students and tutors revealed tremendous ambivalence about what it meant to adapt standard English and an academic expository essay style to their writing and personal communication. DiPardo argued that universities, although well intentioned, need to give more careful thought to the organization and goals of basic writing programs for ethnically and linguistically diverse students. Ogbu (1987) and Fordham (1988) have argued that African American students sometimes develop an oppositional attitude toward school in part because they equate success in school with "acting White." This possibility of learning to act White as a prelude to success in school is inevitably tied to learning to speak standard English and potentially divorcing oneself from appropriate uses of Black English. Marsha Taylor (1982) stresses that "in Black Language, attention is paid not only to *what* is said but *how* it is said, *where* it is said, and *who* is doing the 'saying'" (p. 68). Because the investment in developing competency in a particular language variety is so intimately linked to social competence in a given community as well as to concepts of self, Farr (1991) recommends that schools stress what she calls bidialectism or bilingualism, as well as biculturalism.

Several other studies have investigated how African American English is used in socializing children not only to attitudes about school and about evaluating social realities but also to attitudes toward language. Williams (1991) investigated how a group of middle-class African American families socialized their children about goals for education in conjunction with developing African American cultural identities, many trying to help their young children steer their way through values that may conflict. Potts (1989) analyzed stories of personal experience told by children living in a public housing project in Chicago. The stories were individually and jointly constructed with a parent. Using Labov's (1972) framework for narratives, Potts found the stories to be structurally complex. Heath (1983) conducted ethnographic investigations of two working-class Piedmont communities of the Carolinas, one White and one Black. She found the language socialization patterns and the norms for what constituted a good story very different in the two communities. She also found that expectations about language use and narrative strategies in the two communities differed greatly from those of the school. Within the African American working-class community of Trackton, the rules observed by Heath for turn taking within conversations and for getting the floor, as well as the norms for good narratives, are consistent with the characteristics of Black English usage described earlier. Although this literature on socializing through use of Black English offers great promise, little formal research has been conducted to investigate its practical implications for schooling. Two exceptions are Heath (1983) and Lee (1993, 2001).

Cultural Variables in Learning and Teaching Mathematics

Most of the research and educational practices linking culture to learning have been in humanities-related fields, focusing on relationships between language and literacy or cultural learning styles; too little attention has been paid to the implications of African American cultural knowledge and/or experiences for learning and teaching mathematics. Unfortunately, one of the most widely acknowledged works in this area posits a deficit model. Orr (1987) argues that African American English serves as a barrier impeding Black children's understanding of certain mathematical concepts that she claims are counterintuitively expressed in Black English. In a comprehensive review of issues of culture and mathematics by Stigler and Baranes (1989), the only reference to African American culture and mathematics is the questionable Orr study. Baugh (1988) critiques Orr's argument on these grounds, among others: (a) the fact that the school in which she made these observations catered primarily to wealthy Whites, and thus the faculty was not sufficiently familiar with the language and cultural variables influencing the education of inner-city Black students; (b) weaknesses and contradictions in the pedagogy of the classes; (c) a lack of understanding of Black English vernacular on the part of the author; and (d) an impoverished research design. In addition, Baugh cites criticisms of the work raised by Wolf Wolfram of the Center for Applied Linguistics in Washington, D.C., who served as the primary linguistic consultant on the Orr project. J. A. Jones (1990) offers additional criticisms of the Orr study, focusing on the limitations of the mathematical pedagogy employed.

Culture and mathematical learning are joined in what Stigler and Baranes (1989) refer to as "a new sociology of mathematics [that] has arisen that takes as its premise that the foundations of mathematics are to be found through examination of the cultural practices in which the activities of mathematicians are embedded" (p. 258). Mathematicians, in this sense, are not merely those who have chosen mathematics as a professional study but also all of us who carry out routinized daily activities that involve problem solving related to number, space, time, volume, and probability. Stigler and Baranes argue that culture may influence mathematical understanding and practices through cultural tools, cultural practices, and cultural institutions. The conceptualization of ethnomathematics as a framework in the discipline of mathematics education is now influencing instruction (Ascher, 1991; D'Ambrosio, 1985; Frankenstein, 1990; Stiff & Harvey, 1988; Zaslavsky, 1979, 1993). Nasir (2000; see also Dawson, Saxe, Fall, & Howard, 1996) has powerfully demonstrated the mathematical competencies that African American middle and high school students develop through their participation in routine practices such as playing basketball and dominoes.

Consistent with the National Council of Teachers of Mathematics' *Professional Standards for Teaching Mathematics* (1989), others have called on schools to organize curriculum and instruction around the real-life experiences of culturally diverse students (S. Anderson, 1990; Frankenstein, 1990; Joseph, 1987). Tate (1993) argues that mathematics education should empower African American students and others to protect their rights and interests, particularly in a society where mathematics may be used to stereotype and in which mathematical models are used to represent particular political and economic interests within societal decision making. He asserts that mathematics instruction for African American students should be grounded in a critical base of racial knowledge. Both Tate (1993) and Secada (1993) encourage teachers to engage students in problem solving that is situated in the real-life struggles of the communities in which students live. Martin (2000) offers a comprehensive analysis of the sociohistorical, community, school, and interpersonal sources of support for and challenge to African American students' achievement levels in mathematics.

At least three major projects involving the learning of mathematics by African American students include a cultural frame of reference: the Algebra Project, founded by civil rights activist and mathematician Bob Moses (Moses & Cobb, 2001; Moses, Kamii, Swap, & Howard, 1989); the work of Uri Treisman at the University of California at Berkeley, helping African American students master calculus at the collegiate level (Fullilove & Treisman, 1990); and the historic work of Abdulalim Shabazz at Clark-Atlanta University in Atlanta (Hilliard, 1991a; Kostelecky, 1992). A special issue of the *Journal of Negro Education* (Jones-Wilson, 1990), "Black Students and the Mathematics, Science and Technology Pipeline: Turning the Trickle into a Flood," highlights other projects and approaches that have proven successful for African American students learning mathematics.

Moses explicitly states that he started the Algebra Project to empower African American, Hispanic, and other "minority" youth to master the rudiments of algebra, which serves as the gatekeeper to the study of higher mathematics and sciences (Moses & Cobb, 2001; Moses et al., 1989). The Algebra Project introduces an extensive study of algebra in the middle grades in order to prepare students, predominantly African Americans, to enter high school ready for advanced mathematics. The Algebra Project uses the structure of an urban transit system as a metaphor for the directionality of positive and negative numbers in algebra. The project draws on culturally specific norms by consciously encouraging students to express a descriptive representation of algebraic problems using African American English, Spanish, Creole, or whatever the indigenous language of the student may be (Kamii, 1990; Silva, Moses, Rivers, & Johnson, 1990). Recent extensions of the project in small southern African American communities have included drawing mathematical metaphors for key concepts from African drumming. The project emphasizes a curricular process that draws upon students' existing social knowledge and experiences and links that knowledge to the more fundamental and powerful ideas that undergird the domain of algebra. The project started at the King Elementary School in Cambridge, Massachusetts. As a result of the project, "40% of King's 1989 graduates passed the high school algebra exam and most of the others were placed in honors algebra as freshmen" (Klonsky, 1990, p. 8). The project has now expanded to other large and small school districts across the United States.

The Math Workshop Program at the University of California at Berkeley was established by Philip Uri Treisman. He discovered (Fullilove & Treisman, 1990; Jackson, 1989) that African American students entering the university who had been high achievers in high school were not faring well in calculus. Asian American students, by contrast, were doing exceptionally well. Treisman observed that Asian American students often worked cooperatively in study groups for calculus. African American students, on the other hand, had come from high schools where individual hard work was emphasized and viewed as necessary in order to distance high-achieving students from others who did not appear to value school success. These African American students came to Berkeley thinking it was inappropriate to work together and share knowledge. Drawing in part on the work on cooperative learning that suggests that African American students achieve well in such groupings (Boykin, 1983, 1994; Slavin, 1977; Slavin & Oickle, 1981), Treisman formed the Math Workshop Program to foster cooperative learning. The program has been tremendously successful and received national recognition. Treisman's observations support claims by Irvine and Irvine (1983) and Fordham (1988) that academic success is often interpreted by African American students as requiring cultural and social transformations that are not consistent with more traditional African American values of group cooperation and social responsibility.

Between 1956 and 1963, Abdulalim Shabazz, a Black mathematician at Atlanta University (now Clark-Atlanta University), trained 109 African American students who received master's degrees in mathematics. Hilliard (1991a) states:

It is estimated that nearly 50% of the present African-American mathematicians in the United States (about 200) resulted either directly or indirectly from Atlanta University's 109 master's degree recipients during the seven-year period from 1956 to 1963. . . . Shabazz, directly or indirectly, is linked to the production of more than half the African-American holders of the Ph.D. in mathematics. (p. 31)

Shabazz explicitly states that his approach links a sense of social activism, social responsibility, and cultural awareness and includes a history of African and African American contributions to the history of mathematics (Hilliard, personal communication, October 1993). Shabazz attributes the tremendous success of his program to these cultural focuses.

Teachers and Cultural Contexts for Learning

According to M. Foster (1993, 1997), the literature that examines the effects of the thinking, beliefs, and values of teachers on their delivery of instruction has not investigated the effects of cultural background and racial identity on those beliefs, values, and thinking. The body of literature that specifically looks at African American teachers teaching African American students tends to fall into two broad categories. One portrays African American teachers as uncaring and unable to relate to African American students of working-class backgrounds (Conroy, 1972; Rist, 1970; Spencer, 1986). The second body portrays successful teachers of African American students as professionals who draw upon community norms in order to establish close personal ties with students, emphasizing both cognitive and affective personal development (Lerner, 1972; Lightfoot, 1978; Siddle-Walker, 1993, 1996; Sterling, 1972). Studies of African American teachers from this second body of literature conclude from personal testimonies that such teachers bring their political views into play within the classroom, believing that it is their responsibility to prepare African American students with the explicit knowledge and attitudes they will need to succeed in a racist society (Baker, 1987; S. Clark, 1962; Monroe & Goldman, 1988; see M. Foster, 1993, for a full review). An emerging core of African American researchers has begun to argue that culturally conscious teachers who are effective with African American students espouse a distinct educational philosophy and pedagogy that is rooted in African American cultural norms and political history (M. Foster, 1989, 1993; Henry, 1992; J. E. King, 1991; Ladson-Billings, 1991; Lomotey, 1993; Murrell, 1991).

The arguments of these researchers share much in common with the educational philosophies advocated by DuBois (1973b), Woodson (1933/1969), Bond (1935), and Bethune (1939). The concept of what makes these teachers effective aligns consistently with the expressed philosophy of education that emphasizes acquiring knowledge not only of the world but also specifically about African American history and culture in order to empower students to succeed in an antagonistic world and society. M. Foster (1993) initiates the concept of "community nomination," wherein parents and community members nominate teachers who they determine are outstanding, and these community-nominated teachers become the subjects of research. Ladson-Billings (1990, 1992) introduces the concept of "culturally relevant teaching" and distinguishes it from "assimilationist" teaching. In the former, teachers see their "role as helping students to see the contradictions and inequities that existed in their local community and the larger world" (1992, p. 382). According to Ladson-Billings, culturally relevant teaching involves "a pedagogy that empowers students intellectually, socially, emotionally, and politically by using cultural referents to impart knowledge, skills, and attitudes" (p. 382). Ladson-Billings argues that culturally relevant teaching reflects a state of mind. She documents the teaching style of a teacher whom she labels "biologically White" and "culturally Black" (p. 383). Similar observations have been made by Gay (1993) and Cazden (1976).

The studies cited on African American teachers and teachers who have proven effective in teaching African American students have included ethnographic investigations involving interviews, surveys of community residents, and to a limited extent classroom observations. An elaborate study by Lightfoot (1973) investigated the relationships between the expressed political ideology of two teachers and the social and cognitive development of the African American children they taught. Lightfoot's study involved not only interviews of teachers and extensive classroom observation but also interviews with students in the classrooms. Both teachers in the study expressed desires to prepare their students to succeed in a hostile society, but their beliefs about how best to confront the societal contradictions differed dramatically. Lightfoot concludes that in analyzing how the politics of teachers influences the delivery of instruction, one must also consider their attitudes about student assertiveness, expressiveness, and dissonant reasoning.

Some of the research on African American teachers has investigated the effects of racism on these teachers in desegregated schools (J. Anderson, 1988; Curry, 1981; Ethridge, 1979; Franklin, 1979; Tyack, 1974). M. Foster (1990) notes:

Historically, paid less than their white counterparts, rarely employed except to teach African American pupils, opposed by unions seeking to preserve seniority rights of their largely white constituencies, dismissed in large numbers following the *Brown vs. Board of Education* Decision, and denied access to teaching positions through increased testing at all levels, African American teachers' lives and careers have been seriously affected by racism. (p. 3)

Cultural Appropriations of Technology

Recent research in educational technology use by African Americans has focused on (1) culturally responsive design of software tools, (2) culturally responsive ways that African American students display their adaptation of technology, and (3) using technology as a tool for community empowerment. We have chosen to highlight these research efforts because they stand as meaningful responses to the problems of the digital divide (Goslee, 1998). A more detailed review of these culturally responsive approaches in technology use may be found in Lee (2000a, 2002). In addition to the culturally responsive approaches to technology use and design, there is also significant work incorporating technology in service of science learning in urban school systems serving large proportions of African American students. The Center for Learning Technologies in Urban Schools represents one such effort, a collaboration among Northwestern University, the University of Michigan, the Chicago Public Schools, and the Detroit Public Schools.

Pinkard (1999a, 1999b, 2001) has developed two culturally responsive systems for teaching early literacy skills, with a special focus on African American youngsters: Rappin' Reader and Say, Say Oh Playmate. These systems are currently in use in Detroit area elementary schools. Assessments show significant improvement in sight vocabulary with use of the system. Pinkard has also developed a framework to inform the design of computer-based tools that are responsive to the cultural diversity of users. Her "Lyric Architecture" (Pinkard) is a prototype for such systems.

Hooper (1996) completed a longitudinal study of the culturally responsive ways in which African American students in an African-centered elementary school use Logo Writer multimedia software. Logo Writer is based on Papert's (1993) constructionist claim that children can productively learn mathematical concepts as well as generative strategies and habits of mind by building objects. Using Logo Writer, students wrote stories that they animated with objects representing characters, setting, and so forth, which moved and embodied sounds. The animated multimedia stories were entirely programmed by students. Students had to use knowledge of mathematics and programming procedures to animate their stories. Hooper found the students used the Nguzo Saba (the seven principles celebrated during the African American holiday Kwanzaa) in how they collaborated, in the goals they developed, and in the themes of their stories. This groundbreaking work opens up a new perspective on what it means for culturally diverse groups of students to appropriate technology. Continuing the proposition that computer-based tools will be adapted in culturally responsive ways, Lin (2001) found that a Hong Kong elementary school class adapted the Jasper Series (Cognition and Technology Group at Vanderbilt University, 1997) in ways not anticipated by its designers but rooted in the cultural traditions of Hong Kong classrooms.

Shaw and Pinkett have developed approaches for using technology to enhance community empowerment. Shaw (1996) extends Papert's notion of constructionism with the construct of social constructionism: "Social constructionism extends the constructionist view by explicitly including as constructions the social relations and social activities that become shared outcomes and artifacts at work in the developmental cycle" (p. 177). Shaw took the importance of community empowerment as a serious site of development parallel to that of the school. Shaw designed a networking system that allowed community residents and organizations to communicate electronically around issues of community development. Similar work is currently being carried out by Pinkett (2000). DuPont (2001) works from a similar perspective, building technology rich interventions in out-of-school settings, giving African American high school students opportunities to learn programming skills in service of community-based problems.

MAJOR POLICIES AND STRATEGIES TO IMPROVE AFRICAN AMERICAN EDUCATION: CULTURAL PARADIGM

Educational research and practices that reflect a cultural paradigm emphasize cultural solidarity; education for self-reliance in the African American community; and specific ways in which cultural knowledge, practices, and values that characterize the historic and contemporary African American experience can be drawn upon to improve the education of African Americans (Shujaa, 1993b; Watkins, 1993). Many of the researchers, policy makers, and practitioners operating under this framework explicitly draw upon the educational philosophies of DuBois (1973b), Woodson (1933/1969), Bond (1935, 1976), and Bethune (1939), among others.

The research that informs this question draws in part from work in educational psychology (Boykin, 1982, 1983; Boykin & Allen, 1988; Nobles, 1985; Shade, 1982, 1983, 1986) and in part from work in language socialization patterns (Ward, 1971; Heath, 1983), child socialization patterns (McAdoo, 1988), and narrative traditions (Labov, 1972; Smitherman, 1977) within the African American community. Willis (1989) provides a full review of the research literature on African American learning styles, as do Irvine and York (1995).

Boykin (1979, 1983), Shade (1982), Nobles (1986), and Karenga (1992) each have outlined sets of variables that, in their opinions, characterize African American

culture. Each argues that the origin of these characteristics can be traced to the continuity of African belief systems within African American culture. Herskovits (1958) and DuBois (1903/1968, 1908/1969) have made similar arguments regarding family structure; L. Jones (1963) and Southern (1971) around musical patterns; Vass (1979), Smitherman (1977), and Dillard (1972) around language patterns; and Hale-Benson (1986) and Billingsley (1968) around family socialization.

The critical challenge to this line of research is in defining its implications for classroom practice. One conclusion has been that the mismatches between the styles of learning exhibited by African American students and the behavioral expectations and pedagogical styles of schools result in low levels of achievement among African American students (Allen & Boykin, 1991; Irvine, 1990). According to Hilliard (1989/1990; Allen & Boykin, 1991), such mismatches can lead to underestimation of the intellectual potential of both individuals and groups. This problem has been particularly virulent with regard to language use (Cazden, John, & Hymes, 1972; Cook-Gumperz, 1986; Hilliard, 1983; Taylor & Lee, 1987) and discipline. The high levels of physical activity often attributed to young African American males have led to increased instances of negative discipline (Hale-Benson, 1986), as well as increased grade failures and placement in special education classes (Harry, 1992; Obiakor, 1992). Hilliard (1976) has suggested ways that the culture of the school can change to accommodate learning styles and needs of diverse student populations. He suggests that schools become more flexible, creative, holistic, and people-centered in their teaching strategies.

One line of research that supports the learning-styles argument and informs classroom practice is the work on cooperative learning. Slavin (1977) and Slavin and Oickle (1981) have found that African American students appear to achieve at higher levels when cooperative-learning instructional strategies are used. Boykin, in a series of studies, extends Slavin's findings by positing a cultural argument to account for the success of cooperative learning strategies with African American students (Tuck & Boykin, 1989; see Boykin, 1994, for a full review of related studies). In these studies, Boykin gave middle school African American and White children differing conditions under which to learn a set of materials. These conditions included cooperative groups that worked together for group competition; groups that worked together for no reward; and situations in which the format of the learning was varied, a circumstance that Boykin has labeled *verve*. Boykin found consistently that the African American students preferred to work cooperatively in groups for which there was no external reward. They preferred group work for its intrinsic value and learning environments that were characterized by verve;

they learned more new material under these conditions. Boykin argues that elements of African American cultural norms and socialization influence the success of these strategies with African American students. Ladson-Billings's work on culturally responsive pedagogy (1990, 1992) is consistent with this line of research, which is grounded in the premise of distinctive ways of learning within the African American community.

Current community organizing efforts for African-centered curriculum in both public and private schools are linked directly to educational research and educational philosophies that highlight the relationships among African American cultural norms and knowledge bases and effective learning and teaching of African American students. "In Search of African Liberation Pedagogy: Multiple Contexts of Education and Struggle," a special issue of the *Journal of Education* (J. E. King, 1990), and "Africentrism and Multiculturalism: Conflict or Consonance?" a special issue of the *Journal of Negro Education* (S. Johnson, 1992b), offer in-depth analyses of theoretical and practical issues related to African-centered curriculum and pedagogy. A special issue of *Educational Leadership,* "Whose Culture?" (Brandt, 1991/1992), captures the controversies and disagreements of the debate about the common American culture to be emphasized in the school curriculum, as opposed to curriculum that reflects the distinctive contributions of different groups. Lee, Lomotey, and Shujaa (1990) articulate the need for and offer definitions of African-centered pedagogy, while at the same time acknowledging both its limitations within and contributions to public education. Lee et al. theorize that an effective African-centered pedagogy:

1. legitimizes African stores of knowledge; 2. positively exploits and scaffolds productive community and cultural practices; 3. extends and builds upon the indigenous language; 4. reinforces community ties and idealizes service to one's family, community, nation, race, and world; 5. promotes positive social relationships; 6. imparts a worldview that idealizes a positive, self-sufficient future for one's people without denying the self-worth and right to self-determination of others; 7. supports cultural continuity while promoting critical consciousness. (p. 50)

Similar arguments have been made by Gordon (1993), Shujaa (1993a), King and Wilson (1990), and Ladson-Billings (1992).

There are at least three practical contexts in which such a pedagogy can be observed: (a) independent African-centered schools, (b) African American public school academies (including all-male academies), and (c) community rites-of-passage programs. Each of these educational environments can be found in cities and towns nationwide, although clearly the majority of African American students are enrolled in traditional public school arrangements.

Slaughter and Johnson (1988) provide a comprehensive overview of African Americans in private schools. K–12 private schools attended by African American students generally fall within three broad categories: (a) Catholic schools, (b) predominantly White elite schools, and (c) Black independent schools with either a religious philosophy or an African American cultural orientation. These three categories of institutions differ widely in terms of educational philosophy and the distribution of African American students attending. Franklin and McDonald (1988) present a historical overview of the participation of African Americans in Catholic education. Black parents who choose Catholic schools for their children tend not to be Catholic and select the schools for academic rather than religious reasons (Hoffer, 1988). African American students in Catholic schools perform academically better than their counterparts in public schools, although there is still a gap between Black and White achievement within Catholic schools (Coleman & Hoffer, 1987; Hoffer, Greeley, & Coleman, 1985).

African American students who attend predominantly White elite schools represent a minority in terms of enrollment and face some of the same racist tensions that African Americans face in public schools and the larger society (Speede-Franklin, 1988; Epps, 1988). However, the presence of African American faculty seems to help students overcome these tensions (Epps, 1988). Black parents seriously consider the effects of racial isolation in such schools on the self-image and social development of their children but make their choices on the assumption that the academic benefits will ultimately outweigh the effects of racial isolation (Brookins, 1988).

Private schools owned and operated by African Americans with African American student populations differ in history and philosophy from Catholic and predominantly White private schools. Independent African American schools can be traced back to the late 18th century, including the school founded in Boston by Prince Hall in 1798 and one founded in 1829 in Baltimore by the Oblate Sisters of Providence, an order of Black nuns, which is still functioning today (Ratteray & Shujaa, 1988; Bond, 1976; Franklin, 1979). Among the oldest African American schools still in existence are Piney Woods Country Life School, a residential school in Mississippi in operation since 1909, and Laurinburg Institute in North Carolina, founded in 1909 (Ratteray & Shujaa, 1988).

Ratteray and Shujaa (1987), in a survey of parents whose children attend African American independent schools, analyzed an array of characteristics important to parents choosing this type of schooling. Their data indicate that parents choose African American independent schools for a variety of reasons: 48% for the learning environment, 29% for the academics, 12% for religious education (where applicable), and 7% for the cultural emphasis; 4% were concerned about cost (Ratteray & Shujaa, 1987). Although the survey included 399 parents at 40 schools, in interpreting the results it is important to keep in mind that the low percentages reported for religious education and cultural emphasis may reflect the relative percentages of schools with such emphases within the sample.

The private Black schools that have the greatest emphasis on culture include those in the Council of Independent Black Institutions, or CIBI (Lomotey & Brookins, 1988), founded in 1972, although there are other schools emphasizing African American culture that are not part of the CIBI organization, such as the Marcus Garvey School in Los Angeles and the Chad School in Newark. A special issue of the *Journal of Negro Education* (S. Johnson, 1992a), "African Americans and Independent Schools: Status, Attainment, and Issues," examines successful culturally responsive independent schools (Foster, 1992; Lee, 1992b), as well as the school system of the Nation of Islam (Rashid & Muhammad, 1992).

Although there is a standing tradition of private education that centers on African American cultural foundations, there is a growing movement in public education for public schools to include curriculum content that reflects African American and African historical experiences. Since the late 1980s, this movement has been manifested in two basic thrusts. The first has been to change the content of curriculum and textbooks used by all children (Banks, Chapter 1, this volume). The second has been to focus the organization of certain schools on supporting the explicit development of African American males (Holt, 1991/1992; Leake & Leake, 1992). In some instances, public schools with predominantly African American student populations are being challenged to include African-centered curriculum (Asante, 1991/1992; Hilliard, Payton-Stewart, & Williams, 1990; Shujaa, 1993a).

The critique of curriculum content centers mostly on the representation of African and African American history, particularly in textbooks (J. E. King, 1992; Swartz, 1992). Hilliard et al. (1990) summarize the criticisms:

1. "No significant history of Africans in most academic disciplines before the slave trade."
2. "No 'People' history."
3. "No history of Africans in the African Diaspora."
4. "No presentation of the cultural unity among Africans and the descendants of Africans in the African Diaspora."
5. "Little to no history of the resistance of African people to the domination of Africans through slavery, colonization, and segregation apartheid."
6. "The history of African people that is presented fails to explain the common origin and elements in

systems of oppression that African people have experienced, especially during the last 400 years." (pp. xx–xxi)

King refers to this knowledge base as *Diaspora literacy.* She was intimately involved in the critique of the California History/Social Science Framework of 1988 and the 1990 history textbook adoption policies of the state of California. As a result of this controversy, "at least five communities . . . have refused to buy the books in California" that were recommended by the state (J. E. King, 1992, p. 323; Epstein & Ellis, 1992). According to King, groups of teachers, parents, and students have made similar critiques of the content of curriculum and textbooks:

The Rochester (NY) Public Schools Multicultural Office, TACT (The Association of Chinese Teachers in San Francisco), CURE (Communities United Against Racism in Education in Berkeley), TACTIC (Taxpayers Concerned About Truth in the Curriculum in Sacramento), NABRLE (National Association of Black Reading and Language Educators in Oakland), and the Rethinking Schools Collective (in Wisconsin). (p. 323)

The New York State Board of Regents (Hancock, 1990) has faced similar political battles over its curriculum project to infuse African-centered content into the curriculum and textbooks. Perhaps the most widely cited example of a major urban school district infusing African-centered content into the wider curriculum is Portland, Oregon (O'Neil, 1991/1992). The Portland school system commissioned African American scholars in each of the major academic disciplines to write overviews, known as *baseline essays.* The Portland *African American Baseline Essays* (Hilliard & Leonard, 1990) have been used as references for other school districts, while at the same time resulting in significant controversy (Martel, 1991/1992).

Historians may disagree over interpretations and definitions of what counts as evidence, but few multiculturalists take exception to the need to address gaps in the representation of African and African American history in traditional school curricula and textbooks. Some, in fact, argue that teaching historical controversies may be a powerful way of apprenticing students into the formal study of history as a discipline (Lee et al., 1990; Seixas, 1993; Wineburg, 1991). Perhaps the most controversial of these initiatives in public education has been the call for African-centered all-male academies. These all-male academy initiatives are a result in part of current concern about the appalling statistics describing the low educational achievement and life chances of African American males (Madhubuti, 1990; Wright, 1991/1992). A special issue of the *Journal of Negro Education,* "Focus on Black Males and Education" (S. Johnson, 1992c), explores the political, educational, and economic variables that influence this state of affairs, as well as exploratory programs that seek to empower African American male students. The African American Immersion project in the Milwaukee public school system received much attention in the early 1990s (Holt, 1991/1992; Leake & Leake, 1992). There have been similar efforts to establish African American all-male academies in Detroit, Washington, Baltimore, Dallas, and Brooklyn (Dent, 1989), although several of these efforts have been challenged in court for gender segregation. In these instances, as in Milwaukee, the school systems have reconfigured the proposals to include an emphasis on African American culture and male development but have agreed to include both male and female student populations. These programs often invite members of the community to serve as mentors for male students, modeling the rites-of-passage movement outside of schools.

Insufficient attention has been given to models of academic success in predominantly African American public schools. Sizemore (1985, 1987, 1988) documents organizational features, academic routines, qualities of leadership, and staff support that resulted in sustained academic achievement as measured by standardized tests. Among the features identified by Sizemore (1988) are:

1. The use of staff and teacher expertise, skills, information, and knowledge to conduct problem-directed searches for the resolution of school concerns and dilemmas
2. The involvement of parents in some participatory and meaningful way in the school's program
3. The prompt evaluation of teacher and staff performances and the provision of assistance, help, and inservice where necessary; however, the rating of performances as unsatisfactory where warranted, including persuading such teachers to transfer in spite of central office resistance
4. The demand for the use of material which prove functional for elevating achievement when such are not approved by the Board of Education, especially in the areas of phonics, African American History and Culture, and mathematics problem solving
5. The denial of student placement in Educable Mentally Retarded divisions unless all strategies for regular learning had occurred and had been exhausted
6. The refusal to accept system programs which consumed administration and supervision time normally given to the regular program unless such programs increased the school day. (pp. 244–245)

Although it may not be evident on the surface, Sizemore's analysis includes both cultural and political dimensions. She emphasizes the need for leaders at the school level who are willing to confront bureaucratic restrictions and struggle to institute curriculum, academic routines, and staff necessary to bring about academic achievement in underachieving African American public schools. She also emphasizes the need to include African American history and culture as a foundational component of the academic curriculum. Sizemore (1988) concludes:

While there is much in the literature citing teacher leadership and parent involvement as important criteria for high achievement, our findings do not confirm these notions. It may be that the African American school needs a different mix of ingredients for a successful recipe. Since there has never been a consensus among the American polity around full citizenship for the African American, and since the institutional value of white superiority still dominates the social reality, strong leadership may continue to emerge as the most important factor in the elevation of achievement in African American schools until the education of teachers to include content which reflects the true history and condition of African Americans so that they are enlightened and better prepared to teach African American children. (1988, p. 265)

Strong consideration must be given to Sizemore's analysis, as her work demonstrates evidence of sustained high academic achievement.

According to Warfield-Coppock (1992), community-based rites-of-passage programs have been growing steadily since the 1970s. These programs may be sponsored by community organizations, schools, agencies, churches, or groups of families, or they may function as part of outpatient services in therapeutic environments. Programs in school contexts are still community-driven in that the schools often depend on mentoring from members of the community. The argument is that adolescent rites-of-passage programs can develop cultural and social values and coping strategies that help African American youth develop positive self-concepts and self-esteem, and that promote positive social relationships (Dunham, Kidwell, & Wilson, 1986; Hare & Hare, 1985; Oliver, 1989; Perkins, 1986; Warfield-Coppock, 1992). The self-concept of African American youth is endangered by negative socialization through the media, institutions, and street culture (Hare & Hare, 1985; Ogbu, 1985; M. Spencer, 1990), economic disadvantage (Muga, 1984; M. Spencer, 1987; Oliver, 1989), and racism (M. Spencer). The theoretical underpinning of the rites-of-passage movement has been that a positive ethnic identity is essential to the development of a healthy self-concept and positive functioning in U.S. society, especially for adolescents making the transition to adulthood. There is, however, very little research-based evaluation of such programs. Since the 1960s, the rites-of-passage movement has developed programmatic models that draw on traditional African models of adolescent socialization (Warfield-Coppock, 1990).

IMPLICATIONS FOR FURTHER RESEARCH, POLICY, AND PRACTICE

One of the most immediate needs in future research is to recognize the cultural diversity now present within African American families and communities throughout the United States (Slaughter-Defoe, Nakagawa, Takanishi, & Johnson, 1990). These communities presently include children descended from the entire Caribbean, South American, African, and African American experience. Although these families collectively share the consequences of the political, economic, and social oppression of U.S. Blacks, they have and are devising their own strategies for establishing and maintaining cultural competence. If, as Spencer and colleagues have posited (M. Spencer, Swanson, & Cunningham, 1991), ethnicity and ethnic identity are pivotal to competence formation, then these groups will have overlapping and unique approaches to educational environments that could be informative to those endorsing multicultural educational policies and practices (e.g., Miller-Jones, 1988; Ogbu, 1987, 1988).

Yet another important trend is the growing appreciation for the overriding importance of development and continuity to what and how children learn. When Kenneth Clark published *Dark Ghetto* in 1965, he perceived compensatory programs such as Project Head Start to have mistakenly blamed African American parents and families for their children's educational difficulties. In contrast, he placed blame squarely on teachers and school administrators for not assuming proper responsibility and accountability for the education of lower-income and minority children. In 1991, the contemporary Project Head Start program endorsed a set of "multicultural principles." Further, elementary and secondary educators increasingly acknowledge the importance of family and community as *active, positive* contributors to the educative process both inside and outside the classroom (Lightfoot, 1978; Slaughter-DeFoe, 1991; Strickland & Ascher, 1992). Collaborative partnerships must be established with children's families at all grade levels if the recent academic and learning challenges occasioned by the deepening crises of chronic and persistent poverty are to be ameliorated (Comer, 1988a; McLoyd, 1990; Scott-Jones, 1991; Slaughter, 1988; Slaughter-Defoe, Kuehne, & Straker, 1992; M. N. Wilson, 1989). The ideals of these elementary and secondary educators are very similar to those always held by prevailing Head Start preschool programs. Thus today, preschool, elementary, and secondary teachers increasingly acknowledge that they contribute collectively to the continuities in children's learning and development.

As we enter the 21st century, it is likely that increasing numbers of African American children will be educated with other, culturally different populations in the same school or classroom at both elementary and secondary levels. For example, in a study of the Comer process in Chicago, several participating lower-income elementary schools include Asian, Hispanic, and African American student populations (Cook, Slaughter-Defoe, & Payne, 1994). Given the earlier research on Black-White populations, we are aware that the early experience of desegregation is likely to enhance IQ performance test scores (e.g., see Crain & Mahard, 1981; Moore, 1987). However, we know very little about how these newer intergroup experiences will influence the children's academic and social competencies, including their intellectual and achievement performances. More research in this area is indicated, as well as into how African American parents will effect school choices in the public school arena given the newer options relative to school community composition (Slaughter, Johnson, & Schneider, 1988; Yeakey, 1988).

Finally, the challenges inherent in the education of African American students demand increased investigation by researchers and practitioners into the abiding influences of culture, not from the deficit models of prior decades but rather as an important strand in the ongoing multicultural education project. Such research holds great promise for the emerging disciplines of cultural psychology (Stigler, Schweder, & Herdt, 1990) and everyday cognition (Rogoff & Lave, 1984). Investigations into the roles of culture in learning among African American children and adolescents offer opportunities for new understandings, not only about learning in specific school subject matters but also in issues of socialization and character development (Spencer, 1999). The sociolinguistic research agenda of the 1970s provided significant insights into the complex structures and functions of different language varieties (Gumperz & Hymes, 1986) and their implications for teaching and learning (Cazden, John, & Hymes, 1972), but that research had little impact on instruction in school and nonschool settings (Lee, 1993). The research agenda we are proposing should include both basic and applied research, as well as action research by university-based and school-based researchers. Bridges between theoretical and applied research are needed, for example, to investigate the effects of movements calling for authentic and dynamic assessment of African American achievement in education and opportunities for advanced schooling (Brandt, 1992; Wolf, Bixby, Glenn, & Gardner, 1991). Clearly, the problem of attracting African Americans into the field of education is another area requiring additional research (S. H. King, 1993).

Miller-Jones (1988) argued that research into the development of African American children positively influenced the formulation of new paradigms in child development. We propose that the research directions we have recommended will not only have a similar enriching effect on the quality of the educational experiences for African American students but also influence fundamental understandings about learning and teaching that will support the development of all children.

References

Abrahams, R. (1970). *Deep down in the jungle: Negro narrative folklore from the streets of Philadelphia.* Chicago: Aldine.

Allen, B., & Boykin, A. (1991). The influence of contextual factors on Afro-American and Euro-American children's performance: Effects of movement opportunity and music. *International Journal of Psychology, 26,* 373–387.

Allen, R. (1974). Politics of the attack on Black studies. *Black Scholar, 6*(1), 2–7.

Anderson, J. D. (1975). Education as a vehicle for the manipulation of Black workers. In W. Feinberg & H. J. Rosemont (Eds.), *Work, technology and education: Dissenting essays in the intellectual foundations of American education* (pp. 15–40). Urbana: University of Illinois Press.

Anderson, J. D. (1978, Winter). Northern foundations and southern rural Black education, 1902–1935. *History of Education Quarterly, 18,* 371–396.

Anderson, J. D. (1984). The schooling and achievement of Black children: Before and after Brown v. Topeka, 1900–1980. In M. L. Maehr & D. E. Bartz (Eds.), *The effects of school desegregation on motivation and achievement* (pp. 103–121). Greenwich, CT: JAI Press.

Anderson, J. D. (1988). *The education of Blacks in the south, 1860–1935.* Chapel Hill: University of North Carolina Press.

Anderson, S. (1990). Worldmath curriculum: Fighting Eurocentrism in mathematics. *Journal of Negro Education, 59,* 348–359.

Anson, A., Cook, T., & Habib, F. (1991). The Comer school development program: A theoretical analysis. *Urban Education, 26*(1), 56–82.

Asante, M. (1980). *Afro-centricity: The theory of social change.* Buffalo, NY: Amulefi.

Asante, M. (1987). *The Afrocentric idea.* Philadelphia: Temple University Press.

Asante, M. (1991/1992). Afrocentric curriculum. *Educational Leadership, 49*(4), 28–31.

Ascher, M. (1991). *Ethnomathematics: A multicultural view of mathematical ideas.* Pacific Grove, CA: Brooks/Cole.

Ayers, W. (1991). Perestroika in Chicago's schools. *Educational Leadership, 48*(8), 69–71.

Baker, H. (1987). What Charles knew. In L. Rubin (Ed.), *An apple for my teacher: 12 authors tell about teachers who made the difference* (pp. 123–131). Chapel Hill, NC: Algonquin.

Ball, A. F. (1992). Cultural preference and the expository writing of African-American adolescents. *Written Communication, 9*(4), 501–532.

Banks, J. A. (1992). African American scholarship and the evolution of multicultural education. *Journal of Negro Education, 61*(3), 273–286.

Baron, R., Tom, D., & Cooper, H. (1985). Social class, race and teacher expectations. In J. Dusek (Ed.), *Teacher expectations* (pp. 251–269). Hillsdale, NJ: Erlbaum.

Bastide, R. (1979). *African civilization in the new world.* London: C. Hurst.

Baugh, J. (1988). Twice as less, Black English and the performance of Black students in mathematics and science [Book review]. *Harvard Educational Review, 58,* 395–403.

Beady, C., & Hansell, S. (1981). Teacher race and expectations for student achievement. *American Educational Research Journal, 18,* 191–206.

Bennett, C., & Harris, J. J. (1981). *A study of the causes of disproportionality in suspensions and expulsions of male and black students. Part I: Characteristics of disruptive and non-disruptive students.* Washington, DC: U.S. Office of Education.

Bethune, M. M. (1939). The adaptation of the history of the Negro to the capacity of the child. *Journal of Negro History, 24,* 9–13.

Billingsley, A. (1968). *Black families in White America.* Englewood Cliffs, NJ: Prentice Hall.

Bond, H. M. (1935, April). The curriculum of the Negro child. *Journal of Negro Education, 4*(2), 159–168.

Bond, H. M. (1976). *Education for freedom.* Lincoln, PA: Lincoln University Press.

Boo, K. (1992, October). Reform school confidential. *Washington Monthly,* pp. 17–24.

Boykin, A. W. (1979). Psychological/behavioral verve: Some theoretical explorations and empirical manifestations. In A. W. Boykin, A. Franklin, & J. Yates (Eds.), *Research directions of Black psychologists* (pp. 351–367). New York: Russell Sage Foundation.

Boykin, A. W. (1982). Task variability and the performance of Black and White schoolchildren: Vernistic explorations. *Journal of Black Studies, 12,* 469–485.

Boykin, A. W. (1983). On academic task performance and Afro-American children. In J. Spencer (Ed.), *Achievement and achievement motives* (pp. 324–371). Boston: W. H. Freeman.

Boykin, A. W. (1994). Harvesting culture and talent: African American children and educational reform. In R. Rossi (Ed.), *Educational reform and at risk students.* New York: Teachers College Press.

Boykin, A. W., & Allen, B. (1988). Rhythmic-movement facilitated learning in working-class Afro-American children. *Journal of Genetic Psychology, 149,* 335–347.

Brandt, R. (Ed.). (1991/1992). Whose culture? [Special issue] *Educational Leadership, 49*(4).

Brandt, R. (Ed.). (1992). Using performance assessment. *Educational Leadership, 49*(8).

Brisbane, R. (1974). *Black activism.* Valley Forge, PA: Judson Press

Brookins, G. K. (1988). Making the honor roll: A Black parent's perspective on private education. In D. T. Slaughter & D. J. Johnson (Eds.), *Visible now: Blacks in private schools* (pp. 12–20). New York: Greenwood Press.

Bullock, H. A. (1967). *A history of Negro education in the South: From 1619 to the present.* Cambridge, MA: Harvard University Press.

Butchart, R. E. (1980). *Northern schools, Southern Blacks, and reconstruction: Freedmen's education, 1862–1875.* Westport CT: Greenwood Press.

Butchart, R. E. (1988). Outthinking and outflanking the owners of the world: A historiography of the African-American struggle for education. *History of Education Quarterly, 28*(3), 333–336.

Campbell, E. L. (1982). *School discipline: Policy, procedures, and potential discrimination—A study of disproportionate representation of minority pupils in school suspensions.* New Orleans, LA: Mid-South Educational Research Association.

Campbell, J. R., Hombo, C. M., & Mazzeo, J. (2000). *NAEP 1999 trends in academic progress: Three decades of student performance.* Washington, DC: National Center for Educational Statistics.

Carruthers, J., & Karenga, M. (Eds.). (1986). *Kemet and the African world view: Selected papers of the proceedings of the first and second conferences of the Association for the Study of Classical African Civilization.* Los Angeles: University of Sankore Press.

Carson, C. (1981). *In struggle: SNCC and the Black awakening of the 60s.* Cambridge, MA: Harvard University Press.

Carter, D., & Wilson, R. (1993). *11th annual status report on minorities in higher education.* Washington, DC: American Council on Education.

Cazden, C. (1976). How knowledge about language helps the classroom teacher—or does it: A personal account. *Urban Review, 9*(2), 74–90.

Cazden, C. (1988). *Classroom discourse.* Portsmouth, NH: Heinemann.

Cazden, C., John, V., & Hymes, D. (Eds.). (1972). *Functions of language in the classroom.* New York: Teachers College Press.

Cazden, C., Michaels, S., & Tabors, P. (1985). Spontaneous repairs in sharing time narratives: The intersection of metalinguistic awareness, speech event and narrative style. In S. Freedman (Ed.), *The acquisition of written language: Revision and response.* Norwood, NJ: Ablex.

Champion, T. (1998). Tell me something good: A description of narrative structures. *Linguistics and Education, 9*(3), 251–286.

Chicago schools must do worse. (1991, January 19). *Economist,* p. 26.

Clark, K. (1965). *Dark ghetto.* New York: Harper.

Clark, S. (1962). *Echo in my soul.* New York: Dutton.

Cognition and Technology Group at Vanderbilt. (1997). *The Jasper project: Lessons in curriculum, instruction, assessment, and professional development.* Mahwah, NJ: Erlbaum.

Cole, M., & Keyssar, H. (1985). The concept of literacy in print and film. In D. R. Olson, N. Torrance, & A. Hildyard (Eds.), *Literacy, language and learning: The nature and consequences of reading and writing* (pp. 50–72). New York: Cambridge University Press.

Coleman, J. S., & Hoffer, T. (1987). *Public and private high schools.* New York: Basic Books.

Comer, J. (1980). *School power.* New York: Free Press.

Comer, J. (1988a, November). Educating poor minority children. *Scientific American, 259*(5), 42–48.

Comer, J. (1988b). *Maggie's American dream.* New York: New American Library.

Conroy, P. (1972). *The water is wide.* Boston: Houghton Mifflin.

Cook, T., Slaughter-Defoe, D., & Payne, C. (1994). *Comer school development program in Chicago schools: Unpublished proposal to the MacArthur Foundation.* Evanston, IL: Northwestern University, Center for Urban Affairs and Policy Research.

Cook-Gumperz, J. (Ed.). (1986). *The social construction of literacy.* New York: Cambridge University Press.

Crain, R. L., & Mahard, R. E. (1981). Minority achievement: Policy implications of research. In W. Hawley (Ed.), *Effective school desegregation: Equity, quality, and feasibility* (pp. 55–84). Newbury Park, CA: Sage.

Curry, L. (1981). *The free Black in America 1800–1850.* Chicago: University of Chicago Press.

D'Ambrosio, U. (1985). Ethnomathematics and its place in the history and pedagogy of mathematics. *For the Learning of Mathematics, 5*(1), 44–48.

Darling-Hammond, L. (1985). *Equality and excellence: The educational status of Black Americans.* New York: College Board.

Darling-Hammond, L., & Green, J. (1990). Teacher quality and equality. In J. Goodlad & P. Keating (Eds.), *Access to knowledge: An agenda for our nation's schools* (pp. 237–258). New York: College Entrance Examination Board.

Dawson, V., Saxe, G., Fall, R. & Howard, S. (1996). Culture and children's mathematical thinking. In R. Sternberg & T. Ben-Zeev (Eds.), *The Nature of Mathematical Thinking* (pp. 119–144). Hillsdale, NJ: Erlbaum.

Delain, M., Pearson, P., & Anderson, R. (1985). Reading comprehension and creativity in Black language use: You stand to gain by playing the sounding game. *American Educational Research Journal, 22*(2), 155–173.

Delpit, L. (1986). Skills and other dilemmas of a progressive Black educator. *Harvard Educational Review, 56*(4), 379–385.

Delpit, L. (1988). The silenced dialogue: Power and pedagogy in educating other people's children. *Harvard Educational Review, 58*(3), 280–298.

Dent, D. (1989). Readin', ritin' & rage: How schools are destroying Black boys. *Essence, 20*(7), 54–59.

Designs for Change. (1982). *Caught in the web: Misplaced children in Chicago's classes for the mentally retarded.* Chicago: Author.

Dillard, J. (1972). *Black English.* New York: Random House.

Diop, C. A. (1974). *The African origin of civilization: Myth or reality* (M. Cook, Trans.). New York: Lawrence Hill.

DiPardo, A. (1993). *A kind of passport: A basic writing adjunct program and the challenge of student diversity.* Urbana, IL: National Council of Teachers of English.

Dreeben, R., & Gamoran, A. (1986). Race, instruction, and learning. *American Sociological Review, 51,* 660–669.

DuBois, W.E.B. (1935/1962). *Black reconstruction in America: An essay toward a history of the part which Black folk played in the attempt to reconstruct democracy in America, 1860–1880.* Cleveland: World, Meridian Books. (Original work published 1935)

DuBois, W.E.B. (1903/1968). *The souls of Black folk: Essays and sketches.* Greenwich, CT: Fawcett. (Original work published 1903)

DuBois, W.E.B. (1908/1969). *The Negro American family.* New York: Afro-American Studies, New American Library. (Original work published 1908)

DuBois, W.E.B. (1973a). Education and work. In H. Aptheker (Ed.), *The education of Black people: Ten critiques, 1906–1960* (pp. 61–82). New York: Monthly Review Press.

DuBois, W.E.B. (1973b). *The education of Black people: Ten critiques, 1906–1960* (H. Aptheker, Ed.). New York: Monthly Review Press.

DuBois, W.E.B. (1973c). Whither now and why. In H. Aptheker (Ed.), *The education of Black people: Ten critiques, 1906–1960* (pp. 149–158). New York: Monthly Review Press.

DuBois, W.E.B., & Dill, A. G. (1911). *The common school and the Negro American.* Atlanta: Atlanta University Press.

Dunham, R., Kidwell, J., & Wilson, S. (1986). Rites of passage at adolescence: A ritual process paradigm. *Journal of Adolescent Research, 1,* 139–154.

DuPont, V. (2001, April). Connecting the classroom and community: A design approach to using technology as a mediating tool. Paper presented at the annual meeting of the American Education Research Association, Seattle, WA.

Epps, E. G. (1988). Summary and discussion. In D. T. Slaughter & D. J. Johnson (Eds.), *Visible now: Blacks in private schools* (pp. 86–90). New York: Greenwood Press.

Epps, E. G. (1992). Education of African Americans. In M. C. Alkin (Ed.), *Encyclopedia of educational research* (Vol. 1, pp. 49–60). New York: Macmillan.

Epstein, K., & Ellis, W. (1992). Oakland moves to create its own multicultural curriculum. *Phi Delta Kappan, 73*(3), 635–638.

Ethridge, S. (1979). Impact of the 1954 Brown v. Topeka board of education decision on Black educators. *Negro Educational Review, 30*(3–4), 217–232.

Farr, M. (1991). Dialects, culture and teaching the English language arts. In J. Flood, J. M. Jensen, D. Lapp, & J. R. Squire (Eds.), *Handbook of research on teaching the English language arts* (pp. 365–371). New York: Macmillan.

Fordham, S. (1988). Racelessness as a factor in Black students' school success. *Harvard Educational Review, 58*(1), 54–84.

Foreman, C. (1932). *Environmental factors in Negro elementary education.* New York: Norton.

Foster, G. (1992). New York city's wealth of historically Black independent schools. *Journal of Negro Education, 61*(2), 186–201.

Foster, M. (1989). It's cookin' now: An ethnographic study of a successful Black teacher in an urban community college. *Language in Society, 18*(1), 1–29.

Foster, M. (1993). Educating for competence in community and culture: Exploring the views of exemplary African-American teachers. *Urban Education, 27*(4), 370–394.

Foster, M. (1997). *Black teachers on teaching.* New York: New Press.

Frankenstein, M. (1990). Incorporating race, gender, and class issues into a critical mathematical literacy curriculum. *Journal of Negro Education, 59,* 336–351.

Franklin, V. P. (1979). *The education of Black Philadelphia.* Philadelphia: University of Pennsylvania Press.

Franklin, V. P. (1984). *Black self-determination: A cultural history of the faith of the fathers.* Westport, CT: Lawrence Hill.

Franklin, V. P., & Anderson, J. (Eds.). (1978). *New perspectives on Black educational history.* Boston: G. K. Hall.

Franklin, V. P., & McDonald, E. B. (1988). Blacks in urban Catholic schools in the United States: A historical perspective. In D. T. Slaughter & D. J. Johnson (Eds.), *Visible now: Blacks in private schools* (pp. 93–108). New York: Greenwood Press.

Freeman, K. E., Alfeld, C. & Vo, Q. (2001). *African American teachers: Just the facts.* Fairfax, VA: Frederick D. Patterson Research Institute.

Fullilove, R. E., & Treisman, P. U. (1990). Mathematics achievement among African American undergraduates at the University of California, Berkeley: An evaluation of the math workshop program. *Journal of Negro Education, 59*(3), 463–478.

Gadsden, V. L. (1993). Literacy, education, and identity among African-Americans: The communal nature of learning. *Urban Education, 27*(4), 352–369.

Gates, H. L. (1988). *The signifying monkey: A theory of Afro-American literary criticism.* New York: Oxford University Press.

Gay, G. (1993). Ethnic minorities and educational equality. In J. A. Banks & C. A. M. Banks (Eds.), *Multicultural education: Issues and perspectives* (2nd ed., pp. 171–194). Boston: Allyn and Bacon.

Gee, J. P. (1989). What is literacy? *Journal of Education, 171*(1), 18–25.

Gordon, B. (1993). African-American cultural knowledge and liberatory education: Dilemmas, problems, and potentials in a postmodern American society. *Urban Education, 27*(4), 448–470.

Goslee, S. (1998). *Losing ground bit by bit: Low-income communities in the information age.* Washington, DC: Benton Foundation.

Gould, S. J. (1981). *The mismeasure of man.* New York: Norton.

Grimmett, S., & Garrett, A. (1989). A review of evaluations of Project Head Start. *Journal of Negro Education, 58*(1), 30–38.

Gumperz, J. J., & Hymes, D. (Eds.). (1986). *Directions in sociolinguistics: The ethnography of communication.* New York: Basil Blackwell.

Gutman, H. G. (1979, 17–18 August). *Observations on selected trends in American working-class historiography together with some new data that might affect some of the questions asked by historians of American education interested in the relationship between education and work.* Paper presented at the Conference on the Historiography of Education and Work, Stanford University, Stanford, CA.

Hale-Benson, J. (1986). *Black children: Their roots, culture, and learning styles.* Baltimore, MD: Johns Hopkins University Press.

Hall, W. S., & Guthrie, L. F. (1980). On the dialect question and reading. In R. Spiro, B. Bruce, & W. Brewer (Eds.), *Theoretical issues in reading comprehension: Perspectives from cognitive psychology, linguistics, artificial intelligence and education* (pp. 439–452). Hillsdale, NJ: Erlbaum.

Hancock, L. (1990, April 24). Whose America is this anyway? *Village Voice,* pp. 37–39.

Harding, V. (1981). *There is a river: The Black struggle for freedom in America.* New York: Harcourt Brace Jovanovich.

Hare, N. (1972). The battle of Black studies. *Black Scholar, 3*(9), 32–37.

Hare, N., & Hare, J. (1985). *Bringing the Black boy to manhood: The passage.* San Francisco: Black Think Tank.

Harris, V. (1990). African-American children's literature: The first one hundred years. *Journal of Negro Education, 59,* 540–555.

Harris, V. (1992). Contemporary griots: African-American writers of children's literature. In V. Harris (Ed.), *Teaching multicultural literature in grades K–8* (pp. 55–108). Norwood, MA: Christopher-Gordon.

Harry, B. (1992). *Cultural diversity, families, and the special education system.* New York: Teachers College Press.

Haynes, N., & Comer, J. (1993). The Yale school development program: Process, outcomes, and policy implications. *Urban Education, 28*(2), 166–199.

Head Start Bureau. (1990). *Head Start research and evaluation: A blueprint for the future.* (DHHS Publication No. ACY 91–31195.) Washington, DC: Department of Health and Human Services, Administration for Children, Youth, and Families.

Heath, S. B. (1983). *Ways with words: Language, life and work in communities and classrooms.* New York: Cambridge University Press.

Henry, A. (1992). African Canadian women teachers' activism: Recreating communities of caring and resistance. *Journal of Negro Education, 61*(3), 392–404.

Herskovits, M. J. (1958). *The myth of the Negro past.* Boston: Beacon Press.

Hess, G. A., & Greer, J. (1987). *Bending the twig: The elementary years and the dropout rates in the Chicago Public Schools.* Chicago: Spencer Foundation and Chicago Panel on Public School Policy and Finance.

Hess, G. A., & Lauber, D. (1985). *Dropouts from the Chicago public schools: An analysis of the classes of 1982, 1983, 1984.* Chicago: Lloyd A. Frey Foundation and Chicago Panel on Public School Policy and Finance.

Hilliard, A. G. (1976). *Alternatives to IQ testing: An approach to the assessment of gifted "minority" children* (Final Report to the Special Education Support Unit). Sacramento: California State Dept. of Education. (ERIC Document Reproduction Service no. ED 147 009)

Hilliard, A. G. (1983). Psychological factors associated with language in the education of the African-American child. *Journal of Negro Education, 52*(1), 24–34.

Hilliard, A. G. (Ed.). (1987). Testing African American students [Special issue]. *Negro Educational Review, 38*(2–3).

Hilliard, A. G. (1989/1990, December/January). Teachers and cultural styles in a pluralistic society. *Rethinking Schools*, p. 3.

Hilliard, A. G. (1991a). Do we have the *will* to educate all children? *Educational Leadership, 49*(1), 31–36.

Hilliard, A. G. (Ed.). (1991b). *Testing African American students: Special re-issue of* The Negro Educational Review. Morristown, NJ: Aaron Press.

Hilliard, A. G., & Leonard, C. (Eds.). (1990). *African American baseline essays.* Portland, OR: Portland Public Schools.

Hilliard, A. G., Payton-Stewart, L., & Williams, L. O. (Eds.). (1990). *Infusion of African American content in the school curriculum: Proceedings of the first national conference, October, 1989.* Morristown, NJ: Aaron Press.

Hoffer, T. B. (1988). Catholic schools and Black children: Summary and discussion. In D. T. Slaughter & D. J. Johnson (Eds.), *Visible now: Blacks in private schools* (pp. 157–160). New York: Greenwood Press.

Hoffer, T., Greeley, A. M., & Coleman, J. S. (1985). Achievement growth in public and Catholic schools. *Sociology of Education, 58*(2), 74–97.

Holt, K. C. (1991/1992). A rationale for creating African-American immersion schools. *Educational Leadership, 49*(4), 18–19.

Hooper, P. K. (1996). "They have their own thoughts": A story of constructionist learning in an alternative African-centered community school. In Y. Kafai (Ed.), *Constructionism in practice: Designing, thinking, and learning in a digital world* (pp. 241–254). Mahwah, NJ: Erlbaum.

Howe, F. (1965). Mississippi's freedom schools: The politics of education. *Harvard Educational Review, 35*(2), 144–160.

Hymes, D. (1974). *Foundations in sociolinguistics.* Philadelphia: University of Philadelphia Press.

Hyon, S., & Sulzby, E. (1994). African American kindergarteners' spoken narratives: Topic associating and topic centered styles. *Linguistics and Education, 6*(2), 121–152.

Irvine, J. (1990). *Black students and school failure.* New York: Praeger.

Irvine, J. (2001). Why we need African American teachers. In K. E. Freeman, C. Alfeld, & Q. Vo. (Eds.), *African American teachers: Just the facts.* Fairfax, VA: Frederick D. Patterson Research Institute.

Irvine, J. J., & York, D. E. (1995). In J. A. Banks & C. A. M. Banks (Eds.), *Handbook of research on multicultural education* (pp. 484–497). New York: Macmillan.

Irvine, R. W., & Irvine, J. J. (1983). The impact of the desegregation process on the education of Black students: Key variables. *Journal of Negro Education, 52*(4), 410–422.

Jackson, A. (1989, Spring). Minorities in mathematics: A focus on excellence, not remediation. *American Educator*, pp. 22–27.

Johnson, C. S. (1954). Some significant social and educational implications of the U.S. Supreme Court's decision. *Journal of Negro Education, 23*(3), 364–371.

Johnson, D. (1991). *Telling tales: The pedagogy and promise of African American literature for youth.* Westport, CT: Greenwood Press.

Johnson, S. (Ed.). (1992a). African Americans and independent schools: Status, attainment, and issues [Special issue]. *Journal of Negro Education, 61*(2).

Johnson, S. (Ed.). (1992b). Africentrism and multiculturalism: Conflict or consonance? [Special issue]. *Journal of Negro Education, 61*(3).

Johnson, S. (Ed.). (1992c). Focus on Black males and education [Special issue]. *Journal of Negro Education, 61*(1).

Jones, F. C. (1981). *A traditional model of educational excellence: Dunbar High School of Little Rock, Arkansas.* Washington, DC: Howard University Press.

Jones, J. A. (1990). *Look at math teachers not "Black English"* (Policy Studies on Education series). Washington, DC: Institute for Independent Education.

Jones, L. (1963). *Blues people: Negro music in White America.* New York: Morrow.

Jones-Wilson, F. C. (Ed.). (1990). Black students and the mathematics, science and technology pipeline: Turning the trickle into a flood [Special issue]. *Journal of Negro Education, 59*(3).

Joseph, G. (1987). Foundations of Eurocentrism in mathematics. *Race and Class, 27*, 13–28.

Kamii, M. (1990). Opening the algebra gate: Removing obstacles to success in college preparatory mathematics courses. *Journal of Negro Education, 59*(3), 392–405.

Karenga, M. (1982). *Introduction to Black studies.* Los Angeles: Kawaida.

Karenga, M. (1992). *Afrocentricity and multicultural education: Concept, challenge and contribution.* Unpublished paper, Department of Black Studies, California State University, Long Beach.

Kaufman, P. (1991). *Dropout rates in the United States: 1990.* Washington, DC: National Center for Education Statistics.

King, J. E. (Ed.). (1990). In search of African liberation pedagogy: Multiple contexts of education and struggle [Special issue]. *Journal of Education, 172*(2).

King, J. E. (1991). Black student alienation and Black teachers' emancipatory pedagogy. In M. Foster (Ed.), *Readings on equal education: Vol. 11. Qualitative investigations into schools and schooling* (pp. 245–271). New York: AMS.

King, J. E. (1992). Diaspora literacy and consciousness in the struggle against miseducation in the Black community. *Journal of Negro Education, 61*(3), 317–340.

King, J. E., & Wilson, T. L. (1990). Being the soul-freeing substance: A legacy of hope in Afro humanity. *Journal of Education, 172*(2), 9–27.

King, J. R. (1976). African survivals in the Black community: Key factors in stability. *Journal of Afro-American Issues, 4*(2), 153–167.

King, S. H. (1993). The limited presence of African-American teachers. *Review of Educational Research, 63*(2), 115–149.

Klonsky, M. (1990, October). Civil rights leader promoting algebra for all. *Catalyst, Voices of Chicago School Reform*, pp. 8–9.

Kochman, T. (Ed.). (1972). *Rappin' and stylin' out: Communication in urban Black America.* Urbana: University of Illinois Press.

Kochman, T. (1981). *Black and White: Styles in conflict.* Chicago: University of Chicago Press.

Kostelecky, J. (1992, Summer). The will and the way to educate. *Technos*, pp. 11–14.

Kroll, R. (1980). A meta analysis of the effects of desegregation on academic achievement. *Urban Review, 12*, 211–224.

Labov, W. (1969). *The study of nonstandard English.* Urbana, IL: National Council of Teachers of English.

Labov, W. (1972). *Language in the inner city: Studies in the Black English vernacular.* Philadelphia: University of Pennsylvania Press.

Ladson-Billings, G. (1990). Like lightning in a bottle: Attempting to capture the pedagogical excellence of successful teachers of

Black students. *International Journal of Qualitative Studies in Education, 3*(4), 335–344.

Ladson-Billings, G. (1991). Returning to the source: Implications for educating teachers of Black students. In M. Foster (Ed.), *Readings on equal education: Vol. 11. Qualitative investigations into schools and schooling* (pp. 227–244). New York: AMS.

Ladson-Billings, G. (1992). Liberatory consequences of literacy: A case of culturally relevant instruction for African American students. *Journal of Negro Education, 61*(3), 378–391.

Langer, J. (1984). Literacy instruction in American schools: Problems and perspectives. In N. Stein (Ed.), *Literacy in American schools, learning to read and write* (pp. 111–136). Chicago: University of Chicago Press.

Leake, D. O., & Leake, B. L. (1992). Islands of hope: Milwaukee's African American immersion schools. *Journal of Negro Education, 61*(1), 24–29.

Lee, C. D. (1991). Big picture talkers/words walking without masters: The instructional implications of ethnic voices for an expanded literacy. *Journal of Negro Education, 60*(3), 291–304.

Lee, C. D. (1992a). Literacy, cultural diversity, and instruction. *Education and Urban Society, 24*(2), 279–291.

Lee, C. D. (1992b). Profile of an independent Black institution: African-centered education at work. *Journal of Negro Education, 61*(2), 160–177.

Lee, C. D. (1993). *Signifying as a scaffold for literary interpretation: The pedagogical implications of an African American discourse genre.* Urbana, IL: National Council of Teachers of English.

Lee, C. D. (1995a). A culturally based cognitive apprenticeship: Teaching African American high school students skills in literary interpretation. *Reading Research Quarterly, 30*(4), 608–631.

Lee, C. D. (1995b). Signifying as a scaffold for literary interpretation. *Journal of Black Psychology, 21*(4), 357–381.

Lee, C. D. (1997). Bridging home and school literacies: Models for culturally responsive teaching, A case for African American English. In J. Flood, S. B. Heath, & D. Lapp (Eds.), *A handbook for literacy educators: Research on teaching the communicative and visual arts.* New York: Macmillan.

Lee, C. D. (2000a). *The state of research on Black education.* (Invited paper.) Washington, DC: American Educational Research Association, Commission on Black Education.

Lee, C. D. (2000b). Signifying in the zone of proximal development. In C. D. Lee & P. Smagorinsky (Eds.), *Vygotskian perspectives on literacy research.* New York: Cambridge University Press.

Lee, C. D. (2001). Is October Brown Chinese? A cultural modeling activity system for underachieving students. *American Educational Research Journal, 38*(1), 97–142.

Lee, C. D. (2002). Literacy, technology and culture. (G. Hatano and X. Lin, Special Guest Editors). *Technology, Culture and Education* [Special issue of *Mind, Culture and Activity*].

Lee, C. D., Lomotey, K., & Shujaa, M. (1990). How shall we sing our sacred song in a strange land? The dilemma of double consciousness and the complexities of an African-centered pedagogy. *Journal of Education, 172*(2), 45–61.

Lee, C. D., Mendenhall, R., & Tynes, B. (2000). *Cultural modeling: A framework for scaffolding performance and narrative production for academic narrative writing.* Paper presented at the Annual Meeting of the American Educational Research Association, New Orleans, LA.

Lee, C. D., & Rosenfeld, E. (2001). *Well shut my mouth wide open: Cultural modeling in narrative as a framework for the design of writing curriculum for emergent remedial writers.* Paper presented at the Annual Meeting of the American Educational Research Association, Seattle, WA.

Lerner, G. (Ed.). (1972). *Black women in White America: A documentary history.* New York: Vintage.

Lewis, D., & Nakagawa, K. (1994). *Race and reform in the American metropolis.* Albany: State University of New York Press.

Lightfoot, S. L. (1973). Politics and reasoning: Through the eyes of teachers and children. *Harvard Educational Review, 43*(2), 197–244.

Lightfoot, S. L. (1978). *Worlds apart: Relationships between families and schools.* New York: Basic Books.

Lin, X. (2001). Reflective adaptation of a technology artifact: A case study of classroom change. *Cognition and Instruction, 19*(4), 395–440.

Lincoln, E. (1969). The relevance of education for Black Americans. *Journal of Negro Education, 38*(3), 218–222.

Lomotey, K. (1993). African-American principals: Bureaucrat/administrators and Ethno-humanists. *Urban Education, 27*(4), 395–412.

Lomotey, K., & Brookins, C. C. (1988). Independent Black institutions: A cultural perspective. In D. T. Slaughter & D. J. Johnson (Eds.), *Visible now: Blacks in private schools* (pp. 163–183). New York: Greenwood Press.

Madhubuti, H. (1990). *Black men: Single, dangerous and obsolete.* Chicago: Third World Press.

Mahiri, J. (1991). Discourse in sports: Language and literacy features of preadolescent African American males in a youth basketball program. *Journal of Negro Education, 60*(3), 305–313.

Marshall, J. D. (1990). *Discussions of literature in lower-track classrooms.* (Report Series no. 2.10.) Albany: State University of New York, Center for Learning and Teaching of Literature.

Martel, E. (1991/1992). How valid are the Portland baseline essays? *Educational Leadership, 49*(4), 20–23.

Martin, D. (2000). *Mathematics success and failure among African-American youth: The roles of sociohistorical context, community forces, school influence, and individual agency.* Mahwah, NJ: Erlbaum.

Mbiti, J. (1970). *African religion and philosophy.* New York: Anchor Books.

McAdoo, H. (Ed.). (1988). *Black families.* Beverly Hills, CA: Sage.

McLoyd, V. (1990). The impact of economic hardship on Black families and children: Psychological distress, parenting, and socioemotional development. *Child Development, 61,* 311–346.

Means, B., & Knapp, M. S. (1991). *Teaching advanced skills to educationally disadvantaged students: Final report.* Washington, DC: U.S. Department of Education.

Meier, K. J., Stewart, J. & England, R. E. (1989). *Race, class, and education: The politics of second generation discrimination.* Madison: University of Wisconsin Press.

Michaels, S. (1981). "Sharing time," children's narrative styles and differential access to literacy. *Language in Society, 10,* 423–442.

Michaels, S. (1986). Narrative presentations: An oral preparation for literacy with first graders. In J. Cook-Gumperz (Ed.), *The social construction of literacy* (pp. 94–115). New York: Cambridge University Press.

Miller-Jones, D. (1988). A study of African-American children's development: Contributions to reformulating developmental paradigms. In D. T. Slaughter-Defoe (Ed.), *Black children and poverty: A developmental perspective* (pp. 75–92). San Francisco: Jossey-Bass.

Miller-Jones, D. (1989). Culture and Testing. *American Psychologist, 44*(2), 360–366.

Mitchell-Kernan, C. (1981). Signifying, loud-talking and marking. In A. Dundes (Ed.), *Mother wit from the laughing barrel* (pp. 310–328). Englewood Cliffs, NJ: Prentice-Hall.

Monroe, S., & Goldman, P. (1988). *Brothers: Black and poor, a true story of courage and survival.* New York: Ballantine.

Moore, E. G. (1987). Ethnic social milieu and Black children's intelligence test achievement. *Journal of Negro Education, 56*(1), 44–52.

Moses, R. P. & Cobb, C. (2001). *Radical equations: Math literacy and civil rights.* New York: Beacon Press.

Moses, R. P., Kamii, M., Swap, S. M., & Howard, J. (1989). The Algebra Project: Organizing in the spirit of Ella. *Harvard Educational Review, 59*(4), 423–443.

Moss, B. (1994). Creating a community: Literacy events in African American churches. In B. Moss (Ed.), *Literacy across communities.* Cresskill, NJ: Hampton Press.

Muga, D. (1984). Academic sub-cultural theory and the problematic of ethnicity: A tentative critique. *Journal of Ethnic Studies, 12,* 1–51.

Mullis, I. V., Dossey, J. A., Foertsch, M. A., Jones, L. R., & Gentile, C. A. (1991). *Trends in academic progress: Achievement of U.S. students in science, 1969–70 to 1990, mathematics, 1973 to 1990, reading, 1971 to 1990, writing, 1984 to 1990.* (Prepared by Educational Testing Service.) Washington, DC: U.S. Department of Education, Office of Educational Research and Improvement.

Murrell, P. (1991). Cultural politics in teacher education: What's missing in the preparation of minority teachers. In M. Foster (Ed.), *Readings on equal education, Vol. 11. Qualitative investigations into schools and schooling.* New York: AMS.

Myrdal, G. (1944). *An American dilemma: The Negro problem and modern democracy* (Vols. 1 & 2). New York: Harper and Brothers.

Nasir, N. (2000). Points ain't everything: Emergent goals and average and percent understandings in the play of basketball among African-American students. *Anthropology and Education, 31*(3), 283–305.

National Council of Teachers of Mathematics. (1989). *Professional standards for teaching mathematics.* Reston, VA: Author.

Nobles, W. (1974). African roots and American fruit: The Black family. *Journal of Social and Behavioral Sciences, 20*(2), 52–64.

Nobles, W. (1985). *Africanity and the Black family: The development of a theoretical model.* Oakland, CA: Institute for the Advanced Study of Black Family Life and Culture.

Nobles, W. (1986). *African psychology: Toward its reclamation, reascension and revitalization.* Oakland, CA: Black Family Institute.

Oakes, J. (1985). *Keeping track: How schools structure inequality.* New Haven, CT: Yale University Press.

Oakes, J. (1990). *Multiplying inequalities: The effects of race, social class and tracking on opportunities to learn mathematics and science.* Santa Monica, CA: RAND Corporation.

Obiakor, F. E. (1992). Embracing new special education strategies for African-American students. *Exceptional Children, 59*(2), 104–106.

Ogbu, J. (1985). A cultural ecology of competence among inner-city Blacks. In M. Spencer, G. Brookins, & W. Allen (Eds.), *Beginnings: The social and affective development of Black children* (pp. 45–66). Hillsdale, NJ: Erlbaum.

Ogbu, J. (1987). Opportunity structure, cultural boundaries, and literacy. In J. Langer (Ed.), *Language, literacy and culture* (pp. 149–177). Norwood, NJ: Ablex.

Ogbu, J. (1988). Cultural diversity and human development. In D. T. Slaughter (Ed.), *Black children and poverty: A developmental perspective* (pp. 11–28). San Francisco: Jossey-Bass.

Oliver, W. (1989). Black males and social problems: Prevention through Afrocentric socialization. *Journal of Black Studies, 20,* 15–39.

O'Neil, J. (1991/1992). On the Portland plan: A conversation with Matthew Prophet. *Educational Leadership, 49*(4), 24–27.

Orfield, G., & Ashkinaze, C. (1991). *The closing door: Conservative policy and Black opportunity.* Chicago: University of Chicago Press.

Orr, E. W. (1987). *Twice as less: Black English and the performance of Black students in mathematics and science.* New York: Norton.

Page, R. (1991). *Lower track classrooms: A curricular and cultural perspective.* New York: Teachers College Press.

Papert, S. (1993). *The children's machine.* New York: Basic Books.

Pasteur, A., & Toldson, I. (1982). *Roots of soul: The psychology of Black expressiveness.* Garden City, NY: Doubleday.

Perkins, U. E. (1986). *Harvesting new generations: The positive development of Black youth.* Chicago: Third World Press.

Picott, R. (1976). *A quarter century of elementary and secondary education.* Washington, DC: Association for the Study of Negro Life and History.

Pinkard, N. (1999). *Learning to read in culturally responsive computer environments.* Ann Arbor, MI: Center for the Improvement of Early Reading Achievement.

Pinkard, N. (2001). Rappin' Reader and Say Say Oh Playmate: Culturally relevant beginning literacy computer-based learning environment. *Journal of Educational Computing Research, 25*(1).

Pinkett, R. D. (2000, April 24–28). Bridging the Digital Divide: Sociocultural constructionism and an asset-based approach to community technology and community building. Paper presented at the 81st Annual Meeting of the American Educational Research Association (AERA), New Orleans, LA. (www.media.mit.edu/~rpinkett/papers/index.html)

Porter, D. B. (1936). The organized educational activities of Negro literary societies, 1828–1846. *Journal of Negro Education, 5*(4), 555–576.

Potts, R. (1989, April). *West side stories: Children's conversational narratives in a Black community.* Paper presented at the annual meeting of the Society for Research in Child Development, Kansas City, MO.

Rashid, H. M., & Muhammad, Z. (1992). The Sister Clara Muhammad schools: Pioneers in the development of Islamic education in America. *Journal of Negro Education, 61*(2), 178–185.

Ratteray, J. D., & Shujaa, M. (1987). *Dare to choose: Parental choice at independent neighborhood schools.* Washington, DC: Institute for Independent Education.

Ratteray, J. D., & Shujaa, M. (1988). Defining a tradition: Parental choice in independent neighborhood schools. In D. T. Slaughter & D. J. Johnson (Eds.), *Visible now: Blacks in private schools* (pp. 184–198). New York: Greenwood Press.

Rist, R. (1970). Student social class and teacher expectations: The self-fulfilling prophecy in ghetto education. *Harvard Educational Review, 40*(3), 411–451.

Robinson, J. L. (1988). The social context of literacy. In E. R. Kintgen, B. M. Kroll, & M. Rose (Eds.), *Perspectives on literacy* (pp. 243–253). Carbondale: Southern Illinois University Press.

Rodgers, F. A. (1975). *The Black high school and its community.* Lexington, MA: Heath.

Rogoff, B., & Lave, J. (Eds.). (1984). *Everyday cognition: Its development in social context.* Cambridge, MA: Harvard University Press.

Saville-Troike, M. (1989). *The ethnography of communication.* New York: Basil Blackwell.

Schorr, L. (1988). *Within our reach: Breaking the cycle of disadvantage.* New York: Doubleday.

Scott, T., Cole, M., & Engel, M. (1992). Computers and education: A cultural constructivist perspective. In G. Grant (Ed.), *Review of research in education* (Vol. 18, pp. 191–254). Washington, DC: American Educational Research Association.

Scott-Jones, D. (1991). Adolescent childbearing: Risks and resilience. *Education and Urban Society, 23,* 53–62.

Secada, W. G. (1993). *Towards a consciously-multicultural mathematics curriculum.* Paper presented at the Teachers College Conference on Urban Education, Teachers College, Columbia University, New York.

Seixas, P. (1993). The community of inquiry as a basis for knowledge and learning: The case of history. *American Educational Research Journal, 30*(2), 305–326.

Shade, B. J. (1982). Afro-American cognitive style: A variable in school success? *Review of Educational Research, 52,* 219–244.

Shade, B. J. (1983). Cognitive strategies as determinants of school achievement. *Psychology in the Schools, 20,* 488–493.

Shade, B. J. (1986). Is there an Afro-American cognitive style? *Journal of Black Psychology, 13,* 13–16.

Shaw, A. (1996). Social constructionism and the inner city: Designing environments for social development and urban renewal. In Y. Kafai (Ed.), *Constructionism in practice: Designing, thinking, and learning in a digital world* (pp. 175–206). Mahwah, NJ: Erlbaum.

Shujaa, M. (1993a). Education and schooling: You can have one without the other. *Urban Education, 27*(4), 328–351.

Shujaa, M. (Ed.). (1993b). Social and cultural tensions in the schooling and education of African-Americans: Critical reflections [Special issue]. *Urban Education, 27*(4).

Shujaa, M. (Ed.) (1994). *Too much schooling, too little education: A paradox of Black life in White societies.* Trenton, NJ: Africa World Press.

Siddle-Walker, E. V. (1993). Caswell County Training School, 1933–1969: Relationships between community and school. *Harvard Educational Review, 63*(2), 161–182.

Siddle-Walker, E. V. (1996). *Their highest potential: An African American school community in the segregated south.* Chapel Hill: University of North Carolina Press.

Silva, C. M., Moses, R. P., Rivers, J., & Johnson, P. (1990). The algebra project: Making middle school mathematics count. *Journal of Negro Education, 59*(3), 375–392.

Sizemore, B. A. (1985). Pitfalls and promises of effective schools research. *Journal of Negro Education, 54,* 269–288.

Sizemore, B. A. (1987). The effective African American elementary school. In G. W. Noblit & W. T. Pink (Eds.), *Schooling in social context: Qualitative studies* (pp. 175–202). Norwood, NJ: Ablex.

Sizemore, B. A. (1988). The Madison elementary school: A turnaround case. *Journal of Negro Education, 57*(3), 243–266.

Skinner, E., & Nwokah, O. (1987). Communication and continuity in the diaspora: Some personal reflections on cultural connections. In W. Baber & G. Gay (Eds.), *Expressively Black: The cultural basis of ethnic identity* (pp. 321–344). New York: Praeger.

Slaughter, D. T. (Ed.). (1988). *Black children and poverty: A developmental perspective.* San Francisco: Jossey-Bass.

Slaughter, D. T., & Epps, E. G. (1987). The Black child's home environment and student achievement. *Journal of Negro Education, 56*(1), 3–20.

Slaughter, D. T., & Johnson, D. J. (Eds.). (1988). *Visible now: Blacks in private schools.* Westport, CT: Greenwood Press.

Slaughter, D. T., Johnson, D. J., & Schneider, B. (1988). The educational goals of Black private school parents. In D. T. Slaughter & D. J. Johnson (Eds.), *Visible now: Blacks in private schools* (pp. 224–250). Westport, CT: Greenwood Press.

Slaughter, D. T., Lindsey, R. W., Nakagawa, K., & Kuehne, V. (1989). Who gets involved? Head Start mothers as persons. *Journal of Negro Education, 58*(1), 16–29.

Slaughter, D. T., Washington, V., Oyemade, U. J., & Lindsey, R. (1988). Head Start: A backward and forward look. *Social Policy Report, 3*(2). Washington, DC: Society for Research in Child Development, Washington Liaison Office.

Slaughter-Defoe, D. T. (1991). Parental educational choice: African American dilemmas. *Journal of Negro Education, 60*(3), 354–360.

Slaughter-Defoe, D. T., Kuehne, V., & Straker, J. (1992). African-American, Anglo-American, and Anglo-Canadian grade 4 children's concept of old people and of extended family. *International Journal of Aging and Human Development, 35*(2), 161–178.

Slaughter-Defoe, D. T., Nakagawa, K., Takanishi, R., & Johnson, D. J. (1990). Toward cultural/ecological perspectives on schooling and achievement in African- and Asian-American children. *Child Development, 61*(1), 363–383.

Slavin, R. (1977). *Student team learning techniques: Narrowing the achievement gap* (Report no. 228). Baltimore, MD: Johns Hopkins University, Center for Social Organization of Schools.

Slavin, R., & Oickle, E. (1981). Effects of cooperative learning teams on student achievement and race relations: Treatment by race interactions. *Sociology of Education, 54*(3), 174–180.

Smith, A. (1972a). Markings of an African concept of rhetoric. In A. Smith (Ed.), *Language, communication and rhetoric in Black America* (pp. 363–374). New York: Harper & Row.

Smith, A. (1972b). Socio-historical perspectives of Black oratory. In A. Smith (Ed.), *Language, communication and rhetoric in Black America* (pp. 295–305). New York: Harper & Row.

Smitherman, G. (1977). *Talkin and testifyin: The language of Black America.* Boston: Houghton Mifflin.

Southern, E. (1971). *The music of Black Americans: A history.* New York: Norton.

Sowell, T. (1976). Patterns of Black excellence. *Public Interest, 43,* 26–58.

Speede-Franklin, W. A. (1988). Ethnic diversity: Patterns and implications of minorities in independent schools. In D. T. Slaughter & D. J. Johnson (Eds.), *Visible now: Blacks in private schools* (pp. 21–31). New York: Greenwood Press.

Spencer, D. (1986). *Contemporary women teachers: Balancing school and home.* New York: Longman.

Spencer, M. B. (1987). Black children's ethnic identity formation: Risk and resilience of castelike minorities. In J. Phinney & M. Rotheram (Eds.), *Children's ethnic socialization: Pluralism and development* (pp. 103–116). Newbury Park, CA: Sage.

Spencer, M. B. (1990). Parental values transmission: Implications for the development of African-American children. In H. Cheatham & J. Stewart (Eds.), *Black families: Interdisciplinary perspectives* (pp. 111–130). New Brunswick, NJ: Transaction.

Spencer, M. B. (1999). Social and cultural influences on school adjustment: The application of an identity-focused cultural ecological perspective. *Educational Psychologist, 34*(1), 43–57,

Spencer, M. B., Swanson, D. P., & Cunningham, M. (1991). Ethnicity, ethnic identity, and competence formation: Adolescent transition and cultural transformation. *Journal of Negro Education, 60*(3), 366–387.

Spradley, J. (1980). *Participant observation.* New York: Holt, Rinehart and Winston.

Stein, N., & Policastro, M. (1984). The concept of a story: A comparison between children's and teachers' viewpoints. In H. Mandl, N. Stein, & T. Trabasso (Eds.), *Learning and comprehension of text.* Hillsdale, NJ: Erlbaum.

Sterling, P. (1972). *The real teachers: 30 inner-city schoolteachers talk honestly about who they are, how they teach and why.* New York: Random House.

Stiff, L., & Harvey, W. (1988). On the education of Black children in mathematics. *Journal of Black Studies, 19*(2), 190–203.

Stigler, J., & Baranes, R. (1989). Culture and mathematics learning. In E. Z. Rothkopf (Ed.), *Review of research in education* (Vol. 15, pp. 253–307). Washington, DC: American Educational Research Association.

Stigler, J. W., Shweder, R. A., & Herdt, G. (Eds.). (1990). *Cultural psychology: Essays on comparative human development.* New York: Cambridge University Press.

Stowe, H. B. (1879, June). The education of the freedmen. *North American Review,* pp. 605–615.

Strickland, D. S., & Ascher, C. (1992). Low income African-American children and public schooling. In P. W. Jackson (Ed.), *Handbook of research on curriculum* (pp. 609–625). New York: Macmillan.

Stuckey, S. (1987). *Slave culture.* New York: Oxford University Press.

Swartz, E. (1992). Emancipatory narratives: Rewriting the master script in the school curriculum. *Journal of Negro Education, 61*(3), 341–355.

Tate, W. F. (1993, April). *Can America have a colorblind national assessment in mathematics?* Paper presented at the annual meeting of the American Educational Research Association, Atlanta.

Taylor, D. (1989). Toward a unified theory of literacy learning and instructional practices. *Phi Delta Kappan, 71*(3), 184–193.

Taylor, M. (1982). *The use of figurative devices in aiding comprehension for speakers of Black English.* Unpublished doctoral dissertation, University of Illinois, Urbana-Champaign.

Taylor, O. (1992, June). *Toward a redefinition of standard Black English.* Paper presented at the African American English in Schools and Society Conference, Stanford University, Stanford, CA.

Taylor, O., & Lee, D. (1987). Standardized tests and African-American children: Communication and language issues. *Negro Educational Review, 38*(2/3), 67–80.

Tuck, K., & Boykin, A. (1989). Verve effects: The relationship of task performance to stimulus preference and variability in low-income Black and White children. In A. Harrison (Ed.), *The eleventh conference on empirical research in Black psychology* (pp. 84–95). Washington, DC: National Institute on Mental Health.

Turner, L. (1949). *Africanisms in the Gullah dialect.* Chicago: University of Chicago Press.

Tyack, D. (1974). *The one best system: A history of American urban education.* Cambridge, MA: Harvard University Press.

Urban, W. J. (1993). *Black scholar: Horace Mann Bond 1904–1972.* Athens: University of Georgia Press.

Vass, W. (1979). *The Bantu speaking heritage of the United States.* Los Angeles: University of California, Center for Afro-American Studies.

Ward, M. (1971). *Them children: A study in language learning.* New York: Holt, Rinehart and Winston.

Warfield-Coppock, N. (1990). *Afrocentric theory and applications: Volume 1. Adolescent rites of passage.* Washington, DC: Baobab Associates.

Warfield-Coppock, N. (1992). The rites of passage movement: A resurgence of African-centered practices for socializing African American youth. *Journal of Negro Education, 61*(4), 471–482.

Washington, B. T. (1902). *Up from slavery: An autobiography.* New York: Doubleday.

Washington, V., & Oyemade, U. J. (1987). *Project Head Start: Past, present, and future trends in context.* New York: Garland.

Watkins, W. H. (1993). Black curriculum orientations: A preliminary inquiry. *Harvard Educational Review, 63*(3), 321–338.

Williams, K. (1991). Storytelling as a bridge to literacy: An examination of personal storytelling among Black middle-class mothers and children. *Journal of Negro Education, 60*(3), 399–410.

Willis, M. G. (1989). Learning styles of African American children: A review of the literature and interventions. *Journal of Black Psychology, 16*(1), 47–65.

Wilson, K. R., & Allen, W. (1987). Explaining the educational attainment of young Black adults: Critical familial and extrafamilial influences. *Journal of Negro Education, 56*(1), 64–76.

Wilson, M. N. (1989). Child development in the context of the Black extended family. *American Psychologist, 44*(2), 380–385.

Wineburg, S. (1991). On the reading of historical texts: Notes on the breach between school and academy. *American Educational Research Journal, 28*(3), 495–520.

Wolf, D., Bixby, J., Glenn, J., & Gardner, H. (1991). To use their minds well: Investigating new forms of student assessment. In G. Grant (Ed.), *Review of Research in Education* (Vol. 17, pp. 31–74). Washington, DC: American Educational Research Association.

Woodson, C. G. (1933/1969). *The mis-education of the Negro.* Washington, DC: The Associated Publishers. (Original work published 1933)

Woodson, C. G. (1919/1991). *The education of the Negro prior to 1861.* Salem, NH: Ayer. (Original work published 1919)

Wright, W. J. (1991/1992). The endangered Black male child. *Educational Leadership, 49*(4), 14–16.

Yeakey, C. C. (1988). The public school monopoly: Confronting major national policy issues. In D. T. Slaughter & D. J. Johnson (Eds.), *Visible now: Blacks in private schools* (pp. 284–307). New York: Greenwood Press.

Zaslavsky, C. (1979). *Africa counts: Number and pattern in African culture.* Chicago: Lawrence Hill Books.

Zaslavsky, C. (1993). *Multicultural mathematics: Interdisciplinary cooperative-learning activities.* Portland, ME: J. Weston Walch.

24

EDUCATING MEXICAN AMERICAN STUDENTS

Past Treatment and Recent Developments in Theory, Research, Policy, and Practice

Eugene E. García

Arizona State University

Our understanding of population diversity as it relates to educational endeavors continues to expand in its utilization of diverse theories of language, learning, thinking, teaching, socialization, and culture (Cole & Cole, 2001; E. García, 2001a, 2001b). What was once considered the study of values and behavior (Mead, 1937; Skinner, 1957) has become today an interlocking study of linguistic, psychological, and social domains, each independently significant, but converging in a singular attempt to reconstruct the nature of the cultural experience at the micro (smallest unit of social analysis, such as a speech event) and macro (larger unit of social analysis, such as social class) levels. It is this complex set of understandings upon which an educator must depend when addressing teaching and learning in today's classrooms. For the educator of culturally and linguistically diverse students in general and Mexican American students in particular, the issue of culture—what it is and how it directly and indirectly influences academic learning—becomes particularly important (Ogbu, 1999).

This reality of global diversity and interrelatedness pertains directly to our own nation's heterogeneity and interdependence. The United States is itself a country of incredible cultural and linguistic diversity. This trend of ethnic and racial population diversification continues most rapidly among its young and school-age children. California has already been transformed into a minority-majority state, with 55% of today's students coming from "minority" categories; in fewer than 20 years, 70% of California's students will be non-White, and one-half will speak a language other than English on their first day of

school. Nationwide, White, non-Hispanic student enrollment has decreased since 1976 by 13%, or a total of 5 million students. As the overall total of the U.S. student population has decreased from 43 million to 41 million students (pre-K to grade 12) since 1976, several demographic student indicators have become educationally significant:

- Minority enrollment as a proportion of total enrollment in elementary and secondary education rose from 24% in 1976 to 34% in 1996.
- As a proportion of total enrollment, Hispanics increased from 6.4% in 1976 to 12% in 1996. The number of Hispanic students increased from almost 3 million in 1976 to more than 4.5 million in 1996, an increase of 52%.
- During this same period, Asian/Pacific Islander students increased from 535,000 to 1,158,000, an increase of 116% (National Center for Educational Statistics, 1991).

The new foundations related to the schooling initiatives targeted at Mexican American students in the United States will be the focus of this chapter. I will include an expanded discussion of the issues that bring together research, theory, and educational policy and practice of significance to these students. Even more specifically, the chapter will address educationally related conceptual/theoretical pursuits that attempt to "explain," and therefore lay the foundation for, educational "action."

Within the last few decades, research and practice in culture and education have shifted from a focus on

"Americanization" (Gonzalez, 1990) and educational equity (Ramírez & Castañeda, 1974) to multicultural education (Banks, 1991; Sleeter & Grant, 1987), and more recently to the "culturally" relevant instruction of children from culturally and linguistically diverse groups (E. García, 2001a, 2001b; Moll, 1998; Tharp, 1989). The discussion here introduces the demographic contexts of schooling and the theoretical and empirical knowledge bases related to an understanding of culture and education as they concern Mexican American students. Teaching/learning will be addressed as it relates to linguistic, cognitive, and social research and theory that has developed over the last two decades. Such contributions have reshaped in a dramatic way our view of Americanization, equal educational opportunity, multicultural education, and the overall role of linguistic and cultural "difference" in education by generating responsive teaching and learning environments in U.S. schools.

THE DEMOGRAPHIC CONTEXT

The U.S. Census Bureau never fails to confuse us in its attempts to provide clarifying demographic information. With regard to documenting the racial and ethnic heterogeneity of our country's population, it has arrived at a set of highly confusing terms that place individuals in separate exclusionary categories: White, White non-Hispanic, Black, Hispanic (with some five subcategories of Hispanics). Unfortunately, outside of the census meaning of these terms, they are for the most part highly ambiguous and nonrepresentative of the true heterogeneity that the bureau diligently seeks to document. Therefore, it is important to note at the outset of this discussion that these categories are useful only as the most superficial reflection of our nation's true diversity. I do not know many census-identified "Whites," "Blacks," or "Hispanics" who believe that they are truly "White," "Black," or any other restrictive label. But given the limited responses allowed them in census questionnaires, they are constrained by these choices. Racially and culturally we are not "pure" stock, and any separation by the Census Bureau, the National Center of Educational Statistics, or other social institutions that attempt to address the complexity of our diverse population is likely to impart a highly ambiguous sketch.

Having consented to this significant restriction with regard to efforts aimed at documenting population diversity in this country, I must still conclude that an examination of the available data in this area does provide a fuzzy but useful portrait of our society and the specific circumstances of various groups within our nation's boundaries. The demographic portrait of Mexican Americans in the United States is even more unfocused than

the norm. National data are difficult to obtain in such a specific ethnic format, which is generally concerned with identifying "Hispanics." Although the term *Hispanic* is a relatively new census-related identifier, it is quite evident that populations thus identified (Mexicans, Mexican Americans, Puerto Ricans, Cubans, Chicanos, Latinos, and so forth) are often presumed to be one ethnic group, with little appreciation for the diversity among them. Because of this "forced marriage" of demographic data at the national level, I will use the data on Hispanics whenever it is required by the nature of the information source, but whenever possible I will restrict my analysis to Mexican American populations. Although this is awkward, it is reflective of the problems that exist in using myriad ethnic data sources.

Table 24.1 attempts to summarize present data relevant to the Hispanic subpopulations in the United States. However, because of the difficulties inherent in reporting related data, the table combines these subgroups in focusing on general demographic indicators, as well as on the specific educational character of the population and specific social indexes that mark this population as particularly vulnerable to U.S. institutions. It is quite evident, either independently or comparatively, that the plight of Hispanics (some 60% Mexican American) in the United States is highly problematic; the table depicts consummate vulnerability for Hispanic families, children, and students. On almost every indicator, Hispanic families, children, and students are at risk, likely to fall into the lowest quartile on indicators of well-being: family stability, family violence, family income, child health and development, and educational achievement. Yet this population has grown significantly in the last two decades and will grow substantially in the decades to come.

By most measures, Hispanics lag far behind national educational norms. Of particular concern, at all levels of the educational system, is the fact that Latinos are heavily overrepresented among the nation's least successful students and severely underrepresented among the most successful students. For example, Hispanics tend to have much higher percentages of elementary and secondary students with low scores on standardized tests than Whites and Asian Americans. They also have much higher school dropout rates. From a high-achievement standpoint, relatively few Latinos are among the nation's top high school graduates each year. Hispanics also remain heavily underrepresented among recipients of bachelor's and graduate and professional degrees. Hispanics who do earn a bachelor's or advanced degree are less likely than Whites and Asians to graduate with honors. The next section is a more systematic overview of this low-achievement phenomenon that helps us understand the challenges facing Hispanic students, their families and communities, and those that serve them in U.S. schools.

TABLE 24.1. Hispanic Demographic.

I. General Demographic Character

A. Of the 30.4 million Hispanics in the continental United States, the following characterizes the population's ethnic diversity:

Country/Area of Origin	Number	Percentage
Mexico	19.5 million	64.3
Puerto Rico	3.8 million	10.6
Central/South America	3.0 million	13.4
Cuba	1.1 million	4.7
Other Areas	1.6 million	7.0

B. Ninety-six percent of Hispanics are concentrated in California (31 percent), Colorado (14 percent), Texas (29 percent), and Arizona (22 percent). Other top states occupied by Hispanics are Florida (14 percent), Nevada (15 percent), and New York (14 percent).

C. Average age in 1993 is 26.75 years (compared to 35.5 years for Whites). Hispanics' age increased by 2 years since 1983.

D. About 200,000 Hispanics immigrate legally to the United States yearly, 40 percent of all legal immigrants. (An estimated 200,000 Hispanics immigrate illegally.)

E. The Hispanic population grew 35 percent since 1990, compared to 8 percent growth in the general U.S. population. The census projects that Hispanics will be the largest minority group by the year 2005.

F. Seventeen million Hispanics report speaking Spanish in the home.

G. Ninety percent of Hispanics live in metropolitan areas, 52 percent in central cities.

II. Indices of "Vulnerability"

A. Median family income has increased by 5.8 percent from 1995 to 1996 (to 24,906). In the past, the median income fluctuated for Hispanics (1982, $23,814; 1991, $24,614; 1992, $23,912), remaining below non-Hispanics (1982, $35,075; 1991, $38,127; 1992, $38,015). Since 1972, Hispanic median family income has decreased due to the increasing representation of immigrants in the Hispanic population.

B. In 1996, 29.4 percent of Hispanic families lived below the poverty line, compared to 27.2 percent in 1982.

C. In 1993, 1,239,094 Hispanic families (23.3 percent) were maintained by a female head of household (an increase of 0.5 percent from 1983, which was 22.8 percent or 827,184). Of these households, 48.8 percent lived below the poverty line. The child poverty rate for Hispanics has increased more dramatically than for any other group and is currently about equivalent to that of African Americans.

D. The proportion of Hispanics holding unskilled and semiskilled jobs is 72.9 percent, compared to 50.8 percent of non-Hispanics.

III. Education

A. Approximately 50 percent of Hispanics leave school prior to graduation (70 percent leave by 10th grade). In 1997, about half of Hispanics aged 25 and older did not complete high school.

B. Thirty-eight percent of Hispanics are held back at least one grade.

C. Fifty percent of Hispanics are overaged at grade 12.

D. Ninety percent of Hispanic students are in urban districts.

E. Eighty-two percent of Hispanic students attend segregated schools.

F. Hispanics are significantly below national norms on academic achievement tests of reading, math, science, social science and writing at grades 3, 7, and 11, generally averaging 1–2 grade levels below the norm. At grade 11, Hispanics average a grade 8 achievement level on these tests.

G. Hispanics are placed in special education services six times more often than the general student population.

Sources: Council of Economic Advisers (1998); Reddy (1993); U.S. Census Bureau (1990, 1993, 1996, 1997); U.S. Department of Commerce Census Bureau (1996a, 1996b, 1996c, 1996d); U.S. Immigration and Naturalization Service (1994).

Elementary and Secondary Academic Achievement Patterns

In addition to the low percentage of Latino young adults who have graduated from high school, another obstacle to producing a major increase in the percentage of Latinos who earn an associate, bachelor's, or graduate or professional degree is the low percentage of Hispanics in U.S. schools who are doing well academically at the elementary and secondary levels. Only a small portion of Latino children get off to an excellent start academically during the K-3 years, and they remain heavily underrepresented among above-average and top students throughout their elementary and secondary school careers. Thus, even among those Latinos who graduate from high school, a relatively low percentage are academically well prepared for college.

Table 24.2 presents data for 12th graders from recent National Assessment of Educational Progress (NAEP) tests in reading, math, science, and writing. These tests have three performance levels: advanced, proficient, and basic. A rough way to estimate the share of high school seniors who have the academic skills necessary to pursue higher education successfully is to look at the percentages that score at least at the proficient level. Estimating the share of seniors that will graduate from high school with very weak academic skills can be done by looking at the percentages scoring below the basic level.

Regarding the low-achievement issue, note that on the four subject area tests, between one-third and two-thirds of the Latino seniors scored less than the basic level. On most of these tests, Latinos were about twice as likely to score below basic as Whites. Concerning high achievement, with the exception of reading very small percentages of Latinos (and African Americans and Native Americans) scored at the proficient level on these tests, and virtually none scored at the advanced level. For example, although 27% of the Whites scored at these two levels in science (24% proficient and 3% advanced), only 7% of the Hispanics did so. In the case of math, 20% of the Whites and only 6% of the Latinos did so. Since large numbers of Latino 17-to-18-year-olds have already dropped out of school, these data probably overestimate the percentage of Hispanics who emerge from the K–12 education system well prepared academically for college.

NAEP tests are administered not only to 12th graders but also to 8th graders and 4th graders. One of the striking things about the results for the three grade levels is how similar they are; the percentage of students who

score at the proficient level on these tests in the 4th grade tends to be similar to the percentages that do so on the tests in the 8th and 12th grades. Table 24.3 presents reading, math, science, and writing results for fourth graders for NAEP tests administered between 1996 and 2000. We have reason to believe that these patterns will change relatively little as this age cohort progresses through the K–12 system. This would mean that the percentage of Latinos finishing high school over the next 5 to 10 years that will be academically very well prepared for higher education will be about the same as now. The percentage with very low skill levels may remain fairly similar as well.

Table 24.4 shows first- and third-grade reading and math test score data from another federal source, the Prospects Study, which was based on a large national sample of elementary and middle school students in the early 1990s. Note that Whites were two to three times as likely as Hispanics to score in the top quartile on the reading and math tests at the beginning of the first grade.

These first-grade data are a powerful reminder that the achievement patterns for all racial/ethnic groups are basically established in the early years of school. No racial/ethnic group is currently producing a dramatic increase in the percentage of students who are strong academic performers after the primary grades. This is true for the groups that have the highest percentages of high achievers (Whites and Asians) as well as for those with low percentages of high achievers (Latinos, African Americans, and Native Americans). This reality is of great significance for efforts to expand Latino access and success in higher education. There are some valuable things that can be done at the secondary and college levels to

TABLE 24.2. Percentages of 12th-Grade Students Who Scored Below Basic and Within the Basic, Proficient, and Advanced Ranges on the NAEP 1998 Reading, 1996 Math, 1996 Science, and 1998 Writing Tests.

	Percentage Below Basic				Percentage at Basic			
Race/Ethnicity	Reading	Math	Science	Writing	Reading	Math	Science	Writing
White	17	21	32	16	36	59	41	58
Black	43	62	77	36	40	34	19	56
Hispanic	36	50	67	35	38	44	26	55
Asian/Pacific Islander	25	19	44	22	37	48	34	54
American Indian	35	66	48	42	38	31	42	49

	Percentage at Proficient				Percentage at Advanced			
Race/Ethnicity	Reading	Math	Science	Writing	Reading	Math	Science	Writing
White	40	18	24	25	7	2	3	1
Black	17	4	4	8	1	0	0	0
Hispanic	24	6	6	10	2	0	1	0
Asian/Pacific Islander	33	26	19	23	6	7	3	1
American Indian	24	3	10	9	3	0	0	0

Sources: Donahue (1999); Reece (1997); Bourque (1997); Greenwald (1999).

TABLE 24.3. Percentages of Fourth-Grade Students Who Scored Within the Proficient and Advanced Ranges on the NAEP 2000 Reading, 1996 Math, 1996 Science, and 1998 Writing Tests.

Race/Ethnicity	Percentage Below Basic				Percentage at Basic			
	Reading	Math	Science	Writing	Reading	Math	Science	Writing
White	27	24	21	10	34	48	42	61
Black	64	68	66	31	26	27	27	61
Hispanic	60	59	58	28	26	33	33	62
Asian/Pacific Islander	31	27	34	7	32	47	37	57
American Indian	53	48	41	24	33	44	33	65

Race/Ethnicity	Percentage at Proficient				Percentage at Advanced			
	Reading	Math	Science	Writing	Reading	Math	Science	Writing
White	29	25	33	27	11	3	4	2
Black	10	5	7	8	2	0	0	0
Hispanic	13	8	9	10	3	0	0	0
Asian/Pacific Islander	29	21	25	32	17	5	4	4
American Indian	16	7	24	11	2	1	2	1

Sources: Donahue (2001); Reece (1997); Bourque (1997); Greenwald (1999).

TABLE 24.4. Percentages of First-Grade and Third-Grade Cohorts in Prospects Study Who Scored at or Above the 50th and 75th Percentiles in Reading and Math.

Race/Ethnicity	First Grade Cohort				Third Grade Cohort			
	Reading		Mathematics		Reading		Mathematics	
	50th+	75th+	50th+	75th+	50th+	75th+	50th+	75th+
White	48	22	55	27	58	30	54	29
Black	23	7	25	8	19	6	22	8
Hispanic	25	8	29	12	24	7	27	10

Source: Borman, Stringfield, & Rachuba (2000).

help increase Latino college attendance and graduation rates, but reaching parity with Whites in these areas seems almost certain to require very large improvements in Latino achievement patterns in the early grades. Moreover, a major increase in the percentage of Latino high achievers in college (e.g., those who graduate with honors) is likely to require a large increase in high achievers as far back as the primary grades. Indeed, recent data on school readiness of youngsters who entered kindergarten in 1998 suggest that major improvements need to be made in the preschool years (E. García, 2001a).

Historically, most efforts to raise achievement levels of minority students in the United States have focused on extremely disadvantaged minority youngsters. This has reflected a recognition that low-SES youngsters tend to do less well in school than high-SES youngsters, and much higher percentages of Latino, African American, and Native American youngsters are from disadvantaged circumstances than is the case for the White population. In recent years, however, it has become much more widely recognized that there is a need to help underrepresented minority students from all social classes raise their achievement levels. This is because these groups tend to do significantly less well academically than White and Asian students at each social class level, as measured by parent education and family income.

Gender Differences

Earlier in this proposal, data were presented showing that, although Hispanics as a whole lag far behind Whites and African Americans in high school completion and bachelor's degree rates, the lag is even larger for Latino males than for Latino females. A recently released report on high school dropout rates by the American Association of University Women (AAUW) provides further evidence of this reality. The AAUW report indicates that dropout rates are about 7% for White females and 8% for White males and

13% and 12%, respectively, for Black females and males. For Latinos, however, the dropout rates are 26% for females and 31% for males.

SAT I data also show that Latino males are somewhat more underrepresented among SAT test takers relative to Latino females than is the case for White males relative to White females. For example, among high school seniors in 2000, the female-male split among SAT I test takers was 55% to 45% for Whites, but 58% to 42% each for Mexican Americans, Puerto Ricans, and other Latinos. Only African Americans had a less favorable gender split for males—59% to 41%. (The splits were 52% to 48% for Asians and 54% to 46% for Native Americans.) The less favorable gender split for the Hispanic groups (and for African Americans) relative to Whites was heavily related to social class. This is because, for most groups, low-SES females are much more likely than low-SES males to sit for the SAT I, and much higher percentages of Latino (and Black) SAT I takers than Whites are from low-SES families. For example, among White seniors in 2000 who took the SAT I and who had no parent with a high school diploma, females were 63% and males were 37%. Among Mexican Americans, the gender split in this SES segment was 61% female and 39% male. However, 28% of the Mexican American test takers were in this SES, segment compared to only 1% of the White test takers.

Interestingly, this roughly three-to-two female-to-male split also is often found among participants in high school outreach programs designed to help more disadvantaged secondary students prepare for and enroll in college. This is the case despite the fact that program operators often work hard to include as many males as possible in their programs. (No matter what program operators do, females seem almost always to end up constituting a large majority of participants.)

High School and College Completion Data

Table 24.5 below presents Current Population Survey data on the percentages of White, Black, and Hispanic 25-to-29-year-olds in 1971, 1985, and 1999 who had graduated from high school, as well as the percentages of those who had graduated from high school that also had earned a bachelor's degree or more. This age group has been selected for two reasons. First, most people who complete high school and earn a bachelor's degree do so by their mid-to-late twenties. Second, many individuals in this age group are parents of young children. Thus, educational attainment patterns of this age group tell us a lot about the education levels of parents of the current generation of children in the United States.

Four things stand out about the high school data in Table 24.5:

1. All three groups experienced an increase in the percentage of their 25-to-29-year-olds who had completed high school (or earned a GED) between 1971 and 1999.
2. The Latino gains were essentially in the 1971–1985 period; they made little further progress in this age segment after that year.
3. Consistent with other recent data, Latinos in this age segment still lagged far behind the high school graduation percentages of Whites and African

TABLE 24.5. High School and Bachelor's Degree Percentages for Whites, Blacks, and Hispanics in 1971, 1985, and 1999.

Percentage of 25-to-29-Year-Olds Who Had Completed at Least High School

	White			Black			Hispanic		
Year	Total	Male	Female	Total	Male	Female	Total	Male	Female
1971	81.7	83.0	80.5	58.8	56.7	60.5	48.3	51.3	45.7
1985	89.5	89.2	89.9	80.5	80.6	80.5	61.0	58.6	63.1
1999	93.0	91.9	94.1	88.7	88.2	89.2	61.6	57.4	65.9

Percentage of 25-to-29-Year-Old High School Completers Who Also Had Completed at Least a Bachelor's Degree

	White			Black			Hispanic		
Year	Total	Male	Female	Total	Male	Female	Total	Male	Female
1971	23.1	27.0	19.1	11.5	12.1	10.9	10.5	15.4	5.8
1985	27.3	28.6	26.0	14.4	12.9	15.6	18.2	18.6	17.7
1999	36.1	34.8	37.3	16.9	14.9	18.6	14.4	13.8	15.8

Source: Current Population Surveys for March 1971, 1985, and 1999 of U.S. Census Bureau.

Americans in 1999—only three in five Hispanics had a diploma.

4. Latinos had the largest gender gap in high school completion rates in this age segment, with more than 8% more females than males holding a high school degree in 1999.

I will have more to say about gender differences in a later section of this chapter.

Five points need to be made about the college degree data in the table:

1. Within the 25-to-29-year-old population, all three groups had increases in the 1971–1999 period in the percentage of high school graduates who completed a bachelor's degree or more.

2. Similar to the high school graduation pattern, Latinos collectively did not experience a gain in college degree percentage after 1985. (They may actually have had a drop, but this is not clear owing to sample variations in Current Population Survey results.)

3. For all groups, the biggest gains were for females, with White females leading the way by a huge margin.

4. For Hispanics, the overall percentage gains in the period were due exclusively to advances made by Latino females; Latino males made no progress. That was not the case for Whites and African Americans.

5. The absolute differences between Whites and Latinos (and between Whites and Blacks) in the percentages of high school graduates who completed college grew markedly in the period. In 1971, the gap between Whites and Latinos was 12.6% (23.1% -10.5%); by 1999 it was 21.7% (36.1% -14.4%).

Because the high school graduation rate for Hispanics is so much lower than those of Whites and African Americans, the overall Latino lag in college graduation percentage relative to other groups in the 25-to-29-year-old population is actually somewhat larger than the data in Table 24.5 suggest. Table 24.6 presents data demonstrating this point,

which are drawn from the March 2000 Current Population Survey. Among Whites, 34.0% in that age group had completed at least a bachelor's degree, compared to 17.8% of the Blacks and only 9.6% of the Hispanics. Thus, there was a 24.4% difference (34.0%–9.6%) between Whites and Latinos. Moreover, the Asian-Latino gap was much larger— 44.4%—as 54.0% of all Asians in this age group had completed at least a bachelor's degree.

It also is important to recognize that there were large gaps for Latinos at all attainment levels, not just at high school and bachelor's degree levels. Table 24.5 presents data on this point as well.

Note that not only did 37.2% of the 25-to-29-year-old Latinos in the March 2000 Current Population Survey sample have less than a high school degree; nearly one in five (18.8%) had an eighth-grade education or less. In contrast, just 1% or 2% of the other groups had an eighth-grade education or less.

One immediate reason the high school graduation percentage for 25-to-29-year-old Latinos is very low is that many of the Latinos in this age segment are immigrants who had dropped out of school prior to coming to the United States. Some who arrived as teenagers also may have found it difficult to make the transition to U.S. schools. These patterns seem most severe for immigrants from Mexico. For example, in the 1990 census, only 38% of 25-to-29-year-old Mexican immigrants had completed high school. This compared to 78% of native-born Mexican Americans in that age group that year. In contrast, all other 25-to-29-year-old Latinos collectively had a much smaller (albeit still consequential) difference in high school graduation percentages between immigrants and the native born. In 1990, 78% of other Latinos who had been born in the United States had graduated from high school, compared to 67% of other Latino immigrants. Unless ways are found to help more adolescent and young adult immigrants from Mexico enroll and succeed in U.S. schools, the overall high school graduation rate for Latinos in the United States is likely to remain well below the rates for most other groups for a long time to come. In turn, it will be very difficult for Latinos to move toward

TABLE 24.6. Highest Level of Educational Attainment Among 25-to-29-Year-Olds in 2000, by Race/Ethnicity.

Group	Percentage at Each Attainment Level							
	> 8th Grade	9–11th Grade	High School Degree	Some College, No Degree	Associate Degree	Bachelor's Degree	Master's Degree	Professional or Doctoral Degree
All	3.8	8.1	29.8	20.6	8.7	23.6	4.0	1.4
White	1.0	5.2	29.9	20.4	9.6	28.2	4.4	1.4
Black	1.4	11.8	34.1	26.7	8.2	14.2	2.7	0.9
Hispanic	18.8	18.4	30.0	17.4	5.7	7.6	1.3	0.7
Asian	2.3	4.3	15.5	17.6	6.5	38.5	10.7	4.8

Source: March 2000 Current Population Survey of U.S. Census Bureau.

parity with Whites in associate, bachelor's, master's, professional, and doctoral degree percentages.

Summary

Making sense of demographic data within the realm of education and related domains is like trying to make sense of the economy only by exploring the vast array of statistics that we as Americans compile about our nation. No one can obtain a clear understanding of the economy merely by examining those statistics, no matter how comprehensive, strategic, or ingenious the numbers are. The same is true for the education of Mexican American and Hispanic students in this country. However, much like economics, education is an important part of our social fabric. Most of us have been to school. In fact, most of us have spent a majority of our lives in formal schooling activities. We use demographic statistics (much as we use economic statistics) to help us understand the nature of the enterprise through the description of the status or well-being of students (education) and employees (business). In the demographic analysis presented in this chapter, specific status indicators for specific groups and individuals have been presented with the understanding that such description can add some depth, but not total understanding, to the challenge faced by today's and tomorrow's educators.

What do these descriptive data tell us about that challenge? It is unmistakable that the students who will populate our schools, who will play the "game," will be radically different with regard to race, culture, and language within a relatively short period. In less than two decades, one-half of our students will be non-White and Hispanic, with one-quarter of the total student body speaking a language other than English on their first day of school. A teacher receiving a teaching credential today will probably be responsible for educating a more diverse student body than any teacher at any time in the history of formal education. This will be true at all levels of education. Mexican American students, coming from social and economic circumstances that make them particularly vulnerable, will undertake their schooling with several strikes against them.

Yet these same data unequivocally indicate that the future of our society rests with these students. As they emerge as the majority in the schools, their success is our success and their failure is our failure. They must succeed. We have no other alternative short of disbanding the game. To think of disbanding education in the United States is as impossible as thinking of disbanding the economy. Can education rise to this challenge and accommodate students it has historically underserved? There is no doubt that we have the resourcefulness to meet this challenge. The remainder of this chapter will address aspects of this country's past and more recent educational responses to the education of Mexican American students. It is important to add depth of this type to the demographic understanding of this challenge.

THE EDUCATIONAL RESPONSE

Americanization

Historically, Americanization has been a prime institutional education objective for culturally diverse children (Elam, 1972; Gonzalez, 1990). Americanization schooling practices were adopted whenever the population of these students rose to significant numbers in a community. This adoption led to the establishment of special programs that were applied to both children and adults in urban and rural schools and communities. The desired effect of Americanizing students was to socialize and acculturate the diverse community. In essence, if schools could teach these students English and American values, then educational failure could be averted. Ironically, social economists have argued that this effort was coupled with systematic efforts to maintain disparate conditions between Anglos and "minority" populations. Indeed, more than anything else, past attempts at addressing the "Black, Hispanic, Indian, and Asian educational problem" have actually preserved the political and economic subordination of these communities (Moreno, 1997).

Coming from a sociological theory of assimilation, Americanization has traditionally been recognized as a solution to the problem of immigrants and ethnicity in the modern industrialized United States. Americanization was intended to merge small ethnic and linguistically diverse communities into a single dominant national institutional structure and culture. Thomas and Park (1921) argued that the immigrants' "Old World" consciousness would eventually be overcome by "modern" American values. Rather than provide here a detailed review of the literature regarding the historical circumstances of the many immigrant populations that came to the United States, I will rely on recent analyses by Gonzalez (1990) and San Miguel and Valencia (1998). According to Gonzalez, there were important distinctions between European immigrants and the experiences of other immigrant groups regarding assimilation. First, the Americanization of the non-European community has been attempted in a highly segregated social context that shows little sign of diminishing. Mexican American and other non-White students are more segregated today than three decades ago. Second, assimilation of these groups had both rural and urban aspects, whereas the European experience was overwhelmingly urban. Third, this assimilation was heavily influenced by the regional agricultural economy, which retarded a "natural" assimilation process. Finally, immigrants from Mexico could not escape the effects of the economic and political relationship between the advanced and industrialized United States and a semi-industrialized, semifeudal nation, the latter increasingly under the political and economic sway of the former. This relationship led to a very constrained immigration pool, with only farm and low-skilled labor immigrating continuously to the United States. None of the contributory European nations had such a relationship with the United States, and thus their national cultures tended to be judged more on an equal footing with nations or territories struggling to realize their interests against the nationalism of a rising world power. This factor alone would have made for a significant modification in the objectives and manner in which Americanization was applied to non-European background communities.

It can be argued that Americanization is still the goal of many programs aimed at Mexican American students (Valdes, 1996; E. García, 2001b). Americanization for Mexican American students unfortunately still means the elimination not only of linguistic and cultural differences but also of an undesirable culture. Americanization programs seem to assume a single homogeneous ethnic culture in contact with a single homogenous modern one, and the relationship between the two is not that of equals. The dominant community, enjoying greater wealth and privileges, claims its position by virtue of cultural superiority (Ogbu, 1986, 1999). In one way or another, every Mexican American child, whether born in the United States or in Mexico, is likely to be treated as a foreigner, an alien, or an intruder. Unfortunately, even today the objective is to transform the diversity in our communities into a monolithic English-speaking, American-thinking, and American-acting community. This attitude was articulated by Ken Hill, a California superintendent who has received national and state distinction for his efforts in a district serving a large number of Mexican American students: "We've got to attend to the idea of assimilation and to make sure that we teach English and our values as quickly as we can so these kids can get in the mainstream of American life" (quoted in Walsh, 1990). Hill is echoing the Americanization solution articulated repeatedly over the last century. It is important to note that the dropout rate for Mexican American students in Hill's school district was recently reported as more than 40% (Matute-Bianchi, 1990).

The Americanization solution has not worked. Moreover, it depends on the flawed notion of group culture. The Americanization solution presumes that culturally different children are culturally flawed as a group. To fix them individually, the individuals must be acted on as members of a cultural group. It is assumed that changing the values, language, and culture of the group will be the solution to the educational underachievement of students who represent that group. In essence, the groups should "melt" into one large and more beneficial American culture. But the challenge facing educators with regard to Mexican American students is not to Americanize them. Instead, it is to understand them and act responsively to the specific diversity that they bring and to the educational goal of academic success for all students. Is the adoption of this notion of education equity enough?

Educational Equity

For at least the last four decades, equal access to educational opportunities has served as a basic assumption of U.S. educational activities. This was clearly brought home by the 1954 Supreme Court decision in *Brown v. Board of Education of Topeka*. The landmark case concluded that separate/segregated education for Black Americans was unequal to that education provided for White Americans, and inherently unequal. In essence, the court argued that every effort must be made to address equal access to education regardless of race. This decision was reinforced for Hispanic Americans, Asian Americans, Native Americans, and women in the significant U.S. congressional activity during the War on Poverty era of the 1960s and 1970s. The major legislative act was the Civil Rights Act of 1964, Title IV of which banned discrimination on the grounds of race, color, or national origin in any program receiving federal financial assistance (Title VII of that act addressed educational equity across gender). Not coincidentally, the Elementary and Secondary Act of 1965 began to provide millions of federal dollars in assistance to state and local school systems. If these school systems were to make use of federal funds, they were held accountable to the standard of nondiscrimination.

The 1964 legislation directly banned recipients of federal resources from "restricting an individual in any way in the enjoyment of any advantage or privilege enjoyed by others receiving any service, financial aid or benefit under the [federally] funded program." Moreover, the recipient of federal funds was prohibited from using criteria or methods that would have the effect of impairing accomplishment of the objectives of the federally funded program with respect to individuals of a particular race, color, or national origin. Significantly, other provisions of this legislation provided the possibility of a private cause of action (a lawsuit) against the federally funded institution to rectify issues of discrimination. Students and their parents did not have to wait for the federal government to find funded programs out of compliance; they could move to the courts independently to seek relief. And they did. A barrage of legal action aimed at addressing education equities soon followed passage of the legislation.

In addition to legal action, further administrative and legislative activity also was a consequence of this initial legislative attention to equal educational opportunity, aimed particularly at Mexican American students. In 1970, the Department of Health, Education, and Welfare issued a memorandum, later referred to as the "May 25 Memorandum," that clarified the mandate of the 1964 Civil Rights Act with respect to non–English-speaking populations of students:

Where a liability to speak and understand the English language excludes national origin minority group children from effective participation in the educational program offered by a school district, the district must take affirmative steps to rectify the language deficiency in order to open instructional programs to these students.

The Equal Educational Opportunities and Transportation Act of 1974 placed this administrative protection for language-diverse students into formal law. The act makes "the failure by an educational agency to take appropriate action to overcome language barriers that impede equal participation by its students in its educational programs" an unlawful denial of equal educational opportunities.

Taken together, these legal and legislative initiatives placed the societal values regarding the importance of education into a form of direct relevance to culturally diverse populations. In essence, any child, regardless of race, color, national origin, and language, is equally entitled to the benefits of educational endeavors. This equal educational approach to the growing number of culturally diverse students pervaded our schools for over a decade and is still a part of what drives many educational initiatives for these students. In 2001, the *Secondary School Principal,* a respected publication of this country's professional education community, dedicated its entire September issue to those concerns still presently confronted by efforts of school desegregation and equal educational opportunity. But equal access has not been the only stimulus driving our educational interest for Mexican American students.

Multicultural Education

From the educational establishment and minority groups themselves came another important educational thrust of particular consequence to culturally diverse students. Aimed mostly at curriculum reform, this initiative suggested that curriculum in the United States should reflect the diverse character of the country's cultural and linguistic groups. A *multicultural education* was recommended, for several reasons. First and foremost, the curriculum should represent the actual contributions by various cultural groups to this country's society. Curriculum was criticized for its unbalanced perspectives, which emphasized Western European values, history, literature, and general worldview (Banks, 1984). The United States was not one monolithic culture, and the curriculum should reflect that cultural diversity. Second, a multicultural curriculum would inform "majority" group children of "minority" group contributions, and it would at the same time reaffirm the minority group significance to the society. Third, multicultural education was perceived as a school reform movement aimed at changing the content and process within schools. Its goal was not only to provide equal educational opportunity but also to enhance the schooling experience for all students (Sleeter & Grant, 1987).

The multicultural education concept took on several distinct approaches to instructing students in general and culturally diverse students in particular. However, the major impact of this reform movement has been in the curriculum areas, that is, the area of schooling that addresses the content of instruction. In essence, this major reform attempted to address *what* students should be learning. The reform made it quite clear that we needed to know more about this country's diverse cultural groups, and that after we had uncovered such knowledge we needed to dispense it in our everyday schooling endeavors. This overall agreement about the importance of including curriculum that addressed diversity was quite significant, since there was some disagreement with regard to the goals of such activity.

Sleeter and Grant (1987) have provided an excellent review of these discrepant goals and the overall limited consequences of the multicultural education reform movement for American education. Within a model described as "teaching the multiculturally different," the goal was to assist educators in assisting culturally different students to succeed in mainstream schooling. Although not directly implicating the need to "change" or "assimilate" children of different backgrounds into the mainstream, this goal seemed to serve as a foundation for that form of multicultural education. The prescription was usually subtractive in nature. That is, children with different cultures and languages were asked to leave these attributes behind through the assistance of bridgelike educational programs that promised access to and success in academic and, later, other societal domains. Within this view, multicultural education was seen as a temporary, highly directed educational endeavor that would lead to a melting pot of a successful and more homogeneous student population.

Early vestiges of Head Start reflect this multicultural approach. For preschool children ages three to four, Head Start and its extension for the early elementary student, Follow Through, were perceived as bridges to the mainstream academic environment. Other compensatory education programs such as Title I and now Chapter I programs that address underachievement directly are in this same category of educational programs meant to bridge nonachieving students with achievement. They are temporary in nature, with goals of providing a transition for unsuccessful students to success through a process likened to natural cultural assimilation. In such assimilation, immigrants with very diverse cultures and languages come to embrace mainstream American values and acquire English as their main mode of communication. Schools were asked to serve, positively, as an organized vehicle to hasten this natural form of assimilation.

The bridging goal of some multicultural education efforts was combined with another goal: enhancing human relations (Perry, 1975; Colangelo, Foxley, & Dustin, 1982). Such a goal was seen as best achieved by learning about and with each other. In so doing, diverse populations would be able to understand each other, and the corollary of this better understanding would be enhanced communication and social relations. Distinct from the assimilation and bridging goals and procedures, educational programs reflecting this approach to multicultural education asked students to add knowledge about other groups not like their own and use it in ways that would enhance social accommodation of diversity—("let's learn to get along better"). The most dramatic example of a large-scale program of this type actually occurred in Canada, where French-speaking populations (Francophones) in the province of Quebec were in constant social and economic dispute with English-speaking populations (Anglophones). The solution to this social relations problem was bilingual-bicultural immersion education. Anglophone children were placed in French-only schooling programs for the first three years of their educational experience. Over time, the goal of the program was for children to acquire knowledge of both the language and the culture of Francophones, with the expected product of better human relations. Evaluation of these programs indicate that these expectations were achieved without any cost in academic achievement through children's learning academic content in a language other than their own home language.

Yet another approach to multicultural education has been much more activist in nature. Its goals serve to promote respect for diversity. Beyond just acquiring and disseminating information regarding cultural diversity, this approach is aimed at developing intellectual and societal acceptance of cultural diversity as a goal in and of itself (Banks, 1984, 1988; Fishman, 1989; R. García, 1979; Gay, 1975; Gollnick & Chinn, 1986; G. W. Grant, 1977). This approach has been the most popular and most influential in the past decade and has attempted to bring together issues of race, ethnicity, gender, and social class. The thrust of such initiatives has been to permeate the curriculum with issues of diversity—in literature, social thought, scientific approaches, historical construction—while at the

same time serving up criticism of "standardized" curriculums, particularly those that reflect Western European contributions as the standard. A corollary of this approach is the overall multicultural and social reconstructionist perspective that is also espoused (Appleton, 1983). In essence, students are asked to become social critics, particularly relative to issues of social injustice. Adoption of this multicultural educational approach would rid society of pervasive social injustices inflicted on the basis of race, ethnicity, and gender.

An example of a proactive stance with regard to multicultural education for Mexican Americans has emerged from the bilingual education community in this country. Starting in 1988, "double immersion" programs have been introduced into large Mexican American school districts of California and Texas. The goal of these programs is to produce a student population that is bilingual and bicultural. For Anglo, English-speaking students, the goal is English- and Spanish-language fluency and literacy, with the program beginning in kindergarten. These students are exposed to Spanish-language instruction in classrooms with Latino Spanish-speaking students and to a curriculum that addresses bicultural concerns. The goals for Mexican American students in the programs are the same. These goals are in concert with the notion of actively promoting cultural diversity, with a healthy academic respect for the linguistic and cultural attributes of the diverse students involved. Similar programs in the public schools of San Francisco, San Diego, and Chicago are housed in "magnet" schools. The intent is to have a highly culturally diverse set of students come together around a thematically designed curriculum that is multilingual and multicultural. Such programs attempt to integrate African American, Mexican American, Asian American, and other culturally diverse student populations by recognizing diversity as a potential positive in addressing equal educational opportunity and multicultural education agendas (Grant & Sleeter, 1988).

Attention to multicultural education in this country over the last two decades has produced a series of debates and substantive accomplishments. Publishing companies have launched new curriculum efforts to address concerns of "bias" raised by proponents of multicultural education (Gollnick & Chinn, 1986). Teacher-training programs have been required to provide specific training at the preservice level (California Commission on Teacher Credentialing, 1991). School-based programs such as the magnet and double immersion bilingual education programs already described find their roots, at least partially, in the values and goals of multicultural education.

This discussion has attempted to place multicultural education into three broad categories that are based on the goals of distinct but not necessarily exclusive goal agendas. These goals range from those related to bridging/assimilation for Mexican American students, to enhancing human relations, to actively promoting cultural diversity as a societal goal. Such goals build upon the previous historical and ongoing initiatives dealing with equal educational opportunity—no child should be denied the benefits of education. These two educational initiatives—equal educational opportunity and multicultural education—have individually and together changed the educational response to the growing presence of cultural diversity in our schools.

Beyond the "Simple" Notion of Multicultural Education

Equal educational opportunity and multicultural education, in their more basic curricular and activist forms, have not comprehensively addressed a number of important educational concerns. For the most part, they have lacked strong theoretical foundations, addressed only curriculum (not instructional methods or pedagogy), produced many single-case studies of ethnic groups, and yielded little empirical data to substantiate the positive effects of implementation (E. García, 2001b). Academic achievement in many culturally diverse populations has not been enhanced significantly over the past decades. Equal educational opportunity activity has generated ongoing legislative and legal policy along with concomitant resources to address this core societal value. But such action has not dealt, in any comprehensive manner, with how educational equity should be achieved. Similarly, educational inertia in and around multicultural education has espoused important societal values and has led to advances on a number of educational fronts. But it has not produced a set of comprehensive strategies that address the educational concerns it has raised. Therefore, the result of these educational equity and multicultural reform initiatives has been to raise issues. In accomplishing this outcome, they have been assisted by the demographic reality of a changing, culturally diverse society.

An era of equal educational opportunity and multicultural education has left us with a legacy of some clearly identifiable results. First, educational endeavors related to culturally diverse students have been pragmatically oriented. That is, they have focused on a set of problems—discrimination, desegregation, underachievement, low self-esteem, non-English proficiency—and have forwarded programs to address these problems. However, these efforts have tended to lack any substantive theoretical underpinnings. Instead, the proposed solutions were driven by the social values associated with educational equity and pluralism. A more theoretical approach would still consider the same problems but would attempt first to understand why such problems exist, and then address solutions on the basis of those understandings (E. García, 1991, 1992, 2001a; Tharp, 1989).

More recent conceptualizations related to the multicultural circumstances of Mexican American students have focused on their social circumstances inside and outside of school (Mehan, Villanueva, Hubbard, & Lintz, 1996; Stanton-Salazar, 1997, Valenzuela, 1999). Issues related to social capital such as academic networks (Stanton-Salazar) and related institutional structures, such as tracking (Mehan, Villanueva, Hubbard, & Lintz), have been reported as social variables of significance for Mexican American students. Moreover, external polices have been generated that do not reflect the knowledge base related to the effective schooling of Mexican American students (E. García, 2001a). Of particular significance is California's implementation of Proposition 227 (a policy enacted in 1998 to eliminate the use of native language instruction for non-English speaking students) and the implementation of state accountability systems in California and Texas that rely on high-stakes testing (Alamillo & Viramontes, 2000; E. García & Palmer, 2000; McNeil, 2000; McNeil & Valenzuela, 2001).

In California, since the passage of Proposition 227 in 1998, additional policy shifts including high-stakes testing, supplemental curriculum focused on English acquisition, and high accountability have converged significantly to affect the education of language-minority students. Unfortunately, the effect of these multiple policies has not been positive and the implications not promising (E. García & Palmer, 2000). This impact has limited the services provided for Mexican American English language learners, causing students to fall even further behind. Although principals' philosophical position regarding bilingual education and Proposition 227 factored into how they perceived the relationship between and impact of these multiple policies on language-minority students, nonetheless they resoundingly agreed with teachers that these policies were converging in California's classrooms and their impact was uniformly powerful in a highly negative way (Alamillo & Viramontes, 2000).

California educators' perceptions of the impact of high-stakes testing on their Mexican American students have strong parallels in the research findings of McNeil and Valenzuela (2001). Drawing on emerging research on high-stakes testing and their individual investigations (McNeil, 1988, 2000; Valenzuela, 1999), the authors identify a set of alarming educational trends regarding the impact of the Texas Assessment of Academic Skills (TAAS) testing in Texas. Some of the critical issues identified by McNeil and Valenzuela mirror the set of concerns raised by teachers in our study: TAAS-based teaching and test preparation are usurping a substantive curriculum, and TAAS is divorced from children's experience and culture and is widening the educational gap between rich and poor, between mainstream and language-minority students (McNeil & Valenzuela, 2001).

The educational trends in California and Texas are similar. Both states use one test to determine academic outcomes for students. Both have placed tremendous emphasis on school ranking and are seeing a drastic increase in the implementation of mandated scripted reading programs, at the expense of known effective instructional practices for second language learners. California's educational system is growing more and more prescriptive, just as the system in Texas has, discrediting the cultural and linguistic assets students bring to the classroom. McNeil and Valenzuela argue that the TAAS system in Texas is greatly harming the poorest minority children. Our data indicates that the same is true in California. The combined effects of recent reform attempts will exact a great price on the education of California's poorest minority students. These policies and related practices are not aligned with federal efforts to build additive bilingual/bicultural programs, as opposed to subtractive English-only programs for Mexican American students (E. García, 2001b). Nor are they aligned with empirical information related to optimal and effective schooling for language-minority students (August & Hakuta, 1997). Recent analysis of the SAT 9 scores for Mexican American students in the state continue to show statewide underachievement, with significant achievement gaps among Mexican American, White, and Asian students. This is three years after full implementation of Proposition 227 and two years after implementation of state accountability policies. This statewide underachievement data combined with qualitative analysis present does not provide a positive prognosis for high-level Mexican American student learning in California nor in Texas, neither for the short run nor the long run.

Another legacy of the last three decades of educational activity centered on culturally diverse populations, particularly the result of multicultural education endeavors, has been the extended case-study approach to cultural diversity. The educational community has produced an extensive literature on the characteristics of different racial, ethnic, and ethnolinguistic groups. The goal of this work was to document the cultural and linguistic attributes of groups in the United States so that these attributes could be understood and used to serve these populations better. It was not uncommon to learn early on, as these case studies were reported, that American Indian children were nonverbal (Appleton, 1983), Asian American children were shy (Sue & Okazaki, 1990), Mexican American children were cooperative (E. García, 1983), African American children were aggressive (Boykin, 1986), and Anglo children were competitive (Kagan, 1983). Although this case-study work was meant to advance our understanding of culturally diverse students, it often had the effect of promoting stereotypes. Moreover, it did not recognize the broader, well-understood axiom of social scientists who study culture: there is as much heterogeneity within any cultural group as there is between cultural groups. Unfortunately, descriptively useful indicators took on explanatory values: if that student is Mexican American, she must be cooperative, be field-sensitive, and speak Spanish. Educational programs were developed to address these cultural attributes, only to discover that many Mexican American children were not cooperative, were field-independent, and did not speak Spanish. If all Mexican Americans are not alike, if all African Americans are not alike, and if all American Indians are not alike, then what set of knowledge about those groups is educationally important? What overarching conceptualization of culture is useful in understanding the educational framework of culturally diverse groups?

In summary, over the last five decades, research and practice in language, culture, and education has ranged from a focus on Americanization (Gonzalez, 1990) and educational equity (Ramírez & Castañeda, 1974), to multicultural education (Banks, 1988; Grant & Sleeter, 1988; Banks & Banks, 1995), and more recently to responsive pedagogy (E. García, 2001a, 2001b). Educational responses to cultural diversity are examined here briefly to set the stage for the development of the conceptual framework we propose for addressing cultural and linguistic diversity through a more comprehensive view of its central role in establishing responsive learning communities (RLC) that serve all students optimally.

August and Hakuta (1997) provide a comprehensive review of optimal learning conditions that serve linguistically and culturally diverse student populations—conditions leading to high academic performance. Their reviews of some 33 studies, most involving Mexican American students, indicate that certain attributes were identified by this case study research strategy:

A supportive school-wide climate, school leadership, a customized learning environment, articulation and coordination within and between schools, use of native language and culture in instruction, a balanced curriculum that includes both basic and higher-order skills, explicit skill instruction, opportunities for student-directed instruction, use of instructional strategies that enhance understanding, opportunities for practice, systematic student assessment, staff development, and home and parent involvement. (August & Hakuta, 1997, p. 171)

A more recent report by the National Research Council in March 1999, *Starting Out Right: A Guide to Promoting Children's Success in Reading,* summarizes a large body of research over the last two decades regarding reading and effective reading instruction for students who come to school speaking Spanish as their primary language. The report makes clear that both phonetic analysis and meaning making are important in the beginning stages of reading development. Of significance, the report makes very clear that the body of research available regarding the reading development of English by nonnative English speakers whose first language is Spanish is most effective by instruction in reading in the child's native language.

A series of case studies of exemplary schools throughout the United States serving highly diverse and poor student populations also illustrates what can be done to promote academic excellence (McLeod, 1996). In these studies, selected schools with demonstrated academic success records were subjected to intensive site-by-site study with the goal of identifying specific attributes at each site related to the functioning of the school, as well as a more ambitious effort to identify common attributes across the sites. Schools in four states (Texas, Illinois, California, Massachusetts) were particularly successful in achieving high academic outcomes with a diverse set of students and used these common goals for ensuring high-quality teaching.

- *Fostering English acquisition and the development of mature literacy.* Schools used native language abilities to develop literacy that promoted English literacy development. Programs in these schools were more interested in this mature development than transitioning students quickly into English language instruction. This approach paid off in English language development at levels that allowed students to be successful in English instruction.
- *Delivering grade-level content.* Challenging work in the academic disciplines was perceived and acted on simultaneously with the goals of English language learning. Teachers organized lessons to deliver grade-level instruction through a variety of native language, sheltered English, and ESL activities.
- *Organizing instruction in innovative ways.* Examples of innovations were (a) "schools-within-schools" to more responsively deal with diverse language needs of the students; (b) "families" of students who stayed together for major parts of the school day; (c) "continuum classes" in which teachers remained with their students for two to three years, helping teachers become more familiar with and respond to the diversity in the students; and (d) grouping of students more flexibly on a continuous basis so as to respond to the developmental differences between their native language and second language.
- *Protecting and extending instructional time.* Schools used after-school programs, supportive computer-based instruction, and voluntary Saturday schools and summer academies. These school activities multiplied the opportunities for students to engage in academic learning. Regular teachers or trained tutors were used to extend this learning time. Not surprisingly, a

majority of students took advantage of these voluntary extensions. Care was taken not to erode the daily instructional time that was available—erosion often related to auxiliary responsibilities by teachers that take valuable time away from instruction.

- *Expanding teachers' roles and responsibilities.* Teachers were given much greater roles in curricular and instructional decision making. This decision making was much more collective in nature to ensure cross-grade articulation and coordination. Teachers in these schools became full co-partners. They devised more "authentic" assessments that could inform instruction, developing assessment tools and scoring rubrics in reading and mathematics.
- *Addressing students' social and emotional needs.* Schools were located in low-income neighborhoods serving poor families. Therefore, a proactive stance with regard to issues in these communities was adopted. An after-school activity that was aimed at families, particularly dealing with issues of alcohol and drug abuse, family violence, health care, and related social service needs, brought the school staff together with social service agencies at one school site. Similar examples of actual family counseling and direct medical care were arranged at other sites.
- *Involving parents in their children's education.* Some of the schools were magnet schools, to which parents had chosen to send their children. In such schools, parent involvement was part of the magnet school contract: involvement in school committees, school festivals and celebrations, student field trips, and other activities. In nonmagnet schools, parent outreach services were an integral part of the school operation. In all cases, communication was accomplished on a regular basis in various home languages. Parent participation in governance of the school was a common attribute, although levels of parent participation were highly variable (adapted from McLeod, 1996, pp. 13–33).

In a more intensive case study of two elementary schools and one middle school, Miramontes, Nadeau, and Commins (1997) describe in detail the development of exemplary school attributes with an emphasis on linking decision making to effective programs. Over a period of several years, these schools, serving a majority of Hispanic students, developed local, state, and national recognition for their academic success with very linguistically and culturally diverse student bodies—schools with as many as five languages represented in significant proportion. They conclude that a set of premises (Figure 24.1) were key in guiding the development and reform of the schools' effective programs.

Premise 1: Active learning. Knowledge is best acquired when learners actively participate in meaningful activities that are constructive in nature and appropriate to their level of development.

Premise 2: The primary language foundation. The more comprehensive the use of the primary language, the greater the potential for linguistically diverse students to be academically successful. There are always ways to nurture the primary language regardless of school resources.

Premise 3: The quality of primary language use. There is a difference between token use of the primary language in instruction and its full development as a foundation for thinking and learning.

Premise 4: Strategies for second language development. Second language development creates an added dimension to instructional decision-making. Instruction must reflect specific strategies designed to meet the needs of second language learners.

Premise 5: Contexts for second language development. Second language instruction must be organized to give students the time, experiences, and opportunities they need to fully develop language proficiency. This requires a range of social and academic contexts in which both language and content are emphasized.

Premise 6: First and second language environments. Bilingual academic proficiency requires that clear, distinct, and meaning-enriched contexts for each language be created during instructional time.

Premise 7: Transitions and redesignations. Decisions regarding transition to formal second language reading and redesignations that exit students from programs cannot be made arbitrarily.

Premise 8: Instructional assessment. Instructional assessment must be based on students' first and second language development, rather than on grade level or predetermined criteria. An appropriate assessment plan should address language and literacy development, as well as content knowledge.

Premise 9: Parents and community. Parents and community need to play a major role in the learning and schooling of their children.

Premise 10: Planning for cross-cultural interactions. Instruction must be organized to help students understand and respect themselves and their own culture as well as the cultures of the broader society. Planned cross-cultural interactions are an essential component of programs for all students.

Premise 11: Sociocultural and political implications. Sociocultural factors and political context must be considered in making decisions regarding every aspect of program planning.

Premise 12: Teachers as decision makers. Teachers are decision makers. As part of a learning community, they are all equally responsible for decisions regarding the instructional program for linguistically diverse students.

FIGURE 24.1. Basic Premises of Effective School Reform.

Source: Miramontes, Nadeau, & Commins (1997, pp. 37–38).

In conclusion, information derived from recent research indicates that linguistically and culturally diverse students can be served effectively (Lockwood & Secada, 1999; Romo, 1999; Tashakorri & Ochoa, 1999). These students can achieve academically, at or above the national norm. Instructional strategies that serve these students best acknowledge, respect, and build upon the language and culture of the home. Teachers play the most critical role in students' academic success, and students become important partners with teachers in the teaching and learning enterprise. Although much more research is required, we are not without a knowledge base that can make a difference.

A RESPONSIVE PEDAGOGY AND DEVELOPING RESPONSIVE LEARNING COMMUNITIES

This discussion is framed in a broad educationally relevant theoretical continuum. At one end of this continuum, it is argued that addressing linguistically and culturally diverse populations calls for a deeper understanding of the interaction of a student's language and culture and the prevailing school language and culture (Cole, 1996; E. García, 1999). This cultural significance position is supported by a rich contribution of research suggesting that the educational failure of "diverse" student populations is related to this culture clash between home and school. Evidence for such a position comes from Boykin (1986) for African American students; Heath (1983) for poor White students; Wiesner, Gallimore, and Jordan (1988) for Hawaiian students; Vogt, Jordan, and Tharp (1987) for Navaho students; Romo and Falbo (1996) for Mexican American students; and Rodriguez (1989) for Puerto Rican students. In essence, these researchers have suggested that without attending to the distinctiveness of the contribution of culture, educational endeavors for these culturally distinct students are likely to fail.

To facilitate the discussion of how considerations of cultural diversity can be integrated into the development of a pedagogy and practices that improve the educational conditions of diverse students, Figure 24.2 provides a depiction of the continuum of approaches suggested by the literature reviewed briefly here. Theoretically, students do not succeed because the difference between school culture and home culture leads to an educationally harmful dissonance. The challenge for educators is to identify critical differences between and within ethnic minority groups and individuals within those groups and to incorporate this information into classroom practice. In this manner, the individual and the cultural milieu in which that individual resides receives educational attention.

At the other extreme of the theoretical continuum in Figure 24.2 lies the position that instructional programs must ensure the implementation of appropriate general principles of teaching and learning. The academic failure of any student rests on the failure of instructional personnel to implement what we know works. Using the now common educational analytical tool known as meta-analysis, Walberg (1986) suggests that educational research synthesis has identified indicators of instructional conditions that have academically significant effects across various conditions and student groups. Other reviews (Baden & Maehr, 1986; Bloom, 1984; Slavin, 1989; 1996) have articulated this same position. In this vein, a number of specific instructional strategies—including direct instruction (Rosenshine, 1986), tutoring (Bloom, 1984), frequent evaluation of academic progress (Slavin, Karweit, & Madden, 1989), and cooperative learning (Slavin, 1989, 1996)—have been particular candidates for the what-works category. Expectations play an important role in other formulations of this underachievement dilemma. Levin (1988) and Snow (1990) have suggested that students, teachers, and school professionals in general have low academic expectations of culturally and linguistically diverse students. Raising student motivation in conjunction with enhancing academic expectations with challenging curriculum is a prescribed solution. Implied in this "general principle" position is that the educational failure of "diverse" populations can be eradicated by the systemic and effective implementation of these understood general principles of instruction that work with "all" students.

Interspersed along this continuum are other significant conceptual contributions that attempt to explain the academic underachievement of culturally and linguistically diverse students. Paulo Freire (1970) has argued that educational initiatives cannot expect academic or intellectual success under social circumstances that are oppressive. He and others (Cummins, 1986; Pearl, 1991) suggest that such oppression taints any curriculum or pedagogy, and only a pedagogy of empowerment can fulfill the lofty goals of educational equity and achievement. Similarly, Bernstein (1971), Laosa (1982), and Wilson (1987) point to socioeconomic factors that influence the organization of schools and instruction. Extensive exposure, over generations, to poverty and related disparaging socioeconomic conditions significantly influence the teaching/learning process at

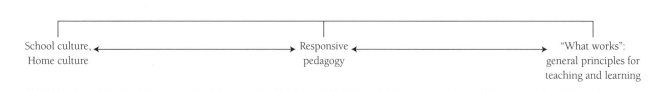

FIGURE 24.2. Addressing Cultural and Linguistic Diversity: A Continuum of Theoretical Perspectives.

home, in the community, and in schools. The result is disastrous, long-term educational failure and social disruption of family and community. Ogbu (1999) offers an alternative, macrosociological perspective with regard to the academic failure of culturally and linguistically diverse students. Such a conceptualization interprets this country's present social approach to several immigrant and minority populations as "castelike." In this theoretical attempt to explain underachievement, these theorists argue that these populations form a layer of our society not expected to excel academically or economically and therefore are treated as a castelike population. As a result, these expectations are transformed into parallel self-perceptions by these populations with academic underachievement and social withdrawal. Soto (1997) has reported that school personnel's reaction to non–English-speaking students is often highly negative. Parents are not respected if they do not speak English and participate in traditional support roles. Valdés (1996) has documented the clear dissonance between the cultural transitions of newly arrived Mexican immigrants and the schooling that they receive.

Clearly, these conceptualizations are not presented here in any comprehensive manner. Moreover, the continuum from cultural dissonance to general principles need not be interpreted as a set of incompatible approaches in the attempt to understand the educational circumstances of culturally diverse students. Instead, this short introduction should make evident that a variety of scholars have seriously dealt with this topic of attempting to understand why so many culturally and linguistically diverse students are not well served by today's educational institutions. These conceptual contributions have attempted to address the issues surrounding the challenges of educating a linguistically and culturally diverse population by searching for explanations for those conditions.

These contributions take into consideration the work of Anyon (1980), Bernstein (1971), Cummins (1979, 1986), Freire (1970), Heath (1986), Levin (1988), Ogbu (1992), Rose (1989), Trueba (1987), and Tharp and Gallimore (1989), who have suggested that the schooling vulnerability of culturally diverse students must be understood within the broader contexts of this society's circumstances for students in and out of school. That is, no quick fix is likely under social and schooling conditions that mark the student for special treatment of his or her cultural difference without consideration for the psychological and social circumstances in which the student resides. This approach warns us against isolating any single attribute (poverty, language difference, learning potential, and so on) as the only variable of importance. This more comprehensive view of the schooling process includes an understanding of the relationship between home and school, the psycho-socio-cultural incongruities between the two, and the resulting effects on learning and achievement (Brown & Campione, 1996; Cole, 1996). Moll (1991, 1996, 1998) has argued forcefully that Mexican American students come to school with "funds of knowledge" that are often ignored in the classroom.

Imbedded in this perspective is the understanding that language, culture, and their accompanying values are acquired in the home and community environment (Cummins, 1986; Goldman & Trueba, 1987; Heath, 1981); that children come to school with some knowledge about what language is, how it works, and what it is used for (Hall, 1987; Goodman, 1980; Smith, 1971); that children learn higher-level cognitive and communicative skills as they engage in socially meaningful activities (Duran, 1987); and that children's development and learning is best understood as the interaction of linguistic, sociocultural, and cognitive knowledge and experiences (Trueba, 1988). A more appropriate perspective of learning, then, is one recognizing that learning is enhanced when it occurs in contexts that are both socioculturally and linguistically meaningful for the learner (Cole, 1996; Diaz, Moll, & Mehan, 1986; Heath, 1986; Moll, 2001; Scribner & Cole, 1981; Wertsch, 1985). Students learn best and teachers feel most satisfied when both are encouraged to become allies in the learning process.

How do we as educators begin to understand such a complex set of interactions? One framework for understanding is founded on the concept of "act psychology." First formulated at the end of the 19th century, the notion of act psychology proposes a model for human cognitive processes, or how we come to know. It focuses on the assertion that the mental functions of perceiving, remembering, and organizing—ultimately, knowing—are all acts of construction. It also asserts that what we know is closely related to the circumstances in which we come to know it.

The term *constructivist* really is apt. The constructivist perspective is rooted in the notion that for humans, knowing is a result of continuous building and rebuilding. Our "construction materials" consist of give-and-take among the organization and content of old information and new information, processes of organizing that information, and the specific physical and social circumstances in which this all occurs. We come to understand a new concept by applying knowledge of previous concepts to the new information we are given. For example, in order to teach negative numbers, a math teacher can use the analogy of digging a hole: the more dirt you take out of the hole, the greater the hole becomes (the more one subtracts from a negative number, the greater the negative number becomes). But a math teacher cannot use this example with children who have no experience digging holes. It won't work. As you can see, this theory of how the mind works implies that continuous revisions (or "renovations," as an architect might say) are to be expected. Therefore, when we organize teaching and learning environments, we must recognize the nature of those environments. As educators, we build teaching and learning environments out of what we know and how we come to know it. We must continue to build; to ignore that need is to discount the relevance of previous educational environments to the ones we are considering now. They got us to *here*, but that does not mean they will get us to *tomorrow.*

Embedded in the constructivist approach to education is the understanding that language and culture, and the values that accompany them, are constructed in both home and community environments (Cummins, 1986; Goldman & Trueba, 1987; Heath, 1981). This approach acknowledges that children come to school with some constructed knowledge about many things (Goodman, 1980; Hall, 1987; Smith, 1971); it points out that children's development and learning is best understood as the interaction of past and present linguistic, sociocultural, and cognitive constructions (Cole & Cole, 2001). A more appropriate perspective of development and learning, then, is one recognizing that development and learning is enhanced when it occurs in contexts that are socioculturally, linguistically, and cognitively meaningful for the learner. These meaningful contexts bridge previous constructions to present constructions (Diaz, Moll, & Mehan, 1986; Heath, 1986; Scribner & Cole, 1981; Wertsch, 1985, 1991; Ladson-Billings, 1994; Cole & Cole, 2001).

Such meaningful contexts have been notoriously inaccessible to linguistically and culturally diverse children. On the contrary, schooling practices often contribute to their educational vulnerability. The monolithic culture transmitted by U.S. schools in the form of pedagogy, curricula, instruction, classroom configuration, and language (Walker, 1987) dramatizes the lack of fit between the culturally diverse student and the school experience. The culture of U.S. schools is reflected in such practices as:

- The systematic exclusion of the histories, languages, experiences, and values of these students from classroom curricula and activities (Banks & Banks, 1995)
- Tracking, which limits access to academic courses and which justifies learning environments that do not foster academic development and socialization (Oakes, 1985) or perception of self as a competent learner and language user
- A lack of opportunity to engage in developmentally and culturally appropriate learning in ways other than teacher-led instruction (E. García, 1999; Grant & Ladson-Billings, 1997)

Responsive Pedagogy and Learning Communities

The implication of this rethinking has profound effects for the teaching/learning enterprise related to culturally diverse students (E. García, 1994). This new pedagogy is one that redefines the classroom as a community of learners in which speakers, readers, and writers come together to define and redefine the meaning of the academic experience. It might be described by some as a pedagogy of empowerment (Cummins, 1986), by others as cultural learning (Heath, 1986; Trueba, 1987), and by still others as a cultural view of providing instructional assistance or guidance (Tharp & Gallimore, 1989). In any case, it argues for the respect and integration of the students' values, beliefs, histories, and experiences and recognizes the active role that students must play in the learning process. It is therefore a *responsive pedagogy*, one that encompasses practical, contextual, and empirical knowledge and a worldview of education that evolves through meaningful interactions among teachers, students, and other school community members. This responsive set of strategies expands students' knowledge beyond their own immediate experiences while using those experiences as a sound foundation for appropriating new knowledge.

Of course, a teaching and learning community that is responsive to the dynamics of social, cultural, and linguistic diversity within the broader concerns for high academic achievement both requires and emerges from a particular schooling environment. Although considerable work has been devoted to restructuring schools and changing the fundamental relationships that exist among school personnel, students, families, and community members, seldom have these efforts included attention to the unique influences of the linguistic and sociocultural dimensions of these same relationships and structures. The environments that potentially support and nurture the development of responsive learning communities are not unlike those promoted by leading school reform and restructuring advocates; however, we further suggest that the incorporation of social, cultural, and linguistic diversity concerns creates a set of educational principles and dimensions that are more likely to address the challenges faced by schools that must attend to the needs of growing populations of diverse students.

Responsive Learning Communities

The learning environments that we consider essential to the development of a responsive pedagogy are referred to as "effective schooling" (E. García, 1994, 1999, 2001b) and "high performance learning communities" (Berman, 1996). The focus on the social, cultural, and linguistic diversity represented by students in today's public schools

TABLE 24.7. Conceptual Dimensions of Addressing Cultural and Linguistic Diversity in Responsive Learning Communities.

Practice/Dimensions

School-wide

- A vision defined by the acceptance and valuing of diversity; Americanization is *not* the goal
- Treatment of classroom practitioners as professionals, colleagues in school development decisions
- Characterized by collaboration, flexibility, enhanced professional development
- Elimination (gradual or immediate) of policies that seek to categorize diverse students, thereby rendering their educational experiences inferior or limiting further academic learning
- Reflection of and connection to surrounding community, particularly with the families of the students attending the school

Teacher/Instructional

- Bilingual/bicultural skills and awareness
- High expectations of diverse students
- Treatment of diversity as an asset to the classroom
- Ongoing professional development on issues of cultural and linguistic diversity and practices that are most effective
- Basis of curriculum development to address cultural and linguistic diversity:
  1. Attention to and integration of home culture/practices
  2. Focus on maximizing student interactions across categories of English proficiency, academic performance, schooling prior to immigration to United States, etc.
  3. Regular and consistent attempts to elicit ideas from students for planning units, themes, activities
  4. Thematic approach to learning activities, with integration of various skills, events, and learning opportunities
  5. Focus on language development through meaningful interactions and communications rather than on grammatical skill building that is removed from its appropriate context

further challenges us to consider the theoretical and practical concerns relative to ensuring educational success for diverse students. That is, responsive learning communities must necessarily address issues of diversity in order to maximize their potential and to sustain educational improvement over time. To further examine this challenge, Table 24.7 summarizes the conceptual dimensions for high-performing responsive learning communities.

Conclusion

In summary, a responsive learning community recognizes that academic learning has its roots in processes both out of school and in school. Such a conceptual framework rejects the Americanization strategy; extends beyond the policy and practice frameworks of equal educational opportunity; and concludes that a focus on broader issues of culture, such as those represented in the multicultural education movement, is useful but not enough for effectively serving culturally diverse students in today's schools. Instead, a focus on responsive instructional engagement encourages students to construct and reconstruct meaning and seek reinterpretations and augmentations to past knowledge within compatible and nurturing schooling contexts. Diversity is perceived and acted on as a resource for teaching and learning, instead of a problem. A focus on what students bring to the schooling process generates an approach that is oriented more toward assets and resources than toward deficit or needs assessment.

Within this knowledge-driven, responsive, and engaging learning environment, skills are tools for acquiring knowledge, not a fundamental target of teaching events (Cole, 1996; E. García, 2001b; Tharp & Gallimore, 1989).

In addition, the search for general principles of learning that work for all students must be redirected. This redirection considers a search for and documentation of particular implementations of general and nongeneral principles of teaching and learning that serve a diverse set of environments, in and out of school. This mission requires an understanding of how individuals with diverse sets of experiences, packaged individually into cultures, make meaning, communicate that meaning, and extend it, particularly in the social context we call school. Such a mission requires in-depth treatment of the processes associated with producing diversity, issues of socialization in and out of schools, coupled with a clear examination of how such understanding is actually transformed into pedagogy and curriculum that results in high academic performance for all students.

A RESEARCH AND POLICY AGENDA THAT CAN HELP ACCELERATE MEXICAN AMERICAN EDUCATIONAL PROGRESS

Given the very large educational attainment and academic achievement gaps described in this chapter, it is likely to take quite a long time for Hispanics, and Mexican Americans in particular, to reach parity with Whites in educational outcomes—probably several decades, even under the best of circumstances. Nonetheless, there is reason to believe that we can increase the rate of progress and produce valuable medium-term gains, not just in the long run. In this regard, one positive aspect of the current situation is that the effort, nearly two decades old, to improve elementary and secondary education in the United States has placed considerable emphasis on raising achievement levels of minority students, especially those from extremely disadvantaged backgrounds. There also is a great deal of interest in improving outcomes for minority students at the level of higher education, despite the rollback of affirmative action in several states. In some respects, the central question is how to build on the efforts in ways that can help educational leaders promote acceleration of the rate of Latino educational advancement more effectively.

Among policy makers, especially in state government, much attention has gone into raising K–12 educational standards. For example, most states have raised high school graduation standards and instituted extensive testing programs to monitor the performance of individual students and schools. Increasingly, these testing programs carry high stakes for both students and educators. Importantly, elementary school students who do not pass state tests may be retained in grade, and secondary school students who do not pass may not be awarded a high school diploma. Among educators, an enormous amount of effort has gone into designing school-level strategies that can raise student achievement via such things as improving curriculum and instruction, strengthening school-level management, and improving home-school relations. One recent count found about 300 "whole school" reform strategies being used in the schools.

From the standpoint of raising Latino achievement at the K–12 level as a means of helping improve Latino higher education access and outcomes, the current school reform movement has several limitations. First, few school-level strategies have been demonstrated in a large number of schools to produce substantial increases in the percentage of Latino (or other) students who are academically well prepared for college as measured by school grades and test scores. Indeed, few school-level strategies have been tested and evaluated rigorously from a high achievement perspective, for example, whether they increase the number of students who score in the top tenth or the top quarter on standardized tests or who earn mainly As or Bs in their courses. For example, it has been common for elementary school evaluations to look at whether they help reduce the number of students who achieve at low levels on standardized tests and increase the number who perform at grade level. At the high school level, evaluations have tended to look at whether students avoid dropping out or whether they complete more college prep courses.

Second, consistent with this "pulling up the bottom" emphasis of many evaluations, much minority-oriented school reform work has focused on schools serving high concentrations of disadvantaged youngsters who are at risk of not doing well academically. Even though such work is of utmost importance, it also means that little attention has been given to testing school reform strategies in settings in which there are significant numbers of middle-class minority students, as in a growing number of suburban schools. Certainly, the school reform movement has yet to engage systematically the within-class achievement differences that continue to exist among groups—although recently several suburban districts have made it clear that they need help closing their minority-majority achievement gaps. Even in disadvantaged settings, few strategies seem to be focused on closing male-female achievement differences, or ensuring that previously high-achieving disadvantaged minority students continue to be high achievers.

Third, the standards-based efforts of state government have often had a basic skills orientation. This means that increases in pass rates on many of these tests have not necessarily been an indication that larger percentages of minority students are reaching high levels of achievement. Also, there is a possibility that, in many schools serving mainly disadvantaged children, much time is being spent teaching to these basic skills tests; in the process, the curriculum is being narrowed markedly. Even when states introduce tests with a genuine capacity to measure high academic performance, it does not always mean that high performance trends will be monitored. Indeed, if large numbers of students are not doing well on such tests and they carry high stakes (such as blocking students from graduating from high school), little attention may be given to the high-achievement question.

For those concerned with advancing a research and policy agenda for improving K–12 outcomes for Mexican Americans in ways that produce greater Hispanic success in higher education, these circumstances suggest a number of priorities:

- Promote a much expanded evaluation effort of educational strategies that would involve assessing programs from the perspective of whether they increase the number of Mexican American elementary and secondary students who are achieving at above-average to very high levels as well as from the perspective of whether they reduce the number of low achievers. Some of this work should involve reviewing existing evaluations to determine which current strategies may have such a capacity. Some of the work also should entail undertaking new evaluations for the specific purpose of gathering information on high-performance questions.

- Encourage the testing of strategies with a broad range of Mexican American students and in a variety of school settings. Priority should be given to testing strategies in ways that ensure that their effectiveness can be determined for male and female Latino students from all social class levels, in schools in urban, suburban, and rural settings. These tests of strategies also should include a large enough number of students and schools (with appropriate control groups) to offer solid information on whether the strategies can help increase the number of above-average and high-achieving students as a means of increasing the pool of students prepared academically for colleges and universities of all levels of selectivity.

- Encourage states to ensure that their standardized tests for monitoring progress assess both basic and higher-level academic skills, and to report results on a highly disaggregated basis, including for student segments defined simultaneously in terms of race/ethnicity, social class, and gender. By conducting studies that analyze state and district results in such a way, researchers can lead policy makers in these directions.

- Encourage states to pull back from the most extreme forms of high-stakes testing. For example, until educators have demonstrated that they know how to help most students in a variety of schools and circumstances reach achievement levels associated with being prepared for college, such performance should not be required for students to receive a diploma. One of the benefits of a much expanded evaluation effort of educational strategies is that it should become much clearer what the real operational knowledge base is for raising student achievement at a given point in time, so that policy makers can set ambitious goals without overreaching at the expense of the students.

- Identify and/or design and test strategies for providing more effective continuing education for teachers in schools serving large numbers of Mexican American children, especially those from disadvantaged backgrounds. Research going back to the middle 1960s has documented (unsurprisingly) that children who have well-educated parents or well-educated teachers have a better chance of doing well academically in school than students who are in the opposite position. Latino students' need for knowledgeable, highly skilled teachers is especially great, because so many have parents with little formal education. Yet many large urban school districts that serve a high percentage of disadvantaged Mexican American (and other minority) youngsters (E. García, 2001b) are having difficulty recruiting and retaining teachers who are well trained in their disciplines. To the extent that the nation's economy remains basically healthy in coming years, this could become an even more difficult problem for urban districts, especially in math and science, because new and experienced teachers with strong backgrounds in these areas will continue to have excellent employment opportunities in the private sector. This suggests that researchers should be giving high priority to identifying affordable and scalable approaches to continuing education that can help many teachers develop much deeper grounding in the fields in which they are teaching. This work may need to extend to a much expanded continuing education effort for early childhood educators who work mainly with disadvantaged Latino children. One recent estimate suggests that by 2015 about three-fifths of youngsters with no parent with a high school diploma will be Hispanic, and nearly half of such youngsters will be from Latino immigrant families.

An underlying theme of the recommendations made here is that the strategies that educators and policy makers use to attempt to improve Mexican Americans' educational outcomes should be as empirically grounded as possible and target a number of student segments.

References

Alamillo, L., & Viramontes, C. (2000). Reflections from the classroom: Teacher perspectives on the implementation of Proposition 227. *Bilingual Research Journal, 24*(1–3), 155–167.

Anyon, S. (1980) Social class and the hidden curriculum. *Journal of Education, 162*(1), 67–91.

Appleton, C. (1983). *Cultural pluralism in education: Theoretical foundations.* New York: Longman.

August, D., & García, E. (1988). *Language minority education in the United States: Research, policy and practice.* Chicago: Charles C. Thomas.

August, D., & Hakuta, K. (Eds.). (1997). *Improving schooling for language-minority children: A research agenda.* Washington, DC: National Academy Press.

Baden, B., & Maehr, M. (1986). Conforming culture with culture: A perspective for designing schools for children of diverse sociocultural backgrounds. In R. Feldman (Ed.), *The social psychology of education* (pp. 289–309). Cambridge, MA: Harvard University Press.

Banks, J. A. (1984). *Teaching strategies for ethnic studies* (3rd ed.). Boston: Allyn and Bacon.

Banks, J. A. (1988). *Multiethnic education: Theory and practice* (2nd ed.). Boston: Allyn and Bacon.

Banks, J. A. (1991). *Teaching strategies for ethnic studies* (5th ed.). Boston: Allyn and Bacon.

Banks, J., & Banks, C.A.M. (1995) *Handbook of research on multicultural education.* New York: Macmillan.

Berman, P. (1996). *High performance learning communities: Proposal to the U.S. Department of Education*. Emeryville, CA: Research, Policy and Practice Associates.

Bernstein, B. (1971). *Class, codes and control* (Vol. 1). London: Routledge & Kegan Paul.

Bloom, B. (1984). The search for methods of group instruction as effective as one-to-one tutoring. *Educational Leadership, 41*(8), 4–17.

Borman, G. D., Stringfield, S., & Rachuba, L. (2000). *Advancing minority high achievement: National trends and promising programs and practices, a report of the National Task Force on Minority High Achievement*. New York: College Board.

Bourque, M. L. (1997). *1996 science performance standards: Achievement results for the nation and the states*. Washington, DC: National Assessment Governing Board.

Boykin, A. (1986). The triple quandary and the schooling of Afro-American children. In U. Neisser (Ed.), *The school achievement of minority children* (pp. 57–92). New York: New Perspectives.

Brown, A. L., & Campione, J. C. (1996). Psychological theory and the design of innovative learning environments: On procedures, principles, and systems. In L. Schauble & R. Glaser (Eds.), *Innovation in learning new environments for education* (pp. 289–325). Mahweh, NJ: Erlbaum.

Brown vs. Board of Education of Topeka, 347 US 483 (1954): 686.

California Commission on Teacher Credentialing. (1991). *Teacher credentialing in California: A special report*. Sacramento: Author.

Colangelo, N., Foxley, C. H., & Dustin, D. (Eds.). (1982). *The human relations experience*. Monterey, CA: Brooks/Cole.

Cole, M. (1996). *Cultural psychology: A once and future discipline*. Cambridge, MA: Belknap Press of Harvard University Press.

Cole, M., & Cole, S. R. (2001). *The development of children*. New York: Worth Publishers.

Council of Economic Advisers. (1998). *Changing America: Indicators of social and economic well-being by race and Hispanic origin*. Washington, DC: U.S. Government Printing Office.

Cummins, J. (1979). Linguistic interdependence and the educational development of bilingual children. *Review of Educational Research, 19*, 222–251.

Cummins, J. (1986). Empowering minority students: A framework for intervention. *Harvard Educational Review, 56*(1), 18–36.

Diaz, S., Moll, L. C., & Mehan, H. (1986). Sociocultural resources in instruction: A context-specific approach. In *Beyond language: Social and cultural factors in schooling language minority students* (pp. 197–230). Sacramento: California State Department of Education, Bilingual Education Office.

Donahue, P. L. (1999). *NAEP 1998 reading report card for the nation and the states*. Washington, DC: U.S. Department of Education.

Donahue, P. L. (2001). *The nation's report card: Fourth-grade reading 2000*. Washington, DC: U.S. Department of Education.

Duran, R. (1987). Factors affecting development of second language literacy. In S. Goldman & H. Trueba (Ed.), *Becoming literate in English as a second language* (pp. 33–55). Norwood, NJ: Ablex.

Elam, S. E. (1972). Acculturation and learning problems of Puerto Rican children. In F. Corradasco & E. Bucchini (Eds.), *Puerto Rican children in mainland schools* (pp. 344–351). Metuchen, NJ: Scarecrow Press.

Fishman, J. (1989). *Language and ethnicity in minority sociolinguistic perspective*. Philadelphia: Multilingual Matters.

Freire, P. (1970). *Pedagogy of the oppressed*. New York: Seabury Press.

García, E. (1983). *Bilingualism in early childhood*. Albuquerque: University of New Mexico Press.

García, E. (1994). Addressing the challenges of diversity. In S. L. Kagan & B. Weissbourd (Eds.), *Putting families first.* (pp. 243–275). San Francisco: Jossey-Bass.

García, E. (1999). *Understanding and meeting the challenge of student cultural diversity* (2nd ed.). Boston: Houghton Mifflin.

García, E. (2001a). *Hispanic education in the United States: Raíces y alas*. Lanham, MD: Rowman and Littlefield.

García, E. (2001b). *Understanding and meeting the challenge of student diversity* (3rd ed.). Boston: Houghton Mifflin.

García, E., & Curry, J. E. (2000). The education of limited English proficient students in California schools: An assessment of the influence of Proposition 227 in selected districts and schools. *Bilingual Research Journal, 24*(1–2), 15–36.

García, E., & Palmer, D. (2000). Voices from the field: Bilingual educators speak candidly about Proposition 227. *Bilingual Research Journal, 24*(1–3), 169–178.

García, R. (1979). *Teaching in a pluralistic society*. New York: Harper & Row.

Gay, G. (1975). Organizing and designing culturally pluralistic curriculum. *Educational Leadership, 33*, 176–183.

Goldman, S., & Trueba, H. (Eds.). (1987). *Becoming literate in English as a second language: Advances in research and theory*. Norwood, NJ: Ablex.

Gollnick, D. M., & Chinn, P. C. (1986). *Multicultural education in a pluralistic society*. New York: Macmillan.

Gonzalez, G. (1990). *Chicano education in the segregation era: 1915–1945*. Philadelphia: Balch Institute.

Goodman, Y. (1980). The roots of literacy. In M. P. Douglass (Ed.), *Reading: A humanizing experience* (pp. 286–301). Claremont, CA: Claremont Graduate School.

Grant, C. A., & Ladson-Billings, G. (1997). *Dictionary of multicultural education*. Phoenix, AZ: The Oryx Press.

Grant, C. A., & Sleeter, C. E. (1988) Race, class and gender and abandoned dreams. *Teachers College Record 90*(1), 19–40.

Grant, G. W. (1977). *In praise of diversity: Multicultural classroom applications*. Omaha: University of Nebraska Press.

Greenwald, E. A. (1999). *NAEP 1998 writing report card for the nation and the states*. Washington, DC: U.S. Department of Education.

Hall, N. (1987). *The emergence of literacy*. Portsmouth, NH: Heinemann Educational Books.

Heath, S. B. (1981). Towards an ethnohistory of writing in American education. In M. Farr-Whitman (Ed.), *Writing: The nature, development and teaching of written communication. (Vol. 1.) Variation in writing: Functional and linguistic-cultural differences* (pp. 225–246). Hillsdale, NJ: Erlbaum.

Heath, S. B. (1983). *Ways with words*. Cambridge, England: Cambridge University Press.

Heath, S. B. (1986). Sociocultural contexts of language development. In *Beyond language: Social and cultural factors in schooling language minority students* (pp. 143–186). Sacramento: California State Department of Education, Bilingual Education Office.

Kagan, S. (1983). Social orientation among Mexican American children: A challenge to traditional classroom structures. In E. García (Ed.), *The Mexican American child* (pp. 163–182). Tempe: Arizona State University.

Ladson-Billings, G., (1994). *The dreamkeepers: Successful teachers of African American children.* San Francisco: Jossey-Bass.

Laosa, L. M. (1982). School, occupation, culture and family: The impact of parental schooling on the parent-child relationship. *Journal of Educational Psychology, 74*(6), 791–827.

Levin, I. (1988). *Accelerated schools for at-risk students.* (CPRE Research Report Series RR-010). New Brunswick, NJ: Rutgers University, Center for Policy Research in Education.

Lockwood A. T., & Secada, W. G. (1999), *Transforming education for Hispanic youth: Exemplary practices, programs, and schools.* Madison: University of Wisconsin Press; New York: Teachers College Press.

Matute-Bianchi, E. (1990). *A report to the Santa Clara County School District: Hispanics in the schools.* Santa Clara, CA: Santa Clara County School District.

McNeil, L. M. (2000). *Contradictions of reform: The educational costs of standardization.* New York: Routledge.

McNeil, L. M., & Valenzuela, A. (2001). The harmful impact of the TAAS system of testing in Texas: Beneath the accountability rhetoric. In M. Kornhaber & G. Orfield (Eds.), *The effects of high stakes testing on minority youth.* New York: Century Foundation.

Mead, M. (1937). *Cooperation and competition among primitive people.* New York: McGraw-Hill.

Mehan, H. Villanueva, I., Hubbard, L., & Lintz, A. (1996). *Constructing school success: The consequences of untracking low-achieving students.* New York: Cambridge University Press.

Miramontes, O., Nadeau, A., & Commins, N. (1997). *Linguistic diversity and effective school reform: A process for decision-making.* New York: Teachers College Press.

Moll, L. (1991). *Funds of knowledge for change: Developing mediating connections between homes and classrooms.* Paper presented at the conference Literacy, Identity and the Mind, University of Michigan, Ann Arbor.

Moll, L. (1996). Educating Latino students. *Language Arts, 64,* 315–324.

Moll, L. (1998). Bilingual classroom studies and community analysis: Some recent trends. *Educational Researcher, 21*(2), 20–24.

Moreno, R. P. (1997). Everyday instruction: A comparison of Mexican American and Anglo mothers and their preschool children. *Hispanic Journal of Behavioral Sciences, 19*(4), 527–539.

National Center for Educational Statistics. (1991). *The condition of education, 1991: Vol. 1. Elementary and secondary education.* Washington, DC: Government Printing Office.

National Research Council. (1999). *Starting out right: A guide to promoting children's success in reading.* Washington, DC: National Academy Press.

Oakes, J. (1985). *Keeping track: How schools structure inequality.* New Haven: Yale University Press.

Ogbu, J. (1986). The consequences of the American caste system. In U. Neisser (Ed.), *The school achievement of minority children: New perspectives* (pp. 19–56). Hillsdale, NJ: Erlbaum.

Ogbu, J. (1992). Understanding cultural diversity and learning. *Educational Researcher, 21*(8), 5–14.

Pearl, A. (1991). Democratic education: Myth or reality. In R. Valencia (Ed.), *Chicano school failure and success* (pp. 101–118). New York: Falmer Press.

Perry, J. (1975). Notes toward a multi-cultural curriculum. *English Journal, 64,* 8–9.

Ramírez, M., III, & Castañeda, A. (1974). *Cultural democracy, bicognitive development and education.* New York: Academic Press.

Reddy, M. A. (1993). *Statistical record of Hispanic Americans.* Detroit, MI: Gale Research.

Reece, C. M. (1997). *NAEP 1996 mathematics report card for the nation and the states.* Washington, DC: U.S. Department of Education.

Rodriguez, C. E. (1989). *Puerto Ricans born in the U.S.A.* Winchester, MA: Unwin Hyman.

Romo, H. (1999). *Reaching out: Best practices for educating Mexican-origin children and youth.* Charleston, WV: Clearinghouse on Rural Education and Small Schools.

Romo, H., & Falbo, T. (1996). *Latino high school graduation: Defying the odds.* Austin: University of Texas Press.

Rose, M. (1989). *Lives on the boundary.* New York: Free Press.

Rosenshine, B. (1986). Synthesis of research on explicit teaching. *Educational Leadership, 43,* 60–69.

San Miguel, G., & Valencia, R. R. (1998). From the Treaty of Guadalupe Hidalgo to "Hopwood": The educational plight of Mexican Americans in the Southwest. *Harvard Educational Review, 68*(3), 353–412.

Scribner, S., & Cole, M. (1981). *The psychology of literacy.* Cambridge, MA: Harvard University Press.

Skinner, B. F. (1957). *Verbal behavior.* Englewood Cliffs, NJ: Prentice-Hall.

Slavin, R. E. (1989). The PET and the pendulum: Fadism in education and how to stop it. *Phi Delta Kappan, 70*(10), 752–759.

Slavin, R. E. (1996). Success for all: A summary of research. *Journal of Education for Students Placed at Risk, 1,* 41–76.

Slavin, R., Karweit, N., & Madden, N. (1989). *Effective programs for students at risk.* Boston: Allyn and Bacon.

Sleeter, C. E., & Grant, C. A. (1987). An analysis of multicultural education in the United States. *Harvard Educational Review, 57*(4), 421–444.

Smith, F. (1971). *Understanding reading.* New York: Holt, Rinehart and Winston.

Snow, C. E. (1990). The development of definitional skill. *Journal of Child Language, 17*(3), 697–710.

Soto, L. D. (1997). *Language, culture, and power: Bilingual families and the struggle for quality education.* Albany: State University of New York Press.

Stanton-Salazar, R. (1997) A social capital framework for understanding the socialization of racial minority children and youths. *Harvard Educational Review, 67*(1), 1–40.

Sternberg, R. J., & Wagner, R. K. (Eds.). (1986). *Practical intelligence.* New York: Cambridge University Press.

Sue, S., & Okazaki, S. (1990). Asian-American educational achievements: A phenomenon in search of an explanation. *American Psychologist, 45*(8), 913–920.

Tashakkori, A., & Ochoa, S. H. (1999) *Education of Hispanics in the United States: Politics, policies, and outcomes.* New York: AMS Press.

Tharp, R. G. (1989). Psychocultural variables and k constants: Effects on teaching and learning in schools. *American Psychologist, 44,* 349–359.

Tharp, R. G., & Gallimore, R. (1989). *Challenging cultural minds.* London: Cambridge University Press.

Thomas, S. V., & Park, B. (1921). *Culture of immigrants.* Cambridge, MA: Newcome Press.

Trueba, H. (1987). *Success or failure? Learning and the language minority student.* New York: Harper & Row.

Trueba, H. (1988). Rethinking learning disabilities: Cultural knowledge in literacy acquisition. Unpublished manuscript, Office for Research on Educational Equity, Graduate School of Education, University of California, Santa Barbara.

U.S. Census Bureau. (1990). *Social and economic characteristics in the U.S.: 1990 census of the population.* Washington, DC: U.S. Government Printing Office.

U.S. Census Bureau. (1993). *The Hispanic population in the United States: March 1993.* Washington, DC: U.S. Government Printing Office.

U.S. Census Bureau. (1997). *The Hispanic Population in the United States: March 1997.* Washington, DC: U.S. Government Printing Office.

U.S. Census Bureau, Population Division. (1997). *Population Division, release PPL-91, United States Population Estimates, by Age, Sex, Race, and Hispanic Origin, 1990 to 1997.* Washington, DC: U.S. Government Printing Office.

U.S. Department of Commerce Census Bureau. (1996a). *Health insurance coverage: 1996.* Washington, DC: U.S. Government Printing Office.

U.S. Department of Commerce Census Bureau. (1996b). *Money income in the United States: 1996.* Washington, DC: U.S. Government Printing Office.

U.S. Department of Commerce Census Bureau. (1996c). *Population projections of the United States by age, sex, race, and Hispanic origin: 1995–2050.* (P25–1130) Washington, DC: U.S. Government Printing Office.

U.S. Department of Commerce Census Bureau. (1996d). *Poverty in the United States: 1996.* Washington, DC: U.S. Government Printing Office.

U.S. Immigration and Naturalization Service. (1994). *Statistical yearbook of the Immigration and Naturalization Service, 1993.* Washington, DC: U.S. Government Printing Office.

Valdés, G. (1996). *Con respeto: Bridging the difference between culturally diverse families and schools.* New York: Teachers College Press.

Valenzuela, Angela. (1999). *Subtractive schooling: U.S.-Mexican youth and the politics of caring.* Albany: State University of New York Press.

Vogt, L., Jordan, C., & Tharp, R. (1987). Explaining school failure, producing school success: Two cases. *Anthropology and Education Quarterly, 18*(4), 276–286.

Walberg, H. (1986). Synthesis of research on teaching. In M. Wittrock (Ed.), *Handbook of research on teaching* (3rd ed., pp. 15–32). New York: Macmillan.

Walker, C. L. (1987). Hispanic achievements: Old views and new perspectives. In H. Trueba (Ed.), *Success or failure? Learning and the language minority student* (pp. 15–32). Cambridge, MA: Newbury House.

Walsh, R. (1990, October 12). Minority students in Santa Clara county continue to deteriorate academically. *San Francisco Examiner,* pp. B1–4.

Wertsch, J. V. (1985). *Vygotsky and the social formation of mind.* Cambridge, MA: Harvard University Press.

Wertsch, J. V. (1991). *Vygotsky and the social formation of the mind.* Cambridge, MA: Harvard University Press.

Wiesner, T. S., Gallimore, R., & Jordan, C. (1988). Unpackaging cultural effects on classroom learning: Native Hawaiian peer assistance and child-generated activity. *Anthropology and Education Quarterly, 19*(4), 327–353.

Wilson, W. J. (1987). *The truly disadvantaged: The inner city, the underclass, and public policy.* Chicago: University of Chicago Press.

25

PUERTO RICAN STUDENTS IN U.S. SCHOOLS

A Troubled Past and the Search for a Hopeful Future

Sonia Nieto

University of Massachusetts, Amherst

Although Puerto Ricans have resided in the United States for more than a hundred years, they have achieved the dubious distinction of being one of the most undereducated ethnic groups in the United States. How this has come to pass is a long story, infused with controversy concerning political status, conflicts over the role of culture and language in school and society, the experience of racism and inequality, and a community's fierce determination to define and defend itself. This chapter is an attempt to document that history, provide some insights into what can be learned from it, and suggest where we go from here.

According to the U.S. Census Bureau, Puerto Ricans living in the United States now number 3,039,000, about 15% of the total Latino population and the second largest Latino ethnic group in the nation (U.S. Census Bureau, 2000). This number is nearly the same as for those who live on the island of Puerto Rico, making their immigration arguably one of the most dramatic diasporas in the world. Yet whether they reside in Puerto Rico or in the United States itself, Puerto Ricans have been "born in the U.S.A." since 1898, because they have been subject to U.S. policies as a result of a change of sovereignty from one colonial power to another (Rodríguez, 1991).

Because of this colonial relationship, Puerto Ricans even in Puerto Rico have attended U.S.-controlled schools since 1898, when the island was taken over by the United States shortly after the Spanish-American War. The U.S. Congress mandated that Puerto Rican children learn English and the "American way of life" as soon as the island was ceded by Spain in 1898 (Cafferty & Rivera-Martínez, 1981; Negrón, 1971). Additionally, U.S. ideals have been instilled through language policies and U.S. textbooks, materials, and methods, as well as through teacher preparation and the celebration of national U.S. holidays— including, ironically, U.S. independence (Osuna, 1949; Walsh, 1991). Juan José Osuna went so far as to suggest that, shortly after 1898, the average Puerto Rican child knew more about George Washington, Abraham Lincoln, and Betsy Ross than the average child in the United States did. This may be an overstatement, but it nevertheless indicates the extent to which Puerto Rican youngsters on both sides of the Atlantic have been indelibly shaped by the U.S. educational system.

Needless to say, Puerto Ricans who have lived in the continental United States have been even more directly affected by U.S. educational policies than those living in Puerto Rico. In the 2000 census, the Latino population slightly surpassed that of African Americans as the "majority minority" in the United States (U.S. Census Bureau, 2000), but few educational gains have accompanied this enormous growth. For Puerto Ricans, current educational data tell a tale of unfulfilled dreams and unrealized expectations not very different from the conditions of 60 or 70 years ago.

The experiences and challenges faced by Puerto Ricans in U.S. schools have been the subject of numerous studies and research reports since the 1930s. In the early years, Puerto Ricans were described for the most part with such terms as "problems," "losers," "culturally deprived," or "disadvantaged," among other labels (see, e.g., Association of Assistant Superintendents, 1948; Gallardo, 1970; Lewis, 1965; Margolis, 1968). In the past three decades, the situation has changed as a greater sensibility concerning the education of Puerto Rican youngsters developed, a sensibility due in no small part to an increase in the number of Puerto Rican and other Latino educational researchers. Since this chapter was first published in 1995, a number of new research reports and studies have appeared. Even more important, a more critical analysis of the education of Puerto Rican and other Latino students has been developing, especially among the growing number of Puerto Rican and Latino scholars. Recent relevant sources demonstrating these new perspectives are included in this revised chapter.

The purpose of this chapter is to document the troubling history of Puerto Rican students in U.S. schools in order to analyze how and why it has occurred, and to explore directions for a more promising future. First, the question Who are the Puerto Ricans? is addressed, with special attention to the use of appropriate ethnic labels and the problem of inconsistency of data. In order to aid understanding of educational attainment among Puerto Rican students, I present a brief history of the Puerto Rican community in the United States. A discussion of recurring themes in the education of Puerto Ricans in the United States, with a focus on the dropout issue, follows. The chapter ends with lessons to be learned from the struggle of Puerto Ricans for equal and quality education.

WHO ARE THE PUERTO RICANS?

The Meaning of Ethnic Labels

A perpetual problem facing researchers and policy makers interested in the education of Puerto Ricans and other Latinos has been that of definition. First, there is the question of which overarching term is most appropriate. Over the years, terms have included *Spanish origin, Hispanic, Latin American,* and *Latino(a)*. Recently debate has focused on whether *Hispanic* or *Latino(a)* is the more relevant term. Why the debate over ethnic labels? As Murguia suggests, "Struggles over ethnic labels are not meaningless. Fundamentally, they are ideological in nature, attempts to define a group and to direct its future" (Murguia, 1991, p. 8). Some have argued that *Latino* is far more accurate, while others have staunchly defended the use of *Hispanic*. The debate is complicated by the tremendous diversity within the Latino/Hispanic community itself. Martha Gimenez (1997) has suggested that both *Hispanic* and *Latino* are inappropriate because they give Latin Americans a "contrived Hispanic ethnicity" (p. 225) because Latin Americans in general have not faced the kinds of oppressive conditions in the United States that Mexicans and Puerto Ricans have encountered. She has suggested several categories: first, Puerto Ricans and Mexicans, the two "minority" groups who have been historically oppressed in the United States; followed by Cuban immigrants; Central American refugees; Central American immigrants; and South American immigrants. According to Gimenez, because each group has a particular historical context that needs to be recognized, the categorizations would recognize the relative privileged positions, time in the United States, race, and other differences among these groups.

There will never be complete agreement concerning ethnic labels. However, there seems to be a growing consensus that the ethnic labels used to describe people are not as important as other issues: how they are treated, the access they have to opportunities, and the tremendous economic and social stratification and inequality that are largely influenced by ethnicity. In her conclusion about ethnic labels, Gimenez uses the example of health care, but she could just as easily be writing about education when she writes: "In the last instance, access to good health care is not a function of race, ethnicity, or language skills; it is a function of social class and location in the socioeconomic stratification system." This truth, she maintains, "bears repeating over and over in a social, academic, and policy-making context that downplays the existence of class differences and their impact upon people's life chances" (p. 236).

Although the terms *Latino(a)* and *Hispanic* may be useful in describing the deep connections among all those who are descendants of the indigenous inhabitants, Spanish and other European colonizers, and enslaved Africans—or any combination of them—these terms are less useful in recognizing the historic, regional, linguistic, racial, social-class, immigration-experience, and other vital differences among Latinos. The tendency in the literature to lump all groups together has resulted in concealing crucial differences that can help explain issues such as poverty, language dominance, political orientation, and school success or failure. It should also be noted that there is a widespread, although certainly not unanimous, preference among Latinos for specific ethnic terms (Puerto Rican, Mexican American, or Guatemalan, for example, rather than either *Latino* or *Hispanic*).

As a subgroup within the Latino population, Puerto Ricans have historically been near the bottom in educational outcomes (Carrasquillo, 1991; Latino Commission on Educational Reform, 1992; Meier & Stewart, 1991; Nieto, 2000a; Pérez & Salazar, 1997). However, specific data are often hidden because Puerto Ricans are generally categorized within the larger framework of *Hispanic* or *Latino(a)*, rather than by their specific national origin. As a result, some data are hard to come by. For instance, Puerto Rican children have the greatest risk of living in poverty of any Latino group: 26.7% of Puerto Rican families live below the official poverty level, compared with 22.7% of other Latinos and just 11.2% of the general population. This fact is not widely known (U.S. Census Bureau, 2000).

General data can nevertheless be helpful because they provide a glimpse into the dismal conditions faced by many Latinos regardless of national origin. For instance, many Latinos besides Puerto Ricans also live in poverty, and the relationship between poverty and schooling tends to be strong. Latinos usually live in and attend schools in big cities, which are chronically underfunded. Urban school systems, which are 27% Latino, spent an average of $5,200 per pupil in 1991, compared with $6,073 for suburban schools (ASPIRA Institute for Policy Research, 1993). As a consequence, less money is spent on Latino students than on other groups of students in the United States. Related to this is the fact that Latinos are now significantly more segregated than African American students; as a result, they experience more concentration in high-poverty schools than any other group of students (Orfield, Bachmeier, James, & Eitle, 1997).

That there is a need to disaggregate the data on Latinos by ethnicity is clear, but it is more easily said than done. In this chapter, data specific to Puerto Ricans are used whenever possible. However, this is not always an option because Puerto Ricans are often studied only in conjunction with other Latinos. At the same time, it is sometimes helpful to consider research that focuses on other Latinos in order to explore specific strategies, programs, or philosophical orientations that have been successful with them. In cases where such research might be useful for the purposes of this chapter, it is included.

Lack of Consistent Data

Another problem associated with the educational attainment of Puerto Ricans is the lack of consistent and reliable data. A 1976 national report by the U.S. Commission on Civil Rights concluded that, in spite of the fact that Puerto Ricans "have been studied to death," the research had been performed largely by social scientists, not policy makers, and government agencies had failed to adequately document socioeconomic data. At the same time, the commission found that the study of "problem groups" such as Puerto Ricans and African Americans amounted almost to "an industry within the social sciences." Their conclusion is as accurate today as it was then: "There is no need for further study to prove that Puerto Rican problems merit special attention, even though the full extent of their problems are inadequately documented. Lack of data is no longer a valid excuse for government inaction" (U.S. Commission on Civil Rights, 1976, p. 1).

A study commissioned by ASPIRA (Margolis, 1968) documented that, as early as 1968, Francesco Cordasco, an Italian American educator with a deep interest in and commitment to the immigrant Italian and Puerto Rican communities, had compiled an impressive bibliography of 450 articles and studies devoted to the issue of Puerto Rican children in U.S. schools. But the literature on the Puerto Rican experience, especially in the early years, was characterized by a lack of a vision for building effective strategies and models for instruction. The problem was not lack of data, but lack of action and will to remedy the many educational problems faced by Puerto Ricans. As this chapter will document, major reports over the past 60 years have defined problems and made recommendations to solve them in remarkably similar ways, but these recommendations have been largely ignored.

PUERTO RICANS IN THE UNITED STATES: A BRIEF HISTORY

It is impossible to understand the Puerto Rican experience in the United States without first understanding what brought Puerto Ricans here in the first place. As U.S. citizens since 1917 (albeit an imposed citizenship that was neither sought nor particularly desired), Puerto Ricans can travel freely to and from the United States, and they have come in large numbers since the beginning of the century to seek better economic opportunities for their families (Acosta-Belén & Sánchez Korrol, 1993; Chenault, 1938/1970; Colón, 1961/1982; Fitzpatrick, 1971, 1987; History Task Force, Centro de Estudios Puertorriqueños, 1979; History Task Force, 1982; Iglesias, 1984; Rodríguez, 1991; Rodríguez & Sánchez Korrol, 1996; Sánchez Korrol, 1983). Between 1940 and 1970, the years of what has come to be known as "the great migration," 835,000 Puerto Ricans moved to the U.S. mainland on a net basis, making it one of the most massive emigration flows occurring anywhere in the 20th century (Rivera-Batíz & Santiago, 1996). At least 20% of Puerto Ricans on the island have lived in the United States at one time or another (Zentella, 1997b). As a result, virtually no Puerto Rican has been untouched by the migration experience.

The Migration Experience

The migration of Puerto Ricans to the United States has been a unique experience for several reasons (History Task Force, 1982; Matos-Rodríguez & Hernández, 2001). Consequently, "[t]raditional paradigms for understanding the experience of other immigrant groups—particularly Europeans—have been of only marginal use in analyzing the Puerto Rican experience" (Matos-Rodríguez & Hernández, 2001). Puerto Ricans represent the first group of newcomers to arrive as citizens; there has been no need for them to focus inordinate attention on the process of becoming citizens or severing ties with the home country, as is customary with other immigrants. Thus the term *migration* rather than *immigration* is more often used to describe this movement.

Second, Puerto Rican migration was the first "jet-age" movement to the United States. Travel to and from the island became relatively easy and inexpensive with the growing accessibility of air travel beginning in the 1940s. Third, the major Puerto Rican migration occurred at a time when a strong back was less important in the United States than technical or professional skills. As a result, the low-skill jobs generally available to earlier immigrants were largely eliminated and the importance of education grew tremendously. That is, in contrast with the experiences of previous immigrants, a high school diploma became a minimum requirement for most jobs, and this slowed down the economic advancement of Puerto Ricans as a group (Fitzpatrick, 1971, 1987).

Finally, the migration has been characterized by a back-and-forth movement closely correlated with economic ups and downs in both the United States and Puerto Rico. For instance, "Operation Bootstrap" (an economic development program in Puerto Rico that began in the 1950s), resulted in tremendous wealth for U.S. companies but a disappointingly low number of jobs for Puerto Rican residents. Paradoxically, even greater immigration to the United States resulted. Between 1946 and 1964, more Puerto Ricans arrived in the United States than ever before or since (Rivera-Batíz & Santiago, 1996). In the words of Pedro Pietri, a "Nuyorican" (Puerto Rican born and raised in New York) poet, "We were all Operation Bootstrap casualties" (C. D. Hernández, 1997, p. 108). Puerto Rican migration has been dubbed "the revolving door," a "circulatory migration" (Bonilla & Campos, 1981), or "a process of Puerto Rican commuting" (Fitzpatrick, 1971). This experience is reflected even in Puerto Rican fiction: in a short story entitled "The Flying Bus," the novelist Luis Rafael Sánchez describes one of the passengers as "a well-poised woman . . . [who] informs us that she flies over *the pond* every month and that she has forgotten on which bank of it she really lives" (L. R. Sánchez, 1987, p. 19, emphasis in original).

Causes of Migration of Puerto Ricans to the United States

Contrary to conventional wisdom, Puerto Ricans are not new migrants. A small number lived in the continental United States nearly two centuries ago. By 1830, there was a *Sociedad Benéfica Cubana y Puertorriqueña* (translated at the time as the Spanish Benevolent Society) comprising primarily Puerto Rican and Cuban merchants in New York City, largely the result of trade among Cuba, Puerto Rico, and the mid-Atlantic states (Sánchez Korrol, 1983). Political activists, especially those supporting independence for

Cuba and Puerto Rico and dedicated to an Antillean federation, found their way to New York City by the 1860s, where they published newspapers and started political and civic organizations. By the early 1900s, both skilled craftspeople and unskilled workers, particularly in the tobacco industry, had migrated to Florida and New York. In 1910, there were more than a thousand Puerto Ricans living in 39 states and Hawaii, and by 1920 Puerto Ricans could be found in 45 states (Sánchez Korrol, 1983).

The major reason for the migration was not simple overpopulation, as has frequently been advanced (Fitzpatrick, 1971), but the effect of dramatic structural economic changes that virtually destroyed traditional patterns of individual land ownership and consolidated the domination of large corporations from the United States (Sánchez Korrol, 1983; Rodríguez, 1991). Structural changes such as these resulted in an increase in unemployment and the growth of a marginal workforce. Hence, the possibility of job opportunities, not overpopulation, is the most important factor encouraging migration to the continental United States.

Puerto Rican migration to the United States has been described as a "push-pull" phenomenon, with the U.S. economy acting as both pull and push factors. A 1950 study documented that from 1908 on, the ups and downs of the U.S. economy and the waves of migration from Puerto Rico were highly correlated (Mills & Goldsen, 1950). Structural changes in the Puerto Rican economy represent an important push factor, and the direct recruitment of Puerto Rican workers beginning early in the 20th century is an example of a pull factor. Such early recruitment efforts took Puerto Ricans as far as Hawaii, where, in 1903, 539 children were enrolled in Hawaiian schools (History Task Force, 1982).

The contract farm worker program that began in 1940 was another important source of migrants, bringing in an average of 20,000 workers every year to harvest crops in states as diverse as Michigan, Connecticut, New Jersey, and Massachusetts. These arrangements continued into the 1970s in formal contracts, and informally into the present. Many Puerto Rican communities in the United States began as a result of former agricultural workers remaining and bringing other family members to join them (Fitzpatrick, 1971, 1987; Glasser, 1997).

Result of Circulatory Migration

There have been two major results of circulatory migration among Puerto Ricans, both of which have significant implications for education. For one, in general Puerto Ricans have continued to identify with their culture and language more than was the case with European immigrants who arrived earlier. In fact, Latinos in general have resisted to a great extent the pressures of the assimilationist ideology that characterized the experiences of European immigrants. Circulatory migration has provided a cultural and linguistic continuity not afforded previous immigrants or even some recent ones, and this has been manifested by a practical need for use of the Spanish language and familiar cultural patterns (Rodríguez & Sánchez Korrol, 1996).

Examples of cultural maintenance among Puerto Ricans abound. The first major study of bilingualism among Puerto Ricans, based on a series of interviews with leaders in the community, revealed that they placed great importance on maintaining and speaking Spanish and identifying as Puerto Rican (Fishman, Cooper, & Ma, 1971). A later study, based on interviews with 100 families, revealed that not one among them identified as exclusively "American"; rather they all continued to identify as either "Puerto Rican" or "Puerto Rican American" (Colleran, Gurick, & Kurtz, 1984). Studies focusing on bilingualism among Puerto Ricans in New York City have generally concluded that there is tremendous allegiance to maintaining the Spanish language as a marker of identity (Attinasi, 1979; Zentella, 1997a).

The second effect of the circulatory migration for Puerto Ricans has been to redefine immigration from "a single life-transforming" experience to "a way of life" (National Puerto Rican Task Force, 1982). Although for the majority of Europeans immigration was a new beginning, albeit an often painful one, for many Puerto Ricans migration has tended to be a series of periodic movements to and from the island. The situation has been disruptive, to be sure, but it has also reframed the migration experience as a normal part of life in which cultural patterns are renewed, transformed, and recreated, and it has redefined Puerto Ricans not as traditional immigrants but as "a community in movement" in "a process of commuting" (Fitzpatrick, 1971).

To understand the disruption caused by migration, one need only look at the immensity of the exodus from the island. By 1957, 550,000, or fully a quarter of the Puerto Rican people, lived in the United States (Rand, 1958), and by 2000, more than 3,000,000 were residents of the mainland, which is almost the same number of Puerto Ricans who lived on the island (U.S. Census Bureau, 2000). Under any definition, this represents a dramatic unsettling of the population and cannot help but influence such issues as educational achievement, employment, and health.

New York City, a "Home Away From Home," and Other Destinations

At the beginning of the 20th century, only 37% of Puerto Ricans living in the United States were concentrated in New York City, but by 1940 fully 85% were residing there (Sánchez Korrol, 1983), making it the preeminent home away from home for most Puerto Ricans. One of the earliest studies of the Puerto Rican community (Chenault, 1938/1970) found that in 1930 half of all Puerto Ricans in the United States were living in East Harlem (soon to be known as *El Barrio,* or Spanish Harlem). The author of that study portrayed Spanish Harlem in 1935 as one might describe it and many other Puerto Rican communities in the years to come:

The community has, to a large degree, taken on the color and customs of the Spanish-speaking countries. In certain sections Spanish is generally spoken. Some of the stores have no signs in English at all, and seem to depend entirely upon Spanish-speaking customers. . . . The entire settlement seems to take on an increased activity at night. There are many people on the streets, Spanish music can be heard from the music and radio shops, dances are in progress, and the bars and restaurants are prosperous. (Chenault, 1938/1970, pp. 129–130)

During this early period, many of the migrants were agricultural workers, domestics, or needleworkers. Others were factory workers, and many worked in one of the two largest employers of Puerto Ricans, a large biscuit company and a pencil factory (Chenault, 1938/1970). By 1948, some 200,000 Puerto Ricans lived in New York City.

The Puerto Rican community in New York was a vibrant and active one even in the early years, when the first wave of migrants, *los pioneros* (the pioneers), made their pilgrimage to the United States (Matos-Rodríguez & Hernández, 2001). As early as 1923, the *Hermandad Puertorriqueña,* a community organization with a focus on mutual assistance, was created, and in the 1930s the Puerto Rican Merchants Association, representing more than 500 small businesses, mostly *bodegas* (small, family-owned grocery stores with Caribbean products), was founded (Sánchez Korrol, 1983).

Although the Puerto Rican community was concentrated in New York City between 1940 and 1960, it later dispersed, primarily throughout the Northeast. Migration to New York City increased 206% between 1940 and 1950, but in other states it increased an astounding 443%. By 1955, it was estimated that there were as many as 175,000 Puerto Ricans in cities outside of New York, with another half million in New York City itself (Padilla, 1958). For example, in Philadelphia the Puerto Rican population doubled to more than 14,000 between 1950 and 1960 (Koss, 1965). This pattern has held true to the present. By the year 2000, just 68.6% of Puerto Ricans lived in the Northeast, while 14.9% lived in the South, 9.4% in the Midwest and 7% in the West (U.S. Census Bureau, 2000). The number of Puerto Ricans living in the United States has increased steadily throughout the century. Although the return migration has sometimes surpassed the number coming into the United States, the annual migration has generally resulted in a net gain (Meléndez, 1991).

The Relationship Between Migration and Education

This brief review of migration has made several points clear. First, it is evident that Puerto Rican migration does not fit neatly within the traditional framework of the immigration of other newcomers. Second, the colonial relationship of Puerto Rico to the United States should not be overlooked in analyzing either the presence of Puerto Ricans or their history of underachievement in U.S. schools. Third, although many Puerto Ricans dream of returning to the island—indeed, migration and return migration are parallel processes—the truth is that many never return. In fact, there are many Puerto Rican families who have lived steadily in the United States for three or more generations. Thus Puerto Ricans as a community are in the United States to stay.

RECURRING THEMES IN THE EDUCATION OF PUERTO RICAN STUDENTS

A number of related themes are interwoven throughout the history of the education of Puerto Ricans in the United States. Inextricably linked to migration, these themes have appeared and reappeared over the past 70 years or so, that is, since Puerto Rican youngsters began attending U.S. schools in substantial numbers. The themes should not be understood as isolated phenomena, but as interconnected issues that sometimes overlap: the legacy of colonialism; the role of racism, ethnocentrism, and linguicism; and the struggle for self-determination. Each is briefly described below and will become evident throughout the remainder of this chapter.

The Legacy of Colonialism

Colonialism has always played an important role in the Puerto Rican experience. Puerto Rico and the United States are connected through colonial ties, and this gives the migration a unique character. According to Rodríguez, the fact that Puerto Rico and the United States were joined as a result of "an act of conquest" is often overlooked or minimized in the literature, with Puerto Ricans perceived as simply one of the latest "newcomers" in the traditional conception of the immigration experience (Rodríguez, 1991). Early writers were especially fond of focusing on the "overpopulation problem" as an overriding reason for the migration (Chenault, 1938/1970; Mills & Goldsen, 1950; Fitzpatrick, 1971), conveniently avoiding U.S. imperialism and the structural changes it brought about in the Puerto Rican economy as contributing factors. Later work by Sánchez Korrol (1983), Rodríguez (1991), Campos and Bonilla (1976), Meléndez (1991), and even Fitzpatrick's own (1987) challenge this analysis as overly simplistic.

The Colonial Impact in Puerto Rico. In Puerto Rico itself, policies and practices in schools and other educational institutions geared toward assimilating the population to U.S. values and ideals have had an enormous impact (Negrón, 1971). Beginning in the earliest grades, English is a required subject in all Puerto Rican public schools. More significantly, Puerto Rican youngsters are barraged with U.S. cultural images not only in schools but also through the media and marketing. For example, children in Puerto Rico learn both the American national anthem and the Puerto Rican anthem; they celebrate the birthdays of U.S. heroes and Puerto Rican heroes; and they hear both salsa (Caribbean music) and rap on the radio. One result is that Puerto Rican youngsters are more familiar and comfortable with mainstream U.S. culture than is the case of other immigrant children. At the same time, the situation has resulted in endless debates about the role of Spanish and English, and the maintenance of Puerto Rican culture, both in the schools and in the society as a whole.

The colonial condition, which makes migration a constant experience, has also created what have been called "the students in between," those who spend time on the island and the mainland (Quality Education for Minorities Project, 1990). It merits mention that since 1973, approximately 35,000 Puerto Ricans annually have returned to live on the island, and at least 10% of the island's school population are characterized as "return migrants," children of former migrants who have returned to the island, sometimes many times over (Zentella, 1997a). Puerto Rican students have suffered discrimination in both places (X. A. Rivera, 2000; Zentella, 1997a). In her study of Puerto Rican students in Puerto Rico and in New York, Zentella (1997a) concluded: "The truth is that Puerto Rican youngsters on both sides of the ocean are trapped in educational systems that produce failure" (p. 313). Special programs and policies to help ease the transition from island to mainland, or vice versa, have been suggested for many years (Gallardo, 1970; Morrison, 1958; X. A. Rivera, 2000; Zentella, 1997a, 1997b).

The Colonial Impact in the United States. Given its status as a colony of first Spain and later the United States, Puerto Rico has been at the mercy of policies and practices over which it has had little control. This powerlessness has also left its mark on the Puerto Rican community in the United States. In this regard, John Ogbu's theory concerning the difference between the educational attainment of *voluntary* and *involuntary* minorities is helpful (Ogbu, 1987). Ogbu classifies Puerto Ricans, Mexican Americans, African Americans, and Native Americans as *involuntary minorities* because of their subjugation and exploitation—through colonization, enslavement, or conquest—by the United States. According to this theory, it is not only a group's cultural background but also its situation in the host society and its perceptions of opportunities available in that society that help explain its educational attainment. For Ogbu, the major problem in the academic performance of involuntary minorities is not that they possess a different language, culture, or cognitive or communication style, but the nature of their relationship with the United States, together with their responses to the relationship. In later research, Signithia Fordham and Ogbu (1996) found that African American students considered academic success to be "acting White," with the implication that the same could be happening with other involuntary minorities.

Recent research among Puerto Ricans has challenged Ogbu's theory, at least as applied wholesale to all involuntary minority groups. Flores-González (2002), in a study of Puerto Rican high achievers in a Chicago high school, found that these students did not associate academic success with "whiteness." On the contrary, although academically successful, the students she studied did not mask their accomplishments, nor did they want to shed their Puerto Rican identity. Flores-González has suggested that a different conception of ethnicity, based on culture rather than race (Rodríguez, 2000), as well as their sociohistorical context, may account for the difference.

Racism, Ethnocentrism, and Linguicism

As in the case of other students of color, Puerto Ricans have faced varying degrees of racism and other forms of ethnocentrism in the schools and out. But because Puerto Ricans are racially mixed, they represent a challenge to the rigid White-Black categorization traditionally employed in the United States. Puerto Ricans tend to identify primarily in cultural ways rather than racially (Rodríguez, 2000). This includes identification with Spanish, their native language. *Linguicism* (Skutnabb-Kangas, 1988), which refers to discrimination based on native language, is a preeminent reality in the Puerto Rican educational experience. It has surfaced time and again and has led to demands for bilingual education and Spanish-language maintenance.

In addition to language discrimination, Puerto Rican children have also had to confront racism in schools. Negative responses of teachers and other educators concerning Puerto Rican students have ranged from being "color-blind" to insensitivity, to outright discriminatory policies, and all have left their mark on students' perceptions of their ability to achieve academic success. Even children's literature has not been exempt, as research on the images of Puerto Ricans in U.S. children's books and school textbooks has documented that they contain stereotypes that are at best misleading and incomplete, and at worst racist, sexist, and assimilationist (Nieto, 1997, 1998).

Early Examples in the Literature

Conflicts in communities where Puerto Ricans live have been documented for many years. As early as the 1920s, near race riots between Puerto Ricans and Jews were reported (Chenault, 1938/1970; Sánchez Korrol, 1983). In Brooklyn, a factory was said to have put up a sign that read, "No Negroes or Porto [sic] Ricans wanted" (Chenault, 1938/1970, p. 79). Another early study quoted two journalists who described Puerto Ricans as

mostly crude farmers, subject to congenital tropical diseases . . . [who are] almost impossible to assimilate and condition . . . [and who] turn to guile and wile and the steel blade, the traditional weapon of the sugar cane cutter, mark of their blood and heritage. (Mills & Goldsen, 1950, p. 80)

Puerto Rican students were often perceived as inheriting their families' negative characteristics, among them impulsiveness, lack of discipline, and destructiveness, all of which purportedly led to an inability to profit from their education. Chenault described Puerto Rican students as "less inclined to seek out educational advantages and follow them up by regular attendance than individuals of some of the other cultural groups" (1938/1970, p. 145). Another sociologist suggested that a high percentage of Puerto Ricans in a school "drags the teaching down almost inevitably, because of the language problem, and when Puerto Rican children are in a majority on a street they can, like any such majority, make life almost unbearable for other children" (Rand, 1958, p. 5).

The inability of many teachers to confront cultural differences has been evident in much of the early literature concerning the education of Puerto Rican youngsters. In an early paper, Margolis (1968) explains: "Because [the teacher] subscribes to the great American abstraction that 'prejudice is bad,' she abhors the more barbarous symptoms of bigotry and allows herself the luxury of feeling tolerant. The tolerance often turns to condescension" (p. 7). In other cases, teachers have sometimes been puzzled by their students' behavior, making remarks that demonstrate an obvious lack of awareness concerning language development, cultural issues, and the importance of relating education to students' experiences. A typical remark is this one made by a teacher in the 1960s:

Things just don't make an impression on these children. We haven't found the way to teach them. For some reason they don't relate to school. The reason is that their whole culture is different. The only way to teach them is to repeat things twenty-five times unless for some reason it means something to them. (Sexton, 1965, p. 58)

Even recent research indicates a continued lack of awareness and sensitivity concerning Puerto Rican students (Darder & Upshur, 1993; Flores-González, 2002; Frau-Ramos & Nieto, 1993). Feelings of marginalization among Latino students have been a chief consequence of the negative perceptions of teachers and others concerning their academic abilities. For example, Virginia Vogel Zanger (1993) found that Latino students in a Boston high school felt excluded, invisible, and subordinate to other students. She also found that some teachers were just as contemptuous of Latinos as the most racist students. One student, for example, described how stunned he was when a teacher called him a "spic" in class.

It is essential to highlight such discriminatory practices and racist attitudes not to focus on past grievances but to understand how such attitudes and practices have influenced students' low academic achievement and high dropout rate. Even in the earliest years of migration, Puerto Rican communities reacted to racism and discrimination by insisting on their right to self-determination.

Self-Determination

The struggle to define their own reality has been a constant theme in the experience of Puerto Ricans in the United States. This was apparent even during the 1920s and 1930s, when the community, in its infancy, formed numerous community agencies and organizations (Sánchez Korrol, 1983) and became more pronounced as professional and grassroots leaders began to emerge during the 1950s.

In those years, even well-meaning non–Puerto Ricans tended to perceive issues quite differently from Puerto Ricans. Thus, although "Americanization" and "cultural adaptation" were called for by early efforts focusing on Puerto Rican educational problems, Puerto Ricans themselves, even at this time, were pressing for some form of Spanish-language maintenance (Morrison, 1958).

Similarly, at about the same time that overwhelming negative perceptions of Puerto Ricans were holding sway, Elena Padilla (1958), a noted anthropologist and a Puerto Rican herself, challenged them squarely by suggesting that the problems of Puerto Ricans are neither unidimensional nor solely of their own doing. Commenting on the cultural strengths of the community and people's ability to confront inequities, she added: "Regarded as a problem in New York City, Puerto Ricans have problems of their own and solutions to them that, while not always recognized or acceptable to the larger society, make their lives tick" (p. 162).

The quest for self-determination became even more apparent in the way Puerto Ricans, particularly the small but growing professional class, began organizing starting in the 1950s. Numerous self-help and advocacy organizations, the trademark of a community resolved to define itself and solve its own problems, invariably centered on issues of education. In the mid-1950s, a group of young Puerto Rican professionals established the Puerto Rican–Hispanic Leadership Forum (now the National Puerto Rican Forum), a communitywide organization to promote their interests in New York City (Fitzpatrick, 1971; ASPIRA Association, 1991). Chief among the organizers was Antonia Pantoja (1921–2002). Born and raised in Puerto Rico, Pantoja was educated first as a teacher on the island and later as a social worker in New York City. During her lifetime, she worked as a factory worker, artist, student, teacher, social worker, and community organizer (ASPIRA Association, 1991; Pantoja, 2002; Perry, 1998). Many educational and social reform efforts of the past half century can be traced to her vision, particularly the organization called ASPIRA.

ASPIRA is a primary example of the kind of organization that reflects the growing self-awareness and incipient spirit of self-determination of these years. A Spanish word meaning "to aspire," ASPIRA was founded in 1961 by the Puerto Rican Forum to promote education among Puerto Rican youths. Pantoja was the guiding force and inspiration for ASPIRA. In her memoirs (Pantoja, 2002), published just days before her death, Pantoja explained one of the primary motivations for the creation of ASPIRA: "We believe that the uprooting of our children from their community has been deadly to their ability to learn and to their sense of worth" (p. 106). Through its long and distinguished history as the primary agency promoting the educational rights of Puerto Ricans, ASPIRA has provided tens of thousands of youths with the support, inspiration, and courage to stay in school and become leaders in their communities and throughout the nation. ASPIRA has also been instrumental in promoting higher education for Puerto Rican youth through the establishment of clubs in high schools (where student members become *aspirantes,* or "those whoaspire"). Many Puerto Ricans who have gone on to become leaders in their communities and the nation trace their success to their involvement with ASPIRA.

Other grassroots educational and political organizations that have emerged over the past three decades echo the theme of self-determination first enunciated in the early part of the 20th century (Iglesias, 1984; Sánchez Korrol, 1983) but most evident in the 1960s. These include the National Puerto Rican Coalition in Washington, D.C., and in what is still the location with the largest and most influential Puerto Rican community, New York City, the Institute for Puerto Rican Policy (now a partner of the Puerto Rican Legal Defense and Education Fund), the Puerto Rican Educators Association, and the National Congress for Puerto Rican Rights. The National Council of La Raza and the Hispanic Policy Development Project, both located in Washington, D.C., although not focused exclusively on Puerto Ricans, include them prominently.

Puerto Ricans' demand to be heard became increasingly militant after the 1960s. Political and community struggles, an outgrowth of the civil rights movement in the United States, were characterized by a growing frustration among students, parents, and other previously disenfranchised segments of the population. This new militancy was evident in numerous struggles for community control; bilingual and ethnic studies education; decentralization of the city's schools; and, in higher education, demands for Puerto Rican studies departments and open enrollment at CUNY, the City University of New York, which eventually led to the development of several such departments and a research center, the Centro de Estudios Puertorriqueños and the Puerto Rican/Latino Education Roundtable (Caballero, 2000; M. E. Sánchez & Stevens-Arroyo, 1987; L. O. Reyes, 2000).

Self-definition and self-determination in the Puerto Rican community have moved in tandem with the growth of the community itself, and they are major themes in the many commissions, reports, studies, and grassroots efforts of the past 40 years. How the self-determination agenda has developed in the political context of this period will be evident in the next section.

THE EDUCATION OF PUERTO RICANS IN U.S. MAINLAND SCHOOLS: FROM "PROBLEM" TO POSSIBILITY

This section begins by considering the dropout crisis, one of the major problems affecting Puerto Rican students since they began attending U.S. schools in substantial numbers. This is followed by a discussion of some of the other recurring issues, problems, and solutions concerning the education of Puerto Rican students in U.S. schools. Prevailing assumptions about Puerto Ricans students are addressed using studies and research projects from the 1930s to the present. The many labels used to characterize Puerto Rican students in U.S. schools are also considered in order to understand how they have reflected particular historical and political contexts.

The Dropout Crisis

Amply documented since the 1960s, although it probably existed even before then, dropping out of high school has been a persistent dilemma in the educational experience of Puerto Ricans. For example, as early as 1920 it was suggested that a major cause of Puerto Rican students' poor academic performance was their inability to understand the language of instruction (Cafferty & Rivera-Martínez, 1981). No doubt contributing to the early dropout crisis were practices such as placing students behind their peers or in "special" classes (such as those

for the mentally retarded or slow learners) because they were Spanish speaking (Sánchez Korrol, 1983).

In one of the first reports on the educational status of Puerto Ricans commissioned by ASPIRA, the dropout crisis was identified; although the data were described as "murky" and accurate statistics could not be provided, the author concluded: "The public schools are like a giant sieve, sifting out all but the strongest, the smartest, or the luckiest" (Margolis, 1968, p. 3).

A low rate of high school completion has been dismally similar over the years wherever Puerto Ricans go to school, with a dropout rate of 71% reported in Chicago (U.S. Commission on Civil Rights, 1976); 70% in Philadelphia and 90% in Boston (Cafferty & Rivera-Martínez, 1981); 80% in New York City (Calitri, 1983); and 72% in Holyoke, Massachusetts (Frau-Ramos & Nieto, 1993).

Dropping out of high school remains one of the most severe problems affecting Latinos. Depending upon measures used, data differ widely, but the fact remains that Latinos in general, and Puerto Ricans in particular, are regarded as having the highest dropout rate of any group. Although the situation improved slightly during the late 1970s and mid-1980s, by the early 1990s more Latinos were dropping out than ever. In 1991, 35.3% of Latinos were high school dropouts, compared to 34.3% in 1972 (ASPIRA Institute for Policy Research, 1993). Although the situation had improved substantially for both Whites and African Americans by 1998, the dropout rate still hovered at the crisis level for Latinos: 30% of Latinos were still dropping out, double the rate for African Americans and more than three times the rate for Whites (National Center for Education Statistics, 1998). Moreover, the high school completion rate of Latinos has not changed very much in several years. As of 1998, the high school completion rate for Latinos was just 63%, compared with 90% for Whites and 81% for African Americans (National Center for Education Statistics, 1998).

The Inadequacy of Traditional Explanations. Tackling the vexing problem of dropouts has been on the Puerto Rican agenda for decades. A number of reasons, explanations, and theories concerning the dropout crisis have been formulated over the years. The National Council of La Raza, or NCLR (1990), for example, described a combination of factors that continue to place many Latinos in a high-risk category for dropping out. The NCLR cited single-parent family status plus low family income, and low parental education plus limited English proficiency, as two significant combinations. Puerto Ricans are more likely to have two or more of these risk factors than other Latinos. In addition, single-parent family status has also been identified as a major risk factor affecting Latino students: the percentage of Puerto Rican children living in a single-parent household (37.2%) is greater than for any other group—even other Latino groups, which have a 23.7% rate of single-headed households (U.S. Census Bureau, 2000).

Traditional research on school failure focused almost exclusively on three areas: student characteristics (social class, race and ethnicity, family structure, native language), school policies related to student behavior (discipline problems, suspension, and absenteeism), and poor academic performance (poor grades and retention). By the mid-1980s, this kind of analysis was being called into question for failing to look more deeply into the role played by schools in actually *promoting* failure (Wehlage & Rutter, 1986). It is equally crucial to note that schools can do little to remedy these conditions. Schools can, however, look at their own policies and practices as aggravating the problem. School policies and practices therefore began to be viewed more critically since much of the research carried out in the 1980s.

A More Comprehensive View of High School Dropouts. New scholars concerned with the question of the education of Puerto Ricans and other Latinos are suggesting a more comprehensive approach to understanding and tackling both the dropout crisis and the general lack of educational attainment. This comprehensive perspective may prove to be more helpful than earlier theories in suggesting strategies to resolve the dropout crisis among Puerto Ricans. That is, the crisis is a reflection of larger societal inequities. Therefore, these broader inequities need to be addressed before substantial can change take place. Although more investment in education is absolutely crucial, educational problems are also influenced by other factors, such as discrimination, family structure, poverty and its consequences, and a lack of a coherent national response to these issues (Pérez & Salazar, 1997).

Looking beyond family, personal, and socioeconomic characteristics to a more holistic explanation of school failure, research over the past two decades has suggested that school policies and practices themselves negatively influence Latino students' academic performance, behavior, and decision to stay in or leave school. For example, Fernández and Shu (1988) found that Latinos had higher dropout rates than their non-Latino peers even when they did not fall into the risk categories. That is, they had higher dropout rates even if their grades were higher than those of other students; they were in academic rather than general tracks; they were not from poor families; they did not have parents with less schooling; or they did not have problems with their teachers. The only possible explanation for this situation that the researchers could suggest was that many Latinos expressed more negative feelings about their schools than did other students.

Another theory posits that certain conditions in schools themselves, termed the school's *holding power,* encourage success or failure (Wehlage & Rutter, 1986). That is, a combination of factors, including student characteristics *and* school conditions, is responsible for academic success or failure. As a result, much of the research that began in the mid-to-late 1980s has focused on not just the student, the family, or cultural background but rather on such factors as grade retention, overage status of the student, placement practices, and student confrontation with school authorities (National Council of La Raza, 1990; Fernández & Vélez, 1990).

Newer voices in scholarship are also proposing wholesale change, not only in schools but in society in general. For example, such activist scholars as Antonia Darder, Rodolfo Torres, and Henry Gutiérrez (1997) maintain that "[i]t is becoming more obvious from a historical analysis that educational restructuring cannot be accomplished independently from radical democratic social and economic reform" (p. xii). A good example of the problem is presented in a study of poor Puerto Rican households in Philadelphia. In this study, Javier Tapia (1998) found that household stability, which is influenced by economic stability, is the most significant factor affecting student learning.

Although the dropout crisis among Puerto Rican and Latino youths has been a major problem, it is by no means the only one. In some ways, it is merely a symptom of deeper issues. For instance, Hispanic students consistently perform below the national average in reading, math, and science in the National Assessment of Educational Progress (NAEP). Disparities begin as early as kindergarten and remain consistent (National Center for Education Statistics, 1999). According to the Educational Testing Service (2000), the average score of Latino youngsters in fourth-grade reading (195) is substantially behind that of White students (225). By age 17, Latino youngsters' scores still lag behind (270 compared to 294 for Whites). Also, average math proficiency for Hispanic 9-year-olds is just 213, compared with 239 for Whites; by the time they reach 17, Latinos score 293, compared with 315 for Whites (Educational Testing Service, 2000). Their performance is directly related to the kinds of math courses they take: only 5.6% of Hispanics take trigonometry, compared with 10% of Whites, and even in lower-level courses such as algebra II their participation (48% compared with 64%) is remarkably low (National Center for Education Statistics, 1997).

In what follows, the various labels that have been used to characterize Puerto Rican students are reviewed. Generally applied from a paradigm of privilege, that is, from the perspective of the dominant White, Anglo-Saxon middle class, the labels have ranged from viewing Puerto Ricans as "problems" and "culturally deprived" to "at risk." Through the years, Puerto Rican and other progressive educators have challenged the use of such terms. The characterizations used here do not always fit neatly into the time frames suggested, but they provide an idea of why particular pedagogical and social policies and strategies have been developed.

Before 1960: The Puerto Rican Student as a "Problem"

The fact that Puerto Ricans face tremendous problems in U.S. schools has been recognized for decades, but how these problems have been identified and defined has varied over the years. The early literature was replete with references to the "Puerto Rican problem," situating the issue squarely on the experiences, culture, language, and social class of Puerto Rican students.

The existence of the "Puerto Rican problem" was defined as early as 1935, with the release of a report from the New York City Chamber of Commerce that claimed Puerto Rican children were "slow learners," on the basis of the results of an experiment in which 240 Puerto Rican children were given intelligence tests (Iglesias, 1984; Sánchez Korrol, 1983, 1996). The release of this report was met by fierce rebuttals from both the community and Congressman Vito Marcantonio, the beloved Italian American politician who represented Spanish Harlem for many years. He challenged the discriminatory effects of standardized tests, concluding that they made inadequate allowances for social, economic, linguistic, and environmental issues in the lives of Puerto Rican children (Sánchez Korrol, 1996).

The Association of Assistant Superintendents (1948) released the first major report on Puerto Ricans in the New York City schools, and in it the "problem" label was once again used. The position of substitute auxiliary teacher (SAT) was created by the New York City Board of Education as a result of this report. The primary duty of SATs—positions filled by Spanish speakers who could qualify for a substitute license—was to assist teachers working with Puerto Rican pupils and parents. By 1949 there were 10 such positions citywide. Other teaching personnel (OTPs)—who were hired to teach English to Puerto Ricans—and Puerto Rican coordinators (teachers at the junior high school level) were later added and numbered 50 citywide by 1954 (Morrison, 1958). Thus, in the first efforts focusing on remedying the educational problems faced by Puerto Rican students, Puerto Rican teachers filled primarily low-level, low-status, and substitute positions.

The Puerto Rican Study, 1953–1957. A massive project conducted by the New York City Board of Education from 1953 to 1957, the Puerto Rican Study was undertaken to investigate the education and adjustment of Puerto Rican students in the public schools, who already numbered more than 53,000 (Morrison, 1958). Although certainly not as negative in tone as previous studies, it still reflected the tendency to focus on perceived deficits of Puerto Rican students. It was also guided, as were many of the early reports, by the assumption that quick Americanization was a primary objective of schooling (Fitzpatrick, 1971).

The major objectives of the Puerto Rican Study were to gather accurate data on the number and characteristics of Puerto Rican pupils in New York City schools, and to determine the most effective methods and materials for teaching them English in order to promote their adjustment. As a result of this extensive, $1 million study, six reports and 16 resource unit volumes were generated, and 23 short-range and long-range recommendations were made, many of which were to be repeated in studies over the next 50 years. Among them were specific recommendations on teaching English, developing closer working relationships with parents, and formulating new policies for working with students who did not speak English. Although bilingual education was not specifically mentioned, the report flirted with the issue of how to use the language skills that Puerto Rican students already had (Morrison, 1958).

Lack of Puerto Rican Involvement in Early Research. Most early reports and studies concerning Puerto Rican students in U.S. schools were conceived, developed, and conducted by non–Puerto Ricans (Association of Assistant Superintendents, 1948; Chenault, 1938/1970; Mills & Goldsen, 1950; Morrison, 1958; Rand, 1958). Even the Puerto Rican Study had only one Puerto Rican member among 17 on the Advisory Panel and one Puerto Rican consultant among nine (Morrison). The lack of Puerto Rican perspectives no doubt colored the way problems were defined and the recommendations that were made.

Nevertheless, one of the major accomplishments of the Puerto Rican Study was to upgrade the teaching of English as a second language (ESL), thus setting the stage for improving services to Puerto Rican students and also increasing the presence of Puerto Ricans in the schools as aides, community liaisons, teachers, and counselors. By 1961, the SAT position was elevated to regular auxiliary teacher (RAT); by 1965, there were 142 such positions in the New York City public schools (Fitzpatrick, 1971). With an increase in personnel came an increase in curriculum development and adaptation of materials to meet the educational needs of Puerto Rican youngsters. This probably signaled the beginning of a real Puerto Rican imprint, particularly of Puerto Rican women educators, on the New York City educational system (Sánchez Korrol, 1996).

In this regard, we should mention another significant educational resource in the lives of children: libraries and librarians. One name stands out above all others. Pura Teresa Belpré (1903–1982) was the first Puerto Rican librarian hired by the New York Public Library. A prolific storyteller and children's book author, she was also a pioneer in establishing what Lisa Sánchez González (2001) termed "bilingual children's librarianship" (p. 75). In addition, she was active in the civil rights movement, working tirelessly to promote children's literature for Puerto Rican children and other children of color and increased services to the Puerto Rican and African American communities (J. L. Hernández, 1992; Sánchez González, 2001).

"The Culture of Poverty," "the Losers," and Tentative Challenges to the Melting Pot: Perspectives from the 1960s

The 1960s ushered in an era characterized by a growing dichotomy between how Puerto Ricans and non–Puerto Ricans interpreted the Puerto Rican experience, a divergence that has continued in some ways to the present. Although not all Puerto Ricans speak with one voice, recommendations and demands made by the Puerto Rican community concerning education have been remarkably consistent over 40 years, while actual policies and practices, generally developed and carried out by non–Puerto Ricans, have lagged behind. This pattern was first established during the 1960s.

The Social and Political Context. We need to keep the social and political context in mind if we are to understand how the educational problems of Puerto Ricans were defined during the 1950s and 1960s. At the same time that the civil rights, Black Power, and other liberation movements were beginning to sweep the nation, a conservative ideology centered on cultural and linguistic differences as deficiencies was taking hold in academia and schools, especially schools serving students of color (Reissman, 1962; Jensen, 1969).

For Puerto Ricans, this paradigm of cultural deficiency was nowhere more devastatingly articulated than in *La Vida* (Lewis, 1965), an extensive study of 100 Puerto Rican families living in poverty in New York City and San Juan, Puerto Rico. In an in-depth study of the Ríos family, described by the author as "closer to the expression of an unbridled id than any other people I have studied" (p. xxvi), Lewis defined "the culture of poverty" and all its negative ramifications for generations to come. A particularly insidious passage in his book reads:

The people in this book, like most of the other Puerto Rican slum dwellers I have studied, show a great zest for life, especially for sex, and a need for excitement, new experiences and adventures. . . . They value acting out more than thinking out, self-expression more than self-constraint, pleasure more than productivity, spending more than saving, personal loyalty more than impersonal justice.

They are fun-loving and enjoy parties, dancing and music. They cannot be alone; they have an almost insatiable need for sociability and interaction. (p. xxvi)

Attitudes such as these were reflected in other studies as well as in the popular imagination of the time. In a sociological study published that same year concerning the Puerto Rican, African American, and Italian populations of Spanish Harlem (Sexton, 1965, p. 11), a youth worker is quoted as saying: "No wonder they can't learn anything in school. . . . They have sex on their minds 24 hours a day." A teacher, referring specifically to Puerto Rican and African American children, stated: "They love to dance and move their bodies. They can't sit still. The ones that do well in school usually don't like to dance or move around."

By the 1960s, few of the recommendations of the Puerto Rican Study had been carried out, and educational opportunities for Puerto Ricans had in fact worsened. For example, by 1960 only 13% of Puerto Ricans 25 and older had completed high school, and more than half had less than an eighth-grade education (Puerto Rican Forum, 1970). A 1961 study of a Manhattan community found that fewer than 10% of Puerto Rican children in third grade were reading at grade level or above (Puerto Rican Forum). In addition, only a small number of Puerto Ricans graduated from a New York City high school with an academic diploma in 1963 (331, or 1.6% of the 21,000 academic diplomas granted), at a time when the total Puerto Rican school-age population was more than 150,000 (Fitzpatrick, 1971). Of these 331, only 28 went on to college (Cafferty & Rivera-Martínez, 1981).

As reported by the Puerto Rican Forum, this dire situation was reflected in other arenas too: a 1964 study found that Puerto Ricans had the highest percentage of poverty in New York City, along with the worst housing and the lowest levels of education and income. Probably not coincidentally, as of 1970 there was no Puerto Rican elected official in the city administration (Puerto Rican Forum, 1970). Outside of New York City, the situation was often worse. For instance, between 1966 and 1969 only four Puerto Rican students graduated from the Boston public schools (Cafferty & Rivera-Martínez, 1981). A 1972 study in Massachusetts estimated that at least 2,500 Puerto Rican children in Boston were not even attending school, and that a third of all students in one Springfield, Massachusetts, junior high school quit before going on to high school (Massachusetts State Advisory Committee to the U.S. Commission on Civil Rights, 1972).

Growing Puerto Rican Involvement in Research and Advocacy. The worsening educational situation for Puerto Ricans led to a change in how these problems were addressed in the community, apparent in three major ways. First, concerned educators and community activists led a more aggressive challenge of the melting-pot and cultural-deprivation models and other negative characterizations of their community. In New York City, boycotts and other protests for quality education were frequent during the 1950s and 1960s. Second, there were initial, although tentative, demands for programs such as bilingual education, ethnic studies, and cross-cultural education; these later grew into major rallying cries for educational equality, signaling a new paradigm of cultural and linguistic inclusion. Third, there arose demands for including more Puerto Rican educators and policy makers in decision making.

It was also clear that reform in teacher preparation was an essential component of the change that was needed. Not only did most teachers know very little about Puerto Rican students, but many espoused stereotypical and racist viewpoints that impeded student learning. In the early 1970s, two educators, Francesco Cordasco and Eugene Bucchioni (1972) created one of the first staff development institutes for teachers of Puerto Rican students in the New York City area. Included in the institute were the study of Puerto Rican history and culture and the Puerto Rican experience in the United States, conversational Spanish, bilingual education, and parent involvement strategies. Moreover, members of the Puerto Rican community were to be centrally involved in the institute's offerings. A major criterion for selection of teachers was a "commitment to the education of Puerto Rican students and to teaching in the Puerto Rican community" (Cordasco & Bucchioni, p. 309). The focus on the kinds of attributes teachers need to develop in order to be effective with Puerto Rican youngsters is a key concern even now (Flores-González, 2002; Mercado & Moll, 2000; Nieto & Rolón, 1997).

Given the grave situation and growing frustration in the Puerto Rican community, the slow trickle of studies begun in the 1930s grew steadily in the 1960s, and the increasing militancy in the community was beginning to be felt to one degree or another in new research. For instance, the next major report on the education of Puerto Ricans in the United States—this time with substantial community involvement—was based on the First Citywide Conference of the Puerto Rican Community, which took place in April 1967 (Office of the Mayor, 1968). A total of 32 recommendations, many similar or identical to those made previously by the Puerto Rican Study, were submitted to the mayor of New York City. This time, however, the new recommendations reflected the changes in the political climate of the 1960s and the prominent Puerto Rican participation in the conference. Among these recommendations were bilingual programs and courses in Puerto Rican culture, literature, and history.

Hemos Trabajado Bien (1968). Bilingual and ethnic studies education were also a feature of the ASPIRA symposium of 1968, *Hemos Trabajado Bien* (ASPIRA of New York, 1968), a conference on the education of Puerto Ricans and Mexican Americans that received widespread national attention and for which another report was commissioned (Margolis, 1968). Titled *The Losers*, the eloquently written document served as a common starting point for understanding the status of the education of Puerto Rican youth. According to its author, *losers* referred to a number of groups, including the children, the community, and society at large. Visiting 16 schools in seven cities with large Puerto Rican communities, Margolis documented major problems, including high dropout and low attendance rates, poor academic achievement, and uninformed and unsympathetic teachers and administrators. The report signaled a new emphasis on parental involvement that was to become a hallmark of all subsequent reports on the education of Puerto Rican youth. Although it did not make any concrete recommendations, the report's findings concerning poor record keeping, biased and unimaginative teaching, and low expectations for Puerto Rican students were compelling.

Especially noteworthy in the ASPIRA report was the fact that it was among the first to challenge the melting-pot ideology prevalent until then. Margolis (1968) maintained that teachers who refused to recognize their students' differences were practicing "a subtle form of tyranny":

They are saying, "All people should pretend to be like everyone else even when they are not." That is how the majority culture imposes its standards upon a minority—a cruel sort of assimilation forced onto children in the name of equality. (p. 7)

This was not the first critique of the melting pot, which had come under serious scrutiny some years before. In a statement with a flavor more of the 1980s than of their day, Mills and Goldsen (1950), writing specifically about Puerto Ricans, roundly condemned this ideology:

With the recent decline of immigration, cultural pluralism, a new approach to the solution of problems arising from the presence of divergent cultures, has been taken seriously by small circles of people. This perspective assumes the bankruptcy of the "melting pot theory," asserting that to attack group values is likely to strengthen them. More importantly, it proposes that each cultural group may have something to contribute to American civilization as a mixed cultural whole. (p. 84)

This kind of thinking marked a turning point in how educational problems were defined and addressed, and it had a great impact on Puerto Rican and other progressive educators.

Pressure Toward Assimilation. In spite of these changes, schools continued (and many continue to this day) to reflect the conventional "melting pot" ideology by stressing the assimilationist role of education. A 1965 ethnographic doctoral study by Bucchioni provides a glimpse into the daily and consistent pressures toward assimilation taking place in New York City schools with large Puerto Rican student bodies (Bucchioni, 1982). Using the case of "Miss Dwight" for detailed analysis and discussion, Bucchioni documented both subtle and obvious assimilationist pressures in her curriculum, teaching methods, and other messages to children about the inherent value of their experiences and culture. The pressures included admonitions about not speaking Spanish, a discussion about what constitutes a good nutritious diet (in which no Puerto Rican foods were included), learning how to do the square dance, and a disturbing discussion about neighborhoods in New York City. In that discussion, Juan, a student who was astonished to learn that some families had their own bathrooms, concluded that only very rich people can live in those places. But he was reassured by Miss Dwight: "Not exactly rich, Juan. But they do work hard, and every day," to which Juan answered "My papa, he say he work hard, every day—eben on Sunday" (p. 210).

It was becoming clear to many educators that the cumulative effect of negative messages through the curriculum and pedagogy, whether intended or unintended, can be disastrous for young people struggling to maintain a sense of integrity in a hostile environment. Miss Dwight's attitudes can best be described as patronizing, while those of one of her fellow teachers were more blatantly ethnocentric and defeatist: "What's the use of worrying about these kids? Between their lousy way of living and their Spanish, we're lost before we begin," she concluded (Bucchioni, 1982, p. 213). The messages in both the expressed and the hidden curriculum emphasized to Puerto Rican youths that everything associated with their lives (native language, foods, lifestyles, music, and even their parents) was somehow lacking and deficient.

Fighting the Labels: A Growing Militancy and Other Perspectives from the 1970s

Labels are not always the result of imposition from above. In the case of Puerto Ricans in the United States, labels sometimes emerged from the tensions of colonialism and migration. For instance, in the 1970s Puerto Ricans from the island tended to view the experience of Puerto Ricans in the United States in a naïve or patronizing way. The growing conflicts between Puerto Rican perspectives from the island and those from the U.S. mainland were exemplified at a 1970 conference, held in Puerto Rico, on the education of Puerto Rican children in the United States (Gallardo, 1970). Conference organizers, largely from Puerto Rico, focused on the so-called problems of Puerto Ricans in the United States. As a result, there was great anger among Puerto Rican participants from the United

States when they heard the conference organizers' characterization of Puerto Rican youngsters in the United States as "pitiful" and "victimized." One U.S. Puerto Rican activist, Joseph Monserrat, criticized the romanticized cultural content of the conference as completely off the mark:

We can talk about "compadrazco" [godparent relationships], and we can talk about extended families, and we can talk about "machismo," and we can talk about the Puerto Rican syndrome [a term used in the mental health literature referring to the behavior of women in stressful situations, characterized by screaming and fainting], and it is interesting to talk about these things. But as long as we talk about the Puerto Rican, we will never talk about the problem, because the problem is not the Puerto Rican. . . . The problem basically is the realities that exist in the communities into which Puerto Ricans move. (Gallardo, 1970, p. 67)

He suggested instead that the task at hand was to break "the monolingual, monocultural barrier" and to challenge the melting-pot ideology. Conference organizers also presented a viewpoint of great naïveté, suggesting that within the next 25 years Puerto Ricans would know English sufficiently well that bilingual programs would no longer be needed (Gallardo, 1970)!

The 1970s thus brought not only internal tensions between Puerto Ricans on the island and U.S. Puerto Rican urban communities but also greater advocacy and determination within the community in the United States. The growing educational militancy can be understood as part of the larger civil rights movement, although civil rights were defined in a particularly Puerto Rican context. Two examples will help illustrate these developments: the struggle for equal educational opportunity in New York City, and the prominence of bilingual education as a rallying point for demands to improve the education of Puerto Rican youths.

Puerto Rican Educational Militancy: Two Cases. Although less well documented than the formal reports or conferences and research studies on Puerto Rican communities, there are in the literature some concrete examples of how more militant demands were manifested in the community. Two of the most fully chronicled cases of Puerto Rican educational militancy occurred as part of the community control and decentralization movements of the mid-1960s and early 1970s. They took place in Intermediate School 201 in Harlem and District 1 on New York's Lower East Side (Fuentes, 1976; Gittell, 1972; Jennings & Chapman, 1996). Along with African Americans, Puerto Ricans had been involved in demanding two-way integration since the 1950s. IS 201, a huge, windowless structure built in 1966 in Harlem, was to be the setting for this integration. Because they feared a White exodus, however, neither the city's mayor nor the New York City

Board of Education pursued integration, thus setting the stage for parent demands to control the school in order to guarantee quality education.

Boycotts and prolonged community activism led to the establishment of three experimental school districts in the summer of 1966 in New York City: IS 201, Two Bridges, and Ocean Hill-Brownsville. Parents and other community members were to have a major voice in the educational decisions affecting their children in these districts (Gittell, 1972). Puerto Rican students were a significant population in each of the schools involved. Combining forces, the Board of Education and the United Federation of Teachers (UFT) crushed these grassroots movements, but the movements nevertheless left an important legacy. For example, one of the first bilingual programs established in the city was set up as a minischool in Ocean Hill-Brownsville in 1968 (Fuentes, 1976; Rubinstein, 1970; Wasserman, 1969). Parents also helped in selecting the staff and determining the focus of the curriculum (Rubinstein; Jennings & Chapman, 1996).

Two Bridges, a community in Lower Manhattan, was the setting for the other important educational movement of the early 1970s in which Puerto Ricans were heavily represented (Fantini & Magat, 1970). This neighborhood, known as Community District 1, became the setting for one of the longest and most bitterly fought campaigns for the rights of Puerto Rican and other community students and parents during the early 1970s (Fuentes, 1976; Jennings & Chapman, 1996). By 1972, parents and other activists secured the majority of seats on the school board and made immediate changes, including hiring Luis Fuentes (principal of the Ocean Hill-Brownsville school, which had begun the bilingual program a number of years before) as community superintendent; hiring other Latino, African American, and Chinese American personnel; and instituting bilingual education and a systematized reading program.

These changes were greeted with skepticism and fear by the educational establishments, including the UFT, which claimed that because of the campaign waged by the community the schools had become "arenas of political extremism, racism and patronage" (Shanker, 1973). The UFT-backed coalition called itself the "Brotherhood Slate," but in the 1973 and 1974 elections its candidates totaled 17 Whites and only 1 Black (in spite of the fact that the district's pupil population was 73% Puerto Rican and only 6% White). None of these candidates had children in the public schools. Grassroots elements of the local Puerto Rican community organized an opposing parent slate consisting of four Puerto Ricans, two African Americans, one Chinese, and one White citizen, all parents of children in the district's public schools. Ironically, this slate was termed "separatist" by the opposition (Fuentes, 1976).

The UFT spent more than $100,000 to the parent slate's $4,000, and by 1974 the community school board was restored to a White majority; the controversial Luis Fuentes, who had been supported by most residents of the community, was fired. In spite of these setbacks, District 1 had struggled and in some ways even flourished as an educational experiment in which new and innovative programs were started, including the hiring of 120 bilingual Chinese- and Spanish-language teachers, the development of interviewing and hiring committees that comprised parents and students, and a school lunch program selected and supervised by parents (Fuentes, 1976). Also for the first time ever, a few Puerto Ricans, including Hernán La Fontaine (principal of P.S. 25, the first bilingual school in the city and the second in the nation), were hired as principals in New York City schools.

A New Era Begins. It was against this backdrop that the U.S. Commission on Civil Rights conducted a series of regional studies and open meetings between 1971 and 1976 and issued an influential national report on the condition of Puerto Ricans in the United States (U.S. Commission on Civil Rights, 1976). This report was noteworthy for a number of reasons. First, with the exception of surveys by the Census Bureau, it represented the first time a federal government agency had focused specifically on the entire population of mainland Puerto Ricans. Second, it was the first effort to document accurately the socioeconomic status of Puerto Ricans throughout the United States. It was found, for example, that as of 1975 more than 1.7 million Puerto Ricans were living in the United States, with an incidence of poverty and unemployment more severe than that of virtually any other ethnic group.

Third, the report comprehensively documented for the first time the educational status of Puerto Ricans in the continental United States. What the commission found was a severely undereducated population and an educational establishment that consistently failed to respond to its needs. For instance, although 62% of all U.S. adults had completed a high school education, only 28.7% of Puerto Ricans had done so. The report also reported chronic underachievement and a catastrophic dropout problem among Puerto Ricans (U.S. Commission on Civil Rights, 1976).

Rather than the traditional explanation of cultural deprivation to account for the educational failure of Puerto Ricans, the report was notable in its insistence that school policies and practices contributed in a significant way to the problem. It documented how tracking, IQ and achievement tests, assignment practices, little support for parent and community involvement, and insensitive teachers and counselors unfairly jeopardized Puerto Rican students, and it highlighted how Puerto Rican students—the majority of whom lived in poverty in comparison to middle-class and wealthier students—had unequal access to quality education. A focus on school policies and practices represented a fundamental shift from the paradigm of cultural deprivation and "blaming the victim" (Ryan, 1972) that had been the norm. The U.S. Commission on Civil Rights report was also significant because it redefined native language and cultural differences as potential assets rather than liabilities. Hernán La Fontaine, now the first director of the Board of Education's Office of Bilingual Education, was quoted as saying:

> Our definition of cultural pluralism must include the concept that our language and culture will be given equal status to that of the majority population. It is not enough simply to say that we should be given the opportunity to share in the positive benefits of modern American life. Instead, we must insist that this sharing will not be accomplished at the sacrifice of all those traits which make us what we are as Puerto Ricans. (U.S. Commission on Civil Rights, 1976, p. 103)

The recommendations made by the commission included the establishment of affirmative action plans to recruit Puerto Rican faculty; the elimination of ability grouping in all but the most absolutely necessary cases; and, most important, bilingual-bicultural education in all school districts with significant enrollments of Puerto Rican and other language-minority students (U.S. Commission on Civil Rights, 1976). This last recommendation was in keeping with the resurgence of bilingual education since the late 1960s as a primary way to improve educational attainment among Puerto Rican students. A brief review of bilingual education will explain how it became a prominent issue in the community's demands for equitable education during the 1970s and beyond.

Bilingual Education in the Puerto Rican Community

Although bilingual education was not a new idea, it resurfaced in the 1960s as an antidote to the many educational problems faced by Puerto Rican and other Latino youngsters. Bilingual education has had a long history in the United States (Crawford, 2000; Cummins, 2000; Ovando & Collier, 1998). The cycle of policies and practices related to languages and language use in society in general, and in schools in particular, reflects the multiple ways the United States has addressed language diversity. These have ranged from "sink or swim" policies (i.e., immersing language-minority students in English-only classrooms to fend for themselves) through the imposition of English as the sole medium of instruction to encouraging the flourishing of bilingual education, such as through German-English bilingual schools in the 1800s (Crawford, 1995). But in the context of the huge influx of new immigrants at the turn of the century, the accompanying xenophobic hysteria, and a policy of isolationism, bilingual education had virtually disappeared between the two world wars. During the late 1960s, renewed demands for bilingual education were heard, another consequence of the civil rights movement.

Bilingual Education as a Remedy for Unequal Education. While school integration remained the primary focus for achieving equality of education in the African American community, Puerto Rican and other Latino communities focused their efforts on language maintenance. One reason was that school desegregation had not led to a greater understanding of Latinos by school administrators or teachers. One study by ASPIRA concluded that desegregation plans needed to distinguish the needs of African Americans and Latinos, and to adhere to state and federal guidelines for bilingual education (ASPIRA of America, 1979). As a result, in the Puerto Rican and other language-minority communities, bilingual education became the cornerstone of educational equality and their major civil rights issue (Báez, Fernández, Navarro, & Rice, 1986). Most language-minority communities viewed bilingual education as the best guarantee that youngsters who did not speak English would be provided education in a language they understood. Without it, they might well be doomed to educational underachievement and severely limited occupational choices in the future.

Bilingual education was also seen as helping to counteract the assimilationist agenda of schooling, which resulted in young people's shifting their cultural and class identification away from their own communities and toward that of the larger society. Parents, community activists, and concerned educators began to fear that through the hidden and expressed curriculum and the educational power of the media, young Puerto Ricans were being taught to reject the values of their own communities, including their language and culture. Bilingual education was seen as one way to respond to this pressure.

Demands for bilingual education should not be understood as outside the American dream, but as part and parcel of it. The main objectives Puerto Ricans envision for education are economic security and what one might call "the good life," objectives not very different from those of the larger society and the educational system. There are, however, some fundamental differences between the ways these objectives are defined. In general, the good life for Puerto Ricans has not included wholesale assimilation or cultural rejection. On the contrary, Puerto Ricans have demonstrated an almost unbridled enthusiasm for education *while at the same time* displaying a fierce tenacity with respect to maintaining their language and culture. In the Puerto Rican community, and in the larger Latino community in general, there has been no contradiction between getting a good education and retaining ethnic and linguistic identity.

Some Results of Demands for Bilingual Education.
Activism for bilingual education in the Puerto Rican community resulted in programs in specific schools, such as in Ocean Hill-Brownsville and P.S. 25 in the Bronx, the latter being the first totally bilingual school in the Northeast, established in 1968 (Fuentes, 1976; La Fontaine et al., 1973). At the national level, protests and demands among activists in the Mexican American, Puerto Rican, American Indian, and other language-minority communities led to passage of the Bilingual Education Act of 1967 (part of the Elementary and Secondary Education Act of 1968), which made funding available for a small number of demonstration projects throughout the country. This act provided for a program of instruction that would enable students to achieve equal proficiency in English and their native language, develop pride in and awareness of their cultural heritage, and aid them in increasing their academic achievement. State-level activism on the part of Puerto Ricans and others in Massachusetts led to the passage of Chapter 71A, the first law to mandate bilingual education, which became the model for virtually every other such state-mandated law in the country (Bureau of Transitional Bilingual Education, 1971).

Recourse to the Courts and Local and Federal Legislatures.
Two key arenas for the political demands of Puerto Rican and other linguistic-minority communities were the legislatures at the state and national levels, and the local and federal courts. In 1969, plaintiffs representing 1,800 Chinese-speaking students sued the San Francisco Unified School District for failing to give non–English-speaking students an equal chance to learn. Although the case was lost at the state level, by 1974 it had reached the Supreme Court. In the landmark *Lau* v. *Nichols* (1974) case, the Court, recognizing the relationship of language to equal educational opportunity, ruled unambiguously that the civil rights of students who did not understand the language of instruction were indeed being violated.

By 1975, the Office for Civil Rights and the Department of Health, Education, and Welfare issued a document popularly known as the "Lau Remedies," which offered guidance in identifying, assessing the language abilities of, and providing appropriate programs for students with limited proficiency in English (Office of Civil Rights, 1975). This document has served as the basis for determining whether or not school systems are in compliance with the findings of the *Lau* decision. Bilingual programs have been the common remedy in most cases.

One of the Puerto Rican community's most important campaigns for educational equity through bilingual education took place in 1972, when the Puerto Rican Legal Defense and Education Fund (PRLDEF) along with ASPIRA of New York, ASPIRA of America (now the ASPIRA Association), and other organizations representing the educational interests of Puerto Rican youngsters sued the New York City Board of Education on behalf of 15 schoolchildren and their parents (Santiago-Santiago, 1986; ASPIRA Association, 1991). The suit, a landmark case in the history of bilingual education because it involved the largest school system in the country and the largest class of plaintiff children (more than 80,000), was based on evidence that Puerto Rican youngsters of limited English proficiency were being denied equal educational opportunity (Santiago-Santiago, 1986). After a great deal of litigation and negotiation, the suit was resolved in August 1974 and resulted in the ASPIRA Consent Decree, mandating bilingual education in the New York City school system (ASPIRA Association, 1991).

According to Santiago-Santiago (1986), the ASPIRA Consent Decree, and bilingual education in the Puerto Rican community in general, need to be placed in the context of the sociopolitical relationship of Puerto Rico to the United States. The special citizenship status of Puerto Ricans is often overlooked in bilingual education literature. Some Puerto Ricans have maintained that specific educational and language policies need to be developed that respond to the conditions of this citizenship status. Thus, although the reasons for bilingual education may be just as urgent in other language-minority communities, the situation of Puerto Ricans is unique in that they are not immigrants but citizens, whether they are born in Puerto Rico or on the U.S. mainland.

It is understandable that in the Puerto Rican community bilingual education became inextricably linked with demands for equal educational opportunity, as demonstrated in numerous reports and studies released in the late 1960s and thereafter (Margolis, 1968; Massachusetts State Advisory Committee to the U.S. Commission on Civil Rights, 1972; National Puerto Rican Task Force, 1982; Puerto Rican Forum, 1970; U.S. Commission on Civil Rights 1976). Although bilingual education continues to be an element in calls for educational reform for Puerto Rican students, it was only one of many strategies recommended during the 1980s and 1990s, to which we will now turn.

Puerto Rican Students "At Risk": Redefining Complex Issues in the 1980s and 1990s

The 1980s represented a period of retrenchment and retreat from the more liberal educational policies of the 1960s and 1970s, a trend no better defined than in the educational reform movement that officially began with the publication of *A Nation at Risk* (National Commission on Excellence in Education, 1983). Educational concerns during the previous two decades had focused on educational equality by challenging the deficit theories popularized in the 1960s and espousing strategies such as busing, integration, ethnic studies, and cross-cultural and multicultural education, but the 1980s ushered in a more conservative era marked by a growing concern that equity had been won at the expense of excellence. This conservative backlash led to calls for higher standards, longer school days and years, reinstatement of the classics, a return to the "basics," and the forging of a common cultural experience for all students (National Commission on Excellence in Education; Bloom, 1987; Hirsch, 1987).

The term *at risk*, referring to students whose socioeconomic, experiential, and cultural characteristics made them likely candidates for school failure, began to be used in the 1980s. Although often meant to point out unequal educational access for youngsters on the basis of their race, language, or social class, the term was frequently used to blame students for perceived shortcomings rather than to attend to the shortcomings of school systems and the society in general.

Puerto Rican activists and professionals, however, embarked on a process of redefining educational equity and excellence through studies and reports centering on the education of Puerto Ricans and other Latinos (National Commission on Secondary Education for Hispanics, 1984; Valdivieso, 1986). Although bilingual education remained a key ingredient in all calls for reform during the 1980s and 1990s, the educational agenda expanded to include a more serious look at other policies and practices leading to educational failure among Puerto Rican youths. For instance, in a review of the ASPIRA Consent Decree more than a decade after it was implemented, Santiago-Santiago (1986) suggested that one of its shortcomings was that it would not ensure equal educational opportunity for fully 60% of Puerto Rican youngsters in New York City because they were not enrolled in bilingual programs. Some of them were youngsters who did not qualify for bilingual education under the consent decree (children who were proficient in English, even if they were also proficient in Spanish, could not qualify for such programs). Hence, bilingual education continued to be identified as a compensatory rather than an enrichment program.

Puerto Rican and other Latino communities began to recognize that lack of English skills alone did not explain poor academic achievement or high dropout rates. For example, Cuban American students, who have the highest educational level of all Latinos, are also the most likely to speak Spanish at home. In their case, middle-class status, with its accompanying access to higher-level education, has been found more salient in promoting academic achievement (Valdivieso & Davis, 1988). In addition, activists in the community began scrutinizing educational policies and practices more carefully, and calls for more political participation were louder than ever before (Caballero, 2000; L. O. Reyes, 2000).

National Commission on Secondary Education for Hispanics. The focus of many of the reports undertaken by Latino advocacy groups during the 1980s and 1990s shifted from defining students as failures to defining the schools they attended as deficient. For instance, in a move that countered the prevailing ideology of reform movement reports, for instance, the National Commission on Secondary Education for Hispanics explored why so many inner-city public high schools were not more successful in educating Latinos. For several months during 1983 and 1984, members of the commission traveled to cities with large Latino communities (New York City, Miami, Los Angeles, Chicago, and San Antonio), visiting schools and holding hearings with students, parents, teachers, administrators, counselors, and business people.

The report chronicled the failure of schools to educate Latino students through data on placement practices, test scores, tracking, and dropouts. Their data revealed that 40% of all Latinos who dropped out did so before 10th grade—information that could be useful in changing the nature of dropout prevention programs, which were generally targeted for high school students and thus too late to be of any help. The commission also found that 25% of all Latino students who entered high school were overage for their grade, and among Puerto Rican students in particular 45% who began high school never finished. The effects of tracking, testing, and low expectations of students were found to be especially severe for Latino students, with 76% of those who took the High School and Beyond (HSAB) achievement tests scoring in the bottom half of national results and with 40% of all Latinos in a general track (National Commission on Secondary Education for Hispanics, 1984).

The commission reported that the schools most successful with Latinos were characterized by strong links to the community, active parent involvement, dedicated principals and teachers who had high expectations for all students, as well as a good number of Latino teachers and other adults in guidance, mentoring, and supervisory roles. In fact, students who testified at the hearings attributed their success in these schools to a quality of "caring"; in the words of one of them, "Teachers lean on us and get on our case but we know they care about us" (National Commission on Secondary Education for Hispanics, 1984, vol. 1, p. 29). Not surprisingly, the major findings of the commission centered on the importance of the quality of life in schools, suggesting that personal attention, contact with adults, and family involvement with the schools are the keys to improving the performance and retention of Latino students.

Other Research Studies and Reports. Also responding to the inadequacy of reforms of the 1980s after the release of *A Nation at Risk* was a report that asked the plaintive question, *Must They Wait Another Generation?* (Valdivieso, 1986). It reported dropout rates for Latinos as high as 70% in Chicago and 80% in New York City in the early 1980s. Among 20-to-24-year-old Puerto Ricans, 46% were not high school graduates, the worst standing of any Latino group. Claiming that current reforms were inadequate for the needs of Latinos because many of the issues important to them had been overlooked, the author suggested such strategies as more sensitive counseling; recognizing the role of work in the lives of Latino high school students; and major changes in the organization of secondary schools, including tracking, ability grouping, and access to high-level curriculum (Valdivieso, 1986).

Because of its history, as well as its large number of Puerto Rican professionals and the size of its Puerto Rican community, New York City still remains in the forefront of many of the educational struggles of the Puerto Rican community. In 1987, ASPIRA of New York established an educational group consisting of the Puerto Rican/Latino Educational Roundtable of the Centro (Center for Puerto Rican Studies) at CUNY, the Puerto Rican Educators Association (PREA), and other organizations concerned with educating Puerto Ricans in New York City. Their report, another response to the national reform movement, made recommendations regarding systematic dropout prevention efforts, bilingual/bicultural programs, parental participation, recruitment of bilingual and Latino professionals at all levels, and affirmation of cultural and linguistic diversity (L. O. Reyes, 1988).

At around the same time, two researchers undertook an extensive quantitative, historical, and legal analysis of 142 U.S. school districts to explore inequities in Latino education and to find suggestions for what can be done about them (Meier & Stewart, 1991). The authors agreed that Latino students were more segregated than African Americans, but they argued that segregation was not the only impediment to equal educational opportunity. Other, more subtle methods were equally effective in denying access to education, among them ethnic disparities in discipline (e.g., dress codes that are more rigidly enforced among Latinos) and academic grouping (through special education, curriculum tracking, ability grouping, and segregated bilingual education). Coined "second-generation educational discrimination" (Bullock & Stewart, 1979), these conditions can induce Latino students to drop out of school, thus attaining a lower quality of education.

Meier and Stewart (1991) also found that second-generation discrimination exists because Latinos lacked the political power to prevent such actions, and that school districts with greater Latino representation on school boards and among teaching faculty experienced significantly less of this discrimination. Calling the situation for low-income Puerto Ricans "especially grim," the authors concluded that they fared the worst of any Latino subgroup because, even though their educational experiences resembled those of African Americans, they did not have the compensating political resources of that group (Meier & Stewart, 1991).

The Latino Commission. Another report in the long history chronicling the education of Puerto Ricans in New York City was released by the Latino Commission on Educational Reform, formed in October 1991 to examine issues of concern to the 334,000 Latino children in the New York City public schools, about 50% of whom were Puerto Rican (Latino Commission on Educational Reform, 1992, 1994). Chaired by Board of Education member Luis O. Reyes, the commission comprised 35 Latino leaders representing community-based organizations, colleges and universities, and government agencies, as well as students, parents, and teachers.

Although some of the concerns they addressed were familiar, the differences between the commission and its predecessor of almost 40 years, the Puerto Rican Study (Morrison, 1958), were striking. Among the similarities were the charge (to make recommendations to help the Board of Education fulfill its commitment to Latino students) and the findings of high dropout rates, poor achievement, and lack of access to rigorous academic programs. In a replay of the dismal educational conditions of the 1950s, Latino students were still found to be attending mostly segregated and underachieving schools and to have a dropout rate 40% higher than all other students. The dropout rate, estimated at 35%, was still the highest among Puerto Ricans (Latino Commission on Educational Reform, 1994).

The Latino Commission report was dramatically different from the Puerto Rican Study for a number of reasons. First, in a marked departure from using such labels as *losers* and *at-risk,* the commission concentrated its efforts on characterizing Latino youngsters as potential "leaders." Its focus was on rigorous academics, high expectations, innovative pedagogy, community service, and empowerment so that students could develop sound skills, a social conscience, a connection to other ethnic groups, and leadership abilities for a pluralistic society.

There were other differences between the two documents as well. In dramatic contrast to the Puerto Rican Study, whose membership was almost entirely non-Latino, all 35 commission members were Latinos. The voices of Latino professionals, parents, and community activists were loud and strong, something that would have been unthinkable 40 years earlier. Latino students were also represented through a series of surveys and interviews carried out by Latino college student researchers from Fordham University, working under the supervision of sociologist Clara Rodríguez. The major findings echoed those of similar research: schools with low Latino dropout rates were characterized by cohesive school spirit and teacher and counselor cultural sensitivity. The interim report concluded: "The respect and value in which students were held was extremely important in separating the schools with low Latino dropout rates from those with high rates" (Latino Commission, 1992, Vol. 2, p. 79).

Research Studies in the 1990s. Feelings of marginalization and alienation among Puerto Rican youths had been evident for many years, but it was during the 1990s that research studies attempted to discern systematically the reasons for low achievement and high dropout rates. More ethnographic studies, focusing on comprehensive analyses of actual school experiences, were carried out during this time than ever before. Darder and Upshur (1993), for instance, in a study of four Boston public schools conducted extensive meetings and interviews with teachers, principals, students, and parents, and they also administered questionnaires and took part in long hours of classroom observation. They found that the overall environment in these schools, which had student bodies that were 45–55% Latino, was inadequate because of physical dilapidation and because the curriculum and instructional strategies were largely irrelevant to the lives of the children.

In the schools they studied, Darder and Upshur (1993) found numerous principals and teachers who believed the cause of Puerto Ricans' educational problems was either in their environment (cultural and socioeconomic) or in the children themselves. The students, on the other hand, located the problems squarely in the school: children wanted more sports activities, better food in the cafeteria, more interesting books, more computers, cleaner bathrooms, teachers who did not yell at them, and a safe environment.

Examples of student marginalization were found in other research during these years as well. For example, an extensive review of school records in Holyoke, Massachusetts, high schools found that Puerto Rican students in nonbilingual programs were more than twice as likely (69% compared to 31%) to drop out as those in bilingual programs (Frau-Ramos & Nieto, 1993). One young man, expressing the views of many other Puerto Ricans over the years, explained his reason for dropping out by saying that he felt like "an outsider," not really belonging

to the community of the school. In another study, Virginia Vogel Zanger (1993), through research based on a panel discussion of 20 high-achieving Latino students in a college-skills course in a Boston high school who were asked to reflect on their school experiences, found that many expressed similar feelings of marginalization. In the words of one student: "They won't accept you if you're not like them. They want to *monoculture* [you]" (p. 169). If even academically successful students feel this way, we can only speculate that low-achieving students feel even more marginalized and disempowered.

The Twenty-First Century: The Search for a More Hopeful Future

Since the end of the 20th century and into the first years of the 21st century, there has been increasing attention to the education of Puerto Ricans in the United States. For instance, since 1990 both Republican and Democratic presidents have signed executive orders focusing on improving educational excellence for Hispanics. With each executive order, a Presidential Advisory Commission was established, with a charge to report its findings to the White House, the Secretary of Education, and the nation. Executive order 12900, signed by President Bill Clinton in 1994, resulted in two reports. The first, *Our Nation on the Faultline: Hispanic American Education* (President's Advisory Commission on Educational Excellence for Hispanic Americans, 1996), documented the dramatic growth of the Hispanic population and described the serious shortcomings of the education system in serving Hispanic students.

The second report was titled *Creating the Will: Hispanics Achieving Educational Excellence* (President's Advisory Commission on Educational Excellence for Hispanic Americans, 2000). Rather than present a series of recommendations as was the case in the first report, the commission instead challenged the nation to focus on one major task: closing the achievement gap by the year 2010. Acknowledging that the achievement gap is the result of many factors (low expectations of Hispanic students; poorly prepared teachers and administrators; poverty; rigid ability tracking; and limited English proficiency, among others), commission members nevertheless urged all sectors of the nation to "create the will" to promote educational excellence among Latinos. Echoing the theme of other recent studies and reports, the report focused on the positive resources of Latino students: "Accepting this challenge [to close the achievement gap] begins with recognizing the many talents Hispanic students bring to the classroom" (Presidential Advisory Commission on Educational Excellence for Hispanic Americans, 2000, p. 4).

Another cause for hope at the close of the 20th century was the increasing attention journals and books were paying to the education of Puerto Rican students. In 1998—for the first time ever—an entire issue of the *Harvard Educational Review* ("Symposium . . .," 1998) was devoted to the question of educating Puerto Ricans in the United States. (It was also notable as the first time an entire issue of a journal, disseminated as a companion issue, was translated into Spanish.) A number of articles in the issue documented the historic educational failure of Puerto Rican youth (Nieto, 1998; Perry, 1998; Walsh, 1998), challenging the view that their culture or values were to blame for educational failure. Other articles centered on the long-standing advocacy of the Puerto Rican community in addressing these problems (del Valle, 1998; Ramos-Zayas, 1998).

In addition, an entire volume on educating Puerto Ricans was released at the dawn of the present century (Nieto, 2000a), with chapters addressing myriad issues: racial, gender, and linguistic identity (Hidalgo, 2000; Rolón, 2000; Walsh, 2000; Zavala, 2000); return migrant students (X. A. Reyes, 2000); community advocacy for educational change (Caballero, 2000; L. O. Reyes, 2000; M. Rivera & Pedraza, 2000); and classroom-based change (Mercado & Moll, 2000; Morales & Tarr, 2000; Torres-Guzmán & Thorne, 2000). The volume also included testimonials of Puerto Ricans from 14 through 52 years of age who were, or had been, "Puerto Rican students in U.S. schools," lending a human face to the research and data presented in the other chapters.

Although a small number of previous volumes had been instrumental in directing attention to the education of Puerto Rican students (Cordasco & Bucchioni, 1972b; Ambert & Alvarez, 1992), a significant feature of this volume was that almost all the authors were Puerto Rican, a striking indication of the growing number of Puerto Rican scholars engaged in educational research. In previous years, most of the research on educating Puerto Rican students had been carried out by non–Puerto Rican scholars. This is not to suggest that only Puerto Ricans are capable of doing such research; rather it is to point out that Puerto Ricans need to be prevalent among those investigating and analyzing these issues.

An example of why an insider's perspective is needed is found in new research by Nilda Flores-González, one of the young Puerto Rican scholars of the 21st century (Flores-González, 2002). Her work builds on earlier research by scholars who suggested that "caring" (a concept whose implications for education was most clearly articulated by Noddings, 1992) is a key ingredient in educating Latinos (Fernández & Shu, 1988; National Commission on Secondary Education for Hispanics, 1984; Nieto, 1998). In Flores-González's ethnographic research among Puerto Rican and other Latino/a students in Chicago, she found that students develop identities as either "school kids" or "street kids" largely on the basis of the relationships they have with teachers

and other adults in the school, as well as on the accommodations made by schools to meet their needs. Research concerning Mexican and Mexican American students has come to similar conclusions (Reyes, Scribner, & Scribner, 1999; Valenzuela, 1999).

The insights of researchers who share a cultural heritage with the students they investigate may be valuable to other researchers, as well as to policy makers and teachers who work with Puerto Rican and other Latino youths. For instance, Nitza Hidalgo (1998) has suggested that research on Puerto Ricans and other Latinos often is based on a deficiency paradigm that is ignorant of Latino family values and perspectives. In contrast to the deficiency paradigm, she has developed one that includes a series of methodological requirements for a Latino family research paradigm based on critical race theory, feminist theory, and Puerto Rican/Latino culture and experience. This paradigm also examines the supposedly neutral role of the researcher, suggesting that research is never totally objective or free of ideology.

A reason for optimism in the new century, therefore, is the growing number of Latinos who are studying their own communities, and the implications of their research for the educational future of Latinos. A recent venture building on this reality is the National Latino Education Research Agenda Project, or NLERAP, spearheaded by Pedro Pedraza of the Puerto Rican Studies Research Center (also known as "the Centro") at Hunter College in New York City in 1998 and funded by a number of leading philanthropic organizations. With a national advisory board primarily of Latino scholars whose research focuses on educating Latinos, the NLERAP hopes to develop a new action-oriented educational research agenda that will identify school and nonschool conditions that support or inhibit Latino/a students' learning and development. The NLERAP also hopes to support specific research projects that incorporate these principles by using a community-based approach that respects indigenous knowledge and culture.

WHAT HAVE WE LEARNED? BUILDING ON THE STRUGGLES AND PREPARING FOR A MORE HOPEFUL FUTURE

A number of lessons that may be helpful in developing a vision and strategies for the future education of Puerto Ricans in the United States can be gleaned from the review presented in this chapter. These lessons are described in three broad contexts.

Building on Family Strengths

The family is a major force in Puerto Rican culture, and it has had a vital influence in the history of the education of Puerto Rican youngsters. Whether it has been through parent involvement, the community control movement, or inclusion of family perspectives in the curriculum, the family can have a positive impact on students' attitudes and achievement. Even so, and although the literature is replete with evidence of the high expectations of Puerto Rican parents for their children's achievement, it has also shown that families have received little direct help in fostering an environment for their children's success (Díaz Soto, 1997; Hidalgo, 2000; Zentella, 1997b).

Special strengths of the Puerto Rican community lie in close family relationships, the conception of community responsibility, and resilience in the face of adversity. Given Puerto Rican parents' high aspirations and stubborn insistence on the rewards of education, it makes sense to use these values in any strategy to improve the education of their children. One example of using the family strengths of Puerto Rican and other children as the core of the curriculum has been described by a teacher working with two professors in western Massachusetts (see Keenan, Willett, & Solsken, 1993). They write, "Unlike other approaches that focus on changes the families must make to support schools, we begin with ways that schools must change to support families" (p. 57). Through classroom visits by families of culturally diverse background, including Puerto Rican families, the researchers documented the range of knowledge, skills, and teaching capabilities parents used with their children at home that can enrich their education in school as well. The work of Carmen Mercado and Luis Moll (2000) with Puerto Rican and Mexican American families echoes this theme. Building on the families' "funds of knowledge," these researchers worked with teachers who visited their students' homes to learn how their home environment could further promote learning.

Research such as this documents how students' experiences, culture, and language are vital sources for curriculum development, and thus for their academic achievement, and can serve as a promising practice for other schools working with a culturally diverse population.

Cultural and Linguistic Maintenance

Throughout much of the history of the education of Puerto Ricans in the United States, cultural and linguistic maintenance has served as both a defense against a hostile environment and as a nonnegotiable demand for educational improvement. Even during periods of Americanization and other assimilationist pressures, Puerto Ricans have insisted on retaining Spanish and their cultural roots, while at the same time learning English and becoming biculturally adept. Nowhere is this more evident than in the demands for bilingual education that

began in the 1960s. Research over the past several decades has reaffirmed the academic and linguistic benefits of maintaining the native language and becoming bilingual (Cummins, 2000; Díaz Soto, 1997).

Other indications of how cultural and linguistic maintenance can promote learning are found in research focusing on the impact on learning of cultural and linguistic maintenance. Ana Celia Zentella (1997a), in research focusing on 19 Puerto Rican families in New York City, discovered that the most successful students in the study were also the most fluent bilinguals. Walsh's (1991) research among Puerto Rican youngsters in a small city in New England found that youngsters maintained their culture and language, albeit in limited ways, even in schools where they were disparaged. She found that fourth-grade Puerto Rican students often maintained cultural nuances in the meanings they gave to words in Spanish but not for the words they used in English. For instance, *neighborhood* in English was described as a place with buildings, while its Spanish equivalent, *comunidad,* was described as "a place where there's a lot of family" (p. 73). This intriguing research points out how children internalize reality from two different worlds and can end up being either enriched or "cultural schizophrenics." This kind of research has valuable implications for the classroom and student learning.

An ethnographic study by María Torres-Guzmán (1992) tells stories of teachers struggling to give hope and create an environment for the empowerment of Latino students. In describing an integrated environmental science curriculum in a New York City alternative high school housed in a community-based organization, she demonstrates how students' experiences were used as the basis for their education and to help them become more active learners. The curriculum described by Torres-Guzmán resulted in the formation of "the Toxic Avengers," a student group that investigated toxic wastes in their Brooklyn neighborhood and eventually instigated the cleanup of a particularly polluted lot. In 1989 the Toxic Avengers received an award from the Citizens' Committee of New York for their efforts. Concludes Torres-Guzmán:

The message of the stories is not complex: incorporating student experiences as a way of giving primacy to students' voices changes the relationships of power and collaboration in the classroom. Learning can become meaningful and purposeful for the individual and can create spaces for exploring what the relationship of the individual is within the broader social context. (p. 488)

These examples point to the importance of linguistic and cultural maintenance, through bilingual and multicultural approaches, as an essential cornerstone of any strategy to improve the education of Puerto Rican youngsters.

Changing School Policies and Practices

Much research on educating Puerto Ricans has emphasized the need to reexamine the impact of school policies and practices on their academic achievement and high school completion. These policies and practices have included inequitable school funding (ASPIRA Institute for Policy Research, 1993; Meier & Stewart, 1991), overcrowding (Darder & Upshur, 1993), ability grouping (Flores-González, 2002), retention (Fernández & Vélez, 1990), testing (Mestre & Royer, 1991), curriculum reform (Latino Commission on Educational Reform, 1994; Nieto, 2000b), disciplinary policies (Wehlage & Rutter, 1986), and the need to promote the participation of Latino students in extracurricular activities, which has been found to have a positive influence on student retention (Flores-González, 2000).

Rather than continuing to focus on Puerto Rican students or their families as the problem, research instead suggests that schools need to look at their own policies and practices in order to improve the education of Puerto Rican students. This in no way minimizes the responsibility of families and communities; it simply reaffirms the traditional responsibility of U.S. schools to educate *all* students, not just those from English-speaking, middle-class, and well-educated families. Rather than focus on conditions about which they can do precious little—poverty, low parental educational level, or single-parent family structure—schools need to focus on what they *can* change. At the same time, Puerto Rican families must play a crucial role in educating their children, and partnerships have to be formed among families, schools, and the larger community in order to tackle the plague of underachievement and the high dropout rate.

CONCLUSION

Puerto Ricans have been attending schools in the continental United States in large numbers since the 1940s, and myriad problems with their educational achievement have been identified throughout these years. In this chapter, a disturbing history of educational underachievement among Puerto Ricans has been reviewed. Three themes characterizing the history of the education of Puerto Ricans in U.S. schools were explored: the legacy of colonialism; the role of racism, ethnocentrism, and linguicism; and the quest for self-determination. This was followed by an extensive review of research on Puerto Ricans' education, documenting the extent of high dropout rates and low achievement. Schools' responsibility in fueling these problems through negative attitudes and low expectations, and through such practices as ability grouping, grade retention, inadequate counseling, and irrelevant curriculum, were also discussed. Finally, lessons drawn from this history were suggested: the need to build on family strengths, facilitate linguistic and cultural maintenance, and reform school policies and practices in order to make schools more accommodating to Puerto Rican students.

The long history of Puerto Rican students in U.S. schools has been one of unfulfilled expectations and broken dreams. The failure of schools to educate this population has jeopardized both students and our society at large. In the meantime, labels used to characterize Puerto Rican students have left in their wake a legacy of neglect and hopelessness. Ironically, the same labels can also be used to describe our schools and our society. As Margolis (1968) so aptly stated nearly four decades ago:

"The Losers"—refers to us all. The children are losing all hopes of learning or succeeding; the schools are losing all hopes of teaching; and the nation is losing another opportunity, perhaps its last, to put flesh on the American dream. (p. i)

The fact that the Latino population has grown tremendously, or that its members have become the new minority, is little solace for the millions of Latinos who continue to be poorly served by U.S. schools. The hope for a brighter future rests not in numbers but in understanding the history and culture that Puerto Rican students bring with them to school; developing welcoming and culturally affirming learning environments for them; and demonstrating in tangible ways that school is a place where they can be who they are and at the same time soar intellectually. All of us—parents and families, students, teachers, schools, policy makers, and our society at large—have important roles to play in reversing the legacy of the past by providing Puerto Rican students with the excellent and equitable education that all youngsters deserve.

References

Acosta-Belén, E., & Sánchez Korrol, V. (Eds.). (1993). *The way it was and other writings.* Houston, TX: Arte Público Press.

Ambert, A. N., & Alvarez, M. D. (Eds.). (1992). Puerto Rican children on the mainland: Interdisciplinary perspectives. New York: Garland.

ASPIRA Association. (1991). *The ASPIRA story: 1961–1991.* Washington, DC: Author.

ASPIRA Institute for Policy Research. (1993). *Facing the facts: The state of Hispanic education, 1993.* Washington, DC: Author.

ASPIRA of America. (1979). *Trends in segregation of Hispanic students in major school districts having large Hispanic enrollments. Final report.* New York: Author.

ASPIRA of New York. (1968). *Hemos trabajado bien. Proceedings of the ASPIRA National Conference of Puerto Ricans, Mexican-Americans, and Educators.* New York: Author.

Association of Assistant Superintendents. (1948). *A program of education for Puerto Ricans in New York City.* Brooklyn: New York City Board of Education.

Attinasi, J. J. (1979). Language attitudes in a New York Puerto Rican community. In *Bilingual education and public policy in the United States* (Ethnoperspectives in bilingual education research, Vol. I) (pp. 408–461). Ypsilanti: Eastern Michigan University Press.

Báez, T., Fernández, R. R., Navarro, R. A., & Rice, R. I. (1986). Litigation strategies for educational equity: Bilingual education and research. *Issues in Education, 3*(3), 198–214.

Bilingual Education Act of 1967. (1968). U.S. Code 20.

Bloom, A. (1987). *The closing of the American mind: How higher education has failed democracy and impoverished the souls of today's students.* New York: Simon & Schuster.

Bonilla, F., & Campos, R. (1981). A wealth of poor: Puerto Ricans in the new economic order. *Daedalus, 110,* 133–176.

Bucchioni, E. (1982). The daily round of life in the school. In F. Cordasco & E. Bucchioni (Eds.), *The Puerto Rican community and its children on the mainland* (3rd rev. ed., pp. 201–238). Metuchen, NJ: Scarecrow Press.

Bullock, C. S., III, & Stewart, J., Jr. (1979). Incidence and correlates of second-generation discrimination. In M. L. Prelley & M. B. Preston (Eds.), *Race, sex, and policy problems* (pp. 115–129). Lexington, MA: Lexington Books.

Bureau of Transitional Bilingual Education. (1971). *Two way: Bilingual bicultural is two-way education.* Boston: Department of Education.

Caballero, E. (2000). The Puerto Rican/Latino education roundtable: Seeking unity in vision and organizing for educational change. In S. Nieto (Ed.), *Puerto Rican students in U.S. schools* (pp. 203–221). Mahwah, NJ: Erlbaum.

Cafferty, P.S.J., & Rivera-Martínez, C. (1981). *The politics of language: The dilemma of bilingual education for Puerto Ricans.* Boulder, CO: Westview Press.

Calitri, R. (1983). *Racial and ethnic high school dropout rates in New York City.* New York: ASPIRA.

Campos, R., & Bonilla, F. (1976). Industrialization and migration: Some effects on the Puerto Rican working class. *Latin American Perspectives, 3*(3), 66–108.

Carrasquillo, A. L. (1991). *Hispanic children and youth in the United States: A resource guide.* New York: Garland.

Chenault, L. R. (1970). *The Puerto Rican migrant in New York City.* New York: Columbia University Press. (Original work published 1938)

Colleran, K., Gurick, D., & Kurtz, M. (1984). *Migration, acculturation, and family processes.* New York: Fordham University, Hispanic Research Center.

Colón, J. (1982). *A Puerto Rican in New York and other sketches.* New York: International. (Original work published 1961)

Cordasco, F., & Bucchioni, E. (Eds.). (1972). The Puerto Rican community and its children on the mainland: A source book for teachers, social workers, and other professionals. Metuchen, NJ: Scarecrow Press.

Crawford, J. (1995). *Bilingual education: History, politics, theory, and practice* (3rd ed.). Los Angeles: Bilingual Educational Services.

Crawford, J. (2000). *At war with diversity: U.S. language policy in an age of anxiety.* Clevedon, England: Multilingual Matters.

Cummins, J. (2000). *Language, power, and pedagogy: Bilingual children in the crossfire.* Clevedon, England: Multilingual Matters.

Darder, A., Torres, R. D., & Gutiérrez, H. (1997). Introduction. In A. Darder, R. D. Torres, & H. Gutiérrez (Eds.), *Latinos and education: A critical reader* (pp. xi–xix). New York: Routledge.

Darder, A., & Upshur, C. (1993). What do Latino children need to succeed in school? A study of four Boston public schools. In R. Rivera & S. Nieto (Eds.), *The education of Latino students in Massachusetts: Research and policy considerations* (pp. 127–146). Boston: Gastón Institute for Latino Public Policy and Development.

Del Valle, S. (1998). Bilingual education for Puerto Ricans in New York City: From hope to compromise. *Harvard Educational Review, 68*(2), 193–217.

Díaz Soto, L. (1997). *Language, culture, and power: Bilingual families and the struggle for quality education.* Albany: State University of New York Press.

Educational Testing Service. (2000). *NAEP trends in educational progress.* Princeton, NJ: Author.

Fantini, M., & Magat, R. (1970). *Community control and the urban school.* New York: Praeger.

Fernández, R. R., & Shu, G. (1988). School dropouts: New approaches to an enduring problem. *Education and Urban Society, 20*(4), 363–386.

Fernández, R. R., & Vélez, W. (1990). Who stays? Who leaves? Findings from the ASPIRA five cities high school dropout study. *Latino Studies Journal, 1*(3), 59–77.

Fishman, J. A., Cooper, R. L., & Ma, R. (Eds.). (1971). *Bilingualism in the barrio.* Bloomington: Indiana University Press.

Fitzpatrick, J. P. (1971). *Puerto Rican Americans: The meaning of migration to the mainland.* Englewood Cliffs, NJ: Prentice-Hall.

Fitzpatrick, J. P. (1987). *Puerto Rican Americans: The meaning of migration to the mainland* (2nd ed.). Englewood Cliffs, NJ: Prentice-Hall.

Flores-González, N. (2000). The structuring of extracurricular opportunities and Latino student retention. *Journal of Poverty, 4*(1 & 2), 85–108.

Flores-González, N. (2002). *School kids, street kids: Identity and high school completion among Latinos.* New York: Teachers College Press.

Fordham, S., & Ogbu, J. U. (1986). Black students' school success: Coping with the "burden of acting White." *Urban Review, 18*(3), 176–206.

Frau-Ramos, M., & Nieto, S. (1993). "I was an outsider": Dropping out among Puerto Rican youths in Holyoke, Massachusetts. In R. Rivera & S. Nieto (Eds.), *The education of Latino students in Massachusetts: Research and policy considerations* (pp. 147–169). Boston: Gastón Institute for Latino Public Policy and Development.

Fuentes, L. (1976). Community control did not fail in New York: It wasn't tried. *Phi Delta Kappan, 57*(10), 692–695.

Gallardo, J. M. (Ed.). (1970). *Proceedings of conference on education of Puerto Rican children on the mainland.* Santurce, PR: Puerto Rico Department of Education.

Gimenez, M. E. (1997). Latino/"Hispanic": Who needs a name? The case against a standardized terminology. In A. Darder, R. D. Torres, & H. Gutiérrez (Eds.), *Latinos and education: A critical reader* (pp. 225–238). New York: Routledge.

Gittell, M. (1972). Decentralization and citizen participation in education. *Public Administration Review, 32,* 670–686.

Glasser, R. (1997). *Aquí me quedo: Puerto Ricans in Connecticut.* Middletown, CT: Connecticut Humanities Council.

Hernández, C. D. (1997). *Puerto Rican voices in English: Interviews with writers.* Westport, CT: Praeger.

Hernández, J. L. (1992). Pura Teresa Belpré, storyteller and pioneer Puerto Rican librarian. *Library Quarterly, 62*(4), 425–440.

Hidalgo, N. M. (1998). Toward a definition of a Latino family research paradigm. *Qualitative Studies in Education, 11*(1), 103–120.

Hidalgo, N. M. (2000). Puerto Rican mothering strategies: The role of mothers and grandmothers in promoting school success. In S. Nieto (Ed.), *Puerto Rican students in U.S. schools* (pp. 167–196). Mahwah, NJ: Erlbaum.

Hirsch, E. D. (1987). *Cultural literacy: What every American needs to know.* Boston: Houghton Mifflin.

History Task Force, Centro de Estudios Puertorriqueños. (1979). *Labor migration under capitalism: The Puerto Rican experience.* New York: Monthly Review Press.

History Task Force, Centro de Estudios Puertorriqueños. (1982). *Sources for the study of Puerto Rican migration: 1879–1930.* New York: Centro de Estudios Puertorriqueños, Hunter College, City University of New York.

Iglesias, C. A. (1984). *Memoirs of Bernardo Vega.* New York: Monthly Review Press.

Jennings, J., & Chapman, F. (1996). Puerto Ricans and the community control movement in New York City's Lower East Side: An interview with Luis Fuentes. *Race Relations Abstracts, 21*(1), 25–40.

Jensen, A. R. (1969). How much can we boost I.Q. and scholastic achievement? *Harvard Educational Review, 39*(1), 1–123.

Keenan, J. W., Willett, J., & Solsken, J. (1993). Constructing an urban village: School/home collaboration in a multicultural classroom. *Language Arts, 70,* 56–66.

Koss, J. D. (1965). *Puerto Ricans in Philadelphia: Migration and accommodation.* Unpublished doctoral dissertation, University of Pennsylvania, Department of Anthropology.

La Fontaine, H., Colón, E., Hernández, M., Meléndez, G., Orta, A., Pagán, M., et al. (1973). Teaching Spanish to the native Spanish speaker. In J. W. Dodge (Ed.), *Sensitivity in the foreign-language classroom: Reports of the working committees* (pp. 63–86). Middlebury, VT: Northeast Conference on the Teaching of Foreign Languages.

Latino Commission on Educational Reform. (1992). *Toward a vision for the education of Latino students: Community voices, student voices. Interim report of the Latino Commission on Educational Reform* (2 vols.). Brooklyn: New York City Board of Education.

Latino Commission on Educational Reform. (1994). *Making the vision a reality: A Latino action agenda for educational reform. Final report of the Latino Commission on Educational Reform* (2 vols.). Brooklyn: New York City Board of Education.

Lau v. Nichols, 414 U.S. 563 (1974).

Lewis, O. (1965). *La vida: A Puerto Rican family in the culture of poverty, San Juan and New York.* New York: Vintage Books.

Margolis, R. J. (1968). *The losers: A report on Puerto Ricans and the public schools.* New York: ASPIRA.

Massachusetts State Advisory Committee to the U.S. Commission on Civil Rights. (1972). *Issues of concern to Puerto Ricans in Boston and Springfield.* Boston: U.S. Commission on Civil Rights.

Matos-Rodríguez, F. V., & Hernández, P. D. (2001). *Pioneros: Puerto Ricans in New York City, 1896–1948.* Charleston, SC: Arcadia.

Meier, K. J., & Stewart, J., Jr. (1991). *The politics of Hispanic education: Un paso pa'lante y dos pa'tras.* Albany: State University of New York Press.

Meléndez, E. (1991). *Los que se van, los que regresan: Puerto Rican migration to and from the United States, 1982–1988.* New York: Commonwealth of Puerto Rico, Department of Puerto Rican Community Affairs.

Mercado, C. I., & Moll, L. C. (2000). Student agency through collaborative research in Puerto Rican communities. In S. Nieto (Ed.), *Puerto Rican students in U.S. schools* (pp. 297–329). Mahwah, NJ: Erlbaum.

Mestre, J. P., & Royer, J. M. (1991). Cultural and linguistic influences on Latino testing. In G. S. Keller, J. R. Deneen, & R. J. Magallán (Eds.), *Assessment and access: Hispanics in higher education* (pp. 39–66). Albany: State University of New York Press.

Mills, C. W., Sr., & Goldsen, R. K. (1950). *The Puerto Rican journey: New York's newest migrants.* New York: Harper & Row.

Morales, M., & Tarr, E. R. (2000). Social action projects: Apprenticeships for change in school and community. In S. Nieto (Ed.), *Puerto Rican students in U.S. schools* (pp. 249–266). Mahwah, NJ: Erlbaum.

Morrison, J. C. (1958). *The Puerto Rican study, 1953–1957.* Brooklyn: New York City Board of Education.

Murguia, E. (1991). On Latino/Hispanic ethnic identity. *Latino Studies Journal, 2*(3), 8–18.

National Center for Education Statistics. (1993). *Dropout rates in the United States: 1993.* Washington, DC: U.S. Department of Education.

National Center for Education Statistics. (1997). *NAEP trends.* Washington, DC: U.S. Department of Education.

National Center for Education Statistics. (1998). *Dropout rates in the United States: 1998.* Washington, DC: U.S. Department of Education.

National Center for Education Statistics. (1999). *The condition of education.* Washington, DC: U.S. Department of Education.

National Commission on Excellence in Education. (1983). *A nation at risk: The imperative for educational reform.* Washington, DC: Government Printing Office.

National Commission on Secondary Education for Hispanics. (1984). *"Make something happen": Hispanics and urban school reform* (2 vols.). Washington, DC: Hispanic Policy Development Project.

National Council of Education Statistics. (1998). *Digest of education statistics.* Washington, DC: U.S. Department of Education.

National Council of La Raza. (1990). *Hispanic education: A statistical portrait, 1990.* Washington, DC: Author.

National Puerto Rican Task Force. (1982). *Toward a language policy for Puerto Ricans in the U.S.: An agenda for a community in movement.* New York: Centro de Estudios Puertorriqueños, Hunter College, City University of New York Research Foundation.

Negrón, A. (1971). *Americanization in Puerto Rico and the public school system, 1900–1930.* Río Piedras, PR: Editorial Edil.

Nieto, S. (1997). We have stories to tell: Puerto Ricans in children's books. In V. J. Harris (Ed.), *Using multiethnic literature in the K-8 classroom* (pp. 59–93). Norwood, MA: Christopher-Gordon.

Nieto, S. (1998). Fact and fiction: Stories of Puerto Ricans in U.S. schools. *Harvard Educational Review, 68*(2), 133–163.

Nieto, S. (Ed.) (2000a). *Puerto Rican students in U.S. schools.* Mahwah, NJ: Erlbaum.

Nieto, S. (2000b). Puerto Rican students in U.S. schools: A brief history. In S. Nieto (Ed.), *Puerto Rican students in U.S. schools* (pp. 5–37). Mahwah, NJ: Erlbaum.

Nieto, S., & Rolón, C. (1997). Preparation and professional development of teachers: A perspective from two Latinas. In J. J. Irvine (Ed.), *Critical knowledge for diverse teachers and learners* (pp. 93–128). Washington, DC: American Association of Colleges of Teacher Education.

Noddings, N. (1992). *The challenge to care in schools: An alternative approach to education.* New York: Teachers College Press.

Office of Civil Rights. (1975). *Task force findings specifying remedies for eliminating past educational practices ruled unlawful under Lau v. Nichols.* Washington, DC: Department of Education.

Office of the Mayor. (1968). *Puerto Ricans confront problems of the complex urban society: A design for change* (Community conference proceedings). New York: Author.

Ogbu, J. U. (1987). Variability in minority school performance: A problem in search of an explanation. *Anthropology and Education Quarterly, 18*(4), 312–334.

Orfield, G., Bachmeier, M. D., James, D. R., & Eitle, T. (1997). Deepening segregation in American public schools: A special report from the Harvard Project on School Desegregation. *Equity and Excellence in Education, 30*(20), 5–24.

Osuna, J. J. (1949). *A history of education in Puerto Rico.* Río Piedras, PR: Editorial de la Universidad de Puerto Rico.

Ovando, C. J., & Collier, V. P. (1998). *Bilingual and ESL classrooms: Teaching in multicultural contexts* (2nd ed.). Boston: McGraw-Hill.

Padilla, E. (1958). *Up from Puerto Rico.* New York: Columbia University Press.

Pantoja, A. (2002). *Memoir of a visionary: Antonia Pantoja.* Houston: Arte Público Press.

Pérez, S. M., & Salazar, D. de la Rosa (1997). Economic, labor force, and social implications of Latino educational and population trends. In A. Darder, R. D. Torres, & H. Gutiérrez (Eds.), *Latinos and education: A critical reader* (pp. 45–79). New York: Routledge.

Perry, W. (1998). Memorias de una vida de obra (Memories of a life of work): An interview with Antonia Pantoja. *Harvard Educational Review, 68*(2), 244–258.

President's Advisory Commission on Educational Excellence for Hispanic Americans. (1996). *Our nation on the faultline: Hispanic American education.* Washington, DC: White House Initiative on Hispanic Education. Available: www.ed.gov/offices/OIIA/Hispanic

President's Advisory Commission on Educational Excellence for Hispanic Americans. (2000). *Creating the will: Hispanics achieving educational excellence.* Washington, DC: White House Initiative on Hispanic Education. Available: www.ed.gov/offices/OIIA/Hispanic

Puerto Rican Forum. (1970). *A study of poverty conditions in the New York Puerto Rican community.* New York: Author.

Quality Education for Minorities Project. (1990). *Education that works: An action plan for the education of minorities.* Cambridge, MA: Author.

Ramos-Zayas, A. Y. (1998). Nationalist ideologies, neighborhood-based activism, and educational spaces in Puerto Rican Chicago. *Harvard Educational Review, 68*(2), 164–192.

Rand, C. (1958). *The Puerto Ricans.* New York: Oxford University Press.

Reissman, F. (1962). *The culturally deprived child.* New York: Harper & Row.

Reyes, L. O. (1988). *Su nombre es hoy.* New York: ASPIRA of New York.

Reyes, L. O. (2000). Educational leadership, educational change: A Puerto Rican perspective. In S. Nieto (Ed.), *Puerto Rican students in U.S. schools* (pp. 73–89). Mahwah, NJ: Erlbaum.

Reyes, P., Scribner, J. D., & Scribner, A. P. (1999). *Lessons from high-performing Hispanic schools: Creating learning communities.* New York: Teachers College Press.

Reyes, X. A. (2000). Return migrant students: Yankee go home? In S. Nieto (Ed.), *Puerto Rican students in U.S. schools* (pp. 39–67). Mahwah, NJ: Erlbaum.

Rivera, M. & Pedraza, P. (2000). The spirit of transformation: An education reform movement in a New York City Latino/a community. In S. Nieto (Ed.), *Puerto Rican students in U.S. schools* (pp. 223–243). Mahwah, NJ: Erlbaum.

Rivera, R., & Nieto, S. (Eds.). (1993). *The education of Latino students in Massachusetts: Research and policy considerations.* Boston: Gastón Institute for Latino Public Policy and Development.

Rivera-Batíz, F. L., & Santiago, C. E. (1996). *Island paradox: Puerto Rico in the 1990s.* New York: Russell Sage Foundation.

Rodríguez, C. E. (1991). *Puerto Ricans: Born in the U.S.A.* Boulder, CO: Westview Press.

Rodríguez, C. E. (2000). *Changing race: Latinos, the census, and the history of ethnicity in the United States.* New York: New York University Press.

Rodríguez, C. E., & Sánchez Korrol, V. (1996). *Historical perspectives on Puerto Rican survival in the United States.* Princeton, NJ: Markus Wiener.

Rolón, C. (2000). Puerto Rican female narratives about self, school, and success. In S. Nieto (Ed.), *Puerto Rican students in U.S. schools* (pp. 141–165). Mahwah, NJ: Erlbaum.

Rubinstein, A. T. (1970). *Schools against children: The case for community control.* New York: Monthly Review Press.

Ryan, W. (1972). *Blaming the victim.* New York: Vintage Books.

Sánchez, L. R. (1987). The flying bus. In A. Rodríguez de Laguna (Ed.), *Images and identities: The Puerto Rican in two world contexts* (pp. 17–25). New Brunswick, NJ: Transaction Books.

Sánchez, M. E., & Stevens-Arroyo, A. M. (Eds.). (1987). *Toward a renaissance of Puerto Rican studies: Ethnic and area studies in university education.* Highland Lakes, NJ: Atlantic Research and Publications.

Sánchez González, L. (2001). *Boricua literature: A literacy history of the Puerto Rican diaspora.* New York: New York University Press.

Sánchez Korrol, V. E. (1983). *From colonia to community: The history of Puerto Ricans in New York, 1917–1948.* Westport, CT: Greenwood Press.

Sánchez Korrol, V. (1996). Toward bilingual education: Puerto Rican women teachers in New York City schools, 1947–1967. In A. Ortiz (Ed.), *Puerto Rican women and work: Bridges intransnational labor* (pp. 82–104). Philadelphia: Temple University Press.

Santiago-Santiago, I. (1986). *ASPIRA v. Board of Education* revisited. *American Journal of Education, 95*(1), 149–199.

Sexton, P. C. (1965). *Spanish Harlem.* New York: Harper & Row.

Shanker, A. (1973, April 29). Where we stand. *New York Times,* p. E11.

Skutnabb-Kangas, T. (1988). Multilingualism and the education of minority children. In T. Skutnabb-Kangas & J. Cummins (Eds.), *Minority education: From shame to struggle* (pp. 9–44). Clevedon, England: Multilingual Matters.

Symposium on colonialism and working-class resistance: Puerto Rican education in the United States [Special issue]. (1998). *Harvard Educational Review, 68*(2).

Tapia, J. (1998). The schooling of Puerto Ricans: Philadelphia's most impoverished community. *Anthropology and Education Quarterly, 28*(3), 297–323.

Torres-Guzmán, M. E. (1992). Stories of hope in the midst of despair: Culturally responsive education for Latino students in an alternative high school in New York City. In M. Saravia-Shore & S. F. Arvizu (Eds.), *Cross-cultural literacy: Ethnographies of communication in multiethnic classrooms* (pp. 477–490). New York: Garland.

Torres-Guzmán, M. E., & Thorne, Y. M. (2000). Puerto Rican/Latino student voices: Stand and deliver. In S. Nieto (Ed.), *Puerto Rican students in U.S. schools* (pp. 269–291). Mahwah, NJ: Erlbaum.

U.S. Census Bureau. (2000). *Statistical abstract of the United States.* Washington, DC: U.S. Department of Commerce.

U.S. Commission on Civil Rights. (1976). *Puerto Ricans in the continental United States: An uncertain future.* Washington, DC: Author.

Valdivieso, R. (1986). *Must they wait another generation? Hispanics and secondary school reform.* New York: Columbia University, Teachers College, Institute for Urban and Minority Education, Clearinghouse on Urban Education.

Valdivieso, R., & Davis, C. (1988). *U.S. Hispanics: Challenging issues for the 1990s.* Washington, DC: Population Trends and Public Policy.

Valenzuela, A. (1999). *Subtractive schooling: U.S.-Mexican youth and the politics of caring.* Albany: State University of New York Press.

Walsh, C. E. (1991). *Pedagogy and the struggle for voice: Issues of language, power, and schooling for Puerto Ricans.* New York: Bergin & Garvey.

Walsh, C. E. (1998). "Staging encounter": The educational decline of U.S. Puerto Ricans in [post]-colonial perspective. *Harvard Educational Review, 68*(2), 218–243.

Walsh, C. E. (2000). The struggle of "imagined communities" in school: Identification, survival, and belonging for Puerto Ricans. In S. Nieto (Ed.), *Puerto Rican students in U.S. schools* (pp. 97–114). Mahwah, NJ: Erlbaum.

Wasserman, M. (1969, June). The I.S. 201 story: One observer's version. *Urban Review, 2,* 3–15.

Wehlage, G., & Rutter, R. (1986). Dropping out: How much do schools contribute to the problem? *Teachers College Record, 87*(3), 374–392.

Zanger, V. V. (1993). Academic costs of social marginalization: An analysis of Latino students' perceptions at a Boston high school. In R. Rivera & S. Nieto (Eds.), *The education of Latino students in Massachusetts: Research and policy considerations* (pp. 170–190). Boston: Gastón Institute for Latino Public Policy and Development.

Zavala, M. V. (2000). Puerto Rican identity: What's language got to do with it? In S. Nieto (Ed.), *Puerto Rican students in U.S. schools* (pp. 115–136). Mahwah, NJ: Erlbaum.

Zentella, A. C. (1997a). *Growing up bilingual: Puerto Rican children in New York.* Oxford, UK: Basil Blackwell.

Zentella, A. C. (1997b). Returned migration, language, and identity: Puerto Rican bilinguals in dos worlds/two mundos. In A. Darder, R. D. Torres, & H. Gutiérrez (Eds.), *Latinos and education: A critical reader* (pp. 302–318). New York: Routledge.

26

ASIAN PACIFIC AMERICAN STUDENTS

Challenging a Biased Educational System

Valerie Ooka Pang
San Diego State University

Peter N. Kiang
University of Massachusetts, Boston

Yoon K. Pak
University of Illinois, Champaign-Urbana

Too few educators are able to recognize and respond to the diversity of educational strengths and needs of Asian Pacific American (hereafter APA) students. To many teachers, counselors, and administrators, Asian Pacific American students are "model minorities" who seem to look and act alike. Educators should challenge a biased educational and social system that often labels APA children and their families as model minorities and/or perpetual foreigners (Suzuki, 2002). Asian Pacific American families have lived in what is now the continental United States since 1763, when Filipinos settled in Louisiana (Cordova, 1983).

Before turning to general discussion of the Asian Pacific American population, a word must be said about the label *Oriental*. Though this term is often used in education to identify students with Asian roots, its use in reference to U.S. citizens and residents ignores the negative connotations of an outgroup status of foreigners, and perhaps even of "yellow peril." The term *Oriental* may also generate Western imperialistic images of rugs and spices, rather than people. One of the historical uses of *Oriental* was devised as a way to distinguish from the *Occident*, to mark the former inferior and the latter superior (Said, 1979). Asian Pacific Americans have resided in the United States for over 200 years, some being able to trace their roots back over 10 generations. Soldiers from the Filipino American community fought in the War of 1812 (Cordova, 1983). "Asian Pacific American" or,

more inclusively, "Asian and Pacific Islander American" is the most appropriate term to describe groups with roots in Asia and the Pacific Islands.

Stereotypes about APA youth can place students at the margins of schools and restrict the opportunities and services APA students receive (Kiang, 2002; Pang & Cheng, 1998; Suzuki, 2002; Yu, Hwang, Schwalberg, Overpeck, & Kogan, 2002). For example, APA students are severely underrepresented in special education programs (See Chapter 34, this volume). Since the passage of Public Law 94–142 in 1975, the Education for All Handicapped Children Act, there has been a steady increase in students in other ethnic groups being served, while Asian Pacific American students are underserved (Watanabe, 1998). Watanabe writes that given the belief that abilities and disabilities are normally distributed, more APA students should be enrolled in special education programs. Parents may also adhere to stereotypical notions of achievement and these values may influence low representation of APA youth. APA parents may respond in a variety of ways when they find out their children need special services. They may demonstrate shock, guilt, denial, depression, fear, and withdrawal and this may result in shame, defensiveness, and the loss of self-esteem (Watanabe, 1998). The model minority myth so prevalent in society may affect parent and teacher expectations of students and contribute to their underrepresentation.

The model minority myth characterizes Asian Pacific Americans as quiet, obedient, and high achieving students with little need for teacher intervention, guidance, or support. Teachers may also stereotype students who have language needs as quiet and nonverbal because English Language Learners (ELLs) may be reticent to engage in conversation so that they will not embarrass themselves (Wong, 1987). If teachers stereotype Asian Pacific American students as shy, they may view the behavior of ELLs as cultural rather than resulting from their limited English proficiency. In fact, Yu and her colleagues (2002) found in their cross-national 1997–1998 World Health Organization Study of Behavior in School Children that Asian American adolescents in their sample who did not speak English at home or spoke two languages faced a higher risk of health, psychosocial, and school issues. Often this was due to parents' limited abilities to speak English and access social services. Language limitations often resulted in linguistic isolation for family members. However, many teachers and other social service professionals may be unaware of this context and view many APA students as members of model minority families.

The experiences of many APA students parallel what psychologist Steele (1999) refers to as "stereotype threat." The image of the model minority shapes the intellectual identity and expected performance of students. APA youth may internalize feelings of inadequacy if they score low on math texts, for example, since the prevailing notion expects Asian Pacific Americans to excel in math and science. Congruently, students may feel the pressure to excel in math- and science-related professions and this limits student interest and development in pursuing careers in other areas such as in the arts, humanities, and social sciences.

One of the most troubling factors in the marginalization of APA students is the use by academic scholars and policy makers of overgeneralizations to describe the academic performance of various Asian Pacific American youth without recognizing their ethnic and socioeconomic diversity (Suzuki, 2002). The use of aggregate data to describe APA educational achievement masks the realities of many students and creates cross-racial/cultural animosity between Asian Pacific American students and students from other underrepresented communities. The divisive pitting of students and families from different racial/ethnic groups against each other is a disturbing practice in the educational community.

The use of disaggregated data for APA populations, therefore, is essential. For example, according to the 1990 Census among Asian immigrants aged 16 and older, one out of four Filipinos and one out of five East Indians had undergraduate degrees, compared with one out of eleven Vietnamese, one out of forty Cambodians, and one out of 85 Hmong. Wide differences exist in the educational achievement among immigrant parents which, in turn, influence the human capital resources that are available to school-age students in various Asian Pacific American communities (Kiang, 2002). The President's Advisory Commission on Asian Americans and Pacific Islanders (2001) noted that in 1997, over 60% of the APA population was born outside of the United States. The Commission also stated more specifically in their report that though the general U.S. poverty rate for all Americans was 10%, Hmong Americans had a rate of 66%, Cambodians had a rate of 47%, Laotian Americans demonstrated a rate of 67%, and Vietnamese Americans were at a rate of 34%.

Decisions about educational policies or resource allocations should not be based solely upon quantitative measures such as test score performance or graduation rates, even if disaggregated. Such data certainly should inform educational policy and practice. However, educators should also consider the sociocultural and emotional needs of students that contribute to intellectual growth. The goal of this chapter is to provide readers with a comprehensive understanding of the diversity and complexities among Asian Pacific American students and to describe ways that educators can respond effectively to the needs of APA youth.

WHO ARE ASIAN PACIFIC AMERICANS?

Asian Pacific American students are members of diverse ethnic and cultural communities. They represent many cognitive strengths and weaknesses, may speak several different languages, have diverse cultural traditions, and include newly immigrated youth as well as those whose families have roots in the United States that date prior to 1776 (Cordova, 1983).

Asian Pacific Americans constitute a number of highly diverse ethnic groups, including those of Asian Indian, Cambodian, Chinese, Filipino, Guamanian/Chamorro, Hawaiian, Hmong, Indonesian, Japanese, Korean, Laotian, Pakistani, Samoan, Thai, Tibetan, and Vietnamese cultural heritages. In the U.S. 2000 census, other groups were also categorized (Table 26.1): Bangladeshi, Bhutanese, Burmese, Carolinian, Chuukese, Fijiian, Indo Chinese, Iwo Jiman, Kosraean, I-Kiribati, Malaysian, Maldivian, Malaysian, Mariana Islander, Marshallese, Melanesian, Micronesian, Nepalese, Okinawan, Palauan, Papua New Guinean, Pohnpeian, Polynesian, Saipanese, Sikkimese, Singaporean, Sri Lankan, Tahitian, Tokelauan, Tongan, Yapese, and other Pacific Islander (U.S. Census Bureau, 2000b, 2000c). Asian Pacific Americans as of the 2000 U.S. Census totaled 12,773,242 (U.S. Census Bureau, 2000b, 2000c).

TABLE 26.1. Asian Pacific Islander and Native Hawaiian (APINH) Population by Detailed Group: Census 2000.

Detailed Group	APINH Alone		APINH in Combination with One or More Other Races		
	One APINH Group Reported[1]	Two or More APINH Groups Reported[2]	One APINH Group Reported	Two or More APINH Groups Reported[2]	APINH Detailed Group Alone or in Any Combination[2]
Total	10,409,017	232,816	1,963,954	167,455	12,773,242
Asian Indian	1,678,765	40,013	165,437	15,384	1,899,599
Bangladeshi	41,280	5,625	9,655	852	57,412
Bhutanese	183	9	17	3	212
Burmese	13,159	1,461	1,837	263	16,720
Cambodian	171,937	11,832	20,830	1,453	206,052
Chinese, except Taiwanese	2,314,537	130,826	201,688	87,790	2,734,841
Filipino	1,850,314	57,811	385,236	71,454	2,364,815
Hmong	169,428	5,284	11,153	445	186,310
Indo Chinese	113	55	23	8	199
Indonesian	39,757	4,429	17,256	1,631	63,073
Iwo Jiman	15	3	60	—	78
Japanese	796,700	55,537	241,209	55,486	1,148,932
Korean	1,076,872	22,550	114,211	14,794	1,228,427
Laotian	168,707	10,396	17,914	1,186	198,203
Melanesian					
Fijian	9,796	169	3,461	155	13,581
Papua New Guinean	135	3	83	3	224
Solomon Islander	12	3	10	—	25
Ni-Vanuatu	6	1	7	4	18
Melanesian, not specified	147	15	149	4	315
Malaysian	10,690	4,339	2,837	700	18,566
Maldivian	27	2	22	—	51
Micronesian					
Guamanian or Chamorro	58,240	1,247	30,241	2,883	92,611
Mariana Islander	60	11	60	10	141
Saipanese	195	122	120	38	475
Palauan	2,228	102	1,004	135	3,469
Carolinian	91	40	30	12	173
Kosraean	157	11	51	7	226
Pohnpeian	486	77	116	21	700
Chuukese	367	50	220	17	654
Yapese	236	13	111	8	368
Marshallese	5,479	183	849	139	6,650
I-Kiribati	90	17	47	21	175
Micronesian, not specified	7,509	411	1,768	252	9,940
Nepalese	7,858	351	1,128	62	9,399
Okinawan	3,513	2,625	2,816	1,645	10,599
Pakistani	153,533	11,095	37,587	2,094	204,309
Polynesian					
Native Hawaiian	140,652	5,157	241,510	13,843	401,162
Samoan	91,029	5,727	28,287	8,238	133,281
Tongan	27,713	2,227	5,675	1,225	36,840
Tahitian	800	199	1,137	1,177	3,313
Tokelauan	129	142	134	169	574
Polynesian, not specified	3,497	1,547	3,005	747	8,796
Singaporean	1,437	580	307	70	2,394
Sri Lankan	20,145	1,219	2,966	257	24,587
Thai	112,989	7,929	27,170	2,195	150,283

| Detailed Group | APINH Alone | | APINH in Combination with One or More Other Races | | |
	One APINH Group Reported[1]	Two or More APINH Groups Reported[2]	One APINH Group Reported	Two or More APINH Groups Reported[2]	APINH Detailed Group Alone or in Any Combination[2]
Vietnamese	1,122,528	47,144	48,639	5,425	1,223,736
Other Asian, not specified[3]	146,870	19,576	195,449	7,535	369,430
Other, Pacific Islander	40,558	1,309	129,038	4,007	174,912

Notes: "—" represents zero.

[1]The total of 10,409,017 APINH respondents categorized as reporting only one APINH group in this table is lower than the total reported in the general census 2000 summary files for the Asian and Native Hawaiian and Other Pacific Islander populations. This table includes more detailed groups. This means that, for example, an individual who reported "Pakistani *and* Nepalese" is shown in this table as reporting two or more Asian groups. However, the same individual is categorized as reporting a single Asian group in general census 2000 summary file no. 1 because both Pakistani and Nepalese are part of the larger "other specified Asian group."

[2]The numbers by detailed APINH group do not add up to the total population. This is because the detailed APINH groups are tallies of the number of APINH responses rather than the number of APINH respondents. Respondents reporting several APINH groups are counted several times. For example, a respondent reporting "Korean and Filipino" would be included in the Korean as well as the Filipino numbers.

[3]Includes respondents who checked the "Other Asian" and "Other Pacific Islander" response categories on the census questionnaire or wrote in a generic term such as "Asian," "Asiatic," or "Pacific Islander."

Source: U.S. Census Bureau (2000b, 2000c). The census conducted separate tabulations for Asian and Native Hawaiian and Other Pacific Islander groups; the numbers are combined in this table.

The category for "Asian" in the 2000 U.S. census refers to people having origins in any of the original peoples of the Far East, Southeast Asia, or the Indian subcontinent. Unlike the 1990 census, the Native Hawaiian or Other Pacific Islander category is listed and analyzed separately from the Asian category and was not combined as an Asian Pacific/Pacific Islander total. However, when including Native Hawaiian, other Pacific Islanders, and multiracial Asians, the census 2000 data counted 12,773,242 Asian Pacific Americans, representing an increase of 73% from the 1990 census (U.S. Census Bureau, 2000b, 2000d). The APA population of 2000 constituted more than 4% of the total U.S. population (Youngberg, 2001). In the 2000 census, the proportion of individuals who indicated a multiracial Asian identity was 14% of the total Asian population, which was significantly higher than the proportion of multiracial Whites of 2.5% and Blacks of 5% (U.S. Census Bureau, 2000b, 2000d). Ong and Hee (1993) project that by the year 2020 the Asian Pacific American population will number 20.2 million.

The Asian Pacific American student population has grown dramatically since 1980. During the 1980s the number of Asian Pacific American students increased from approximately 900,000 to 1.7 million, almost doubling (Kiang & Lee, 1993). Day (1996) predicted that the number of APA children and young adults, ages 0–24, will increase by an additional 150% from 1990 to 2020. In states like California, New York, New Jersey, and Pennsylvania, the number of Asian Pacific school-age students grew at a rate of over 100% during the 1980s. In many local school districts, the magnitude of population growth has been even more dramatic. In Lowell, Massachusetts, for example, the influx from refugee secondary migration was so rapid during 1987 that between 35 and 50 new Cambodian and Laotian students entered the Lowell public schools each week (Kiang & Lee, 1993).

Midwest states such as Minnesota and Wisconsin have witnessed a dramatic increase of Hmong American residents (U.S. Census Bureau, 2000c). Neighboring states of Illinois, Michigan, and Iowa also reflect the growth trends of APA communities. Furthermore, growth is occurring outside of urban, metropolitan areas. In Illinois the largest increase in the APA population occurred outside the Chicago city limits. Currently DuPage County (outside Chicago) and Champaign County (which contains more rural farm towns as well as a flagship university) represent some of the geographic diversity in the resettlement patterns of APAs (U.S. Census Bureau, 2000a, 2000c). The challenges that face immigrant families and some of the resulting conflicts that occur between parents and offspring become heightened in places where there is a lack of community and social service support. Knowing how to access services or respond to discrimination, even in schools, has been a continuous struggle for many Southeast Asian residents in the Midwest, in part because of their isolation in the region (Lee, 1996).

An additional factor contributing to the increasing number and complexity of APA students is the adoption of Asian children by U.S. families (Chan, 1991). Tessler, Gamache, Liu, and Weber (1997) reported that 10,630 Chinese children had been adopted by U.S. families by 1997. Minneapolis-St. Paul is considered the center for Korean American adoption, with over 10,000 Korean adoptees in 2000. Issues of identity development and cultural awareness can become isolating in the lives of students who do not feel that they belong to either the Korean American community or mainstream culture. Such feelings also become problematic when they are one of few ethnic minority students in school and are asked or forced to "represent" Korean culture.

Multiracial and Multiethnic Realities

Asian multiracial students and families have been part of the Asian American population since the first Filipino immigrants made Louisiana their home in 1763 and wed outside their ethnic community (Cordova, 1983). In fact every year since 1989 more than 100,000 biracial children have been born in the United States (Wardle, 2000). The term *multiracial,* or *biracial,* refers to students whose parents are from differing racial groups. Table 26.2 presents first the total multiracial Asian population for the United States (U.S. Census Bureau, 2000a), when for the first time, the 2000 census allowed the option of selecting one or more race categories to indicate racial identities (Grieco & Cassidy, 2001). The second portion of the table presents mixed race numbers for Asian Pacific Americans (U.S. Census Bureau, 2000b, 2000d). (In 2000, a separate Pacific Islander category was included because some Pacific Islanders argued that their realities were more aligned with those of Native American and indigenous populations than others APAs.)

Resulting from and also in resistance to exclusion and anti-miscegenation laws, small numbers of multiracial Asian families have historic roots across several generations in the United States, including Sikh-Mexican families in the West (Leonard, 1992) and Chinese African Americans in the South (Loewen, 1988). Mixed race families and students also resulted from the military involvement of U.S. personnel in Japan, Korea, Vietnam, and the Philippines from 1945 to the present. For example, an increase in mixed-parentage students came about from the military involvement of U.S. soldiers in Korea from the beginning of the Korean War in 1950 until 1990. Many Korean women became wives of soldiers, and their children added to the increase of interracial children (Chan, 1991). Many Amerasian children and their mothers' families from Vietnam entered the United States under the Amerasian Homecoming Act of 1987, which allowed those born from 1962 through 1975 to be admitted to the country (Bass, 1996). Many mixed race students conceived during the Vietnam War were rejected both in Vietnam, because of their American roots, and in the United States, because of their Vietnamese background (Carlin & Sokoloff, 1985). In addition, many Asian Americans, particularly among Japanese and Filipino Americans, have married outside of their ethnic groups during the past 30 years (Lee & Yamanaka, 1990). Their children and their children's children also add significantly to the number of Asian Americans with multiple ethnic and racial roots.

Increasing numbers of multiethnic Asian Pacific Americans will continue. Of the over 12 million Asian Pacific Americans, 232,816 reported they were members of two or more Asian Pacific American groups (U.S. Census Bureau, 2000b, 2000d). Multiethnic Asian Pacific Americans must not only deal with common APA stereotypes in society, they must also manage a dual or integrated multiethnic identity. Along with their biethnic or multiethnic identification, they also must cope with societal forces to culturally assimilate.

The increased recognition of multiracial and multiethnic realities in U.S. society, especially among Asian Americans, are reflected in media portrayals of individual stars

TABLE 26.2. Multiracial Asian Pacific Islander and Native Hawaiian Populations for the United States, 2000.

Population	Number	Percentage
Asian American alone	10,242,998	86.0
Asian in combination with one or more other races	1,655,830	14.0
Asian and White	868,395	7.3
Asian and Native Hawaiian and other Pacific Islander	138,802	1.2
Asian and Black or African American	106,782	0.9
Asian and all other combinations	541,851	4.6
Asian alone or in combination with one or more races	11,898,828	100.0
Asian Pacific Islander and Native Hawaiian alone (APINH)	10,641,833	83.0
APINH in combination with one or more other races	2,131,409	17.0
APINH total	12,773,242	100.0

Sources: U.S. Census Bureau (2000a, 2000b). The census conducted separate tabulations for Asian and Native Hawaiian and Other Pacific Islander groups; the numbers are combined in this table.

like Tiger Woods, the golfer, and Kimora Lee Simmons, the designer, as well as a growing number of popular, artistic, and scholarly publications and Internet-based resources (Gaskins, 1999; Houston & Williams, 1997; Wardle, 2000; Williams-León & Nakashima, 2001; Worral & Ardeña, 2000). The needs, voices, and contributions of mixed race Asian Americans are becoming increasingly important to educators, not only because of their growing numbers, but also because their presence demands a deeper appreciation for how identities are constructed and situated in complex, and sometimes, contradictory ways. Developing such an awareness is healthy for and helpful to all student populations, and has important implications for curriculum development and teacher preparation, as well as intercultural/interracial relations in schools (Wardle, 2000). In a landmark anthology, psychologist Maria Root (1996) outlined a "Bill of Rights for Racially Mixed People" that is a clear set of guidelines for educators to embrace when working with multiracial students:

I have the right: not to justify my existence in this world; not to keep the races separate within me; not to be responsible for people's discomfort with my physical ambiguity; not to justify my ethnic legitimacy. *I have the right:* to identify myself differently than strangers expect me to identify; to identify myself differently than how my parents identify me; to identify myself differently than my brothers and sisters; to identify myself differently in different situations. *I have the right:* to create a vocabulary to communicate about being multiracial; to change my loyalties over my lifetime—and more than once; to have loyalties and identify with more than one group of people; to freely choose whom I befriend and love. (1996, pp. 3–14)

These guidelines should also assist educators in understanding the needs of multiethnic Asian Pacific Americans.

The Consequences of High-Stakes Assessment and Aggregate Data Collection

Reports on the academic achievement of Asian American students have typically labeled them as "whiz kids" because of their high test scores (Brand, 1987). This portrayal does not accurately reflect the actual achievement levels found across various groups within the APA population. Consequently, the high stakes testing movement hampers the ability of school officials to respond to the actual needs of APA youth.

In the early 1990s learner-centered approaches to assessment, such as portfolios of student work collected over time and exhibitions that demonstrate students' learning and application of knowledge in a variety of domains, signaled a hopeful phase of education reform. However, these approaches have been overturned in recent years by a coalition of governors, state legislatures, and business leaders who positioned high stakes standardized testing as both the ends and the means of demanding accountability for teaching and learning (Vinson, Gibson, & Ross, 2001). What makes these tests high stakes is their life-affecting decisions of student tracking, placement, and graduation, as well as teacher evaluation and school funding tied to test results. The evidence of test validity and reliability have rarely been provided for high stakes tests (U.S. Department of Education Office for Civil Rights, 1999).

In principle, the purpose of student assessment and evaluation is to identify areas of weakness that can be strengthened through the targeting of appropriate services and strategies. Once targeted, resources should be mobilized to enable all students to overcome identified weaknesses in order to achieve their full potential. In practice, assessment policies, particularly those based on standardized testing, have led to the inequitable distribution of educational resources, accompanied by the sorting and labeling of students, often according to race, socioeconomic status, gender, and English proficiency (First, Kellogg, Almeida, & Gray, 1991).

The unfair consequences of using aggregate data to describe Asian American educational achievement is nowhere more clear than in the widely cited report, *Reaching the Top,* by the College Board's National Task Force on Minority High Achievement (Miller, 1999). While calling for comprehensive, targeted support for African American, Latino, and Native American students from pre-K through higher education, the report also asserts that Whites and Asians are succeeding academically and, therefore, do not need comparable attention or interventions.

In a separate report also commissioned by the College Board's National Task Force on Minority High Achievement, however, Patricia Gándara (1999), a specialist in educational policy and Chicano student achievement, critically explains:

Data are not disaggregated by the College Board for Asian groups; indeed the College Board lumps all Asians with Pacific Islanders, and this obscures wide differences within the group. The typical standard deviation for SAT scores of Asian students is almost one fourth of a standard deviation larger than for whites and about one fifth of a standard deviation greater than for other minority groups, suggesting that some Asian students are performing much higher than others. (p. 9)

Massachusetts data support Gándara's analysis of SAT scores. For example, while White, African American, Puerto Rican, and American Indian students' SAT I math and Verbal scores in 1999 all have standard deviations of between 100 to 109, the standard deviations for Asian American students' math and verbal SAT scores are 132 and 138—the highest of all groups reported and nearly one third more variable than others (Miller, 1999). Clearly the Asian American sample is heterogeneous. In questioning the validity of using Asian American aggregate data, Gándara (1999) echoes other warnings that appear in every major study or literature review on Asian American educational issues produced during the past two decades (Kiang & Lee, 1993; Lee, 1996; Nakanishi & Nishida, 1995; Olsen, 1997; Pang & Cheng, 1998; Park & Chi, 1999; Suzuki, 1988; Trueba, Cheng, & Ima, 1993; Trueba, Jacobs, & Kirton, 1990; Weinberg, 1997). It is unfortunate that research of the scale and significance of the College Board's National Task Force could ignore such longstanding and clearly articulated concerns.

Ironically, while the discourse that compels high stakes testing is framed in terms of accountability, the policies and policy makers have been completely unaccountable to Asian American communities and other communities of color, for whom standardized testing continues to serve as a system of sorting and exclusion. Public policy commitments to high stakes testing in Massachusetts, for example, have led to the imposition of statewide testing at the 3rd, 4th, 8th, and 10th grades (Massachusetts Department of Education, 2000). Students must achieve passing scores at the 10th-grade level in order to receive a high school diploma. However, statewide results from the 1998 tests show 26% of Asian American 10th graders failing in English and 40% failing in math. Furthermore, Black and Latino students failed at twice those rates. The projected drop-out and force-out rates of high school age youth of color as a consequence of these assessment policies have grave implications for many other areas of public policy related to poverty, crime, and social services that K–12 policymakers have ignored or neglected (Uriarte & Chavez, 1999).

The Massachusetts case clearly shows why it is essential to disaggregate data for Asian American populations—a step that Massachusetts education officials have not taken. Aggregate Massachusetts Comprehensive Assessment System (MCAS) scores for Asian Americans statewide conceal the dramatic differences between urban and suburban school districts and the realities of the specific Asian American populations who reside within them. By examining MCAS scores in Table 26.3 from the 15 school districts in Massachusetts with the largest numbers of Asian American students, location can be used as a proxy for ethnicity, particularly for Southeast Asian American populations who are overwhelmingly concentrated (Cambodians in Lowell, Lynn, and Revere; Hmong in Fitchburg; Vietnamese in Boston, Springfield, and Worcester). In fact, it is exactly those same school districts where mean scaled scores show that Asian 10th-grade students are receiving failing scores (220). In contrast, other school districts with large numbers of Asian students (primarily Chinese and Indian) have mean scaled scores at the proficient level (240+). Using the MCAS as a graduation requirement clearly has a disparate impact on Southeast Asian American populations, though this is hidden when statewide aggregate Asian scores are reported.

TABLE 26.3. 1999 Massachusetts Comprehensive Assessment System Test, 10th-Grade Asian American Student Scaled MCAS Scores and Percentage of Failing Massachusetts School Districts with Greater Than 500 Asian American Students, 1999 MCAS Results for Asian Students.

	Asian Students		English		Math		Science/Technology	
City	Percentage	Number	Percentage Failing	Score	Percentage Failing	Score	Percentage Failing	Score
Boston	8.9	5,617	33	228	35	232	38	225
Brookline	17.0	1,021	4	246	17.7	246	4	241
Cambridge	9.9	722	32	232	38	232	43	227
Fall River	5.4	663	38	223	64	214	56	221
Fitchburg	10.8	652	48	219	80	211	57	218
Lexington	12.1	705	0	247	9	250	6	246
Lowell	31.3	5,098	52	219	69	215	60	217
Lynn	14.0	2,112	47	221	65	215	61	219
Malden	19.7	1,124	28	232	28	239	30	230
Newton	9.7	1,100	4	247	14	251	10	242
Quincy	22.1	2,011	26	232	34	229	26	230
Randolph	12.3	512	29	234	44	227	37	225
Revere	11.8	707	50	222	69	21	63	217
Springfield	2.1	554	48	220	54	219	47	222
Worcester	7.6	1,942	38	225	46	222	46	221

Notes: MCAS scaled score levels: advanced = 260–280, proficient = 240–259, needs improvement = 220–239, failing = 200–219.

Source: Massachusetts Department of Education (2000).

Fortunately, some disaggregated information is currently being gathered by a few school districts around the country. Their data clearly show that there are both successful and failing Asian Pacific American students and that it is critical for districts to gather disaggregated data. San Diego City Schools is one such district. Their data indicate the difference in academic performance of students from various Asian Pacific American groups. In the 1999–2000 school year, San Diego City Schools consisted of 140,744 students who were 37.2% Hispanic, 27.4% White, 16.6% African American, 2.8% Asian, 8.0% Filipino, 6.4 Indochinese, 1.0 Pacific Islander (total Asian Pacific Islander, 18.2%), and .6% Native Americans. Tables 26.4 and 26.5 show the performance of English-speaking students in the district on the Stanford Achievement Test. In 1998 the Indochinese American student score of 28.5% was similar to the African American score of 27.0% on the reading portion of the instrument. In both populations only a little more than one quarter of

the students scored at the 50th percentile or above on the Stanford Achievement Test 9. This is in comparison to 61.7% for the Asian score and 67.3% for White students. In contrast, only 33% of the Pacific Islander American students scored at or above the 50th percentile. APA students performed at a higher level on the language portion of the SAT 9 in comparison to the reading section, and the scores of the different groups greatly varied.

The data from the San Diego City School District demonstrate that disaggregated data must be used in order for school personnel to clearly identify the specific needs of APA youth. Though most organizations continue to use aggregated data, it is evident from detailed statistics that many Asian Pacific American students have academic needs. For example, the Admissions Testing Program of the College Board collected data for five years (1980–1985) on college-bound seniors (Ramist & Arbiter, 1986). The 1985 sample included the responses of 1,052,351 high school seniors. Among them were

TABLE 26.4. 1998–2000 SAT 9 Test Results in San Diego City Schools, All Students by Racial/Ethnic Group, with Percentage of Students Scoring at or Above the 50th Percentile in Reading.

	1998		1999		2000		
Racial/Ethnic Group	Number and Percentage		Number and Percentage		Number and Percentage		Change
African American	13,790	27.0	14,507	30.3	14,303	34.9	7.9
Asian	2,489	61.7	2,617	65.6	2,700	69.4	7.8
Filipino	7,956	53.0	8,134	55.3	8,275	59.5	6.5
Hispanic	26,943	21.0	29,980	23.3	32,120	26.4	5.3
Indochinese	6,550	28.5	6,605	33.4	6,286	38.7	10.2
Native American	563	58.6	606	58.9	576	64.2	5.6
Pacific Islander	873	33.0	902	37.8	947	42.9	9.9
White	25,724	67.3	26,507	69.7	26,040	73.6	6.3
Total	84,888	41.2	89,876	43.4	91,247	46.7	5.6

Source: San Diego School District (2001).

TABLE 26.5. 1998–2000 SAT 9 Test Results in San Diego City Schools, All Students by Racial/Ethnic Group, with Percentage of Students Scoring at or Above the 50th Percentile in Language.

	1998		1999		2000		
Racial/Ethnic Group	N	%	N	%	N	%	Change
African American	13,899	31.8	145,657	35.3	14,308	39.9	8.1
Asian	2,497	69.0	2,611	72.8	2,720	76.4	7.4
Filipino	7,956	62.9	8,154	66.6	8,290	70.3	7.4
Hispanic	27,395	27.0	30,208	30.2	32,205	33.8	6.8
Indochinese	6,622	40.2	6,613	46.7	6,282	51.2	11.0
Native American	563	60.0	604	61.8	574	65.9	5.8
Pacific Islander	873	41.9	914	45.0	963	49.5	7.6
White	25,781	69.6	26,502	72.2	26,004	75.2	5.6
Total	85,586	46.6	90,263	49.4	91,346	52.7	6.1

Source: San Diego School District (2001).

42,637 Asian Pacific American students, or 4% of all candidates, which was almost a 50% increase from the beginning of the study in 1980. The sample represented a broad spectrum of Asian communities. On the Scholastic Aptitude Test in 1985, the Asian Pacific American verbal mean score of 404 was below the national average of 431, but the mathematics mean of 518 was above the national average of 475. There was a significant decrease in the average verbal scores of Asian Pacific American students during the years 1976 through 1984. The most dramatic drop in mean scores of Asian Pacific students came in 1978, 1979, and 1982 school years, when their average scores were 396, 396, and 395, respectively. These scores may reflect the lower scores obtained by the large number of refugee students who entered U.S. schools speaking languages other than English during the first and second waves of migration from Southeast Asia.

The observed trend of Asian Pacific American students doing better in mathematics than in verbal areas has been reported in the past (Stodolsky & Lesser, 1967), but few researchers have identified specific strengths or weaknesses within these broad subject areas. However, the Admissions Testing Program did provide information about the SAT reading comprehension and vocabulary subscores (Ramist & Arbeiter, 1986). On the reading comprehension subscale, Asian Pacific Americans scored 40.7, in contrast with the White American mean of 44.9. On the vocabulary subscale, the scores were 40.4 for Asian Pacific Americans and 45.0 for White Americans.

Of the 1985 Asian Pacific American high school seniors who indicated that English was not their best language, the SAT verbal median score was a low 272; the median for APAs who reported English as being their best language was 434, still lower than the mean of 449 for White Americans. The large number of Asian Pacific American students who have migrated to the United States since the 1970s, many of whose families have home languages other than English, may account for these findings. Program development in both oral and written communication skills for Asian Pacific American students is an area that educators, policy makers, and researchers need to address. This need is perceived by Asian Pacific American seniors themselves. Even though 73% rated themselves high on mathematics abilities, only 56% rated themselves high on oral expression, in comparison with 64% for all students (Ramist & Arbeiter, 1986). Some Asian Pacific American students seem to have "communication anxiety," they reveal a fear of writing and speaking. Such apprehension in itself may cause students to select technical and scientific fields of study. This suggests that teachers and districts should be systematically targeting programs for APA students to develop writing and other communication skills as forms of "stereotype threat" may occur (Steele, 1999).

The high stakes testing movement and the use of aggregate data are serious obstacles to equal educational opportunity. For APA students the standardized testing movement assumes the existence of a body of knowledge that must be learned by all students. Dewey clearly wrote that subject-matter knowledge is not fixed nor should it be disconnected from the lives of students as standardized tests present (Vinson, Gibson, & Ross, 2001). Testing also dehumanizes the learning process. Students are placed under severe anxiety and stress to perform. Since many Asian Pacific American students exhibit high levels of test anxiety (Pang, 1991), this anxiety can exacerbate the pressures students feel to excel in order to please their parents and teachers and lead to mental health problems. These pressures are compounded when in states like Massachusetts graduation from high school may depend on the performance of APA students on tests which are culturally and linguistically biased.

One of the most disturbing aspects of testing is its use as a tool of oppression that serves to pit one group against another for resources and services. This has been a continual and constant national problem (Pang & Cheng, 1998). Aggregate test scores do not serve the needs of APA youth and overgeneralized scores are used to denigrate the performance of students from other ethnic communities. This often promotes conflicts between students of various racial and ethnic communities.

Given that one of the most pressing needs of APA youth is language development, the following section presents historical information regarding the leadership roles Asian Americans have played in demanding and sustaining bilingual education.

Bilingual Education and Language Needs

Asian Pacific American students bring a wide range of languages to schools that should be considered as assets (Wong, 1987). More than half of all Asian Pacific American students come to school with a home language other than English (Trueba et al., 1993). The first language of Asian Pacific American students may be one of the following: Burmese, Cantonese, Chamorro, English, Farsi, Fijian, Hawaiian, Hindi, Hmong, Indonesian, Japanese, Khmer, Korean, Lao, Mandarin, Polynesian, Samoan, Tagalog, Thai, Urdu, or Vietnamese. These languages are extremely diverse and come from five broad language roots: Sino-Tibetan, Altaic, Malayo-Polynesian, Austro-Asiatic, and Indo-European (Cheng, 1991). The immigration and resettlement of various APA populations in the past thirty years reveal that more suburban and rural parts of the United States are witnessing changing student profiles. Between 1980 and 1990, sharp increases in Asian language speakers emerged among Koreans (135%), Chinese (109%), Filipinos (90%), Vietnamese (160%), and Japanese (27%; Waggoner, 1993). For example, the Martin Luther King, Jr. Elementary School in Urbana, Illinois has students from over 50 different countries who speak more than 40 languages a majority of whom are APA students (for more information about this school, see www.cmi.k12.us/Urbana/king/). King elementary is representative of the rich diversity schools are experiencing and suggests the range of knowledge on which teachers and administrators need to draw daily.

In many immigrant families, a power reversal occurs between immigrant parents and their U.S.-born or -educated children (Shoho, 1990). In many cases immigrant parents must rely on their children to interpret and communicate information between home and school. In this situation, students' status is heightened in the communication process. The child is able to filter messages between home and school, allowing the meaning of messages to be distorted.

Language issues affecting Asian Pacific Americans have a long history in the United States. Prior to the landmark 1974 Supreme Court case *Lau* v. *Nichols,* many schools implemented English-only programs in order to assimilate immigrant students and to instill cultural domination (Spring, 2001). For APA students, in particular, English-only instruction was often symptomatic of larger sociopolitical factors stemming from race prejudice (Tamura, 1993). Where greater fear arose, local communities fought for segregated schooling. Early 20th-century fears of the "yellow peril" and subsequent concerns over "race-mixing" in the public schools of California and beyond extended the practice of segregated schooling with "separate but equal" facilities first enacted through the 1896 case of *Plessy* v. *Ferguson* (Takaki, 1989). The present-day issues of recognizing language and culture with the need for bilingual instruction results in part from the Asian American pioneers who resisted segregated schooling.

In San Francisco, the 1885 Supreme Court case, *Tape* v. *Hurley,* and *Aoki* v. *Deane,* which resulted in the 1907 "Gentlemen's Agreement" that restricted the migration of Japanese laborers to the U.S. mainland, contested policies and beliefs which held that American students of Asian ancestry had no legal right to attend regular public schools in the United States (Wollenberg, 1995). The Chinese and Japanese immigrant parents argued that as taxpayers and as guaranteed under the Fourteenth Amendment, their children had the right to attend public schools with White students. Even in Mississippi, Gong Lum, the father of Martha Lum, fought on his daughter's behalf in 1927 for her to attend the local White public school [*Gong Lum* v. *Rice,* 275 U.S. 78 (1927)]. While these court cases primarily addressed arguments of school segregation, they were also directly tied to racial prejudice and fears of the presence of Asian languages in schools. As Asian American students and their families

demanded to be included in public schools, their growing presence from the early 20th century to the present made it necessary for school officials to address diverse linguistic needs.

English-only movements and the 100% Americanization of immigrants in the early decades of the 20th century were advocated by nativist and political groups to inculcate a narrow view of Americanism and "political fundamentalism" in schools (Tyack & Thomas, 1987). Students were often teased by teachers and peers for speaking English with an accent and were often forced to Anglicize their names (Cohen & Mohl, 1979; Paik Lee, 1990). De facto and de jure segregation served to filter out the "negative" or "undesirable" elements of society. Later progressive educators emerged who began to recognize the connections between students' cultural and linguistic backgrounds and democratic relationships (Pak, 2002). But in communities where ethnic language schools were operating apart from regular day schools, many questioned what they perceived to be the promotion of divided loyalties. This became especially difficult for Japanese language schools in the aftermath of Japan's attack on Pearl Harbor.

Japanese language schools along the West Coast were established by *Issei,* immigrant Japanese parents, concerned with the language gulf between themselves and their more English-speaking *Nisei,* second-generation students. While their initial purpose was to prepare offspring for formal education in Japan, *Issei* parents soon realized that the United States was their children's home. The main purpose of Japanese language schools then shifted to affirm *Nisei* identities within the United States (Ichioka, 1988; Pak, 2002; Tamura, 1994). Although many White community members feared that Japanese language schools promoted loyalties to the Japanese emperor, most attendees of language schools only learned the rudiments of the Japanese alphabet and viewed these schools primarily as a social gathering place consistent with Americanization and acculturation (Miyamoto, 1939; Shoho, 1993).

In 1970 a class action suit, brought by Kinney Lau and 11 other Chinese American students against Alan Nichols and the San Francisco Board of Education, further asserted the language needs of Asian students in public schools (Kiang & Lee, 1993). This suit led to the historic 1974 *Lau* v. *Nichols* Supreme Court decision that ruled that all students are entitled to an equal education. The San Francisco School Board argued that the district was providing equal education because the instruction, materials, and teachers were the same for all students. The Chinese American community argued that equal education was not possible in a classroom where students were Cantonese-speaking and instruction was in English. The Supreme Court ruled that the students were not receiving equal treatment. This decision provided the foundation for the nation's bilingual education mandates. The court unanimously concluded in 1974 (cited in Wang, 1980) that "there is no equality of treatment merely by providing students with the same facilities, textbooks, teachers, and curriculum; for students who do not understand English are effectively foreclosed from any meaningful education" (p. 186).

Like *Brown* v. *Board of Education,* the Supreme Court's decision in the *Lau* case fundamentally reformed U.S. educational policy. Because of the leadership of Chinese American students and parents, the educational rights of limited-English speaking students of all nationalities were formally recognized and protected. Educators should recognize the importance of providing APA English language learners (ELLs) with a comprehensive approach toward language learning (Cheng, 1998; Fung, 1998; Wong, 1987). Students are often bombarded with complex and conflicting social messages because of friction with mainstream cultural values, trauma from family, refugee camp experiences, and lack of social networks. Learning English involves both affective and cognitive development. The ability of students to learn English matures as they more fully understand and make adjustments to new social contexts and when literacy development is nurtured in their native language.

Thomas and Collier (1997) studied ten years of data collected from schools across the United States and found that developmental bilingual education programs are the most effective program model for English language learners. Long-term programs are the most lasting for bilingual learners and should be at least 3 to 5 years in length. They also studied more than 3,500 immigrant students in English as a Second Language classes, of which over 65% were Asian and 20% were Hispanic, and found that students from ages 8 to 11 who were taught in their home language for 2 to 5 years took 5 to 7 years to develop academic or more conceptual language. For immigrant students in the study who began school before the age of 8 and did not receive instruction in their home language, their academic language skills took 7 to 10 years to develop. Thomas and Collier wrote, "The only difference between the two groups was that the younger children had received little or no formal schooling in their first language (L1), and this factor appeared to be a significant predictor" (p. 33). Their research reinforced the importance of developmental and two-way bilingual education programs for Asian Pacific American students. However, two-way bilingual education programs are more difficult for schools with Asian populations to fund because APA students use multiple languages while Latino populations from various countries and cultures share the Spanish language.

Federal mandates and an enormous body of research demonstrate how various bilingual program strategies are effective and appropriate in promoting cognitive development and academic achievement among English language learners (Hakuta & Pease-Alvarez, 1992; McKay & Wong, 1988; Ramirez, 1991). However, the ideological attacks on bilingual education have succeeded through well-funded ballot initiatives in eliminating or severely undermining the opportunities for students to learn or maintain any languages other than English in numerous states throughout the United States (Crawford, 1992).

The elimination of bilingual instruction and support run directly counter to the findings of the U.S. Commission on Civil Rights (1992), which, in its review of educational programs provided for Asian American English language learners, concluded:

Many Asian American immigrant children, particularly those who are limited English proficient (LEP), are deprived of equal access to educational opportunity. These children need to overcome both language and cultural barriers before they can participate meaningfully in the educational programs offered in public schools. . . . Our investigation has revealed that these needs of Asian American LEP students are being drastically underserved. In particular, there is a dire national shortage of trained bilingual/ESL teachers and counselors. (pp. 193–194)

Other studies indicate that some school districts have responded to the needs of Asian immigrant students by incorrectly classifying them as learning disabled instead of providing them with appropriate bilingual instruction as required by law (National Education Association, 1987). School research reveals similar findings. For example, ethnographers Trueba, Jacobs, and Kirton (1990), in their study of Hmong elementary school students, observe: "Illiteracy in English continues to be the most frequently recorded reason for classifying minority students as 'learning disabled'" (p. 11). At the same time, immigrant students, particularly from low SES backgrounds, are also being denied federally mandated Chapter 1 compensatory education services, according to a June 1992 report from the U.S. Department of Education (Schmidt, 1992).

As numbers of U.S.-born students with immigrant parents continue to increase significantly in the coming years, one of the most important dynamics affecting the experiences of Asian American students in school is the intergenerational relationship with their families and their struggle to bridge the often conflicting worlds of home and school. Findings from the National Education Longitudinal Study of 1988 (NELS:88) database, which surveyed 1,505 Asian Pacific eighth-graders in a sample of 25,000 eighth-graders in 1,000 public and private schools, are instructive (National Center for Education Statistics, 1992). Roughly 52% of the NELS:88 Asian sample were U.S.-born and 48% were foreign-born. Disaggregated by ethnicity, the sample included 20% Filipinos,

17% Chinese, 13% Southeast Asians, 11% Korean, 9% Pacific Islanders, 9% South Asians, 6% Japanese, and 15% others. Nearly three out of four students in the sample came from bilingual households, although only 12% indicated a high proficiency in their home language.

Several important findings correlated with socioeconomic status are revealed by the NELS:88 study. Socioeconomic status (SES) was associated with English proficiency and with reading and math performance levels. Of the Asian students from bilingual homes, for example, 78% of the high SES students had a high English proficiency compared to 50% of low SES students. Moreover, nearly 40% of the low SES students failed to achieve basic performance levels for both reading and math compared with less than 15% of the high SES students. In addition, when SES was controlled, students with low English proficiency were less confident about graduating from high school compared to those with greater proficiency (60% versus 83%). Confidence levels differed by ethnic group as well. For example, 86% of South Asians, 72% of Filipinos, and 67% of Pacific Islanders were sure about graduating from high school (National Center for Education Statistics, 1992).

Furthermore, even though three-fourths of the Asian student population came from bilingual families, nearly 60% indicated that they have low proficiency in their home language compared to 66% who have high proficiency in English. Interestingly, only 6% of those students from bilingual families reported attending a bilingual program of instruction during their first two years of school in the U.S. And, although the study noted that 73% of the Asian students came from bilingual homes, only 27% were identified as such by at least one of their teachers—suggesting that many linguistic and cultural issues faced by students in moving between their dual worlds of home/family and school are not recognized or addressed.

This is cause for concern, given detailed findings by Wong Fillmore (1991b) and colleagues in a landmark study providing evidence that as language minority students learn English in the U.S., they lose their native language and, by extension, their culture—the younger the age, the greater the effect—due to the dominant status of English in early childhood education programs and the larger society. Wong Fillmore clearly shows that as the home language and culture are lost in the process of acquiring English, family relations erode. The following example reported by Wong Fillmore (1991a) may well represent the future of inter-generational relations projected for many Asian American families with immigrant parents and American-born students:

An interviewer told the story of a Korean immigrant family in which the children had all but lost the ability to speak their native language after just a few years in American schools. The parents could speak English only with difficulty, and the grandmother who lived with the family could neither speak nor understand it. She felt isolated and unappreciated by her grandchildren. The adults spoke to the children exclusively in Korean. They refused to believe that the children could not understand them. They interpreted the children's unresponsiveness as disrespect and rejection. It was only when the interviewer, a bilingual Korean-English speaker, tried to question the children in both languages that the parents finally realized that the children were no longer able to speak or understand Korean. The father wept as he spoke of not being able to talk to his children. One of the children commented that she did not understand why her parents always seemed to be angry. (p. 2)

It is ironic that the strengths and cultural values of family support that are so often praised as explanations for the academic achievement of Asian American students are severely undercut by the lack of programmatic and policy support for broad-based bilingual instruction and native language development, particularly in early childhood education. The unfortunate cost of such policies is the sacrifice of substantive communication and meaningful relationships across generations within many Asian American families and the squandering of linguistic and cultural resources within the United States.

Knowing the Historical Roots of APA Communities: The Example of Korean Americans

Each APA community has its own historical roots. For example, many teachers are not aware of the role of Christian churches in the history of Korean immigration and their influence on the belief systems of Korean American youth. The first wave of Korean immigration occurred around the turn of the 20th century between 1903 and 1907 and the second after the 1965 immigration act (Chan, 1991; Patterson & Kim, 1992; Takaki, 1989). The first group of Korean settlers were political exiles who fled their native country. A sizable community developed first in Hawaii and then in southern California. Their early adjustment period in the United States was also tied to activist work on behalf of Korean liberation from Japan.

Christian churches assisted in coordination efforts to maintain ties to Korea in the fight for independence. Early Korean immigrants felt a strong sense of nationalism and pride in their home country in light of the political turmoil that plagued Korea for much of the 20th century. The strong feelings of transnationalism that many Korean Americans feel today have direct connections to the history of Korean nationalist struggle. Recent immigrants felt first-hand the effects of Japanese colonialism, Chinese communism in North Korea, and the subsequent effects of the Korean War. Many Korean Americans recall the times of intense uncertainty and being uprooted from their homes with vivid descriptions. Such oral accounts told by elder Koreans have been passed down to the younger generations (Kim, 1980). Consequently residual feelings of animosity toward Japan and China have also been passed through the generations. And those sentiments have been internalized by a number of younger generations of Korean American youth. Hence many Korean Americans may identify as "Korean" rather than as "Korean American" or "Asian American." The nationalist ties to Korea thus reflect the history of struggle experienced by family members and the feeling of expressing pride in one's ethnicity and culture over a tradition of domination and oppression. While it is important to recognize the history of Korea and the Korean American struggle and to understand the context of nationalist sentiments, it is also important to teach the younger generation of Korean Americans the importance of developing a more pan-Asian American identity. Similar patterns of intergenerational and transnational relationships can be identified with other APA populations.

Self-Concept and Mental Health Issues

To many U.S. educators, Asian Pacific American students appear to have fewer and less severe personal problems than other students. Though teachers are often aware of language needs of Southeast Asian American students, educators may not be aware of their emotional and social needs. It is sometimes easier for educators to identify language proficiency problems, but more difficult for them to identify students' internal conflicts such as acculturative stress, posttraumatic stress disorder (PTSD), or depression (Chun & Sue, 1998). In addition, research indicates that Asian Pacific Americans underuse mental health care delivery systems (Sue, Fujino, Hu, Takeuchi, & Zane, 1991).

Though there is limited research on the mental health needs of Asian Pacific American students, several issues arise from what is known (Chun & Sue, 1998). Some Asian Pacific American students have a higher incidence of depression than their European American peers. For example, parents of Chinese American young males reported them to be more withdrawn (L. Chang, Morrissey, & Koplewicz, 1995). These young people demonstrated more interpersonal conflict and insecurities regarding their social capabilities. A survey conducted by the Federal Center for Disease Control and Prevention points to the need for more attention to the mental health needs of Filipino American students (Lau, 1995). In 1993, a random sample of 1,788 high school students completed a survey in the San Diego Unified School District. More Filipino American females indicated that they had seriously considered attempting suicide within the past 12 months of the survey than any other group (Pang, 1998). In this study 45.6% of the Filipino American women who filled out the survey had seriously

considered suicide; this compared with 33.4% among Hispanic females, 26.2% among Caucasian and 25.3% among Black females. In addition, 39.2% of the Filipino females had made plans about how they would attempt suicide and 23.3% had attempted suicide. These numbers were higher than any other group (Lau, 1995). The medical examiner's office in San Diego reported that six Filipino males under 19 years of age had committed suicide in the past five years, in comparison to one Filipina during the same time period. The data signaled a serious and complicated issue. Though more females indicated they had thought about suicide and attempted it, more males completed suicide.

The results of the survey deeply disturbed members of the Filipino American community and school personnel. Filipino American counselors indicated that the findings of the survey reinforced their beliefs that Filipino American adolescents are uncertain about how to cope with cultural conflicts and social pressures to assimilate. Parents realized that by working two to three jobs, they were providing a middle-class living for their children, but they were not home to direct and guide them. Villa (personal communication, March 31, 1995) pointed out that many Filipino immigrant parents operated at a survival mode level and believed it was necessary for them to work as hard as possible to provide their children with opportunities they did not have in the Philippines (D. Villa, interview, San Diego, 1995).

Other groups within the Asian Pacific American communities also have mental health needs that are important for educators and health professionals to consider. Many Southeast Asian refugee and immigrant parents have experienced severe and multiple trauma due to war in their homelands, dangerous escapes, lengthy stays in refugee camps, and poverty as well as racial violence following resettlement in the United States (Chun & Sue, 1998; Nidorf, 1998). Second-generation effects of posttraumatic stress are now being documented (Ko, 2001).

Another challenge for Asian Pacific American students is identity development. This issue is especially important during adolescence when a child develops a sense of who he or she is, separate and independent from his or her family. Identity development can be confusing for youth who come from collective societies where individualism is strongly discouraged and independence is allowed outside of the family and not within it (Chun & Sue, 1998). Students must also deal with the stressors of racism and conflicting cultural messages communicated by media images as well as teacher expectations of Asian Pacific Americans (Pang, Colvin, Tran, & Barba, 1992). Asian Pacific Americans are "nerds" who raise the grading curve, not football stars or cheerleaders. Students who do well must cope with this social image. Yet they often come from families in which education is highly valued. Many

Asian Pacific parents will sacrifice material comfort in order to provide the best educational experience for their children (Mordkowitz & Ginsburg, 1986). Some parents expect not only "good grades," but exceptionally high grades from their offspring (Pang, 1991). Thus, students who feel pressure from their families must deal simultaneously with possible rejection from their peers.

On the other hand, there are Asian Pacific American students who are not intellectually gifted and cannot reach the high academic standards that parents or teachers assume and expect. These students have a difficult time dealing with negative feelings of being a "loser." One *sansei* (third-generation Japanese American) high school student said about himself, "My folks just gave up on me because I didn't get into college." Unfortunately, this message was reiterated by his teacher, who told the student, "Your sister was an A student. How come you only get C's? You're not trying" (Pang & Cheng, 1998). The model minority image can be a liability for students who are not academically inclined, especially when teachers assume that students from certain Asian Pacific American groups will be top achievers. Mixed messages regarding their status in school and mainstream society can be frustrating and burdensome.

The impact of both sociocultural and racial marginalization can also have a forceful effect on the developing self-image of students. The findings from several studies investigating the self-concept of Asian Pacific American youth reveal a disturbing pattern of generally lower levels of self-esteem than students from other groups. For example, Tidwell (1980) found that Asian American students had lower levels of self concept than their Caucasian and African American peers. Oanh and Michael (1977) found that Vietnamese American students scored lowest on overall self-concept in comparison to non-Vietnamese Asian, Caucasian, African American, and Mexican American students. Similarly, T. Chang (1975) and Fox and Jordan (1973) reported that Korean American and Chinese American students did not feel as positive about their physical self-image as African American or White American students. Pang, Mizokawa, Morishima and Olstad (1985) studied the general self-concept of Japanese American students in the 4th through 5th grades and found that lower physical self-concept scores were offset by high academic self-image scores, making the aggregate scores more problematic to interpret. These findings may be surprising to many educators who believe that Asian Pacific Americans are well-adjusted, competent students. Such studies point to the need for schools, colleges, and universities to take steps to help Asian Pacific American students develop more positive perceptions of themselves.

The self-concept of many students is tied to their achievement in schools. Pang (1991) found that the level of parental support felt by middle school students of Chinese, Filipino, Korean, and East Indian heritages was predictive of mathematics grades. However, these students were also more test anxious than their White American counterparts because of their desire to please their parents. The side effect of high parental expectations and students' need for parental approval may be achievement and test anxiety. In comparison with their White American peers, Asian Pacific American students report more support and encouragement from their parents. Asian Pacific American parents, more than their White American counterparts, believe that their children try to please them. The socialization of Asian Pacific American students, then, follows a complex interpersonal process that transforms into an intrapersonal one (Cole, John-Steiner, Scribner, & Souberman, 1978). The quest for approval through doing well becomes internalized, though students are typically unaware of the process. Moreover, it may be that the support felt by Asian Pacific American students helps them to diffuse, to an extent, the pressure of high parental academic expectations (Pang, 1991).

Impact of Prejudice

Ethnic and racial prejudice can be powerful influences in the development of self-concept, racial identity, and social skills. Asian Pacific American students report frustrating experiences in dealing with prejudicial attitudes and remarks. For example, after the terrorist attacks against the Pentagon and the World Trade Center on September 11, 2001, reports throughout the United States in cities such as New York and Los Angeles have documented cases of harassment of South Asian American students and families, particularly Asian Indians, Sikhs, and Pakistanis, who have been swept into the racist backlash against Arab Americans, Arabs, and Muslims (Goodstein & Lewin, 2001; Reyes, 2002).

Racism is also documented historically and across all Asian Pacific American communities. For instance, Kim (1980) found 30% of the Korean American students she studied reporting discrimination at school in the form of harassment or name calling. Such incidents involved not only other students but also some school personnel. She recounted an incident in which a 5-year-old boy said, "They [his classmates] call me Chinese!" Apparently this child was hurt because he was singled out for his difference in physical appearance. In addition, many Asian Pacific American students who are not Chinese resent being automatically identified as a member of this group. Often people use the category of Chinese as a generic Asian label because they do not know how many different groups exist in the Asian Pacific American community. This plays into the stereotype that all Asians look the same. When others do not understand the diversity of

APA groups, students may feel frustrated and disturbed when they are labeled inappropriately. Matute-Bianchi (1986) reported similar concerns expressed by Japanese American high school students in central California. Many were upset because of the perceived image their peers had of Japanese Americans. As a ninth grader said: "They [the school community] think we're all smart and quiet. We're not, but they think we are." Another student indicated that Japanese-American "students have a reputation for being really good in science and math." And another student said he was not particularly "good" in math but "the teacher expected me to do good in it" (p. 247).

To more fully understand the experiences of Southeast Asian American students in the San Diego city schools in California, the district surveyed 521 junior high students and found strong resentment against Southeast Asian Americans (Rumbaut & Ima, 1988). Approximately 30% of the nonrefugee students made disturbing remarks such as: "Get rid of the Cambodians"; "I think the Blacks and Whites get along great but it's the Vietnamese we can't stand"; "Move some Nips to other schools" (p. 59). Bigotry against Asian Pacific Americans has resulted in the death of students. In 1987 in Lowell, Massachusetts, during a period of community unrest surrounding busing and anti-immigration sentiment, an 11-year-old White male beat up Vandy Phorng, a 13-year-old Cambodian student. Phorng was pushed into a canal, where he drowned (Kiang, 1990). In January 1989 in Stockton, California, a White male shot and killed five Southeast Asian American students at Cleveland School (Kiang, 1990). The violence against Asian Pacific American students is a shocking expression of the prejudice that exists in American society. It is also tragic, given that many parents left their home countries to escape violence.

Southeast Asian American students in San Diego and Boston provided recommendations for improving intercultural relationships (Rumbaut & Ima, 1988; Kiang & Kaplan, 1994). They wanted school staff to do something about, among other things, the name calling, as it often escalated into physical violence between Vietnamese and nonrefugee students. Cambodian American students were greatly offended by derogatory remarks that abusers considered to be casual statements. In addition, several Southeast Asian American youth felt teachers, who were biased against them, made negative statements about Vietnam or punished them unfairly. The biases expressed in school experiences can greatly affect the emerging bicultural identity of Asian Pacific American youth. Educators need to understand the choices and dilemmas such students face in the cultural assimilation process, and to help them to develop the personal confidence and coping skills needed to deal with the ethnic discrimination they will most likely encounter. Students may withdraw from the school community or fight back, verbally or physically, if they feel powerless to deal with prejudicial situations (Kiang, 1994).

Commitments to Youth Development

With the doubling of the school-age population of Asian Pacific Americans during the 1990s, the unmet needs of APA youth have escalated in schools and communities throughout the United States. In most settings, adults with professional responsibilities for supporting APA students, including teachers, counselors, and administrators, do not share their ethnic, linguistic, and racial backgrounds. Constrained by limited resources, an increasingly hostile, anti-immigrant climate, and their own stereotypical assumptions that often reflect popular media images which portray APA young people either as hardworking over-achievers or as violent gangbangers, many educators and adult professionals have been unable to respond effectively to the full range of academic, social, and personal challenges that face growing numbers of APA youth (Kiang, 2001; Lee, 1996). In addition Asian Pacific American females must also fight the "Suzie Wong" or "dragon lady" sexual stereotypes still pervasive in movies, television, and print media.

At the same time, due to linguistic barriers, cultural differences, and economic pressures, APA parents, most of who are immigrants, typically do not participate or intervene consistently in their children's schooling, even if they express high expectations at home for their children's educational success. Indeed, despite the rhetoric and rationalizations articulated by many immigrant adults that their decisions to come to the U.S. reflect their commitments to do what they think is best for their children's futures, it is clear from research that Asian American parents understand little about their children's actual daily lives, struggles, and dreams (Kiang, 2001). Thus, Asian Pacific American students are often left on their own to manage and mediate their experiences in school and society.

A wide range of APA youth organizations, programs, and projects have emerged in recent years that deal with school, family, and community. Many APA social and cultural student clubs, for example, operate as "extracurricular" activities within schools. Although these are typically organized as after-school activities, educators should examine how to integrate lessons and learning from these student-initiated activities into the traditional curriculum of the regular school day. Youth service initiatives have also been established as programs within larger community-based and/or mainstream institutions such as churches, neighborhood centers, and multi-service agencies. Some, like the Filipino Youth Activities (FYA) of Seattle (Cordova, 1998), represent legacies of more than four decades of community-based commitments to develop youth empowerment while others come and go within a few months. A few, like the East Bay Asian Youth Center in Berkeley, have elaborate funding streams and staffing patterns, while others, such as the youth education and empowerment program of the Filipino American National Historical Society (Cordova, 1998) in cities like Seattle, Washington, National City, California, and Hampton Roads, Virginia, survive strictly through the commitments of volunteers. Only a handful of Asian Pacific American youth organizations, however, such as South Asian Youth Action! (SAYA!) in Queens, New York, have explicit missions to develop leadership and ethnic pride, together with practices of empowerment. Even fewer, such as the Coalition for Asian Pacific American Youth (CAPAY) in Massachusetts, are consciously youth-run in governance and pan-Asian in representation (Kiang, 1998).

The roles and impact of these various APA youth organizations are vital, especially in teaching APA youth how to participate more fully in the policy-making process. These few youth organizations provide young people opportunities to gain skills, experiences, resources, and visions related to issues and dynamics of power, representation, and identity. It is important for various APA youth organizations throughout the country to share lessons, strategies and resources while striving to articulate a collective youth agenda. Funders such as the Ford Foundation, together with national advocacy organizations like the Children's Defense Fund and National Coalition of Advocates for Students, and most importantly, the youth-led and youth-serving Asian American organizations, are moving in this direction.

Implications for Research and Practice

The historical misrepresentation of Asian Pacific American students as model minorities and the manipulations of aggregated statistics, in particular, have created a large under-served student population. Despite constant reminders in the literature that APAs represent diverse ethnicities with a historical legacy to the late 1700s, the capstone image of all Asians as being academically successful persists, much like the historical stereotype that "all Orientals look the same." Though it seems as if a positive stereotype like the "model minority" would be more desirable than the deficit label saddled on other students of color, any stereotype hampers the ability of school officials to respond to the individual needs found within the APA population.

Many educators also mistakenly believe that APA students come with strong Confucian values that set the stage for academic success. However, teachers may confuse the pragmatic and resourceful actions of many Asian Pacific American students to combat racial prejudice as cultural values (Sue & Abe, 1988). Many researchers

mistakenly view Confucian values as compatible with American mainstream values (Sue & Abe, 1988). Trueba et al. (1993) reported, however, that some Asian Pacific American students found cultural values of humility, obedience, moderation, and harmony dysfunctional in U.S. society that is individualistic and capitalistic. Researchers have failed to recognize and examine the cultural conflicts students must cope with in the cultural assimilation and educational achievement processes.

Policy makers also seem unable to accept the idea that individual differences in Asian cultures exist and that students from these diverse communities are in need of targeted services. The uncritical acceptance by some academics and educators of these images result in *a priori* conclusions that deny resources for APA youth who need support in schools. Students who do poorly are seen as misfits and atypical of the APA educational experience (Lee, 1996). In fact, many students require school support services such as English language tutoring, assistance in writing, college career counseling, and orientation to an educational system to which their families are wholly unfamiliar (Park & Chi, 1999).

Much research on ethnic and cultural differences has compared African American and White American samples (Goodman, 1952; Spencer, 1982). Not until the 1990 Census did the U.S. government report on Asian Pacific Americans in many of their comprehensive population tables. In the past Asian Pacific Americans were classified with various groups into an "other" category or were not included. This explains the invisibility of Asian Pacific American students in many research projects. Research by Mizokawa and Rychman (1990) demonstrated how the aggregation of data hid critical differences among cultural groups. Mizokawa and Rychman found in their study of six Asian Pacific American student groups that distinguishing patterns arose on four attributional choices of ability, effort, luck, and task ease in success and failure situations. Their sample of 2,511 students included 836 Chinese, 562 Filipino, 232 Japanese, 166 Korean, 344 Vietnamese, and 371 other Southeast Asian youth. The authors found that Asian Pacific American students believed that effort was more important than ability in explaining success or failure. Of the six groups studied, Korean Americans had the highest attribution scores, followed by Filipino Americans, Chinese Americans, Japanese Americans and Southeast Asian Americans; Vietnamese American students scored the lowest. Clearly, disaggregated data collection and analysis are necessary for quality research. In addition, some research on Asian Pacific American students has limited generalizability because of small sample sizes and the grouping of diverse Asian groups into one gross category like ethnicity or race. It is important for researchers to examine characteristics such as gender, religious affiliation, generation in the United States, home language, English-language proficiency, socioeconomic status, gender, gender-role expectations, family values, neighborhood/geographical location, parents' education, and occupation of parents.

Though there seems to be a growing body of knowledge about the historical experience of Asian Pacific Americans, there is much less research on educational issues such as learning styles, motivational styles, sociocultural communication styles, effective language strategies, and metacognitive processing. One of the few researchers who is examining learning styles among APA students is Park (1999). She found Korean American secondary students to demonstrate minor preferences for auditory, visual, tactile, and individual learning. They were also found to have a major preference for kinesthetic learning, but a negative preference for group learning. This line of study assists teachers in understanding the importance of providing a range of educational activities. More research is needed to examine the learning patterns of various Asian Pacific American groups, but it is also important for researchers to examine the impact of individual differences (Slaughter-Defoe, Nakagawa, Takanishi, & Johnson, 1990). In addition, the researchers have customarily studied middle-class college students rather than younger youth; research that centers upon Asian Pacific American children is rare. Longitudinal studies of Asian Pacific American students are also scarce.

The general image of Asian Pacific American youth includes the complex combination of the model minority myth, the perennial foreigner and the "good minority" (Cheung, 1993). However, APA females are confronted with pervasive and conflicting stereotypes in society such as being quiet, obedient, conforming "Suzy Wong" sexual objects, and/or "dragon ladies." These images objectify adolescent Asian Pacific American females. The educational community should consider the struggle and educational needs of Asian Pacific American females and many APA students. APA students in general are marginalized in school; APA females are often more invisible than their male counterparts. They may be called on less frequently in class discussions. In addition, the devaluing of Asian Pacific women students may be found in family relationships. Some traditional APA families are traditional and patriarchal (Uba, 1994). The father may be distant in his relationships with his children, while the mother plays the nurturing role and communicates the concerns and wants of children to their father. Uba writes that in this traditional structure, males are more valued. Researchers should consider the influence that families and schools have on the social, psychological, emotional, and academic development of young women.

Teacher Training and Recruitment

Students and teachers are cultural beings. However in schools, culture is often ignored because teachers are unable to see elements of culture in their own lives (Pang, 2001). Even when educators are aware that their students speak Vietnamese, Farsi, Russian, or Cambodian at home, they often do not comprehend the powerful force culture, of which language is a major component, plays in shaping students' perspectives, behaviors, expectations, and values.

Teacher education researchers have found that many educators are unprepared to teach culturally diverse students (Gay, 2000; Irvine, 1995). These teachers do not do well, in part, because their knowledge base of culturally relevant teaching is nonexistent or limited. Gay argues that in order to reach many young people, it is essential that educators communicate with culturally diverse students in affirming and appropriate ways. Cultural competence is a powerful skill for teachers to develop and use in the learning process. When a teacher is culturally competent, she or he will create a learning environment that builds on APA students' cultural knowledge, social interaction patterns, and belief systems.

One of the most successful program models involving Asian Pacific American students was the Kamehameha Elementary Education Program (KEEP) for native Hawaiian students (Tharp & Gallimore, 1988). A 10-year study of the program involving 3,345 students demonstrated significant achievement in reading. Influenced by Vygotsky's sociocultural theory of learning, the KEEP program focused on teacher/student and student/student interactions to facilitate literacy development and cognition. The program was grounded in the sociocultural experiences of students and the ways youth shared those experiences as a close community. One of the culturally responsive teaching/learning strategies used in KEEP's learning centers was "talk story" (Au, 1980). Through a "talk story" pedagogy, students developed literacy skills through "overlapping speech, joint performance (cooperative production of responses), and informal turn-taking" (Tharp & Gallimore, 1988, p. 151). Using this culturally familiar method of communication as an alternative to highly structured teacher-directed instruction enabled students to develop language and literacy skills in a natural context.

Teachers may not have the ability to create a comprehensive program like KEEP; however, they can seek out APA resources. A wide range of Asian American studies curriculum materials is now available in print, video, and on-line (Asian American Curriculum Project, 2002; Asian American Studies Center, 2002). Since many teachers are not familiar with these resources and do not have sufficient background knowledge or training to adopt them effectively for classroom use, training is essential. Recent findings by the National Commission on Asia in the Schools (2001) concluded that Americans have a huge knowledge gap about Asia, despite their recognition of the economic, political, social, and cultural importance of the region. The commission's report reveals significant weaknesses in the existing K–12 curriculum and published textbooks concerning Asia as well as a glaring absence of attention to Asia-related content in university teacher preparation programs. Among its conclusions, the commission stated that in every aspect of K–12 education—from curriculum frameworks and material resources to teacher preservice and in-service courses and programs—current scholarship on Asia and Asian American content should be integrated (National Commission on Asia in the Schools).

This is also a larger policy issue for regional and national accrediting bodies such as the National Council for the Accreditation of Teacher Education (NCATE) that currently makes no mention of Asian or Asian American content in any of its policy guidelines.

The urgency for teacher training and professional development to address these issues is intensified by policies such as California Proposition 227 and parallel initiatives in other states that seek to eliminate bilingual education. These initiatives require English-only instruction for English language learners with the goal of a limit of one year of English instruction. The generational turnings from recent immigrant students to 1.5- and second-generation students, combined with local and national attacks on bilingual education programs have resulted in a decline in the numbers of Asian students enrolled in bilingual classrooms. For example, Boston Public Schools data show that in the decade between 1989 and 1999, the number of Asian students enrolled in Boston's bilingual education programs (Chinese, Vietnamese, Cambodian, and Lao) declined from 1,853 (20% of all students in bilingual programs) to 1,423 (15%). Cambodian and Lao student numbers especially dropped from 151 to 25 and from 61 to only 1, respectively—resulting in the demise of both the Khmer and Lao bilingual programs in Boston (Boston Redevelopment Authority, 1999). As the elimination of bilingual programs becomes more widespread, all teachers and school personnel, not just the bilingual teachers, should become fully responsible for establishing learning environments that support the diverse, multicultural populations of immigrant students in school.

In addition to developing policies and programs that can more effectively prepare all teachers, a related and equally urgent need is to produce more APA teachers. Asian Pacific Americans constitute nearly 4% of the nation's school-age students, but only 1% of the nation's teachers, and an even smaller percentage of school administrators, guidance counselors, educational researchers, and policy makers (U.S. Department of Education, 1997b). This is true at the local level as well. In Boston, for example, the student body is 15% White, 49% Black, 27% Latino, and 9% Asian while the faculty is 61% White, 26% Black, 9% Latino, and only 4% Asian (Boston Foundation, 2000).

Furthermore, Asian Pacific Americans are proportionately less apt to choose the field of education than all other groups in the graduate degree pipeline. Roughly 30% of those who received master's degrees in 1994 did so in the field of education (White 29%, Black 33%, Hispanic 30%, Native American 36%). Only 10% of APA master's degrees were earned in education. Similarly, at the doctoral level, only 7.5% of APA doctorates were in education in 1994, compared to much higher percentages for all other racial groups (White 20%, Black 38%, Hispanic 22%, Native American 31%) (U.S. Department of Education, 1997a). Most Asian Pacific Americans are choosing degree pathways that are professionally distant from educational practice or policy. This is a tremendous irony because APA families believe in educational institutions, but have left the shaping of those institutions to others. While it may be imperative for schools of education to develop more effective outreach and recruitment mechanisms, it is undeniable that APA families and communities must also take the lead in addressing this severe under-representation of professionals in education. Parents should consider encouraging their children to consider education for their careers.

SUMMARY

The United States has an educational system that continues to have difficulty dealing with students who come to school with varying languages, beliefs, perspectives, and ideas. This system tends to subordinate groups like Asian Pacific Americans from the majority. Social stereotypes serve to confirm misconceptions and dehumanize APA youth. These beliefs are often used to justify why educators have not created comprehensive educational programs for APA students. In order to provide equal educational opportunities for Asian Pacific American students, many teachers and teacher educators must reevaluate and change their beliefs and practices. APA students are often ignored or neglected, and their education is marginalized by an educational system where racial harassment and discrimination from peers and educational personnel continue to hamper them (Suzuki, 2002).

Many educators participate in the creation of educational inequities that Asian Pacific American students experience by perpetuating misconceptions through the uncritical use of aggregate data and a deep ideological investment in the model minority youth. These beliefs and practices continue to seriously hamper efforts to provide needed programs for APA students. Many teachers have little knowledge of Asian languages or culture, even though culture clearly plays a pivotal role in the learning process. Schools of education should be assisting teachers to develop an in-depth knowledge base such as APA values, philosophical orientations, history, learning styles, and immigration patterns. Cultural competence should be addressed in all education courses from policy development to writing methods in order for teachers to be comprehensively prepared to serve Asian Pacific American students and their families. Students should be encouraged to be involved in all aspects of their schooling from sports to leadership positions. Educational opportunities and the promise of democratic life are increased when faculty are guided by accurate information and believe in education that liberates students rather than limits them.

References

Asian American Curriculum Project. (2002). *Spring Catalogue.* San Mateo, CA: Author.

Asian American Studies Center. (2002). Asian American Studies Center Homepage. Los Angeles: UCLA, Author. Available: www.sscnet.ucla.edu/aasc/.

Au, K. (1980). Participation structures in a reading lesson with Hawaiian children: Analysis of a culturally appropriate instructional event. *Anthropology and Education Quarterly, 11*(2), 91–115.

Bass, T. A. (1996). *Vietnamerica: The war comes home.* New York: Soho Press.

Boston Foundation. (2000). *The wisdom of our choices: Boston's indicators of progress, change and sustainability 2000.* Boston: Boston Foundation.

Boston Redevelopment Authority. (1999). *Gateway City: Boston's Immigrants 1988–1998.* Boston: City of Boston.

Brand, D. (1987, August 31). The new whiz kids. *Time,* pp. 42–51.

Carlin, J., & Sokoloff, B. (1985). Mental health treatment issues for Southeast Asian refugee children. In T. Owen (Ed.), *Southeast Asian mental health: Treatment, prevention, services, training and research* (DHHS Publication no. ADM 85–1399, pp. 91–112). Washington, DC: U.S. Department of Health and Human Services.

Chan, S. (1991). *Asian Americans: An interpretive history.* Boston: Twayne.

Chang, L., Morrissey, R. F., & Koplewicz, H. S. (1995). Prevalence of psychiatric symptoms and their relation to the adjustment of Chinese-American youth. *Journal of American Academy of Child and Adolescent Psychiatry, 34,* 91–99.

Chang, T. (1975). The self-concept of children in ethnic groups: Black American and Korean American. *Elementary School Journal, 76,* 52–58.

Cheng, L. (1991). *Assessing Asian language performance: Guidelines for evaluating limited-English-proficient students.* Oceanside, CA: Academic Communications Associates.

Cheng, L. (1998). Language assessment and instructional strategies for limited English proficient Asian and Pacific Islander American children. In V. Pang & L. L. Cheng (Eds.), *Struggling to be heard: The unmet needs of Asian Pacific American children* (pp. 181–196). Albany: State University of New York Press.

Cheung, K. (1993). *Articulate silences: Hisaye Yamamoto, Maxine Hong Kingston, Joy Kogawa.* Ithaca, NY: Cornell University Press.

Chun, C., & Sue, S. (1998). Mental health issues concerning Asian Pacific American children. In V. Pang & L. L. Cheng (Eds.), *Struggling to be heard: The unmet needs of Asian Pacific American children* (pp. 75–87). Albany: State University of New York Press.

Cohen, R. D., & Mohl, R. A. (1979). *The paradox of progressive education: The Gary Plan and urban schooling.* Port Washington, NY: Kennikat Press.

Cole, M., John-Steiner, V., Scribner, S., & Souberman, E. (Eds.). (1978). *Mind in society.* Cambridge, MA: Harvard University Press.

Cordova, F. (1983). *Filipinos: Forgotten Asian Americans.* Dubuque, IA: Kendall/Hunt.

Cordova, F. (1998). The legacy: Creating a knowledge base on Filipino Americans. In V. Pang & L. L. Cheng (Eds.), *Struggling to be heard: The unmet needs of Asian Pacific American children* (pp. 165–180). Albany: State University of New York Press.

Crawford, J. (1992). *Hold your tongue: Bilingualism and the politics of "English only."* Reading, MA: Addison-Wesley.

Day, J. C. (1996). Population projections of the United States by age, sex, race, and Hispanic origin: 1995 to 2050. In U.S. Census Bureau, *Current Population Reports, P25–1130.* Washington, DC: U.S. Government Printing Office.

First, J., Kellogg, J. B., Almeida, C.A., & Gray, R., Jr. (1991). *The good common school: Making the vision work for all children.* Boston: National Coalition of Advocates for Students.

Fox, D., & Jordan, V. (1973). Racial preference and identification of American Chinese, Black and White children. *Genetic Psychology Monographs, 88,* 220–286.

Fung, G. (1998). Meeting the instructional needs of Chinese American and Asian English language development and at-risk students. In V. Pang & L. L. Cheng (Eds.), *Struggling to be heard: The unmet needs of Asian Pacific American children* (pp. 197–220). Albany: State University of New York Press.

Gándara, P. (1999). *Priming the pump: Strategies for increasing the achievement of underrepresented minority undergraduates.* Washington, DC: College Board.

Gaskins, P. F. (1999). *What are you? Voices of mixed-race young people.* New York: Henry Holt.

Gay, G. (2000). *Culturally responsive teaching: Theory, research, and practice.* New York: Teachers College Press.

Goodman, M. E. (1952). *Race awareness in young children.* New York: Collier.

Goodstein, L., & Lewin, T. (2001, September 19). A nation challenged: Violence and harassment; Victims of mistaken identity, Sikhs pay a price for turbans. *New York Times,* sec. A, p. 1.

Grieco, E. M., & Cassicy, R. C. (2001, March). *Overview of race and Hispanic origin, Census 2000 brief.* Washington, DC: U.S. Department of Commerce.

Hakuta, K., & Pease-Alvarez, L. (Eds.). (1992). [Special issue on bilingual education.] *Educational Researcher, 21*(2).

Houston, V. H., & Williams, T. (1997). No passing zone: The artistic and discursive voice of Asian-descent multiracials. *Amerasia Journal, 23,* vii-xii.

Ichioka, Y. (1988). *The Issei: The world of the first-generation Japanese immigrants, 1885–1924.* New York: Free Press.

Irvine, J. J. (1995). *Critical knowledge for diverse teachers and learners.* Washington, DC: American Association of Colleges for Teacher Education.

Kiang, P. N. (1990). Southeast Asian parent empowerment: The challenge of changing demographics in Lowell, Massachusetts. *Asian American Policy Review, 1*(1), 29–37.

Kiang, P. N. (1993). When know-nothings speak English only: Analyzing Irish and Cambodian struggles for community development and educational equity. In K. Aguilar-San Juan (Ed.), *The state of Asian America: Activism and resistance in the 1990s* (pp. 125–145). Boston: South End Press.

Kiang, P. N. (1998). We could shape it: Organizing for Asian Pacific American student empowerment. In V. Pang and L. L. Cheng (Eds.), *Struggling to be heard: The unmet needs of Asian Pacific American children* (pp. 243–264). Albany: State University of New York Press.

Kiang, P. N. (2001). Pathways for Asian Pacific American youth political participation. In G. H. Chang (Ed.), *Asian Americans and politics: Perspectives, experiences, prospects* (pp. 230–257). Stanford, CA: Stanford University Press and Woodrow Wilson Center Press.

Kiang, P. N. (2002). K-12 education and Asian Pacific American youth development. *Asian American Policy Review, 10,* 31–47.

Kiang, P. N., & Kaplan, J. (1994). Where do we stand? Views of racial conflict by Vietnamese American high school students in a Black-and-White context. *Urban Review, 26*92), 95–119.

Kiang, P. N., & Lee, V. W. (1993). Exclusion or contribution? Education K-12 policy. In K. Aguilar-San Juan (Ed.), *The state of Asian Pacific America: A public policy report: Policy issues to the year 2020* (pp. 25–48). Los Angeles: LEAP Asian Pacific American Public Policy Institute, and UCLA, Asian American Studies Center.

Kim, B. (1980). *The Korean-American child at school and at home.* Washington, DC: U.S. Department of Health, Education, and Welfare.

Ko, S. (2001). Examining the contributions of ethnic attitudes, collective self-esteem, and spirituality to delinquent behavioral outcomes among Cambodian adolescents. *Dissertation Abstracts International,* B62/11.5379.

Lau, A. (1995, February 11). Teen and suicide. *San Diego Union-Tribune,* p. A-19.

Lee, S. (1996). *Unraveling the "model minority" stereotype: Listening to Asian American youth.* New York: Teachers College Press.

Lee, S., & Yamanaka, K. (1990). Patterns of Asian American intermarriage and marital assimilation. *Journal of Comparative Family Studies, 21*(2), 287–305.

Leonard, K. I. (1992). *Making ethnic choices: California's Punjabi Mexican Americans.* Philadelphia: Temple University Press.

Loewen, J. W. (1988). *The Mississippi Chinese: Between Black and White* (2nd ed.). Prospect Heights, IL: Waveland Press.

Massachusetts Department of Education. (2000). *Report of 1999 Massachusetts and local school district MCAS results by race/ethnicity.* Boston: Author.

Matute-Bianchi, M. (1986). Ethnic identities and patterns of school success and failure among Mexican-descent and Japanese-American students in a California high school: An ethnographic analysis. *American Journal of Education, 94,* 233–255.

McKay, S. L., & Wong, S. C. (1988). *Language diversity: Problem or resource?* New York: Newbury House.

Miyamoto, F. (1939). Social solidarity among the Japanese in Seattle. *University of Washington Publications in the Social Sciences, 11*(2), 57–130.

Mizokawa, D., & Rychman, D. (1990). Attributions of academic success and failure: A comparison of six Asian-American ethnic groups. *Journal of Cross-Cultural Psychology, 21*(4), 434–451.

Mordkowitz, E., & Ginsburg, H. (1986, April). The academic socialization of successful Asian Pacific American college students. Paper presented at the annual meeting of the American Educational Research Association, San Francisco.

Nakanishi, D. T., & Nishida, T. Y. (1995). *The Asian American educational experience.* New York: Routledge.

National Center for Education Statistics. (1992). *Language characteristics and academic achievement: A look at Asian and Hispanic eighth graders in NELSS:88.* Washington, DC: U.S. Department of Education.

National Commission on Asia in the Schools. (2001). *Asia in the schools: Preparing young Americans for today's interconnected world.* New York: Asia Society.

National Education Association. (1987, June). *Report of the Asian and Pacific Islander concerns study committee.* Washington, DC: Author.

Nidorf, J. (1998). Mental health and refugee youths: A model for diagnostic training. In T. Owan & E. Choken (Eds.), *Southeast Asian mental health: Treatment, prevention, services, training and research* (pp. 391–429). Washington, DC: U.S. Department of Health and Human Services.

Oanh, N. T., & Michael, W. B. (1977). The predictive validity of each of ten measures of self-concept relative to teacher's ratings of achievement in mathematics and reading of Vietnamese children and of those from five other ethnic groups. *Educational and Psychological Measurement, 37,* 1005–1016.

Olsen, L. (1997). *An invisible crisis: The educational needs of Asian Pacific American youth.* New York: Asian Americans/Pacific Islanders in Philanthropy.

Ong, P., & Hee, S. (1993). The growth of the Asian Pacific American population: Twenty million in 2020. In *The state of Asian Pacific America: A public policy report: Policy issues to the year 2020.* Los Angeles: LEAP Asian Pacific American Public Policy Institute, and UCLA, Asian American Studies Center.

Paik Lee, M. (1990). *Quiet odyssey: A pioneer Korean American woman in America.* Seattle: University of Washington Press.

Pak, Y. K. (2002). *"Wherever I go I will always be a loyal American": Schooling Seattle's Japanese Americans during World War II.* New York: RoutledgeFalmer.

Pang, V. O. (1991). The relationship of test anxiety and math achievement to parental values in Asian-American and European-American middle school students. *Journal of Research and Development in Education, 24*(4), 1–10.

Pang, V. O. (1998). Educating the whole child: Implications for teachers. In V. Pang & L. L. Cheng (Eds.), *Struggling to be heard: The unmet needs of Asian Pacific American children* (pp. 265–304). Albany: State University of New York Press.

Pang, V. O. (2001). *Multicultural education: A caring-centered, reflective approach.* Boston: McGraw-Hill.

Pang, V. O., & Cheng, L. L. (1998). *Struggling to be heard: The unmet needs of Asian Pacific American children.* Albany: State University of New York Press.

Pang, V. O., Colvin, C., Tran, M., & Barba, R. (1992). Beyond chopsticks and dragons: Selecting Asian-American literature for children. *Reading Teacher, 46*(3), 216–224.

Pang, V. O., Mizokawa, D., Morishima, J., & Olstad, R. (1985). Self-concepts of Japanese-American children. *Journal of Cross-Cultural Psychology, 16*, 99–109.

Park, C. C. (1999). Struggling for Korean-American students: A sociocultural perspective. In C. C. Park & M. Chi (Eds.), *Asian American education: Prospects and challenges* (pp. 47–70). Westport, CT: Bergin & Garvey.

Park, C. C., & Chi, M. (1999). *Asian American education: Prospects and challenges.* Westport, CT: Bergin & Garvey.

Patterson, W., & Kim, H. C. (1992). *Koreans in America.* Minneapolis: Lerner.

President's Advisory Commission on Asian Americans and Pacific Islanders. (2001). Asian Americans and Pacific Islanders: A people looking forward: Action for access and partnerships in the 21st century. In D. Nakanishi & J. Lai (Eds.), *2001–02 National Asian Pacific American Almanac* (pp. 65–79). Los Angeles: UCLA, Asian American Studies Center.

Ramirez, J. D. (1991). *Final report: Longitudinal study of structured English immersion strategy, early-exit and late-exit transitional bilingual programs for language minority children.* Washington, DC: Office of Bilingual Education.

Ramist, L., & Arbeiter, S. (1986). *Profiles: College-bound seniors 1985.* New York: College Entrance Examination Board.

Reglin, G., & Adams, D. (1990). Why Asian-American high school students have higher grade point averages and SAT scores than other high school students. *The High School Journal, 73*(3), 143–149.

Reyes, D. (2002, April 12). O.C. [Orange County] Reports of Anti-Arab bigotry soared after 9/11. *Los Angeles Times*, pp. B1, B3.

Root, M. A. (1996). *The multiracial experience: Racial borders as the new frontier.* Thousand Oaks, CA: Sage.

Rumbaut, R., & Ima, K. (1988). *The adaptation of Southeast Asian refugee youth: A comparative study.* Washington, DC: U.S. Department of Health and Human Services, Family Support Administration, Office of Refugee Resettlement.

Said, E. (1979). *Orientalism.* New York: Vintage Books.

San Diego School District. (2001). *1998–2000 SAT 9 Test Results: Accountability and research report.* [On-line]. Available: www2.sandi.net/research/reports/sat9_3yr_Ethnic/index.htm.

Schmidt, P. (1992, June 17). LEP students denied remedial help, study finds. *Education Week*, pp. 11.

Shoho, A. (1990). *Americanization through public education of Japanese Americans in Hawaii: 1930–1941.* Unpublished doctoral dissertation, Arizona State University, Tempe.

Shoho, A. (1993, April). *Japanese language school: Aid or hindrance to the Americanization of Japanese Americans in Hawaii?* Paper presented at the Annual Meeting of the American Educational Research Association.

Slaughter-Defoe, D., Nakagawa, K., Takanishi, R., & Johnson, D. (1990). Toward cultural/ecological perspectives on schooling and achievement in African- and Asian-American children. *Child Development, 61*, 363–383.

Spencer, M. B. (1982). Personal and group identity of Black children: An alternative synthesis. *Genetic Psychology Monographs, 106*, 59–84.

Spring, J. (2001). *The American school: 1642–2000* (5th ed.). New York: McGraw-Hill.

Steele, C. M. (1999). A threat in the air: How stereotypes shape intellectual identity and performance. In E. Y. Lowe (Ed.), *Promise and dilemma: Perspectives on racial diversity and higher education* (pp. 92–128). Princeton, NJ: Princeton University Press.

Stodolsky, S., & Lesser, G. (1967). Learning patterns in the disadvantaged. *Harvard Educational Review, 37*, 546–593.

Sue, S., & Abe, J. (1988). *Predictors of academic achievement among Asian-American and White students* (Report no. 88–11). New York: College Entrance Examination Board.

Sue, S., Fujino, D., Hu, L., Takeuchi, D. T., & Zane, N. (1991). Community mental health services for ethnic minority groups: A test of the culturally responsive hypothesis. *Journal of Consulting and Clinical Psychology, 59*, 533–540.

Suzuki, B. (1988, April). *Asian Americans in higher education: Impact of changing demographics and other social forces.* Paper presented at the National Symposium on the Changing Demographics of Higher Education, Ford Foundation, New York.

Suzuki, B. (2002). Revisiting the model minority stereotype: Implications for student affairs practice and higher education. *New Directions for Student Services, 97*, 21–32.

Takaki, R. (1989). *Strangers from a different shore.* Boston: Little, Brown.

Tamura, E. (1993). The English-only effort, the anti-Japanese campaign, and language acquisition in the education of Japanese Americans in Hawaii, 1915–40. *History of Education Quarterly, 33*, 37–57.

Tamura, E. (1994). *Americanization, acculturation, and ethnic identity: The Nisei generation in Hawaii.* Urbana: University of Illinois Press.

Tessler, R., Gamache, G., Liu, L., & Weber, D. (1997, April). *The experiences of American parents who adopted children from China.* (Occasional paper.) Boston: Institute for Asian American Studies.

Tharp, R., & Gallimore, R. (1988). *Rousing minds to life.* New York: Cambridge University Press.

Thomas, W. P., & Collier, V. P. (1997). *School effectiveness for language minority students.* Washington, DC: National Clearinghouse for Bilingual Education.

Tidwell, R. (1980). Gifted students' self-images as a function of identification process, race and sex. *Journal of Pediatric Psychology, 5*, 57–69.

Trueba, H., Cheng, L., & Ima, K. (1993). *Myth or reality: Adaptive strategies of Asian Americans in California.* Washington, DC: Falmer Press.

Trueba, H., Jacobs, L., & Kirton, E. (1990). *Cultural conflict and adaptation: The case of Hmong children in American society.* Basingstroke, UK: Falmer Press.

Tyack, D., & Thomas, J. (1987). Moral majorities and the school curriculum: Making virtue mandatory, 1880–1930. In D. Tyack & J. Thomas (Eds.), *Law and Shaping of Public Education* (pp. 154–176). Madison: University of Wisconsin.

Uba, L. (1994). *Asian Americans: Personality patterns, identity, and mental health.* New York: Guilford Press.

Uriarte, M., & Chavez, L. (1999). *Latino students and the Massachusetts public schools.* Boston: University of Massachusetts, Gaston Institute.

U.S. Census Bureau. (2000a). *Census 2000 Redistricting Summary File.* (Table PL1.) Washington, DC: Government Printing Office.

U.S. Census Bureau. (2000b). *The Native Hawaiian and other Pacific Islander population: 2000.* (Table 4.) Washington, DC: Government Printing Office. [On-line]. Available: www.census.gov/prod/2001pubs/c2kbr01–14.pdf

U.S. Census Bureau. (2000c). *Rankings and comparisons population and housing tables* (PHC-T Series). [On-line]. Available:

www.census.gov/population/www/cen2000/phct16.html and www.census.gov/population/www/cen2000/phct6.html.

U.S. Census Bureau. (2000d). *Special tabulations: The Asian populations: 2000.* (Table 4.) Washington, DC: Government Printing Office. (www.census.gov/prod/2002pubs/c2kbr01–16.pdf).

U.S. Commission on Civil Rights. (1992). *Civil rights issues facing Asian Americans in the 1990s.* Washington, DC: Commission on Civil Rights.

U.S. Department of Education. (1997a). Table 26.3. In *Digest of Education Statistics 1996.* Washington, DC: National Center for Educational Statistics.

U.S. Department of Education. (1997b). Table 67. In *Digest of Education Statistics.* Washington, DC: National Center for Educational Statistics.

U.S. Department of Education Office for Civil Rights. (1999, December 14). *Non-discrimination in high stakes testing: A resource guide.* Washington, DC: U.S. Government Printing Office.

Vinson, K., Gibson, R., & Ross, E. W. (2001, Winter). High-stakes testing and standardization: The threat to authenticity. *Progressive Perspectives* [University of Vermont], *3,* 1–13.

Waggoner, D. (1993). The growth of multilingualism and the need for bilingual education: What do we know so far? *Bilingual Research Journal, 17,* 1–12.

Wang, L. (1980). Lau v. Nichols: History of struggle for equal and quality education. In R. Endo, S. Sue, & N. Wagner (Eds.), *Asian-Americans: Social and psychological perspectives* (Vol. 2, pp. 181–216). Palo Alto, CA: Science and Behavior Books.

Wardle, F. (2000). Multiracial and multiethnic students: How they must belong. *Multicultural Perspectives, 2*(4), 11–16.

Watanabe, A. (1998). Asian American and Pacific Islander American families with disabilities. In V. Pang & L. L. Cheng (Eds.), *Struggling to be heard: The unmet needs of Asian Pacific American children* (pp. 151–163). Albany: State University of New York Press.

Weinberg, M. (1997). *Asian-American education: Historical background and current realities.* Mahwah, NJ: Erlbaum.

Williams-León, T., & Nakashima, C. (2001). *The sum of our parts: Mixed heritage Asian Americans.* Philadelphia: Temple University Press.

Wollenberg, C. M. (1995). "Yellow peril" in the schools (I and II). In D. T. Nakanishi & T. Y. Nishida (Eds.), *Asian American education: A source book for teachers and students* (pp. 3–29). New York: Routledge.

Wong, S. C. (1987). The language needs of school-age Asian immigrants and refugees. In W. A. Van Horne (Ed.), *Ethnicity and language* (pp. 124–159). Milwaukee: University of Wisconsin System, Institute on Race and Ethnicity.

Wong Fillmore, L. (1991a, Spring). Preschoolers and native language loss. *Massachusetts Association for Bilingual Education Newsletter,* p. 2.

Wong Fillmore, L. (1991b). When learning a second language means losing the first. *Early Childhood Research Quarterly, 6,* 323–347.

Worral, B. L., & Ardeña, J. L. (2000). *Too mixed up.* Los Angeles: Mixt Up Productions and Isangmahal Arts Kollective.

Youngberg, F. L. (2001). Census 2000: Asian Pacific American Americans changing the face of America at a rapid pace. In *2001–02 National Asian Pacific American political almanac* (pp. 42–64). Los Angeles: UCLA, Asian American Studies Center.

Yu, S., Huang, Z. J., Schwalberg, R., Overpeck, M., & Kogan, M. (2002). Association of language spoken at home with health and school issues among Asian American adolescents. *Journal of School Health, 72,* 192–198.

LANGUAGE ISSUES

27

LANGUAGE ISSUES IN MULTICULTURAL CONTEXTS

Masahiko Minami

San Francisco State University

Carlos J. Ovando

Arizona State University

Over the last four decades, scholarship in such fields as linguistics, psychology, and education has emphasized the continuous and ongoing process through which immigrant children are acculturated into new societies. In particular, scholarship undertaken from a multicultural/bilingual perspective has had a significant impact on the understanding of why immigrant children are not always successful in school settings, and it has emphasized how to create a learning environment that is responsive to these children's needs. The major goal of this chapter is to serve as a resource for those who are interested in language issues in multicultural contexts. We find that although the scholarship of the 1960s and 1970s tended to be influenced by the Chomskyan revolution, the 1980s and 1990s saw a major shift from generative theory to sociocultural theory, that is, the view that language, literacy, and multicultural/bilingual education are the products of socioculturally mediated processes among individuals and groups in school and nonschool settings.

The theoretical-linguistic nature of language studies in the 1960s and 1970s reflected the influence of Noam Chomsky's (1957) revolution, which demonstrated the importance of conceptualizing links between the role of language and the human mind. Since the latter half of the 1970s, however, language studies have addressed more social and pragmatic linguistic concerns, focusing on literacy and multiculturalism/bilingualism within a sociocultural framework. The shift in language studies is perhaps a reflection of the demographic changes that began in the United States in the second half of the 20th century.

Although the United States has always been diverse, that diversity was constrained by U.S. immigration policies between 1923 and 1965. During the last three decades in particular, U.S. society has again become increasingly multicultural as well as multilingual. At the dawn of the new millennium, it is no longer news that the United States is becoming even more racially, culturally, and linguistically diverse (Ovando, 2001a). The 1990s, for instance, witnessed a rapid influx of immigrants from Asia and Latin America. A survey conducted by the U.S. Census Bureau recently provided a new estimate of 11–12 million immigrants, which surpassed an earlier projection by at least 2.5 million, and offered more proof of the growing demographic diversity of the nation. The Census Bureau also increased its estimate of the country's total foreign-born population in 2000, from 28.3 million to approximately 30 million, which roughly corresponds to 11% of the nation's 281 million residents (Armas, 2001). This difference was largely attributable to a higher-than-expected count of Hispanics; the 2000 census count of 35.3 million Hispanics nationwide was approximately 2.5 million higher than had originally been estimated. Also, according to a report on demographic changes summarized by the *San Francisco Examiner* (McCormick, 2000), a survey conducted by the U.S. Census Bureau projects

We are grateful to James A. Banks, Jim Cummins, Terrence Wiley, and Jeff MacSwan for their helpful comments on an earlier draft of the chapter.

that San Francisco will soon become the second major U.S. city (Honolulu was the first) to have a higher Asian population than White. With increased immigration, the number of second- and third-generation Latino and Asian Americans who want to maintain the language of their forebears is also increasing. Absent this factor, maintenance of heritage languages might not be successful.

The upswing in immigration has also resulted in a large number of school entrants whose first language is not English. Most educational learning environments to date, however, have tended to reflect the discourse practices of mainstream society, with often unfortunate results for nonmainstream students, including many language-minority students (Cazden, 1988; Gee, 1990; Michaels, 1981). According to John Gumperz (1996), the Eurocentric notion of relatively homogeneous and largely monolingual societies will soon be obsolete. With regard to school populations in particular, linguistic minorities will soon outnumber monolingual English speakers in many places in the United States; as a consequence, students will inevitably encounter more than one grammatical and cultural system in the process of socialization. Deploring the fact that U.S. educators are not well prepared to work effectively in such diverse contexts, Gumperz urges teachers to learn something about their students' cultural background in order to make themselves understood. Although some foreign-language teachers do attempt to achieve such understanding, many foreign-language courses have failed to make systematic efforts to deal with this issue. Gumperz stresses the need to introduce cultural content into second-language instruction curricula. It is crucial that we acknowledge the socioculturally embedded nature of language learning. As Gumperz (1996) suggests, we should realize that (a) "cooperating in a foreign language requires more than just knowledge of grammar and lexicon" and (b) "to the extent that cultures differ, communication tends to become more and more problematic" (p. 469). Accordingly, we should modify classroom discourse patterns, interactional patterns, and participation structures.

There are positive as well as negative aspects with regard to the recent trends in bilingual and multicultural education. A positive aspect is that between 1987 and 1997, the proportion of elementary schools in the United States offering foreign language instruction rose from 22% to 31% (Rhodes & Branaman, 1999). This substantial increase reflects a growing recognition of the importance of knowing more than one language, and of the cognitive and academic benefits of learning another language in the early grades (Gilzow, 2001). Unfortunately, a disturbing fact remains: the educational achievement gap has continued to widen between Latino, African American, and Native American students and middle- and upper-class European American students.

Focusing on home-school *match-mismatch*, some linguists (for example, Cook-Gumperz & Gumperz, 1982; Erickson & Mohatt, 1982; Heath, 1983; Mehan, 1991; Philips, 1982) have postulated that language-minority students do not prosper academically in such contexts because the discursive practices of their homes do not match the discursive practices of the school environment, where European American middle-class teachers with very limited multicultural and multilingual competencies and experiences are the majority. This mismatch tends to limit language-minority students' access to and participation in higher educational and occupational opportunities (Spener, 1988). In other words, children from middle- and upper-class cultural and speech communities are sociolinguistically advantaged in the school environment, but children from poor, non-English, and nonstandard English speech communities are more likely to be disadvantaged, and even at risk of being marginalized, in school environments. In light of this conflict between the lived experiences of students and their teachers, there is an urgent need for U.S. schools—especially public schools—to improve the teaching and learning environment for neglected student populations (Larson & Ovando, 2001; Ovando & McLaren, 2000). Through language studies in multicultural contexts, researchers have addressed in a variety of ways the language issues that have emerged since the 1960s in relation to such students. These studies have the potential to help educators working with those who are from distinct cultural and speech communities. Reviewing the research on language diversity, ethnic minorities, and learning is therefore important for many reasons.

The most influential studies can be organized into three types, as presented here in interrelated sections: classic theoretical approaches to language, language as a socioculturally mediated product, and multicultural and bilingual issues in relation to language. Specifically, the first section presents an overview of the classic theoretical approaches to language studies, connecting two disciplines of linguistics: generative grammar, represented by Noam Chomsky; and sociolinguistic studies, represented by Dell Hymes, William Labov, and Basil Bernstein. The second section, which emphasizes sociocultural aspects, discusses language-related issues in different societies. The third section further extends the issues discussed in the second section to multicultural and bilingual educational settings within a culturally diverse society such as the United States.

Through these three interrelated sections, we will be examining these key questions:

1. What does past research tell us about cross-cultural differences in the process of language acquisition and literacy skills development?
2. Does the linguistic match-mismatch conception adequately capture the relationships between the primary speech community in which an individual was raised and the secondary speech community represented by the school?
3. If languages—standard school languages in particular—are conceptualized as social *possessions,* with literacy thus being perceived from a sociocultural standpoint, what significance does this realization have for education in multicultural/bilingual contexts?

CLASSIC THEORETICAL APPROACHES TO LANGUAGE

The Chomskyan Revolution and Its Influence on Language Studies

One issue critical to understanding human development is the centuries-old debate between heredity (nature) and environment (nurture). These alternatives have been particularly salient in the study of language acquisition. According to B. F. Skinner (1957), language learning is based upon experience. Skinner's empiricist view stands in striking contrast to Noam Chomsky's (1959, 1965) innatist view that humans have a biological endowment enabling them to discover the framework of principles and elements common to human languages. Chomsky (1965) called this biological endowment a language acquisition device (LAD). The LAD includes basic knowledge about the nature and structure of human language, which is termed "universal grammar" (UG). Although grammatical rules of sentence structure are limited, no one could exhaust all the possible sentences of language; triggered by input, this internalized system of rules can generate an infinite number of grammatical sentences. Considering language a "mental organ," Chomsky (1985) thus believed in a self-charged or innate "bioprogram" whereby language acquisition is autonomous.

The linguistic revolution originated by Chomsky in the late 1950s and the early 1960s has exerted an enormous influence on contemporary studies (e.g., see Slobin, 1985). Brown and Bellugi (1964), for example, stress the rule-governed nature of language acquisition. Similarly, Carol Chomsky (1969), examining elementary schoolchildren's language development, found a relationship between oral language development and reading. With particular emphasis on humans' innate mechanism for language learning, she suggests that this natural process of language development continues actively into children's elementary school years. (Her finding that schoolchildren are still in the process of their first-language acquisition serves as a strong logical foundation for supporting "late-exit" bilingual programs that encourage students to continue to develop their first-language skills, both oral and written, while adding English to their first language. Programs of this type are discussed in this chapter under "Multicultural and Bilingual Issues in Relation to Language.") Carol Chomsky's study ignores sociocultural differences and does not emphasize conversational or social interactions; thus it is illustrative of the theoretical-linguistic focus of this period. Influenced by Noam Chomsky's (1965) conception of an innate LAD, her study focuses only on inborn linguistic competence and analyzes the underlying rule-governed nature of the target language. Sociocultural differences and social interactions, however, play a major role in the school environment in relation to a realignment of the function of language, from oral language used in everyday life to written language with fewer nonlinguistic and situational cues. Because of the need to address such issues, studies of a more sociolinguistic nature emerged in the 1970s.

Sociolinguistic Studies of the 1970s

Noam Chomsky's corrective emphasis on a biological foundation for language acquisition was an oversimplification just as extreme as the Skinnerian emphasis on behavioral operant conditioning, though on the opposite end of the nature-nurture debate. The notion of competence in generative transformational grammar (as represented by Chomsky) was challenged by sociolinguists because of the necessity of reconceptualizing childhood environments in other societies and cultures. Chomsky (1965), using the *langue-parole* distinction originally proposed by the Swiss linguist Ferdinand de Saussure (1915/1959), presented the dichotomy of competence (a person's internalized grammar of a language) and performance (the actual use of language in concrete situations). Challenging this dichotomy of competence and performance, Dell Hymes (1974a), an ethnographer of communication, introduced the concept of "communicative competence," the ability not only to apply the grammatical rules of a language in order to construct grammatically correct sentences but also to know when, where, and with whom to use these correct sentences in a given sociocultural situation.

Claiming that Chomsky's bifurcation of competence and performance is misleading, Hymes suggests—in contrast to the innatist position—that sociocultural differences affect the process of language acquisition and later language skills development at a number of levels. In other words, Chomsky focuses on the universal nature of language acquisition but Hymes stresses characteristic features of the outcome of language acquisition in a specific sociocultural context. Hymes's work is an example of how researchers in the 1960s and 1970s—whether they agreed with Chomsky or not—were greatly influenced by the Chomskyan revolution.

Although, as Hymes suggests, language development includes communicative interactions that are outside the child's developing linguistic competence, such as the ability to participate fully in a set of social practices, those who support generative grammar still explain the process of language acquisition very differently. For example, when applying the theory of generative grammar to standard English and to nonmainstream varieties of American English such as African American vernacular English (AAVE), it is possible to claim that, despite different surface features and expressions, they share the same underlying (deep) structure. The double negative—for example, compare "We want *neither* one of you" with "We do*n't* want *neither* one of y'all" (Labov, 1972, p. 185)—is a feature of AAVE that is frequently stigmatized, particularly in school settings (Orr, 1987). To show that there are no logical foundations for such stigmatization, according to the innatist position, multiple negation can be explained as a result of acquiring a different rule-governed system; that is, AAVE is rule-governed, and exposure to a distinct set of examples in early childhood leads to different types of unconscious rules for sentence production. In this way, those who support generative grammar conclude that "Standard English is better because we assume it to be better" (Robinson, 1990, p. 63).

As reviewed above, following Hymes, learning a language is much more than learning syntax. Like Hymes, William Labov (1972), in studying performance, has shifted a paradigm from isolated linguistic form (i.e., the grammatical sentences of a language) to linguistic form in human context and analyzed the sequential use of language. While studying the structure of AAVE in order to show that nonstandard dialects are also highly structured systems, Labov has taken a very different route from that of the innatist. Labov's (1972) particular solution to the problem was to examine how people use AAVE in a natural context. In interviewing inner-city youth, he used so-called "danger-of-death" prompts, such as "Were you ever in a situation where you were in serious danger of being killed?" (1972, p. 363), to elicit narratives. Labov and his colleagues define narrative technically as "one method of recapitulating past experience by matching a verbal sequence of clauses to the sequence of events which (it is inferred) actually occurred" (Labov, 1972, pp. 359–360). Using this high-point analysis, Labov presents the

linguistic techniques employed to evaluate experience within a speaker's particular cultural set, such as AAVE, and to study the basic structure of narrative within a particular culture. In other words, these researchers stress that some linguistic variables, such as structural components in story or narrative, are under the strong influence of sociocultural variation (which, as later sections will reveal, is a significant factor in multicultural educational settings).

The British sociologist Basil Bernstein (1971) interprets competence-performance in a more sociocultural way. According to him, "competence refers to the child's tacit understanding of the rule system," but "performance relates to the essentially social use to which the rule system is put" (p. 173). Bernstein thus reframes performance by combining Chomsky's notion of "performance" and Hymes's conception of "communicative competence."

Bernstein (1971) further claims that there is substantial evidence suggesting the effects of sociocultural variables. He investigated the question of why many children of working-class families could not keep up academically and dropped out of school. According to Bernstein, working-class and middle-class people use different linguistic codes. Middle-class speakers in England employ an *elaborated code* that facilitates the verbal elaboration of subjective intent, while working-class speakers, to a greater or lesser degree, employ a *restricted code,* a speech mode in which it is unnecessary for the speaker to elaborate subjective intent verbally. Bernstein stated that the communication style characterized by a restricted code put children from families of lower socioeconomic status at a disadvantage in schools, where an unfamiliar elaborated code was prevalent. However, Bernstein's notion of codes has been criticized because it fails to acknowledge an overriding concern with collaborative message construction by working-class speakers; for instance, working-class speakers are more likely to use affective nonreasoning strategies (Hemphill, 1989). Furthermore, because his conception has often been regarded as a "verbal-deficit" theory that attempts to explain differences in social-class language behavior, it has tended to be misused, especially in the United States (Brandt, 1990), where it was employed as a mechanism to explain the academic failure of children of linguistically nonmainstream backgrounds (including children from working-class homes). Despite these criticisms, as later sections will reveal, his theory greatly influenced those studies in the 1980s that examined how children deal with tasks in school settings.

In summary, tracing the pros and cons of the innatist explanations for language development is important because such debate influenced the direction of later language studies. For Chomsky (1985), for instance, language is nothing but principles and parameters. Although criticizing Chomsky, who tends to ignore the significance of language performance, Brown (1973) still tries to measure competence through children's performance data. At the same time, Hymes's (1974a) notion of "communicative competence" lays the foundation for work of the 1980s, especially in the educational arena. Cook-Gumperz and Gumperz (1982) summarize:

The task of exploring the cultural transmission of knowledge as communicative competence requires us to see the interactional face-to-face relationship of teacher to student as embedded interactively within a context of the procedures of classroom practices within schools, which themselves are part of an institutional system of education policies and ideology. (pp. 19–20)

As this statement illustrates, those theories that were developed in the 1960s and 1970s were incorporated into studies in the 1980s and 1990s. As regards communicative competence in particular, the next section will focus on socialization, the process whereby children acquire the ability to recognize and interpret the types of social activities that are taking place in their culture-specific environment.

LANGUAGE AS A SOCIOCULTURALLY MEDIATED PRODUCT

Starting in the latter half of the 1970s, and increasingly in the 1980s and 1990s, the shift toward more social and pragmatic concerns deepened the sociocultural focus of many language studies. Specifically, studies of language acquisition and socialization in a variety of settings flourished during this period, exploring issues related to language within a sociocultural framework. The core assumption of these studies was the social interaction paradigm, which was built upon the work of the Russian psychologist Lev Vygotsky (1978) and other major cognitive-developmental theorists such as Jerome Bruner (1977).

According to this social interaction theory, a child's communicative competence, reflecting a certain cultural identity, develops in accordance with socially accepted rules. This communicative style will be important when the child enters school, which may require a realignment of language use. This realignment is often necessary because there is a difference between the language use of the primary speech community (generally the oral language style used at home) and the language use of the secondary speech community (school literacy, in addition to a certain type of oral language used at school).

More specifically, literacy can be defined in more than one way. Some researchers (see Garton & Pratt, 1989) define literacy as both spoken and written language because of their belief that a strong connection exists between learning to talk and learning to read and write. This theory assumes that early oral language development is directly related to the later development

of written language. In this hypothesis, literacy can be defined as "the mastery of spoken language *and* reading and writing" (Garton & Pratt, 1989, p. 1). Likewise, Deborah Tannen (1982, 1987) criticizes simplistic orality-literacy contrasts; because spoken discourse sometimes takes on literate forms and functions just as written texts sometimes resemble the forms and functions of talk, Tannen advocates that orality and literacy be treated as a continuum. Catherine Snow (1983) defines oral language and literacy in another way: whereas language simply means "all oral forms of communication, speaking and listening," literacy includes "the activities and skills associated with the use of print—primarily reading and writing" (p. 166). Exploring the relationship between young children's oral language acquisition and the later years of their language skills development, however, Snow regards oral and written language as forming a continuum rather than a dichotomy. Many researchers therefore seem to agree that continuity exists between oral and written language. To represent the idea that "the contextual clues to interpretation are in the text itself" (Scollon & Scollon, 1981, p. 48), we use the term *decontextualization* throughout.

The Social Interaction Approach: A Theoretical Background

Studies of language development and language skills acquisition have increasingly focused on communicative social interactions in the earliest stages of children's speech patterns. Since there are remarkably wide individual differences (Nelson, 1981) as well as cultural differences (Schieffelin & Ochs, 1986), researchers have come to view children not as passive beneficiaries of their environments but as active agents in their own socialization throughout life. The progress in this viewpoint is predicated on the theory that individuals and society construct one another through social interaction (Ochs, 1996).

Vygotsky's (1978) ideas form a basis for the view of language as a socioculturally mediated product. Vygotsky defined the "zone of proximal development (ZPD)" as "the distance between the actual development as determined by independent problem solving and the level of potential development as determined through problem solving under adult guidance or in collaboration with more capable peers" (p. 86). Vygotsky's ZPD, in other words, means the level at which, through supportive interpersonal interactions with adults (or experts), learners can almost perform a task on their own. This enabling process is referred to by other researchers as "scaffolding" (Bruner, 1977), "apprenticeship" (Lave, 1991), "peripheral participation" (Lave & Wenger, 1991), or "assisted performance" (Tharp & Gallimore, 1991).

When applied to the use of language, the social interaction paradigm suggests a culturally ideal adult-child relationship. For example, children acquire their first language through interactions with more competent individuals, usually mothers (see, for instance, Snow, 1983). When one applies the social interaction approach to the classroom context, an ideal situation can be conceptualized as one in which, through constructive dialogue between teacher and student, the teacher fully understands the student's needs and assists his or her internalization of subject matter (Tharp & Gallimore, 1991). In multicultural contexts, an ideal situation would be one in which, through interactive processes of teaching and learning, the teacher's questions scaffold the child's constructing process of knowledge on the basis of his or her own cultural identity. The ZPD was initially conceptualized as an interactional space in which a child's activity is supported by an adult or more capable individual, but interactions among peers promote the provision of help from child to child that results in assisted performance. It is through social interaction that the ZPD is formed.

Overall, Vygotsky's ZPD suggests that language learners and those they interact with (including teachers and peers) should be viewed as a dynamic system in which each actively interacts with and influences the other. Even infants and small children are influential in socializing other members of their family, as well as their peers. For instance, later-born children are said to tend toward slower language development than firstborn children, perhaps because of parental attitudinal changes such as shortening of conversation directed at later-born children, and because siblings are not good language models for later-born children (Ochs, 1986). Similarly, it is easy to imagine that children socialize their peers into gender-specific modes of action and communication that they have acquired through social interactions such as game situations (Cook-Gumperz, 1992). According to Cook-Gumperz and Scales (1996), for instance, gender is an important component of children's construction of their social identity even in their preschool years. Girls spend a considerable amount of time in social interactions with other girls, such as playing in the kitchen or playing with dolls, and they develop same-sex friendships. In contrast, boys are more independent, playing with toy trucks and doing more outside activities. By the end of the preschool years, boys' behavior and girls' behavior become different in many respects. It is therefore possible to assume that the links between gender and linguistic practices are culturally constructed (Borker, 1980) and, more important, developed through early social interactions. In this way, the social interactionist paradigm has thus greatly influenced language studies in the 1980s and 1990s.

Language Socialization in Diverse Cultural Contexts: Becoming a Member of a Speech Community

As discussed earlier in this chapter, Hymes (1974a) stresses that from early childhood on, children are learning the appropriate use of their language, as well as its grammar and vocabulary. The acquisition of a culture-specific communicative competence thus plays a significant role in the process of language acquisition and the development of language skills. Peggy Miller (1982) describes a variety of culture-specific routinized interactions between mothers and their children in South Baltimore. As a matter of fact, different cultures have different priorities with respect to caring for, socializing, and educating young children. The primary intent of Miller's (1982) study is to suggest that although children from lower-class families in South Baltimore are being taught distinct styles of language, they are not linguistically deprived. In different cultural settings, people can observe dissimilarities in parental expectations and their resultant communicative styles. From observations of "sharing time" classes (an oral language activity in early elementary classrooms), Sarah Michaels (1981) distinguished the differing ways that African American and White (or European American) children describe past events in their narratives during sharing time. Similarly, Shirley Brice Heath's (1983) work is an ethnographic study of the ways in which literacy is embedded in the cultural context of three communities. She found that children growing up in White middle-class, White working-class, and African American working-class families in Appalachia have distinct experiences with literacy and thus develop different expectations concerning the behavior and attitudes that surround reading and writing events. The communicative style of each community reflects a unique culture-specific perspective of socialization. Therefore, not only the nature of language usage that children encounter in their early experiences but also the types of early interaction in which they are engaged play an important role in shaping their language styles to (appropriately) reflect divergent sociocultural and communicative functions. Furthermore, these two factors interact with each other in the development of literacy skills.

According to Hymes (1982), among the Chinook and some other North American Indian tribes newborn babies were believed not to be babbling but to be speaking a special language that they shared with the spirits. Ochs and Schieffelin (1984) claim that "what a child says and how she or he says it will be influenced by local cultural processes, in addition to biological and social processes that have universal scope" (p. 277). Accepting N. Chomsky's (1965) notion of a highly abstract core of structures that is applicable to any language, these researchers put particular emphasis on the influence of environmental and sociocultural factors. Two claims proposed by Schieffelin and Ochs (1996) clearly support Hymes's notion of "communicative competence":

1. The process of acquiring language is deeply affected by the process of becoming a competent member of society.
2. The process of becoming a competent member of society is realized to a large extent through language, by acquiring knowledge of its functions, social distribution, and interpretations in and across socially defined situations, i.e., through exchanges of language in particular social situations (p. 252).

Through different processes, from a very early age children are socialized into culturally specific modes of organizing knowledge, thought, and communicative style. Language acquisition and socialization are thus two sides of the same coin.

Through investigation of the language acquisition and socialization process of the Kaluli of Papua, New Guinea, Schieffelin and her colleagues (Ochs & Schieffelin, 1984; Schieffelin, 1986; Schieffelin & Eisenberg, 1984) find another example of the strong dependence of language on social patterns. According to these researchers, Kaluli mothers do not recast their children's utterances; nor do they modify their own language to fit the linguistic ability of the young child. During the first 18 months or so, very little sustained dyadic verbal exchange takes place between adult and infant. The infant is only minimally treated as an addressee and is not treated as a communicative partner in dyadic exchanges.

In her attitude toward her child's language development, the Kaluli mother presents a remarkable contrast to the Anglo-American middle-class mother, who accommodates situations to the child from birth on. Kaluli mothers consider finely tuned child-directed speech (sometimes called "motherese") inappropriate. Instead, they train their children to imitate adult forms of speech, believing that complex adult speech will thereby be tuned into the child's comprehension. The Anglo-American middle-class mother treats her young child as an addressee in social interaction; she simplifies her speech to match more closely what she considers to be the communicative competence of the young child (Ninio & Snow, 1996; Snow, 1983; Snow & Ninio, 1986). Note, however, that since communicative competence is culturally shaped, it represents culture-specific norms and aspirations. In other words, because differing environmental and sociocultural factors are operating in the Anglo-American middle-class and Kaluli speech communities, the communicative competence required for each community is consequently

different. Therefore, arguing whether finely tuned child-directed speech and recasts contribute universally to an optimal course of language development is obviously irrelevant.

In summary, cross-cultural studies have suggested that the pattern of social interaction differs with the environment. This is especially true with respect to language socialization, which is the critical area of socialization for the propagation of culture-specific communicative competence. Language studies in the 1980s thus emphasize that children from different cultures are driven in divergent directions by models endorsed by the adults around them, and that, following culturally specific norms, different language goals and plans are implemented in a variety of forms.

The Relationship Between Oral Language and Literacy: Consequences of Literacy

This section has thus far examined, from a linguistic point of view, how socialization serves to produce members of a society who are competent in socioculturally specific ways. An individual is socialized from infancy on, with the primary agent of socialization being the family. However, once a child has started schooling, which is widespread in modern societies, the main agent of socialization changes from the primary speech community—the family and the local community in which the child was raised—to the secondary speech community—the school, in which the child's narrative discourse style and subsequent literacy practices are often reshaped.

Regarding this point, David Olson (1977) has stated that the development of literacy proceeds from context-dependent (that is, contextualized), oral ways of thinking to the acquisition of context-free (decontextualized), logical, message-focused skills, such as reasoning and problem solving. Olson claims that as the representation of meaning becomes more unambiguous and autonomous, the evolution progresses not only historically and culturally but also developmentally, from what he terms *utterance* to *text*. Olson concludes that one of the major roles of schooling is to facilitate children's smooth mastery of this "language as text." In other words, Olson equates the acquisition of literacy with that of higher-level critical-thinking skills, claiming that the function of schooling is to make children's language skills increasingly explicit and decontextualized. (As will be seen later, Cummins, 1980, integrated this notion into his work but called it "context reduced" language.)

Some researchers, such as Heath (1983, 1986) and Snow (1983), suggest many similarities between learning to talk (language acquisition) and learning to read and write (literacy) in the early stages of the child's development. These researchers, in other words, imply that family support and early exposure to literacy have profound influence on the child's development of literacy skills. According to Snow (1983), for instance, the specific oral discourse style employed by middle-class families at home, which has the characteristic features of being decontextualized and detached, closely matches school language use, a factor that accounts for the later literacy success of children from these homes. In other words, since Snow regards early oral language development as having a direct influence on the development of later language skills, her emphasis is naturally placed on the importance of the continuity between oral language and literacy. Recall that, according to Tannen (1987), any particular instance of discourse uses a ratio of both orality and literacy.

This hypothesis suggests that oral language skills acquired at home are a necessary precursor to later literacy skills in an educational context. Conversely, it can be seen that if conversational interactions at home do not parallel those at school, a child's academic success may be jeopardized. This is the match-mismatch formulation of literacy mentioned earlier. The conflict between contextualized home language use and decontextualized school language use was a recurrent issue throughout the 1980s and 1990s, and even toward the beginning of the 21st century (see Cummins, 2000). We will discuss this topic from a slightly different angle in relation to bilingual education in the next section of this chapter.

Some researchers have opposed the literacy-as-development view and its resulting match-mismatch formulation of literacy. On the basis of their research, Scribner and Cole (1981) have challenged Olson's (1977) view, in which literacy, in combination with schooling, is supposed to equip children with the skills necessary for the transition from context-dependent thought (characteristic of oral language used in everyday life) to decontextualized abstract thinking (characteristic of literacy). Scribner and Cole studied the unschooled but literate Vai people of Liberia, who invented a syllabic writing system to represent their language. They suggest that in the case of the Vai, literacy is not associated with decontextualized thought. Scribner and Cole's argument is supported by other studies, such as research on the Cree-speaking people's syllabic script in northern Canada (Bennett & Berry, 1991). These research findings conclude that the relationship between higher-order intellectual skills and literacy practices is very complex, as is the relationship between literacy and schooling. Research conducted in other cultures thus warns that how various modes of learning usually considered to be related to one another in Western societies function may vary with the culture and society.

There is another criticism of the notion that language use develops from context-bound orality to context-free literacy (Robinson, 1990). According to Deborah Brandt (1989, 1990), Olson's (1977) "strong-text" view of literacy, which is based on the oral-literate dichotomy (an "explicit," elaborated literate style as opposed to an "ambiguous," restricted oral style), in fact originates in Bernstein's (1971) theory of codes, which has been used to explain why some children do better in school than others (Torrance & Olson, 1985). The oral-literate dichotomy is considered dangerous because it is likely to be connected with the deficit hypothesis, which assumes that parents in some sociocultural groups fall short of the skills necessary to promote their children's success at school. For example, examining literacy programs that support low-income, minority, and immigrant families, Elsa Auerbach (1989) warns that the so-called transmission of school practices model, which promotes parents' efforts toward school-like literacy practices in the home, functions under the deficit hypothesis. Since this hypothesis ether implicitly or explicitly blames children's environmental, sociocultural, or linguistic background for their failure in the classroom context, it implies that the family, not the teacher, is responsible for providing adequate educational support. The oral-literate dichotomy has thus served as a basis for the match-mismatch formulation of literacy and its resulting deficit hypothesis. As Brandt (1990) puts it, "in match-mismatch formulations, students are deemed at risk in school literacy performance to the extent to which their home language is at odds with the so-called explicit, decontextualized language of the school" (p. 106).

To counter criticism that the match-mismatch formulation of literacy has tended to be confounded with social class, Snow, Barnes, Chandler, Goodman, and Hemphill (1991) examined home and classroom environments and family-school relationships "within social class." Believing that it is "necessary to look elsewhere to understand the differences between the children who did well and those who did poorly" (p. 3), they restricted their study to children from low-income families. They found that frequent parent-teacher contact was one of the most important factors contributing to children's academic growth (discussed at the end of the next section under "Parental Participation"). Overall, the match-mismatch formulation of literacy has been dominant, although it has remained controversial because of its close association with the oral-literate dichotomy, which is easily confounded with social class and, above all, the deficit hypothesis.

Yet the match-mismatch formulation still sheds light on the role of socialization and reflects the relationships between the primary speech community in which an individual was raised and the secondary speech community represented by the school. In order to capture the mutual relationships, narrative study, which Labov (1972) has stressed, plays an important role, because a specific narrative discourse style not only reflects the language socialization process but also represents a fundamental structure that has been socioculturally cultivated.

Earlier in this chapter, we introduced Heath's (1983) ethnographic study of three communities, which revealed three distinct environments for literacy development; although parents in all three communities placed a high value on their children's academic success, only the children from White middle-class families tended to be successful in school. Heath thus concludes that children's acquisition of literacy is influenced by sociocultural conditions. Similarly, Michaels (1981) distinguishes how African American and White (or European American) children describe past events in their narratives, such as those used during sharing time at school. According to Michaels, White middle-class teachers who are accustomed to a discourse with a clearly identifiable topic (topic-centered) tend to misunderstand African American children, whose culture encourages them to use a discourse consisting of a series of implicitly associated personal anecdotes (topic-associating). Susan Philips (1972) describes how, because of differences in unconscious interactional norms, the verbal as well as nonverbal communicative style of Native American students causes conflict and misunderstanding in interaction with Anglo teachers.

An extension of such contrast may be described this way: through socialization, children from some cultures may be more accustomed to an analytic or deductive style, while children from other cultures may feel more comfortable with an inductive style of talking, in which the main theme of the talk must be inferred from a series of concrete examples. Thus, by describing how children's habitual ways of communicating at home may not necessarily work in the school setting, Michaels (1981) and Philips (1972) suggest that educators who are sensitive to and supportive of children's linguistic and communicative styles will be better able to understand children from different cultures.

To understand culture-specific patterns of narrative, James Gee (1985) has used stanza analysis, which has been applied successfully to narratives from various cultures (Minami & McCabe, 1991, 1995). Introducing the concept of stanza, Hymes (1982) cites a short story from the Zuni, a Native American tribe in New Mexico, and develops his argument about a culture-specific pattern of narrative structure. Extending Hymes's work (1981, 1990), Gee's (1985) verse analysis specifies the notion of stanza as an ideal structure containing "lines," each of which is generally a simple clause; overall, a stanza consists of a group of lines about a single topic.

Applying this stanza analysis to the sharing-time data (Cazden, 1988; Michaels, 1981), Gee (1985, 1986b)

illustrates differences in narrative between an African American girl and a White (or European American) girl. He categorizes the former as an oral-strategy (or poetic) narrative and the latter as a literate-strategy (or prosaic) narrative. Gee (1986b) then attributes this difference to whether a society is founded on an orality-oriented culture or a literacy-oriented culture and concludes that a so-called residually oral community, less influenced by written-language styles than the White middle-class community, still retains ties to an oral tradition with a particular narrative pattern.

Gee (1990) has made another contribution to language studies by rejecting the traditional view of literacy, which has been construed as an individual's ability to read and write in order to achieve an autonomous, higher-level cognitive skill. Gee claims that this traditional view is too naïve to capture the sociocultural role of literacy. Rather, following Brazilian educator Paulo Freire's (1970) conceptualization of literacy acquisition as an emancipatory process, Gee argues that language is always a social possession, and that the notion of "literacy" has been used to oppress nonliterate individuals and underrepresented groups, thus consolidating the preestablished social hierarchy, especially in Western societies. Culture-related domains for the mastery of communicative competence include discourse, appropriateness, paralinguistics, pragmatics, and cognitive-academic language proficiency (Ovando, 1993). Gee's (1990) notion of "Discourse" with a capital *D*, including more than sequential speech or writing, represents a sociocultural aggregate model that consists of "words, acts, values, beliefs, attitudes, social identities, as well as gestures, glances, body positions and clothes" (p. 142). Rather than simply using the linguistic match-mismatch conception, Gee argues that diverse sociocultural variables unfairly influence children's school success and failure. In other words, North American mainstream literacy practices are in effect playing a gatekeeping role, which fails to recognize and build on the literacy skills and cultures that minority students bring to school from their homes and local communities.

In summary, an examination of studies of social interaction, socialization, and the resulting acquisition of communicative competence in diverse cultural contexts suggests the many complex relationships between oral language and literacy. Above all, the issue of ambiguous oral discourse contrasted with explicit literate discourse has received a lot of attention, particularly in the United States. As Gee (1986a) argues, however, "the oral-literate contrast makes little sense because many social groups, even in high-technology societies, fall into such mixed categories as residual orality" (p. 737). This argument by Gee corresponds to Heath's (1983) statement that "the traditional oral-literate dichotomy does not capture the ways other cultural patterns in each community affect the uses of oral and written language" (p. 344), as well as to Hymes's (1974b) view that "it is impossible to generalize validly about 'oral' vs. 'literate' cultures as uniform types" (p. 54).

As Kieran Egan (1987) suggests, since language development should be understood as developing from orality to a composite of orality and literacy, effective use of children's orality during the early school years should then lead to their subsequent development of literacy. By emphasizing this composite model of orality and literacy, the Kamehameha Early Education Program (KEEP) in Hawaii has been successful. KEEP is founded on the premise that teachers from mainstream culture should appreciate minority children's early socialization patterns and home discourse practices without trying to mold those children into the patterns of Anglo-American middle-class children (Au & Jordan, 1981; Jordan, 1984; Jordan, Vogt, & Tharp, 1993). Educators can facilitate students' academic success by combining new areas of linguistic knowledge with the communicative skills the students have already acquired at home. With the establishment of culturally compatible classroom practices, home language can further facilitate children's effective participation in school activities.

This section has also emphasized that narrative discourse styles, which represent communicative competence, mirror the society in which they are employed. Studies on cultural settings within and outside U.S. society have identified a number of communicative styles. As Gee (1985) puts it, "Just as the common core of human language is expressed differently in different languages, so the common core of communicative style is expressed differently in different cultures" (p. 11). Cazden (1988) states that "narratives are a universal meaning-making strategy, but there is no one way of transforming experience into a story" (p. 24). This line of thinking is further advanced by Bruner (1990), who suggests that the meaning-creation process in narrative discourse is closely related to a specific style of cultural representation.

What is problematic is that, since it is based on the oral-literate dichotomy and its resulting match-mismatch formulation of literacy, the essayist style of literacy—which is assumed to be the cultural norm of mainstream schooling—is performing a gatekeeping role in Western societies. Scollon and Scollon (1981) observed that their 2-year-old daughter Rachel, a product of a mainstream U.S. environment, was already on her way to Western literacy even though she could not yet read and write. In contrast, a 10-year-old Athapaskan girl in Alaska talked and wrote in a way that, despite its being grammatical, was regarded by her teachers as oral and nonliterate. The Athapaskan girl's style, which was ambiguous, was considered inappropriate according to the Western norm of literacy.

Along similar lines, African American children who are accustomed to disambiguating pronouns in oral narrative discourse by means of prosody (largely depending on intonation contours such as vowel elongation) are assumed by teachers to produce ambiguous, poorly written narratives (Michaels & Collins, 1984). In U.S. society, unfortunately, such ambiguity tends to be confounded with preliteracy skills and further connected with social class, with little consideration of cultural differences. Therefore, it is not the match-mismatch formulation per se that is responsible for the controversy. Rather, the real issue is that, coupled with biases against minorities, there seems to be a general assumption in mainstream U.S. society that an oral style is ambiguous and should be valued negatively, whereas a literate style is explicit and should be characterized positively.

MULTICULTURAL AND BILINGUAL ISSUES IN RELATION TO LANGUAGE

Because of rapid social diversification, multicultural and bilingual education are playing an increasingly important role in U.S. schools. In the past, however, immigrant communities in many bilingual and multilingual societies have undergone a shift to the dominant language in the course of two to four generations (Blum-Kulka, 1997). The language shift to English is now so advanced that people at times cannot maintain informal intergenerational interactions in their heritage languages even within the confines of the family (Fishman, 1991). Many children from immigrant families lose their native tongue entirely, even though they may have retained some sense of ethnic identity or cultural vitality. Some immigrant children who successfully maintain their native language do so only in connection with diglossic situations in which the dominant language spoken in school (English, for instance) and a less widely used language or nonstandard dialect spoken at home coexist but do not overlap. The American public as a whole is becoming more sensitive to and aware of cultural and ethnic differences; yet cross-cultural miscommunications and misunderstandings are not uncommon and still lead to confusion and anger. To make matters worse, bilingual education tends to be seen by some people as a threat to the traditional conception of the United States as a melting pot. For instance, California decided in 1998 to eliminate bilingual education from the public schools, and other states are poised to follow suit. Although recent reports seem to indicate an improvement in the academic performance of California's students with limited English proficiency since the implementation of this policy, the underlying research is replete with methodological flaws, such as the lack of scientifically valid controlled studies, rendering the results highly questionable (Krashen, in press; "A Rush to Judgment on Bilingual Education," 2000). Overall, therefore, educational settings are becoming increasingly multicultural, particularly in urban areas, but educators are often ill-prepared to work effectively in such culturally and linguistically diverse contexts. There is thus an urgent need for research that increases our understanding of bilingualism and literacy so that teachers and public policy makers, using accurate information, can arrive at sound decisions about how to educate language-minority children most effectively.

In this section, we will look more specifically at bilingual and multicultural education and discuss further the socioculturally embedded nature of language acquisition and mastery of language skills. Although this section includes bilingual education, we do not intend to lump first-language proficiency and bilingualism together. It is certainly true that second-language acquisition (or bilingualism) is influenced by knowledge of the first language. At the same time, however, second-language acquisition (or bilingualism) is, like first-language acquisition, influenced by active hypothesis testing under the control of a rule-governed system (N. Chomsky, 1965). This section and the preceding one constitute a continuum in the sense that even if the same language is spoken, if the manner of presentation and interaction style differ communication may be difficult; and if different languages are spoken, communication problems may become even more serious. The potential problems that are raised in these sections, therefore, are the same: (a) What happens when a child who has acquired a certain paradigm for communication in one culture enters another cultural setting? (b) Since the habitual way of communicating in one cultural setting does not necessarily work in a new setting, what should educators keep in mind (and moreover do) for these children?

Misconceptions Regarding Bilingualism

More than half a million immigrants from nearly 100 countries and cultures enter the United States every year, most speaking languages other than English (Crawford, 1989). To help immigrant children master the new language, those who speak little or no English are placed in a variety of programs, such as maintenance bilingual education (MBE) or additive/late-exit, transitional bilingual education (TBE) or early-exit, or English as a second language (ESL). Researchers, policy makers, administrators, the public, and those actively involved in bilingual and ESL programs have been engaged for the past 25 years in heated debate for and against bilingual education. For example, Baker and de Kanter's (1981, 1983) evaluation studies generally conclude that bilingual programs are no more effective in promoting language and academic skills than alternative programs—such as structured immersion,

in which content-area instruction is provided through a monolingual English approach with modified use of ESL techniques. In contrast to Baker and de Kanter, Willig (1985), Ramírez, Yuen, and Ramey (1991), and Rosier and Holm (1980) found evidence supporting the efficacy of bilingual programs. That is, bilingual education promotes the learning processes of bilingual children; moreover, programs with substantial native-language components seem effective in promoting education achievement by minority students.

Differences exist even among those who support bilingual programs. Some advocate an MBE program, claiming that this approach gives children an opportunity to become proficient in English while maintaining their home language. Others recommend a TBE program—the approach used in most bilingual education programs in the United States (Crawford, 1989)—the purpose of which is to help LEP children become familiar with subject matter temporarily through their native language while also developing English proficiency. However, since many TBE programs provide only a very limited period of native-language instruction and do not guarantee the mastery of English, these programs may prevent LEP children from attaining proficiency in either their native language or English (Spener, 1988).

Reflective of the large number of early-exit TBE (as opposed to MBE) programs, there seems to be widespread sentiment throughout the United States that language-minority children should use as little of their home language as possible, under the assumption that this will lead to quicker proficiency in English (Hakuta, 1986; Huddy & Sears, 1990). As a matter of fact, bilingualism has sometimes been considered a handicap. In the early literature, in the 1920s and 1930s in particular, a generally pessimistic view of bilingualism can be found; it was alleged that mastery of two languages would lead to mental confusion. In a study of a group of Hawaiian children, for example, Madorah Smith (cited in Hakuta, 1986) concluded that bilingualism caused retardation and that second-language learning in childhood is arduous, handicapping, and fraught with problems. Barry McLaughlin (1992) notes several myths about bilingualism, which cause people to support programs that use as little of the home language as possible: (a) "Children learn second languages quickly and easily"; (b) "The younger the child, the more skilled in acquiring a second language"; (c) "The more time students spend in a second language context, the quicker they learn the language"; (d) "Children have acquired a second language once they can speak it"; and (e) "All children learn a second language in the same way" (pp. 1–7). These misunderstandings, based on simplistic and erroneous assumptions, have been employed to argue against the use of children's home language in school settings.

In sharp contrast, research by Peal and Lambert (1962) refuted the pessimistic view of bilingualism and instead showed bilinguals to be intellectually normal and, especially in the domain of "mental/cognitive flexibility," superior to monolinguals. A variety of research findings in the late 1970s, the 1980s, and the 1990s further refute the arguments against bilingual education. Contextualized language used mainly for conversational purposes is quite different from decontextualized language used for school learning. Furthermore, the former develops earlier than the latter (Cook-Gumperz & Gumperz, 1982). In the context of bilingual education in the United States, this means that children become conversantly fluent in English before they develop the ability to use English in an academic situation (Cummins, 1991). As can be inferred from the passage of Proposition 227, under which the postbilingual age began in California, bilingual programs are commonly criticized for retaining students for too long a period after they begin to develop English skills. Jim Cummins (1979), however, suggests that even though children may pick up conversational fluency in as little as two years (as measured on standardized tests), it may take five to seven years to acquire the decontextualized language skills necessary to function successfully in an all-English classroom (that is, native-like oral skills do not instantly lead to native-like literacy skills). To represent these two separate skills—contextualized or context-embedded communication and decontextualized or context-reduced language—Cummins (1980) originally proposed basic interpersonal communicative skills (BICS) and cognitive/academic language proficiency (CALP). According to him, BICS is the communicative capacity to function well in everyday interpersonal and social (thus contextualized or context-embedded) contexts, whereas CALP is related to language skills required for cognitively demanding tasks such as literacy (thus decontextualized or context-reduced). Cummins suggests that because it quickly reaches a developmental plateau (in both L1 and L2), conversational fluency is largely unrelated to academic achievement. BICS and CALP, therefore, correspond respectively to what Olson (1977) terms *utterance* and *text*. (Note, however, that the concepts formerly called BICS and CALP have more recently been labeled simply as conversational- and academic-language proficiency.)

Cummins (1979, 1991) and Cummins et al. (1984) suggest that first-language and second-language proficiency are interdependent, and that a strong native-language foundation therefore acts as a support in learning English, making the process easier and faster. Moreover, using the concept of common underlying proficiency (CUP), Cummins (1991) argues that since most of the learning that goes on in the native language transfers readily to a second language, transfer of academic knowledge from the first language to a second language in an educational context is highly probable. For example, once decontextualization skills have been acquired in one's first language, they are available for use in a second language (Snow, 1990; Snow, Cancino, De Temple, & Schley, 1991). In this way, once the basic principles of reading are mastered in the home language, such reading skills transfer quickly to a second language (Cummins, 1991). Collier (1987) found that five-, six-, and seven-year-old arrivals to the United States, because of limited literacy skills in their first language, tend not to acquire English academic skills as easily as older arrivals, who can transfer knowledge of reading in their native language to reading in English. Studies examining language-minority students' long-term academic achievement in the United States generally confirm that students who have been in late-exit programs perform better than those who exited bilingual programs early (Collier, 1992; Ramírez et al., 1991). Stephen Krashen (in press) writes:

> Quality bilingual programs introduce English right away and teach subject matter in English as soon as it can be made comprehensible, but they also develop literacy in the first language and teach subject matter in the first language in early stages. Developing literacy in the first language is a short cut to English literacy. It is much easier to learn to read in a language one understands, and once a child can read in the primary language, reading ability transfers rapidly to English. Teaching subject matter in the first language stimulates intellectual development and provides students with valuable knowledge that will help the child understand instruction when it is presented in English.

The premise of interdependence between the two languages thus supports bilingual programs that develop proficiency in English while maintaining minority children's first language.

It is important to consider the educational arrangements that either support or demand bilingualism, but there are other complicated factors that we also need to take into consideration. Wallace Lambert (1975) argued that bilingual programs may be "additive," in which, as in MBE programs, children's first language is maintained and supported; or "subtractive," in which the first language is gradually replaced by a socially more prestigious one but without developing the second one fully. Whether bilingual children can fully develop their academic language proficiency depends on whether they are in an environment that can give them extensive opportunity to develop their first- and second-language skills in a manner that is compatible with the language-use expectations of the school.

Recall our discussion that mainstream middle-class children often acquire school-based literacy skills through experiences in their home before and during school; children from nonmainstream homes often do not get such opportunities in their home prior to school, mainly because of their parents' lack of access to such skills. In other words, before entering school mainstream middle-class children may already have been primed more appropriately for participating in the classroom discourse. Therefore mainstream middle-class children and teachers do not have conflict in terms of their communicative styles. Rather than appealing to a presumed weakening of the home language, Krashen (1996) posits "socioeconomic status (SES) as 'de facto' bilingual education." In Krashen's view, many language-minority children do not do well in an all-English instructional environment because they cannot understand the teacher for some time after entering school. Krashen notes that immigrant children who do well in all-English classrooms are generally of higher SES, who either immigrated to the United States with prior educational experience or have parents who are better prepared to assist with schoolwork; hence they may do well even in the absence of native language instruction. Note, however, that academic language for Krashen is the actual code, with more complex syntax, expanded vocabulary, and use—such as use of the composing process in writing to solve problems—and that Krashen's views on the relation between "language" and "academic content" do not necessarily differ from those of Cummins.

This explanation, at least in part, seems to apply to many other bilingual situations as well. Examining Japanese American bilingual children, the first author of this chapter (Minami, 2001) found that increasing language ability in either language (English or Japanese) used by bilingual children can accelerate their progress in the other language as well. However, although the case studies of Japanese families suggest the positive effects of being bilingual, we should not forget the part played in this success by both the relatively high prestige of the Japanese language and the instrumental benefits associated with high proficiency in that language (i.e., instrumental motivation, as mentioned above), particularly on the West Coast (where knowledge of Japanese is useful for a future career).

Cummins's (1991) model, as a matter of fact, helps explain why ongoing academic instruction in the first language is beneficial to language-minority children. Research in Canada, for example, suggests that although students immersed in a second language at an older age (secondary school) showed less native-like communicative competence than students immersed in the second language at a younger age (Hart, Lapkin, & Swain, 1991), the second-language skills shown by late-immersion students are far ahead of the skills of early-immersion students in some academic discourse domains (Harley, 1991). Similarly, Genesee (1983) reports that only one year of immersion in a second-language classroom in the seventh grade provides as much development in the

second language as three years of immersion starting in the first grade; that is, late-immersion students show a high level of communicative competence, particularly in academic settings. Therefore, the commonsense notion that it is beneficial to immerse children in their second language as soon as possible is not a well-founded idea.

It may be difficult to make any conclusive statements concerning the long-term comparison between transitional and maintenance programs because of such variables as district differences (Cazden, 1992), but the research of the 1980s and 1990s tends to suggest the effectiveness of maintenance programs for children's first- as well as second-language development. Furthermore, research findings from Canada in particular refute the linguistic match-mismatch hypothesis discussed in the preceding section. Comparison of late-immersion and early-immersion students does not support the theory that the conflict between home-language use and school-language use results in academic difficulties; children exposed to a home-language switch experienced no academic retardation (Cummins, 1991). Research into late-immersion programs in Canada demonstrates that ideal bilingual education programs increase fluency in both languages by treating a nonmainstream first language as an asset rather than a handicap. Therefore, maintenance bilingual programs hold the edge in helping to educate children to be confident and capable in the academic environment.

Empowerment of Minority Students, Parents, and Communities

Facing diverse approaches to educating LEP children, many researchers have recently begun to support maintenance programs. Two-way (or interlocking) bilingual/immersion education programs have attracted particular attention. In these programs, non-English-background students and English monolingual students are placed together in a bilingual classroom to learn each other's language and work academically in both languages. For instance, while an English-speaking child is learning Spanish, a Spanish-speaking child is learning English in the same classroom; they study the content areas in each other's language (Lindholm, 1992; Ovando, 1990; Ovando & Pérez, 2000). Similarly, in a partial-immersion program adopted by the Japanese language program in Portland, Oregon, the student's day is divided in half by language: one class studies in English in the morning and switches to Japanese after lunch, whereas the other class has the reverse schedule (Gilzow, 2001). There is no isolation of language-minority students in this educational setting, and children have the opportunity to play and talk together in each other's language (Morison, 1990). Thus, two-way bilingual education plays a crucial role in helping language-minority children maintain their ethnic identity, and at the same time exposing majority children to a minority language and culture.

The story is not such a simple one, however. In some bilingual programs, majority children learn virtually none of the second language, even when minority students outnumber the majority children in the program. For example, it has been reported in evaluations of the bilingual program in Culver City, California, that immersion students who began the program as English monolinguals had not attained mastery of Spanish even after six years of immersion in the language (Genesee, 1985; Wong Fillmore & Valadez, 1986). Similarly, the bilingual component of the Brookline Early Education Project (BEEP) in Massachusetts, in which language-majority (English) and language-minority (Spanish) children were brought together, reports that even though all Spanish-speaking children eventually learned English while maintaining Spanish, the effects of the program on English-speaking children's proficiency were not as evident (Hauser-Cram, Pierson, Walker, & Tivnan, 1991). Although the Culver City program and BEEP may have played an important role in sensitizing language-majority children to different cultures, the findings in terms of second-language proficiency are educationally disappointing.

The clue to understanding this problem may be found in studies on language and literacy on the Navajo reservation, where about two-thirds of school-age Navajo children are currently attending public schools (Holm & Holm, 1990) but a diglossic situation still exists. Two languages coexist, each encompassing its own range of social functions (D. McLaughlin, 1990). English is generally used in schools and churches and is thus regarded as a language with greater social prestige. Navajo, used primarily in informal situations such as family conversation, has been relegated to vernacular status and consequently is considered less prestigious. Though accepting the use of vernacular Navajo in formal situations, schools and churches limit its use; the message they are conveying to Navajo children is the stigmatized image of their indigenous language. The case on the Navajo reservation may explain why language-majority children in some bilingual programs do not attain mastery of a minority language. It may be that adults, administrators, and teachers in those programs are sending children a conscious or unconscious negative message about minority languages and cultures.

As these examples indicate, although the home environment and family-school relationships are important (Snow, Barnes, et al., 1991), many researchers have tended to discuss students' school success and failure simply in terms of the match-mismatch formulation of literacy and discourse patterns. Children's academic success should be studied and emphasized differently.

Cummins (1986) has long examined the pattern of minority students' academic success and failure; he stressed ways in which educators can promote the empowerment of minority students and their parents and communities so that those children can become confident and capable in the academic environment. To provide a balanced view, we should acknowledge that some researchers (Edelsky et al., 1983; MacSwan, 2000; Martin-Jones & Romaine, 1986; Wiley, 1996) disagree with Cummins. Carole Edelsky (1991), for instance, strongly criticizes Cummins on the grounds that his analysis of the social and cognitive nature of children's language skills relies heavily on test scores. According to Edelsky, though Cummins advocates the empowerment of minority students he is in reality using culturally biased conventional test scores to measure their academic progress. Edelsky claims that what Cummins is measuring has nothing to do with the extent to which minority children have become truly confident and capable in the academic environment. She concludes that Cummins's ideal and practice are contradictory. In response to this criticism, Cummins (2000) points out that the construct of academic language proficiency entails no reliance on test scores as support for either its construct validity or its relevance to education.

Consequently, equitable assessment is necessary to monitor bilingual children's progress not only in language development but also in the development of language skills such as literacy. It is certainly true that standardized tests do not always serve as an accurate or fair measure of language-minority students' diverse strengths (Edelsky, 1991; McCloskey & Enright, 1992). Yet, as Cummins emphasizes, the function of educators and policy makers should be to create contexts of empowerment for minority students. Moreover, as Collier (1992) argues, ignoring minority students' performance on standardized tests means denying those students "access to a meaningful education and equal opportunity to benefit in life from their education" (p. 194). Additionally, as a recent trend, the Bilingual Verbal Ability Tests (BVAT), which reflect ideas developed by Cummins (1980, 1991)—particularly the notion of CALP (cognitive/academic language proficiency)—were developed by researchers, educators, and classroom teachers (Muñoz-Sandoval, Cummins, Alvarado, & Ruef, 1998). The tests are administered to (a) measure an individual child's English language proficiency, (b) measure a child's bilingual verbal ability (e.g., verbal cognitive ability in English and Japanese combined), and (c) predict a child's academic progress. The major objective of the BVAT is therefore to measure the unique combination of cognitive and academic language abilities possessed by bilingual individuals in English and another language.

The importance of minority students' empowerment is further clarified in the writing of Freire (1970), who suggests that the literacy process should be conceptualized as playing a central role in empowering those who are, in many ways, oppressed in a given social system, so that those people can participate fully in the system. Similarly, Williams and Snipper (1990) have broken literacy down into three levels. *Functional literacy* indicates the minimum skills necessary for an individual to function in everyday life in a given society, such as the ability to read signs on the street or at the railroad station. *Cultural literacy,* which is not in line with E. D. Hirsch, Jr.'s (1988) cultural literacy project (1998), emphasizes cultural ties and traditions in a given society. *Critical literacy* identifies political elements intrinsic to reading and writing events, involving the ability to use print for empowerment in society. Thus the ultimate goal of literacy education is to achieve a practice based on authentic dialogue between equally well-informed individuals.

These three levels differ from one another, but they are similar in their conceptualization of literacy as reflecting the relationship between an individual and the society in which he or she lives, and in their implication that literacy should equip an individual to function well and above all to fight against the inequity prevalent in society. It has been observed that many students may need at least four years of second-language study to reach functional literacy in the second language (Collier, 1992). Having arrived at this level, students can then proceed toward cultural and critical literacy. (Note that this evidence supports Cummins's [1979] threshold hypothesis, which attempts to incorporate children's proficiency levels into predictions about the effects of bilingualism. In this hypothesis, Cummins claims there is a threshold level of linguistic competence that must be attained in each language if bilinguals are to avoid cognitive deficits and benefit cognitively from their bilingualism.)

In considering the empowerment of language-minority students, one must take into account the circumstances of their presence in the majority society. As John Ogbu (1992) puts it, "To understand what it is about minority groups, their cultures and languages that makes crossing cultural boundaries and school learning difficult for some but not for others, we must recognize that there are different types of minorities" (p. 8). Ogbu (1990, 1992) classifies minorities into two groups: castelike or involuntary minorities, and immigrant or voluntary minorities. For example, whereas African Americans and Native Americans belong to involuntary minorities, Chinese, Koreans, Japanese, and other Asians are representative of voluntary or immigrant minorities. According to Ogbu, because the history of African Americans and Native Americans in the United States is utterly different

from that of other racial and ethnic minority groups, they try to preserve linguistic and cultural differences as symbolic of their ethnic identity and their separation from the oppressive mainstream culture. In contrast, Ogbu argues, voluntary minorities generally believe that life in the United States is better than life in their native country. They are therefore more likely to succeed than involuntary minorities are, particularly in academic achievement. Voluntary minorities' positive appraisal of their situation is thus likely to have a positive influence on their overall performance. However, the monolithic view of Asian Americans as academic high achievers, which derives from the model-minority stereotype, is oversimplified. By examining the experiences of adolescents from East Asian backgrounds in U.S. high schools, the first author of this chapter (Minami, 2000) found that voluntary minorities at times feel the same way that involuntary minorities do.

Lisa Delpit (1988) provides some suggestions for overcoming such social injustice. According to Delpit, children from middle-class communities are advantaged because they know what she calls the codes or culture of power; children from lower-class communities or African American communities are disadvantaged because they lack this knowledge. Delpit claims that social injustice is embedded in the social norms of communicative interaction of the dominant group. Her argument parallels Bernstein's (1971) codes and the match-mismatch formulation of literacy. To empower minority students, Delpit argues that teachers should make the rules of the "culture of power" explicit and teach those rules to all students as a first step toward a fairer education and society. This concept corresponds to the idea proposed by Jay Robinson (1990), who advocates that all students should be given equal opportunities to practice and develop language competencies in response to concrete situations, especially in the classroom.

Those who advocate minority students' empowerment do not necessarily agree about what exactly, in the domains of language and literacy, offers such empowerment. For example, recall that Freire (1970) argues for educational practice based on an authentic dialogue between teachers and learners as equally knowing subjects. He sharply criticizes the use of social norms held by the dominant culture to legitimate only a few modes of communication, because this restrictive approach leads to the devaluation and thus subtle oppression of minority-language speakers and speakers of nonmainstream varieties of language. Instead, Freire strongly advocates that the literacy process should play a key role in empowering those who are oppressed within the system, and thus function as a means of cultural action for freedom.

In contrast to Freire (1970), Delpit (1988), in her discussion of the debate over the process-oriented or whole-language approach versus the skills-oriented approach to education, stresses that educators, particularly those who support whole language, do not adequately provide minority students with knowledge of the rules needed to function in the culture of power. Whole-language classrooms are usually characterized as valuing students' home cultures and thus accepting a plurality of literacies (Edelsky, 1991). Under this pedagogical ideal, the teacher's role is different than it would be in a traditional teacher-centered, skills-oriented classroom; in whole-language classrooms, teachers are guides, participants, and (above all) learners in their own domains. Delpit has been criticized for her lack of sensitivity to the diversity within the whole-language and process-writing movements (Reyes, 1992). She emphasizes, however, that it is the educators, and not minority children's homes, that should constitute a beneficial environment for those children and facilitate their academic performance.

In summary, language researchers have shown in a variety of ways how children's home environment and language community affect their academic development. How a teacher perceives this background can be crucial to the child's academic success or failure. For example, Snow, Barnes, et al. (1991) report parent-teacher miscommunications and misunderstandings, as well as teachers' biases against low-income families and their children, as factors hindering those children's academic growth. It may be true that some children, especially minority children, arrive at school with distinct external disadvantages when compared with peers whose home environment has afforded them ample opportunities to learn the language used in school. No one can deny that children need good environmental support for learning. Moreover, Ogbu (1992) criticizes multicultural education for tending to emphasize changes in teacher attitude and practice instead of focusing on the minority students' own responsibility for their academic performance. However, when one looks at the language research that shows the great variation in linguistic styles and functions, it becomes apparent that educators do need a good understanding of the potential difficulties that language differences can produce, but without lowering their expectations for children who come from linguistically nonmainstream backgrounds.

Lessons from Successful Cases

Our discussion of minority students' empowerment has stressed that sociocultural and linguistic differences alone cannot account for their academic success or failure. There are many elements that should be taken into consideration, such as teacher-student or peer collaborative learning, positive self-image, and the level of teachers' expectations for students. This subsection will discuss factors in minority students' success.

Parental Participation. As Eugene García (1991) aptly states, lessons from successful cases will "provide important insights with regard to general instructional organization, literacy development, academic achievement, and the perspectives of students, teachers, administrators, and parents" (p. 2). Reporting on language-minority students' success in secondary schools, Lucas, Henze, and Donato (1990) identify eight factors as related to successful outcomes with language-minority students:

1. Value is placed on the students' languages and cultures
2. High expectations of language-minority students are made concrete
3. School leaders make the education of language-minority students a priority
4. Staff development is explicitly designed to help teachers and other staff serve language-minority students more effectively
5. A variety of courses and programs for language-minority students is offered
6. A counseling program gives special attention to language-minority students through counselors [who understand those students linguistically as well as culturally]
7. Parents of language-minority students are encouraged to become involved in their children's education
8. School staff members share a strong commitment to empower language-minority students through education (pp. 324–325).

As can be seen, one of the factors in language-minority students' success is parental involvement, which is also exemplified in successful late-exit programs (Cazden, 1992), as well as in the Japanese-language magnet program in Portland, Oregon, where the parent support organization serves parents for the entire K–12 program and creates opportunities for the families involved to develop a sense of community and mutual support (Gilzow, 2001). Similarly, Snow, Barnes, et al. (1991) report a positive correlation between parental expectations and low-income children's academic achievement. At the same time, however, these researchers warn that a dangerous situation is created when parents are not as involved with teachers at the high school level as they were with teachers at the elementary school level, because of increased parent-teacher miscommunications and misunderstandings, as well as teachers' biases against children with certain backgrounds.

Community Participation. The second factor in minority students' academic success is a community's active participation in school curriculum design in order to accommodate the needs of a particular student population. The second author of this chapter (Ovando, 1984) reports such efforts in Nulato, a remote indigenous Athapaskan village in Alaska. According to Ovando, Nulato students and their parents believe that one of the important reasons for getting an education is to learn about Athapaskan traditions. Thus they have worked actively with administrators to see that the curriculum includes Native culture and that an effort is made to hire Native teachers. The community's efforts have resulted in a positive school environment in which there is little conflict in socialization patterns between the primary speech community (home) and the secondary speech community (school).

Another positive outcome of the community's participation in school curriculum takes the form of preserving that community's traditions. Various traditional customs are still alive, but language loss was a serious issue in Nulato in the 1990s. Since parents in the current generation of better-schooled, English-speaking Athapaskans have experienced an intergenerational language communication gap with their own parents, they are trying to find ways to preserve their ancestral language and culture (Ovando, 1994). To solve or lessen this critical issue, the community and the school are currently exploring the creation of ecological niches in the school environment in which grandparents can promote the use of the Athapaskan language with schoolchildren. The lessons from Nulato indicate that the school and the community can work together to explore ways to encourage preservation of the language and culture of children's primary speech community without sacrificing their academic prosperity. In the past, local community movements have played a major role in the development of national language policies, such as the formulation and passage of the Native American Languages Act (Hale, 1992). In this sense, language-maintenance programs that involve the community and the school are a good lesson for those who seek empowerment of minority students, parents, and communities.

In summary, schools need to create a learning environment that is culturally and linguistically responsive while simultaneously expanding the horizons of their students. If the majority of teachers, staff, administrators, and community members share the same cultural and linguistic heritage, there will be a close match between the cultural and linguistic values and norms of the communities and the school's practices. There are lessons to be learned from successful cases. In these schools, (a) teachers treat their students as if they were their own biological children in social, emotional, physical, and academic matters; (b) teachers and school administrators believe in contacting family members or caregivers whenever it is necessary to do so; and (c) schools, parents, and community leaders jointly embrace the philosophy that all students can learn (Ovando, 2001b). Overall, therefore, educators need to promote the empowerment of minority students, their parents, and communities. We also should not forget that the quality of multicultural/bilingual education programs varies with the teachers. Teachers also need to experience the elements necessary to empower language-minority students (Ada, 1986). In this sense, not only minority students, their parents, and communities but teachers themselves should be empowered.

CONCLUSION AND IMPLICATIONS

Throughout this chapter, we have suggested that the social nature of language be considered seriously in educating those who are not from mainstream middle-class families, particularly language-minority children. Guided by the questions posed at the outset of this chapter, we have extended the traditional discussion of language issues to multicultural educational settings by looking at how language shapes and is shaped by diverse cultural experiences:

- What does past research tell us about cross-cultural differences in the process of language acquisition and literacy skills development?
- Does the linguistic match-mismatch conception adequately capture the relationships between the primary speech community in which an individual was raised and the secondary speech community represented by the school?
- If languages—standard school languages in particular—are conceptualized as social possessions, with literacy thus being perceived from a sociocultural standpoint, what significance does this realization have for education in multicultural/bilingual contexts?

With regard to the first question, this review of existing studies shows that the acquisition of culture-specific communicative competence and socialization patterns plays a significant role in the process of language acquisition and the development of language skills. Because of the differences in social structure and practices, direct comparison among differing speech communities may not be possible. The findings and implications presented in this chapter, however, suggest that U.S. educators should reconsider their cultural approaches and assumptions.

With regard to the second question, the linguistic match-mismatch conception does not adequately capture the primary and secondary speech community relationships. The second section has discussed biases that are often operating behind the match-mismatch hypothesis. The third section has further identified rebutting evidence from the Canadian immersion bilingual program. Thus, the emphasis throughout this chapter has been that regardless of their home environment, children can learn to internalize new expectations of classroom life.

Obviously, our answers to questions one and two are intricately related to question three. As reviewed in the third section, empowerment of language-minority students and their parents and communities is an issue that cannot be ignored in discussing successful language development for language-minority students. To achieve this end, the importance of teacher-student interaction (and peer interaction in the case of two-way bilingual education programs) should be conceptualized and put into practice by using the framework presented by Vygotsky (1978) and Bruner (1977). The nature of the teacher-student interaction is particularly relevant to the promotion of minority children's academic success. Teachers who understand the linguistic issues, so that they can develop communicative competence in response to meaningful situations in the classroom, will be better prepared to provide equal opportunities to all students. As we have seen through the research, there are many potential obstacles to smooth teacher-student interactions. For example, even if interlocutors exchange ideas about a particular topic and acknowledge each other's comments, they may define the same discourse or narrative topic somewhat differently if they have differing cultural backgrounds, and communication may eventually break down. Thus cultural components play a crucial role in keeping a collaborative activity on track.

Biases against socioculturally disadvantaged groups should not be ignored. Take mathematics and science classrooms, for example. Following the Sapir-Whorf hypothesis (Whorf, 1956)—that the language one speaks profoundly affects the manner in which one thinks about the world—Orr (1987) erroneously concludes that AAVE serves as a barrier to African American students' success in mathematics and science; the deficit hypothesis condemning African American children's home environment is operating behind her argument. Similarly, it has been reported that teachers tend to miss many opportunities to include female students in discussions. Through choice of language, the teacher may not provide clear or explicit instructions to female students or may tend to call on White middle-class male students much more frequently than minority working-class female students (Lemke, 1990). Unequal time allocation between males and females in the classroom may be attributed not only to differences in gender-specific language socialization (Maltz & Borker, 1982; Tannen, 1990) but also to the fact that women tend to be kept silent and powerless in society (Lakoff, 1990).

Considering all of these obstacles, the result is that classroom teachers do tend to interact differently with children from a variety of sociocultural backgrounds

(Cazden, 1988; Michaels, 1981), and that some do lower their expectations for those minority students' academic achievement (see Cummins, 1986). As anthropological sociolinguists (for example, Schieffelin & Ochs, 1986) claim, there are behavioral similarities for children of a given age in each cultural setting. Rather than accepting species-specific characteristics, such as the language acquisition process claimed by Noam Chomsky (1965), finding such population-specific characteristics is necessary for understanding what language socialization is all about.

Some classroom teachers tend to view minority students as a group, simply ignoring their individual differences. To make matters worse, in such classrooms the "we" (mostly White middle-class teachers) and "they" (minority students as a bundle) notion of multiculturalism may also exist. Not only is it true that even if they speak the same first language (for example, Spanish) children from one community (Mexico, for instance) and those from another (Puerto Rico) are different; it is also necessary that each minority student from each community be perceived as a distinct individual. If classroom teachers attribute Hispanic children's discipline problems to their parents and home environments, in statements such as "The Hispanic students come from restrictive environments; when they arrive in school they go wild" (Penfield, 1987, p. 31), the teachers' view delineates, on the basis of the deficit hypothesis, a bias against minority students. A one-size-fits-all approach never applies in any sense (Reyes, 1992). As Floden, Buchmann, and Schwille (1987) stress, today's schools are responsible for presenting students with a series of options for living and thinking, and providing them with diverse experiences and disciplinary concepts. Thus, contrary to the deficit hypothesis, it is the teacher, not the family, who has the main responsibility for adequate educational support.

Unfortunately, North American mainstream practices are, in effect, playing a gatekeeping role, which fails to recognize and build on the literacy skills and cultures that minority children bring to school from their home and local community. Those who were raised in North American mainstream culture misinterpret cultural differences in discourse style as deficits and, moreover, impose their mainstream norms on minority children. Miscommunications are certainly inevitable, because we tend to view and interpret the behavior of others through our own cultural filters. As we grow, we add more and more layers to our cultural filters, and as a result we rely on stereotypical misconceptions. These filters are like lenses that allow us to perceive the world in a certain way. Mainstream teachers, however, should break such stereotyped misconceptions, because literacy in the United States should be understood and addressed in consideration of the diverse cultures represented in U.S. schools.

The classroom teacher's major responsibility is, then, as Carol Winkelman (1990) puts it, to perform the role of an "experienced participant in the community rather than sole authority" and to facilitate classroom discourse, so that all "students feel more comfortable about being innovative and taking risks with their language" (p. 117). To create such an interactive classroom, the teacher needs to understand the interwoven relationship among language-minority students' linguistic, sociocultural, and cognitive processes (Ovando & Collier, 1998). On the basis of this understanding, a classroom, a school, and above all education can then become a forum in which—regardless of race, ethnicity, social background, and gender—everyone is treated equally, so that children from different sociocultural backgrounds can fully nurture their identity and self-esteem.

References

Ada, A. F. (1986). Creative education for bilingual teachers. *Harvard Educational Review, 56*(4), 386–394.

Armas, G. C. (2001, March 22). *Census data shows more immigrants in U.S.* Associated Press [On-line]. http://www.stolaf.edu/people/welchb/courses/es137/articles/articles/census_immigrants.htm.

Au, K. H., & Jordan, C. (1981). Teaching reading to Hawaiian children: Finding a culturally appropriate solution. In H. Trueba, G. P. Guthrie, & K. H. Au (Eds.), *Culture in the bilingual classroom: Studies in classroom ethnography* (pp. 139–152). Rowley, MA: Newbury House.

Auerbach, E. R. (1989). Toward a social-contextual approach to family literacy. *Harvard Educational Review, 59*(2), 165–181.

Baker, K. A., & de Kanter, A. A. (1981). *Effectiveness of bilingual education: A review of the literature.* Washington, DC: U.S. Department of Education, Office of Planning, Budget and Evaluation.

Baker, K. A., & de Kanter, A. A. (1983). Federal policy and the effectiveness of bilingual education. In K. A. Baker & A. A. de Kanter (Eds.), *Bilingual education* (pp. 33–86). Lexington, MA: Lexington Books.

Bennett, J. A., & Berry, J. W. (1991). Cree literacy in the syllabic script. In D. R. Olson & N. Torrance (Eds.), *Literacy and orality* (pp. 90–104). New York: Cambridge University Press.

Bernstein, B. (1971). *Class, codes and control: Vol. 1. Theoretical studies towards a sociology of language.* London: Routledge & Kegan Paul.

Blum-Kulka, S. (1997). *Dinner talk: Cultural patterns of sociability and socialization in family discourse.* Mahwah, NJ: Erlbaum.

Borker, R. (1980). Anthropology. In S. McConnell-Ginet, R. Borker, & N. Furman (Eds.), *Women and language in literature and society* (pp. 26–44). New York: Praeger.

Brandt, D. (1989). The medium is the message: Orality and literacy once more. *Written Communication, 61,* 31–44.

Brandt, D. (1990). *Literacy as involvement: The acts of writer, reader, and texts.* Carbondale: Southern Illinois University Press.

Brown, R. (1973). *A first language.* Cambridge, MA: Harvard University Press.

Brown, R., & Bellugi, U. (1964). Three processes in the child's acquisition of syntax. *Harvard Educational Review, 34*(2), 133–151.

Bruner, J. (1977). Early social interaction and language development. In H. R. Schaffer (Ed.), *Studies in mother-child interaction* (pp. 271–289). London: Academic Press.

Bruner, J. (1990). *Acts of meaning.* Cambridge, MA: Harvard University Press.

Cazden, C. B. (1988). *Classroom discourse: The language of teaching and learning.* Portsmouth, NH: Heinemann.

Cazden, C. B. (1992). *Language minority education in the United States: Implication of the Ramírez report* (Educational Practice Report no. 3). Santa Cruz, CA: National Center for Research on Cultural Diversity and Second Language Learning.

Chomsky, C. (1969). *The acquisition of syntax in children from 5 to 10.* Cambridge, MA: MIT Press.

Chomsky, N. (1957). *Syntactic structure.* The Hague: Mouton & Co.

Chomsky, N. (1959). Review of *Verbal Behavior* by B. F. Skinner. *Language, 35*(1), 26–58.

Chomsky, N. (1965). *Aspects of the theory of syntax.* Cambridge, MA: MIT Press.

Chomsky, N. (1985). *Knowledge of language: Its nature, origin, and use.* New York: Praeger.

Collier, V. P. (1987). Age and rate of acquisition of second language for academic purposes. *TESOL Quarterly, 21*(4), 617–641.

Collier, V. P. (1992). A synthesis of studies examining long-term language-minority student data on academic achievement. *Bilingual Research Journal, 16*(1 & 2), 187–212.

Cook-Gumperz, J. (1992). Gendered talk and gendered lives: Little girls being women before becoming (big) girls. In K. Hall, M. Buchholtz, & B. Moonwomon (Eds.), *Locating power: Proceedings of the 1992 Berkeley Women and Language Conference* (Vol. 1, pp. 68–79). Berkeley: University of California, Berkeley Women and Language Group.

Cook-Gumperz, J., & Gumperz, J. J. (1982). Communicative competence in educational perspective. In L. C. Wilkinson (Ed.), *Communicating in the classroom* (pp. 13–24). New York: Academic Press.

Cook-Gumperz, J., & Scales, B. (1996). Girls, boys, and just people: The interactional accomplishment of gender in the discourse of the nursery school. In D. I. Slobin, J. Gerhardt, A. Kyratzis, & J. Guo (Eds.), *Social interaction, social context, and language: Essays in honor of Susan Ervin-Tripp* (pp. 513–527). Mahwah, NJ: Erlbaum.

Crawford, J. (1989). *Bilingual education: History, politics, theory, and practice.* Trenton, NJ: Crane.

Cummins, J. (1979). Linguistic interdependence and the educational development of bilingual children. *Review of Educational Research, 49,* 222–251.

Cummins, J. (1980). The cross-lingual dimensions of language proficiency: Implications for bilingual education and optimal age issue. *TESOL Quarterly, 14*(2), 175–187.

Cummins, J. (1986). Empowering minority students: A framework for intervention. *Harvard Educational Review, 56*(1), 18–36.

Cummins, J. (1991). Language development and academic learning. In L. M. Malavé & G. Duquette (Eds.), *Language, culture and cognition* (pp. 161–175). Clevedon, England: Multilingual Matters.

Cummins, J. (2000). *Language, power and pedagogy: Bilingual children in the crossfire.* Clevedon, England: Multilingual Matters.

Cummins, J., Swain, M., Nakajima, K., Handscombe, J., Green, D., & Tran, C. (1984). Linguistic interdependence among Japanese and Vietnamese immigrant students. In C. Rivera (Ed.), *Language proficiency and academic achievement* (pp. 60–81). Clevedon, England: Multilingual Matters.

Delpit, L. D. (1988). The silenced dialogue: Power and pedagogy in educating other people's children. *Harvard Educational Review, 58*(3), 280–298.

Edelsky, C. (1991). *With literacy and justice for all.* Bristol, PA: Falmer Press.

Edelsky, C., Hudelson, S., Flores, B., Barkin, F., Altweger, J., & Jilbert, K. (1983). Semilingualism and language deficit. *Applied Linguistics, 4,* 1–22.

Egan, K. (1987). Literacy and the oral foundation of education. *Harvard Educational Review, 57*(4), 445–472.

Erickson, F. D., & Mohatt, G. (1982). Cultural organization of participation structures in two classrooms of Indian students. In G. D. Spindler (Ed.), *Doing the ethnography of schooling: Educational anthropology in action* (pp. 132–175). New York: Holt, Rinehart, & Winston.

Fishman, J. A. (1991). *Reversing language shift.* Clevedon, England: Multilingual Matters.

Floden, R. E., Buchmann, M., & Schwille, J. R. (1987). Breaking with everyday experience. *Teachers College Record, 88*(4), 485–506.

Freire, P. (1970). *Pedagogy of the oppressed.* New York: Seabury Press.

García, E. (1991). *Education of linguistically and culturally diverse students: Effective instructional practices* (Educational Practice Report no. 1). Santa Cruz, CA: National Center for Research on Cultural Diversity and Second Language Learning.

Garton, A., & Pratt, C. (1989). *Learning to be literate: The development of spoken and written language.* New York: Basil Blackwell.

Gee, J. P. (1985). The narrativization of experience in oral style. *Journal of Education, 167,* 9–35.

Gee, J. P. (1986a). Orality and literacy: From the savage mind to ways with words. *TESOL Quarterly, 20*(4), 719–746.

Gee, J. P. (1986b). Units in the production of narrative discourse. *Discourse Processes, 9,* 391–422.

Gee, J. P. (1990). *Social linguistics and literacies: Ideologies in discourse.* Bristol, PA: Falmer Press.

Genesee, F. (1983). Bilingual education of majority-language children: The immersion experiments in review. *Applied Psycholinguistics, 4,* 1–46.

Genesee, F. (1985). Second language learning through immersion: A review of U.S. programs. *Review of Educational Research, 55*(4), 541–561.

Gilzow, D. F. (2001). Japanese immersion: A successful program in Portland, Oregon. *ERIC News Bulletin, 24*(1 & 2), 1–3.

Gumperz, J. J. (1996). On teaching language in its sociocultural context. In D. I. Slobin, J. Gerhardt, A. Kyratzis, & J. Guo (Eds.), *Social interaction, social context, and language: Essays in honor of Susan Ervin-Tripp* (pp. 469–480). Mahwah, NJ: Erlbaum.

Hakuta, K. (1986). *Mirror of language: The debate on bilingualism.* New York: Basic Books.

Hale, K. (1992). On endangered languages and the safeguarding of diversity. *Language, 68*(1), 1–3.

Harley, B. (1991). The acquisition of some oral second language skills in early and late immersion. In L. M. Malavé & G. Duquette (Eds.), *Language, culture and cognition* (pp. 232–249). Clevedon, England: Multilingual Matters.

Hart, D., Lapkin, S., & Swain, M. (1991). Secondary level immersion French skills: A possible plateau effect. In L. M. Malavé & G. Duquette (Eds.), *Language, culture and cognition* (pp. 250–265). Clevedon, England: Multilingual Matters.

Hauser-Cram, P., Pierson, D. E., Walker, D. K., & Tivnan, T. (1991). *Early education in the public schools: Lessons from a comprehensive birth-to-kindergarten program.* San Francisco: Jossey-Bass.

Heath, S. B. (1983). *Ways with words: Language, life and work in communities and classrooms.* New York: Cambridge University Press.

Heath, S. B. (1986). Social contexts of language development. In California State Department of Education (Ed.), *Beyond language: Social and cultural factors in schooling* (pp. 143–186). Los Angeles: California State University.

Hemphill, L. (1989). Topic development, syntax, and social class. *Discourse Processes, 12,* 267–286.

Hirsch, E. D., Jr. (1988). Comments on *Profession 88. Profession 88.* New York: Modern Language Association.

Holm, A., & Holm, W. (1990). Rock Point, a Navajo way to go to school: A valediction. In C. B. Cazden & C. E. Snow (Eds.), *English plus: Issues in bilingual education* (pp. 170–184). Newbury Park, CA: Sage.

Huddy, L., & Sears, D. O. (1990). Qualified public support for bilingual education: Some policy implications. In C. B. Cazden & C. E. Snow (Eds.), *English plus: Issues in bilingual education* (pp. 119–134). Newbury Park, CA: Sage.

Hymes, D. (1974a). *Foundations in sociolinguistics: An ethnographic approach.* Philadelphia: University of Pennsylvania Press.

Hymes, D. (1974b). Speech and language: On the origins and foundations of inequity among speakers. In E. Haugen & M. Bloomfield (Eds.), *Language as a human problem* (pp. 45–71). New York: Norton.

Hymes, D. (1981). *"In vain I tried to tell you": Studies in Native American ethnopoetics.* Philadelphia: University of Pennsylvania Press.

Hymes, D. (1982). Narrative as a "grammar" of experience: Native Americans and a glimpse of English. *Journal of Education, 2,* 121–142.

Hymes, D. (1990). Thomas Paul's Sametl: Verse analysis of a (Saanich) Chinook jargon text. *Journal of Pidgin and Creole Languages, 5*(1), 71–106.

Jordan, C. (1984). Cultural compatibility and the education of Hawaiian children: Implications for mainland educators. *Education Research Quarterly, 8*(4), 59–71.

Jordan, C., Vogt, L., & Tharp, R. G. (1993). Explaining school failure, producing school success: Two cases. In E. Jacob & C. Jordan (Eds.), *Minority education: Anthropological perspectives* (pp. 53–65). Norwood, NJ: Ablex.

Krashen, S. (1996). *Under attack: The case against bilingual education.* Culver City, CA: Language Education Associates.

Krashen, S. (in press). Proposition 227 and skyrocketing test scores: An urban legend from California. *Journal of the Texas Association for Bilingual Education.*

Labov, W. (1972). *Language in the inner city.* Philadelphia: University of Pennsylvania Press.

Lakoff, R. T. (1990). *Talking power.* New York: Basic Books.

Lambert, W. E. (1975). Culture and language as factors in learning and education. In A. Wolfgang (Ed.), *Education of immigrant students: Issues and answers* (pp. 55–83). Toronto: Ontario Institute for Studies in Education.

Larson, C. L., & Ovando, C. J. (2001). *The color of bureaucracy: The politics of equity in multicultural school communities.* Belmont, CA: Wadsworth.

Lave, J. (1991). Situating learning in communities of practice. In L. B. Resnick, J. M. Levine, & S. D. Teasley (Eds.), *Perspectives on socially shared cognition* (pp. 63–82). Washington, DC: American Psychological Association.

Lave, J., & Wenger, E. (1991). *Situated learning: Legitimate peripheral participation.* New York: Cambridge University Press.

Lemke, J. (1990). *Talking science: Language, learning, and values.* Norwood, NJ: Ablex.

Lindholm, K. J. (1992). Two-way bilingual/immersion education: Theory, conceptual issues, and pedagogical implications. In R. V. Padilla & A. H. Benavides (Eds.), *Critical perspectives on bilingual education research* (pp. 195–220). Tempe, AZ: Bilingual Press/Editorial Bilingüe.

Lucas, T., Henze, R., & Donato, R. (1990). Promoting the success of Latino language-minority students: An exploratory study of six high schools. *Harvard Educational Review, 60*(3), 315–340.

MacSwan, J. (2000). The threshold hypothesis, semilingualism, and other contributions to a deficit view of linguistic minorities. *Hispanic Journal of Behavior Sciences, 20*(1), 3–45.

Maltz, D., & Borker, R. (1982). A cultural approach to male-female miscommunication. In J. Gumperz (Ed.), *Language and social identity* (pp. 195–216). New York: Cambridge University Press.

Martin-Jones, M., & Romaine, S. (1986). Semilingualism: A half-baked theory of communicative competence. *Applied Linguistics, 7,* 26–38.

McCloskey, M. L., & Enright, D. S. (1992). America 2000: A TESOL response. In *TESOL resource packet* (pp. 1–9). Alexandria, VA: TESOL.

McCormick, E. (2000, September 3). Asians will soon be biggest S.F. group. *San Francisco Examiner,* A1, A12.

McLaughlin, B. (1992). *Myths and misconceptions about second language learning: What every teacher needs to learn* (Educational Practice Report no. 5). Santa Cruz, CA: National Center for Research on Cultural Diversity and Second Language Learning.

McLaughlin, D. (1990). The sociolinguistics of Navajo literacy. *Journal of Navajo Education, 7*(2), 28–36.

Mehan, H. (1991). *Sociological foundations supporting the study of cultural diversity* (Research Report no. 1). Santa Cruz, CA: National Center for Research on Cultural Diversity and Second Language Learning.

Michaels, S. (1981). "Sharing time": Children's narrative styles and differential access to literacy. *Language in Society, 10,* 423–442.

Michaels, S., & Collins, J. (1984). Oral discourse styles: Classroom interaction and the acquisition of literacy. In D. Tannen (Ed.), *Coherence in spoken and written discourse* (pp. 219–244). Norwood, NJ: Ablex.

Miller, P. (1982). *Amy, Wendy, and Beth: Language acquisition in South Baltimore.* Austin: University of Texas Press.

Minami, M. (2000). Crossing borders: The politics of schooling Asian students. In C. J. Ovando & P. McLaren (Eds.), *The politics of multiculturalism and bilingual education: Students and teachers caught in the cross fire* (pp. 188–207). New York: McGraw-Hill.

Minami, M. (2001, April). *Holding onto a native tongue: Retaining bilingualism for school-age children of Japanese heritage.* Paper presented at the American Educational Research Association 2001 annual meeting, Seattle, WA.

Minami, M., & McCabe, A. (1991). Haiku as a discourse regulation device: A stanza analysis of Japanese children's personal narratives. *Language in Society, 20,* 577–600.

Minami, M., & McCabe, A. (1995). Rice balls and bear hunts: Japanese and North American family narrative patterns. *Journal of Child Language, 22,* 423–445.

Morison, S. H. (1990). A Spanish-English dual-language program in New York City. In C. B. Cazden & C. E. Snow (Eds.), *English plus: Issues in bilingual education* (pp. 160–169). Newbury Park, CA: Sage.

Muñoz-Sandoval, A. F., Cummins, J., Alvarado, C. G., & Ruef, M. L. (1998). *Bilingual verbal ability tests: Comprehensive manual.* Itasca, IL: Riverside.

Nelson, K. (1981). Individual differences in a language development: Implications for development and language. *Psychological Bulletin, 17,* 170–187.

Ninio, A., & Snow, C. E. (1996). *Pragmatic development.* Boulder, CO: Westview Press.

Ochs, E. (1986). Introduction. In B. B. Schieffelin & E. Ochs (Eds.), *Language socialization across cultures* (pp. 1–13). New York: Cambridge University Press.

Ochs, E. (1996). Linguistic resources for socializing humanity. In J. J. Gumperz & S. C. Levinson (Eds.), *Rethinking linguistic relativity* (pp. 407–437). New York: Cambridge University Press.

Ochs, E., & Schieffelin, B. B. (1984). Language acquisition and socialization: Three developmental stories. In R. Schweder & R. LeVine (Eds.), *Culture theory: Essays on mind, self and emotion* (pp. 276–320). New York: Cambridge University Press.

Ogbu, J. U. (1990). Cultural model, identity, and literacy. In J. W. Stigler, R. A. Shweder, & G. Herdt (Eds.), *Cultural psychology: Essays on comparative human development* (pp. 520–541). New York: Cambridge University Press.

Ogbu, J. U. (1992). Understanding cultural diversity and learning. *Educational Researcher, 21*(8), 5–14.

Olson, D. R. (1977). From utterance to text: The bias of language in speech and writing. *Harvard Educational Review, 47*(3), 257–281.

Orr, E. W. (1987). *Twice as less: Black English and the performance of Black students in mathematics and science.* New York: Norton.

Ovando, C. J. (1984). School and community attitudes in an Athapaskan bush village. *Educational Research Quarterly, 8*(4), 12–29.

Ovando, C. J. (1990). Politics and pedagogy: The case of bilingual education. *Harvard Educational Review, 60*(3), 341–356.

Ovando, C. J. (1993). Language, diversity, and education. In J. A. Banks & C. A. M. Banks (Eds.), *Multicultural education: Issues and perspectives* (2nd ed., pp. 215–235). Boston: Allyn & Bacon.

Ovando, C. J. (1994). Change in school and community attitudes in an Athapaskan village. *Peabody Journal of Education, 69*(2), 43–59.

Ovando, C. J. (2001a). Beyond "blaming the victim": Successful schools for Latino students. *Educational Researcher, 30*(3), 29–31, 39.

Ovando, C. J. (2001b). Language diversity and education. In J. A. Banks & C. A. M. Banks (Eds.), *Multicultural education: Issues and perspectives* (4th ed., pp. 268–291). Boston: Allyn and Bacon.

Ovando, C. J., & Collier, V. P. (1998). *Bilingual and ESL classrooms: Teaching in multicultural contexts* (2nd ed.). Boston: McGraw-Hill.

Ovando, C. J., & McLaren, P. (2000). *The politics of multicultural and bilingual education: Students and teachers caught in the cross fire.* Boston: McGraw-Hill.

Ovando, C. J., & Pérez, R. (2000). The politics of bilingual immersion programs. In C. J. Ovando & P. McLaren (Eds.), *The politics of multiculturalism and bilingual education: Students and teachers caught in the cross fire* (pp. 148–165). New York: McGraw-Hill.

Peal, E., & Lambert, W. E. (1962). The relation of bilingualism to intelligence. *Psychological Monographs, 76*(27, Whole No. 546), 1–23.

Penfield, J. (1987). ESL: The regular classroom teacher's perspective. *TESOL Quarterly, 21*(1), 21–39.

Philips, S. U. (1972). Participant structures and communicative competence: Warm Springs children in community and classroom. In C. B. Cazden, V. P. John, & D. Hymes (Eds.), *Functions of language in the classroom* (pp. 370–394). Prospect Heights, IL: Waveland Press.

Philips, S. U. (1982). *The invisible culture: Communication in classroom and community on the Warm Springs Indian reservation.* New York: Longman.

Ramírez, J. D., Yuen, S. D., & Ramey, D. R. (1991). *Longitudinal study of structured English immersion strategy, early-exit and late-exit transitional bilingual education programs for language-minority children. Final report to the U.S. Department of Education.* (Executive Summary and Vols. 1 & 2). San Mateo, CA: Aguirre International.

Reyes, M. L. (1992). Challenging venerable assumptions: Literacy instruction for linguistically different students. *Harvard Educational Review, 62*(4), 427–446.

Rhodes, N. C., & Branaman, L. E. (1999). *Foreign language instruction in the United States: A national survey of elementary and secondary schools.* McHenry, IL, and Washington, DC: Delta Systems and Center for Applied Linguistics.

Robinson, J. L. (1990). *Conversations on the written word: Essays on language and literacy.* Portsmouth, NJ: Heinemann.

Rosier, P., & Holm, W. (1980). *The Rock Point experience: A longitudinal study of a Navajo school program.* Washington, DC: Center for Applied Linguistics.

A rush to judgment on bilingual education. (2000, September 3). *San Francisco Chronicle,* p. 6.

Saussure, F. de. (1959). *Course in general linguistics* (W. Baskin, trans.). New York: McGraw-Hill. (Original work published 1915)

Schieffelin, B. B. (1986). Teasing and shaming in Kaluli children's interactions. In B. B. Schieffelin & E. Ochs (Eds.), *Language socialization across cultures* (pp. 165–181). New York: Cambridge University Press.

Schieffelin, B. B., & Eisenberg, A. R. (1984). Cultural variation in children's conversations. In B. B. Schieffelin & J. Picker (Eds.), *The acquisition of communicative competence* (pp. 378–420). Baltimore, MD: University Park Press.

Schieffelin, B. B., & Ochs, E. (Eds.). (1986). *Language socialization across cultures.* New York: Cambridge University Press.

Schieffelin, B. B., & Ochs, E. (1996). The microgenesis of competence: Methodology in language socialization. In D. I. Slobin, J. Gerhardt, A. Kyratzis, & J. Guo (Eds.), *Social interaction, social context, and language: Essays in honor of Susan Ervin-Tripp* (pp. 251–263). Mahwah, NJ: Erlbaum.

Scollon, R., & Scollon, S. (1981). *Narrative, literacy and face in interethnic communications.* Norwood, NJ: Ablex.

Scribner, S., & Cole, M. (1981). *The psychology of literacy.* Cambridge, MA: Harvard University Press.

Skinner, B. F. (1957). *Verbal behavior.* Englewood Cliffs, NJ: Prentice-Hall.

Slobin, D. I. (1985). Introduction: Why study acquisition crosslinguistically? In D. I. Slobin (Ed.), *The crosslinguistic study of language acquisition: Vol. 1. The data* (pp. 3–24). Hillsdale, NJ: Erlbaum.

Snow, C. E. (1983). Literacy and language: Relationships during the preschool years. *Harvard Educational Review, 53*(2), 165–189.

Snow, C. E. (1990). The development of definitional skill. *Journal of Child Language, 17,* 697–710.

Snow, C. E., Barnes, W. S., Chandler, J., Goodman, I. F., & Hemphill, L. (1991). *Unfulfilled expectations: Home and school influences on literacy.* Cambridge, MA: Harvard University Press.

Snow, C. E., Cancino, H., De Temple, J., & Schley, S. (1991). Giving formal definitions: A linguistic or metalinguistic skill? In E. Bialystok (Ed.), *Language processing in bilingual children* (pp. 90–112). New York: Cambridge University Press.

Snow, C. E., & Ninio, A. (1986). The contracts of literacy: What children learn from learning to read books. In W. Teale & E. Sultzby (Eds.), *Emergent literacy: Written and reading* (pp. 116–138). Norwood, NJ: Ablex.

Spener, D. (1988). Transitional bilingual education and the socialization of immigrants. *Harvard Educational Review, 58*(2), 133–153.

Tannen, D. (1982). The myth of orality and literacy. In W. Frawley (Ed.), *Linguistics and literacy. Proceedings of the Delaware Symposium on Language Studies* (pp. 37–50). New York: Plenum.

Tannen, D. (1987). The orality of literature and literary conversation. In J. A. Langer (Ed.), *Language, literacy and culture: Issues of society and schooling* (pp. 67–88). Norwood, NJ: Ablex.

Tannen, D. (1990). *You just don't understand: Women and men in conversation.* New York: Morrow.

Tharp, R. G., & Gallimore, R. (1991). *Rousing minds to life: Teaching, learning, and schooling in social context.* Cambridge, England: Cambridge University Press.

Torrance, N., & Olson, D. R. (1985). Oral and literate competencies in the early school years. In D. R. Olson, N. Torrance, & A. Hildyard (Eds.), *Literacy, language, and learning: The nature of consequences of reading and writing* (pp. 256–284). New York: Cambridge University Press.

Vygotsky, L. S. (1978). *Mind in society: The development of higher psychological processes.* Cambridge, MA: Harvard University Press.

Whorf, B. L. (1956). *Language, thought, and reality: Selected writings* (J. B. Carroll, Ed.). Cambridge, MA: MIT Press.

Williams, J. D., & Snipper, G. C. (1990). *Literacy and bilingualism.* New York: Longman.

Willig, A. C. (1985). A meta-analysis of selected studies on the effectiveness of bilingual education. *Review of Educational Research, 55,* 269–317.

Wiley, T. (1996). *Literacy and language diversity in the United States.* McHenry, IL: Center for Applied Linguistics and Delta Systems.

Winkelman, C. L. (1990). Talk as text: Students on the margins. In J. L. Robinson (Ed.), *Conversations on the written word: Essays on language and literacy* (pp. 115–128). Portsmouth, NJ: Heinemann.

Wong Fillmore, L., & Valadez, C. (1986). Teaching bilingual teachers. In M. C. Wittrock (Ed.), *Handbook of research on teaching* (3rd ed., pp. 648–684). New York: Macmillan.

28

TRENDS IN TWO-WAY IMMERSION RESEARCH

Kelly Bikle

Stanford University

Kenji Hakuta

Stanford University

Elsa S. Billings

Stanford University

On January 8, 2002, President George W. Bush signed into law the No Child Left Behind Act of 2001, a reauthorization of the Elementary and Secondary Education Act. In this new law, the Bilingual Education Act (Title VII) was renamed the English Language Acquisition, Language Enhancement, and Academic Achievement Act (Title III), and the Office of Bilingual Education and Minority Languages Affairs (OBEMLA) was renamed the Office of English Language Acquisition, Language Enhancement, and Academic Achievement for Limited English Proficient Students, thus bringing to an end a 24-year period in American history when the term *bilingual education* was codified in U.S. law and the institution of government.

During this period, bilingual education was a projective test of the many hopes and fears surrounding language policy in the United States. Advocates for English learners saw hope in developing local capacity to implement programs to deliver access to English language acquisition and appropriate content instruction, thus meeting the requirements of the Supreme Court decision *Lau* v. *Nichols* (1974), which required modifications to instruction to meet the needs of English learners. Advocates for bilingualism saw the potential for developing a national language policy to promote bilingualism, especially through leveraging the many linguistic resources brought by immigrants. Conservatives who feared the balkanization of the United States and a continuing need for Americanization of immigrants argued against anything officially bilingual—bilingual ballots, bilingual drivers' tests, and bilingual education programs—and expressed their fears through advocacy for codification of

English as the official language of the United States (Hayakawa, 1992; U.S. English, 1992).

During these 24 years, Title VII supported programs running the full gamut of variations. The most common were transitional bilingual education programs, in which the native language is used for a short period of time as a crutch until children develop proficiency in English. Some of these programs further tried to maintain the native language even after the students had acquired English. But also supported were English-only programs, with names such as special alternative instructional programs, structured immersion, and sheltered instruction (see August & Hakuta, 1997). Fierce battles were waged, especially during the Reagan administration with William Bennett as secretary of education, over the relative proportion of funds that supported these bilingual versus English-only programs (Crawford, 1999).

In the waning years of the Bilingual Education Act, there emerged a growing interest in a new type of bilingual program: two-way immersion (hereafter, TWI, also varyingly called dual immersion or developmental bilingual education). In TWI programs, students from language-majority and language-minority backgrounds are brought together with the common goals of attaining a high level of proficiency in both languages, meeting academic standards, and developing cross-cultural understanding. This chapter puts the spotlight on TWI programs as a way of telling a complex story about the interplay of policy, politics, education, and research in language education.

The first part of this chapter describes the framework of TWI programs and then discusses how they sit at the intersection of two significant bodies of theory and research in language learning: the education of nonnative speakers of English and foreign language education, focusing on language immersion programs for native English speakers. In the second part of this chapter, recent research on TWI programs is discussed. This includes a presentation of statistics on program descriptions, language allocation, student characteristics and demographics, approaches to literacy, and student outcomes. Finally, the concluding section suggests new lines of research to broaden the understanding of the linguistic, academic, and social outcomes for students in TWI programs.

TWO-WAY IMMERSION PROGRAMS

Two-way immersion programs are designed with the lofty aim of integrating language-majority and language-minority students in classrooms with the goal of bilingualism, biliteracy, and high academic achievement for all. Students enrolled in TWI programs learn content through two languages, developing both language skills and academic competencies simultaneously. Since the lessons are not translated and students are encouraged to use the language of instruction, students have the opportunity to serve both as a language model (during instruction in their native language) and as a language learner (during instruction in their second language). Native English speakers are integrated with speakers of a minority language to draw on the combined linguistic resources of the two language groups. Finally, TWI approaches have been celebrated by some (Cazabon, Lambert, & Hall, 1993) as a means of balancing inequalities inherent in some segregated programs that separate students by language.

The first program that served as an early model for TWI in the United States began at the Coral Way School in Dade County, Florida, in 1963. The program, which provided equal amounts of instruction in English and Spanish for all students, was a response to the desire of Cuban political refugees, largely from the professional classes, to maintain their language and culture. Open to both English and Spanish speakers, both groups showed above-average achievement in English reading, and the Cuban children maintained a high level of Spanish as well (Hakuta, 1986; Mackey & Beebe, 1977).

In the 30 years following Coral Way, however, the growth of TWI programs was slow. Although federal funding was available to support bilingual education programs through Title VII, the focus was mainly on transitional bilingual education. The intent of Title VII was primarily remedial. There was limited support for bilingual enrichment, but the majority of these programs were aimed exclusively at language-minority students. One exception to the compensatory model was a TWI program established in San Diego, California (Lindholm-

Leary, 2001). Although there is no published record of the early years of the program, the district produced a handbook that was influential as similar programs emerged (ESEA Title VII Bilingual Demonstration Project, 1982, as cited in Lindholm-Leary, 2001).

The past decade has seen rapidly growing interest in TWI programs. In 1990, there were fewer than 40 programs nationwide; by 2000, 253 programs in 24 states were in operation (Center for Applied Linguistics, 2001). In California, 91 programs in 47 districts offered TWI programs. Texas, New York, Illinois, New Mexico, Arizona, and Massachusetts each boasted between 13 and 34 programs. The vast majority of these are Spanish/English immersion, but a few Chinese/English, Korean/English, French/English, and Navajo/English programs are also in operation (Center for Applied Linguistics, 2001).

As a developing pedagogical approach to language and content area education, the definition of TWI continues to evolve. As such, a range of programs that include all types of enriched language education have come to be considered as two-way approaches. However, in recent years, increasing interest and discussion about the characteristics of TWI has led to proposed criteria for an "official" TWI designation. The Center for Applied Linguistics, or CAL (2001), defines these programs as those that meet three criteria: (a) integration, where language-minority and language-majority students must be integrated for at least 50 percent of the day at all grade levels; (b) instruction, wherein content and literacy instruction in both languages is provided to all students; and (c) population, meaning within the program there is a balance of language-minority and language-majority students, with each group making up between one-third and two-thirds of the total student population. Working with this definition, the center has compiled a database of TWI programs based on a self-reported questionnaire (Center for Applied Linguistics, 2001).

TWI programs are often thought to serve students from poor Hispanic backgrounds and middle-class English-speaking students. This may be true for many programs, but there also exists considerable diversity. Although the national minority population in TWI consists of more low-income students than the majority population, the programs do serve a large number of low-income majority-language speakers as well. Approximately 30 percent of programs report that more than half of their students receive free or reduced lunch, a commonly used indicator of low socioeconomic status. Additionally, among the TWI programs in the CAL database, about half report no clear ethnic or racial majority among the native English speakers (Howard & Sugarman, 2001).

The vast majority of TWI programs are at the elementary school level, beginning in kindergarten or first grade and extending through fifth grade. Although a growing number of programs have appeared at the middle and high school levels, districts continue to struggle with implementing articulated programs across elementary, middle, and high schools (Christian, 1994).

A large number of language-enrichment programs are in operation that do not meet CAL's criteria for two-way designation. Many programs across the country are dedicated to providing language-enrichment education to their students; however, because of issues such as limited budgets, philosophical differences, staffing constraints, or student population, the programs may not meet the language instruction or integration requirements to be considered TWI programs by CAL. Although a review of these programs is outside the scope of this chapter, it should be noted that many more programs dedicated to viewing language diversity as a resource are in operation than those identified as TWI.

HISTORY OF SECOND LANGUAGE PEGAGOGY AND POLICY

Educators have long grappled with language education, both English language development for language-minority students and foreign language education for native English speakers. Historically, these two fields have been largely separate, each pursuing its own goals. In the case of language-minority students, programs ranging from English as a second language (ESL) to bilingual education emerged from the civil rights era in an attempt to provide equitable education and access to the curriculum. For native speakers of English, however, foreign language educators have battled to raise the public profile as well as the pedagogical effectiveness of foreign language education. One program model, immersion education, based on the highly popular French immersion programs in Canada (Genesee, 1983; Lambert & Tucker, 1972; Swain & Lapkin, 1982), has shown a relatively high rate of success in developing both language and academic competencies (Genesee, 1985; Snow, 1990; Snow, Padilla, & Campbell, 1988).

TWI programs sit at the intersection of bilingual programs for nonnative speakers of English and immersion programs for native English speakers. Thus, although English and foreign language education are far apart in terms of goals and the populations they serve, TWI programs work to unite these two very different language learning domains. It is the complexity and challenges that arise in bringing these two fields together that make TWI an interesting topic for a chapter on multicultural education.

Minority Language Speakers Learning English: Programs and Paradigms

In the 1950s and 1960s, ESL instruction began as a response to the growing number of refugee and immigrant children entering the United States and to the increase of international students coming to the United States to study. Prior to ESL instruction, students who spoke languages other than English were placed in traditional classrooms with native English speakers and "submersed" in English language instruction for all content areas. Often referred to as a sink-or-swim approach, submersion had become the norm across the United States (Ovando & Collier, 1985).

Despite improvements in recent decades, many of the programs offered to English language learners (ELLs) are largely based on a compensatory view of minority languages, with students' first language (L1) viewed as a problem or deficit to overcome, or, in some cases, used as a support to more quickly attain English proficiency. This is not surprising given that the programs are the result of impetus from the 1974 U.S. Supreme Court decision on the case of *Lau* v. *Nichols* (1974), a lawsuit filed on behalf of Kenny Lau that charged the San Francisco Unified School District with failure to provide its ELLs with an opportunity to learn English as well as meaningful access to an education. The Supreme Court ruled in favor of *Lau,* concluding that "there is no equality of treatment merely by providing students with the same facilities, textbooks, teachers, and curriculum; for students who do not understand English are effectively foreclosed from any meaningful education" (*Lau* v. *Nichols, 1974*). The court asserted that in order for students with a limited proficiency in English to participate in the education process, they must first understand the English language. Although ruling in favor of Lau, the Supreme Court decision simply guaranteed equal access to education and did not go so far as to mandate bilingual instruction (Crawford, 1999).

The *Lau* decision was supported by another lawsuit, *Castaneda* v. *Pickard* (1981), which outlined the requirements for establishing a program appropriate for ELLs. Although the decision did not advocate for a particular program, it did establish three criteria that a program must meet. First, the program must be based on "sound" educational theory. Second, it must be, "implement[ed] effectively" with appropriate resources and personnel. Finally, it must be evaluated for effectiveness after a trial period of implementation.

In the policy realm, the development of bilingualism as enrichment was a stealth goal of Title VII–supported efforts, especially during the 1970s. One evaluation during this period found that 86% of bilingual education directors surveyed said that native language maintenance was an important goal of their program (Dandoff, 1978), leading politicians such as President Ronald Reagan to respond with alarm: "It is absolutely wrong and against American concept to have a bilingual education program that is now openly, admittedly dedicated to preserving their native language and never getting them adequate in English so they can go out into the job market" (quoted in Hakuta, 1986, p. 207). Because of this tension, political support for maintenance programs has never really taken root, in part because these programs are perceived as separatist and lacking in native English speaking models to assist with the development of English. Although there are no recent estimates of the number of maintenance programs (also called "late exit programs"), they are rare and with few exceptions have not been systematically evaluated (see Ramirez, Yuen, Ramey, & Pasta, 1991, for the best effort to evaluate such programs).

By the 1980s, the larger educational policy arena in the United States was marked by a standards-setting movement, in an attempt to explicitly define grade-level competencies. In an effort to include the needs of ELLs, which had been overlooked (Short, 1997), national ESL standards were developed through TESOL (Teachers of English to Speakers of Other Languages). This was the first time that the needs of ELLs had been systematically addressed, focusing on their needs across the grade levels as well as language proficiency levels.

Today, there are mainly two types of ESL instructional programs. The first is often referred to as ESL or English language development (ELD). ESL and ELD programs offer English learners specialized English language instruction that is based upon the students' individualized levels of English proficiency (Lindholm-Leary, 2001). Sheltered English instruction is another type of English language program for ELLs, which develops English proficiency through specialized content instruction adapted to the proficiency level of the students (Rennie, 1993).

Considerable research energy during the 1970s and 1980s went into the race between the relative effectiveness of bilingual education over English-only or ESL programs. Research funding patterns during this period showed a significant shift from basic and program-based research to efforts at program evaluation (Moran & Hakuta, 2001). Much of the work is summarized in August and Hakuta (1997), Greene (1997), Meyer and Fienberg (1992), and Willig (1985). On the basis of these reports, one can draw these conclusions: (a) most of the comparisons were between transitional bilingual programs and ESL programs, and very little investment was made in looking at maintenance programs; (b) meta-analyses of the evaluations show significant advantages of bilingual over ESL approaches; (c) the size of the effect is generally considered small (less than half a standard deviation); and (d) the magnitude of the program differences are small when compared to the magnitude of the achievement gap between socioeconomically advantaged and disadvantaged students. Thus one might say that transitional bilingual programs are effective, but much more is needed if socioeconomically driven inequities are to be reduced. One might also say that the political heat generated by the bilingual issue has distracted policy makers from paying attention to the myriad socioeconomic issues associated with educating English language learners.

After reviewing the evidence, the most recent National Academy of Sciences report (August & Hakuta, 1997) concluded that evaluations comparing transitional bilingual and ESL programs are unlikely to produce additional knowledge, and that an important line of work to be pursued would be theory-driven evaluations that go beyond simple language of instruction, and include various factors at the school level (August & Hakuta, 1997). Especially important in the theoretical components of programs to be investigated are factors identified in case studies of schools that are considered successful in meeting the needs of English learners. In this context, the language of instruction is just one of a number of other important factors, such as the school leadership and climate, a coherent curriculum, and systematic student assessment that support clearly articulated instructional goals. Since these are features that are lacking in many high-poverty schools in which most English learners are found, systematic research into the relevance of these factors and how they can be promoted is extremely important in school improvement.

Majority Language Speakers and Foreign Language Education: Programs and Paradigms

Despite a long history of foreign language education for majority language speakers, the field has been marked by apathy and lack of educational policy. The elementary school programs in the United States and Canada that are in operation have followed three basic program models. Models that approach language education as either supplemental or enrichment education seek to expose children to a second language or teach language skills in isolation. These models have been largely unsuccessful (Branaman & Rennie, 1998). Immersion education, an approach developed in Canada in which Anglophone students are educated through the medium of French, has shown promising results (Genesee, 1987; Lambert & Tucker, 1972). There has been cross-fertilization, albeit often misinformed, as to the relevance of Canadian research in French immersion to the possibility of providing English immersion to language-minority students in the United States.

Foreign Language Education in the United States: 1950-Present. The years following World War II saw a dramatic increase in the number of foreign language education programs available in elementary schools, although many of the programs available were of poor quality (Andersson, 1969) or based on inappropriate theory (Met & Rhodes, 1990). In the 1950s and 1960s, language learning was approached from a behaviorist standpoint. The audiolingual method, which mimicked the manner in which a first language was learned, was considered the most appropriate instructional approach. However, the excessive repetition, rote memorization, and lack of attention to cognitive development proved unsuccessful in producing the desired result of foreign language fluency (Heining-Boynton, 1990).

Spurred by the public's discontent with education and disappointing outcomes in proficiency levels, as well as by changing ideas about learning theory, the conception of foreign language instruction moved away from a focus on grammar and toward a more interactive and communication-based model (Bruning, Flowerday, & Trayer, 1999; Schulz, 1998; Thompson, Christian, Stansfield, & Rhodes, 1990). In the late 1970s, a presidential commission report brought foreign language education under political scrutiny and was highly critical of international education in general. The report stated, "American's scandalous incompetence in foreign languages" was viewed as the key impediment to graduates' "dangerously inadequate understanding of world affairs" (President's Commission on Foreign Languages and International Studies, 1979, p. 7). This report spurred a dialogue on the goals of language study, appropriate assessment, and public awareness of the importance of foreign language education (Thompson et al., 1990).

During the 1980s and 1990s, the emergence of professional organizations along with changing conceptions of programs and pedagogical approaches changed the model of language education to be more interactive and communication-based (Lipton, 1998; Met & Rhodes, 1990; Rennie, 1998). Associations such as the American Council on the Teaching of Foreign Languages began to play a larger role in providing training and support for classroom teachers, developing standards and assessments (see National Standards in Foreign Language Education Project, 1996), and advocating for an increased national focus on foreign language education. New pedagogical approaches incorporated Vygotsky's (1986) social cognitive theory. Despite the focus on developing communication skills in 1997, only half of all public high school students and less than 15% of elementary school students were enrolled in any type of foreign language program (Branaman, Rhodes, & Rennie, 1998).

Foreign Language Programs in the Elementary School: FLES and FLEX. Foreign language in the elementary school programs (FLES), the most common type of language education in U.S. elementary schools, approach foreign language teaching as a separate subject that is typically taught three to five times a week. Classes vary in length from 20 to 50 minutes and focus on the four communication areas—listening, speaking, reading, and writing—as well as culture. Some programs may incorporate academic themes into the instruction (Branaman & Rennie, 1998). With sufficient time and practice, students who remain in long-term FLES programs do show substantial progress in second language proficiency (Curtain & Pesola, 1994, as cited in Branaman & Rennie, 1998).

Foreign language experience programs (FLEX), on the other hand, place more emphasis on languages and cultures as general concepts instead of developing skills in the second language. On average, FLEX programs are taught less often and for shorter duration than FLES programs. The emphasis is not on gaining proficiency in any one language, but on exposing students to one or more languages. FLEX programs are controversial in the research community because some believe that exposure to language is better than no language education, while others believe that if proficiency is not the goal, the students do not gain from their time in the program (Branaman & Rennie, 1998).

Foreign Language in the Elementary School: Immersion Models. Immersion is a form of language and content instruction in which students who speak the majority language of a society receive part of their instruction through the medium of a second language, and part through their first language. Both languages are used to teach and learn content material in familiar school subjects such as math, science, and history. Each lesson is taught in only one language; instruction is not translated (Genesee, 1987). In the immersion model, then, the second language is not the subject of instruction but rather the medium through which content knowledge is acquired (Met, 1993).

Modern immersion programs have their roots in the politics surrounding the use and status of the French language in Quebec, Canada. Dissatisfied with the amount of French instruction that their English-speaking children were receiving in school (20–30 minutes), and the emphasis on grammatical approaches to language education, a group of parents in St. Lambert, Quebec, with the support of Wallace Lambert, established an experimental immersion kindergarten in 1965 (Genesee, 1987; Lambert & Tucker, 1972). Immersion programs have also been implemented in the United States (Fortune & Jorstad, 1996; Genesee, 1985). These programs differ from TWI programs in that they are designed only for English-speaking children to learn a second language.

Early research in immersion education in Canada focused on the impact on academic attainment when learned through a second language (Lapkin, Swain, & Shapson, 1990). These studies have shown that the Canadian immersion models yield positive results on academic and language measures (Curtain & Pesola, 1988; Genesee, 1987; Swain, 1985, 2000).

In a study of four immersion programs across the United States, Genesee (1985, 1987) found similar trends.

In terms of first-language development, no long-term deficits have been noted as a result of majority language speakers' participation in immersion programs. With respect to academic levels, students demonstrated no difficulty in learning content through a second language. In terms of the second language, students in all of the programs attained functional proficiency. Although they did not demonstrate nativelike mastery of the target language, even after several years in the program, their linguistic irregularities did not impede their ability to communicate proficiently.

In the 1980s, the focus in immersion research in Canada broadened to include issues such as instructional aspects, qualitative language assessment, and program design (Lapkin et al., 1990). Researchers focused on understanding components of an effective immersion program by understanding the experience of students enrolled in immersion courses. What became apparent was that language instruction integrated with content instruction is a more effective approach to second language instruction than direct teaching of the language. Snow, Met, and Genesee (1989) posit four main reasons for this. First, language is acquired most readily in situations in which it is learned for communication in a significant, meaningful situation. In school, academic learning can provide such a basis as students work together to discuss, explain, argue, or develop their understandings. Second, the classroom learning situation gives students an "authentic" situation in which to develop and practice their language skills. Sustained exposure to the language of the classroom offers adequate opportunities to learn the patterns of the language and sufficient context in which to acquire new information. Third, integrating content with language for instruction allows for language learning to become a natural part of cognitive and social development in schools. Finally, learning and using a language across their academic subjects allows students to practice using their language in a variety of contexts.

One of the main weaknesses of the immersion model, however, is that students are not exposed to the target language as it is used by children who are native speakers. Furthermore, Swain (1988) found that teachers tended to simplify their language in teaching, used a restricted set of grammatical forms, and gave students little opportunity to engage in extended discourse. Additionally, since students did not often have peers who were native speakers of the target language, there was little chance for them to develop age-appropriate varieties of it.

Recent research has addressed this issue from a variety of perspectives. Some have examined the effectiveness of teaching form (grammar and vocabulary) to students as part of their content lessons (Day & Shapson, 1991; Swain, 2000). Lyster (1996) examined language learning from a sociolinguistic perspective to assess the efficacy of teaching sociolinguistic variation (polite and informal, use of indirect questions and conditional forms in French, and the like). From still another perspective, student interaction about language at the metalinguistic level has been shown to be an important factor in language development (Swain & Lapkin, 1998). The positive outcomes in student language that are due to instruction and interaction lend credence to the authors' claim that students in immersion programs will not acquire nativelike proficiency on their own; rather, they need to receive feedback from peers and their teacher on the appropriateness, accuracy, and coherence of the language they employ.

These results point not only to the need for systematic planning in terms of language objectives so that students are challenged to learn increasingly complex linguistic skills but also to the added benefit native speakers could provide in terms of naturalistic use of language. In immersion models, new grammatical structures, vocabulary, and idioms are introduced largely by the teacher, since all of the students are language learners. Two-way programs, then, with their inclusion of native speakers from each language group in which language is learned through content study, have the potential to counter these drawbacks.

THEORETICAL FOUNDATIONS OF TWO-WAY IMMERSION PROGRAMS

TWI emerges at the intersection of policy and theory of immersion education for language-majority speakers and educational approaches for minority language speakers. Broadly speaking, the programs base themselves on sociolinguistic theory, second language acquisition theory, and cognitive theory (Lindholm, 1992). The greater emphasis placed on the minority language during the early years in some program models is based on sociolinguistic theory about the importance of the status of languages, and the observation that greater attention needs to be paid the language less likely to be developed and retained. The theory of second language development as most successfully accomplished through real communication and comprehensible input is based on second language acquisition theory. There is attention paid to the findings from cognitive research indicating the cognitive benefits of bilingualism and the transfer of cognitive structures and knowledge across languages (Reynolds, 1991).

TWI programs generally seek to promote specific objectives: (a) bilingual education as an enrichment program for all students rather than as a compensatory education mode for English language learners; (b) better understanding between two linguistic communities in a given school community; (c) access to equal education for all students; and (d) educational excellence for all students (ERIC Clearinghouse on Languages and Linguistics, 1990; National Clearinghouse for Bilingual Education, 1990).

Although these goals reflect the ideology of the people they serve, they also are based on theories of first and second language learning and academic development for second language learners.

PROGRAM MODELS

Program models for TWI vary most notably in the allocation of language and the approach to literacy instruction. Two common ones are the "90/10" model and the 80/20 model, in which the first number refers to the percentage of instructional time in kindergarten conducted in the minority language and the second number is the percentage of instructional time in English. As students progress through the grades, the ratio of language changes until it reaches 50/50, usually by the fourth grade (Lindholm, 1997). Other programs are "balanced," maintaining an equal split between the two languages throughout the program (Center for Applied Linguistics, 2001). Programmatic decisions rest largely on the community beliefs about language education (Lindholm-Leary, 2000). Those who choose 90/10 or 80/20 may believe that more Spanish is necessary because all students have more opportunities to practice speaking English outside of school; native English speakers have no other opportunities to use their developing Spanish abilities.

Programs that choose the 50/50 model may do so out of a desire to promote equity between the two languages throughout the program, fear of lower academic outcomes in English, or lack of staffing capacity for a 90/10 program. Some programs, however, have found that the native English speakers do not achieve as highly in Spanish with less exposure to the language (Lindholm-Leary, 2001; Christian, Montone, Lindholm, & Carranza, 1997). In fact, recent research has revealed that more instructional time spent in the minority language increases the second language skills of the majority speakers without sacrificing achievement in English for either group (Christian et al., 1997; Lindholm-Leary).

Literacy instruction is most commonly approached in one of three ways. Some programs introduce literacy instruction in the minority language to all students first, while others introduce literacy in both languages at the same time. Still other programs separate students by language group for the literacy portion of the day. Until recently, there was little research to guide the conceptualization of literacy instruction in two-way programs; instead, many of these decisions were guided by local policies, priorities, and student enrollments. Emerging research suggests that young children are quite capable of handling literacy instruction in both languages simultaneously (C. Snow, 1994, as cited in Christian et al., 1997).

Language of instruction can be allocated by time, content area, or person, or by a combination of all three (Christian, 1994). If allocated by time, the language of instruction is changed on a schedule that can alternate (such as day, morning, or afternoon). If altered by content area, decisions are made as to the language of instruction in content areas such as science, math, and social studies. One consistent language is used for each specific area. Finally, if altered by person, students have two teachers, one of whom provides instruction in the minority language and the other in the majority language.

EMERGING RESULTS

Research on the effectiveness of the three goals of TWI programs is quickly emerging. A growing body of literature points to the heightened interest in the efficacy of TWI programs (see, e.g., Lindholm-Leary, 2001). Over the past decade, emerging evidence supports the assertion that two-way programs foster a high level of academic achievement, language development in both languages, and positive cross-cultural understandings for students from both language groups (Cazabon et al., 1993; Christian et al., 1997; Lindholm-Leary, 2001). Recent work has aimed to widen the scope of assessment in both language and academic achievement (Center for Applied Linguistics, 2001; Lindholm, 1993; Rhodes, 1996). At the same time, cautionary notes about issues such as mainstream language and school structure dominance and language testing have emerged in the literature to guide future research and program development.

Academic Achievement

A growing body of evidence indicates the success of two-way programs in terms of traditional measures of school achievement, most notably standardized test results. Data from academic achievement measures reveals a trend of positive effects for both language groups in two-way programs. Evaluation reports (Lindholm & Gavlek, 1994, as cited in Christian, 1994) and case studies (Christian et al., 1997; Cazabon, Nicoladis, & Lambert, 1998), indicate that students are demonstrating consistent growth and achievement in both languages across mathematics and language arts, although there is considerable variation among and between programs. Although there is still a considerable achievement gap between the majority and minority language populations in TWI programs in the United States, English learners in TWI programs do tend to outperform their peers in other programs (Lindholm-Leary, 2001).

In 1993, Cazabon et al. conducted one of the first major evaluations of a two-way program that had been established for a substantial amount of time. Their evaluation of the Amigos Program, in operation since 1986 in Cambridge, Massachusetts, describes the academic achievement of students as well as their attitudes toward diversity and language learning. The researchers compared the Amigos pupils to control groups of native English and native Spanish speakers enrolled in regular (English speaker) and transitional bilingual (Spanish speaker) programs at the same school. All students were given a test of nonverbal intelligence (Raven's Progressive Matrices) and matched in terms of their Raven's scores. Achievement was defined as standardized test scores in reading/language and math on the California Achievement Test in English.

Despite spending the majority of instructional time in Spanish, the English Amigos scored at or above the level of their native English-speaking peers enrolled in the regular education program in both reading/language and math. Similarly, both English- and Spanish-speaking students performed better on the English math assessment than the Spanish control group. In Spanish, the English Amigos showed steady gains in their reading and math abilities. Spanish speakers scored slightly below the Spanish controls in Spanish reading, but higher in Spanish math.

Other researchers have approached the issue of measuring achievement by using standardized test data for both Spanish and English speakers to make direct comparisons not only between language groups and between programs within a school but also to national norms. Using this approach, at Francis Scott Key Elementary School in Arlington, Virginia, results have indicated that students generally show good academic progress, regardless of the fact that half of the instruction was in Spanish and the test in English (Christian et al., 1997). English speakers tended to outscore Spanish speakers, but no test was given in Spanish to determine if the opposite pattern would emerge. Similarly, standardized test scores for students at the River Glen Elementary School in San Jose, California, reveal that students score at or above average in all areas except in English reading. The low scores in English reading are not surprising since students are not exposed to English literacy instruction before the third grade (Christian et al.).

In an in-depth longitudinal study of 20 schools over a period of approximately 15 years, Lindholm-Leary (2001) found academic outcome results that "clearly show that both English-speaking and Spanish-speaking students benefited from instruction in DLE (Dual Language Education) . . . regardless of the students' background characteristics (ethnicity, socioeconomic class, gender, language background, grade level), program type (90:10, 50:50), or school characteristics" (p. 302). Furthermore, in her evaluation of mathematics achievement, students not only achieved at grade level but also showed evidence that content learned in one language was also available in the other language.

In addition to outcomes seen through standardized measures, there have been important attempts to examine more broadly and deeply student outcomes through nontraditional measures. These attempts aim to address difficulties of assessing English learners (e.g., see Hill, 2000; and Valdés & Figueroa, 1994). A portfolio assessment developed by Lindholm (1993) for language arts assessment was a response to a sense among staff and parents that students' test scores underestimated their abilities in the two languages in reading and writing. Additionally, teachers wanted a systematic method of recording and understanding their students' language arts levels (Lindholm, 1993). The contents of Lindholm's portfolio include results from oral and written language testing, reading observations, and parent and student questionnaires.

Other approaches to portfolios place greater emphasis on the learner's perception of his or her own achievement and areas of challenge (see, for example, Fernandez & Baker, 1993). Mirroring the change in educational theory from a behaviorist to a sociocognitive approach, there is more emphasis on the role of the learner in selecting pieces to include in the portfolio, assessing the learner's own work, and discussing evaluations with the teacher (Hancock, 1994).

One limitation to locally developed portfolio assessments is that outcomes cannot easily be compared across programs. A recent study conducted by the Center for Applied Linguistics (2001) collected a narrative writing sample, a written self-assessment, a cloze reading assessment, and parent questionnaires from 344 students enrolled in eleven TWI programs throughout the United States over a period of three years. Results from their preliminary analysis suggest that students from both language backgrounds showed growth in language and literacy. Native Spanish speakers tended to have fairly balanced literacy skills, while native English speakers tended to remain dominant in English. These results not only strengthen the evidence that students in TWI programs are progressing academically but also show the potential for developing alternative assessments that can be used to compare different programs.

What is clear from a review of the literature on academic outcomes is that two-way programs are, in general, a successful approach for both language groups. When compared with the academic achievement of their respective peers, standardized test data reveal that both native English and minority language students in TWI programs achieve at or above the level of their peers in other programs (Lindholm-Leary, 2001).

A final important point to note is the difference in the approaches to the two language groups in terms of measuring the success of TWI programs. For the native English-speaking students, parents and educators are concerned about the possible impact that learning through a second language has on academic indicators. Their test scores are compared to national averages among other native English-speaking students in their age group, and there is great relief to discover that learning a second language does not impair academic growth in the first language. In general, there is considerably more focus on achievement in English than on content understanding in the minority language, as evident in the attention paid to the English standardized and language test results (Amrein & Peña, 2001). In contrast, the level of achievement of nonnative English speakers is measured more by their scores in English than by scores obtained in their first language.

Test scores for the nonnative English speakers are significantly better than for their nonnative English-speaking peers in other program types, but they are not, in the vast majority of cases, approaching national averages for native English speakers. The English learners' significantly higher achievement in English as compared with peers in the other types of programs has been used as a strong indicator of the success of the programs. Although these higher academic outcomes may indicate an improved approach to the education of English-learning students, it is also important to be mindful of the significant gap that still remains between native English-speaking and English-learning children in the United States (Hakuta, Goto-Butler, & Witt, 2000) when evaluating TWI outcomes.

Language Development

TWI programs aim to develop a high level of biliteracy for all students. Indeed, outcomes on commonly used language assessment show students are acquiring second language skills. Some researchers have begun to search for more effective means of measuring language development. Others have examined the practical implementation issues of using two languages in the classroom, and some researchers are concerned with sociopolitical issues surrounding language equity and attitudes toward language.

Language Assessment. Language assessments yield promising results for the language proficiency of students in TWI programs. Oral language proficiency has most often been measured with standardized language instruments, such as the Student Oral Language Observation Matrix (SOLOM), the Language Assessment Scale (LAS), and the Idea Proficiency Test (IPT), although researchers are now investigating new methods of assessing language, such as the Student Oral Proficiency Assessment (SOPA), which attempts to capture a more accurate picture of language knowledge and use.

Lindholm-Leary (2001) found that on the SOLOM all students scored at or near fluent in their first language; by the upper elementary years, almost all students were rated as proficient in both languages. These results are consistent with earlier findings, such as those of Lindholm and Gavlek (1994) and Mahrer and Christian (1993), that indicate TWI programs are providing a context in which students are becoming increasingly proficient in their first and second languages.

Commonly used language assessments, like standardized academic measures, have come under criticism for their inability to capture the breadth and depth of a child's linguistic ability (Valdés & Figueroa, 1994). In an attempt to capture the language skills that educators hope are the outcomes of learning in a two-way classroom, educators have grappled with this question in different ways. Some programs have integrated language assessment into student portfolios. Although traditional measures, such as the SOLOM, are still used, the results can be examined in conjunction with a student's writing and reading samples to gain a broader understanding of the student's language usage in academic contexts (Fernandez & Baker, 1993; Lindholm, 1993).

Other researchers have attempted to develop new language measures that more effectively evaluate the language proficiency of TWI students. The Center for Applied Linguistics developed a pilot measure of oral proficiency and listening comprehension specifically for first to fourth graders in TWI Spanish programs (Rhodes, 1996). The SOPA aims to encourage students to produce as much language as possible in a short time period so that evaluators have ample data on which to base their global ratings. The assessment is an oral interview in which students are asked to talk about a range of concepts, from personal information to science to storytelling. Evaluators feel that the elicited language more accurately reflects students' use of language in the classroom as compared to other measures of oral proficiency (Rhodes, 1996).

The SOPA differs from other oral proficiency measures because the goal is to elicit the student's natural use and range of language, instead of attempting to capture specific usages of morphology, tense, or vocabulary. Among the second graders included in the pilot, the students of Spanish language background demonstrated growth and proficiency in their native language. Their native English-speaking classmates show a growing proficiency level in Spanish (Rhodes, 1996). These results seem to indicate that the SOPA was able to capture growth in Spanish that oral measures focusing on specific vocabulary or grammatical forms overlook.

Language Use in the Classroom. Research on the use of language in the classroom has focused on three main areas: allocation of language for instruction, patterns of teacher talk, and patterns of student talk. Two main foci have emerged; some studies examine overt language use in the classroom (Christian et al., 1997; M. A. Snow et al., 1989), while others examine underlying issues of language equity that arise in the schools and classrooms (Amrein & Peña, 2001; Valdés, 1997). Some studies have considered student use of language in the classroom in terms of educational allocation and choice (Griego-Jones, 1994), while others have considered student attitudes and feelings toward learning a second language and becoming bilingual (Cazabon et al., 1998).

The issue of student talk is complex. Students live in the dominant culture that promotes the value of English over other languages. It is important to consider how this becomes salient in TWI programs and how teachers and parents can help students come to value the minority language. Many educators are diligent in their attempts to promote the two languages as equitable, but data from research studies in a variety of domains point to the great difficulty of this task (Amrein & Peña, 2001; Freeman, 1996).

Researchers have documented better results with language learning when instruction is provided through content than when language itself is the object of study (Short, 1993; M. A. Snow et al., 1989). For this reason, one of the main tenets of TWI programs is a concerted effort to separate the two languages by teacher, by topic, or by time. In classrooms, however, there is wide variation in how strictly this guideline is followed. In some schools, such as River Glen in San Jose and Francis Scott Key School in Arlington, observations did not reveal any instances of teachers switching or mixing languages. At Inter-American Magnet School (IAMS) in Chicago, however, teachers were occasionally observed translating for students who were struggling (Christian et al., 1997).

This tension within theory and practice points to an important unknown in TWI research. On the one hand, educators believe that students must focus on one language at a time in order to build competency, especially in their second language (Lindholm-Leary, 2000). Creating opportunities for students to focus on expressing themselves in the language that is more difficult (with the assistance of native-speaking peers) is one way of assisting them (Lindholm-Leary, 2001). On the other hand, the forced separation of the two languages can be viewed as a false one for the students. Although no research has been conducted in TWI programs, numerous studies exist on the use of two languages in bilingual or linguistically diverse classrooms (see, for example, Brice, Mastin, & Perkins, 1998; Duran, 1994; Garcia, 1998; Huerta-Macias

& Quintero, 1992). Research on code switching has shown that bilingual students who employ two languages simultaneously do so not as a result of confusion but in a manner that is strategic (Zentella, 1997), is patterned (Brice et al., 1998), and has academic (Garcia, 1998) and social (Huerta-Macias & Quintero, 1992) purposes. Furthermore, requiring students to speak in only one of their languages may reduce the creative value and natural tendency (Duran, 1994) of drawing on their bilingual competencies to express their understandings and ideas. Future research could investigate the place of code switching within a TWI program.

A TWI approach allows the language-majority and language-minority groups to have ample interaction and promote both languages equally. In this way, both groups are afforded the opportunity to serve as the language experts, which builds self-esteem and provides native-speaker language models to the language learning group. However, in order to make the language comprehensible to students acquiring it, teachers may modify their vocabulary, grammatical structure, or the conceptual difficulty of the lessons. Concerns have been raised about modifying language to respond to students' learning needs. Valdés (1997) speculates that such a situation might result in both language groups receiving less-than-full exposure to school language. As she points out, this is an area that has not been investigated, but it is also a crucial question since language is a primary focus of the program.

These issues point to the multitude of important questions around teacher education for TWI programs. For example, it is known that teachers need to have a high level of proficiency in the minority language to provide appropriate instruction through that language. Additionally, they must have an understanding of the cognitive, social, and affective theories of language development to successfully integrate content area and language development objectives into the curriculum (Lindholm-Leary, 2001). Finally, they must deal with the fundamental difficulties of promoting equity between the two languages. The teacher plays a crucial role in either colluding with or challenging mainstream language ideologies (Amrein & Peña, 2001; McCollum, 1999).

Language Equity. Some researchers have attempted to understand how students in TWI programs come to value English over Spanish through hidden messages in the curriculum. These studies draw on the social theory posited by Bourdieu (1977)—that institutions, such as schools, reward the cultural capital of mainstream students and devalue that of nonmainstream groups. In a study of one program, McCollum (1999) notes the "double bind" of many Spanish-speaking students in that they are not fluent in English and speak a version of Spanish that is not of the "high" variety, and they are often corrected in both languages. This stands in contrast to the mainstream English that many of their classmates bring to school and the praise this group receives for attempting to use their Spanish (Valdés, 1997). Similar issues were notable in the greater attention to the English standardized test than the Spanish, as well as the practice of delivering announcements in English first. In another study of a TWI program in Texas, Amrein and Peña (2001) found that many of the English teachers were monolingual, unlike the Spanish teachers, who were fluent in both Spanish and English. The unequal proficiencies of the teachers meant that the needs of the English-dominant students were much more easily met, in that both the English- and Spanish-speaking teachers could respond to their questions even when the question was asked in English. However, the Spanish-speaking students were forced to use English in their interactions with the English-speaking teachers. The inequity in languages understood and spoken by the TWI staff clearly led to inequity in interactions with students.

Student Language Attitudes. Two-way immersion is designed to "promote positive attitudes toward both languages and cultures and is supportive of full bilingual proficiency for both native and non-native speakers of English" (Christian, 1994, p. 1). Emerging evidence points to the successes and the complexities of fostering the value of two languages, particularly given the high status of English and the lower status of the other minority languages used in TWI programs. Analysis of student attitude surveys and case studies of TWI students reveals that even though both minority and majority students generally have positive attitudes toward becoming bilingual, they are also well aware that English is the language of power and status in the United States.

Among upper elementary students in a TWI program, Hayashi (1998, as cited in Cazabon et al., 1998) found that students held positive views toward their own bilingualism and perceived instruction in Spanish as both valuable and necessary for their continued academic achievement in both languages. Cazabon et al. (1998) conducted a survey of students as well as two case studies on student attitudes toward becoming bilingual in a two-way program. Results indicate that students enjoy learning in two languages, although there is a decrease in satisfaction in the upper-elementary years—perhaps, the authors suggest, because students begin to see English as the language necessary for their future or because general satisfaction with school begins to decline at that age. The two girls included in the case study indicated their satisfaction with learning in two languages. Both were native Spanish speakers and addressed the importance of

maintaining and developing Spanish for the purpose of communicating with their families and increasing their economic opportunities in the future, as well as personal satisfaction with being bilingual (Cazabon et al., 1998).

Some research results, however, caution against assuming that all children will automatically value biliteracy, even when the two languages are equally promoted in the classroom. In a small study of kindergarten students, Griego-Jones (1994) found that students preferred English to Spanish. English was perceived as the language of higher status and achievement. This was most evident in writing activities, where students described their "writing" as English, regardless of their oral English proficiency. Students' attitudes are a crucial element in language learning. These findings point to the importance of including an assessment of and attention to the linguistic attitudes of students in a two-way program if the highest level of biliteracy is to be achieved.

Cross-Cultural Understanding

Of the three major goals of TWI programs, the extent to which cross-cultural understandings are fostered between majority and minority language speakers is the least understood. This is unfortunate since such outcomes are possibly the most desirable ones.

Only a few studies have considered issues such as students' and parents' perceptions of native speakers of the other language, and how to promote positive relationships between two groups that often differ not only in linguistic and cultural backgrounds but also in socioeconomic status. Of prime importance is the status of the minority language speakers in the school institution. If TWI seeks to promote positive cross-cultural relationships, it is crucial that both groups value and respect the language and cultural resources gained from their interaction.

Results from some studies indicate that positive psychosocial attitudes and a high level of self-esteem may be fostered by TWI programs, although the reality of social interactions and attitudes among the students are much more complex. In an examination of social networks in a classroom, Cazabon et al. (1993) found that friendships did not depend on ethnicity or cultural background in most cases. Students preferred to have friends from both minority and majority language groups. Interestingly, at one of the two grade levels studied, no ethnic bias was found in questions addressing the student's best friend in class, but students tended to self-segregate in choosing a lunch partner and whom to sit next to in class or invite to a party. Majority-group children tended to favor other majority-group children over all minority groups. However, minority-group children (mostly African American) and the Hispanic children appeared to favor one another's groups over the majority. The authors concluded that the Hispanic children did not self-segregate in response to the emphasis on their language and culture.

Amrein and Peña (2001) examined self-segregation patterns among students by language level. They found that students tended to self-segregate on the basis of language competencies whenever students were not grouped by the teacher. Additionally, those students who served as translators for their peers, and who were expected to assist peers in the language learning process, were not equally accessible to all students. In fact, the authors observed, the language brokers, most often language-minority students, were more likely to interact with other language brokers or with majority-group children, as opposed to the monolingual Spanish-speaking children. Amrein and Peña argue that "these students hastened their assimilation into the dominant language group" (p. 12). Furthermore, they argue, the highly bilingual minority-group students preferred to associate with bilingual majority-group students because they were viewed as possessing "enhanced bilingual proficiency" (p. 12). This preference for cross-cultural association that is dependent on language proficiency and status reveals the difficulty of fostering an environment in which true cross-cultural understandings can grow, and the necessity of a deeper understanding of the social and school contexts that influence students' understandings of their own culture and the cultures of others.

Freeman's studies (1994, 1996) of the Oyster Bilingual School in Washington, D.C., show how one school has worked to address some of these issues. The Oyster School defines the problem for language-minority students as "mainstream U.S. educational and societal discrimination against minority languages and minority peoples" (p. 7). The goals for a TWI program developed under this social view are multiple. First, minority and majority students are socialized and positioned to view each other's language and culture as equal through attention to language, culture, and identity in the multicultural curriculum. Second, students are given opportunities to recognize, discuss, and try out refuting discriminatory practices as a social responsibility. This approach to cross-cultural understanding is a proactive stance in which students are socialized differently from the mainstream U.S. educational discourse and at the same time taught about their own potential role in social change. Despite a great deal of attention to developing a language and identity plan, and a stated commitment to the goals just outlined, Oyster School still deals with many of the same issues outlined by Cazabon et al. (1993), such as students self-segregating at lunch tables (Freeman, 1996), an indication of the difficulty of overcoming the norms of interaction in the larger society.

FUTURE DIRECTIONS

Research on TWI programs thus far has given the field important information about TWI school characteristics, students attending TWI programs, and TWI outcomes in terms of students' language proficiencies and academic performance. Because many TWI studies have tended to be descriptive and small-scale in nature, the data collected have been extremely rich, yielding much-needed information on TWI and helping us understand the many complex variables involved with TWI implementation and effectiveness (Christian et al., 1997; Cazabon et al., 1998).

These data have helped to define the TWI field, giving it a foundation upon which to discuss and develop TWI theory, research, and practice across programs. It has served as a basis for researchers such as Lindholm-Leary (2001) and the Center for Applied Linguistics to push beyond small-scale and purely descriptive studies to longitudinal studies that seek to compare outcomes across programs. Additionally, with the trend toward nontraditional academic and language assessment, other researchers have begun to push for new and deeper understandings of TWI.

Building on the current research foundation, future work should continue to focus on the complex theoretical issues surrounding TWI implementation, student attainment, and social issues. Thus, even though there is a need for and much value inherent in descriptive studies, there is also a need to develop studies that pose theoretical questions to address some of the issues that are described next. Three overarching issues that should be addressed by future research are the match between program ideology and implementation, how TWI schools address or fail to address issues of language equity, and issues of assessment.

The first issue centers on the match between stated program objectives and actual implementation. Much of the TWI literature describes the objectives of TWI and the theories that support these objectives; however, to date almost no studies have sought to research the practicality of implementing the ideologies that drive TWI. A model for studying TWI implementation comes from research by Amrein and Peña (2001). Their theoretical framework of asymmetry offers a unique perspective on the balance, fairness, and equality of a TWI school, including both intentions and implementation of instruction, resources, and student body. Amrein and Peña (2001) ask an interesting theoretical question about the actual effects of TWI on intergroup relations. TWI literature has well documented the ideological perspectives of promoting cross-cultural relations among its students and faculty, which places it in a unique and interesting position in terms of its potential to overcome racial, ethnic, and linguistic segregation. Amrein and Peña's (2001) work presents an example of a research model that pushes beyond TWI intentions and analyzes actual behavior. Their findings raise serious concerns about the degree to which integration actually occurs, and the impact this has on TWI students, particularly language-minority students.

Amrein and Peña (2001) raise additional questions and issues to be addressed through future research on TWI intergroup relations: What are mainstream children's attitudes toward minority children? What impact may these attitudes have on minority children? What impact do societal linguistic expectations have on both groups of students? For instance, Amrein and Peña (2001) argue that for mainstream students learning a second language is applauded; however, for minority children acquiring English is expected. They suspect that with these very different expectations must come very different treatments.

Valdés (1997) also believes that we need to understand how TWI theory is implemented into practice. For instance, although TWI promotes a language-enrichment perspective, Valdés raises concerns over the lack of research on the quality of instruction in the minority language. She advocates a research agenda that investigates the impact of modified language on the linguistic and academic/cognitive development of native speakers of the language. A number of questions should be addressed in this line of research: Will native Spanish speakers acquire nativelike academic Spanish? Will they learn as much and as rapidly as they might in standard bilingual programs? Will they develop the cognitive academic proficiency that is claimed (by Cummins, 1991) to undergird the development of similar proficiencies in the second language? Furthermore, on the basis of Amrein and Peña's (2001) theory of asymmetry and with support from findings in their study, research needs to more widely address instructional asymmetry in two-way-immersion programs.

Another program issue for study centers on one of the main tenets of practice in many TWI programs, the prevailing theory that separation of language during class time leads to higher, more nativelike proficiencies. Separation of language is a common programmatic feature in TWI programs, but there is much research to suggest that the use of two languages simultaneously or interchangeably, referred to as code switching (Duran, 1994), is a natural linguistic phenomena that occurs in bilingual communities. Moreover, research shows that code switching is not random; rather, it is purposeful and grammatical (Brice et al., 1998; Zentella, 1997). Given these findings, research on code switching in the classroom would help expand the field's understanding of the appropriateness of the current TWI practice of separating languages and the theory that supports this practice.

Therefore, an important research question to address is, given the research that acknowledges code switching as a positive and natural language form in bilinguals, whether there should be space for it in the TWI classroom.

The second overarching topic that TWI research should address is that of language equity. Research should examine how TWI schools address issues of language equity, as seen in the curriculum, student and faculty language use, and parent voice and involvement, as well as other manifestations. Ideologically, TWI programs strive to empower students using an enrichment perspective to promote cultural pride, as well as bilingualism and biliteracy for all students. Once again, it is not clear whether behavior actually follows ideology in this area. Freeman (1994, 1996) and Amrein and Peña (2001) point to the need to understand how school communities can overcome the societal biases toward English, to help children value their two languages equally. Criticism from researchers within a critical language awareness perspective (Bhatt & Martin-Jones, 1992, as cited in Valdés, 1997) asks "whether societal inequalities can be overcome by curriculum and teaching practices" (Valdés, p. 418). Given the earlier concern of asymmetry, this question looms even larger.

The third overarching topic that calls for research centers on assessment tools used to evaluate TWI effectiveness and student learning. Most TWI literature that discusses program effectiveness and student learning cites outcomes on standardized tests in English. Overall, it appears that, using these tools, students in TWI programs are faring better than their peers (Cazabon et al., 1993; Lindholm-Leary, 2001). However, because most assessments are conducted in English, several issues remain unclear. More information is needed about language-minority students' development of content understanding in their native language, and language-majority students' proficiency in the second language. Furthermore, even though standardized assessments yield one form of important data with which to make comparisons across TWI and other programs, their true strength lies within the assessment of monolingual English speakers. Such assessments are not developed with the bilingual student as the target and thus do not yield information on those skills developed by bilinguals. To fully understand both the potential and effectiveness of two-way-immersion programs in developing bilingual and biliterate children, research is needed that identifies the special skills of the bilingual and works toward a theory of an assessment tool that captures these skills.

One final and important note is about the feasibility of two-way programs on a large scale. Of the myriad bilingual program models in existence, TWI programs are the elite. Research is revealing the strength and efficacy of the model, but TWI is not an easy answer to the difficult issues surrounding the education of English language learners. Issues of capacity, in terms of adequately trained teachers and community desires for education, will always be a roadblock in some communities. Furthermore, many schools would have difficulty recruiting a population that makes a TWI program possible; de facto segregation poses an enormous challenge. In communities where TWI programs are feasible, the model has great potential; the literature described in this chapter provides a wealth of knowledge to assist educators in facing the challenges of establishing such a program.

References

Amrein, A., & Peña, R. A. (2001). Asymmetry in dual language practice: Assessing imbalance in a program promoting equality. *Education Policy Analysis Archives, 8*(8), 2–18.

Andersson, T. (1969). *Foreign languages in the elementary school: A struggle against mediocrity.* Austin: University of Texas Press.

August, D., & Hakuta, K. (Eds.). (1997). *Improving schooling for language-minority children: A research agenda.* Washington, DC: National Academy Press.

Bhatt, A., & Martin-Jones, M. (1992). Whose resource? Minority languages, bilingual learners and language awareness. In N. Fairclough (Ed.), *Critical language awareness* (pp. 285–302). London: Longman.

Bourdieu, P. (1977). Cultural reproduction and social reproduction. In J. Karabel & A. H. Halsey (Eds.), *Power and Ideology in Education* (pp. 487–511). Oxford, England: Oxford University Press.

Branaman, L., & Rennie, J. (1998). Many ways to learn: Elementary school foreign language program models. *Eric Review, 6*(1) [On-line]. Available: www.eric.ed.gov/resources/ericreview/vol6no1/models.html.

Branaman, L., Rhodes, N., & Rennie, J. (1998). A national survey of K-12 foreign language education. *Eric Review, 6*(1) [On-line]. Available: www.eric.ed.gov/resources/ericreview/vol6no1/survey.html.

Brice, A., Mastin, M., & Perkins, C. (1998). English, Spanish, and code-switching use in the ESL classroom: An ethnographic study. *Journal of Children's Communication Development, 19*(2), 11–20.

Bruning, R., Flowerday, T., & Trayer, M. (1999). Developing foreign language frameworks: An evaluation study. *Foreign Language Annals, 32*(2), 159–176.

Castañeda v. Pickard, 648 F.2nd 989 (1981).

Cazabon, M., Lambert, W., & Hall, G. (1993). *Two-way bilingual education: A progress report on the Amigos program* (Research Report no. 7). Washington, DC: National Center for Research on Cultural Diversity and Second Language Learning [On-line]. Available: www.ncbe.gwu.edu/miscpubs/ncrcdsll/rr7/index.htm.

Cazabon, M., Nicoladis, E., & Lambert, W. (1998). *Becoming bilingual in the Amigos two-way immersion program.* Santa Cruz, CA: Center for Research on Education, Diversity & Excellence [On-line]. Available: www.cal.org/crede/pubs/research/rr3.htm.

Center for Applied Linguistics (2001). *Directory of two-way bilingual immersion programs in the U.S.* Washington, DC [On-line]. Available: www.cal.org/twi/directory.

Christian, D. (1994). *Two-way bilingual education: Students learning through two languages.* Washington, DC: National Center for Research on Cultural Diversity and Second Language Learning [On-line]. Available: www.ncbe.gwu.edu/miscpubs/ncrcdsll/epr12/.

Christian, D., Montone, C., Lindholm, K., & Carranza, I. (1997). *Profiles in two-way immersion education.* McHenry, IL: Delta Systems.

Crawford, J. (1999). *Bilingual education: History, politics, theory and practice* (4th ed.). Los Angeles: Bilingual Education Services.

Cummins, J. (1991). The role of primary language development in promoting educational success for language minority students. In California State Department of Education (Ed.), *Schooling and language minority students: A theoretical framework.* Los Angeles: California State University, Evaluation, Dissemination and Assessment Center.

Curtain, H. A., & Pesola, C. A. (1988). *Languages and children: Making the match.* Reading, MA: Addison-Wesley.

Curtain, H., & Pesola, C. (1994). *Languages and children: Making the match* (2nd ed.). White Plains, NY: Longman.

Dandoff, M. N. (1978). *Evaluation of the impact of ESEA Title VII Spanish-English bilingual education programs* (Technical Report). Washington, DC: American Institutes for Research.

Day, E., & Shapson, S. (1991). Integrating formal and functional approaches to language teaching in French immersion: An experimental study. *Language Learning, 51*(1), 47–80.

Duran, L. (1994). Toward a better understanding of code-switching and interlanguage in bilinguality: Implications for bilingual instruction. *Journal of Educational Issues of Language Minority Students, 14,* 69–88.

ERIC Clearinghouse on Languages and Linguistics. (1990). *Two-way language development programs.* Washington, DC: Office of Educational Research and Improvement. (ERIC Document Reproduction no. ED 321 589)

ESEA Title VII Bilingual Demonstration Project. (1982). *An Exemplary approach to bilingual education: A comprehensive handbook for implementing an elementary-level Spanish-English language immersion program.* (Publication no. I-B-82–58.) San Diego, CA: Unified School District.

Fernandez, E., & Baker, S. (1993). *Assessment portfolio, grades K-5. Two-way Spanish partial immersion program.* Arlington, VA: Arlington Public Schools.

Fortune, T., & Jorstad, H. L. (1996). US immersion programs: A national survey. *Foreign Language Annals, 29*(2), 163–190.

Freeman, R. (1994). Language planning and identity planning: An emergent understanding. *Working Papers in Educational Linguistics, 10*(1), 1–20.

Freeman, R. (1996). Dual-language planning at Oyster Bilingual School: "It's much more than language." *TESOL Quarterly, 30*(3), 557–582.

Garcia, G. (1998). Mexican-American bilingual students' metacognitive reading strategies: What's transferred, unique, problematic? *National Reading Conference Yearbook, 47,* 253–63.

Genesee, F. (1983). Bilingual education of majority language children: The immersion experiments in review. *Applied Psycholinguistics, 4*(1), 1–46.

Genesee, F. (1985). Second language learning through immersion: A review of U.S. programs. *Review of Education Research, 55,* 541–546.

Genesee, F. (1987). *Learning through two languages.* Cambridge, MA: Newbury House.

Greene, J. (1997). A meta-analysis of the Rossell & Baker review of bilingual education research. *Bilingual Research Journal, 21*(2–3), 103–122.

Griego-Jones, T. (1994). Assessing students' perceptions of biliteracy in two-way bilingual classrooms. *Journal of Educational Issues of Language Minority Students, 13,* 79–93.

Hakuta, K. (1986). *Mirror of language.* New York: Basic Books.

Hakuta, K., Goto-Butler, Y., & Witt, D. (2000, January). *How long does it take English learners to attain proficiency?* University of California Linguistic Minority Research Institute Policy Report, 2000–1 [On-line]. Available: www.stanford.edu/~hakuta/Docs/HowLong.pdf.

Hancock, C. (1994*). Alternative assessment and second language study: What and why?* ERIC Digest ED376695.

Hayakawa, S. I. (1992). The case for official English. In J. Crawford (Ed.), *Language loyalties* (pp. 94–100). Chicago: University of Chicago Press.

Hayashi, A. (1998). *Attitudes toward bilingualism: A comparative study of attitudes of children in the two different bilingual education programs: The two-way bilingual program and the transitional bilingual education program.* Unpublished manuscript, School of Education, Boston University.

Heining-Boynton, A. (1990). Using FLES history to plan for the present and future. *Foreign Language Annals, 23*(6), 503–509.

Hill, C. (2000). *Children and reading tests.* Stamford, CT: Ablex.

Howard, E., & Sugarman, J. (2001, March). *Two-way immersion programs: Features and statistics.* Center for Applied Linguistics. (ERIC Digest EDO-FL-01–01) [On-line]. Available: www.cal.org/ericcll/digest/0101twi.html.

Huerta-Macias, A., & Quintero, E. (1992). Code-switching, bilingualism and biliteracy: A case study. *Bilingual Research Journal, 16*(3–4), 69–90.

Lambert, W. E., & Tucker, G. R. (1972). *The bilingual education of children: The St. Lambert experiment.* Rowley, MA: Newbury House.

Lapkin, S., Swain, M., & Shapson, S. (1990). French immersion research agenda for the 1990s. *Canadian Modern Language Review, 46*(4), 638–674.

Lau v. Nichols, 414 U.S. 563 (1974).

Lindholm, K. (1992). Two-way bilingual/immersion education: Theory, conceptual issues, and pedagogical implications. In R. Padilla & A. Benavides (Eds.), *Critical perspectives on bilingual education research* (pp. 195–220). Tempe, AZ: Bilingual Press.

Lindholm, K. (1993). *Two-way bilingual language arts portfolio.* Paper presented at the American Educational Research Association. (ERIC Document Reproduction Service no. ED 369 856)

Lindholm, K. (1997). Two-way bilingual education programs in the United States. *Encyclopedia of language and education. Vol. 5: Bilingual education.* Netherlands: Kluwer Academic.

Lindholm-Leary, K. (2000). *Biliteracy for a global society: An idea book on dual language education.* Washington, DC: Office of Bilingual Education and Minority Language Affairs.

Lindholm-Leary, K. J. (2001). *Dual language education.* Clevedon, England: Multilingual Matters.

Lindholm, K. J., & Gavlek, K. (1994). *California DBE projects: Project-wide evaluation report, 1992–1993.* San Jose, CA: Author.

Lipton, G. (1998). A century of progress: A retrospective on FLES program: 1898–1998. *Hispania, 81,* 75–87.

Lyster, R. (1996). Question forms, conditionals, and second-person pronouns used by adolescent native speakers across two levels of formality in written and spoken French. *Modern Language Journal, 80*(2), 165–182.

Mackey, W. F., & Beebe, V. N. (1977). *Bilingual schools for a bilingual community: Miami's adaptation to the Cuban refugees.* Rowley, MA: Newbury House.

Mahrer, C., & Christian, D. (1993). *A review of findings from two-way bilingual educational evaluation reports.* Washington, DC: National Center for Research on Cultural Diversity and Second Language Learning.

McCollum, P. (1999). Learning to value English: Cultural capital in a two-way bilingual program. *Bilingual Research Journal, 23*(2–3), 113–134.

Met, M. (1993). *Foreign language immersion programs.* Eric Digest [On-line]. Available: www.cal.org/ericcll/digest/met00001.html.

Met, M., & Rhodes, N. (1990). Elementary school foreign language instruction: Priorities for the 1990s. *Foreign Language Annals, 23*(6), 433–443.

Meyer, M. M., & Fienberg, S. E. (Eds.). (1992). *Assessing evaluation studies: The case of bilingual education strategies.* Panel to Review Evaluation Studies of Bilingual Education, Committee on National Statistics, National Research Council. Washington, DC: National Academy Press.

Moran, C., & Hakuta, K. (2001). Bilingual education: Broadening research perspectives. In J. A. Banks & C.A.M. Banks (Eds.), *Handbook of research on multicultural education* (pp. 445–462). New York: Macmillan.

National Clearinghouse for Bilingual Education. (1990, January). *Two-way language development programs.* San Francisco: Jossey-Bass.

National Standards in Foreign Language Education Project. (1996). *Standards for foreign language learning: Preparing for the 21st century.* Lawrence, KS: Allen Press.

No Child Left Behind Act of 2001, Pub. L. No. 107–110.

Ovando, C. J., & Collier, V. P. (1985). *Bilingual and ESL classrooms: Teaching in multicultural contexts.* New York: McGraw-Hill.

President's Commission on Foreign Languages and International Studies. (1979). *Strength through wisdom: A critique of U.S. capability.* Washington, DC: Government Printing Office.

Ramirez, D. J., Yuen, S. D., Ramey, D. R., & Pasta, D. J. (1991). *Final report: National longitudinal study of structured-English immersion strategy, early-exit and late-exit transitional bilingual education programs for language-minority children: Vol. I and II. Technical Report.* San Mateo, CA: Aguirre International.

Rennie, J. (1993). *ESL and bilingual program models.* Washington DC: ERIC Clearinghouse on Languages and Linguistics. (ERIC Document Reproduction Service no. ED362072)

Rennie, J. (1998). Current trends in foreign language assessment. *Eric Review, 6*(1) [On-line]. Available: www.eric.ed.gov/resources/ericreview/vol6no1/trends.html.

Reynolds, A. (1991). The cognitive consequences of bilingualism. In A. Reynolds (Ed.), *Bilingualism, multiculturalism, and second language learning.* Hillsdale, NJ: Erlbaum.

Rhodes, N. (1996). *Alternative assessment for immersion students: The Student Oral Proficiency Assessment (SOPA)*. Paper presented at the European Conference on Immersion Programmes. (ERIC Document Reproduction Service no. ED 416 677)

Schulz, R. (1998). Foreign language education in the united states: Trends and challenges. *Eric Review, 6*(1) [On-line]. Available: www.eric.ed.gov/resources/ericreview/vol6no1/trends.html.

Short, D. (1993). *Integrating language and content in middle school American history classes*. (Educational Practice Report no. 8). Washington, DC: National Center for Research on Cultural Diversity and Second Language Learning.

Short, D. (1997). The ESL standards for pre-K-12 students [On-line]. Available: www.tesol.org/assoc/k12standards/it/02.html.

Snow, C. (1994, March). *Learning to read a second time: Influence of L1 and L2 oral proficiency*. Paper presented at the annual meeting of the American Association for Applied Linguistics, Baltimore, MD.

Snow, M. A. (1990). Language immersion: An overview and comparison. In A. M. Padilla, H. H. Fairchild, & C. M. Valadez (Eds.), *Foreign language education: Issues and strategies* (pp. 109–26). Newbury Park, CA: Sage.

Snow, M. A., Met, M., & Genesee, F. (1989). A conceptual framework for the integration of language and content in second/foreign language instruction. *TESOL Quarterly, 23,* 201–217.

Snow, M. A., Padilla, A. M., & Campbell, R. (1988). Patterns of second language retention of graduates of a Spanish immersion program. *Applied Linguistics, 9,* 182–197.

Swain, M. (1985). Communicative competence: Some roles of comprehensible input and comprehensible output in its development. In S. Gass & C. Madden (Eds.), *Input in second language acquisition* (pp. 235–253). Rowley, MA: Newbury House.

Swain, M. (1988). Manipulating and complementing content teaching to maximize second language learning. *TESL Canada Journal, 6,* 68–83.

Swain, M. (2000). French immersion research in Canada: Recent contributions to SLA and applied linguistics. *Annual Review of Applied Linguistics, 20,* 199–212.

Swain, M., & Lapkin, S. (1982). *Evaluating bilingual education: A Canadian case study*. Clevedon, England: Multilingual Matters.

Swain, M., & Lapkin, S. (1998). Interaction and second language learning: Two adolescent French immersion students working together. *Modern Language Journal, 82,* 320–337.

Thompson, L., Christian, D., Stansfield, C., & Rhodes, N. (1990). Foreign language instruction in the United States. In A. Padilla, H. Fairchild, & C. Valadez (Eds.), *Foreign language education: Issues and strategies* (pp. 22–35). Newbury Park: CA: Sage.

U.S. English. (1992). In defense of our common language. In J. Crawford (Ed.), *Language loyalties* (pp. 143–147). Chicago: University of Chicago Press.

Valdés, G. (1997). Dual-language immersion programs: A cautionary note concerning the education of language-minority students. *Harvard Education Review, 67,* 391–429.

Valdés, G., & Figueroa, R. (1994). *Bilingualism and testing: A special case of bias*. Norwood, NJ: Ablex.

Vygotsky, L. S. (1986). *Thought and language*. Cambridge, MA: MIT Press.

Willig, A. C. (1985). A meta-analysis of selected studies on the effectiveness of bilingual education. *Review of Educational Research, 55*(3), 269–317.

Zentella, A. (1997). *Growing up bilingual*. Oxford, England: Blackwell.

PART IX

ACADEMIC ACHIEVEMENT

Approaches, Theories, and Research

29

WHAT HAPPENS TO A DREAM DEFERRED?

The Continuing Quest for Equal Educational Opportunity

Linda Darling-Hammond

Stanford University

As a consequence of structural inequalities in access to knowledge and resources, students from racial and ethnic "minority" groups in the United States continue to face persistent and profound barriers to educational opportunity. This chapter documents these inequalities, identifies some of their sources, describes their consequences for the nature and quality of education provided to various groups of students in the United States, and suggests policy changes needed to correct continuing inequities. The chapter argues that documentation of and serious policy attention to these ongoing, systematic inequalities are critical for improving the quality and outcomes of education for all students. Without acknowledgment that students experience very different educational realities, policies will continue to be based on the presumption that it is students, not their schools or classroom circumstances, that are the sources of unequal educational attainment.

I begin with a brief discussion of the history and current state of segregation and exclusion confronting historically designated minority groups within the U.S. public education system. It is this isolation that creates the conditions for systematically unequal access to learning opportunities. In the second section, I describe the role played by funding inequities in perpetuating unequal access to resources and knowledge. In the third section, I explore questions of access to educational resources, including qualified teachers, courses, curriculum materi-

als, and equipment. The fourth section addresses how tracking serves to exacerbate existing discrepancies by further rationing curricular opportunities. In the final section, I offer recommendations concerning school finance equalization, professional teaching policies, curriculum and testing reforms, and governmental roles in improving access to knowledge and educational resources for all students in the United States.

THE STRUCTURE OF INEQUALITY IN U.S. EDUCATION

Institutionally sanctioned discrimination in access to educational resources is older than the American nation itself. In his history of 18th-century colonial education, Lawrence Cremin (1970) writes:

For all of its openness, provincial America, like all societies, distributed its educational resources unevenly, and to some groups, particularly those Indians and Afro-Americans who were enslaved and even those who were not, it was for all intents and purposes closed. . . . For the slaves, there were few books, few libraries, [and] few schools . . . the doors of wisdom were not only not open, they were shut tight and designed to remain that way. . . . [B]y the end of the colonial period, there was a well-developed ideology of race inferiority to justify that situation and ensure that it would stand firm against all the heady rhetoric of the Revolution. (pp. 411–412)

This chapter was prepared with the assistance of Ali Borjian; it updates an earlier chapter ("Inequality and Access to Knowledge") in the first edition of this *Handbook*.

Indeed, the legacy of discrimination did persist: "While [19th-century] publicists glorified the unifying influence of common learning under the common roof of the common school, black Americans were rarely part of that design" (Tyack, 1974, p. 110). From the time Southern states made it illegal to teach an enslaved person to read, throughout the 19th century and into the 20th, African Americans faced de facto and de jure exclusion from public schools throughout the nation, as did Native Americans and, frequently, Mexican Americans (Kluger, 1976; Meier, Stewart, & England, 1989; Tyack, 1974).

Twentieth-century statistics reveal the long-term effects of this pattern. African Americans and Hispanic Americans have, on the whole, completed significantly fewer years of school than Whites. In 1940 only 7% of African Americans over 25 had graduated from high school, as compared to 24% of Americans generally (U.S. Census Bureau, 1992). By 1998, 87% of White American adults had completed 12 or more years of school, compared to 76% of African Americans and 56% of Hispanics (National Center for Education Statistics [NCES], 2000). Similar patterns are true for Native Americans, although comparable data are less frequently available.

Although overall educational attainment for people of color in the United States increased between 1960 and 1990, this trend is reversing as more states have imposed graduation exams and as resources to city schools have continued to decline. By 1998, 88% of African Americans and 63% of Hispanics between the ages of 25 and 29 had completed high school with a diploma or an equivalency (NCES, 2000), beginning to close the gap with White Americans. However, even though dropout rates for 16-to-24-year-old Black male students declined steadily between 1975 and 1990, they have been increasing since, growing from 11.9% in 1990 to 15.5% in 1998 (NCES, 2000), while the dropout rate for Hispanic males in this age group has remained above 30%.

The advent of high-stakes testing reforms requiring students to achieve specific test score standards in order to advance in grade or graduate from school has occurred while educational experiences for minority students continue to be substantially separate and unequal. In contrast to European and Asian nations that fund schools centrally and equally, the wealthiest 10% of school districts in the United States spend nearly 10 times more than the poorest 10%, and spending ratios of three to one are common within states. Poor and minority students are concentrated in the less well funded schools, most of them located in central cities and funded at levels substantially below those of neighboring suburban districts. Recent analyses of data prepared for school finance cases in Alabama, California, New Jersey, New York, Louisiana, and Texas have found that on every tangible measure—from qualified teachers to curriculum offerings—schools serving a greater number of students of color had significantly fewer resources than schools serving mostly White students.

This inequality in resource allocation was supported by the increasing resegregation of schools over the decades of the 1980s and 1990s. In 1998–99, almost a half century after *Brown* v. *Board of Education,* 70% of the nation's Black students attended predominantly minority schools, up significantly from the low point of 63% in 1980. The proportion of students of color in intensely segregated schools also increased. More than a third of African American and Latino students (36.5% and 36.6%, respectively) attended schools with a minority enrollment of 90–100%. Furthermore, racially segregated schools (for all groups except Whites) are almost always schools with a high concentration of poverty. The average Black or Latino student attends a school with more than twice as many poor classmates than the average White student does (Orfield, 2001).

African American and Hispanic American students continue to be concentrated in central city public schools, many of which have become majority "minority" over the past decade while their funding has fallen further behind that of their suburbs. As of 1997, students of color constituted more than 55% of those served by school districts of more than 15,000 students (National Center for Education Statistics, 2000). As we describe later, central city schools are typically funded at levels substantially below those of neighboring suburban districts. The continuing segregation of neighborhoods and communities intersects with funding formulas and school administration practices that create substantial differences in the educational resources made available in different communities. Together, these conditions produce ongoing inequalities in educational opportunity by race and ethnicity.

Not only do funding systems and other policies create a situation in which urban districts receive fewer resources than their suburban neighbors, but schools with a high concentration of minority students receive fewer resources than other schools within these districts. Tracking systems also exacerbate these inequalities by segregating many minority students within schools, allocating still fewer educational opportunities to them at the classroom level. Later we describe how these layers of inequality are constructed.

The Legacy of Funding Inequality

In 1857, a group of African American leaders testified before a state investigating committee about the striking discrepancies between the finances allocated to White and to Black students. The New York Board of Education spent $16 per White child for sites and school buildings, but the comparable figure per Black child was one cent; Black students occupied school buildings described as "dark and cheerless" in neighborhoods "full of vice and filth," but White students had access to schools that were "splendid, almost palatial edifices, with manifold comforts, conveniences, and elegancies" (Tyack, 1974, p. 119).

Over a century later, after the Supreme Court had already declared "separate but equal" education to be a violation of the 14th Amendment, James Bryant Conant's *Slums and Suburbs* (1961), Francis Keppel's *The Necessary Revolution in American Education* (1966), and Richard Kluger's *Simple Justice* (1976) documented continuing disparities in educational opportunity. These disparities existed—and continue to exist—between predominantly White and minority schools even within the same district. In 1967, the Washington, D.C., District Court found that Black and poor children were denied equal educational opportunity not only because of de facto segregation in Washington's schools but because of unequal spending as well. The court held that

If Whites and Negroes, rich or poor, are to be consigned to separate schools, pursuant to whatever policy, the minimum the Constitution will require and guarantee is that for their objectively measurable aspects these schools be run on the basis of real equality, at least unless any inequalities are adequately justified. (*Hobson v. Hansen*, 269 F. Supp. 401, 496, D.D.C. 1967)

The court subsequently ordered a program of massive reallocation of school resources, ranging from textbooks to teachers and facilities construction. In 1990, the Los Angeles City School District was sued on similar grounds (*Rodriguez et al.* v. *Los Angeles Unified School District*, 1992). Students there in predominantly minority schools, which are overcrowded and less well funded than other schools, were found to be disproportionately assigned to inexperienced and unprepared teachers hired on emergency credentials. In 2001, students in California's highest minority schools were still five times more likely to have an uncertified teacher than those in largely White schools (Shields et al., 2001). This unequal assignment of teachers creates ongoing differentials in expenditures and access to curriculum opportunities, including the knowledge well-prepared teachers rely on in offering high-quality instruction.

Jonathan Kozol's *Savage Inequalities* describes the striking differences between public schools in urban settings—schools whose population is between 95 and 99% non-White—and their suburban counterparts. Chicago public schools spent just over $5,000 per student in 1989, while nearby Niles Township High School spent $9,371 per student. Central city Camden, New Jersey, schools spent $3,500 that year, but affluent suburban Princeton spent $7,725 per student. Schools in New York City spent $7,300

in 1990, while those in nearby suburbs such as Manhasset and Great Neck spent over $15,000 per student for a population with many fewer special needs (Kozol, 1991).

Savage Inequalities is replete with familiar yet poignant stories: the description of East St. Louis Senior High School, whose biology lab had no laboratory tables or usable dissecting kits, contrasted with neighboring suburban schools that enjoyed features like a 27-acre campus; an athletic program featuring golf, fencing, ice hockey, and lacrosse; and a computer hookup to Dow Jones to study stock transactions. Such disparities can still be seen across the country and have not lessened in the last decade. The plaintiffs' brief in the recently filed *Williams* v. *State of California* (2001) lawsuit includes this description of a school serving low-income students of color in San Francisco:

At Luther Burbank, students cannot take textbooks home for homework in any core subject because their teachers have enough textbooks for use in class only. . . . Some math, science, and other core classes do not have even enough textbooks for all the students in a single class to use during the school day, so some students must share the same one book during class time. . . . For homework, students must take home photocopied pages, with no accompanying text for guidance or reference, when and if their teachers have enough paper to use to make homework copies. . . . The social studies textbook Luther Burbank students use is so old that it does not reflect the breakup of the former Soviet Union. Luther Burbank is infested with vermin and roaches and students routinely see mice in their classrooms. One dead rodent has remained, decomposing, in a corner in the gymnasium since the beginning of the school year. The school library is rarely open, has no librarian, and has not recently been updated. Luther Burbank classrooms do not have computers. Computer instruction and research skills are not, therefore, part of Luther Burbank students' regular instruction in their core courses. The school no longer offers any art classes for budgetary reasons. Two of the three bathrooms at Luther Burbank are locked all day, every day. The third bathroom is locked during lunch and other periods during the school day, so there are times during school when no bathroom at all is available for students to use. Students have urinated or defecated on themselves at school because they could not get into an unlocked bathroom. . . . When the bathrooms are not locked, they often lack toilet paper, soap, and paper towels, and the toilets frequently are clogged and overflowing. . . . Ceiling tiles are missing and cracked in the school gym, and school children are afraid to play basketball and other games in the gym because they worry that more ceiling tiles will fall on them during their games. . . . The school heating system does not work well. In winter, children often wear coats, hats, and gloves during class to keep warm. Eleven of the 35 teachers at Luther Burbank have not yet obtained regular, nonemergency credentials, and 17 of the 35 teachers only began teaching at Luther Burbank this school year. (*Williams* v. *State of California*, Superior Court, San Francisco; see www.decentschools.org)

That this kind of school setting is the reality for hundreds of thousands of children in the wealthiest nation on earth would be a surprise to many U.S. citizens. Yet, as we describe later in this chapter, measurable and compounded inequalities leave most minority children with fewer and lower-quality books, materials, computers, labs, and other accoutrements of education, as well as less-qualified and less-experienced teachers, fewer counselors, and social service providers working under greater stress with larger loads. It all adds up.

Such discrepancies in resource allocation are a function of how public education in the United States is funded. In most cases, education costs are supported by a system of general taxes—primarily local property taxes, along with state grants-in-aid (Guthrie, Garms, & Pierce, 1988). Because these funds are typically raised and spent locally, districts with higher property values have greater resources with which to fund their schools, even when poorer districts tax themselves at a proportionally higher rate. In Texas, for instance, the 100 wealthiest districts taxed their local property at an average rate of $0.47 per $100 of assessed worth in 1989; at that level of effort, they were able to spend more than $7,000 per student. Meanwhile, the 100 poorest districts, taxing themselves at a rate of more than $0.70 per $100, were able to raise only enough to spend some $3,000 per student (Kozol, 1991).

Differences of the same kind exist among states, with per-pupil expenditures ranging from more than $10,000 in New Jersey in 1996–97 to only $4,000 in Utah (NCES, 2000). Although states generally provide fiscal aid that has a modest equalizing effect on spending among districts, the federal government thus far plays no such role with respect to differentials among states in wealth and ability to pay for education.

These disparities translate into real differences in the services provided in schools: higher-spending districts have smaller classes, higher-paid and more experienced teachers, and greater instructional resources, as well as better facilities, more up-to-date equipment, and a wider range of course offerings (Educational Testing Service, 1991). Districts serving a large proportion of poor children have fewer resources (NCES, 1998). Thus, those students least likely to encounter an array of educational resources at home are also least likely to encounter them at school (Berne, 1992; Betts, Rueben, & Danenberg, 2000; ETS, 1991; New York Study Group on Outcome Equity, 1993).

The Legality of Unequal School Funding

Although concern about unequal school funding was expressed as early as the turn of the century (Cubberly, 1906; Updegraff & King, 1922), it was not until the mid-1960s that the legality of traditional inequities of school finance was subjected to judicial review. In 1965, Arthur Wise published an article challenging the constitutionality of school finance schemes that produce radically disparate per-pupil expenditures within states. Arguing that such unequal spending leads to unequal educational opportunities, he suggested that this might constitute a denial by the state of equal protection under the law (see also Wise, 1972).

A number of lawsuits were filed on these grounds, and in 1973, in *Robinson* v. *Cahill*, the New Jersey Supreme Court declared the state's school financing system to be in violation of the New Jersey constitution's education clause, which called for a "thorough and efficient system of free public schools" for all children between the ages of 5 and 18 (Wise & Gendler, 1989, p. 14). That same year, in *San Antonio Independent School District* v. *Rodriguez* (1973), however, the U.S. Supreme Court rejected the argument that education constitutes a fundamental right under the federal Constitution, thus stemming further federal court challenges of educational funding inequities.

Although hopes for a sweeping indictment of school funding traditions on federal grounds were dashed by the *San Antonio* decision, state-level challenges continued in several dozen state courts during the 1970s (Taylor & Piche, 1991). In 1976, in *Serrano* v. *Priest*, California's Supreme Court ended nearly a decade of debate by ruling that the state's system of school finance violated both the federal Constitution's 14th Amendment and California's own equal protection clause (Guthrie et al., 1988; Wise & Gendler, 1989). Other victories were achieved in West Virginia and Connecticut. However, most of the challenges were unsuccessful. Taylor and Piche note the differences in how state courts have approached similar problems:

In each case, the state court was confronted with significant fiscal disparities, but the opinions reflect that they each engaged in their own unique legal reasoning, applying different standards, and ultimately drawing different conclusions. The indisputable impact then of the "Federalist" approach, forged by the Supreme Court in *Rodriguez,* is that children in the poor districts of states like Connecticut and West Virginia are guaranteed some measure of equity, while those who live in the property-poor and urban districts of states like New York and Maryland are condemned to inferior educations. (Taylor & Piche, 1991, p. 67)

Large disparities in funding ratios of three to one between high- and low-spending districts are common within states in which challenges have been both successful and unsuccessful. These disparities create differences among students' educational opportunities as a function of race and socioeconomic status as well as geography. As Taylor and Piche (1991) observe:

Inequitable systems of school finance inflict disproportionate harm on minority and economically disadvantaged students. On an interstate basis, such students are concentrated in states, primarily in the South, that have the lowest capacities to finance public education. On an intra-state basis, many of the states with the widest disparities in educational expenditures are large industrial states. In these states, many minorities and economically disadvantaged students are located in property-poor urban districts which fare the worst in educational expenditures. In addition, in several states economically disadvantaged students, white and black, are concentrated in rural districts which suffer from fiscal inequity. (pp. xi–xii)

Furthermore, this connection between inadequate funding and the race and social status of students exacerbates the difficulties of creating either integrated or adequately funded schools. The vicious cycle was described early on in the fight for school funding reform:

School inequality between suburbia and central city crucially reinforces racial isolation in housing; and the resulting racial segregation of the schools constantly inhibits progress toward funding a therapeutic answer for the elimination of school inequality. If we are to exorcise the evils of separateness and inequality, we must view them together, for each dimension of the problem renders the other more difficult to solve—racially separate schools inhibit elimination of school inequality, and unequal schools retard eradication of school segregation. (Silard & Goldstein, 1974, p. 324)

Courts that have found their state's school finance scheme to be unconstitutional have done so on one of three grounds: the federal Constitution's 14th Amendment, the state constitution's equal opportunity clause, or the state constitution's education article (McUsic, 1991). A series of state challenges in the 1970s were followed by a decade of little activity, during which time there remained substantial variation in the share of school funding provided by states, with less activism aimed at equalization in states in which judicial pressure had been absent (Wong, 1989). The issue was rejoined in the late 1980s, when successful finance suits were brought in New Jersey, Texas, Montana, Kentucky, and Tennessee (ETS, 1991) and continued into the 1990s with lawsuits in Alabama, New York, California, and elsewhere arguing a new "adequacy" theory. These suits seek to demonstrate how access to concrete learning opportunities is impaired by differential access to money, and how these learning opportunities translate into academic achievement for students.

As standards are used to articulate what students need to learn to function in today's society and what schools need to do to support these levels of learning, lawsuits like one recently won in Alabama may be linked to definitions of the quality of education that is adequate to meet the state's expectations for student achievement. Such cases are requiring remedies that link the level of funding to minimum standards of learning, teaching, and resources. For example, the trial judge in the New York case (which was on appeal in 2003) stated, in deciding for the plaintiffs:

This court has held that a sound basic education mandated by the Education Article consists of the foundational skills that students need to become productive citizens capable of civic engagement and sustaining competitive employment. In order to ensure that public schools offer a sound basic education the State must take steps to ensure at least the following resources, which, as described in the body of this opinion are for the most part currently not given to New York city's public school students: 1) Sufficient numbers of qualified teachers, principals, and other personnel; 2) Appropriate class sizes; 3) Adequate and accessible school buildings . . .; 4) Sufficient and up to date books, supplies, libraries, educational technology, and laboratories; 5) Suitable curricula, including an expanded platform of programs to help at risk students . . .; 6) Adequate resources for students with extraordinary needs; and 7) A safe orderly environment. (*Campaign for Fiscal Equity et al.* v. *State of New York,* 187 Misc. 2d 1; 719 N.Y.S.2d 475; January 9, 2001)

Although the legal intricacies by which the courts have made their decisions are beyond the scope of this chapter, some of the conceptual grounds on which opponents of such decisions rest their arguments are not. In particular, opponents of school finance reform often argue that (a) concerns about local control outweigh concerns about equalizing funding across districts; and (b) differences in per-pupil expenditures are irrelevant to issues of equity, since financial input does not affect the quality of education a district offers. For example, in overturning the CFE decision cited above, an appellate panel concluded that New York City's lower levels of funding had no proven bearing on student achievement and that, in any event, students could get by as low-level workers on an 8th- or 9th-grade education. The state, the court said, has no constitutional responsibility to ensure they can reach the new graduation standards laid down by the State Board of Regents. It remains to be seen whether the State Court of Appeals will agree with this view that, although children are accountable to the state for specific levels of achievement, the state is not accountable to children to provide the means to reach these levels.

Proponents of the argument that "money doesn't make a difference" suggest that low-cost attitudinal and administrative changes contribute more than financial resources to educational quality within districts, and that no definitive correlation has been shown between money spent and educational quality. Advocates of finance reform argue that although money *can* be misspent, and although significant changes can be made without maximum resources, the question must be considered within the larger framework of the possibilities that are created and constrained at differing levels of resources. Within that framework, money makes a substantial difference (Minow, 1991; Murnane, 1991).

In response to the local control argument, defenders of school finance reform have pointed out that local control of schools has already been subjected to such erosion that, as the Texas Supreme Court wrote in its 1988 *Edgewood* v. *Kirby* decision,

the only element of local control that remains undiminished is the power of wealthy districts to fund education at virtually any level they choose, as contrasted with property-poor districts who enjoy no such local control. . . . Most of the incidents in the education process are determined and controlled by state statute and/or State Board of Education rule, including such matters as curriculum, course content, textbooks, hours of instruction, pupil-teacher ratios, training of teachers, administrators and board members, teacher testing, and review of personnel decisions and policies. (quoted in Wise & Gendler, 1989, p. 16)

Although local control in the form of parental and community involvement in the schools remains an important factor in education, it does not justify radically inequitable allocation of financial resources. Indeed, a more equitable distribution of resources might be a precondition for genuine local control (Yudof, 1991).

HOW MONEY MAKES A DIFFERENCE

The relationship between educational funding and educational achievement was placed in question in 1966, when James Coleman and a team of researchers issued *Equality of Educational Opportunity* (Coleman et al., 1966), which later came to be known as the Coleman report. Although the report argued that sources of inequality that it identified should be remedied, its statement that "schools bring little influence to bear on a child's achievement that is independent of his background and general social context" (quoted in Ferguson, 1991, p. 468) became widely viewed as a claim that school funding does not affect school achievement. As later analyses pointed out, it is in part the high correlation between students' backgrounds and their schools' resources that makes it difficult in macroanalytic studies to identify an independent effect of schooling on achievement (see, e.g., MacPhail-Wilcox & King, 1986).

Nonetheless, although the Coleman report did not say so, the received view became the belief that additional resources play no role in producing better-educated students. Other studies have sought to confirm this view (e.g., Hanushek, 1990; Jencks et al., 1972), while newspapers have reported the counterintuitive conclusion that "money doesn't buy better education. . . . The evidence can scarcely be clearer" (*Wall Street Journal*, June 27, 1989, cited in Kozol, 1991, p. 133).

More recent studies, however, have provided empirical justification for the view that money *does* make a difference. Analyzing a set of data on Texas school districts even larger than that available to Coleman and his team of researchers, Ronald Ferguson (1991) found that the most important measurable cause of increased student learning was teacher expertise, measured by teacher performance on a statewide recertification exam, teacher experience, and a master's degree. He also found that class size, at a teacher-student ratio of 1:18, is also a statistically significant determinant of student outcomes.

Both of these findings have been confirmed elsewhere. As described in the next section, a large number of studies have found positive effects of teacher expertise on student achievement. In addition, smaller class size (below a threshold that is often in the low 20s or below) can make a substantial difference in achievement, especially in the early grades and for low-income students (Educational Research Service, 1980; Glass, Cahen, Smith, & Filby, 1982; Walberg, 1982).

Ferguson demonstrated that if regional cost differentials are accounted for, school district operating expenditures exert a significant positive effect on student achievement. The strength of effects on achievement increases as funding moves closest to direct instruction of students. All are significant, but proportionally equivalent investment in teachers' salaries produces higher marginal gains in student performance than investment in general instructional expenditures, and investment in instructional expenditures produces higher marginal gains in achievement than proportional increases in general operating expenditures. Money makes a difference, and the difference increases as it is spent on instructionally crucial resources.

Ferguson (1991) notes that this finding "strongly supports the conventional wisdom that higher-quality schooling produces better reading skills among public school students, and that when targeted and managed wisely, increased funding can improve the quality of public education" (p. 488). Furthermore, "what the evidence here suggests most strongly is that teacher quality matters and should be a major focus of efforts to upgrade the quality of schooling. Skilled teachers are the most critical of all schooling inputs" (p. 490). The effects of teacher quality were so strong, and the variations in teacher expertise so great, that after controlling for socioeconomic status the large disparities in achievement between Black and White students were almost entirely accounted for by differences in the qualifications of their teachers.

Ferguson and Helen Ladd (1996) repeated this analysis in Alabama with a data set that included rougher proxies for teacher knowledge (master's degree and ACT scores instead of teacher licensing examination scores), and they still found sizable influences of teacher qualifications and smaller class size on student achievement gains in mathematics and reading when the data were analyzed at both the district and the school levels. They found that 31% of the predicted difference in district mathematics scores in the top and bottom quartiles was explained by teacher qualifications and class size, while 29.5% was explained by poverty, race, and parent education.

A similar study (Strauss & Sawyer, 1986) found that student test performance in North Carolina districts was strongly associated with teachers' average scores on the most commonly used teacher licensing examination, the National Teacher Examinations. (The NTE Core Battery, in use in North Carolina at that time, included components measuring basic skills, general knowledge, and professional teaching knowledge.) Taking into account per-capita income, student race, district capital assets, student plans to attend college, and pupil-teacher ratios, teachers' test scores had a strikingly large effect on student failure rate on the state competency examinations: a 1% increase in teacher quality (as measured by NTE scores) was associated with a 3% to 5% decline in the percentage of students failing the exam. This effect was much larger than the effect of student race. The authors' conclusion was similar to Ferguson's:

Of the inputs which are potentially policy-controllable (teacher quality, teacher numbers via the pupil-teacher ratio and capital stock), our analysis indicates quite clearly that improving the quality of teachers in the classroom will do more for students who are most educationally at risk, those prone to fail, than reducing the class size or improving the capital stock by any reasonable margin which would be available to policy makers. (p. 47)

As I describe next, the evidence is increasingly clear that equal educational opportunity must include access to quality teachers and teaching.

ACCESS TO GOOD TEACHING

In "Closing the Divide," Robert Dreeben (1987) describes the results of his study of reading instruction and outcomes for 300 Black and White first graders across seven schools in the Chicago area. He found that differences in reading outcomes among students were almost entirely explained not by socioeconomic status or race but by the quality of instruction the students received:

Our evidence shows that the level of learning responds strongly to the quality of instruction: having and using enough time, covering a substantial amount of rich curricular material, and matching instruction appropriately to the ability levels of groups. . . . When black and white children of comparable ability experience the same instruction, they do about equally well, and this is true when the instruction is excellent in quality and when it is inadequate. (p. 34)

However, the study also found that the quality of instruction received by African American students was, on average, much lower than that received by White students, thus creating a racial gap in aggregate achievement by the end of first grade. In fact, the highest ability group in Dreeben's sample was in a school in a low-income African American neighborhood. However, these students learned less during first grade than their lower-ability White counterparts. Why? Because their teacher was unable to provide the kind of appropriate and challenging instruction this highly talented group deserved.

Another study of African American high school youths randomly placed in public housing in the Chicago suburbs rather than in the city found similar results (Kaufman & Rosenbaum, 1992). Compared with their comparable city-placed peers, who were of equivalent income and initial academic attainment, the students who were enabled to attend largely White and better-funded suburban schools had better educational outcomes across many dimensions; they were substantially more likely to have the opportunity to take challenging courses, receive additional academic help, graduate on time, attend college, and secure good jobs.

These examples are drawn from carefully controlled studies that confirm what many other studies have suggested: much of the difference in school achievement found between African American students and others is due to the effects of substantially different school opportunities, in particular greatly disparate access to high-quality teachers and teaching (see, e.g., Barr & Dreeben, 1983; College Board, 1985; Dreeben & Barr, 1987; Dreeben & Gamoran, 1986; Oakes, 1990).

The Unequal Distribution of Teachers

Minority and low-income students in urban settings are most likely to find themselves in a classroom staffed by an inadequately prepared, inexperienced, and ill-qualified teacher because funding inequities, distribution of local power, and labor market conditions conspire to produce teacher shortages of which they bear the brunt. In almost every field, schools with the largest number of low-income and minority students are much more likely than other schools to report that they have difficulty filling vacancies (NCES, 1997). These schools are also much more likely than others to fill vacancies with unqualified teachers, substitutes, or teachers from other fields, or to expand class sizes or cancel course offerings when they cannot find teachers.

These "shortages," though, are largely a problem of distribution rather than of absolute numbers. Wealthy districts that pay high salaries and offer pleasant working conditions rarely experience a shortage in any field. Districts that serve low-income and minority students tend to pay teachers less and offer larger class sizes and pupil loads, fewer materials, and less desirable teaching conditions, including less professional autonomy (Darling-Hammond, 1997; NCES, 1999). They also often have cumbersome and inefficient hiring systems that make the selection process particularly slow and grueling for candidates. For obvious reasons, they have more difficulty recruiting and retaining teachers.

As a consequence of these conditions, teachers working in schools serving a larger number of low-income and minority students generally have a substantially lower level of education and are more often unprepared for their teaching assignments than those in economically advantaged schools (NCES, 1999; Oakes, 1990). In California, where these differentials are among the most striking, schools serving the greatest proportion of low-income and minority students are four to five times more likely to hire teachers without full certification. Unqualified teachers are also concentrated in the lowest-achieving schools (Shields et al., 2001). In a national study of mathematics and science teaching, Oakes found that students in the highest-minority schools have only a 50% chance of being taught by a math or science teacher who is certified and holds a degree in the subject area(s) taught (Figure 29.1). She concludes:

Our evidence lends considerable support to the argument that low-income, minority, and inner-city students have fewer opportunities. . . . They have considerably less access to science and mathematics knowledge at school, fewer material resources, less-engaging learning activities in their classrooms, and less-qualified teachers. . . . The differences we have observed are likely to reflect more general patterns of educational inequality. (pp. x–xi)

Just as Dreeben (1987) found in his study of early reading teaching, Oakes (1990) also discovered that "high-ability students at low-socioeconomic status, high-minority schools may actually have fewer opportunities than low-ability students who attend more advantaged schools" (p. vii). The pattern of systematic underexposure to good teaching tends to put all children in high-minority schools at risk.

Teacher shortages subvert the quality of education in a number of ways. They make it hard for a district to be selective about the quality of teachers it hires, and they often result in hiring teachers who do not have content background for the fields they teach and have not completed (or sometimes even begun) their pedagogical training. Thus districts serving the greatest concentration of poor children, minority children, and children of immigrants are also those in which incoming teachers are least likely to have learned about up-to-date teaching methods or about what to do if they are having difficulties. In addition, when faced with a shortage, a district must often hire substitutes, assign teachers outside their fields of qualification, expand class sizes, or cancel course offerings. No matter what strategies are adopted, the quality of instruction suffers.

According to the most recent national data, at least 100,000 teachers in 1999–2000 were underqualified for their teaching assignments, and most of them were assigned to the most disadvantaged central city or rural schools, where working conditions are least attractive and the turnover rate highest (Schools and Staffing Surveys, 1999-2000, teacher survey data; tabulations conducted by Richard Ingersoll and John Luczak for the National Commission on Teaching and America's Future). Since many of the more expert and experienced teachers transfer to more desirable schools and districts when they are able, new teachers are typically given the most difficult teaching assignments in schools that offer the fewest supports (Murnane, Singer, Willett, Kemple, & Olsen, 1991; Wise, Darling-Hammond, & Berry, 1987). Because of these challenges, attrition rates for new teachers, especially in cities, average between 30% and 40% over the first five years of teaching (Grissmer & Kirby, 1987; Ingersoll, 2002).

High attrition rates add problems of staff instability to the already difficult circumstances in which central city youths attend school. Where shortages are acute and enduring, many children are taught by a parade of short-term substitute teachers, inexperienced teachers without support, and underqualified teachers who know neither their subject matter nor effective teaching methods. This sets up the school failure that society predicts for low-income and minority children—a failure that it helps to create for them by its failure to deal effectively with the issues of teacher supply and quality.

What Matters in Teaching?

Over the last 20 years, educational research has exploded the myths that any teaching is as effective as any other, and that unequally trained and experienced teachers are equally advantageous to students. In a study documenting the positive influence of teaching experience on teaching effectiveness, Murnane and Phillips (1981) note:

The question of whether teachers become more productive as they gain teaching experience has been of interest to policymakers for many years. One reason is that schools serving children from low-income families have typically been staffed with less experienced teachers than schools serving middle-class children. This has led to court tests of whether the uneven distribution of teaching experience constitutes discrimination against low-income children. (pp. 453–454)

Although the correlation between teacher experience and effectiveness is not unvarying over the course of a career, studies consistently find that new teachers—those with fewer than three years of experience—tend to be much less effective than more experienced teachers (Betts et al., 2000; McNeil, 1974; Murnane & Phillips, 1981; Rottenberg & Berliner, 1990). Especially in the unsupported

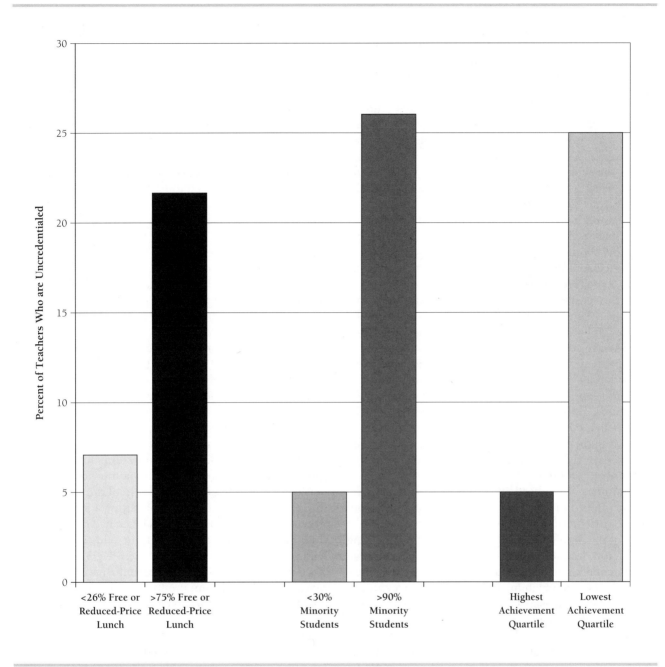

FIGURE 29.1. Distribution of Underqualified Teachers.

Source: Shields et al. (2001).

environment most encounter, beginning teachers experience a range of problems in learning to teach; problems with classroom management, motivating students, being aware of and dealing appropriately with individual learning needs and differences, and developing a diverse repertoire of instructional strategies are among the most commonly noted (Johnston & Ryan, 1983; Rottenberg & Berliner; Veenman, 1984).

Having confirmed that teacher experience does make a difference, researchers are now identifying what expert veterans do in the classroom that distinguishes their teaching from that of novices. Among other things, expert teachers are much more sensitive to students' needs and individual differences; they are more skilled at engaging and motivating students; and they can call upon a wider repertoire of instructional strategies for addressing student needs (see e.g., Berliner, 1986; Grossman, 1990; Shulman, 1987). Much of this research also demonstrates the importance of teacher education for acquiring knowledge and skills that improve the caliber of instruction and the success of students (Darling-Hammond, 2000a, 2000b; Wilson, Floden, & Ferrini-Mundy, 2001). Studies have found significant relationships between student achievement and measures of teacher education and certification at the level of the individual teacher (Goldhaber & Brewer, 2000; Hawk, Coble, & Swanson, 1985; Monk, 1994), the school (Betts et al., 2000; Fetler, 1999), the school district (Ferguson, 1991; Strauss & Sawyer, 1986), and the state (Darling-Hammond, 2000b).

This is particularly important in light of the fact that policy makers have nearly always answered the problem of teacher shortages by lowering standards so that people who have had little or no preparation for teaching can be hired. These teachers are disproportionately assigned to teach the least enfranchised students. Although this practice is often excused by the assumption that virtually anyone can figure out how to teach, a number of research reviews have concluded that fully prepared and certified teachers are more highly rated and more successful with students than teachers without preparation (Ashton & Crocker, 1986, 1987; Darling-Hammond, 1992; Evertson, Hawley, & Zlotnik, 1985; Druva & Anderson, 1983). Thus, policies that resolve a shortage in a poor district by supporting the hiring of unprepared teachers serve only to exacerbate the inequalities experienced by low-income and minority children.

A number of studies have found that teachers who enter without full preparation are less able to plan and redirect instruction to meet students' needs (and less aware of the need to do so), less skilled in implementing instruction, less able to anticipate students' knowledge and potential difficulties, and less likely to see it as their job to do so, often blaming students if their teaching is not successful (Bledsoe, Cox, & Burnham, 1967; Grossman, 1990; Rottenberg & Berliner, 1990). Furthermore, teachers who enter teaching with little or no training leave at a very high rate. In California, just over 40% of emergency permit teachers leave the profession within a year, and two-thirds never receive a credential. The California Commission on Teacher Certification (CCTC) reports one-year attrition rates for emergency credentialed teachers of 35% for elementary recruits and 48% for secondary recruits (CCTC Emergency Permit Persistence Data, 1996-97, compiled by Certification and Waiver Division, January 1, 1998, on first-time multiple and single-subject long-term emergency permits). National data from the Recent College Graduates Survey indicates that about two-thirds of unprepared entrants leave teaching within their first year (Stowe, 1993). Other national data indicate that about 60–65% of entrants who enter

through short-term alternative certification routes have left within three years (Darling-Hammond, 2000a). An NCES report notes that 29% of new teachers who had not had student teaching left teaching within five years, as compared to only 15% of those who had had student teaching (Henke, Chen, & Geis, 2000).

In the context of today's higher standards and the growing diversity of students in schools, the lack of adequate teacher preparation for so many teachers in urban and poor rural schools is troubling. Teachers not only need the skills to impart content knowledge in an accessible way, they also need to be able to reach the growing number of students whose first language is not English and the large number of students with special learning needs. The National Center for Education Statistics estimates that, in 1993–94, only 30% of teachers instructing limited English proficient (LEP) students had any training to do so, and fewer than 3% of teachers with LEP students had earned a degree in teaching English as a second language or in bilingual education. Fewer than 50% of LEP students in middle and high schools receive any kind of ESL or bilingual education support (Ruiz de Velasco & Fix, 2000). Meeting the needs of this growing segment of the student population—and many others with particular learning needs—requires much more knowledge about teaching and learning. At the same time, many teachers whose teaching assignments require the greatest expertise have the least.

More than ever before in our nation's history, education is the ticket not only to economic success but to basic survival. Whereas a high school dropout in 1970 had two chances out of three of getting a job, by 1993 a recent school dropout who was Black had only a one-in-four chance of being employed; the odds for his White counterpart were about 50% (NCES, 1995). Those who do not succeed in school are becoming part of a growing underclass, cut off from productive engagement in society. Because the economy can no longer absorb many unskilled workers at decent wages, lack of education is increasingly linked to crime and welfare dependency. Women who have not finished high school are much more likely than others to be on welfare, while men are much more likely to be in prison.

In 1993, there were more African American citizens on probation, in jail, in prison, or on parole (1,985,000) than there were in college (1,412,000; U.S. Department of Commerce, 1996). More than half the adult prison population has literacy skills below those required by the labor market (Barton & Coley, 1996), and nearly 40% of adjudicated juvenile delinquents have treatable learning disabilities that went undiagnosed and untreated in the schools (Gemignani, 1994).

Meanwhile, schools have changed slowly. Most are still organized to prepare only about 20% of their students for "thinking work"—those students who are tracked very early into gifted and talented, "advanced," or honors courses. These opportunities are least available to African American, Latino, and Native American students.

Access to Courses, Curriculum Materials, and Equipment

In addition to being taught by less qualified teachers than their suburban counterparts, urban students face dramatic differences in courses, curriculum materials, and equipment. For example, Kozol (1991) noted that, although Goudy Elementary School, which serves a predominantly African American student population in Chicago, uses "15-year-old textbooks in which Richard Nixon is still president" and has "no science labs, no art or music teachers . . . [and] two working bathrooms for some 700 children," the neighboring town of New Trier (more than 98% White) provides its high school students with "superior labs . . . up-to-date technology . . . seven gyms [and] an Olympic pool" (1991, pp. 63–65).

From a more wide-ranging statistical vantage point, Oakes (1990) found in a study of access to mathematics and science-related educational resources that

> students in low-income, high-minority schools have less access than students in other schools to computers and to the staff who coordinate their use in instruction, to science laboratories, and to other common science-related facilities and equipment. (p. ix)

Oakes and Saunders (2002) point out that in science, learning materials and workspaces that permit hands-on science activities are increasingly necessary for student achievement in inquiry-based science education, and that opportunities for laboratory inquiry lead to higher achievement and more equitable achievement among students of different socioeconomic backgrounds (Von Secker & Lissitz, 1999). Inadequate facilities and equipment and lack of money to purchase supplies create larger gaps among advantaged and disadvantaged students because these shortages lead to students in disadvantaged schools having fewer opportunities for scientific inquiry.

Disparities also exist in access to other kinds of materials, including textbooks, supplies, and computers. Analyzing data from a California school survey, Oakes and Saunders (2002) found that schools serving a large population of low-income or minority students had less access to every category of instructional resources than did schools serving a population with few low-income or minority students. For example, although 88% of teachers working at schools serving fewer minority students (less than 30%) indicated that textbooks were always available, only 68% of teachers working at schools serving more minority students (more than 90%) indicated that

they always had access to textbooks. Similarly, 83% of teachers working at schools serving a small percentage of low-income students indicated that they always had access to textbooks, versus only 57% of teachers who worked at schools serving a large population of low-income students.

Although the Clinton administration's E-rate program made important strides in closing the gap between rich and poor schools in access to technology—a gap that exacerbates the gap in access to technology across affluent and low-income households—there are still noticeable disparities in students' access to computers and the Internet. In 2000, even though 98% of schools had some kind of Internet access, schools with a high concentration of students in poverty had fewer classrooms connected to the Internet (60% as opposed to 82% in higher income schools) and higher ratios of students to computers (9:1, in contrast with the 6:1 ratio in more affluent schools; NCES, 2001c).

In predominantly minority schools, 23% of classrooms had no computers available (as compared to between 11% and 16% in predominantly White schools), and in high-poverty schools the proportion of classrooms with no computer access was 18% (as compared to 13% in low-poverty schools; Smerdon et al., 2000). Furthermore, research has found that in predominantly minority schools and classrooms, microcomputers have been used much more frequently for drill and practice and much less frequently to teach students to program, access data, and solve problems using the computer as a tool, rather than as a master (Sutton, 1991; Smerdon et al.).

Even more important are deep-seated inequalities in access to curriculum. High-minority schools have traditionally been much less likely to offer advanced and college preparatory courses in mathematics and science than schools that serve affluent and largely White populations (Oakes, 1990; Oakes, Joseph, & Muir, Chapter 4, this volume). In many parts of the country, conditions of this kind have not changed. Schools with the fewest resources in terms of teaching expertise typically also have fewer resources of all other kinds as well. A Public Policy Institute study in 2000 discovered that large disparities in teachers' experience, general education (degree level), and preparation for teaching (as measured by certification status) across California schools are associated with equally large disparities in access to curriculum. Teacher quality and curriculm indicators as measured by the percentage of high school courses that satisfy entrance requirements at the University of California (the "a-f" courses) and advanced placement courses. Both of these are strongly related to students' socioeconomic status (Betts et al., 2000; see Table 29.1). Low-income schools are also more likely to be large and overcrowded, sometimes operating on multitrack, year-round schedules, all of which pose disadvantages both for student learning and for attracting and retaining well-qualified teachers.

TABLE 29.1. Disparities in Curriculum and Teaching Resources, by School Socioeconomic Status.

Characteristics of Teaching Force and Curriculum in Schools	Lowest SES Schools (Bottom Quintile)	Highest SES Schools (Top Quintile)
Percentage with 0–2 years' experience (K–6)	23.8	17.2
Percentage with 10 or more years' experience (K–6)	43.3	53.3
Percentage with bachelor's degree or less (K–6)	32.6	8.8
Percentage with master's degree or more (K–6)	21.7	27.0
Percentage not fully certified (K–6)	21.7	2.0
Percentage "a-f" classes (9–12)	51.8	63.2
Percentage AP classes	2.0	3.2

Source: Betts et al. (2000, Table B1).

When high-minority, low-income schools offer any advanced or college preparatory courses, they typically offer them to only a very tiny fraction of students. Thus, at the high school level, African Americans, Hispanics, and American Indians have traditionally been underrepresented in academic programs and overrepresented in vocational education programs, where they receive fewer courses in areas such as English, mathematics, and science (College Board, 1985). As Oakes (1992) explains:

The extraordinarily complex connections between tracking and social stratification play out in two ways. First, schools with predominantly low-income and minority student populations tend to be "bottom heavy." That is, they offer smaller academic tracks and larger remedial and vocational programs than do schools serving whiter, more affluent student bodies. . . . The second link between tracking and students' race and social class is forged in racially mixed schools through the disproportionate assignment of African-American and Latino students to low-track classes. (p. 13)

Long-standing gaps in access to and participation in academic coursework have continued. In 1998, for example, 45% of White high school graduates had taken advanced courses in mathematics, while the proportions for Black and Hispanic graduates were 30% and 26%, respectively (NCES, 2001a). Although 31% of White high school graduates had taken advanced courses in English, the proportions for Black, Hispanic, and Native American graduates were 27%, 22%, and 17%, respectively (NCES, 2001b, p. 61). Black, Hispanic, and Native American students were also 50–90% more likely to have taken English courses that were categorized as "low academic level."

Unequal access to high-level courses and challenging curriculum explains much of the difference in achievement between minority students and White students. For example, analyses of data from the High School and Beyond surveys demonstrate that, for students of all racial and ethnic groups, course taking is strongly related to achievement; among students with similar course-taking records, achievement test score differences by race or ethnicity narrow substantially (College Board, 1985; Jones, 1984; Jones, Burton, & Davenport, 1984; Moore & Smith, 1985; Pelavin & Kane, 1990).

TRACKING AND THE RATIONING OF CURRICULUM

The same forces that produce the flow of good teachers and rich educational resources to advantaged schools, and the ebb of opportunities from disadvantaged schools and students, are at work within schools wherever tracking persists. Tracking—that is, the practice of placing students into course streams that differentiate the kind and amount of content to which they will have access —has endured in the face of evidence that it does not substantially benefit high achievers and tends to put low achievers at a disadvantage (Hoffer, 1992; Kulik & Kulik, 1982; Oakes, 1985, 1986; Slavin, 1990), in part because good teaching is a scarce resource and thus must be allocated. Scarce resources tend to get allocated to the students whose parents, advocates, or representatives have the most political clout. This results—not entirely, but disproportionately—in the most highly qualified teachers teaching the most enriched curricula to the most advantaged students. (Tracking can be distinguished from other forms of grouping in several ways. Tracking affects a student's possibility of accessing content since it differentiates content within courses and establishes a long-term course "stream" that follows from a given track assignment, as with honors, college preparatory, general, vocational, remedial or special education, and in some states, ESL "sheltered." Other forms of grouping for instruction may occur to take account of student interests or current achievement levels without predicting or precluding their long-range access to content.)

Evidence suggests that teachers themselves are tracked, with those judged to be the most competent, the most experienced, or with the highest status assigned to the top ranks (Finley, 1984; Talbert, 1990). In one study of secondary school curriculum, for example, 42% of teachers of remedial, vocational, and general mathematics had been teaching for five years or less, compared with 19% of those in the pre-algebra and algebra sections (McDonnell, Burstein, Ormseth, Catterall, & Moody, 1990, cited in Wheelock, 1992). Expert, experienced teachers who are in great demand are rewarded with opportunities to teach the students who already know a lot. New teachers, unprepared teachers, and those teaching outside their field of preparation are often assigned to the students and the classes that others do not care to teach, which leaves them practicing on the students who would benefit most from the skills of the expert, experienced teachers.

Another major reason for the persistence of this practice is the kind of preparation teachers receive generally. Managing a heterogeneous classroom requires preparation that relatively few teachers receive and skills that relatively few of them acquire (Darling-Hammond, 1990b; Wheelock, 1992). It requires refined diagnostic ability, a broad repertoire of teaching strategies, and the ability to match strategies to varied learning styles and prior levels of knowledge. It requires skill in using inquiry and cooperative learning strategies, as well as skills in classroom management even more considerable than those required in a homogeneous classroom. Because relatively few teachers are prepared to manage heterogeneous classrooms effectively, tracking persists.

Tracking in elementary and middle school is much more extensive in U.S. schools than in most other countries. Even those countries that differentiate high schools typically provide a common core curriculum prior to high school. In the United States, tracking often starts in elementary school with designation of instructional groups and programs, such as "gifted and talented" or "compensatory" classes, on the basis of test scores and recommendations. These distinctions generally become highly formalized by junior high school. The result of this practice is that challenging curricula are rationed to a very small proportion of students, and far fewer U.S. students ever encounter the kinds of curriculum typically experienced by students in other countries (McKnight et al., 1987; Useem, 1990; Usiskin, 1987; Wheelock, 1992). Although advanced course taking has increased, in 1998 it was still the case that 62% of U.S. high school students had not taken advanced mathematics courses of the kind taken by most students in the highest-achieving countries (NCES, 2001b).

Students placed in lower tracks are typically exposed to a more limited, rote-oriented curriculum; ultimately they achieve less than students of similar aptitude who are placed in academic programs or untracked classes (Gamoran, 1990; Gamoran & Mare, 1989; Oakes, 1992). Teacher interaction with students in lower-track classes has been found to be less motivating and less supportive, as well as less demanding of higher-order reasoning and responses (Good & Brophy, 1987). Presentations are often less clear and less focused on higher-order cognitive goals (Oakes, 1985). These interactions are also less academically oriented and more likely to focus on behavioral criticisms, especially for minority students (Eckstrom & Villegas, 1991).

These curricular differences are widespread, and they explain much of the disparity between the achievement of White and minority students, and between higher and lower income levels (Lee & Bryk, 1988; Oakes, 1985). Studies over more than two decades have found that when students of similar background and initial achievement level are exposed differentially to either more or less challenging curriculum material, those given the richer curriculum opportunities outperform those placed in less challenging classes (Alexander & McDill, 1976; Gamoran & Berends, 1987; Oakes, 1985). Most studies have estimated effects statistically based on naturalistic occurrences of different tracking policies. However, one study that randomly assigned seventh-grade at-risk students to remedial, average, and honors mathematics classes found that, at the end of the year, the at-risk students who took the honors class offering a pre-algebra curriculum outperformed all other students of similar background (Peterson, 1989, cited in Levin, 1992).

Tracking exacerbates differential access to knowledge. As Oakes (1986) notes, assignment of poor and minority students to lower tracks is predictable. Though test scores and prior educational opportunities may offer one reason for these differential placements, race and socioeconomic status play a distinct role. Oakes and Lipton (1998) report on their findings in racially mixed school systems, that African American and Latino students are much less likely than White or Asian students *with the same test scores* to be placed in a high-ability class. In one West Coast district they studied, White and Asian students with average scores on standardized tests were more than twice as likely to be placed in an accelerated class as Latino students with the same scores. Although 93% of high-scoring Whites were in accelerated classes, only 56% of high-scoring Latinos with comparable scores were in these classes.

Gamoran (1992) also found that race and socioeconomic status determine assignment to high school honors courses even after test scores are controlled. This is true in part because of prior placement of students in upper tracks in earlier grades, in part because of counselors' views that they should advise students in a way that is "realistic" about their future, and in part because of the greater effectiveness of parent intervention in tracking decisions for higher-SES students. For similar reasons, race and socioeconomic status also affect students' placement in vocational and academic programs and in more or less challenging courses within them (Oakes, Selvin, Karoly, & Guiton, 1992; Useem, 1990). The seeds of this tracking are planted in "ability grouping" in elementary school; students' placements are well established long before high school begins (Moore & Davenport, 1988).

From "gifted and talented" programs at the elementary level through advanced courses in secondary schools, teachers who are generally the most skilled offer rich, challenging curricula to select groups of students, on the theory that only a few students can benefit from such curricula. Yet the distinguishing feature of such programs, particularly at the elementary level, is not their difficulty but their quality. Students in these programs are given opportunities to integrate ideas across fields of study. They have opportunities to think, write, create, and develop projects. They are challenged to explore. Though virtually all students would benefit from being similarly challenged, the opportunity for this sort of schooling remains acutely restricted.

Statistical patterns are brought alive by descriptions of sorting such as this one, offered by Kozol (1991), of a school in New York City: "The school is integrated in the strict sense that the middle- and upper-middle class white children here do occupy a building that contains some Asian and Hispanic and black children; but there is little integration in the classrooms"(p. 93).

Kozol describes how minority children are disproportionately assigned to special education classes that occupy small, cramped corners and split classrooms, while classes of the gifted and talented, almost exclusively White with a few Asian students, occupy the most splendid spaces, filled with books and computers, where they learn, in the children's words, "logical thinking," "problem-solving," "respect for someone else's logic," and "reasoning." Students are recommended for these classes by their teachers and parents as well as by their test scores. Kozol wrote in his notes: "Six girls, four boys. Nine white, one Chinese. I am glad they have this class. But what about the others? Aren't there ten black children in the school who could enjoy this also?" (p. 97).

Testing and Tracking

These differential allocations of resources are maintained and justified in substantial measure by the continued use of standardized testing for allocating curriculum opportunities. Over many decades, standardized tests have been used to define both teaching goals and students' opportunities to learn. As a tool for tracking students into different courses, levels, and kinds of instructional programs, testing has been a primary means for limiting or expanding students' life choices and their avenues for demonstrating competence. Increasingly, these uses of tests are recognized as having the unintended consequence of limiting students' access to further learning opportunities (Darling-Hammond, 1991; Glaser, 1990; Oakes, 1985).

For more than 100 years, standardized testing has been a tool used to exert control over the schooling process and to make decisions about educational entitlements for students (Kornhaber, Chapter 5 of this volume). Testing proved a convenient instrument of social control for those late-19th-century superintendents who sought to create

the "one best system" of education (Tyack, 1974). It also proved enormously useful as a means of determining how to slot students for either more or less rigorous (and costly) curricula when public funding of education and compulsory attendance vastly increased access to schools in the early 20th century.

Given the massive increase in students, the limits of public budgets, and the relatively meager training of teachers, strategies were sought to codify curriculum and to group students for differential instruction. IQ tests were widely employed as a measure of educational input (with intelligence viewed as the "raw material" for schooling) to sort pupils so they could be efficiently educated according to their future roles in society (Cubberly, 1919; Cremin, 1961). The tests were frequently used to exclude students from schooling opportunities altogether (Glaser, 1981).

Though many proponents argued that the use of these tests as a tool for tracking students would enhance social justice, the rationales for tracking—like those for using scores to set immigration quotas into the United States— were often frankly motivated by racial and ethnic politics. Just as Goddard "proved" with his testing experiments in 1912 that 83% of Jews, 80% of Hungarians, 79% of Italians, and 87% of Russians were feeble-minded, so did Terman "prove" in the early 1900s that "Indians, Mexicans, and negroes . . . should be segregated in special classes. . . . They cannot master abstractions, but they can often be made efficient workers" (Kamin, 1974; Terman, quoted in Oakes, 1985, p. 36).

Terman found many performance inequalities among groups on his IQ test, adapted from Binet's work in France. Most, but not all, seemed to confirm what he, and presumably every "intelligent" person, already knew: that various groups were inherently unequal in their mental capacities. However, when girls scored higher than boys on his 1916 version of the Stanford-Binet, he revised the test to correct for this apparent flaw by selecting items to create parity among genders in the scores (Mercer, 1989). Other inequalities—between urban and rural students, higher- and lower-SES students, native English speakers and immigrants, Whites and Blacks—did not occasion such revision, since their validity seemed patently obvious to the test makers.

The role of testing in reinforcing and extending social inequalities in educational opportunity has by now been extensively researched (Gould, 1981; Kamin, 1974; Mercer, 1989; Oakes, 1985) and widely acknowledged. For low-income and minority students, testing has mostly been a tool for denying access to challenging curriculum rather than improving the quality of education they receive (Watson, 1996). Use of tests for placement and promotion ultimately reduces the amount of learning achieved by students placed in lower tracks or held back in grade (Darling-Hammond, 1991). Minority students are disproportionately subject to both of these outcomes of testing.

Neither outcome ultimately improves achievement. Students who are retained in grade fall consistently behind on both achievement and social-emotional measures when compared with students of equivalent achievement levels who are promoted (Holmes & Matthews, 1984; Shepard & Smith, 1986). Furthermore, the practice of retaining students is a major contributor to increased dropout rates (Mann, 1987; Wehlage, Rutter, Smith, Lesko, & Fernandez, 1990). One of the more recent large-scale grade retention policies reconfirmed these repetitive findings. In Chicago, where a policy requiring test passage at grades 3, 6, and 8 led to the retention of more than 20,000 students in 1997 and 1998, an evaluation by the Consortium on Chicago School Research concluded that

retained students did not do better than previously socially promoted students. The progress among retained third graders was most troubling. Over the two years between the end of second grade and the end of the second time through third grade, the average Iowa Test of Basic Skills (ITBS) reading scores of these students increased only 1.2 GEs (grade equivalents) compared to 1.5 GEs for students with similar test scores who had been promoted prior to the policy. Also troubling is that one-year dropout rates among eighth graders with low skills are higher under this policy. . . . In short, Chicago has not solved the problem of poor performance among those who do not meet the minimum test cutoffs and are retained. Both the history of prior attempts to redress poor performance with retention and previous research would clearly have predicted this finding. Few studies of retention have found positive impacts, and most suggest that retained students do no better than socially promoted students. (Roderick, Bryk, Jacob, Easton, & Allensworth, 1999, pp. 55–56)

The negative consequences of these policies have been exacerbated by sanctions attached to schools' average test scores. Because these scores are sensitive to changes in the population of students taking the test and such changes can be induced by manipulating admissions, dropouts, and pupil classifications, schools have been found to label a large number of low-scoring students for special education placement so that their scores won't "count" in school reports, retain students in grade so that their relative standing will look better on "grade-equivalent" scores, exclude low-scoring students from admission to "open enrollment" schools, and encourage such students to leave school or drop out (Allington & McGill-Franzen, 1992; Darling-Hammond, 1991; Figlio & Getzler, 2002; Haney, 2000; Smith & Shepard, 1987; Smith et al., 1986). In all of these cases, low-income students and students of color are most likely to be harmed by the consequences of such policies. Smith and colleagues explained the widespread engineering of student populations that they found in their study of New York

City's implementation of test-based accountability as a basis for school level sanctions:

[S]tudent selection provides the greatest leverage in the short-term accountability game. . . . The easiest way to improve one's chances of winning is (1) to add some highly likely students and (2) to drop some unlikely students, while simply hanging on to those in the middle. School admissions is a central thread in the accountability fabric. (Smith et al., 1986, pp. 30–31)

Finally, many studies have found that students placed in the lowest tracks or in remedial programs—disproportionately low-income and minority students—are most apt to experience instruction geared only to multiple-choice tests, working at a low cognitive level on test-oriented tasks that are profoundly disconnected from the skills they need to learn. Rarely are they given the opportunity to talk about what they know; to read real books; to write; or to construct and solve problems in mathematics, science, or other subjects (Cooper & Sherk, 1989; Davis, 1986; Oakes, 1985). In short, they have been denied the opportunity to develop the capacities they will need for the future, in large part because commonly used tests are so firmly pointed at educational goals of the past.

Enriching an Impoverished Curriculum

Cooper and Sherk (1989) describe how worksheet-based instruction focused on the discrete "skill" bits featured on multiple-choice tests impedes students' progress toward literacy:

When hundreds of these worksheets, each of which presents a small, low-level skill related to reading, have been completed, children are said to have completed the "mastery" skills program. Often, these children still cannot read very well, if one defines reading as the ability to discern connected prose for comprehension. [Furthermore], worksheets are devised in such a way, teachers are told, that the material teaches itself. As a result, the amount of oral communication between pupil and teacher and between pupil and pupil is drastically reduced. . . . [Yet] if children are to learn language, a part of which is reading, they must interact and communicate. They must have some opportunity to hear words being spoken, to pose questions, to conjecture, and to hypothesize. (p. 318)

Their discussion of what teachers should be able to do to support children's literacy development maps onto more general principles of effective instruction. Teachers must be able to construct active learning opportunities involving student collaboration and many modes of oral and written language use; help students access prior knowledge that will frame for them the material to be learned; structure learning tasks so that students have a basis for interpreting the novel experiences they encounter; and stimulate and engage students' higher-order thought processes, including their capacities to hypothesize, predict, evaluate, integrate, and synthesize ideas (Cooper & Sherk, 1989; see also Braddock & McPartland, 1993; Garcia, 1993; Resnick, 1987).

In recent years, the school reform movement has engendered widespread efforts to transform how students' work and learning are organized and assessed in schools. These alternatives are frequently called performance-based, or "authentic," assessments because they engage students in "real world" tasks rather than multiple-choice tests and evaluate them according to criteria that are important for actual performance in that field (Wiggins, 1989). Such assessments include oral presentation or exhibition, along with collection of students' written products and their solutions to problems, experiment, debate, constructions and models, videotapes of performances and other learning occasions, and results of scientific and other inquiries (Archbald & Newman, 1988).

Much of the rationale for these initiatives is based on growing evidence that traditional norm-referenced, multiple-choice tests fail to measure complex cognitive and performance abilities. Furthermore, when used for decision making, such tests encourage instruction that tends to emphasize decontextualized, rote-oriented tasks imposing low cognitive demands rather than meaningful learning. Thus efforts to raise standards of learning and performance must rest in part on efforts to transform assessment practices. A number of studies have found increases in performance on both traditional standardized tests and performance measures for students in classrooms that offer a problem-oriented and performance-based curriculum that regularly features performance assessment. For example, in a study of more than 2,000 students within 23 restructured schools, most of them in urban areas, Newmann, Marks, and Gamoran (1995) found much higher levels of achievement on complex performance tasks for students who experienced what these researchers termed "authentic pedagogy": instruction focused on active learning in real-world contexts calling for higher-order thinking, consideration of alternatives, extended writing, and an audience for student work. A recent analysis of NELS data found that students in restructured schools where authentic instruction was widespread experienced greater achievement gains on conventional tests (Lee, Smith, & Croninger, 1995).

When accompanied by skilled teaching that is appropriate to the curriculum goals, these practices have been found to reduce inequalities in student performance generally associated with socioeconomic status (see, e.g., Lee & Smith, 1995; Lee, Smith, & Croninger, 1995; Newmann & Wehlage, 1995). The findings of these large-scale studies are further illuminated by case study research on extraordinarily successful schools, such as Central Park East Secondary School, International High School, the Urban Academy, and others that serve low-income, minority, and recent immigrant students who would normally fail in central city schools. Using personalized approaches coupled with performance assessments that set high standards and enable continuous improvement, these schools—and newer schools launched on the same design—have achieved graduation and college-going rates of more than 90% and a much higher level of academic achievement than schools serving similar student populations (Darling-Hammond, Ancess, & Ort, 2002).

If performance-based assessments that are currently being developed point at more challenging learning goals for all students, they may ameliorate some of the current test-induced sources of inequality (Glaser, 1990). However, this will be true only to the extent that teachers are able to teach in the ways demanded by these assessments—that is, so as to support the development of higher-order thinking and performance skills and diagnose and build upon individual learners' strengths and needs. Equalization of educational opportunities must rest as much on improving the caliber of teaching encountered by students of color as it does on changing the testing instruments or other technologies of schooling to which they are subject.

POLICY FOR EQUALITY: TOWARD EQUALIZATION OF EDUCATIONAL OPPORTUNITY

The common assumption about educational inequality is that it resides primarily in those students who come to school with inadequate capacity to benefit from what education the school has to offer. In line with the sorting philosophy described earlier, students must prove themselves worthy to receive a rich, challenging, and thoughtful curriculum. If they do not, the fault is thought to be in their own capacity as learners, not in the schools' capacity to teach them. Too few policy makers, educators, and members of the public at large presume that students are entitled to such a curriculum as a matter of course. In fact, some state defendants have countered school finance cases arguing for equalization of school expenditures with the assertion that equalization is not required unless it can be proven that equal expenditures will produce equal outcomes.

The fact that U.S. schools are structured such that students routinely receive dramatically unequal learning opportunities on the basis of their race and social status is simply not widely recognized. If the academic outcomes for minority and low-income children are to change, aggressive action must be taken to change the caliber and quantity of learning opportunities they encounter. These efforts must include equalization of financial resources; changes in curriculum and testing policies and practices;

and improvement in the supply of highly qualified teachers for all students.

Resource Equalization

Progress in equalizing resources to students will require attention to inequality at all levels—among states; districts; schools within districts; and students differentially placed in classrooms, courses, and tracks that offer substantially disparate opportunities to learn. As a consequence of systematic inequalities at each level, minority and low-income students are not only frequently at risk from poverty or community factors but also placed further at risk by the schools they attend.

Special programs such as compensatory or bilingual education will never be effective at remedying underachievement so long as these services are layered on a system that educates minority and low-income children so poorly to begin with. The presumption that "the schools are fine, it's the children who need help" is flawed. Schools serving a large concentration of low-income students of color are generally not fine, and many of their problems originate with district and state policies and practices that place the schools at risk as well.

The inherently unequal effect of current policies should be considered as attention focuses on the special circumstances of the students put in greatest jeopardy by those policies. Current initiatives to create special labels and programs for at-risk children and youth are unlikely to succeed if they do not attend to the structural conditions of schools that place children at risk, not only from their home or community circumstances but from their school experiences as well. Pressures are great to respond to special circumstances with special categorical programs, and the tradition of succumbing to those pressures in an add-on fashion is well established in education as in other areas of national life. But special programs, with all their accoutrements of new rules and procedures; separate budgets; and fragmented, pull-out programs will be insufficient so long as the status quo remains unchanged in more significant ways.

As the 1992 interim report of an independent commission on Chapter 1 observes: "Given the inequitable distribution of state and local resources, the current notion that Chapter 1 provides supplemental aid to disadvantaged children added to a level playing field is a fiction" (Commission on Chapter 1, 1992, p. 4). The commission proposed that each state be held accountable for assuring comparability in "vital services" among all its districts as well as in all schools within each district. Among these vital services, perhaps the most important is highly qualified teachers, not just for specific Chapter 1 services but for all classrooms.

The new wave of school finance lawsuits that are challenging both within-state and within-district resource allocation disparities are also promising. These suits are increasingly able to demonstrate how access to concrete learning opportunities is impaired by differential access to money, and how these learning opportunities translate into academic achievement for students. As standards are used to articulate clearer conceptions of what students need to learn to function in today's society and what schools need to do to support this level of learning, lawsuits like one recently won in Alabama may be linked to definitions of the quality of education that is "adequate" to meet the state's expectations for student achievement. Such cases suggest remedies that link the level of funding to minimum standards of learning and teaching. As suits brought on the adequacy theory establish that learning experiences depend on resources and influence outcomes, they establish a principle of "opportunity to learn" that could allow states to define a curriculum entitlement that becomes the basis for both funding and review of school practices.

The idea of "opportunity to learn" standards was first developed by the National Council on Education Standards and Testing (NCEST), which proposed that states collect evidence on the extent to which schools and districts provide the opportunity to learn the curricula implied by content and performance standards before using tests for school graduation or other decisions (NCEST, 1992).

Opportunity-to-learn standards would establish, for example, that if a state's curriculum frameworks and assessments outline standards for science learning that require (a) laboratory work and computers, (b) certain kinds of coursework, and (c) particular knowledge for teaching, resources must be allocated and policies must be fashioned to provide for these entitlements. Such a strategy would leverage both school improvement and school equity reform, establishing a basis for state legislation or litigation where opportunities to learn are not adequately funded.

Such standards would define a floor of core resources, coupled with incentives for schools to work toward professional standards of practice that support high-quality learning opportunities. Enacted through a combination of funding commitments, educational indicators, and school review practices, such standards could be a basis for information about the nature of the teaching and learning opportunities made available to students in different districts and schools across the state; state legislation and, if necessary, litigation that supports greater equity in funding and in distributing qualified teachers; and incentives for states and school districts to create policies that ensure adequate and equitable resources, curriculum opportunities, and teachers to children in all schools.

The goal of these activities should be to ensure that, at least at the state level, where constitutional responsibility for education resides, all students have access—both across and within districts—to equal financial resources, adjusted for student poverty and cost-of-living differentials. Ferguson's (1991) recommendation that equalization focus on district capacity to hire high-quality teachers is an important one with empirical support. In addition to the weight of evidence indicating how centrally important qualified teachers are to student learning, there is real-world experience with the positive effects of such policies on teacher quality and distribution. When Connecticut raised and equalized beginning teacher salaries under its 1986 Education Enhancement Act, shortages of teachers including those that had plagued urban areas, evaporated. By 1989, many teaching fields showed a surplus. Improvements in teacher education, licensing, and mentoring, along with investment in professional development, led to sharply increasing achievement in Connecticut throughout the 1990s. In this state, with large proportions of students of color and language minority students in public schools, student achievement scores increased to the point where the state ranks at or near number one in reading, writing, mathematics, and science on the National Assessments of Educational Progress (Baron, 1999; Wilson, Darling-Hammond, & Berry, 2001). Connecticut's approach is a useful beginning point for other policies aimed at ensuring access to good teaching.

Curriculum and Assessment Reform

When the school reform movement was launched in the early 1980s, many studies pointed out that the curriculum offered to most students in U.S. schools is geared toward lower-order rote skills (Boyer, 1983; Goodlad, 1984; Sizer, 1984), and that it is far less challenging than that encountered by the majority of students in many other countries (McKnight et al., 1987). As in times of past national concern—for example, the post-Sputnik years—major curriculum reform projects have been launched by the federal government as well as by many states.

These efforts to create a "thinking curriculum" for all students are important to individual futures and to our national welfare. They are unlikely to pay off, however, unless other critical changes are made as well. Among these are changes in how U.S. schools track students in order to differentiate curriculum, and how teachers are prepared and supported. Although mounting evidence indicates the problems with watered-down, low-track classes, these inadequate learning experiences will be difficult to reform until there is an adequate supply of well-trained teachers. Such teachers must be prepared both to teach the more advanced curriculum that U.S. schools now fail to offer most students and to assume the challenging task of teaching many kinds of students with diverse needs, interests, aptitudes, and learning styles in an integrated classroom setting.

Other important changes concern the types and use of achievement tests in U.S. schools. As a 1990 study of the implementation of California's new mathematics curriculum framework points out, when a curriculum reform aimed at problem solving and the development of higher-order thinking skills encounters an already-mandated rote-oriented basic skills testing program, the tests win out (Darling-Hammond, 1990a). As one teacher put it:

Teaching for understanding is what we are supposed to be doing . . . [but] the bottom line here is that all they really want to know is how are these kids doing on the tests. . . . They want me to teach in a way that they can't test, except that I'm held accountable to the test. It's a Catch 22. (S. Wilson, 1990, p. 318)

Initiatives to develop more complex and authentic modes of assessment may begin to offset this problem. But the bigger issue for enhancing learning opportunities is how tests are used. Many current proposals for performance-based assessment view this new kind of test as serving the same screening and tracking purposes as more traditional tests, assuming that more "authentic" assessments would both motivate and sort students more effectively. Others see a primary goal of assessment reform as transforming the purposes and uses of testing as well as its form and content. They argue for shifting the use of assessment from a sorting device to a tool for identifying student strengths and needs so that teachers can adapt instruction more successfully (Glaser, 1981, 1990).

Assessment initiatives that hope to embed authentic assessment in the ongoing processes of teaching and curriculum development share the view offered by Glaser (1990) that schools must move from a selective mode to an adaptive mode. They must shift from an approach "characterized by minimal variation in the conditions for learning" in which "a narrow range of instructional options and a limited number of paths to success are available" (p. 16), to one in which "conceptions of learning and modes of teaching are adjusted to individuals—their backgrounds, talents, interests, and the nature of their past performances and experiences" (p. 17). Fundamental agreement with this view leads to a rejection of the traditional use of testing, even performance-based testing, as an externally controlled tool for allocating educational opportunities. If teachers are to engage in the pursuit of "individually configured excellence" (Gardner, 1991, p. 17) for all students, they must be able to employ multiple pathways to learning. As students are offered wider opportunities for learning, and assessment of their achievement becomes an integral part of learning and teaching, assessments must afford multidimensional views of performance that inform ever more effective instruction.

The outcomes of the current wave of curriculum and assessment reforms will depend in large measure on the extent to which assessments are developed and used to serve teaching and learning rather than sorting and selecting; pursue broader reforms to improve and equalize access to educational resources and opportunities; and support the professional development of teachers along with the organizational development of schools, so that assessment is embedded in teaching and learning and is used to inform more skillful and adaptive teaching that enables more successful learning for all students.

Investing in Good Teaching for All Students

A key corollary to this analysis of inequality is that improved opportunities for students of color will rest in part on policies that professionalize teaching by increasing the knowledge base for teaching, and on the mastery of this knowledge by all teachers permitted to practice. This means providing *all* teachers with a stronger understanding of how children learn and develop, how a variety of curricular and instructional strategies can address their needs, and how changes in school and classroom organization can support their growth and achievement.

There are two reasons for this assertion. First, the professionalization of an occupation raises the floor below which no entrants will be admitted to practice. It eliminates practices of substandard or irregular licensure that allow untrained entrants to practice disproportionately on underserved and poorly protected citizens. Second, professionalization increases the overall knowledge base for the occupation, thus improving the quality of services for all clients, especially those most in need of high-quality teaching (Darling-Hammond, 1990c).

The students who have, in general, the poorest opportunities to learn—those attending the central city schools that are compelled by the current incentive structure to hire a disproportionate number of substitute teachers, uncertified teachers, and inexperienced teachers, and that lack resources for mitigating the uneven distribution of good teaching—are the students who will benefit most from measures that raise the standards of practice for all teachers. They will also benefit from targeted policies that provide quality preparation programs and financial aid for highly qualified prospective teachers who will teach in central cities and poor rural areas.

Investment in better-prepared teachers is also needed to support current education reforms that envision greater teacher responsibility in educational decisions at all levels. Restructured schools require changes in the nature of teaching work and knowledge, including a more active, integrated, and intellectually challenging curriculum, and a broader range of roles for teachers in developing curriculum and assessment of student performance, coaching and mentoring other teachers, and working more closely with families and community agencies. Because restructured schools are also redesigning classroom organization so that "push-in" rather than "pull-out" methods are more likely to be used for children with special needs, and so that interdisciplinary approaches to a thinking curriculum are more common, teachers will need to know more about both subjects and students than they have in the past.

Finally, school-based management and shared decision-making initiatives rely for their success on the capacity of education practitioners to make knowledgeable judgments about curriculum and assessment, school organization, and program evaluation. Teachers will need to be prepared to make such decisions responsibly. Teacher preparation and licensing should reflect the demands of teachers' evolving roles. In addition, providing equity in the distribution of teacher quality requires changing policies and long-standing incentive structures in education so that schools serving low-income and minority students are not disadvantaged in recruiting and retaining good teachers by lower salaries and poorer working conditions.

Building and sustaining a well-prepared teaching force will require local, state, and federal initiatives. To recruit an adequate supply of teachers, states and localities will need to upgrade teachers' salaries to a level competitive with those of college graduates in other occupations, who currently earn 25–50% more, depending on the field. This should occur as part of a general restructuring effort that places more resources as well as decision-making authority at the school level and allocates a greater share of education dollars to classrooms than to the large bureaucracies that oversee them (see, e.g., Darling-Hammond, 1990b).

States must also strengthen teacher education and certification. In almost all colleges and universities, teacher education is more poorly funded than other schools or departments (Ebmeier, Twombly, & Teeter, 1990). It has long been used as a revenue producer for programs that train engineers, accountants, lawyers, and future doctors. Rather than bemoaning the quality of teacher training, policy makers must invest in its improvement.

Accreditation and licensing are two major quality-control mechanisms for any profession. In the field of teaching, these mechanisms have historically been weak. Although all of the other established professions require graduation from an accredited school as one condition of the license to practice, most states do not require departments or schools of education to be accredited, nor do they require candidates for licensure to have graduated from such a school. The National Council for Accreditation of Teacher Education (NCATE) accredits approximately 600 of more than 1,300 institutions that prepare teachers. Meanwhile, "the generally minimal state-prescribed criteria remain subject to local and state political influences, economic conditions within the state, and historical conditions which make change difficult" (Dennison, 1992, p. A40).

The historic lack of rigorous standard setting in teaching is changing, however. A growing number of states are improving teacher education programs by encouraging their accreditation under the new, more rigorous standards that are being implemented by NCATE. The foundation of the new accreditation system is the body of growing knowledge about teaching and learning, including understandings about how to teach diverse learners well. A National Board for Professional Teaching Standards has set high and rigorous standards for accomplished teachers, and many states are rewarding teachers for meeting them. California awards large additional bonuses to teachers who will teach in low-performing schools, which are overwhelmingly those that serve low-income and minority students.

Improvement of teacher education depends as well on major changes in the content and governance of teacher licensing. Few believe that historic state licensing requirements have offered meaningful standards of teacher knowledge and competence—not the public, not the profession, not even the policy makers who are themselves responsible for setting the requirements. Their willingness to avoid their own regulations by creating emergency, temporary, and alternative routes to certification has been the most obvious indictment of the system they have established. Meaningful standards must be established and then met by all entrants to the profession. Shortages must be met by offering enhanced incentives to teach rather than by lowering standards, especially for those who teach children in central cities and poor rural schools. Accreditation will improve the quality of teacher education, but professional licensing, coupled with targeted financial supports for recruitment, is needed to ensure that every child will have access to a well-prepared teacher.

The federal government must play a leadership role in providing an adequate supply of well-qualified teachers, just as it has in making available an adequate supply of well-qualified physicians. When shortages of physicians were a major national problem more than 40 years ago, Congress passed the 1963 Health Professions Education Assistance Act to support and improve the caliber of medical training, create and strengthen teaching hospitals, offer scholarships and loans to medical students, and create incentives for physicians to train in shortage specialties and to locate in underserved areas. In an important departure from the tradition of supplying the least-well-qualified teachers to the most needy children, the No Child Left Behind Act (the reauthorization of ESEA) requires that all children in Title I schools be taught by fully certified teachers with strong content knowledge by 2005. However, this important goal will not be achieved without support for equalizing resources for these schools. As in medicine, federal initiatives in education should seek to:

1. *Recruit new teachers,* especially in shortage fields and in shortage locations, through service scholarships and forgivable loans for high-quality teacher education
2. *Strengthen and improve teachers' preparation* through improvement incentive grants to schools of education and supports for certification reform
3. *Improve teacher retention and effectiveness* by improving clinical training and support during the beginning teaching stage, when 30% of new teachers drop out; this would include funding internship programs for new teachers in which they receive structured coaching and mentoring, preferably in urban schools supported to provide state-of-the-art practice.

If the interaction between teachers and students is the most important aspect of effective schooling, then reducing inequality in learning has to rely to a large extent on policies that ensure equal access to competent, well-supported teachers. The public education system ought to be able to guarantee that every child who is required by public law to go to school is taught by someone who is prepared, knowledgeable, competent, and caring. That is real accountability. As Grant (1989) puts it, "Teachers who perform high-quality work in urban schools know that, despite reform efforts and endless debates, it is meaningful curricula and dedicated and knowledgeable teachers that make the difference in the education of urban students" (p. 770). When it comes to equalizing opportunities for students to learn, that is the bottom line.

References

Alexander, K. L., & McDill, E. L. (1976). Selection and allocation within schools: Some causes and consequences of curriculum placement. *American Sociological Review, 41,* 963–980.

Allington, R. L., & McGill-Franzen, A. (1992). Unintended effects of educational reform in New York. *Educational Policy, 6*(4), 397–414.

Archbald, D. A., & Newman, F. M. (1988). *Beyond standardized testing: Assessing authentic academic achievement in the secondary school.* Reston, VA: National Association of Secondary School Principals.

Ashton, P., & Crocker, L. (1986). Does teacher certification make a difference? *Florida Journal of Teacher Education, 38*(3), 73–83.

Ashton, P., & Crocker, L. (1987). Systematic study of planned variations: The essential focus of teacher education reform. *Journal of Teacher Education, 38*(3), 2–8.

Barr, R., & Dreeben, R. (1983). *How schools work.* Chicago: University of Chicago Press.

Barton, P. E., & Coley, R. J. (1996). *Captive students: Education and training in America's prisons.* Princeton, NJ: Educational Testing Service.

Berliner, D. C. (1986). In pursuit of the expert pedagogue. *Educational Researcher, 15*(7), 5–13.

Baron, J. B. (1999). *Exploring high and improving reading achievement in Connecticut.* Washington, DC: National Educational Goals Panel.

Berne, R. (1992). Educational input and outcome inequities in New York State. In *The road to outcome equity.* Albany: New York State Education Department.

Betts, J. R., Rueben, K. S., & Danenberg, A. (2000). *Equal resources, equal outcomes? The distribution of school resources and student achievement in California.* San Francisco: Public Policy Institute of California.

Bledsoe, J. C., Cox, J. V., & Burnham, R. (1967). *Comparison between selected characteristics and performance of provisionally and professionally certified beginning teachers in Georgia.* Washington, DC: U.S. Department of Health, Education and Welfare.

Boyer, E. (1983). *High school.* New York: Harper & Row.

Braddock, J., & McPartland, J. M. (1993). Education of early adolescents. In L. Darling-Hammond (Ed.), *Review of research in education* (Vol. 19, pp. 135–170). Washington, DC: American Educational Research Association.

Campaign for Fiscal Equity et al. v. State of New York, 719 N.Y.S.2d 475 (2001).

Coleman, J. S., Campbell, E. Q., Hobson, C. J., McPartland, J., Mood, A. M., Weinfeld, F. D., et al. (1966). *Equality of educational opportunity.* Washington, DC: Government Printing Office.

College Board. (1985). *Equality and excellence: The educational status of Black Americans.* New York: College Entrance Examination Board.

Commission on Chapter 1. (1992). *High performance schools: No exceptions, no excuses.* Washington, DC: Author.

Conant, J. B. (1961). *Slums and suburbs.* New York: McGraw-Hill.

Cooper, E., & Sherk, J. (1989). Addressing urban school reform: Issues and alliances. *Journal of Negro Education, 58*(3), 315–331.

Cremin, L. (1961). *The transformation of the school: Progressivism in American education, 1876–1957.* New York: Vintage Books.

Cremin, L. (1970). *American education: The colonial experience 1607–1783.* New York: Harper & Row.

Cubberly, E. P. (1906). *School funds and their apportionment.* New York: Teachers College Press.

Cubberly, E. P. (1919). *Public education in the United States: A study and interpretation of American educational history.* Boston: Houghton Mifflin.

Darling-Hammond, L. (1990a). Instructional policy into practice: "The power of the bottom over the top." *Educational Evaluation and Policy Analysis, 12*(3), 233–242.

Darling-Hammond, L. (1990b). Teacher professionalism: Why and how. In A. Lieberman (Ed.), *Schools as collaborative cultures: Creating the future now* (pp. 25–50). Philadelphia: Falmer Press.

Darling-Hammond, L. (1990c). Teacher quality and equality. In J. Goodlad & P. Keating (Eds.), *Access to knowledge: An agenda for our nation's schools* (pp. 237–258). New York: College Entrance Examination Board.

Darling-Hammond, L. (1991). The implications of testing policy for quality and equality. *Phi Delta Kappan, 73*(3), 220–225.

Darling-Hammond, L. (1992). Teaching and knowledge: Policy issues posed by alternate certification for teachers. *Peabody Journal of Education, 67*(3), 123–154.

Darling-Hammond, L. (1997). *Doing what matters most: Investing in quality teaching.* New York: National Commission on Teaching and America's Future.

Darling-Hammond, L. (1999). *Educating teachers for California's future.* San Francisco: James Irvine Foundation.

Darling-Hammond, L. (2000a). *Solving the dilemmas of teacher, supply, demand, and quality.* New York: National Commission on Teaching and America's Future.

Darling-Hammond, L. (2000b). Teacher quality and student achievement: A review of state policy evidence. *Educational Policy Analysis Archives, 8*(1). Available: http://epaa.asu.edu/epaa/v8n1.

Darling-Hammond, L., Ancess, J., & Ort, S. (2002). Reinventing high school: An evaluation of the Coalition Campus Schools Project. *American Educational Research Journal, 39*(3), 639–673.

Davis, D. G. (1986, April). *A pilot study to assess equity in selected curricular offerings across three diverse schools in a large urban district.* Paper presented at the annual meeting of the American Educational Research Association, San Francisco.

Dennison, G. M. (1992). National standards in teacher preparation: A commitment to quality. *Chronicle of Higher Education, 39*(15), A40.

Dreeben, R. (1987). Closing the divide: What teachers and administrators can do to help Black students reach their reading potential. *American Educator, 11*(4), 28–35.

Dreeben, R., & Barr, R. (1987, April). *Class composition and the design of instruction.* Paper presented at the annual meeting of the American Education Research Association, Washington, DC.

Dreeben, R., & Gamoran, A. (1986). Race, instruction, and learning. *American Sociological Review, 51*(5), 660–669.

Druva, C. A., & Anderson, R. D. (1983). Science teacher characteristics by teacher behavior and by student outcome: A meta-analysis of research. *Journal of Research in Science Teaching, 20*(5), 467–479.

Ebmeier, H., Twombly, S., & Teeter, D. (1990). The comparability and adequacy of financial support for schools of education. *Journal of Teacher Education, 42*(3), 226–235.

Eckstrom, R., & Villegas, A. M. (1991). Ability grouping in middle grade mathematics: Process and consequences. *Research in Middle Level Education, 15*(1), 1–20.

Edgewood Independent School District v. Kirby, 777 S.W.2d 391 (Texas 1989).

Educational Research Service. (1980). *Class size: A summary of research.* Reston, VA: Author.

Educational Testing Service. (1991). *The state of inequality.* Princeton, NJ: Author.

Evertson, C., Hawley, W., & Zlotnick, M. (1985). Making a difference in educational quality through teacher education. *Journal of Teacher Education, 36*(3), 2–12.

Ferguson, R. F. (1991). Paying for public education: New evidence on how and why money matters. *Harvard Journal on Legislation, 28*(2), 465–498.

Ferguson, R. F., & Ladd, H. F. (1996). How and why money matters: An analysis of Alabama schools. In H. Ladd (Ed.), *Holding schools accountable* (pp. 265–298). Washington, DC: Brookings Institution.

Fetler, M. (1999, March 24). High school staff characteristics and mathematics test results. *Education Policy Analysis Archives, 7.* Available: http://epaa.asu.edu.

Figlio, D. N., & Getzler, L. S. (2002, April). *Accountability, ability, and disability: Gaming the system?* Cambridge, MA: National Bureau of Economic Research. Available: http://papers.nber.org/papers/w9307.

Finley, M. K. (1984). Teachers and tracking in a comprehensive high school. *Sociology of Education, 57,* 233–243.

Gamoran, A. (1990, April). *The consequences of track-related instructional differences for student achievement.* Paper presented at the annual meeting of the American Educational Research Association, Boston.

Gamoran, A. (1992). Access to excellence: Assignment to honors English classes in the transition from middle to high school. *Educational Evaluation and Policy Analysis, 14*(3), 185–204.

Gamoran, A., & Berends, M. (1987). The effects of stratification in secondary schools: Synthesis of survey and ethnographic research. *Review of Educational Research, 57,* 415–436.

Gamoran, A., & Mare, R. (1989). Secondary school tracking and educational inequality: Compensation, reinforcement or neutrality? *American Journal of Sociology, 94*(5), 1146–1183.

Garcia, E. (1993). Language, culture, and education. In L. Darling-Hammond (Ed.), *Review of research in education* (Vol. 19, pp. 51–98). Washington, DC: American Educational Research Association.

Gardner, H. (1991). *The unschooled mind.* New York: Basic Books.

Gemignani, R. J. (1994, October). Juvenile correctional education: A time for change. Update on research. (*Juvenile Justice Bulletin.*) Washington, DC: U.S. Department of Justice, Office of Juvenile Justice and Delinquency Prevention.

Glaser, R. (1981). The future of testing: A research agenda for cognitive psychology and psychometrics. *American Psychologist, 39*(9), 923–936.

Glaser, R. (1990). *Testing and assessment: O tempora! O mores!* Pittsburgh: University of Pittsburgh, Learning Research and Development Center.

Glass, G. V., Cahen, L. S., Smith, M. L., & Filby, N. N. (1982). *School class size: Research and policy.* Beverly Hills, CA: Sage.

Goldhaber, D. D., & Brewer, D. J. (2000). Does teacher certification matter? High school certification status and student achievement. *Educational Evaluation and Policy Analysis, 22*(2), 129–145.

Good, T. L., & Brophy, J. (1987). *Looking in classrooms.* New York: Harper & Row.

Goodlad, J. (1984). *A place called school: Prospects for the future.* New York: McGraw-Hill.

Gould, S. J. (1981). *The mismeasure of man.* New York: Norton.

Grant, C. A. (1989). Urban teachers: Their new colleagues and curriculum. *Phi Delta Kappan, 70*(10), 764–770.

Grissmer, D. W., & Kirby, S. N. (1987). *Teacher attrition: The uphill climb to staff the nation's schools.* Santa Monica, CA: RAND.

Grossman, P. L. (1990). *The making of a teacher: Teacher knowledge and teacher education.* New York: Teachers College Press.

Guthrie, J. W., Garms, W. I., & Pierce, L. C. (1988). *School finance and education policy: Enhancing educational efficiency, equality and choice* (2nd ed.). Englewood Cliffs, NJ: Prentice Hall.

Haney, W. (2000). The myth of the Texas miracle in education. *Education Policy Analysis Archives, 8*(41). Available: http://epaa.asu.edu/epaa/v8n41/.

Hanushek, E. A. (1990, March). *The impact of differential expenditures on school performance.* (Issue analyses.) Washington, DC: American Legislative Exchange Council.

Hawk, P., Coble, C. R., & Swanson, M. (1985). Certification: It does matter. *Journal of Teacher Education, 36*(3), 13–15.

Henke, R. R., Chen, X., & Geis, S. (2000). *Progress through the teacher pipeline: 1992–93 college graduates and elementary/secondary school teaching as of 1997.* Washington, DC: U.S. Department of Education, National Center for Education Statistics.

Hobson v. Hanson, 269 F. Supp. 401, 496 (D.D.C. 1967).

Hoffer, T. B. (1992). Middle school ability grouping and student achievement in science and mathematics. *Educational Evaluation and Policy Analysis, 14*(3), 205–227.

Holmes, C. T., & Matthews, K. M. (1984). The effects of nonpromotion on elementary and junior high school pupils: A meta-analysis. *Review of Educational Research, 54*(2), 225–236.

Ingersoll, R. (2002, June). The teacher shortage: A case of wrong diagnosis and wrong prescription. *NASSP Bulletin, 86,* 16–31.

Jencks, C., Smith, M., Acland, H., Bane, M. J., Cohen, D., Gintis, H., et al. (1972). *Inequality: A reassessment of the effect of family and schooling in America.* New York: Basic Books.

Johnston, J. M., & Ryan, K. (1983). Research on the beginning teacher. In K. R. Howie & W. E. Gardner (Eds.), *The education of teachers: A look ahead* (pp. 136–162). New York: Longman.

Jones, L. V. (1984). White-Black achievement differences: The narrowing gap. *American Psychologist, 39*(11), 1207–1213.

Jones, L. V., Burton, N. W., & Davenport, E. C. (1984). Monitoring the achievement of Black students. *Journal for Research in Mathematics Education, 15,* 154–164.

Kamin, L. (1974). *The science and politics of IQ.* New York: Wiley.

Kaufman, J. E., & Rosenbaum, J. E. (1992). Education and employment of low-income Black youth in White suburbs. *Educational Evaluation and Policy Analysis, 14*(3), 229–240.

Keppel, F. (1966). *The necessary revolution in American education.* New York: Harper & Row.

Kozol, J. (1991). *Savage inequalities.* New York: Crown.

Kluger, R. (1976). *Simple justice.* New York: Knopf.

Kulik, C. C., & Kulik, J. A. (1982). Effects of ability grouping on secondary school students: A meta-analysis of evaluation findings. *American Education Research Journal, 19*(3), 415–428.

Lee, V. E., & Bryk, A. (1988). Curriculum tracking as mediating the social distribution of high school achievement. *Sociology of Education, 61*(2), 78–94.

Lee, V. E., & Smith, J. (1995). Effects of high school restructuring and size on gains in achievement and engagement for early secondary school students. *Sociology of Education, 68*(4), 241–270.

Lee, V. E., Smith, J., & Croninger, R. (1995). Another look at high school restructuring. In *Issues in Restructuring Schools, No. 9.* Madison: University of Wisconsin, Center on Organization and Restructuring of Schools.

Levin, H. M. (1992). The necessary and sufficient conditions for achieving educational equity. In R. Berne (Ed.), *New York equity study.* Unpublished report of the Equity Study Group, New York State Education Department, Albany.

MacPhail-Wilcox, B., & King, R. A. (1986). Resource allocation studies: Implications for school improvement and school finance research. *Journal of Education Finance, 11*(4), 416–432.

Mann, D. (1987). Can we help dropouts? Thinking about the undoable. In G. Natriello (Ed.), *School dropouts: Patterns and policies* (pp. 3–19). New York: Teachers College Press.

McKnight, C. C., Crosswhite, J. A., Dossey, J. A., Kifer, E., Swafford, S. O., Travers, K. J., et al. (1987). *The underachieving curriculum: Assessing U.S. school mathematics from an international perspective.* Champaign, IL: Stipes.

McNeil, J. D. (1974). Who gets better results with young children—Experienced teachers or novices? *Elementary School Journal, 74,* 447–451.

McUsic, M. (1991). The use of education clauses in school finance reform litigation. *Harvard Journal on Legislation, 28*(2), 307–340.

Meier, K. J., Stewart, J., Jr., & England, R. E. (1989). *Race, class, and education: The politics of second-generation discrimination.* Madison: University of Wisconsin Press.

Mercer, J. R. (1989). Alternative paradigms for assessment in a pluralistic society. In J. A. Banks & C.A.M. Banks (Eds.), *Multicultural education* (pp. 289–303). Boston: Allyn and Bacon.

Minow, M. (1991). School finance: Does money matter? *Harvard Journal on Legislation, 28*(2), 395–400.

Monk, D. H. (1994). Subject matter preparation of secondary mathematics and science teachers and student achievement. *Economics of Education Review, 13*(2), 125–145.

Moore, D., & Davenport, S. (1988). *The new improved sorting machine.* Madison, WI: National Center on Effective Secondary Schools.

Moore, E. G., & Smith, A. W. (1985). Mathematics aptitude: Effects of coursework, household language, and ethnic differences. *Urban Education, 20*(3), 273–294.

Murnane, R. J. (1991). Interpreting the evidence on "Does money matter?" *Harvard Journal on Legislation, 28*(2), 457–464.

Murnane, R. J., & Phillips, B. R. (1981). Learning by doing, vintage, and selection: Three pieces of the puzzle relating teaching experience and teaching performance. *Economics of Education Review, 1*(4), 453–465.

Murnane, R. J., Singer, J. D., Willett, J. B., Kemple, J. J., & Olsen, R. J. (1991). *Who will teach? Policies that matter.* Cambridge, MA: Harvard University Press.

National Center for Education Statistics. (1995). *The condition of education, 1995.* Washington, DC: U.S. Department of Education.

National Center for Education Statistics. (1997). *America's teachers: Profile of a profession.* Washington, DC: U.S. Department of Education.

National Center for Education Statistics. (1998). *Inequalities in public school district revenues.* Washington, DC: U.S. Department of Education.

National Center for Education Statistics. (1999). *Teacher quality: A report on the preparation and qualifications of public school teachers.* Washington, DC: U.S. Department of Education.

National Center for Education Statistics. (2000). *Digest of educational statistics, 1999.* Washington, DC: U.S. Department of Education.

National Center for Education Statistics (2001a). *The condition of education 2000 in brief.* Washington, DC: U.S. Department of Education.

National Center for Education Statistics (2001b). *The condition of education 2001.* Washington, DC: U.S. Department of Education.

National Center for Education Statistics. (2001c). *Internet access in U.S. public schools and classrooms: 1994–2000.* Washington, DC: U.S. Department of Education.

National Council on Education Standards and Testing (NCEST). (1992). *Raising standards for American education.* Washington, DC: Government Printing Office.

Newmann, F. M., and Wehlage, G. G. (1995). *Successful school restructuring.* Madison: University of Wisconsin, Center on Organization and Restructuring of Schools.

Newmann, F. M., Marks, H. M., & Gamoran, A. (1995). Authentic pedagogy: Standards that boost study performance. In *Issues in Restructuring Schools, No. 8.* Madison, WI: Center on Organization and Restructuring of Schools.

New York Study Group on Outcome Equity. (1993). *The road to outcome equity: Final report of the study group on outcome equity* (R. Berne, Ed.). Albany: New York State Education Department.

Oakes, J. (1985). *Keeping track.* New Haven: Yale University Press.

Oakes, J. (1986). Tracking, inequality, and the rhetoric of reform: Why schools don't change. *Journal of Education, 168*(1), 60–86.

Oakes, J. (1990). *Multiplying inequalities: The effects of race, social class, and tracking on opportunities to learn mathematics and science.* Santa Monica, CA: RAND.

Oakes, J. (1992). Can tracking research inform practice? Technical, normative, and political considerations. *Educational Researcher, 21*(4), 12–21.

Oakes, J., & Lipton, M. (1994). Tracking and ability grouping: A structural barrier to access and achievement. In J. I. Goodlad & P. Keating (Eds.), *Access to knowledge: The continuing agenda for our nation's schools* (pp. 187–204). New York: College Entrance Examination Board.

Oakes, J., & Lipton, M. (1998). *Teaching to change the world.* New York: McGraw-Hill.

Oakes, J., & Saunders, M. (2002). *Access to textbooks, instructional materials, equipment, and technology: Inadequacy and inequality in California's public schools.* Los Angeles: University of California at Los Angeles.

Oakes, J., Selvin, M., Karoly, L., & Guiton, G. (1992). *Educational matchmaking: Academic and vocational tracking in comprehensive high schools.* Santa Monica, CA: RAND.

Orfield, G. F. (2001). *Schools more separate: Consequences of a decade of resegregation.* Cambridge, MA: Harvard Civil Rights Project. Available: www.law.harvard.edu/civilrights.

Pelavin, S. H., & Kane, M. (1990). *Changing the odds: Factors increasing access to college.* New York: College Entrance Examination Board.

Resnick, L. B. (1987). *Education and learning to think.* Washington, DC: National Academy Press.

Robinson v. Cahill, 303 A. 2d 273, 294 (1971).

Roderick, M., Bryk, A. S., Jacob, B. A., Easton, J. Q., & Allensworth, E. (1999). *Ending social promotion: Results from the first two years.* Chicago: Consortium on Chicago School Research.

Rodriguez et al. v. Los Angeles Unified School District, Superior Court of the County of Los Angeles, no. C611358 (consent decree filed Aug. 12, 1992).

Rottenberg, C. J., & Berliner, D. C. (1990, April). *Expert and novice teachers' conceptions of common classroom activities.* Paper presented at the annual meeting of the American Educational Research Association, Boston.

Ruiz de Velasco, J., & Fix, M. (2000). *Overlooked and underserved: Immigrant students in U.S. secondary schools.* Washington, DC: Urban Institute.

San Antonio Independent School District v. *Rodriguez,* 411 U.S. 483 (1973).

Serrano v. *Priest,* 487 P. 2d 1241 (1971).

Shepard, L., & Smith, M. L. (1986). Synthesis of research on school readiness and kindergarten retention. *Educational Leadership, 44*(3), 78–86.

Shields, P. M., Humphrey, D. C., Wechsler, M. E., Riel, L. M., Tiffany-Morales, J., Woodworth, K., et al. (2001). *The status of the teaching profession 2001.* Santa Cruz, CA: Center for the Future of Teaching and Learning.

Shulman, L. S. (1987). Knowledge and teaching: Foundations of the new reform. *Harvard Educational Review, 57*(1), 1–22.

Silard, J., & Goldstein, B. (1974, July). Toward abolition of local funding in public education. *Journal of Law and Education, 3,* 324.

Sizer, T. (1984). *Horace's compromise: The dilemma of the American high school.* Boston: Houghton Mifflin.

Slavin, R. E. (1990). Achievement effects of ability grouping in secondary schools: A best evidence synthesis. *Review of Educational Research, 60*(3), 471–500.

Smerdon, B., Cronen, S., Lanahan, L., Anderson, J., Iannotti, N., & Angeles, J. (2000, Winter). Teachers' tools for the 21st century: A report on teachers' use of technology. *Education Statistics Quarterly, 2*(4), 48–52.

Smith, F., et al. (1986). *High school admission and the improvement of schooling.* New York: New York City Board of Education.

Smith, M. L., & Shepard, L. (1987). What doesn't work: Explaining policies of retention in the early grades. *Phi Delta Kappan, 69*(2), 123–124.

Stowe, P. (1993, October). *New teachers in the job market. 1991 update.* Washington, DC: National Center for Education Statistics.

Strauss, R. P., & Sawyer, E. A. (1986). Some new evidence on teacher and student competencies. *Economics of Education Review, 5*(1), 41–48.

Sutton, R. E. (1991). Equity and computers in the schools: A decade of research. *Review of Educational Research, 61*(4), 475–503.

Talbert, J. E. (1990). *Teacher tracking: Exacerbating inequalities in the high school.* Stanford, CA: Stanford University, Center for Research on the Context of Secondary Teaching.

Taylor, W. L., & Piche, D. M. (1991). *A report on shortchanging children: The impact of fiscal inequity on the education of students at risk.* Prepared for the Committee on Education and Labor, U.S. House of Representatives. Washington, DC: Government Printing Office.

Tyack, D. B. (1974). *The one best system.* Cambridge, MA: Harvard University Press.

U.S. Census Bureau. (1992). *Statistical abstract of the United States: 1992* (112th ed.). Washington, DC: U.S. Department of Commerce.

U.S. Department of Commerce (1996). *Statistical abstract of the United States: 1996* (116th ed.). Washington, DC: U.S. Census Bureau.

Updegraff, H., & King, L. A. (1922). *Survey of the fiscal policies of the state of Pennsylvania in the field of education.* Philadelphia: University of Pennsylvania.

Useem, E. L. (1990). You're good, but you're not good enough: Tracking students out of advanced mathematics. *American Educator, 14*(3), 24–27, 43–46.

Usiskin, Z. (1987). Why elementary algebra can, should, and must be an eighth grade course for average students. *Mathematics Teacher, 80,* 428–438.

Veenman, S. (1984). Perceived problems of beginning teachers. *Review of Educational Research, 54*(2), 143–178.

Von Seeker, C., & Lissitz, R. W. (1999). Estimating the impact of instructional practices on student achievement in science. *Journal of Research in Science Teaching, 36*(10), 1110–1126.

Walberg, H. (1982). What makes schooling effective. *Contemporary Education: A Journal of Review, 1,* 22–34.

Watson, B. C. (1996). *Testing: Its origins, use, and misuse.* New York: National Urban League.

Wehlage, G. G., Rutter, R. A., Smith, G. A., Lesko, N., & Fernandez, R. R. (1990). *Reducing the risk: Schools as communities of support.* New York: Falmer Press.

Wheelock, A. (1992). *Crossing the tracks.* New York: New Press.

Wiggins, G. (1989). Teaching to the (authentic) test. *Educational Leadership, 46*(7), 41–47.

Williams et al. v. *State of California, Superior Court,* San Francisco, No. 312236. Available: http://www.decentschools.org.

Wilson, S. (1990). A conflict of interests: Constraints that affect teaching and change. *Educational Evaluation and Policy Analysis, 12*(3), 309–326.

Wilson, S., Darling-Hammond, L., & Berry, B. (2001). *A case of successful teaching policy: Connecticut's long-term efforts to improve teaching and learning.* Seattle: University of Washington, Center for the Study of Teaching and Policy.

Wilson, S. M., Floden, R. E., & Ferrini-Mundy, J. (2001). *Teacher preparation research: Current knowledge, gaps, and recommendations.* Seattle: University of Washington, Center for the Study of Teaching and Policy.

Wise, A. E. (1965, Spring). Is denial of equal educational opportunity constitutional? *Administrator's Notebook, 13,* 1–4.

Wise, A. E. (1972). *Rich schools, poor schools: The promise of equal educational opportunity.* Chicago: University of Chicago Press.

Wise, A. E., Darling-Hammond, L., & Berry, B. (1987). *Effective teacher selection: From recruitment to retention.* Santa Monica, CA: RAND.

Wise, A. E., & Gendler, T. (1989). Rich schools, poor schools: The persistence of unequal education. *College Board Review, 151,* 12–17, 36–37.

Wong, K. K. (1989). Fiscal support for education in American states: The "parity-to-dominance" view examined. *American Journal of Education, 97*(4), 329–357.

Yudof, M. G. (1991). School finance reform in Texas: The Edgewood saga. *Harvard Journal on Legislation, 28*(2), 499–505.

30

RESEARCH ON FAMILIES, SCHOOLS, AND COMMUNITIES

A Multicultural Perspective

Nitza M. Hidalgo
Westfield State College

Sau-Fong Siu
Wheelock College

Joyce L. Epstein
Johns Hopkins University

Studies of school, family, and community partnerships have grown broader and deeper over the past two decades, to address important questions about the nature and extent of family and community involvement in children's education. Researchers are examining not only what families do to influence their children's development, or what schools do to educate youngsters, but also what schools and families do together and with others in the community to support and motivate children to succeed in school.

The field of study now includes researchers from many disciplines studying numerous topics of school, family, and community connections from infancy through adolescence, and across grade levels from preschool through high school. Questions have broadened, measures have deepened, and methods of analyses have improved over time to increase the quality of research on partnerships.

Local and regional studies have produced information on program implementation and results of partnerships. Nationwide data such as the National Education Longitudinal Survey (NELS) and the National Household Education Survey (NHES) have provided researchers with large, representative samples of diverse populations so as to explore the nature of selected family and community involvement activities and results for students (Catsambis & Beveridge, 2001; S. Lee, 1994; Simon, 2001). The newly initiated Early Childhood Longitudinal Study (ECLS), which will follow a national sample of kindergarten children and their families through many years of schooling, offers new opportunities for research on the types and effects of partnership (West, Denton, & Reaney, 2000).

This research was supported by grants from the U.S. Department of Education's Office of Educational Research and Improvement (OERI) to the Center for Research on the Education of Students Placed at Risk (CRESPAR), and prior grants to the Center on Families, Communities, Schools, and Children's Learning. The authors thank Nancy Chavkin for her helpful suggestions. The research and opinions are the authors' and do not necessarily represent the positions of the funding agency.

PROGRESS IN RESEARCH ON SCHOOL, FAMILY, AND COMMUNITY PARTNERSHIPS

The Importance of Family Environments and Involvement

For many decades, studies have shown that children benefit when their parents support and encourage their education. On average, parents with more formal education tend to be more involved in schools and with their children's formal education. Studies are accumulating, however, that show family practices and involvement activities are more important for helping students succeed in school than are family structure; socioeconomic status; or characteristics such as race, parent education, family size, and age of child (Becker & Epstein, 1982; Clark, 1983; Comer, 1980, 1988; Davies, 1991; Epstein, 1986, 1990; Hoover-Dempsey et al., 2001; S. Lee, 1994; Scott-Jones, 1986, 1987; Simon, 2000; Van Voorhis, 2000). This is true regardless of parents' formal education, income level, family culture, language spoken at home, or student ability or grade level. Many families compensate for the lack of material or economic resources by drawing upon their strengths in attitude and energy to support and monitor their children's education at home and at school.

The Importance of School Programs and Practices to Involve All Families

Early studies of the importance of family environments for students' success led to a new research question: *If family involvement and encouragement is important,* how can schools and communities help all families become involved in a way that helps their children succeed in school? Research results are accumulating that show school leaders can take steps to develop and implement practices enabling more parents to become, and remain, involved in their children's education. Evidence is also growing that if schools develop effective programs of partnership, families appreciate the assistance; more families become involved; and more students improve their achievement, attitude, and behavior (Davies, 1990; Dornbusch & Ritter, 1988; Epstein, 1991; Epstein & Dauber, 1991; Lopez, Scribner, & Mahitivanichcha, 2001; Sanders, 1999; Swap, 1993).

These and other studies indicate that the more a school does to organize programs and practices to involve families, the more parents respond, regardless of family background variables. Also, studies indicate that schools can implement targeted activities to involve parents in particular ways that help students reach specific learning and behavior goals (Epstein & Sheldon, 2002; Sheldon & Epstein, 2001; Simon, 2001; Van Voorhis, 2001).

The Importance of Community Involvement

New attention is being given to the influence of community in improving schools, assisting families, and increasing student learning and success (Boyd & Crowson, 1993; Sanders, 2001). Just as families are important for student success, communities have resources that combine with and extend beyond the school or family to help improve student learning and success (Boyd & Crowson; Heath & McLaughlin, 1987). School-community partnerships may be established with businesses, universities, governmental agencies, health care organizations, faith-based organizations, senior citizen groups, cultural groups, and other groups (Adger, 2001; Dryfoos, 1994; Epstein, 1995; Sanders). Viable school-community partnerships that focus on student learning, however, require honest and frequent communication and negotiation between educators and community leaders (Sanders & Harvey, 2000).

Studies are beginning to identify that all communities have important strengths in the human talent and social resources of local people, programs, and organizations. More than low or high rankings on demographic or economic characteristics, the human qualities in a neighborhood may more accurately predict and explain the success of students, the strengths of a school program, and the capacities of families to guide and assist their children. That is, in all communities adult-coach-teacher-tutors may be organized to share their varied skills, knowledge, and talents with children, such as making repairs, gardening, butchering, cooking, using transportation, obtaining needed services, public speaking, chess, sports, music, dance, art, science, and other competencies (Benson, 1997; Dryfoos, 1998; Epstein & Sanders, 2000; Gonzalez et al., 1995; Moll, Amanti, Neff, & Gonzalez, 1992).

A Theory of Multiple Influences on Student Learning and Development

Research on schools' practices of family involvement conducted in the 1980s began to challenge prevailing theories of social organization, which assumed that organizations were most effective when they operated independently and separately (Waller, 1932; Weber, 1947). On the basis of results of several studies, Epstein (1987) developed a model of "overlapping spheres of influence" of family and school and extended it (1994, 2001) to include community influences in order to account for the major contexts that affect students at all age levels. This social-organizational perspective integrates and extends the ecological model of Bronfenbrenner (1979, 1986), Leichter's (1974) educational insights of families as educators, the sociological perspectives on connections of professional and nonprofessional institutions and individuals of Litwak and Meyer (1974), the emphasis on shared responsibility of Seeley (1981), and a long tradition of sociological and psychological research on school and family environments and their effects. The model diagrams where and how "social capital" is developed (Coleman, 1988), as parents, educators, and community members exchange information, assist one another, and help students succeed in school.

The model of overlapping spheres of influence includes both external and internal structures. The external structure represents the multiple contexts of home, school, and community, which overlap more or less, depending on the philosophies and practices of families, schools, and communities. The model takes into account the age or grade level of the student, which may affect the contexts, participants, and practices of partnership. The internal structure of the model presents paths of interaction of educators, families, and community members within and across contexts at the institutional and individual levels.

It is assumed that the child's success in school is the reason for the connections of home, school, and community. The child is therefore placed at the center of the model, to recognize the central role that students play in their own education and in the interaction of parents, teachers, and community partners. Students are often the main conductors of two-way communication between school and home and interpreters for the family of information about school and community activities.

Overall, the external and internal structures of overlapping spheres of influence recognize the interlocking histories of institutions that motivate, socialize, and educate children, and the changing and accumulating skills and interactions of the individuals in those contexts. The general model promotes research on the relationships and actions of parents, teachers, and others in the community who may affect children's learning and development (Simon & Epstein, 2001).

Continuing Questions

Although progress has been made in research on the connections of home, school, and community, this is a very young field with many questions to address in rigorous quantitative and qualitative studies (Baker & Soden, 1997; Chavkin, 2001; Epstein & Sanders, 2000; Honig, Kahne, & McLaughlin, 2001; Jordan, Orozco, & Averett, 2002; Knapp, 1995). In particular, more research is needed to increase knowledge and improve practices of school partnerships with families from diverse backgrounds in diverse communities. Research to date has

built an important base of information on how parents with different educational and cultural backgrounds teach their children and communicate with their children's schools (Borman & Baber, 1998; Chavkin, 1993). This includes studies of African American families (Boykin, 1994; Clark, 1983; Comer, 1980, 1988; Dauber & Epstein, 1993; Epstein & Dauber, 1991; Epstein, Herrick, & Coates, 1996; McAdoo, 1981; Scott-Jones, 1987); studies of Asian families (Caplan, Choy, & Whitmore, 1992; Collingnon, Men, & Tan, 2001; S. J. Lee, 2001; Pang, 1995; Rong & Brown, 2002; Sung, 1987; L. C. Wong, 1990); and studies of Latino families (Canino, Earley, & Rogler, 1989; Chavkin, 1996; Delgado & Humm-Delgado, 1982; Delgado-Gaitan, 1990; Delgado-Gaitan & Trueba, 1991; E. E. Garcia, 1995; Henderson, 1997; Hidalgo & Nevárez-La Torre, 1997; Lucas, Henze, & Donato, 1990; Moll & Greenberg, 1990; Valdés, 1996).

These and other studies confirm that families from all cultural groups are interested in their children's education and desire closer and better connection with educators in their children's school. Many questions remain, however, about patterns of family influence as children progress through school, and about the strategies schools need to implement in order to reach, inform, and involve diverse families in their children's education.

About This Chapter

This chapter summarizes information from studies of family influence and family-school-community connections of two ethnic groups in the Boston area. An earlier version of this chapter, in the first edition of the *Handbook,* also included attention to African American and Irish American families and students (Hidalgo, Bright, Siu, & Swap, & Epstein, 1995). Here, we follow Latino and Chinese families as examples of ethnic groups in American schools that are dramatically increasing in number and in diversity. Nitza Hidalgo extends her review of the influence of Latino families on children's education. Sau-Fong Siu updates her work on Chinese American families. Joyce Epstein introduces and discusses the chapter, drawing from her research on school and family partnerships in diverse communities.

Hidalgo and Siu each followed ten families to learn how Latino and Chinese American parents, respectively, supported their children's school success from kindergarten through grade two; how definitions of success change from year to year as children proceed through the grades with new teachers; and how families respond to their children's development and to new teachers' demands and expectations. These studies are important because educators need to know whether family involvement in children's education prevents a student from failing in school and increases the number of students who succeed at a high level. One must understand how these processes work for students from different ethnic minority groups in economically distressed communities. It may be that communication and collaborative action of parents, educators, and community groups help motivate minority and immigrant children to learn and succeed in school. If this is true, it is necessary to help schools establish programs that build and extend partnerships to include all families and benefit all students.

The next two sections give a brief history of immigration patterns of Latino and Chinese American families in the United States, including the treatment of the early immigrants and their experiences with education in the United States. Each section discusses family influence on children's education and family involvement in education at home, at school, and in the community. The summary and discussion section identifies several cross-cutting themes of similarities and differences of Latino and Chinese American family involvement and partnerships with schools. It also raises questions for future research to improve knowledge of family influence as well as school, family, and community partnerships of diverse race and ethnic groups. The summary presents ideas for new and needed connections of multicultural education and school, family, and community partnerships to improve the quality and success of both elements in school programs.

PUERTO RICAN FAMILY INVOLVEMENT IN EDUCATION

Research on home-school connections has shown positive relationships between parental involvement and children's school achievement (Davies, 1993; Díaz-Soto, 1990; Jones & Velez, 1997). The positive effects are found in low-income and middle-income populations and among racial/ethnic groups (Comer, 1986; Dauber & Epstein, 1993; Delgado-Gaitan, 1990; Epstein & Dauber, 1991; Robledo Montecel, 1993).

In the past, studies that were grounded on White, middle-class definitions of parental involvement in schools tended to lack sensitivity to cultural variations within Latino groups and miss subtle aspects of Latino parent involvement. (The term *Latino* is used interchangeably with *Puerto Rican* in this paper. Studies that address issues related to only Puerto Ricans will be so noted.) In her review of research on Latino families, Hurtado (1995) perceived that many studies stemmed from an assimilationist model that compared Latinos to other immigrant groups of the past, who arrived during different economic times in the United States and whose goals were to achieve White, middle-class behavior patterns. Changes in Latino

families' behavior away from supposed deficiencies were interpreted to be movement toward "normal" behavior (Hurtado).

The low achievement rate of Latino students was blamed, in part, on a deficit interpretation of Latino families' and communities' culturally specific child rearing and school involvement practices. Many educators consider Latino parents "hard to reach" or not interested in their children's education (Commins, 1992; Davies, 1993; H. Garcia & Donato, 1991). Such perspectives ignore the role that school policies and practices play in fostering parental involvement (Davies, 1993). School policies and practices may create barriers to involvement for Latino parents on several levels (R. Rivera, 1993). Lack of bilingual staff or information packets that are difficult to understand are institutional barriers. School staff may have different conceptions of parental responsibilities concerning the education of children leading to cultural barriers. There are also socioeconomic and sociodemographic barriers. Low-income parents may experience stresses associated with poverty or may have limited time off from low-wage jobs, resulting in less involvement. Single parents with small children to care for may have difficulty participating in a school. R. Rivera also states that parents with a low level of education may not be able to translate their high expectations for their children into concrete help.

A conceptual model sensitive to patterns of Puerto Rican family involvement in children's schooling includes the meaning and function of the extended family; the values and practices of a family within particular contexts of home, school, and community; and family adaptations to daily structural constraints. As applied to parental involvement, a social-contextual approach uses parental knowledge, values, beliefs, and at-home practices to reconstruct the concept of family involvement (Auerbach, 1989; Hidalgo, 2000; Volk, 1992).

Auerbach (1989) suggests that researchers look at the socially and culturally meaningful activities in daily family life that may promote school achievement. She notes that researchers have used the model of school as the framework for defining the activities parents should conduct at home, deeming school-like practices as most beneficial for academic success. Research that is conceptualized on Latino practices and beliefs expands the view of beneficial practices for educational success to those found in Latino homes. Thus Latino family organization and practices are not seen as deficits but as strengths and potential resources for building teacher and parent partnerships.

This section reviews literature on Puerto Rican parental involvement in the home, school, and community. After a brief review of background information on Puerto Rican families in the United States, the definition of family is examined closely using the Puerto Rican model. Two criteria were applied. First, studies of Puerto Ricans were chosen for this review if the focus on parental involvement embraced cultural and social-contextual considerations—that is, if they incorporated cultural beliefs and practices into their investigative paradigms. Second, because Puerto Rican parents also may be limited in English proficiency, the review includes literature on Latino parents' relations to bilingual programs in schools to broaden an understanding of Puerto Rican parental involvement.

Background Information

The 2000 U.S. census shows the Latino population grew by 57% from 1990 to 2000. Latinos in the United States are one of the fastest growing ethnic groups, numbering more than 35 million, or 12.5% of the total U.S. population (U.S. Census Bureau, 2001).

In 2000, Puerto Ricans were 9.6% of the total national Latino population (U.S. Census Bureau, 2001). Puerto Ricans, whose median age was 25, numbered more than 3,406,000 in the continental United States. Only 64% of Puerto Ricans aged 25 and older had graduated from high school in 2000, and only 10.6% aged 25 and older had completed four years of college. Twenty-five percent of Puerto Ricans lived below the 2000 poverty level.

Although a small number of Puerto Ricans have lived in the United States since the 19th century, their mass migration began in the 1940s. During the 1960s and 1970s, although many Puerto Ricans continued to arrive in the United States, reverse migration to the island exceeded the number of arrivals (Torres & Velázquez, 1998). The back-and-forth movement of families continues to date. There are three distinct categories of Puerto Ricans in the United States: recently arrived migrants in search of employment; migrant workers moving back and forth as work demands; and U.S.-born second-, third-, and fourth-generation Puerto Ricans (Santiestevan & Santiestevan, 1984).

Puerto Rican Family Organization

Variations on Puerto Rican family composition are evident in the United States. Mizio (1974) wrote that "the Puerto Rican family system must be viewed on a continuum. At one end is an extended family system with traditional Puerto Rican values, and at the other end the nuclear family system with an American value system" (p. 78).

The Puerto Rican family may include the mother, father, their children, the children of other unions, and the children of friends. Extended families may include parents, children, and grandparents, with frequent visits from aunts and uncles. According to Harry (1992a), extended families may be seen as an "integral part of the family's identity and authority structure" (p. 388).

The extended family serves various functions. It is a source of ethnic identification and language maintenance for children (Zentella, 1997), a source of caring and affection for children (Hidalgo, 1994), a provider of child care (Bird & Canino, 1982), and a fountain of emotional support for family members in times of crisis (Delgado, 1995). An economic analysis of Latino extended family households (Angel & Tienda, 1982) yielded evidence of the importance of extension as a financial coping strategy, which may not be solely related to cultural preferences.

Harry (1992b) found that Puerto Rican "parents spoke of their children's strengths and weaknesses in terms of family characteristics" (p. 32). She found that Puerto Ricans share a collective identity in which the achievements or conditions ascribed to one member, such as a child, reflect back to the family as a whole. The parents trace the child's characteristics to particular family members, as traits inherited from adults in the family. A sense of family identification is holistic in nature and not individualized.

Hurtado (1995) found that Latinos retain a strong ethnic identification. She stated that "the endpoint of immigrant children's adaptation to the United States is not a total rejection of their ethnic origins and complete assimilation to the Anglo mainstream; rather the endpoint is stable biculturalism" (p. 48).

Thus, when inquiring into family structures of Puerto Ricans, one should ensure that parental-involvement models are inclusive of the extended family (see Epstein, 1992, for an expanded formulation of parental involvement). Insight into ethnic/racial differences in the definition of family should lead investigators to study the active and multiple roles played by extended family members.

Parental Involvement in the Home

Discerning the influence of Puerto Rican families on school achievement requires an understanding of the particular mechanisms of socialization that exist within the culture. The literature on Puerto Rican culture reveals a number of values and child-rearing practices that have been preserved and maintained in some form despite the transition to the United States. Close communication, connections to the island, the existence of the extended family, and the back-and-forth movement of families are the mechanisms facilitating maintenance of cultural values and practices. Strong family unity and a preference for extended family networks are primary Latino cultural values.

Family obligation is deeply ingrained in Puerto Rican culture, in which the fundamental obligations are to family and friends. Inner self-worth and sense of integrity come from doing what is expected, especially with regard to family obligations. Sabogal, Marín, Otero-Sabogal, Marín, and Pérez-Stable (1987) found Latinos seek close geographical proximity to family members and prefer a lot of family support.

Family unity and interdependency are highly valued, and close and frequent contacts among family members are expected (Mizio, 1974). Genuine expression of generosity toward others and concern about closeness and caring are part of interpersonal relationships in which one is expected to reciprocate kindness. Reciprocity is taught by the example of parents and by oral expressions that are repeated during the childhood years, such as the saying *Hoy por tí, mañana por mí* (Today for you, tomorrow for me). Reciprocity is most significant and expected among family members and neighbors.

Interdependence among family members is expected and viewed positively. No one is expected to do everything alone (Mizio, 1974). Sánchez-Ayéndez (1988) stated that "the interdependency framework conceptualizes the individual as unable to do everything or to do everything well and therefore in need of others for assistance" (p. 177). The interdependency framework provides a support system for individuals.

Child-rearing behavior reflects the value of respect. Lauria (1972) differentiates between the two varieties of respect (*respeto*) in Puerto Rican culture. The first definition refers to respect for human dignity in a general sense, or "generalized deference" (p. 38). Respect of this kind is a precondition for all social relations. The second form of respect, according to Lauria, is respect for another's authority and stature, "particularized forms of *respeto*" (p. 38), which stem from certain types of social relations. Respect of the second kind encompasses particular kinds of regard for others according to status.

Children are expected to be obedient and dedicated to the family. The Puerto Rican family is "one with close emotional and psychological ties in which the child becomes well-acquainted with the hierarchy of power and the role expectations of each family member" (Nieves Falcón, quoted in Salgado, 1985, p. 40). Although mothers control decisions on child rearing, children are taught to have unquestioned respect for both parents, especially for the father's authority.

There are many subtle ways in which parents positively influence their children that are often overlooked in studies of ethnic family involvement in education. Díaz-Soto (1990), in her study of 57 Puerto Rican families of high- and low-achieving students, found that "parents acted as facilitators within an organized framework of expectations" (p. 19). Díaz-Soto found a number of recurrent themes in relation to language, aspirations, and discipline in the homes of high achievers. Parents used both Spanish and English in communicating with their children, parents held high expectations for their children's future career, and parents employed consistent controlling strategies.

Volk (1992), in a study that directly addresses Puerto Rican parental involvement, investigated the parent-child home interactions of kindergarten children. Employing the social-contextual model (Auerbach, 1989), Volk found both formal and informal learning activities in the home. She concluded that even parents who did not employ teacher-like talk with their children made available various learning activities (such as natural conversation strategies) that stimulated children's development.

Longitudinal research on Puerto Rican parent involvement practices reveals a number of strategies employed by working-class Puerto Rican mothers and the conditions that necessitated the strategies (Hidalgo, 2000). The mothers employed four strategies to promote their children's academic success: monitoring, communicating, motivating, and protecting. Monitoring strategies are actions related to the academic learning of the child. Communicating strategies are processes that aim to foster open, nurturing family relationships. Motivating strategies stimulate the child's interest in school. Protecting strategies are actions geared to maintaining child safety.

The parenting strategies of the working-class mothers stemmed both from their cultural traditions and their neighborhood context—one in which the physical safety of their children was not ensured. The mothers devised elaborate protection strategies in an effort to control negative social influences upon their children. From a Eurocentric perspective often found in schools, the mothers' strategies would be interpreted as overprotective, but from the Puerto Rican mothers' point of view the strategies were common sense.

Much of the research on the influence that the home exerts on Puerto Rican student achievement focuses on the differences between child-rearing practices in the home and the teaching practices in schools. Research on the discontinuities of home and school that judge differences by nonethnic paradigms may miss insight as to how cultural beliefs shape home practices. Differences between home and school, when understood within a social-contextual model, are seen as cultural boundaries (Erickson, 1987), which are not negatively charged by dominant cultural definitions.

Parental Involvement in the School

Research exposes how families of different backgrounds structure the academic socialization of their children. Some strategies that parents employ may be missed by a parental involvement definition if the teacher does not consider the activities that parents conduct at home among family members. For example, teachers may not observe parents' activities that address unique cultural issues, such as reading the Spanish Bible with their children to foster Spanish language fluency. Marttila and Kiley (1995), in a cross-cultural study, found that less affluent Latino and African American parents tended to spend more time on home activities, such as reading to children and helping with homework. The parents perceived the at-home work to have a direct link to school achievement, while in-school activities, such as attending a play, held a less evident relationship to school achievement.

Vázquez-Nutall and Romero-García (1989) looked at differences between how Puerto Rican girls are taught in the home and the expectations of U.S. teachers for student behavior. They found that the teachers promoted individual achievement, while the Puerto Rican approach emphasized family satisfaction. Puerto Rican parents value interdependence and nurture cooperation in children.

In a study of low-income Puerto Rican families' interactions with the special education system, Harry (1992a, 1992b) examined how ethnicity influenced parents' understanding of their children's placement in special education. She found that Puerto Rican parents used a broader definition of normal child development than the definitions used by educators. Harry also found ethnic differences in defining family, parenting styles and discipline strategies, and parent-child interactions.

Jones and Velez (1997) studied 9 Puerto Rican families in a sample of 20 Latino families. They found all Latino parents held high expectations for their children, but the parents reported a lack of effective communication from schools. Schools tended to send correspondence (such as form letters) that did not contain specific information about the Latino children. The Puerto Rican parents in the study perceived Puerto Rican teachers to be more "warm and caring" than the teachers at their children's schools.

The nature of parent-teacher interactions is influenced by how parents are approached by the school staff (Moe, 1994). Violand-Sánchez, Sutton, & Ware (1991) reviewed effective bilingual programs. They concluded that all written communication between schools and parents, including all newsletters and notes, should be translated into the native language(s) of the home. Native language communication, however, was necessary but not sufficient to promote Latino parental involvement. Moe created and evaluated a school-to-home communication project whose purpose was to improve student achievement. Although student achievement was not significantly improved at the classroom level, individual students fared better when parents participated and followed through on school remedies. The study recommended that in initial contact with parents with limited English proficiency, teachers should seek to establish personal rapport and not require a high level of parental commitment, which may overwhelm parents. Thus positive interactions require establishing rapport that involves more than just communication in the parents' native language (Violand-Sánchez et al., 1991). Successful outreach efforts include "personal, face to face conversations with parents; meetings that have social components, not just formal events; and meetings that respond to parents' needs and concerns" (Inger, 1992, p. 3).

Some studies have focused on differences in the underlying cultural assumptions of teachers and parents. In a case study of immigrant bilingual and English-speaking parents' views on education, Allexsaht-Snider (1992) found differences in parents' and teachers' cultural forms of knowledge of schooling. Her investigation of parent-teacher conferences revealed subtle differences in interpretation of information between what the teacher intended and what the parent understood about the communication. The teachers assumed that the parents' understanding of terms and concepts was similar to their own. By contrast, the parents, whose communication style was nonconfrontational, did not push for a full explanation even if they were unfamiliar with the technical terms that teachers used.

A longitudinal, cross-cultural ethnographic study on parental influences on children's school success found (1) a lack of agreement among teachers in the same school and between teachers and parents about what constitutes success, (2) a lack of opportunity for teachers and parents from diverse cultures to share their expectations and definitions of school success, and (3) differences in parents' and teachers' definitions of parental involvement (Bright, Hidalgo, Siu, & Swap, 1995). For example, Chinese American and Puerto Rican families made important distinctions between involvement in the school and involvement in their children's education. The families may not have participated actively in the life of the school or in classrooms, but they invested tremendous energy and time in their children's education at home, and the Chinese American families also invested in activities in their community.

Rubio (1995), using qualitative measures, studied Puerto Rican parents' volunteer activities in elementary schools. She found that some schools promoted parental involvement by hiring parent coordinators, whose responsibilities were to encourage parent participation and conduct outreach activities, such as home visits. A key feature was the availability of funds to offer limited pay for parent liaison positions, which met their financial needs and helped parents become "insiders" within the school structure.

Research on the social and cultural influences on parent-teacher communication and interaction points to subtle language and cultural differences that can be a barrier to effective communication between teachers and Latino parents. Parents want useful information containing specific details that they can use to instruct their children. Schools need to structure opportunities in which teachers and parents can develop rapport and trust, share their expectations of children, and create partnerships.

Parental Involvement in the Community

Latino parent groups have organized nationally and locally to promote equal educational opportunity and appropriate bilingual educational programs. On the national level, Latinos have created organizations such as the National Council of La Raza and ASPIRA to conduct research, advocacy, and political lobbying activities and to disseminate information on and about the Latino condition in the United States. Latinos have a long history of organizational development, especially in labor unions, to support their community (Acuña, 1988). Projects to promote Latino parental involvement in schools have been created by many Latino agencies, including the ASPIRA Association (Weiser Ramírez, 1990), the Hispanic Policy Development Project (Nicolau & Ramos, 1990), and the Intercultural Development Research Association (Robledo Montecel, 1993).

On the community level, movements and community activists work to uplift Latino neighborhoods. Historically, many Latino political movements have "used the family to symbolize the need for unity, strength and struggle with adversity" (Bonilla-Santiago, 1992, 25). Návarez-La Torre (1997) found household-based educational networks that were maintained on the value of *confianza* (trust) between neighborhood residents. Community programs often become an extension of family (K. Rivera, 1999). The El Barrio Popular Education Program in New York (K. Rivera, 1999) used Spanish language literacy, critical pedagogy, and popular research to help low-income Puerto Rican and Dominican women gain critical awareness of oppressive social structures affecting their families and communities.

Pardo (1990) documented the community activism of Mexican American mothers in East Los Angeles and found that the women used their traditional responsibilities as nurturers of children and families to network with other women who were concerned with quality-of-life issues in their community. According to Pardo, the mothering role was transformed into community caring, where concern for family and community meshed into one motivating entity. Thus Latino families historically have fought for equal educational opportunities for their children.

Patterns of Parental Involvement: Implications for Educators, Administrators, and Researchers

To encourage the active participation of Puerto Rican families in schools, educators should note some unique Puerto Rican interrelational patterns. The interpersonal style of communication views directness as rude; diplomacy in communicating with parents is advised. Educators should consider extending personal attention and outreach to parents, especially through using Spanish, with such actions as employing bilingual front office staff, building social components into school meetings, and addressing parents' specific concerns. Educators are encouraged to employ home-school-community liaisons that have established their validity as community members. Furthermore, teachers and administrators should treat members of the extended family with the same respect and authority as parents (Robledo Montecel, 1993) because they are legitimate representatives of family interests. Successful outreach to Latino parents requires "personal outreach, non-judgmental communication, and respect for parents' culture" (Inger, 1992, p. 2).

Davies (1993) presented several recommendations from his Schools Reaching Out Project, which studied parents from low-socioeconomic background and their relation to schools. He concluded that (a) schools should attract mental health and social service organizations to the school to assist families and children, (b) they should free one teacher's time to be a "school-community specialist" to create linkages with families and community-based organizations, (c) districts could provide funding for teachers to develop materials that may be used at home to support instructional goals, and (d) school districts could offer funding for in-service opportunities so teachers may begin to change their way of thinking about parent-teacher partnerships.

This section reviewed research on the influences of Puerto Rican families on their children in the home, in the school, and in the community. The conceptualization of family was expanded to include both nuclear and extended families, as these are authentic definitions for Puerto Rican families. The review defined a framework for reviewing literature that included the influence of ethnicity in the study of family involvement. Puerto Rican cultural values and child-rearing practices were described to give a more complete picture of how these families structure the learning environment for their children. Research studies that examined the subtle variations of Puerto Rican and other Latino families' expectations and strategies to ensure school achievement were highlighted. Future examinations of Puerto Rican family involvement in education should include the meaning of parental practices and cultural values in order to identify and explain important ethnically derived contributions made by families.

CHINESE AMERICAN FAMILY INVOLVEMENT IN EDUCATION

A comprehensive review of literature on family processes and educational achievement (Dornbusch & Wood, 1989) found that better school performance is associated with frequent parental participation in school functions, but this finding is not generalizable to Asian American student populations. Asian American parents generally care deeply about their children's education and contribute substantially to the child's learning environment, but parental support may take forms differing from those of other cultures. To acknowledge the tremendous diversity among Asian Americans and to avoid overgeneralization, this section of the chapter focuses on Chinese Americans, the largest Asian American ethnic group and the one with the longest history in the United States. (From here on, the terms "Chinese parents" and "Chinese families" will refer to those in the United States, unless otherwise specified.)

According to the 2000 census (U.S. Census Bureau, 2000), the nation's 2.4 million Chinese Americans constitute 0.087% of the population. This is a 48% increase since the 1990 census (Banerjee, 2001). If trends in the last three decades are any indication, and barring any drastic change in immigration policy, the number of Chinese Americans is expected to increase. They are concentrated in urban areas of 10 states, in descending order by size of Chinese American population: California, New York, Texas, New Jersey, Massachusetts, Illinois, Washington, Hawaii, Pennsylvania, and Maryland. Immigrants outnumber American-born Chinese by roughly two to one.

Large-scale Chinese immigration did not occur until the gold rush in 1848. Largely due to an economic downturn and racism, an anti-Chinese movement swept across the country, culminating in the Chinese Exclusion Act of 1882. From the late 1880s to World War II, access to American education was limited for some Chinese and nonexistent for others (Chang, 1983; McCunn, 1988; Siu, 1992b). Public schools seemed to be far more interested in finding ways to exclude Chinese children from the schools and to fight Chinese parents than in building home-school partnerships with the parents. Despite more than a century of severe discrimination in immigration, employment, housing, education, citizenship, marriage, and social life, Chinese Americans as a group have taken advantage of educational and career opportunities that opened up after World War II. With changes in the immigration law in 1965 favoring the professionally trained,

the educational profile of Chinese Americans has been transformed. Since the 1970s, Chinese students have been perceived by the American public as superachievers or math whiz kids. On a number of commonly accepted indicators of educational achievement—such as dropout rate, college enrollment rate, and college graduation rate—Chinese Americans as a group have indeed fared well, even outperforming Whites (M. Wong, 1995; S. C. Wong & Lopez, 2000).

However, aggregate data do not tell the whole story. The diversity in country of origin, language, socioeconomic status, educational background, and degree of acculturation makes it extremely difficult to generalize about the contemporary Chinese American community. The "30% uptown Chinese and 30% downtown Chinese" pattern first identified by Kwong (1987) still holds true today, and this bimodal distribution must be kept in mind when discussing achievement and family involvement, or any other characteristic of Chinese Americans.

The literature examining the educational achievement of Chinese Americans is vast. (See Siu, 1992b, for a literature review and bibliography on this subject.) Although the "model minority" myth about Asian Americans has been debunked (Hu, 1989; Kim & Chun, 1992; Suzuki, 1977) and the adequacy of the cultural thesis to explain school success has been challenged (Ogbu, 1983; Siu, 1992b; Sue & Okazaki, 1990), the public as well as the professional community continue to be deeply interested in the role of Chinese culture in children's academic achievement.

Current Research and Gaps

Given the amount of attention to how Chinese family structure, practices, and values influence children's educational achievement, the dearth of research studies on Chinese family involvement in education is surprising. The one book that examines the relationship between Asian parents and schools does not cover Chinese parents but focuses instead on Filipino and Southeast Asian parents (Te, Cordova, Walker-Moffat, & First, 1997). Journal articles that address the issue of Asian parental involvement with education are few and far between (F. Y. Lee, 1995; Yao, 1985, 1988). There is even less on the relationship between Chinese (not generic Asian) parents and public schools. Available information about Chinese parental involvement tends to be limited and anecdotal, although there is a growing body of knowledge on the topic, mostly from qualitative studies of small samples. For example, L. Y.-F. Wong (1992) carried out field work for three months in Los Angeles, New York City, and San Francisco in 1987, using observation and interviews. The focus of her study was educational initiatives of the Chinese, namely, Chinese language/culture schools and community-based supplementary schools offering tutoring classes of mainstream English-medium curriculum. Of the 104 people she interviewed, only two were Chinese parents and 22 were Chinese pupils. The pilot study conducted by Wu (2001) used the focus group technique to collect data in Chinese language schools in Massachusetts from 38 Mandarin-speaking parents, mostly immigrants. The focus of her study was on parenting experiences and challenges, with education being one of several topics for the focus group discussions.

A five-year project in Boston funded by the U.S. Department of Education (Siu & Feldman, 1996) encompassed a longitudinal ethnographic study of 10 Chinese families of American-born young children in monolingual classrooms of public schools, and a survey of 90 Chinese parents of young children of various backgrounds in bilingual as well as monolingual classrooms. The project focused on family support of young children's educational success (Siu, 1992a, 1992b, 1994a, 1994b, 1996, 2001, 2002; Siu & Feldman, 1995, 1996).

Parental Involvement in the Home

The literature is replete with references to the value Chinese parents place on education. Although valuing education is by no means a claim unique to Chinese Americans, what is distinctive is the tendency for Chinese Americans to define their cultural identity in terms of academic achievement (Lau, 1988; P. S. Lee, 1983); to be a scholar and do well in school is to be Chinese. Education is also seen as an important avenue, and perhaps the only one, for upward social mobility (Wu, 2001). Unlike in the West, educational attainment to the Chinese is more a matter of enhancement of the family than of individual achievement (Sue, 1997).

Findings from studies of family socialization patterns conducted in China, Taiwan, and Hong Kong, as well as those conducted in the United States (e.g., Chao, 1994; Chen & Uttal, 1988; Hess, Chang, & McDevitt, 1987; D.Y.F. Ho, 1986; Lin, 1988; Schneider & Lee, 1990; Sue & Sue, 1971; Yao, 1985), suggest commonalities among parents of Chinese heritage. When compared with their American Caucasian counterparts, Chinese parents tend to monitor their children more closely, moralize more often, emphasize a greater sense of family obligation, value grades more than general cognitive achievement, evaluate more realistically a child's academic and personality characteristics, be less easily satisfied with a child's accomplishments, and believe more in effort and less in innate ability as a factor in school success. It should be pointed out, however, that the studies cited here do not include second-generation or third-generation Chinese born in the United States, who tend to exhibit very

different parenting styles and espouse very different socialization goals for their children. Recognition of within-group diversity among Chinese parents is imperative (Fong & Wu, 1996; Siu & Feldman, 1996).

According to Epstein (1992), one type of school and family partnership consists of "basic parental obligations to make children ready for school" (p. 1145). This is the type of child-centered involvement with which Chinese parents feel most comfortable and in which they probably excel. As Epstein notes, the term *parental involvement* needs to be conceptualized broadly as "school and family partnerships" to include members of the extended family. What is clear from the current literature is that Chinese parents are not the only ones who involve themselves with the children's education. Grandparents, aunts, uncles, cousins, and even older siblings are sometimes key players in a child's schooling, whether or not they live under the same roof (Siu, 1994b, 2001; Siu & Feldman, 1996). Furthermore, in the last 20 years the phenomenon of "little foreign students" has caught the attention of school personnel (Yuan, 1987, as cited in S. C. Wong & Lopez, 2000). Large numbers of Chinese children and teenagers are sent to America by well-to-do families from Taiwan and Hong Kong to live with relatives, or in some cases paid caregivers, while attending local public schools. *Parental involvement* therefore needs to be conceptualized broadly to include members of the extended family, which assumes great significance in Chinese culture.

How do Chinese parents support their children's school performance? A review of the literature (Schneider & Lee, 1990; Siu, 1994b, 2001; Siu & Feldman, 1996; Slaughter-DeFoe, Nakagawa, Takanishi, & Johnson, 1990; L. C. Wong, 1990; Wu, 2001) reveals many ways: reducing the number of household chores for children, using Chinese proverbs and folk stories to motivate children to study, purchasing workbooks, establishing study times, scheduling children's free time, taking children to the library, teaching the three R's before children enter kindergarten, enrolling children in language schools and music classes on weekends or after school, and assisting them with homework. These practices are not limited to families that are educated and affluent. The ethnographies of both L. C. Wong (1990) and Siu (2001) have documented the considerable amount of money, time, and energy put in by low-income, non–English-proficient Chinese parents to help their children get good grades. Creating homework, for example, seems to be a common strategy. This is prompted by a firm belief that practice makes perfect, a desire to keep children occupied, and a need to compensate for the perceived lax situation of the American public schools.

This positive picture of active family involvement in the child's education must be counterbalanced by the one portrayed in a comprehensive study of new immigrant children in New York City's Chinatown (Sung, 1987). Sung concluded that "parental absence is a pervasive phenomenon" (p. 224). The poorer new immigrant Chinese American family has in fact delegated many of its functions (feeding, medical attention, providing supervision, monitoring homework) to the school or to an after-school program. Older children take jobs to supplement family income; in many instances, education takes a back seat to the economic survival of the family (Sim, 1992; Sung).

Parental Involvement in the School

Whereas many Chinese parents are actively engaged in the home with their children's education, there is not a matching interaction between school personnel and parents. "A Cool Response to School Activities; a Hiding of Dissatisfaction Deep in the Heart" is the title of the lead article of a Chinese newspaper's special issue on Chinese parental involvement in the schools (Ho & Fong, 1990, p. 1). These two phrases perhaps best capture the general state of the Chinese parent-school relationship. A survey (Ho & Fong) in New York City of a broad spectrum of parents with regard to educational level, children's age, and length of residency in the United States yields some disturbing findings. The child's report card was, for many, the only means of school-home communication, but only 42% of all respondents could read and understand everything without the help of a dictionary or translator, and 1% of the parents surveyed did not read the report card. Most claimed that parental involvement was necessary to improve education for children, but only 27% regularly attended parent-teacher conferences and other school functions; only 11% voted in parents' council elections or on school issues.

Although school participation was minimal across the board, parents who had only an elementary school level of education had the least amount of participation, presumably because of the long working hours necessary for their survival. These respondents also did not believe their involvement could have an impact on the quality of their children's education.

Lack of English proficiency is often cited by school personnel as well as parents as the chief barrier to more active involvement in the schools (First & Carrera, 1988). Limited ability to speak English, as F. Y. Lee (1995) learned from her study of 40 Asian (including Chinese) parents in California and Colorado, can lead to "feelings of inferiority, uncertainty, fear, and awkwardness" (p. 8). Although language barriers can indeed be formidable, attitudinal and other factors cannot be discounted since available data suggest that involvement in the school remains low even when the parents can understand and speak English, or when Chinese-speaking teachers and counselors are available and all notices are written in both

Chinese and English (Ming Sum, 1990; Yao, 1985, 1988). Siu (1988), on the basis of a review of the literature, identifies a range of explanations for the minimal Chinese immigrant parents' presence in the schools as volunteer assistants, attendees of meetings, advocates for their own children, or participants in policy making: unwillingness to appear to challenge school authority, unfamiliarity with established protocols for scheduling appointments with the teacher, skepticism about the efficacy of speaking out, and others. Other factors that could make parents uncomfortable in school or unable to visit the school are the lack of any schooling in one's homeland, preoccupation with economic survival, inflexible or overcrowded work schedules, and in the case of undocumented immigrants fear of deportation resulting from being too involved with official institutions such as schools.

Could the low level of participation indicate complete trust in the school? It is true that Chinese parents tend to accord legitimacy to the school and the teacher, but it does not automatically follow that they are satisfied with them. Ogbu's (1983) assertion that Chinese immigrants tend to think of this country's education as superior to that in the home country refers to access to educational opportunities, not necessarily to the quality of education. Although many Chinese parents see higher education as more accessible in the United States—a perception that is sometimes the motivation for immigration—they have grave concerns about the lax discipline in the schools, lack of moral education, poor mathematics training, and insufficient homework (Chan, 1991; K. Ho & Fong, 1990; Kenny Lai, as cited in J.F.J. Lee, 1991; Siu & Feldman, 1995, 1996; Wu, 2001). Instead of complaining to school authorities, the prevailing Chinese parental strategy is to take compensatory measures—inventing homework, sending children to church or to Chinese-language school to learn discipline and moral values, and enrolling children in after-school tutoring classes and specialized programs such as Kumon math workshops (Siu, 2001; L. Y.-F. Wong, 1992; Wu, 2001). L.Y.-F. Wong attributes the prevalence of community tutoring classes to the parents' lack of confidence in the public school's ability to meet the needs of their children.

American-born Chinese parents seem to display a different pattern of involvement with the school, one that can be explained by familiarity and comfort with the school system and perception of their secure status in the United States. Where work schedules permit, these parents are active and vocal in the school (Siu & Feldman, 1995, 1996). One encouraging development in the last 10 years has been the election of long-time immigrant as well as American-born Chinese parents to school committees in a number of California and New York communities.

The lack of fit between beliefs and values held by teachers and those held by Chinese parents is an area of concern. Cheng (1999) has outlined eight major differences in expectation between American teachers and Chinese parents regarding the nature of teaching and learning and the respective roles of teachers and students. For example, American teachers expect students to question the teacher, whereas Chinese parents expect students not to challenge the teacher. Again, here as elsewhere, one should not lose sight of the within-group diversity. A chart highlighting these differences in Chinese parents' definition of "good" teachers, conceptualization of the goal of education, and perception of parents' role in education can be found in the work by Siu and Feldman (1996).

One of the few studies of teachers' perception of Chinese parents of kindergarten and first-grade children in public schools (Siu, 1994a) finds no mention of partnership or teamwork in discussing parent-school relationships. Teachers and parents did not always see eye to eye with regard to homework, classroom management, and other issues. Furthermore, after school is over, teachers and parents move in different communities.

Some strategies to get Chinese parents involved have been tried by schools and found somewhat useful: setting up telephone networks (New York City Board of Education, 1980); offering ESL classes in the schools (New York City Board of Education, 1990); cosponsoring with local colleges a guest speaker program featuring prominent Chinese Americans from various fields (Young, Scorza, & Sica, 1984); and offering a course called Parent, Child, and the School to learn about the school system (Patel & Kaplan, 1994).

School personnel often use parental presence in the school building as an indicator of parental interest in the child's education. This is a questionable practice because available research consistently points to the school success of Chinese children whose parents do not participate actively in school functions and policy-making bodies. Obviously, one needs to look more closely at, and appreciate, the day-to-day contributions that parents and other family members make to their children's education at home and in the community.

Parental Involvement in the Community

Historically, maintenance of the Chinese language and culture has been important to Chinese communities across the nation, as evidenced by the growth of community-based Chinese language schools, often started and staffed by Chinese parents. A number of research studies (among them X. Wang, 1996; L. Y.-F. Wong, 1992; S. C. Wong & Lopez, 2000) have examined the goals, structure, and effects of these schools. In large cities with a concentration of Chinese immigrants, social service agencies have emerged to provide needed services, such as day care and supplementary schools offering tutoring classes, but the supply cannot keep up with the demand (Sim, 1992; L. Y.-F. Wong.

The famous Supreme Court decision Lau v. Nichols in 1974 (414 U.S. 563) is perhaps the best-known illustration of how Chinese parents mobilized themselves to demand appropriate education for non–English-proficient students. When the San Francisco Unified School District delayed implementation of this court ruling, parents formed a citizens' task force to develop a master plan for bilingual/bicultural education. Concluding his account of the history of the Chinese community's struggle for equal and quality education, L.L.C. Wang (1976) placed the Lau decision in the same league as the 1954 Brown v. Board of Education decision that outlawed school segregation. The Lau decision was a contribution "toward recognizing the rights of non–English speaking Americans and has helped put together a strong coalition of minority communities in San Francisco, California and nation-wide to fight for meaningful change in our social institutions" (p. 258).

The Chinese community has learned at least four valuable lessons from the long, hard struggle to make bilingual/bicultural education a reality. First, reliance on a legal remedy, such as a class action suit, is not enough because there are local political and legal forces that can pose great obstacles to implementing a good principle. Second, the best way to combat resistance to reform from the public school system is to develop well-planned community action to put pressure on those in power. Third, the participation of other minority groups in developing a master plan for bilingual/bicultural education is crucial to the success of the struggle. The Citizens Task Force on Bilingual Education, with its 27 members, reflected the ethnic composition of the student body in the San Francisco Unified School District. There were representatives from the Chinese, Filipino, Japanese, and Spanish-speaking communities and five additional seats for speakers of other groups, such as Samoan, Korean, and Hindu communities. L.L.F. Wang (1976) identified this as "the first time that such a coalition of minority communities had come together to work on a common cause," (p. 250). Furthermore, each committee within the task force included at least one person from each language caucus. Fourth, collaboration with other groups cannot be overlooked. The task force had worked cooperatively with the professional staff of the Center for Applied Linguistics and with minority teachers in the American Federation of Teachers and the California Teachers Association.

A more recent case of community action is that of Ho v. San Francisco Unified School District. In 1994, several schoolchildren of Chinese descent filed the Ho action, challenging the school district's school assignment policy as being based on racial quotas ("A Diversity Plan," 2001). The consent decree of 1999 ruled in favor of the

Chinese families and required the SFUSD to modify a policy that has placed Chinese students at a disadvantage for many years.

One of the most successful information and referral services set up by and for Chinese parents is the Chinese American Parents' Association of New York City, which has a membership of more than 800 in seven districts. Its hotline handles 1,500 or more calls per year from parents. In addition, the organization offers newsletters and workshops to familiarize recent immigrants with the American educational system, and it mediates disputes between school systems and Chinese parents. There are other local and national community groups that support Chinese family involvement in the schools or advocate for Chinese students (Siu, 2002).

Chinese parental involvement in education is largely uncharted territory, ripe for exploration. First, more is known about parental involvement in the home than about involvement in school governance and advocacy. Second, little data exist on the effects that the degree and type of involvement have on school achievement. Finally, more is known about the involvement of overseas-born Chinese parents than about American-born Chinese parents, primarily because research access is made easier by the concentration of Chinese immigrants in Chinatowns. We know relatively little about involvement patterns of Chinese parents who are scattered in suburban communities and whose children are not enrolled in bilingual programs. Shoho's (1992) study of three generations of parental involvement among Japanese Americans in Hawaii is instructive. First-generation Japanese American parents show a different pattern of family-school partnership from that of third-generation parents, with the latter being more directly and actively involved in the schools. Results from the Boston project (Siu & Feldman, 1996) suggest that such a pattern may also be true of Chinese Americans.

Swap (1993) offers a useful typology of four models of home-school relationships: the protective model, the school-to-home transmission model, the curriculum enrichment model, and the partnership model. It is fair to say that most of the literature on the relationships between Chinese families and public schools reflects the school-to-home transmission model. There are hardly any data on the partnership model as it applies to Chinese parents.

Four lines of inquiry could prove fruitful and close the gaps in the literature: (a) a comparison of immigrant and native-born parental involvement, (b) a study of the effects of differential involvement on student achievement, (c) a comparison of family-school relationships of several generations of Chinese Americans, and (d) evaluation of various models of home-school relationships as applied to Chinese parents.

SUMMARY AND DISCUSSION

Crosscutting Themes

We draw six conclusions from these summaries of Latino and Chinese American family influence and school partnerships.

On Common Beliefs and Behaviors. *Latino and Chinese American families share some common beliefs and behaviors concerning their children's education.* Families in both groups:

- Love and care for their children
- Have historically valued and supported their children's education
- Have traditionally drawn from the strengths of their extended family and community for support, guidance, and motivation in raising and educating their children
- Have made and continue to make personal sacrifices and investments so that their children will have the education they need to succeed in mainstream U.S. society

Other studies reveal that these beliefs and actions also are true for other cultural groups (Borman & Baber, 1998; Noguera, 2001; see also sections on African American and Irish American families in Hidalgo et al., 1995).

Historically, Latino and Chinese American immigrants experienced prejudice and discrimination in the United States because of their race, culture, and language. Yet through their support for education over time, families in both groups have guided their children away from poverty toward greater prosperity, and away from disdain toward greater respect. *Hoy por tí, mañana por mí* sounds very much like the commitments of other early immigrant groups, in which parents and older siblings worked overtime and on several jobs so that children (sons, at first; daughters, later) could graduate from high school and attend college (Azmitia & Cooper, 2001). The first generation of college-goers in every racial and ethnic group has been celebrated by their families and communities (Henderson, 1997; Portes & Rumbaut, 2001).

On Within-Group Differences. *Differences within racial and ethnic groups may be greater than differences between groups on all family factors, including support for children's education, use of extended families and community networks, and involvement in schools.* This chapter describes intragroup differences that show how wrong it is to generalize about any particular group (Nieto, 2000). Not all Asian American families and children are model minorities. Indeed, no group could fulfill such expectations. Of course, negative labels are no more correct or useful than positive stereotypes (S. J. Lee, 2001; Rong & Brown, 2002; Siu, 2001).

Members of every group did, do, and will vary widely in social class, recency of immigration, English- and native-language competencies, family educational background, area of residence, ethnicity of neighborhood, age of parents, intermarriage, family structure, parental employment, level of poverty or prosperity, and other measures of assimilation or acculturation.

Puerto Rican family attitudes and practices in children's education also may be affected by the locale of parents' and students' early years and education, migration patterns, and the intensity of family connections with the island or home country. Students in all ethnic groups respond differently to these variations in family situations, making some students more resilient than others to stressors (Rong & Brown, 2002; Winfield, 1991). Equally interesting, some children are nonresponsive to *advantages* that are offered by their families.

This chapter's overviews of Latino and Chinese American families suggest that there are many variables of family life and learning that are as important as (or more important than) country of origin, race, or ethnicity when it comes to influencing family attitudes and actions about education and connection with their children's school.

On Researching Success. *Most research on diverse families and school practice has focused on children's and families' failures, but more will be learned by understanding their successes.* Many studies of Latino children and families have been conducted in a way that perpetuates negative stereotypes and that contributes to educators' low expectations for family involvement or children's success. In the past, this also was true for Chinese American children. The two overviews in this chapter, however, indicate that when research asks questions about family influence on student *success,* results reveal some common behaviors that override other conditions. Thus, regardless of family cultural or linguistic background, children are more successful with the presence of reading matter at home; family praise and guidance for being a good student and getting good grades; and family support for literacy activities such as reading, writing, word games, poetry, and stories (E. E. García, 1995; Lucas et al., 1990).

On Multiple Family Membership. *Families teach their children about their multiple memberships.* The studies of Latino and Chinese American families highlight another similarity across ethnic groups that remains an important variable for future research. Latino and Chinese American families help their children develop bicultural identity, including understanding their own ethnicity and their membership in mainstream America. Boykin (1994), Bright (in Hidalgo et al., 1995), and Perry (1993) describe how African American parents teach their children to exercise their multiple memberships. These researchers and others recognize that Latino, Chinese, and African American youngsters hold several racial, ethnic, and mainstream memberships. This perspective has broad importance and implications. European American children also need to be aware of their own multiple memberships in order to understand their families—and understand students who are different from themselves. Although this task is portrayed as a burden for minority or immigrant groups, it actually is everyone's burden and opportunity.

Research is needed to gain a fuller account of how families within and across cultural groups are similar and different in their attitudes, behaviors, and influences on children's learning and development. These variables include and go beyond the racial and ethnic characteristics of students and their families.

On the Role of the School. *Schools play an important role in whether and how all families become involved in their children's education.* The reviews of Latino and Chinese American families show that, although just about all parents value education, most have not been given much information from schools to help them support their children at every grade level. The lack of timely and understandable information affects all parents, but it is particularly serious for parents who do not speak or read English fluently or who are unfamiliar with the schools their children attend.

Until recently, parents have been left on their own to learn about their children's development, educational programs, and how to become involved at school. New research is showing, however, that school leadership and actions to develop programs of partnership make a difference in whether all families (including those with diverse educational and cultural backgrounds) become and remain effective partners in their children's education (Chavkin, 1996; Durán, Durán, Perry-Romero, & Sanchez, 2001; Epstein, 2001; Lopez et al., 2001; Sanders, 1999; Swap, 1993; Valdez, 1996). The reviews of Latino and Chinese American families featured in this chapter make important distinctions between family experiences with and readiness for involvement at home and at school. As other studies also show, most parents want to know how to help their own child at home each year (Epstein, 2001; Hoover-Dempsey et al., 2001). Yet most schools still focus heavily on parents' visits to the school building. As educators learn how to develop comprehensive and inclusive programs of partnership, they will be better able to implement feasible, family-friendly activities that enable parents to become involved at home and at school.

On Partnership. *The concept of partnership acknowledges that neither the family nor the school alone can socialize and educate children for success in school or in society.* Increasingly, research, policy, and practice show that the family, school, and community need to work together to help children succeed in school and solve learning and development problems that may arise throughout the school years (Collingnon et al., 2001; Epstein, 2001; Hidalgo & Nevárez-La Torre, 1997; Sanders, 1999, 2001; Siu, 2002). School, family, and community partnerships make it more likely that ideas, energy, and resources will be combined and targeted to improve schools, strengthen families, and increase students' chances for success. Two-way communications are needed to help families understand school programs, and to help schools understand families' cultures, strengths, and goals. In short, educators and families need to exchange information about the children they share. Children need to know that their families and their teachers are communicating with each other and have similar expectations for them to work hard in the role of student.

Questions for Future Research

The reviews of Latino and Chinese American families in this chapter suggest that differences in family involvement in children's education are not the result of fixed, unchangeable, culturally determined values and practices. Rather, family involvement and influence are likely to be explained by variations in family factors, community contexts, and school programs and practices of partnership. More research on these alterable variables is needed, to learn how much is similar and how much is different between and among families of cultural groups. This chapter's reviews raise many questions that need to be addressed to deepen understanding of diverse families. Here are a few examples of comparative questions that require targeted, rigorous quantitative and qualitative studies to extend research on school, family, and community partnerships and to help improve school practice.

Do Puerto Rican parents value interdependence and cooperation more than other parents? Or is this a quality that varies within groups as much as or more than between them? Various researchers have reported that Hispanic Americans, African Americans, Native Americans, and Native Hawaiians value cooperation, interdependence, and exchange. Other studies indicate that cooperation and interaction are general teaching tools that help all children learn (Slavin, 1995). How should these features guide school programs to inform and involve families in their children's education?

Do Chinese American families manage their children's education more closely than do other parents, or does this skill vary among families of all races and ethnicities? Is the degree to which parents guide and manage their children's education determined by parents' education and experiences with schools, as some studies report (Baker & Stevenson, 1986; Gutman & McLoyd, 2000; Useem, 1992), or by schools' practices that guide parents to monitor and discuss schoolwork and homework with their youngsters (Dauber & Epstein, 1993; Epstein, 1986)?

Do Chinese American families make more explicit than other groups do their desire that their children become fully competent in mainstream U.S. society, or do otherwise similar families in all cultural groups make that goal equally explicit? How do families help their children become competent in mainstream America? How do schools help families select and conduct these activities? How is this goal affected or balanced by family goals and actions to help children retain and benefit from their cultural identities?

Do Puerto Rican families value home life more than other families, or do these values and behaviors vary among families in all groups? Many families in various ethnic groups stress the importance of religiosity and ties to their church (Sanders, 1998). Families in all ethnic groups emphasize the importance of their relatives and connection with their community. It is likely that there are similarities and variations among families in all groups in warmth, hospitality, and other qualities of home life. How do these qualities affect children's attitudes toward teachers, behavior in school, friendships with peers, and other indicators of school success?

Is the Puerto Rican concept of *respeto* similar to or different from the African American emphasis on reciprocity, the Chinese concept of harmony in relationships, and the Irish American emphasis on respect and respectability, or other groups' attention to the golden rule? How is the concept of respect for students' views represented in various cultures? Do family teachings on these concepts prepare children for interactions with teachers and other children in school and in the community? Does lack of such training explain problems that students have in school? How do these factors help educators and parents develop and maintain the mutual respect that is needed for their partnerships in children's education?

Implications for Schools' Programs of Partnership and Multicultural Education

The studies reviewed in this chapter raise many questions about whether and how families of varying cultural backgrounds are alike or different in their hopes for their children, their approaches to learning, the information they need from schools, and how they connect with and communicate with teachers and their children about education. Knowledge to date suggests four important implications for a school's program of partnership.

Offering Many Activities. *Effective school programs of partnership need to include activities to meet the similar and different goals and needs of diverse families.* Common practices of partnership are needed to construct a sense of community for all families, children, and educators at school without regard to cultural or other differences. All families need to feel welcome at the school their children attend. All families need and want good and useful information to maintain their involvement and influence in their children's lives. The same information may be needed in different forms or languages.

Some educators still consider families with a variety of cultural, racial, and language backgrounds hard to reach. They consider family language or cultural differences as a barrier to communication. Other educators have implemented policies and practices that enable them to reach out to all families (Davies, 1991; Sanders & Epstein, 2000). New knowledge is making it possible for all schools to draw from a wide repertoire of practices to involve all families in their children's education at home and at school (Epstein et al., 2002; see also www.partnershipschools.org and the section there called "In the Spotlight").

Some practices that schools initiate must be common for all families, such as invitations to join the PTA or PTO. Other practices must be tailored to the group in order to attain common goals, such as translations needed to communicate with families who do not speak English, or meetings or conferences that must be scheduled at night to reach parents who work during the day. Still other practices must be unique if they are to respond to family situations and needs, such as special meetings with new immigrant families to welcome and orient them to the school, or family literacy programs that are conducted for parents who want to learn or improve English or reading skills.

The reviews of Latino and Chinese American families in this chapter also point to the need to connect the fields of school, family, and community partnerships and multicultural education. The connections need to flow in both directions, as is discussed next.

Partnership in Multicultural Education. *Multicultural education must incorporate school and family partnerships to ensure student success in school and the success of multicultural programs.* The reviews of Latino and Chinese American families in this chapter should help redirect the debate about multicultural education by revealing why *schools* must take stronger leadership to develop clear, inclusive, and excellent programs in three areas: curriculum and instruction; interpersonal and race relations; and school, family, and community partnerships. The first two areas have been traditional components of multicultural education. The third—school, family, and community partnerships—must be addressed in new ways.

In a well-designed program of partnership, all families are guided to help their own children at home and other children in school develop pride in their history and culture, bolster self-esteem, and contribute to a sense of community. When parents of different cultural groups work together at school and in the community, they send powerful images and messages to children about the importance of the family in education and about cooperation among adults.

By contrast, a weak or poorly designed program excludes families who are from various cultures, labels them hard to reach, ignores their strengths, avoids their cultures and customs, denies their aspirations for their children or their knowledge of their children's talents, and treats them as part of (or as the cause of) their children's problems in school. Research suggests that if this happens, children suffer, the school and community lose the skills and investments of potential participants, and families become isolated from each other and from their children's work as students.

Strong programs of school and family partnerships improve the chances of reaching three goals of multicultural education: increase knowledge, reduce prejudice, and strengthen the school social structure (J. A. Banks, 1993a, 1993b). For example, family reflections and experiences may be incorporated in school activities and homework assignments to contribute to students' construction of cultural knowledge. It is hard to imagine a deep sense of empowerment for students *unless* they know that their families are accepted and valued in the school culture and social structure.

C.A.M. Banks (1993) notes that students from various groups must "cross barriers of language, values, cognitions and culture" (p. 43) in school. This is another way of recognizing the multiple memberships that individuals exercise to succeed in mainstream society. Such barriers may be crossed if schools establish and sustain programs that are more "congruent" with students' families (C.A.M. Banks; Nieto, 2000; Torres-Guzmán, 1990). Epstein (1987, 2001) calls these congruent constructions "school-like families" and "family-like schools." Her theory of overlapping spheres of influence suggests that the home, school, and community should be restructured through the use of partnership activities that support children as students. Only then will educators, families, and community members be aware of, responsive to, appreciative of, and able to work with each other.

Undoubtedly, students' self-acceptance and self-confidence as learners are affected by how the school accepts, respects, and appreciates them and their families. By participating in their children's education, families can help students develop pride without prejudice. This includes helping children gain knowledge about their heritage and culture; participating at their children's school; and contributing, with other families, to the school culture and community. Although involving families and community partners in schools complicates multicultural education by requiring educators to pay attention to and work with families, this hard work is needed to attain the main goals of multicultural education: to improve learning and help all youngsters function effectively in a culturally and ethnically diverse nation and world (J. A. Banks, 1993b).

Incorporating Multicultural Education. *School and family partnerships must incorporate multicultural education in order to ensure student success in school, and to involve all families successfully.* Topics and approaches of multicultural education must be added to the design and implementation of programs of school, family, and community partnerships. This includes drawing from results of research to understand various cultural groups, and selecting common and different practices that involve all families in their children's education.

Starting in the mid-1980s, Epstein (1992, 1995) began to tailor and test her framework of major types of involvement to address the needs of families with limited English skills and immigrant families. Now, six types of involvement guide schools in developing comprehensive programs of partnership (Epstein, 1992, 1995). Practices for each type of involvement may be selected or designed to accommodate families of students with diverse cultural backgrounds, accounting for the parents' language of proficiency or level of English reading skills.

In the framework for comprehensive partnership programs, type one (parenting) practices involve families in workshops or other activities that help families *understand child and adolescent development* and create *home conditions that support student learning*. These topics, often addressed in workshops at school, should be offered to all families, not just to those proficient in English. For example, at one workshop for parents translators in three languages and sign language worked simultaneously with different sections of an audience as the main speakers were talking. This clearly conveyed the message that all parents were welcome at the event. Most schools have low attendance at workshops and other meetings at school. It is not surprising that participation is low in places where parents are neither understood nor made welcome through communication in their own language. If tape recordings, videos, summaries of workshops, and other information on child development and parenting are provided to families, they too need to be translated for use by families who do not speak English.

Type one or parenting activities also include ways for families to share their culture and customs with their children's school. For example, in Saint Paul, Minnesota, an elementary school celebrated the Hmong New Year with schoolwide presentations, dances, songs, feasts, costumes, and other activities, and with families invited. The celebration demonstrated the school's awareness of the importance of extending learning and sharing the joy of a day that is important in the lives of many students and families (National Network of Partnership Schools, 2001).

Type two (communicating) activities provide *information about school programs and children's progress* to all families. Letters, memos, notices, report cards, and other materials that are sent home must be translated by educators or volunteers in a school or school district if families do not read English at all or not well. This can be accomplished without losing information and without patronizing families. Conferences at school or telephone calls to and from school may require translators to ensure that parents and teachers can communicate effectively with each other about the children they share. California is a state leader in requiring communications in three languages (English, Spanish, and Chinese) to reach all students' families. Other states and districts have or are developing similar responsive policies.

Type three (volunteering) activities organize and prepare parents and other volunteers to assist teachers, administrators, and students in various ways. Volunteering also includes parents as an *audience* for student presentations and events at school. Although most parents cannot come to the school very often because of their own work and family schedules, others—particularly those from diverse cultural and language groups—may not come because they do not feel welcome or have not been properly invited. Parents who live far from the school and those whose own school experiences were negative and who feel insecure in school tend to stay away from the school building unless they are specifically invited to volunteer and participate. In a well-designed partnership program, all families—regardless of the language they speak at home—are asked to volunteer their time and talent to assist teachers, administrators, and students at home or at school, and to come to school as the audience for student events.

Schools may conduct surveys or make phone calls in the parents' language to obtain volunteers. A bilingual parent, volunteer, or school faculty or staff member may be needed to welcome and effectively instruct new volunteers on particular tasks. Some schools establish "parent rooms" or "parent centers" where families and others can conduct volunteer activities and communicate with other families and teachers in a setting other than the classroom (Johnson, 1993). Similarly, when parents come as an audience for a student performance or assembly, other parents or students with bilingual skills may be needed to welcome and assist those who are not familiar with or comfortable at school.

Type four (learning-at-home) activities involve families with their own children on homework and in discussion about courses or academic matters to boost students' progress, skills, and talents. The reviews of Latino and Chinese American families in this chapter indicate that parents from all backgrounds want to monitor and influence their children's education at home, but they need information about how to do this from year to year as students proceed through the grades. In type four activities, educators share information with parents using clear language about what the children are learning; the skills needed to pass the grade; how to encourage and assist their children in reading, math, science, or other skills at home; how to supervise homework; and other connections to curriculum and learning. Families need to know that the school wants them to support, monitor, encourage, and interact with their children about homework, and that they can do so in the language that is used at home, even as the students study or complete their homework in English.

Type five (decision-making) activities refer to parent representation on a school committee or council to bring parents' voices to the table on decisions about school policies; programs for students; and plans for school, family, and community partnerships. It is not enough to involve token representatives of bilingual or economically disadvantaged families in a limited decision-making role, or to include parents only on a committee about bilingual or Title I programs. Parent representatives must be trained and guided to make contact with all of the families they represent so that all parents can have input to school decisions that affect their children. For example, an elementary school in Connecticut that serves families who speak nearly a dozen languages developed "neighborhood representatives," local parent leaders who inform parents who live near them about school policies, activities, and events (Salinas & Jansorn, 2001). The representatives are parent leaders who serve as volunteers, communicate with others about school programs, and increase parent input to decision making.

Type six (collaborating-with-the-community) activities are conducted with various groups, organizations, and individuals to improve school programs and students' success. Also, some community agencies and advocacy groups include bilingual staff or volunteers to help families gain information about community programs and services that may help them and their children. Schools may arrange various type six activities to help children, families, and the schools to learn about community strengths and resources. For example, one New York elementary school conducted field trips to compile a neighborhood "portrait" that identified many resources in the neighborhood that educators and families had previously overlooked (Goode, 1990). Also, community cultural groups may serve as "brokers" to help families negotiate and communicate effectively with schools (Collingnon et al., 2001; Durán et al., 2001).

The framework of six types of involvement can be used to link school, family, and community partnerships to multicultural education. Plans for activities that include all types of involvement can be tailored, as has been described, to help strengthen multicultural education programs by understanding, respecting, and increasing the involvement of families with diverse cultural and linguistic backgrounds. This approach has been used to help schools, districts, and state departments of education develop effective programs of partnerships with highly diverse family and student populations (Sanders & Epstein, 2000).

The connections of school and family partnerships with multicultural education suggest a need to reword and reinterpret the historic *Lau* v. *Nichols* decision that altered education for children with limited English proficiency. In a modest proposal, Epstein (2001) suggested that the *Lau* decision should be reworded to reflect the results of research on school, family, and community partnerships:

Where the inability of (*parents of*) school children to speak and understand the English language *excludes the children* from effective participation in the education program, *the school district* must take affirmative steps *to open its instructional program to these* (*parents and their*) children. (2001, p. 34; words in parentheses and in italics added for emphasis)

The proposed revision recognizes that language barriers between parents and teachers—just like barriers between children and teachers—impede the equal participation of children in educational programs. If parents cannot understand their children's teachers, classroom programs, and communications from the school, then parents cannot effectively guide their children, monitor their work and progress, raise questions or concerns with teachers, or advocate for their children. Without clear and understandable communications, parents cannot effectively evaluate the quality of the schools or the education of their children.

Language barriers impede equal participation and eliminate some parents from school, family, and community partnerships. The *Lau* decision focuses on equal protection of children's educational opportunities, but it is clear that parents need equal protection too, to understand the school and classroom programs and effectively communicate with teachers, counselors, and administrators about their children.

Whether or not this reinterpretation is accepted, these comments about *Lau* v. *Nichols* raise some general questions about schools' responsibilities to communicate with all parents, including those whose English is limited.

Partnership in Education Programs. *These perspectives and directions linking school and family partnership and multicultural education should be added to preservice, advanced, and in-service education programs for teachers and administrators.* The nation is becoming more diverse as immigration continues to increase (Jamieson, Curry, & Martinez, 2001). It is estimated that by 2040 about 50% of all school-aged children in the United States will come from racial and ethnic minority families (Olson, 2000), making minorities the majority in public schools. Most students and their families will live in central cities, and most of them will be poor. Most of their teachers will be White.

These facts and projections make it necessary to ask, How will all teachers be prepared to work with diverse students and their families? How, when, and where will educators learn about the various cultures, values, and histories of the families of students they may teach during their careers, and the particular families in their present school? How will educators learn to communicate with all families so that parents will understand the schools and their children's programs each year?

This chapter's reviews of Latino and Chinese American families testify loudly to the need for educators to have better information about the similarities and differences of family backgrounds, cultures, histories, languages, strengths, values, and goals for their children (Goodwin, 2002; Nieto, 2000). Educators must understand the similarities of families' need for information and the differences in how information must be conveyed, and the connections of multicultural education with school and family partnerships, including the common, tailored, and unique practices for all six types of involvement that can be used to engage all families in their children's education. Because these goals have neither been set nor met in the past, most teachers and administrators are confused by and less successful with children and families who have different backgrounds (Epstein, 2001). If these goals are to be met, future teachers and administrators will need specific preservice and advanced education in the new forms of school, family, and community partnerships as a component of multicultural education.

CONCLUSION

This chapter's reviews of Latino and Chinese American families and discussion confirm that the family is an inevitable, continuous, and important influence in children's lives in school and out. All families—whatever their background, culture, or language—want and need assistance from schools in helping their children succeed each year. Studies confirm that families from all cultural groups influence their children's learning and development, from preschool through high school. Other studies show that school programs are important for determining whether and which families become productively involved in their children's education. The sections of this chapter converge in suggesting that two main connections must be made and strengthened. First, the field of multicultural education needs to be more explicit about the involvement of families and communities in students' learning and development. Second, the field of school, family, and community partnerships has to be more explicit about the contributions of multicultural education to improve and increase the involvement of all families. In U.S. schools in the new century, this combination of educational restructuring could help many more students of all cultural backgrounds succeed in school.

References

Acuña, R. (1988). *Occupied America*. New York: HarperCollins.

Adger, C. T. (2001). School-community-based organization partnerships for language minority students' school success. *Journal of Education for Students Placed at Risk (JESPAR), 6,* 7–25.

Allexsaht-Snider, M. (1992, April). *Bilingual parents' perspectives on home-school linkages.* Paper presented at the annual meeting of the American Educational Research Association, San Francisco.

Angel, R., & Tienda, M. (1982). Determinants of extended household structure: Cultural pattern or economic need? *American Journal of Sociology, 87,* 1360–1383.

Auerbach, E. (1989). Toward a social-contextual approach in family literacy. *Harvard Educational Review, 59*(2), 165–181.

Azmitia, M., & Cooper, C. R. (2001). Good or bad? Peer influences on Latino and European American adolescents' pathways through school. *Journal of Education for Students Placed at Risk (JESPAR), 6,* 45–71.

Baker, A.J.L., & Soden, L. M. (1997). *Parent involvement in children's education: A critical assessment of the knowledge base.* New York: National Council of Jewish Women's Center for the Child.

Baker, D. P., & Stevenson, D. L. (1986). Mothers' strategies for children's school achievement: Managing the transition to high school. *Sociology of Education, 59,* 156–166.

Banerjee, N. (2001, May 17). Census releases data on Asian subgroups. *Asian Week,* p. 8.

Banks, C.A.M. (1993). Restructuring schools for equity: What have we learned in two decades? *Phi Delta Kappan, 75*(1), 42–48.

Banks, J. A. (1993a). The canon debate, knowledge construction and multicultural education. *Educational Researcher, 22*(5), 4–14.

Banks, J. A. (1993b). Multicultural education: Historical development, dimensions and practice. In L. Darling-Hammond (Ed.), *Review of research in education* (pp. 3–50). Washington, DC: American Educational Research Association.

Becker, H. J., & Epstein, J. L. (1982). Parent involvement: A study of teacher practices. *Elementary School Journal, 83,* 85–102.

Benson, P. L. (1997). *All kids are our kids: What communities must do to raise caring and responsible children and adolescents.* San Francisco: Jossey-Bass.

Bird, H., & Canino, G. (1982). The Puerto Rican family: Cultural factors and family intervention strategies. *Journal of the American Academy of Psychoanalysis, 10,* 257–268.

Bonilla-Santiago, G. (1992). *Breaking ground and barriers: Hispanic women developing effective leadership.* San Diego, CA: Marin.

Borman, K. M., & Baber, M. Y. (1998). *Ethnic diversity in communities and schools: Recognizing and building on strengths.* Stamford, CT: Ablex.

Boyd, W. L., & Crowson, R. L. (1993). Coordinated services for children: Designing arks for storms and seas unknown. *American Journal of Education, 101,* 140–179.

Boykin, A. W. (1994). Harvesting culture and talent: African American children and educational reform. In R. Rossi (Ed.), *Educational reform and at risk students.* New York: Teachers College Press.

Bright, J., Hidalgo, N., Siu, S. F., & Swap, S. (1995, April). *Five-year review: Research on families, communities, schools, and children's Learning.* Paper presented at the annual meeting of the American Educational Research Association, San Francisco.

Bronfenbrenner, U. (1979). *The ecology of human development: Experiment by nature and design.* Cambridge, MA: Harvard University Press.

Bronfenbrenner, U. (1986). Ecology of the family as a context for human development: Research perspectives. *Developmental Psychology, 22,* 723–742.

Canino, I., Earley, B., & Rogler, L. (1989). *The Puerto Rican child in New York City: Stress and mental health* (Monograph no. 4). Bronx, NY: Hispanic Research Center.

Caplan, N., Choy, M. H., & Whitmore, J. K. (1992). Indochinese refugee families and academic achievement. *Scientific American, 263*(5), 36–42.

Catsambis, S., & Beveridge, A. A. (2001). Does neighborhood matter? Family, neighborhood, and school influences on eighth grade mathematics achievement. *Sociological Focus, 34,* 435–457.

Chan, C. K. (1991, September). Is American education suitable for your children? *Sing Tao Daily* (New York City, in Chinese), p. 13.

Chang, P. M. (1983). *Continuity and change: A profile of Chinese-Americans.* New York: Vantage Press.

Chao, R. K. (1994). Beyond parent control and authoritarian parenting style: Understanding Chinese parenting through the cultural notion of training. *Child Development, 65,* 1111–1119.

Chavkin, N. (Ed.). (1993). *Families and schools in a pluralistic society.* Albany: State University of New York Press.

Chavkin, N. F. (1996). Involving migrant families in their children's education: Challenges and opportunities for schools. In J. L. Flores (Ed.), *Children of la frontera: Binational efforts to serve Mexican migrant and immigrant students* (pp. 325–339). Charleston, WV: ERIC Clearinghouse on Rural Education and Small Schools.

Chavkin, N. F. (2001). Recommendations for research on the effectiveness of school, family, and community partnerships. In S. Redding & L. G. Thomas (Eds.), *The community of the school* (pp. 83–96). Lincoln, IL: Academic Development Institute.

Chen, C., & Uttal, D. H. (1988). Cultural values, parents' beliefs, and children's achievement in the United States and China. *Human Development, 31,* 351–358.

Cheng, L. L. (1999). Sociocultural adjustment of Chinese-American students. In C. C. Clark & M. M.-Y. Chi (Eds.), *Asian-American education: Prospects and challenges* (pp. 1–17). Westport, CT: Bergin & Garvey.

Clark, R. M. (1983). *Family life and school achievement: Why poor Black children succeed or fail.* Chicago: University of Chicago Press.

Coleman, J. S. (1988). Social capital in the creation of human capital. *American Journal of Sociology, 94,* 95–120.

Collingnon, F., Men, M., & Tan, S. (2001). Finding ways in: Community-based perspectives on Southeast Asian family involvement with schools in a New England state. *Journal of Education for Students Placed at Risk (JESPAR), 6,* 27–44.

Comer, J. P. (1980). *School power: Implications of an intervention project.* New York: Free Press.

Comer, J. (1986). Parent participation in schools. *Phi Delta Kappan, 67,* 442–446.

Comer, J. P. (1988). Educating poor minority children. *Scientific American, 259*(5), 42–48.

Commins, N. (1992). Parents and public schools. *Equity and Choice, 8*(2), 40–45.

Dauber, S. L., & Epstein, J. L. (1993). Parents' attitudes and practices of involvement in inner-city elementary and middle schools. In N. Chavkin (Ed.), *Families and schools in a pluralistic society* (pp. 53–71). Albany: State University of New York Press.

Davies, D. (1990). Shall we wait for revolution? A few lessons from the Schools Reaching Out Project. *Equity and Choice, 6*(3), 68–73.

Davies, D. (1991). Schools reaching out: Family, school and community partnerships for students' success. *Phi Delta Kappan, 72*(3), 376–382.

Davies, D. (1993). Benefits and barriers to parental involvement: From Portugal to Boston to Liverpool. In N. Chavkin (Ed.), *Families and schools in a pluralistic society* (pp. 205–216). Albany: State University of New York Press.

Delgado, M. (1995, April). *Five-year review: Research on families, communities, schools, and children's learning.* Paper presented at the annual meeting of the American Educational Research Association, San Francisco.

Delgado, M., & Humm-Delgado, D. (1982). Natural support systems: Source of strength in Hispanic communities. *Social Work, 27,* 81–90.

Delgado-Gaitan, C. (1990). *Literacy for empowerment: The role of parents in children's education.* New York: Falmer Press.

Delgado-Gaitan, C., & Trueba, H. (1991). *Crossing cultural borders.* New York: Falmer Press.

Díaz-Soto, L. (1990). *Families as learning environments: Reflections on critical factors affecting differential achievement.* (ERIC Document Reproduction Service no. ED 315 498)

A diversity plan for S.F. schools. (2001, January 5). *Asian Week.*

Dornbusch, S. M., & Ritter, P. L. (1988). Parents of high school students: A neglected resource. *Educational Horizons, 66,* 75–77.

Dornbusch, S. M., & Wood, K. D. (1989). Family processes and educational achievement. In W. Weston (Ed.), *Education and the American family: A research synthesis* (pp. 66–95). New York: New York University Press.

Dryfoos, J. (1994). *Full-service schools*. San Francisco: Jossey-Bass.

Dryfoos, J. (1998). *Safe passage: Making it through adolescence in a risky society*. New York: Oxford University Press.

Durán, R., Durán, J., Perry-Romero, D., & Sanchez, E. (2001). Latino immigrant parents and children learning and publishing together in an after-school setting. *Journal of Education for Students Placed at Risk (JESPAR), 6*, 95–113.

Epstein, J. L. (1986). Parents' reactions to teacher practices of parent involvement. *Elementary School Journal, 86*, 277–294.

Epstein, J. L. (1987). Toward a theory of family-school connections: Teacher practices and parent involvement. In K. Hurrelman, F. Kaufman, & F. Losel (Eds.), *Social intervention: Potential and constraints* (pp. 121–136). New York: De Gruyter.

Epstein, J. L. (1990). Single parents and the schools: Effects of marital status on parent and teacher interactions. In M. Hallinan (Ed.), *Change in societal institutions* (pp. 91–121). New York: Plenum.

Epstein, J. L. (1991). Effects on student achievement of teacher practices of parent involvement. In S. Silvern (Ed.), *Literacy through family, community, and school interaction* (pp. 261–276). Greenwich, CT: JAI Press.

Epstein, J. L. (1992). School and family partnerships. In M. Alkin (Ed.), *Encyclopedia of educational research* (6th ed., pp. 1139–1151). New York: Macmillan.

Epstein, J. L. (1994). Theory to practice: School and family partnerships lead to school improvement and student success. In C. Fagnano & B. Werber (Eds.), *School, family, and community interaction: A view from the firing lines* (pp. 39–52). Boulder, CO: Westview.

Epstein, J. L. (1995). School/family/community partnerships: Caring for the children we share. *Phi Delta Kappan, 76*, 701–712.

Epstein, J. L. (2001). *School, family, and community partnerships: Preparing educators and improving schools*. Boulder, CO: Westview Press.

Epstein, J. L., & Dauber, S. L. (1991). School programs and teacher practices of parent involvement in inner-city elementary and middle schools. *Elementary School Journal, 91*(3), 289–303.

Epstein, J. L., Herrick, S. C., & Coates, L. (1996). Effects of summer home learning packets on student achievement in language arts in the middle grades. *School Effectiveness and School Improvement, 7*, 93–120.

Epstein, J. L., & Sanders, M. G. (2000). School, family, and community connections: New directions for social research. In M. Hallinan (Ed.), *Handbook of sociology of education* (pp. 285–306). New York: Plenum.

Epstein, J. L., Sanders, M. G., Simon, B. S., Salinas, K. C., Jansorn, N. R., & Van Voorhis, F. L. (2002). *School, family, and community partnerships: Your handbook for action*. Thousand Oaks, CA: Corwin Press.

Epstein, J. L., & Sheldon, S. B. (2002). Present and accounted for: Improving student attendance through family and community involvement. *Journal of Education Research, 95*(5), 308–318

Erickson, F. (1987). Transformation and school success: The politics and culture of educational achievement. *Anthropology & Education Quarterly, 18*(4), 335–356.

First, J. M., & Carrerra, J. W. (1988). *New voices: Immigrant students in U.S. public schools*. Boston: National Coalition of Advocates for Students.

Fong, R., & Wu, D. Y. (1996). Socialization issues for Chinese American children and families. *Social Work in Education, 8*(2), 71–83.

García, E. E. (1995). Educating Mexican American students: Past treatment and recent developments in theory, research policy and practice. In J. A. Banks & C.A.M. Banks (Eds.), *Handbook of research on multicultural education* (pp. 372–387). New York: Macmillan.

Garcia, H., & Donato, R. (1991, September). Language minority parental involvement within middle class schooling boundaries. *Community Education Journal, 22–23*.

Gonzalez, N., Moll, L., Floyd-Tenery, M., Rivera, A., Rendon P., Gonzalez, R., et al. (1995). Funds of knowledge for teaching in Latino households. *Urban Education, 29*, 444–471.

Goode, D. A. (1990). The community portrait process: School community collaboration. *Equity and Choice, 6*(3), 32–37.

Goodwin, A. L. (2002). Teacher preparation and the education of immigrant children. *Education and Urban Society, 34*, 156–172.

Gutman, L. M., & McLoyd, V. C. (2000). Parents' management of their children's education within the home, at school, and in the community: An examination of African-American families living in poverty. *Urban Review, 32*, 1–24.

Harry, B. (1992a). Developing cultural self-awareness: The first steps in values clarification for early interventionists. *Topics in Early Childhood Special Education, 12*(3), 333–350.

Harry, B. (1992b). Making sense of disability: Low-income Puerto Rican parents' theories of the problem. *Exceptional Children, 59*(1), 27–40.

Heath, S. N., & McLaughlin, M. W. (1987). A child resource policy: Moving beyond dependence on school and family. *Phi Delta Kappan, 68*, 576–580.

Henderson, R. W. (1997). Educational and occupational aspirations and expectations among parents of middle school students of Mexican descent: Family resources for academic development and mathematics learning. In R. D. Taylor & M. C. Wang (Eds.), *Social and emotional adjustment and family relationships in ethnic minority families* (pp. 99–131). Mahwah, NJ: Erlbaum.

Hess, R. D., Chang, C.-M., & McDevitt, T. M. (1987). Cultural variations in family beliefs about children's performance in mathematics: Comparisons among Peoples' Republic of China, Chinese American, and Caucasian-American families. *Journal of Educational Psychology, 79*(2), 179–188.

Hidalgo, N. M. (1994). Profile of a Puerto Rican family's support for school achievement. *Equity and Choice, 10*(2), 14–22.

Hidalgo, N. M. (2000). *Latina/o families epistemology*. Paper presented at Latinos in the 21st Century: Mapping the Research Agenda conference, Harvard University. Cambridge, MA.

Hidalgo, N. M., Bright, J., Siu, S., Swap, S., & Epstein, J. (1995). Research on families, schools, and communities: A multicultural perspective. In J. Banks and C.A.M. Banks (Eds.), *Handbook of research on multicultural education* (1st ed., pp. 498–524). New York: Macmillan.

Hidalgo, N. M., & Nevárez-La Torre, A. (1997). Latino communities: Resources for educational change. *Education and Urban Society, 30* [entire issue].

Ho, D.Y.F. (1986). Chinese patterns of socialization: A critical review. In M. H. Bond (Ed.), *The psychology of the Chinese people* (pp. 1–36). Hong Kong: Oxford University Press.

Ho, K., & Fong, M. (1990). A cool response to school activities: A hiding of dissatisfaction deep in the heart. *Herald* [New York City, special issue on Chinese American parent involvement, in Chinese], *3*(9), 1.

Hoover-Dempsey, K. V., Battiato, A. C., Walker, J. M., Reed, R. P., DeJong, J. M., & Jones, K. P. (2001). Parental involvement in homework. *Educational Psychologist, 36,* 195–210.

Honig, M. I., Kahne, J., & McLaughlin, M. W. (2001). School-community connections: Strengthening opportunity to learn and opportunity to teach. In V. Richardson (Ed.), *Handbook of research on teaching* (4th ed.). Washington, DC: American Educational Research Association.

Hu, A. (1989). Asian-Americans: Model minority or double minority? *Amerasia Journal, 15,* 243–257.

Hurtado, A. (1995). Variations, combinations, and evolutions: Latino families in the United States. In R. Zambrana (Ed.), *Understanding Latino families* (pp. 40–61). Thousand Oaks, CA: Sage.

Inger, M. (1992, August). Increasing the school involvement of Hispanic parents. (ERIC Clearinghouse on Urban Education, pp. 1–5). New York: Teachers College.

Jamieson, A., Curry, A., & Martinez, G. (2001). School enrollment in the United States: Social and economic characteristics of students. *Current Population Reports P20–533.* Washington, DC: U.S. Census Bureau, Government Printing Office.

Johnson, V. R. (1993). *Parent/family centers in schools: Expanding outreach and promoting collaboration* (Center Report 200). Baltimore, MD: Center on Families, Communities, Schools, and Children's Learning.

Jones, T. G., & Velez, W. (1997, March). *Effects of Latino parental involvement on academic achievement.* Paper presented at the annual meeting of the American Educational Research Association, Chicago.

Jordan, C., Orozco, E., & Averett, A. (2002). *Emerging issues in school, family, & community connections.* Austin, TX: Southwest Educational Development Laboratory.

Kim, U., & Chun, M.B.J. (1992, April). *Educational "success" of Asian Americans: An indigenous perspective.* Paper presented at the annual meeting of the American Educational Research Association, San Francisco.

Knapp, M. S. (1995). How shall we study comprehensive, collaborative services for children and families? *Educational Researcher, 24*(4), 5–16.

Kwong, P. (1987). *The new Chinatown.* New York: Hill & Wang.

Lau, G.M.H. (1988). *Chinese American early childhood socialization in communication.* Unpublished doctoral dissertation, Stanford University.

Lauria, A. (1972). Respeto, relajo and interpersonal relations in Puerto Rico. In F. Cordasco & E. Buccioni (Eds.), *The Puerto Rican community and its children on the mainland* (pp. 36–48). Metuchen, NJ: Scarecrow Press.

Lee, F. Y. (1995). Asian parents as partners. *Young Children, 5*(3), 4–9.

Lee, J.F.J. (1991). *Asian American experiences in the United States.* Jefferson, NC: MacFarland.

Lee, P. S. (1983). *Intraethnic diversity: An exploratory study of ethnic identity of Chinese-American adolescents.* Unpublished doctoral dissertation, Oregon State University, Corvallis.

Lee, S. (1994). *Family-school connections and students' education: Continuity and change of family involvement from the middle grades to high school.* Doctoral dissertation, Department of Sociology, Johns Hopkins University.

Lee, S. J. (2001). More than "model minorities" or "delinquents": A look at Hmong American high school students. *Harvard Educational Review, 71,* 505–528.

Leichter, H. J. (1974). *The family as educator.* New York: Teachers College Press.

Lin, C.-Y. C. (1988). *A comparison of childrearing practices among Chinese, Chinese-American, and non-Asian American parents.* Unpublished doctoral dissertation, Virginia Polytechnic Institute and State University, Blacksburg.

Litwak, E., & Meyer, H. J. (1974). *School, family, and neighborhood: The theory and practice of school-community relations.* New York: Columbia University Press.

Lopez, G. R., Scribner, J. D., & Mahitivanichcha, K. (2001). Redefining parental involvement: Lessons from high-performing migrant-impacted schools. *American Educational Research Journal, 38,* 253–288.

Lucas, T., Henze, R., & Donato, R. (1990). Promoting the success of Latino language-minority students: An exploratory study of six high schools. *Harvard Educational Review, 60,* 315–340.

Marttila, T., & Kiley, L. (1995). *A study of attitudes among the parents of primary-school children.* Washington, DC: Institute for Educational Leadership.

McAdoo, H. (1981). *Black families.* Newbury Park, CA: Sage.

McCunn, R. L. (1988). Chinese American portraits: Personal histories: 1828–1988. San Francisco: Chronicle Books.

Ming Sum. (1990). Why does the school emphasize parent participation? *Herald* [New York City, special issue on Chinese-American parent involvement, in Chinese], *3*(9), 12.

Mizio, E. (1974). Impact of external systems on the Puerto Rican family. *Social Casework, 55*(2), 76–85.

Moe, B. (1994). *Home-school communication [ninth grade].* Master's thesis, Saint Xavier University.

Moll, L. C., Amanti, C., Neff, D., & Gonzalez, N. (1992). Funds of knowledge for teaching: Using a qualitative approach to connect homes and classrooms. *Theory into Practice, 31,* 132–141.

Moll, L. C., & Greenberg, J. B. (1990). Creating zones of possibilities: Combining social contexts for instruction. In L. C. Moll (Ed.), *Vygotsky and education* (pp. 319–348). Cambridge, England: Cambridge University Press.

National Network of Partnership Schools. (2001). *Working together for student success* (Video). Baltimore, MD: Johns Hopkins University, Center on School, Family, and Community Partnerships.

Návarez-La Torre, A. (1997). Influencing Latino education: Church-based community programs. *Education and Urban Society, 30*(1), 58–74.

New York City Board of Education. (1980). *Comprehensive high school bilingual program, 1979–80, final evaluation report.* Brooklyn, NY: New York City Board of Education, Office of Educational Evaluation. (ERIC Document Reproduction Service, no. ED 206 749.)

New York City Board of Education. (1990). *Chinese opportunities in career education (Project Choice), 1989–90, final evaluation report.* Brooklyn, NY: New York City Board of Education, Office of Research, Evaluation, and Assessment. (ERIC Document Reproduction Service no. ED 331 926)

Nicolau, S., & Ramos, C. (1990). *Together is better: Building strong relationships between schools and Hispanic parents.* Washington, DC: Hispanic Policy Development Project.

Nieto, S. (2000). *Affirming diversity* (3rd ed.). New York: Longman.

Noguera, P. A. (2001). Racial politics and the elusive quest for excellence and equity in education. *Education and Urban Society, 34,* 18–41.

Ogbu, J. (1983). Minority status and schooling in plural societies. *Comparative Education Review, 27*(2), 168–190.

Ogbu, J. U. (1990). Overcoming racial barriers to equal access. In J. Goodlad (Ed.), *Access to knowledge: An agenda for our nation's schools* (pp. 59–89). Princeton, NJ: College Entrance Examination Board.

Olson, L. (2000, September 27). Children of change: Minority groups to emerge as a majority in U. S. schools. *Education Week, 31,* 34–35.

Pang, V. O. (1995). Asian Pacific American students: A diverse and complex population. In J. A. Banks & C.A.M. Banks (Eds.), *Handbook of research on multicultural education* (1st ed., pp. 412–424). New York: Macmillan.

Pardo, M. (1990). Mexican American women grassroots community activists: "Mothers of East Los Angeles." *Frontiers, 11*(1), 1–7.

Patel, N., & Kaplan, J. (1994). Literacy programs for immigrant families. *New Voices, 4*(1), 6.

Perry, T. (1993). *Toward a theory of African American school achievement* (Center Report 16). Baltimore, MD: Center on Families, Communities, Schools and Children's Learning.

Portes, A., & Rumbaut, R. G. (2001). *Legacies: The story of the immigrant second generation.* Berkeley: University of California Press.

Rivera, K. (1999). Popular research and social transformation: A community-based approach to critical pedagogy. *TESOL Quarterly, 33*(3), 485–500.

Rivera, R. (1993). Barriers to Latino parental involvement in the Boston public schools. In R. Rivera & S. Nieto (Eds.), *The education of Latino students in Massachusetts: Issues, research, and policy implications* (pp. 77–87). Boston: Mauricio Gastón Institute for Latino Community Development and Public Policy.

Robledo Montecel, M. (1993). *Hispanic families as valued partners: An educator's guide.* San Antonio, TX: Intercultural Development Research Association.

Rong, X. L., & Brown, F. (2002). Socialization, culture, and identities of black immigrant children: What educators need to know and do. *Education and Urban Society, 34,* 247–273.

Rubio, O. (1995). 'Yo soy voluntaria': Volunteering in a dual-language school. *Urban Education, 29*(4), 396–409.

Sabogal, F., Marín, G. Otero-Sabogal, R., Marín, B.V.O., & Pérez-Stable, E. J. (1987). Hispanic familism and acculturation: What changes and what doesn't? *Hispanic Journal of Behavioral Sciences, 9,* 397–412.

Salgado, R. (1985). The Puerto Rican family. In L. Nuñez (Ed.), *Puerto Ricans in the mid '80s: An American challenge* (pp. 29–44). Alexandria, VA: National Puerto Rican Coalition.

Salinas, K. C., & Jansorn, N. R. (2001). Promising partnership practices 2001. Baltimore, MD: Johns Hopkins University, Center on School, Family, and Community Partnerships.

Sánchez-Ayéndez, M. (1988). The Puerto Rican American family. In C. Mindel, R. Habenstein, & R. Wright (Eds.), *Ethnic families in America* (pp. 173–195). New York: Elsevier.

Sanders, M. G. (1998). The effects of school, family and community support on the academic achievement of African-American adolescents. *Urban Education, 33,* 385–409.

Sanders, M. G. (1999). School membership in the National Network of Partnership Schools: Progress, challenges, and next steps. *Journal of Educational Research, 92,* 220–230.

Sanders, M. G. (2001). The role of "community" in comprehensive school, family, and community partnership programs. *Elementary School Journal, 102,* 19–34.

Sanders, M. G., & Epstein, J. L. (2000). The National Network of Partnership Schools: How research influences educational practice. *Journal of Education for Students Placed at Risk (JESPAR), 5,* 61–76.

Sanders, M. G., & Harvey, A. (2000, April). *Developing comprehensive programs of school, family, and community partnerships: The community perspective.* Paper presented at the annual meeting of the American Educational Research Association, New Orleans, LA.

Santiestevan, H., & Santiestevan, S. (Eds.). (1984). *The Hispanic Almanac.* Washington, DC: Hispanic Policy Development Project.

Schneider, B., & Lee, Y. (1990). A model for academic success: The school and home environment of East Asian students. *Anthropology and Education Quarterly, 21*(4), 358–377.

Scott-Jones, D. (1986). The family. In J. Hannaway & M. E. Lockheed (Eds.), *The contributions of the social sciences to educational policy and to practice, 1965–1985* (pp. 11–31). Berkeley, CA: McCutchan.

Scott-Jones, D. (1987). Mother-as-teacher in the families of high- and low-achieving low-income Black first graders. *Journal of Negro Education, 56,* 21–34.

Seeley, D. S. (1981). *Education through partnership: Mediating structures and education.* Cambridge, MA: Ballinger.

Sheldon, S. B., & Epstein, J. L. (2001). *Focus on math achievement: Effects of family and community involvement.* Baltimore, MD: Johns Hopkins University, Center for Research on the Education of Students Placed at Risk (CRESPAR).

Shoho, A. R. (1992, April). *An historical comparison of parental involvement in three generations of Japanese Americans (isseis, niseis, sanseis) in the education of their children.* Paper presented at the annual meeting of the American Educational Research Association, San Francisco.

Sim, S. C. (1992). Social service needs of Chinese immigrant high school students in New York City. *Asian American Policy Review, 3,* 35–54.

Simon, B. S. (2000). *Predictors of high school and family partnership and the influence of partnerships on student success.* Unpublished dissertation, Department of Sociology, Johns Hopkins University.

Simon, B. S. (2001). Family involvement in high school: Predictors and effects. *NASSP Bulletin, 85,* 8–19.

Simon, B. S., & Epstein, J. L. (2001). School, family, and community partnerships: Linking theory and practice. In D. Hiatt-Michaels (Ed.), *Promising practices for family involvement in schools* (pp. 1–24). Greenwich, CT: Information Age.

Siu, S.-F. (1988, November). *Reaching out to new American families.* Paper presented at the Annual Conference of National Association for the Education of Young Children, Anaheim, CA.

Siu, S.-F. (1992a). How do family and community characteristics affect children's educational achievement? The Chinese American experience. *Equity and Choice, 8*(2), 46–49.

Siu, S.-F. (1992b). *Toward an understanding of Chinese-American educational achievement: A literature review* (Center Report 2). Baltimore, MD: Center on Families, Communities, Schools and Children's Learning.

Siu, S.-F. (1994a, April). *The meaning of home support: Perspective of teachers with Chinese American children in their classrooms.* Paper presented in Interactive Symposium, Home-School Connections with Parents from Diverse Backgrounds in Kindergarten and First Grade, at the annual meeting of the American Educational Research Association, New Orleans, LA.

Siu, S.-F. (1994b). Taking no chances: A profile of a Chinese-American family's support for school success. *Equity and Choice, 10*(2), 23–32.

Siu, S.-F. (1996). *Questions and answers: What research says about Chinese American children.* Baltimore, MD: Center on Families, Communities, Schools and Children's Learning.

Siu, S.-F. (2001). An ethnographic study of Chinese American family involvement in young children's education. In C. C. Park, A. L. Goodwin, & S. J. Lee (Eds.), *Research on the education of Asian and Pacific Americans* (pp. 105–128). Greenwich, CT: Information Age.

Siu, S.-F. (2002). Toward building home-school partnerships: The case of Chinese American families and public schools. In E. H. Tamura, V. Chattergy, & R. Endo (Eds.), *Asian and Pacific Islander American education: Social, cultural, and historical contexts* (pp. 59–84). South El Monte, CA: Pacific Asia Press.

Siu, S.-F., & Feldman, J. A. (1995). *Success in school: The journey of two Chinese American families.* (Center Report 31). Baltimore, MD: Center on Families, Communities, Schools and Children's Learning.

Siu, S.-F., & Feldman, J. A. (1996). *Patterns of Chinese American family involvement in young children's education: Final report* (Center Report 36). Baltimore, MD: Center on Families, Communities, Schools and Children's Learning.

Slaughter-DeFoe, D. T., Nakagawa, K., Takanishi, R., & Johnson, D. J. (1990). Toward cultural/ecological perspectives on schooling and achievement in African- and Asian-American children. *Child Development, 61,* 363–383.

Slavin, R. E. (1995). *Cooperative learning: Theory, research, and practice* (2nd ed.) Boston: Allyn & Bacon.

Sue, D. W. (1997). Counseling strategies for Chinese Americans. In C. C. Lee (Ed.), *Multicultural issues in counseling: New approaches to diversity* (2nd ed., pp. 173–187). Alexandria, VA: American Counseling Association.

Sue, S., & Okazaki, S. (1990). Asian-American educational achievement: A phenomenon in search of an explanation. *American Psychologist, 45*(8), 913–920.

Sue, S., & Sue, D. W. (1971). Chinese American personality and mental health. *Amerasia Journal, 1*(2), 36–49.

Sung, B. L. (1987). *The adjustment experience of Chinese immigrant children in New York City.* New York: Center for Migration Studies.

Suzuki, B. H. (1977). Education and the socialization of Asian Americans: A revisionist analysis of the "model minority" thesis. *Amerasia Journal, 4*(2), 23–51.

Swap, S. M. (1993). *Developing home-school partnerships: From concepts to practice.* New York: Teachers College Press.

Te, B., Cordova, J. M., Walker-Moffat, W., & First, J. (1997). *Unfamiliar partners: Asian parents and U.S. public schools: A report from the National Coalition of Advocates for Students.* Boston: National Coalition of Advocates for Students.

Torres, A., & Velázquez, J. E. (Eds.). (1998). *The Puerto Rican Movement.* Philadelphia: Temple University Press.

Torres-Guzmán, M. E. (1990). Recasting frames: Latino parent involvement. In C. Faltis & M. McGroary (Eds.), *In the interest of language: Contexts for learning and using language* (pp. 529–552). The Hague, Netherlands: Mouton.

U.S. Census Bureau. (2000). *Table DP-1. Profile of general demographic characteristics for the United States: 2000.* Available: www.census.gov/Press-Release/www//tables/dp_us_2000.pdf

U.S. Census Bureau. (2001). *Hispanic population in the United States. Current population reports, population characteristics* (pp. 2–8). Washington, DC: Government Printing Office.

Useem, E. L. (1992). Middle schools and math groups: Parents' involvement in children's placement. *Sociology of Education, 65,* 263–279.

Valdés, G. (1996). *Con respeto: Bridging the distance between culturally diverse families and schools: An ethnographic portrait.* New York: Teachers College Press.

Van Voorhis, F. L. (2000). *The effects of interactive (TIPS) and non-interactive homework assignments on science achievement and family involvement of middle grade students.* Unpublished doctoral dissertation, University of Florida, Gainesville.

Van Voorhis, F. L. (2001). Interactive science homework: An experiment in home and school connections. *NASSP Bulletin, 85*(627), 20–32.

Vázquez-Nutall, E., & Romero-García, I. (1989). From home to school: Puerto Rican girls learn to be students in the United States. In C. García Coll & M. de Lourdes Mattei (Eds.), *The psychosocial development of Puerto Rican women* (pp. 60–83). New York: Praeger.

Violand-Sanchez, E., Sutton, C. P., & Ware, H. W. (1991). *Fostering home-school cooperation: Involving language minority families as partners in education.* Washington, DC: National Clearinghouse for Bilingual Education.

Volk, D. (1992, April). *A case study of parental involvement in the homes of three Puerto Rican kindergartners.* Paper presented at the annual meeting of the American Educational Research Association, San Francisco.

Waller, W. (1932). *The sociology of teaching.* New York: Russell and Russell.

Wang, L. L.-C. (1976). *Lau v. Nichols:* History of a struggle for equal and quality education. In E. Gee (Ed.), *Counterpoint: Perspectives on Asian America* (pp. 240–263). Los Angeles: UCLA, Asian American Studies Center.

Wang, X. (Ed.). (1996). *A view from within: A case study of Chinese heritage community language schools in the United States.* Washington, DC: National Foreign Language Center.

Weber, M. (1947). *The theory of social and economic organization.* New York: Oxford University Press.

Weiser Ramírez, E. (1990). *Hispanic community organizations: Partners in parental involvement.* Washington, DC: ASPIRA Association.

West, J., Denton, K., & Reaney, L. (2000). *The Kindergarten Year (NCES–023) (ECLS-K).* U.S. Department of Education, NCES. Washington, DC: U.S. Government Printing Office.

Winfield, L. F. (Ed.). (1991). Resilience, schooling and development in African-American youth [Special issue]. *Education and Urban Society, 24*(1).

Wong, L. C. (1990). *An ethnographic study of literacy behaviors in Chinese families in an urban school community.* Unpublished doctoral dissertation, University of Michigan, Ann Arbor.

Wong, L. Y.-F. (1992). *Education of Chinese children in Britain and the USA.* Clevedon, England: Multilingual Matters.

Wong, M. (1995). Chinese Americans. In P. G. Min (Ed.), *Asian Americans: Contemporary trends and issues* (pp. 58–94). Newbury Park, CA: Sage.

Wong, S. C., & Lopez, M. (2000). English language learners of Chinese background. In S. L. McKay & S. C. Wong (Eds.), *New immigrants in the United States* (pp. 263–305). New York: Cambridge University Press.

Wu, S.-J. (2001). Parenting in Chinese American families. In N. B. Webb (Ed.), *Culturally diverse parent-child and family relationships* (pp. 235–260). New York: Columbia University.

Yao, E. L. (1985). A comparison of family characteristics of Asian-American and Anglo-American high achievers. *International Journal of Comparative Sociology, 26*(3–4), 198–207.

Yao, E. L. (1988). Working effectively with Asian immigrant parents. *Phi Delta Kappan, 70*(3), 223–225.

Young, J., Scorza, M. H., & Sica, M. (1984, April). *Evaluation report of Newtown High School project capable, 1982–83.* Brooklyn: New York City Board of Education, Office of Educational Evaluation. (ERIC Document Reproduction Service no. ED 250 432.)

Zentella, A. C. (1997). *Growing up bilingual.* Malden, MA: Blackwell.

31

SOCIAL CLASS AND SCHOOLING

Michael S. Knapp
University of Washington, Seattle

Sara Woolverton
Seattle Public Schools, Washington

Teachers do it with class.

—Popular bumper sticker

The familiar slogan, a variant on a decades-old risqué theme, could be edited slightly to express, or at least hint at, the theme of this chapter: "Teachers do it with social class." But the amended phrasing would never make it in contemporary American society, either as humor or as a statement about the role of educators in society. We prefer not to see social class permeating institutions so long associated with social mobility. If anything, Americans would rather cling to the notion of school as the great social equalizer, offering a set of experiences that permit individuals to transcend the boundaries of social class. But our ideologies are not our realities, and no amount of wishing will eliminate the pervasiveness of social-class dynamics in the lives of teachers and learners. Educators and the educated alike need clarity and insight regarding the presence, interplay, and power of social class in their encounters with one another.

The purpose of this chapter is to illuminate these social-class dynamics within educational institutions. We address this topic with the system of schooling from preschool through high school primarily in mind, but with attention to postsecondary institutions as well. To shed light on the roles played by social class in these institutions, we draw together diverse threads of theory and scholarship over the last half century. In essence, we are answering the question, What is known—and thought— about the relationship of social class and schooling by scholars who have studied that relationship? Our review is thus both a conceptual and an empirical effort to synthesize concepts, frameworks, and evidence that shed light on the question at hand. As will quickly become evident, our review does not assume a unified body of

knowledge about the topic, but rather a set of claims and conceptions that are often at odds with one another. Somewhere in the diversity of views lies the great, gray truth, as best we know it to date, and the ground for future discoveries.

Although we have attempted to approach the topic in a comprehensive fashion, we make no claim to exhaustiveness. Rather than think of the review task as a meta-analyst might, we have conceived of our role as builders of useful conceptual frameworks. In this regard, we have leaned heavily on qualitative literature, as we find it more concerned with the meanings and fine detail of connections between schooling and social class. In so doing, we have not done justice to a substantial body of quantitative work that has dominated particular aspects of the territory we are exploring—for example, research on status attainment, compositional effects, or tracking (see Gamoran, 1992; Lucas, 1999).

To accomplish our goal of framework building, we have drawn on various bodies of work. Most are in some respect, if not in name, sociological—the social science field most directly and continuously concerned with social class—though we have also borrowed heavily from work in anthropology and psychology or social psychology. More specifically, we have concentrated on classical and modern branches of the sociology of education drawing on writing in the functionalist tradition, neo-Marxist and non-Marxist conflict theory, interpretivist tradition, and various critical perspectives (Apple, 1978; LeCompte & Dworkin, 1988). We have focused on seminal work, both conceptual and empirical, and recent syntheses of work in the field. In addition, we have relied on educational research aimed at understanding inequality and educational opportunity, disadvantagement, the nature of curriculum, the phenomenon of learner differences, the profession of teaching, and the nature of the teacher's work. (Our watershed includes other tributaries, among them a review of key journals such as *Sociology of Education* and a search of the ERIC database for work that bears descriptors related to both social class and schooling.)

We embark on this review in full recognition of the fact that it is hard—perhaps impossible, in some respects—to disentangle social class from other categorical social descriptors such as race, ethnicity, and gender; from culture (viewed as the set of shared meanings held by social groups); and from ideology (the system of values and beliefs to which societies subscribe and that serve as a justification for actions). The interactions between race and class, for example, are an ongoing topic of research (see Banks, 1993) and the subject of various discussions elsewhere in this *Handbook*. A growing number of researchers, primarily in the critical theory tradition, are beginning to attend to gender as a social-class issue (for example, Weiler, 1988). The interactions between culture and class, as they bear on education, are the topic of various lines of research, for example, in recent work on the working class (Weis, 1990), classic analysis of cultural capital (Bourdieu & Passeron, 1977), and older work on the "culture of poverty" (Lewis, 1966). The relationship between ideology and class permeates (and often clouds) the work of scholars, as it does the vision of many individuals in society. Nonetheless, we will proceed on the assumption that conceptual distinctions are at least possible and probably helpful, if never entirely clear. Empirical distinctions are less easily made but instructive, and so we bring them into discussion wherever relevant.

Given that it is entwined with other social conditions, why does social class as a force in educational institutions deserve the scrutiny we will give it? We believe the scrutiny is essential for a number of reasons. First, decades of sociological work and the intuitions of thoughtful people suggest that social class is fundamental to understanding the workings and consequences of educational institutions. Second, social class is hidden, in schooling and elsewhere. American mythologies obscure the fact of social class, hide its potential or actual influence on other aspects of educational or social life, and limit our capacity to see and understand social conflicts related to class. Third, the continued omission of social class from discussions among educators and in teacher preparation programs risks continuation of class-based differential teaching, to the detriment of children, school systems, and ultimately our nation. Fourth, social class is central to social inequality. Whether or not one accepts inequalities as inevitable or necessary (and most Americans would not), they are deeply rooted in the social order. To imagine greater equality, and the role that education might play in bringing that about, one must come to terms with the meanings and dynamics of social class. The matter takes on some urgency at the present time, when social inequalities in America are apparently increasing and, along with them, the shape of the social-class structure is changing.

Finally, education is implicated in both the conception and the measurement of social class. Put another way, it is hard to talk about the former without the latter, whether one is simply referring to indices of social-class position (which often use educational level as one component), describing the process by which individuals attain a position within the social order (which almost always involves their path through a succession of educational institutions), or identifying the educational institutions' overt or covert roles in guiding individual development (which typically imply "opportunities" for "advancement" and "preparation" for a place in the occupational structure).

We have organized our review in five parts that reflect a thematic rather than a chronological review of work. First, to clarify key terms and paradigms within which ideas are located, we discuss the concept of social class and alternative perspectives adopted by scholars in considering the relationships between society and schools. We then examine the enduring correlation between measures of social class and most measures of educational outcomes.

The succeeding three sections attempt to "unpack" the correlation by considering, in turn, how social class is related to (a) the community context of schools, the social organization of the student population, and the teaching force; (b) the learner; and (c) the nature of curriculum and instruction. We conclude the chapter with a review of the principal explanations for the pattern of differentiated schooling that emerges in these discussions, followed by an examination of promising directions for new research.

CONCEPTIONS OF SOCIAL CLASS AND THE PURPOSES OF SCHOOLING

To understand the relationship of social class and schooling, one must first recognize that reasonable scholars have differing views of social class, the purposes of schooling, and the relationship between the two. We review the range of conceptions for each and sketch a working definition that enables us to think productively about the topic at hand.

Thinking About Social Class

All societies are *stratified* in some degree; members of societies view themselves and each other as occupying differing social positions that are hierarchically ordered, from those who have more of some socially desired goods to those with less. The geological metaphor of *strata,* or layers, of people suggests a more concrete, fixed, and visible phenomenon than is typically the case (though there are instances of fixed and visible stratification); nonetheless, the fact of stratification is evident to all members of the society. They may disagree with one another about where (or whether) to draw boundaries between the strata, where to place themselves or others, and what meaning to attach to their social positioning, but all accept the existence of some social ranking.

To begin with, the social classes in a stratification system are distinguished in economic terms, with those individuals having greatest wealth or access to resources typically occupying the "highest" classes. There are other, less tangible grounds for distinguishing class, including political power, status prestige, and what might be referred to as "cultural power." These social "goods" can be thought of as both determinants and consequences of one's social-class position. The distribution of these social goods and hence social position is rarely fixed, except in the most rigid caste systems, because most social stratification systems permit mobility across class boundaries. Thus, except for members of a caste, one's social position at birth need not determine one's social position later in life.

Intellectual traditions in the social sciences approach the conceptual definition of *social class* differently. Although they all recognize the economic roots of class, they give it different meaning and, in varying degrees, attach to the concept other social, political, and cultural baggage. Following the ideas of Weber (1946), many social theorists and scholars see social class as deriving from relative economic power, resulting in a *positional* ranking of occupations in terms of their presumed social value and corresponding rewards. Marxist and neo-Marxist scholars assert an alternative, "objective" basis for class rooted in the *relationship* of people to the means of production (Dahrendorf, 1970), though more recent formulations in this tradition (e.g., McLaren, 1989) speak of class more broadly, including within the concept economic, social, and political relationships affecting how people in a social order live their lives. Contemporary elaborations of this theme address production as a multilevel concept that includes the relationship of the individual to systems of ownership, the structure of authority, and the process of one's own work activity (Anyon, 1981). Non-Marxist conflict theorists (e.g., Collins, 1979) are more apt to emphasize the cultural basis of social class, whereby members of society distinguish one another on the basis of tastes, preferences, and manners as much as anything else. Scholars approaching the matter from one or another critical perspective (e.g., Apple, 1978) are also likely to assert that social class has a cultural as well as economic basis and is intimately connected to the individual's construction of a social identity.

Reflecting the differences in intellectual tradition, the precise number, boundaries, and character of social classes remain in dispute. Sociologists operating from a positional view of social class tend to identify three to six classes (Bensman & Vidich, 1971), while Marxists distinguish three to four (Wright & Perrone, 1977). The great majority of empirical work is done with a positional breakdown of classes: working class, lower-middle class, middle class, and so on, or, more simply, high, middle, and low positions on some scale such as socioeconomic status (SES).

These distinctions among classes, and the analytic work based on them, may objectify social class more than is warranted. We prefer to think of social classes and one's own position within them as socially constructed, and reconstructed, to reflect changing conditions within society and changing views of the way society works. In this sense, social class is a fiction, albeit a powerful and constraining one. Such fictions change slowly when held by many people, and though one may exert influence over one's own class consciousness one has little control over others' views. In this sense, people are captured by their own and others' shared sense of their social class positioning within society.

In ways that will become apparent as the discussion unfolds, education is inextricably part of the layering of society into distinct classes. At the least, social class is an attribute of all individuals engaged in the enterprise of schooling, of educators as well as learners. In addition, the communities served by schools can be characterized in terms of their aggregate social-class position (and also in terms of variability within them). But these characterizations are static and do not reveal the heart of the processes by which the social positions of participants in education influence schooling, and in turn are influenced by it. To describe these processes, we must first acknowledge that differing assumptions may be made about society and the role(s) that formal schooling may play within it.

Thinking About the Purposes of Schooling

To consider the relationship between social class and schooling, one must make assumptions about the purposes of schooling, and also about the nature of society and the role of schools in preparing individuals for lives in the larger social context. These assumptions set the stage for interpretation of class-related phenomena in the context of schools.

In a pluralistic, democratic society such as that of the United States, it is commonplace to recognize that there are multiple and competing purposes for education. There are as well competing assumptions made by analysts who wish to make sense of the behavior and results of schooling. We distinguish three sets of assumptions, or perspectives, that have been especially prominent in the scholarship of the last half century related to schooling in a social context: functionalist, conflict, and interpretive and critical perspectives.

Functionalist Perspectives. Functionalist thinking visualizes society as analogous to an organism, containing institutions that carry out vital functions. The vital function of schools is the transmission of mainstream culture and the preparation of citizens for the technical demands of modern society (deMarrais & LeCompte, 1999).

Within functionalism, however, transmission of culture is not conceived in narrow terms solely as the teaching of mainstream cultural skills, values, and behavioral norms. Functionalists also see schooling as an arena for sorting and selecting individuals for various future roles. Modern-day society is thought of as an *expert society,* relying on highly trained individuals for economic and social growth, as well as a *meritocracy* in which ability and effort count for more than privilege and inherited social position (Hurn, 1993). Schools are viewed as instruments of this meritocratic expert society, in that they allow the best and the brightest to rise to the top. Theoretically, those who demonstrate the most ability and expend the most effort receive expert training in order to take high-status positions in the social and economic structure—regardless of race, gender, or social-class origins. Tracking and other forms of institutionalized differential treatment are justified by this notion of specific educational needs for individuals of different (greater or lesser) abilities to perform different types of occupation. Schools are thus perceived to be the link between an individual's cognitive abilities and his or her later jobs or social class.

In simplistic form, functionalism's view of social class is tied to the notion of meritocracy. If social and occupational status are dependent primarily on merit, then social class must, in some sense, be a reflection of effort and ability. Functionalists believe that upper classes comprise the exceptionally capable and motivated, lower classes the least capable and industrious. Social-class boundaries are seen as permeable; highly capable and motivated lower-class individuals may move upward through the class structure by diligence and intelligence, while individuals of upper-class origins may experience downward socio-economic mobility in the absence of ability and effort. Schooling is thus viewed as the sorter and selector of human talent, and in that role it is perceived as mainstream culture's instrument of upward social and economic mobility for the lower classes.

Conflict Perspectives. Arising initially from Marxist thought, conflict perspectives offer an alternative view of society and education, focusing on the unequal property and power distribution in modern society (deMarrais & LeCompte, 1999). Like functionalism, conflict perspectives presume a transmission theory of schooling. Unlike functionalism, however, conflict theorists believe that schools transmit unequal power relationships and the value systems of the elite rather than shared popular culture, values, and skills. Building on the work of Bowles and Gintis (1976) in the Marxist tradition and others in non-Marxist traditions (such as Collins, 1979), conflict theorists have argued that, through (a) use of the language and behavioral expectations of the dominant elite, (b) differential treatment systems such as tracking, and (c) the reinforcing of the social and political status quo, schools serve the interests of the elite (deMarrais & LeCompte). Rather than transmitting only intellectual and academic skills that prepare one for the workplace, schools inculcate the attitudes and values sought by future employers—among them loyalty, compliance, promptness, submission to authority, and docility—and the credentials and status culture that are the ticket of admission to positions in the societal hierarchy. Through mechanisms such as ability grouping and tracking (between and within schools) *different* knowledge, skills, and values are transmitted to students from different social classes. Middle- and upper-class students are given the tools to enter lucrative high-status positions, while working-class students are trained in the knowledge and values that are required for blue-collar jobs (deMarrais & LeCompte; Hurn, 1993). Schools are thus viewed by conflict theorists as institutions that reinforce class inequality in modern society.

From this perspective, social-class position arises inescapably by virtue of one's current economic, political, and cultural relationship to those who control the means of production in the society and, along with it, the status culture of elite groups. Because elites control production and organize society to foster their own interests, members of other social classes are likely to stay where they are, unless the inevitable struggle among the classes effects a new hierarchy (or, in the original Marxist ideal view, which has yet to appear, a classless society).

Interpretive and Critical Perspectives. Functionalism and conflict theory are both theories of cultural transmission, though they differ in notions of what schools transmit. Interpretive and critical theories, on the other hand, focus on cultural transformation by viewing individuals within social settings as active, rather than passive, participants in the social construction of their own realities (deMarrais & LeCompte, 1999).

Growing out of the phenomenological tradition, interpretive theory focuses on the construction of meanings in social interaction. Unlike functionalism and conflict theories, which typically rely on quantitative research and concentrate on macro issues of culture and society, interpretivists use qualitative methods and center their attention on the actual interactions of teachers, students, and peers in the construction of the school experience at the micro level. The concern of interpretivists is the meaning brought to social interactions by all parties, the behavior of individuals based on those meanings, and the resultant relationships formed and new meanings constructed in student interactions in schools.

Critical theory combines elements of the works of neo-Marxist conflict theorists and interpretivists; it was developed to explain both macro- and micro-level phenomena of education. Like interpretive theory, critical perspectives emphasize the social construction of meaning; like conflict perspectives, critical theory attends to questions of power in the larger social structure, particularly around social, economic, and political inequality. Thus one of the primary concerns of critical theory is injustice and oppression in modern society. Gramsci's (1971) work on the imposition of the worldview of the elite, a phenomenon he named "hegemony," and Freire's (1970) emphasis on the ways in which state hegemony structured the lives of Brazilian peasants, reflect critical theory's attention to the role of elite ideology in shaping meanings that support the domination and oppression of the lower social classes. The institution of formal schooling, according to critical theorists, is a societal force that contributes to domination and oppression by mirroring the worldview of the elite, and by instruction that results in differential outcomes that support the elite worldview.

Although this sounds much like conflict theory, critical perspectives go a step further by visualizing individuals and schools in a more transformative way (Apple, 1980). Central to critical perspectives is the assumption that individuals and social groups construct their own reality regardless of the oppressive elite-dominated social hierarchy in which they exist, and thereby they have the capacity to resist and reconstrue their relationship to it. Learners are not passive recipients of curriculum, whether overt or covert. Meanings created in school, which typically reflect the elite worldview, grow out of actions, reactions, and interactions among students, teachers, and others involved in the educational process. These meanings are open to change and reinterpretation by any of the parties to the meaning-construction process. Social stratification as an outcome of schooling tends to continue not because lower-class students passively accept their lower status in schools but because, in the struggle over ideology, meaning, and social position in classrooms, middle-class teachers and hegemonic curricula (reinforced by mass media) are significantly more powerful than low-status students. Some lower-class students can and do succeed beyond teacher and societal expectations under these conditions, but many do not.

Social class, from this point of view, is more a subjective construction than objective reality. The class consciousness that may develop is a stimulus to, and basis for, class-based resistance to oppressive conditions.

Analysts approaching the question of social class and schooling bring to their quest fundamentally different assumptions about the phenomenon. Nonetheless, virtually all agree on a few central facts regarding the strong and enduring association between social class (however measured) and the outcomes of education. As in much of the debate among researchers from the various perspectives, we take these facts, described in the next section, as the starting point for our examination.

SOCIAL CLASS AND THE OUTCOMES OF SCHOOLING

There is an enduring correlation between social class and educational outcomes. It is almost universally true that averages of educational attainment—measured by years in school or the rate of dropping out—and educational achievement—measured by grades and test scores—vary by social class (Coleman et al., 1966; Jencks, 1972; Natriello, McDill, & Pallas, 1990). In general, higher-class status correlates with high levels of educational attainment and achievement, low social class correlates with low levels of educational attainment and achievement, and the middle classes fall somewhere in between (Coleman et al.; Goldstein, 1967; Mayeske et al., 1972; Persell, 1977, 1993). The possession of educational credentials also follows this pattern, with upper-class individuals on average holding more credentials than members of the middle class, who in turn possess more than lower-class individuals (Coleman et al.; Goldstein; Mayeske et al.; Persell).

These correlations hold over time and across cultures (Hurn, 1993; Persell, 1977). There has been ample research documenting the fact that despite an increase in the availability of schooling, the rate of change in the correlation between social class and educational outcomes has been inconsequential (Boudon, 1974; Hurn; Thurow, 1972). Hurn reviews literature on a number of European studies demonstrating the enduring link between educational attainment and measures of social class, primarily fathers' income, occupation, and educational attainment (see Boudon, 1974, for a review of European data; Garnier & Raffalovich, 1984, regarding France; and Halsey, Heath, & Ridge, 1980, regarding Great Britain). Students in Europe and the United States from higher-social-class backgrounds are most likely, for example, to pursue postsecondary education, to do so in four-year institutions, and to go to private colleges and universities. Students from lower-social-class backgrounds are not only less likely than their middle- and upper-class peers to graduate from high school but also less likely to go on to college (Sewell & Shaw, 1967). If they seek postsecondary education, they are more likely to attend a two-year or vocational institution rather than a four-year college or university (Karabel, 1972) and are less likely to pursue a graduate degree (Sewell & Hauser, 1976). One recent review of literature pertinent to the link between educational attainment and social class concludes, "The most powerful predictor of how much education individuals obtained was the social class background of their parents, as measured by their income level, occupation, and education" (deMarrais & LeCompte, 1999, p. 214).

The correlational research base has some limitations. It tells us only about a certain set of outcomes: those valued enough by the mainstream social scientific community to be well studied. The research also depends heavily on quantifiable measures. Further, like most social scientific research it has focused primarily on White males and may not be generalizable to interclass differences between females or non-Whites (Ayella & Williamson, 1976; Rosenfeld, 1980). Finally, most correlational data have focused on paternal status as a measure of social class and may not adequately reflect the impact on social class of mothers' education and occupation (deMarrais & LeCompte, 1999).

Educational attainment, achievement, and credentialing are the most commonly studied direct outcomes of schooling. Other outcomes of schooling that have been overlooked by the research community when considering the link between social class and educational outcomes may be equally important in the long run. Many of them, such as self-esteem, expectancy of success, and aspirations, fall into what might be termed the *affective* domain. Persell (1993), for instance, in reviewing literature pertinent to the link between students' social status and self-esteem concluded that the length of time in school is negatively correlated with lower-class student self-esteem. Aspirations for educational success and occupational roles also vary by social class, with lower-class students reporting lower aspirations on average than those of their peers in the middle and upper classes (Cicourel & Kitsuse, 1963; Hurn, 1993; Kahl, 1953; Sewell & Hauser, 1976). Students' expectations for their own success correlate with both teacher feedback and student history of success or failure in school settings (Weiner, 1985), both of which correlate with social class. Because the affective dimension of schooling appears to be more extensively studied with reference to female students, and in light of Weiler's (1988) suggestion that gender is a class issue, the research base offered by studies of gender might offer great opportunities for studying the links between social class and affective outcomes.

The centrality of the enduring correlation between social class and the direct outcomes of the educational process is of clear relevance in a discussion of social class and schooling. Also relevant to the discussion—though a detailed examination of these correlations is beyond the scope of this chapter—are the relationships between social class and occupational outcomes, which are always mediated by the outcomes of schooling.

Occupational and economic outcomes of schooling are often considered the most salient of the correlates of social class. Though the relative impact of social class and education on occupational outcomes has not been definitively established (and may never be), it cannot be denied that both education (Sewell & Shaw, 1967) and social class (Wright & Perrone, 1977) play some role in occupational attainment and earnings. Education is most clearly linked to occupational outcomes in situations in which credentials are required for job acquisition. Collins (1979) maintains that education constitutes a kind of "cultural capital" that allows the holder to "purchase" certain roles in society; the currency that allows the acquisition of higher-status jobs is the credential. Meyer (1977) asserts that it is not necessarily education that gives individuals an advantage in the job market, but the wider societal belief that educated people are better able to perform jobs. Regardless of the relationship between education and the tasks of the job, education is used as a criterion in allocating individuals to occupations.

It is difficult to sort the contributions of social class from those of education in their influence on occupation because social class, as is argued in this chapter, is itself a contributor to educational outcomes such as achievement, attainment, and credentials. Wright and Perrone (1977), in seeking to determine the relative influence of education and social class, looked at occupational stratification in Marxist terms and concluded that social class is better than educational attainment as a predictor of future occupational status. Bennett and LeCompte (1990) summarize the findings of this study as follows:

Class matters more than education, and even overrides the effects of education. Thus, even with high levels of education, working class children will not achieve as much prestige as children from the upper classes. This is because working class children are handicapped by their background; they cannot translate their education into as much occupational prestige and economic success as can upper and middle class children with the same or inferior levels of education. (p. 171)

The research reviewed here establishes the correlation between social class and occupational outcomes, but it does little to explain *how* the two are linked. If one envisions schooling as a black box into which students of a given social class enter and from which emerge individuals of varying educational attributes, one must examine this black box to understand the subtle role social class may play in shaping educational and occupational outcomes.

SOCIAL CLASS IN THE COMMUNITY CONTEXT, STUDENT POPULATION, AND THE TEACHING FORCE OF SCHOOLS

We investigate the relationship between social class and the outcomes of schooling from the outside in—that is, we start in this section with the community context of schools, then examine the social organization of the student population, and finally discuss the teaching force. In subsequent sections, we proceed to the nature of the learner and to instruction itself (including both formal and hidden curricula).

Our understanding of community context, social organization, and the teaching force comes from various sources. Along with large-scale studies of community demography, ethnographic and observational studies of schools and school-community relations provide the most useful insight into how the social class of the community conditions what school people do. Research on tracking is especially helpful in revealing the sorting processes at the heart of the school's macro social organization. Studies of the demography of the teaching force and the teacher in workplace contexts help illuminate the social-class nature of the educator.

Drawing on these sources, we describe three sets of linkage between social class and educational outcomes. First, the character of the community served by the school is shaped to a large extent by social class, and this in turn defines the social makeup of the student population, the community's expectations of that population, and the resources available to schools. Second, in part reflecting the social topography of communities, schools serve populations—and within schools, particular programs serve subpopulations—that are surprisingly homogeneous in social-class composition. This homogeneity comes about over time as schools in effect sort young people by social class. Third, the teaching force brings to the school certain class-based sensibilities rooted in their own social origins and life trajectory, as well as in the class-related positioning of teaching within the occupational structure.

Social Class and the Community Context of Schooling

The starting point for understanding the role of social class in schooling is to recognize that schools serve communities, and that community is more than a defined geographical place. Rather, communities reflect "patterned social interaction" and exhibit a "collective identity" (Hunter, 1975, as cited in Louis, 1990). From the perspective of both community members and outsiders, community interaction and identity are suffused with the social class of community members. More often than not,

one broad social-class identity predominates; we routinely refer to a particular community as a working-class town, or an upper-middle-class suburb, and so on.

Although this labeling of communities usually masks a complex social structure, it hints at a basic fact of U.S. social topography: residential arrangements are profoundly segregated by social class. There is historical evidence that, in the wake of World War II, social-class segregation has increased (Kantor & Brenzel, 1992) with the relocation of middle-class and upper-middle-class groups from diverse central-city areas to the patchwork of suburbs that constitute the nation's metropolitan areas. Segregation by social class is especially noticeable when one considers the immediate community served by a given school, defined by its attendance area. Thus a given high school serves a "poor area of town" or an elementary school draws its students primarily from a "wealthy professional neighborhood." Alternatively, where people of different social classes live in close proximity to one another, as in some urban areas, segregation results from parental choice when, for example, large proportions of the affluent send their children to private schools (Persell, 1993).

Besides the obvious effects on the nature of the student population, the social-class makeup of the community influences what it expects of the schools and what it expects of its young people. The community embodies a value system (Louis, 1990) and a "social class culture" (McLaughlin, Talbert, & Bascia, 1990) to which educators must respond. Communities "develop a common consciousness" that constitutes a class-based context in which teachers and administrators do their work, and these contexts can differ considerably from one another depending on the social composition of the community (Anyon, 1980, 1981; Connell, Ashenden, Kessler, & Dawsett, 1982; Metz, 1990). A rich account of these influences emerges from recent ethnographic research on high schools in communities of varying SES level:

It is clear that class issues get into the schools primarily through community pressures and through the students. The three communities [in this study] had different priorities for their schools' goals and daily practice. All the schools' staffs, especially principals, took community priorities seriously. These priorities were visibly a part of each school's life, particularly in the overall policies of each school, but also to a significant degree in the classroom teaching. (Metz, 1990, p. 92)

According to this and other studies (such as Anyon, 1981; Hemmings & Metz, 1990; and Wilcox, 1982), communities varying by social class want different things for their children. For example, the predominantly working-class communities in the Metz study placed a high priority on acquiring credentials and following rules, whereas the higher-SES communities, in which wealthier business and professional families were the dominant social group, placed emphasis on students' gaining particular kinds of knowledge and skills.

Observational research makes clear, however, that broad class characterizations of communities and what they expect of schools or students are oversimplified and not particularly useful if the subtle variations within social-class groupings are not considered (Metz, 1990). Among communities of the same social class, for example, there is considerable diversity in priorities and expectations, reflecting various factors, including generational differences (how recently community members arrived at their current class position), the basis of high or low status (education, occupation, wealth), and a community's cohesiveness or "functional integration" (Coleman, 1990). In addition, within broad social-class groupings (and to an extent cutting across class lines), other social markers shape the character of the community and its relationship to its schools. As studies of desegregation demonstrate, race and ethnicity play an especially prominent role in this regard, as do other factors (for example, religious beliefs and political interests) that define the culture of a community. Social class is only one condition among many that give a community its flavor, distinctive character, and propensity to pressure the schools in a particular way.

The social class of the community translates into other important influences on schools. The first is simply a matter of resources. Higher-social-class communities generally have the wherewithal to provide teachers with ample resources to do their work, whereas chronic shortages of resources and less adequate facilities are common in schools serving communities lower in the social-class hierarchy (Kozol, 1991; Metz, 1990; Persell, 1993).

The power of well-resourced schools in affluent communities to raise the achievement of even low-SES students is suggested by Caldas and Bankston (1997):

The effect of schoolmates' family social status on achievement is significant and substantial, and only slightly smaller than an individual's own family background status. Thus, attending school with classmates who come from higher SES backgrounds does tend to positively raise one's own academic achievement, independent of one's own SES background, race, and other factors. (p. 275)

Although the evidence for such "compositional" effects is debated and the relative contribution of school versus family social class is not well established (Gamoran, 1992), there is nonetheless a reasonable possibility that schoolmates' social status could influence lower-SES classmates' performance in various ways, even indirectly—for example, through favorable resource conditions for teachers' work (Louis, 1990).

Furthermore, higher-status communities are not passive in their relationship with schools but rather take active steps to advocate their interests, either as a group or on behalf of individual children, and they have the political clout to make themselves heard. Middle-class and upper-class parents have "interconnected" (as opposed to working-class parents' "separated") relationships with schools (Lareau, 2000). They know how to gain access to elite programs for their children, and they frequently oppose school reform efforts aimed at reducing tracking and other forms of inequitable distribution of educational resources (Ball & Vincent, 2001; Oakes, Quartz, Ryan, & Lipton, 2000). Lower-status groups lack such easy and entitled relationships with schools and have less political voice (though there are notable exceptions); generally they are easily ignored, or simply not heard at all. Social-class position is thus intimately linked to the distribution and exercise of power.

The Social Organization of the Student Population

Across schools or within them, the student population is not consciously or intentionally organized along social-class lines. If anything, quite the opposite is the case: educators intend to organize schools, and programs within them, to address particular kinds of learning needs, convey certain kinds of knowledge to those who can make best use of them, and prepare students for further educational experiences of various kinds. On the face of it, entry into a school or a program within a school is based on geography, parental preferences, students' interests, or some measure of the students' aptitude or ability.

But beneath the surface, social class plays several potentially major roles in the social organization of the school population, both across and within schools, with the net result that students are progressively sorted into groupings that are relatively homogeneous by social class (Persell, 1977, 1993).

Much of this sorting across schools can be said to happen by default, as a result of parental choice (in the case of private and parochial schools) or the residential segregation described earlier. Especially at the elementary level, public schools (and, to a lesser extent, many private schools) serve a residential area with a particular social-class composition. In the simplest case, the neighborhood school serves a residential area that is largely homogeneous in social-class terms. In more complex cases, the attendance area of the school embraces different neighborhoods, thus diversifying the aggregate class character of the student population, but usually a particular social class predominates. Thus students are likely to go to school with people like themselves, that is, who share a common social-class identity (Persell, 1993).

Such characterizations gloss over diversity and do not describe well the socially heterogeneous nature of some magnet schools; certain private schools; and large schools serving complex, transitional attendance areas.

As students progress up the ladder from elementary to senior grade levels through schools that serve ever-wider attendance areas, the overall social-class diversity of the student population is likely to increase. The social heterogeneity of such instances can be compounded by parental choice, but in all probability when parents opt for private schools they are selecting a social group for their children that more closely resembles their own than the public school options available to them.

Within schools, especially those with larger, socially heterogeneous student populations, further sorting by social class takes place (Persell, 1977). Here the role of social class is both subtle and profound; it is part of a complex story describing assignment of students to declared or de facto tracks, classrooms, groupings within classrooms, or supplemental services for individuals with a specialized learning need. The story changes somewhat at different levels of schooling.

In the elementary grades, some social-class sorting takes place whenever students are assigned by "ability" (either among or within classrooms). In the younger years, when ability (or achievement) is harder to assess, the teacher's *perception* of ability predicts placement more accurately than do standardized scores (deMarrais & LeCompte, 1999). The most telling forms of social-class grouping probably occur *within* the classroom in the form of ability grouping. Classic ethnographic studies (for example, Rist, 1970) have demonstrated that class-related characteristics of kindergarten children—their appearance, behavior, and parents' welfare status—are important determinants of teacher expectations for the children's performance and hence of their placement in high- or low-ability groups for reading instruction in first grade. Other research suggests that similar factors, such as degree of politeness and willingness to follow the teacher's directions—which are related to class-based upbringing—play an important role in early ability-group assignment (Mackler, 1969, as cited in Hurn, 1993). However, in research relying on cruder quantitative measures, which so far has failed to find a direct effect of social class on ability-group assignment at the elementary level (Haller & Davis, 1981), these observational results have not yet been substantiated.

The research reviewed so far establishes only that, in the absence of concrete information about performance, *initial* assignment to a group draws heavily on traits that are closely linked to children's social class. As the years go on, teachers rely increasingly on measures of achievement (though some degree of teacher judgment is always part of the grouping decisions). But because grouping assignments have considerable permanence (see, for instance, Rist, 1970), and because of the differentiated nature of instruction in ability groups (described later in this chapter), initial group assignments can exert an enduring influence on students' progress through school.

The pattern in the secondary grades, described in research on tracking (Findley & Bryan, 1975; Heyns, 1978; Oakes, 1985), continues the sorting processes begun in elementary school. At the secondary level, the explicit bases for track assignment are three (Oakes): (a) student test-score performance, (b) teacher and counselor recommendations, and (c) student and parental choice. Social class and ethnicity are likely to be a further consideration, though not conscious or deliberate (Persell, 1993), especially in the perceptions and actions of teachers and counselors. For example, in research at the junior high school level, even when ability and teacher recommendations are similar, social class has been found to be directly related to track assignments (Kariger, 1962, as cited in Persell). Observational research has documented that markers of social-class identity—among them speech patterns, clothing, and behavior—are important considerations in counselors' grouping decisions at the high school level (Cicourel & Kitsuse, 1963). Drawing on this and other studies, a recent review concludes, "Secondary students from different backgrounds are given different types of information, advice, and counselor attention and . . . social, class-based placements are produced in the advising process" (Oakes, Gamoran, & Page, 1992, p. 577). It is plausible that high school teachers make judgments about students that draw subliminally on the same sort of factors (Oakes, 1985). In addition, for reasons that are deeply embedded in their nature as cultural beings, students tend to choose (or parents choose for them) to be with students who are most like themselves. Though not the only factor, the ability to be among peers with a similar social background is likely to rank high in the choice of courses or program placements.

There are forms of grouping within a school other than assignment to ability group in the elementary grades or tracks at the secondary level. Assignment to specialized educational services such as compensatory or special education reflects class-related characteristics and hence can be considered a subsidiary sorting mechanism that isolates students for part or all of the school day in groupings with students of similar social-class backgrounds. Federal and state compensatory education programs, for example, are explicitly targeted to low-performing students in schools that serve a concentration of low-income children (Birman et al., 1987). Poverty level, which is for obvious reasons closely related to social class, is considered a major indicator of educational disadvantagement or "at-riskness" and hence a focus of many specialized services (Natriello et al., 1990). Special education labeling and program assignments reflect class-based differences both in the disproportionate number of lower-social-class students served and in the differential labeling of students with perceived learning and behavioral handicaps. For example, learning disabilities, the largest category of educational handicap, originated as a less stigmatizing response to demands by middle-class parents to meet the educational needs of their underachieving children, though over the years this category has become a repository for children from lower-status groups (Sleeter, 1991). In addition, social class and class-based resistance are implicated in the debate over the inclusion of "socially maladjusted" students in programs serving the behaviorally disordered (Nelson, Rutherford, Center, & Walker, 1991).

Social Class and Educators

Having considered the community and the social organization of the student population in and among schools, we have one other category of participant in the social drama of education: the educators themselves. Rarely considered in research on schooling, the social-class background and identity of teachers, administrators, and specialists within the school building is a potentially influential element in the interactive story of teaching, learning, and credentialing. To the extent that the encounter between students and educators is a central part of that story (as we argue in subsequent sections of this chapter), it is important to know where *both* parties to the encounter are coming from.

Educators hold dual class identities, one deriving from their class of origin and the other from their current occupational position as teacher, administrator, counselor, or other role. In many cases, the two are one and the same; in crude positional terms, teachers are considered middle-class, occupying a rung in the middle of the occupational status hierarchy, and large numbers of them come from middle-class families (deMarrais & LeCompte, 1999; Lortie, 1975). The same is not true of all teachers; for many, teaching is a means to improve social status. This was especially so in the past; as recently as 1960, more than half of all teachers were from farm or blue-collar families (Betz & Garland, 1974, cited in deMarrais & LeCompte, 1999). Thus, though teachers occupy a relatively common station in the stratification of society, they arrive from very different places.

No discussion of the class-based nature of the teaching force can ignore the fact that teaching is a segmented labor market that has been largely feminized at the lower levels, and increasingly so at the secondary level—a pattern that has long historical roots in U.S. schools. In this respect, the class-based dynamics of the teaching profession differ markedly for men and women (Weiler, 1988). Teaching offers men, for example, a better avenue of continuing upward mobility than it does women (deMarrais & LeCompte, 1999). More recent formulations of the issues from a feminist perspective treat the feminization of teaching as another instance of a dual class system in

which women tend to end up with lower-status occupations and higher-status occupations tend to be reserved for men (Weiler), though it is clear that the increasing feminization of teaching depresses the social status of the profession for both men and women. A prominent critical perspective argues that all teachers, male and female, are placed in subordinate positions in the labor structure; increasingly, these positions have been deprived of professional discretion ("deskilled") by a patriarchal power structure (Apple, 1986).

Educators bring class-based sensibilities to their work—a curious omission of the teacher socialization literature (Zeichner & Gere, 1990), which focuses on the influence of formally designated agents of socialization such as teacher-preparation institutions. These sensibilities derive in part from the teachers' class of origin, in part from their professional and life trajectory, and in part from their current patterns of association outside of school. Ethnographic research on the workplace context of high school teachers highlights the phenomenon this way:

> Teachers participate in communities and in kinship and friendship networks that also are part of the social class system. While teachers have formally similar educational credentials and participate in a single, undifferentiated occupation, they not only come from a range of social class backgrounds but participate as adults in networks that vary significantly in their social class. We were struck with the differences in attitude, lifestyle, and associates, among [the teachers we studied]. . . .
> Teachers' own class affected their definitions of their work. Teachers who associated with managers and professionals defined their responsibilities more in terms of being sure to do a good job, whatever that required, while those with working class associates defined their responsibilities more in terms of conscientiously putting in required hours. (Metz, 1990, pp. 94–95)

Seen from this perspective, teachers' past and current social-class affiliations are part of what equips them to cope with the varied demands of educating young people. It certainly shapes their views of their role as educators, but it also may predispose them to perceive, and interact with, students in certain ways (Weiler, 1988). In many instances, teachers' social-class identities equip them poorly to deal with youngsters whose social-class origins differ from their own (deMarrais & LeCompte, 1999). This is not to say that teachers deal more effectively with students who match them in social-class background, though such is often the case; rather, teachers who have become multicultural are more likely to do well with a student population that represents a variety of backgrounds. At present, the institutions that prepare people for teaching do little to instill multicultural perspectives, knowledge, and skills. The bulk of today's teacher workforce was trained in a time when issues of diversity and multicultural teaching skills were not comprehensively addressed (Gay, 1986).

One further dynamic reinforces the influence that educators' social class has on schooling: some evidence suggests that teachers, like students, are subtly sorted by class background among schools and, within a school, among programs (for example, Anyon, 1980, 1981; Metz, 1990). Social class is not the only variable controlling where educators are assigned, nor is it the most powerful. Teachers are not passive participants in their assignment to one school or another, as the sorting metaphor implies; depending on the individual and the school system, a great deal of active choice may enter into the process. But whether or not they are active agents, the net effect is the same. Teachers are likely to gravitate to teaching situations in which their colleagues' social-class sensibilities resemble their own. (Over time, faculties construct shared sensibilities as well.) Thus the cadre of teachers at a typical working-class school and those serving predominantly upper-middle-class students are likely to look very different.

Implications for Educational Outcomes

The preceding discussion explores the connections between social class and the community context, social organization of students, and staffing of schools; it argues that, in each realm, social class contributes to stratification within and across schools. We have argued that social class is an important influence on these realms, and that in turn each realm conditions the work of the school. We have not yet established that these influences change the outcomes of education, nor does most of the research we have reviewed so far purport to do so. At best, the class-based expectations of the community, the social sorting of students into relatively homogeneous groupings by class, and the class-based sensibilities of educators are indirect influences that can affect outcomes only by a chain of events. In the next two sections, we carry the argument forward, tracing that chain of events as learners enter the school building, interact with educators, and engage in—or resist—instruction.

SOCIAL CLASS AND THE LEARNER

As individuals and in peer groups, learners enter the school building with a worldview, language, values, and apparent intellectual capacities. Various lines of research help us see how social class may shape the learner's approach to the intellectual and social work of school. The research base for this discussion draws on sociological and anthropological studies focusing on cultural differences and cultural discontinuities. In addition, literature on peer groups and student resistance is also helpful, as is psychological work on testing and student responses to adverse conditions in schooling.

It must be remembered, in any discussion of social class and children, that young people embark on their journey through schooling bearing the social class of their parents. Children and youths are thus assigned social-class membership on the basis of their parents' or guardians' occupation, educational attainment, earnings, lifestyle, or other markers; they gradually acquire class culture and, as adults, attain a social-class status that may differ from that of their parents. The learner's social class is thus not fixed for life but rather reflects a process of social-class identity development.

This section begins with the relationship between social class and the learners' "intelligence," which is often assumed to explain class-based differences in schooling outcomes. The inadequacies of intelligence concepts and measures lead us to examine the role of social class in the learner's approach to intellectual work. Following that, we consider how the learner confronts the gap between the social and linguistic codes of home and those of school. Next, we examine the role of social class in adult and peer perceptions of learners and their capabilities, and then we consider social class in the peer culture.

Social Class and the Learner's Intelligence

Attuned as they are to cognitive functioning, educators are soon aware that students appear to display differing capacities for intellectual work. Generations of educators and scholars have assumed that this meant differences in the learners' intelligence, and they have settled for intelligence quotient (IQ) measures as a reasonable proxy for the expression of these differences. These measures have a long history in efforts to understand the relationship between social class and schooling because (a) indicators of social class (such as SES) are highly correlated with IQ and (b) IQ is highly predictive of most schooling outcomes (see, for example, Coleman et al., 1966; Jencks, 1972).

A long-standing assertion in educational sociology is that IQ is the principal means by which social-class influences schooling outcomes (Christopher Hurn, personal communication, October 1993). Put in the simplest and baldest terms, this argument holds that, on average, individuals born into higher social classes either grow up with more optimal conditions for cognitive development (better nutrition, more cognitive stimulation, and so on), inherit greater cognitive potential (because over time smart people are assumed to gravitate to high-status positions in society), or both. These conditions are assumed to produce young people who score higher on IQ tests. Because IQ tests capture how well students do on tasks related to the cognitive work of schooling, these individuals are more likely to succeed in school. Their success in school is likely to be rewarded with higher-status jobs and social circumstances, and the cycle then repeats itself. This position has been most recently and forcefully expressed by the authors of *The Bell Curve* (Hernnstein & Murray, 1994).

Many scholars (ourselves included) view this assertion and the premises on which it rests as problematic (Ballantine, 1993; Davis, 1951; Knapp, Kronick, Marks, & Vosburgh, 1996; Reissman, 1962). First, it is unclear exactly what IQ tests measure, and there is considerable doubt that these tests measure intelligence in any absolute sense. To compound matters, the scholarly community has yet to agree on a definition of intelligence, or even to establish that a single mental ability is involved; multiple abilities are included in many definitions of intelligence (for instance, Gardner, 1987). More than four decades ago, an analysis of IQ testing put the matter this way:

Intelligence tests measure how quickly people can solve relatively unimportant problems making as few errors as possible, rather than measuring how people grapple with relatively important problems, making as many productive errors as necessary with no time factor. (Murray, 1960, quoted in Reissman, 1962, p. 49)

Second, there is reason to doubt the stability of the tests. They are supposed to produce a constant score, and most often this is the case. But there have been numerous demonstrations in which the scores of individuals, particularly those from a lower-status background, have risen dramatically following some coaching in test-taking strategies (Haggard, 1954; Heber, 1979, cited in Ballantine, 1993). Third, the content and format of IQ tests reflect particular culturally based experiences, thereby favoring certain social and ethnic groups over others (Ballantine). Fourth, it is not clearly established that higher-status positions are awarded on the basis of talent (Hurn, 1993), as noted earlier in this chapter in the discussion of conflict and critical perspectives on schooling and its relationship to society.

Finally, this line of argument conspicuously ignores the possibility that powerful social forces and conditions might shape an individual's performance in a testing situation. Despite an enormous reference base, the authors of *The Bell Curve*, for example, are conspicuously silent about both theory and evidence regarding structural determinants of social mobility, social roots of poverty, and the role that statistical and institutional racism can play in shaping individual performance (Knapp et al., 1996).

We find it more productive to look at IQ testing in the same way that we examine everything else involved in the relationship between social class and schooling. IQ testing—the activity that produces IQ scores—is a *social*

act governed by the same norms and cultural rules that guide most of what goes on in school (Reissman, 1962). From the student's perspective, it is intellectual work that results in a performance, as with many things done in school or school-like contexts. Students come to these contexts with different social and linguistic codes, cultural understandings, presentations of self, and peer affiliations. As the ensuing discussion demonstrates, these factors all influence how students engage in intellectual tasks, what they produce as a result of this engagement, and how they are viewed by others.

Put another way, rather than social class being a natural correlate and consequence of intelligence, it is just as likely that apparent intelligence levels are "assigned," in part on the basis of social-class position. No doubt there are still *individual* variations in intelligence (by a more satisfactory definition of the concept) within social groups and across the population as a whole, but there is little compelling evidence that clear *group* differences in intelligence (by the same definition) exist or are passed on from one generation to the next (Hurn, 1993). In sum, trying to explain the relationship between social class and schooling in terms of how smart people are is a fruitless task; more satisfactory explanations emerge from closer examination of the characteristics of the learner that are clearly class-based.

Social Class and the Learner's Approach to Intellectual Work

Students are born into a social environment formed, in varying degrees, by family and community; that environment comprises a complex web of social and linguistic patterns (Delpit, 1988; Haviland, 1990; Heath, 1983; McDermott, 1987). From these patterns grow expectations that inform the behaviors and interactions of members of each family and community. These social and linguistic "codes" are determined by numerous factors, including elements of culture grown up around ethnicity, gender, religious beliefs, and position in the social-class hierarchy (Haviland). Secondary factors arise out of interaction between family and community and the larger sociopolitical milieu, including the type and level of education attained and available, familial and community history, and the perceived employment opportunities available to family and community members (Delpit; Ogbu, 1979).

The defining elements of social class—relationship to economic resources, work roles, access to power, and the cultural resources (including education) that govern entry to status positions—are thus all present in the learner's experience outside of school. Regardless of formal schooling, a child in a given community learns language and behaviors that suit her or him to take up adult roles specific to females or males in that family or community.

In the broadest sense, children are taught by the culture of family and community how to think, behave, and communicate. Research and theory have yet to develop a full account of the roles of social class in defining this culture; class and culture are, after all, distinct and should not be equated with one another. But three themes emerge from work to date, each of which contributes to our understanding of the learner's approach to the intellectual work of schooling. First, the social class of home and community shapes the learner's approach to authority, especially as manifested in work roles. Second, social class contributes to a particular kind of meaning system embedded in linguistic codes. Third, class-based conditions offer varying degrees of material security, which influences children's physical reality and attendant anxiety or contentment.

With regard to authority and work roles, the social class of family and community members can offer children an initial definition of their future places in the larger occupational structure. This definition helps to shape students' aspirations and expectations, and it results in behaviors and interactive patterns that optimize the chance for success in occupations common to their parents' social class. There is some evidence that middle-class and upper-class parents, as a group, exhibit parenting styles that foster independence, creativity, and problem-solving and reasoning skills, while lower-class parenting methods are said to emphasize docility and obedience in the face of authority and a passive learning style (Bernstein, 1970, 1977; deMarrais & LeCompte, 1999; Ogbu, 1979). These class-related parenting styles do not indicate success or failure in socializing children adequately. Rather, parenting styles reflect adaptations that maximize the chances of a child growing up to find employment in a job typical of the social class of origin (Ogbu). By this argument, working-class parents socialize their children to be responsive to authority and receptive to subservience because those are competencies required in many working-class jobs. Middle-class parents socialize their children in the competencies of reasoning, questioning, and independence because those are skills thought to be required for middle-class jobs.

With regard to class-based linguistic meaning systems, a number of researchers have focused on the nature of linguistic patterns that vary by social class. Bernstein (1977), for example, found that working-class life—organized around authority based on age, class, and gender—generates communicative codes characterized by a "particularistic" meaning system. The resulting verbal shorthand reflects the assumption that listeners are familiar with intent and meaning. Meaning is usually not made explicit

by the speaker, and directives are grounded in authority rather than rational explanation. In contrast, middle-class families tend to use a "universalistic" language code in which meaning and context are more elaborately spelled out. Working-class linguistic codes may be entirely satisfactory in the home and community, but students who do not know the nuances of universalistic communication are at a disadvantage in a school system, in which universalistic patterns predominate and middle-class teachers may be unfamiliar with lower-class students' intent and meaning.

Research focused on the linguistic teaching of nonmainstream cultural groups—which occupy lower levels of the social-class hierarchy—arrives at similar conclusions. Consider, for example, work on interrogative patterns (Heath, 1983) and the learning of "the culture of power" (Delpit, 1988). Although such research does not single out social class as the primary source of linguistic meaning systems, there is good reason to understand it as an important contributing condition.

Other factors related to the economic and social concomitants of social class can also affect a student's ability to learn. At least one in four American students live in poverty and are faced with somatic concerns revolving around unmet physical needs. Hunger, inadequate clothing, insufficient medical care, transient status, a dangerous community, and overcrowded or substandard housing are part of daily life for a growing percentage of children (Children's Defense Fund, 1991; deMarrais & LeCompte, 1999; Natriello et al., 1990; Payne & Biddle, 1999; Vail, 1996). Psychological distress arising from uncertainty about daily needs, cultural incongruence with the school, the social stigma of poverty, and a high level of familial stress is commonplace for impoverished children (Kozol, 1991; National Commission on Children, 1991; Rafferty & Shinn, 1991; Schorr, 1988). Anxiety generated by uncertainty in physical, emotional, and social survival detracts from capacity to learn, in that anxious students must devote a portion of their energy and intellectual capacity to coping with physical and emotional concerns unrelated to the academic tasks of school (Tobias, 1979). There are many social, emotional, and physical stressors that affect learners of all social classes, but lower-class students are far more likely to experience anxiety due to the economic realities of social class than are their middle-class and upper-class peers. The effects of poverty on children not only play a central role in school achievement but also affect a growing number of young people. One recent study estimated that "as a result of 'welfare reform,' 1.1 million *more* children will shortly be added to the poverty rolls in the United States" (Payne & Biddle, 1999, p. 7). On the other hand, some learners from the upper classes may face a greater degree of pressure than their middle-class and lower-class peers to succeed in intellectual tasks, and this pressure may result in personal anxiety that affects ability to learn.

The Match or Mismatch Between Social Class of Learners and of School

As the earlier discussion of educators' social class suggests, schools display a way of thinking, behaving, and communicating that is shaped by social class. Students walking through a classroom door are entering a well-established culture, complete with linguistic codes, behavioral expectations, and assumptions about the nature of teaching and learning. Most of these communicative and behavioral codes reflect the values, power dynamics, and knowledge base of mainstream middle-class or upper-class cultures (Bourdieu & Passeron, 1977; Delpit, 1988; Hurn, 1993; Nelson-Barber & Meier, 1990; Persell, 1977). To the degree to which learners have been raised in family and community environments with similar middle-class assumptions and expectations, students have a good chance of experiencing cultural congruence between family and school; that is, mainstream students in mainstream schools are more likely to understand overt communications and expectations, as well as the unspoken rules of middle-class behavior. To the degree that learners' linguistic and behavioral codes and expectations differ from those of the mainstream, students may experience cultural incongruity.

Researchers have begun to identify communicative code differences that arise in situations of cultural incongruence. Students and teachers

produce communicative breakdowns by simply performing routine and practical everyday activities in ways their subcultures define as normal and appropriate. Because behavioral competence is differently defined by different social groups, many children and teachers fail in their attempts to establish rational, trusting and rewarding relationships across ethnic, racial or class boundaries in the classroom. (McDermott, 1987, p. 173)

According to McDermott's theory of cultural incongruence (1987), school failure for lower-class children is built of the culturally incongruent actions, reactions, and interactions between middle-class teachers and lower-class "pariah" students. Because many researchers studying cultural incongruence (scholars such as Delpit, McDermott, and Ogbu) have studied populations in which race and class differences intersect, it is not always possible to disentangle the effects of one or the other of these characteristics. However, it is possible to make a good argument about the class-based nature of much racially generated cultural incongruence by demonstrating that middle-class members of racial minorities experience a greater degree

of cultural harmony with mainstream schools than do lower-class racial minorities.

Another way of looking at the match between the class-based cultures of students and schools is suggested by the work of Bourdieu (Bourdieu & Passeron, 1977), who observed, primarily in French schools, the teaching of the superiority of elite culture, especially as reflected in familiarity with the arts and use of elegant language forms. Hurn summarizes the essential argument:

Students who lack familiarity with this style, who lack what Bourdieu calls "cultural capital," will appear dull, plodding, and (at best) merely earnest, and they will be consistently typed as worthy members of the middle or lower class but as unsuitable for elite positions. . . . Schools work to conceal the real character of domination by teaching that there is only one legitimate culture and one form of approved consciousness—that of the highly educated elite. (1993, p. 197)

Lower-class children frequently lack the "cultural capital" that is valued in schools, in that they use different language forms and bring to school familiarity with different (not necessarily classical) art forms. The cultural capital that working-class children bring to school constitutes a sort of foreign currency that is undervalued in the mainstream school context (Bourdieu & Passeron, 1977).

Social Class as a Basis for Perceptions of the Learner's Capabilities

The match between what the learner brings to school—class-based modes of thinking, behaving, and communicating—and the prevailing class-based culture of the school conditions other people's perceptions of the child. In particular, adults in the school, other learners, and the students' own parents ascribe capabilities and characteristics to the student when there is no direct or objective evidence on which to base these perceptions. Here, once again, social class is closely entwined with matters of race, ethnicity, and culture. But the underlying pattern is clear: learners who are identifiably from a lower-class background (regardless of race) tend to be perceived negatively, as less capable than they probably are, while those from families and communities located higher in the social-class hierarchy tend to be perceived positively (McDermott, 1987; Persell, 1977, 1993; Rosenholtz & Rosenholtz, 1981).

Adults' Perceptions of the Learners' Capabilities. Historically, educators, researchers, and educational policy makers have tended to attach notions of deficit and asset to differences in culture, language, behavioral norms, and educational preparedness (for instance, Baratz & Baratz, 1970; also see review discussions in deMarrais &

LeCompte, 1999, and Hurn, 1993). Not surprisingly, mainstream cultural values, standard English, compliant but inquisitive behaviors, and a functional knowledge of mainstream school norms and academic skills have been considered assets for students. When educators speak about educational preparedness, socialization, or enculturation, they are often referring to this or a similar set of skills, and to standards (Nelson-Barber & Meier, 1990). To the extent that students possess *different* qualities, languages or dialects, behaviors, and knowledge, they have been considered deficient. This deficit model has worked to the disadvantage of lower-class learners in that they often have been viewed as culturally deprived or culturally disadvantaged, and the learning environment from which they originate (their families and communities) has been considered culturally impoverished:

By characterizing the environment of lower-class children as deprived, disorganized, or pathological, the cultural deprivation argument shifted attention away from the failings of the schools and of biased testing instruments to the supposed failure of poor people to bring up their children correctly. (Hurn, 1993, p. 152)

This assumption of deficit in the lives and academic readiness of lower-class students has been reified in the form of policies and programs that objectify economic disadvantage or cultural deprivation. The Head Start program, for example, was created to overcome the deprivation of disadvantage perceived to be symptomatic of low-income families (Hurn, 1993; Baratz & Baratz, 1970). Through repeated use of such terms as "economic disadvantage" or "cultural deprivation," educators and policy makers have objectified the conception of learner deficit due to low social class as something real and all but inevitable (Bloom, Davis, Hess, & Silverman, 1965; Reissman, 1962). This objectification of learner deficit slipped into the unconscious assumptions of educators; most teachers automatically assume deficiencies in the skills and abilities of lower-class students (Persell, 1977, 1993). These assumptions are compounded by the influence on teachers of "information" about students gleaned from academic records, test scores, and narrative accounts—all influenced by social class. This is significant because "much of the information teachers gain about low income children seems to be negative" (Persell, 1993, p. 80). As discussed elsewhere in this chapter, unconscious and conscious assumptions of deficit on the part of school personnel can have a profound impact on the treatment of learners through such mechanisms as differential classroom treatment (Brophy & Good, 1970; Chaikin, Sigler, & Derlega, 1974; Rosenholtz & Rosenholtz, 1981), labeling (Rist, 1977), tracking (Oakes, 1985), and career counseling. Furthermore, teacher modeling of low expectations for students is a factor in students' evaluations of their peers' skills and abilities, as discussed next (Cohen, 1986b).

Peers' Perceptions of the Learners' Capabilities. The influence of social status on perceptions of learner skills, abilities, and characteristics in the school environment is not limited to adults. Students are actively engaged in rank-ordering each other and forming social hierarchies. Although the process of peer stratification and establishing dominance is more characteristically a male than a female phenomenon (Daniels-Bierness, 1989), most students do form opinions about each other's characteristics and abilities, and frequently these opinions are initially fashioned on the basis of "diffuse status characteristics" such as race, gender, and perceived social class (Cohen, 1982, 1986b). Cohen has demonstrated that peer perceptions of learners' abilities influence social dynamics in the classroom in such a way that low-status peers are given fewer opportunities to participate meaningfully in group activities, while high-status peers tend to participate more, be listened to, and be allowed to take authority roles. Lack of low-status student participation in group activities reduces not only learning opportunities for these students but social opportunities as well by eliminating the chance for them to demonstrate skills and abilities. When students do or do not demonstrate skills and abilities, peers evaluate them differently on the basis of student social status in order to avoid what Hymel (1986) terms "affective incongruence." High-status peers are given the benefit of the doubt when not behaving as expected, while low-status student behavior tends to be negatively valued regardless of its actual content. Although it must be emphasized that *social status* and *social class* are conceptually distinct, these findings are important because, as mentioned earlier, perceived social class is one of the diffuse status characteristics used by students in assessment and assignment of social status.

Given the predictable way in which the perceptions of adults and peers in the school building are shaped by social class and other factors that bear little relationship to capabilities, it is no wonder that efforts to reform the schooling available to lower-status children have targeted the deficit model just described. "Accelerated schools" (Levin, 1988) and "complex instruction" (Cohen, 1986a), to mention only two reform proposals, have created approaches to schooling and curriculum that assume a multidimensional "asset model" of the learner. Other efforts to promote academically challenging instruction in schools serving a high concentration of low-status children are also explicit about the need to reconceive the learner (Knapp & Shields, 1990; Means, Chelemer, & Knapp, 1991).

Parents' Perceptions of the Learners' Capabilities. Parents' perceptions of student capabilities and opportunities must also be considered in a discussion of social class. Parents of any social class may have faith in their children's intellectual capabilities, but lower-class parents frequently do not trust the schools' ability to elicit the cognitive capacities of their children. That is, many lower-class parents are cognizant that the abilities of their children may not be the ones valued by middle-class teachers and anticipated by school curricula, and many understand that their children do not possess some of the skills valued by mainstream culture. The ensuing cultural mismatch can result in mutual distrust between parents and teachers and loss of hope on the part of lower-class parents that schools will educate their children adequately (Comer, 1988).

Social Class in the Peer Culture

Students in schools group themselves into peer groups of like individuals, and one of the dimensions of familiarity influencing peer-group formation is social class. Research and theory points to important effects of class-based peer culture on educational outcomes.

Because students form peer groups with others who are like themselves, speak in familiar languages (and vernaculars), behave in predictable ways, and are perceived to be academically similar, social-class sensibilities are a large determinant (though certainly not the only one) of peer-group membership. It is not inconceivable that the shared experiences of peer-group members along social-class lines in a school context may be the primary factor in setting the tone for the peer-group response to the institution of schooling. Even peer groups explicitly formed along lines of race and gender inevitably invoke class issues, through the inextricable relationships between these two characteristics and social class. It is known, for example, that disaffection with and resistance to schooling is far more common among individuals and groups of lower-class origin than among those from upper-class and middle-class families and communities (Fordham, 1988; Solomon, 1992). Of course, there are exceptions to this pattern among individuals and groups; that lower-class students are the most likely to be disaffected does not mean that most lower-class children *are* disaffected. Contented and discontented students exist at all levels of the social-class hierarchy.

The peer culture provides a sense of community and belonging to students (Fordham & Ogbu, 1986). In essence, one's peer culture is analogous to one's family within the school; it plays a similar role in offering models, shaping aspirations, establishing expectations, and forming identity. As students get older and less dependent on adult approval, peer-group influence strengthens. Indeed, any casual observer of youth is likely to note that the opinions of peers are a great deal more salient to adolescents than those of school staff.

One of the common tasks of a peer culture within a school is to define its members' response to the social and academic learning environment. If the school is a safe, stimulating, validating, and reinforcing environment for members of the peer group, the spoken or unspoken standards of the group may well emphasize success within the social and academic parameters of the school. For instance, some middle-class and upper-class peer groups may consist of successful students who are active in the formal extracurricular culture of school, including participation in athletics, cheerleading, debate club, chess club, student government, or other sanctioned school activities. Conversely, peer groups consisting of students who find school an unfamiliar, unfair, unstimulating, or hostile environment may develop a culture that is centered around or includes elements of resistance to the formal culture of the school (Anyon, 1980; McDermott, 1987; Neufeld, 1991). This resistance may take many forms, among them noncompliance or nonparticipation in the classroom, outright defiance of school staff and school regulations, cutting class, dropping out, or engaging in illegal activities on or off school grounds (Solomon, 1992).

How the Learner's Social Class Relates to Educational Outcomes

When one brings the learner into focus, the web of potential influences on educational outcomes becomes more interconnected and richly textured. Differing social-class backgrounds condition learners' approaches to the intellectual work of schooling. The gap between the class-based world from which the learner comes and the essentially middle-class culture of the school compounds the matter; teachers and learners may misunderstand each other in their daily interactions, and both adults and other students will form impressions of the learner's capabilities based on visible class-related characteristics, among other traits. Finally, peer groups form, in part influenced by the learners' social class, and may provide a united response to schooling, whether supportive or resistant.

Taken together, these class-based dynamics predispose learners from a higher-social-class background to perform more effectively in the typical school setting, and those from a lower-class background to perform less so, regardless of their innate abilities. However, student performance also reflects the nature of instruction itself, to which we now turn.

SOCIAL CLASS AND THE NATURE
OF INSTRUCTION

We have considered the role of social class in setting the community and school context for instruction and in shaping what the principal participants—teachers and learners—bring to instructional interactions. In this section, we turn to instruction itself by examining first what is taught (content) and second how it is taught (pedagogy) in the class contexts that result from the sorting processes described earlier in the chapter. In our analysis of instruction, we include both the formal and the hidden curricula of schooling. In organizing our discussion by what is taught and how it is taught, we acknowledge the difficulty of separating content from pedagogy. Nonetheless, the distinction is analytically useful in ways that will become apparent as we proceed.

What we know about the relationship of social class and instruction comes from various sources, especially from the growing literature on "curriculum differentiation" (see Oakes et al., 1992, for a recent comprehensive review) and from interpretive research on the sociology of the curriculum (see deMarrais & LeCompte, 1999, for a review of this work). Even within these traditions, relatively few studies have attempted to trace the links between social class and instruction in any detail and with any attention to the complexities inherent in the concept of class. More often, one encounters SES or parental income level as one among many variables predicting, or correlated with, some feature of content and pedagogy. Such quantitative research offers the statistical power of larger samples and presents clues to the puzzle, but it does not produce a compelling account of the mechanisms by which social class connects with instruction. To trace such links, we must rely more extensively on observational and ethnographic research (Anyon, 1980, 1981; Metz, 1990; Wilcox, 1982).

Research on the relationship between social class and instruction reveals a consistent pattern. Both content and pedagogy vary systematically with the class context of schooling. Put simply, the instruction available to students lower down on (any) social-class scale is, on average, academically less challenging, more repetitive, and more dominated by a concern for social control than that offered to students of higher-social-class background. Thus, in the aggregate, learners from different social-class backgrounds are typically taught different content and are taught it in a distinctive manner.

What Is Taught (Content)

When considering what is taught, one must examine the content of both the formal curriculum and the hidden curriculum embedded in instructional materials and the design of learning tasks. We include within the content of the formal curriculum the kinds of information and knowledge—and also the implied conception of knowledge and its sources—conveyed by materials, learning tasks, direct instruction, articulation of content across grades, and the array of informational resources to which learners have predictable access. These sources offer explicit statements of values, beliefs, and ideologies that are also part of the formal curriculum content. The content of the hidden curriculum includes values, norms, and beliefs regarding the organization of society, authority, work, the economy, achievement, success or failure, the purpose of learning, and the place of the individual in relation to these concerns. This content is implied rather than stated and is conveyed in myriad ways, most subconscious.

Social class enters the examination of curricular content in two ways. First, the curriculum teaches *about* class—what it is, how social classes relate to one another. Second, the curriculum *reflects* (some would argue, is tailored to) the social-class context of instruction. Put another way, systematic differences in the curriculum *are associated with* the social-class composition of the student population.

Social Class as Part of the Content of Instruction. Regarding social class as a focus or topic of study, the formal curriculum says relatively little. Systematic reviews of leading textbooks, for example, reveal remarkably little about social class in any subject area (Anyon, 1979; Sleeter & Grant, 1991). Rather, instructional materials in common use are "class-blind," conveying the message that social class is not a significant feature of life. In examining the kinds and conceptions of knowledge taught in differing class contexts, Anyon's classic research (1980, 1981) found that upper-elementary children were taught little about the history, prevalence, or operation of class-related phenomena in the United States. Thus the curriculum teaches about social life as much by what it excludes as what it includes. The same phenomenon has been noted in studies of the treatment of gender (see Sadker, Sadker, & Long, 1993).

If anything, the formal curriculum systematically underrepresents the experience of individuals living at either extreme of the social-class hierarchy, as well as the variety of perspectives that can be brought to bear on these experiences or the hierarchy as a whole. Conversely, the curriculum typically overrepresents the experience and worldview of middle-class America, in line with prevailing ideologies of the nation as an egalitarian society in which individual effort counts most. The class-blind character of the curriculum thus mirrors what has long been a fact of life in U.S. society: that the lives of the poor and rich are relatively invisible to the great majority of Americans (deMarrais & LeCompte, 1999).

Differentiation of Content by Social Class. Regarding the correspondence between curricular content and the social-class composition of the student population, most of what has been learned derives from careful comparative inquiry into what is taught in different social-class contexts. Such research (at the elementary level, see Anyon, 1980, 1981; Wilcox, 1982; at the secondary level, Oakes, 1985) reveals a pattern of formal content differentiated on at least these dimensions: focus on "advanced" versus "basic" skills, focus on conceptual understanding, range and variety of academic tasks, degree of repetition, extent of topical coverage, and attention to "practical" knowledge (i.e., with immediate vocational applications). In broad strokes, the content taught to learners in higher-status class contexts is typically more conceptual, varied, challenging, wide ranging, and focused on advanced skills than the content taught in lower-status class contexts, and at the same time less repetitive and less focused on knowledge with immediate practical application.

Underlying these differences are divergent conceptions of knowledge itself. Consider, for example, how Anyon (1981) characterizes the prevailing conception of knowledge in two working-class elementary schools:

What counts as knowledge in these two working class schools is not knowledge as concepts, cognitions, information or ideas about society, language, math, or history, connected to conceptual principles or understandings of some sort. Rather, it seems that what constitutes school knowledge here is (1) fragmented facts, isolated from context and connection to each other or wider bodies of meaning, or to activity or biography of the students; and (2) knowledge of "practical" rule-governed behaviors—procedures by which the students carry out tasks that are largely mechanical. Sustained conceptual or "academic" knowledge has only occasional, symbolic presence here. (p. 12)

These conceptions contrast sharply with those that predominated in an elementary school serving children mostly from affluent professional families:

Knowledge in the affluent professional school is not only conceptual, but is open to discovery, construction, and meaning making; it is not always given. Knowledge is often concepts and ideas that are used to make sense, and that thus have personal value. Although knowledge may result from personal creativity and independent thinking, there are constraints and directives on what counts as answers. Knowledge has individualistic goals, but it also may be a resource for social good. It is analytical and more realistic about society than knowledge in the middle class and working class schools. The children are also getting a good dose of two dominant ideologies: that the system itself will be made more humane by expressions of concern for the less fortunate, and that individuals, not groups, make history. (p. 23)

These differences in formal content are accompanied and reinforced by a hidden curriculum of values, norms, and beliefs related to society, work roles, and the students' relationship to these roles. One comparative ethnographic study of first-grade classrooms in both a lower-middle-class and an upper-middle-class elementary school identifies clear differences in lessons about the child's self-presentation skills, relationship to authority, and images of self at present and in the future (Wilcox, 1982). In the lower-status school, children were taught to see themselves as part of an externally controlled hierarchical system, given limited opportunities to develop self-presentation skills, and focused on the present with little reference to their future. Their counterparts in the upper-middle-class school were taught to internalize control over their actions, given daily practice in self-presentation skills, and helped to develop images of their prospects for the future (in second grade, for example, but also in the distant future, at college and beyond).

A parallel pattern pertains at the secondary level, though with differences that relate to the organization of schooling at this level. Unlike the elementary level, where the official scope and sequence of subject matter to be taught in the respective schools were relatively similar, the formal and hidden content of what is taught in secondary schools is, in varying degrees, formally differentiated by tracks (or their equivalent) that are designed for learners with presumably different educational and occupational futures (Oakes, 1985; Oakes et al., 1992; Page, 1991). The differentiated pattern occurs both across tracks (college prep, general, vocational) and, within track, by ability (the top, middle, and lower English classes within a given grade). The variable array of elective courses is itself deployed informally along a continuum from more to less demanding.

There are various ways for the differences in content to be associated with class context at the secondary level. First, as in the case of elementary schools, high schools serve attendance areas that reflect some residential segregation by class, which gives the schools as a whole a distinctive class-related character (Metz, 1990). Second, within high schools, learners from different social classes are unequally distributed among tracks (and even within tracks), and these disparities grow with time (Oakes et al., 1992). Predictably and consistently, learners from lower-status social backgrounds are concentrated in lower-track classrooms. In general terms, such placement means a pronounced departure from what is taught in "more advanced" courses; less material is covered overall, the knowledge is more fragmented, and less is asked of the learner. Although nominally addressing the same subject matter as more advanced classrooms (and generating the same credit toward graduation), low-track classrooms may offer "less detail" (that is, less demanding content), "practical skill building" (reading skills rather than substance), "relevance" (topics chosen for their appeal to disaffected adolescents), or some combination of these components (Page, 1991, p. 181).

The ostensible basis for selecting course content (and for track placement, as discussed earlier in the chapter) is the learner's presumed or demonstrated level of ability and achievement. It is thus easy to assume, as many educators do, that social background plays no real part in these differences. By this argument, the unequal social distribution of learners is simply an unfortunate side effect.

There is no clear empirical evidence to resolve the matter, but there are grounds for a counterposition. First, the contrasts in curriculum across schools of differing social-class context are striking. Unless one assumes that whole populations of learners are simply less capable overall—a dubious assumption in the light of advanced placement calculus results from "turnaround" inner-city high schools (Matthews, 1988)—then there is likely to be less matching of curriculum with actual ability than educators claim. Second, because differential grouping by ability appears to compound the measured differences in achievement over time, any intrusion of social background factors in the process will be carried forward over time (Goodlad & Oakes, 1988). Third, the correspondence between what is taught and the knowledge requirements of the work roles of learners' parents is remarkably close. If one makes the assumptions that (a) society needs an array of skilled and unskilled workers in roughly similar proportions to the present, and (b) in the absence of good information teachers will assume that learners' capabilities and occupational futures resemble those of their parents, then the correspondence between what is taught and social-class background is not accidental but instead highly functional (Wilcox, 1982). Without necessarily intending to do so, teachers and schools thus tailor curriculum to social-class background (this linkage is still an association more than a clear causal claim).

To put this argument in some perspective, there are many similarities in curriculum across class contexts, perhaps more than the ethnographic research base suggests. Analysts find, for example, a great deal of repetition in the curriculum at all levels, emphasis on coverage of factual material, and relatively little intellectual challenge (Gehrke, Knapp, & Sirotnik, 1992). Interpretive research on high school lower-track classrooms finds them "paradoxically different *and* similar . . . as versions of a particular school's regular classes, rather than as readily distinguishable phenomena" (Page, 1991, p. 237).

We should point out that differences in the formal and hidden curricula across class contexts often reflect more than social class. Race, ethnicity, and gender, among other social factors, also appear to be implicated in the differentiation of content, in ways that are analytically distinct from, though often intertwined with, social class. Nonmainstream ethnic backgrounds and experiences, for example, are systematically underrepresented in curriculum materials or selection of content and, by implication, are undervalued. In many instances in which minority-group members are concentrated in lower-status groupings, instructional content is differentiated concurrently by ethnicity and social class.

How the Content Is Taught (Pedagogy)

The manner in which curricular content is taught also differs systematically by class context and reinforces the messages embedded in instructional materials, learning tasks, and the scope and sequence of content. Pedagogy conveys overt and covert lessons about learners' intrinsic worth, prospects for success in school, and relationships with authority and control. For our purposes, *pedagogy* includes the teacher's approach to teaching subject matter, classroom management (to the extent this can be distinguished from content-specific pedagogy), personal style of interacting with learners, and control over learning tasks. We assume that pedagogy, as we have defined it, is interactive and thus jointly constructed by teachers and learners.

The prevailing pattern of instruction in lower-class and working-class contexts emphasizes "transmission" teaching (for example, Hargreaves, 1988; Knapp & Shields, 1991; Oakes, 1990); tight control of classroom interactions; heavy-handed discipline; teacher control of learning tasks; reliance on seat work and worksheet activities; and an impersonal, authoritarian style that is often disrespectful of learners. This instructional style responds to, and in reciprocal fashion aggravates, the often-identified pattern of resistance to schooling by students in such contexts (Anyon, 1981; deMarrais & LeCompte, 1999; Erickson, 1987). This approach to pedagogy teaches students that little is expected of them (except perhaps minimal compliance), they are not highly valued, they cannot be trusted to guide their own learning or conduct themselves responsibly in the classroom, and they must accept low-level positions in a rigidly controlled hierarchy.

The prevailing pattern in higher-status social-class contexts contrasts in predictable ways. Teachers in such schools tend to rely less on transmission modes of teaching (though there is still plenty of it), employ a wider range of approaches to classroom control and discipline, and offer more opportunities for learner control of learning tasks (see Oakes et al., 1992, for a review of studies related to this point). Teachers tend to interact with learners in a more personalized and respectful way. On their part, learners are more outwardly cooperative (Metz, 1990) and accepting of the school's implicit premise (LeCompte & Dworkin, 1988). Both obviously and subtly, this pedagogical pattern encourages students to develop a greater sense of self-worth, higher expectations for school success, and a broader range of possibilities for fitting into hierarchies of control at different levels.

Though it probably describes much of what teachers and learners experience in school at all levels, this stark contrast in pedagogy by class context masks some complexities and ambiguities. First, though most closely matched with the culture of the school and most likely to be accepting of schooling, learners from middle-class and affluent families are not the only ones who buy into the teaching and learning patterns they encounter in the school building. For example, the children of recent immigrant families and refugees, though often positioned in a lower social class, are typically highly responsive to schooling, transmission teaching and all (deMarrais & LeCompte, 1999). Second, the learners' experience of lower-track and upper-track pedagogy is more varied than the preceding scenario suggests. In some instances, learners do not find the former pedagogy oppressive and may even feel that it facilitates academic learning, while the latter can be highly routinized and skill-based (Oakes et al., 1992). The distinctive culture of the school may provide remarkably different meanings to lower-track participation, as in this summary by Oakes et al. of findings from Metz's study of two desegregated junior high schools (1978):

In one school, lower-track placement was stigmatizing, exacerbated racial divisions, and provoked uneasy truces or classroom mayhem. At the other school, lessons proceeded and there were more positive relations between and among teachers and students. Worksheets predominated in both schools' lower-track curriculum, but in one context they signified the teachers' distance from and control of students, whereas in the second, they signified the provision of manageable assignments, shelter from public failure, and reassuring routine. (Oakes et al., 1992, p. 588)

Consequences for Learning and Credentialing

Differentiated instruction entails various consequences for learning. Because the curricula are received by learners with divergent social-class profiles, the net effect is for these students to absorb, on average, different kinds and amounts of knowledge. Not surprisingly, learning outcomes vary by learners' social class. At least three kinds of effect have been considered in research to date: normative and attitudinal learning, cognitive learning, and credentialing.

Regarding the learning of specific norms and attitudes, the discussion of differentiated instruction has already summarized the principal evidence available. Because normative learning is subtle, subliminal, and pervasive, no large-scale database presents satisfactory evidence for assessing claims in this regard. We must rely on more closely examined small-scale studies, which suggest in

effect that divergent norms—ranging from obedience and respect for external authority at the lower end of the social-class hierarchy to independence and individual initiative at the upper end—are communicated and learned by students in their respective class contexts. The evidence also suggests that learners are by no means passive and compliant in this regard; for example, students in lower-track contexts may internalize norms of resistance as much as they come to accept external control. Similarly, most researchers agree that learners form distinctive attitudes about schooling that vary with social-class context, with those in higher-status contexts forming generally more positive attitudes. However, the sources of these attitudes are much in dispute. In all probability, differentiated instruction is only one of a complex of forces both inside and outside the school that contribute to their formation.

Regarding cognitive learning, the predominant bodies of research rely on large-scale quantitative databases in which achievement-test scores are the principal dependent variable (see Hurn, 1993, and Oakes et al., 1992, for reviews of this evidence base). The evidence base is mixed, but on the whole it appears to demonstrate that learners in higher-ability groups or track placements gain more than those lower in the school stratification system. Furthermore, considerable evidence indicates that the disparities in cognitive achievement increase with time, suggesting that there are cumulative effects of differentiated instruction.

Regarding persistence in school and the acquisition of credentials, the evidence is relatively consistent and strong: participation in higher-track programs and experiences increases the likelihood that learners will persist in school and attain higher-status educational credentials (Hurn, 1993; Oakes et al., 1992). It is a reasonable inference, then, that the differentiated instruction available to learners of differing social-class backgrounds contributes in no small measure to these outcomes.

PUTTING THE STORY TOGETHER

This chapter suggests a broad general argument about the nature of the relationship between social class and schooling. In brief, we have argued that social class contributes to an increasingly differentiated pattern of schooling over time, and that this differentiation is one determinant of educational outcomes. Drawing on the alternative perspectives noted at the beginning of the chapter, we review the principal explanations offered to date for this pattern and its consequences. These explanations and the research base on which they rest leave a number of issues for future research to explore, which we suggest at the close of the chapter.

Explanations for the Differentiation of Schooling and Its Consequences

Each of the realms we have examined—the community context, social organization of the student population, the teaching force and the conditions under which it works, the learners as individuals and peer groups, and instruction—appears to contribute to class-related differentiation in the learner's schooling experience. Associated with these experiences are systematic differences in educational outcomes. To what extent can the differentiated pattern and its consequences be attributed to social class? Put another way, is it plausible, theoretically and empirically, that social class exerts an influence on outcomes? If so, how does it do so?

Explaining the differentiation of schooling and its consequences is not an easy matter and depends heavily on the analyst's framework. The explanations typically offered combine one or more of (a) the composition and expectations of the communities served by schools, (b) the capabilities and background of the teaching force, (c) the conditions under which teachers work, (d) the nature of the students and their response to schooling, and (e) the explicit intentions of powerful interests inside and outside the school system.

The Nature of Communities Served by the Schools. Communities that differ in social-class profile demand different things of schools and their children. Reflecting differences in power and the ability to advocate their interests both individually and collectively, community members express and press their demands more or less effectively. Furthermore, whatever community members actually feel about the school, school personnel tend to perceive the communities' wants differently, depending on social-class context. Finally, communities that are higher in social class typically have greater collective resources to offer educational institutions, as well as greater individual resources to enable (private) school choice. As detailed earlier in the chapter, lower-class and working-class contexts are less likely to make active and sustained demands for academically challenging instruction; are more likely to expect tight control of instruction and student behavior; are less likely, on average, to encourage high academic achievement, or at least to model the meaning of high academic achievement; are more likely to be perceived as preferring tight control and caring less about academic challenges; and are more likely to perceive the school as a hostile institution (the role of social class in this pattern of hostility is complicated in mixed-race situations).

Social class thus plays a major role in shaping parents' aspirations for their children, parental access to school personnel, ability to bring pressure to bear on the schools, expectations for instructional behavior, perceptions of community demands, and resources for school support or school choice. The more homogeneous in terms of social class one assumes that a community is, the stronger this argument becomes. The more diverse the school community, the more it is likely to send mixed signals and raise for school people the question of which signals to attend.

The Nature and Capabilities of the Teaching Force. A second set of explanations holds that schooling differs by class context and produces outcomes that differ with the kind of teacher working in each context. Seen with a functionalist lens, teachers in lower- and working-class contexts are less capable, on average, than those in a higher-social-class context. Teachers of talent are drawn to schools serving a higher-social-class population by greater rewards, improved working conditions (discussed next), and enhanced prestige that come with higher-status students. Viewed from a critical perspective, the matter is less one of teaching ability and more the match between the teachers' own social-class sensibilities and the individuals they teach. Teachers gravitate (by choice, assignment, or both) to a social-class context in which they feel most at home or at least are more closely matched with the student population they are teaching. Thus teachers in lower-status schools are more likely to originate from lower-class and working-class backgrounds and hence are more likely to be guided by the aspirations and styles typical of individuals from these backgrounds.

Here, social class serves either as a source of prestige to which people of talent are attracted, or as a primary consideration, conscious or unconscious, in the sorting of teachers by social-class context.

Conditions Under Which Teachers Work. From this perspective, differentiated schooling and unequal outcomes reflect variations in the conditions of work (defined by the resource environment, rewards and incentives, degree of professional autonomy, and collegial culture), which are in part shaped by the social class of communities, students, and teachers. Teachers in lower-class and working-class contexts are more likely to experience severe resource constraints, receive fewer rewards for good work, see fewer incentives to work hard, have less autonomy, and work within a professional culture that discourages complex forms of teaching. Hence it is understandable that teachers gravitate to the least demanding forms of teaching (such as transmission teaching), and plausible that these forms of teaching should produce lower educational outcomes, on average.

Social class enters into this set of explanations in complex ways—for example, by shaping the availability of resources (for rewards, facilities, or materials), influencing teachers' assessment of the quality of their work lives, or influencing the formation of a collegial culture within the school.

The Nature of the Students and Their Response to Schooling. This explanation holds that students are increasingly segregated by social class as they progress through the grades, within schools (by program or track) and somewhat across schools (where schools differentially prepare students for different kinds of occupational outcomes). The social composition of the students in a given ability group, classroom, track, or school shapes perceptions of ability, expectations for success, the education offered to them, and their way of responding to it. In comparison with higher-status contexts, lower-class and working-class contexts present teachers with a student population that uses communicative codes different from those of the teachers, appears to be less capable in a mainstream context, and is arguably more difficult to teach. Such populations include a higher proportion of students with specialized learning needs. Students in such contexts are more likely to manifest active or passive forms of resistance, as discussed earlier in the chapter. Given the typical mismatch in cultural and social-class terms between these students and the school, they are likely to appear deficient and be judged less capable. As a consequence, instruction that demands less and controls more is a natural (default) approach to the teaching task. It is natural, even inevitable, that students who are asked for less will achieve less on conventional measures of educational outcomes.

Here, social class affects instructional outcomes by influencing how students are perceived, distributing specialized learning needs unequally, encouraging class-based grouping, and encouraging resistance to schooling. This explanation is complicated by the tendency for lower-class and working-class contexts to present the teacher with greater ethnic and cultural diversity.

The Intentions of Powerful Interests Inside and Outside the School System. The fifth set of explanations posits a driving force that is external to teachers, students, and the interaction among them. In this view, the mandates, requirements, and other decisions of educational leaders respond to key constituencies for education (for instance, corporate interests) and in so doing encourage different curricula to be taught to children with different class origins. From this perspective, lower-class and working-class contexts tend to be targeted by corporate interests as a source of unskilled and semiskilled labor; viewed as deficient in basic skills by the educational establishment, hence needing a less challenging curriculum; or viewed as too numerous for, or less deserving of, exposure to the status culture, which would lose its meaning if too many people acquired it.

Here, social class acts as a marker of appropriateness for particular niches in the social and occupational hierarchy, where appropriateness is judged by those with greater power in society. The argument rests on a demonstration of intentionality on the part of various powerful interests and the degree of confluence between their interests or desires and educational practices.

Using Different Perspectives to Weigh These Explanations. The three frameworks presented at the beginning of the chapter combine elements of these five explanations in several ways, and are more or less convincing in particular respects.

Critical perspectives leave the most room for individual and group construction of the meaning of social-class position; acknowledge power differentials explicitly; explain resistance patterns well; and demonstrate clearly how class consciousness might be passed on from parents to children, among peers in school, and to a limited extent by teachers who come from similar social origins. Critical perspectives assert the greatest role for social class in the subjective experience of the individual.

Conflict accounts offer the most satisfactory explanation of the unequal power distribution among social groups and the consequences of these power disparities for the kinds of schooling available to members of these groups. Conflict accounts also identify pervasive influences of social class in the schooling process, particularly with regard to sorting, tracking, and streaming. These accounts, however, tend to assume tighter coupling of schooling to societal outcomes and greater, more direct control of schooling by power elites than is warranted by the evidence to date. In addition, conflict accounts do a better job of describing social prospects in the aggregate than at the individual level.

Functional accounts are the weakest of the three in explaining the prevailing patterns of peer interaction, sorting, and instructional differentiation when these are viewed as group phenomena. Functional explanations do a better job of explaining individual mobility across social-class lines at the margins, and incremental shifts in social-group prospects over time. Functional accounts assert that social-class-related forces have the least to do with the processes of schooling itself. Like conflict accounts, functional arguments insist on greater coupling between schooling and society than the existing evidence suggests.

Challenges for Future Research

Existing research and theory leave many puzzles for scholars. In particular, research and theory should:

1. *Explore how existing scholarship can be informed and elaborated by feminist views of class and views rooted in*

race and ethnicity. The connections among class, race, and gender are numerous and deserve to be more fully explored than they have been to date (an exploration of these connections has not been attempted in this chapter). But the task is greater than merely disentangling highly correlated variables or demonstrating instances in which two or more of these variables form a reinforcing social pattern. The task involves a reconsideration of the meaning of class—as, for example, in light of feminist thinking, which approaches class in a way that departs markedly from conventional positional conceptions of stratification systems.

2. *Investigate multiple meanings of social class and the variability within social class categories.* Understandings of the role of social class in educational processes are still too dependent on empirical work relying on crude categorical markers of class identity, which assumes a high degree of constancy of composition or meaning within any particular class category. Further research could productively explore the differences among working-class communities or affluent professional communities, to identify and describe the development of distinctive class-based relationships with schooling. Students' class sensibilities probably vary within broad social-class groupings in important ways that are as yet unexplored, reflecting the subtle variations in the meaning of social class in the communities from which they come. Interpretive research aimed at uncovering these meanings could make a significant contribution to current understandings.

3. *Study educators' responses to social class.* Research to date tells us that educators are generally socialized to ignore social class (especially their own), or else to operate from crude stereotypes based on the perceived class of their students. As awareness grows of the profound and subtle workings of class in the interaction among learners, teachers, and subject matter, educators are likely to develop more sophisticated frameworks for understanding social class dynamics and to adapt their programs to minimize limitations on young people's learning or futures. Research that looks closely at such programs, in comparison with other forms of schooling, may help to establish the possibilities for educators to alter the normal trajectory of social class in the educational process.

4. *Examine the intersection of policy, poverty, and schooling.* Recent and foreseeable policy actions have the potential to affect substantially both the economic circumstances of children's lives and the conditions of their schooling. Research is needed that will consider how particular policies—or the policy environment, more generally—affect the encounter between educators and young people of different social classes. For example, by minimizing or accentuating tracking, giving parents greater choice over their children's schooling options, or restructuring school programs, policies may reshape the interaction among learners, teachers, and content, and the resulting academic and social learning. Furthermore, policies may directly affect the economic circumstances of young people's lives (welfare reform policies) as well as their prospects for completing school and attaining credentials (high-stakes accountability policies). The "natural experiment" afforded by rapidly changing economic conditions and by policy experimentation by state and federal governments are an important opportunity to explicitly understand the workings of social class in schooling.

In closing, we urge a touch of humility in the aspirations and claims of those who study social class and schooling. The goal is not to identify simple, powerful relationships between discrete variables but rather to understand the subtle yet profound roles of a pervasive social condition in the lives of educators and those they educate. In this vein, we find ourselves subscribing to the view argued by Metz (1990) and others that

class positions are not simply determinative of either attitude or action. Every school will have students, teachers, and administrators who bring a somewhat distinctive mix of class (and racial and gender) perspectives to the social life inside a school building. While class is a crucial element in constituting the life of every school, it never determines that life in any simple or complete sense. (p. 99)

References

Anyon, J. (1979). Ideology and United States history textbooks. *Harvard Educational Review, 49*(3), 361–386.

Anyon, J. (1980). Social class and the hidden curriculum of work. *Journal of Education, 162,* 67–92.

Anyon, J. (1981). Social class and school knowledge. *Curriculum Inquiry, 11*(1), 3–42.

Apple, M. (1978). The new sociology of education: Analyzing cultural and economic reproduction. *Harvard Educational Review, 48,* 495–503.

Apple, M. (1980). The other side of the hidden curriculum: Correspondence theories and the labor process. *Journal of Education, 162,* 47–66.

Apple, M. (1986). *Teachers and texts: A political economy of class and gender relations in education.* New York: Methuen.

Ayella, M. E., & Williamson, J. B. (1976). The social mobility of women: A causal model of socioeconomic success. *Sociological Quarterly, 17,* 334–354.

Ball, S. & Vincent, C. (2001). New class relations in education: The strategies of the "fearful" middle classes. In J. Demaine (Ed.), *Sociology of education today.* New York: Palgrave.

Ballantine, J. H. (1993). *The sociology of education: A systemic analysis* (3rd ed.). Englewood Cliffs, NJ: Prentice-Hall.

Banks, J. A. (1993, April). *What does it mean to integrate race, ethnicity, class, and gender in theory and research?* Paper presented at the annual meeting of the American Education Research Association, Atlanta.

Baratz, S. S., & Baratz, J. C. (1970). Early childhood intervention: The social science base of institutional racism. *Harvard Educational Review, 40,* 29–50.

Bennett, K., & LeCompte, M. (1990). *The way school works.* New York: Longman.

Bensman, J., & Vidich, A. J. (1971). *The new American society: The revolution of the middle class.* Chicago: Quadrangle Books.

Bernstein, B. (1970). *Class, codes and control: Vol. I. Theoretical studies towards a sociology of language.* London: Routledge & Kegan Paul.

Bernstein, B. (1977). *Class, codes and control: Vol. III. Towards a theory of educational transmission.* London: Routledge & Kegan Paul.

Betz, M., & Garland, J. (1974). Intergenerational mobility rates of urban school teachers. *Sociology of Education, 47,* 511–522.

Birman, B. F., Orland, M. E., Jung, R., Anson, R. J., Garcia, G. N., Moore, M. T., et al. (1987). *The current operation of the Chapter 1 program.* Washington, DC: U.S. Department of Education.

Bloom, B. S., Davis, A., Hess, R. D., & Silverman, S. B. (1965). *Compensatory education for cultural deprivation.* New York: Holt, Rinehart, & Winston.

Boudon, R. (1974). *Education, opportunity and social inequality.* New York: Wiley.

Bourdieu, P., & Passeron, J. (1977). *Reproduction in education, society and culture.* London: Sage.

Bowles, S., & Gintis, H. (1976). *Schooling in capitalist America: Educational reform and the contradictions of economic life.* New York: Basic Books.

Brophy, J. E., & Good, T. L. (1970). Teachers' communication of differential expectations for children's classroom performance: Some behavioral data. *Journal of Educational Psychology, 61,* 365–374.

Caldas, S. J., & Bankston, C., III (1997). Effect of school population socioeconomic status on individual academic achievement. *Journal of Educational Research, 90(5),* 269–277.

Chaikin, A. L., Sigler, E., & Derlega, V. J. (1974). Nonverbal mediators of teacher expectancy effects. *Journal of Personality and Social Psychology, 30,* 144–149.

Children's Defense Fund. (1992). *The state of America's children, 1992.* Washington, DC: Author.

Cicourel, A. V., & Kitsuse, J. (1963). *The educational decision makers.* Indianapolis: Bobbs-Merrill.

Cohen, E. G. (1982). Expectation states and interracial interaction in school settings. *Annual Review of Sociology, 8,* 209–235.

Cohen, E. (1986a). *Designing groupwork: Teaching strategies for heterogeneous classrooms.* New York: Teachers College Press.

Cohen, E. (1986b). On the sociology of the classroom. In J. H. Hannaway & M. E. Lockheed (Eds.), *The contributions of the social sciences to educational policy and practice: 1965–1985* (pp. 127–162). Berkeley, CA: McCutchan.

Coleman, J. S. (1990). *Equality and achievement in education.* Denver: Westview Press.

Coleman, J. S., Campbell, E. Q., Hobson, C. J., McPartland, J., Mood, A. M., Weinfeld, F. C., et al. (1966). *Equality of educational opportunity.* Washington, DC: Government Printing Office.

Collins, R. (1979). *The credential society.* New York: Academic Press.

Comer, J. P. (1988). Educating poor minority children. *Scientific American, 259(5),* 42–48.

Connell, R. W., Ashenden, D. J., Kessler, S., & Dawsett, G. W. (1982). *Making the difference.* Sydney: George Allen & Unwin.

Dahrendorf, R. (1970). Marx's theory of class. In M. Tumin (Ed.), *Readings on social stratification* (pp. 3–16). Englewood Cliffs, NJ: Prentice-Hall.

Daniels-Bierness, T. (1989). Measuring peer status in boys and girls: A problem of apples and oranges? In B. Schneider, G. Attili, J. Nadel, & R. Weissber (Eds.), *Social competence in developmental perspective* (pp. 107–120). The Netherlands: Kluwer Academic Press.

Davis, A. (1951). Socio-economic influences on learning. *Phi Delta Kappan, 32,* 253–256.

Delpit, L. D. (1988). The silenced dialogue: Power and pedagogy in educating other people's children. *Harvard Educational Review, 58,* 280–298.

deMarrais, K. B., & LeCompte, M. D. (1999). *The way schools work* (3rd ed.). New York: Longman.

Erickson, F. (1987). Transformation and school success: The politics and culture of educational achievement. *Anthropology and Education Quarterly, 18,* 335–356.

Findley, W., & Bryan, M. (1975). *The pros and cons of ability grouping.* Washington, DC: National Education Association.

Fordham, S. (1988). Racelessness as a factor in Black students' school success: Pragmatic strategy or Pyrrhic victory? *Harvard Educational Review, 58,* 54–84.

Fordham, S., & Ogbu, J. (1986). Black students' school success: Coping with the burden of acting White. *Urban Review, 18,* 176–206.

Freire, P. (1970). *Pedagogy of the oppressed.* New York: Continuum.

Gamoran, A. (1992). Social factors in education. In M. Alkin (Ed.), *Encyclopedia of Educational Research* (pp. 1222–1229). New York: Macmillan.

Gardner, H. (1987). The theory of multiple intelligences. *Annual Dyslexia, 37,* 19–35.

Garnier, M., & Raffalovich, L. (1984). The evolution of equality of educational opportunities in France. *Sociology of Education, 57,* 1–10.

Gay, G. (1986). Multi-cultural teacher education. In J. A. Banks & J. Lynch (Eds.), *Multicultural education in Western societies* (pp. 154–177). London: Holt, Rinehart, & Winston.

Gehrke, N., Knapp, M. S., & Sirotnik, K. (1992). In search of the school curriculum. In G. Grant (Ed.), *Review of Research in Education* (Vol. 18, pp. 51–110). Washington, DC: American Educational Research Association.

Goldstein, B. (1967). *Low-income youth in urban areas: A critical review of the literature.* New York: Holt, Rinehart, & Winston.

Goodlad, J., & Oakes, J. (1988). We must offer equal access to knowledge. *Educational Leadership, 45,* 16–22.

Gramsci, A. (1971). *Selections from the prison notebooks*. New York: International.

Haggard, E. A. (1954). Social status and intelligence. *Genetic Psychology Monographs, 49,* 141–186.

Haller, E. J., & Davis, S. A. (1981). Teacher perceptions, parental social status, and grouping for reading instruction. *Sociology of Education, 54,* 162–173.

Halsey, A. H., Heath, A. F., & Ridge, J. M. (1980). *Origins and destinations: Family, class, and education in modern Britain*. Oxford: Clarendon Press.

Hargreaves, A. (1988). Teaching quality: A sociological analysis. *Journal of Curriculum Studies, 20*(3), 211–231.

Haviland, W. A. (1990). *Cultural anthropology*. Fort Worth, TX: Holt, Rinehart, & Winston.

Heath, S. B. (1983). *Ways with words: Language, life, and work in communities and classrooms*. Cambridge, England: Cambridge University Press.

Heber, R. (1979). Sociocultural mental retardation—A longitudinal study. Paper cited in Hoult, T. F. (1979). *Sociology for a new day* (2nd ed.). New York: Random House.

Hemmings, A. E., & Metz, M. H. (1990). Real teaching: How high school teachers negotiate societal, local community, and student pressures when they define their work. In R. Page & L. Valli (Eds.), *Curriculum differentiation: Interpretive studies in U.S. secondary schools* (pp. 91–112). Albany: State University of New York Press.

Herrnstein, R. J., & Murray, C. (1994). *The bell curve: Intelligence and class structure in American life*. New York: Free Press.

Heyns, B. (1978). Social selection and stratification within schools. *American Journal of Sociology, 79,* 1434–1451.

Hunter, A. (1975). The loss of community: An empirical test through replication. *American Sociological Review, 40,* 537–552.

Hurn, C. (1993). *The limits and possibilities of schooling* (3rd ed.). Boston: Allyn and Bacon.

Hymel, S. (1986). Interpretations of peer behavior: Affective bias in childhood and adolescence. *Child Development, 57,* 431–445.

Jencks, C. (1972). *Inequality: A reassessment of the effect of family and schooling in America*. New York: Basic Books.

Kahl, J. H. (1953). Educational and occupational aspirations of "common man" boys. *Harvard Educational Review, 53,* 186–203.

Kantor, H., & Brenzel, B. (1992). Urban education and the "truly disadvantaged": The historical roots of the contemporary crisis, 1945–1990. *Teachers' College Record, 42,* 521–562.

Karabel, J. (1972). Community colleges and social stratification: Submerged class conflict in American higher education. *Harvard Educational Review, 42,* 521–562.

Kariger, R. B. (1962). *The relationship of lane grouping to the socioeconomic status of parents of seventh-grade pupils in three junior high schools*. (Doctoral dissertation, Michigan State University). *Dissertation Abstracts, 23,* 4586.

Knapp, M. S., & Shields, P. (1990). Reconceiving academic instruction for the children of poverty. *Phi Delta Kappan, 71*(10), 752–758.

Knapp, M. S., & Shields, P. (1991). *Better schooling for the children of poverty*. Berkeley, CA: McCutchan.

Knapp, P., Kronick, J., Marks, B., & Vosburgh, M. (1996). *The assault on equality*. Westport, CT: Praeger.

Kozol, J. (1991). *Savage inequalities: Children in America's schools*. New Haven, CT: Yale University Press.

Lareau, A. (2000). *Home advantage: Social class and parental intervention in elementary education*. New York: Rowman and Littlefield.

LeCompte, M. D., & Dworkin, A. G. (1988). Educational programs: Indirect linkages and unfulfilled expectations. In H. R. Rodgers, Jr. (Ed.), *Beyond welfare: New approaches to the problem of poverty in America* (pp. 135–167). Armonk, NY: M. E. Sharpe.

Levin, H. M. (1988). Accelerating elementary education for disadvantaged students. In Council of Chief State School Officers (Ed.), *School success for students at risk* (pp. 209–226). Orlando, FL: Harcourt Brace Jovanovich.

Lewis, O. (1966). The culture of poverty. *Scientific American, 215*(4), 19–25.

Lortie, D. (1975). *Schoolteacher*. Chicago: University of Chicago Press.

Louis, K. S. (1990). Social and community values and the quality of teacher work life. In M. W. McLaughlin, J. E. Talbert, & N. Bascia (Eds.), *The context of teaching in secondary schools: Teachers' realities* (pp. 17–39). New York: Teachers College Press.

Lucas, S. R. (1999). *Tracking inequality: Stratification and mobility in the American high school*. New York: Teachers College Press.

Mackler, B. (1969). Grouping in the ghetto. *Education and Urban Society, 2,* 80–96.

Matthews, J. (1988). *Jaime Escalante: The best teacher in America*. New York: Holt.

Mayeske, G. W., Wisler, D. E., Beaton, A. E., Weinfeld, F. D., Cohen, W. M., Okada, T., et al. (1972). *A study of our nation's schools*. Washington, DC: Government Printing Office.

McDermott, R. (1987). Achieving school failure: An anthropological approach to illiteracy and social stratification. In G. Spindler (Ed.), *Education and cultural process* (2nd ed., pp. 173–209). Prospect Heights, IL: Waveland Press.

McLaren, P. (1989). *Life in schools*. New York: Longman.

McLaughlin, M. W., Talbert, J. E., & Bascia, N. (Eds.). (1990). *The context of teaching in secondary schools: Teachers' realities*. New York: Teachers College Press.

Means, B., Chelemer, C., & Knapp, M. S. (1991). *Teaching advanced skills to at-risk students*. San Francisco: Jossey-Bass.

Metz, M. H. (1978). *Classrooms and corridors: The crisis of authority in desegregated secondary schools*. Berkeley: University of California Press.

Metz, M. H. (1990). How social class differences shape teachers' work. In M. W. McLaughlin, J. E. Talbert, & N. Bascia (Eds.), *The context of teaching in secondary schools: Teachers' realities* (pp. 40–107). New York: Teachers College Press.

Meyer, J. W. (1977). The effects of education as an institution. *American Journal of Sociology, 83,* 55–77.

Murray, W. (1960). Some major assumptions underlying the development of intelligence tests. Unpublished paper cited in F. Reissman (1962), *The culturally deprived child*. New York: Harper & Brothers.

National Commission on Children. (1991). *Speaking of kids: A national survey of children and parents*. Washington, DC: Author.

Natriello, G., McDill, E. L., & Pallas, A. M. (1990). *Schooling disadvantaged children: Racing against catastrophe*. New York: Teachers College Press.

Nelson, C. M., Rutherford, R. B., Center, D., & Walker, H. (1991). Do public schools have an obligation to serve troubled children and youth? *Exceptional Children, 57*(5), 406–415.

Nelson-Barber, S., & Meier, T. (1990, Spring). Multicultural context: A key factor in teaching. *Academic Connections*, 1–9. Princeton, NJ: College Entrance Examination Board.

Neufeld, B. (1991). Classroom management and instructional strategies for the disadvantaged learner: Some thoughts about the nature of the problem. In M. S. Knapp & P. M. Shields (Eds.), *Better schooling for the children of poverty: Alternatives to conventional wisdom* (pp. 257–272). Berkeley, CA: McCutchan.

Oakes, J. (1985). *Keeping track: How schools structure inequality*. New Haven, CT: Yale University Press.

Oakes, J. (1990). *Multiplying inequalities: The effects of race, social class and teaching*. Santa Monica, CA: Rand.

Oakes, J., Gamoran, A., & Page, R. N. (1992). Curriculum differences: Opportunities, outcomes, and meanings. In P. Jackson (Ed.), *Handbook of research on curriculum* (pp. 570–608). New York: Macmillan.

Oakes, J., Quartz, K. H., Ryan, S., & Lipton, M. (2000). Becoming good American schools: The struggle for civic virtue in education reform. *Phi Delta Kappan, 81*(8), 568–575.

Ogbu, J. (1979). Social stratification and the socialization of competence. *Anthropology & Education Quarterly, 10*(1), 3–20.

Page, R. N. (1991). *Lower-track classrooms: A curricular and cultural perspective*. New York: Teachers College Press.

Payne, K. J., & Biddle, B. J. (1999). Poor school funding, child poverty, and mathematics achievement. *Educational Researcher, 28*(6), 4–13.

Persell, C. H. (1977). *Education and inequality: The roots and results of stratification in America's schools*. New York: Free Press.

Persell, C. H. (1993). Social class and educational equality. In J. Banks & C.A.M. Banks (Eds.), *Multicultural education: Issues and perspectives* (2nd ed., pp. 71–89). Boston: Allyn and Bacon.

Rafferty, Y., & Shinn, M. (1991). The impact of homelessness on children. *American Psychologist, 46*, 1170–1179.

Reissman, F. (1962). *The culturally deprived child*. New York: Harper & Brothers.

Rist, R. C. (1970). Student social class and teacher expectations: The self-fulfilling prophecy in ghetto education. *Harvard Educational Review, 40*, 411–451.

Rist, R. C. (1977). On understanding the processes of schooling: The contributions of labeling theory. In J. Karabel & A. H. Halsey (Eds.), *Power and ideology in education* (pp. 292–305). New York: Oxford University Press.

Rosenfeld, R. A. (1980). Race and sex differences in career dynamics. *American Sociological Review, 45*, 583–609.

Rosenholtz, S., & Rosenholtz, S. (1981). Classroom organization and the perception of ability. *Sociology of Education, 54*, 134–140.

Sadker, M., Sadker, D., & Long, L. (1993). Gender and educational equality. In J. A. Banks & C.A.M. Banks (Eds.), *Multicultural education: Issues and perspectives* (2nd ed., pp. 111–128). Boston: Allyn and Bacon.

Schorr, L. B. (1988). *Within our reach: Breaking the cycle of disadvantage*. New York: Doubleday.

Sewell, W. H., & Hauser, R. M. (1976). Causes and consequences of higher education: Modes of the attainment process. In W. H. Sewell, R. M. Hauser, & D. L. Featherman (Eds.), *Schooling and achievement in American society* (pp. 9–28). New York: Academic Press.

Sewell, W. H., & Shaw, V. P. (1967). Socioeconomic status, intelligence, and the attainment of higher education. *Sociology of Education, 40*, 1–23.

Sleeter, C. (1991). Learning disabilities: The social construction of a category. In S. Sigmon (Ed.), *Critical voices on special education: Problems and progress concerning the mildly handicapped* (pp. 21–34). Albany: State University of New York Press.

Sleeter, C., & Grant, C. (1991). Race, class, gender, and disability in current textbooks. In M. Apple & L. K. Christian-Smith (Eds.), *The politics of the textbook* (pp. 78–110). London: Routledge & Kegan Paul.

Solomon, R. P. (1992). *Black resistance in high school*. Albany: State University of New York Press.

Thurow, L. C. (1972, Summer). Education and economic equality. *Public Interest, 72*, 66–81.

Tobias, S. (1979). Anxiety research in educational psychology. *Journal of Educational Psychology, 71*, 573–582.

Vail, K. (1996). Learning on the move. *American School Board Journal, 183*(12), 20–25.

Weber, M. (1946). *From Max Weber: Essays in sociology*. New York: Oxford University Press.

Weiler, K. (1988). *Women teaching for change: Gender, class, and power*. New York: Bergin & Garvey.

Weiner, B. (1985). An attributional theory of achievement motivation and emotion. *Psychological Review, 92*, 548–573.

Weis, L. (1990). *Working class without work*. New York: Routledge.

Wilcox, K. (1982). Differential socialization in the classroom: Implications for equal opportunity. In G. Spindler (Ed.), *Doing the ethnography of schooling: Educational anthropology in action* (pp. 268–309). New York: Holt, Rinehart, & Winston.

Wright, E. O., & Perrone, L. (1977). Marxist class categories and income inequality. *American Sociological Review, 42*, 32–55.

Zeichner, K. M., & Gere, J. M. (1990). Teacher socialization. In W. R. Houston (Ed.), *Handbook of research on teacher education* (pp. 329–348). New York: Macmillan.

32

A THREAT IN THE AIR

How Stereotypes Shape Intellectual Identity and Performance

Claude M. Steele

Stanford University

A general theory of domain identification is used to describe achievement barriers still faced by women in advanced quantitative areas and by African Americans in school. The theory assumes that sustained school success requires identification with school and its subdomains; that societal pressures on these groups (e.g., economic disadvantage, gender roles) can frustrate this identification; and that in school domains where these groups are negatively stereotyped, those who have become domain identified face the further barrier of stereotype threat, the threat that others' judgments or their own actions will negatively stereotype them in the domain. Research shows that this threat dramatically depresses the standardized test performance of women and African Americans who are in the academic vanguard of their groups (offering a new interpretation of group differences in standardized test performance), that it causes disidentification with school, and that practices that reduce this threat can reduce these negative effects.

From an observer's standpoint, the situations of a boy and a girl in a math classroom or of a Black student and a White student in any classroom are essentially the same. The teacher is the same; the textbooks are the same; and in better classrooms, these students are treated the same. Is it possible, then, that they could still experience the classroom differently, so differently in fact as to significantly affect their performance and achievement

there? This is the central question of this chapter, and in seeking an answer it has both a practical and a theoretical focus. The practical focus is on the perhaps obvious need to better understand the processes that can hamper a group's school performance and on what can be done to improve that performance. The theoretical focus is on how societal stereotypes about groups can influence the intellectual functioning and identity development of individual group members. To show the generality of these processes and their relevance to important outcomes, this theory is applied to two groups: African Americans, who must contend with negative stereotypes about their abilities in many scholastic domains, and women, who must do so primarily in math and the physical sciences. In trying to understand the schooling outcomes of these two groups, the theory has a distinct perspective, that of viewing people, in Sartre's (1946/1965) words, as "first of all beings in a situation" such that if one wants to understand them, one "must inquire first into the situation surrounding [them]" (p. 60).

The theory begins with an assumption: that to sustain school success one must be identified with school achievement in the sense of its being a part of one's self-definition, a personal identity to which one is self-evaluatively accountable. This accountability—that good self-feelings depend in some part on good achievement—translates into sustained achievement motivation. For

Reprinted with permission of the American Psychological Association and the author from *American Psychologist*, 52(6), 613–629, 1997.

such an identification to form, this reasoning continues, one must perceive good prospects in the domain, that is, that one has the interests, skills, resources, and opportunities to prosper there, as well as that one belongs there, in the sense of being accepted and valued in the domain. If this relationship to schooling does not form or gets broken, achievement may suffer. Thus, in trying to understand what imperils achievement among women and African Americans, this logic points to a basic question: What in the experience of these groups might frustrate their identification with all or certain aspects of school achievement?

One must surely turn first to social structure: limits on educational access that have been imposed on these groups by socioeconomic disadvantage, segregating social practices, and restrictive cultural orientations, limits of both historical and ongoing effect. By diminishing one's educational prospects, these limitations (e.g., inadequate resources, few role models, preparational disadvantages) should make it more difficult to identify with academic domains. To continue in math, for example, a woman might have to buck the low expectations of teachers, family, and societal gender roles in which math is seen as unfeminine as well as anticipate spending her entire professional life in a male-dominated world. These realities, imposed on her by societal structure, could so reduce her sense of good prospects in math as to make identifying with it difficult.

But this article focuses on a further barrier, one that has its effect on the already identified, those members of these groups who, having survived structural obstacles, have achieved identification with the domain (of the present groups, school-identified African Americans and math-identified women). It is the social-psychological threat that arises when one is in a situation or doing something for which a negative stereotype about one's group applies. This predicament threatens one with being negatively stereotyped, with being judged or treated stereotypically, or with the prospect of conforming to the stereotype. Called *stereotype threat*, it is a situational threat—a threat in the air—that, in general form, can affect the members of any group about whom a negative stereotype exists (e.g., skateboarders, older adults, White men, gang members). Where bad stereotypes about these groups apply, members of these groups can fear being reduced to that stereotype. And for those who identify with the domain to which the stereotype is relevant, this predicament can be self-threatening.

Negative stereotypes about women and African Americans bear on important academic abilities. Thus, for members of these groups who are identified with domains in which these stereotypes apply, the threat of these stereotypes can be sharply felt and, in several ways, hampers their achievement.

First, if the threat is experienced in the midst of a domain performance—classroom presentation or test-taking, for example—the emotional reaction it causes could directly interfere with performance. My colleagues and I (Spencer, Steele, & Quinn, 1999; C. M. Steele & Aronson, 1995) have tested this possibility with women taking standardized math tests and African Americans taking standardized verbal tests. Second, when this threat becomes chronic in a situation, as for the woman who spends considerable time in a competitive, male-oriented math environment, it can pressure *disidentification,* a reconceptualization of the self and of one's values so as to remove the domain as a self-identity, as a basis of self-evaluation. Disidentification offers the retreat of not caring about the domain in relation to the self. But as it protects in this way, it can undermine sustained motivation in the domain, an adaptation that can be costly when the domain is as important as schooling.

Stereotype threat is especially frustrating because, at each level of schooling, it affects the vanguard of these groups, those with the skills and self-confidence to have identified with the domain. Ironically, their susceptibility to this threat derives not from internal doubts about their ability (e.g., their internalization of the stereotype) but from their identification with the domain and the resulting concern they have about being stereotyped in it. (This argument has the hopeful implication that to improve the domain performance of these students, one should focus on the feasible task of lifting this situational threat rather than on altering their internal psychology.) Yet, as schooling progresses and the obstacles of structure and stereotype threat take their cumulative toll, more of this vanguard will likely be pressured into the ranks of the unidentified. These students, by not caring about the domain vis-à-vis the self, are likely to underperform in it regardless of whether they are stereotype-threatened there. Thus, although the identified among these groups are likely to underperform only under stereotype threat, the unidentified (casualties of sociocultural disadvantage or prior internalization of stereotype threat) are likely to underperform and not persist in the domain even when stereotype threat has been removed.

In these ways, then, the present analysis sees social structure and stereotypes as shaping the academic identities and performance outcomes of large segments of society. But first, for the two groups under consideration, what are these outcomes?

As is much discussed, these outcomes are in a crisis state for African Americans. Although Black students begin school with standardized test scores that are not too far behind those of their White counterparts, almost immediately a gap begins to appear (e.g., Alexander & Entwistle, 1988; Burton & Jones, 1982; Coleman et al.,

1966) that, by the sixth grade in most school districts, is two full grade levels (Gerard, 1983). There have been encouraging increases in the number of African Americans completing high school or its equivalence in recent years: 77% for Black students versus 83% for White students (American Council on Education, 1995–96). And there have been modest advances in the number of African American high school graduates enrolling in college, although these have not been as substantial as in other groups (American Council on Education). Perhaps most discouraging has been the high dropout rate for African American college students: those who do not finish college within six years are 62%, compared with a national dropout rate of 41% (American Council on Education). And there is evidence of lower grade performance among those who do graduate, on average two-thirds of a letter grade lower than for those of other graduating students (Nettles, 1988). On predominantly White campuses, Black students are also underrepresented in math and the natural sciences. Although historically Black colleges and universities now enroll only 17% of the nation's Black college students, they produce 42% of all Black B.S. degrees in natural science (Culotta & Gibbons, 1992). At the graduate level, although Black women have recently shown modest gains in Ph.D.s received, the number awarded to Black men has declined over the past decade more than for any other subgroup in society (American Council on Education, 1995–96).

Women clearly thrive in many areas of schooling. But in math, engineering, and the physical sciences, they often endure lesser outcomes than men. In a meta-analysis involving over 3 million participants, Hyde, Fennema, and Lamon (1990), for example, found that through elementary and middle school, there are virtually no differences between boys and girls in performance on standardized math tests but that a trend toward men doing better steadily increases from high school (SD = .29) through college (SD = .41) and into adulthood (SD = .59). And, as their college careers begin, women leave these fields at a rate two and a half times that of men (Hewitt & Seymour, 1991). Although White women constitute 43% of the U.S. population, they earn only 22% of the B.S. degrees and 13% of the Ph.D.s and occupy only 10% of the jobs in physical science, math, and engineering, where they earn only 75% of the salary paid to men (Hewitt & Seymour, 1991).

These inequities have compelled explanations ranging from the sociocultural to the genetic. In the case of African Americans, for example, past and ongoing socioeconomic disadvantage, cultural orientations (see, e.g., Ogbu, 1986), and genetic differences (Herrnstein & Murray, 1994; Jensen, 1969) have all been proposed as factors that, through singular and accumulated effect, could undermine their performance. In the case of women's performance in math and the physical sciences,

there are parallel arguments: structural and cultural gender role constraints that shunt women away from these areas; culturally rooted expectations (e.g., Eccles, 1987; Eccles-Parsons et al., 1983); and, again, genetic limitations (Benbow & Stanley, 1980, 1983). But, like crumbs along the forest floor, several findings lead away from these analyses as fully sufficient.

For one thing, minority student achievement gaps persist even in the middle and upper socioeconomic classes. Using data from the Coleman report (Coleman et al., 1966) and a more recent College Board study of Scholastic Aptitude Test (SAT) scores, Miller (1995, 1996) found that the gaps in academic performance (grades as well as standardized test scores) between Whites and non-Asian minorities (e.g., African Americans, Hispanics, and Native Americans) were as large in the upper and middle classes (as measured by parental education and occupation) as in the lower classes, or larger. Group differences in socioeconomic status (SES), then, cannot fully explain group differences in academic performance.

Another point is that these differences are not even fully explained by group differences in skills. This is shown in the well-known *overprediction* or *underperformance* phenomenon of the test bias literature. Overprediction occurs when, at each level of performance on a test of preparation for some level of schooling (e.g., the SAT), students from one group wind up achieving less—getting lower college grades, for example—than other students with the same beginning scores. In this sense, the test scores of the low-performing group overpredict how well they will actually achieve, or, stated another way, the low-performing group underperforms in relation to the test's prediction. But the point here is that because the students at each test-score level have comparable initial skills, the lower eventual performance of one group must be due to something other than skill deficits they brought with them.

In the case of African Americans, overprediction across the academic spectrum has been so reliably observed as to be almost a lawful phenomenon in American society (e.g., Jensen, 1980; Vars & Bowen, 1997). Perhaps the most extensive single demonstration of it comes from a recent Educational Testing Service study (Ramist, Lewis, & McCamley-Jenkins, 1994) that examined the predictiveness of the SAT on 38 representative college and university campuses. As is typically the case, the study found that the predictive validity to the SAT—its correlation with subsequent grades—was as good for African American, Hispanic, and Native American students as for White and Asian students. But for the three non-Asian minority groups, there was sizable overprediction (underperformance) in virtually all academic areas. That is, at each level of preparation as measured by the SAT, something further depressed the grades of these groups once they arrived on campus.

As important, the same study found evidence of SAT overprediction for female students (i.e., women performing less well than men at comparable SAT levels) in technical and physical science courses such as engineering, economics, and computer science but not in nontechnical areas such as English. It is interesting, though, that women in this study were not overpredicted in math per se, a seeming exception to this pattern. The overprediction of women's college math performance has generally been unreliable, with some studies showing it (e.g., Benbow & Arjmand, 1990; Levin & Wyckoff, 1988; Lovely, 1987; Ware, Steckler, & Leserman, 1985) and others not (Adelman, 1991; DeBoer, 1984; Ware & Dill, 1986). However, a recent study (Strenta, Elliott, Adair, Scott, & Matier, 1993) involving over 5,000 students at four prestigious northeastern colleges identified a pattern of effects that suggests why these different results occur: underperformance reliably occurred among women who were talented in math and science and who, perhaps for that reason, took courses in these areas that were intended for majors, whereas it did not occur among women with less math and science preparation who took courses in these areas intended for non-majors. Thus, women may be reliably overpredicted in math and the physical sciences, just as Black students are more generally, but only when the curriculum is more advanced and only among women who are more identified with the domain. Among this vanguard, though, something other than skill deficits depresses their performance. What are these further processes?

SOCIAL AND STEREOTYPE STRUCTURE AS OBSTACLES TO ACHIEVEMENT IDENTIFICATION

The proposed answer is that at least one of these processes is a set of social psychological phenomena that obstruct these groups' identification with domains of schooling.[1] I turn first to school identification.

Academic Identification

As noted, this analysis assumes that sustained school achievement depends, most centrally, on identifying with school, that is, forming a relationship between oneself and the domains of schooling such that one's self-regard significantly depends on achievement in those domains. Extrinsic rewards such as better career outcomes, personal security, parental exhortation, and so on can also motivate school achievement. But it is presumed that sustaining motivation through the ebb and flow of these other rewards requires school identification. How, then, is this identification formed?

Not a great deal is known about the process. But several models (e.g., Schlenker & Weigold, 1989; C. M.

Steele, 1988; Tesser, 1988) share an implicit reasoning, the first assumption of which is that people need positive self-regard, a self-perception of "adaptive and moral adequacy" (C. M. Steele, 1988, p. 289). Then, the argument goes, identification with a given domain of life depends, in large part, on the self-evaluative prospects it offers. James (1890/1950) described the development of the self as a process of picking from the many, often incompatible, possible selves, those "on which to stake one's salvation" (p. 310). This choice and the assessment of prospects that goes into it are, of course, multifaceted: Are the rewards of the domain attractive or important? Is an adequate opportunity structure available? Do I have the requisite skills, talents, and interests? Have others like me succeeded in the domain? Will I be seen as belonging in the domain? Will I be prejudiced against in the domain? Can I envision wanting what this domain has to offer? and so on. Some of these assessments undergird a sense of efficacy in the domain (e.g., Bandura, 1977, 1986). Others have to do with the rewards, importance, and attractiveness of the domain itself. And still others have to do with the feasibility and receptiveness of the domain. The point here is that students tacitly assess their prospects in school and its subdomains, and, roughly speaking, their identifications follow these assessments: increasing when they are favorable and decreasing when they are unfavorable. As for the two groups under consideration, then, this analysis suggests that something systematically downgrades their assessments of, and thus their identification with, critical domains of schooling.

Threats to Academic Identification

Structural and Cultural Threats. Both groups have endured and continue to endure sociocultural influences that could have such effects. Among the most replicable facts in the schooling literature is that SES is strongly related to school success and cognitive performance (e.g., Coleman et al., 1966; Miller, 1996). And because African Americans have long been disproportionately represented in lower socioeconomic classes, this factor surely contributes to their achievement patterns in school, both through the material limitations associated with lower SES (poor schools, lack of resources for school persistence, etc.) and through the ability of these limitations, by downgrading school-related prospects, to undermine identification with school. And beyond socioeconomic structure, there are cultural patterns within these groups or in the relation between these groups and the larger society that may also frustrate their identification with school or some part of it, for example, Ogbu's (1986) notion of a lower-class Black culture that is "oppositional" to school achievement or traditional feminine gender roles that eschew math-related fields (e.g., Eccles-Parsons et al., 1983; Linn, 1994).

Stereotype Threat. Beyond these threats, waiting for those in these groups who have identified with school, is yet another threat to their identification, more subtle perhaps but nonetheless profound: that of stereotype threat. I define it as follows: the event of a negative stereotype about a group to which one belongs becoming self-relevant, usually as a plausible interpretation for something one is doing, for an experience one is having, or for a situation one is in, that has relevance to one's self-definition. It happens when one is in the *field* of the stereotype, what Cross (1991) called a "spotlight anxiety" (p. 195), such that one can be judged or treated in terms of a racial stereotype. Many analysts have referred to this predicament and the pressure it causes (e.g., Allport, 1954; Carter, 1991; Cose, 1993; Goffman, 1963; Howard & Hammond, 1985; E. E. Jones et al., 1984; Sartre, 1946/1965; C. M. Steele, 1975; C. M. Steele & Aronson, 1995; S. Steele, 1990). The present definition stresses that for a negative stereotype to be threatening, it must be self-relevant. Then, the situational contingency it establishes—the possibility of conforming to the stereotype or of being treated and judged in terms of it—becomes self-threatening. It means that one could be limited or diminished in a domain that is self-definitional. For students from groups in which abilities are negatively stereotyped in all or some school domains and yet who remain identified with those domains, this threat may be keenly felt—felt enough, I argue, to become a further barrier to their identification with the domain.

There is, however, a more standard explanation of how negative stereotypes affect their targets. Beginning with Freud (as cited in Brill, 1938) in psychology and Cooley (1956) and Mead (1934) in sociology, treatises on the experience of oppression have depicted a fairly standard sequence of events: through long exposure to negative stereotypes about their group, members of prejudiced-against groups often internalize the stereotypes, and the resulting sense of inadequacy becomes part of their personality (e.g., see Allport, 1954; Bettelheim, 1943; Clark, 1965; Erikson, 1956; Fanon, 1952/1967; Grier & Coobs, 1968; Kardiner & Ovesey, 1951; Lewin, 1941).

In recent years, the tone of this argument has constructively lightened, replacing the notion of a broad self-hatred with the idea of an inferiority anxiety or low expectations and suggesting how situational factors contribute to this experience. S. Steele's (1990) essays on *racial vulnerability* (i.e., a vulnerability of both Blacks and Whites that stems, in part, from the situational pressures of reputations about their groups) offered an example. This work depicts the workings of this anxiety among African Americans in an interconnected set of ideas: *integration shock* that, like Goffman (1963), points to settings that integrate Blacks and Whites as particularly anxiety arousing; *objective correlatives* or race-related situational cues that can trigger this anxiety; and the inherent sense of risk, stemming from an internalized *inferiority anxiety* and from a *myth of inferiority* pervading integrated settings, of being judged inferior or of confirming one's own feared inferiority. Howard and Hammond (1985) earlier made this argument specifically in relation to the school achievement of Black students. They argued that once "rumors of inferiority" about Black students' abilities pervade the environment—through, for example, national debates over the genetic basis of racial differences in IQ—they can intimidate Black students; become internalized by them; and, in turn, lead to a low sense of self-efficacy, demotivation, and underperformance in school. Analogous arguments have been applied to women interested in math-related areas (cf. Eccles-Parsons et al., 1983).

These models recognize the situational influence of negative stereotypes (e.g., Allport, 1954; Howard & Hammond, 1985; S. Steele, 1990) but most often describe it as a process in which the stereotype, or more precisely the possibility of being stereotyped, triggers an internalized inferiority doubt or low expectancy. And because this anxiety is born of a socialization presumed to influence all members of the stereotyped group, virtually all members of the group are presumed to have this anxiety, to one degree or another.

Stereotype threat, in contrast, refers to the strictly situational threat of negative stereotypes, the threat that does not depend on cueing an internalized anxiety or expectancy. It is cued by the mere recognition that a negative group stereotype could apply to oneself in a given situation. How threatening this recognition becomes depends on the person's identification with the stereotype-relevant domain. For the domain-identified, the situational relevance of the stereotype is threatening because it threatens diminishment in a domain that is self-definitional. For the less domain-identified, this recognition is less threatening or not threatening at all, because it threatens something that is less self-definitional.

Stereotype threat, then, as a situational pressure "in the air," so to speak, affects only a subportion of the stereotyped group and, in the area of schooling, probably affects confident students more than unconfident ones. Recall that to be identified with schooling in general, or math in particular, one must have confidence in one's domain-related abilities, enough to perceive good prospects in the domain. This means that stereotype threat should have its greatest effect on the better, more confident students in stereotyped groups, those who have not internalized the group stereotype to the point of doubting their own ability and have thus remained identified with the domain—those who are in the academic vanguard of their group.[2]

Several general features of stereotype threat follow:

1. Stereotype threat is a general threat not tied to the psychology of particular stigmatized groups. It affects the members of any group about whom there exists some generally known negative stereotype (e.g., a grandfather who fears that any faltering of memory will confirm or expose him to stereotypes about the aged). Stereotype threat can be thought of as a subtype of the threat posed by negative reputations in general.

2. That which turns stereotype threat on and off, the controlling "mechanism" so to speak, is a particular concurrence: whether a negative stereotype about one's group becomes relevant to interpreting oneself or one's behavior in an identified-with setting. When such a setting integrates stereotyped and nonstereotyped people, it may make the stereotype, as a dimension of difference, more salient and thus more strongly felt (Frable, Blackstone, & Sherbaum, 1990; Goffman, 1963; Kleck & Strenta, 1980; Sartre, 1946/1965; S. Steele, 1990). But such integration is neither necessary nor sufficient for this threat to occur. It can occur even when the person is alone, as for a woman taking an important math test alone in a cubicle but under the threat of confirming a stereotyped limitation of ability. And, in integrated settings, it need not occur. Reducing the interpretive relevance of a stereotype in the setting, say in a classroom or on a standardized test, may reduce this threat and its detrimental effects even when the setting is integrated.[3]

3. This mechanism also explains the variabilities of stereotype threat: the fact that the type and degree of this threat vary from group to group and, for any group, across settings. For example, the type and degree of stereotype threat experienced by White men, Black people, and people who are overweight differ considerably, bearing on sensitivity and fairness in the first group, on school performance in the second, and on self-control in the third. Moreover, for any of these groups, this threat will vary across settings (e.g., Goffman, 1963; S. Steele, 1990). For example, women may reduce their stereotype threat substantially by moving across the hall from math to English class. The explanation of this model is straightforward: different groups experience different forms and degrees of stereotype threat because the stereotypes about them differ in content, in scope, and in the situations to which they apply.

4. To experience stereotype threat, one need not believe the stereotype nor even be worried that it is true of oneself. The well-known African American social psychologist James M. Jones (1997) wrote: "When I go to

the ATM machine and a woman is making a transaction, I think about whether she will fear I may rob her. Since I have no such intention, how do I put her at ease? Maybe I can't . . . and maybe she has no such expectation. But it goes through my mind" (p. 262).

Jones felt the stereotype threat in this situation even though he did not believe that the stereotype characterized him. Of course, this made it no less a life-shaping force. One's daily life can be filled with recurrent situations in which this threat pressures adaptive responses.

5. The effort to overcome stereotype threat by disproving the stereotype—for example, by outperforming it in the case of academic work—can be daunting. Because these stereotypes are widely disseminated throughout society, a personal exemption from them earned in one setting does not generalize to a new setting where either one's reputation is not known or where it has to be renegotiated against a new challenge. Thus, even when the stereotype can be disproven, the need to do so can seem Sisyphean, everlastingly recurrent. And in some critical situations, it may not be disprovable. The stereotypes considered in this work allege group-based limitations of ability that are often reinforced by the structural reality of increasingly small group representations at more advanced levels of the schooling domain. Thus, for group members working at these advanced levels, no amount of success up to that point can disprove the stereotype's relevance to their next, more advanced performance. For the advanced female math student who has been brilliant up to that point, any frustration she has at the frontier of her skills could confirm the gender-based limitation alleged in the stereotype, making this frontier, because she is so invested in it, a more threatening place than it is for the nonstereotyped. Thus, the work of dispelling stereotype threat through performance probably increases with the difficulty of work in the domain, and whatever exemption is gained has to be rewon at the next new proving ground.

EMPIRICAL SUPPORT FOR A THEORY OF STEREOTYPE THREAT AND DISIDENTIFICATION

In testing these ideas, the research done by my colleagues and me has had two foci: the first is on intellectual performance in the domain in which negative group stereotypes apply. Here, the analysis has two testable implications. One is that for domain-identified students, stereotype threat may interfere with their domain-related intellectual performance. Analysts have long argued that behaving in a situation in which one is at risk of confirming a negative stereotype about one's group, or of being seen or treated stereotypically, causes emotional distress and pressure (Cross, 1991; Fanon, 1952/1967; Goffman, 1963; Howard & Hammond, 1985; Sartre, 1946/1965; C. M. Steele & Aronson, 1995; S. Steele, 1990). The argument here is that for those who identify with the domain enough to experience this threat, the pressure it causes may undermine their domain performance. Disruptive pressures such as evaluation apprehension, test anxiety, choking, and token status have long been shown to disrupt performance through a variety of mediating mechanisms: interfering anxiety, reticence to respond, distracting thoughts, self-consciousness, and so on (Baumeister & Showers, 1984; Geen, 1991; Lord & Saenz, 1985; Sarason, 1980; Wine, 1971). The assumption of this model is that stereotype threat is another such interfering pressure. The other testable implication is that reducing this threat in the performance setting, by reducing its interfering pressure, should improve the performance of otherwise stereotype-threatened students.

The second research focus is the model's implication that stereotype threat, and the anticipation of having to contend with it unceasingly in school or some domain of schooling, should deter members of these groups from identifying with these domains, and, for group members already identified, it should pressure their disidentification.[4]

Stereotype Threat and Intellectual Performance

Steven Spencer, Diane Quinn, and I (Spencer et al., 1999) first tested the effect of stereotype threat on intellectual performance by testing its effect on the standardized math test performance of women who were strong in math.

The Stereotype Threat of Women Performing Math. At base, of course, the stereotype threat that women experience in math-performance settings derives from a negative stereotype about their math ability that is disseminated throughout society. But whether this threat impaired their performance, we reasoned, would depend on two things. First, the performance would have to be construed so that any faltering would imply the limitation of ability alleged in the stereotype. This means that the performance would have to be difficult enough so that faltering at it would imply having reached an ability limit but not so difficult as to be nondiagnostic of ability. And second, as has been much emphasized, the women in question would have to be identified with math, so that faltering and its stereotype-confirming implication would threaten something they care about, their belongingness

and acceptance in a domain they identify with. Of course, men too (at least those of equal skill and identification with math) could be threatened in this situation; faltering would reflect on their ability too. But their faltering would not carry the extra threat of confirming a stereotyped limitation in math ability or of causing them to be seen that way. Thus, the threat that women experience, through the interfering pressure it causes, should worsen their performance in comparison to equally qualified men. Interestingly, though, these otherwise confident women should perform equally as well as equally qualified men when this situational threat is lessened.

To explore these questions, Spencer, Quinn, and I (Spencer et al., 1997) designed a basic research paradigm: we recruited female and male students, mostly college sophomores, who were good at math and who strongly identified with it in the sense of seeing themselves as strong math students and seeing math as important to their self-definition. We then gave them a very difficult math test one at a time. The items were taken from the advanced math Graduate Records Examination (GRE) and we assumed would frustrate the skills of these students without totally exceeding them. As expected, and presumably reflecting the impairing effects of stereotype threat, women significantly underperformed in relation to equally qualified men on this difficult math test. But more important, in another condition of this experiment in which the test was an advanced literature test rather than a math test and in which participants had been selected and matched for their strong literature skills and identification, women performed just as well as equally qualified men. This happened, we reasoned, because women are not stereotype-threatened in this area.

A second experiment replicated women's underperformance on the difficult math test and showed that it did not happen when the test was easier, that is, when the items, taken from the regular quantitative section of the GRE, were more within the skills of these strong math students. The lack of performance frustration on this easier test, presumably, reduced women's stereotype threat by making the stereotype less relevant as an interpretation of their performance.

Stereotype Threat Versus Genes. So went our interpretation. But an alternative was possible: the biological limits of women's math ability do not emerge until the material tested is difficult. It is this very pattern of evidence that Benbow and Stanley (1980, 1983) used to suggest a genetic limitation in women's math ability. Thus, the first two experiments reproduced the gender effects on math performance reported in the literature: that women underperform primarily in math and mainly when the material is difficult. But they fall short of establishing our interpretation.

To do this, we would need to give women and men a difficult math test (one capable of producing women's underperformance) but then experimentally vary stereotype threat, that is, vary how much women were at risk of confirming the stereotype while taking the test. A third experiment did this by varying how the test (the same difficult one used in the earlier experiments) was represented. Participants were told either that the test generally showed gender differences, implying that the stereotype of women's limitations in math was relevant to interpreting their own frustration, or that it showed no gender differences, implying that the gender stereotype was not relevant to their performance and thus could not be confirmed by it on this particular test. The no-gender-differences representation did not challenge the validity of the stereotype; it simply eliminated the risk that the stereotype could be fulfilled on this test. In the gender-differences condition, we expected women (still stereotype-threatened) to underperform in relation to equally qualified men, but in the no-gender-differences condition, we expected women (with stereotype threat reduced) to perform equal to such men. The genetic interpretation, of course, predicts that women will underperform on this difficult test regardless of how it is represented.

In dramatic support of our reasoning, women performed worse than men when they were told that the test produced gender differences, which replicated women's underperformance observed in the earlier experiments, but they performed equal to men when the test was represented as insensitive to gender differences, even though, of course, the same difficult "ability" test was used in both conditions (see Figure 32.1).

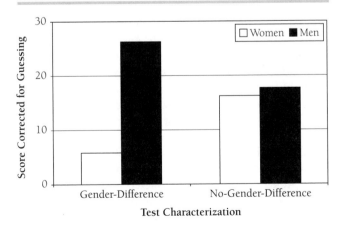

FIGURE 32.1. Mean Performance on a Difficult Math Test as a Function of Gender and Test Characterization.

Genetic limitation did not cap the performance of women in these experiments. A fourth experiment showed that reducing stereotype threat (through the no-gender-differences treatment) raised women's performance to that of equally qualified men, even when participants' specific performance expectancies were set low, that is, when participants were led to expect poor test performance. Also, a fifth experiment (that again replicated the treatment effects of the third experiment) found that participants' posttreatment anxiety, not their expectancies or efficacy, predicted their performance. Thus, the disruptive effect of stereotype threat was mediated more by the self-evaluative anxiety it caused than by its lowering of performance expectations or self-efficacy.

Internal or Situational Threat. These findings make an important theoretical and practical point: the gender-differences conditions (including those in which the possibility of gender differences was left to inference rather than stated directly) did not impair women's performance by triggering doubts they had about their math ability. For one thing, these women had no special doubts of this sort; they were selected for being very good at math and for reporting high confidence in their ability. Nor was this doubt a factor in their test performance. Recall that the math test was represented as an ability test in all conditions of these experiments. This means that in the no-gender-differences conditions, women were still at risk of showing their own math ability to be weak—the same risk that men had in these conditions. Under this risk (when their own math ability was on the line), they performed just as well as men. Whatever performance-impairing anxiety they had, it was no greater than that of equally qualified men. Thus, the gender-differences conditions (the normal condition under which people take these tests) could not have impaired their performance by triggering some greater internalized anxiety that women have about their own math ability—an anxiety acquired, for example, through prior socialization. Rather, this condition had its effect through situational pressure. It set up an interpretive frame such that any performance frustration signaled the possible gender-based ability limitation alleged in the stereotype. For these women, this signal challenged their belongingness in a domain they cared about and, as a possibly newly met limit to their ability, could not be disproven by their prior achievements—thus its interfering threat.

The Stereotype Threat of African Americans on Standardized Tests. Joshua Aronson and I (C. M. Steele & Aronson, 1995) examined these processes among African

American students. In these studies, Black and White Stanford University students took a test composed of the most difficult items on the verbal GRE exam. Because the participants were students admitted to a highly selective university, we assumed that they were identified with the verbal skills represented on standardized tests. The first study varied whether or not the stereotype about Black persons' intellectual ability was relevant to their performance by varying whether the test was presented as *ability—diagnostic,* that is, as a test of intellectual ability, or as *ability—nondiagnostic,* that is, as a laboratory problem-solving task unrelated to ability and thus to the stereotype about ability. Analysis of covariance was used to remove the influence of participants' initial skills, measured by their verbal SAT scores, on their test performance. This done, the results showed strong evidence of stereotype threat: Black participant greatly underperformed White participants in the diagnostic condition but equaled them in the nondiagnostic condition (see Figure 32.2).

A second experiment produced the same pattern of results with an even slighter manipulation of stereotype threat: whether or not participants recorded their race on a demographic questionnaire just before taking the test (described as nondiagnostic in all conditions). Salience of the racial stereotype alone was enough to depress the performance of identified Black students (see Figure 32.3).

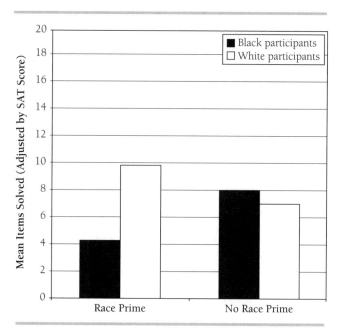

FIGURE 32.3. Mean Performance on a Difficult Verbal Test as a Function of Whether Race Was Primed.

Note: SAT = Scholastic Aptitude Test.

The Cognitive Mediation of Stereotype Threat. Stereotype threat, then, can impair the standardized test performance of domain-identified students; this effect generalizes to several ability-stereotyped groups, and its mediation seems to involve anxiety more than expectancies. But do these manipulations cause a specific state of stereotype threat, that is, a sensed threat specifically about being stereotyped or fitting the stereotype? To address this question, Aronson and I (C. M. Steele & Aronson, 1995) tested two things: whether manipulating stereotype threat actually activates the racial stereotype in the thinking and information processing of stereotype-threatened test takers and whether it produces in them a specific motivation to avoid being seen stereotypically. Again, Black and White participants were run in either an ability-diagnostic or ability-nondiagnostic condition, except that just after the condition instructions and completion of the sample test items (so that participants could see how difficult the items were) and just before participants expected to take the test, they completed measures of stereotype activation and avoidance. The stereotype-activation measure asked them to complete 80 word fragments, 10 of which we knew from pretesting could be completed with, among other words, words symbolic of African American stereotypes (e.g., _ _ce [race], la_ _ [lazy], or _ _ or [poor]) and 5 of which could be completed with, among other words, words signifying self-doubts (e.g., lo_ _ _ [loser], du_ _ [dumb], or sha_ _ [shame]). The measure of participants' motivation to avoid being seen stereotypically simply

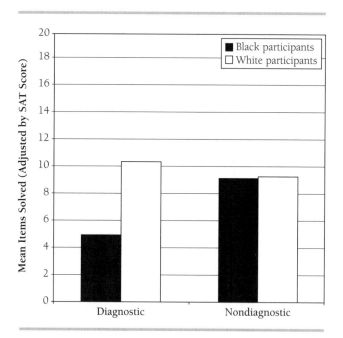

FIGURE 32.2. Mean Performance on a Difficult Verbal Test as a Function of Race and Test Characterization.

Note: SAT = Scholastic Aptitude Test.

asked them how much they preferred various types of music, activities, sports, and personality traits, some of which a pretest sample had rated as stereotypic of African Americans.[5]

If expecting to take a difficult ability-diagnostic test is enough to activate the racial stereotype in the thinking of Black participants and to motivate them to avoid being stereotyped, then these participants, more than those in the other conditions, should show more stereotype and self-doubt word completions and fewer preferences for things that are African American. This is precisely what happened. Black participants in the diagnostic condition completed more word fragments with stereotype- and self-doubt-related words and had fewer preferences for things related to African American experience (jazz, basketball, hip-hop) than Black participants in the nondiagnostic condition or White participants in either condition, all of whom were essentially the same (see Figure 32.4).

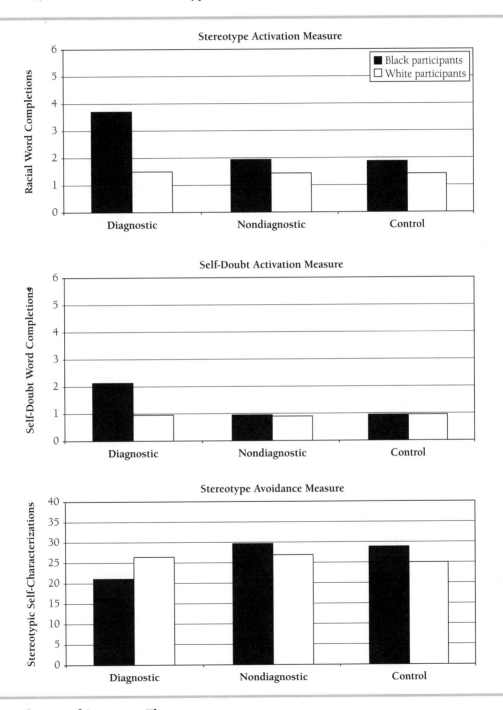

FIGURE 32.4. Indicators of Stereotype Threat.

Also, as a last item before participants expected to begin the test, they were given the option of recording their race, a measure we thought might further tap into an apprehension about being viewed stereotypically. Interestingly, then, all of the Black participants in the nondiagnostic condition and all of the White participants in both conditions listed their race, whereas only 25% of the Black participants in the diagnostic condition did so.

Self-Rejection or Self-Presentation? A troubling implication of the earlier mentioned internalization models (Allport, 1954; Bettelheim, 1943; Clark, 1965; Erikson, 1956; Fanon, 1952/1967; Grier & Coobs, 1968; Kardiner & Ovesey, 1951) is that negative stereotypes about one's group eventually become internalized and cause rejection of one's own group, even of oneself—*self-hating* preferences. The famous finding of Clark and Clark (1939) that Black children preferred White dolls over Black dolls has been interpreted this way. The preferences of Black participants in the diagnostic condition fit this pattern; with negative stereotypes about their group cognitively activated, they valued things that were African American less than any other group. But the full set of results suggests a different interpretation. In those conditions in which Black participants did not have to worry about tripping a stereotypic perception of themselves, they valued things that were African American more strongly than did other participants. Thus, rather than reflecting self- or own-group rejection, their devaluing of things that were African American in the diagnostic condition was apparently a strategic self-presentation aimed at cracking the stereotypic lens through which they could be seen. So it could be, then, in the general case, rather than reflecting real self-concepts, behavior that appears group-rejecting or self-rejecting may reflect situation-bound, self-presentational strategies.

Stereotype Threat and Domain Identification. Not being identified with a domain, our theory (C. M. Steele & Aronson, 1995) reasons, means that one's experience of stereotype threat in the domain is less self-threatening. Although we have yet to complete a satisfactory test of this prediction, partially completed experiments and pretests show that stereotype threat has very little, if any, effect on participants not identified with the domain of relevance. Most typically, these participants give up and underperform on the difficult test regardless of whether they are under stereotype threat. Although not yet constituting a complete test of this implication of the theory, these data do emphasize that the above results generalize only to domain-identified students.

Stereotype Threat and the Interpretation of Group Differences in Standardized Test Performance. Inherent to the science of quantifying human intelligence is the unsavory possibility of ranking societal groups as to their aggregated intelligence. It is from this corner of psychology that the greatest controversy has arisen, a controversy that lasted throughout the 20th century and that is less about the fact of these group differences than about their interpretation (cf. Herrnstein & Murray, 1994; Kamin, 1974). To the set of possible causes for these group differences, our findings (C. M. Steele & Aronson, 1995) add a new one: the differential impact of stereotype threat on groups in the testing situation itself. Thus, stereotype threat may be a possible source of bias in standardized tests, a bias that arises not from item content but from group differences in the threat that societal stereotypes attach to test performance. Of course, not every member of an ability-stereotyped group is going to be affected by stereotype threat every time they take a test. As our research has shown, the experience of success as one takes the test can dispel the relevance of the stereotype. Nonetheless, among the most identified test takers in the stereotype-threatened group—those in its academic vanguard who have the greatest confidence and skills—this threat can substantially depress performance on more difficult parts of the exam. And this depression could contribute significantly to the group's underperformance in comparison with nonstereotype-threatened groups.[6]

Reaction of Disidentification

Stereotype threat is assumed to have an abiding effect on school achievement—an effect beyond its impairment of immediate performance—by preventing or breaking a person's identification with school, in particular, those domains of schooling in which the stereotype applies. This reasoning has several implications for which empirical evidence can be brought to bear: the resilience of self-esteem to stigmatization; the relationship between stigmatized status and school achievement; and, among ability-stigmatized people, the relationship between their school performance and self-esteem.

Self-Esteem's Resilience to Stigmatization. In a recent review, Crocker and Major (1989) were able to make a strong case for the lack of something that common sense suggests should exist: a negative effect of stigmatization on self-esteem. Following the logic of the internalization models described above and viewing stigmatization as, among other things, an assault to self-esteem, one might expect that people who are stigmatized would have lower self-esteem than people who are not. Yet, as Crocker and Major reported, when the self-esteem of stigmatized groups (e.g., Blacks, Chicanos, the facially disfigured, obese people, etc.) is actually measured, one finds that their self-esteem is as high as that of the nonstigmatized.

Crocker and Major (1989) offered the intriguing argument that stigma itself offers esteem-protective strategies. For example, the stigmatized can blame their failures on the prejudice of out-group members, they can limit their self-evaluative social comparisons to the in-group of other stigmatized people, and they can devalue the domains in which they feel devalued. Other models have also described esteem-saving adaptations to stigma. For example, models that assume internalization of stereotype-related anxieties often posit compensatory personality traits (e.g., grandiosity) that protect self-esteem but leave one poorly adapted to the mainstream (Allport, 1954; Clark, 1965; Grier & Coobs, 1968; Kardiner & Ovesey, 1951; S. Steele, 1990). In the present reasoning, stigmatization stems from stereotype threat in specific domains. Thus, it adds to the list of stigma adaptations the possibility of simple domain disidentification, the rescuing of self-esteem by rendering as self-evaluatively irrelevant the domain in which the stereotype applies. Herein may lie a significant source of the self-esteem resilience shown in stigmatized groups. This idea also implies that once domain disidentification is achieved, the pressure for adaptations of attribution and personality may be reduced.

A Universal Connection Between Stigmatization and Poor School Achievement. If disidentification with school, and the resulting underachievement, can be a reaction to ability-stigmatizing stereotypes in society, then it might be expected that ability stigmatization would be associated with poor school performance wherever it occurs in the world. Finding such a relationship would not definitively prove the present theory; the direction of causality could be quarreled with, as could the mediation of such a relationship. Still, it would be suggestive, and, in that respect, Ogbu (1986) reported an interesting fact: among the caste-like minorities in industrial and nonindustrial nations throughout the world (e.g., the Maoris of New Zealand, the Buraku of Japan, the Harijans of India, the Oriental Jews of Israel, and the West Indians of Great Britain), there exists the same 15-point IQ gap between them and the nonstigmatized members of their society as exists between Black and White Americans. These groups also suffer poorer school performance, higher dropout rates, and related behavior problems. Moreover, these gaps appear even when the stigmatized and nonstigmatized are of the same race, as in the case of the Buraku and other Japanese. What these groups share that is capable of explaining their deficits is a caste-like status that, through stereotypes in their societies, stigmatizes their intellectual abilities—sowing the seeds, I suggest, of their school disidentification.

The Disassociation of Self-Esteem and School Achievement. If the poor school achievement of ability-stigmatized

groups is mediated by disidentification, then it might be expected that among the ability-stigmatized, there would be a disassociation between school outcomes and overall self-esteem. Several kinds of evidence suggest this process among African Americans. First, there is the persistent finding that although Black students underperform in relation to White students on school outcomes from grades to standardized tests (e.g., Demo & Parker, 1987; Simmons, Brown, Bush, & Blyth, 1978; C. M. Steele, 1992), their global self-esteem is as high as or higher than that of White students (e.g., Porter & Washington, 1979; Rosenberg, 1979; Wylie, 1979). For both of these facts to be true, some portion of Black students must have acquired an imperviousness to poor school performance.

Several further studies suggest that this imperviousness is rooted in disidentification. In a study of desegregated schools in Champaign, Illinois, Hare and Costenell (1985) measured students' school achievement; overall self-esteem; and self-esteem in the specific domains of home life, school, and peer-group relations. Like others, they found that although Black students performed less well than White students, they still had comparable levels of overall self-esteem. Their domain-specific measures suggested why: although Black students were lower than White students in school and home-life self-esteem, Blacks slightly exceeded Whites in peer-group self-esteem. Here then, perhaps, was the source of their overall self-regard: disidentification with domains in which their evaluative prospects were poor (in this case, school and home life) and identification with domains in which their prospects were better (i.e., their peers).

A recent study suggests that this may be a not-uncommon phenomenon. Analyzing data available from the National Educational Longitudinal Survey (National Center for Educational Statistics, 1992, a nationally representative longitudinal survey begun in 1988), Osborne (1994) found that from the 8th through 10th grades Black students had lower achievement and somewhat higher self-esteem than White students, which replicated the general pattern of findings described above. But more than this, he found evidence of increasing Black students' disidentification over this period: the correlation between their school achievement and self-esteem for this period decreased significantly more for Black than for White students. Also, using a scale measure of school disidentification, Major, Spencer, Schmader, Wolfe, and Crocker (1998) found that Black students were more disidentified than White students in several college samples and that for disidentified students of both races, negative feedback about an intellectual task had less effect on their self-esteem than it did for identified students. Major et al. further showed that when racial stereotypes were primed, neither negative nor positive feedback affected Black students' self-esteem, whereas the self-esteem of White students followed the direction of the feedback. Ability stigmatization of the sort experienced by African Americans, then, can be associated with a protective "disconnect" between performance and self-regard, a disconnect of the sort that is consistent with disidentification theory.

Can stereotype threat directly cause this disconnect? To test this question, Kirsten Stoutemeyer and I varied the strength of stereotype threat that female test takers (Stanford students) were under by varying whether societal differences between women and men in math performance were attributed to small but stable differences in innate ability (suggesting an inherent, gender-based limit in math ability) or to social causes such as sex-role prescriptions and discrimination (suggesting no inherent, gender-based limit in math ability). We then measured their identification with math and math-related careers, either before or after they took a difficult math test. Regardless of when identification was measured, women under stronger stereotype threat disidentified with math and math-related careers more than women under weaker stereotype threat. Although domain identification has several determinants, these findings suggest that stereotype threat is an important one of them.

"WISE" SCHOOLING: PRACTICE AND POLICY

As a different diagnosis, the present analysis comes to a different prescription: the schooling of stereotype-threatened groups may be improved through situational changes (analogous to those manipulated in our experiments) that reduce the stereotype threat these students might otherwise be under. As noted, psychological diagnoses have more typically ascribed the problems of these students to internal processes ranging from genes to internalized stereotypes. On the face of it, at least, internal states are more difficult to modify than situational factors. Thus, the hope of the present analysis, encouraged by our research, is that these problems might be more tractable through the situational design of schooling, in particular, design that secures these students in the belief that they will not be held under the suspicion of negative stereotypes about their group. Schooling that does this, I have called wise, a term borrowed from Irving Goffman (1963), who borrowed it from gay men and lesbians of the 1950s. They used it to designate heterosexuals who understood their full humanity despite the stigma attached to their sexual orientation: family and friends, usually, who knew the person beneath the stigma. So it must be, I argue, for the effective schooling of stereotype-threatened groups.

Although "wisdom" may be necessary for the effective schooling of such students, it may not always be sufficient. The chief distinction made in this analysis (between those of these groups who are identified with the relevant school domain and those who are not) raises a caution. As noted, stereotype threat is not keenly felt by those who identify little with the stereotype-threatening domain. Thus, although reducing this threat in the domain may be necessary to encourage their identification, it may not be sufficient to build an identification that is not there. For this to occur, more far-reaching strategies that develop the building blocks of domain identification may be required: better skills, greater domain self-efficacy, feelings of social and cultural comfort in the domain, a lack of social pressure to disidentify, and so on.

But for the identified of these groups, who are quite numerous on college campuses, the news may be better than is typically appreciated. For these students, feasible changes in the conditions of schooling that make threatening stereotypes less applicable to their behavior (i.e., wisdom) may be enough. They are already identified with the relevant domain, they have skills and confidence in the domain, and they have survived other barriers to identification. Their remaining problem is stereotype threat. Reducing that problem, then, may be enough to bring their performance on par with that of nonstereotyped persons in the domain.

This distinction raises an important and often overlooked issue in the design of schooling for stereotype-threatened students, that of triage, the issue of rendering onto the right students the right intervention. Mistakes can easily be made. For example, applying a strategy to school-identified students (on the basis of their membership in a stereotype-threatened group) that assumes weak identification, poor skills, and little confidence could backfire. It could increase stereotype threat and underperformance by signaling that their abilities are held under suspicion because of their group membership. But the opposite mistake could be made by applying a strategy that assumes strong identification, skills, and confidence to those who are actually unidentified with the relevant domain. Merely reducing stereotype threat may not accomplish much when the more primary need of these students is to gain the interests, resources, skills, confidences, and values that are needed to identify with the domain.

Some wise strategies, then, may work for both identified and unidentified students from these groups, but others may have to be appropriately targeted to be effective. I offer some examples of both types.

For both domain-identified and domain-unidentified students:

1. *Optimistic teacher-student relationships.* The prevailing stereotypes make it plausible for ability-stigmatized students to worry that people in their schooling environment will doubt their abilities. Thus, one wise strategy, seemingly suitable for all students, is to

discredit this assumption through the authority of potential-affirming adult relationships. The Comer (1988) Schools Project (1988) has used this strategy with great success at the elementary school level, and Johnides, von Hippel, Lerner, and Nagda (1992) have used it in designing a mentoring program for incoming minority and other students at the University of Michigan. In analogous laboratory experiments, Geoffrey Cohen, Lee Ross, and I (Cohen, Steele, & Ross, 1997) found that critical feedback to African American students was strongly motivating when it was coupled with optimism about their potential.

2. *Challenge over remediation.* Giving challenging work to students conveys respect for their potential and thus shows them that they are not regarded through the lens of an ability-demeaning stereotype. Urie Treisman (1985) used this strategy explicitly in designing his successful group-study workshops in math for college-aged women and minorities. Taking students where they are skillwise, all students can be given challenging work at a challenging, not overwhelming, pace, especially in the context of supportive adult-student relationships. In contrast, remedial work reinforces in these students the possibility that they are being viewed stereotypically. And this, by increasing stereotype threat in the domain, can undermine their performance.

3. *Stressing the expandability of intelligence.* The threat of negative-ability stereotypes is that one could confirm or be seen as having a fixed limitation inherent to one's group. To the extent that schooling can stress what Carol Dweck (1986) called the *incremental* nature of human intelligence—its expandability in response to experience and training—it should help to deflect this meanest implication of the stereotype. Aronson (1996) recently found, for example, that having African American college students repeatedly advocate the expandability of intelligence to their elementary school tutees significantly improved their own grades.

For domain-identified students:

1. *Affirming domain belongingness.* Negative-ability stereotypes raise the threat that one does not belong in the domain. They cast doubt on the extent of one's abilities, on how well one will be accepted, on one's social compatibility with the domain, and so on. Thus, for students whose primary barrier to school identification is stereotype threat, direct affirmation of their belongingness in the domain may be effective. But it is important to base this affirmation on the students' intellectual potential. Affirming social belonging alone, for those under the threat of an ability stereotype, could be taken as begging the question.

2. *Valuing multiple perspectives.* This refers to strategies that explicitly value a variety of approaches to both academic substance and the larger academic culture in which that substance is considered. Making such a value public tells stereotype-threatened students that this is an environment in which the stereotype is less likely to be used.

3. *Role models.* People from the stereotype-threatened group who have been successful in the domain carry the message that stereotype threat is not an insurmountable barrier there.

For domain-unidentified students:

1. *Nonjudgmental responsiveness.* Research by Lepper, Woolverton, Mumme, and Gurtner (1993) has identified a distinct strategy that expert tutors use with especially poor students: little direct praise, Socratic direction of students' work, and minimal attention to right and wrong answers. For students weakly identified with the domain, who are threatened by a poor reputation and who probably hold internalized doubts about their ability, this Socratic strategy has the wisdom of securing a safe teacher-student relationship in which there is little cost of failure and the gradual building of domain efficacy from small gains.

2. *Building self-efficacy.* Based on Bandura's (1977, 1986) theory of self-efficacy, this strategy attempts to build the student's sense of competence and self-efficacy in the schooling domain. Howard and Hammond (1985) have developed a powerful implementation of this strategy for African American and other minority students, especially in inner-city public schools.

CONCLUSION

In social psychology, we know that as observers looking at a person or group we tend to stress internal, dispositional causes of their behavior, whereas when we take the perspective of the actor, now facing the circumstances they face, we stress more situational causes (e.g., E. E. Jones & Nisbett, 1972; Ross, 1977). If there is a system to the present research, it is that of taking the actor's perspective in trying to understand the intellectual performance of African American and female students. It is this perspective that brings to light the broadly encompassing condition of having these groups' identification with domains of schooling threatened by societal stereotypes. This is a threat that in the short run can depress their intellectual performance and, over the long run, undermine the identity itself, a predicament of serious consequence. But it is a predicament—something in the interaction between a group's social identity and its social psychological context, rather than something essential to the group itself. Predicaments can be treated, intervened on, and it is in this respect that I hope the perspective taken in this analysis and the early evidence offer encouragement.

Notes

1. Other factors may also contribute. For example, there are persistent reports of women and minorities being treated differently in the classroom and in other aspects of schooling (e.g., Hewitt & Seymour, 1991). This treatment includes both the "chilly-climate" sins of omission—the failure to call on them in class or to recognize and encourage their talents, and so on—and, in the case of low-income minorities, sins of commission—disproportionate expulsion from school, assignment to special education classes, and administration of corporal punishment ("National Coalition of Advocates for Students Report," 1988).

2. The point is not that negative stereotypes are never internalized as low self-expectancies and self-doubts. It is that in such internalization, disidentification is the more primary adaptation. That is, once the stereotype-relevant domain—for instance, math—is dropped as a self-definition, the negative stereotype—for example, that women are limited in math—can be accepted as more self-descriptive, that is, internalized, without it much affecting one's self-regard, as for the woman who, not caring about math, says she is lousy at it. But this internalization is probably resisted (Crocker & Major, 1989) until disidentification makes it less self-threatening. Once this has happened, the person is likely to avoid the domain because of both disinterest and low confidence regardless of whether stereotype threat is present.

3. As a process of social devaluation, stereotype threat is both a subform of stigmatization and something more general. It is that form of stigmatization that is mediated by collectively held, devaluing group stereotypes. This means that it does not include stigmatization that derives from nonstereotyped features such as a facial disfigurement or, for example, what Goffman (1963) called abominations of the body. Stereotype threat is a situational predicament. And, in this sense, it is also more general than stigmatization. It is a threat that can befall anyone about whom a negative reputation or group stereotype exists.

4. Moreover, a protective avoidance of identification can become a group norm. In reaction to a shared sense of threat in school, for example, it can become a shared reaction that is transmitted to group members as the normative relation to school. Both research (Ogbu, 1986; Solomon, 1992) and the media have documented this reaction in minority students from inner-city high schools to Harvard University's campus. Thus, disidentification can be sustained by normative pressure from the in-group as well as by stereotype threat in the setting.

5. Participants did not actually take the test in this experiment, as completing these measures would likely have activated the stereotype in all conditions.

6. Those who are less domain-identified in the stereotype-threatened group may also underperform on standardized tests. Because they care less about the domain it represents, they may be undermotivated or they may withdraw effort in the face of frustration. And for all of the reasons I have discussed, the greater portion of the stereotype-threatened group may be academically unidentified. This fact too, then, may contribute to the group's overall weaker performance on these tests in comparison with nonstereotype-threatened groups.

References

Adelman, C. (1991). *Women at thirty-something: Paradoxes of attainment.* Washington, DC: U.S. Department of Education, Office of Research and Development.

Alexander, K. L., & Entwistle, D. R. (1988). Achievement in the first two years of school: Patterns and processes. *Monographs of the Society for Research in Child Development, 53*(2).

Allport, G. (1954). *The nature of prejudice.* New York: Doubleday.

American Council on Education. (1995–1996). *Minorities in higher education.* Washington, DC: Office of Minority Concerns.

Aronson, J. (1996). Advocating the malleability of intelligence as an intervention to increase college grade performance. Unpublished manuscript, University of Texas.

Bandura, A. (1977). Self-efficacy: Toward a unifying theory of behavior change. *Psychological Review, 84,* 191–215.

Bandura, A. (1986). *Social foundations of action: A social-cognitive theory.* Englewood Cliffs, NJ: Prentice Hall.

Baumeister, R. F., & Showers, C. J. (1984). A review of paradoxical performance effects: Choking under pressure in sports and mental tests. *European Journal of Social Psychology, 16,* 361–383.

Benbow, C. P., & Arjmand, O. (1990). Predictions of high academic achievement in mathematics and science by mathematically talented students: A longitudinal study. *Journal of Educational Psychology, 82,* 430–441.

Benbow, C. P., & Stanley, J. C. (1980). Sex differences in mathematical ability: Fact or artifact? *Science, 210,* 1262–1264.

Benbow, C. P., & Stanley, J. C. (1983). Sex differences in mathematical reasoning ability: More facts. *Science, 222,* 1029–1031.

Bettelheim, B. (1943). Individual and mass behavior in extreme situations. *Journal of Abnormal and Social Psychology, 38,* 417–452.

Brill, A. A. (Ed.). (1938). *The basic writings of Sigmund Freud.* New York: Random House.

Burton, N. W., & Jones, L. V. (1982). Recent trends in achievement levels of Black and White youth. *Educational Researcher, 11,* 10–17.

Carter, S. (1991). *Reflections of an affirmative action baby.* New York: Basic Books.

Clark, K. B. (1965). *Dark ghetto: Dilemmas of social power.* New York: Harper & Row.

Clark, K. B., & Clark, M. K. (1939). The development of consciousness of self and the emergence of racial identification of Negro school children. *Journal of Social Psychology, 10,* 591–599.

Cohen, G., Steele, C. M., & Ross, L. (1997). Giving feedback across the racial divide: Overcoming the effects of stereotypes. Unpublished manuscript, Stanford University.

Coleman, J. S., Campbell, E. Q., Hobson, C. J., McPartland, J., Mood, A. M., Weinfield, F. D., & York, R. L. (1966). *Equality of educational opportunity*. Washington, DC: U.S. Government Printing Office.

Comer, J. (1988, November). Educating poor minority children. *Scientific American, 259*, p. 42.

Cooley, C. H. (1956). *Human nature and the social order*. New York: Free Press.

Cose, E. (1993). *The rage of a privileged class*. New York: Harper-Collins.

Crocker, J., & Major, B. (1989). Social stigma and self-esteem: The self-protective properties of stigma. *Psychological Review, 96*, 608–630.

Cross, W. E., Jr. (1991). *Shades of black: Diversity in African-American identity*. Philadelphia: Temple University Press.

Culotta, E., & Gibbons, A. (Eds.). (1992, November 13). Minorities in science [Special section]. *Science, 258*, 1176–1232.

DeBoer, G. (1984). A study of gender effects in science and mathematics course-taking behavior among students who graduated from college in the late 1970s. *Journal of Research in Science Teaching, 21*, 95–103.

Demo, D. H., & Parker, K. D. (1987). Academic achievement and self-esteem among Black and White college students. *Journal of Social Psychology, 4*, 345–355.

Dweck, C. (1986). Motivational processes affecting learning. *American Psychologist, 41*, 1040–1048.

Eccles, J. S. (1987). Gender roles and women's achievement-related decisions. *Psychology of Women Quarterly, 11*, 135–172.

Eccles-Parsons, J. S., Adler, T. F., Futterman, R., Goff, S. B., Kaczala, C. M., Meece, J. L., & Midgley, C. (1983). Expectations, values, and academic behaviors. In J. I. Spence (Ed.), *Achievement and achievement motivation* (pp. 75–146). New York: Freeman.

Erikson, E. (1956). The problem of ego-identity. *Journal of the American Analytical Association, 4*, 56–121.

Fanon, F. (1967). *Black skins, white masks*. New York: Grove Press. (Original work published 1952)

Frable, D., Blackstone, T., & Sherbaum, C. (1990). Marginal and mindful: Deviants in social interaction. *Journal of Personality and Social Behavior, 59*, 140–149.

Geen, R. G. (1991). Social motivation. *Annual Review of Psychology, 42*, 377–399.

Gerard, H. (1983). School desegregation: The social science role. *American Psychologist, 38*, 869–878.

Goffman, E. (1963). *Stigma: Notes on the management of spoiled identity*. New York: Touchstone.

Grier, W. H., & Coobs, P. M. (1968). *Black rage*. New York: Basic Books.

Hare, B. R., & Costenell, L. A. (1985). No place to run, no place to hide: Comparative status and future prospects of Black boys. In M. B. Spencer, G. K. Brookins, & W. Allen (Eds.), *Beginnings: The social and affective development of Black children* (pp. 201–214). Hillsdale. NJ: Erlbaum.

Herrnstein, R. A., & Murray, C. (1994). *The bell curve*. New York: Grove Press.

Hewitt, N. M., & Seymour, E. (1991). *Factors contributing to high attrition rates among science and engineering undergraduate majors*. Unpublished report to the Alfred P. Sloan Foundation.

Howard, J., & Hammond, R. (1985, September 9). Rumors of inferiority. *New Republic, 72*, 18–23.

Hyde, J. S., Fennema, E., & Lamon, S. J. (1990). Gender differences in mathematics performance: A meta-analysis. *Psychological Bulletin, 107*, 139-155.

James, W. (1950). *The principles of psychology* (Vol. 1). New York: Dover. (Original work published 1890)

Jensen, A. R. (1969). How much can we boost IQ and scholastic achievement? *Harvard Educational Review, 39*, 1–123.

Jensen, A. R. (1980). *Bias in mental testing*. New York: Free Press.

Johnides, J., von Hippel, W., Lemer, J. S., & Nagda, B. (1992, August). *Evaluation of minority retention programs: The undergraduate research opportunities program at the University of Michigan*. Paper presented at the 100th Annual Convention of the American Psychological Association, Washington, DC.

Jones, E. E., Farina, A., Hastorf, A. H., Markus, H., Miller, O. T., & Scott, R. A. (1984). *Social stigma: The psychology of marked relationships*. New York: Freeman.

Jones, E. E., & Nisbett, R. E. (1972). The actor and the observer: Divergent perceptions of the causes of behavior. In E. E. Jones, D. E. Kanouse, H. H. Kelley, R. E. Nisbett, S. Valins, & B. Weiner (Eds.), *Attribution: Perceiving the causes of behavior* (pp. 79–94). Morristown, NJ: General Learning Press.

Jones, J. M. (1997). *Prejudice and racism* (2nd ed.). New York: McGraw-Hill.

Kamin, L. (1974). *The science and politics of I.Q.* Hillsdale, NJ: Erlbaum.

Kardiner, A., & Ovesey, L. (1951). *The mark of oppression: Explorations in the personality of the American Negro*. New York: Norton.

Kleck, R. E., & Strenta, A. (1980). Perceptions of the impact of negatively valued physical characteristics on social interactions. *Journal of Personality and Social Psychology, 39*, 861–873.

Lepper, M. R., Woolverton, M., Mumme, D. L., & Gurtner, J.-L. (1993). Motivational techniques of expert human tutors: Lessons for the design of computer-based tutors. In S. P. Lajoie & S. J. Derry (Eds.), *Computers as cognitive tools* (pp. 75–104). Hillsdale, NJ: Erlbaum.

Levin, J., & Wyckoff, J. (1988). Effective advising: Identifying students most likely to persist and succeed in engineering. *Engineering Education, 78*, 178–182.

Lewin, K. (1941). *Resolving social conflict*. New York: Harper & Row.

Linn, M. C. (1994). The tyranny of the mean: Gender and expectations. *Notices of the American Mathematical Society, 41*, 766–769.

Lord, C. G., & Saenz, D. S. (1985). Memory deficits and memory surfeits: Differential cognitive consequences of tokenism for tokens and observers. *Journal of Personality and Social Psychology, 49*, 918–926.

Lovely, R. (1987, February). *Selection of undergraduate majors by high ability students: Sex difference and attrition of science majors*. Paper presented at the annual meeting of the Association for the Study of Higher Education, San Diego, CA.

Major, B., Spencer, S., Schmader, T., Wolfe, C., & Crocker, J. (1998). Coping with negative stereotypes about intellectual performance: The role of psychological disengagement. *Personality and Social Psychology Bulletin, 24*, 34–50.

Mead, G. H. (1934). *Mind, self and society*. Chicago: University of Chicago Press.

Miller, L. S. (1995). *An American imperative: Accelerating minority educational advancement*. New Haven, CT: Yale University Press.

Miller, L. S. (1996, March). *Promoting high academic achievement among non-Asian minorities*. Paper presented at the Princeton University Conference on Higher Education, Princeton, NJ.

National Center for Educational Statistics. (1992). *National Educational Longitudinal Study of 1988: First follow-up. Student component data file user's manual*. Washington, DC: U. S. Department of Education, Office of Educational Research and Improvement.

National Coalition of Advocates for Students Report. (1988, December 12). *Ann Arbor News*, pp. Al, A4.

Nettles, M. T. (1988). *Toward undergraduate student equality in American higher education*. New York: Greenwood.

Ogbu, J. (1986). The consequences of the American caste system. In U. Neisser (Ed.), *The school achievement of minority children: New perspectives* (pp. 19–56). Hillsdale, NJ: Erlbaum.

Osborne, J. (1994). Academics, self-esteem, and race: A look at the underlying assumption of the disidentification hypothesis. *Personality and Social Psychology Bulletin, 21*, 449–455.

Porter, J. R., & Washington, R. E. (1979). Black identity and self-esteem: A review of the studies of Black self-concept, 1968–1978. *Annual Review of Sociology, 5*, 53–74.

Ramist, L., Lewis, C., & McCamley-Jenkins, L. (1994). *Student group differences in predicting college grades: Sex, language, and ethnic groups* (College Board Report no. 93-1, ETS no. 94.27). New York: College Entrance Examination Board.

Rosenberg, M. (1979). *Conceiving self*. New York: Basic Books.

Ross, L. (1977). The intuitive psychologist and his shortcomings: Distortions in the attribution process. In L. Berkowitz (Ed.), *Advances in experimental social psychology* (Vol. 10, pp. 337–384). New York: Academic Press.

Sarason, I. G. (1980). Introduction to the study of test anxiety. In I. G. Sarason (Ed.), *Test anxiety: Theory, research, and applications* (pp. 57–78). Hillsdale, NJ: Erlbaum.

Sartre, J. P. (1965). *Anti-Semite and Jew*. New York: Schocken Books. (Original work published 1946)

Schlenker, B. R., & Weigold, M. F. (1989). Goals and the self-identification process: Constructing desired identities. In L. A. Pervin (Ed.), *Goals concepts in personality and social psychology* (pp. 243–290). Hillsdale, NJ: Erlbaum.

Simmons, R. G., Brown, L., Bush, D. M., & Blyth, D. A. (1978). Self-esteem and achievement of Black and White adolescents. *Social Problems, 26*, 86–96.

Solomon, R. P. (1992). *Forging a separatist culture*. Albany: State University of New York Press.

Spencer, S. J., Steele, C. M., & Quinn, D. M. (1999). Stereotype threat and women's math performance. *Journal of Experimental Social Psychology, 35*, 4–28.

Steele, C. M. (1975). Name-calling and compliance. *Journal of Personality and Social Psychology, 31*, 361–369.

Steele, C. M. (1988). The psychology of self-affirmation: Sustaining the integrity of the self. In L. Berkowitz (Ed.), *Advances in experimental social psychology* (Vol. 21, pp. 261–302). New York: Academic Press.

Steele, C. M. (1992, April). Race and the schooling of Black Americans. *Atlantic Monthly*, pp. 68–78.

Steele, C. M., & Aronson, J. (1995). Stereotype threat and the intellectual test performance of African Americans. *Journal of Personality and Social Psychology, 69*, 797–811.

Steele, S. (1990). *The content of our character*. New York: St. Martin's Press.

Strenta, A. C., Elliott, R., Adair, R., Scott, J., & Matier, M. (1993). *Choosing and leaving science in highly selective institutions*. Unpublished report to the Alfred P. Sloan Foundation.

Tesser, A. (1988). Toward a self-evaluation maintenance model of social behavior. In L. Berkowitz (Ed.), *Advances in experimental social psychology* (Vol. 21, pp. 181–227). New York: Academic Press.

Treisman, U. (1985). A study of mathematics performance of Black students at the University of California, Berkeley. Unpublished report.

Vars, E. E., & Bowen, W. G. (1997). *SAT scores, race, and academic performance: New evidence from academically successful colleges*. Pittsburgh, PA: Mellon Foundation.

Ware, N. C., & Dill, D. (1986, March). *Persistence in science among mathematically able male and female college students with pre-college plans for a scientific major*. Paper presented at the annual meeting of the American Educational Research Association, San Francisco.

Ware, N. C., Steckler, N. A., & Leserman, J. (1985). Undergraduate women: Who chooses a science major? *Journal of Higher Education, 55*, 73–84.

Wine, J. (1971). Test anxiety and direction of attention. *Psychological Bulletin, 76*, 92–104.

Wylie, R. (1979). *The self-concept* (Vol. 2). Lincoln: University of Nebraska Press.

33

ENGAGING LIFE

A Funds-of-Knowledge Approach to Multicultural Education

Luis C. Moll
University of Arizona

Norma González
University of Utah

Es indispensable instrumentar didácticamente a la escuela para trabajar con la diversidad. Ni la diversidad negada, ni la diversidad aislada, ni la diversidad simplemente tolerada. Pero tampoco la diversidad asumida como un mal necesario, o celebrada como un bien en si mismo. . . . Transformar la diversidad conocida y reconocida en una ventaja pedagógica: ese me parece el gran desafío para el futuro.

—E. Ferreiro (1994)

If teachers are not learning much from their students, it is probable that their students are not learning much from them.

—Cummins (1996)

This chapter addresses, from a particular sociocultural perspective, the points mentioned in these two epigraphs. The first one, in our translation, reads: "It is indispensable to tool (*instrumentar*) the schools didactically to work with diversity. Neither diversity denied, nor diversity isolated, nor diversity simply tolerated. But also not diversity assumed as a necessary evil, or celebrated as good in and of itself. . . . To transform diversity that is known and recognized into a pedagogical advantage: that seems to me the greatest challenge for the future." Ferreiro (1994) suggests that the great challenge for the future of schooling is how to transform diversity into a pedagogical asset. (In this chapter, we use the terms *diversity* and *multiculturalism* interchangeably as affirming the pluralism that teachers, students, and their communities represent; see Nieto, 1997, 2000.) This transformation of diversity represents the greatest challenge ("el gran desafío") not just because the future is now, given the unavoidable presence of diversity in schools. It is a challenge, Ferreiro writes, because a fundamental historical function of schools, especially in their nation-building mission, has been to negate differences, to deal with diversity by ignoring it or by forging uniformity.

Three recent policy developments in U.S. education underscore Ferreiro's (1994) point that the school, on its own, is an unlikely place for addressing diversity as a resource. One is the onset of mass (high-stakes) testing as a reform strategy (Heubert & Hauser, 1999). Despite the lack of evidence that such testing facilitates school reform, especially in terms of narrowing the achievement gap between majority and minority students, these tests are being developed and mandated in virtually all states. A consequence of these tests is that, for a prolonged period of time, teaching is reduced to preparing students for the test, usually by increasing rote instruction on a narrow (English-only) group of subjects (Popham, 2000). Another consequence is that the overwhelming emphasis on administering these tests leaves little or no room for more formative types of assessment that may inform the professional development of teachers (Shepard, 2002). That is, the professional development that is needed for schools to address equity issues, or for that matter the needs of a multicultural student population, is not on the contemporary reform agenda (Orfield, 2000).

A second policy development involves highly restrictive and regimented phonics reading programs generally imposed on schools by law (Allington & Haley, 1999; Taylor, 1998). These reading programs, which are being implemented widely in urban districts, focus primarily on children pronouncing phonemes in isolation as the principal if not sole pedagogy of early reading, severely curtailing or even prohibiting alternative (meaning-driven) instructional approaches. As Smith (1999), a particularly insightful critic of this phonics nonsense, has put it:

Anything that mandates a specific course of behavior for teachers—even if it were relatively enlightened—constitutes a threat to education. People who care professionally about reading do not normally attempt to assert their views through legislation and litigation. On the other hand, people whose aim is to transform schools into more technological and commercial enterprises are likely to pick reading as a particularly soft and profitable target. Passions are easily swayed, simplistic solutions seem realistic, and teachers can be demonized and deprofessionalized. (p. 154)

The third policy, implemented by fiat through popular vote on political propositions, seeks to banish bilingual education, under penalty of law, and teachers or administrators are threatened with lawsuits if Spanish is used in schools (Gándara, 2002; García, 2000). These oppressive laws are now in place in California and Arizona and are being considered in other states, such as Colorado and New York, all having significant Latino student populations. Consider the coercive ideological context that such a law perpetuates, establishing Spanish as a pariah language in the schools while privileging English exclusively. In our view, these propositions have little to do with children learning English but much to do with coercive relations of power, especially given the changing demographics in the United States.

The extent to which these propositions represent methods of social control imposed through schools on the Latino population, a time-tested strategy of coercion (Spring, 1997), is made clear by voting patterns. In both California and Arizona, Latinos (and American Indians), against whom such propositions are specifically aimed, voted overwhelmingly against the propositions (63% against in California; similar figures estimated for Arizona). However, the propositions passed by a clear majority in both states (67% in California; 61% in Arizona). The intent of the vote in favor, in other words, was primarily to show Latinos who is in charge. As Sleeter (1999) has observed, the dominant assumption guiding such actions is that

monolingual Anglo members of the general public are perfectly capable of deciding what kind of educational programming is best for non-Anglo language minority children . . . and are better able to make such decisions than are bilingual education teachers or the communities the children come from. (pp. xv–xvi)

Schools, then, are faced with a sort of "multicultural paradox." On the one hand, administrators and teachers recognize the importance of cultural diversity in today's schooling (Nieto, 2000; Phillips & Crowell, 1994). How can they not, given the changing characteristics of children in their midst? Many schools, it should be emphasized, have responded with innovative programs to address student diversity (see Gándara, 2000; Mehan, Villanueva, Hubbard, & Lintz, 1996; Rivera & Pedraza, 2000). On the other hand, especially in the current societal context, this same diversity has motivated the present emphases on narrow practices; parochial monolingual visions; and conservative, reactionary policies (Hubbard & Mehan, 1999). Therefore, if we are to appropriate pedagogically the richness of diversity, including its multiculturalism, it is certainly insufficient to simply acknowledge diversity. Instead, it is indispensable, as Ferreiro (1994) suggests, to provide schools with the "didactic" tools to work with diversity. (This is what Ferreiro refers to as "instrumentar didácticamente a la escuela" in the opening epigraph. The term *didactic* or *didactical* has a broader meaning in Spanish than in English. In (U.S.) English it is routinely used to refer to rote instruction; in Spanish it has a pedagogical meaning that may include expert and novel teaching strategies.)

A major purpose of the "funds-of-knowledge" approach summarized in this chapter is to give teachers theoretical and methodological equipment to address diversity through a process of engagement with the everyday conditions of life (González et al., 1995; Moll, Amanti, Neff, & González, 1992). Our approach, building on anthropological methods, centers on visiting students' households for the purpose of developing social relations with family members that allow the documentation of their knowledge. We use the term *funds of knowledge* to refer to the knowledge base that underlies the productive and exchange activities of households. But those visits are only part of the story. We also create social settings, or study groups, to help teachers and researchers, working collaboratively, think about the meaning and implications of their work. Our claim is that the theoretical orientation of the approach, the empirical research with families, and the process of data analysis and interpretation help teachers re-present their students' households, and by implication the school's community, in terms of the social and cultural resources they possess.

Another consequence of our work is to help teachers think about how to use such resources for instruction. Our stance here is captured by Cummins's (1996) aphorism presented at the opening of the chapter. It calls for teachers, as a basic principle of teaching, to learn from their students. We believe that documenting funds of knowledge, and getting to know children and their families in contexts other than school, as part of a broader social world, helps recontextualize students for the teachers (Patterson & Baldwin, 2001). In so doing, the teachers become aware of resources and opportunities for teaching that are made apparent by establishing such social relations (López, 2001). That is, the student is no longer defined solely by what happens in the classroom, a reduced social context. The student is now understood as a person who partakes in a broader social life, which also includes the school and classroom.

This emphasis on studying social life moves us away from an understanding of culture as a "bounded" normative concept (González, 2001). It is quite common, especially in education, to think of culture as a well-defined entity that helps differentiate entire groups of people; for example, one says, "The French are like this; but the British are like that." Or one hears the claim that "Anglos do this, but Latinos do that." These statements imply a concept of culture as a well-bounded, cohesive entity whose traits and values are shared, in one way or another, by all members of a particular group. Given the great diversity that exists *within* groups, such cohesiveness is unlikely to exist. Rather than focus on cultural norms, then, and how people live by these norms, we chose instead to focus on practices, on how people "live culturally," to borrow a turn from Ingold (1994). This emphasis means that we attempt to understand, by interacting with families, the strategies and adaptations that households have developed over time and the multiple dimensions of the lived experiences of families and students, including the funds of knowledge they have produced. It is especially important in this work, therefore, to learn how to think about culture as dynamic and changing, never fixed or static, and full of agency and versatility, especially in response to the many circumstances of material life. This approach, then, places a high premium on respecting and understanding cultural diversity in life, and the multiculturalism implied by this diversity in schools.

This chapter is divided into four parts. We first elaborate the concept of funds of knowledge, and related theoretical notions, borrowing examples as needed from our previous work. The examples help illustrate the ethnographic approach central to our work, the collaborative arrangement with teachers, the methods of study, and what is learned by conducting such team research with teachers. In the second part we address what this concept and the approach we have developed contribute to multicultural research in education. Rather than provide generalizations, we rely on presenting specific examples on how the work has been done by others, in different locations, and with people living in different circumstances. We then review how teachers have used what they learned in practice and present, as a conclusion, possibilities for extending our approach to address other topics central to multicultural education, such as language variation, social class, and immigration.

THE ORIGINS OF THE APPROACH

The research on funds of knowledge has had many iterations—as many iterations, we could say, as there have been teachers involved in the work. However, all of them occurred within two primary phases of study. The first phase of study, from about 1987 to 1990, included development of the basic design of the work, and the first systematic attempt to collect household data based on the concept of funds of knowledge. The term *funds of knowledge* was coined by James Greenberg and Carlos Vélez-Ibáñez, borrowing in part from Eric Wolf's (1966) analysis of nonmarket forms of exchange among households (see Greenberg, 1989; Vélez-Ibáñez, 1988; and Vélez-Ibáñez, 1996, Chapter 4). This phase is reviewed in González, Moll, and Amanti (in press), so we do not elaborate on it here, except to point out that it featured a sustained collaboration among anthropologists, educational researchers, and classroom teachers that has become one of the hallmarks of this approach (Moll, 1992; Moll & Greenberg, 1990). The research design coordinated three interrelated activities: (a) ethnographic analysis of household dynamics, (b) examination of classroom practices, and (c) development of after-school study groups with teachers. These study groups, collaborative ventures between teachers and researchers, are settings within which we discuss our developing understanding of households and classrooms. These study groups also function as "mediating structures" for developing novel classroom practices that involve strategic connections between these two other entities (Moll, 1997).

During this first phase, however, the university-based researchers and graduate students in education and anthropology collected all of the household data, the gist of which was then presented to teachers in an attempt to influence their practice (Moll & Greenberg, 1990). Hence the teachers were involved minimally in the collection of funds-of-knowledge data, but they took the lead in developing classroom practices and helped establish the importance of study groups in conducting this type of research.

The second phase of study (1991 to present) featured teachers involved in all aspects of study, including the collection and analysis of household data (González et al., in press; González et al., 1995; Moll et al., 1992). Involving teachers in all aspects of the work was a key change in its design. This change helped involve teachers intellectually in the design and conduct of the study, and it helped us understand how the development of social relations itself, a methodological necessity in this type of work, becomes an important outcome of study for the teachers. That is, it was not only the collection and transformation of funds-of-knowledge data that became important for teachers but the formation of social relations with the students' families, relations that would not have developed otherwise. This change, involving teachers firsthand in all aspects of study, means that teachers need not depend on second-hand generalities made by academic researchers about Mexican Americans, African Americans, Native Americans, or any other cultural group. Instead, they are learning, as ethnographers would, directly from interviews, observations, and other firsthand experiences. Our claim is that these qualitative methods of study can become the "tools" necessary for the teachers' development of *theoretical knowledge*. This theoretical knowledge, in turn, helps teachers formulate a pedagogy that is specific to their situations and that builds strategically on the social relations and cultural resources of their school's community.

COLLECTION AND ANALYSIS OF FUNDS OF KNOWLEDGE

The theoretical orientation of the research, then, is toward documenting the productive (and other) activities of households and what they reveal about families' knowledge. Particularly important in this work has been analysis of households as "strategizing units": how they function as part of a wider economy, and how family members obtain and distribute their material and intellectual resources through strategic social ties or networks, or through other adaptive arrangements. We have learned that in contrast to the classroom, a household never functions alone or in isolation; it is always connected to other households and institutions through diverse social networks. These social networks not only facilitate various forms of economic assistance and labor cooperation but serve important emotional and service functions, providing assistance of different types, for example, in finding jobs, with child care and rearing, or other problem-solving functions.

Teachers participating in the project in its various iterations were primarily elementary school teachers, although middleschool teachers have also participated, and from a variety of backgrounds and ranges of teaching experience. (It is a common misperception that only Latino teachers have participated in this work. This is simply not accurate; we estimate that about half of the teachers are Latino, most not well acquainted initially with the communities in which they conducted their research or with any families, and thus having scant knowledge of the families of their students. In our experience, most teachers do not live within the community in which they teach, particularly if the neighborhood is low income.) We make it a point to work only with

teachers who volunteer to collaborate with us. This strategy obviously presents a sampling bias, for those teachers are already predisposed to make the necessary time and intellectual commitment to participate in the study. Thus they may be unusually dedicated teachers, something we acknowledge. However, selecting teachers randomly or otherwise requiring their participation involuntarily is likely to create considerable hostility and resistance, and it would be perceived as a further imposition on teachers. We therefore work only with teachers who volunteer to participate in the study or those who enroll in our graduate courses patterned after the study. (Although the work we describe in this paper has been conducted in schools, we also have taught a graduate field research course patterned after this work. The requirements of the course mimic the field research activities. Participants are required to visit a household at least three times during the course of the semester, read theoretical and methodological articles and related case studies, record and expand observations in writing, and write a final paper. The nature of the relationship between university professors and classroom teachers is different under the graduate course arrangement than if the study is conducted at a school site, given the usual course requirements and professor-student relationships. We have found that the relationships become more symmetrical in the school-based studies when no grading takes place. For further comments on such classroom arrangements as part of conducting funds-of-knowledge research, see Mercado, in press.)

Generally, we first make a visit to the school, often at the behest of teachers, to present details of the study, how we do the work, and its potential benefits. We then invite teachers to collaborate with us and, when possible, remunerate them for their participation. As we completed more studies, the approach to ethnographic training shifted as we learned more about what makes sense in each situation. Not surprisingly, what works is exactly our basic assumption. The more that teachers can identify and engage with the topic of study, the more interest and motivation they have. What does not work is an approach that avoids engaging life, the hallmark of a personal ethnographic encounter.

Consequently, certain important points are the key in adopting such an anthropological lens. The first is to read ethnographic literature. Teachers are given a reader that contains numerous examples of ethnographic work relating to educational settings (e.g., Heath, 1983). The second is to role-play and practice (we ask teachers to interview each other) and discuss a nonevaluative, nonjudgmental stance to the fieldwork they will be conducting. We may not always agree with what we hear or see, but our role is to understand how others make sense of their lives. This sense-making process may be contradictory or ambiguous, but in one way or another, understanding what makes sense to others is what we try to achieve. The third point is to pay attention to detail, for we are interested in the particulars, in the concrete practices of life.

Preparing for the visits therefore begins long before actually entering the homes. (Portions of this description of the ethnographic training of teachers appeared in McIntyre, Rosebery, and González, 2001.) As the teachers drive down the street, we urge them to observe the neighborhood, the surrounding area, and the external markers of what identifies a particular neighborhood. We look for material clues to possible funds of knowledge: in gardens (botanical knowledge?), patio walls (masonry?), restored automobiles (mechanical knowledge?), or ornaments displayed or murals (artists?). During our initial "training" sessions, we often show a video with short segments or vignettes of ordinary community or household scenes and ask participants to discuss what they notice. The first video, for example, contains a family yard sale with a great deal of activity going on at once. We emphasize that this is usually what happens on a household visit, since life doesn't stand still in these homes for us to observe it. The vignette usually elicit comments on what is being sold, such as wooden doll furniture, which might indicate carpentry skills. It might be the interactions involved where older siblings are caring for younger babies, indicating cross-age care taking. Another could be the particular uses of language and how code switching between Spanish and English may be evident throughout, or the presence of literacy in two languages. Through this process of interpretation, we point out how our own interests and funds of knowledge often determine what we observe.

Another video segment we use is particularly revealing of potential curricular applications. It shows a nine-year-old boy in a backyard workshop, working with his father to build a barbecue grill. The scene is replete with measurement, estimation, geometry, and a range of other household mathematical practices. Because we do not often think of routine household activities as containing mathematics, this slice of life helps to suggest the academic potential of household knowledge.

Finally, and perhaps most important, we emphasize asking respectful questions and learning to listen to answers. The dialogue that comes about in the face-to-face interaction of the ethnographic interview is vital in building relationships between households and schools, and between parents and teachers. It is important to point out that the interviews emerge as a type of conversation, rather than a sequential survey or research format.

On the basis of our previous experience in household interviews and observations, we distilled critical topics into three basic areas. These areas correspond to three questionnaires that are generally covered in three household visits. Using questionnaires as a tool is useful for the teacher/ethnographer to signal a shift in approaching the household, not necessarily as a teacher but as a learner. Entering the household with questions, rather than answers, creates the context for an inquiry-based visit. These questionnaires are used as a guide rather than a strict protocol, suggesting possible areas to explore and using previous information as a platform to formulate new questions. Teachers generally conclude that the questionnaires help guide the conversations.

The first interview is based on a family and labor history. The questions are open-ended, as we invite stories about families. We often begin by asking how and when the family happened to be in their present location. This generally leads to a conversation about family background, tracing the movements of the family from locale to locale. We also ask about other households in the region with which they might be in regular contact. This helps us conceptualize the social networks within which the family operates, including kin relations. For example, we have heard many stories of families who followed other family members to a particular region of the country. They were then able to tap into knowledge that others had accumulated about the area, especially about its job markets. The narratives that emerge from these household histories are often testimony to the resiliency and resources of people whose lives may be lived at the economic margins.

We find that labor history is a very rich source of the funds of knowledge that a household possesses. The jobs that people have had often provide them with a varied and extensive wealth of information. However, the types of jobs and labor histories that are common within a particular location are linked to the region's political economy. In the Southwest, for example, we find funds of knowledge consolidated in the ecologically pertinent arenas of mining and metallurgy, ranching and animal husbandry, ethnobotany, and transborder transactions. For those who do not have relocation as an option, the economic climate of the region drives households into a breadth of marketable skills in multiple areas, often as a strategy for economic survival. Children are exposed not only to the funds of knowledge that these labor shifts engender but also to strategic shifts in employment goals. These children become aware that survival is often a matter of making the most of scarce resources and adapting to a situation in innovative and resourceful ways.

The second interview focuses on regular household activities. Children are often involved in ongoing household practices, such as car repair, gardening, home improvement, child care, or working in a family business or hobby. One child, for example, participated in bicycle repairs and was able to acquire a high level of competency in this area. We asked about music practices, sports, shopping with coupons, and other aspects of a child's life, which helped us develop a composite and complex image of the range of possible funds of knowledge.

The third interview asks questions about parenthood, raising children, and the experience of being a parent. Parents are asked about their own school experiences, and how they contrasted with those of their children. Immigrant parents are asked about school experiences in their home country, and to contrast it with the educational system in the United States. There are also questions about language use for bilingual families, including when a particular language is spoken, read, or written, and under what circumstances.

It is important to remember that questions are not asked intrusively or in strict sequence, and any question that seems inappropriate is simply not asked. The teacher-researcher, then, develops a set of skills in asking questions within a conversation in a way that everyone involved finds comfortable. None of the questions are prescriptive, and there is wide latitude in how the interview is conducted. The main purpose of the interview is to establish a relationship, and the discovery of funds of knowledge is a benefit or consequence of that social relationship.

There is considerable latitude as well in how families are selected to participate in the study. Teachers can select any child. Some select a name at random, while others identify particular households because they had previous contact with them, or because they have an interest in getting to know the family better. It is important, of course, that the family be willing to participate, that they are informed that they can withdraw from the study at any time, and that they are aware that it involves a time commitment. We have experienced very few refusals and little reticence to participate from the families. If anything, the opposite is true. Children often request that their home be visited, and teachers are welcomed as honored guests and with the utmost respect and courtesy. Once teachers are in the home, conversations about family histories often elicit picture albums and elaborate family histories. Topics about work and hobbies often produce handcrafted items or tours of the house or apartment. It has also been our experience that teachers are often invited to participate in other family gatherings or church and community functions. When there is a truly engaged and interested listener, telling their story became an important and valued experience for the families. This willingness for families to tolerate and even enjoy our visits has been our experience.

In what follows, we present excerpts adapted from field note narratives developed in the study. The first excerpt is from Moll and Greenberg (1990) and Moll and González (1997); the second excerpt is from Browning-Aiken (in

press), and the third one is from unpublished project materials. All names are pseudonyms, and some details have been modified to preserve confidentiality. The intent is to illustrate the amount and types of information that can be gathered from the interviews and how one gets to the documentation of funds of knowledge.

The Zavala Household

The Zavalas are an urban working-class family. They have seven children. Mr. Zavala is best characterized as an entrepreneur. He works as a builder, part-time, and owns some apartments in working-class neighborhoods in Tucson and properties in Nogales, Arizona. Mrs. Zavala was born in Albuquerque, New Mexico, in 1950 but came to Tucson as a young child. She left school in the 11th grade. Mr. Zavala was born in Nogales, Sonora (México), in 1947, where he lived until he finished the 6th grade. His father too was from Nogales (Sonora). His father had little education and began to work at the age of nine to help support the family. His family then moved to Nogales, Arizona, where he went to school for another two years. When he was 17, Mr. Zavala left home and joined the army, spending two years stationed on military bases in California and Texas. After his discharge, he returned to Nogales (Arizona) and worked for a year installing television cable and heating and cooling ducts. In 1967, Mr. Zavala came to Tucson, first working as a house painter for six months and then in an airplane repair shop, where he worked for three years. In 1971, he opened a washing machine and refrigerator repair shop, a business he had for three years. Since 1974, Mr. Zavala has worked in construction part-time, builds and sells houses, and owns four apartments (two of which he built in the backyard of his house).

Everyone in the Zavala household, including the children, is involved in informal-sector economic activities to help the family. Juan, for example, who is in the sixth grade, has a bicycle shop in the back of the house. He buys used bicycle parts at a swap meet and assembles them to build bicycles, which he sells at the yard sales his family holds regularly. He is also building a go-cart and says he is going to charge kids 15 cents per ride. His sisters, Carmen and Conchita, sell their schoolmates candies that their mother buys in Nogales. The children used the money they earned to buy the family a VCR.

In Tucson, Mr. Zavala has a set of younger brothers who live in a house owned by his mother. Ana Zavala, an older sister, also rents a house (at a discount) from her grandmother on the same block. As is typical of such household clusterings of kin, Mr. Zavala's youngest brother and Ana are very close, and he does many favors for his niece, such as grocery shopping. As well, one of Mr. Zavala's sisters is married to a junior high school teacher. When his children have difficulties with their homework, they often seek assistance from their uncle. Although most of Mrs. Zavala's relatives live in California, she also has a brother in Phoenix. When he comes to visit, because he knows of Juan's interest in building bicycles, he buys parts for him.

The Hernández Household

The Hernández household consists of Miriam (the student), age 13; her mother, Maria, age 47; her brothers, Carlos, age 11, and Marco, Jr., age 14; and her father Marco, Sr., age 50. Originally from Cananea, Sonora, they moved a few years ago to Nogales (Sonora), where Miriam's father worked in a general store. After a year, the family moved to Tucson for better educational and employment opportunities for their children and to be closer to relatives living in Tucson and Phoenix.

Miriam's mother was a nurse in a doctor's office in Cananea. In Tucson, she worked as a volunteer home nurse and as a monitor in Miriam's school. Marco, Jr., worked in his father's store in Nogales and did yard work for relatives in Tucson. Although Miriam and Carlos did not have paying jobs, they were responsible for specific tasks in the home and at their uncle's house in Cananea. In Cananea, three of Miriam's uncles on both sides of the family worked or had worked in copper mines. Those who were no longer doing so received settlements after the mines closed. However, two other uncles had been working in Arizona copper mines between Tucson and Phoenix.

In Tucson, Miriam had a maternal cousin with four children close in age to her and her brothers. The two families participated in frequent visits and joint activities and provided mutual support in child raising and household concerns. Her mother also had a friend in Tucson whom she regarded as a sister, and a sister-in-law in Cananea whom she described as her best friend. Miriam's family returned every summer to visit her mining relatives in Mexico and had been on mine tours with them. In addition, conversations about family photographs and about travel back and forth across the border revealed a familiarity with past problems in the mining industry, such as wage disputes and hazardous working conditions. They were familiar with the history of Cananea as the cradle of the Mexican Revolution, so called because of the 1906 miners' strike against the American mine owner William Greene and against the economic policies of Porfirio Díaz.

The Gómez Household

There are six people living in the Gómez household: Mr. and Mrs. Gómez and their four children. Abel, at 19, the oldest, is attending a community college in town; Victor is in his second year of high school; Oscar is a sixth grader; and Lupita is a fifth grader. All the children were born in México but have attended school in the United States since their early elementary school years, except Abel, who entered in sixth grade.

Mr. Gómez was born in Hermosillo, Sonora (México). His brother lives in Hermosillo and is a teacher and vice-principal of a school. His sister lives in Guadalajara. His mother also lives in Hermosillo, and the whole Gómez family visits often, at least once a month. His father, who worked on the railroads, passed away at the age of 85. He was born in Jalisco but came to the United States during the Mexican revolution. He did not receive any formal schooling but did learn to read and write. His mother attended school until about fifth grade in México.

Mr. Gómez states that he has had to work like a "burro" since he came to the United States. In México he was a technical draftsman for the Banco de Crédito Rural (a bank that lends money to farmers) and shows with pride the drafting instruments he has retained. He says in that job he sat comfortably at a desk all day "como un maestro" ("like a teacher"). He was involved in drawing survey maps for well drillers, among other tasks. But after coming to the United States he was not able to get a job within that field and has been working as a roofer for the past eight years, for different companies. He feels working as a roofer has been so hard on his hands that he has no skills left in them for drafting. He did not work on the day of our visit, to be able to participate in the interview.

Mrs. Gómez, a homemaker, also born in México, has eleven brothers and sisters. Her parents recently moved to Tucson from México and live close to the Gómez household. All but two brothers, who live in a border town in México, live in Arizona. Other family members live in California and Texas. For Mrs. Gómez, Tucson is the family center, now that her parents are in town, and their presence has motivated other family members to come to visit frequently, especially for the holidays.

The Gómez children are the first generation to speak English. The two youngest children accompany their parents whenever they go shopping to translate for them. Mr. Gómez, however, seems to have developed a working English vocabulary and interjects such words as "boss" and "Mexican paper" into his Spanish conversation. In the home, the children speak only in Spanish with their parents, but Mr. Gómez states that they speak English among themselves.

Mr. Gómez considers that his two oldest children have a very good command of English, not only in speaking but also in reading and writing. The oldest son was in and out during the interview and spoke to us in English. Mr. Gómez is not as certain about his two youngest children's abilities in reading and writing English and states that the two oldest brothers help them when they need assistance with their English homework. Everyone in the family can also read and write in Spanish, a fact that is very important to Mr. Gómez. He feels it is a shame that there are many families of Mexican origin here that do not continue the use of Spanish or teach it to their children. He believes is very important for children to know their roots, including being able to communicate in Spanish.

He feels, however, that there is a difference between the Spanish spoken in México and the Spanish spoken by people born in the United States—or "pochos," as he says they are called. To him, Spanish speakers from the United States do not speak Spanish well, and he says on occasion he corrects the Spanish that Oscar (the sixth grader) is speaking. An example of incorrect Spanish that he has heard is the verb *paniquear,* from the word *panic* (*pánico,* in Spanish). He says this is not a real word, nor a verb that can be conjugated, and no one would know what it meant in México.

SPECIFYING FUNDS OF KNOWLEDGE

Even these cursory and superficial examples reveal substantial funds of knowledge that a teacher could document and use in instruction, as well as knowledge about the family's strategies to cope with economic circumstances. We can specify that these families (collectively) have knowledge about purchasing, constructing, renting, and maintaining apartments (business knowledge); installing cable TV and heating and cooling ducts; and repairing washing machines, refrigerators, and even airplanes, as well as professional knowledge about painting houses. There is also knowledge about building and repairing bicycles, and about sales (of candy purchased in México) and savings. In addition, there is knowledge about mining, drafting and surveys, and nursing.

The families' history also reveals the cross-border character (and knowledge) of the family, typical of many Mexican families in Tucson. Their social networks place them in contact with considerable knowledge about other matters, for example, what they know about formal schooling from a relative, who is a teacher, or about copper mining or history. We also learn about issues related to learning both English and Spanish, including instrumental and affective factors, and the relation of Spanish and specific varieties of Spanish to issues of cultural identity.

The case examples obviously do not exhaust the nature of household funds of knowledge, their development and formation, or the forms of exchange that these households are capable of producing. Our analysis also suggests that each exchange of information, or of other resources, includes a didactic component that is part of the activity of sharing. Sometimes this teaching is quite explicit, as when teaching someone how to build a room or a machine (such as a bicycle) or how to use a new gadget; at other times it is implicit and depends on the participation or observation of the learner, as when the children assist the father in building an addition to the house. What we are calling a didactic component to the exchange is part of any household's pedagogy. People must teach and learn new knowledge and skills to deal with a changing reality. In many instances, the children are involved in these activities and may be the recipients of the exchange, as observers or participants.

It should be obvious, then, that these households are not socially or intellectually barren. They contain knowledge; people use reading, writing, and mathematics; they mobilize social relationships; and they teach and they learn on the basis of their lived experiences, including their schooling. From the documentation and (theoretical) analysis of funds of knowledge, one learns not only about the extent of the knowledge found among these working-class households but also about the special importance of the social and cultural world, and of social relations, in the development of knowledge.

MULTICULTURAL CONNECTIONS

Although these examples are all taken from Mexican-origin families in Tucson, they display the *within-culture heterogeneity* that we have come to expect. This diversity is produced in a number of ways, among them the age of the family members; whether they are first- or second-generation (or more) in the United States; their history of schooling and work; the division of labor within the household; the nature of their social networks; whether these networks extend into México or not; their involvement with schools or other social institutions; and the languages and varieties of those languages they speak, read, or write. In addition to Mexican families, we have also conducted research (not reported here) in households with African American, Native American, and White families.

In this section, we establish the multicultural relevance of the funds-of-knowledge approach by borrowing selectively from the work of colleagues who have used the approach in other locations and for other purposes. (For additional and varied examples, see Andrade & González Le Denmat, 2001; Brenden, in press; González, Andrade, Civil, & Moll, 2001; González Angiulo, 1998; Gregory, 1997; McIntyre et al., 2001; Medd & Whitmore, 2000; Moje, 2000; Olmedo, 1997; Patterson & Baldwin, 2001; and Villenas & Moreno, 2001; see also Villegas & Lucas, 2002.) We begin with the work of Mercado (in press; Mercado & Moll, 1997, 2000; see also Mercado, 2001), conducted in collaboration with teachers in New York City. Working through her graduate courses, Mercado has engaged about 100 teachers in theoretical analysis, household visits, and documentation in both Long Island and East Harlem, the latter among the poorest neighborhoods in the city. The second example is from the work of McIntyre and colleagues (e.g., McIntyre, Kyle, Moore, Sweazy, & Greer, 2001; McIntyre & Stone, 1998; see also McIntyre, Rosebery, & González, 2001) in Kentucky, where they have done long-term household research with both Appalachian-descent and African American families. This work highlights, more than other studies, the contradictions of doing this type of research, where one engages the lives of different families, documenting both positive and negative details of daily life.

The third example is drawn from the work of Allen and colleagues in Georgia, featuring teachers (and student teachers) who work with varied student populations (Allen et al., 2002; Allen & Labbo, 2001). Their innovation, a novel approach to multicultural teacher education, involves combining a funds-of-knowledge approach with photographing and writing narratives about the scenes, events, or persons depicted photographically. (The three studies summarized in this section were conducted independently of our efforts. We greatly appreciate these colleagues' sharing their work with us, including some of their unpublished materials.)

New York City

We start with the study of funds of knowledge in New York City because it is a revealing comparison to the work conducted in Arizona. In addition to changes in regional setting and study population, there were differences in the backgrounds of the teachers who participated, and the social and economic diversity of the households studied. However, as Mercado (in press) has observed:

The power of this comparative perspective is that it shows that no matter how different our journeys were, we reached a common destination. We learned the value of all students' homes as rich contexts for learning with enormous pedagogical possibilities for teachers. (pp. 1–2)

In terms of diversity, Mercado cites Davis (2000) to point out that in New York City there are no less than 21 major Latino neighborhoods within four boroughs, including eleven predominantly Puerto Rican areas, two majority Dominican neighborhoods, and two mixed South American enclaves in Queens. (For readers unfamiliar with New York City, it has a total of five boroughs or divisions: Manhattan, Brooklyn, Bronx, Queens, and Staten Island. The largest and oldest Puerto Rican neighborhood is located in East Harlem and is usually known simply as

"El Barrio.") This distribution of the Latino population (without even mentioning the many other ethnic groups in the city) means that a teacher's experience of diversity depends upon the particular neighborhood within which a school is located. The study's participants (n = 59) were primarily bilingual teachers (many 30 to 40 years old) with classroom experience in low-performing schools where the student population was primarily Latino and African American.

The teachers who participated in the study were enrolled in a required graduate course that Mercado taught. In the course, dialogue among participants became central to knowledge construction, combined with lectures and assignments, as is often necessary with such course arrangements. Mercado (in press) explains the process as follows:

I had to be able to do a careful, on-the-spot reading of students' discourse when presenting progress reports and when planning, analyzing and comparing experiences in small and large groups. My challenge was to focus our discussions to advance understanding through a cross-case comparison (essential to highlight similarities and differences across households that mitigate against the formation of ethnic stereotypes) and to provide timely support within each session to build confidence, make the work manageable and to sustain momentum. (p. 8)

As the teachers were able to document during their household visits, the content of knowledge and the range of activities in Puerto Rican and other Latino households are both rich and variable, dispelling a number of stereotypes about these low-income households, notably that they lack resources for learning. The teachers were impressed that each household is distinct in composition, living arrangements, and beliefs and practices. In the process of documenting this diversity, the teachers "confronted the popular view guiding teachers' pedagogical practices: that all members of a group share a normative and integrated view of their own culture" (Mercado & Moll, 2000, p. 301).

The economic realities of the families were equally striking to the teachers, as they came face-to-face with the dire reality of what it means to have an income far below national and state medians, as is quite evident in the living conditions of many of the families. The teachers found this poverty most affecting when they first visited the students' homes; they were jolted by the realization of how little they really knew about their students' economic conditions. Consider these comments:

"I've often said I know my students' stories because I've been there. Well, I was wrong. . . . Times have changed and the conditions for many of these children are worse than expected."
"There exists a poverty I only thought existed in other places of the world, but not in America."

"Children . . . live in fear of what could happen to them and their families." (Mercado & Moll, 2000, p. 301)

The teachers also learned, however, a key point of the work: that within these conditions of poverty there can also be many riches—in emotional support, resilience, love, and funds of knowledge. As the teachers stated:

"I learned from the García family about love, despair, pain, hope, survival and happiness. Mrs. García is a fighter, a woman of tremendous courage."

"Learning is constantly taking place in Ita's home. She is a collector of antiques, photographs, tools, paintings, books, [and] magazines. . . . She is a historian and a storyteller."

"My greatest surprise in this research was not that the family had much to offer, it was that Jacklyn . . . had a virtual classroom in her home. . . . I feel that she adopted the classroom model for home management." (Mercado & Moll, 2000, p. 303)

The teachers gained an understanding not only of how much they share with the families but of the injustices that many of the families experience. The emotional impact of the visits was obvious, and it strengthened the teachers' identification with the students, as some stated:

"I have learned that I can't pass judgment; I don't know what's happening in the home."

"My mother's life and [my student's mother's] life are very similar."

"She was very similar to me."

"I see my own mother in a different light" (Mercado & Moll, 2000, p. 305).

Nevertheless, not all household assets were so easy to document, and some teachers could not initially detect funds of knowledge in certain households:

Going through the experience and listening in class . . . made me feel something was missing or I was doing something wrong. Everyone was finding and reporting rich experiences and funds of knowledge while I seemed not to be looking at what was probably there. *No podía ver lo que estaba ahí* (I could not see what was there). (Mercado & Moll, 2000, p. 303; emphasis in original)

Commenting on such differences, Mercado (in press) writes as follows:

Initially I thought it was because of the relative brevity of the home visits, but I have come to believe otherwise. With every cycle of activities we have found variability in the quantity and quality of social networks across households having limited economic resources. (p. 17)

That is, although some households had strong ties with other households and institutions, others appeared to have much weaker ties. Because these networks strategically connect a household to other households and institutions, they make vital intellectual, emotional, and economic resources accessible to a household with restricted income. Thus this variability in the development of social networks has consequences for the quantity and quality of funds of knowledge that are potentially accessible to a household.

Mercado (in press) traced this variation among households to "core" values and beliefs that marked or characterized the ethos of each particular household, which she labeled as a household's "ideology." The idea is that a household's ideology is captured by its core values and beliefs; just as ideologies guide and mediate human being's actions and practices, a household's ideology guides its activities and shapes its relationships. However, because they emerge from and are influenced and transformed by the lived experiences of each household, these ideologies are *fluid* as they reflect and are shaped by the particular social, economic, and historical conditions of living. Recognizing a household's ideology provides a theoretical extension of the approach that may enable teachers to understand household activities and thereby the nature of its social networks and funds of knowledge.

Kentucky

The work of McIntyre and colleagues involves a long-term collaboration with teachers, families, and schools in rural Kentucky (McIntyre & Stone, 1998). The project is multifaceted, studying curriculum and instruction in multiage primary classrooms as part of a broader reform initiative in the state (McIntyre, Kyle, Hovda, & Stone, 1999). Here we concentrate primarily on the study of families conducted by nine of the teachers in the study. In all, the teachers (and researchers) visited 45 families, with a core group of 30 families visited from 4 to 15 times. As has also been our experience, the families readily agreed to collaborate with the teachers, with only a few families reluctant to participate in the study. During these visits, the teacher-researchers collected demographic data as well as data on family histories, family routines and practices, views on education, and educational aspirations (McIntyre & Stone, 1998).

These researchers report that many teachers still hold denigrating stereotypes about Appalachian families and culture, even if they have never met the families. As they report it, the "folk wisdom" about the poor and working-class families in Kentucky is that they do not care about education, or that the parents do not care about the children, or even that they do not have a language (see also Purcell-Gates, 1995). These stereotypes are, of course, commonly held about other poor or working-class families in the rest of the country.

Their "family visits," as they called them, lead both researchers and teachers to appreciate the diversity of family life (McIntyre, Kyle, et al., 2001). They wrote as follows:

As we analyzed fieldnotes, and discussed what the data meant, our concepts of "culture" began to disintegrate. We discovered what seemed like an infinite number of home routines, literacy acts, and funds of knowledge, some of which remained stable and others which changed over the course of the three years we worked with the families. (p. 264–265)

The Appalachian families identified themselves mostly as "country" or "small town" people. All of the children spoke English, many in a variety of English or dialect associated with the Appalachian areas, one often stigmatized by other people. Religion played a major role in their lives, with numerous church-related activities occurring during the year, providing an important social network for many of the families. In general, the families were rooted to their communities, reluctant to live elsewhere, and appreciated living within extended family. These extended family connections afforded social, emotional, and financial support, and children's lives were embedded within these extended family environments. Several of the families desired to own farmland one day, although farming, a traditional source of work, has become a diminished option of employment in a changing regional economy. In addition, given financial problems related to the scarcity of employment, some adults have had to seek work outside the community in other trades. In any case, their work included tenant farming, assembly line work, clerk, cook, auto mechanic, construction, and retail worker, all in the working-class segment of the economy.

Much of the knowledge of the families was thus related to farming procedures, especially tobacco cultivation and dairy farming. There was also knowledge about crafts and cooking (major parts of cultural life in Appalachia), about religious beliefs and procedures, and about art. In addition, the visits to document these funds of knowledge helped improve relationships between teachers and parents, especially as teachers realized that the parents, as they expressed in various ways, valued education and school success. Like parents everywhere, these parents want their children to get better educated, make more money, respect themselves and others, be hard working and moral persons, and avoid mistakes that the parents have made. The knowledge gained about students from the visits helped furnish teachers with many instances, especially through the selection of literature, to connect curriculum with the students in a more personal way (McIntyre, Sweazy, & Greer, 2001).

Serious problems were also documented, many related to conditions of financial stress, including violence, alcohol-related problems, and even abuse. The families varied in terms of levels of education, but about half the parents had not completed high school. A combination of factors therefore left the poor and working-class children lacking certain "educational capital," as the authors put it, especially as related to knowledge about print (McIntyre et al., 1999). They write: "It seems to us (as outsiders to some extent) that their lives have both positive and negative consequences for school success, despite how teachers use the information to enhance the curriculum" (p. 56).

In engaging the families more intimately, McIntyre, Kyle, et al. write, one faces both positive and disagreeable situations (2001):

We have come away from some visits depressed and unable to help, even unsure how to help. To do this kind of work, we must be prepared to be a little depressed at times. Of course, just as often, we come away exhilarated at the love and humor we find in the homes. (p. 270)

As McIntyre and colleagues put it, in appreciating differences among families there are relatively simple differences—related, for example, to how often they read or watch television. However, there are also more striking differences, not only among the families but between the families and the researchers, such as the prevalence of racist beliefs or differing approaches to child discipline. How to understand and document these differences or the details of family life always involves a "moral" choice of how one chooses to represent families for others or for what purposes. "Our guiding principle," McIntyre, Kyle, et al. (2001) write, "has been to share only what may end up benefiting that child or family or others like them" (p. 270).

Georgia

Allen and colleagues (2002) report on a project called PhOLKs (which stands for photographs of local knowledge sources). In this study, teachers gave students cameras to photograph "things that were important to them in their homes or neighborhood" (p. 313). With the help of teachers, and the permission of families, the students generated the subjects of their photographs—family members, particular events, favorite activities. The students then wrote or dictated a story about each picture, and a family member also wrote a narrative on another picture that offered an additional, personal perspective on everyday life. The goal of the study became to "reenvision" the students in contexts other than the class-room, and in relation to other adults or children in their lives. In so doing, the centrality of social relationships in learning, and in developing classroom communities, became readily apparent. As the authors report:

We began this project with the express purpose of connecting home and school communities. We thought those connections would be curricular, that we would learn about children and family 'funds of knowledge' and that we would design units, learning experiences, and instructional strategies based on what was important to children, as Moll et al. had done. But as we pored over pictures, laughed and cried over narratives, read and reread field notes, family notebooks, and transcripts of our meetings, formal curriculum was not central—relationships were. (p. 314)

Sharing and discussing photographs, and the narratives about them, among teachers and with the students led to a number of insights about the children's social worlds—what they called "kid culture"—that most teachers can never access (see also Andrade, 1994). Teachers also learned about the children's relationships with various family members, their interests away from school, and ways of accessing resources and mediating problems. For example, Hattie, an African American teacher, learned about her Hispanic children's home lives and about their strengths:

[The teacher] felt at a disadvantage with her Hispanic students because of language and cultural differences with her own experiences as an African American. The photographs and narratives helped Hattie realize the similarities between African American and Hispanic children: they shared interests, family seemed to be their number one priority, and most lived with extended families. (Allen et al., 2002, p. 317–318)

This teacher also learned that parents expected her, as part of her teacher's role, to discipline their children if necessary. In general, then, these teachers discovered, as we have during our household visits, that parents are "eager to share their lives, hopes, concerns, and insights about children" (Allen et al., 2002, p. 321), and that they live their lives in the contexts created by multiple social relationships, and that forming such social relationships also builds a foundation for teachers to learn more about children and their families.

In a related study, Allen and Labbo (2001) describe a similar methodology (taking photographs and writing narratives) in helping 27 White, middle-class, under-graduate students in a teacher education program examine details of their lives. The goal was to produce reflections through writing "cultural memoirs" and study how such insights would shape the (preservice) teachers' interactions and reflections of their work with elementary students of diverse backgrounds. Interestingly, most of the teachers felt that culture was a concept applicable to other people's lives but not necessarily to their own; similarly,

most resisted examining their own privilege, as afforded by their race, schooling, and social class characteristics. Initially, the authors report, most of the writing was super-ficial, not delving critically into the details of what experiences have shaped their lives and identities. Pro-gressively, as they gained practice in making themselves objects of inquiry, the student teachers produced consid-erable insights, analyzing both positive and negative influ-ences in their development.

A related task was for these teachers to emulate the process with children in their classrooms during a four-week field experience, where they asked students to take photographs and write analogous cultural memoirs. On the basis of what they learned, these teachers were then asked to plan instruction or approach the parents of the students to discuss what they had learned. They also had to discuss through letter writing what they had learned from the combined project experiences:

The most critical aspect of the process occurred when we asked stu-dents to write a letter (to us, to their parents, or to the parents of future students) that made explicit connections between deep reflec-tions on their own cultures and what it meant to teach children from a variety of cultural heritages. (Allen & Labbo, 2001, p. 44)

These reflective letters proved candid and revealing, reaf-firming their commitment to teaching and permitting an "understanding that their students too, come from valued and diverse cultural backgrounds, and if they are to reach each student they must connect with them" (Allen & Labbo, 2001, p. 50). In at least one case, however, a student decided to pursue other life experiences before entering the teaching profession and withdrew from the program. The authors themselves were changed by the experience, gaining knowledge about these preservice teachers as people with life experiences and values that belie simple stereotypes, and admiring "their remarkable strength in interrogating some of their tacit cultural influ-ences" (Allen & Labbo, p. 50).

They closed their article, as we do this section, by quoting selectively from Susan, one of their preservice students, and her powerful reflections about her upbring-ing and changes in her thinking. The letter is a glimpse of the possibilities for critical analysis and for change that their methods facilitate:

. . . I don't think anyone told me to dislike black people, but I was raised that I was better.
Our maid is black. Our yardman is black. The trashmen on our street are black. The janitors and cooks at my school are black. . . . The man at the bank is white. My teachers are white. My doctor is white. . . . My parents friends are white. Are the black people bad people? No. Do I want their jobs? No. I was never told that blacks are inferior, but the ones that I came in contact with had jobs and lives that I did not want. . . . I did not imagine them when I thought about what I wanted to do when I grew up. (Allen & Labbo, 2001, p. 51)

After considerable elaboration, including describing her experiences in a high school where Whites were the minority, she writes about examining critically her attitudes and thinking. Let us quote again from her letter:

I convinced myself that there was a difference between black people and niggers, just like there is a difference between white people and white trash. . . . I cannot tell you when all this changed. . . . It may have been when I had my first placement in a school. It may have been when I was reading articles for classes. It may have been repeatedly listening to people blanketly refer to all black people as niggers. Regardless, something snapped. I could no longer take it. . . . I figured out how unfair it is to have a class of mixed ethnicities, mixed cultures, mixed socioeconomic classes and for me to think that I, and everyone like me, is better. What makes me better? Because I have had more opportunities, more privileges, I am better? Because my dad made more money, I am better? That makes no sense. What is better about me than these children whose parents work their tails off to give their children clothes and food? . . . Because we never really struggled, I am better? That makes no sense. *It makes no sense.* . . . I cannot continue to think that I am better if I want to be a successful teacher or citizen. (Allen & Labbo, 2001, p. 51; emphasis in original)

Pedagogical Implications

We have, so far, presented details of a funds-of-knowledge approach, with examples drawn from our field studies. We have also made a case for the multicultural relevance of the approach by summarizing the research of colleagues working in other locations with teachers and families of different backgrounds. In this section, we want to address pedagogical implications. We have explored such implications in a number of ways but have generally followed the lead of teachers who participated in the studies, learning from their efforts (González et al., in press; González et al., 1995).

In what follows, we discuss two general types of implication. The first one involves concrete changes in the way of teaching, with teachers making use of data on funds of knowledge as inspiration for transforming lessons within their particular circumstances. The second one, more subtle and indirect—but, we believe, more enduring—involves altering the perceptions of diversity held by teachers in terms of funds of knowledge. We claim that both are important in addressing multicultural issues in education.

The first implication derives from the attempts of teachers to apply what they have learned in classroom practice. These attempts, collectively, share three prominent features. One is that they challenge the usual encapsulation of schooling by transcending the classroom walls to develop lessons based on knowledge drawn from households or other locations. Usually, the goal is to enhance a particular curricular objective or activity, but these lessons may be long-term or open-ended inquiries, going beyond the original intent of the curriculum, and

taking into account and expanding the students' interests and experiences. In our view, no classroom innovation will last unless teachers are able to overcome the intellectual limits of the encapsulation of schooling for low-income children. A major limitation of most classroom innovations is that they do not require (or motivate) teachers or students to go beyond the classroom walls to make instruction work. Consequently, sooner or later the classroom comes under the control of a restrictive status quo. Capitalizing on cultural resources for teaching allows both teachers and students to continuously challenge the status quo, especially in terms of how the students are using literacy as a tool for inquiry and thinking, and to refurbish their learning with new topics, activities, and questions.

A second feature is that the external (to the classroom) funds of knowledge can be related to different types of literature that the children can read or write as part of the activity. As McIntyre and Stone (1998) have also emphasized, literature represents a primary source for further contextualizing instruction in relation to funds of knowledge. The teachers in their studies, they wrote, "found books they knew particular children would enjoy because of what they had learned about the children during family visits" (p. 214), such as using books about grandparents in recognition of the strong social relationships many of the children had established with their grandparents.

The third feature is the participation of parents and others from the local community as intellectual resources for lessons. In the example that follows, for instance, the teacher developed a series of theme-related units in which she invited about 20 people from the school's community to contribute in numerous ways to the pedagogical activities. To take another example, Hensley (in press) describes the extended participation and transformation of an African American father, whose artistic talents were discovered by the teacher during a household visit (see also McIntyre, Sweazy, & Greer, 2001).

A revealing case example that formed part of one of our initial collaborations comes from the work of a teacher, Hilda González Le Denmat (called "Ina" in the article; for details, see Moll & Greenberg, 1990). On the basis of study group discussions, she initiated classroom activities to explore the theme of construction of structures. This topic was chosen deliberately as a way to integrate knowledge prevalent within the broader community, especially in the experiences of some of the families of the children, and a way to integrate additional reading, writing, and mathematical activities as part of the same lessons. Central to this extended lesson was the students' doing research on the topic, building models of structures, gathering books and articles as supplementary information, and writing essays on their explorations (see also Ayers, Fonseca, Andrade, & Civil, 2001).

A key addition to these theme units, in ways analogous to the household dynamics studied, was the teacher's attempts to tap into the social networks of the students (and others) to identify parents and other community members who could contribute substantively to the lessons. The intent here was for parents and others to contribute intellectually to the activity, sharing their knowledge, expertise, and experiences with the students. With the initial success of the parent visits, forming social networks to help address academic goals became a regular feature of instruction in this classroom.

The second type of implication involves shaping perceptions of diversity by developing the teachers' possibilities for theorizing about social practices, be they in the classroom or the household. The teachers in funds-of-knowledge studies visit their students' households to learn from the families, and with a theoretical perspective that seeks to understand how people generate knowledge as they engage life. An important implication of this work is that of debunking ideas of a low-income household as lacking worthwhile knowledge and experiences, replacing it with a perspective that is able to identify, document, and access for teaching the knowledge and experiences of the children and their families. This view of the household as possessing ample resources for learning changes radically, we claim, how the students are perceived, talked about, and taught.

It is the documentation of the particulars of life through the social relations we establish with families that creates new possibilities for theorizing and for pedagogical actions. Our strategy therefore has been to get close to the phenomenon of household life by making repeated visits in our role as learners. These visits, however, must be supplemented by the theoretical work done in study-group settings expressly created for the purpose, and by developing case studies of specific households. Here is where the concept of funds of knowledge plays a major role as a "theoretical tool," in the Vygotskian sense, by helping mediate the teachers' comprehension of social life within the households they study. The concept is intended to make obvious the wealth of resources available within any single household and its social networks, resources that may not necessarily be obvious to teachers or even to the families themselves.

However, documenting funds of knowledge or making cultural resources obvious is also a theoretical activity. The empirical information that teachers collect from households is the starting point; expanding and sharing insights from these visits with other teachers is part of the theoretical work done at the study-group setting. In other words, through the visits, and through deliberately elaborating the concept of funds of knowledge, we appropriate theoretically the families' lived experiences. As such, as with any theoretical enterprise, our conclusions are always tentative, temporary, and subject to revision by further study or scrutiny (González et al., in press).

DISCUSSION

In this final section, we address how a funds-of-knowledge approach may help address other issues of diversity, including the changing ethnic, racial, and cultural diversity of schools. We have argued that such an approach helps a school, through the work of its teachers, by shaping perceptions and ways of working with diversity. In other words, the approach helps a school accommodate "organically" to the knowledge and practices of local neighborhood cultures (Corson, 1998). "This means," Corson writes, "that the schools, in their formal curriculum and in their informal message systems, recognize and respect any important aspects of the neighborhood cultures that seem educationally relevant" (pp. 111–112).

Any such alteration of the status quo, however, also involves alteration in the relations of power that constitute a school as a social setting (see in particular Sarason, 1991). After all, to conduct this work at any school involves negotiations not only with the teachers and parents—social relations we have emphasized in this chapter, for obvious reasons—but also with the principal, who has the power to either facilitate or deny access to the school grounds, or to help reorganize (or not) the instructional schedule to give teachers time and space to meet as a study group. It is also necessary to negotiate access with the school district and the administrator(s) in charge of the region in which the school is located. In some regions, it has also entailed negotiating with the teachers' union.

Such negotiations are now more difficult than ever, given that teachers have become virtually powerless in making pedagogical decisions of importance in addressing diversity. Consider that the three educational policies discussed at the beginning of this chapter—high-stakes testing, mandated reading curricula, and English-only restrictions—are impositions in which teachers (and much less parents) have no participation or voice. These policies are also impositions that exacerbate the encapsulation of schooling and the enclosure of teachers and students, an enclosure that a funds-of-knowledge approach tries to remedy.

Nevertheless, it is possible to create space for the social (and cultural) practices that characterize such an approach. There is an advantage to preserving an after-school location for study-group settings, rather than subjecting it entirely to school norms. Being at the margin of school routine allows alternative discourse, knowledge, and representation about neighborhoods, households, and schools to flourish, and it permits production of alternative pedagogical actions, as we have illustrated in this chapter.

We suggest, then, that the same study-group arrangement, and collaborative thinking among teachers, researchers, and others, can be used strategically to serve multiple purposes (González et al., in press). For example, given the importance of social class to the schooling of children and the work of teachers, one could treat social class as a primary theoretical or conceptual tool, exactly the way we have treated the concept of funds of knowledge. After all, we did not just casually introduce the teachers to this concept (funds of knowledge) and then walk into homes to discover what we could find. Instead, we prepared diligently to conduct the work by doing the required theoretical and methodological readings to establish the ethnographic nature of the concept. As part of this preparation, we highlighted the relation of funds of knowledge to the history of labor of the families and to the extant household economy, with the understanding that both were related primarily to the working-class segment of the labor market.

Ideally, we could have also developed a more sophisticated understanding of social class as it conditions household and classroom dynamics, production of knowledge, and the relationships between these settings. Therefore, just as the teachers developed (appropriated) a theoretical language about funds of knowledge in the process of redefining their understandings of households and communities, and in taking action to make those funds of knowledge pedagogically viable, they (and we) could have also developed a language to talk about class relations as the major source of inequality in education.

Similarly, several topics or themes are also essential to understanding the changing diversity of schools that could be addressed within such study-group spaces. One such issue is immigration. Few if any preservice or inservice courses for teachers address immigration issues and dynamics. Teachers are thus usually left to deal with media-driven stereotypes about immigration and its influence on education, views that ignore the great diversity of immigrant social and schooling experiences (see, e.g., Portes & Rumbaut, 2001; Suárez-Orozco & Suárez-Orozco, 2001). However, immigration does more than simply alter the ethnic character of a school; it also changes the social context of a neighborhood. In particular, it produces new conditions for interethnic relations, as is the case with Latino and African American students, who are the majority in most urban school districts in the country. Recent studies reveal negative interethnic perceptions and potential serious conflict among groups (e.g., Johnson, Farrell, & Guinn, 1999). Nevertheless, Latino and African American relations may vary considerably depending on the urban area and specific social issues (Mollenkopf, 1999; Rodríguez, 1999). Issues of immigration therefore are already of great significance if one is to understand the changing character of diversity in education and the funds of knowledge needed for successful adaptation to society and school. School personnel should address immigration dynamics with the seriousness that they deserve, especially because these dynamics shape the character of diversity.

The role of gender in a funds-of-knowledge analysis is another important issue. It is evident to us that women play the central role in the formation of the critical social ties and networks of the household. It has also been evident that if we were to establish enduring or reciprocal relations between households and classrooms, the role of women, as the key participants in both settings, is critical. Although we often took note of the nature of a household's division of labor, we did not develop an analysis of gender as central to a funds-of-knowledge approach. Such an analysis is not simply a matter of highlighting the role of women in household dynamics or in school life. It is a matter of developing a theoretical analysis of the role of gender or of gender relations in constituting household and classroom settings. Here the gender scholarship in understanding immigration dynamics is again important (Hondagneu-Sotelo, 2001). For example, within certain contexts labor markets may tend to favor women over men, helping women exceed the earnings and job stability of men (Hondagneu-Sotelo, 1994). It is feasible that diverse and changing employment locations and remuneration may then shape not only gender relations within the household but also social relations outside the household, with important consequences for the formation of funds of knowledge.

The point is that an emphasis on gender relations may yield a more diverse and nuanced understanding of funds-of-knowledge formation and deployment, just as it is providing more sophisticated understanding of immigrant dynamics and of the potential for home-school relations within changing contexts of work. It is also likely to be a topic of considerable interest to teachers, most of whom are women, and for the possibilities of their sustained activism in education.

It has become clear that the simple presence of student diversity in schools is insufficient to provoke change in education. If anything, the presence of diversity has served to reaffirm entrenched views of schooling that tend to preserve the status quo. We have described an approach that presents both theory and methods for teachers to conceptualize diversity as an asset by addressing its substance, the varied ways people engage life, and the funds of knowledge these engagements produce. We have also indicated the importance of restructuring schools so that teachers, within their specific social circumstances, can create settings to think, reflect upon important issues influencing schools, and connect with others to garner resources for positive changes in practice.

References

Allen, J., Fabregas, V., Hankins, K., Hull, G., Labbo, L., Lawson, H., et al. (2002). PhOLKS Lore: Learning from photographs, families and children. *Language Arts, 79*(4), 312–322.

Allen, J., & Labbo, L. (2001). Giving it a second thought: Making culturally engaged teaching culturally engaging. *Language Arts, 79*(1), 40–52.

Allington, R., & Haley, W. J. (1999). The politics of literacy teaching. *Educational Researcher, 28*(8), 4–12.

Andrade, R. (1994). *Children's constructive social worlds: Existential lives in the balance.* Unpublished doctoral dissertation, University of Arizona, Tucson.

Andrade, R., & González Le Denmat, H. (2001). The formation of a code of ethics for Latina/Chicana scholars. The experience of melding personal experiences into professional ethics. *Frontiers: A Journal of Women's Studies, 20*(1), 151–160.

Ayers, M., Fonseca, J. D., Andrade, R., & Civil, M. (2001). Creating learning communities: The "build your dream house" unit. In E. McIntyre, A. Rosebery, & N. González (Eds.), *Classroom diversity: Connecting curriculum to students' lives* (pp. 92–99). Portsmouth, NH: Heinemann.

Brenden, M. (in press). Funds of knowledge and team ethnography. In N. González, L. C. Moll, & C. Amanti (Eds.), *Theorizing practices: Funds of knowledge in households and classrooms.* Mahwah, NJ: Erlbaum.

Browning-Aiken, A. (in press). Border crossings: Funds of knowledge within a Mexican American family. In N. González, L. C. Moll, & C. Amanti (Eds.), *Theorizing practices: Funds of knowledge in households and classrooms.* Mahwah, NJ: Erlbaum.

Corson, D. (1998). *Changing education for diversity.* Buckingham, England: Open University Press.

Cummins, J. (1996). *Negotiating identities: Education for empowerment in a diverse society.* Los Angeles: California Association for Bilingual Education.

Davis, M. (2000). *Magical urbanism.* New York: Verso.

Ferreiro, E. (1994, July). *Diversidad y proceso de alfabetización: De la celebración a la toma de conciencia* [Diversity and the process of alphabetization: From celebration to the gaining of consciousness.] Opening plenary session presented at the 15th World Congress of the International Reading Association, Buenos Aires, Argentina.

Gándara, P. (2000). *Final report of the evaluation of High School Puente: 1994–1998* (Rev. ed.). Report prepared for the Carnegie Corporation of New York.

Gándara, P. (2002). Learning English in California: Guideposts for the nation. In M. Suárez-Orozco & M. Páez (Eds.), *Latinos: Remaking America* (pp. 339–358). Berkeley: University of California Press.

García, E. (2000). Implementation of California's Proposition 227: 1998–2000. (Editor's introduction.) *Bilingual Research Journal, 24*(1 & 2), 1–3.

González, N. (2001). *I am my language: Discourses of women and children in the borderlands.* Tucson: University of Arizona Press.

González, N., Andrade, R., Civil, M., & Moll, L. C. (2001). Bridging funds of distributed knowledge: Creating zones of practice in mathematics. *Journal of Education for Students Placed at Risk, 6*(1), 115–132.

González, N., Moll, L. C., & Amanti, C. (Eds.). (in press). *Theorizing practices: Funds of knowledge in households and classrooms.* Mahwah, NJ: Erlbaum.

González, N., Moll, L. C., Floyd-Tenery, M., Rivera, A., Rendón, P., & Gonzales, R. (1995). Funds of knowledge for teaching in Latino households. *Urban Education, 29*(4), 443–470.

González Angiulo, H. (1998). *Las Señoras: Moving from funds of knowledge to self-discovery.* Unpublished doctoral dissertation, University of Arizona, Tucson.

Greenberg, J. B. (1989, April). *Funds of knowledge: Historical constitution, social distribution, and transmission.* Paper presented at the annual meeting of the Society for Applied Anthropology, Santa Fe, NM.

Gregory, E. (1997). *One child, many worlds: Early learning in multicultural communities.* New York: Teachers College Press.

Heath, S. B. (1983). *Ways with words: Language, life, and work in communities and classrooms.* New York: Cambridge University Press.

Hensley, M. (in press). From untapped potential to creative realization: Empowering parents of multi-cultural backgrounds. In N. González, L. C. Moll, & C. Amanti (Eds.), *Theorizing practices: Funds of knowledge in households and classrooms.* Mahwah, NJ: Erlbaum.

Heubert, J. P., & Hauser, R. M. (Eds.). *High stakes: Testing for tracking, promotion, and graduation.* Washington, DC: National Academy Press.

Hondagneu-Sotelo, P. (1994). *Gendered transitions: Mexican experiences of immigration.* Berkeley: University of California Press.

Hondagneu-Sotelo, P. (2001). Immigrant women and paid domestic work: Research, theory, and activism. In J. Blau (Ed.), *The Blackwell companion to sociology* (pp. 423–436). Oxford: Blackwell.

Hubbard, L., & Mehan, H. (1999). Race and reform: Educational "niche picking" in a hostile environment. *Journal of Negro Education, 68*(2), 213–226.

Ingold, T. (1994). Introduction to culture. In T. Ingold (Ed.), *Companion encyclopedia of anthropology: Humanity, culture and social life* (pp. 329–349). London: Routledge.

Johnson, J. H., Jr., Farrell, W. C., Jr., & Guinn, C. (1999). Immigration reform and the browning of America: Tensions, conflict, and community instability in metropolitan Los Angeles. In C. Hirschman, P. Kasinitz, & J. DeWind (Eds.), *The handbook of international migration: The American experience* (pp. 390–411). New York: Russell Sage Foundation.

López, G. (2001). The value of hard work: Lessons on parent involvement from an (im)migrant household. *Harvard Educational Review, 71*(3), 416–437.

McIntyre, E., Kyle, D., Hovda, R., & Stone, N. (1999). Nongraded primary programs: Reform for Kentucky's children. *Language Arts, 78*(3), 264–272.

McIntyre, E., Kyle, D., Moore, G., Sweazy, R. A., & Greer, S. (2001). Linking home and school through family visits. *Language Arts, 78*(3), 264–272.

McIntyre, E., Rosebery, A., & González, N. (Eds.). (2001). *Classroom diversity: Connecting curriculum to students' lives.* Portsmouth, NH: Heinemann.

McIntyre, E., & Stone, N. (1998). Culturally contextualized instruction in Appalachian-descent and African-American classrooms. *National Reading Conference Yearbook, 47*, 209–220.

McIntyre, E., Sweazy, R. A., & Greer, S. (2001). Agricultural field day: Linking rural cultures to school lessons. In E. McIntyre, A. Rosebery, & N. González (Eds.), *Classroom diversity: Connecting curriculum to students' lives* (pp. 76–84). Portsmouth, NH: Heinemann.

Medd, S. K., & Whitmore, K. (2000). What's in *your* backpack? Exchanging funds of language knowledge in an ESL classroom. In P. Smith (Ed.), *Talking classrooms: Shaping children's learning through oral language instruction* (pp. 42–56). Newark, DE: International Reading Association.

Mehan, H., Villanueva, I., Hubbard, L., & Lintz, A. (1996). *Constructing school success.* Cambridge, UK: Cambridge University Press.

Mercado, C. (2001). The learner: "Race," "ethnicity," and linguistic difference. In V. Richardson (Ed.), *Handbook of research on teaching* (4th ed., pp. 668–694). Washington, DC: American Educational Research Association.

Mercado, C. (in press). Reflections of the study of households in New York City and Long Island: A different route, a common destination. In N. González, L. C. Moll, & C. Amanti (Eds.), *Theorizing practices: Funds of knowledge in households and classrooms.* Mahwah, NJ: Erlbaum.

Mercado, C., & Moll, L. C. (1997). The study of funds of knowledge: Collaborative research in Latino homes. *Centro, 9*(9), 26–42.

Mercado, C., & Moll, L. C. (2000). Student agency through collaborative research in Puerto Rican communities. In S. Nieto (Ed.), *Puerto Rican students in US schools* (pp. 297–329). Mahwah, NJ: Erlbaum.

Moje, E. (2000). Circles of kinship, friendship, position, and power: Examining the community in community-based literacy research. *Journal of Literacy Research, 32*(1), 77–112.

Moll, L. C. (1992). Literacy research in community and classrooms: A sociocultural approach. In R. Beach, J. Green, M. Kamil, & T. Shannahan (Eds.), *Multidisciplinary perspectives in literacy research* (pp. 211–244). Urbana, IL: National Conference on Research in English.

Moll, L. C. (1997). The creation of mediating settings. *Mind, Culture, and Activity, 4*(3), 192–199.

Moll, L. C., Amanti, C., Neff, D., & González, N. (1992). Funds of knowledge for teaching: A qualitative approach to connect households and classrooms. *Theory into Practice, 31*(2), 132–141.

Moll, L. C., & González, N. (1997). Teachers as social scientists: Learning about culture from household research. In P. M. Hall (Ed.), *Race, ethnicity and multiculturalism* (pp. 89–114). New York: Garland.

Moll, L. C., & Greenberg, J. (1990). Creating zones of possibilities: Combining social contexts for instruction. In L. C. Moll (Ed.), *Vygotsky and education* (pp. 319–348). Cambridge: Cambridge University Press.

Mollenkopf, J. H. (1999). Urban political conflicts and alliances: New York and Los Angeles compared. In C. Hirschman, P. Kasinitz, & J. DeWind (Eds.), *The handbook of international migration: The American experience* (pp. 412–422). New York: Russell Sage Foundation.

Nieto, S. (1997). Diversity: What do teachers need to know? In J. Paul, M. Churton, H. Rosselli-Kostor, W. Morse, K. Marfu, C. Lavely, et al. (Eds.), *Foundations of special education* (pp. 187–201). Pacific Grove, CA: Brooks/Cole.

Nieto, S. (2000). *Affirming diversity: The sociopolitical context of multicultural education* (3rd ed.). New York: Longman.

Olmedo, I. (1997). Voices of our past: Using oral history to explore funds of knowledge within a Puerto Rican family. *Anthropology and Education Quarterly, 28*(4), 550–573.

Orfield, G. (2000). Policy and equity: Lessons of a third of a century of educational reforms in the United States. In F. Reimers (Ed.), *Unequal schools, unequal chances: The challenges to equal opportunity in the Americas* (pp. 400–426). Cambridge, MA: Harvard University Press and David Rockefeller Center for Latin American Studies.

Patterson, L., & Baldwin, S. (2001). A different spin on parent involvement: Exploring funds of knowledge within a systems perspective. In W. Goodman (Ed.), *Living and teaching in an unjust world* (pp. 113–126). Portsmouth, NH: Heinemann.

Phillips, D., & Crowell, N. (1994). *Cultural diversity and early education.* (Workshop report.) Washington, DC: National Academy Press.

Popham, W. J. (2000, November). *Educational mismeasurement: How high stakes testing can harm our children (and what we might do about it).* Paper presented at the conference of the National Staff Association for Legislative and Political Specialists in Education, National Education Association, Sanibel Island, FL.

Portes, P., & Rumbaut, R. (2001). *Legacies.* Berkeley: University of California Press.

Purcell-Gates, V. (1995). *Other people's words: The cycle of low literacy.* Cambridge, MA: Harvard University Press.

Rivera, M., & Pedraza, P. (2000). The spirit of a Latino/a quest: Transforming education for community self-determination and social change. In S. Nieto (Ed.), *Puerto Rican students in US schools* (pp. 223–243). New York: Erlbaum.

Rodríguez, N. (1999). U.S. immigration and changing relations between African Americans and Latinos. In C. Hirschman, P. Kasinitz, & J. DeWind (Eds.), *The handbook of international migration: The American experience* (pp. 423–432). New York: Russell Sage Foundation.

Sarason, S. (1991). *The predictable failure of educational reform.* San Francisco: Jossey-Bass.

Shepard, L. (2002, January). *The contest between large-scale accountability testing and assessment in the service of learning: 1970–2001.* Paper presented at the Spencer Foundation's 30th Anniversary Conference, Chicago.

Sleeter, C. (1999). Foreword. In A. Valenzuela, *Subtractive schooling* (pp. xv–xviii). Albany: State University of New York Press.

Smith, F. (1999). Why systematic phonics and phonemic awareness instruction constitute an educational hazard. *Language Arts, 77*(2), 150–155.

Spring, J. (1997). *Deculturalization and the struggle for equality* (2nd ed.). New York: McGraw-Hill.

Suárez-Orozco, C., & Suárez-Orozco, M. (2001). *Children of immigration.* Cambridge, MA: Harvard University Press.

Taylor, D. (1998). *Beginning to read and the spin doctors of science.* Urbana, IL: National Council of Teachers of English.

Vélez-Ibáñez, C. G. (1988). Networks of exchange among Mexicans in the U.S. and Mexico: Local level mediating responses to national and international transformations. *Urban Anthropology, 17*(l), 27–51.

Vélez-Ibáñez, C. (1996). *Border visions: Mexican cultures of the southwest United States.* Tucson: University of Arizona Press.

Villegas, A., & Lucas, T. (2002). Educating culturally responsive teachers: A coherent approach. Albany: State University of New York Press.

Villenas, S., & Moreno, M. (2001). To *valerse por si misma* between race, capitalism, and patriarchy: Latina mother-daughter pedagogies in North Carolina. *International Journal of Qualitative Studies in Education, 14*(5), 671–687.

Wolf, E. (1966). *Peasants.* Englewood Cliffs, NJ: Prentice-Hall.

34

CULTURALLY DIVERSE STUDENTS IN SPECIAL EDUCATION

Legacies and Prospects

Alfredo J. Artiles
Vanderbilt University

Stanley C. Trent
University of Virginia

John D. Palmer
Colgate University

As the United States ventures into the 21st century, there is one factor that appears to remain constant nationwide: the shift toward a more culturally and linguistically diverse population. As the White population decreased from 80% in 1990 to 75%, all other races increased their overall percentages (U.S. Census Bureau, 2000b). In the public schools, the minority student population grew from 22% to more than 37%, with the Hispanic population growing substantially from 5.8% to 15.1% during the same period (U.S. Department of Commerce, 1972–1998). Further, the foreign-born population grew significantly from 1970 to 2000. From 1970 to 1979, 4.6 million immigrants arrived in the United States, in comparison to the 11.2 million who arrived in the years from 1990 to 2000 (U.S. Census Bureau, 2000a). Consequently, one of the fastest growing sectors of the U.S. student population is made up of English Language Learners (ELLs). According to Smith (2000), ELL students made up more than 10% of the overall student population in 2000, and 80% of this group was Spanish-speaking.

Unfortunately, these demographic changes, especially more language diversity, have been regarded as a problem and this narrow view has contributed to the construction of inequalities in our educational system. For example, many students, because of race, language, or lower socioeconomic status, continue to fail in school at a rate that is significantly higher than for White students. Moreover, many of these students are referred, placed, and served in special education programs at a disproportionately higher level than White students. In identifying these circumstances, we do not purport that culturally and linguistically diverse students should never be placed in special education. Nor do we contend that school districts and schools are solely responsible for the dismal educational outcomes for a significant number of culturally and linguistically diverse students. Clearly, poverty can have nefarious effects on students' physical and intellectual development. However, discriminatory practices within the larger society and schools have influenced the perpetuation of poverty and affected the quality of instruction in schools many culturally and linguistically diverse students attend. Hence, we argue for a more comprehensive analysis of problems and solutions, one that does not focus preeminently on the deficits that reside

We are indebted to Beth Harry, Russell Gersten, and the editors of the *Handbook* for their feedback on earlier versions of this manuscript. Writing of this chapter was supported by the COMRISE Project at the University of Virginia under grant no. H326M990001 and the National Center for Culturally Responsive Educational Systems (NCCREST) under grant no. H326E020003, awarded by the U.S. Department of Education, Office of Special Education Programs.

within children but that instead views the child within the context of broader cultural historical communities (Trent, Artiles, Fitchett-Bazemore, McDaniel, & Coleman-Sorrell, 2002).

In light of these current circumstances and the focus of this *Handbook*, the purpose of this chapter is to examine broadly the role special education has played in educators' attempts to meet the needs of diverse or minority students. The term *minority* is generally used to describe group representation in a "numerical" sense. However, some U.S. racial or linguistic groups have become the majority in certain regions, states, and cities. The term *minority* is also sometimes used to signal the oppressed status of groups even if they represent a numerical majority. An extreme example is the black minority during the apartheid in South Africa. We used the term in this chapter in the latter sense, to signal their oppressed status.

First we examine special education historically, with emphasis on how its genesis and development in the U.S. may have set the stage for sustaining the problems just identified. Second, we emphasize contemporary salient trends (that is, after 1990) in assessing and instructing culturally diverse students. Third, we identify contemporary challenges and future directions for theory, research, and practice. We focus on high-incidence disabilities (mild mental retardation, emotional and/or behavioral disorders, learning disabilities) because this is the largest group of students in the special education field and it is where minority students are more visible (see Table 34.1 for definitions of these disabilities). Also, we allude to family issues whenever relevant.

HISTORICAL SKETCH OF SPECIAL EDUCATION AND DIVERSE STUDENTS

Historically, special education laws were created through sustained advocacy, litigation, and legislation on the part of certain constituents and their advocates. Moreover, the gains made by the efforts of one group have often spawned social action by another group. For example, many scholars and policy analysts have concluded that African American parents served as a major impetus for special education advocacy, litigation, and legislation (Hunt & Marshall, 2002). During the Civil Rights movement of the 1950s and 1960s, these parents fought for equal educational opportunities for their children. Public demonstrations, marches, and confrontations with government officials and educators eventually resulted in the 1954 *Brown* v. *Board of Education* Supreme Court decision. This ruling led to legislation that mandated an end to school segregation on the basis of race. According to Kirk, Gallagher, and Anastasiow (2000), after observing the

evolution of the Civil Rights movement, "[s]upporters of people with disabilities were working to translate abstract legal rights into tangible social action through the judicial system" (p. 75). For example, in *Pennsylvania Association for Retarded Citizens (PARC)* v. *Commonwealth of Pennsylvania* (1972), parents fought for the rights of their children with mental retardation to receive a free appropriate public education, and the courts ruled in favor of the parents. These and other court cases led to the passage of Public Law 94–142, the Education for All Handicapped Children Act (1975, now referred to as the Individuals with Disabilities Education Act or IDEA). This law ensures the rights of students with disabilities and their families and gives this population access to special education and related services that address their unique needs. The law also assists state and local education agencies (SEAs and LEAs respectively) to provide for the education of these students and oversee the effectiveness of efforts to serve this population.

Also included in IDEA were several assurances designed to protect the rights of students with disabilities. Specifically, SEAs and LEAs were mandated to screen and identify all students with disabilities (zero reject) and provide them with a free and appropriate education. In addition, they were charged to offer nondiscriminatory evaluations appropriate to students' cultural and linguistic backgrounds; develop an individualized education program (IEP) for each student based on unique needs; and, to the fullest extent possible, provide services in the least restrictive environment (LRE). In addition, the law established guidelines to protect parental rights and the rights of SEAs and LEAs. For example, due process procedures were created to settle disputes between parents and school divisions. Furthermore, parental participation in all aspects of the assessment, IEP, and placement processes were included and considered essential to the success of the law (Hallahan & Kauffman, 2000; see Table 34.2 for a list of acronyms used in this chapter).

IDEA has been amended three times. It was first amended in 1986 (PL 99–547) and renamed the Education of the Handicapped Act Amendments. These amendments extended the age limits for service delivery for all eligible students between the ages three and five. SEAs also received federal funding to develop early intervention programs for children from birth through three who were at risk for developing disabilities (Hunt & Marshall, 2002). In 1990, the law was amended again and renamed the Individuals with Disabilities Education Act (IDEA). The terminology was changed from "handicapped children" to "individuals with disabilities," which placed more emphasis on person-first rather than disability-first language. In addition, these amendments addressed more substantively the needs of individuals with disabilities

Table 34.1. Definitions of Disability Categories Covered in This Chapter.

Disability Category	Acronym	Definition
Mental retardation	MR	According to the American Association on Mental Retardation (AAMR, 1992, cited in Smith, 2000): Mental retardation refers to substantial limitations in present functioning. It is characterized by significantly subaverage intellectual functioning, existing concurrently with related limitations in two or more of the following applicable adaptive skill areas: communication, self-care, home living, social skills, community use, self-direction, health and safety, functional academics, leisure, and work. Mental retardation manifests itself before age 18 (p. 230).
Mild mental retardation	MMR	The AAMR divides mental retardation into four levels: mild, moderate, severe, and profound. An MMR student is less severe and is typically identified as a person whose IQ is approximately 55–70 (Smith, 2000).
Emotional/behavior disorders	E/BD	According to the federal government, E/BD is: [A] condition exhibiting one or more of the following characteristics over a long period of time and to a marked degree, which adversely affects educational performance: • An inability to learn which cannot be explained by intellectual, sensory, or health factors. • An inability to build or maintain satisfactory interpersonal relationships with peers and teachers. • Inappropriate types of behavior or feelings under normal circumstances. • A general pervasive mood of unhappiness or depression. • A tendency to develop physical symptoms or fears associated with personal or school problems. The term also includes children who are schizophrenic. The term does not include children who are socially maladjusted, unless it is determined that they are emotionally disturbed (cited in Smith, 2000, p. 324).
Learning disabilities	LD	The federal government defines a specific learning disability as: A disorder in one or more of the basic psychological processes involved in understanding or in using language, spoken or written, that may manifest itself in an imperfect ability to listen, think, speak, read, write, spell, or to do mathematical calculations, including conditions [such] as perceptual disabilities, brain injury, minimal brain dysfunction, dyslexia, and developmental aphasia. The term does not include learning problems that are primarily the result of visual, hearing, motor disabilities, mental retardation, emotional disturbance, or environmental, cultural, or economic disadvantages (cited in Smith, 2000, p. 128). An LD student can be described as one who unexpectedly underachieves and does not learn in the same way or at the same rate as a nondisabled student (Smith, 2000).
Language learning disabilities	LLD	A student identified as LLD has met school district criteria for both a learning disability and a language disorder. In identifying the student's learning disability, factors such as second language acquisition should be taken into consideration. In identifying the student's language disorder, the criteria should assess the student's oral language development in her or his more proficient language (Fletcher, Bos, & Johnson, 1999).

beyond childhood. For example, one amendment required LEAs to develop individualized transition plans (ITP) designed to help people with disabilities make smoother transitions from high school to work.

The most recent amendments to IDEA were made in 1997. These amendments placed more attention on student outcomes, performance on statewide testing, effective instructional practices, and discipline. In addition, significant emphasis was placed on the needs of culturally and linguistically diverse students. For instance, authors of the amendments highlighted the increased ethnic and racial diversity in the United States and the public schools. They also noted that, unfortunately, this population increase has been accompanied by unfavorable

Table 34.2. Acronyms Used in the Chapter.

Acronym	Definition and Description
EHCA	*Education for All Handicapped Children Act.* Passed in 1975 and renamed in 1986 the Education of the Handicapped Act Amendments. In 1990 renamed Individuals with Disabilities Education Act.
IDEA	*Individuals with Disabilities Education Act.* In 1990, P.L. 94–142, the Education for All Handicapped Children Act (EHCA) changed its name to IDEA. Amendments added in 1997 called for a free and appropriate public education (FAPE; see below) to ensure the rights of children with disabilities, to assist states and localities (SEAs and LEAs; see below) to "provide for the education of all children with disabilities, and to assess and assure the effectiveness of efforts to educate children with disabilities" (as cited in Yell, 1998, p. 72).
FAPE	*Free and Appropriate Public Education.* A provision established in IDEA "that ensures that children with disabilities receive necessary education and services without cost to the child and family" (Smith, 2000, p. 54).
LRE	*Least Restrictive Environment.* A principle outlined in IDEA that requires that a student with disabilities "be integrated with nondisabled peers as much as possible and included in the mainstream of society" (Smith, 2000, p. 55).
LEA	*Local Education Agency.* Also regarded as the local school district, the LEA complies with the federal and state requirements regarding the provisions set forth by IDEA and is monitored by the State Education Agency (SEA; see below). The LEA is authorized by the board of education, the superintendent, assistant superintendent, principal, and assistant principal (Podemski, Marsh, Smith, & Price, 1995).
SEA	*State Education Agency.* A monitoring agency that ensures the provisions of IDEA "are implemented appropriately" (Podemski et al., 1995, p. 20).
IEP	*Individualized Education Plan.* "A requirement of IDEA that guarantees a specifically tailored program to meet the individual needs of each student with disabilities. . . . The IEP is a management tool designed to ensure that school children with special needs receive the special education and related services appropriate to their needs" (Smith, 2000, p. 55, 65).
ITP	*Individualized Transition Plan.* An ITP is provided to a child with disabilities as "a statement of the transitional services required for the coordination and delivery of services as the student moves to adulthood" (Smith, 2000, p. 549).
ESL	*English as a Second Language.* "Students receive specified periods of instruction aimed at the development of English-language skills, with primary focus on grammar, vocabulary, and communication, rather than academic content areas" (August & Hakuta, 1997, p. 19).
ELL	*English Language Learner.* "Students who come from language backgrounds other than English and whose English proficiency is not yet developed to the point where they can profit fully from English-only instruction" (August & Hakuta, 1997, p. 15).
AAVE	*African American Vernacular English.* Ebonics, Black English, and/or African American language "is rooted in the Black American Oral Tradition and represents a synthesis of African (primarily West African) and European (primarily English) linguistic-cultural traditions" (Smitherman, 1998, p. 30).
CBM	*Curriculum-Based Measurement.* CBM is an assessment procedure that examines the student's performance against the teacher's assessment of his or her own practice as well as evaluates the student's daily and weekly progress (Smith, 2000).
PRT and TAT	*Prereferral Team and Teacher Assistance Team.* The team is formed by teachers, special administrators, parents, personnel from outside agencies, school psychologists, and social workers that not only assist teachers in developing and monitoring effective educational interventions for students prior to the initiation of a special education referral but also work directly with an individual student who may be experiencing learning or behavior problems.

outcomes for many students from culturally and linguistically diverse backgrounds. These unfavorable outcomes include discrepancies in special education referrals and placements for ELL students, disproportionate representation of minority students in special education on the basis of their representation in the general population, and higher dropout rates for minority students (Individuals with Disabilities Education Act Amendments, 1997).

Some of the 1997 amendments to IDEA were designed to address these unfortunate circumstances. For the first time since the passage of the law, SEAs and LEAs are now required to assess the efficacy of educational and transitional services for culturally and linguistically diverse students with disabilities. Specifically, they must provide annual data on the number of minority children referred for special education assessment, the number of minority students receiving special education, the extent to which they are served, high school graduation rates, and performance on state assessments.

At first glance, these amendments represent substantial energy, enthusiasm, and commitment to culturally and linguistically diverse students with disabilities. However, we are not convinced that these measures alone will lead to more equitable practices for these students. To attain this goal, we believe that educators and policy makers must examine the problems identified earlier in this chapter from a broader, cultural-historical perspective. We support our position in the next section.

Examining the Problem from a Cultural-Historical Perspective

Why did the "minority problem" remain after the desegregation mandates and the passage of IDEA? We believe that a partial answer to this question lies in the failure to examine teaching, learning, and schooling from a cultural-historical perspective (Engeström, 1999). According to Trent et al. (2002), proponents of cultural-historical theory view "human development and learning as culturally and historically situated and dialogically based" (p. 12). In other words, if educators, researchers, and policy makers are to develop more efficacious policies and practices for culturally and linguistically diverse students, they must begin to examine the evolution of educational policies and practices historically, contextually, and from multiple perspectives (Kalyanpur, Harry, & Skrtic, 2000). In this vein, historical factors that have distinguished the powerful from the powerless among service providers and stakeholders must be considered throughout the implementation process. In addition, new policies and reforms must be implemented with full consideration of preexisting policies and how old policies will interact with new ones. As we have learned from history, failure to examine

education from this standpoint may very well result in cosmetic changes that do not significantly improve outcomes for the majority of those the policy was intended to help in the first place. We now return to the interactions between desegregation mandates and IDEA to support these beliefs.

As we stated above, policy advocacy on the part of parents of students with disabilities came on the heels of policy advocacy to gain equal access and educational equity for African American students. Mandates emanating from this advocacy were monumental and did create new educational opportunities for African American students and students with disabilities. However, more careful analysis of the interactions between these two mandates reveals that neither policy advocates nor policy makers considered historically and contextually how desegregation and special education mandates might have negative effects on culturally and linguistically diverse learners placed in special education (Trent, Artiles, & Englert, 1998). Why? For one, educators and policy makers tend to forget that an educational system is merely a microcosm of the larger society and that "schooling is 'embedded' in the habits and patterns of our national life" (Tyack & Hansot, 1984, p. 34), particularly the patterns of life of mainstream culture. In the United States, this perspective often results in devaluation of the patterns of life of non-Europeans and supports ethnicity theory, which, according to Sleeter (2001), "is based on an analysis of the experience of European ethnic groups in the United States, and examines mainly the extent to which groups retain distinct cultures while becoming structurally assimilated into the dominant society" (p. 86). Non-Europeans are simply appended to this theory, with little or no consideration given to the influence of color, class, and language on opportunity and advancement. Hence, on the basis of a Western rational model, many proponents of desegregation concluded that integration of African American children alongside European American children would end exclusivity and differentiated educational opportunities. They failed to realize that desegregation mandates placed African American students (and later, other culturally and linguistically diverse students) in the very settings that extolled and maintained supremacist beliefs, racial discrimination, and inequitable educational opportunities (Akbar, 1985).

Enactment of IDEA complicated matters further. Although one law mandated racial integration, the other mandated special education services in a variety of settings, including self-contained classrooms. Once again, deeply embedded beliefs about racial superiority and inferiority paved the way for continued inequity manifested in the form of de facto segregation in overtly integrated schools and the continued loss of power and advocacy among minority teachers and minority and economically disadvantaged parents (Lazerson, 1983). Researchers have presented concrete examples of this circumstance. Harry, Allen, and McLaughlin (1996) conducted a three-year qualitative study to determine if beliefs about the most effective instructional approaches differed between teachers and 18 low- to middle-class African American parents of students who were at risk for school failure These researchers did find differences between the two groups. Teachers preferred more constructivist, process-oriented approaches for teaching reading and math, while parents believed that explicit instruction, the instruction that many of them received in school, would render the best results for their children. Harry and colleagues discussed implications of these differences for the dominant and dominated cultures. They expressed concerns that, without exploring the views of minority parents more substantively, educators might view parents' beliefs as limited and unworthy of consideration for instructional purposes. Moreover, they concluded that even though African American parents did meet with teachers to discuss their children's progress, they may have feared for their students' well-being and felt less empowered than White parents because of racist practices that have historically characterized schools and the larger society.

From this study and similar ones, researchers have begun to develop frameworks emanating from sociocultural and cultural-historical theory to explain more systematically how these beliefs and practices are maintained in society. For instance, Kalyanpur et al. (2000) contend that the mandate for parental involvement in the special education process is flawed because it does not account for hierarchical structures within schools and between parents and teachers. They also argue that this situation may be even more difficult for culturally different and economically disadvantaged parents. Harry, Rueda, and Kalyanpur (1999) assert that without cultural reciprocity or the ability to "view discrepant beliefs through multiple cultural lenses" (p. 125), it will be difficult for school personnel to move beyond their own viewpoints and consider critically the viewpoints of minority teachers and parents who may think differently.

In summary, as we identify problems that exist for culturally and linguistically diverse students with disabilities, it is imperative that we do so from a broader, more holistic perspective. No longer can we afford to create mandates and policies that emanate solely from a Western rational model and fail to consider how sociocultural and historical factors affect outcomes for these students. In the next section of this chapter, we continue this discussion and support these conclusions with information about disproportionate representation of culturally diverse students in special education programs.

Overrepresentation of Culturally Diverse Students

Minority students are disproportionately represented in special education. Artiles and Trent (2000) write, "This phenomenon refers to unequal proportions of culturally diverse students in these special programs. Two patterns are associated with disproportionality, namely over- and under-representation" (p. 514). Historically, racial minorities have been overrepresented in high-incidence disabilities. Lloyd Dunn (1968) first acknowledged this problem in a highly visible journal, and despite the attention received over the years it is still a major source of debate in the field. Two National Research Council panels (Donovan & Cross, 2002; Heller, Holtzman, & Messick, 1982), resolutions, statements, and actions from major professional organizations such as the Council for Exceptional Children (CEC, 1997, 2002), litigation and pressure from advocacy and family groups, and efforts from a relatively small group of researchers have not been sufficient to significantly reduce this problem.

Explanations of overrepresentation can be grouped in two categories: outcome-based and process-oriented. Outcome-based overrepresentation has received the greatest attention in the literature. It focuses on the outcome of the special education process: placing minorities in disability categories or programs. One such explanation stresses the deficits of minority students as a result of the negative consequences of poverty. Some have even taken issue with the assumption about "equal proportions" that underlies the overrepresentation debate. These individuals suggest disabilities might be unequally distributed, with minorities disproportionately represented given the higher incidence of poverty and health threats that affect these populations. Indeed, poverty can have devastatingly negative consequences on family and children's lives that can in turn disable children's development. However, this kind of deficit-based explanation ignores the protective forces that can buffer children's development even in the most adverse circumstances (McLoyd, 1998). It also overlooks the structural conditions that are correlated with poverty, such as meager school resources, low teacher quality, poor instructional practices, and negative school climate. Perhaps more important, the explanation that focuses solely on the role of poverty does not raise the question, What are the historical, cultural, and structural *antecedents* of the systematic link between poverty, race, and disability?

Process-oriented explanations concentrate on the precursors of minority placement in special education. One strand of scholarship is grounded in a social reproduction thesis suggesting that the special education system is essentially discriminatory; that is, minority overrepresentation in special education is merely a reflection of minorities' oppressed status in the larger society (Patton, 1998). This scholarship tends to be theoretical. An alternative line of work aims to document contextual, technical, structural, or ideological factors in the processes that ultimately lead to placement decisions, specifically referral, assessment, and decision-making processes in eligibility meetings (Mehan, Hartwick, & Meihls, 1986). Examples of this kind of work include how the variability in eligibility and placement criteria across states affects overrepresentation, the role of teacher factors (gender, race, classroom management ability, beliefs) in referral and placement bias, and the influence of examiner and test content and development biases in disability diagnoses (see Donovan & Cross, 2002, for a summary of this work).

Although there are multiple ways to calculate overrepresentation, most scholars use three indicators. The more widely used method is called the "composition index," which compares the proportion of students from a group (racial, linguistic) within a disability category or special education program with the proportion of the same group of students in the general school population (Donovan & Cross, 2002). The rule of thumb is that a group is considered overrepresented if their enrollment in special education is equal to or greater than 10% of their proportion in general education (Chinn & Hughes, 1987). The second way to calculate overrepresentation is called the "risk index," which is calculated by dividing the number of students from the target group (e.g., African American) placed in a disability category or program (e.g., MR, or mental retardation; see Table 34.1) by the total number of students in that group enrolled in the school population.

An interesting example of the insights gained from both indicators is found in Artiles, Rueda, Salazar, and Higareda (2000). These authors assessed English learner representation in special education in several large urban districts in California. Artiles and colleagues (2000) found that although the risk index for English learners was similar to the index for the entire district (7.6% and 7.2%, respectively), various overrepresentation patterns emerged as they calculated the composition indices across programs, grade levels, subgroups of English learners, and disability categories. For instance, overrepresentation was not observed when the data were aggregated at the district level for the entire population of English learners, but these students were clearly overrepresented in secondary grades, and a subgroup of English learners was most affected: those students designated as having limited proficiency in their first *and* second languages. It is important, therefore, that the composition *and* risk indices be calculated to gain a more complete understanding of overrepresentation patterns. The third indicator is the odds ratio: [It] "divides the risk index of one racial/ethnic group (e.g., Black) by the risk index of another racial/ethnic

group (e.g., White) and thereby provides a comparative index of risk" (Donovan & Cross, 2002, p. 43).

Several placement patterns have been consistently observed over the history of this problem. More specifically, African Americans and Native Americans have been overrepresented at the national level: African Americans in the MR and E/BD (emotional and behavioral disorder; see Table 34.1) categories and Native Americans in the LD (learning disability) category. Another consistent finding is that Asian Americans are underrepresented in disability categories (with the occasional exception of speech and language impairments). Latinos have been overrepresented in the MR and LD categories at the state and district levels. The level at which data are examined (national, state, district, school), the size of the district, and the representation of a group in the district also mediate overrepresentation patterns (see Donovan & Cross, 2002, and Heller et al., 1982, for examples). With some exceptions, longitudinal analyses are rare; we know little about the potential influence of general education reforms on overrepresentation in special education (e.g., elimination of bilingual education, accountability) and contextual forces (e.g., social class level of district, school, and individual student; school climate), though a new generation of research is beginning to offer intriguing evidence. Some emerging findings are discussed in the next section.

Emergent Findings from a New Generation of Research on Overrepresentation

Minority students tend to be placed in restrictive settings (Parrish, 2000; Skiba, Wu, Kohler, Chung, & Simmons, 2001). In California, for example, where there is a long history of litigation around issues of overrepresentation and one would expect close monitoring of systemic bias, African American students are less likely to be placed in regular classrooms and more likely to "be designated as requiring intensive services than White students (29% vs. 23%) and are more likely to be placed in such restrictive settings as special education self-contained classrooms (37% vs. 24%)" (Parrish, 2000, p. 16). Parrish also found that African American students are less likely to receive related services such as speech, occupational, and physical therapy than their White peers. Greater segregation, as reflected in placement in the juvenile justice and correctional systems, has been reported for African Americans and Hispanics (Parrish, 2000). As research indicates, the special educational needs of individuals are not always well addressed in these systems. For example, citing the National Longitudinal Transition Study and state-reported data, Hehir (2000) pointed out that "disabled students in cities [where minorities constitute the largest segment of school populations] are almost three times more likely to be segregated in separate schools and far more likely to be kept out of challenging academic programs than their suburban counterparts" (p. 16).

School location seems to have a mediating effect on overrepresentation patterns. The documented difficulties and constraints of urban schools seem to have a devastating influence on poor minority students (Kozol, 1991). For example, Hehir (2000), when comparing urban students to suburban students, found disproportionate placement of urban students in special schools, more segregation of these students outside of general education, and fewer opportunities for them to participate in general education activities.

Researchers are also beginning to document interactions between school location, disability category, ethnic group, poverty, and proportion of minority school enrollment. Oswald, Coutinho, and Best (2000) reported African American MR overrepresentation declined as poverty level of community increased. In contrast, poverty level and African American and Latino overrepresentation in LD and E/BD had a positive relationship. Oswald et al. (2000) reported that as "communities become increasingly NONWHITE . . . White students are substantially less likely to be identified as LD. For Black students, particularly Black male students, living in a community with few NONWHITE students is a substantial risk factor for MR and [E/BD] overrepresentation" (p. 8). American Indian students tend to be overrepresented, particularly in E/BD, if they live in predominantly non-White communities.

Standards, high-stakes testing, and discipline measures dominate contemporary education policy discussions. Although it has been argued these reform movements will have a disproportionately negative influence on poor and minority students (Advancement Project & Civil Rights Project, 2000), there is a dearth of research on their impact on minority representation in special education. Indeed, the data are scarce and equivocal. Heubert (2000) reported that although it is difficult to find data on the performance of students with disabilities on high-stakes tests, there is some evidence that these students

pass state tests in higher numbers over time. . . . On the other hand, 1998 data from fourteen states show gaps remain quite high: Students with disabilities consistently fail state graduation tests at rates 35 to 40 percentage points higher than those for nondisabled students. (p. 3)

Heubert argues that even if the graduation rate improved, the question arises as to whether such a rate reflects an improvement in the quality of teaching and learning for students with disabilities and minority and poor students. He recommends that results of high-stakes tests be scrutinized in the context of factors such as (a) dropout rate, (b) grade retention rate, (c) whether students who leave school to obtain general equivalency diplomas are included in the calculation of dropout rate, and (d) whether exempted groups are included (e.g., ELLs, students with disabilities). He also suggests high-stakes test results be interpreted in relation to the overlap between the covered curriculum and the standards content, whether tests were applied and used according to best practice standards, and whether improper test accommodations could inflate test results (see also Skiba et al., 2001; and Thurlow & Liu, 2000).

The availability of alternative programs such as bilingual education has been mentioned as a factor that can shape the magnitude and even the existence of overrepresentation. Finn (1982) found that MR overrepresentation was significant in school districts with sizable Latino enrollment (i.e., greater than 70%), particularly in small districts with high Latino enrollments. Finn also found that districts with the highest overrepresentation had a small proportion of students in bilingual programs. The question arises as to whether language differences are being misunderstood as cognitive or learning disabilities. Unfortunately, the knowledge base on ELLs with special needs is thin; hence, few research-based guidelines are available (Ortiz, 1997).

Although Artiles et al. (2000) did not focus on this question, their descriptive analysis of districts in California reflects a troubling increase in ELL special education placement from 1993 to 1998, the year when bilingual education programs were abolished. They also report that ELLs had a higher chance of being placed in special education as the level of language support diminished. Indeed, there is an urgent need to conduct more research on these reform trends, particularly as they intersect with other large-scale reforms such as high-stakes testing. For example, Thurlow and Liu (2000) express concern that exclusion of certain disability categories may result in increased placements in special education, thus eliminating these students from counts. It is therefore urgent to study further the impact of current reforms on minority overrepresentation.

Funding is another understudied area, particularly as it influences overrepresentation. Parrish (2000) found most states devote more resources and special education to districts with higher levels of poverty and minority enrollment; however, "this pattern seems only weakly linked to patterns of overrepresentation" (p. 18). Certain types of funding formulas can affect overrepresentation. Parrish identified 6 states (out of 28 with enough data to conduct analyses) with funding formulas that placed "higher premiums on higher cost disabilities, such as mental retardation . . . ; [these states were] much more likely to over identify minority students as mentally retarded, and at the same time to under fund them" (p. 14). The states were South Carolina, Delaware, New Jersey, Florida, Indiana, and Ohio. Further quantitative analyses of state datasets as well as in-depth case studies of districts where funding formulas vary by category of disability are certainly warranted.

Bias is often mentioned in discussions about overrepresentation, but the empirical evidence is scarce. Lack of evidence, however, does not mean bias does not exist or is not a problem; the dearth of evidence is most likely explained by the lack of attention to this issue in the research community. Some of the emerging research summarized here suggests bias may be playing a role in some aspects of overrepresentation. Future research needs to acknowledge bias is not restricted to the actions and decisions of individuals; bias can also take the form of historical residue and be found in the social structures of educational settings and institutional regulations and practices that shape institutional discrimination. For these reasons, bias should be examined throughout the entire special education process, including prereferral interventions, referrals, assessment, eligibility and placement decisions, and delivery of services.

Just as it is critical that we examine evidence indicating possible bias, discrimination, and inadequate practice that affect poor minority students, it is equally important to acknowledge that progress has been made. National organizations such as the Council for Exceptional Children, the U.S. Department of Education, and legislators have paid more attention to the problem of overrepresentation in the last decade than in previous decades. As a result, task forces and panels have been created to examine the extant literature, such as the most recent National Research Council panel appointed in 1997 (Donovan & Cross, 2002). Funds for research and technical assistance have been allocated (e.g., creation of the Center of Minority Research in Special Education); practices to reduce disproportionate representation are being disseminated (e.g., Artiles & Ortiz, 2002); and new mandates and regulations have been included in federal legislation (e.g., protections against inappropriate identification of minority students, requirements to monitor and intervene where overrepresentation occurs) (Hehir, 2000).

At the same time, several important gaps must be addressed in the near future to better understand and find viable solutions to this problem. One such gap is the availability and quality of data. There is an urgent need for datasets that are nationally representative and include enough information to conduct comprehensive analyses. Until recently, for example, the Office for Civil Rights survey used different sampling procedures over time, and the demographic profiles of schools varied from one survey to the next (Reschly, 1997). Moreover, the Office for Civil Rights survey did not include until recently information on student (e.g., language proficiency level) and context (e.g., teacher beliefs, quality of instruction, school climate) variables that would enhance the quality and mean-

ingfulness of future studies. To address the shortcomings of existing datasets, researchers often use multiple datasets; unfortunately, this complicates the work of investigators, who do not always have ready access to multiple databases or may lack technical expertise to merge and carry out analyses with several multilevel datasets (Artiles et al., 2000). In addition, monitoring and enforcement of IDEA's current mandates about overrepresentation must be strengthened. For this purpose, some of the recommendations are to (a) influence the Office of Special Education Programs (OSEP) monitoring activities with states, for example, through advocate pressure to include complaints in monitoring reports and corrective action plans; (b) use states' complaint processes, such as formal complaints about noncompliance with IDEA; and (c) have a clear vision of the change one wants to see, which includes a sophisticated "benefit" analysis to gauge how to maximize positive impact and reduce unintended consequences that could deny minority students the protection of disability legislation (Hehir, 2000).

Overrepresentation is a multifaceted problem in need of more and better research. Ultimately, this problem is about making appropriate decisions regarding students' potential and needs, the consequences of such decisions for program placement, students' opportunities to learn, and the quality of services offered to them. Heller et al. (1982) believe that overrepresentation is a problem

(1) if children are invalidly placed in programs for mentally retarded students; (2) if they are unduly exposed to the likelihood of such placement by virtue of having received poor quality regular instruction; and (3) if the quality and academic relevance of the special instruction programs block students' educational progress, including decreasing the likelihood of their return to the regular classroom. (p. 18; also see Artiles, 2003, and Donovan & Cross, 2002, for discussions on research needs)

In the next section, we review the research on assessment and instruction for minority students.

OVERVIEW OF RESEARCH ON ASSESSMENT AND INSTRUCTION

Notwithstanding the disproportionate representation of poor minority students in programs for language-based reading difficulties (Snow, Burns, & Griffin, 1998) and in high-incidence disability categories and programs (Donovan & Cross, 2002), the research on assessment and instruction of these students is alarmingly scarce.

The lack of attention to minority students in special education research has been noted in recent comprehensive reviews of the literature and discussions about the future of the field. For instance, Artiles, Trent, and Kuan (1997) conducted a review of the empirical literature published in a 22-year period (1975–1994) in four highly visible peer-reviewed journals. The results indicate that less than 3% of the empirical studies in these four major journals disaggregated the data by racial group; this finding was recently reiterated by the National Research Council report (Donovan & Cross, 2002). The small number of studies published in this period also lacked basic information that would enhance the replicability of this work, such as sample selection procedures, social class of participants, procedures to diagnose disabilities, types of disabilities, and investigators' race. Also, Asian American and American Indian students were noticeably underrepresented in study samples. We now summarize trends in this miniscule research base.

Assessment

Assessment practices used to place culturally and linguistically diverse students in special education programs have been a source of controversy before and since the passage of the Individuals with Disabilities Education Act. However, most assessment research has been devoted to assessment for referral and placement into special education programs. In addition, this work has focused on the degree to which standardized measures of intelligence are culturally biased and do not appropriately measure the intellectual abilities of culturally diverse students (Ortiz, 1997). We believe that research on assessment for referral and placement is needed because, as we have stated previously in this chapter, many culturally diverse learners are disproportionately referred and placed in special education programs. However, in addition to this type of research, we should also study assessment practices *prior to* and *after* special education placement. Such a focus moves beyond a deficit perspective and views learning as being situated within cultural-historical contexts. In other words, the onus for learning is not placed solely on the child, but on the interaction of the child with other members and mediating artifacts (e.g., instructional interventions) that exist within the classroom and school cultures (see Donovan & Cross, 2002, for a discussion of this vision). Here, we focus specifically on these three aspects of assessment.

Prereferral Interventions. Currently, the inclusive education movement is gaining more momentum in special education. This focus on serving students with disabilities in general classroom settings has prompted implementation of prereferral teams (PRTs), designed to decrease the number of referrals made to special education (Hallahan & Kauffman, 2000). Also, according to Chalfant and Pysh (1989), PRTs or teacher assistance teams (TATs) create in-house professional development opportunities for teachers and help general education teachers develop and monitor effective educational interventions for students prior to initiating a special education referral. TATs, developed by Chalfant and Pysh, consist of general education teachers, special education teachers, administrators, parents, and staff from outside agencies who may be working with the student experiencing learning or behavior problems. Participants may also include parents, school psychologists, social workers, and other ancillary personnel. Chalfant and Pysh have developed a 30-minute problem-solving strategy designed to identify and describe the student's academic and behavioral performance, the child's strengths, antecedents and consequences that accompany the behaviors, and possible interventions that might improve learning and behavioral outcomes. With assistance from colleagues, the referring teacher selects an intervention that is acceptable and manageable. After the meeting, roles and responsibilities and dates for evaluation of the intervention are established.

From a rational standpoint, PRTs or TATs represent a promising intervention that may result in decreased special education referrals and improved educational outcomes (see Donovan & Cross, 2002, for a review of this research). In fact, although very little research has been conducted on the efficacy of PRTs and TATs, researchers have found that "(1) they do cut down on the number of referrals to special education; and (2) team members and administrators report that they are effective" (Schram et al., 1984, as cited in Hallahan & Kauffman, 2000, p. 62). Moreover, Ortiz (1997) supports the use of PRTs and believes that this model may serve as an effective intervention for culturally and linguistically diverse learners. However, before accepting this practice as effective, researchers should examine its implementation more holistically. For example, two assumptions about the model are that (a) with little preparation and facilitation, educators can work together effectively to meet the needs of an increasingly diverse student population; and (b) educators hold high expectations for all students and view parents as equal partners during the implementation and evaluative process.

Furthermore, we know that approaches such as PRT require collaboration consisting of sustained discourse, reflection, development of common goals and language, and the ability to engage in constructive criticism (Englert, Raphael, & Mariage, 1998). Also, just as it is for any educational reform, in order to create and sustain collaborative approaches such as PRTs educators must address systemic constraints that may impede development and sustainability. For example, Englert et al. (1998) found teacher study groups to be very effective in developing and sustaining a literacy curriculum for students with and without disabilities in urban schools. The primary goal of the Early Literacy Project was not to decrease special education referrals but to address issues of instruction, improve the quality of literacy instruction for all students, and bring teachers together around a common theme. In their longitudinal research in urban multicultural schools, Englert et al. found that teachers took ownership of the project because they were given the choice to establish individual goals and choices. Over time, teachers' isolated reflections and activities were made visible to the entire group through sustained discourse during biweekly meetings, videotaped lessons, and sharing of instructional materials and student products. Interventions and ideas were then borrowed, modified, refined, and transformed on the basis of the unique needs of teachers and their students. In order to facilitate and sustain this recursive process, the researchers had to garner support from administrators to restructure the school day and allow early dismissal of teachers to attend the meetings. These researchers have longitudinally documented the stages of development that led to sustained and mutually satisfying collaborative relationships among educators and improved literacy outcomes for students with disabilities served in pullout and self-contained settings. This documentation included a focus on roles and responsibilities, goals, outcomes, and the mediating artifacts or tools that were used to develop the literacy curriculum, and student outcomes.

In the future, researchers should also identify how childhood experiences, professional training, race, gender, and class among team members mediate group dynamics (e.g., Who maintains power, and why?), discursive rules, and problem-solving processes. To keep these issues at the forefront, researchers and implementers of PRTs should ask such questions as (a) What are the theoretical premises of team members' beliefs, and what are the historical antecedents of such beliefs? (b) How do team members define teaching and learning, and what are the basic assumptions and points on which they agree and disagree? and (c) "How can we strategically, through our discourse and use of other mediating artifacts, integrate these different beliefs and theories in ways that will help us accomplish desired outcomes for all of our students and ourselves?" (Trent et al., 2002, p. 19). As we addressed earlier in this chapter, researchers and implementers of PRTs must also examine their beliefs about parents who are different from them in race, ethnicity, religion, education, and class, and how willing they are to accept them as valuable, viable members of the problem-solving team.

Assessment for Referral and Placement. As has been indicated, most of the research on assessment and culturally diverse students has focused on referral and placement (Ortiz, 1997). This has been due in large part to the controversies surrounding the use and appropriateness of standardized tests. For example, just before and after the passage of the Individuals with Disabilities Act, many

minority parents once again advocated and initiated litigation to protect the rights of their children, who they believed were being inappropriately placed in special education largely due to biased assessment practices. Two such cases were the highly influential *Diana* v. *California Board of Education* (1970) and *Larry P.* v. *Riles* (1979). *Diana* involved parents of Mexican American students who sued the California Department of Education for placement in MMR (mild mental retardation; see Table 34.1) programs that were based on biased testing practices (Spanish-speaking students were tested with English instruments). Eventually, California settled the suit. *Larry P.* was brought about by parents of African American students and focused on issues of culture. It was argued that intelligence tests were culturally (instead of linguistically) biased. Unlike *Diana*, the case was not settled out of court and went to trial. The judge commented that classes for the mildly retarded were "dead end" programs that resulted in few if any positive outcomes for African American students. He ruled that "IQ tests could not be used to identify African American students with mental retardation" (Hunt & Marshall, 2002, p. 23). Other important rulings in these cases were that (a) biased assessment explained the overrepresentation of Latinos and Black students in mental retardation programs, (b) alternative means were needed to assess these students' capacities and potential, and (c) these minority students should be retested and reclassified (see Reschly, Kicklighter, & McKee, 1988, and Valdés & Figueroa, 1994, for discussions of these cases).

More attention is now being devoted to alternative assessment procedures for culturally diverse students. Work done with ELL students has substantiated the need for these new procedures and demonstrated that using the same procedure for all students is not necessarily equitable. For example, Ortiz and her colleagues "found that the intelligence, achievement, and language tests used to assess Hispanic students referred because of suspected learning disabilities were essentially the same as those used to assess their Anglo peers" (as cited in Ortiz, 1997, p. 325). Similar findings have been documented for African American students who speak African American Vernacular English (AAVE). For example, as Keulen, Weddington, and DeBose (1998) reported:

Speech-language pathologists knowledgeable of African American English have found that the assessment procedures in which they have been trained frequently led them to conclude that the speech of certain African American children was defective, when it was apparent that the conclusion had resulted from the use of biased criteria. (p. 6)

These authors propose a model for alternative assessment of AAVE speakers that includes standardized, dynamic, informal, and criterion-referenced testing (see Donovan & Cross, 2002; García & Pearson, 1994; and Valdés & Figueroa, 1994 for discussions of assessment models with diverse populations). In addition, interviews are conducted with parents to glean perspectives about aspects of their culture, including language, that may be different from mainstream culture. Pathologists, in turn, are encouraged to examine parental beliefs within the context of what they themselves believe and how they can consider another perspective that will inform the effectiveness of their interventions. This kind of assessment needs to become more prevalent among researchers and educators interested in improving academic and social outcomes for culturally and linguistically diverse learners.

To conclude, the National Research Council report concluded student referral and assessment processes for special education are not identifying "the right students" (i.e., "students who need and can benefit from those programs"; Donovan & Cross, 2002, p. 5). These issues must continue to be addressed. In addition, future investigations need to stress the role of instruction, classroom context, and opportunity to learn in student achievement.

Performance Monitoring After Placement. Effective prereferral interventions and culturally appropriate assessment for referral and placement may preclude the need for special education. However, if culturally diverse students are found eligible for special education through appropriate assessment procedures, their academic and behavioral performance should be monitored regularly, not just through pretesting and posttesting at the beginning and end of the academic year (Marston, 1989). For several years, an ongoing assessment procedure referred to as curriculum-based measurement (CBM) has proven effective with many students with disabilities (Marston, 1989). Rather than focusing on isolated skill development or skill clusters, CBM focuses on global outcomes based on the curriculum being used. Student performance is measured weekly and examined against the teacher's assessment of his or her own practice. There has been little research conducted focusing solely on the use of this practice with culturally diverse students. Still, it holds promise as an effective means to monitor outcomes for students and teacher effectiveness.

According to Hilliard (1992), another promising assessment approach for use with culturally and linguistically diverse students is a system consisting of connected diagnosis and remediation procedures. Developed by Reuven Feuerstein and emanating largely from Piagetian psychology, "dynamic assessment" is used to diagnose deficient cognitive functions; "instructional enrichment" consists of a set of mediational strategies designed to remediate identified deficits. Like CBM, this approach requires ongoing assessment of student and teacher performance. Unlike CBM, the dynamic assessment and instructional enrichment components of Feuerstein's (1979) model represent a recursive process that includes student-teacher discourse, observation, and continual provision of scaffolds that support students in their efforts to become self-regulated learners.

Though these are two promising assessment approaches, researchers and practitioners should not assume that their use will affect significantly the intellectual and social development of culturally and linguistically diverse learners with disabilities if they are not cognizant and reflective about the cultural-historical issues we have discussed throughout this chapter. For example, they should consider how discontinuities between the majority culture and students' cultures might affect negatively the beliefs and expectations they hold for these students. Otherwise, just as might happen with more traditional pretest and posttest procedures, educators may interpret poor performance among culturally and linguistically diverse students as substantiation of their limited intellectual abilities and see no need to examine critically the assumptions and effectiveness of their own practices (Delpit, 1995).

Instruction

There is a strong tradition of instructional research in special education. Gersten, Baker, Pugach, Scanlon, and Chard (2001) concluded that a vibrant research community has produced a solid corpus of special education instruction based on cognitive strategies and scaffolds, content enhancement strategies, direct instruction, and, more recently, models that integrate various instructional approaches (e.g., explicit instruction and situated cognition strategies).

Notwithstanding these advances, instructional research with minority students is distressingly sparse, even in areas that have been extensively investigated; in this vein, as the National Research Council report recently concluded, "The committee is not aware of any published studies that compare the quality of special education programs or the efficacy of specific instructional practices among various racial/ethnic groups" (Donovan & Cross, 2002, p. 338). More intense versions of effective instructional models for nondisabled students are often useful for students with disabilities. At the same time, although some instructional approaches used with nonminority students with special needs are also effective with culturally diverse learners, core issues in the education of minorities are undertheorized in such approaches, as with definitions of culture, the link between culture and learning, and how culture is incorporated in the design of the approach. Special education research stands in stark contrast to the increasing attention given to culturally responsive instruction in general education (Gallego, Cole, & LCHC, 2001). Prescriptions for culturally responsive or relevant instruction generally focus on two groups of students: racial/ethnic and linguistic minorities.

Instruction for Racial/Ethnic Minorities. Instructional approaches for racial minorities often target African Americans and tend to rely on a cultural discontinuity argument (i.e., it is purported that instruction should bridge the gap between the culture of African Americans and the White middle-class culture of schools). Although the original empirical evidence for this instructional model was generated with nondisabled populations (e.g., Heath, 1983), many special educators concerned with the education of minority exceptional learners recommend its use (Anderson & Webb-Johnson, 1995; Byrd, 1995).

Although the cultural discontinuity hypothesis has merits, instructional models based on the thesis are limited in at least three respects. First, the hypothesis stresses cultural homogeneity over within-group diversity. This lends itself to production of overgeneralizations and stereotypes about various culturally diverse groups. The diversity found within any cultural group tends to be overlooked. This violates a basic tenet of special education, namely, individualization. Evidence about minority parents' beliefs and perceptions of instruction suggests there is considerable diversity within and between cultural groups (Harry et al., 1996). Second, the cultural mismatch hypothesis might inadvertently emphasize a static view of minority cultures. This literature tends to discuss the traits of "African American culture" or "Latino(a) culture" as if those groups have had and will always have the same culture. The dynamic nature of cultures and the perpetual processes of cultural changes are not acknowledged. Again, the result might be stereotyping of groups. Third, these instructional models seem to assume classrooms are populated by two racial groups, for example, White and one minority group. In such a scenario, making instruction culturally congruent with the culture of the one minority group is feasible. But how would a teacher go about this task in a classroom where multiple cultural groups are represented?

The literature on culturally responsive pedagogy in general education is beginning to address these shortcomings by focusing on principles of practice that are adapted to local circumstances. These principles touch upon not only instructional activities and strategies but also teacher knowledge, dispositions, and habits of mind (e.g., Ladson-Billings, 1995). In addition, there is research in special education based on a social constructivist view of learning (Trent et al., 1998). This research is promising because it emphasizes the social origins of development and honors the cultural basis of human development. Although the bulk of this work has not examined instructional issues with racially diverse students, some researchers are beginning to conduct it in multicultural classrooms (e.g., Gutierrez & Stone, 1997).

Instruction for Linguistic Minorities. Just as the work on instructional models for racial minority students in general education informs the special education community, research on ELLs and bilingual education for nondisabled students (August & Hakuta, 1997) is used for populations with disabilities. As with the instructional research reviewed thus far, few studies have been conducted in this area. Gersten and Baker (2000b) identified only *two* experimental studies in the 1990s. Research on current practices suggests that ELLs' learning difficulties may be due in part to inadequate instructional practices (e.g., less opportunity to learn, less active engagement in academic tasks, communication difficulties in the classroom; Donovan & Cross, 2002). For instance, Arreaga-Mayer and Perdomo-Rivera (1996) examined the types of language use and academic behavior in which ELLs were engaged by observing elementary school English as a Second Language (ESL) and regular classrooms. The researchers observed 14 ESL and regular classrooms in three urban schools. The Ecobehavioral System for the Contextual Recording of Interactional Bilingual Environments (ESCRIBE) was used to examine these learning environments. ESCRIBE can be used to assess ecobehavioral processes for individual students during single sessions or an entire school day in both special and general education contexts. The data collected with this system can be summarized to offer molar (for instance, percentage of time spent on various types of activity, grouping and language use patterns) and molecular (behavioral or linguistic patterns during various types of activities or grouping formats) descriptions of programs. The system also allows educators to conduct process-product analyses of ecobehavioral processes with student outcomes (see Arreaga-Mayer & Perdomo-Rivera, 1996). The researchers found little difference in student academic engagement and language use between the two classroom types. Overall, the data revealed a low level of opportunity for ELLs to partake in language development and academic behaviors during a typical school day. Furthermore, there was minimal teacher attention to language development. The majority of instruction was through whole-class and lecture formats.

Three questions are recurrent in policy and research discussions about the education of ELLs (Gersten & Baker, n.d.): (a) What is the optimal age at which to expose ELLs to academic instruction in English? (b) What is the impact of native-language instruction on ELLs' cognitive and academic development? and (c) What is the most effective instructional method for ELLs? According to Gersten and Baker (n.d.), research has failed to provide conclusive answers to the first two questions, though some evidence offers preliminary answers to the third.

Gersten and Baker (2000a) conducted a comprehensive literature review spanning 12 years (1985–1997) in grades K-8 to address the third question. Three sources of evidence were examined in the research review: intervention research, descriptive studies, and professional work groups (n = 44 across five states). Eight intervention studies met these criteria, and an exploratory meta-analysis was conducted.

Descriptive studies that focused on classroom learning environments were selected if data were gathered via structured or naturalistic observation systems (that is, high- and low-inference systems); 15 such studies were located. Gersten and Baker (2000a) explained: "We did not weigh the findings from highly subjective or interpretative research as heavily as we did research conducted with valid experimental designs and reliable measures or qualitative that seemed to provide a more dispassionate analysis of issues raised" (p. 33). The five work groups were heterogeneous with regard to the professional backgrounds represented (bilingual, special, and general education teachers, administrators, researchers, psychologists, and staff development specialists).

Gersten and Baker (2000a) concluded there is a very thin knowledge base on effective instruction for ELLs and that the few studies identified do not render clear patterns. Studies lacked information about how interventions were implemented, whether they were implemented as originally planned, information about the language used during intervention, and other contextual variables. Gersten and Baker (2000a) also suggested that research on effective instruction should differentiate between the development of language and academic growth; despite the lack of evidence, they explained it is often assumed that greater language use increases academic growth. Gersten and Baker (2000a) recommend that English-language development include three components: increased English proficiency and fluency (including social and academic communication competence), adequate use of conventional English grammar, and learning new academic content. Although content and language acquisition are merged, the demands for content should be higher. According to these researchers, an effective program for special education students ought to include these three components. Gersten and Baker (2000a) and Fletcher, Bos, and Johnson (1999) proposed a number of principles of effective practice that should be adapted to schools' local circumstances:

1. *Build and use vocabulary as a curricular anchor.* The number of new words introduced should be relatively small (e.g., seven), and words should be selected on the basis of their centrality, usefulness, and relevance in relation to the content being taught and the lives of students. This approach should allow students to develop deep understanding of words and concepts.

2. *Use visuals to reinforce concepts and vocabulary.* Visual aids such as concept and story maps, word banks, and graphic organizers assist students in visualizing abstract notions and help them learn more efficiently via processing, reflecting on, and integrating concepts and vocabulary. However, visuals are helpful only if teachers use them to assist students in engaging in higher-order thinking when learning concepts and words.

3. *Use cooperative learning and peer tutoring strategies.* Teachers can capitalize on activities that rely on collaboration or that require students to shift roles (novice, expert) to develop language or learn content.

4. *Make strategic use of a student's first language.* Teachers must rely on students' cultural and linguistic capital during instruction. One effective way is to use English at levels that are accessible to ELLs, while native language can be used to teach complex notions.

5. *Carry out strategic orchestration of cognitive and language demands.* Although the empirical support for this principle is thin, it was strongly advocated by the professional work groups. The recommendation is that teachers strategically modulate during instruction the cognitive and linguistic demands of activities to achieve particular goals. For example, the linguistic requirements of oral communication would be lowered if students are expected to grapple with complex notions, whereas in other instances the cognitive demands of tasks could be reduced to facilitate students' prolonged use of English skills.

6. *Contextualize teaching and learning to infuse students' language, while also considering students' disabilities.*

7. *Collaborate with other teachers and specialists and mentor novice teachers.*

Another persistent issue in the education of ELLs is whether knowledge and skills learned in a native language transfer to English. August, Calderón, and Carlo (2000) reported preliminary findings that address this issue. They conducted the study in three Success for All schools (Boston, El Paso, and Chicago) in which a balanced approach that emphasizes phonics and meaning was implemented. (Success for All is a school model that targets at-risk students in early elementary grades. The model includes reading tutors; a program facilitator; emphasis on reading, language arts and writing, and math; periodic assessments; individual academic plans; small class size (n = 25 in grades one through three); preschool program; family support team; special education; and advisory and steering committees (Slavin, Madden, & Karweit, 1989). The sample included 127 native Spanish-speaking students who were followed from the end of second to the end of third grade, the year at which most students are transitioned out of bilingual programs. Students were placed in three types of reading programs:

Spanish-only instruction, combined use of language (two years of Spanish instruction and one year of English instruction), and instruction in English only. The researchers controlled statistically for the potential influence of ability, oral English proficiency, and number of years of formal instruction in English reading. The preliminary findings suggest that

Spanish phonemic awareness, Spanish letter identification, Spanish word recognition, and fluency in letter and word identification in Spanish were reliable predictors of English performance on parallel tasks in English at the end of third grade. The effect of Spanish phonemic awareness on English phonemic awareness emerged for all students. However, the effect of Spanish word decoding on English word decoding emerged only for students who had received formal instruction in Spanish reading. (August et al., 2000, p. 4)

August et al. (2000) also reported that the level of Spanish literacy or the level of oral English proficiency did not influence the effect of Spanish literacy on English literacy.

To conclude, instructional research for cultural and linguistic minority students is scarce. Although special educators can benefit from the literature generated for nondisabled students, there is a critical need for studies that include minority populations with disabilities. Moreover, as suggested in the historical review of the field, it is necessary that instructional research acknowledge the societal context in which minorities live and are educated (Cummins, 1989). For example, instructional research must attend explicitly to opportunity to learn issues and build into the design of interventions the supports needed by the personnel that work in the communities where minority students attend school, since "how well any child meets the demands of schooling will be determined both by that child *and* by the school context itself. . . . The weight of the burden in improving school outcomes for minority students, then, falls on the interactions in the classroom" (Donovan & Cross, 2002, pp. 209–210, emphasis in original).

DIRECTIONS FOR FUTURE RESEARCH

At least three conclusions can be made on the basis of this review of the literature. First, the education of culturally diverse students has the potential to be informed by two critical traditions in the struggle for civil rights: the social justice movements for people with disabilities and racial/linguistic minority individuals. Second, notwithstanding the growing presence of culturally diverse people in society and in the educational system (including special education programs), they are largely invisible in special education scholarship. Third, given this state of affairs, it is not surprising that the educational needs of students of color are not being fully addressed. Consistent

with the focus of this volume, we discuss the need for programmatic research that bridges the gaps identified in this review. We argue that such a research program should be characterized by three interrelated sets of practices that ultimately improve the education of minority students with and without disabilities: historical imagination, complexity, and mapping of the spaces of practice. We explain these practices in the next sections.

Historical Imagination: Toward a Cultural Theory of Difference in a Democratic Society

Future research should be concerned with better serving minority students who need special education as well as differentiating between cultural differences and disabilities. As our brief historical review suggests, researchers cannot ignore that compelling socioeconomic, political, and cultural forces have shaped and continue to shape the experiences of minorities' existence. Minorities and those who make up the majority should not erase from their memories and existential stance that they live in a society that (a) accumulated wealth and privileged status for White citizens through the free labor of African American slaves and the appropriation of land that had been populated for centuries by indigenous groups, (b) denied minorities voting rights and access to the same basic social services and institutions (including education) until the 1950s, (c) exploited and oppressed immigrant groups for economic gain (e.g., Mexican and Chinese workers), (d) eliminated programs that increased minorities' access to better employment and educational opportunities, (e) prohibited the use of minorities' native language for instructional purposes, and (f) inequitably distributed financial and professional resources to schools that serve minority-populated schools. Indeed, these historical events and experiences shape the collective perception of who is and who is not "different" in the United States. As Minow (1990) reminds us, difference is a comparative notion ("different from whom?"). As we know, culturally specific understandings of what is "competent performance," "normal development," and "natural ability" are based on White middle-class parameters.

It is critical, therefore, that researchers be mindful of this historical reality in order to better understand the schooling experiences of minority students (Artiles, 1998). Recognition of the past as well as the present realities of people of color in the United States helps researchers understand, for example, that the resistance stance toward schools, educators, and authority that some minority students embrace may encode communicative goals (Abowitz, 2000); the questions then become, what is being communicated, to whom, in which context, and for what purposes? This means researchers should change several practices. For instance, future intervention and descriptive studies in special education should include minority samples and urban schools that typically serve these students. The invisibility of minorities in programs of research at this time in history is unjustifiable. Research should also tap families' and students' perceptions and beliefs about instructional innovations and reforms and about overrepresentation of children of color in special education. Just as researchers strive to gather the views of teachers, administrators, and fellow researchers to improve research and practice, minority families and students should be given the opportunity to project their voices and thus contribute to generating a knowledge base. By the same token, it is important for researchers to make explicit in study reports their views about culture and their theories about minority student performance.

Attention to history in research practices also implies that researchers document the potential role of bias and discrimination in the education of minority students. Disenfranchised individuals experience bias and discrimination every day. But we should remember bias and discrimination are not located only in the behavior or thoughts of individuals but also in the regulations, requirements, expectations, and organization of institutions.

At the same time, research with a historical imagination should look to the future. As practitioners and researchers learn from the past to build a better present, research efforts should be informed by a vision of an ideal state of affairs. Little attention has been given in special education to envisioning the nature and shape of services for students with disabilities in a pluralistic democratic society. Scholars need to theorize and test models of exemplary practice in schools that are mindful of both cultural differences and students' unique educational needs that require specialized intense interventions.

Embrace Complexity: Interdisciplinary Research on the Intersection of Culture, Learning, and Disability

Gersten and Baker (2000a) concluded, "There is no question that there is a limited understanding of the difficulty and complexity of this type of research. The U.S. Department of Education should be made aware of the lack of research and of the difficulties of doing good research in [special education]" (p. 73). Future research needs to embrace complexity to honor the schooling experiences of minority students in a pluralistic society. The first step in this direction is to ground research in sound theoretical frameworks. Albert Einstein said that "it is the theory which decides what we can observe" (as cited in Minow, 1990, pp. 59–60). Hence, a research program on diverse students in special education should draw from theories that systematically link learning and culture. We

are partial to a cultural historical framework that gives explicit attention to the social origins of learning, the cultural mediation of human activity, and the requirement that human development be studied historically (Trent et al., 1998). This framework enables researchers to understand that student competence and performance as well as pedagogical processes are immersed in culture. At the same time, we realize it is important to promote the use of multiple theoretical frameworks, as long as they account systematically for culture and history.

The definition of culture is critical in implementing future research. Culture has been defined in past research from a fairly static perspective as encoded in the values, beliefs, and worldviews of "different" students. Thus, educators have emphasized models that are sensitive to the "cultures in the classroom"—as reflected in the distinctive characteristics or patterns of groups defined by the race, ethnicity, language, social class, and gender of students and teachers. A sound definition of culture should also encompass both within-group variability and the classroom cultures that are socially created and shaped by the historically charged contexts of schools. We are referring to the classroom cultures that define what it takes to be competent, what counts as being articulate or smart, and the cultural capital required to navigate and use institutional resources for individual advancement (e.g., how to ask questions, how to negotiate course placement decisions with counselors, how to challenge authority in sanctioned ways, and so on). Klingner and Vaughn (1996) offer an example of research that enhances our understanding of within-group variability, in this case ELLs with LD.

Through use of a view of culture that accounts for classroom cultures and the cultures in the classroom (Gallego et al., 2001), the next generation of special education research will transcend dichotomies (e.g., is minority student low achievement due to cultural deprivation or cultural discontinuity?). We are arguing for a more fluid and instrumental view of culture in which students and teachers are not boxed in categorical identities (e.g., "poor Latino low-achieving student"). This means we need (a) intervention research that takes into account students' cultural toolkits as defined by both their group heritage and unique life histories and (b) descriptive inquiries that document how classroom cultures enhance or constrain the implementation of interventions in multicultural classrooms. This way, instructional research will not aim to identify the most effective model to teach English to ELLs. Instead, research questions will be concerned with the strategies and conditions that promote bilingualism and proficiency in multiple literacies across contexts (Artiles, 2002; Ruiz, 1995; Varenne & McDermott, 1999).

Map the Spaces of Practice: Focus on Processes and Outcomes Across Activity Systems

One consequence of using a multiparadigmatic approach to research is that studies conducted under controlled as well as naturalistic conditions will be carried out. Experimental research aims to map out the outcomes of alternative strategies for various groups of students under distinct conditions. The ultimate test of good experimental research is its application in the contexts where practitioners and families work and live. Such experimental findings, however, are used in schools where multiple and often-contradictory reforms exert pressure on administrators and school personnel to change their practices. For instance, many teachers are now required to use certain reading instructional approaches but without relying on students' native language. They are also expected to show improvement in learning outcomes as measured by standardized tests, and as they work in inclusive classrooms where more students with disabilities are placed.

This layering of reforms is having an impact on school practice, as many teachers are now required to spend an increasing amount of time preparing for high-stakes tests. This change in the allocation of time often comes at the expense of opportunity to learn subject matter, particularly in high-poverty schools that serve culturally diverse students. Other unfortunate consequences of the current reform climate include lower teacher morale and injury to student emotional well-being and cultural or linguistic identity. For example, in the months after Proposition 227 mandated elimination of bilingual programs in California,

teachers reported being completely confused because they didn't know if it was still legal to use the methods and materials they had always used. . . . We observed children's confusion about what language to use and why they could no longer use their primary language. Some older students worried that their teachers would be arrested for using Spanish in class and other children reported feeling sad and afraid about being in school. (Gutierrez et al., 2002, p. 331)

It is clear that the political dimension of education is most evident as reforms shape the daily practices and demands placed on teachers and administrators. In addition, minority students and their families come to schools with histories that position them in trajectories qualitatively and meaningfully different from those of White middle-class students. As Luis Moll recently suggested, "Propositions 227 and 203 weren't about bilingual education. They were about broader ideological and political concerns, especially in the context of the changing demographics" (cited in Gutierrez et al., 2002, p. 341). Current educational reforms and societal attitudes toward minorities have triggered dramatically disparate reactions to accommodate, resist, or assimilate the mandated changes depending on the particular sociopolitical realities of schools. Intervention and descriptive research cannot afford to ignore this reality. Future research needs to focus on the processes of intervention implementation as educators grapple with layering reforms that tend to differentially affect poor minority communities and families (Artiles, 1999). It is equally important to track minority student outcomes in ever-changing reform climates, particularly those placed in special education, for the literature suggests their outcomes are dismal: 73% of students with LD are involved in work or educational activities after high school, only 50% of students with E/BD are employed, dropout rates for students with LD and E/BD are staggering, and almost one-third of these two groups of students fail to graduate (Donovan & Cross, 2002).

Future research should also concentrate on documenting exemplary practices that beat the odds faced by poor minority students in school. Gutierrez et al. (2002) suggested that what people do to improve the schooling of culturally and linguistically diverse students is not only the result of artful implementation of educational interventions; "it's [also] a political achievement" (p. 338). Thus we must trace and understand better the conditions that nurture multiple literacies; the forces that counter the oppressive weight of subtractive schooling; and the cognitive, social, emotional, and political resources that allow a school to build a culture of trust between families, students, and personnel, increase academic achievement, and give students access to better postschool opportunities.

References

Abowitz, K. K. (2000). A pragmatist revisioning of resistance theory. *American Educational Research Journal, 37,* 877–907.

Advancement Project, & Civil Rights Project. (2000). *Opportunities suspended: The devastating consequences of zero tolerance and school discipline policies.* Cambridge, MA: Civil Rights Project, Harvard University. [On-line].Available: www.law.Harvard.edu/groups/civilrights/conferences/zero/zt_report2.html.

Akbar, N. (1985). Our destiny: Authors of a scientific revolution. In H. P. McAdoo & J. L. McAdoo (Eds.), *Black children: Social, educational, and parental environments* (pp. 17–31). Newbury Park, CA: Sage.

Anderson, M. G., & Webb-Johnson, G. (1995). Cultural contexts, the seriously emotionally disturbed classification, and African American learners. In B. A. Ford, F. E. Obiakor, & J. M. Patton

(Eds.), *Effective education of African American exceptional learners* (pp. 151–187). Austin, TX: Pro-ed.

Arreaga-Mayer, C., & Perdomo-Rivera, C. (1996). Ecobehavioral analysis of instruction for at-risk language minority students. *Elementary School Journal, 96,* 245–258.

Artiles, A. J. (1998). The dilemma of difference: Enriching the disproportionality discourse with theory and context. *Journal of Special Education, 32,* 32–36.

Artiles, A. J. (1999, October). *Toward a theory of teacher learning about diversity: Preliminary evidence from a novice teacher.* Paper presented at the National Academy of Education annual meeting's Fellows Forum, University of Pittsburgh.

Artiles, A. J. (2002). Culture in learning: The next frontier in reading difficulties research. In R. Bradley, L. Danielson, & D. P. Hallahan (Eds.), *Identification of learning disabilities: Research to policy* (pp. 693–701). Mahwah, NJ: Erlbaum.

Artiles, A. J. (2003). Special education's changing identity: Paradoxes and dilemmas in views of culture and space. *Harvard Educational Review, 73,* 164–202.

Artiles, A. J., & Ortiz, A. (Eds.). (2002). *English language learners with special needs: Identification, placement, and instruction.* Washington DC: Center for Applied Linguistics.

Artiles, A. J., Rueda, R., Salazar, I., & Higareda, J. (2000, November). *Factors associated with English learner representation in special education: Emerging evidence from urban school districts in California.* Paper presented at the Conference on Minority Issues in Special Education in Public Schools, Harvard University, Cambridge, MA.

Artiles, A. J., & Trent, S. C. (2000). Representation of culturally/linguistically diverse students. In C. R. Reynolds & E. Fletcher-Jantzen (Eds.), *Encyclopedia of special education, Vol. 1* (2nd ed., pp. 513–517). New York: Wiley.

Artiles, A. J., Trent, S. C., & Kuan, L. A. (1997). Learning disabilities empirical research on ethnic minority students: An analysis of 22 years of studies published in selected refereed journals. *Learning Disabilities Research and Practice, 12,* 82–91.

August, D., Calderón, M., & Carlo, M. (2000). *Transfer of skills from Spanish to English: A study of young learners: Report for practitioners, parents, and policymakers.* [On-line]. Available: www.cal.org/pubs/articles/skillstransfer.pdf.

August, D., & Hakuta, K. (1997). *Improving schooling for language-minority students: A research agenda.* Washington, DC: National Academy Press.

Byrd, H. B. (1995). Curricular and pedagogical procedures for African American learners with academic and cognitive disabilities. In B. A. Ford, F. E. Obiakor, & J. M. Patton (Eds.), *Effective education of African American exceptional learners* (pp. 123–150). Austin, TX: Pro-ed.

Chalfant, J., & Pysh, M. V. (1989). Teacher assistance teams: Five descriptive studies on 96 teams. *Remedial and Special Education, 10*(6), 49–58.

Chinn, P. C., & Hughes, S. (1987). Representation of minority students in special education classes. *Remedial and Special Education, 8*(4), 41–46.

Council for Exceptional Children (CEC). (1997, April 12). Resolution on disproportionate representation. *CEC Today, 5*(9). [On-line.] Available: www.cec.sped.org/bk/cectoday/1999/dispres_june99.html.

Council for Exceptional Children (CEC). (2002, January 17). *Need for funding and role of bias downplayed in new study on the over-identification of children from diverse backgrounds for special education.* [On-line]. Available: www.cec.sped.org/spotlight/cec_response/press_01–22–02.html.

Cummins, J. (1989). A theoretical framework for bilingual special education. *Exceptional Children, 56,* 111–119.

Delpit, L. (1995). *Other people's children: Cultural conflict in the classroom.* New York: New Press.

Diana v. State Board of Education, Civil Action No. C-7037RFP (N. D. Cal. Jan. 7, 1970, June 18, 1973).

Donovan, S., & Cross, C. (Eds.). (2002). *Minority students in special and gifted education.* Washington, DC: National Academy Press.

Dunn, L. (1968). Special education for the mildly retarded: Is much of it justifiable? *Exceptional Children, 35,* 5–22.

Engeström, Y. (1999). Activity theory and individual and social transformation. In Y. Engeström, R. Miettinen, & R. Punamaki (Eds.), *Perspectives on activity theory* (pp. 19–36). New York: Cambridge University Press.

Englert, C. S., Raphael, T. E., & Mariage, T. V. (1998). A multi-year literacy intervention: Transformation and personal change in the community of the Early Literacy Project. *Teacher Education and Special Education, 21,* 255–277.

Feuerstein, R. (1979). *The dynamic assessment of retarded performers: The learning potential assessment device, theory, instruments, and techniques.* Baltimore: University Park Press.

Finn, J. D. (1982). Patterns in special education placement as revealed by the OCR surveys. In K. A. Heller, W. H. Holtzman, & S. Messick (Eds.), *Placing children in special education: A strategy for equity* (pp. 322–381). Washington, DC: National Academy Press.

Fletcher, T. V., Bos, C. S., & Johnson, L. M. (1999). Accommodating English language learners with language and learning disabilities in bilingual education classrooms. *Learning Disabilities Research and Practice, 14,* 80–91.

Gallego, M. A., Cole, M., & Laboratory of Comparative Human Cognition (LCHC). (2001). Classroom cultures and cultures in the classroom. In V. Richardson (Ed.), *Handbook of research on teaching* (4th ed., pp. 951–997). Washington, DC: American Educational Research Association.

García, G. E., & Pearson, P. D. (1994). Assessment and diversity. *Review of Research in Education, 20,* 337–391.

Gersten, R., & Baker, S. (2000a). The professional knowledge base on instructional practices that support cognitive growth for English-language learners. In R. Gersten, E. P. Schiller, & S. Vaughn (Eds.), *Contemporary special education research: Synthesis of the knowledge base on critical instructional issues* (pp. 31–79). Mahwah, NJ: Erlbaum.

Gersten, R., & Baker, S. (2000b). What we know about effective instructional practices for English-language learners. *Exceptional Children, 66,* 454–470.

Gersten, R., & Baker, S. (n.d.). *Practices for English-language learners: An overview of instructional practices for English-language learners: Prominent themes and future directions.* National Institute for Urban School Improvement Topical Summary. [On-line]. Available: www.edc.org/urban/topical/ts_eng.pdf.

Gersten, R., Baker, S., Pugach, M., Scanlon, D., & Chard, D. (2001). Contemporary research on special education teaching. In V. Richardson (Ed.), *Handbook of research on teaching* (4th ed., pp. 695–722). Washington, DC: American Educational Research Association.

Gutierrez, K., Asato, J., Pacheco, M., Moll, L. C., Olson, K., Horng, E. L., et al. (2002). "Sounding American": The consequences of new reforms on English language learners. *Reading Research Quarterly, 37*(3), 328–343.

Gutierrez, K., & Stone, L. D. (1997). A cultural-historical view of learning and learning disabilities: Participating in a community of learners. *Learning Disabilities Research & Practice, 12,* 123–131.

Hallahan, D. P., & Kauffman, J. M. (2000). *Exceptional learners: Introduction to special education* (8th ed.). Boston: Allyn and Bacon.

Harry, B., Allen, N., & McLaughlin, M. (1996). "Old-fashioned, good teachers": African American parents' views of effective early instruction. *Learning Disabilities Research & Practice, 11,* 193–201.

Harry, B., Rueda, R., & Kalyanpur, M. A. (1999). Cultural reciprocity in sociocultural perspective: Adapting the normalization principle for family collaboration. *Exceptional Children, 66,* 123–136.

Heath, S. B. (1983). *Ways with words: Language, life and work in communities and classrooms.* Cambridge, England: Cambridge University Press.

Hehir, T. (2000, November). *IDEA and disproportionality: Federal enforcement, strategies for change.* Paper presented at the Conference on Minority Issues in Special Education in Public Schools, Harvard University, Cambridge, MA.

Heller, K. A., Holtzman, W. H., & Messick, S. (Eds.). (1982). *Placing children in special education: A strategy for equity.* Washington, DC: National Academy Press.

Heubert, J. P. (2000, November). *High-stakes testing: Opportunities and risks for students of color, English-language learners, and students with disabilities.* Paper presented at the Conference on Minority Issues in Special Education in Public Schools, Harvard University, Cambridge, MA.

Hilliard, A. G. III. (1992). Behavioral style, culture, and teaching and learning. *Journal of Negro Education, 61*(3), 370–377.

Hunt, N., & Marshall, K. (2002). *Exceptional children and youth* (3rd ed.). New York: Houghton Mifflin.

Individuals with Disabilities Education Act Amendments of 1997, P.L. 105–17, 105th 10 Cong., 1st Sess. (1997).

Kalyanpur, M., Harry, B., & Skrtic, T. (2000). Equity and advocacy expectations of culturally diverse families' participation in special education. *International Journal of Disability, Development and Education, 47*(2), 119–136.

Keulen, J. E., Weddington, G. T., & DeBose, C. E. (1998). *Speech, language, learning, and the African American child.* Boston: Allyn and Bacon.

Kirk, S. A., Gallagher, J. J., & Anastasiow, N. J. (2000). *Educating exceptional children* (3rd ed.). New York: Houghton Mifflin.

Klingner, J. K., & Vaughn, S. (1996). Reciprocal teaching of reading comprehension strategies for students with learning disabilities who use English as a second language. *Elementary School Journal, 96,* 275–293.

Kozol, J. (1991). *Savage inequalities: Children in America's schools.* New York: Crown.

Ladson-Billings, G. (1995). Toward a theory of culturally relevant pedagogy. *American Educational Research Journal, 32,* 465–491.

Larry P. v. Riles. (1979). C-71–2270, FRP Dist. Ct.

Lazerson, M. (1983). The origins of special education. In J. G. Chambers & W. T. Hartman (Eds.), *Special education policies: Their history, implementation, and finance* (pp. 15–47). Philadelphia: Temple University Press.

Marston, D. B. (1989). A curriculum-based measurement approach to assessing academic performance: What it is and why do it. In

M. R. Shinn (Ed.), *Curriculum-based measurement: Assessing special children* (pp. 18–78). New York: Guilford.

McLoyd, V. C. (1998). Socioeconomic disadvantage and child development. *American Psychologist, 53,* 185–204.

Mehan, H., Hartwick, A., & Meihls, J. L. (1986). *Handicapping the handicapped: Decision-making in students' educational careers.* Stanford, CA: Stanford University Press.

Minow, M. (1990). *Making all the difference: Inclusion, exclusion, and American law.* Ithaca, NY: Cornell University Press.

Ortiz, A. A. (1997). Learning disabilities occurring concomitantly with linguistic differences. *Journal of Learning Disabilities, 30,* 321–332.

Oswald, D. P., Coutinho, M. J., & Best, A. M. (2000, November). *Community and school predictors of overrepresentation of minority children in special education.* Paper presented at the Conference on Minority Issues in Special Education in Public Schools, Harvard University, Cambridge, MA.

Parrish, T. (2000, November). *Disparities in the identification, funding, and provision of special education.* Paper presented at the Conference on Minority Issues in Special Education in Public Schools, Harvard University, Cambridge, MA.

Patton, J. M. (1998). The disproportionate representation of African Americans in special education: Looking behind the curtain for understanding and solutions. *Journal of Special Education, 32,* 25–31.

Pennsylvania Association for Retarded Citizens (PARC) v. Commonwealth of Pennsylvania. (1972). 343 F., Supp. 279.

Podemski, R. S., Marsh, G. E., II, Smith, T.E.C., & Price, B. J. (1995). *Comprehensive administration of special education* (2nd ed.). Englewood Cliffs, NJ: Prentice-Hall.

Reschly, D. J. (1997). *Disproportionate minority representation in general and special education: Patterns, issues, and alternatives.* Des Moines: Iowa Department of Education.

Reschly, D. J., Kicklighter, R., & McKee, P. (1988). Recent placement litigation, part III: Analysis of differences in Larry P., Marshall and S-1 and implications for future practices. *School Psychology Review, 17,* 39–50.

Ruiz, N. T. (1995). The social construction of ability and disability: II. Optimal and at-risk lessons in bilingual special education classrooms. *Journal of Learning Disabilities, 28,* 491–502.

Skiba, R. J., Wu, T. C., Kohler, K., Chung, C., & Simmons, A. B. (2001). *Disproportionality and discipline among Indiana's students with disabilities.* Status report to the Indiana Department of Education Division of Special Education. Bloomington: Indiana University, Indiana Education Policy Center.

Slavin, R. E., Madden, N. A., & Karweit, N. L. (1989). Effective programs for students at risk: Conclusions for practice and policy. In R. E. Slavin, N. L. Karweit, & N. A. Nadden (Eds.), *Effective programs for students at risk* (pp. 355–372). Boston: Allyn and Bacon.

Sleeter, C. (2001). An analysis of the critiques of multicultural education. In J. A. Banks and C.A.M. Banks (Eds.), *Handbook of research on multicultural education* (1st ed., pp. 81–94). San Francisco: Jossey-Bass.

Smith, D. D. (2000). *Introduction to special education: Teaching in an age of opportunity* (4th ed.). Boston: Allyn & Bacon.

Smitherman, G. (1998). Black English/Ebonics: What it be like? In T. Perry & L. Delpit (Eds.), *The real Ebonics debate: Power, language, and the education of African-American children* (pp. 29–37). Boston: Beacon Press.

Snow, C. E., Burns, M. S., & Griffin, P. (Eds.). (1998). *Preventing reading difficulties in young children.* Washington, DC: National Academy Press.

Thurlow, M. L., & Liu, K. K. (2000, November). *State and district assessment as an avenue to equity and excellence for English language learners with disabilities.* Paper presented at the Conference on Minority Issues in Special Education in Public Schools, Harvard University, Cambridge, MA.

Trent, S. C., Artiles, A. J., & Englert, C. S. (1998). From deficit thinking to social constructivism: A review of special education theory, research and practice. *Review of Research in Education, 23,* 277–307.

Trent, S. C., Artiles, A. J., Fitchett-Bazemore, K., McDaniel, L., & Coleman-Sorrell, A. (2002). Addressing theory, ethics, power, and privilege in inclusion research and practice. *Teacher Education and Special Education, 25,* 11–22.

Tyack, D., & Hansot, E. (1984). Hard times, then and now: Public schools in the 1930s and 1980s. *Harvard Educational Review, 54,* 34–67.

U.S. Census Bureau. (2000a). *Foreign-born population by world region of birth, citizenship and year of entry.* [On-line]. Available: www.census.gov/population/socdemo/foreign/p20–534/ tab0206.pdf.

U.S. Census Bureau. (2000b). *Overview of race and Hispanic origin 2000.* [On-line]. Available: www.census.gov/prod/ 2001pubs/c2kbr01–1.pdf.

U.S. Department of Commerce, Bureau of the Census. (1972–1998). *Current Population Survey, 1972–1998.* [On-line]. Available: http://nces.ed.gov/pubs2000/coe2000/section1/s_table4_1.html.

Valdés, G., & Figueroa, R. (1994). *Bilingualism and testing: A special case of bias.* Norwood, NJ: Ablex.

Varenne, H., & McDermott, R. (Eds.). (1999). *Successful failure: The school America builds.* Boulder, CO: Westview Press.

Yell, M. L. (1998). *The law and special education.* Englewood Cliffs, NJ: Prentice-Hall.

35

EQUITY IN HETEROGENEOUS CLASSROOMS

Elizabeth G. Cohen
Stanford University

Rachel A. Lotan
Stanford University

Multilingual, multicultural, multiethnic classrooms are here to stay. They are not a passing phenomenon. These are frequently classrooms where students have wide-ranging academic achievement and differing levels of English proficiency. Unless strong steps are taken, such academic and linguistic heterogeneity can result in serious inequity for students. Traditional methods of teaching consign some students to failure, and to the perception that they are intellectually incompetent.

The multicultural classroom should be an equitable classroom. This chapter takes the position that fundamental change of the social system of the classroom can produce a more equitable situation where each student makes valued intellectual contributions and where teachers intervene to overcome status differences that impede learning. Teachers must find ways to provide access to intellectually challenging instruction and grade-appropriate curriculum for all students.

The first section of the chapter begins with a brief documentation of the increasing diversity of American classrooms. Following this demographic analysis is a discussion of the special problems teachers face in adapting instruction for heterogeneous classes. The second section of the chapter, after defining *equitable classroom*, introduces the dimensions of the social system of the classroom. These dimensions are used to describe how teachers and students function in an equitable classroom. The third section opens with an analysis of status problems in the multicultural classroom along with a summary of research evidence on the consequences of status problems for learning outcomes. Following is the theoretical background necessary for understanding the occurrence of status problems in the classroom. This section

concludes with theory and research evidence concerning how traditional task and evaluation structures in the classroom help to create a hierarchy of perceived intellectual competence.

The fourth and fifth sections include detailed evidence on how teachers can transform the social system and create equitable classrooms. The fourth section describes and documents how teachers have been able to change expectations for competence so that interaction in small groups of students is closer to "equal status." In the fifth section are the required changes in the role of the teacher and the interaction among the students, the learning tasks, and the evaluation practices. The final section contrasts our approach to the diverse classroom with the approach based on individual differences and the goal of meeting individual needs. Recommendations for future research and for current multicultural practice conclude the chapter.

INCREASING CLASSROOM DIVERSITY

The demography of the school population of the United States reflects greater diversity than ever before. According to the most recent census data, 35% of U.S. children are members of minority groups and 20% come from a household headed by immigrants ("Children of Change," 2000). Orfield and Yun (1999) report that there are already five states (notably California and Texas) where the majority of all public school students are from minority backgrounds. Although the minority population will remain concentrated in a handful of states, demographers predict that all but two states will see an increase in minority enrollment between now and 2015 ("Children of Change"). The flow of immigrants and new ethnic groups across the country will produce marked changes in the student enrollment of many school districts. A special tabulation of census data in the same issue of *Education Week* shows 1,485 counties with an increase in minority enrollment greater than 30% between 1990 and 1998.

Along with this demographic change has come an increase in ethnic and racial segregation of schools and classrooms (Orfield & Yun, 1999). Despite this worrisome trend, the sheer size of the minority school population and the current tendency for that population to move into new areas of the country mean that a relatively high percentage of U.S. classrooms have a mix of racial and ethnic groups. An examination of the Common Core of Data (National Center for Educational Statistics, 2001) for the 1999–2000 school year shows that in 39% of all U.S. public schools the population of second graders represents three or more minority groups. In this analysis, minority groups are defined as Blacks, Hispanics, Asian and Pacific Islanders, and American Indians. Moving to the third-grade population, the percentage of multiracial/multiethnic schools (using the same definition) is 40%. A further analysis shows that in 25% of all schools, 20–60% of second and third graders are from minority backgrounds. In other words, a quarter of these schools are diverse rather than segregated.

The focus of this chapter is on these multiracial, multiethnic classrooms rather than on segregated classrooms. The issue of diversity in the classroom is also a pressing one for Europe, Canada, and Australia. Ethnic groups are on the move all over the world. There is also racial diversity because residents of former colonies have moved to countries that used to be colonizers.

Racially and ethnically diverse classrooms are not necessarily economically diverse. In addition to problems of linguistic and racial segregation, the United States also faces serious problems of economic segregation of schools. Areas such as inner cities where most people are poor are also areas where new immigrants, Latinos, Southeast Asians, and African Americans live in the same school district. Suburbs where many central-city families have migrated, looking for safer conditions and better schools, ring the great cities. Today, many of these suburban areas are also relatively poor and have great ethnic diversity. Thus diverse classrooms are frequently made up of students from families who face poverty and who struggle to make ends meet. Missing from many of these classrooms are children of highly educated parents who are well versed in academic language and who know how to respond to academic requirements.

Teachers of diverse classrooms must address differences in students' linguistic, cultural, and educational backgrounds as well as foster positive intergroup relations. Beyond these challenges, they face the difficult problem of choosing a suitable technology of teaching. If they assume that their students only need to acquire basic skills through routine drill, they will deprive these students of grade-appropriate content and the chance to move up the educational ladder. In this case, students will not be prepared for higher education and better jobs. If teachers maintain high standards and use reading and discussion focused on conceptual learning, they run the risk of losing many of the students who cannot understand the textbooks and are not proficient in English. The necessity of working with diversity is inseparable from the necessity to present intellectually challenging and grade-appropriate content in such a way that students experience academic success.

THE EQUITABLE CLASSROOM

Creating equitable classrooms for multicultural school populations is a fundamental educational goal. Students should not only appreciate the differing perspectives and cultures of their classmates but also feel that they are on an equal footing with each other intellectually and academically. There are a number of key features of an equitable classroom. First, teachers and students view each student as capable of learning both basic skills and high-level concepts. All students have equal access to challenging learning materials; the teacher does not deprive certain students of tasks demanding higher-order thinking because they are perceived as "not ready"; classmates readily share instructional materials and give others a chance to use such tools as Cuisenaire rods, computers, or laboratory equipment. Teachers create opportunities for students who do not read at grade level or understand the language of instruction to complete activities and use materials. Secondly, the interaction among students is equal-status, that is, all students are active and influential participants and their opinions matter to their fellow students. Finally, despite wide variation in previous academic achievement, the instruction in an equitable classroom does not produce comparable variation in learning outcomes among the students. Although the more academically successful students continue to do well, the less successful students are closely clustered around the mean achievement of the classroom rather than trailing far out on the failing end of the distribution. Thus there is a higher mean and a lower variance of achievement scores in a more equitable classroom than in a less equitable classroom.

THE CLASSROOM AS A SOCIAL SYSTEM

The sociologist views the classroom as a social system rather than a collection of individuals with their own backgrounds and needs. Dimensions of that system include how teachers use their authority, how they organize the class for work, how they evaluate students, and how students perceive and rank each other on academic ability and popularity.

In the social system of an equitable classroom, the roles of teachers and students as well as the nature of learning tasks and evaluation methods are fundamentally different from those of the traditional classroom. In addition to the traditional role of direct supervision, the teacher knows how to delegate authority to groups of students while holding them accountable. Students talk and work together, treating each other as academic and linguistic resources for learning. Learning tasks require creative problem solving and a range of human intellectual abilities. Interaction among students is equal-status; the work in groups is not dominated by certain students, and everyone participates. The evaluation system works so that students know the criteria used to evaluate their work in groups and their individual products. Because of this knowledge, they are able to discuss their group products in a self-critical manner while focusing on the academic content of their group activities. Once these basic changes have occurred, internal mechanisms keep them functioning, so that classrooms do not require constant intervention and "treatment."

STATUS PROBLEMS IN THE HETEROGENEOUS CLASSROOM

The culturally and linguistically diverse classroom is at risk of developing serious inequities on the basis of difference in student status. A range of previous academic achievement makes it very likely that students will form a social ranking that is based on the academic ability they perceive each other to have (Cohen, Lotan, & Leechor, 1989). New immigrants arrive with variable schooling experience, leading to variation in the academic skills of reading, writing, and computation. Students whose parents have little formal education often have difficulty with schoolwork, since the parents are less likely to prepare their children for school by reading books to them, teaching them numbers and letters, and speaking standard English at home. These differences in preliteracy activity, in use of standard English, and in knowledge of academic discourse lead to differences in academic success. Some students have attended preschool while many have not; formal preschool experience is also a strong predictor of

early academic success (Duncan, & Brooks-Gunn, 2001). Because the central task of the classroom in a low-income area is teaching basic skills, there is a narrow definition of what it means to do well in school. Initial differences among the students in family background and preschool experience all too quickly convert into performance differentials in basic skills and a strong status order in which students rank each other on intellectual ability, using perceived achievement in basic skills as an indicator.

Once these status orders have formed, they have negative consequences for behavior and learning. For example, when the teacher uses small groups for cooperative learning, those children who are seen as having high academic status will do much more talking and their opinions will count more heavily than those children who are seen as having low status (Cohen, 1997). Some of these high-status students will actually take over the small-group tasks, telling everyone what to do and insisting that only they have the right answers. In the meantime, low-status students will have a hard time voicing their opinions and persuading the rest of the group to even listen to them or let them have access to the learning materials given to the group.

Many teachers are distressed to observe that newcomers and some minority students are virtual nonparticipants in the group. This is not what they hoped would be the outcome of cooperative learning. They intended that students would learn, from the group experience, that each of their classmates has something worthwhile to contribute to the discussion.

Consequences for Learning

When teachers use cooperative learning techniques, there are many excellent results in terms of academic achievement, trust, and interracial friendliness. Students in cooperative groups perform better than students working alone or in a competitively structured classroom (Johnson & Johnson, 1990). According to Slavin's (2001) review of research, when students work in ethnically mixed cooperative-learning groups, they gain in cross-ethnic friendships. Moreover, the effects are long lasting. However, if difference in status causes some students to fail to participate, that reduced rate of interaction affects learning outcomes. Access to interaction is critical in a classroom featuring cooperative learning.

Cohen and Lotan, along with their colleagues, have developed a model of cooperative learning that specifically treats problems arising from status difference. This model is called "complex instruction." In classrooms using complex instruction, they have carried out studies on the relationship of status, interaction in small groups, and learning (Cohen & Lotan, 1997b). As in all classrooms using complex instruction, the groupwork task was one requiring that students exchange ideas and information to arrive at a group product. The groups were not given a task that is usually assigned to individuals and told to help each other arrive at correct answers. Instead, they worked on what is called a true group task, a task that one person could not easily carry out unassisted.

Studies of these true group tasks consistently find that *the more students talk and work together, the greater are their learning gains.* This proposition holds at the elementary and middle school levels and for a variety of subject matters. At the elementary school level, the more students in a classroom talked and worked together, the higher were their gains on a standardized achievement test in mathematics ($r = .72$, $p < .05$ for 1982–83, and $r = .52$, $p < .05$ for 1984–85; Cohen, Lotan, & Holthuis, 1997). At the middle school level, the higher the percentage of students talking and working together, the greater were the gain scores on a social studies test ($r = .50$; $p < .01$). In a study of 56 students in sixth-grade science classes (Bianchini, 1995), the correlation between the average rate of talk and a gain score summed over several unit tests was $r = .453$ ($p < .001$). A most dramatic finding comes from Israel, where Ben-Ari (1997) showed that the process of students talking and working together on challenging group tasks led to significant gains on a standardized test of reasoning.

These findings are at the classroom level, but the relationship between interaction and achievement also holds at the individual level. Leechor (1988) assessed the effects that talking with peers has on individual learning in elementary school. He found that the student's average rate of task-related talk in the group was a significant predictor of posttest score, holding constant pretest score and student status.

Explaining How and Why Status Problems Occur

Why do some students dominate small groups while others barely participate? It is not enough to say, "Well, that's because of status problems." Giving something a name is not really the same as a sound explanation of the source of these behavioral differences among group members and an understanding of the process that produces differences in prominence within the small group.

Berger, Cohen, and Zelditch (1966, 1972) have developed a theory of status characteristics explaining this phenomenon, a theory that has proved very useful in developing ways to produce more equal-status behavior in the classroom. According to this theory, the observed difficulty starts with differences in status characteristics that are socially perceived rankings, where everyone feels that it is better to have a high rank than a low rank. The multicultural, multiracial classroom contains many potential status characteristics, among them race, social class,

proficiency in English, and gender. Beyond these more general or "diffuse status characteristics," there are also local status characteristics peculiar to the classroom, such as academic and peer status. Academic status has already been introduced; equally important in the classroom is peer status, or the relative popularity of students. In addition, there are also specific status characteristics in classrooms such as being good with computers or being able to calculate numbers rapidly. Their effect on the behavior of group members is similar to the effect of other kinds of status characteristics described earlier. Because most situations involve differences on multiple status characteristics, one cannot, in advance of knowing the composition of the group in which a person is working, decide that someone is inherently a high-status or low-status person. The very same person may be high-status in one situation and low-status in another.

Such differences among students would not present a problem were it not for the differing expectations of competence that are attached to being high and low on the status characteristic. Most familiar are the differences in expectations attached to race and gender. These are often referred to as racist or sexist beliefs, whereby some people think that Whites and males are more intelligent than Blacks or females. What is not so obvious is that there are parallel expectations for competence at a range of tasks attached to having high academic status or high peer status in a classroom.

When the teacher (or anyone else) composes a group of students who differ on one or more of these characteristics and gives that group a task where they must work together, the stage is set for differential expectations for competence to spread to the new task. *Status generalization* (Berger, Cohen, & Zelditch, 1966, 1972) is the process by which status characteristics affect interaction and influence so that the prestige and power order of the group reflects the initial differences in status. (For a full description of this process, see Berger, Rosenholtz, & Zelditch, 1980.) Those students who are high on one or more of the status characteristics are expected to be more competent at the new cooperative assignment, while those who are low on the status characteristic(s) are expected to be less competent. In other words, expectations that were initially attached to differences in status become the basis for expectations for competence at the new task, *even when there is no rational basis* for expecting these particular students to excel at the new task. Once the expectations are in place, different behaviors occur. Those who are high status talk more than those who are low status. Moreover, group members find what high-status members have to say more important than what low-status members say. A self-fulfilling prophecy takes place in which those who were initially expected to be more competent become more active and influential and are seen by all members of the group as having had better ideas and as having done more to guide the group. Those who were expected to be less competent participate less, and when they do speak up people tend not to listen to them; they are regarded as having few important ideas and as having done little to guide the group.

In the classroom, the most important status characteristics are academic and peer status or popularity. Classroom studies at the elementary, middle school, and secondary school level have demonstrated that students who are higher on a combined measure of academic and peer status participate significantly more in small groups than students of lower status (Bower, 1997; Cohen, 1997). In analyzing the data on social background, academic and peer status, and participation in task groups, once academic and peer status are taken into account, one finds that the fact that some students are also of a low-status group in the larger society (such as being Black, Brown, or female) may not contribute anything additional to predicting participation (Lloyd & Cohen, 1999). Yet diffuse status characteristics such as race and ethnicity have repeatedly shown strong effects on participation in laboratory groups (Cohen, 1982).

Many educators and social scientists focus so strongly on race and ethnicity that they find it difficult to believe these are not the major predictors of behavior in the classroom. Teachers often assume that characteristics such as darkness of skin color, proficiency in English, or recent immigration are the most important sources of status difference among the students. Because the classroom is a powerful social system, it has the power to create status orders that are more directly relevant to the classroom situation. Status orders such as academic and peer status (popularity) can be much stronger than race, ethnicity, and recent immigration in affecting behavior in groups. Thus teachers should not assume that newcomers or children of color will have low social status among their classmates. The consequences of such an assumption may be lowered expectations for competence held by the teacher for children from these backgrounds.

Diffuse status characteristics such as social class, race, and ethnicity are often closely correlated with local status characteristics such as academic status, and sometimes with peer status. For example, children of migrant laborers are often stigmatized and isolated so that they have low peer status. They also hold low academic status because of the lack of formal education of their parents. Also, their itinerant lifestyle makes it difficult for them to be highly successful in school. In multiracial classrooms, students of color are often very popular and have high peer status. Because members of the group combine all the status information in forming expectations for competence at the new cooperative task, the positive effects of student popularity act to cancel out negative effects of

low academic status (Humphreys & Berger, 1981). When all the positive and negative factors are combined, classroom status orders frequently do not present a mirror image of status orders of the society at large.

When there are multiple status characteristics, as in the case of a heterogeneous classroom, the statuses most relevant to the task have the greatest weight. For example, if the task is technology-based, those students who are high on the specific status characteristic of expertise with computers dominate the group gathered around the computer. Because this specific status characteristic is highly relevant to the task at hand, it has more weight than any other status characteristic in determining behavior in the group. Academic status is highly relevant for any school-type task. This is especially so because ability at schoolwork is seen as unidimensional (ranging from "smart" to "dumb") rather than made up of many specific abilities. As a result, students do not view each other as being good at some important skills and less skilled at other tasks. Instead, they expect students with high academic status to be good at all school tasks. Even when the new task is something like creating a role-play or building a model and is not directly linked to traditional academic skills, those with high academic status are expected to be more competent. Even less rational is the expectation that the most popular student in the group will automatically be the most knowledgeable.

Determination of who is high-status and low-status always depends on the status of other people in the group. Therefore, being low-status is a relative, not an absolute, characteristic of a student in a given classroom. If the group contains the highest-status student in the classroom, then a student who is in the middle of the rank order on academic status can be a low-status actor (Lloyd & Cohen, 1999; Rosenholtz, 1985). If a student holds low status in the group, it is very important to understand that this is not a personality characteristic that will appear in all situations. The same student could act otherwise in a differently composed group or in groups with another type of task. There is no substitute for teachers observing groups freshly and carefully, without preconceptions based on race or language, to see who is behaving as a low-status actor.

How Classrooms Create an Academic Status Order

How does academic status order arise in the classroom? There is an important connection between how the teacher organizes the classroom and evaluates students and the development of a strong status order based on perceived differences in ability. The task and evaluation practices in many classrooms help to build inequity through a process of social comparison through which students see each other arrayed on a single dimension of ability in schoolwork. Social comparison shapes students' ideas about where they stand on the dimension of ability (Rosenholtz & Simpson, 1984). Students compare themselves to each other as they complete tasks and when they hear the teacher make public evaluations. The net result of this process of social comparison is an agreed-upon rank order by teachers and students as to the relative "smartness" of each member of the class.

In classrooms where opportunities for social comparison are common, students show a high level of agreement with each other and with the teacher regarding who belongs where in the rank order of perceived academic ability (Rosenholtz & Wilson, 1980; Simpson, 1981). According to Rosenholtz and Simpson (1984), intellectual ability is a socially constructed concept. A high level of agreement on each person's "ability" within a class indicates a consensual judgment arising from joint experiences in the classroom.

In studying the features of the classroom that create an agreed-upon ranking on ability, Rosenholtz and Simpson (1984) stressed the "dimensionality" of classroom organization. Unidimensional organization of instruction establishes conditions that facilitate "ability formation." In a unidimensional classroom, daily activities encourage comparison and they imply a single underlying dimension of ability. The first feature of the unidimensional classroom is an undifferentiated task structure. All students work on similar tasks, or with a narrow range of materials and methods. For example, the unidimensional class requires reading for successful performance on most tasks and relies mostly on paper-and-pencil tasks. This task structure facilitates social comparison; students can easily tell how well they are doing in comparison to others.

A second feature of the unidimensional classroom is a low level of student autonomy and little variety in tasks. If students have few choices as to what tasks they carry out and how to carry out those tasks, they must rely only on the teacher's evaluations. Third, the unidimensional classroom uses whole-class instruction or clear-cut ability groups. Either of these most common ways of organizing the classroom makes one's relative standing very clear. In whole-class instruction, the teacher's evaluation of recitation makes all of one's mistakes public knowledge. Fourth, a unidimensional class relies on competitive marking and grading as the major method of evaluation and the principal source of feedback to the students.

In contrast, the multidimensional classroom has varied materials and methods, a higher degree of student autonomy, more individual tasks, varied grouping patterns, and less reliance on grading. Examples of a multidimensional task structure are multiple learning centers each with its own tasks, or small groups of students working on various projects, or even an individualized classroom where students work on very different tasks.

In a comparison of these two classroom types, researchers found that students' self-reported ability levels were more widely dispersed in unidimensional classrooms (Rosenholtz & Rosenholtz, 1981; Simpson, 1981). In unidimensional classrooms, there were more students who ranked themselves below average, whereas in multidimensional classrooms most students ranked themselves average or above, thus restricting the distribution of self-evaluations. In other words, the self-rankings were more tightly clustered in the multidimensional classrooms and more spread out in the unidimensional classrooms. Student reports of their peers' ability levels were also more dispersed in unidimensional classes. Moreover, students agreed much more closely on ranks in the unidimensional classroom, and their self-ratings were much more in line with ratings by peers and the teacher.

Classroom tasks affect not only ranking on academic ability but also rankings on popularity and desirability as a friend. In studies of friendship choices, many classrooms exhibit an unequal number of choices: a few "sociometric stars" receive many choices while most of the other children receive few choices, and a significant number of students are social isolates, receiving no choices. Sociometric studies of the 1950s and 1960s claimed that this pattern was universal for elementary children. When students have more opportunity to walk around, talk with others, choose seats and activities, and work in small groups, the pattern of peer status changes (Cohen, 1994b; Epstein & Karweit, 1983; Hallinan, 1976). There is a less hierarchical distribution of choices and fewer social isolates and sociometric stars. In ethnically diverse fourth-grade classrooms, Plank (2000) found that those classrooms with a narrow range of academic tasks and reward structure had much more hierarchical distribution of peer choices, with many more social isolates. In review, this body of research shows how the choice of classroom tasks and how the teacher evaluates and rewards students helps to create academic and peer status orders in the classroom. Once they are created, the undesirable effects of status generalization on participation, effort, and learning follow.

CHANGING EXPECTATIONS FOR COMPETENCE

Using status characteristic theory, it has been possible to derive, develop, and test classroom interventions designed to improve expectations for competence for low-status students. Teachers can modify status processes by altering the expectations for competence that students hold for themselves, as well as the expectations that students hold for one another. "Status treatment" is the shorthand term for an intervention designed to create equal-status interaction. Two status treatments have proved effective and are widely implemented: the multiple ability treatment and assigning competence to low-status students (Cohen & Lotan, 1997a).

Multiple Ability Treatment

One way to minimize the problem of unequal access and learning for low-status students is to broaden the conception of what it means to be smart. The multiple ability treatment requires the teacher's public recognition of a wealth of intellectual abilities that are relevant and valued in the classroom and in daily life. Rather than assuming that all students can be ranked along a single dimension of intelligence, the multiple ability treatment highlights specific skills and abilities that students need for their particular tasks. Each student has personal strengths and weaknesses among these multiple abilities. For example, the highly verbal student may have difficulty with tasks that require spatial and visual competence. Likewise, the student who scores poorly on a vocabulary test may be an astute scientific observer. This view of ability is compatible with work in psychology that views intelligence as multidimensional (Gardner, 1983; Sternberg, 1985, 1998).

A multiple ability treatment typically occurs during orientation to the day's work in groups. The teacher starts by naming the skills and abilities necessary for successful completion of an activity and then explains the relevance of these abilities to the tasks assigned to the groups. An effective multiple ability treatment convinces students that the tasks they are about to undertake are fundamentally different from traditional classroom tasks because they rely on many kinds of intellectual ability. For example, a teacher introducing a complex instruction unit on the concept of the afterlife in ancient Egypt might say, "Let me remind you that for these activities you need many abilities. You will read, write, sing, and draw. You need to be able to analyze the pictures and have the ability to visualize what the ancient gods were like. Finally, you will need to be imaginative to build a three-dimensional model of a tomb."

The next step in the treatment is to create a mixed set of expectations for each student. It is essential that each student perceive that he or she will be strong on some of the abilities and weaker on others. A successful treatment never omits this statement: "Remember—no one of us has all these abilities, but each one of us has some of the abilities we will need today." Herein lies a central premise of creating equal-status interaction: each individual brings valuable and differing abilities to the task. For the group to be successful, all members must contribute.

Theoretically, this treatment works because the teacher has helped the students understand there are a number of specific status characteristics that are directly relevant to the task they are about to undertake. As was already explained, specific status characteristics, such as the ability to observe and compare, work the same way as academic status or race. Those students who are felt to rank highly on this ability will be more active and influential on all aspects of the task than those who are not ranked so highly. By breaking up the task so that students perceive that there are many relevant abilities, the teacher breaks up the assumption that only general academic status or a student's relative popularity predicts competence at this task. Further, telling students that no one is good at all of these abilities but that everyone is good on at least one means that each student has a mixed set of expectations for competence rather than uniformly high or uniformly low expectations. Because the teacher has pointed to specific status characteristics that are directly relevant to the task at hand, they will be stronger than academic or peer status characteristics. The new mixed set of expectations softens the effects of a person's standing on academic, peer status, racial, or ethnic status. The net effect is improved participation and performance on the new task by low-status students.

Assigning Competence to Low-Status Students

Assigning competence is a public statement that specifically recognizes the intellectual contribution a student has made to the group. Teachers can assign competence to any student, but it is especially important and effective to focus attention on those who are behaving as low-status students within their group. Teachers must first identify who is acting as a low-status member. Then they must watch for important intellectual contributions by low-status members to the group.

Assigning competence is a positive, truthful evaluation. Theoretically, the teacher has assigned the low-status student a high state on a specific status characteristic. This treatment derives from status characteristics theory and from source theory (Webster & Sobieszek, 1974). In the language of source theory, the higher the status of an individual, the greater is the likelihood of that individual becoming a source of important evaluations. The high-status individual can thus influence one person's self-evaluation relative to another. If the teacher, as a high-status source, positively evaluates a student's performance, that student comes to believe that his or her ability is consistent with the teacher's evaluation.

To not only change the student's expectations for competence but also raise the group's expectations for the student, the teacher must assign competence publicly, so that both the student and the classmates hear it. Assigning competence must also be specific so that the student and the group know exactly what the student can do well. Finally, it must make the intellectual ability demonstrated by the student relevant to the work of the group. If the specific status characteristic is relevant to the work of the group, it has more power in raising the expectations for competence for the low-status student than the other status characteristics that caused the group to treat the student as a low-status individual. The group now expects that the formerly low-status student will have something to contribute. They make greater efforts to listen and find out what the student is thinking. (See Cohen, 1994c, for a videotape of teachers using the treatments.)

Candida Graves, a fourth-grade teacher of a bilingual classroom, describes what happened when she assigned competence to a low-status student:

One day I had a student named Juan. He was extremely quiet and hardly ever spoke. He was not particularly academically successful and didn't have a good school record. He had just been in the country for two or three years and spoke just enough English to be an LEP (limited English proficient) student. I didn't notice that he had many friends, but not many enemies either. Not that much attention was paid to him.

We were doing an activity that involved decimal points and I was going around and noticed he was the only one of his group that had all the right answers. I was able to say, "Juan! You have figured out all of this worksheet correctly. You understand how decimals work. You really understand that kind of notation. Can you explain it to your group? I'll be back in a minute to see how you did." And I left. I couldn't believe it; he was actually explaining it to all the others. I didn't have faith it was going to work, but in fact he explained it so well that all of the others understood it and were applying it to their worksheets. They were excited about it. So then I made it public among the whole class, and from then on they began calling him "the smart one." This spread to the area where he lived, and even today kids from there will come tell me about the smart one, Juan. I thought, "All of this started with a little intervention!" (Graves & Graves, 1991, p. 14)

In a study of 13 elementary schools, Cohen and Lotan (1995) found that status interventions boosted the participation of low-status students while not suppressing the contributions of high-status students. The more frequently the teacher used the multiple ability treatment and assigned competence to low-status students, the more the low-status students spoke up and were active in their groups. The overall status problems in such classrooms were observably weaker than in classrooms where teachers used these treatments less frequently. Research has shown the power of these newly assigned expectations for competence to transfer to new task situations (Berger, Rosenholtz, & Zelditch, 1980; Webster & Foschi, 1988). Therefore teachers do not have to assign competence repeatedly to the same students. The students themselves recognize the competence of their classmates on the previous task, and this new specific status characteristic affects their expectations for his or her competence on the next task.

TRANSFORMING THE CLASSROOM

In the equitable classroom, the teacher strives to change the students' expectations for each other's intellectual competence by using the interventions for status equalization already described. In addition, the teacher reorganizes the classroom in ways that allow students to recognize each other's critical contributions to the work of their group when the task calls for many abilities and skills. In an equitable classroom, students serve as academic and linguistic resources for one another as they work on intellectually challenging learning tasks, and the assessment of their products is sound and authentic. The next section addresses three aspects of the classroom that are important to consider when the goal is to change its traditional social structure: instructional strategies that affect student interactions and the role of the teacher, features of the learning tasks, and the evaluation of students' individual as well group products.

Instructional Strategies: Fostering Interaction Among Students

Cooperative learning is a central feature of an equitable classroom. Cooperative learning is a well-documented and highly recommended strategy for enhancing academic, cognitive, social, and attitudinal outcomes for students. As mentioned earlier, researchers have demonstrated that a cooperative learning group produces higher learning gains in basic academic skills as well as in conceptual understanding when compared to students in a traditional whole-class setting (Johnson & Johnson, 1990). Students who learn in a group also show enhanced social skills and improved intergroup relations (Slavin, 2001). Increasingly, educators and researchers are also interested in the potential for language development in linguistically heterogeneous classrooms that use cooperative learning strategies and that establish an authentic communicative context. For example, Wong Fillmore (1991) found that students who are English language learners showed growth in the language of instruction when they had the opportunity to interact with native or nativelike speakers and when they had access to a language-rich classroom environment.

A further challenge for English learners in linguistically heterogeneous, mainstream classrooms is the development of academic and subject-specific discourse as well as mastery of grade level content. Arellano (2002) conducted a study in a sixth-grade bilingual social studies classroom where the teacher used complex instruction, a specific model of small-group instruction. Arellano documented the processes by which students concurrently mastered the content of the social studies curriculum and developed their academic linguistic competencies. Students made significant gains on test scores for social studies content. During small-group interactions, they increased their use of academic language functions over time. Furthermore, an examination of students' written products revealed growth in the students' ability to use language in the most academically challenging context: the final unit essay.

When students engage in meaningful group activities, they pose interesting and original questions, discuss ideas, deliberate decisions on how to accomplish the task, and learn to resolve intellectual and social conflicts. In the company of others, students construct deeper understandings of concepts, while social interactions support their continued learning. In a diverse classroom, students have differing intellectual strengths, levels of prior academic achievement, and relevant skills; they bring to the group varying experiences and different, yet equally valuable, repertoires of problem-solving strategies. By serving as academic and linguistic resources for one another, students can benefit from such intellectual diversity and richness. When they work on a problem that has an uncertain outcome or many paths to a solution, the more the students talk and work together, the more they learn.

Organizational theory has proved to be a useful way of explaining and predicting how structural arrangements such as peer interaction and the teacher's use of his or her authority might affect levels of learning in a classroom. In his early work, Perrow (1967), an organizational sociologist, argued that to maintain effectiveness, increased complexity of the task requires increased complexity of the work arrangements and structures. If workers face uncertain tasks, work arrangements must shift from direct supervision (a simple organizational structure) to delegation of authority to the workers. Furthermore, to address the uncertainty of the tasks effectively, workers must make extensive use of lateral relations, that is, they need to communicate with one another.

Applying this theory, peer relations become critical to the learning process when the learning task is complex and uncertain. Students help each other with reading and understanding the learning tasks; they explain basic concepts and procedures to each other; they work together to plan and build models, design experiments, and perform role-plays. If such interaction is crucial for academic achievement, then the teacher needs to shift from direct supervision to delegating authority to the students, while holding them accountable for their own and their group members' engagement and learning. When students work in groups, the teacher is no longer the focal point in the classroom, the only source of information and knowledge, constantly regulating and closely directing students' behavior and learning. Instead, students become responsible for their own learning and for that of their groupmates.

Cohen (1994a) calls this process "delegation of authority," meaning that the teacher delegates to the groups and to the individuals in these groups the authority and responsibility for managing the group, for ensuring the group members' engagement in learning, and for completing the task.

Unless the teacher delegates authority and teaches students how to work cooperatively in small groups, uncertain tasks will create serious problems. Faced with uncertainty, many students become frustrated; they pressure the teacher to give the "right" answers. If the teacher succumbs to this pressure, he or she short-circuits students' creative problem solving, thereby preventing students from learning how to work together to find solutions and how to build intellectual and social consensus.

Many teachers struggle with delegating authority and the fear of losing control. They worry that without direct and constant supervision, the classroom might deteriorate into chaos; students will not understand what needs to be done, they will make too many mistakes, they won't complete their assignments, and they will become disengaged. A system of cooperative group norms and student roles assists the teacher in delegating authority and supports the changed roles of the teacher and of the students during small-group instruction. Like the teacher, the students need to learn to adjust to delegation of authority. New ways of interacting with peers require new norms of behavior and new ways of talking to one another.

In a diverse classroom, it is particularly important to educate students to avoid negative, insensitive behavior in small groups. Available research suggests that investing in team building, developing awareness of desirable group processes, and giving specific feedback on cooperative behavior can make for more productive groups (Johnson, Johnson, Stanne, & Garibaldi, 1990; Lew, Mesch, Johnson, & Johnson, 1986; Swing & Peterson, 1982). To be effective, learned cooperative behaviors must not only be specific but also directly relevant to desired behaviors in particular tasks, rather than a more general human relations approach that emphasizes the development of sensitivity, receptivity, openness, and reciprocity (Miller & Harrington, 1990). For example, Johnson et al. (1990) emphasized several behaviors as particularly pertinent for cooperative groups: summarizing ideas and information of all group members, encouraging active oral participation of all members, and checking for agreement among members each time a decision is made.

Cohen (1994a) recommends that teachers use skill builders designed to teach students specific norms for cooperative behaviors that support delegation of authority, such as students serving as resources for one another or taking responsibility for each other's engagement and learning. For example, students learn that one has the right to ask for help and the duty to assist when asked for help. To improve the constructive quality of group conversation, students learn how to justify their arguments and how to explain procedures to others rather than doing the work for someone else.

Also to support teachers as they delegate authority, students assume specific procedural roles. By playing these roles, students manage the groups and themselves; they take over the responsibility for some of the practical, yet mundane, functions and duties of the traditional teacher role. Thus, in each group the facilitator sees to it that all members understand the instructions to the task and that they all get a turn. The facilitator also acts as the liaison between the teacher and the group. At the end of the time for the group task, the reporter presents what the group found out, introduces or describes the group product, and often evaluates how group members worked together. The materials manager collects the manipulatives, props, tools, and supplies as needed and oversees the cleanup. Depending on the task and the teacher's priorities, additional roles may be assigned: timer, peace maker, safety officer, or resource person.

These procedural roles are different from "content" roles such as theorist, questioner, or explainer, which reflect metacognitive functions necessary for groupwork; they are also different from "professional" roles such as artist, musician, or director—roles that potentially lead to a strict division of labor. Although division of labor is often an efficient way to get the job done, it also reduces interaction. Since peer interaction produces learning gains, there needs to be a healthy balance between division of labor and interdependence.

Each student in the group has a role to play, and roles rotate. In addition to participating fully in the content-specific, substantive work of the group, all students learn how to play all roles competently and develop important social skills highly relevant for adult life.

Broadening the Curriculum

Often, when teachers plan their curriculum for an academically heterogeneous classroom, they modify the activities or assignments to fit what they perceive to be the academic ability of individual students or various groups of students in the classroom. Such modifications run the risk of creating more challenging curriculum for some students than for others, and of creating differential expectations for performance from students in the same classroom. In many linguistically heterogeneous classrooms, teachers assign different textbooks and expect lesser-quality work from students who are learning English, thereby watering down the content of the lessons for these students. To avoid such a problematic situation of in-class tracking or ability grouping, the curriculum needs to be redesigned to allow all students access to abstract concepts and vital information in multiple ways. If students have multiple opportunities and many avenues for accessing the task, the information, and the supporting materials, the probability of understanding increases. Multiple ability curricula used in complex instruction present students with up to five group tasks, each task representing a different way to understand the major idea underlying the unit. As students interact during these varied tasks, they act as academic and linguistic resources for one another.

Uncertainty

Educators distinguish between problem-solving, open-ended, "ill structured" tasks (e.g., examples are designing an experiment, explicating a text, solving mathematical problems in real-life contexts, reconciling contrasting points of view) and routine tasks (e.g., decoding, recalling factual information, completing worksheets, and so on). Others distinguish between purely linguistic tasks or tasks that require only traditional academic skills (reading, writing, computing) and tasks that require many intellectual abilities for successful completion.

Routine tasks have clearly defined procedures or steps that need to be followed, and usually a right or wrong answer. Students can carry out such tasks by conscientiously heeding instructions, completing sentences, applying familiar algorithms and formulas, or by finding and memorizing information. Groupwork might not be essential for completing such tasks, but it can benefit many students. Some researchers (e.g., see Webb, 1982) have documented the academic benefits for those students who help their peers by explaining, modeling, and practicing these skills while accomplishing such routine paper-and-pencil tasks. In contrast, when students engage in problem solving, open-ended, and hands-on activities, they grapple with many uncertainties; they explore alternatives and often come up with legitimately different solutions. In a synthesis of research, Qin, Johnson, and Johnson (1995) found that cooperation on hands-on activities enhances problem solving when compared to linguistic tasks, that is, tasks that rely on verbal interaction exclusively.

Sound group tasks are as close as possible to a real-life situation, a genuine problem, or an authentic dilemma. True group tasks that cannot easily be accomplished by a single person are uncertain both in their outcome and in how one can go about identifying strategies and finding solutions. Open-ended questions and problem-solving activities ask for students' experiences, opinions, and interpretations. Beyond the who, where, and what, students reflect on why and how things happened and whether they could have happened differently. In such activities, students analyze and evaluate, discuss cause and effect, explore controversial issues, and draw conclusions. Lotan (1997) argues that "by assigning tasks that are open-ended in their process and in their outcome, teachers effectively delegate intellectual authority to the students" (p. 110). However, this delegation of intellectual authority is often difficult for teachers who might be confronted by their students' unexpected and sometimes uncomfortable answers or solutions. Many teachers try to maintain control of their students' intellectual enterprise through tight supervision of the learning task, by overspecifying instructions or preteaching the assignment to remove much of the uncertainty. As the sine qua non of group tasks, uncertainty of the outcome and multiplicity of ways to complete the task or resolve a problem challenge students' as well as the teacher's (and often parents') conceptions of learning. This challenge can produce great anxiety and even resistance. A second-grade teacher shared her experiences with groupwork and concluded her case with this statement:

The room was quieter and more orderly with large group instruction. Students called the more traditional reading and question-answer activities "real learning." Hands-on groupwork often required interaction that sent the room through increasingly uncomfortable noise levels amplified by the wooden ceiling and walls, threatening classroom order. Students didn't associate groupwork—even when successful—with real learning. I wonder if students feel less secure generating their own questions and findings answers from multiple resources than they are working with questions and "real" answers from a textbook. What can I do to expand their concept of "real learning?" (Shulman, Lotan, & Whitcomb, 1998, pp. 19–20)

Multiple Intellectual Abilities

The notion of multiple abilities is central to true group tasks and crucial for successful status treatments. It sets the stage for changing the teacher's and the students' expectations for competence and their view of what it is to be smart in an equitable classroom. Multiple-ability tasks are different from traditional classroom activities for which students use a narrow range of intellectual abilities such as listening to a lecture, reading a textbook, memorizing information, or filling in blanks.

Rich group tasks require many skills and multiple intellectual abilities for their successful completion. Such tasks allow students to contribute their various talents, multiple intelligences, or diverse repertoire of problem-solving strategies; they also give students the opportunity to develop these strengths further and acquire new ones. When tasks are multidimensional, more students have opportunities to show intellectual competence. By making tasks multidimensional rather than unidimensional (requiring only basic academic skills), educators are redefining not only the learning task but also the traditional social system of the classroom. Multidimensional, multiple-ability tasks are a precondition for providing more opportunity for more students to show "smarts" and be perceived as smart by the teacher and their peers.

Group tasks that include multiple abilities can serve an additional purpose: they attract more students to the task and entice them to participate, thus opening additional avenues for students to gain access to the learning task. Students who are still learning to read might be drawn to a multiple ability task by examining and analyzing a photograph or a video clip. Some students might be lured to the task and respond more readily when listening to an audiotape of a song, a speech, or a story. Students who are in the process of learning the language of instruction might understand a task better as they work with real objects, manipulatives, or three-dimensional models in addition to attending to verbal information. Students who still have difficulty reading might access information related to the activity from a graph, matrix, cartoon, or diagram—information that has traditionally been conveyed exclusively through text.

As more students who have poor academic skills gain access to the task and participate more, they read, write, and compute in the context of group activities. They use basic skills in a meaningful, relevant context; they use language to communicate and solve problems. Indeed, reading comprehension increases and writing becomes more fluent along with gains in conceptual understanding (Bower, 1997).

Assessment of Group and Individual Performance

Cooperative learning in the multicultural classroom can improve intergroup relations *and* achieve cognitive goals. Group activities can call on basic skills and provide extensive academic content while also teaching general concepts. The most difficult and abstract concepts are more efficiently and effectively taught in groups than as individual exercises. Schultz (1999) demonstrated that individual performance in science as a result of group activities in complex instruction was superior to performance as a result of individual work in the same active learning tasks on the topic of ecology. The students in her study who had worked in groups showed a much deeper understanding of hypothesis testing than those who had worked through the same exercises as individuals.

Teachers who use group tasks to attain academic objectives need to know how to assess learning in such a way that they (and parents and administrators) can be sure that students are making solid academic gains. It is not enough to administer a test at the end of groupwork. As the groups proceed, the teacher needs to know whether students are gaining from the rich academic content of the group tasks. Students benefit from the teacher's feedback prior to test taking on how their understanding of the concepts is progressing. One of the most difficult parts of teaching concepts through the use of groupwork is feedback to groups presenting the results of their work. If the task is creative and open-ended, there is no way of knowing in advance what the group will present; teachers are often at a loss as to how to provide specific, constructive feedback on the academic content of the group product.

Powerful assessment is particularly challenging for active and constructivist tasks. According to experts, assessment should be directly aligned with instruction. Articulation between content and the performance used to measure it is critical to student achievement (Solomon, 1998). In the absence of a clear connection between content and performance, students foster "a keen indifference to investing in the assessment" (Wolf & Reardon, 1996, p. 19). Another condition for powerful assessment is that students should be aware of criteria that are being used for evaluation (Frederiksen & Collins, 1989). Expectations should be visible to students, and students should be active in evaluating their own work (Shepard, 2000). Without explicit criteria, students will be unclear on how to demonstrate mastery and consequently "will not be able to participate fully in managing their own learning" (Brookhart, 1999, p. iii).

A practical way to meet these conditions for powerful assessment is to create evaluation criteria that are unique to each group product. In language appropriate to the students, these criteria inform them as to what constitutes an exemplary group product. In doing so, the criteria do not shut down the open-ended constructivist nature of the task. Some of the criteria can refer to the multiple abilities required by the task. Criteria can require that the students integrate the academic content in the task with their group presentations to the class. Other criteria can require that the product or presentation be firmly linked to the underlying abstract concepts of the unit. Students can be instructed to use the criteria in discussing their potential product and in providing feedback to other groups who are making presentations.

Researchers in complex instruction have experimented with creating such evaluation criteria. For example, in a unit on ancient Egypt for the sixth grade, there is an activity on the Weighing of the Heart Ceremony in which the students are asked to create a skit of this ceremony, which was believed to take place as each dead soul entered the afterlife. Among the resources available to the group are primary source excerpts translated from the ancient Egyptian Book of the Dead. One contains spells to protect the heart of the deceased on the way to the Hall of Judgment. Another lists 15 of the confessions the deceased was required to make to each of the 42 lesser deities, or

judges, along the way.

The evaluation criteria for this task require the students to integrate their study of the resource materials with their creation of the skit:

- Skit includes at least two sins, two virtues, and one spell.
- Skit gives good reasons for whether or not the deceased entered the afterlife.
- Script is well rehearsed and believable.

Research on the effectiveness of the use of these evaluation criteria compared three complex instruction classrooms that made use of the criteria with two classrooms that did not (Cohen, Lotan, Abram, Scarloss, & Schultz, 2002). All five sixth-grade self-contained classrooms were multiethnic, mixed SES, and multilingual. The teachers, who were well-trained in complex instruction, all used the same multiple ability units.

Audiotapes of the group discourse and presentations, digital photographs of the products, and a final essay on the unit made up the body of data. Each source of data was systematically scored. The use of evaluation criteria affected the nature of the group conversations, the character of the group products, and the quality of the final essay students wrote about the unit. Groups that had evaluation criteria were more self-critical about their products, more task-focused, and less likely to be disengaged. Scarloss (2001) found that groups with evaluation criteria also spent much more time making sense of their assignment and their product, a group behavior that had a favorable impact on their essay scores.

Evaluation criteria had a strongly favorable effect on the quality of the group product (Cohen et al., 2002). Criteria act as a direct and suitable form of assessment of the daily work of the groups. The group products and presentation become the "assessment performance," which exactly parallels the content of the group tasks. With explicit criteria, both students and teachers have guidance as to what counts as a good product. Teachers who have evaluation criteria provide much more feedback on group products that is specific and concrete than teachers who lack these criteria (Schultz et al., 2000). In complex instruction, the whole class hears feedback to each group on tasks that some groups subsequently carry out. This feedback prepares the groups doing particular tasks the next day to do a better job at meeting the criteria. Teachers state that they feel so much more confident in providing relevant feedback to groups when they have specific criteria to look at and upon which they can base their comments.

In the analysis of the five sixth-grade classrooms (Cohen et al., 2002), superior group products and more self-critical group conversations had a direct and favorable impact on the grasp of facts and major ideas displayed by the students in their essays. This was true of the average scores on the essays of each group as well as of the individual essay scores. Those individuals who were in a group that had a superior product and that was more self-critical and task-focused in its conversation had higher scores on the essays than those individuals who were in a less effective group. Thus the use of more powerful assessment strategies can directly affect the quality of the discourse and performance in groups, and it can have an indirect impact on the caliber of individual achievement in a heterogeneous classroom.

CONCLUSION

Altering the social system of the classroom by changing the task and evaluation structure is a liberating idea for the teacher of heterogeneous classrooms. The prospect of having to devise different approaches for each individual depending on his or her personal and cultural characteristics is a daunting one. Instead, this strategy allows the teacher to organize the task structure of the classroom so that there are many ways to understand central concepts. Moreover, students have the benefit of peers in helping them make sense of the assignments and assist in creating a successful performance while being able to make important contributions to the group product. These changes in the situation permit more students with differing previous academic achievement to be successful.

With the tools developed from status characteristic theory, it is possible to produce equal-status interaction. Low-status students are able to participate more and thus learn more. Finally, the shift to feedback based on objective criteria that is provided for groups and individuals can free the teacher from overemphasis on competitive marking and grading.

Proponents of intercultural education in Europe and Francophone Canada see the principles underlying complex instruction as a vital tool for their major concerns. These principles have been integrated into work at centers of intercultural education in Denmark and Belgium. In addition, Pieter Batelaan has adapted the approach for the European context. Batelaan and van Hoof (1996) write about the particular pertinence of this model of cooperative learning for intercultural education. Fernand Ouellet of the University of Sherbrooke in Quebec, Canada, finds this approach particularly promising for intercultural education because it does not isolate cultural heterogeneity from other forms of heterogeneity (such as social class or academic achievement). The development of social skills becomes a way to reinforce the learning of academic materials and the mastery of conceptual skills

at a high level. Not only does the work attach a great importance to the scholarly success of at-risk pupils, but it gives teachers a means of helping these students (Ouellet, 2002).

Overlap of Agendas

There are significant areas of overlap between these recommendations and the work of other educational researchers. For example, the constructivist view of the importance of social interaction in the classroom has many parallels with our research on the importance of talking and working together for learning. The requirements for successful groupwork incorporated in complex instruction are similar to those used by many other researchers and developers of cooperative learning. The recommendation of introducing multiple abilities into the curriculum shares with Gardner (1983) and Sternberg (1985, 1998) the conception of multiple dimensions of human intelligence. The idea of making the criteria for evaluation transparent to the student is a truism in the assessment literature (although systematic evidence for the effectiveness of criteria has been lacking). There are two features of complex instruction that are unique: the emphasis on treating problems of status through changing expectations for competence, and its completeness as a model that works with the total social system of the classroom.

Alternatives to the Full Model

Practitioners (especially new teachers) may feel that the full model of complex instruction, with its elaborate multiple ability curricula and use of different tasks in simultaneous operation, is overwhelming. The fundamental ideas behind an equitable classroom can be implemented without the feeling that absolute fidelity to the full model is required. This is why the authors of this chapter have tried to present the underlying theory as more important than the details of the particular set of strategies of complex instruction. For example, teachers can develop a single multiple ability task for cooperative learning and implement that task in groups with appropriate norms and roles. To ensure equal-status interaction, they can use the two status treatments; see Cohen (1994a) for more on these strategies. Last, the development of specific evaluation criteria for the task is not difficult or onerous and will prove practical as a way for teachers to improve the feedback provided for students.

Future Research

The social system of the classroom and its effects on intergroup relations, academic achievement, and peer relations are a rich and fertile area for research for the multicultural specialist. With a curriculum featuring multiple perspectives and multiple ability group tasks, one could examine many of the outcome variables of interest to the multicultural educator. There should be strong effects on peer relations, intergroup relations, and achievement.

The emphasis on learning to meet standards is often regarded as a threat to both multicultural education and use of cooperative learning. These two fields are often seen as preoccupied with process rather than with academic learning and therefore irrelevant to the standards movement. However, by providing numerous ways with multiple abilities that the students can grasp and display understanding of central concepts and with the use of peers as resources, one can make accessible to a range of learners the most demanding of concepts. By combining emphasis on social studies or science objectives with learning academic English and writing expository prose, one can simultaneously meet standards in social studies or science and the language arts. With the use of evaluation criteria, one can gain the maximum benefit from including academic content in group tasks. From a policy perspective, research in the multicultural classroom that demonstrates this way of attaining curriculum standards is a vital necessity.

In conclusion, the currently available strategies for the multicultural educator for changing attitudes, teacher-student relationships, and intergroup relations, and for empowering parents and the community, represent necessary but not sufficient conditions for achieving equitable classrooms. Reshaping the classroom social system, including the status relations among the students, should make it possible to attain the desired state of interpersonal and intercultural understanding along with the goals of equity in interpersonal relations and access to academic achievement.

References

Arellano, A. (2002). *Bilingual students, acquisition of academic language in a complex instruction classroom.* Unpublished doctoral dissertation, Stanford University, Stanford, CA.

Batelaan, P., & van Hoof, C. (1996). Cooperative learning in intercultural education. *European Journal of Intercultural Studies, 7*(3), 5–16.

Ben-Ari, R. (1997). Complex instruction and cognitive development. In E. G. Cohen & R. A. Lotan (Eds.), *Working for equity in heterogeneous classrooms: Sociological theory in practice* (pp. 193–206). New York: Teachers College Press.

Berger, J. B., Cohen, B. P., & Zelditch, M., Jr. (1966). Status characteristics and expectation states. In J. Berger, M. Zelditch, Jr., & B. Anderson (Eds.), *Sociological theories in progress* (Vol. 1, pp. 9–46). Boston: Houghton-Mifflin.

Berger, J. B., Cohen, B. P., & Zelditch, M., Jr. (1972). Status characteristics and social interaction. *American Sociological Review, 37*(3), 241–255.

Berger, J. B., Rosenholtz, S. J., & Zelditch, M., Jr. (1980). Status organizing processes. *Annual Review of Sociology, 6,* 479–508.

Bianchini, J. (1995). *How do middle school students learn science in small groups? An analysis of scientific knowledge and social process construction.* Unpublished doctoral dissertation, Stanford University, Stanford, CA.

Bower, B. (1997). Effects of the multi-ability curriculum in secondary social studies classrooms. In E. G. Cohen & R. A. Lotan (Eds.), *Working for equity in heterogeneous classrooms: Sociological theory in practice* (pp. 117–133). New York: Teachers College Press.

Brookhart, S. (1999). The art and science of classroom assessment: The missing part of pedagogy. *ASHE ERIC Higher Education Report.* Washington, DC: George Washington University Press.

Children of change. (2000, September 27). *Education Week,* p. 31.

Cohen, E. G. (1982). Expectation states and interracial interaction in school settings. *Annual Review of Sociology, 8,* 209–235.

Cohen, E. G. (1994a). *Designing groupwork: Strategies for heterogeneous classrooms* (Rev. ed.). New York: Teachers College Press.

Cohen, E. G. (1994b). Restructuring the classroom: Conditions for productive small groups. *Review of Educational Research, 64*(1), 1–35.

Cohen, E. G. (Producer). (1994c). *Status treatments for the classroom.* [Video]. (Available from Teachers College Press, 1234 Amsterdam Ave., New York, NY 10027)

Cohen, E. G. (1997). Understanding status problems: Sources and consequences. In E. G. Cohen & R. A. Lotan (Eds.), *Working for equity in heterogeneous classrooms: Sociological theory in practice* (pp. 61–76). New York: Teachers College Press.

Cohen, E. G., & Lotan, R. A. (1995). Producing equal-status interaction in the heterogeneous classroom. *American Educational Research Journal, 32,* 99–120.

Cohen, E. G., & Lotan, R. A. (1997a). Raising expectations for competence: The effectiveness of status interventions. In E. G. Cohen & R. A. Lotan (Eds.), *Working for equity in heterogeneous classrooms: Sociological theory in practice* (pp. 77–91). New York: Teachers College Press.

Cohen, E. G., & Lotan, R. A. (Eds.). (1997b). *Working for equity in heterogeneous classrooms: Sociological theory in practice.* New York: Teachers College Press.

Cohen, E. G., Lotan, R. A., Abram, P., Scarloss, B., & Schultz, S. E. (2002). Can groups learn? *Teachers College Record, 104,* 1045–1068.

Cohen, E. G., Lotan, R. A., & Holthuis, N. C. (1997). Organizing the classroom for learning. In E. G. Cohen & R. A. Lotan (Eds.), *Working for equity in heterogeneous classrooms: Sociological theory in practice* (pp. 31–43). New York: Teachers College Press.

Cohen, E. G., Lotan, R. A., & Leechor, C. (1989). Can classrooms learn? *Sociology of Education, 62,* 75–94.

Duncan, G., & Brooks-Gunn, J. (2001). Poverty, welfare reform, and children's achievement. In B. Biddle (Ed.), *Social class, poverty, and education: Policy and practice* (pp. 49–75). New York: Routledge Falmer.

Epstein, J. S., & Karweit, N. (1983). *Friends in school: Patterns of selection and influence in secondary schools.* New York: Academic Press.

Frederiksen, J. R., & Collins, A. (1989). A systems approach to educational testing. *Educational Researcher, 18*(9), 27–32.

Gardner, H. (1983). *Frames of mind: The theory of multiple intelligences.* New York: Basic Books.

Graves, N., & Graves, T. (1991). Candida Graves: Complex teamwork in action. *Cooperative Learning, 12*(1), 12–16.

Hallinan, M. J. (1976). Friendship patterns in open and traditional classrooms. *Sociology of Education, 49*(4), 254–265.

Humphreys, P., & Berger, J. (1981). Theoretical consequences of status characteristic formation. *American Journal of Sociology, 86*(15), 953–983.

Johnson, D., & Johnson, R. (1990). Cooperative learning and achievement. In S. Sharan (Ed.), *Cooperative learning: Theory and research* (pp. 23–37). New York: Praeger.

Johnson, D., Johnson, R., Stanne, M., & Garibaldi, A. (1990). Impact of group processing on achievement in cooperative groups. *Journal of Social Psychology, 129*(4), 507–516.

Leechor, C. (1988). *How high and low achieving students differentially benefit from working together in cooperative small groups.* Unpublished doctoral dissertation, Stanford University, Stanford, CA.

Lew, M., Mesch, D., Johnson, D., & Johnson, R. (1986). Positive interdependence, academic and collaborative skills, group contingencies, and isolated students. *American Educational Research Journal, 23*(3), 476–488.

Lloyd, P., & Cohen, E. G. (1999). Peer status in the middle school: A natural treatment for unequal participation. *Social Psychology of Education, 4*(1), 1–24.

Lotan, R. A. (1997). Principles of a principled curriculum. In E. G. Cohen & R. Lotan (Eds.), *Working for equity in heterogeneous classrooms: Sociological theory in practice* (pp. 105–116). New York: Teachers College Press.

Miller, N., & Harrington, H. J. (1990). A situational identity perspective on cultural diversity and teamwork in the classroom. In S. Sharan (Ed.), *Cooperative learning: Theory and research* (pp. 39–75). New York: Praeger.

National Center for Educational Statistics [Department of Education]. (2001). *Common core of data. Public elementary/secondary school universe survey: School year 1999-2000.* [Electronic data file]. Washington, DC: Author.

Orfield, G., & Yun, J. T. (1999). *Resegregation in American schools.* Cambridge, MA: Harvard University, Civil Rights Project.

Ouellet, F. (2002). *Les défis du pluralisme en éducation. Essais sur la formation interculturelle* [The challenges of pluralism in education. Essays on intercultural education]. Québec: Presses de l'Université Laval/Paris, L'Harmattan.

Perrow, C. (1967). A framework for the comparative analysis of organizations. *American Sociological Review, 32*(2), 194–208.

Plank, S. (2000). *Finding one's place: Teaching styles and peer relations in diverse classrooms.* New York: Teachers College Press.

Qin, Z., Johnson, D. W., & Johnson, R. T. (1995). Cooperative vs. competitive efforts and problem solving. *Review of Educational Research, 65*(2), 129–143.

Rosenholtz, S. J. (1985). Treating problems of academic status. In J. Berger & M. Zelditch, Jr. (Eds.), *Status, rewards, and influence* (pp. 445–470). San Francisco: Jossey-Bass.

Rosenholtz, S. J., & Rosenholtz, S. H. (1981). Classroom organization and the perception of ability. *Sociology of Education, 54*(2), 132–140.

Rosenholtz, S. J., & Simpson, C. (1984). The formation of ability conception: Developmental trend or social construction? *Review of Educational Research, 54*(1), 31–63.

Rosenholtz, S. J., & Wilson, B. (1980). The effect of classroom structure on shared perceptions of ability. *American Educational Research Journal, 17*(1), 75–82.

Scarloss, B. (2001). *Sensemaking, interaction, and learning in student groups.* Unpublished doctoral dissertation, Stanford University, Stanford, CA.

Schultz, S. E. (1999). *To group or not to group: Effects of groupwork on students' declarative and procedural knowledge in science.* Unpublished doctoral dissertation, Stanford University, Stanford, CA.

Schultz, S. E., Scarloss, B., Lotan, R. A., Abram, P. L., Cohen, E. G., & Holthuis, N. C. (2000, April). Let's give 'em somethin' to talk about: Teacher's talk to students in open-ended group tasks. Paper presented to the AERA Annual Meeting, New Orleans.

Shepard, L. (2000). The role of assessment in a learning culture. *Education Researcher, 29*(7), 4–14.

Shulman, J., Lotan, R. A., & Whitcomb, J. A. (1998). *Groupwork in diverse classrooms: A Casebook for educators.* New York: Teachers College Press.

Simpson, C. (1981). Classroom structure and the organization of ability. *Sociology of Education, 54*(3), 120–132.

Slavin, R. E. (2001). Cooperative learning and intergroup relations. In J. A. Banks & C.A.M. Banks (Eds.), *Handbook of research on multicultural education* (pp. 628–634). San Francisco: Jossey-Bass.

Solomon, P. G. (1998). *The curriculum bridge: From standards to actual classroom practice.* Thousand Oaks, CA: Corwin Press.

Sternberg, R. J. (1985). *Beyond IQ: A triarchic theory of human intelligence.* Cambridge, England: Cambridge University Press.

Sternberg, R. (1998). Abilities are forms of developing expertise. *Educational Researcher, 27*(3), 11–20.

Swing, S., & Peterson, P. (1982). The relationship of student ability and small-group interaction to student achievement. *American Educational Research Journal, 19*(2), 259–274.

Webb, N. (1982, March). *Interaction patterns: Powerful predictors of achievement in small groups.* Paper presented at the annual meeting of the American Educational Research Association, New York.

Webster, M., Jr., & Foschi, M. (1988). Overview of status generalization. In M. Webster, Jr., & M. Foschi (Eds.), *Status generalization: New theory and research* (pp. 1–20). Stanford, CA: Stanford University Press.

Webster, M., Jr., & Sobieszek, B. (1974). *Sources of self-evaluation: A formal theory of significant others.* New York: Wiley.

Wolf, D. P., & Reardon, S. F. (1996). Access to excellence through new forms of student assessment. In J. B. Baron & Wolf, D. P. (Eds.), *Performance-based student assessment: Challenges and possibilities.* Chicago: University of Chicago Press.

Wong Fillmore, L. (1991). Second language learning in children: A model of language learning in social context. In E. Bialystok (Ed.), *Language processing in bilingual children* (pp. 49-69). Cambridge, England: Cambridge University Press.

INTERGROUP EDUCATION
APPROACHES TO SCHOOL REFORM

36

INTERCULTURAL AND INTERGROUP EDUCATION, 1929–1959

Linking Schools and Communities

Cherry A. McGee Banks

University of Washington, Bothell

Schools are linked to communities through school boards, volunteers, funding, and other formal and informal networks. These linkages provide opportunities for members of the community and educators to share information, engage in deliberations, and learn from each other. Parents, who are often children's first and most important teachers, are a critical part of the link between schools and communities. Parents directly or indirectly help shape their children's value system, orientation toward learning, and view of the world (Cook, 1938; Perrone, 1998). They can help teachers extend their knowledge and understanding of the students in their classrooms. Through that knowledge and understanding, teachers can improve student learning (Henderson, 1987; C.A.M. Banks, 2003; Hidalgo, Siu, & Epstein, Chapter 30, this volume).

The challenge of linking schools to communities, which is ongoing, was particularly salient at the dawn of the 20th century, when millions of immigrants from southern and eastern Europe entered the United States. With few choices before them, many immigrant parents enrolled their children in public schools, where the dominant ideology was Americanization. The implicit curriculum in those schools suggested that their parents' ways of speaking, behaving, and thinking were inferior to what they were taught in school (Carlson, 1987). Although some parents saw Americanization as a means to achieve upward mobility and wanted their children to assimilate into mainstream American society as soon possible, many were alienated by the Americanization process. They were put off by the public schools and saw them as autonomous institutions staffed by people who were strangers in their communities. For the most part, public school teachers didn't live in immigrant communities, know their students' parents, or share their students' values (Carlson; C.A.M. Banks, 2003). Many Italian parents, for example, were concerned that instead of teaching students to "respect and obey their elders and perform traditional family roles, American schools stressed individualism and self-expression" (Seller, 1977, p. 142). Boys and girls could freely interact with each other and seemingly participate in activities without regard to gender. Parents were also concerned that their students were being "taught useless subjects such as drawing and physical education" instead of skills that could lead to good jobs (p. 142).

In a study highlighting the public's demands on public schools, Waller (1932) concluded that parents and teachers lived in a state of mutual distrust, and even hostility. Waller was referring to the tension between parents and teachers that resulted from ongoing efforts of citizen groups to influence school curricula, course offerings, and school texts. At that time, educators and parents, especially immigrant parents, did not see themselves as partners working together to educate students. Each viewed the other with suspicion. Educators saw themselves as trained professionals who should not be interfered with by outsiders. Many immigrants, on the other hand, believed they were misrepresented or deliberately left out of the school curriculum (Zimmerman, 1999).

Immigrants at the turn of the 20th century, as well as White ethnics in midcentury, frequently experienced discontinuity between their home culture and the culture of the school. Some parents were able to reduce the language, religious, and other forms of discontinuity between home and school by sending their children to parochial schools (Troen, 1975). Others worked with civic, ethnic, and religious groups to pressure decision makers to include more ethnic content in the school curriculum, provide opportunities for students to study their mother tongue, and revise textbooks to reflect their groups' interpretation of historical events and actors (Zimmerman, 1999).

This chapter is about the role that public school educators played in the early and mid-1900s to establish links between the school and the community. Those linkages strengthened the relationship between the school and the home and allowed educators to work more effectively with students and parents as they helped students learn to appreciate diversity, reject prejudice and discrimination, and actualize democratic values. Many of the educators who were involved in establishing those linkages worked from outside as well as inside the school for change. Outsiders within are characterized by their values, perspectives, religions, ethnicities, or other traits, which are different from those of the dominant group in their organization (Collins, 1990). As outsiders within, they had to navigate the gap between their values, ideals, and identities and those of the dominant school culture. Within the school, they offered professional insights and direction on curricular change, as well as parent involvement, informed by their understanding and appreciation of immigrant life and values. Outside the school, in their role as citizens, they were active members of civic groups that advocated for school change. These educators, who were outsiders within, along with social scientists and social activists, formed what became known as the intercultural education movement.

The chapter begins with an overview of the social context in which intercultural education began. Divergent views within intercultural education, intragroup diversity, and funding for the movement are discussed as major characteristics of intercultural education. Next, three important initiatives in intercultural education—the Service Bureau for Education in Human Relations, the Springfield Plan, and the Project in Intergroup Education in Cooperating Schools—are described and discussed. That section is followed by a look inside Benjamin Franklin High School, which was an important site of intercultural education in the 1930s and 1940s. The chapter ends with a discussion of the waning influence of intercultural education. A major goal of this chapter is to help contemporary educators gain a better understanding of the enduring characteristics of intergroup tensions in

the United States and how educators have worked to reduce them.

Two terms, *intercultural education* and *intergroup education,* are used interchangeably throughout the chapter to describe the work of educators during the 1900s seeking to help students reduce their prejudice and increase their understanding and appreciation of ethnic, racial, and religious diversity. The term *intercultural education* was officially coined in 1935 after the Progressive Education Association (PEA) established the Commission on Intercultural Education. However, by the 1940s, the term *intergroup education* was in common use to describe efforts that were previously called intercultural education.

The two terms, to a great degree, reflected similar concerns and efforts. Intercultural education developed as a response to nativist perspectives and attitudes that were widespread during the early 20th century. Intercultural educators primarily focused their attention on immigrants and issues related to ethnic and religious diversity (C.A.M. Banks, 1996). Intergroup educators were also concerned with those issues, but they focused more directly on prejudice reduction. Reducing prejudice and discrimination became a major concern because of two historical events: the Holocaust and the great migration of African Americans from the South to New York, Detroit, Cleveland, Chicago, Pittsburgh, and other northern industrial cities. Intergroup tensions intensified and resulted in riots and widespread discrimination as large numbers of African Americans who had migrated from the South, in search of greater economic opportunities during World War II, competed with White ethnics for jobs and housing (Crew, 1987; Marks, 1989). Intergroup tensions associated with the great migration, in conjunction with an understanding that anti-Semitism resulted in the extermination of six million Jews in the Holocaust, increased awareness and concern about the extreme consequences of intolerance, prejudice, and discrimination (Clinchy, 1942). Consequently, with fears of the nation fracturing into competing ethnic and religious groups, intergroup educators placed greater emphasis on similarities among groups and prejudice reduction than intercultural educators.

THE SOCIAL CONTEXT IN WHICH INTERCULTURAL EDUCATION BEGAN

Between 1881 and the beginning of World War I, almost 22 million immigrants arrived in the United States (Hutchinson, 1949). Immigration continued at an unprecedented rate throughout the early 20th century, peaking in 1914, when 1,218,480 immigrants entered the country (U.S. Census Bureau, 1975). The new immigrants were ethnically and religiously diverse. Unlike mainstream

Americans, who were primarily Protestant, the new immigrants were Catholics, Jews, Muslims, and members of the Greek and Russian Orthodox churches. More than a half million of the immigrants who arrived in 1914 came from Russia, the Baltic States, and Italy (U.S. Census Bureau).

The new immigrants were frequently viewed with suspicion by mainstream Americans. They spoke alien languages and had political beliefs, religious practices, and cultural characteristics that were viewed as un-American. As immigration increased, anti-alien sentiments and fears escalated (Hutchinson, 1949). Even though earlier immigrants, such as the Germans and Irish, were also victims of prejudice and discrimination when they first arrived in the United States, many of them expressed nativist sentiments. Nativists opposed immigration because they believed that American values and institutions were threatened by immigrants and minorities (Higham, 1972). They were also concerned about the growing levels of labor unrest and unemployment after World War I (Ziegler, 1953). In addition, the Bolshevik Revolution, which resulted in the overthrow of the czar in Russia, increased concerns about the ability of immigrants to understand and appreciate American democracy (Ross, 1914). Nativists used fears about the stability of American institutions and their vulnerability to outside radical forces to argue for restrictions on immigration. The American Protective Association, a nativist organization, also used the availability of newer and less expensive forms of transatlantic transportation to raise fears; it argued that unrestricted immigration would flood American institutions with "$9.60 steerage slime" (Ziegler, 1953, p. 7). Nativism became full-blown in the early 1900s in organizations such as the Ku Klux Klan, which was anti-Catholic, anti-Jewish, anti-foreigner, and anti-Black.

In addition to politicians and opportunists, some university professors also embraced nativist sentiments. Henry Pratt Fairchild, a well-known sociologist, expressed nativist sentiments in two books: *The Melting Pot Mistake* and *Immigration: A World Movement and Its American Significance* (Fairchild, 1913, 1926). Fairchild argued that immigrants were responsible for lowering the American standard of living, increasing crime, and burdening society with a disproportionate number of people in insane asylums, as well as for the general decline in the quality of American life. Commenting on crime, he noted that two forms in particular, the Mafia and White slave traffic, were associated with immigration. He associated the Mafia with Italians and White slave traffic with Jewish, French, and Belgian immigrants. He was particularly concerned about native-born children of immigrants and used statistics to argue that the second generation had a much higher inclination toward criminal behavior than mainstream native Whites. Although acknowledging the complex causes of juvenile delinquency, he concluded,

"Whatever the cause, this tendency toward lawlessness among the second generation of immigrants is indisputable, and is one of the most disturbing elements in the whole situation" (Fairchild, 1953, p. 49).

Nativists' perspectives, such as those articulated by Fairchild, were incorporated into school textbooks, materials, and curricula. This statement from a 1931 curriculum guide for social studies teachers in Houston is an example of nativist ideas in the curriculum:

Migration from the foreign countries has become a problem. The immigrants who were so freely welcomed as long as land was abundant became a menace to our higher standards of living when they remained in cities where already there were more persons than jobs. Consequently, the number of immigrants that may enter our country in any one year has been cut to a very small fraction of the number of persons from any given country who were in the U.S. in 1890. This regulation has tended to lessen the immigration from southern Europe. Before 1890 most of our immigrants had come from England, Germany, Sweden, and other countries of northern Europe. (Houston Curriculum Guide, 1931, p. 7)

The Houston Curriculum Guide gave teachers a rationale for explaining why immigration was restricted and a way to draw a distinction between mainstream Americans, whose ancestors generally settled in rural areas and started small family farms, and the new immigrants, who settled in cities, lived in ethnic communities, and took jobs in mines and factories. Interestingly, these distinctions between old and new immigrants were the same ones used by nativists to justify immigration restrictions.

Support for Immigrants

Not all Americans accepted ideas such as those articulated by Fairchild and reflected in the Houston Curriculum Guide. Nativist ideas were challenged by academics such as Horace Kallen (1924) as well as by immigrants themselves (Zimmerman, 1999). Kallen and a small group of like-minded scholars (Bourne, 1917; Drachsler, 1920) argued that it was possible for immigrants to assimilate into American society while maintaining important elements of their ancestral cultures. Kallen and his colleagues called this idea *cultural pluralism* (Cremin, 1961). Nativist perspectives were also challenged by immigrants along with African Americans and others who argued that diversity could enrich American society. Through groups such as the Knights of Columbus, White ethnics fought for American textbooks to include the voices and perspectives of a range of racial, ethnic, religious, and civic groups (Zimmerman, 1999).

Rachel Davis DuBois (1928), a teacher at Woodbury High School in Woodbury, New Jersey, also rejected the idea that the new immigrants were inferior to mainstream Americans. (She was not related to W.E.B. DuBois, the renowned social scientist. However, they did know each other and maintained a close relationship for many years. Their relationship is discussed in David Levering Lewis's biography [2000] of W.E.B. DuBois.) In the late 1920s, she began developing school assembly programs on local ethnic groups. DuBois also worked with parents and members of the community to identify artifacts that could be displayed in the school, and to solicit speakers who could present information on local ethnic groups. The assembly programs were designed to affirm the values, customs, and contributions of ethnic students, improve intergroup relations, and dispel negative images of the ethnics (DuBois, 1928). DuBois's assembly programs at Woodbury High School, which were an early example of the linkage between school and community, served as a prototype for what later became known as intercultural education.

Major Characteristics of Intercultural and Intergroup Education

Intergroup education was a broadly conceptualized movement. (The terms *intercultural education* and *intergroup education* are used in equivalence in this chapter. However, in this section, for ease of reading the term *intergroup* is used to refer to both intergroup and intercultural education. Readers should note, however, that the term *intercultural education* was used mainly prior to 1940 and *intergroup* generally after 1940.) It involved curriculum innovation, teacher training, program development, and other forms of school improvement. Even though it focused on education, intergroup education wasn't limited to schools. Intergroup educators recognized that education took place in the community as well as the classroom (Cook, 1938). Intergroup education programs were implemented in community organizations such as the YMCA and the YWCA, as well as entire cities, one example being Springfield, Massachusetts, where the famous Springfield Plan was initiated.

Even though intercultural education was an applied field, it wasn't limited to classroom practice. It also involved research. Intergroup educators researched ways to help teachers gain the skills and knowledge they needed to work with diverse students (Cook, 1950; Taba, 1953; Cook & Cook, 1957) and reduce student prejudice (Trager & Yarrow, 1952). The many variations of intergroup education representing numerous populations, sites, strategies, and activities shared several common threads: a clear focus on education as a means to address intergroup tensions, the centrality of democratic values and responsibilities in American life, and the recognition that education took place in the community as well as in schools.

The commitments of intergroup educators were reflected in the books and articles (Adamic, 1934, 1940, 1944; Vickery & Cole, 1943), workshops and college courses (Taba & VanTil, 1945; Cook & Cook, 1954), research projects (Taba, Brady, Robinson, & Vickery, 1951), and strategies they designed to help teachers learn how to teach about ethnic, racial, and religious groups and work more effectively with diverse students, parents, and communities (Covello, 1936; DuBois, 1930, 1939). By 1945, there were more than 200 organizations working in the field of intergroup education (Giles, 1945). The number of intergroup organizations mushroomed after riots in Detroit and Los Angeles in 1943. Most organizations involved in intergroup education, such as the Bureau for Intercultural Education, the National Conference of Christians and Jews, and the American Council on Race Relations, were national in scope; others were local and regional. In a survey identifying intergroup organizations throughout the United States, H. Harry Giles (1945) found that 60 were located in the Northeast, 51 in the South, 44 in the Midwest, and 20 were in the Far West.

Intergroup programs were most extensively implemented in New York City. The demographics of the population there made it a logical center for intergroup education. Millions of immigrants landed at Castle Garden in New York Harbor and at Ellis Island during the later part of the 19th century and the early part of the 20th. Approximately 97% of the Italians who entered the United States after 1880 arrived in and remained in New York (Nelli, 1983).

Intergroup education was also popular in Chicago, Philadelphia, Syracuse, Los Angeles, and other cities that had large immigrant and minority populations (Committee on the Study of Teaching Materials in Intergroup Relations, 1949; Taba, Brady, Jennings, & Robinson, 1949). However, it was not implemented for as long a period or in as comprehensive a manner in these cities as it was in New York City.

The New York City schools provided intergroup training for teachers, developed intercultural curricula, and purchased intercultural materials for teachers to use in their classrooms. The implementation of intergroup education in New York, however, was not consistent or steady. It had peaks and valleys reflecting the politics of diversity in New York, as well as the school board's concerns about the quality and impact of intergroup education (Chase, 1940). Community groups also influenced the speed and scope of the implementation of intercultural education in New York. For example, the American Jewish Committee clashed with intercultural educators over content on Jews. Intercultural educators taught about Jews as an ethnic group; the American Jewish Committee wanted Jews to be presented as a religious group (Montalto, 1982). Catholics and Protestants also had concerns about the way they were presented in intercultural education programs and materials (Zimmerman, 1999). When Mary L. Riley, who worked for the New York City Board of Education, received a list of speakers for an upcoming intercultural education program, she protested the inclusion of Bishop G. Bromley Oxnam. In a letter to Lily Edelman of the East-West Association, Riley (1945) noted that Oxnam had made offensive remarks about the Roman Catholic Church and that he shouldn't be included on the program. Riley went on to recommend other, more acceptable speakers. (Oxnam, who was a bishop in the New York Methodist Church, became embroiled in a bitter controversy between Protestant and Catholic leaders regarding accusations of bigotry in the Catholic Church when he gave a series of lectures on the topic.) These and other conflicts resulted in one group or the other exerting political pressure on the schools or withdrawing support for intergroup programs.

Divergent Views in Intercultural Education

Leaders in intercultural education did not speak with a single voice. They expressed diverse perspectives and points of view about the purpose, direction, and audience for intergroup education. Louis E. Yavner, the commissioner of investigations of the City of New York, expressed concern about divergent views in intercultural education in his influential report on intercultural education in the New York City public schools. Yavner (1945) concluded that there wasn't agreement among intercultural educators on acceptable practices and procedures. (Yavner wasn't the only person who was concerned about intercultural leadership in the New York city Schools. A Mrs. Leder, a member of the Council for Community Action, wrote a letter [n.d.] to Jacob Greenberg, associate superintendent, to complain that no one person seemed to be coordinating or running the intercultural program. Moreover, there didn't seem to be a clear relationship between the intercultural committee and the school program. Leder felt there was a breakdown in communication.)

This was somewhat of an overstatement, given the number of books written in the field and the published definitions of intercultural education, but Yavner's critique captured the elastic quality of the movement. That quality had both positive and negative implications for intercultural education. On the positive side, its broad base enabled intercultural educators to focus their attention on interrelated efforts, ranging from curriculum development to parent involvement and from teacher training to reducing intergroup tension in the community. A negative implication was that the broad base of intercultural

education made it difficult to identify its center. Without a clearly defined focus, intercultural education was difficult to evaluate. Consequently, its quality and impact could easily be called into question.

Yavner (1945) also observed that intercultural education had taken on the character of a social movement. This statement captured concerns that such intercultural educators as the Service Bureau's director, Stewart Cole, and Bruno Lasker, a noted social scientist, had raised in the early 1940s about the field's focus on cultural contributions (Chase, 1940). Even though Yavner's report had political overtones and was used to undermine the influence of intergroup educators who embraced cultural pluralism, it revealed an important element of dissention within the movement.

One point of dissension among intergroup educators concerned the audience for their programs. Rachel Davis DuBois argued that intercultural programs should be directed to members of ethnic, racial, and religious groups. In that way, the programs could improve the self-esteem of the group members. Ruth Benedict, who was a well-known anthropologist and author of *Patterns of Culture,* had a different point of view. Benedict's perspective mattered because she was a member of the Progressive Education Association's advisory board and chaired the Commission on Intercultural Education (Caffrey, 1989). Benedict saw intercultural education as a way to help calm the fears and concerns of mainstream Americans about minorities and immigrants. She wanted intercultural educators to reach people who lived in "those areas where most Poles, Italians, and Negroes never go except as servants" (Benedict, 1942, p. 22). The nation was at war, and she was concerned about the social upheaval and chaos that could result from intergroup tensions. Benedict supported intercultural programs that helped mainstream students understand that prejudice and discrimination were incompatible with democratic ideals. She argued that intercultural programs based on human worth would be more effective in changing the attitudes of mainstream students than presentations on ethnic "folk" culture.

A related point of dissension among intergroup educators was the degree of ethnic affirmation they were willing to endorse. Intercultural educators recognized that some degree of ethnic affirmation was necessary to support a sensitive and humane transition into American society. They did not, however, agree on the level of ethnic affirmation that was needed. Frank Trager, who was an administrator with the American Jewish Committee and a member of the Service Bureau board along with William Kilpatrick (the noted progressive educator and Service Bureau board chair), and Stewart Cole (director of the Service Bureau) were among the intercultural educators who argued that problems associated with nativism would disappear as immigrants and their children assimilated into American society. They supported a weak level of ethnic affirmation to help speed the assimilation process, not programs and materials that focused on isolated ethnic histories and contributions. They were concerned that isolated ethnic histories and contributions would highlight differences instead of similarities among groups. Immigrants were encouraged to learn English and take on the social and cultural practices of mainstream Americans while holding on to symbolic elements of their ethnic group. Once assimilated, it was assumed that the sons and daughters of immigrants would be indistinguishable from mainstream Americans. Kilpatrick held a similar position with respect to African Americans. His biographer, John A. Beineke (1998), notes that Kilpatrick "believed that desegregation would be fully won only when the black population as a whole became more fully integrated throughout the entire country" (p. 377).

Other intercultural educators, such as Rachael Davis DuBois; George Graff, a bureau field worker; and Leonard Covello, principal at Benjamin Franklin High School in East Harlem, embraced a stronger form of ethnic affirmation. Although they agreed that immigrants needed to experience some degree of assimilation, they didn't believe the newcomers should completely abandon their cultures. Covello wanted immigrants to learn English but also to maintain their mother tongue. He worked to get Italian listed as one of the languages that would satisfy the high school foreign language requirement in the New York City schools (Zimmerman, 1999). Covello believed ethnics would be able to maintain important elements of their culture and history, such as language, music, and art, if those elements were incorporated into the U.S. national identity. He and his colleagues not only supported ethnic affirmation but also worked to incorporate ethnic content into the curriculum. They believed that ethnic content in the regular school curriculum would send a message to both ethnic and mainstream students that the school valued information about American ethnic groups.

Intercultural educators also used varying strategies and approaches. Rachael DuBois focused her work on issues related to culture, race, and religion. She and like-minded colleagues believed students needed to have accurate information about ethnic groups and their cultures. They provided students and teachers with information on the contributions and cultures of ethnic and minority groups. Hugh Hartshorne, a board member of the Service Bureau for Intercultural Education, and Bruno Lasker raised two major concerns about intergroup materials. Hartshorne was concerned about the impact of the materials; he argued that focusing on ethnic studies would be divisive and potentially lead to separatist tendencies (Chase, 1940). Lasker was concerned about the quality of the

Bureau's materials on ethnic groups. He thought they were superficial, emphasized insignificant contributions, and included inaccurate information on the role ethnics and minorities played in U.S. history (Chase, 1940). Intergroup educators who shared Hartshorne's and Lasker's perspectives preferred for students to focus on issues related to brotherhood, prejudice, and discrimination. In that way, educators would be able to refute claims of racial superiority as well as teach students about how prejudice undermined democracy (Vickery & Cole, 1943; Cole, 1946). These intergroup educators focused on providing teachers with the skills and knowledge they needed to reduce student prejudice and increase positive intergroup relations.

The continuum of views within intercultural education ranged from cultural pluralism to assimilation. Intergroup programs, materials, and practices, however, rarely reflected either end of the continuum. They generally incorporated elements of both cultural pluralism and assimilation. For example, "Americans All—Immigrants All," a nationally broadcast intercultural radio program, reflected both assimilationist and cultural pluralist perspectives. By highlighting the contributions minorities and immigrants made to American society, the program embraced the cultural pluralist goal of legitimizing immigrant groups. However, it also helped calm mainstream Americans' concerns about minorities and ethnic culture by creating an atmosphere of tolerance for diversity. This was an important goal for assimilationists. Advocates of assimilation and cultural pluralism both found a home in intercultural education.

Intragroup Diversity

In addition to divergent voices within intergroup education, there were also differing perspectives, concerns, and allegiances within ethnic communities. To the outsider, an ethnic community was a monolith composed of people who essentially looked and acted the same way. Ethnics, however, were very aware of their differences. Italian Americans, for example, did not constitute a single group. The time period in which they emigrated to the United States as well as the region in Italy they called home were important markers of difference among Italian immigrants. Four-fifths of the Italians who came to the United States came from the *mezzogiorno* (that part of the peninsula below Rome) or from Sicily. More than half were between 14 and 49 years old. Between 1881 and 1910, four-fifths of the immigrants were male, and between 1911 and 1930 about two-thirds were male. Most of those individuals were unskilled, transient agricultural workers in the *mezzogiorno*.

Immigrants from northern Italy, most of whom arrived in the United States before 1880, were comfortably settled when immigrants from southern Italy began arriving in large numbers. When the northern Italians came to the United States, they brought marketable skills. Many were "well-educated professionals, stonecutters and masons" (Allen & Turner, 1988, p. 122). Their background in northern Italy, which was the most prosperous region of the country, offered a strong foundation for their assimilation into the U.S. mainstream. Over time, they were integrated into the social and civic life of the communities in which they lived. Their hard-earned status, however, was threatened by the arrival of their poor and uneducated cousins from southern Italy and Sicily. Instead of embracing the newcomers, they were ashamed of their cultural characteristics and held them in disdain.

Northern Italians and mainstream Americans may have seen the southern Italians as a single group, but the southern Italians didn't see themselves as a holistic group. From their perspective, their differences were salient. To them, nationality was less important than region. Southern Italians identified with their region or village. Italy, after all, did not become a unified nation until 1871.

Southern Italians came together in U.S. neighborhoods that were often made up of people from the same region or village in Italy (Allen & Turner, 1988). There was a sense of kinship among people from the same region that didn't extend to people from other regions. People from different regions often spoke dialects and couldn't easily communicate with each other. Dialects and other regional variations resulted in allegiances as well as animosities within the Italian American community. Over time, regional distinctions became less important and ethnicity became a unifying concept. The ancestral village was less important to the second and third generations than it was for their fathers and mothers. As subsequent generations interacted with Italian Americans from the several regions as well as people outside the Italian American community, their identity began to shift from the village to a larger Italian American identity.

Intragroup diversity can be invisible to outsiders who don't have a deep understanding of the ethnic or racial group. Leonard Covello (1936), the immigrant Italian who became principal of Benjamin Franklin High School, used his understanding of intragroup differences in the Italian American community to gain legitimacy with parents and to secure community support for his educational program. As an outsider within, he was able to help the teachers at Benjamin Franklin become aware of and respond sensitively to intragroup differences within the Italian American community in East Harlem.

Funding for Intergroup Education

Diversity within intercultural education mirrored its funding sources. Funding for the intercultural education

movement came primarily from organizations that were concerned with groups on the margins of U.S. society. The American Council on Education, the American Jewish Committee, the Council on Cooperation in Teacher Education, the Julius Rosenwald Fund, and the National Conference of Christians and Jews were among the organizations that provided funding for intercultural education (DuBois, 1984; Montalto, 1982; Vickery & Cole, 1943). A number of other organizations, among them the National Association for the Advancement of Colored People (NAACP), the National Urban League, the China Institute, and the Japan Institute, carried out periodic funding (Montalto, 1982). The membership of these civic and civil rights groups was primarily made up of ethnic and racial minorities.

The specific goals of the funding organizations varied, but overall they were dedicated to social justice and civil rights. Intercultural education was a means for the organizations to promote social justice in U.S. society through the schools. Even though individual members of groups such as the American Jewish Committee and the National Conference of Christians and Jews were financially successful, they were members of social groups that were on the margins of U.S. society. Their ability to be included and fully participate in American society depended, in large part, on the acceptance of their social group. Intergroup education was a way to influence school knowledge and consequently reduce the stigma associated with their social groups. As groups moved closer to the mainstream, they were less interested in the issues of people on the margins of society. Over time, for example, Jewish groups became less supportive of intergroup educators who promoted ethnic affirmation more strongly than religious tolerance and prejudice reduction. Intercultural programs that emphasized ethnic groups and cultural contributions were seen by some Jewish organizations as highlighting differences rather than similarities; they ran the risk of eliciting old animosities and anti-Semitic feelings (Montalto, 1982).

Major Initiatives in Intercultural Education

The three initiatives discussed in this section each present an important view of intercultural education.

The Service Bureau for Education in Human Relations was the first intercultural education organization with a national audience. The Bureau is an example of an advocacy group. Its founder, Rachael Davis DuBois, was a New England Quaker and a social activist who was committed to linking schools with communities.

The Springfield Plan was a citywide effort to promote brotherhood and assimilation. It is offered as an example of how city and school officials cooperated with a civil rights organization to create a prototype of a city free of prejudice and discrimination. The Springfield Plan illustrates the power of social networks in the community and the role that schools have played in social change.

The last program discussed is the Intergroup Education in Cooperating Schools Project, directed by Hilda Taba. Unlike the social activist perspectives that grounded the Service Bureau for Intercultural Education and the social network of the Springfield Plan, Taba's work reflected her stance as a professional educator and scholar. Her work focused on prejudice reduction through research, curriculum development, and professional development for teachers.

Service Bureau for Education in Human Relations

In 1933, Professor Mabel Carney of Teachers College, Columbia University, invited 16 academic and community leaders to a luncheon to discuss establishing a service bureau for education in human relations. Carney opened the luncheon discussion by emphasizing the need for schools to address intergroup tensions, and by making reference to the school assembly programs that Rachel Davis DuBois had begun implementing in 1929 ("Minutes of luncheon meeting," 1933).

The luncheon ended with a consensus that the group would constitute an advisory board and work to establish a service bureau. By 1934, only months after their first meeting, the advisory group established the Service Bureau for Education in Human Relations. The bureau grew out of the advisory board's vision for a place where educators and community leaders could turn for information and resources on intercultural education (Advisory Board, 1934).

Rachel Davis DuBois, who served as the first executive secretary of the bureau, became a major figure in intercultural education. She helped establish the bureau and the successors as the premier organizations in intercultural education. DuBois and her colleagues implemented intercultural education programs that included the study of ethnic groups, assembly programs, and club activities in a number of cities (Englewood, New Jersey; Washington, DC; Philadelphia; New York City; and elsewhere). They disseminated newsletters, articles, and reading lists on intercultural education to a national audience, developed and disseminated curriculum materials, offered in-service courses for teachers, served as a network for individuals interested in working in intercultural education, and advocated for intercultural education with school and community leaders ("History of the Service Bureau . . .," 1935).

The goals and direction of the bureau were guided by its funding sources and the intellectual orientation of its leaders. Bureau leaders were well connected through their positions on influential boards and organizations. Eight members of the 25 on the advisory board that established

the bureau were faculty or staff members at Columbia University or Teachers College, Columbia University. They provided the intellectual leadership necessary for the intercultural education movement to have academic legitimacy. They also had connections to the American Jewish Committee and National Conference of Jews and Christians, groups that funded the bureau.

Financial and intellectual factors influenced the bureau throughout its existence. The bureau's funders were a major factor in the change in emphasis from programs on cultural contributions to programs that had a more direct connection to prejudice reduction. How monetary and intellectual factors influenced the bureau is illustrated in its relationship with the Progressive Education Association.

When the bureau experienced difficulty funding programs, it was able to use connections with faculty at Teachers College to receive support from the PEA. The association supported the bureau's work by establishing a Commission on Intercultural Education (DuBois, 1984; Montalto, 1982). As a commission of the PEA, the bureau's programs came under greater scrutiny; tensions developed between DuBois and the PEA over the appropriate focus for intercultural education programs. DuBois believed that intercultural education should focus on the contributions various ethnic groups had made to American life and on building immigrants' self-esteem. She argued that by focusing on the contributions of immigrants, mainstream Americans would develop a more sympathetic and tolerant attitude toward them (DuBois, 1942). The PEA was more interested in reducing prejudice than in building the self-esteem of White ethnics. Ideological tensions, as well as DuBois's inability to draw large audiences at PEA meetings, resulted in her leaving the commission.

Even though there were tensions between DuBois and the PEA about the appropriate focus of intercultural education, there was still a demand for it. Consequently, DuBois was able to find support to continue her work. She revived the Service Bureau for Education in Human Relations under a new name, the Service Bureau for Intercultural Education. One of her first projects was to prepare research on ethnic groups for the radio program "American All—Immigrants All" (DuBois, 1984; Montalto, 1982). The program, which provided information on the cultures and contributions of various ethnic and racial groups, was broadcast on CBS on Sunday afternoons. The popular program reached an estimated three million listeners. The bureau gave educators recordings of the program as well as supporting materials for use in their intercultural education activities (Covello, 1938; Service Bureau for Intercultural Education, 1939).

Over the years, the name of the bureau changed three times. It was originally called the Service Bureau for Education in Human Relations, later the Service Bureau for

Intercultural Education, and finally the Bureau for Intercultural Education. Under each name, the bureau provided intercultural support to schools from 1934 until closing its doors in 1954. DuBois was associated with the bureau under all three names; however, with each name change she moved further from the center of decision making within the bureau. She also saw more of her ideas about the centrality of ethnic contributions to American life, self-esteem, and cultural maintenance seriously challenged. To promote her ideas and play a larger role in decision making, DuBois left the bureau in 1941 and, later that year, founded the Intercultural Education Workshop, which was also known as the Workshop for Cultural Democracy.

The Service Bureau is an important organization to examine because it illustrates how intercultural education was influenced by both internal and external forces. Whereas funding and intellectual factors illustrate the power external forces influenced over the direction of the bureau (Davis, 1999), the strong resolve and leadership of Rachel Davis DuBois exemplified an *internal* force that helped shape the bureau. Most important, the ebb and flow of support for the bureau paralleled the assimilation of White ethnics into mainstream society. The saliency of the bureau also served as a harbinger of the eventual demise of the intercultural education movement. By the 1960s, when civil unrest threatened to paralyze a number of U.S. cities, the intergroup education movement was only a dim memory (C.A.M. Banks, 1996). The grandchildren of immigrants had settled comfortably into the suburbs as mainstream Americans. The narrative of their parents' and grandparents' experiences in the United States in the early 20th century had been rewritten as the attainment of the American Dream. DuBois moved on from her work in intercultural education to become an associate of Dr. Martin Luther King, Jr., and an advocate for civil rights.

The Springfield Plan

The Springfield Plan was a community-based plan designed in 1939 by citizens in Springfield, Massachusetts, to combat intergroup tensions through education. Leaders in Springfield were concerned about intergroup tensions because they recognized that limiting the ability of some citizens to fully participate in society could undermine democracy and limit everyone's freedom. Reflecting prevalent progressive education sentiments of the day, the designers of the plan saw the school as a place where students should not only learn about but also practice democratic values. The plan included community and school components and was designed to help young people and adults acquire the skills, attitudes, and behaviors needed to embrace the principles of democracy in a

multicultural society (Alland & Wise, 1945; Chatto, 1944; Chatto & Halligan, 1945).

The idea for the Springfield Plan came out of a suggestion by Professor Clyde R. Miller of Teachers College, Columbia University, to identify a city that could serve as a laboratory to determine if it was possible for people to be accepted regardless of their ethnic, racial, religious, or social-class background. Miller had spent time in war-torn Germany and was an active member of the National Conference of Christians and Jews. In August 1939, the National Conference of Christians and Jews completed a survey indicating that counterpropaganda was not effective in reducing prejudice. The conference decided to take Miller's recommendation and look for a community where the school system could work with the community to implement democratic practices and reduce prejudice. Miller and officials of the National Conference of Christians and Jews met with John Granrud, superintendent of schools in Springfield, to discuss implementing an intercultural education program there. Granrud enthusiastically supported the idea.

Springfield was selected as the site for the program because it had many of the characteristics of middle-sized American communities whose demographic profiles had changed as a result of immigration and migration. Of the 130,000 people in Springfield in 1939, about 30% to 40% were considered "old" immigrants; their descendents had come to North America in the 1600s and 1700s (Green, 1886). The rest of the population were considered "new" immigrants. That portion of the population included individuals who were Jewish, Irish, Italian, Polish, and Greek, as well as Chinese and Filipino immigrants and Mexican Americans and African Americans. Springfield was also religiously diverse, with Catholics constituting approximately 60% of the population. The remaining 40% included Jews, Orthodox Greeks, and Protestants (Alland & Wise, 1945; Douglass, 1926).

Although segregated housing and people with anti-Catholic and anti-Semitic feelings were present in Springfield, prejudice and discrimination weren't rampant. They were at a level that was typical for most northern communities of the day. The city also had several positive characteristics; Miller (1944) cited Springfield's high rating in Edward L. Thorndike's study of cities as one of the reasons Springfield was selected. In his study, Thorndike (1939) gave the city a high rating on his "goodness index" for its civic spirit, good newspapers, and strong school system. (Ironically, a high percentage of Black families in a city was considered a negative factor on Thorndike's scale.)

Superintendent of Schools John Granrud is credited with providing the leadership for organizing and implementing the Springfield Plan. He appointed the Committee on Education for Democracy to develop an action plan to reduce prejudice and intolerance among students. The committee studied the issue and concluded that if students were to appreciate and understand democracy they had to experience it in their schools and classrooms. They also concluded that prejudice among students could not be addressed effectively by focusing exclusively on students. An effective program to reduce prejudice had to include the entire community. The committee also recommended that provisions for teacher training be part of the plan. It was understood that teachers would need additional training to design and implement the curricular changes necessary to implement the plan (Alland & Wise, 1945).

After the committee issued its report, the Council on Adult Education and the Council of Social Agencies were formed. These groups, made up of clergy of different faiths and members of business organizations, unions, and civic and social agencies, were responsible for the actual development of the plan (Alland & Wise, 1945). In addition to an extensive educational program for students and in-service training for teachers, the plan offered adult evening classes on subjects ranging from the duties and privileges of citizenship to ethnic cooking. It also created opportunities for members of the community to attend musical concerts and forums on local and national civic problems. Perhaps most important, the plan gave an opportunity to people from diverse racial, ethnic, and religious groups to identify common goals and work together to achieve them.

Almost immediately after it was implemented, the Springfield Plan won national acclaim as a prime example of the way to fight intolerance. The League for Fair Play, an organization based in New York City, was largely responsible for publicizing the plan. The league, working with its educational consultant Clyde R. Miller, found speakers, printed materials, and produced information on the plan's organizational procedures. Miller also personally conducted roundtable discussions for educators and members of civic groups. Articles about the plan were published in popular magazines such as *Parents' Magazine* and *Vogue* as well as in professional journals such as the *Journal of Education* and the *National Elementary Principal*. The plan was covered in newspapers around the country and was the subject of a Warner Brothers film. It was considered a model for other cities to emulate. School officials from Pittsburgh and other cities sent representatives to Springfield to study the plan as they contemplated implementing their own versions of it.

The plan began to come under more critical evaluation during the mid-1940s. Prior to that time, most accounts of the plan were designed to describe or promote it. An early critique noted that describing it as a "plan" was inaccurate (Payne, 1946). The term *Springfield Plan* became popular after it was used in a *New York Times* article. In actuality, the plan included several independent components, such as the authorization of a single salary schedule for teachers, the use of newsletters, an adult education program to foster stronger school-community ties, and the use of an examining board made up of administrators and members of the three major religions to select teachers (Bresnahan, 1971).

In the early 1950s, rumors undermined the rudiments of the plan by connecting it to subversive activities. Bresnahan (1971) reported that "a witness before the Senate's internal security subcommittee revealed that in a 1947 course for New York teachers she was told that the Plan was introduced as 'a softening up process done so carefully that to oppose it would have seemed sinful'" (p. 157). Granrud was no longer superintendent, and the plan didn't have a local- or national-level person championing it. (Amid controversy regarding the plan, Granrud resigned under pressure in the fall of 1945. The following summer, Alden H. Blankenship was hired to replace him.) The plan did, however, have critics in the Catholic community who were vying for more control of the schools. (Catholic leaders were interested in recruiting more students into parochial schools. In a series of articles in Catholic publications, they condemned public school education and promoted parochial education; see issues of the *Catholic Viewpoint* and the *Catholic Mirror* of the time.) Also by the 1950s, most White ethnics in Springfield had assimilated into mainstream society and did not want to be reminded of their former second-class status or associated with the ethnic and racial differences that were highlighted in the plan.

In the 1960s, some elements of the plan, such as the policies on staff selection and the single salary schedule, which had been incorporated into standard practice in the school district, were still in place. Other aspects of the plan, such as its intercultural education program, had faded. There were efforts to resurrect the term *Springfield Plan* to address some of the new aspects of intergroup tensions related to African Americans during the 1960s. However, those efforts failed to revive the plan. The intellectual and monetary support that was at the center of creation of the Springfield Plan had moved on to other issues. The individuals who were trying to revive the plan did not have the social network necessary to finance, promote, and legitimize its resurrection.

Center for Intergroup Education

Hilda Taba founded the Center for Intergroup Education at the University of Chicago in 1948. It continued in operation until 1951. Taba entered intercultural education when the focus in the movement was shifting from White ethnics to racial minorities. Racial unrest and the ongoing assimilation of White ethnics into the mainstream precipitated that shift. The Detroit race riot in June 1943 focused the nation's attention on the deep racial divide that existed in U.S. society. Foundations and educational institutions stepped forward to respond to the widespread prejudice and discrimination that were highlighted by the riots in Detroit and other U.S. cities. Taba found strong support for the intellectual rigor that she brought to what was considered a national problem.

Taba (1945) approached her work in intergroup education as a curriculum theorist and scholar. She argued that intercultural issues were complex and that teachers needed to bring "the sharp tools of logic and intellectual analysis" to their work (p. 126). She feared that without a firm grasp of social science knowledge, teachers would turn to "superficial sentimentalism and the musical comedy variety of pageantry in place of a fundamental, systematic education" (p. 126).

Staff at the Center for Intergroup Education were especially interested in experimental programs in schools and communities that could help teachers diagnose the human relations needs of their students. Center programs were based on the belief that "only by studying what children know, understand, feel, and can do, can teachers decide what they need to learn next" (Taba et al., 1951, p. 1). Center staff reported, in professional journals and texts, their findings on effective ways to learn about the cultural backgrounds of students and the communities in which they lived. Taba and her colleagues also wrote about how to evaluate methods used to reduce prejudice. One of their most important contributions was a series of books called Studies in Intergroup Education, in which *Diagnosing Human Relations Needs* was the first volume.

Taba and her colleagues implemented their ideas on intergroup education and continued to research them through a series of leadership training workshops, which were held at the University of Chicago from 1945 to 1950. Beginning in 1946, workshops were also held at Mills College in California and at Syracuse University in upstate New York (Taba, 1953). Eighteen school districts participated in the leadership training workshops.

Taba brought an appreciation for interdisciplinary approaches to her work in intercultural education. Key concepts and ideas from anthropology, sociology, psychology, and other social sciences were brought to bear on the educational challenge of reducing intergroup tensions. Her workshops varied from those focusing on theoretical perspectives and content to those emphasizing practice and application. All of the workshops, however, had several common characteristics. They concentrated on teacher concerns and were organized around issues that grew out of teachers' classroom experiences. When working with teachers, Taba made sure that they had direct access to project staff, subject matter specialists, and the information needed to refine their questions; they didn't

have to go through an intermediary. Teachers were encouraged to expand their understanding of human values by participating in community-based activities in which they came into contact with people who held differing values and perspectives on issues. Workshop experiences were designed to promote cooperation among the teachers in planning and implementing projects (Taba, 1945).

In her evaluation of three years of intercultural workshops, Taba found that teachers needed to be actively involved with intercultural information. Simply amassing information was insufficient for reducing intolerance and creating an environment of understanding. It was important to create opportunities for teachers to experience what they were studying through role-playing or some other experiential avenue in which they could take on the perspectives of people who were different from them and "feel" what they were experiencing. Taba (1945) noted that the intergroup workshops could be markedly improved if teachers had "an opportunity to first plan, secondly to practice [the planned activities] under supervision, and thirdly to re-plan in terms of practical experience" (p. 128). She also noted that provision should be made for some component of the workshop to be conducted in a community setting where members of the community would be able to work with teachers to develop and refine the plan. Taba's carefully researched approach toward intergroup education supported the efforts of such intercultural educators as Leonard Covello and John Granrud, who worked to link schools to the communities in which they were located.

The Project in Intergroup Education in Cooperating Schools was also implemented at the University of Chicago. Taba served as the director of the project from the time it began in January 1945 until it ended in September 1948. The Project in Intergroup Education was one of the best-known programs developed by intergroup educators. During its height, more than 250 local projects were involved, in 72 schools and with 2,500 teachers, school administrators, and community members (Brady, 1992). The American Council on Education sponsored the project, with financial support from the National Conference of Christians and Jews. Project staff worked cooperatively with classroom teachers to develop materials, approaches, and techniques to reduce prejudice and to identify ways to mobilize school and community resources to improve human relations and promote intergroup understanding (Taba et al., 1949).

Taba eventually left the University of Chicago and moved to California, where she became curriculum coordinator for the school district in Contra Costa County. By 1959, she had moved to San Francisco State University, where she was a professor. She remained on the faculty until her untimely death in 1967 (Krull & Martis, 1992).

Hilda Taba was an influential leader and decisive voice in the intergroup education movement (Brady, 1992). Her biographical journey in many ways marked her as an outsider within. She was a woman in a man's world, an intellectual in a field characterized by social action, and an immigrant who by many standards succeeded in mainstream America. As an outsider within, and like other intercultural educators who were immigrants or members of the second generation, she had firsthand experience with prejudice and discrimination. She was also aware that gender discrimination existed in schools. Yet there is little evidence in her writing that she saw herself as a feminist or believed that education could be a force for social change for women (Bernard-Powers, 1999).

Benjamin Franklin High School

Benjamin Franklin High School (BFHS)is an example of a school that implemented intercultural education. It is included in this chapter as an example of how intercultural education looked in practice.

BFHS was established in 1934 in East Harlem, New York. In the 1930s, East Harlem was an immigrant community, with Italian Americans as one of the dominant groups. In neighborhood studies, teachers and students at BFHS collected information on the ethnic and racial background of the people in the community. They found that in 1930, 233,400 people lived in East Harlem. Whites of foreign stock and members of the second generation totaled 169,519 people. The native White population (people born in the United States of American-born parents) numbered 33,888, with 14,000 of that number identified as Puerto Ricans. Approximately 80,000 of those individuals were Italians. The remaining population included 28,000 Jews, 19,000 Irish, 5,000 British, 4,000 Slavs, 4,000 Scandinavians, and 1,500 Greeks. Blacks constituted 29,422, and the remaining 571 were members of other ethnicities (Covello, 1935).

Leonard Covello, an Italian immigrant, served as the first principal of the school. He was raised in an Italian American community and understood the people in East Harlem. Under his leadership, BFHS received national attention for its vision and compelling mission in addressing the problems of the second generation. Covello (1939) believed that America could be "enriched by the cultural heritage of all the world without sacrificing any degree of that which is essentially American" (p. 11). He used intercultural education as a means to create understanding, appreciation, and comradeship among people who were different from one another and to link BFHS to its East Harlem community. Covello's work was based on his understanding that schools weren't isolated from the community and that the school shouldn't ignore tensions and conflicts that existed in the wider community.

One of the problems that Covello faced in implementing intercultural education at BFHS was teacher preparation. Many of them were concerned about discrimination and prejudice and were aware of intercultural tensions; however, for the most part, they were subject matter specialists who did not know how to deal with issues related to race and culture in the classroom. As a first step, Covello encouraged teachers to meet with parents at community sites. Parent conferences were held at places such as the East Harlem Health Center, the Neighborhood Music School, and Union Settlement House. These conferences enabled parents who were uncomfortable with attending meetings at school to meet on "neutral" territory. It also gave teachers an opportunity to gain firsthand experience with a broad range of people in the community. Covello (1936) also used a more formal, two-prong approach to increase the intercultural skills, knowledge, and attitudes of his teachers and administrators. He implemented a schoolwide in-service training program, which included teacher training as well as activities, materials, and assembly programs for students. He also implemented a series of committees that linked the school and the community.

BFHS Committees

Covello used committees to get teachers actively involved in the community. In that way, they could learn about the community in which their students lived and make valuable personal contacts with parents and community members. One of the first committees that Covello established was one to promote racial understanding and cooperation (Covello, 1958). The committee:

- Met periodically to maintain open lines of communication between the school and the community
- Organized a group of speakers who visited various community organizations to make presentations (in the language of the group) on the intercultural goals of BFHS
- Presented radio addresses on intercultural education designed to reach individuals who very likely would not attend community meetings
- Placed articles on intercultural education in local foreign-language publications

In addition to working with community members and parents to gain support for the school's goals, Covello wanted his teachers to be advocates for positive change in the community. This aspect of Covello's philosophy was reflected in the establishment of the Housing Committee and the Guidance Committee and Placement Bureau.

In the 1930s, East Harlem was a congested area where many students lived in old tenement houses. The Housing Committee's charge was to help secure better housing for low-income families in the community. The committee conducted a study of housing needs in East Harlem and used the findings to advocate for a low-income housing project.

The Guidance Committee and Placement Bureau worked with students to help prepare them for the world of work and contacted businessmen in the city to identify job openings. This was particularly helpful given the scarcity of jobs. According to Covello (1958), the school developed such a good reputation that when job openings occurred employers would call the school for qualified applicants.

Serving on a school committee meant working long hours and taking on extra work. By October 1937, it was becoming increasingly clear that the strain on teachers was too great. In addition to carrying a heavy teaching load, teachers were also chairing or serving on school-community committees. Covello appointed a subcommittee to review the entire community-school committee structure. The subcommittee recommended that the committees be reorganized and that committees that overlapped be eliminated. Committees doing similar work were merged and others no longer needed were sunset. The reduction in committees helped alleviate some of the stress and strain that teachers experienced, but it did not eliminate them. As a high-energy person committed to the community, Covello assumed that his teachers and administrators were willing and able to keep up with him. Some, such as Rita Morgan, were able to do so. Morgan established herself as an expert on implementing intercultural education in schools and became a respected administrator in the New York public schools. Other teachers and administrators resisted efforts to embrace intercultural education and community schooling.

Intercultural Training at Benjamin Franklin High School

Covello worked with the Service Bureau for Education in Human Relations to provide intercultural training for teachers at BFHS. Teachers and administrators from BFHS met in Covello's office with representatives from the Service Bureau (DuBois, 1937). Together they designed the school's first intercultural education in-service training plan. It had teacher and student components; the former involved small group meetings with representatives from the bureau, during which teachers discussed intercultural perspectives on issues, read material on the contributions of immigrant groups, and were trained in the intercultural program that would be implemented with students. The program included three approaches, which were designed and promoted by Rachael Davis DuBois:

1. An emotional approach. This included assemblies with guest speakers and performances. The goal was to give students an opportunity to see the rich cultural traditions of their classmates.

2. A situational approach. Informal conversations with community members who could talk about ethnic or cultural issues were arranged so students could get to know people personally who were from a different ethnic group. Each guest was met and introduced by students from an ethnic group other than the speaker's.

3. An intellectual approach. During the homeroom period, students read and discussed information about ethnic groups that wasn't available in school texts. The information was in pamphlets and booklets produced by the Service Bureau.

Intercultural content was also incorporated into the curriculum in several areas, notably biology, mathematics, and English. "Living Together with Others," "Mankind Grows Up," "Understanding America," and "The Literature of Moral Attitudes and Social Problems" were themes woven through the English curriculum. The themes were a basis for exploring issues related to race relations, nationality, prejudice, stereotypes, and the interrelationship of world religions (Covello, 1939).

Language Issues at BFHS. Even with Covello's efforts to increase his teachers' skill and knowledge about intercultural education and to link the school to the community, teachers at Benjamin Franklin faced a tremendous challenge in involving parents in the school. Many of their students' parents were foreign-born and did not speak English; they couldn't understand letters or school brochures that were written in English. Moreover, they weren't interested in attending meetings where all of the business was conducted in a language they didn't understand. In addition to language barriers, some parents, as a result of negative experiences at school or the formality of the school setting, did not feel welcome at Benjamin Franklin.

In an effort to break down those barriers, communications to parents were sent out in several languages (English, Italian, Spanish, German, Yiddish, and others). Covello and other educators at Benjamin Franklin who were bilingual made presentations to community groups in the language of the group. Not everyone at BFHS agreed with this approach. Some were afraid that it would not encourage immigrants to learn English. Covello did not yield to the opposition he encountered. He recognized that in order for parents to ultimately support the goals of the school, they had to understand them. Therefore, when possible, the mother tongue of the student's family was used during school conferences. Use of the family's language, according to Covello, reduced parental tension during conferences and created an environment where parents and teachers could work together.

Looking Back. Covello's commitment to community schooling was embraced by many (though not all) of the teachers at Benjamin Franklin High School. Through the strength of his personality, leadership skills, and respect in the school system, Covello maintained links with the community throughout his tenure as principal at BFHS. However, by the late 1940s, when African Americans and Puerto Ricans became a more sizable component of the student population, the focus on community schooling began to wane. By the late 1950s, community schooling was only a shadow of what it had been in the 1930s and early 1940s (Johanek, 1995).

The innovations at Benjamin Franklin High School were achieved as a result of an actively involved community, a dedicated and committed group of socially minded teachers, and the visionary leadership of Leonard Covello. Human values were paramount at Benjamin Franklin. Covello argued that students should not be seen as clay to be molded in the hands of skilled craftsmen. They were alive, vibrant, ever-changing young people who were being shaped by forces both within and outside the school (Covello, 1939). Leadership through values was at the base of Covello's work at Benjamin Franklin High School. This was a difficult kind of leadership because values are often in conflict. As the community and student population changed, it became harder for Covello and the teachers at Benjamin Franklin to identify and use common values to motivate people to come together.

CYCLES OF CHANGE: THE WANING INFLUENCE OF INTERCULTURAL EDUCATION

Intercultural education began at a time of tremendous social, economic, and cultural change. Nativist sentiments, lynching, and race riots were widespread. Intercultural educators responded to social unrest and intergroup tension by incorporating ethnic content and celebrations into the curriculum, examining prejudice and discrimination, and providing sympathetic support for White ethnics and racial minorities as they underwent cultural assimilation into U.S. society. Both people of color and White ethnics, for the most part, welcomed their efforts. Unlike White ethnics, however, racial minorities did realize the full benefits of intergroup education. Intercultural educators focused their attention on creating the conditions for tolerance and brotherhood, but they did not address segregation and other institutional barriers that prevented racial minorities from gaining access to good schools and meaningful curricula.

Responding to segregated schools and communities, school texts and materials that misrepresented racial minorities, and teachers and administrators who used discriminatory hiring practices required more than verbal commitment to tolerance and brotherhood. It meant action based on an understanding of the need to unravel the deep structure of prejudice and discrimination that had been built up over generations: a structure into which not only mainstream Americans were socialized but immigrants as well. Intercultural educators for the most part did not seem to recognize or were not prepared to address the enormous problem of minority discrimination. Today multicultural educators are addressing these and other related issues.

THE MORE THINGS CHANGE, THE MORE THEY STAY THE SAME

The groups that were excluded from full participation in U.S. society have changed since the 1930s, but exclusion continues to exist. By the beginning of the 21st century White ethnics, whose ancestors were on the margins of U.S. society in the early 20th century, had largely moved into the mainstream. The margins, however, didn't disappear. They continued to be filled by indigenous groups and by new waves of immigrants.

The actual number of immigrants from 1991 to 1999 was almost identical to the number from 1901 to 1910 (U.S. Census Bureau, 1975, 2000). A major difference between the two time periods was that almost 92% of the immigrants who came during the first decade of the 20th century were from Europe, while only 14.8% came from Europe during the last decade of that century (Gibson & Lennon, 1999). At the beginning of the 20th century, U.S. immigrants were primarily from Italy, Russia, and other southern and eastern European countries. However, by the end of the century they were primarily from the Caribbean, Central America, South America, Mexico, and Asian countries (China, India, Korea, the Philippines; Gibson & Lennon, 1999).

The origin of U.S. immigrants changed from the beginning to the end of the 20th century, but attitudes toward newcomers remained skeptical, unsure, and in some cases fearful. Patrick Buchanan (2002) captured those concerns in his best-selling book *The Death of the West: How Dying Populations and Immigrant Invasions Imperil Our Country and Civilization*. It is ironic that Buchanan, a person whose religion would have placed him in the margins of society at the beginning of the 20th century, was able a century later to use rhetoric similar to that of Henry Pratt Fairchild in the early 1900s to raise concerns about new immigrants.

One of the characteristics of movement from the margins to the center is the adoption of mainstream rhetoric.

Once people have experience structural assimilation, it is not uncommon for them to become gatekeepers and defenders of the status quo who try to limit access for other groups. They frequently use the same arguments against other groups that were used to discriminate against their ancestors only a few generations before (Ignatiev, 1995).

Educators today, like intergroup educators in the past, can intervene in this cycle of exclusion with curricula, strategies, and programs designed to reduce intergroup tensions and help students develop the skills, attitudes, and values necessary to become active participants in a multicultural democratic society. However, what educators believe about the schooling of immigrants in the past can influence their understanding of and their expectations for recent immigrants as well as indigenous minority groups (Olneck, Chapter 19 of this volume). If their understanding of the immigrant experience is based on the idea that immigrants were able to overcome hardship and adversity through hard work, determination, and perseverance, they may feel that other groups will simply have to do the same if they want to enter the mainstream.

Better understanding of what teachers were taught about intergroup education can help bring historical perspective to contentious debate about the importance of acknowledging and responding to ethnicity, language, and other forms of student diversity. Information on the intergroup education movement suggests that educators took seriously their responsibility to prepare students to live in a democracy. They didn't ignore prejudice and discrimination; they addressed it in their classrooms. Most important, they went out into the community to make connections with their students' parents and worked to reduce individual prejudice and discrimination head on.

As members of the second generation, many of the teachers who established links between the school and community in the 1930s and 1940s understood ethnic communities and had some affection for their residents. Today students of color are primarily taught by teachers who do not have a personal connection to the communities in which they teach. Encouraging and supporting teachers to reach out to communities less well known to them requires teacher training and a commitment to building strong community relations.

As the ethnic and racial texture of our society deepens and as social class, language, and other forms of diversity become more salient, linking schools to communities can help teachers better understand their students and increase their ability to draw on the community as a rich resource. Intergroup educators established links between schools and communities as an important step in reducing intergroup tension and actualizing democratic ideals. Their shortcomings, struggles, and victories can yield important insights for educators today.

References

Adamic, L. (1934, November). Thirty million new Americans. *Harper's, 169,* 684–694.

Adamic, L. (1940). *From many lands.* New York: Harper.

Adamic, L. (1944). *A nation of nations.* New York: Harper.

Advisory Board, Service Bureau for Education in Human Relations. (1934). *First report of the Advisory Board.* MSS 40, folder 50/9, Covello Papers, Balch Institute.

Alland, A., & Wise, J. W. (1945). *The Springfield Plan.* New York: Viking Press.

Allen, J. P., & Turner, E. J. (1988). *We the people: An atlas of America's ethnic diversity.* New York: Macmillan.

Banks, C.A.M. (1996). The intergroup education movement. In J. A. Banks (Ed.), *Multicultural education, transformative knowledge, and action: Historical and contemporary perspectives* (pp. 251–277). New York: Teachers College Press.

Banks, C.A.M. (2003). Parents and teachers: Partners in school reform. In J. A. Banks and C.A.M. Banks (Eds.), *Multicultural education: Issues and perspectives* (Updated 4th ed., pp. 402–420). New York: Wiley.

Beineke, J. A. (1998). *And there were giants in the land: The life of William Heard Kilpatrick.* New York: Peter Lang.

Benedict, R. (1942). American melting pot, 1942 model. In Department of Supervisors and Directors of Instructors of the National Education Association, National Council of Teachers of English, and Society for Curriculum Study. *Americans all: Studies in intercultural education* (pp. 14–24). Washington, DC: National Education Association, Department of Supervisors and Directors of Instruction.

Bernard-Powers, J. (1999). Composing her life: Hilda Taba and social studies history. In M. S. Crocco & O. L. Davis, Jr. (Eds.), *Bending the future to their will: Civic women, social education, and democracy* (pp. 185–206). New York: Rowman & Littlefield.

Bourne, R. S. (1917). *Education and living.* New York: Crowell.

Brady, E. H. (1992). Intergroup education in public schools, 1945–51. In *Jubilee conference: Hilda Taba-90* (pp. 15–29). Tartu, Estonia: Tartu University.

Bresnahan, D. (1971). *The Springfield Plan in retrospect.* Unpublished doctoral dissertation, Teachers College, Columbia University.

Buchanan, P. J. (2002). *The death of the West: How dying populations and immigrant invasions imperil our country and civilization.* New York: Thomas Dunne.

Caffrey, M. M. (1989). *Ruth Benedict: Stranger in this land.* Austin: University of Texas Press.

Carlson, R. (1987). *The Americanization syndrome: A quest for conformity.* New York: St. Martin's Press.

Carney, M. (1933, October 18). Letter to Leonard Covello. MSS 40, folder 50/9, Covello Papers, Balch Institute.

Chase, G. (1940). *Report of the committee for evaluation of the work of the Service Bureau for Intercultural Education.* New York: New York City School Board.

Chatto, C. I. (1944). Education for democratic living. *Journal of Education, 127*(6), 189–191.

Chatto, C. I., & Halligan, A. L.(1945). *The story of the Springfield Plan.* New York: Barnes & Noble.

Clinchy, E. R. (Ed.). (1942). *The world we want to live in.* New York: Doubleday.

Cole, S. G. (1946). What is intercultural education? In G. B. deHuszar (Ed.), *Anatomy of racial intolerance* (pp. 175–182). New York: H. W. Wilson.

Collins, P. H. (1990). *Black feminist thought: Knowledge, consciousness, and the politics of empowerment.* New York: Routledge.

Committee on the Study of Teaching Materials in Intergroup Relations. (1949). *Intergroup relations in teaching materials: A survey and appraisal.* Washington, DC: American Council on Education.

Cook, L. A. (1938). *Community backgrounds of education.* New York: McGraw-Hill.

Cook, L. A. (1950). *College programs in intergroup relations.* Washington, DC: American Council on Education.

Cook, L. A., & Cook, E. (1954). *Intergroup education.* New York: McGraw-Hill.

Cook, L. A., & Cook, E. (1957). *School problems in human relations.* New York: McGraw-Hill.

Covello, L. (1935). *Neighborhood studies.* L. MM40, Covello 54/22, Covello Papers, Balch Institute.

Covello, L. (1936). A high school and its immigrant community: A challenge and an opportunity. *Journal of Educational Sociology, 9*(2), 331–346.

Covello, L. (1938, December 9). Letter to the faculty at Benjamin Franklin High School. MSS 40, folder 4/12, Covello Papers, Balch Institute.

Covello, L. (1939). *Paper presented at intercultural conference.* Unpublished manuscript, Balch Institute.

Covello, L., with D'Agostino, G. (1958). *The heart is the teacher.* New York: McGraw-Hill.

Cremin, L. (1988). *American education: The metropolitan experience, 1876–1980.* New York: Harper & Row.

Crew, S. R. (1987). *Field to factory: Afro-American migration 1915–1940.* Washington, DC: Smithsonian Institution.

Davis, O. L., Jr. (1999). Rachel Davis DuBois: Intercultural education pioneer. In M. S. Crocco & O. L. Davis, Jr. (Eds.), *Bending the future to their will: Civic women, social education, and democracy* (pp. 169–184).New York: Rowman & Littlefield.

Douglass, H. P. (1926). *The Springfield church survey: A study of organized religion with its social background.* New York: George H. Doran.

Drachsler, J. (1920). *Democracy and assimilation: The blending of immigrant heritages in America.* Westport, CT: Negro Universities Press.

DuBois, R. D. (1928). *Education in worldmindedness: A series of assembly programs given by students at Woodbury High School, Woodbury, New Jersey, 1927–1928.* Philadelphia.

DuBois, R. D. (1930). *The contributions of racial elements to American life* (2nd ed.). Philadelphia: Women's International League for Peace and Freedom.

DuBois, R. D. (1936). Exploring sympathetic attitudes towards people. *Journal of Educational Sociology, 9,* 391–394.

DuBois, R. D. (1937). Intercultural education at Benjamin Franklin High School. *High Points, 19,* 23–29.

DuBois, R. D. (1939). *Adventures in intercultural education: A manual for secondary school teachers.* New York: Intercultural Education Workshop.

DuBois, R. D. (1942). Conserving cultural resources. In Department of Supervisors and Directors of Instructors of the National Education Association, National Council of Teachers of English, and Society for Curriculum Study. *Americans all: Studies in intercultural education* (pp. 148–159). Washington, DC: National Education Association, Department of Supervisors and Directors of Instruction.

DuBois, R. D., with Okorodudu, C. (1984). *All this and something more: Pioneering in intercultural education.* Bryn Mawr, PA: Dorrance.

Fairchild, H. P. (1913). *Immigration: A world movement and its American significance.* New York: Macmillan.

Fairchild, H. P. (1926). *The melting-pot mistake.* Boston: Little, Brown.

Fairchild, H. P. (1953). Conditions in America as affected by immigration. In B. M. Ziegler (Ed.), *Immigration: An American dilemma* (pp. 34–49). Boston: Heath.

Gibson, C., & Lennon, E. (1999). *Region of birth of the foreign-born population.* Washington, DC: U.S. Census Bureau, Population Division.

Giles, H. H. (1945). Organizations in the field of intercultural relations. *Harvard Educational Review, 15*(2), 87–92.

Gordon, M. (1964). *Assimilation in American life.* New York: Oxford University Press.

Green, M. A. (1886). *Springfield 1636–1886: History of town and city.* Boston: Rockwell and Churchill.

Henderson, A. (1987). *The evidence continues to grow: Parent involvement improves student achievement.* Columbia, MD: National Committee for Citizens in Education.

Higham, J. (1972). *Strangers in the land: Patterns of American nativism 1860–1925.* New York: Atheneum.

History of the Service Bureau for Education in Human Relations. (1935). MSS 40, folder 50/9, Covello Papers, Balch Institute.

Houston Curriculum Guide. (1931). *Life on the American frontier: A study of the westward movement in American history* (Unit III). Houston: Houston Public Schools.

Hutchinson, E. P. (1949). *Immigration policy since World War I. Annuals, 262,* 15–21.

Ignatiev, N. (1995). *How the Irish became White.* New York: Routledge.

Johanek, M. C. (1995). *The public purposes of public education: The evolution of community-centered schooling at Benjamin Franklin High School, 1934–1944.* Unpublished doctoral dissertation, Teachers College, Columbia University.

Kallen, H. M. (1924). *Culture and democracy in the United States.* New York: Boni and Liveright.

Krull, E., & Marits, A. (1992). Hilda Taba and Estonian educational science. Taba's childhood, schooling, and the acceptance of her educational ideas in Estonia. In *Jubilee conference: Hilda Taba—90* (pp. 51–59). Tartu, Estonia: Tartu University.

Leder, [Mrs.]. (n.d.). Letter to Jacob Greenberg. Series 562, folder 3, Board of Education N, New York Public Schools, Special Collections of Milbank Memorial Library, Teachers College, Columbia University.

Lewis, D. L. (2000). *W.E.B. DuBois: The fight for equality and the American century, 1919-1963.* New York: Henry Holt.

Locke, A., & Stern, B. J. (Eds.). (1942). *When peoples meet: A study in race and culture contacts.* New York: Progressive Education Association.

Marks, C. (1989). *Farewell-we're good and gone: The great Black migration.* Bloomington: Indiana University Press.

Miller, C. (1944). Country wages total war on prejudice. *Nation's Schools, 33,* 16–18.

Minutes of luncheon meeting. (1933, October 18). MSS 40, folder 50/9, Covello Papers, Balch Institute.

Montalto, N. V. (1982). *A history of the intercultural education movement 1924–1941.* New York: Garland.

Nelli, H. S. (1983). *From immigrants to ethnics: The Italian Americans.* New York: Oxford University Press.

Payne, E. G. (1946). The Springfield Plan. *Journal of Educational Sociology, 14,* 395–397.

Perrone, V. (1998). *Teacher with a heart.* New York: Teachers College Press.

Riley, M. L. (1945, September 26). Letter to Lily Edelman. Series 562, folder 1, Board of Education, New York Public Schools, Special Collections of Milbank Memorial Library, Teachers College, Columbia University.

Ross, E. A. (1914). Immigrants in politics: The political consequences of immigration. In B. M. Ziegler (Ed.), *Immigration: An American dilemma* (pp. 71–77). Boston: D. C. Heath.

Seller, M. (1977). *To seek America: A history of ethnic life in the United States.* Englewood, NJ: J. S. Ozer.

Service Bureau for Intercultural Education. (1939). *Human beings are making America.* New York: Service Bureau for Intercultural Education,

Taba, H. (1945). The contributions of workshops to intercultural education. *Harvard Educational Review, 15*(2), 122–128.

Taba, H. (1953). *Leadership training in intergroup education.* Washington, DC: American Council on Education.

Taba, H., Brady, E. H., Jennings, H. H., & Robinson, J. T. (1949). *Curriculum intergroup relations: Case studies in instruction for secondary schools.* Washington, DC: American Council on Education.

Taba, H., Brady, E., Robinson, J., & Vickery, W. R. (1951). *Diagnosing human relations needs.* Washington, DC: American Council on Education.

Taba, H., & VanTil, W. (Eds.). (1945). *Democratic human relations: Promising practices in intergroup and intercultural education in the social studies.* Washington, DC: National Council for the Social Studies.

Thorndike, E. L. (1939). American cities and states: Correlation in institutions, activities, and the personal qualities of residents. *Annuals of the New York Academy of Sciences, 39,* 213–298.

Trager, H. G., & Yarrow, M. R. (1952). *They learn what they live: Prejudice in young children.* New York: Harper & Brothers.

Troen, S. K. (1975). *The public and the schools: Shaping the St. Louis schools system, 1838-1920.* Columbia: University of Missouri Press.

U.S. Census Bureau. (1975). *Historical statistics of the United States, colonial times to 1970, bicentennial edition, Part 2.* Washington, DC: U.S. Government Printing Office.

U.S. Census Bureau. (2000). *Statistical abstract of the United States: 2000* (120th ed.). Washington, DC: U.S. Government Printing Office.

Vickery, W. E., & Cole, S. G. (1943). *Intercultural education in American schools: Proposed objectives and methods.* New York: Harper & Brothers.

Waller, J. F. (1932). *Outside demands and pressures on the public schools.* New York: Columbia University, Teachers College.

Yavner, L. E. (1945). *Administration of human relations programs in New York City schools.* New York: New York Public Schools.

Ziegler, B. M. (Ed.). (1953). *Immigration: An American dilemma.* Boston: Heath.

Zimmerman, J. (1999). Storm over the schoolhouse: Exploring popular influences upon the American curriculum, 1890–1941. *Teachers College Record, 100*(3), 602–626.

37

INTERGROUP CONTACT

Theory, Research, and New Perspectives

Thomas F. Pettigrew

University of California, Santa Cruz

Both multicultural education and intergroup contact advance methods designed to reduce intergroup prejudice, ignorance, and conflict. Although multicultural efforts usually involve didactic procedures and intergroup contact interactive procedures, the two approaches are fully compatible and often combined. Indeed, it proves useful to distinguish between those multicultural methods that are most appropriate to single-group settings and those most appropriate for mixed-group settings. Stephan and Stephan (2001), in their important book *Improving Intergroup Relations,* found it necessary to discuss separately the processes used in multicultural education in segregated settings as opposed to those used in integrated settings.

This chapter discusses intergroup contact—its enormous theoretical and research literature, new theoretical advances, and practical implications for reducing intergroup prejudice. The central thesis is that when multicultural education is combined with optimal intergroup contact, its advantages are greatly enhanced. Moreover, when multicultural instruction occurs in multigroup contexts, major criticisms of multicultural education lose force. In short, the two approaches together have greater potential for improving intergroup relations than either approach alone.

HISTORICAL DEVELOPMENT OF INTERGROUP CONTACT THEORY AND RESEARCH

Early Studies

The newly emerging discipline of social psychology of the 1930s soon began to study intergroup contact. This interest followed logically from the field's emphases on intergroup relations and the interaction between people. Researchers at the University of Alabama were among the first to conduct a study directly focused on contact (Sims & Patrick, 1936). Not surprisingly, given the negative contact conditions, these initial results were not encouraging. With each year that students from the North remained at the southern university, their anti-Black attitudes increased. Since the university's faculty and student body were then all White, these students met only lower-status Blacks and behaved according to Alabama's racist norms of that period.

Later studies investigated Black-White contact under more favorable conditions. After the desegregation of the Merchant Marine in 1948, genuine bonds developed between Black and White seamen on the ships and in the maritime union (Brophy, 1946). Consequently, the more

I am indebted to Linda Tropp of Boston College for her extensive and persistent work on our meta-analysis of intergroup contact's effects on prejudice (Pettigrew & Tropp, 2000, 2002).

voyages the White seamen took with Blacks, the more positive their racial attitudes became. Similarly, White police in Philadelphia who had worked with Black colleagues differed sharply from other White policemen on the force (Kephart, 1957). They had fewer objections to Blacks joining their previously all-White police districts, teaming with a Black partner, and taking orders from qualified Black officers.

Robin Williams's Initial Formulation

American theorists and practitioners began to speculate about interracial contact before there was a research base to guide them. Some writers, like Baker (1934), thought contact between the races under conditions of equality would breed only "suspicion, fear, resentment, disturbance, and at times open conflict" (p. 120). Greater optimism characterized the speculations following World War II. Lett (1945) held that shared interracial experiences with a common objective led to "mutual understanding and regard" (p. 35). Brameld (1946) went further. When groups "are isolated from one another," he asserted, "prejudice and conflict grow like a disease" (p. 245).

The Social Science Research Council then asked Robin Williams, Jr., the distinguished Cornell University sociologist, to review what was known about group relations. Williams's (1947) monograph, *The Reduction of Intergroup Tensions,* remains a classic work. His booklet offers 102 testable "propositions" on intergroup relations and a host of suggestions for future research. Williams (1947) presents the initial formulation of intergroup contact theory in his propositions.

Williams (1947) looked carefully at the early studies. He stressed that many variables would influence contact's effects on prejudice—such as the status of the participants, the social milieu, the level of prior prejudice, the duration of the contact, and the amount of intergroup competition in the situation. In particular, he held that intergroup contact would maximally reduce prejudice when (1) the two groups share similar status, interests, and tasks; (2) the situation fosters personal, intimate intergroup contact; (3) the participants do not fit the stereotyped conceptions of their groups; and (4) the activities cut across group lines. Later research supports all of Williams's insightful contentions.

The New York Field Studies

By 1950, research began to test the theory more rigorously. Major field studies of public housing projects by New York researchers provided the strongest evidence. Indeed, these studies mark the introduction of large-scale field research in social psychology with rigorous research designs that Campbell and Stanley (1963) later called "quasi-experiments."

Deutsch and Collins (1951) took advantage of a social experiment. Two biracial housing projects in New York City made apartment assignments regardless of race or personal preference. Two comparable projects in Newark, New Jersey, assigned Black and White residents to separate buildings. Striking differences emerged in interviews of White housewives in the two sets of projects. Not surprisingly, the desegregated women had far more optimal contact with their Black neighbors—in the building and at laundry and grocery facilities. And they held their Black neighbors in higher esteem and expressed greater support of interracial housing (75% to 25%). When asked to name Black faults, they listed such personal issues as feelings of inferiority. The segregated White women typically voiced such stereotypes as "rowdy" and "dangerous."

Further public housing research by Wilner, Walkley, and Cook (1955) extended these findings. They found the intimacy of interracial contact to be critical. Favorable racial attitudes developed among only a third of the White tenants who did not interact with their African American neighbors beyond casual greetings. However, half of those who had street conversations with their Black neighbors and three fourths of those who had many types of interactions developed more favorable racial views. In short, those Whites who acted like neighbors felt like neighbors. This sequence of changed behavior leading to changed attitudes is a vital means by which optimal intergroup contact has positive effects. Follow-up research by Works (1961) showed that the same principles operate for African Americans. He found that increased equal-status interracial contact in a public housing project related to both more positive feelings and attitudes toward White Americans.

Gordon Allport's Influential Formulation

Armed with Williams's (1947) initial effort and the rich findings of the New York studies, Gordon Allport (1954) introduced the most influential statement of contact theory in his famous book, *The Nature of Prejudice.* His formulation has guided research on the phenomenon for the past half-century. He noted the contrasting effects of intergroup contact—often reducing but sometimes exacerbating prejudice. To explain these findings, Allport adopted a "positive factors" approach. Reduced prejudice will result, he held, when four positive features of the contact situation are present: equal status of the groups in the situation, common goals, intergroup cooperation, and the support of authorities, law, or custom. Consider each of these conditions.

Equal Group Status in the Situation. Relevant research supports the importance of this factor, although "equal status" is difficult to define and researchers have used it in different ways (Cagle, 1973; Riordan, 1978). It is important that both groups expect and perceive equal status in the situation (Cohen, 1982; Cohen & Lotan, 1995; Riordan & Ruggiero, 1980; Robinson & Preston, 1976). Some writers emphasize equal group status coming into the situation (Brewer & Kramer, 1985). Thus, Jackman and Crane (1986) uncovered negative effects from contact with out-group members of lower status. But Patchen (1982), in research on racially desegregated high schools, found equal status in the situation to be more important.

Common Goals. Passive contact between groups is of little use. To reduce prejudice, contact must involve an active effort toward a goal that the groups share. Athletic teams furnish a prime example (Chu & Griffey, 1985; Miracle, 1981; Patchen, 1982). In striving to win, intergroup teams need each other—which leads to Allport's third condition.

Intergroup Cooperation. Attainment of the groups' common goals should be an interdependent effort without intergroup competition (Bettencourt, Brewer, Rogers-Croak, & Miller, 1992). Sherif (1966) demonstrated this principle vividly in his famous Robbers Cave field study. Intergroup cooperation in schools, often involving a multicultural curriculum, provides the strongest evidence (Brewer & Miller, 1984; Desforges et al., 1991; Johnson, Johnson, & Maruyama, 1984; Schofield, 1989; Slavin, 1983; Slavin & Madden, 1979). Guided by Allport's contentions, Aronson's jigsaw classroom technique (Aronson & Patnoe, 1997) structures intergroup classrooms so that students strive cooperatively for common goals. This direct application of contact theory has led to positive results for children around the globe: in Australia (Walker & Crogan, 1998), Germany (Eppler & Huber, 1990), Japan (Araragi, 1983), and the United States (Aronson & Gonzalez, 1988).

Support of Authorities, Law, or Custom. Allport's final condition focuses on the auspices of the contact. Backed by explicit social sanction, intergroup contact is more readily accepted and has more positive effects. Authority support establishes norms of acceptance. Field research has demonstrated its importance in military (Landis, Hope, & Day, 1984), business (Morrison & Herlihy, 1992), and religious settings (Parker, 1968).

Problems with Allport's Intergroup Contact Theory

Although Allport's formulation has served researchers well, its weaknesses have become more apparent over the years. In particular, four problems have emerged that we must address (Pettigrew, 1998). (1) First, there is the problem of causal sequence: Does contact reduce prejudice, or does prejudice reduce contact? (2) The theory risks being an open-ended, ever expanding list of necessary positive conditions. (3) It also says little about the processes by which contact leads to changed attitudes and behavior. Finally, (4) the theory does not specify how contact's effects will generalize beyond the immediate situation. These points highlight the complexity of the intergroup contact phenomenon.

The Causal Sequence Problem. Determining causation is one of social science's most difficult tasks (Pettigrew, 1996). And in many of the investigations of contact's effects, the causal direction is not clear. The theory interprets the results to mean that optimal contact causes improved intergroup attitudes. Yet the opposite causal sequence also could explain these results. The unprejudiced may seek and the prejudiced avoid intergroup contact. This selection bias could by itself create the negative association between contact and prejudice. Indeed, there is evidence that such a selection bias does operate.

There are several ways to overcome this limitation. (1) Research can eliminate the selection bias by restricting the choice of subjects; when bigots cannot avoid the contact, the bias cannot operate. In the Merchant Marine and police studies mentioned earlier, there was little choice available to the seamen and police. (2) Longitudinal research offers an ideal way to overcome selection bias (Pettigrew, 1996). Over-time designs measure the dependent variable repeatedly, starting before the contact and following through after the contact. Such studies are expensive and difficult to conduct, so there are few such contact examples. An outstanding exception is Sherif's Robbers Cave field experiment (1966). Finally, (3) statistical methods can evaluate the two causal paths (contact lowers prejudice and prejudice decreases contact) even in research that is not longitudinal (Pettigrew, 1997a; Powers & Ellison, 1995). All these methods indicate that both causal paths operate, but the contact reducing prejudice path is the stronger. (Other methods too have reached the same conclusion; see Irish, 1952; Link & Cullen, 1986; and Wilson, 1996. Springer's thesis research [1996] is the lone exception, although it did not employ direct measures of prejudice.)

An Ever Expanding List of Necessary, Positive Conditions. Allport's approach risks being an open-ended laundry list of conditions—ever expandable and thus eluding falsification (Pettigrew, 1986, 1998; Stephan, 1987). To the four original conditions, researchers have added many other factors. Thus, from Germany, Wagner and Machleit (1986) conclude that a common language, voluntary contact, and prosperous economic times are necessary. From

Israel, Ben-Ari and Amir (1986) hold that positive effects will not occur if the groups' initial attitudes toward each other are too negative. From the United States, Cook (1978) maintains that the out-group must have characteristics that disconfirm their negative stereotype before positive effects will occur. And Pettigrew (1997a) regards as critical the potential of the situation for cross-group friendships to form.

This growing list of limiting conditions threatens to remove all practical interest from the theory. Too many factors risk making it a lengthy list of necessary conditions that excludes most intergroup situations. In that event, the theory would rarely predict positive results from intergroup contact—although research contradicts this possibility. The problem is that writers often confuse facilitating with essential conditions, a point to which we shall return in the reformulation of the theory.

Failure to Specify the Processes by Which Intergroup Contact Diminishes Prejudice. The theory predicts only when contact will lead to positive change, not how and why the change occurs. Later work suggests four broad and interrelated types of processes: (1) learning about the out-group, (2) generating affective ties, (3) changing behavior, and (d) reappraising the in-group (Pettigrew, 1998):

1. *Learning about the out-group.* Early writers thought that learning about the out-group is the major process by which intergroup contact diminishes prejudice. Their reasoning was that this new learning would counter negative views of the out-group and thus reduce prejudice. But there is an array of cognitive mechanisms that causes us to deny or explain away evidence that disconfirms our prejudicial thinking (Pettigrew, 1979; Rothbart & John, 1985).

    Nonetheless, new information about the out-group has the potential to improve attitudes. Stephan and Stephan (1984) studied two junior high schools in New Mexico and found that contact allowed the Anglo students to learn more about Chicano culture. This new understanding led to more positive attitudes toward their Chicano classmates. "Ignorance," maintain Stephan and Stephan (1984), "promotes prejudice" (p. 238). We fear and reject what we do not understand. So social psychologists have devised various methods to help people learn more about other cultures. The typically positive results of these techniques show that learning more about the out-group can improve intergroup attitudes. Indeed, this postulate is fundamental to multicultural education.

2. *Generating affective ties.* Emotion is an important element in intergroup contact. Optimal contact often evokes positive feelings toward the out-group, especially when it involves cross-group friendship

(Pettigrew, 1997a; Pettigrew & Tropp, 2000, 2002). Negative emotions, such as anxiety, also play a role. Contact's potential to reduce intergroup anxiety is often involved in the improvement of attitudes. In reformulating the theory, we shall see that affect plays a central role in contact's potential to reduce prejudice.

3. *Changing behavior.* Conventional wisdom holds that people must be persuaded to engage in new behavior, that attitude change must precede behavioral change. But hundreds of social psychological studies have shown the efficacy of precisely the opposite causal sequence: behavior change is often the precursor of attitude change. This sequence is important for intergroup contact effects. New situations with new norms require us to behave differently, to conform to new expectations. When these expectations include acceptance of out-group members, this behavior itself can produce attitude change. Our old prejudices conflict with our new behavior. We can resolve this cognitive dissonance by altering our old attitudes. Optimal intergroup contact offers a means of behavior modification, with new behavior leading to changed attitudes.

    The behavior change process also benefits from repeated contact. Repetition makes the formerly strange intergroup encounter seem comfortable, even "right." Indeed, repetition itself leads to liking (Zajonc, 1968). Repeated rewards for the new behavior enhance the positive effects further.

4. *Reappraising the in-group.* A fourth process of positive contact effects involves in-group reappraisal. Optimal intergroup contact provides insight about in-groups as well as out-groups. In-group norms and customs turn out not to be the only ways to manage the social world. This new perspective provides a less provincial perspective on other groups as well. Indeed, several studies have uncovered evidence of intergroup contact leading to diminished prejudice against out-groups not involved in the contact (Pettigrew, 1997a).

Part of this in-group reappraisal process involves having less contact with the in-group as a result of interacting more with the out-group. Wilder and Thompson (1980) found that in-group contact influenced bias toward an out-group. They covaried both contact with the in-group and out-group in an experiment using student subjects. Although it had no impact on in-group ratings, less in-group contact led to less bias toward the out-group.

Do Contact Effects Generalize Beyond the Immediate Situation? If contact led only to improved attitudes toward the immediate out-group members in the situation, the theory's practical value would be extremely limited. Hence, for optimal contact to improve intergroup relations, its effects must generalize beyond the situation and those involved in the contact. This issue first arose from a U.S. Army study during World War II (Stouffer, Schuman, DeVinney, Star, & Williams, 1949). In the Battle of the Bulge during the severe winter of 1944–1945, U.S. Army commanders called up Black infantry platoons comprising volunteers. They joined White infantry companies with whom they fought throughout the war's final months. This situation met Allport's key criteria handsomely. Black and White soldiers fought side by side on equal terms. They had common goals: staying alive and winning the battle. Their contact was maximally interdependent and noncompetitive, and the army's high command supported it.

Stouffer and his colleagues collected data as soon as the fighting ended and found dramatic contact effects (Stouffer et al., 1949). Whether officers or enlisted men, whether southern or northern, the White soldiers sharply changed their attitudes toward African Americans as soldiers. Seventy-seven percent said the experience had made them more favorable toward Black Americans. More than 80% thought the Black troops performed "very well," and 90% thought that as infantrymen, they were as good as or better than Whites. To show that the changes resulted from the contact, Stouffer compared these attitudes with those of Whites who were not in the racially desegregated companies. The farther the soldiers serving as the control comparisons were from the desegregated companies, the greater their dislike of such contact.

Dramatic as these changes are, however, they did not immediately generalize to new situations. Thus, attitudes toward interracial post exchanges did not change. These military stores were then racially segregated, and many Whites whose attitudes about Black soldiers had radically changed still thought that the stores should stay separate. Only after the army offered many types of optimal interracial situations could it conclude that its program of racial desegregation "works" (U.S. Department of Defense, 1955).

Another type of generalization involves projecting one's new views and feelings toward the out-group individuals in the situation to the whole out-group itself. A host of cognitive factors restrict such generalization. We can explain away positive out-group behavior (Pettigrew, 1979). We can maintain our negative stereotypes and prejudice toward the out-group by regarding our positive contact experience as an exceptional instance. We like this particular out-group member, but "she is different"— the exception that proves the rule. In recent years, social psychologists have learned that generalization to the entire out-group from intergroup experiences is importantly shaped by just how the groups are categorized by the contact participants.

Three Models of Group Categorization

To overcome the cognitive barriers to generalization, group membership must be salient. Only then will contact effects routinely generalize to the entire out-group (Hewstone & Brown, 1986). When participants view each other as group representatives, the contact becomes an intergroup encounter. With this salient categorization condition, intergroup contact effects generalize beyond the immediate out-group members. Thus, contact effects generalize best when those involved are seen as typical members of their groups (Wilder, 1984; Weber & Crocker, 1983). As typical members, their group memberships are salient.

This raises a problem for understanding contact effects. Typical members of two groups will be different in many ways. Yet "birds of a feather flock together"; that is, people with similar social status and experiences often seek each other out. Consequently, people from different groups who have contact are more likely to share similar interests and values. In this vein, Brewer and Miller (1984) advocate decategorization. The exact opposite of salient categorization, it holds that intergroup contact is most effective when group saliency is low and personalization is maximized.

Contradictory as they seem, both the decategorization and salient categorization strategies are possible if they occur sequentially (Pettigrew, 1998). The initiation of effective intergroup contact needs the perception of similarities; later stages need the appreciation of group differences. The reduced salience of group categories is helpful in the first stages of contact. After such contact is firmly established, salient categorization is needed for the effects to generalize to the intergroup level.

In time, a third strategy, recategorization, becomes possible (Gaertner & Dovidio, 2000). After extended contact, people can think of themselves in a larger group perspective. Both the Dutch and Germans are Europeans. Black and White Americans are all Americans. All of us are human beings. Recategorization involves adopting broad, inclusive categories. Such categories highlight the similarities, rather than the differences, between groups and obscure the old boundary between us and them.

TESTING THE THEORY: A META-ANALYTIC REVIEW OF INTERGROUP CONTACT RESEARCH

Intergroup contact theory has inspired extensive research over the past half-century (Pettigrew, 1998). But past narrative reviews of this extensive literature have been subjective and incomplete. As is often the case with such reviews, they reach sharply conflicting conclusions: in support of the theory (Pettigrew, 1971, 1998; Riordan, 1978), mixed (Forbes, 1997; Stephan, 1987), and in opposition to the theory (Ford, 1986). Thus, a meta-analysis is required that statistically evaluates as much of this literature as it is possible to obtain. Linda Tropp and I have recently completed such a meta-analysis to measure intergroup contact's effects on prejudice. It uses 516 individual studies with 716 independent samples and 1,367 nonindependent tests. In total, 250,000 subjects from 38 different nations participated in this research (Pettigrew & Tropp, 2000, 2002).

Meta-Analytic Inclusion Rules

Before we review the results of this analysis, we must first note the definition of contact and the inclusion rules for accepting studies that the meta-analysis employed. We defined intergroup contact as *actual face-to-face interaction between members of clearly distinguishable and defined groups*. From this definition flow five inclusion criteria. The analysis includes only empirical studies in which (1) intergroup contact acts as a causal, independent variable; (2) there is contact between members of discrete, clearly distinguishable groups; (3) there is some degree of direct intergroup interaction; (4) the prejudice-dependent variables are collected on individuals rather than simply as a total aggregate outcome; and (5) there are comparative data to evaluate any changes in prejudice.

Basic Meta-Analytic Findings

Intergroup Contact Typically Reduces Intergroup Prejudice. The average mean effect across these varied studies is a correlation of –.23. (The meta-analysis employed DSTAT software; Johnson, 1993.) All effect sizes were weighted for sample size. In addition, maximum ceilings were applied for more conservative estimates. The results reported here derive from an analysis that capped especially large studies, $n > 5,000$; samples, $n > 3,000$; and tests, $n > 2,000$.) There is, however, great variation in effect sizes across the many studies even though only 4% of the studies found that contact led to increased prejudice. Just as intergroup contact theory predicts, the varying conditions under which contact takes place shape this vast heterogeneity. For example, intergroup contact that occurs in recreational settings (mean $r = -.23$) diminishes prejudice significantly more than such contact in tourist settings (mean $r = -.13$).

This Empirically Established Link Between Intergroup Contact and Less Prejudice Is Not an Artifact. The meta-analysis allows a direct test of the causal sequence (or selection bias) problem. Research studies that allowed

their participants no choice whatsoever in engaging in intergroup contact eliminate the possibility of the more bigoted avoiding such contact. And these studies actually obtain significantly larger reductions in prejudice (mean $r = -.28$) than studies that allowed choice (mean $r = -.20$). Similarly, the meta-analytic results render the possibility of a publication bias highly unlikely. It would require 7,287 unattained studies that average no contact-prejudice effect whatsoever to eliminate the overall result from occurring at the 5% level of confidence. This "failsafe" estimate is almost three times the tolerance guideline (5×516 studies + 10 = 2,590) suggested by Rosenthal (1991). Moreover, unpublished studies in the meta-analysis (mean $r = -.24$) actually yield significantly larger, not smaller, effects than published studies (mean $r = -.19$).

Intergroup Contact Effects Typically Generalize Beyond the Out-Group Members in the Immediate Situation to the Entire Out-Group. The research literature provides an unequivocal answer to the generalization problem. Extensive generalization to the entire out-group typically occurs. The average effect for reduced prejudice toward the entire out-group (mean $r = -.20$) approaches that of reduced prejudice toward the immediate out-group members (mean $r = -.21$).

The More Rigorous the Research, the More It Demonstrates That Contact Reduces Prejudice. Hence, experimental studies (mean $r = -.27$) obtain significantly larger effects than surveys (mean $r = -.20$). And when prejudice is measured with reliable (alpha > .69) scales or ratings, a significantly larger average effect size (mean $r = -.24$) is attained than when it is measured with a single item or a scale with low reliability (mean $r = -.18$).

Changes Wrought by Contact Are Broad. Intergroup Contact Reduces Many Different Manifestations of Prejudice. The affective components of prejudice are especially improved (mean $r = -.25$), but substantial improvements are also recorded for biased beliefs (mean $r = -.21$), favorability ratings (mean $r = -.20$), and social distance preferences (mean $r = -.21$). Two types of indicators, however, revealed much smaller effects: stereotypes (mean $r = -.13$) and sociometric choices (mean $r = -.08$).

The Effectiveness of Intergroup Contact to Lessen Prejudice Varies Across Different Types of Groups. Contact reduces prejudice against homosexuals (mean $r = -.25$) and ethnic and racial groups (mean $y = -.22$) significantly more than it reduces prejudice against the mentally ill (mean $\Omega = -.15$) and retarded (mean $r = -.13$). Since multicultural education focuses on cultural, ethnic, and racial groups, this finding suggests that contact effects are likely to be stronger than average in those settings most common to multicultural efforts. In addition, the effects are typically smaller for minority subjects (mean $r = -.15$) than for majority subjects (mean $r = -.21$).

Optimal Conditions Increase Contact's Reduction of Prejudice. The meta-analysis employed two global variables to test the importance of the optimal conditions specified by Allport. First, did the contact lead to cross-group friendship? Friendship typically involves frequent contacts under optimal conditions. As expected, these contacts revealed a significantly greater effect (mean $r = -.27$) than other types of contact (mean $r = -.18$). Likewise, those studies in which most of Allport's optimal conditions operated provided a significantly larger effect (mean $r = -.28$) than that of other studies (mean $r = -.20$).

NEW THEORETICAL PERSPECTIVES

A Reformulated Intergroup Contact Theory

These meta-analytic findings point to a reformulated intergroup contact theory that addresses its major problems. We have already introduced parts of this new formulation—the four hypothesized processes that undergird contact's effects and the three-part sequence of group categorization. But the meta-analytic results go further in suggesting a reverse approach to the issue adopted by Allport (1954).

Instead of the "positive conditions" of Allport's (1954) classic conception, the meta-analytic findings imply a "negative conditions" approach. That is, it is far more problematic when contact increases prejudice than when it decreases prejudice. Hence, the research literature strongly indicates a greater focus on the negative conditions of intergroup contact that lead to enhanced prejudice. More specifically, this reformulation consists of the following three components:

1. There is a small basic effect of intergroup contact reducing prejudice.
2. If there are positive facilitating factors, this basic effect of intergroup contact is enhanced. But these facilitating factors are not necessary conditions.
3. For intergroup contact to increase prejudice, there must be strong negative factors operating in the situation, such as high anxiety and threat.

Consider the specific evidence from the meta-analysis relevant to these basic contentions:

1. *There is a small basic effect of intergroup contact reducing prejudice.* Theorists in both sociology and psychology have long held that contact generally leads to liking. Homans (1950), in his influential book *The Human Group*, maintained that contact between individuals typically results in liking. And Zajonc (1968) has shown experimentally how familiarity itself leads to liking.

Consistent with these contentions, the meta-analysis consistently uncovered a negative relationship between intergroup contact and prejudice, with only 4% of the studies showing that contact led to greater prejudice. This result emerged despite the fact that more than half of the studies involve questionnaires that rely on the respondents' reporting prior out-group contact without information concerning the conditions of the contact.

While revealing a negative relationship between contact and prejudice, many of these studies conspicuously lack the positive conditions long held critical. Consider several examples to illustrate the point. Van Dyk (1990) found that rural Afrikaans-speaking White housewives who had had close contact with their African domestic workers had more favorable attitudes toward Africans in general ($r = -.09$). Conducted during the final days of South Africa´s apartheid policy, this contact situation sharply violates Allport's (1954) key conditions, especially that of equal status. Similarly, Crain and Weisman (1972) found that adult African Americans who reported having played with Whites as children were somewhat less anti-White ($r = -.08$) even though their neighborhoods and elementary schools had been racially segregated.

Shafer and his colleagues (1989) investigated a similarly impoverished contact situation. They found modest reductions in prejudice toward the mentally retarded ($r = -.09$) among employees who only worked together with retarded employees but rarely had social contact with them. Even a one-time tour of a residential facility for the mentally retarded improved the attitudes of high school students (Sellin & Mulchahay, 1965: $r = -.10$). And a few visits with an elderly person modestly modified the negative stereotypes held by college students of the aged (Eddy, 1986: $r = -.12$).

Like these examples, many of the meta-analysis's 516 studies clearly lack most of Allport's (1954) key conditions for positive contact and yet report some reduction in prejudice. This finding leads to the second contention.

2. *If there are positive facilitating factors, this basic effect of intergroup contact is enhanced. But these facilitating*

factors are not necessary conditions. Although many studies demonstrate that Allport's (1954) positive conditions are not in themselves determining, the meta-analytic results also show that such factors are important in enhancing contact's negative relationship with prejudice. We have seen that when the contact measure involves cross-group friendship, prejudice significantly declines. Friendship necessarily includes most of the positive conditions specified by social psychologists over the past half-century. Studies of intergroup programs directly structured to feature most of the optimal conditions favored by social psychologists provide a more direct test. Once again, the negative average effect sizes are markedly larger for the structured programs (mean $r = -.28$ compared to mean $r = -.20$ for unstructured contact).

3. *For intergroup contact to increase prejudice, there must be strong negative factors operating in the situation, such as high anxiety and threat.* Such negative factors are more likely to operate for minority groups than for the more powerful majority groups. And we saw that the average effect size for contact reducing the prejudice of majority samples is far greater than for minority samples. This marked difference underlines the fact that these negative factors are not simply objective features of the contact situation, as many have misinterpreted Allport's (1954) positive factors. Rather, majorities and minorities may perceive the same objective situation in contrasting ways. For example, what may appear as equal group status in the contact situation to majority members may well seem to minority members as quite unequal group status.

Negative factors play three roles in the process. Initially, they act to discourage intergroup contact. And when intergroup contact does occur, these factors create situations likely to increase rather than decrease prejudice. Finally, the reduction of these factors in the contact situation can serve as mediators of the contact's potential for diminishing prejudice. Put differently, the power of contact to ameliorate such negative factors as anxiety is directly related to the contact situation's potential for eventually reducing prejudice. Each of these three roles of negative factors emerges in the meta-analytic findings.

First, negative factors discourage intergroup contact from taking place. Opportunity is by far the largest predictor of intergroup contact. If two groups are separated in housing, education, and employment, few opportunities will arise for contact, especially contact under optimal conditions. Within this social context, however, individual-level variables, such as high anxiety and perceived threat, also restrict intergroup contact. Numerous

studies show that those most anxious about contact with an out-group are understandably less likely to engage in such interaction. For instance, Brown (1997) found that intergroup anxiety toward African Americans among her 190 University of Georgia White student subjects related strongly to both the frequency ($r = -.48$) and the quality ($r = -.50$) of their interracial contact.

Next, negative factors cause contact to be associated positively with prejudice. We noted that a mere 20 of the 516 (4%) studies find contact and prejudice positively related. And these few studies are distinctive in numerous ways. Thirty-five percent of them measured stereotypes compared with only 14% of the other studies. In addition, these 20 exceptional cases were less rigorous investigations. None were experiments, and they employed less adequate control groups and measures of both contact and prejudice.

Specific studies serve as prototypes of these rare instances when intergroup contact heightened prejudice. One of these investigations involved four- and five-year-old children visiting elders in a nursing home once a week for a full year. Using a between-group design with 30 children in each group, Seefeldt (1987) uncovered an overall r of +.36 with her various measures of stereotypes. Hence, the experimental group rated the elderly more "passive," "terrible," and "unfriendly." In addition, the experimental children adopted a more negative view of their own aging. Although some of Seefeldt's measures had low reliabilities, the key factor appears to be threat. The elderly in the study were quite impaired and thus often confirmed rather than countered existing stereotypes of the elderly.

Threat is often involved in these 20 "error cases." In another investigation on attitudes toward the elderly, Auerbach and Levenson (1977) investigated the changes among young college students caused by classroom interaction with elderly fellow students. With a measure of prejudice of unstated reliability, these researchers found that the experimental group became considerably more negative to the elderly over the course of a semester ($r = +.52$). These students typically viewed the elderly as unfair competitors. They perceived their older competitors as putting "an inordinate amount of time and energy" (p. 365) on their class work and using their age to usurp the attention of the instructor (Auerbach & Levenson, 1977).

Finally, the amelioration of negative factors by contact can act as mediators of the process, leading to less prejudice. Affect, both positive and negative, is often involved. Consider the role of anxiety, a negative factor emphasized by Stephan and Stephan (1985, 1992). Contact tends to ease intergroup anxiety, and this benefit in turn is part of the process of contact reducing prejudice.

Advantages of This Reformulation

This reformulation of intergroup contact theory and its emphasis on negative factors has four distinct advantages in comparison with the traditional approach:

1. *It is shaped directly by the meta-analytic summary of a large research literature.* Allport (1954) based his initial contact hypothesis on the limited literature available a half-century ago. Now we can exploit an enormous research literature on intergroup contact that involves a wide variety of interacting groups. The present meta-analysis with its surprising conclusions provides an opportunity to reformulate the theory based on a far larger empirical base.

2. *It builds on Allport's emphasis on positive factors.* We have seen that there is considerable support for the importance of these and additional factors—but not as necessary conditions. Viewed instead as facilitating factors, the reformulation incorporates this supporting research while avoiding the logical pitfall that arose for the traditional theory. As noted earlier, an ever-extending list of positive conditions threatened the viability of contact theory (Pettigrew, 1986, 1998; Stephan, 1987). Once viewed as facilitating but unnecessary conditions, however, this expansive list no longer poses a problem.

3. *There is greater attention to process.* Allport (1954) did not specify the processes that are involved in intergroup contact reducing prejudice. The chapter has suggested four such processes. In addition, as described above, an intensive focus on negative conditions sheds light on three different stages of the intergroup contact process. To contribute maximally to the development of the theory, future work should attend more closely to specifying these processes. The meta-analytic results suggest several promising leads. First, emotion emerges as pivotal. The mean contact effects for affective indicators of prejudice are by far the largest, while those for stereotypes are among the smallest. It appears that contact can lead to liking without significant shifts in the images held of the out-group. The stereotype remains, but its affective tone may shift—"lazy" becomes "laid back," "cheap" becomes "thrifty."

Second, such negative factors as anxiety and threat operate at three stages of the intergroup contact process: avoiding contact, limiting its effects, and mediating its effects. Indeed, the lack of opportunity for and resistance to intergroup contact are major ways group prejudice is developed and maintained throughout the world. Future research should focus on the effects of the lack of contact as an integral part of the process. In addition, future work would benefit by following the lead of Stephan and Stephan (1985, 1992) and focusing on the mediation of contact's effects by such factors as anxiety and threat.

4. *It locates intergroup contact theory in a broader net of social psychological theory.* While popular over the past half-century, intergroup contact theory—like many other theories in social psychology—has remained largely isolated from the discipline's other theories. The present reformulation places the theory in a wider context and invites connections with other bodies of theory.

Links with the theories of Homans, Zajonc, and Stephan and Stephan have been noted. And the renewed emphasis on affect places the reformulation in the mainstream of recent thinking about the phenomenon of prejudice (Pettigrew, 1997b). Elliot Smith (1993) has argued for defining prejudice as an emotion, and recent research reveals the greater predictive power of affect than stereotypes (Esses, Haddock, & Zanna, 1993; Stangor, Sullivan, & Ford, 1991). In addition, this reformulation invites direct links with the long-term close relationship literature, especially when friendship is involved (Pettigrew, 1997a; Wright & Van Der Zande, 1999; Wright et al., 2000).

PRACTICAL IMPLICATIONS OF CONTACT THEORY FOR MULTICULTURAL EDUCATION

Intergroup Contact Addresses Three Major Criticisms of Multicultural Education

Critics of multicultural education advance numerous, often conflicting, criticisms of multicultural education (Banks, 1993; Sleeter, 1995; Stephan & Stephan, 2001). However, once such instruction joins intergroup contact, at least three of these criticisms lose their force:

- *Too didactic.* Some critics believe that multicultural education is too didactic, too cognitive, too removed from realistic intergroup interaction to be effective. But multicultural instruction employed in intergroup settings is not subject to this criticism. Mixed-group interaction is experiential, not didactic. And we have noted that its principal effects are affective, not cognitive, in nature. In this sense, each approach supplies what the other lacks.

- *Does not promote structural reform.* Critics also have viewed multicultural education as attempting to address intergroup tensions without making needed structural changes. Indeed, some large urban school systems, trying a variety of schemes, have in fact used multicultural training in segregated settings to avoid racial desegregation of their schools. But desegregating schools and using multicultural instruction are not substitutes for one another. And when combined, the two methods answer this criticism directly.

- *Fails to promote cultural cohesion and national identity.* Once again, critics cannot sustain this point when multicultural instruction takes place in intergroup classrooms. As Banks and his colleagues (2001) emphasize, effective multicultural education programs in intergroup settings encourage students to develop superordinate, cross-cutting group memberships and identities. What, one might ask, could promote cultural cohesion more directly? Critics typically overlook the unifying possibilities of diversity.

Advantages of Combining Intergroup Contact and Multicultural Education

Joining the two approaches together also has positive advantages beyond simply countering key criticisms of multicultural instruction. Neither intergroup contact nor multicultural education proffers a panacea for intergroup relations. But each offers a promising means of alleviating intergroup prejudice, discrimination, and conflict. Together, they are even more promising.

While contact has particular effects of increasing liking and decreasing anxiety, multicultural education is better suited for supplying information and countering negative stereotypes. Moreover, Stephan and Stephan (2001) point out that mixed groups working together cooperatively have marked advantages over multicultural efforts in segregated settings. Intergroup dialogues are possible, and cross-group friendships can form. Highly involving cross-group exercises are easier to devise. And there are more opportunities for students to unlearn their stereotypes. Events that celebrate a particular group have more meaning and greater impact when the group being celebrated is present. Knowing how personally important Dr. Martin Luther King, Jr., is to your friend is incomparably more influential than hearing a speech on King's birthday.

CONCLUSIONS

Contact offers a significant means of reducing intergroup prejudice. A vast social scientific research literature demonstrates contact's value across many different types of groups, nations, and settings. A meta-analysis of this research shows that selection and publication biases cannot explain away this result. Moreover, the positive effects of contact generalize widely, even to out-groups not involved in the initial contact. Intergroup contact can also increase prejudice, but for this negative result to happen, there must be sharply negative factors, such as threat, operating in the contact situation.

As an established phenomenon, intergroup contact constitutes an important complement to multicultural education. When combined with multicultural techniques, many of the objections to multicultural efforts lose force. And multicultural instruction in intergroup settings has positive advantages for the nature of the intergroup contact.

References

Allport, G. W. (1954). *The nature of prejudice*. Reading, MA: Addison-Wesley.

Araragi, C. (1983). The effect of the jigsaw learning method on children's academic performance and learning attitude. *Japanese Journal of Educational Psychology, 31,* 102–112.

Aronson, E., & Gonzalez, A. (1988). Desegregation, jigsaw, and the Mexican-American experience. In P. A. Katz & D. A. Taylor (Eds.), *Eliminating racism: Profiles in controversy* (pp. 301–314). New York: Plenum.

Aronson, E., & Patnoe, S. (1997). *The jigsaw classroom: Building cooperation in the classroom* (2nd ed.). Reading, MA: Addison-Wesley.

Auerbach, D. N., & Levenson, R. L. (1977). Second impressions: Attitude change in college students toward the elderly. *Gerontologist, 17,* 362–366.

Baker, P. E. (1934). *Negro-White adjustment*. New York: Association Press.

Banks, J. A. (1993). Multicultural education and its critics: Britain and the United States. *New Era, 65*(3), 58–64.

Banks, J. A., Cookson, P., Gay, G., Hawley, W. D., Irvine, J. J., Nieto, S., Schofield, J. W., & Stephan, W. G. (2001). *Diversity within unity: Essential principles for teaching and learning in a multicultural society*. Seattle: Center for Multicultural Education, University of Washington.

Ben-Ari, R., & Amir, Y. (1986). Contact between Arab and Jewish youth in Israel: Reality and potential. In M. Hewstone & R. Brown (Eds.), *Contact and conflict in intergroup encounters* (pp. 45–58). Oxford: Blackwell.

Bettencourt, B. A., Brewer, M. B., Rogers-Croak, M. R., & Miller, N. (1992). Cooperation and the reduction of intergroup bias: The role of reward structure and social orientation. *Journal of Experimental Social Psychology, 28,* 301–319.

Brameld, T. (1946). *Minority problems in the public schools*. New York: HarperCollins.

Brewer, M. B., & Kramer, R. M. (1985). The psychology of intergroup attitudes and behavior. *Annual Review of Psychology, 36,* 219–243.

Brewer, M. B., & Miller, N. (1984). Beyond the contact hypothesis: Theoretical perspectives on desegregation. In N. Miller & M. B.

Brewer (Eds.), *Groups in contact: The psychology of desegregation* (pp. 281–302). Orlando, FL: Academic Press.

Brophy, I. N. (1946). The luxury of anti-Negro prejudice. *Public Opinion Quarterly, 9,* 456–466.

Brown, S. A. (1997). *Intergroup anxiety in Whites: The impact of the motivation to control prejudice and Black ethnic identity.* Unpublished doctoral dissertation, University of Georgia, Athens, GA.

Cagle, L. T. (1973). Interracial housing: A reassessment of the equal-status contact hypothesis. *Sociology and Social Research, 57,* 342–355.

Campbell, D. T., & Stanley, J. C. (1963). *Experimental and quasi-experimental designs for research.* Skokie, IL: Rand McNally.

Chu, D., & Griffey, D. (1985). The contact theory of racial integration: The case of sport. *Sociology of Sport Journal, 2,* 323–333.

Cohen, E. G. (1982). Expectation states and interracial interaction in school settings. *Annual Review of Sociology, 8,* 209–235.

Cohen, E. G., & Lotan, R. A. (1995). Producing equal-status interaction in the classroom. *American Educational Research Journal, 32,* 99–120.

Cook, S. W. (1978). Interpersonal and attitudinal outcomes in cooperating interracial groups. *Journal of Research and Development in Education, 12,* 97–113.

Crain, R. L., & Weisman, C. S. (1972). *Discrimination, personality, and achievement: A survey of northern Blacks.* New York: Seminar Press.

Desforges, D. M., Lord, C. G., Ramsey, S. L., Mason, J. A., Van Leeuwen, M. D., West, S. C., & Lepper, M. R. (1991). Effects of structured cooperative contact on changing negative attitudes toward stigmatized social groups. *Journal of Personality and Social Psychology, 60,* 531–544.

Deutsch, M., & Collins, M. (1951). *Interracial housing: A psychological evaluation of a social experiment.* Minneapolis: University of Minnesota Press.

Eddy, D. M. (1986). Before and after attitudes toward aging in a BSN program. *Journal of Gerontological Nursing, 12,* 30–34.

Eppler, R., & Huber, G. L. (1990). Wissenserwerb im Team: Empirische Untersuchung von Effekten des Gruppen-Puzzles [Knowledge acquisition in a team: Empirical investigation of the effects of group puzzles]. *Psychologie in Erziehung und Unterricht, 37,* 172–178.

Esses, V. M., Haddock, G., & Zanna, M. P. (1993). Values, stereotypes, and emotions as determinants of intergroup attitudes. In D. M. Mackie & D. L. Hamilton (Eds.), *Affect, cognition, and stereotyping: Interactive processes in group perception* (pp. 137–166). Orlando, FL: Academic Press.

Forbes, H. D. (1997). *Ethnic conflict: Commerce, culture, and the contact hypothesis.* New Haven, CT: Yale University Press.

Ford, W. S. (1986). Favorable intergroup contact may not reduce prejudice: Inconclusive journal evidence, 1960–1984. *Sociology and Social Research, 70,* 256–258.

Gaertner, S. L., & Dovidio, J. F. (2000). *Reducing intergroup bias: The common ingroup identity model.* Philadelphia: Psychology Press.

Hewstone, M., & Brown, R. (Eds.). (1986). *Contact and conflict in intergroup encounters.* Oxford: Blackwell.

Homans, G. C. (1950). *The human group.* New York: Harcourt, Brace.

Irish, D. P. (1952). Reactions of Caucasian residents to Japanese-American neighbors. *Journal of Social Issues, 8*(1), 10–17.

Jackman, M. R. & Crane, M. (1986). "Some of my best friends are Black . . . .": Interracial friendship and Whites' racial attitudes. *Public Opinion Quarterly, 50,* 459–486.

Johnson, B. T. (1993). *DSTAT: Software for the meta-analytic review of research literatures.* Mahwah, NJ: Erlbaum.

Johnson, D. W., Johnson, R. T., & Maruyama, G. (1984). Goal interdependence and interpersonal-personal attraction in heterogeneous classrooms: A meta-analysis. In N. Miller & M. B. Brewer (Eds.), *Groups in contact: The psychology of desegregation* (pp. 187–212). Orlando, FL: Academic Press.

Kephart, W. M. (1957). *Racial factors and urban law enforcement.* Philadelphia: University of Pennsylvania Press.

Landis, D., Hope, R. O., & Day, H. R. (1984). Training for desegregation in the military. In N. Miller & M. B. Brewer (Eds.), *Groups in contact: The psychology of desegregation* (pp. 258–278). Orlando, FL: Academic Press.

Lett, H. A. (1945). Techniques for achieving interracial cooperation. *Proceedings of the Institute on Race Relations and Community Organization.* Chicago: University of Chicago and the American Council on Race Relations.

Link, B. G., & Cullen, F. T. (1986). Contact with the mentally ill and perceptions of how dangerous they are. *Journal of Health and Social Behavior, 27,* 289–303.

Miracle, A. W. (1981). Factors affecting interracial cooperation: A case study of a high school football team. *Human Organization, 40,* 150–154.

Morrison, E. W., & Herlihy, J. M. (1992). Becoming the best place to work: Managing diversity at American Express travel related services. In S. E. Jackson and Associates (Eds.), *Diversity in the workplace: Human resources initiatives* (pp. 203–226). New York: Guilford Press.

Parker, J. H. (1968). The interaction of Negroes and Whites in an integrated church setting. *Social Forces, 46,* 359–366.

Patchen, M. (1982). *Black-White contact in schools.* West Lafayette, IN: Purdue University Press.

Pettigrew, T. F. (1971). *Racially separate or together?* New York: McGraw-Hill.

Pettigrew, T. F. (1979). The ultimate attribution error: Extending Allport's cognitive analysis of prejudice. *Personality and Social Psychology Bulletin, 5,* 461–476.

Pettigrew, T. F. (1986). The contact hypothesis revisited. In M. Hewstone & R. Brown (Eds.), *Contact and conflict in intergroup encounters* (pp. 169–195). Oxford: Blackwell.

Pettigrew, T. F. (1996). *How to think like a social scientist.* New York: HarperCollins.

Pettigrew, T. F. (1997a). Generalized intergroup contact effects on prejudice. *Personality and Social Psychology Bulletin, 23,* 173–185.

Pettigrew, T. F. (1997b). The affective component of prejudice: Empirical support for the new view. In S. A. Tuch & J. K. Martin (Eds.), *Racial attitudes in the 1990s: Continuity and change* (pp. 76–90). New York: Praeger.

Pettigrew, T. F. (1998). Intergroup contact theory. *Annual Review of Psychology, 49,* 65–85.

Pettigrew, T. F., & Tropp, L. R. (2000). Does intergroup contact reduce prejudice? Recent meta-analytic findings. In S. Oskamp (Ed.), *Reducing prejudice and discrimination: Social psychological perspectives* (pp. 93–114). Mahwah, NJ: Erlbaum.

Pettigrew, T. F., & Tropp, L. R. (2002). A meta-analytic test and reformulation of intergroup contact theory. Unpublished manuscript, University of California, Santa Cruz, CA.

Powers, D. A., & Ellison, C. G. (1995). Interracial contact and Black racial attitudes: The contact hypothesis and selectivity bias. *Social Forces, 74,* 205–226.

Riordan, C. (1978). Equal-status interracial contact: A review and revision of the concept. *International Journal of Intercultural Relations, 2*, 161–185.

Riordan, C., & Ruggiero, J. (1980). Producing equal-status interracial interaction: A replication. *Social Psychology Quarterly, 43*, 131–136.

Robinson, J. W., & Preston, J. D. (1976). Equal status contact and modification of racial prejudice: A reexamination of the contact hypothesis. *Social Forces, 54*, 911–924.

Rosenthal, R. (1991). *Meta-analytic procedures for social research* (Rev. ed.). Thousand Oaks, CA: Sage.

Rothbart, M., & John, O. P. (1985). Social categorization and behavioral episodes: A cognitive analysis of the effects of intergroup contact. *Journal of Social Issues, 41*, 81–104.

Schofield, J. W. (1989). *Black and White in school: Trust, tension, or tolerance?* New York: Teachers College Press.

Seefeldt, C. (1987). The effects of preschoolers' visits to a nursing home. *Gerontologist, 27*, 228–232.

Sellin, D., & Mulchahay, R. (1965). The relationship of an institutional tour upon opinions about mental retardation. *American Journal of Mental Deficiency, 70*, 408–412.

Shafer, M. S., Rice, M. L., Metzler, H.M.D., & Haring, M. (1989). A survey of nondisabled employees' attitudes toward supported employees with mental retardation. *Journal of the Association for Persons with Severe Handicaps, 14*, 137–146.

Sherif, M. (1966). *In common predicament.* Boston: Houghton Mifflin.

Sims, V. M., & Patrick, J. R. (1936). Attitude toward the Negro of northern and southern college students. *Journal of Social Psychology, 7*, 192–204.

Slavin, R. E. (1983). *Cooperative learning.* White Plains, NY: Longman.

Slavin, R. E., & Madden, N. A. (1979). School practices that improve race relations. *American Educational Research Journal, 16*, 169–180.

Sleeter, C. E. (1995). An analysis of critiques of multieducational education. In J. A. Banks & C.A.M. Banks (Eds.), *Handbook of research on multicultural education* (pp. 81–94). San Francisco: Jossey-Bass.

Smith, E. R. (1993). Social identity and social emotions: Toward new conceptions of prejudice. In D. M. Mackie & D. L. Hamilton (Eds.), *Affect, cognition, and stereotyping: Interactive processes in group perception* (pp. 241–272). Orlando, FL: Academic Press.

Springer, L. (1996). *Applying the contact hypothesis to research on intergroup relations among college students.* Unpublished doctoral dissertation, Pennsylvania State University, University Park, PA.

Stangor, C., Sullivan, L. A., & Ford, T. E. (1991). Affective and cognitive determinants of prejudice. *Social Cognition, 9*, 359–380.

Stephan, C. W., & Stephan, W. G. (1992). Reducing intercultural anxiety through intercultural contact. *International Journal of Intercultural Relations, 16*, 89–106.

Stephan, W. G. (1987). The contact hypothesis in intergroup relations. In C. Hendrick (Ed.), *Review of personality and social psychology: Group processes and intergroup relations* (Vol. 9, pp. 13–40). Thousand Oaks, CA: Sage.

Stephan, W. G., & Stephan, C. W. (1984). The role of ignorance in intergroup relations. In N. Miller & M. B. Brewer (Eds.), *Groups in contact: The psychology of desegregation* (pp. 229–255). Orlando, FL: Academic Press.

Stephan, W. G., & Stephan, C. W. (1985). Intergroup anxiety. *Journal of Social Issues, 41*, 157–175.

Stephan, W. G., & Stephan, C. W. (2001). *Improving intergroup relations.* Thousand Oaks, CA: Sage.

Stouffer, S. A., Schuman, E. A., DeVinney, L. C., Star, S. A., & Williams, R. M., Jr. (1949). *The American soldier: Adjustment during army life* (Vol. 1). Princeton, NJ: Princeton University Press.

U.S. Department of Defense (1955). *A progress report on integration in the armed services.* Washington, DC: U.S. Government Printing Office.

Van Dyk, A. C. (1990). Voorspellers van etniese houdings in 'n noue kontaksituasie [Determinants of ethnic attitudes in a close contact situation]. *South African Journal of Psychology, 20*, 206–214.

Wagner, U., & Machleit, U. (1986). "Gastarbeiter" in the Federal Republic of Germany: Contact between Germans and migrant populations. In M. Hewstone & R. Brown (Eds.), *Contact and conflict in intergroup encounters* (pp. 59–78). Oxford: Blackwell.

Walker, I., & Crogan, M. (1998). Academic performance, prejudice, and the jigsaw classroom: New pieces to the puzzle. *Journal of Community and Applied Social Psychology, 8*, 381–393.

Weber, R., & Crocker, J. (1983). Cognitive processes in the revision of stereotypic beliefs. *Journal of Personality and Social Psychology, 45*, 961–977.

Wilder, D. A. (1984). Intergroup contact: The typical member and the exception to the rule. *Journal of Experimental Social Psychology, 20*, 177–194.

Wilder, D. A., & Thompson, J. E. (1980). Intergroup contact with independent manipulations of in-group and out-group interaction. *Journal of Personality and Social Psychology, 38*, 589–603.

Williams, R. M., Jr. (1947). *The reduction of intergroup tensions.* New York: Social Science Research Council.

Wilner, D. M., Walkley, R. P., & Cook, S. W. (1955). *Human relations in interracial housing: A study of the contact hypothesis.* Minneapolis: University of Minnesota Press.

Wilson, T. C. (1996). Prejudice reduction or self-selection? A test of the contact hypothesis. *Sociological Spectrum, 16*, 43–60.

Works, E. (1961). The prejudice-interaction hypothesis from the point of view of the Negro minority group. *American Journal of Sociology, 67*, 47–52.

Wright, S. C., & Van Der Zande, C. C. (1999). *Bicultural friends: When cross-group friendships cause improved intergroup attitudes.* Paper presented at the annual meeting of the Society for Experimental Social Psychology, St. Louis, MO.

Wright, S. C., Van Der Zande, C. C., Ropp, S. A., Tropp, L. R., Young, K., Zanna, M., & Aron, A. (2000). *Cross-group friendships and reduced prejudice: Experimental evidence of a causal direction.* Unpublished manuscript, University of California, Santa Cruz, CA.

Zajonc, R. B. (1968). Attitudinal effects of mere exposure. *Journal of Personality and Social Psychology Monographs, 9*(2), pt. 2, 1–27.

38

INTERGROUP RELATIONS IN MULTICULTURAL EDUCATION PROGRAMS

Walter G. Stephan
New Mexico State University

Cookie White Stephan
New Mexico State University

One of the primary goals of multicultural education is improving relations among racial, ethnic, religious, cultural, and other types of groups (Banks, 1997, 2001). Improving intergroup relations is a formidable task because the negative elements of these relations are deeply embedded in the history of every society and, without intervention, tend to be replicated across generations. Fortunately, over the course of the past 50 years, a great deal has been learned about how to alter relations between groups using educational techniques. Although the research indicates that these techniques are generally successful in leading to improvements in intergroup relations, much less is understood about the processes that underlie these changes (Stephan, Renfro, & Stephan, in press; Stephan & Stephan, 2001).

The primary goal of this chapter is to explore the underlying processes that provide the basis for changing prejudice, stereotypes, and discrimination. Understanding these processes will make it possible to design and implement even better multicultural education programs in the future by allowing educators to create curricula that explicitly take advantage of these processes and maximize opportunities to bring about beneficial changes in cognitions, affect, and behavior.

The approaches used to understand the processes underlying improvements in intergroup relations are based largely on social psychological research and theory. For decades, social psychologists have sought to understand the causes of prejudice, stereotyping, and discrimination. During the same period, educators were developing multicultural education and other programs

to improve intergroup relations. Both groups were working in relative isolation, and neither fully benefited from the work of the other group. This chapter is an attempt to join the approaches to intergroup relations from these two disciplines to the advantage of both. Multicultural educators need a better understanding of the social psychological processes underlying their techniques, and social psychologists would benefit from a greater understanding of how these processes operate in educational settings.

This chapter begins with a brief discussion of three central intergroup relations concepts: prejudice, stereotyping, and discrimination. In order to understand the processes underlying changes in attitudes and behaviors, theories of the causes of prejudice, stereotyping, and discrimination are explored. After the discussion of each set of theories, the focus is on social psychological processes that can be used to reduce prejudice, stereotypes, and discrimination in multicultural education settings. Finally, research findings on the effects of multicultural education programs on intergroup relations are discussed.

PREJUDICE

Prejudice may be defined as "negative attitudes toward social groups" (Stephan, 1985, p. 600). Prejudice occurs when individuals are prejudged and disliked based on their group memberships. Prejudice can be founded on any group-based characteristic; race, ethnicity, national origin, sex, age, social class, caste, handicapped status,

782

sexual orientation, religion, language, and region are common sources of prejudice in today's world. Prejudice can occur in the absence of powerful social or historical differences, and physical differences are not necessary for prejudice to occur (Rothbart & John, 1996). Nonetheless, visible markers such as race and sex do provide potent sources of prejudice, due to their visibility and the beliefs associated with these physical manifestations of alleged "natural" biological differences (Rothbart & Taylor, 1992).

STEREOTYPES

The basis of stereotyping is the categorization of people into groups (Allport, 1954; Tajfel, 1978). Stereotypes consist of the characteristics attributed to categories of people. They have roots in the history of relations between groups and are transmitted through socialization agents, including the mass media. Unfortunately, stereotypes are all too often overgeneralized, inaccurate, and negative. Thus, the stereotypes of members of one group (the in-group) about the members of other groups (the out-groups) typically reveal contempt and a failure to recognize the diversity within out-groups. Regrettably, stereotypes are frequently used to dominate, disparage, or dehumanize members of out-groups. Whereas some researchers believe that stereotypes are automatically activated in nearly all members of society (Devine, 1989), others have found that they are activated primarily among individuals who are high in prejudice (Lepore & Brown, 1999).

DISCRIMINATION

Discrimination is the behavioral component of the attitude of prejudice. It consists of "a selectively unjustifiable behavior toward members of [a] target group" (Dovidio & Gaertner, 1986, p. 3). Traditionally, it has been argued that stereotypes lead to prejudice and that prejudice leads to discrimination. However, research findings have shown only moderate relationships among these factors (Dovidio, Brigham, Johnson, & Gaertner, 1996). In addition, neither of these causal links is always found. Theories of stereotypes, prejudice, and discrimination and their reduction posit a wide variety of relations among and between these concepts. For example, it has been argued that stereotypes cause discrimination (Dovidio et al., 1996; Jussim & Fleming, 1996; Snyder, 1992) and that discrimination induces stereotyping (Allport, 1954; Jost & Banaji, 1994). Having introduced the basic concepts of intergroup relations, we next examine theories that explain prejudice.

THEORIES OF PREJUDICE

Eight causal theories of prejudice are briefly discussed. The first, social identity theory, is based on cognitive processes. The next three theories—symbolic racism, aversive racism, and ambivalence-amplification—share the idea that prejudice has become more subtle as blatant prejudice has become less acceptable. Four final theories explore the role of social structures as causes of prejudice: realistic group conflict, integrated threat, social dominance, and control theory.

Cognitive Theory

Social Identity. Social identity theory is based on the idea that social categorization is both a natural cognitive process and functional for adaptation in a complex world (Tajfel, 1978, 1982; Tajfel & Turner, 1986). Social identity theorists believe that the self is composed of multiple identities. Personal identity consists of aspects of the self based on individual characteristics (e.g., personality traits), whereas social identity consists of components of the self based on group memberships (for example, sex, race, ethnicity). Social interactions can be placed on a continuum from purely interpersonal, dependent exclusively on individual characteristics, to purely intergroup, contingent completely on social identities. Personal and social identities are evoked by the specific situation. When individuals are categorized on the basis of their group memberships, social identity creates and maintains attitudinal and behavioral distinctions favoring the in-group through the mere process of categorization. Many prejudice-reduction processes make use of these basic ideas from social identity theory.

Subtle Racism Theories

Symbolic Racism. Symbolic racism consists of negative affect toward an out-group plus the belief that members of that group violate some of the traditional values the in-group holds dear, such as the values of individualism and self-reliance widely held by U.S. Whites (Kinder & Sears, 1981; Sears, 1988). Symbolic racism theory suggests that this combination of factors leads to opposition to race-based social policies, such as affirmative action.

Aversive Racism. Aversive racism theorists argue that a contradiction exists between individuals' values and feelings (Dovidio, Kawakami, & Gaertner, 2000; Gaertner & Dovidio, 1986). From this perspective, people experience unacknowledged negative affect toward minority groups, but struggle to avoid having these feelings reflected in their behavior because they also hold egalitarian values and regard themselves as nonprejudiced. These complex beliefs and feelings lead to anxiety and avoidance of out-group members.

Ambivalence-Amplification Theory. Ambivalence-amplification theory focuses on the ambivalence created by simultaneously experiencing incompatible feelings: sympathy for the suffering of members of disadvantaged out-groups and an aversion toward them (Katz & Hass, 1988; Katz, Wackenhut, & Hass, 1986). In situations in which the aversion overrides sympathy, negative attitudes and behaviors are directed toward out-group members.

Social Structural Theories

Realistic Group Conflict Theory. Realistic group conflict theory postulates that group antagonisms arise from competition for scarce resources, such as territory, wealth, or natural resources (LeVine & Campbell, 1972; Sherif, 1966). Greater threats due to competition are thought to lead to increased prejudice.

Integrated Threat Theory. Integrated threat theory asserts that four types of threat can lead to prejudice (Stephan & Stephan, 2000). Out-groups are disliked if they are perceived to pose realistic or value threats to the in-group, if in-group members are anxious about interacting with the out-group because they expect negative outcomes from such interactions, or if negative stereotypes of out-groups are threatening. Perceived threats are often unrealistic or exaggerated.

Social Dominance Theory. Social dominance theory views prejudice as an outcome of belief systems that enable dominant groups to legitimize the power, privileges, and prestige they enjoy (Sidanius & Pratto, 1993, 1999). Research supports the idea that people who have a more hierarchical conception of society tend to be more prejudiced (Sidanius & Pratto, 1999).

Control Theory. In control theory, it is argued that dominant ethnic groups work to institutionalize their expropriation of resources from subordinate ethnic groups (Jackman, 1994). They also encase these institutions in a moral code that sanctifies them not as discriminatory but as rational, benevolent, protective, and even as being for the good of the oppressed group.

Summary of the Theories of Prejudice

Taken together, these theories of prejudice suggest that prejudice begins with the natural cognitive process of categorization. Prejudice is a complex attitude that is often based on contradictory emotions, some of which are

unacknowledged. Although negative attitudes toward social groups are sometimes openly acknowledged and expressed as hatred, hostility, or resentment, they are just as often expressed in a more subtle form, for instance, as opposition to policies favoring out-groups. Negative attitudes may exist and exert subtle effects on many people's behaviors, but they may be unaware of their underlying attitudes. In such cases, prejudice may be evidenced in avoidance of out-group members or awkwardness during interactions with out-group members and in behavior that is patronizing, condescending, and overly solicitous (for example, too formal). Prejudice can be founded in feelings of threat as well as the desire to legitimize the power, privileges, and prestige that dominant groups enjoy. The complexity of prejudice and the multiplicity of its causes make it a formidable enemy. Nonetheless, a number of techniques have been developed to reduce prejudice.

PREJUDICE-REDUCTION PROCESSES

Some prejudice-reduction processes are designed to influence behaviors, whereas others are designed to influence cognitive processes. Still others have an impact on affect. Thirteen processes underlying techniques of changing prejudice are discussed. This section starts with three behavioral processes: the contact hypothesis, reinforcing and modeling positive behaviors, and increasing self-disclosure. It then examines five cognitive processes: increasing perceptions of similarity, personalization, creating multiple identities and cross-cutting categories, recategorization, and creating common in-group identities. Next, one process designed to directly manipulate affect, reducing threat, is considered. Last, four processes involving more than one factor are explained: creating empathy, using dissonance to create attitude change, making value-behavior discrepancies explicit, and modifying associations between cognitions and affect.

Behavioral Processes

Contact. The original statement of the contact hypothesis suggested that the necessary conditions for contact to improve intergroup relations are equal-status interactions, the pursuit of common goals, support by authority figures, and a perception of common interests and humanity (Allport, 1954; Amir, 1976; Pettigrew, 1971). Other theorists have added a large number of features that can also affect the outcomes of contact. A recent meta-analysis of over 2,000 published studies of the effect of face-to-face interaction on prejudice found that overall, intergroup contact led to a moderate decline in prejudice (see Chapter 37, this volume). Multicultural education programs often include components of successful contact, including cooperation, equal status interactions, and teacher support for the process.

Cooperative learning groups are sometimes used in multicultural education programs. Cooperative learning techniques usually place students in small groups where the task and the reward structure require face-to-face interaction in a situation in which students are interdependent. Typically, students from two or more ethnic groups, both sexes, and of varying academic abilities are brought together in groups of four to six to learn academic materials that have been tailored for these groups. Cooperation guides the within-group interaction. Cooperative learning techniques have been shown to lead to significant improvements in intergroup relations in classrooms diverse in race and ethnicity, nationality, and performance levels (Slavin, 1995; Stephan & Stephan, 2001). In addition, cooperative learning techniques increase student achievement, especially the achievement of minority students and low-achieving students.

Reinforcing and Modeling Positive Behaviors. Social learning theory highlights the role that reinforcements and modeling play in changing behaviors (Bandura, 1986). People who find interacting with out-group members rewarding are likely to change their behavior and attitudes toward them. Rewarding students for nonprejudiced behaviors is a powerful tool in multicultural education classrooms (Hauserman, Walen, & Behling, 1973).

Likewise, people's behavior is affected by the models to whom they are exposed. When the behavior of a model leads to rewards, others imitate their actions. In many multicultural education programs, teachers and administrators from a variety of groups model behavior toward one another that they wish their students to imitate. In a study of modeling among students, pairing high-prejudice White primary school students to talk about racial issues with low-prejudice friends decreased prejudice in the former and did not increase prejudice in the latter (Aboud & Doyle, 1996).

Increasing Self-Disclosure. In some multicultural education programs, participants are provided with opportunities for personal self-disclosure. Self-disclosure often leads to liking because it creates an atmosphere of trust and it is usually reciprocal (Derlega, Metts, Petronio, & Margulis, 1993). In the context of multicultural education programs, both enhanced in-group identity and acceptance of out-group identity are potential benefits of self-disclosure (Davidman, 1995).

During multicultural education programs, as individuals from different groups come to know one another better, the depth of their self-disclosure increases, and its basis changes from demographic to personal characteristics. Many of the properties of multicultural education programs, such as their duration, openness of communication, informality, and the presence of multiple goals, foster a climate in which self-disclosure can become more intimate and result in intergroup benefits (Brewer & Miller, 1984).

Dialogue groups are facilitated discussions among members of two groups with a history of conflict in which participants are encouraged to listen carefully to one another and in the process to correctly understand the others' values and beliefs (DuBois & Hutson, 1997). Self-disclosures are common in these groups. In one study, they were shown to lead to increased racial understanding in college students that persisted three years after the groups had ended (Gurin, Peng, Lopez, & Nagda, 1999).

Cognitive Processes

Increasing Perceptions of Similarity Among Groups. From the perspective of social identity theory, changing the belief that the out-group differs from the in-group in ways that are integral to self-identity should lead to reductions in prejudice. Considerable evidence indicates that increasing perceptions of the similarity of others to the self increases liking for these others (Byrne, 1971; Rokeach, Smith, & Evans, 1960). Thus, in multicultural education programs, information and experiences that erode the assumed dissimilarity between groups can potentially play a significant role in reducing prejudice. It is therefore valuable in multicultural education programs to balance information about group differences with information about group similarities.

Personalization. Categorization of self and others into groups leads to category-based interactions, interactions in which individuals are predominantly viewed as members of the in-group or the out-group (Brewer & Miller, 1984; Dovidio, Gaertner, Isen, Rust, & Guerra, 1998; Miller, Brewer, & Edwards, 1985). However, if the salience of group categories is reduced, students can get to know each other as individuals. The use of small group interaction in multicultural education programs provides an opportunity to personalize out-group members. Personalized interactions break down prejudice by providing accurate information about out-group members and increasing the perceived variability within these out-groups. Two studies have found decreased prejudice in elementary school students as a result of personalization (Aboud & Fenwick, 2000; Katz & Zalk, 1978).

Multiple Identities and Cross-Cutting Categories. The tendency to see the world in terms of dichotomies (for example, racial or ethnic categories) can be reduced by reminding people of other important sources of identity (Brewer, 2000; Dovidio, Gaertner, Isen, Rust, & Guerra,

1998; Dovidio et al., 2000; Hewstone, Islam, & Judd, 1993). Prejudice based on a single category is attenuated when even one other important cross-cutting in-group/out-group category is made salient. Multicultural education programs can employ multiple identity exercises to blur the distinctions between racial, ethnic, and cultural groups.

Recategorization. A third way to reduce the power of categorization is by inducing members of differing groups to think of themselves as members of one superordinate group (Gaertner, Dovidio, Nier, Ward, & Banker, 1999; Gaertner, Mann, Murrell, & Dovidio, 1989; Sherif, 1966). Attitudes toward former out-group members then become more positive through a process of superordinate in-group favoritism. Multicultural education programs can promote recategorization into superordinate categories through the use of activities that promote recategorization (for example, projects involving the whole class, identification with the school or community).

Creating Common In-Group Identity. The common in-group identity model combines several social categorization processes (Dovidio et al., 1998; Gaertner, Dovidio, Anastasio, Bachman, & Rust, 1993). It is argued that the creation of a superordinate group, personalization, and a strategy of dual identification can all be effective in reducing prejudice. Dual identification is created by maintaining attachments to one's subgroup at the same time one identifies with a superordinate group that includes one's in-group and other subgroups (Gaertner, Rust, Dovidio, Bachman, & Anastasio, 1994, but see Wittig & Molina, 2000). Dual identification also decreases bias through the process of in-group favoritism.

Some theorists argue that intergroup contact has sequential effects that unfold over time: it first leads to liking for the individuals involved in the contact, creating interpersonal liking (Pettigrew, 1998; Hewstone, 1996; Hewstone & Brown, 1986). This process often involves decategorization or personalization, that is, thinking of people as individuals rather than as members of a group. Next, the positive effects of contact generalize to the group, creating intergroup liking. In addition, positive contact can ultimately lead to the perception that individuals are part of an overarching group. Many multicultural education programs already include components that enhance these processes (Stephan & Stephan, 2001).

Affective Process

Reducing Threat. Integrated threat theory argues that feelings of threat are a cause of prejudice. Multicultural education programs can reduce feelings of threat, and therefore prejudice, by providing accurate information on group similarities and differences. Films, videos, plays, readings, field trips, guest lectures, group discussions, and role playing are among the multicultural materials that have been used to present positive and accurate information about out-group members (Bigler, 1999; Graves, 1999). They can also reduce threat by creating conditions for positive face-to-face interaction with out-group members, thereby reducing anxiety regarding future interactions.

Processes Involving Multiple Factors

Creating Empathy. Creating empathy in multicultural education programs can also result in prejudice reduction. Research has demonstrated that empathizing with out-group members can lead to decreased prejudice (Batson et al., 1997; Stephan & Finlay, 1999). When people empathize with out-groups, their empathic reactions can take two forms, the first of which is cognitive empathy. Individuals experience cognitive empathy when they take the role of another and view the world from that person's perspective. Cognitive empathy is promoted by acquiring knowledge about the out-group, including their worldview and their practices, norms, and values. It may also help people to learn about the way the out-group views the in-group. One way in which cognitive empathy has been successfully induced in college communication classes is through the integration of cultural diversity topics into public speaking assignments (Carrell, 1997).

The second empathic reaction involves emotional empathy. In multicultural education programs, emotional empathy consists primarily of compassion-related emotions that arise from a feeling of concern for the suffering of others. According to Batson and his colleagues (1997), emotional empathy causes people to value the welfare of the out-group, leading to more positive attitudes toward the group. Finlay and Stephan (2000) suggest that emotional empathy can also lead to attitude change by undercutting the tendency to blame the victims of discrimination for the difficulties they suffer. In multicultural education programs, reading information about the experiences of another group or listening to the members of an out-group describe their experiences can create both cognitive and emotional empathy for that group. Role-playing exercises may also arouse emotional empathy for out-groups (Weiner & Wright, 1973). Role playing of race-related issues has been shown to be effective in reducing prejudice and discrimination in students of all ages (McGregor, 1993).

Using Dissonance to Create Attitude Change. In dissonance theory, it is argued that when people behave in ways that are inconsistent with their customary views of themselves, they become uncomfortable about this discrepancy

(Aronson, 1997). This discomfort is labeled dissonance, and it can motivate people to change their former attitudes in order to maintain a consistent view of themselves. Thus, if people who are prejudiced, ethnocentric, or biased toward members of another group behave in positive ways toward members of this group, they will be motivated to change their previously prejudicial attitudes to be consistent with their current behavior (Gray & Ashmore, 1975; Leippe & Eisenstadt, 1994). Dissonance can have powerful effects on attitudes in multicultural education programs that motivate students to behave in positive ways toward members of previously disliked groups.

Making Value-Behavior Discrepancies Explicit. Valuing egalitarianism is associated with low levels of prejudice (Katz, Wachenhut, & Hass, 1986). Studies have shown that because most Americans believe in equality, confronting them with the discrepancy between their beliefs in equality and their biased attitudes and behaviors toward out-group members leads to changes in these attitudes and behaviors (Grube, Mayton, & Ball-Rokeach, 1994; Monteith, 1993; Rokeach, 1971). Many multicultural education programs have an emphasis on egalitarian and humanistic norms as one component of the program (Stephan & Stephan, 2001). Making the discrepancies between their values and their biased behaviors explicit can help students further reduce prejudice by leading them to confront these discrepancies directly (Altemeyer, 1994).

Modifying Associations Between Cognitions and Affect. Social learning theory emphasizes the learned associations between objects and emotions, including associations between social groups and affective responses to them (Bandura, 1986). All too often, people have learned to link certain social groups with negative affect through socialization, exposure to the media, and direct experience. As a consequence, some out-groups are feared, disliked, and avoided. In multicultural education programs, it is possible to modify the associations between out-groups and negative affect by providing students with positive experiences and information about out-groups.

Summary of Prejudice-Reduction Processes

Behavioral, cognitive, and affective processes are all effective in reducing prejudice. Creating the conditions of the contact hypothesis should be a goal in all multicultural education classrooms with racially heterogeneous student populations: interacting students should have equal status in the classroom, be engaged in cooperative interaction that provides information about the students as individuals, and be supported by school authorities such as teachers and administrators. Other behavioral

processes can be added through classroom procedures and experiential assignments. A variety of cognitive processes can be used to break down the perception of monolithic out-groups. Affective processes can both decrease negative affect and increase positive affect. In addition, processes that combine nonbiased cognitions, values, affect, and behaviors may have especially broad and long-lasting effects on prejudice. In the next section, theories of stereotyping are examined.

THEORIES OF STEREOTYPING

Six theories of the causes of stereotyping are briefly discussed in this section. Five cognitive theories of stereotypes are explored: category-based information processing, expectancy theory, cognitive bias theories, identity formation, and one theory suggesting that social structural issues underlie stereotyping, motivation to stereotype, and power maintenance.

Cognitive Theories

Category-Based Information Processing and Stereotyping. Fiske and her colleagues (Fiske, 2000; Fiske & Neuberg, 1990) believe that impression-formation processes lie on a continuum from category based (for example, impressions based on stereotypes) to individuated (for example, impressions based on the individual's unique traits). They argue that stereotypic thinking often has priority and is likely to be used, particularly if the individual from the out-group appears to present attributes that match the group stereotype. However, if the perceiver's attention can be drawn to the target's unique attributes, stereotypes lose their strength.

Expectancy Theories. A number of theorists have argued that stereotypes function to create order out of the chaos of social reality. Stereotypes provide guidelines for social interaction and explanations for the behavior of others. When people attribute a set of characteristics to an out-group, they then have a basis for expectations about their behaviors. People commonly base their own behavior toward out-group members on such stereotype-related expectancies. The members of the out-group often respond to being treated in this manner by acting in ways that confirm the initial expectancies, thus creating a self-fulfilling prophecy (Snyder, 1992; Snyder, Tanke, & Berscheid, 1977).

Stereotypes are maintained in part by the tendency to better remember expectancy-confirming than expectancy-disconfirming information about social groups (Fyock & Stangor, 1994; Stangor & McMillan, 1992). These biases affect the information that is noticed, placed in short-term memory, stored in long-term memory, and subsequently recalled (Bodenhausen & Wyer, 1985; Stangor & McMillan, 1992). Even the language used to encode information facilitates the stereotyping of out-group members. Individuals have been shown to encode desirable in-group and undesirable out-group behaviors at a higher level of abstraction than undesirable in-group and desirable out-group behaviors (Maass, Salvi, Arcuri, & Semin, 1989). The higher the level of abstraction, the more resistant the impressions are to disconformation.

Cognitive Bias Theories. The "ultimate attribution error" occurs when people explain the negative behaviors of out-group members in terms of their internal traits (Pettigrew, 1979; Stephan, 1977). People fail to take situational causes of negative behaviors into consideration when they should, resulting in stronger negative stereotypes of out-groups than the evidence warrants (Schaller, Asp, Rosell, & Heim, 1996; Schaller & O'Brien, 1992).

The "illusory correlation" leads people to remember that members of minority groups have engaged in negative behaviors more frequently than they actually have (Hamilton & Rose, 1980).

Identity Formation. Stereotypes also enable in-groups to perceive that they are distinctive from out-groups, thus contributing to group identity (Oakes, Haslam, & Turner, 1994). In the process of forming social categories, the differences between groups tend to be accentuated, and variability within the out-group tends to be minimized. The perception of out-groups as homogeneous is most likely to occur for negative traits, and majority groups seem more prone to display this bias than minority groups.

Motivation to Stereotype. Bodenhausen and his colleagues (Bodenhausen, Macrae, & Garst, 1998) believe that activating stereotypes sows the seeds of discrimination. Stereotypes are often activated through such characteristics as physical appearance (Gilbert & Hixon, 1991; Moreno & Bodenhausen, 1999) when sufficient cognitive capacity is available and the motivation to stereotype exists (Bodenhausen et al., 1998). Once activated, stereotypes influence judgments regarding the meaning of ambiguous behaviors (Wyer & Srull, 1989).

Social Structural Theory

Stereotypes and Power Maintenance. Dominant groups use negative stereotypes to justify and maintain their power (Jost & Banaji, 1994). Stereotypes are partly a product of the history of relations between groups. The content of stereotypes also tends to reflect the current role and status relations between the groups (LeVine & Campbell, 1972). Groups often differ in beliefs, norms, and behaviors, and these differences are rarely evaluated neutrally. When relations between groups involve conflict or disparities in status, out-group stereotypes are particularly likely to be negative.

Summary of the Theories of Stereotyping

Taken together, these theories suggest that stereotyping is a result of natural tendencies to categorize objects in the environment. Group-level categorizations based on stereotypes are likely to be used when perceiving others. Biases in cognitive information processing also result in stereotyping. Moreover, stereotypes are employed to create positive social identities for in-groups by making them seem distinctive from other groups. Stereotypes are most likely to be employed when people have sufficient cognitive capacity and are motivated to stereotype. Like prejudice, stereotypes are commonly used to maintain the social dominance of some groups over others. Having explored a number of explanations for the creation of stereotypes, we now examine suggestions for their reduction.

STEREOTYPE-REDUCTION PROCESSES

Stereotypes are resistant to change, but a number of techniques have been developed to counteract them. Five processes involved in stereotype change are briefly discussed. First a behavioral process, creating interdependence, is explored. Because stereotypes consist of cognitions concerning the characteristics of out-groups, many of the processes involved in changing them are cognitive in nature. Three such processes are reviewed here: differentiating the out-group, overcoming ignorance, and counteracting expectancies. Finally, an affective process, creating compunction, is discussed.

Behavioral Processes

Creating Interdependence. Fiske (Fiske, 2000; Fiske & Neuberg, 1990) has argued that individual-level interdependence (outcome dependency) motivates people to attend to stereotype-inconsistent information and make dispositional attributions about it. Individuals are motivated to focus on new information (for example, counter-stereotypic attributes) rather than their stereotypes because it is of obvious benefit to them to accurately understand the other person. Multicultural education programs commonly create interdependence among students through techniques such as the use of cooperative learning groups. Many cooperative learning theorists believe that the creation of positive goal interdependence is a major factor in the success of cooperative learning groups (Deutsch, 1962; Johnson & Johnson, 1994).

Cognitive Processes

Differentiating the Out-Group. People sometimes avoid changing their stereotypes by subtyping. That is, they break a larger group down into smaller subcategories when they come upon out-group members who do not fit their stereotypes. They then form a subtype that encompasses the exceptions. Thus, subtyping preserves the stereotype of the larger group.

The presentation of information about out-group members that is very discrepant from the stereotype often results in subtyping. However, the presentation of information about out-group members who fit the stereotype in some ways but are discrepant from it in others has been shown to produce subgrouping (Richards & Hewstone, 2001; Hewstone & Lord, 1998). In subgrouping, stereotype change occurs, creating a more differentiated view of the out-group.

The tendency to subtype can be undercut by providing contact with a number of different out-group members (Rothbart & John, 1985). This type of differentiation results when so many new categories are created that subtyping becomes impossible (Langer, 1989). The conditions for differentiation of the out-group to take place can be created in multicultural education programs through contact with or learning about diverse out-group members. Multiple identities can also be used to break down monolithic stereotypes. In a study of elementary school students, Bigler and Liben (1992) demonstrated that training in multiple classifications of individuals reduced students' tendencies to stereotype.

Counteracting Ignorance. Information about other groups attacks one of the main causes of stereotypes: ignorance (Stephan & Stephan, 1984). In the absence of knowledge about other groups, people tend to rely on stereotypes in their interactions. The information about out-groups that is such an integral part of multicultural materials puts a human face on out-groups that may have been previously viewed in a stereotypical and dehumanized way. In addition, learning about other groups can also counteract the tendency to make unfavorable attributions for their behaviors. Multicultural education programs can accomplish these goals by presenting information on group differences in norms, beliefs, and values in a positive light. Most programs include curricular materials about a variety of groups not typically fully represented in regular classes. However, it is clear that materials must be selected carefully, ideally with input from the groups represented. Children's literature and even multicultural education readers may consist of materials that inadvertently reinforce stereotypes; distort history; convey subtle support for racism, sexism, or colonialism; and demean or disparage certain groups (Harris, 1992). Some elementary and secondary schools use courses in anthropology to teach cultural diversity issues (Dynneson, 1998).

Counteracting Expectancies. Negative out-group stereotypes can be weakened if people engage in conscious, thoughtful processing of expectancy-disconfirming information and then attribute the causes of the disconfirming behaviors to internal factors (Crocker, Hannah, & Weber, 1983). Internal trait attributions are most likely to be made if a number of different out-group members engage in the disconfirming behavior and it occurs frequently in a variety of settings (Mackie, Allison, Worth, & Asuncion, 1992; Rothbart & John, 1985). It is also helpful if the people displaying the disconfirming behavior are otherwise seen as typical out-group members (Rothbart & Lewis, 1988). The self-fulfilling effects of negative expectancies also tend to disappear when people want out-group members to like them (Neuberg, 1996).

Multicultural education programs often create situations in which students' negative expectancies about outgroups are disconfirmed. Face-to-face interaction, experiential exercises, and information about within-group diversity can all help to increase the ability of students to make attributions to out-group members' behaviors that are similar to those the out-group members themselves make (Stephan & Stephan, 2001). Cohen and her colleagues (Cohen & Lotan, 1997) have had considerable success with two interventions to counteract negative expectancies associated with lower-status students. In one intervention, teachers give lower-status students a new status inconsistent with their general status, by informing all of the students that the lower-status students will be good at the new task to be completed and the higher-status students will not be as good at the task. In a second intervention, teachers tell students that the new task requires many abilities, no one possesses high abilities in all the areas, and everyone possesses high ability in at least one of them.

Affective Processes

Creating Compunction. Compunction theory maintains that many people believe that stereotyping is wrong and experience guilt or self-criticism (compunction) when they think in stereotypic ways (Devine, 1989; Devine, Monteith, Zuwerink, & Elliot, 1991). Although stereotypes can be automatically activated, people can learn to put self-regulatory processes into effect so that triggering stereotypes evokes guilt (Monteith, Zuwerink, & Devine, 1994). If people are motivated to overcome stereotyping, these guilt feelings lead to the suppression of stereotype-related behaviors (Montieth, 1993). The steps by which compunction is achieved are accepting nonprejudiced norms, internalizing them, learning to inhibit automatic, prejudice-related responses, and finally replacing them with belief-based controlled responses (Devine, Plant, & Buswell, 2000). Many multicultural education programs not only emphasize equality and fairness, but also attempt to put these values into practice, thus beginning a process that can result in compunction. Some programs also take active steps to teach students to counteract stereotypes when activated. These programs could be even more effective if they explicitly addressed the steps involved in the self-regulation of stereotypes. However, some researchers have found that suppressing a thought can make it more accessible in memory and thus more likely to be manifest (Bodenhausen & Macrae, 1996; Wegner & Erber, 1992), so care must be exercised in creating feelings of compunction.

Summary of Stereotype-Reduction Processes

The tendency to stereotype can be undercut by providing contact with a number of different out-group members who exhibit a variety of characteristics. Stereotypes can be disconfirmed through the reduction of ignorance about the characteristics of out-groups. They are also reduced when individuals interact with out-group members who display stereotype-disconfirming behaviors. This technique is particularly useful when the individual has an opportunity to carefully process the expectancy-disconfirming information and when the individuals' outcomes are interdependent. In addition, the tendency to stereotype can be arrested if individuals are taught to experience guilt when the stereotype is activated. In the last set of theories, explanations for discriminatory acts are discussed.

THEORIES OF DISCRIMINATION

Three social psychological theories that explain the causes of discrimination are explored. The theory of reasoned action and the MODE model are both based in part on the idea that reason and attention to social norms influence behavior. Power maintenance theory invokes social structural elements as causes of discrimination.

Attitude and Norm Theories

Theory of Reasoned Action. The theory of reasoned action captures the interplay between the role of attitudes, such as prejudice, and social norms as determinants of behavior (Fishbein & Ajzen, 1975). According to this theory, people's intentions to behave are a function of their attitudes toward the act and their subjective norms. The relevant attitudes toward the act are twofold: beliefs about the value of the outcomes of the possible behavior and beliefs about the probability that these outcomes will occur. Subjective norms are the perceptions people have

of the attitudes of others who are important to them. The effect of subjective norms on behavior is influenced by the degree to which people are motivated to comply with the wishes of these significant others.

MODE Model. Fazio (Fazio, 1990; Schuette & Fazio, 1995) has argued that two types of relationship between attitudes and behavior exist. Which one prevails depends on the extent to which behavior is based on conscious deliberation or is a spontaneous reaction to perceptions of the immediate situation. When behavior is spontaneous, the likelihood that it will be consistent with attitudes is based on the accessibility of the attitude. If prejudiced attitudes are highly accessible, discrimination is likely to follow. People will behave spontaneously unless they are motivated to deliberately process information and given an opportunity to do so. When behavior is based on deliberation, the theory of reasoned action applies; attitudes and subjective norms produce behavioral intentions which lead to actions.

Social Structural Elements

Racism and Power Maintenance. Operario and Fiske (1998) start with the social identity perspective that prejudice and stereotyping are basic, perhaps universal, phenomena that have some functional and adaptive aspects. Although such affective and cognitive biases are common to all people, only some individuals have the power to impose their biases on others. Thus, in this view, prejudice combined with social power creates discrimination against the less powerful.

Summary of Theories of Discrimination

When people have the cognitive resources and the motivation to use them, whether discrimination occurs is based on a combination of one's attitudes, the perceived outcomes of the discriminatory behavior, and the perceived probability that these outcomes will occur, plus the attitudes of important others and the motivation to comply with those attitudes. When people lack the cognitive resources or the motivation to use them, discrimination may be based on a spontaneous reaction to an immediate situation in conjunction with accessible and relevant attitudes. In both cases, the higher the individuals' social power, the more capable they are of acting on their attitudes. In the following section, processes that can reduce discrimination are discussed.

DISCRIMINATION-REDUCTION PROCESSES

The components of the theory of reasoned action suggest two cognitive processes by which discrimination can be reduced: modifying attitudes about behavioral outcomes and altering perceptions of subjective norms. In addition, behavioral interventions to alter power structures in the schools and the society may be effective in reducing discrimination.

Cognitive Processes

Modifying Attitudes About Behavioral Outcomes. School personnel should create and enforce clear norms regarding the inappropriateness of discriminatory behavior and derogatory speech. If discrimination is negatively sanctioned, students' attitudes about the consequences of discrimination will be altered along with their perceptions of the probability of receiving these negative sanctions. Creating a positive climate for diversity can also change the perceptions of the outcomes of discrimination. If nondiscriminatory behavior is rewarded, attitudes about behavioral outcomes will be further modified. In some schools, children are both rewarded for caring acts in their educational community and taught to reward others' caring acts (Davidson & Davidson, 1994).

Codes of conduct detailing basic human rights for all personnel and students can be a helpful tool in improving intergroup relations. These codes can be generated through school meetings involving representatives from administrators, teachers, students, parents, and other staff members. Multicultural education curricula can reinforce these messages by emphasizing equal rights and treatment of all students, training students to empathize with victims of discrimination, and providing ways to respond to discrimination when it occurs.

Altering Perceptions of Subjective Norms. As new norms valuing diversity take hold and the school climate becomes more tolerant and egalitarian, subjective perceptions of what students believe significant others wish them to do will also change. If teachers and administrators model nondiscriminatory behavior, students will be better able to recognize that members of their reference groups are opposed to discriminatory behavior (Hauserman et al., 1973). At the individual level, the Aboud and Doyle (1996) method of pairing high-prejudice students to talk about racial issues with low-prejudice friends should also influence the perception of subjective norms in a positive manner.

Altering Power Structures in the Schools and the Society. Teaching students about racism and other systems of oppression is a first step in altering such systems. Dialogue groups provide an example of a technique used on college campuses to teach about oppression (DuBois & Hutson, 1997). Some schools have created educational democracies in which everyone has an equal voice in making rules and in which the validity of the rules is judged by their fairness to all interested parties (Power, Higgins, & Kohlberg, 1989). These schools have also involved older children in changing society's social structures by teaching them about social stratification and human oppression and involving them in local human rights actions. If students are encouraged to publicly state their intentions to behave in nondiscriminatory ways, the chances that students will follow through on their commitments to change their behaviors will increase.

Summary of Discrimination-Reduction Processes

A combination of changing the climate for diversity through modifying behavioral outcomes and the creation of policies favoring diversity, altering perceptions of subjective norms, instituting systems of caring and justice, and teaching students to recognize oppression and fight against it should reduce instances of discrimination in the school system.

PROCESSES TO REDUCE PREJUDICE, STEREOTYPING, AND DISCRIMINATION: DEVELOPMENTAL CONCERNS

Although a number of the processes discussed in this chapter have been studied among students of different age levels, the bulk of the research on these processes has been conducted with college students. As a result, the degree to which these processes influence younger students is not always clear. Most should apply relatively straightforwardly to secondary school students, but the age at which these processes can be initially introduced is often unknown. Some research indicates that the processes associated with contact theory, as well as interdependence, personalization, superordinate groups, similarity, empathy, dissonance, learning theory, identity formation, and correcting attributional biases, can be effective with primary school students. However, there is less evidence on the extent to which the processes associated with multiple identities, threat, compunction, expectancies, and cognitive biases are suitable for use with young children. Additional research is needed to determine at which age all these processes can be most effectively employed. The final section reviews the research findings on the effects of multicultural education programs on intergroup relations.

EFFECTS OF MULTICULTURAL EDUCATION PROGRAMS ON INTERGROUP RELATIONS

Despite the widespread use of multicultural education programs, only a limited number of studies has examined its effects on intergroup relations (for more detail on these findings, see Stephan et al., in press; Stephan & Stephan, 2001). Only published, statistically analyzed quantitative studies of multicultural education programs are reviewed here. These studies had a range of goals and a variety of corresponding outcome measures, including attitudes, knowledge, behaviors, racial awareness, and self-reported competencies. Student programs were included only if they lasted two weeks or longer; teacher programs were reviewed if they continued for a weekend or longer. Published studies reporting qualitative data, shorter interventions, quantitative data not subjected to statistical testing, and laboratory studies are excluded from this review. (Dozens of studies have examined the short-term effects of specific components of multicultural programs, such as readings, films and videos, role playing, and discussions. Although most of these studies indicate that the components of these programs typically have positive effects on intergroup attitudes and behaviors, they are not discussed here because there are reasons to be skeptical of these studies; see Stephan & Stephan, 2001, for a review. The immediate measures of the effects of a single technique are subject to demand characteristics: the participants may know what outcome the researcher wishes to find and simply give the desired responses. Furthermore, the immediate effects may well decay, so the immediate effects may make the component appear more effective than it actually is.)

Four settings have been studied. Some research has explored the effects of multicultural education programs on intergroup relations in primary and secondary schools. Other studies have considered the effects of teacher education on multicultural topics. A third set of studies has detailed the effects of multicultural education courses on college students. Finally, there are studies of the effects of multicultural education graduate courses for counseling psychologists.

Studies of Primary and Secondary School Students

Two of the ten studies conducted in primary and secondary schools found that multicultural education programs had only positive effects on measures of intergroup relations (Litcher & Johnson, 1969; Yawkey & Blackwell, 1974). Another five studies found a mixture of positive and no effects (mostly positive effects were found for Aboud & Fenwick, 2000, study 1, and Verma & Bagley, 1973; mostly null effects were obtained by Avery, Bird, Johnstone, Sullivan, & Thalhammer, 1982, Colca, Lowen, Colca, & Lord, 1982, and Wittig & Molina, 2000, study 2). Two studies reported no effects (Lessing & Clarke, 1976; Yawkey, 1973), and another, negative effects (Wittig & Molina, 2000, study 1). Only two studies of the effects of multicultural education on pre-school students were

found. One study showed a combination of null and negative effects (Kowalski, 1998), and the other yielded no effects (Best, Smith, Graves, & Williams, 1975).

Studies of College Teacher Training Courses

In many schools of education, prospective teachers are required to take multicultural education courses to prepare them to teach students from diverse backgrounds. In addition, some teachers attend in-service education programs. Two of the four studies of the effects of these courses indicate that multicultural teacher training programs initially improved intergroup relations (Grant & Grant, 1985; Henington, 1981). However in one, the effects had dissipated after 26 days (Henington, 1981). Another found positive effects for White teachers and no effects for Black teachers immediately and after 16 months (Robinson & Preston, 1976). The final study found no effects of training (Washington, 1981).

Studies of General Undergraduate Courses

In studies of undergraduate courses, the effects of multicultural education courses were entirely positive in three out of seven cases (Astin, 1993; Katz & Ivey, 1977; Robinson & Bradley, 1997). Two studies found a mixture of positive and no effects (Carrell, 1997; Richards & Gamache, 1979), another reported no effects (Neville & Furlong, 1994), and one had negative effects (Van Soest, 1996).

Studies of Counseling Graduate Students and Counselors

A final set of 10 studies targeted graduate students in counseling psychology and practicing counselors. Two studies reported exclusively positive effects (Ota Wang, 1998; Parker, Moore, & Neimeyer, 1998), including one in which the positive results were maintained for seven months (Ota Wang, 1998). Four studies found a mixture of positive and no effects on intergroup relations measures (Brooks & Kahn, 1990; Brown, Parham, & Yonker, 1996; Byington, Fischer, Walker, & Freedman, 1997; D'Andrea, Daniels, & Heck, 1991). In one, White but not Black practitioners showed more positive attitudes after interracial training (Lefley, 1985).

In four studies of self-reported multicultural competencies, two found positive results (Diaz-Lazaro & Cohen, 2001; Neville et al., 1996), and in one of these, the positive results persisted for a year (Neville et al., 1996). The third showed mixed positive and no effects of multicultural training (Sodowsky, Kuo-Jackson, Richardson, & Corey, 1998). One study found positive effects for women but not men (Constantine & Yeh, 2001). Of course, self-reported competence may be different from actual competence.

Analysis of the Findings

Since all these multicultural programs were different, it is difficult to use the results of these studies to draw conclusions about how to make programs more successful. In addition, the studies employed different measures of intergroup relations (for example, attitudes toward out-groups, multicultural skills, knowledge of out-groups). The validity and reliability of many of these measures have not been well established, so their use may have led to inaccurate assessments of the programs in some cases. Moreover, the programs were conducted in different regions of the country using participants who differed widely in age and other demographic characteristics, and the contexts in which these programs were conducted were very different from one another, and this also complicates interpretation.

Few of the studies examined programs that are as comprehensive as most multicultural programs in place today, and none of them lasted longer than half a school year. The majority examined the effects of multicultural education only on Whites. Only a few of the longer studies included Blacks, and they show mixed results. It is not clear if the Blacks, who were often shown in these studies to be less prejudiced, should have been expected to change attitudes dramatically, particularly with materials designed for Whites. Even fewer studies have examined the effects of multicultural education on other minority groups. It is possible that current multicultural education programs have different effects on Whites and members of minority groups, but until further research is done, it is impossible to know.

The outcomes of most of the programs were measured immediately, increasing the chances of finding positive results. Furthermore, none of these studies investigated long-term effects of multicultural education such as choosing to live in integrated housing, working in integrated environments, friendship selection, voting patterns, racial and ethnic attitudes, attitudes toward public policies, or participation in organizations devoted to improving intergroup relations. These potential long-term effects of multicultural education should be assessed.

Little information on program content was presented in the manuscripts. Clearly, more information on the outcomes of multicultural education programs is needed. Every evaluation should provide detailed information on the programs and the outcomes of the programs. In addition, research that attempts to identify mediators of the programs and assess the efficacy of the proposed mediators is almost unknown in the literature and is greatly needed. Until researchers are certain they understand why their programs produced the outcomes that were found, they will have less information than they should have to make their programs maximally effective. Finally, very few comparative studies exist. Information regarding the outcomes of two or more programs in the same population would be invaluable to researchers and teachers in selecting ideal programs.

Summary of the Intergroup Relations Effects of Multicultural Education Programs

Any conclusions formed on the basis of these studies must be regarded as extremely tentative. Despite the widespread use of multicultural education programs, only a limited number of studies has examined its effects on intergroup relations. With these reservations in mind, it appears that most multicultural education programs achieve some success in improving attitudes toward out-group members, increasing knowledge of out-groups, and improving multicultural skills (see Table 38.1). However, it appears that many of them do not fully achieve the goals they were designed to achieve, and in a small number of cases, they actually lead to negative outcomes. One of the most common findings in these studies is a mixture of positive effects and no effects. Clearly, there is room for improvement in the implementation of many of these programs. Since authors are more likely to submit—and journals are more likely to publish—evaluations with positive and significant findings, it is likely that these few studies are not representative of the entire pool of evaluations conducted on multicultural education. The results reported here undoubtedly overstate the positive nature of the outcomes of intergroup relations programs.

All multicultural education programs should document their effects on intergroup relations. A program that seems to be doing the right thing may in fact be promoting

Table 38.1. Summary of Intergroup Relations Effects of Multicultural Education Programs.

Type of Program	Positive Effects	Mixed Positive and No Effects	No Effects	Mixed Negative and No Effects	Negative Effects
Nursery school			1	1	
Primary/secondary	2	5	2	1	1
Teacher training	2	1	1		
College students	3	2	1		1
Counselors	4	6			
All programs	11 (33%)	14 (42%)	5 (15%)	1 (3%)	2 (16%)

stereotypes or worsening relations between group members. In the area of multicultural education, the best of intentions does not guarantee positive outcomes. Ideally, this evaluation would include both qualitative and quantitative data. The ideal quantitative analysis would be longitudinal, to determine if short-term gains endure over time. It would also use a control group, preferably with individuals randomly assigned to training and nontraining groups. In addition, the measures used to assess the program should be carefully examined to make certain that they actually assess the concepts they are intended to measure. Ultimately, mediating variables need to be specified. Many programs are known to have specific effects, but it is not clear what aspects of the program create the effects and why.

Most multicultural education programs attempt to change the attitudes and behaviors of individuals in the hopes that by changing individuals, the society itself can be changed. But prejudice, stereotyping, and discrimination also need to be attacked at the structural level. All multicultural education programs should have as one of their goals modifying the structure and procedures of the school to reflect the egalitarian emphasis of the curriculum. Programs are most effective when they transform the entire organization into a caring, inclusive, egalitarian one and involve students in actions to make their communities more humane. The ultimate goal should be total societal change.

The values transmitted in multicultural education classes can be reinforced by other programs and practices that promote the same values. For example, cooperative learning techniques have been shown to lead to significant improvements in intergroup relations in classrooms diverse in race and ethnicity, nationality, and performance levels (Slavin, 1995; Stephan & Stephan, 2001). Moreover, cooperative learning techniques increase student achievement, especially the achievement of minority students and low-achieving students. Cooperative learning groups could be one important component of multicultural education. In addition, evaluations of general school-based conflict resolution and peer mediation programs show that these programs are typically effective in teaching students integrative negotiation and mediation procedures and that trained students tend to use these procedures to reach constructive solutions to conflict (Carruthers, Sweeney, Kmitta, & Harris, 1996; Johnson & Johnson, 1996; Lam, 1989). Peer mediation training appears to be successful among children as young as kindergarten age (Johnson & Johnson, 1996). The positive academic messages of multicultural education programs could be reinforced by mediation techniques designed to lower the level of intergroup conflict in the schools.

SUMMARY

In this chapter, it is argued that improving intergroup relations in multicultural education programs requires attention to the concepts of prejudice, stereotyping, and discrimination. Educators need to understand the causes of prejudice, stereotyping, and discrimination, as well as the processes by which they can be reduced. Knowledge of these concepts and processes will help educators improve negative intergroup relations by changing aspects of the schools that promote prejudice, stereotyping, and discrimination and creating the conditions in which ameliorating processes can occur. Preliminary data have shown that multicultural education programs can be successful in reducing prejudice, stereotyping, and discrimination, but most programs appear to be less successful than they could be.

References

Aboud, F. E., & Doyle, A. B. (1996). Does talk of race foster prejudice or tolerance in children? *Canadian Journal of Behavioural Science, 28,* 161–170.

Aboud, F. E., & Fenwick, V. (2000). Exploring and evaluating school-based interventions to reduce prejudice. *Journal of Social Issues, 55,* 767–786.

Allport, G. W. (1954). *The nature of prejudice.* Reading, MA: Addison-Wesley.

Altemeyer, B. (1994). Reducing prejudice in right-wing authoritarians. In M. P. Zanna & J. M. Olson (Eds.), *The psychology of prejudice: The Ontario symposium* (Vol. 7, pp. 131–148). Mahwah, NJ: Erlbaum.

Amir, Y. (1976). The role of intergroup contact in change of prejudice and race relations. In P. Katz & D. A. Taylor (Eds.), *Towards the elimination of racism* (pp. 245—308). New York: Pergamon.

Aronson, E. (1997). The theory of cognitive dissonance: The evolution and vicissitudes of an idea. In E. Harmon-Jones & J. S. Mills (Eds.), *Cognitive dissonance theory: Revival with revisions and controversies* (pp. 20–35). Oxford: Blackwell.

Astin, A. (1993). Diversity and multiculturalism on campus: How are students affected? *Change, 25,* 44–49.

Avery, P. G., Bird, K., Johnstone, S., Sullivan, J. L., & Thalhammer, K. (1992). Exploring political tolerance with adolescents. *Theory and Research in Social Education, 20,* 386–420.

Bandura, A. (1986). *The social foundations of thought and action.* Englewood Cliffs, NJ: Prentice Hall.

Banks, J. A. (1997). *Educating citizens in a multicultural society.* New York: Teachers College Press.

Banks, J. A. (2001). Multicultural education: Historical development, dimensions, and practice. In J. A. Banks & C.A.M. Banks

(Eds.), *Handbook of research on multicultural education* (pp. 617–627). San Francisco: Jossey-Bass.

Batson, C. D., Polycarpou, M. P., Harmon-Jones, E., Imhoff, H. J., Mitchener, E. C., Bednar, L. L., Klein, T. R., & Highberger, L. (1997). Empathy and attitudes: Can feeling for a member of a stigmatized group improve feelings toward the group? *Journal of Personality and Social Psychology, 72,* 105–118.

Best, D. L., Smith, S. C., Graves, D. J., & Williams, J. E. (1975). The modification of racial bias in preschool children. *Journal of Experimental Child Psychology, 20,* 193–205.

Bigler, R. S. (1999). The use of multicultural curricula and materials to counter racism in children. *Journal of Social Issues, 55*(4), 767–786.

Bigler, R. S., & Liben, L. S. (1992). Cognitive mechanisms in children's gender stereotyping: Theoretical and educational implications of a cognitive-based intervention. *Child Development, 63,* 1351–1363.

Bodenhausen, G. V., & Macrae, C. N. (1996). The self-regulation of intergroup perception: Mechanisms and consequences of stereotype suppression. In C. N. Macrae, C. Stangor, & M. Hewstone (Eds.), *Stereotypes and stereotyping* (pp. 227–253). New York: Guilford.

Bodenhausen, G. V., Macrae, C. N., & Garst, J. (1998). Stereotypes in thought and deed: Social-cognitive origins of intergroup discrimination. In C. Sedikides, J. Schopler, & C. A. Insko (Eds.), *Intergroup cognition and intergroup behavior* (pp. 311–335). Mahwah, NJ: Erlbaum.

Bodenhausen, G. V., & Wyer, R. S., Jr. (1985). Effects of stereotypes on decision making and information processing strategies. *Journal of Personality and Social Psychology, 48,* 267–282.

Brewer, M. B. (2000). Reducing prejudice through cross-categorization: Effects of multiple social identities. In S. Oskamp (Ed.), *Reducing prejudice and discrimination* (pp. 165–183). Mahwah, NJ: Erlbaum.

Brewer, M. B., & Miller, N. (1984). Beyond the contact hypothesis: Theoretical perspectives on desegregation. In N. Miller & M. B. Brewer (Eds.), *Groups in contact: The psychology of desegregation* (pp. 281–302). Orlando, FL: Academic Press.

Brooks, G. S., & Kahn, S. E. (1990). Evaluation of a course in gender and cultural issues. *Cultural Education and Supervision, 30,* 66–76.

Brown, S. P., Parham, T. A., & Yonker, R. (1996). Influence of cross-cultural training course on racial identity attitudes of White women and men: Preliminary perspectives. *Journal of Counseling and Development, 74,* 510–516.

Byington, K., Fischer, J., Walker, L., & Freedman, E. (1997). Evaluating the effectiveness of a multicultural counseling ethics and assessment training. *Journal of Applied Rehabilitation Counseling, 28,* 234–248.

Byrne, D. (1971). *The attraction paradigm.* Orlando, FL: Academic Press.

Carrell, L. J. (1997). Diversity in the communication curriculum: Impact on student empathy. *Communication Education, 46,* 234–244.

Carruthers, W. L., Sweeney, B., Kmitta, D., & Harris, G. (1996). Conflict resolution: An examination of the research literature and a model for program evaluation. *School Counselor, 44,* 5–18.

Cohen, E. G., & Lotan, R. A. (1997). Raising expectations for competence: The effectiveness of status interventions. In E. G. Cohen & R. A. Lotan (Eds.), *Working for equity in heterogeneous classrooms: Sociological theory in practice* (pp. 77–91). New York: Teachers College Press.

Colca, C., Lowen, D., Colca, L., & Lord, S. A. (1982). Combating racism in the schools. *Social Work and Education, 21,* 5–15.

Constantine, M. G., & Yeh, C. J. (2001). Multicultural training, self-construals, and multicultural competence of school counselors. *Professional School Counseling, 4,* 202–207.

Crocker, J., Hannah, D. B., & Weber, R. (1983). Person memory and causal attributions. *Journal of Personality and Social Psychology, 44,* 55–66.

D'Andrea, M., Daniels, J., & Heck, R. (1991). Evaluating the impact of multicultural counseling training. *Journal of Counseling and Development, 70,* 143–150.

Davidman, L. (1995). Multicultural education: A movement in search of meaning and positive connections. *Multicultural Education, 2,* 8–12.

Davidson, F. H., & Davidson, M. M. (1994). *Changing childhood prejudice: The caring work of the schools.* Westport, CT: Greenwood Press.

Derlega, V. J., Metts, S., Petronio, S., & Margulis, S. T. (1993). *Self-disclosure.* Thousand Oaks, CA: Sage.

Deutsch, M. (1962). Cooperation and trust: Some theoretical notes. In M. R. Jones (Ed.), *Nebraska Symposium on Motivation,* (Vol. 10, pp. 275–319). Lincoln: University of Nebraska Press.

Devine, P. (1989). Stereotypes and prejudice: Their automatic and controlled components. *Journal of Personality and Social Psychology, 56,* 5–18.

Devine, P. G., Monteith, M. J., Zuwerink, J. R., & Elliot, A. J. (1991). Prejudice with and without compunction. *Journal of Personality and Social Psychology, 60,* 817–830.

Devine, P. G., Plant, E. A., & Buswell, B. N. (2000). Breaking the prejudice habit: Progress and obstacles. In S. Oskamp (Ed.), *Reducing prejudice and discrimination* (pp. 185–208). Mahwah, NJ: Erlbaum.

Diaz-Lazaro, C. M., & Cohen, B. B. (2001). Cross-cultural contact in counseling training. *Multicultural Counseling and Development, 29,* 41–56.

Dovidio, J. F., Brigham, J. C., Johnson, B. T., & Gaertner, S. (1996). Stereotyping, prejudice, and discrimination: Another look. In C. N. Macrae, C. Stangor, & M. Hewstone (Eds.), *Stereotypes and stereotyping* (pp. 276–319). New York: Guilford.

Dovidio, J. F., & Gaertner, S. L. (1986). Prejudice, discrimination, and racism: Historical trends and contemporary approaches. In J. F. Dovidio & S. L. Gaertner (Eds.), *Prejudice, discrimination, and racism* (pp. 1–34). Orlando, FL: Academic Press.

Dovidio, J. F., Gaertner, S. L., Isen, A. M., Rust, M., & Guerra, P. (1998). Positive affect, cognition, and the reduction of intergroup bias. In C. Sedikides, J. Schopler, & C. A. Insko (Eds.), *Intergroup cognition and intergroup behavior* (pp. 337–366). Mahwah, NJ: Erlbaum.

Dovidio, J. F., Kawakami, K., & Gaertner, S. L. (2000). Reducing contemporary prejudice: Combating explicit and implicit bias at the individual and intergroup level. In S. Oskamp (Ed.), *Reducing prejudice and discrimination* (pp. 137–163). Mahwah, NJ: Erlbaum.

DuBois, P. M., & Hutson, J. J. (1997). *Intergroup dialogues across America.* Hadley, MA: Common Wealth Printing.

Dynneson, T. L. (1998). Precollegiate anthropology: Its potential for the twenty-first century. *Social Studies, 89,* 118–122.

Fazio, R. H. (1990). Multiple processes by which attitudes guide behavior: The MODE model as an integrative framework. In M. Zanna (Ed.), *Advances in experimental social psychology* (Vol. 23, pp. 75–109). Orlando, FL: Academic Press.

Finlay, K. A., & Stephan, W. G. (2000). Reducing prejudice: The effects of empathy on intergroup attitudes. *Journal of Applied Social Psychology, 30,* 1722–1736.

Fishbein, M., & Ajzen, I. (1975). *Belief, attitude, intention, and behavior: An introduction to theory and research.* Reading, MA: Addison-Wesley.

Fiske, S. T. (2000). Interdependence and the reduction of prejudice. In S. Oskamp (Ed.), *Reducing prejudice and discrimination* (pp. 115–136). Thousand Oaks, CA: Sage.

Fiske, S. T., & Neuberg, S. L. (1990). A continuum model of impression formation, from category-based to individuating processes: Influences of information and motivation on attention and interpretation. In M. P. Zanna (Ed.), *Advances in experimental social psychology* (Vol. 23, pp. 1–74). Orlando, FL: Academic Press.

Fyock, J., & Stangor, C. (1994). The role of memory biases in stereotype maintenance. *British Journal of Social Psychology, 33,* 331–343.

Gaertner, S. L., & Dovidio, J. F. (1986). The aversive form of racism. In J. F. Dovidio & S. L. Gaertner (Eds.), *Prejudice, discrimination, and racism* (pp. 61–90). Orlando, FL: Academic Press.

Gaertner, S. L., Dovidio, J. F., Anastasio, P. A., Bachman, B., & Rust, M. C. (1993). The Common Ingroup Identity Model: Recategorization and the reduction of intergroup bias. In W. Stroebe & M. Hewstone (Eds.), *European review of social psychology* (Vol. 4, pp. 1–26). New York: Wiley.

Gaertner, S. L., Dovidio, J. F., Nier, J. A., Ward, C. M., & Banker, B. S. (1999). Across cultural divides: The value of superordinate identity. In D. A. Prentice & D. T. Miller (Eds.), *Cultural divides: Understanding and overcoming group conflict* (pp. 173–212). New York: Russell Sage Foundation.

Gaertner, S. L., Mann, J., Murrell, A., & Dovidio, J. F. (1989). Reducing intergroup bias: The benefits of recategorization. *Journal of Personality and Social Psychology, 57,* 239–249.

Gaertner, S. L., Rust, M. C., Dovidio, J. F., Bachman, B. A., & Anastasio, P. A. (1994). The contact hypothesis: The role of a common ingroup identity on reducing intergroup bias. *Small Group Research, 25,* 224–249.

Gilbert, D. T., & Hixon, J. G. (1991). The trouble of thinking: Activation and application of stereotypic beliefs. *Journal of Personality and Social Psychology, 60,* 509–517.

Grant, C. A., & Grant, G. A. (1985). Staff development and education that is multicultural. *British Journal of In-Service Education, 12,* 6–18.

Graves, S. B. (1999). Television and prejudice reduction: When does television as a vicarious experience make a difference? *Journal of Social Issues, 55,* 707–727.

Gray, D. B., & Ashmore, R. D. (1975). Comparing the effects of informational, role-playing, and value-discrepant treatments of racial attitudes. *Journal of Applied Social Psychology, 5,* 262–281.

Grube, J. W., Mayton, D. M., & Ball-Rokeach, S. J. (1994). Inducing change in values, attitudes, and behaviors: Belief system theory and the method of value self-confrontation. *Journal of Social Issues, 50,* 1253–1273.

Gurin, P., Peng, T., Lopez, G., & Nagda, B. R. (1999). Context, identity, and intergroup relations. In D. Prentice & D. Miller (Eds.), *Cultural divides: The social psychology of intergroup contact* (pp. 133–170). New York: Russell Sage Foundation.

Hamilton, D. L., & Rose, T. (1980). Illusory correlation and the maintenance of stereotype beliefs. *Journal of Personality and Social Psychology, 39,* 832–845.

Harris, V. J. (Ed.). (1992). *Teaching multicultural literature in grades K-8.* Norwood, MA: Christopher-Gordon Publishers.

Hauserman, N., Walen, S. R., & Behling, M. (1973). Reinforced racial integration in the first grade: A study of generalization. *Journal of Applied Behavioral Analysis, 6,* 193–200.

Henington, M. (1981). Effect of intensive multicultural non-sexist instruction on secondary student teachers. *Educational Research Quarterly, 6,* 65–75.

Hewstone, M. (1996). Contact and categorization. In C. N. Macrae, C. Stangor, & M. Hewstone (Eds.), *Foundations of stereotypes and stereotyping* (pp. 323–368). New York: Guilford.

Hewstone, M., & Brown, R. (1986). Contact is not enough: An intergroup perspective on the contact hypothesis. In M. Hewstone & R. Brown (Eds.), *Contact and conflict in intergroup encounters* (pp. 1–44).Oxford: Blackwell.

Hewstone, M., Islam, M. R., & Judd, C. M. (1993). Models of crossed categorization and intergroup relations. *Journal of Personality and Social Psychology, 64,* 779–793.

Hewstone, M., & Lord, C. G. (1998). Changing intergroup cognitions and intergroup behavior: The role of typicality. In C. Sedikides, J. Schopler, & C. A. Insko (Eds.), *Intergroup cognition and intergroup behavior* (pp. 367–392). Mahwah, NJ: Erlbaum.

Jackman, M. R. (1994). *The velvet glove: Paternalism and conflict in gender, class, and race relations.* Berkeley: University of California Press.

Johnson, D. W., & Johnson, R. T. (1994). Learning together. In S. Sharan (Ed.), *Handbook of cooperative learning methods* (pp. 51–65). Westport, CT: Greenwood Press.

Johnson, D. W., & Johnson, R. T. (1996). Conflict resolution and peer mediation programs in elementary and secondary schools: A review of the research. *Review of Educational Research, 66,* 459–506.

Jost, J. T., & Banaji, M. R. (1994). The role of stereotyping in system-justification and the production of false consciousness. *British Journal of Social Psychology, 33,* 1–27.

Jussim, L., & Fleming, C. (1996). Self-fulfilling prophecies and the maintenance of social stereotypes: The role of dyadic interaction and social forces. In N. Macrae, C. Stangor, & M. Hewstone (Eds.), *Stereotypes and stereotyping* (pp. 161–192). New York: Guilford Press.

Katz, I., & Hass, R. G. (1988). Racial ambivalence and American value conflict: Correlational and priming studies of dual cognitive structures. *Journal of Personality and Social Psychology, 55,* 893–905.

Katz, I., Wackenhut, J., & Hass, R. G. (1986). Racial ambivalence, value duality, and behavior. In J. F. Dovidio & S. L. Gaertner (Eds.), *Prejudice, discrimination, and racism* (pp. 35–60). Orlando, FL: Academic Press.

Katz, J. H., & Ivey, A. (1977). White awareness: The frontier of racism awareness training. *Personnel and Guidance Journal, 55,* 485–489.

Katz, P. A., & Zalk, S. R. (1978). Modification of children's racial attitudes. *Developmental Psychology, 14,* 447–461.

Kinder, D. R., & Sears, D. O. (1981). Prejudice and politics: Symbolic racism versus racial threats to the good life. *Journal of Personality and Social Psychology, 40,* 414–431.

Kowalski, K. (1998). The impact of vicarious exposure to diversity on preschoolers' emerging ethnic/racial attitudes. *Early Child Development and Care, 146,* 41–51.

Lam, J. A. (1989). *The impact of conflict resolution programs on schools: A review and synthesis of the evidence.* Amherst, MA: National Association for Mediation in Education.

Langer, E. (1989). *Mindfulness*. Reading, MA: Addison-Wesley.

Lefley, H. P. (1985). Impact of cross-cultural training on Black and White mental health professionals. *International Journal of Intercultural Relations, 9*, 305–318.

Leippe, M. R., & Eisenstadt, D. (1994). Generalization of dissonance reduction: Decreasing prejudice through induced compliance. *Journal of Personality and Social Psychology, 67*, 395–413.

Lepore, L., & Brown, R. (1999). Exploring automatic stereotype activation: A challenge to the inevitability of prejudice. In D. Abrams & M. A. Hogg (Eds.), *Social identity and social cognition* (pp. 141–163). Oxford: Blackwell.

Lessing, E. E., & Clark, C. C. (1976). An attempt to reduce ethnic prejudice and assess its correlates in a junior high school sample. *Educational Research Quarterly, 1*, 3–16.

LeVine, R. A., & Campbell, D. T. (1972). *Ethnocentrism: Theories of conflict, ethnic attitudes, and group behavior*. New York: Wiley.

Litcher, J. H., & Johnson, D. W. (1969). Changes in attitudes toward Negroes of white elementary school students after use of multicultural readers. *Journal of Educational Psychology, 60*, 148–152

Maass, A., Salvi, D., Arcuri, L., & Semin, G. (1989). Language use in intergroup contexts: The linguistic intergroup bias. *Journal of Personality and Social Psychology, 57*, 981–993.

Mackie, D. M., Allison, S. T., Worth, L. T., & Asuncion, A. G. (1992). Social decision making processes: The generalization of outcome-biased counter-stereotypic inferences. *Journal of Experimental Social Psychology, 28*, 23–42.

McGregor, J. (1993). Effectiveness of role playing and antiracist teaching in reducing student prejudice. *Journal of Educational Research, 86*, 215–226.

Miller, N., Brewer, M. B., & Edwards, K. (1985). Cooperative interaction in desegregated settings: A laboratory analogue. *Journal of Social Issues, 41*, 63–81.

Monteith, M. J. (1993). Self-regulation of prejudiced responses: Implications for progress in prejudice-reduction efforts. *Journal of Personality and Social Psychology, 65*, 469–485.

Monteith, M. J., Zuwerink, J. R., & Devine, P. G. (1994). Prejudice and prejudice reduction: Classic challenges, contemporary approaches. In P. G. Devine, D. L. Hamilton, & T. M Ostrom (Eds.), *Social cognition: Impact on social psychology* (pp. 324–346). Orlando, FL: Academic Press.

Moreno, K. N., & Bodenhausen, G. V. (1999). Resisting stereotype change: The role of motivation and attentional capacity in defending social beliefs. *Group Processes and Intergroup Relations, 2*, 5–16.

Neuberg, S. L. (1996). Social motives and expectancy-tinged thoughts. In R. M. Sorrentino & E. T. Higgins (Eds.), *Handbook of social cognition* (Vol. 3, pp. 225–261). New York: Guilford.

Neville, H., & Furlong, M. (1994). The impact of participation in a cultural awareness program on the racial attitudes and social behaviors of first-year college students. *Journal of College Student Development, 35*, 371–377.

Neville, H. A., Heppner, M. J., Louie, C. E., Thompson, C. E., Brocks, L., & Baker, C. E. (1996). The impact of multicultural training on white racial identity attitudes and therapy competencies. *Professional Psychology: Research and Practice, 27*, 83–89.

Oakes, P. J., Haslam, S. A., & Turner, J. C. (1994). *Stereotyping and social reality*. Oxford: Blackwell.

Operario, D., & Fiske, S. T. (1998). Racism equals power plus prejudice: A social psychological equation for racial oppression. In J. L. Eberhardt & S. T. Fiske (Eds.), *Confronting racism: The problem and the response* (pp. 33–53). Thousand Oaks, CA: Sage.

Ota Wang, V. (1998). Curriculum evaluation and assessment of multicultural genetic counseling. *Journal of Genetic Counseling, 7*, 87–111.

Parker, W. M., Moore, M. A., & Neimeyer, G. J. (1998). Altering White racial identity and interracial comfort through multicultural training. *Journal of Counseling Development, 76*, 302–310.

Pettigrew, T. F. (1971). *Racially separate or together?* New York: McGraw-Hill.

Pettigrew, T. F. (1979). The ultimate attribution error: Extending Allport's cognitive analysis of prejudice. *Personality and Social Psychology Bulletin, 5*, 461–476.

Pettigrew, T. F. (1998). Intergroup contact theory. *Annual Review of Psychology, 49*, 65–85.

Pettigrew, T. F., & Tropp, L. R. (2000). Does intergroup contact reduce prejudice: Recent meta-analytic findings. In S. Oskamp (Ed.), *Reducing prejudice and discrimination* (pp. 93–114). Mahwah, NJ: Erlbaum.

Power, F. C., Higgins, A., & Kohlberg, L. (1989). *Lawrence Kohlberg's approach to moral education*. New York: Columbia University Press.

Richards, H. C., & Gamache, R. (1979). Belief polarity: A useful construct for studies of prejudice. *Educational and Psychological Measurement, 39*, 791–801

Richards, Z., & Hewstone, M. (2001). Subtyping and subgrouping: Processes for the prevention and promotion of stereotype change. *Personality and Social Psychology Review, 5*, 52–73.

Robinson, B., & Bradley, L. J. (1997). Multicultural training for undergraduates: Developing knowledge and awareness. *Journal of Multicultural Counseling and Development, 25*, 281–289.

Robinson, J. W., Jr., & Preston, J. D. (1976). Equal status contact and modification of racial prejudice: A reexamination of the contact hypothesis. *Social Forces, 54*, 911–924.

Rokeach, M. (1971). Long-range experimental modification of values, attitudes and behavior. *American Psychologist, 26*, 453–459.

Rokeach, M., Smith, P. W., & Evans, R. I. (1960). Two kinds of prejudice or one? In M. Rokeach (Ed.), *The open and closed mind* (pp. 132–168). New York: Basic Books.

Rothbart, M., & John, O. P. (1985). Social categorization and behavioral episodes: A cognitive analysis and the effects of intergroup contact. *Journal of Social Issues, 41*, 81–104.

Rothbart, M., & John, O. P. (1996). Intergroup relations and stereotype change: A social-cognitive analysis and some longitudinal findings. In P. M. Sniderman, P. E. Tetlock, & E. G. Carmines (Eds.), *Prejudice, politics, and the American dilemma* (pp. 32–59). Stanford, CA: Stanford University Press.

Rothbart, M., & Lewis, S. (1988). Inferring category attributes from exemplar attributes: Geometric shapes and social categories. *Journal of Personality and Social Psychology, 55*, 157–178.

Rothbart, M., & Taylor, M. (1992). Category labels and social reality: Do we view social categories as natural kinds? In G. R. Semin & K. Fiedler (Eds.), *Language, interaction, and social cognition* (pp. 13–36). Thousand Oaks, CA: Sage.

Schaller, M., Asp, C. H., Rosell, M. C., & Heim, S. J. (1996). Training in statistical reasoning inhibits the formation of erroneous group stereotypes. *Personality and Social Psychology Bulletin, 22*, 829–844.

Schaller, M., & O'Brien, M. (1992). "Intuitive analysis of covariance" and group stereotype formation. *Personality and Social Psychology Bulletin, 18*, 776–785.

Schuette, R. A., & Fazio, R. H. (1995). Attitude accessibility and motivation as determinants of biased processing: A test of the

MODE model. *Personality and Social Psychology Bulletin, 21,* 704–710.

Sears, D. O. (1988). Symbolic racism. In P. A. Katz & D. A. Taylor (Eds.), *Eliminating racism: Profiles in controversy* (pp. 53–84). New York: Plenum.

Sherif, M. (1966). *In common predicament: Social psychology of intergroup conflict and cooperation.* London: Routledge.

Sidanius, J., & Pratto, F. (1993). The inevitability of oppression and the dynamics of social dominance. In P. M. Sniderman & P. E. Tetlock (Eds.), *Prejudice, politics, and the American dilemma* (pp. 173–211). Stanford, CA: Stanford University Press.

Sidanius, J., & Pratto, F. (1999). *Social dominance: An intergroup theory of social hierarchy and oppression.* Cambridge: Cambridge University Press.

Slavin, R. E. (1995). *Cooperative learning: Theory, research, and practice* (2nd ed.). Needham Heights, MA: Allyn & Bacon.

Snyder, M. (1992). Motivational foundations of behavioral confirmation. In M. Zanna (Ed.), *Advances in experimental social psychology* (Vol. 25, pp. 67–114). Orlando, FL: Academic Press.

Snyder, M., Tanke, E., D., & Berscheid, E. (1977). Social perception and interpersonal behavior: On the self-fulfilling nature of social stereotypes. *Journal of Personality and Social Psychology, 35,* 656–666.

Sodowsky, G. R., Kuo-Jackson, P. Y., Richardson, M. R., & Corey, A. T. (1998). Correlates of self-reported multicultural competencies: Counselor multicultural social desirability, race, social inadequacy, locus of control, racial ideology, and multicultural training. *Journal of Counseling Psychology, 45,* 256–264.

Stangor, C., & McMillan, D. (1992). Memory for expectancy-congruent and expectancy-incongruent information: A review of the social and social developmental literatures. *Psychological Bulletin, 111,* 42–61.

Stephan, C. W., Renfro, L., & Stephan, W. G. (in press). The evaluation of intergroup relations programs: Techniques and a meta-analysis. In W. G. Stephan & W. P. Vogt (Eds.), *Intergroup Relations Programs.* New York: Teachers College Press.

Stephan, W. (1977). Cognitive differentiation in intergroup perception. *Sociometry, 40,* 50–58.

Stephan, W. G. (1985). Intergroup relations. In G. Lindzey & E. Aronson (Eds.), *Handbook of social psychology* (Vol. 3, pp. 599–658). Reading, MA: Addison-Wesley.

Stephan, W. G., & Finlay, K. A. (1999). The role of empathy in improving intergroup relations. *Journal of Social Issues, 55,* 729–744.

Stephan, W. G., & Stephan, C. W. (1984). The role of ignorance in intergroup relations. In N. Miller & M. B. Brewer (Eds.), *Groups in contact: The psychology of desegregation* (pp. 229–257). Orlando, FL: Academic Press.

Stephan, W. G., & Stephan, C. W. (2000). An integrated threat theory of prejudice. In S. Oskamp (Ed.), *Reducing prejudice and discrimination* (pp. 225–46). Mahwah, NJ: Erlbaum.

Stephan, W. G., & Stephan, C. W. (2001). *Improving intergroup relations.* Thousand Oaks, CA: Sage.

Tajfel, H. (Ed.). (1978). *Differentiation between social groups: Studies in the social psychology of intergroup relations.* Orlando, FL: Academic Press.

Tajfel, H. (1982). *Social identity and intergroup relations.* Cambridge: Cambridge University Press.

Tajfel, H., & Turner, J. C. (1986). The social identity theory of intergroup behavior. In S. Worchel & W. G. Austin (Eds.), *Psychology of intergroup relations* (2nd ed., pp. 33–47). Chicago: Nelson-Hall.

Van Soest, D. (1996). Impact of social work education on student attitudes and behavior concerning oppression. *Journal of Social Work Education, 32,* 191–202.

Verma, G. K., & Bagley, C. (1973). Changing racial attitudes in adolescents. *International Journal of Psychology, 8,* 55–58.

Washington, V., (1981). Impact of antiracism/multicultural education training on elementary teachers' attitudes and classroom behavior. *Elementary School Journal, 81,* 186–192.

Wegner, D. M., & Erber, R. (1992). The hyperaccessibility of suppressed thoughts. *Journal of Personality and Social Psychology, 45,* 74–83.

Weiner, M. J., & Wright, F. E. (1973). Effects of undergoing arbitrary discrimination upon subsequent attitudes toward a minority group. *Journal of Applied Social Psychology, 3,* 94–102.

Wittig, M., & Molina, L. (2000). Moderators and mediators of prejudice reduction in multicultural education. In S. Oskamp (Ed.), *Reducing prejudice and discrimination* (pp. 295–318). Mahwah, NJ: Erlbaum.

Wyer, R. S., Jr., & Srull, T. K. (1989). *Memory and cognition in its social context.* Mahwah, NJ: Erlbaum.

Yawkey, T. D. (1973). Attitudes toward Black Americans held by rural and urban White early childhood subjects based upon multi-ethnic social studies materials. *Journal of Negro Education, 42,* 164–169.

Yawkey, T. D., & Blackwell, J. (1974). Attitudes of 4 year old urban Black children toward themselves and Whites based upon multiethnic social studies materials and experiences. *Journal of Educational Research, 67,* 373–377.

39

FOSTERING POSITIVE INTERGROUP RELATIONS IN SCHOOLS

Janet Ward Schofield

University of Pittsburgh

Two facts make attention to the issue of how to improve intergroup relations among children and youth from different racial and ethnic backgrounds vital. First, despite the marked improvement in many aspects of intergroup relations in the United States since the 1950s, serious problems still exist (Hurtado, 1992; Katz & Kofkin, 1997; Levin & McDevitt, 1993; Magner, 1989; Mays, Bullock, Rosenweig, & Wessells, 1998). Second, minority-group members are becoming an increasingly large proportion of the U.S. population (Riche, 2000). Thus, patterns of prejudice or discrimination that persist will exact an increasing social and economic toll, in terms of both the number of minority-group members affected and the loss of their potential contribution to the broader society. Furthermore, the potential for increased political power inherent in growing numbers makes it likely that minority-group members will be able to pursue their interests more effectively than in the past. While this may have many benefits, it may well also exacerbate intergroup tensions as majority-group members have to adjust to new realities and members of different minority groups vie with each other as well as with Whites for social and economic power (Charp & Soukamneuth, 1999). Thus, the question of how to build and maintain positive relations among the increasingly diverse racial and ethnic groups in the United States is an issue of major importance and will remain so in the foreseeable future.

Because of the pervasive residential segregation in our society (Farley, 1996), children frequently have their first relatively extended opportunity for contact with those from different racial or ethnic backgrounds in school. Hence, whether hostility and stereotyping grow or diminish may be critically influenced by the experiences children have there. For this reason, this chapter will focus on exploring policies and practices that are conducive to improving intergroup relations in schools.

Much of the research on intergroup relations in schools stems from the late 1970s and the 1980s (Gerard & Miller, 1975; Hawley et al., 1983; Hewstone & Brown, 1986; Patchen, 1982; Prager, Longshore, & Seeman, 1986; Rist, 1979; Schofield, 1989). This work has three important limitations. First, much of it is correlational, which leaves open the question of the causal direction of empirical links found between school policies and student outcomes (Schofield, 1991). Second, much of it focuses exclusively on improving relations between Whites and African Americans rather than on the more multifaceted situations common today. Third, this work fails to reflect the societal and generational changes in intergroup attitudes and behavior that have occurred since it appeared (Schuman, Steeh, Bobo, & Krysan, 1997), as well as recent progress in conceptualizing and measuring prejudice, stereotyping, and discrimination (see Devine, Plant, & Blair, 2001; Dovidio, Kawakami, & Beach, 2001;

l

This chapter is adapted from a prior chapter published in Willis D. Hawley and Anthony Jackson (Eds.), *Realizing Our Common Destiny: Improving Race and Ethnic Relations in America* (San Francisco: Jossey-Bass, 1995). A section of this chapter originally appeared in J. W. Schofield, "Promoting Positive Peer Relations in Desegregated Schools," *Educational Policy,* 7(3), 297–317, copyright 1993 by Corwin Press. This chapter appears here with permission from Jossey-Bass and Corwin Press.

Operario & Fiske, 2001; Rothbart, 2001). In spite of these weaknesses, there is much to be learned from this work. Thus, while this review draws to the extent possible on recent work, it depends heavily on earlier research where more recent work is not available.

MATCHING THE APPROACH TO IMPROVING INTERGROUP RELATIONS TO THE CURRENT STATE OF SUCH RELATIONS

Before discussing what we know about improving intergroup relations in schools, some conceptual distinctions should be made because the strategies that are likely to be effective in meeting this goal vary substantially depending on a number of factors. The first of these is the current state of relations among the groups in question. Strategies that might work well where there is some tension and hostility, but no major ongoing overt conflict, are quite different from those that would be needed if two or more groups are engaged in intense conflict (Ben-Ari & Amir, 1986). Second, it is important to distinguish between approaches that emphasize ongoing structural features of the school and those that emphasize circumscribed "human relations" interventions, such as special assembly programs or festivals. Third, the goal of reducing negative intergroup attitudes or behaviors and the goal of increasing positive intergroup attitudes and behaviors are not identical. Indeed, quite different factors may be related to changes in the amount of positive and negative intergroup behavior that occurs (Patchen, 1982; Schofield, 1989). To take a simple example, one can stop a fight by physically separating the combatants, at least temporarily eliminating this negative behavior. However, this action in and of itself does not foster positive relations between members of the groups involved. Furthermore, intergroup attitudes and intergroup behaviors do not always change in a consistent manner (Schofield, 1989).

The goal of this chapter is to review strategies aimed at fostering positive relations and inhibiting negative relations among members of different racial and ethnic groups in situations in which intergroup isolation or tensions exist, although they have not precipitated major persistent conflict. This state of affairs characterizes many racially and ethnically mixed schools. This chapter focuses primarily on ongoing structural factors and policies rather than specific "human relations" or individually oriented change efforts for insertion into the curriculum because attention to pervasive everyday policies and practices is likely to have a greater impact on intergroup relations than a focus on more limited special-purpose interventions. However, both approaches are likely to be useful (Hawley, Banks, Padilla, Pope-Davis, & Schofield, 1995). Indeed, recent studies suggest that a number of modular approaches, such as perceptual training designed to reduce the assumption that physical similarities imply psychological ones or training designed to foster perspective taking, critical thinking, and moral decision making, may be quite helpful in improving aspects of intergroup relations (Aboud & Fenwick, 1999; Katz, Barrett, & Arango, 1998; Levy, 1999; McGregor, 1993; Schultz, Barr, & Selman, 2001).

RESEGREGATION: A COMMON BARRIER TO IMPROVED INTERGROUP RELATIONS

The first question to ask about intergroup relations in any racially or ethnically mixed school is the extent to which there is any kind of meaningful intergroup contact. Achieving intergroup contact is especially a challenge in situations involving groups of youth whose native tongues are different from each other. It is perfectly possible for a school that has a diverse ethnic and racial makeup to be one in which individuals from the various groups have little or no contact with each other, a situation that virtually all scholars who have dealt with the issue agree is not conducive to improved intergroup relations. Such resegregation can be extreme. For example, in one racially mixed school, a student remarked, "All the segregation in this city was put in this school," reflecting the fact that although students from different backgrounds all attended that school, they had little contact with each other (Collins & Noblit, 1978, p. 195). So it is important to be aware of the possibility of resegregation and to plan actively to avoid or minimize it.

How does this resegregation occur? A number of common educational practices lead, often inadvertently, to resegregation within desegregated schools. The most widespread of these are practices designed to reduce academic heterogeneity within classrooms. A whole host of social, economic, as well as psychological factors such as stereotype threat (Aronson, Fried, & Good, 2002; Steele, Spencer, & Aronson, 2002) contribute to the fact that minority–group students in desegregated schools often perform less well in academic subjects than their White peers. Thus, schools that group students into classes or tracks on the basis of standardized tests, grades, or related criteria tend to have resegregated classrooms (Epstein, 1985; Hughes, 1998; Oakes, 1996).

Although much resegregation in schools stems from policies such as tracking or ability grouping, it is undeniable that students often voluntarily resegregate themselves in classrooms, in lunchrooms, and on playgrounds. The extent of such voluntary resegregation is sometimes remarkable. For example, one set of studies of seating patterns in the cafeteria of a school whose student body was about half African American and half White reported that on a typical day, roughly 5% to 10% of the students sat next to someone of the other race (Schofield, 1979; Schofield & Sagar, 1977) in spite of the fact that there was little overt racial friction. Other studies have reported similarly marked cleavage by race (Gerard, Jackson, & Conolley, 1975; Rogers, Henningan, Bowman, & Miller, 1984).

There is nothing inherently deleterious to intergroup relations about children who share particular interests, values, or backgrounds associating with each other to achieve valued ends. However, when grouping by race or ethnic groups stems from fear, hostility, and discomfort or is not balanced by students' participation in diverse settings, it is incompatible with the goal of breaking down barriers between groups and improving intergroup relations. Stephan and Stephan's (1985) work suggests that anxiety about dealing with out-group members is prevalent and can direct behavior in unconstructive ways. Other studies (Scherer & Slawski, 1979; Schofield, 1989) suggest numerous ways in which such anxiety can cause problems, including resegregation, in desegregated schools.

The importance of avoiding resegregation, whether it stems from formal institutional policies or informal behavior patterns, is made clear by theoretical and empirical work in social psychology and sociology (Hallinam & Smith, 1985; Khmelkov & Hallinam, 1999; Pettigrew, 1969; Schofield, 1983, 1989). For example, a large body of work on social identity theory (Bourhis & Gagnon, 2001) suggests that when individuals are divided into groups they tend to favor the in-group and discriminate against the out-group, even though these groups have no previous history of antipathy. If one creates racially or ethnically homogeneous groups through school policies that resegregate students, already existing tendencies toward stereotyping and discrimination are likely to be magnified.

Thus, care should be taken to avoid policies that lead to resegregation and to adopt policies that undercut children's tendency to cluster in racially homogeneous groups because of fear, hostility, or uncertainty. The specific policies employed to discourage such resegregation would depend on the particular situation. However, some policies and practices that undercut resegregation can be easily implemented. For example, teachers can assign seats in a way that fosters interracial contact rather than letting students resegregate themselves. Specifically, teachers can assign students' seats alphabetically rather than letting students select their own seats and then institutionalizing the segregated pattern that often results from students' voluntary behavior with a seating chart (Schofield, 1979, 1989). The impact of such simple procedures is demonstrated by Wellisch, Marcus, MacQueen, and Duck (1976), who found more interracial mixing in informal settings among elementary school children whose teachers used classroom seating assignment policies that resulted in a lot of cross-race proximity than among children whose teachers

tended to group their students by race in class. Furthermore, something as simple as occasionally changing assigned seats increases the number of friends students are likely to make during the school year (Byrne, 1961).

Another policy that can help to avoid resegregation is active planning to encourage both minority and majority students to participate in extracurricular activities, since there is evidence suggesting both that White students are more likely than minority students to participate in such activities and that those students who do participate tend to cluster in activities in which their groups are disproportionately represented (Clotfelter, 2002). Participation in such activities with those of different backgrounds is important because it can play a constructive role in improving intergroup relations (Braddock, Dawkins, & Wilson, 1995; Hallinan & Teixeira,1987; Slavin & Madden, 1979). Yet sometimes after-school activities become the province of either minority or majority students so that one group participates extensively and the other hardly participates at all (Trent & McPartland, 1981). Another common pattern is for particular activities to become associated with students from a particular background, so that although all groups of students participate in some activities, there are few activities in which students from different backgrounds participate jointly (Collins, 1979; Scherer & Slawski, 1979; Sullivan, 1979). Again, the way to prevent these outcomes clearly depends on the specific situation. But helpful policies can be adopted. For example, if one group of students does not participate because transportation poses a problem, special arrangements for transportation can be made. Similarly, if adult sponsors of school-based clubs take steps to encourage students from various backgrounds to participate before these activities get a reputation as "belonging" to one group, they are much more likely to succeed than if they wait until the resegregation is complete and well known among the students before trying to encourage diversity of membership.

Some resegregation may be an inevitable consequence of policies designed to advance important goals. For example, it is often hard to provide an education for children for whom English is not a first language without a certain amount of resegregation (Stepick & Bowie, 1998). However, constructive ways to deal with this situation have been suggested (California State Department of Education, 1983; Carter, 1979; Carter & Chatfield, 1986; Cazabon, Lambert, & Hall, 1993; Genesee & Gándara, 1999; Heleen, 1987; Lindholm, 1992, 1994; Minami & Ovando, 1995; Morison, 1990). Similarly, although the past decade or so has seen some movement away from the traditional ready acceptance of tracking policies on the part of policy makers and educators (Carnegie Council on Adolescent Development, 1989; National Governors' Association, 1990), many difficult and complex pedagogical and political issues remain to be resolved about how best to serve students in classrooms or schools in which skill levels vary widely (Oakes, 1992). In addition, there may be certain extracurricular activities, such as gospel choirs and swimming teams, that are likely to be both highly valued by some parts of the community and more attractive to students from certain backgrounds than others. Finally, single-race groups sometimes function as a kind of "safe space" (Tatum, 1997, p. 82) in which students can most effectively deal with problems and issues of identity development specific to those of a given background. In spite of the preceding, schools serving children of diverse racial or ethnic backgrounds need to address the issue of resegregation and devote serious attention to seeing that it does not undermine the school's potential to help students learn through interacting with those of differing backgrounds.

CONDITIONS CONDUCIVE TO IMPROVING INTERGROUP RELATIONS

Of course, the mere absence of resegregation is not enough to create a set of experiences that foster constructive outcomes among children from different backgrounds (Allport, 1954; Cohen, 1997; Eddy, 1975; Pettigrew, 1998; Schofield, 1983). The quality of those experiences is crucial, as Pettigrew (1969) pointed out in making his classic distinction between mere desegregation, which refers to the existence of a racially mixed environment, and true integration, which refers to the creation of a setting conducive to the development of positive relations among members of different groups.

There are a great many things that schools serving diverse clienteles can do to promote positive intergroup relations and minimize intergroup conflict (Aboud & Levy, 1999; Banks et al., 2001; Chesler, Bryant, & Crowfoot, 1981; Cohen & Lotan, 1997; Epstein, 1985; Forehand & Ragosta, 1976; Hallinan & Smith, 1985; Hallinan & Teixeira, 1987; Hawley, 1981; Hawley et al., 1983; Miller, 1980; Patchen, 1982; Sagar & Schofield, 1984; Slavin & Madden, 1979; Stephan, 1999; Stephan & Stephan, 2001). Precisely which practices are suitable depends on factors such as the students' ages, the institution's racial and ethnic mix, and the degree to which racial and ethnic background are related to socioeconomic status. Because space limitations make it impractical to discuss each of the myriad of possibilities separately, this chapter will discuss what theory and research suggest about the general underlying conditions that are conducive to building and maintaining positive intergroup relations.

The most influential social psychological perspective on the conditions that are necessary to lead to positive outcomes is the contact hypothesis. Since 1954, when

Allport first proposed it, this approach has stimulated a great deal of research that generally supports its basic elements (material reviewing, extending, and revising the contact hypothesis can be found in Brewer & Gaertner, 2001; Brewer & Miller, 1984; Hewstone & Brown, 1986; Pettigrew, 1998; and Pettigrew & Tropp, 2000). Basically, Allport (1954) argued that three aspects of the contact situation are particularly important in determining whether positive intergroup relations develop: (1) equal status within the situation for members of all groups, (2) an emphasis on cooperative activities focused on common goals rather than competitive activities, and (3) the explicit support of relevant authority figures, laws, and customs for positive relations. In discussing these factors, this chapter will illustrate briefly the types of school policies and procedures that flow from them.

Equal Status

First, Allport argues that the contact situation must be structured in a way that gives equal status to all groups. He argues that if one does not do this, existing stereotypes and beliefs about the superiority or inferiority of the groups involved will be likely to persist. Although other theorists have argued that equal status is not absolutely essential for improving intergroup relations, they generally see it as quite helpful (Amir, 1969; Brown, 1995; Riordan, 1978). In a school, roles are ordered in a status hierarchy. Those on top, like the superintendent at the system level or the principal at the school level, have more power and prestige than those who serve under them. Allport's argument suggests that it is important that individuals from all groups be distributed throughout the status hierarchy rather than being concentrated at one level. For example, majority- and minority-group members do not have equal status in a school if the administrators and the faculty are almost all majority-group members and the teachers' aides are generally minority-group members.

Even if a school does its best to see that the formal status of the members of various racial and ethnic groups is equal, it is undeniably true that members of the different groups are likely to have very different statuses outside that setting. This can create serious difficulties for achieving equal status within the setting For example, disparities in education between majority- and minority-group members contribute to making it difficult for schools to hire minority faculty and administrators in numbers proportionate to their representation in the population (Boyer & Baptiste, 1996). Furthermore, given the sizable and stubborn link between social class and academic achievement, it is likely that unequal status of various groups in the larger society will translate into unequal distribution of students from different racial and ethnic backgrounds into the more and less advanced tracks in schools that have academic tracks. Even if schools eschew tracking, students' performance levels may well still differ in ways that affect their informal statuses within the school and their peer groups (Schofield, 1980).

Finding effective ways to keep the unequal status of various groups in the larger society from creating unequal status within the school is not easy. However, concerted efforts to achieve this do appear to make a difference. For example, much has been written about the way in which textbooks and other curriculum components have either ignored or demeaned the experiences and contributions of minority-group members (McAdoo & McAdoo, 1985; National Alliance of Black School Educators, 1984; Oakes, 1985). This hardly creates an equal-status environment. Although there are many barriers to remedying this situation (Boateng, 1990) and efforts to change it do not always have the intended impact (Bigler, 1999), change is possible and can have constructive effects. For example, Stephan and Stephan's (1984) review of the research on multiethnic curriculum components concludes that a substantial, if incomplete and methodologically flawed, set of studies generally suggests that multiethnic curricula have a positive effect on intergroup relations, at least when the program elements are of some reasonable complexity and duration.

A controversial issue relating to both equal status and resegregation is the issue of the grouping of students based on their academic performance. As mentioned previously, when desegregated schools group students on the basis of test scores, they often end up with heavily White high-status accelerated groups and heavily minority lower-status groups. This means that students are not only resegregated, but are resegregated in a way that can reinforce traditional stereotypes and engender hostility. Tracking is often instituted or emphasized in schools with heterogeneous student bodies as a mechanism for coping with diversity in achievement levels. However, studies have not yielded any consistent support for the idea that tracking generally benefits students academically (Gamoran & Berends, 1988; Mosteller, Light, & Sachs, 1996). Furthermore, it may sometimes undermine the achievement and motivation of students in the lower tracks and have a negative effect on intergroup relations (Collins & Noblit, 1978; National Opinion Research Center, 1973; Oakes, 1992; Schofield, 1979). Epstein's (1985) study of grouping practices in desegregated elementary schools found a clear positive link between equal-status programs (e.g., programs that emphasize the equality and importance of both Black and White students and that avoid inflexible, academically based grouping) and higher achievement for African American students. Furthermore, equal-status programs positively influenced both White and Black students' attitudes toward desegregated schooling.

Although tracking is one of the most visible ways in which status differentials from outside the school get reinforced and formalized inside the school, there are also many other ways in which this happens. Awareness of this issue can suggest seemingly minor, but nonetheless worthwhile, changes in practice. For example, schools can add the practice of honoring students who have shown unusually large amounts of improvement in their academic performance to the traditional practice of honoring students whose absolute level of achievement is outstanding. This reinforces academic values while being more inclusive than traditional practice.

Such practices are trivial in some respects. Yet students often are very sensitive to such matters. For example, Schofield (1989) reports an incident in which a racially mixed classroom of sixth graders was shown a televised quiz show in which a team of students from their school competed against a team from another school. A usually well-behaved African American child refused to watch. Later, he explained that he did not want to see the program because the team from his school, which had a student body that was just over half African American, consisted entirely of White children. He said bitterly, "They shouldn't call this school Wexler [a pseudonym]; they should call it White School" (p. 220).

Cooperative Interdependence

Allport (1954) argues that in addition to creating a situation that gives members of all groups equal status, it is also extremely important that the activities required in the situation be cooperative rather than competitive. Given that discrimination is both a historical fact and a present reality in many spheres of life, the results of competition will frequently support traditional stereotypes. In addition, competition between groups can lead to stereotyping, unwarranted devaluation of other groups' accomplishments, and hostility, even when these groups initially have no history predisposing them to negative reactions to each other (Sherif, Harvey, White, Hood, & Sherif, 1961). It is reasonable to expect that this tendency for intergroup competition to lead to hostility and negative beliefs would be reinforced when the groups involved have a history that makes initial hostility or at least suspicion likely.

Both theory and research suggest that the type of cooperation most likely to improve intergroup relations is cooperation toward achieving a shared goal that cannot be accomplished without the contribution of members of all groups (Johnson & Johnson, 1992; Sherif et al., 1961). Examples of activities likely to foster this type of cooperation in schools would be the production of a play, participation in team sports, or participation in choral or instrumental groups. The important feature of these situations is that each student is able to make a contribution to a whole that individuals could not possibly achieve without cooperation. Although different students may contribute different skills, each is necessary to the final product. A caveat to keep in mind is that such situations are more likely to result in improved intergroup relations when the group is successful in achieving its goal. Indeed, experimental work by Worchel, Andreoli, and Folger (1977) demonstrated that for groups with a history of competition and conflict, successful cooperation increased intergroup attraction whereas unsuccessful cooperation decreased liking for out-group members.

Schools in the United States have historically stressed competition, so they may not be milieus particularly conducive to promoting cooperation. However, this emphasis on competition is not inevitable or completely unchangeable. First, with the advent of self-paced instructional approaches and work on mastery learning, there has been an increasing acceptance of the idea that children may benefit from working at their own pace. Second, in the past two decades, there have been more and more voices speaking in favor of increasingly emphasizing the importance of teaching children how to work cooperatively with others to achieve a joint end product (Hertz-Lazarowitz & Miller, 1992; Johnson & Johnson, 1987; Johnson, Johnson, & Maruyama, 1984; Slavin & Cooper, 1999). Certainly this trend is sensible given the increasing bureaucratization and complexity of our society, which means that, as adults, individuals are increasingly likely to work with others as part of an organization rather than as individual craftspeople or entrepreneurs.

The use of student teams to create joint projects comes very close to being the type of cooperation toward shared goals that appears to be so important for improving intergroup relations. A large number of experiments using a variety of cooperative structures suggest that this does indeed have a positive effect. (Aronson & Gonzales, 1988; Aronson & Patnoe, 1997; Johnson & Johnson, 1982; Johnson et al., 1984; Slavin, 1995). One important feature of such cooperative groups is that they not only appear to foster improved intergroup relations but also have positive academic consequences (Slavin & Cooper, 1999).

Although cooperative activities in schools and classrooms hold great potential for improving intergroup relations, such cooperation must be carefully structured (Hertz-Lazarowitz, Kirkus, & Miller, 1992; Miller & Harrington, 1992; Slavin, 1992). It is important that the young people involved contribute to the group efforts in effective ways that do not reinforce traditional modes of interaction between members of different groups. For example, when White and African American children who are equally capable interact with each other in certain kinds of situations, the White students tend to be more active and influential even though there is no rational basis for their dominance. Only after a carefully planned program of activities that includes having the African American children teach their White peers new skills does this tendency diminish or disappear (Cohen, Lockheed, & Lohman, 1976). Hence, it is vital to be constantly aware of the need to find ways to ensure that all children contribute to the group's final products rather than assuming that the existence of a cooperative group in and of itself will motivate all children to contribute and to allow others to contribute to the group's work.

The precise dynamics that lead cooperation to have a positive effect on intergroup relations are far from fully understood, although considerable attention has been devoted to the issue (see Hertz-Lazarowitz & Miller, 1992). However, there appear to be a number of contributing factors that are worth individual consideration because, although they are likely to be found in cooperative situations, they are neither inevitable aspects of all cooperative situations nor strictly limited to situations in which cooperation is a salient element.

Fostering Superordinate and Crosscutting Social Identities. Strategies that create and emphasize meaningful shared social category memberships for youths of different racial and ethnic backgrounds, as many cooperative activities do, should help to improve intergroup relations. In fact, research by Gaertner and Dovidio and their colleagues (Gaertner, Mann, Murrell, & Dovidio, 1989; Gaertner, Rust, Dovidio, Bachman, & Anderson, 1994) suggests that bias between two initially separate groups can be mitigated when they later function in a new situation that gives them a superordinate unified identity. Thus, the creation of signs and symbols that promote shared identity (ranging from school T-shirts and traditions to special songs and the like) should be helpful in improving intergroup relations. Indeed, a qualitative study conducted in a desegregated school that forged such shared identities in a number of ways suggested that it did play an important role in improving intergroup relations (Schofield & McGivern, 1979).

It also appears that the tendency of individuals to show bias toward out-group members can sometimes be undermined by creating what are called cross-cutting social categories (Brewer, Ho, Lee, & Miller, 1987; Schofield & McGivern, 1979; Vanbeselaere, 1991). The importance of any one basis of social categorization, such as race or ethnicity, can be mitigated by creating or making salient other orthogonal bases of social categorization. Thus, for example, having African American and White students on each of two different cooperative learning teams means that racial background and team membership are crosscut. That is, students from different racial backgrounds now share something (i.e., team membership) with some members of the racial out-group and simultaneously differ on that dimension from some members of their racial in-group. To the extent that the social category that cross-cuts racial or ethnic background is valued and salient, it may well undermine the tendency to discriminate based on the former. However, some questions about the impact of cross-cutting categories remain since some research suggests that they can actually increase bias toward individuals who are out-group members on both dimensions (Hewstone, Islam, & Judd, 1993).

Personalization of Out-Group Members. Cooperative activities by their very nature require individuals to work together, thus providing the opportunity for them to come to know each other in ways they might not otherwise. This potential for cooperative work to lead to the development of relatively close personal relationships with members of out-groups is frequently cited as one of its advantages (Miller & Harrington, 1992). The development of such personal relations and the accompanying tendency to increasingly see the out-group members as individuals with their own particular set of personality traits, skills, and experiences is potentially important for several reasons. First, it can lead to the discovery of unexpected similarities between oneself and out-group members, and there is clear evidence that perceptions of similarity play a strong role in attraction to others (Berscheid & Reis, 1998). Indeed, low-prejudiced peers' comments about the similarity of members of different ethnic groups to their own group increase tolerance in their more prejudiced peers (Aboud & Doyle, 1996; Aboud & Fenwick, 1999). Second, to the extent the out-group members behave in ways that are contrary to stereotypes of that group's behavior, such stereotypes may be weakened. This is, however, far from a simple process. Behaviors tend to be perceived in ways that are consistent with stereotypes (Rothbart & John, 1985; Sagar & Schofield, 1980). This appears to be due to the fact that stereotypes lead to the biased processing of social information (Bodenhausen, 1988; Greenberg & Pyszczynski, 1985; Hamilton & Trolier, 1986). Individuals may perceive those who act in ways unexpected for their group as "exceptions" whose existence does not challenge the validity of the basic stereotype (Johnston & Hewstone, 1992; Kunda & Oleson, 1995). Third, ongoing experience with several members of the out-group may help to undermine the strong tendency to see out-group members as relatively similar to each other compared to in-group members, who are typically perceived to be much more varied (Judd & Park, 1988; Linville, Fischer, & Salovey, 1989). Research by Ryan, Judd, and Park (1996) demonstrates that a tendency to perceive out-group members as quite homogeneous affects judgments of the characteristics of specific individuals belonging to that group in ways consistent with one's initial expectations. Thus, experiences that lead students to think of out-group members as individuals who vary in many respects should be helpful in weakening

stereotypes and lessening their impact on interactions with members of the out-group.

The Development of Intergroup Friendships. Both increasing perceptions of similarity between in-group and out-group members and increasing awareness of the individual characteristics of out-group members seem likely to contribute to the development of friendships between in-group and out-group members. At first, it may seem tautological to argue that increased friendship between students of different backgrounds helps to account for the positive impact of cooperation on intergroup relations since many of the measures used to assess the impact of cooperation on intergroup relations are measures of friendship. However, two facts must be kept in mind. First, some studies of the impact of cooperation on intergroup relations use other indicators of improved intergroup relations, such as changes in racial attitudes. Second, and more important, there is increasingly strong reason to believe that the development of friendships between members of different groups can improve important aspects of intergroup relations above and beyond the improvement indicated by the development of such friendships. Specifically, a set of surveys conducted in seven countries in Europe demonstrated that individuals with friends from racial or other out-groups showed less prejudice than did those without such friendships. More important, the statistical path from friendship to prejudice was stronger than the path going in the other direction, suggesting that out-group friendships are conducive to reduced prejudice, rather than just reflecting the tendency of the unprejudiced to have out-group members among their friends (Pettigrew, 1998). Furthermore, laboratory research has demonstrated that experiences that create feelings of friendship toward out-group members also predict positive change in intergroup attitudes (Wright, Ropp, & Tropp, 1998). Finally, there is evidence that when schoolchildren think that in-group members are friends with out-group members, they become more positive toward the out-group, suggesting that the existence of cross-group friendships can have an impact on those who are aware of their existence but not involved in them (Liebkind & McAlister, 1999). Thus, the existence of intergroup friendships augers well for changes in other aspects of intergroup relations. It is for this reason that Pettigrew (1998) has suggested that the formation of positive affective ties between in-group and out-group members may be one of the important processes through which contact can lead to improved intergroup relations.

Support of Authorities for Positive Relations

Finally, Allport (1954) suggests that the support of authority, law, and custom for positive equal-status relationships among members of all groups is vital to producing constructive change in intergroup attitudes and behavior as a result of intergroup contact. Certainly, a court ruling that requires desegregation (or a decision on the part of a school system to desegregate) is a very important sign of authorities' support for this policy. However, in and of themselves, such events are not nearly enough. For school children, the most relevant authorities are probably their school's principal, their teachers, and their parents. Religious leaders can also be important authorities for some children. In addition, as children move from their early years into adolescence, their peers become increasingly important arbiters of opinion and exert a more and more potent influence on their behavior. Thus, although Allport clearly did not mean to include peers in his definition of "authorities," it seems sensible at least to point out that finding ways to mobilize the peer group to support positive intergroup relations could be a rather powerful approach, as demonstrated by Blanchard, Lilly, and Vaughn (1991), whose work shows that peers influence each other's expression of racist opinions. Similarly, Patchen (1982) found that individuals' avoidance of outgroup members was clearly related to negative racial attitudes among their same-race peers, which suggests that concerns about peer disapproval of intergroup contact can contribute to resegregation.

In schools, the principal is an important authority who can facilitate improved intergroup relations in numerous ways (Hawley et al., 1995). Principals play at least four important roles in influencing desegregation's outcomes through their actions toward teachers, students, and parents. First, they play an enabling function; that is, they make choices that facilitate or impede practices that promote positive intergroup relations. For example, the principal can encourage teachers to adopt cooperative learning techniques by providing appropriate training or can create multiethnic committees designed to identify and solve problems before they turn into polarizing crises. Second, the principal's behavior can serve a modeling function. There is no guarantee others will follow the principal's example, but it is likely to be helpful. Third, the principal can play a sensitizing function. The principal is in a good position to argue for the importance of paying attention to the quality of intergroup relations and to put this matter in an important place on the school's list of priorities. Finally, of course, the principal can serve a sanctioning function by actively rewarding positive practices and behaviors and punishing negative ones. This can be important in at least two respects. First, to the extent that the existence of such sanctions influences behavior, they are important, since there is reason to believe that changes in intergroup behavior may well lead to changes in intergroup attitudes (Pettigrew, 1998). Second, the prevention of negative intergroup behaviors is an issue of utmost

importance because negative incidents can stimulate other negative behaviors in an escalating spiral. Research demonstrating that one of the strongest predictors of unfriendly intergroup contact for both White and African American students is the students' general aggressiveness (Patchen, 1982) suggests the importance of the principal's role in creating a well-ordered environment in which aggressive behavior of any sort is minimized.

Teachers are also vital authority figures in the school. They too can facilitate or impede the development of positive relations at the classroom level through the processes of enabling, modeling, sensitizing, and sanctioning. For example, with regard to enabling, teachers often have it within their power to create conditions that are likely to improve intergroup relations among students. Epstein (1985) demonstrates that teachers with positive attitudes toward desegregation tend to use equal-status instructional programs more than others and that students in such classrooms have more positive attitudes toward desegregation than peers in classrooms not using such approaches. Similarly, teachers with negative attitudes are more likely to use within-class ability grouping. Teachers, like principals, can also model respect for and equitable treatment of both ingroup and out-group members. Indeed, Patchen (1982) found a clear relation between negative teacher intergroup attitudes and White students' tendency to avoid their African American classmates. More recently, Flanagan (2000) found that students whose teachers promoted a democratic and tolerant climate at school were more likely than others to report on a survey that it was personally important to them to try to promote equality.

With regard to sanctioning, teachers and others in authority can make an important contribution to fostering positive intergroup relations by clearly articulating their expectation that children will respect each other's rights and by backing up their stated expectations with disciplinary measures. It is especially important that the expectation that individuals will treat each other with respect be made clear from the very beginning so that children know that they cannot violate others' rights with impunity. If the expectation of harmony and respect is not made clear at the beginning, students are more likely to try to test the limits of the system and to feel they are being treated unfairly when they are held accountable for that behavior. Greenfield's (1998) study of multiethnic sports teams in California high schools suggests how important setting norms of respect can be. The coach of the team that ended up having the fewest racial and ethnic tensions meted out immediate public punishment to the team when one student spoke disrespectfully to a teammate of another race, whereas the coach of the team that ended up rife with conflict dealt with such matters in a private and individual way, thus failing to set clear norms against such behavior.

One important way in which authorities such as principals and teachers can foster the development of positive intergroup relations through sensitizing is for them to be aware that individuals in a desegregated school may misunderstand others' motives or intentions, either because of cultural differences or because of fears and uncertainties about out-group members (Sagar & Schofield, 1980; Schofield, 1989). Using this awareness constructively can help to deal with problems that arise. Although effectively supporting the development of positive intergroup relations is far from a simple task for principals and teachers, increasingly resources are available to assist them in that task (Banks et al., 2001; Hawley et al., 1995; Stephan & Stephan, 2001; Tatum, 2000; Tatum & Brown, 1998).

Parents too are important authority figures for most children, especially in their younger years. Their potential impact on desegregated schools is made clear by Patchen (1982), who found that negative parental attitudes are likely to be associated with students' intergroup avoidance and unfriendly intergroup encounters, whereas positive parental attitudes are associated with students' friendly intergroup contact. Thus, finding ways to encourage parents to involve their children in racially or ethnically diverse settings and to play a constructive role in encouraging positive intergroup contact is very important. A recent review of the literature by Aboud and Amato (2001) points out that parents often do not discuss race with their children. Furthermore, although a modest relation between parents' and children's racial attitudes is found when the topic is discussed, not surprisingly, there is no such correlation when parents do not explicitly discuss race with their children. Thus, parents, through their silence, may miss the opportunity to have a positive though modest impact on their children's attitudes. In the context of desegregated schools, practices designed to foster positive reactions on the part of parents, such as involving them early in the planning process, creating school and communitywide multiethnic committees involving parents, teachers, and students, and providing information and opportunities for contact with the school, all seem helpful in creating better relations among students (Hawley et al., 1983). For instance, Doherty, Cadwell, Russo, Mandel, and Longshore (1981) found that parent involvement in school activities can create more positive attitudes toward majority-group members on the part of minority-group students. Issues relating to their children's safety are likely to be very salient to parents, especially in communities in which tensions are high. Thus, practices that promote safety and information about these practices might also be useful in encouraging positive attitudes.

It is common for principals, teachers, and other authority figures involved with racially or ethnically diverse settings to feel that the best and fairest thing they can do is to adopt a point of view sometimes called the color-blind perspective (Rist, 1974). This perspective sees racial and ethnic group membership as irrelevant to the way individuals are treated. Taking cognizance of such group membership in decision making is perceived as illegitimate and likely to lead to discrimination against minority-group members or to reverse discrimination. Two factors make serious consideration of the color-blind perspective worthwhile. First, it is widely endorsed as a desirable perspective in institutions as diverse as the schools and the judicial system (Gillborn, 1992; Jervis, 1996; Pollock, 2000; Schofield, 2001; Sleeter, 1993). Second, although the color-blind perspective is appealing in many ways—and consistent with a long-standing American emphasis on the importance of the individual—it easily leads to misrepresentation of reality in ways that encourage discrimination against minority-group members (Bonilla-Silva, 2003).

The color-blind perspective may have some positive effects. It can reduce, at least in the short term, the potential for overt racial or ethnic conflict by generally deemphasizing the salience of race and encouraging the evenhanded application of rules to all students (Miller & Harrington, 1992). It may also reduce the potential for discomfort or embarrassment in racially or ethnically mixed schools by vigorously asserting that race does not matter.

However, this perspective also has a number of potentially negative effects. Most important, the decision to try to ignore group membership, to act as if no one notices or should notice race or ethnicity, means that policies that are disadvantageous to minority groups are often accepted without examination or thought (Schofield, 2001). For example, disproportionate suspension rates for minority students may not be seen as a sign of the need to examine discipline policies if school faculty and staff think of students only as individuals rather than facing the difficult issue of whether the school may be treating certain categories of students differently from others. Similarly, a color-blind perspective can easily lead to ready adoption or tolerance of policies that lead to resegregation. Furthermore, this perspective makes it easy for a school to use textbooks and curricular materials that inadequately reflect the perspectives and contributions of minority group members. In addition, there is some evidence that discussions of race between more and less prejudiced students can actually reduce prejudice in the former without increasing it in the latter (Aboud & Doyle, 1996; Aboud & Fenwick, 1999), a fact that suggests the color-blind perspective may undercut the potential of such discussions to improve intergroup relations. A final disadvantage of the color-blind perspective is that it seems likely to lead to "colormuteness," the reluctance of teachers and administrators to discuss race in certain situations, which Pollock (2001) suggests can impede progress toward the constructive resolution of problems in schools with diverse student populations.

However, recognition that the color-blind perspective has some clear disadvantages does not imply that it is desirable to remind students constantly of their group membership and to emphasize group differences continually. Both theory and experimental work suggest that practices that enhance the salience of such category memberships can harm rather than help intergroup relations (Miller & Harrington, 1992). For example, a study by Miller, Brewer, and Edwards (1985) found that when participants in cooperative groups believed that social category membership was the basis for assignment, they were less likely to respond with favorable evaluations of the out-group members than when they believed assignment to the groups was on the basis of each individual's attitudes. Furthermore, research suggests that teachers' explicit functional use of categories in classrooms, such as lining students up for recess on the basis of a biological difference like hair color or an arbitrary difference like the color of their T-shirts, fosters in-group bias (Bigler, Jones, & Lobliner, 1997). Thus, the best course of action may be to do what one can to encourage students to deal with each other as individuals while recognizing in setting policies and making decisions that attention to how various groups are faring is not only appropriate but likely to be constructive. The apparent contradiction here is mitigated by the fact that one of the things that is likely to make group identities salient to students is the perception that their group is not being treated fairly in comparison to others. To the extent that group outcomes are equitable because attention is paid to this issue in setting policies and making decision, one important source of polarization between members of different groups is lessened.

SUMMARY

This chapter has discussed factors that theory and research in social psychology suggest are important in structuring racially and ethnically mixed environments in ways that will foster positive relations and minimize negative relations among different groups of students. First, it is important to avoid resegregation, which can occur as a result of numerous factors, including school policies, students' negative attitudes toward members of other groups, or students' anxiety about interacting with unfamiliar others. However, avoiding resegregation is not enough. Policies and practices need to be closely examined to ensure that, insofar as possible, they promote equal status and cooperative interdependence between members of different groups. Efforts to heighten a sense of connection to superordinate group identities that include members of the various groups represented in a situation or to create cross-cutting group memberships are likely to be beneficial, as are practices that encourage individuals to participate with out-group members in experiences that help participants to come to know each other as individuals. Those in positions of authority can support the development of positive intergroup relations by enabling others, as well as through modeling, sensitizing, and sanctioning. Recognizing that improving intergroup relations is likely to require some attention to how groups as well as individuals are faring in a given setting should help those in authority to perform these functions in an effective manner. However, in general, practices that heighten the salience of group membership should be avoided unless they are the only way to make sure that other vital goals are obtained.

References

Aboud, F. E., & Amato, M. (2001). Developmental and socialization influences on intergroup bias. In R. Brown & S. Gaertner (Eds.), *Blackwell handbook of social psychology: Intergroup processes* (pp. 65–88). Malden, MA: Blackwell.

Aboud, F. E., & Doyle, A. B. (1996). Does talk of race foster prejudice or tolerance in children? *Canadian Journal of Behavioral Science, 28*(3), 161–170.

Aboud, F. E., & Fenwick, V. (1999). Exploring and evaluating school-based interventions to reduce prejudice. *Journal of Social Issues, 55*(4), 767–785.

Aboud, F. E., & Levy, S. R. (Eds.). (1999). Reducing racial prejudice, discrimination, and stereotyping: Translating research into programs [Special issue]. *Journal of Social Issues, 55*(4), 621–815.

Allport, G. W. (1954). *The nature of prejudice.* Reading, MA: Addison-Wesley.

Amir, Y. (1969). Contact hypothesis in ethnic relations. *Psychological Bulletin, 71,* 319–342.

Aronson, E., & Gonzalez, A. (1988). Desegregation, jigsaw, and the Mexican-American experience. In P. A. Katz & D. A. Taylor (Eds.), *Eliminating racism: Profiles in controversy* (pp. 301–314). New York: Plenum.

Aronson, E., & Patnoe, S. (1997). *The jigsaw classroom: Building cooperation in the classroom* (2nd ed.). New York: Addison Wesley Longman.

Aronson, J., Fried, C., & Good, C. (2002). Reducing the effects of stereotype threat on African American college students by shaping theories of intelligence. *Journal of Experimental Social Psychology, 38*(2), 1–13.

Banks, J. A., Cookson, P., Gay, G., Hawley, W. D., Irvine, J. J., Nieto, S., Schofield, J. W., & Stephan, W. G. (2001).

Diversity within unity: Essential principles for teaching and learning in a multicultural society. *Phi Delta Kappan, 83*(3), 196–203.

Ben-Ari, R., & Amir, Y. (1986). Contact between Arab and Jewish youth in Israel: Reality and potential. In M. Hewstone & R. Brown (Eds.), *Contact and conflict in intergroup encounters* (pp. 45–58). Oxford: Blackwell.

Berscheid, E., & Reis, H. T. (1998). Attraction and close relationships. In D. T. Gilbert, S. T. Fiske, & G. Lindzey (Eds.), *The handbook of social psychology* (Vol. 2, pp. 193–281). New York: McGraw-Hill.

Bigler, R. E. (1999). The use of multicultural curricula and materials to counter racism in children. *Journal of Social Issues, 55*(4), 687–705.

Bigler, R. S., Jones, L. C., & Lobliner, D. B. (1997). Social categorization and the formation of intergroup attitudes in children. *Child Development, 68*(3), 530–543.

Blanchard, F. A., Lilly, T., & Vaughn, L. A. (1991). Reducing the expression of racial prejudice. *Psychological Science, 2,* 101–105.

Boateng, F. (1990). Combatting deculturalization of the African American child in the public school system: A multi-cultural approach. In K. Lomotey (Ed.), *Going to school: The African American experience* (pp. 73–84). Albany: State University of New York Press.

Bodenhausen, G. V. (1988). Stereotypic biases in social decision making and memory: Testing process models of stereotype use. *Journal of Personality and Social Psychology, 55,* 726–737.

Bonilla-Silva, E. (2003). *Racism without racists: Color-blind racism and the persistence of racial inequality in the United States.* Lanham, MD: Roman & Littlefield.

Bourhis, R. Y., & Gagnon, A. (2001). Social orientations in the minimal group paradigm. In R. Brown & S. Gaertner (Eds.), *Blackwell handbook of social psychology: Intergroup processes* (pp. 89–111). Malden, MA: Blackwell.

Boyer, J. B., & Baptiste, H. P., Jr. (1996). The crisis in teacher education in America: Issues of recruitment and retention of culturally different (minority) teachers. In J. Sikula, T. J. Buttery, & E. Guyton (Eds.), *Handbook of research on teacher education* (2nd ed., pp. 779–794). New York: Macmillan.

Braddock, J. H., Dawkins, M. P., & Wilson, G. (1995). Intercultural contact and race relations. In W. D. Hawley & A. J. Jackson (Eds.), *Toward a common destiny: Improving race and ethnic relations in America* (pp. 423–434). San Francisco: Jossey-Bass.

Brewer, M. B., & Gaertner, S. L. (2001). Toward reduction of prejudice: Intergroup contact and social categorization. In R. Brown & S. Gaertner (Eds.), *Blackwell handbook of social psychology: Intergroup processes* (pp. 451–472) Oxford: Blackwell.

Brewer, M. B., Ho, H., Lee, J., & Miller, N. (1987). Social identity and social distance among Hong Kong schoolchildren. *Personality and Social Psychology Bulletin, 13,* 156–165.

Brewer, M. B., & Miller, N. (1984). Beyond the contact hypothesis: Theoretical perspectives on desegregation. In N. Miller & M. B. Brewer (Eds.), *Groups in contact: The psychology of desegregation* (pp. 281–302). Orlando, FL: Academic Press.

Brown, R. (1995). *Prejudice: Its social psychology.* Malden, MA: Blackwell.

Byrne, D. (1961). The influences of propinquity and opportunities for interaction on classroom relationships. *Human Relations, 14,* 63–69.

California State Department of Education. (1983). *Desegregation and bilingual education—partners in quality education.* Sacramento: Author.

Carnegie Council on Adolescent Development. (1989). *Turning points: Preparing American youth for the 21st century.* Washington, DC: Carnegie Corporation of New York.

Carter, T. P. (1979). *Interface between bilingual education and desegregation: A study of Arizona and California.* Washington, DC: National Institute of Education. (ERIC Document Reproduction Service No. ED 184 743)

Carter, T., & Chatfield, M. L. (1986). Effective bilingual schools: Implications for policy and practice. *American Journal of Education, 95,* 200–232.

Cazabon, M., Lambert, W. E., & Hall, G. (1993). *Two-way bilingual education: A progress report on the Amigos Program.* Santa Cruz, CA: National Center for Research on Cultural Diversity.

Charp, H. L., & Soukamneuth, S. (1999). *Towards a more critical understanding of White students' racial attitudes in multiracial schools.* Paper presented at the annual meeting of the American Educational Research Association, Montreal.

Chesler, M., Bryant, B., & Crowfoot, J. (1981). *Making desegregation work: A professional guide to effecting change.* Beverly Hills, CA: Sage.

Clotfelter, C. T. (2002). Interracial contact in high school extracurricular activities. *Urban Review, 34*(1), 25–46.

Cohen, E. G. (1997). Understanding status problems: Sources and consequences. In E. G. Cohen & R. A. Lotan (Eds.), *Working for equity in heterogeneous classrooms: Sociological theory in practice* (pp. 61–76). New York: Teachers College Press.

Cohen, E. G., Lockheed, M., & Lohman, M. (1976). The Center for Interracial Cooperation: A field experiment. *Sociology of Education, 49,* 47–58.

Cohen, E. G., & Lotan, R. A. (1997). Raising expectations for competence: The effectiveness of status interventions. In E. G. Cohen & R. A. Lotan (Eds.), *Working for equity in heterogeneous classrooms: Sociological theory in practice* (pp. 77–91). New York: Teachers College Press.

Collins, T. W. (1979). From courtrooms to classrooms: Managing school desegregation in a Deep South high school. In R. C. Rist (Ed.), *Desegregated schools: Appraisals of an American experiment* (pp. 89–114). New York: Academic Press.

Collins, T. W., & Noblit, G. W. (1978). *Stratification and resegregation: The case of Crossover High School, Memphis, Tennessee.* Washington, DC: National Institute of Education.

Devine, P. G., Plant, E. A., & Blair, I. V. (2001). Classic and contemporary analyses of racial prejudice. In R. Brown & S. Gaertner (Eds.), *Blackwell handbook of social psychology: Intergroup processes* (pp. 198–217). Malden, MA: Blackwell.

Doherty, W. J., Cadwell, J., Russo, N. A., Mandel, V., & Longshore, D. (1981). *Human relations study: Investigations of effective human relations strategies* (Vol. 2). Santa Monica, CA: System Development Corporation.

Dovidio, J. F., Kawakami, K., & Beach, K. R. (2001). Implicit and explicit attitudes: Examination of the relationship between measures of intergroup bias. In R. Brown & S. Gaertner (Eds.), *Blackwell handbook of social psychology: Intergroup processes* (pp. 175–197). Malden, MA: Blackwell.

Eddy, E. (1975). Educational innovation and desegregation: A case study of symbolic realignment. *Human Organization, 34*(2), 163–172.

Epstein, J. L. (1985). After the bus arrives: Resegregation in desegregated schools. *Journal of Social Issues, 41*(3), 23–43.

Farley, R. (1996). *The new American reality: Who we are, how we got here, where we are going.* New York: Russell Sage Foundation.

Flanagan, C. (2000, July 23–28). Schools as mini polities: How teens learn about membership and tolerance. In K. Boehnke (Chair), *We and the other: The political psychology of in-group favoritism, nationalism, and xenophobia.* Symposium at the XXVII International Congress of Psychology, Stockholm.

Forehand, G. A., & Ragosta, M. (1976). *A handbook for integrated schooling.* Washington, DC: U.S. Department of Health, Education and Welfare.

Gaertner, S. L., Mann, J., Murrell, A., & Dovidio, J. F. (1989). Reducing intergroup bias: The benefits of recategorization. *Journal of Personality and Social Psychology, 57,* 239–249.

Gaertner, S. L., Rust, M. C., Dovidio, J. F., Bachman, B. A., & Anastasio, P. A. (1994). The contact hypothesis: The role of a common ingroup identity in reducing intergroup bias. *Small Group Research, 25,* 224–249.

Gamoran, A., & Berends, M. (1988). The effects of stratification in secondary schools: Synthesis of survey and ethnographic research. *Review of Educational Research, 57*(4), 415–435.

Genesee, F., & Gándara, P. (1999). Bilingual education programs: A cross-national perspective. *Journal of Social Issues, 55*(4), 665–686.

Gerard, H. B., Jackson, D., & Conolley, E. (1975). Social context in the desegregated classroom. In H. B. Gerard & N. Miller (Eds.), *School desegregation: A long-term study* (pp. 211–214). New York: Plenum.

Gerard, H. B., & Miller, N. (Eds.). (1975). *School desegregation: A long-term study.* New York: Plenum.

Gillborn, D. (1992). Citizenship, race and the hidden curriculum. *International Studies in Sociology of Education, 2*(1), 57–73.

Greenberg, J., & Pyszczynski, T. (1985). The self-serving attributional bias: Beyond self-presentation. *Journal of Experimental Social Psychology, 21,* 61–72.

Greenfield, P. (1998). *How can sports teams promote racial tolerance and positive intergroup relations? Key lessons from recent research.* Paper presented at the Workshop on Research to Improve Intergroup Relations Among Youth, National Research Council, Washington, DC.

Hallinan, M. T., & Smith, S. S. (1985). The effects of classroom racial composition on students' interracial friendliness. *Social Psychology Quarterly, 48*(1), 3–16.

Hallinan, M. T., & Teixeira, R. A. (1987). Students' interracial friendships: Individual characteristics, structural effects and racial differences. *American Journal of Education, 95,* 563–583.

Hamilton, D. L., & Trolier, T. K. (1986). Stereotypes and stereotyping: An overview of the cognitive approach. In J. F. Dovidio & S. L. Gaertner (Eds.), *Prejudice, discrimination, and racism* (pp. 127–163). Orlando, FL: Academic Press.

Hawley, W. D. (1981). *Effective school desegregation: Equity, quality, and feasibility.* Beverly Hills, CA: Sage.

Hawley, W. D., Banks, J. A., Padilla, A. M., Pope-Davis, D. B., & Schofield, J. W. (1995). Strategies for reducing racial and ethnic prejudice: Essential principals for program design. In W. D. Hawley & A. J. Jackson (Eds.), *Toward a common destiny: Improving race and ethnic relations in America* (pp. 423–434). San Francisco: Jossey-Bass.

Hawley, W. D., Crain, R. L., Rossell, C. H., Schofield, J. W., Fernandez, R., & Trent, W. P. (1983). *Strategies for effective desegregation: Lessons from research.* Lexington, MA: Lexington Books.

Heleen, O. (Ed.). (1987). Two-way bilingual education: A strategy for equity [Special issue]. *Equity and Choice, 3*(3).

Hertz-Lazarowitz, R., Kirkus, V. B., & Miller, N. (1992). Implications of current research on cooperative interaction for classroom application. In R. Hertz-Lazarowitz & N. Miller (Eds.), *Interaction in cooperative groups* (pp. 253–280). Cambridge: Cambridge University Press.

Hertz-Lazarowitz, R., & Miller, N. (Eds.). (1992). *Interaction in cooperative groups.* Cambridge: Cambridge University Press.

Hewstone, M., & Brown, R. (Eds.). (1986). *Contact and conflict in encounters.* Oxford: Blackwell.

Hewstone, M., Islam, M. R., & Judd, C. M. (1993). Models of crossed categorization and intergroup relations. *Journal of Personality and Social Psychology, 64,* 779–793.

Hughes, D. (1998). *The Early Adolescent Development Study.* Paper presented at the Workshop on Research to Improve Intergroup Relations Among Youth, National Research Council, Washington, DC.

Hurtado, S. (1992). The campus racial climate: Contexts of conflict. *Journal of Higher Education, 63*(5), 539–569.

Jervis, K. (1996). How come there are no brothers on that list? Hearing the hard questions all children ask. *Harvard Educational Review, 66*(3), 546–576.

Johnson, D. W., & Johnson, R. T. (1982). The study of cooperative, competitive, and individualistic situations: State of the area and two recent contributions. *Contemporary Education, 1*(1), 7–13.

Johnson, D. W., & Johnson, R. T. (1987). *Learning together and alone* (2nd ed.). Englewood Cliffs, NJ: Prentice-Hall.

Johnson, D. W., & Johnson, R. T. (1992). Positive interdependence: Key to effective cooperation. In R. Hertz-Lazarowitz & N. Miller (Eds.), *Interaction in cooperative groups* (pp. 174–199). Cambridge: Cambridge University Press.

Johnson, D. W., Johnson, R. T., & Maruyama, G. (1984). Goal interdependence and interpersonal attraction in heterogeneous classrooms: A meta-analysis. In N. Miller & M. B. Brewer (Eds.), *Groups in contact: The psychology of desegregation* (pp. 187–212). Orlando, FL: Academic Press.

Johnston, L., & Hewstone, M. (1992). Cognitive models of stereotype change: Subtyping and the perceived typicality of disconfirming group members. *Journal of Experimental Social Psychology, 28*(4), 360–386.

Judd, C. M., & Park, B. (1988). Outgroup homogeneity: Judgments of variability at the individual and group levels. *Journal of Personality and Social Psychology, 54,* 778–788.

Katz, P., Barrett, M., & Arango, S. (1998). *Fostering positive intergroup attitudes in young children.* Paper presented at the Workshop on Research to Improve Intergroup Relations Among Youth, National Research Council, Washington, DC.

Katz, P. A., & Kofkin, J. A. (1997). Race, gender, and young children. In S. S. Luthar, J. A. Burack, D. Cicchetti, & J. Weisz (Eds.), *Developmental psychopathology: Perspectives on adjustment, risk, and disorder* (pp. 51–74). New York: Cambridge University Press.

Khmelkov, V. T., & Hallinan, M. T. (1999). Organizational effects on race relations in schools. *Journal of Social Issues, 55*(4), 627–645.

Kunda, Z., & Oleson, K. C. (1995). Maintaining stereotypes in the face of disconfirmation: Constructing grounds for subtyping deviants. *Journal of Personality and Social Psychology, 68,* 565–579.

Levin, J., & McDevitt, J. (1993). *Hate crimes: The rising tide of bigotry and bloodshed.* New York: Plenum.

Levy, S. R. (1999). Reducing prejudice: Lessons from social-cognitive factors underlying perceiver differences in prejudice. *Journal of Social Issues, 55*(4), 745–765.

Liebkind, K., & McAlister, A. L. (1999). Extended contact through peer modeling to promote tolerance in Finland. *European Journal of Social Psychology, 29,* 765–780.

Lindholm, K. (1994). Promoting positive cross-cultural attitudes and perceived competence in culturally and linguistically diverse classrooms. In R. C. DeVillar, C. Faltis, & J. Cummins (Eds.), *Cultural diversity in schools* (pp. 189–206). Albany: State University of New York Press.

Lindholm, K. J. (1992). Two-way bilingual/immersion education: Theory, conceptual issues, and pedagogical implications. In R. V. Padilla & A. H. Benavides (Eds.), *Critical perspectives on bilingual education research* (pp. 195–220). Tempe, AZ; Bilingual Press/Editorial Bilingüe.

Linville, P. W., Fischer, G. W., & Salovey, P. (1989). Perceived distributions of characteristics of ingroup and outgroup members: Empirical evidence and a computer simulation. *Journal of Personality and Social Psychology, 57,* 165–188.

Magner, D. K. (1989, April 26). Blacks and Whites on the campuses: Behind ugly racist incidents, student isolation and insensitivity. *Chronicle of Higher Education,* 28–31.

Mays, V. M., Bullock, M., Rosenweig, M. R., & Wessells, M. (1998). Ethnic conflict: Global challenges and psychological perspectives. *American Psychologist, 53,* 737–742.

McAdoo, H. P., & McAdoo, J. W. (Eds.). (1985). *Black children: Social, educational and parental environments.* Beverly Hills, CA: Sage.

McGregor, J. (1993). Effectiveness of role-playing and antiracist teaching in reducing student prejudice. *Journal of Educational Research, 86,* 215–226.

Miller, N. (1980). Making school desegregation work. In W. G. Stephan & J. R. Feagin (Eds.), *School desegregation: Past, present, and future* (pp. 309–348). New York: Plenum.

Miller, N., Brewer, M. B., & Edwards, K. (1985). Cooperative interaction in desegregated settings: A laboratory analogue. *Journal of Social Issues, 41*(3), 63–79.

Miller, N., & Harrington, H. J. (1992). Social categorization and intergroup acceptance: Principles for the design and development of cooperative learning teams. In R. Hertz-Lazarowitz & N. Miller (Eds.), *Interaction in cooperative groups* (pp. 203–227). Cambridge: Cambridge University Press.

Minami, M., & Ovando, C. J. (1995). Language issues in multicultural contexts. In J. A. Banks & C. A. M. Banks (Eds.), *Handbook of research on multicultural education* (pp. 427–444). New York: Macmillan.

Morison, S. H. (1990). A Spanish-English dual-language program in New York City. In C. B. Cazden & C. E. Snow (Eds.), *English plus: Issues in bilingual education* (pp. 160–169). Thousand Oaks, CA: Sage.

Mosteller, F., Light, R. J., & Sachs, J. A. (1996). Sustained inquiry in education: Lessons from skill grouping and class size. *Harvard Educational Review, 66*(4), 797–842.

National Alliance of Black School Educators. (1984). *Saving the African American child.* Washington, DC: Author.

National Governors' Association. (1990). *Educating America: State strategies for achieving the national educational goals.* Washington, DC: Author.

National Opinion Research Center. (1973). *Southern schools: An evaluation of the effects of the Emergency School Assistance Program and of school desegregation* (Vols. 1–2). Chicago: Author.

Oakes, J. (1985). *Keeping track: How schools structure inequality.* New Haven, CT: Yale University Press.

Oakes, J. (1992). Can tracking research inform practice? Technical, normative, and political considerations. *Educational Researcher, 21*(4), 12–21.

Oakes, J. (1996). Two cities' tracking and within-school segregation. In E. C. Lagemann & L. P. Miller (Eds.), *Brown v. Board of Education: The challenge for today's schools* (pp. 81–90). New York: Teachers College Press.

Operario, D., & Fiske, S. T. (2001). Stereotypes: Content, structures, processes, and context. In R. Brown & S. Gaertner (Eds.), *Blackwell handbook of social psychology: Intergroup processes* (pp. 22–44). Malden, MA: Blackwell.

Patchen, M. (1982). *Black-White contact in schools: Its social and academic effects.* West Lafayette, IN: Purdue University Press.

Pettigrew, T. F. (1969). The Negro and education: Problems and proposals. In I. Katz & P. Gurin (Eds.), *Race and the social sciences* (pp. 49–112). New York: Basic Books.

Pettigrew, T. F. (1998). Intergroup contact theory. *Annual Review of Psychology, 49,* 65–85.

Pettigrew, T. F., & Tropp, L. R. (2000). Does intergroup contact reduce prejudice: Recent meta-analytic findings. In S. Oskamp (Ed.), *The Claremont Symposium on Applied Social Psychology* (pp. 93–114). Mahwah, NJ: Erlbaum.

Pollock, M. (2000). *Racing, de-racing, and erasing: The paradoxes of racial description in school.* Unpublished doctoral dissertation, Stanford University.

Pollock, M. (2001). How the question we ask most about race in education is the very question we most suppress. *Educational Researcher, 30*(19), 2–12.

Prager, J., Longshore, D., & Seeman, M. (Eds.). (1986). *School desegregation research: New directions in situational analysis.* New York: Plenum.

Riche, M. F. (2000). America's diversity and growth: Signposts for the 21st century. *Population Bulletin, 55*(2), 1–43.

Riordan, C. (1978). Equal-status interracial contact: A review and revision of the concept. *International Journal of Intercultural Relations, 2*(2), 161–185.

Rist, R. C. (1974). Race, policy, and schooling. *Society, 12*(1), 59–63.

Rist, R. C. (Ed.). (1979). *Desegregated schools: Appraisals of an American experiment.* New York: Academic Press.

Rogers, M., Henningan, K., Bowman, C., & Miller, N. (1984). Intergroup acceptance in classrooms and playground settings. In N. Miller & M. B. Brewer (Eds.), *Groups in contact: The psychology of desegregation* (pp. 213–227). New York: Academic Press.

Rothbart, M. (2001). Category dynamics and the modification of outgroup stereotypes. In R. Brown & S. Gaertner (Eds.), *Blackwell handbook of social psychology: Intergroup processes* (pp. 45–64). Malden, MA: Blackwell.

Rothbart, M., & John, O. P. (1985). Social categorization and behavior episodes: A cognitive analysis of the effects of intergroup contact. *Journal of Social Issues, 41,* 81–104.

Ryan, C. S., Judd, C. M., & Park, B. (1996). Effects of racial stereotypes on judgments of individuals: The moderating role of perceived group variability. *Journal of Experimental Social Psychology, 32,* 71–103.

Sagar, H. A., & Schofield, J. W. (1980). Racial and behavioral cues in Black and White children's perceptions of ambiguously aggressive acts. *Journal of Personality and Social Psychology, 39,* 590–598.

Sagar, H. A., & Schofield, J. W. (1984). Integrating the desegregated school: Problems and possibilities. In M. Maehr & D. Bartz (Eds.), *Advances in motivation and achievement: A research manual* (pp. 203–242). Greenwich, CT: JAI Press.

Scherer, J., & Slawski, E. (1979). Color, class, and social control in an urban school. In R. C. Rist (Ed.), *Desegregated schools: Appraisals of an American experiment* (pp. 117–153). New York: Academic Press.

Schofield, J. W. (1979). The impact of positively structured contact on intergroup behavior: Does it last under adverse conditions? *Social Psychology Quarterly, 42,* 280–284.

Schofield, J. W. (1980). Cooperation as social exchange: Resource gaps and reciprocity in academic work. In S. Sharon, P. Hare, C. Webb, & R. Hertz-Lazarowitz (Eds.), *Cooperation in education* (pp. 160–181). Provo, UT: Brigham Young University Press.

Schofield, J. W. (1983). Black-White conflict in the schools: Its social and academic effects. *American Journal of Education, 92,* 104–107.

Schofield, J. W. (1989). *Black and White in school: Trust, tension, or tolerance?* New York: Teachers College Press.

Schofield, J. W. (1991). School desegregation and intergroup relations: A review of the research. In G. Grant (Ed.), *Review of research in education* (Vol. 17, pp. 335–409). Washington, DC: American Educational Research Association.

Schofield, J. W. (2001). The colorblind perspective: Causes and consequences. In J. A. Banks & C. A. M. Banks (Eds.), *Multicultural education: issues and perspectives* (4th ed., pp. 247–267). New York: Wiley.

Schofield, J. W., & McGivern, E. P. (1979). Creating interracial bonds in a desegregated school. In R. G. Blumberg & W. J. Roye (Eds.), *Interracial bonds* (pp. 106–119). Bayside, NY: General Hall.

Schofield, J. W., & Sagar, H. A. (1977). Peer interaction patterns in an integrated middle school. *Sociometry, 40,* 130–138.

Schultz, L. H., Barr, D. J., & Selman, R. L. (2001). The value of a developmental approach to evaluating character development programmes: An outcome study of *Facing History and Ourselves. Journal of Moral Education, 30*(1), 3–27.

Schuman, H., Steeh, C., Bobo, L., & Krysan, M. (1997). *Racial attitudes in America: Trends and interpretations.* Cambridge, MA: Harvard University Press.

Sherif, M., Harvey, O. J., White, B. J., Hood, W. R., & Sherif, C. (1961). *Intergroup cooperation and competition: The Robbers Cave experiment.* Norman, OK: University Book Exchange.

Slavin, R. E. (1992). When and why does cooperative learning increase achievement? Theoretical and empirical perspectives. In R. Hertz-Lazarowitz & N. Miller (Eds.), *Interaction in cooperative groups* (pp. 145–173). Cambridge: Cambridge University Press.

Slavin, R. E. (1995). Cooperative learning and intergroup relations. In J. A. Banks & C. A. M. Banks (Eds.), *Handbook of research on multicultural education* (pp. 628–634). New York: Macmillan.

Slavin, R. E., & Cooper, R. (1999). Improving intergroup relations: Lessons learned from cooperative learning programs. *Journal of Social Issues, 55*(4), 647–663.

Slavin, R. E., & Madden, N. A. (1979). School practices that improve race relations. *American Educational Research Journal, 16,* 169–180.

Sleeter, C. E. (1993). How White teachers construct race. In C. McCarthy & W. Crichlow (Eds.), *Race identity and representation in education* (pp. 157–175). London: Routledge.

Steele, C. M., Spencer, S. J., & Aronson, J. (2002). Contending with group image: The psychology of stereotype and social identity threat. In M. P. Zanna (Ed.), *Advances in experimental social psychology* (Vol. 34, pp. 379–440). San Diego, CA: Academic Press.

Stephan, W. G. (1999). *Reducing prejudice and stereotyping in schools.* New York: Teachers College Press.

Stephan, W. G., & Stephan, C. W. (1984). The role of ignorance in intergroup relations. In N. Miller & M. B. Brewer (Eds.), *Groups in contact: The psychology of desegregation* (pp. 229–255). Orlando, FL: Academic Press.

Stephan, W. G., & Stephan, C. W. (1985). Intergroup anxiety. *Journal of Social Issues, 41*(3), 157–175.

Stephan, W. G., & Stephan, C. W. (2001). *Improving intergroup relations.* Thousand Oaks, CA: Sage.

Stepick, A., & Bowie, S. L. (1998). *Immigrant and native minority adolescent interaction: Miami.* Paper presented at the Workshop on Research to Improve Intergroup Relations Among Youth, National Research Council, Washington, DC.

Sullivan, M. L. (1979). Contacts among cultures: School desegregation in a polyethnic New York City high school. In R. C. Rist (Ed.), *Desegregated schools: Appraisals of an American experiment* (pp. 201–240). New York: Academic Press.

Tatum, B. D. (1997). *"Why are all the Black kids sitting together in the cafeteria?" and other conversations about race.* New York: Basic Books.

Tatum, B. D. (2000). Examining racial and cultural thinking. *Educational Leadership, 57,* 54–57.

Tatum, B. D., & Brown, P. C. (1998). Breaking the silence: Talking about race in schools. *Knowledge Quest, 27*(2), 12–16.

Trent, W., & McPartland, J. (1981). *Race comparisons of student course enrollment and extracurricular membership in desegregated and resegregated high schools.* Paper presented at the American Educational Research Association meeting, Los Angeles.

Vanbeselaere, N. (1991). The different effects of simple and crossed social categorizations: A result of the category differentiation process or of differential category salience? *European Review of Social Psychology, 2,* 247–278.

Wellisch, J. B., Marcus, A. C., MacQueen, A. H., & Duck, G. A. (1976). *An in-depth study of Emergency School Aid Act (ESAA) schools: 1974–1975.* Santa Monica, CA: System Development Corporation.

Worchel, S., Andreoli, V. A., & Folger, R. (1977). Intergroup cooperation and intergroup attraction: The effect of previous interaction and outcome of combined effort. *Journal of Experimental Social Psychology, 13,* 131–140.

Wright, S. C., Ropp, S. A., & Tropp, L. R. (1998). *Intergroup contact and the reduction of prejudice: Findings in support of the friendship hypothesis.* Paper presented at the meeting of the American Psychological Association, San Francisco.

40

MULTICULTURAL COUNSELING AND THERAPY (MCT) THEORY

Derald Wing Sue

Teachers College, Columbia University

We are rapidly becoming a multiethnic, multiracial, and multilingual society. Referred to as "the diversification of the United States" or, literally, "the changing complexion of society" (Atkinson, Morten, & D. W. Sue, 1998), the demographic transformation has meant that racial and ethnic minorities will become a numerical majority in several decades (U.S. Bureau of the Census, 2001). The diversification is fueled primarily by changes in immigration laws that have allowed large numbers of racial minorities to enter the United States and by higher birthrates among the minority populations when compared to their White counterparts (D. W. Sue et al., 1998). For example, the 2000 U.S. Census reveals that racial or ethnic minorities make up more than one third of the population, and they made up approximately 45% of the students in public schools. The changing complexion of society is also reflected in the world of work, where some 75% of those people currently entering the labor force are racial and ethnic minorities and women (D. W. Sue Parham, & Bonilla-Santiago, 1998). Some states have for some time had to cope with the changing demographics. In California, for example, students of color composed more than 50% of the school-age population in 1988.

Demands for cultural relevance, need for inclusion, and equal access and opportunities have forced changes at individual, professional, institutional, and societal levels (D. W. Sue, 2001). Training institutions are being challenged to produce culturally competent practitioners; organizations must develop new policies, practices, and structures to accommodate the diversity of society; and our social, economic, and political systems seem inadequate and often ill prepared to deal with the challenges posed by racial and ethnic minority groups and communities. With such demands have also come misunderstandings, resistance, and societal conflicts. Cries for multicultural and bilingual education have become political hot potatoes, and concepts of multiculturalism, diversity, and affirmative action have evoked strong emotional reactions as well. Never has there been a greater need for understanding the psychology of race, diversity, and multiculturalism than now. Mutual intergroup understanding, the need to build multicultural alliances, and promoting social justice must be top priorities for our society.

The need for the counseling and mental health professions to address issues of race, culture, and ethnicity has also never been more urgent (Pedersen, 1999; D. W. Sue & D. Sue, 1999). It is increasingly difficult for any helping professional not to encounter students, clients, and client groups who differ from them on these important dimensions. It is important for counselors to recognize that traditional psychological concepts and theories were developed from a predominantly Euro-American context and may be limited in application to the emerging racial and cultural diversity in the United States (D. W. Sue, Bingham, Porche-Burke, & Vasquez, 1999). Yet it appears that counselors are ill prepared to deal with the changing characteristics of the U.S. population (Ponterotto, Casas, Suzuki, & Alexander, 2001). Developing culturally effective helping strategies has met with much resistance. Several major obstacles seem to stand in the way of such a movement. First, the monocultural nature of education and training has taught mental health professionals an ethnocentric perspective of the helping process, an approach that is often antagonistic to the life experiences and values of their culturally different clients. Second, the counseling profession has often ignored the culture-bound nature of traditional theories of counseling and psychotherapy. The assumption of universal application to all populations and problems is highly questionable (D. W. Sue, 2001). Third, the profession has been slow in developing a conceptual framework that incorporates culture as a central core concept of the counseling process (Pedersen, 1999; D. W. Sue & D. Sue, 1999). This has seriously hindered the development of culturally relevant strategies, programs, and practices in working with racial and ethnic minority clients.

The failure to deliver relevant services to diverse groups seems to lie in the Euro-American definitions of what constitutes counseling and therapy. Many forms of counseling, for example, (1) occur in a one-to-one relationship, (2) take place in an office setting, (3) are aimed at remediation rather than prevention, (4) treat the individual as the psychosocial unit of operation, (5) dictate a relatively inactive role on the part of the counselor, (6) place the onus of change on the client, (7) adhere to standards of practice that apply equally to all clients and helping relationships, and (8) use talking as the primary medium of help. These traits are challenged by the definition of multicultural counseling and therapy (MCT) proposed by D. W. Sue (2001):

Multicultural counseling and therapy can be defined as both a helping role and process that uses modalities and defines goals consistent with the life experiences and cultural values of clients, recognizes client identities to include individual, group and universal dimensions, advocates the use of universal and culture-specific strategies and roles in the healing process, and balances the importance of individualism and collectivism in the assessment, diagnosis and treatment of client and client systems. (p. xx)

The concept of MCT therefore is in marked contrast to traditional definitions of counseling and psychotherapy. Analyzing this definition reveals significant differences:

1. MCT broadens the helping roles counselors play and expands the repertoire of therapy skills considered helpful and appropriate in counseling. The more passive and objective stance taken by counselors is seen as only one method of helping. Other roles like teaching, consulting, and advocacy can supplement the conventional counselor or therapist role.
2. MCT advocates using modalities and defining goals for culturally diverse clients that are consistent with their racial, cultural, ethnic, gender, and sexual orientation backgrounds. Thus, traditionally taboo behaviors like giving advice and suggestions may be effective and appropriate in use with some client populations.
3. MCT acknowledges our existence and identity as being composed of individual (uniqueness), group, and universal dimensions. Any form of helping that fails to recognize the totality of these dimensions negates important aspects of a person's identity.
4. MCT supports the notion that different racial and ethnic minority groups might respond best to culture-specific strategies of helping. For example, research seems to support the belief that Asian Americans are more responsive to directive and active approaches and that African Americans appreciate helpers who are authentic in their self-disclosures (Pedersen, Draguns, Lonner, & Trimble, 2002).
5. MCT broadens the perspective of the helping relationship by balancing the individualistic approach with a collectivistic reality that acknowledges our embeddedness in families, significant others, communities, and cultures. In many ways, multicultural group counseling is more appropriate across cultures than individual counseling (A. Ivey, Pedersen, & M. Ivey, 2002).
6. MCT assumes a dual role in helping clients. For example, in many cases, focusing on the individual client and encouraging him or her to achieve insights and learn new behaviors are appropriate. However, when problems of clients of color reside in prejudice, discrimination, and racism of employers, educators, and neighbors or in organizational policies or practices in schools, mental health agencies, government, business, and our society, the traditional therapeutic role appears ineffective and inappropriate. The focus for change must shift to changing client systems rather than individual clients.

The purpose of this chapter is to begin the process of proposing a theory of MCT that incorporates those features described above. Such an attempt is filled with hazards and may be a culturally biased attempt in itself. Such a criticism is inescapable, however, as all theories are necessarily culture specific. Thus, an attempt will be made to minimize such a danger by (1) analyzing the weaknesses and culture-bound biases of traditional mental health practices, (2) reviewing the literature associated with factors identified as important in MCT and "minority" mental health, and (3) proposing tentative propositions consistent with developing a theory of multicultural counseling and psychotherapy.

CHARACTERISTICS OF COUNSELING AND PSYCHOTHERAPY

For the purposes of this chapter, traditional counseling may be defined as the systematic application of techniques derived from predominantly Eurocentric psychological principles by a trained and experienced professional counselor or therapist for the purpose of helping psychologically troubled people. It is difficult to be more succinct or precise without getting involved in specific types of counseling. Depending on their perspectives and theoretical orientations, counselors may seek to modify attitudes, thoughts, feelings, or behaviors; facilitate the patient's self-insight and rational control of his or her own life; cure mental disorders; enhance mental health and self-actualization; make clients "feel better"; remove a cause of a psychological problem; change a self-concept; or encourage adaptation. Counseling is practiced by many different kinds of people in many different ways—a fact that seems to preclude establishing a single set of standard therapeutic procedures (D. Sue, D. W. Sue, & S. Sue, 2000). And, despite the Euro-American emphasis on the scientific basis of counseling, in practice it is often more art than science.

Diverse Eurocentric counseling approaches seem to share some common therapeutic factors. In a study of 50 publications on psychotherapy and counseling, investigators found the most common attributes to be (1) development of a therapeutic alliance, (2) opportunity for catharsis, (3) acquisition and practice of new behaviors, and (4) the clients' positive expectancies (Grencavage & Norcross, 1990).

First, counseling offers the client a chance to relearn—more specifically, a chance to unlearn, relearn, develop, or change—certain behaviors or levels of functioning.

Second, counseling helps generate the development of new, emotionally important experiences. It involves the experiencing of emotions that clients may have avoided, along with the painful and helpless feelings fostered by these emotions. This experiencing allows relearning as well as emotional and intellectual insight into problems and conflicts.

Third, there is a therapeutic relationship. Counselors have been trained to listen, show sympathetic concern, be objective, value the client's integrity, communicate understanding, and use professional knowledge and skills. Counselors may provide reassurance, interpretations, self-disclosures, reflections of the client's feelings, or information, each at appropriate times. As a team, counselors and clients are better prepared to venture into frightening areas that clients would not have faced alone.

Finally, clients in counseling have certain motivations and expectations. Most people enter counseling with both anxiety and hope. They are frightened by their emotional difficulties and by the prospect of treatment, but they expect or hope that counseling will be helpful.

The goals and general characteristics of counseling as described seem admirable, and most people consider them so. However, counseling itself has been criticized as being biased and inappropriate to the lifestyles of many clients, such as members of minority groups (Lewis, Lewis, Daniels, & D'Andrea, 1998; Locke, 1998; Paniagua, 1998; D. W. Sue & D. Sue, 1999). Indeed, the process and goals of counseling and psychotherapy have often been likened to forms of cultural oppression (Katz, 1985; D. W. Sue, 1978).

COUNSELING THEORIES AND WORLDVIEWS

Elsewhere, a worldview has been broadly defined "as how a person perceives his or her relationship to the world (nature, institutions, other people, things, etc.). Worldviews are highly correlated with a person's cultural upbringing and life experiences" (D. W. Sue, 1978, p. 419). While worldviews have traditionally been applied to individuals (microunit of analysis) in how they construe meaning in the world, the concept has been increasingly applied to larger units, such as gender, race, and culture (macroanalysis). A. Ivey (1981, 1986) has referred to the different theories of counseling and psychotherapy as "temporary cultures" with their own assumptions about the nature of people, how problems arise, and what methods must be employed to be effective. These temporary cultures are, indeed, different worldviews (Ibrahim, Roysircar-Sodowsky, & Ohnishi, 2001; A. Ivey, M. Ivey, & Simek-Morgan, 1997), associated with different theoretical orientations. A number of multicultural scholars (Baruth & Manning, 1999; A. Ivey, 1993; Locke, 1998; Parham, White, & Ajamu, 1999; Pedersen, 1999; D. W. Sue & S. Sue, 1999) have already made a strong case that the worldviews implicit in the psychodynamic, cognitive-behavioral, existential-humanistic, and other schools of thought might conflict with the worldviews of racial and ethnic minority clients.

To be fair, most practicing clinicians consider themselves eclectics. They contend that relying on a single theory and a few techniques is correlated with inexperience; the more experienced the clinician is, the greater are the diversity and resourcefulness used in a session (Corey, 2001; Norcross & Prochaska, 1988). Therapeutic eclecticism has been defined as the "process of selecting concepts, methods, and strategies from a variety of current theories which work" (Brammer & Shostrom, 1982, p. 35). An example is the early "technical eclecticism" of Lazarus (1967). This approach has now been refined into a theoretical model called multimodal behavior therapy (Lazarus, 1976, 1984). Although behavioral in basis, it embraces many cognitive and affective concepts as well. Yet it is important to note that for counselors to draw from the available current theories (most of which are Eurocentric) still leaves a great void. While the behavioral schools of thought see us as behaving beings, the cognitive schools as thinking beings, the humanistic schools as feeling beings, and the psychoanalytic as historic and unconsciously motivated beings, it is important to note that we are all of these and more. D. W. Sue (1992) has stated,

The problem with traditional theories is that they are culture-bound and often recognize and treat only one aspect of the human condition: the thinking self, the feeling self, the behaving self, or the social self. Few include the totality of the human experience, and few include the cultural and political self. (p. 32)

COUNSELING AND CULTURAL BIAS

Racial and ethnic minorities have frequently criticized counseling as being a "handmaiden of the status quo," a "transmitter of society's values," and an "instrument of oppression." Rather than helping people reach their full potential, critics say, it has often been used to subjugate the very people it was meant to free. The meaning of such statements is clear: the process and goals of counseling are culture bound and thus culturally biased against people whose values differ from those of Western societies. The following generic characteristics of counseling, which seem to be common to most schools of thought, often conflict with clients' cultural values (Paniagua, 1998; Pedersen, 1999; D. W. Sue & D. Sue, 1999):

1. *Focus on the individual.* Most forms of counseling and psychotherapy stress the importance and uniqueness of the individual, an attitude reflected in the concept of the I-thou relationship, the one-to-one encounter, and the belief that the client must take responsibility for himself or herself. In many cultural groups, however, the basic psychosocial unit of operation is not the individual but the family, the group, or the collective society. For example, many Asians and Hispanics define their identities within the family constellation. Whatever a person does reflects not only on that person but on the entire family as well. Important decisions are thus made by the entire family rather than by the individual (McGoldrick, Giordano, & Pearce, 1996; Szapocznik & Kurtines, 1993).

Counselors who work with people from such cultures may see their clients as "dependent," "lacking in maturity," or "avoiding responsibility." These negative labels do much harm to the self-esteem of minority-group members, especially when they become part of a diagnosis.

2. *Verbal expression of emotions.* The psychotherapeutic process works best for clients who are verbal, articulate, and able to express their feelings and be assertive. The major medium of communication is the spoken word (in standard English). Those who tend to be less verbal, who speak with an accent, or who do not use standard English are placed at a disadvantage. In addition, many cultural groups (including Asians and Native Americans) are brought up to conceal rather than verbalize their feelings; counselors often perceive them as "inhibited," "lacking in spontaneity," or "repressed." Thus, the counseling process, by valuing expressiveness, may not only force minority clients to violate their cultural norms but also label them as having negative personality traits. Counseling and psychotherapy also fail to realize major differences in communication styles and the use of nonverbal forms of communication. Asian Americans, African Americans, Hispanic and Latino Americans, and American Indians seem to rely much more on nonverbal communication or to use contextual cues more than their White counterparts (Dana, 1998; Herring, 1999).

3. *Openness and intimacy.* Self-disclosure and discussion of the most intimate and personal aspects of one's life are hallmarks of counseling. However, cultural and sociopolitical factors may make some clients unwilling or unable to engage in such self-disclosure (Ridley, 1984; D. W. Sue & S. Sue, 1999). For example, the "cultural paranoia" that many African Americans have developed as a defense against discrimination and oppression may be a healthy distrust that would make them reluctant to disclose their innermost thoughts and feelings to a White counselor (Grier & Cobbs, 1968, 1971). Unfortunately, counselors who encounter this reluctance might perceive their clients as suspicious, guarded, and paranoid. Likewise, many counselors do not understand the cultural implications of disclosure among Asians, who discuss intimate matters only with close acquaintances and not with strangers, which counselors may well be.

4. *Insight.* Most closely associated with the psychodynamic approach but valued in many theoretical orientations, insight is the ability to understand the basis of one's motivations, perceptions, and behavior. But many cultural groups do not value insight. In China, for example, a depressed or anxious person may be advised to avoid the thoughts that are causing the distress. This contrasts sharply with the Western belief

that insight is always helpful in counseling (Hong & Domokos-Cheng Ham, 2001). Interestingly, the rise in popularity of cognitive counseling approaches, such as those advocated by Ellis (1962, 1989), Beck (1976, 1985), and Meichenbaum (1985), now reveals that "healthy denial" or avoidance of "morbid thinking" is a useful counseling strategy; this is a method that has traditionally run counter to the belief in insight.

5. *Competition versus cooperation.* In Western society, competitiveness is a highly valued trait. This is clearly reflected in our educational system, where competition among persons is created by having children sit in neatly arranged rows of individual desks; where asking and answering questions occur by raising one's hand to seek individual recognition; where a bell-shaped curve is used to grade students (for someone to get an A, others have to obtain Bs, Cs, Ds, and Fs). Some groups such as American Indians and Hispanics value and prefer more cooperative efforts in the classroom (Comas-Diaz, 1990). Counselors may perceive such cultural differences as indicative of passivity, noncompetitiveness, or lack of assertiveness. One of the reasons that American Indians have the highest dropout rates in our educational system may be that to achieve they must violate basic values of their cultures (Banks, 1993).

6. *Linear-static time emphasis.* The United States operates by "clock time," which tends to view time as static and linear. Statements such as "Time is money" and "Don't be late" indicate the importance of time consciousness. In counseling and psychotherapy, appointments are traditionally once a week, 50 minutes out of the hour. Yet many cultural groups possess a much more dynamic, flowing, and harmonious perception of time (circular versus linear and flowing versus rigid), or they tend to mark time by events rather than by the clock (Ho, 1987; Inclan, 1985; Kluckhohn & Strodtbeck, 1961; Spiegel & Papajohn, 1983). Such differences in temporal perspectives can lead to major misunderstandings and difficulties. A client whose cultural background differs from that of the counselor and who shows up late for an appointment may be perceived by the counselor as passive-aggressive or irresponsible (D. W. Sue, 1990; D. W. Sue & D. Sue, 1999).

7. *Nuclear versus extended family.* Although it is no longer the norm in the United States, the nuclear family is still held to be the ideal from which we conceptualize and practice family counseling. The unit of the family usually includes the husband, wife, and immediate offspring. The definition of the family in many cultural groups may be quite different from that of their White counterparts. For example, extended family systems that include aunts, uncles, godparents, and even deceased members (ancestor worship of certain Asian groups) appear to be the norm for Mexican Americans and Asian Americans (Ho, 1987; McGoldrick et al., 1996); among African Americans and American Indians, the concept *family* may extend not only to aunts and uncles but to neighbors and tribal members (Franklin, 1988; Ho, 1987; McGoldrick et al., 1996; Red Horse, 1983; Thomas & Dansby, 1985). Thus, the counselor or therapist may need to redefine family counseling in an extended manner.

8. *Locus of responsibility.* Traditional counseling stresses that responsibility for change resides with the individual and that the locus of the problem is generally internal. Thus, much of counseling is aimed at having clients explore their own conflicts, achieve insight, and become healthy in some manner. Racial and ethnic minorities, however, often view the problem as residing outside the person and believe that change must occur in the system rather than solely in t he individual (Parham et al., 1999; D. W. Sue, 2001; D. W. Sue, A. Ivey, & Pedersen, 1996). Racism, discrimination, and prejudice are seen as system stressors that call for new roles for counselors (e.g., change agent, advocate, or facilitator of indigenous healing; Atkinson, Thompson, & Grant, 1993).

9. *Scientific empiricism.* The field of counseling and the broader field of psychology attempt to mimic the physical sciences. The process of asking and answering questions about the human condition is based on the value placed on symbolic logic (D. W. Sue & D. Sue, 1999), and the valued approach is an atomistic, quantitative, and reductionistic analysis of phenomena that are believed to be related by cause and effect (S. Sue, 1999). Many cultural groups believe in a more nonlinear, holistic, and harmonious approach to the world. The counselor is often trained to engage in linear, rational, and objective thinking in helping clients to resolve problems and difficulties (Katz, 1985; Pedersen, 1999). As a result, a counselor's desire to help may unwittingly be at odds with that of the culturally different client.

The solution to this cultural gap is obvious: counselors need to do three things. First, they should begin the process of becoming more aware of their own cultural values, biases, stereotypes, and assumptions about human behavior (Pedersen, 2000; D. W. Sue, Arredondo, & McDavis, 1992; D. W. Sue et al., 1982; D. W. Sue, Carter, 1998). They need to ask: What are the worldviews we bring to the counseling encounter? What value system is inherent in our theory of helping? What values underlie the strategies and techniques used in counseling? Without such an awareness and understanding, counselors may inadvertently assume that everyone shares their worldview. When this happens, they may become guilty of cultural oppression, imposing values on their culturally different clients (D. W. Sue, 1978).

Second, counselors should begin the process of acquiring knowledge and understanding of the worldviews of minority or culturally different clients (D. W. Sue et al., 1992). Counselors need to reflect on these questions about ethnic groups of color: What are their values, biases, and assumptions about human behavior? How similar or dissimilar are they to those of the helping professional's value system? Are there such things as African American, Asian American, Latino and Hispanic American, and Native American worldviews?

Third, counselors should begin the process of developing culturally appropriate intervention strategies in the counseling process (D. W. Sue, 1990). This involves developing not only individual counseling and communication skills but system intervention skills as well. Although not discussed in this chapter, indigenous healing practices and help-giving networks of different cultures and minority communities are crucial to the provision of relevant mental health services (Das, 1987; Harner, 1990; Lee, Oh, & Mountcastle, 1992; D. W. Sue et al., 1996).

RACIAL AND ETHNIC MINORITY COUNSELING RESEARCH: IMPORTANT THEMES

In building a theory of MCT, knowledge of the limitations and weaknesses of current models is essential, which is one of the reasons this chapter has devoted a considerable amount of space to analyzing the culture-bound limitations of current theories. Another useful path is to review the current racial and ethnic minority counseling research to identify important themes, concepts, and findings of relevance to multicultural counseling. This chapter will extract some of these key concepts and findings and attempt to draw out their implications for MCT.

Centrality of Culture to Theories of Counseling

All counseling theories arise from a cultural context and as such are highly culture bound (Ivey et al., 1997; Parham et al., 1999; Pedersen, 1999). Yet the counseling profession continues to ignore this fact and act as if counseling theories are equally applicable to all people regardless of differences in race, culture, and ethnicity. The multicultural counseling literature suggests that failure to understand and take into consideration the cultural assumptions of counseling may result in ineffectiveness or cultural oppression. For example, minorities are often the victims of psychological helping models that view

them as inferior, deprived, or deficient in desirable characteristics (Parham et al., 1999; Ponterotto & Casas, 1991; Robinson & Howard-Hamilton, 2000; D. W. Sue & D. Sue, 1999). This generally occurs because the counseling professional is unaware of the cultural values, biases, and assumptions of the theories.

Szapocznik and Kurtines (1993) reconceptualize family psychology and counseling to include the concept of embeddedness. This paradigm studies the individual within the context of family, which is in turn embedded in a cultural context (A. Ivey et al., 1997). There are two important things to note in this new formulation. First, an effective counseling approach does not view the individual in the context of family and culture as though they were separate, isolated dimensions. Rather, contexts are embedded and act on one another. Szapocznik and Kurtines (1993) state, "We have found it useful to extend our concern for culture to include the concept of the nesting of the individual within the family and the family within the culture" (p. 401). Second, the cultural context in which nesting occurs is not a monocultural one. The model does not apply solely, for example, to a Cuban cultural context (a very monocultural view in itself). Rather, in the United States, contexts are embedded within a culturally pluralist milieu, a recognition of multiculturalism. While Cuban American children may be raised in a Cuban community in Florida, they are eventually and ultimately exposed to the Eurocentric culture of the United States as well as others.

Minority Identity Development

Multicultural specialists are increasingly recognizing the importance of racial and cultural identity development of clients in the counseling process. Researchers disagree on whether we are talking about a stage model (Atkinson et al., 1998; Cross, 1971, 1991; Hardiman, 1982; Helms, 1984, 1986, 1990; Jackson, 1975; Parham, 1989; Parham & Helms, 1981) or a social-learning one (Rowe, Bennett, & Atkinson, 1994). Nevertheless, these models strongly imply that the stage or level of identity attained by the minority individual may dictate different counseling strategies and approaches. They also give strong emphasis to sociopolitical factors in the formation of racial and cultural identity.

Perhaps the most influential of the Black identity development models was the one proposed by Cross (1971, 1987, 1991). He proposed a four-stage process (originally five) in which Blacks in the United Sates moved from a White frame of reference: preencounter, encounter, immersion-emersion, and internalization. The preencounter stage is characterized by Blacks who devalue their own Blackness in favor of White values and ways. Adopting White Eurocentric values and ways through assimilation in and acculturation to White society is the overriding goal. In the encounter stage, a two-step process begins to occur. The person may encounter an event (for example, the slaying of Martin Luther King, Jr.) or a series of events that produce a profound challenge to the individual's previous way of thinking and behaving; this is followed by a reinterpretation of the world and a personal shift in worldviews. Anger and guilt may move the Black person to the third stage of development, immersion-emersion. Here Blacks may withdraw from the dominant culture and immerse themselves in Black culture and tradition. There may be a rise in Black pride. The final stage, internalization, is characterized by inner security as conflicts between the old and new identities are resolved.

Because many other minority groups seem to move through similar identity processes, several multicultural psychologists (Atkinson et al., 1998; D. W. Sue & D. Sue, 1999) have attempted to analyze the many similarities that seem to exist among them. They identify five stages through which racial and ethnic minorities may move: conformity, dissonance, resistance and immersion, introspection, and integrative awareness. Each stage has its corresponding attitudes and behaviors. For example, the conformity stage is characterized by the minority individual's unequivocal preference for dominant cultural values over those of the minority culture. Dominant cultural ways are viewed favorably, while those of one's own cultural heritage are viewed with disdain. To make sense of this stage and others requires an understanding of the dominant-subordinate relationship between two different cultures and the concept of "cultural racism" (D. W. Sue & D. Sue, 1999). Each stage represents a part of the development that oppressed people experience as they struggle to understand themselves in terms of their own culture, the dominant culture, and the oppressive relationship between the two. In counseling, a minority client at the conformity stage may prefer a White counselor, while one at the resistance and immersion stage (characterized by a focus on White racism as the problem) might prefer a counselor of his or her own race. Minority identity development models hold much promise for improving the delivery of culturally appropriate mental health services to racial and ethnic minorities.

White Identity Development

Within the past few years, an increasing number of multicultural counseling scholars have turned their attention to studying what has become known as "White identity development" (Hardiman, 1982; Helms, 1984, 1990; Rowe et al., 1994; Sabnani, Ponterotto, & Borodovsky, 1991). Most of these models seem to share some common assumptions. D. W. Sue and D. Sue (1999) state:

First, racism is a basic and integral part of U.S. life and permeates all aspects of our culture and institutions. Second, Whites are socialized into U.S. society and, therefore, inherit the biases, stereotypes, and racist attitudes, beliefs, and behaviors of the society. In other words, all Whites are racist whether knowingly or unknowingly. Third, how Whites perceive themselves as racial beings seems to follow an identifiable sequence that can be called stages. Fourth, the stage of White racial identity development in a cross-cultural encounter (counseling minorities, counselor training, etc.) affects the process and outcome of an interracial relationship. Last, the most desirable stage is the one where the White person not only accepts his/her Whiteness, but also defines it in a nondefensive and nonracist manner. (p. 113)

Like their minority counterparts, a White counselor at the conformity stage (belief in the superiority of White culture over all others) may do great damage to culturally different clients. Part of effective counselor training would consist of an attempt to move the White counselor from an ethnocentric-oppressive bias to a nonracist self-affirming White identity. The conclusion we can draw is fairly straightforward. It is important to understand not only minority identity development but the racial and cultural identity of the White counselor as well.

CULTURALLY APPROPRIATE INTERVENTION STRATEGIES

In the field of counseling, increasing importance is being placed on how culture, race, ethnicity, and gender affect communication styles (A. Ivey, 1981, 1986; A. Ivey et al., 1997; D. W. Sue, 1977, 1991a, 1991b; D. W. Sue & D. Sue, 1999). A body of literature suggests that counseling style is influenced by communication style, which in turn is affected by worldviews. Different theories of counseling represent different worldviews and may greatly influence the counseling styles and strategies used by the helping professional. Process and content analysis of counseling sessions employing strategies such as Rogerian, rational emotive, and gestalt reveals major counseling style differences generally consistent with their theoretical orientations (Dolliver, Williams, & Gold, 1980; Edwards, Boulet, Mahrer, Chagnon, & Mook, 1982; Lee & Uhlemann, 1984; Meara, Pepinsky, Shannon, & Murray, 1981; Weinrach, 1986).

A. Ivey (1981, 1986) has repeatedly emphasized the fact that different theories of counseling are concerned with generating different constructs, sentences, and helping responses. Because counseling and psychotherapy are predominantly White middle-class activities, clients who differ in race, culture, ethnicity, and class may be placed at a disadvantage in the helping relationship. The process of counseling may be antagonistic to the cultural styles of helping deemed appropriate for that particular group. For example, some studies suggest that certain groups of Asian Americans, African Americans, American Indians, and Hispanic Americans may prefer more active counseling approaches than nonactive ones (Herring, 1999; Hong & Domokos-Cheng Ham, 2001; A. Ivey et al., 1997; Locke, 1998; Paniagua, 1998; Ponterotto et al., 2001; D. W. Sue & D. Sue, 1999). Traditional approaches that use a much more nondirective and egalitarian relationship may be experienced negatively by the culturally different client. As a result, minority clients may perceive the session as unhelpful and may prematurely terminate (D. W. Sue & D. Sue, 1999). Multicultural specialists are beginning to realize the need for developing culturally appropriate intervention strategies in working with racial and ethnic minority clients and groups.

SYSTEMS INTERVENTION ROLES

One of the strongest criticisms of counseling approaches has been aimed at the traditional role of the counselor itself (Atkinson, Morten, & D. W. Sue, 1998; Atkinson et al., 1993). While some have argued that conventional counseling can be effective across cultural groups, others are critical for a number of reasons. First, conventional counseling focuses on the individual and may perceive the problem as residing in the person rather than in the oppressive environment. Attempting to change the person to adjust to the sick environment is to blame the victim. Second, conventional counseling roles concentrate on the development of one-to-one interpersonal skills. It is characterized by a helping professional sitting in an office engaging in verbal self-exploration of the client. Clients are asked to take responsibility for their own actions, and all treatment is confined to an office setting. Few counselors have been trained to change systems. Thus, if the problem resides in oppressive environmental conditions, counselors are ill prepared to act as social or environmental change agents. Third, the use of helping approaches indigenous to the client's ancestral culture receives minimal study in counselor education or counseling psychology programs. Even the study of multiculturalism in the United States is predominantly Eurocentric; Afrocentric and Asian-centric perspectives are all but missing (D. W. Sue & D. Sue, 1999).

BASIC ASSUMPTIONS IN A THEORY OF MCT

The literature on MCT makes clear that the field is on the verge of what Kuhn (1970) has referred to as a major paradigm shift. Such a shift occurs when (1) ideas, concepts, and data cannot be adequately accounted for by the science and theory of the day and (2) a new and competing perspective better accommodates the existing data. This chapter's review of cultural biases inherent in the theories, processes, and goals of counseling and psychotherapy points out the inadequacy of current models, and the competing multicultural perspective seems better positioned to accommodate the existing data. Pedersen (1999) has coined the phrase "multiculturalism as a fourth force in counseling," which recognizes that a major change is in the works for the profession. It is probably accurate to say that this change will be one of the most important ones to occur in the 21st century and is likely to be quite revolutionary. It will alter how we think about the nature of reality and how we define counseling, force us to reconceptualize our theories, and broaden our definition of what constitutes helping strategies. Multiculturalism will have a major impact on the education, training, and practice of mental health professionals. It also points to a new direction toward which research will be steered, and it may require different research strategies.

While no one has developed a generally accepted or overarching theory of MCT, there are numerous perspectives that seem to possess some common assumptions and propositions. Many of these perspectives have already been reviewed, and it appears that a developed theory of MCT is not far off. The development of a new perspective (paradigm shift) from which to view the field of counseling will occur only when MCT establishes itself as a viable theoretical perspective. In their attempt to lay the foundations of MCT theory, D. W. Sue et al. (1996) propose some propositions most likely to be incorporated into such a theory. The remaining portion of this chapter will outline propositions based more on assumptions than axioms (truths).

Proposition 1

MCT is a metatheory of counseling and psychotherapy. It is a theory about theories and offers an organizational framework for understanding the numerous helping approaches that humankind has developed. It recognizes that theories of counseling and psychotherapy developed in the Western world and those indigenous helping models intrinsic to non-Western cultures are not inherently right or wrong or good or bad. Each theory represents a different worldview.

As mentioned earlier, the centrality of culture in all theories of counseling and psychotherapy needs to be acknowledged and made explicit. Criticisms about counseling and psychotherapy being culture bound would become less compelling and problematic once the cultural assumptions were stated. For example, a counselor with a rational-emotive counseling orientation would realize that the emphasis on individual, rational decision making might be inappropriate with a Chinese client who may have a collectivist approach to solving life problems.

MCT uses the theoretical approach most consistent with the experiences and cultural perspectives of the client. In some cases, it may be best to incorporate a psychoanalytic perspective. With one client, it may mean a cognitive-behavioral perspective. And with yet another, it may mean an organic-biological one. In most cases, however, it means a systematic integration of numerous theoretical concepts, in recognition of the complexity of the human condition. Part of the complexity is the realization that we are products of our environments (familial, social, cultural, and political). In situations where integration is not possible (concepts of the models are epistemologically conflicting), a synergetic formation of a new theory or model may be called for. This is especially true when we realize that we live in a global world where indigenous and non-Western healing approaches are often the preferred means of help. Counseling is growing very rapidly outside the United States, and MCT itself will not be limited to the domestic counseling process but will be relevant around the world. Thus, international, indigenous, and alternative therapies must be acknowledged and integrated into our helping models.

Proposition 2

MCT recognizes that both counselor and client identities are formed and embedded in multiple levels of experiences (individual, group, and universal) and contexts (individual, family, and cultural milieu). The totality and interrelationship of experiences and contexts must be the focus of treatment.

In simple terms, human beings possess three levels of identity. At the individual level, we are all unique. Because no two individuals share the same biology (even if they are identical twins) or experiences, no two individuals are ever the same. At the group level of identity, we share commonalities with others by virtue of membership in some reference group (for example, race, culture, ethnicity, gender, religion). The universal level of identity suggests that we all belong to the species *Homo sapiens*. Like the Shakespearean character who asks, "When I cut myself, do I not bleed?" we all share many characteristics. Unfortunately, most forms of counseling and psychotherapy appear to focus on either the individual or universal level of identity to the exclusion of the group level. Two reasons seem to account for this fact: (1) counseling bias in theories that value the uniqueness or universal qualities of the human condition and (2) sociopolitical discomfort in recognizing group characteristics and differences (D. W. Sue, 2001). MCT recognizes the totality of the person's multiple identities and does not prefer one to the other. The guiding principle is one of salience.

Psychology has traditionally studied the individual as an isolated entity, separate and apart from external influences (A. Ivey et al., 1997; D. W. Sue & D. Sue, 1999; Szapocznik & Kurtines, 1993). This orientation is being challenged because it fails to recognize the interaction between the person and the larger environment. One of these challenges is the contextualist movement, which simply states that behavior cannot be understood outside the context in which it occurs (Bronfenbrenner, 1986; Steenbarger, 1991; D. W. Sue, 1991b). The context includes not only the individual but also the family and culture. The new contextualist paradigm being proposed is that working with the individual requires understanding of how the person is embedded in the family, which in turn requires understanding of how the family is affected by being embedded in a pluralistic (not a singular) culture (Szapocznik & Kurtines, 1993).

Proposition 3

Cultural identity development is a major determinant of both counselor and client attitudes toward the self, others of the same group, others of a different group, and others of the dominant group. These attitudes, which may be manifested in affective and behavioral dimensions, are strongly influenced not only by cultural variables but also by the dynamics of a dominant-subordinate relationship among culturally different groups. The level or stage of racial and cultural identity will influence how clients and counselors define the problem and will dictate what they believe to be appropriate counseling goals and processes.

An understanding of the level of identity consciousness displayed by the culturally different client is crucial to the provision of appropriate mental health services. Models of cultural identity development make a strong case that not all members of a minority group are the same and that within-group differences may be moderated by many variables (Atkinson et al., 1998). Among the more important ones is minority status in a society. Here we refer to the dominant-subordinate relationship between two different cultures, one of which is oppressed. As a result, counseling needs to acknowledge the importance of sociopolitical dynamics on the experiences of culturally different groups in a society. The manifestation of so-called psychological problems may actually be a manifestation of oppression.

Likewise, the majority-group counselor is also embedded in his or her own culture and equally affected by the sociopolitical climate (D'Andrea et al., 2001; Katz, 1985). White identity development theories stress, for example, that White counselors (members of the majority culture) need to deal with their concepts of Whiteness and examine their own biases and prejudices, as well as the roles they play in oppression. These roles include not only individual acts of bias and discrimination but also the overprivileged roles that are seemingly granted to Whites in our society (McIntosh, 1989). McIntosh states, "As a white person, I realized I had been taught about racism as something which puts others at a disadvantage, but had been taught not to see one of its corollary aspects, white privilege, which puts me at an advantage" (p. 8).

Proposition 4

MCT effectiveness is most likely enhanced when the counselor uses modalities and defines goals consistent with the life experiences and cultural values of the client. No one helping approach or intervention strategy is equally effective across all populations and life situations. The ultimate goal of multicultural counselor and therapist training is to expand the repertoire of helping responses available to the professional, regardless of theoretical orientation.

Helping is administered differently in different cultural groups and societies (Das, 1987; Lee et al., 1992). Eurocentric methods such as self-disclosure, nondirectiveness, and verbal participation for clients have been found to be antagonistic to many culturally different groups. It is not that these techniques or strategies are wrong or bad; rather, they are simply inappropriate and, when applied indiscriminately, can be constricting and oppressive. If counseling is intended to liberate individuals to the possibilities of life consistent with their culture, then helping styles need to be compatible with the experiences and values of the client.

It appears that the wider the repertoire of responses the counselor possesses, the better the helper is likely to be (Nwachuku & A. Ivey, 1991; D. W. Sue, 1990; D. W. Sue et al., 1992). Relying on a very narrow and limited number of skills in counseling restricts the effectiveness of counseling. Theories of counseling and psychotherapy have been shown to be differentially associated with characteristic responses. The work of Ivey and colleagues (A. Ivey, 1986, 1988; A. Ivey & Authier, 1978; A. Ivey et al., 1997) on the relationship of microskills and theoretical orientation of the counselor is compelling and convincing in this regard. Rogerians, for example, are likely to use predominantly attending skills, while those with a behavioral orientation will use many more influencing skills. While these skills may be inherently consistent with the worldview of the theory, what happens if the culturally different client does not share that view? A traditional Chinese American client who expects advice or suggestions from the counselor (perceived as a knowledgeable and "wise" expert) might find a more nondirective approach (withholding advice and suggestions) confusing and unhelpful. Termination of the relationship is highly probable, although the need for help is still present.

MCT advocates cultural flexibility in the helping process. It recognizes that we are all thinking, feeling, behaving, social, cultural, and political beings. Those counselors who are most able to shift their counseling styles to meet the needs of their clients are in the best position to provide needed help. This concept has been labeled cultural intentionality by A. Ivey et al. (1997). They state:

The person who acts with intentionality has a sense of capability. She or he can generate alternative behaviors in a given situation and "approach" a problem from different vantage points. The intentional, fully functioning individual is not bound to one course of action but can respond in the moment to changing life situations and look forward to longer-term goals. (p. 8)

Proposition 5

MCT stresses the importance of multiple helping roles developed by many culturally different groups and societies. These roles often involve not simply a one-to-one encounter aimed at remediation in the individual but involve larger social units, systems intervention, and prevention. The conventional roles of counseling and psychotherapy are seen as only one of many others available to the helping professional.

As indicated previously, increasing emphasis is being placed on the need for counselors to adapt themselves to work within the client's culture rather than demanding that the culturally different adjust to the counselor's culture. With respect to racial and ethnic minorities in the United States, for example, counselors may be more effective if they leave their offices and meet a client in the client's environment (Atkinson et al., 1993, 1998). Several important reasons dictate such an orientation.

First, conventional counseling roles may unintentionally reinforce the belief that the problem resides within the individual. When in reality the problem resides outside the person (in the environment), we may become guilty of blaming the victim. A Latino client who may be unemployed and having difficulty finding a job may be blamed for his or her life circumstance when it may be due to discrimination or prejudice on the part of employers. An African American student who frequently gets into fights in school may be the victim of racist comments from and attitudes of White peers. The fighting behavior may actually be a product of a pathological situation in the school system.

Second, if the basis of the client's troubles is located in the social structure or system, the most appropriate form of intervention may call for the counselor to change the environment, a role that calls for the counselor to become active in community and social problems. The counselor may be required to act as a change agent, consultant, teacher, or community worker.

Third, the traditional counseling role is one of remediation (Atkinson et al., 1998; Katz, 1985). It tends to be reactive rather than proactive. Counselors who view the social system as a major contributor to problems of their clients would direct their energies toward prevention. As such, the orientation is to change the social environment that oppresses. Egan (1985) advocates that a counselor assume the role of a change agent, which he defines as someone "who plays an important part in designing, redesigning, running, renewing, or improving any system, subsystem, or program" (p. 12).

Fourth, movement into the client's environment has the additional advantage of allowing the counselor to observe directly the environmental factors that contribute to the client's dilemmas; direct observation promotes better understanding of the client and of what he or she believes is helpful, and it enhances the counselor-client relationship. The counselor comes to understand that helping roles have evolved within cultural contexts and that they are helpful because members of the culture believe in their efficacy. For example, it appears that the *curranderismo* (Mexican folk healer), practitioner of Santeria, acupuncturist or Tai Chi Chuan teacher, Sufis of Islamic countries, Alfas of Nigeria, and the Hakeem and Motwaas of Saudi Arabia are viewed by their respective cultures as legitimate healers dispensing potent forms of treatment (Das, 1987; Harner, 1990; Kakar, 1982; Lee et al., 1992).

Atkinson et al. (1993) have proposed a three-dimensional model of counselor roles. The selection of an appropriate counseling role depends on three major variables: (1) locus of the problem (internal vs. external), (2) level of acculturation, and (c) counseling goals or objectives (remediation vs. prevention). From this conceptual framework, they identify the following roles of importance to counseling: adviser, advocate, facilitator of indigenous support systems, facilitator of indigenous healing systems, consultant, change agent, counselor, and psychotherapist. No one role is considered more important than the others.

Proposition 6

Multicultural counselor competence involves the continual development of attitudes and beliefs, knowledges, and skills related to (1) awareness of own assumptions, values, and biases; (2) understanding of the worldview of the culturally different client; and (3) culturally appropriate intervention strategies and techniques.

For the past several decades, cultural competence has become one of the leading issues facing the profession (American Psychological Association, 1993; Constantine & Ladany, 2001; D. W. Sue, 2001). Based on the work of D. W. Sue and colleagues (D. W. Sue et al., 1982, 1992; D. W. Sue, Carter et al., 1998), multicultural counseling competencies have been described along a tripartite framework: (1) beliefs and attitudes, (2) knowledges, and (3) skills. The first involves attitudes and beliefs of counselors with respect to racial and ethnic minorities, the need to check stereotypes and biases, and the need to develop a positive orientation toward multiculturalism. The second recognizes that counselors need thorough understanding of their own worldviews and specific knowledge of the cultural groups with which they work. The last dimension involves the acquisition of specific skills (intervention techniques and strategies) needed to work effectively with minority groups.

While debate continues regarding whether the three-domain model accounts fully for all the components of cultural competence (Sodowsky, 1996; Vinson & Neimeyer, 2000), most multicultural specialists agree to its conceptual usefulness. Indeed, these competencies and their earlier derivatives have been incorporated into instruments attempting to measure cross-cultural counseling competencies: the Cross-Cultural Counseling Inventory—Revised (LaFromboise, Coleman, & Hernandez, 1991), Multicultural Counseling Awareness Scale—Form B: Revised Self Assessment (Ponterotto, Sanchez, & Magids, 1991), Multicultural Counseling Inventory (Sodowsky, Taffe, Gutkin, & Wise, 1994), and the Multicultural Awareness-Knowledge-and-Skills Survey (D'Andrea, Daniels, & Heck, 1991). Several recent studies (Ottavi, Pope-Davis, & Dings, 1994; Sodowsky et al., 1994) are impressive in documenting the existence of these competency factors. Thus, in keeping with our definition of MCT and its theoretical base, I proposed the following definition of cultural competence (D. W. Sue, 2001):

Cultural competence is the ability to engage in actions or create conditions that maximize the optimal development of client and client systems. Multicultural counseling competence is defined as the counselor's acquisition of awareness, knowledge, and skills needed to function effectively in a pluralistic democratic society (ability to communicate, interact, negotiate, and intervene on behalf of clients from diverse backgrounds), and on an organizational/societal level, advocating effectively to develop new theories, practices, policies and organizational structures that are more responsive to all groups. (p. 802)

RESEARCH IMPLICATIONS

Any theory of counseling, including MCT theory, is ultimately linked to research findings that either confirm or disconfirm its assumptions and basic tenets. This review of counseling research casts doubts on the adequacy of current models developed by primarily Eurocentric-trained psychologists to explain, predict, or treat the mental health problems of the diversity of peoples in this world. Thus, it speaks strongly to the development of a more inclusive model of helping. A theory of MCT has clear implications for research strategies (methodology and techniques) and focus. The development of MCT theory points to promising but previously neglected areas for future research.

First, research has traditionally emphasized a cause-and-effect orientation based on symbolic logic and empiricism (Morrow, Rakhsha, & Castaneda, 2001; Quintana, Troyano, & Taylor, 2001; D. W. Sue & D. Sue, 1999). The reductionistic and quantitative approach to asking and answering questions so valued by the counseling profession is often not amenable to the complex study of the human condition. Furthermore, many cultures value a more holistic and experiential approach in studying human interactions. Increasingly, multicultural researchers are recognizing the importance of such matters and advocating the use of qualitative methodology or alternative research paradigms to investigate counseling theory and practice. They have described qualitative research as (1) descriptive in nature, (2) inductive, (3) holistic, (4) flexible, and (5) clinically significant (see the detailed discussion in Ponterotto & Casas, 1991). It appears that the counseling profession would benefit greatly from using the following qualitative research strategies borrowed from anthropology and sociology: participant observation, in-depth interviewing, and life histories and case studies. The point to keep in mind is that both quantitative and qualitative research have their own strengths and limitations. One is not better than the other, but they should complement one another.

Second, MCT theory suggests that traditional Eurocentric theories of counseling and psychotherapy are culture bound and represent worldviews that are different from those of non-European cultures. Adopting a theory of helping inevitably ties the observers to the values and assumptions implicit in the model. When raised and socialized in the particular culture as well, the researcher may possess a biased perspective of cultural differences.

This matter was considered of sufficient importance that *Counseling Psychologist,* the official publication of the Division of Counseling Psychology, ran a special issue entitled "White American Researchers and Multicultural Counseling" (Mio, Iwamasa, Ponterotto, Ivey et al., 1993). Unfortunately, early in the 21st century, these criticisms continue to hold true. In a series of persuasive articles, multicultural specialists argued that:

- The contributions of minority professionals doing cross-cultural counseling research are often ignored and given less importance than those of their White counterparts (A. Ivey, 1993; Parham, 1993; Ponterotto, 1993).
- Research has presented a picture of racial and ethnic minorities as deviant and pathological (Casas & San Miguel, 1993; D. W. Sue, 1993). This has led to the development of genetic inferiority models, cultural deficit models, or cultural deficiency models applied to racial minorities.
- By far the most powerful statement was the need for White researchers to begin considering how their own resolved issues of race and ethnicity color their cross-cultural perceptions (Helms, 1993; Ponterotto, 1993).

Helms (1993) believes that much of the cross-cultural research now in existence is culturally biased. She states, "To the extent that White researchers have been the primary gatekeepers of cross-cultural research (e.g., journal editors, dissertation advisers), then it is possible that those with restricted worldviews encourage constricted study of cultural diversity issues" (p. 242).

It is important to note that Helms (1993) believes many minority researchers are also victims of primarily Western European training. They can also be culturally encapsulated and can inherit the biases of the larger society. It appears that individuals (majority and minority) conducting research on multicultural areas need to understand themselves as racial and cultural beings and the possible biases, stereotypes, and assumptions about human behavior they possess (D. W. Sue, 1993).

Last, it is important to echo again the call for greater consideration and, indeed, research into indigenous models of counseling and mental health. Non-Western models of helping are unfamiliar to most Western-trained counselors and researchers. There is therefore a huge void in our knowledge base. Ironically, a theory of multicultural counseling and psychotherapy that recognizes culture specificity (emic) has the greatest chance of being universal (etic).

CONCLUSIONS

We are experiencing a revolution in the counseling and educational fields. It is clear that multiculturalism can no longer be treated as ancillary; rather, it is an integral part of counseling. The challenge before us is not an easy one, for it means revising our theories and expanding our definitions of the helping process. Many mental health scholars continue to hold Eurocentric theories of counseling and psychotherapy as sacred cows that can be universally applied. Many of them continue to be ethnocentric and culture bound. Many may resist change because it threatens the very foundations of their belief systems and may mean a redistribution of power in our society. Yet to ignore the social reality of multiculturalism is to deny reality itself. If we are to provide equal access and opportunities for all, then the recognition of cultural diversity is essential to our survival.

Likewise, the survival of the counseling profession depends on its ability to respond to the challenge of providing appropriate mental health services to a culturally diverse population. The MCT movement offers hope in that direction. The next step is for us to begin constructing a theory of MCT. This chapter has outlined six propositions that seem to form the foundations of such an endeavor. Future work needs to delineate basic tenets from each proposition and to translate them into a working theory of MCT.

References

American Psychological Association. (1993). Guidelines for providers of psychological services to ethnic, linguistic, and culturally diverse populations. *American Psychologist, 48*(1), 45–48.

Atkinson, D. R., Morten, G., & Sue, D. W. (Eds.). (1998). *Counseling American minorities* (5th ed.). New York: McGraw-Hill.

Atkinson, D. R., Thompson, C. E., & Grant, S. K. (1993). A three-dimensional model for counseling racial/ethnic minorities. *Counseling Psychologist, 21*(2), 257–277.

Banks, J. A. (1993). Multicultural education: Characteristics and goals. In J. A. Banks & C. A. M. Banks (Eds.), *Multicultural education* (2nd ed., pp. 3–28). Boston: Allyn & Bacon.

Baruth, L. G., & Manning, M. L. (1999). *Multicultural counseling and psychotherapy*. Columbus, OH: Merrill.

Beck, A. (1976). *Cognitive therapy and the emotional disorders*. New York: International Universities Press.

Beck, A. (1985). Cognitive therapy, behavior therapy, psychoanalysis, and pharmacology: A cognitive continuum. In M. Mahoney & A. Freeman (Eds.), *Cognition and psychotherapy* (pp. 325–347). New York: Plenum.

Brammer, L. M., & Shostrom, E. (1982). *Therapeutic psychology: Fundamentals of counseling and psychotherapy* (4th ed.). Upper Saddle River, NJ: Prentice-Hall.

Bronfenbrenner, U. (1986). The ecology of the family as a context for human development. *Developmental Psychology, 22,* 723–742.

Casas, J. M., & San Miguel, S. (1993). Beyond questions and discussions, there is a need for action: A response to Mio and Iwamasa. *Counseling Psychologist, 21*(2), 233–239.

Comas-Diaz, L. (1990). Hispanic Latino communities: Psychological implications. *Journal of Training and Practice in Professional Psychology, 1,* 14–35.

Constantine, M. G., & Ladany, N. (2001). New visions for defining and assessing multicultural counseling competence. In J. G. Ponterotto, J. M. Casas, L. A. Suzuki, & C. M. Alexander (Eds.), *Handbook of multicultural counseling* (2nd ed., pp. 482–498). Thousand Oaks, CA: Sage.

Corey, G. (2001). *Theory and practice of counseling and psychotherapy*. Stamford, CT: Brooks/Cole.

Cross, W. E. (1971). The Negro-to-Black conversion experience: Toward a psychology of Black liberation. *Black World, 20,* 13–27.

Cross, W. E. (1987). A two-factor theory of Black identity: Implications for the study of identity development in minority children. In J. S. Phinney & M. J. Rotheram (Eds.), *Children's ethnic socialization: Pluralism and development* (pp. 117–133). Newbury Park, CA: Sage.

Cross, W. E. (1991). *Shades of Black: Diversity in African American identity*. Philadelphia: Temple University Press.

Dana, R. H. (1998). *Understanding cultural identity and intervention and assessment*. Thousand Oaks, CA: Sage.

D'Andrea, M. D., Daniels, J., Arredondo, P. Ivey, M. B., Ivey, A. E., Locke, D. C., O'Bryant, B., Parham, T. A., & Sue, D. W. (2001). Fostering organizational changes to realize the revolutionary potential of the multicultural movement: An updated case study. In J. G. Ponterotto, J. M. Casas, L. A. Suzuki, & C. M. Alexander (Eds.), *Handbook of multicultural counseling* (2nd ed., pp. 222–253). Thousand Oaks, CA: Sage.

D'Andrea, M., Daniels, J., & Heck, R. (1991). Evaluating the impact of multicultural training. *Journal of Counseling and Development, 70*(1), 143–150.

Das, A. K. (1987). Indigenous models of therapy in traditional Asian societies. *Journal of Multicultural Counseling and Development, 15,* 25–37.

Dolliver, R. H., Williams, E. L., & Gold, D. C. (1980). The art of gestalt therapy or: What are you doing with your feet now? *Psychotherapy: Theory, Research and Practice, 17,* 136–142.

Edwards, H. P., Boulet, D. B., Mahrer, A. R., Chagnon, G. J., & Mook, B. (1982). Carl Rogers during initial interviews: A moderate and consistent therapist. *Journal of Counseling Psychology, 29,* 14–18.

Egan, G. (1985). *Change agent skills in helping and human service settings*. Monterey, CA: Brooks/Cole.

Ellis, A. (1962). *Reason and emotion in psychotherapy*. New York: Stuart.

Ellis, A. (1989). Rational-emotive therapy. In R. J. Corsini & D. Weddings (Eds.), *Current psychotherapies* (pp. 197–238). Itasca, IL: Peacock.

Franklin, J. A. (1988). A historical note on Black families. In H. P. McAdoo (Ed.), *Black families* (pp. 23–26). Newbury Park, CA: Sage.

Grencavage, L. M., & Norcross, J. C. (1990). Where are the commonalities among the therapeutic common factors? *Professional Psychology: Research and Practice, 21*(5), 372–378.

Grier, W., & Cobbs, P. (1968). *Black rage*. New York: Basic Books.

Grier, W., & Cobbs, P. (1971). *The Jesus bag*. New York: McGraw-Hill.

Hardiman, R. (1982). *White identity development: A process-oriented model for describing the racial consciousness of White Americans* (Doctoral dissertation, University of Massachusetts, 1982). *Dissertation Abstracts International, 43,* 104A. (University Microfilms No. 82–10330).

Harner, M. (1990). *The way of the shaman: A guide to power and healing* (10th ed.). San Francisco: Harper.

Helms, J. E. (1984). Toward a theoretical model of the effects of race on counseling: A Black and White model. *Counseling Psychologist, 12,* 153–165.

Helms, J. E. (1986). Expanding racial identity theory to cover counseling process. *Journal of Counseling Psychology, 33,* 62–64.

Helms, J. E. (Ed.). (1990). *Black and White racial identity: Theory, research, and practice*. Westport, CT: Greenwood Press.

Helms, J. E. (1993). I also said, "White racial identity influences White researchers." *Counseling Psychologist, 21*(2), 240–243.

Herring, R. D. (1999). *Counseling with Native Americans and Alaska Natives.* Thousand Oaks, CA: Sage.

Hong, G. K., & Domokos-Cheng Ham, M. (2001). *Psychotherapy and counseling with Asian American clients.* Thousand Oaks, CA: Sage.

Ho, H. K. (1987). *Family therapy with ethnic minorities.* Thousand Oaks, CA: Sage.

Ibrahim, F. A., Roysircar-Sodowsky, G., & Ohnishi, H. (2001). Worldview: Recent developments and needed directions. In J. G. Ponterotto, J. M. Casas, L. A. Suzuki, & C. M. Alexander (Eds.), *Handbook of multicultural counseling* (2nd ed., pp. 425–456). Thousand Oaks, CA: Sage.

Inclan, J. (1985). Variations in value orientations in mental health work with Puerto Ricans. *Psychotherapy, 22,* 324–334.

Ivey, A. E. (1981). Counseling and psychotherapy. *Counseling Psychologist, 9*(2), 81–98.

Ivey, A. E. (1986). *Developmental therapy.* San Francisco: Jossey-Bass.

Ivey, A. E. (1988). *Intentional interviewing and counseling.* Pacific Grove, CA: Brooks/Cole.

Ivey, A. E. (1993). On the need for reconstruction of our present practice of counseling and psychotherapy. *Counseling Psychologist, 21*(2), 225–228.

Ivey, A. E., & Authier, J. (1978). *Microcounseling: Innovations in interviewing training.* Springfield, IL: Thomas.

Ivey, A. E., Ivey, M. B., & Simek-Morgan, L. (1997). *Counseling and psychotherapy: A multicultural perspective.* Boston: Allyn & Bacon.

Ivey, A. E., Pedersen, P. B., & Ivey, M. B. (2002). *Intentional group counseling: A microskills approach.* Belmont, CA: Brooks/Cole.

Jackson, B. (1975). Black identity development. *Journal of Educational Diversity, 2,* 19–25.

Kakar, S. (1982). *Shamans, mystics, and doctors: A psychological inquiry into India and its healing traditions.* New York: Knopf.

Katz, J. (1985). The sociopolitical nature of counseling. *Counseling Psychologist, 13,* 615–624.

Kluckhohn, F. R., & Strodtbeck, F. L. (1961). *Variations in value orientations.* Evanston, IL: Row, Peterson.

Kuhn, T. S. (1970). *The structure of scientific revolutions* (2nd ed.). Chicago: University of Chicago Press.

LaFromboise, T. D., Coleman, H., & Hernandez, A. (1991). Development and factor structure of the cross-cultural counseling inventory—revised. *Professional Psychology: Research and Practice, 22*(5), 380–388.

Lazarus, A. A. (1967). In support of technical eclecticism. *Psychological Reports, 21,* 415–416.

Lazarus, A. A. (Ed.). (1976). *Multimodal behavior therapy.* New York: Springer.

Lazarus, A. A. (1984). Multimodal therapy. In R. J. Corsini (Ed.), *Current psychotherapies* (pp. 508–544). Itasca, IL: Peacock.

Lee, C. C., Oh, M. Y., & Mountcastle, A. R. (1992). Indigenous models of helping in nonwestern countries: Implications for multicultural counseling. *Journal of Multicultural Counseling and Development, 20,* 1–10.

Lee, D. Y., & Uhlemann, M. R. (1984). Comparison of verbal responses of Rogers, Shostrom, and Lazarus. *Journal of Counseling Psychology, 32,* 91–94.

Lewis, J. A., Lewis, M. D., Daniels, J. A., & D'Andrea, M. J. (1998). *Community counseling.* Pacific Grove, CA: Brooks/Cole.

Locke, D. C. (1998). *Increasing multicultural understanding.* Newbury Park, CA: Sage.

McGoldrick, M., Giordano, J., & Pearce, J. (Eds.). (1996). *Ethnicity and family therapy.* New York: Guilford.

McIntosh, P. (1989, July/August). White privilege: Unpacking the invisible knapsack. *Peace and Freedom,* 8–10.

Meara, N. M., Pepinsky, H. B., Shannon, J. W., & Murray, W. A. (1981). Semantic communication and expectations for counseling across three theoretical orientations. *Journal of Counseling Psychology, 28,* 110–118.

Meichenbaum, D. (1985). *Stress inoculation training.* New York: Pergamon Press.

Mio, J. S., Iwamasa, G., Ponterotto, J. G., Ivey, A. E., et al. (1993). To do, or not to do: That is the question for White cross-cultural researchers. *Counseling Psychologist, 21* (2), 197–212.

Morrow, S. L., Rakhsha, G., & Castaneda, C. L. (2001). Qualitative research methods for multicultural counseling. In J. G. Ponterotto, J. M. Casas, L. A. Suzuki, & C. M. Alexander (Eds.), *Handbook of multicultural counseling* (2nd ed., pp. 575–603). Thousand Oaks, CA: Sage.

Norcross, J. C., & Prochaska, J. O. (1988). A study of eclectic (and integrative) views revisited. *Professional Psychology, 19,* 170–174.

Nwachuku, U., & Ivey, A. (1991). Culture specific counseling: An alternative approach. *Journal of Counseling and Development, 70*(1), 106–111.

Ottavi, T. M., Pope-Davis, D. B., & Dings, J. G. (1994). Relationship between White racial identity attitudes and self-reported multicultural counseling competencies. *Journal of Counseling Psychology, 41*(2), 149–154.

Paniagua, F. A. (1998). *Assessing and treating culturally diverse clients.* Thousand Oaks, CA: Sage.

Parham, T. A. (1989). Cycles of psychological nigrescence. *Counseling Psychologist, 17*(2), 187–226.

Parham, T. A. (1993). White researchers conducting multicultural counseling research: Can their efforts be "mo betta"? *Counseling Psychologist, 21*(2), 250–256.

Parham, T. A., & Helms, J. E. (1981). The influence of Black students' racial attitudes on preferences for counselor's race. *Journal of Counseling Psychology, 28,* 250–257.

Parham, T. A., White, J. L., & Ajamu, A. (1999). *The psychology of Blacks: An African-centered perspective* (3rd ed.). Upper Saddle River, NJ: Prentice Hall.

Pedersen, P. B. (1999). *Multiculturalism as a fourth force.* Philadelphia: Taylor & Francis.

Pedersen, P. (2000). *A handbook for developing multicultural awareness* (3rd ed.). Alexandria, VA: American Counseling Association.

Pedersen, P., Draguns, J., Lonner, W., & Trimble, J. (Eds.). (2002). *Counseling across cultures* (5th ed.). Thousand Oaks, CA: Sage.

Ponterotto, J. G. (1993). White racial identity and the counseling professional. *Counseling Psychologist, 21*(2), 213–217.

Ponterotto, J. G., & Casas, J. M. (1991). *Handbook of racial/ethnic minority counseling research.* Springfield, IL: Thomas.

Ponterotto, J. G., Casas, J. M., Suzuki, L. A., & Alexander, C. M. (Eds.). (2001). *Handbook of multicultural counseling.* Thousand Oaks, CA: Sage.

Ponterotto, J. G., Sanchez, C. M., & Magids, D. M. (1991, August). *Initial development and validation of the Multicultural Counseling Awareness Scale (MCAS).* Paper presented at the annual meeting of the American Psychological Association, San Francisco.

Quintana, S. M. Troyano, N., & Taylor, G. (2001). Cultural validity and inherent challenges in qualitative methods for multicultural research. In J. G. Ponterotto, J. M. Casas, L. A. Suzuki, & C. M. Alexander (Eds.), *Handbook of multicultural counseling* (2nd ed., pp. 604–630). Thousand Oaks, CA: Sage.

Red Horse, J. (1983). Indian family values and experiences. In G. J. Powell, J. Yamamoto, A. Romero, & K. A. Morales (Eds.), *The psychosocial development of minority group children* (pp. 258–272). New York: Brunner/Mazel.

Ridley, C. R. (1984). Clinical treatment of the nondisclosing Black client. *American Psychologist, 39,* 1234–1244.

Robinson, T. L., & Howard-Hamilton, M. F. (2000). *The convergence of race, ethnicity, and gender.* Columbus, OH: Merrill.

Rowe, W., Bennett, S., & Atkinson, D. R. (1994). White racial identity consciousness: A social learning analysis. *Counseling Psychologist, 22*(1), 129–146.

Sabnani, H. B., Ponterotto, J. G., & Borodovsky, L. G. (1991). White racial identity development and cross-cultural counselor training. *Counseling Psychologist, 19*(1), 76–102.

Sodowsky, G. R. (1996). The Multicultural Counseling Inventory: Psychometric properties and some uses in counseling training: A stage model. In G. R. Sodowsky & J. Impara (Eds.), *Multicultural assessment in counseling and clinical psychology* (pp. 123–154). Lincoln, NE: Buros Institute of Mental Measurements.

Sodowsky, G. R., Taffe, R. C., Gutkin, T. B., & Wise, S. L. (1994). Development of the multicultural counseling inventory: A self-report measure of multicultural competencies. *Journal of Counseling Psychology, 41*(2), 137–148.

Spiegel, J., & Papajohn, J. (1983). *Final report: Training program on ethnicity and mental health.* Waltham, MA: Florence Heller School, Brandeis University.

Steenbarger, B. (1991). All the world is not a stage: Emerging contextualist themes in counseling and development. *Journal for Counseling and Development, 70*(2), 288–299.

Sue, D., Sue, D. W., & Sue, S. (2000). *Understanding abnormal behavior* (6th ed.). Boston: Houghton Mifflin.

Sue, D. W. (1977). Barriers to effective cross-cultural counseling. *Journal of Counseling Psychology, 24,* 420–429.

Sue, D. W. (1978). Eliminating cultural oppression in counseling: Toward a general theory. *Journal of Counseling Psychology, 25,* 419–428.

Sue, D. W. (1990). Culture specific techniques in counseling: A conceptual framework. *Professional Psychology: Research and Practice, 21*(6), 424–433.

Sue, D. W. (1991a). A conceptual model for cultural diversity training. *Journal of Counseling and Development, 70*(2), 99–105.

Sue, D. W. (1991b). A diversity perspective on contextualism. *Journal of Counseling and Development, 70,* 300–301.

Sue, D. W. (1992). The challenge of multiculturalism: The road less traveled. *American Counselor, 1,* 7–14.

Sue, D. W. (1993). Confronting ourselves: The White and racial/ethnic minority researcher. *Counseling Psychologist, 21*(2), 244–249.

Sue, D. W. (2001). Multidimensional facets of cultural competence. *Counseling Psychologist, 29*(6), 790–821.

Sue, D. W., Arredondo, P., & McDavis, R. J. (1992). Multicultural counseling competencies and standards: A call to the profession. *Journal of Counseling and Development, 70*(4), 477–486.

Sue, D. W., Bernier, J. B., Durran, M., Feinberg, L., Pedersen, P., Smith, E., & Vasquez-Nuttall, E. (1982). Position paper: Cross-cultural counseling competencies. *Counseling Psychologist, 10,* 45–52.

Sue, D. W., Bingham, R., Porche-Burke, L., & Vasquez, M. (1999). The diversification of psychology: A multicultural revolution. *American Psychologist, 54*(12), 1061–1069.

Sue, D. W., Carter, R. T., Casas, J. M., Fouad, N. A., Ivey, A. E., Jensen, M., LaFromboise, T., Manese, J. E., Ponterotto, J. G., & Vasquez-Nuttall, E. (1998). *Multicultural counseling competencies: Individual and organizational development.* Thousand Oaks, CA: Sage.

Sue, D. W., Ivey, A. E., & Pedersen, P. B. (1996). *A theory of multicultural counseling and therapy.* Pacific Grove, CA: Brooks/Cole.

Sue, D. W., Parham, T. A., & Bonilla-Santiago, G. (1998). The changing face of work in the United States: Implications for individual, institutional, and societal survival. *Cultural Diversity and Mental Health, 4*(3), 153–164.

Sue, D. W., & Sue, D. (1999). *Counseling the culturally different: Theory and practice.* New York: Wiley.

Sue, S. (1999). Science, ethnicity and bias: Where have we gone wrong? *American Psychologist, 54*(12), 1070–1077.

Szapocznik, J., & Kurtines, W. M. (1993). Family psychology and cultural diversity: Opportunities for theory, research, and application. *American Psychologist, 48*(4), 400–407.

Thomas, M. B., & Dansby, P. G. (1985). Black clients: Family structures, therapeutic issues, and strengths. *Psychotherapy, 22,* 398–407.

U.S. Bureau of the Bureau. (2001). *Statistical abstract of the United States: 2001.* Washington, DC: U.S. Government Printing Office.

Vinson, T. S., & Neimeyer, G. J. (2000). The relationship between racial identity development and multicultural counseling competency. *Journal of Multicultural Counseling and Development, 28,* 177–192.

Weinrach, S. G. (1986). Ellis and Gloria: Positive or negative model? *Psychotherapy, 23,* 642–647.

41

THE EFFECTS OF SCHOOL DESEGREGATION

Jomills Henry Braddock II
University of Miami

Tamela McNulty Eitle
University of Miami

Early advocates expected that school integration would bring about equitable access for African American students to the resources, experiences, and connections that facilitate full and equal participation in mainstream American society. However, as Wells (2002) recently pointed out, much of the social science research subsequent to *Brown* v. *Board of Education* has not matched the rationale of the plaintiffs in seeking or the Supreme Court in granting that historic 1954 decision. Specifically, in *Brown,* and especially in the higher education cases (*Sweatt* v. *Painter* and *McLauren* v. *Oklahoma State Regents for Higher Education*) that preceded *Brown,* emphasis was on the negative effects on African American students of not only the resource inequalities experienced by segregated African American schools, but also because of their status in society and the social networks of faculty and students within them (Wells, 2002). Unfortunately, early social science research on school desegregation was not grounded in the same set of understandings that guided the plaintiffs and the Court.

Research examining the effects of school desegregation can be distinguished by studies that focus on short-term effects—what happens to students while they are still in school as a result of intergroup contact (Bankston & Caldas, 1998; Coleman et al. 1966; Crain & Mahard 1978a; Mickelson, 2001; Pride & Woodard, 1985)—and studies that focus on long-term effects—what happens to students as they move into adulthood as a result of their intergroup experiences in elementary and secondary schools (Braddock, 1980; Braddock & McPartland 1980, 1989b; McPartland & Braddock, 1981).

The earliest and most voluminous body of school desegregation research addressed short-term outcomes for students, that is, achievement, attitudes, and aspirations (for reviews of these studies see Cook, 1984a, 1984b; Mahard & Crain, 1983; St. John, 1975; Schofield, 2001; Wells, 1995). In contrast, more recent studies have focused increasingly on long-term benefits, that is, improved life chances and lifestyles (for reviews of this research, see Braddock, 1985; Braddock, Crain, & McPartland, 1984; Braddock & Dawkins, 1984; Braddock & McPartland, 1988; Dawkins & Braddock, 1994; Schofield, 2001; Wells, 1995, 2002; Wells & Crain, 1994).

Attention to long-term effects expands our understanding of school desegregation. However, in examining long-term effects, both researchers and reviewers have juxtaposed studies focusing on the short- and long-term effects of school desegregation such that their logical and empirical connection has been obscured. Thus, we have learned that school desegregation affects academic achievement and psychosocial outcomes for elementary and secondary students (Hallinan, 1998; Hallinan & Teixeria, 1987; Mickelson, 2001; Schofield & Sagar, 1983). And we have learned that future educational and career attainments of African Americans and to some extent Hispanic students are affected as well by school desegregation (Braddock, 1980; Braddock, Dawkins, & Trent 1994; Crain, 1970). What has not been adequately addressed, however, is how the long-term outcomes of school desegregation may be affected by the short-term outcomes, or how the short-term outcomes may themselves

We thank Amy Stuart Wells, Willis Hawley, and James A. Banks for their thoughtful comments and suggestions on earlier drafts of this chapter.

be interrelated. Just as important, as a result of a dearth of research on White and Latino students, we have very limited comparative evidence regarding short- and especially long-term outcomes of school desegregation. The lack of comparable studies of White students is striking in the light of the fact that the Appendix to the Appellant's Briefs, prepared by social scientists for *Brown* v. *Board of Education,* also cited harms of segregation to Whites as well as to African Americans (Clark, 1988).

This chapter summarizes the empirical evidence and describes a conceptual framework that links the research literature on the short-term and long-term effects of school desegregation. Many of the studies reviewed focus on African American students; however, evidence pertaining to White and Latino students is included where available. Specifically, we examine research on short-term achievement, socialization and intergroup relations' outcomes, and long-term social inclusion and social mobility outcomes of school desegregation. Building on previous reviews (see Braddock, 1985; Braddock & McPartland, 1988; Braddock et al., 1984; Braddock & Dawkins, 1984; McPartland, 1978; Wells & Crain, 1994; Wells, 1995, 2002; Schofield, 2001) and the conceptual framework of Dawkins and Braddock (1994), this chapter suggests that short-term effects of school desegregation can operate as important mediators of long-term outcomes.

We argue that elementary and secondary school desegregation experiences may affect students' interracial attitudes, aspirations, self-esteem, and locus of control, as well as their standardized tests, grades, and class rank. These socialization experiences and academic credentials in turn may affect students' postsecondary attainments and experiences, along with their access to networks and affiliations. Finally, both higher postsecondary attainments and social networks and affiliations directly affect adult career outcomes, including income, job status, and diversity. More specifically, the effects of elementary and secondary desegregated school experiences on long-term outcomes are mediated through their effects on key intervening short-term outcomes. And while short-term outcomes such as locus of control and academic achievement are interrelated, if not interdependent, the focus of this review is on their independent connections to critical long-term schooling outcomes, including educational and career success. A model outlining these relationships is presented later in the chapter.

SHORT-TERM ACADEMIC ACHIEVEMENT EFFECTS

Much of the early research on school desegregation focused on whether African American and White students' achievement test scores rise or fall following desegregation. Unfortunately, early research in this area was often guided by cultural deficit theories, which assumed that mere exposure to White classmates would create the possibility for lateral transmission of values that might in turn raise African American achievement. As such, these early studies of achievement lacked any theoretical basis linked to the rationale for *Brown,* such as examining access to learning opportunities (Epstein, 1985; Oakes, 1990) or other mediating mechanisms (for example, high teacher expectations, positive school climate) that are related to academic success (Ferguson, 1998; Rist, 1970, 1978; Slavin 1995; Schofield, 1995). Unfortunately, this remains true for many recent studies as well (Mickelson, 2001, represents a notable exception). This is especially ironic given that even in the 1950s, the social scientists who wrote the famous social science statement (Clark, "Effects of Segregation," 1953) that led to the *Brown* decision understood that school desegregation had to be accompanied by changes in school organization and practice (Clark, 1954; Cook, 1979).

Extensive research and careful and increasingly sophisticated reviews show that the academic performances of Whites and African Americans are not harmed in desegregated schools and that African Americans typically show achievement gains, especially in reading, as a result of school desegregation (Crain & Mahard, 1978a, 1978b, 1981; Prager & Seeman, 1986). Although the magnitude of African American student gains has been subject to debate among experts, virtually all of the research results are in a positive direction, whether they are drawn from case studies of schools and school districts or from comparative studies across large numbers of schools or school systems (Hawley & Rosenholtz, 1986).

Crain and Mahard's (1981) comprehensive review of research published through 1980 examined a large number of case studies, input-output analyses, and longitudinal correlations. Although they found mixed evidence, they concluded that overall, desegregation is associated with modest gains in the academic achievement of African Americans, particularly when students initially attend desegregated schools in the early grades. Like Schofield (2001) more recently, Crain and Mahard found virtually no evidence that the achievement of Whites was affected one way or another by desegregation. Mahard and Crain's (1980) review of the limited evidence on the effects of desegregation on the academic performance of Hispanics concluded that desegregation enhanced their achievement.

In 1982, the U.S. Department of Education commissioned seven politically diverse researchers representing different disciplines to examine a subset of 19 of the existing studies. The consensus among these researchers was that desegregation had a small, positive effect on the African American students' reading achievement but no consistent effects on math achievement (Cook, 1984b). Crain's (1984a) comprehensive syntheses of case studies, which included 93 inquiries and employed rigorous and sophisticated statistical techniques, concluded that the school desegregation effect is significant. Of 20 studies comparing the academic achievement of African Americans who had experienced desegregation since kindergarten or first grade to the achievement of African Americans who had never experienced desegregation, 16 showed significantly positive effects of desegregation, and only 2 showed negative effects. Of those 20 studies that used randomized experiments, all showed relatively large gains related to desegregation (Crain, 1984a).

Unfortunately, research on the academic consequences of desegregation has been limited since the early 1980s because of sparse government and foundation funding. Pride and Woodward (1985) and Carsrud (1984) found evidence that African American achievement was enhanced by desegregation. Arias (1989) found that the achievement of African Americans and Hispanics was enhanced by desegregation in San Jose, California, but only if desegregation raised the overall socioeconomic status (SES) of the student body. Two studies that examined the busing of African American children from Hartford, Connecticut, to desegregated schools in the suburbs (Bennett & Easton, 1988; Gable & Iwanicki, 1986) found little effect of desegregation on the student test scores.

Mayer and Jencks's (1989) comprehensive review of research dealing with racially and socioeconomically mixed schools and neighborhoods concluded that (1) the first year of attending a desegregated school usually has a small positive effect on the reading, but not the math, achievement of African American elementary students; (2) twelve years in a predominantly White northern school probably has a substantial effect on African American students' academic achievement; and (3) the effects on African American students of attending desegregated schools in the South and the effects of desegregation on White students in the North and South are uncertain.

Since the mid-1990s, several district-, state-, and national-level studies have offered generally consistent results indicating that students who attend racially diverse schools achieve at higher levels than similar students attending schools that are predominantly one race. For example, at the district level, Mickelson's (2001) unique comprehensive study of school segregation and student achievement in Charlotte-Mecklenburg, North Carolina, found that the proportion of elementary education spent in racially identifiable African American schools had direct negative effects on end-of-course test scores and high school track placement, holding constant students' sixth-grade test scores and other variables associated with achievement. In addition to these direct effects, segregation in elementary school also has indirect effects through sixth-grade standardized test scores and high school track placement on later academic outcomes like Scholastic Aptitude Test (SAT) scores and high school grade point average (GPA; Mickelson, 2001). This pattern was observed for both African American and White students, but since African American students are more likely than Whites to be found in racially identifiable African American elementary schools, they suffer the disproportionate harm of this form of racial isolation.

In a different type of study, Ludwig, Ladd, and Duncan (2001) examined Baltimore data from the Department of Housing and Urban Development's Moving to Opportunity (MTO) housing mobility experiment and found that despite some evidence of increased problem behavior among teens in the treatment groups, moving low-income families from high- to low-poverty neighborhoods increased the achievement test scores of African American children in elementary schools. Studies of the Gautreaux program in Chicago, which relocated African American public housing residents into different parts of the metropolitan area, also found that compared with those who moved to other parts of the city, suburban movers had lower dropout rates and higher rates of college attendance (Rosenbaum, 1995). Similarly, in his analysis of the link between neighborhood racial composition and school desegregation in New Castle County, Delaware, Darden (1985) found that student gains in California Achievement Test (CAT) scores were related to neighborhood racial diversity.

Bankston and Caldas's (1996) analysis of statewide data from Louisiana concluded that holding constant family-, individual-, and school-level influences on achievement, both African American and White students scored lower in schools with high concentrations of minority students and that African American students' achievement increased as the proportion of their schoolmates who were White increased. In a subsequent analysis of these data, Bankston and Caldas (1998) concluded that the high proportion of African American students who lived in poor, one-parent families explained poor achievement in predominantly African American schools.

Other recent state-level analyses of minority concentration and standardized achievement test performance in Texas also found that a higher percentage of African American schoolmates had a strong adverse effect on African American achievement, and these effects were concentrated in the upper half of the ability distribution. In contrast, racial composition had a smaller effect on achievement among Whites, Latinos, and lower-performing African Americans (Hanushek, Kain, & Rivkin, 2001). Hoxby's (2002) analysis of Texas data found that African American, Latino, and White third graders all tended to perform worse in reading and math when they were in classes that had a larger share of African American students. In assessing the "power of peers," Hoxby noted that peer effects operated most strongly within racial and ethnic groups, and having more African American peers appeared to be most damaging to other African American students. Analyzing data from Texas metropolitan areas, Kain and O'Brien (2000) found that school quality—as measured by mean test scores for individual campuses and grades—had a significant effect on the performance of individual students from all racial and ethnic groups; however, this effect was more substantial for African American students. They estimated that a substantial portion of the racial gap in achievement test scores could be eliminated by providing African American students increased access to suburban quality schools. Grissmer, Flanagan, and Williamson (1998) examined changes in state test scores on the National Assessment of Educational Progress (NAEP) and attributed significant increases in the academic achievement of African American students in some states and not others to desegregation.

At the national level, Schiff, Firestone, and Young (1999) examined students' NAEP scores in math and reading and found that both African American and White students who attended desegregated schools where Whites were in the majority outperformed students who attended predominantly African American or predominantly White schools. Also at the national level, Brown (1999) examined data from the National Educational Longitudinal Study and concluded that schools with the highest academic achievement overall, and with the smallest gap between students of different races and ethnicities, were between 61% and 90% White or Asian American and between 10% and 39% African American and Hispanic. The last two studies cited here are unique in their focus on the effects on students of all races and ethnicities of attending schools that were virtually all White.

The results of desegregation-achievement studies are difficult to summarize. Studies employ widely varying methods, lack of consistent definitions of "desegregation" variables, and they are based on different theories—if they have a theoretical base. Moreover, as Schofield (2001) points out, other problems also complicate drawing definitive conclusions. Most studies occurred in the first years of program implementation. Almost all studies focused on the effects of desegregation on only African Americans and Whites. And little attention was given to the school and district context (e.g., were students resegregated within schools?). Nevertheless, research on the effects of desegregation on student academic achievement, measured by standardized tests, seems to support the proposition that African American and Hispanic students learn somewhat more in schools that are majority White as compared to their academic performance in schools that are predominantly non-White.

This general conclusion regarding the achievement benefits of school desegregation is further supported by indirect evidence showing that during the 1980s, for example, improved test performance among African Americans accounted for roughly 40% of overall gains in SAT scores (Wainer, 1986). And although improvement in African American student test scores occurred nationwide, as then president of the Educational Testing Service (ETS) Gregory Anrig noted, the most significant gains were achieved in the South, where school desegregation probably had its greatest impact (Anrig, 1985).

SHORT-TERM SOCIALIZATION AND INTERGROUP RELATIONS OUTCOMES

Clearly, closing the test score achievement gap is an important goal, and the research suggests that school desegregation has had an important impact in this regard. Nevertheless, developing academic skills is only one of many functions of public education. Schools also socialize youth for responsible adult social roles, and it is in this realm that the effects of school desegregation have been most impressive. Especially at the elementary and secondary levels, schools play an important role as socializing institutions in transmitting society's culture and values to its young as well as preparing them with appropriate knowledge and skills for leading productive and fulfilling adult lives.

For nearly 50 years, the contact hypothesis has been a principal formulation in the study of intergroup relations (see Chapter 37, this volume). In addressing the primary question raised by this hypothesis (whether contact improves intergroup relations), the cumulative evidence from decades of research in different settings supports assumptions posited by Allport (1954) and others regarding factors necessary for contact to improve intergroup relations. These factors include: (1) equal status contact between individuals from majority and minority groups in pursuit of common goals, (2) contact that is sanctioned by institutional supports (authority figures), and (3) the opportunity for minority- and majority-group members to interact as individuals.

Several studies of the contact hypothesis focused on schools as the setting for studying intergroup contact (Aronson & Patnoe 1997; Slavin, 1979). These studies underscore the importance of cooperation in intergroup contact. The most important way through which young people learn the dispositions and skills that result in positive intergroup relations is intergroup interaction. Sociologists, social psychologists, and educational psychologists have focused for many years on proximity as an important correlate of interracial perceptions, attitudes, and behaviors. Pettigrew and Troop's (2000) recent comprehensive meta-analytic review of more than 200 empirical studies provides strong support of the contact hypothesis. Among several important theoretical implications of this body of research, the authors noted that face-to-face contact is significantly related to reduced prejudice, prejudice reduction resulting from intergroup contact is generalizable across different situations, and intergroup contact affects a broad range of outcomes (Pettigrew & Troop, 2000). Patchen (1982), for example, suggested that the racial composition of the classroom is more important than the racial composition of the school as a whole in influencing cross-racial interaction. Therefore, to fully understand the benefits and outcomes of racially diverse schools, especially outcomes related to intergroup interaction, it is critically important to understand students' experiences in the classroom and other school environments (Metz, 1978; Schofield, 1989; Schofield & Sagar, 1977, 1983; Wells & Crain, 1996).

Research on intergroup contact between children of different racial and ethnic backgrounds in desegregated schools has produced mixed results. Some early reviews of the literature indicated that the majority of studies on interracial contact in desegregated schools showed few positive effects on intergroup relations (Armor, 1972; St. John, 1975; Stephan, 1978). However, more recent studies of the impact of desegregated classrooms have shown that children exposed to racially diverse peers in the classroom exhibited reduced adherence to racial stereotypes (Hallinan & Teixeria, 1987; Schofield, 2001; Sonleitner & Wood, 1996) and reduced racial prejudice (Hallinan, 1998; Schofield & Sagar, 1983; Sonleitner & Wood, 1996).

Although the impact and outcomes of classroom desegregation have not been extensively examined, several studies provide indications about what it may mean. Schofield and Sagar (1977) provided a particularly striking example of voluntary cross-race peer interaction. They studied student interaction in a prestigious middle school in which seventh-grade classes were racially mixed, but eighth-grade classes were more homogeneous due to tracking based on standardized test scores (one eighth-grade class group was composed of 80% White students, and another class group was composed of predominantly African American students). Through a five-month observation of voluntary peer interactions in the school cafeteria, the researchers found that the number of seventh graders who sat next to or across from students of another race tripled, while the number of eighth graders who sat next to or across from students of another race declined. They concluded that the daily exposure in the classroom to students of a different race was directly related to students' willingness to engage in voluntary interactions with peers of a different race.

There is also some indication that the effects of desegregated classrooms on intergroup relations may be long term. For example, Sonleitner and Wood (1996) studied 292 White adults who were children when desegregation

plans were implemented in Oklahoma school districts and found that past interracial contact had significant negative association with both anti-Black prejudice and adherence to stereotypes. Other evidence indicates that students from racially diverse school environments develop an increased likelihood of supporting continued and widespread desegregation initiatives (Sigelman, Bledso, Welch, & Combs 1996).

Desegregated classroom environments can also promote a range of positive cross-race attitudes and interactions. These include development of tolerance, understanding, and positive attitudes toward different racial and ethnic groups, increased voluntary cross-race peer interactions, and interracial friendliness (Hallinan & Teixeria, 1987; Hallinan & Williams, 1989; Schofield, 1989; Kurlaender, 2001). Friendliness implies an even deeper level of engagement than voluntary cross-race interaction, and numerous researchers have found that racially desegregated classroom environments can also have a positive impact on interracial friendliness. These findings generally fall into two groups: those relating to generally friendly interracial contact (Hallinan & Smith, 1985; Hallinan & Teixeria, 1987; Patchen, 1982) and cross-race best friendships (Hallinan & Smith, 1985). In studying African American and White cross-race best friendships, Hallinan and Smith (1985) found that students of one racial group were friendlier toward students of another racial group as the proportion of the racial group increased. They conclude that racially balanced classrooms maximize the interracial friendliness of both African Americans and Whites.

LONG-TERM EFFECTS ON SOCIAL INTEGRATION AND MINORITY CAREER SUCCESS

Social science research on long-term adult outcomes establishes a broader rationale for school desegregation policies. Instead of focusing only on how desegregation may benefit individuals by increasing student test scores or changing attitudes, this research considers how desegregation contributes to the structure of opportunities in adult life. These studies find that racial isolation in present-day American education is delaying progress on the problem of race inequalities in adult career success and perpetuating adult segregation in communities and in mainstream social institutions.

Questions concerning the long-term effects of school desegregation have been less extensively examined by social scientists and for a much shorter period of time. The focal concern of the long-term studies has been whether school desegregation, independent of social class and academic credentials, enhances status attainment outcomes for African Americans and Hispanics and whether, for all students, school desegregation contributes to more pluralistic and diverse adult social relationships and experiences in educational, housing, and workplace settings. This more comprehensive focus in school desegregation research assumes that a genuinely meaningful assessment of desegregation as a national social policy must consider its impact on the full range of outcomes (long term as well as immediate) of elementary and secondary schooling in the United States.

Perpetuation of Segregation from Elementary and Secondary School to College

One of the most important and compelling aspects of racial segregation is the tendency for it to become self-perpetuating. There has been an accumulation of strong and consistent research evidence that both majority and minority individuals whose childhood experiences, in schools and neighborhoods, take place in largely segregated environments are likely to also lead their adult lives in largely segregated settings (Braddock et al., 1994; Crain, 1970; U.S. Commission on Civil Rights, 1967). The earliest empirical documentation of the perpetuation of segregation showed that African Americans who attended desegregated schools were more likely to function in desegregated environments in later life (Crain, 1970; Crain & Weisman, 1972). As adults, they were more frequently found to live in desegregated neighborhoods, to have children who attended desegregated schools, and to have close friends of the other race than did adults of both races who had attended segregated schools (Crain, 1970; Crain & Weisman, 1972). This research broke new ground in studying the long-term effects of school desegregation and in theorizing about important intervening causal mechanisms that may break down barriers to integration-assimilation.

Several subsequent investigations of the long-term effects of school desegregation have produced additional evidence that both minority and majority segregation tends to be perpetuated over stages of the life cycle and across institutional settings (Braddock, 1980, 1986; Braddock & McPartland, 1980, 1987, 1989b; Braddock, McPartland, & Trent, 1984; Green, 1982a, 1982b; McPartland & Braddock, 1981; McPartland & Crain, 1980; Braddock, Dawkins, & Trent, 1994). Much of this evidence is based on analyses of longitudinal studies that permit meaningful assessments of educational and early career attainments. Furthermore, the analyses in the later studies typically use national longitudinal data, and findings from these data have, to a large extent, ruled out one key alternative explanation that the results hold only for a certain subset of students, for example, those students especially sensitive to the effects of desegregation or those who were desegregated in some particular way.

School Segregation and Postsecondary Outcomes

Results suggest that early desegregation is related to the type of postsecondary education that African Americans receive. Three studies provide evidence on the effects of elementary and secondary school desegregation on African American attendance at predominantly White colleges and universities (Braddock, 1980, 1986; Braddock & McPartland, 1980). These studies concluded that African Americans who have been educated in desegregated elementary and secondary schools are more likely to attend predominantly White colleges.

Braddock (1980) analyzed survey data obtained in 1972 from 253 African American students attending two predominantly African American and two predominantly White colleges (matched on Standard Metropolitan Statistical Area location and public versus private control) in a single southern state. The results revealed a strong positive association between high school and college desegregation, after controlling for academic credentials, social class, and college inducements such as offers of financial aid. This study, however, was geographically restricted and excluded two-year colleges.

More compelling evidence that earlier school desegregation affects attendance at predominantly White colleges was provided by a national study that included statistical controls for the students' region, social class background, college admissions credentials (high school grades and test scores), and residential proximity to alternative colleges (Braddock & McPartland, 1982). Using National Longitudinal Survey data from over 3,000 Black 1972 high school graduates, this study found both direct and indirect effects of earlier school desegregation on attendance at predominantly White colleges. This relationship was strongest for those African American students who had also attended desegregated elementary schools. In addition, it was found that among African American students who were enrolled in desegregated colleges, those who had also attended desegregated elementary and high schools, controlling for differences in social class and ability, were more likely to continue in college and fare better academically than those students who had attended segregated schools (Braddock & McPartland, 1982).

Using data from the African American sample from the High School and Beyond survey, Braddock (1986) confirmed earlier findings of the effect of attendance at desegregated high schools on subsequent attendance at predominantly White colleges. Braddock (1986) also found that in predominantly White two-year colleges, African Americans who had attended desegregated schools were more likely to major in the higher-paying technical or scientific fields than were graduates of segregated high schools. These results are consistent with earlier studies suggesting that high school racial composition has an impact on African Americans' aspirations to enter career fields where they have traditionally been underrepresented (Dawkins, 1983).

School Segregation and Adult Labor Market Outcomes

Social scientists have noted that the racial employment and income gap is not solely due to differences in the level of education attained by African Americans relative to Whites (especially in the light of the dramatic closing of the gap in years of school completed). African Americans and Whites who earn similar amounts of education continue to show substantial differences in earned income and employment rates. A key reason for these persisting disparities lies in the types of occupations in which African Americans are employed and the way in which employers fill and workers seek jobs.

Desegregation can affect the occupational attainments of African Americans and other students of color in two ways. First, school desegregation is positively related to the jobs and occupations to which African Americans aspire and have access. And second, school desegregation positively affects the resources that African Americans have available to seek a job. Thus, desegregation in education directly affects not only the type of job obtained, but also whether any job is obtained. Specifically, desegregation can increase the pool of contacts and informants from whom African Americans can obtain information about available jobs. Such informational networks are highly important not only for providing specific job information and referrals, but also for providing information about job-seeking strategies. In addition, desegregated education may provide credentials that are more likely to be accepted at face value by White employers.

Research indicates that school racial composition contributes to (1) the development and persistence of plans by African American students to enter professional and nontraditional occupations where they are underrepresented (Braddock, 1986; Crain, 1970; Dawkins, 1983); (2) employer preferences for hiring African Americans from desegregated schools over African Americans (similarly qualified) from segregated schools (Braddock, Crain, McPartland, & Dawkins, 1986; Crain, 1984b); and (3) being employed in ethnically diverse work environments (Green, 1982a, 1982b; Braddock et al., 1984, 1994; Braddock & McPartland, 1989b).

Green (1982a, 1982b) analyzed follow-up data collected in 1980 by the American Council on Education from a national sample of African Americans who had been freshmen in 1971. He found that high school racial composition was positively associated with the racial composition of adult coworker and informal friendship groups. Braddock and McPartland (1989b) used data from the National Longitudinal Survey's Youth Cohort

(NLS-YC) to study the effects of high school racial composition on employment segregation. They found that for African Americans in the North, high school racial composition was the strongest predictor of coworker racial composition. However, in the South, they found community racial composition to be the major predictor of coworker racial composition. They suggest that the strong association between community and school desegregation in the South makes it difficult to disentangle the unique and joint effects of school and community desegregation.

Braddock et al. (1984) used data from the African American and White subsamples of the National Longitudinal Study of 1972 (NLS-72) merged with survey data from their subjects' 1976 and 1979 employers. They found that both African Americans and Whites from desegregated schools were more likely to work in racially diverse firms than were their counterparts from segregated all–African American and all-White schools. This finding was replicated by Braddock et al. (1994) using data from three national surveys: the 1979–1980 National Survey of Black Americans (NSBA), a 1987 follow-up of the NLS-YC, and a national survey of the 1976 and 1979 employers of NLS-72 participants. They found that White, African American, and Hispanic graduates of desegregated schools were more likely than their ethnic peers from segregated all–African American, all-White, or all-Hispanic high schools to be employed in ethnically diverse firms or coworker groups. Crain (1984b) examined employment decisions in a national survey of more than 4,000 employers of NLS-72 respondents and found that employers gave preference in hiring decisions to African American graduates of desegregated high schools.

CONNECTING RESEARCH ON THE SHORT-TERM AND LONG-TERM EFFECTS OF SCHOOL DESEGREGATION

When school desegregation is viewed in the context of the long-term functions of education, it is important to examine whether it promotes the social integration of Whites and African Americans and leads to African Americans' full and equal participation in the social, economic, and political life of the society. Thus, assessments of school desegregation effects, like other assessments of school effects, should examine life consequences such as career attainments and adult social roles as well as immediate student outcomes such as achievement, aspirations, and personality development (Levin, 1975; McPartland, Epstein, Karweit, & Slavin, 1976).

Taken together, impressive evidence suggests that segregation is perpetuated from elementary and secondary schools to college and the workplace. Earlier desegregated schooling breaks this self-perpetuating cycle by making

African American attendance at predominantly White colleges and being employed in interracial employment settings more likely. The studies described above estimate the association between the extent of desegregation experienced in one institution earlier in life and the extent of desegregation experienced in another institution later in life. The results imply that earlier desegregation in schools foreshadows later desegregation in adult life. Whites who have desegregated school experiences with either African American or Hispanic students are more likely to have African American or Hispanic coworkers. African American and Hispanic students who have attended desegregated schools are more likely to have White coworkers.

There are several possible causal explanations for the consistent association found for African Americans and Whites between the racial composition of their social environments early and later in life. One explanation involves social psychological processes—social inertia and avoidance learning. A second explanation involves structural mechanisms—social networks. A third involves the racial demography of local areas that could produce the observed linkages without any social psychological processes operating.

The racial demography explanation is based on the possibility that the observed associations with desegregation are spuriously created by a common ecological factor that has nothing to do with any structural or individual socialization process. For example, localities with different racial population mixes will produce different random chances of interracial contact (e.g., African Americans in mostly White communities have a greater random chance of encountering Whites than do African Americans in mostly African American communities, and vice versa). Aside from the community differences in random probabilities for cross-race contact, there is evidence that local communities differ in political and structural factors that influence institutional desegregation (see, for example, Pearce, 1980). Such community ecological factors could also produce the observed associations without any individual socialization processes at work.

Most of the studies reviewed above address the possibility that observed associations between different measures of desegregation are a spurious consequence of demographic features of different communities by including statistical controls on the racial composition of the community before estimating the linkage between desegregation across institutions or across stages of the life cycle. Thus, they strengthen the argument that social psychological processes (e.g., attitudes) *and* social structural factors (e.g., social networks) produce and reinforce desegregation across institutional settings and stages of the life cycle.

Social psychological processes are based on changes in the behavioral orientations or attitudes of individuals resulting from their exposure to intergroup contact. For example, among African Americans, aversive behavioral orientations to seeking or sustaining memberships in desegregated groups would be greater for those individuals who have expectations of hostile reactions from Whites, have less confidence that they can function successfully in an interracial situation, or have greater difficulty dealing with the strains that may accompany interpersonal contacts across racial lines. If earlier experiences by African Americans in desegregated settings generally reduce or eliminate these social psychological barriers—by creating clearer and more accurate expectation of White reactions, building confidence in one's ability to succeed in racially mixed environments, or providing practice with dealing with the strains of cross-race contact—then one would expect less avoidance or withdrawal from desegregated experiences in later life.

Similarly, social psychological barriers to interracial contact among White adults may be broken down by early experiences in cross-race situations. If cross-racial contacts in desegregated schools serve to reduce White students' negative racial stereotypes and fears of hostility in interracial situations, then some foundations would have been laid to weaken White resistance toward interracial contacts when these White students become adults. Scott and McPartland's (1982) tabulations of racial attitude questions from national surveys of African American and White students do suggest that there is an average positive effect of school desegregation on both African Americans' and Whites' orientations toward future interracial situations. In addition, more recent analyses from in-home interviews with 1,124 African American and White adult residents of the Detroit metropolitan area show that for both groups, early school desegregation experiences are positively related to casual interracial contacts and to close interracial friendships (Sigelman et al., 1996).

Sociologists have called attention to several structural and institutional processes linked to segregation that support the inference that elementary and secondary school as well as college desegregation can have positive long-term social and economic consequences for African American, and possibly Latino, students. These intervening processes include (1) access to effective social networks of job information, contacts, and sponsorship; (2) exposure and socialization experiences that may broaden students' aspirations for entry into nontraditional major-fields and career lines offering higher income returns; (3) development of interpersonal skills and comfort level in interracial settings; (4) reduced social inertia—increased tolerance of and willingness to participate in desegregated environments; (5) opportunities to earn credentials that are valued by White employers or admissions officers; and (6) avoidance of negative attributions that are often associated with "African American" institutions (see Banks, 1984; Braddock, 1980; Braddock & Dawkins, 1984; Braddock & McPartland, 1982; Crain, 1970; Crain & Weisman, 1972; McPartland & Crain, 1980; Wells, 1995; Wells & Crain, 1994).

These processes are difficult to measure and investigate directly, and there exists no comprehensive data set with appropriate indicators to allow comprehensive and simultaneous examination of each set of processes. Moreover, even if a single longitudinal data set with appropriate measures were available, many of the intervening processes are likely to be so strongly intercorrelated that problems of multicolinearity would present a challenge to single-model analyses. Some of these connections have been made in a piecemeal fashion. For example, the national longitudinal High School & Beyond data have provided in disparate studies consistent evidence on key short-term and long-term outcomes. These data, for example, were used in the Hallinan and Williams (1989) study that found a significant link between propinquity in classrooms and students' interracial friendship patterns and several studies linking segregation in elementary and secondary schools to adult postsecondary and workplace segregation (Braddock, 1986; Braddock et al., 1984, 1994). Nevertheless, the intervening processes clearly identify factors that may produce aggregate differences in adult educational and career success of students of color, as well as in enhanced interracial contact for adults of all racial and ethnic backgrounds with earlier experiences in desegregated schools.

Both theory and research suggest that the learning, socialization, and social networking experiences associated with school desegregation can have a major impact on adult outcomes, including social mobility and social integration. Consequently, the consistently observed positive association between elementary and secondary school desegregation and a diverse array of long-term outcomes might best be understood by examining the varied mediating channels through which interracial contact in schools can affect such outcomes. Dawkins and Braddock (1994) identify elements of a conceptual framework that specifies several key mediating causal connections between elementary and secondary school desegregation and adult career success. Figure 41.1 provides a heuristic model of the potential relations between this set of factors and is an adaptation of the earlier framework.

The model posits that elementary and secondary school desegregation experiences may affect two broad categories of short-term student outcomes: socialization and personal development outcomes (interracial attitudes, aspirations, self-esteem, locus of control) and academic credentials (standardized tests, grades, class rank). Both socialization and personal development experiences and academic credentials influence postsecondary attainment (matriculation, desegregation, major field) and systemic

or structural barriers to racial equity (social networks, negative employer or college admissions attributions). Finally, both higher postsecondary attainments and systemic barriers directly affect adult career outcomes (income, job status, and ethnic diversity). Put differently, the effects of elementary and secondary desegregated school experiences on long-term outcomes are mediated through their effects on key intervening short-term outcomes.

Desegregation, Academic Credentials, and Social Mobility Outcomes

Researchers examining the impact of school desegregation on student achievement have typically focused attention on standardized test scores. In seeking explanations for the narrowing earnings gap between African Americans and Whites, some economists have speculated that this income convergence may be a consequence of increasing proportions of African Americans who graduate from majority-White schools and especially colleges (Smith & Welch, 1977). Based on the human capital perspective, this view assumes that African American graduates of predominantly White schools and colleges receive a better education—assumed to be reflected in average test score differences between majority African American and majority White schools. Thus, White employers attribute enhanced productivity functions to African American graduates of desegregated (majority White) schools that are later reflected in higher earnings and job status.

Thus, the economic perspective rests on the assumption that employers attribute higher-quality ratings to majority-White schools and colleges than to majority–African American schools and colleges. This has implications for our model connecting long- and short-term effects of school desegregation. On the one hand, as noted earlier, evidence indicates that there is some tangible standardized achievement benefits that accrue to African Americans enrolled in desegregated schools (Bankston & Caldas, 1996; Crain & Mahard, 1981; Mickelson, 2001). Although research suggests that such benefits may be modest, they do exist, and they can have direct consequences with regard to the human capital or academic credentials that college-bound African American high school graduates bring to the postsecondary application and admissions process and non-college-bound African American high school graduates bring to the labor market. Enhanced academic credentials or human capital should result in greater access to college and employment opportunities. On the other hand, otherwise qualified African Americans may often not be selected in the admissions or hiring process due to statistical discrimination. Many employers do not invest heavily in obtaining extensive information about job applicants

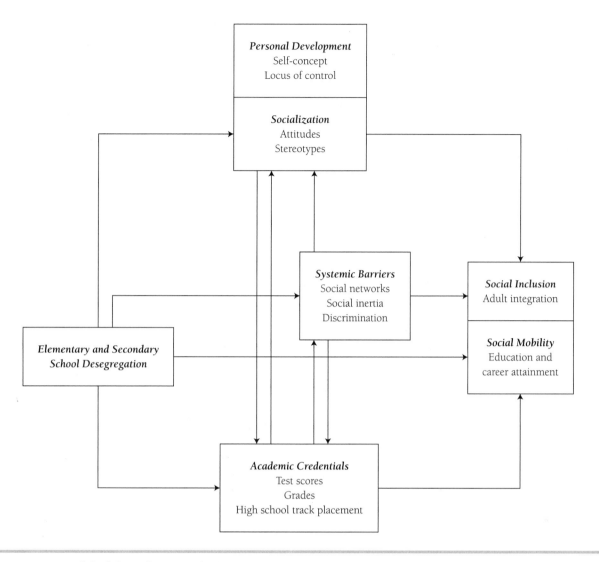

Figure 41.1. A Model of the Influences of School Desegregation on African Americans.

(especially for jobs requiring less than college), and as a result they may rely on group identifiers, such as sex or race, in their hiring decisions. For example, statistical discrimination can occur when such an employer selects a White applicant over a similarly qualified African American applicant based on a belief in average group differences in SAT scores (Bielby & Baron, 1986; Braddock et al. 1986; Thurow, 1975).

The sociological perspective also suggests there may be related indirect processes associated with systemic barriers to equality of opportunity operating here as well. In this regard, the model suggests that African American students attending majority–African American institutions may lack extensive social networks with connections to rewarding career opportunities, or they may confront negative attributions and stigma associated with the racial composition of their school independent of their achieved

personal academic credentials. While the networking hypothesis has not been extensively examined, Braddock and McPartland (1989a) presented evidence that the earnings advantage of African American graduates of predominantly White colleges is related to the use of social networks in the job-seeking process. With regard to statistical discrimination at the institutional level, a national survey-experiment provides evidence that when employers make hiring decisions for jobs requiring a high school education, they exhibit a significant preference for African American males from suburban (desegregated) schools over African American males from inner-city (segregated) schools (Braddock et al., 1986; Crain, 1984b). In the national survey-experiment, Braddock et al. (1986) found that White personnel officers tend to assign African American male high school graduates to significantly lower-paying (approximately $1,000 less in annual mean income) positions than those assigned to White male high school graduates. However, among the same White hiring officials, other things being equal, African American male graduates of suburban schools are assigned jobs averaging nearly six and one-half percentage points higher in prestige than those of African American male graduates of inner-city schools. This study demonstrates potential indirect systemic barriers through which African American male students attending majority–African American institutions may pay a cost associated with the racial composition of their school independent of their tangible human capital or any achieved personal academic credentials.

It is helpful to consider the early desegregation to postsecondary and beyond outcomes in stages. Consider again the connection between elementary and secondary school desegregation and achievement test performance of African Americans. This generally positive association suggests the potential accrual of human capital or academic credentials that might, in the higher education pipeline, favor African American graduates of desegregated elementary and secondary school over graduates of majority–African American elementary and secondary schools. While evidence in this area is both limited and mixed, Crain (1970) found that African Americans who attended desegregated schools are more likely to have finished high school and to attend and finish college. Crain and Mahard (1978b) reported similar results but found that high school desegregation had positive effects on college enrollment and persistence in the North but negative results on the same outcomes in the South.

Further analyses revealed that when the negative effects of grading practices and faculty racial composition are taken into account, the remaining net effect of desegregated schools on college enrollment and persistence is no longer negative in the South and is more strongly positive in the North. Put differently, the effect of desegregated schools on college enrollment and persistence may have been suppressed by two key factors: (1) African American students' relatively lower grades in desegregated high schools (despite higher standardized test scores compared to African Americans in segregated high schools) and (2) higher proportions of White teachers in desegregated schools who may be less likely to encourage African American students to attend college or to attend colleges where they are likely to persist beyond two years.

Success in college, in addition to access and persistence, is also important. Braddock and Dawkins (1981), using the NLS-72 data, found that after taking into account the effects of gender, SES, high school track, high school grades, standardized tests, and study habits, African American students who had attended desegregated high schools earned better grades than did their counterparts from segregated high schools. This relationship was found to be positive across levels and

types of colleges. Studies have shown that student attrition and graduation rates are related to college racial composition (Braddock, 1981; Braddock & McPartland, 1989a). Although the effects of elementary and secondary school desegregation on college success were typically positive, these studies found that African American students at predominantly White colleges are more likely to drop out or fail to graduate on schedule than their counterparts at predominantly African American colleges. However, Braddock and McPartland (1989a) also found that among African American students who were enrolled in desegregated colleges, those who had also attended desegregated elementary and high schools, controlling for differences in social class and ability, were more likely to continue in college and fare well academically than those students who had attended segregated schools. Overall, these findings indicate that one advantage of early desegregated education is that it may cumulatively produce the skills (academic, social, and psychological) necessary for success and coping in desegregated situations, thus increasing the likelihood of future positive desegregated experiences.

DISCUSSION AND IMPLICATIONS

Advocates of desegregation tend to find the modest positive effects of desegregation on African American (and, to some extent, Hispanic) student achievement to be encouraging. They argue that it is surprising to find the positive effects that are discovered given that desegregation is seldom accompanied by major efforts to enhance teacher capabilities or adapt curriculum and school structures in ways that would provide minority students with increased learning opportunities. This is especially true in the light of advances in evaluation research showing that the measurable effects of any intervention are strongly dependent on the strength and fidelity of the implementation. Much research-based practical knowledge has been established about how to create the optimal conditions in desegregated schools to obtain these desirable outcomes (Hare & Levine, 1984; Hawley, Banks, Padilla, Pope-Davis, & Schofield, 1995; Hawley & Jackson, 1995; Hawley & Rosenholtz, 1986). There has been considerable advancement in developing and identifying research-based practices in such areas as pedagogy (Cohen, 1980; Slavin, 1979, 1985, 1990, 1995) and curriculum content (Banks et al., 2001).

Indeed, one might argue that the claims of formal contact theory might be too modest with respect to school desegregation. Despite frequent failures of desegregated experiences to meet the criteria specified in the contact hypothesis, the positive effects of school desegregation appear to be far reaching and include lifelong social integration and occupational attainment. While demographic and human-capital factors may often be connected to school desegregation, adult social integration and career success evidence shows that the very dimensions in which contact theorists have been interested (for example, attitudes, friendship, and social networks) help mediate these positive outcomes in significant ways. And as contact theory would predict, these seem to be early links in a chain of beneficial effects.

There appears to be growing agreement among researchers that the opportunity to learn with and from people from different racial and ethnic backgrounds can, under the right conditions, enhance students' academic achievement and cognitive development, increase cross-cultural competence, and promote dispositions and behaviors that will have economic and social consequences for individuals and communities. This emerging consensus is built on theories grounded on a large number of studies of learning and group behavior in different contexts. However, research that directly links learning in diverse schools to student outcomes—both long term and short term—is not extensive, and much of this research was conducted many years ago and deals largely with African American–White relationships.

This review, like other recent reviews (Braddock & Dawkins, 1994; Schofield, 1995; Wells & Crain, 1994; Wells, 1995, 2002), highlights the need for systematic longitudinal research on the varied outcomes of school desegregation. There is a dearth of longitudinal research that measures students' long-term experiences in desegregated schools. In other words, most work exploring both short- and long-term outcomes of school desegregation measures the racial context of the school or district the student attends at one point in time (often during the high school experience). Data that document the racial context of the school environment students experience throughout their educational careers have been more difficult to obtain and hence prevent the exploration of whether students who have consistently attended desegregated schools from kindergarten until they leave school differ from students who have had less consistent desegregation experiences. This seems to be an important question since research has indicated that the effect size of school desegregation on achievement is greater for students in elementary school and decreases thereafter (Cook, 1984b; Mahard & Crain, 1983). Most of the studies exploring the impact of school desegregation on postsecondary education and occupational outcomes are also limited by a focus only on whether the student attended a predominantly African American high school. Future studies should attempt to measure students' experiences with school desegregation throughout their elementary and secondary education.

There is also a need for contextualization of desegregation in long-term outcome studies (Wells & Crain, 1996). Studies exploring the postsecondary educational and occupational outcomes of school desegregation have focused almost exclusively on the effects of the racial composition of students' schools or districts on various outcomes. Measures of desegregation need to be enhanced in order to better reflect the varied social contexts in which students experience desegregated schooling. Studies of the long-term outcomes of school desegregation have almost exclusively measured a student's school desegregation experience as the racial composition of their high school. This measure is theoretically appropriate because these studies argue that desegregated schools (with larger White enrollments) provide better access to social networks and enhanced social mobility for African Americans than schools that have majority African American enrollments. However, it assumes that African American students who attend high schools with more Whites will have a greater opportunity to test their racial beliefs and thus become more comfortable in integrated environments than students who attend high schools with fewer Whites. In fact, there may be a great deal of variation in these opportunities for cross-race contact even in schools with majority White enrollments (Feld & Carter, 1998; Clotfelter, 2002). In other words, access itself may not be enough to ensure what Granovetter (1989) termed "weak ties" or informal interpersonal networks. The conditions of access to school desegregation may also be an important area for study. Access achieved through voluntary or involuntary means, contested in any way or accompanied by some racially relevant response (like resegregation within schools), may be more or less likely to result in weak ties that can facilitate mobility opportunities.

There is a need to extend the long-term research to include outcomes for White students and students from other racial minority groups. Most of the long-term school desegregation studies have focused disproportionately on outcomes for African American students. The same outcomes (educational and occupational) that have been explored for African American students should be examined for other racial and ethnic groups. Additional long-term outcomes should be considered to study the impact of school desegregation on adults' attitudes about a broad range of racially related experiences, policies, and beliefs. Such studies might be particularly important for examining the potential for school desegregation to challenge racial stereotypes and promote intergroup relations in the long term. For example, future research could more fully consider whether adults who attended desegregated schools are more likely to see attendance at a multiracial school as a priority for their own children, choose to live in an integrated neighborhood, or have adult relationships (personal or work) with individuals of other racial backgrounds.

Perpetuation theory posits a relationship between macrostructures of segregation and racial isolation and microprocesses of identity and attitude formation that need to be more fully examined. Wells (1995) has emphasized network analysis focusing on how desegregated schools provide access to informal interpersonal networks that might help African American students access opportunities to go to college, live, and work in desegregated schools, neighborhoods, and occupations. Studies of the long-term affect of school desegregation should include a micro- and macrolevel analysis that considers how school desegregation influences students' identities, attitudes, and future decisions about college, residence, and occupation and how micro- and macroconnections facilitate the flow of information and opportunities to previously excluded groups. Research is needed to examine systematically whether these processes result in the greater incorporation of excluded groups into important interpersonal networks.

The goals of equal opportunity and fair competition are deeply rooted in American society. Thus, a better understanding of conditions that inhibit equal access to career opportunities is especially useful for constructive public policy debates. In particular, public discussions about school desegregation policies can be significantly enriched with information showing how desegregation opens adult opportunity structures for minorities that may otherwise be available only to Whites. State or federal agencies and policy makers concerned with employment inequities and discrimination do not usually propose solutions to reduce the unintentional exclusionary processes embedded in labor market and organizational structures. These agencies ordinarily are more concerned with reducing overt or intended discrimination in the labor market by establishing and enforcing fair employment practices. Thus, public officials concerned with equalizing adult career opportunities seldom consider racial segregation of schools as part of the problem. In the current environment, where school districts across the country are being declared unitary and being released from their court-ordered desegregation requirements, it is critical for not just educational professionals and researchers but also public agencies and officials concerned with employment issues to broaden their understanding of the role of desegregation in providing fair access to a variety of adult opportunities.

References

Allport, G. (1954). *The nature of prejudice.* Cambridge, MA: Addison-Wesley.

Anrig, G. (1985). Educational standards, testing, and equity, *Phi Delta Kappan, 66,* 623–625.

Arias, M. B. (1989). Compliance Monitor's Fifth-Annual Report Vasques v. San Jose (CA), Unified School District. Submitted to Honorable Robert F. Perkham, Chief U.S. District Judge, San Francisco.

Armor, D. J. (1972). The evidence on busing. *Public Interest, 28,* 90–126.

Aronson, E. B., & Patnoe, S. (1997). *The jigsaw classroom: Building cooperation in the classroom* (2nd ed.). Reading, MA: Addison-Wesley.

Banks, J. A. (1984). Black youths in predominantly White suburbs: An exploratory study of their attitudes and self-concepts. *Journal of Negro Education, 53*(1), 3–17.

Banks, J. A., Cookson, P., Gay, G., Hawley, W. D., Irvine, J. J., Nieto, S., Schofield, J. W., & Stephan, W. G. (2001). *Diversity within unity: Essential principals for teaching and learning in a multicultural society.* Seattle: Center for Multicultural Education, University of Washington.

Bankston, C., & Caldas, C. (1996). Majority African American schools and social injustice: The influence of de facto segregation on academic achievement. *Social Forces, 75,* 535–552.

Bankston, C., & Caldas, C. (1998). Family structure, schoolmates, and racial inequalities in school achievement. *Journal of Marriage and the Family, 60,* 715–723.

Bennett, A., & Easton, J. Q. (1988). *Voluntary transfer and student achievement: Does it help or hurt?* Paper presented at the annual meeting of the American Educational Research Association, New Orleans.

Bielby, W., & Baron, J. (1986). Men and women at work: Sex segregation and statistical discrimination. *American Journal of Sociology, 91,* 759–799.

Braddock, J. H., II (1980). The perpetuation of segregation across levels of education: A behavioral assessment of the contact-hypothesis, *Sociology of Education, 53*(7), 178–186.

Braddock, J. H., II (1981). Desegregation and Black student attrition. *Urban Education, 15*(1), 403–418.

Braddock, J. H., II (1985). School desegregation and Black assimilation, *Journal of Social Issues, 41,* 9–22.

Braddock, J. H., II (1986). *Black student attendance at segregated schools and colleges: More evidence on the perpetuation of segregation across levels of education.* Paper presented at the National Conference on School Desegregation Research, University of Chicago, Chicago.

Braddock, J. H., II, Crain, R. L., & McPartland, J. M. (1984). A long-term view of school desegregation: Some recent studies of graduates as adults, *Phi Delta Kappan, 66*(4), 259–264.

Braddock, J. H., II, Crain, R., McPartland, J., & Dawkins, R. (1986). Applicant race and job placement decisions: A national survey experiment, *International Journal of Sociology and Social Policy, 6,* 3–24.

Braddock, J. H., II, & Dawkins, M. P. (1981). Predicting Black academic achievement in higher education, *Journal of Negro Education, 80,* 319–327.

Braddock, J. H., II, & Dawkins, M. P. (1984). Long-term effects of school desegregation on southern Blacks. *Sociological Spectrum, 4*, 365–381.

Braddock, J. H., II, Dawkins, M. P., & Trent, W. (1994). Why desegregate? The effect of school desegregation on adult occupational desegregation of African Americans, Whites and Hispanics. *International Journal of Contemporary Sociology, 31*, 273–283.

Braddock, J. H., II, & McPartland, J. M. (1980). Assessing school desegregation effects: New directions in research. In R. Corwin (Ed.), *Research in sociology of education and socialization* (Vol. 3, pp. 209–282). Greenwich, CT: JAI.

Braddock, J. H., II, & McPartland, J. M. (1982). Assessing school desegregation effects: New directions in research. *Research in Education and Socialization, 41*(3), 259–282.

Braddock, J. H., II, & McPartland, J. M. (1987). Social science evidence and affirmative action policies: A response to the commentators. *Journal of Social Issues, 43*, 133–143.

Braddock, J. H., II, & McPartland, J. M. (1988). The social and academic consequences of school desegregation. *Equity and Choice, 4*(2), 5–10, 63–73.

Braddock, J. H., II, & McPartland, J. M. (1989a). Some cost and benefit considerations for Black college students attending predominantly White and predominantly Black universities. In M. Nettles (Ed.), *The Black experience in American higher education* (pp. 87–104). Westport, CT: Greenwood Press.

Braddock, J. H., II, & McPartland, J. M. (1989b). Social psychological processes that perpetuate racial segregation: The relationship between school and employment desegregation. *Journal of Black Studies, 19*, 267–289

Braddock, J. H., II, McPartland, J. M., & Trent, W. (1984). *Desegregated schools and desegregated work environments*. Paper presented at the American Educational Research Association Annual Meeting, New Orleans.

Brown v. Board of Education of Topeka Kansas, 347 U.S. 483 (1954).

Brown, S. (1999). *High school racial composition: Balancing excellence and equity*. Paper presented at the meeting of the American Sociological Association, Chicago.

Carsrud, K. B. (1984). *Does pairing hurt Chapter I students?* Austin, TX: Independent School District, Office of Research and Evaluation.

Clark, K. B. (1953). The effects of segregation and the consequences of desegregation: A social science statement. Appendix to appellants' brief: *Brown v. Board of Education of Topeka, Kansas. Minnesota Law Review, 37*, 427–439.

Clark, K. B. (1954). Some principles related to the problem of desegregation. *Journal of Negro Education, 23*(3), 339–347.

Clark, K. B. (1988). The *Brown* decision: Racism, education, and human values. *Journal of Negro Education, 57*(2), 125–132.

Clotfelter, C. T. (2002). Interracial contact in high school extracurricular activities. *Urban Review, 34*(1), 25–46.

Cohen, E. G. (1980). Design and redesign of the desegregation school: Problems of status, power, and conflict. In W. G. Stephan & J. R. Feagin (Eds.), *School desegregation: Past, present, and future* (pp. 251–278). New York: Plenum.

Coleman, J. S., Campbell, E. Q., Hobson, C. J., McPartland, J., Mood, A. M., Weinfeld, F. D., & York, R. L. (1966). *Equality of educational opportunity*. Washington, DC: U.S. Government Printing Office.

Cook, S. (1979). Social science and school desegregation: Did we mislead the Supreme Court? *Personality and Social Psychology Bulletin, 5*, 420–437.

Cook, T. D. (1984a). *School desegregation and black achievement*. Washington, DC: U.S. Department of Education, National Institute of Education.

Cook, T. D. (1984b). What have Black children gained academically from school integration? Examination of the meta-analytic evidence. In T. Cook, D. Armor, R. Crain, N. Miller, W. Stephan, H. Walberg, & P. M. Wortman (Eds.), *School desegregation and Black achievements* (pp. 6–42). Washington, DC: National Institute of Education.

Crain, R. L. (1970). School integration and occupational achievement of Negroes. *American Journal of Sociology, 75*, 593–606.

Crain, R. L. (1984a). *Is nineteen really better than ninety-three?* Washington, DC: National Institute of Education.

Crain, R. L. (1984b). *The quality of American high school graduates: What employers say and do about it* (Rep. No. 354). Baltimore, MD: Center for Social Organization of Schools, Johns Hopkins University.

Crain, R. L., & Mahard, R. E. (1978a). Desegregation and Black achievement: A review of the research. *Problems, 42*(17), 16.

Crain, R. L., & Mahard, R. E. (1978b). School racial composition and Black college attendance and achievement test performance. *Sociology of Education, 51*, 81–101.

Crain, R. L., & Mahard, R. E. (1981). The consequences of controversy accompanying institutional change: The case of school desegregation. *American Sociological Review, 47*(6), 697–708.

Crain, R. L., & Weisman, C. (1972). *Discrimination, personality and achievement*. New York: Seminar Press.

Darden, J. (1985). Neighborhood racial composition and school desegregation in New Castle County, Delaware. In R. Green (Ed.), *Metropolitan desegregation* (pp. 123–142). New York: Plenum.

Dawkins, M. P. (1983). Black students' occupational expectations: A national study of the impact of school desegregation. *Urban Education, 18*, 98–113.

Dawkins, M. P., & Braddock, J. H., II (1994). The continuing significance of desegregation: School racial composition and African American inclusion in American society. *Journal of Negro Education, 63*(3), 394–405.

Epstein, J. (1985). After the bus arrives: Resegregation in desegregated schools. *Journal of Social Issues, 41*, 23–43.

Feld, S., & Carter, W. (1998). When desegregation reduces interracial contact. *American Journal of Sociology, 103*(5), 1165–1186.

Ferguson, R. (1998). Teachers' perceptions and expectations and the Black-White test score gap. In C. Jencks & M. Phillips (Eds.), *The Black-White test score gap* (pp. 273–317). Washington, DC: Brookings Institute Press.

Gable, R., & Iwanicki, E. (1986). The longitudinal effects of a voluntary school desegregation program on the basic skill programs of participants. *Metropolitan Education, 1*, 76–77.

Granovetter, M. (1989). The microstructure of school desegregation. In D. Prager, D. Longshore, & M. Seeman (Eds.), *School desegregation research: New directions in situational analysis* (pp. 81–110). New York: Plenum.

Green, K. C. (1982a). *The impact of neighborhood and secondary school integration on educational and occupational attainment of college bound Blacks*. Unpublished doctoral dissertation, University of California, Los Angeles.

Green, K. (1982b). *Integration and attainment: Preliminary results from a national longitudinal study of the impact of school desegregation*. Paper presented at the American Educational Research Association, Los Angeles.

Grissmer, D., Flanagan A., & Williamson, S. (1998). Why did the Black-White score gap narrow in the 1970s and 1980s? In C. Jencks & M. Phillips (Eds.), *The Black-White test score gap* (pp. 182–226). Washington, DC: Brookings Institute Press.

Hallinan, M. T. (1998). Diversity effects on student outcomes: Social science evidence. *Ohio State Law Journal, 59*(3), 733–754.

Hallinan, M. T., & Smith, S. S. (1985). The effects of classroom racial composition on students' interracial friendliness. *Social Psychology Quarterly, 48*(1), 3–16.

Hallinan, M. T., & Teixeria, R. A. (1987). Opportunities and constraints: Black-White differences in the formation of interracial friendships. *Child Development, 58*(5), 1358.

Hallinan, M. T., & Williams, R. (1989). Interracial friendship choices in secondary schools. *American Sociological Review, 54*(1), 67–78.

Hanushek, E., Kain, J., & Rivkin, S. (2001). *New evidence about Brown v. Board of Education: The complex effects of school racial composition on student achievement.* Working paper, Green Center for the Study of Science and Society, University of Texas, Dallas.

Hare, B., & Levine, D. (1984). *Toward effective desegregation.* Washington, DC: National Institute for Education

Hawley, W. D., Banks, J. A., Padilla, A. M., Pope-Davis, D. B., & Schofield, J. W. (1995). Strategies for reducing racial prejudice: Essential principles for program design toward a common destiny. In W. Hawley & A. Jackson (Eds.), *Toward a common destiny: Improving race relations in American society* (pp. 423–433). San Francisco: Jossey-Bass.

Hawley, W. D., Crain, R. L., Rossell, C. H., Smylie, M. A., Fernandez, R. R., & Schofield, J. W. (1983). *Strategies for effective desegregation: Lessons from research.* Lexington, MA: Lexington Books.

Hawley, W. D., & Jackson, A. W. (Eds.) (1995). *Toward a common destiny: Improving race relations in American society.* San Francisco: Jossey-Bass.

Hawley, W. D., & Rosenholtz, S. (1986). *Achieving quality integrated education.* Washington, DC: National Education Association.

Hoxby, C. (2002, Summer). The power of peers. *Education Next, 39,* 217–239.

Kain, J., & O'Brien, D. (2000). *Black suburbanization in Texas metropolitan areas and its impact on student achievement.* Working paper, Green Center for the Study of Science and Society, University of Texas, Dallas.

Kurlaender, M. (2001). *The impact of school racial composition on students' attitudes towards living and working in multiracial settings.* Qualifying paper, Graduate School of Education, Harvard University, Cambridge, MA.

Levin, H. M. (1975). Education, life chances, and the courts: The role of social science evidence. *Law and Contemporary Problems, 39*(2), 217–239.

Ludwig, J., Ladd, H., & Duncan, G. (2001). Urban poverty and educational outcomes. In W. Gale & J. Pack (Eds.), *Brookings-Wharton Papers on Urban Affairs* (pp. 147–201). Washington, DC: Brookings Institution.

Mahard, R. E., & Crain, R. L. (1980). *The influence of high school racial composition on the academic achievement and college attendance of Hispanics.* Paper presented at the annual meeting of the American Sociological Association, New York.

Mahard, R. E., & Crain, R. L. (1983). Research on minority achievement in desegregation schools. In I.C.H. Rossell & W. D. Hawley (Eds.), *The consequences of school desegregation.* Philadelphia: Temple University Press.

Mayer, S. E., & Jencks, C. (1989). Growing up in poor neighborhoods: How much does it matter? *Science, 243*(4897), 1441–1445.

McLaurin v. Oklahoma State Regents, 339 U.S. 637 (1950).

McPartland, J. M. (1978). Desegregation and equity in higher education and employment: Is progress related to the desegregation of elementary and secondary schools? *Law and Contemporary Problems, 43*(3), 108–132.

McPartland, J. M., & Braddock, J. H., II (1981). Going to college and getting a good job: The impact of desegregation. In W. D. Hawley (Ed.), *Effective school desegregation* (pp. 141–154). New York: Studies by the National Review Panel on School Desegregation Research, Sage.

McPartland, J. M., & Crain, R. L. (1980). Racial discrimination, segregation, and processes of social mobility. In V. T. Covello (Ed.), *Poverty and public policy.* New York: G. K. Hall.

McPartland, J. M., Epstein, J., Karweit, N., & Slavin, R. (1976). *Productivity of schools: Conceptual and methodological frameworks for research* (Rep. No. 218). Baltimore: Center for Social Organization of Schools, Johns Hopkins University.

Metz, M. (1978). *Classrooms and corridors: The crisis of authority in desegregated secondary schools.* Old Tappan, NJ: Macmillan.

Mickelson, R. A. (2001). Subverting *Swann:* Tracking and second generation segregation in Charlotte-Mecklenburg schools. *American Educational Research Journal, 38*(2), 215–252.

Oakes, J. (1990). *Multiplying inequalities: The effects of race, social class, and ability grouping on opportunities to learn mathematics and science.* Old Tappan, NJ: Macmillan.

Patchen, M. (1982). *Black-White contact in schools: Its social and academic effects.* West Lafayette, IN: Purdue University Press.

Pearce, D. (1980). *Breaking down the barriers: New evidence on the impact of metropolitan school desegregation on housing patterns.* Washington, DC: National Institute of Education.

Pettigrew, T., & Troop, L. (2000). Does intergroup contact reduce prejudice? In S. Oskamp (Ed.), *Reducing prejudice and discrimination* (pp. 93–114). Mahwah, NJ: Erlbaum.

Prager, J., & Seeman, M. (1986). *School desegregation research: New directions in situational analysis.* New York: Plenum.

Pride, D., & Woodard, D. (1985). *The burden of busing: The politics of desegregation in Nashville.* Knoxville: University of Tennessee Press.

Rist, R. (1970). Student social class and teacher expectations: The self-fulfilling prophecy in ghetto education. *American Harvard Educational Review, 40,* 411–452.

Rist, R. (1978). *The invisible children.* Cambridge, MA: Harvard University Press.

Rosenbaum, J. (1995). Changing the geography of opportunity by expanding residential choice: Lessons from the Gautreaux Program. *Housing Policy Debate, 6*(1), 231–270.

Schiff, J., Firestone, W., & Young, J. (1999). *Organizational context for student achievement: The case of student racial composition.* Paper presented at the meeting of the American Educational Research Association, Montreal, Canada.

Schofield, J. W. (1989). *Black and White in school: Trust, tension, or tolerance?* New York: Teachers College Press.

Schofield, J. W. (1995). Promoting positive intergroup relations in school settings. In W. Hawley & A. Jackson (Eds.), *Toward a common destiny: Improving race relations in American society* (pp. 257–289). San Francisco: Jossey-Bass.

Schofield, J. W. (2001). Review of research on school desegregation's impact on elementary and secondary school students. In J. A. Banks & C.A.M. Banks (Eds.), *Handbook of research on multicultural education* (pp. 597–616). San Francisco: Jossey-Bass.

Schofield, J. W., & Sagar, W. A. (1977). Peer interaction patterns in an integrated middle school. *Sociometry, 40*(21), 130–139.

Schofield, J. W., & Sagar, W. A. (1983). Desegregation, school practices and student race relations. In C. Russell & W. D. Hawley (Eds.), *The consequences of school desegregation* (pp. 58–102). Philadelphia: Temple University Press.

Scott, R., & McPartland, J. M. (1982). Desegregation as national policy: Correlates of racial attitudes. *American Educational Research Journal, 19*, 397–414.

Sigelman, L., Bledso, T., Welch, S., & Combs, M. (1996). Making contact? Black-White social interaction in an urban setting. *American Journal of Sociology, 101*(5), 1306–1332.

Slavin, R. (1979). Effects on biracial learning teams on cross-racial friendships. *Journal of Educational Psychology, 71*(3), 1979.

Slavin, R. (1990). Achievement effects of ability groups in secondary schools: A best evidence synthesis. *Review of Educational Research, 60*, 471–499.

Slavin, R. (1995). Enhancing intergroup relations in schools: Cooperative learning and other strategies. In W. Hawley & A. Jackson (Eds.), *Toward a common destiny: Improving race relations in American* society (pp. 291–314). San Francisco: Jossey-Bass.

Smith, J., & Welch, F. (1977). Black-white male wage ratios: 1960–1970. *American Economic Review, 67*, 397–414.

Sonleitner, N., & Wood, P. B. (1996). The effect of childhood interracial contact on adult antiblack prejudice. *International Journal of Intercultural Relations, 20*(1), 1–17.

St. John, N. (1975). *School desegregation: Outcomes for children.* New York: Wiley.

Stephan, W. (1978). School desegregation: An evaluation of predictions made in *Brown* v. *Board of Education. Psychological Bulletin, 85*, 217–238.

Sweatt v. Painter, 339 U.S. 629 (1950).

Thurow, L. (1975). *Generating inequality.* New York: Basic Books.

U.S. Commission on Civil Rights. (1967). *Racial isolation in the public schools* (Appendix C5). Washington, DC: U.S. Government Printing Office.

Wainer, H. (1986). Minority contributions to the SAT turnaround: An example of Simpson's paradox. *Journal of Educational Statistics, 11*, 239–244.

Wells, A. S. (1995). Reexamining social science research on school desegregation: Long- versus short-term effects. *Teachers College Record, 94*(4), 691–706.

Wells, A. S. (2002). The "consequences" of school desegregation: The mismatch between the research and the rationale. *Hastings Constitutional Law Quarterly, 28*(4), 771–797.

Wells, A. S., & Crain, R. L. (1994). Perpetuation theory and the long-term effects of school desegregation. *Review of Educational Research, 64*, 531–556.

Wells, A. S., & Crain, R. L. (1996). *Stepping over the colorline.* New Haven, CT: Yale University Press.

HIGHER EDUCATION

42

RESEARCH ON RACIAL ISSUES IN AMERICAN HIGHER EDUCATION

Christine I. Bennett

Indiana University

Nearly ten years ago, this review of racial issues in American higher education identified the quest for community amid diversity as the major challenge facing colleges and universities at the time. This quest was evident in the heated controversy over multiculturalism in the curriculum, the rise of racial incidents on campuses across the country, and the declining percentages of minority high school graduates who entered college, even as our population was becoming more ethnically diverse. Today, the focus of theory and research has changed as a result of lessons learned from over three decades of research on racial diversity issues on college campuses and the increasing numbers of college students of color at predominantly White institutions (PWIs). The new conversation centers on the importance of making public the benefits of diversity and of creating campus climates that affirm and support racially diverse student populations. For example, the *Seventeenth Annual Status Report of Minorities in Higher Education* (Wilds, 2000) includes a special focus section that "discusses the growing body of research that demonstrates that racial and ethnic diversity benefits individuals, colleges and universities, the economy, and society. This section also emphasizes the importance of institutional context and climate in optimizing the benefits of racial and ethnic diversity in higher education" (p. v). And the Preface to *Understanding the Difference Diversity Makes: Assessing Campus Diversity Initiatives* (Musil et al., 1999) states:

While higher education has long been one of the contested sites of experimentation with diversity, the past three decades have been witness to an historically defining moment. Campuses have been the cauldron where newly expanded access has converged with intellectual ferment. In the heat of transmuting its central educational mission, the academy has brimmed with the challenge of making democratic promises become actual practice. Policy innovations, scholarly innovations, and practical experiments have coalesced into what is becoming known as the "campus diversity movement." This movement has focused new attention on access, recruitment, admission, and retention; diversifying faculty, staff, and administrations; restructuring the curriculum; re-evaluating counseling, career planning, and residential life; and re-configuring the relationship between the campus and the community. (p. vii)

The review of research for this chapter reflects these changes in the literature. The first section provides an overview of trends in college participation rates and educational attainment. The second section provides a synthesis of theory and research on racial issues in higher education that is organized around a new conceptual framework for understanding four dimensions of campus climate developed by major scholars in the field: an institution's historical legacy of inclusion or exclusion, structural diversity in terms of the representation of racial and cultural groups on campus, the psychological dimension of climate, and the behavioral climate dimension (Hurtado, Milem, Clayton-Pedersen, & Allen, 1998, 1999). The conclusion focuses on integrated pluralism as an ideal and a practical framework for campus interventions that affirm the benefits of racial and cultural diversity.

TRENDS IN COLLEGE PARTICIPATION RATES AND EDUCATIONAL ATTAINMENT

Ten years ago, this review of educational attainment among African Americans, American Indians, Asian Americans, and Hispanics was limited by several factors.

Researchers lacked a national database that is representative of American Indians, Asian Americans, and Latinos; reports ignored diversity such as different socioeconomic backgrounds and geographic regions within the various ethnic groups; and findings led to contradictory conclusions when trends were reported in terms of college enrollments (the actual head counts provided by colleges and universities each fall) rather than college participation rates (the percentage of a given age group that is currently enrolled in college or has attended for one or more years) (Carter & Wilson, 1991). Today these limitations persist, raising questions about the trends reported in this section and casting a shadow of incompleteness regarding the data.

College enrollment trends are revealed in Table 42.1, showing undergraduate enrollments reported for 1976, 1980, 1984, 1991, and 1997. College enrollments grew steadily for all ethnic groups between 1976 and 1997, with the exception of Whites, whose enrollments have declined since 1991 due to their decline in the population. College enrollment increases are most dramatic for Asian Americans and Hispanics. However, as seen in Table 42.2, the trends look somewhat different when expressed in proportion of high school graduates enrolled in college rather than actual numbers. Based on the 18- to 24-year-old age cohorts in 1976, 1984, 1989, 1992, and 1999, Table 42.2 reports the number and percentage of high school graduates, the number and participation rate of high school graduates in college, and the ever-enrolled-in-college rates for high school graduates between the ages of 18 and 24. The figures are shown by race and ethnicity and sex for African Americans, Latinos, and Whites.

High School Graduation and Dropout Rates

The traditional college-going cohort of 18 to 24 year olds decreased by nearly 4 million students between 1984 and 1992, but increased by close to a half million by 1997 due to increases in the number of students of color. Likewise, after a decline in the number of high school graduates by about 3 million between 1984 and 1992, the number of high school graduates increased nearly half a million by 1997. Between 1976 and 1992, the high school completion rate for African Americans increased from 71.8% to 76.8% for females and from 62.3% to 72.2% for males; in 1997, the completion rate increased again for females (77.5%) but decreased slightly for males (71.4%). An even more pronounced gender difference is evident in the trends for Latinos: high school completion rates rose for females from 56.8% in 1976 to 62.3% in 1984, remained at 62.8% in 1992, and increased to 65.7% in 1997. Among males, the high school graduation rates rose from 53.9% in 1976 to 57.4% in 1984, dropped to 52.0% in 1992, and dropped again in 1997 to 49.2%. High school completion rates for Whites remained stable during this time period, with 84.8% of females and 80.6% of males graduating in 1997 (down slightly for males from 1992 rates).

The increased high school graduation rates among African American and Latina students are consistent with high school dropout trends among 16 to 24 year olds (National Center for Education Statistics, 1993, 1998). The overall dropout rate fell between 1972 and 1992, especially for African Americans. In 1972, 14.6% of all 16 to 24 year olds were not enrolled in school and had neither graduated from high school nor received general equivalency diploma (GED) credentials. (The dropout

TABLE 42.1. Undergraduate Enrollment in Higher Education by Race and Ethnicity, 1976, 1980, 1984, 1991, and 1997.

	All Students	White	Total Minority	Asian[a]	Black	Hispanic	Native American[b]
Fall 1976	8,432,240	6,899,743	1,402,487	152,533	865,147	323,540	61,267
Fall 1980	9,262,820	7,465,722	1,606,192	214,989	932,055	390,440	68,708
Fall 1984	9,063,178	7,293,747	1,579,267	284,897	830,986	399,333	64,051
Fall 1991	12,439,000	9,508,000	2,698,000	559,000	1,220,000	804,000	106,000
Fall 1997	12,451,000	8,784,000	3,399,000	744,000	1,398,000	1,126,000	131,000
			Percentage Change				
1976–1980	9.9	8.2	14.5	40.9	7.7	20.7	12.1
1980–1984	−2.2	−2.3	−1.7	32.5	−10.8	2.3	−6.8
1990–1991	3.9	2.4	NA	11.2	−7.1	10.7	10.7
1988–1997	10.1	−1.4	55.0	70.3	34.6	78.4	52.3

[a]Includes Pacific Islanders.

[b]Includes Alaskan Natives and American Indians.

Sources: 1976–1984: Fields (1988). 1990–1991: U.S. Department of Education, 1997: Wilds (2000).

TABLE 42.2. High School Completion Rates and College Participation Rates by Race and Ethnicity and by Sex, 1976, 1984, 1989, 1992, and 1997 (in thousands).

	All Persons		African American		Hispanic		White	
	(n)	(%)	(n)	(%)	(n)	(%)	(n)	(%)
1976 pop. 18–24 years	26,919		3,315		1,551		23,119	
Female	13,907		1,813		850		11,840	
Male	13,012		1,503		701		11,279	
High school graduates	21,677	80.5	2,239	67.5	862	55.6	19,045	82.4
Female	11,365	81.7	1,302	71.8	483	56.8	9,860	83.3
Male	10,312	79.2	936	62.3	378	53.9	9,186	81.4
Enrolled in college	7,181	33.1	749	33.5	309	35.8	6,276	33.0
Female	3,508	30.9	417	32.0	160	33.1	3,026	30.7
Male	3,673	35.6	331	35.4	150	39.7	3,250	35.4
% ever college enrolled		53.4		50.4		48.9		53.5
Female		51.4		50.3		46.5		51.3
Male		55.7		50.3		51.8		55.9
1984 pop. 18–24 years	28,031		3,862		2,018		23,347	
Female	14,287		2,052		1,061		11,826	
Male	13,744		1,811		956		11,521	
High school graduates	22,870	81.6	2,885	74.7	1,212	60.1	19,373	83.0
Female	11,956	83.7	1,613	78.6	661	62.3	10,026	84.8
Male	10,914	79.4	1,272	70.2	549	57.4	9,348	81.1
Enrolled in college	7,591	33.2	786	27.2	362	29.9	6,256	33.7
Female	3,662	30.6	419	26.0	207	31.3	3,120	31.1
Male	3,929	36.0	367	28.9	154	28.1	3,406	36.4
% ever college enrolled		53.0		45.2		46.0		53.8
Female		52.4		45.1		46.6		53.4
Male		53.6		45.2		45.7		54.2
1989 Pop. 18–24 years	25,261		3,559		2,818		20,825	
Female	12,936		1,905		1,377		10,586	
Male	12,325		1,654		1,439		10,240	
High school graduates	20,461	81.0	2,708	76.1	1,576	55.9	17,089	82.1
Female	10,758	83.2	1,511	79.3	823	59.8	8,913	84.2
Male	9,700	78.7	1,195	72.2	756	52.5	8,177	79.9
Enrolled in college	7,804	38.1	835	30.8	453	28.7	6,631	38.8
Female	4,085	38.0	511	33.8	244	29.6	3,409	38.2
Male	3,717	38.3	324	27.1	211	27.9	3,223	39.4
% ever college enrolled		57.9		49.1		43.6		58.9
Female		58.6		51.8		44.5		59.2
Male		57.2		45.8		42.7		58.5
1992 Pop. 18–24 years	24,278		3,521		2,754		19,671	
Female	12,313		1,845		1,369		9,928	
Male	11,965		1,676		1,384		9,744	
High school graduates	19,921	82.1	2,625	74.6	1,578	57.3	16,379	83.3
Female	10,344	84.0	1,417	76.8	860	62.8	8,468	85.3
Male	9,576	80.0	1,211	72.3	720	52.0	7,911	81.2
Enrolled in college	8,343	41.9	886	33.8	586	37.1	6,916	42.2
Female	4,429	42.8	531	37.5	339	39.4	3,625	42.8
Male	3,912	40.9	356	29.7	247	34.3	3,291	41.6
% ever college enrolled		65.6		53.3		55.0		67.0
Female		66.9		56.6		57.4		68.1
Male		64.1		49.4		52.2		65.8

TABLE 42.2. High School Completion Rates and College Participation Rates by Race and Ethnicity and by Sex, 1976, 1984, 1989, 1992, and 1997 (in thousands). *(continued)*

	All Persons		African American		Hispanic		White	
	(n)	(%)	(n)	(%)	(n)	(%)	(n)	(%)
1997 Pop. 18–24 years	24,973		3,650		3,600		20,020	
Female	12,460		1,949		1,669		9,847	
Male	12,513		1,701		1,937		10,173	
High school graduates	20,338	81.4	2,726	74.7	2,236	62.0	16,557	82.7
Female	10,403	83.5	1,511	77.5	1,697	65.7	8,352	84.8
Male	9,933	79.4	1,214	71.4	1,140	58.9	8,204	80.6
Enrolled in college	9,204	45.2	1,085	39.8	806	36.0	7,495	45.3
Female	4,820	46.4	659	43.6	436	39.7	3,863	46.3
Male	4,374	44.0	425	35.0	371	32.5	3,633	44.3
% ever college enrolled		67.3		60.0		54.3		67.7
Female		69.6		63.0		59.6		70.1
Male		64.9		56.3		49.2		65.3

Sources: 1976–1992: Carter & Wilson (1994). 1997: Wilds (2000).

rate was 12.3% for Whites, 21.3% for Blacks, and 34.3% for Latinos.) By 1992, the overall dropout rate had fallen to 11.0%, with rates at 7.7% for Whites, 13.7% for Blacks, and 29.4% for Latinos; the trend remained steady in 1998 (National Center for Educational Statistics, 1998). While the dropout difference between Blacks and Whites has narrowed, the dropout rate for Latinos remains high, at nearly 30% in 1998 (National Center for Educational Statistics, 1998, p. 13).

College Participation Rates

After a dramatic improvement in high school completion rates, African American college participation rates began to increase after 1992, particularly among females. College participation rates among African American females dropped from 32% in 1976 to 26% in 1984, increased to 37.5% in 1992, and reached a high of 43.6% in 1997. Among African American males, there was a steady decline from 35.4% in 1976 to 29.7% in 1992, followed by an increase to 35% in 1997. Among Latinos, however, the college participation rates have not improved significantly, although females show an increase that is matched by the decrease for males. The Latina college participation rate dropped from 33.1% in 1976 to 29.6% in 1989; the drop was even more significant among males, who fell from 39.7% in 1976 to 27.9% in 1989. In 1992, the Latina participation rate increased to 39.4% and remained at 39.7% in 1997. For males, the rates increased to 34.3% but decreased to 32.5% in 1997. Among White students, college participation rates of 18 to 24 year olds increased for females from 30.7% in 1976 to 42.8% in 1992 and increased again to 46.3% in 1997. White male students

increased their college participation rates from 35.4% in 1976 to 41.6% in 1992, and increased further to 44.3% in 1997.

Overall, since the late 1980s, the college enrollments of students of color have increased by 57.2%, including 16.1% between 1992 and 1997 (Wilds, 2000). Latinos and Asian Americans show the most dramatic enrollment increase. American Indians have also increased their college enrollments, although their graduation rates remain the lowest of all groups (Wilds, 2000). The increase in college enrollments for students of color and decrease in college enrollments for White students resulted in a stable or stagnant overall college enrollment throughout the 1990s (Wilds, 2000).

College participation rates as well have increased for all groups (participation rates are not reported for American Indians), although African Americans and Latinos still lag behind Whites and Asian Americans in terms of college participation rates for high school graduates ages 18 through 24 (Wilds, 2000). By 1997, the college participation rates of African American females, Latinas, and European American males and females attained new highs. African American and Latino males gained less than females, and the Latino college participation rate in 1997 was actually lower than in 1976. College graduation rates are highest for Asian Americans (65%), followed by Whites (58%), Latinos (45%), African Americans (38%), and American Indians (37%) (Wilds, 2000, p. 81). Although the college enrollments, participation rates, and college graduation rates among Asian Americans continue to be the highest of all groups (Wilds, 2000), the figures vary dramatically by nation of origin (Hune & Chan, 1997).

Trends in Graduate and Professional School Enrollment

Graduate school enrollment, for both Whites and all minorities, has slowly increased since 1978 (see Table 42.3). The only exception to the steady increase is a drop in enrollments for Hispanics between 1986 and 1988; however, increases are noted in 1991 and 1997, and the percentage increase between 1988 and 1997 is 99.3%. The percentage increases in enrollments between 1988 and 1997 per ethnic group are as follows: White, non-Hispanic, 9.4%; African American, 80%; Latino, 72%; Asian American, 99.3%; American Indian, 67.3%; and international students, 25.1%. Enrollments in professional schools between 1978 and 1988 declined slightly for Whites and increased slightly for minorities; in 1991 and 1997, there are larger increases for African Americans, Hispanics, and Asian Americans, while American Indian enrollments remain the same and Whites continue to decline. (See Table 42.4.)

The proportion of minority and White students enrolled in undergraduate, graduate, and professional schools since 1976 is shown in Table 42.5. The proportion of students of color in the overall population of college students has increased at all levels of higher education, most dramatically in professional schools. In contrast, the proportion of Whites has steadily declined at all levels. Enrollments grew at the highest rates for Asian American students. The proportion of Hispanics has also increased in the undergraduate, graduate, and professional student populations. American Indians have gained slightly in undergraduate education and have maintained the same proportion of graduate and professional school enrollments since 1976. The proportions of African Americans in the undergraduate and graduate student population have declined since 1976, although there has been a slight increase in the professional school population.

In contrast to this trend of increasing proportions of minority students in the higher education student population, a very different trend is also evident in the school populations shown in Table 42.5. For each year shown, the proportion of White students in the graduate and professional levels usually exceeds the proportion of Whites in the undergraduate student population. In contrast, minority representation usually decreases. Minorities contributed 16.6% of the undergraduate population in 1976 but only 10% of the graduate school student population

TABLE 42.3. Graduate Enrollment in Higher Education by Race and Ethnicity: Biennially, Fall 1978–Fall 1988, 1991, and 1997 (in thousands).

	1978	1980	1982	1984	1986	1988	1991	1997
Total	1,219	1,250	1,235	1,344	1,435	1,472	1,639	1,753
White, non-Hispanic	1,019	1,030	1,002	1,087	1,133	1,153	1,258	1,262
Total minority	120	125	123	141	167	167	205	302
African American non-Hispanic	68	66	61	67	72	76	89	132
Hispanic	24	27	27	32	46	39	51	79
Asian American[a]	24	28	30	37	43	46	58	83
American Indian	4	4	5	5	5	6	7	9
Nonresident alien	80	94	108	115	136	151	177	189

[a]Asian American includes Pacific Islanders.

Source: Carter & Wilson (1991).

TABLE 42.4. Professional School Enrollment in Higher Education by Race and Ethnicity: Biennially, Fall 1978–Fall 1988, 1991, and 1997 (in thousands).

	1978	1980	1982	1984	1986	1988	1991	1997
Total	255	277	278	278	270	267	281	298
White, non-Hispanic	229	248	246	243	231	223	224	220
Total minority	22	26	29	32	36	39	50	70
African American non-Hispanic	11	13	13	13	14	14	17	21
Hispanic	5	7	7	8	9	9	11	14
Asian American[a]	5	6	8	9	11	14	21	33
American Indian	1	1	1	1	1	1	1	2
Nonresident alien	3	3	3	3	4	5	6	7

[a]Asian American includes Pacific Islanders.

Source: Carter & Wilson (1991).

TABLE 42.5. Enrollment by Race and Ethnicity as a Percentage of Total Undergraduate, Graduate, and Professional Enrollments: 1976, 1980, 1984, 1988, and 1991.

	1976	1980	1984	1988	1991
White					
Undergraduate	81.8	80.6	80.5	78.8	76.4
Graduate	83.9	81.9	80.5	78.4	76.7
Professional	90.1	89.3	87.1	83.6	79.8
Minorities					
Undergraduate	16.6	17.3	17.4	19.2	21.8
Graduate	10.0	10.2	9.8	11.4	12.4
Professional	8.6	9.6	11.6	14.7	18.1
Asian[a]					
Undergraduate	1.8	2.3	3.1	3.6	4.5
Graduate	1.7	2.1	2.6	3.1	3.5
Professional	1.7	2.2	3.4	5.4	7.4
Black					
Undergraduate	10.3	10.1	9.2	9.2	9.9
Graduate	6.1	5.5	4.8	5.2	5.4
Professional	4.5	4.6	4.9	5.4	6.1
Hispanic					
Undergraduate	3.8	4.2	4.4	5.6	6.5
Graduate	1.9	2.2	2.2	2.7	3.1
Professional	1.9	2.4	2.9	3.5	4.1
Native American[b]					
Undergraduate	0.7	0.7	0.7	0.8	0.9
Graduate	0.4	0.4	0.3	0.4	0.4
Professional	0.5	0.4	0.4	0.4	0.5

[a]Includes Pacific Islanders.

[b]Includes Alaskan Natives and American Indians.

Sources: For 1988 and 1991: National Center for Education Statistics (1993). For 1976–1984: U.S. Department of Education, 1987).

and 8.6% of the professional school student population. By 1991, minorities accounted for 21.8% of all undergraduates (with over half enrolled in two-year community colleges) but only 12.4% of graduate students; however, their proportion of the professional school student population increased to 18.1%. Asian American students are an exception to the trend: percentages in graduate and professional school populations are close to or exceed undergraduate percentages.

Explanations of Lower College Enrollments, Participation Rates, and Persistence Among Students of Color

A full review of the research on access to and persistence in higher education and the complex reasons for disparities among college students of color is beyond the scope of this chapter. However, this section discusses several reviews of the research, provides a brief overview of main themes in the literature, and discusses a sample of the relevant studies.

A review by Baker and Velez (1996) on access to and opportunity in postsecondary education from the 1960s into the 1990s identifies key racial and ethnic differences in educational attainment that relate to background factors, academic integration, social integration, external factors, institutional factors, and financial aid. Important reasons for college enrollment declines among African Americans and Latinos are increasing segregation in elementary and secondary schools, rising college costs, inadequate assistance to less-well-prepared students, and a lack of commitment by postsecondary institutions to the educational needs of minorities (Baker & Velez, 1996). Changes in financial aid policies since the 1960s that come "increasingly in the form of repayable loans" rather than grants are another factor in college enrollment declines among students of color, who are less willing to assume loans "because of their sense that their lifetime earnings from a college education may not repay the costs incurred from their indebtedness" (Baker & Velez, 1996, p. 87). According to St. John and Noell (1989), financial aid has a greater impact on college attendance for African Americans and Latinos than for Whites, and all types of financial aid are effective. Other evidence shows the significant positive impact of financial aid in the form of grants and fellowships and questions the effectiveness of repayable loans as a means to improve equitable access (Baker & Velez, 1996).

A comprehensive study of the effects of financial aid on college student persistence that controlled for student academic ability, motivation, college integration, and commitment concluded that financial aid has a significant but indirect impact. Apparently, financial aid allows "its recipients more freedom to engage in social activities, removes the anxieties associated with looking for funds to finance their education, and makes it easier to engage in academic activities that enhance academic performance" (Baker & Velez, 1996, p. 95). Thus, financial aid may help facilitate the social integration of students of color at PWIs, provided that the campus climate reflects conditions of democratic pluralism (a concept discussed later in this chapter).

Among students of color, weak academic preparation related to increasing segregation in elementary and secondary schools and attendance in inferior urban public schools is a background factor that affects college access and persistence. The poor academic preparation provided many Alaskan Natives, American Indians, African Americans, Mexican Americans, and Puerto Ricans in our nation's schools is well documented (College Board, 1985; Kozol, 1991; National Coalition of Advocates for Students, 1985; National Council of La Raza, 1990; Oakes, 1985; Wells, 1997). They are overrepresented in general in vocational tracks, in classes for the mentally retarded, and in schools that have outdated books and inadequate facilities. In fact, the authors of a 1988 report on Indian elementary school children found that only 53% were termed not handicapped (O'Brien, 1992a). Inadequate precollegiate education, coupled with rising standards in college entrance exams and a lack of counseling and remedial support, contributes to the declines in college access and academic success (Durán, 1994; Wright, 1987). Traditional criteria for college admission, such as standardized test scores and high school grades, are not good predictors of college potential for many minorities, especially Hispanic students (Durán, 1986), yet alternatives have not been developed. Some scholars point out that a disrespect for and denial of students' home cultures and communities, and an expectation that students of color assimilate into the White cultural milieu in order to succeed, are also important explanations (e.g., Tierny, 1999).

In an exemplary study of minority and nonminority access to higher education, Orfield (1988) developed a case study of declining college access and public policy in Los Angeles since the early 1970s. He points out that nearly a fifth of the nation's Hispanics live in the greater Los Angeles area, as do many African Americans and Asians. His data on dropouts, high school achievement levels, college access and retention, and job training programs are part of the Metropolitan Opportunity Project, which has been collecting large quantities of education data in five locations: Chicago, Houston, Philadelphia, Atlanta, and Los Angeles. Orfield found that African American and Hispanic students attend schools that are inferior to those serving Whites and Asians and that the college-going pool is shrinking for African American and Hispanic youth due to high school dropouts (43% for African Americans and Hispanics compared to 25% for Whites and 15% for Asians) and failure to obtain admission into four-year colleges because only the top 7% of high school graduates are eligible for the University of California system. Most African Americans or Hispanics "are entitled to nothing but a community college system from which few earn degrees or certificates and few transfer successfully and eventually win a B.A. degree" (p. 512). Orfield (1988) writes:

The educational policies needing close examination include those that increase high school dropouts, that increase the burdens on low-income families desiring a college education, that increase standards for admission to public four-year colleges and universities, that increase reliance on community colleges to prepare successful transfer students, that reduce and de-emphasize minority recruitment and retention programs, and that curtail civil rights enforcement. (p. 157)

He is particularly critical of California's 1960 Master Plan, which established "a huge system of public higher education on the basis of a highly selective system of access to the four-year college" (p. 157) and relies on two-year community colleges for everyone else. Orfield argues that because "high school education is unequal, and [because] there are tremendous racial differences in eligibility for public education . . . low-income minority families are paying state taxes that very heavily subsidize the universities which few of their children may attend" (p. 157), especially because the state funding of community colleges is declining.

Moreover, enrollment in community colleges is a factor that appears to decrease the chances of college graduation, especially among Latinos, who constitute about 57% of the two-year college population, compared to 39% of all students (Baker & Velez, 1996). The transfer process to four-year schools is often difficult to negotiate. In addition, "Such factors as language, culture, historical orientation to particular institutions, and degree of acceptance into the university community are believed to lead to different rates of completion for American Indians, African Americans, and Latinos" (p. 92). And a study of African American students in community college that examined the impact of the student's community found "considerable tension between the strong collective tradition of the African American community and the official notions of individualism embedded in the expectations of the community college, as well as between the belief in the value of knowledge and education and distrust of and skepticism toward school" (p. 93).

The voluminous literature focused on similarities and differences in issues related to college access and persistence among and within particular ethnic groups can only be touched on in this chapter. *Minorities in Higher Education* (Justiz, Wilson, & Bjork, 1994) is one excellent example. Chapters on Latino student access and persistence focus on standardized testing and educational attainment (Durán, 1994) and long-term (1975–1991) community and schooling factors that affect Latino student education attainment (de los Santos & Rigual, 1994). Chapters focused on African American college students discuss the role of historically Black colleges and universities (HBCUs), the community college experience, and the need to improve public education in large urban schools (Wilson, 1994), and the persistent importance of HBCUs in the 21st century (Payne, 1994). Another chapter surveys the history of American Indian participation in postsecondary education and explores the tensions between acculturation and maintaining traditional Native American community values and traditions (Kidwell, 1994). And a chapter by Suzuki (1994) corrects common misconceptions about Asian Americans as a monolithic model minority and discusses the urgent need for colleges and universities to address issues of Asian college student preparation, access, academic development, and achievement, as well as their experiences related to the college curriculum and pedagogy, the sociopsychological environment, college and university hiring and promotion practices, and returns on higher education.

Sections of the *Annual Status Reports of Minorities in Higher Education* (American Council on Education) are other examples of research reports focused on specific ethnic groups in higher education (e.g., Chapa, 1991; Hune & Chan, 1997). A special report on Hispanics stresses the complex interaction of social, economic, and demographic factors, as well as influences from elementary and secondary education (Chapa, 1991). Hispanics have a high proportion of younger age cohorts, and as one of the largest and fastest-growing minority groups in the United States, they will have an important role in the nation's workforce. Yet their high school completion rates are among the nation's lowest, and "their participation in higher education is much lower than their proportion of the college age population. . . . In fact, the rapid growth of the population masks increased attrition from the educational system" (Chapa, 1991, p. 13).

Efforts to address educational inequities among Latinos are hindered by a lack of knowledge about Latino students (Olivas, 1986). Much of the research on Latino college students has lumped them into a "minority population" with African Americans and has overlooked substantive linguistic differences and cultural experiences. Educational researchers and program evaluators measure Latino children with instruments and methodologies evolved from studies of majority students (Olivas, 1986) and tend to blame Latinos for their own school failure.

According to Olivas (1986), "In 1982 Hispanic children attended schools that were more segregated than in 1970 . . . [and] are less likely than majority or even most minority students to complete high school or graduate with their age groups" (p. 1). Bilingual education programs remain inadequate in most states; schools lack appropriate means of diagnosing students' linguistic competence and cognitive abilities, and they lack bilingual curricula and personnel. Olivas writes that these early failures of education are "mirrored in post secondary institutions. Here, issues of limited access, discriminatory employment practices, and high attrition disproportionately affect Hispanic students" (p. 3).

Decades of research show that many African American students do not fare well at predominantly White colleges and universities (Garibaldi, 1997). In a major study of Black college students, Fleming (1984) compared their experience in historically Black and predominantly White colleges. Her cross-sectional research was designed to "be large-scale enough to approximate a survey but intensive enough to approximate a case study" and explored general issues of student development while addressing "the importance of sex, race, and individual differences in the college experience" (p. 27). In her sample were 1,455 Black students at historically Black schools and 1,062 Black students and 388 White students at predominantly White schools, for a total of 1,752 freshmen and 971 seniors. Among African American students in her sample, 58.4% were female and 41.6% were male. Among White students in her sample, 57% were male and 43% were female. The survey research was conducted in several phases on 14 different campuses, administered in personalized group settings, and followed up with personalized interviews where feasible. Analyses of the massive amounts of data gathered in the study were organized into four factors displayed according to campus and race: academic adjustment, adjustment to college, career development, and psychosocial adjustment. Fleming concluded that African American students may be better served on Black campuses in terms of their personal, social, and cognitive development. Despite the generally superior resources and facilities on White campuses and despite the fact that Black students attending White schools tend to have stronger college-entry-level skills, Black students attending Black schools achieve greater academic success and personal development. Fleming attributes this to a friendlier, more supportive atmosphere for Blacks on Black campuses.

These findings are especially significant because since the 1960s, there has been a dramatic increase in the numbers of Black students attending predominantly White colleges and universities. Prior to 1950, over 75% of Black college students attended historically Black colleges due to segregation laws and the absence of open-admission policies. By 1973, that proportion was down to 25% and declined to less than 20% in the mid-1980s (Anderson, 1988; Garibaldi, 1991). Nevertheless, an average of 37% of the bachelor's degrees and about 30% of master's degrees earned by African Americans are awarded by HBCUs (Wilson & Carter, 1989), even though they represent barely 3% of the more than 3,000 colleges and universities in the United States (Garibaldi, 1997).

Deborah La Fountaine, director of development for the American Indian Science and Engineering Society (AISES), is appalled at the college retention figures for American Indian students. She accuses colleges and universities of recruiting students for funding purposes and then ignoring the problem of high attrition rates. As a result, she says, "All of our AISES programs deal with retention. . . . In Indian communities the community comes first. We teach them to reconcile the two worlds" (quoted in Rodriguez, 1992, p. 25). AISES stresses leadership training, curriculum development for grades 8 through 12, and teacher training because many teachers are non-Indians teaching on Indian reservations and do not relate well to their students.

In their history of American Indians in higher education, Wright and Tierney (1991) describe the centuries of efforts to Christianize and "civilize" the Indians. Throughout this history of miseducation, Indians have resisted pressures to give up their cultural identity. The tribal colleges that developed in the 1970s are for the most part a "response to the unsuccessful experience of Indian students on mainstream campuses" (p. 17). According to Paul Boyer, author of a Carnegie Foundation study on tribal colleges, "Tribal colleges are doing so well because they recognize these differences [between tribal and mainstream values] and stress tribal values and history in the curriculum" (quoted in O'Brien, 1992c, p. 28).

Some educators hypothesize that Indian students who attend public schools rather than Bureau of Indian Affairs (BIA) schools do better in mainstream colleges, but there is no research to support this theory. According to Boyer, Indians who do best in college are those who have the "strongest sense of self-identity and connections to Indianness." Students who live on reservations are more likely to develop these connections, although they also experience culture shock on White campuses. Indians who live in urban areas are not necessarily assimilated into White culture, and many suffer from "cultural homelessness"

(quoted in O'Brien, 1992c, p. 30). Because American Indians are a "minority among minorities," there is a danger that most colleges and universities will continue to be unresponsive to their needs (p. 15).

With the exception of Asian Americans, the proportion of minorities in higher education is lower than what would be expected if access to college were equitable. According to the 2000 census, African Americans account for 12.3% of the total population, Hispanics 12.5%, Asian Americans and Pacific Islanders 4.5%, and American Indians about 1.5% (U.S. Bureau of the Census, 2000). Their percentage of the undergraduate, graduate, and professional school student population is substantially less, especially when over half the minority student undergraduates are enrolled in community colleges from which most will not transfer on to four-year colleges. It should be noted, however, that the disparities between the proportion of minorities in the general and higher education populations have lessened since 1991, due in large part to affirmative action programs (Chang, Witt, Jones, & Hakuta, 2003) and various campus initiatives in higher education (Hurtado et al., 1999). Current attacks on affirmative action, the clear trend toward school resegregation at the precollegiate level (Garibaldi, 1997; Orfield, 1999), and increasing economic disparities between the wealthy and poor across ethnic groups all threaten to undo the progress made in equitable educational access and attainment during the past decade, as well as hinder future efforts to maximize the benefits of racial and cultural diversity on college campuses.

CREATING CAMPUS CLIMATES THAT RESPECT AND SUPPORT RACIALLY AND CULTURALLY DIVERSE STUDENT POPULATIONS

In their introduction to "Enhancing Campus Climates for Racial/Ethnic Diversity: Educational Policy and Practice," Hurtado, Milem et al. (1998) write,

Probably few policy areas of higher education have received more recent attention than the issue of race on campus. Evidence appears in policies and programs related to college admissions, financial aid, affirmative action, discrimination and harassment, and desegregation. Yet, at the same time, probably no area of campus life has been so devoid of policy initiatives as the racial climate at individual institutions. Until recently, there has been no common framework for understanding the campus racial climate in a way that helps develop policies and practices that can be used to enhance the campus climate. (p. 279)

They propose four explanations for this lack of attention to the racial climate on college campuses. First, there exists a laissez-faire approach wherein campus administrators have assumed that people on campus will work things out on their own and that interventions in student interactions are inappropriate. Second, faculty and administrators have been uncertain about their role as agents of socialization and the extent to which they should "try consciously to shape society" (p. 280). Third, although research documents the important role college and university faculty play as agents of socialization, university officials have been reluctant to address faculty attitudes and behaviors that may result in racial and cultural discrimination. And fourth, until recently, the field of higher education has overlooked or ignored several decades of research on issues that affect the racial climate on college campuses. The authors assert, "Perhaps at no other time in our history have higher education scholars had the opportunity to provide evidence of the educational outcomes of diversity in a way that puts the benefits of diversity at the center of the educational enterprise" (p. 280). Guided by this hopeful perspective, the following section begins with a discussion of the benefits of diversity, including a conceptual framework for understanding these benefits, and continues with a conceptual framework for understanding campus climate and related research.

Affirming the Benefits of Racial and Cultural Diversity on Campus

At a time when college and university administrators and academics, as well as national education associations, recognize that

> racial and ethnic diversity expands and enriches teaching and learning in colleges and universities . . . and that the ability to enroll a diverse student body and to hire a diverse faculty and staff are essential to the mission of colleges and universities across the nation . . . more and more constraints are being placed on campus leaders' ability to make decisions that ensure that racial and ethnic diversity is part of their institutions. (Milem & Hakuta, 2000, p. 40)

Scholars in higher education argue that it is imperative to inform the public about the benefits of racial and cultural diversity on college campuses (e.g., Hurtado, 1999; Kurlaender, & Orfield, 1999; Chang et al., in press; Hurtado, Milem et al., 1998, 1999; Milem, in press).

According to Milem and Hakuta (2000) four misconceptions about racial diversity on college campuses threaten to undermine progress already made to redress a legacy of racial discrimination and unequal access in education. First, there is a mistaken view that racial and ethnic minorities and low-income students no longer experience inequities in educational access and opportunities. Second is the misconception that student merit can be defined by standardized test scores, such as the Scholastic Aptitude Test (SAT) and the American College

Test (ACT). Third is the mistaken view that a "color-blind" or "race-neutral" policy is the best approach to achieve fairness and educational equity. And fourth is the misconception that only students of color (and not White students) benefit from policies and practices designed to strengthen racial and ethnic diversity on campus. Building on scholarly work in higher education (e.g., Milem & Hakuta, 2000; Hurtado et al., 1998, 1999), Milem and Hakuta (2000) identify three interrelated aspects of campus diversity: structural diversity (representation of diverse racial and ethnic groups in the student population), diversity-related initiatives (for example, multicultural curricula, workshops), and diverse interactions ("students' exchanges with racially and ethnically diverse people as well as diverse ideas, information, and experiences," p. 43). They also provide a "Conceptual Framework for Understanding the Educational Benefits of Diversity," which is an excellent summary of research that documents the benefits of racial and ethnic diversity on college campuses (Milem & Hakuta, 2000; Hurtado et al., 1998, 1999). Four major benefits of diversity on college campuses are identified: student learning and development, transformations of colleges and universities in terms of their missions, preparation of students for work in a global economy, and societal benefits in terms of preparing students for a racially diverse democratic society, such as civic and professional development and meeting society's needs for diversification of the medical profession (Milem & Hakuta, 2000). Student benefits are discussed below as an illustration of these benefits.

Research indicates that all students, not only students of color, benefit when increases in racial and cultural diversity are accompanied by appropriate campus policies. For example, studies indicate that racial and cultural diversity on college campuses (including cultural awareness workshops and opportunities to interact with diverse peers) are associated with better critical thinking skills, reductions in ethnocentrism, and better preparation for living in a pluralistic democratic society. Patricia Gurin (cited in Milem & Hakuta, 2000) discovered that students who are exposed to diverse ideas and people were more motivated and more engaged in higher-level thinking; for Whites, diverse ideas, new knowledge, and peer interactions were most important. African Americans benefited from interactions with diverse peers, but they benefited most when same-race interaction and same-race friendships were also part of their college experience. Research by Chang (reported in Milem & Hakuta, 2000, pp. 46–47) discovered that "socializing across race and discussing racial/ethnic issues have a positive effect on the learning outcomes of retention, intellectual self-concept, and social self-concept." Chang's research shows that increased structural diversity (greater representation of racially diverse students) improves the chances for cross-racial experience; however, if structural diversity is not accompanied by opportunities for cross-racial interactions (presumably positive interaction), students of color are likely to report less overall satisfaction with their college experience.

A Framework for Understanding Campus Climate

In a major review of recent and classic studies of student diversity and college environments, Hurtado and colleagues identify four interactive dimensions of the college campus climate that provide a "conceptual handle for understanding elements of the environment that were once thought to be too complex to comprehend" (1998, p. 281). Educational programs and practices at any one institution create a context, an institutional climate, that can be examined through these dimensions: (1) the historical legacy of inclusion or exclusion of various racial and ethnic groups, (2) structural diversity in terms of the numerical representation of various racial and ethnic groups, (3) the psychological climate comprising perceptions and attitudes between and among groups, and (4) intergroup relations on campus, or the behavioral climate.

Historical Legacy of Inclusion or Exclusion. Most PWIs have a history of limited access for students of color and are likely to have evolved in ways that benefit White students (Hurtado et al., 1998). Hurtado and associates (1998) argue that although "colleges and universities cannot change their past histories of exclusion (nor should they deny this past) . . . they can take steps to insure that diversity becomes a central value of their educational enterprise" (p. 284). Furthermore,

Campus leaders should not assume that members of their community (particularly incoming students) know these histories, nor should they assume teaching about these histories will lead to dissatisfaction. By being clear about an institution's past history of exclusion and the detrimental impact that this history has had on the campus, colleges and universities may garner broader support for their efforts to become more diverse through affirmative action programs and other programs and services designed to improve the climate for diversity. Moreover, acknowledging a past history of exclusion implies an institutional willingness to actively shed its exclusionary past. (p. 284–285)

Addressing legacies of exclusion rooted in institutional racism on campus is a major challenge. In a pioneering book that distinguishes between individual and institutional racism, Knowles and Prewitt (1969) state that individual acts of racism, as well as racist institutional policies, can sometimes occur unintentionally, without conscious prejudice, and can be based on ignorance. The authors explain the hidden power of institutions to reward and penalize people in such areas as career opportunities,

health care, educational development, political participation, treatment under the law, housing, and employment opportunities. Feagin and Feagin (1978) extend these early works in their writings about institutionalized racism and sexism in terms of direct discrimination and indirect discrimination. Examples of direct institutional racism in education include the "legally required or informally prescribed practices" that result in ethnic minority children being segregated into inferior public schools (p. 30). Direct institutional discrimination leads to indirect institutional discrimination when poorly educated minorities cannot compete with Whites and do not qualify for advanced education and employment even though school officials and employers may be eager to recruit ethnic minorities.

Bullock and Rogers (1976) explain how both direct and indirect institutional racism operate in higher education, particularly in admissions policies that base acceptance for undergraduate, graduate, and professional education on standardized tests that are geared to the curricula of White, middle-class schools. Many colleges now use affirmative action procedures in an attempt to redress past discrimination. Affirmative action procedures have, however, alienated many White students and faculty, who regard such programs as "reverse discrimination," even though the programs may also target low-income Whites. Perceptions of reverse discrimination, particularly among White males, may have contributed to the rise in racial incidents on college campuses in the 1980s and 1990s, and many minorities are themselves becoming disenchanted with campus affirmative action programs because they often stigmatize students and faculty who are erroneously perceived as less qualified than nonminorities on campus (Altbach & Lomotey, 1991; Altbach, Lomotey, & Kyle, 1999; Feagin & Feagin, 1993; Jones, 1981).

Cultural racism refers to the "elevation of the White Anglo-Saxon Protestant cultural heritage to a position of superiority over the cultural experiences of ethnic minority groups" (Gay, 1973, p. 33). Cultural racism combines ethnocentrism, the view that other cultures are inferior to the Anglo-European, and the power to suppress or eradicate manifestations of non-Anglo-European cultures. The legacy of cultural racism can be found in the formal curriculum, in tests, media, and course offerings. It can also be detected in the hidden, informal curriculum, as in low expectations for minority student achievement held by White faculty, ethnic and racial myths and stereotypes held by students and faculty in the university community, and an unfamiliar, unsupportive, unfriendly, or hostile campus environment.

Individual, institutional, and cultural racism are interactive on college campuses. In a sense, because colleges and universities are institutions, racism in higher education can be viewed simply as institutional racism. However, distinctions between types of racism, particularly individual versus cultural and institutional, help pinpoint the sources of racism and clarify approaches to reform. Because Whites are in control of campus life, institutional and cultural racism, even though it may be unintentional, is likely in the absence of campus-based self-scrutiny and conscious antiracist policy making. In the Foreword to *Latino College Students,* Madrid (1986) writes:

Racism can enter the school curriculum through written texts which depict minorities negatively or ignore them altogether. Intelligence tests may be considered a form of racism, since they measure one's knowledge of middle class culture. . . . The result of racism, in the educational system is continual segregation of Hispanics, . . . as demonstrated [also] by the concentration of Hispanics in two-year colleges as opposed to four-year colleges. (p. xvii)

The monocultural curriculum in place in most of the nation's colleges and universities is an example of persistent racism and exclusion. Gordon (1992) argues that even as Americans become

increasingly less European and more global in origin, . . . there has been a subtle but systematic insistence on the examination and celebration of a "single American heritage" and its assumed "universal perspective," both of which are the result of northern European cultural traditions having gained hegemony in North America. The dominance of these cultural traditions has proceeded simultaneously with a reduction in opportunities for the examination and celebration of other heritages as the rigid boundaries of ethnic communities and ghettos have weakened. (p. 235)

Indeed, conflict over the curriculum emerged in the 1980s as a major multicultural issue in higher education. In a crisp description of the polemics, Levine and Cureton (1992) wrote:

The competing claims about multiculturalism boom loudly today. Some say the college curriculum has been largely impermeable to multiculturalism: that it remains unalterably "Eurocentric," ignoring—or, at best, marginalizing—diversity concerns. Others counter that higher education has sold its soul in the name of multiculturalism, that the academy currently is purging the curriculum of its historic Western canon and replacing it willy-nilly with non-Western, ethnic, and gender studies. (p. 25)

Levine and Cureton (1992) surveyed a random sample of 270 colleges and universities stratified by Carnegie type to be representative of American higher education. They focused on whether, and to what extent, these institutions engaged in specific multicultural activities. The researchers concluded that a third of all colleges and universities have a multicultural general education requirement and offer course work in ethnic and gender studies, over half (54%) have introduced multiculturalism into some of their departmental course offerings (particularly English, history, and the social sciences), and a majority

are seeking to increase the ethnic diversity of their faculty (36% are actively recruiting, and another 22% report passive efforts). Efforts to put multiculturalism into the curriculum are uneven; they are evident in "public institutions more than private, four-year schools more than two-year schools, research universities more than other types of colleges, and middle Atlantic and western schools more than southern and northeastern institutions" (p. 29). The researchers argue that neither the view that the curriculum is unalterably "Eurocentric" nor the view that multiculturalism has replaced the historic Western canon is correct. "Multiculturalism is widespread in higher education today," but it lacks cohesion and "so far is only a beginning of what is likely to be a very long process" (p. 29). Although Levine and Cureton do not make the point, it seems noteworthy that approximately two thirds of the schools surveyed did not report any multicultural general education requirements, nearly half did not report any departments that are including multicultural content, and over half are not actively recruiting ethnic minority faculty.

Structural Diversity and Its Impact on Students. Structural diversity refers to the representation of racially and ethnically diverse students, faculty, and staff at a particular institution. Research indicates that increasing the representation of people of color is a necessary, though insufficient, "step toward improving the campus climate for diversity" (Hurtado et al., 1998, p. 287). Affirmative action programs that are most successful in enhancing minority student access and attainment are those that base selection criteria on both individual merit and group membership (Levin, 2003). Different criteria to select students from underrepresented minority groups and the majority group may be necessary because of inequities in precollegiate educational and economic opportunities linked with group status and the history of institutional racism; however, individual achievement-related characteristics must also be considered to ensure that affirmative action is procedurally fair and affirms the self-confidence and esteem of beneficiaries.

Two policy areas that can produce immediate increases in the proportion of students of color on campus are admissions and financial aid, as well as other strong affirmative action programs. For example, a study of college application behaviors of ethnically diverse students based on data from the National Longitudinal Study (NELS) and the Beginning Postsecondary Student Longitudinal Study (BPS) found that "increasing the diversity of the student body in terms of racial/ethnic backgrounds and family incomes becomes a more difficult task under conditions of weak affirmative action programs and diminished student financial aid—two of higher education's main redistributive measures aimed at assuring greater college access" for African Americans and Latinos (Hurtado, Inkelas, Briggs, & Rhee, 1997, p. 66). In addition to affirmative action related to financial aid and admissions, recruitment and retention of Native American college students must also include culturally appropriate strategies, begin in elementary and middle school, and involve Native communities (Thomason & Thurber, 1999).

In a review of issues associated with testing and assessment in equitable college access, Astin (1994) makes a case for revised college admission policies to increase the enrollments of students of color. His talent development approach defines excellence in terms of what colleges and universities do for students once they are admitted, rather than the criteria of average standardized test scores for entering students. In an attempt to ascertain the impact on minority student representation on college campuses, Astin and a colleague conducted a simulation study using national college admissions test data, wherein the current emphasis on high school grades, test scores, and other assessment data was modified. Their major findings include the following:

- Both African Americans and Hispanics are put at a competitive disadvantage when high school grades and standardized admissions test scores are used in making admissions decisions. Test scores pose a greater handicap than high school grades do, especially for African Americans.
- The handicap resulting from the use of test scores and grades becomes greater as the selection ratio increases. A simple combination of test scores and grades produces an 80% underrepresentation of African Americans when the selection ratio is one and four, but only a 65% under representation when the selection ratio is one in two.
- Much of the handicap posed by the use of test scores and grades can be mitigated by the use of a "disadvantagement index" based on the income and educational level of the student's parents. This index gives special credit for students whose parents are poor and/or relatively uneducated.
- Underrepresented minorities benefit differently from the use of a disadvantagement index, but such an index must be given substantial weight to overcome the handicap imposed by test scores and grades.
- Given the considerable handicap posed by standardized test scores, the use of a disadvantagement index benefits minority students more if it is combined with grades alone rather than with grades and test scores. (Astin, 1994, pp. 61–62)

Oliver and Etchevery (1987) conducted a longitudinal study of factors that influence academically talented Black students to attend college. They surveyed 82% of the African American students with a cumulative grade point average of B or above who graduated from a Midwestern high school during a five-year period, for a total of 184 respondents. Five influence variables that discriminated between college attendees and nonattendees were identified as significant and accounted for 42.7% of the variance. These were, in descending order of importance, career objectives, availability of financial aid, job availability, contact with professionals working in the field of interest, and peers. The researchers recommended that college recruitment efforts should be focused on jobs and careers, should include concrete information on financial aid, should use prospective students' local networks, and should strengthen connections with professionals in students' fields of interest.

According to Genevieve M. Ramirez (quoted in Fields, 1988), professor of Mexican American studies at California State University at Long Beach:

The research conducted on large cross-sections of college students nationwide offers us the following facts as significant enhancements of academic success: good high school preparation, good study habits, high self-esteem, relatively well-educated and somewhat affluent family background, entry from high school directly to a four-year institution, residence on campus, receipt of financial aid grants or scholarships and no need to work, and enrollment at a selective institution. (p. 25)

She added, "Hispanic-origin students nationwide, except the limited numbers of immigrants coming from affluent refugee families, are almost item-for-item the exact opposite" (quoted in Fields, 1988, p. 25). When asked to identify the two main reasons that they or their peers must withdraw from the university, Ramirez said that Hispanic "students most highly rated the following factors, in order: need to support self or family financially, lack of interest/motivation/goals, time conflicts with job or family obligations, emotional inability to cope with college demands, academic under-preparedness, and poor academic performance" (p. 25).

There is an urgent need for researchers to develop knowledge of college achievement predictors for Hispanic students (Durán, 1986). Although he realizes that high school grades and college admission test scores will continue to be used in the foreseeable future, Durán proposes that the following factors also be reviewed for Hispanic college applicants: (1) language background and proficiency in English; (2) exposure to schooling in Spanish and academic achievement in Spanish contexts; (3) high aspirations and motivation to achieve combined with lower-than-expected high school grades and admissions test scores; (4) high school grades and test scores that are higher than would be expected based on family socio-economics (i.e., severe financial or family obligations during high school coupled with higher-than-expected grades and test scores); (5) involvement in significant school, home, or community activities that require academic skills; and (6) the development of significant literacy skills in Spanish and the ability to use these skills at advanced levels.

In a federally funded study aimed at identifying factors that help minority students succeed in college, six lessons emerged from the case studies of 10 public universities (Richardson, Simmons, & de los Santos, 1987). The universities were selected because of their strong records for awarding baccalaureate degrees to one or more of three underrepresented minority groups in higher education: African Americans, Latinos, and Native Americans. Other criteria for selection included a commitment to providing opportunities to minorities and willingness to share their experiences (the case studies are not disguised), diverse missions and geographic locations, and a predominantly White or multicultural student population. The authors write: "While all of the universities offered some form of intervention strategies such as summer bridge programs, early outreach, remediation, tutoring, and counseling support, none believed that these special programs captured the essence of their efforts to graduate minorities" (p. 20). In their attempt to understand the perspectives of these "very diverse" institutions, the researchers identified six common themes that help explain their successes in minority student achievement. First, "minority achievement is viewed as a preparation problem rather than a racial problem" (p. 21). For the short run, these schools waive regular admission standards to achieve "acceptable levels of representation," but they are also working to expand the admissions pool of regularly qualified high school graduates through early outreach programs in the elementary and junior high schools. Second, the importance of a positive campus climate is recognized. These universities recognize the connection between student involvement in campus life and their academic success. In multicultural settings, such as Memphis State University or Florida International University, a positive environment seems to emerge on its own. One faculty member succinctly described the shift that had taken place as minority enrollments grew from tolerance ("they're here") to acceptance ("let's work with them") (Richardson et al., 1987, p. 23). At predominantly White schools, where minority student enrollments are closer to 10%, considerable attention is given to building a hospitable environment.

The four remaining lessons reflect a strong commitment from campus authority figures to strengthening diversity: (1) concerns about small numbers of minorities on the faculty and the underinvolvement of all faculty in equal opportunity strategies; (2) strong, visible leadership and commitment from the administration; (3) comprehensive and systematic (rather than fragmented and sporadic) strategies for promoting the academic success of minorities, with an emphasis on achievement rather than retention; and (4) a favorable state policy environment (though this was not present in 2 of the 10 schools). The researchers conclude with some intriguing questions that also emerged from the study. Is there a minimum presence a minority group must attain to become a vital part of the campus community? Do individuals from marginally represented groups or multicultural campuses experience the same problems as they would in predominantly White schools? Which early intervention strategies are most effective in expanding the pool of qualified minority students? What kinds of contributions from minority communities can be reasonably expected?

In a later phase of the study (Skinner & Richardson, 1988), 107 spring 1986 minority graduates from the 10 schools were interviewed by telephone. "Rich portraits of minority student achievement" (p. 37) emerged through open-ended interviews that focused on precollegiate preparation, family backgrounds, and university experiences. Although every story is unique, four student types emerged:

1) well-prepared, second generation college-goers with a lifelong commitment to higher education; 2) first generation students who also grew up with a strong belief in education, but whose preparation was inadequate; 3) first and second generation students who questioned the value of education in their lives, despite adequate preparation; and 4) first generation college students with little preparation who had grown up never intending to go to college. (p. 38)

In the discussion of implications from their research, Skinner and Richardson (1988) argue that the institution must take steps to accommodate student diversity. When there is a mismatch between a student's background and university expectations, the authors state:

To the extent that institutions expect students to do all or most of the adjusting, they limit the range of minority students they can serve responsibly to those who resemble traditional college-goers in preparation and opportunity orientation. . . . Given the current socioeconomic status of blacks, Hispanics, and American Indians—the disparities in parental education and income, the deficiencies in schooling, and so on—relatively few minority students will fit the profile of the well-prepared students in category one. (p. 42)

The 10 case study universities in their research recognize this fact and take steps to prevent discrimination and create a positive campus climate. Overall, Skinner and Richardson (1988) show that "minorities can succeed in a variety of settings—when the *institution* accepts responsibilities for improving its environment as well as working to improve the preparation and opportunity orientations of its students" (p. 42).

The Psychological Dimension of Climate and Its Impact on Students. The psychological climate of an institution refers to student, faculty, and staff perceptions of racial and ethnic tension; perceptions of discrimination; attitudes; and reduction of prejudice (Hurtado et al., 1999). There exists ample research evidence that campus climate has a major impact on the success or failure of students in college (Sedlacek, Helm, & Prieto, 1997). The success of a campus program depends on the degree to which all groups on campus perceive the value of diversity, power relations among groups are equal, and diversity programs are based on prior research (Sedlacek et al., 1997). And research grounded in theories of ethnic identity development indicates that a student's sense of ethnic identity is an important factor in mediating the psychological dimension of campus climate.

A prevalent theme in the research on minority students attending predominantly White colleges and universities is the feeling of "culture shock" (Fiske, 1988) and alienation due to conflicts between the students' home cultures and university expectations (Chew & Ogi, 1987; O'Brien, 1992b; Pounds, 1987; Quevedo-Garcia, 1987). Boateng (1990) refers to the deculturalization process many minority children experience in public school. The process continues at the postsecondary level. Farrell and Jones (1988) write that

the behaviors, lifestyles, and values of minority students are likely to be substantially different from those of whites, [making it difficult for those students] to successfully negotiate the university environment. . . . Universities, on the other hand, have made limited adjustments in their organizational and administrative structures and practices to accommodate the diverse and complex needs of their minority student populations, especially Blacks, Hispanics and American Indians. (p. 212)

As a result, many minority students have dropped out of school or found needed peer support in voluntary segregation, a phenomenon that is often resented and feared by White students, adding to racial tensions and misunderstandings.

There is overwhelming evidence that college students of color on White campuses feel more alienated than their White peers and less satisfied with many aspects of academic and social life (Allen, 1987; Fleming, 1984; Feagin & Sikes, 1995). Beginning in 1981, the National Study of Black College Students (NSBCS), directed by Walter Allen, has tracked the achievements, experiences, attitudes, and backgrounds of African American undergraduates at a variety of historically Black and predominantly White colleges and universities. The research conducted by Allen and his associates reveals that attrition rates of Black students on predominantly White college campuses are five to eight times higher than the attrition rates of White students on the same campuses. African American students also report more dissatisfaction and alienation than White students. In contrast, Black students at HBCUs experience more academic success and are portrayed as more "satisfied, engaged in campus life, and well-adjusted" (Allen, 1987, p. 28).

A study of the unique stresses experienced by minority students at PWIs explored the possibility that college freshmen of color experience difficulties beyond the generic adjustment problems that are common to all incoming students, such as academics, social support networks, and financial worries (Smedley, Myers, & Harrell, 1993). African American students in particular appear to experience minority status stresses related to "experiences with racism and questions about their right to be on campus" that constitute an additional stress load beyond the usual college freshman experience (Smedley et al., 1993, p. 435). A number of other studies lend support to this conceptualization of minority status stress. For example, in a case study that compared the attitudes and characteristics of minority and nonminority persisters with attitudes and characteristics of nonpersisters at one predominantly White university, Bennett and Okinaka (1990) found that Asian and African American persisters felt less satisfied with the university, felt more trauma, and experienced less positive interracial contact on campus than did the nonpersisters. Among Anglos and Latinos on this campus, those who felt most negative had dropped out. It appeared that the longer African American and Asian students remained on campus, the more dissatisfied and socially alienated they felt.

This study did not provide answers as to why this was the case. But possibly it is because these groups are the most easily identified as racially distinct from the White majority. Neither entry-level skills nor academic performance on campus explained the high levels of dissatisfaction and social alienation because Asians were at the higher end of the continuum of grade point averages and SAT and ACT scores, and African Americans were at the lower end, although the highest-achieving African American students also dropped out at a high rate. Yet Asian and African American persisters on that campus felt more alienated and dissatisfied than did their Hispanic or White classmates.

The myth of the model minority contributes to stereotypes that create special problems for Asian Americans on college campuses. For example, Suzuki (1989) writes that "large numbers [of Asian Americans] are encountering personal or academic difficulties; many, especially those who have recently immigrated, are struggling to learn English . . . [and] many Asian students are undergoing extreme psychological stress and alienation" (p. 18). Stereotypes of the "successful student" mislead teachers and counselors who overlook language problems and pressures to achieve that are experienced by many Asian students.

A growing body of qualitative research describes cultural conflict among American Indian students in college. For example, a two-year ethnographic study for the Ford Foundation (Tierney, 1991) found that Native American college students experienced problems that are also faced by non-Indians, such as lack of academic preparation and feelings of loneliness. He identified other problems unique to Indian students, such as

native beliefs about science that might conflict with what is taught in a biology class, or the feeling that one must return home for specific ceremonies even if it means a class must be missed or an exam skipped. Family obligations are paramount for most Indian students. (p. 36)

Two studies have identified stress encountered in college as an important factor for understanding Latino undergraduates (Muñoz, 1986; Muñoz & García-Bahne, 1977). Both studies consisted of three phases: a one-hour structured interview (one-to-one), a paper-and-pencil demographic questionnaire, and administration of the College Environmental Stress Index. The second study (Muñoz, 1986) was conducted with samples of 342 Chicano students and 120 Anglo students enrolled in four California universities. The results showed that Latino college students experienced more stress than did Anglo students; Chicanas reported greater stress than did Chicanos, while Anglo men and women were similar in the stress they encountered. Despite their higher stress scores, however, Chicanas were more academically successful than Chicano students. Chicana students received less family support than Chicanos and experienced greater sex role conflicts. Furthermore, the primary support systems for Chicanas appeared to be Chicana discussion groups and campus organizations. A third study (Chacón, Cohen, & Strover, 1986) found that time spent on domestic tasks became barriers to higher education among Chicanas, a trait not encountered to the same degree among Chicanos or the Anglo women studied.

In a review of research on Black students at PWIs that are "largely run by Whites for Whites," Sedlacek (1987) argues that a strong sense of ethnic identity is related to positive academic experiences and social interactions on campus. *Ethnic identity* refers to the degree to which a person feels connected with a racial or culture group, one's familial ethnic group while growing up. (An ethnic group is a community of people within a larger society that is socially distinguished or set apart, by others or by itself, primarily on the basis of racial or cultural characteristics, such as religion, language, a shared history, and tradition [Gordon, 1966]. The central factor is the idea of being set apart from the larger society, based on physical or cultural attributes or both. Thus, American ethnic groups are socially constructed categories based on both race, that is, innate physical or biological attributes, and culture, that is, an acquired worldview, attitudes, values, beliefs, norms, verbal and nonverbal communication, and so forth.) Ethnic identity is a complex cluster of factors "including self-labeling, a sense of belonging, positive evaluation, preference for the group, ethnic interest and knowledge, and involvement in activities associated with the group" (Phinney, 1996, p. 923). The strength or degree of one's ethnic identity is significantly influenced by factors such as language spoken in the home, ethnic composition of the neighborhood, and percentage of friends who are in the same ethnic group. There are developmental differences within an individual over the span of a lifetime, as well as tremendous variability within any one ethnic group in terms of the strength of ethnic identification, the adherence to familial cultural values and norms, and experiences in the predominantly White society.

A number of scholars have explored racial and ethnic identity development among students of color at the college level (Dalton, 1991; Ethier & Deaux, 1994; Harris & Nettles, 1991; Mitchell & Dell, 1992; Parham & Helms, 1985; Taylor & Howard-Hamilton, 1995). This research reveals that ethnic identity plays a significant role in a student's college experience, particularly with regard to social integration. For instance, Rooney (1985) argues that ethnic identity among ethnic minority students at PWIs influences their ability to adjust both academically and socially and to develop institutional relationships that contribute to their integration into campus life. Likewise, Gerdes and Mallinckrodt (1994) argue that social factors are as important as, and in some cases more important than, academic factors in the college persistence and development of minority students. Research has shown that a student's level of ethnic identity plays a significant role in her or his social interactions with college peers, faculty, and administrators (Bennett, 1984; Dalton, 1991; Ethier & Deaux, 1994; Harris & Nettles, 1991; Mitchell & Dell, 1992; Parham & Helms, 1985; Stage, 1989; Taylor & Howard-Hamilton, 1995). This phenomenon is intensified for ethnic minority students at PWIs and influences their ability to succeed academically and to develop social relationships that contribute to their integration into campus life (Rooney, 1985).

One of the most prevalent theories of racial identity pertaining to African American students is the Nigrescence Model introduced by William Cross (1971). Nigrescence is defined by Cross (1971) as "the process of developing a Black identity." Cross argues that there are five psychological stages of Nigrescence: pre-encounter, encounter, immersion-emersion, internalization, and internalization-commitment. Personal identity development may or may not include a highly salient ethnic identity and influences the perceptions and interactions of African Americans in predominantly White settings, such as most college and university environments (Cross, 1989; Cross, Strauss, & Fhagen-Smith, 1999).

While numerous studies have focused on the ethnic identity of African American college students, substantially less is written about the college experiences and ethnic identity of Latinos, Asians, or American Indians. However, two recent studies provide helpful insights regarding ethnic identity development among Latino and Latina students in college (Ethier & Deaux, 1994; Fiske, 1988). Fiske (1988) argues that for many Latino students, the most serious problems are those they confront once they arrive on campus, not barriers they encounter getting into college. He argues that "even those from secure and privileged backgrounds are often thrown off-balance by finding themselves identified as belonging to a 'minority' group for the first time" (p. 29). In his study of 10 Latino students at 10 different predominantly White universities across the country, Fiske (1988) concluded:

The problem of how to balance participation in two cultures is a continuing one, and each Hispanic student must make his or her own decision. Some join Hispanic social or political groups and affirm their heritage as overtly as possible. Others become "coconuts"—brown on the outside, white on the inside—but this leads to charges of selling out. (p. 31)

In a longitudinal study of first-year Latino students at a predominantly White university, Ethier and Deaux (1994) identified two very different processes of ethnic identity development. Students who entered college with a strong sense of ethnic identity made choices that continued their involvement in ethnic activities and resulted in stronger ethnic group identification. Students who came in with a weak sense of ethnic identity showed more signs of stress with resultant lower self-esteem and negative feelings about their ethnicity. Family background, high school friends, and neighborhood context all contributed to a strong sense of ethnic identity. Latino students who came from communities with high concentrations of Latinos, spoke Spanish in their homes, and had a high percentage of Latino friends during high school were more likely to make friends with other Latinos and join Latino organizations at college. Students who did not possess these precollegiate characteristics and did not identify strongly with their ethnic group generally felt conflicted about being categorized as Hispanics by the university. Furthermore, these students were more likely to perceive threats to their identity and have a lower sense of self-esteem. Strategies for addressing these issues for Latino students at PWIs, particularly in university counseling centers, have been identified and are being implemented on some college campuses (e.g., Gloria & Rodriguez, 2000).

Overall, researchers conclude that minority students succeed at unprecedented rates when optimal levels of student social psychological components such as the following are present: (1) supportive relationships with peers and institutional agents (e.g., faculty), (2) social outlets and friends (e.g., parties and social outings), (3) self-confidence and self-esteem, (4) psychological comfort and sense of belonging, and (5) a sense of empowerment and ownership (Allen, 1992).

The Behavioral Dimension of Climate and Its Impact on Students. There exists abundant research on the negative experiences of minority students at PWIs concerning nonminority faculty and student peers (e.g., Allen, 1992; Burrell, 1980; Cole, 1999; Kraft, 1991). This evidence shows that classroom climates at PWIs are often not accepting of students of color. For example, in one study of student contact with college faculty, African American students reported fewer interactions with faculty within and outside the classroom than did their White classmates. They attributed this to racial prejudice and discrimination on the part of their instructors and nonminority peers (Nettles, Thoeny, & Gosman, 1986). Other researchers have noted the importance of student perceptions of racism on campus and how these perceptions influence their college experience and persistence (Nettles et al., 1986). As would be expected, minority student perceptions of racism negatively influenced their interactions with faculty and peers at PWIs (Kraft, 1991; Nora & Cabrera, 1996). In a study of 338 minority students at five PWIs, Burrell (1980) found that almost one third of the students reported that they were not called on enough by teachers to participate in class discussions. Half of these students stated that the teacher assumed minority students "were the experts on the minority experience and history" (Burrell, 1980, p. 25) and said they were often asked to elaborate on the perspectives of minority students and the conditions of race relations. Only a few students perceived that their faculty spent sufficient class time in dealing with the experiences of ethnic minorities related to the subject matter. In other studies, minority students report the direct effects of racist assumptions in class and conclude that faculty were less willing to interact with them, even when dealing with their academic concerns (Allen, 1992; Burrell, 1980; Kraft, 1991). Minority students who lacked significant contact with faculty wondered if race were the reason (Kraft, 1991; Nettles et al., 1986).

Moreover, Nettles (1991) shows that college progression rates of African American college students increase when college instructors use a "nontraditional teaching style" (i.e., lecture is deemphasized) and are perceived to be equitable and nondiscriminatory (no such connections were discovered for White students at PWIs). And research at a small public university in California highlights the importance of quality teaching and faculty accessibility as components contributing to the success of minority students (Loo & Rolison, 1986). Small class size, noncompetitive classroom environments, diverse curriculum, and limited objective exams were related to student perceptions of extensive faculty and peer interaction and subsequent satisfaction with their academic programs. For these minority students, nonminority faculty and peer support, faculty accessibility, and other social psychological factors were important in their development as college students.

A study of teaching styles and classroom climate in postsecondary education identifies five distinctive styles of teaching that provide conceptual clarity for thinking about "traditional" and "nontraditional" teaching: Expert, Formal Authority, Personal Model, Facilitator, and Delegator (Grasha, 1994). It supports other research that indicates the benefits of nontraditional teaching for many students of color in particular. An *Expert* teaching style is content-driven teaching, where the primary goal is knowledge transmission; students may enjoy having access to a knowledgeable "high-status" faculty member, but they may also feel intimidated and view the teacher as aloof. Similarly, a *Formal Authority* teaching style poses the teacher as the source of knowledge, whose primary role is to create classroom rules and establish learning objectives and expectations for student learning. While students may appreciate receiving critical feedback from their instructor, they may also perceive their teacher to be rigid and insensitive. In the *Personal Model* style, the teacher leads by example and emphasizes a hands-on approach through role modeling. This style presents the teacher's way as the best and may leave some students feeling inadequate in comparison. In contrast, a *Facilitator* style emphasizes the development of teacher-student and student-student interactions. The facilitator's primary goal is to develop the student as an independent and responsible learner. This style is highly flexible, but can be time-consuming and ineffective at times when a direct approach is necessary. *Delegators* stress the development of student autonomy; they act primarily as a resource person but may have difficulty in gauging students' readiness for autonomy in their learning.

These styles appear in faculty teaching behavior in varying degrees, primarily in four main combinations (Grasha, 1994): Expert/Formal Authority (Combination 1), Expert/Personal Model/Formal Authority (Combination 2), Expert/Facilitator/Personal Model (Combination 3), and Expert/ Facilitator/Delegator (Combination 4). Some of the combinations create a more comfortable learning environment where students are actively engaged and interact with each other, while others do not. For instance, Combination 1 (Expert/Formal Authority), which consists of lectures, term papers, and some guest presentations, creates the least comfortable environment for developing faculty-student and peer interactions. In contrast, Expert/Facilitator/Delegator (Combination 4), composed primarily of student-designed group projects, independent research projects, and cooperative learning

activities, is the most conductive for developing faculty-student and peer interactions. Research suggests that students of color may learn best in settings that favor Combination 3 (Expert/Facilitator/Personal Model) with its emphasis on small group discussions, debates, case studies, and problem-based learning as the primary teaching techniques (e.g., Bennett, Cole, & Thompson, 1999; Loo & Rolison, 1986).

CONCLUSIONS: INTEGRATED PLURALISM AND CAMPUS CLIMATE

Integrated pluralism is a theoretical ideal that provides a conceptual framework to create campus climates where students and faculty of every cultural and racial background feel welcome and are encouraged to reach their highest potential. School desegregation research shows that good race relations, high standards of academic achievement, and personal development among all students are most likely when school policies are based on the model of integrated pluralism rather than on that of assimilation or business as usual (Forehand & Ragosta, 1976). Most of the desegregation research has been conducted in public schools (K–12), but there is every reason to assume that these findings would apply in desegregated colleges and universities as well.

Integrated pluralism refers to a school setting characterized by equity and mutual respect among the diverse racial and cultural groups on campus. In contrast to assimilation or business as usual, in which all students on campus are expected to conform to White middle-class culture, Sagar and Schofield (1984) write:

Integrated pluralism affirms the equal value of the school's various ethnic groups, encouraging their participation, not on majority defined terms, but in an evolving system, which reflects the contributions of all groups. However, integrated pluralism goes beyond mere support for the side-by-side coexistence of different group values and styles. It is integrationist in the sense that it affirms the educational value inherent in exposing all students to a diversity of perspectives and behavioral repertoires and the social value of structuring the school so that students from previously isolated and even hostile groups can come to know each other under conditions conducive to the development of intergroup relations. . . .

Integrated pluralism takes an activist stance in trying to foster interaction between different groups of students rather than accepting resegregation as either desirable or inevitable. (pp. 231–232)

The concept of integrated pluralism has developed out of social contact theory and interracial contact situations such as desegregated schools, housing, and workplaces that bring ethnically encapsulated groups together for the first time. According to social contact theorists, positive racial attitudes develop out of positive interracial contacts if certain conditions in the contact situations exist (Allport, 1954; Byrne, 1961; Cohen, 1976; DeVries & Edwards, 1974; Sagar & Schofield, 1984; Wiser & Cook, 1971). Based on the original work of Gordon Allport, four conditions are necessary if these contacts are to be positive: (1) an equal-status environment for minorities and nonminorities, especially in classrooms and in cocurricular activities; (2) a social climate that supports interracial association, especially as modeled by authority figures such as teachers, principals, superintendents, and college administrators; (3) contacts among minorities and nonminorities that lead to in-depth knowledge and understandings of each other's similarities and differences; and (4) opportunities for minorities and nonminorities to work together cooperatively to achieve common goals.

Most colleges and universities in the United States represent a classic interracial contact situation in that many undergraduates have grown up in ethnically encapsulated environments (Banks, 1991). Whether they are from rural areas, small towns, inner cities, or the suburbs, most students have been isolated from some of the other ethnic groups on campus and often hold fears, myths, and stereotypes about them. This contributes to racial unrest when neither the curriculum nor campus life provides opportunities to unlearn these negative prejudices and misunderstandings. Casual observation shows that for most students, ethnic encapsulation continues on campus, often through unconscious or voluntary separation. A lack of integration may contribute to the high rate of attrition among African Americans, Latinos, and American Indians attending predominantly White colleges and universities.

However, it must also be emphasized that opportunities for peer interactions and friendships within one's ethnic group are a necessary component of integrated pluralism, especially on predominantly White campuses, where less than 10% of the students and 3% of the faculty are minorities. Many forms of intragroup self-segregation or isolation have existed throughout the history of higher education without destroying the sense of campus community (Cortés, 1991). Social segregation is based on the same gender, as in sororities and fraternities; shared religious beliefs, as in a Hillel or a Newman Center; common social goals, as in volunteer tutoring programs; and ethnic-based student organizations where people "gather periodically in ethnic comfort zones of shared experiences, identities, and concerns" (Cortés, 1991, p. 11). It is when students, faculty, or staff of "visibly similar ethnic appearance" gather that critics proclaim this as evidence of "Balkanization" or "tribalism" (p. 11). Furthermore, numerous studies point out the benefits of intragroup organizations and supports for minority students on White campuses (Allen, 1988; Bennett, 2002; Bennett et al., 1999; Hurtado et al., 1999; Kuh et al., 1991; Milem & Hakuta, 2000; Muñoz & García-Bahne, 1977).

Finally, the idea of integrated pluralism captures the spirit of conversation and research on racial issues in higher education today. It affirms arguments to transform old notions of academic and social integration in college student success:

Rather than demand that students of color attending mainstream institutions of higher education undergo initiation rites that inevitably led to their cultural suicide, a more protean cultural model of academic life should prevail. Such a model should contend that students of color on predominantly White campuses be able to affirm, rather than reject, who they are. Campuses that adopt this model will not be sites of assimilation but, instead, sites of contestation and multiple interpretations. Individuals on these campuses will not struggle over the presently static model of culture but over more fluid and dynamic notions. In such settings, students of color will not only have greater likelihood of gaining access to institutional capital, but the campuses themselves will become more democratic spheres of educational opportunity. (Tierney, 1999, p. 89)

References

Allen, W. R. (1987). Black colleges vs. White colleges: The fork in the road for Black students. *Change, 19*(3), 28–34.

Allen, W. R. (1988a). Black students in U.S. higher education: Toward improved access, adjustment, and achievement. *Urban Review, 20*, 165–188.

Allen, W. R. (1992). The color of success: African-American college student outcomes at predominantly White and historically Black public colleges and universities. *Harvard Educational Review, 62*(1), 26–44.

Allport, G. (1954). *The nature of prejudice*. Reading, MA: Addison-Wesley.

Altbach, P. G., & Lomotey, K. Eds. (1991). *The racial crisis in American higher education*. Albany: State University of New York Press.

Altbach, P. G., Lomotey, K., & Kyle, S. R. (1991). Race in higher education: The continuing crisis. In P. G. Altbach, R. O. Berdahl, & P. J. Gumport (Eds.), *American higher education in the twenty-first century: Social, political, and economic challenges* (pp. 448–466). Baltimore: Johns Hopkins University Press.

Anderson, J. (1988). *The education of Blacks in the South, 1820–1935*. Chapel Hill: University of North Carolina Press.

Astin, A. (1994). Educational equity and the problem of assessment. In M. J. Justiz, R.M. Wilson, & L. G. Bjork (Eds.), *Minorities in higher education* (pp. 44–63). Phoenix, AZ: American Council on Education/Oryx Press.

Baker, T. L., & Velez, W. (1996). Access to and opportunity in postsecondary education in the United States: A review. *Sociology of Education (extra issue)*, 82–101.

Banks, J. A. (1991). Teaching multicultural literacy to teachers. *Teaching Education, 4*(1), 135–144.

Bennett, C. I. (1984). Interracial contact experience and attrition among Black undergraduates at a predominantly White university. *Theory and Research in Social Education, 12*(2), 19–47.

Bennett, C. I. (2002). Enhancing ethnic diversity at a big ten university through Project TEAM: A case study in teacher education. *Educational Researcher, 31*(2), 21–29.

Bennett, C., Cole, D. & Thompson, J. (1999, April). Teacher education in a collaborative multicultural classroom: Implications for critical-mass-minority and all-minority classes at a predominantly White university. In C. Bennett (Chair), *Project TEAM.* Symposium conducted at the meeting of the American Educational Research Association, Montreal, Canada.

Bennett, C. I., Cole, D., & Thompson, J. N. (2000). Preparing teachers of color at a predominantly White university: A case study of Project TEAM. *Teaching and Teacher Education, 16,* 445–464.

Bennett, C. I., & Okinaka, A. (1990). Factors related to persistence among Asian, Black, Hispanic, and White undergraduates at a predominantly White university: Comparison between first and fourth year cohorts. *Urban Review, 22*(1), 33–60.

Boateng, F. (1990). Combatting deculturalization of the African-American child in the public school system: A multicultural approach. In K. Lomotey (Ed.), *Going to school: The African American experience* (pp. 73–84). Albany: State University of New York Press.

Bullock, C. S., III, & Rodgers, H. R. (1976). Institutional racism: Prerequisites, freezing, and mapping. *Phylon, 37*(3), 212–223.

Burrell, L. F. (1980). Is there a future for black students on predominantly White campuses? *Integrated Education, 18*(5–6), 23–27.

Byrne, D. (1961). The influence of propinquity and opportunities for interaction on classroom relationships. *Human Relations, 14,* 63–69.

Carter, D. J., & Wilson, R. (Eds.). (1991). *Ninth annual status report: Minorities in higher education.* Washington, DC: American Council on Education.

Carter, D. J., & Wilson, R. (Eds.). (1994). *Twelfth annual status report: Minorities in higher education.* Washington, DC: American Council on Education.

Carter, D. J., & Wilson, R. (Eds.). (1997). *Fifteenth annual status report: Minorities in higher education.* Washington, DC: American Council on Education.

Chacón, M. A., Cohen, E. G., & Strover, S. (1986). Chicanas and Chicanos: Barriers to progress in higher education. In M. S. Olivas (Ed.), *Latino college students* (pp. 296–324). New York: Teachers College Press.

Chang, M. J., Witt, D., Jones, J., & Hakuta, K. (Eds.). (in press). *Compelling interest: Examining the evidence on racial dynamics in higher education.* Washington, DC: American Educational Research Association and Stanford University Press.

Chapa, J. (1991). Special focus: Hispanic demographic and educational trends. In D. J. Carter & R. Wilson (Eds.), *Ninth annual status report: Minorities in higher education* (pp. 11–17). Washington, DC: American Council on Education.

Chew, C. A., & Ogi, A. Y. (1987). Asian American college student perspectives. In D. J. Wright (Ed.), *Responding to the needs of today's minority students* (pp. 39–48). San Francisco: Jossey-Bass.

Cohen, E. (1976, April). *Status equalization in the desegregated school.* Paper presented at the annual meeting of the American Educational Research Association, San Francisco.

Cole, D. (1999). *Faculty-student interactions of African American and White college students at predominantly White institutions.* Unpublished doctoral dissertation, Indiana University.

College Board. (1985). *Equality and excellence: The educational status of Black Americans.* New York: Author.

Cortés, C. E. (1991). Pluribus and unum: The quest for community amid diversity. *Change, 23*(5), 8–13.

Cross, W. (1971). The Negro-to-Black conversion experience. *Black World, 20*(9), 17–27.

Cross, W. (1989). Nigrescence: A nondiaphanous phenomenon. *Counseling Psychologist, 17*(2), 273–276.

Cross, W., Strauss, L., & Fhagen-Smith, P. (1999). African American identity development across the life span: Educational implications. In R. H. Sheets & E. R. Hollins (Eds.), *Racial and ethnic identity in school practices: Aspects of human development* (pp. 29–47). Mahwah, NJ: Erlbaum.

Dalton, J. C. (1991). Racial and ethnic backlash in college peer culture. *New Directions for Student Services, 56,* 3–12.

De los Santos, A., Jr., & Rigual, A. (1994). Progress of Hispanics in American higher education. In M. J. Justiz, R. Wilson, & L. G. Bjork (Eds.), *Minorities in higher education* (pp. 173–194). Phoenix, AZ: American Council on Education/Oryx Press.

DeVries, D., & Edwards, K. (1974). Student teams and learning games: Their effects on cross-race and cross-sex interaction. *Journal of Educational Psychology, 66,* 741–749.

Durán, R. P. (1986). Prediction of Hispanics' college achievement. In M. S. Olivas (Ed.), *Latino college students* (pp. 221–245). New York: Teachers College Press.

Durán, R. P. (1994). Hispanic student achievement. In M. J. Justiz, R. Wilson, & L. G. Bjork (Eds.), *Minorities in higher education* (pp. 151–172). Phoenix, AZ: American Council on Education/Oryx Press.

Ethier, K. A., & Deaux, K. (1994). Negotiating social identity when contexts change: Maintaining identification and responding to threat. *Journal of Personality and Social Psychology, 67*(2), 243–251.

Farrell, W. C., & Jones, C. K. (1988). Recent racial incidents in higher education: A preliminary perspective. *Urban Review, 20*(3), 211–225.

Feagin, J. R., & Feagin, C. B. (1978). *Discrimination American style: Institutional racism and sexism.* Englewood Cliffs, NJ: Prentice Hall.

Feagin, J. R., & Feagin, C. B. (1993). *Racial and ethnic relations* (4th ed.). Englewood Cliffs, NJ: Prentice Hall.

Feagin, J. R., & Sikes, M. P. (1995). How Black students cope with racism on White campuses. *Journal of Blacks in Higher Education, 8,* 91–97.

Fields, C. M. (1988). The Hispanic pipeline: Narrow, leaking, and needing repair. *Change, 20*(3), 20–27.

Fiske, E. B. (1988). The undergraduate Hispanic experience: A case of juggling two cultures. *Change, 20*(3), 29–33.

Fleming, J. (1984). *Blacks in college.* San Francisco: Jossey-Bass.

Fleming, J. (1990). Standardized test scores and the Black college environment. In K. Lomotey (Ed.), *Going to school: The African American experience* (pp. 143–154). Albany: State University of New York Press.

Forehand, G. A., & Ragosta, M. (1976). *A handbook for integrated schooling.* Princeton, NJ: Educational Testing Service.

Garibaldi, A. M. (1991). The role of historically Black colleges in facilitating resilience among African-American students. *Education and Urban Society, 24*(1), 103–112.

Garibaldi, A. M. (1992). Educating and motivating African American males to succeed. *Journal of Negro Education, 61*(1), 4–11.

Garibaldi, A. M. (1997). Four decades of progress and decline: An assessment of African American educational attainment. *Journal of Negro Education, 66*(2), 105–120.

Gay, G. (1973). Racism in America: Imperatives for teaching ethnic studies. In J. A. Banks (Ed.), *Teaching ethnic studies: Concepts and strategies* (pp. 27–49). Washington, DC: National Council for the Social Studies.

Gerdes, H., & Mallinckrodt, B. (1994). Emotional, social, and academic adjustment of college students: A longitudinal study of retention. *Journal of Counseling and Development, 72,* 281–288.

Gloria, M. G., & Rodriguez, E. R. (2000). Counseling Latino university students: Psychosociocultural issues for consideration. *Journal of Counseling and Development, 78,* 145–153.

Gordon, E. W. (1992). Conceptions of Africentrism and multiculturalism in education: A general overview. *Journal of Negro Education, 61,* 235–236.

Gordon, M. M. (1966). *Assimilation in American life.* New York: Oxford University Press.

Grasha, A. F. (1994). A matter of style: The teacher as expert, formal authority, personal model, facilitator, and delegator. *College Training, 42*(4), 142–149.

Gurin, P. (1999). Expert report of Patricia Gurin. In Gratz et al. v. Bollinger et al., *The compelling need for diversity in higher education.* No. 97–75321 (E.D. Mich.) Ann Arbor: University of Michigan.

Harris, S. M., & Nettles, M. T. (1991, Winter). Racial differences in student experiences and attitudes. *New Directions for Student Services,* no. 56, 25–38.

Hune, S., & Chan, K. C. (1997). Special focus: Asian Pacific American demographic and educational trends. In D. J. Carter & R. Wilson (Eds.), *Fifteenth annual status report: Minorities in higher education* (pp. 39–67). Washington, DC: American Council on Education.

Hurtado, S., Inkelas, K. K., Briggs, C., & Rhee, B.-S. (1997). Differences in college access and choice among racial/ethnic groups: Identifying continuing barriers. *Research in Higher Education, 38*(1), 43–75.

Hurtado, S., Milem, J. F., Clayton-Pedersen, A. R., & Allen, W. (1998). Enhancing campus climates for racial/ethnic diversity: Educational policy and practice. *Review of Higher Education 21*(3), 279–302.

Hurtado, S., Milem, J. F., Clayton-Pedersen, A. R., & Allen, W. (1999). *Enacting diverse learning environments: Improving the climate for racial/ethnic diversity in higher education.* Washington, DC: George Washington University/ERIC Clearinghouse on Higher Education.

Jones, J. M. (1981). The concept of racism and its changing reality. In B. P. Bowser & R. G. Hunt (Eds.), *Impacts of racism on White Americans* (pp. 27–49). Thousand Oaks, CA: Sage.

Justiz, M. J., Wilson, R., & Bjork, L. G. (Eds.). (1994). *Minorities in higher education.* Phoenix, AZ: American Council on Education/Oryx Press.

Kidwell, C. S. (1994). Higher education issues in Native American communities. In M. J. Justiz, R. Wilson, & L. G. Bjork (Eds.). *Minorities in higher education* (pp. 239–257). American Council on Education/Oryx Press.

Knowles, L. L., & Prewitt, K. (1969). *Institutional racism in America.* Englewood Cliffs, NJ: Prentice Hall.

Kozol, J. (1991). *Savage inequalities: Children in America's schools.* New York: Crown.

Kraft, C. L. (1991). What makes a successful Black student on a predominantly White campus. *American Educational Research Journal, 28*(2), 423–443.

Kuh, G. D., Schuh, J., Whitt, E., Andrea, R., Lyons, J., Strange, C., et al. (1991). *Involving colleges: Successful approaches to fostering student learning and development outside the classroom.* San Francisco: Jossey-Bass.

Kurlaender, M., & Orfield, G. (1999). In defense of diversity: New research and evidence from the University of Michigan. *Equity and Excellence in Education, 32*(3), 31–35.

Levin, S. (2003). Social psychological evidence on race and racism. In M. J. Chang, D. Witt, J. Jones, & K. Hakuta (Eds.). *Compelling interest: Examining the evidence on racial dynamics in higher education* (pp. 1–20). Palo Alto, CA: Stanford University Press.

Levine, A., & Cureton, J. (1992). The quest revolution: Eleven facts about multiculturalism and the curriculum. *Change, 24*(1), 25–29.

Loo, C., & Rolison, G. (1986). Alienation of ethnic minority students at a predominantly White university. *Journal of Higher Education, 57*(1), 58–77.

Madrid, A. (1986). Foreword. In M. S. Olivas (Ed.), *Latino college students* (pp. ix–xvii). New York: Teachers College Press.

Milem, J. F. (in press) The educational benefits of diversity: Evidence from multiple sectors. In M. J. Chang, D. Witt, J. Jones, & K. Hakuta (Eds.), *Compelling interest: Examining the evidence on racial dynamics in higher education.* Palo Alto: Stanford University Press.

Milem, J. F., & Hakuta, K. (2000). Special focus: The benefits of racial and ethnic diversity in higher education. In D. Wilds (Ed.), *Seventeenth annual status report: Minorities in higher education, 1999–2000* (pp. 39–67). Washington, DC: American Council on Education.

Mitchell, S. L., & Dell, D. M. (1992). The relationship between Black students' racial identity attitude and participation in campus organizations. *Journal of College Student Development, 33,* 39–43.

Muñoz, D. G. (1986). Identifying areas of stress for Chicano undergraduates. In M. S. Olivas (Ed.), *Latino college students* (pp. 131–156). New York: Teachers College Press.

Muñoz, D. G., & García-Bahne, B. (1977). *A study of the Chicano experience in higher education.* Washington, DC: National Institute of Mental Health.

Musil, C. M., Garcia, M., Hudgins, C. A., Nettles, M. T., Sedlecek, W. E., & Smith, D. G. (1999). *To form a more perfect union: Campus diversity initiatives.* Washington, DC: Association of American Colleges & Universities.

National Center for Education Statistics. (1993). *Trends in enrollment in higher education by racial/ethnic category: Fall 1982 through fall 1991.* Washington, DC: U.S. Office of Education.

National Center for Education Statistics. (1998). *Trends in enrollment in higher education by racial/ethnic category: Fall 1988 through fall 1997.* Washington, DC: U.S. Office of Education.

National Coalition of Advocates for Students. (1985). *Barriers to excellence: Our children at risk.* Boston: Author.

National Council of La Raza. (1990). *Hispanic education: A statistical portrait 1990.* Washington, DC: Author.

Nettles, M. T. (1991). Racial similarities and differences in the predictors of college student achievement. In W. R. Allen, E. G. Epps, & N. Z. Haniff (Eds.), *College in Black and White: African American students in predominantly White and in historically Black public universities* (pp. 75–94). Albany: State University of New York Press.

Nettles, M., Thoeny, A., & Gosman, E. (1986). Comparative and predictive analyses of Black and White students' college achievement and experiences. *Journal of Higher Education, 57*(3), 289–318.

Nora, A., & Cabrera, A. (1996). The role and perceptions of prejudice and discrimination on the adjustment of minority students to college. *Journal of Higher Education, 67*(2), 119–148.

O'Brien, E. M. (1992a). The demise of Native American education. *Black Issues in Higher Education, 7*(1), 15–22.

O'Brien, E. M. (1992b). A foot in each world: Striving to succeed in higher education. *Black Issues in Higher Education, 7*(1), 27–31.

O'Brien, E. M. (1992c). Tribal colleges thrive amid hardship: Building nations and preserving cultural heritage. *Black Issues in Higher Education, 7*(1), 37–39.

Oakes, J. (1985). *Keeping track: How schools structure inequality.* New Haven, CT: Yale University Press.

Olivas, M. S. (Ed.). (1986). *Latino college students.* New York: Teachers College Press.

Oliver, J., & Etchevery, R. (1987). Factors influencing the decisions of academically talented Black students who attend college. *Journal of Negro Education, 56,* 152–161.

Orfield, G. (1988). Exclusion of the majority: Shrinking college access and public policy in metropolitan Los Angeles. *Urban Review, 20*(3), 147–163.

Parham, T. A., & Helms, J. E. (1985). Attitudes of racial identity and self-esteem of black students: An exploratory investigation. *Journal of College Student Personnel, 26*(2), 143–147.

Payne, N. J. (1994). Maintaining the competitive tradition. In M. J. Justiz, R. Wilson, & L. G. Bjork (Eds.), *Minorities in higher education* (pp. 210–238). Phoenix, AZ: American Council on Education/Oryx Press.

Phinney, J. (1996). When we talk about ethnic groups, what do we mean? *American Psychologist, 51*(9), 918–927.

Pounds, A. W. (1987). Black students' needs on predominantly White campuses. In D. J. Wright (Ed.), *Responding to the needs of today's minority students* (pp. 23–38). San Francisco: Jossey-Bass.

Quevedo-Garcia, E. L. (1987). Facilitating the development of Hispanic students. In D. J. Wright (Ed.), *Responding to the needs of today's minority students* (pp. 49–63). San Francisco: Jossey-Bass.

Richardson, R. C., Simmons, H., & de los Santos, A. (1987). Graduating minority students. *Change, 19*(3), 20–27.

Rodriguez, R. (1992). Professional groups create an educational continuum. *Black Issues in Higher Education, 8*(24), 26–27.

Rooney, G. D. (1985). Minority students' involvement in minority student organizations: An exploratory study. *Journal of College Student Personnel, 26*(5), 450–456.

Sagar, H. A., & Schofield, J. W. (1984). Integrating the desegregated school: Problems and possibilities. In D. E. Bartz & M. L. Maehr (Eds.), *Advances in motivation and achievement* (pp. 204–242). Greenwich, CT: JAI Press.

Sedlacek, W. E. (1987, November). Black students on White campuses: 20 years of research. *Journal of College Student Personnel,* 484–495.

Sedlacek, W. E., Helm, E. G., & Prieto, D. O. (1997). *The relationship between attitudes toward diversity and overall satisfaction on university students by race* (Research Rep. No. UMC-PR-3-97).

Orono: University of Maryland Counseling Center. (ERIC Document Reproduction Service No. 411 754)

Skinner, E. F., & Richardson, R. C., Jr. (1988). Making it in a majority university: The minority graduate perspective. *Change, 20*(3), 37–42.

Smedley, B. D., Myers, H. F., & Harrell, S. P. (1993). Minority-status stresses and the college adjustment of ethnic minority freshmen. *Journal of Higher Education, 64*(4), 434–452.

St. John, E. P., & Noell, J. (1989). The effects of student financial aid on access to higher education: An analysis of progress with special consideration of minority enrollment. *Research in Higher Education, 30*(6), 563–581.

Stage, F. K. (1989). Reciprocal effects between the academic and social integration of college students. *Research in Higher Education, 30*(5), 450–456.

Suzuki, R. H. (1989). Asian Americans as the "model minority." *Change, 21*(6), 13–19.

Suzuki, R. H. (1994). Higher education issues in the Asian American community. In M. J. Justiz, R. Wilson, & L. G. Bjork (Eds.), *Minorities in higher education* (pp. 258–285). Phoenix, AZ: American Council on Education/Oryx Press.

Taylor, C. M., & Howard-Hamilton, M. F. (1995). Student involvement and racial identity attitudes among African American males. *Journal of College Student Development, 36*(4), 330–336.

Thomason, T. C., & Thurber, H. J. (1999). *Strategies for the recruitment and retention of Native American students.* Flagstaff: Northern Arizona University, Institute for Human Development. (ERIC Document Reproduction Service No. ED 453 514)

Tierney, W. G. (1991). Native voices in academe: Strategies for empowerment. *Change, 23*(2), 36–39.

Tierny, W. G. (1999). Models of minority college-going and retention: Cultural integrity versus cultural suicide. *Journal of Negro Education, 68*(1), 80–91.

U.S. Bureau of the Census. (2000). *Statistical abstract of the United States: 2000.* Washington, DC: U.S. Government Printing Office.

U.S. Department of Education. (1987). Fall enrollment in colleges and universities surveys, 1976, 1980, and 1984. *Change: Trendlines, 19*(1), 29–34.

Wells, R. N. (1997). *The Native American experience in higher education: Turning around the cycle of failure II.* Washington, DC: U.S. Department of Education. (ERIC Document Reproduction Service No. ED 414 108)

Wilds, D. J. (Ed.). (2000). *Seventeenth annual status report: Minorities in higher education, 1999–2000.* Washington, DC: American Council on Education.

Wilson, R. (1994). The participation of African Americans in American higher education. In M. J. Justiz, R. Wilson, & L. G. Bjork (Eds.), *Minorities in higher education* (pp. 195–209). Phoenix, AZ: American Council on Education/Oryx Press.

Wilson, R., & Carter, D. J. (Eds.). (1989). *Eighth annual status report: Minorities in higher education.* Washington, DC: American Council on Education.

Wiser, P., & Cook, S. (1971). The impact of cooperative learning experiences on cross-ethnic relationships and attitudes. *Journal of Social Issues, 31,* 219–244.

Wright, B., & Tierney, W. G. (1991). American Indians in higher education: A history of cultural conflict. *Change, 23*(2), 11–18.

Wright, D. J. (1987). Minority students: Developmental beginnings. In D. J. Wright (Ed.), *Responding to the needs of today's minority students* (pp. 5–21). San Francisco: Jossey-Bass.

43

ETHNIC STUDIES IN U.S. HIGHER EDUCATION

History, Development, and Goals

Evelyn Hu-DeHart

Brown University

Fire insurance, meaning political settlement or appeasement, is a term sometimes used to describe the decision by U.S. colleges and universities to create Black Studies and other ethnic studies programs on their campuses (Hayes, 1992). The reasons hark back to the history of militant student activism in the last quarter century and to the rise of Black Power, Brown Power, and Yellow Power.

BRIEF HISTORY AND CURRENT STATUS OF ETHNIC STUDIES

In the late 1960s, inspired by the civil rights movement and further buoyed by the energies of the antiwar movement, a generation of college students throughout the United States invaded and occupied administration offices on their campuses and startled, and no doubt terrified, a few presidents, deans, and professors.

The demonstrations occurred mainly on large, predominantly White campuses, private and public. Led by students of color—then called "Third World" students in solidarity with the imperialized Third World and from whence so many of their forebears came as slaves, coolies, or immigrants—the activists demanded some fundamental changes in higher education. The faculty and administration then were still almost exclusively White and slightly less so male. Although more women and minorities were admitted to colleges in the 1960s, student bodies were only somewhat less monolithic than were the faculties

and administrations. The curriculum had been fairly static since the first decades of the century, and the idea of multiculturalism had not yet emerged.

Beginning in 1968 at San Francisco State and University of California campuses such as Berkeley and Santa Barbara—then spreading to many campuses across the nation during the course of the next quarter century to the present day—students of color have been demanding greater access to higher education, recruitment of more faculty of color, and the creation of programs that have come to be collectively known as ethnic studies and separately by a variety of names: Black Studies (also Afro-American Studies, African American Studies, Africana Studies); Chicana/o, Mexican American, and Puerto Rican Studies (also Latina/o Studies); American Indian (or Native American) Studies; and Asian American Studies. These programs formed the beginning of multicultural curricular reform in higher education.

For 25 years, despite fits and starts, peaks and valleys, ethnic studies programs and departments have survived and proliferated hundreds-fold from their origins in California to all parts of the nation. After some serious cutbacks in the budgetary crisis of the mid-1970s to the mid-1980s, they are now back bigger and stronger than ever before, revitalized, reorganized, and in some cases reconceptualized, increasingly institutionalized, and definitely here to stay. They have produced a prodigious amount of new scholarship, which, as in all other disciplines and fields of learning, contains some bad, some mediocre, and much work that is good and innovative.

I thank my colleagues Tim Fong and Gregory Mark of California State Sacramento Ethnic Studies Department for their critical reading, comments, and suggestions.

The new perspectives are intended not only to increase our knowledge base but in time to transform all scholarship. Their deep and widespread influence is definitely being felt and debated.

At the beginning of the 1990s, there were over 700 programs and departments throughout the United States (Butler, 1991), and the numbers have ebbed and flowed around that level since then. They come in various forms, shapes, and sizes. The largest and most powerful are the departments, followed by centers or institutes that focus on research but may also have a curricular component. The smallest, weakest, and most problematic programs tend to be those described as "interdisciplinary"—in the sense that they draw their faculty from traditional disciplinary departments—yet this is also by far the most common model, for reasons that are discussed in this chapter.

The various components of ethnic studies are in turn represented by four major professional associations: the National Council of Black Studies, the National Association of Chicano Studies, the Asian American Studies Association, and the National Association of Ethnic Studies. The American Indian Studies Association, organized around 1980, has been inactive. A number of smaller and more specifically focused professional associations have also been formed over the years, such as the Puerto Rican Studies Association in 1992. Women's Studies was born during the same time and out of similar dynamics generated by the women's movement (see Chapter 44, this volume). However, it was in origin and remains to this day dominated by White and middle-class feminist academics and students.

Given their history, it is not surprising that a disproportionate number of ethnic studies programs are located in public institutions, which are more susceptible to public pressure. Most are also in the western region of the United States, which has a fast-growing, diverse population. The biggest and most powerful programs are found in four public universities in the West. They incorporate more than one ethnic-specific focus, adopt a comparative approach, and have a research emphasis in addition to teaching (undergraduate and graduate). They have full or near department status, with graduate programs in place or anticipated. They also offer variations in organizational structures and approaches.

One of the oldest, largest, and probably the best-known ethnic studies programs is at the University of California, Berkeley. It was founded in 1969, in the crucible of protracted student demonstrations, as an autonomous department reporting directly to the chancellor. Originally, it had four programs: Black Studies, Chicano Studies, Asian American Studies, and Native American Studies, each offering its own undergraduate degree. In the mid-1970s, the Black Studies faculty (since renamed African-American Studies) voted to move out of the ethnic studies department and into arts and sciences as a separate department in its own right. It continues to cooperate with other ethnic studies programs on programmatic issues, such as the creation of comparative ethnic studies B.A., M.A., and Ph.D. programs (Wang, n.d.).

In the 1990s, the four ethnic studies programs together offered over 150 different courses and enrolled over 8,000 students a year, turning away another 1,000 students each semester. In 1983, Berkeley became the first and in 1992 remained the only university to offer a Ph.D. in ethnic studies. Ten years later, it had over 80 doctoral candidates enrolled, and all seven graduates had been placed in academic positions (Wang, n.d.).

The University of Washington's Department of American Ethnic Studies, the next largest multiethnic program, is relatively new. It was created in 1985 by bringing together existing or new programs in Black Studies, Chicano Studies (which had been shunted off to the social work school), and Asian American Studies. The small Native American Studies faculty chose to remain within the department of anthropology. An undergraduate degree-granting department, it expected to offer an M.A. degree by the mid-1990s, but as of 2003, the graduate program is still on hold.

The University of California, San Diego's Department of Ethnic Studies, created in 1990, is also relatively new. It emphasizes the comparative approach and has no ethnic-specific foci or separate degrees (University of California, San Diego, 1990).

The University of Colorado, Boulder's Center for Studies of Ethnicity and Race in America was created in 1987 by consolidating existing programs in Black Studies (renamed Afro-American Studies) and Chicano Studies, with new programs in Asian American and American Indian Studies. In 1996, the Department of Ethnic Studies was created out of the center. The faculty converted the Black Studies major into an ethnic studies major and minor, with ethnic-specific concentrations. Students in the new major are required to take core courses in theory and methods, do a community-based practicum, and finish with a capstone senior seminar, in addition to choosing a primary and secondary ethnic-specific concentration. In 2002, the small American Studies program merged with the Department of Ethnic Studies and became the fifth comparative American cultures concentration.

In addition to these four research universities in the West, the University of California, Los Angeles (UCLA), established yet another model in the 1960s. On this campus, there are four separate and distinct research centers devoted to the study of African Americans, Asian Americans, Chicanas/os, and Native Americans.

Outside the West, Bowling Green State University in Ohio has one of the oldest ethnic studies departments, founded in 1979. Like the University of California, San

Diego, it does not have ethnic-specific foci. Among four-year or nonresearch institutions, San Francisco State has one of the oldest and still largest ethnic studies departments, with four distinct foci and degrees. The largest of the programs on this campus is Asian American Studies, which was founded in 1969, making it also the oldest (Hirabayashi & Alquizola, 1992). San Francisco State has retained the original, still unique, and politically charged name of La Raza Studies for what elsewhere is called Chicana/o or Mexican American Studies.

Other than these big, multifoci, or comparative programs, almost all ethnic studies programs are ethnic specific. Foremost among them, for historical reasons, are Black Studies (Hine, 1992), now increasingly renamed Afro American or African American. More than 60 of them (Adams, 1993) have department status, some in conjunction with a research center. Notable among them are long-standing programs at flagship state institutions, such as Ohio State University; the University of Wisconsin, Madison; the University of Michigan, Ann Arbor; and the University of California, Berkeley. Temple University, a public research institution in Philadelphia, has one of the oldest, largest, and most distinctive Black Studies departments. For many years, under the guidance of its founder, Molefi Asante, it is also the foremost Afrocentric or African-centered program and the first to offer a Ph.D. degree (Asante, 1992). (Asante has recently stepped down as chair.)

Among elite private universities, Cornell, Brown, and the University of Pennsylvania have well-established centers and departments, with Harvard and Princeton relative latecomers. Yale had one of the preeminent Black Studies programs until the late 1970s, when it largely disintegrated with the departure (due in part to denial of tenure) of some of its most distinguished faculty members and the subsequent decrease of institutional support. In 2000, the program has been revitalized and elevated to department status under the leadership of British-educated black scholar Hazel Carby.

On a few West Coast research university campuses, such as the University of California, Davis, and the University of California, Santa Barbara—where Chicana/o Studies was formally launched in 1968 with the militant student document entitled El Plan de Santa Bárbara—Chicana/o Studies has also achieved department status (Keller, Magallan, & Garcia, 1989). The department has been authorized to offer a Ph.D. in the field. The biggest and one of the oldest Chicana/o Studies departments is located on the California State University, Northridge campus. Founded in 1969 by Rudolfo Acuña, a preeminent first-generation Chicano Studies scholar-activist, it is primarily teaching and community oriented.

Leading the development of Puerto Rican Studies on the East Coast is the Centro de Estudios Puertorriqueños at Hunter College of the City University of New York (CUNY), which is research and community oriented. A number of other CUNY campuses, such as Lehman College, Brooklyn College, and John Jay College, have Puerto Rican Studies departments. Both Chicana/o and Puerto Rican Studies are linked with other educational equity programs, such as bilingual education, that address the needs of largely Spanish-speaking immigrant groups. The rise of Puerto Rican Studies cannot be divorced from Puerto Rico's neocolonial relationship with the United States. The rise of La Raza and Chicana/o Studies is inextricably linked to the emergence of various Chicano social movements, notably César Chávez's Farm Workers Movement (Acuña, 1988).

Asian American Studies has had an interesting trajectory. Although two major programs that rapidly became departments were founded in the late 1960s in California, at the University of California, Berkeley, and San Francisco State, the rest of the country was slow to follow suit. It was not until the 1980s, with the dramatic rise of immigration from Asia, that Asian American Studies gained renewed impetus. The new immigrants not only swelled the total numbers of peoples of Asian descent in the United States, from under 1 million in 1965 to over 10 million by 2000, it also diversified the Asian American population well beyond the dominant groups of Chinese and Japanese, to include Filipinos, Koreans, Asian Indians, Vietnamese, and other Southeast Asian ethnicities (Omatsu, 1989; Ong & Hee, 1993). The University of California, Santa Barbara, the University of Colorado at Boulder, and Queens College on the East Coast have relatively new Asian American Studies programs, research centers, or departments.

The least developed of the ethnic studies programs is American Indian, or Native American, Studies (Ortiz, 1980). This is no doubt related to the isolation of Native peoples of the United States from mainstream society and institutions, including higher education, resulting in the absolute paucity of Native Americans with much postsecondary academic training. In the 2000s, more than any other ethnic studies foci, Native American Studies is still closely tied to student services. UCLA has one of the few centers devoted to research; it also edits and publishes the *American Indian Culture and Research Journal*, one of several academic journals devoted to Native American issues. In the East, Cornell University has perhaps the most significant Native American Studies programs, which combines student support services with curriculum. Hawaiian Studies at the University of Hawaii shares common issues with Native Americans on the mainland, its growth linked to the burgeoning Hawaiian sovereignty movement and international indigenous peoples' rights.

Historically, there are several models or routes for introducing and implementing ethnic studies into the curriculum. In the beginning, the first ethnic studies courses were often offered not by academic departments or by regular faculty members. Rather, community activists and minority student counselors in student service units, such as educational opportunity programs (EOPs), began teaching courses on various and distinct minority experiences, with or without academic credit. These courses gradually gave way to more formally constituted programs located on the academic side of campus. However, some of the early instructional staff, including many community activists, were retained on the faculty.

On campuses where ethnic studies was originally established as strictly research units, such as the four ethnic-specific research centers at UCLA, these centers have been compelled to start offering courses, undergraduate and graduate, although not necessarily degree programs. At UCLA, the Asian American Studies Center appears to have responded most actively and comprehensively to student needs. It offers not only a range of undergraduate courses, but since the 1980s a well-received M.A. degree as well (although still no B.A. degree). By contrast, the lack of attention paid on this campus to the development of an undergraduate curriculum and degree in Chicana/o Studies prompted a large number of mostly Chicana/o students and a few faculty members to mount a hunger strike at the beginning of summer 1993, resulting in the 1994 creation of the César E. Chávez Center for Interdisciplinary Instruction in Chicana and Chicano Studies.

On most other campuses, American Studies (or its variants, such as American cultures) seems to be the most common vehicle to integrate some aspect of ethnic studies into the curriculum. This model is frequently used on campuses where there is already an established African American Studies program and mounting pressure—primarily from non-Black minority students, whose numbers are swelling on our campuses and in many cases exceeding Black students, to offer additional ethnic-specific or comparative ethnic courses. If forcing these new ethnic foci into the existing African American Studies department or program is not feasible (for political and structural reasons), then American Studies generally emerges as the most amenable unit to incorporate the new courses. Such has been the case even at large research universities such as Yale and the University of Michigan, Ann Arbor (Garcia, 1992). American Studies is also attractive for small colleges that cannot afford to create new academic units.

Yet another model is the merging of ethnic studies with existing or new area studies programs. This arrangement is particularly common for African Studies and African American Studies, which, by using the African diaspora paradigm, has found it politically and structurally feasible to work as one academic unit. These units are often named African and African American Studies or, more simply, Africana Studies. It should be noted that such units, staffed as is the case with other Black Studies programs predominantly by African, African American, and occasionally Caribbean and African scholars, are quite distinct from traditional African area studies programs, which draw their faculty from traditional disciplines and are mostly White (Okihiro, 1991).

Latino and Latin American Studies is another model, although not a common arrangement, because the merger seems to arise partially out of administrative expediency. One example is the City College of New York's (CCNY) Puerto Rican Studies department, which changed its name in the late 1980s to the Department of Latin American and Hispanic Caribbean Studies. Besides offering courses on and a major in Latin America, it retains the major in Puerto Rican Studies while adding a sequence in Dominican Studies, in view of Upper Manhattan's swelling Dominican immigrant population. At about the same time, Rutgers University decided to bring together Puerto Rico (a U.S. dependency) and the independent Spanish-speaking countries of the Caribbean into a new department of Puerto Rican and Spanish Caribbean Studies. This formulation appears to make historical, political, and cultural sense, sharing as they do a historical colonial relationship to Spain and a contemporary neocolonial relationship with the United States.

There is no known instance of Asian American Studies merging with Asian Studies, although on some campuses, the first Asian American Studies courses could well have been offered through the Asian Studies program. Some changes are afoot, as scholars such as Arif Dirlik and Sucheta Mazumdar of Duke University attempt to formulate an Asian-Pacific paradigm (Dirlik, 1993; Mazumdar, 1991). For over a decade, a growing number of scholars have worked with the more global concept of the "Asian diaspora" (Hirabayashi & Hu-DeHart, 2003; Hu-DeHart, 1991).

WHY ETHNIC STUDIES?

Although the study of the Black experience in America has been an old community-based practice, led by the work of African American scholars such as Carter G. Woodson and his Association for the Study of Afro-American Life and History (Adams, 1993), the rationale for establishing formal Black Studies programs almost 30 years ago was, first and foremost, to recognize the growing presence of African American students on historically White U.S. campuses.

These students wanted what most other students want out of an education: to study the experiences and contributions of their community to U.S. society and culture and to use the resources of the university to help solve community problems. The guiding principle was that "knowledge was to be socially relevant." In other words, the ideals of "academic excellence" and "social responsibility" were conceived as compatible and complementary (Adams, 1993, p. 27). The other side of this argument was an explicit challenge to the Eurocentric curriculum and the prevailing, but unwritten, assumption that Western civilization was superior and universal and that its values and norms are applicable to all peoples at all times.

Since the founding and subsequent proliferation of Black Studies programs, the call for the establishment of Chicana/o, Puerto Rican, Asian American, and Native American Studies has increased in intensity while subscribing to the same guiding principles. The reasons have much to do with the changing nature of American society since the mid-1960s. The civil rights movement might have removed the last vestiges of legal apartheid in the United States, but the rich and powerful and their political surrogates have merely invented other means to continue to segregate, divide, exclude, and in many other ways deny equal opportunity to the historically marginalized communities of color.

Two and a half decades after the issuance of the Kerner Commission report in 1968, which spoke of two Americas, one rich, one poor, one White, one Black, the gulf between these two Americas has grown wider than ever, especially during the Reagan-Bush years. To be more specific, by 1992, 1% of the U.S. population had gained control of more wealth than 90% of this society, a situation that parallels the intolerable inequality of much of the Third World (Muwakkil, 1992; Nasar, 1992). According to one recent study of assets in America, by 1998 the top 20% of Americans held 90.9% of the country's financial wealth; the top 1% held 47.3% of total wealth (Shapiro & Wolff, 2001).

Dramatic and significant demographic changes have also overtaken the United States during this same quarter century. Since 1965, when U.S. immigration laws eliminated the national origins quotas, which had clearly favored Europeans, many new immigrants from Asia, Latin America, and the Caribbean have greatly outnumbered the traditional White European immigrants for the first time in history (Barringer, 1991; Usdansky, 1992). Additional impetus for accelerated immigration from Asia and Central America and the Caribbean have come as consequences of U.S. economic, political, and military interventions during the post-World War II era. From 1965 into the 1990s, non-Europeans composed over 80% of all new immigrants (Usdansky, 1992). Almost 9 million came in a great surge in the 1980s. This new wave of immigration accounted for the doubling of Asian Americans and the increase of Latinos by 60% between 1980

and 1990 (Ong & Hee, 1993; Usdansky, 1992). These trends have continued into the 21st century.

The upshot of these new immigration patterns is that the U.S. population is fast becoming "colored" and ever more diverse—by race, ethnicity, religion, language, food, music, art, literature, and many other cultural expressions. In fact, with over half of its population already highly diverse in 1992, California gives us a glimpse of the national future, which is projected to become by 2050, using an oxymoronic phrase, "majority minority." The relatively high reproductive rates of minority Americans as well as their lower age distribution mean that peoples of color will increasingly characterize the nation's classrooms and workforce.

In order to bring about a truly pluralistic democracy, our educational system at all levels must not only reflect this diversity of Americans in its student body, faculty, and curriculum but must seek to achieve comparable educational outcomes for all groups in American society. To reach this end, the variety of educational reforms that are gathered under the broad rubric of "multiculturalism" include the integration of ethnic studies into the college and university curriculum. It also means that all students, not just those of color, should be exposed to the histories and cultures of Americans of non-European descent. In other words, ethnic studies is not for minorities only.

ETHNIC STUDIES DEFINED

With the exceptions discussed above regarding the emerging of some ethnic studies with certain area studies, a common mistake is to confuse or conflate ethnic studies in general with global or international studies, on the basis that they are both "non-Western" and are usually organized as nondepartmental interdisciplinary programs.

Area studies arose out of the context of U.S. imperialism in the Third World and bear names such as African Studies, Asian Studies, and Latin American/Caribbean Studies. Their original founding purpose was to focus on U.S.–Third World relations and to train specialists to uphold U.S. hegemony in those regions of the world in which the United States had heavy economic and political investments. Although area studies scholars have become far more critical of U.S.–Third World relations since the antiwar movement of the 1960s, and many have adopted Third World perspectives in their work, they are still predominantly White male scholars entrenched in established departments, using conventional disciplinary methodologies, subscribing to disciplinary epistemologies, and benefiting from traditional patterns of distributing power and rewards in the academy, including those underwritten by private foundations and the U.S. government (Hu-DeHart, 1991; Hune, Kim, Fugita, & Ling,

1991; Mazumdar, 1991; Okihiro, 1991). Rather than truly interdisciplinary, these programs can better be described as multidisciplinary.

Ethnic studies, on the other hand—having grown out of student and grassroots community challenges to the prevailing academic power structure and Eurocentric curriculum of U.S. colleges and universities—were insurgent programs with a subversive agenda from the outset. Hence, they were suspect and illegitimate even as they were grudgingly allowed into the academy. The founders of ethnic studies—students, faculty, and community supporters alike—did not mask their objective of systematically examining and dismantling institutional racism.

Within the academy, ethnic studies scholars attempt to define a distinct epistemology, struggle consciously to break or transcend the bounds of traditional disciplines in their search for new methodologies, and wrestle more deliberately to articulate a genuinely interdisciplinary approach to the discovery of new knowledge. They argue for a holistic or organic approach to the understanding of minority experiences in America and for an emic, or insider, approach. In American Indian Studies, for example, the faculty speak of an "indigenous model" (Jaimes, 1987, p. 1).

Program definitions vary from campus to campus and change over time. The curriculum or course offerings are not uniform and do not conform to a prescribed pattern, although they generally fall within the broad categories of historical, sociological, and cultural. What they have in common is a specific or comparative focus on groups socially constructed as "minorities" in U.S. society, a status that results from these groups' shared history of having been racially constructed as distinct from European immigrants and their descendants. The latter have dominated the United States and defined its identity as White, Western, and superior; they see differences among themselves as strictly "cultural," or ethnic. The racially defined, non–European-descended groups in the United States have a "social trajectory and outcome quite diverse from that of people categorized only by cultural standards" (Liu, 1989, p. 275), that is, Irish Americans, Jewish Americans, Italian Americans, and Polish Americans.

By recognizing this distinction between race and ethnicity, ethnic studies scholars confront the irony that the very name of their intellectual and political project is problematic. "The term Ethnic Studies is a misleading one, confusing our students, and lending itself to much mischievous hostility by those academics who would rather not have studies of people of color in the university at all," notes Rhett Jones of Brown University, who concludes the field should be renamed "race studies" (Jones, 1993, p. 6).

John Liu (1989), in presenting his case for the consideration of ethnic studies as a separate and distinct discipline, begins with this crucial difference: "Race and ethnicity represented divergent experiences, with never the twain to meet because of institutionalized racism" (p. 276). He argues that race, ethnicity, and institutionalized racism form the central core disciplinary concepts of ethnic studies. This assertion is sharply at odds with the views of certain influential social scientists—such as Nathan Glazer and Daniel Moynihan (1975), Alejandro Portes and Robert Bach (1985), and Thomas Sowell (1981)—who maintain that race is merely one type of ethnicity and that all groups plunge into the "melting pot" and become Americans in due time (Liu, 1989).

In advancing its own coherent methodological orientation, the ethnic studies approach to knowledge, described as interdisciplinary, must be more than "simply separate applications of discipline-based methodology" (Butler, 1991, p. 28). Furthermore, unlike traditional disciplines, which are long divorced from any community base or origins, ethnic studies scholars must ask the question, Why do research and for whom? since its raison d'être is to correct the omissions and distortions in mainstream academia. Ethnic studies must "give voice to the excluded" and "involve racial groups in the articulation of their own existences through various means" (Liu, 1989, p. 279). Therefore, oral history and participatory research are important tools in ethnic studies research. Furthermore, "the enunciation of a people's voice has led many ethnic scholars to organize their research around communities" (Liu, 1989, p. 280).

Ethnic studies scholars also dispute the assertion that good scholarship is necessarily "objective" and nonpolitical, again in contrast to values in traditional disciplines. On the contrary, they openly acknowledge a moral and political purpose in their work because they are simultaneously committed to scholarship and social change, to a "more equitable social order," and to "creating new social realities" (Liu, 1989, pp. 281–282).

A good definition of comparative race and ethnic studies can be found in the University of California, San Diego, Ethnic Studies Department's founding document. The purpose is to focus "on immigration, slavery, and confinement, those three processes that combined to create in the United States a nation of nations. Ethnic studies intensively examines the histories, languages and cultures of America's racial and ethnic groups in and of themselves, their relationships to each other, and particularly, in structural contexts of power" (University of California, San Diego, 1990, p. 2). The attention here is on the recovery of knowledge denied or submerged and on the construction of new knowledge from the perspectives of historically marginalized and powerless groups.

To many in ethnic studies, its purpose also has to include a fundamental and explicit challenge to the dominant paradigms of academic practices. While he was specifically addressing the goals of Puerto Rican studies, Frank Bonilla, founder and director of Hunter College's Centro de Estudios Puertorriqueños, expressed guiding principles applicable to all ethnic studies:

We have set out to contest effectively those visions of the world that assume or take for granted the inevitability and indefinite duration of the class and colonial oppression that has marked Puerto Rico's history. All the disciplines that we are most directly drawing upon—history, economics, sociology, anthropology, literature, psychology, pedagogy—as they are practiced in the United States are deeply implicated in the construction of that vision of Puerto Ricans as an inferior, submissive people, trapped on the underside of relations from which there is no foreseeable exit. (quoted in Vázquez, 1988, p. 25)

In the words of another scholar, ethnic studies is a "liberating educational process" (Vázquez, 1988, p. 26) that challenges the triumph of Western civilization on U.S. soil—Eurocentrism—and its claims to objectivity and universalism. In ethnic studies, peoples of color are constructed not as mere objects to study but as "creators of events" and agents of change.

Ethnic studies scholars recognize the importance of perspective and that "perspectives . . . are always partial and situated in relationship to power" (University of California, San Diego, 1990, pp. 5–6). Putting it concretely, "it is both practically and theoretically incorrect to use the experience of white ethnics as a guide to comprehend those of nonwhite, or so-called 'racial' minorities" (Chaufauros, 1991, p. 25).

Another expression of the distinctive nature of ethnic studies scholarship is provided by Johnnella Butler, former chair of the Department of American Ethnic Studies at the University of Washington, Seattle. She proposes a "matrix model"—that is, "looking at the matrix of race, class, ethnicity and gender . . . within the context of cultural, political, social, and economic expression" (Butler, 1991, p. 29). The purpose of this new academic field is to recover and reconstruct the lived historical experiences and memories of those Americans whom history has neglected, to identify and credit the contributions of these Americans to the making of U.S. society and culture, to chronicle protest and resistance, and, finally, to establish alternative values and visions, institutions, and cultures.

CURRENT DEBATES AND ISSUES WITHIN ETHNIC STUDIES

The above discussion should not convey the idea that ethnic studies is totally stabilized, institutionalized, harmonious, or monolithic. In fact, it is in a state of flux and transition, structurally, organizationally, intellectually, and ideologically. There is no automatic uniformity between and among any of the 700 or so mostly ethnic-specific programs and departments across the nation. In part, the conversations and discussions within ethnic studies are no different from ongoing debates among biologists, anthropologists, and historians as their fields grow and change. At the same time, while the discussions among ethnic studies practitioners have not become vituperative and destructive, they can become heated and reflect the state of development of a still young field and discipline. The following comments by no means exhaust the list of issues but should convey some sense of the concerns and stakes. This discussion should also suggest the likely directions that ethnic studies will take as the field and discipline move into the future.

Twenty-five years after its inception, ethnic studies finds its key issue to be a structural and organizational one on the surface, which in turn fundamentally impinges on the larger issues of governance, academic or curricular legitimacy, professional certification, and educational mission: in short, the heart and soul of any academic enterprise (Hirabayashi & Alquizola, 1992). Should ethnic studies continue largely to be an interdisciplinary program along the model of area studies, drawing faculty from established departments and disciplines? Or should it push for autonomy and department status, given its self-identity as a distinctive new academic field, complete with disciplinary definition and methodology? Should it now concentrate on establishing intellectual credentials and credibility while loosening or severing ties forged in its early days with minority student services? Should the professional associations impose some clear definition of the field, clarify the necessary qualifications or credentials for the faculty, and in general impose some sort of "quality control" over the curriculum and educational mission?

Of all these issues, the most crucial one to understand is the difference between programs and departments. As programs relying on other departments for faculty and courses, ethnic studies has no control over faculty hiring or resources and minimal influence on course offerings, thus very little power to define itself intellectually and academically. It becomes nearly impossible to build a sound, coherent, and intellectually challenging program through a rather haphazard and random sampling of whatever courses may be made available through established departments. The unfortunate result of such efforts, well intentioned though they may be, is that they fuel the argument of skeptics and critics of ethnic studies that it lacks intellectual rigor and legitimacy.

Hence, in practice, such programs at best function as a mere coordinating body of a loosely related set of courses around an ethnic-specific or comparative ethnic theme, entirely reliant on the goodwill, positive attitude, and depth of understanding and appreciation of the mission of ethnic studies by traditional departments. Most often, the relationship between ethnic studies programs and academic departments is tenuous and uneasy, if not outright hostile. Built on attitudes of turf protection, competition for scarce resources, and, frankly, outright racism on the part of some traditional scholars who cannot shake off perceptions of illegitimacy and inferiority about ethnic studies as a field (and by extension ethnic studies scholars), this relationship becomes largely unmanageable. Being the weaker of the partnership, the ethnic studies program suffers disproportionately. During periods of financial constraints, such programs can be easily—both in the structural and political sense—cut back or disbanded, which is what happened to many of them during the budgetary crisis of the 1970s.

Departments, on the other hand, control budgets, do their own faculty hiring, and, most important, determine the course of study and hence define the field, including issues of pedagogy, research, and publication (both the type and place). In short, they have status and, at least structurally, enjoy equality with other disciplines and fields of study. Departments can also readily create and sponsor graduate programs. This is why there is really little dispute within ethnic studies about the desirability in theory of department over program.

However, political expediency as well as practical and financial matters often dictate the less ideal course of action. In public institutions, a program can be created by administrative fiat, whereas the creation of new departments requires extensive review and discussion by the general faculty and layers of higher education oversight bodies, a long, drawn-out process that can become contentious.

Also, in view of the limited resources of most colleges and universities, a situation that is likely to get worse in the financial crises of the early 21st century, a program is still the most common model, being the easiest and least costly way to start ethnic studies. Furthermore, on campuses where administrators have yielded to the department model, these ethnic studies departments usually have very small, and often mostly untenured, faculty. Thus, they are still reduced to a weak and marginal status within the specific college or university.

Despite these dilemmas, in the 1980s and into the 1990s, administrators were often eager to establish some kind of ethnic studies presence on their campuses, for the simple reason that it is an easy way to make a positive statement of commitment to diversity and multiculturalism. If they can go the extra mile and create an ethnic studies department with its own faculty lines, they also know it is the fastest route to diversifying the faculty. Ethnic studies scholars and supporters, having been stranded on the margins for so long, see any movement toward the center as acceptable, hence their tendency sometimes to settle for less.

Whether as program or department, the undeniable fact of ethnic studies proliferation, along with the general push toward multiculturalism and diversity, however these concepts are understood, means that ethnic studies has been acknowledged and is becoming institutionalized. A further step toward its institutionalization is linked to efforts within curriculum reform movements to "integrate" ethnic studies perspectives and scholarships into the mainstream curriculum and mainstream scholarship. This entails not only hiring ethnic studies scholars within traditional departments, such as history, sociology, psychology, political science, and literature, but also to encourage non–ethnic studies scholars to integrate the scholarship and perspectives from ethnic studies into their courses. Finally, a current debate among students and faculty on many campuses concerns the desirability of requiring an ethnic studies course as part of the core or general undergraduate education program.

Thus, beginning in the mid-1980s with faculty in-service workshops typically described as curriculum integration projects, campuses have embarked on the voluntary reeducation of willing and self-selected existing faculty. With institutional and foundation support such as that from the Ford Foundation, the workshops have become more ambitious and recently redesignated as "curriculum transformation" (Butler & Walter, 1991). This should be, and by and large is, good news for ethnic studies. With institutionalization and widespread influence come respect and legitimacy.

Nevertheless, uneasiness has set in around these recent developments. Does the campus push for multiculturalism threaten to swallow up or co-opt ethnic studies? Would the fading argument (very audible at the inception of ethnic studies and women's studies) more than 20 years ago, that these are stopgap or transitory measures that would eventually and automatically go out of existence once the campus is integrated, be revived in order to justify reduction or withdrawal of resources from ethnic studies?

Even as some applaud the inevitable spillover of ethnic studies into the rest of the curriculum, they also note the tension between ethnic studies and traditional fields "as people try to locate the boundaries between the two" (Magner, 1991, p. A11). In short, as summarized by the headline of a major discussion of this issue in the May 1, 1991, Chronicle of Higher Education: "Push for Diversity in Traditional Departments Raises Questions About the Future of Ethnic Studies" (Magner, 1991, p. A11). This explains the wariness and opposition on the part of the Black Studies faculty of San Francisco State University's School of Ethnic Studies to the hiring by the department of political science of an African American faculty member to teach Black politics—a clear struggle over boundary lines.

The dispute over boundaries raises a larger issue, which will be even more hotly debated in the 21st century. When Jesse Vázquez (1988), director of Queens College's Puerto Rican studies program, noted that "even traditional academic departments, formerly resolute in their refusal to include ethnic studies courses in their curriculum, now cross-list, and in many instances generate their own version of ethnic studies courses in direct competition with existing ethnic studies programs" (p. 23), he also sounded a warning that these multicultural curricular reforms may have "effectively managed to co-opt some of the more socially and politically palatable aspects of the ethnic studies movement of the late 1960s and early 1970s" (p. 24). At the same time, Vázquez continues,

these latest curricular trends seem to be moving us away from the political and social urgency intended by the founders of ethnic studies and toward the kind of program design which conforms to and is consistent with the traditional academic structures. Certainly, the struggle to legitimize these programs academically has taken the edge and toughness out of the heart of some of our ethnic studies curriculum. (p. 24)

The question is, Does the drive for legitimacy and institutionalization entail trade-offs for ethnic studies that may, ironically, weaken it in the long run? Should ethnic studies be seduced and lulled into believing that institutionalization translates into authentic acceptance and full acknowledgment and signals a change in traditional faculty attitudes, behavior, and values? Vázquez thinks not.

Neither does E. San Juan, Jr., educated at Harvard in Western literature. An incisive and vociferous critic of U.S. racial politics as manifested through issues of multiculturalism and ethnic studies (San Juan, 1992), he is concerned that (n.d., n.p.) "gradual academization" of ethnic studies would force it into the dominant European orthodoxy, which emphasizes ethnicity to the exclusion of race, and therefore "systematically [erases] from the historical frame of reference any perception of race and racism as causal factors in the making of the political and economic structure of the United States. If race and racism should remain the analytical core of the ethnic studies project, then would not total retreat into the academy be a contradiction, for how could it separate itself from the ongoing, real-life struggles of peoples of color in the United States today?"

San Juan also seeks to recapture the "activist impulse" that had propelled the creation of ethnic studies in the first place. He and other scholars characterize this challenge as the integration of theory (or critique) and praxis. Others put it even more simply and directly: how to reconcile the academic project of ethnic studies (i.e., the production of knowledge) with the original commitment to liberating and empowering the communities of color. Asks San Juan (n.d.): "Will it try to recuperate its inaugural vision as part of wide-ranging popular movements for justice and equality, for thoroughgoing social transformation?" Or will it settle for being just another respected academic unit?

ATTEMPTS TO UNDERMINE ETHNIC STUDIES

Throughout the 1980s and early 1990s, ethnic studies became caught up in the political maelstrom of the cultural war in which neoconservative and liberal critics of multiculturalism accused ethnic studies scholars, students, and supporters, among other multicultural educational reformers, of committing terrible crimes against truth (Simpson, 1991). Multiculturalists are charged with promoting "ethnic particularism" at the expense of national unity and a "common culture." (In Chapter 13, this volume, Sleeter and Delgado Bernal offer a more thorough discussion of the critiques of multicultural education.)

Those who mounted the political correctness campaign can be described as "triumphalists" (a term borrowed from Bell-Villada, 1990), a closely knit group of academics and scholars, writers, journalists and editors, political pundits and commentators, and highly placed members of the Reagan-Bush administrations (Aufderheide, 1992; Berman, 1992). Most of them are conservatives and neoconservatives but can increasingly count on old liberals joining their ranks. Binding them together is the fear that multiculturalism is changing—too fast, too profoundly, and in negative directions—U.S. history, society, and culture as they know and cherish and in some cases have helped to construct them.

The writings and public pronouncements of triumphalists—polemicists such as William Bennett (Beyers, 1991; Gordon, 1992), Dinesh D'Souza (1991), Lynne Cheney (1992), Irving Kristol (1991), George Will (1991), Roger Kimball (1990), and academics such as Allan Bloom (1987), even liberal ones such as Arthur Schlesinger (1991, 1992), Eugene Genovese (1991), and C. Vann Woodward (1991)—expose their motives. It seems quite clear that their problem really boils down to a refusal to even consider, let alone meet, the challenge mounted by multiculturalists against the claim that they, the triumphalists, make for Western universalism, objectivity, and timeless truths.

As ethnic studies has entered the 21st century and the fourth decade of its existence, it finds itself in a paradoxical situation surrounded by growing hostility around multiculturalism, as exemplified by unrelenting attacks on affirmative action, along with certain mixed messages. On the one hand, the field boasts some long-established programs and departments, and in the case of Black/African American Studies, new Ph.D. programs spearheaded by Ivy League institutions such as Harvard and Yale. On the other hand, it is still intellectually marginalized, its necessity in the academy acknowledged, but its centrality and scholarly merits still debated (JBHE, 2001).

In other words, the very success of ethnic studies appears to have brought about a backlash, not only in the highly visible and contested arena of cultural politics briefly described above, but, even more troubling, from institutional forces that seek to weaken the innovative programs in ethnic studies they have engendered in the first place. Why is ethnic studies beleaguered even as it continues to spread on U.S. campuses? Why is it both promoted and undermined?

On most campuses, administrators have denied ethnic studies the one academic currency it most needs: recognition and respect as a legitimate scholarly field that constructs, disseminates, and imparts knowledge in a distinctive way. This is accomplished primarily by withholding respect for ethnic studies scholars and their work, which they have largely failed to appreciate and whose approach to scholarship they have difficulty fully comprehending. Knowing they need ethnic studies because it is one clear manner to demonstrate commitment to multiculturalism—it is the surest way to put color into the curriculum, and its largely non-White faculty promotes faculty diversity more rapidly than hiring in traditional disciplinary departments—these administrators also appear to distrust ethnic studies. Once an ethnic studies unit is established and administrators have taken public relations credit for doing so, they often refuse to build it up. They appear to be afraid of strengthening a force that they never really wanted to create: a critical mass of free-thinking, independent-minded faculty of color with an intellectual base of their own in ethnic studies. With academic roots in traditional disciplines, most deans and provosts have never bothered to become familiar with the knowledge produced by ethnic studies scholars. It is little wonder, then, that few of them identify collegially with ethnic studies faculty and intellectually with ethnic studies scholarship.

The undermining of ethnic studies has taken shape with alarming consistency across the country. Common practices include installing weak and pliable program directors and department chairs, sometimes after rejecting strong scholars selected by the faculty. They include refusing to hire more than a handful of full-time faculty members in an ethnic studies department and then swelling its ranks with part-time or nonethnic studies–oriented personnel, who may then be given voting rights to dilute the strength of the legitimate, full-time ethnic studies faculty. Sometimes the research component is separated from the teaching faculty, for example, by setting up distinct units for research and for instruction, and then ethnic studies faculty are denied control over the research center. The administrative decisions can be especially fatal to the legitimacy of ethnic studies in research universities. Such was the predictable fate of the César Chávez Center for Interdisciplinary Studies at UCLA, organized in haste in 1995 by a beleaguered administration in response to intense student hunger strikers who protested the lack of

degree programs in Chicano/a studies in the middle of Los Angeles. The problem was that at a premier research institution, an autonomous undergraduate unit with no organic link to the well-established Chicano Studies Research Center was doomed to flounder. Administrators are also likely to use the shrinking budget to justify reneging on promised resources for ethnic studies to grow, even on those campuses where they have thrived. Ethnic studies programs have every reason to fear a reprise of what happened in the budget crisis of the mid-1970s, when many universities nearly gutted or outright decimated ethnic studies programs (at that time mainly Black and Chicano Studies). Again, in a budgetary crisis, those programs that have secured departmental status and a strong, tenured faculty are in a much better position to defend themselves, compete with other departments for institutional resources, and fight back.

FUTURE DIRECTIONS AND CHALLENGES FOR ETHNIC STUDIES

Thirty years after its founding, a generational split between the original cohort and a new wave of scholars is evident and occasionally tense (Hirabayashi & Alquizola, 1992). This dichotomy between "cultural nationalists" and those ethnic studies scholars who work by the race, class, and gender matrix proposed by Butler and discussed above is especially sharp in Black or African American studies, represented by Afrocentrists on one end (of whom Molefi Asante of Temple University and Leonard Jeffries of the City College of the City University of New York are only two variants on a broad spectrum) and, on the other end, liberals (such as Henry Louis Gates of Harvard), feminists (such as bell hooks of CUNY), Marxists, and other critical theorists (such as Manning Marable of Columbia University). In 1992, the National Council of Black Studies appeared to have weighed in on this issue by naming its new journal the *Afrocentric Scholar.* However, in his introduction to the first issue, the editor, William A. Little, adopts a very broad approach to Afrocentrism, defining it in opposition to the "Eurocentric perspective" and as "an effort to illuminate the contributions of African people to world culture and to provide an alternative intellectual framework to the study of African people" (Little, 1992, p. i).

On another front, the relationship with practically all other new interdisciplinary systems of inquiry are being fruitfully explored: ethnic studies and women studies, cultural studies and queer studies; with diaspora, transnational, and postcolonial studies; with performance studies and media studies; with environmental studies and policy studies; with professional schools, especially law, education, and health (Butler, 2001; Butler & Walter,

1991; Crenshaw, Gotanda, Peller, & Thomas, 1995; Delgado 1995; Miller, 2001; Wing, 1997.) Furthermore, those working within diasporic, transnational, and postcolonial frameworks are steadily globalizing ethnic studies, in ways that distinguish it from international affairs or area studies (Hu-DeHart, 1999; Hune et al., 1991). Also broached is the question, Can White scholars teach ethnic studies? (Some already do, and increasingly more are prepared by education, political, and intellectual inclination to do so, especially with the recent development of "Whiteness" studies and critical race studies discussed below.)

Another significant new development is the accelerated alliance or merger of ethnic studies with American Studies, in the process revitalizing one of the first interdisciplinary programs in the humanities whose founding principle of American exceptionalism is being supplanted by a multicultural and comparative approach across the Americas. Indeed, noted ethnic studies scholars such as George Lipsitz, George Sanchez, and Steven Sumida, chairs of their respective ethnic studies departments (University of California, San Diego, University of Southern California, and University of Washington), have all heeded the clarion call of Cornell historian Mary Washington, recent president of the American Studies Association, to diversify American Studies (Washington, 1998). At the University of Colorado at Boulder, the small American Studies program asked to be merged with the larger and more institutionalized Ethnic Studies Department, a proposal that took some administrators by surprise but eventually was approved by the general arts and sciences faculty.

With ethnic studies in these pace-setting public institutions taking the lead toward integrating postnationalist American Studies (Rowe, 2000) on their campuses with global and comparative ethnic studies, they in effect reversed the earlier pattern whereby established American Studies departments expanded to incorporate aspects of ethnic studies largely as a matter of convenience for administrators under student pressure to implement ethnic studies. In this older model, the marriage has not been equally satisfying to both partners, with the weaker of the two, ethnic studies, often feeling tokenized, if not exactly neglected. As a result, ethnic studies has not been adequately served, leading to serious discussions on some of these campuses about an amicable parting. Nevertheless, despite evidence that forcing ethnic studies under the traditional paradigm of American Studies without having first transformed American Studies itself cannot produce a felicitous union, universities such as Princeton responded to student demonstrations in the 1990s for ethnic studies by adopting precisely this awkward model.

Another innovative direction defined by the new generation of American Studies scholars, such as David Roediger and Ruth Frankenberg, is the study of Whiteness and its historical and social construction as a racial category (Frankenberg, 1993; Roediger, 1991; Stowe, 1996). Roediger's project links race with class, as he carefully traces the historical construction of whiteness by and for the White working class in America. By equating Whiteness with freedom, this default racial identity is thus framed against the unfreedom of Black Americans and other Americans defined as non-White. Furthermore, with race trumping class, Roediger argues that Whiteness blunts class consciousness among America's White working class, in effect encouraging solidarity among Whites across class differences against all non-Whites. Frankenberg examines the intersection of race and gender, in her case how race as whiteness shapes White women's lives in America. While ethnic studies scholars have long laid out the intersections of race, class, and gender, it took White scholars such as Roediger and Frankenberg to realize that whiteness is also a racial formation that is historically contingent and socially constructed. By opening up ethnic studies to include whiteness, the field is now more comfortably accessible to White scholars interested in the same questions that have intrigued ethnic studies scholars. Established ethnic studies scholars such as George Lipsitz (1998) have eagerly engaged the study of Whiteness.

Whiteness studies also intersects with another new project that is both political and academic, this one launched by left legal scholars, some White but mostly of color, who equate their work with a movement and call it critical race theory (CRT). Led by law professors such as Derrick Bell and Kimberle Crenshaw (African Americans), Richard Delgado and Ian Haney Lopez (Latinos), and Neil Gotanda (Asian American), this new legal scholarship offers a critique of liberalism and challenges head on comfortable liberal premises embedded in the law and the legal academy (Delgado, 1995; Crenshaw et al., 1995). Far from being neutral and objective, these scholars argue that legal scholarship and the law itself, including civil rights law and discourse, are inevitably political and actually complicit in maintaining White supremacy and the basic myths of American meritocracy. They make a distinction between the formal equality underpinning civil rights race reform legislation and subtle forms of racism that remain deeply entrenched in American culture and institutions. So they set about to reexamine familiar terrains of legal scholarship, such as federal Indian legislation and antidiscrimination laws, from a critical race perspective, as well as to create new, oppositionist accounts of race.

Ethnic studies has benefited enormously and in many ways energized and challenged to rethink some of its own premises by the steady stream of innovative scholarship coming out of Whiteness studies and critical race studies. They share a commitment not only to the production of new knowledge, but simultaneously an unabashed and unapologetic acknowledgment that scholarship is necessarily about power and should be dedicated to the goal of social justice and human liberation.

CONCLUSION

While the rhetoric of the eighties led by neoconservative ideological warriors Lynne Cheney and William Bennett (not coincidentally, both former Republican-appointed directors of the National Endowment for the Humanities) have cooled in recent years, the assault on America's racialized communities has only accelerated with time. The battle has not been abandoned but has shifted to the arena of public policy, where affirmative action, bilingual education, and curricular reform first come under severe scrutiny and then are systematically emasculated and decimated. In the face of the backlash, the challenge for ethnic studies in this new century is to remain steadfast in its founding mission, for it has the unique opportunity to reinvent and thus to redefine America through its scholarship and teaching. In the new millennium, America's options are clear. It can retain its traditional self-image as an expression of Western triumphalism, an identity largely unchanged since the days of the founding fathers and reinforced by a social structure that historian Alexander Saxton bluntly describes as "white supremacist" and "intolerant of racial diversity" (Saxton, 1990, p. 10). The alternative is for this nation to move seriously toward racial and cultural democracy.

To do so, education in the United States must begin by rectifying an official history that has been exclusive, and therefore incomplete and distorted. As long as ethnic studies and multicultural education in general remain within the confines of "sensitivity training" and "celebrating diversity," it is safe and uncontested. But the minute ethnic studies and multicultural educators take seriously the edict that education's highest purpose is to liberate and empower (as opposed to socialize), then it becomes controversial and, frankly, threatening to the status quo. However, this is precisely what makes ethnic studies so exciting and powerful, given its location at the crux of this monumental but necessary project to rethink and reimagine America.

References

Acuña, R. (1988). *Occupied America: A history of Chicanos* (3rd ed.). New York: HarperCollins.

Adams, R. L. (1993). African-American studies and the state of the art. In M. Azevedo (Ed.), *Africana studies: A survey of Africa and the African diaspora*. Durham, NC: Carolina Academic Press.

Asante, M. K. (1992). The Afrocentric metatheory and disciplinary implications. *Afrocentric Scholar, 1*(1), 98–117.

Aufderheide, P. (Ed.). (1992). *Beyond PC: Toward a politics of understanding*. St. Paul, MN: Graywolf Press.

Barringer, F. (1991, March 11). Census shows profound change in racial makeup of the nation. *New York Times*, p. A1.

Bell-Villada, G. (1990). Critical appraisals of American education: Dilemmas and contradictions in the work of Hirsch and Bloom. *International Journal of Politics, Culture, and Society, 3*(4), 485–511.

Berman, P. (Ed.). (1992). *Debating PC: The controversy over political correctness on college campuses*. New York: Dell.

Beyers, B. (1991, June 19). Machiavelli loses ground at Stanford; Bible holds its own. *Chronicle of Higher Education*, B2.

Bloom, A. (1987). *Closing of the American mind*. New York: Simon & Schuster.

Butler, J. (1991). Ethnic studies: A matrix model for the major. *Liberal Education, 77*(2), 26–32.

Butler, J. (Ed.). (2001). *Color-line to borderlands: The matrix of American ethnic studies*. Seattle: University of Washington Press.

Butler, J., & Walter, J. (Eds.). (1991). *Transforming the curriculum: Ethnic studies and women's studies*. Albany: State University of New York Press.

Chaufauros, E. A. (1991). New ethnic studies in two American universities: A preliminary discussion. Unpublished manuscript, Yale University, Program on Non-Profit Organizations, New Haven.

Cheney, L. (1992). *Telling the truth: A report on the state of the humanities in higher education*. Washington, DC: National Endowment for the Humanities.

Crenshaw, K., Gotanda, N., Peller, G., & Thomas, K. (Eds.). (1995). *Critical race theory: The key writings that formed the movement*. New York: New Press.

Delgado, R. (Ed.). (1995). *Critical race theory: The cutting edge*. Philadelphia: Temple University Press.

Dirlik, A. (1993). The Asia-Pacific in Asian-American perspective. In A. Dirlik (Ed.), *What is in a rim? Critical perspectives on the Pacific region idea* (pp. 305–329). Boulder, CO: Westview Press.

D'Souza, D. (1991). *Illiberal education: The politics of race and sex on campus*. New York: Free Press.

Frankenberg, R. (1993). *White women, race matters: The social construction of whiteness*. Minneapolis: University of Minnesota Press.

Garcia, M. T. (1992). Multiculturalism and American studies. *Radical History Review, 54*, 49–58.

Genovese, E. D. (1991, April 15). An argument for counterterrorism in the academy: Heresy, yes—sensitivity, no. *New Republic*, pp. 30–35.

Glazer, N., & Moynihan, D. P. (Eds.). (1975). *Ethnicity: Theory and experience*. Cambridge, MA: Harvard University Press.

Gordon, D. (1992). Inside the Stanford mind. *Perspectives, 30*(4), 1–8.

Hayes, F. W., III (Ed.). (1992). *A turbulent voyage: Readings in African American studies*. San Diego, CA: Collegiate Press.

Hine, D. C. (1992). The Black studies movement: Afrocentric-traditionalist-feminist paradigms for the next stage. *Black Scholar, 22*(3), 11–19.

Hirabayashi, L., & Alquizola, M. (1992). Asian American studies and the politics of association. Unpublished manuscript.

Hu-DeHart, E. (1991). From area studies to ethnic studies: The study of the Chinese diaspora in Latin America. In S. Hune, H. Kim, S. Fugita, & A. Ling (Eds.), *Asian Americans: Comparative and global perspectives* (pp. 5–16). Pullman: Washington State University Press.

Hu-DeHart, E. (1999). *Across the Pacific: Asian Americans and globalization.* Philadelphia: Temple University Press.

Hune, S., Kim, H., Fugita, S., & Ling, A. (Eds.). (1991). *Asian Americans: Comparative and global perspectives* (pp. 1–4). Pullman: Washington State University Press.

Jaimes, M. A. (1987). American Indian studies: Toward an indigenous model. *American Indian Culture and Research Journal, 11*(3), 1–16.

JBHE. (2001, Spring). A JBHE survey: Is Black studies central to the mission of a great university? *Journal of Blacks in Higher Education, no. 31,* p. 38.

Jones, R. (1993). Ethnic studies—beyond myths and into some realities: A working paper. Unpublished manuscript, Brown University, Center for the Study of Race and Ethnicity in America, Providence.

Keller, G., Magallan, R. J., & Garcia, A. M. (Eds.). (1989). *Curriculum resources in Chicano studies.* Tempe, AZ: Bilingual Review/Press.

Kimball, R. (1990). *Tenured radicals: How politics has corrupted our higher education.* New York: HarperCollins.

Kristol, I. (1991, July 31). The tragedy of multiculturalism. *Wall Street Journal,* p. A12.

Lipsitz, G. (1998). *The possessive investment in whiteness: How White people profit from identity politics.* Philadelphia: Temple University Press.

Little, W. (1992). Introduction. *Afrocentric Scholar, 1*(1), i.

Liu, J. (1989). Asian American studies and the disciplining of ethnic studies. In G. Nomura, S. Sumida, & R. Long (Eds.), *Frontiers of Asian American studies* (pp. 273–283). Pullman: Washington State University Press.

Magner, D. (1991, May 1). Push for diversity in traditional disciplines raises questions about the future of ethnic studies. *Chronicle of Higher Education,* p. A11.

Mazumdar, S. (1991). Asian American studies and Asian studies: Rethinking roots. In S. Hune, H. Kim, S. Fujita, & A. Ling (Eds.), *Asian Americans: Comparative and global perspectives* (pp. 29–44). Pullman: Washington State University Press.

Miller, T. (Ed.). (2001). *A companion to cultural studies.* London: Blackwell.

Muwakkil, S. (1992, May 27–June 9). L.A. lessons go unlearned. *In These Times,* p. 1.

Nasar, S. (1992, March 5). *The 1980s: A very good time for the very rich.* New York Times, p. A1.

Okihiro, G. (1991). African and Asian American studies: A comparative analysis and commentary. In S. Hune, H. Kim, S. Fujita, & A. Ling (Eds.), *Asian Americans: Comparative and global perspectives* (pp. 17–28). Pullman: Washington State University Press.

Omatsu, G. (Ed.). (1989). Commemorative issue—Salute to the 60s and 70s: Legacy of the San Francisco State strike. *Amerasia Journal, 15*(1).

Ong, P., & Hee, S. J. (1993). The growth of the Asian Pacific American population: Twenty million in 2020. In *The state of Asian Pacific America—a public policy report: Policy issues to the year 2020* (pp. 11–23). Los Angeles: LEAP Asian American Public Policy Institute and UCLA Asian American studies Center.

Ortiz, R. D. (1980). *Final report from the round table of Native American studies directors in forming the Native American Studies Association.* Albuquerque: University of New Mexico, Institute for Native American Development.

Portes, A., & Bach, R. (1985). *Latin journal: Cuban and Mexican immigrants in the United States.* Berkeley: University of California Press.

Roediger, D. R. (1991). *The wages of whiteness: Race and the making of the American working class.* London: Verso.

Rowe, J. C. (Ed.). (2000). *Post-nationalist American studies.* Berkeley: University of California Press.

San Juan, E., Jr. (1992). *Racial formations/critical transformations: Articulations of power in ethnic and racial studies in the United States.* Atlantic Highlands, NJ: Humanities Press International.

San Juan, E., Jr. (n.d.). Multiculturalism versus hegemony: Ethnic studies, Asian Americans, and U.S. racial politics. Unpublished manuscript, University of Connecticut, Storrs.

Saxton, A. (1990). *The rise and fall of the White republic.* London: Verso.

Schlesinger, A. M., Jr. (1992). *The disuniting of America: Reflections on a multicultural society.* New York: Norton.

Shapiro, T. M., & Wolff, E. N. (2001). *Assets for the poor.* New York: Russell Sage Foundation.

Sowell, T. (1981). *Ethnic America: A history.* New York: Basic Books.

Stowe, D. W. (1996, September–October). Uncolored people: The rise of Whiteness studies. *Lingua Franca,* pp. 68–77.

University of California, San Diego. (1990, January 25). Proposal for the creation of a department of ethnic studies at the University of California, San Diego. Unpublished manuscript, University of California, San Diego.

Usdansky, M. (1992, May 29–31). "Diverse" fits nation better than "normal." *USA Today,* p. 1A.

Vázquez, J. (1988). The co-opting of ethnic studies in the American university: A critical view. *Explorations in Ethnic studies, 11*(1), 23–34.

Wang, L. L. (n.d.). Ethnic studies and curriculum transformation at UC Berkeley: Our past, present and future. Unpublished manuscript, University of California, Berkeley, Department of Ethnic Studies.

Washington, M. (1998). Disturbing the peace: What happens to American studies if you put African American studies at the center? Presidential address to the American Studies Association, October 29, 1997. *American Quarterly, 50*(1), 1–23.

Wing, A. (Ed.). (1997). *Critical race feminism: A reader.* New York: NYU Press.

Woodward, C. V. (1991). Freedom and the universities. In P. Aufderheide (Ed.), *Beyond PC: Toward a politics of understanding* (pp. 27–49). St. Paul, MN: Graywolf Press.

44

WOMEN'S STUDIES AND CURRICULUM TRANSFORMATION IN THE UNITED STATES

Betty Schmitz
University of Washington, Seattle

Johnnella E. Butler
University of Washington, Seattle

Beverly Guy-Sheftall
Spelman College

Deborah Rosenfelt
University of Maryland, College Park

Women's studies has created theories about gender and the intersections of gender, race, ethnicity, class, and sexuality that offer important analytical frameworks for developing multicultural curricula. In this chapter, we focus our discussion on multicultural aspects of women's studies, that is, on how gender intersects with race, ethnicity, class, sexuality, and other variables, rather than on theoretical debates about the meanings of gender. We also review the progress of women's studies as a catalyst for transformation of U.S. higher education curricula.

THE EVOLUTION OF WOMEN'S STUDIES: CREATING A NEW FIELD

There are today more than 615 women's studies programs in the United States, enrolling more students than any other interdisciplinary field (Buhle, 2000). The impetus for the formation of women's studies programs and departments, like African American studies and other ethnic studies, can be traced to the social protest and political dissent of the civil rights movement and accompanying Black Power, Chicano, American Indian, and women's movements. Students and faculty members engaged with these concerns pushed for greater access to education and courses on groups that had been historically invisible in the curriculum. Feminists in the academy critiqued the content of the academic disciplines, the patriarchal structure of educational institutions, and the relationship of education to dominant cultural, political, economic, and social systems.

The far-reaching objectives of women's studies are well stated in the 1977 founding preamble to the National Women's Studies Association (NWSA): "to promote and sustain 'the educational strategy of a break-through in consciousness and knowledge' that would 'transform' individuals, institutions, relationships, and ultimately the whole of society" (Boxer, 1982, p. 661). NWSA articulated a transformative vision of "a world free not only from sexism, but also from racism, classism, ageism, heterosexism—from all the ideologies and institutions that have consciously or unconsciously oppressed and exploited some for the advantage of others" (p. 662). The development of a field of study that would have a social change as well as an academic mission was an idea present from the beginning.

We gratefully acknowledge Christy Flores for the research assistance she provided in revising this chapter, especially the section on Chicana/Latina studies. We also thank our editors, James A. Banks and Cherry A. McGee Banks, and colleagues Suzanne Benally, Kathy Friedman, David Silver, and Mary Kay Tetreault for their helpful suggestions.

Developing and Institutionalizing Women's Studies Programs

Women's studies as a distinct programmatic unit within higher education began in 1970 at San Diego State University and grew rapidly. By 1976, there were more than 270 programs nationwide and 15,000 courses spread across 1,500 institutions. Women's caucuses began to appear within disciplinary-based professional associations. Other scholarly supports—journals (*Feminist Studies* and *Women's Studies Quarterly* in 1972 and *Signs: A Journal of Women in Culture and Society* in 1975), research centers, libraries, archives, and textbooks—developed to serve scholars and teachers. The Feminist Press, founded in 1970, published syllabi and other resources from women's studies courses in *Female Studies VI* (Hoffman, Secor, & Tinsley, 1973) and *Female Studies VII* (Rosenfelt, 1973); foundational texts for diversity among women, *All the Women Are White, All the Blacks Are Men, But Some of Us Are Brave* (Hull, Scott, & Smith, 1982); and *Lesbian Studies* (Cruikshank, 1982). Stimpson refers to this early period of women's studies as the "take-off phase," where "submerged and marginalized traditions" emerged "explosively" (1992, p. 1967). Indeed, in the 1960s, the Library of Congress documented 269 new titles in women's history, 1,534 in the 1970s, 3,862 in the 1980s, but 1,743 titles from 1990 to 1991 alone (Ruthdotter, cited in Westbrook, 1999, p. 57).

Women's studies built on the presence in traditional departments of a significant number of women interested in feminist issues and gender analysis. The "founding mothers" of women's studies were the "come-back" generation of women in higher education after the 1950s when women's enrollment hit a low point (Buhle, 2000, p. xvi). Often in part-time positions and junior in rank, these women nevertheless risked their academic careers to establish the field, as reported in *The Politics of Women's Studies: Testimony from 30 Founding Mothers* (Howe, 2000). Women's studies tended to emerge as programs, building curricula around departmentally based courses. Many women's studies units pursued departmental status since it is difficult to mount coherent curricula and engage in long-term planning when faculty members owe allegiance to more powerful departments that make tenure and promotion decisions and when program directors must negotiate with department heads to develop and schedule courses. Faculty members also sometimes feel divided between different sets of service obligations and different scholarly imperatives.

Women's studies requires familiarity with a range of texts and ideas that transcend disciplinary boundaries and question disciplinary assumptions (Hesse-Biber, Gilmartin, & Lydenberg, 1999; Westbrook, 1999). The dependence of women's studies on disciplinary-based scholarship as well as interdisciplinary work is reflected in the structure of the major (Butler, Coyner, Homans, Longenecker, & Musil, 1991). A typical women's studies major takes 35 semester hours, including an introductory course, usually thematically arranged around topics such as the cultural representation of women, work, family, sexuality, and cultural diversity; a series of electives in the humanities and social sciences; and a final capstone course in the form of a senior seminar, field study, or independent study. Many majors now require courses in feminist theory, and one-third of programs surveyed required a course or courses on race, ethnicity, or cross-cultural perspectives. Lee (2000) notes that requiring a single course on "women of color" in the women's studies major institutionalizes the marginality of women of color.

A significant development in women's studies in the past decade has been the evolution of graduate programs. Women's studies programs began to offer M.A.s and graduate certificates or emphases in women's studies in the 1980s. Since the late 1990s, a small but growing number of departments have developed a Ph.D. program, consciously oriented toward training the next generation of interdisciplinary feminist scholars. Work on the challenges of and need for interdisciplinarity in research on a wide range of issues affecting women from diverse backgrounds has been important in inspiring and supporting this evolution (Allen & Kitch, 1998; Forum, 2001). Some Ph.D. degrees are offered jointly with specific departments; for example, at the University of Michigan, students may obtain a Ph.D. in women's studies and English or women's studies and psychology. Others, such as those at the University of Maryland and the University of Washington, are deliberately conceived as interdisciplinary programs.

The Development of Inclusive Feminist Scholarship

Feminist scholarship emerged both within specific academic disciplines and through the interdisciplinary work encouraged by women's studies programs, centers for research on women, and activist women outside the academy. Feminist scholars in disciplinary fields began to document and critique male bias embedded in their fields (Andersen, 1987). DuBois, Kelly, Kennedy, Korsmeyer, and Robinson (1985) analyzed how "feminist scholarship from a multiplicity of disciplines is beginning to converge" (p. 6) by examining the dialectics of oppression and liberation, victimization and agency as central axes of inquiry. An extensive literature of critique of the concepts, methods, and perspectives in traditional disciplines emerged (Bleier, 1986; Harding, 1986; Hartman & Messer-Davidow, 1991; Hermann & Stewart, 1994; Hubbard, 1982; Minnich, 1990; Sherman & Beck, 1979; Spender, 1981; Stanton & Stewart, 1995).

In its earlier manifestations, from the late 1960s to the mid-1970s, women's studies focused on the unity of women's experience. As Boxer (1998) notes and Howe's volume on founding mothers (2000) demonstrates, the originators of women's studies programs and early theorists were largely White. Much of the influential theoretical work in this period sought universal explanations, structural and psychological, for the origins and persistence of patriarchal patterns—for example, Millett's (1970) *Sexual Politics*, which identified a relatively undifferentiated pattern of sexist imagery in male-authored literature, explained with references to male domination in virtually all societies; Rubin's (1975) "The Traffic in Women," which drew on structural anthropology and Lacanian psychoanalysis to originate the term *sex-gender system;* Rosaldo's (1974) "Women, Culture, and Society: A Theoretical Overview," which proposed a structural model that related aspects of psychology and social organization to what she posited as a "public/private" split in male/female orientations; Ortner's (1974) "Is Female to Male as Nature Is to Culture?" which proposed a universal structure of perception; Chodorow's (1978) *The Reproduction of Mothering: Psychoanalysis and the Sociology of Gender*, which drew on object-relations theory to posit crucial developmental differences between women and men; and Gilligan's (1982) *In a Different Voice*, which implied universal differences between women and men in their cognitive and moral development.

Also during the 1980s, a tendency already present in the late 1970s gained primacy: an emphasis on difference and diversity among women. Two conflicting theoretical and pedagogical concepts of "difference" emerged: (1) as primarily gender difference that united women as distinct from men and (2) as an index of incommensurability among women of different races, classes, ethnicities, abilities, sexualities, and nationalities. Thus, while Jardine (1988) in her prelude to *The Future of Difference* heard among feminists "a common voice, which crosses cultural, political, and linguistic boundaries" in its inquiry into fundamental gender dichotomy (pp. xxv–xxvii), and Morgan (1984), in *Sisterhood Is Global*, reiterated the universality of violence against women, poverty among women, women's limited access to social and economic power, and women's resistance in a global feminist movement as signs of women's underlying unity, simultaneously, writers in *This Bridge Called My Back: Writings by Radical Women of Color* (Moraga & Anzaldúa, 1981) and *But Some of Us Are Brave* (Hull et al., 1982) offered critiques of White feminism. These writers demonstrated that in both theory and pedagogical practice, gender alone could not define women and explored through multiple perspectives the simultaneity of oppressions in women's lives and the intersections between and among gender, class, race, ethnicity, religion, and sexual orientation.

Lorde (1981) observed that the "oppression of women knows no ethnic or racial boundaries, true, but that does not mean it is identical within those boundaries. . . . To deal with one without even alluding to the other is to distort our commonality as well as our difference" (p. 97). Sánchez (1983) called for an end to tokenism of Native American women in women's studies, given the "hundreds of resource lists or Indian-run agencies, hundreds of Indian women in organizations all over the country" (p. 153). And Zinn, Cannon, Higginbotham, and Dill (1986) noted that those holding the "gatekeeping positions" at major feminist scholarly journals were as White as those at any mainstream social science or humanities publication.

This critique emerged from the development of autonomous movements of women of color throughout the world, spurred by new perspectives on the global political economy of women arising within the context of the United Nations Decade for Women (Albrecht & Brewer, 1990). The term *womanist* became current in the early 1980s in the writings of some African American women who wished to define their perspective as different from feminism in its incorporation of racial, cultural, national, economic, and political considerations, but similar in its critical perception of and reaction against patriarchy and sexism (Ogunyemi, 1985; Walker, 1983). The work of White feminists who critiqued hegemonic feminist theory also helped to transform the field (Bunch, 1983; Culley, 1985; Frye, 1983; Palmer, 1983; Spelman, 1988).

Women from working-class backgrounds have also felt marginalized within women's studies. Helmbold (1987), hooks (1984, 2000), and Tokarczyk and Fay (1993) wrote of the chasm between academic environments and the backgrounds of working-class women. Others critiqued the bias of feminist discourses that ignored class differences or that spoke abstractly of class while objectifying the experiences of working-class women of all races and ethnicities, and simultaneously offered new paradigms for changing pedagogy and personal politics (Fisher-Mannick, 1981; Zandy, 1990, 2001).

Lesbian feminists critiqued institutionalized heterosexism and the relative invisibility of lesbian experience within women's studies (Bulkin, 1980; Cruikshank, 1982); Muslim women spoke about their invisibility (Ahmed, 1980; al-Hibri, 1983); Jewish women criticized anti-Semitism within the women's movement and women's studies scholarship (Beck, 1988; Pogrebin, 1982); women with disabilities raised issues of access, bias, and the intersection of gender and disability (Fine & Asch, 1988; Hillyer, 1992; Wendell, 1996); and a critique of ageism in women's studies (Copper, 1988; Macdonald & Rich, 1983) generated theory about women and aging (Gannon, 1999; Pearsall, 1997; Porter, 1989; Wheeler, 1997; Woodward, 1999).

Another source of challenge to the idea of unity among women, postmodernism also interrogated the idea of unity in subjectivity and textuality, emphasizing the partiality and situational nature of all knowledge. It "deconstructed" binary oppositions, including those between male and female, positing a plurality of subject positions in their stead. Postmodern theory has maintained a steady hostility to "biologism" and "essentialism" as ontological errors misreading the symbolic, culturally constructed nature of identity, including gender, race, and national identity (Barrett & Phillips, 1992; Haraway, 1991; Nicholson, 1990).

New Fields of Study

An immense literature focusing on women's lives and experiences has emerged from academic and activist women's studies, but it is primarily the work of women of color and women of different ethnicities and sexualities that has contributed to the development of multicultural paradigms.

Black Women's Studies. Black women's studies emerged in part because of the failure of both Black studies and women's studies to address adequately the experiences of women of African descent. This field provided the conceptual frameworks for moving women of color out of the margins of women's studies. Cade edited a collection of works about African American women in 1970; *The Black Woman* was as important in the development of feminist theory as Millett's *Sexual Politics,* though rarely cited in this context by White feminists. Cade's (1970) work preceded Lerner's 1973 *Black Women in White America,* which is often cited as having ushered in Black women's studies.

Equally important was *The Afro-American Woman: Struggles and Images* (Terborg-Penn & Harley, 1978), which provided important feminist historical perspectives. Many other critical works followed in the formative years of African American women's studies (Davis, 1981; Dill, 1979; Jones, 1985; Lorde, 1984; Stack, 1984; Sterling, 1984; White, 1985). Giddings's (1984) history of Black women, *When and Where I Enter,* underscored the significance of the argument that Black women's history and experiences are inextricably related to that of the entire community.

A critical component in the development of Black women's studies was the emergence of Black feminist literary criticism, a response to Black women's exclusion from both African Americanist and feminist critical canons. Smith's "Toward a Black Feminist Criticism" (1977) was the first theoretical essay attempting to define a Black feminist aesthetic, followed by work by McDowell (1980), Christian (1980, 1988), and Carby (1987). Bell, Parker, and Guy-Sheftall (1979) and Washington

(1975, 1980, 1987) edited anthologies of African American women writers for classroom use. Black women's studies expanded considerably in the 1990s. New histories of African American women in America include Hine (1990, 1998), Hine, King, and Reed (1995), White (1999), Hunter (1997), Robnett (1997), and Terborg-Penn (1998).

One of the most exciting developments is the emergence of Black feminist theory and histories of Black feminist thought, which began with the now-classic "Combahee River Collective Statement" (1977), penned by members of the Boston Black Feminist Collective (Hull et al., 1982), and the pioneering work of hooks in *Ain't I a Woman* (1981), *Feminist Theory: From Margin to Center* (1984), and later *Where We Stand* (2000). Despite its ideological diversity, the most distinguishing characteristic of Black feminist theory and other antiracist feminisms is the complex ways in which they interrogate the social constructions of race, gender, class, nation, and sexuality and how they operate as interlocking systems of oppression. Black feminist theory explicates the multiple ways that gender operates in relationship to other identity markers and argues that women's different social locations matter with respect to their experience of womanhood. See Collins, *Black Feminist Thought* (2000) and *Fighting Words* (1998); James and Farmer, *Spirit, Space and Survival* (1993); James and Busia, *Theorizing Black Feminisms* (1993); Guy-Sheftall, *Words of Fire: An Anthology of African American Feminist Thought* (1995); J. James and Sharpley-Whiting, *The Black Feminist Reader* (2000); White, *Dark Continent of Our Bodies: Black Feminism and the Politics of Respectability* (2001); and Mullings, *On Our Own Terms: Race, Class and Gender in the Lives of African American Women* (1997).

The global reach of Black women's studies is also manifested in a new subfield, African diaspora women's studies, whose foundational texts are Steady's (1981) *The Black Woman Cross Culturally* and Terborg-Penn, Harley, and Rushing's (1987) *Women in Africa and the African Diaspora.* This field includes work on women in Africa, the Caribbean, Black Britain, Brazil, and the Americas. Important theoretical texts include Davies, *Black Women, Writing and Identity: Migrations of the Subject* (1994); Davies and Ogundipe-Leslie, *Moving Beyond Boundaries: Black Women's Diasporas* (1995); and Nnaemeka, *Sisterhood, Feminisms and Power: From Africa to the Diaspora* (1998).

American Indian Women's Studies. Twelve American Indian women held a special meeting in 1977 at the NWSA to formalize a network of academic Indian women. They identified the need for work on Indian women that represented their own perspectives, for increased attention to Indian women's survival networks and relationships between them and White women, and to focus on modern life rather than the past (Green, 1979). Green's *Native American Women: A Contextual Bibliography* (1983a) and *That's What She Said: Contemporary Fiction and Poetry by Native American Women* (1983b), along with such works as *American Indian Women: Telling Their Lives* (Bataille & Sands, 1984) and *A Gathering of Spirit: Writing and Art by Native North American Women* (Brant, 1988), documented the scope and cultural diversity of writings by and about Native women for whom women's issues are linked to issues of tribal sovereignty and Indian self-determination. These and more recent works make clear that "feminist" issues such as reproductive rights, health care, and employment remain rooted in concerns for the survival of Indian peoples and their cultures and issues of land, natural resources, and treaty rights (LaDuke, 1999; Mihesuah, 2000; Tohe, 2000; Trask, 1993). American Indian women's activism has arisen primarily out of tribal activism rather than out of the feminist movement (Crow Dog, 1990, 1993; Jaimes & Halsey, 1992; Witt, 1976).

For her bibliography, Green (1983a) reviewed more than 700 bibliographic items and 200 years of writing on Native North American women, two thirds of which were written between 1960 and 1980. Although she finds some of the earlier "as told to" narratives useful today (Lurie, 1961), she faults researchers and scholars in anthropology and history for preferring to study those tribes and topics that remain visibly traditional and fit existing models. Thus, more early scholarship may exist proportionally on American Indian women than other groups of U.S. women of color, but it is selective, stereotypical, and romanticized. Donaldson (1999) criticizes the appropriation of American Indian traditions as alternative sources of knowledge and spirituality by some strands of feminism and challenges feminist scholars to conduct more sophisticated study of cultural misappropriation.

The historical and cultural studies by scholars such as Albers and Medicine (1983), Allen (1986), Kidwell (1979, 1994), and Medicine (1981, 1987) illustrate how American Indian women have conceptualized their struggles with tradition and change, defined contemporary familial and societal structures, and acted on behalf of the survival of their communities. Important new work on the boarding school experience (Lomawaima, 1994; Mihesuah, 1993) and gender and sexuality (Jacobs, Thomas, & Lang, 1997; Woodsum, 1995) expands the thematic focus of scholarship on American Indian women. Contemporary biographical and autobiographical works document women's lives in different tribal contexts (see especially Mankiller, 1993; Perdue, 1998, 2001; and Shoemaker, 1995). American Indian women's literary texts intertwine contemporary and past oral traditions and treat themes of community, loss, and continuance; resistance to assimilation; attention to the sacredness of language;

concern for the land; and affirmation of tribal sovereignty and cultural traditions (Brant, 1996; Campbell, 1993; Dunn & Comfort, 1999; Gould, 1995; Harjo & Bird, 1997; Hernandez-Avila, 1995; Hungry Wolf, 1982; Katz, 1995; Perreault & Vance, 1993; Trafzer, 1996).

Asian American and Pacific Islander Women's Studies. Asian American women's studies emerged within activist women's movements and within the struggles of Asian American communities, providing complex analyses of the intersections of race, class, and gender (Cheung, 1997; Le Espiritu, 1997; Lowe, 1996; Yamada, 1981). In 1974, faculty members teaching Asian American women's studies classes in eight California universities convened to discuss the connections between theoretical orientations and activism in a field in which there was a paucity of scholarship (Chu, 1986). The diversity of immigration experiences among Chinese, Japanese, Filipino, Korean, Pacific Islander, and the newer South and Southeast Asian women enlarged the field with studies of intergenerational conflicts and issues of assimilation and language, ways to address intolerance of women's issues within the Asian communities, and ways to maintain courses within academic curricula without a scholarly precedent (Chai, 1988; Chow, 1987; Chu, 1986; Lai, 1992; Lim, 1991). Aguilar-San Juan (1983) and Tsui (1983) pioneered work on Asian American and Pacific Islander lesbians.

Wong and Santa Ana (1999) identify three periods of treatment of gender and sexuality in Asian American literature. In the first period, violence and "deviance," spanning the 1850s to the 1950s, works by Sui Sin Far, Hisaye Yamamoto, and others appeared in small literary magazines. In the second period, self-definition and self-representation (1960s–1980s), women's writing took off. Writers such as Hagedorn, Mirikitani, Lim, N. Wong, and Yamada critiqued oppression of Asian American women, expressed solidarity with Third World women in Asia, challenged stereotypes of "lotus blossom" and "dragon lady," reconstructed female ancestors' forgotten lives, and explored generational differences (Wong & Santa Ana, 1999). The work of these writers is anthologized in such collections as *Asian and Pacific American Experiences: Women's Perspectives* (Tsuchida, 1982); *Making Waves* (Asian Women United of California, 1989); *Forbidden Stitch* (Lim & Tsutakawa, 1989); *Home to Stay* (Watanabe & Bruchac, 1990); and *Unbroken Thread* (Uno, 1993). Kim (1982) pioneered studies of gender in Asian American literature, including analyses of the exoticization and demonization of Asian women and emasculation of Asian men.

Feminist writers in the final period identified by Wong and Santa Ana (multiple selves, sites, transgressions—late 1980s to the present) treat gender and sexuality in postmodern perspective (Minh-ha, 1989; Mohanty, 1991) and exhibit a greater willingness to explore sexuality (Eng & Hom, 1998; Kim, Villanueva, & Asian Women United of California, 1997; Lim-Hing, 1994; Leong, 1996; Nam, 2001; Shah, 1997). There is an emphasis also on the heterogeneity of Asian American and Pacific Islander experiences (Dasgupta, 1998; Gupta, 1999; Hagedorn, 1997; Ho, 1999; Song & Moon, 1998; Williams-León & Nakashima, 2001; Women of South Asian Descent Coalition, 1993).

The historical work of Glenn (1986), Hune, Kim, Fugita, and Ling (1991), and Chan (1991) has strengthened the scholarly underpinnings of Asian American and Pacific Islander women's studies.

Chicana/Latina Studies. Chicana studies, Puerto Rican women's studies, and other Latina studies emerged from autonomous women of color movements and from the context of community struggles and the creation of Chicano studies, Latino studies, and Puerto Rican studies. Chicana/Latina feminists critiqued women's studies for its exclusionary practices and lack of attention to diversity among women (González, 1977; Rebolledo, 1985). Their theoretical work and creative writing bring new themes and paradigms to women's studies, illustrating how issues of race, class, sexuality, cultural identity, and gender subordination intersect and coexist. A central task is to name their subject in the face of linguistic and geographical boundaries and classification systems ("Hispanic," "Spanish speaking") that do not define their reality. Through their analyses of silence and voice within the context of bilingualism, they challenge monolingual English-speaking feminists to experience their own limitations and create new definitions of self through the creative use of both languages (Anzaldúa, 1987; Gómez, Moraga, & Romo-Carmona, 1983; Horno-Delgado, Ortega, Scott, & Sternbach, 1989). Galindo and Gonzales's edited volume (1999) examines linguistic phenomena such as code switching, bilingualism, and transgressive language.

Chicana feminism implicitly or explicitly informs Chicana studies (De la Torre & Pesquera, 1993). Chicana theorists developed the paradigm of borderland consciousness to describe their experiences living in multiple and contradictory realities based on ethnicity, nationality, sexuality, and language. Anzaldúa (1987, 1990) writes of her identities as a Chicana writer in a Euro-American literary tradition, as a woman in patriarchal societies, and as a lesbian in a heterosexist culture; she does not seek unity for this fragmented self-hood but rather a manifold subjectivity. Chicanas see borderland consciousness as a powerful, transformative state rather than an oppressive one. Likewise, Chicana theorists break new ground in dealing with lesbian sexuality (Alarcon, Castillo, & Moraga, 1993; Trujillo, 1991, 1998) and sexual violence (Zavella, 1998).

Another common thread is a commitment to relating academic knowledges to *la comunidad* (the Chicano/a community), as well as relating *la comunidad* to academic knowledges (Anzaldúa, 1990). Chicana studies scholarship then often blurs the boundaries between "practical" and "theoretical" as scholars continue to examine their relationship to both feminism (Segura & Pesquera, 1993) and Chicano studies to seek self-determination, often through the formation of grassroots associations such as Mujeres Activas en Letras y Cambio Social (MALCS) and the Chicana caucus of the National Association of Chicano Studies (NACS). *Chicana Feminist Thought: The Basic Historical Writings* (García, 1997) contains a comprehensive collection of Chicana writings about political grassroots movements, historical accounts, Chicana feminist theories, and creative, personal pieces, representing the complexity and multiplicity of Chicana voices.

Current scholarship within Chicana studies encompasses numerous fields and disciplines: history (Perez, 1999; Ruíz, 1987), literary studies (Alarcón, 1993; Herrera-Sobek, 1985; McCracken, 1999; Rebolledo, 1995; Rebolledo & Rivero, 1993; Saldívar-Hull, 2000), the social sciences (Galindo & Gonzales, 1999; Pardo, 1998), and cultural studies (Yarbro-Bejarano, 1994). Chicanas in theater and media also continue to enjoy considerable attention (Fregoso, 1993; Herrera-Sobek & Viramontes, 1995; Maciel, Ortiz, & Herrera-Sobek, 2000; Ramirez, 2000). Although Chicanas in the workplace have been of continuing interest (Segura, 1989; Segura & Pierce, 1992), in the 1990s scholarship in Chicana studies broadened to include the transnational examination of the role of female Mexican nationals/Mexican immigrant women as workers—or *maquiladoras*—on both the literal and figurative U.S.-Mexico border (Hondagneu-Sotelo, 2001; Iglesias-Prieto, 1997; Peña, 1997; Romero, 1992).

Acosta-Belén's (1986) edited collection, *The Puerto Rican Woman: Perspectives on Culture, History, and Society*, first published in 1979, is a critical source for the study and understanding of Puerto Rican women's reality both on the island and in the continental United States. Scholarship that has contributed substantially to our knowledge about Puerto Rican women includes historical analysis (Azize-Vargas, 1990; Matos-Rodriquez & Delgado, 1998), workplace and labor (Browne, 1999; Ortiz, 1996), and community and family (Lamberty & García-Coll, 1994; Muniz, 1998). Acosta-Belén, Bose, and Sjostrom (1994) have developed an interdisciplinary guide for research and curriculum on Puerto Rican women (1994).

Jewish Women's Studies. The field of Jewish women's studies has explored the history, literature, experiences, and religious dilemmas of Jewish women worldwide (Antler, 1997, 1998; Baskin, 1999; Elwell, 1992; Hyman

& Moore, 1997; Kantrowitz & Klepfisz, 1989). Jewish women's studies emerged simultaneously within women's studies and Jewish studies, having to critique anti-Semitism in one and sexism in the other and to negotiate visibility in both. Although Jewish women were influential participants in and shapers of women's studies since its inception, they were not always visible as Jews. Beck (1988) suggested that Jewish women's invisibility reflected less a deliberate anti-Semitism than a reliance on a set of variables—race, class, and gender—that obscured Jewish women's ethnic and religious identities. Hyman (1998) more recently documented areas of convergence and divergence between Jewish feminism and the American women's movement.

Within Jewish studies and Jewish community life, Jewish women have struggled with a central dilemma: Can one be simultaneously a feminist and a Jew? A lesbian and a Jew? Jewish women's efforts to resolve these questions have generated a critique of patriarchal practices in Jewish cultures (Baskin & Tenenbaum, 1994; Cantor, 1995; Davidman & Tenenbaum, 1994; Kornbluth & Kornbluth, 2000; Levitt, 1997; Plaskow, 1990; Rudavsky, 1995; Sacks, 1995) and scholarship on balancing lesbianism and Jewish faith (Alpert, 1998; Beck, 1989).

Jewish women's studies also includes biblical analysis and reinterpretation of biblical texts (Ostriker, 1993; Pardes, 1992); historical work on Jewish women in specific historical periods (Antler, 1997; Friedman-Kasaba, 1996; Glenn, 1990; Prell, 1999); work, often with Palestinian women, on peace in the Middle East (Rosenwasser, 1992; Sharoni, 1995); and scholarship on the contradictions between religious-ethnic identity and feminist consciousness with women in other religious traditions (Manning, 1999).

Contemporary American Jewish women's studies has seen a rise in scholarly attention to diversity, questioning Jewish women's shifting identities in relation to class, race, and ethnicity, including studies of Sephardic Jews, Mizrahi Jews, Jewish women of color, working-class Jewish women, and Orthodox and Hasidic women (Brodkin, 1998; Davidman, 1991; Ruttenberg, 2001). Important bibliographic resources include Herman (1998), Masnik (1996), and Weisbard (2002).

Muslim and Arab American Women's Studies. Muslim, Arab, and Arab American women's studies emerged within the United States as immigrant women and feminist scholars from Arab countries attempted to find a home for their work within women's studies programs in the United States. Scholars have documented the emergence of feminist movements around the world, including the Middle East, particularly in local liberation struggles and religious reform movements, including Islamic reform movements. In fact, the term *Islamic*

feminism became visible in the 1990s in various Middle Eastern countries; this evolving Islamic feminist discourse attempts to capture notions of gender equality and social justice within an Islamic paradigm (Ahmed, 1992; Mernissi, 1991; Spellberg, 1994). The basic argument of Islamic feminist discourse is that the Qur'an affirms equality among all human beings, but gender equality has been subverted by patriarchal ideologies and practices within Muslim societies and Islamic fundamentalist states. Yamani (1996) writes about Qur'anically mandated gender equality in *Feminism and Islam*, which fuels continuing debates about the status of Muslim women, and McCloud (1995) describes African American Islam and its gender politics.

Muslim and Arab feminists in the United States have had to combat stereotypes and preoccupation of American feminists in the academy with issues of the veil and excision (Mernissi, 1992), on one level, and the desires on the part of some U.S. feminists to quell critiques of Zionism and racism (Naber, Desouky, & Baroudi, 2001). The Egyptian feminist Nawal El Saadawi was the most read and anthologized, and for a long time the only, Arab feminist on U.S. women's studies syllabi. The reception of the *Hidden Face of Eve* (1980) encouraged representations of Arab women solely as victims of oppression. Newer works by Ahmed (1999), El Saadawi (1997), Kadi (1994), Shakir (1997), and Webb (2000) provide multiple perspectives on Muslim and Arab American women.

Lesbian Studies. While lesbians were central theorists of women's studies from its beginnings, the publication of *Lesbian Nation* (Johnston, 1973); *This Bridge Called My Back* (Moraga & Anzaldúa, 1981); *Conditions, Volume 5* (Bethel & Smith, 1979); *Nice Jewish Girls: A Lesbian Anthology* (Beck, 1982, 1989); *Lesbian Studies: Present and Future* (Cruikshank, 1982); *Home Girls: A Black Feminist Anthology* (Smith, 1983); and the "Lesbian Issue" of *Signs* (Freedman et al., 1984) made visible to wider audiences literary, historical, sociological, and critical work by lesbians that had been largely ignored by women's studies in the academy. Works like these recovered the history of lesbians; gave voice to the variety of lesbian experiences defined by race, ethnicity, and class; and defined heterosexism as a structural form of oppression and homophobia as a form of prejudice. These works also provided curricular and pedagogical approaches for creating lesbian studies as a legitimate field within women's studies and for integrating lesbian studies into other fields.

The "coming-out" literature of the 1970s and 1980s, with its concurrent activism within the academy that led to antidiscrimination policies and partner benefits, paved the way for a proliferation of research and writing by and about lesbians in the 1990s. New scholarly trends included more complex analyses of the intersections of difference in lesbian experiences (Aguilar-San Jose, 1993; Brant, 1993; Gomez, 1993; Kennedy & Davis, 1993; McNaron, Anzaldúa, Argüelles, & Kennedy, 1993; Mason-John, 1995; Trujillo, 1991, 1998). Zimmermann and McNaron's (1996) *The New Lesbian Studies* and Garber's (1994) *Tilting the Tower* (1994) present the complexity of women's lives as defined by sexuality, age, race, class, ethnicity, and nationality. These volumes, along with *Straight Studies Modified* (Griffin & Andermahr, 1997), demonstrate how lesbian studies has become more institutionalized in the academy and has transformed content and pedagogy in the classroom.

The emergence of queer theory in the early 1990s (Butler, 1990; De Lauretis, 1991; Fuss, 1990) posed new theoretical challenges to lesbian studies and provided alternative pathways for scholarly work by lesbians in the academy. Like postmodernism, queer theory questions the existence of categories, identities, and labels, including that of "lesbian," and challenges the binary lesbian/straight by positing queer as fluid and performative. Furthermore, by taking sexuality as its focus, it separates sexuality from gender and hence erases lesbian specificity, one of its most problematic theoretical premises for lesbian feminists (Ristock & Taylor, 1998; Walters, 1996). Garber (1994), while acknowledging that queer theory has made some straight women take sexuality seriously as an analytic category for the first time, cautions that lesbian studies might become subsumed under queer studies. While some lesbians of color, such as Anzaldúa (1991) and Moraga (1997), find affinity with queer studies, others, such as Smith (1993) and Hammonds (1997), critique queer theory for the same exclusionary practices and normative whiteness that have characterized gay and lesbian studies.

Postcolonial and Transnational Feminist Studies. In the 1990s, as women's organizations and movements proliferated internationally and became more influential, the need to integrate international perspectives and issues into the curriculum became increasingly compelling. One important influence has been the changing tone and nature of women's engagements with the United Nations women's conferences and nongovernmental organization forums as they evolved from 1975 in Mexico City to 1995 in Beijing: to become more consistently inclusive of the experiences, voices, and strategies for change of women around the world. Rupp (1997) and Smith (2000) provide useful overviews.

Bringing the lens of gender to bear on international issues and global processes has entailed two related but not identical questions: how to think and teach comparatively and relationally about women's lives and gender arrangements in locations around the world, and how to bring international perspectives to bear on women's lives and gender arrangements in any given location, including the United States. Work at the intersections of women's studies and an internationalized ethnic studies examining heritages, migrations, diasporas, and political struggles across borders has been especially productive (Acosta-Belén, 2003; Guy-Sheftall, 2003). Spivak's (1999) work in the establishment of postcolonial feminist studies was instrumental in theorizing the connections between feminism, Marxism, postmodernism, imperialism, and decolonization. Sandoval's (2000) "theory of oppositional consciousness" characterizes U.S. Third World feminism as struggles against gender domination but also as struggles against race, class, and cultural hierarchies. Studies of gender, colonialism, and empire have proliferated (Alexander & Mohanty, 1997; Basu & McGrory, 1995; Bhavnani, 2001; Chaudhuri & Chaudhuri, 1992; Kaplan, Alarçon, & Moallem, 1999; Midgley, 1995; Strobel, 1994).

According to Grewal and Kaplan (1994), transnational feminist practices need "to address the concerns of women around the world in the historicized particularities of their relationship to multiple patriarchies as well as to international economic hegemonies . . . and to compare multiple, overlapping and discrete oppressions rather than to construct a theory of hegemonic oppression under a unified category of gender" (pp. 17–18). Transnational discourse challenges the local/global paradigm that emerged in Western conceptualizations of international feminisms as this binary fails to encompass the complex intersections of identity, community, region, nation, and world (Moghadam, 1994; Mohanty, 1991; Mohanty, Russo, & Torres, 1991; Shohat, 1998).

The expansion of the women's movement around the world and global feminist theories are bringing fresh perspectives on such issues as women and development, structural adjustment, the debt crisis, violence against women, reproductive rights and technologies, militarism, sex tourism, racism, refugees, and work and family (Alarcón, Kaplan, & Moallem, 1999; Fenton & Heffron, 1987). Acosta-Belén and Bose (1990) argue that feminist theory must remain connected to the everyday struggles of women and articulate solutions to complex and basic survival issues, as do Chow and Berheide (1994).

Whiteness Studies and Men's Studies. Antiracist scholars and activists have generated a new discourse within feminist theory called whiteness studies. Arguing that racial categories are socially constructed, they analyze the meanings and maintenance of Whiteness and the idea of White racial identity within feminist analytical frameworks. Feminist scholars writing about the history and meanings of whiteness, the systems that maintain it, and how to resist power and privileges of whiteness include

Frankenberg (1993, 1997), Ware (1992), Frye (1983), Fine (1997), Segrest (1994), Cuomo and Hall (1999), and Razack (1998).

Heavily influenced by feminist theory and practice, the field of men's studies rejects the traditional paradigm of male experience as normative. It focuses on men's lives "as men" and the social, historical, and cultural construction of masculinities (August, 1994; Berger, Wallis, & Watson, 1995; Brod, 1987; Byrd & Guy-Sheftall, 2000; Clatterbaugh, 1997; hooks, 1992; Kimmel, 1987, 1996; Kimmel & Messner, 1998). Many of its areas of interest are the same as women's studies, interrogating meanings of gender, difference, power relations, sexuality, violence, and intersections among gender, race, class, ethnicity, age, and nationality. There are men's studies journals (*Journal of Men's Studies* and *Men and Masculinities*), a national professional association (American Association of Men's Studies), and a growing number of courses. Debates have inevitably accompanied the development of the field, as women's studies claims similar scholarly and teaching priorities.

Feminist Pedagogy

The 1970s produced serious interest in developing theory about the dynamics of feminist classrooms. The challenge of women paralleled discussions about the impact of opening up classrooms to previously excluded groups of students and social change–oriented pedagogies influenced by Freire's (1970) *Pedagogy of the Oppressed*. Freire conceived of "liberatory pedagogy" as mutually supported learning whose goal is to empower learners to act on behalf of social justice, a goal of feminist pedagogy as well (hooks, 1994; Weiler, 1994).

The now-classic *Gendered Subjects*, edited by Culley and Portuges (1985), collected work from the 1970s and early 1980s and remains unusual in its attention to the dynamics of race, class, sexuality, age, and ethnicity as they intersect with gender in the classroom. The volume critiques feminist pedagogy for its inattention to gender and race, analyzes the paradox of "female authority" in the classroom, and redefines the uses of authority to empower students (see also Rich, 1979). It draws connections between feminist scholarship and interactive learning, treats the dynamics of interaction among women situated differently in relation to power, and connects knowledge to social action.

In the 1990s, pedagogical researchers and theorists influenced by postmodernism interrogated the initial emphasis of feminist pedagogy on a set of practices emphasizing collaborative and experiential learning, a nonhierarchical classroom, and an exploration of the personal in its relationship to the political. Gore (1993), for example, worries that feminist pedagogies, like other radical pedagogies, manifest totalizing tendencies that approximate what Foucault (1980) called "regimes of truth." A number of critics observe that, as Gore states it, "'micro' level analyses of classrooms, more characteristic of traditional conceptions of pedagogy, have tended to ignore the constitutive role of power in pedagogy. Radical pedagogies, on the other hand, have tended to focus on the 'macro' level of ideologies and institutions while down playing the instructional act" (p. xiv).

Contemporary feminists' preoccupation with poststructuralism and with the intersection of feminism and critical pedagogy has also served to narrow attention to difference. An emphasis on empowerment of an undifferentiated "woman student" or of the "female subject"— still an important theme (e.g., the Lacanian analysis by Finke, 1993)—ignores crucial race and class differences among women and men. *Feminisms and Critical Pedagogy* (Luke & Gore, 1992) includes only rare citations to the work of women of color and on occasion cites them as if they were concerned solely with gender (see Lewis's 1992 reference to hooks, pp. 183–184).

Developing an antiracist, critical feminist pedagogy remains a necessary goal for women's studies (Ng, Staton, & Scane, 1995). In *The Feminist Classroom*, Maher and Tetreault (2001) examine how assumptions of Whiteness shape the construction of knowledge as it is produced and resisted in the classroom and how students' constructions of gender, class, ethnicity, and race are informed by unacknowledged assumptions of whiteness. Keating and Ramamurthy (personal communication, 2002) call for work that will expand the range of pedagogies that can be called "feminist." In particular, they see the need for pedagogies that extend the possibility of feminist pedagogies from individual empowerment to "social empowerment"—how to make the process of decentering individual privilege an intellectual project that is socially accountable and empowering of all students. Issues of international political economy and the intersections of race, class, gender, and nation require this shift in the locus of power.

The pedagogical dilemmas raised in efforts to teach international perspectives are particularly challenging, since the classroom must always negotiate between the extremes of absolutism or universalism, on the one hand (we are all alike inside, and the same legal, political, and ethical practices and values should apply across cultures), and cultural relativism, on the other (any practice is defensible on the basis of cultural traditions). "Culturally challenging practices" (Gunning, 1997) such as *sati*, clitoridectomy, arranged marriage, and veiling present especially difficult pedagogical challenges, provoking North American students to cast women who participate in such customary practices as "the other," exoticized, pitied, and viewed as victims. A number of the essays in

Lay, Monk, and Rosenfelt (2002) propose teaching strategies to encourage U.S. students to situate such practices in cultural and historical contexts, compare them with more familiar ones in the West, and study women's forms of agency and resistance in specific societies.

Women's Studies and the Web

Electronic forms of communication have transformed access to information by and about women and women's studies. The World Wide Web offers an enormous collection of on-line documents useful for conducting research on women (Atkinson & Hudson, 1990; Hudson & Turek, 1994; University of Wisconsin System, 2002); developing women's studies courses, curricula, and programs (Korenman, 1994–2002; University of Maryland, 2002); guides to Internet usage for students of women's studies (McCaughey, Koella, & Keene, 2001); and fast dissemination of information useful to women in their everyday lives (Goodloe, 1996–1999; Wwwomen, Inc., 1996–2001). The Web pages of the National Women's Studies Association (2002), individual women's studies programs, and women's studies faculty provide access to curricular planning documents, programmatic and research directions, and current curricula and courses. The Internet also provides access to listservs and chatrooms where subscribers with special interests can exchange resources, strategies, and ideas (Korenman, 1997).

The Web has been hailed as a site of feminist empowerment. "Cyberfeminism," defined by Millar (1998, p. 200) is "a woman-centred perspective that advocates women's use of new technologies for empowerment." Hawthorne and Klein (1999) see in cyberfeminism a philosophy that at once acknowledges that there are differences in power in digital discourse and that feminists want to change this situation. They analyze the cultural practices of the powerful in their description of cyberculture, raising questions about who makes decisions about digitizing knowledge for on-line uses. Will voices of women of color, lesbians, disabled people, and poor people be made accessible? The editors of wired_women acknowledge that "none of the few women of color we were able to find online were available to write, a mirror of the extremely white nature of the medium at this time" (Cherny & Weise, 1996, p. xv). Balsamo (1996) and O'Brien (1999) both describe how the Web, heralded as a gender-free zone, reproduces gendered, race-marked bodies.

Feminist critiques of these electronic structures of communication emphasize the Web and cyberculture as built by and for men (Millar, 1998), where women are rendered invisible or subjected to denigration. Dietrich (1997) characterizes the Web as both a site of conservative gender politics and a subversive feminist space. Like Haraway, who in *Simians, Cyborgs and Women* (1991) conceives of political empowerment as constituted from textuality, Dietrich believes that community can be formed within cyberspace as women respond to one another's ideas through electronic circuitry. Harcourt in *women@internet* (1999) chronicles the work of Women on the Net, set up by the Society for International Development to create a women's agenda for cyberspace and to use the Internet as a political tool.

Impact of Women's Studies on Students

The focus of most experimental research in the 1970s and 1980s centered on assessing changes in students' attitudes toward sex roles and sex stereotyping and on the impact of women's studies courses on student self-esteem, career aspirations, and feminist identity development (Bargad & Hyde, 1991). A comprehensive study on student learning in women's studies published in 1992 responds to this need and demonstrates that women's studies contributes to central goals of both liberal and multicultural education. Musil's (1992a) *The Courage to Question* explores the intellectual and personal changes that occur when students take course work in women's studies and attempts to relate outcomes of student learning with the claims the field has traditionally made about its impact. Based on multiple methods of data collection and analysis at seven colleges and universities over a three-year period, this report suggests that women's studies, far from imposing a monolithic ideology based on "oppression studies," as critics have charged, provides students with many of the intellectual and personal skills central to calls for reform in undergraduate education. For example, this research indicates that women's studies helps students create personalized learning by linking the intellectual and the experiential and that students find women's studies to be more intellectually rigorous because it challenges them to incorporate new knowledge into their lives (Musil, 1992b). It helps students develop a critical perspective: students in women's studies classes debate issues far more frequently both in and out of class, and women's studies professors encourage divergent points of view that challenge students to form their own opinions. Regarding social change, a central goal of women's studies, this research shows that women's studies students move from voice to self-empowerment to social responsibility, that they want to improve things for others as well as themselves, and that they translate these desires into citizen action.

This report also suggests that women's studies aids in the furthering of central goals of multicultural education. Women's studies courses heighten students' awareness of diversity and difference, and students report significant change in the way they think about people who are different from themselves. In addition, "many students developed an analysis of larger systems in which differences were embedded, reinforced, and defined and from which unequal power was allocated and perpetuated" (Musil, 1992b, p. 5). Men students, while often resisting the content of women's studies, increase their number of female friends when they take women's studies courses and develop awareness of gendered power relations. Stake and Hoffman (2001) conducted a study of women's studies students at 32 colleges and universities and found that they increased their egalitarian attitudes, awareness of sexism and other forms of discrimination, and commitment to social justice to a larger extent than students who did not take women's studies courses.

Luebke and Reilly (1995) undertook a study of the outcomes of the women's studies major. The 89 survey respondents (25% of the sample) from 43 campuses mentioned similar effects: "being empowered; developing self-confidence; learning to think critically; understanding differences; discovering the intersections among racism, homophobia, sexism, classism, ableism, anti-Semitism, and other forms of oppression; and experiencing community" (p. 199). An important aspect of this study is that it chronicles the professional choices of these graduates, hence demonstrating the wide range of employment options for women's studies majors.

Women's studies and feminist scholarship continue to gain in importance to undergraduate curricula. Graff (1992) cites feminism as one of several major advances in humanistic scholarship over the past three decades. Astin (1993) suggests that offering women's studies courses has positive effects on self-reported improvements in general knowledge, student retention, and affective outcomes, while the presence of a women's or gender studies requirement had a negative effect on student satisfaction with general education requirements.

CHALLENGING AND CHANGING THE CURRICULUM

Curriculum transformation brings new scholarship, conceptual frameworks, and pedagogies from fields of women's studies, American ethnic studies, and other comparative cultural studies to faculty members who teach in other disciplines. It also focuses on the development of inclusive frameworks in women's studies, American ethnic studies, and area studies. Butler (1991), arguing that ethnic studies and women's studies can provide the transformative content and pedagogy for the liberal arts, calls for paradigm shifts in women's studies and in American ethnic studies by developing what she calls generative scholarship. This scholarship would include (1) the identification of the connections between and interactions among the disciplines; (2) the study and definition of the experience and aesthetics of neglected groups of people, studied not in comparison to the dominant group and not as problems to the dominant group but in and of themselves and in relation to one another; (3) the correction of distortions in the study of all groups; and (4) the defining and structuring of a curriculum that through its content and pedagogy affirms the interconnectedness of human life, experience, and creativity.

Beginnings

In the mid-1970s to the early 1980s, major curricular change efforts began on many campuses with support from the Ford Foundation, the Mellon Foundation, the Women's Educational Equity Act Program, the National Endowment for the Humanities, the Fund for the Improvement of Postsecondary Education, and others (Schmitz, 1985). The impetus for creation of a national curriculum change movement based in women's studies was provided in 1981. The Workshop on Integrating Women's Studies into the Curriculum, organized and sponsored by the Southwest Institute for Research on Women, brought together directors from 17 projects around the country to exchange information and assess current theory and practice in feminist curriculum change. These projects varied greatly in scope and purpose, those with large, external grants attempting more widespread change. Campuses that pioneered faculty development projects aimed at curriculum transformation include Wheaton College (Spanier, Bloom, & Boroviak, 1984); California State University, Hayward (Pointer & Auletta, 1990); the University of Arizona (Aiken, Anderson, Dinnerstein, Lensink, & MacCorquodale, 1988; Andersen, 1987); Montana State University (Schmitz, 1985); Lewis and Clark College (Arch & Kirschner, 1984); and Smith College (Schuster & Van Dyne, 1985). Projects aimed at reevaluating and transforming the disciplines themselves included the Reconstructing American Literature Project of the Feminist Press (Lauter, 1983, 1991) and the Black Studies/Women's Studies Faculty Development Project (Butler, 1985).

Leaders of these projects identified effective strategies and chronicled successes and failures (Butler & Walter, 1991). In recruiting faculty members, they relied almost entirely on faculty interest rather than institutional mandate, yet still often met with resistance from participants (see especially Aiken et al., 1988). Normally, project leaders secure funds and solicit applications from which they choose a group of participants and provide incentives for course development, such as stipends or release time. Project leaders recommend a balance of participants—by rank, discipline, gender, and race—to ensure that various perspectives are brought into play in curriculum and course design. Emphasis on pedagogy as well as content in the choice of readings and in course design is essential.

The dissemination of information about these early projects through national educational media and national professional associations resulted in the proliferation of projects. As the fiscal restraints of the 1980s began to result in retrenchment, campuses explored more cost-effective strategies, such as concentrating on more limited areas of the curriculum, piggybacking on institutional processes, and working with faculty already interested in change. Consortial models emerged in which several campuses shared resources from a major grant. For example, in 1988, Towson State University began a consortial project with five community colleges in the Baltimore-Washington, D.C., area (Goldenberg & Parry, 1996).

Developing Inclusive Curricular Frameworks

Shrinking resources for women's studies and curriculum transformation in the 1980s generated serious debate about the best focus for women's studies work in the academy. Women's studies faculty raised questions about the impact of curriculum change projects: What happens to feminist perspectives when taught by nonfeminists? Will women again become invisible within mainstream scholarship? Can the interdisciplinary knowledge explored in women's studies ever fit in traditional disciplines, and what resonances among texts and voices are lost in this process? How will mainstreaming efforts influence the already fragile alliances among women separated by race, class, sexual orientation, and ethnicity (Bowles & Klein, 1983; Rosenfelt, 1984)?

In this climate, the development of truly inclusive theory and practice for women's studies became a more compelling agenda for many women's studies scholars and teachers than curriculum transformation efforts aimed elsewhere (Butler, 1984). Without such inclusiveness, transformation of the academy risked replicating the conceptual and political errors of "White" women's studies, which Butler characterized as having to divest itself of White skin privilege, racism, and the insistence on gender as a primary category of analysis, and of "male" ethnic studies, which needs to divest itself of sexism and homophobia. The collaborative project between Black Studies and Women's Studies at the University of Massachusetts and Smith College (Butler, 1985) attempted to make such interconnections among race, class, gender, and ethnicity. In 1983, with support from the Ford Foundation, Spelman College, the oldest historically Black college for women, began a two-year project to integrate African American women's studies materials into general education courses at Spelman and to carry out faculty development activities at four other institutions: Clark, Morehouse, Agnes Scott, and Kennesaw Community College (Guy-Sheftall, 1986).

Rosenfelt and Williams (1992) describe how a curriculum transformation project funded at the University of Maryland at College Park to focus on women and gender has evolved to focus on race and gender. They describe how they explicitly use dynamics that occur in the seminar to discuss the gendered, interracial, and intercultural nature of social interactions. The Mainstreaming Minority Women's Studies Project (Fiol-Matta & Chamberlain, 1994) supported 13 women's research centers to conduct faculty development activities aimed at transformation of the undergraduate curriculum. The projects emphasized different groups of women of color in the United States, depending on the expertise of the sponsoring institution and the demographic composition of its location. Most notably, the program funded at the State University of New York, Albany, focused on Puerto Rican women and established collaborative working relationships with campuses in Puerto Rico to develop "transnational approaches that link the study of cultural and socioeconomic systems on both ends of the continuum of the migratory process" (Acosta-Belén, 1993, p. 181).

Current Strategies and Approaches

More and more institutions are beginning projects with internal funding, using existing faculty development programs or funds. These new programs have benefited from more than two decades of work and have developed intellectually and pedagogically sound curricula for faculty development that take into account the diversity of women's experiences.

Teaching the Intersections. Intersectional analysis, pioneered in the writing of women of color, now stands at the forefront of contemporary theory and practice not just in women's studies, but also in feminist cultural studies, racial and ethnic studies, and multiculturalism. Intersectional analysis is the overriding theoretical framework underpinning calls for inclusionary theory and practice. As Dill, Nettles, and Weber point out (2001), the systematic study of intersectionality is "flexible enough to consider large-scale, historically constructed and hierarchical power systems and the politics of personal interactions, including meanings and representations in the experience of individuals" (p. 4). Weber, Higginbotham, and Dill (1994) pioneered early work on intersectionality in curriculum transformation through the Center for Research on Women of Color and Southern Women at the University of Memphis.

Crenshaw, in her influential essay, "Mapping the Margins: Intersectionality, Identity Politics, and Violence against Women of Color" (1994), distinguishes "structural intersectionality," in which the location of women of color at the intersection of race and gender makes experiences of rape, domestic violence, and remedial reform qualitatively different from that of White women, and "political intersectionality," in which antisexist and antiracist rhetoric operate in tandem to marginalize the issue of violence against women. Essed (1991) develops intersectional analysis as a tool to identify intertwined gender, race, ethnic, economic, and educational factors in shaping specific expressions of everyday injustices. Intersectional analysis, and particularly Crenshaw's and Essed's work, has become influential as a policy framework in the arena of international women's rights with organizations such as the Committee to End All Discrimination Against Women of the United Nations.

The Ford Foundation has funded two projects on curriculum transformation focused specifically on intersectionality: the Consortium on Race, Gender and Ethnicity at the University of Maryland (2002), which focuses on funding collaborative research projects, and the Curriculum Transformation Project at the University of Washington (2002), which focuses on funding new courses that teach about intersectionality. Many textbooks and anthologies exist for faculty use in teaching the intersections of gender, race, class, ethnicity, and other constructs (Andersen & Collins, 1992; Romero & Stewart, 1999; Rothenberg, 1992; Ruíz & DuBois, 1990; Young & Dickerson, 1994; Zinn & Dill, 1994). Of particular interest are Weber's (2001) two-volume *Understanding Race, Class, Gender, and Sexuality*, Rosenblum and Travis's (2000) *The Meaning of Difference: American Constructions of Race, Sex and Gender, Social Class, and Sexual Orientation*, and Belkhir's (1999) comprehensive bibliography on intersectionality as a cognitive framework for multicultural education, women's studies, racial and ethnic studies, social class studies, and within the disciplines.

International Perspectives. A number of societal and institutional tendencies have converged to encourage the internationalization of women's studies and the consideration of gender issues in international contexts across the curriculum. Some curriculum change projects made efforts as early as the 1980s to internationalize women's studies and bring women's issues and gender relations into internationally oriented fields across the disciplines, but these were relatively rare (see *Women's Studies International Forum*, 1991, and the recent texts updated from an earlier Organization of American Historians project: Berger & White, 1999; Nashat & Tucker, 1999; Navarro & Sanchez-Korrol, 1999; and Ramusack & Sievers, 1999).

In the mid-1990s, a national initiative supported by the Ford Foundation and initially coordinated by the National Council for Research on Women began to encourage curriculum transformation efforts aimed at internationalizing the study of women in the United States. In 1995, these groups launched the Women's Studies, Area Studies, and International Studies curriculum integration project (WSAIS) designed to link programs in and the insights of women's studies, area studies, and international studies, and to facilitate the curricular inclusion of materials concerning women and gender especially in the non-Western world (Chamberlain, 1996). Thirteen campuses or consortia received grants and hosted a series of regional, national, and international conferences.

The courses and writings generated by the WSAIS initiative suggest that there are certain key issues of gendered, internationalized inquiry: the changing material and economic circumstances that affect women's experiences in work and family life; questions of identity, subjectivity, cultural representation, and cultural production; issues of women's rights, citizenship, and political representation in relation to the state; the historical and current forms of women's resistance and activism; questions of language and power (both the power-laden designations—"international," "global," "Western," "non-Western," "Northern," "Southern," "Third World," "developing"—necessarily used in discussion, and the power-fraught hierarchies that privilege some languages over others). Crucially underlying issues of epistemology and ethics are: Who is the "we" doing the thinking, the knowing, the writing? Such questions about knowledge and power are inseparable from histories of colonization, anticolonialist struggle, decolonization, and neocolonialism, and these histories themselves must command the attention of those attempting to think across borders (Monk & Rosenfelt, 2000).

The Impact of Curriculum Transformation. Rosenfelt (1990) reports that faculty participants in an eight-week summer institute at the University of Maryland felt that it contributed to their greater sensitivity to issues of difference as they affect human interactions and that half of the participants indicated they expected their work in the institute to have an impact on their future research. The 26 faculty members and teaching assistants who participated in a year-long University of Washington Curriculum Transformation Project, 1992–1993, developed new materials and new pedagogical strategies and revised at least one undergraduate course. Faculty members reported that although they had made changes in themes and texts, the major difference they noted was in the change in their approach. They reported using comparative approaches and interactive pedagogies and placing a stronger emphasis on critical thinking. Many expressed a new confidence in students' capacity to learn and welcomed conflict and tension as a means to developing intellectual enlightenment and maturity. They also reported that they had expanded their scope of reading and the kinds of questions they ask in their teaching and research, and had developed new collegial relationships that resulted in team teaching or teaching in one another's classes (University of Washington, 2003).

Since most of these projects have focused on large, introductory courses central to the liberal arts curriculum and have favored required courses over electives, large numbers of students on these campuses are engaged in the study of material on women and gender. Lewis and Clark College, which has both a Gender Studies Program and an institutional priority and commitment to "balanced exploration of the perspectives, traditions, and contributions of women and men," provides a source of comparison for the relative impact on students of these complementary educational strategies. Finke, Maveety, Shaw, and Ward (1992) report that there is a crucial difference between the integration of gender across the curriculum and the kind of systematic investigation of gender that the gender studies minor allows; and that even the most gender-balanced courses do not provide the intensity of study or the same level of skill development as the gender-focused courses. They conclude also that the strength of gender integration is in reaching students who choose not to take a course in the Gender Studies Program.

The University of Washington Curriculum Transformation Project involves students as codevelopers of courses with faculty members. Undergraduate students participate in the seminars, conduct research for faculty members, and provide perspectives on effective teaching approaches. Student evaluations in the project indicated that the project provided a way for students to contribute their own expertise and validate their classroom experiences in the past that had been unwelcoming to them (University of Washington, 2002).

Other researchers have focused inquiry on understanding student resistance to inclusive perspectives in the curriculum and strategies faculty members can use to overcome opposition when students encounter inclusive perspectives in the classroom (Chan & Treacy, 1996; Higginbotham, 1996).

Institutionalization of Curriculum Transformation

We estimate that curriculum transformation has reached to varying degrees one-quarter of U.S. institutions of higher education. On many campuses, alliances between women's studies and ethnic studies and renewed student activism in the face of anti–affirmative action initiatives have resulted in institutionally funded curriculum transformation projects and diversity requirements. Nonetheless, disciplines still resist interdisciplinary scholarship and teaching, ethnic studies is regarded as suspect, and institutionalized women studies struggles to maintain its radical critiques. Faculty and administrators in curriculum transformation programs are providing analyses of their experiences in higher education that will prove useful in designing projects in the future (Butler & Walter, 1991; Lim & Herrera-Sobek, 2000; Mohanty, 1997).

The foundations, federal programs, and states that have supported curriculum transformation have ensured its continuation through the creation of permanent centers and projects. Curriculum transformation became a central priority of the Campus Diversity Initiative of the Ford Foundation, which funded the Association of American Colleges and Universities to become a clearinghouse of diversity initiatives. It now offers annual conferences on diversity in higher education, develops resources, and maintains a comprehensive Web site in collaboration with the University of Maryland (Association of American Colleges and Universities and University of Maryland, 1996–2000). The National Center for Curriculum Transformation Resources on Women (2000) received grants from the Ford Foundation and the Fund for the Improvement of Postsecondary Education to develop resources to support curriculum transformation, including a planning guide (Hedges, 1997), bibliographies (Coulter, n.d.), and disciplinary analyses. By 1990, New Jersey, which initiated a statewide project to support curriculum transformation in 1986, had placed $1.5 million into gender integration projects. This project involves all two- and four-year public and private colleges and universities in the state; supports them in integrating gender, race, class, ethnicity, and sexual orientation into the curriculum (Friedman, Kolmar, Flint, & Rothenberg, 1996); and publishes a journal, *Transformations*. The Illinois Board of Education has funded an Expanding Cultural Diversity Project that includes an annual curriculum transformation institute and has published a collection of essays (Adams & Welsch, 1999).

FUTURE DIRECTIONS FOR WOMEN'S STUDIES AND CURRICULUM TRANSFORMATION

Leaders in curriculum transformation agree that continued support for transformation is necessary to expand research and teaching about differences among women and the exploration of the plurality of feminist approaches and paradigms worldwide (Goings et al., 2000). Collaboration is even more essential as women's studies attempts to develop theory, policy analysis, and pedagogy related to intersectionality. For such development to occur, however, women's studies must attend to its demographics. Can women's studies do a better job attracting students of color and hiring and tenuring faculty of color? Can women's studies faculty and faculty of color in various spaces in academe forge better coalitions?

While some women's studies programs have developed links to programs in American ethnic studies and international area studies programs, the relationship of women's studies to multiculturalism has yet to be institutionalized. The founding of transnational consortia among women's studies programs at the graduate level already underway can facilitate such efforts. Ideally, such consortia will ensure that women's studies in the United States can transcend its provincial origins and equip students with the intensive training in language and culture necessary for a genuinely transnational grasp of women's issues.

In addition to strengthening programs where they already exist, women's studies must be extended to other kinds and levels of education, where it is rare: to community colleges, historically Black institutions, tribally controlled colleges, high schools and secondary education, and graduate and professional education.

Finally, collaborations across these institutional and national boundaries can help bridge a growing rift in U.S. women's studies between those doing "high theory" and those interested in empirical data and activist engagement. This is an old tension in women's studies (see McDermott, 1994; Bell & Klein, 1996). It can become a productive one as scholars and teachers from different geographic, institutional, and racial and ethnic origins speak to each other across the fault lines of difference. What are the implications for women's studies as a field of critical and antiracist pedagogies, queer theory, and critical approaches to embodiment and disability?

Curriculum transformation faces similar challenges. The majority of participating faculty have come from the social sciences and humanities. While literary studies have been largely transformed and social sciences are making significant progress, women's studies also must extend its influence to the sciences, business, and technical fields (MacNabb, Cherry, Popham, & Prys, 2001). Few projects have been conducted in community colleges (see models provided in Fiol-Matta, 1996; Schmitz & Dinnerstein, 1991), which enroll large percentages of women and minority students. Graduate and professional education has been virtually untouched by women's studies in any of its forms.

Curriculum transformation will undoubtedly take new forms as we become clearer about the convergences of the various studies entering the academy—cultural studies, queer studies, disability studies, transnational studies, postcolonial studies—and American studies and other area studies that are striving toward multiculturalism. Expanded efforts will take place in a climate of decreased resources. Imaginative and far-reaching collaborations at many levels, across various institutional structures and touching a variety of fields, are now both possible and essential. Collaboration among women's studies and ethnic studies programs, schools of education, state boards of education, and K–12 teachers and administrators could substantially expand the impact of curriculum change efforts.

References

Acosta-Belén, E. (Ed.). (1986). *The Puerto Rican woman: Perspectives on culture, history, and society* (2nd ed.). New York: Praeger.

Acosta-Belén, E. (1993). Defining common ground: The theoretical meeting of women's, ethnic, and area studies. In E. Acosta-Belén & C. E. Bose (Eds.), *Researching women in Latin America and the Caribbean* (pp. 175–186). Boulder, CO: Westview Press.

Acosta-Belén, E. (2003). Ethnic and gender encounters: A hemispheric approach to Latin American and U.S. Latino(a) studies. In M. Lay, J. Monk, & D. Rosenfelt (Eds.), *Encompassing gender.* New York: Feminist Press.

Acosta-Belén, E., & Bose, C. E. (1990). From structural subordination to empowerment: Women in development in Third World contexts. *Gender and Society, 4*(3), 299–320.

Acosta-Belén, E., Bose, C. E., & Sjostrom, B. R. (1994). Focus on Puerto Rican studies. In L. Fiol-Matta & M. K. Chamberlain (Eds.), *Women of color and the multicultural curriculum* (pp. 341–386). New York: Feminist Press.

Adams, J. Q., & Welsch, J. R. (1999). *Cultural diversity: Curriculum, classroom, and climate.* N.p.: Illinois Staff and Curriculum Developers Association.

Aguilar-San Juan, K. (1993). Landmarks in literature by Asian American lesbians. *Signs, 18*(4), 936–943.

Ahmed, L. (1980). Encounter with American feminism: A Muslim woman's view of two conferences. *Women's Studies Quarterly, 8*(3), 7–9.

Ahmed, L. (1992). *Women and gender in Islam: Historical roots of a modern debate.* New Haven, CT: Yale University Press.

Ahmed, L. (1999). *A border passage: From Cairo to America.* New York: Farrar, Straus & Giroux.

Aiken, S. H., Anderson, K., Dinnerstein, M., Lensink, J. N., & MacCorquodale, P. (1988). *Changing our minds: Feminist transformations of knowledge.* Albany: State University of New York Press.

Alarcón, N. (Ed.). (1993). *Chicana critical issues.* Berkeley, CA: Third Woman Press.

Alarcón, N., Castillo, A., & Moraga, C. (Eds.). (1993). *The sexuality of Latinas.* Berkeley, CA: Third Woman Press.

Alarcón, N., Kaplan, C., & Moallem, M. (Eds.). (1999). *Between woman and nation: Nationalisms, transnational feminisms, and the state.* Durham, NC: Duke University Press.

Albers, P., & Medicine, B. (Eds.). (1983). *The hidden half: Studies of Plains Indian women.* Washington, DC: University Press of America.

Albrecht, L., & Brewer, R. M. (Eds.). (1990). *Bridges of power: Women's multicultural alliances.* Philadelphia: New Society Publishers and the National Women's Studies Association.

Alexander, M. J., & Mohanty, C. T. (Eds.). (1997). *Feminist genealogies, colonial legacies, democratic futures.* New York: Routledge.

al-Hibri, A. (1983). Unveiling the hidden face of racism: The plight of Arab American women. *Women's Studies Quarterly, 9*(3), 10–11.

Allen, J. A., & Kitch, S. L. (1998). Disciplined by disciplines? The need for an interdisciplinary research mission in women's studies. *Feminist Studies, 24*(2), 275–299.

Allen, P. G. (1986). *The sacred hoop: Recovering the feminine in American Indian traditions*. Boston: Beacon Press.

Alpert, R. (1998). *Like bread on the Seder plate*. New York: Columbia University Press.

Andersen, M. L. (1987). Changing the curriculum in higher education. *Signs, 12*(2), 222–254.

Andersen, M. L., & Collins, P. H. (Eds.). (1992). *Race, class, and gender: An anthology*. Belmont, CA: Wadsworth.

Antler, J. (1997). *The journey home: Jewish women and the American century*. New York: Free Press.

Antler, J. (Ed.). (1998). *Talking back: Images of Jewish women in American popular culture*. Waltham, MA: Brandeis University Press.

Anzaldúa, G. (1987). *Borderlands/La frontera: The new mestiza*. San Francisco: Aunt Lute.

Anzaldúa, G. (1990). *Making face, making soul, haciendo caras: Creative and critical perspectives by feminists of color*. San Francisco: Aunt Lute.

Anzaldúa, G. (1991). To(o) queer the writer: *Loca, escritora y chicana*. In B. Warfield (Ed.), *Inversions: Writing by dykes, queers and lesbians* (pp. 249–63). Vancouver: Press Gang Publishers.

Arch, E. C., & Kirschner, S. (1984). Gender balancing as a catalyst for institutional change. *Educational Record, 66*(2), 48–52.

Asian Women United of California. (Eds.). (1989). *Making waves: An anthology of writings by and about Asian American women*. Boston: Beacon Press.

Association of American Colleges and Universities and the University of Maryland. (1996–2003). *Diversity web: An interactive resource hub for higher education*. Available on-line: http://diversityweb.org. Retrieved March 9, 2003.

Astin, A. W. (1993). *What matters in college? Four critical years revisited*. San Francisco: Jossey-Bass.

Atkinson, S. D., & Hudson, J. (Eds.). (1990). *Women online: Research in women's studies using online databases*. New York: Haworth Press.

August, E. R. (1994). *The new men's studies: A selected and annotated interdisciplinary bibliography* (2nd ed.). Upper Saddle River, NJ: Prentice Hall.

Azize-Vargas, Y. (1990). The roots of Puerto Rican feminism. *Radical America, 23*(1), 71–80.

Balsamo, A. (1996). *Technologies of the gendered body: Reading cyborg women*. Durham, NC: Duke University Press.

Bargad, A., & Hyde, J. S. (1991). Women's studies: A study of feminist identity development in women. *Psychology of Women, 15*(2), 181–201.

Barrett, M., & Phillips, A. (Eds.). (1992). *Destabilizing theory: Contemporary feminist debates*. Stanford: Stanford University Press.

Baskin, J. R. (Ed.). (1999). *Jewish women in historical perspective*. Detroit: Wayne State University Press.

Baskin, J., & Tenenbaum, S. (Eds.). (1994). *Gender and Jewish studies: A curriculum guide*. New York: Biblio Press.

Basu, A., with McGrory, E. (Eds.). (1995). *The challenge of local feminisms: Women's movements in global perspective*. Boulder, CO: Westview Press.

Bataille, G. M., & Sands, K. M. (1984). *American Indian women: Telling their lives*. Lincoln: University of Nebraska Press.

Beck, E. T. (1988). The politics of Jewish invisibility. *NWSA Journal, 1*(1), 93–102.

Beck, E. T. (Ed.). (1989). *Nice Jewish girls: A lesbian anthology* (rev. ed.). Boston: Beacon Press. (Original work published 1982)

The Beijing declaration and the platform for action. (1996). New York: United Nations Department of Public Information.

Belkhir, J. A. (1999). *Race, class, and gender bibliography*. Available on-line: http://www.suno.edu/sunorgc/. Retrieved March 9, 2003.

Bell, D., & Klein, R. (1996). *Radically speaking: Feminism reclaimed*. Victoria, Australia: Spinifex.

Bell, R. P., Parker, B. J., & Guy-Sheftall, B. G. (1979). *Sturdy Black bridges: Visions of Black women in literature*. New York: Doubleday.

Berger, I., & White, E. F. (1999). *Women in sub-Saharan Africa: Restoring women to history*. Bloomington: Indiana University Press.

Berger, M., Wallis, B., & Watson, S. (Eds). (1995). *Constructing masculinity*. New York: Routledge.

Bethel, L., & Smith, B. (Eds.). (1979). The Black women's issue [Special issue]. *Conditions, 5.*

Bhavnani, K. (Ed.). (2001). *Feminism and "race."* New York: Oxford University Press.

Bleier, R. (1986). *Feminist approaches to science*. New York: Pergamon Press.

Bowles, G., & Klein, R. D. (Eds.). (1983). *Theories of women's studies*. New York: Routledge.

Boxer, M. J. (1982). For and about women: The theory and practice of women's studies in the United States. *Signs, 7*(3), 661–695.

Boxer, M. J. (1998). *When women ask the questions*. Baltimore: Johns Hopkins University Press.

Brant, B. (Ed.). (1988). *A gathering of spirit: A collection by North American Indian women*. Ithaca, NY: Firebrand Books.

Brant, B. (1993). Giveaway: Native lesbian writers. *Signs, 18*(4), 944–947.

Brant, B. (1996). The good red road: Journeys of homecoming in Native women's writings. In B. Brant & S. Laronde (Eds.), *Sweetgrass grows around her* (pp. 82–90). Toronto: Native Women in the Arts.

Brod, H. (Ed.). (1987). *The making of masculinities: The new men's studies*. Boston: Allen & Unwin.

Brodkin, K. (1998). *How Jews became White folks and what that says about race in America*. New Brunswick, NJ: Rutgers University Press.

Browne, I., (Ed.). (1999). *Latinas and African American women at work: Race, gender, and economic inequality*. New York: Russell Sage Foundation.

Buhle, M. J. (2000). Introduction. In F. Howe (Ed.), *The politics of women's studies: Testimony from 30 founding mothers* (pp. xv-xxvi). New York: Feminist Press of the City University of New York.

Bulkin, E. (1980, Nov.). Heterosexism and women's studies. *Radical Teacher*, no. 17, 25–31.

Bunch, C. (1983). Not by degrees: Feminist theory and education. In C. Bunch & S. Pollack (Eds.), *Learning our way: Essays in feminist education* (pp. 248–260). Trumansburg, NY: Crossing Press.

Butler, J. (1990). *Gender trouble: Feminism and the subversion of identity*. New York: Routledge.

Butler, J. E. (1984). Minority studies and women's studies: Do we want to kill a dream? *Women's Studies International Quarterly, 7*(3), 135–138.

Butler, J. E. (1985). Complicating the question: Black studies and women's studies. In M. R. Schuster & S. R. Van Dyne (Eds.), *Women's place in the academy: Transforming the liberal arts curriculum* (pp. 73–86). Totowa, NJ: Rowman & Allanheld.

Butler, J. E. (1991). Difficult dialogues. In J. E. Butler & J. C. Walter (Eds.), *Transforming the curriculum: Ethnic studies and women's studies* (pp. 1–19). Albany: State University of New York Press.

Butler, J. E., Coyner, S., Homans, M., Longenecker, M., & Musil, C. M. (1991). *Liberal learning and the women's studies major.* College Park, MD: National Women's Studies Association.

Butler, J. E., & Walter, J. C. (Eds.). (1991). *Transforming the curriculum: Ethnic studies and women's studies.* Albany: State University of New York Press.

Byrd, R., & Guy-Sheftall, B. (Eds.). (2000). *Traps: African American men on gender and sexuality.* Bloomington: Indiana University Press.

Cade, T. (Ed.). (1970). *The Black woman.* New York: Signet Books.

Campbell, J. H. (1993). *Bloodlines: Odyssey of a native daughter.* New York: Random House.

Cantor, A. (1995). *Jewish women/Jewish men: The legacy of patriarchy in Jewish life.* San Francisco: HarperSanFrancisco.

Carby, H. V. (1987). *Reconstructing womanhood: The emergence of the Afro-American woman novelist.* New York: Oxford University Press.

Chai, A. Y. (1988). Women's history in public: "Picture brides" of Hawaii. *Women's Studies Quarterly, 16*(1&2), 51–62.

Chamberlain, M. K. (1996). Introduction. *Women's studies, area and international studies curriculum project.* New York: National Council for Research on Women.

Chan, C. S., & Treacy, M. J. (1996). Resistance in multicultural courses. *American Behavioral Scientist, 40*(2), 212–221.

Chan, S. (1991). *Asian Americans: An interpretive history.* Boston: Twayne.

Chaudhuri, N., & Strobel, M. (Eds.). (1992). *Western women and imperialism: Complicity and resistance.* Bloomington: Indiana University Press.

Cherny, L., & Weise, E. R. (Eds.). (1996). *Wired_women: Gender and new realities in cyberspace.* Seattle: Seal Press.

Cheung, K.-K. (1997). *An interethnic companion to Asian American literature.* Cambridge: Cambridge University Press.

Chodorow, N. (1978). *The reproduction of mothering: Psychoanalysis and the sociology of gender.* Berkeley: University of California Press.

Chow, E. N. (1987). The development of feminist consciousness among Asian American women. *Gender and Society, 1*(3), 284–299.

Chow, E. N., & Berheide, C. W. (Eds.). (1994). *Women, the family, and policy: A global perspective.* Albany: State University of New York Press.

Christian, B. (1980). *Black women novelists: The development of a tradition, 1892–1976.* Westport, CT: Greenwood Press.

Christian, B. (1988). The race for theory. *Feminist Studies, 14*(1), 67–79.

Chu, J. (1986). Asian American women's studies courses: A look back at our beginnings. *Frontiers, 8*(3), 96–101.

Clatterbaugh, K. (1997). *Contemporary perspectives on masculinity: Men, women and politics of modern society* (2nd ed.). Boulder, CO: Westview Press.

Collins, P. H. (2000). *Black feminist thought: Knowledge, consciousness, and the politics of empowerment* (Rev. ed.). Boston: Unwin and Hyman.

Collins, P. H. (1998). *Fighting words: Black women and the search for justice.* Minneapolis: University of Minnesota Press.

Copper, B. (1988). *Over the hill: Reflections on ageism between women.* Freedom, CA: Crossing Press.

Coulter, S. (n.d.) *Introductory bibliography for curriculum transformation.* Available on-line: http://pages.towson.edu/ncctrw/publications/introbib.html. Retrieved March 9, 2003.

Crenshaw, K. W. (1994). Mapping the margins: Intersectionality, identity politics, and violence against women. In M. A. Fineman & R. Mykituik (Eds.), *The public nature of private violence* (pp. 93–129). New York: Routledge.

Crow Dog, M. (1990). *Lakota woman.* New York: Grove Weidenfeld.

Crow Dog, M. (1993). *Ohitika woman.* New York: Grove Press.

Cruikshank, M. (Ed.). (1982). *Lesbian studies: Present and future.* New York: Feminist Press.

Culley, M. (1985). Anger and authority in the introductory women's studies classroom. In M. Culley & C. Portuges (Eds.), *Gendered subjects: The dynamics of feminist teaching* (pp. 209–218). New York: Routledge.

Culley, M., & Portuges, C. (Eds.). (1985). *Gendered subjects: The dynamics of feminist teaching.* New York: Routledge.

Cuomo, C. J., & Hall, K. Q. (1999). *Whiteness: feminist philosophical reflections.* Lanham, MD: Rowman & Littlefield.

Dasgupta, S. D. (Ed.). (1998). *Patchwork shawl: Chronicles of South Asian women in America.* New Brunswick, NJ: Rutgers University Press.

Davidman, L. (1991). *Tradition in a rootless world: Women turn to orthodox Judaism.* Berkeley: University of California Press.

Davidman, L., & Tenenbaum, S. (Eds.). (1994). *Feminist perspectives on Jewish studies.* New Haven, CT: Yale University Press.

Davies, C. B. (1994). *Black women, writing, and identity: Migration of the subject.* New York: Routledge.

Davies, C. B., & Ogundipe-Leslie, M. (Eds.). (1995). *Moving beyond boundaries.* Trenton, NJ: Africa World Press.

Davis, A. Y. (1981). *Women, race, and class.* New York: Vintage.

De la Torre, A., & Pesquera, B. M. (1993). *Building with our hands: New directions in Chicana studies.* Berkeley: University of California Press.

De Lauretis, T. (Ed.). (1991). Queer theory: Lesbian and gay sexualities [Special issue]. *differences, 3*(2).

Dietrich, D. (1997). (Re)-fashioning the techno-erotic woman: Gender and textuality in the cybercultural matrix. In S. G. Jones (Ed.), *Virtual culture: Identity and communication in cybersociety* (pp. 169–184). Thousand Oaks, CA: Sage.

Dill, B. T. (1979). The dialectics of Black womanhood. *Signs, 4*(3), 543–555.

Dill, B. T., Nettles, S. M., & Weber, L. (2001, Spring). Defining the work of the consortium: What do we mean by intersections? *Connections: Newsletter of the Consortium on Race, Gender, and Ethnicity,* p. 4.

Donaldson, L. E. (1999). On medicine women and White shamans. *Signs, 24*(3), 677–696.

DuBois, E. C., Kelly, G. P., Kennedy, E. L., Korsmeyer, C. W., & Robinson, L. S. (1985). *Feminist scholarship: Kindling in the groves of academe.* Urbana: University of Illinois Press.

Dunn, C., & Comfort, C. (Eds.). (1999). *Through the eye of the deer: An anthology of Native American women writers.* San Francisco: Aunt Lute.

El Saadawi, N. (1980). *The hidden face of Eve: Women in the Arab world.* London: Zed.

El Saadawi, N. (1997). *The Nawal El Saadawi reader.* London: Zed.

Elwell, S. L. (1992). Jewish women's studies. In B. Holtz (Ed.), *The Schocken guide to Jewish books.* New York: Schocken.

Eng, D., & Hom, A. (Eds.). (1998). *Q & A: Queer in Asian America.* Philadelphia: Temple University Press.

Essed, P. (1991). *Understanding everyday racism: An interdisciplinary theory.* Thousand Oaks, CA: Sage.

Fenton, T. P., & Heffron, M. J. (Eds.). (1987). *Women in the Third World: A directory of resources.* Maryknoll, NY: Orbis Books.

Fine, M. (Ed.). (1997). *Off white: Readings on race, power, and society.* New York: Routledge.

Fine, M., & Asch, A. (Eds.). (1988). *Women with disabilities: Essays in psychology, policy, and politics.* Philadelphia: Temple University Press.

Finke, L. (1993). Knowledge as bait: Feminism, voice, and the pedagogical unconscious. *College English, 55*(1), 7–27.

Finke, L., Maveety, E., Shaw, C., & Ward, J. (1992). Lewis and Clark College: A single curriculum. In C. M. Musil (Ed.), *The courage to question: Women's studies and student learning* (pp. 43–81). Washington, DC: Association of American Colleges and National Women's Studies Association.

Fiol-Matta, L. (Ed.). (1996). Curriculum transformation in community colleges [Special issue]. *Women's Studies Quarterly, 24*(3&4).

Fiol-Matta, L., & Chamberlain, M. K. (Eds.). (1994). *Women of color and the multicultural curriculum: Transforming the college curriculum.* New York: Feminist Press of the City University of New York.

Fisher-Mannick, B. (1981). Race and class: Beyond personal politics. In *Building feminist theory: Essays from Quest* (pp. 149–160). New York: Longman.

Forum: Doing feminism in interdisciplinary contexts. (2001). *Feminist Studies, 27*(2), 499–531.

Foucault, M. (1980). Truth and power. In C. Gordon (Ed.), *Power and knowledge: Selected interviews and other writings, 1972–1977* (pp. 109–133). New York: Pantheon Books.

Frankenberg, R. (1993). *White women, race matters: The social construction of whiteness.* Minneapolis: University of Minnesota Press.

Frankenberg, R. (Ed.). (1997). *Displacing whiteness: Essays in social and cultural criticism.* Durham, NC: Duke University Press.

Freedman, E., Gelpi, B. C., Johnson, S. L., & Weston, K. M. (1984). The lesbian issue [Special issue]. *Signs, 9*(4).

Fregoso, R. L. (1993). *The bronze screen: Chicana and Chicano film culture.* Minneapolis: University of Minnesota Press.

Freire, P. (1970). *Pedagogy of the oppressed.* (M. B. Ramos, Trans.). New York: Seabury Press.

Friedman, E. G., Kolmar, W. K., Flint, C. B., & Rothenberg, P. (Eds.). (1996). *Creating an inclusive college curriculum: A teaching sourcebook from the New Jersey Project.* New York: Teachers College Press.

Friedman-Kasaba, K. (1996). *Memories of migration: Gender, ethnicity, and work in the lives of Jewish and Italian women in New York, 1870–1924.* Albany: State University of New York Press.

Frye, M. (1983). *The politics of reality.* Trumansburg, NY: Crossing Press.

Fuss, D. (Ed.). (1990). *inside/out: Lesbian theories, gay theories.* New York: Routledge.

Galindo, D. L., & Gonzales, M. (Eds.). (1999). *Speaking Chicana: Voice, power and identity.* Tucson: University of Arizona Press.

Gannon, L. (1999). *Women and aging: Transcending the myths.* New York: Routledge.

Garber, L. (Ed.). (1994). *Tilting the tower: Lesbians, teaching, queer subjects.* New York: Routledge.

García, A. M. (Ed.). (1997). *Chicana feminist thought: The basic historical writings.* New York: Routledge.

Giddings, P. (1984). *When and where I enter: The impact of Black women on race and sex in America.* New York: Morrow.

Gilligan, C. (1982). *In a different voice: Psychological theory and women's development.* Cambridge, MA: Harvard University Press.

Glenn, E. K. (1986). *Issei, nisei, war bride: Three generations of Japanese American women in domestic service.* Philadelphia: Temple University Press.

Glenn, S. (1990). *Daughters of the shtetl: Life and labor in the immigrant generation.* Ithaca, NY: Cornell University Press.

Goings, K. W., Rothenberg, P., Bernstein, A., Minnich, E. K., Anderson, M., Fiol-Matta, L., Baker, J., & Rosenfelt, D. (2000). The next decade of curriculum transformation. *Transformations, 9*(2), 120–127.

Goldenberg, M., & Parry, S. C. (1996). Faculty development: A consortial model. *Women's Studies Quarterly, 24*(3&4), 23–29.

Gómez, A., Moraga, C., & Romo-Carmona, M. (Eds.). (1983). *Cuentos: Stories by Latinas.* Brooklyn: Kitchen Table/Women of Color Press.

Gómez, J. (1993). Speculative fiction and Black lesbians. *Signs, 18*(4), 948–955.

González, S. (1977). The White feminist movement: The Chicana perspective. *Social Science Journal, 14*(2), 67–76.

Goodloe, A. (1996–1999). *Lesbian.org: Promoting lesbian visibility on the internet.* Available on-line: http://www.lesbian.org. Retrieved March 9, 2003.

Gore, J. (1993). *Struggles for pedagogies: Critical and feminist discourses as regimes of truth.* New York: Routledge.

Gould, J. (1995). American Indian women's poetry: Strategies of rage and hope. *Signs, 20*(4), 797–817.

Graff, G. (1992). *Beyond the culture wars: How teaching the conflicts can revitalize American education.* New York: Norton.

Green, R. (1979). American Indian women meet in Lawrence. *Women's Studies Newsletter, 7*(3), 6–7.

Green, R. (1983a). *Native American women: A contextual bibliography.* Bloomington: Indiana University Press.

Green, R. (Ed.). (1983b). *That's what she said: Contemporary fiction and poetry by Native American women.* Bloomington: Indiana University Press.

Grewal, I., & Kaplan, C. (Eds.). (1994). *Scattered hegemonies: Postmodernity and transnational feminist practices.* Minneapolis: University of Minnesota Press.

Griffin, G., & Andermahr, S. (Eds.). (1997). *Straight studies modified: Lesbian interventions in the academy.* Washington, DC: Cassell.

Gunning, I. R. (1997). Arrogant perception, world traveling, and multicultural feminism. In A. K. Wing (Ed.), *Global critical race feminism.* New York: New York University Press.

Gupta, S. R. (Ed.). (1999). *Emerging voices: South Asian American women redefine self, family, and community.* Walnut Creek, CA: Sage.

Guy-Sheftall, B. (1986). Women's studies at Spelman College: Reminiscences from the director. *Women's Studies International Quarterly, 9*(2), 151–156.

Guy-Sheftall, B. (Ed.). (1995). *Words of fire: An anthology of African-American feminist thought.* New York: New Press.

Guy-Sheftall, B. (2003). "Shifting contexts: Integrating Black, gender, and African diaspora studies." In M. M. Lay, J. Monk, & Rosenfelt, D. S. (Eds.), *Encompassing gender.* New York: Feminist Press.

Guy-Sheftall, B., with Heath, S. (1995). *Women's studies: A retrospective.* New York: Ford Foundation.

Hagedorn, J. (1997). The exile within: The question of identity. In B. Schneider (Ed.), *Race: An anthology in the first person* (pp. 43–49). New York: Crown.

Hammonds, E. (1997). Black (w)holes and the geometry of Black female sexuality. In E. Weed & N. Schor (Eds.), *Feminism meets queer theory* (pp. 136–156). Bloomington: Indiana University Press.

Haraway, D. J. (1991). *Simians, cyborgs, and women: The reinvention of nature.* New York: Routledge.

Harcourt, W. (Ed.). (1999). *Women@internet: Creating new cultures in cyberspace.* New York: Zed Books.

Harding, S. (1986). *The science question in feminism.* Ithaca, NY: Cornell University Press.

Harjo, J., & Bird, G. (1997). *Reinventing the enemy's language: Contemporary Native women's writing of North America.* New York: Norton.

Hartman, J. E., & Messer-Davidow, E. (1991). *(En)gendering knowledge: Feminists in academe.* Knoxville: University of Tennessee Press.

Hawthorne, S., & Klein, R. (Eds.). (1999). *Cyberfeminism: Connectivity, critique and creativity.* North Melbourne: Spinifex Press.

Hedges, E. (1997). *Getting started: Planning curriculum transformation.* Towson, MD: National Center for Curriculum Transformation Resources on Women.

Helmbold, L. R. (1987). Feminists pretend to deal with class. *Sojourner, 13*(1), 33–34.

Herman, F. (Comp.). (1998). *A bibliography of works on Jewish women's history, with references to works on Jewish gender studies, Jewish masculinity and Jewish sexuality.* Waltham, MA: Hadassah International Research Institute on Jewish Women. Available on-line: http://www.brandeis.edu.hirjw/pdf/history.pdf. Retrieved March 9, 2003.

Hermann, A. C., & Stewart, A. J. (1994). *Theorizing feminism: Parallel trends in the humanities and social sciences.* Boulder, CO: Westview Press.

Hernandez-Avila, I. (1995). Relocations upon relocations: Home, language and Native American women's writings. *American Indian Quarterly, 19*(4), 491–507.

Herrera-Sobek, M. (Ed.). (1985). *Beyond stereotypes: A critical analysis of Chicana literature.* Binghamton, NY: Bilingual Press.

Herrera-Sobek, M., & Viramontes, M. (Eds.). (1995). *Chicana (w)rites: On word and film.* Berkeley: Third Woman Press.

Hesse-Biber, S., Gilmartin, C., & Lydenberg, R. (Eds.). (1999). *Feminist approaches to theory and methodology: An interdisciplinary reader.* New York: Oxford University Press.

Higginbotham, E. (1996). Getting all students to listen. *American Behavioral Scientist, 40*(2), 203–211.

Hillyer, B. (1992). Women and disabilities. *NWSA Journal, 4*(1), 106–114.

Hine, D. C. (Ed.). (1990). *Black women in United States history* (Vols. 1–16). Brooklyn, NY: Carlson.

Hine, D. C. (1998). *A shining thread of hope: The history of Black women in America.* New York: Broadway Books.

Hine, D. C., King, W., & Reed, L. (Eds.). (1995). *"We specialize in the wholly impossible": A reader in Black women's history.* Brooklyn, NY: Carlson.

Ho, W. (1999). *In her mother's house: The politics of Asian-American mother-daughter writing.* Walnut Creek, CA: Alta Mira Press.

Hoffman, N., Secor, C., & Tinsley, A. (Eds.). (1973). *Female studies VI: Closer to the ground, women's classes, criticism, programs-1972* (2nd ed.). New York: Feminist Press.

Hondagneu-Sotelo, P. (2001). *Doméstica: Immigrant workers cleaning and caring in the shadows of affluence.* Berkeley: University of California Press.

hooks, b. (1981). *Ain't I a woman: Black women and feminism.* Boston: South End Press.

hooks, b. (1984). *Feminist theory: From margin to center.* Boston: South End Press.

hooks, b. (1992). *Black looks, race and representations.* Boston: South End Press.

hooks, b. (1994). *Teaching to transgress: Education as the practice of freedom.* New York: Routledge.

hooks, b. (2000). *Where we stand: Class matters.* New York: Routledge.

Horno-Delgado, A., Ortega, E., Scott, N. M., & Sternbach, N. S. (Eds.). (1989). *Breaking boundaries: Latina writing and critical readings.* Amherst: University of Massachusetts Press.

Howe, F. (Ed.). (2000). *The politics of women's studies: Testimony from 30 founding mothers.* New York: Feminist Press of the City University of New York.

Hubbard, R. (1982). *Women look at biology looking at women.* New York: G. K. Hall.

Hudson, J., & Turek, K. A. (1994). *Electronic access to research on women: A short guide* (2nd ed.). Albany, NY: Institute for Research on Women.

Hull, G. T., Scott, P. B., & Smith, B. (Eds.). (1982). *All the women are White, all the Blacks are men, but some of us are brave.* New York: Feminist Press.

Hune, S., Kim, H., Fugita, S. S., & Ling, A. (Eds.). (1991). *Asian Americans: Comparative and global perspectives.* Pullman: Washington State University Press.

Hungry Wolf, B. (1982). *The ways of my grandmothers.* New York: Quill.

Hunter, T. W. (1997). *To joy my freedom: Southern Black women's lives and labors after the Civil War.* Cambridge, MA: Harvard University Press.

Hyman, P. E. (1998). *Jewish feminism faces the American women's movement: Convergence and divergence.* David W. Belin Lecture in American Jewish Affairs, University of Michigan.

Hyman, P. E., & Moore, D. D. (Eds.). (1997). *Jewish women in America: An historical encyclopedia.* New York: Routledge.

Iglesias-Prieto, N. (1997). *Beautiful flowers of the maquiladora: Life histories of women workers in Tijuana.* Austin: University of Texas Press, Institute of Latin American Studies.

Jacobs, S. E., Thomas, W., & Lang, S. (Eds.). (1997). *Two-spirit people: Native American gender identity, sexuality, and spirituality.* Urbana: University of Illinois Press.

Jaimes, M. A., & Halsey, T. (1992). American Indian women: At the center of indigenous resistance in North America. In M. A. Jaimes (Ed.), *The state of Native America* (pp. 311–344). Boston: South End Press.

James, J., & Farmer, R. (Eds.). (1993). *Spirit, space survival: African American women in (White) academe.* New York: Routledge.

James, J., & Sharpley-Whiting, T. D. (Eds.). (2000). *The Black feminist reader.* New York: Blackwell.

James, S., & Busia, A. (Eds.). (1993). *Theorizing Black feminisms.* New York: Routledge.

Jardine, A. (1988). Prelude: The future of difference. In H. Eisenstein & A. Jardine (Eds.), *The future of difference* (pp. xxv–xxvii). New Brunswick, NJ: Rutgers University Press.

Johnston, J. (1973). *Lesbian nation: The feminist solution*. New York: Simon & Schuster.

Jones, J. (1985). *Labor of love, labor of sorrow: Black women, work, and the family from slavery to the present*. New York: Basic Books.

Kadi, J. (Ed.). (1994). *Food for our grandmothers: Writings by Arab American and Arab Canadian feminists*. Boston: South End Press.

Kantrowitz, M. K., & Klepfisz, I. (Eds.). (1989). *The tribe of Dina: A Jewish women's anthology*. Boston: Beacon Press.

Kaplan, C., Alarcón, N., & Moallem, M. (Eds.). (1999). *Between woman and nation: Nationalisms, transnational feminisms, and the state*. Durham, NC: Duke University Press.

Katz, J. (Ed.). (1995). *Messengers of the wind: Native American women tell their stories*. New York: Ballantine.

Kennedy, E. L., & Davis, M. D. (1993). *Boots of leather, slippers of gold: A history of a lesbian community*. New York: Routledge.

Kidwell, C. S. (1979). The power of women in three American Indian societies. *Journal of Ethnic Studies, 6*(3), 113–121.

Kidwell, C. S. (1994). What would Pocahontas think now? Women and cultural persistence. *Callaloo, 17*(1), 149–159.

Kim, E. H. (1982). *Asian American literature: An introduction to the writings and their social context*. Philadelphia: Temple University Press.

Kim, E. H., Villanueva, L. V., & Asian Women United of California. (Eds.). (1997). *Making more waves: New writings by Asian American women*. Boston: Beacon Press.

Kimmel, M. (Ed.). (1987). *Changing men: New directions in research on men and masculinity*. Beverly Hills, CA: Sage.

Kimmel, M. S. (1996). *Manhood in America: A cultural history*. New York: Free Press.

Kimmel, M., & Messner, M. A. (Eds.). (1998). *Men's lives* (4th ed.). Old Tappan, NJ: Macmillan.

Korenman, J. (1997). *Internet resources on women: Using electronic media in curriculum transformation*. Towson, MD: National Center for Curriculum Transformation Resources on Women.

Korenman, J. (1994–2002). *Women's studies online resources*. Available on-line: http://www.research.umbc.edu/~korenman/wmst/. Retrieved March 9, 2003.

Kornbluth, S. T., & Kornbluth, D. (Eds.). (2000). *Jewish women speak out about Jewish matters*. Detroit: Targum/Feldheim.

LaDuke, W. (1999). *All our relations: Native struggles for land and life*. Boston: South End Press.

Lai, T. (1992). Asian American women: Not for sale. In M. L. Andersen & P. H. Collins (Eds.), *Race, class, and gender: An anthology* (pp. 163–171). Belmont, CA: Wadsworth.

Lamberty, G., & García-Coll, C. (1994). *Puerto Rican women and children: Issues in health, growth and development*. New York: Plenum Press.

Lauter, P. (Ed.). (1983). *Reconstructing American literature: Courses, syllabi, issues*. New York: Feminist Press.

Lauter, P. (1991). *Canons and contexts*. New York: Oxford University Press.

Lay, M., Monk, J., & Rosenfelt, D. (Eds.). (2003). *Encompassing gender*. New York: Feminist Press.

Le Espiritu, Y. (1997). *Asian American women and women: Labor, laws, and love*. Thousand Oaks, CA: Sage.

Lee, R. (2000). Notes from the (non)field: Teaching and theorizing women of color. *Meridians, 1*(1), 85–109.

Leong, R. (Ed.). (1996). *Asian American sexualities*. New York: Routledge.

Lerner, G. (Ed.). (1973). *Black women in White America: A documentary history*. New York: Pantheon.

Levitt, L. (1997). *Jews and feminism: The ambivalent search for home*. New York: Routledge.

Lewis, M. (1992). Interrupting patriarchy: Politics, resistance and transformation in the feminist classroom. In C. Luke & J. Gore (Eds.), *Feminisms and critical pedagogy* (pp. 167–191). New York: Routledge.

Lim, S. G. (1991). Asian American daughters rewriting Asian maternal texts. In S. Hune, H. Kim, S. S. Fugita, & A. Ling (Eds.), *Asian Americans: Comparative and global perspectives* (pp. 239–248). Pullman: Washington State University Press.

Lim, S. G., & Herrera-Sobek, M. (Eds.). (2000). *Power, race, and gender in academe: Strangers in the tower?* New York: Modern Language Association.

Lim, S. G., & Tsutakawa, M. (Eds.). (1989). *The forbidden stitch: An Asian American women's anthology*. Corvallis, OR: Calyx Books.

Lim-Hing, S. (1994). *The very inside: An anthology of writing by Asian and Pacific Islander lesbian and bisexual women*. Toronto: Sister Vision Press.

Lomawaima, K. T. (1994). *They called it Prairie Light: The story of Chilocco Indian School*. Lincoln: University of Nebraska Press.

Lorde, A. (1981). An open letter to Mary Daly. In C. Moraga & G. Anzaldúa (Eds.), *This bridge called my back: A collection of writings by radical women of color* (pp. 94–97). Watertown, MA: Persephone Press.

Lorde, A. (1984). *Sister outsider: Essays and speeches*. Trumansburg, NY: Crossing Press.

Lowe, L. (1996). *Immigrant acts: On Asian American cultural politics*. Durham, NC: Duke University Press.

Luebke, B. F., & Riley, M. E. (1995). *Women's studies graduates: The first generation*. New York: Teachers College Press.

Luke, C., & Gore, J. (Eds.). (1992). *Feminisms and critical pedagogy*. New York: Routledge.

Lurie, N. O. (1961). *Mountain Wolf Woman, sister of Crashing Thunder, a Winnebago Indian*. Ann Arbor: University of Michigan Press.

Maciel, D. R., Ortiz, I. D., & Herrera-Sobek, M. (Eds.). (2000). *Chicano renaissance: Contemporary cultural trends*. Tucson: University of Arizona Press.

Macdonald, B., & Rich, C. (1983). *Look me in the eye: Old women, aging and ageism*. San Francisco: Spinsters, Ink.

MacNabb, E. L., Cherry, S. L., Popham, S. L., & Prys, R. P. (Eds.). (2001). *Transforming the disciplines: A women's studies primer*. New York: Haworth Press.

Maher, F., & Tetreault, M.K.T. (2001). *The feminist classroom* (2nd ed.). Lanham, MD: Rowman & Littlefield.

Mankiller, W. P. (1993). *Mankiller: A chief of her people*. New York: St. Martin's Press.

Manning, C. (1999). *God gave us the right: Conservative Catholic, evangelical Protestant, and orthodox Jewish women grapple with feminism*. New Brunswick, NJ: Rutgers University Press.

Masnik, A. S. (1996). *The Jewish woman: An annotated selected bibliography*. New York: Biblio Press.

Mason-John, V. (Ed.). (1995). *Talking Black: Lesbians of African and Asian descent speak out*. New York: Cassell.

Matos-Rodriquez, F., & Delgado, L. (Eds.). (1998). *Puerto Rican women's history: New perspectives*. Armonk, NY: M. E. Sharpe.

McCaughey, M., Koella, J. C., & Keene, M. (2001). *The Mayfield quick view guide to the Internet for students of women's studies.* Mountain View, CA: Mayfield.

McCloud, A. B. (1995). *African American Islam.* New York: Routledge.

McCracken, E. (1999). *New Latina narrative: The feminine space of postmodern ethnicity.* Tucson: University of Arizona Press.

McDermott, P. (1994). *Politics and scholarship: Feminist academic journals and the production of knowledge.* Urbana: University of Illinois Press.

McDowell, D. (1980). New directions for Black feminist criticism. *Black American Literature Forum, 14*(3), 153.

McNaron, T.A.H., Anzaldúa, G., Argüelles, L., & Kennedy, E. L. (Eds.). (1993). Theorizing lesbian experience [Special issue]. *Signs, 18*(4).

Medicine, B. (1981). Contemporary literature on Indian women: A review essay. *Frontiers, 6*(3), 122–125.

Medicine, B. (1987). Indian women and the renaissance of traditional religion. In R. J. DeMallie & D. R. Parks (Eds.), *Sioux Indian religion: Tradition and innovation.* Norman: University of Oklahoma Press.

Mernissi, F. (1991). *The veil and the male elite: A feminist interpretation of women's rights in Islam.* Reading, MA: Addison-Wesley.

Mernissi, F. (1992). *Beyond the veil* (2nd ed.). Rochester, VT: Schenkman.

Midgley, C. (1995). *Gender and imperialism.* Manchester: Manchester University Press.

Mihesuah, D. A. (1993). *Cultivating the rosebuds: The education of women at Cherokee Female Seminary, 1851–1909.* Urbana: University of Illinois Press.

Mihesuah, D. A. (2000). A few cautions at the millennium on the merging of feminist studies with American Indian women's studies. *Signs, 25*(4), 1247–1252.

Millar, M. S. (1998). *Cracking the gender code: Who rules the wired world?* Toronto: Second Story Press.

Millett, K. (1970). *Sexual politics.* New York: Doubleday.

Minh-ha, T. T. (1989). *Women, native, other: Writing postcoloniality and feminism.* Bloomington: Indiana University Press.

Minnich, E. K. (1990). *Transforming knowledge.* Philadelphia: Temple University Press.

Moghadam, V. M. (Ed.). (1994). *Identity politics and women: Cultural reassertions and feminisms in international perspective.* Boulder, CO: Westview Press.

Mohanty, C. T. (1991). Under Western eyes: Feminist scholarship and colonial discourses. In C. T. Mohanty, A. Russo, & L. Torres (Eds.), *Third World women and the politics of feminism* (pp. 50–80). Bloomington: Indiana University Press.

Mohanty, C. T. (1997). Dangerous territories, territorial power, and education. In L. G. Roman & E. Eyre (Eds.), *Dangerous territories: Struggles for difference and equality in education* (pp. ix–xvii). New York: Routledge.

Mohanty, C. T., Russo, A., & Torres, L. (Eds.). (1991). *Third World women and the politics of feminism.* Bloomington: Indiana University Press.

Monk, J., & Rosenfelt, D. (2000). *Internationalizing the study of women and gender.* Towson, MD: National Center for Curriculum Transformation Resources on Women.

Moraga, C. (1997). *Waiting in the wings: Portrait of a queer motherhood.* Ithaca, NY: Firebrand Books.

Moraga, C., & Anzaldúa, G. (Eds.). (1981). *This bridge called my back: A collection of writings by radical women of color.* Watertown, MA: Persephone Press.

Morgan, R. (Ed.). (1984). *Sisterhood is global: The international women's movement anthology.* New York: Doubleday.

Mullings, L. (1997). *On our own terms: Race, class, and gender in the lives of African American women.* New York: Routledge.

Muniz, V. (1998). *Resisting gentrification and displacement: Voices of Puerto Rican women of the barrio.* New York: Garland.

Musil, C. M. (Ed.). (1992a). *The courage to question: Women's studies and student learning.* Washington, DC: Association of American Colleges and National Women's Studies Association.

Musil, C. M. (1992b). *The courage to question: Executive summary.* Washington, DC: Association of American Colleges.

Naber, N., Desouky, E., & Baroudi, L. (2001). *The forgotten "-ism": An Arab American women's perspective on Zionism, racism and sexism.* San Francisco: Arab American Women's Solidarity Association. Available on-line: http://www.nadyalec.com/zionism.pdf. Retrieved March 9, 2003.

Nam, V. (Ed.). (2001). *Yell-oh girls: Emerging voices explore culture, identity, and growing up Asian American.* New York: Quill.

Nashat, G., & Tucker, J. E. (1999). *Women in the Middle East and North Africa.* Bloomington: Indiana University Press.

National Center for Curriculum Transformation Resources on Women. (2000). Available on-line: http://pages.towson.edu/ncctrw. Retrieved March 9, 2003.

National Women's Studies Association. (2002). Available on-line: http://www.nwsa.org. Retrieved March 9, 2003.

Navarro, M., & Sanchez-Korrol, V. (1999). *Women in Latin America and the Caribbean.* Bloomington: Indiana University Press.

Ng, R., Staton, P., & Scane, J. (Eds.). (1995). *Anti-racism, feminism and critical approaches to education.* Westport, CT: Greenwood Press.

Nicholson, L. (Ed.). (1990). *Feminism/postmodernism.* New York: Routledge.

Nnaemeka, O. (Ed.). (1998). *Sisterhood, feminisms, and power: From Africa to the diaspora.* Trenton, NJ: Africa World Press.

O'Brien, J. (1999). Writing in the body: Gender (re)production in online interaction. In M. A. Smith & P. Kollock (Eds.), *Communities in cyberspace* (pp. 76–104). New York: Routledge.

Ogunyemi, C. O. (1985). Womanism: The dynamics of the contemporary Black female novel in English. *Signs, 11*(1), 63–80.

Ortiz, A. (Ed.). (1996) *Puerto Rican women and work: Bridges in transnational labor.* Philadelphia: Temple University Press.

Ortner, S. (1974). Is female to male as nature is to culture? In L. Lamphere & M. Z. Rosaldo (Eds.), *Women, culture and society* (pp. 67–87). Stanford: Stanford University Press.

Ostriker, A. S. (1993). *Feminist revision and the Bible.* Cambridge, MA: Blackwell.

Palmer, P. M. (1983). White women/Black women: The dualism of female identity and experience in the United States. *Feminist Studies, 9*(1), 151–170.

Pardes, I. (1992). *Countertraditions in the Bible: A feminist approach.* Cambridge, MA: Harvard University Press.

Pardo, M. (1998). *Mexican American women activists: Identity and resistance in two Los Angeles communities.* Philadelphia: Temple University Press.

Pearsall, M. (Ed.). (1997). *The other within us: Feminist explorations of women and aging.* Boulder, CO: Westview Press.

Pena, D. G. (1997). *The terror of the machine: Technology, work, gender, and ecology on the U.S.-Mexico border.* Austin: Center for Mexican American Studies, University of Texas.

Perdue, T. (1998). *Cherokee woman: Gender and culture change, 1700–1835.* Lincoln: University of Nebraska Press.

Perdue, T. (Ed.). (2001). *Sifters: Native American women's lives*. New York: Oxford University Press.

Perez, E. (1999). *The decolonial imaginary: Writing Chicanas into history*. Bloomington: Indiana University Press.

Perreault, J., & Vance, S. (Eds.). (1993). *Writing the circle: Native women of western Canada*. Norman: University of Oklahoma Press.

Plaskow, J. (1990). *Standing again at Sinai: Judaism from a feminist perspective*. New York: HarperCollins.

Pogrebin, L. C. (1982). Anti-Semitism in the women's movement. *Ms., 10*(12), 45–49.

Pointer, B. P., & Auletta, G. S. (1990). Restructuring the curriculum: Barriers and bridges. *Women's Studies Quarterly, 18*(1&2), 86–94.

Porter, N. (1989). The art of aging: A review essay. *Women's Studies Quarterly, 17*(1&2), 97–108.

Prell, R.-E. (1999). *Fighting to become Americans: Jews, gender, and the anxiety of assimilation*. Boston: Beacon Press.

Ramirez, E. (2000). *Chicanas/Latinas in American theatre: A history of performance*. Bloomington: Indiana University Press.

Ramusack, B. N., & Sievers, S. (1999). *Women in Asia*. Bloomington: Indiana University Press.

Razack, S. (1998). *Looking white people in the eye: Gender, race, and culture in courtrooms and classrooms*. Toronto: University of Toronto Press.

Rebolledo, T. D. (1985). Chicana studies: The missing text. In *Curriculum integration: Revising the literary canon* (Working Paper No. 20). Tucson: University of Arizona, Southwest Institute for Research on Women.

Rebolledo, T. (1995). *Women singing in the snow: A cultural analysis of Chicana literature*. Tucson: University of Arizona Press.

Rebolledo, T. D., & Rivero, E. S. (Eds.). (1993). *Infinite divisions: An anthology of Chicana literature*. Tucson: University of Arizona Press.

Rich, A. (1979). *On lies, secrets, and silences: Selected prose, 1966–1978*. New York: Norton.

Ristock, J. L., & Taylor, C. G. (Eds.). (1998). *Inside the academy and out: Lesbian/gay/queer studies and social action*. Toronto: University of Toronto Press.

Robnett, B. (1997). *How long? How long? African-American women in the struggle for civil rights*. New York: Oxford University Press.

Romero, M. (1992). *Maid in the U.S.A.* New York: Routledge.

Romero, M., & Stewart, A. (Eds.). (1999). *Untold stories: Breaking silence, talking back, voicing complexity*. New York: Routledge.

Rosaldo, M. Z. (1974). Women, culture, and society: A theoretical overview. In M. Z. Rosaldo & L. Lamphere (Eds.), *Women, culture, and society* (pp. 17–42). Stanford: Stanford University Press.

Rosenblum, K. E., & Travis, T-M. C. (2000). *The meaning of difference: American constructions of race, sex and gender, social class, and sexual orientation*. New York: McGraw-Hill.

Rosenfelt, D. S. (Ed.). (1973). *Female studies VII: Going strong, new courses/new programs*. New York: Feminist Press.

Rosenfelt, D. S. (1984). What women's studies programs do that mainstreaming can't. *Women's Studies International Forum, 7*(3), 167–175.

Rosenfelt, D. S. (1990). *Curriculum transformation project at UMCP: Report on the 1989 Summer Faculty Institute*. Unpublished manuscript, College Park: University of Maryland, Curriculum Transformation Project.

Rosenfelt, D. S., & Williams, R. (1992). Learning experience: The curriculum transformation project at the University of Maryland at College Park. *Women's Review of Books, 9*(5), 33–35.

Rosenwasser, P. (Ed.). (1992). *Voices from the promised land: Palestinian women and Israeli peace activists speak their hearts*. Willimantic, CT: Curbstone Press.

Rothenberg, P. S. (Ed.). (1992). *Race, class, and gender in the United States: An integrated study* (2nd ed.). New York: St. Martin's Press.

Rubin, G. (1975). The traffic in women: Notes on the "political economy of sex." In R. Reiter (Ed.), *Toward an anthropology of women* (pp. 157–210). New York: Monthly Review Press.

Rudavsky, T. M. (Ed.). (1995). *Gender and Judaism: The transformation of tradition*. New York: New York University Press.

Ruíz, V. (1987). *Cannery women, cannery lives: Mexican women, unionization, and the California food processing industry, 1930–1950*. Albuquerque: University of New Mexico Press.

Ruíz, V. L., & DuBois, E. C. (Eds.). (1990). *Unequal sisters: A multicultural reader in U.S. women's history*. New York: Routledge.

Rupp, L. J. (1997). *Worlds of women: The making of an international women's movement*. Princeton, NJ: Princeton University Press.

Ruttenberg, D. (2001). *Yentl's revenge: The next wave of Jewish feminism*. Seattle: Seal Press.

Sacks, M. (Ed.). (1995). *Active voices: Women in Jewish culture*. Urbana: University of Illinois Press.

Saldívar-Hull, S. (2000). *Feminism on the border: Chicana gender politics and literature*. Berkeley: University of California Press.

Sánchez, C. L. (1983). Sex, class and race intersections: Visions of women of color. In B. Brant (Ed.), A gathering of spirit: A collection by North American Indian women [Special issue]. *Sinister Wisdom, 22–23*, 150–154.

Sandoval, C. (2000). *Methodology of the oppressed*. Minneapolis: University of Minnesota Press.

Schmitz, B. (1985). *Integrating women's studies into the curriculum: A guide and bibliography*. New York: Feminist Press.

Schmitz, B., & Dinnerstein, M. (1991). Incorporating scholarship on women into the community college curriculum. *AAWCJC Journal, 5*–11.

Schuster, M. R., & Van Dyne, S. R. (Eds.). (1985). *Women's place in the academy: Transforming the liberal arts curriculum*. Totowa, NJ: Rowman & Allanheld.

Segrest, M. (1994). *Memoir of a race traitor*. Boston: South End Press.

Segura, D. A. (1989). Chicana and Mexican immigrant women at work. *Gender and Society, 3*(1), 37–52.

Segura, D. A., & Pesquera, B. M. (1993). Beyond indifference and antipathy: The Chicana feminist movement and Chicana feminist discourse. *Aztlán, 19*(2), 69–88.

Segura, D. A., & Pierce, J. L. (1992). Chicano/a family structure and gender personality: Chodorow, feminism, and psychoanalytic sociology revisited. *Signs, 19*(1), 62–91.

Shah, S. (Ed.). (1997). *Dragon ladies: Asian American feminists breathe fire*. Boston: South End Press.

Shakir, E. (1997). *Bint Arab: Arab and Arab American women in the United States*. New York: Praeger.

Sharoni, S. (1995). *Gender and the Israeli-Palestinian conflict: The politics of women's resistance*. Syracuse, NY: Syracuse University Press.

Sherman, J. A., & Beck, E. T. (Eds.). (1979). *The prism of sex: Essays in the sociology of knowledge*. Madison: University of Wisconsin Press.

Shoemaker, N. (Ed.). (1995). *Negotiators of change: Historical perspectives on Native American women*. New York: Routledge.

Shohat, E. (Ed.) (1998). *Talking visions: Multicultural feminism in a transnational age*. Cambridge, MA: MIT Press.

Smith, B. (Ed.). (1977). Towards a Black feminist criticism [Special issue]. *Conditions, 2.*

Smith, B. (Ed.). (1983). *Home girls: A Black feminist anthology.* New York: Kitchen Table/Women of Color Press.

Smith, B. (1993). Queer politics: Where's the revolution? *Nation, 257*(1), 14.

Smith, B. (2000). *Global feminisms since 1945.* New York: Routledge.

Song, Y. I., & Moon, A. (Eds.). (1998). *Korean American women: From tradition to modern feminism.* New York: Praeger.

Spanier, B., Bloom, A., & Boroviak, D. (1984). *Toward a balanced curriculum: A sourcebook for initiating gender integration projects.* Rochester, VT: Schenkman.

Spellberg, D. (1994). *Politics, gender, and the Islamic past.* New York: Columbia University Press.

Spelman, E.V. (1988). *Inessential woman: Problems of exclusion in feminist thought.* Boston: Beacon Press.

Spender, D. (Ed.). (1981). *Men's studies modified: The impact of feminism on the academic disciplines.* New York: Pergamon Press.

Spivak, G. C. (1999). *A critique of postcolonial reason: Toward a history of the vanishing present.* Cambridge, MA: Harvard University Press.

Stack, C. (1984). *All our kin: Strategies for survival in a Black community.* New York: HarperCollins.

Stake, J. E., & Hoffman, F. L. (2001). Changes in student social attitudes, activism, and personal confidence in higher education: The role of women's studies. *American Educational Research Journal, 38*(2), 411–436.

Stanton, D. C., & Stewart, A. J. (Eds.). (1995). *Feminisms in the academy.* Ann Arbor: University of Michigan Press.

Steady, F. C. (Ed.). (1981). *The Black woman cross-culturally.* Rochester, VT: Schenkman.

Sterling, E. (Ed.). (1984). *We are your sisters: Black women in the nineteenth century.* New York: Norton.

Stimpson, C. R. (1992). Women's studies. In B. R. Clark & G. R. Neave (Eds.), *Encyclopedia of Higher Education* (pp. 1965–1976). New York: Pergamon Press.

Strobel, M. (1994). *Gender, sex, and empire.* Washington, DC: American Historical Association.

Terborg-Penn, R. (1998). *African American women in the struggle for the vote, 1850–1920.* Bloomington: Indiana University Press.

Terborg-Penn, R., & Harley, S. (Eds.). (1978). *The Afro-American woman: Struggles and images.* Port Washington, NY: National University Publications.

Terborg-Penn, R., Harley, S., & Rushing, A. B. (1987). *Women in Africa and the African diaspora.* Washington, DC: Howard University Press.

Tohe, L. (2000). There is no word for feminism in my language. *Wicazo Sa Review, 15*(2), 103–110.

Tokarczyk, M. M., & Fay, E. A. (Eds.). (1993). *Working-class women in the academy.* Amherst: University of Massachusetts Press.

Trafzer, C. E. (Ed.). (1996). *Blue earth, red dawn: New Native American storytellers.* New York: Doubleday.

Trask, H. (1999). *From a native daughter: Colonialism and sovereignty in Hawai'i.* Honolulu: University of Hawai'i Press.

Trujillo, C. (Ed.). (1991). *Chicana lesbians.* Berkeley: Third Woman Press.

Trujillo, C. (1998). *Living Chicana theory.* Berkeley, CA: Third Woman Press.

Tsuchida, N. (Ed.). (1982). *Asian and Pacific American women's perspectives.* Minneapolis: University of Minnesota, Asian/Pacific American Learning Resource Center and General College.

Tsui, K. (1983). *Words of a woman who breathes fire.* San Francisco: Spinsters, Ink.

University of Maryland. (2002). *Women's studies database website.* Available on-line: http://www.mith2.umd.edu/WomensStudies/. Retrieved March 9, 2003.

University of Washington. (2002). Center for Curriculum Transformation Web site. http://depts.washington.edu/tp/fsctpsuccess.htm. Retrieved March 9, 2003.

University of Wisconsin System. Women's Studies Librarian. (2003). Women's studies librarian Web site. http://www.library.wisc.edu/libraries/WomensStudies. Retrieved March 9, 2003.

Uno, R. (Ed.). (1993). *Unbroken thread: An anthology of plays by Asian American women.* Amherst: University of Massachusetts Press.

Ware, V. (1992). *Beyond the pale: White women, racism, and history.* New York: Verso.

Walker, A. (1983). *In search of my mothers' gardens: Womanist prose.* San Diego: Harcourt.

Walters, S. D. (1996). From here to queer: Radical feminism, postmodernism, and the lesbian menace (or, why can't a woman be more like a fag?). *Signs, 21*(4), 830–869.

Washington, M. H. (Ed.). (1975). *Black-eyed Susans: Classic stories by and about Black women.* New York: Doubleday.

Washington, M. H. (Ed.). (1980). *Midnight birds: Stories by contemporary Black women writers.* New York: Doubleday.

Washington, M. H. (1987). *Invented lives: Narratives of Black women, 1860–1960.* New York: Doubleday.

Watanabe, S., & Bruchac, C. (Eds.). (1990). *Home to stay: Asian American women's fiction.* Greenfield Center, NY: Greenfield Review Press.

Webb, G. (Ed.). (2000). Windows of faith: Muslim women scholars/activists in North America. Syracuse, NY: Syracuse University Press.

Weber, L. (2001). *Understanding race, class and gender.* New York: McGraw-Hill.

Weber, L., Higginbotham, L., & Dill, B. T. (1994). *Sisterhood as collaboration: The Memphis State University Center for Research on Women* (Working paper). Memphis, TN: University of Memphis, Center for Research on Women.

Weiler, K. (1991). Freire and a feminist pedagogy of difference. *Harvard Educational Review, 61*(4), 449–474.

Weisbard, P. H. (Comp.). (2002). *Annotated bibliography and guide to archival resources on the history of Jewish women in America.* Available on-line: http://www.utoronto.ca/wjudaism/journal/journal_index.html. Retrieved March 9, 2003.

Wendell, S. (1996). *The rejected body: Feminist philosophical reflections on disability.* New York: Routledge.

Westbrook, L. (1999). *Interdisciplinary information seeking in women's studies.* Jefferson, NC: McFarland.

Wheeler, H. R. (1997). *Women and aging: A guide to the literature.* Boulder, CO: Westview Press.

White, D. G. (1985). *Ar'n't I a woman? Female slaves in the plantation South.* New York: Norton.

White, D. G. (1999). *Too heavy a load: Black women in defense of themselves, 1894–1994.* New York: Norton.

White, E. F. (2001). *Dark continent of our bodies: Black feminism and the politics of respectability.* Philadelphia: Temple University Press.

Williams-León, T., & Nakashima, C. L. (Eds.). (2001). *The sum of our parts: Mixed-heritage Asian Americans.* Philadelphia: Temple University Press.

Witt, S. H. (1976). The brave-hearted women: The struggle at Wounded Knee. *Akwesasne Notes, 8*(2), 16–17.

Women of South Asian Descent Collective. (Eds.). (1993). *Our feet walk the sky: Women of the South Asian diaspora.* San Francisco: Aunt Lute Books.

Women's Studies International Forum. (1991). *14*(4), 285–294.

Wong, S. C., & Santa Ana, J. (1999). Review essay: Gender and sexuality in Asian American literature. *Signs, 25*(1), 171–226.

Woodsum, J. A. (1995, Fall). Gender and sexuality in Native American societies: A bibliography. *American Indian Quarterly, 19,* 527–554.

Woodward, K. (1999). *Figuring age: Women, bodies, generations.* Bloomington: Indiana University Press.

Wwwomen, Inc. (1996–2001). *Electronic guide to research on women.* Available on-line: http://www.wwwomen.com/. Retrieved March 9, 2003.

Yamada, M. (1981). Asian Pacific American women and feminism. In C. Moraga & G. Anzaldúa (Eds.), *This bridge called my back: A collection of writings by radical women of color* (pp. 71–75). Watertown, MA: Persephone Press.

Yamani, M. (1996). *feminism and Islam.* New York: New York University Press.

Yarbro-Bejarano, Y. (1994). *Feminism and the honor plays of Lope de Vega.* West Lafayette, IN: Purdue University Press.

Young, G., & Dickerson, B. J. (Eds.). (1994). *Color, class and country: Experiences of gender.* London: Zed Books.

Zandy, J. (Ed.). (1990). *Calling home: Working-class women's writings: An anthology.* New Brunswick, NJ: Rutgers University Press.

Zandy, J. (Ed.). (2001). *What we hold in common: An introduction to working-class studies.* New York: Feminist Press at the City University of New York.

Zavella, P. (1998). When Jesus came the Corn Mothers went away: Marriage, sexuality and power in New Mexico, 1500–1846. *Aztlan, 23*(2), 239.

Zimmerman, B., & McNaron, T.A.H. (Eds.). (1996). *The new lesbian studies: Into the twenty-first century.* New York: Feminist Press.

Zinn, M. B., Cannon, L. W., Higginbotham, E., & Dill, B. T. (1986). The costs of exclusionary practices in women's studies. *Signs, 11*(2), 290–303.

Zinn, M. B., & Dill, B. T. (Eds.). (1994). *Women of color in U.S. society.* Philadelphia: Temple University Press.

45

MULTICULTURALISM AND CORE CURRICULA

Ann K. Fitzgerald
American Museum of Natural History

Paul Lauter
Trinity College

When we wrote this chapter for the previous edition of this book, we began by asserting that "both of the terms of our title—*multiculturalism* and *core curricula*—represent highly contested grounds in education (see, for example, Carnochan, 1993; Geyer, 1993). Indeed . . . their very definitions have been matters of conflict." In the intervening decade, things have changed, at least in some degree. Even relatively intransigent conservatives, including the president of the United States, have since September 11, 2001, acknowledged, indeed celebrated, the diversity of American society, however suspicious they might remain about devoting significant collegiate study to the cultural and social manifestations of that diversity. At the same time, requirements that all students learn about American diversity have spread, such that what was once a point of curricular conflict has become, if not a norm, at least a commonplace. Encouraged by national organizations like the American Association of Colleges and Universities, the financial support of local and national foundations, and a student culture that supports, or at least does not seriously object to, diversity requirements, a majority of institutions of higher education have established such core requirements. Although multiculturalism and core curriculum are not precisely married, in many places around the nation, they do cohabit.

All the same, many of the tensions that have marked this relationship continue. We will elaborate on these later. But it is useful to have in mind from the beginning the stresses that have helped shape the landscape this chapter attempts to map. These include, first, a certain contradiction between ideas of presumed universality and of particular phenomena (race, gender, ethnicity, and the like) as central to core curricula. This distinction often plays out in terms of whether a core program focuses on the "monuments of unaging intellect" dear to the hearts of humanities traditionalists, or on historically contingent conflicts more familiar to social scientists. The distinction also manifests itself in whether a core course is shaped around a theme—the riddle of human justice, beauty is its own excuse for being, women's health issues—or is focused on historically contingent events and circumstances. A second tension has to do with whether courses that explore difference are most suggestively focused on American society in the 21st (or 20th) century or on diversity as it is expressed across international borders—in other words, in American minority or in non-Western societies and cultures. A third tension has to do with whether core courses ought to be organized on the basis of where students are perceived to be coming from in terms of their own cultural assumptions and needs, or around the learnings—ideas, books, symbols—we as faculty and as representatives of institutional purpose believe they ought to know. This tension is often played out in terms of classroom priorities: Do we focus on presumably crucial texts or on the real lives of the real people who constitute the classroom? This is not an abstract question, for the experience of studying difference can be profoundly unsettling for students and faculty alike. Is that a good thing or a bad thing? Should the objective of core curricula be, in Emerson's phrase, to "unsettle all things," or should it be the traditional one of the liberal arts: passing on to ever new generations of students the received wisdom of their culture? Is it really the objective of core curricula to change students' values and outlooks or to reinforce what they, and we, already share? Such questions inform this chapter and have led us to present the case studies that follow.

Core curricula are often taken to represent a single course or sequence of courses taken by all undergraduates or all those enrolled toward a particular degree. For an older generation of faculty and for many in the nonacademic public, the model is that proposed by Harvard's 1945 report, *General Education in a Free Society,* also known as the "Redbook," and implemented in many colleges around the nation (though not at Harvard) during the 1950s (Bell, 1966). The model evokes the picture of a large auditorium in which an entire freshman class would attend two or three lectures a week, as well as discussion sections focused on common texts—the Bible or works from Greek and Roman civilization. The underlying idea, much touted during the 1980s, especially by the chairpersons of the National Endowment for the Humanities (Boyer & Levine, 1981; Cheney, 1989), was to provide undergraduate students with what a generation earlier had been presented as a "common experience," a "core of unity" (President's Commission on Higher Education, 1947), exposure to a set of shared texts taken to represent the shared heritage of Western culture.

On closer examination, however, few, if any, programs actually conform to this idealized stereotype. As the authors of one of the few studies of contemporary general education practice comment:

"Core" is not used with the consistency the advocates expect. Often it is a very loose collection of electives set out in very general categories. In the public arena the idea of a common core of general studies reaching across all institutions is proposed as a solution to all sorts of societal shortcomings. At the campus level such "one-size-fits-all" encounters realities of schedules, professional preparation requirements, and local traditions. (Toombs, Amey, & Chen, 1991, p. 112)

We will consequently use a relatively broad definition of *core curriculum,* including within this rubric a range of curricular formats. At one pole, rarely put into practice, are core programs that mandate that all students take one required course or a series of them. The most thoroughgoing implementation of this pattern has been at St. John's College, in Annapolis, Maryland, which has mandated the entire four-year curriculum, organized around some 120 "great books" (Rudolph, 1977). In the early 1990s, such course sequences accounted "for less than 5 percent of all undergraduate general education programs" (Astin, 1993, p. 425); others estimate that of the 34% of colleges and universities that had at that time a multicultural general education requirement, only 13% could have been called core curricula in this sense (Levine & Cureton, 1992). That proportion has decreased in the intervening decade. At the other pole, conceptions of "core" slide off into generalized distribution requirements, courses of study in which students are expected to take a number of general

education offerings from outside their majors. These are likely to include at least introductory-level courses in the various disciplines—courses such as American literature or psychology. Between these poles are a variety of tight and loose models of core curricular organization. Some institutions require students to choose from among a relatively restricted number of courses focused on issues (such as racial or sexual discrimination) or skills (such as computer or mathematical literacy) or from among a limited number of thematic tracks (Levine & Cureton, 1992, estimated that 68% of general education requirements including multicultural materials followed this model). Others offer opportunities for much broader student selection among courses gathered into loosely drawn categories such as "cultural diversity" or "scientific ways of knowing." Mount Saint Mary's College, to use one concrete example of an institution that created a core in the 1980s, required 61 hours, about half the curriculum, of general education:

The first two years are devoted to study in the humanities and sciences of Western civilization. The third year explores the American and Christian heritages, with emphasis on the Catholic tradition. The fourth year includes an examination of one non-Western culture and reflection about contemporary moral problems, with the aid of ethical theories. (Campbell & Flynn, 1990, p. 10)

We choose a somewhat eclectic strategy for discussing core curricula, not only because it better reflects the variety of collegiate practices than any narrow definition might, but also because the traditional definition of core curriculum as unitary course of study—"today is October 5 and we are all working on Thucydides"—generally contains within itself a conclusion about the virtues of this particular form of curricular organization (Brann, 1993). Part of our intent in this chapter, however, is to interrogate various methods of providing students with a core educational experience in relation to our second conflicted term, *multiculturalism.*

That term, as this *Handbook* and the sheer variety and number of books and articles indicate (e.g., Banks & Banks, 1993; Ch'maj, 1993; Nordquist, 1992; Goldberg, 1994; Gordon & Newfield, 1996; Ball, Berkowitz, & Mzamane, 1998; Mio & Awakuni, 2000; Narayan & Harding, 2000; Susser & Patterson, 2001), embraces an increasing range of curricular, pedagogical, and organizational practices at every level of education (Humphreys, 1997). In its weaker manifestations, it can represent little more than a celebration of cultural differences, as these are displayed in dress, foodways, art, and language. These are not inconsequential matters, to be sure; they constituted the central elements of the popular 1930s folk festivals promoted by leaders of the intercultural educational movement of that time (Montalto, 1982). But they seem to us of less educational weight in this historical moment than forms of study that raise issues of differences in power and questions of hybridization and change in the study of cultural and social heterogeneity (Baumann, 1999; Barry, 2001).

A second set of tensions concerns the different ways in which the term *multiculturalism* is used: To what groups does it refer (Biale, Galchinsky, & Heschel, 1998)? Should the term properly be restricted to diversity rooted in race and ethnicity? Does it also encompass differences based on national origin, gender, class, sexual orientation, and other terms of analysis and identity formation, including "exceptionality"? Can multiculturalism be equated with non-Western or other international studies? A growing consensus among multicultural theorists distinguished early in the discussion between multicultural education, which is primarily focused on issues of race, class, and gender, and global education (Banks & Banks, 1993; Gaff, 1992). While we concentrate primarily on race and ethnicity, our analysis deals as well with certain other categories, particularly gender and class, because, implicitly or explicitly, these are seldom absent from curricula or academic discussions concerned with multiculturalism (Rothenberg, 1998). It might be theoretically helpful to be able to draw a line between considerations, say, of race and of gender, but in practice such categories turn out to be mutually constitutive (Spelman, 1988), as can be seen by the very fragility of generalizations about all Black people or all women (Gaskell & Willinsky, 1995). Furthermore, in practice, among colleges and universities that have multicultural general education requirements, a growing number focused on what Levine and Cureton (1992) called "domestic diversity," more emphasized "global multiculturalism," and most included both.

HISTORICAL DETERMINANTS: SPECIALIZED AND GENERAL EDUCATION

In the 20th century, American collegiate curricula responded to alternating pulls from advocates of specialized and of general education. The elective system, developed primarily at Harvard toward the end of the 19th century under the leadership of President Charles W. Eliot, enabled students to pursue virtually any course of study they chose; of equal significance, perhaps, it allowed faculty to teach whatever was of primary interest to them (Kerr, 1964; Spurr, 1970). Increasingly influenced by the German model of the research institution, introduced at Johns Hopkins University in 1876, faculty found specialization in teaching and research to be in both their intellectual and material self-interest (Bisesi, 1982).

Not surprisingly, therefore, reformers from the general education movement of the 1920s (Gruber, 1975; Rudolph, 1962) to those of the 1940s (*General Education in a Free Society,* 1945) and the last quarter century (Association of American Colleges, 1985; Rosovsky, 1978; Cuban 1999) have decried faculty specialization as a main bar to sustaining viable forms of general education. Periodically, reformers have mounted campaigns to provide "coherence" and "direction" to the curriculum by exposing undergraduates to "a body of common knowledge," or—as an originator of Columbia's Contemporary Civilization program put it—to "introduce into our education a liberalizing force which will give to the generations to come a common background of ideas and commonly understood standards of judgment" (Gruber, 1975, p. 238). Just as regularly, student preoccupation with job preparation and faculty recognition that teaching outside their disciplines offered few direct professional rewards— and could present significant professional encumbrances (Lauter, 1991)—have led to the reemphasis of departmental and thus of specialized concerns.

Such an account is accurate, so far as it goes, but it tends, like many histories focused chiefly on educational institutions, to portray developments at colleges and universities in isolation from forces at work in the wider society (a problem illustrated by Allardyce, 1982). In fact, educational reforms generally, and efforts to foster core curricula most particularly, always reflect broader social forces (Hall & Kevles, 1982). Skeptics answer the *Jeopardy*-style question, "What is the problem for which core curriculum is an answer?" by citing "political, moral, ethical, and social" rather than strictly educational issues (Kaplan, 1982; Deats & Lenker, 1994; Foster & Herzog, 1994; Fullinwider, 1996). And they point to the need to deconstruct ideological terms such as *coherence* and *direction,* which often mask the political mandates that energize educational reforms.

Indeed, the alternating calls for general and specialized education have embedded within them certain common social imperatives. General education during and after World War I, for example, was supported in significant measure as a countervailing cultural force to the disintegrating tendencies some commentators saw in the influence of immigrants, Bolsheviks, women's suffrage, and other expressions of change in ethnic, class, and gender norms. Core courses such as Columbia's War Issues—the predecessor to Contemporary Civilization—mandated by the U.S. War Department, served to gather up fragments of European history against the ruin of the war-wracked culture bemoaned by modernist writers and critics like T. S. Eliot and Oswald Spengler. Not incidentally, such programs buttressed the cultural authority of the traditionally educated classes by valorizing what was assumed to be their heritage (Bell, 1966, offers a rather more benign view of these origins).

Similarly, in our own time, core curricula focused particularly on the Western tradition have been posed as an antidote to the disuniting tendencies critics located in multiculturalism, feminism, and Black studies (Bloom, 1987; Schlesinger, 1991; Roy, 1996). Their opponents have, by contrast, proposed that efforts to reconstruct narrowed general education cores correspond to the broader retreat in the 1980s from the commitments of earlier decades to educational experimentation dedicated "to equal opportunity, to openness, to multivalent validations," that core curricula represent, in practice, "a genteel way to retract the social commitment of the 1960s" (Kaplan, 1982, pp. 8–9; Willett, 1998). In short, a history of general education and its discontents in 20th-century America can too easily become a social history of 20th-century America. That is not our intent. It remains important, nevertheless, not to take at face value the terms, objectives, and claims to disinterestedness deployed by each cadre of educational reformers in behalf of their plans. Curricular coherence, for example, may be a significant virtue—or it may not, depending on the basis on which coherence is obtained (fundamentalism? Jihad? Aryanism? Stalinism?) and what is sacrificed to obtain it. Similarly, "the lack of a common intellectual experience is problematic only to the extent that it is held as an institutional value" (Jones & Ratcliff, 1991, p. 100). Our aim in the narratives that follow is not to promote any one model for relating core curricula and multiculturalism—though we do conclude that certain strategies can be seen to produce particular effects—but to portray the play of social, cultural, and political forces that have marked that uneasy relationship in our time.

CHANGING PATTERNS OF THE PAST TWENTY-FIVE YEARS

We have suggested a regular pattern of alternating tacks in 20th-century America toward general and specialized education. But history does not repeat itself. A measure of the distance between the general education reforms of the 1920s and those of the 1980s—and an observation to which we will return—is the extent to which most new or revised core programs, however much they might initially have focused on traditional ideas of Western civilization, soon took on additional but significant multicultural or non-Western elements (Schmitz, 1992a). The reasons for this development can be seen through a close reading of social and consequent educational changes usually attributed to "the Sixties." And these may, in turn, usefully be seen in relation to core curricula widely developed,

in response to the Harvard Redbook, during the previous decade.

One such core course, which can be taken to stand for many, was the Western Civilization program implemented during the 1950s at Hobart and William Smith colleges, mainly by faculty trained at Harvard. The first year of the course was required of all students, the second year required of those pursuing bachelor of arts degrees. Year one was divided into four units: the Hebrew Bible; Greek epic, history, and drama; Roman literature and history; and the New Testament. Elaborate briefings had been prepared for faculty teaching the course on each of the texts—and much of the content—to be taught, and the staff gathered every Friday afternoon over sherry to discuss the following week's work, the upcoming lectures, the briefings, and strategies for conducting the discussion sections.

From one point of view, such meetings, the lectures themselves—delivered in the main by senior colleagues—and the briefing books not only furnished a wonderful education for younger, new faculty, but they provided a commonality of experience for the students. As a recent dean at Hobart put it about another college's new (and different) core courses: "To separate ourselves into twelve separate courses would end the intellectual community that we, the faculty, are becoming within the program. While commonality can become a straightjacket that crushes creativity and spontaneity, we must continue to risk that our collective common sense will prevent the strangulation of intellectual growth among the program faculty" (Schmitz, 1992a, p. 50). From another point of view, however, all the efforts at coordination, in addition to the usual academic pressures toward conformity, operated to acculturate teachers, and through them students, to the course's ideological "line." That was expressed with disarming, if stunning, clarity in the 1950s course subtitle: "The Origins of Christian Civilization." In significant ways, the course pursued that central path: it certainly never deviated into Boasian comparative cultural study by considering, for example, originary stories or epics from outside the Western framework, nor did it for a moment ponder the implications, or even the facts, of Greek and Roman, much less American, slavery. Indeed, the course did not focus on what William H. McNeill has claimed to be the original "great idea" of such programs: Western history as the evolution of human freedom (McNeill, 1977). In fact, it was so constructed that Christianity seemed to spring ex nihilo as a climax less to history than to theology.

In about 1961, Lauter, then a young professor assigned to teach the course, mildly raised the great historical gap yawning between the Old and New testaments: Wasn't that worth discussing, even if the books were, in traditional

Protestant fashion, considered "Apocrypha"? Weren't there Jewish influences on early Christianity, on its theology as well as its culture, that might be of particular interest, among others, to the increasing number of Jewish students making their way through "Christian Civilization"? The older colleagues were considerate, judicious. Perhaps there ought to be a lecture on intertestamental literature; perhaps Lauter ought "to deliver it, as the one, ah, most concerned in it." Thus was expressed one fundamental dynamic of academic multiculturalism: if you are "it," you are *it*. That is, what you are supposed to know and be concerned about is, for many well-meaning people, derived from what you are in terms of race, gender, or ethnicity. From such essentialist assumptions arise the notions that women scholars are necessarily resident experts on women and ethnics on ethnicity.

More fundamentally, perhaps, this episode illustrates an early instance of the critique of general education curricula and core courses in particular that became widespread later in the 1960s. The problem, this critique maintained, was that existing curricula were incomplete, narrow, perhaps even biased. In the effort to construct a coherent, progressive narrative, they omitted too much, left out rather more of society, history, and culture than they put in. Earlier advocates of general education were rather more frank about this process of selection than some of its current champions. James Harvey Robinson (1926), in many respects the intellectual father of the 1920s Western civilization programs, wrote of his own development:

He then saw that if history was to fulfill its chief function and become an essential explanation of how our own civilization came to take the form it has, and present the problems that it does, a fresh selection from the records of the past would have to be made. Much that had been included in historical manuals would of necessity be left out as irrelevant or unimportant. Only those considerations would properly find a place which clearly served to forward the main purpose of seeing more and more distinctly how this, our present Western civilization, in which we have been born and are now immersed, has come about. (p. 4)

In the 1960s the early civil rights movement raised the demand to be let in—in to the front of the bus, to public accommodations, to the ballot box. Just so, the demand began to be raised for admission, open admission to decent schools, to all colleges, even to the curriculum. "Where," civil rights activists and students asked of courses of study, especially at mostly White institutions, "where are the Blacks?" And later, "Where are the women?" "Where are *we* in your texts, your bookshelves, your syllabi, your classrooms and faculties?"

These questions, raised with increasing intensity by the 1960s movements for social change, confronted the dominantly White and male academic establishment with dilemmas, exacerbated by the widening ruptures in the society over the war on Vietnam, the transition from civil rights to Black Power, and the advent of a new wave of feminist militancy. The intellectual basis for general education programs of any sort had been eroding since the response to *Sputnik* in 1957 accelerated a return to specialization. It became harder and harder to achieve consensus about what students ought to know—or at least to study. "When there is no longer *a* history, when history ceases to have a central narrative, there is no longer a logical necessity for students to know either the same facts or the same history" (Allardyce, 1982, p. 720). Indeed, grand narratives, whether those of Christianity, Marx, liberal democracy, or other traditions, would soon come under attack by deconstructionist critics. At the same time, partly in response to the perceived threat of Soviet technology, partly for other reasons, colleges and universities were rapidly expanding, thus providing unprecedented advancement opportunities to faculty (and administrators). Most faculty perceived that such opportunities were more likely to be available to those who pursued disciplinary specialties, who established professional reputations by publishing and speaking, than to those who devoted long hours to the variety of subjects with which one needed to work to teach in serious core programs (Bell, 1966). Many faculty were only too happy to see general education requirements dissolve and thus free them, guiltless, to pursue disciplinary self-advancement. In addition, the student movement of the 1960s demanded not only free speech but much freer choices in living arrangements and academic study. With the call for "relevance," students raised questions about the relation between the classroom and their lives; they decried the arbitrary powers of administrations and faculty, including those over curriculum, pointing to the (often) direct links between academic institutions and a government seemingly committed to war (Flacks, 1971; Long, 1969; one often-cited example was the Army Mathematics Research Center at the University of Wisconsin). Student questioning of the sources of this academic "illegitimate authority" accelerated the movement away from requirements altogether.

Furthermore, it would have been no easy task to reconstruct established core courses of study to be more inclusive, polycentric, responsive to a world of increasing diversity. What needed to be asked and what, therefore, omitted? On what educational or political bases could such judgments be grounded? For many faculty members, answering such questions felt rather like relearning the disciplinary alphabet. And, to be truthful, what we shall call the new scholarship on women and minority men was not very well developed by the late 1960s.

Important texts were not yet widely available, commentaries on them were few, historical narratives that linked new and traditional texts were just being disseminated or formulated. Educators had barely begun to consider the more fundamental changes in the underlying paradigms of disciplinary knowledge and therefore of curricula, of the existing structures of courses of study, that the new scholarship increasingly seemed to imply. And while the movements for social change systematically linked curricular change to opening the educational system to minority and female students *and* faculty, those links were not widely accepted within academe, and their implications were not systematically considered. All of these centrifugal forces contributed to the processes that, by the mid-1970s, had eliminated much of general education, and almost all core courses, from the academic landscape.

Meanwhile, a strategy of deepening and institutionalizing the new scholarship was pursued by advocates of Black studies, women's studies, and the other forms of ethnic minority programs that began to appear in the academy. This is not the place to examine these developments in detail (see Chapter 44, this volume). Broadly speaking, in its first stage, the new scholarship tried to answer with increasing detail the questions, "Where are the Blacks?" and "Where are the women?" It focused on a process of rediscovering history and culture that had largely been buried or forgotten, reexamining social, political, and economic structures that had marginalized women and minority men. And it concentrated on making the fruits of its searches available to scholars, students, and the wider public through new journals and presses—many of which were founded in the late 1960s or early 1970s—and in new courses such as those on women's history, African American literature, or the psychology of sex and gender differences. Syllabi of such new courses were shared in conferences as well as through publications such as the Female Studies series published alternatively by KNOW, Inc., and The Feminist Press. And academic structures such as Chicano studies, women's studies, and Black studies programs were created, or at least proposed, to accommodate such courses.

From these beginnings, advocates of the new scholarship had two curricular goals. One, of course, concerned establishing new courses, of the sort just mentioned, devoted to the primary concerns of feminist and multicultural scholarship. The other curricular goal had to do with transforming existing mainstream courses, like those in American history or introductory psychology, to include materials on minorities and White women (Howe & Lauter, 1980). The objective was simple: creating a course on women writers or on African American history might satisfy the goal of beginning to institutionalize the study of these subjects, but it also ran the risk of

ghettoizing them, along with the faculty and students interested in them. How, then, could one offer the fruits of the new scholarship to the wider academic community *except* by transforming in some measure the whole curriculum? This long-term effort, begun in the late 1970s, has continued unabated (Messer-Davidow, 2002). It has taken at least three forms that are of concern to us here. First, it has been directed at transforming baseline disciplinary courses (e.g., Berger, 1994; Foster & Herzog, 1994; Jarratt & Worsham, 1998; Katsiaficas & Kiros, 1998; Mahalingham & McCarthy, 2000), which often do double duty satisfying general education requirements, and the textbooks on which such courses generally depend. We will use as our example the Reconstructing American Literature project (c. 1978–1984) and the revisionist *Heath Anthology of American Literature* (first published in 1990; now, published by Houghton Mifflin, in its fourth edition), which was developed from that project. Second, efforts to broaden the impact of the new scholarship have taken the form of developing new required core courses that deal with matters of central concern to multicultural study, such as racial and sexual discrimination. We will use as our initial example Denison University's first-in-the-nation requirement, established in 1979. Third, attempts to transform curricula have been directed at existing as well as at new core requirements. We will use as our initial example the struggle between 1986 and 1988 over Stanford University's Western Culture program.

Before we turn to these specific examples, however, it will be useful to note that the events we will be chronicling took place during the second wave of the new scholarship (see Chapter 44, this volume). In this phase, the fundamental issue shifted from inclusion in existing curricular and intellectual paradigms to altering the paradigms and curricular structures themselves (Spanier, Bloom, & Boroviak, 1984). Literary, historical, economic, even religious canons came to be seen not as permanent fixtures of some transcendent culture, but as social constructions, mutable, historically contingent, subject to reformulation and reconstruction *by* people *in* time. Needless to say, such challenges to the long-standing norms of disciplinary study have been met with serious—at times hysterical—resistance. Moreover, as the postmodernism of commentators such as Fredric Jameson and Jean-François Lyotard challenged all overarching narratives—Christian, communist, Western, Islamic—reaction outside the academy against prophets of disbelief also heightened. It is within such an increasingly skeptical outlook and the initially enraged responses and later stiff accommodations to it, on the one hand, and an intensifying narcissistic and venal political economy of the 1980s and 1990s, on the other—in short, within a deeply conflicted society—that this early stage of the encounter of multiculturalism with core curricula has emerged and developed.

PARADIGM 1: TEXTBOOKS AND DISCIPLINARY-BASED CHANGE

The strategy one adopts to provide a core educational experience depends very much on how one defines that experience. For many reformers whose work was rooted in the new scholarship, one curricular goal has been wide student exposure to texts and materials on minorities and on White women, particularly in introductory courses, both formative for study in the major and available for general education credit. Such exposure, it has been expected, would help bring minority and female concerns into collegiate culture generally and into more advanced courses in the major in particular. This may, on the face of it, seem a modest goal indeed, especially compared with the name, *curriculum transformation*, given it. But narrative evidence suggests that in cultural study, including at least literature and writing, some students feel, as Victor Doyno of the State University of New York (SUNY), Buffalo, has put it, "authorized" by discovering "authors" like themselves who provide them with a sense of the "authority" necessary to write or to speak with conviction and power (Kennedy, 1991). It may be that for some students, perhaps for a majority in any given classroom, such processes of identification are relatively unimportant. Nevertheless, for some and perhaps many students, especially those from previously marginalized cultures, the effects of role model identification can be very significant (see, for example, McQuillen, 1992; Zaborowska, 1998). Moreover, as Cary Nelson (1993) has put it, a "priority placed on multicultural representation in the classroom helps persuade students about the priority of multicultural representation on the faculty and in the student body" (p. 47) and, implicitly, within the body politic.

Moreover, the goal of exposing most, or all, students to a particular set of ideas or texts does not altogether differ in intent—though certainly in content—from the objectives of those who have promoted Western civilization courses. They too assimilated general education to introductory disciplinary courses, especially in history, which they wished to fill with the varied content they named "Western civilization" (Allardyce, 1982).

The empirical evidence developed by Alexander Astin (1993) establishes significant correlations between certain collegiate environmental factors and desirable outcomes in student attitudes and behaviors. Astin writes:

As far as institutional policies and practices are concerned, this study has included two major indicators: Institutional Diversity Emphasis (having to do primarily with affirmative action and promotion of multiculturalism on campus), and Faculty Diversity Orientation (having to do mainly with the content both of the research that faculty members do and of the courses that they teach). The study also included several indicators of the individual student's direct experience with diversity activities: taking women's or ethnic or third world courses, participating in racial or cultural awareness workshops, discussing racial or ethnic issues, and socializing with someone from another racial or ethnic group. Generally speaking all these institutional and individual environmental experiences were associated with greater self-reported gains in cognitive and affective development (especially increased cultural awareness), with increased satisfaction in most areas of the college experience, and with increased commitment to promoting racial understanding. The same variables are also negatively associated with the development of materialistic values and with the belief that the individual can do little to change society. (pp. 430–431; Musil, 1992)

To be sure, "associated with" does not necessarily imply causality, and Astin does point out that the direct effects of curricula that emphasize minority, Third World, or women's studies materials, while not inconsequential, are not strong, especially as compared with peer relationships and student involvement with course content. But curricular choices do not take place in an institutional vacuum. Those active in developing multicultural and gender-fair courses recognized from the outset that efforts to translate the new scholarship into course work would influence and be affected by other institutional processes, including affirmative action hiring, departmental practices of curricular and personnel review (Dinnerstein, O'Donnell, & MacCorquodale, 1981; Spanier et al., 1984), recruitment of more diverse student bodies, and, perhaps most important, forms of pedagogy (Culley & Portuges, 1985; Maher, 1987; Sleeter & McLaren, 1995; Mayberry & Rose, 1999). Indeed, campus discussions of altering curricula would, over time, help engage more fundamental issues of institutional purposes and priorities. Thus, the modest goal of inclusion, as its conservative critics came to recognize, implied more, say, than adding to the American literature survey a Black and a woman and stirring lightly (Fiol-Matta & Chamberlain, 1994).

Two main bars to such curricular change appeared early in the process: the limits of knowledge even among faculty sympathetic to change and the lack of appropriate, available textbooks and other curriculum materials. The first problem, which lies beyond the scope of this chapter (see Schmitz, 1992a), has continued to be addressed in a variety of faculty development formats, though increasingly widespread changes in graduate programs have helped produce younger faculty more familiar with cultural diversity. The second issue—that of texts—has been engaged in most humanities and social science disciplines. For example, the Curriculum

Analysis Project in the Social Sciences, funded by the Women's Educational Equity Act from 1979 to 1981, developed content modules on sex and gender for use in introductory sociology, psychology, and microeconomics courses (Gappa & Pearce, n.d.). The American Anthropological Association brought scholars together with textbook authors to produce an *Introduction to Cultural Anthropology*. The Organization of American Historians produced a series of packets, directed to college faculty, for integrating material on women into a variety of history survey courses and into courses on Western civilization (Organization of American Historians, 1988; Fox-Genovese & Stuard, 1983). Led by Johnnella Butler and Margo Culley, a project at Amherst, Hampshire, Mount Holyoke, and Smith colleges and the University of Massachusetts published a collection of syllabi and other materials titled *Black Studies/Women's Studies: An Overdue Partnership* (Spanier et al., 1984). While significant research has now been published examining the impact of diversity requirements on institutions (Musil, Garcia, Moses, & Smith, 1995) and on students (Smith, 1997), we know of no comparably systematic evaluation of the impact of these and similar projects to disseminate curriculum materials (but see Musil et al., 2000). However, our experience indicates that, particularly in earlier stages of course change and before commercial publishers are willing to issue significantly altered textbooks, these projects have provided helpful models and otherwise unavailable materials.

Historical precedent also suggests something about the importance of such textbooks. "From the start," Gilbert Allardyce (1982) writes, "Western Civ traveled by textbook, and it was the success of particular works that helped standardize the course across the country" (p. 714). A similar conclusion may hold about the spread of multiculturalism, especially in certain disciplines such as literary study. The availability of a particular textbook may in fact underlie the construction of an entire course, as was the case in the Special Sections on Cultural Legacies of Tennessee State University's freshman composition course (Schmitz, 1992a; the text was *American Mosaic: Multicultural Readings in Context*, edited by Barbara Roche Rico and Sandra Mano). Moreover, as Cary Nelson (1993) has written:

The admissions policy embodied in the anthology makes an implicit comment on the admissions policy appropriate to the institution as a whole. Nor is it much of a leap to make a connection with the nation's admission policy—its immigration statutes and their mixed history of openness and racism. The problems of ethnic, racial, and gender representation in an anthology devoted to a national literature . . . speak quite directly to questions about representation in public debate and in legislative bodies. Anthologies empower students to make these connections whether or not teachers choose to make them explicit. (pp. 47–48)

Inversely, as Margaret Wilkerson (1992) has written, "When students who are members of those groups left out of our intellectual life are present on our campuses, their invisibility calls into question their right to be there, their intellectual capacities, and their very existence" (p. 59).

The Reconstructing American Literature (RAL) project, from which *The Heath Anthology of American Literature* developed, offers an instance in which such a disciplinary-based effort of curriculum transformation can be linked to both commercial development of the product and specific alteration of a variety of courses in American literature and American studies. The project, initiated at The Feminist Press in 1978, was initially supported by the federal Fund for the Improvement of Post-Secondary Education (FIPSE), and later by the Lilly Endowment and the Rockefeller Foundation, as well as by a number of colleges and universities. The project's objectives, more modest than its title, were summarized by its slogan: "So that the work of Frederick Douglass, Mary Wilkins Freeman, Agnes Smedly, Zora Neale Hurston and others is read with the work of Nathaniel Hawthorne, Henry James, William Faulkner, Ernest Hemingway and others."

In practice, RAL carried out a number of tasks. In June 1982, it held a two-week institute at Yale involving over 50 scholars focused on the theoretical and practical issues of transforming American literature courses. The institute helped establish a network of scholars working in the field, a process accelerated in subsequent years when, under the project's auspices, a number of workshops on the issues were held in different parts of the country. In addition, The Feminist Press published the project's collection of syllabi, essays, and other helpful materials as *Reconstructing American Literature* (Lauter, 1983).

The ultimate task of the project was to produce a seriously altered anthology of American literature that would include significant numbers of African American, Latino and Spanish, Native American, Asian American, and White women writers, as well as the canonical figures. To carry out that task, the editors adopted a number of innovations. Until this project, no person who was not White and only two who were not male had ever served on editorial boards of American literature anthologies. The fourteen-person editorial board for the RAL anthology was uniquely diverse: half of its members were White, half people of color, and half were male, half female; they came from every part of the country and from most kinds of collegiate institutions. But they were chosen not so much for their representational characteristics as for their expertise. By 1982, the field called American literature had grown so quickly and in so many new directions that no small group, certainly no one individual, could possibly have kept abreast of the new scholarship, much less the accelerating changes in disciplinary paradigms. A second innovation involved asking the literary profession at large, through mailings and meetings, which writers teachers wished to see included in such an anthology. The editors were thus able to draw on the expertise of literally hundreds of American literature scholars instead of being limited to what other anthologies had traditionally included or to their own graduate school training. Furthermore, this inclusive strategy helped widen the network of faculty interested in the project, develop their sympathies with the process of change in which it was implicated, and—not so incidentally—organize a constituency for the anthology once it was actually marketed.

Eight years elapsed between the beginning of the effort to edit an anthology and its actual publication as *The Heath Anthology of American Literature* (Lauter et al., 1990). During that period, the field of American literature continued to change in terms of both the texts that were seen to constitute it and the structure of history and culture used to frame and interpret them. It is probably fair to say that the *Heath Anthology* mainly confirmed the reality of these changes by embodying them in printed form and by gaining wide acceptance within the literary profession. The ongoing work of the project and then the very existence of the anthology and the differences in teaching it made possible accelerated change. It is, of course, hard to measure influence or to confirm causality in movements of culture. What is easy to demonstrate, however, are the differences in curricula before and after the *Heath Anthology* became available. *Reconstructing American Literature* contained American literature course syllabi that, for their time (1982–1983), were markedly advanced in terms of their inclusion of works by White women and African American writers. Compared with many of the syllabi now regularly published in the *Heath Anthology Newsletter* (probably the most widely circulated "journal" in the field of American literature), they appear extraordinarily limited, if not downright backward—at least with respect to multicultural content. A dramatic example of curricular change is provided by syllabi for two courses offered by Sherry Sullivan at the University of Alabama, Birmingham, in 1980 and then in 1990 using the *Heath Anthology* (Ch'maj, 1993).

To be sure, it is impossible to estimate the role of a single textbook in a much larger movement to alter one corner of the educational landscape, any more than one can trace out specifically curricular impacts on student thinking or values isolated from a variety of collegewide influences such as peer pressures, exposure to a diverse student body, or public commitments to creating an equitable environment. And it is logically fallacious to assume that what came after the publication of the *Heath Anthology* was caused by it. For all that, the instance offered by Sullivan's two syllabi is suggestive of the role a teaching tool can play in altering what actually is studied, and thus validated, in widely enrolled and culturally influential courses that help define campus climate as well as emphases in major study. Furthermore, the visibility of the anthology—it was, for example, the subject of a front-page story in the *Los Angeles Time,* a full-page story in the *Chronicle of Higher Education,* and reviews in *TLS,* the *Nation,* and other nonacademic journals—its marketplace success in a market-driven culture, and its subsequent imitation by other textbooks have helped to validate multicultural approaches to literary study and make them easier to carry out in practice.

PARADIGM 2: A DIVERSITY REQUIREMENT

In 1979, 11 years before the *Heath Anthology* was published, Denison University adopted a requirement in its core general education curriculum that focused on themes, topics, and texts central to multiculturalism: the results of racial and sexual discrimination. This requirement—stated in the University Senate minutes of May 15, 1978, as one in "Minority Studies/Women's Studies"—was the first of its kind in the nation.

The requirement was described (in institutional documents like the catalogue) in these terms:

Every Denison student enrolled in BA or BS programs shall complete a course dealing primarily with some or all of the following:

The nature and effects of discrimination against women and minority groups in America; the roles and significant contributions of women and minority groups in American society; the ways in which historical factors have shaped women's and minorities' participation in American life; the unique experiences, identity and art that these important groups have contributed to American culture; an examination of the moral values central to these issues.

The character of this requirement and the processes of its adoption provide a number of significant insights to understanding the relation of multiculturalism and core curricula.

Denison University seems, at first, an unlikely site for the emergence of so controversial a requirement. The student movements for change enacted at Berkeley, Columbia, and elsewhere had by the mid-1970s not produced analogous action at small, primarily conservative institutions like Denison. Yet a series of student actions informed by those political movements emerged on the Denison campus. And while no curricular models for multicultural and feminist changes in core curricula then existed, the experimental spirit of the times had filtered down even to small-town Ohio. Most important, perhaps, an unusual conjunction of factors at the university in the mid- and late 1970s proved enabling of the changes.

First, in terms of its influence on the development of the requirement, a strong, popular (highly enrolled) interdisciplinary women's studies course had been established by Ann Fitzgerald and Joan Straumanis in 1972 and taught every year. From the onset, this course had undergraduate teaching assistants (TAs) who led weekly discussion groups; the TAs took a seminar (for credit) that dealt with the readings for the course, pedagogy, and campus politics. Modeled as a graduate-level women's studies course, the seminar included the unusual element of self-consciously recognizing and discussing the fact that the students were employees of the university and therefore, in some sense, responsible for its shaping. The director of the women's studies course purposefully chose students for these roles who were campus leaders (often presidents of sororities or fraternities), thus creating a certain cachet for the course among students. The seminar, and in many respects the course itself, became an intriguing blend of controversy and trendiness, as, by extension, did the women's studies program. The visible student TAs, moreover, attracted other students in large numbers to the course, well over 100 in any given semester, on a campus that generally had 25 in a class. Given the residential nature of the campus, course topics spilled into dorm discussions and programs; the director of women's studies worked closely with the Dean of Students Office and residence hall assistants to ensure continuity between the curricular and residence life programs. A Women's Resource Center provided an additional hub of feminist activity. Feminist ideas were thus widely disseminated on an otherwise conservative campus.

Second, a Black studies program had been established in 1969 with a director and a number of departmental offerings. Thus, there existed a locus for the examination of curricular ideas focused on race, especially in its American manifestations. Together with the establishment of Black studies, a number of influential White and tenured faculty had instituted courses on these issues within their own departments. Once again, therefore, educational ideas about race and racism had been widely disseminated across the campus, at least among the faculty.

Closely related to the Black studies program, though independent from it, was the Black Student Union, a student organization provided with both a lounge and meeting space and a budget by the Denison administration. The Black Student Union had the ability, demonstrated during the final stages of the debate over the requirement, to mobilize its members to respond to incidents of campus racism. Within the student community, in fact, a cadre of Black and feminist students organized through the Black Student Union, the Women's Resource Center, and the TA program in women's studies played a significant leadership role. The large majority of students at the university were White, upper middle class, and unused to thinking about power; nevertheless, as the process of pushing for a requirement went on, they became increasingly intrigued by the power they began to find they could wield.

Third, ongoing administrative leadership was provided by the provost, Louis Brakeman, and the president, Robert Good, both political scientists with substantial academic and political backgrounds in global education and policy and well informed about and committed to the importance of multiculturalism and affirmative action. They helped to encourage a campus climate of self-reflection and self-criticism. They also fostered a widely felt need to grapple with the problem of creating a sense of community, a need forced by the reality of Denison's being a small residential college in a small Ohio town. And they provided material support to the development both of curricular innovations such as Black and women's studies and departures in student activities such as the Black Student Union.

Fourth, Denison's faculty was, in keeping with its commitment to undergraduate teaching, involved in the problem of student development both inside and outside the classroom and alert to the connections. The faculty were, not surprisingly, inclined to be more progressive than the students. Moreover, many shared an educational philosophy fostering interdisciplinary study of global education and some experience in its implementation.

Last, but by no means least, Denison retained a well-established and rather unquestioned system of general education core requirements. Unlike most other colleges of its kind, Denison had maintained traditional requirements throughout the turbulent 1960s and 1970s, so there was, rather ironically, an existing educational core and mission statement, which the proponents of multiculturalism could invoke.

The factors we have listed influenced the debates leading to adoption of the requirement and to the particular character of its final shape. Yet many or most of these factors have, we think, been critical in the development of virtually all multicultural core requirements.

The idea for proposing what became the "minority studies/women's studies" requirement grew out of a series of meetings convened by members of the women's studies, Black studies, and Latin American studies staffs to discuss their differences and disagreements and to express common concerns about the racism and sexism on the Denison campus, primarily among students. The original core requirement proposed by that coalition of groups was a course focused "on the nature and effects of discrimination in the United States." Local reality, the sense of urgency forced by the prejudices evident in everyday campus life, thus shaped the design. For example, the "American multiculturalists" saw the "internationalists" as diverting attention away from the conditions of campus and community life and thus pushed for the explicit focus on the United States. The result was, in the long run, a requirement that emphasized America—a word repeated no fewer than four times in four (out of the five) final criteria for the course.

The proposal also specified that "this requirement shall be added to the existing General Education requirements," at that time all departmental, disciplinary courses designed to provide breadth for students. This provision signaled the special nature of this requirement: women and minorities were to be included, added to the existing core curriculum in the form of distinct courses, much the way that women's studies and Black studies had been added as separate programs, alongside the traditional departments. At the same time, this provision took advantage of the fundamental tendency in American higher education to innovate by addition. The new did not displace the existing core requirements but extended them into realms increasingly seen as important to the educational program.

Once an initial proposal to establish a requirement was submitted to the growing Academic Affairs Committee in December 1977, a combination of normal academic procedures and unusual political activities influenced its shaping and final passage. This link was hardly distinctive in its time—or, indeed, as the example of Stanford suggests, in later moments. Discussion centered on the criteria to be used to determine which courses might count toward satisfying the requirement and on what body would administer the criteria and thus effectively oversee implementation of the requirement. The issues have become familiar: Should courses dealing with societies and events outside the United States count? Should courses whose content is primarily cultural or artistic rather than social or political be included? Similarly, should the requirement be administered by those most deeply involved—the faculty of Black studies and women's studies—by a presumptively objective group, or by some combination thereof? Even within the best-intentioned faculty, such discussions can slow movement to a flypaper crawl. However, a series of particularly vivid and campus-shattering racial incidents in the spring of 1978 precipitated final action.

One of these incidents—hardly unique to fraternity practice—occurred the day prior to the first student hearing on the proposal, sponsored by the Academic Affairs Committee. The incident had involved a group of White fraternity members appearing at a spring event in blackface; members of the Black Student Union confronted them. Five days after that hearing, women's studies students attended the annual meeting of the Great Lakes Colleges Association Women's Studies Conference, where the events on the Denison campus were a major focus. After this conference, the women's studies students initiated meetings with the Black Student Union, and, together in teams, they met with each member of the Academic Affairs Committee. A second hearing for student response to the proposed requirement was held later in April, followed by the first demonstration held on the Denison campus in 10 years. Students argued with recalcitrant faculty that they, the students, needed the requirement, that more needed to be done to eradicate the pervasive racism and sexism from the campus, that the curriculum was a logical place for addressing this educational need, and that it was all right with them to add another requirement. Although there was sufficient administrative and faculty support to pass the requirement, it was finally student pressure that brought it out of the contentious slough of institutional haggling into an unusually popular reality.

This part of the process was, to be sure, deeply inflected by quite local events. At the same time, these events serve to dramatize the general importance of student involvement in creating curricular—in this case, multicultural—change. Indeed, they raise a question about the viability of recent administrative efforts to impose such requirements or related codes of campus speech. At Denison, top-level administrative support was critical to inaugurating the requirement, but the decisive word here is *support,* not initiation. Senior administrators helped foster respect for the work being done in women's studies and Black studies, and they provided funds not only to set up a Women's Resource Center and a Black Student Union, but also for faculty research on women and minorities and for teaching about them. But the major initiatives arose from coalitions of concerned faculty and students.

The Denison process also calls attention to the deep connection between race and gender discrimination and the development of such "minority studies/women's studies" general education requirements. As the student arguments put it: "What do you do about racism and sexism in an educational community? You teach about them." While few, if any, argued that the requirement did not have a strong basis in scholarly information and ideas, the engine behind the students' self-expressed desire for the course was not pure academic knowledge but social issues. Thus, the central criterion determining whether a course might count toward this requirement was whether its major focus—in the language of the day—was the "nature and effect of discrimination against women and/or minorities."

One may draw a number of other conclusions from this brief narrative. A central one involves change within departments. Certain courses already in place, administered and staffed by the existing women's studies and Black studies programs, had a multicultural and/or feminist focus; they offered a base and perspective, a locus of momentum and expertise for developing the requirement. But these programs were small and interdisciplinary—for example, they depended on individual departments to house separate courses—and thus could provide only a few of the 15 or so courses that came to count toward satisfying the requirement. Thus, the traditional departments themselves had to assume primary responsibility for developing and staffing the courses. Departmental involvement was entirely optional; no department was ever mandated to change courses, develop new ones, or contribute staff for the requirement. However, there was considerable encouragement, and at times pressure, to do so from the segments of the community that had helped initiate the requirement: faculty, administration, and students (Gold, 1997). Furthermore, the dynamics of academic cost accounting encouraged departments to participate: required courses meant student enrollments, and increased enrollments meant increased budgets.

In order to fulfill the requirement, departmental courses had to meet the specified criteria existing outside departmental structures under the umbrella of general education. Therefore, if they wanted to participate in this component of the core curriculum, departments had to develop a bipolar vision, working both inside and outside their own educational and political paradigms. In order to accomplish this, departments could transform existing offerings or, alternatively, develop new courses. As the requirement was being put into practice, the latter strategy—designing new departmental courses to fulfill the requirement and hiring faculty to teach them—became the dominant one. It was initially more expedient than facing the resistance of some traditional faculty and the inertia of courses entrenched in the catalogue; it did, however, mean that departments were forced to rethink their hiring priorities (Talburtt, 1988) since additional lines of funding were not made available to them. That process, it would appear, had effects that could not initially have been anticipated. With certain other internal and external factors, it fostered the institutionalization of knowledge about the teaching of materials on women and minorities within the traditional departments that constitute the basic framework of the academy. The graduation requirement thus became a major factor in producing a striking degree of curricular and research change at Denison (Talburtt, 1988).

What has been less subject to research analysis until recently was the impact of the requirement on student and faculty culture (see Appel, Cartright, Smith, & Wolf, 1996; Musil et al., 1995; Smith, 1997). As we indicated above, a number of factors, including the campus leadership roles played by women's studies TAs, helped bring the academic concerns of women's studies courses in particular into the residential life of the student population at large. For a significant number of students, that linkage helped foster what Alexander Astin (1993) has pointed to as critical to changing student attitudes and ideas: peer group engagement. It is unclear, however, whether this phenomenon has persisted over the years, although the anecdotal evidence related at a 10th anniversary celebration of the

"minority studies/women's studies" requirement at Denison suggested that it had. Still, continuing study of the long-term impacts of such requirements on faculty and student culture and performance seems to us important to understanding their value as a major interface of multiculturalism with core curricula. The James Irvine Foundation has supported such studies through the Office of Diversity, Equity and Global Initiatives of the American Association of Colleges and Universities, initially to examine the variety of campus diversity requirements and their impacts (Humphreys, 2000), and more recently to evaluate the foundation's Campus Diversity Initiatives project and other curriculum diversity efforts (American Association of Colleges and Universities, 2002).

PARADIGM 3: RECONSTRUCTING "WESTERN CIVILIZATION"

In our third model of a core curriculum, students take a mandated sequence of courses, the content of which, in this century, has generally focused on Western civilization. Such courses, it has usually been said, provide students with a common intellectual experience by exposing them to a unified narrative of America's inherited Western culture, a narrative conveyed usually by a set of core texts, often referred to as "great books" (Brann, 1993), and by a series of lectures traditionally delivered by members of history departments. Debates about Western civilization and the curricula devised to represent it to undergraduates have, we have noted, waxed and waned throughout the 20th century, subject to changing social and intellectual imperatives and to the economic and ideological needs of the nation and the university. Thus, the curricula of such courses are always potentially in a state of flux, subject to the normal academic process of review, revision, and change (Bell, 1966). The logic internal to the curricular process mandates that widely taken courses—core courses absorbing vast amounts of institutional resources—be routinely reevaluated and that questions concerning common intellectual experiences be openly debated. This is the work expected of faculty, administrators, and, increasingly, students.

Yarmolinsky (1992) has noted the importance of the process by which faculty in particular determine curricula:

The faculty cannot always, or even usually, be expected to agree on what should go into the syllabus. But they must be free to reach their own decisions by their own processes, without interference from outsiders of whatever political persuasion. . . . Whatever their political differences, faculty members are forced by the nature of the academy to argue them out in what purports to be rational terms. And they are further required to reach at least a second-order agreement—to agree on the nature and extent of their disagreements so that the institution can function. (p. 74)

What happened at Stanford University, then, between 1986 and 1988 during its revision of the Western Culture program was not in itself remarkable as an instance of the process of curricular change, nor was the questioning of the existing core along multicultural lines, which had been a hallmark of curricular debate for at least two decades, at Stanford as well as at numerous other colleges and universities across the nation (Bell, 1966).

Rather, what was remarkable about these somewhat routine academic processes was that they reached the front pages of *Time* and *Newsweek*, the *New York Times*, and the *Wall Street Journal* (Hitchens, 1988). In a prolonged and well-orchestrated media campaign generated primarily by William Bennett, then secretary of education and later President George H. W. Bush's general in the war on drugs, and supported by neoconservative politicians and commentators, the "Stanford controversy" came to be less an educational debate about core curricula than one of national political identity. The very questioning of the existing core list of readings and the suggestion that it be altered to reflect minority, female, and non-Western cultures and voices, texts, and paradigms was deemed to augur the fall of Western civilization, the destruction of all that was best and brightest ("The Changing Curriculum: Then and Now," 1991; Hook, 1989). What occasioned this alarm at the national level and what fueled the media coverage was the recognition that general education (e.g., a core curriculum) was to be taken seriously as a form of public policy (Parekh, 2000). Bennett used Stanford to indicate that the government had needs to fulfill in educating and shaping its citizens; his actions, speeches, and writings (and those of other neoconservative commentators such as Allan Bloom, Sidney Hook, and George Will) all served to underscore the fact that a core curriculum, especially at one of the nation's elite universities, has far-reaching political implications (Bossman, 1991; McNew, 1992; Slevin, 1996). The national media reflected the real politics of diversity the nation faced (encoded in the proposed multicultural curricular components for the Stanford core curriculum)—at this near end-of-the-century—by mourning in 20th-century words and pictures the death, yet again, of Socrates, this time under the sunny skies of California, amid the palms of Stanford's campus. Stanford's story was used as synecdoche: the part taken for the whole of what was going awry with the nation at large, beset with a plurality of groups with competing identities and claims for inclusion, and even demands for a fundamental shift in America's national story (Ravitch, 1990). As the politicians, commentators, and media all pointed out in alarm, the center of the core was not holding.

In light of this national controversy spawned by the pedestrian academic processes at Stanford, it is important to see what really happened on the campus that occasioned such attention. The center of attention was a year-long, three-quarter course entitled "Western Culture," required of all freshman and transfer students. As was the case with many other similar programs across the country, this one had historical antecedents in an earlier core course on Western civilization, established in 1935 and taught (in large lectures) primarily by the history department until the course, along with most other requirements, was eliminated in the late 1960s. Efforts to restore a similar requirement were begun in 1975 by members of the faculty in the humanities, a two-year pilot was launched in 1978, and the program was fully implemented in 1980. The shape of the program was the result of much debate, compromise, and political trading on the part of all of the parties and departments involved; there were, in fact, seven other competing proposals for a cultural requirement. The ground, then, on which the program was developed was already heavily contested (Carnochan, 1993).

Unlike its Western civilization predecessor, "Western Culture" offered students a choice among eight different tracks or sequences, each housed and staffed in different departments within the humanities (many of the details of this history are drawn from Thomas, 1991; she was administrator of the program during this period). The course would generally have over half of its five weekly meetings in seminar discussion groups (a pedagogical factor allowing for even more variation among the groups within a given track than, say, a series of common lectures for all students in that track). Lectures were generally given by specialists in the departments housing the track, and the seminar discussions were led by younger Ph.D.s, hired in national searches to teach exclusively in the Western Culture program. Because these seminar leaders were employed on nontenure track contracts, the resulting turnover in staff undoubtedly led to a diversity in viewpoints and intellectual priorities within the program. It is important to recognize that one of the ostensible goals of the course, the creation of a "common intellectual experience," was thus vitiated from the start.

What gave these different tracks their common bond was a core list of readings, 15 required and 18 strongly recommended. Each track would weave around these works other materials related to the particular theme devised by the department offering the track. The list itself then became the true core, rather than the particular uses to which that list might be put, pedagogically, educationally, or politically. Ironically (especially in the light of the way the program changes were described by Bennett and others), the very list was not even conceived of as a canon; initially, the program's designers envisioned the core list as changing and evolving on some regular basis under the direction of an academic oversight committee. This did not in fact happen because participants who developed the list reported that "the difficulty of negotiating the list was one source of its permanence: the process had been so painful and so lacking in intellectual integrity that no one expressed the slightest desire to repeat it" (Pratt, 1990, p. 12).

The 15 required works that rose quietly to canonized stature in the Western Culture program were the following:

Ancient World
Hebrew Bible, *Genesis*
Plato, *Republic,* major portions of books 1–7
Homer, major selections from *Iliad, Odyssey,* or both
At least one Greek tragedy
New Testament, selections including a Gospel

Medieval and Renaissance
Augustine, *Confessions,* 1–9
Dante, *Inferno*
More, *Utopia*
Machiavelli, *The Prince*
Luther, *Christian Liberty*
Galileo, *The Starry Messenger, The Assayer*

Modern
Voltaire, *Candide*
Marx and Engels, *Communist Manifesto*
Freud, *Outline of Psychoanalysis, Civilization and Its Discontents*
Darwin, selections

This is the list that, together with its companion group of 18 "strongly recommended" works, was so enthusiastically defended and whose demise was so heatedly contested in the national arena (e.g., Phillips, 1988). The list reveals a lack of specificity (*a* "Greek tragedy" on the required list and *a* "Shakespearean tragedy" and *a* "nineteenth-century novel" on the recommended) juxtaposed with a highly specific Eurocentric focus.

When this list was constituted in 1980 and the Western Culture program begun, the program had already built into it the opportunity for significant variation. For example, in 1986, the seven tracks of the program were: History; Humanities; Conflict and Change in Western Culture; Philosophy; Great Books; Structured Liberal Education; and Technology, Science, and Society (Thomas, 1991). Given this range of focuses, there was considerable difference among the sequences and quite different intellectual and pedagogical contexts in which the core list could be read and interpreted. Nevertheless, the core list served as the locus for the ideological definition of the program for both those who supported retaining it and those arguing for change (McNew, 1992). In the case of the former, the list offered a universally agreed-on

narrative of "our" American heritage, based on the works of Western civilization tested by time and conveying truths that transcended a particular ethnic heritage or historical moment (Hook, 1989). For the latter, the list displayed a narrow canonical "Eurocentric paradigm" (Pratt, 1990) and an equally narrow sense of Europe, along with a "monumentalist attitude" to the texts themselves.

The process of change, then, took place against a backdrop of continuing debate and centered on something allegedly concrete: "The List." And as we have noted, there were from the beginning a series of factors opening the Western Culture program to modification and rational disagreement: the variation among the tracks, the potential for the list to be changed, the different faculty members and different pedagogical formats used within a given track, and the oversight committee's disregard of the increasing reluctance of some faculty to teach all of the required works.

The local academic and institutional context also played an enabling role in the process of reform. Stanford had an established series of minority and women's studies courses and faculty members who themselves were leading scholars in the educational movements to transform intellectual paradigms along multicultural lines; some of these scholars were the new Ph.D.s teaching in the Western Culture program. Students, 40% of whom were minorities, were also quite active on campus, coming together in relatively strong organizations with a willingness to form coalitions. The initial, formal, public move to openly question the Western Culture program and its canon came from the students in the form of a statement from the Black Student Union. The statement issued to the faculty and administration called for the inclusion of issues of race, sex, and ethnicity in the core list of readings: The "current program is a disservice to the Stanford community because of its failure to acknowledge the contributions [to] and impact of women and people of color on American and European culture" (Thomas, 1991, p. 10). This call resonated in a world of existing student activism (e.g., Rainbow Coalition organizing, antiapartheid protests) and increasing faculty discontent with the narrowness of the core list (a discontent made manifest by the fact that not all were using the readings). There was thus a union of unmet needs.

In response to these concerns, in October 1986, a university task force was formed to review the entire program. The committee released an interim report in the autumn of 1987 specifying that the course be renamed "Cultures, Ideas, and Values" (CIV) and that it focus on issues relating to class, ethnicity, race, religion, gender, and sexual orientation; courses were to examine at least one European and one non-European culture. A final draft of the report then passed to the faculty senate, where it was debated during the spring of 1988. Throughout this period, the faculty-staff newspaper, *Campus Report*, printed all letters and recorded speeches related to the controversy, and the senate carried on its debate in open forums, allowing all visitors with prepared statements to speak. Thus, the members of the Stanford community were engaged in an open, if heated, exchange about a core syllabus and course objectives—surely "a faculty prerogative as well as an obligation" (Yarmolinsky, 1992, p. 74). Indeed, the senate, composed of 55 senior faculty and former administrators (for the most part, White male faculty from science and professional schools), would pass the final verdict. Before it could do so, however, what had been an academic process exploded into the national press when Bennett (1984) described the process as "curriculum by intimidation."

The entry into this academic process of Bennett, Hook, conservative commentators, and the national print and television media cast the debate as itself something unnatural, undesirable, and dangerous. The introduction of multicultural components in the core course became synonymous with what Bennett called the "dropping of the West" and others deplored as "leaving students ignorant of the works of genius that lie at the heart of their own civilization." In this respect, political outsiders to the ongoing discussion succeeded in interfering with the university's processes and shaping its politics. In another, perhaps more significant, sense, the revisions of Stanford's core curriculum became an arena in which differing political visions of America's cultural heritage were contested.

It was finally the faculty in the program itself that crafted a compromise, a "second-order agreement," that enabled the senate to break an increasingly conflicted deadlock and vote in favor of the new CIV. The course would provide a "common intellectual experience" by focusing on certain common elements (issues, authors, texts, or themes) that would be decided on each spring by those teaching the course. Each year the core would change, the canon thereby ceasing to exist. The process of compromise emphasizes how critical to the harmonious functioning of core curricula is the involvement of the faculty charged with its implementation.

But one might draw other lessons as well. One is that core curricula are never free of political agendas (Jackson & Solís, 1995; Mio & Awakuni, 2000). Although the prominence of Stanford undoubtedly occasioned the amount of national attention drawn to its revisions, any such discussion will contain, covertly or openly, conflicting political agendas. These can, of course, be minimized; yet there may be significant educational value in opening to reasoned discussion the connections between political and curricular objectives.

Moreover—a point to which we will return below—in practice, the final shape of the CIV program deviated remarkably little from its Western Culture ancestor. From this fact, one might draw a number of different conclusions. Conservatives succeeded in minimizing what were to them objectionable changes; inertial forces within a university are remarkably strong; Western civilization contains within itself enormous gravitational forces that may, in practice, conflict with the development of significant multicultural study. Whatever the balance of truth in these hypotheses, the Stanford experience adumbrates many of the issues with which advocates of core curricula on the Western Civilization model must contend.

SOME INFERENCES

In large measure, the many intersections of core curricula with multiculturalism can be framed within one or another of the paradigmatic cases we have discussed—or by some combination of them.

In institutions that define core learning experiences loosely as those provided by a range of introductory courses, some combination of which is mandated by a breadth requirement, the issue for those concerned with multiculturalism is the extent to which the content of such courses has been significantly affected by the new scholarship (see Butler & Walter, 1991). American literature or American history can be mandated as requirements for students, but that does not at all guarantee that the concerns of multiculturalism will be addressed. Even the wide popularity of the *Heath Anthology* and the significantly enhanced diversity of its main competitor, the *Norton Anthology*, do not guarantee that faculty will assign or students read what continue to be perceived as non-canonical works.

The impact of the *Heath Anthology* and of analogous revisionary textbooks in other fields has been primarily within particular academic disciplines. But as these have changed, as once marginalized writers like Frederick Douglass, Harriet Jacobs, Charlotte Perkins Gilman, or José Martí have found places in literary curricula, the possibilities for multicultural approaches to core curricula have accelerated. Faculty knowledge, student interest, and textbook validation developed within majors and in graduate study pay off in changes in what is acceptable and, more to the point, what is really possible in general education. Widespread changes in academic majors—at least in the humanities and the social sciences—have an additional impact: they go a significant way in overcoming the problem that students come to regard diversity as a kind of curricular hurdle they must overcome by completing some required core course. To transform the major is to reinforce the fundamental message of the multicultural core curriculum rather than ghettoizing it as yet one more tedious requirement. Thus, revisionary textbooks play roles in both the alteration of academic specialties and in core sequences in which they might not, or might, be used.

Other institutions define the core educational experience as classroom exposure to issues directly affecting women, minority men, or non-Westerners. Estimates were that as of 1990, a useful base year, 46% of four-year colleges and universities (fewer among two-year institutions—Levine & Cureton, 1992) required a course on world civilizations and at least 20% a course with racial or ethnic content (El-Khawas, 1991, cited by Carnegie Foundation for the Advancement of Teaching, 1992). These figures represent a marked increase from earlier trends noted by the Carnegie Foundation for the Advancement of Teaching. In 1985, its report indicated that "international/global education" requirements had increased to 14.6% of institutions, up from 4.5% in 1970; that in the same time period, "Third World studies" requirements were up from 2.9% to 7.9%, and "women's studies" requirements up from zero to 1.6% of institutions reporting (Carnegie Foundation for the Advancement of Teaching, 1992). By 2000, a survey by the American Association of Colleges and Universities showed that 54% of U.S. institutions had a diversity requirement in place (mainly a single course), and another 8% were in the process of developing one (Humphreys, 2000). For institutions planning or examining such requirements, the Denison experience may be helpful, as may a variety of American Association of Colleges and Universities publications (including Musil et al., 1995; American Association of Colleges and Universities, 1998).

An increasing number of institutions have devised, or are trying to develop, mandated core sequences, usually with a significant emphasis on aspects of Western civilization. The studies we have just cited show an increase from 43.1% of institutions reporting in 1970, to 48.5% in 1985, to 53% in 1990 (Carnegie Foundation for the Advancement of Teaching, 1992; Gaff & Wasescha, 1991). For the many colleges and universities moving in this direction, the debates at Stanford may prove relevant, as is the issue of universality versus particularism, to which we will turn in a moment.

In the remainder of this chapter, we will examine what seem to us some of the central tensions, introduced earlier, that emerge in efforts to sustain or develop forms of core educational experience significantly inflected by multiculturalism.

MULTICULTURALISM AND CORE CURRICULA: TENSIONS AND POSSIBILITIES

An instructor from the Western civilization courses of 50 years ago coming to most of today's crop would be surprised, perhaps even shocked, to discover the little role

that history now plays. Where once "European history [was] the integrating discipline of general education programs" (Allardyce, 1982, p. 709), today's courses are organized mainly along thematic or conceptual lines, rather like those at the University of Chicago in the 1930s. There, "artistic works were studied not within the flux of historical change, where everything was relative to time and to place, but within genres, forms, or topics that were deemed to be timeless or recurring in human creative production" (p. 711). For example, an administrator at Fairleigh Dickinson University described the rationale for Core II, "The American Experience: The Quest for Freedom," in the following terms:

In Core II, we begin with an analysis of the sacred texts of the American "Western Tradition": the Bill of Rights, the Declaration of Independence, the Gettysburg address, the Battle Hymn of the Republic, and King's "I Have a Dream" speech. As we read these works, we ask our students, who are "all men"? What is the basis of individual rights? Are we a religious people? What is the American dream and who is included in it? (cited in Schmitz, 1992a, p. 16)

Similarly, the University of Richmond's interdisciplinary core course was organized around themes such as "Moral Order," "Social Order," and "Familiar Order." The "Social Order" unit brought together quite diverse texts—*Sundiata,* Mencius, Rousseau's *Discourse on the Origins of Inequality,* and Freud's *Civilization and Its Discontents* (Schmitz, 1992a)—necessarily removed from any deeply informative historical context (other similar strategies are illustrated in "Exploring the Complexities of Culture," 1991). It is not that history has disappeared, but as Schmitz put it, "nearly all the new courses [associated with the 'Cultural Legacies' project of the Association of American Colleges] are interdisciplinary, based on primary texts, and thematically organized" (p. 41).

The contraction of the role of history in most Western civilization and similar mandated core courses has itself to be seen historically in relation to the intense debate—the so-called culture wars—carried on in the 1980s and 1990s over the issue of universality and particularism in the curriculum. Many new Western civilization programs have been supported and significantly encouraged by the National Endowment for the Humanities, two of whose chairpersons in the 1980s and 1990s were strong partisans of a great books approach to core humanities study. That strategy poses the value of such texts precisely in terms of their universal qualities, their ability to transcend the vagaries of time and place. They are best studied, therefore, in their own terms or perhaps in relation to other isolated texts; implied herein is a formalist methodology linked to a great ideas focus of the sort popularized by Bennett (1984). The revival of historicized study in literature, the arts, and other areas of culture has not only been associated with Marxist and poststructuralist ideologies but has insisted on examining the cultural work that texts perform in specific historical moments. Indeed, new historicists argue that the very meaning of a text will change in changing circumstances; thus, texts need to be read within the particular contexts they inhabit (Kennedy, 1991). The role of the interpreter is not primarily to discover the universal in the particularities of a text, but to understand "what forces, social, economic, aesthetic, technological, have come together to produce this thing in this place at this time" (Lauter, 2001, p. 15).

This phenomenon is partly a legacy of the history of general education programs: those grounded in the humanities, where, as we have pointed out, the study of "monuments of unaging intellect" has been traditional, are less likely to focus on social issues such as difference than programs based in the social sciences. If one wishes to emphasize issues and problems of difference—multiculturalism, gender, sexual orientation, class, disability, age—in the core educational experience presented to students, one is more likely to build courses around specific historical and social problems. For example, "American cultures courses," like that adopted at Temple, "cover the evolution of such ideas as equality of opportunity, classlessness, social mobility, and equality under the law. Studies in Race courses examine the impact of race and racism on social, cultural, and political institutions" (Humphreys & Schneider, 1997). Such courses may be exemplified by SUNY Buffalo's sophomore-level "American Pluralism and the Search for Equality"; by the University of California at Berkeley's Ethnic Studies course "Racial Inequality in America: A Comparative Historical Perspective," initially taught by Ronald Takaki (1991) and later by Herb Green (1996; cf. Wilkerson, 1992); or by Oregon State's (2002) "Difference, Power, and Discrimination Program," which "works to create a more inclusive curriculum that addresses issues of race, class, gender, sexual orientation, and other institutionalized systems of inequality" (http://www.osu.orst.edu/dept/dpd/). The SUNY Buffalo course was designed to deal with race, ethnicity, gender, class, and religion and to "provide undergraduate students with an intellectual awareness of the causes and effects of structured inequalities and prejudicial exclusion in the United States and of processes leading to a more equitable society." Its various sections used books that emphasize the social sciences and history, like Paula Rothenberg's *Race, Class, and Gender in the United States* and Ronald Takaki's *A Different Mirror: A History of Multicultural America*, as well as individual texts like speeches by Sojourner Truth and essays by Simone de Beauvoir and Studs Terkel ("Exploring the Complexities of Culture," 1991).

Along similar lines, Rockland (New York) Community College adopted as a graduation requirement for all associate degree students an approved three-credit "course on pluralism and diversity in America." The basic course designed to satisfy this requirement, "Pluralism and Diversity in America," was described in the catalogue as follows:

Course designed to engage the student in the increasingly important issues of cultural, ethnic and racial diversity in America. The student will explore: acculturation; class; communication and the interrelationships between culture and language; cultural customs; family, gender and sexuality; heritage; race and ethnicity; religion and ideology; and stereotypes.

Most, though not all, of the readings were drawn from social science disciplines, and the frequently used videos focused on subjects such as "American Tongues," "Customs," "Gender," and "Racism 101." But such approaches are not necessarily neutral either. The Western heritage can be universalized by devoting major institutional resources (and student time) to it in the form of studying presumably cosmic texts, existing in the grand isolation of an aesthetic empyrean; by contrast, the cultural heritage of "others" may be approached through social scientific analyses, which, by embedding them in particular societies and histories, implicitly deny their "universality" (cf. Schmitz, 1992b).

A historically organized "Survey of Western Civilization Since 1648" at William Patterson College presented something of a middle ground but also underlined the tensions we have been exploring. An instructor faced two problems in revising the course: how to "engage our students in a relationship with their collective past" (a telling variation from the traditional objectives of Western civilization courses) and how to integrate material on women and minorities into the course (Tirado, 1987). She noted that certain topics elicited high levels of participation among her often resentful (because the course is required), busy (because a large majority work 20 and more hours per week), heterogeneous, and poorly prepared students. These included "economic and social changes of European society," "the relationship between slavery and the Western economics," and "changes in women's roles and the character of the family" (p. 36). Retaining a familiar organization for the survey course, the instructor shifted significantly the questions she asked students to pursue. For example,

Traditionally, we ask what factors explain the Industrial Revolution's birth in England? Further, we ask what the relationship was between industrialization and the Agricultural Revolution, with its higher yields, enclosures, and the freeing of agricultural labor for incorporation into other sectors of the economy. But we may also ask what the links were between the slave trade and the English textile industry, the heart of the English Industrial Revolution. What were the implications of this first industrial revolution for the non-Western world? Non-Western nations became providers of raw materials and labor and consumers of European manufactured goods. The textile industry benefited from a seemingly ever-expanding market, which gave the impetus for further industrial growth. How were non-European countries, such as India, once a major producer of textiles, de-industrialized? Students were assigned essays on women's roles in the Industrial Revolution. Specifically, they were to analyze the separation between the public and private spheres and how that separation affected women's position in society. (p. 40)

In the course, students read a number of texts they might also have found in more traditional great books formats: Hobbes's *Leviathan,* Locke's "Treatise of Civil Government," Montesquieu's "Spirit of the Laws," Wollstonecraft's "Vindication of the Rights of Woman," *The Communist Manifesto,* excerpts from Ruskin's *Sesame and Lillies.* But these were encountered in a changed intellectual framework that reflected the desire of state education authorities to encourage a "gender perspective" in traditional courses (Braun, 1987).

Coming from a traditionally defined discipline, this course evokes questions similar to those raised above about the tension between thematic and historicized organizational principles and the relationship of this problem to including multicultural and gender concerns. It suggests that the issue can be less—or, at any rate, not only—the texts themselves than the structures within which they are framed. Mount Holyoke's "Pasts and Presences in the West" has explored classical texts and "Western heritages as a series of problems and values to be analyzed and reinterpreted, not as a sequence of ideas and institutions," or as a set of sacred documents. It used Adrienne Rich's "Toward a Woman-Centered University" and David Tracy's *Plurality and Ambiguity* to introduce a unit on the ancient Greeks that presents Herodotus, Thucydides, and *Antigone* as performing significant cultural work in fifth-century Athens and today ("Exploring the Complexities of Culture," 1991, p. 47).

The tension we are outlining is by no means new. Daniel Bell poses a similar conflict between history and analysis as one of three antinomies—the others are between past and present and between East and West—central to the future of liberal arts education (Bell, 1966). Both historicized and thematic study have their virtues and limitations: both can engage students, both can be superficial though in different ways. But the choice between them is not ideologically neutral; on the contrary, it is choice that may well have important ramifications for multicultural study.

An ironic replay of this debate has recently been taking place within the SUNY system. There, a board of trustees dominated by activist conservatives mandated in 2000 that all SUNY students take a minimum of one American history course. At the same time, the board has rejected at least some proposed courses focused on American diversity as inappropriate to satisfy this

requirement. Here, the universality-particularism debate has been transformed into one between teaching putatively core American values and historical developments against focusing course work on concerns seen as particular to certain groups. The outcome of this debate is not at all clear, but it obviously has far-reaching implications for the relationship of core courses to multiculturalism.

Closely related to such issues is that of whether core courses should focus on primarily domestic problems of difference and prejudice or on difference encountered long ago or far away ("Exploring the Complexities of Culture," 1991). Schmitz (1992a) was concerned that

fewer institutions in the Cultural Legacies project—about 25 percent of the total—include or propose a required course on pluralism within the United States as part of the core. It may be easier and less threatening to engage difference at a distance—where it is expected and anticipated and where one has no permanent responsibility as a citizen—than at home. (p. 29)

American Association of Colleges and Universities surveys showed that the trend in the 1990s was toward courses with more of a focus on domestic issues of difference and especially prejudice. Still at 44% of the institutions responding in 2000, a student could fulfill the diversity requirement without taking a single course dealing with issues of diversity in the United States (Humphreys, 2000). Schmitz may well be right that at least before September 11, 2001, it was somewhat easier to encounter difference abroad.

Schmitz (1992b) has cogently analyzed the problematics of even the best-intentioned strategies for relating Western cultural and political traditions to those of "others." Rigidly distinguishing West and non-West will very likely establish the kind of hierarchy generally implicit in such binaries (and falsify continuing cultural interactions) as well as the separation between "we" and "they" inimical to serious study of non-Western or minority cultures. Similarly, viewing other cultures only, or primarily, within the frameworks established for the study of the West can seriously misrepresent "others" or reduce them to points of contrast for illuminating—and implicitly validating—Western norms. Stating the problems and sensitizing planners to them do not, however, guarantee solutions, for as the Stanford example suggests, deeply held political and personal systems of value are involved. More to the point perhaps, few educational tasks are finally more difficult—or more vital—than learning to see one's own culture from another; these are, one might argue, the end points rather than the beginnings of curriculum.

An interesting model that tries to bridge the gap between domestic and overseas difference may be provided by "The Global Search for Justice," a requirement at the College of St. Catherine ("Diversity and Social

Justice," 1998). Different versions of the course focus on different problems of justice—for example, women and health, the environment, dissent—as well as on different regions of the world. In general, however, students must examine "issues of social justice that cut across two or more cultures, including a culture outside of North America/Europe or a minority culture within our dominant culture." Iowa State has taken a different approach: one of the goals stated in its 2001–2003 *Bulletin* is "to prepare its students to meet the challenges of responsible citizenship and effective professional roles in a culturally diverse global community. To help achieve this goal, all undergraduate students must fulfill graduation requirements in two areas: U.S. Diversity and International Perspectives."

A different kind of bridge between global and domestic issues may be provided by the "Cross Cultural Inquiry" (CCI) requirement of Duke University's (1998) Curriculum 2000 initiative. The rationale for the requirement was stated in the report formulated by the committee charged with developing the new curriculum as follows:

CCI provides an academic engagement with the dynamics and interactions of culture(s) in a comparative or analytic perspective. This type of inquiry provides a scholarly, comparative, and integrative study of political, economic, aesthetic, social and cultural differences. It seeks to provide students with the tools to identify culture and cultural difference across time or place, between or within national boundaries. . . . CCI encourages critical and responsible attention to issues of identity, diversity, globalization, and power so that students may evaluate complex and difficult issues from multiple perspectives. In fulfilling the CCI requirement, students are encouraged to undertake comparisons that extend beyond national boundaries and their own national cultures and to explore the impact of increasing globalization. (http://www.aas.duke.edu/admin/curriculum2000/report/focused.html)

Of course, it remains to be seen how such aspirations will be translated into curricular practice over time and in a variety of general education courses that might deal with "political economies, scientific understandings, social and aesthetic representations," among other topics. Still, the requirement, one of a number in Duke's new curriculum, represents a significant commitment of institutional resources to an effort to translate multicultural as well as global issues into a set of core courses.

The problem we are addressing may be rooted in where one begins core experiences, institutionally and personally. The approach of one of the colleges in the Engaging Cultural Legacies project, LeMoyne-Owen, illustrates this point. There, students began "by examining the African and African American heritage in a year-long interdisciplinary course, historical in approach; the course explores African roots, diaspora, and the varied experiences of Africans in the western hemisphere." Starting in the sophomore year, students then looked at other

major civilizations, "beginning with Egypt and Mesopotamia" (Schmitz, 1992a, p. 26). An analogous strategy seems to be implicit in Fisk's humanities sequence, which began with "The African American Heritage" and later used that, in part, to compare "classic texts from the Greek and Roman empire and from various religious traditions . . . with works by African Americans"—for example, Plato's *Apology, Crito,* and *Phaedo* with Martin Luther King, Jr.'s "Letters from the Birmingham Jail" ("Exploring the Complexities of Culture," 1991). These programs may be taken to engage the debate over Afrocentric curricular approaches (Asante & Ravitch, 1991; Petrie, 1991). These have often been criticized as ahistorical and exaggerated, and no doubt some are. Orlando Patterson (1991) has proposed that African American history vitally recapitulates the core experiences of Western civilization. Rooted in slavery—as in Athens and Rome, central to economic and political development—African American culture has been energized, as in the classical period among slaves and their descendants, by the struggle for freedom. According to Patterson, the result—again in ways deeply similar to what occurred in the classical and Renaissance Italian states—has been a transformation of both the slaves' and the masters' cultures (Patterson, 1991). Like the LeMoyne-Owen course, Patterson's paradigm is suggestive of what may be perceived by placing multicultural experiences at the center rather than at the margins of historical study, including that of the West.

Still, given the emphasis that core curriculum planners have placed on local circumstances and particular bodies of students, programs such as those at LeMoyne-Owen and Fisk may be confronted with the question of whether they are appropriate only to a traditionally Black college. One might ask in response whether they could, in fact, be even more important to schools whose predominantly White student bodies are likely to be largely ignorant of African and African American cultures and histories. More generally, should core sequences be designed differently for different student bodies, or should students, however diverse, be expected to adapt themselves to core curricula designed, like the Hobart and William Smith course described earlier or Columbia's Contemporary Civilization (Bell, 1966), to communicate an institution's vision of a collective legacy? That "there is no one right answer to such questions" is a truism that does not mitigate the tensions the questions produce in any effort to design a core sequence that honestly grapples with cultural multiplicity and difference.

These questions, in fact, evoke a critical antinomy: whether one formulates a core experience from "what we wish students to learn" or from "who the students are," a version of "Do we teach bodies of knowledge or people?" To be sure, these are hardly independent variables, but they lead in somewhat different directions, especially if a main concern—as it needs to be—is classroom dynamics. The work of Frances Maher and Mary Kay Tetreault (Maher, 1987; Maher & Tetreault, 1994; cf. Deats & Lenker, 1994) strongly suggests that the single most dominant factor in shaping patterns of classroom discussion is the mix (or relative uniformity) of people *in* the classroom. Thus "who the students are" emerges with the texts and structures of curriculum as critical to learning. For example, it is certainly desirable for an institution to consider its location and its constituency in planning the kinds of core experiences it wishes to provide. As two successful core planners correctly put it, "The search for a universal core curriculum, we believe, is a quixotic quest. Today's core curriculum must be rooted in each college's own academic focus, its special approach to the world, and the kind of students it enrolls" (Campbell & Flynn, 1990, p. 10). But at some point, what seems locally engaging and happily familiar to students can become what is parochial. Indeed, the Denison example suggests the importance of challenging a local institutional culture precisely for the sake of gender and racial equity.

These are not abstract issues, especially because students have increasingly come to be aware of the subject positions through which they encounter readings and discussions. Indeed, in the 1980s and early 1990s, courses engaging multiculturalism were often driven by issues of identity politics. Here the concern is often not multiculturalism as distanced by texts, by history, or by social analysis, but racial, ethnic, and gender tensions in the real space called a classroom or a college (Giroux, 1993; Harris, 1995). Some earlier courses in what came to be called multiculturalism emphasized the need to rediscover voices and perspectives long excluded from the curriculum, and the ways in which students from related racial, ethnic, and sexual backgrounds engaged such voices. More recently, however, courses devoted primarily to examining identity categories have given way to those exploring "prejudice and discrimination" (Humphreys & Schneider, 1997). Moreover, newer courses emphasizing comparative approaches to ethnic, racial, sexual, and other categories of identity and analysis have increasingly come into prominence (Lauter, 1991; Diversity and Social Justice, 1998). (It needs to be pointed out, of course, that many of the early practitioners of multicultural requirements, as at Denison, were from the beginning focused not on issues of identity but of discrimination and often organized their course work from comparative perspectives.) Still, undergraduates are always to some extent deeply involved with identity questions; they are, after all, young people, perhaps especially so in the United States. To what extent, then, might a movement away from such personal issues and toward more abstract analysis undercut the effectiveness of core diversity requirements?

Teaching core multicultural courses also raises certain personal issues for faculty. As a number of core participants have noted, the departure of faculty members from their home disciplines into the less-known territory of core curricula turns them from expert instructors into co-learners with their students. In this new position, faculty *can* become more open to collaborative learning endeavors with their students (Wilkerson, 1992), and these, the research suggests, can be particularly fruitful (Goodsell, Maher, & Tinto, 1992). Likewise, when instructors move from positions of expertise into collaboration, they may be more inclined to replace traditional classroom hierarchies with more open-ended pedagogies (Wilkerson, 1992). Indeed, Astin's (1993) findings suggest that "how the students *approach* general education (and how the faculty actually *deliver* the curriculum) is far more important than the formal curricular content and structure" (p. 425).

At the same time, a classroom significantly engaged with multicultural and gender issues can be a tense, even a repressed, location, especially when unexamined racial, ethnic, gender, and class differences exist between teacher and students or among the students themselves. In such a context, as Teresa McKenna suggested at the 1993 seminar on multicultural literature at Pennsylvania State University, difference itself needs to become the source of commonality among classroom participants and the differences in subject position the subject matter, in some degree, of classroom as well as out-of-class discussion. Then, however, particularly in heavily structured core courses mandating set curricula, one encounters the ongoing imperatives of syllabi. If exposure to a set of common texts lies at the heart of the syllabus, one cannot but be caught up in the tension between covering what is laid out there as distinct from focusing on what is going on here in the classroom.

In addition, the encounters with diversity in the classroom can be seriously unsettling experiences, especially for students from relatively parochial or ethnocentric backgrounds. One researcher who has systematically explored this problem encourages faculty teaching diversity courses to adjust them according to students' levels of intellectual and personal development. He hopes that "classrooms can be safe spaces for the cognitive and personal challenges that diversity presents," providing that "the encounters are carefully sequenced and students are helped to learn how to be reflective about their own thinking and that of others" (Knefelkamp, 2000). These are admirable goals, to be sure. But whether classrooms can ever be seen as safe spaces remains an open question. They are, after all, public spaces within which different agendas and differently situated individuals (e.g., the syllabus and the experience, the teacher and the student, the articulate major and the insecure general education draftee) compete for space and control. *Safety* is thus a relative term and needs to be explored and defined, not assumed.

One also needs to account for Astin's (1993) finding that what he calls a true-core curriculum (in which all students take exactly the same courses) is the only one among general education programs that appears to have any significant effects on student cognitive or affective behavior. Astin suggests that the "beneficial effects of true-core curriculum may be mediated by the peer group" (p. 425), an impact he attributes to how common experiences can spark student discussions out of class and provide intellectual bases for peer bonding. Ironically, a major source of student discussion out of class appears to be comparison of how instructors present the same material, which, if so, may tend to push faculty back toward more presentational modes, in the tradition of the Harvard general education approach (Bell, 1966). More important, perhaps, common multicultural experiences in core programs provide distinctively valuable sources of bonding, animated discussion, and shared work in an institution committed to equity, as the early years of the Denison experience suggest.

One final set of tensions, also related to this finding, concerns the relative value of diffuse as distinct from highly focused models of core curricula. The virtues of the tight, true-core model is apparent in Astin's (1993) findings. The value of more and less diffuse models may be harder to establish. We have pointed to a number of these in connection with the Denison case: for example, diffusion of concern for equity issues among departments. The Pennsylvania State University cultural diversity requirement offers certain other values. In the first place, its statement of purpose, widely disseminated in a booklet listing courses that fulfill the requirement and distributed to all students statewide, declared as an institutional goal that

> every United States citizen should understand both the progress made in eliminating discrimination and prejudice from our society and the gaps between national ideas and national performance. Diversity courses consider: (1) the concerns and contributions of women and minorities (defined by race, ethnicity, religion, and sexual orientation), and (2) a national need for more tolerant cooperation within a complex and increasingly global community.

A participant in the faculty senate debate over the requirement framed other of its uses this way: "A requirement underscores the value of a category of learning. It directs students to a wide range of clearly important areas of study. It promotes course development. It feeds information and ideas into the intellectual life of the campus."

To be sure, the category of "diversity-focused" courses is rather loosely drawn. The courses listed in Penn State's 1991–1992 brochure included, for example, "Rape and Sexual Violence," "Arts of Africa, Oceania, and Indian America," "Gender and Geography," and "Cultural Aspects of Food." Such courses satisfy quite different student needs and intellectual purposes. Drawn together under a single rubric of diversity, they may suggest a lack of definition, a politics of low-level inclusion. That does not mean, however, that a diffuse core model has no meaningful impacts. On the contrary, recent research at a university much like Penn State suggests that "completing a diversity course requirement significantly reduced students' level of racial prejudice" (Chang, 2000). Indeed, Chang's findings "also suggest that learning about one significant difference in U.S. society (i.e., gender or class differences) might also transfer well to thinking about other differences and subsequently reduce multiple types of prejudice."

NEW DIRECTIONS

The question of impact seems to us a critical problem, for colleges and universities have, we believe, lost substantial cultural authority in the recent decade. Increasingly, students gain a sense of the world from the entertainment industry, the mass media, and other commercial institutions. They see reflected in these what they infrequently found examined in the university, even in relatively innovative global cultures programs ("Exploring the Complexities of Culture," 1991): "the experience of profound unsettlement," the violence attendant on the vast migrations of people, the breaking down of existing borders and categories, the increasing creolization of global mass culture. "Such experience," Michael Geyer (1993) has written, "requires the study of unsettlement, rather than settlement" (p. 553). A multicultural general education able to engage what students now experience and to enable them to function as rational and cooperative human beings in what was then the next century will, he argued,

> need to overcome the limits of civilization—and settlement-bound approaches, whether they argue for civilization writ large or for plural civilizations as autonomous units of identity. Rather than concentrating on the achievements of settlement, we should keep our eyes open for regions, times, and peoples of unsettlement, for the ceaseless struggle to think and create orders and to provide meanings. (p. 533)

Geyer's proposal was and remains a challenge to virtually all current core curricula, and especially those on Western cultures, which do tend to focus on the moments in which settled societies flower in classic written texts. His idea of concentrating on "unsettlement" adds a further set of conflicting priorities to efforts to design any core curriculum, particularly one that takes multiculturalism seriously.

In many respects, however, the aftermath of September 11, 2001, has outrun even such radical ideas. Since those events, many conservatives have accepted the idea, once excoriated, that a wide diversity, embracing many heretofore invisible groups, is a key element in American democracy. Meanwhile, traditional centers of liberalism, like labor unions, have become increasingly suspicious of one main source of that diversity: immigration. The porous borders of the United States have, from this perspective, come to seem threatening, not only because they present problems of security to Americans but because the flow of workers into the United States, and of jobs and corporate home bases out of the United States, undercuts domestic employment. In short, older political alignments, as well as older curricular paradigms, have come into question, even as the imperative for understanding difference and even ethnic conflict has markedly increased. In fact, general education, including core courses, has often been presented as the venue within which curricular responses to September 11 can be deployed.

Given academic calendars and the glacial pace of curricular reform, it is far too early to predict the directions that new initiatives might take. But we suspect that at least some of the many new courses now being taught about Islam, Arabs in America, oil and immigration, and the like will find their ways into general education programs directed at students puzzled and often frightened by events—and, at the same time, anxious to build a better and safer world. One might pose as a rubric for these programs "America in the World and the World in America." Such a framework may offer a kind of bridge between courses directed outward, so to speak, toward comprehending difference as it is enacted around our violent planet, and courses directed inward, toward sorting out the often tense interrelationships between diversity and unity in a democratic society. After all, one priority that has been thrust on us is clarifying how events "outside" are shaped by and heavily shape events "inside." A sign of the times is that the 2002 conference of the National MultiCultural Institute was titled "Thinking Globally: Broadening the Context of Multicultural Dialogue and Action." But whether a rubric connecting multiculturalism and global issues comes into prominence, it is clear that the academic year 2001–2002 saw the push for bringing the concerns of multiculturalism into general education emerge with new urgency.

In this light, certain lessons that might be drawn from our case studies take on additional significance. First, institution-wide core requirements, like those at Denison, focused on diversity and even ethnic and religious conflict, can produce changes in campus culture and departmental priorities. To be sure, students tend to resist additional requirements, but it is not clear how deeply that resistance runs, especially if students are directly involved in the formulation of such new programs. Moreover, many students have themselves demanded, indeed helped formulate, new courses about the issues of diversity. Similarly, the professional basis of faculty hesitation about general education needs to be respected. At the same time, material aid to faculty in changing what they teach and concrete rewards for such change can turn resistance into its opposite (Wilkerson, 1992). In this connection, it is vital to recognize, as the wide adoption of *The Heath Anthology of American Literature* suggests and as the enthusiasm for its use confirms, that multicultural teaching and scholarship can be enormously rewarding for faculty, *providing* they have time for study; opportunities in conferences, seminars, and institutes to interact with colleagues; and access to new books and journals. Moreover, the pedagogical implications of multicultural syllabi need to be taken seriously, as does the study of collaborative, experiential, and service learning, flexible classroom arrangements, and other departures fostered within academic communities often indifferent to such "educational" issues. In fact, there is increasing evidence from conference programs in the humanities that such pedagogical study is newly popular.

It might be asked, Aren't these prescriptions, however seemingly modest, altogether utopian at a time in which higher education is under severe fiscal constraint and has, not coincidentally, lost much of its cultural and civil authority? The Denison experience shows that meaningful multicultural departures can be accomplished without significant outside funding. That does not mean that changing patterns of curricula and scholarship comes free. On the contrary, one main criticism of the efforts of the SUNY Board of Trustees to mandate American history courses has been their refusal to provide funds for faculty development or for necessary additional positions. Institutions do need, in one or another form, to invest their resources, especially in areas like faculty development, if they wish to respond to changing intellectual priorities and help shape a multicultural future—as was explicitly done by Oregon State to implement its "Difference, Power, and Discrimination Program."

The Stanford experience suggests the need for honest, even if heated, debate about the political issues underlying educational departures such as multiculturalism. While some differences are not likely to be resolved, at least a level of civil discourse, important to establishing community on campus, can be modeled. In any case, multiculturalism, as we have suggested, cannot be divorced from issues of difference, not just in appearance or food or customs, but of power.

Finally, we have come to view the post–September 11 situation not only in terms of the threats it represents but as an opportunity. Especially in view of the low esteem in which Americans have come to view many of this nation's institutions—business (think Enron), politics (think Florida), the justice system (think FBI)—it may well be that the path linking general education and a broadly conceived multiculturalism is the only one that might lead to reestablishing the cultural authority universities should ideally wield and that democratic education seems to us to require.

References

Allardyce, G. (1982). The rise and fall of the Western civilization course. *American Historical Review, 87,* 695–725.

American Association of Colleges and Universities. (1998). *Diversity blueprint: A planning manual for colleges and universities.* Washington, DC: Author.

American Association of Colleges and Universities. (2002). James Irvine Foundation Campus Diversity Initiative Evaluation Project. [On-line]. Available: http://www.aacu edu.org/irvinediveval/overview.cfm.

Appel, M., Cartwright, D., Smith, D. G., & Wolf, L. E. (1996). *The impact of diversity on students: A preliminary review of the research literature.* Washington, DC: American Association of Colleges and Universities.

Asante, M. K., & Ravitch, D. (1991). Multiculturalism: An exchange. *American Scholar, 60,* 267–277.

Association of American Colleges. (1985). *Integrity in the college curriculum: A report to the academic community.* Washington, DC: Author.

Astin, A. W. (1993). *What matters in college? Four critical years revisited.* San Francisco: Jossey-Bass.

Ball, H., Berkowitz, S. D., & Mzamane, M. (Eds.). (1998). *Multicultural education in colleges and universities: A transdisciplinary approach.* Mahwah, NJ: Erlbaum.

Banks, J. A., & Banks, C.A.M. (Eds.). (1993). *Multicultural education: Issues and perspectives* (2nd ed.). Needham Heights, MA: Allyn & Bacon.

Barry, B. M. (2001). *Culture and equality: An egalitarian critique of multiculturalism.* Cambridge, MA: Harvard University Press.

Baumann, G. (1999). *The multicultural riddle: Rethinking national, ethnic, and religious identities.* New York: Routledge.

Bell, D. (1966). *The reforming of general education: The Columbia College experience in its national setting.* New York: Columbia University Press.

Bennett, W. (1984). *To reclaim a legacy: A report on the humanities in higher education.* Washington, DC: National Endowment for the Humanities.

Berger, M. (Ed.). (1994). *Modern art and society: An anthology of social and multicultural readings.* New York: Icon Editions.

Biale, D., Galchinsky, M., & Heschel, S. (1998). *Insider/outsider: American Jews and multiculturalism.* Berkeley: University of California Press.

Bisesi, M. (1982). Historical developments in American undergraduate education: General education and the core curriculum. *British Journal of Educational Studies, 30,* 199–212.

Bloom, A. (1987). *The closing of the American mind.* New York: Simon & Schuster.

Bossman, D. M. (1991). Cross-cultural values for a pluralistic core curriculum. *Journal of Higher Education, 62,* 661–681.

Boyer, E. L., & Levine, A. (1981). *A quest for common learning.* Washington, DC: Carnegie Foundation for the Advancement of Teaching.

Brann, E.T.H. (1993). The canon defended. *Philosophy and Literature, 17,* 193–218.

Braun, R. J. (1987, February 15). State aims at "gender perspective" in public, private college courses. *Newark Star-Ledger.*

Butler, J. E., & Walter, J. C. (Eds.). (1991). *Transforming the curriculum: Ethnic studies and women's studies.* Albany: State University of New York Press.

Campbell, J., & Flynn, T. (1990). Can colleges go back to a core curriculum? *Planning for Higher Education, 19,* 9–15.

Carnegie Foundation for the Advancement of Teaching. (1992). Signs of a changing curriculum. *Change, 24,* 50–52.

Carnochan, W. B. (1993). *The battleground of the curriculum: Liberal education and American experience.* Stanford: Stanford University Press.

Chang, M. (2000, Winter). Measuring the impact of a diversity requirement on students' level of racial prejudice. *Diversity Digest.* [On-line]. Available: http://www.diversityweb.org/Digest/W00/research2.html.

The changing curriculum: Then and now. (1991). *Partisan Review, 58,* 249–281.

Ch'maj, B.E.M. (Ed.). (1993). *Multicultural America: A resource book for teachers of humanities and American studies—Syllabi, essays, projects, bibliography.* Lanham, MD: University Press of America.

Cheney, L. V. (1989). *Fifty hours: A core curriculum for college students.* Washington, DC: National Endowment for the Humanities.

Cuban, L. (1999). *How scholars trumped teachers: Change without reform in university curriculum, teaching, and research, 1890–1990.* New York: Teachers College Press.

Culley, M., & Portuges, C. (Eds.). (1985). *Gendered subjects: The dynamics of feminist teaching.* New York: Routledge.

Deats, S. M., & Lenker, L. T. (Eds.). (1994). *Gender and academe: Feminist pedagogy and politics.* Lanham, Md.: Rowman & Littlefield.

Dinnerstein, M., O'Donnell, S. R., & MacCorquodale, P. (1981). *Integrating women's studies into the curriculum: A report to the Association of American Colleges on the SIROW conference "Integrating Women's Studies into the Liberal Arts Curriculum" (Princeton, NJ, August 27–30).* Tucson, AZ: Southwest Institute for Research on Women.

Diversity and social justice in general education: New curricular models. (1998, Fall). *Diversity Digest.* [On-line]. Available: http://www.diversityweb.org/digest/F98/models.html.

Duke University. (1998). *Curriculum 2000: Report.* [On-line]. Available: http://www.aas.duke.edu/admin/curriculum2000/report/focused.html.

Exploring the complexities of culture. (1991). *Liberal Education, 77,* 40–60.

Fiol-Matta, L., & Chamberlain, M. K. (Eds.). (1994). *Women of color and the multicultural curriculum: Transforming the college classroom.* New York: Feminist Press at the City University of New York.

Flacks, R. (1971). *Youth and social change*. Chicago: Markham.

Foster, L., & Herzog, P. (Eds.). (1994). *Defending diversity: Contemporary philosophical perspectives on pluralism and multiculturalism*. Amherst: University of Massachusetts Press.

Fox-Genovese, E., & Stuard, S. M. (1983). *Restoring women to history: Materials for Western civilization I and II*. Bloomington, IN: Organization of American Historians.

Fullinwider, R. K. (Ed.). (1996). *Public education in a multicultural society: Policy, theory, critique*. Cambridge: Cambridge University Press.

Gaff, J. G. (1992). Beyond politics: The educational issues inherent in multicultural education. *Change, 24*, 31–35.

Gaff, J. G., & Wasescha, A. (1991). Assessing the reform of general education. *JGE: The Journal of General Education, 40*, 51–68.

Gappa, J. M., & Pearce, J. (n.d.). *Sex and gender in the social sciences: Reassessing the introductory course*. Washington, DC: American Sociological Association/American Psychological Association. San Francisco: Judith Gappa.

Gaskell, J., & Willinsky, J. (Eds.). (1995). *Gender in/forms curriculum: From enrichment to transformation*. Ontario: Oise Press; New York: Teachers College Press.

General Education in a Free Society. (1945). Cambridge, MA: Harvard University Press.

Geyer, M. (1993). Multiculturalism and the politics of general education. *Critical Inquiry, 19*, 499–533.

Giroux, H. A. (1993). *Living dangerously: Multiculturalism and the politics of difference*. New York: P. Lang.

Gold, P. (1997). Faculty collaboration for a new curriculum. *Liberal Education, 83*, 46–49.

Goldberg, D. T. (1994). *Multiculturalism: A critical reader*. Cambridge, MA: Blackwell.

Goodsell, A., Maher, M., Tinto, V. (with Smith, B. L., & MacGregor, J.). (1992). *Collaborative learning: A sourcebook for higher education*. Syracuse, NY: National Center on Postsecondary Teaching, Learning and Assessment.

Gordon, A., & Newfield, C. (Eds.). (1996). *Mapping multiculturalism*. Minneapolis: University of Minnesota Press.

Green, H. (1996). *Racial inequality in America: A comparative historical perspective*. [On-line]. Available: http://learning.berkeley.edu/AC/archive/syllabi/EthStd130AC_Green.html.

Gruber, C. S. (1975). *Mars and Minerva: World War I and the uses of higher learning in America*. Baton Rouge: Louisiana State University Press.

Hall, J. W., & Kevles, B. L. (1982). The social imperatives for curricular change in higher education. In J. W. Hall & B. L. Kevles (Eds.), *Opposition to core curriculum: Alternative models for undergraduate education* (pp. 13–38). Westport, CT: Greenwood Press.

Harris, D. A. (Ed.). (1995). *Multiculturalism from the margins: Nondominant voices on difference and diversity*. Westport, CT: Bergin & Garvey.

Hitchens, C. (1988, Mar. 4–10). Whose culture, what civilization? *Times Literary Supplement*, p. 246.

Hollinger, D. A. (1995). *Postethnic America: Beyond multiculturalism*. New York: Basic Books.

Hook, S. (1989). Curricular politics. *Partisan Review, 56*, 201–213.

Howe, F., & Lauter, P. (1980). *The impact of women's studies on the campus and the disciplines*. Washington, DC: National Institute of Education.

Humphreys, D. (1997). *General education and American commitments: A national report on diversity courses and requirements*. Washington, DC: American Association of Colleges and Universities.

Humphreys, D. (2000, Fall). National survey finds diversity requirements common around the country. *Diversity Digest*. [On-line]. Available: http://www.diversityweb.org/Digest/F00/survey.html.

Humphreys, D., & Schneider, C. G. (1997, Winter). Curricular change gains momentum: New requirements focus on diversity and social responsibility. *Diversity Digest*. [On-line]. Available: http://www.diversityweb.org/Digest/W97/newreqs.html.

Jackson, S., & Solís, J. (Eds.). (1995). *Beyond comfort zones in multiculturalism: Confronting the politics of privilege*. Westport, CT: Bergin & Garvey.

Jarratt, S. C., & Worsham, L. (Eds.). (1998). *Feminism and composition studies: In other words*. New York: Modern Language Association of America.

Jones, E. A., & Ratcliff, J. L. (1991). Which general education curriculum is better: Core curriculum or the distributional requirement? *JGE: The Journal of General Education, 40*, 70–101.

Kaplan, M. (1982). The wrong solution to the right problem. In J. W. Hall & B. L. Kevles (Eds.), *Opposition to core curriculum: Alternative models for undergraduate education* (pp. 3–12). Westport, CT: Greenwood Press.

Katsiaficas, G., & Kiros, T. (Eds.). (1998). *The promise of multiculturalism: Education and autonomy in the 21st century: A new political science reader*. New York: Routledge.

Kennedy, A. (1991). Memory and values: Disengaging cultural legacies. *Liberal Education, 77*, 34–39.

Kerr, C. (1964). *The uses of the university*. Cambridge, MA: Harvard University Press.

Knefelkamp, L. (2000, Spring–Summer). Encountering diversity on campus and in the classroom: Advancing intellectual and ethical development. *Diversity Digest*. [On-line]. Available: http://www.diversityweb.org/digest/SpSm00/development.html.

Lauter, P. (Ed.). (1983). *Reconstructing American literature: Courses, syllabi, issues*. New York: Feminist Press.

Lauter, P. (1991). *Canons and contexts*. New York: Oxford University Press.

Lauter, P. (2001). *From Walden Pond to Jurassic Park: Activism, culture, and American studies*. Durham, NC: Duke University Press.

Lauter, P., Bruce-Novoa, J., Bryer, J., Hedges, E., Ling, A., Littlefield, D. F., Jr., et al. (Eds.). (1990). *The Heath anthology of American literature* (2 vols.). Boston: Houghton Mifflin.

Levine, A., & Cureton, J. (1992). The quiet revolution: Eleven facts about multiculturalism and the curriculum. *Change, 24*, 25–29.

Long, P. (Ed.). (1969). *The new left: A collection of essays*. Boston: Porter Sargent.

Mahalingam, R., & McCarthy, C. (Eds.). (2000). *Multicultural curriculum: New directions for social theory, practice and policy*. New York: Routledge.

Maher, F. (1987). Toward a richer theory of feminist pedagogy. *Journal of Education, 169*, 91–99.

Maher, F., & Tetreault, M.K.T. (1994). *The feminist classroom*. New York: Basic Books.

Mayberry, M., & Rose, E. C. (Eds.). (1999). *Meeting the challenge: Innovative feminist pedagogies in action*. New York: Routledge.

McNeill, W. H. (1977). Beyond Western civilization: Rebuilding the survey. *History Teacher, 10*, 509–515.

McNew, J. (1992). Whose politics? Media distortions of academic controversies. *Virginia Quarterly Review, 68*, 1–23.

McQuillen, J. S. (1992). Role models in education: Their relation to students' perceived competence, stress and satisfaction. *Education, 112,* 403–407.

Messer-Davidow, E. (2002). *Disciplining feminism: From social activism to academic discourse.* Durham, NC: Duke University Press.

Mio, J. S., & Awakuni, G. I. (2000). *Resistance to multiculturalism: Issues and interventions.* New York: Brunner/Mazel.

Montalto, N. V. (1982). *A history of the intercultural educational movement, 1924–1941.* New York: Garland.

Musil, C. M. (Ed.). (1992). *The courage to question: Women's studies and student learning.* Washington, DC: Association of American Colleges and National Women's Studies Association.

Musil, C. M., Garcia, M., Hudgins, C. A., Nettles, M. T., Sedlack, W. E., & Smith, D. G. (2000). *A diversity research agenda.* Washington, DC: American Association of Colleges and Universities.

Musil, C. M. (with Garcia, M., Moses, Y. T., & Smith, D. G.). (1995). *Diversity in higher education: A work in progress.* Washington, DC: American Association of Colleges and Universities.

Narayan, U., & Harding, S. (Eds.). (2000). *Decentering the center: Philosophy for a multicultural, postcolonial, and feminist world.* Bloomington: Indiana University Press.

National Institute of Education. (1984). *Involvement in learning: Realizing the potential of American higher education.* Washington, DC: Author.

Nelson, C. (1993). Multiculturalism without guarantees: From anthologies to the social text. *Journal of the Midwest Modern Language Association, 26,* 47–57.

Nordquist, J. (1992). *The multicultural education debate in the university: A bibliography.* Santa Cruz, CA: Reference and Research Service.

Oregon State University. (2002). *Difference, power, and discrimination program.* [On-line]. Available: http://oregonstate.edu/dept/dpd/.

Organization of American Historians. (1988). *Restoring women to history: Packets for integrating women's history into courses on Africa, Asia, Latin America, the Caribbean, and the Middle East.* Bloomington, IN: Author.

Parekh, B. C. (2000). *Rethinking multiculturalism: Cultural diversity and political theory.* Cambridge, MA: Harvard University Press.

Patterson, O. (1991). *Freedom in the making of Western culture.* New York: Basic Books.

Petrie, P. (1991, August). Afrocentrism in a multicultural democracy. *American Visions,* pp. 20–26.

Phillips, W. (Ed.). (1988). Stanford documents. *Partisan Review, 55,* 653–674.

Pratt, M. L. (1990). Humanities for the future: Reflections on the Western culture debate at Stanford. *South Atlantic Quarterly, 89,* 7–25.

President's Commission on Higher Education. (1947). *Higher education for American democracy.* Washington, DC: U.S. Government Printing Office.

Ravitch, D. (1990). Multiculturalism: E pluribus plures. *American Scholar, 59,* 337–354.

Rico, B. R., & Mano, S. (Eds.). *American mosaic: Multicultural readings in context.* Boston: Houghton Mifflin.

Robinson, J. H. (1926). *The ordeal of civilization.* New York: HarperCollins.

Rosovsky, H. (1978, February 15). Report on the core curriculum. Memorandum to Harvard Faculty of Arts and Sciences, Harvard University.

Rothenberg, P. S. (Ed.). (1998). *Race, class, and gender in the United States: An integrated study* (4th ed.). New York: St. Martin's Press.

Roy, D. H. (1996). *The reuniting of America: Eleven multicultural dialogues.* New York: Peter Lang.

Rudolph, F. (1962). *The American college and university.* New York: Vintage.

Rudolph, F. (1977). *Curriculum: A history of the American undergraduate course of study since 1936.* San Francisco: Jossey-Bass.

Schlesinger, A. M., Jr. (1991). *The disuniting of America.* Knoxville, TN: Whittle Direct Books.

Schmitz, B. (1992a). *Core curriculum and cultural pluralism: A guide for campus planners.* Washington, DC: Association of American Colleges.

Schmitz, B. (1992b). Cultural pluralism and core curricula. In M. Adams (Ed.), *Promoting diversity in college classrooms: Innovative responses for the curriculum, faculty, and institutions* (pp. 61–69). San Francisco: Jossey-Bass.

Sleeter, C. E., & McLaren, P. L. (Eds.). (1995). *Multicultural education, critical pedagogy, and the politics of difference.* Albany: State University of New York Press.

Slevin, J. (1996, Fall). Politics of curricular change: The story behind media attacks on Georgetown. *Diversity Digest.* [On-line]. Available: http://www.diversityweb.org/Digest/F96/georgetown.html.

Smith, D. G. (1997). *Diversity works: The emerging picture of how students benefit.* Washington, DC: American Association of Colleges and Universities.

Spanier, B., Bloom, A., & Boroviak, D. (Eds.). (1984). *Toward a balanced curriculum: A sourcebook for initiating gender integration projects.* Rochester, VT: Schenkman.

Spelman, E. V. (1988). *Inessential woman: Problems of exclusion in feminist thought.* Boston: Beacon Press.

Spurr, S. (1970). *Academic degree structures: Innovative approaches.* New York: McGraw-Hill.

Susser, I., & Patterson, T. C. (Eds.). (2001). *Cultural diversity in the United States: A critical reader.* Cambridge, MA: Blackwell.

Takaki, R. (1991). The value of multiculturalism. *Liberal Education, 77,* 8–10.

Talburtt, M. A. (1988). *Including women in the curriculum: A study of strategies that make it happen.* Ann Arbor, MI: Formative Evaluation Research Associates.

Thomas (Rosenstock), M. (1991). *Gender, race, and the curriculum: The Western culture controversy at Stanford.* Unpublished manuscript.

Tirado, I. A. (1987). Integrating issues of gender in the survey of Western civilization since 1648. In *Initiating curriculum transformation in the humanities: Integrating women and issues of race and gender.* Wayne, NJ: William Patterson College.

Toombs, W., Amey, M. J., & Chen, A. (1991). General education: An analysis of contemporary practice. *JGE: Journal of General Education, 40,* 102–118.

Wilkerson, M. (1992). Beyond the graveyard: Engaging faculty involvement. *Change, 24,* 59–63.

Willett, C. (Ed.). (1998). *Theorizing multiculturalism: A guide to the current debate.* Cambridge, MA: Blackwell.

Yarmolinsky, A. (1992). Loose canons: Multiculturalism and humanities 101. *Change, 24,* 6–9, 74–75.

Zaborowska, M. J. (Ed.). (1998). *Other Americans, other Americas: The politics and poetics of multiculturalism.* Aarhus, Denmark: Aarhus University Press.

46

MULTICULTURAL TEACHER EDUCATION

Research, Practice, and Policy

Marilyn Cochran-Smith

Boston College

Danné Davis

Boston College

Kim Fries

University of New Hampshire

The strikingly different racial, cultural, and linguistic profiles of the nation's student and teaching populations, coupled with continuing disparities among racial and cultural groups in school achievement and completion rates, poverty levels, and opportunities to learn from qualified teachers, have been highlighted for some time now as a pressing—if not the most pressing—issue for teacher preparation research, practice, and policy. Efforts to make teacher education "multicultural" and more attentive to diversity through governmental and nongovernmental policies, curriculum reform, recruitment and selection of students and faculty, and institutional and organizational change constitute the major professional responses to this critical issue.

This chapter reviews the literature on multicultural teacher education as it shapes and is shaped by educational practice and policy during the last decade of the twentieth century and the early years of the twenty-first. The chapter situates the literature within current political and professional contexts, analyzes key syntheses that already exist on the topic, and examines both conceptual and empirical research from 1992 through 2001. The chapter concludes by commenting on the future of multicultural teacher education, including research programs and approaches that have received little attention thus far.

THE BEST AND WORST OF TIMES

In the early years of the twenty-first century, it is the best and worst of times for multicultural teacher education.

On the one hand, it is a time for celebration and hope—a time of heightened attention to issues of diversity and schooling. For example, presidential candidate George W. Bush, a self-identified conservative, made "leaving no child behind" a major part of his election campaign, emphasizing nationwide school accountability for raising the academic standards and performance of every child. True to his promise, President George Bush led an ultimately bipartisan effort to reauthorize the Elementary and Secondary Education Act (ESEA), called the No Child Left Behind Act to pay homage to his campaign slogan. ESEA directly targets poor students and struggling schools by shifting funding formulas and makes schools accountable by tracking test results, reporting to parents, and disaggregating results by race, gender, and other factors. Another example of the "good" news about multicultural teacher education is the fact that although national professional organizations did not address multicultural issues until the 1970s, all of the major professional organizations related to the preparation, licensing, and certification of teachers and/or the accreditation of programs now have consistent standards or recommendations regarding teachers' competency to produce learning gains for all students, including those from diverse backgrounds (National Commission on Teaching and America's Future, 1997).

Along related lines, as Donna Gollnick's (1995) policy analysis of national and state initiatives related to multicultural education indicates, by 1993, 16 of the 17 national curriculum guidelines approved by the National Council for the Accreditation of Teacher Education

931

(NCATE) had incorporated multicultural guidelines. Similarly, 35 states referred to ethnicity and/or the importance of understanding cultural influences on learning and schooling in their policies regarding teacher candidates, and 40 states required that schools or teacher education programs include the study of ethnic groups, cultural diversity, human relations, or multicultural and bilingual education (Gollnick, 1995). Furthermore, over the past decade, teacher preparation programs at colleges and universities across the country have revised courses, curriculum, fieldwork experiences, and policies to include attention to diversity and multicultural education (Ladson-Billings, 1995; Zeichner & Hoeft, 1996). Also attesting to "the best" of times, there is now a larger body of research and scholarship related to multicultural education in general (see Banks & Banks, 1995) and multicultural teacher education in particular (see Sleeter, 2001a, 2001b) than there was a decade ago when multicultural theorists noted the dearth of research in these areas (Grant, 1992; Grant & Secada, 1990). Finally, there is some evidence that certain alternate routes into teaching—especially those in urban areas—are attracting more teachers of color into the teaching profession (Wilson, Floden, & Ferrini-Mundy, 2001; Zeichner & Schulte, 2001) and that policies that permit alternate entry points may be helping to diversify the teaching force in some areas (Lauer, 2001).

Despite these and other examples of heightened attention to diversity in schooling, however, it is also the worst of times for multicultural teacher education—a time for grave concern and urgency. In many areas of the country, there is a significant backlash against affirmative action, bilingual and other language education programs, and race-based admissions and scholarship policies in higher education (Gordon, 2001b). In some states, new ways of assessing teacher quality and successful schools are burying issues of diversity under technical notions of equity defined as opportunities for all to be held equally accountable to the same high-stakes tests, despite grossly unequal resources and opportunities to learn. This is the situation Robert Schaeffer of FairTest was referring to when he suggested the new ESEA would be more accurately nicknamed the "No Child Left Untested Act" (Toppo, 2002). Furthermore, as many critics have pointed out, although there have been local pockets of dramatic change and exemplary programs at certain institutions (e.g., Haberman, 1988; Ladson-Billings, 1999), there has been little broad-based fundamental change in education policies (Gollnick, 1995) or teacher education programs (Irvine, 2001; Ladson-Billings, 1999). By and large, teachers continue to be prepared from a monocultural perspective (Zeichner & Hoeft, 1996) that eschews the pervasive impact of race, class, linguistic background, culture, gender, and ability (King & Castenell, 2001a) and

emphasizes instead a universal knowledge base for teaching, learning, and schooling (Grant & Wieczorek, 2000; Nieto, 2001). Along these lines, critics suggest that some of the most widespread reforms in teacher education (for example, the addition of a course in multicultural education, new requirements for field placements in "diverse" settings) have been more rhetorical than real, piecemeal and optional rather than infused into a coherent multicultural curriculum (Villegas & Lucas, 2002a; Zeichner & Hoeft, 1996).

Also indicative of the "worst" of times, is the fact that a major government-funded synthesis of the research on teacher preparation (Wilson et al., 2001), intended to guide policy initiatives as well as research funding under the Bush administration, is organized around five major questions deemed central to the preparation of teachers. Not one of these questions has to do with preparing teachers for diverse populations or for the special problems of urban schools that are most in need of teachers. Furthermore, although some alternate routes into teaching do seem to be attracting more teachers of color than traditional preparation programs, there is also evidence that many teachers who enter through alternate routes leave teaching after two years (Lauer, 2001; Raymond, Fletcher, & Luque, 2001). Perhaps worst of all, in some states, a significant influence on teacher certification and/or program approval regulations is the assumption that multicultural education is a pernicious political agenda that is anti-White, anti-intellectual, and anticapitalist. (See Cochran-Smith, 2001c, and Cochran-Smith & Fries, 2001, for descriptions of two such instances; also see Stotsky, 1999.)

It is with the understanding that this is both the best and worst of times for multicultural teacher education that this chapter examines the literature. The chapter is organized into six sections: (1) the current state of teacher education practice and policy, including the competing agendas for reform and accountability that have dominated the discourse about teaching quality and teacher preparation; (2) changing patterns in the multicultural teacher education research and scholarship according to the research syntheses published since the 1970s when attention first turned to these issues; (3) a conceptual framework for understanding the multiple meanings of multicultural teacher education, which is used in the chapter to analyze the literature; (4) key ideas in the theoretical frameworks, definitions, conceptual frames, models, approaches, and typologies published from 1992 to 2001 and widely used to conceptualize multicultural teacher education; (5) current trends and issues in multicultural teacher education, based on a review of the empirical studies from 1992 to 2001; and (6) conclusions and directions forward, including discussion of what has so far been missing from the literature. Taken together, the parts of this chapter are intended to provide an overview of research, practice, and policy in multicultural teacher education in the United States early in the 21st century.

Across its sections, the chapter is based on several key assumptions. First, it is assumed that all efforts to make teacher education multicultural occur within the complex political, social, and professional contexts that are dominant during a given period. Thus, the chapter locates the literature in relation to the educational agendas that prevail at state and national levels, as well as to larger social and political contexts. A second assumption underlying the chapter is that teacher education, like teaching, is an enterprise that cannot be adequately conceptualized as either theoretical or practical but is instead located at the intersections of the theoretical and practical worlds. Whether explicit or not, coherent or not, theoretical frameworks and underlying assumptions are the filters through which practice and policy are mediated, as well as the moorings to which practices and policies with multiple interpretations are attached and given specific form and meaning. For this reason, the chapter is not limited only to empirical research designed to provide evidence of the effectiveness of particular strategies for multicultural education, although this kind of research is certainly needed. Instead, the chapter reviews empirical as well as theoretical and conceptual scholarship, arguing that key concepts and theories contribute to the development of multicultural teacher education practice and policy and, reciprocally, that emergent practices and policies contribute to the development of new theories.

Although this chapter focuses on the initial preparation of teachers (and thus does not include in-service education and professional development for experienced teachers), a third idea animating the chapter is that learning to teach begins prior to formal teacher preparation and continues across the professional life span. The chapter therefore includes literature on selection and recruitment, as well as on the background knowledge and beliefs that prospective teachers bring with them as they begin formal preparation. The chapter also includes research about understandings and knowledge that may emerge during initial teacher preparation and during fieldwork experiences, when teachers act on what they have learned in classrooms. Finally, the chapter recognizes that "multicultural teacher education" is a term with many everyday meanings and as many formal definitions and categorical schemes. In keeping with the premises about multicultural education on which this book is based, the literature search for this chapter began with a broad conceptualization of multicultural teacher education, reviewing literature that is classified under terms such as *teacher preparation* (or *teacher education* or *teacher training*) for a multicultural society, for underserved populations, for cultural diversity, for social change and social justice, for antiracist schools and society, for urban schools and classrooms, and so on.

THE TEACHER EDUCATION CONTEXT

It is impossible to understand the current state of multicultural teacher education research, practice, and policy without understanding the larger context of teacher education. Ladson-Billings (1995) made a similar point in the teacher education chapter in the first edition of this *Handbook*: "The responsibility of multicultural teacher education, then, is to ensure that it is placed squarely within the debate about teacher education in general" (p. 749). Three important aspects of the current debates about teacher education are changing demographics, competing agendas for teacher education reform, and challenges to the research base.

The Demographic Imperative

The phrase "the demographic imperative" (Banks, 1995; Dilworth, 1992) has been used to draw the conclusion—both essential and inescapable—that the educational community must take action in order to alter the disparities deeply embedded in the American educational system. Evidence for the demographic imperative includes statistics and other information in three areas: the diverse student population, the homogeneous teaching force, and "the demographic divide" (Gay & Howard, 2000), or the marked disparities in educational opportunities, resources, and achievement among student groups that differ from one another racially, culturally, and socioeconomically.

Drawing on information collected for the 2000 census, the noted educational demographer Harold Hodgkinson (2001, 2002) points out that although some 40% of the school population is now from racially and culturally diverse groups, this varies dramatically (from 7% to 68%), depending on the state. Hodgkinson (2002) explains anticipated demographic changes:

Future population growth in the United States continues to be uneven—61% of the population increase in the next 20 years will be Hispanic and Asian, about 40% Hispanic and 20% Asian; but then, as now, 10 states will contain 90% of the Hispanic population, 10 will contain 90% of the Asian population, and 7 will do both. Half of all Mexican Americans live in California! In fact, most of this increased diversity will be absorbed by only about 300 of our 3,000 [U.S.] counties. . . .

If we look at what changes America, it is 1 million immigrants a year, 4 million births, 2 million deaths, and 43 million people moving each year. Transience is a major factor in crime rates, poor health care, and poor-performing schools and states. . . . The worst performing states in terms of the percentage of 19-year-olds who have both graduated from high school and been admitted to a college . . . also are the states with the most transience and the highest crime rates. (pp. 103–104)

If projections are accurate, children of color will constitute the statistical majority of the student population by 2035 and account for 57% by 2050 (U.S. Department of Commerce, 1996, as cited in Villegas & Lucas, 2002a).

The most recent information available on the nation's teaching force suggests a profile that is quite different from the student profile, with White teachers currently accounting for some 86% of the teaching force and with teachers of color collectively accounting for only 14% (National Center for Education Statistics, 1997). This pattern reflects a modest increase in the percentage of minority teachers since a low point of only 7% in 1986. Information about who is currently preparing to teach indicates a pattern that is generally similar to that of the current teaching force (American Association of Colleges for Teacher Education, 1997, 1999; Dilworth, 1992; Howey, 1994), with White students representing the vast majority (80-93%) of students enrolled in collegiate education programs, depending on institution and location. Hodgkinson (2002) and others have pointed out that declines since the 1960s in enrollments among African American students in teacher education programs are related in part to proportionate increases in enrollments in business administration majors. Although there is some evidence that teacher education programs may be becoming somewhat more diverse (American Association of Colleges for Teacher Education, 1999) and some alternate route programs are attracting more minority students (Lauer, 2001), it seems clear that the teaching force will remain primarily White European American for some time to come.

As has been pointed out, the demographic implications for education are far greater than the obvious numerical differences between student and teaching populations. There are also marked differences in the biographies and experiences of most teachers who are White European Americans from middle-class backgrounds who speak only English, on the one hand, and the many students who are people of color, and/or live in poverty, and/or speak a first language that is not English, on the other hand (Gay, 1993; Irvine, 1997a). Teachers tend not to have the same cultural frames of reference and points of view as their students because, as Gay (1993) suggests, "they live in different existential worlds" (p. 287) and thus often have difficulty functioning as role models for students (Villegas & Lucas, 2002a) or as cultural brokers and cultural agents (Gay, 1993; Goodwin, 2000) who help students bridge home-school differences. They also often have difficulty constructing curriculum, instruction, and interactional patterns that are culturally responsive

(Irvine, 2001; Ladson-Billings, 1995), which means that the students in the greatest academic need are least likely to have access to educational opportunities congruent with their life experiences. Perhaps most serious, many White middle-class teachers understand diversity as a deficit to be overcome and have low expectations and fears about students who are different from themselves, especially those in urban areas (Gay & Howard, 2000; Irvine, 1990; Valenzuela, 2002; Weiner, 1993; Yeo, 1997).

The third part of the demographic imperative has to do with the staggering disparities in educational outcomes and conditions for students with and without the advantages conferred by race, culture, language, and socioeconomic status. Villegas and Lucas (2002a) offer a chilling and detailed discussion of these disparities based on standard sources of education statistics as well as original analyses. They point out that the United States has the highest rate of children living in poverty among advanced nations worldwide (Children's Defense Fund, 2000, as cited in Villegas & Lucas, 2002a) and that the percentage of Black and Hispanic children living in poverty (42% and 40%, respectively) far exceeds the percentage of White children (16%) (Kilborn, 1996, as cited in Villegas & Lucas, 2002a). Furthermore, they note that the achievement levels of Black and Hispanic students on the National Assessment of Educational Progress (NAEP) mathematics and reading assessments are consistently and markedly lower than levels for White students (NCES, 1997b, 1998, 1999, as cited in Villegas & Lucas, 2002a) as are high school graduation rates (Educational Research Service, 1995, as cited in Villegas & Lucas, 2002a; National Education Goals Panel, 1994, as cited in Villegas & Lucas, 2002a). Villegas and Lucas conclude that "the consistent gap between racial/ethnic minority and poor students and their White, middle-class peers . . . is indicative of the inability of the educational system to effectively teach students of color as schools have traditionally been structured" (p. 9).

As has long been documented, there are also staggering disparities in allocation of resources (for example, equipment, supplies, physical facilities, books, access to computer technology, and class size) to urban, suburban, and rural schools (Darling-Hammond, 1995; Kozol, 1991). A California lawsuit filed in 2000 by the American Civil Liberties Union (ACLU) on behalf of public school children in 18 California school districts reflects continuation of this pattern. The suit charges that children who attend schools that lack basic learning tools such as books, materials, functioning toilet facilities, safe and infestation-free buildings and grounds, trained teachers, and enough seats for all students are deprived of fundamental educational opportunities. In the plaintiffs' schools, 96.4% of the student population is children of color, compared with 59% across the state (American

Civil Liberties Union, 2000). Along these same lines, there is growing evidence that children of color and children who live in urban or poor areas are the most likely to have teachers who are not fully qualified or licensed to teach (Darling-Hammond, 2000; Darling-Hammond & Sclan, 1996).

What does all this add up to? What is the demographic imperative for teacher education? In short, it is the recognition that bridging the chasm between the school and life experiences of those with and without social, cultural, racial, and economic advantages requires fundamental changes in the ways teachers are educated. This does not mean that changing teacher education will—in and of itself—change the schools or fix what is wrong with American education. Weiner (1993) has argued extensively that teacher preparation cannot change schools, despite some expectations to the contrary. (Also see Weiner, 1990, 1993, 2000; Earley, 2000; and Yeo, 1997, for discussions along these lines.) Teachers can, however, join with others to work for change. This is not a new idea, of course. Unfortunately, however, despite the fact that the demographic imperative has now been widely acknowledged and meticulously well documented, there is still great need. The early part of the 21st century is dominated by a conservative political environment, a relentless focus on high-stakes tests, a growing underclass that many fear will be permanent, and a convergence of factors that places the least well-qualified teachers in schools with students in the greatest peril. These are good—and appalling—reasons to conclude that the demographic imperative is even more imperative now than it was a decade ago.

Competing Agendas for Reform

A second important aspect of the current context for teacher education is the interplay between two larger national agendas for educational reform in general and teacher education reform in particular. These intensely political agendas are overlapping in certain ways but simultaneously competing and even contradictory in others (Apple, 2000, 2001; Cochran-Smith, 2001a, 2001b; Cochran-Smith & Fries, 2001; Earley, 2000). The agenda to professionalize teaching and teacher education, which is linked to the K-12 curriculum standards movement, has been spearheaded by Linda Darling-Hammond and the National Commission on Teaching and America's Future and forwarded through the joint efforts of NCATE, the National Board for Professional Teaching Standards (NBPTS), and the Interstate New Teacher Assessment and Support Consortium (Gallagher & Bailey, 2000). These projects reflect a broad-based effort to develop a consistent approach to teacher education nationwide based on high standards for the initial preparation, licensing, and certification of teachers. Supported by foundations including the Carnegie Corporation, the Pew Charitable Trusts, the Ford Foundation, and the DeWitt Wallace Reader's Digest Fund, proponents of professionalization advocate standards- and knowledge-based teacher preparation and professional development, as well as teacher assessments based on school and classroom performance, across the professional life span.

In direct opposition to the professionalization agenda, however, is the well-publicized movement to deregulate teacher preparation by dismantling teacher education institutions and breaking up the monopoly that the profession has "too long" enjoyed. Supported by conservative political groups and private foundations including the Fordham Foundation, the Heritage Foundation, the Pioneer Institute, and the Manhattan Institute, the deregulation agenda begins with the premise that the requirements of state licensing agencies and schools of education are unnecessary hurdles that keep bright young people out of teaching and focus on social goals rather than academic achievement. Advocates of deregulation push for alternate routes into teaching and high-stakes teacher tests as the major gatekeeper for the profession. Part of a larger conservative political agenda for the privatization of education (Whitty, Power, & Halpin, 1998) and a market-based approach to educational reform (Apple, 2001), the deregulation agenda intersects in certain ways with the standards movement, particularly in the widespread implementation of high-stakes testing programs that purportedly reflect newer, higher teaching and learning standards for all students and, increasingly, all teachers.

These two agendas are shaping the way teacher education reforms are being constructed, debated, and implemented in many states. In some states, there are unprecedented actions to control teacher education and limit the role of colleges and universities by establishing new state-level requirements that regulate nearly every aspect of the teacher education curriculum. In some states and cities, particularly where there are or will be severe teacher shortages, there are major efforts to establish alternate entry routes into teaching, some of which bypass colleges and universities altogether, while others are linked to alternative programs at higher education institutions. In a number of states, there are simultaneous—and contradictory—initiatives at the state level, especially tighter control of existing college- and university-based teacher preparation programs coupled with preferred alternate entry routes into teaching that reward those who have had no college- and university-based programs at all.

Challenges to the Research Base

The third major aspect of the teacher education context in the early years of the 21st century is intense scrutiny—and some would say direct attack—of the research basis for college- and university-based teacher preparation. First made visible in the debates about the evidence for professionalization versus deregulation as policy options (Ballou & Podgursky, 2000; Darling-Hammond, 2000; Education Commission of the States, 2000), these arguments have grown increasingly heated and, in some cases, ad hominem. (See Abell Foundation, 2001a, 2000b; Darling-Hammond, 2001; also see Cochran-Smith & Fries, 2001, for an analysis of these debates). Policy makers have become intensely interested in whether there is a research basis justifying various policies in terms of bottom-line, value-added impact on teacher quality and student achievement. The synthesis of empirical research on teacher preparation sponsored by the Office of Educational Research and Improvement (OERI) (Wilson et al., 2001), for example, concluded that the research base for teacher education is thin. The report pointed out that although there are many peer-reviewed and published articles about teacher preparation, most do not meet accepted criteria for disciplined inquiry: rigorous methods of investigation and analysis as well as findings described sufficiently to assess validity. Along similar lines, the Education Commission of the States sponsored a secondary analysis of the same set of studies reviewed by Wilson et al., but with a particular focus on policy-related questions (Lauer, 2001). This report also concludes that the research base is inadequate and that there is a clear need for research that accounts for context, draws on complementary research methods, and examines the impact of various policy options regarding teacher preparation on student learning.

The intense scrutiny of the empirical research basis for teacher education is part of the much larger accountability zeitgeist that dominates education early in the 21st century, with its emphasis on outcomes, impacts, evidence, bottom lines, results, effectiveness, and added value. This emphasis is bolstered by what appears to be the new orthodoxy of federally funded research about "what works" or what is "evidence based" in terms of reading and other instructional areas. Consistent with the production imagery embedded in the language of outcomes and effects is the definition of scientific research certified by the federal government in the reauthorization of the Elementary and Secondary Education Act (ESEA). According to the federal government, "scientific research" is to be evaluated "using experimental or quasi-experimental designs . . . with appropriate controls to evaluate the effects of the condition of interest, with a preference for random-assignment experiments" (No Child Left Behind Act of 2001, 2002). This definition of educational research contrasts with the one put forward in the National Research Council's recent report, *Scientific Inquiry in Education* (Shavelson & Towne, 2002), which emphasizes that it is not a particular method that makes research scientific but a particular inquiry process guided by scientific principles. According to the report, this means that many paradigms of educational research can be scientific, although asking different kinds of questions. Debates about research paradigms, the research basis for teacher education, and what kinds of research are worthy of government funding figure largely in the teacher education context.

This is the complex context within which the literature on multicultural teacher education must be considered in the early years of the 21st century: changing demographics that exacerbate the divide between privileged and disadvantaged groups, competing agendas for educational reform with privatization a pivotal issue, and serious challenges to the research basis in all areas of education.

SYNTHESIZING THE SYNTHESES

In 1972, the first Commission on Multicultural Education of the American Association of Colleges for Teacher Education (AACTE) made three key assertions: (1) cultural diversity is a valuable resource, (2) multicultural education preserves and extends the resource of culture diversity rather than merely tolerating it or making it "melt away," and (3) a commitment to cultural pluralism ought to permeate all aspects of teacher preparation programs (Baptiste & Baptiste, 1980). In 1976, NCATE added multicultural education to its standards, requiring that institutions seeking accreditation show evidence that multicultural education was planned for (by 1979) and then provided (by 1981) in all programs of teacher preparation (Gollnick, 1992). Since that time, a number of key syntheses of the research literature have reported on the state of multicultural teacher education research, practice, and policy.

The Task of Synthesis

As Grant and Graue (1997) point out, the task of a synthesis is not straightforward and unchanging, but is rather "constantly recreated and nurtured by the opportunities, possibilities, and visions of the scholarship of that particular time period" (p. 1). Sleeter (2001a) makes a similar point in the introduction to her review of research on preservice teacher preparation for underserved populations: "The question, 'What is a review?' is disconcertingly complex. . . . Equally complex is the question 'What counts as research?'" (p. 209). These comments make it clear that a synthesis of the literature on multicultural teacher education requires a host of decisions. Arguably, even the simplest version of the question, What does the research say about multicultural teacher education? requires decision rules about (1) how "the problem" of multicultural teacher education is constructed and framed, (2) what body of research is to be examined and excluded, (3) what conceptions of multicultural education are to be used, and (4) what conceptions of teacher education are to be used. In addition, some synthesizers work from a particular theoretical or disciplinary perspective that they regard as a rich or heretofore missing approach to sorting out the literature. A synthesis of syntheses, which is the intention here, complicates the review task considerably by making its own decision rules and at the same time attempting to make sense of the decisions made by previous synthesizers.

This synthesis of syntheses includes 14 reviews published between 1980 and 2001. These appeared primarily in the major reviewing outlets in education—four in handbooks of research, two in the *Review of Research in Education (RRE),* and three in *Review of Educational Research (RER)*—as well as in other outlets—two in technical reports, one in an edited book, one in a journal, and one a book itself. Each of these focuses on the initial recruitment or preparation (or both) of teachers for a multicultural society and is intended to be synthetic of a particular body of work. It should be noted that syntheses of multicultural education in general or of K-12 classroom teaching for diversity are not included here, nor are edited books related to multicultural teacher education, individual studies or analyses, or models and conceptual frameworks. Many of these references, however, are analyzed or referred to in other sections of this review.

Multicultural Teacher Education Syntheses, 1980–2001

This synthesis of syntheses begins with the 1980 report of AACTE's Commission on Multicultural Education (Baptiste & Baptiste, 1980), which was intended to clarify the meaning and intent of NCATE's new multicultural standard. The commission report opened with an unequivocal statement about the task of teacher education:

The authors believe that teachers and other education personnel can deliver educational equity in our schools. However, the mandate of teacher education programs must be to prepare teachers with the necessary skills to deliver education to all students equitably once they are in the classroom. This, of course, implies that teacher educators must examine their own programs to determine how well they are currently delivering such skills. This will probably necessitate the redesigning of portions of current programs. (p. 1)

The commission's overview brought together nine research-based articles, selected from 103 proposals. These drew on a wide range of literature, almost all of it from the 1970s and reflecting to a certain extent that era's

emphasis on competency-based teacher education. Although little of this literature examined the effectiveness of particular approaches, it explored an array of topics: teacher recruitment, intergroup relations, ethnic studies, bilingual and bicultural education, learning styles, family socialization patterns, bidialectalism, interpersonal skills, disproportionate minority discipline, and multicultural curriculum theories and models. This report and the three commission volumes that followed it helped to prompt attention to these issues in teacher education for the next 25 years.

In Figure 46.1, the 14 syntheses are arranged chronologically as follows: Baptiste and Baptiste (1980), Grant and Secada (1990), Gollnick (1992), King (1993), Weiner (1993), Zeichner (1993a), Ladson-Billings (1995), Haberman (1996), Zeichner and Hoeft (1996), Ladson-Billings (1999), McAllister and Irvine (2000), Weiner (2000), and Sleeter (2001a, 2001b). Each of the syntheses is analyzed according to how the problem is constructed; the specific questions posed or the purpose of the review (or both); the body of research considered; the definition of multicultural education or the conceptual and theoretical frameworks (or both) used to structure the synthesis; and its findings and recommendations.

Below is more detail about eight of the reviews that are widely cited in teacher education, including two instances where two closely related reviews by the same author are combined and considered together. These illustrate some of the major threads in the ongoing conversation about multicultural teacher education. Of the eight reviews highlighted here, four address general issues in multicultural teacher preparation and recruitment, two address urban teacher preparation specifically, one considers the epistemological basis of multicultural teacher education research, and one considers teacher education from the perspective of critical race theory.

Grant and Secada's (1990) review appeared in the first *Handbook of Research on Teacher Education.* They framed the topic of preparing teachers for diversity in terms of three content domains—multicultural education, sex equity, and second language learning—and used Grant and Sleeter's (1985) typology to categorize the studies. Compared with other syntheses in this area, theirs takes the most limited approach (some would say rigid, others would say, rigorous, depending on point of view) to what counts as research, ultimately reviewing only 23 empirical research studies that provided external objective support for claims. Grant and Secada (1990) concluded that there was a surprising and unacceptable paucity of empirical research, reflecting "the marginal status and low importance that has been given to research" on this topic (p. 404). They also concluded that experiences with diverse perspectives and populations—the more intensive, the better—were good for teachers but difficult to

TABLE 46.1. Synthesis of the Syntheses on Multicultural Education, 1980–2001.

Major Syntheses	How the "Problem" of Cultural Diversity in Teacher Education Is Constructed	Question Addressed and/or Purpose of the Review	Body of Research Reviewed	Definition of Multicultural Education and/or Conceptual Framework Used to Organize the Literature	Findings and Recommendations
1980: Baptiste, Baptiste, & Gollnick	The increasing cultural diversity in schools requires revision of TE programs	Purpose: To clarify meaning and intent of new NCATE and AACTE multi-cultural standards	1970s research on MCTE: Recruitment, MC theories, ethnic studies, interpersonal relationships, bidialectalism, learning styles, teachers' inter-personal skills	AACTE 1972 definition of MCE: Education that values cultural pluralism and sees cultural diversity as a resource	TE must examine programs to see how well they prepare teachers to deliver equitable education TE must redesign portions of current programs to meet new standards
1990: Grant & Secada	There is growing discontinuity between the teaching force and student diversity	Purpose: to review the empirical research on TE in the domains of multi-cultural education, sex equity, and second-language learning	Literature on preparing teachers for diversity, 1964-1988. From larger pool, reviews 23 studies with objective support for claims	Adaptation of Grant & Sleeter's (1985) typology for classifying MCE studies	Paucity of empirical research in MCTE Need more studies that examine impact of recruitment models, cut across contexts, define and measure pro-gram outcomes
1992: Gollnick	Institutions do not seem to have taken MCE and MCTE mandates seriously	Purpose: To review policies related to cultural pluralism and MCE in TE	Major national policies and practices in preparation programs for educators and their implemen-tation in higher education, mid-1970s to 1990	Lynch's (1986) typology of policy options related to MCE and Grant & Sleeter's (1989) approaches to MC teaching	The only national policies that govern MCTE are voluntary After 12 years of required MCE, institutions have not accepted or integrated this across curriculum Serious difficulties recruiting students and faculties of color

TABLE 46.1. Synthesis of the Syntheses on Multicultural Education, 1980–2001. (*continued*)

Major Syntheses	How the "Problem" of Cultural Diversity in Teacher Education Is Constructed	Question Addressed and/or Purpose of the Review	Body of Research Reviewed	Definition of Multicultural Education and/or Conceptual Framework Used to Organize the Literature	Findings and Recommendations
1993: King	There is a severely limited presence of African American teachers in the workforce	Purpose: To provide a comprehensive review of literature that explores general trends in the teaching profession and factors that contribute to limited presence of African American teachers	1980s and 1990s literature related to the need for African American teachers, including supply and demand trends, explanations for limited presence of AA teachers	General framework that combines historical, pedagogical, demographic, and sociological analyses	Despite small gains in 1991, presence of AA teachers is limited, with small numbers entering and staying in teaching Factors influencing numbers of AAs in teaching include desegregation, school enrollment trends, increased alternate job opportunities, role of historically black colleges, and teacher competency tests Need more complex research on why AAs enter teaching, what experiences they have, and why they are important
1993: Weiner	The preparation of teachers is completely inadequate for urban schools	Purpose: To review school reform literature related to preparation of teachers for urban schools	Social science educational research related to urban teacher preparation, 1960-1990	Ecological perspective on schools and schooling. A definition of "urban" more complex than "diversity," including hierarchical structures of schools, bureaucratic features, social conditions of urban areas	Need specific focus on preparing urban teachers, not general MCTE Has been a shift over 30 years from educating teachers to teach the disadvantaged, to competency-based TE, to using understandings of urban schools to change TE programs

TABLE 46.1. Synthesis of the Syntheses on Multicultural Education, 1980–2001. *(continued)*

Major Syntheses	*How the "Problem" of Cultural Diversity in Teacher Education Is Constructed*	*Question Addressed and/or Purpose of the Review*	*Body of Research Reviewed*	*Definition of Multicultural Education and/or Conceptual Framework Used to Organize the Literature*	*Findings and Recommendations*
1993: Zeichner	A major policy issue in TE is dealing with the discrepancy between diverse school population and white, culturally encapsulated TE students	Purpose: To report on how teacher educators have attempted to improve the preparation of teachers to teach students who have been failed by the school system	Published and fugitive literature that suggests alternative approaches to preparation of teachers for diversity	Preparation for teaching as a combination of the knowledge, skills, and dispositions for successful teaching of diverse populations	Key elements of TE for diversity: •Knowledge of and about culture(s) •Historical knowledge about school and societal inequities •How to learn about students' cultures •Diverse community and field experiences •How to create culturally appropriate curriculum, instruction, assessment
1995: Ladson-Billings	There is a great need for fundamental, paradigmatic change in teacher education for diversity	Purpose: To reexamine the literature of MCTE to suggest linkages between theory and practice	43 studies within MCTE literature, 1989-19921	Banks's (1993) dimensions of MCE paradigms	Must analyze MCTE within larger context of TE challenges

Quantity does not equal quality in MCTE programs or research

Need to include "new scholarship" in MCTE that reveals knowledge based on the experience of teacher educators |

TABLE 46.1. Synthesis of the Syntheses on Multicultural Education, 1980–2001. (*continued*)

Major Syntheses	How the "Problem" of Cultural Diversity in Teacher Education Is Constructed	Question Addressed and/or Purpose of the Review	Body of Research Reviewed	Definition of Multicultural Education and/or Conceptual Framework Used to Organize the Literature	Findings and Recommendations
1996: Haberman	There is enormous and increasing difficulty recruiting and preparing competent teachers for urban schools	Purpose: To conceptualize the major issues related to recruitment and selection of urban teachers	Literature related to recruitment of urban teachers, primarily from 1980s	Epistemological basis of TE programs: universal vs. contextual approaches	Most TE programs have an universalistic approach to preparing teachers Instead, we need a specific focus on urban context TE for urban teachers is evolving outside the university (by default)
1996: Zeichner & Hoeft	A major policy issue in TE is how to prepare all teachers with the knowledge, skill, and dispositions to teach all students well	Purpose: To examine the research on the socialization of teachers for cultural diversity in three areas: recruitment and selection, curriculum and instruction, and institutional change	Literature on TE for diversity from 1990s, including in-service and occupational socialization in other professions	Four dimensions of MCTE: infusion and segregation, culture-specific and culture-general, interacting with and studying about culture, program as model	There are trends in TE strategies used, but evidence of their effectiveness is weak Paucity of literature on in-service MCTE Lack of evidence for long-term impact of institutional strategies
1999: Ladson-Billings	Adequately preparing teachers for diverse learners within current public school systems and current TE programs is extremely improbable	Purpose: To reframe the task of the research review to include paradigmatic underpinnings and practical strengths of previous literature	More than 30 MCTE articles since 1992 plus exemplary efforts by teacher educators and programs with critical race theory perspectives	Critical race theory as a new prism for considering MCTE efforts	MCTE continues to conceptualize diversity as a problem with the solution appendages to the main program Recent literature restates need for MCTE without evidence; knowing what the literature says is not enough Can use critical race theory to understand how innovative programs challenge the system

TABLE 46.1. Synthesis of the Syntheses on Multicultural Education, 1980–2001. *(continued)*

Major Syntheses	*How the "Problem" of Cultural Diversity in Teacher Education Is Constructed*	*Question Addressed and/or Purpose of the Review*	*Body of Research Reviewed*	*Definition of Multicultural Education and/or Conceptual Framework Used to Organize the Literature*	*Findings and Recommendations*
2000: McAllister & Irvine	Teachers who work in MC schools need to develop cross-cultural competence	Purpose: To examine the research base for process-oriented models that are applicable to TE for teachers who work in MC schools	12 studies from 1980s and 1990s that used three cross-cultural models to study teachers' development of cross-cultural competency	Helms's (1984, 1990) model of racial identity, Banks's (1994) typology of ethnicity, Bennett's (1993) developmental model of intercultural sensitivity	The most useful process models focus on how people grow in cultural identity and in worldview Process models can help teacher educators sequence course content; understand teachers' responses, resistance, and growth; create productive learning environments
2000: Weiner	There are continuing and mounting problems recruiting and preparing teachers to work in urban schools	Purpose: Building on Weiner's 1993 study, to synthesize research on changed economic, political, social, and educational contexts of urban teacher preparation	Educational scholarship from 1990s (in psychology, social foundations, policy, curriculum and instruction) with implications for urban TE	Ecological perspective on schools and schooling; complex definition of "urban" (see Weiner, 1993)	There is a notable absence of analysis of how political and economic conditions influence research on teaching, teachers, TE General thrust of education reform in 1990s has been how to harness education in service to economy Urban TE research has failed to study how school structures and organization mediate teacher-student learning (partly there is the assumption that "urban" equals "diversity")

TABLE 46.1. Synthesis of the Syntheses on Multicultural Education, 1980–2001. *(continued)*

Major Syntheses	How the "Problem" of Cultural Diversity in Teacher Education Is Constructed	Question Addressed and/or Purpose of the Review	Body of Research Reviewed	Definition of Multicultural Education and/or Conceptual Framework Used to Organize the Literature	Findings and Recommendations
2001a: Sleeter	There are growing gaps between teachers and students in terms of culture, race, economic backgrounds	Purpose: To examine research on the preparation of teachers for MC or historically under-served populations from the perspective of epistemology	119 published articles on recruitment and preparation of teachers for underserved populations with some form of data, late 1970s through 1990s	Epistemological perspectives underlying research: positivism, phenomenology, narrative research, and emancipatory research	There is a strong mismatch between those going into teaching and the current student population Many MCTE studies are weak methodologically; the research base is still thin Most research is small-scale, not producing coherent body of work Community-based experiences for TE students seem promising Alternative TE programs remain marginal Traditional TE programs discourage and silence TE students of color who bring different experiences

TABLE 46.1. Synthesis of the Syntheses on Multicultural Education, 1980–2001. *(continued)*

Major Syntheses	How the "Problem" of Cultural Diversity in Teacher Education Is Constructed	Question Addressed and/or Purpose of the Review	Body of Research Reviewed	Definition of Multicultural Education and/or Conceptual Framework Used to Organize the Literature	Findings and Recommendations
2001b: Sleeter	TE students of color bring more diverse experiences than white TE students, but both need to develop teaching skills to work with underserved populations	Purpose: To review research about two approaches to preparing teachers for underserved students: recruitment and selection, developing attitudes and MC knowledge base in teachers	Draws on Sleeter (2001a), 80 published studies with data on TE for under-served populations	Approaches used in TE to address diversity issues: recruitment and selection, community-based experience, MCE course work and fieldwork, program interventions	There is an "over-whelming pres-ence of whiteness" in MCTE— focuses on prepar-ing White teachers for diversity, which may discourage TE students of color
					Need research that follows TE gradu-ates into classroom
					Need more community-based links and experi-ences for TE students

Note: The following abbreviations are used: TE, teacher education; MCE, multicultural education; MCTE, multicultural teacher education; AA, African American.

translate into classroom practice. They called for research that went beyond changing teachers' attitudes on a self-reported, short-term basis and instead examined the impact of teachers' expectations on students' learning. They also called for studies of the effects of recruitment and preparation models and outcome-based definitions of program goals, which would allow for generalizations across programs, institutions, and locations.

Ladson-Billings's (1995) synthesis, which appeared in the first edition of this *Handbook,* was framed as a "reex-amination" of the literature, intended to explore linkages between theory and practice. She observed that despite increases in quantity of attention to multicultural issues, few changes in quality had been accomplished. Ladson-Billings used Banks's (1993) typology of multicultural education to categorize the literature, asserting that this typology reconceptualized multicultural teacher educa-tion as a field of scholarly inquiry rather than in terms of a deficit paradigm. Ladson-Billings suggested that any review needed to include "new scholarship in teacher education," especially more qualitative case studies based on "careful documentation of practice" (p. 753), and tap

into the wisdom of practice. Along these lines, she sug-gested several trends in teacher education practice, including the use of autobiography, restructured field experiences, situated pedagogies, and returning to the classrooms of experts. Ladson-Billings concluded that multicultural teacher education mediated between theory and practice and thus might "well be the determiner of the fate of multicultural education. . . . [It must] assume a pro-active leadership role or else risk a marginalization that will have dire consequences" (p. 756).

A synthesis of the literature on teacher socialization for cultural diversity by Zeichner and Hoeft (1996) was pub-lished in the second *Handbook of Research on Teacher Edu-cation.* Building on Zeichner's earlier synthesis (1993a) of what teachers need to know to be culturally responsive, Zeichner and Hoeft's review examined three areas—the selection and recruitment of teachers, curriculum and instruction in teacher education, and efforts to strengthen the higher education institutional environment. Zeichner and Hoeft also included literature on the professional development of experienced teachers for diversity, an aspect of teacher education not included in most other reviews (exceptions are Grant & Secada, 1990; McAllister & Irvine, 2000), as well as the literature on occupational socialization in other human services. Like Ladson-Billings (1995) and despite the fact that the empirical evidence was weak, Zeichner and Hoeft included the work of teacher education practitioners by identifying and offering examples of strategies that appeared to be common. Zeichner and Hoeft pointed out the dearth of empirical studies in many areas of teacher education, particularly those that examine the short- and long-term impact of recruitment and selection, curriculum and instruction, and institutional strategies. They noted several gaps in the literature: how program structures and components are connected to teaching practices, how cultural knowledge influences cultural competency in the workplace, and how experiences in teacher education are connected (or not) to personal and professional changes in teachers.

Ladson-Billings's (1999) review, which appeared in *RRE*, focused on preparing teachers for diversity from the perspective of critical race theory. Her review, like the two by Weiner (1993, 2000) described below, used the tool of the research synthesis to create "a new prism," or to do what Graue and Grant (2002) describe as using "the genre of the research review, which seem[s] to many to be a conservative force in the generation of knowledge, to open up the notion of research and make new understandings" (p. 268). Ladson-Billings argued that to date, multicultural teacher education had not been rethought or reframed. Drawing on tenets from critical race theory, she argued that diversity continued to be seen as a deficit in teacher education, and thus its solution continued to be appendages to the curriculum rather than a fundamental paradigmatic shift. In doing so, Ladson-Billings "reframe[d] notions of preparing teachers for teaching diverse learners so that we might understand the 'improbability' of such a task in public school systems that actively work at achieving school failure" (p. 211). Ladson-Billings described six teacher educators or programs with critical race theory perspectives, arguing that we need to know how teacher educators and programs understand issues of diversity by examining critically efforts that do (or do not) challenge the status quo.

Weiner's two reviews of research (1993, 2000) are closely tied to multicultural teacher education. The first, a book published by Teachers College Press, synthesized educational social science literature related to urban teacher preparation from 1960 to 1990; the second, which appeared in *RER*, built on the first, examining research from the 1990s. Weiner worked from an ecological perspective on school reform and a complex definition of "urban" that included highly diverse populations, complex school bureaucracies, consistent underfunding, and

"unitary and objective" notions of intelligence and achievement. Emphasizing the conditions of urban schools, Weiner traced research in four areas over the 40-year period: the skills and attitudes necessary to teach disadvantaged students, how teacher preparation should be revised to provide those skills, how the structures of urban school systems influenced teaching and learning, and how teacher education could use understanding of these to develop urban teacher preparation programs. Weiner found that although there was some change during the 1990s, researchers had generally failed to account for the ways in which political and economic conditions influenced research and the ways in which school structures mediated teaching and learning. Weiner concluded that this shift had been long in coming because researchers continued to equate "urban" simply with cultural diversity.

Finally, Sleeter (2001a, 2001b) published two related reviews on the preparation of teachers for historically underserved populations, one in *RER* and the other in the *Journal of Teacher Education*. Sleeter's reviews sorted out and synthesized the "diverse epistemologies" used to examine multicultural teacher education in more than 100 articles that drew on some kind of data. Based on her analysis of underlying epistemological assumptions, Sleeter concluded that much of the research had been rooted in positivist assumptions, with a fair amount of research based on phenomenological and narrative assumptions and almost no research that could be termed emancipatory. Sleeter demonstrated that different aspects of the same topic could be usefully studied in epistemologically different ways, but also pointed out the disadvantages of many small-scale studies that do not add up to a coherent body of knowledge in the field. She concluded that at the turn of the century, the research base for multicultural teacher education was still thin, with many studies methodologically weak, despite epistemological bases. Across epistemologies, she suggested that there was an "overwhelming presence of Whiteness" (p. 94) that discouraged or silenced teachers of color and nontraditional teacher recruits.

Looking Across the Syntheses

Across the syntheses, there are a number of interesting issues related to the potential of multicultural teacher education to accomplish its goals as well as to varying visions of scholarship and knowledge generation. One of the most striking conclusions is that basic changes in teacher education are necessary but have not occurred despite more than a quarter-century of attention. The caution in the 1980 synthesis by Baptiste and Baptiste, quoted earlier, that teacher education would probably need to redesign "portions of current programs" seems both remarkably wise in its early call for self-reflexive examination and remarkably naïve about the scope of the task, which now seems so clearly to demand fundamental reinvention rather than incremental modification. Along these lines, several of the syntheses—notably Gollnick's (1992), Haberman's (1996), Ladson-Billings's (1999), Weiner's (1993, 2000), and Sleeter's (2001a)—specifically propose new lenses to illuminate heretofore omitted or silenced issues and stimulate new approaches to the "improbable" (Ladson-Billings, 1999) work of reinvention. Also along these lines is the continuing thread in the syntheses, first pointed out in Grant and Secada's (1990) review, that research in multicultural teacher education has been consistently marginalized. From the perspective of policy, Gollnick (1992) makes this point emphatically, charging that after twelve years of NCATE's requiring multicultural education, "institutions still have not taken seriously its incorporation into its programs and practices" and that "equality and cultural diversity are not central to their missions" (p. 237). Consistent marginalization in mission, funding, and urgency helps explain the lack of longitudinal studies and concentrated efforts to develop clear impact measures. It also sheds light on the large number of small-scale, short-term studies that are conducted by individual teacher educators.

Based on 40 years of research on urban teacher preparation, Weiner (2000) makes explicit the connection between how research problems are prioritized, on the one hand, and economic and social conditions, on the other:

Although funding for research on urban school reform and teacher preparation was sparked by the civil rights movements' agitation for equal opportunity for Black Americans, this fact was hardly noted in scholarship of the 60s and 70s. Yet it is critical for understanding why, suddenly, researchers became interested in a problem that had existed for decades before. Similarly the diminution of research on urban teacher preparation and educational research in the 90s can only be understood in light of ideological and economic changes in the society. (p. 372)

Marginalization and underfunding help explain why there has been little change in multicultural teacher education practice and teacher education. The synthesizers argue persuasively that well-developed and thoughtful impact measures are needed that allow for comparisons of recruitment and selection strategies, as well as comparisons of the pedagogies of teacher education. These impact measures need to link teacher preparation strategies with the school-based cultural competencies of teachers and prospective teachers, on the one hand, and the performance of K-12 students, on the other. This kind of research, however, as this chapter suggests in its conclusion,

requires funding, institutional infrastructure, and research skills in a variety of methods and approaches.

Another theme that threads through several of the syntheses is the need to move beyond traditional notions of evidence, effectiveness, and impact in reviewing the multicultural teacher education literature. Ladson-Billings (1995) included "the wisdom of practice" in her synthesis, and Zeichner and Hoeft (1996) included the "most common strategies" in teacher education, even though they also commented that the empirical evidence about the effectiveness of these was weak. In her second review, Ladson-Billings (1999) included descriptions of six exemplary educators and the programs with which they were involved. Sleeter (2001a) also included the writing of teacher education practitioners that provides "some form of data" (p. 213), much of which would not have withstood the criteria for empirical research explicated by Grant and Secada in their 1990 review. Part of what may account for this trend of teacher education practitioner researchers studying their own practice are increased expectations, even at colleges and universities not traditionally focused on research, that teacher educators conduct and publish research. But another explanation has to do with the intentional blurring or reconceptualization of roles in teacher education over the past 15 years or so. A number of teacher educators have been working to invent new roles in teacher education that privilege neither scholarship nor practice but instead depend on a rich dialectic of the two. This in no way suggests that this kind of work should not be held accountable to high standards of scholarship, but it does suggest that there may be different notions of what high standards look like.

THE MULTIPLE MEANINGS OF MULTICULTURAL TEACHER EDUCATION: A CONCEPTUAL FRAMEWORK

Despite the fact that most teacher education programs report that they have now incorporated multicultural perspectives and content into the curriculum, external examinations often prove to the contrary (Gollnick, 1995), and, as noted above, synthesizers consistently conclude that nothing much has "really" changed. These discrepancies suggest that there are multiple meanings for the ideas related to multiculturalism and multiple instantiations of what "multicultural teacher education" actually means.

There are a number of frameworks available for examining teacher education generally, including Feiman-Nemser's (1990) "structural and conceptual alternatives," "traditions of practice" (Liston & Zeichner, 1991; Zeichner, 1993b), and Cochran-Smith and

Lytle's (1999) "relationships of knowledge and practice." In addition, there are several conceptions and typologies for multicultural education generally that have been applied to teacher education, including Sleeter and Grant's typology for classifying multicultural education studies (Grant & Sleeter, 1985; Sleeter & Grant, 1987), Banks's (1993, 1994) typology for approaches to multicultural curricular reform, Lynch's (1986) typology of the ideological orientations to policy options, and Jenks, Lee, and Kanpol's (2001) versions of multiculturalism, which point out similarities and differences among previous conceptions. More specific to teacher preparation, Zeichner and Hoeft (1996) suggest that all teacher education programs take positions on four issues related to multicultural education: infusion versus segregation, culture-specific versus culture-general, interacting with versus studying about cultures, and whether a program itself is a model of what it espouses. There are also a number of models or program approaches to multicultural teacher education described in the literature (e.g. Bennett, 1995; Villegas & Lucas, 2002a).

In this chapter, Cochran-Smith's (2003b) theoretical framework for understanding "the multiple meanings of multicultural teacher education" is used. (Earlier versions of this framework are described in Cochran-Smith, 1997, 1998; also see Cochran-Smith, 2000, 2001a, 2001b.) This framework (see Figure 46.1) may be applied to any existing or envisioned teacher preparation approach, whether a college or university program, an alternate route, a for-profit provider, or a school-based on-the-job program. It can also be used, as has been done here, to analyze the literature related to multicultural teacher education.

Cochran-Smith's (2002) framework is based on the premise that any given approach to teacher preparation implicitly (or explicitly) answers and acts on the answers to eight questions that are related to multicultural issues: the diversity question, the ideology question, the knowledge question, the teacher learning question, the practice question, the outcomes question, the recruitment and selection question, and the coherence question. The *diversity question* has to do with how the demographic imperative is constructed as a "problem" for teacher education and what are understood to be desirable "solutions" to the problem. The *ideology question* has to do with ideas, ideals, values, and assumptions about the purposes of schooling, the social and economic history of the nation, and the role of public education in a democratic society, particularly with regard to prevailing images of American society as meritocratic or hegemonic. The *knowledge question* has to do with the knowledge, interpretive frameworks, beliefs, and attitudes that are considered necessary to teach diverse populations effectively, particularly knowledge and beliefs about culture and its role in schooling. The *teacher learning question* has to do with

general assumptions about how, when, and where adults learn to teach, including particular pedagogies and strategies that facilitate this learning. The *practice question* involves the competencies and pedagogical skills teachers are assumed to need to teach diverse populations effectively, particularly with regard to cultural competence, culturally responsive teaching, and ways of working with families and communities. The *outcomes question* has to do with the appropriate consequences of teacher preparation as well as how, by whom, and for what purposes these outcomes are demonstrated and measured. The *recruitment and selection question* has to do with perspectives on which candidates should be recruited and selected for the teaching force. The seven questions described so far are encompassed by an eighth, the *coherence question,* or the degree to which the first seven are connected to and coherent across one another and also

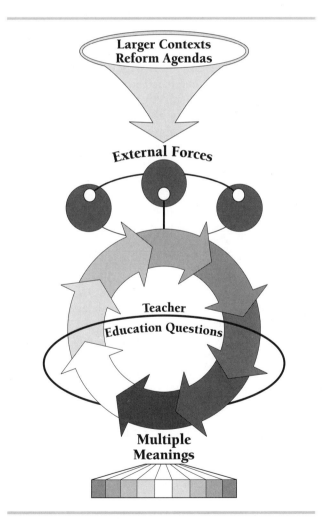

FIGURE 46.1. Understanding the Multiple Meanings of Multicultural Teacher Education.

with how multicultural issues are positioned in relation to other issues.

Cochran-Smith's (2002) framework for understanding the multiple meanings of multicultural teacher education also focuses on the forces that are somewhat external to teacher education programs but shape how the eight questions are answered: institutional capacity, relationships with local communities, and governmental and nongovernmental regulations, all of which are embedded within larger societal contexts. *Institutional capacity* has to do with the organization of institutions and institutional constraints and supports for a teacher education that is multicultural, as well as its relationship to larger institutional missions and goals. *Relationships with local communities* has to do with the interactions and relationships between a teacher preparation program and local families, neighborhoods, schools, communities, community agencies, and cities, towns and regions, including perspectives about the value of community contributions. *Governmental and nongovernmental regulations* refers to the requirements regarding teacher preparation stipulated by the agencies that govern and evaluate programs and approaches, either nonvoluntarily or voluntarily. The *larger societal context* refers to the conditions of schools and the larger social, historical, economic, and political contexts in which all of the above are embedded, including agendas for educational reform.

This chapter uses Cochran-Smith's (2002) framework to examine a decade of conceptual and empirical literature on multicultural teacher education. Ladson-Billings's (1995) chapter on the multicultural teacher education literature, published in the first edition of this *Handbook,* examined the empirical literature published between 1989 and 1992. The current chapter takes Ladson-Billings's ending point, 1992, as its starting point and uses 2001 as its ending point.

To establish the database for the next two sections of this chapter, initial Boolean searches (database searches for references that contain both of two or more key descriptors) were conducted on the *ERIC* and *Educational Abstracts* databases, combining "teacher education" (or "teacher preparation," or "preservice education," or "teacher recruitment") with "multicultural education" (or "diversity," or "cultural diversity," or "underserved populations," or "social justice," or "urban education," or "race"). The literature base yielded from these initial searches was supplemented with manual searches of key publications, professional recommendations, and Library of Congress searches for the same combined descriptors in order to locate books and chapters that were pertinent. References yielded by these searches that were on topics not within the scope of this chapter (such as in-service education, the preparation of bilingual or special education teachers, and international teacher education) were

eliminated. Also eliminated were a very small number of items that could not be located, unpublished papers and dissertations, program descriptions that did not include data and analyses, articles with tips or ideas for teachers and teacher educators, conference proceedings, and position papers. In sum, the final database for the next two sections of this chapter, which review the conceptual and the empirical multicultural teacher education literature, includes journal articles, books, and book chapters published or in press between 1992 and 2001 that deal with the initial recruitment and selection and preparation of teachers for a multicultural society in the United States. The section on the conceptual and theoretical literature reviews 93 references, and the section on the empirical and data-based literature reviews 153 studies. (These are in addition to the 59 citations referenced in the other sections of the chapter.)

NEW PARADIGMS FOR MULTICULTURAL EDUCATION? THE CONCEPTUAL LITERATURE, 1992–2001

Given the "improbability" of change under current societal and institutional conditions (Ladson-Billings, 1999), there have been many calls for new paradigms of multicultural teacher education or new ways of conceptualizing and building teacher preparation policy, practice, and research that respond to the nation's diversity. This section reviews the literature from 1992 to 2001 that speaks to paradigms, theories, conceptions, theoretical frameworks, typologies, and schema for multicultural teacher education.

Reviewing the Conceptual Literature

Although previous syntheses have generally used one or more frameworks to categorize the empirical literature, they have not reviewed the conceptual scholarship per se. As pointed out in the introduction to this chapter, however, underlying conceptions and theories mediate practice and policy, giving specific form and interpretation to approaches that have multiple meanings and possibilities. This is the case because teacher education, like teaching, is both a theoretical and a practical enterprise, even though there has long been an artificial distinction between the two, a point well explicated by Carr (1987):

Past efforts to understand the concept of practice within the field of education have tended to follow the natural sciences model in which theorizing is regarded as something distinct from the phenomena studied . . . . But to make such a division between theory and practice is to misunderstand the nature of practice. . . . By making the twin assumptions that all theory is non-practical and all practice is non-theoretical, this approach always underestimates the extent to which those engaged in educational practices have to reflect upon, and hence theorize, what, in general, they are trying to do. (Carr, 1987, pp. 13–14, as cited in Cochran-Smith & Lytle, 1998)

Our analysis of the conceptual literature related to multicultural teacher education is thematic rather than categorical. That is, the analysis cuts across the conceptual literature to examine how multicultural teacher education is conceptualized rather than assigning each article to one of the categories of Cochran-Smith's (2002) framework. This is particularly appropriate given that most of the conceptual literature deals with multiple issues and their interrelationships.

The View Since 1992: The Conceptual Literature

Most of the conceptual and theoretical literature over the decade advocates "new" ways of mapping out the conceptual contours of a teacher preparation that is multicultural. There are different ideas, however, about what "new" means and about where the lines are drawn between rearranging and adding pieces to already existing structures that remain fundamentally unchanged, on the one hand, and truly altering perspectives by beginning with quite different assumptions, on the other. Ladson-Billings (1999) argues that it is extremely difficult to do the latter because "the norms and folkways of teacher education have occluded our abilities to institute real change" (p. 224). Trying to assess which recent conceptual work is "really" new and which is simply old wine in new bottles is not a useful pursuit. Instead, the chapter uses Cochran-Smith's framework to identify points of agreement, of which there are many, as well as points of divergence in the conceptual literature.

The Diversity Question. There is a clear consensus in the conceptual literature that the "problem" of diversity in teacher preparation has historically been constructed from a deficit perspective about the education of minority students, particularly African Americans (Ladson-Billings, 1994b). Ladson-Billings (1999) calls this the "perversity of diversity" (p. 216), where White is normative and diversity is equated with depravity, disadvantage, and deficiency. Along related lines, Weiner (1993) suggests that the major flaw in reforms for urban teacher preparation is that "urban" has been consistently co-mingled with "at risk," and Villegas and Lucas (2002a) suggest that for the many prospective teachers who are relatively privileged members of society, it is difficult not to see diversity as a deficit. Solorzano (1997) and Solorzano and Yosso (2001) suggest that a critical race theory perspective can interrupt the deficit perspectives that underlie most teacher education programs, Ladson-Billings (1999) concurs:

We define a critical race theory in teacher education as a framework that can be used to theorize and examine the ways in which race and racism impact on the structures, processes, and discourses within the teacher education context. This framework challenges dominant ideology, which supports deficit notions about students of color. (Solorzano & Yosso, 2001, p. 3)

In a complete condemnation of traditional teacher preparation, Yeo (1997) suggests that multicultural teacher education does little more than perpetuate the status quo, since it "has been shaped and contorted by both ethnicity and deficiency theoretical understandings . . . [and] the result has been a shallow and instrumental applicability of multicultural knowledge" (pp. 164–165). As these comments suggest, the diversity question is closely linked to the ideology question in the conceptual literature.

The Ideology Question. Several of the conceptual articles reviewed here argue that a "seamless ideological web" (Weiner, 2000, p. 381) threads through most teacher preparation programs, taking for granted "the seamless tale of triumph, conquest, and the inevitability of America as a great nation" (Ladson-Billings, 1999, p. 224). This ideological web weaves together these assumptions: American schooling (and indeed most of American life) is meritocratic (Sleeter, 1995b) and thus subtly reinforces the idea that failure for certain individuals or groups is "normal" (Goodwin, 2001); racism and sexism (and other forms of oppression) are old problems that have for the most part been solved (Gay & Howard, 2000); the purpose of schooling is to help all students assimilate into the mainstream and thus produce workers who can help maintain America's dominance in the global economy (Grant & Wieczorek, 2000; Weiner, 1993); and high-stakes tests and other standard measures are neutral and objective means of assessing merit (Gordon, 2001b). Cary (2001) refers to the everyday discourse of teacher preparation as part of the "normalizing practices that maintain the status quo despite their best intentions for social change" (p. 405), and Grant and Wieczorek (2000) suggest that it helps maintain "naturalized universals in the reasoning of actors working in education today" (p. 925). A theme in the conceptual literature is that powerful and transformative learning experiences are needed for both teacher educators and prospective teachers in order to interrupt these ideological assumptions (Jenks et al., 2001; Sleeter, 1995b; Yeo, 1997).

Although some of the literature along these lines explicitly critiques the social and economic conditions of schooling, particularly those that subvert success in urban schools (Haberman, 1996; Weiner, 1993, 2000; Yeo, 1997), much of the recent conceptual work emphasizes race. This includes the need to help prospective teachers interrogate Whiteness, privilege, and power, especially in relation to knowledge and knowledge construction (Cary, 2001; Ewing, 2001; Grant & Wieczorek, 2000). The stronger theme in the conceptual literature, however, is the need for teacher educators to deal directly with issues of race and racism (Gay & Howard, 2000; Ladson-Billings, 1995), recognizing that part of "contemporary racism" is failure to talk about it (Goodwin, 2001) and that "postmodern racism" includes attacks on affirmative action, the dissolution of programs for linguistic minorities, and the resurgence of standardized tests as the primary indicators of competence (Gordon, 2001a, 2001b). King and Castenell's (2001b) monograph, *Racism and Racial Inequality: Implications for Teacher Education*, makes this point unqualifiedly:

[This] monograph addresses a case for the centrality of antiracism in teacher education at the front and center of the teacher education reform agenda. . . . We argue that teacher education institutions need to understand that to prepare teachers with the will and the strategies to teach all children, fighting racism has to be the bottom line. (pp. 9–10)

Several themes along these lines are evident in the conceptual literature, including the need for antiracist teacher preparation (Kailin, 1999; Tatum, 2001), a curriculum that includes the history of White resistance (Fennimore, 2001), and examination of teachers' expectations for children from the perspective of race and racism (Goodwin, 2001).

The Knowledge Question. Over the past two decades, teacher education as a field has moved away from emphasizing what effective teachers do to what they know and need to know, sources of knowledge, and how they organize and use knowledge generally and in specific content areas. Those conceptualizing multicultural teacher education do not dispute the fact that teachers ought to know much of what is typically included in "the knowledge base," particularly that they ought to have broad and deep knowledge of the subject areas they teach. But the multicultural teacher education literature also explicates what teachers need to know about the knowledge base and what else they need to know, including the attitudes and beliefs needed to teach diverse populations successfully. Grant (1997) suggests that the traditional knowledge base concentrates on the canon and omits many other "cultural funds" of knowledge. Along these lines, several whole volumes, published recently, have attempted to develop (Hollins, King, & Hayman, 1994; Irvine, 1997a; King, Hollins, & Hayman, 1997) or have summarized (Pritchy-Smith, 1998) what Irvine (1997b) calls a "specific and more comprehensive knowledge base" (p. 217) for preparing teachers for diversity. These efforts are

intended to challenge the idea of the traditional knowledge base, including voices traditionally excluded (see, for example, many specific examples in the three volumes noted above from African American, Puerto Rican, Native American, Asian, and other perspectives).

This approach also challenges the universality of the traditional knowledge base and instead exposes how it is "socially moored," or connected to "circulations of power [and] tied to race, class, and gender issues" (Grant & Wieczorek, 2000, p. 932), which limits what can be known and results in what Sleeter (2001b), noted earlier, calls the "overwhelming presence of Whiteness" among those who are "knowers" or legitimate knowledge producers in the field. Haberman (1996) makes a strong case against a universal approach to teacher education in favor of a contextual one, pointing out that because the theoretical constructs of teacher education derive primarily from psychology, where the unit of analysis is the individual, prospective teachers do not learn alternative theories where other units are used. He suggests that the debate is "whether factors such as urban poverty, race, or membership in a particular cultural group demand new forms of teacher preparation and practice" (p. 749). Along similar lines, Fox and Gay (1995) contend that there is no such thing as general knowledge because knowledge is "inseparable from social and historical contexts" (p. 66). Both Au (2002) and Oakes, Franke, Quartz, and Rogers (2002) argue, respectively, that contextual knowledge is essential to preparing teachers for Native Hawaiian students and for urban schools.

One of the strongest themes in the recent conceptual literature is the importance of knowledge and information about culture itself. In a text for prospective teachers, for example, Hollins (1996) points out that "culture is the medium for cognitive learning for all human beings, not just ethnic minorities and low income children" (p. 71); she asserts that understanding the "deep meaning of culture in school learning" constitutes a "new paradigm" for teacher preparation. Hollins and others (e.g., Cochran-Smith, 1997; Garibaldi, 1992; Villegas & Lucas, 2002a) argue that teachers need to know the meaning of culture; the impact of culture on learning and schooling; the ways in which schools and classrooms function as "cultures"; the nature of ethnic, racial, and urban cultures different from their own; and the role of culture in patterns of socialization, interaction, and communication. The literature also suggests that prospective teachers need to learn about their own cultures and think of themselves as cultural beings (Gay, 1993; Goodwin, 2000; Grant, 1991) at the same time they learn positive attitudes toward students with different cultural backgrounds (Irvine, 2001; Villegas & Lucas, 2002a). Gay and Howard (2000) refer to many of these ideas collectively as "critical cultural consciousness," and Villegas and Lucas (2002a, 2002b) refer to them as "sociocultural consciousness." The importance of teachers' knowing how to act on cultural knowledge in order to construct culturally sensitive curriculum and pedagogy is also critical; this is discussed below under the "practice question."

The Teacher Learning Question. The teacher learning question is addressed in two closely related ways in the conceptual literature: how in general teachers learn to teach for diversity, and what in particular are the pedagogies of teacher preparation (for example, course work assignments, readings, discussion) that make this learning possible. The enormity of the task of teachers' learning to teach for diversity is elegantly expressed by Villegas and Lucas (2002a):

Because many teachers-to-be enter teacher education believing that schools are impartial institutions, that cultural diversity is problematic, that knowledge is objective and neutral, that learning consists of passively absorbing new information and repeating it by rote, and that teaching entails dispensing information, preparing them to be culturally responsive requires a complete resocialization. (p. xix)

Part of resocialization is becoming self-reflective and developing self-knowledge about teaching and learning (Breault, 1995; Hollins, 1995). Cochran-Smith and Lytle (1992; Cochran-Smith, 1997, 1999) argue that inquiry-based teacher preparation, rather than the "training" or transmission models that prevail in many places, are the most promising approaches for preparing teachers to be lifelong learners who can work effectively in diverse settings:

We take the more radical position that learning from teaching ought to be regarded as the primary task of teacher education across the professional life span. By "learning from teaching," we mean that inquiry ought to be regarded as an integral part of the activity of teaching and . . . that classrooms and schools ought to be treated as research sites. . . . This argument is based in part on the assumption that the increasing diversity of America's schools and schoolchildren and the increasing complexity of the tasks educators face render global solutions to problems and monolithic strategies for effective teaching impossible. (Cochran-Smith & Lytle, 1992, pp. 63–64)

Inquiry-based conceptions of teacher learning, which focus on question posing and continuous learning over the professional life span, are in keeping with current research about how people learn more generally (Bransford, Brown, & Cocking, 2000) and with the literature on teacher learning communities (Cochran-Smith & Lytle, 1999).

The conceptual literature mentions autobiography, restructured field experiences, situated pedagogies, and returning to the classrooms of experts as part of teacher education pedagogy for diversity (Ladson-Billings, 2000). Similarly, Zeichner (1993a) argues for using cases of successful teachers with high expectations for diverse students, as well as cases of failure that highlight how school conditions structure failure. He also recommends biography, self-examination of attitudes, field experiences in diverse settings, developing cultural knowledge, and community immersion.

The Practice Question. In much of the recent literature on multicultural teacher education, teaching practice is conceptualized to include teachers' roles as members of school communities, school leaders, and theorizers of practice. This image of practice includes responsibilities to families and transformed relationships with students (Ladson-Billings, 1994a, 1995; Irvine, 2001), as well as deeper and altered connections to communities (Haberman, 1996).

Questions about how experienced teachers work successfully with diverse groups of students are among the most well researched in the multicultural literature, with culturally responsive teaching and many related conceptions now well known (see, for example, Gay, 2000; Irvine, 2001; Irvine & Armento, 2001; Ladson-Billings, 1994a, 1995; Villegas, 1991). Teaching prospective teachers to construct culturally responsive curriculum and pedagogy is emphasized in the conceptual literature as a critical part of preparation. It is included among Zeichner's (1993a) "key elements" and among Villegas and Lucas's (2002a) orienting "strands" for coherent teacher preparation. Gay (2000) describes this as "power pedagogy," and Ladson-Billings (1994a) suggests that culturally relevant teaching allows students to choose both academic success and maintenance of their own cultural identities, an approach that differs markedly from assimilationist teaching (Ladson-Billings, 1995). There are interesting and important differences among the various multicultural theorists' conceptions of culturally responsive teaching, but that discussion, which concentrates on K-12 teaching, is not within the scope of this chapter.

Another important theme in the conceptual literature is that prospective teachers need to develop cultural competence to work effectively with parents and families, draw on community and family resources, and know how to learn about the cultures of their students (Gay, 1993; Goodwin, 2000; Villegas & Lucas, 2001a, 2001b; Zeichner, 1993a). Gay suggests that each teacher needs to be prepared to be a "cultural broker" who

thoroughly understands different cultural systems, is able to interpret cultural symbols from one frame of reference to another, can mediate cultural incompatibilities, and knows how to build bridges or establish linkages across cultures that facilitate the instructional process. (p. 293)

The practice question is closely related to the outcomes question.

The Outcomes Question. As noted above, the outcomes question has to do with the consequences of teacher preparation as well as how and why these are documented. In teacher preparation generally, there has been a shift from focusing primarily on curriculum- or program-oriented standards to emphasizing performance-based standards and long-term impacts (Imig et al., 2000; Wise, 1999). At the same time, there has been considerable public pressure to define outcomes narrowly in terms of the achievement test scores of the K-12 students whom teachers teach. Analyses of this kind are intended to demonstrate that the teachers prepared by a given program or institution or who hold a particular teaching credential produce demonstrable learning gains (or not) in the students they teach (Cochran-Smith, 2001a). In the recent literature on multicultural teacher education, it is clear that high expectations, high standards, and high levels of achievement for all K-12 students ought to be an explicit outcome of teacher preparation. However, there is also a strong theme of resistance in the conceptual literature to narrow conceptions of outcomes. The fear is that defining achievement only as higher test scores has what Valenzuela (2002) calls a "subtractive" effect on students' cultural identities and perpetuates the cycle of failure for students of color, poor students, and students from linguistic minorities (Cochran-Smith, 2001a, 2001b; Gordon, 2001a, 2001b).

There is also strong agreement in the conceptual literature that an appropriate outcome of teacher education is teachers who understand culture, are culturally competent, and are prepared to teach in culturally responsive ways, as discussed above. There is divergence, however, about the unit of analysis for measuring outcomes, where to look for evidence, and the nature of that evidence itself. For example, Cochran-Smith (1991, 1995a, 1995b, 1998) argues that we need to prepare teachers to work against the grain of common practice, to be agents for social change, and to teach for social justice. Smylie, Bay, and Tozer (1999) suggest that in order to be agents of change, teachers-to-be should examine the dilemmas of schooling, particularly competing notions of "the public good." Along related lines, Ladson-Billings (1995) asserts that learning to construct culturally relevant pedagogy includes learning to raise questions about the systematic ways schooling fails many students from diverse backgrounds. She contends that if pedagogy does not affirm K-12 students' own cultures while simultaneously teaching them to critique the system, then it is neither culturally relevant nor appropriate. This suggests that one outcome of teacher preparation is how prospective teachers use what they have learned to raise questions, critique

common practices, and work for social justice in actual schools.

From an ecological perspective on school reform, however, Weiner (1993) takes a different view about the outcomes of teacher preparation. She argues that teacher education and professional development are not the key to K-12 school reform, pointing out that changes in school structures and political changes outside schools must come first. She asserts that "teacher preparation can make modest improvements in the ways people teach, but that it cannot reform schools, as many teacher preparation programs have demanded" (p. 8). In his critique of multicultural education generally, Yeo (1997) too suggests that teacher preparation should look beyond individual teachers' practices or curriculum to assess outcomes. He argues that the integration of cultural knowledge into the curriculum (K-12 or teacher preparation) is not an appropriate goal; rather, he suggests that "community empowerment is the purpose of education" (p. 131). These issues are related to larger theoretical discussions about multicultural education and critical pedagogy, which are beyond the scope of this chapter. (For insightful discussions of these issues, see especially Banks, 1994; Kanpol & McLaren, 1995; and Sleeter, 1996a, 1996b, 1996c, 1996d.)

The Selection and Recruitment Question. For some time now, two arguments have been made about the selection and recruitment of teachers in order to meet the needs of diverse populations. One has to do with the value of diversifying the teaching force: to give children of color the opportunity to work with teachers who are like them in terms of cultural, racial, or linguistic background (Chinn & Wong, 1992); to provide role models for minority students (Sianjina, Cage, & Allen, 1996); and to enrich the learning opportunities of all students because of the diverse life experiences and knowledge perspectives that others bring (Eubanks & Weaver, 1999; Villegas & Lucas, 2002a). The second has to do with recruiting teachers who are more likely to succeed in high-need areas, particularly in urban centers, because of their experiences or their maturity, or both (Haberman, 1996; Clewell & Villegas, 2001c; Shumann, 1992). Other educators have advocated for programs that rely on early recruitment of young people into the teaching profession, targeting middle and high school students, connections to community colleges, and parent information campaigns (Riley, 1998; Sianjina et al., 1996).

Haberman, who has written well-known analyses of issues related to recruitment and selection of teachers (Haberman, 1991, 1996; Haberman & Post, 1998), has argued for a long time that the critical point of reform in multicultural teacher education is selection and recruitment of teachers more likely to succeed in urban schools instead of revising curriculum and instruction for young middle-class White women. He asserts that adolescents (the young college students who constitute the majority of students in many preservice teacher education programs) are simply not developmentally capable of the kind of learning and unlearning required to teach diverse populations within the conditions of urban centers. He argues for jettisoning traditional selection criteria associated with a universal approach to teacher preparation and instead recruiting older adults who already have the traits and experiences associated with urban success.

Villegas and colleagues (Clewell & Villegas, 2001a, 2001b, 2001c; Villegas et al., 1995; Villegas & Lucas, 2002a) have also argued in many venues for new ways of thinking about recruiting and selecting teachers who are prepared to teach in today's schools. They argue that more diversity among the life experiences and knowledge perspectives of college and university participants creates an enriched intellectual climate and enhances the education of all participants (Villegas & Lucas, 2002a). They also argue that recruiting teachers from nontraditional pools (such as teacher aides or assistants, minority college graduates seeking a career change, and noncertified teachers) is a particularly effective way both to increase the diversity of the teaching force and to provide fully qualified teachers for high-need areas (Clewell & Villegas, 2001a, 2001b, 2001c; Villegas et al., 1995). This line of reasoning has been studied through an extensive program of empirical research, which is discussed below.

The Coherence Question. A very strong theme in the conceptual literature is that multicultural issues must be central, not peripheral, to the rest of the teacher education curriculum, mandatory rather than optional for all prospective teachers, infused throughout courses and fieldwork experiences rather than contained in a single course, and a major part of how teachers and programs are evaluated. Nieto (2000; Nieto & Rolen, 1997) asserts that teacher education must be transformed by placing issues of equity "front and center" rather than on the side, at the bottom, or at the end of everything else that matters. Villegas and Lucas (2002a, 2002b) also make it clear that coherence is a top priority by incorporating the idea directly into the title of their book, *Educating Culturally Responsive Teachers: A Coherent Approach.* They caution that when one or two courses (often optional) are added on to the curriculum, many students as well as faculty assume they are not responsible for these issues, and a multicultural focus is ultimately undermined. They write: "In the absence of a broad vision for preparing culturally responsive teachers, such courses can be contradicted by the rest of the curriculum, marginalizing those individual efforts to address diversity issues (Villegas & Lucas, 2002a, p. xiii)."

Institutional Capacity. A number of scholars directly discuss the impact of institutional environment on multicultural teacher education (Melnick & Zeichner, 1997; Villegas & Lucas, 2002a; Zeichner & Hoeft, 1996), particularly the need to examine programs in light of larger university policies on race and affirmative action (Elijah, 2001; Villegas et al., 1995), as well as larger institutional agendas and missions (O'Loughlin, 2001; Zeichner & Hoeft, 1996). Villegas and Lucas (2002a) and Cochran-Smith (2003a) also suggest that department, school, and institutional approaches to faculty development must be considered as part of institutional capacity. Along related lines, Wallace (2000) calls for a complete paradigm shift in multicultural training at graduate schools of education as a whole, with self-examination, review, revision, and refinement of all programs and approaches central. Similarly, Talbert-Johnson and Tillman (1999) identify multiple and prominent university problems related to race and offer a series of proposals about the recruitment, mentoring, and support of faculty of color with increased attention to equity issues. Villegas and Lucas (2002a) devote an entire chapter of their book to institutional context, stating that change in teacher education does not and will not happen without significant organizational and institutional reform:

Institutions . . . would do well to acknowledge that colleges and universities, like elementary and secondary schools, were not traditionally designed to promote the value of diversity or to serve a racially/ethnically diverse student population. Such an admission spares the institution the waste of valuable time and resources rationalizing policies and practices that contradict the goal of diversity. (p. 151)

Themes in the conceptual literature make it clear that institutional capacity is closely related to other aspects of multicultural teacher education, particularly diversity and ideology.

Other External Forces and Contexts. There is little emphasis in the conceptual literature on the other external forces that influence the multiple meanings of multicultural teacher education, although there is some empirical work along these lines, as is discussed in the next section. Some theorists focus on the relationship of multicultural teacher education to local communities (Haberman, 1996; Weiner, 1993; Yeo, 1997), primarily by critiquing the lack of connection between most teacher preparation programs and their immediate neighborhoods and communities, a failing that reflects the universal rather than contextual approach that is dominant in teacher preparation (Haberman, 1996; Valenzuela, 2002). Many of the conceptual pieces suggest that community-based experiences may be critical but are often missing from teacher preparation (Oakes et al., 2002; Sleeter,

2001a; Yeo, 1997; Zeichner, 1993a; Zeichner & Hoeft, 1996). A few theorists comment on the impact of governmental and nongovernmental regulations on teacher education and on the relationships of multicultural teacher education to the larger social, economic, and political contexts. Gollnick (1992, 1995), for example, theorizes multicultural teacher education in terms of the larger ideological orientations that legitimize particular governmental and nongovernmental regulations at the national and international levels. Other scholars locate teacher preparation within larger historical contexts, linking research, practice, and policy in teacher education to broader social and political movements and to the conditions of schooling (Liston & Zeichner, 1991; Weiner, 1993, 2000). Along these lines, the future of multicultural teacher education has been analyzed in relation to market-based educational reform agendas that support the privatization of education (Apple, 2000, 2001) and undermine the goals of social justice (Cochran-Smith, 2001a, 2001b).

A New Multicultural Teacher Education?

Although there is some divergence in viewpoints, the conceptual literature over the past decade calls for a "new multicultural teacher education," that is, a teacher education that does not add on to or supplement existing structures and paradigms but fundamentally reinvents them. This new paradigm answers the eight critical questions of teacher education and builds on understandings of the external forces and contexts of teacher education in the ways elaborated above. Radical new ways to conceptualize the preparation of teachers for a diverse society are intended to interrupt conventional teacher education discourse and tradition that have become ingrained and institutionalized in spite of the fact that they are unable to meet the challenges of the 21st century. Although a "new multicultural teacher education" may indeed be envisioned as the way to meet the needs of students and families in the real world, it is far removed from the demands and traditions of another real world: the institutional reality of colleges and universities, which supports and maintains the status quo. Ladson-Billings (1995) alluded to this disparity in the first edition of this *Handbook,* heading one of the sections of her chapter on multicultural teacher education, "Real Reform or Rhetoric?"

Gay (1995) wisely reminds us that the multicultural teacher education theory-practice disparity is not so surprising given that in general the development of multicultural theory has far outstripped the development of multicultural practice, with refinements of theory depending more on proposals for what should be than on conceptualizing the lessons learned from what has been. She suggests that the evolution (or reinvention?) of multicultural teacher education might better be regarded developmentally than hierarchically, as do Jenks et al. (2001), who allow that most teacher educators themselves have not had the transformative learning experiences required to provide these for their students. Notwithstanding Weiner's (1993) caution that teacher education cannot change schools, Cochran-Smith (1995a) has addressed the new paradigm issue explicitly:

> To alter a system that is deeply dysfunctional, we need teachers who regard teaching as a political activity and embrace social change as part of the job, teachers who enter the profession not expecting to carry on business as usual but prepared to join other educators and parents in major reforms. . . . Teacher educators cannot carry on business as usual either. (p. 494)

The next section of this chapter reviews the empirical and data-based literature on multicultural teacher education. Although the published literature does not represent all that is occurring in practice, it does provide some notion of trends in the field and offers one lens for considering whether multicultural teacher education reflects the new paradigms envisioned in the conceptual literature or is really just "business as usual."

BUSINESS AS USUAL? EMPIRICAL AND DATA-BASED LITERATURE, 1992–2001

We turn now to empirical studies and data-based inquiries related to multicultural teacher education, published or in press between 1992 and 2001. Using Cochran-Smith's (2003b) framework as an organizing tool, this section reviews the research that speaks to various aspects of multicultural teacher education and also reveals which issues have received more and less attention over the last decade. Although this review reveals that there is a great deal of research about prospective teachers' attitudes and learning experiences in courses and programs, it also makes clear that there is very little empirical attention to the outcomes of multicultural teacher education, in terms of either prospective and new teachers' teaching practices or K–12 students' learning. In addition, this section points out the considerable differences in emphases between the conceptual and the empirical literature.

Reviewing the Empirical and Data-Based Literature

As this chapter has noted, questions about what literature to "count" as empirical research are not completely straightforward, and previous syntheses have used different decision rules along these lines. The following section of this chapter reviews each piece of literature that met three criteria: it was an educational inquiry with questions posed and analyses offered; it drew on what Sleeter (2001b) has called "some form of data" (experimental, survey, observation, and interview data), as well as "the data of experience," to construct the analyses; and it related directly to the initial selection or preparation of U.S. teachers for a multicultural society. As Sleeter (2001a) has pointed out, research on this topic has been conducted from a variety of epistemological positions. In coupling Sleeter's notion of data with a broad definition of educational inquiry, this chapter assumes that there are multiple forms of inquiry that inform multicultural teacher education.

Thus, this chapter includes and attempts to assess appropriately the value of studies that involve very small samples, use data from a single course, and/or take the researcher's own professional context as the site for research. This decision reflects some of the current tensions in the field. On the one hand, there is burgeoning interest among teacher educators in studying their own practice (Zeichner, 1999). Generally, this seems a healthy and productive development, which reflects the commitment of teacher educators to getting better at what they do through systematic self-reflection (Hamilton, 1998) and provides inside perspectives on multicultural teacher education that may be inaccessible to outside researchers (Cochran-Smith & Lytle, 1993). In addition, close studies of specific sites may lead to the development of conceptual frameworks, theories, and practices that are useful well beyond the original site (Lytle & Cochran-Smith, 1992). On the other hand, there is criticism and sometimes dismissal of practitioner inquiry since it is obviously "biased" in the traditional sense of desired researcher separation from what is being researched (Huberman, 1996) and seems to use different criteria for making knowledge claims from those used in traditional formal research (Fenstermacher, 1994). In addition, it is difficult to assess the cumulative meaning of many little studies (Sleeter, 2001a) or to draw conclusions from analyses of single courses (Wilson et al., 2001). Finally, in practitioner inquiries of various kinds, there is sometimes inadequate attention to the issues of power and coercion that obtain when a course instructor (who is also the researcher) draws on the words of students (who are also the research participants or informants) to assess what has been learned from an experience in which the instructor or researcher has a vested interest.

The fact that the value of practitioner inquiry is contested, however, does not alter the reality that a substantial body of this work does exist, has been presented and published in highly regarded and peer-reviewed journals,

and presumably is being read by those interested in preparing teachers for diversity. In this sense, it *is* part of the literature of multicultural teacher education, and it seems important to identify and include it in a review of this kind.

The View Since 1992

To prepare the following analysis, the empirical and data-based literature was categorized topically according to the 12 aspects of Cochran-Smith's framework, with each piece assigned to one of the teacher education questions (diversity, ideology, knowledge and beliefs, teacher learning, practice, outcomes, selection, coherence) or one of the external forces (institutional capacity, community-school relationships, governmental and nongovernmental regulations), or to the category of larger social, political, historical, and economic contexts. The literature sorted relatively easily into these categories. Even when a given article was informed by several perspectives or addressed more than one topic, it was usually clear what the primary focus was. For example, a number of articles examined teachers' attitudes about diverse groups by distributing a survey to the students in a course. When the study went beyond the survey and focused also on what prospective teachers learned or how their attitudes and beliefs changed by interacting with course content, the study was categorized as "teacher learning." When the researcher used a course as convenient access to a sample of students to assess their attitudes, the study was categorized under "knowledge and beliefs."

The Diversity Question. There are several topics related to the diversity question discussed later in this review: attitudes and knowledge about diversity are examined under "the knowledge question"; recruitment of a diverse teaching force is included with "the selection and recruitment question"; and the relationship of teacher education to larger institutional missions regarding diversity is included under "institutional capacity." In addition to these topics, some literature pertains directly to how notions of diversity are conceptualized and instantiated in teacher education programs and projects. Fuller (1992) and the Holmes Group Equity and Excellence Committee, for example, conducted a census of the 19 institutions that were members of the Midwest Holmes Group. They found that although all but one institution offered a multicultural education course, only half required it; they also found that faculty and students were overwhelmingly White and middle class, with most field experiences occurring in schools serving White populations. Along related but somewhat different lines, Kitano, Lewis, Lynch, and Graves (1996) asked a stratified random sample of faculty members in one college of education (n = 56 with 86% return) to respond to a vignette about what teachers with diverse classes needed to know; they found significant variability in extent of faculty knowledge, information, and depth of understanding.

As noted earlier, critics claim that most teacher education programs promote the status quo through a curriculum where White is normative and diversity issues are addressed shallowly. This issue has been addressed by a number of studies that examine the actual experiences of minority students in teacher preparation programs that are primarily, if not overwhelmingly, White. All were based on interviews and other qualitative data from relatively small numbers of preservice students (ranging from a case study of one student over a two-year period to interviews with 24 students in two different institutions). Studies of Asian students (Pailliotet, 1997; Su, Goldstein, & Suzuki, 1997) revealed that the teacher education students themselves had had positive school experiences, but also felt isolated from the mainstream and were aware of unequal educational opportunities for children of color. Some had difficulties with discourse forms, abstract teaching styles, and values different from their own. Studies of African American teacher candidates (Agee, 1998; Guyton, Saxton, & Wesche, 1995; Hood & Parker, 1994; Kornfeld, 1999; Meacham, 2000; Parker & Hood, 1995) indicated that, unlike their White peers, most were committed to teaching for social justice and planned to teach in diverse communities. African American candidates perceived that multicultural issues were relegated to electives or foundations courses and that methods courses failed to provide information relevant to culturally diverse groups. African American students also felt silenced and like outsiders; they were put off by the implicit White middle-class focus and dysconscious racism they perceived in their programs, including stereotypes about language and intelligence. One study (Burant, 1999) concentrated on Mexican American students as part of a larger study and found similar experiences in terms of silencing and discomfort.

The Ideology Question. There were very few studies in the literature base that dealt specifically with the underlying ideologies of schools and society or with challenging the dominant history of the nation as a meritocracy. In some studies, which are included below under "teacher learning," issues of this kind were mentioned, but the emphasis was on a particular strategy for teaching these issues. Three studies (Cochran-Smith, 1995b; Cooney & Akintude, 1999; Graham & Young, 2000) examined explicitly how teacher candidates made sense of race, racism, gender inequity, and other forms of institutionalized oppression by documenting, respectively, responses to course readings and discussions, debriefing sessions for

field experiences, and written responses to a symposium on inequity. In all three, the researchers were also teacher educators directly engaged in the work. They described the difficulty of "open[ing] the unsettling discourse of race" (Cochran-Smith, 1995a, p. 541) or "ripp[ing] open the silence" (Cooney & Akintude, 1999, p. 9) about hitherto taboo topics. Based on reaction papers by 75 students, Cooney and Akintude also pointed out that many teacher candidates initially understood these issues in terms of personal blame and guilt rather than as societal and systemic. Along similar lines, drawing on transcriptions of course conversations and students' writing, both Cochran-Smith and Graham and Young cautioned that in order to get beneath the surface, teacher educators themselves must engage in unflinching self-examination about underlying ideology in much the same way that they urge for teacher candidates.

The Knowledge Question. The knowledge question is not just about knowledge, but also involves the interpretive frameworks, beliefs, attitudes, expectations, and conceptions that are related to teaching diverse populations. A number of empirical studies fell into this category, seeming to operate from this assumption:

Historically, colleges of education have developed programs based on the notion that competence is mainly a function of knowledge and skills. Programs driven by this theory have failed to recognize the important and powerful role teacher beliefs and attitudes play in eliminating educational discrepancies and developing democratic and culturally responsive schools. (Pohan, 1996, p. 65)

The studies in this category addressed three major questions: What are preservice teachers' attitudes, beliefs, and conceptions about diversity? What experiences and other factors seem to influence those beliefs? Do beliefs change after program experiences intended to enhance capacity to deal with diversity?

Eight studies (Avery & Walker, 1993; Barry & Lechner, 1995; Easter, Schultz, & Neyhart, 1999; Montecinos & Rios, 1999; Neuharth-Pritchett, Reiff, & Pearson, 2001; Shultz, Neyhart, & Reck, 1996a, 1996b; Tettegah, 1996) surveyed moderate to relatively large numbers of preservice teachers (n = 73–380) using paper-and-pencil questionnaires to assess basic attitudes about diversity, urban teaching, multicultural education, gender, and racial consciousness. Results, reported primarily through simple descriptive statistics, indicated that preservice teachers had had few experiences with diversity but did anticipate diverse classrooms, held traditional expectations for "good students" as well as some stereotypical views about racial and cultural groups, and did not understand the structural underpinnings of inequity, but wanted to teach all students effectively. There were mixed responses about whether teacher candidates felt prepared by their preparation programs to do so.

These results are quite consistent with those obtained differently. For example, using factor analysis to study teaching efficacy with regard to teaching African American students, Pang and Sablan (1998) found that preservice teachers scored higher in personal efficacy than in-service teachers did, that neither group had much experience with or knowledge of African Americans, and that many teachers felt unable to teach African Americans, whom they believed did not care about education. Goodwin (1994), Neuharth-Pritchett et al. (2001), and Ross and Yeager (1999) used content analysis of preservice teachers' writing to conclude, respectively, that they had unsophisticated notions about multiculturalism, diversity, and democracy. Based on written responses to critical incidents, Goodwin (1997) also found that preservice teachers had concerns about race but no models for how to deal with racial issues. Similarly, based on qualitative and quantitative analysis of survey data, Taylor and Sobel (2001) found that preservice teachers wanted to teach all students well but had limited experience. Rios and Montecinos (1999) surveyed 28 ethnically diverse preservice teachers and found that they had fairly sophisticated understandings of multicultural education practices and agreed that teaching and schooling should address social inequities. Similarly, Montecinos (1994) interviewed 18 students of color at a primarily White institution and discovered that although they had had few experiences with multicultural curriculum in their own K-12 experience, they were committed to offering this to their future students.

Five studies (Canella & Reif, 1995; Kesner, 2000; Pohan, 1996; Smith, Moallem, & Sherrill, 1997; Zulich, Bean, & Herrick, 1992) examined factors that influenced prospective teachers' growth and explored how their beliefs interacted with program experiences. Pohan surveyed 429 preservice teachers using two belief scales, a knowledge test, and open-ended questions. The strongest correlations were between personal and professional beliefs. Canella and Reif reached the same conclusion based on an ethnographic case study of one student teacher. Drawing on students' journals and autobiographical papers, Zulich, Bean, and Herrick and Smith and Mosallen concluded that personal experiences and program characteristics interacted to shape beliefs and practices. Taking a related but somewhat different tack, Kesner found that preservice teachers' histories of personal attachment to others had a significant impact on their self-reported relationships with K-5 children during fieldwork.

Finally, six studies (Aaronsohn, Carter & Howard, 1995; Cabello & Burstein, 1995; Deering & Stanutz, 1995; Huber & Klein, 1993; Pattnaik, 1997; Ross & Smith, 1992) examined whether preservice students' knowledge, beliefs, or attitudes about diversity changed following program experiences. Looking across very different research designs and assumptions, these studies indicated that program experiences—overall program designed for diversity, courses on cultural diversity, fieldwork experiences in a diverse setting—had modest or uneven effects depending on teachers' backgrounds and quality of supervision and facilitation. In a unique study, Pattnaik examined the views of the preservice students in her class about having an Asian instructor; pre- and postcourse writing indicated that students' views changed over time from naïve stereotypes to more complex understandings.

The Teacher Learning Question. The literature in this area has to do with the pedagogies teacher educators used to help prospective teachers learn to teach for diversity. As noted above, much of the research on this topic is based on what Sleeter (2001a) calls the "data of experience," wherein teacher educators themselves study practice by examining their own and students' writing, course discussions, and program and course materials. Often the intent in this kind of inquiry is not to measure the impact of specific pedagogies but to explore the pedagogies themselves by investigating how preservice teachers interact with course and program content and how they make sense of their experiences. One study (Solomon, 2000) examined the impact of cross-race dyads as an organizational structure for learning to teach by pairing members of racial minority groups with persons from dominant racial groups. Solomon found that this exposed some of the inequities of an educational system where racial difference was perceived as deficiency and that the dyads were more beneficial for White students than for students of color. Across the studies in this area, four general pedagogies were examined: inquiring into one's own experience and practice, reading about the experiences and practices of others, studying multicultural education itself, and using computer-assisted communication and games. In addition, some studies examined the impact of innovative programs as a whole.

Research on learning to teach through inquiring into or researching one's own experiences and practices included autobiographical writing (Clarke & Medina, 2000; Curtis, 1998), teacher research on classroom instruction and curriculum (Cochran-Smith, 1995b; Cochran-Smith & Lytle, 1992), dialogue journals and oral inquiries about practice (Garmon, 1998; Gomez, 1996), and portfolios that represented practice and reflection over time (Pleasants, Johnson, & Trent, 1998). Based on qualitative analyses of preservice teachers' written and oral inquiries, many of these accounts provide a "proof of possibility" that inquiry can promote preservice teachers' explorations of school culture and the larger contexts that structure school lives (Curtis) as well as culturally responsive practice (Cochran-Smith). In addition, these studies speak to the power of narrative to connect personal history, academic content, and school-based teaching experiences (Clark & Medina; Garmon; Gomez) and the important role of teacher communities in sustaining teacher learning (Gomez; Pleasants, Johnson, & Trent).

Learning to teach by reading about others' experiences includes using teaching and learning cases (Boyce, 1996; Greenleaf, Hull, & Reilly, 1994), biographies and nonfiction accounts of schooling and inequities (Holm, 1995; McFalls & Cobb-Roberts, 2001; Roberts, Jensen, & Hadjiyianni, 1997), children's books (Laframboise & Griffiths, 1997), and ethnic autobiography (Florio-Ruane, 1994, 2001). Like the studies noted above, much of this work reveals the power of reading about the practices and lives of others. Two studies go beyond the individual teacher educator's studying his or her own work. Greenleaf, Hull, and Reilly analyzed discussions in five different in-service and preservice contexts to critique the interpretive frames teachers used to make sense of cases of K-12 students' school experiences. Florio-Ruane combined the role of researcher and facilitator-participant in a book club with preservice teachers who read ethnic autobiographies. Both studies concluded that these pedagogies had the potential to broaden teachers' understandings of diversity, culture, and teaching and learning.

A number of inquiries focused on how preservice teachers learned by studying multicultural education itself. Using questionnaires or pre- postcourse surveys, some of these studies conclude that students reported changed views about diverse groups, appropriate curriculum, multicultural awareness, and language and learning (Morales, 2000; Peterson, Cross, Johnson, & Howell, 2000; Torok & Aguilar, 2000; Tran, Young, & DiLella, 1994; Warring, Keim, & Rau, 1998). Other studies concluded from self-reports, students' writing, and pre- and postsurveys that there had been little change in attitudes or deep understandings (Greenman & Kimmel, 1995; Guillaume, Zuniga-Hill, & Yee, 1995; Reed, 1993; Rudney, Marxen, & Risku, 1999). Based on various combinations of interviews, student writing, and observations, several researchers concluded that using multicultural material in social studies (McCall, 1995a, 1995b), science (Bullock, 1997), and special education (Donovan, Rovegno, & Dolly, 2000) had some impact on preservice teachers' views about diversity and schooling. Based on participant questionnaires, Kea and Bacon (1999) concluded that students from traditionally White and historically Black institutions developed new respect for cultural differences from opportunities to talk together at two conferences on multicultural issues, and Scott (1995) saw improvements in attitudes toward diverse groups after students participated in multicultural laboratory demonstrations.

Cabello, Eckmier, and Baghieri (1995) and Cabello and Eckmier (1995) examined the impact of an innovative program explicitly intended to prepare teachers for diversity drawing on interviews and questionnaires. They found that school-university collaboration, a cadre of faculty, extensive pre–student teaching fieldwork, and opportunities to reflect with a cohort group were factors in success; systemic differences between school and university cultures were obstacles.

Several studies examined computer-assisted communications and computer simulations and games as a form of multicultural teacher education pedagogy. Harrington and Hathaway (1995), as well as Sernak and Wolfe (1998), examined computer conferences and e-mail, respectively, as ways to open conversations about multicultural issues, as did Appelbaum and Enomoto (1995) in a study with over 400 students. Although all three suggest that computer-assisted communication has the potential to open discussions that are otherwise difficult because participants may retain anonymity, they also report difficulty "breaking cultural myths of teaching and the ideology of professionalism embraced by preservice teachers" (Appelbaum & Enomoto, p. 49). A few educators document other particular strategies in teacher education courses, such as the use of card games or simulations (Frykholm, 1997), multimedia units (Anderson, 1998), and issues exchanges (Marshall, 1998) to promote cultural understanding.

The Practice Question. As indicated above, there is a fair amount of empirical research on teacher candidates' attitudes, beliefs, and developing knowledge about diversity. Surprisingly, though, there are few empirical studies or data-based inquiries that describe or assess the actual practice of teacher candidates when they work in schools and classrooms. Only 10 such studies occurred in the literature base for this chapter (Canning, 1995; Cochran-Smith, 1999; Corbett, Kilgore, & Sindelar, 1998; Ladson-Billings, 2001; Lawrence, 1997; Rodriguez & Sjostrom, 1995; Smith, 2000; Tellez, 1999; Valli, 1995; Vavrus, 1994). Lawrence's study was based on interviews with three students (studied previously in terms of levels of racial identity) after their 15-week full-time student teaching experience, Tellez interviewed four students during their final semester in a year-long professional development program, and Cochran-Smith analyzed six teacher candidates' classroom studies in which they posed questions and documented children's learning. The other seven studies used some combination of classroom fieldwork observation and various qualitative data sources, such as instructional profiles, reflections and lesson plans, and assessments by school-based faculty.

Corbett et al. (1998) found that students in a combined special and elementary education program focused on diversity were able to overlook theoretical conflicts between faculty members and manage classrooms effectively. Cochran-Smith (1999) found that elementary student teachers were able to construct some classroom practices in keeping with the major principles of teaching for social justice identified in the literature. Valli (1995) found that nine student teachers who worked in Black and multicultural settings wrestled with the dilemma of understanding issues of race and teaching influenced by efforts both to be color-blind and to see students' color; she concluded that student teachers benefited by eventually acknowledging the dialectical relationship of these ideas. Canning (1995) found that Anglo secondary teacher candidates from the Midwest were able to work successfully with Mexican American students in the Southwest depending on their open-mindedness, communication skills, and the support of bicultural mentors.

In four other studies, researchers examined the extent to which teacher candidates engaged in multicultural and antiracist pedagogy; they found that the extent depended on prior levels of racial identity (Lawrence, 1997), the availability of experienced teacher models (Rodriguez & Sjostrom, 1995), and their own personal backgrounds, including race, gender, social class, and experiences with diversity (Smith, 2000). Vavrus (1994) found that most of the 107 student teachers he studied used an "additive" or "contributions" approach to multicultural education (Banks, 1994) with little evidence of "infusion" of multicultural material or perspectives into the curriculum. On another note, however, Tellez (1999) found that four Mexican American students were generally unable to use their cultural knowledge in the classroom, despite the fact that their program suggested the importance of doing so, because the curriculum at their schools was predetermined and there was little opportunity or encouragement of this.

Ladson-Billings (2001) conducted a year-long ethnographic study of one cohort of student teachers enrolled in an experimental teacher preparation program for diversity. As participant observer, she commingled the roles of supervisor and researcher, using as data notes on meetings with students, classroom observations, lesson plans, students' personal statements, and interviews. Her study provides a close and complex look at student teachers in the process of trying to put into practice three tenets of culturally relevant teaching: maintaining high expectations for all students, acting on cultural competence, and developing sociopolitical consciousness. The study provides detail about what success (and failure) at implementing these abstract notions look like in the context of school life.

The Outcomes Question. As previous syntheses have consistently pointed out, there are few empirical studies that examine the consequences or impact of multicultural teacher preparation on teachers' actual work in schools after they complete preservice preparation, and virtually none that examines the learning opportunities and achievements of the K-12 students they teach. Only five studies focused on outcomes. Artiles, Barreto, McClafferty, and Pena (1998) conducted a longitudinal case study of two bilingual education teachers in urban schools. Qualitative and quantitative analyses were completed using data collected before and after a multicultural education course as well as during the teachers' first two years of teaching; data included concept maps, interviews, and surveys developed by the National Center for Research on Teacher Learning at Michigan State University. Researchers found that the relationships between prior knowledge, beliefs, and decision making were complex, and that classroom and school contexts influenced attempts to instantiate constructivist and social justice principles. Fuller (1994) studied 26 "monocultural" elementary teachers who were teaching in multicultural settings and were recent graduates of a teacher preparation program with a "social reconstructionist" perspective. Based on a survey, interviews, and classroom observations, Fuller concluded that although most of the graduates said they had benefited from the program, their teaching strategies during the first year of teaching were not "culturally informed" and they were not able to select relevant teaching strategies for a multicultural environment. Causey, Thomas, and Armento (2000) selected two graduates who had evidenced "cognitive restructuring" as a result of "the treatment" of a multicultural class taught by one of the researchers coupled with an intensive field experience in an urban school and studied these teachers three years later. Based on interviews, classroom observations, and reanalysis of their writing during the preservice program, the researchers found that one graduate, currently teaching in a diverse lower-middle-class school, had not maintained her altered views, while the other, who was teaching in a White suburban school, had maintained her "restructured paradigm." Powell (1997) followed one White student teacher who had demonstrated cultural sensitivity during the preservice period over five years. Based on observations and interviews, he found a number of themes in the teacher's development and practice that were generally consistent with Ladson-Billings's (1994a) culturally relevant pedagogy. However Powell did not analyze how these were linked to the teacher's preservice preparation.

Yeo's (1997) book is part personal narrative about teaching in an urban middle school, part critical theory–based rejection of multiculturalism, and part ideological and practical condemnation of teacher education.

He concludes:

> While I am loath to place significant responsibility at the doors of urban teachers, I am not reluctant to blame teacher education and teacher educators. Thus I intend to assert the direct culpability of teacher education for the styles and results of teaching in urban schools. This chapter can and should be taken for a candid condemnation of mainstream teacher education, which . . . [is] committed to positivism and ethnicity theory . . . and blind faith in the ultimate triumph of the American middle class way of life through assimilation and deculturalization. (p. 146)

Although no documentation of his own or other teacher education programs is offered beyond his own recollections, Yeo makes generalizations about "mainstream" teacher education and seems to work from a deterministic view of the impact of teacher preparation on how teachers teach that, curiously, fails to account for the conditions of urban schooling as a mediating factor between teacher preparation and teaching practice.

The Recruitment and Selection Question. A number of empirical studies in the literature base directly address the teacher recruitment and selection question. These studies address two major questions: What kinds of models, programs, and structural arrangements are effective in recruiting and preparing a more diverse teaching force? Why are various minority groups selecting or not selecting teaching as a career path?

Some of the most extensive work related to the first question has been conducted by Ana Maria Villegas and Beatrice Clewell (Clewell & Villegas, 2001a, 2001b, 2001c; Villegas & Clewell, 1998; Villegas et al., 1995). Villegas and colleagues (1993) studied efforts by the Ford Foundation Minority Education Demonstration Project and the Educational Testing Service Teaching Programs Council to develop models to increase the supply of minority teachers. Based on data from site visits, program literature, and completion and retention rates, they identified several key strategies: targeting students while in middle and high school, establishing formal agreements with financial support for transfer students from community colleges, recruiting teaching assistants from local schools, recruiting minority college graduates interested in career changes, and developing innovative curricula (also see Villegas & Clewell, 1998). One Ford Foundation project designed to recruit Latino and Navajo teachers was successful due to targeted recruitment of para-educators, a needs-based curriculum, and close collaboration among all parties (Becket, 1998). Gonzalez (1997) visited six sites funded by the Ford Foundation. Based on interviews with student teachers, program documents, and evaluation reports, Gonzalez found several key strategies in keeping with the findings of Villegas, including the "human dimension" of personal caring and interaction, peer recruitment, early school experiences, and monitoring and academic support.

Clewell and Villegas (2001a, 2001b, 2001c) studied the Wallace–Reader's Digest Fund Pathways Program, a $50 million national initiative to recruit well-qualified teachers for high-need areas by tapping into nontraditional pools of teacher candidates. Based on surveys and performance, retention, and completion data from more than 50 projects over six years, Clewell and Villegas found that the Pathways model recruited more than 2,500 minority teachers with rates higher than national averages for diversity, program completion, entry into teaching in high-need areas, teaching performance evaluations by principals, and retention in high-need areas after three years. Keys to success were targeted recruitment of paraprofessionals and noncertified teachers, adequate financial and other family and academic support, flexible curriculum with diversity a central value, strong partnerships between school districts and universities, and commitment over the long haul. One Pathways program in Norfolk, Virginia, designed to recruit paraprofessionals, had early success because of collaboration, commitment, concern for students, and the development of an innovative curriculum (Littleton, 1998).

A number of other studies analyzed individual institutional efforts to select minorities into redesigned or alternative teacher education programs and to support them in innovative ways. Using data from student interviews and program completion, for example, Arends, Clemson, and Henkelman (1992) analyzed a successful University of Maryland effort; Shade, Boe, Garner, and New (1998) provided data about a program for minority career changers at University of Wisconsin–Parkside; Contreras and Willis (1993) evaluated a summer bridge project at the University of North Texas to recruit minority students from high school and community and junior colleges; and Haberman (1993) concluded that his urban teaching interview process, developed over two decades of alternative programs for urban schools, could be used to predict success in urban schools. In addition, three case studies of innovative minority recruitment and retention programs drew on some combination of interviews, students' writing, autobiographical assignments, journal entries, and instructors' reflections: Bennett, Cole, and Thompson (2000) examined Project TEAM, Brennan and Bliss (1998) analyzed the Teaching Opportunity Program for career changers sponsored by the Kentucky Department of Education, and Dillard (1994) examined a summer institute for minority education students at Ohio State University. Across these individual institutional efforts, one of the strongest themes was the importance of community building and of making space for open discussions through cohort groups, honors seminars, summer programs, and alternate programs for minority students only. Obstacles to success included the difficulty in recruiting minority candidates in general, finding appropriate cooperating teachers, and—especially for career changers—dealing with the extensive length of time required for program completion.

Along different lines, Yopp, Yopp, and Taylor (1992) pointed out that the Teacher Track Project had created interest in teaching careers among Hispanic high school students and aides, although aides would require many years of education before being ready for teacher preparation programs. Following postulates proposed by John Goodlad for educational renewal, Jacobowitz (1994) studied the initial efforts of teacher education faculty at Montclair State University to analyze and then alter their admissions policies in keeping with a commitment to preparing teachers for a democratic society. A number of other entries in the literature base provided descriptions of interesting and innovative programs designed to promote minority recruitment into teaching but did not pose research questions, gather data to address those questions, or offer analyses based on these and thus are not reviewed here. (See, for example, Dandy, 1998; Hegler, 1997; Hrabowski, Lee, & Martello, 1999; Love & Greer, 1995; Torres-Karna & Krustchinsky, 1998; and Wenzlaff & Thrond, 1995.)

Our literature search yielded five studies (Gordon, 1994, 2000a, 2000b; King, 1993; Su, 1996) that explored why minority groups do or do not choose to enter teaching as a profession. Gordon, who has done some of the most extensive work along these lines, concluded that calls for greater representation and diversity of voices in the education of minority youth is in tension with resistance to encouraging youth to enter teaching. Based on interviews with more than 200 people of color, she compared differences in reasons for African American, Asian American, Latino, and Native American resistance to teaching. Reasons for Asian Americans included low pay and low respect for teachers, lack of encouragement and resistance from family, language issues, diversity, cultural differences, and racism and discrimination (Gordon, 2001a, 2000b). African Americans did not choose teaching because of low return in terms of pay and educational investment, lack of encouragement, more opportunities in other careers, negative experiences with school, and little support from higher education. Latinos did not perceive teaching as a low-status or low-paying job, but had little preparation or opportunity and were concerned about language issues and discrimination. For Native Americans, the issues were poor academic preparation, low high school graduation rates, and racism (Gordon, 1994, 2000b).

Along different but related lines, Su (1996) compared the profiles and entry perspectives of some 150 teacher candidates, about 60 of them minorities. He found that minority candidates had lower socioeconomic status and parents' educational levels than White candidates. He also found different perceptions of supports and obstacles for entering teaching. White students were not discouraged by families, had had positive school experiences themselves, and did not see the low status of teaching as an obstacle. Minority students lacked early information and recruitment, experienced family resistance due to the low status and low pay of teaching (especially among Asian students), and were especially conscious of social justice reasons for entering teaching. King (1993) studied 41 minority African American students who were recent graduates of a selective teacher education institution and found that only 18% planned teaching careers. The major reason for entering teaching was the opportunity to work with young people; the major deterrents were working conditions and the opportunities available in other careers.

The Coherence Question. Although the conceptual literature asserts that coherence may well be the most critical aspect of multicultural teacher education (Nieto, 2000; Villegas & Lucas, 2002a), there is very little empirical research on this topic. Davis (1995) conducted a two-year ethnographic study of the cultural and societal views 30 students brought to their preservice program in relation to what they learned from the courses, professors, and program experiences about these. Based on analysis of the "cultural community" using tape-recorded classes, interviews, and course materials, Davis concluded that students came with a meritocratic view of society that was reinforced by the conceptions of IQ, difference, and the larger social order implicit in most faculty courses. As part of the Teacher Education Learning to Teach study at the National Center for Research of Teacher Education, Tatto (1996) drew on survey data from nine teacher education programs, including 113 faculty members, 552 students upon program entry, and 265 students upon exit. Using hierarchical linear modeling to analyze responses, she found that "constructivist teacher education" programs had more coherent visions about what students needed to know to teach diverse student populations and that more coherent programs were more influential than conventional programs that focused on transmission of knowledge.

Institutional Capacity. Institutional capacity refers to organization-level policies, procedures, and practices that indirectly or directly influence teacher education for diversity, including faculty development, recruitment and reward systems, and institutional cultures. The studies in this category include three topics: general institutional climate or support, institutional strategies that support or constrain teacher preparation for diversity, and what happens when higher education faculty members engage in professional development related to diversity. Although there have been many calls for stepped-up efforts to recruit a more diverse teaching force (Chinn & Wong, 1992; Eubanks & Weaver, 1999; Riley, 1998; Shumann, 1992; Villegas & Lucas, 2002a), many questions have been raised about whether this is a real priority for most higher education institutions that prepare teachers. AACTE's RATE VI study (Howey, 1994) of the context for teacher education reform, for example, indicated that more than 60% of deans surveyed said their central administration supported their efforts to recruit diverse candidates, but fewer than 10 of some 200 deans and faculty surveyed said that lack of minority faculty and students was among the most severe problems constraining efforts to improve teacher education.

Examining institutional obstacles and supports, Melnick and Zeichner (1997, 1998) identified the positive institutional strategies of three exemplary teacher education programs as part of an NCRTL study on educating teachers for diversity: active recruitment of faculty of color, staff development for teacher educators, partnerships between institutions with and without diverse populations, and consortia. Building on this work, Price and Valli (1998) examined self-report information on "The Diversity Web," an electronic hub connecting 300 institutions. They identified three dimensions of institutional support for diversity: institutional leadership and change, recruitment and retention efforts, and curriculum transformation.

Pang, Anderson, and Martuza (1997) investigated the experiences of a 15-member consortium intended to "train university professors" in multicultural and bilingual education. They identified three key elements that supported faculty growth—transformative learning opportunities, experiential learning, and problem-posing dialogue—but also found key obstacles: institutional power structures, conflicting expectations and agendas, and the cultures of institutions. Merryfield (2000) examined personal and professional profiles written by 80 teacher educators nominated as exemplary in multicultural and global education. She concluded that childhood and family life, early experiences crossing cultures, and learning from the felt contradictions of one's own work were significant dimensions of professional development. Similarly, Paccione (2000) surveyed 330 members of the National Association for Multicultural Education about the development of multicultural education commitment. Based on a 30% response rate, she found that family and childhood experiences, mentors, education, cultural immersion, and critical incidents were related factors and that commitments developed in stages. Gallavan (2000) analyzed surveys from 18 university instructors who taught diversity courses. Obstacles to their success

included student resistance, students' desire for universal solutions to educational questions, and lack of institutional support. Support included talking with others, reading and writing, and listening to students. Respondents also reported higher-than-usual attrition rates for those teaching diversity courses.

An often overlooked but important aspect of institutional capacity is the professional development opportunities that are available for (or created by) faculty members for teacher education programs for diversity. A number of teacher educators have looked closely at these opportunities and at their own learning processes through self-studies or practitioner inquiries. These vary considerably in terms of systematicity and kind and extent of data sources. Some are based on loose narrative descriptions of personal growth based on journals (Dillard, 1996), while others are analyses of students' writing, responses to questionnaires, and discussions in relation to course syllabi and instructor reflections (Cochran-Smith, 2000; Cockrell, Placier, Cockrell, & Middleton, 1999; Obidah, 2000). Others offer analyses of written reflections and transcribed discussions among pairs or small groups of faculty interrogating key conceptions such as social justice, the role of interpretation, and the use of inquiry in learning to teach for diversity (Cochran-Smith, in press; Cochran-Smith et al., 1999; Conle, 1999; Lesko & Bloom, 1998; Zollers, Albert, & Cochran-Smith, 2000).

Across these inquiries, several themes are indicated: it is difficult for faculty members themselves to acknowledge inconsistencies between what they intend or espouse and what is instantiated in their own everyday practice; despite intentions to provide transformative learning experiences for preservice students, actual practice may be embedded in positivist or universalistic assumptions about learning and schooling; and institutionally supported public spaces are needed to identify and exchange differing interpretations that are otherwise assumed to be the same. In addition, some of this work indicates that while collaborative faculty self-study is useful, it may also have unintended consequences and risks for individuals, such as influencing promotion and tenure decisions or taking time away from individual research and publication.

Relationships with Local Communities. The literature base for this chapter included a number of empirical studies or data-based inquiries related to the role of community experience in teacher preparation. In many of these, preservice teachers engaged in community service learning in communities different from their own as part of specific course or program requirements (Potthoff, Dinsmore, & Stirtz, 2000). As part of literacy or methods courses, for example, preservice teachers worked in family literacy or tutoring programs (Murtadha-Watts, 1998;

Patton, Silva, & Myers, 1999), programs or schools for the children of homeless families (Barton, 1999; Gustafson & Cichy, 1996), and urban projects sponsored by churches or community agencies (Bollin, 1996; Boyle-Baise, 1998; Vadeboncoeur, Rahm, Aguilera, & LeCompte, 1996). Two studies described cultural immersion experiences, which are quite different from community experiences connected to courses: semester-long student teaching on an American Indian reservation (Zeichner & Melnick, 1996) and four and a half weeks living in a Mexican American community and creating an arts enrichment program there (Aguilera & Pohan, 1998). Several researchers examined the impact of urban field experiences and conducting ethnographic studies in urban communities and schools (Fry & McKinney, 1997; Marxen & Rudney, 1999; Narode, Rennie-Hill, & Peterson, 1994; Olmedo, 1997).

In this group of studies, two closely related questions were asked: What meaning do preservice teachers make of particular community-based experiences? What impact does community experience have on preservice teachers' understandings about culture, attitudes, and expectations? Generally, findings are in keeping with previous conclusions (Larke, Wiseman, & Bradley, 1990; Sleeter, 2001b; Zeichner & Hoeft, 1996) that experiences in diverse communities are promising but somewhat uneven strategies in teacher preparation. Vadeboncoeur et al. (1996) combined a pre- and postcourse and community experience survey with analysis of students' journal entries to compare explanations for social issues related to the development of a "democratic character." All of the other studies use various combinations of qualitative and narrative data, including students' inquiry projects, reflective essays, journals, interviews, observations, program and course literature, and evaluation materials to assess the impact of community experience on teachers' understandings. The strength and face validity of researchers' conclusions vary, depending on the number of preservice students included in the sample, the quality and duration of the experiences, and the power of the preservice students' words—which are used in all of the studies—to make the case about changes in attitudes or understandings. Generally, this body of research suggests that experiences in diverse communities, including student teaching or other fieldwork experiences, have an impact on the complexity of students' views of culture, their cultural understandings, their appreciation of family resources, and their ability to contextualize the concepts they are learning. The quality and extent of the learning seem to depend on the quality and extent of reflection and reading that are connected to the community experience, the duration and quality of the experience itself, and the facilitation or support that preservice teachers have as they make sense of the experiences. In addition, one

study (Potthoff et al., 2000) found that students were more satisfied than faculty were with community service learning. Some studies also noted that students do not necessarily engage in more social critique and activism or see the links to larger conditions just because they work in diverse communities (Boyle-Baise, 1998; Duesterberg, 1998; Vadeboncoeur et al., 1996). In fact, some of the literature suggests that without appropriate guidance, some community experiences may actually reinforce deficit notions of diversity or bolster stereotypes (Boyle-Baise; Duesterberg).

Governmental and Nongovernmental Regulations. Only a few of the empirical studies in our literature base focused on governmental and nongovernmental regulations for teacher education programs, either nonvoluntary or voluntary. Gollnick's policy studies have provided the most consistent work in this area. In 1992, Gollnick concluded that the only national standards teacher preparation programs were accountable to were voluntary standards, including those of NCATE and the affiliated professional organizations. Based on an analysis of the first 59 institutions reviewed according to 1987 NCATE standards regarding diversity, Gollnick found that only 13.6% were in full compliance, and that after 12 years with NCATE requiring multicultural education, this was still not seriously incorporated into programs. Gollnick's 1995 study of national and state initiatives for multicultural education concluded that 16 of the 17 NCATE curriculum areas had multicultural guidelines and that the number of states with requirements related to multicultural education had increased. She also concluded, however, that since 1977, there had been little change in the substance and focus of policies, with most limited to working with students with disabilities or from diverse backgrounds. Based on a survey of state departments of education in all 50 states plus the District of Columbia, Evans, Torrey, and Newton (1997) found that only half of the states required multicultural education course work as part of their certification and credentialing process. They also concluded that most requirements were isolated, with little evidence of infusion throughout the program.

Larger Social, Economic, Historical, and Political Contexts. Although a number of studies in our literature base acknowledged the larger contexts in which teacher preparation for a diverse society was embedded, no empirical studies directly addressed these contexts. Some recent discussions of larger educational agendas and the discourse of teacher education reform come the closest to this perspective (see Apple, 2001; Cochran-Smith, 2001a, 2001b; Cochran-Smith & Fries, 2001; Fenstermacher, 2003; Furlong, 2003), but none of these was designed to address specifically multicultural issues.

Business as Usual?

As this review indicates, there has been a great deal of empirical research and data-based inquiry about multicultural teacher education over the past decade. A growing amount of this research has been conducted by teacher educators themselves, who have engaged in practitioner inquiry, narrative research, or self-study, taking their own professional programs and projects as sites for inquiry. This trend in the research suggests that multicultural teacher education is not business as usual, with traditional approaches simply taken for granted. To the contrary, many teacher educators appear to take their work seriously, self-consciously posing questions and then investigating those questions by gathering and analyzing the data of practice. The focus of most of this work is what preservice teachers learn from course and program experiences—how their knowledge, attitudes, and beliefs may change; how they interact with program content; and how particular pedagogies provide different kinds of learning opportunities. Along these lines, a particularly promising teacher preparation pedagogy appears to be community-based experience, which offers teacher candidates new understandings about culture, families, and ways of life that are different from their own. In addition, opportunities to engage in inquiry—about the teacher candidate's own assumptions as well as experiences and emerging practices and about the experiences and practices of others—seem to provide particularly rich sites for learning. This also appears to be true for teacher educators themselves, with a growing number of studies focusing on how teacher educators learn within communities.

At the conclusion of their review of the research on teacher preparation, Wilson et al. (2001) noted that there was little research about what and how teachers-to-be learn from teacher preparation courses. This conclusion holds, however, only if reviewers eliminate at the outset any inquiry that is based on a single course or conducted by a teacher educator or researcher. This decision rule may increase the generalizability of the research reviewed, but it ignores a number of rich accounts that provide insights into how preservice teachers (and teacher educators) construct questions, develop interpretive frameworks, and attempt to make sense of new ideas about diversity, culture, and society. Inquiry into how and what preservice teachers learn is not good or bad simply because the research site is a single course. In many other professional areas, there is a long tradition of research that has yielded important insights based on very small samples that take the practitioner's own professional context as the research site. In teacher education, given the tremendous variation across sites, instructors, materials, and students, it may ultimately be impossible to regard teacher preparation programs or courses as unvarying

"treatments." This suggests that individual inquiries may be important; they need to be examined more closely, and distinctions about their quality need to be made according to the quality and usefulness of the insights they offer rather than the site of the research in the first place.

In considering whether teacher education today is business as usual, it is also important to note that there is very little research on the practice or outcomes of multicultural teacher education. As noted above, only a few studies examine what preservice teachers actually do with what they learn in courses by following student teachers into classrooms and investigating classroom practice, and even fewer follow teacher candidates after they conclude teacher preparation programs and begin to work as full-fledged teachers in schools. As this chapter argues in its conclusion, much more research is needed along these lines. As a field, we need research that maps forward from the teacher preparation period by following preservice teachers into the classroom; we also need research that maps backward to teacher preparation by investigating what the preservice educational experiences and opportunities were for those teachers who are particularly effective working in diverse settings. Research that maps forward to and backward from teacher preparation requires rich and sensitive notions of outcomes, as is noted below.

Finally, there is little empirical or data-based research that concentrates directly on how the diversity and ideology questions of multicultural teacher education are instantiated in programs and how particular programs are coherent (or not) across courses, fieldwork, and other structures. The small amount of work that exists in these areas seems to suggest that with some notable exceptions, many of the fundamental assumptions about the purposes of schooling and the meritocratic nature of American society that have long been implicit in teacher education remain unchallenged and undermined by the weight of other aspects of preparation.

Is it the case, then, that multicultural teacher education is business as usual? No, not completely. There are local pockets of change and a number of individual teacher educators strongly committed to interrogating their own practice and preparing teachers for a diverse society. But the new multicultural teacher education paradigm envisioned by the theorists and reviewed in the conceptual section of this chapter is certainly not in place.

MULTICULTURAL TEACHER EDUCATION IN THE 21ST CENTURY: CONCLUSIONS AND DIRECTIONS FORWARD

This chapter locates the multicultural teacher education literature within teacher education more broadly and within the larger educational and political contexts of the time. The chapter suggests that at the end of the first few years of the 21st century, making teacher preparation more multicultural and more responsive to the needs of the children who are actually in the schools is more precarious than ever before. A "conservative multiculturalism" (Jenks et al., 2001) dominates the political landscape wherein "leaving no child untested" is being mistaken for "leaving no child behind," where equal accountability to the same high-stakes tests is being mistaken for equity of access to learning opportunity, and where heavy pressure to assimilate all schoolchildren into mainstream values and knowledge perspectives is being mistaken for preparing all young people to participate in a democracy. Higher education in a more general sense is also at a crossroads. There has been considerable erosion of public confidence in education and an "increasing clamor to apply quantitative measures of academic outcomes to guarantee educational quality for consumers" (Graham, Lyman, & Trow, 1995, p. 7). This is reflected in the enlarged—and some would say, intrusive—federal role in education, including the imposition of a definition of what counts as research about educational problems by key government agencies that control the purse strings.

It is within this context that the conceptual and empirical literature related to multicultural teacher education have been reviewed. One major conclusion across these two major sections of the chapter is that there is no longer a paucity of research in this area, as was the case at the time of the early syntheses, but this is a reasonable conclusion only if the definition of research stipulated at the outset includes inquiries that draw on many different kinds of data, including the data of experience and including the work of practitioners who are studying their own courses and programs. A second conclusion is that there is promising work in a number of areas, as elaborated above. A third conclusion across the conceptual and empirical work is that the two are disparate in certain important ways. To a great extent, the conceptual research theorizes a new paradigm of multicultural teacher education that is coherent and radical. Yet although the empirical research and data-based inquiries suggest promising practices and several areas of heightened attention, they continue, to a great extent, to study the individual pieces of traditional teacher education.

Directions Forward

Where do we go from here? As a field of scholarly inquiry, multicultural teacher education needs studies linking theory and practice. Particularly, we need to know what is happening to notions of multiculturalism, diversity, equity, and social justice in the face of intense emphasis on standards, high-stakes testing, and narrow views of what counts as research. We need to know more about

how teacher educators themselves theorize the practice of multicultural teacher education, including the range and variation across and among teacher educators. We also need to know more about the impact of competing agendas for teacher education reform on the development and revision of programs. For example, in light of simultaneous efforts to professionalize and deregulate teacher education, what is happening to multicultural programs, practices, and policies?

Along related lines, we need to know how teacher education programs are responding to the new accountability systems that differ from state to state. Are there systematic variations in the impact of these on multicultural aspects of programs? There is little empirical evidence about the impact of national accreditation systems on programs and practices. For example, what happens to multicultural education and teaching for social justice in the face of new NCATE regulations, stipulating that teacher education programs must provide evidence that all teachers certified can produce demonstrable learning gains in all K-12 students? We need research that examines whether these regulations are regarded as consistent or conflicting with existing state and other regulations related to preparing teachers for diversity, as well as research that examines how new regulations interact with the changing missions and goals of institutions.

In the concluding section of their report on the research base for teacher preparation, Wilson et al. (2001) suggest a number of "strategic investments" in research initiatives that might move teacher education forward. Among these, they include linking individual studies into multisite research programs, as well as conducting large-scale national studies. As noted earlier, the Wilson et al. review says virtually nothing about preparing teachers for diverse populations, a failing that was perhaps inevitable given the questions stipulated by OERI. However, the idea of linking individual studies is very applicable to research on multicultural teacher education. Particularly given the increasing number of teacher educators who are interested in engaging in research on their own practice and who seem committed to some of the tenets of multicultural education, there are very promising possibilities here. Multisite research programs in this area could capitalize on the natural laboratory of variations in program types, structures, and arrangements and perhaps lead to findings generalizable beyond the individual site. Of course, this kind of research requires considerable funding and research capacity, which are not readily available at most of the sites where teacher educators have been struggling to research their own programs. As Grant (1992) pointed out a decade ago, research in multicultural education has been consistently marginalized and underfunded. Nonetheless, with appropriate funding, there is great potential in the area of multisite research.

The Missing Research Program: Mapping Forward, Mapping Back

In 1986, in a review of paradigms and research programs in the study of teaching, Lee Shulman suggested that a missing program of research was how teachers understood and used subject matter knowledge. He wrote:

The general public and those who set educational policy are in general agreement that teachers' competence in the subjects they teach is a central criterion of teacher quality. They remain remarkably vague, however, in defining what sort of subject-matter knowledge they have in mind . . . . Ironically, little is known about such matters empirically because these questions have fallen between the cracks in the research-on-teaching field. (pp. 25–26)

Many researchers took Shulman's call and the calls of other researchers along these same lines seriously. Over the next 15 years, several major programs of research were developed about teachers' subject matter expertise, pedagogical content knowledge, and the ways teachers transform knowledge of subject matter into effective classroom practice. The research program on teachers' cognition and knowledge use, as well as its documentation through portfolios and its assessment through NBPTS certification, was in fact so successful that Shulman (2002) himself was prompted to comment more recently about what it left out: the connection between teacher knowledge and K-12 student achievement. Shulman wrote, "If our national board work reflected the theoretical importance of the three Cs of content, cognition, and context, it continued to ignore a fourth C, consequences for students" (p. 251).

The contrast between Shulman's comments in 1986 and 2002 is instructive in terms of needed directions in teacher education research related to diversity. The missing research program in multicultural teacher education is research that examines the links among teacher preparation for diversity and teachers' own learning, their professional practices, and their K-12 students' learning. Research of this kind would examine the connections and linkages that obtain (or not) among these, criss-crossing back and forth between the diversity question, the teacher learning question, the practice question, and the outcomes question. The call in this chapter for research that addresses the outcomes and effectiveness of teacher preparation is certainly not new. Grant and Secada concluded in 1990 that we needed "more information about the scope of effective educational practice and the combinations of practice that result in optimal outcomes" (p. 413). Every major synthesis since 1990 has said something similar to what Grant and Secada wrote.

Why then don't we already have research that examines these connections in multicultural teacher education? One reason is certainly the historical marginalization and underfunding of research related to diversity and education in general, as noted already. Another is the heavy emphasis in the field of teacher education over the past 15 years on the knowledge base for teaching, with research on teacher knowledge, teacher thinking, and more recently teacher learning in communities overshadowing other topics. But a third reason this research has not yet developed is that it is difficult to do, and particularly difficult to do well. If there is one thing that the research on diversity and teaching has made clear, it is the importance of social and cultural contexts and of local meanings in all aspects of school and schooling. In contrast, studies that focus on outcomes are intended, almost by definition, to produce evidence of the impact of isolatable variables that are generalizable across variations in contexts. Along these lines, Weiner (2000) argues that a sign of progress in research on urban teaching and teacher preparation was the gradual move in the 1990s away from reductionist studies of single factors. She writes, "A significant shift occurred away from studies that attempted to find explanations for school failure that focused on student and teacher characteristics in isolation from one another and from schools" (p. 384).

A promising way to develop the missing program of research in multicultural teacher education is through studies that map forward from teacher preparation to student outcomes, as well as those that map backward from successful outcomes for students to quality and kind of teacher preparation. Studies that map forward from initial teacher preparation would feature longitudinal designs that follow up on the experiences, successes, and problems and failures of new teachers who have been prepared in various ways as they embark (or not) on teaching careers. They would also track teachers' performances in diverse settings over some part of the professional life span. Studies that map backward from successful teaching in diverse settings would begin with successful classroom practice and trace the connections back to teacher learning experiences and varying modes of teacher preparation. Sleeter (2001a) makes a similar point, suggesting that "rather than starting with the question of what teacher education looks like, we should start with the question of what good teachers look like and then work backward" (p. 242).

The most critical aspect of research that maps either forward or back is the definition of "good teaching" or "successful practice" that guides the research. Definitions of successful teaching that rely only on teachers' presumed impact on K-12 students' scores on high-stakes tests will simply exacerbate the historical problems for students of color when competence is conceptualized in this narrow way and will reify the notion that learning equals test scores. This kind of approach is certainly not in keeping with the fundamental tenets of multicultural education. But definitions of teaching success that rely on principals' or colleagues' evaluations of teachers and on parents' and community nominations while ignoring the outcomes of high-stakes assessments will fail to account for the current political context and risk being dismissed by most of the major power brokers in education. Furthermore, neither of these considers as part of teaching "success" the development of classroom pedagogy that is aligned with curriculum and teaching standards in the various subject matter areas, a critical aspect of teaching that arguably reflects cutting-edge research on how people learn disciplinary knowledge. This needs to be included in notions of success. Finally, none of the conceptualizations of outcomes mentioned so far directly includes social activism and participation in larger community and professional movements for social change. These are also vital to teaching for diversity.

The major challenge in establishing the missing program of research in multicultural teacher education is to develop rich and sensitive outcomes measures that take all of these aspects of "successful teaching" for diversity into account and then map forward from, or backward to, teacher preparation. Early in the 21st century, this is especially challenging but also especially imperative work. As an educational community, we cannot afford *not* to take up the challenge.

References

Aaronsohn, E., Carter, C., & Howard, M. (1995). Preparing mono-cultural teachers for a multicultural world. *Equity and Excellence in Education, 29*(1), 5–9.

Abell Foundation. (2001a, Oct.). *Teacher Certification Reconsidered: Stumbling for Quality.* Baltimore, MD: Abell Foundation. [On-line]. Available: http://www.abell.org.

Abell Foundation. (2001b, Nov.). *Teacher Certification Reconsidered: Stumbling for Quality. A Rejoinder.* Baltimore, MD: Abell Foundation. [On-line]. Available: http://www.abell.org.

Agee, J. (1998). Confronting issues of race and power in the culture of schools. In M. Dilworth (Ed.), *Being responsive to cultural differences* (pp. 21–38). Thousand Oaks, CA: Corwin Press.

Aguilar, T., & Pohan, C. (1998). A cultural immersion experience to enhance. *Sociotam, 8*(1), 30–49.

American Association of Colleges for Teacher Education. (1997). *Selected data from the 1995 AACTE/NCTE joint data collection system.* Washington, DC: Author.

American Association of Colleges for Teacher Education. (1999). *Teacher education pipeline IV: Schools, colleges, and departments of education enrollments by race, ethnicity, and gender.* Washington, DC: Author.

American Civil Liberties Union. (2000). *ACSL-Southern California Docket: Williams et al. v. State of California et al.* [On-line]. Available: http://www.aclu-sc.org.

Anderson, S. (1998). Integrating multicultural materials into an educational psychology course. *Journal of Technology and Teacher Education, 6*(2–3), 169–182.

Appelbaum, P., & Enomoto, E. (1995). Computer-mediated communication for a multicultural experience. *Educational Technology, 35,* 49–58.

Apple, M. (2000). Can critical pedagogies interrupt rightists' policies? *Educational Theory, 50*(2), 229–254.

Apple, M. (2001). Markets, standards, teaching, and teacher education. *Journal of Teacher Education, 52*(3), 182–195.

Arends, R., Clemson, S., & Henkelman, J. (1992). Tapping non-traditional sources of minorities in teaching talent. In M. Dilworth (Ed.), *Diversity in teacher education* (pp. 160–180). San Francisco: Jossey-Bass.

Artiles, A., Barreto, R., McClafferty, K., & Pena, L. (1998). Pathways to teacher learning in multicultural contexts. *Remedial and Special Education, 19*(2), 70–90.

Au, K. (2002). Communities of practice: Engagement, imagination, and alignment in research on teacher education. *Journal of Teacher Education, 53*(3), 222–227.

Avery, P., & Walker, C. (1993). Prospective teachers' perceptions of ethnic and gender differences in academic achievement. *Journal of Teacher Education, 44*(1), 27–37.

Ballou, D., & Podgursky, M. (2000). Reforming teacher preparation and licensing: What is the evidence? *Teachers College Record, 102*(1), 5–27.

Banks, J. (1993). Approaches to multicultural curriculum reform. In J. Banks & C.A.M. Banks (Eds.), *Multicultural education: Issues and perspectives* (2nd ed., pp. 195-214). Needham Heights, MA: Allyn & Bacon.

Banks, J. (1994). *An introduction to multicultural education.* Needham Heights, MA: Allyn & Bacon.

Banks, J. (1995). Multicultural education: Historical development, dimensions, and practice. In J. Banks & C.A.M. Banks (Eds.), *Handbook of research on multicultural education* (pp. 3–24). Old Tappan, NJ: Macmillan.

Banks, J., & Banks, C.A.M. (Eds.). (1995). *Handbook of Research on Multicultural Education.* Old Tappan, NJ: Macmillan.

Baptiste, H., & Baptiste, M. (1980). Competencies toward multiculturalism. In H. Baptiste, M. Baptiste & D. Gollnick (Eds.), *Multicultural teacher education: Preparing teacher educators to provide educational equity* (Vol. 1). Washington, DC: American Association of College for Teacher Education.

Barry, N., & Lechner, J. (1995). Preservice teachers' attitudes about the awareness of multicultural teaching and learning. *Teaching and Teacher Education, 11,* 149–161.

Barton, A. (1999). Crafting a multicultural science teacher education: A case study. *Journal of Teacher Education, 50,* 303–314.

Becket, N. (1998). Increasing the number of Latino and Navajo teachers in hard-to-staff schools. *Journal of Teacher Education, 49*(3), 196–205.

Bennett, C. (1995). Preparing teachers for cultural diversity and national standards of academic excellence. *Journal of Teacher Education, 46,* 259–265.

Bennett, C., Cole, D., & Thompson, J. (2000). Preparing teachers of color at a predominantly White university: A case study of project TEAM. *Teaching and Teacher Education, 16*(4), 445–464.

Bollin, G. (1996). Using multicultural tutoring to prepare preservice teachers for diverse classrooms. *Educational Forum, 61*(1), 68–76.

Boyce, B. (1996). Dealing with student diversity through the case-study approach. *Journal of Physical Education, Recreation, and Dance, 67*(5), 46–50.

Boyle-Baise, M. (1998). Community service learning for multicultural education: An exploratory study with preservice teachers. *Equity and Excellence in Education, 31*(2), 52–60.

Bransford, J., Brown, A., & Cocking, R. (Eds.). (2000). *How people learn: Brain, mind, experience, and school.* Washington, DC: National Academy Press.

Breault, R. (1995). Preparing preservice teachers for culturally diverse classrooms. *Educational Forum, 59,* 265–275.

Brennan, S., & Bliss, T. (1998). Increasing minority representation in the teaching profession through alternative certification: a case study. *Teacher Educator, 34*(1), 1–11.

Bullock, L. (1997). Efficacy of a gender and ethnic equity in science education curriculum for preservice teachers. *Journal of Research in Science Teaching, 34,* 1019–1038.

Burant, T. (1999). Finding, using, and losing (?) voice: A preservice teacher's experience in an urban educative practicum. *Journal of Teacher Education, 50,* 209–219.

Cabello, B., & Burstein, N. (1995). Examining teachers' beliefs about teaching in culturally diverse classrooms. *Journal of Teacher Education, 46,* 285–294.

Cabello, B., & Eckmier, J. (1995). Looking back: teachers' reflections on an innovative teacher preparation program. *Action in Teacher Education, 17,* 33–42.

Cabello, B., Eckmier, J., & Baghieri, H. (1995). The comprehensive teacher institute: Successes and pitfalls of an innovative teacher preparation program. *Teacher Educator, 31*(1), 43–55.

Canning, C. (1995). Getting from the outside in: Teaching Mexican Americans when you are an "Anglo." *High School Journal,* 195–205.

Carr, W. (1987). What is an educational practice? *Journal of the Philosophy of Education, 21*(2), 163–175.

Cary, L. (2001). The refusals of citizenship: Normalizing practices in social educational discourses. *Theory and Research in Social Education, 29*(3), 405–430.

Causey, V., Thomas, C., & Armento, B. (2000). Cultural diversity is basically a foreign term to me: The challenges of diversity for preservice teacher education. *Teaching and Teacher Education, 19*(1), 33–45.

Chinn, P., & Wong, G. (1992). Recruiting and retaining Asian/Pacific American teachers. In M. Dilworth (Ed.), *Diversity in teacher education.* San Francisco: American Association of Colleges for Teacher Education and Jossey-Bass.

Clarke, C., & Medina, C. (2000). How reading and writing literacy narratives affect preservice teachers' understandings of literacy, pedagogy, and multiculturalism. *Journal of Teacher Education, 51*(1), 63–76.

Clewell, B., & Villegas, A. (2001a). *Ahead of the class: A handbook for preparing new teachers from new sources.* Washington, DC: Urban Institute.

Clewell, B., & Villegas, A. (2001b). *Absence unexcused: Ending teacher shortages in high-need areas.* Washington, DC: Urban Institute.

Clewell, B., & Villegas, A. (2001c). *Evaluation of the DeWitt Wallace-Reader's Digest Fund's Pathways to Teacher Careers program.* New York: Wallace Reader's Digest Fund.

Cochran-Smith, M. (1991). Learning to teach against the grain. *Harvard Educational Review, 51*(3), 279–310.

Cochran-Smith, M. (1995a). Color blindness and basket making are not the answers: Confronting the dilemmas of race, culture, and language diversity in teacher education. *American Educational Research Journal, 32*(3), 493–522.

Cochran-Smith, M. (1995b). Uncertain allies: Understanding the boundaries of race and teaching. *Harvard Educational Review, 65*(4), 541–570).

Cochran-Smith, M. (1997). Knowledge, skills, and experiences for teaching culturally diverse learners: A perspective for practicing teachers. In J. Irvine (Ed.), *Critical knowledge for diverse learners and teachers.* Washington, DC: American Association of Colleges for Teacher Education.

Cochran-Smith, M. (1998). Teaching for social change: Toward a grounded theory of teacher education. In A. Hargreaves, A. Lieberman, M. Fullan, D. Hopkins (Eds.), *The international handbook of educational change* (pp. 916–951). Norwell, MA: Kluwer.

Cochran-Smith, M. (1999). Learning to teach for social justice. In G. Griffin (Ed.), *The education of teachers: Ninety-eighth yearbook of the National Society for the Study of Education* (pp. 114–144). Chicago: University of Chicago Press.

Cochran-Smith, M. (2000). Blind vision: Unlearning racism in teacher education. *Harvard Educational Review, 70*(2), 157–190.

Cochran-Smith, M. (2001a). Constructing outcomes in teacher education: Policy, practice and pitfalls. *Educational Policy Analysis Archives, 9*(11).

Cochran-Smith, M. (2001b). *Learning and unlearning: Educating teacher educators from an inquiry stance.* Paper presented at the Annual Meeting of the American Educational Research Association, Seattle, WA.

Cochran-Smith, M. (2001c). The outcomes question in teacher education. *Teaching and Teacher Education, 17*(5), 527–546.

Cochran-Smith, M. (2003a). Learning and unlearning: The education of teacher educators. *Teaching and Teacher Education, 19,* 5–28.

Cochran-Smith, M. (2003b). *The multiple meanings of multicultural teacher education. Teacher Education Quarterly, 30*(2), 7–26.

Cochran-Smith, M., Dimattia, P., Dudley-Marling, C., Freedman, S., Friedman, A., Jackson, J., Jackson, R., Loftus, F., Mooney, J., Neisler, O., Peck, A., Pelletier, C., Pine, G., Scanlon, D., & Zollers, N. (1999). *Seeking social justice: A teacher education faculty's self study, Year III.* Paper presented at the Annual Meeting of the American Educational Research Association, Montreal, Canada.

Cochran-Smith, M., & Fries, K. (2001). Sticks, stones, and ideology: The discourse of teacher education. *Educational Researcher, 30*(8), 3–15.

Cochran-Smith, M., & Lytle, S. (1992). Interrogating cultural diversity: Inquiry and action. *Journal of Teacher Education, 43*(2), 104–115.

Cochran-Smith, M., & Lytle, S. (1993). *Inside/outside: Teacher research and knowledge.* New York: Teachers College Press.

Cochran-Smith, M., & Lytle, S. (1998). Teacher research: The question that persists. *International Journal of Leadership in Education, 1*(1), 19–36.

Cochran-Smith, M., & Lytle, S. (1999). Relationship of knowledge and practice: Teacher learning in communities. In A. Iran-Nejad & C. D. Pearson (Eds.), *Review of research in education* (Vol. 24, pp. 249–306). Washington, DC: American Educational Research Association.

Cockrell, K., Placier, P., Cockrell, D., & Middleton, T. (1999). Coming to terms with "diversity" and "multiculturalism" in teacher education: Learning about our students, changing our practice. *Teaching and Teacher Education, 15*(4), 351–366.

Conle, C. (1999). Moments of interpretation in the perception and evaluation of teaching. *Teaching and Teacher Education, 15*(7), 801–814.

Contreras, G., & Willis, N. (1993). Attracting minority community/junior college students to teaching. *Action in Teacher Education, 15*(1), 1–7.

Cooney, M., & Akintude, O. (1999). Confronting white privilege and the "color blind" paradigm in teacher education. *Multicultural Education, 7*(2), 9–14.

Corbett, N., Kilgore, K., & Sindelar, P.(1998). "Making sense" in a collaborative teacher education program: Lessons from Project PART students. *Teacher Education and Special Education, 21*(4), 293–305.

Curtis, A. (1998). Creating culturally responsive curriculum: Making race matter. *Clearinghouse, 71*(3), 135–139.

Dandy, E. (1998). Increasing the number of minority teachers, tapping the paraprofessional pool. *Education and Urban Society, 31*(1), 89–103.

Darling-Hammond, L. (1995). Inequality and access to knowledge. In J. A. Banks & C.A.M. Banks (Eds.), *Handbook of research on multicultural education.* Old Tappan, NJ: Macmillan.

Darling-Hammond, L. (2000). Reforming teacher preparation and licensing: Debating the evidence. *Teachers College Record, 102*(1), 28–56.

Darling-Hammond, L. (2001). The research and rhetoric on teacher certification: A response to "Teacher certification reconsidered." [On-line]. Available: http://www.nctaf.org. Retrieved Oct. 2001.

Darling-Hammond, L., & Sclan, E. M. (1996). Who teaches and why. In J. Sikula (Ed.), *Handbook of research on teacher education* (pp. 67–101). New York: Simon & Schuster.

Davis, K. (1995). Multicultural classrooms and cultural communities of teachers. *Teaching and Teacher Education, 11,* 553–563.

Deering, T., & Stanutz, A. (1995). Preservice field experience as a multicultural component of a teacher education program. *Journal of Teacher Education, 46,* 390–394.

Dillard, C. (1994). Beyond supply and demand: Critical pedagogy, ethnicity, and empowerment in recruiting teachers of color. *Journal of Teacher Education, 45*(1), 9–17.

Dillard, C. (1996). From lessons of self to lessons of others: Exploring the role of autobiography in the process of multicultural learning and teaching. *Multicultural Education, 4*(2), 33–37.

Dilworth, M. (Ed.). (1992). *Diversity in teacher education.* San Francisco: Jossey-Bass.

Donovan, C., Rovegno, I., & Dolly, J. (2000). Teaching development and diversity in field-based methods courses. *Action in Teacher Education, 22*(3), 37–46.

Duesterberg, L. (1998). Rethinking culture in the pedagogy and practices of preservice teachers. *Teaching and Teacher Education, 14*(5), 497–512.

Earley, P. (2000). Finding the culprit: Federal policy and teacher education. *Educational Policy, 14*(1), 25–39.

Easter, L., Shultz, E., & Neyhart, T. (1999). Weighty perceptions: A study of the attitudes and beliefs of preservice teacher education students regarding diversity and urban education. *Urban Review, 31*(2), 205–220.

Education Commission of the States. (2000). *Two paths to quality teaching: Implicaiton for policy makers.* [On-line]. Available: http://www.edexcellence.net.

Elijah, R. (2001). Untold stories: Implications for understanding minority preservice teachers' experiences. In S. King & L. Castenell (Eds.), *Racism and racial inequality: Implications for teacher education.* Washington, DC: American Association of Colleges for Teacher Education.

Eubanks, S., & Weaver, R. (1999). Excellence through diversity: connecting the teacher quality and teacher diversity agendas. *Journal of Negro Education, 68*(3), 451–459.

Evans, E., Torrey, C., & Newton, S. (1997). Multicultural education requirements in teacher certification. *Multicultural Education, 4*(3), 9–11.

Ewing, N. (2001). Teacher education: Ethics, power, and privilege. *Teacher Education and Special Education, 24*(1), 13–24.

Feiman-Nemser, S. (1990). Teacher preparation: Structural and conceptual alternatives. In W. Houston (Ed.), *Handbook of Research on Teacher Education.* Old Tappan, NJ: Macmillan.

Fennimore, B. (2001). Historical white resistance to equity in public education: A challenge to white teacher educators. In S. King & L. Castenell (Eds.), *Racism and racial inequality: Implications for teacher education.* Washington, DC: American Association of Colleges for Teacher Education.

Fenstermacher, G. (1994). The knower and the known: The nature of knowledge in research on teaching. In L. Darling-Hammond (Ed.), *Review of research in education* (Vol. 20, pp. 3–56). Washington, DC: American Educational Research Association.

Fenstermacher, G. (2003). Reconsidering the teacher education reform debate: A commentary on Cochran-Smith and Fries. *Educational Researcher, 31*(6), 20–22.

Florio-Ruane, S. (1994). The future teachers' autobiography club: Preparing educators to support literacy learning in culturally diverse classrooms. *English Education, 26*(1), 52–66.

Florio-Ruane, S. (2001). *Teacher education and the cultural imagination.* Mahwah, NJ: Erlbaum.

Fox, W., & Gay, G. (1995). Integrating multicultural and curriculum principles in teacher education. *Peabody Journal of Education, 70,* 64–82.

Fry, P., & McKinney, L. (1997). A qualitative study of preservice teachers' early field experiences in an urban, culturally different school. *Urban Education, 32*(2), 184–201.

Frykholm, J. (1997). A stacked deck: Addressing issues of equity with preservice teachers. *Equity and Excellence in Education, 30*(2), 50–58.

Fuller, M. (1992). Monocultural teachers and multicultural students: A demographic clash. *Teaching Education, 4* (2), 87–93.

Fuller, M. (1994). The monocultural graduate in the multicultural environment: A challenge for teacher educators. *Journal of Teacher Education, 45*(4), 269–277.

Furlong, J. (2003). Ideology and reform in teacher education in England: Some reflections on Cochran-Smith and Fries. *Educational Researcher, 31*(6), 23–25.

Gallagher, K., & Bailey, J. (2000). The politics of teacher education reform: Strategic philanthropy and public policy making. *Educational Policy, 14*(1), 11–24.

Gallavan, N. (2000). Multicultural education at the academy: Teacher educators' challenges, conflicts and coping skills. *Equity and Excellence in Education, 33*(3), 5–11.

Garibaldi, A. (1992). Preparing teachers for culturally diverse classrooms. In M. Dilworth (Ed.), *Diversity in teacher education* (pp. 23–39). San Francisco: Jossey-Bass.

Garmon, M. (1998). Using dialogue journals to promote student learning in a multicultural teacher education course. *Remedial and Special Education, 19*(1), 32–45.

Gay, G. (1993). Building cultural bridges: A bold proposal for teacher education. *Education and Urban Society, 25*(3), 285–289.

Gay, G. (1995). Bridging multicultural theory and practice. *Multicultural Education, 3*(1), 4–9.

Gay, G. (2000). *Culturally responsive teaching: Theory, research and practice.* New York: Teachers College Press.

Gay, G., & Howard, T. (2000). Multicultural teacher education for the 21st century. *Teacher Educator, 36*(1), 1–16.

Gollnick, D. (1992). Multicultural education: Policies and practices in teacher education. In C. Grant (Ed.), *Research and multicultural education: From the margins to the mainstream* (pp. 218–239). Bristol, PA: Falmer Press.

Gollnick, D. (1995). National and state initiatives for multicultural education. In J. Banks and C.A.M. Banks (Eds.), *Handbook of research on multicultural education*. Old Tappan, NJ: Macmillan.

Gomez, M. (1996). Telling stories of our teaching, reflecting on our practices. *Action in Teacher Education, 18*(3), 1–12.

Gonzalez, J. (1997). Recruiting and training minority teachers: Student views of the preservice program. *Equity and Excellence in Education, 30*(1), 56–64.

Goodwin, A. (1994). Making the transition from self to other: What do preservice teachers really think about multicultural education? *Journal of Teacher Education, 45*(2), 119–130.

Goodwin, A. (1997). Multicultural stories: Preservice teachers' conceptions of and responses to issues of diversity. *Urban Education, 32*(1), 117–145.

Goodwin, A. (2000). Teachers as (multi)cultural agents in schools. In R. Carter (Ed.), *Addressing cultural issues in organizations: Beyond the corporate context* (pp. 104–114). Thousand Oaks, CA: Sage.

Goodwin, A. (2001). Seeing with different eyes: Reexamining teachers' expectations through racial lenses. In S. King & L. Castenell (Eds.), *Racism and racial inequality: Implications for teacher education*. Washington, DC: American Association of Colleges for Teacher Education.

Gordon, B. (2001a). Knowledge construction, competing critical theories, and education. In J. Banks & C.A.M. Banks (Eds.), *Handbook of research on multicultural education* (pp. 184–202). San Francisco: Jossey-Bass.

Gordon, B. (2001b). The criticality of racism in education at the dawn of the new millennium. In S. King & L. Castenell (Eds.) *Racism and racial inequality: Implications for teacher education* (pp. 15–32). Washington, DC: American Association of Colleges for Teacher Education.

Gordon, J. (1994). Preparing future teachers for diversity. *Urban Review, 26*(1), 25–34.

Gordon, J. (2000a). Asian American resistance to selecting teaching as a career: the power of community and tradition. *Teachers College Record, 102*(1), 173–196.

Gordon, J. (2000b). *The color of teaching.* London: Routledge.

Graham, P., Lyman, R., & Trow, M. (1998). *Accountability of colleges and universities: An essay.* New York: Columbia University Press.

Graham, R., & Young, J. (2000). Talking practice: The debriefing session in multicultural teacher education curriculum. *Journal of Educational Thought, 34*(2), 165–182.

Grant, C. (1991). Culture and teaching: What do teachers need to know? In M. Kennedy (Ed.), *Teaching academic subjects to diverse learners* (pp. 237–256). New York: Teachers College Press.

Grant, C. (Ed.). (1992). *Research and multicultural education: From margins to the mainstream.* Bristol, PA: Falmer Press.

Grant, C. (1997). Critical knowledge, skills, and experiences for the instruction of culturally diverse students: A perspective for the preparation of preservice teachers. In J. Irvine (Ed.), *Critical knowledge for diverse teachers and learners* (pp. 1–26). Washington, DC: American Association of Colleges for Teacher Education.

Grant, C., & Graue, E. (1997). Editor's introduction: The charge and the challenge. *Review of Educational Research, 67*(1), 1–2.

Grant, C., & Secada, W. (1990). Preparing teachers for diversity. In W. R. Houston, M. Haberman, & J. Sikula (Eds.), *Handbook of research on teacher education* (pp. 403–422). Old Tappan, NJ: Macmillan.

Grant, C., & Sleeter, C. (1985). The literature on multicultural education: Review and analysis. *Educational Studies, 12,* 47–71.

Grant, C., & Wieczorek, K. (2000). Teacher education and knowledge in "the knowledge society": The need for social moorings in our multicultural schools. *Teachers College Record, 102*(5), 913–935.

Graue, E., & Grant, C. (2002). Questions, calls, and conversations for researchers in teacher education. *Journal of Teacher Education, 52*(2).

Greenleaf, C., Hull, G., & Reilly, B. (1994). Learning from our diverse students: Helping teachers rethink problematic teaching and learning situations. *Teaching and Teacher Education, 10*(5), 521–541.

Greenman, N., & Kimmel, E. (1995). The road to multicultural education: Potholes of resistance. *Journal of Teacher Education, 46*(5), 360–368.

Guillaume, A., Zuniga-Hill, C., & Yee, I. (1995). Prospective teachers' use of diversity issues in a case study analysis. *Journal of Research and Development in Education, 28,* 69–78.

Gustafson, J., & Cichy, S. (1996). Teaching homeless children: Exemplary field experiences for teacher education candidates. *Educational Forum, 61*(1), 24–29.

Guyton, E., Saxton, R., & Wesche, M. (1995). Experiences of diverse students in teacher education. *Teaching and Teacher Education, 12*(6), 643–652.

Haberman, M. (1988). *Preparing teachers for urban schools.* Bloomington, IN: Phi Delta Kappan Educational Foundation.

Haberman, M. (1991). Rationale for training adults as teachers. In C. Sleeter (Ed.), *Empowerment through multicultural education* (pp. 275–286). Albany: SUNY Press.

Haberman, M. (1993). Predicting the success of urban teachers (the Milwaukee trials). *Action in Teacher Education, 15*(3), 1–5.

Haberman, M. (1996). Selecting and preparing culturally competent teachers for urban schools. In J. Sikula, T. Buttery, & E. Guyton (Eds.), *Handbook of research on teacher education* (2nd ed., pp. 747–760). Old Tappan, NJ: Macmillan.

Haberman, M., & Post, L. (1998). Teachers for multicultural schools: The power of selection. *Theory into Practice, 37*(2), 96–104.

Hamilton, M. (Ed.). (1998). *Reconceptualizing teaching practice: Self-study in teacher education.* Bristol, PA: Falmer Press.

Harrington, H., & Hathaway, R. (1995). Illuminating beliefs about diversity. *Journal of Teacher Education, 46,* 275–284.

Hegler, K. (1997). Collaboration for diversity. *Action in Teacher Education, 19,* 74–79.

Hodgkinson, H. (2001). Educational demographics: What teachers should know. *Educational Leadership, 58*(4), 6–11.

Hodgkinson, H. (2002). Demographics and teacher education. *Journal of Teacher Education, 53*(2), 102–105.

Hollins, E. (1995). Revealing the deep meaning of culture in school learning: Framing a new paradigm for teacher preparation. *Action in Teacher Education, 17*(1), 70–79.

Hollins, E. (1996). *Culture in school learning: Revealing the deep meaning.* Mahwah, NJ: Erlbaum.

Hollins, E., King, J., & Hayman, W. (Eds.). (1994). *Teaching diverse populations: Formulating a knowledge base.* Albany, NY: SUNY Press.

Holm, G. (1995). Cultural awareness through biographies. *College Teaching, 43*(2), 72–75.

Hood, S., & Parker, L. (1994). Minorities, teacher testing, and recent US Supreme Court holdings: A regressive step. *Teachers College Record, 92*(4), 603–618.

Howey, K. (1994). *RATE VI: The context of the reform of teacher education.* Washington, DC: American Association of Colleges for Teacher Education.

Howey, K., Arends, G., Yarger, S. & Zimpher, N. (1994). *RATE VI: The context of the reform of teacher education.* Washington, DC: American Association of Colleges for Teacher Education.

Hrabowski, F., Lee, D., & Martello, J. (1999). Educating teachers for the 21st century: Lessons learned. *The Journal of Negro Education, 68*(3), 293–305.

Huber, T., & Klein, F. (1993). Attitude toward diversity: Can teacher education programs really make a difference? *Teacher Educator, 29*, 15–23.

Huberman, M. (1996). Focus on research moving mainstream: Taking a closer look at teacher research. *Language Arts, 73*(2), 124–140.

Imig, D., Cochran-Smith, M., Diez, M., Murrell, P., Pankratz, R., & Schalock, D. (2000). *Shifting the paradigm: Professionalizing teaching through accountability for student progress in learning.* Paper presented at the American Association of Colleges for Teacher Education, Chicago.

Irvine, J. (1990). *Black students and school failure.* Westport, CT: Greenwood Press.

Irvine, J. (Ed.). (1997a). *Critical knowledge for diverse teachers and learners.* Washington, DC: American Association of Colleges for Teacher Education.

Irvine, J. (1997b). Location, location, location: A synthesis perspective on the knowledge base for urban teacher education. In J. Jordan-Irvine (Ed.), *Critical knowledge for diverse teachers and learners* (pp. 217–222). Washington, DC: American Association of Colleges for Teacher Education.

Irvine, J. (2001). *Caring, competent teachers in complex classrooms.* Paper presented at the Charles W. Hunt Memorial Lecture for American Association of Colleges for Teacher Education, Dallas.

Irvine, J., & Armento, B. (2001). *Culturally responsive teaching: Lesson planning for elementary and middle schools.* New York: McGraw-Hill.

Jacobowitz, T. (1994). Admission to teacher education programs: Goodlad's sixth postulate. *Journal of Teacher Education, 45*(1), 46–49.

Jenks, C., Lee, J., & Kanpol, B. (2001). Approaches to multicultural education in preservice teacher education: Philosophical frameworks and models for teaching. *Urban Review, 33*(2), 87–105.

Kailin, J. (1999). Preparing urban teachers for schools and communities: An anti-racist perspective. *The High School Journal, 82*(2), 80–87.

Kanpol, B., & McLaren, P. (Eds.). (1995). *Critical multiculturalism.* Westport, CT: Bergin and Garvey.

Kea, C., & Bacon, E. H. (1999). Journal reflections of preservice education students on multicultural experiences. *Action in Teacher Education, 21*(2), 34–50.

Kesner, J. (2000). Teacher characteristics and the quality of child-teacher relationships. *Journal of School Psychology, 38*(2), 133–149.

King, J., Hollins, E., & Hayman, W. (1997). *Preparing teachers for cultural diversity.* New York: Teachers College Press.

King, S. (1993). The limited presence of African-American teachers. *Review of Educational Research, 63*(2), 115–149.

King, S., & Castenell, L. (Eds.). (2001a). *Racism and racial inequality: Implications for teacher education.* Washington, DC: American Association of Colleges for Teacher Education.

King, S., & Castenell, L. (2001b). Tenets to guide antiracist teacher education practice. In S. King & L. Castenell (Eds.), *Racism and racial inequality: Implications for teacher education.* Washington, DC: American Association of Colleges for Teacher Education.

Kitano, M., Lewis, R., Lynch, E., & Graves, A. (1996). Teaching in a multicultural classroom: Teacher educators' perspectives. *Equity and Excellence in Education, 29*(3), 70–77.

Kornfeld, J. (1999). Sharing stories: A study of African American students in a predominantly white teacher education program. *Teacher Educator, 35*(1), 19–40.

Kozol, J. (1991). *Savage inequalities: Children in America's schools.* New York: HarperCollins.

Ladson-Billings, G. (1994a). *The dream keepers: Successful teachers of African-American children.* San Francisco: Jossey-Bass.

Ladson-Billings, G. (1994b). Who will teach our children: Preparing teachers to successfully teach African American students. In E. Hollins, J. King, & W. Hayman (Eds.), *Teaching diverse populations: Formulating a knowledge base* (pp. 129–142). Albany, NY: SUNY Press.

Ladson-Billings, G. (1995). Multicultural teacher education: Research, practice, and policy. In J. A. Banks & C.A.M. Banks (Eds.), *Handbook of research on multicultural education* (pp. 747–761). Old Tappan, NJ: Macmillan.

Ladson-Billings, G. (1999). Preparing teachers for diverse student populations: A critical race theory perspective. In A. Iran-Nejad & D. Pearson (Eds.), *Review of research in education* (Vol. 24, pp. 211–248). Washington, DC: American Educational Research Association.

Ladson-Billings, G. (2000). Fighting for our lives: Preparing teachers to teach African American students. *Journal of Teacher Education, 51*(3), 206–214.

Ladson-Billings, G. (2001). *Crossing over to Canaan: The journey of new teachers in diverse classrooms.* San Francisco: Jossey-Bass.

Laframboise, K., & Griffith, P. (1997). Using literature cases to examine diversity issues with preservice teachers. *Teaching and Teacher Education, 13*(4), 369–382.

Larke, P., Wiseman, D., & Bradley, C. (1990). The minority mentorship project: Changing attitudes of preservice teachers for diverse classrooms. *Action in Teacher Education, 12*(3), 5–11.

Lauer, P. (2001). *A secondary analysis of a review of teacher preparation research.* Denver: Education Commission of the States.

Lawrence, S. (1997). Beyond race awareness: White racial identity and multicultural teaching. *Journal of Teacher Education, 48*(2), 108–117.

Lesko, N., & Bloom, L.(1998). Close encounters: Truth, experience and interpretation in multicultural teacher education. *Journal of Curriculum Studies, 30*(4), 375–395.

Liston, D., & Zeichner, K. (1991). *Teacher education and the social conditions of schooling.* New York: Routledge.

Littleton, D. (1998). Preparing professionals as teachers for the urban classroom: A university/school collaborative model. *Action in Teacher Education, 19*(4), 149–158.

Love, F., & Greer, R. (1995). Recruiting minorities into teaching. *Contemporary Education, 67*(1), 30–32.

Lynch, J. (1986). *Multicultural education: Principles and practices.* New York: Routledge.

Lytle, S., & Cochran-Smith, M. (1992). Teacher research as a way of knowing. *Harvard Educational Review, 62*(4), 447–474.

Marshall, P. (1998). Toward developmental multicultural education: Case study of the issues exchange activity. *Journal of Teacher Education, 49*(1), 57–65.

Marxen, C., & Rudney, G. (1997). An urban field experience for rural preservice teachers. *Teacher Education Quarterly, 26,* 61–74.

McAllister, G., & Irvine, J. (2000). Cultural competency and multicultural teacher education. *Review of Educational Research, 70*(1), 3–24.

McCall, A. (1995a). Constructing conceptions of multicultural teaching: Preservice teachers' life experiences and teacher education. *Journal of Teacher Education, 46*(5), 340–350.

McCall, A. (1995b). We were cheated! Students' responses to a multicultural, social reconstructionist teacher education course. *Equity and Excellence in Education, 28*(1), 15–24.

McFalls, E., & Cobb-Roberts, D. (2001). Reducing resistance to diversity through cognitive dissonance instruction: Implications for teacher education. *Journal of Teacher Education, 52*(2), 164–172.

Meacham, S. (2000). Black self-love, language, and the teacher education dilemma: The cultural denial and cultural limbo of African American preservice teachers. *Urban Education, 34*(5), 571–596.

Melnick, S., & Zeichner, K. (1997). Enhancing the capacity of teacher education institutions to address diversity issues. In E. Hollins, J. King, & W. Hayman (Eds.), *Teaching diverse populations: Formulating a knowledge base* (pp. 23–39). Albany, NY: SUNY Press.

Melnick, S., & Zeichner, K. (1998). Teacher education's responsibility to address diversity issues: Enhancing institutional capacity. *Theory into Practice, 37*(2), 88–95.

Merryfield, M. (2000). Why aren't teachers being prepared to teach for diversity, equity and global interconnectedness? A study of lived experiences in the making of multicultural and global educators. *Teaching and Teacher Education, 16*(4), 429–443.

Montecinos, C. (1994). Teachers of color and multiculturalism. *Equity and Excellence in Education, 27*(3), 34–42.

Montecinos, C., & Rios, F. (1999). Assessing preservice teachers' zones of concern and comfort with multicultural education. *Teacher Education Quarterly, 26*(3), 7–24.

Morales, R. (2000). Effects of teacher preparation experiences and students' perceptions related to developmentally and culturally appropriate practices. *Action in Teacher Education, 22*(2), 67–75.

Murtadha-Watts, K. (1998). Teacher education in urban school-based multiagency collaboratives. *Urban Education, 32*(5), 616–631.

Narode, R., Rennie-Hill, L., & Peterson, K. (1994). Urban community study by preservice teachers. *Urban Education, 29*(1), 5–21.

National Center for Education Statistics. (1997). *Digest of educational statistics.* Washington, DC: U.S. Government Printing Office.

National Commission on Teaching and America's Future. (1997). *Doing what matters most: Investing in quality teaching.* New York: Author.

Neuharth-Pritchett, S., Reiff, J., & Pearson, C. (2001). Through the eyes of preservice teachers: Implications for the multicultural journey from teacher education. *Journal of Research in Childhood Education, 15*(2), 256–269.

Nieto, S. (2000). Placing equity front and center: Some thoughts on transforming teacher education for a new century. *Journal of Teacher Education, 51*(3), 180–187.

Nieto, S. (2001). What keeps teachers going? And other thoughts on the future of public education. *Equity and Excellence in Education, 34*(1), 6–15.

Nieto, S., & Rolen, C. (1997). Preparation and professional development of teachers: A perspective from two Latinos. In J. Irvine (Ed.), *Critical knowledge for diverse teachers and learners* (pp. 89–124). Washington, DC: American Association of Colleges for Teacher Education.

Oakes, J., Franke, M., Quartz, K., & Rogers, J. (2002). Research for high quality urban teaching: Defining it, developing it, assessing it. *Journal of Teacher Education, 53*(3), 228–234.

Obidah, J. (2000). Mediating boundaries of race, class, and professional authority as a critical multiculturalist. *Teachers College Record, 102*(5), 1035–1060.

Olmedo, I. (1997). Challenging old assumptions: Preparing teachers for inner schools. *Teaching and Teacher Education, 13,* 245–258.

O'Loughlin, M. (2001). Seven principles underlying socially just and ethnically inclusive teacher preparation. In S. King & L. Castenell (Eds.), *Racism and racial inequality: Implications for teacher education.* Washington, DC: American Association of Colleges for Teacher Education.

Paccione, A. (2000). Developing a commitment to multicultural education. *Teachers College Record, 102*(6), 980–1005.

Pailliotet, A. (1997). I'm really quiet: A case study of an Asian language minority preservice teacher's experience. *Teaching & Teacher Education, 13,* 675–690.

Pang, V., Anderson, M., & Martuza, V. (1997). Removing the mask of academic institutions collaborating in the struggle for equity. In E. Hollins, J. King, & W. Hayman (Eds.), *Teaching diverse populations: Formulating a knowledge base* (pp. 53–70). Albany, NY: SUNY Press.

Pang, V., & Sablan, V. (1998). Teacher efficacy. In M. Dilworth (Ed.), *Being responsive to cultural differences* (pp. 39–58). Thousand Oaks, CA: Corwin Press.

Parker, L., & Hood, S. (1995). Minority students vs. minority faculty and administrators in teacher education: Perspectives on the clash of cultures. *Urban Review, 27*(2), 159–174.

Pattnaik, J. (1997). Cultural stereotypes and preservice education: moving beyond our biases. *Equity and Excellence in Education, 30*(3), 40–50.

Patton, M., Silva, C., & Myers, S. (1999). Teachers and family literacy: Bridging theory to practice. *Journal of Teacher Education, 50*(2), 140–146.

Peterson, K., Cross, L., Johnson, E. & Howell, G. (2000). Diversity education for preservice teachers: Strategies and attitude outcomes. *Action in Teacher Education, 22*(2), 33–38.

Pleasants, H., Johnson, C., & Trent, S. (1998). Reflecting, reconceptualizing, and revising: The evolution of a portfolio assignment in a multicultural teacher education course. *Remedial and Special Education, 19*(1), 46–58.

Pohan, C. (1996). Preservice teachers' beliefs about diversity: Uncovering factors leading to multicultural responsiveness. *Equity and Excellence in Education, 29*(3), 62–69.

Potthoff, D., Dinsmore, J., & Stirtz, G. (2000). Preparing for democracy and diversity: The impact of a community-based field experience on preservice teachers' knowledge, skills, and attitudes. *Action in Teacher Education, 22*(1), 79–92.

Powell, R. (1997). Then the beauty emerges: A longitudinal case study of culturally relevant teaching. *Teaching and Teacher Education, 13,* 467–484.

Price, J., & Valli, L. (1998). Institutional support for diversity in preservice teacher education. *Theory into Practice, 27*(2), 114–120.

Pritchy-Smith, G. (1998). *Common sense about uncommon knowledge: The knowledge bases for diversity.* Washington, DC: American Association of Colleges for Teacher Education.

Raymond, M., Fletcher, S., & Luque, J. (2001). *Teach for America: An evaluation of teacher differences and student outcomes in Houston, Texas.* Washington, DC: Thomas B. Fordham Foundation.

Reed, D. (1993). Multicultural education for preservice students. *Action in Teacher Education, 15*(3), 27–34.

Riley, R. (1998). Our teachers should be excellent, and they should look like America. *Education and Urban Society, 31*(1), 18–29.

Rios, F., & Montecinos, C. (1999). Advocating social justice and cultural affirmation. *Equity and Excellence in Education, 32*(3), 66–76.

Roberts, S., Jensen, S., & Hadjiyianni, E. (1997). Using literature study groups in teacher education courses: Learning through diversity. *Journal of Adolescent and Adult Literacy, 41*(2), 124–133.

Rodriguez, Y., & Sjostrom, B. (1995). Culturally responsive teacher preparation evident in classroom approaches to cultural diversity: A novice and an experienced teacher. *Journal of Teacher Education, 46,* 304–311.

Ross, D., & Smith, W. (1992). Understanding preservice teachers' perspectives on diversity. *Journal of Teacher Education, 43*(2), 94–103.

Ross, D., & Yeager, E. (1999). What does democracy mean to prospective elementary teachers? *Journal of Teacher Education, 50*(4), 255–266.

Rudney, G., Marxen, C., & Risku, M. (1999). Preservice teachers' growth in multicultural understanding: Assessing the assessment. *Action in Teacher Education, 20*(1), 32–46.

Scott, R. (1995). Helping teacher education students develop positive attitudes toward ethnic minorities. *Equity and Excellence in Education, 28*(2), 69–73.

Sernak, K., & Wolfe, C. (1998). Creating multicultural understanding and community in preservice education classes via email. *Journal of Technology and Teacher Education, 6*(4), 303–329.

Shade, B., Boe, B., Garner, O., & New, C. (1998). The road to certification: A different way. *Teaching and Change, 5*(3–4), 261–275.

Shavelson, R., & Towne, L. (Eds.). (2002). *Scientific research in education.* Washington, DC: National Academy Press.

Shulman, L. (1986). Paradigms and research programs in the study of teaching: A contemporary perspective. In M. C. Wittrock (Ed.), *Handbook of research on teaching.* New York: Macmillan.

Shulman, L. (2002). Truth *and* consequences: Inquiry and policy in research on teacher education. *Journal of Teacher Education, 53*(3), 248–253.

Shultz, E., Neyhart, K., & Reck, U. (1996a). Swimming against the tide: A study of prospective teachers' attitudes regarding cultural diversity and urban teaching. *Western Journal of Black Studies, 20*(1), 1–7.

Shultz, E., Neyhart, K., & Reck, U. (1996b). Uphill all the way: An investigation of attitudinal predispositions of preservice teachers toward diversity in urban classrooms. *Teacher Educator, 32,* 22–36.

Shumann, A. (1992). Learning to teach Hispanic students. In M. Dilworth (Ed.), *Diversity in teacher education* (pp. 112–133). San Francisco: Jossey-Bass.

Sianjina, R., Cage, B., & Allen, V. (1996). African-Americans' participation in teacher education programs. *Educational Forum, 61,* 30–33.

Sleeter, C. (1995a). An analysis of the critiques of multicultural education. In J. Banks & C.A.M. Banks (Eds.), *Handbook of research on multicultural education* (pp. 81–96). Old Tappan, NJ: Macmillan.

Sleeter, C. (1995b). White preservice students and multicultural education coursework. In J. Larkin & C. Sleeter (Eds.) *Developing multicultural teacher education curricula.* (pp. 17–29). Albany, NY: SUNY Press.

Sleeter, C. (1996a). *Multicultural education as social activism.* Albany, NY: SUNY Press.

Sleeter, C. (1996b). Multicultural education, social positionality, and whiteness. In C. Sleeter (Ed.), *Multicultural education as social activism* (pp. 133–153). Albany, NY: SUNY Press.

Sleeter, C. (1996c). Reflections on my use of multicultural and critical pedagogy when students are White. In C. Sleeter (Ed.), *Multicultural education as social activism* (pp. 117–134). Albany, NY: SUNY Press.

Sleeter, C. (1996d). Resisting racial awareness: How teachers understand the social order from their social locations. In C. Sleeter (Ed.), *Multicultural education as social activism* (pp. 65–89). Albany, NY: SUNY Press.

Sleeter, C. (2001a). Epistemological diversity in research on preservice teacher preparation for historically underserved children. In W. Secada (Ed.), *Review of research in education* (Vol. 25, pp. 209–250). Washington, DC: American Educational Research Association.

Sleeter, C. (2001b). Preparing teachers for culturally diverse schools: Research and the overwhelming presence of Whiteness. *Journal of Teacher Education, 52*(2), 94–106.

Sleeter, C., & Grant, C. (1987). An analysis of multicultural education in the United States. *Harvard Educational Review, 57*(4), 421–444.

Smith, R. (2000). The influence of teacher background on the inclusion of multicultural education: A case study of two contrasts. *Urban Review, 32*(2), 155–176.

Smith, R., Moallem, M., & Sherrill, D. (1997). How preservice teachers think about cultural diversity. *Educational Foundations, 11*(2), 41–62.

Smylie, M., Bay, M., & Tozer, S. (1999). Preparing teachers as agents of change. In G. Griffin (Ed.), *The education of teachers: Ninety-eighth yearbook of the National Society for the Study of Education* (pp. 18–62). Chicago: University of Chicago Press.

Solomon, R. (2000). Exploring cross-race dyad partnerships in learning to teach. *Teachers College Record, 102*(6), 953–979.

Solorzano, D. (1997). Images and words that wound: Critical race theory, racial stereotyping, and teacher education. *Teacher Education Quarterly, 24,* 5–19.

Solorzano, D., & Yosso, T. (2001). From racial stereotyping and deficit discourse toward a critical race theory in teacher education. *Multicultural Education, 9*(1), 2–8.

Stotsky, S. (1999). *Losing our language: How multicultural classroom instruction has undermined our children's ability to read, write, and reason.* New York: Free Press.

Su, Z. (1996). Why teach: Profiles and entry perspectives of minority students as becoming teachers. *Journal of Research and Development in Education, 29*(3), 117–133.

Su, Z., Goldstein, S., & Suzuki, G. (1997). Socialization of Asian Americans in human service professional schools: A comparative study. *Urban Education, 32*(2), 279–303.

Talbert-Johnson, C., & Tillman, B. (1999). Perspectives on color in teacher education programs: Prominent issues. *Journal of Teacher Education, 50*(3), 200–208.

Tatto, M. (1996). Examining values and beliefs about teaching diverse students: Understanding the challenges for teacher education. *Educational Evaluation and Policy Analysis, 18*(2), 155–180.

Tatum, B. (2001). Professional development: An important partner in antiracist teacher education. In S. King & L. Castenell (Eds.), *Racism and racial inequality: Implications for teacher education.* Washington, DC: American Association of Colleges for Teacher Education.

Taylor, S., & Sobel, D. (2001). Addressing the discontinuity of students' and teachers' diversity: A preliminary study of preservice teachers' beliefs and perceived skills. *Teaching and Teacher Education, 17*(4), 487–503.

Tellez, K. (1999). Mexican-American preservice teachers and the intransigency of the elementary school curriculum. *Teaching and Teacher Education, 15,* 555–570.

Tettegah, S. (1996). The racial consciousness attitudes of white prospective teachers and their perceptions of the teachability of students from a different racial/ethnic background: Findings from a California study. *Journal of Negro Education, 65*(2), 151–163.

Toppo, G. (2002, Jan. 7). Bush to sign education bill, but the debate over required testing goes on. *Washington Post.*

Torok, C., & Aguilar, T. (2000). Changes in preservice teachers' knowledge and beliefs about language issues. *Equity and Excellence in Education, 33*(2), 24–31.

Torres-Karna, H., & Krustchinsky, R. (1998). The early entry program. An innovative program for recruiting and training new bilingual teachers. *Teacher Education and Practice, 14*(1), 10–19.

Tran, M., Young, R., & DiLella. (1994). Multicultural education courses and the student teacher: Eliminating stereotypical attitudes in our ethnically diverse classroom. *Journal of Teacher Education, 45*(3), 183–189.

Vadeboncoeur, J., Rahm, J., Aguilera, D., & LeCompte, M. (1996). Building democratic character through community experiences in teacher education. *Education and Urban Society, 28*(2), 189–207.

Valenzuela, A. (2002). Reflections on the subtractive underpinnings of education research and policy. *Journal of Teacher Education, 53*(3), 235–241.

Valli, L. (1995). The dilemma of race: Learning to be color blind and color conscious. *Journal of Teacher Education, 46*(2), 120–129.

Vavrus, M. (1994). A critical analysis of multicultural education infusion during student teaching. *Action in Teacher Education, 16*(3), 45–57.

Villegas, A. (1991). *Culturally responsive pedagogy for the 1990s and beyond.* Princeton, NJ: Educational Testing Service.

Villegas, A., & Clewell, B. (1998). Increasing teacher diversity by tapping the paraprofessional pool. *Theory into Practice, 37*(2), 121–130.

Villegas, A., Clewell, B., Anderson, M., Goertz, M., Joy, F., Bruschi, B., & Irvine, J. (1995). *Teaching for diversity: Models for expanding the supply of minority teachers.* Princeton, NJ: Educational Testing Service.

Villegas, A., & Lucas, T. (2002a). *Educating culturally responsive teachers: A coherent approach.* Albany, NY: SUNY Press.

Villegas, A., & Lucas, T. (2002b). Preparing culturally responsive teachers: Rethinking the curriculum. *Journal of Teacher Education, 53*(1), 20–32.

Wallace, B. (2000). A call for change in multicultural training at graduate schools of education: Education to end oppression and for social justice. *Teachers College Record, 102*(6), 1086–1111.

Warring, D., Keim, J., & Rau, R. (1998). Multicultural training for students and its impact. *Action in Teacher Education, 20*(2), 56–83.

Weiner, L. (1990). Preparing the brightest for urban schools. *Urban Education, 25*(3), 258–273.

Weiner, L. (1993). *Preparing teachers for urban schools: Lessons from 30 years of school reform.* New York: Teachers College Press.

Weiner, L. (2000). Research in the 90s: Implications for urban teacher preparation. *Review of Educational Research, 70*(3), 369–406.

Wenzlaff, T., & Thrond, M. (1995). The role of teachers in a cross-cultural drama. *Journal of Teacher Education, 46*(5), 334–339.

Whitty, G., Power, S., & Halpin, D. (1998). *Devolution and choice in education: The school, the state, and the market.* Melbourne, Australia: Australian Council for Educational Research.

Wilson, S., Floden, R., & Ferrini-Mundy, J. (2001). *Teacher preparation research: Current knowledge, gaps, and recommendations.* Washington, DC: Center for the Study of Teaching and Policy.

Wise, A. (1999). *Standards or no standards? Teacher quality in the 21st century.* [On-line]. Available: http://www.ncate.org. Retrieved Oct. 1999.

Yeo, F. (1997). Teacher preparation and inner-city schools: Sustaining educational failure. *Urban Review, 29,* 127–143.

Yopp, R., Yopp, H., & Taylor, H. (1992). Profiles and viewpoints of minority candidates in a teacher diversity project. *Teacher Education Quarterly, 19*(3), 29–48.

Zeichner, K. (1993a). *Educating teachers for cultural diversity.* East Lansing, MI: Michigan State University. (ERIC Document Reproduction Service No. ED 359 167)

Zeichner, K. (1993b). Traditions of practice in U.S. preservice teacher education programs. *Teaching and Teacher Education, 9,* 1–13.

Zeichner, K. (1999). The new scholarship of teacher education. *Educational Researcher, 28*(9), 4–15.

Zeichner, K., & Hoeft, K. (1996). Teacher socialization for cultural diversity. In J. Sikula & T. Buttery & E. Guyton (Eds.), *Handbook of research on teacher education* (2nd ed., pp. 525–547). Old Tappan, NJ: Macmillan.

Zeichner, K., & Melnick, S. (1996). The role of community field experiences in preparing teachers for cultural diversity. In K. Zeichner & S. Melnick & M. Gomez (Eds.), *Currents of reform in preservice teacher education* (pp. 176–198). New York: Teachers College Press.

Zeichner, K., & Schulte, A. (2001). What we know and don't know from peer-reviewed research about alternative teacher certification programs. *Journal of Teacher Education, 52*(4), 266–282.

Zollers, N., Albert, L., & Cochran-Smith, M. (2000). In pursuit of social justice: Collaborative research and practice in teacher education. *Action in Teacher Education, 29*(1), 1–12.

Zulich, J., Bean, T., & Herrick, J. (1991). Charting stages of preservice teacher development and reflection in a multicultural community through dialogue journal analysis. *Teaching and Teacher Education, 8*(4), 345–360.

INTERNATIONAL PERSPECTIVES ON MULTICULTURAL EDUCATION

47

MULTICULTURAL EDUCATION IN AUSTRALIA

Historical Development and Current Status

Bob Hill

Charles Sturt University, Bathurst

Rod Allan

Charles Sturt University, Bathurst

Australia's first inhabitants were the Aborigines, hunters and gatherers who occupied the continent, according to non-Aboriginal archeologists (Fullagar, Price & Head, 2001), over 100,000 years ago. They were attracted to the fertile and well-watered country of the coastal fringe, especially in the south and east of the continent. At the time of the British invasion that began in the 1830s, the Aboriginal population is estimated to have been between 300,000 (Reynolds, 1982) and 750,000 (Butlin, 1983), and by this stage they had developed distinctive cultures that were finely tuned to the environment.

During the 17th century, a number of European explorers, principally Portuguese and Dutch, journeyed to the northwestern and southern sections of the continent. It was not until 1770 that a British navigator, Captain James Cook, sighted the east coast of Australia. Although his account of the voyage aroused considerable interest in Britain, no attempt was made to colonize the land until the American colonies were lost in the Revolutionary War. One hundred and sixty-seven years after the Pilgrims arrived in America, a fleet of 11 ships under the command of Captain Arthur Phillip sailed from Britain on May 13, 1787, with 1,030 people on board, 736 of them convicts (Ward, 1976). The initial settlement of Botany Bay was abandoned after one week, and on January 26, 1788, the fleet sailed into Port Jackson, the site today of the country's largest city, Sydney.

Historically, the colonization of Australia has been downplayed by non-Aboriginal historians who have preferred the term *settlement* to *invasion*, despite the dramatic impact the arrival had through war and disease on the indigenous inhabitants. While the dominant ethos of White Australia at the opening of the postwar immigration boom was one of assimilation, the ancestors of contemporary Anglo Australians were too ethnocentric to have ever considered assimilating into Aboriginal culture. Few Whites bothered to learn local languages and then usually only with the motivation of converting the indigenous population.

By the end of the 19th century, the Aborigines, like many indigenous peoples in the Americas, had been all but decimated. The prevailing policy of "soothe the dying pillow" was designed to make their demise comparatively humane. However, the Aboriginal people declined to fulfill the objectives of this policy, and, partly as a result of legal attempts to end the genocide and partly as a result of their development of resistance to European diseases, the Aboriginal population increased from about 70,000 in the early 1930s to around 160,000 in 1981, 1% of the population. Their current demographic profile inclines toward youth, and Aborigines now constitute 3.2% of the school population, though their numbers are unevenly distributed throughout the country's schools (McRae et al. 2000).

While recent policies of education authorities share a number of similarities in their attitudes toward Aboriginal education and multicultural education, and a common interest in antiracism, cultural studies, and strategies

We express our appreciation for the constructive criticisms provided by Brian Bullivant, Michael Garbutcheon Singh, and Anthony Welch on various drafts of this chapter. We also acknowledge the assistance of the New South Wales Department of Education and Training.

designed to create greater equality of educational opportunity, most Aboriginal educators are adamant about distinguishing Aboriginal education from multicultural education. They argue that to conceptually incorporate indigenous Australians with immigrant Australians and their descendants is to deny Aboriginal people their unique identity and unique claim to a place in Australian education. Partly as a result of this preference, the term *multicultural education* in Australia is normally understood to exclude Aborigines. Government departments and institutions responsible for multiculturalism have rarely solicited Aboriginal participation. Institutions responsible for Aboriginal education, now increasingly Aboriginal controlled, have pursued a different, although often parallel, agenda (National Aboriginal Education Committee [NAEC], 1982). This chapter continues that tradition and, in deferring to the arguments of Aboriginal educators such as Miller (1985), will not incorporate a discussion of Aboriginal education or Aboriginal studies.

Although this chapter will concentrate on the educational response to the massive post–World War II immigration program, a wide range of ethnic groups contributed to Australian demographics and culture throughout the 19th and early 20th centuries. While the earliest immigrants to Australia in the first 40 years of British settlement were convicts and Irish political dissidents, the availability of land led to an influx of "free" settlers, not all of them British. German Lutherans, victims of political persecution in their homeland, came to South Australia under a privately financed scheme as refugees. A small number of Indians, Chinese, and Malays were imported by some pastoralists in New South Wales as "coolie" workers. In 1851, gold was discovered in New South Wales and Victoria, and before long, the goldfields had a multinational flavor. Gold seekers came in numbers from southern China, provoking much resentment, which was to have a considerable and long-term impact on the attitudes of Australians. Some 20 years after the gold rush, sugar growers in northern Queensland began conscripting labor to their fledgling industry with the often forcible recruitment of people from the Pacific Islands. As pressure against this practice increased, Italians came as a new source of labor, thus beginning a process of chain migration. This process also brought Greek and Spanish immigrants. By the turn of the 20th century, there was a range of ethnic groups in Australia, but the overwhelming majority were of British origin. This is not to imply that the British were ethnically homogeneous. As Sherington (1991) points out, Britons identified themselves as Irish, Scots, English, Welsh, and Cornish; maintained their religious differences; and entrenched them in the nascent school system.

For the first half of the 20th century, immigrants, albeit in small numbers, continued to arrive, mainly from Britain. Partly because of two world wars, there developed a more distinctive Australian identity, although one that was embedded in British institutions and social mores to the extent that cultural differences, particularly languages, were regarded as "un-Australian."

POSTWAR MIGRATION

Despite the image of a homogeneous country and its people, an image often promoted by the Australian mass media, Australia is one of the most ethnically diverse nations in the world, with a higher proportion of its population born overseas than any other country except Israel (Kalantzis, Cope, Noble, & Poynting, 1990). Australia's population is 19 million (Department of Immigration and Multicultural Affairs [DIMA], 2002), more than double the number at the end of World War II. This increase reflects the influx of new settlers from an extensive immigration program. Twenty-three percent of the population has been born overseas and a further one in five has at least one parent born overseas (DIMA, 2002). Almost 6 million migrants from over 100 countries have settled in Australia since 1945. Over 25% of Australia's population is of non–English-speaking background. In both absolute terms and in relation to population, Australia is one of the leading resettlement countries for refugees. Since World War II, over 590,000 people have arrived as displaced persons or refugees under Australia's humanitarian program. They include 170,000 from Europe as a result of World War II and its aftermath; 14,000 Hungarians who fled during the uprising of 1956; 5,700 Czechoslovakians after Dubcek's removal in 1968; 70,000 Indochinese since the end of the Vietnam War in 1975; and 13,000 Eastern European political dissidents who have sought asylum (DIMA, 2002).

In 1945, Australia's population was 7 million, 97% of whom had ancestors from the British Isles. Australia had been through the traumatic experience of having, for the first and so far only time of British settlement, its shores attacked by hostile forces: the Japanese bombed Darwin, and their midget submarines sank a ferry in Sydney harbor. The nation's psyche was shattered: Australians were made suddenly aware that the protective umbrella of Britain no longer extended to the Pacific. The capitulation of Singapore destroyed the cherished belief that membership in the British Empire was sufficient to ensure security from external menace. The prime minister, J. B. Chifley, articulated a widely held belief that the most effective means of survival was to increase the nation's population, for otherwise "we will not be able to justify before the world our retention of such a great country" (Crisp, 1961, p. 319). However, such a natural increase was unlikely, given the limitations of population size despite the enticing cry of Australia's first minister for immigration, Arthur Calwell, who decreed that Australia must "ennoble motherhood" for we must either "populate the country or sooner or later be overrun by Asiatic peoples" (Wilton & Bosworth, 1984, p. 7). Realistic assessments showed that the need for an immigration policy based on pragmatism and humanitarianism was long overdue. Not that in developing such a policy was a multicultural nation ever envisaged. The cornerstone was to be the immigrant from Britain: "It is my hope that for every foreign migrant there will be ten from the United Kingdom," proclaimed Calwell (Wilton & Bosworth, 1984, p. 11). Seven years later, his successor to the portfolio of immigration, Harold Holt, saw no reason to disagree: "Australia, in accepting a balanced intake of other British people, can still build a truly British nation on this side of the world" (Wilton & Bosworth, 1984, p. 17).

Although there was strong community support for such principles, the reality was that Australia's immigration policies proved to be far more flexible than envisaged, as evidenced by the ethnic pluralism of today. However, community opinion about desirable sources of immigration has consistently lagged behind government policy. The United Kingdom and Ireland traditionally have been the largest source, but the number of immigrants from other countries has fluctuated over time. From the mid-1950s and 1960s, southern European were predominant, particularly those from Italy and Greece, followed soon after by Lebanese and Turkish immigrants. From the mid-1970s, refugees and migrants have come from Southeast Asia and other Asian countries, and more recently from South America and the Pacific rim. In 1998–1999, the major sources were New Zealand, the

United Kingdom, and China. These trends are illustrated in Table 47.1.

Foster (1988) notes that Australian immigration was characterized by the offering of inducements to preferred immigrants. However, the definition of "preferred" widened from British to northern European, then to southern European as economic conditions in those source countries altered. The Australian economy also dictated the flow of immigration, with additional quotas in good economic years and substantial reductions in times of increased unemployment. Similar economic push-pull factors operated in Western Europe during the same period. The critical difference, however, was that in Western Europe, immigrants generally arrived as guest workers to fulfill labor contracts with a view to returning to their country of origin. In Australia, however, it had always been accepted that arrivals came not as guest workers but as permanent settlers, that is, as "New Australians." By the 1990s, however, the number of people coming on short-term business and student visas had become significant (DIMA, 2002).

RESPONSES TO IMMIGRATION

Popular Reaction to Postwar Immigration, 1945–1972

The reaction of Australians to this change in demographic patterns has been complex. Many historians and social commentators assert that Australia suffers an identity crisis. Its traditional roots are British, its modern popular cultural orientation is toward the United States, and its major export market is Japan. The country is a geographic

TABLE 47.1. Top 10 Countries of Birth for Australian Immigrants.

1976–1977			1991–1992			2001–2002		
Country of Birth	*No.*	*%*	*Country of Birth*	*No.*	*%*	*Country of Birth*	*No.*	*%*
UK and Ireland	19,220	27.1	UK	14,465	13.5	New Zealand	15,663	17.6
Lebanon	12,190	17.2	Hong Kong	12,913	12.0	UK	8,749	9.8
New Zealand	4,840	6.8	Vietnam	9,952	8.9	China	6,708	7.5
Cyprus	2,770	3.9	New Zealand	7,242	6.7	South Africa	5,714	6.4
Malaysia	1,770	2.5	Philippines	5,917	5.5	India	5,091	5.7
Philippines	1,680	2.4	India	5,608	5.2	Indonesia	4,221	4.7
Yugoslavia	1,650	2.3	China	3,388	3.2	Philippines	2,837	3.2
Greece	1,530	2.2	Taiwan	3,172	3.0	Yugoslavia	2,082	2.3
Italy	1,320	1.9	Malaysia	3,123	2.9	Sri Lanka	2,011	2.3
USA	1,220	1.7	Sri Lanka	2,777	2.6	Malaysia	<u>1,939</u>	<u>2.2</u>
Subtotal	48,190	67.9	Subtotal	68,197	63.5			
Other	<u>22,730</u>	<u>32.1</u>	Other	<u>39,194</u>	<u>36.5</u>			
Total	70,920	100.0	Total	107,391	100.0	Total	88,900	100.0

Source: Bureau of Immigration Research (1992); DIMA (2002).

extension of Southeast Asia, and that is where its probable economic future lies.

Russel Ward (1958) argued that the beliefs held by the dominant force in 19th-century Australia, the White Anglo Saxon male, still permeated society at the time when the country was accepting a large proportion of new settlers. Ward identified twin ideals of "mateship" and "egalitarianism" as unifying and pervasive factors. These ideals had been challenged during the gold rush era of the 19th century by the arrival of Chinese indentured labor. The Chinese people were regarded as an affront: they worked for a pittance, "invaded" claims after White diggers had vacated them, spoke a different language, and, importantly, were of a different color. Violence does not figure prominently in Australian history, except in the treatment of Aborigines, yet the goldfields were witness to scenes of vicious racial clashes. One result of the gold rush era was that various state legislatures passed restrictive laws aimed at curtailing immigration of Asian labor. The Immigration Restriction Act, passed after the federation of Australian states came into being in 1901, soon became known as the "White Australia policy." Based substantially on the U.S. Chinese Exclusion Act (1884), it prohibited the immigration of colored peoples and institutionalized the nation's xenophobia (Ward, 1958).

If we are to accept Ward's (1958) proposition, then it is reasonable to suggest that the logical outcome of institutionalized resentment to colored immigration would be extended to other immigration as well. Elements of egalitarianism and xenophobia have persisted in the reactions of Australians to the substantial immigration of the 1950s and 1960s. Such attitudes were perceptively analyzed by Jean Martin (1972), who identified a fundamental set of beliefs held by Anglo-Australians about the ways in which immigrants could and should be incorporated into Australian society. She termed these beliefs the "ideology of settlement." It is an assimilationist ideology underpinned by elements that are not exclusive to Australia. It depicts Australia as a peculiarly egalitarian society, a "lucky country" whose immigrants should be grateful for the opportunity to live there. It is a society that can cope with immigration without necessitating radical structural change, and certainly without any special privileges being extended to the newly arrived. The success of this assimilation process depends fundamentally on the goodwill of individual immigrants and individual Australians.

Throughout the 1960s, these attitudes were mirrored in government policy, which was one of assimilation and attendant ethnocentrism. Immigrants were expected to submit to a dominant culture and in so doing divest themselves of their cultural distinctiveness and, in particular, their languages. This policy had public and political support, but in practice it simply did not work.

The Advent of Multiculturalism, 1972–1986

By the end of the 1960s, the non–English-speaking ethnic communities had become more vocal and better organized to challenge the dominant paradigm of assimilation. A groundswell of opinion in the broader community was reacting against the policies developed during two decades of conservative rule.

The election of the reformist Whitlam Labor government in 1972 hastened the demise of assimilation and introduced the nation to a decade of sweeping multicultural initiatives. The catalyst for change was the minister for immigration, Al Grassby (1979), a flamboyant and publicity-conscious personality, whose view was that the cultural resources of immigrants should be seen as an integral part of Australian society. Grassby constantly spoke about "the family of the nation" and in so doing placed immigration firmly in the public arena. Labor's focus was welfare oriented, and immigrants were acknowledged as suffering both socioeconomic disadvantage and discrimination. The dismantling of the Department of Immigration and the siting of its functions within the Departments of Labor, Social Security, and Education was indicative of this approach (Kalantzis et al., 1990). During his brief tenure of 18 months, Grassby began oversight of the transition to multiculturalism. Labor effectively dismantled the White Australia policy by removing race as an explicit criterion for immigration selection, thus emulating the Canadian initiative of a decade earlier (Samuda, 1986). A commitment to refugee settlement was maintained as well.

The Labor government was short-lived. Whitlam's successor, the leader of a conservative coalition, Malcolm Fraser, was confronted with a crisis. A dramatic change in the ethnic composition of the immigrant intake sat uneasily with the residual cultural racism that had underpinned the White Australia Policy (M. Garbutcheon Singh, personal communication, 2002). Fraser commissioned the Galbally report, *Report of the Review of Post-Arrival Programs and Services for Migrants* (Galbally, 1978). Galbally identified the basic principles to be applied in the selection of immigrants and in program development and services for them. They were equality of opportunity, cultural maintenance with integration, transitional positive discrimination, and programs designed and operated in full consultation with the clients intended.

The acceptance of these principles by Fraser and subsequent governments led to the establishment of adult and child migrant education programs, interpreter services within government departments and statutory authorities, Disadvantaged Schools Programs (DSP), the development of the Special Broadcasting Service (SBS) with its multilingual media outlets, the Multicultural Education Program (MEP), and the Australian Institute of Multicultural Affairs (AIMA).

The Galbally principles were also embodied in two other influential reports, the Australian Ethnic Affairs Council's (AEAC) *Australia as a Multicultural Society* (Australian Ethnic Affairs Council, 1977) and the Schools Commission Committee on Multicultural Education's *Education for a Multicultural Society* (1979).

The Economic Imperative, 1986 to the Present

The return to power of the Australian Labor Party in 1983 under Bob Hawke saw support for these initiatives maintained until an economic downturn three years later necessitated severe budget cuts. AIMA was closed, although it was later replaced by the Office of Multicultural Affairs within the Department of the Prime Minister. Funds were withdrawn from MEP, and English as a Second Language (ESL) teaching programs suffered substantial decreases in funding. Coinciding with these fiscal measures was the release of a national inquiry, *The Review of Migrant and Multicultural Programs and Services: Don't Settle for Less* (Jupp, 1986). This report enunciated basic rights of equity and access in the economic, social, cultural, and political life of the nation and advocated the inalienable right for all to enjoy their own culture, practice their own religion, and use their own language.

These themes were taken up by the Office of Multicultural Affairs when in 1989 it launched the *National Agenda for a Multicultural Australia* (Office of Multicultural Affairs, 1989). The agenda had three dimensions: cultural rights, social justice, and economic efficiency. The last of these acknowledged that immigration policies must address economic issues; otherwise, there would be the potential for social division and perhaps conflict.

In political terms, the most interesting aspect about the immigration program has been the bipartisanship it has attracted from the major political parties. Even during the Blainey debate in 1984, when the eminent historian Geoffrey Blainey warned of the "Asianization" of Australia, little political capital was made by the opposition. During the 1987 federal election campaign, the opposition leader, John Howard, sought to exploit immigration as an issue, although he did not pursue it for long. The issue, however, was rekindled with the release of the Fitzgerald report, *Immigration: A Commitment to Australia* (Fitzgerald, 1988). The report, although supporting an increased immigrant intake, was critical of the current immigration program, claiming that there was a decline of community confidence in immigration because the program was perceived to be no longer in the public interest. Fitzgerald argued for a sharper economic focus in selection and

stressed that immigration must serve national economic needs with greater emphasis on skills, English-language proficiency, and youth and less on family reunion. The report was particularly critical of multiculturalism, which was seen as divisive and threatening; what the community required was a strong sense of Australian identity.

In the last decade of the 20th century, the consensus on immigration was challenged. An economic downturn led to increased unemployment and the inevitable cries for reduced immigration to shore up domestic job opportunities. Many Australians were alienated as a result of economic and cultural changes brought about by globalization. Those who had not benefited from the changing conditions were ripe for exploitation by those who blamed levels and sources of immigration as the primary cause of alienation. A new political entity, the One Nation party, and its leader, Pauline Hanson, exploited this discontent. As a newly elected member of federal parliament, Hanson used her maiden speech to attack political correctness and the politically bipartisan consensus on Aboriginal affairs and multiculturalism. In particular, she reserved her venom for targeted financial assistance aimed at overcoming Aboriginal and immigrant disadvantage (Hanson, 1996). Her speech was followed by saturation coverage in the media. She served as a lightning rod for those groups most disaffected by the changes that accompanied globalization and economic rationalism. As levels of unemployment stayed high, Aborigines and Asian immigrants in particular served as useful scapegoats.

Despite One Nation's erratic performance, it would be imprudent to ignore the deep and underlying emotions that Hanson touched in the Australian community and the effect that she had on policy decisions. A telling example of this has been the government's overreaction to the recent arrival of asylum seekers, whom they refer to as "illegal immigrants." Since the end of the Vietnam War, a fluctuating number of people have arrived independently in Australia seeking asylum, but the numbers have been relatively small by international standards. Yet recently, the government's zero tolerance response to these "illegals" arriving from the Middle East via Southeast Asia has generated wide media coverage (Hill & Allan, 2001). In the lead-up to the 2001 federal election, the conservative government exploited two events. The *MV Tampa*, a Norwegian container ship, rescued a sinking boatload of predominantly Afghani and Iraqi asylum seekers off the northwestern Australian coast. The government refused permission for these people to set foot on Australian soil. In a hastily devised operation, now called the Pacific Solution, these people were transferred to neighboring countries pending assessment of their refugee status. One month later, a stricken vessel carrying more asylum seekers was intercepted by an Australian naval vessel. The government issued press releases claiming that children were thrown overboard and cynically exploited this by demonizing these people as being unfit to be considered for Australian citizenship. A Senate Select Committee into the affair conducted after the elections revealed that no children had been thrown overboard. The government's reelection indicated that there was strong community support for its antirefugee stance, which complemented the rhetoric of One Nation (Skehan & Clennell, 2002).

In summary, this period was characterized by economic rationalism, which affected multicultural initiatives. For example, there was a marked change from cultural to economic justification for multiculturalism, as evidenced in the shift of emphasis from community languages to Asian ones, which was justified by the potential expansion of trade and tourism. Early in the 21st century, like most of the rest of the industrial world, Australia faces difficult economic conditions. With high levels of unemployment (7% in 2001), underemployment, and an increase in the proportion of the workforce employed on casual rather than full-time, tenured conditions, there is strong public and political support for reduced immigration and a resentment of government resources being channeled to special interest groups. In a climate of fiscal restraint, multicultural programs are likely to be funded only if universal economic benefits can be demonstrated. The *National Agenda,* with its assumption that multiculturalism is a means of maintaining cultural and economic stability, will be tested.

THE EDUCATIONAL RESPONSE

This section, which focuses largely on primary (elementary) and secondary school education, identifies three discernible periods relating to multicultural education in Australia. The first canvasses the postwar years through to the end of a 23-year period of conservative government in 1972. It was during this time that Australia received its greatest number of immigrants, and the educational response was clearly an assimilationist one. The years from 1972 to 1986 saw successive governments of different political persuasion involved in the transition from "migrant education" to an era of multiculturalism in which the ethnic diversity of the nation was celebrated. This was an interventionist time when the federal government encouraged and financed educational initiatives by way of grants to states for specified purposes. The period since 1986 has been characterized by fiscal restraint as Australia struggles to combat the harsh economic conditions that have beset much of the industrialized world.

From Passive to Active Assimilation, 1945–1972

The initial postwar period was characterized by passive assimilation in education. Policies consistent with Martin's ideology of settlement were implemented. These policies required immigrant children to adapt to existing school and curriculum organization. There was a minimum of structural change in the bureaucracy and schools. A statement by a school principal in 1951 typified official thinking. He described his staff as "teachers who have no special training for this work, nor do they use any foreign language, but they have met their peculiar problems with commendable initiative, patience and skill" (Martin, 1978, p. 85). Immigrant children were defined as "problems" that would be solved over time with goodwill rather than by special programs. The little educational research conducted in this early period focused on immigrant children's deficits (Roper, 1971).

The late 1960s saw a change in perspective driven by the concerns of teachers who were having difficulty in coping with non–English-speaking background (NESB) children at a time when student numbers were growing beyond the capacity of staffing and building programs. While the implicit objective of educational commitment remained assimilation, programs were introduced to pursue that aim more actively. To comprehend the dynamic behind this change to active assimilation, it is important to understand the nature of Australian federalism. Like the United States and Canada, Australia has a federal constitution. While the national government controls immigration, the states (provinces) have responsibility for education. From the early 1970s, the federal government's advantaged fiscal base enabled it increasingly to set the educational agenda by allocating grants to the states for specified programs. A crucial example of this was the Child Migrant Education Program (CMEP), launched initially as an interim measure in 1970. This program subsidized the provision of special ESL withdrawal classes in those primary and secondary schools with high immigrant density and provided funding for teachers, short training courses, and language laboratories. This paradigm of active assimilation was accompanied by a growing body of literature designed to provide teachers with information about the cultural background and learning difficulties of immigrant children (Bullivant, 1973; Kovacs & Cropley, 1975). However, by far the major thrust of child immigrant education was teaching English as a second language.

From Immigrant to Multicultural Education, 1972–1986

The election in 1972 of a Labor government after 23 years of conservative rule ushered in an era of great expectation for change. This accelerated the trend to greater federal involvement in ethnic affairs and also resulted in a spectacular increase in resources for education. Most important, it signaled a rejection of the old paradigm of assimilation with its focus on migrant education for a celebration of Australia's ethnic diversity. Grassby (1979), the former minister for immigration, summed up the new ethos:

We are not talking about "migrant" children. We are talking about Australian children of many different backgrounds. Certainly it is irrelevant to talk about migrant education. What we are really talking about is education of all children to fit them for a life in a multicultural and polyethnic society.

The change was not instant and was often honored by rhetoric rather than reality. However, by the early 1980s, all Australian states had adopted multicultural education policies, typified by that of the numerically largest state, New South Wales, which enunciated its objectives in 1978 in this philosophical position:

In a multicultural society each person has a right to cultural integrity, to a positive self-image, and to an understanding and respect for differences. Not only should each person be exposed to positive feelings about his or her own heritage, but must experience like feelings about the heritage of others. (New South Wales Department of Education, 1978, p. 3)

A ministerial policy statement (New South Wales Ministry of Education, 1979) was released the following year that formed the basis for the *Multicultural Education Policy Statement* (New South Wales Department of Education, 1983) and support documents:

The aims of multicultural education encompass the provision of educational experiences which will develop in all children:

a) an understanding and appreciation that Australia has been multicultural in nature throughout its history both before and after European colonization
b) an awareness of the contribution which people of many different cultural backgrounds have made and are making to Australia
c) intercultural understanding through the consideration of attitudes, beliefs and values related to multiculturalism
d) behaviour that fosters interethnic harmony
e) an enhanced sense of personal worth through an acceptance and appreciation not only of their Australian national identity but also of their specific Australian ethnic identity in the context of a multicultural society. (New South Wales Department of Education, 1983, p. 4)

Support documents were produced in the specific areas of ESL education, community languages education, ethnic studies, intercultural education, and multicultural

perspectives to the curriculum. The last two were to be mandatory components for all schools.

In December 1972, the New South Wales Department of School Education released its *Multicultural Education Plan, 1993–1997*. This plan provides schools with a significant range of multicultural initiatives in order to "safeguard equality of access to educational opportunity for students from non–English-speaking backgrounds within the wider brief of providing all students with an understanding of the relevance of multiculturalism to their personal lives and in their future as responsible adults" (New South Wales Department of School Education, 1992b, p. 3).

This conceptualization of multiculturalism as a component of every child's education had radical curriculum implications. A wealth of teaching resources dealing with the lifestyles and cultures of Australian ethnic groups was produced (National Advisory and Coordinating Committee on Multicultural Education [NACCME], 1987). A plethora of literature demonstrating the potential for incorporating a multicultural perspective in a variety of subject areas, including English (Kable, 1987), religion (Goosen, 1985), social studies (Mannix, 1985), and history (Cigler, 1987; Kalantzis, 1987), appeared.

Multicultural perspectives across the curriculum were explicitly designed to foster interethnic harmony. This was a belated response to the changing ethnic composition of Australian immigrants, a change accelerated by the introduction of a nondiscriminatory entry policy in 1973 and the admission of relatively large numbers of Indochinese refugees.

Another characteristic of this period was a changed focus on language. Whereas CMEP had seen ESL as a major strategy to assist the assimilation of immigrant children, the focus now was on community languages and bilingual programs as a means of overcoming educational disadvantage, strengthening ethnic identity, and preserving community languages as a national asset. Community languages became emblematic of ethnic group identity (LoBianco, 1988). There was an expansion in most states of community language electives for final-year secondary students (Department of Education and Training [DET], 1991).

Most state education departments developed language policies either separately or as a component of their multicultural education policy. There was a growing convergence in the terminology used and a concern about lack of resources, and complaints about the destabilizing effects of short-term tied federal funding were common. Policies of different states reflected their demography and educational traditions and were often seen to be written for different audiences. In Queensland, for example, the policy documents seemed designed to reduce the threat of Languages Other Than English (LOTE) in the minds of decision makers. In Victoria, the policy reflected the strength of the ethnic lobby and pressure for language maintenance (Andreoni & Ozolins, 1985).

Administrative difficulties in staffing such subjects, caused by the geographical distribution of students and the fact that only a small minority of Australian teachers could speak a community language, resulted in the contentious solution of increasing government funding to ethnic community-controlled schools operating outside normal school hours. Encouraged by the Galbally report, the number of ethnic schools increased; Noorst (1982) reported the existence of 1,045 separate schools involving more than 85,000 students. Government support of these schools was criticized for being potentially divisive and allowing mainstream schools to avoid responsibility for the provision of community languages. Noorst (1982) strongly supported these schools, arguing that they were crucial in the maintenance and development of language and the preservation and promotion of cultural heritage. Bullivant (1982) was critical of the way the schools selected and transmitted culture. He argued for dual ethnic schools that might produce a "hyphenated ethnic" (Greek-Australian, Italian-Australian), although he acknowledged the difficulty in achieving this, especially as far as smaller ethnic groups were concerned. Lewins (1982) claimed that the funding of ethnic schools could not be justified on the grounds of affirmative action. Smolicz (1984) saw such schools as contributing to ethnic separatism. Yet by 1991, the federal government had funded 196,000 enrollments through more than 500 ethnic organizations at a cost of $A6.9 million (DET, 1991).

Three major criticisms have been raised concerning the emphasis on culture during this multicultural phase. Although state policies exhorted teachers to incorporate multicultural perspectives, implementation, particularly in schools with few immigrant students, was commonly tokenistic. This reflected Cahill's finding that, nationally, Australian teachers' knowledge about Australia's ethnic groups was "seriously deficient" (Cahill, 1984, p. xiii). Typical activities such as "national" days stressed traditional cultures' externalities such as food, dress, music, and dance. Bullivant (1981b) argued that to equate culture with heritage was a dangerous oversimplification that ignored the adaptive and evolutionary nature of a group's culture and the extent to which cultural convergence had taken place.

Second, curriculum implementation across the country was uncoordinated and unsystematic, a problem that was recognized by the establishment of the NACCME in 1984 in an attempt to counter the duplication of resource development in different states and the ad hoc distribution of teaching materials (Foster, 1988). There was a lack of professionalism in the production values of many of the resources produced with government funding, and rarely did resource development budgets provide funds for training teachers to use the resources (Cahill, 1984). Earlier, the *Report of the National Inquiry into Teacher Education* (Auchmuty, 1980) had criticized teacher training institutions for their inability to prepare students adequately to understand and implement programs that catered to the diverse nature of Australian society.

Finally, there was a developing criticism that the emphasis on culture promoted by Grassby (1979) and Galbally (1978) had ignored the structural underpinnings of racism in Australian society. A growing body of critics called for a greater emphasis on affirmative action and a curriculum for working-class immigrant children aimed at achieving equal outcomes and empowering them for participation in the workforce rather than singing in their community language while they danced in the dole queue (Kalantzis, 1987).

The Economic Imperative, 1986 to the Present

In 1986, MEP was abolished. The 1984 *Review of the Commonwealth Multicultural Education Program* was critical of MEP's failure to achieve substantial and lasting change in Australian schooling. The review described a lack of national coordination, an unimpressive project completion rate, and widespread lack of awareness about the scheme (Cahill, 1984). Economic constraints were to dominate educational decision making in the ensuing period. Resources for multicultural education were less plentiful and more carefully targeted to meet goals of access and equity. With a half million Australian adults identified as having major literacy problems (LoBianco, 1988), ESL teaching was seen as crucial to the demands of a more sophisticated workforce. Whereas a generation before, non–English-speaking immigrants would have been consigned as "factory fodder," there developed a greater willingness to upgrade and recognize immigrant qualifications with ESL programs complementing this process. The National Office of Overseas Skills Recognition (NOOSR) was established in 1989, and an access-and-equity strategy for Commonwealth government instrumentalities was adopted (Cope, Castles, & Kalantzis, 1991).

A national policy on languages was announced in April 1987, partly in response to figures suggesting that three years earlier, only 10.5% of final-year secondary students matriculated with a second language, a decrease from 44% in 1967 (LoBianco, 1987). Programs funded by the language policy included the Australian Second Language

Learning Program, which allocated funds to state education systems for language instruction; the Asian Studies Program, which developed curricula in Asian languages and culture; and the Cross-Cultural Supplementation Program, for training professionals and paraprofessionals in cross-cultural communication (Clyne, 1991). Under this policy, the desirability of using mainstream schools to encourage language maintenance took less prominence than arguments for learning the languages of Asian trading partners.

The production of classroom resources concerning cultural difference, which peaked in the early 1980s, reflected the change in national priorities. The bicentenary of British colonization in 1988 resulted in an avalanche of teaching materials (NACCME, 1987) and a renewed commitment to Australian studies. However, by the end of the decade, the emphasis had rapidly moved to the promotion of Asian studies, seen by some as reflecting the ascendancy of economic rationalism in educational decision making.

This brief summary of the educational response to ethnic diversity since the end of World War II has attempted to identify the major components of educational change. It should be stressed, however, that in a conservative institution such as education, national or state policies have not always been implemented in the classroom.

RESEARCH

The changing educational paradigms and government policies identified previously had direct and indirect impacts on the amount and nature of educational research related to cultural diversity in Australia. Most of this research is government funded, but the amount of funding since 1986 has been considerably reduced. This section examines significant research relating to the educational outcomes of immigrant children, the incorporation of multicultural perspectives into the curriculum, the creation of harmonious interethnic relations, and language teaching in Australian schools.

Educational Performance of Immigrant Children

A major focus of research in Australian multicultural education has been the outcomes experienced by immigrant students. The most commonly used measures have been performance on standardized educational tests, retention rates, admission to tertiary education, and indicative vocations. Comparing the findings of these studies is fraught with difficulty for a number of reasons. Definitions of immigrants vary. In some studies, the criterion used is the

country of birth of the child; in other cases, it is the country of birth of one or both parents. In others, the term is restricted to immigrants from non–English-speaking countries. Some studies clearly identify the specific ethnic group membership, while others combine subjects from quite different ethnic groups and categorize them as immigrants. Generalizations are difficult because of complex interactions between gender, class, and ethnicity. Nor do official statistics, which categorize immigrants according to their country of origin, accurately identify ethnicity. For example, among immigrants from Indonesia are Dutch colonials, political refugees from East Timor, ethnic Chinese businesspersons, as well as ethnic Indonesians who arrived in the country originally as Australian government-sponsored students (Da Costa, 1992). With these qualifications, we turn to the studies.

In a major Sydney study of immigrant in-school retention rates, Meade (1983) compared the rate of secondary school completion of children whose parents were born in a non–English-speaking country with those whose parents were born in an English-speaking country (including Australia). Forty-one percent of NESB students completed secondary school, a significantly higher proportion than that of Anglo students who completed secondary schooling (30%). This result still held when the IQs and socioeconomic status of both groups of students were controlled. Williams (1980, cited in Marsh, 1988) had arrived at a similar conclusion in an earlier study, conducted in Melbourne, that found that children whose fathers were born in a non–English-speaking country were more likely to complete secondary school than were those whose fathers were born in either Australia or an English-speaking country. Burke and Davis (cited in Marsh, 1988) demonstrated that the proportion of second-generation immigrant children entering tertiary institutions is higher than that of Anglo Australians. However, despite common difficulties confronted by NESB children, the results for different ethnic groups were uneven. Martin and Meade (cited in Sturman, 1985) showed that Lebanese, Maltese, Italian, and Yugoslav students tended to remain at school for shorter periods than children from other ethnic groups. Furthermore, the Australian Schools Commission pointed out that there is frequently a strong interaction between ethnicity and gender; in many ethnic groups, educational aspirations do not extend as strongly to girls. There was no evidence that the daughters of immigrant parents perform any less well than the sons, but at both 16- and 18-year-old levels in 1971, girls born in Greece, Italy, and Yugoslavia were markedly more likely to have left the educational system than were Australian girls or boys of similar background (Sturman, 1985). Keceli and Cahill (1998), in a case study involving interviews with seventy second-generation Turkish-Australian secondary school students, found that while their performance was superior to that of their parents, they attended the types of schools less geared to university entry. They suffered covert discrimination within the school environment, and as a consequence few sought entrance to university, a contributing factor to the high level of unemployment among this generation.

With qualifications about ethnic and gender differences, these findings suggest that at least among a significant number of ethnic groups, there is high pressure for academic success and a willingness to make the financial sacrifice that might be required to ensure educational retention. The higher valuation placed on education by families from some ethnic groups may receive a more positive response from teachers (Bullivant 1988a; Nicklin Dent & Hatton, 1996). There is some evidence that teacher support for immigrant students has affected career choices. Abraham (1992) reports that the number of female teachers of Greek descent is higher than that of any other ethnic group in Sydney. He saw the impetus being the introduction in 1973 of modern Greek to the secondary syllabus, which may have encouraged Greek students to pursue that career, coupled with the imprimatur of Greek parents who saw teaching as an acceptable profession for their daughters.

In summarizing a number of research investigations into parental attitudes, Marsh (1988) uncovered clear evidence of strong preferences for a traditional academic curriculum. Connell, Connell, Sinclair, and Stroobant (1975) recorded that their immigrant respondents wished their children to be taught more science and have fewer confusing subject choices. DiFerranti (cited in Marsh, 1988) reported that immigrant parents expressed criticism about too little homework and the absence of languages in the curriculum of Australian schools. Jakubowicz and Wolf (cited in Marsh, 1988) noted among immigrant parents a desire for stricter schooling. Spearritt and Colman (cited in Marsh, 1988) interviewed refugee parents who were appreciative of their children's opportunities to attend school and learn English but felt too much time was wasted by playing games and sport. Both Burke and Davis (cited in Marsh, 1988) and Sturman (1985) suggested that Catholic schools seem to be more closely aligned with the educational values of many immigrant parents than are schools in the state system. Taft and Cahill (1978), in a study of Maltese, British, and South American immigrant children, ascertained that the British and Maltese children found their Australian schooling less difficult than in their own country of origin, and majorities from all three groups found Australian schools less difficult than they had expected. Solman (1987), in a survey of an urban state high school community with a high ethnic population, found a strong correlation between parental and student views about what should be taught (literacy, numeracy, and precise information about sex and drugs). However, there were differences between teachers and immigrant parents and children concerning the school's role. Although the overwhelming majority of parents and students believed that it was the responsibility of the school to encourage students to complete their full six years of secondary schooling, only 20% of teachers agreed.

It is dangerous to overgeneralize about the educational performance of immigrant children because the pattern varies among ethnic groups. In a major study, Marjoribanks (1979) surveyed 850 Adelaide families from five ethnic or social class groups (Greek, Italian, Yugoslav, Anglo middle, and Anglo working class) who had children in primary school. Using multiple regression analysis, he demonstrated the complex nature of the correlates of children's achievement with a range of variables, including parental aspirations, parental instrumental and expressive orientations, and ethnicity and class. He found that students from Italian, Greek, and Yugoslav families scored less well, particularly in the literacy components of the study, than did Australian students of similar-class background.

Taft and Cahill (1978) found quite different patterns of academic progress among their South American, Maltese, and British subjects. In their longitudinal study of students' academic progress, they found a slight reduction in the proportion of South American children rated as "slow learners" by their teachers over the two-year period. By contrast, the proportion of Maltese children who were rated as "slow learners" at the end of their second year was three times as high as the proportion rated as such in their first at the school.

Hewitt (cited in Sturman, 1985) compared the performance of 10- and 14-year-old immigrant and Australian children on a number of reading and mathematics tests. Although there was no significant ethnic difference on the mathematics tests, 59% of 10-year-old and 43% of 14-year-old immigrant children failed to achieve 80% mastery on the reading test as compared to 47% and 28%, respectively, of the Australian children. Williams, Batten, Girling-Butcher, and Clancy (cited in Sturman, 1985) concluded that NESB immigrants were disadvantaged in their scores on word knowledge, literacy, and numeracy, and these unsurprising findings are supported by others that suggest, however, that immigrant students' deficit in language tests are reduced as the students progress through secondary school (Marsh, 1988).

In 1996, the Australian Council for Education Research conducted a national school English literacy survey analyzing the reading and writing standards of elementary students in years 3 and 5 (average age eight and ten). The results showed that students from a language background other than English performed only slightly below the norm but marginally higher than students from low socioeconomic status and dramatically better than indigenous students (McRae et al., 2000).

The category of immigration may also be a predictor of educational performance. Following the war in Indochina, many of the Asian immigrants were refugees who came generally without resources and without qualifications recognized in Australia. Spearritt and Colman (1983, cited in Marsh, 1988) assessed the performance of a group of Indochinese refugee students in language and numeration before they undertook an educational reception program. They retested the students three and eight months later and found that the Laotian and Cambodian children (but not the Vietnamese) were significantly below norms on all aspects of the test. The posttests revealed that the educational deficit was maintained in all groups in literacy and numeracy despite some increase in oral proficiency and essay writing. Bullivant (cited in Marsh, 1988) provides evidence that longer-term Chinese immigrants are less academically motivated than are short-stay immigrants. According to this perspective, the longer that immigrant children are in Australia, the more they are "contaminated" by values less supportive of education (Marsh, 1988).

With restrictions on numbers of immigrants during the economic recession of the late 1980s and early 1990s, an increasing proportion of immigrants were in the category of business and professional immigration. Most of these people spoke English, had qualifications in demand, and arrived with some financial security. Increasing numbers came from Hong Kong as the British mandate over that colony approached its end. The children of these immigrants appear to have met with considerable academic success. The Australian media have projected the stereotype of Asian students as particularly conscientious and successful. For example, in New South Wales, articles highlighting the fact that the top two students in the higher school certificate (matriculation) exam were Chinese Australians featured prominently. So too was evidence of the large proportion of Asian scholars among the top 200 students (Diaz, 1992). Later research by Fan and Karnilowicz (2000) showed Chinese migrant adolescent high school girls performed better in mathematics than their Anglo Australian peers. Asians who have come as refugees without the same favorable economic circumstances appear not to have fared as well in the educational system (Chan, 1987).

Multicultural Perspectives in Curriculum

In most states of Australia, curriculum was centralized and highly prescriptive until the mid-1970s. Subsequently, a trend emerged empowering schools to develop curricula targeted to the specific needs of the children in relation to their location and circumstance. This made it difficult to ascertain the extent to which multicultural perspectives had been incorporated in the curriculum and to evaluate the influence of such programs on student knowledge and attitudes. The 1990s saw a collaborative move toward greater consistency in curriculum among states. In the future, generalizations about the multicultural nature of Australian curricula should be easier.

It would seem that few schools in Australia have been untouched by multicultural perspectives. The production of classroom resources reflected education department policies. The NACCME (1987) produced a directory of multicultural classroom resources that listed some 300 materials in English and 200 written in community languages. Cope (1987) analyzed 650 history and social studies texts published since 1945 and discovered a fundamental paradigm shift from homogeneous Australian identity oriented toward Britain to an identity that celebrated ethnic diversity. He describes a trend from 1945 texts, which provide a narrative of progress and development in which cultural differences are described in terms of superiority and inferiority, dominance and suppression, to a new pattern in the late 1980s, in which cultures are depicted as relative, cultural difference is celebrated, and senses of superiority are challenged as ignorant and insensitive. The risk Cope warns of is that the materials, in their patronizing niceness, may exaggerate and construct stereotypes of cultural differences, thereby providing grist for the racist mill and ignoring the potential for cultural change and convergence. Garbutcheon Singh (1987) shares Cope's concern that even some of the best multicultural material has focused on the externalities of cultural difference (food, dress, songs, and dances) and ignored the broader sociopolitical context that constrains the way in which individuals from different ethnic groups construct their lives. By omission, these materials deny issues of justice, rights, power, and participation.

Another criticism of the resources developed for multicultural perspectives was the lack of professionalism in their production values and the failure of the development budgets to provide funds for training teachers in the use of the resources. One organization to have addressed these criticisms is the federally funded Asia Education Foundation (AEF) founded in 1992. The AEF has produced a range of print and electronic classroom resources and teaching plans dealing with contemporary Asian societies. To maximize the effectiveness of these resources, the AEF has introduced a network of 1,500 magnet schools, which provide professional development for teachers in the use of resources (AEF, 2001).

Cahill (1984), in a study of teacher attitudes in the state of Victoria, found widespread endorsement of multicultural education. Only 14% of teachers considered it to be a "passing fad." In a later study of Queensland primary teachers, Sachs (1989) found their concept of culture to be remarkably consistent with that of the Queensland Department of Education multicultural policy document. Alcorso and Cope (1986) found that most state curricula advocated against multiculturalism being taught as a separate subject, instead requiring a multicultural perspective across the entire curriculum. Despite finding widespread acceptance of multiculturalism among teachers, the rapid expansion of classroom resources, and the changing image of Australia in history and social science texts, Cahill (1984) also uncovered a general lack of understanding by teachers concerning ethnicity. Teachers' knowledge about ethnic groups was deficient, and they tended to exclude students of non-Anglo background from the concept "Australian."

In 1977–1978, D. McInerney (1987) surveyed teachers' attitudes toward different aspects of multicultural curriculum development. He found that while teachers were favorably disposed to minority children maintaining their ethnic identity, they were not supportive of schools being actively involved in teaching ethnic languages or extending multicultural curricula. Over twenty years later, a follow-up study of 345 New South Wales teachers reported little change in the enthusiasm for multiculturalism, especially among younger teachers (V. McInerney et al., 2001; D. McInerney, Cincotta, Totaro, & Williams, 2001). Earlier, Maddock and Ramsland (1985) administered an attitude scale measuring support for multicultural values to secondary students in the Hunter Valley of New South Wales. Results varied among classes in the school, and there was no clear pattern of interaction of attitudes with gender, religion, or parental occupation. While attitudes toward multiculturalism were generally favorable, they were considerably less supportive than those of secondary students in Florida and Hawaii, the subjects of a previous comparable study. This led the authors to conclude that multicultural values were more deeply embedded in the curricula of American high schools and that American teachers were more consistently active in promoting these values. Walker (1987), in an ethnographic study of a secondary school with high immigrant density, demonstrated the persistence of assimilationist values in a peer group culture despite a manifest commitment to multiculturalism within the school.

Antiracism

Sachs and Poole (1989) claim that the term *antiracism* has been less frequently used in Australia than in Great Britain. They approvingly quote Humphrey McQueen: "Silence has been a source of sustenance to racism and it has not gone away just because we have not had to articulate it" (quoted in Sachs and Poole, 1989, p. 14). Most research described in this section has focused on describing the extent of racism; there is a lamentable absence of studies evaluating school-based programs to combat racism.

Rosenthal and Morrison (1979) looked at the effect of ethnic mix within the classroom on a range of attitudes and abilities using year 6 (12-year-old) children in three categories of elementary schools in Melbourne with a high, medium, and low proportion of NESB children. The results showed no significant difference between the groups in attitudes to immigrants, with one exception. In the high-immigrant school, immigrant children recorded more positive attitudes than did the nonimmigrant children. Another study investigating interethnic attitudes was conducted by Jones and de Lacey (1979) in Wollongong, an industrial city within commuting distance from Sydney. The subjects, 50 immigrant and 100 Australian-born students, completed an instrument containing multiple-choice and open-ended items relating to attitudes held toward immigrants. The authors concluded that although negative attitudes among Australian-born students were lessening, the students were not making strong efforts to incorporate immigrants. By contrast, the immigrant students were initiating most of the intergroup interaction. Cahill and Ewen (1987; Cahill, 1984), in a major study of 1,346 year 8 students in 50 secondary schools, found friction scores tended to be higher in schools with high immigrant density in low socioeconomic locations.

Immigrant students have not been the only victims of racism in schools. Interviews with student and practicing teachers from Asian ethnic backgrounds indicate that the teachers had experienced racist incidents from students and received little support from colleagues and school administrators in dealing with the problem (Santoro, 1999; Kamler, Reid, & Santoro, 1999).

Findings from studies designed to investigate interethnic attitudes among school students empirically were not widely distributed, nor did they appear to have much impact on policy. For example, the impetus for antiracism programs—the Combating Prejudice in Schools Project (Skelton, 1986) and *Human Rights in Education* (Human Rights and Equal Opportunity Commission and New South Wales Department of Education, 1988)—came more from media reports of racist incidents in the community and pressure from ethnic organizations responding to the concerns of their members. These concerns were elaborated in the *Report of the National Inquiry into Racist Violence in Australia* (Human Rights and Equal Opportunity Commission, 1991), which concluded that the main victims of racist violence were Aborigines, Asians, and members of the Islamic community. This report found comparatively little physical violence in schools but gave detailed accounts of verbal abuse and harassment, often inadequately dealt with by teachers. While recommending various measures that school authorities could take to prevent racism, the commissioners accurately summarized the state of research into Australian schools: "At present there appears to be little information available to school management and staff about who experiences racism, in what forms, and from whom; or how schools can successfully accommodate students from different cultural backgrounds" (p. 349).

During 1991–1992, the New South Wales Department of School Education conducted two whole-school antiracism pilot projects, one in a rural area with a high proportion of Aboriginal students and the other in an urban area of high NESB density. The strategies employed and lessons learned as part of this Whole School Anti-Racism Project were widely disseminated and used in school development programs across the state (Foster, 1995). Building on this experience, the renamed Department of Education and Training now employs 13 antiracism consultants across the state. Another action research project, Dracon, trains 13- to 18-year-old students in conducting drama workshops among their peers exploring conflict, often racial conflict, and its resolution. This project was successfully trialed in a rural school that was the scene of interracial tensions and is currently part of a collaborative project with schools in Malaysia, the Philippines, and Sweden (Hill & Allan, 2001).

At a national level, all states and school systems have cooperated in a federally funded antiracist project entitled, Racism: No Way. This involves the production of a national Web site with information about legislation, the history of racism, resources for understanding it, examples of innovative teaching, interviews with well-known Australians, and strategies for cooperation. The federal government, through the Department of Immigration and Multicultural Affairs' Living in Harmony program, funds a wide variety of community-based projects designed to improve community relations, many of which involve schools (Hill & Allan, 2001).

English as a Second Language

ESL has been the least controversial and most generously and consistently funded component of multicultural education programs in Australia. Nonetheless, some critics argue that these programs have been implicitly assimilationist, aiming to replace rather than supplement the students' first language (Garbutcheon Singh, 2002). A number of studies have attempted to evaluate the success of federal ESL programs since the inception of CMEP. The Schools Commission Committee on Multicultural Education (1979) reported that only one third of students classified as "migrant and in need of special language

assistance" were being helped under the program. Many such students were reluctant to participate because of the social stigma attached to ESL withdrawal classes. Campbell and McMeniman (1985, cited in Collins, 1990) found that ESL tuition was often withdrawn before children had attained the necessary language skills. Ninety percent of ESL staff were only generalist teachers, most with inadequate in-service preparation. Moreover, nearly half the children who needed ESL teaching were not receiving it (Collins, 1990).

Intensive Language Centres (ILC) for newly arrived immigrants were established to remedy the inefficiencies of decentralized reception. In New South Wales in 1977, the first center was opened, and by 1992 there were 17 centers attached to secondary schools operating in the Sydney metropolitan area. These varied in size, but by 1988 they were servicing 3,500 students whose average stay was 6 months before transferring to mainstream schools (Wren and Johnson, 1992). The function of each center was to assess children's English-language level and maximize their chances of successful transition to secondary-school study. Yet there was no central New South Wales education policy on their status and role, no standard curriculum, and no recognized credentials for students on completion of the program.

Wren and Johnson (1992) summarized the limited research on the effectiveness of these programs. Campbell and McMeniman (cited in Wren and Johnson, 1992) found that students who attended for longer periods were initially more successful in senior high school studies and initially better able to understand lessons and textbooks than those who had attended two terms or less. Not surprisingly, students who had experienced the greatest difficulty in transition had previously been illiterate, slow learners, refugees, or older. Gaffey (cited in Wren and Johnson, 1992) found that students who began ILC courses at a younger age and with some formal school background were more successful in the transition to mainstream classes. Kassim (cited in Wren and Johnson, 1992) found that ILC graduates were performing well in mathematics but experienced difficulty with language-embedded subjects such as geography, art, and science. Ferguson (cited in Wren and Johnson, 1992) confirmed that ILC graduates had difficulty in mainstream classrooms because they did not receive enough opportunity to write or interact with fluent English speakers and were not given texts to assist their private study. In their own research, Wren and Johnson (1992) uncovered common concerns among stakeholders in the ILC program. There was a strong desire for a uniform national instrument to assess English-language proficiency and a need for recognized credentialing of graduates from these centers. There was a demand for more proactive and less ad hoc policymaking for ILCs. The administrative relationship between ILCs and the secondary schools they serviced required clarification. Teachers in mainstream schools needed to be better prepared to adjust to the different learning styles and expectations of students who were coming from ILCs.

In a national evaluation of ESL provision, the authors in Herriman (1992) noted that resources tended to be allocated in favor of recent arrivals; fewer resources were directed to the transition of students from reception centers to mainstream schools. They discovered a great variation in the qualifications of ESL teachers and found that ESL teachers were occupationally marginalized, with few promotion prospects. Like Wren and Johnson (1992), they noted a need for assessment instruments that could assist in evaluating the effectiveness of ESL programs in order to enhance diagnosis and educational planning.

Languages Other Than English

Smolicz and Secombe (1977) conducted an analysis of submissions to a federal government inquiry into the teaching of immigrant languages in schools. The majority of the submissions were from ethnic organizations, and the remainder could not be seen as representative of Australian public opinion. The findings suggest a coalescence between increasing political influence of the ethnic lobby and a move among influential Anglo Australians to value the existence of ethnic cultures and advocate strategies that facilitated their maintenance. Ethnic languages were seen to play a major role not only in maintaining cultural heritage but in providing the benefits of cultural interaction. Submissions from the smaller ethnic groups saw support for ethnic schools as the most realistic means of language maintenance. Over half the submissions from ethnic organizations preferred the introduction of ethnic languages and cultures as separate subjects in Australian schools. While these two strategies were concerned with ethnic structural maintenance, half of those submissions that advocated bilingualism saw it as a transitional rather than a maintenance strategy.

Kalantzis, Cope, and Slade (1986) compared attitudes toward language maintenance and language competence of students and parents from two ethnic groups in the Wollongong area: German and Macedonian. The research methodology included group interviews with parents, attitudinal questionnaires with primary and secondary students from seven Wollongong schools, and tests of their first-language competence. The German community was deemed to represent more established immigrant groups who had achieved a generally higher socioeconomic status and English-language proficiency. The Macedonians tended to be more recently arrived immigrants,

less proficient in English, and more likely to use Macedonian in the home. Both groups of parents gave a high priority to their children's obtaining a high degree of competence in English. There were, however, differences in the parental groups' attitudes to language maintenance in schools. German respondents generally believed that they had little personal need for German-language instruction, as they felt quite competent in English. They believed in principle that German, as an important international and scientific language, merited being taught in schools. The Macedonian parents were keen to have more resources devoted to their language but were divided as to whether those resources should be allocated to mainstream or after-hours ethnic schools. In common with other ethnic groups, their reasons for advocating language maintenance were not cognitive or pedagogical but related to the prestige of their community. At the primary school level, German students tended to be indifferent to language maintenance, though most took the opportunity to study it when offered. Those Macedonians who studied their language in school increased their proficiency and developed a more positive attitude toward Macedonian. By secondary school, the majority felt that while Macedonian should be offered and while it might provide employment opportunities, they themselves would prefer to study languages of greater prestige such as French and German. Favorable attitudes toward Macedonian were positively correlated with the number of Macedonian students in the school. The findings on language proficiency were quite disturbing. Unsurprisingly, both NESB groups gained lower scores in English than the English-speaking control group. However, their first-language proficiency was also low, and the students felt that their experiences of mother-tongue learning at community or Department of Education Saturday language schools were unsatisfactory.

The most comprehensive research into the teaching of languages other than English in schools was conducted by the Commonwealth Department of Education in 1986. The main findings are summarized below.

Almost half of Australian students had never studied a language other than English. Only 11.7% of students from homes where a LOTE was spoken were studying that language at school. At any one time, only 17.3% of all students studied one or more non-English languages. Fewer than one third of Australian schools teach one or more languages. Only 10% of elementary schools taught a second language. Fifteen percent of secondary schools did not teach any languages other than English. Schools that did not teach other languages were more likely to be small and rural. Students who elected to study languages were more likely to be girls (20%) than boys (14.6%), and students with at least one parent from a non–English-speaking country were more likely to study a language than students from an English-speaking background. The median hours per week allocated to study a language in schools ranged from 1.0 in primary, to 2.7 in lower secondary, to 3.9 in upper secondary. Only a minute number of students (0.1%) studied the language of Australia's major trading partner, Japan (LoBianco, 1987). By 1990, almost 21,000 students were studying a LOTE in their final year of secondary education (11.7% of year 12 students), the five most popular of which were French, German, Japanese, Italian, and Mandarin (DET, 1991). Since this study, different state education departments have attempted to promote the teaching of LOTE. In New South Wales, under the Community Languages Program in Primary Schools, there were over 20,000 primary children in 73 government schools studying 1 of 11 community languages. An Ethnic Schools Board was established by the state government in 1992 to assist with the efficient operation of ethnic ("Saturday") schools. In 2000, the federal government provided grants of $A15 million for the states to distribute for ESL insertion programs in mainstream schools, Saturday schools run by state authorities, and language schools run by ethnic organizations (Hill & Allan, 2001). This reduced funding in real terms reflects a change in federal government language policy of reducing emphasis on community languages to encouraging the use of those of Australia's trading partners. Under its policy of productive diversity, the federal government has prioritized 14 languages and generously subsidizes states that are teaching Asian languages (Clyne, 1997). The current federal goal is that 60% of Australian children should learn an Asian language from year 3 (8 years of age). The response from the states to these targets has varied.

CONCLUSION

In Australia until recently, immigration and ethnic affairs have generally been characterized by bipartisan consensus. Multiculturalism has not represented a threat to the dominant social institutions but has been confined to the private and the cultural sphere of Australian life. Indeed, as Bullivant (1981a) argues, Australia has been polyethnic rather than multicultural, where Anglo Australians could appreciate the "color" that ethnic diversity provided—as long as diversity did not involve radical redistribution of life chances and did not require Anglo Australians to change their lifestyle significantly. Meanwhile, 50 years since the beginning of the immigration program, control of the country is still largely invested in Anglo Australian hands. English is the uncontested national language, and, despite the momentum toward republicanism, the dominant social structures of the country remain unchallenged.

We believe that three discernible trends may affect this area in Australia: increased government financial restraint coupled with economic pragmatism, a growing involvement of the national government in the centralization of curriculum design, and a devolution to local communities of school management.

Research into multicultural education has seldom been the driving force of educational policy. Policy changes have rarely used the language or findings of the research literature. Most Australian educational research is government funded, and, in the short term, resources for research into multicultural education will be significantly reduced. Economic pragmatism seems likely to determine the research agenda, and we anticipate that the two areas where funding will be concentrated are the relationship between education and workforce participation of immigrant children and the effectiveness of language teaching, particularly Asian languages, in Australian schools.

A number of wider changes in Australian education will affect multicultural education. In some states, there has been a trend toward greater participation of local communities in the governance of their schools, with the primary intentions of this involvement being to access community resources and to reduce administration costs. While this may provide opportunities for more established ethnic groups to influence the direction of schools, it might tend to marginalize newer arrivals further.

The past decade has seen a national government increasingly involved in coordination of education. This increased role may lead to efficiencies, especially in nationally accredited instruments for ESL teaching, distance education curriculum materials for languages, and ethnic studies materials targeted to national curricula. Nonetheless, in a time of significant educational and social change, we suggest that multiculturalism in schools has been supplanted by other priorities.

References

Abraham, D. (1992, December 10). Platonic love: The Greek passion for teaching. *Sydney Morning Herald,* p. 16.

Alcorso, C., & Cope, B. (1986). *A review of Australian multicultural education policy, 1979–1986* (National Advisory Co-ordinating Committee on Multicultural Education Commissioned Research Paper, No. 6). Canberra: Australian Government Publishing Service.

Andreoni, H., & Ozolins, U. (1985). *Three language policy statements: Two evaluations.* Canberra: Australian Government Publishing Service.

Asia Education Foundation. (2001). *School programs* [On-line]. Available: http://www.asialink.unimelb.edu.au/aef/schools/index. html. Accessed July 18, 2001.

Auchmuty, J. J. (1980). *Report of the national inquiry into teacher education.* Canberra: Australian Government Publishing Service.

Australian Ethnic Affairs Council. (1977). *Australia as a multicultural society.* Canberra: Australian Government Publishing Service.

Blainey, G. (1984). *All for Australia.* North Ryde: Methuen Haynes.

Bullivant, B. M. (1973). *Educating the immigrant child: Concepts and cases.* Sydney: Angus and Robertson.

Bullivant, B. M. (1981a). *The pluralist dilemma in education: Six case studies.* North Sydney: George Allen and Unwin.

Bullivant, B. M. (1981b). *Race, ethnicity and curriculum.* South Melbourne: Macmillan.

Bullivant, B. M. (1982). Are ethnic schools the solution to ethnic children's accommodation to Australian society? *Journal of Intercultural Studies, 3*(2), 17–35.

Bullivant, B. M. (1986). Multicultural education in Australia: An unresolved debate. In J. A. Banks & J. Lynch (Eds.), *Multicultural education in Western societies* (pp. 98–124). New York: Holt, Rinehart, & Winston.

Bullivant, B. M. (1988a). Missing the empirical forest for the ideological trees: A commentary on Kalantzis and Cope. *Journal of Intercultural Studies, 9*(1), 58–69.

Bureau of Immigration Research. (1992). *Immigration update.* Canberra: Australian Government Printing Service.

Butlin, N. G. (1983). *Our original aggression: Aboriginal populations in south eastern Australia, 1788–1850.* Sydney: George Allen and Unwin.

Cahill, D. B. (1984). *Review of the commonwealth multicultural education program.* Melbourne: Phillip Institute of Technology.

Cahill, D. B., & Ewen, J. (1987). *Ethnic youth: Their assets and aspirations.* Canberra: Australian Government Publishing Service.

Chan, H. (1987). *The adaptation, life satisfaction and academic achievement of Chinese senior school students in Melbourne.* Unpublished doctoral dissertation, Monash University, Australia.

Cigler, M. (1987). Community history for young Australians. *Australian History Teacher, 14,* 9–12.

Clyne, M. (1991). Australia's language policies: Are we going backwards? *Current Affairs Bulletin, 68*(6), 13–20.

Clyne, M. (1997). Language policy in Australia: Achievements, disappointment, prospects. *Journal of Intercultural Studies, 18*(1), 63–71.

Collins, J. (1990). *Migrant hands in a distant land.* Sydney: Pluto Press.

Connell, W. F., Connell, R. W., Sinclair, K., & Stroobant, R. (1975). *12 to 20: Studies of city youth.* Sydney: H. Smith.

Cope, B. (1987). *Racism, popular culture and Australian identity in transition: A case study of change in school textbooks since 1945* (Occasional Paper No. 14). Wollongong: University of Wollongong, Centre for Multicultural Studies.

Cope, B., Castles, S., & Kalantzis, M. (1991). *Immigration, ethnic conflicts and social cohesion.* Canberra: Bureau of Immigration Research.

Crisp, L. F. (1961). *Ben Chifley.* Sydney: Angus and Robertson.

Da Costa, H. (1992, September). Indonesians in Australia. *Inside Indonesia, 32,* 19–20.

Department of Aboriginal Affairs. (1984). *Aboriginal social indicators.* Canberra: Australian Government Publishing Service.

Department of Education and Training. (1991). *Australia's language: The Australian language and literacy policy.* Canberra: Australian Government Publishing Service.

Department of Immigration and Multicultural Affairs. (2002). DIMA fact sheets [On-line]. Available: http://www.immi.gov.au/facts/index2.htm#research.

Diaz, T. (1992, January 14). Coincidentally, they are also very clever. *Sydney Morning Herald,* p. 3.

Fan, C., & Karnilowicz, W. (1997) The measurement of definitions of success among Chinese and Australian girls. *Journal of Cross-Cultural Psychology, 28,* 589–599.

Fitzgerald, S. (1988). *Immigration: A commitment to Australia.* Canberra: Australian Government Publishing Service.

Foster, D. (Ed.). (1995). *Whole school anti-racism project.* Sydney: New South Wales Department of School Education.

Foster, L. E. (1988). *Diversity and multicultural education: A sociological perspective.* North Sydney: Allen and Unwin.

Fullagar, R.L.K., Price, D. M., & Head, L. M. (2001, June). Early human occupation of Australia: Archeology and thermoluminescence dating of Jinmium rock-shelter, Northern Territory. *Antiquity* [On-line]. Available: http://intarch.ac.uk/antiquity/fullagar.html.

Galbally, F. (1978). *Report of the review of post-arrival programs and services for migrants.* Canberra: Australian Government Publishing Service.

Garbutcheon Singh, M. (1987). Towards a strategic redefinition of intercultural studies. *Discourse, 7*(2), 69–85.

Goosen, G. (1985). How multicultural is your R.E. curriculum? *Journal of Christian Education, 83,* 13–19.

Grassby, A. J. (1979). It's time for migrant education to go. In P. R. de Lacey & M. E. Poole (Eds.), *Mosaic or melting pot: Cultural evolution in Australia* (pp. 278–282). Sydney: Harcourt Brace Jovanovich.

Herriman, M. L. (Ed.). (1992). *An evaluative study of the commonwealth ESL program.* Perth: University of Western Australia.

Hill, B., & Allan, R. (2001). Immigration policy and multicultural policy in Australia: Charting the changes. In F. Salili & R. Hoosain (Eds.), *Multicultural education: Issues, policies and practice.* Greenwich, CT: Information Age Publishing.

Human Rights and Equal Opportunity Commission. (1991). *Report of the national inquiry into racist violence in Australia.* Canberra: Australian Government Publishing Service.

Human Rights and Equal Opportunity Commission and the New South Wales Department of Education. (1988). *Human rights in education.* Sydney: New South Wales Department of Education.

Jones, J. M., & de Lacey, P. R. (1979). Natives and newcomers: Mutual attitudes. In P. R. de Lacey & M. E. Poole (Eds.), *Mosaic or melting pot: Cultural evolution in Australia* (pp. 163–172). Sydney: Harcourt Brace Jovanovich.

Jupp, J. (1986). *The review of migrant and multicultural programs and services: Don't settle for less.* Canberra: Australian Government Publishing Service.

Kable, J. (1987). Connecting literature and life. *Idiom, 22*(1), 12–18.

Kalantzis, M. (1987). Racism and pedagogy. *Teaching History, 20*(4), 45–48.

Kalantzis, M., Cope, B., Noble, G., & Poynting, S. (1990). *Cultures of schooling: Pedagogies for cultural difference and social access.* Basingstoke: Falmer Press.

Kalantzis, M., Cope, B., & Slade, D. (1986). *The language question: The maintenance of languages other than English* (Vols. 1–2). Canberra: Department of Immigration and Ethnic Affairs.

Kamler, B., Reid, J., & Santoro, N. (1999). Who's asking the questions? Researching race, ethnicity and teachers. *Australian Educational Researcher, 26*(1), 55–74

Keceli, B., & Cahill, D. (1998). Education and inequality: A case study of second generation Turkish-Australians. *Journal of Intercultural Studies, 19*(2), 207–213.

Kelly, P. (1992). *The end of certainty: The story of the 1980s.* Sydney: Allen and Unwin.

Kovacs, M. L., & Cropley, A. J. (1975). *Immigrants and society: Alienation and assimilation.* Sydney: McGraw-Hill.

Lewins, F. (1982). The political implications of ethnic schools. *Journal of Intercultural Studies, 3*(2), 36–47.

LoBianco, J. (1987). *National policy on languages.* Canberra: Australian Government Publishing Service.

LoBianco, J. (1988). Multiculturalism and the national policy on languages. *Journal of Intercultural Studies, 9*(1), 25–38.

Maddock, M., & Ramsland, J. (1985). Attitudes towards multiculturalism in schools in an industrial area: A study in the Hunter Valley, New South Wales. *Journal of Intercultural Studies, 6*(3), 16–42.

Mannix, C. (1985, May). Teaching about different cultures to students in a multicultural setting. *Newsletter (Victorian Association for Multicultural Education), 103,* 14–17.

Marjoribanks, K. (1979). *Ethnic families and children's achievements.* North Sydney: Allen and Unwin.

Marsh, C. J. (1988). *Policy options paper on access and success of school children from non-English speaking backgrounds.* Canberra: Office of Multicultural Affairs.

Martin, J. (1972). *Migrants: Equality and ideology.* Melbourne: LaTrobe University.

Martin, J. (1978). *The migrant presence.* Sydney: Allen and Unwin.

McInerney, D. M. (1987). Teacher attitudes to multicultural curriculum development. *Australian Journal of Education, 31*(2), 129–144.

McInerney, V., McInerney, D. M., Cincotta, M., Totaro, P., & Williams, D. (2001, April 10–14). *Teachers' attitudes to, and beliefs about, multicultural education: Have there been changes over the last twenty years?* Paper presented at the 82nd Conference of the American Educational Research Association, Seattle, WA.

McRae, D., Ainsworth, G., Cumming, J., Hughes, P., Mackay, T., Price, K., Rowland, M., Warhurst, J., Woods, D., & Zbar, V. (2000). *What works? Explorations in improving outcomes for indigenous students.* Canberra, Australian Curriculum Studies Association & National Curriculum Services.

Meade, P. (1983). *The educational experience of Sydney high school students: Comparative study of migrant students of non-English speaking origin and students whose parents were born in a non-English speaking country.* Canberra: Australian Government Publishing Service.

Miller, J. (1985). *Koori: A will to win.* Sydney: Angus and Robertson.

National Aboriginal Education Committee. (1982). Rationale, aims and objectives in Aboriginal education. In J. Sherwood (Ed.), *Aboriginal education: Issues and innovations* (pp. 61–66). Perth: Creative Research.

National Advisory and Co-ordinating Committee on Multicultural Education. (1987). *Resource materials directory.* Canberra: Australian Government Publishing Service.

New South Wales Department of Education. (1978). *Multicultural education: A consultative document.* Sydney: Government Printer.

New South Wales Department of Education. (1983). *Multicultural education policy statement.* Sydney: Government Printer.

New South Wales Department of School Education. (1992a). *Antiracism policy statement.* Sydney: Government Printer.

New South Wales Department of School Education. (1992b). *Multicultural education plan, 1993–1997.* Sydney: Government Printer.

New South Wales Ministry of Education. (1979). *Multicultural education policy statement.* Sydney: Government Printer.

Nicklin Dent, J., & Hatton, E. (1996). Education and poverty: An Australian primary school case study. *Australian Journal of Education, 40*(1), 42–60.

Noorst, M. (1982). Ethnic schools: What are they and what would they like to be? *Journal of Intercultural Studies, 3*(2), 6–16.

Office of Multicultural Affairs. (1989). *National agenda for a multicultural Australia.* Canberra: Australian Government Publishing Service.

Reynolds, H. (1982). *The other side of the frontier: Aboriginal resistance to the European invasion of Australia.* Melbourne: Penguin.

Roper, T. (1971). *The myth of equality.* Melbourne: Heinemann.

Rosenthal, D., & Morrison, S. (1979). On being a minority in the classroom: A study of the influence of ethnic mix on cognitive functioning and attitudes in working-class children. In P. R. de Lacey & M. E. Poole (Eds.), *Mosaic or melting pot: Cultural evolution in Australia* (pp. 140–154). Sydney: Harcourt Brace Jovanovich.

Sachs, J. (1989). Match or mismatch: Teachers' conceptions of culture and multicultural education policy. *Australian Journal of Education, 33*(1), 19–33.

Sachs, J., & Poole, M. (1989). Multicultural education policies in Australia and Britain: Social transformation or status quo? *Education and Society, 7*(1), 9–19.

Samuda, R. J. (1986). Social and educational implications of multiculturalism. *Education and Society, 4*(2), 63–68.

Santoro, N. (1999). Relationships of power: An analysis of school practicum discourse. *Journal of Intercultural Studies, 20*(1), 31–42.

Schools Commission Committee on Multicultural Education. (1979). *Education for a multicultural society.* Canberra: Schools Commission.

Sherington, G. (1991). Australian immigration, ethnicity and education. *History of Education Review, 20*(1), 61–72.

Skehan, C., & Clennell, A. (2002, May 4). Reith "talked of retracting boat children photos." *Sydney Morning Herald,* p. 4.

Skelton, K. (1986). Educating for cultural understanding: The work of the Combating Prejudice in Schools project. *Youth Studies, 5*(3), 36–39.

Smolicz, J. J. (1984). Who's afraid of bi-lingualism? *Education News, 18*(5), 36–39.

Smolicz, J. J., & Secombe, M. J. (1977). Mosaic or melting pot: Cultural evolution in Australia. *Australian Journal of Education, 21*(1), 1–24.

Solman, R. T. (1987). A survey of the needs of an urban high school's community. *Australian Journal of Education, 31*(2), 145–160.

Sturman, A. (1985). *Immigrant Australians, education and the transition to work.* Canberra: National Advisory and Co-ordinating Committee on Multicultural Education.

Taft, R., & Cahill, D. (1978). *Initial adjustment to schooling of immigrant families.* Canberra: Australian Government Publishing Service.

Walker, J. C. (1987). School sport, ethnicity and nationality: Dimensions of male youth culture in an inner-city school. *Australian Journal of Education, 31*(3), 303–316.

Ward, R. B. (1958). *The Australian legend.* Melbourne: Oxford University Press.

Ward, R. B. (1976). *Australia: A short history.* Sydney: Ure Smith.

Wilton, J., & Bosworth, R. (1984). *Old words and new Australia.* Melbourne: Penguin.

Wren, H., & Johnson, N. (1992). The role of intensive English language centres. *Journal of Intercultural Studies, 13*(1), 33–54.

48

MULTICULTURAL EDUCATION IN THE UNITED KINGDOM

Historical Development and Current Status

Peter Figueroa

University of Southampton

This chapter provides a review of the development of education for a multicultural society in postwar Britain, and particularly in England, the largest part of the union with the largest minority ethnic population. The chapter seeks to give a broad and balanced picture, but selection is inevitable since the literature is truly extensive.

Some brief initial definition of the field seems appropriate. There has been much disagreement about multicultural and antiracist education and related issues in Britain as elsewhere. Multicultural societies and the related educational issues are complex. With Nieto (1992), multicultural education may be characterized as a process of basic education and of educational reform at all levels and for all students. It combats racism, affirms pluralism, and promotes social justice. It should permeate all aspects of the education system from education officers to classroom teachers, including policy, strategy, and structure; curriculum, pedagogy, and materials; assessment, allocation, rewards, and punishment; interactions among teachers, students, and parents; the physical environments; and teacher education (see Gay, 2001; Figueroa, 1991, 1999).

Philosophical questions are involved, for instance, about the meanings of key concepts (e.g., pluralism, citizenship, and racism) and about core values (e.g., equality, justice, freedom, concord, and inclusiveness). Related

to these are issues of human rights and obligations. There are sociological issues, such as the social structure, power and hierarchies, and social networks and discrimination. At least four key characteristics of British society, and the related concepts and values, must be understood if a consequential multicultural antiracist education is to be developed: diversity, inequality, racism, and democracy. Moreover, a historical understanding and a grasp of current supranational and global contexts and forces is necessary. So are specific monitoring and auditing of contemporary realities and situations in schools and in the wider society (see Figueroa, 1999, 2000a).

THE HISTORICAL CONTEXT

Immense social change, including decolonization and extensive labor migration, took place worldwide after World War II. Europeans sought new lives in other parts of the world. People from Africa, the Caribbean, the Indian subcontinent, and other areas—overwhelmingly colonials and ex-colonials—sought new lives in Europe and elsewhere.

The links of such peoples with Europe extend back across centuries of European expansion and ancient trading links, but it has been mainly during the past 500 years

Thanks to James A. Banks, John Eggleston, David Gillborn, Robin Grinter, and Gillian Klein for making many helpful comments on drafts of this chapter.

that Britain became involved with Africa, the Caribbean, and the Indian subcontinent and that a significant non-European population grew up in Britain. The transatlantic slave trade, the American colonies, the Raj, and expansion into Africa were key factors, with Asian and especially African people being brought to England largely through the slave trade from about the mid- to late 1500s (see Fryer, 1984; Little, 1948). By the 19th century, a substantial Black population "permeated most ranks of society, through the length and breadth" of Britain (Walvin, 1973, p. 72).

The Industrial Revolution in Britain was funded largely through the slave trade and the exploitation of the colonies (Williams, 1944). The British Empire, with White people ruling non-Europeans, was at its height in the 19th century. The dogma of racism offered a justification. This long history of British domination of non-European peoples and the growth of nationalism and capitalism account largely for the postwar migrations into Britain, the position of the visible minorities there, and British attitudes toward them and multiculturalism.

MAJOR CHARACTERISTICS OF MULTICULTURAL POSTWAR BRITAIN

Britain has long been culturally diverse and characterized by other fundamental and crisscrossing differences—for instance, those of gender, status, privilege, power, social class, education, age, and region. The United Kingdom consists of Great Britain (England, Scotland, and Wales) and Northern Ireland—four very different regions with different but intertwined histories. The education systems of Northern Ireland and Scotland are quite different from those of England and Wales, whose systems are closely linked, although Wales, unlike England, is officially bilingual. Recently, a peace process and a national assembly have been established in Northern Ireland, a parliament in Scotland, and an assembly in Wales. In the postwar era, the diversity in Britain, particularly the cultural (and regional) diversity, gained new social and political importance, especially with substantial labor in-migration in a period of reconstruction.

Visible minorities, especially those of Caribbean and Indian subcontinent background, have been seen as problematic. This visible minority population is relatively small. The 1991 census put it at only 5.5% (3.1 million) of Great Britain's population of 54.9 million and 6.3% of the population in England (Owen, 1992). The 2001 census data show that this minority ethnic population had increased. It was now 4.6 million, or about 7.9% of the United Kingdom's total population of 58.8 million and to 8.0% of the population in England (Office for National Statistics, 2002). Although this population is spread across Britain, there are substantial concentrations in the conurbations. Also, the visible minority population is relatively young and accounts for about 11% of the school population. There is a great deal of diversity across and within these visible minority groups. There is also a great deal of diversity within the majority population (based on region, social class, and gender, for example). Furthermore, there are significant "invisible" ethnic minorities (that is, White minority ethnic groups), originating in Ireland, North America, continental Europe, South Africa, Australia, and New Zealand. (There is no satisfactory terminology. As a shorthand, "minority ethnic" or "visible minority" is used here to refer without differentiation to the "visible minority ethnic" population.)

Despite the great diversity, the various visible minority groups do share some interests and even similarities, such as each having a strong sense of a distinctive identity, but each aspiring to be "fully accepted as equal members" of British society (Department of Education and Science [DES], 1985, p. 760). Also, each experiences inequality and racism in various forms (DES, 1985; Figueroa, 1991, 1999; Modood et al., 1997). The notion that Britain is a racist society (Brandt, 1986) has often been misunderstood. However, there is much evidence of different forms of racism in postwar Britain, including in schools (Brown, 1984; Brown & Gay, 1985; Daniel, 1968; Fryer, 1984; Gillborn, 1995; Modood et al., 1997; Smith, 1977; Troyna & Hatcher, 1992). Much of this will emerge in what follows.

HISTORICAL DEVELOPMENT OF MULTICULTURAL AND ANTIRACIST EDUCATION

Several different policy approaches relating to education and the presence of minority ethnic people in the United Kingdom in the postwar era can be identified, although these approaches have not appeared in some neat historical order. (See, for instance, Brandt, 1986; DES, 1985; Little & Willey, 1981; Mullard, 1982; Rose et al., 1969; Troyna & Williams, 1986.) They make different assumptions about what the important issues are, their conceptualization, social and educational values, and the action required. They also entail assumptions about self and other, about Britain and who the British are, about "immigrants," and in particular about "non-White" and "White" people—in short, about identity and nation. As with any other social issue of significance, there is hardly a matter of importance concerning education for a multicultural society that is not contested. Similarly, diverse terminology has been used, with terms often having diverse meanings.

In education, the main, partly overlapping and interrelating, approaches have been laissez-faire, immigrant education, assimilationism, integrationism, multiculturalism and pluralism, Black studies, antiracism, and multicultural antiracism. Other approaches or terms partly overlapping with these are color-blind education, compensatory education, education for the disadvantaged, ethnic minority education, multiracial education, multiethnic education, intercultural education, and education for all.

Laissez-Faire

The approach during the early postwar period is often seen as laissez-faire. According to this, everyone is equal before a color-blind law, and the presence of immigrants calls for no special provisions. The British Nationality Act of 1948 conferred equal citizenship rights in the United Kingdom on citizens of the Commonwealth and colonies (Table 48.1 lists the major acts, events, and developments). All that was needed, some believed, was the proclamation of this equality (Rose et al., 1969).

Kirp (1979) typified the preferred education policy approach in this period, and even until the late 1970s, as "racial inexplicitness." There was a common belief that everything would sort itself out in time and that it was best to keep quiet about race. He thought that this inexplicitness helped the minority ethnic population: it was "doing good by doing little" (p. 53). In fact, because of unstated assumptions, for example, of cultural superiority or not recognizing relevant differences, it permitted discriminatory practices to operate unchallenged (see Troyna & Williams, 1986).

Troyna and Williams (1986) argue that "nonracialized discourse" is a better typification than "racial inexplicitness" of education policy at the time. Actually, neither of these terms or laissez-faire is entirely satisfactory. The vocabulary of the day, even in educational connections, did include racial category words such as colored. Also, immigrant was commonly used to mean "colored resident." Furthermore, a body like the Royal Commission on Population (1949) could reject increased immigration because Britain could hardly "absorb immigrants of alien race and religion" (p. 225).

Rose et al. (1969) consider that the Commonwealth Immigrants Act of 1962 and the 1965 white paper, Immigration from the Commonwealth, marked the end of the general laissez-faire period. About then, explicit education policies on immigrants began to emerge. In 1963, Sir Edward Boyle, the minister of education, rejected a "laissez faire acceptance of . . . .de facto segregation between immigrant . . . .and native schools" (House of Commons, 1963–1964, col. 439).

Assimilationism and Immigrant Education

Rose et al. (1969) define assimilation as the merging of an immigrant group into the host society, with complete loss of separate identity (see also Patterson, 1963). British assimilationist thinking tends to assume that there is a unitary British way of life, often that it is superior to anything the immigrants bring with them, and that they should adapt totally to it. Yet they may still not be accepted.

Notting Hill Anti-Black Riot, 1958. After World War I, there had been serious race riots in which White people attacked Black people and their property (Fryer, 1984; Little, 1948; Walvin, 1973). After World War II, there were similar incidents starting in 1948 (Fryer, 1984; Walvin, 1973). The worst such riots took place in Notting Hill, London, in 1958. Slogans used included "We'll kill the Blacks" (Fryer, 1984; Glass & Pollins, 1960; Hiro, 1971; Walvin, 1973). The following year Kelso Cochrane, a West Indian carpenter, was fatally stabbed in Notting Hill.

These events had a great impact, with a strong reaction from those who wanted Asian and Black immigration stopped and such people repatriated. But those, White and non-White, who stood for equality, greater harmony, and an end to discrimination also reacted strongly. Lord Justice Salmon, a Jew, told the nine White youths found guilty of assault during the Notting Hill riots: "Everyone, irrespective of the colour of their skin, is entitled to walk through our streets with their heads erect and free from fear" (Rose at al., 1969, p. 214). Self-organization among minority ethnic people increased (see Sivanandan, 1982).

Introduction of the Control of Minority Ethnic Immigration. Immigration controls were the first notable consequence of these events and of the burgeoning pressure groups opposed to Black and Asian immigration (Rose et al., 1969). The Commonwealth Immigrants Act 1962, passed by a Conservative government, was designed to control the entry into Britain of such people although they held British passports, albeit issued abroad.

This act was only the first of many that, along with various administrative arrangements including many changes to immigration rules, progressively removed existing rights from Asian and Black people and limited their immigration (Macdonald & Blake, 1991). Ironically, the 1962 act had the immediate effect of increasing immigration as many, especially from the Indian subcontinent, sought "to beat the ban." People who had come as temporary immigrants decided to settle and bring their families.

Dispersal of Immigrant Pupils. In 1963, White parents of children at two primary schools in Southall, West London, organized a protest against the presence of immigrant pupils (Rose et al., 1969). One of these schools was 60% immigrant (mainly Indians and Pakistanis). Sir Edward Boyle met the parents and later "regretfully" told

TABLE 48.1. The Historical Development of Multicultural Education in the United Kingdom.

Pluralist, Antiracist, Equitable, or Democratic Developments	Antipluralist, Racist, Anti-Immigrant, Untargeted Developments, or Disorderly Events
1215: Magna Carta.	1523: An act to regulate stranger craftsmen.
1679: The Habeas Corpus Act.	1562: English transatlantic slave trade starts.
1789: Olaudah Equiano, ex-slave, publishes autobiography as part of abolitionist campaign.	1596: Queen Elizabeth I orders deportation of "Blackamoores."
1807: Abolition of British slave trade.	1793: An Aliens Act.
1839: Committee of Council for Education formed, a step toward a state system of education in England and Wales.	1905: Aliens Act.
1889: Britain's first mosque opens.	1919: Anti-Black riots especially in Cardiff, Liverpool, and East London (where riots were also anti-Chinese).
1944: Disabled Persons (Employment) Act.	1948: Anti-Black riots in Liverpool.
1948: British Nationality Act.	1958: Anti-Black riots in Nottingham and especially Notting Hill, London.
1952: Institute of Race Relations (IRR) established.	1959: Kelso Cochrane, West Indian, fatally stabbed in Notting Hill.
1962: Association of Teachers of English to Pupils from Overseas formed, later National Association for Multiracial Education (NAME), then National Antiracist Movement in Education.	1961: Anti-Black riots in Middlesbrough.
1964: National Committee for Commonwealth Immigrants (NCCI) established.	1962: First Commonwealth Immigrants Act, restricting entry to U.K. of British citizens with passports issued abroad. Created Commonwealth Immigrants Advisory Council (CIAC).
1965: First Race Relations Act passed. Establishes Race Relations Board.	1963: Second, assimilationist, Report of CIAC.
1965: Campaign Against Racial Discrimination (CARD) founded.	1963: Ministry of Education published assimilationist English for Immigrants.
1966: Local Government Act, section 11 of which provided support for education in "immigrant" areas.	1965: Department of Education and Science Circular 7/65 states policy of dispersal.
1966: NCCI conference for educators, Towards a Multi-Racial Society.	1965: Assimilationist white paper, Immigration from the Commonwealth, published.
1967: Political and Economic Planning & Research Services report, Racial Discrimination, published.	
1967: Universal Coloured People's Association founded.	
1967: Educational Priority Areas initiated in deprived areas, including "immigrant" areas.	
1968: Runnymede Trust founded with focus on "racial" equality and justice.	1968: Enoch Powell's "rivers of blood" speech incites hostility to visible minorities.
1968: Second Race Relations Act; created Community Relations Commission.	1968: Second Commonwealth Immigrants Act restricting entry of British citizens of Asian East African origin. Incorporated "patriality" principle.

TABLE 48.1. The Historical Development of Multicultural Education in the United Kingdom. *(continued)*

Pluralist, Antiracist, Equitable, or Democratic Developments	*Antipluralist, Racist, Anti-Immigrant, Untargeted Developments, or Disorderly Events*
1968: Urban Aid Programme, providing help to deprived areas.	
1969: IRR publishes *Colour and Citizenship,* a Survey of Race Relations.	1969: Racist murder of several "Asians" in 1969–1970.
1969: Select Committee on Race Relations and Immigration (SCRRI) produces report, *The Problems of Coloured School-Leavers.*	1971: Immigration Act entrenching "patriality" and removing previous rights of "Commonwealth" immigrants.
1974: Muslim Institute established.	
1975: Sex Discrimination Act; created Equal Opportunities Commission.	1976: Gurdip Singh Chaggar, 18 years old, fatally stabbed in Southall, West London.
1976: Third Race Relations Act; set up the Commission for Racial Equality.	1979: Blair Peach, apparently killed by police during protest against National Front march in Southall.
1977: SCRRI report, *The West Indian Community,* published.	1980: "Riots" in Bristol, with mainly Black people attacking police and property.
1977: Inner London Education Authority (ILEA) policy statement on multiethnic education.	1981: British Nationality Act, defines three classes of British citizens, removing rights "Commonwealth" citizens previously held.
1981: Rampton report, *West Indian Children in Our Schools,* published.	1981: Riots in Brixton, London, and across England, mainly by Black people.
1981: Scarman report, *The Brixton Disorders,* appeared.	
1981: *Racial Disadvantage,* Home Affairs Committee report.	1985: Riots in Handsworth, Birmingham, and elsewhere, mainly by Black people.
1985: Swann report, *Education for All,* published.	1986: Racist murder of Ahmed Iqbal Ullah in a Manchester school playground.
1986: Public Order Act strengthening laws against incitement to racial hatred.	1987: Immigration (Carriers' Liability) Act, introducing fines even for unwitting carriers.
1989: Children Act including provisions for care services to heed children's religion, "race," culture, and language.	1988: Immigration Act, tightening regulations.
1989: Macdonald report, *Murder in the Playground,* on Ahmed Iqbal Ullah's killing.	1988: Salman Rushdie's *The Satanic Verses* published.
1991: Football (Offences) Act partly addressing racism in football.	1988: Education Reform Act introduces a national curriculum, neglecting multiculturalism.
1992: Education (Schools) Act, including inspection criteria on equality of opportunity.	1989: The *fatwa,* or "death sentence," issued against Salman Rushdie.
1995: Disability Discrimination Act; establishes Disability Rights Commission.	1991: Riots in Cardiff, Birmingham, Oxford, and on Tyneside, mainly by Black people.
1996: Review by Gillborn and Gipps, *Recent Research on the Achievements of Ethnic Minority Pupils,* published.	1993: Racist murder of Stephen Lawrence in Southeast London. Several "Asians" were also murdered in 1992 & 1993.
1997: *Ethnic Minorities in Britain,* the fourth national survey, by Modood et al., is published.	1993: Asylum and Immigration Appeals Act tightens regulations.
1997: Social Exclusion Unit established.	1994: Education (Initial Teacher Education and Student Unions) Act increases central control.

TABLE 48.1. The Historical Development of Multicultural Education in the United Kingdom. (*continued*)

Pluralist, Antiracist, Equitable, or Democratic Developments	*Antipluralist, Racist, Anti-Immigrant, Untargeted Developments, or Disorderly Events*
1997: Special Immigration Appeals Commission Act establishes a means of appeal in security expulsion cases.	1995: Riots by "Asian" youth in Bradford.
1998: Human Rights Act.	1996: Asylum and Immigration Act tightens regulations.
1998: Crime and Disorder Act, including measures to tackle racial violence.	1998: Schools Standard and Framework Act to raise standards but weak on multiculturalism, antiracism, and equal opportunities.
1999: Ethnic Minority Achievement Grant (EMAG) replaces section 11 of 1966 act.	1999: Restrictive Immigration and Asylum Act introduces dispersal and vouchers.
1999: Macpherson Report on Stephen Lawrence case.	2000: Terrorism Act.
1999: Guidelines issued for Citizenship Education: nonstatutory for primary schools and statutory for secondary schools (effective September 2002).	2001: Riots in Bradford, Oldham, Burnley, and Leeds mainly by "Asian" people.
2000: Race Relations (Amendment) Act.	2001: An asylum seeker fatally stabbed on Glasgow council estate.
2000: Report of the Runnymede Trust's Commission on The Future of Multi-Ethnic Britain.	2001: Anti-terrorism, Crime, and Security Act.
2001: Cantle and other reports on 2001 riots.	2002: Nationality, Immigration, and Asylum Act further tightens controls.

Note: This table is not intended to be comprehensive. See Kershaw and Pearsall (2000) on some of the earlier information.

the House of Commons that "one school . . . must be regarded now as irretrievably an immigrant school" and that he opposed such schools "in the interests of . . . racial integration." He offered his "strongest support" for local education authorities (LEAs) adopting a noncompulsory dispersal policy, asserting that on "educational grounds . . . no . . . school should have more than about 30 per cent of immigrants" (House of Commons, 1963–1964, cols. 439–442). Southall then adopted a policy of dispersal for new admissions, having appointed the first "teacher for immigrants" in 1957 (Power, 1967).

English for Immigrants. Immediately after this parliamentary debate, the first official education publication relating to immigrants in Britain, *English for Immigrants,* was published (Ministry of Education, 1963). Earlier, the Ministry of Education (1954) had asserted that English literature and language were "the central expression of English life and culture and . . . the central subject in the education of every English child" (p. 49).

English for Immigrants stressed the acquisition of English above all, and suggested separate English classes by withdrawing "immigrants" from regular classes or placing new arrivals in special classes or centers (Ministry of Education, 1963). It took an assimilationist approach,

suggesting that such temporary segregation would facilitate eventual integration. However, it cautioned against too quick a demand for conformity, recognizing that many immigrant parents did not want their children to abandon their culture (Ministry of Education, 1963). Soon various LEAs had instituted centers, itinerant teachers, or reception schools to teach English to immigrant children (see House of Commons, 1963–1964; Rose et al., 1969).

English for Immigrants highlighted the "problems" of "immigrants" and "immigrants as problems": the greater their proportion, the greater the "problem." It stated that British parents wanted reassurance "that the progress of their own children is not being impeded" (Ministry of Education, 1963, p. 10). It dismissed the notion of color prejudice in schools and suggested (incorrectly—see, for instance, Davey, 1983; Milner, 1975) that younger children are "unconscious of colour differences." However, it called for "positive steps" to help young people "not succumb . . . to . . . irrational prejudices" after leaving school (Ministry of Education, 1963, p. 11).

The Commonwealth Immigrants Advisory Council. The Commonwealth Immigrants Act of 1962 also set up the Commonwealth Immigrants Advisory Council (CIAC) to advise the home secretary on matters "affecting the welfare of Commonwealth immigrants . . . and their integration into the community" and "to examine the arrangements made by local authorities . . . to assist immigrants to adapt . . . to British habits and customs" (CIAC, 1963, p. 2).

CIAC's second report (1964) was strongly assimilationist, asserting that a national system of education "cannot be expected to perpetuate the different values of immigrant groups" (p. 5). It emphasized the "problem" of the "large number of immigrant children," giving ominous warnings of "very grave" social and educational consequences of "predominantly immigrant schools" (p. 10). It stressed the learning of English, hinting at a linguistic and cultural deficit theory to account for "educational backwardness" (p. 5). It favored dispersal, even if that meant overriding (minority ethnic) parental choice, since segregation was to be avoided "at all costs" (p. 1). Yet it stated that Britain was "becoming a multi-racial society," consisting of "individuals with equal rights," and saw no problem with the segregation resulting from separate reception centers and classes (p. 3).

Twin Policies of "Immigration" Controls and "Integration." In 1965, the new Labour government passed the first Race Relations Act against racial discrimination in public places and against "incitement to racial hatred." This act also established a Race Relations Board to oversee the implementation of the law. Like the act, this board was weak. Simultaneously, the government pursued policies very similar to those of its predecessor: dispersal, English for immigrants, and limitation of Black and Asian immigration.

The policy of dispersal was stated officially in Circular 7/65 by the Department of Education and Science (DES) (1965), the successor to the Ministry of Education, and in a white paper incorporating Circular 7/65 and repeating the earlier concerns (Prime Minister, 1965). The only italicized sentence stressed that "*parents of non-immigrant children*" should see that "*the progress of their own children is not being restricted,*" although there was no evidence that it was (DES, 1965, p. 5). Race, color, prejudice, racism, and discrimination were not mentioned, but everyone knew that "immigrant" meant "non-White." About half of the white paper dealt with immigration and more stringent immigration controls. The rest was preoccupied with an assimilationist approach to "problems" in "housing, education, employment and health" (Prime Minister, 1965, p. 10).

Assimilationist views were also common among LEAs. Some education officers used stereotypes and racialized language. But there were divergent views too, accepting pluralism (see Power, 1967). According to Power, Circular 7/65 encouraged "less inhibited discussion and more

constructive local policies than . . . hitherto" (p. 7). But Rose et al. (1969) stated that the "dispersal proposals . . . tended to reinforce popular views about the danger of English children being held back" (p. 270).

The National Committee for Commonwealth Immigrants (NCCI), created in 1964, absorbed CIAC in 1965. It backed a stronger Race Relations Act, sponsoring a national survey with the Race Relations Board. Carried out by Political and Economic Planning (PEP) and Research Services, this survey demonstrated the widespread existence of color discrimination and boosted the case for a stronger Race Relations Act (NCCI, n.d., ca. 1967; PEP & Research Services, 1967; Taylor, 1974).

In 1966, Labour, having "established its restrictionist *bona fides* with the voters" through the 1965 white paper, won a landslide victory at new general elections (Hiro, 1971, p. 221). The Local Government Act 1966 was passed. Section 11 provided support for staffing in "immigrant" areas for the teaching of English language and, later, "community languages," and even for general multicultural education.

Integrationism and Immigrant Education

In 1966, Roy Jenkins, then home secretary, gave his famous definition of integration. He described immigration "not as a flattening process of assimilation but as equal opportunity, accompanied by cultural diversity, in an atmosphere of mutual tolerance" (Jenkins, 1966). Many commentators have seen this as marking a shift from assimilationism to integrationism, in which minority cultures were given some recognition and respect, with "integration" meaning that the "incoming" group, although adapting in important ways, was able to retain some distinctiveness (see Patterson, 1963). As Mullard (1982) has argued, however, the ideological and practical differences between assimilationism and integrationism (and indeed pluralism) were not great (see also Brandt, 1986). The onus of adaptation remained with the immigrants, with British culture and society being seen as superior and as retaining dominance.

From the early 1960s, courses, workshops, and seminars for teachers of immigrant children began to appear (see Power, 1967; Rose et al., 1969). The Association of Teachers of English to Pupils from Overseas, founded in 1962, was active in this field. It became the National Association for Multiracial Education (NAME) in 1973 and the National Antiracist Movement in Education in 1985. This last change caused a virtually fatal split.

An NCCI conference for educators in 1966 focused on integration and on exposing the "mythology of race" so as to promote equality (NCCI, n.d., ca. 1966, p. 5). The conference report (NCCI, n.d., ca. 1966) showed that assimilationism was not universally accepted: multiculturalism and even antiracism were stirring. However, immigrant children as a "problem" and English language as a priority remained salient.

At this conference, Philip Mason, director of the Institute of Race Relations (IRR), set up in 1952 with a mainly international rather than British focus, stated that everyone "must belong to some race" (NCCI, n.d., ca. 1966, p. 7). Yet, "race" is a highly problematic concept (Miles, 1982), being simultaneously an ideological construct, a product of racist thinking, and a social reality produced, defined, and reproduced by racist social forces (see Figueroa, 1991; Miles, 1982).

Also at this conference, Kenneth Little, the doyen of studies in race relations in Britain, found little difference "in the treatment of coloured people in Britain today and some 200 years ago" (NCCI, n.d., ca. 1966, p. 26). He called for the presentation of the total culture of other peoples, not just of the bizarre. Dipak Nandy, executive member of the Campaign Against Racial Discrimination (CARD), pointed beyond personal racism without using the concept of institutional racism. He spoke of "systematic, impersonal patterns of discrimination," arguing that the "problem" may not be one "which would disappear if only people were kinder to each other." "Race relations" was not an "immigrant problem," he added, and "the native community" needed educating at least as much as "the immigrant community" did (NCCI, n.d., ca. 1966, pp. 32–33). However, around the same time, the Schools Council (established in 1964) was taking an assimilationist approach, rejecting bilingualism and stressing the teaching of English for "cultural and social assimilation" (1967, p. 4).

Multicultural Education

The developments in multicultural, and later antiracist, education came more from the bottom than the top, through the efforts of both White and non-White people. Factors stimulating action included the shock of the 1958 riots; the shift in status among the visible minorities from immigrants to settlers, which the Commonwealth Immigrants Act 1962 hastened; the dissatisfaction especially of Afro-Caribbean people with the education of their children; and the negative messages from control of immigration. Also, visits by American civil rights leaders made an impact: Martin Luther King, Jr., in 1964, Malcolm X (especially important) in 1965, and Stokely Carmichael in 1967. The findings of extensive discrimination (PEP & Research Services, 1967) also sparked Black power supporters, who formed the Universal Coloured People's Association in 1967.

The movements from below among the visible minorities included supplementary schools; representations, demonstrations, and agitation; and action through various bodies, such as CARD, NAME, the Commission for Racial Equality (CRE), the IRR, and the Runnymede Trust (see Sivanandan, 1982). Research and publications by minority ethnic scholars also played an important role. (The list of such works is extensive and includes Hill, 1967; Figueroa & McNeal, 1969; Figueroa, 1991; John, 1970; Coard, 1971; Hiro, 1971; Verma & Bagley, 1975, 1993a, 1993b; Hall, 1978, 1992; Hall, Critcher, Jefferson, Clarke, & Roberts, 1978; Nandy, 1981; Stone, 1981; Sivanandan, 1982; Mullard, 1984; Brandt, 1986; Parekh, 1986; Wright, 1986; Gilroy, 1987; Duncan, 1989; Mirza, 1992; Modood et al., 1997; Sewell, 1997; Osler, 1997; Osler & Morrison, 2000; Osler & Starkey, 2000; Blair et al., 1998; Blair, 2001; Bhavnani, 2001.)

Significant Events. An Inner London Education Authority (ILEA) report (1967) showed that Afro-Caribbean children were overrepresented in schools for the "educationally subnormal" (ESN). Another very influential ILEA study (1968) concluded, despite methodological problems, that "minority" groups, especially Afro-Caribbean children, were "underachieving" (see Figueroa, 1991).

Rose et al. (1969) stated that at first it was "not uncommon" (p. 285) for all immigrant pupils to be placed with the remedial teacher. Coard (1971) argued that West Indian children were being *made* educationally subnormal in the British educational system. Subsequently, Tomlinson (1982) provided some evidence supporting this view. As Craft (1986) says, the assimilationist thinking of the 1950s and early 1960s meant that there was a tendency to disregard linguistic and "cultural differences in the ability testing of immigrant pupils" (p. 80), who were thus often misplaced. The minority ethnic community responded by campaigning on the political and social front, setting up supplementary schools (Brandt, 1986; Tomlinson, 1983), and calling for action in state schools, such as the teaching of Black studies (see Taylor, 1974).

A development that "severely" shook the "immigrant" communities and organizations (Rose et al., 1969, p. 619) and increased their protests was the passing in record time of the racist Commonwealth Immigrants Act 1968 to keep out Kenyan "Asians," who were actually British citizens with British passports. Jo Grimond, leader of the Liberal Party, condemned this measure as being directed purely against "coloured people" (cited by Rose et al., 1969, p. 614).

Also about this time, Sandys and Powell, senior Conservative members of Parliament, were making racist comments or speeches, but the attorney general refused to charge them under the Race Relations Act 1965. Apart from Colin Jordan, a leader of the fascist British National Socialists, the only convictions on incitement to racial hatred between 1965 and 1976 were, ironically, of minority ethnic people (Macdonald, 1977).

Yet in 1969, the many recommendations of the influential report of the Survey of Race Relations (sponsored by the IRR and funded by the Nuffield Foundation) gave little attention to such matters. The focus remained on disadvantage and deprivation, the culture of immigrant communities, immigrant education, the teaching of English, compensatory education, and "adjustment to . . . an alien culture" (Rose et al., 1969, p. 698). A recommendation on student teachers being instructed "about inheritance, cultural variation, and the sources of prejudice" (p. 702) did not mention racism.

Select Committee on Race Relations and Immigration, 1969. Partly through the influence of CARD (1965–1967), the NCCI, and the report by PEP and Research Services (1967), a much wider, though still weak, Race Relations Act was passed in 1968. This act replaced the NCCI with the Community Relations Commission (CRC) to coordinate the policy on race relations and to promote "harmonious community relations between Commonwealth immigrants and the host population" (Taylor, 1974, p. 19).

In November 1968, a parliamentary Select Committee on Race Relations and Immigration (SCRRI) was established to review policies on immigration and the expanded Race Relations Act. It took evidence, and the Caribbean and "Asian" communities made representations to it. J. Crawford, active in the Caribbean community, told the committee that basically there was "no immigrant problem in schools," but there was a "white problem"—"hostility and . . . overt racialism" against Black people, in school and beyond (SCRRI, 1969c, p. 1017).

By contrast, the written evidence of the DES (SCRRI, 1969a, pp. 150–152) focused on "problems" "caused" by the "concentration" of "immigrants" in certain areas and on lack of English or its "limited or defective" nature. This DES evidence included circulars 7/65 and 8/67. The latter emphasized "integration," counterposed to "segregation." The DES referred to courses in colleges of education concerning "the problem of a multi-cultural society" (SCRRI, 1969a, p. 169). One of the earliest uses of the term *multicultural* by the DES, this focused on the education of immigrants, seeing foreign cultural traditions as a handicap. Although the DES denied the aim of assimilation, it sought to further the immigrants' integration into "an alien society by assisting them to take full advantage of our system of education" (p. 152). There was no hint that any adjustment on the part of the system might be desirable.

Sir Herbert Andrew, permanent under secretary of state, DES, rejected prejudice reduction and race relations as the job of schools (SCRRI, 1969c, p. 1180). Although he accepted that "any colour discrimination" by an LEA would constitute a contravention of the 1968 Race Relations Act, he clearly did not think that the DES needed to have any specific policy or strategy for this (SCRRI, 1969c). He asserted, incorrectly, that "problems of discrimination and of social tension . . . do not arise within schools or colleges, and the educational system could do nothing about such problems in the wider society" (p. 1194). He seemed to blame the immigrants, not the system, for any "difficulties." These had to do with English-language competence, little "familiarity with English [sic] culture, social customs," and living in "run-down areas" (SCRRI, 1969c, pp. 1193–1194). "Colour" was not a problem, and once the children received all of their education in Britain, there would be "no problem at all" (p. 1194).

In its report, SCRRI (1969d) focused on the "problems" of immigrants and made the usual points about deprivation, culture shock, the need for English, and the need for immigrants to learn English customs. But SCRRI also acknowledged the bias of normal IQ tests and stated that schools "should prepare all their children for adult life in a multi-racial society" (p. 41). All school leavers should be taught "the main features of race relations," and all children could be given a "better understanding of the national and cultural background of immigrants" (p. 41). A fundamental need was to recognize the "bitterness of coloured [sic] prejudice" and that "the main obligation for improving race relations rests with the indigenous [sic] people" of Britain (p. 20).

Here, then, is a shift from immigrant education to a broader focus incorporating something of multicultural education, and perhaps even of antiracism. Unfortunately, however, in seeking bridges "between cultures and communities," the committee mentioned only "West Indian songs, or . . . Indian art, jewelry and costumes" (SCRRI, 1969d, pp. 40–42). Besides, racism was conceptualized in the limited, individual sense of "colour prejudice."

Other Developments. A 1968 survey found that attention was being given to the education of children from immigrant communities, but much less to teaching in a multicultural society generally (Millins, 1970). Hence the CRC and the Association of Teachers in Colleges and Departments of Education (ATCDE) produced in 1974 a report, *Teacher Education for a Multi-cultural Society.* It considered that the ethnocentric curriculum was "dangerously inappropriate" (CRC & ATCDE, 1974, pp. 9–10, 44). Student teachers needed to confront the issues of prejudice and institutional discrimination, as well as those of low performance and English as a second language (pp. 10–14). Unfortunately, even today, teacher education has still hardly addressed such issues (see also Siraj-Blatchford, 1990).

A 1975 CRC study in eight urban multiracial areas found that none of the LEAs had made a comprehensive review of its services focusing on "the needs of a multi-racial area" (Wallis, 1977, p. 43). The policy makers in these LEAs stressed English as a second language, integration, and equality of opportunity and tended not to see mother tongue and minority cultures as school matters (Wallis, 1977).

The teachers too saw English language as "the major priority" but mentioned a "wider range of issues" (p. 42): minority underachievement, identity difficulties, and difficulties after leaving school, including racial discrimination. They also tended not to see "the preservation of minority cultures" (p. 43) as a matter for schools. A minority of teachers were "hostile to ethnic minorities" (p. 45). Several teachers thought prejudice and discrimination rare in schools and that it was best not to draw attention to such (difficult) issues.

The majority of parents were generally satisfied. A minority "considered the teachers to be racially biased or unsympathetic to their children" (Wallis, 1977, p. 45). There was quite a strong demand for minority ethnic teachers, and some Asian parents wanted instruction in their own religions and languages.

The notion of multicultural education gained prominence in the 1970s through conferences, research, publications, and the media, despite the DES (CRC, 1971; Milner, 1975; Taylor, 1974; Twitchin, 1978; Verma & Bagley, 1975). A 1972 Schools Council pamphlet distinguished between the needs in multiracial classrooms and the needs of all children in all schools to help them understand that Britain had become a multiracial and multicultural society. A notable Schools Council project at the time was the Humanities Curriculum Project (1967–1972). It proposed a "neutral chair" procedure for the teacher in dealing with controversial issues such as race (Stenhouse, 1975).

In 1972, Sivanandan, IRR's long-serving librarian became its director through a palace revolution (Sivanandan, 1974). Since then the IRR has promoted antiracism from a socialist position.

Follow-Up to the SCRRI Report of 1969. After the SCRRI inquiry, the DES commissioned the National Foundation for Educational Research (NFER) to investigate the "educational arrangements for schools with immigrant pupils" (Townsend, 1971, p. 15). It was found that almost half of the LEAs in England had made some special arrangements, mainly for the teaching of English. The focus on "deprivation" and compensatory education continued (p. 10). Secondary schools often, but primary schools seldom, included some treatment of race relations (Townsend & Brittan, 1972). Culture-bound measures of ability and attainment were being inappropriately used. Also, some head teachers declared that one should

"let . . . sleeping dogs lie" (p. 111)—in other words, do nothing.

Furthermore, Her Majesty's Inspectorate (HMI) carried out a "pilot survey . . . into current practice and opinion concerning the educational assessment of pupils from overseas" (DES, 1971b, p. 1). The DES also produced a survey of the "education of immigrants" (DES, 1971a) and another "pilot study" of secondary school "immigrant pupils" (DES, 1972). In these studies, the foci were still the education of "immigrants," their "disabilities" and "problems," and the teaching of English.

The DES (1971a), however, acknowledged that teachers were "no less prone than anyone else to feelings of prejudice or even acts of discrimination," but explained this through lack of knowledge of the pupils' backgrounds and "bewilderment . . . at not knowing how to set about . . . teaching these pupils" (p. 11). This report also provided a rather rosy view of children of "different ethnic groups and cultural backgrounds" living "together happily," and an image of "immigrants" integrated as equals into a "cohesive, multi-cultural society," and permitted "the expression of differences of attitudes, beliefs and customs, language and culture . . . which may eventually enrich the main stream of our cultural and social tradition" (pp. 119–120). In discussing the substantial over-representation of immigrant pupils, mainly African Caribbean, in ESN schools, this report continued to insist, without providing any evidence, that there are "some immigrant children who are too disadvantaged educationally to prosper in . . . ordinary classes. They need special arrangements . . . where they do not displace native born children" (pp. 68–69).

The SCRRI Report of 1973. This SCRRI report was critical of the DES, but itself focused mainly on the education of immigrants, English as a second language, and what it referred to as "handicaps" (SCRRI, 1973, p. 4). However, it acknowledged that the term *immigrant* was unsatisfactory and recommended phasing it out. Besides, it quoted the National Union of Teachers (NUT) as calling for "education directed towards the needs of a multiracial society" and not simply towards educating "immigrants" for assimilation (SCRRI, 1973, p. 21).

Noting "no consensus about the future nature of the multiracial society," the committee saw "the first task for schools as equipping their pupils with awareness of an increasingly diverse society" so that they could "develop their own attitudes" to it (p. 25). It agreed that "the history, geography and cultures of the . . . minorities . . . are worthy of study . . . not least by indigenous children" (p. 28), but rejected the notion of "black studies." It accepted "unity through diversity," not "through uniformity" (p. 28). But DES thinking remained within the perspectives of the "problems of immigrants" and "educational disadvantage" (DES, 1974, p. 5).

Schools Council on Education for a Multiracial Society.
Between 1973 and 1976, the Schools Council funded research in primary and secondary schools on education for a multiracial society. This study found that a majority of head teachers agreed that schools should prepare pupils for life in a multiracial society. Nevertheless, a large proportion of schools did little about this, many not regarding it as part of their job (Townsend & Brittan, 1973).

A 1981 Schools Council report produced from this study referred to the then current notion of a continuum from assimilationism to pluralism. Rejecting assimilationism, and speaking of "racial minorities" or "minority ethnic groups" instead of "immigrants," this report took a pluralist stance, according to which "minority cultures retain their essential identities and stand in a relationship of equality and mutual respect to the cultural mainstream" (Schools Council, 1981, p. 15). The objectives of multiracial education included knowledge of "the main cultures . . . in Britain," acceptance of "the principles of equal rights and justice," recognition "that prejudice and discrimination are widespread in Britain" and are damaging to "the rejected group," acknowledgment of "the possibility of developing multiple loyalties," and the development of "a positive self-image," mother-tongue skills, and English language skills (pp. 16–17). Nevertheless, the assumptions seemed to persist that minority cultures were problematic and that the mainstream would remain essentially unchanged. Furthermore, the report addressed racism cautiously in terms of prejudice and stereotypes. A more direct and vivid section of five chapters on racism by the project team was vetoed.

Immigration Control. Meanwhile, central government policy on immigration was still, and increasingly, control oriented. The wide-ranging Immigration Act 1971 was passed by a Conservative government to "rationalize" the laws governing Commonwealth immigrants and aliens and in preparation for joining the European Economic Community. This law put on a permanent basis and expanded the provisions of the Commonwealth Immigrants Act 1962, which had required annual renewal. It incorporated and refined the principle of "patriality," which means an "ancestral connection," originally through the father or father's father, to the U.K. This principle had been introduced into the Commonwealth Immigrants Act 1968 to permit the entry of "patrial" (White) noncitizens, while excluding "non-White" people ("nonpatrials") holding British passports issued abroad. This is racially discriminatory (Macdonald & Blake, 1991). It

was also in the implementation of this act that the inexcusable vaginal examination of Asian women entering Britain to marry was introduced as part of immigration controls to confirm their virginity.

The reaction of the minority ethnic communities and their sympathizers to the 1971 law was one of horror and increased militancy. The chairperson of the CRC, no radical, stated that this law would "adversely affect the establishment of harmonious community relations" and "acutely increase the insecurity which coloured people . . . already feel" (CRC, 1971, p. 43). As Fryer (1984) states, even before this bill was introduced, many "Asians and West Indians . . . went in daily fear of their lives" (p. 385). The visible minorities have always found that, far from facilitating integration, tightening "immigration" controls encourages racism.

The policy of strict immigration controls continued, and 10 years later, the British Nationality Act 1981, another racist law (Macdonald & Blake, 1991), was passed by a Conservative government. This major act essentially retained the principle of patriality, further refining it. It divided British nationality into three categories, British overseas citizens, British dependent territories citizens, and British citizens, the last being the only category to have freedom of entry to and the right of abode in the U.K., rights previously enjoyed by people covered by the other two categories as well. Over the years, in particular since the 1962 act, the rights of such people, mainly Black and Asian, have been progressively removed. Yet such rights have not been taken away from the major source of immigrants, the White citizens of the Irish Republic, or from patrial (mainly White) citizens of independent Commonwealth countries, although birth in the U.K. no longer guarantees a right to British citizenship. Furthermore, British overseas citizens, largely non-White people, could find themselves in effect stateless. The Conservative government's Immigration Act 1988 introduced even tougher regulations, and the Labour government has followed suit more recently.

Equal Opportunities Legislation. A Labour government was returned (with a very small majority) in 1974, and equal opportunities became prominent on the agenda. The Sex Discrimination Act 1975 was passed, which created the Equal Opportunities Commission (gender). In 1976, a much-strengthened Race Relations Act was passed, outlawing, in a wide range of spheres, including education, both direct and indirect discrimination on grounds of race, color, nationality, citizenship, and ethnic or national origins. This act also set up the Commission for Racial Equality (CRE) to take over the functions of the Race Relations Board and the CRC. However, the state, including the police, was largely exempt from the provisions of this act, and its implementation arrangements remained relatively weak. The Conservative government's Public Order Act 1986 remedied some of the defects of previous laws against incitement to racial hatred, while its Football (Offences) Act 1991 addressed racism in football (that is, soccer). It was not until 1995 that the Disability Discrimination Act was passed. Although somewhat comparable to the legislation against gender and race discrimination, this act is weaker.

Recommendation of the SCRRI Report of 1977 for Committee of Inquiry. SCRRI (1977) in its report, *The West Indian Community*, eventually recommended "as a matter of urgency" that the government establish an inquiry "into the causes of the underachievement of children of West Indian origin" (vol. 1, p. xx, paragraph 57). At about the same time, a government consultative paper (DES, 1977) was asserting, finally, that the curriculum should be multicultural. Although the government still stressed the learning of English and compensating for "difficulties" facing immigrants, it stated too that in its content, values, and assumptions, the curriculum "must reflect the wide range of cultures, histories and lifestyles in our multiracial society" (Home Office, 1978, p. 6). It saw "racial disadvantage" as caused partly by "cultural difference" but largely by "the complex and pervasive nature of racial discrimination" (p. 4).

The Labour government (Home Office, 1978) welcomed the report of 1977. Committing itself to racial equality and equal opportunities in education and speaking of "ethnic minorities," not "immigrants," it established an inquiry in 1979, chaired by Anthony Rampton. The wide brief encompassed "the needs of all pupils for education for life in a multi-racial society" (Home Office, 1978, p. 7). Thus, the agitation of the Caribbean community in the 1960s and 1970s about their children's education had had some effect (DES, 1985). Although the Conservatives under Margaret Thatcher won a landslide victory later in 1979, the inquiry proceeded, producing an interim report in 1981. Rampton resigned amid controversy, and Lord Swann was appointed as the new chairperson, the final report appearing in 1985.

Policy Developments and Debates. The first LEA policy statement on multiethnic education was produced by the ILEA (1977) shortly after the 1976 Race Relations Act was passed, largely in response to the concerns of the ethnic minorities, especially the African Caribbeans, about the education of their children. Until then, the ILEA had been largely assimilationist, stressing the acquisition of English and seeing the immigrants' situation simply as one of disadvantage (see Troyna & Williams, 1986). The

new policy statement focused on the particular cultural backgrounds of the underachieving groups so as to improve their performance (Troyna & Williams, 1986). By contrast, a 1980 multicultural education policy statement from Manchester was more concerned with promoting understanding and acceptance of cultural differences among all students (see Troyna & Williams, 1986). Teaching unions also produced policy statements and guidance on multicultural education or even on addressing racism (NUT, 1978).

In 1978, the BBC televised extracts from five lectures on race and racism in what it referred to as "multiracial" Britain (Twitchin, 1978). In one of these, Alan Little identified two sets of issues: (1) the "majority" versus the "minorities" and (2) the "special educational needs" of the "minorities." But he wanted to eradicate the notions of "minorities," and especially of "immigrants" (Little, 1978, pp. 56, 57). Among other things, he highlighted "racial hostility . . . and . . . prejudice" in school and beyond (pp. 58–64).

However, in 1981, in the middle of a summer of race riots, the DES (1981a) was blandly stating that schools must "reflect" the "multicultural" nature of "our society." The House of Commons Home Affairs Committee (which had replaced the SCRRI) was sharply critical of the DES for inaction and for not separating out "multiracial education" concerns from "the whole range of educational disadvantage arising from social deprivation" (Home Affairs Committee, 1981, p. xx). It also stated that "the fraught relationship between the police and young blacks had its . . . origins in . . . social and economic disadvantage," especially disadvantage "in education and employment" (pp. vii, liv). However, it stressed that discrimination, although very important, was "possibly not the prime factor," and racism was not "a sufficient explanation" of minority ethnic "educational problems" (pp. xiv, liv, lv). None of its recommendations for education addressed racism specifically. They focused instead on promoting "multicultural education" and targeting the "problems" of "ethnic minorities." The committee reiterated the importance of (English) "language training" (but not mother-tongue teaching in schools) and made the usual error of stating that "West Indian" children "have no ready-made culture of their own," presumably because Caribbean cultures are closer to British ones than are Asian cultures (pp. xvi, lv).

Thatcher's government took no action. Protesting that it was "wholly committed to a multiracial society in which there is full equality of opportunity irrespective of colour, race or religion," the government simply asserted the general thesis that "the creation of a stronger and more prosperous economy where new real jobs are created . . . and unemployment falls . . . is the most potent means of combatting . . . racial disadvantage" (Home Office, 1982, pp. 3, 6).

Lynch (1983) argued for multicultural education, understood as an "initiation of children into critical-rational acceptance of cultural diversity" (p. 15) and as a challenging of bias, stereotyping, and discrimination. The basic principle was "respect for persons" or "mutuality" (Lynch, 1983, 1986). Lynch (1987) later emphasized "prejudice reduction" and a whole school approach, including multiethnic staffing, and an explicit statement that "racist, sexist and credist behaviour is totally unacceptable" (p. 72; see Lynch, 1986). However, he saw racism primarily as an individual phenomenon. He also tended, like Craft (1984), to highlight the supposed "dilemma" of cohesion versus diversity. But it is too simple to pose a stark dichotomy between cultural diversity and social cohesion, to stress diversity as the cause of fragmentation and conflict or to see conflict as necessarily negative.

1981. As Craft (1984) has observed, the year 1981 was significant for the development of multicultural (and antiracist) education. Several important publications appeared, some of which have already been referred to. In April 1981, Brixton ablaze was flashed across the nation's television screens as "a few hundred young people—most . . . black—attacked the police on the streets" of South London (Home Office, 1981a, p. 1). Similar disturbances took place throughout the country that summer, notably in Toxteth (Liverpool). Another "race riot" had taken place one year earlier in Bristol. One year before that, Blair Peach had been killed, apparently "from a blow to the head . . . by a police officer with an unauthorized . . . weapon" (Unofficial Committee of Enquiry, 1980, p. 86), during a confrontation between the police and protesters against a National Front meeting in Southall, West London. There have been many other "race riots" over the years: in 1985 in Handsworth (Birmingham); in 1991 in Cardiff, Birmingham, Oxford, and on Tyneside; in 1995 in Bradford; and in 2001 in northern towns, the last two involving mainly Asian youth.

From October 1981, television screens also carried a BBC series on multicultural education (see Twitchin & Demuth, 1985), understood as meeting "special needs," especially for English as a second language; bringing minority cultures into the classroom and supporting self-esteem; providing a "global perspective" for all children; and contributing "to good race relations" (pp. 6, 7). However, up to the early 1980s at least, there was still a wide gap between rhetoric and educational practice, as documented by a Schools Council study in all LEAs (Little & Willey, 1981; Willey, 1984b). Most LEAs with few minority ethnic students did not see multicultural education as a concern of theirs. Most other LEAs focused on English

as a second language (Little & Willey, 1981). Eggleston, Dunn, and Purewal (1981) found in-service teacher education similarly wanting.

Of the many publications in 1981, however, probably the two most significant were the Rampton (DES, 1981b) and Scarman (Home Office, 1981a) reports. Scarman, charged with inquiring into the Brixton riot, identified "racialism and discrimination against black people—often hidden, sometimes unconscious" as "a major source of social tension and conflict" (Home Office, 1981a, p. 110). This contributed to "racial disadvantage," including housing shortages and unemployment, which, along with oppressive policing, was a significant cause of the "Brixton disorders." Scarman asserted, however, that "institutional racism" did "not exist in Britain" (Home Office, 1981a, p. 135). Besides, almost all of his recommendations on education focused on ethnic minority education, including the usual stress on English language. Moreover, action on his recommendations was disappointing (see Solomos, 1986).

The Rampton and Swann Reports. The Rampton report (DES, 1981b) concentrated on the "academic underachievement" of West Indian children, but within the context of "the education of *all* children," the issues being "relevant to *every school* and *every teacher*" (pp. 4, 5). This report concluded that "West Indian children as a group are failing in our education system" (DES, 1981b, p. 70), the causes being complex, but "racism, both intentional and unintentional," being one of the important factors (p. 12). Rampton was critical of the "lack of leadership" of the DES and of its subsuming "ethnic minority" children's needs under "educational disadvantage" (p. 73). The report recommended a "multi-cultural approach throughout education" (p. 79) and that all LEAs should designate a multicultural education adviser. It called on "teachers to play a leading role . . . to bring about a change in attitudes . . . towards ethnic minority groups" (pp. 14, 78). But despite this report's highlighting racism, not one of its many recommendations referred specifically to racism. It paid particular attention to (English) language, special education, and disruptive units. Four years later, the Swann report (DES, 1985) lamented that the only recommendation to which the DES had made a formal response concerned "the collection of educational statistics on an ethnic basis" (p. 218).

The Swann report (DES, 1985) itself traced developments through the phases of assimilation, integration, and multicultural education, plus some demands for antiracist education. Swann observed that multicultural education had not been clearly defined, in practice had targeted ethnic minorities primarily, and made an impact only in multiethnic schools.

Swann argued for a pluralist approach, with the basic principle of "diversity within unity" (DES, 1985). The report propounded "education for all." This meant "educating all children" to understand "the shared values" of the society; to appreciate and respect cultural diversity and "the multi-racial nature of society, free from . . . inaccurate myths and stereotypes"; to be committed to "the principles of equality and justice"; to have "confidence in their own cultural identities"; and to realize their full potential (pp. 226, 316, 320, 321, 323). Education must cater to all individual educational needs, including any particular minority ethnic needs.

Furthermore, "the major obstacle" to the "pluralist society" was racism, that is, "individual attitudes and behaviour" and the "more pervasive 'climate' of racism," including "institutional policies and practices" (DES, 1985, pp. 8, 36). Hence, a good education must combat racism and remove "those practices and procedures" in the educational system that "work, directly or indirectly, and intentionally or unintentionally, against pupils from any ethnic group" (p. 320). Swann also advocated political education.

The report itself is obviously a compromise document. The politics of the whole undertaking was extremely complex, reflecting social realities. Not surprisingly, then, there is a deep ambiguity within the text. Rhetorically, it is pluralist, but with a deep undercurrent of conformity. Also, despite the references to "institutional racism," its conception of racism is primarily the limited one of individual attitudes, stereotypes, and ignorance.

The report, however, contained many rich appendixes. Also, several major publications appeared in conjunction with it, including four substantial reviews of research into the education of minority ethnic pupils (Taylor, 1981, 1987, 1988; Taylor & Hegarty, 1985). Unfortunately, there was no comparable review of the education of White pupils for a multicultural and antiracist society. Another linked publication, based on research funded by the DES, was *Education for Some* (Eggleston, Dunn, Anjali, & Wright, 1986), which revealed "pervasive racism at both institutional and personal levels" (Klein, 1993, p. 71), including "complex processes . . . which can disadvantage black young people and . . . particularly those of Afro-Caribbean origin" (Wright, 1986, p. 178).

The inquiry was a major event that stimulated much evidence and discussion before and after the publication of the report. Whereas very few LEAs had multicultural or antiracist policies in the early 1980s, by the end of the decade, 80 of 115 had adopted such policies, including many LEAs without a large minority ethnic population. Although the Conservative government accepted few of the many recommendations, limited funds were provided for various projects, including the in-service training of teachers.

Antiracist Education

There were many critics, from left and right, of multiculturalism, variously understood (Banks, 1984). Many antiracists were among its most vigorous critics. The Institute of Race Relations (IRR) (1980), in its submission on "anti-racist not multicultural education" to the Swann committee, argued sharply that "an ethnic or cultural approach to the educational needs . . . of racial minorities evades the fundamental reasons for their disabilities . . . the racialist attitudes and the racist practices in the larger society and in the educational system itself" (p. 82). According to Sivanandan (1982), antiracism grew out of the "Black" experience. Mullard (1984) holds with some justification that antiracist education had always been present but emerged formally in the early 1960s in reaction to the racism of immigrant education and "within the framework of the Black Consciousness Movement" (p. 24). It had its "efflorescence" in the early 1980s as a "largely 'black' response to the ethnicism of multicultural education" (p. 12), ethnicism being a culturalist, perhaps covert, form of racism. The antiracist education perspective gained legitimacy partly through the SCRRI, Scarman, Rampton, and Swann inquiries, which were all influenced by the evidence of the minority ethnic community.

Antiracist Thinking and Local Policy Statements. Quintin Kynaston Comprehensive School in London provides an early example of an antiracist school policy, adopted in 1980. Also, in 1980, Bradford became the first LEA to run an in-service racism awareness workshop for teachers (Twitchin & Demuth, 1985). Twitchin and Demuth, in discussing this workshop, identified individual, cultural, and institutional racism and provided ideas for exercises to raise awareness. They stressed that "racism is not just a matter of overt colour prejudice and discriminatory attitudes," but also of "racial disadvantage [and] . . . unwitting racist attitudes . . . embedded in our language and culture; and . . . institutionalised racism" (p. 7).

Neither the ILEA nor the Manchester policy statement mentioned above referred explicitly to racism, but by 1979, the ILEA had added a section on "teaching against racism," and Manchester started developing an antiracist policy after 1981 (Troyna & Williams, 1986). In 1982, a pack for teachers published by Birmingham LEA stated that a "subtle but endemic racism . . . permeates our society and . . . culture," and "white racism is a white problem" (Rudell & Simpson, 1982, quoted by Hatcher & Shallice, 1983, p. 3). In 1983, the ILEA and the NUT published antiracist guidelines.

A 1982 Berkshire policy document called for an emphasis on "equality and justice, and combating racism" rather than on "diversity and pluralism" (Advisory Committee for Multicultural Education, 1982, pp. 5, 8). It identified three main perspectives in "race relations and education." These emphasized respectively:

1. Integration of a problematic "Black" community
2. Cultural diversity, with racism seen merely as "a set of mental prejudices"
3. Equality and the "pervasive influence of racism," understood as a "combination of discriminatory practices, unequal relations and structures of power, and negative beliefs and attitudes" (pp. 7, 9).

This third perspective, which the document endorsed, was "not indifferent to cultural differences and diversity" (p. 8). In 1983, the Berkshire Education Committee formally adopted a policy on education for "racial equality and justice" and opposed to "racism in all its forms" (Royal County of Berkshire LEA, 1983, reproduced in DES, 1985, pp. 366–370).

Mullard's Analysis of Antiracist Education. One of the most influential statements on antiracist education was made by Mullard in 1984 at the NAME annual conference. Mullard (1984) identified four main dominant "racial" forms of education—immigrant (1950s and 1960s), multiracial (1960s and early 1970s), multiethnic (late 1970s), and multicultural (late 1970s and 1980s)—and one dominated "racial" form: antiracist education. The four dominant forms were all racist, the first two focusing on race as a structural phenomenon and the last two focusing on race as a cultural phenomenon. Immigrant education was assimilationist, multiracial education was integrationist; multiethnic and multicultural education were pluralist. The object of antiracist education was justice, a restructured structural-cultural order, for it focused on both structure and culture. Antiracist education was thus "a struggle against racism [and ethnicism] in education in which the specific-educational relations of social liberation and change as opposed to . . . control are . . . developed" (p. 38). Antiracist and multicultural education were "currently oppositional and antagonistic forms" (p. 12).

Many other antiracists besides Mullard, such as Brandt (1986), also argued the incompatibility of multicultural and antiracist education. They tended to see multicultural education as a containing reaction by White society and the White educational system to the Black struggle against racism and inequality. It was a "cooling-out" process (Stone, 1981). Grinter (1990, 1992), abandoning an earlier position, maintained that multicultural and antiracist education were "incompatible philosophies" (1992, p. 95). Multicultural education believed in the assimilation of the various cultures into a "social consensus with

shared values" (p. 101). Far from being, as the right wing considered, "the thin edge of an antiracist wedge," it was a "racist philosophy" that "attempts to divert . . . the black struggle" (Grinter, 1990, p. 212). Overemphasizing the personal aspects and neglecting the "political dimension and power structures," it saw racism as resting on "misunderstanding and ignorance" (Grinter, 1992, p. 95, 1990, p. 212). Antiracist education, by contrast, saw conflict as central "in a social system that concentrates power in white, middle-class and male hands," dominant values being imposed on disempowered, unvalued groups (Grinter, 1992, p. 101). It understood racism as "an ideology . . . based on learnt attitudes of white superiority to . . . groups that Europe . . . exploited" so that "an unequal distribution of power . . . is accepted as natural" (p. 94).

Mullard's (1984) argument sharply analyzed multiculturalism and antiracism, understood that racism is as "serious and pervasive" as sexism and classism in "white Western history" (p. 58), and grasped the need to face reality critically, deconstructing institutionalized racism and racist practice and reconstructing relationships. However, the argument leaves much insufficiently defined and undeveloped. Also, there is perhaps a tendency to reify sharp dichotomies. First, despite the oppositional relationships, and therefore the oppositional interests, between the White dominant "group" and the Black dominated "group," these groups nevertheless share some interests. This is one of the inescapable contradictions of social reality, and Mullard's rejection of "'mutual interests' (à la Brandt)" (p. 15) is too hasty. Second, multiculturalism tended to become for Mullard, in sharp opposition to antiracism, not just in some forms of usages but inherently and irretrievably, an instrument of control. The understanding, however, of multiculturalism put forward by Mullard, Grinter, and some other antiracists is at best a partial one. The social reality that must be faced is multicultural as well as racist, and culture and structure interpenetrate, so antiracism must encompass antiracist multiculturalism.

Attack on Antiracism. In the 1980s, the growing acceptance of antiracism by some in education came under severe attack by some academics and public figures and much of the national media. One of the key critics, Jeffcoate (1984), rejected as too wide the antiracists' use of the term *racism* to include beliefs, hostile prejudices, discrimination, violence, and institutional racism, which he found particularly "obscure" (p. 145). But his main contention was that antiracism was "illiberal," "authoritarian," and prone to "indoctrination."

He argued that apart from the question of "separating truth from falsehood, myth from reality, rationality from irrationality," there was "a vast area of opinion and belief, represented by the ideology of racism . . . and the politics of immigration control and race relations" (p. 161) and that students were entitled to hold such opinions and beliefs. Jeffcoate apparently considered it inherently indoctrinatory for the teacher to question such "opinions" and to offer an alternative view or to question the underlying assumptions. To seek to change "opinions and attitudes" (such as National Front opinions) as distinct from "misinformation and faulty logic," apparently even by persuasion, was considered by Jeffcoate to "infringe" on the pupil's "autonomy" (pp. 159, 160). He contended that if, despite having "the relevant facts, some children argue that white people are as a group intellectually superior to black people, . . . we have to accept that as their privilege. . . . As teachers, our job is not to combat opinions we do not like but to uphold democratic principles and procedures" (p. 161).

Does not this last sentence itself simply represent an "opinion," and if some young people do not share our opinions about upholding democratic principles and procedures, is that not their "privilege"? Jeffcoate has not addressed basic issues about values. Education is not only about truth and falsity and how to "test" them. Besides, opinions may also raise questions of truth and falsity, and facts and arguments can be adduced to show the likely consequences of given opinions. Some opinions at least are not simply a matter of liking or disliking. Besides, democracy is not simply a matter of noting what the majority or any individual likes but rather of rational dialogue. Moreover, education is about the growth of the whole person as an individual who is a social being, and hence about values and whether there is any way of "testing" them. It is, too, about exercising one's rights and privileges without infringing on, and with sensitivity to, the rights and privileges of others. If democracy is to be upheld, so must antiracism and multiculturalism.

The media often took delight in portraying antiracists as "loony lefties." One of the most striking cases concerned the report *Murder in the Playground* (Macdonald, Bhavani, Kahn, & John, 1989), which looked into the fatal stabbing at Burnage High School, Manchester, in September 1986 of Ahmed Iqbal Ullah, a 13-year-old Muslim of Bangladeshi background. Manchester City Council was to publish the report but kept putting this off, citing advice from libel lawyers. Finally, in April 1988, the *Manchester Evening News* published the final chapter of conclusions and recommendations.

The national media, perhaps reading these out of context, launched an onslaught on antiracism, blaming it for Ahmed Ullah's murder. The report's authors had to call a press conference to

repudiate totally any suggestion that the anti-racist education policy . . . led . . . to the death of Ahmed Ullah. . . . The work of all

schools should be informed by a policy that recognizes the pernicious and all-pervasive nature of racism in the lives of students, teachers and parents, black and white, and the need to confront it. . . . This is not only a task facing schools in inner cities or in . . . "immigrant" areas. . . . The report . . . points out how dangerous . . . a "colour-blind" approach to racism is. (Macdonald et al., 1989, p. xxiv)

The full report, finally published in 1989, highlighted the complexities of the issues and was critical of simplistic notions of multicultural and antiracist education. It concluded that Ahmed Ullah's murder was racist but that other factors were also involved. It found that Burnage school did have an antiracist policy, but was critical of its conceptualization and implementation and of the senior management team and its top-down approach. The report rejected racism awareness training as playing simply on the guilt of White people, and any symbolic, moralistic, or simplistic, Black versus White notion of antiracism. It also criticized the notion that racism in Britain is "caused by . . . cultural misunderstanding" (Macdonald et al., 1989, p. 345) but mistakenly saw this view as a "central tenet of multi-cultural education" (p. 344) rather than as one, unsatisfactory, understanding of it by some. Racism, it stressed, is not just a matter of individual prejudice, but of structural and social realities and power relations. The report offered an example of good antiracist education practice: a project of curricular innovation that consisted of "a large mixed group of white and black students from three schools" in Manchester (Macdonald et al., 1989, p. 360) researching and producing a play on Len Johnson, a local son of an African father and Irish mother. Notable features of this project were

the integration of the issues of race, class and gender with the students' lives, the linking of the different parts of their own experience (e.g. as Irish, as women) and their resulting critical questioning and growing self confidence. (Macdonald et al., 1989, pp. 363–364)

The report had a great impact on the debate about antiracist and multicultural education and helped to move thinking forward.

About the same time, another rather different publication, Salman Rushdie's *Satanic Verses,* which appeared in 1988, caused a national uproar. This book was a heavy satire of all that Muslims hold most holy. It was vigorously condemned by Muslims (Semseddin, 1989). Much debate ensued, especially after Ayatollah Khomeini issued a *fatwa,* or death sentence, in February 1989 against Salman Rushdie and the publisher. Muslims in Britain became much more self-aware.

The Muslim Institute was founded in 1973–1974, largely through the efforts of Kalim Siddiqui (Institute of

Contemporary Islamic Thought [ICIT], 2000). Subsequent to the *fatwa*, the Muslim Institute published in 1990 the Muslim Manifesto, largely the work of Siddiqui, setting out the problems facing Muslims in Britain and their duties and responsibilities. He then established the controversial Muslim Parliament in 1992. Although these bodies have declined since his death in 1996, they have had an important impact on the situation of the Muslim community in Britain (see ICIT, 2000). Chazan (1998) has also expressed the view that "concerns over the growth of anti-Islamic feeling in the UK . . . are . . . galvanising the Muslim community" (p. 1).

Multicultural and Antiracist Education

Despite the arguments in the 1980s that multiculturalism and antiracism are opposed to each other, there is no inherent contradiction between these concepts. Both are needed. Entrenched as racism is, it is not the only relevant cause of social conflict or the only significant feature of society that needs addressing. Cultural difference, although a resource, can also occasion conflict, and cross-cultural communication also needs addressing. Besides, multicultural education is not only descriptive; it can be informed by a structural understanding of racism. Above all, it is not inherently racist. Furthermore, antiracist education can be multicultural, as even Grinter (1990) and the IRR (1980) seem to imply. Even Mullard (1984) states that "anti-racist education . . . attempts to absorb certain aspects of multiracial and multicultural education" (p. 18).

In fact, in the 1980s and 1990s, there were attempts to effect a synthesis between multicultural and antiracist education (see, for instance, Leicester, 1986, 1989). Figueroa (1991) argued that "education in Britain needs to be both multicultural and antiracist," since "Britain is both culturally diverse *and* racist . . . while nevertheless . . . containing important antiracist forces" and a long democratic tradition (p. 50; see also Parekh, 1986 and of Table 48).

The social and the educational situations are complex. The school, like the society, is structured by class, gender, race, culture, and other factors. The society is riven and yet held together by contradictions in the sense that any one sector might have to embrace opposing strategies (see Hatcher & Shallice, 1983) and that there are many different, and unequal, "interest groups" with conflicting but also shared interests. Different tendencies and imperatives operate constantly within the dominant group itself (Hatcher & Shallice, 1983; Whitty, 1990), as also within each minority group, although one tendency might come more to the fore for a while and then another. Social and education policy and practice must take account of and address this complex, dynamic reality.

Figueroa (1991, 1998, 1999, 2000a) has also argued that multicultural antiracist education is pertinent to every aspect and level of education and the education system and must take account of and address racism, diversity and identity, inequality and justice, democracy, and human rights and obligations. In this, it is important to be not only reactive but also proactive: to raise awareness, promote democratic values, and help develop skills of challenging racism, promoting justice, avoiding miscommunication, and reducing or even benefiting from conflict. Underpinning this must be quality educational entitlement for each child.

ZIGZAGS OF HISTORY

The reality, however, was a retreat from the late 1980s in developments in multicultural antiracist education and related matters. The Conservative government was well established, and the right wing was dominant.

Retreat

The Education Reform Act 1988 (ERA), introduced by a Conservative government, ushered in radical changes and turbulence. The Education Act 1944 had provided a national state education system with different types of schools and strong LEAs, but no national curriculum. It had also instituted the Ministry of Education, which became the Department of Education and Science in 1964. However, central government played little formal role in education, although it increasingly controlled funding. Individual schools had much autonomy, under the control of an LEA.

The Education Reform Act and After. ERA introduced a quasi-market in education within tight central controls, a detailed national curriculum, plus compulsory religious education (RE), and testing at ages 7, 11, 14, and 16. It endowed the secretary of state for education and science with numerous and wide-ranging new powers, simultaneously reducing the power and status of LEAs (see Mitchell, 1996). It abolished the influential Labour-controlled ILEA, which had played a leading role in multicultural and antiracist education. ERA also created the National Curriculum Council (NCC) and the Schools Examinations and Assessment Council, later amalgamated, first as the School Curriculum and Assessment Authority (SCAA), and then the Qualifications and Curriculum Authority (QCA), which also replaced the National Council for Vocational Qualifications.

Many of ERA's (1988) provisions may at first glance seem beneficial to minority ethnic students. For example, it requires that the curriculum be "balanced and broadly based," promote the "cultural . . . development of pupils . . . and of society," and prepare "pupils for the opportunities, responsibilities and experiences of adult life" (part 1, chap. 1, section 1(2)(a),(b), in, of course, a multicultural society and world. Furthermore, a national curriculum, with the implication of an educational entitlement for all and greater accountability for schools, could perhaps, in benefiting all students, bring significant improvements for visible minorities. There is, too, scope within the individual national curriculum subjects and RE for multicultural and antiracist education (see, for instance, Fyfe & Figueroa, 1993; Klein, 1993; Pumfrey & Verma, 1993a, 1993b; Verma & Pumfrey, 1993a, 1993b). In RE, although ERA gives priority to the Christian tradition, it also requires that the "other principal religions" in Britain be taken account of (ERA, 1988 section 8(3)). Moreover, the DES (1989) guidance to schools post-ERA stressed that coverage of multicultural and gender issues should be included across the curriculum. The NCC developed the idea of cross-curricular elements and dimensions, such as equal opportunities and multicultural education (NCC, 1990a, 1990b). These dimensions were to "permeate the curriculum and are the responsibility of all teachers" (NCC, 1992, p. 15). Education for citizenship was identified as a cross-curricular theme, with "roles and relationships in a pluralist society," as one of its main components (NCC, 1990b).

Nevertheless, many concerns have been expressed "that national policies since 1988 will not promote racial equality" (Basini, 1996, p. 94). ERA was passed in an antiegalitarian climate. Its stress on market forces and competition between schools, along with the associated funding regime, in effect rewarded schools for avoiding certain students, including some visible minorities, since these are often seen as behavioral problems or low academic achievers (see Gewirtz, 1996; Gillborn & Youdell, 2000). Furthermore, the notion that entitlement and the regular assessment of pupils would equally benefit all is dubious. Those with greater advantages in the first place, including greater dominant cultural capital, could be expected to benefit more. Besides, entitlement has been undermined by such strategies as the tiering of subjects for the General Certificate of Secondary Education (GCSE) (Gillborn & Youdell, 2000).

ERA ignored the Swann Report and marked a step backward from the modest progress in multicultural and antiracist education to that date (Swann, 1993). There was a notable lack of a clear lead and support from the center on multicultural and antiracist education despite the greater centralization. There was virtually no mention of racism or antiracism in the vast official post-ERA documentation. The relatively infrequent references to

multiculturalism were mainly in brief, nonmandatory documents. The working groups that developed the curricular recommendations for each subject were required to take account of ethnic and cultural diversity and of the promotion of equal opportunities regardless of ethnic origin and gender, but this was hardly reflected in the statutory orders.

The national curriculum tended to be narrowly British and monocultural (see Pumfrey & Verma, 1993a, 1993b; Verma & Pumfrey, 1993a, 1993b). The cross-curricular approach to multicultural issues meant in practice that they were largely disregarded, since the national curriculum is strongly subject based, and the multicultural and antiracist possibilities offered by subjects were largely ignored. Taylor (1992) found in a study into LEA policy and practice in multicultural and antiracist education since ERA that over one third of advisers thought things had either stayed "much the same" or even "slipped backwards" (p. 4). Multicultural and antiracist education was often perceived as irrelevant in mainly white areas and seemed to be poorly understood and to have a low priority. Her Majesty's Inspectorate also found a wide gap in 1990–1991 between policy and practice in equality of opportunity (DES, 1992). Many studies have indicated that for years, the education system has failed certain minority ethnic groups, especially Afro-Caribbean boys, Bangladeshi pupils, Gypsies, and some others (DES, 1981b, 1985; Drew & Gray, 1991; Figueroa, 1991; Kysel, 1988; Taylor, 1981, 1987, 1988; Taylor & Hegarty, 1985; Tomlinson, 1983). The review by Gillborn and Gipps (1996) of research on the educational achievement of minority ethnic pupils confirmed this picture post-ERA. It also found a considerable increase in school exclusions, that is, suspensions or expulsions, in recent years, with especially African Caribbean boys substantially overrepresented (Gillborn & Gipps, 1996). This review by Gillborn and Gipps was funded by the Office for Standards in Education (OFSTED) and had a direct influence on DFEE policy.

Important factors in the disproportionate exclusion and poor performance of some visible minorities include social class, the schools attended, aspects of culture and cultural difference, and racism, especially institutional racism and racist frames of reference (Figueroa, 1991; Gillborn, 1995; Smith & Tomlinson, 1989; Troyna & Hatcher, 1992). However, there was a vigorous debate throughout the 1990s between those who rejected the soundness of research providing evidence of racism in schools (Foster, 1990; Foster, Gomm, & Hammersley, 1996; Hammersley, 1993) and those who defended such research (Connolly, 1992; Figueroa, 2000b; Troyna, 1991, 1995).

Since the passing of the Education Reform Act 1988, there have been very many other education acts, such as the massive Education Acts 1994 and 1996, many continuing to increase central control. Many other developments have followed, including the reorganization of the DES into the Department for Education (DFE) in 1992, the Department for Education and Employment (DFEE) in 1994, and the Department for Education and Skills (DFES) in 2001.

Moreover, in the 1990s, the scope of section 11 funding was progressively reduced, so that eventually neither community languages nor multicultural and antiracist education were supported, but only English as a second language. Bagley (1992) noted that this amounted to a reaffirmation in the 1990s of the assimilationism of the 1960s.

There were also some very negative signals from the NCC and its successor, SCAA. In 1989, the NCC set up a Multicultural Task Group to prepare nonstatutory guidance "on multicultural education in the National Curriculum" (Tomlinson, 1993, pp. 29, 23). But the NCC, apparently because of right-wing political interference, did not publish the quite moderate report (Graham & Tytler, 1993; NCC Multicultural Task Group, n.d.; Tomlinson, 1993). As a result the Runnymede Trust (1993) published the useful *Equality Assurance in Schools*.

Also, multiculturalism and antiracism were neglected at the important SCAA conference in 1994. This was organized leading up to national consultation on draft revised national curriculum orders because teachers had boycotted assessment procedures in protest. There is, too, very little evidence of a cross-curricular, multicultural, or antiracist focus in the 1995 post-Dearing slimmed-down national curriculum.

Teacher Education. In the 1980s and 1990s, teacher education too was increasingly the object of right-wing-inspired central government control and reform (see Judd & Crequer, 1993). In the 1980s, the relevant bodies, including the DES, had begun to recognize the need for multicultural and even antiracist teacher education. But after ERA, the focus was on the delivery of the subject-based national curriculum. Also, increasingly since the early 1990s, initial teacher education courses have been required to work within very tight time constraints and to have primarily a practical orientation. They thus provide very limited opportunities for multicultural and antiracist issues to be adequately explored.

In the 1990s, the Teacher Training Agency (TTA) and OFSTED were established and given key roles, along with Her Majesty's Chief Inspector of Schools, in inspecting and controlling teacher education institutions. The framework that OFSTED and TTA produced in 1996 for accreditation of teacher education largely ignored multicultural and antiracist teacher education.

Not surprisingly, student teachers, and no doubt teacher educators, often were (and still are) inadequately aware of multicultural and antiracist education issues and often tend to share the myths of the wider society (see DES, 1985; Figueroa, 1991; Higher Education Funding Council for England [HEFCE], 1995; and Siraj-Blatchford, 1993). The underrepresentation of minority ethnic groups among student teachers, and even more among teacher educators, does not help (DES, 1985; HEFCE, 1995).

Murder of Stephen Lawrence and Others. There have been incidents of extreme racist violence in schools and beyond. Some murders have already been mentioned. Others include racist murders of Asians in 1969–1970 and the fatal stabbing of Gurdip Singh Chaggar, an 18 year old, in 1976 in Southall (Ashrif, 2001). Fryer (1984, p. 395) states: "Between 1976 and 1981, 31 black people in Britain had been murdered by racists." "The Runnymede Trust" (1994) named 12 people, mostly South Asians, who died in 1992 and 1993 as a result of apparently racist attacks. One of these was Stephen Lawrence. An innocent 18-year-old Englishman of African Caribbean heritage, he was gratuitously killed in a racist attack in 1993 at a bus stop in Southeast London (Macpherson, 1999). But the policing and legal systems failed. This became a celebrated case and is dealt with later.

Persisting Disadvantage and Some Improvement

The Policy Studies Institute (PSI), with Social and Community Planning Research, undertook the fourth national survey of ethnic minorities in 1994. They investigated ethnic minorities' lifestyles, cultural identities, and quality of life, including discrimination and disadvantage in employment, income, housing, health, and education. The sample consisted of 2,867 White people and 5,196 people of African Asian, Indian, Pakistani, Caribbean, Bangladeshi, and Chinese origins in England and Wales.

The overall conclusion was that although there continue to be "diversity and divergence between ethnic groups" (Modood et al., 1997, p. 342), there has been "some improvement for most groups by most measures," but also "persisting disadvantage" (p. 346). Many interacting factors, including differential stereotyping, prejudice, and discrimination, have been important.

Nearly a quarter of the ethnic minority sample "worried about being racially attacked" (p. 284). On average, 13% (ranging from 15% of Caribbeans to 9% of Bangladeshis) reported being "subjected to . . . racial harassment" in the previous 12 months (Modood et al., 1997, p. 266). The majority of perpetrators were male and the great majority White. Extrapolating from the figures would suggest that in 1993–1994, "racially" motivated harassment consisted of 20,000 people being attacked, 40,000 having their property damaged, and 230,000 being insulted. These estimates compare with "10,000 incidents reported to the police and . . . 130,000 identified by the British Crime Survey" (p. 267). According to a Home Office report (1981b), Asians were 50 times and African Caribbeans 36 times more likely than White people to suffer "racial" victimization. The Runnymede Bulletin (No. 268, p. 4, 1993 & No. 294, p. 8, 1996–1997) also found a substantial increase in reported racially motivated attacks. Modood et al. (1997, p. 350) note "the rise of anti-Muslim prejudice," with Islamophobia being highlighted by the Runnymede Trust (Conway, 1997).

On education, Modood et al. (1997) confirmed and elaborated previous findings that some minority ethnic groups were highly qualified, while others, in particular Caribbeans and Bangladeshi, were much less likely to be qualified. Among those between the ages 16 to 24, the ethnic minorities, except perhaps Bangladeshi and Pakistani women, showed a particularly strong commitment to postcompulsory education. Referring to other studies, Modood et al. (1997) note that

there is considerable evidence that . . . teachers, fellow pupils and others have encouraged black [that is, African Caribbean] males to excel in sports and discouraged them from commitment to academic goals. . . . Young black men have been stereotyped as violent and disruptive, challenging the authority of teachers and the police; or they have been praised and emulated as macho, "cool" and exemplars of youth culture. (p. 347)

New Developments

In May 1997, after eighteen years of Tory rule, New Labour won a landslide victory in the general elections on a platform with education as its highest priority. Its first white paper, *Excellence in Schools,* spoke of "excellence for everyone," thus implying perhaps a "levelling up" (DFEE, 1997). However, this New Labour government persisted with much of the Conservative education program and largely with "neutral" policies for "everyone" rather than targeted policies for particular groups with particular needs, such as minority ethnic groups.

The white paper did mention minority ethnic groups several times and spoke of monitoring "ethnic minority pupils' performance" and promoting "racial harmony" (p. 35). It even mentioned "cultural richness and diversity" (p. 34) and "tackling racial harassment and stereotyping" (p. 35). It underlined the fundamental importance of equality of opportunity. However, there was a tendency to associate ethnic minorities primarily with problems, and there was little focus on the positive development of multiculturalism or antiracism. Equal opportunities specifically targeted on ethnic minorities were not explored, nor was education for citizenship in a plural society.

This Labour government passed the major Schools Standard and Framework Act in 1998. This contained several measures aimed at raising standards, including Education Action Zones, which are meant to be partnerships between businesses, parents, schools, and LEAs. An OFSTED (2001) review found that these "are making some useful contributions to raising standards" (p. 2), especially in primary schools, and also to involving parents more in their children's education. This act addressed discipline and exclusion specifically but contained no express commitment to antiracist, multicultural, or even equal opportunities education and no measures targeted at improving achievement or reducing exclusions specifically among the groups at risk, such as Afro-Caribbean boys. Besides, the act had a distinctly top-down character and the appeals procedure against exclusions remained distinctly weighted in favor of schools.

The New Labour government introduced a plethora of other initiatives, such as the Literacy Hour in primary schools, the Numeracy Strategy, Regional Development Agencies, Urban Regeneration, the New Deals, and Excellence in Cities. Such schemes might be expected to benefit ethnic minorities, especially since these overwhelmingly live in urban conurbations, but they are not targeted programs. Another undertaking was the setting up of a Social Exclusion Unit in the Cabinet Office, which has been positively reviewed (Runnymede Bulletin, No. 308, p. 8 1997–1998; Cabinet Office, 1999). However, there remains a danger of pathologizing minority ethnic groups. It is essential to address the rights and needs of all groups equitably, positively, and in targeted ways within mainline education.

Advances

The Advisory Group on Raising the Achievement of Ethnic Minority Pupils, which the previous government had recently instituted, was retained by the New Labour government. The new employment minister, Andrew Smith (1997–1998, p. 3), asserted commitment through this group to "raising minority pupils' achievement" and to giving "guidance on . . . tackling racial harassment and stereotyping . . . and reducing exclusion."

The 1996 OFSTED report by Gillborn and Gipps had indicated that schools were failing some minority ethnic groups. The DFEE thus produced in September 1996 a 10-point action plan to raise the achievement of these groups. The research project, *Making the Difference* (Blair & Bourne, 1998), was the realization of one of these action points. It was designed to investigate and disseminate good practice in multiethnic schools.

Blair and Bourne (1998) note that there are many key school characteristics that are necessary but "not sufficient to raise the attainment of all students" (p. 2). Schools have to grapple with "the complexity of their own local . . . circumstances" (p. 2). However, the authors identified two "significant additional and transferable key characteristics" of effective multi-ethnic schools: being a "listening" school and having "the resources . . . to achieve . . . flexibility in the deployment of their staffing" (p. 2). "Listening schools"

took time to talk with students and parents; . . . were prepared to consider and debate values as well as strategies; . . . and . . . used this learning to reappraise, and . . . change, their practices and . . . build a more inclusive curriculum. These schools . . . incorporate not only a respect for individuals but also for . . . group identities. (Blair & Bourne, 1998, p. 2)

Critical were "an approach linking performance to a pastoral system which embraces group as well as individual needs and concerns" (p. 176); "recognition of group . . . needs, strengths, disadvantages and perceptions"; attention to specific needs and situations; and "structures and strategies for the support of vulnerable students" (p. 170). Related key characteristics of schools successful with visible minorities included "a strong and committed headteacher" (p. 173), "clear and effective whole school organisation," a "strong . . . lead on equal opportunities . . . by the headteacher," and "consistently high expectations of students" (p. 169).

In 1999, the section 11 scheme was replaced with the Ethnic Minority Achievement Grant (EMAG), a targeted scheme under the auspices of the DFEE, with a sharper focus on raising the achievement of minority ethnic pupils than the section 11 provisions. But it still does not have the wider remit of multicultural antiracist education for all pupils (see DFEE, 1999). There is a separate grant relating to Travelers' children (mainly Gypsies).

On a wider front, the Special Immigration Appeals Commission Act 1997, in response to a finding against the British government by the European Court of Human Rights, established a special commission to consider appeals against security exclusions and expulsions (Webber, 2001). Also, the government included measures to tackle racial violence in the Crime and Disorder Act 1998 (see Runnymede Bulletin, No. 308, p.10, 1997–1998). Most notably, it has, through the Human Rights Act 1998, finally, after 50 years, incorporated into British law the European Convention on Human Rights. This act came into force in October 2000. Although a great advance, it still leaves the government much scope for restricting civil liberties or interfering with basic rights, such as in fighting crime, illegal immigration, or (suspected) terrorism (see Webber, 2001). The Anti-terrorism, Crime and Security Act 2001 illustrates this.

The Macpherson Report. Stephen Lawrence's murder in 1993 eventually led, through the campaigning especially of his parents, to a public inquiry established by the New Labour government in 1997. This resulted in February 1999 in the famous Macpherson Report, which aroused the highest expectations.

Macpherson (1999) concluded that "institutional racism affects the MPS [Metropolitan Police Service], and Police Services elsewhere." Moreover, "Collective failure is apparent" in many "other institutions and organizations," "including the Criminal Justice system." Hence, "It is incumbent upon every institution to examine their policies and the outcome of their policies and practices to guard against disadvantaging any section of our communities" (p. 321). Macpherson specifically included in this connection agencies "dealing with housing and education" (p. 33). The inquiry received evidence of "a divide between policy and practice": LEAs "had anti-racist policies," but they "were often not implemented." Furthermore, there was much concern that the national curriculum failed "to reflect adequately the needs of a diverse multi-cultural and multi-ethnic society" and that "the number of exclusions from school . . . were apparently disproportionate to the ethnic mix of the pupils" (p. 313).

Macpherson's (1999) general definition of racism was "conduct or words or practices which disadvantage or advantage people because of their colour, culture, or ethnic origin. In its more subtle form it is as damaging as in its overt form" (p. 20). Moreover, after stressing that the report "will not produce a definition cast in stone," (p. 20), Macpherson delineates institutional racism as

the collective failure of an organisation to provide an appropriate and professional service to people because of their colour, culture, or ethnic origin. It can be seen or detected in processes, attitudes and behaviour which amount to discrimination through unwitting prejudice, ignorance, thoughtlessness and racist stereotyping which disadvantage minority ethnic people. (Macpherson, 1999, p. 28)

For Macpherson (1999), institutional racism seems to be unwitting discrimination and indirect racism flowing from the collective reality of an organization, as distinct from deliberate discrimination and overt racism on the part of an individual. This analysis is incomplete.

Macpherson (1999) made 70 recommendations. These included training for the police in "racism awareness and valuing cultural diversity" (p. 332) and three recommendations specifically relating to schools: that consideration should "be given to amendment of the National Curriculum aimed at valuing cultural diversity and preventing racism"; LEAs and school governors should "have the duty to create and implement strategies in their schools to prevent and address racism"; and OFSTED inspections should "include examination of the implementation of such strategies." Finally, "local Government and relevant agencies should specifically consider implementing community and local initiatives aimed at promoting cultural diversity and addressing racism" (pp. 334–335).

In presenting this report to Parliament, the home secretary, Jack Straw, stated, "Any long-established, White dominated organisation is liable to have procedures, practices and a culture that tend to exclude or to disadvantage non-White people" (House of Commons, 1998–1999, col. 391). He also announced that the 1976 Race Relations Act would be extended to cover public services. The government later produced an action plan (Home Office, 1999). For education, this concerned:

- Review of the national curriculum
- Introduction of citizenship education
- Schools having strategies to tackle "racial" harassment
- Strategies to address overrepresentation of ethnic minorities in school exclusions
- Additional language support and mentoring for ethnic minorities
- Training of teachers and head teachers to meet the needs of ethnic minorities
- School inspection to ensure implementation (see Osler & Morrison, 2000, pp. 12–13)

The Race Relations (Amendment) Act 2000 finally rectified some of the weaknesses that remained in the 1976 act. In particular, the act now covers public authorities, including government departments, the police, schools, colleges, and LEAs. It also places a statutory duty (which became fully operational in 2002) on all such public authorities to promote racial equality. However, it still exempts the spheres of immigration and asylum seeking (see CRE, 2001a).

Citizenship Education. One of the most significant recent educational initiatives is the introduction of citizenship education, which secondary schools had to provide beginning in September 2002. Nonstatutory guidelines were also issued for primary schools to incorporate citizenship education into the existing personal, social, and health education program (DFEE & QCA, 1999b).

The statutory guidelines for citizenship education in secondary schools (DFEE & QCA, 1999a, 1999c) prescribe knowledge and understanding about, for instance, rights and responsibilities, diversity and mutual respect, active democracy, resolving conflict fairly, and the global community. They also prescribe skills of inquiry, communication, and responsible action, among others. However, there is hardly mention of antiracism and no sharp focus on the meaning of citizenship in a plural Britain.

Nevertheless, citizenship education offers much potential for multicultural antiracist education (see Figueroa, 2000a, 2003; Osler & Starkey, 2000).

The Future of Multi-Ethnic Britain. The Runnymede Trust's Commission on the Future of Multi-Ethnic Britain (2000) took up the theme of citizenship in plural Britain. This commission illustrates some of the positive multicultural and antiracist forces in British society today. Its brief was "to analyse the current state of multi-ethnic Britain and to propose ways of countering racial discrimination and disadvantage and making Britain a confident and vibrant multicultural society at ease with its rich diversity" (p. viii).

The commission's (2000) report envisages Britain as a democratic, inclusive, dynamic, cosmopolitan, outward-looking community of communities. It believes that the "national story" needs rethinking so as to be truly inclusive, and genuinely to recognize the diversity that is Britain, which "is not and never has been the unified, conflict-free land of popular imagination" (p. 26). On education, the report points out that there was still "inadequate direction from government on issues of equality and diversity in education" and "still a dearth of straightforward information," for instance, on minority ethnic educational achievement (p. 143). It further notes:

African-Caribbean children start school . . . at much the same standard as the national average. By the age of 10, however, they have fallen behind. . . .

Bangladeshi and Pakistani pupils achieve below the national average, but steadily close the gap . . . in the course of their education. . . .

Gypsy and Traveller pupils are particularly at risk. . . . In 1996 it was estimated that . . . 10,000 . . . of secondary school age were not even registered for education. (p. 146)

The commission's (2000) report makes many recommendations, including over 20 on education, ranging across schools, higher education, LEAs, and central government. One recommendation is that a handbook should be produced "for schools on issues of race equality and cultural diversity" (p. 149). In fact, the Runnymede Trust's *Equality Assurance in Schools* (1993) was updated and comprehensively reedited (Runnymede Trust, 2003). Another recommendation is that "work financed under the auspices of the EMAG grant be independently evaluated" (p. 150). In fact, the DFEE invited tenders for this in 2001.

Facing Both Ways

Despite the advances, Bourne (2001), in discussing the Macpherson Report, argues that the promise it "appeared to hold out is not being met" (p. 13). She finds that the government faces both ways: while it "is apparently tackling racism with one hand, it is introducing new forms of institutional racism with the other" (p. 13; see also Table 48.1). Besides, local authorities and voluntary bodies have not risen to the challenge of "a fundamental rethinking of how racism came to be embedded in their organisations" (p. 15). Meanwhile, the right dismisses multiculturalism, antiracism, and the Macpherson Report as so much nonsense.

The problem, Bourne (2001) argues, lies partly with Macpherson's attempt to define institutional racism, which he does not clearly distinguish from personal racism:

He correctly identifies an organization's collective failure . . . as the crux of the problem, . . . [but] fails to locate such failure in the structure, workings and culture of an organization, which includes not only processes, behaviour, policies, practices and procedures, but also the organic relationship between them and the dynamics that that throws up. Instead, he attributes this collective failure, in part, to people's attitudes and behaviour. And, by going on to use words like "unwitting prejudice" and "thoughtlessness", he further compounds the confusion between personal and institutional racism. (p. 17)

The CRE (2001b) also found that although there had been progress in implementing the Macpherson recommendations, there was still quite a shortfall. Specifically, in relation to education, "There was little evidence either of any change in the employment of ethnic minority staff or of measures aimed to address the needs of ethnic minority pupils" (p. 5). Osler and Morrison (2000) stress that "the lead responsibility in monitoring the implementation of race equality initiatives within schools and local education authorities [was] given to OFSTED" (p. 13) but up at least to when they were writing, OFSTED had hardly taken this role seriously.

Anti-Immigration and Asylum Seekers Acts. Despite apologists for a twin track approach, developments like the Immigration (Carriers' Liability) Act 1987, the Immigration Act 1988, the Asylum and Immigration Appeals Act 1993, the Asylum and Immigration Act 1996, and the Immigration and Asylum Act 1999 do not assist toward the goal of citizenship for plural Britain. Instead, politicians of the two major parties seem to vie with each other about who is tougher on asylum seekers and people hoping to improve their lives through immigration (see Mynott, 2000). This, in turn, seems to feed through to a more negative approach toward minority ethnic people by many in Britain (Miles, 1993; Mynott, 2000). These acts continue the long-standing trend toward making legal entry into Britain increasingly difficult. The appeals process available to those whose application for asylum is turned down has been severely hedged around and limited by the 1993, 1996, and 1999 acts. The very

possibility of qualifying for refugee status seems to be reduced.

The 1999 act created new offenses and increased the powers of police and immigration officers in regard to "illegal immigrants." It instituted dispersal of asylum applicants across the country and vouchers exchangeable for goods, in particular, for food (Mynott, 2000; Shah, 2000; Webber, 2001). According to Webber (2001), these controversial and degrading arrangements engendered "racism . . . in local communities" (p. 88) to which asylum seekers were dispersed. Asylum seekers experienced racist harassment, and in August 2001 an asylum seeker was fatally stabbed on a council estate in Glasgow, where he had been housed. Webber (2001) states that despite the Human Rights Act, "institutionally racist measures such as the treatment of asylum seekers under the 1999 . . . Act are beyond the reach of the courts" (p. 88). However, one concession that this act included was the right of appeal on human rights grounds in view of the Human Rights Act (Webber, 2001). Nevertheless, the tightening of asylum and immigration controls continues with the Nationality, Immigration and Asylum Act 2002.

Antiterrorism Acts. Somewhat similar to the anti-immigration, anti–asylum seekers acts, recent antiterrorism acts send out messages to the majority and to minorities that hardly assist toward the goal of citizenship for plural Britain. The Terrorism Act 2000 incorporated the broadest ever definition of terrorism to that date. It was first used in March 2001 to proscribe 21, mostly Muslim, organizations (Fekete, 2001). Peirce, an experienced civil rights lawyer, notes that it affects extensive communities: "More than one million people from refugee communities . . . involved in liberation movements, movements of self-determination, resistance against tyrannies, are now . . . criminalized" (Fekete, 2001, p. 97).

Peirce also argues that this act is incompatible with the new Human Rights Act, in particular with the fundamental rights to freedom of association, speech, and expression, and especially with that act's "ban on these rights being withheld on a discriminatory basis, on the basis of religion, politics or ethnic origin" (Fekete, 2001, p. 102). Moreover, the Terrorism Act "cuts off all potential for intelligent political argument . . . about any politics that involves a proscribed organization" (Fekete, 2001, p. 98), such as the Kurdish Worker's Party, which must be involved in any debate about the future of the Kurds in Turkey.

After the terrorist attacks on the World Trade Center and the Pentagon on September 11, 2001, an even more draconian Anti-terrorism, Crime and Security Act 2001, which circumscribes even further the fundamental rights of noncitizens, was rushed through Parliament. Even with amendments that were secured, indefinite detention of noncitizens on the suspicion of their involvement in international terrorism is allowed, where their deportation is not possible. Yet internment, introduced in 1971 in Northern Ireland, was ineffectual in deterring terrorism and was actually counterproductive (Taylor, 2002). However, one important successful amendment is that detained suspects will have their cases reviewed by the Special Immigration Appeals Commission, which will have a raised status (Anti-terror Act, 2001).

The home secretary, David Blunkett, was intemperate, in Parliament and subsequently on the radio, in his attack on those who, within the democratic processes of the Houses of Parliament, raised objections to the 2001 bill ("Blunkett pays price," 2001). This could be seen as undermining the very democratic processes of scrutiny of government proposals.

Troubles

In 2001, around the general elections of June 6, "race riots" reappeared in Britain. There were disturbances in Bradford in mid-April and then in Oldham (Manchester) in May, followed by disturbances in other northern towns. These areas are all ethnically mixed. The main ethnic composition of Oldham in percentages is White, 77.4; Pakistani, 6.9; Kashmiri, 2.7; and Bangladeshi, 2.4 (Ritchie, 2001, p. 79, appendix 7). The Caribbean, Irish, and Indian heritage populations are each less than about 0.4%. Almost 10% is of "other" or unknown ethnicity.

Labour won a second term with another landslide victory (but on a low turnout), and because of these disturbances, the new home secretary established the Community Cohesion Review Team, chaired by Cantle (n.d.), "to identify good practice, key policy issues and new . . . thinking in the field of community cohesion" (p. 5). Local inquiries were also established. Ritchie (2001) chaired one in Oldham.

The Ritchie (2001) report shows that racism is widespread there. In the 2001 general elections, the far right British National Party (BNP) received a much larger share of the vote in Oldham West (16%) than it usually does. The BNP explicitly put its racist policies to the Ritchie inquiry team, arguing for voluntary "repatriation" of Pakistanis and Bangladeshis since "multi-culturalism has never worked" (Ritchie, 2001, p. 6). Commenting on this, the report stresses that "this policy constitutes a fundamental breach of the human rights of British citizens, designed . . . to intimidate, and . . . is as unworkable as it is disreputable. . . . These communities are as much British as any others" (Ritchie, 2001, p. 6).

This report makes many useful recommendations across a wide range. Recommendations on education focus, for instance, on raising the achievement of minority ethnic pupils, promoting the integration of pupils from different backgrounds, monitoring the effectiveness of equal opportunity and racial harmony policies, and promoting the knowledge of English where needed. The report on Bradford (Ouseley, 2001) also highlights education, in particular, citizenship education.

The Cantle (n.d.) team "was particularly struck by the depth of polarization"; many communities, it noted, lived "parallel lives," which "often do not seem to touch at any point, let alone . . . promote any meaningful interchanges" (p. 9). Cantle also noted the failure to attempt "to develop clear values" focusing on the meaning of being "a citizen of . . . multi-racial Britain." Many still looked "backwards to some supposedly halcyon days of a mono-cultural society, or alternatively . . . to their country of origin for some form of identity" (p. 9). Moreover,

the programmes . . . to tackle the needs of many disadvantaged and disaffected groups . . . often seemed to institutionalise the problems. The plethora of initiatives and programmes, with their baffling array of . . . conditions, seemed to ensure divisiveness and a perception of unfairness in virtually every section of the communities. (Cantle, n.d., p. 10)

Cantle (n.d.) articulated two aims: (1) "to promote community cohesion, based upon a greater knowledge of, contact between, and respect for, the various cultures" and (2) "to establish a greater sense of citizenship, based on . . . common principles . . . shared . . . by all," while placing "a higher value on cultural differences" (p. 10).

Cantle (n.d.) called for a national debate "to develop some shared principles of citizenship" and for a local community cohesion plan, which "should include the promotion of cross cultural contact . . ., foster understanding and respect, and break down barriers" (p. 11). They also listed several items that they think important, including an emphasis on the English language, a recognition of "the contribution of all cultures to this Nation's development throughout its history," but "a clear primary loyalty to this Nation," "formalised into a . . . statement of allegiance" (p. 20). It is not clear whether this is intended to apply only to new immigrants, minority ethnic communities generally, or all citizens. Moreover, there is no evidence that visible minorities hold any less loyalty to the United Kingdom than others.

Cantle (n.d.) made numerous other recommendations on many issues, including the quality of education, and contacts and understanding across cultures within each school, including faith-based schools, and across schools and beyond. Required also, Cantle notes, are more minority ethnic teachers and the training of teachers for diversity.

FUTURE OUTLOOK AND CONCLUSION

What, then, is the outlook? There have been many positive developments, including a greater official acknowledgment of racism since the Macpherson Report. But there are still strong forces for a narrow view of Britain, including the continuing legacy of the conservative reforms of the 1980s.

Of the key issues of diversity, inequality, and racism, the focus even at the level of policy rhetoric, and to the extent that the issues have been addressed, seems to have been on inequality, and the approach seems to be mainly corrective. As far as racism is concerned, the understanding has often been narrow and the emphasis also corrective. Even issues relating to diversity are often only vaguely indicated by general references to multiculturalism, even in the new citizenship education. The valuable contribution of the Commission on the Future of Multiethnic Britain, which encouraged a national debate, was ridiculed in much of the press. Also, despite the call of the Cantle report, there is hardly yet any concerted national attempt to address coherently the wide-ranging and complex issues, whether in social policy and programs generally or specifically in education.

There have been various constant or recurring themes through the decades: visible minorities seen as problematic, a stress on English language, an assimilationist tendency, integration counterposed to segregation, the assumption of a unitary British way of life, poor educational achievement and exclusion of African Caribbean boys and some other minorities, a paucity of multicultural antiracist education and of multicultural antiracist teacher education, often general rather than targeted approaches, often a discounting of racism, and a "twin track" approach stressing immigration controls but also promoting democratic values and developing antiracist, egalitarian, and human rights legislation.

Research findings, social facts, and social analysis suggest a need for a greater understanding not only of the cultural and ideological aspects but of the material realities and forces, along with a much more inclusive vision of the future and practical measures across a broad front. The social and structural roots of the problems need addressing. This requires concrete social programs to redress the disadvantages of visible minorities and of White disadvantaged groups. The state also needs to be overtly just, egalitarian, pluralist, and antiracist and to avoid all hint of racism or unfairness in its policies and arrangements. The Race Relations (Amendment) Act and the Human Rights Act must be fully used. The messages that public figures and the media transmit are critical.

A plural society requires a national identity that includes and values diversity. It is crucial "to formulate an explicit ideal of multicultural citizenship appropriate to Britain" based on "difference" *and* "shared experiences" (Modood et al., 1997, p. 359), recognizing the rightful place in Britain of all its cultures. Along with legislation and social programs, antiracism that goes to the structural and cultural roots, and consequential multicultural antiracist education and teacher education are essential. Important tasks for education include exploring and promoting an appropriate multicultural citizenship and helping people to identify and appreciate the best in every strand of plural British culture and to recognize and combat all racism. A broad view of education is essential: for social well-being, economic prosperity, and individual fulfillment.

References

Advisory Committee for Multicultural Education, Royal County of Berkshire. (1982). *Education for equality: A paper for discussion in Berkshire.* Reading: Author.

Ashrif, S. (2001). Charting the development of multi-ethnic Britain. *Multicultural Teaching, 19*(3), 6–11.

Bagley, C. A. (1992). *Back to the future—Section 11 of the Local Government Act 1966: LEAs and multicultural/antiracist education.* Slough, Berkshire: National Foundation for Educational Research in England and Wales.

Banks, J. A. (1984). Multicultural education and its critics: Britain and the United States. *New Era, 65*(3), 58–65.

Basini, A. (1996). Race. In J. Docking (Ed.), *National school policy: Major issues in education policy for schools in England and Wales, 1979 Onwards* (pp. 86–99). London: David Fulton.

Bhavnani, R. (2001). *Rethinking interventions in racism.* Stoke on Trent: Trentham Books.

Blair, M. (2001). *Why pick on me? School exclusion and black youth.* Stoke on Trent: Trentham Books.

Blair, M., & Bourne, J. with Coffin, C., Creese, A., & Kenner, C. (1998). *Making the difference: Teaching and learning strategies in successful multi-ethnic schools* (Research Report No. 59). London: Department for Education and Employment.

Blunkett pays price for his bill. (2001, December 14) [On-line]. Available: http://news.bbc.co.uk/hi/english/uk_politics/newsid_1710000/1710848.stm.

Bourne, J. (2001). The life and times of institutional racism. *Race and Class, 43*(2), 7–22.

Brandt, G. L. (1986). *The realization of anti-racist teaching.* London: Falmer.

Brown, C. (1984). *Black and white Britain: The Third PSI Survey.* London: Heinemann Educational Books.

Brown, C., & Gay, P. (1985). *Racial discrimination: Seventeen years after the act.* London: Policy Studies Institute.

Cabinet Office. (1999, December). *Review of the Social Exclusion Unit* [On-line]. Available: http://www.cabinet-office.gov.uk/seu/1999/review.htm#SUMMARY.

Cantle, T. (n.d., ca. 2001). *Community cohesion: A report of the Independent Review Team.* London: Home Office [On-line]. Available: http://www.guardian.co.uk/racism/.

Chazan, Y. (1998, September 16). UK press "fuels Islamophobia" [On-line]. Available: http://news.bbc.co.uk/hi/english/uk/newsid_172000/172782.stm.

Coard, B. (1971). *How the West Indian child is made educationally subnormal in the British school system.* London: New Beacon Books.

Commission for Racial Equality. (2001a, Spring). New law, new rights, new responsibilities. *Connections, 3.*

Commission for Racial Equality. (2001b, Spring). Reforms fall short of Macpherson recommendations. *Connections, 5.*

Commonwealth Immigrants Advisory Council. (1963). *Report* (Cmnd. 2119). London: Her Majesty's Stationery Office.

Commonwealth Immigrants Advisory Council. (1964). *Second report* (Cmnd. 2266). London: Her Majesty's Stationery Office.

Community Relations Commission. (1971). *Report of the Community Relations Commission for 1970–71.* London: Her Majesty's Stationery Office.

Community Relations Commission and Association of Teachers in Colleges and Departments of Education. (1974). *Teacher education for a multi-cultural society.* London: Authors.

Connolly, P. (1992). Playing it by the rules: The politics of research in "race" and education. *British Educational Research Journal, 18*(2), 133–48.

Conway, G. (1997). *Islamophobia: A challenge for us all.* London: Runnymede Trust.

Craft, M. (1984). Education for diversity. In M. Craft (Ed.), *Education and cultural pluralism* (pp. 5–25). Lewes, Sussex: Falmer.

Craft, M. (1986). Multicultural education in the United Kingdom. In J. A. Banks & J. Lynch (Eds.), *Multicultural education in Western societies* (pp. 76–97). London: Holt, Rinehart and Winston.

Daniel, W. W. (1968). *Racial discrimination in England.* Harmondsworth: Penguin.

Davey, A. (1983). *Learning to be prejudiced: Growing up in multiethnic Britain.* London: Arnold.

Department for Education and Employment. (1997). *Excellence in schools* [White Paper]. London: Her Majesty's Stationery Office.

Department for Education and Employment. (1999). *The Standards Fund 2000–2001* (Circular 16/99). London: Author.

Department for Education and Employment and Qualifications and Curriculum Authority. (1999a). *The national curriculum: Handbook for secondary teachers in England (Key stages 3 and 4).* London: Author.

Department for Education and Employment and Qualifications and Curriculum Authority (1999b). *The national curriculum: Handbook for primary teachers in England (Key stages 1 and 2).* London: Author.

Department for Education and Employment and Qualifications and Curriculum Authority (1999c). *Citizenship: The national curriculum for England (Key stages 3 and 4).* London: Author.

Department of Education and Science. (1965). *The education of immigrants* (Circular 7/65). London: Author.

Department of Education and Science. (1971a). *The education of immigrants* (Education Survey No. 13). London: Her Majesty's Stationery Office.

Department of Education and Science. (1971b). *Potential and progress in a second culture* (Education Survey No. 10). London: Her Majesty's Stationery Office.

Department of Education and Science. (1972). *The continuing need of immigrants* (Education Survey No. 14). London: Her Majesty's Stationery Office.

Department of Education and Science. (1974). *Educational disadvantage and the needs of immigrants* (Cmnd. 5720). London: Her Majesty's Stationery Office.

Department of Education and Science. (1977). *Education in schools: A consultative document.* London: Her Majesty's Stationery Office.

Department of Education and Science. (1981a). *The school curriculum.* London: Her Majesty's Stationery Office.

Department of Education and Science. (1981b). *West Indian children in our schools* (Cmnd. 8273). London: Her Majesty's Stationery Office.

Department of Education and Science. (1985). *Education for all* (Cmnd, 9453). London: Her Majesty's Stationery Office.

Department of Education and Science. (1989). *National curriculum: From policy to practice.* London: Her Majesty's Stationery Office.

Department of Education and Science. (1992). *Education in England 1990–1991.* London: Her Majesty's Stationery Office.

Drew, D., & Gray, J. (1991). The black-white gap in examination results: A statistical critique of a decade's research. *New Community, 17*(2), 159–72.

Duncan, C. (1989). *Pastoral care: An antiracist multicultural perspective.* London: Blackwell.

Education Reform Act. (1988). (England and Wales, c. 40). London: Her Majesty's Stationery Office.

Eggleston, J., Dunn, D., & Anjali, M. (1986). *Education for some: The educational and vocational experiences of fifteen- to eighteen-year-old members of minority ethnic groups.* Stoke-on-Trent: Trentham Books.

Eggleston, J., Dunn, D., & Purewal, A. (1981). *In-service teacher education in a multiracial society.* Keele: University of Keele.

Fekete, L. (2001) The Terrorism Act 2000: An interview with Gareth Peirce. *Race and Class, 43*(2), 95–103.

Figueroa, P. (1991). *Education and the social construction of "race."* London: Routledge.

Figueroa, P. (1998). Intercultural education in Britain. In K. Cushner (Ed.), *International perspectives on intercultural education* (pp. 122–44). Mahwah, NJ: Erlbaum.

Figueroa, P. (1999). Multiculturalism and anti-racism in a new ERA: A critical review. *Race, Ethnicity and Education. 2*(2), 281–301.

Figueroa, P. (2000a). Citizenship education for a plural society. In A. Osler (Ed.), *Citizenship and democracy in schools: Diversity, identity, equality* (pp. 47–62). Stoke-on-Trent: Trentham Books.

Figueroa, P. (2000b). Researching education and racialization: Virtue or validity? In H. Simons & R. Usher (Eds.), *Situated ethics in educational research* (pp. 82–100). London: Routledge.

Figueroa, P. (2003). Diversity and citizenship education in England. In J. A. Banks (Ed.), *Diversity and citizenship education: Global perspectives* (pp. 219–244). San Francisco: Jossey-Bass.

Figueroa, P., & McNeal, J. (1969, February 19). Summary of material in Figueroa's study and detailed study of Figueroa's material. In Select Committee on Race Relations and Immigration, *The problems of coloured school-leavers* (pp. 198–9, 207–13). London: Her Majesty's Stationery Office.

Foster, P. (1990). *Policy and practice in multicultural and anti-racist education.* London: Routledge.

Foster, P., Gomm, R., & Hammersley, M. (1996). *Constructing educational inequality: An assessment of research on school processes.* Falmer: London.

Fryer, P. (1984). *Staying power: The history of Black people in Britain.* London: Pluto Press.

Fyfe, A., & Figueroa, P. (1993). *Education for cultural diversity: The challenge for a new era.* London: Routledge.

Gay, G. (2001) Curriculum theory and multicultural education. In J. A. Banks & C. A. M. Banks (Eds.), *Handbook of research on multicultural education* (pp. 25–43). San Francisco: Macmillan.

Gewirtz, S. (1996). Market discipline versus comprehensive education: A case study of a London comprehensive school struggling to survive in the education market place. In J. Ahier, B., Cosin, B. & M. Hales (Eds.), *Diversity and change: Education, policy and selection* (pp. 289–311). London: Routledge.

Gillborn, D. (1995). *Racism and antiracism in real schools: Theory, policy, practice.* Buckingham: Open University Press.

Gillborn, D., & Gipps, C. (1996). *Recent research on the achievements of ethnic minority pupils* (OFSTED Reviews of Research). London: Her Majesty's Stationery Office.

Gillborn, D., & Youdell, D. (2000). *Rationing education: Policy, practice, reform and equity.* Buckingham: Open University Press.

Gilroy, P. (1987). *There ain't no black in the Union Jack.* London: Hutchinson.

Glass, R., & Pollins, H. (1960). *Newcomers: The West Indians in London.* London: Allen and Unwin.

Graham, D., & Tytler, D. (1993). *A lesson for us all: The making of the national curriculum.* London: Routledge.

Grinter, R. (1990). Developing an antiracist national curriculum: Constraints and new directions. In P. Pumfrey & G. K. Verma (Eds.), *Race relations and urban education: Contexts and promising practices* (pp. 199–213). London: Falmer.

Grinter, R. (1992). Multicultural or antiracist education: The need to choose. In J. Lynch, S. Modgil, & C. Modgil (Eds.), *Education for cultural diversity: Convergence and divergence* (pp. 95–111). London: Falmer.

Hall, S. (1978). Racism and reaction. In J. Twitchin (Ed.), *Five views of multi-racial Britain: Talks on race relations broadcast by BBC TV.* London: Commission for Racial Equality.

Hall, S. (1992). New ethnicities. In J. Donald & A. Rattansi (Eds.), *"Race," culture and difference* (pp. 252–259). London: Sage and Open University Press.

Hall, S., Critcher, C., Jefferson, T., Clarke, J., & Roberts, B. (1978). *Policing the crisis.* London: Macmillan.

Hammersley, M. (1993). Research and "anti-racism": The case of Peter Foster and his critics. *British Journal of Sociology, 44*(3), 429–48.

Hatcher, R., & Shallice, J. (1983). The politics of anti-racist education. *Multiracial Education, 12*(1), 3–21.

Higher Education Funding Council for England. (1995). *Special initiative to encourage widening participation of students from ethnic minorities in teacher training.* Bristol: Author.

Hill, C. S. (1967). *How colour prejudiced is Britain?* London: Panther.

Hiro, D. (1971). *Black British, White British.* London: Eyre and Spottiswoode.

Home Affairs Committee. (1981). *Racial disadvantage* (fifth report of the committee, session 1980–81, HC 424, 1–4, Vol. 37). London: Her Majesty's Stationery Office.

Home Office. (1978). *The West Indian community: Observations on the report of the Select Committee on Race Relations and Immigration* (session 1977–78, Cmnd. 7186, Vol. 50). London: Her Majesty's Stationery Office.

Home Office. (1981a). *The Brixton disorders, April 10–12, 1981: Report of an inquiry* (Cmnd. 8427). London: Her Majesty's Stationery Office.

Home Office. (1981b). *Racial attacks.* London: Her Majesty's Stationery Office.

Home Office. (1982). *Racial disadvantage: The government reply to the fifth report from the Home Affairs Committee, session 1980–1981 HC 424* (session 1981–82, Cmnd. 8476, Vol. 51). London: Her Majesty's Stationery Office.

Home Office. (1999). *Stephen Lawrence inquiry: Home Secretary's action plan.* London: Author.

House of Commons. (1963–1964). *Parliamentary debates* (Hansard, 1963, November 27, fifth series, Vol. 685, cols. 433–444). London: Her Majesty's Stationery Office.

House of Commons. (1998–99). *Parliamentary debates* (Hansard, 1999, February 24, sixth series, Vol. 326, col. 391). London: Her Majesty's Stationery Office.

Inner London Education Authority. (1967). *Immigrant children in ESN schools: Survey report.* London: Author.

Inner London Education Authority. (1968). *The education of immigrant pupils in primary schools* (February, Report 959). London: Author.

Inner London Education Authority. (1977). *Multi-ethnic education.* London: Author.

Inner London Education Authority. (1983). *Race, sex, and class: Antiracist statement and guidelines.* London: Author.

Institute of Contemporary Islamic Thought. (2000, April 17). *Dr Kalim Siddiqui biography.* London: Author [On-line]. Available: http://www.islamicthought.org/ks-bio.

Institute of Race Relations. (1980). Anti-racist not multiracial education: IRR statement to the Rampton Committee on Education. *Race and Class, 22*(1), 81–83.

Jeffcoate, R. (1984). *Ethnic minorities and education.* London: HarperCollins.

Jenkins, R. (1966). Address given by the Home Secretary to a meeting of the Voluntary Liaison Committees, 23 May 1966. London: National Committee for Commonwealth Immigrants.

John, A. (1970). *Race in the inner city: A report from Handsworth, Birmingham.* London: Runnymede Trust.

Judd, J., & Crequer, N. (1993). The right tightens its grip on education. In C. Chitty & B. Simon (Eds.), *Education answers back: Critical responses to government policy* (pp. 120–125). London: Lawrence and Wishart.

Kershaw, R., & Pearsall, M. (2000). *Immigrants and aliens: A guide to sources on UK immigration and citizenship* (Readers' Guide No. 22). Richmond: Public Record Office.

Kirp, D. (1979). *Doing good by doing little.* Berkeley: University of California Press.

Klein, G. (1993). *Education towards race equality.* London: Cassell.

Kysel, F. (1988). Ethnic background and examination results. *Educational Research, 30*(2), 83–89.

Leicester, M. (1986). Multicultural curriculum or antiracist education: Denying the gulf. *Multicultural Teaching, 4*(2), 4–7.

Leicester, M. (1989). *Multicultural education: From theory to practice.* Windsor, Berkshire: NFER-Nelson.

Little, A. (1978). Schools and race. In J. Twitchin (Ed.), *Five views of multi-racial Britain: Talks on race relations broadcast by BBC TV* (pp. 56–65). London: Commission for Racial Equality.

Little, A., & Willey, R. (1981). *Multi-ethnic education: The way forward* (Schools Council Pamphlet 18). London: Schools Council.

Little, K. (1948). *Negroes in Britain: A study of racial relations in English society.* London: Routledge & Kegan Paul.

Lynch, J. (1983). *The multicultural curriculum*. London: Batsford Academic and Educational.

Lynch, J. (1986). *Multicultural education: Principles and practice*. London: Routledge & Kegan Paul.

Lynch, J. (1987). *Prejudice reduction and the schools*. London: Cassell.

Macdonald, I. (1977). *Race relations: The new law*. London: Butterworths.

Macdonald, I., Bhavnani, R., Khan, L., & John, G. (1989). *Murder in the playground: The Burnage report* (The report of the Macdonald Inquiry into Racism and Racial Violence in Manchester Schools). London: Longsight Press.

Macdonald, I., & Blake, N. J. (1991). *Immigration law and practice in the United Kingdom* (3rd ed.). London: Butterworths.

Macpherson of Cluny, W. (1999). *The Stephen Lawrence inquiry* (Home Department, CM 4262-I). London: Her Majesty's Stationery Office.

Miles, R. (1982). *Racism and migrant labour*. London: Routledge & Kegan Paul.

Miles, R. (1993). *Racism after "race relations."* London: Routledge.

Millins, P.K.C. (1970). *Education for a multi-cultural society: Syllabuses*. London: Community Relations Commission.

Milner, D. (1975). *Children and race*. Harmondsworth: Penguin.

Ministry of Education. (1954). *Language* (Pamphlet No. 26). London: Her Majesty's Stationery Office.

Ministry of Education. (1963). *English for immigrants* (Pamphlet No. 43). London: Her Majesty's Stationery Office.

Mirza, H. S. (1992). *Young, female and black*. London: Routledge.

Mitchell, P. (1996). Implementing multicultural education as seen from a number of different perspectives. *European Journal of Intercultural Studies, 7*(1), 11–19.

Modood, T., Berthoud, R., Lakey, J., Nazroo, J., Smith, P., Virdee, S., & Beishon, S. (1997). *Ethnic minorities in Britain: Diversity and disadvantage*. London: Policy Studies Institute.

Mullard, C. (1982). Multiracial education in Britain: From assimilation to cultural pluralism. In J. Tierney, P. Dickinson, M. Syer, C. Mullard, J. Gundara, C. Jones & K. Kimberley (Eds.), *Race, migration and schooling* (pp. 120–133). London: Holt, Rinehart and Winston.

Mullard, C. (1984). *Antiracist education: The three O's*. Cardiff: National Association for Multi-Racial Education.

Mynott, E. (2000, June). The asylum debate—haunted by the ghost of Enoch Powell? *Runnymede Bulletin*, No. 322, pp. 17–18.

Nandy, D. (1981). *A review and assessment of Black studies in London schools*. Social Science Research Council report lodged with the British Library lending division.

National Committee for Commonwealth Immigrants. (n.d., ca. 1966). *Towards a multi-racial society*. London: Author.

National Committee for Commonwealth Immigrants. (n.d., ca. 1967). *Report for 1966*. London: Author.

National Curriculum Council. (1990a). *Curriculum guidance three: The whole curriculum*. York: Author.

National Curriculum Council. (1990b). *Curriculum guidance eight: Education for citizenship*. York: Author.

National Curriculum Council. (1992). *Starting out with the national curriculum: An introduction to the national curriculum and religious education*. York: NCC.

National Curriculum Council, Multicultural Task Group. (n.d., ca. 1990). *Multicultural education*. Unpublished manuscript, National Curriculum Council, York, England.

National Union of Teachers. (1978). *All our children*. London: Author.

National Union of Teachers. (1983). *Combating racism in schools: A union policy statement—Guidance for members*. London: Author.

Nieto, S. (1992). *Affirming diversity: The sociopolitical context of multicultural education*. New York: Longman.

Office for National Statistics. (2003). National statistics. [On-line]. Available: http://www.statistics.gov.uk/census2001/profiles/.

Office for Standards in Education. (2001, February). *Education action zones: Commentary on the first six zone inspections* [On-line]. Available: http://www.ofsted.gov.uk/public/docs01/eaz-commentry.pdf.

Osler, A. (1997). *The education and careers of Black teachers: Changing identities, changing lives*. Buckingham: Open University Press.

Osler, A., & Morrison, M. (2000). *Inspecting schools for race equality: OFSTED's strengths and weaknesses—A report for the Commission of Racial Equality*. Stoke-on-Trent: Trentham Books.

Osler, A., & Starkey, H. (2000). Citizenship, human rights and cultural diversity. In A. Osler (Ed.), *Citizenship and democracy in schools: Diversity, identity, equality* (pp. 3–17). Stoke-on-Trent: Trentham Books.

Ouseley, H. (2001, July). *Community pride not prejudice: Making diversity work in Bradford* [On-line]. Available: http://www.guardian.co.uk/racism/.

Owen, D. (1992). *Ethnic minorities in Great Britain: Settlement patterns* (1991 Census Statistical Paper No. 1). Coventry: University of Warwick, Centre for Research in Ethnic Relations, National Ethnic Minority Data Archive.

Parekh, B. (1986). The concept of multicultural education. In S. Modgil, G. K. Verma, K. Mallick, & C. Modgil (Eds.), *Multicultural education: The interminable debate* (pp. 19–31). London: Falmer.

Patterson, S. (1963). *Dark strangers: A sociological study of the absorption of a recent West Indian migrant group in Brixton, South London*. London: Tavistock.

Political and Economic Planning and Research Services. (1967). *Racial discrimination*. London: Political and Economic Planning.

Power, J. (1967). *Immigrants in school: A survey of administrative policies*. London: Councils and Education Press.

Prime Minister. (1965). *Immigration from the Commonwealth* (Cmnd. 2739). London: Her Majesty's Stationery Office.

Pumfrey, P., & Verma, G. K. (Eds.). (1993a). *Cultural diversity and the curriculum: The foundation subjects and religious education in primary schools*. London: Falmer.

Pumfrey, P., & Verma, G. K. (Eds.). (1993b). *Cultural diversity and the curriculum: The foundation subjects and religious education in secondary schools*. London: Falmer.

Ritchie, D. (2001, Dec.). *Oldham independent review: One Oldham, one future*. Oldham [On-line]. Available: http://www.guardian.co.uk/racism/.

Rose, E.J.B., Deakin, N., Abrams, M., Jackson, V., Peston, M., Vanags, A. H., Cohen, B., Gaitskell, J., & Ward, P. (1969). *Colour and citizenship: A report on British race relations*. London: Oxford University Press.

Royal Commission on Population. (1949). *Report* (session 1948–49, Cmnd. 7695, Vol. 19). London: Her Majesty's Stationery Office.

Royal County of Berkshire Local Education Authority. (1983). *Education for racial equality: Policy paper 1*. Reading: Author.

Rudell, D., & Simpson, M. (1982). *Recognising racism*. Birmingham: City of Birmingham Education Department.

Runnymede Bulletin, no. 268. (1993, September). *Racial violence* (p. 4). London: Newsletter of the Runnymede Trust.

Runnymede Bulletin, no. 299. (1996/97, December–January). *Racial violence and fear* (p. 8). London: Newsletter of the Runnymede Trust.

Runnymede Bulletin, no. 308. (1997/98, December–January*). Bid to tackle racial violence* (p. 10). London: Newsletter of the Runnymede Trust.

Runnymede Bulletin, no. 308. (1997/98, December–January). *Social exclusion unit launched* (p. 8). London: Newsletter of the Runnymede Trust.

Runnymede Trust. (1993). *Equality assurance in schools: Quality, identity, society—A handbook for action planning and school effectiveness.* London: Trentham Books.

Runnymede Trust. (1994, September). *Multi-ethnic Britain: Facts and trends* (Report compiled for the conference on "The Future of Multi-Ethnic Britain"). London: Trentham Books.

Runnymede Trust. (2003). *Complementing teachers: A practical guide to promoting race equality in schools.* London: Granada Learning.

Runnymede Trust Commission on the Future of Multi-Ethnic Britain. (2000). *The future of multi-ethnic Britain* (The Parekh Report). London: Profile Books.

Schools Council. (1967). *English for the children of immigrants* (Working Paper No. 13). London: Her Majesty's Stationery Office.

Schools Council. (1972). *Race relations and the curriculum.* London: Author.

Schools Council. (1981). *Education for a multiracial society: Curriculum and context 5–13.* London: Author.

Select Committee on Race Relations and Immigration. (1969a). *The problems of coloured school-leavers: Minutes of evidence, Thursday, 13th February, 1969* (session 1968–69, 13 Feb., 58, 6, Vol. 17). London: Her Majesty's Stationery Office.

Select Committee on Race Relations and Immigration. (1969b). *The problems of coloured school-leavers: Minutes of evidence, Wednesday, 19th February, 1969* (session 1968–69, 19 Feb., 58, 7, Vol. 17). London: Her Majesty's Stationery Office.

Select Commission on Race Relations and Immigration. (1969c). *The problems of coloured school-leavers: Minutes of evidence* (session 1968–69, 413, 3, Vol. 20). London: Her Majesty's Stationery Office.

Select Commission on Race Relations and Immigration. (1969d). *The problems of coloured school-leavers: Report and proceedings of the committee* (session 1968–69, 413, 1, Vol. 19). London: Her Majesty's Stationery Office.

Select Committee on Race Relations and Immigration. (1973). *Education* (session 1972–73, 405, 1–3, Vols. 30 & 31). London: Her Majesty's Stationery Office.

Select Committee on Race Relations and Immigration. (1977). *The West Indian community* (session 1976–77, H.C. 180, 1–3, Vol. 43). London: Her Majesty's Stationery Office.

Semseddin, T. (1989, February 28). Satanic Verses is libel against Islam. *The Tech,* 109(7), 4 [On-line]. Available: http://the-tech.mit.edu/V109/N7/turkoz.07o.html.

Sewell, T. (1997). *Black masculinities and schooling: How Black boys survive modern schooling.* Stoke-on-Trent: Trentham Books.

Shah, P. (2000, June). Asylum in the new age. *Runnymede Bulletin.* No. 322, pp. 23–24.

Siraj-Blatchford, I. (1990). Positive discrimination: The underachievement of initial teacher education. *Multicultural Teaching,* 8(2), 14–19.

Siraj-Blatchford, I. (1993). Social justice and teacher education in the UK. In G. K. Verma (Ed.), *Inequality and teacher education: An international perspective* (pp. 89–99). Falmer Press: London.

Sivanandan, A. (1974). *Race and resistance: The IRR story.* London: Race Today Publishers.

Sivanandan, A. (1982). *A different hunger: Writings on black resistance.* London: Pluto Press.

Smith, A. (1997/1998, December–January). Time to make equality a reality. *The Runnymede Bulletin.* No. 308, p. 3.

Smith, D. J. (1977). *Racial disadvantage in Britain.* Harmondsworth: Penguin.

Smith, D. J., & Tomlinson, S. (1989). *The school effect: A study of multi-racial comprehensives.* London: Policy Studies Institute.

Solomos, J. (1986). *Riots, urban protest and social policy: The interplay of reform and social control* (Policy Papers in Ethnic Relations, No. 7). Coventry: University of Warwick, Centre for Research in Ethnic Relations.

Stenhouse, L. A. (1975). Problems of research in teaching about race relations. In G. K. Verma, & C. Bagley (Eds.), *Race and education across cultures* (pp. 305–321). London: Heinemann.

Stone, M. (1981). *The education of the black child in Britain: The myth of multiracial education.* Glasgow: Fontana.

Swann, L. (1993). Education for all: A personal view. In A. Fyfe & P. Figueroa (Eds.), *Education for cultural diversity: The challenge for a new era* (pp. 1–8). London: Routledge.

Taylor, F. (1974). *Race, school and community: A survey of research and literature on education in multi-racial Britain.* Windsor: NFER Publishing Company.

Taylor, M. J. (1981). *Caught between: A review of research into the education of pupils of West Indian origin.* Windsor: NFER-Nelson.

Taylor, M. J. (1987). *Chinese pupils in Britain: A review of research into the education of pupils of Chinese origin.* Windsor: NFER-Nelson.

Taylor, M. J. (1988). *Worlds apart? A review of research into the education of pupils of Cypriot, Italian, Ukrainian and Vietnamese origin, Liverpool Blacks and Gypsies.* Windsor: NFER-Nelson.

Taylor, M. J. (1992). *Equality after ERA? Concerns and challenges for multicultural antiracist education.* Slough: NFER.

Taylor, M. J., & Hegarty, S. (1985). *The best of both worlds . . . ? A review of research into the education of pupils of South Asian origin.* Windsor: NFER-Nelson.

Taylor, P. (2002, January 1). Heath's fateful decision. *Guardian,* p. 14.

Tomlinson, S. (1982). *A sociology of special education.* London: Routledge & Kegan Paul.

Tomlinson, S. (1983). *Ethnic minorities in British schools: A review of the literature, 1960–82.* London: Heinemann.

Tomlinson, S. (1993). The multicultural task group: The group that never was. In A. S. King & M. J. Reiss (Eds.), *The multicultural dimension of the national curriculum* (pp. 21–29). London: Falmer.

Townsend, H.E.R. (1971). *Immigrant pupils in England: The LEA response.* Slough: National Foundation for Educational Research in England and Wales.

Townsend, H.E.R., & Brittan, E. M. (1972). *Organization in multiracial schools.* Slough: National Foundation for Educational Research in England and Wales.

Townsend, H.E.R., & Brittan, E. M. (1973). *Multiracial education: Need and innovation* (Schools Council Working Paper 50). London: Evans and Methuen.

Troyna, B. (1991). Underachievers or underrated? The experience of pupils of South Asian origin in a secondary school. *British Educational Research Journal, 17*(4), 361–76.

Troyna, B. (1995). Beyond reasonable doubt? Researching "race" in educational settings. *Oxford Review of Education, 21*(4), 395–408.

Troyna, B., & Hatcher, R. (1992). *Racism in children's lives: A study of mainly-white primary schools.* London: Routledge.

Troyna, B., & Williams, J. (1986). *Racism, education and the state: The racialisation of education policy.* London: Croom Helm.

Twitchin, J. (Ed.). (1978). *Five views of multi-racial Britain: Talks on race relations broadcast by BBC TV.* London: Commission for Racial Equality.

Twitchin, J., & Demuth, C. (Comp). (1985). *Multi-cultural education: Views from the classroom* (2nd ed.). London: BBC.

Unofficial Committee of Enquiry. (1980). *Southall 23 April 1979: The report of the Unofficial Committee of Enquiry* (Chair: M. Dummett). London: National Council for Civil Liberties.

Verma, G. K., & Bagley, C. (Eds.). (1975). *Race and education across cultures.* London: Heinemann.

Verma, G. K., & Pumfrey, P. (Eds.). (1993a). *Cultural diversity and the curriculum: Cross curricular contexts, themes and dimensions in primary schools.* London: Falmer.

Verma, G. K., & Pumfrey, P. (Eds.). (1993b). *Cultural diversity and the curriculum: Cross curricular contexts, themes and dimensions in secondary schools.* London: Falmer.

Wallis, S. (1977). *The education of ethnic minority children: From the perspectives of parents, teachers and education authorities.* London: Community Relations Commission.

Walvin, J. (1973). *Black and white: The Negro in English society, 1555–1945.* London: Allen Lane.

Webber, F. (2001). The Human Rights Act: A weapon against racism? *Race and Class, 43*(2), 77–94.

Whitty, G. (1990). The new right and the national curriculum: State control or market forces? In B. Moon (Ed.), *New curriculum—national curriculum* (pp. 15–22). London: Hodder and Stoughton.

Willey, R. (1984). *Race, equality and schools.* London: Methuen.

Williams, E. (1944). *Capitalism and slavery.* Chapel Hill: University of North Carolina Press.

Wright, C. (1986). School processes: An ethnographic study. In J. Eggleston, D. Dunn, M. Anjali & C. Wright (Eds.), *Education for some: The educational and vocational experiences of fifteen- to eighteen-year-old members of minority ethnic groups* (pp. 127–179). Stoke-on-Trent: Trentham Books.

49

CHALLENGES FOR POST-APARTHEID SOUTH AFRICA

Decolonizing Education

Kogila A. Moodley

University of British Columbia

In apartheid South Africa, "difference" was constructed in hierarchical terms and color coded within a carefully crafted, politically legitimated pigmentocracy. These constructions were scaffolded by ideologies of cultural difference, which Kuper (1969) described as "an almost invariable phenomenon in race relations. They convey racial characterizations from which principles of race relations are derived. They are linked to the structure of society generally either supporting or challenging domination" (p. 12). Segregated and unequal educational opportunities were conceived of as part of a commonsense understanding of the natural order of a society divided by race, ethnicity, and class with differential political inclusion.

From 1948 to 1990, the apartheid system structured social, political, and economic life on the basis of race. Individuals were categorized by the Population Registration Act of 1950 as falling into one of four hierarchically organized groups: Whites, Coloreds, Asians, and Africans. Each of the three "non-White" groups was confined to its "own areas," where they were supposed to have a voice in decision making but were disenfranchised nationally. When *race* became a discredited term through studies in the biological sciences and in the aftermath of the racist policies of Hitler, "social theorists of the ruling group resorted to the theory of 'ethnic groups'" (Alexander, 1985, p. 44). A series of laws, referred to as petty apartheid, prevented groups from mixing across the color line in all spheres of life from birth to death. All of this was to change between 1990 and 1994 when, after acrimonious negotiations, an unprecedented negotiated settlement was concluded (Adam & Moodley, 1993). After the first nonracial elections in April 1994, Nelson Mandela, a political prisoner for 27 years, became the president of the new nonracial South Africa.

The end of apartheid meant the collapse of legislated identities, and the vision of an overarching South African "rainbow nation" emerged. Race or ethnicity was to become an irrelevant factor in the public realm. Peaceful coexistence of different communities with equal rights for all citizens and common loyalty to a shared state stood out as a promise. The language of political transformation was one of compromise, emphasizing reconciliation at the expense of justice and retribution. The slogan became "one nation, many cultures." The three core concepts of nation building, nonracialism, and reconciliation were to express the consensual alternative to the previously imposed separation and interracial antagonisms.

These changes can be comprehended fully only against a historical background, which needs to be known in order to understand the present.

To attempt a coherent account of such a complex history over centuries is foolhardy at best. To ground recent developments by recounting state attempts at legislating racial segregation, though providing a sequential and well-documented coherence, would be to neglect the role of resistance movements, the role of students, parents, and other ordinary citizens who constantly challenged a state-sponsored hegemony. Such an analysis must be conscious of the fluidity and ambiguity of developments, as Bundy (2000) points out so well.

Cognizant of these dilemmas and shortcomings in approaching a mammoth brief, this chapter explores, with very broad brush strokes, (1) how the South African state during the apartheid era used ethnicity and race in order to legitimize the maintenance of privilege and power through the policy of separate development; (2) how the post-apartheid era developed contrary and counteracting discourses, deemphasizing "race," culture, and ethnicity in favor of a common society; (3) the demise of ethnically segregated educational institutions under the new government's policy of nonracialism; (4) the challenges faced by educational institutions in addressing the legacy of apartheid while developing the ideal of a common nonracial South Africa with the mantra of nation building as the binding glue; and (5) newer approaches and insights into addressing inequality and diversity.

APARTHEID IDEOLOGIES: HISTORICAL BACKGROUND

At the turn of the 20th century, Afrikaner-inspired "Christian National Education" developed as a formal response to counter the supremacist effects of British colonialism of the previous century. Afrikaans language and culture flourished in opposition to Anglicization attempts. The aim of Christian National Education was to preserve the Afrikaans language and culture, which Afrikaners viewed as being eroded through policies of Anglicization. This was to constitute the underpinnings of the political ideology of apartheid. The Christian National Education movement, which was so instrumental in the cultural and linguistic valorization of Afrikanerdom in its resistance to British colonialism, formed the basis of subsequent policies of racial segregation in education. From these beginnings as a tool of survival for a threatened group's fledgling culture, apartheid projected Afrikaner communalism and nationalism onto other groups. Perceiving and promoting different African "tribes" conveniently divided the Black majority on the basis of ethnicity. Social-anthropological notions of culture in the 1920s and 1930s took the place of a preceding "civilizing mission" of British colonialism. The overall term *Bantu culture* was used to refer to a distinctive homogenized African way of life. Rationalizations motivated the need for separation based on constructions of essentialist, cultural, and intellectual divides between White and Black. These were followed by ideologies of "cultural preservation." Racial segregation was considered essential for "community development." "The invention and reinvention of symbols and images that emphasized difference and the need for separateness in cultural and educational institutions of whites and blacks" (Cross,

1999, p. 289) resulted from this worldview of an ascending nationalist minority.

Segregated education was not a Nationalist Party invention. It existed as customary practice prior to the Nationalist Party's ascension to power in 1948. However, from 1948 to 1990, the Nationalist Party government formalized, entrenched, and streamlined education to socialize the population into ideologies of racialized and ethnicized separation, thereby consolidating the goals of apartheid. Resources were never separate but equal. They were differentially allocated together with access. Unequal resources were evident in compulsory and free schools for Whites only. Vast discrepancies of per capita state expenditure on education for Blacks, Whites, Coloreds, and Indians prevailed. The apartheid state sought to dissimilate an increasingly integrated urban population from the late 1940s to the 1980s. Through demographic engineering, the Black population was ethnicized, denationalized, and fragmented, while the White population was racialized by unifying those of different national and cultural backgrounds simply as "Whites" (Adam & Moodley, 1993). Race and class became critical polarized theoretical lenses through which apartheid education was viewed. They constituted an ongoing debate in subsequent analyses of educational reform (Christie & Collins, 1984; Nolutshungu, 1982).

Language was another pivotal area around which controversy centered. All the different groups were expected to gain mastery of Afrikaans as one of two official languages. Black students especially found this an aggressive imposition on speakers of African languages, since it meant that Afrikaans, besides English, would be the third language they would have to master. Black students associated Afrikaans, as a hegemonic "tainted" language of the dominant group, with their own degradation and powerlessness. It was also viewed as limiting their international access to opportunities. The imposition of these requirements and restriction of opportunities resulted in the Soweto students' rebellion in 1976. Not surprisingly, the use of ethnic and linguistic labels for the different groups was discredited among those who resisted apartheid. Ethnicity and race were viewed as stigmatizing state categorization.

The mirror image of the Afrikaner desire for cultural preservation in the light of British colonial dominance was imposed on Africans. Despite political exclusion, non-Whites were expected to be proud of their distinctiveness. Heavily laced with paternalism, ensuing educational policies developed the idea of "Bantu culture" and implemented it through a new curriculum. Education was geared to the perceived communal needs of Africans. Educational priorities for Africans were geared to the specific market niches envisioned to sustain a racialized division of labor (Wolpe, 1988). Similar programs of segregated education were also organized for the two middle groups, the so-called Coloreds (10% of the population of mixed descent) and South Africans of Indian origin (3%).

In the name of continued "sound" race relations, the African majority and the middle groups, all of whom were initially labeled "non-Whites," were excluded from political participation at the national level yet encouraged to administer their "own affairs" through compliant councils or homeland reservations. The apartheid state valued cultural diversity and cultural self-determination along the lines it specified and controlled, as long as it fragmented the numerically stronger majority and privileged the White community. State educational initiatives, above all, sought to elevate the Afrikaner community to the higher educational levels of English-speaking Whites. This meant offering compulsory education to all White children and special vocational programs for the upliftment and mobility of mostly Afrikaner working-class White children. Bilingual education was to placate the demands of Afrikaans and English speakers, while at the same time fostering a common racial consciousness as Whites across the linguistic and class divides. Pervasive in this worldview was the essential need for separate schools for each group to retain cultural specificities (Adam & Giliomee, 1979).

Earlier, the 1943 Christian National Education policy had articulated nationalist views on the relationship of culture, language and racial identity:

Our culture must be carried into the school and that cannot be done merely by having our language as a medium. More is needed. Our Afrikaans schools must not merely be mother-tongue schools; they must be places where our children will be imbued with the Christian and national spiritual and cultural material of our nation. . . . We wish to have no mixing of languages, no mixing of cultures, no mixing of religions and no mixing of races. We are winning the struggle over medium. The struggle for Christian and national schools lies before us. (Instituut vir Christelike-Nasionale Onderwys, Christelike-Nasionale Onderwys, cited in Cross, 1999, p. 43)

Educational policy in the 1950s and 1960s developed as an explicit tool to implement political apartheid. The state maintained exclusive control of education in a highly centralized, bureaucratized, and racially exclusive manner. Each population group had its own department of education. The Bantu Education Act of 1953 (Horrell, 1968) was subsequently replaced in 1979 by the Education and Training Act. The Department of Education and Training controlled African schools outside the homelands and regulated the quality of education that would be offered to Africans. Although this initially resulted in a great increase in African school attendance, it was mitigated by a very high dropout rate. Christie (1994) writes, "Until the 1970s about 70% of Africans in school were in the first four years. . . . Less than 1% of Africans at school were in matric [the final high school leaving examination]" (p. 7). This profile changed in the 1970s with the increasing numbers of Black students graduating, due to a skill shortage in an expanding economy. Of the total number of African pupils, about 70% of Africans were schooled in the homelands and rural areas, which were under the control of collaborating Black administrations.

The Department of Colored Affairs, which was created in 1963, was responsible for the education of Coloreds, and the Indian Education Act of 1965 delegated control over Indian education to the Department of Indian Affairs. This was accomplished through differential infrastructures, graduated per capita funding, and separate curricula based on so-called differing cultural needs. In practice, this led to limited access to the study of science and mathematics for non-White groups, higher pupil-teacher ratios for non-White schools especially for Africans, and very high proportions of underqualified teachers in African schools in contrast to White schools with negligible numbers of unqualified teachers (National Education Policy Investigation, 1994).

The 1959 passage of the euphemistically titled Extension of University Education Act was experienced by recipients as restriction of educational opportunity. Tertiary institutions were formally segregated with the development of separate universities not just for racial groups but for each ethnic group. Non-White students were generally prohibited entry into White universities, except for the study of a few subjects not taught at ethnic institutions. It also made the education of Blacks cheaper while simultaneously creating a new critical mass of educated young people in separate institutions. Bundy (2000) shows how "Black school enrollment rose from 1m in 1955 to more than 2.5m in 1969" (p. 67). These segregated institutions were to politicize students now exposed to the harsh realities of apartheid in contrast to the official intention to depoliticize them through separation and isolation. Anticipation of these trends was outlined by Moodley (1971). Similarly, Karis and Gerhart (1997) refer to the creation of "hothouse conditions for the growth of a new spirit of resistance" (p. 90).

THE CHALLENGE OF BLACK CONSCIOUSNESS

The history of South African education has been highly conflicted. Restrictive governmental measures were constantly contested. Bundy (2000) outlines the dramatic walkout by Black students from the liberal nonracial National Union of South African Students (NUSAS) conference in 1967 in protest against the segregated housing offered them. This sparked the rise of the Black consciousness movement and led to the formation, two years later, of the South African Students' Organization (SASO) (Moodley, 1991). Other high points of student resistance were the 1976 Soweto students' uprising against Bantu education and the imposition of Afrikaans as a medium of instruction, the 1979 formation of the Congress of South African Students (COSAS), and the 1980 Cape School boycotts. The inspiration for some of these actions came from the Black consciousness movement within South Africa, as well as the exiled African National Congress (ANC), the banned liberation party, which currently rules the country with a 66% majority. Resistance to apartheid was mobilized with different strategies by activists who disagreed among themselves about the most effective way to challenge the state.

The Black consciousness movement grew out of the South African Students' Organization—not as a return to African specificities and a narrow cultural revitalization, as its name suggests, but aspiring to be a unifying force among the politically disenfranchised—and excluded against a colonial, Eurocentric curriculum of apartheid education. It drew African, Indian, and Coloured youth together in an antioppression stance. It was initially headed by Steve Biko, whose underlying philosophy was to shape a movement of self-reliance and psychological liberation. Biko's idea is outlined in his 1978 selection of writings, appropriately entitled, *I Write What I Like.* Mentorship came from Black intellectuals such as the Algerian psychoanalyst Franz Fanon who in his writing *The Wretched of the Earth* (1963) and *Black Skin, White Masks* (1967) captured the moral outrage against French colonialism. Julius Nyerere, then president of Tanzania, served as an inspiration through his emphasis on freedom from dependency, as well as his use of the indigenous philosophy of Ujamma to further national development through traditional structures in community development (Hyden, 1983). These ideas resonated well with the South African philosophy of Ubuntu (Ramphele, 1991). The anticolonialist leader and first president of independent Senegal, Leopold Senghor, who developed the idea of negritude (Fanon, 1986), and Freire's (1972) work on conscienticization in Latin America also related directly to South African conditions.

The Black consciousness movement stimulated the development of theater and literary work as a form of political activity in the 1970s (Mzamane, 1991). Various forms of critical pedagogical materials were produced. Multimedia art and dramatic productions were developed with the aim of infiltrating apartheid education with consciousness of protest, ridicule, and resistance. This movement, however, was soon squelched by the government

by placing the young leaders in detention and assassinating its chief ideologue, Steve Biko, while he was in solitary confinement in prison. The process of alternative identity construction to that envisioned by the state also points to racial group membership or identity politics, ironically, as a possible source of strength and psychological liberation. Denigration is reversed in the proud self-identification with one's group. The Black consciousness movement of the 1970s insisted on this reclaimed liberated identity at the height of apartheid. (For a detailed discussion of this movement, see Adam, 1973; Gerhart, 1978; Moodley, 1991.)

Black consciousness was received with some ambivalence among many critics of apartheid due to the stigma of using the same criterion, racial consciousness, by which the state repressed, enslaved, and dehumanized the majority (Alexander, 1991). However, as Greenstein (1993) argues:

> To stay at the level of moral condemnation of racism is not enough. . . . One need not endorse any form of racialism (let alone regard race [as] a valid biological category) to realize that life in a racially-structured world shapes in critical ways the conceptions that people have about themselves, about others, and about the social relations in which they are embedded. Furthermore, its unsavory historical origins notwithstanding, race *can* and frequently *does* become an affirmative principle underlying individual and collective identities, partially overlapping and partially competing with other foci of identity. Racial identification can thus become a basis for political and cultural empowerment, allowing people to confront exclusion and marginalization by promoting a positive sense of their own identity which may or may not conform to official categories. In other words, discussions of race need not be confined forever within the restrictive framework imposed on them by the historical experiences of racism and discrimination, crucially important as these have been to our understanding of the meaning of race. (pp. 3–4)

Socialist activists criticized Black consciousness for its focus on attitudes and racialization of culture at the expense of economic transformation (Alexander, 1991). White antiapartheid liberals objected to the self-segregation of Black consciousness students (Budlender, 1991). Both critics failed to appreciate the importance of the psychological liberation of colonized minds.

The 1976 revival of visible protest after the banning of all liberation movements in 1960 was specifically targeted against apartheid education. The Soweto students' resistance took place in an oppositional climate directed against Bantu education, a depressed economy, having to study in an inferior educational system, overcrowded schools and classrooms with teacher-to-student ratios of 100:1, and underqualified teachers (Molobi, 1988). The final straw that led to their mobilization against the state was its imposition of Afrikaans as a medium of instruction.

The state viewed this collective action as revolutionary and endangering stability, though it was essentially democratic in nature. The peaceful march of 20,000 students on June 16, 1976, led to the killing of several hundred students in country-wide uprisings and to the bannings of 14 organizations. All student political activity was outlawed (Gerhart, 1978).

In this climate, new linkages developed among students, community organizations, and labor unions. Student demands focused on

the release of detained students; the recognition of Student Representative Councils; the reconstruction of damaged schools; the provision of proper school facilities; the provision of free textbooks; the unbanning of the Congress of South African Students (COSAS); the reinstatement of dismissed teachers; the total scrapping of Bantu Education. (Molobi, 1988, p. 156)

The state responded with its heavily armed presence outside schools and sometimes even in classrooms, threatening both students and teachers. Expulsions for political involvement were common. This turned schools into highly politicized, chaotic, and unsafe spaces. It is little wonder that schools viewed as centers of state indoctrination were places to be vandalized and destroyed by learners, which made no sense to outsiders. "Liberation before education" emerged as a subsequent slogan, marginalizing a whole generation of undereducated activists (Motlhabi, 1984; Nzimande, 1994; South African Institute of Race Relations, 1985, 1986, 1990).

In response to these challenges as well as the needs of a changing economy, the government-appointed De Lange Commission investigated education in 1980. In 1981, the commission recommended revised educational structures, a unitary education department for all South Africans, six years of compulsory schooling, and the provision of equitable basic education for all. Although De Lange was a member of the Broederbond, the tightly knit think tank of Afrikanerdom, the ruling group was increasingly split over reformist measures. The De Lange Commission was viewed by many analysts as being related to the crisis faced by the South African state as well as the skills shortage (see Chisholm, 1984; Saul & Gelb, 1981). Yet these were contentious recommendations; only some were acceptable for the government of the day, and certainly not the introduction of a single education system. Instead, each group—Blacks, Coloreds, Asians, and Whites—had educational administrations set up under its "own affairs" departments. African education was administered under the Department of Education and Training, and each of the nine homelands was responsible for its own education. The debate was soon overtaken by the 1985 state of emergency, when various student organizations were again banned. The politicization of education created a

niche for the framing of alternative forms of education, most notable of which was "People's Education" (Sizulu, 1986).

THE VISION OF PEOPLE'S EDUCATION

In sharp contrast to Bantu education, which Blacks rejected as oppressor education, People's Education was "an integral part of the struggle for a non-racial, democratic South Africa." This alternative vision entailed:

- The democratisation of education, involving a cross-section of the community in decisions on the content and quality of education.
- The negation of apartheid in education by making education relevant to the democratic struggles of the people.
- The achievement of a high level of education for everyone.
- The development of a critical mind that becomes aware of the world.
- The bridging of the gap that exists between theoretical knowledge and practical life.
- The closing of the chasm between natural science and the humanities, between mental and manual labor, with emphasis on worker education and the importance of production. (Molobi, 1988, p. 159)

Molobi (1988) rejected the often-used label "alternative education" to describe initiatives such as People's Education since he found it a voguish depoliticizing label aimed at an apolitical Black middle class.

People's Education was not a new movement but merely a new label. As early as in the mid-1950s, similar ideas were framed as "Democratic, liberatory education[,] . . . democratic in control, organisation and purpose[,] . . . . to equip people and the youth to fulfill the historic task of liberating themselves" (Hyslop, 1999, p. 71). However, due to a lack of supportive infrastructure and obstacles faced by labeling it subversive education, People's Education did not materialize as a coherent alternative (see Muller, 1987; Sisulu, 1986; Unterhalter & Wolpe, 1991). Liberatory educational movements resembled the socialist utopia of international class solidarity. They were celebrated for their inclusiveness; they did not aim at ethnic specific privileging and were notable for forging theoretical alliances among groups. In a segregated repressive society, these progressive visions faced insurmountable obstacles.

During a prolonged state of emergency and heightened township confrontation from the mid-1980s, concerned teachers and parents constituted themselves nevertheless as groups, such as the Soweto Parents' Crisis Committee (SPCC), to be followed by other support groups, such as the National Education Crisis Committee (NECC). These moves were punctuated by the banning of activists and organizations as well as counteracting alternative education programs. (For in-depth reading on these organizational developments, see Kallaway, 1984; Nasson & Samuel, 1990; Nkomo, 1990.)

With the slow breakdown of apartheid ideology under economic imperatives, the curriculum could no longer continue with a crude form of racialization (see Norval, 1996, for an expanded discussion of this issue). The debate soon focused not only on new educational content but also on the differential allocation of expenditure and the most appropriate organization of the segregated system for an integrated economy (Adam & Moodley, 1986). Attempts to integrate schooling had begun in the 1970s. Notable in these initiatives were the open schools movement, which was introduced at a South African bishops' conference, followed by initiatives sponsored by corporate interests, such as Anglo American (Christie, 1990b). The role of the Christian churches is discussed in the report of the Education Commission on Christianity in South Africa (Study Project on Christianity in Apartheid Society, 1971). Some White public schools also began very gradual integration of a few non-White students, though these were met with bureaucratic barriers, such as the need to obtain formal permission before "nonconforming" students could be admitted.

Liberalization of admission policies continued as the demise of apartheid became inevitable. In 1990, White government schools were finally allowed to admit all groups, subject to parental approval. Schools were offered the choice of declaring themselves Model A, B, or C schools. Model A schools were those that declared themselves to be private and were allocated a subsidy of 45% per school, to be phased out over three years. Model B enabled schools to operate as they were and decide on their own admission policies, provided that the character and ethos of the school remained that of the majority White population. Model C schools were free to admit other groups, became state aided, and received funding for teachers' salaries and some operating costs (South African Institute of Race Relations, 1992).

For the most part, formerly all-White schools were in no danger of losing their cultural ethos or character, first because of their commitment to a Eurocentric curriculum as the only guarantors of standards, and second, because privileged Black parents readily bought into this model as a certain insurance for their children's upward mobility. Included in this group were some of the children of the late Steve Biko and Mamphela Ramphele, both Black consciousness activists. Similarly, Chris Hani, a prominent leader of the Communist Party, sent his child to a private school offering Greek and Latin. Overall, English or Afrikaans still continue as the medium of instruction. African languages, though used widely, remained in a vibrant oral tradition, since these were not considered to be high-status languages that would provide currency in the marketplace other than as an added asset. Most predominantly White schools, however, do teach the dominant African language of the province as a third language.

Blacks in South Africa consequently dismiss any attempts at cultural retention as part of a divisive ideology. Instead, they see access to political and economic power as the central issue. Concerns about cultural differences are firmly and emphatically rejected in favor of a general, nonracial inclusiveness that transcends different ethnicities. The former South African opposition struggled to transform an undemocratic, authoritarian indoctrination into a participatory and politically relevant education. Their vision for a post-apartheid society embraced a common society rather than an explicitly plural one. Since 1990, the post-apartheid state has strongly endorsed the goals of integrated schooling, as embodied in the South African Schools Act of 1996, which formalized a unified national school system (South African Institute of Race Relations, 1997).

EDUCATION IN THE POST-APARTHEID PERIOD

Post-apartheid education seeks a balance between respect for different languages in use and the project of nation building. New policies in the development of curriculum and the teaching of history demonstrate changing priorities, programs, and school arrangements in grappling with the legacy of racialization (Ministry of Education, 2001). Neville Alexander, a long-time Trotskyist activist, has advocated language planning in South Africa as an aid to the creation of national unity (Alexander, 1990). He promotes the unification of African languages in much the same way that the German language is used by Austrians and Swiss. Alexander (1989, 1992) aims at giving African languages greater prominence in the public arena and increased accessibility as a language of instruction.

"Difference" is heavily intertwined with politics in South Africa. With the demise of apartheid, negotiations around education opened up as well. Chisholm (1992) describes two emerging concerns: "the need for new policy to guide and change developments" and "the resolution of the schools crisis" (p. 279). At the heart of the predicament lie the problems of how to address past inequality under the banner of nonracialism when inequality is racially based and how to create opportunities in a recessionary economy with an increasing unemployment rate among mainly Black youth. The gravity of the problem is perhaps best illustrated by 1995 education figures, which encapsulate what the post-apartheid government inherited. Asmal and James (2001) conclude that

19 percent of the population had no formal education at all. Within this group, Black Africans accounted for a staggering 92% of the uneducated. Most of these uneducated black Africans were in the rural and poorer provinces of the Eastern Cape, Mpumalanga, the North West and Northern provinces. The majority of the formally uneducated—16 percent—were women. (p. 187)

How does a society maintain the quality of education in pockets of privilege, usually White, and not be viewed as excluding the less privileged who are noncompetitive? Asmal and James (2001) write, "One consequence of a negotiated change is that reforms must proceed with inherited assets and liabilities. The deracialization of schooling had to be evolutionary" (p. 187).

These dilemmas can be understood only by the backlog suffered from the heavy politicization of African education during the apartheid era. Schools became the battlefields of the apartheid era, when activist students embarrassed parents for their political passivity and when slogans such as "liberation before education" became the rallying cry. The resulting belief in the illegitimacy of authority led to schools' becoming sites of lawlessness, struggle, and resistance. Many schools became wastelands, where learning was considered an individually motivated "bourgeois" activity. Like all other aspects of society in South Africa, politicization of schools was racially differentiated, affecting African students most and White students least, with other groups, such as Asians and Coloreds, in between. These politically engaged students came to be known as the "lost generation" due to the price they paid in lost schooling (Hyslop, 1988).

The consequences of apartheid are manifest in the high rates of illiteracy and innumeracy, lack of high-level skills, underresourced and understaffed schools, and Black school curricula favoring occupations requiring low levels of scientific and technological skills. Chisholm (1992) notes:

In 1988, Blacks (including Coloreds and Indians) constituted but 3.8 percent of all engineers, 10.9 percent of all scientists, 12.5 percent of all technicians and technologists, 11.8 percent of accountants and auditors and 6.7 per cent of all administrative occupations. (p. 281)

At the heart of all these trends, the schools crisis was an issue that desperately called for resolution, especially in the context of national negotiations. New policies were needed to guide future practice. In 1991, Nelson Mandela called together a 35-member team to work toward resolution and redress. Recognizing the daunting nature of the task in addressing the infrastructural basis for mass schooling, President Mandela and the National Educational Crisis Committee formally launched the Culture of Learning and Teaching campaign in February 1997. It

followed along the lines of earlier "back-to-school" and "intensive learning" campaigns. This approach was criticized for being motivated by concerns about law and order and the need to attract foreign investment (Chisholm, 1992). However, what also becomes apparent is that from the perspective of the state, attitudinal change on the part of the victims lies at the heart of the problem. The improvement of infrastructure and conditions of learning and reduction of the high unemployment rates that affect Black family life were given short shrift. Clearly, the answer lies in a combination of these forces; neither alone can bring about effective change.

President Thabo Mbeki's (1996) speech "I am an African" launched the theme of "African renaissance," which resonated a need of a formerly colonized majority to demonstrate that an undervalued and unrecognized continent can rule itself successfully. As long as the African renaissance includes every citizen who identifies with the land and the new constitutional order, it can be a useful mobilizing vision. However, if it is interpreted racially to benefit only a self-styled "patriotic bourgeoisie," the desirable African renaissance repeats the divisive patronage of the past. Nation building and patriotism easily conflate corporate interest with the common good. This class-blind appeal of the national project promises to be even more problematic the more that Black entrepreneurs join the established White corporate order through empowerment deals and affirmative procurement policies. The new nation is on its way to being successfully transformed at the top but left even more hopelessly impoverished at the bottom. (For further elaboration of this debate, see Adam, Slabbert, & Moodley, 1998.)

The "culture of learning" and "back-to-school" slogans smacked of a philosophical locus akin to the American ethos of "back to basics." Yet it was followed by the launching of Curriculum 2005 in March 1997, which introduced a progressive outcomes-based approach to learning to revamp the authoritarian, discriminatory content and processes of the past (South African Institute of Race Relations, 1997). In essence, it echoed what People's Education earlier had aimed to do but was a more structured program. It called for a shift from traditional subject areas to broader learning areas: arts and culture, language, literacy and communications, mathematical literacy, mathematics and mathematical sciences, human and social sciences, natural sciences, technology, economic and management sciences, and life orientation. Vally and Dalamba (1999) summarize the focus of Curriculum 2005 as being based on two kinds of outcomes,

the first of which is critical cross-field outcomes. These are general in nature and are generated across different learning areas rather than in any specific area. They include among others: the identification and solution of problems, teamwork, the organisation and analysis of information, effective communication, social and environmental responsibility, understanding of the interrelated nature of the world. The second kind of outcomes is specific to each learning area and forms the basis for evaluation of progress and effectiveness of learning programmes. Specific outcomes are evaluated through the use of a continuous assessment model that is meant to be ongoing and formative or developmental in nature. (p. 17)

State-of-the-art curriculum models, despite their obvious appeal, face an uphill battle when over a third of the teaching force is underqualified and ill equipped or textbooks fail to arrive in schools on time. Furthermore, the new curriculum challenges the core of an authoritarian education system and is hampered by a teaching force itself ill educated and therefore lacking the will to work in this mode. (For further details, see Asmal & James, 2001.) The *Mail and Guardian* (March 22–27, 2002) reports:

South Africa's schools are heading for a crisis that could already be too late to avert completely. No new curriculum is yet in place for next year's grade 10 learners; and it follows that no teacher training at this level has taken place, and no new textbooks and other support materials have been developed. (p. 12)

To add to these administrative glitches, Jansen (2001a) refers to poor planning and inadequate preparation of teachers for working with Curriculum 2005 in poorly resourced classrooms. Grave concerns are being expressed by school personnel about the ineffective transmission of training. Vast differences in capacity and teaching experience have inhibited effective implementation. This situation has invariably led to the return to traditional methods by teachers who feel unprepared even to attempt the new approach to teaching and learning.

EDUCATION FOR RECONCILIATION

Despite poor implementation of progressive ideas, new visions of the post-apartheid nation emerged from the widely publicized hearings of the Truth and Reconciliation Commission (TRC) between 1996 and 1998. In South Africa, it is not a depoliticized concern with cultural maintenance that threatens nation building, but how past beneficiaries and victims of discrimination can live together under a new dispensation. One axis along which a new nation may be built is through grappling with a shared horrendous history marked by human rights violations involving all groups. A new nation emerges from the ashes of the past depicted as "another country" in the report of the TRC, the country's attempt to achieve reconciliation through an open airing of the crimes committed.

The commission's recommendations focused on the promotion of national unity to consolidate democracy and build a culture of human rights. More specifically, the TRC *Report* (1998) argues in favor of "human rights curricula [being] introduced in formal education, [as well as] specialized education and the training of law enforcement personnel. These curricula must address issues of . . . racism, gender discrimination, conflict resolution and the rights of children" (p. 5).

On the issue of reparation and rehabilitation, the TRC highlights "raising the consciousness about the public's moral responsibility to participate in healing the wounded and facilitating nation building" (p. 15). Among its recommendations for educational purposes were the building of monuments and memorials and the development of museums to commemorate past events. In this regard, De Kok (1998) describes how individuals, institutions, and communities have collaborated in mapping the past and recording personal histories. Educational endeavors such as these reveal the need to continue vigilance based on knowledge about the active perpetration of evil, passive complicity, and experiences of the victimized through an informed, critical, and introspective historical awareness.

The TRC was a noble attempt to forge unity out of an unsavory past and to reconcile perpetrators and victims. In the conclusion to its *Report,* the commission (1998) states: "The full disclosure of truth and an understanding of why violations took place encourage forgiveness" (Vol. 5, p. 36). However, the reactions to the comprehensive report also indicated that South Africans across the political spectrum remain far from the required acknowledgment and forgiveness of past violations. Virtually all political groupings, from the far right Afrikaner parties and the Inkatha Freedom Party (IFP) to the ANC and Pan African Congress (PAC) on the left, united to denounce their own stated responsibility. Although there now exists "a minimum willingness to co-exist and work for the peaceful handling of continuing differences," the required "readiness to accept responsibility" is absent on all sides to a greater or lesser degree (Truth and Reconciliation Commission, 1998, Vol. 5, p. 36). On the contrary, the TRC *Report* has turned out to be a weapon in the party political competition for all groupings rather than an opportunity for "learning from and redressing past violations for the sake of our shared present and our children's future" (vol. 5, p. 36).

THE CHALLENGE OF POLITICAL EDUCATION

The project of unifying nation building through political education should not be abandoned as wishful thinking. However, the limits of the TRC's idealistic dream should be recognized. There is always the danger of taking the moral high ground through censorious admonitions. A more effective way to create critical political literacy is to address the underlying motivations of contending groups. Above all, it cannot be assumed, as the TRC does, that a moral universe is shared by all citizens in a deeply divided country. Different life experiences in legislated discrimination have resulted in different value systems, perspectives, and identities derived from conflicting interests. These differences cannot be dissolved or subsumed under a theologically inspired concept of reconciliation that may apply to interpersonal relations but mystifies objective, collective antagonisms. For example, the interests of capital and labor, White business and Black unions, cannot be reconciled permanently except through temporary trade-offs and continuous bargaining.

In this regard, Goduka (1999) argues in favor of using the TRC as a way to initiate introspective narratives, an innovative approach that links the historical and political. The personal domain is extended beyond lifestyle and "difference" to come to grips with the past in order to move ahead.

The more modest goal of political education in this context requires cognizance of the role of different identities, as well as the significance of conflicting moral claims, as Adam (2000) has suggested. Democratic ways of conflict resolution rather than the idealistic clamoring for unifying national values become more salient. Teaching of negotiation skills and tolerance of and respect for political opponents contribute more to democratic nation building than does a utopian common memory or an official history about a divisive past. Such a minimalist goal has a greater chance of success than expressions of moral indignation and normative educational endeavors shared only at a very abstract and superficial level.

With the end of apartheid in 1994, the new state-of-the-art constitution formally entrenched the fundamental right to an education and equality of access to all citizens. This is easier said than done in view of such a horrendous legacy. Asmal and James (2001) point to three dilemmas faced in implementation:

First as the government seeks to distribute resources fairly, it finds growing inequality to be a barrier. Second, the South African population is ill equipped in Science, Math and Technology and therefore poorly prepared to meet the challenges of globalization. Third, the sustainability of quality schools depends in large measure on the sustainability of a democratic ethos in civic life and, therefore, thriving partnerships between the core institutions of civil society. Many sectors of our society are bereft of a democratic culture and simply lack the core institutions of civil society. (p. 186)

In a similar vein, Carrim (2001) sees the need for deepening democracy, which the current practices of centralization in educational decision making, their progress from the previous era notwithstanding, fail to address

effectively. Deepening democracy means broadening citizens' participation in decision making where such decisions affect their lives. In contrast, all trends in South Africa point to fewer people making decisions for the many, who are encouraged to be passive consumers. When groups are assumed to be internally coherent and homogeneous, leadership of a traditional kind is favored. Under these conditions, the space for different voices within groups to express themselves becomes constrained.

When difference in the form of "race" coincides with continued inequality of opportunity in a fragile democratic culture, it poses a real threat to sound intergroup relations. On the question of continuing racialization of educational opportunity and outcome, Jansen (2001a) maintains that

the sheer scale of backlogs left by the apartheid legacy, combined with very modest economic growth forecasts, foreclose any revolutionary or radical reform of the status quo as far as education is concerned. . . . We should expect an increasingly divided schooling system to be more evident in class terms though still distinguishable in racial terms. (p. 283)

Supportive arguments are put forward by Soudien, Jacklin, and Hoadley (2001), who reflect on the move from race-based choice of schooling in the past to one increasingly based on consumer choice. This marks the shift, they maintain, from the "public right to education" (p. 79), which is much touted in the state-of-the-art constitution, to "education as a private good" (p. 91). Parental choice is increasingly influenced by income, geography, and location.

The unquestioning way in which the logic of privatization has been accepted is of concern to many progressive educators. Privatization casts doubt on the genuineness of the official state discourse about equity and redress. The counter-logic of consumer choice does exactly the opposite: it reinforces the existing class and, consequently, race divide. It also reinforces the discrepancy between the sophisticated policy formulation and implementation, which relegates policy to having no more than a symbolic role (see Jansen, 2001a, 2001b).

DESEGREGATED SCHOOLS: LESSONS FOR FUTURE PUBLIC SCHOOL INTEGRATION

Schools all over the world are the laboratories for racial harmony or conflict, a microcosm of the society at large, challenged to transcend institutional and educational racism with alternatives of multicultural or antiracist education. To what extent has desegregation of schools led to a new nonracial order in South Africa? To what extent have past imbalances been addressed? Research from the

United States, Canada, and Britain that seeks to improve intergroup or race relations in their schools raises our awareness that mere desegregation of schools does not necessarily alter the relations of domination. The South African experience demonstrates that merely changing the color of the political power holders or having a racially integrated leadership does not automatically improve the way in which students of once powerless groups now see themselves or are seen by previously advantaged groups (Dawes & Finchilescu, 1993; Gaganakis, 1991).

The experience of the Catholic Church in South Africa with "open schools" is instructive. Despite their outspoken criticism of racist practices, Catholic schools were segregated until 1976. Seizing on a government request in 1973 to offer integrated schooling opportunities for the children of Black diplomats, they strategized to broaden this offering and formally resolved to integrate schools. Although very limited numbers of students attended these schools, they aroused considerable interest as lenses into what the new South Africa might resemble. Christie and Butler (1988) outline in greater depth various attempts to experiment with approaches to teaching and curriculum. The actual interrelationships between the students in these open schools raised great interest in a society with entrenched group biases. The racist attitudes of some White students toward their fellow students from other groups were frequently reported as problematic (Christie & Butler, 1988). After all, mere integration in an artificial environment vastly different from the society outside could hardly be expected to end racial assumptions abruptly.

One study concluded that "the racial composition of the school influenced White students' views on racial mixing." Christie (1992) is worth quoting at length:

White students in schools with no black students responded least favourably on issues of racial mixing, and their views were significantly different from their counterparts in schools with 3% to 14% black enrollments. White students in schools with 18% to 29% black enrollments were most in favour of mixing, and the difference between them and other students was statistically significant. However, this trend was reversed in schools with black enrollments of over 35% suggesting that a different dynamic came into play when a critical mass of black students was reached. At this stage, it is likely that schools could no longer be taken-for-granted terrain of white students, and this resulted in less positive views among white students. This suggests that open schools did indeed challenge racial assumptions among white students. (p. 70)

Experience in private, high-quality, resource-rich open schools provided valuable lessons for racially integrated public schools in post-apartheid South Africa. It is clear that racial assumptions, even under the best conditions, will need to be addressed on an ongoing basis.

Gaganakis's (1991) insightful analysis of the marginal position endured by Black students who attend high-quality desegregated schools needs to be addressed more prominently in studies of school integration. Critics of the "multicultural schools," as desegregated schools were inaccurately referred to, had argued that Black children placed in an integrated school environment would be alienated "from both their home community and township peers, because of their perceived social status and educational opportunity" (p. 76). Black students refer to "being Black" or "falling between two cultures" as part of their school experience (p. 78). Gaganakis, however, interprets this cultural explanation as an overstatement. Instead, she maintains that the notion of difference expressed refers to the "differential worlds of experience between dominant and subordinate groups." The "home," characterized by violence, poverty, and inferior housing, stands in stark contrast to the "safety" of the trouble-free zone of the "White" school. The social distance between Black and White pupils outside school reinforces the perception of Black students as a "usurpationary group" who are taking advantage of White privilege and opportunity to which others in their ranks do not have access.

In South Africa, democratization has also brought in its wake the rapid desegregation of formerly White, Indian, and Colored public schools. James (2001) points out:

In 1997, 28% of all schools were racially integrated and in 1996 . . . African children made up 27% of all students in Gauteng's [a province of South Africa] formerly white schools, 31% in its formerly coloured schools, and 45% in its formerly Indian schools. Five years later, African students are the majority in all these schools. (p. 58)

However, of the 12 million students in about 30,000 South African schools in 2001, the overwhelming majority were still in all-Black schools. Impoverished township schools in particular are experiencing adverse learning conditions due to the African middle-class exodus into formerly all-White, Colored, and Indian schools (James, 2001). These 5,000 institutions, together with independent (private) schools, are now more integrated in the sense that their demographic composition is more diverse. Nationally, an average of 15% of all African students and a significant number of Colored and Indian students are now enrolled in formerly White establishments. However, White students have not enrolled in formerly Black schools (James, 2001).

A comprehensive 1999 report by the South African Human Rights Commission (Vally & Dalamba, 1999) selected a sample of 90 schools, 10 from each province, for an in-depth evaluation of racism, racial integration, and desegregation in public secondary schools. To the question of having experienced racial incidents or "examples of racism in your school," 62% of the students surveyed answered in the affirmative, typically describing derogatory name calling or forms of racial harassment, sometimes resulting in physical altercations. Given the extreme apartheid racialization, one would in fact expect a much higher percentage, particularly since only half of South Africa's schools have formal antiracist policies or programs in place (Vally & Dalamba, 1999). While it cannot be assumed that mere desegregation eliminates racism, the slow physical integration of urban White, Indian, and Colored schools has proceeded rather smoothly on the whole. After all, racial incidents and friction between students are not uncommon in multiethnic classrooms the world over. However, the long apartheid experience may not have sensitized teachers in South Africa to be more introspective about their biases. By contrast, their counterparts in North America and the United Kingdom have been steadily exposed to multicultural and antiracism education (Banks & Banks, 2001; Gillborn, 1995; Yon, 2000).

In virtually all desegregated schools, the newcomers are expected to adjust to the ethos of the dominant ethnicity rather than the school's making allowances for different cultural traditions. In practice, that means an unchanged, often authoritarian school culture. The minorities, in most cases, are either merely tolerated or expected to conform and assimilate. The superiority of "White standards" is taken for granted. Black learners are welcomed as long as they "fit in" and do not threaten the religious character, linguistic predominance, or other cherished cultural tradition. Assimilation is also guaranteed by the racial composition of teachers, as 98% of educators in former White schools remain White, according to the South African Human Rights Commission Report (Vally & Dalamba, 1999).

Ironically, many of the Black parents who send their children to formerly all-White or all-Indian schools at great cost and effort to themselves endorse the Eurocentric notions of what constitutes a proper education. The experience with underresourced township schools and underqualified, unmotivated Black teachers has added to the quest of a growing African middle class to ensure the best White education for their children. Even if the codes of conduct are alien, the language of instruction is not in the mother tongue, school fees are difficult to afford, and the staff is prejudiced, such an education is still sought by people keen to secure success and mobility for the next generation.

Once predominantly White postsecondary institutions now face the challenge of providing an equitable education to students who are differentially prepared due to past apartheid injustices. Sixty-five percent of University of Witwatersrand students are Black. Paradoxically, at the same time, the Black student dropout rate is very high at most universities (Reid, 2002). University presidents are faced with the balancing act of maintaining high morale and public confidence in their ability as they also try to retain high academic standards. Presidents also try to avoid the language of "deficit" and "drain" when describing the past legacies of iniquitous education that affect the performance of most Black students. More innovative approaches to admission are sought to transcend the narrow matriculation examination now in operation. The University of Cape Town has in place a "potential"-based exercise as part of its admission procedure, geared to assessing students' capacities to grasp the essence of selected material being taught. This is markedly different from the University of the Western Cape's partial lottery system of admission. Reid (2002), the vice chancellor of University of Witwatersrand, in her installation speech questioned traditional modes of teaching in higher education in favor of more "interactive and individualized forms of learning which will benefit all students" (p. 5). She views this decade as "a time for rebirth—academic innovation in the pedagogy and the curriculum, a new discourse between higher education and government, cultural change in higher education, new relations with students, [and] exploration of new ways to access" (p. 5). Noticeable is the inclusive way in which these transformative practices are framed, avoiding the "cultural differences" approach frequently used in North American diversity education.

Some contradictory forces are evident on the fate of "race," ethnicity, and identity within the context of a state that speaks of African Renaissance and nation building. More recently, cultural studies and postmodernist theories have stimulated greater interest in racial discourse analysis and constructions of identity (Hall, 1995; McCarthy, & Crichlow, 1993). The introduction of open schools in the mid-1980s gave rise to some excellent studies probing experiences with school integration, such as Christie's (1989, 1990b) study of Catholic school desegregation. Similarly, Soudien (1994, 1998) studied the impact of integrated schooling on the identity production of African and Colored students in a Cape Town public school. Carrim (1992) examined desegregation in Colored and Indian schools in Johannesburg. Several other studies now address the issue of White self-concept (Dolby, 2001; Steyn, 2001), as well as the topic of Colored identity. Paradoxically, with the demise of apartheid, instead of the disappearance of state-imposed identity, there are indications of greater assertions of self-chosen, new group identities, which might have been expected. The formation of new group identities is a factor that warrants more careful observation and study, as does the relationship between relative privilege and identity formation.

CONCLUSIONS

This chapter has traced the changing attempts at apartheid educational indoctrination. Imposing colonial values and worldviews on rightless indigenes ultimately failed, partly because of strenuous resistance by the subjects themselves and partly because of economic imperatives. The need for skills and higher education of the majority could not be reconciled with their disenfranchisement.

In the post-apartheid state, political empowerment and formal equality still have to confront the legacy of past educational neglect. Progressive educational policies are challenged by ingrained conditions and habits of racial domination. Despite the formidable task of equalizing opportunities, encouraging beginnings have been made and the problems clearly identified. Progressive South Africans of all groups and ideological traditions have negotiated a peaceful settlement of their seemingly intractable conflict. All indicators point to similar success in solving the educational crisis with imaginative new policies.

References

Adam, H. (1973). The rise of Black consciousness in South Africa. *Race, 15*(2), 149-165.

Adam, H. (2000). Divided memories: Confronting the crimes of previous regimes. *TELOS, 118,* 87–108.

Adam, H., & Giliomee, H. (1979). *Ethnic power mobilized.* New Haven, CT: Yale University Press.

Adam, H., & Moodley, K. (1986). *South Africa without apartheid: Dismantling racial domination.* Berkeley: University of California Press.

Adam, H., & Moodley, K. (1993). *The opening of the apartheid mind: Options for the new South Africa.* Berkeley: University of California Press.

Adam, H., Slabbert, V., & Moodley, K. (1998). *Comrades in business: Post-liberation politics in South Africa.* Cape Town, South Africa: Tafelberg.

Alexander, N. (1985). *Sow the wind: Contemporary speeches.* Johannesburg, South Africa: Skotaville.

Alexander, N. (1989). *Language policy, and national unity in South Africa/Azania: An essay.* Cape Town, South Africa: Buchu Books.

Alexander, N. (1990). *Education and the struggle for national liberation in South Africa.* Johannesburg, South Africa: Skotaville.

Alexander, N. (1991). Black consciousness: A reactionary tendency? In N. B. Pityana, M. Ramphele, M. Mpumlwana, & L. Wilson (Eds.), *Bounds of possibility: The legacy of Steve Biko and the Black consciousness movement in South Africa* (pp. 238–252). Cape Town, South Africa: David Philip.

Alexander, N. (1992). Language policy research in South Africa. *Transformation, 18/19,* 175–178.

Asmal, K., & James, W. (2001). Education and democracy in South Africa today. *Daedalus, 130*(1), 185–205.

Banks, J., & Banks, C. M. (Eds.). (2001). *Handbook of research on multicultural education.* San Francisco: Jossey-Bass.

Budlender, G. (1991). Black consciousness: A reactionary tendency? In N. B. Pityana, M. Ramphele, M. Mpumlwana, & L. Wilson (Eds.), *Bounds of possibility: The legacy of Steve Biko and the Black consciousness movement in South Africa* (pp. 238–252). Cape Town, South Africa: David Philip.

Bundy, C. (2000). A rich and tangled skein: Strategy and ideology in anti-apartheid struggles. In Comparative Human Relations Initiative (Eds.), *Beyond racism: Embracing an interdependent future: Three nations at the crossroads* (pp. 60–67). Atlanta, GA: Southern Education Foundation.

Carrim, N. (1992). *Desegregation in Coloured and Indian schooling.* Johannesburg: Education Policy Unit, University of Witwatersrand.

Carrim, N. (2001) Democratic participation, decentralisation and educational reform. In Y. Sayed & J. Jansen (Eds.), *Implementing education policies: The South African experience* (pp. 98–109). Cape Town, University of Cape Town Press.

Chisholm, L. (1984). Redefining skills: Black education in South Africa in 1980s. In P. Kallaway (Ed.), *Apartheid and education: The education of Black South Africans* (pp. 387–409). Johannesburg, South Africa: Ravan Press.

Chisholm, L. (1992). South African education in the era of negotiation. In G. Moss & I. Obery (Eds.), *South African review 6, from Red Friday to Codesa* (pp. 279-293). Johannesburg, South Africa: Ravan Press.

Christie, P. (1989). Desegregating schools in South Africa: The case of the Catholic open schools. *Discourse, 10*(1), 37-48.

Christie, P. (1990a). Reforming the racial curriculum: Curriculum change in desegregated schools in South Africa. *British Journal of Sociology of Education, 11*(1), 37–49.

Christie, P. (1990b). *Open schools: Racially mixed Catholic Schools in South Africa, 1976–1986.* Johannesburg, South Africa: Ravan Press.

Christie, P. (1992). An open system within the system: Catholic schools in South Africa, 1976–1986. In D. Freer (Ed.), *Towards open schools possibilities and realities for non-racial education in South Africa* (pp. 57–73). Manzini, South Africa: University of Witwatersrand Press.

Christie, P. (1994). *The right to learn: The struggle for education in South Africa.* Braamfontein, South Africa: Ravan Press.

Christie, P., & Butler, D. (1988). *Witness through schooling.* Pretoria, South Africa: SACBC.

Christie, P., & Collins, C. (1984). Bantu education: Apartheid ideology and labor reproduction. In P. Kallaway (Ed.), *Apartheid and education: The education of Black South Africans* (pp. 160–183). Johannesburg, South Africa: Ravan Press.

Cross, M. (1999). *Imagery of identity in South African education, 1880–1990.* Durham, NC: Carolina Academic Press.

Dawes, A., & Finchilescu, G. (1993). *Adolescents' perspectives on South African society.* Cape Town: Project of the Co-Operative Programme on Youth.

De Kok, I. (1998). Cracked heirlooms: Memory on exhibition. In S. Nuttall & C. Coetzee (Eds.), *Negotiating the past: The making of memory in South Africa* (pp. 57–74). Cape Town, South Africa: Oxford University Press.

Dolby, N. E. (2001). *Constructing race: Youth, identity and popular culture in South Africa.* Albany: State University of New York Press.

Fanon, F. (1963). *The wretched of the earth.* New York: Grove Press.

Fanon, F. (1967). *Black skin, White masks.* New York: Grove Press.

Freire, P. (1972). *Pedagogy of the oppressed.* Harmondsworth, England: Penguin.

Gaganakis, M. (1991). Opening up the closed school: Conceptualizing the presence of Black pupils in White schools. In D. Freer (Ed.), *Towards open schools possibilities and realities for non-racial education in South Africa* (pp. 73–93). Manzini, Swaziland: Macmillan.

Gerhart, G. (1978). *Black power in South Africa: The evolution of an ideology.* Berkeley: University of California Press.

Gillborn, D. (1995). *Racism and antiracism in real schools: Theory, policy, and practice.* Philadelphia: Open University Press.

Goduka, M. I. (1999). *Affirming unity in diversity in education: Healing with Ubuntu.* Cape Town, South Africa: Juta.

Greenstein, R. (1993). Racial formation: Towards a comparative study of collective identities in South Africa and the United States. *Social Dynamics, 19*(2), 1–12.

Hall, S. (1995). New ethnicities. In B. Ashcroft, G. Griffith, & H. Tiffin (Eds.), *The post-colonial studies reader* (pp. 223-227). London: Routledge.

Horrell, M. (1968). *Bantu education to 1968.* Johannesburg, South Africa: South African Institute of Race Relations.

Hyden, G. (1983). *No short-cuts to progress: African development management in perspective.* Berkeley: University of California Press.

Hyslop, J. (1988). School student movements and state education policy: 1972–87. In W. Cobbett & R. Cohen (Eds.), *Popular struggles in South Africa* (pp. 183–209). Trenton, NJ: Africa World Press.

Hyslop, J. (1999). *The classroom struggle: Policy and resistance in South Africa, 1940-1990.* Pietermaritzburg, South Africa: University of Natal Press.

James, W. (Ed.). (2001). *Manifesto on values: Education and democracy.* Pretoria, South Africa: Ministry of Education.

Jansen, J. D. (2001a). Explaining non-change in education reform after apartheid: Political symbolism and the problem of policy implementation. In Y. Sayed & J. D. Jansen (Eds.), *Implementing education policies: The South African experience* (pp. 272–292). Cape Town, South Africa: University of Cape Town Press.

Jansen, J. D. (2001b). The race for education policy after apartheid. In Y. Sayed & J. D. Jansen (Eds.), *Implementing education policies: The South African experience* (pp. 12–24). Cape Town, South Africa: University of Cape Town Press.

Kallaway, P. (Ed.). (1984). *Apartheid and education: The education of Black South Africans.* Johannesburg, South Africa: Ravan Press.

Karis, T., & Gerhart, G. (1997). *From protest to challenge: A documentary history of African politics in South Africa, 1882–1990, Vol. 5: Nadir and resurgence, 1964–1979.* Bloomington: Indiana University Press.

Kuper, L. (1969). *Race, class and power: Ideology and revolutionary change in plural societies.* London: Aldine.

Mbeki, T. (1996, May 8). Statement of Deputy President TM Mbeki on behalf of the African National Congress on the occasion of the adoption by the constitutional assembly of "The Republic of South Africa Constitution Bill 1996" [On-line]. Available: http://www.anc.org.za/ancdocs/history/mbeki/1996/sp960508. html.

McCarthy, C., & Crichlow, W. (1993). *Race, identity and representation in education.* New York: Routledge.

Ministry of Education. (2001). *Manifesto on values: Education and democracy.* Cape Town, South Africa: Department of Education.

Molobi, E. (1988). From Bantu education to people's education. In W. Cobbett & R. Cohen (Eds.), *Popular struggles in South Africa* (pp. 155–208). Braamfontein, South Africa: Ravan Press.

Moodley, K. (1971). The dialectic of higher education for the colonized. In H. Adam (Ed.), *South Africa: Sociological perspectives* (pp. 197–213). Oxford: Oxford University Press.

Moodley, K. (1991). The continued impact of Black consciousness. In N. B. Pityana, M. Ramphele, M. Mpumlwana, & L. Wilson (Eds.), *Bounds of possibility: The legacy of Steve Biko and the Black consciousness movement in South Africa* (pp. 238–252). Cape Town, South Africa: David Philip.

Motlhabi, M. (1984). *Black resistance to apartheid.* Johannesburg, South Africa: Skotaville.

Muller, J. (1987). People's education. *South African Review, 4,* 18–32.

Mzamane, M. V. (1991). The impact of Black consciousness on culture. In N. B. Pityana, M. Ramphele, M. Mpumlwana, & L. Wilson (Eds.), *Bounds of possibility: The legacy of Steve Biko and the Black consciousness movement in South Africa* (pp. 238–252). Cape Town, South Africa: David Philip.

Nasson, B., & Samuel, J. (1990). *Education: From poverty to liberty.* Cape Town, South Africa: David Philip.

National Education Policy Investigation. (1994). *The framework report and final report summaries.* Cape Town, South Africa: Oxford University Press.

Nkomo, M. (1990). *Pedagogy of domination: Toward a democratic education in South Africa.* Trenton, NJ: Africa World Press.

Nolutshungu, S. (1982). *Changing South Africa: Political considerations.* Manchester, England: Manchester University Press.

Norval, A. (1996). *Deconstructing apartheid discourse.* New York: Verso.

Nzimande, B. (1994). Schooling in the context of violence. In V. Maphai (Ed.), *South Africa: The challenge of change* (pp. 241–269). Harare, South Africa: Sapes Books.

Ramphele, M. (1991). Empowerment and symbols of hope: Black consciousness and community development. In N. B. Pityana, M. Ramphele, M. Mpumlwana, & L. Wilson (Eds.), *Bounds of possibility: The legacy of Steve Biko and the Black consciousness movement in South Africa* (pp. 238–252). Cape Town, South Africa: David Philip.

Reid, N. (2002, February 22). Facing the challenges of tertiary education. *Business Day.*

Saul, J. S., & Gelb, S. (1981). *The crisis in South Africa: Class defence, class revolution.* New York: Zed Press.

Sisulu, Z. (1986). People's education for people's power. *Transformation, 1,* 106–113.

Soudien, C., Jacklin, H., & Hoadley, U. (2001). Policy values: Problematizing equity and redress in education. In Y. Sayed & J. Jansen (Eds.), *Implementing education policies: The South African experience* (pp. 78–91). Cape Town, South Africa: University of Cape Town Press.

Soudien, C. (1994). Dealing with race: Laying down patterns for multiculturalism in South Africa. *Interchange, 25*(3), 281–294.

Soudien, C. (1998). We know why we're here: The experience of African children in a "coloured" school in Cape Town, South Africa. *Race, Ethnicity and Education, 1*(1), 7–29.

South African Institute of Race Relations. (1985). *Race relations survey 1985.* Johannesburg, South Africa: South African Institute of Race Relations.

South African Institute of Race Relations. (1986). *Race relations survey 1986.* Johannesburg, South Africa: South African Institute of Race Relations.

South African Institute of Race Relations. (1990). *Race relations survey 1989/90.* Johannesburg, South Africa: South African Institute of Race Relations.

South African Institute of Race Relations. (1992). *Race relations survey, 1991/92.* Johannesburg, South Africa: South African Institute of Race Relations.

South African Institute of Race Relations. (1997). *South Africa survey 1996/1997.* Johannesburg, South Africa: South African Institute of Race Relations.

Steyn, M. (2001). *Whiteness just isn't what it used to be: White identity in a changing South Africa.* Albany: State University of New York Press.

Straker, G. (1992). *Faces in the revolution: The* Study Project on Christianity in Apartheid Society. (1971). *Education beyond apartheid: Report of the Education Commission on Christianity in Apartheid Society.* Johannesburg, South Africa: Christian Institute of South Africa.

Truth and Reconciliation Commission. (1998). *Report.* Cape Town, South Africa: Juta.

Unterhalter, E., & Wolpe, H. (1991). *Apartheid education and popular struggles.* London: Zed Books.

Vally, S., & Dalamba, Y. (1999). *Racism, "racial integration" and desegregation in South African public secondary schools: A report on a study by the South African Human Rights Commission.* Johannesburg, South Africa: South African Human Rights Commission.

Wolpe, H. (1988). *Race, class and the apartheid state.* Paris: UNESCO Press.

Yon, D. (2000). *Elusive culture: Schooling, race and identity in global times.* Albany: State University of New York Press.

NAME INDEX

A

Abe, J., 557
Abelmann, N., 337
Abi-Nader, J., 189
Aboud, F. E., 16, 17, 23, 235, 785, 791, 792, 805, 807
Abowitz, K. K., 730
Abraham, D., 988
Abt-Perkins, D., 194
Achilles, C. M., 133
Acosta-Belén, E., 303, 305, 306, 887, 889
Acuña, R., 4, 12, 14, 234, 274, 638
Ada, A. F., 583
Adair, J., 220
Adam, H., 1027, 1028, 1029, 1030, 1032, 1033, 1035
Adamic, L., 756
Adams, B. S., 43
Adams, D. W., 442, 446, 447
Adams, J. Q., 895
Adams, R. L., 871, 872, 873
Adelman, C., 71, 76, 82
Adler, P. A., 161
Adorno, T. W., 7, 10
Agar, M., 161
Agbayani-Siewert, P., 340
Agnes, M., 17, 233
Aguilar, T., 963
Aguilar-San Juan, K., 889
Aguilera, D., 963
Ahmed, L., 884, 888
Aiken, S. H., 892
Ajamu, A., 139
Ajzen, I., 790
Akbar, N., 720
Akintude, O., 956
Alamillo, L., 502
Alarcón, N., 277, 887, 889
Alarcón, R., 268, 279
Alatorre Alva, S., 130, 139
Alba, R. D., 149, 338
Albers, P., 886
Albrecht, L., 884
Aldridge, D. P., 351, 356, 362
Aleinikoff, T. A., 60
Alers, O., 303
Alexander, C. M., 813
Alexander, K. L., 619, 683
Alexander, N., 1027, 1030, 1032
Alexie, S., 119, 315
Alfeld, C., 469

al-Hibri, A., 884
Alinsky, S., 357
Aliotta, J. J., 304
Allan, R., xv, 979–993, 983, 990
Alland, A., 761, 762
Allardyce, G., 910, 912, 913, 921
Allen, J., 707, 709, 710, 711
Allen, J. A., 883
Allen, J. P., 759
Allen, N., 721, 728
Allen, P. G., 886
Allen, R., 471
Allen, R. I., 71, 77
Allen, R. L., 211, 220
Allen, V., 952
Allen, W. R., 8, 857, 861, 863
Allensworth, E., 621
Allexsaht-Snider, M., 637
Allington, R., 700
Allison, S. T., 788
Allman, K. M., 117
Allport, G. W., 8, 9, 10, 18, 44, 128, 232, 686, 771, 772, 776, 777, 778, 783, 784, 802, 803, 805, 831
Almaguer, A., 277
Almaguer, T., 268, 274, 276
Almeida, C. A., 547
Alorsco, C., 990
Alpert, R., 888
Alquizola, M., 871, 875, 878
Alred, G. J., 253
Alt, M. N., 421
Altemeyer, B., 787
Alumkal, A., 337
Alvarado, C. G., 580
Alvarado, M., 223
Alvarez, C., 303
Alvarez, M. D., 535
Alves, M. J., 195
Alvord, J. W., 464
Alwood, E., 214
Amanti, C., 363, 700, 701, 711, 712, 713
Amato, M., 807
Ambert, A. N., 535
Ambler, M., 320
Ameisen, E. R., 149
Amey, M. J., 907
Amir, Y., 773, 784, 800, 802
Amrein, A., 597, 598, 599, 600, 601
Amrein, A. L., 99, 101
Anastasio, P. A., 786, 804
Anastasiow, N. J., 717

Ancess, J., 614, 622
Andermahr, S., 889
Anders, G. C., 320
Andersen, M. L., 883, 892
Anderson, B., 146, 150, 160
Anderson, J., 187–188, 197, 198, 466, 855
Anderson, J. D., 8, 9, 463, 464, 465, 467
Anderson, J. E., 36
Anderson, K., 892
Anderson, M. G., 728, 962
Anderson, R., 293, 473–474
Anderson, S., 475, 958
Andersson, T., 592
Andrade, R., 710, 711
Andreoli, V. A., 804
Andreoni, H., 986
Andrew, H., 1005
Andrews, S., 464
Angel, R., 635
Anjali, M., 1010
Anrig, G., 831
Anthony, M., 280
Antler, J., 887, 888
Antonsen, P. J., 305
Anyon, J., 75, 658, 662, 666, 671, 672, 673, 674
Anzaldúa, G., 54, 61, 277, 884, 887, 888, 889
Aparicio, F., 302–303
Apodaca, P., 453
Appel, M., 917
Appelbaum, P., 958
Appiah, A., 428
Apple, M. W., 37, 59, 168, 186, 241, 243, 656, 658, 660, 665, 954, 955
Applebaum, A. P., 185
Appleton, C., 501, 503
Appleton, N., 451
Aptheker, H., 230, 359
Aragón, G., 277
Aragón, T., 275
Aran, K., 13
Araragi, C., 772
Arbeiter, S., 549, 550
Arce, C. H., 281
Arch, E. C., 892
Archbald, D. A., 622
Archuleta, M. L., 446, 448
Arcuri, L., 788
Arellano, A., 743
Arellano, A. R., 130
Arends, R., 960
Arensberg, C., 146